Amerada Hess Corporation

Recommendation: SELL ★ ★ ☆ ☆ ☆   12-Month Target Price: **$72.00** (as of July 08, 2004)

Business Summary August 24, 2004

As an integrated oil and gas company emphasizing exploration and production (20% of 2003 operating revenues and 56% of income from continuing operations), Amerada Hess Corp. has exposure to the refining and marketing (80%; 44%) segment. As of May 2003, the Hess family and related interests owned about 14% of the common shares.

The company engages in exploration and production activities in the U.S. (26% of 2003 barrel oil equivalent (BOE) production, 18% of 2003 year end proved BOE reserves) and Europe (55%, 42%), with the remainder in Africa, Asia and other regions. At 2003 year end, AHC had 1,035 million BOE (68% developed, 62% crude oil, condensate and natural gas liquids), down 13% from 1,195 million BOE (67%, 65%) a year earlier. Upstream production dropped 17%, to 373,000 BOE per day in 2003, reflecting a 20% drop in liquids and a 9.4% drop in natural gas. About 60% of the reduction in production was due to asset sales and swaps, with the remainder due to natural declines and poorer than expected performance of certain fields in the U.S. and Equatorial Guinea. Production is expected to decline in 2004 by about 13% due to the 2003 asset sales and swaps, and natural declines in its remaining fields. The company is funding 12 developments that are expected to provide over 100,000 BOE/day in 2006. Unit cost per barrel totaled $17.32 in 2003, $15.11 in 2002, and $13.11 in 2001; AHC estimates that its 2004 unit costs will approximate the 2003 amount. In June 2004, AHC formed a joint venture with an affiliate of Poten & Partners, to be known as Hess LNG.

AHC manufactures, purchases, transports, trades and markets refined petroleum

products. One of its largest single operations is a 50%-owned refining joint venture, HOVENSA, formed in October 1998 with Petroleos de Venezuela S.A. (PdVSA) in the U.S. Virgin Islands. PdVSA supplies 155,000 b/d of Venezuelan Mesa heavy crude oil to HOVENSA under a long-term (through 2008) crude oil supply contract, and a second long-term supply contract with PdVSA to purchase 115,000 b/d of Venezuelan Merey heavy crude oil. The remaining crude oil is purchased mainly under contracts of one year or less from third parties and through spot purchases on the open market. After sales of refined products by HOVENSA to third parties, the company purchases 50% of HOVENSA's remaining production at market prices. HOVENSA refined an average of 440,000 b/d of crude oil in 2003, versus 361,000 b/d in 2002. In August 2002, the coking unit at HOVENSA commenced operation, and rates averaged 53,000 b/d in 2003. AHC also owns and operates a fluid catalytic cracking (FCC) facility in Port Reading, NJ, which operates at 54,000 b/d and produces substantially all gasoline and heating oil.

The company primarily markets refined petroleum products on the U.S. East Coast. At the end of 2003, it had 1,195 HESS gasoline stations, of which about 68% were company-operated. In early 2004, a 50%-owned joint venture acquired a chain of gasoline stations, adding about 50 HESS retail outlets. AHC owns about 50% of the properties on which the stations are located. Refined product sales averaged 419,000 b/d (50% obtained from HOVENSA and Port Reading) in 2003, versus 383,000 b/d (46%) in 2002.

Company Financials Fiscal Year ending December 31

Per Share Data ($)

(Year Ended December 31)	2003	2002	2001	2000	1999	1998	1997	1996	1995	1994
Tangible Bk. Val.	40.86	36.50	44.10	43.76	33.51	29.96	35.16	36.35	28.60	33.33
Cash Flow	16.83	12.50	21.13	19.30	12.07	2.20	7.40	15.52	5.37	10.77
Earnings	5.17	-2.48	10.25	11.38	4.85	-5.12	0.08	7.09	-4.24	0.79
S&P Core Earnings	5.24	-3.84	9.76	NA	NA	NA	NA	NA	NA	NA
Dividends	1.20	1.20	1.20	0.60	0.60	0.60	0.60	0.60	0.60	0.60
Payout Ratio	23%	NM	12%	5%	12%	NM	NM	8%	NM	76%
Prices - High	57.20	84.70	90.40	76.25	66.31	61.06	64.50	60.50	53.62	52.62
- Low	41.14	49.40	53.75	47.81	43.75	46.00	47.37	47.50	43.25	43.75
P/E Ratio - High	11	NM	9	7	14	NM	NM	9	NM	67
- Low	8	NM	5	4	9	NM	NM	7	NM	55

Income Statement Analysis (Million $)

	2003	2002	2001	2000	1999	1998	1997	1996	1995	1994
Revs.	14,480	12,093	13,413	11,993	7,039	6,590	8,234	8,272	7,302	6,602
Oper. Inc.	2,127	2,382	2,399	2,264	1,214	475	910	1,306	1,149	1,312
Depr. Depl. & Amort.	1,053	1,320	967	714	648	657	673	783	893	928
Int. Exp.	293	269	194	162	158	153	136	166	247	245
Pretax Inc.	781	-51.0	1,438	1,672	702	-514	127	1,014	-352	236
Eff. Tax Rate	40.2%	NM	36.4%	38.8%	37.6%	NM	93.7%	34.9%	NM	68.7%
Net Inc.	467	-218	914	1,023	438	-459	8.00	660	-394	74.0
S&P Core Earnings	468	-339	870	NA	NA	NA	NA	NA	NA	NA

Balance Sheet & Other Fin. Data (Million $)

	2003	2002	2001	2000	1999	1998	1997	1996	1995	1994
Cash	518	197	37.0	312	41.0	74.0	91.0	113	56.0	53.0
Curr. Assets	3,186	2,756	3,946	4,115	1,828	1,887	2,204	2,427	1,963	1,722
Total Assets	13,983	13,262	15,369	10,274	7,728	7,883	7,935	7,784	7,756	8,338
Curr. Liab.	2,669	2,553	3,718	3,538	1,579	1,797	1,740	1,737	1,605	1,201
LT Debt	3,868	4,976	5,283	1,985	2,287	2,476	2,003	1,712	2,587	3,235
Common Equity	5,326	8,498	4,907	3,883	3,038	2,643	3,216	3,384	2,660	3,100
Total Cap.	10,352	14,518	11,301	6,378	5,767	5,603	5,781	5,712	5,850	6,882
Cap. Exp.	1,358	1,404	2,501	938	797	1,439	1,346	861	692	596
Cash Flow	1,515	1,102	1,881	1,737	1,086	198	681	1,443	499	1,002
Curr. Ratio	1.2	1.1	1.1	1.2	1.2	1.1	1.3	1.4	1.2	1.4
% LT Debt of Cap.	37.4	34.3	46.7	31.1	39.7	44.2	34.6	30.0	44.2	47.0
% Ret. on Assets	3.4	NM	7.1	11.4	5.6	NM	0.1	8.5	NM	0.9
% Ret. on Equity	9.7	NM	20.8	29.6	15.4	NM	0.2	21.8	NM	2.4

Data as orig reptd.; bef. results of disc opers/spec. items. Per share data adj. for stk. divs.; EPS diluted. E-Estimated. NA-Not Available. NM-Not Meaningful. NR-Not Ranked. UR-Under Review.

Office: 1185 Avenue of the Americas, New York, NY 10036.
Telephone: 212-997-8500.
Email: investorrelations@hess.com
Website: http://www.hess.com
Chrmn & CEO: J.B. Hess.
EVP & CFO: J.Y. Schreyer.
EVP & General Counsel: J.B. Collins II.

VP & Treas: R.J. Vogel.
VP & Secy: G.C. Barry.
VP & Investor Contact: J.R. Wilson 212-536-8940.
Dirs: N. F. Brady, J. B. Collins II, J. B. Hess, E. E. Holiday, T. H. Kean, C. G. Matthews, J. J. O'Connor, F. A. Olson, J. Y. Schreyer, R. N. Wilson, E. H. von Metzsch.

Founded: in 1920.
Domicile: Delaware.
Employees: 11,481.
S&P Analyst: T. Vital/PMW/GG

Ameren Corp.

Recommendation: **HOLD** ★ ★ ★ ★ ☆
SELL | SELL | HOLD | BUY | BUY

12-Month Target Price: $47.00
(as of October 25, 2004)

AEE has an approximate 0.09% weighting in the **S&P 500**

Sector: Utilities
Sub-Industry: Electric Utilities
Peer Group: Electric & Gas - Mid-sized & Smaller

Summary: AEE is the holding company for the largest electric utility in the state of Missouri.

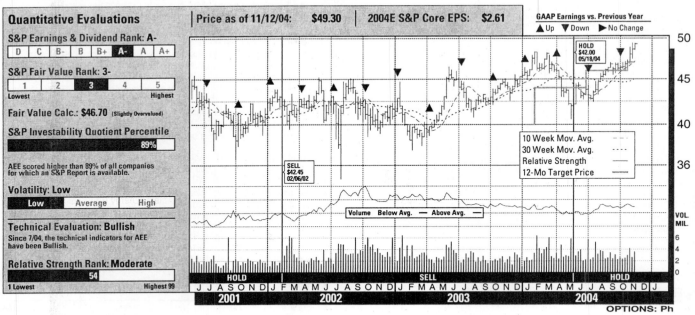

Quantitative Evaluations

S&P Earnings & Dividend Rank: A-

| D | C | B- | B | B+ | A- | A | A+ |

S&P Fair Value Rank: 3-

| 1 | 2 | 3 | 4 | 5 |
| Lowest | | | | Highest |

Fair Value Calc.: $46.70 (Slightly Overvalued)

S&P Investability Quotient Percentile
89%

AEE scored higher than 89% of all companies for which an S&P Report is available.

Volatility: Low

| Low | Average | High |

Technical Evaluation: Bullish
Since 7/04, the technical indicators for AEE have been Bullish.

Relative Strength Rank: Moderate
54
1 Lowest | Highest 99

Price as of 11/12/04: $49.30
2004E S&P Core EPS: $2.61

GAAP Earnings vs. Previous Year
▲ Up ▼ Down ▶ No Change

10 Week Mov. Avg.
30 Week Mov. Avg.
Relative Strength
12-Mo Target Price

Volume Below Avg. — Above Avg.

HOLD $42.00 05/18/04
SELL $42.45 02/06/02

OPTIONS: Ph

Analyst commentary prepared by Justin McCann/MF/BK

Highlights October 01, 2004

- After an anticipated 5% decline in 2004 (from 2003 operating EPS of $2.95), we expect EPS to grow about 5% in 2005. The expected decline in 2004 partially reflects the issuance of stock related to the planned acquisition of Illinois Power (IP). Assuming the anticipated regulatory approvals, the acquisition of IP is expected to be completed by the end of 2004, and to be accretive to 2005 EPS by $0.05 to $0.10.

- Following the January 2003 acquisition of CILCORP, the Illinois Power acquisition (valued at $2.3 billion) would increase AEE's customer base by 46%, to 3.2 million, with 60% in Illinois. All significant integration activities related to CILCORP have been completed, and the acquisition added $0.04 to 2003 EPS on approximately 10% more shares.

- In addition to the impact of new Illinois Power-related share issuances, we expect 2004 EPS to be restricted by higher costs for employee benefits, insurance, and plant security. AEE plans to use stock issuance proceeds to pay the $500 million cash portion of the purchase price for Illinois Power, and to reduce assumed IP debt ($1.8 billion).

Investment Rationale/Risk October 01, 2004

- We view the shares as being fully valued at a better than 13% premium to the average P/E multiple of 13.5X our 2005 estimates of AEE's electric and gas utility peers. In our view, the premium is warranted due to a dividend yield (recently around 5.5%) that is well above the industry average. With the federal tax on dividends having been reduced from the earned rate to a 15% rate, this would indicate an after-tax yield of nearly 4.7%.

- Risks to our recommendation and target price include Ameren's failure to get regulatory approval for the acquisition of Illinois Power, as well as a sharp reduction in the average P/E multiple of AEE's peer group as a whole.

- Although we do not expect Ameren's dividend to be increased (it has not been raised since 1997), we view it as stable, despite the well above average payout ratio of 91% of our EPS estimate for 2004. Based on our view that the shares will continue to trade at around the current premium to peers, but that the P/E multiple will remain relatively flat, our 12-month target price is $46.

Key Stock Statistics

S&P Core EPS 2005E	2.85	52-week Range	$49.44-40.55
S&P Oper. EPS 2004E	2.75	12 Month P/E	18.5
P/E on S&P Oper. EPS 2004E	17.9	Beta	0.11
S&P Oper. EPS 2005E	2.95	Shareholders	89,970
Yield (%)	5.2%	Market Cap (B)	$ 9.6
Dividend Rate/Share	2.54	Shares Outstanding (M)	194.3

Value of $10,000 invested five years ago: **$ 17,685**

Dividend Data Dividends have been paid since 1906

Amount ($)	Date Decl.	Ex-Div. Date	Stock of Record	Payment Date
0.635	Feb. 13	Mar. 08	Mar. 10	Mar. 31 '04
0.635	Apr. 27	Jun. 07	Jun. 09	Jun. 30 '04
0.635	Aug. 27	Sep. 07	Sep. 09	Sep. 30 '04
0.635	Oct. 08	Dec. 06	Dec. 08	Dec. 31 '04

Revenues/Earnings Data Fiscal year ending December 31

Revenues (Million $)

	2004	2003	2002	2001	2000	1999
1Q	1,216	1,108	1,115	1,025	723.1	735.9
2Q	1,152	1,088	1,111	1,057	940.3	859.9
3Q	1,317	1,350	1,232	1,432	1,195	1,193
4Q	—	1,047	823.0	992.7	894.8	734.4
Yr.	—	4,593	3,841	4,506	3,856	3,524

Earnings Per Share ($)

	2004	2003	2002	2001	2000	1999
1Q	0.55	0.52	0.42	0.48	21.00	0.40
2Q	0.65	0.68	0.80	0.69	0.83	0.63
3Q	1.20	1.70	1.63	1.94	1.87	1.82
4Q	E0.35	0.24	-0.20	0.34	0.19	-0.04
Yr.	E2.75	3.14	2.60	3.45	3.33	2.81

Next earnings report expected: early-February Source: S&P, Company Reports
EPS Estimates based on S&P Operating Earnings; historical GAAP earnings are as reported.

Ameren Corporation

Stock Report
November 13, 2004
NYSE Symbol: **AEE**

Recommendation: **HOLD** ★★★☆☆   12-Month Target Price: **$47.00** (as of October 25, 2004)

Business Summary October 01, 2004

Ameren Corp. is the St. Louis-based holding company for AmerenUE, AmerenCIPS, AmerenCILCO, and AmerenEnergy Generating Co.

The holding company was formed on December 31, 1997, through the merger of AmerenUE, the holding company for Union Electric Co., and CIPSCO, the holding company for Central Illinois Public Service Co.

On February 3, 2004, AEE agreed to acquire Illinois Power Co. from Dynegy Inc., in a transaction valued at $2.3 billion, including the assumption of $1.8 billion in debt. Illinois Power serves about 590,000 electric and 415,000 natural gas customers in Illinois. The purchase would include Dynegy's 20% interest in Electric Energy, Inc. (EEI). AEE already has a 60% interest in EEI, which operates electric generation and transmission facilities in Illinois..

On January 31, 2003, AEE acquired CILCORP, the holding company for Central Illinois Light Co. (CILCO), in a transaction valued at $1.4 billion, including the assumption of about $900 million of CILCORP debt and preferred stock. CILCO, which now operates as AmerenCILCO, serves about 203,000 electric and 208,000 natural gas customers.

AmerenUE is the largest electric utility in Missouri. It serves 1.2 million electric customers and 123,000 gas customers Missouri and portions of Illinois. AmerenCIPS serves 323,000 electric customers and 169,000 natural gas customers in central and southern Illinois.

AmerenEnergy Generating Company was formed in May 2000, when, as a result of

Illinois deregulation, AmerenCIPS transferred its Illinois power plants (2,900 megawatts of capacity) to the new, unregulated electric generating subsidiary.

In 2003, AEE's electric operations accounted for 85.7% of consolidated revenues (91.6% in 2002); the natural gas operations for 14.1% (8.2%); and other 0.2% (0.2%).

Ameren's electric revenues by customer segment in 2003 were: residential 31.7% (34.1% in 2002), commercial 28.3% (29.1%); industrial 18.6% (14.5%); wholesale 7.5% (8.3%); interchange 7.5% (5.7%); and other 6.4% (8.3%).

Coal accounted for 85% of Ameren's electric fuel supply in 2003 (82% in 2002); nuclear 13% (13%), oil 1% (1%); hydro 1% (2%), and natural gas 0% (2%).

AEE's natural gas revenues by customer segment in 2003 were: residential 52.9% (61.0% in 2002); commercial 21.9% (23.8%); industrial 19.0% (11.7%); off system sales 0.9% (1.3%); and other 5.2% (2.2%).

The company's other businesses include AmerenEnergy Resources Company, a non-regulated Illinois holding company for AmerenEnergy Generating Co., AmerenEnergy Marketing Co., and AmerenEnergy Fuels and Services Co., which manages fuel purchases for the Ameren companies; AmerenEnergy, Inc., a Missouri corporation serving as an energy trading and marketing agent for AmerenUE and AmerenEnergy Generating Co.; and Ameren Services Co., which provides shared support services for AEE and its subsidiaries.

Company Financials Fiscal Year ending December 31

Per Share Data ($)

(Year Ended December 31)	2003	2002	2001	2000	1999	1998	1997	1996	1995	1994
Tangible Bk. Val.	23.19	24.95	24.26	23.34	22.55	22.27	21.92	22.86	22.18	21.64
Earnings	3.14	2.60	3.45	3.33	2.81	2.82	2.82	2.86	2.95	3.01
S&P Core Earnings	3.28	2.36	2.81	NA	NA	NA	NA	NA	NA	NA
Dividends	2.54	2.54	2.54	2.54	2.54	2.54	2.54	2.51	2.46	2.40
Payout Ratio	81%	98%	74%	76%	90%	90%	90%	88%	83%	80%
Prices - High	46.50	45.25	46.00	46.93	42.93	44.31	43.75	44.12	42.00	39.50
- Low	42.55	34.72	36.53	27.56	32.00	35.56	34.50	36.00	34.62	30.75
P/E Ratio - High	15	17	13	14	15	16	16	15	14	13
- Low	14	13	11	8	11	13	12	13	12	10

Income Statement Analysis (Million $)

	2003	2002	2001	2000	1999	1998	1997	1996	1995	1994
Revs.	4,593	3,841	4,506	3,856	3,524	3,318	3,327	2,260	2,103	2,056
Depr.	519	431	406	382	351	348	346	241	233	226
Maint.	NA	NA	382	368	371	312	310	224	222	198
Fxd. Chgs. Cov.	3.61	4.04	4.65	4.86	4.48	NA	4.08	4.25	4.34	4.45
Constr. Credits	4.00	11.0	20.8	14.0	14.0	12.0	12.7	13.5	13.0	11.0
Eff. Tax Rate	37.3%	38.3%	38.7%	39.7%	40.2%	40.9%	38.0%	39.3%	40.0%	39.0%
Net Inc.	506	382	475	457	385	386	387	305	314	321
S&P Core Earnings	530	347	387	NA	NA	NA	NA	NA	NA	NA

Balance Sheet & Other Fin. Data (Million $)

	2003	2002	2001	2000	1999	1998	1997	1996	1995	1994
Gross Prop.	17,511	15,745	14,962	13,910	13,056	12,531	12,273	9,040	8,930	8,454
Cap. Exp.	682	787	1,103	929	571	325	381	376	354	345
Net Prop.	10,917	8,914	8,427	7,706	7,165	6,928	6,987	5,383	5,435	5,345
Capitalization:										
LT Debt	4,273	3,626	3,071	2,980	2,683	2,525	2,506	1,799	1,764	1,823
% LT Debt	49.5	48.6	47.8	48.3	46.5	45.2	43.5	41.0	41.0	42.3
Pfd.	Nil	Nil	Nil	Nil	Nil	NA	235	219	219	219
% Pfd.	Nil	Nil	Nil	Nil	Nil	NA	4.10	5.00	5.10	5.10
Common	4,354	3,842	3,349	3,196	3,089	3,056	3,019	2,355	2,319	2,269
% Common	50.5	51.4	52.2	51.7	53.5	54.8	52.4	54.0	53.9	52.6
Total Cap.	10,653	9,339	8,144	7,884	7,441	7,285	7,507	5,851	5,826	5,834
% Oper. Ratio	83.9	81.0	85.2	83.4	84.1	82.8	82.5	81.1	79.0	78.1
% Earn. on Net Prop.	10.7	7.2	8.2	8.6	8.0	8.2	8.4	8.0	8.4	8.5
% Return On Revs.	11.0	9.9	10.6	11.9	10.9	11.6	11.6	13.5	14.9	15.6
% Return On Invest. Capital	7.4	8.1	8.6	8.5	7.7	11.3	7.7	7.4	7.6	7.9
% Return On Com. Equity	12.3	10.6	14.5	14.5	12.5	12.7	12.8	12.5	13.1	13.8

Data as orig reptd.; bef. results of disc opers/spec. items. Per share data adj. for stk. divs.; EPS diluted. E-Estimated. NA-Not Available. NM-Not Meaningful. NR-Not Ranked. UR-Under Review.

Office: 1901 Chouteau Avenue, St. Louis, MO 63103.
Telephone: 314-621-3222.
Email: invest@ameren.com
Website: http://www.ameren.com
Chrmn & CEO: G.L. Rainwater.
EVP & CFO: W.L. Baxter.

SVP, Secy & General Counsel: S.R. Sullivan.
VP & Treas: J.E. Birdsong.
Investor Contact: B. Steinke 314-554-2574.
Dirs: W. E. Cornelius, S. S. Elliott, C. L. Greenwalt, T. A. Hays, R. A. Liddy, G. R. Lohman, R. A. Lumpkin, J. P. MacCarthy, P. L. Miller, Jr., C. W. Mueller, D. R. Oberhelman, G. L. Rainwater, H. Saligman.

Founded: in 1881.
Domicile: Missouri.
Employees: 7,650.
S&P Analyst: Justin McCann/MF/BK

The **McGraw·Hill** Companies

American Electric Power

Recommendation: **HOLD** ★★★☆☆
SELL | SELL | HOLD | BUY | BUY

12-Month Target Price: **$34.00**
(as of November 11, 2004)

Stock Report
November 15, 2004
NYSE Symbol: **AEP**

AEP has an approximate 0.13% weighting in the **S&P 500**

Sector: Utilities
Sub-Industry: Electric Utilities
Peer Group: Electric Cos. (Domestic) - Very Large

Summary: This Ohio-based electric utility holding company has subsidiaries operating in 11 states in the U.S.

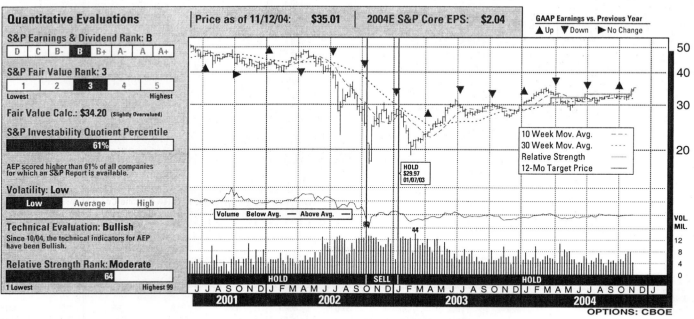

Quantitative Evaluations

S&P Earnings & Dividend Rank: B
D | C | B- | **B** | B+ | A- | A | A+

S&P Fair Value Rank: 3
1 | 2 | **3** | 4 | 5
Lowest | | | | Highest

Fair Value Calc.: $34.20 (Slightly Overvalued)

S&P Investability Quotient Percentile
61%

AEP scored higher than 61% of all companies for which an S&P Report is available.

Volatility: Low
Low | Average | High

Technical Evaluation: Bullish
Since 10/04, the technical indicators for AEP have been Bullish.

Relative Strength Rank: Moderate
64
1 Lowest | Highest 99

Price as of 11/12/04: **$35.01**   **2004E S&P Core EPS:** **$2.04**

GAAP Earnings vs. Previous Year
▲ Up ▼ Down ▶ No Change

- 10 Week Mov. Avg.
- 30 Week Mov. Avg.
- Relative Strength
- 12-Mo Target Price

HOLD $29.97 01/07/03

Volume Below Avg. — Above Avg.

HOLD | SELL | HOLD

J J A S O N D | J F M A M J J A S O N D | J F M A M J J A S O N D | J F M A M J J A S O N D | J
2001 | **2002** | **2003** | **2004**

OPTIONS: CBOE

Analyst commentary prepared by Justin McCann/PMW/JWP

Highlights 15-NOV-04

- We expect 2005 EPS to increase about 4% from anticipated operating EPS of $2.30 in 2004. Operating results in 2004 follow a year that was marred by impairments for non-core businesses and losses of $0.34 a share from the discontinued operations. We expect the utility operations to earn about $2.55 a share in 2004, and see the holding company and non-regulated investments reporting a loss of about $0.25.
- With the divestiture of non-core businesses (with proceeds expected to be used for debt reduction), we believe AEP will be able to concentrate on its regulated operations, including continued reduction of O&M costs and achieving a rate stabilization plan in Ohio by the end of 2004. Results in 2004 and 2005 are also expected to reflect an improving economy.
- In the 2004 third quarter, AEP completed the divestiture of its U.K. operations, which had been hurt by the weakness in the U.K. wholesale market. One-time items, mainly gains from asset sales, added $0.54 to third quarter reported EPS. The company's ongoing operations contributed $0.80 to the third quarter and $1.91 to the first nine months of 2004.

Investment Rationale/Risk 15-NOV-04

- We expect the stock, which underperformed the S&P Index of Electric Utilities in 2003, to perform in line with peers in 2004. We view the company's exit from the U.K. as a major positive factor. In addition to removing the adverse impact on earnings, proceeds from the sale of this and other assets should enable AEP to further strengthen its balance sheet and to maintain the current stable outlook for its investment grade credit ratings, in our view.
- Risks to our recommendation and target price include the potential for weaker than anticipated results from wholesale operations, and a sharp decline in the average peer P/E multiple of the group as a whole.
- In light of what we see as the company's improved financial profile, we expect AEP to explore the possibility of an increase in the dividend (which was cut 42% with the June 2003 payment) in 2005. With the dividend yield about equal to the average for AEP's electric utility peers, we expect the shares to trade at an approximate peer P/E multiple of about 14.2X our EPS estimate for 2005. Our 12-month target price is $34. Currently yielding 4.1%, we would hold the shares on a total return basis.

Key Stock Statistics

S&P Core EPS 2005E	2.31	52-week Range	$35.10-26.69
S&P Oper. EPS 2004E	2.30	12 Month P/E	42.7
P/E on S&P Oper. EPS 2004E	15.2	Beta	0.37
S&P Oper. EPS 2005E	2.40	Shareholders	150,000
Yield (%)	4.0%	Market Cap (B)	$ 13.9
Dividend Rate/Share	1.40	Shares Outstanding (M)	395.7

Value of $10,000 invested five years ago: **$ 14,095**

Dividend Data Dividends have been paid since 1909

Amount ($)	Date Decl.	Ex-Div. Date	Stock of Record	Payment Date
0.350	Jan. 28	Feb. 06	Feb. 10	Mar. 10 '04
0.350	Apr. 27	May. 06	May. 10	Jun. 10 '04
0.350	Jul. 27	Aug. 06	Aug. 10	Sep. 10 '04
0.350	Oct. 26	Nov. 08	Nov. 10	Dec. 10 '04

Revenues/Earnings Data Fiscal year ending December 31

Revenues (Million $)

	2004	2003	2002	2001	2000	1999
1Q	3,300	4,080	3,169	14,165	3,021	1,694
2Q	3,368	3,669	3,575	14,528	3,169	1,643
3Q	3,752	4,109	3,870	18,385	3,915	1,914
4Q	—	3,300	3,941	14,179	3,589	1,665
Yr.	—	14,500	14,555	12,767	13,694	6,916

Earnings Per Share ($)

	2004	2003	2002	2001	2000	1999
1Q	0.70	0.72	0.49	0.83	0.43	0.79
2Q	0.38	0.46	0.49	0.87	-0.06	0.46
3Q	1.04	0.65	1.14	1.25	1.25	0.90
4Q	E0.40	-1.82	-2.01	0.17	-0.68	0.55
Yr.	E2.30	1.35	0.06	3.11	0.94	2.69

Next earnings report expected: early-February Source: S&P, Company Reports
EPS Estimates based on S&P Operating Earnings; historical GAAP earnings are as reported.

The **McGraw·Hill** Companies

American Electric Power Company, Inc.

Recommendation: **HOLD** ★ ★ ★ ☆ ☆   12-Month Target Price: **$34.00** (as of November 11, 2004)

Business Summary 15-NOV-04

In June 2000, American Electric Power completed the acquisition of Central and South West Corp. (CSW), a Dallas-based holding company with four electric utilities in the Southwest and one in the U.K.

U.S. utilities acquired from CSW, now serving about 1.8 million customers in portions of Texas, Oklahoma, Louisiana and Arkansas, included Central Power & Light, Public Service of Oklahoma, Southwestern Electric Power, and West Texas Utilities. In addition to territories acquired from CSW, AEP provides electricity through seven other utility subsidiaries to about 3.1 million customers in portions of Ohio, Indiana, Michigan, Virginia, West Virginia, Kentucky and Tennessee.

On September 28, 2004, AEP sold its 50% interest in the holding company for Shoreham Power Station in the U.K., for about $47 million. The transaction completed the company's divestiture of its U.K. assets. Earlier, on July 30, 2004, AEP sold two coal-fired power plants in the U.K. (Fiddler's Ferry and Ferrybridge), for $248 million, and a number of related commodities contracts, for an additional $208 million.

In July 2002, the company sold SEEBOARD, a U.K. utility acquired in the CSW merger, for $1.05 billion and the buyer's assumption of $1.13 billion of debt. In April 2001, AEP sold (for $383 million and the buyer's assumption of $2 billion of debt) its 50% interest in the holding company for U.K.-based Yorkshire Electricity Group. In August 2002, the company sold CitiPower, based in Melbourne, Australia, for $181 million and the purchaser's assumption of $674 million of debt.

In September 2004, AEP agreed to sell its 25.2% interest in the South Texas Project nuclear plant to two separate purchasers. The transactions, with a combined value of $332 million, are expected to close in late 2004 or early 2005. Earlier, on April 1, 2004, the company sold its Louisiana Interstate Gas (LIG) pipeline assets for $76.2 million. In August 2004, it agreed to sell its LIG storage assets for $94.3 million, in a transaction expected to close by the end of 2004.

Following the sale of 4,497 megawatts (mw) of its generating assets in Texas (required by Texas restructuring legislation), the company's electric utility subsidiaries own or lease generating stations with total generating capacity of about 33,850 megawatts. With the final sales agreement reached in March 2004, the total purchase price for all of the assets to be sold was $805 million. At the end of 2001, the combined net book value for the assets was about $1.8 billion.

In 2003, AEP spent $217 million ($364 million in 2002) on investments related to the improvement of the environmental performance of its power generating facilities and its compliance with air and water quality standards. The company projected environmental-related investments of about $301 million in 2004.

System fuel sources in 2003 were: coal, 80% (78% in 2002, 74% in 2001); gas, 7% (8%, 12%); nuclear, 9% (11%, 11%); and hydroelectric and other, 4% (3%, 3%).

Non-regulated operations include the Houston Pipeline Co., which operates a 4,200-mile intrastate gas pipeline in Texas with daily capacity of about 2.4 Bcf., and the Memco Barge Line subsidiary, which is engaged in transportation of coal and dry bulk commodities, mainly on the Ohio, Illinois, and lower Mississippi rivers.

Company Financials Fiscal Year ending December 31

Per Share Data ($)

(Year Ended December 31)	2003	2002	2001	2000	1999	1998	1997	1996	1995	1994
Tangible Bk. Val.	19.74	19.67	20.92	20.72	25.80	25.21	24.62	23.96	23.08	22.67
Earnings	1.35	0.06	3.11	0.94	2.69	2.81	3.28	3.14	2.85	2.71
S&P Core Earnings	1.47	0.07	2.17	NA	NA	NA	NA	NA	NA	NA
Dividends	1.65	2.40	2.40	2.40	2.40	2.40	2.40	2.40	2.40	2.40
Payout Ratio	NM	NM	77%	255%	89%	85%	73%	76%	84%	89%
Prices - High	31.51	48.80	51.20	48.93	48.18	53.31	52.00	44.75	40.62	37.37
- Low	19.01	15.10	39.25	25.93	30.56	42.06	39.12	38.62	31.25	27.25
P/E Ratio - High	23	NM	16	52	18	19	16	14	14	14
- Low	14	NM	13	28	11	15	12	12	11	10

Income Statement Analysis (Million $)

	2003	2002	2001	2000	1999	1998	1997	1996	1995	1994
Revs.	14,545	14,555	61,257	13,694	6,916	6,346	6,161	5,849	5,670	5,505
Depr.	1,299	1,377	1,383	1,062	600	580	591	601	593	572
Maint.	NA	NA	NA	NA	NA	543	483	503	542	544
Fxd. Chgs. Cov.	2.18	2.83	2.61	1.95	2.23	2.86	3.17	3.15	2.76	2.62
Constr. Credits	NA	NA	NA	NA	NA	NA	NA	NA	NA	NA
Eff. Tax Rate	39.8%	79.3%	35.9%	66.4%	33.3%	32.8%	32.5%	33.9%	33.1%	25.9%
Net Inc.	522	21.0	1,003	302	520	536	620	587	530	500
S&P Core Earnings	573	21.1	699	NA	NA	NA	NA	NA	NA	NA

Balance Sheet & Other Fin. Data (Million $)

	2003	2002	2001	2000	1999	1998	1997	1996	1995	1994
Gross Prop.	36,033	37,857	40,709	38,088	22,512	23,718	21,181	18,970	18,496	18,175
Cap. Exp.	1,358	1,722	1,832	1,773	867	792	760	578	606	643
Net Prop.	22,029	21,684	24,543	22,392	13,362	15,302	13,217	11,420	11,385	11,348
Capitalization:										
LT Debt	12,459	9,329	10,230	10,092	6,500	6,974	5,167	4,832	4,920	4,687
% LT Debt	61.3	56.9	55.4	55.6	56.6	59.0	51.6	48.4	49.6	48.1
Pfd.	Nil	Nil	Nil	Nil	Nil	Nil	174	600	663	824
% Pfd.	Nil	Nil	Nil	Nil	Nil	Nil	1.80	6.00	6.70	8.50
Common	7,874	7,064	8,229	8,059	4,992	4,841	4,677	4,545	4,340	4,230
% Common	38.7	43.1	44.6	44.4	43.4	41.0	46.7	45.6	43.7	43.4
Total Cap.	24,290	21,523	24,523	23,554	14,563	14,767	13,053	13,024	13,010	12,669
% Oper. Ratio	86.8	86.8	97.0	NA	84.9	84.1	75.5	82.8	83.0	83.1
% Earn. on Net Prop.	7.7	16.1	10.2	6.3	7.9	6.7	7.6	8.8	8.5	8.3
% Return On Revs.	3.6	0.1	1.6	2.2	7.5	8.4	10.1	10.0	9.3	9.1
% Return On Invest. Capital	10.2	9.2	8.3	8.5	7.2	9.9	7.7	7.8	7.7	7.4
% Return On Com. Equity	7.0	0.3	12.3	3.6	10.6	11.3	13.4	13.2	12.4	11.9

Data as orig reptd.; bef. results of disc opers/spec. items. Per share data adj. for stk. divs. Bold denotes primary EPS - prior periods restated. E-Estimated. NA-Not Available. NM-Not Meaningful. NR-Not Ranked. UR-Under Review.

Office: 1 Riverside Plaza, Columbus , OH 43215-2373.
Telephone: 614-716-1000.
Email: corpcomm@aep.com
Website: http://www.aep.com
Chrmn, Pres & CEO: M. G. Morris.
EVP & CFO: S. Tomasky.

COO: T. V. Shockley III.
EVP: H. W. Fayne.
Investor Contact: Kathleen Kozero (614-716-2819).
Dirs: E. R. Brooks, D. M. Carlton, J. P. DesBarres, R. W. Fri, W. R. Howell, L. A. Hudson, Jr., L. J. Kujawa, M. G. Morris, L. L. Nowell III, R. L. Sandor, T. V. Shockley III, D. G. Smith, L. G. Stuntz, K. D. Sullivan.

Founded: in 1906.
Domicile: New York.
Employees: 22,075.
S&P Analyst: Justin McCann/PMW/JWP

American Express

Recommendation: HOLD ★★★☆☆
SELL | SELL | HOLD | BUY | BUY

12-Month Target Price: $56.00
(as of July 26, 2004)

AXP has an approximate 0.64% weighting in the **S&P 500**

Sector: Financials
Sub-Industry: Consumer Finance
Peer Group: Consumer Finance - Credit Cards

Summary: AXP, a leader in travel-related services, is also active in investment services, expense management services, and international banking.

Quantitative Evaluations

S&P Earnings & Dividend Rank: A-

| D | C | B- | B | B+ | A- | A | A+ |

S&P Fair Value Rank: 4+

| 1 | 2 | 3 | 4 | 5 |
| Lowest | | | | Highest |

Fair Value Calc.: $55.50 (Fairly Valued)

S&P Investability Quotient Percentile
95%

AXP scored higher than 95% of all companies for which an S&P Report is available.

Volatility: Low

| Low | Average | High |

Technical Evaluation: Bullish
Since 8/04, the technical indicators for AXP have been Bullish.

Relative Strength Rank: Moderate
61
1 Lowest — Highest 99

Price as of 11/12/04: $55.63 | **2004E S&P Core EPS:** $2.54

GAAP Earnings vs. Previous Year
▲ Up ▼ Down ► No Change

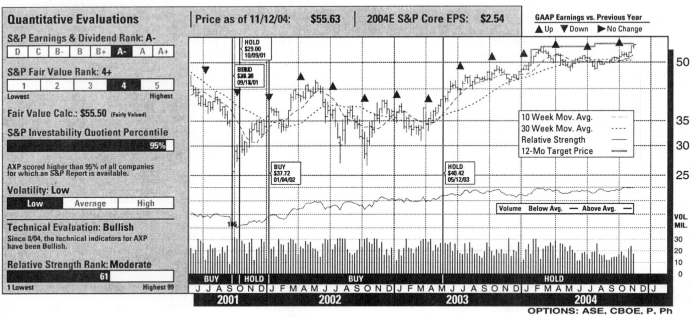

Analyst commentary prepared by Evan Momios, CFA /MF/JWP

Highlights August 19, 2004

- Strong average cardmember spending, growth in cards in force and acquisition benefits allowed the company to exceed its long-term revenue growth target of 8% in the first half of 2004. Expense control, combined with solid credit quality, further boosted the bottom line.

- We believe economic conditions are likely to remain favorable in the 2004 second half, and look for continued corporate and consumer spending to support Travel and Related Services (TRS) revenue growth while increases in marketing expenses should moderate net income growth. In our view, results at AXP's fund unit, American Express Financial Advisors (AEFA), should benefit from what we see as stable market conditions for the rest of the year and the acquisition of Threadneedle Asset Management (completed in the fourth quarter of 2003). We do not expect the announced issuance of American Express cards by MBNA (KRB: $24) to have a meaningful impact on 2004 EPS.

- Overall, we see EPS rising to $2.70 in 2004 and $3.04 in 2005, from $2.31 in 2003. Our 2004 and 2005 Standard & Poor's Core earnings per share estimates are $2.54 and $2.88, respectively, reflecting employee stock option expense.

Investment Rationale/Risk August 19, 2004

- We would hold existing positions. We believe the current valuation fairly reflects the company's strong brand name and growth prospects.

- Risks to our recommendation and target price include a possible deterioration of consumer confidence that could impact domestic consumer spending, a rise in unemployment that could pressure credit quality, a drop in investor confidence, and a serious geopolitical event that could impact domestic equity markets.

- Our 12-month target price of $56 values the stock at 18.5X our 2005 EPS estimate, which we think is an appropriate valuation multiple based on the company's positive operating outlook and average historical valuation. At recent levels, the shares trade at approximately 18.5X our 2004 EPS estimate, compared to about 17X and 22X 12-month forward EPS on average during the past three years and five years, respectively.

Key Stock Statistics

S&P Core EPS 2005E	2.88	52-week Range	$55.63-43.53
S&P Oper. EPS 2004E	2.73	12 Month P/E	21.2
P/E on S&P Oper. EPS 2004E	20.4	Beta	1.16
S&P Oper. EPS 2005E	3.05	Shareholders	47,967
Yield (%)	0.9%	Market Cap (B)	$ 69.8
Dividend Rate/Share	0.48	Shares Outstanding (M)	1255.2

Value of $10,000 invested five years ago: **$ 11,487**

Dividend Data Dividends have been paid since 1870

Amount ($)	Date Decl.	Ex-Div. Date	Stock of Record	Payment Date
0.100	Nov. 18	Dec. 30	Jan. 02	Feb. 10 '04
0.100	Mar. 22	Mar. 31	Apr. 02	May. 10 '04
0.100	May. 25	Jun. 30	Jul. 02	Aug. 10 '04
0.120	Sep. 27	Oct. 06	Oct. 08	Nov. 10 '04

Revenues/Earnings Data Fiscal year ending December 31

Revenues (Million $)

	2004	2003	2002	2001	2000	1999
1Q	6,910	6,023	5,759	5,719	5,657	4,971
2Q	7,258	6,356	5,945	5,268	5,970	5,298
3Q	7,202	6,419	5,907	5,724	5,981	5,311
4Q	—	7,068	6,196	5,871	6,067	5,699
Yr.	—	25,866	23,807	22,582	23,675	21,278

Earnings Per Share ($)

	2004	2003	2002	2001	2000	1999
1Q	0.66	0.53	0.46	0.40	0.48	0.42
2Q	0.68	0.59	0.51	0.13	0.54	0.47
3Q	0.69	0.59	0.52	0.22	0.54	0.47
4Q	E0.70	0.60	0.52	0.22	0.50	0.44
Yr.	E2.73	2.31	2.01	0.98	2.07	1.81

Next earnings report expected: late-January Source: S&P, Company Reports
EPS Estimates based on S&P Operating Earnings; historical GAAP earnings are as reported.

American Express Company

Recommendation: **HOLD** ★ ★ ★ ☆ ☆   12-Month Target Price: **$56.00** (as of July 26, 2004)

Business Summary August 19, 2004

American Express, probably best known for its flagship charge card and travelers cheque products, also offers travel related services, financial advisory services, and international banking services. The company's growth strategy focuses on three principal themes: expanding its international presence, strengthening the charge card network, and broadening financial services offerings. AXP's long-term internal financial targets include 8% annual revenue growth, 12% to 15% annual earnings per share growth, and 18% to 20% return on equity.

Travel Related Services (TRS, 81% of 2003 managed basis revenues) markets travelers cheques and the American Express Card, including the Gold Card, the Platinum Card, the Corporate Card, and the Optima Card. At the end of 2003, cards in force worldwide aggregated $60.5 million, up 5.6% from the level a year earlier. Growth was driven by greater card acquisition activities in the consumer and small business segments, and improved customer retention. Managed charge card receivables totaled $28.4 billion at the end of 2003, up from $26.3 billion a year earlier. The company believes that TRS has the largest card issuing business in the world, based on charge volume. In 2003, TRS's charge volume was $352 billion, with about 26% coming from cardmembers domiciled outside the U.S. Cards are currently issued in 45 currencies, including cards issued by third-party banks and other qualified institutions.

TRS has introduced several new revolving credit card products and features designed to meet the needs of specific customer segments, and to increase consumer loans outstanding. It has also expanded its Membership Rewards program to include a broader range of travel rewards and retail merchandise and gourmet gifts. The program remains an important part of TRS's strategy to increase cardmember spending and loyalty.

Financial Advisors (17%) provides financial products including financial planning and advice, insurance and annuities, investment products such as certificates, mutual funds and limited partnerships, investment advisory services, trust and employee plan administration services, personal auto and homeowners' insurance, and retail securities brokerage services. At the end of 2003, AXP had a sales force of more than 12,121 financial planners. Managed and administered assets totaled $365.3 billion, up from $230.6 billion a year earlier.

American Express Bank Ltd. (3%) offers personal financial and private banking services to customers outside the U.S. At the end of 2003, American Express Bank had loans totaling $6.5 billion, up from $5.6 billion at the end of 2002, and deposits totaling $10.8 billion, up from $9.5 billion a year earlier.

In October 2003, AXP acquired Rosenbluth International, a global travel management company, for an undisclosed amount. In September 2003, the company acquired Threadneedle Asset Management Holdings LTD from Zurich Financial Services Group, for about $565 million in cash.

Company Financials Fiscal Year ending December 31

Per Share Data ($)

(Year Ended December 31)	2003	2002	2001	2000	1999	1998	1997	1996	1995	1994
Tangible Bk. Val.	11.93	10.62	9.04	8.81	7.53	7.18	6.84	6.01	5.53	4.19
Earnings	2.31	2.01	0.98	2.07	1.81	1.54	1.38	1.30	1.04	0.89
S&P Core Earnings	2.09	1.68	0.73	NA	NA	NA	NA	NA	NA	NA
Dividends	0.38	0.32	0.32	0.32	0.30	0.30	0.30	0.38	0.30	0.31
Payout Ratio	16%	16%	33%	15%	17%	19%	22%	29%	29%	35%
Prices - High	49.11	44.91	57.06	63.00	56.29	39.54	30.50	20.12	15.04	11.04
- Low	30.90	26.55	24.20	39.83	31.62	22.33	17.87	12.87	9.66	8.33
P/E Ratio - High	21	22	58	30	31	26	22	15	15	12
- Low	13	13	25	19	18	14	13	10	9	9

Income Statement Analysis (Million $)

	2003	2002	2001	2000	1999	1998	1997	1996	1995	1994
Cards in Force	60.5	57.3	55.2	51.7	46.0	42.7	42.7	41.5	37.8	36.3
Card Chg Volume	352,200	311,400	298,000	296,700	254,100	227,500	209,200	184,000	163,000	141,000
Premium Inc.	1,366	802	674	575	517	469	424	395	735	783
Commissions	16,550	15,463	15,816	16,407	3,626	3,304	4,386	2,540	2,542	8,591
Int & Div.	3,063	2,991	3,049	4,277	4,679	4,631	2,750	4,357	4,531	4,120
Total Revs.	25,866	23,807	22,582	23,675	16,599	14,501	17,760	16,237	15,841	14,282
Net Bef. Taxes	4,247	3,727	1,596	3,908	3,438	2,925	2,750	2,664	2,183	1,891
Net Inc.	3,000	2,671	1,311	2,810	2,475	2,141	1,991	1,901	1,564	1,380
S&P Core Earnings	2,723	2,245	986	NA	NA	NA	NA	NA	NA	NA

Balance Sheet & Other Fin. Data (Million $)

	2003	2002	2001	2000	1999	1998	1997	1996	1995	1994
Total Assets	175,001	157,253	151,100	154,423	148,517	126,933	120,003	108,512	107,405	97,006
Cash Items	5,726	10,288	7,222	8,487	7,471	4,092	4,179	2,677	3,200	3,433
Investment Asset:										
Bonds	Nil	Nil	Nil	Nil	Nil	Nil	Nil	Nil	36,772	23,026
Stocks	Nil	Nil	Nil	Nil	Nil	Nil	Nil	Nil	Nil	Nil
Loans	33,411	29,003	27,401	26,884	24,332	21,861	20,816	18,518	21,595	29,830
Total	57,067	53,638	46,488	43,747	43,052	41,299	59,757	56,857	58,652	54,830
Accounts Receivable	31,269	29,087	29,498	30,543	26,467	22,224	21,774	20,491	19,914	17,147
Cust. Deposits	21,250	18,317	14,557	13,870	12,197	10,398	9,444	9,555	9,885	10,013
Travel Cheques Outst	6,819	6,623	6,190	6,127	6,213	5,823	5,634	5,838	5,697	5,271
Debt	30,809	16,819	8,288	5,211	6,495	7,519	7,873	6,552	7,570	7,162
Common Equity	56,499	51,210	44,800	11,466	10,095	9,698	9,574	8,528	8,020	6,233
% Ret. on Assets	1.8	1.7	0.9	1.9	1.8	1.7	1.7	1.8	1.5	1.4
% Ret. on Equity	5.6	5.6	3.0	26.6	25.0	22.2	22.0	22.9	21.3	18.6

Data as orig reptd.; bef. results of disc opers/spec. items. Per share data adj. for stk. divs. Bold denotes primary EPS - prior periods restated. E-Estimated. NA-Not Available. NM-Not Meaningful. NR-Not Ranked. UR-Under Review.

Office: 200 Vesey Street, New York, NY 10285-4814.
Telephone: 212-640-2000.
Website: http://www.americanexpress.com
Chrmn & CEO: K.I. Chenault.
Vice Chrmn: J.S. Linen.
EVP & CFO: G. Crittenden.

EVP & General Counsel: L.M. Parent.
SVP & Treas: P.H. Hough.
SVP & Investor Contact: R. Stovall 212-640-5574.
Dirs: D. F. Akerson, C. Barshefsky, W. G. Bowen, U. M. Burns, K. I. Chenault, P. R. Dolan, F. R. Johnson, V. E. Jordan, Jr., J. Leschly, R. A. McGinn, E. D. Miller, F. P. Popoff, R. D. Walter.

Founded: in 1868.
Domicile: New York.
Employees: 78,236.
S&P Analyst: Evan Momios, CFA /MF/JWP

American Int'l Group

Recommendation: **BUY** ★★★★☆
SELL | SELL | HOLD | BUY | BUY

12-Month Target Price: **$72.00**
(as of October 26, 2004)

AIG has an approximate 1.44% weighting in the **S&P 500**

Sector: Financials
Sub-Industry: Multi-line Insurance
Peer Group: Insurers - Multi-Line - Larger

Summary: One of the world's leading insurance organizations, AIG provides property, casualty and life insurance, as well as other financial services, in 130 countries and territories.

Quantitative Evaluations

Price as of 11/12/04: $61.03 | **2004E S&P Core EPS:** $4.35

S&P Earnings & Dividend Rank: A+

| D | C | B- | B | B+ | A- | A | A+ |

S&P Fair Value Rank: 3

| 1 | 2 | 3 | 4 | 5 |
| Lowest | | | | Highest |

Fair Value Calc.: $58.40 (Slightly Overvalued)

S&P Investability Quotient Percentile
99%

AIG scored higher than 99% of all companies for which an S&P Report is available.

Volatility: Average

| Low | Average | High |

Technical Evaluation: Bearish
Since 9/04, the technical indicators for AIG have been Bearish.

Relative Strength Rank: Weak
14
1 Lowest | Highest 99

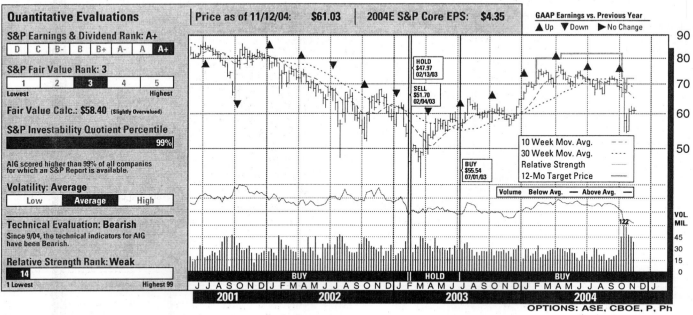

GAAP Earnings vs. Previous Year
▲ Up ▼ Down ► No Change

HOLD $47.97 02/13/03
SELL $51.70 02/04/03
BUY $55.54 07/01/03

10 Week Mov. Avg.
30 Week Mov. Avg.
Relative Strength
12-Mo Target Price

Volume Below Avg. — Above Avg.

BUY | HOLD | BUY
J J A S O N D | J F M A M J J A S O N D | J F M A M J J A S O N D | J F M A M J J A S O N D | J
2001 | 2002 | 2003 | 2004

OPTIONS: ASE, CBOE, P, Ph

Analyst commentary prepared by Catherine A. Seifert/DC/JWP

Highlights August 30, 2004

- Our estimate of 14% revenue growth in 2004 assumes that property-casualty earned premiums will climb at least 24% amid stable prices and continued favorable terms for most lines, particularly large, specialized types of coverage.

- We also expect AIG's significant overseas life insurance franchise to continue to be a core contributor to operating profits. AIG is well positioned, in our view, to exploit growth opportunities that exist in a number of Asian economies. We see a partial offset in more modest growth for U.S.-based life insurance operations. We think continued strength in equity markets will likely spur demand for equity-based investment and savings products, such as variable annuities.

- Our operating EPS estimates of $4.50 for 2004 and $5.10 for 2005 assume a normal level of catastrophe losses and no significant loss reserve additions. AIG expects claims from Hurricane Charley to be $80-$100 million. We estimate the per share impact to be $0.03 to $0.04.

Investment Rationale/Risk August 30, 2004

- We continue to view the shares as modestly undervalued, relative to their historical valuation on both a forward price/earnings and price/book basis. We believe AIG possesses a number of competitive advantages, including its financial strength and its low property-casualty underwriting expense ratio. We believe these strengths leave AIG well positioned, despite an operating environment marked by plateauing property-casualty insurance rates and a stagnant equity market. AIG's unmatched global franchise, particularly in Asia, is also a key competitive advantage, in our opinion. Our outlook is tempered by the fact that AIG's business mix has shifted to a more life insurance-based model in recent years, and life insurance stocks tend to trade at a P/E multiple discount relative to the broader market. We believe investors' near-term appetite for property-casualty insurance stocks may not be particularly hearty amid concerns over heightened premium price competition.

- Risks to our opinion and target price include the possibility of a significant deterioration in claim trends and loss reserve levels, another terrorist attack in the U.S., and a sharp downturn in the U.S. equity markets.

- We derive our 12-month target price of $82 by using a sum-of-the-parts analysis, and assuming a modest expansion of the stock's current P/E multiple.

Key Stock Statistics

S&P Oper. EPS 2004E	4.30	52-week Range	$77.36-54.28	
P/E on S&P Oper. EPS 2004E	14.2	12 Month P/E	14.7	
S&P Oper. EPS 2005E	5.10	Beta	0.87	
Yield (%)	0.5%	Shareholders	60,000	
Dividend Rate/Share	0.30	Market Cap (B)	$159.0	
Shares Outstanding (M)	2604.6			

Value of $10,000 invested five years ago: **$ 8,805**

Dividend Data Dividends have been paid since 1969

Amount ($)	Date Decl.	Ex-Div. Date	Stock of Record	Payment Date
0.065	Nov. 12	Mar. 03	Mar. 05	Mar. 19 '04
0.065	Mar. 17	Jun. 02	Jun. 04	Jun. 18 '04
0.075	May. 19	Sep. 01	Sep. 03	Sep. 17 '04
0.075	Sep. 15	Dec. 01	Dec. 03	Dec. 17 '04

Revenues/Earnings Data Fiscal year ending December 31

Revenues (Million $)

	2004	2003	2002	2001	2000	1999
1Q	23,637	18,927	16,137	—	9,702	9,825
2Q	23,809	19,891	16,662	—	10,157	10,195
3Q	25,411	20,306	17,150	—	13,601	9,638
4Q	—	22,179	17,533	—	12,510	10,998
Yr.	—	81,303	67,482	52,852	45,970	40,656

Earnings Per Share ($)

	2004	2003	2002	2001	2000	1999
1Q	1.08	0.74	0.75	0.65	0.57	0.51
2Q	1.09	0.87	0.68	0.69	0.60	0.54
3Q	0.95	0.89	0.70	0.15	0.60	0.54
4Q	—	1.03	-0.03	0.70	0.64	0.56
Yr.	—	3.53	2.10	2.07	2.41	2.15

Next earnings report expected: mid-February Source: S&P, Company Reports
EPS Estimates based on S&P Operating Earnings; historical GAAP earnings are as reported.

American International Group, Inc.

Recommendation: **BUY** ★ ★ ★ ★ ☆   12-Month Target Price: **$72.00** (as of October 26, 2004)

Business Summary August 30, 2004

New York City-based AIG is one of the world's leading insurance organizations, providing an array of property-casualty, life insurance and retirement savings products in the U.S. and about 130 other countries. It also engages in airline leasing and currency trading. Revenues totaled $81.3 billion in 2003, with general insurance accounting for 42%, life insurance 44%, financial services 9%, and asset management and other 5%. The Far East provided 28% of 2003 revenues, domestic operations 56%, and other foreign 16%.

The General Insurance division underwrites virtually all lines of property-casualty insurance. Net written premiums totaled $35.2 billion in 2003, up 28.4% from $27.4 billion in 2002. Of the 2003 written premiums, the Domestic Brokerage Group accounted for 57%, Foreign General 21%, Domestic Personal Lines 11%, Reinsurance 9%, and Mortgage Guaranty 2%.

The Domestic Brokerage Group markets property-casualty insurance products through insurance brokers to corporations in the U.S. and Canada. Lines of coverage offered consist of so-called standard lines, including commercial property insurance, excess liability, inland marine, and workers' compensation insurance. The unit also offers more specialized lines of coverage, including directors' and officers' liability, kidnap-ransom insurance, export credit and political risk, and various professional errors and omissions coverages. AIG maintains a majority ownership in Transatlantic Holdings (TRH), through which it underwrites rein-

surance. Transatlantic Holdings is a property-casualty reinsurer. The Foreign General division conducts AIG's international property-casualty operations. The Domestic Personal Lines division engages in mass marketing of personal lines insurance, primarily auto insurance. In 2003, AIG acquired the U.S.-based auto and home insurance business of General Electric Co. (GE). The unit also includes 21st Century Industries (TW), a California-based direct writer of personal auto insurance, which was approximately 63% owned at year-end 2003. During 2003, UGC, a division of the General Insurance division, commenced providing guaranty insurance to providers of student loans. UGC had approximately $22 billion of guaranty risk in force at December 31, 2003.

Life insurance subsidiaries offer individual and group life annuity and accident and health policies. Life insurance operations in foreign countries comprised approximately 78% of life premium income in 2003. AIG increased its presence in the U.S. life insurance and retirement savings market via the January 1999 acquisition of SunAmerica, Inc., for 187,543,737 common shares and the August 2001 acquisition of American General Corp. (AGC) for about $23 billion.

Financial service operations include interest rate and currency swaps, cash management, premium financing, airline leasing, asset management, and private banking.

Company Financials Fiscal Year ending December 31

Per Share Data ($)

(Year Ended December 31)	2003	2002	2001	2000	1999	1998	1997	1996	1995	1994
Tangible Bk. Val.	24.39	20.32	19.94	16.98	14.33	13.78	12.20	11.13	9.91	8.22
Oper. Earnings	NA	NA	NA	2.45	2.13	1.87	1.64	1.43	1.23	1.06
Earnings	3.53	2.10	2.07	2.41	2.15	1.91	1.68	1.46	1.26	1.09
S&P Core Earnings	3.89	2.63	2.06	NA	NA	NA	NA	NA	NA	NA
Dividends	0.22	0.18	0.16	0.14	0.13	0.11	0.10	0.09	0.08	0.07
Relative Payout	6%	8%	8%	6%	6%	6%	6%	6%	6%	6%
Prices - High	66.35	80.00	98.31	103.75	75.25	54.73	40.02	27.58	22.63	15.92
- Low	42.92	47.61	66.00	52.37	51.00	34.60	25.24	20.88	15.19	12.91
P/E Ratio - High	19	38	47	43	35	29	24	19	18	15
- Low	12	23	32	22	24	18	15	14	12	12

Income Statement Analysis (Million $)

	2003	2002	2001	2000	1999	1998	1997	1996	1995	1994
Life Ins. In Force	NA	1,324,451	1,228,501	583,059	584,959	499,167	436,573	421,983	376,097	333,379
Prem. Inc.: Life A & H	NA	20,320	19,243	13,610	11,942	10,247	9,926	8,978	8,038	6,724
Prem. Inc.: Cas./Prop.	NA	24,269	19,365	17,407	15,544	14,098	12,421	11,855	11,406	10,287
Net Invest. Inc.	16,662	15,034	14,628	9,824	8,723	5,424	4,750	4,365	3,811	3,184
Total Revs.	81,303	67,482	52,400	40,703	36,356	29,939	27,246	25,298	25,875	22,442
Pretax Inc.	13,908	8,142	8,139	8,349	7,512	5,529	4,731	4,013	3,466	2,952
Net Oper. Inc.	NA	NA	NA	5,737	4,999	3,689	49,662	45,965	38,217	34,141
Net Inc.	9,265	5,519	5,499	5,636	5,055	3,766	3,332	2,897	2,510	2,176
S&P Core Earnings	10,208	6,931	5,476	NA	NA	NA	NA	NA	NA	NA

Balance Sheet & Other Fin. Data (Million $)

	2003	2002	2001	2000	1999	1998	1997	1996	1995	1994
Cash & Equiv.	5,881	1,165	698	256	132	1,874	87.0	3,265	3,574	3,402
Premiums Due	14,166	13,088	11,647	11,832	12,737	11,679	10,283	9,617	9,410	8,802
Invest. Assets: Bonds	309,254	243,366	200,616	102,010	90,144	61,906	51,566	48,625	42,901	35,431
Invest. Assets: Stocks	9,584	7,066	7,937	7,181	6,714	5,893	5,209	6,006	5,369	5,099
Invest. Assets: Loans	21,249	19,928	18,092	12,243	12,134	8,247	7,920	7,877	7,861	5,353
Invest. Assets: Total	449,657	339,320	357,602	140,910	185,882	141,923	116,221	103,982	91,627	73,388
Deferred Policy Costs	26,398	22,256	17,443	10,189	9,624	7,647	6,593	6,471	5,768	5,132
Total Assets	678,346	561,229	492,982	306,577	268,238	194,398	163,971	148,431	134,136	114,346
Debt	57,877	50,076	34,503	5,801	23,795	31,093	25,260	23,521	17,990	17,519
Common Equity	152,620	130,407	113,471	39,619	88,842	27,131	24,002	22,044	19,827	16,422
Comb. Loss-Exp. Ratio	NA	106.0	100.7	96.7	96.4	96.4	96.2	96.9	97.0	98.8
% Return On Revs.	11.4	8.2	10.5	13.8	13.9	12.6	14.8	11.2	9.7	9.7
% Ret. on Equity	6.5	4.5	5.1	15.5	5.9	14.7	14.5	13.8	13.9	13.7
% Invest. Yield	4.1	4.8	4.5	7.4	4.9	4.9	4.3	4.5	4.6	4.7

Data as orig reptd.; bef. results of disc opers/spec. items. Per share data adj. for stk. divs.; EPS diluted. E-Estimated. NA-Not Available. NM-Not Meaningful. NR-Not Ranked. Oper. EPS est. excl. inv. gains/losses; historical EPS data incl. them.

Office: 70 Pine Street, New York, NY 10270-0094.
Telephone: 212-770-7000.
Website: http://www.aig.com
Chrmn & CEO: M.R. Greenberg.
Vice Chrmn: E.S. Tse.
Vice Chrmn: F.G. Wisner.

Vice Chrmn: J.A. Frenkel.
Vice Chrmn: T.R. Tizzio.
Dirs: M. B. Aidinoff, P. Chia, M. A. Cohen, W. S. Cohen, M. S. Feldstein, E. V. Futter, M. R. Greenberg, C. A. Hills, F. J. Hoenemeyer, R. C. Holbrooke, H. I. Smith, M. J. Sullivan, E. S. Tse, J. S. Wintrob, F. G. Wisner, F. G. Zarb.

Founded: in 1967.
Domicile: Delaware.
Employees: 86,000.
S&P Analyst: Catherine A. Seifert/DC/JWP

American Power Conversion

Recommendation: SELL ★ ★ ☆ ☆ ☆
SELL SELL HOLD BUY BUY

12-Month Target Price: $18.00
(as of October 29, 2004)

APCC has an approximate 0.04% weighting in the **S&P 500**

Sector: Industrials
Sub-Industry: Electrical Components & Equipment
Peer Group: Power Supply - Larger

Summary: APCC manufactures uninterruptible power supply (UPS) products that protect data in PCs and other electronic devices from disruptions or surges in electric power.

Quantitative Evaluations

S&P Earnings & Dividend Rank: B+

| D | C | B- | B | B+ | A- | A | A+ |

S&P Fair Value Rank: 2

| 1 | 2 | 3 | 4 | 5 |
| Lowest | | | | Highest |

Fair Value Calc.: $19.10 (Slightly Overvalued)

S&P Investability Quotient Percentile
57%

APCC scored higher than 57% of all companies for which an S&P Report is available.

Volatility: High

| Low | Average | High |

Technical Evaluation: Bullish
Since 11/04, the technical indicators for APCC have been Bullish.

Relative Strength Rank: Strong
88
1 Lowest   Highest 99

Price as of 11/12/04: $20.74   **2004E S&P Core EPS:** $0.69

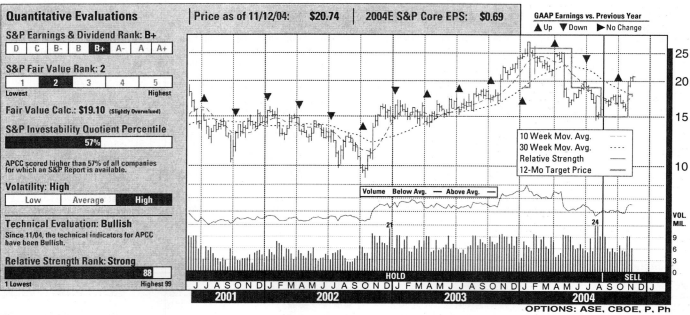

GAAP Earnings vs. Previous Year
▲ Up ▼ Down ► No Change

10 Week Mov. Avg.
30 Week Mov. Avg.
Relative Strength
12-Mo Target Price

Volume Below Avg. — Above Avg.

OPTIONS: ASE, CBOE, P, Ph

Analyst commentary prepared by Markos N. Kaminis/MF

Highlights November 01, 2004

- We project 2004 revenue growth of 14%, as we anticipate that APCC will continue its efforts to gain market share on low end products through price reductions, boosting revenues. We believe the company will also benefit from heightened global awareness of the impact of power disturbances. For 2005, we forecast revenue growth of 8%.

- We expect gross margins to narrow by about 150 basis points in 2004 and 60 points in 2005, as price cuts outweigh the impact of past product cost consolidation efforts, including a transition to lower cost production facilities, and lower costs from suppliers. We forecast continued spending on R&D and higher SG&A in 2004, as the company sees a necessity to leverage its financial strength in an effort to gain market share. SG&A should also be affected by marketing efforts for new products and costs associated with increasing international business. We anticipate SG&A will decrease on a percentage of sales basis in 2005. We expect operating margins to narrow by more than 300 basis points in 2004, before widening modestly in 2005.

- We forecast 2004 EPS of $0.85, down about 3%, excluding a 2003 reversal of a product recall estimate. We project 2005 EPS growth of 13%.

Investment Rationale/Risk November 01, 2004

- We believe many corporations have delayed information technology upgrades. We continue to regard APCC's long-term revenue growth outlook and balance sheet as solid, with substantial cash and no debt. However, although we believe the company's efforts to strengthen its longer-term cash flow at the cost of near-term profitability may prove the right course of action, we view the shares as overvalued compared to our 12-month target price.

- Risks to our recommendation and target price include the possibility that costs incurred for the product recall of selected Back-UPS CS models could be lower than anticipated; APCC's potential ability to more effectively align operating expenses and production capacity with demand; and a lessening of competitive pricing pressures.

- At 23X our 2004 EPS estimate, the shares are valued slightly above those of electrical components and equipment peers in the S&P 1500, which are trading at 22X. We calculate the industry P/E multiple to growth (PEG) ratio at 1.7X, below APCC's 1.8X (based on our longer-term growth projection of 13%). Applying the industry PEG to our forward 12-month EPS forecast of $0.93 and our long-term growth view, we value the stock at $19. Our 12-month target price of $18 is based on a blend of that and our DCF analysis, which assumes a weighted average cost of capital of 15.3%.

Key Stock Statistics

S&P Core EPS 2005E	0.84	52-week Range	$27.42-14.55
S&P Oper. EPS 2004E	0.85	12 Month P/E	22.5
P/E on S&P Oper. EPS 2004E	24.4	Beta	1.99
S&P Oper. EPS 2005E	0.96	Shareholders	1,916
Yield (%)	1.9%	Market Cap (B)	$ 4.0
Dividend Rate/Share	0.40	Shares Outstanding (M)	191.3

Value of $10,000 invested five years ago: **$ 8,997**

Dividend Data Dividends have been paid since 2003

Amount ($)	Date Decl.	Ex-Div. Date	Stock of Record	Payment Date
0.080	Feb. 09	Feb. 23	Feb. 25	Mar. 17 '04
0.080	Apr. 12	May. 24	May. 26	Jun. 16 '04
0.100	Jun. 14	Aug. 24	Aug. 26	Sep. 16 '04
0.100	Oct. 25	Nov. 22	Nov. 24	Dec. 15 '04

Revenues/Earnings Data Fiscal year ending December 31

Revenues (Million $)

	2004	2003	2002	2001	2000	1999
1Q	351.8	309.0	296.7	359.7	311.2	277.2
2Q	395.7	331.5	308.2	364.5	368.0	315.5
3Q	441.7	393.7	337.1	360.9	397.0	355.9
4Q	—	430.6	358.0	348.1	407.3	388.7
Yr.	—	1,465	1,300	1,433	1,484	1,337

Earnings Per Share ($)

	2004	2003	2002	2001	2000	1999
1Q	0.17	0.15	0.08	0.14	0.24	0.18
2Q	0.13	0.17	0.15	0.18	0.17	0.22
3Q	0.34	0.28	0.21	0.11	0.22	0.32
4Q	E0.27	0.28	0.14	0.15	0.20	0.34
Yr.	E0.85	0.88	0.59	0.58	0.83	1.05

Next earnings report expected: early-February Source: S&P, Company Reports
EPS Estimates based on S&P Operating Earnings; historical GAAP earnings are as reported.

American Power Conversion Corporation

Recommendation: **SELL** ★★ ☆☆☆   12-Month Target Price: **$18.00** (as of October 29, 2004)

Business Summary November 01, 2004

American Power Conversion manufactures power protection and management solutions for computer, communications and electronic applications worldwide. The company aims to capitalize on increased awareness of the costs and lost productivity associated with power failures, surges or sags in electrical power. Its products are used with sensitive electronic devices like PCs, high performance computer workstations, servers, communications and internetworking equipment, and other sensitive electronic devices that rely on electric utility power.

APCC believes the growth of the power protection industry has been fueled by demand for information systems to be accessible as much as 24 hours a day, and by the proliferation of microprocessor-based equipment and related systems in the corporate marketplace and the small office/home office environment. It has become necessary to ensure that hardware and data stored in and traveling through networks are protected from fluctuations in utility power. A UPS protects against this by providing continuous power automatically and virtually instantaneously after the electric power supply is interrupted or sags. It also provides line filtering and protection against surges while the electric utility is operating. APCC offers a broad range of U.S. and international UPS models, ranging from 325 volt-amps to 1.6 megawatts, with end user list prices of $29.99 to $210,000.

The company operates primarily in one industry, and has three reportable operating segments: Small Systems, Large Systems, and Other. The Small Systems segment develops power devices and accessories for servers and networking

equipment commonly used in local area and wide area networks and for personal computers and sensitive electronics. Major product offerings include the Smart-UPS, Matrix-UPS, Symmetra Power Array, and the Back-UPS family of UPSs. Also included are the SurgeArrest surge suppressors as well as cabling and connectivity products. Products are sold to home and commercial users primarily through an indirect selling model consisting of computer distributors and dealers, value added resellers, mass merchandisers, catalog merchandisers, e-commerce vendors, and strategic partnerships.

The Large Systems segment produces products that provide back-up power, power distribution and cooling for data centers, facilities, and communications equipment for both commercial and industrial applications. Product offerings include major components of InfraStruXure systems, Silcon UPSs, NetworkAIR precision cooling equipment, DC and broadband power systems, and services. Products are sold to commercial users primarily through an indirect selling model consisting of value added resellers and strategic partnerships. The Other segment principally consists of desktop and notebook computer accessories and replacement batteries.

Sales outside the U.S. accounted for 55% and 52% of net sales in 2003 and 2002, respectively. Two computer distributor customers, Tech Data Product Management and Ingram Micro accounted respectively for 14.1% and 10.0% of net sales in 2003 (14.4% and 13.2% in 2002).

Company Financials Fiscal Year ending December 31

Per Share Data ($)

(Year Ended December 31)	2003	2002	2001	2000	1999	1998	1997	1996	1995	1994
Tangible Bk. Val.	7.28	6.34	5.67	5.00	4.42	3.31	2.74	2.08	1.56	1.15
Cash Flow	1.11	0.79	0.86	1.03	1.21	0.88	0.73	0.56	0.43	0.42
Earnings	0.88	0.59	0.58	0.83	1.05	0.76	0.64	0.49	0.37	0.39
S&P Core Earnings	0.77	0.46	0.33	NA	NA	NA	NA	NA	NA	NA
Dividends	0.16	Nil	Nil	Nil	Nil	Nil	Nil	Nil	Nil	Nil
Payout Ratio	18%	Nil	Nil	Nil	Nil	Nil	Nil	Nil	Nil	Nil
Prices - High	24.69	16.60	19.39	48.84	29.37	24.78	17.18	14.06	12.93	15.25
- Low	13.72	9.06	10.25	9.50	13.09	11.75	7.62	3.93	4.56	7.25
P/E Ratio - High	28	28	33	59	28	33	27	29	35	40
- Low	16	15	18	11	12	15	12	8	12	19

Income Statement Analysis (Million $)

	2003	2002	2001	2000	1999	1998	1997	1996	1995	1994
Revs.	1,465	1,300	1,433	1,484	1,337	1,126	873	707	515	378
Oper. Inc.	277	191	201	298	310	235	189	147	114	112
Depr.	47.5	39.7	55.9	40.9	30.6	23.0	17.7	13.5	10.1	6.11
Int. Exp.	Nil	Nil	Nil	Nil	Nil	Nil	Nil	Nil	0.30	Nil
Pretax Inc.	239	162	159	233	293	216	178	139	105	109
Eff. Tax Rate	26.0%	28.0%	28.5%	29.0%	29.5%	31.6%	31.5%	33.5%	33.5%	34.8%
Net Inc.	177	117	113	166	206	148	122	92.4	69.5	71.3
S&P Core Earnings	157	91.6	64.8	NA	NA	NA	NA	NA	NA	NA

Balance Sheet & Other Fin. Data (Million $)

	2003	2002	2001	2000	1999	1998	1997	1996	1995	1994
Cash	252	209	288	283	456	220	270	153	39.0	41.5
Curr. Assets	1,498	1,277	1,067	961	900	675	540	424	278	211
Total Assets	1,806	1,605	1,421	1,317	1,107	872	641	504	347	265
Curr. Liab.	281	277	183	206	194	181	114	106	51.9	50.3
LT Debt	Nil	Nil	Nil	Nil	Nil	Nil	Nil	Nil	Nil	Nil
Common Equity	1,511	1,312	1,221	1,097	902	681	522	392	290	212
Total Cap.	1,525	1,327	1,238	1,111	913	691	528	398	295	215
Cap. Exp.	21.6	19.6	47.9	73.7	36.0	55.7	37.2	25.0	24.0	35.9
Cash Flow	224	156	169	207	237	171	140	106	79.6	77.4
Curr. Ratio	5.3	4.6	5.8	4.7	4.6	3.7	4.8	4.0	5.4	4.2
% LT Debt of Cap.	Nil	Nil	Nil	Nil	Nil	Nil	Nil	Nil	Nil	Nil
% Net Inc.of Revs.	12.1	9.0	7.9	11.2	15.4	13.1	13.9	13.1	13.5	18.8
% Ret. on Assets	10.4	7.7	8.3	13.7	20.8	19.5	21.3	21.7	22.8	33.4
% Ret. on Equity	12.5	9.2	9.8	16.6	26.0	24.5	26.7	27.1	27.8	41.2

Data as orig reptd.; bef. results of disc opers/spec. items. Per share data adj. for stk. divs. Bold denotes primary EPS - prior periods restated. E-Estimated. NA-Not Available. NM-Not Meaningful. NR-Not Ranked. UR-Under Review.

Office: 132 Fairgrounds Road, West Kingston, RI 02892-1517.
Telephone: 401-789-5735.
Email: investorrelations@apcc.com
Website: http://www.apc.com
Chrmn, Pres & CEO: R.B. Dowdell, Jr.

SVP & CFO: D.M. Muir.
Investor Contact: D. Hancock 800-788-2208.
Dirs: R. B. Dowdell, Jr., J. D. Gerson, J. G. Kassakian, J. F. Keane, Sr., E. E. Landsman, E. F. Lyon, N. E. Rasmussen, E. B. Richstone.
Auditor: KPMG.

Founded: in 1981.
Domicile: Massachusetts.
Employees: 6,365.
S&P Analyst: Markos N. Kaminis/MF

STANDARD &POOR'S

American Standard

Stock Report
November 13, 2004
NYSE Symbol: ASD

Recommendation: **BUY** ★★★★★ 12-Month Target Price: **$49.00**
SELL | SELL | HOLD | BUY | BUY
(as of October 18, 2004)

ASD has an approximate 0.08% weighting in the **S&P 500**

Sector: Industrials
Sub-Industry: Building Products
Peer Group: Heating/Air Conditioning/Plumbing

Summary: This company is a leading worldwide manufacturer of air conditioning systems and bathroom and kitchen fixtures and a major European producer of commercial vehicle braking systems.

Quantitative Evaluations

S&P Earnings & Dividend Rank: B-

| D | C | B- | B | B+ | A- | A | A+ |

S&P Fair Value Rank: 1+

| 1 | 2 | 3 | 4 | 5 |
| Lowest | | | | Highest |

Fair Value Calc.: $25.30 (Overvalued)

S&P Investability Quotient Percentile
98%

ASD scored higher than 98% of all companies for which an S&P Report is available.

Volatility: Low

| Low | Average | High |

Technical Evaluation: Neutral
Since 11/04, the technical indicators for ASD have been Neutral.

Relative Strength Rank: Moderate
48
1 Lowest   Highest 99

| Price as of 11/12/04: | $39.20 | 2004E S&P Core EPS: | $2.12 |

GAAP Earnings vs. Previous Year
▲ Up   ▼ Down   ► No Change

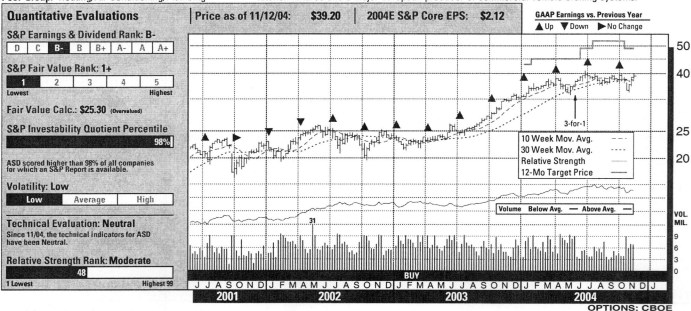

10 Week Mov. Avg. - - -
30 Week Mov. Avg. - - - -
Relative Strength ......
12-Mo Target Price ———

Volume Below Avg. ▒▒ — Above Avg. ———

BUY

J J A S O N D | J F M A M J J A S O N D | J F M A M J J A S O N D | J F M A M J J A S O N D | J
2001 | 2002 | 2003 | 2004 | J

OPTIONS: CBOE

Analyst commentary prepared by Michael W. Jaffe/CB/BK

Highlights October 26, 2004

- Sales should rise about 7% in 2005, on an expected moderate upturn in all of ASD's operating segments. Following the modest revival that was being seen in commercial air conditioning sales in 2004, after a lengthy period of weakness, we expect ongoing growth in that area in 2005, on our outlook for an ongoing upturn in the U.S. economy. We also see the U.S. residential air conditioning and bath and kitchen businesses being aided by what we expect to be continued solid levels of home purchases and remodeling activity during the year, while Europe's larger kitchen and bath operation should also see slightly higher sales on some likely economic pickup in that region. We also see solid volume gains in vehicle controls in 2005, on our forecast of a solid increase in truck builds in markets served and more product content per vehicle.

- Net margins should widen in 2005. We see this forecasted improvement driven by the better demand we see, the likely benefits of productivity and materials purchasing initiatives, and our view of a calming of materials costs after a big run-up that was seen in 2004. These factors should outweigh the likely costs of the implementation of new streamlining activities, plus expected outlays for ongoing new product development and marketing programs .

- Our 2004 EPS forecast excludes net credits of $0.03 a share in the first nine months of the year. Our S&P Core Earnings forecasts for 2004 and 2005 each fall $0.11 a share below our operating estimate, and reflect projected stock option expense and net pension costs, with 2004 also including net credits.

Investment Rationale/Risk October 26, 2004

- We expect ASD's primary commercial air conditioning segment to stage a slightly more robust revival over the coming year. What we view as strong brand names and a well run business also leave us positive about ASD's long-term outlook. Based on these views and valuation considerations, we recommend buying ASD shares.

- Risks to our recommendation and target price include an unexpected downturn in the U.S. economy and a slower than anticipated firming of the European economy.

- The shares recently traded at 14X our 2005 EPS forecast, a small discount to the S&P 500. We think a premium is warranted, as our positive view of ASD's business model and operating prospects should outweigh any discount merited by a highly leveraged ($1.6 billion long-term debt at September 30, 2004) but improving balance sheet. Applying a multiple of 19X to our 2005 EPS estimate suggests appreciation potential to $48 over the next 12 months. Using discounted cash flow, and assuming 6% average free cash flow growth for the next 15 years, 2.5% growth in perpetuity, and a 9% weighted average cost of capital, we arrive at 12-month appreciation potential to $51. Using a blend of these metrics, our 12-month target price is $49.

Key Stock Statistics

S&P Core EPS 2005E	2.44	52-week Range	$40.93-31.64
S&P Oper. EPS 2004E	2.23	12 Month P/E	17.9
P/E on S&P Oper. EPS 2004E	17.6	Beta	0.73
S&P Oper. EPS 2005E	2.55	Shareholders	33,000
Yield (%)	Nil	Market Cap (B)	$ 8.4
Dividend Rate/Share	Nil	Shares Outstanding (M)	214.5

Value of $10,000 invested five years ago: **$ 29,726**

Dividend Data

Amount ($)	Date Decl.	Ex-Div. Date	Stock of Record	Payment Date
3-for-1	Feb. 05	May. 28	May. 18	May. 27 '04

Revenues/Earnings Data Fiscal year ending December 31

Revenues (Million $)

	2004	2003	2002	2001	2000	1999
1Q	2,185	1,951	1,762	1,791	1,822	1,649
2Q	2,575	2,265	2,087	2,039	2,046	1,911
3Q	2,396	2,234	2,070	1,885	1,961	1,876
4Q	—	2,118	1,877	1,750	1,769	1,754
Yr.	—	8,568	7,795	7,465	7,598	7,190

Earnings Per Share ($)

	2004	2003	2002	2001	2000	1999
1Q	0.38	0.29	0.26	0.30	0.27	0.23
2Q	0.73	0.61	0.57	0.54	0.49	0.43
3Q	0.71	0.55	0.52	0.41	0.41	0.36
4Q	E0.44	0.38	0.34	0.09	0.27	0.21
Yr.	E2.23	1.83	1.68	1.35	1.45	1.21

Next earnings report expected: late-January Source: S&P, Company Reports
EPS Estimates based on S&P Operating Earnings; historical GAAP earnings are as reported.

American Standard Companies Inc.

Recommendation: **BUY** ★★★★★   12-Month Target Price: **$49.00** (as of October 18, 2004)

Business Summary October 27, 2004

American Standard Companies is a major global maker of air conditioning systems, bathroom and kitchen fixtures and fittings, and commercial vehicle control systems.

ASD derived 58% of sales and 62% of operating profits (before one-time items) in 2003 from its air conditioning business; 26% and 17% from bath and kitchen products; and 16% and 21% from vehicle control systems.

Brands include Trane and American Standard for air conditioning; American Standard, Ideal Standard, Porcher, Jado, Armitage Shanks, Dolomite and Borma for bath and kitchen products; and Wabco for vehicle control systems.

Operations in Europe accounted for 31% of sales and 30% of operating profits in 2003. Other foreign operations contributed 16% and 17%, respectively.

The company is a leading maker of air conditioning systems, with factories in the U.S. and foreign markets. American Standard derived 25% of the division's sales outside the U.S. in 2003. ASD makes unitary systems, which are factory-assembled central air conditioning systems; and applied systems, which are custom-engineered for commercial use. Some 73% of segment sales came from commercial markets in 2003, and about 60% of air conditioning sales for the year came from replacement, renovation and repair markets.

ASD is a leading maker in Europe, the U.S. and several other nations of bathroom and kitchen fixtures and fittings. It supplies these products to residential and commercial markets through retail and wholesale sales channels. Markets include replacement and remodeling, and new construction. About 66% of bath and kitchen segment sales in 2003 were from non-U.S. operations.

The company is a leading producer, in Europe and Brazil, of braking and control systems for the worldwide commercial, luxury and utility vehicle sectors. The division generated 78% of its 2003 sales in Europe.

Under a program initiated in December 2000, which was targeted at eliminating redundant work and enhancing productivity, ASD reduced its workforce by about 1,750 positions. The company saw the overall program generating $40 million in annual cost savings, with full realization in 2003.

To combat the impact of a weak global economy, the company initiated a program in 2001's fourth quarter to reduce its workforce by another 1,700 (up from 1,000 announced in October 2001). It also recorded $36 million of after-tax expenses ($0.49 a share) to reflect the costs of the plan. ASD expected $55 million of annual pretax savings from these additional staff cuts.

ASD recorded $0.37 a share of after-tax job elimination expenses in 2003's fourth quarter for actions taken to reduce its labor force by 870 more workers. It expects to recognize $36 million of annual savings from these actions as of 2005. Also in that quarter, it recorded a $0.36 a share net benefit mostly from the resolution of a German tax audit.

Company Financials Fiscal Year ending December 31

Per Share Data ($)

(Year Ended December 31)	2003	2002	2001	2000	1999	1998	1997	1996	1995	1994
Tangible Bk. Val.	NM	NM	NM	NM	NM	NM	NM	NM	NM	NA
Cash Flow	2.95	2.36	2.40	2.44	2.14	1.01	1.24	0.42	1.27	NA
Earnings	1.83	1.68	1.35	1.45	1.21	0.15	0.52	-0.20	0.63	NA
S&P Core Earnings	1.85	1.44	1.07	NA	NA	NA	NA	NA	NA	NA
Dividends	Nil	Nil	Nil	Nil	Nil	Nil	Nil	Nil	Nil	NA
Payout Ratio	Nil	Nil	Nil	Nil	Nil	Nil	Nil	Nil	Nil	NA
Prices - High	34.00	26.33	23.63	16.58	16.47	16.41	17.20	13.25	10.66	NA
- Low	21.27	19.40	15.58	11.43	10.37	7.20	11.54	8.50	6.54	NA
P/E Ratio - High	19	16	18	11	14	NM	33	NM	17	NA
- Low	12	12	12	8	9	NM	22	NM	10	NA

Income Statement Analysis (Million $)

	2003	2002	2001	2000	1999	1998	1997	1996	1995	1994
Revs.	8,568	7,795	7,465	7,598	7,190	6,654	6,008	5,805	5,221	NA
Oper. Inc.	924	842	886	916	839	748	711	665	624	NA
Depr.	247	150	232	213	202	190	164	146	143	NA
Int. Exp.	117	129	169	199	188	188	192	202	217	NA
Pretax Inc.	549	556	476	509	452	167	247	57.6	239	NA
Eff. Tax Rate	26.2%	33.3%	38.1%	38.1%	41.5%	79.0%	47.4%	NM	35.6%	NA
Net Inc.	405	371	295	315	264	33.6	120	-46.7	142	NA
S&P Core Earnings	408	319	234	NA	NA	NA	NA	NA	NA	NA

Balance Sheet & Other Fin. Data (Million $)

	2003	2002	2001	2000	1999	1998	1997	1996	1995	1994
Cash	112	96.6	82.1	85.4	61.2	64.8	28.8	59.7	89.0	NA
Curr. Assets	2,491	2,014	1,896	1,878	1,726	1,591	1,394	1,386	1,295	NA
Total Assets	5,879	5,144	4,831	4,745	4,686	4,156	3,669	3,520	3,520	NA
Curr. Liab.	2,034	1,666	1,688	1,807	2,287	2,351	1,841	1,237	1,307	NA
LT Debt	1,627	1,918	2,142	2,376	1,887	1,528	1,551	1,742	1,770	NA
Common Equity	714	230	-90.1	-393	-497	-701	-610	-380	-390	NA
Total Cap.	2,559	2,257	2,137	2,028	1,445	875	941	1,430	1,425	NA
Cap. Exp.	171	165	167	219	274	255	245	212	164	NA
Cash Flow	652	521	527	529	466	224	284	99	285	NA
Curr. Ratio	1.2	1.2	1.1	1.0	0.8	0.7	0.8	1.1	1.0	NA
% LT Debt of Cap.	63.6	85.0	100.2	117.1	130.5	174.6	165.0	121.0	124.2	NA
% Net Inc.of Revs.	4.7	4.8	4.0	4.1	3.7	0.5	2.0	NM	2.7	NA
% Ret. on Assets	7.4	7.4	6.2	6.7	6.0	0.9	3.3	NM	4.3	NA
% Ret. on Equity	85.9	531.1	NM	NM	NM	NM	NM	NM	NM	NA

Data as orig reptd.; bef. results of disc opers/spec. items. Per share data adj. for stk. divs.; EPS diluted.E-Estimated. NA-Not Available. NM-Not Meaningful. NR-Not Ranked. UR-Under Review.

Office: One Centennial Avenue, Piscataway, NJ 08855-6820.
Telephone: 732-980-6000.
Website: http://www.americanstandard.com
Chrmn & CEO: F.M. Poses.
SVP & CFO: G. D'Aloia.

SVP, Secy & General Counsel: J.P. McGrath.
VP & Treas: R.S. Massengill.
VP & Investor Contact: B. Fisher 732-980-6000.
Dirs: S. E. Anderson, J. L. Cohon, P. J. Curlander, S. F. Goldstone, E. E. Hagenlocker, J. F. Hardymon, R. Marshall, F. M. Poses.

Founded: in 1899.
Domicile: Delaware.
Employees: 60,000.
S&P Analyst: Michael W. Jaffe/CB/BK

The McGraw-Hill Companies

AmerisourceBergen

Recommendation: HOLD ★ ★ ★ ★ ★
SELL SELL HOLD BUY BUY

12-Month Target Price: $62.00
(as of July 22, 2004)

ABC has an approximate 0.06% weighting in the **S&P 500**

Sector: Health Care
Sub-Industry: Health Care Distributors
Peer Group: Pharmaceuticals & Health Products

Summary: This distributor of pharmaceutical products and related health care services was formed via the August 2001 merger of AmeriSource Health Corp. and Bergen Brunswig Corp.

Quantitative Evaluations

S&P Earnings & Dividend Rank: A-

| D | C | B- | B | B+ | A- | A | A+ |

S&P Fair Value Rank: 3

| 1 | 2 | 3 | 4 | 5 |
| Lowest | | | | Highest |

Fair Value Calc.: $55.40 (Slightly Overvalued)

S&P Investability Quotient Percentile
This company does not meet the inclusion criteria required for calculating an IQ value.

Volatility: Average

| Low | Average | High |

Technical Evaluation: Bullish
Since 11/04, the technical indicators for ABC have been Bullish.

Relative Strength Rank: Moderate

65

1 Lowest — Highest 99

| Price as of 11/12/04: | $59 | 2005E S&P Core EPS: | $4.05 |

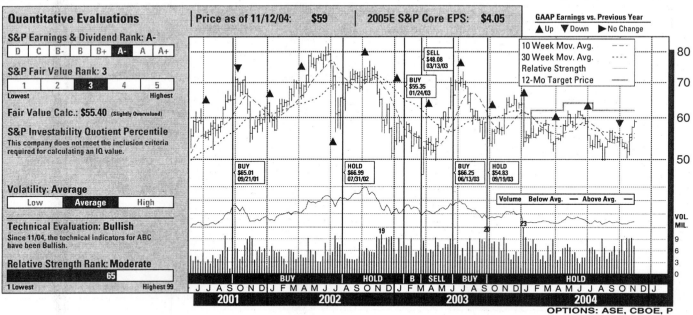

GAAP Earnings vs. Previous Year
▲ Up   ▼ Down   ► No Change

- - - 10 Week Mov. Avg.
······ 30 Week Mov. Avg.
······ Relative Strength
—— 12-Mo Target Price

SELL $48.08 03/13/03
BUY $55.35 01/24/03
BUY $65.01 09/21/01
HOLD $66.99 07/31/02
BUY $66.25 06/13/03
HOLD $54.83 09/19/03

Volume   Below Avg. —— Above Avg.

VOL. MIL.
9 6 3 0

BUY | HOLD | B | SELL | BUY | HOLD
J J A S O N D J F M A M J J A S O N D J F M A M J J A S O N D J F M A M J J A S O N D J
2001 2002 2003 2004

OPTIONS: ASE, CBOE, P

Analyst commentary prepared by Phillip M. Seligman/CB/JWP

Highlights 15-NOV-04

- We expect FY 05 (Sep.) operating revenues to be essentially flat with FY 04's $48.9 billion, as new accounts and increased sales from existing accounts compensate for the loss of the large Department of Veterans Affairs and AdvancePCS contracts and other top-line pressures. These include the lack of price hikes by drugmakers, a continued transition of drugmaker and distributor inventory management to a fee-for-service model, and the potential impact on physician customers, particularly oncologists, of newly proposed Medicare reimbursement regulations. We see revenue growth starting to revive in the FY 05 fourth quarter, on easier comparisons.

- We see gross margins under more pressure than usual until the end of the 2005 third quarter, while ABC adjusts its operations to account for the loss of the two major customers and the continued transition of the business model. After that, while we expect gross margin pressures to continue, mainly due to ongoing competition, we think they will lighten somewhat.

- For FY 05, we expect EBIT (earnings before interest and taxes) to be flat with FY 04. Our FY 05 EPS estimate of $4.30 is up from FY 04's $4.06, almost solely due to lower interest costs and ABC's $500 million share repurchase program. Our FY 04 and FY 05 Standard & Poor's Core Earnings estimates, including projected stock option expense and pension plan adjustments, are $3.86 and $4.05 a share, respectively.

Investment Rationale/Risk 15-NOV-04

- We are encouraged by ABC's wider operating margins, despite gross margin pressures, and by sharply higher operating cash flow, as its inventory management agreements mean that less working capital is required. Moreover, we see EPS continuing to benefit from the rationalization of its distribution centers, which should continue to raise efficiencies. We believe these positive factors reflect good management execution following the loss of AdvancePCS and the Department of Veterans Affairs contracts. However, due to our outlook for flat revenue and EBIT growth, we would not add to positions.

- Risks to our recommendation and target price include intensified price competition, which could outweigh savings realized through internal efforts such as technological upgrades. We believe ABC, which is strictly a drug distribution business, is more sensitive to a possible price war than many of its peers.

- We see only modest EPS growth for most of FY 05, but expect EPS to return to more normalized growth afterward. We think the stock warrants a forward P/E multiple at a small discount to that of the S&P 500. Our 12-month target price of $62 is based on a P/E multiple of 13.5X applied to our calendar 2005 EPS estimate of $4.60.

Key Stock Statistics

S&P Oper. EPS 2005E	4.30	52-week Range	$66.37-49.74
P/E on S&P Oper. EPS 2005E	13.7	12 Month P/E	14.5
Yield (%)	0.2%	Beta	-0.32
Dividend Rate/Share	0.10	Shareholders	3,208
Shares Outstanding (M)	112.4	Market Cap (B)	$ 6.6

Value of $10,000 invested five years ago: **$ 45,174**

Dividend Data Dividends have been paid since 2001

Amount ($)	Date Decl.	Ex-Div. Date	Stock of Record	Payment Date
0.025	Jan. 21	Feb. 11	Feb. 16	Mar. 01 '04
0.025	May. 07	May. 14	May. 18	Jun. 07 '04
0.025	Aug. 11	Aug. 19	Aug. 23	Sep. 07 '04
0.025	Nov. 11	Nov. 18	Nov. 22	Dec. 07 '04

Revenues/Earnings Data Fiscal year ending September 30

Revenues (Million $)

	2004	2003	2002	2001	2000	1999
1Q	13,355	12,435	11,069	3,307	2,839	2,375
2Q	13,364	12,163	10,944	3,481	2,842	2,385
3Q	13,072	12,421	11,621	3,519	2,932	2,469
4Q	13,388	12,640	11,601	5,884	3,032	2,579
Yr.	53,179	49,657	45,235	16,191	11,645	9,807

Earnings Per Share ($)

	2004	2003	2002	2001	2000	1999
1Q	0.94	0.84	0.63	0.49	0.42	0.36
2Q	1.23	1.03	0.84	0.57	0.47	0.41
3Q	1.09	0.99	0.82	0.57	0.48	0.41
4Q	0.81	1.04	0.86	0.48	0.53	0.21
Yr.	4.06	3.89	3.16	2.10	1.90	1.38

Next earnings report expected: late-January Source: S&P, Company Reports
EPS Estimates based on S&P Operating Earnings; historical GAAP earnings are as reported.

AmerisourceBergen Corporation

Recommendation: **HOLD** ★ ★ ★ ☆ ☆   12-Month Target Price: **$62.00** (as of July 22, 2004)

Business Summary 15-NOV-04

AmerisourceBergen Corp. is one of the largest U.S. pharmaceutical distributors. The company began operations in August 2001, following the merger of Ameri-iSource Health Corp. and Bergen Brunswig Corp. Since AmeriSource shareholders owned 51% of ABC's common stock after the merger (with Bergen Brunswig shareholders owning the remaining 49%), ABC accounted for the merger as an acquisition by AmeriSource of Bergen. The board of directors initially included four former directors from each company.

ABC believes it is the largest distributor of pharmaceuticals to independent community drug stores and regional drugstore and food combo chains, which together account for its retail market segment (44% of FY 03 (Sep.) operating revenues), and to the hospital/acute care, mail order and specialty pharmaceuticals markets, which together comprise its institutional market segment (53%). The company's specialty health care distribution business (more than $4 billion in annual sales) supplies goods and services to physicians in the nephrology, oncology, plasma, primary care and vaccine health care segments. The PharMerica division, with a network of 125 pharmacies at the end of FY 03, provides institutional pharmacy care, pharmacy management services, and direct pharmaceutical services to workers' compensation and catastrophic care patients. The American Health Packaging division repackages drugs from bulk to unit dose, unit of use, blister pack, and standard bottle sizes.

ABC's goals through 2007 include achieving annual revenue growth in line with the pharmaceutical market, which is expected to expand 10% to 13%; continuing to expand the operating margin; and increasing annual EPS growth by at least 15%, before merger and acquisition costs. ABC sees growth aided by favorable demographics, and by pharmaceuticals capturing an expanding portion of the health care dollar.

The company expected to achieve $150 million in annual synergies within three years of the merger, with the majority of savings occurring in the second and third years. Savings were expected from consolidation of distribution centers ($50 million), enhanced efficiency of remaining distribution facilities ($30 million), procurement ($30 million), administration and information technology ($35 million), and other ($5 million). Upon completion, ABC expected to have 30 highly automated distribution centers, with an average annual volume per facility of about $1.2 billion, down from 51 centers, with average annual volume of $700 million. About four to six distribution centers were expected to be closed in the first year. In addition, six new facilities were to be built. However, on December 31, 2003, the company lost its Department of Veterans Affairs contract, representing over $3 billion in annual operating revenue, and expiring March 31, 2004. ABC expected to move quickly to take out costs associated with the contract.

In July 2002, ABC acquired AutoMed Technologies, a provider of pharmacy automated prescription fulfillment and distribution systems. In January 2003, it acquired Bridge Medical, Inc., a maker of bedside patient drug scanning system, and US Bioservices Corp., a provider of high-value, complex therapies and reimbursement support.

Company Financials Fiscal Year ending September 30

Per Share Data ($)

(Year Ended September 30)	2004	2003	2002	2001	2000	1999	1998	1997	1996	1995
Tangible Bk. Val.	NA	14.42	10.43	3.59	4.81	2.88	1.50	0.29	NM	NM
Cash Flow	NA	4.42	3.62	2.31	2.21	1.71	1.35	1.19	1.11	0.98
Earnings	4.06	3.89	3.16	2.10	1.90	1.38	1.04	0.97	0.92	0.77
S&P Core Earnings	NA	3.72	3.05	1.69	NA	NA	NA	NA	NA	NA
Dividends	0.10	0.10	0.10	Nil	Nil	Nil	Nil	Nil	Nil	Nil
Payout Ratio	2%	3%	3%	Nil	Nil	Nil	Nil	Nil	Nil	Nil
Prices - High	61.93	73.44	82.85	72.00	53.68	41.37	40.37	33.18	22.87	17.12
- Low	49.74	45.65	50.20	40.12	12.00	11.00	22.23	20.62	13.93	9.87
P/E Ratio - High	15	19	26	34	28	30	39	34	25	22
- Low	12	12	16	19	6	8	21	21	15	13

Income Statement Analysis (Million $)

	2004	2003	2002	2001	2000	1999	1998	1997	1996	1995
Revs.	NA	49,657	45,235	16,191	11,645	9,760	8,575	7,816	5,552	4,669
Oper. Inc.	NA	963	804	302	217	191	166	132	107	105
Depr.	NA	71.0	61.2	21.6	16.1	17.4	14.8	12.4	9.20	7.63
Int. Exp.	NA	145	141	45.7	41.9	39.0	42.1	41.6	36.0	52.3
Pretax Inc.	NA	726	572	202	160	119	82.8	78.0	61.9	45.5
Eff. Tax Rate	NA	39.2%	39.7%	38.6%	38.0%	40.6%	39.0%	39.2%	31.1%	38.0%
Net Inc.	NA	441	345	124	99	70.9	50.5	47.4	42.7	28.2
S&P Core Earnings	NA	421	333	100	NA	NA	NA	NA	NA	NA

Balance Sheet & Other Fin. Data (Million $)

	2004	2003	2002	2001	2000	1999	1998	1997	1996	1995
Cash	NA	800	663	298	121	59.5	85.5	68.9	71.2	46.8
Curr. Assets	NA	8,859	8,350	7,513	2,321	1,920	1,418	1,625	1,115	773
Total Assets	NA	12,040	11,213	10,291	2,459	2,061	1,552	1,745	1,188	839
Curr. Liab.	NA	6,256	6,100	5,532	1,751	1,327	1,015	1,130	786	530
LT Debt	NA	1,723	1,756	1,872	413	559	454	590	434	436
Common Equity	NA	4,005	3,316	5,677	565	166	75.3	14.3	-36.8	-136
Total Cap.	NA	5,728	5,073	7,549	978	725	529	604	397	300
Cap. Exp.	NA	90.6	64.2	23.4	16.6	15.8	10.4	15.9	15.7	13.6
Cash Flow	NA	512	406	145	115	88.3	65.3	59.9	51.8	35.8
Curr. Ratio	NA	1.4	1.4	1.4	1.3	1.4	1.4	1.4	1.4	1.5
% LT Debt of Cap.	NA	30.1	34.6	24.8	42.3	77.1	85.8	97.7	109.3	145.3
% Net Inc.of Revs.	NA	0.9	0.8	0.8	0.9	0.7	0.6	0.6	0.8	0.6
% Ret. on Assets	NA	3.8	3.2	1.9	4.4	3.9	3.1	3.2	4.2	3.6
% Ret. on Equity	NA	12.1	11.2	4.0	22.1	58.8	112.7	NM	NM	NM

Data as orig reptd.; bef. results of disc opers/spec. items. Per share data adj. for stk. divs.; EPS diluted. E-Estimated. NA-Not Available. NM-Not Meaningful. NR-Not Ranked. UR-Under Review.

Office: 1300 Morris Drive, Chesterbrook, PA 19087-5594.
Telephone: 610-727-7000.
Email: investorrelations@amerisourcebergen.com
Website: http://www.amerisourcebergen.com
Chrmn: J. R. Mellor.
CEO: R. D. Yost.

Pres & COO: K. J. Hilzinger.
SVP & CFO: M. D. DiCandilo.
Investor Contact: Michael N. Kilpatrick (610-727-7118).
Dirs: R. H. Brady, C. H. Cotros, R. C. Gozon, E. E. Hagenlocker, J. E. Henney, J. R. Mellor, F. G. Rodgers, J. L. Wilson, R. D. Yost.

Founded: in 1985.
Domicile: Delaware.
Employees: 14,800.
S&P Analyst: Phillip M. Seligman/CB/JWP

Amgen

Recommendation: BUY ★★★★   **12-Month Target Price: $80.00**
(as of July 22, 2004)

AMGN has an approximate 0.69% weighting in the **S&P 500**

Sector: Health Care
Sub-Industry: Biotechnology
Peer Group: Biotech Therapeutics - Larger Capitalization

Summary: The world's leading biotech company, AMGN has major treatments for anemia, neutropenia, rheumatoid arthritis, psoriatic arthritis, and psoriasis.

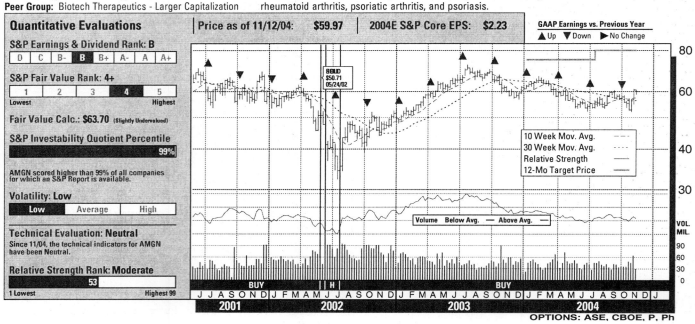

| Quantitative Evaluations | Price as of 11/12/04: $59.97 | 2004E S&P Core EPS: $2.23 |

S&P Earnings & Dividend Rank: B
D   C   B-   **B**   B+   A-   A   A+

S&P Fair Value Rank: 4+
1   2   3   **4**   5
Lowest   Highest

Fair Value Calc.: $63.70 (Slightly Undervalued)

S&P Investability Quotient Percentile
99%
AMGN scored higher than 99% of all companies for which an S&P Report is available.

Volatility: Low
Low   Average   High

Technical Evaluation: Neutral
Since 11/04, the technical indicators for AMGN have been Neutral.

Relative Strength Rank: Moderate
53
1 Lowest   Highest 99

GAAP Earnings vs. Previous Year
▲ Up   ▼ Down   ▶ No Change

- 10 Week Mov. Avg.
- 30 Week Mov. Avg.
- Relative Strength
- 12-Mo Target Price

Volume   Below Avg.   Above Avg.

OPTIONS: ASE, CBOE, P, Ph

Analyst commentary prepared by Frank DiLorenzo, CFA /CB/GG

Highlights October 26, 2004

- Third quarter pro forma EPS of $0.64 (before acquisition-related charges) was $0.02 above our estimate. Enbrel sales of $496 million were $41 million above our projection and 45% above the 2003 quarter. Combined sales of Aranesp and Epogen were $1.289 billion, which was $45 million higher than our forecast and 21% greater than the 2003 period. Combined Neulasta and Neupogen sales of $752 million were $29 million above our projection and up 16% from 2003.

- In October, AMGN announced positive Phase II results for AMG 162 for the treatment of osteoporosis. The company initiated two Phase III trials of the drug in August. We preliminarily estimate that Amgen may be able to file for FDA approval of AMG 162 by the end of 2007. In June, AMGN filed for FDA approval of Palifermin to treat mucositis in patients with hematologic malignancies that are undergoing high-dose chemotherapy. We assume peak annual global sales of Palifermin of $1 billion by 2012.

- We expect combined 2004 Aranesp and Epogen sales of $5.0 billion, with 2005 sales seen at $5.4 billion. We see Neulasta and Neupogen sales of $2.9 billion in 2004 and $3.4 billion in 2005. Enbrel sales are forecasted at $1.8 billion for 2004 and $2.3 billion for 2005. We project 2004 Sensipar sales of $51 million, with 2005 sales rising to $150 million. We forecast total revenues of $10.4 billion in 2004, representing a 25% increase over 2003 levels, and $12.1 billion in 2005. We estimate 2004 pro forma EPS of $2.43, up from our prior $2.40 view. We still estimate 2005 EPS at $2.90.

Key Stock Statistics

S&P Core EPS 2005E	2.76	52-week Range	$66.88-52.00
S&P Oper. EPS 2004E	2.43	12 Month P/E	35.5
P/E on S&P Oper. EPS 2004E	24.7	Beta	0.62
S&P Oper. EPS 2005E	2.90	Shareholders	16,000
Yield (%)	Nil	Market Cap (B)	$ 76.2
Dividend Rate/Share	Nil	Shares Outstanding (M)	1270.1

Value of $10,000 invested five years ago: **$ 14,251**

Dividend Data

No cash dividends have been paid.

Investment Rationale/Risk October 26, 2004

- We are maintaining our buy opinion on AMGN shares as we see continued strong growth in EPS coupled with an attractive valuation and discounted pipeline. Relative to most other biotech stocks and pharmaceutical shares, as well as the S&P 500, AMGN trades at what we view as a very reasonable P/E to growth (PEG) ratio. We assume the FDA will approve Palifermin by the second quarter of 2005, with AMGN launching the drug shortly thereafter. We think AMGN has neglected smaller opportunities, including Kineret for rheumatoid arthritis and Novantrone, a drug obtained through its acquisition of Immunex and with rights subsequently transferred to Serono. All told, we believe the company's business development decisions over the past few years have been questionable, at best.

- Risks to our recommendation and target price include disappointing sales of AMGN's marketed products, increased competition, pipeline failures, changes in Medicare reimbursement in 2005 that could have a negative impact on sales and EPS, and potential generic erythropoietin in Europe by 2006 that could adversely impact EU Aranesp sales.

- With a PEG ratio of 0.9, based on our 2005 EPS estimate, versus a PEG of 1.4 for S&P's biotech peer group (excluding AMGN), we consider the shares attractive. Our DCF model analysis assumes initial 20.6% annualized cash flow growth declining to 4% at year 15, and 4% thereafter, with a 9.7% discount rate, yielding a 12-month target price of $80.

Revenues/Earnings Data Fiscal year ending December 31

Revenues (Million $)

	2004	2003	2002	2001	2000	1999
1Q	2,343	1,761	1,009	901.6	814.1	745.5
2Q	2,585	2,041	1,250	986.7	914.4	820.5
3Q	2,713	2,207	1,499	1,003	949.5	847.2
4Q	—	2,346	1,766	1,124	9,451	926.9
Yr.	—	8,356	5,523	4,016	3,629	3,340

Earnings Per Share ($)

	2004	2003	2002	2001	2000	1999
1Q	0.52	0.37	0.32	0.28	0.25	0.23
2Q	0.57	0.45	0.38	0.30	0.28	0.25
3Q	0.18	0.46	-2.10	0.30	0.33	0.28
4Q	E0.61	0.41	0.34	0.15	0.19	0.26
Yr.	E2.43	1.69	-1.21	1.03	1.05	1.02

Next earnings report expected: late-January   Source: S&P, Company Reports
EPS Estimates based on S&P Operating Earnings; historical GAAP earnings are as reported.

Amgen Inc.

Recommendation: **BUY** ★★★★★   12-Month Target Price: **$80.00** (as of July 22, 2004)

Business Summary October 26, 2004

Amgen, the world's largest biotech company, makes and markets five of the world's best selling biotech drugs.

Epogen is a genetically engineered version of human erythropoietin (EPO), a hormone that stimulates red blood cell production in bone marrow. Its primary market is dialysis patients suffering from chronic anemia. AMGN has EPO rights to the U.S. dialysis market, and has licensed to Johnson & Johnson (JNJ) U.S. rights to all other indications. JNJ also has ex-U.S. rights. Epogen sales were $2.4 billion in 2003.

Neupogen (filgrastim) is a recombinant version of human granulocyte colony stimulating factor (G-CSF), a protein that stimulates production of neutrophils (white blood cells that defend the body against bacterial infection). Its principal use is to build neutrophil levels in cancer patients whose natural neutrophils were destroyed by chemotherapy. AMGN has marketing rights to Neupogen in the U.S. and the EU. Neupogen sales were $1.3 billion in 2003.

In September 2001, Aranesp, a non-naturally occurring recombinant protein that stimulates production of red blood cells in pre-dialysis and dialysis patients, was approved by the FDA to treat anemia associated with chronic renal failure. EU approval was granted in June 2001. In July 2002, Aranesp was approved by the FDA to treat cancer patients with anemia due to chemotherapy use. EU approval was granted in August 2002. Aranesp sales were $1.5 billion in 2003. AMGN is also developing AMG 114, a third generation EPO product that is currently in early stages of development.

In January 2002, the FDA approved Neulasta, a long-acting white blood cell stimulant used to protect chemotherapy patients from infection. Neulasta was approved in the EU in August 2002. Neulasta posted 2003 sales of $1.3 billion.

Enbrel, acquired through AMGN's July 2002 acquisition of Immunex, recorded 2003 sales of $1.3 billion. It is approved to treat rheumatoid arthritis (RA), juvenile RA, and psoriatic arthritis. In addition, in July 2003, the FDA approved Enbrel to treat the spinal condition ankylosing spondylitis. In May 2004, the FDA approved Enbrel to treat adult patients with moderate-to-severe chronic plaque psoriasis.

In March 2004, Sensipar was approved by the FDA to treat secondary hyperparathyroidism in patients on dialysis, and hypercalcemia in patients with parathyroid carcinoma. In June 2004, AMGN filed for FDA approval of Palifermin to treat oral mucositis in hematologic malignancy patients undergoing chemotherapy followed by bone marrow transplant. Phase III trials of AMG 162, a treatment for osteoporosis, commenced in August 2004. In January 2004, a Phase III trial of Panitumumab (ABX-EGF) to treat advanced stage colorectal cancer patients was begun. The drug is being developed with partner Abgenix.

In August 2004, AMGN acquired Tularik for aproximately $1.3 billion, net of cash and AMGN's initial 21% stake in the company. AMGN had previously formed a collaboration with Tularik to discover and develop therapeutics against oncology targets. Tularik has five compounds in clinical development targeted in the areas of oncology, diabetes, inflammation, and obesity. The lead drug candidate is T67, in Phase III studies to treat liver cancer.

Company Financials Fiscal Year ending December 31

Per Share Data ($)

(Year Ended December 31)	2003	2002	2001	2000	1999	1998	1997	1996	1995	1994
Tangible Bk. Val.	4.06	2.80	4.99	4.16	2.97	2.52	2.07	1.80	1.57	1.20
Cash Flow	2.19	-0.82	1.28	1.24	1.18	0.95	0.69	0.70	0.56	0.35
Earnings	1.69	-1.21	1.03	1.05	1.02	0.82	0.59	0.60	0.48	0.29
S&P Core Earnings	1.50	-1.46	0.87	NA	NA	NA	NA	NA	NA	NA
Dividends	Nil	Nil	Nil	Nil	Nil	Nil	0.00	Nil	Nil	Nil
Payout Ratio	Nil	Nil	Nil	Nil	Nil	Nil	NM	Nil	Nil	Nil
Prices - High	72.37	62.94	75.06	80.43	66.43	27.25	17.34	16.62	14.93	7.53
- Low	48.09	30.57	45.43	50.00	25.68	11.65	11.21	12.84	7.01	4.34
P/E Ratio - High	43	NM	73	77	65	33	30	27	31	26
- Low	28	NM	44	48	25	14	19	21	15	15

Income Statement Analysis (Million $)

	2003	2002	2001	2000	1999	1998	1997	1996	1995	1994
Revs.	8,356	5,523	4,016	3,629	3,340	2,718	2,401	2,240	1,940	1,648
Oper. Inc.	3,758	2,501	2,003	1,761	1,638	1,338	1,103	1,058	881	801
Depr.	687	447	266	212	177	144	117	100	84.2	74.5
Int. Exp.	31.5	44.2	13.6	Nil	15.2	10.0	3.70	10.4	20.0	15.8
Pretax Inc.	3,173	-685	1,686	1,674	1,566	1,224	861	962	794	588
Eff. Tax Rate	28.8%	NM	33.6%	32.0%	30.0%	29.5%	25.2%	29.4%	32.3%	45.7%
Net Inc.	2,260	-1,392	1,120	1,139	1,096	863	644	680	538	320
S&P Core Earnings	2,006	-1,683	936	NA	NA	NA	NA	NA	NA	NA

Balance Sheet & Other Fin. Data (Million $)

	2003	2002	2001	2000	1999	1998	1997	1996	1995	1994
Cash	5,123	4,664	2,662	2,028	1,333	201	239	1,077	1,050	697
Curr. Assets	7,402	6,404	3,859	2,937	2,065	1,863	1,544	1,503	1,454	1,116
Total Assets	26,177	24,456	6,443	5,400	4,078	3,672	3,110	2,766	2,433	1,994
Curr. Liab.	2,246	1,529	1,003	862	831	887	742	643	584	536
LT Debt	3,080	3,048	223	223	Nil	223	229	59.0	177	183
Common Equity	19,389	18,286	5,217	4,315	3,024	2,562	2,139	1,906	1,672	1,274
Total Cap.	23,930	22,927	5,440	4,538	3,024	2,785	2,368	2,122	1,849	1,458
Cap. Exp.	1,357	659	442	438	304	408	388	267	163	131
Cash Flow	2,946	-945	1,386	1,350	1,273	1,007	761	780	622	394
Curr. Ratio	3.3	4.2	3.8	3.4	2.5	2.1	2.1	2.3	2.5	2.1
% LT Debt of Cap.	12.9	13.3	4.1	4.9	Nil	8.0	9.7	2.8	9.6	12.6
% Net Inc.of Revs.	27.0	NM	27.9	31.4	32.8	31.8	26.8	30.4	27.7	19.4
% Ret. on Assets	8.9	NM	18.9	24.0	28.3	25.5	21.9	26.2	24.3	17.1
% Ret. on Equity	12.0	NM	23.5	31.0	39.3	36.7	30.7	38.0	34.5	26.3

Data as orig reptd.; bef. results of disc opers/spec. items. Per share data adj. for stk. divs.; EPS diluted. E-Estimated. NA-Not Available. NM-Not Meaningful. NR-Not Ranked. UR-Under Review.

Office: One Amgen Center Drive, Thousand Oaks, CA 91320-1799.
Telephone: 805-447-1000.
Email: investor.relations@amgen.com
Website: http://www.amgen.com
Chrmn, Pres & CEO: K.W. Sharer.
EVP & CFO: R. Nanula.

SVP, Secy & General Counsel: D.J. Scott.
VP & Investor Contact: A. Sood 805-447-1060.
Dirs: D. Baltimore, F. J. Biondi, J. D. Choate, E. Fritzky, F. W. Gluck, F. P. Johnson, Jr., S. Lazarus, G. S. Omenn, J. C. Pelham, J. P. Reason, D. B. Rice, L. D. Schaeffer, K. W. Sharer, P. C. Sueltz.

Founded: in 1980.
Domicile: Delaware.
Employees: 12,900.
S&P Analyst: Frank DiLorenzo, CFA /CB/GG

AmSouth Bancorporation

Recommendation: **BUY** ★★★★☆
SELL SELL HOLD BUY BUY

12-Month Target Price: $27.00
(as of June 17, 2004)

ASO has an approximate 0.09% weighting in the **S&P 500**

Sector: Financials
Sub-Industry: Regional Banks
Peer Group: Southeast Major Regional Banks

Summary: This bank holding company, with about $50 billion in assets, operates more than 670 banking offices in six southeastern states.

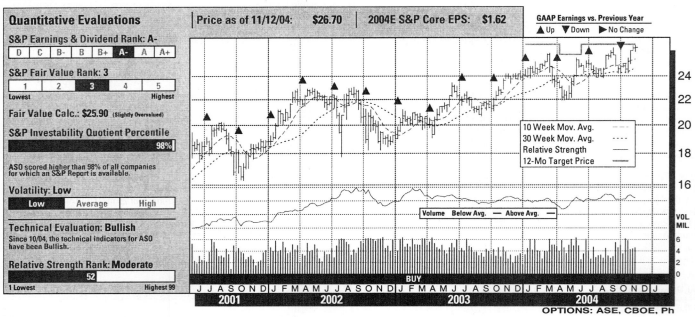

Quantitative Evaluations

S&P Earnings & Dividend Rank: A-
| D | C | B- | B | B+ | A- | A | A+ |

S&P Fair Value Rank: 3
| 1 | 2 | 3 | 4 | 5 |
Lowest — Highest

Fair Value Calc.: $25.90 (Slightly Overvalued)

S&P Investability Quotient Percentile
98%
ASO scored higher than 98% of all companies for which an S&P Report is available.

Volatility: Low
| Low | Average | High |

Technical Evaluation: Bullish
Since 10/04, the technical indicators for ASO have been Bullish.

Relative Strength Rank: Moderate
52
1 Lowest — Highest 99

Price as of 11/12/04: **$26.70**   **2004E S&P Core EPS:** **$1.62**

GAAP Earnings vs. Previous Year
▲ Up   ▼ Down   ▶ No Change

10 Week Mov. Avg.
30 Week Mov. Avg.
Relative Strength
12-Mo Target Price

Volume Below Avg. — Above Avg.

BUY
J J A S O N D | J F M A M J J A S O N D | J F M A M J J A S O N D | J F M A M J J A S O N D | J
2001   2002   2003   2004

OPTIONS: ASE, CBOE, Ph

Analyst commentary prepared by Erik J. Eisenstein/CB/GG

Highlights October 21, 2004

- We see 8% average earning asset growth for ASO in 2005, aided by projected improved demand for commercial credit. We expect relatively flat net interest margin, and also expect an 8% gain in net interest income. Aided by anticipated continued economic recovery, we see credit quality improving modestly throughout 2005. ASO also appears to be well reserved, in our view. As a result, we forecast that loan loss provisions will increase only 6%, less than projected loan growth.

- We estimate that non-interest income will advance 5% in 2005, despite a reduction in mortgage income, paced by increased deposit fees and higher trust income. We expect only a fractional increase in operating expenses, benefiting from the absence of $54.0 million in charges and related professional fees incurred in the third quarter of 2004. These costs relate to agreements with regulators arising out of deficiencies in ASO's compliance with The Bank Secrecy Act. We don't see these settlements having a material net impact on EPS in 2005.

- All told, we forecast a 20% gain in EPS in 2005, to $2.10, from $1.74 seen in 2004. Our 2004 and 2005 Standard & Poor's Core Earnings projections are $1.62 and $1.95 a share, respectively.

Investment Rationale/Risk October 21, 2004

- In our opinion, ASO should generate EPS growth of 10% in the five years beyond 2005, somewhat above the rate of its regional banking peers. This projection reflects our view of the company's position in what we regard as attractive geographic markets, as well as the growth potential of its wealth management and commercial banking businesses. Moreover, we see ASO's profitability as more consistent than in the past, as we believe that the company has improved its interest rate and credit risk profiles.

- Risks to our recommendation and target price include interest rate risk, as well as the risk that ASO will fail to comply with its obligations under the regulatory settlements, which could in turn restrict the company's expansion activities or lead to regulatory prosecution.

- Our 12-month target price of $27 is derived by applying a peer-level regional bank P/E multiple to growth (PEG) ratio of 1.3X to our 2005 EPS and five-year EPS growth estimates. Based on our view of ASO's potential appreciation, and on the stock's above-peer dividend yield of about 3.8%, we recommend accumulating the shares.

Key Stock Statistics

S&P Core EPS 2005E	1.95	52-week Range	$27.00-21.91
S&P Oper. EPS 2004E	1.75	12 Month P/E	15.7
P/E on S&P Oper. EPS 2004E	15.3	Beta	0.38
S&P Oper. EPS 2005E	2.10	Shareholders	27,291
Yield (%)	3.7%	Market Cap (B)	$ 9.5
Dividend Rate/Share	1.00	Shares Outstanding (M)	355.1

Value of $10,000 invested five years ago: **$ 13,326**

Dividend Data Dividends have been paid since 1943

Amount ($)	Date Decl.	Ex-Div. Date	Stock of Record	Payment Date
0.240	Jan. 15	Mar. 16	Mar. 18	Apr. 01 '04
0.240	Apr. 15	Jun. 15	Jun. 17	Jul. 01 '04
0.240	Jul. 15	Sep. 15	Sep. 17	Oct. 01 '04
0.250	Oct. 21	Dec. 16	Dec. 20	Jan. 03 '05

Revenues/Earnings Data Fiscal year ending December 31

Revenues (Million $)

	2004	2003	2002	2001	2000	1999
1Q	745.1	730.5	754.8	882.1	1,003	444.2
2Q	742.9	733.2	760.1	866.2	1,004	455.6
3Q	763.4	734.0	758.3	840.7	813.2	474.4
4Q	—	744.6	720.3	793.7	919.6	240.6
Yr.	—	2,942	2,993	3,383	3,740	3,780

Earnings Per Share ($)

	2004	2003	2002	2001	2000	1999
1Q	0.45	0.44	0.40	0.34	0.35	0.39
2Q	0.47	0.44	0.42	0.36	0.26	0.42
3Q	0.33	0.45	0.43	0.37	-0.10	0.44
4Q	E0.50	0.45	0.44	0.38	0.34	-0.16
Yr.	E1.75	1.77	1.68	1.45	0.86	0.86

Next earnings report expected: mid-January Source: S&P, Company Reports
EPS Estimates based on S&P Operating Earnings; historical GAAP earnings are as reported.

Recommendation: **BUY** ★★★★☆   12-Month Target Price: **$27.00** (as of June 17, 2004)

Business Summary October 21, 2004

At December 31, 2003, ASO operated more than 650 banking offices, in Alabama, Florida, Georgia, Louisiana, Mississippi and Tennessee, with $46 billion in assets. Operations are divided into Consumer Banking, Commercial Banking, and Wealth Management (which offers fiduciary, retirement and investment management services). the company has opened nearly 100 branches in the last five years. In 2003, ASO opened 41 new branches, including 31 in Florida, where it maintains a strategic focus. As of February 2004, the company intended to open at least 30 new branches annually.

After completing a three-year strategic plan in 2003, directors approved a new plan for the years 2004 to 2006, focusing on seven initiatives: to sustain growth in Consumer Banking; continue aggressive growth in Business Banking; expand Commercial Banking with improved credit quality; double the pretax contribution from Wealth Management; double Florida's pretax contribution; enhance sales productivity, service quality, and consumer retention; and leverage technology across all lines of business.

In May 2000, AmSouth Bancorporation completed the integration of First American Corp., a Nashville, TN, financial services company acquired in a 1999 stock transaction valued at about $6.3 billion. In the 2000 third quarter, the bank completed a financial restructuring to reduce interest rate sensitivity, mitigate the effects of steep interest rate increases, and address emerging credit quality

issues. In connection with the restructuring, ASO recorded pretax charges of $260 million, and sold $5 billion in lower-yielding investment securities, selected auto loans, and certain syndicated loans. In addition, it increased reserves associated with syndicated loans remaining in its portfolio. Also in the third quarter, the bank sold IFC Holdings, a provider of insurance and investment products, in keeping with its focus on southeastern markets.

Poor asset quality can have a significant impact on bank profitability. Banks reserve for existing and potential nonperforming assets on a regular basis. At December 31, 2003, the allowance for loan losses covered 1.31% of net loans, versus 1.40% a year earlier. Asset quality improved in 2003; nonperforming assets decreased to 0.50% of loans, from 0.72%.

A majority of the bank's income is derived from interest on loans. In 2003, loans, net of unearned income, were up 7.2%, to $29.3 billion. Loans (by type) at the end of 2003 were divided as follows: consumer 52% (52% in 2002), commercial 32% (32%), commercial real estate 16% (16%).

In April 2003, directors authorized the repurchase of 25 million common shares (7%). During the first six months of 2004, the company bought back 2.1 million shares.

Company Financials Fiscal Year ending December 31

Per Share Data ($)

(Year Ended December 31)	2003	2002	2001	2000	1999	1998	1997	1996	1995	1994
Tangible Bk. Val.	9.18	8.82	8.14	7.52	7.56	8.05	7.65	7.38	7.16	4.90
Earnings	1.77	1.68	1.45	0.86	0.86	1.45	1.21	0.96	0.89	0.67
S&P Core Earnings	1.66	1.51	1.27	NA	NA	NA	NA	NA	NA	NA
Dividends	0.93	0.89	0.85	0.81	0.67	0.53	0.51	0.48	0.46	0.42
Payout Ratio	53%	53%	59%	94%	78%	37%	42%	50%	51%	64%
Prices - High	24.62	23.06	20.24	20.06	34.58	30.41	25.36	15.07	12.25	10.33
- Low	19.05	17.75	15.00	11.68	18.75	20.45	14.00	10.18	7.62	7.51
P/E Ratio - High	14	14	14	23	40	21	21	16	14	15
- Low	11	11	10	14	22	14	12	11	9	11

Income Statement Analysis (Million $)

	2003	2002	2001	2000	1999	1998	1997	1996	1995	1994
Net Int. Inc.	1,415	1,473	1,395	1,379	1,508	699	676	652	596	567
Tax Equiv. Adj.	44.4	51.0	63.7	62.7	4.84	5.64	7.04	9.38	12.4	14.6
Non Int. Inc.	856	739	748	669	848	347	266	235	232	205
Loan Loss Prov.	174	214	187	228	166	58.1	67.4	65.2	40.1	30.1
Exp./Op. Revs.	52.1%	49.8%	53.7%	64.7%	69.8%	55.4%	55.8%	59.5%	61.0%	66.4%
Pretax Inc.	891	872	771	455	541	405	349	288	275	193
Eff. Tax Rate	29.7%	30.1%	30.4%	27.6%	37.1%	35.2%	35.1%	36.6%	36.4%	34.2%
Net Inc.	626	609	536	329	340	263	226	183	175	127
% Net Int. Marg.	3.78	4.37	4.20	3.75	4.02	3.92	4.09	3.93	3.88	4.14
S&P Core Earnings	588	547	472	NA	NA	NA	NA	NA	NA	NA

Balance Sheet & Other Fin. Data (Million $)

	2003	2002	2001	2000	1999	1998	1997	1996	1995	1994
Money Mkt. Assets	42.9	138	453	2,226	205	39.0	20.4	18.9	4.75	159
Inv. Securities	12,054	9,170	8,832	8,559	13,015	5,176	4,780	4,935	4,647	3,720
Com'l Loans	13,940	13,050	13,075	13,918	14,715	3,693	3,854	3,668	3,112	2,699
Other Loans	16,149	15,012	12,777	11,170	11,551	9,177	8,384	8,412	8,708	8,927
Total Assets	45,616	40,571	38,600	38,936	43,407	19,902	18,622	18,407	17,739	16,778
Demand Deposits	12,458	5,495	5,281	4,934	4,739	2,216	2,063	1,952	1,835	1,902
Time Deposits	17,983	21,821	20,886	21,689	23,173	11,068	10,882	10,516	11,574	11,165
LT Debt	7,650	6,009	6,117	5,883	5,603	3,240	1,633	1,436	448	386
Common Equity	3,230	3,116	2,955	2,813	2,959	1,428	1,385	1,396	1,383	1,310
% Ret. on Assets	1.5	1.5	1.4	0.8	0.8	1.4	1.2	1.0	1.0	0.8
% Ret. on Equity	19.7	20.1	18.6	11.4	11.0	18.7	16.3	13.1	13.0	10.2
% Loan Loss Resv.	1.3	1.4	1.4	1.5	1.4	1.4	1.5	1.5	1.5	1.5
% Loans/Deposits	96.7	100.2	97.1	92.8	94.7	96.9	95.7	96.9	87.6	88.5
% Equity to Assets	7.4	7.7	7.4	7.0	7.3	7.3	7.5	7.7	7.8	8.2

Data as orig reptd.; bef. results of disc opers/spec. items. Per share data adj. for stk. divs.; EPS diluted. E-Estimated. NA-Not Available. NM-Not Meaningful. NR-Not Ranked. UR-Under Review.

Office: 1900 5th Ave N, Birmingham, AL 35203.
Telephone: 205-320-7151.
Website: http://www.amsouth.com
Chrmn, Pres & CEO: C.D. Ritter.
EVP & CFO: B.E. Mooney.

EVP, Secy & General Counsel: S.A. Yoder.
Investor Contact: P.G. Brashier 205-583-4439.
Investor Contact: M.L. Underwood, Jr. 205-801-0265
Dirs: E. W. Deavenport, Jr., M. R. Ingram, R. L. Kuehn, Jr., J. R. Malone, C. D. McCrary, C. B. Nielsen, C. D. Ritter, C. Thomas, Jr.

Founded: in 1970.
Domicile: Delaware.
Employees: 12,385.
S&P Analyst: Erik J. Eisenstein/CB/GG

Anadarko Petroleum

Recommendation: HOLD ★ ★ ★ ☆
SELL SELL HOLD BUY BUY

12-Month Target Price: $70.00
(as of November 04, 2004)

APC has an approximate 0.15% weighting in the **S&P 500**

Sector: Energy
Sub-Industry: Oil & Gas Exploration & Production
Peer Group: Exploration & Production - Large

Summary: APC is an international oil and natural gas exploration and production company with associated businesses in marketing and trading, and minerals.

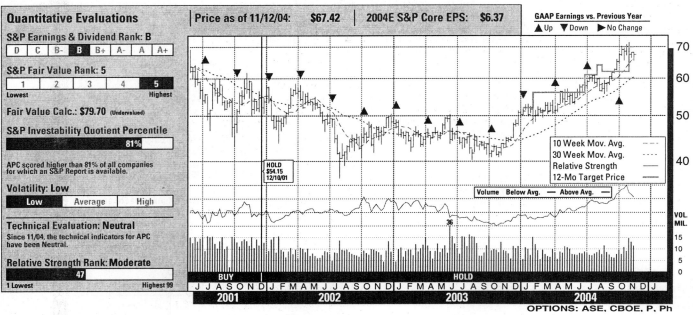

Quantitative Evaluations

S&P Earnings & Dividend Rank: B

| D | C | B- | B | B+ | A- | A | A+ |

S&P Fair Value Rank: 5

| 1 | 2 | 3 | 4 | 5 |
| Lowest | | | | Highest |

Fair Value Calc.: $79.70 (Undervalued)

S&P Investability Quotient Percentile

81%

APC scored higher than 81% of all companies for which an S&P Report is available.

Volatility: Low

| Low | Average | High |

Technical Evaluation: Neutral

Since 11/04, the technical indicators for APC have been Neutral.

Relative Strength Rank: Moderate

47

1 Lowest   Highest 99

Price as of 11/12/04: $67.42   **2004E S&P Core EPS:** $6.37

GAAP Earnings vs. Previous Year
▲ Up ▼ Down ► No Change

- 10 Week Mov. Avg.
- 30 Week Mov. Avg.
- Relative Strength
- 12-Mo Target Price

Volume Below Avg. — Above Avg. —

HOLD $54.15 12/10/01

VOL. MIL.

BUY | HOLD
J J A S O N D | J F M A M J J A S O N D | J F M A M J J A S O N D | J F M A M J J A S O N D | J
2001 | 2002 | 2003 | 2004

OPTIONS: ASE, CBOE, P, Ph

Analyst commentary prepared by Charles LaPorta, CFA /DC/BK

Highlights August 24, 2004

- Second quarter EPS were $1.59, exceeding our estimate by $0.09 on better than expected natural gas revenue. Hydrocarbon production declined 4.9% sequentially, well below our estimate, on production declines in South Louisiana and the Gulf of Mexico shelf.

- Operating expenses rose sequentially due to increased oil recovery activity in the western U.S. and higher operating taxes on higher commodity prices. We are forecasting increased per-unit operating costs for APC in 2004 and 2005, in line with those experienced with other E&P companies. Despite its recent success in drilling in East Texas and North Louisiana, we project 2004 production growth of 2% before giving effect to the sale of producing assets. We expect production gains at Marco Polo and K2 to contribute toward 2005 production growth of 5%.

- We look for an increase of 18% in 2004 EBITDA to $4.3 billion, primarily on strong pricing and adequate cost control, and a decline in 2005 EBITDA to $3.9 billion, on projected lower pricing. Our forecasts for S&P Core EPS are greater than our operating estimates due to the removal of pension losses.

Investment Rationale/Risk August 24, 2004

- APC recently refocused its corporate strategy to emphasize probable returns from development activities. As a result, the company has assembled a set of non-core properties for sale that it internally values at $2.5 billion, which the company plans to use for share repurchases. APC's 2004 capital budget, which stresses the development of its deepwater properties, could reach $3.0 billion. At June 2004, the company's debt to capitalization ratio was 36%.

- Risks to our recommendation and target price include events that would cause substantial and sustained declines in oil and gas prices; a persistent inability by APC to replace its reserves; and acts of terrorism on APC's production facilities.

- Given its weak but improving production profile and the uncertainty surrounding the reshuffling of its asset portfolio, we view APC as a turnaround story. The company appears committed to supporting the stock via share repurchases financed by asset sales. However, we believe these sales will mitigate potential volume growth and, combined with lower 2005 hydrocarbon price expectations, will preclude substantial fundamental improvements. Our $62 target price is based on a forward P/E multiple of 12X, a slight discount to peers.

Key Stock Statistics

S&P Core EPS 2005E	5.23	52-week Range	$71.55-43.92
S&P Oper. EPS 2004E	6.77	12 Month P/E	11.5
P/E on S&P Oper. EPS 2004E	10.0	Beta	0.66
S&P Oper. EPS 2005E	6.55	Shareholders	20,000
Yield (%)	0.8%	Market Cap (B)	$ 16.7
Dividend Rate/Share	0.56	Shares Outstanding (M)	247.3

Value of $10,000 invested five years ago: $ 24,707

Dividend Data Dividends have been paid since 1986

Amount ($)	Date Decl.	Ex-Div. Date	Stock of Record	Payment Date
0.140	Oct. 31	Dec. 08	Dec. 10	Dec. 24 '03
0.140	Feb. 06	Mar. 08	Mar. 10	Mar. 24 '04
0.140	May. 06	Jun. 07	Jun. 09	Jun. 23 '04
0.140	Aug. 09	Sep. 03	Sep. 08	Sep. 22 '04

Revenues/Earnings Data Fiscal year ending December 31

Revenues (Million $)

	2004	2003	2002	2001	2000	1999
1Q	1,460	1,255	790.0	3,009	661.0	136.4
2Q	1,443	1,249	1,002	2,238	748.0	161.5
3Q	1,562	1,340	951.0	1,743	1,871	179.9
4Q	—	1,278	1,117	1,379	2,406	223.3
Yr.	—	5,122	3,860	8,369	5,686	701.1

Earnings Per Share ($)

	2004	2003	2002	2001	2000	1999
1Q	1.55	1.45	0.34	2.52	0.37	-0.19
2Q	1.59	1.20	0.93	1.50	0.48	0.06
3Q	1.58	1.09	0.74	-5.41	1.03	0.15
4Q	E2.05	1.17	1.21	0.41	1.75	0.22
Yr.	E6.77	4.91	3.21	-0.73	4.25	0.25

Next earnings report expected: late-January Source: S&P, Company Reports
EPS Estimates based on S&P Operating Earnings; historical GAAP earnings are as reported.

STANDARD &POOR'S

Anadarko Petroleum Corporation

Stock Report
November 13, 2004
NYSE Symbol: **APC**

Recommendation: **HOLD** ★ ★ ★ ☆ ☆   12-Month Target Price: **$70.00** (as of November 04, 2004)

Business Summary August 24, 2004

As one of the world's largest international exploration and production companies, Anadarko Petroleum's operational focus extends from the deepwater Gulf of Mexico to Texas, Louisiana and Mid-Continent Basins, through the western U.S. and Canadian Rockies, and to the North Slope of Alaska. The company also has production in Algeria, Venezuela, and Qatar, and has exploration programs in several other countries. APC has business segments in oil and gas exploration and production (96% of 2003 sales, 98% of 2003 segment earnings), marketing and trading (3%, 1%), and minerals (1%, 1%).

The company's reserves have grown 22% over the past three years, primarily due to the acquisitions of Berkley Petroleum Corp. and Gulfstream Resources Canada Ltd. in 2001, and Howell Corp. in 2002, and to substantial crude oil and natural gas reserves discovered in the Gulf of Mexico, Canada, and onshore U.S., crude oil reserves added in Algeria and Alaska, and acquisitions of producing properties.

All-in reserve replacement was 196% in 2003, versus a five-year average of 310%; excluding acquisitions, the ratio was 176%, versus 164%. Proved reserved totaled 2.513 billion barrels of oil equivalent (BOE) in 2003, versus 2.328 billion in 2002. Proved oil, condensate and NGL reserves totaled 1.226 billion barrels (bbl.; 61% developed; 56% U.S., 29% Algeria, 5% Canada, and 10% elsewhere) at the end of 2003, versus 1.131 billion bbl. (61% developed; 51% U.S., 33% Algeria, 6% Canada, and 10% elsewhere) at the end of 2002. Proved natural gas reserves totaled 7.724 trillion cubic feet (Tcf; 76% developed; 79% U.S., 19% Canada, and 2% elsewhere)

at the end of 2003, versus 7.18 Tcf (74% developed; 79% U.S., 19% Canada, and 2% elsewhere) a year earlier. Excluding mergers and acquisitions, APC's finding cost was $7.47 per BOE in 2003, versus a five-year average of $8.10. Natural gas sales volumes averaged 643 Bcf in 2003 (692 Bcf in 2002), oil and condensate sales volumes averaged 67 million barrels (MMbbl.; 75 MMbbl.), and NGL volumes averaged 17 MMbbl. (15 MMbbl.). The average sales price for natural gas was $4.43 per Mcf in 2003 ($2.85), $26.55 per bbl. for oil and condensate ($22.44), and $21.18 per bbl. for NGLs ($14.80).

The marketing unit manages sales of the company's oil and gas through Anadarko Energy Services Co., Anadarko, Anadarko Canada Corp., and Anadarko Holdings.

APC owns and operates seven major gas gathering systems (more than 3,100 miles of pipeline, connecting about 3,450 wells, and averaging more than 800 milllion cubic feet (MMcf) per day in 2003) in the U.S.

The company's minerals properties contribute to operating income through non-operated joint venture and royalty arrangements in several coal, trona (natural soda ash) and industrial mineral mines located on lands in and adjacent to its Land Grant holdings. The Land Grant is an 8 million acre strip running through portions of Colorado, Wyoming and Utah, where APC owns most of its fee mineral rights. In addition, the company owns a 50% non-operating interest in Black Butte Coal Co., which produces about 3 million tons per year of coal.

Company Financials Fiscal Year ending December 31

Per Share Data ($)

(Year Ended December 31)	2003	2002	2001	2000	1999	1998	1997	1996	1995	1994
Tangible Bk. Val.	27.93	22.02	19.17	20.99	10.30	8.65	25.10	8.38	7.58	7.64
Cash Flow	10.03	7.48	4.18	7.29	2.00	1.29	2.55	2.26	1.58	1.82
Earnings	4.91	3.21	-0.73	4.25	0.25	-0.41	0.89	0.85	0.18	0.35
S&P Core Earnings	4.95	3.06	-0.97	NA	NA	NA	NA	NA	NA	NA
Dividends	0.44	0.33	0.23	0.20	0.20	0.19	0.15	0.15	0.15	0.15
Payout Ratio	9%	10%	NM	5%	80%	NM	17%	18%	83%	43%
Prices - High	51.72	58.55	73.97	75.95	42.75	44.87	38.37	34.43	27.06	29.25
- Low	40.27	36.77	43.00	27.56	26.25	24.75	25.37	23.37	17.81	18.50
P/E Ratio - High	11	18	NM	18	NM	NM	43	41	NM	84
- Low	8	11	NM	6	NM	NM	29	27	NM	53

Income Statement Analysis (Million $)

	2003	2002	2001	2000	1999	1998	1997	1996	1995	1994
Revs.	5,122	3,860	8,369	5,686	701	560	673	569	434	482
Oper. Inc.	3,648	2,585	3,702	2,190	421	267	402	349	232	267
Depr. Depl. & Amort.	1,297	1,121	1,227	593	218	204	199	167	165	173
Int. Exp.	253	203	92.0	Nil	74.1	57.7	41.0	56.0	53.0	41.6
Pretax Inc.	1,974	1,207	-390	1,426	105	-65.1	164	158	29.3	64.7
Eff. Tax Rate	36.9%	31.2%	NM	42.2%	59.4%	NM	34.7%	36.2%	28.0%	36.4%
Net Inc.	1,245	831	-176	824	42.6	-42.2	107	101	21.0	41.1
S&P Core Earnings	1,248	785	-243	NA	NA	NA	NA	NA	NA	NA

Balance Sheet & Other Fin. Data (Million $)

	2003	2002	2001	2000	1999	1998	1997	1996	1995	1994
Cash	62.0	34.0	37.0	199	44.8	17.0	8.91	15.0	17.0	6.50
Curr. Assets	1,324	1,280	1,201	1,894	356	230	219	270	163	139
Total Assets	20,546	18,248	16,771	16,590	4,098	3,633	2,992	2,584	2,267	2,142
Curr. Liab.	1,715	1,861	1,801	1,676	387	289	252	285	190	128
LT Debt	5,058	5,171	4,638	3,984	1,443	1,425	956	731	674	629
Common Equity	8,510	6,673	6,262	6,586	1,335	1,059	1,117	1,014	910	900
Total Cap.	17,909	15,578	14,454	10,770	3,555	3,208	2,620	2,244	2,034	1,968
Cap. Exp.	2,772	2,388	3,316	1,708	680	917	686	427	331	423
Cash Flow	2,537	1,946	1,044	1,406	250	155	306	268	186	214
Curr. Ratio	0.8	0.7	0.7	1.1	0.9	0.8	0.9	0.9	0.9	1.1
% LT Debt of Cap.	28.2	33.2	32.1	37.0	40.6	44.4	36.5	32.6	33.1	32.0
% Ret. on Assets	6.4	4.7	NM	8.0	1.1	NM	3.8	4.2	1.0	2.0
% Ret. on Equity	16.1	12.8	NM	20.5	2.6	NM	10.1	10.5	2.3	4.7

Data as orig reptd.; bef. results of disc opers/spec. items. Per share data adj. for stk. divs. Bold denotes primary EPS - prior periods restated. E-Estimated. NA-Not Available. NM-Not Meaningful. NR-Not Ranked. UR-Under Review.

Office: 1201 Lake Robbins Drive, The Woodlands, TX 77380-1046.
Telephone: 832-636-1000.
Website: http://www.anadarko.com
Chrmn: R.J. Allison, Jr.
Pres & CEO: J.T. Hackett.
SVP & CFO: J.R. Larson.

VP & Treas: A.L. Richey.
VP & Secy: S. Suter.
VP & Investor Contact: D.R. Larson 832-636-3265.
Dirs: C. P. Albert, R. J. Allison, Jr., L. Barcus, J. L. Bryan, J. R. Butler, Jr., H. P. Eberhart, P. M. Geren III, J. R. Gordon, J. T. Hackett, J. W. Poduska, Sr.

Founded: in 1985.
Domicile: Delaware.
Employees: 3,500.
S&P Analyst: Charles LaPorta, CFA /DC/BK

Recommendation: HOLD ★★★☆☆
SELL · SELL · HOLD · BUY · BUY

12-Month Target Price: **$42.00**
(as of October 21, 2004)

ADI has an approximate 0.14% weighting in the **S&P 500**

Sector: Information Technology
Sub-Industry: Semiconductors
Peer Group: Semiconductors - Analog

Summary: ADI manufactures high-performance integrated circuits (ICs) used in analog and digital signal processing applications.

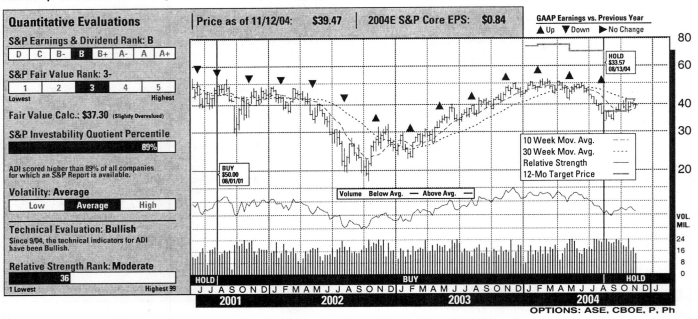

Quantitative Evaluations

S&P Earnings & Dividend Rank: B

| D | C | B- | **B** | B+ | A- | A | A+ |

S&P Fair Value Rank: 3-

| 1 | 2 | **3** | 4 | 5 |
| Lowest | | | | Highest |

Fair Value Calc.: $37.30 (Slightly Overvalued)

S&P Investability Quotient Percentile

89%

ADI scored higher than 89% of all companies for which an S&P Report is available.

Volatility: Average

| Low | **Average** | High |

Technical Evaluation: Bullish
Since 9/04, the technical indicators for ADI have been Bullish.

Relative Strength Rank: Moderate

36

| 1 Lowest | | Highest 99 |

Price as of 11/12/04: **$39.47**
2004E S&P Core EPS: **$0.84**

GAAP Earnings vs. Previous Year
▲ Up ▼ Down ► No Change

- 10 Week Mov. Avg.
- 30 Week Mov. Avg.
- Relative Strength
- 12-Mo Target Price

Volume Below Avg. — Above Avg.

BUY $50.00 08/01/01

HOLD $33.57 08/13/04

HOLD | BUY | HOLD

J J A S O N D | J F M A M J J A S O N D | J F M A M J J A S O N D | J F M A M J J A S O N D | J
2001 | 2002 | 2003 | 2004

OPTIONS: ASE, CBOE, P, Ph

Analyst commentary prepared by Amrit Tewary/DC/BK

Highlights October 25, 2004

- We expect revenues to increase 29% in FY 04 (Oct.) and to grow 6.4% in FY 05, based on our expectations that overall chip industry sales will be robust in calendar 2004, before moderating in 2005, during what we expect will be the last year of the current up cycle. New orders in the FY 04 third quarter were about equal to sales, but a relatively large number of customer cancellations resulted in a book-to-bill ratio of about 0.8, well below the level seen in the previous three quarters.

- We believe higher volumes and a recent move to larger wafer sizes will drive operating margins to 27% in FY 04 and 31% in FY 05, from 19% in FY 03.

- We project operating EPS of $1.45 for FY 04 and $1.70 for FY 05. We estimate Standard & Poor's Core Earnings of $0.84 for FY 04 and $1.08 for FY 05, with the difference from our operating earnings projections mainly reflecting estimated stock option expense.

Investment Rationale/Risk October 25, 2004

- We would hold the shares of ADI. Despite a year-to-date decline in the share price, we believe the stock is adequately valued at current levels, in light of what we see as above-average near-term macroeconomic and competitive risks. We believe consumer spending on electronics during the upcoming holiday season will likely be dampened somewhat by high energy prices, slow job growth, and the prospect of higher interest rates. Also, we are concerned about what we see as relatively weak near-term company guidance, in comparison with ADI's high-end analog peers Maxim Integrated Products (MXIM: $44; accumulate) and Linear Technology (LLTC: $36; buy).

- Risks to our opinion and target price include fluctuations in demand for semiconductors, industry cyclicality, competition, above-average share price volatility, and reliance on stock-based compensation.

- Our 12-month target price of $42 is based on P/E multiple and price to sales ratio analyses. Our target price is derived by applying a P/E multiple of 27X, below historical norms, to our forward 12-month EPS estimate of $1.57, and by applying a price to sales ratio of 5.9X, below historical norms, to our FY 05 sales per share estimate.

Key Stock Statistics

S&P Core EPS 2005E	**1.08**	52-week Range	**$52.37-31.36**
S&P Oper. EPS 2004E	**1.45**	12 Month P/E	**29.5**
P/E on S&P Oper. EPS 2004E	**27.2**	Beta	**NA**
S&P Oper. EPS 2005E	**1.70**	Shareholders	**4,867**
Yield (%)	**0.6%**	Market Cap (B)	**$ 14.9**
Dividend Rate/Share	**0.24**	Shares Outstanding (M)	**378.4**

Value of $10,000 invested five years ago: **$ 13,617**

Dividend Data Dividends have been paid since 2003

Amount ($)	Date Decl.	Ex-Div. Date	Stock of Record	Payment Date
0.040	Nov. 18	Nov. 25	Nov. 28	Dec. 17 '03
0.040	Feb. 17	Feb. 25	Feb. 27	Mar. 17 '04
0.060	May. 14	May. 26	May. 28	Jun. 16 '04
0.060	Aug. 12	Aug. 25	Aug. 27	Sep. 15 '04

Revenues/Earnings Data Fiscal year ending October 31

Revenues (Million $)

	2004	2003	2002	2001	2000	1999
1Q	605.4	467.4	393.0	772.3	490.3	300.5
2Q	678.5	501.9	413.4	601.4	581.0	340.1
3Q	717.8	520.5	445.4	479.9	700.7	378.8
4Q	—	557.5	455.7	423.3	805.6	431.0
Yr.	—	2,047	1,708	2,277	2,578	1,450

Earnings Per Share ($)

	2004	2003	2002	2001	2000	1999
1Q	0.30	0.16	0.06	0.50	0.25	0.09
2Q	0.39	0.19	0.04	0.27	0.32	0.11
3Q	0.43	0.21	0.08	0.10	0.22	0.15
4Q	E0.34	0.38	0.09	0.06	0.52	0.20
Yr.	E1.45	0.78	0.28	0.93	1.59	0.55

Next earnings report expected: mid-November Source: S&P, Company Reports
EPS Estimates based on S&P Operating Earnings; historical GAAP earnings are as reported.

STANDARD &POOR'S

Analog Devices, Inc.

Recommendation: **HOLD** ★★★☆☆   12-Month Target Price: **$42.00** (as of October 21, 2004)

Business Summary October 25, 2004

Analog Devices designs, manufactures and markets a broad line of high-performance analog, mixed-signal and digital signal processing (DSP) integrated circuits (ICs) that address a wide range of real-world signal processing applications. Real-world phenomena that these applications are designed for include temperature, pressure, sound, images, speed, acceleration, position and rotation; these phenomena are specifically analog in nature, consisting of continuously varying information. Analog chips accounted for 78% of FY 03 (Oct.) sales, and DSP chips for 22%.

The company's analog products are typically general purpose in nature, and are used in a wide variety of equipment and systems. Accordingly, they tend to have long life cycles. ADI markets several thousand products; its 10 largest products by revenue accounted for 18% of FY 03 total revenues. A substantial number of products are proprietary, while equivalents to most other products are available from only a limited number of suppliers. These factors, together with greater product price stability and less intense Asian competition, have allowed the company to post more stable operating results than those of most semiconductor makers. The semiconductor industry has displayed sharp cyclicality over its 40-year history.

ADI's products are sold both to OEMs and to customers building their own equipment. Key markets are industrial, which accounted for 35% to 40% of sales in FY 03, communications 35% to 40%, computers 15%, and high-end consumer electronics 10%. The customer base is fairly broad: the 20 largest customers

accounted for 26% of sales in FY 02, and the largest customer accounted for about 3%.

The expansion of broadband and wireless communications applications helps drive demand for analog and DSP chips. ADI's products are built into data and digital subscriber lines (DSL) modems, wireless telephones, base station equipment, and remote access servers.

The company's chips are increasingly sold to PC and digital entertainment markets, as consumer equipment to handle voice, video and images becomes increasingly complex, and sells to a wider audience. ADI's chips are used in end-products that include digital televisions, DVD recorders/players, and digital camcorders and cameras.

Sales are diversified globally, with North America accounting for 26% of FY 03 sales, and the remainder coming from Europe 19%, Japan 18%, and Southeast Asia and other markets 37%. The company maintains direct sales offices in 19 countries, including the U.S. Distributors handle a significant portion of sales.

ADI operates wafer fabrication facilities in California, Massachusetts and Ireland. The company also outsources some wafer production to foundries in the Far East.

In late FY 03, the company paid off its long-term debt. In FY 04 ADI paid its first quarterly cash dividend.

Company Financials Fiscal Year ending October 31

Per Share Data ($)

(Year Ended October 31)	2003	2002	2001	2000	1999	1998	1997	1996	1995	1994
Tangible Bk. Val.	8.42	7.50	7.20	5.90	4.54	3.47	3.50	2.67	2.09	1.67
Cash Flow	1.22	0.90	1.48	2.00	0.94	0.69	0.79	0.74	0.58	0.44
Earnings	0.78	0.28	0.93	1.59	0.55	0.36	0.52	0.52	0.38	0.24
S&P Core Earnings	0.20	-0.32	0.44	NA	NA	NA	NA	NA	NA	NA
Dividends	Nil	Nil	Nil	Nil	Nil	Nil	Nil	Nil	Nil	Nil
Payout Ratio	Nil	Nil	Nil	Nil	Nil	Nil	Nil	Nil	Nil	Nil
Prices - High	50.35	48.84	64.00	103.00	47.25	19.81	18.34	13.31	9.87	6.12
- Low	22.58	17.88	29.00	41.31	12.18	6.00	10.31	6.37	5.00	3.89
P/E Ratio - High	65	NM	69	65	86	56	35	26	26	26
- Low	29	NM	31	26	22	17	20	12	13	16

Income Statement Analysis (Million $)

	2003	2002	2001	2000	1999	1998	1997	1996	1995	1994
Revs.	2,047	1,708	2,277	2,578	1,450	1,231	1,243	1,194	942	773
Oper. Inc.	552	405	675	924	391	289	337	311	222	163
Depr.	168	238	210	157	143	128	104	83.8	64.1	61.3
Int. Exp.	32.2	44.5	62.5	5.84	8.07	11.2	12.5	11.3	4.20	7.15
Pretax Inc.	382	140	507	866	258	150	236	231	159	96.9
Eff. Tax Rate	21.9%	25.0%	29.7%	29.9%	23.6%	20.6%	24.4%	25.5%	25.2%	23.1%
Net Inc.	298	105	356	607	197	119	178	172	119	74.5
S&P Core Earnings	74.2	-118	170	NA	NA	NA	NA	NA	NA	NA

Balance Sheet & Other Fin. Data (Million $)

	2003	2002	2001	2000	1999	1998	1997	1996	1995	1994
Cash	518	1,614	1,365	1,736	356	263	290	300	151	182
Curr. Assets	2,886	3,624	3,435	3,168	1,379	904	895	820	526	505
Total Assets	4,093	4,980	4,885	4,411	2,218	1,862	1,764	1,516	1,002	816
Curr. Liab.	463	484	528	650	479	321	274	270	254	206
LT Debt	Nil	1,274	1,206	1,213	16.2	341	349	354	80.0	80.0
Common Equity	3,288	2,900	2,843	2,304	1,616	1,128	1,147	863	656	522
Total Cap.	3,305	4,197	4,100	3,568	1,672	1,501	1,517	1,233	741	605
Cap. Exp.	67.7	57.4	297	275	77.5	167	179	234	213	90.9
Cash Flow	467	343	567	764	339	247	282	256	183	136
Curr. Ratio	6.2	7.5	6.5	4.9	2.9	2.8	3.3	3.0	2.1	2.5
% LT Debt of Cap.	Nil	30.4	29.4	34.0	1.0	22.7	23.0	28.7	10.8	13.2
% Net Inc.of Revs.	14.6	6.2	15.7	23.6	13.6	9.7	14.3	14.4	12.7	9.6
% Ret. on Assets	6.6	2.1	7.7	18.3	9.6	6.6	10.9	13.7	13.1	9.9
% Ret. on Equity	9.6	3.7	13.8	31.0	14.3	10.5	17.7	22.6	33.9	15.5

Data as orig reptd.; bef. results of disc opers/spec. items. Per share data adj. for stk. divs. Bold denotes primary EPS - prior periods restated. E-Estimated. NA-Not Available. NM-Not Meaningful. NR-Not Ranked. UR-Under Review.

Office: One Technology Way, Norwood, MA 02062-9106.
Telephone: 800-262-5643.
Email: investor.relations@analog.com
Website: http://www.analog.com
Chrmn: R. Stata.
Pres & CEO: J.G. Fishman.

VP, CFO & Chief Acctg Officer: J.E. McDonough.
Treas: W.A. Martin.
Clerk: M.G. Borden.
Investor Contact: M. Tagliaferro 781-461-3282.
Dirs: J. Champy, J. L. Doyle, J. G. Fishman, C. King, F. G. Saviers, K. Sicchitano, R. Stata, L. C. Thurow.

Founded: in 1965.
Domicile: Massachusetts.
Employees: 8,400.
S&P Analyst: Amrit Tewary/DC/BK

Andrew Corp.

Recommendation: **HOLD** ★★★☆☆
SELL | SELL | HOLD | BUY | BUY

12-Month Target Price: $15.00
(as of October 28, 2004)

ANDW has an approximate 0.02% weighting in the **S&P 500**

Sector: Information Technology
Sub-Industry: Communications Equipment
Peer Group: Microwave Equipment

Summary: Andrew Corp. is a global supplier of communications products and systems, with emphasis on wireless communications.

Quantitative Evaluations

S&P Earnings & Dividend Rank: B

| D | C | B- | **B** | B+ | A- | A | A+ |

S&P Fair Value Rank: 4-

| 1 | 2 | 3 | **4** | 5 |
| Lowest | | | | Highest |

Fair Value Calc.: $14.40 (Slightly Overvalued)

S&P Investability Quotient Percentile
85%

ANDW scored higher than 85% of all companies for which an S&P Report is available.

Volatility: High

| Low | Average | **High** |

Technical Evaluation: Bullish
Since 10/04, the technical indicators for ANDW have been Bullish.

Relative Strength Rank: Strong
80
1 Lowest — Highest 99

| Price as of 11/12/04: | $14.75 | 2005E S&P Core EPS: | $0.51 |

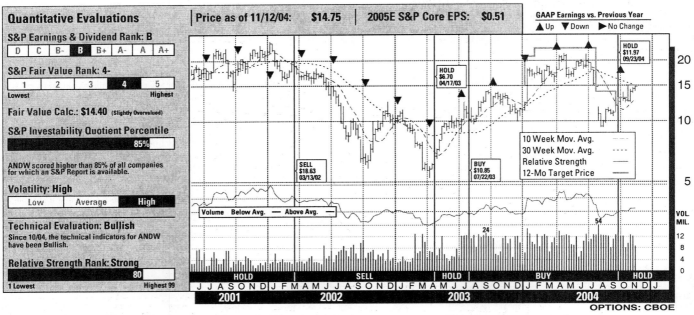

GAAP Earnings vs. Previous Year
▲ Up ▼ Down ► No Change

10 Week Mov. Avg.
30 Week Mov. Avg.
Relative Strength
12-Mo Target Price

Volume Below Avg. — Above Avg.

OPTIONS: CBOE

Analyst commentary prepared by Kenneth M. Leon/PMW/JWP

Highlights November 02, 2004

- Following a total sales increase of 81% in FY 04 (Sep.), including the July 2003 acquisition of Allen Telecom, we estimate normalized sales growth of 11% in FY 05. We believe ANDW's wireless markets should post growth in the low teens in FY 05, but the company sees FY 05 first quarter sales down 4% to 10% sequentially, with slower North America wireless capital spending by Cingular, a major customer. We think Cingular is delaying new cell site expansion and next generation upgrades until it can integrate AT&T Wireless's network operations, which were acquired in late October. Both companies have been major customers for ANDW's base station and antenna equipment products.

- The company estimates FY 05 first quarter revenues of $440 million and $470 million, with operating EPS of $0.07 to $0.10, excluding one-time items. We expect FY 05 gross margins of 23%, versus 24.5% in 2004, as we see a weaker product mix shift and higher raw material costs, especially in copper-related cables. ANDW has said it is not sure how much of the higher material costs can be passed on to customers through price increases.

- After posting operating EPS of $0.44 in FY 04, including the Allen Telecom merger, our respective FY 05 and FY 06 EPS estimates are $0.55 and $0.70. Our S&P Core EPS estimates are $0.51 for FY 05 and $0.66 for FY 06, reflecting projected stock option expense and pension adjustments.

Key Stock Statistics

S&P Core EPS 2006E	0.66	52-week Range	$21.67-9.30
S&P Oper. EPS 2005E	0.55	12 Month P/E	73.8
P/E on S&P Oper. EPS 2005E	26.8	Beta	2.05
S&P Oper. EPS 2006E	0.70	Shareholders	4,214
Yield (%)	Nil	Market Cap (B)	$ 2.4
Dividend Rate/Share	Nil	Shares Outstanding (M)	160.8

Value of $10,000 invested five years ago: **$ 12,844**

Dividend Data

No cash dividends have been paid.

Investment Rationale/Risk November 02, 2004

- Despite our disappointment with the company's guidance for weaker than expected FY 05 first quarter results, we would hold the shares, currently at a discount to peers, with an enterprise value of 1.2X our FY 05 sales projection and 8X our FY 05 EBITDA estimate. ANDW is the leading supplier of radio frequency (RF) equipment for wireless communication infrastructure, and we think the company should benefit from stronger demand evident in the global wireless handset market.

- Risks to our recommendation and target price include a failure to successfully expand the product platform to foreign markets so that the company becomes the leading global wireless sub-system supplier; the failure for sales to rebound after the anticipated completion of Cingular's planned merger with AWE (expected by year end, subject to approvals); lack of anticipated margin benefits from a shift of most manufacturing to overseas facilities; and a move by key OEMs to manufacture their own wireless sub-systems or to select an alternative sub-system supplier as a systems partner.

- Applying an assumed price to sales ratio of 1.4X to our FY 05 sales per share estimate, and a price to book value of 1.8X, below the peer average of 3X, we arrive at our 12-month target price of $15.

Revenues/Earnings Data Fiscal year ending September 30

Revenues (Million $)

	2004	2003	2002	2001	2000	1999
1Q	410.8	254.5	199.9	284.1	233.6	218.6
2Q	447.1	201.3	189.3	239.1	242.7	172.0
3Q	493.0	213.7	203.8	245.1	259.2	186.1
4Q	487.8	344.9	271.8	281.2	283.7	215.1
Yr.	1,839	1,014	864.8	1,050	1,019	791.7

Earnings Per Share ($)

	2004	2003	2002	2001	2000	1999
1Q	0.02	0.07	0.22	0.26	0.21	0.28
2Q	0.06	-0.02	0.04	0.10	0.21	-0.25
3Q	0.11	0.09	0.05	0.15	0.26	0.18
4Q	Nil	-0.01	-0.19	0.25	0.30	0.16
Yr.	0.20	0.11	0.12	0.76	0.98	0.37

Next earnings report expected: early-February Source: S&P, Company Reports
EPS Estimates based on S&P Operating Earnings; historical GAAP earnings are as reported.

Andrew Corporation

Recommendation: **HOLD** ★ ★ ★ ☆ ☆   12-Month Target Price: **$15.00** (as of October 28, 2004)

Business Summary November 02, 2004

Andrew Corp., the successor to a partnership formed in 1937, supplies communications products and systems to commercial, industrial and governmental customers. ANDW's products are related to the company's core competency: the radio frequency (RF) path. Its products are sold principally to three key markets: wireless infrastructure, fixed-line telecommunications networks, and government and broadcast. Sales trends are mostly influenced by the wireless infrastructure market, which account for the majority of the company's sales. International sales accounted for 43% of total sales in FY 04 (Sep.), down from 56% in FY 03.

Cable products accounted for 30% of total sales in FY 04. Coaxial cable is a two-conductor, radio-frequency transmission line with the smaller of the two conductors located inside a larger, tubular conductor. It is used principally to carry radio-frequency signals at frequencies of up to 2 GHz. In addition to bulk cable, ANDW's cable systems include cable connectors, accessories and assemblies. Semiflexible cables and elliptical waveguides are sold under the trademark HELIAX.

Antennas products (27%) include base station antennas, terrestrial microwave antennas, earth station antennas, and multi-band antennas. ANDW is a market leader for base station antennas, a critical piece of wireless infrastructure, which captures the wireless signal from the user handset and sends it to operator's base stations. Base station antennas are marketed under the trade name DECIBEL. The company is also an industry leader in high performance antennas for wireless communications and global positioning system applications.

Base station subsystems (26%) are integral components of wireless base stations and include products such as power amplifiers, filters, duplexers and combiners. These products cover all the major wireless standards and frequency bands and are sold individually or as part of integrated subsystems. ANDW has recently developed two new integrated product offerings that include an integrated radio and amplifier and, in addition, an integrated radio, amplifier and receiver.

Network solutions (10%) includes geolocation, engineering and consulting services, and test and measurement products. ANDW is one of the two recognized suppliers of network based geolocation systems capable of providing wireless E-911 service. Wireless innovations (7%) are used to extend the coverage of wireless networks in areas where signals are difficult to send or receive and include both complete systems and individual components.

In July 2003, ANDW completed a merger with Allen Telecom; it expected to realize substantial synergies and cost savings as a result. Allen is a supplier of filters, base station antennas, network geolocation solutions, repeaters and in-building solutions. ANDW believed the merger would extend its global presence in the wireless subsystems market, expand its customer base, and diversify its product lines. In the FY 04 fourth quarter, the 25 largest customers accounted for 68% of total consolidated sales, with AT&T Wireless as the only customer accounting for more than 10% of total sales. Major OEMs accounted for 37% of total sales in the fourth quarter. Orders for the fourth quarter were $457 million, up 33%, year to year, but the book-to-bill ratio was less than 1.0.

Company Financials Fiscal Year ending September 30

Per Share Data ($)

(Year Ended September 30)	2004	2003	2002	2001	2000	1999	1998	1997	1996	1995
Tangible Bk. Val.	NA	3.16	4.09	6.85	6.22	5.63	5.75	5.40	4.56	3.57
Cash Flow	NA	0.79	0.77	1.42	1.56	0.84	1.60	1.61	1.36	1.05
Earnings	0.20	0.11	0.12	0.76	0.98	0.37	1.18	1.18	0.99	0.77
S&P Core Earnings	NA	-0.01	-0.07	0.68	NA	NA	NA	NA	NA	NA
Dividends	Nil	Nil	Nil	Nil	Nil	Nil	Nil	Nil	Nil	Nil
Payout Ratio	Nil	Nil	Nil	Nil	Nil	Nil	Nil	Nil	Nil	Nil
Prices - High	21.67	14.25	24.88	27.37	42.06	22.87	30.06	42.58	42.16	28.66
- Low	9.30	5.23	5.84	13.18	17.00	11.00	10.37	20.12	12.55	15.11
P/E Ratio - High	NM	NM	NM	36	43	62	25	36	43	37
- Low	NM	NM	NM	17	17	30	9	17	13	20

Income Statement Analysis (Million $)

	2004	2003	2002	2001	2000	1999	1998	1997	1996	1995
Revs.	NA	1,014	865	1,049	1,019	792	853	869	794	664
Oper. Inc.	NA	97.3	90.6	152	176	117	197	208	180	140
Depr.	NA	74.4	56.3	54.4	47.7	39.2	37.5	39.3	34.3	25.8
Int. Exp.	NA	5.67	5.08	7.41	8.86	5.33	6.06	5.00	5.18	5.64
Pretax Inc.	NA	23.3	13.1	90.6	117	49.2	157	166	141	5.64
Eff. Tax Rate	NA	19.8%	19.7%	32.0%	32.0%	38.1%	34.0%	35.0%	36.0%	36.1%
Net Inc.	NA	18.7	10.5	61.6	79.6	30.4	104	108	90.4	70.0

Balance Sheet & Other Fin. Data (Million $)

	2004	2003	2002	2001	2000	1999	1998	1997	1996	1995
Cash	NA	286	84.9	112	44.9	38.3	78.4	93.8	31.3	46.0
Curr. Assets	NA	889	477	556	525	414	437	460	402	323
Total Assets	NA	2,073	1,124	858	817	666	683	691	631	505
Curr. Liab.	NA	274	237	179	174	110	117	127	117	95.6
LT Debt	NA	301	13.4	39.9	65.8	48.8	38.0	35.7	40.4	45.3
Common Equity	NA	1,415	845	601	543	484	509	509	456	356
Total Cap.	NA	1,725	859	641	618	538	552	554	496	402
Cap. Exp.	NA	31.9	40.5	72.1	83.5	51.4	58.5	49.1	52.5	48.1
Cash Flow	NA	86.6	66.8	116	127	69.6	141	147	125	95.8
Curr. Ratio	NA	3.2	2.0	3.1	3.0	3.8	3.7	3.6	3.4	3.4
% LT Debt of Cap.	NA	17.5	1.6	6.2	10.7	9.1	6.9	6.5	8.1	11.3
% Net Inc.of Revs.	NA	1.8	1.2	5.9	7.8	3.8	12.2	12.4	11.4	10.8
% Ret. on Assets	NA	1.2	1.1	7.4	10.7	4.5	15.1	16.3	15.9	NA
% Ret. on Equity	NA	1.1	1.5	10.8	15.5	6.1	20.4	22.3	22.2	NA

Data as orig reptd.; bef. results of disc opers/spec. items. Per share data adj. for stk. divs.; EPS diluted. E-Estimated. NA-Not Available. NM-Not Meaningful. NR-Not Ranked. UR-Under Review.

Office: 10500 West 153rd Street, Orland Park, IL 60462-3071.
Telephone: 708-349-3300.
Email: investorrelations@andrew.com
Website: http://www.andrew.com
Chrmn: F.L. English.
Pres & CEO: R. Faison.
Vice Chrmn & CFO: C.R. Nicholas.

VP & Chief Acctg Officer: M.A. Olson.
VP & Treas: M.J. Gittelman.
Investor Contact: L. Nickless 800-232-6767.
Dirs: J. G. Bollinger, P. W. Colburn, T. A. Donahoe, R. E. Faison, J. D. Fluno, W. O. Hunt, C. R. Nicholas, R. G. Paul, G. A. Poch, G. O. Toney, D. L. Whipple.

Founded: in 1937.
Domicile: Delaware.
Employees: 7,228.
S&P Analyst: Kenneth M. Leon/PMW/JWP

Anheuser-Busch

Recommendation: **BUY** ★★★★☆ SELL | SELL | HOLD | BUY | BUY
12-Month Target Price: **$56.00**
(as of September 27, 2004)

BUD has an approximate 0.37% weighting in the **S&P 500**

Sector: Consumer Staples
Sub-Industry: Brewers
Peer Group: Beer Companies

Summary: BUD, the parent company of the world's largest brewer, also has interests in entertainment operations.

Quantitative Evaluations

| Price as of 11/12/04: | **$51.06** | 2004E S&P Core EPS: | **$2.66** |

S&P Earnings & Dividend Rank: A+

| D | C | B- | B | B+ | A- | A | **A+** |

S&P Fair Value Rank: 1+

| **1** | 2 | 3 | 4 | 5 |
| Lowest | | | | Highest |

Fair Value Calc.: $36.90 (Overvalued)

S&P Investability Quotient Percentile
98%

BUD scored higher than 98% of all companies for which an S&P Report is available.

Volatility: Low

| Low | Average | High |

Technical Evaluation: Bearish
Since 9/04, the technical indicators for BUD have been Bearish.

Relative Strength Rank: Moderate

| 31 | |
| 1 Lowest | Highest 99 |

GAAP Earnings vs. Previous Year
▲ Up ▼ Down ► No Change

10 Week Mov. Avg.
30 Week Mov. Avg.
Relative Strength
12-Mo Target Price

Volume Below Avg. — Above Avg.

VOL. MIL.

BUY

J J A S O N D | J F M A M J J A S O N D | J F M A M J J A S O N D | J F M A M J J A S O N D | J
2001 | 2002 | 2003 | 2004

OPTIONS: CBOE, P, Ph, ASE, CBOE, P

Analyst commentary prepared by Anishka Clarke/PMW/DRJ

Highlights November 04, 2004

■ We expect net sales (after excise taxes) to rise about 5% in 2005, following the 6% gain that we project for 2004. We believe the beer pricing environment will remain favorable over the next six months, allowing net revenue per barrel gains of 2.5% to 3%, on price increases. We see worldwide shipment volumes rising in the mid-single digits reflecting acquisitions. U.S. sales in 2004 should benefit from product and packaging innovations and increased marketing efforts, particularly in the premium-and-above categories. We expect further improvements in mix.

■ Operating margins should widen by 30 basis points, as likely gains in efficiencies outweigh higher ingredient costs, packaging costs and marketing. We also look for margin expansion in the entertainment and packaging divisions. With higher equity income expected from Grupo Modelo, Mexico's largest brewer, and improving profitability for international operations, net income should grow 8.0% in 2005, following a projected 7.5% increase in 2004.

■ Aided by an expected 2% reduction in shares outstanding, we see 2005 EPS up 11%, to $3.04, from an estimated $2.75 in 2004. We project 2004 S&P Core EPS of $2.66, reflecting estimated stock option and pension expenses.

Investment Rationale/Risk November 04, 2004

■ We recommend accumulating the shares, based on valuation. We expect moderate growth in net revenue per barrel, but we see a less favorable pricing environment beyond mid-2005. We look for strengthening competition from SAB Miller and the spirits and wines categories to put pressure on near-term volume growth. However, we believe BUD's brand strength and effective marketing will enable it to maintain market share, at least in the premium-and-above categories. We also expect benefits to start accruing from investments in China within the next 18 months.

■ Risks to our recommendation and target price include an inability to increase market share, due to an aggressive marketing campaign by direct competitor SAB Miller; and the impact of a surge in popularity of wine and spirits in the 21- to 27-year-old demographic.

■ Our 12-month target price of $56 is based on a blend of our DCF and our P/E multiple analyses, giving more weight to the latter. Our DCF model calculates intrinsic value of $64, assuming an 8.5% cost of capital. We expect near-term pressures on beverage trading multiples, and apply a P/E multiple of 18X (below the historical average) to our 2005 EPS estimate of $3.04 to derive our target price of $56.

Key Stock Statistics

S&P Core EPS 2005E	2.96	52-week Range	$54.74-49.42
S&P Oper. EPS 2004E	2.75	12 Month P/E	18.8
P/E on S&P Oper. EPS 2004E	18.6	Beta	-0.06
S&P Oper. EPS 2005E	3.04	Shareholders	56,094
Yield (%)	1.9%	Market Cap (B)	$ 40.3
Dividend Rate/Share	0.98	Shares Outstanding (M)	790.1

Value of $10,000 invested five years ago: **$ 15,021**

Dividend Data Dividends have been paid since 1932

Amount ($)	Date Decl.	Ex-Div. Date	Stock of Record	Payment Date
0.220	Jan. 14	Feb. 05	Feb. 09	Mar. 09 '04
0.220	Apr. 28	May. 06	May. 10	Jun. 09 '04
0.245	Jul. 28	Aug. 05	Aug. 09	Sep. 09 '04
0.245	Oct. 27	Nov. 05	Nov. 09	Dec. 09 '04

Revenues/Earnings Data Fiscal year ending December 31

Revenues (Million $)

	2004	2003	2002	2001	2000	1999
1Q	3,477	3,281	3,137	3,044	2,812	2,685
2Q	4,010	3,770	3,626	3,452	3,266	3,081
3Q	4,080	3,881	3,706	3,522	3,398	3,222
4Q	—	3,215	3,098	2,893	2,787	2,716
Yr.	—	14,147	13,566	12,911	12,262	11,704

Earnings Per Share ($)

	2004	2003	2002	2001	2000	1999
1Q	0.67	0.57	0.51	0.43	0.38	0.33
2Q	0.83	0.75	0.66	0.58	0.52	0.45
3Q	0.85	0.80	0.71	0.62	0.56	0.49
4Q	E0.42	0.36	0.32	0.26	0.23	0.21
Yr.	E2.75	2.48	2.20	1.89	1.69	1.47

Next earnings report expected: early-February Source: S&P, Company Reports
EPS Estimates based on S&P Operating Earnings; historical GAAP earnings are as reported.

STANDARD &POOR'S

Anheuser-Busch Companies, Inc.

Stock Report
November 13, 2004
NYSE Symbol: **BUD**

Recommendation: **BUY** ★ ★ ★ ★ ☆   12-Month Target Price: **$56.00** (as of September 27, 2004)

Business Summary November 08, 2004

Anheuser-Busch Cos. is the holding company parent of the largest U.S. brewer, Anheuser-Busch, Inc. (ABI), which dates back to 1875, Anheuser-Busch International, Inc. (ABII), and other subsidiaries that conduct various other business operations.

Major beer brands include Budweiser, Bud Light, Bud Dry, Bud Ice (Light), Michelob, Michelob Light, Michelob Golden Draft (Light), Michelob Black & Tan Lager, Michelob Amber Bock, Michelob Honey Lager, Michelob Hefe-Weizen, Michelob Marzen, Busch, Busch Light, Busch Ice, Natural Light, Natural Ice, King Cobra, "Doc's" Hard Lemon, and Tequiza, and non-alcoholic malt beverages O'Doul's and Busch NA. In 2002, the company introduced Bacardi Silver, Michelob Ultra, and American Red.

BUD operates 12 breweries, strategically located across the U.S., to serve its distribution system economically. Worldwide sales of the company's beer brands in 2003 totaled 111.0 million barrels (up 1.1% from 109.8 million barrels in 2002). U.S. sales totaled 102.6 million barrels in 2003 (up 0.8%), or about 50% of U.S. industry sales. Through various subsidiaries, the company is involved in a number of beer-related operations that help to insulate it from occasional rises in packaging and ingredient costs. These operations include can manufacturing, metalized paper printing, and barley malting. Packaging operations accounted for 8.7% of total net sales in 2003.

ABII oversees the marketing and sale of Budweiser and other ABI brands outside the U.S., operates breweries in the U.K. and China, negotiates and administers license and contract brewing agreements on behalf of ABI with various foreign brewers, and negotiates and manages equity investments in foreign brewing partners. BUD's beer products are being sold in more than 80 countries and U.S. territories. International beer volume was 8.4 million barrels in 2003, up 3.8% from 8.0 million barrels in 2002. BUD currently holds a 50.2% direct and indirect interest in Diblo, the operating subsidiary of Modelo (Mexico's largest brewer), a 29% direct and indirect ownership interest in the Argentinian subsidiary of Chilean-based Compania Cerveccias Unidas S.A. (CCU), and a 9.9% equity interest in Tsingtao Brewery Company, Ltd. In October 2002, the company agreed to increase its ownership of Tsingtao to 27% over the next seven years. In the first half of 2004, BUD acquired China's fifth largest brewer, Harbin Brewery, for about $650 million. Combined with its interest in Tsingtao, this was expected to result in significant exposure in China, the world's largest beer market.

Through Busch Entertainment Corp., the company operates nine theme parks, including Busch Gardens in Florida and Virginia; Sea World parks in Florida, Texas and California; water parks in Florida and Virginia; and an educational play park in Pennsylvania. It also operates the Baseball City Sports Complex in Florida. Through a Spanish affiliate, BUD owns a 13.6% equity interest in Port Aventura S.A., a theme park near Barcelona; Spain. Busch Entertainment contributed 6.5% of total net sales in 2003.

Company Financials Fiscal Year ending December 31

Per Share Data ($)

(Year Ended December 31)	2003	2002	2001	2000	1999	1998	1997	1996	1995	1994
Tangible Bk. Val.	2.74	3.61	4.15	4.11	3.80	3.96	3.69	3.61	3.93	3.82
Cash Flow	3.53	3.16	2.82	2.56	1.47	2.02	1.86	1.73	1.41	1.57
Earnings	2.48	2.20	1.89	1.69	1.47	1.27	1.18	1.14	0.62	0.98
S&P Core Earnings	2.33	1.96	1.67	NA	NA	NA	NA	NA	NA	NA
Dividends	0.83	0.75	0.69	0.63	0.58	0.54	0.50	0.46	0.42	0.38
Payout Ratio	33%	34%	37%	37%	39%	43%	42%	40%	67%	39%
Prices - High	53.84	55.00	46.95	49.87	42.00	34.12	24.12	22.50	17.00	13.84
- Low	45.30	43.65	36.75	27.31	32.21	21.46	19.25	16.18	12.68	11.78
P/E Ratio - High	22	25	25	30	29	27	20	20	27	14
- Low	18	20	19	16	22	17	16	14	20	12

Income Statement Analysis (Million $)

	2003	2002	2001	2000	1999	1998	1997	1996	1995	1994
Revs.	14,147	13,566	12,912	12,262	11,704	11,245	11,066	10,884	10,341	12,054
Oper. Inc.	4,077	3,827	3,540	3,299	3,080	2,862	2,737	2,623	2,359	2,527
Depr.	877	847	835	804	777	738	684	594	566	628
Int. Exp.	377	351	334	315	290	265	219	233	226	221
Pretax Inc.	3,169	2,975	2,618	2,380	2,165	1,937	1,883	1,893	1,462	1,707
Eff. Tax Rate	34.5%	35.0%	34.9%	34.8%	35.2%	36.3%	37.4%	38.9%	39.3%	39.5%
Net Inc.	2,076	1,934	1,705	1,552	1,402	1,233	1,179	1,156	887	1,032
S&P Core Earnings	1,952	1,722	1,507	NA	NA	NA	NA	NA	NA	NA

Balance Sheet & Other Fin. Data (Million $)

	2003	2002	2001	2000	1999	1998	1997	1996	1995	1994
Cash	191	189	163	160	152	225	147	94.0	94.0	156
Curr. Assets	1,630	1,505	1,550	1,548	1,601	1,640	1,584	1,466	1,511	1,862
Total Assets	14,690	14,120	13,862	13,085	12,640	12,484	11,727	10,464	10,591	11,045
Curr. Liab.	1,857	1,788	1,732	1,676	1,987	1,730	1,501	1,431	1,242	1,669
LT Debt	7,285	6,603	5,984	5,375	4,881	4,719	4,366	3,271	3,270	3,078
Common Equity	2,712	4,013	4,062	4,128	3,921	4,216	4,042	4,029	4,434	4,415
Total Cap.	11,459	11,962	11,334	10,876	10,147	10,238	9,701	8,508	8,837	8,752
Cap. Exp.	993	835	1,022	1,075	856	818	1,199	1,085	953	785
Cash Flow	2,953	2,781	2,539	2,356	1,402	1,971	1,863	1,750	1,453	1,660
Curr. Ratio	0.9	0.8	0.9	0.9	0.8	0.9	1.1	1.0	1.2	1.1
% LT Debt of Cap.	63.6	55.2	52.8	49.4	48.1	46.1	45.0	21.4	37.0	35.2
% Net Inc.of Revs.	14.7	14.3	13.2	12.7	12.0	11.0	10.7	10.6	8.6	8.6
% Ret. on Assets	14.4	13.8	12.7	12.1	11.2	10.2	10.6	11.0	8.4	9.6
% Ret. on Equity	72.0	45.3	41.6	38.6	34.5	29.9	29.2	27.3	20.0	24.2

Data as orig reptd.; bef. results of disc opers/spec. items. Per share data adj. for stk. divs.; EPS diluted. E-Estimated. NA-Not Available. NM-Not Meaningful. NR-Not Ranked. UR-Under Review.

Office: One Busch Place, St. Louis, MO 63118.
Telephone: 314-577-2000.
Website: http://www.anheuser-busch.com
Chrmn: A.A. Busch III.
Pres & CEO: P.T. Stokes.
VP & CFO: W.R. Baker.
VP & Treas: W.J. Kimmins, Jr.

VP & Secy: J.G. Brown.
Investor Contact: D. Sauerhoff 314-577-2000.
Dirs: A. A. Busch III, B. A. Edison, C. G. Fernandez, J. J. Forese, J. E. Jacob, J. R. Jones, C. F. Knight, V. R. Loucks, Jr., V. S. Martinez, W. P. Payne, J. M. Roche, H. H. Shelton, P. T. Stokes, A. C. Taylor, D. A. Warner III, E. E. Whitacre, Jr.

Founded: in 1852.
Domicile: Delaware.
Employees: 23,316.
S&P Analyst: Anishka Clarke/PMW/DF

The McGraw-Hi

Please rea
Redistribution or rep

Anthem, Inc.

Recommendation: **HOLD** ★★★☆☆
SELL | SELL | HOLD | BUY | BUY

12-Month Target Price: $103.00
(as of November 09, 2004)

ATH has an approximate 0.12% weighting in the **S&P 500**

Sector: Health Care
Sub-Industry: Managed Health Care
Peer Group: Managed Care - Large

Summary: This Blue Cross and Blue Shield licensee is one of the largest managed health organizations in the U.S., serving more than 12.7 million members in nine states.

Quantitative Evaluations

S&P Earnings & Dividend Rank: NR

D	C	B-	B	B+	A-	A	A+

S&P Fair Value Rank: 5

1	2	3	4	5
Lowest				Highest

Fair Value Calc.: $134.10 (Undervalued)

S&P Investability Quotient Percentile
94%

ATH scored higher than 94% of all companies for which an S&P Report is available.

Volatility: Average

Low	Average	High

Technical Evaluation: Bearish
Since 10/04, the technical indicators for ATH have been Bearish.

Relative Strength Rank: Strong
83

1 Lowest	Highest 99

Price as of 11/12/04:	**$94.76**	2004E S&P Core EPS:	**$5.94**

GAAP Earnings vs. Previous Year
▲ Up ▼ Down ► No Change

BUY $69.90 10/17/02

- - - 10 Week Mov. Avg.
· · · 30 Week Mov. Avg.
—— Relative Strength
—— 12-Mo Target Price

Volume Below Avg. — Above Avg.

BUY   HOLD

J J A S O N D J F M A M J J A S O N D J F M A M J J A S O N D J F M A M J J A S O N D J
2001   2002   2003   2004

Analyst commentary prepared by Phillip M. Seligman/CB/JWP

Highlights November 02, 2004

- ATH has agreed to acquire larger Blues peer WellPoint Health Networks (WLP: hold, $99) in a transaction originally slated to close in mid-2004, subject to necessary approvals. Until the closing, which we think will be delayed, we will follow the company in its current configuration. For 2005, we look for operating revenues to rise about 11%, to $20.4 billion, from the $18.4 billion we project for 2004. Supporting this growth are 6% to 7% higher enrollment and a premium yield that would cover 9.5% to 10.5% cost trends, as the company expects, similar to 2004 trends.

- We project that the benefits expense ratio will remain near 2004's level, which we see near the high end of ATH's projected range of 81.5% to 82.5%. We expect the SG&A expense ratio to continue to decline, on systems development and more sales of high-margin specialty products.

- We look for 2005 EPS of $7.60, up from 2004's projected operating EPS of $6.60. Our 2004 and 2005 Standard & Poor's Core EPS estimates, which reflect projected stock option expense and pension and post-retirement adjustments, are 9.5% and 9.9%, respectively, below our operating EPS estimates.

Investment Rationale/Risk November 02, 2004

- Despite our positive view of ATH's prospects, we think its profit progress may cause customers to balk at steep rate hikes and health care providers to demand higher payments. We also think the shares are being increasingly viewed by investors from the standpoint of the proposed merger. In this regard, we think the California Insurance Commissioner's decision to oppose the merger will open investor eyes to corporate governance issues. He sees WLP executive compensation as excessive, and the deal not improving the availability and quality of health care. Recently, three other states began to reconsider their approvals, albeit for other reasons. We expect any deal, if it occurs, to be postponed and restructured.

- Risks to our recommendation and target price include increased competition, higher-than-expected medical costs and/or lower-than-expected premium yields, a weakened job market, and failure to consummate the WLP merger. Other risks include expansion of the insurance industry probe by New York Attorney General Spitzer and other state attorneys general into the health insurance industry.

- Given the uncertainties surrounding the insurance probes and planned merger, we see a rise in stock volatility and, hence, a likelihood of valuation compression. By lowering our estimated forward P/E to the peer level, our 12-month target price is $88, based on our 2005 EPS estimate.

Key Stock Statistics

S&P Oper. EPS 2004E	6.60	52-week Range	$95.60-67.28
P/E on S&P Oper. EPS 2004E	14.4	12 Month P/E	13.7
S&P Oper. EPS 2005E	7.60	Beta	NA
Yield (%)	Nil	Shareholders	181,701
Dividend Rate/Share	Nil	Market Cap (B)	$ 13.2
Shares Outstanding (M)	138.8		

Value of $10,000 invested five years ago: **NA**

Dividend Data

No cash dividends have been paid.

Revenues/Earnings Data Fiscal year ending December 31

Revenues (Million $)

	2004	2003	2002	2001	2000	1999
1Q	4,574	4,100	2,812	2,561	—	—
2Q	4,605	4,114	2,900	2,558	—	—
3Q	4,803	4,262	3,579	2,664	—	—
4Q	—	4,295	3,900	2,662	—	—
Yr.	—	16,771	12,991	10,445	8,544	—

Earnings Per Share ($)

	2004	2003	2002	2001	2000	1999
1Q	2.08	1.36	0.95	0.68	—	—
2Q	1.66	1.25	1.01	0.70	—	—
3Q	1.70	1.38	1.29	10.70	—	—
4Q	E1.68	1.47	1.19	0.85	—	—
Yr.	E6.60	5.45	4.51	3.30	2.10	—

Next earnings report expected: late-January Source: S&P, Company Reports
EPS Estimates based on S&P Operating Earnings; historical GAAP earnings are as reported.

STANDARD &POOR'S

Anthem, Inc.

Recommendation: **HOLD** ★ ★ ★ ☆ ☆   12-Month Target Price: **$103.00** (as of November 09, 2004)

Business Summary November 02, 2004

Anthem is one of the largest U.S. health benefits companies. It went public in November 2001, after conversion from a mutual insurance company to a stock insurance company, and became a wholly owned subsidiary of Anthem, Inc., a holding company formed in connection with the demutualization. At December 31, 2003, it served more than 11.9 million members. Anthem is the Blue Cross and Blue Shield licensee for Indiana, Kentucky, Ohio, Connecticut, New Hampshire, Maine, Colorado, Nevada and Virginia, excluding the Northern Virginia suburbs of Washington, DC.

The product portfolio includes a diversified mix of managed care products, including health maintenance organizations (HMOs), preferred provider organizations (PPOs), and point of service (POS) plans, as well as traditional indemnity products. The company also offers administrative and managed care services and partially insured products for employer self-funded plans, including underwriting, stop loss insurance, actuarial services, provider network access, medical cost management, claims processing and other administrative services. In addition, ATH offers group life, disability, prescription management, workers compensation, dental and vision.

At December 31, 2003, health benefits membership by product was as follows: PPO, 47.6%; traditional indemnity, 10.9%; HMO, 13.3%; POS, 4.6%; and BlueCard, 23.6%.

The prescription management services subsidiary is a wholly owned pharmacy benefit manager providing pharmacy network management, pharmacy benefits and mail order prescription services.

ATH offers an array of group life insurance and disability benefit products to both large and small group customers. At December 31, 2003, it had over $29.1 billion of life insurance in force, insuring more than 41,000 groups with more than 830,000 employees.

Vision and dental care programs are primarily for customers enrolled in its Blue Cross and Blue Shield health plans. In addition, the company offers dental third-party administration services. ATH is also a fiscal intermediary for Medicare in certain states.

At December 31, 2003, membership broke down as follows: local large group (contracts with 51 or more eligible employees, but excluding national business contracts), 38.6% of operating revenue and 32.4% of members; small group (contracts with one to 50 employees), 20.1% and 10.5%; individual policies (under age 65 and Medicare Supplement), 13.6% and 10.1%; Medicare+Choice (age 65 and over), 4.1% and 0.8%; Federal Employee Program, 12.5% and 5.9%; national business, including BlueCard (mainly self-insured and sold through brokers and consultants), 5.1% and 38.5%; and Medicaid, 2.9% and 1.8%.

Company Financials Fiscal Year ending December 31

Per Share Data ($)

(Year Ended December 31)	2003	2002	2001	2000	1999	1998	1997	1996	1995	1994
Tangible Bk. Val.	16.88	11.51	15.42	15.31	NA	NA	NA	NA	NA	NA
Cash Flow	7.18	5.80	4.46	3.09	NA	NA	NA	NA	NA	NA
Earnings	5.45	4.51	3.30	2.10	NA	NA	NA	NA	NA	NA
S&P Core Earnings	4.99	3.85	2.32	NA	NA	NA	NA	NA	NA	NA
Dividends	Nil	Nil	Nil	NA	NA	NA	NA	NA	NA	NA
Payout Ratio	Nil	Nil	Nil	NA	NA	NA	NA	NA	NA	NA
Prices - High	82.90	75.50	51.90	NA	NA	NA	NA	NA	NA	NA
- Low	53.00	46.40	36.00	NA	NA	NA	NA	NA	NA	NA
P/E Ratio - High	15	17	16	NA	NA	NA	NA	NA	NA	NA
- Low	10	10	11	NA	NA	NA	NA	NA	NA	NA

Income Statement Analysis (Million $)

	2003	2002	2001	2000	1999	1998	1997	1996	1995	1994
Revs.	16,773	13,282	10,445	8,771	NA	NA	NA	NA	NA	NA
Oper. Inc.	1,595	1,093	733	487	NA	NA	NA	NA	NA	NA
Depr.	245	157	121	102	NA	NA	NA	NA	NA	NA
Int. Exp.	131	99	60.2	69.6	NA	NA	NA	NA	NA	NA
Pretax Inc.	1,219	808	525	315	NA	NA	NA	NA	NA	NA
Eff. Tax Rate	36.1%	31.6%	35.0%	30.8%	NA	NA	NA	NA	NA	NA
Net Inc.	774	549	342	216	NA	NA	NA	NA	NA	NA
S&P Core Earnings	708	467	240	NA	NA	NA	NA	NA	NA	NA

Balance Sheet & Other Fin. Data (Million $)

	2003	2002	2001	2000	1999	1998	1997	1996	1995	1994
Cash	523	744	406	421	NA	NA	NA	NA	NA	NA
Curr. Assets	8,865	7,877	5,300	5,025	NA	NA	NA	NA	NA	NA
Total Assets	13,439	12,293	6,277	6,021	NA	NA	NA	NA	NA	NA
Curr. Liab.	4,772	4,449	2,963	2,784	NA	NA	NA	NA	NA	NA
LT Debt	1,663	1,659	818	789	NA	NA	NA	NA	NA	NA
Common Equity	6,000	5,362	2,060	2,055	NA	NA	NA	NA	NA	NA
Total Cap.	8,188	7,412	2,878	2,844	NA	NA	NA	NA	NA	NA
Cap. Exp.	111	123	70.4	NA	NA	NA	NA	NA	NA	NA
Cash Flow	1,019	706	463	318	NA	NA	NA	NA	NA	NA
Curr. Ratio	1.9	1.8	1.8	1.8	NA	NA	NA	NA	NA	NA
% LT Debt of Cap.	20.3	22.4	28.4	27.7	NA	NA	NA	NA	NA	NA
% Net Inc.of Revs.	4.7	50.8	35.6	2.5	NA	NA	NA	NA	NA	NA
% Ret. on Assets	6.0	5.9	5.7	NA	NA	NA	NA	NA	NA	NA
% Ret. on Equity	13.6	14.8	17.2	NA	NA	NA	NA	NA	NA	NA

Data as orig reptd.; bef. results of disc opers/spec. items. Per share data adj. for stk. divs.; EPS diluted. Pro forma data in 2000, bal. sheet & book val. as of Jun. 30, 2001. E-Estimated. NA-Not Available. NM-Not Meaningful. NR-Not Ranked.

Office: 120 Monument Circle, Indianapolis, IN 46204-4903.
Telephone: 317-488-6000.
Email: anthem.corporate.communications@anthem.com
Website: http://www.anthem.com
Chrmn, Pres & CEO: L.C. Glasscock.
EVP, CFO & Chief Acctg Officer: M.L. Smith.

EVP & General Counsel: D.R. Frick.
VP & Investor Contact: T. Durle 317-488-6390.
Dirs: L. D. Baker, Jr., S. B. Bayh, L. C. Glasscock, W. B. Hart, A. B. Hubbard, V. S. Liss, L. B. Lytle, W. G. Mays, J. W. McDowell, Jr., D. W. Riegle, Jr., W. J. Ryan, G. A. Schaefer, Jr., J. Sherman, Jr., D. J. Sullivan, Jr., J. M. Ward.

Founded: in 1944.
Domicile: Indiana.
Employees: 20,130.
S&P Analyst: Phillip M. Seligman/CB/JWP

Aon Corp.

Recommendation: **SELL** ★★☆☆☆
SELL | SELL | HOLD | BUY | BUY

12-Month Target Price: **$16.00**
(as of October 20, 2004)

AOC has an approximate 0.06% weighting in the **S&P 500**

Sector: Financials
Sub-Industry: Insurance Brokers
Peer Group: Insurance Brokers & Related Services

Summary: This holding company is comprised of a family of insurance brokerage, consulting and insurance underwriting subsidiaries.

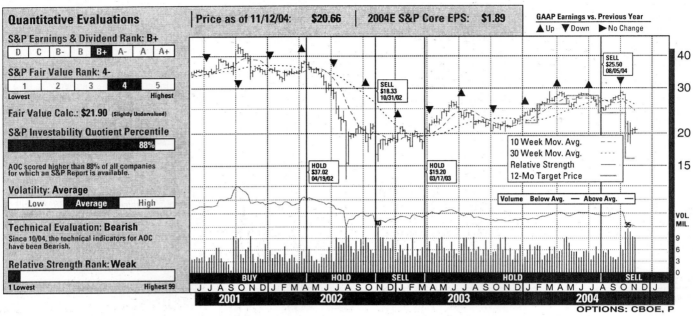

Quantitative Evaluations

S&P Earnings & Dividend Rank: B+

D | C | B- | B | **B+** | A- | A | A+

S&P Fair Value Rank: 4-

1 | 2 | 3 | **4** | 5
Lowest — Highest

Fair Value Calc.: $21.90 (Slightly Undervalued)

S&P Investability Quotient Percentile — 88%

AOC scored higher than 88% of all companies for which an S&P Report is available.

Volatility: Average

Low | **Average** | High

Technical Evaluation: Bearish
Since 10/04, the technical indicators for AOC have been Bearish.

Relative Strength Rank: Weak

1 Lowest — Highest 99

Price as of 11/12/04: $20.66   **2004E S&P Core EPS:** $1.89

GAAP Earnings vs. Previous Year
▲ Up   ▼ Down   ► No Change

- 10 Week Mov. Avg. ---
- 30 Week Mov. Avg. ·····
- Relative Strength ——
- 12-Mo Target Price

Volume   Below Avg. — Above Avg.

SELL $25.50 08/05/04
SELL $18.33 10/31/02
HOLD $37.02 04/19/02
HOLD $19.20 03/17/03

BUY | HOLD | SELL | HOLD | SELL
J J A S O N D J F M A M J J A S O N D J F M A M J J A S O N D J F M A M J J A S O N D J
2001 | 2002 | 2003 | 2004

OPTIONS: CBOE, P

Analyst commentary prepared by Gregory Simcik, CFA /CB/GG

Highlights October 21, 2004

- We expect total revenue to rise 3.9% in 2004, as higher commissions, fees and premiums outweigh lower investment income. Including intersegment revenues, we see risk and brokerage services revenues up 0.5%, with consulting revenues and insurance underwriting revenues increasing 5.5% and 11%, respectively.

- We estimate that total pretax expenses will rise 4.4% in 2004, on growth in policyholder benefits, general expenses and interest expense. As a result, we expect consolidated pretax margins to narrow, with income before income tax and minority interest remaining essentially flat. We project that 2004 EPS from continuing operations, excluding unusual items, will rise 4.3%, to $2.17 (after preferred dividends), on lower income taxes and minority interest, offset somewhat by 4.7% more shares.

- We expect EPS from continuing operations to decline 24% in 2005, to $1.65. Our 2005 estimate assumes a 10% decline in brokerage commissions and fees, including the elimination of contingent commissions and some revenue loss due to client defections. We also assume pretax operating profit margins will fall by roughly 200 basis points due to operating cost deleveraging.

Investment Rationale/Risk October 21, 2004

- We recommend avoiding the shares. We believe additional news related to investigations into insurance broker contingent commissions could continue to pressure AOC stock price and that AOC could see client defections based on negative publicity surrounding the investigation. We also think that the property and casualty market is softening, which could dampen revenue growth for insurance brokers.

- Risks to our recommendation and target price include a favorable resolution of the insurance broker investigation for AOC, faster than expected growth for consulting and/or underwriting services, higher insurance brokerage commission rates, greater than anticipated acquisition activity, market share gains, and the possibility that brokerage volume could increase due to more favorable insurance pricing for clients.

- Our 12-month target price of $16 is based on a trailing P/E multiple of 9.9X our 2005 EPS estimate for continuing operations. We use a multiple at a discount to the historical multiple of 12.2X to account for added risk that we see due to investigations.

Key Stock Statistics

S&P Core EPS 2005E	1.60	52-week Range	$29.44-18.15
S&P Oper. EPS 2004E	1.93	12 Month P/E	10.0
P/E on S&P Oper. EPS 2004E	10.7	Beta	0.85
S&P Oper. EPS 2005E	1.65	Shareholders	11,777
Yield (%)	2.9%	Market Cap (B)	$ 6.5
Dividend Rate/Share	0.60	Shares Outstanding (M)	316.5

Value of $10,000 invested five years ago: **$ 5,900**

Dividend Data Dividends have been paid since 1950

Amount ($)	Date Decl.	Ex-Div. Date	Stock of Record	Payment Date
0.150	Jan. 16	Feb. 06	Feb. 10	Feb. 24 '04
0.150	Apr. 16	Apr. 30	May. 04	May. 17 '04
0.150	Jul. 16	Jul. 30	Aug. 03	Aug. 16 '04
0.150	Oct. 08	Oct. 29	Nov. 02	Nov. 15 '04

Revenues/Earnings Data Fiscal year ending December 31

Revenues (Million $)

	2004	2003	2002	2001	2000	1999
1Q	2,573	2,384	2,088	1,811	1,810	1,699
2Q	2,545	2,434	2,122	1,917	1,819	1,723
3Q	2,402	2,391	2,246	1,912	1,785	1,770
4Q	—	2,601	2,366	2,036	1,961	1,878
Yr.	—	9,810	8,822	7,676	7,375	7,070

Earnings Per Share ($)

	2004	2003	2002	2001	2000	1999
1Q	0.60	0.49	0.57	0.07	0.47	0.19
2Q	0.54	0.48	Nil	0.11	0.49	0.57
3Q	0.36	0.44	0.46	0.26	0.53	0.52
4Q	E0.45	0.67	0.59	0.30	0.33	0.05
Yr.	E1.93	2.08	1.64	0.73	1.82	1.33

Next earnings report expected: mid-February Source: S&P, Company Reports
EPS Estimates based on S&P Operating Earnings; historical GAAP earnings are as reported.

Aon Corporation

Recommendation: **SELL** ★ ★ ☆ ☆ ☆    12-Month Target Price: **$16.00** (as of October 20, 2004)

Business Summary October 21, 2004

Aon Corp. is a global provider of insurance brokerage, insurance products, risk and insurance advice as well as other consulting services. At the end of 2003, the company believed it was the world's second largest insurance broker, the largest independent provider of extended warranty products, the third largest employee benefit consultant, and the fifth largest employee benefit consultant in the U.S., based on total revenues.

U.S. operations accounted for 53% of revenues in 2003 (57% in 2002), the U.K. 19% (18%), continental Europe 15% (13%), and the rest of the world 13% (12%).

AOC classifies its businesses into three operating segments: risk and insurance brokerage, consulting, and insurance underwriting. The risk and insurance broker-age segment accounted for 58% of total operating segment revenues in 2003, the consulting segment accounted for 12% and the insurance underwriting segment for 30%.

The risk and insurance brokerage segment includes retail, reinsurance, and wholesale brokerage operations and related insurance services, such as under-writing and captive insurance company management services, claims services, and premium financing. The consulting segment provides a full range of human capital management services, in five major practices: employee benefits, compen-sation, management consulting, communications, and human resource outsourc-ing. The insurance underwriting segment provides specialty insurance products including supplemental accident, health, and life insurance, extended warranty, credit and select property and casualty insurance products.

The company also reports results from a fourth segment, corporate and other, that includes investment income from assets associated with the insurance underwriting segment that exceed policyholder liabilities, gains and losses on disposals of all securities held by AOC, as well as administrative and information technology costs.

In 2003, AOC contributed $217 million to its major defined benefit pension plans, an increase of $141 million from the level of contributions in 2002. At the end of 2003, the company believed that it would need to make cash contributions of $195 million to its major pension plans in 2004.

During the 2003 first quarter, AOC assigned to another company temporary office space that it had leased in Manhattan at a pretax cost of $46 million following the September 11 terrorist attacks on the World Trade Center. In November 2003, the company reached a final settlement of about $200 million for its overall World Trade Center property insurance claim, and received a final cash payment of $92 million; $108 million had been received previously. The settlement resulted in a pretax gain of $60 million, recognized in 2003 results.

In April 2004, AOC received a subpoena from the New York Attorney General seeking information regarding compensation agreements between insurance bro-kers and insurance companies.

In 2003, the company completed several acquisitions, mostly related to insurance brokerage operations, for a total of $56 million in cash and $8 million in common stock.

Company Financials Fiscal Year ending December 31

Per Share Data ($)

(Year Ended December 31)	2003	2002	2001	2000	1999	1998	1997	1996	1995	1994
Tangible Bk. Val.	NM	NM	NM	NM	NM	NM	NM	4.93	5.99	2.88
Oper. Earnings	NA	NA	NA	NA	NA	NA	1.53	1.09	1.13	1.38
Earnings	2.08	1.64	0.73	1.82	1.33	2.07	1.12	1.10	1.14	1.40
S&P Core Earnings	2.05	1.00	-0.06	NA	NA	NA	NA	NA	NA	NA
Dividends	0.60	0.83	0.90	0.87	0.81	0.73	0.68	0.63	0.60	0.56
Relative Payout	29%	50%	123%	48%	61%	35%	61%	57%	52%	40%
Prices - High	26.79	39.63	44.80	42.75	46.66	50.37	39.25	28.77	22.61	15.88
- Low	17.41	13.30	29.75	20.68	26.06	32.16	26.77	21.11	13.94	13.00
P/E Ratio - High	13	24	61	23	35	24	35	26	20	11
- Low	8	8	41	11	20	16	24	19	12	9

Income Statement Analysis (Million $)

	2003	2002	2001	2000	1999	1998	1997	1996	1995	1994
Life Ins. In Force	26,784	28,136	31,454	28,170	22,011	16,163	19,262	21,301	81,168	75,222
Prem. Inc.: Life A & H	1,680	1,628	1,350	1,233	1,137	1,084	1,081	1,105	1,254	1,684
Prem. Inc.: Cas./Prop.	869	732	672	673	671	589	528	421	173	250
Net Invest. Inc.	317	252	213	508	577	590	494	384	329	760
Total Revs.	9,810	8,822	7,676	7,375	7,070	6,493	5,751	3,888	3,466	4,157
Pretax Inc.	1,110	793	399	854	635	931	542	446	458	538
Net Oper. Inc.	NA	NA	NA	NA	NA	NA	402	283	301	NA
Net Inc.	663	466	203	481	352	541	299	292	304	360
S&P Core Earnings	652	281	-19.4	NA	NA	NA	NA	NA	NA	NA

Balance Sheet & Other Fin. Data (Million $)

	2003	2002	2001	2000	1999	1998	1997	1996	1995	1994
Cash & Equiv.	540	506	439	1,118	837	786	1,085	479	268	642
Premiums Due	1,504	1,213	953	1,278	1,116	1,120	863	989	580	637
Invest. Assets: Bonds	2,751	2,089	2,149	2,337	2,497	3,103	4,841	4,092	7,687	7,927
Invest. Assets: Stocks	42.0	62.0	382	492	574	768	806	879	1,006	939
Invest. Assets: Loans	Nil	Nil	Nil	Nil	NA	Nil	Nil	87.2	858	782
Invest. Assets: Total	7,324	6,587	6,146	6,019	6,184	6,452	5,922	5,213	10,639	9,783
Deferred Policy Costs	1,021	882	704	656	636	573	549	599	1,262	1,182
Total Assets	27,027	25,334	22,386	22,251	21,132	19,688	18,691	13,723	19,736	17,922
Debt	2,095	1,721	2,494	1,848	1,811	1,380	2,201	475	498	496
Common Equity	4,498	3,895	3,521	3,388	3,051	3,017	2,822	2,827	2,666	2,246
Comb. Loss-Exp. Ratio	NA	NA	NA	NA	NA	NA	NA	NA	NA	NA
% Return On Revs.	6.8	5.3	2.6	6.5	5.0	8.3	5.2	7.6	8.8	8.7
% Ret. on Equity	15.7	12.6	5.8	14.8	11.5	18.4	10.1	11.5	11.4	14.5
% Invest. Yield	4.6	4.0	3.5	8.3	9.1	9.5	8.9	4.9	3.6	7.8

Data as orig reptd.; bef. results of disc opers/spec. items. Per share data adj. for stk. divs.; EPS diluted. E-Estimated. NA-Not Available. NM-Not Meaningful. NR-Not Ranked. UR-Under Review.

Office: 200 East Randolph Street, Chicago, IL 60601-6436.
Telephone: 312-381-1000.
Website: http://www.aon.com
Chrmn & CEO: P.G. Ryan.
Pres & COO: M.D. O'Halleran.
EVP & CFO: D.P. Bolger.

EVP & General Counsel: D.C. Findlay.
VP & Secy: K.M. Cooke.
VP & Investor Contact: S. O'Neill .
Dirs: E. D. Jannotta, P. J. Kalff, L. B. Knight, J. M. Losh, R. E. Martin, A. J. McKenna, R. S. Morrison, R. C. Notebaert, M. D. O'Halleran, J. W. Rogers, Jr., P. G. Ryan, G. A. Schaefer, C. Y. Woo.

Founded: in 1919.
Domicile: Delaware.
Employees: 54,000.
S&P Analyst: Gregory Simcik, CFA /CB/GG

Apache Corp.

Recommendation: **BUY** ★★★★ ☆   12-Month Target Price: **$60.00**
SELL SELL HOLD BUY BUY
(as of October 06, 2004)

APA has an approximate 0.15% weighting in the **S&P 500**

Sector: Energy
Sub-Industry: Oil & Gas Exploration & Production
Peer Group: Exploration & Production - Large

Summary: This international independent exploration and production company explores for, develops and produces natural gas, crude oil and natural gas liquids.

Quantitative Evaluations

| Price as of 11/12/04: | $50.52 | 2004E S&P Core EPS: | $5.19 |

S&P Earnings & Dividend Rank: B+

| D | C | B- | B | **B+** | A- | A | A+ |

S&P Fair Value Rank: 3

| 1 | 2 | **3** | 4 | 5 |
| Lowest | | | | Highest |

Fair Value Calc.: $50.70 (Fairly Valued)

S&P Investability Quotient Percentile

100%

APA scored higher than 100% of all companies for which an S&P Report is available.

Volatility: Average

| Low | **Average** | High |

Technical Evaluation: Bullish

Since 9/04, the technical indicators for APA have been Bullish.

Relative Strength Rank: Moderate

| 44 | |
| 1 Lowest | Highest 99 |

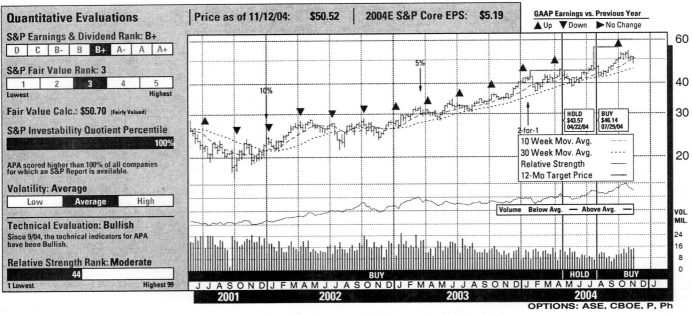

GAAP Earnings vs. Previous Year
▲ Up ▼ Down ► No Change

HOLD $43.57 04/22/04   BUY $46.14 07/29/04

2-for-1

10 Week Mov. Avg.
30 Week Mov. Avg.
Relative Strength
12-Mo Target Price

Volume ▬ Below Avg. — Above Avg.

BUY   HOLD   BUY
J J A S O N D J F M A M J J A S O N D J F M A M J J A S O N D J F M A M J J A S O N D J
2001   2002   2003   2004

OPTIONS: ASE, CBOE, P, Ph

Analyst commentary prepared by Charles LaPorta, CFA /CB/BK

Highlights August 13, 2004

- Second quarter EPS was $1.13, versus $0.74 last year, and well above our estimate of $0.89, on exceptional cost control. APA reduced its direct lifting costs in the North Sea 19% while increasing its production there 7% sequentially. Egyptian operations averaged a production rate of over 100,000 bbl. per day for the first time, and gas production came in at 293 Mmcf per day. Overall second quarter hydrocarbon production grew 3% sequentially. We are expecting production to increase 7% in 2004 and 4% in 2005.

- EBITDA margins expanded to 76%, from 73.9% last year. We expect a 17% increase in 2004, on improved price realizations and cost control, before an anticipated decline of about 5% in 2005, on projected lower pricing.

- In July 2004, APA announced a test that extends the recoverable resources in its Qasr field in Eqypt, the largest onshore gas discovery in the company's history. APA and ExxonMobil reached a broad agreement to jointly develop and produce hydrocarbons in Canada, the Permian Basin and the Gulf of Mexico.

Investment Rationale/Risk August 13, 2004

- APA recently enhanced its competitive position, in our view, by reaching sweeping agreements on major hydrocarbon development projects in Egypt and with ExxonMobil (XOM: $45) in North America. Given these deals and its disclosed drilling activity level, we expect about $2.0 billion in 2004 capital expenditures, up from about $1.5 billion last year. As of June 30, 2004, debt was equal to 23.2% of capitalization.

- Risks to our recommendation and target price include events that would cause substantial and sustained declines in oil and gas prices; a persistent inability by APA to replace its reserves; and acts of terrorism on APA's production facilities.

- Based on a blend of our DCF and market valuations, using our estimate of APA's production growth discussed above, and our oil and gas price projections, our 12-month target price is $56, representing a forward P/E multiple of 15X our FY 05 EPS estimate, a premium to peer levels. We see the premium as justified, based on our view of APA's above-average production growth at below-average costs.

Key Stock Statistics

S&P Core EPS 2005E	5.94	52-week Range	$54.35-34.60
S&P Oper. EPS 2004E	5.25	12 Month P/E	11.8
P/E on S&P Oper. EPS 2004E	9.6	Beta	0.45
S&P Oper. EPS 2005E	6.00	Shareholders	157,000
Yield (%)	0.6%	Market Cap (B)	$ 16.5
Dividend Rate/Share	0.32	Shares Outstanding (M)	326.5

Value of $10,000 invested five years ago: **$ 32,423**

Dividend Data Dividends have been paid since 1965

Amount ($)	Date Decl.	Ex-Div. Date	Stock of Record	Payment Date
0.120	Dec. 18	Jan. 20	Jan. 22	Feb. 23 '04
0.060	Feb. 24	Apr. 20	Apr. 22	May. 21 '04
0.060	May. 26	Jul. 20	Jul. 22	Aug. 23 '04
0.080	Sep. 16	Oct. 20	Oct. 22	Nov. 22 '04

Revenues/Earnings Data Fiscal year ending December 31

Revenues (Million $)

	2004	2003	2002	2001	2000	1999
1Q	1,150	966.6	528.0	795.1	448.2	187.7
2Q	1,241	1,054	656.3	800.4	486.4	281.6
3Q	1,407	1,105	645.2	652.4	618.5	385.4
4Q	—	1,065	730.4	543.1	730.8	445.8
Yr.	—	4,190	2,560	2,791	2,284	1,301

Earnings Per Share ($)

	2004	2003	2002	2001	2000	1999
1Q	1.06	0.97	0.26	0.93	0.42	-0.02
2Q	E1.13	0.75	0.48	0.67	0.51	0.12
3Q	1.31	0.85	0.48	0.52	0.68	0.26
4Q	E1.75	0.80	0.59	0.25	0.85	0.35
Yr.	E5.25	3.35	1.80	2.37	2.48	0.74

Next earnings report expected: late-January Source: S&P, Company Reports
EPS Estimates based on S&P Operating Earnings; historical GAAP earnings are as reported.

Apache Corporation

Recommendation: **BUY** ★★★★★   12-Month Target Price: **$60.00** (as of October 06, 2004)

Business Summary August 13, 2004

As an independent exploration and production company, Apache explores for, develops and produces natural gas, crude oil, and natural gas liquids (NGLs). In North America, its exploration and production interests focus on the Gulf of Mexico, the Gulf Coast, the Permian Basin, the Anadarko Basin, and the Western Sedimentary Basin of Canada. Internationally, APA has exploration and production interests in offshore Western Australia, offshore and onshore Egypt, offshore China, and onshore Argentina, and exploration interests in Poland.

In 2003, APA replaced an all-in 330% of production, versus 155% through exploration and development alone. Proved crude oil, condensate and NGLs reserves were 843.9 million barrels (MMBbls; 46% U.S., 20% Canada, 18% North Sea, 9% Egypt, 6% Australia, and 1% elsewhere) at the end of 2003, versus 636.8 million barrels (MMBbls; 52% U.S., 26% Canada, 12% Egypt, 8% Australia, and 2% elsewhere) a year earlier. Proved natural gas reserves totaled 4.88 trillion cubic feet (Tcf; 42% U.S., 33% Canada, 14% Australia, 11% Egypt, and elsewhere), versus 4.05 Tcf (44% U.S., 33% Canada, 14% Australia, 9% Egypt, and elsewhere). At the end of 2003, estimated reserves were 49% natural gas and 51% oil. Estimated proved developed reserves comprised 71% of total estimated proved reserves at December 31, 2003. Oil, condensate and NGL production averaged 214.5 thousand barrels per day (Mbpd) in 2003 (versus 161.4 Mbpd in 2002). Natural gas production averaged 1.22 billion cubic feet (Bcf) in 2003 (1.08 Bcf). In 2003, 55% of barrel of oil equivalent (BOE) production came from outside the U.S., down from 58% in 2002. During 2003, lease operating costs averaged $4.59 per

BOE ($3.67). The average price received from oil sales was $27.76 per Bbl in 2003 ($24.78); from NGL sales was $21.28 per Bbl ($14.69); and from natural gas price was $4.61 per Mcf ($2.87).

In January 2003, the company agreed to purchase certain of BP plc's oil and gas properties in the North Sea (for about $630 million for estimated proved reserves of 147.6 million BOE) and the Gulf of Mexico (GOM; adjusted purchase price about $509 million for estimated proved reserves of 72.2 million BOE). The GOM portion of the deal closed in March 2003, and the U.K. North Sea Forties field acquisition closed in April 2003. The BP acquisition added the North Sea as a new core area for APA, and the GOM assets, according to the company, were synergistic with existing properties, and made APA the fourth largest producer and second largest acreage holder in GOM waters to 1,200 ft. In January 2003, in conjunction with the BP acquisition agreement, the company sold publicly 9.9 million common shares, including 1.3 million shares for an underwriters' over-allotment option, at $58.10 each. Net proceeds of about $554 million were used to repay debt or were held in short-term investments for the BP acquisition.

In July 2003, APA acquired 26 fields (proved reserves of 124.6 Bcf of natural gas, 6.6 million Bbl of oil) on the Outer Continental Shelf of the Gulf of Mexico from Shell Exploration and Production Co., for about $200 million, subject to normal post-closing adjustments, including preferential rights. The company planned to operate 15 of the fields, with 91% of the production.

Company Financials Fiscal Year ending December 31

Per Share Data ($)

(Year Ended December 31)	2003	2002	2001	2000	1999	1998	1997	1996	1995	1994
Tangible Bk. Val.	19.25	15.33	14.69	12.07	8.97	7.54	8.02	7.30	6.11	5.75
Cash Flow	6.67	4.55	5.30	4.46	2.51	2.20	2.37	2.20	1.92	2.00
Earnings	3.35	1.80	2.37	2.48	0.74	-0.58	0.72	0.61	0.12	0.30
S&P Core Earnings	3.29	1.73	2.28	NA	NA	NA	NA	NA	NA	NA
Dividends	0.21	0.19	0.12	0.09	0.12	0.12	0.12	0.12	0.12	0.12
Payout Ratio	6%	11%	5%	4%	16%	NM	17%	20%	100%	40%
Prices - High	41.67	28.87	31.54	32.11	21.61	16.77	19.50	16.39	13.42	12.66
- Low	26.26	21.12	16.55	13.90	7.63	9.11	13.04	10.55	9.63	9.63
P/E Ratio - High	12	16	13	13	29	NM	27	27	NM	42
- Low	8	12	7	6	10	NM	18	17	NM	32

Income Statement Analysis (Million $)

	2003	2002	2001	2000	1999	1998	1997	1996	1995	1994
Revs.	4,190	2,560	2,777	2,283	1,300	876	1,176	977	751	538
Oper. Inc.	3,241	1,048	2,146	1,310	870	509	712	577	411	327
Depr. Depl. & Amort.	1,073	844	821	584	443	630	388	315	297	240
Int. Exp.	127	133	132	109	84.6	70.4	68.7	89.8	88.1	36.0
Pretax Inc.	1,922	899	1,199	1,204	345	-188	259	200	38.1	64.0
Eff. Tax Rate	43.0%	38.3%	39.7%	40.1%	41.7%	NM	40.1%	39.4%	39.0%	33.5%
Net Inc.	1,095	554	723	721	201	-129	155	121	20.2	42.8
S&P Core Earnings	1,069	524	681	NA	NA	NA	NA	NA	NA	NA

Balance Sheet & Other Fin. Data (Million $)

	2003	2002	2001	2000	1999	1998	1997	1996	1995	1994
Cash	33.5	51.9	35.6	37.2	13.2	14.5	9.69	13.2	13.6	15.1
Curr. Assets	899	767	698	630	343	227	348	268	208	135
Total Assets	12,416	9,460	8,934	7,482	5,503	3,996	4,139	3,432	2,681	1,879
Curr. Liab.	820	532	522	553	337	306	344	310	230	148
LT Debt	2,327	2,159	2,244	2,193	1,880	1,343	150	1,236	1,072	657
Common Equity	6,434	4,826	4,112	3,448	2,361	1,703	1,729	1,519	1,092	816
Total Cap.	8,860	7,083	7,655	5,948	4,549	3,416	3,586	3,010	2,345	1,630
Cap. Exp.	1,595	1,037	1,525	1,011	591	700	732	124	1,133	494
Cash Flow	2,163	1,387	1,525	1,284	629	499	543	436	318	283
Curr. Ratio	1.1	1.4	1.3	1.1	1.0	0.7	1.0	0.9	0.9	0.9
% LT Debt of Cap.	26.3	30.5	29.3	36.9	41.3	39.3	41.9	41.1	45.7	40.3
% Ret. on Assets	10.0	6.0	8.8	11.1	4.2	NM	4.1	3.9	0.9	2.5
% Ret. on Equity	19.4	12.2	18.6	24.1	9.2	NM	9.5	9.3	2.0	5.3

Data as orig reptd.; bef. results of disc opers/spec. items. Per share data adj. for stk. divs.; EPS diluted. E-Estimated. NA-Not Available. NM-Not Meaningful. NR-Not Ranked. UR-Under Review.

Office: 2000 Post Oak Boulevard, Houston, TX 77024-7001.
Telephone: 713-296-6000.
Website: http://www.apachecorp.com
Chrmn: R. Plank.
Pres, CEO & COO: G.S. Farris.
EVP & CFO: R.B. Plank.

VP & Treas: M.W. Dundrea.
VP & General Counsel: A. Lannie.
VP & Investor Contact: R.J. Dye 713-296-6662.
Dirs: F. M. Bohen, G. S. Farris, R. M. Ferlic, E. C. Fiedorek, A. D. Frazier, Jr., P. A. Graham, J. A. Kocur, G. D. Lawrence, Jr., F. H. Merelli, R. D. Patton, C. J. Pitman, R. Plank, J. A. Precourt.

Founded: in 1954.
Domicile: Delaware.
Employees: 2,353.
S&P Analyst: Charles LaPorta, CFA /CB/BK

Apartment Investment and Mgmt.

Recommendation: **SELL** ★★★★★
SELL | SELL | HOLD | BUY | BUY

12-Month Target Price: **$33.00**
(as of November 04, 2004)

AIV has an approximate 0.03% weighting in the **S&P 500**

Sector: Financials
Sub-Industry: Real Estate Investment Trusts
Peer Group: REITs - Residential

Summary: This REIT is the largest U.S. owner and manager of multifamily apartment properties.

Quantitative Evaluations

S&P Earnings & Dividend Rank: B

| D | C | B- | **B** | B+ | A- | A | A+ |

S&P Fair Value Rank: NR

| 1 | 2 | 3 | 4 | 5 |
Lowest ——————————————— Highest

Fair Value Calc.: NA

S&P Investability Quotient Percentile

69%

AIV scored higher than 69% of all companies for which an S&P Report is available.

Volatility: Average

| Low | **Average** | High |

Technical Evaluation: Bullish
Since 10/04, the technical indicators for AIV have been Bullish.

Relative Strength Rank: Moderate

67
1 Lowest ——————————————— Highest 99

| Price as of 11/12/04: | **$38.22** | 2004E S&P Core EPS: | **$0.57** |

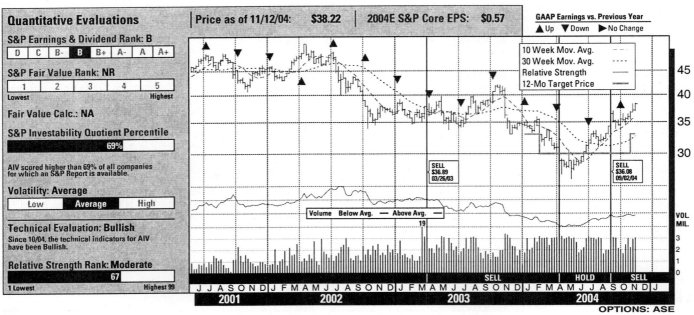

Analyst commentary prepared by Raymond Mathis/PMW/BK

Highlights September 07, 2004

- We forecast continued deterioration in same-property results, as we see an imbalance of supply and demand continuing. Home ownership is at a record high, and with home sales running at a near-record pace and mortgage rates near historically low levels (and below year-earlier levels), we believe tenants will continue to be drawn away from apartments. We also think that a glut of new apartment supply being delivered will outstrip household formation.

- AIV has sought to counteract soft demand by reducing rents, and has tried to bolster earnings through acquisitions. We see sequentially lower occupancy and soft rental rates, and do not expect a meaningful recovery at least until mid-2005.

- Although this could dilute earnings over the longer term, we believe the trust will sell a substantial number of its older properties in an effort to unlock likely capital gains for debt reduction and dividend payments. We see a 2004 operating loss per share of $0.62, and FFO of $2.97 a share. We see the loss narrowing to $0.52 a share in 2005, with FFO of $3.09.

Investment Rationale/Risk September 07, 2004

- We recently downgraded the shares to avoid, from hold. AIV's dividend payout ratio has risen significantly over the past two years. However, the trust reduced the quarterly dividend by 27%, from $0.82 to $0.60, in the 2003 fourth quarter. Since then, operating results have continued to deteriorate. After subtracting projected capital expenditures, we forecast that cash from operations will be insufficient to cover the new dividend, perhaps through mid-2005.

- Risks to our recommendation and target price include the possibility of stronger than expected employment growth stimulating new household formation, or faster than expected interest rate increases, which could slow home sales.

- Assuming no additional dividend reduction, with growth gradually resuming in 2006, we see intrinsic value of $29, based on our dividend discount model. We believe net asset value per share is about $31, despite the decline in average rents. The shares traded recently at 12.3X our 2004 FFO per share estimate, a discount to the 13.1X peer average. We believe this discount is justified, based on our view of weak fundamentals and heightened risk assumptions with regard to dividend security. Our 12-month target price is $30.

Key Stock Statistics

S&P Oper. EPS 2004E	-0.62	52-week Range	$38.38-26.45
P/E on S&P Oper. EPS 2004E	NM	12 Month P/E	24.3
S&P Oper. EPS 2005E	-0.52	Beta	0.19
Yield (%)	6.3%	Shareholders	3,847
Dividend Rate/Share	2.40	Market Cap (B)	$ 3.6
Shares Outstanding (M)	94.8		

Value of $10,000 invested five years ago: **$ 13,393**

Dividend Data Dividends have been paid since 1994

Amount ($)	Date Decl.	Ex-Div. Date	Stock of Record	Payment Date
0.600	Jan. 30	Feb. 18	Feb. 20	Feb. 27 '04
0.600	Apr. 30	May. 14	May. 18	May. 28 '04
0.600	Jul. 29	Aug. 18	Aug. 20	Aug. 31 '04
0.600	Oct. 29	Nov. 17	Nov. 19	Nov. 30 '04

Revenues/Earnings Data Fiscal year ending December 31

Revenues (Million $)

	2004	2003	2002	2001	2000	1999
1Q	376.4	397.4	340.9	322.2	224.3	112.6
2Q	380.2	378.4	373.4	323.8	258.1	116.2
3Q	334.1	377.4	380.4	323.8	271.1	120.4
4Q	—	381.9	411.5	328.0	297.5	204.3
Yr.	—	1,516	1,506	1,298	1,051	640.1

Earnings Per Share ($)

	2004	2003	2002	2001	2000	1999
1Q	-0.15	0.01	0.45	-0.07	0.17	0.01
2Q	-0.18	Nil	0.47	0.11	-0.04	0.14
3Q	-0.02	-0.13	0.24	0.02	0.20	0.07
4Q	E-0.13	-0.12	-0.17	0.16	0.18	1.15
Yr.	E-0.62	-0.25	0.94	0.23	0.52	0.38

Next earnings report expected: mid-February Source: S&P, Company Reports
EPS Estimates based on S&P Operating Earnings; historical GAAP earnings are as reported.

Apartment Investment and Management Company

Recommendation: **SELL** ★ ★ ☆ ☆ ☆   12-Month Target Price: **$33.00** (as of November 04, 2004)

Business Summary September 07, 2004

Apartment Investment and Management Co. is one of the largest U.S. multi-family residential REITs in terms of units. At December 31, 2003, it owned, held an equity interest in, or managed a geographically diversified portfolio of 1,629 properties, including about 287,560 apartment units, located in 47 states, the District of Columbia, and Puerto Rico.

The trust conducts substantially all its business, and owns all its assets, through AIMCO Properties, L.P., of which AIV owns approximately an 89% interest. AIV operates in two segments: the ownership, operation and management of apartment properties; and the management of apartment properties for third parties and affiliates. Income from consolidated property operations grew to $803 million in 2003, from $777 million in 2002. Service businesses, which provide management services to properties and partnerships, produced 2003 income of $19.9 million, versus 2002's $31.4 million.

AIV's principal objective is to increase long-term stockholder value, which it believes results from increasing asset values, increasing operating cash flows and long-term, predictable funds from operations (FFO) per share. The trust's operating and financial strategies include operating diversified types of apartments in markets in which population and employment growth are expected to exceed the national average, and in which AIV believes it can become a regionally significant owner or manager of properties; maintaining a portfolio of proper-

ties that is diversified both geographically and among price points; and acquiring properties at less than replacement cost. The trust emphasizes long-term, fixed rate, self-amortizing debt, to minimize refinancing risk.

The trust's property operations are divided into two business components: conventional and affordable. At December 31, 2003, AIV's conventional properties included 632 properties and 178,397 units, and were divided (by number of units as percentage of portfolio) by region as follows: Michigan 5.8%; Tampa/Orlando, FL, 5.6%; Columbia, SC, 5.5%; Dallas, TX, 5.5%; and Rockville, MD, 5.0%. Affordable properties included 488 properties with 58,598 units, and accounted for 19% of the portfolio; properties managed but not owned 18%; and properties owned but not currently managed 2.9%.

In 2003, AIV sold 72 consolidated properties, one land parcel, and 37 unconsolidated properties, for total net proceeds of $309.6 million. In 2002, the trust purchased a portfolio of 11 conventional garden and mid-rise apartment properties, containing 4,323 units, located in the greater Boston area, for $500 million. It also acquired Casden Properties, a Los Angeles-based REIT that owned 6,356 conventional units in Southern California, 11,027 affordable apartments located in 25 states, and a subsidiary that as general partner controlled more than 400 properties with about 41,000 units. The transaction was valued at $1.1 billion.

Company Financials Fiscal Year ending December 31

Per Share Data ($)

(Year Ended December 31)	2003	2002	2001	2000	1999	1998	1997	1996	1995	1994
Tangible Bk. Val.	20.57	22.88	18.90	23.33	24.27	20.26	19.02	14.56	13.59	13.71
Earnings	-0.25	0.94	0.23	0.52	0.38	0.80	1.08	1.04	0.86	0.42
S&P Core Earnings	-0.32	0.89	0.19	NA	NA	NA	NA	NA	NA	NA
Dividends	3.06	3.28	3.12	2.80	2.50	2.25	1.85	1.70	1.66	0.29
Payout Ratio	NM	NM	NM	NM	NM	NM	171%	163%	193%	69%
Prices - High	42.05	51.46	50.12	50.06	44.12	41.00	38.00	28.37	21.25	18.62
- Low	33.00	33.90	39.25	36.31	34.06	30.00	25.50	18.37	17.12	16.25
P/E Ratio - High	NM	55	NM	96	NM	51	35	27	25	44
- Low	NM	36	NM	70	NM	37	24	18	20	39

Income Statement Analysis (Million $)

	2003	2002	2001	2000	1999	1998	1997	1996	1995	1994
Rental Income	1,446	1,292	1,298	1,051	534	377	193	101	74.9	24.9
Mortgage Income	Nil	Nil	Nil	Nil	43.5	Nil	Nil	Nil	Nil	Nil
Total Income	1,516	1,506	1,464	1,101	577	377	193	101	74.9	28.2
General Exp.	729	664	652	485	406	190	88.2	42.6	49.3	18.8
Interest Exp.	373	340	316	270	140	89.4	51.4	24.8	13.3	1.58
Prov. for Losses	Nil	Nil	Nil	Nil	Nil	Nil	Nil	Nil	Nil	Nil
Depr.	328	289	364	330	151	93.4	37.7	20.0	15.0	4.88
Net Inc.	70.7	175	107	99	83.7	64.5	28.9	12.9	13.4	7.14
S&P Core Earnings	-29.2	77.1	13.8	NA	NA	NA	NA	NA	NA	NA

Balance Sheet & Other Fin. Data (Million $)

	2003	2002	2001	2000	1999	1998	1997	1996	1995	1994
Cash	98.0	97.0	820	1,068	1,123	127	37.1	13.1	19.4	7.14
Total Assets	10,113	10,317	8,323	7,700	5,685	4,268	2,101	835	479	417
Real Estate Invest.	10,601	10,227	8,416	7,012	4,509	2,803	1,657	865	477	404
Loss Reserve	Nil	Nil	Nil	Nil	Nil	Nil	Nil	Nil	Nil	Nil
Net Invest.	8,753	8,616	6,796	6,099	4,092	2,574	1,504	745	448	391
ST Debt	Nil	Nil	214	329	630	460	53.0	205	32.6	21.8
Capitalization:										
Debt	6,198	5,529	4,670	4,031	2,525	1,350	755	318	236	120
Equity	2,005	2,218	1,592	1,664	1,622	1,110	910	223	169	140
Total	9,580	9,180	7,904	7,037	5,181	2,795	1,948	610	435	260
% Earn & Depr/Assets	3.9	5.0	5.9	1.5	4.7	4.7	4.6	4.9	6.4	3.5
Price Times Book Value:										
Hi	2.0	2.3	2.6	2.1	1.8	2.0	2.0	1.9	1.6	1.4
Low	1.6	1.5	2.1	1.6	1.4	1.5	1.3	1.3	1.3	1.2

Data as orig. reptd.; bef. results of disc.opers. and/or spec. items. Per share data adj. for stk. divs.; EPS diluted (primary prior to 1998). Revs. & total income incl. rental prop. opers. only. E-Estimated. NA-Not Available. NM-Not Meaningful. NR-Not Ranked.

Office: 4582 South Ulster Street Parkway, Denver, CO 80237.
Telephone: 303-757-8101.
Email: investor@aimco.com
Website: http://www.aimco.com
Chrmn & CEO: T. Considine.
Pres & Vice Chrmn: P.K. Kompaniez.

EVP & CFO: P.J. McAuliffe.
EVP, Secy & General Counsel: M. Cortez.
SVP & Chief Acctg Officer: T.M. Herzog.
VP & Investor Contact: J. Martin 303-691-4440.
Trustees: J. N. Bailey, T. Considine, R. S. Ellwood, P. K. Kompaniez, J. L. Martin, T. L. Rhodes.

Founded: in 1994.
Domicile: Maryland.
Employees: 7,500.
S&P Analyst: Raymond Mathis/PMW/BK

STANDARD &POOR'S

Recommendation: HOLD ★★★☆☆
SELL SELL HOLD BUY BUY

12-Month Target Price: $70.00
(as of November 03, 2004)

APOL has an approximate 0.13% weighting in the **S&P 500**

Sector: Industrials
Sub-Industry: Diversified Commercial Services
Peer Group: Educational Services

Summary: This leading provider of higher education programs for working adults offers educational programs and services at more than 80 campuses and nearly 140 learning centers.

Quantitative Evaluations

S&P Earnings & Dividend Rank: B+

D	C	B-	B	B+	A-	A	A+

S&P Fair Value Rank: 3

1	2	3	4	5
Lowest				Highest

Fair Value Calc.: $61.60 (Overvalued)

S&P Investability Quotient Percentile

97%

APOL scored higher than 97% of all companies for which an S&P Report is available.

Volatility: Average

Low	Average	High

Technical Evaluation: Bearish
Since 9/04, the technical indicators for APOL have been Bearish.

Relative Strength Rank: Moderate

40

1 Lowest		Highest 99

Price as of 11/12/04: $74.20 | **2005E S&P Core EPS: $2.32**

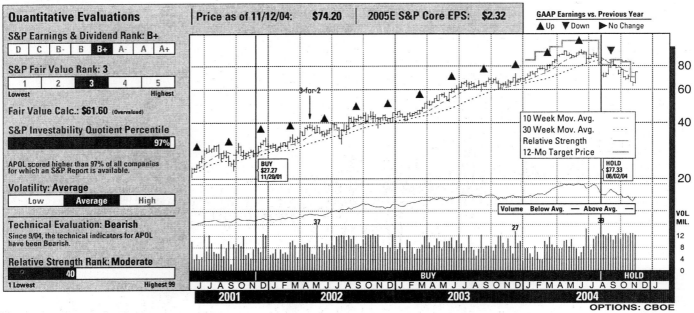

GAAP Earnings vs. Previous Year ▲ Up ▼ Down ► No Change

10 Week Mov. Avg.
30 Week Mov. Avg.
Relative Strength
12-Mo Target Price

BUY $27.27 11/20/01

HOLD $77.33 08/02/04

3-for-2

Volume Below Avg. — Above Avg.

VOL. MIL.

BUY | HOLD

J J A S O N D J F M A M J J A S O N D J F M A M J J A S O N D J F M A M J J A S O N D J
2001 | 2002 | 2003 | 2004

OPTIONS: CBOE

Analyst commentary prepared by Michael W. Jaffe/CB/JWP

Highlights November 05, 2004

- We expect revenues to climb about 25% in FY 05 (Aug.), driven by a strong increase that we see for University of Phoenix enrollments, especially in its online program. APOL's revenues should also benefit from its ongoing addition of physical campuses, and from projected mid-single digit tuition hikes.

- We believe net margins will widen slightly in FY 05, as results should be aided by the leveraging of instructional and service costs, and by cost controls. These factors will likely be partly offset by a higher proportion of selling and promotional costs, as we expect the company's campus openings and expanded student base to lead to more enrollment advisers and greater advertising costs.

- Our FY 05 Standard & Poor's Core Earnings estimate is $0.08 a share below our operating income forecast, reflecting projected stock option expense.

Investment Rationale/Risk November 05, 2004

- We expect adult education markets to remain robust for some time, and think the company has a strong brand name. Based on our belief that it will record ongoing high levels of free cash flow, we think Apollo should be able to continue its active expansion program. However, stocks of for-profit educators have fallen sharply out of favor in recent months, in our view on allegations of dishonest business practices and slower growth trends. APOL paid a $9.8 million fine to the Department of Education in FY 04's fourth quarter, related to its recruiting practices. Combined with valuation considerations, we would not add to positions.

- Risks to our recommendation and target price include a failure to attract and retain students; and the potential further impact on sector valuations of allegations of dishonest practices at APOL and its peers.

- The shares traded recently at 27X our FY 05 EPS forecast of $2.40, a large premium to the level of the S&P 500. However, at 1.35X the 20%-plus EPS gains we see for the next few years, the stock was at a discount to the S&P 500's estimated 1.6X multiple (using S&P's forecast of 10% EPS growth). Although the strong continued growth that we see for APOL has historically caused us to believe that a premium valuation is warranted, the current uncertain conditions in the for-profit education sector make us believe that Apollo's P/E-to-growth ratio should be at a discount to the S&P 500. Our 12-month target price is $70.

Key Stock Statistics

S&P Oper. EPS 2005E	2.40	52-week Range	$98.01-62.55
P/E on S&P Oper. EPS 2005E	30.9	12 Month P/E	96.4
S&P Oper. EPS 2006E	2.95	Beta	0.20
Yield (%)	Nil	Shareholders	94,000
Dividend Rate/Share	Nil	Market Cap (B)	$ 14.3
Shares Outstanding (M)	192.9		

Value of $10,000 invested five years ago: **$ 59,209**

Dividend Data

No cash dividends have been paid.

Revenues/Earnings Data Fiscal year ending August 31

Revenues (Million $)

	2004	2003	2002	2001	2000	1999
1Q	411.8	308.9	228.2	177.1	143.4	115.7
2Q	396.9	295.2	222.6	163.0	134.0	109.4
3Q	497.0	364.2	276.4	214.3	167.6	138.1
4Q	492.8	371.3	282.3	215.1	165.0	135.7
Yr.	1,798	1,340	1,009	769.5	610.0	498.9

Earnings Per Share ($)

	2004	2003	2002	2001	2000	1999
1Q	0.44	0.30	0.18	0.14	0.10	0.08
2Q	0.35	0.24	0.15	0.09	0.07	0.06
3Q	0.56	0.39	0.27	0.19	0.12	0.11
4Q	-0.59	0.37	0.26	0.17	0.12	0.09
Yr.	0.77	1.30	0.87	0.60	0.41	0.33

Next earnings report expected: mid-December Source: S&P, Company Reports
EPS Estimates based on S&P Operating Earnings; historical GAAP earnings are as reported.

Apollo Group, Inc.

Recommendation: **HOLD** ★★★☆☆   12-Month Target Price: **$70.00** (as of November 03, 2004)

Business Summary November 07, 2004

Apollo Group, through subsidiaries, is a leading provider of higher education programs for working adults. Subsidiaries include the University of Phoenix, Inc. (UOP), the Institute for Professional Development (IPD), the College for Financial Planning Institutes Corp. (CFPI), and Western International University, Inc. (WIU). Consolidated enrollment in the company's educational programs would make it the largest private U.S. institution of higher education. As of September 2004, APOL offered programs and services at 82 campuses and 137 learning centers, in 39 states, Puerto Rico, and Vancouver, BC. Combined enrollment at all divisions totaled 255,600 at FY 04 (Aug.) year end, up from 200,100 at August 31, 2003, and 157,800 at the end of FY 02.

Based on its enrollment of 108,900 adult students at August 31, 2004, up 14%, year to year, UOP was one of the largest regionally accredited private universities in the U.S. UOP focuses on the working adult education market, but plans to start targeting the 18-to-23-year-old group in the coming year. The company has typically sought to add four to six campuses a year, but brought nine new campuses on board in FY 04 (six in the prior year); it also plans to open 8 to 11 in FY 05. UOP's centrally developed bachelors and masters degree programs, including business, education, information technology, criminal justice and nursing, are taught in small classroom settings by non-tenured faculty with work experience. Revenues generated through in-class instruction at UOP accounted for about 50% of total revenues in FY 03 (latest available).

Based on surveys of incoming students in FY 03's first half, APOL believed the average age of UOP students was in the mid-30s.

At August 31, 2004, UOP offered its educational degree programs to another 118,900 students (up 50% from a year earlier) worldwide through University of Phoenix Online (UOPX), a computerized educational delivery system. UOPX provides password protected lectures that can be viewed weekly at the student's convenience, and allows some class discussion. At the end of FY 03 (latest available), about 50% of all UOP students were receiving some level of tuition reimbursement from their employers. Effective August 27, 2004, APOL converted all outstanding shares of UOPX into Apollo Group Class A shares, at the rate of 1.1527 Apollo shares for each UOPX share, or a total of about 16.7 million shares. UOPX had been partly spun off as a tracking stock in March 2000, and APOL held an 85.5% stake at November 30, 2003. The transaction resulted in a non-cash stock-based compensation charge of $123.5 million in FY 04's fourth quarter, plus a $114.2 million charge related to the premium paid for the conversion.

IPD provides program development and management services to regionally accredited private colleges and universities interested in expanding or developing their programs for working adults. IPD shares in tuition revenues generated from these programs.

As one of the largest U.S. providers of financial planning education programs, including the Certified Financial Planner Professional Education Program, CFPI began piloting its non-degree programs at several UOP campuses in 1999. The company offers these services to UOP students.

WIU offers graduate and undergraduate degree programs to 2,000 students at one campus and three learning centers, with a focus on international students.

In FY 04's fourth quarter, APOL accrued $9.8 million related to the resolution of a review by the U.S. Department of Education, which had examined the company's compensation and sales practices.

Company Financials Fiscal Year ending August 31

Per Share Data ($)

(Year Ended August 31)	2004	2003	2002	2001	2000	1999	1998	1997	1996	1995
Tangible Bk. Val.	NA	5.23	3.60	2.47	1.39	1.10	0.91	0.71	0.46	NA
Cash Flow	NA	1.62	1.12	0.81	0.57	0.45	0.33	0.23	0.15	0.10
Earnings	0.77	1.30	0.87	0.60	0.41	0.33	0.26	0.19	0.12	0.08
S&P Core Earnings	NA	1.22	0.79	0.52	NA	NA	NA	NA	NA	NA
Dividends	Nil	Nil	Nil	Nil	Nil	Nil	Nil	Nil	Nil	Nil
Payout Ratio	Nil	Nil	Nil	Nil	Nil	Nil	Nil	Nil	Nil	Nil
Prices - High	98.01	73.09	46.15	33.30	22.63	15.22	19.22	14.55	10.14	5.33
- Low	62.55	40.72	28.13	19.33	8.16	7.80	9.11	6.81	3.96	0.77
P/E Ratio - High	NM	56	53	56	55	46	73	77	81	67
- Low	81	31	32	32	20	23	35	36	32	10

Income Statement Analysis (Million $)

	2004	2003	2002	2001	2000	1999	1998	1997	1996	1995
Revs.	NA	1,340	1,009	769	610	499	385	279	211	161
Oper. Inc.	NA	428	293	194	141	113	82.9	57.2	36.6	22.2
Depr.	NA	40.3	35.2	32.7	27.4	20.6	12.8	6.55	4.65	2.75
Int. Exp.	NA	Nil	Nil	Nil	Nil	Nil	Nil	Nil	Nil	0.10
Pretax Inc.	NA	402	266	175	120	98.0	76.3	55.0	35.0	21.8
Eff. Tax Rate	NA	38.5%	39.4%	38.4%	40.8%	39.8%	39.3%	39.3%	38.9%	42.3%
Net Inc.	NA	247	161	108	71.2	59.0	46.3	33.4	21.4	12.6
S&P Core Earnings	NA	218	140	90.1	NA	NA	NA	NA	NA	NA

Balance Sheet & Other Fin. Data (Million $)

	2004	2003	2002	2001	2000	1999	1998	1997	1996	1995
Cash	NA	653	689	402	160	117	75.0	106	76.5	62.6
Curr. Assets	NA	950	730	487	247	198	174	144	109	84.0
Total Assets	NA	1,378	980	680	405	348	305	195	138	102
Curr. Liab.	NA	335	264	182	131	109	95.6	67.4	54.8	45.1
LT Debt	NA	Nil	15.5	14.8	9.97	4.22	3.80	2.48	1.77	1.70
Common Equity	NA	1,027	699	482	261	231	200	124	80.6	55.4
Total Cap.	NA	1,027	715	497	272	237	205	127	83.0	57.0
Cap. Exp.	NA	55.8	36.7	44.4	34.8	44.7	30.9	12.8	10.4	9.90
Cash Flow	NA	287	196	141	99	79.6	59.1	40.0	26.0	15.4
Curr. Ratio	NA	2.8	2.8	2.7	1.9	1.8	1.8	2.1	2.0	1.9
% LT Debt of Cap.	NA	Nil	2.2	3.0	3.7	1.8	1.9	2.0	2.1	2.9
% Net Inc.of Revs.	NA	18.4	16.0	14.0	11.7	11.8	12.0	12.0	10.1	7.8
% Ret. on Assets	NA	20.9	19.4	19.9	18.9	18.1	18.5	20.1	17.8	17.3
% Ret. on Equity	NA	28.6	29.3	29.0	28.9	27.4	28.6	32.6	31.5	40.2

Data as orig reptd.; bef. results of disc opers/spec. items. Per share data adj. for stk. divs.; EPS diluted. E-Estimated. NA-Not Available. NM-Not Meaningful. NR-Not Ranked. UR-Under Review.

Office: 4615 East Elwood Street, Phoenix, AZ 85040-1958.
Telephone: 480-966-5394.
Website: http://www.apollogrp.com
Chrmn, Pres & CEO: T.S. Nelson.
CFO, Treas & Secy: K.B. Gonzales.

Chief Acctg Officer: D.E. Bachus.
Investor Contact: J. Pasinski 800-990-2765.
Dirs: J. Blair, D. J. DeConcini, H. F. Govenar, T. S. Nelson, J. R. Norton III, J. G. Sperling, P. V. Sperling.

Founded: in 1981.
Domicile: Arizona.
Employees: 8,036.
S&P Analyst: Michael W. Jaffe/CB/JWP

Apple Computer

Recommendation: **HOLD** ★ ★ ★ ★ ★
SELL SELL HOLD BUY BUY

12-Month Target Price: **$48.00**
(as of October 27, 2004)

AAPL has an approximate 0.20% weighting in the **S&P 500**

Sector: Information Technology
Sub-Industry: Computer Hardware
Peer Group: Computer Hardware - Large System Vendors

Summary: This leading maker of PCs and related products has made a transition to a new line of personal computer products powered by the PowerPC microprocessor.

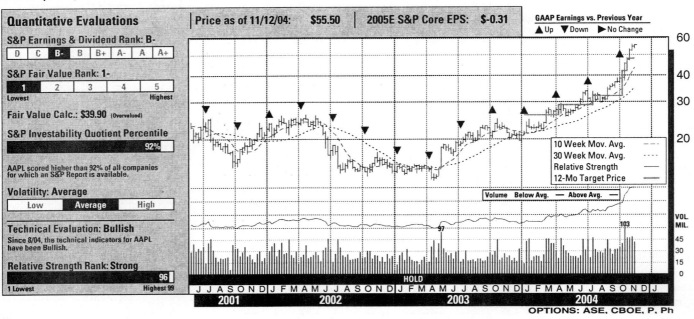

Quantitative Evaluations

S&P Earnings & Dividend Rank: B-

| D | C | B- | B | B+ | A- | A | A+ |

S&P Fair Value Rank: 1-

| 1 | 2 | 3 | 4 | 5 |
Lowest — Highest

Fair Value Calc.: $39.90 (Overvalued)

S&P Investability Quotient Percentile
92%

AAPL scored higher than 92% of all companies for which an S&P Report is available.

Volatility: Average

| Low | Average | High |

Technical Evaluation: Bullish
Since 8/04, the technical indicators for AAPL have been Bullish.

Relative Strength Rank: Strong
96
1 Lowest — Highest 99

Price as of 11/12/04: $55.50   **2005E S&P Core EPS:** $-0.31

GAAP Earnings vs. Previous Year
▲ Up ▼ Down ▶ No Change

- 10 Week Mov. Avg.
- 30 Week Mov. Avg.
- Relative Strength
- 12-Mo Target Price

Volume Below Avg. — Above Avg.

VOL MIL

J J A S O N D J F M A M J J A S O N D J F M A M J J A S O N D J F M A M J J A S O N D J
2001 **2002** **2003** **2004**

HOLD

OPTIONS: ASE, CBOE, P, Ph

Analyst commentary prepared by Megan Graham-Hackett/MF/BK

Highlights October 29, 2004

- We project revenue growth of 36% for FY 05 (Sep.), following a 33% increase in FY 04. We believe trends that helped revenue growth in FY 04 will carry through in FY 05, including the ongoing economic recovery and benefits of new product introductions (specifically the iPod and iPod mini), as well as additional retail store openings. The company's new iBook has been selling relatively well, but its Power Mac sales have been somewhat disappointing, in our view, but we think reflect component availability issues.

- We note that AAPL continues to open retail stores in an effort to introduce new users to its platform. The company plans to have 100 retail stores open by the end of calendar year 2004. We expect FY 05 gross margins to remain flat with FY 04's level, at approximately 27.3%, with benefits from higher volumes being adversely affected by product mix, as the iPod and mini iPod sales weigh on the overall gross margin.

- We project FY 05 EPS of $1.60. However, we note our FY 05 Standard & Poor's Core Earnings projection is a loss of $0.31, reflecting our estimate of the impact of stock option expense.

Key Stock Statistics

S&P Oper. EPS 2005E	1.60	52-week Range	$56.11-19.25
P/E on S&P Oper. EPS 2005E	34.7	12 Month P/E	78.2
Yield (%)	Nil	Beta	1.80
Dividend Rate/Share	Nil	Shareholders	29,015
Shares Outstanding (M)	387.9	Market Cap (B)	$ 21.5

Value of $10,000 invested five years ago: **$ 12,392**

Dividend Data

Cash payments began in 1987 and were discontinued in February 1996.

Investment Rationale/Risk October 29, 2004

- We continue to recommend holding the shares. Despite what we see as a difficult computer hardware environment, reflecting the impact of a weak economy and excessive spending in 1999 and 2000, we think that AAPL has maintained a strong balance sheet and has focused on asset management. We think that the company's FY 04 fourth quarter results showed clear indications that new products and new strategy investments for new retail stores are paying off in terms of earnings growth.

- Risks to our opinion and target price include a deterioration of technology spending levels, challengers to AAPL's successful iPod line, and market share losses in PCs.

- Our 12-month target price of $48 is based on our price to sales ratio analysis, as well as our P/E valuation metric. AAPL has about $13 a share in cash and short-term investments. With the stock trading at a price to sales ratio and P/E multiple that are at the higher end of peer levels, we think the shares are fairly valued, and already reflect the potential for upside earnings surprises based on the success of the iPod.

Revenues/Earnings Data Fiscal year ending September 30

Revenues (Million $)

	2004	2003	2002	2001	2000	1999
1Q	2,006	1,472	1,375	1,007	2,343	1,710
2Q	1,909	1,475	1,495	1,431	1,945	1,530
3Q	2,014	1,545	1,429	1,475	1,825	1,558
4Q	2,350	1,715	1,443	1,450	1,870	1,336
Yr.	8,279	6,207	5,742	5,363	7,983	6,134

Earnings Per Share ($)

	2004	2003	2002	2001	2000	1999
1Q	0.17	-0.02	0.11	-0.61	0.52	0.48
2Q	0.12	0.04	0.11	0.12	0.64	0.42
3Q	0.16	0.05	0.09	0.17	0.55	0.60
4Q	0.26	0.11	-0.13	0.19	0.47	0.32
Yr.	0.71	0.19	0.18	-0.11	2.18	1.81

Next earnings report expected: mid-January Source: S&P, Company Reports
EPS Estimates based on S&P Operating Earnings; historical GAAP earnings are as reported.

STANDARD &POOR'S

Apple Computer, Inc.

Recommendation: **HOLD** ★ ★ ★ ☆ ☆   12-Month Target Price: **$48.00** (as of October 27, 2004)

Business Summary October 29, 2004

Apple Computer has recovered from a dramatic decline in its market share in the worldwide personal computer (PC) markets. Its share was cut by about two-thirds over the four years between 1993 and 1997. The company believes that the decrease was linked to strides made by the Windows platform in narrowing the edge held by the company's products, which were noted for their ease of use, innovative applications, and greater stability. Apple first introduced Macintosh PCs in 1984. All Macintosh products use the PowerPC RISC-based chip, which was developed by an alliance of Apple, IBM and Motorola.

Under a restructuring program introduced in 1996 and enhanced in 1997, Apple presented a new business model to restore sustained profitability. It trimmed its workforce and operating cost structure to reflect its lower sales base. The company also refreshed its product line to match the competition in price/performance metrics. Some of these efforts were initiated by former chairman and CEO Dr. G. Amelio, who was asked by directors to resign in July 1997. The turnaround strategy achieved its current momentum under Apple's co-founder, Steve Jobs, now CEO. The company now has cash and short-term investments totaling more than $5 billion, with gross margins of about 27% to 28%.

The Power Macintosh family is the company's most advanced line, intended for businesses and academics. As part of Apple's simplification strategy, entry-level Power Macs supplanted the former Performa line, targeted at first-time users. In addition, a new, low-priced, consumer-oriented platform, the iMac, was launched in 1998. The iMac has since been refreshed and now features a flat panel display. Rounding out the strategy is the PowerBook portable computer, aimed at the mobile user, recently augmented with the iBook, a consumer laptop. In addition, the company entered the consumer device market with the iPod in 2001. Apple divested its Newton hand-held computer in early 1998. In 2003, the company enabled the iPod to work with PCs based on the Windows operating environment. In early 2004, the company signed an agreement with Hewlett Packard Co., which undertook to sell its own music device based on the iPod.

The company has simplified its software strategy, changing its Mac OS operating system roadmap. Based on industry data, the Mac OS has about 3% market share (based on units sold). Apple's latest version is Mac OS X (read 10), which the company says has a compelling and easier graphical user interface, and, since it is based on the Unix operating system, is more robust. In 2003, Apple introduced iTunes, its offering for digital music downloads from the Internet. As of January 2004, the company estimated that iTunes had a 70% share of the legal download music market. Also in January 2004, Apple announced that HP planned to bundle software in its PCs that directed users to Apple's iTunes site for downloading music.

Apple initiated a retail strategy in 2001. The company had 74 stores at the end of FY 03 (Sep.), and plans to have 100 open at the end of calendar year 2004. Its goal is to drive traffic through its stores, and to expand its installed base of customers by showcasing its products in a user-friendly environment in the stores.

In FY 97, the company purchased its Mac OS license from Power Computing Corp., its largest licensee.

Company Financials Fiscal Year ending September 30

Per Share Data ($)

(Year Ended September 30)	2004	2003	2002	2001	2000	1999	1998	1997	1996	1995
Tangible Bk. Val.	NA	11.21	11.08	11.17	12.00	9.18	5.53	4.10	8.27	11.80
Cash Flow	NA	0.00	0.51	0.19	2.42	1.97	1.25	-3.68	-2.67	2.24
Earnings	0.71	0.19	0.18	-0.11	2.18	1.81	1.05	-4.15	-3.30	1.73
S&P Core Earnings	NA	-0.33	-0.38	-1.43	NA	NA	NA	NA	NA	NA
Dividends	Nil	Nil	Nil	Nil	Nil	Nil	Nil	Nil	0.06	0.24
Payout Ratio	Nil	Nil	Nil	Nil	Nil	Nil	Nil	Nil	NM	14%
Prices - High	56.11	25.01	26.17	27.12	75.18	59.00	21.87	14.87	17.75	25.06
- Low	21.18	12.72	13.36	14.43	13.62	16.00	6.75	6.37	8.00	15.81
P/E Ratio - High	79	NM	NM	NM	34	33	21	NM	NM	15
- Low	30	NM	NM	NM	6	9	6	NM	NM	9

Income Statement Analysis (Million $)

	2004	2003	2002	2001	2000	1999	1998	1997	1996	1995
Revs.	NA	6,207	5,742	5,363	7,983	6,134	5,941	7,081	9,833	11,062
Oper. Inc.	NA	138	72.0	-231	704	471	379	-285	-1,048	788
Depr.	NA	113	118	102	84.0	85.0	111	118	156	127
Int. Exp.	NA	16.0	11.0	16.0	21.0	47.0	62.0	71.0	60.0	48.0
Pretax Inc.	NA	92.0	87.0	-52.0	1,092	676	329	-1,045	-1,295	674
Eff. Tax Rate	NA	26.1%	25.3%	NM	28.0%	11.1%	6.10%	NM	NM	37.1%
Net Inc.	NA	68.0	65.0	-37.0	786	601	309	-1,045	-816	424
S&P Core Earnings	NA	-119	-137	-465	NA	NA	NA	NA	NA	NA

Balance Sheet & Other Fin. Data (Million $)

	2004	2003	2002	2001	2000	1999	1998	1997	1996	1995
Cash	NA	3,396	2,252	2,310	1,191	1,326	1,481	1,230	1,745	952
Curr. Assets	NA	5,887	5,388	5,143	5,427	4,285	3,698	3,424	4,515	5,224
Total Assets	NA	6,815	6,298	6,021	6,803	5,161	4,289	4,233	5,364	6,231
Curr. Liab.	NA	2,357	1,658	1,518	1,933	1,549	1,520	1,818	2,003	2,325
LT Debt	NA	Nil	316	317	300	300	954	951	949	303
Common Equity	NA	4,223	4,095	3,920	4,031	2,954	1,492	1,050	2,058	2,901
Total Cap.	NA	4,223	4,640	4,503	4,870	3,612	2,769	2,415	3,361	3,906
Cap. Exp.	NA	164	174	232	107	47.0	46.0	53.0	67.0	159
Cash Flow	NA	181	183	65.0	870	686	420	-927	-660	551
Curr. Ratio	NA	2.5	3.2	3.4	2.8	2.8	2.4	1.9	2.3	2.2
% LT Debt of Cap.	NA	Nil	6.8	7.0	6.2	8.3	34.5	39.4	28.2	7.8
% Net Inc.of Revs.	NA	1.1	1.1	NM	9.8	9.8	5.2	NM	NM	3.8
% Ret. on Assets	NA	1.0	1.1	NM	13.1	12.7	7.3	NM	NM	7.4
% Ret. on Equity	NA	1.6	1.6	NM	22.5	27.0	24.3	NM	NM	16.0

Data as orig reptd.; bef. results of disc opers/spec. items. Per share data adj. for stk. divs. Bold denotes primary EPS - prior periods restated. E-Estimated. NA-Not Available. NM-Not Meaningful. NR-Not Ranked. UR-Under Review.

Office: 1 Infinite Loop, Cupertino, CA 95014.
Telephone: 408-996-1010.
Email: investor_relations@apple.com
Website: http://www.apple.com
CEO: S.P. Jobs.

SVP & CFO: P. Oppenheimer.
SVP, Secy & General Counsel: N.R. Heinen.
Investor Contact: N. Paxton 408-974-5420.
Dirs: F. D. Anderson, W. V. Campbell, M. S. Drexler, A. Gore, Jr., S. P. Jobs, A. D. Levinson, J. B. York.

Founded: in 1977.
Domicile: California.
Employees: 13,566.
S&P Analyst: Megan Graham-Hackett/MF/BK

The McGraw·Hill Companies

Applera - Applied Biosystems Group

Recommendation: **HOLD** ★ ★ ★
SELL | SELL | HOLD | BUY | BUY

12-Month Target Price: $21.00
(as of May 04, 2004)

ABI has an approximate 0.04% weighting in the S&P 500

Sector: Health Care
Sub-Industry: Biotechnology
Peer Group: Life Science R&D - Larger Capitalization

Summary: ABI (formerly PE Corp. - PE Biosystems Group) supplies instrument systems, reagents, software and related services for life science research applications.

Quantitative Evaluations

S&P Earnings & Dividend Rank: B

| D | C | B- | **B** | B+ | A- | A | A+ |

S&P Fair Value Rank: 5+

| 1 | 2 | 3 | 4 | **5** |
| Lowest | | | | Highest |

Fair Value Calc.: $22.70 (Slightly Undervalued)

S&P Investability Quotient Percentile
89%

ABI scored higher than 89% of all companies for which an S&P Report is available.

Volatility: Average

| Low | **Average** | High |

Technical Evaluation: Bullish
Since 11/04, the technical indicators for ABI have been Bullish.

Relative Strength Rank: Moderate
48
1 Lowest | Highest 99

Price as of 11/12/04: **$20.02** | **2005E S&P Core EPS:** **$0.49**

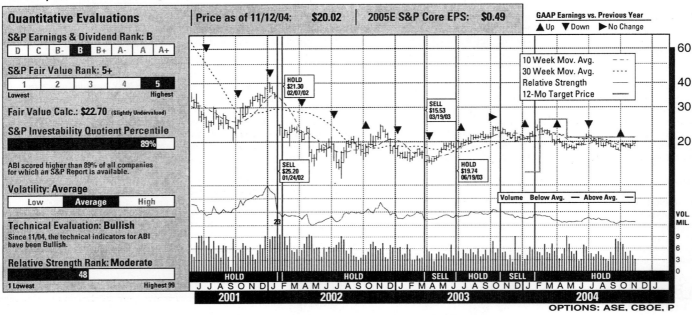

GAAP Earnings vs. Previous Year
▲ Up ▼ Down ▶ No Change

- 10 Week Mov. Avg.
- 30 Week Mov. Avg.
- Relative Strength
- 12-Mo Target Price

HOLD $21.30 02/07/02
SELL $15.53 03/19/03
SELL $25.20 01/24/02
HOLD $19.74 06/19/03

Volume Below Avg. — Above Avg. —

HOLD | HOLD | SELL | HOLD | SELL | HOLD
J J A S O N D|J F M A M J J A S O N D|J F M A M J J A S O N D|J F M A M J J A S O N D|J
2001 | 2002 | 2003 | 2004

OPTIONS: ASE, CBOE, P

Analyst commentary prepared by Jeffrey Loo, CFA /MF/GG

Highlights August 24, 2004

- We see FY 05 (Jun.) sales increasing 4.5%, to about $1.82 billion, on continued strength in the Mass Spectrometry (MS) and Real-time PCR/Other Applied Genomics (formerly sequence detection systems/applied genomics) product lines, partially offset by continued weakness in DNA Sequencing and Core DNA Synthesis & PCR (PCR). We forecast industrywide MS sales growth of about 10% a year over the next three years, but think ABI could grow this segment at a higher rate on its dominant position and new products. We see ABI's MS segment growing 14%, on robust sales of its 4000 Q TRAP and API 4000 LC/MS/MS systems. We see Real-time PCR sales growing about 8%, Core DNA Synthesis sales flat, and DNA Sequencing sales declining about 3%.

- We believe ABI's ongoing strategic and product portfolio review could limit its sales growth, but it may improve margins slightly in 2005 and should have a greater impact in 2006. We see a small but gradual shift to more consumables and higher margin new instruments resulting in a slight improvement in gross margins, partially offset by higher SG&A expenses from enterprise system software upgrades and increased litigation expenses. We forecast a 60 basis point improvement in operating margins.

- Utilizing a 28% tax rate, and aided by share repurchases, our FY 05 EPS estimate is $0.96. Using S&P's Core Earnings methodology, we estimate FY 05 EPS at $0.49, primarily reflecting estimated stock option expense.

Key Stock Statistics

S&P Oper. EPS 2005E	0.96	52-week Range	$24.44-17.76
P/E on S&P Oper. EPS 2005E	20.9	12 Month P/E	22.2
Yield (%)	0.8%	Beta	1.46
Dividend Rate/Share	0.17	Shareholders	6,090
Shares Outstanding (M)	196.0	Market Cap (B)	$ 3.9

Value of $10,000 invested five years ago: **$ 5,693**

Dividend Data Dividends have been paid since 1971

Amount ($)	Date Decl.	Ex-Div. Date	Stock of Record	Payment Date
0.043	Nov. 21	Nov. 26	Dec. 01	Jan. 02 '04
0.043	Jan. 16	Feb. 26	Mar. 01	Apr. 01 '04
0.043	Apr. 05	May. 27	Jun. 01	Jul. 01 '04
0.043	Aug. 19	Aug. 30	Sep. 01	Oct. 01 '04

Investment Rationale/Risk August 24, 2004

- We see improving industry conditions for companies that provide tools and supplies to the life science industry. However, we have concerns that government funding issues, such as the transition of universities to Independent Administrative Agency Status in Japan and the decelerating growth of the NIH budget in the U.S., may constrain sales, particularly of instruments. We believe companies with a high percentage of consumable sales will benefit the most from improving conditions and will be the least affected by government funding issues. We believe ABI's academic and government funded customer base is significant at about 40%. ABI is also in the midst of an organizational and product portfolio restructuring that we believe may constrain sales growth in 2005.

- Risks to our recommendation and target price include ABI's greater reliance on big ticket instrument sales and related services (about 65% combined); its large customer base being dependent on government funding, which may limit its ability to fully benefit from improving conditions; and potential limited acceptance of its new products.

- Our 12-month target price of $21 is based on a blend of our discounted cash flow analysis, which assumes decreased share volatility, a WACC of 10%, and a terminal growth rate of 3%, along with our P/E to growth analysis, utilizing a 1.5X PEG ratio, in line with peers.

Revenues/Earnings Data Fiscal year ending June 30

Revenues (Million $)

	2005	2004	2003	2002	2001	2000
1Q	390.3	382.7	382.7	366.6	363.6	292.3
2Q	—	458.4	444.7	411.2	411.0	335.9
3Q	—	439.6	409.4	409.0	363.1	368.1
4Q	—	460.5	432.9	417.3	481.8	391.8
Yr.	—	1,741	1,683	1,604	1,620	1,388

Earnings Per Share ($)

	2005	2004	2003	2002	2001	2000
1Q	0.18	0.16	0.16	0.15	0.22	0.14
2Q	E0.25	0.25	0.14	0.23	0.26	0.21
3Q	E0.25	0.22	0.19	0.23	0.26	0.26
4Q	E0.28	0.20	0.46	0.18	0.22	0.27
Yr.	E0.96	0.83	0.95	0.78	0.96	0.83

Next earnings report expected: late-January Source: S&P, Company Reports
EPS Estimates based on S&P Operating Earnings; historical GAAP earnings are as reported.

Please read the Required Disclosures and Reg. AC certification on the last page of this report.

The McGraw·Hill Companies

Applera Corporation - Applied Biosystems Group

Recommendation: **HOLD** ★ ★ ★ ☆ ☆   12-Month Target Price: **$21.00** (as of May 04, 2004)

Business Summary August 24, 2004

Applera Corp. - Applied Biosystems Group (formerly PE Corp. - PE Biosystems Group) was formed in May 1999 through a reorganization that resulted in two publicly traded entities with their own common stock: ABI and Celera Genomics Group (CRA). ABI manufactures and sells instrument systems, reagents, software, and related services for life science research applications such as human disease research; genetic analysis; drug discovery, development and manufacturing; human identification; agriculture; and food and environmental testing. Operating revenues were up 5% in FY 03 (Jun.), to $1.68 billion, from $1.60 billion in FY 02.

In FY 01, ABI restructured its organization from operating separate business units for specific technologies, to a more integrated approach entailing focused development and marketing of the company's overall product and services offerings. It created three new operating divisions. The Applications and Products (AP) group is responsible for marketing ABI's broad range of technology platforms, supporting products, and services. The division's marketing activities are split between an applications marketing unit, a platform marketing unit, a global services unit, and a brand marketing unit. The AP group is also responsible for R&D of application-specific products, such as assays for DNA sequencing.

The Platform Products R&D group is involved in researching and developing platform technologies, which include polymerase (PCR) chain reaction amplification instruments, genetic analysis equipment, mass spectrometers, chromatography workstations, protein sequencers, and supporting software.

The Global Operations group manufactures, distributes, and insures the quality control for all of ABI's products. In order to improve manufacturing efficiencies, the company has separate operating units for its instrument, consumables, and oligonucleotide product offerings.

In the U.S., the company's products are sold largely through its own sales force, although some offerings are marketed through independent distributors. Outside the U.S., ABI employs its own sales team, and also uses representative and distributorship agreements in some countries.

In April 2001, ABI and sister company CRA formed Celera Diagnostics, a joint venture that was to develop and commercialize diagnostic products. In December 2002, Celera Diagnostics received FDA marketing clearance for its ViroSeq HIV-1 Genotyping System. ViroSeq is designed to detect mutations in the HIV-1 virus genome that result in HIV drug resistance. The joint venture currently markets a cystic fibrosis diagnostic test.

In April 2002, the company reached an agreement with CRA whereby ABI markets and distributes CRA's genomic database (Celera Discovery System), with CRA entitled to financial payments and royalties.

In 2004, ABI introduced its AB Expression Array System, consisting of a genetic analyzer to scan data from a whole human genome microarray used in conjunction with reagents, and software to analyze the results. Scientists could use these data to characterize levels of gene expression in normal and diseased tissue. This competitive market is led by Affymetrix and Agilent.

Company Financials Fiscal Year ending June 30

Per Share Data ($)

(Year Ended June 30)	2004	2003	2002	2001	2000	1999	1998	1997	1996	1995
Tangible Bk. Val.	6.36	6.63	5.38	NM	NM	NM	2.86	2.49	1.89	1.81
Cash Flow	-1.29	1.45	1.16	1.16	1.11	0.93	0.55	0.85	0.32	0.63
Earnings	0.83	0.95	0.78	0.96	0.86	0.72	0.28	0.65	0.08	0.39
S&P Core Earnings	0.30	0.31	0.34	0.32	NA	NA	NA	NA	NA	NA
Dividends	0.17	0.17	0.17	0.17	0.17	0.17	0.17	0.17	0.17	0.17
Payout Ratio	20%	18%	22%	18%	20%	24%	61%	26%	NM	43%
Prices - High	24.44	24.00	39.28	94.25	160.00	62.93	25.17	21.53	14.06	10.06
- Low	17.76	14.90	13.00	18.49	42.81	21.96	13.62	14.46	9.40	6.43
P/E Ratio - High	29	25	50	98	NM	87	90	33	NM	26
- Low	21	16	17	19	NM	31	49	22	NM	16

Income Statement Analysis (Million $)

	2004	2003	2002	2001	2000	1999	1998	1997	1996	1995
Revs.	1,741	1,683	1,604	1,619	1,388	1,222	1,531	1,277	1,163	1,064
Oper. Inc.	-306	324	318	347	270	234	220	189	166	132
Depr.	96.8	106	81.2	66.8	54.5	44.3	53.1	36.0	41.2	40.7
Int. Exp.	Nil	Nil	0.89	1.30	8.13	4.50	4.91	2.30	4.97	8.20
Pretax Inc.	-240	239	238	304	276	192	101	157	35.5	82.3
Eff. Tax Rate	28.2%	19.6%	29.1%	30.2%	32.5%	15.9%	38.4%	26.8%	60.7%	19.0%
Net Inc.	-172	200	168	212	186	148	56.4	115	13.9	66.9
S&P Core Earnings	63.8	63.3	72.9	71.7	NA	NA	NA	NA	NA	NA

Balance Sheet & Other Fin. Data (Million $)

	2004	2003	2002	2001	2000	1999	1998	1997	1996	1995
Cash	505	602	441	392	395	237	82.9	196	96.6	73.0
Curr. Assets	1,110	1,232	1,072	1,014	998	918	796	794	641	602
Total Assets	1,948	2,127	1,819	1,678	1,698	1,348	1,334	1,105	941	893
Curr. Liab.	518	541	522	508	603	644	508	455	441	374
LT Debt	Nil	Nil	Nil	Nil	36.1	31.5	Nil	33.6	0.89	34.1
Common Equity	1,244	1,388	1,129	1,041	934	534	565	437	323	305
Total Cap.	1,244	1,388	1,129	1,041	970	566	608	471	324	339
Cap. Exp.	60.4	132	88.3	144	94.4	82.5	101	62.2	32.4	28.9
Cash Flow	-269	306	250	279	241	193	110	151	55.2	108
Curr. Ratio	2.1	2.3	2.1	2.0	1.7	1.4	1.6	1.8	1.5	1.6
% LT Debt of Cap.	Nil	Nil	Nil	Nil	3.7	5.6	Nil	7.1	0.3	10.1
% Net Inc.of Revs.	9.9	11.9	10.5	13.1	13.4	12.1	3.7	9.0	1.2	6.3
% Ret. on Assets	8.5	10.1	9.6	12.6	12.2	12.0	4.6	11.3	1.5	7.5
% Ret. on Equity	13.1	15.9	15.5	21.5	25.4	27.0	11.3	30.3	4.4	22.5

Data as orig reptd.; bef. results of disc opers/spec. items. Per share data adj. for stk. divs.; EPS diluted (primary prior to 1998). E-Estimated. NA-Not Available. NM-Not Meaningful. NR-Not Ranked. UR-Under Review.

Office: 301 Merritt 7, Norwalk, CT 06856-5435.
Telephone: 203-840-2000.
Website: http://www.appliedbiosystems.com
Chrmn, Pres & CEO: T.L. White.
SVP & CFO: D.L. Winger.
SVP & General Counsel: W.B. Sawch.

Treas: J.S. Ostaszewski.
Secy: T.P. Livingston.
Investor Contact: L. Greub 650-554-2349.
Dirs: R. H. Ayers, J. Belingard, R. H. Hayes, A. J. Levine, W. H. Longfield, T. E. Martin, C. W. Slayman, O. R. Smith, J. R. Tobin, T. L. White.

Founded: in 1937.
Domicile: Delaware.
Employees: 4,400.
S&P Analyst: Jeffrey Loo, CFA /MF/GG

Applied Materials

Recommendation: **BUY** ★★★★☆   12-Month Target Price: **$21.00**
SELL · SELL · HOLD · BUY · BUY
(as of August 11, 2004)

AMAT has an approximate 0.25% weighting in the **S&P 500**

Sector: Information Technology
Sub-Industry: Semiconductor Equipment
Peer Group: Semiconductor Equipment - Larger Front-end

Summary: This company is the world's largest manufacturer of wafer fabrication equipment for the semiconductor industry.

Quantitative Evaluations

S&P Earnings & Dividend Rank: B-

| D | C | B- | B | B+ | A- | A | A+ |

S&P Fair Value Rank: 5

| 1 | 2 | 3 | 4 | 5 |
| Lowest | | | | Highest |

Fair Value Calc.: $19.30 (Undervalued)

S&P Investability Quotient Percentile

96%

AMAT scored higher than 96% of all companies for which an S&P Report is available.

Volatility: Average

| Low | Average | High |

Technical Evaluation: Neutral
Since 11/04, the technical indicators for AMAT have been Neutral.

Relative Strength Rank: Weak

21

1 Lowest   Highest 99

Price as of 11/12/04: $16.17   **2004E S&P Core EPS:** $0.37

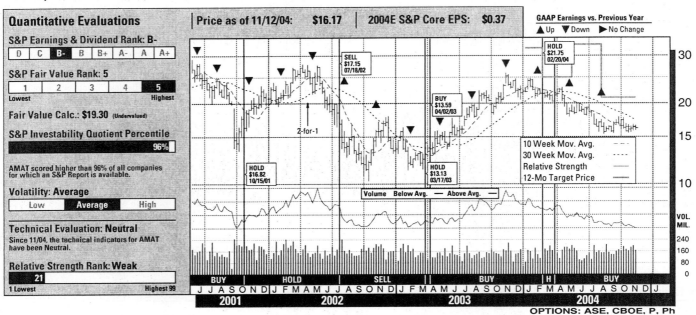

GAAP Earnings vs. Previous Year
▲ Up ▼ Down ► No Change

10 Week Mov. Avg.
30 Week Mov. Avg.
Relative Strength
12-Mo Target Price

Volume Below Avg. — Above Avg.

OPTIONS: ASE, CBOE, P, Ph

Analyst commentary prepared by Colin McArdle/CB/GG

Highlights August 12, 2004

- We see capital spending by chipmakers growing 40% in calendar 2004, following an estimated 5% rise in 2003. With semiconductor fab capacity utilization estimated above 90%, chipmakers began ordering equipment in earnest.

- Applied saw its orders rise 32% in each of the January and April quarters. For the July quarter, AMAT expects to report that orders increased between 5% and 10% sequentially. We believe Applied's order trends indicate that the semiconductor equipment market is in an upturn.

- We also believe share gains are occurring in deposition and etch, Applied's largest markets. We note that 73% of April quarter sales came from Asia, an increasingly important market in which Applied has historically been strong. All told, we forecast that FY 04 (Oct.) sales will rise by over 85%, and estimate EPS of $0.82, growing to $1.24 in FY 05.

Investment Rationale/Risk August 12, 2004

- We believe the semiconductor industry is in the early stages of a sustainable upturn, and that Applied Materials has the technological advantage and economies of scale to capture this global trend. We have an accumulate recommendation on AMAT shares.

- Risks to our recommendation and target price include the possibility that the recent surge in capacity additions could result in a leveling of orders in the July quarter and possibly the October quarter. In addition, we think the industry and AMAT have limited visibility into future orders, and a global economic slowdown could materially affect AMAT results.

- AMAT trades at 5.7X trailing sales, above the historical average of 4.3X, but at a more modest 4.0X our FY 04 sales estimate. On a P/E basis, the shares trade at 20X our calendar 2004 EPS estimate of $0.94, well below the peer average of 35X. On a P/E to growth basis, the shares trade at 1.7X, versus 1.6X for the S&P 500. We apply a conservative, risk-weighted P/E multiple of 18X to our 12-month forward EPS of $1.15, versus $1.24 previously, and derive a $21 price target, from $33 previously.

Key Stock Statistics

S&P Core EPS 2005E	0.95	52-week Range	$24.75-15.36
S&P Oper. EPS 2004E	0.84	12 Month P/E	30.5
P/E on S&P Oper. EPS 2004E	19.3	Beta	2.30
S&P Oper. EPS 2005E	1.24	Shareholders	6,995
Yield (%)	Nil	Market Cap (B)	$ 27.5
Dividend Rate/Share	Nil	Shares Outstanding (M)	1698.2

Value of $10,000 invested five years ago: **$ 6,644**

Dividend Data

No cash dividends have been paid.

Revenues/Earnings Data Fiscal year ending October 31

Revenues (Million $)

	2004	2003	2002	2001	2000	1999
1Q	1,555	1,054	1,000	2,731	1,667	742.5
2Q	2,018	1,107	1,156	1,909	2,190	1,118
3Q	2,236	1,095	1,460	1,334	2,732	1,434
4Q	—	1,221	1,446	1,265	2,920	1,566
Yr.	—	4,477	5,062	7,343	9,564	4,859

Earnings Per Share ($)

	2004	2003	2002	2001	2000	1999
1Q	0.05	-0.04	-0.03	0.33	0.20	0.04
2Q	0.22	-0.04	0.03	0.14	0.27	0.09
3Q	0.26	-0.02	0.07	0.02	0.35	0.15
4Q	E0.25	0.01	0.09	-0.05	0.39	0.17
Yr.	E0.84	-0.09	0.16	0.46	1.20	0.46

Next earnings report expected: mid-November Source: S&P, Company Reports
EPS Estimates based on S&P Operating Earnings; historical GAAP earnings are as reported.

Applied Materials, Inc.

Recommendation: **BUY** ★ ★ ★ ☆   12-Month Target Price: **$21.00** (as of August 11, 2004)

Business Summary August 13, 2004

Applied Materials leads the semiconductor capital equipment market, with 2002 sales nearly twice those of its nearest competitor, Tokyo Electron. AMAT sells equipment to the front end of the semiconductor fabrication process, which consists of those steps necessary to build the transistors and wiring needed to form integrated circuits (IC).

The company produces a broad range of equipment, and holds dominant positions in deposition (with a 45% share of a $5.3 billion market in 2002), etch (25% share; $2.0 billion market) and chemical mechanical planarization, or CMP (60% share; $768 million market). It also holds a 25% share of the ion implantation market ($681 million) and a 25% share of the smaller ($298 million) mask exposure equipment market. Other markets in which AMAT sells tools include rapid thermal processing, wafer wet cleaning, metrology and wafer/reticle inspection, and deposition for flat panel displays (through its AKT subsidiary).

In deposition, in which thin films of conductive or insulating material are deposited to form an IC, Applied introduced the SlimCell ECP system for copper electroplating in FY 03 (Oct.). Applied's previous product in this important market had not performed well versus competitors, and Applied believes the SlimCell will enable the company to capture significant market share.

In etch, the company offers tools for selectively removing thin films of three different types of materials: metal, silicon, and dielectric thin films. In FY 03, Applied introduced the Centura Enabler etch system, which performs etch strip and clean steps in a single chamber, designed to reduce operating costs for chip designs at 65nm and below.

Applied's ion implant products are used to change the conductive properties of silicon, and thereby create active electronic components, by bombarding them with beams of ions.

Chemical-mechanical polishing products are used to polish the surface of a wafer following deposition in order to facilitate subsequent processing steps. In FY 03, AMAT introduced the Applied Reflexion LK system for polishing delicate copper/low-k interconnects, a process that has created significant difficulties for chipmakers.

Metrology and inspection tools are used to measure critical process parameters (such as the thickness of deposited films) and find and classify defects. In this market, Applied offers critical dimension and defect review scanning electron microscopes (CD-SEMs and DR-SEMs) and wafer inspection tools.

Through its AKT subsidiary, Applied offers deposition tools and array test systems for flat panel displays. In FY 03, the company introduced its sixth-generation PECVD system (for deposition), the AKT-25K, which addresses demand for large flat panels greater than one square meter.

Sales by geographic region in FY 03 were North America 29%, Japan 26%, Europe 15%, Taiwan 15%, Asia-Pacific 9%, and Korea 6%. Intel Corp. accounted for 13% and Samsung America for 12% of AMAT's sales in FY 03.

Company Financials Fiscal Year ending October 31

Per Share Data ($)

(Year Ended October 31)	2003	2002	2001	2000	1999	1998	1997	1996	1995	1994
Tangible Bk. Val.	4.62	4.87	4.67	4.20	2.59	2.11	2.00	1.64	1.24	0.72
Cash Flow	0.14	0.39	0.69	1.41	0.63	0.38	0.48	0.51	0.39	0.20
Earnings	-0.09	0.16	0.46	1.20	0.46	0.19	0.33	0.41	0.32	0.16
S&P Core Earnings	-0.33	-0.04	0.33	NA	NA	NA	NA	NA	NA	NA
Dividends	Nil	Nil	Nil	Nil	Nil	Nil	Nil	Nil	Nil	Nil
Payout Ratio	Nil	Nil	Nil	Nil	Nil	Nil	Nil	Nil	Nil	Nil
Prices - High	25.94	27.95	29.55	57.50	32.25	11.75	13.54	5.59	7.48	3.40
- Low	11.25	10.26	13.29	17.06	10.71	5.39	4.33	2.71	2.31	2.26
P/E Ratio - High	NM	NM	65	48	70	77	41	14	23	22
- Low	NM	NM	29	14	23	35	13	7	7	14

Income Statement Analysis (Million $)

	2003	2002	2001	2000	1999	1998	1997	1996	1995	1994
Revs.	4,477	5,062	5,096	9,564	4,859	4,042	4,074	4,145	3,062	1,660
Oper. Inc.	440	683	1,272	3,149	1,257	910	1,429	1,078	777	396
Depr.	382	388	387	362	275	285	219	149	83.2	58.5
Int. Exp.	93.8	49.4	47.6	51.4	47.1	45.3	20.7	20.7	21.4	16.0
Pretax Inc.	-212	341	1,104	2,948	1,056	438	799	922	699	331
Eff. Tax Rate	NM	21.0%	29.8%	30.0%	31.3%	34.0%	37.6%	35.0%	35.0%	35.4%
Net Inc.	-149	269	775	2,064	726	289	498	600	454	214
S&P Core Earnings	-562	-65.2	558	NA	NA	NA	NA	NA	NA	NA

Balance Sheet & Other Fin. Data (Million $)

	2003	2002	2001	2000	1999	1998	1997	1996	1995	1994
Cash	1,365	1,285	1,356	1,648	823	575	448	404	769	422
Curr. Assets	8,371	8,073	7,782	8,839	5,060	3,519	3,770	2,693	2,312	1,231
Total Assets	10,312	10,225	9,829	10,546	6,707	4,930	5,071	3,638	2,965	1,703
Curr. Liab.	1,641	1,501	1,533	2,760	1,669	1,118	1,402	935	862	496
LT Debt	456	574	565	573	584	617	623	275	280	209
Common Equity	8,068	8,020	7,607	7,104	4,337	3,121	2,942	2,370	1,784	966
Total Cap.	8,524	8,594	8,172	7,677	4,954	3,749	3,613	2,658	2,075	1,187
Cap. Exp.	265	383	711	383	204	449	339	453	266	186
Cash Flow	233	657	1,162	2,426	1,001	573	718	748	547	272
Curr. Ratio	5.1	5.4	5.1	3.2	3.0	3.1	2.7	2.9	2.7	2.5
% LT Debt of Cap.	5.4	6.7	6.9	7.5	11.8	16.4	17.3	10.3	13.5	17.6
% Net Inc.of Revs.	NM	5.3	15.2	21.6	14.9	7.1	12.2	14.4	14.8	12.9
% Ret. on Assets	NM	2.7	7.6	23.5	12.5	5.8	11.4	18.1	19.5	14.9
% Ret. on Equity	NM	3.4	10.5	35.3	19.5	9.5	18.8	28.9	33.0	26.8

Data as orig reptd.; bef. results of disc opers/spec. items. Per share data adj. for stk. divs.; EPS diluted. E-Estimated. NA-Not Available. NM-Not Meaningful. NR-Not Ranked. UR-Under Review.

Office: 3050 Bowers Avenue, Santa Clara, CA 95054, United States.
Telephone: 408-727-5555.
Email: investor_relations@appliedmaterials.com
Website: http://www.appliedmaterials.com
Chrmn & CEO: J.C. Morgan.
Pres & CEO: M. Splinter.

EVP & CFO: N.H. Handel.
VP & Treas: G. Davis.
Dirs: M. H. Armacost, D. A. Coleman, H. M. Dwight, Jr., P. V. Gerdine, P. R. Low, D. Maydan, S. L. Miller, J. C. Morgan, G. Parker, W. P. Roelandts, S. Shih, M. R. Splinter.

Founded: in 1967.
Domicile: Delaware.
Employees: 12,050.
S&P Analyst: Colin McArdle/CB/GG

Applied Micro Circuits

Recommendation: **HOLD** ★ ★ ★ ★ ★
SELL SELL HOLD BUY BUY

12-Month Target Price: $4.00
(as of September 22, 2004)

AMCC has an approximate 0.01% weighting in the **S&P 500**

Sector: Information Technology
Sub-Industry: Semiconductors
Peer Group: Semiconductors Communications IC

Summary: Applied Micro Circuits designs, develops, manufactures and markets semiconductors for the communications market.

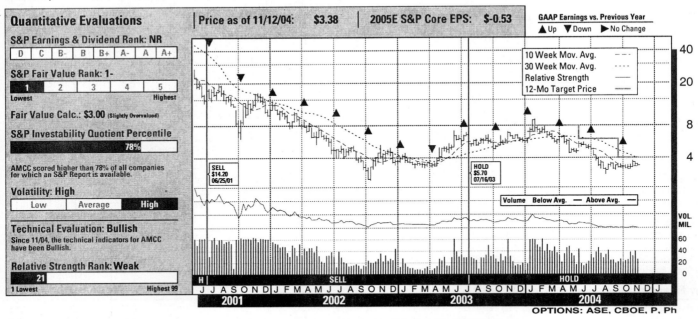

| Quantitative Evaluations | Price as of 11/12/04: $3.38 | 2005E S&P Core EPS: $-0.53 |

S&P Earnings & Dividend Rank: NR
D | C | B- | B | B+ | A- | A | A+

S&P Fair Value Rank: 1-
1 | 2 | 3 | 4 | 5
Lowest — Highest

Fair Value Calc.: $3.00 (Slightly Overvalued)

S&P Investability Quotient Percentile
78%

AMCC scored higher than 78% of all companies for which an S&P Report is available.

Volatility: High
Low | Average | **High**

Technical Evaluation: Bullish
Since 11/04, the technical indicators for AMCC have been Bullish.

Relative Strength Rank: Weak
21
1 Lowest — Highest 99

GAAP Earnings vs. Previous Year
▲ Up ▼ Down ▶ No Change

10 Week Mov. Avg.
30 Week Mov. Avg.
Relative Strength
12-Mo Target Price

Volume Below Avg. — Above Avg.

OPTIONS: ASE, CBOE, P, Ph

Analyst commentary prepared by Zaineb Bokhari/PMW/BK

Highlights November 05, 2004

- We expect revenues to nearly double in FY 05 (Mar.), to $252 million, reflecting acquisitions, a flat third quarter sequentially, and modestly higher revenues in the fourth quarter. We expect continued softness in Asian markets through the remainder of calendar 2004, with a modest uptick thereafter. We expect key OEM customers to continue to work through excess inventory, as we see the market environment remaining challenging through the remainder of FY 05.

- The markets that the company serves continue to show low visibility. For AMCC, we see this compounded by acquisitions, and, as a result, a shifting mix of new products and entry into newer markets. We expect the company to continue to focus on realizing cost synergies from its acquisitions. We expect gross margins to widen to 61.8% in FY 05, from 60.5% in FY 04. We project an operating loss in FY 05, although smaller than in FY 04.

- Overall, we project a pro forma loss per share of $0.03 for FY 05, versus a pro forma loss of $0.08 in FY 04. We see S&P Core Earnings as a loss of $0.53 a share. The difference, due to estimated stock option expense, indicates to us below-average earnings quality.

Investment Rationale/Risk November 05, 2004

- We see the company as a well positioned supplier of integrated circuits, particularly to the communications segment. However, we would not add to positions until visibility improves. The stock traded recently at about 1.2X tangible book value, its average annual low for the past decade. AMCC has little long term debt, and holds about $860 million in cash and short-term investments. We therefore view it as a likely survivor and consolidator through hard times for its industry.

- Risks to our recommendation and target price include fierce competition from larger competitors, acquisition integration risks, and ongoing pricing pressures that are common among technology companies in general and semiconductor manufacturers in particular.

- Our 12-month price target of $4 is derived by applying a peer group P/E multiple of 20X to our FY 06 EPS projection of $0.20. The multiple is within the stock's historical range. At nearly 6X trailing 12-month sales per share, the shares are at the high end of the range for chipmakers.

Key Stock Statistics

S&P Oper. EPS 2005E	-0.03	52-week Range	$9.20-2.79
P/E on S&P Oper. EPS 2005E	NM	12 Month P/E	NM
S&P Oper. EPS 2006E	0.20	Beta	NA
Yield (%)	Nil	Shareholders	795
Dividend Rate/Share	Nil	Market Cap (B)	$ 1.0
Shares Outstanding (M)	308.1		

Value of $10,000 invested five years ago: **$ 1,784**

Dividend Data

No cash dividends have been paid.

Revenues/Earnings Data Fiscal year ending March 31

Revenues (Million $)

	2005	2004	2003	2002	2001	2000
1Q	67.40	20.52	30.16	41.21	74.19	31.64
2Q	61.07	25.12	30.22	41.30	97.01	37.90
3Q	—	38.19	21.11	40.22	143.3	45.76
4Q	—	47.35	20.10	30.11	121.1	57.05
Yr.	—	131.2	101.6	152.8	435.5	172.3

Earnings Per Share ($)

	2005	2004	2003	2002	2001	2000
1Q	-0.07	-0.18	-1.01	-11.18	0.02	0.03
2Q	-0.06	-0.08	-0.24	-0.32	0.13	0.04
3Q	E-0.01	-0.09	-0.13	-0.27	-0.95	0.05
4Q	E-0.01	-0.01	-0.76	-0.30	-0.65	0.08
Yr.	E-0.03	-0.34	-2.14	-12.08	-1.63	0.21

Next earnings report expected: late-January Source: S&P, Company Reports
EPS Estimates based on S&P Operating Earnings; historical GAAP earnings are as reported.

Applied Micro Circuits Corporation

Recommendation: **HOLD** ★★★☆☆   12-Month Target Price: **$4.00** (as of September 22, 2004)

Business Summary November 05, 2004

Applied Micro Circuits aims to be to be the leading supplier of technology products for the transport, switching, routing and storage of information worldwide. The company's strategy includes a focus on the key OEM product families in the communications and storage markets, the acquisition of complementary businesses, products or technologies, increasing the number of products it provides to address specific protocols and networking functions, increasing its market share in Non-Solaris storage environments, and providing a time-to-market and development cost advantage its communications equipment OEM customers

AMCC aims to blend its systems and software expertise with high-performance, high-bandwidth silicon integration to deliver communications ICs and software for global communication networks, fibre channel HBAs (host bus adapters) for SANs (storage area networks) and hardware and software solutions for high-growth storage markets. The company believes that by understanding the systems into which its products are designed, its is better able to anticipate and develop solutions optimized for the various cost, power and performance trade-offs faced by its customers and develop more comprehensive, interoperable solutions.

Rapid growth of the Internet and wireless communications and the emergence of new applications, such as wireless web devices, the increase in demand for high speed, higher bandwidth and remote network access have increased network bandwidth requirements. The increase in volume and complexity of this network traffic has led to the development of new technologies for use in these networks, such as SONET/SDH and dense wavelength division multiplexing (DWDM) systems. AMCC's semiconductor products are used in a wide variety of communications equipment, including routers, optical and digital cross connects, next-generation voice and media gateways, add/drop multiplexers (ADMs), and digital subscriber line access multiplexers (DSLAMs) and wireless base stations and access points.

The communications segment accounted for 79% of FY 04 (Mar.) revenues, up from 65% in FY 03. Storage, a new business for the company, accounted for 10% of FY 04 revenue. Other non-communication segments accounted for 11% of FY 04 revenue. Non-communications chip products are geared toward the automatic test equipment, high-speed computing, and military markets.

AMCC's largest end-use customers are Sanmina - SCI (11% of FY 04; less than 10% in FY 03) and Insight Electronics (14%, less than 10%). By geography, North America accounted for 46% of FY 04 sales, up from 35% of FY 03 sales.

The company made a transition to a fabless production model in FY 03, after closing its San Diego, CA, wafer fabrication plant. AMCC expects a fabless strategy to let it focus fully on its competitive strengths in design technique, while avoiding the costs of direct fab ownership.

AMCC has continued to make a large commitment to research and development of new products, in an attempt to maintain technological leadership. In FY 04, the R&D budget was equal to 86% of net revenue down from 130% in FY 03 and 101% in FY 02.

Company Financials Fiscal Year ending March 31

Per Share Data ($)

(Year Ended March 31)	2004	2003	2002	2001	2000	1999	1998	1997	1996	1995
Tangible Bk. Val.	2.83	3.61	3.93	4.10	4.16	0.57	0.51	0.05	NA	NA
Cash Flow	-0.24	-2.03	-10.98	-1.57	0.24	0.11	0.13	0.29	NA	NA
Earnings	-0.34	-2.14	-12.08	-1.63	0.21	0.08	0.09	NA	NA	NA
S&P Core Earnings	-1.42	-1.84	-5.84	-2.55	NA	NA	NA	NA	NA	NA
Dividends	Nil	Nil	Nil	Nil	Nil	Nil	Nil	NA	NA	NA
Payout Ratio	Nil	Nil	Nil	Nil	Nil	Nil	Nil	NA	NA	NA

Cal. Yrs.	2003	2002	2001	2000	1999	1998	1997	1996	1995	1994
Prices - High	7.18	13.68	88.25	109.75	32.09	5.07	1.68	NA	NA	NA
- Low	3.20	2.45	6.01	25.26	4.11	1.53	1.03	NA	NA	NA
P/E Ratio - High	NM	NM	NM	NM	NM	66	18	NA	NA	NA
- Low	NM	NM	NM	NM	NM	20	11	NA	NA	NA

Income Statement Analysis (Million $)

	2004	2003	2002	2001	2000	1999	1998	1997	1996	1995
Revs.	131	102	153	436	172	105	76.6	57.5	NA	NA
Oper. Inc.	-75.4	-249	-278	-275	69.2	33.3	19.9	12.2	NA	NA
Depr.	30.5	31.8	328	16.1	8.04	7.04	5.17	5.18	NA	NA
Int. Exp.	Nil	Nil	Nil	Nil	Nil	Nil	Nil	0.03	NA	NA
Pretax Inc.	-107	-643	-3,687	-437	74.0	27.4	15.6	6.97	NA	NA
Eff. Tax Rate	NM	NM	NM	NM	34.3%	37.4%	2.60%	9.45%	NA	NA
Net Inc.	-105	-643	-3,606	-436	48.6	17.1	15.2	6.32	NA	NA
S&P Core Earnings	-435	-554	-1,743	-682	NA	NA	NA	NA	NA	NA

Balance Sheet & Other Fin. Data (Million $)

	2004	2003	2002	2001	2000	1999	1998	1997	1996	1995
Cash	861	151	336	58.2	170	13.5	6.46	5.49	NA	NA
Curr. Assets	909	1,074	1,117	1,301	1,005	125	94.5	30.2	NA	NA
Total Assets	1,188	1,225	1,829	5,453	1,047	151	113	41.8	NA	NA
Curr. Liab.	67.6	52.4	56.8	92.9	27.8	21.4	17.1	10.9	NA	NA
LT Debt	Nil	Nil	1.15	1.05	5.29	7.56	4.09	NA	NA	NA
Common Equity	1,121	1,172	1,771	5,238	1,014	122	91.6	27.7	NA	NA
Total Cap.	1,121	1,172	1,772	5,359	1,019	129	95.7	NA	NA	NA
Cap. Exp.	13.4	4.91	31.3	78.2	22.8	16.5	11.3	NA	NA	NA
Cash Flow	-74.4	-612	-3,278	-420	56.7	24.2	20.4	11.5	NA	NA
Curr. Ratio	13.5	20.5	19.7	14.0	36.2	5.8	5.5	2.8	NA	NA
% LT Debt of Cap.	Nil	Nil	0.1	0.0	0.5	5.8	4.3	NA	NA	NA
% Net Inc.of Revs.	NM	NM	NM	NM	28.2	16.3	19.9	11.0	NA	NA
% Ret. on Assets	NM	NM	NM	NM	8.1	13.0	19.7	NA	NA	NA
% Ret. on Equity	NM	NM	NM	NM	8.6	16.1	25.5	NA	NA	NA

Data as orig reptd.; bef. results of disc opers/spec. items. Per share data adj. for stk. divs.; EPS diluted. E-Estimated. NA-Not Available. NM-Not Meaningful. NR-Not Ranked. UR-Under Review.

Office: 6290 Sequence Drive, San Diego, CA 92121-4358.
Telephone: 858-450-9333.
Email: ir@amcc.com
Website: http://www.amcc.com
Chrmn, Pres & CEO: D.M. Rickey.
Vice Chrmn: R.A. Smullen, Sr.

COO: T.L. Tullie.
SVP, CFO & Secy: S.M. Smith.
Investor Contact: T. Hume .
Dirs: C. Cesaratto, F. P. Johnson, Jr., K. N. Kalkhoven, L. W. Price, D. M. Rickey, R. A. Smullen, Sr., D. C. Spreng, A. B. Stabenow, H. P. White.

Founded: in 1979.
Domicile: Delaware.
Employees: 723.
S&P Analyst: Zaineb Bokhari/PMW/BK

Archer-Daniels-Midland

Recommendation: **HOLD** ★★★☆ 12-Month Target Price: **$21.00**
SELL · SELL · HOLD · BUY · BUY
(as of October 29, 2004)

ADM has an approximate 0.12% weighting in the **S&P 500**

Sector: Consumer Staples
Sub-Industry: Agricultural Products
Peer Group: Agricultural Products

Summary: This company is a major processor and merchandiser of agricultural commodities, including oilseeds, corn and wheat.

Quantitative Evaluations

Price as of 11/12/04:	$20.54	2005E S&P Core EPS:	$1.14

S&P Earnings & Dividend Rank: B+

| D | C | B- | B | **B+** | A- | A | A+ |

S&P Fair Value Rank: 4-

| 1 | 2 | 3 | **4** | 5 |
| Lowest | | | | Highest |

Fair Value Calc.: $20.10 (Slightly Overvalued)

S&P Investability Quotient Percentile

96%

ADM scored higher than 96% of all companies for which an S&P Report is available.

Volatility: Average

| Low | **Average** | High |

Technical Evaluation: Bullish
Since 10/04, the technical indicators for ADM have been Bullish.

Relative Strength Rank: Strong

| **90** | |
| 1 Lowest | Highest 99 |

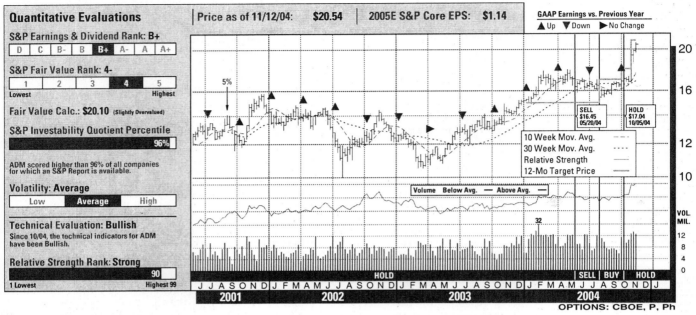

GAAP Earnings vs. Previous Year
▲ Up ▼ Down ► No Change

10 Week Mov. Avg.
30 Week Mov. Avg.
Relative Strength
12-Mo Target Price

Volume Below Avg. — Above Avg.

SELL $16.45 05/20/04   HOLD $17.04 10/05/04

HOLD   SELL | BUY   HOLD
J J A S O N D | J F M A M J J A S O N D | J F M A M J J A S O N D | J F M A M J J A S O N D J
2001   2002   2003   2004

OPTIONS: CBOE, P, Ph

Analyst commentary prepared by Joseph Agnese/MF/JWP

Highlights October 05, 2004

- We expect revenues to increase in the mid- to upper single digits in FY 05 (Jun.), on higher prices due to increased volumes, reflecting continued strong improvement in worldwide demand. We believe corn processing margins will widen, as increased demand for ethanol and high fructose corn syrup offsets higher net corn costs due to low commodity supply levels. Ethanol results should benefit as additional states switch to ethanol as an additive in gasoline, and from increased price support due to higher crude oil prices.

- We expect soybean crush margins to narrow as international oilseed markets rebound from adverse trading conditions. Oilseed margins narrowed in the FY 04 fourth quarter as Chinese defaults on oilseed contracts resulted in the sale of end-products at reduced prices. However, we expect more favorable market conditions in FY 05, reflecting a more favorable supply environment in the U.S. due to increased oilseed production levels in the U.S.

- On an improved mix of supply and demand for ADM's products, we estimate FY 05 operating EPS of $1.25, up 7.8% from $1.16 in FY 04.

Investment Rationale/Risk October 05, 2004

- We recently downgraded the shares to hold, from accumulate, based on valuation. We view recent adverse market conditions as a near term issue, and look for improving environmental conditions in FY 05. We expect a more favorable supply environment in FY 05 based on recent USDA estimates of increased corn and soybean production levels in the U.S. Additionally, we expect end-product demand to remain strong, as ADM sees increased production levels and lower prices resulting in increased demand.

- Risks to our recommendation and target price include the possibility for losses resulting from fluctuations in worldwide commodity supply and demand levels. The company tries to mitigate commodity risks through the use of hedging contracts, which may result in gains or losses.

- We believe the shares will trade in line with their historical P/E average, based on our expectation for an improving commodity environment in FY 05. As such, our 12-month target price is $18, based on 14X our FY 05 EPS estimate of $1.25 and an estimated long-term growth rate of 12%.

Key Stock Statistics

S&P Core EPS 2006E	1.40	52-week Range	$20.73-14.05
S&P Oper. EPS 2005E	1.65	12 Month P/E	21.9
P/E on S&P Oper. EPS 2005E	12.4	Beta	0.37
S&P Oper. EPS 2006E	1.65	Shareholders	24,394
Yield (%)	1.5%	Market Cap (B)	$ 13.4
Dividend Rate/Share	0.30	Shares Outstanding (M)	654.5

Value of $10,000 invested five years ago: **$ 20,330**

Dividend Data Dividends have been paid since 1927

Amount ($)	Date Decl.	Ex-Div. Date	Stock of Record	Payment Date
0.075	Feb. 05	Feb. 11	Feb. 13	Mar. 09 '04
0.075	May. 07	May. 14	May. 18	Jun. 10 '04
0.075	Aug. 05	Aug. 18	Aug. 20	Sep. 10 '04
0.075	Nov. 04	Nov. 17	Nov. 19	Dec. 10 '04

Revenues/Earnings Data Fiscal year ending June 30

Revenues (Million $)

	2005	2004	2003	2002	2001	2000
1Q	8,972	7,968	6,944	5,504	4,635	3,221
2Q	—	9,189	7,807	5,554	4,941	3,420
3Q	—	9,309	7,909	5,326	5,130	3,112
4Q	—	9,686	8,048	7,069	5,345	3,124
Yr.	—	36,151	30,708	23,454	20,051	12,877

Earnings Per Share ($)

	2005	2004	2003	2002	2001	2000
1Q	0.41	0.23	0.17	0.20	0.16	0.05
2Q	E0.45	0.34	0.20	0.23	0.19	0.15
3Q	E0.44	0.35	0.18	0.18	0.14	0.15
4Q	E0.35	-0.16	0.15	0.17	0.09	0.09
Yr.	E1.65	0.76	0.70	0.78	0.58	0.46

Next earnings report expected: late-January Source: S&P, Company Reports
EPS Estimates based on S&P Operating Earnings; historical GAAP earnings are as reported.

Archer-Daniels-Midland Company

Recommendation: **HOLD** ★ ★ ★ ☆ ☆   12-Month Target Price: **$21.00** (as of October 29, 2004)

Business Summary October 05, 2004

Archer-Daniels-Midland (ADM) calls itself "supermarket to the world." Within a network of more than 270 domestic and internationally based plants, cereal grains and oilseeds are processed into a multitude of products used in food, beverage, nutraceutical, industrial and animal feed markets worldwide.

Most of the company's business involves converting raw soybeans, corn and wheat into further-processed ingredients for the food manufacturing industry in the U.S. and abroad. In FY 04 (Jun.), oilseeds processing contributed 33% of revenues (32% in FY 03); corn processing 11.1% (10%); agricultural services 43% (44%); and other 12% (14%).

ADM is one of the world's largest processors of oilseeds (soybeans, cottonseed, sunflower seeds, canola, peanuts, flaxseed and corn germ), which are processed to provide vegetable oils and meals principally for the food and feed industries. Crude vegetable oil is sold to others or refined and hydrogenated to produce oils for margarine, shortening, salad oils and other food products. Oilseed meals supply more than one-half of the high protein ingredients used in the manufacture of commercial livestock and poultry feeds.

The company is the world's largest corn processor. The corn processing segment is involved in corn wet and dry milling operations. Wet milling products include

syrup, starch, glucose, dextrose, crystalline dextrose, high-fructose sweeteners, crystalline fructose, corn gluten feed and ethyl alcohol. Dry milled products include ethanol, distilled grains, meal and grits. In gasoline, ethanol increases octane and is used as an extender and oxygenate.

ADM is vertically integrated, with its agricultural services segment utilizing grain elevators and transportation networks to buy, store, clean and transport agricultural commodities such as oilseeds, corn, wheat milo, oats and barley. In addition to supplying its processing operations, these commodities are resold primarily as food or feed ingredients. Over the past five years, ADM spent $3.0 billion to construct new plants, expand existing plants and acquire plants and transportation equipment. ADM owns 80% of A.C. Toepfer International, one of the world's largest trading companies specializing in agricultural commodities and processed products.

ADM's other operations include the processing of wheat, corn and milo into flour, which is used in both food and industrial products. The company also produces a wide range of edible soy protein products and consumer and institutional health foods based on its soy products.

Company Financials Fiscal Year ending June 30

Per Share Data ($)

(Year Ended June 30)	2004	2003	2002	2001	2000	1999	1998	1997	1996	1995
Tangible Bk. Val.	11.31	10.43	10.39	9.56	9.21	9.23	9.48	9.26	9.37	8.75
Cash Flow	1.82	1.69	1.64	1.44	1.35	1.26	1.36	1.19	1.55	1.63
Earnings	0.76	0.70	0.78	0.58	0.46	0.41	0.60	0.55	0.99	1.10
S&P Core Earnings	1.14	0.61	0.55	0.58	NA	NA	NA	NA	NA	NA
Dividends	0.27	0.24	0.20	0.19	0.14	0.13	0.17	0.16	0.14	0.07
Payout Ratio	36%	34%	25%	32%	30%	32%	29%	28%	14%	7%
Prices - High	20.73	15.24	14.85	15.80	14.46	14.73	19.43	20.25	18.11	14.92
- Low	14.90	10.50	10.00	10.23	7.79	10.37	12.79	13.32	12.21	10.66
P/E Ratio - High	27	22	19	27	32	35	33	37	18	14
- Low	20	15	13	18	17	25	21	24	12	10

Income Statement Analysis (Million $)

	2004	2003	2002	2001	2000	1999	1998	1997	1996	1995
Revs.	36,151	30,708	23,454	20,051	12,877	14,283	16,146	13,853	13,314	12,672
Oper. Inc.	1,432	1,423	1,424	1,272	1,094	1,116	1,247	1,071	1,309	1,598
Depr.	686	644	567	572	604	585	527	446	394	385
Int. Exp.	Nil	Nil	356	397	377	326	293	238	213	203
Pretax Inc.	718	631	719	522	353	420	610	644	1,054	1,182
Eff. Tax Rate	31.1%	28.5%	28.9%	26.6%	14.7%	33.1%	33.8%	41.4%	34.0%	32.6%
Net Inc.	495	451	511	383	301	281	404	377	696	796
S&P Core Earnings	739	397	363	382	NA	NA	NA	NA	NA	NA

Balance Sheet & Other Fin. Data (Million $)

	2004	2003	2002	2001	2000	1999	1998	1997	1996	1995
Cash	1,412	765	844	676	477	1,461	346	728	1,355	1,119
Curr. Assets	10,339	8,422	7,363	6,150	6,162	5,790	5,452	4,284	4,385	3,713
Total Assets	19,369	17,183	15,416	14,340	14,423	14,030	13,834	11,354	10,450	9,757
Curr. Liab.	6,750	5,147	4,719	3,867	4,333	3,840	3,717	2,249	1,634	1,172
LT Debt	3,740	3,872	3,111	3,351	3,277	3,192	2,847	2,345	2,003	2,070
Common Equity	7,698	7,069	6,755	6,332	6,110	6,241	6,505	6,050	6,145	5,854
Total Cap.	12,092	11,485	10,498	10,327	9,948	10,053	9,985	8,993	8,710	8,463
Cap. Exp.	509	420	350	273	429	671	703	780	754	559
Cash Flow	1,180	1,095	1,078	955	905	866	931	823	1,090	1,181
Curr. Ratio	1.5	1.6	1.6	1.6	1.4	1.5	1.5	1.9	2.7	3.2
% LT Debt of Cap.	30.9	33.7	29.6	32.4	32.9	31.8	28.5	26.1	23.0	24.5
% Net Inc.of Revs.	1.4	1.5	2.2	1.9	2.3	2.0	2.5	2.7	5.2	6.3
% Ret. on Assets	2.7	2.8	3.4	2.7	2.1	2.0	3.2	3.5	6.9	8.7
% Ret. on Equity	6.7	6.5	7.8	6.2	4.9	4.4	6.4	6.2	11.6	14.8

Data as orig reptd.; bef. results of disc opers/spec. items. Per share data adj. for stk. divs. Bold denotes primary EPS - prior periods restated. E-Estimated. NA-Not Available. NM-Not Meaningful. NR-Not Ranked. UR-Under Review.

Office: 4666 Faries Parkway, Decatur, IL 62525.
Telephone: 217-424-5200.
Website: http://www.admworld.com
Chrmn & CEO: G.A. Andreas.
Pres & COO: P.B. Mulhollem.

EVP, Secy & General Counsel: D.J. Smith.
Investor Contact: C. Renshaw 212-424-4647.
Dirs: G. A. Andreas, M. H. Carter, R. S. Joslin, P. J. Moore, M. B. Mulroney, O. G. Webb, K. R. Westbrook.

Founded: in 1898.
Domicile: Delaware.
Employees: 26,317.
S&P Analyst: Joseph Agnese/MF/JWP

STANDARD &POOR'S

Ashland Inc.

Recommendation: **HOLD** ★★★☆☆
SELL SELL HOLD BUY BUY

12-Month Target Price: **$58.00**
(as of November 14, 2004)

Stock Report
November 17, 2004
NYSE Symbol: **ASH**

ASH has an approximate 0.04% weighting in the **S&P 500**

Sector: Energy
Sub-Industry: Oil & Gas Refining, Marketing & Transportation
Peer Group: Refining and/or Marketing

Summary: This supplier of highway construction products/services and specialty chemicals has agreed to sell its 38% interest in Marathon Ashland Petroleum LLC to Marathon Oil Corp.

Quantitative Evaluations

S&P Earnings & Dividend Rank: B

| D | C | B- | B | B+ | A- | A | A+ |

S&P Fair Value Rank: 2-

| 1 | 2 | 3 | 4 | 5 |
| Lowest | | | | Highest |

Fair Value Calc.: $54.10 (Slightly Overvalued)

S&P Investability Quotient Percentile

64%

ASH scored higher than 64% of all companies for which an S&P Report is available.

Volatility: Low

| Low | Average | High |

Technical Evaluation: Bullish
Since 9/04, the technical indicators for ASH have been Bullish.

Relative Strength Rank: Moderate

55

| 1 Lowest | Highest 99 |

| Price as of 11/15/04: | **$58.01** | 2005E S&P Core EPS: | **$4.56** |

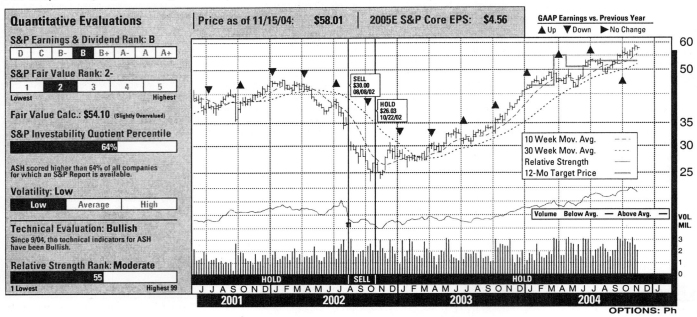

GAAP Earnings vs. Previous Year
▲ Up ▼ Down ▶ No Change

- 10 Week Mov. Avg.
- 30 Week Mov. Avg.
- Relative Strength
- 12-Mo Target Price

Volume — Below Avg. — Above Avg.

OPTIONS: Ph

Analyst commentary prepared by T. Vital/PMW/JWP

Highlights 17-NOV-04

- A strong performance by ASH's road construction and chemicals businesses boosted FY 04 (Sep.) fourth quarter operating earnings 121%, to $148 million, or $2.05 a share, $0.61 a share above our estimate. FY 04 results exclude a tax benefit of $48 million ($0.67 a share) related to prior years, a $6 million pretax gain on the sale of land ($0.05 after tax), and $5 a million pretax reversal to a job loss reserve ($0.05 after tax).
- EBITDA climbed 204% in FY 04, reflecting a strengthening U.S. economy that boosted earnings for chemicals and APAC. We project that FY 05 EBITDA will increase 25%, on continued growth in chemicals and APAC (on a backlog of $1.746 billion at September 30, 2004, versus $1.745 billion in 2003). Funding new growth, particularly in chemicals, boosted capital spending to $210 million in FY 04, from $112 million in FY 03. In November 2004, ASH agreed to purchase, subject to necessary approvals, the DERAKANE epoxy vinyl ester resin business from The Dow Chemical Co., for about $92 million.
- With the proposed transfer of the company's 38% interest in MAP to MRO for about $3 billion under way, we expect ASH to increase its presence in specialty chemicals through organic growth and acquisitions, and in APAC through development of large project design. However, we see high feedstock and utility costs continuing to put pressure on results at APAC and Chemicals.

Investment Rationale/Risk 17-NOV-04

- We see some risk with regard to a favorable IRS tax ruling on the proposed tax-free MAP deal, but we believe the transaction will likely go through. Subject to necessary approvals (the FTC approved the deal on June 2), closing is expected by April 2005. We estimate that about $300 million in earnings contributions will be removed, but this would be offset by a cash position of about $1.3 billion, and a debt-free capital structure (asbestos and pension obligations would remain). If the deal proceeds, ASH expects to focus spending on organic growth and small- to mid-sized acquisitions. However, this spending may take time, and the large cash position expected from the MAP transaction could make ASH a takeover target.
- Risks to our recommendation and target price include risk associated with the proposed transfer of ASH's interest in MAP to MRO, and the company's exposure to asbestos-related claims. As of the FY 04 fourth quarter, ASH had 195,600 open asbestos-related claims, down 3,500 sequentially. As of FY 03, the reserve for asbestos claims was $610 million, versus an insurance receivable of $429 million.
- A blend of our DCF, market and peer multiples valuations leads to our 12-month target price of $58, equal to 18X our FY 05 EPS estimate, a premium to peers. We would hold the shares.

Key Stock Statistics

S&P Oper. EPS 2005E	3.19	52-week Range	**$59.19-38.16**
P/E on S&P Oper. EPS 2005E	18.1	12 Month P/E	10.7
Yield (%)	1.9%	Beta	0.65
Dividend Rate/Share	1.10	Shareholders	16,800
Shares Outstanding (M)	71.1	Market Cap (B)	$ 4.1

Value of $10,000 invested five years ago: **NA**

Dividend Data Dividends have been paid since 1936

Amount ($)	Date Decl.	Ex-Div. Date	Stock of Record	Payment Date
0.275	Jan. 28	Feb. 19	Feb. 23	Mar. 15 '04
0.275	May. 20	May. 26	May. 28	Jun. 15 '04
0.275	Jul. 14	Aug. 19	Aug. 23	Sep. 15 '04
0.275	Nov. 04	Nov. 18	Nov. 22	Dec. 15 '04

Revenues/Earnings Data Fiscal year ending September 30

Revenues (Million $)

	2004	2003	2002	2001	2000	1999
1Q	1,974	1,846	1,812	1,878	1,897	1,646
2Q	1,812	1,736	1,598	1,659	1,822	1,503
3Q	2,425	2,125	2,047	1,567	2,103	1,796
4Q	2,334	2,130	2,086	2,129	2,140	1,856
Yr.	8,301	7,865	7,543	7,719	7,961	6,801

Earnings Per Share ($)

	2004	2003	2002	2001	2000	1999
1Q	0.56	0.04	0.55	0.84	-2.32	-0.14
2Q	-0.16	-0.50	-0.31	0.37	0.19	1.16
3Q	2.35	1.03	0.93	0.53	1.83	1.35
4Q	2.81	0.89	0.68	1.77	1.38	1.57
Yr.	5.59	1.37	1.83	5.77	4.10	3.89

Next earnings report expected: late-January Source: S&P, Company Reports
EPS Estimates based on S&P Operating Earnings; historical GAAP earnings are as reported.

Please read the Required Disclosures and Reg. AC certification on the last page of this report.

Redistribution or reproduction is prohibited without written permission. Copyright © 2004 The McGraw-Hill Companies, Inc.

The McGraw·Hill Companies

Recommendation: **HOLD** ★ ★ ★ ☆ ☆   12-Month Target Price: **$58.00** (as of November 14, 2004)

Business Summary 17-NOV-04

In March 2004, Ashland agreed to transfer its 38% interest in Marathon Ashland Petroleum (MAP) and two other businesses to Marathon Oil Corp. in a deal valued at nearly $3 billion in cash and stock. The other businesses are ASH's maleic anhydride operations, and 61 Valvoline Instant Oil Change (VIOC) centers in Michigan and northwestern Ohio, valued at about $94 million. Subject to necessary approvals, completion is expected by April 2005.

The APAC group of companies (32% of FY 03 (Sep.) revenues; an operating loss of $42 million) is the largest U.S. asphalt and concrete paving company. It performs contract construction work and services, including highway paving, resurfacing and repair, as well as excavation, grading and bridge construction. The segment conducts business through 24 units that operate in 14 southern and midwestern states. About 77% of APAC's FY 03 revenues were from construction, and 23% from materials. About 84% of APAC's FY 03 construction revenues were derived from highway and public sector sources, with 16% from industrial and commercial customers. Construction backlog at September 30, 2003, was $1,745 million, up from $1,691 million a year earlier.

Through Ashland Distribution (37%; $32 million), the company distributes chemicals, plastics, reinforcements and resins, and fine ingredients in North America, and plastics in Europe. Ashland Distribution specializes in providing mixed truckloads and less-than-truckload quantities to customers in a wide range of industries. Deliveries are performed through a network of owned or leased facilities, including about 120 locations in North America. Distribution of thermoplastic resins in Europe is conducted through 17 third-party warehouses in 13 foreign countries.

Ashland Specialty Chemical (15%; $31 million) focuses on two primary chemistries: thermoset and water. Ashland Specialty Chemical makes specialty chemicals for the automotive, building and construction, foundry, marine, paint, paper, ink and flexible packaging industries. The division owns and operates 38 manufacturing facilities, and participates in 12 manufacturing joint ventures in 20 countries. In August 2003, ASH sold its electronic chemicals business, for about $300 million.

With sales in more than 120 countries, Valvoline (16%; $87 million) markets premium-branded automotive and commercial oils, automotive chemicals, automotive appearance products, and automotive services. At September 30, 2003, it also operated a fast oil change business (VIOC) through 357 company-owned and 372 franchised service centers, in 38 states.

The company's crude oil refining and marketing business (NA; $263 million) is conducted through Marathon Ashland Petroleum LLC (MAP), a 38%-owned joint venture with Marathon Oil Co. MAP operates seven refineries with a capacity of 935,000 barrels per day (bpd). At September 30, 2003, 66% of MAP's production of lubricating oils had been purchased by Valvoline, and 41% of its production of petrochemicals (excluding polypropylene) by Ashland Distribution. Retail sales of gasoline and diesel fuel are made primarily through MAP's 1,791 retail outlets in nine midwestern states, operating under the Speedway and SuperAmerica names. In addition, MAP supplies 3,850 independent dealer locations, using the Marathon and Ashland names.

Company Financials Fiscal Year ending September 30

Per Share Data ($)

(Year Ended September 30)	2004	2003	2002	2001	2000	1999	1998	1997	1996	1995
Tangible Bk. Val.	NA	25.44	24.29	24.61	20.40	27.50	25.40	25.39	21.89	19.50
Cash Flow	NA	4.32	4.99	9.37	7.45	6.91	4.99	10.63	9.14	7.94
Earnings	5.59	1.37	1.83	5.77	4.10	3.89	2.63	2.51	2.97	0.08
S&P Core Earnings	NA	1.73	1.45	5.25	NA	NA	NA	NA	NA	NA
Dividends	1.10	1.10	1.10	1.10	1.10	1.10	1.10	1.10	1.10	1.10
Payout Ratio	20%	80%	60%	19%	27%	28%	42%	44%	37%	NM
Prices - High	59.19	44.55	46.98	46.54	37.18	50.62	57.93	54.87	48.87	38.37
- Low	43.73	25.91	23.60	34.39	28.62	30.31	42.25	39.25	34.25	30.37
P/E Ratio - High	11	33	26	8	9	13	22	22	16	NM
- Low	8	19	13	6	7	8	16	16	12	NM

Income Statement Analysis (Million $)

	2004	2003	2002	2001	2000	1999	1998	1997	1996	1995
Revs.	NA	7,518	7,543	7,719	7,961	6,801	6,534	14,200	13,130	12,167
Oper. Inc.	NA	123	309	273	433	400	229	943	703	613
Depr. Depl. & Amort.	NA	204	220	250	237	228	181	572	402	487
Int. Exp.	NA	128	138	170	188	140	130	170	169	171
Pretax Inc.	NA	138	58.0	681	483	482	317	335	311	34.0
Eff. Tax Rate	NA	31.9%	NM	40.4%	39.5%	39.8%	36.0%	35.5%	29.6%	Nil
Net Inc.	NA	94.0	129	406	292	290	203	192	211	24.0
S&P Core Earnings	NA	120	103	371	NA	NA	NA	NA	NA	NA

Balance Sheet & Other Fin. Data (Million $)

	2004	2003	2002	2001	2000	1999	1998	1997	1996	1995
Cash	NA	223	90.0	236	67.0	110	34.0	268	77.0	52.0
Curr. Assets	NA	2,085	1,925	2,213	2,131	2,059	1,828	2,995	2,740	2,575
Total Assets	NA	7,006	6,725	6,945	6,771	6,424	6,082	7,777	7,269	6,992
Curr. Liab.	NA	1,484	1,511	1,497	1,699	1,396	1,361	2,261	2,279	2,094
LT Debt	NA	1,512	1,606	1,786	1,899	1,927	1,507	1,639	1,784	1,828
Common Equity	NA	2,253	2,339	2,399	1,965	2,200	2,137	2,024	1,527	1,362
Total Cap.	NA	4,056	4,201	4,625	4,152	4,353	3,644	3,936	3,836	3,239
Cap. Exp.	NA	110	185	205	232	248	274	431	510	444
Cash Flow	NA	298	349	656	529	518	384	755	594	492
Curr. Ratio	NA	1.4	1.3	1.5	1.3	1.5	1.3	1.3	1.2	1.2
% LT Debt of Cap.	NA	37.3	38.2	38.6	45.7	44.3	41.4	41.6	46.5	56.4
% Ret. on Assets	NA	1.4	1.9	5.9	4.4	4.6	2.9	2.6	3.0	0.4
% Ret. on Equity	NA	4.2	5.4	17.9	14.0	13.4	9.8	10.3	13.4	0.4

Data as orig. reptd.; bef. results of disc. opers. and/or spec. items. Per share data adj. for stk. divs. as of ex-div. date. Revs in Inc. Statement tbl. incl. excise taxes; revs. in quarterly table may incl. oth. inc. Bold denotes basic EPS (FASB 128). E-Estimated. NA-Not Available. NM-Not Meaningful. NR-Not Ranked.

Office: 50 East RiverCenter Boulevard, Covington, KY 41012-0391.
Telephone: 859-815-3333.
Email: investor_relations@ashland.com
Website: http://www.ashland.com
Chrmn & CEO: J. J. O'Brien.
SVP: G. M. Higdem.

SVP & CFO: J. M. Quin.
Investor Contact: William E. Henderson III (859-815-4454).
Dirs: E. H. Drew, R. W. Hale, B. P. Healy, M. L. Jackson, K. Ligocki, P. F. Noonan, J. J. O'Brien, J. C. Pfeiffer, W. L. Rouse, Jr., G. A. Schaefer, Jr., T. M. Solso, M. J. Ward.

Founded: in 1918.
Domicile: Kentucky.
Employees: 22,500.
S&P Analyst: T. Vital/PMW/JWP

Recommendation: **HOLD** ★★★☆☆
SELL | SELL | HOLD | BUY | BUY

12-Month Target Price: **$16.00**
(as of June 29, 2004)

T has an approximate 0.13% weighting in the **S&P 500**

Sector: Telecommunication Services
Sub-Industry: Integrated Telecommunication Services
Peer Group: Telecommunications (Long Distance)

Summary: AT&T, the largest U.S. long-distance provider, is beginning to focus on business customers over consumers.

Quantitative Evaluations

S&P Earnings & Dividend Rank: B

| D | C | B- | **B** | B+ | A- | A | A+ |

S&P Fair Value Rank: 4

| 1 | 2 | 3 | **4** | 5 |
| Lowest | | | | Highest |

Fair Value Calc.: $18.10 (Fairly Valued)

S&P Investability Quotient Percentile

72%

T scored higher than 72% of all companies for which an S&P Report is available.

Volatility: Average

| Low | **Average** | High |

Technical Evaluation: Bullish
Since 10/04, the technical indicators for **T** have been Bullish.

Relative Strength Rank: Strong

86
1 Lowest — Highest 99

Price as of 11/12/04: **$18.25** **2004E S&P Core EPS:** **$1.06**

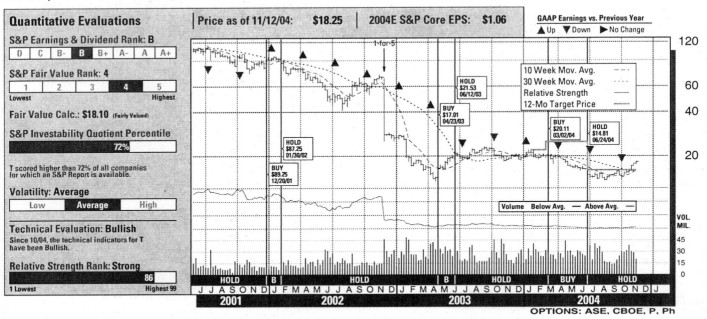

GAAP Earnings vs. Previous Year
▲ Up ▼ Down ▶ No Change

Chart legend: 10 Week Mov. Avg., 30 Week Mov. Avg., Relative Strength, 12-Mo Target Price

HOLD $87.25 01/30/02
BUY $89.25 12/20/01
BUY $17.01 04/23/03
HOLD $21.53 06/12/03
BUY $20.11 03/02/04
HOLD $14.81 06/24/04

Volume Below Avg. — Above Avg.

VOL. MIL. 45 30 15 0

HOLD | B | HOLD | B | HOLD | BUY | HOLD
J J A S O N D | J F M A M J J A S O N D | J F M A M J J A S O N D | J F M A M J J A S O N D | J F M A M J J A S O N D | J
2001 | 2002 | 2003 | 2004

OPTIONS: ASE, CBOE, P, Ph

Analyst commentary prepared by Todd Rosenbluth/PMW/GG

Highlights October 28, 2004

- We see 2005 revenues declining 10%, with an expected drop of about 22% in the Consumer unit, as the Baby Bells win back the majority of the 4.5 million local customers that T gained using access to the Bell network. In July, the company stopped marketing its local and long-distance services to consumers. We expect T to continue to serve most of its existing consumer long-distance customers. We see business revenues declining 6% in 2005, a narrower drop than the 10% revenue reduction we see for 2004, despite continued pricing pressures.

- The company expects $700 million in ongoing marketing savings and $1.2 billion in savings once its 20% workforce cuts are done. However due to lower call volumes and a decline in revenues, we see 2005 EBITDA margins narrowing to 19%, from an expected 22% in 2004. We see depreciation charges declining sharply, due to the long-distance asset writedown, and expect lower interest expense following a debt repurchase program.

- We project operating EPS of $1.86 for 2004 and $1.50 for 2005. EPS in the 2004 third quarter included one-time charges of $0.84 for restructuring and $8.86 for asset impairment. Our 2004 S&P Core EPS projection of $1.06 a share reflects estimated stock option expense and pension adjustments.

Key Stock Statistics

S&P Core EPS 2005E	0.89	52-week Range	$22.10-13.59
S&P Oper. EPS 2004E	1.86	12 Month P/E	NM
P/E on S&P Oper. EPS 2004E	9.8	Beta	0.72
S&P Oper. EPS 2005E	1.50	Shareholders	2,700,000
Yield (%)	5.2%	Market Cap (B)	$ 14.5
Dividend Rate/Share	0.95	Shares Outstanding (M)	795.9

Value of $10,000 invested five years ago: **NA**

Dividend Data Dividends have been paid since 1881

Amount ($)	Date Decl.	Ex-Div. Date	Stock of Record	Payment Date
0.238	Dec. 17	Dec. 29	Dec. 31	Feb. 02 '04
0.238	Mar. 17	Mar. 29	Mar. 31	May. 03 '04
0.238	Jun. 23	Jun. 28	Jun. 30	Aug. 02 '04
0.238	Sep. 24	Sep. 28	Sep. 30	Nov. 01 '04

Investment Rationale/Risk October 28, 2004

- We expect T's dominance in the consumer market to continue to slip, due to wireless and Baby Bell competition, but we anticipate relative strength in the enterprise market, as the company's breadth of services and network quality remain important to large businesses. We see the expected decline in revenues putting pressure on profitability in 2005, but we believe that a reduced workforce and a more limited marketing budget will help T to support and possibly to raise its dividend in the near term.

- Risks to our opinion and target price include rising wholesale rates that the company must pay to provide competitive local service, aggressive pricing competition, greater wireless substitution, and weaker demand for telecom services.

- With declining earnings prospects, we think the stock trades at a justified discount to peers, based on our P/E multiple and enterprise value to projected EBITDA analyses, in light of T's weaker margins and lack of a wireless offering. Our DCF analysis assumes a weighted average cost of capital of 7.9% and operating cash flow declines of 10% to 30% over the next four years before we see cash flow beginning to stabilize in 2008. Our calculation results in intrinsic value of nearly $17 a share. Our blended 12-month target price is $16. The dividend yield is about 5.9%.

Revenues/Earnings Data Fiscal year ending December 31

Revenues (Million $)

	2004	2003	2002	2001	2000	1999
1Q	7,990	8,986	9,548	13,551	15,836	14,096
2Q	7,636	8,795	9,580	13,326	16,221	15,691
3Q	7,638	8,649	9,409	13,087	16,975	16,270
4Q	—	8,099	9,290	12,586	16,884	16,334
Yr.	—	34,529	37,827	52,550	65,981	62,391

Earnings Per Share ($)

	2004	2003	2002	2001	2000	1999
1Q	0.38	0.67	0.63	-0.85	2.70	1.90
2Q	0.14	0.68	0.80	-0.50	2.65	2.45
3Q	-8.99	0.58	0.67	-3.45	1.75	2.50
4Q	E0.56	0.43	-0.79	-1.95	-2.25	1.80
Yr.	E1.86	2.36	1.26	-6.65	4.40	8.70

Next earnings report expected: late-January Source: S&P, Company Reports
EPS Estimates based on S&P Operating Earnings; historical GAAP earnings are as reported.

AT&T Corp.

Recommendation: **HOLD** ★ ★ ★ ☆ ☆   12-Month Target Price: **$16.00** (as of June 29, 2004)

Business Summary October 28, 2004

In October 2000, AT&T (Ma Bell) announced restructuring plans to split its Wireless, Broadband, Business and Consumer units into separately investable units. In July 2001, AT&T Wireless (AWE) was split off into a separate stock company. In August 2001, T completed the spinoff of Liberty Media Corp. (L) as an independent, publicly traded company. In December 2001, AT&T agreed to a $72 billion deal for Comcast (CMCSK), the third largest U.S. cable operator, to merge with AT&T Broadband. The sale, in which 0.3235 of a CMCSK share was exchanged for every pre-split T share, was completed in November 2002; due to a decline in stock price, it was worth an aggregate of about $60 billion. T effected a one-for-five reverse stock split following the completion of the Comcast transaction.

The AT&T Business division (72% of T's 2003 revenues) provides regular and custom voice services, data and Internet Protocol services, hosting, outsourcing and other consulting services to more than 4 million small, mid-sized, and large U.S. and multinational businesses. The segment's network comprises 54,000 route miles of long-haul backbone fiber-optic cable, plus another 19,600 route miles of local fiber cable of carrying high speed traffic. The Business division also has 18 Internet Data Centers, with a capacity of more than 1.8 million sq. ft. of web hosting space.

The Consumer unit (28%) is the largest U.S. provider of consumer long-distance services. The division offers inbound and outbound U.S. and international long-distance, transaction-based long-distance services (operator assistance and prepaid phone cards), local calling offers, and dial-up Internet service through AT&T WorldNet Service. The Consumer segment is also the leading provider of U.S. prepaid calling card services, with the majority of sales made to Wal-Mart Stores.

As of June 2004, AT&T was serving 4.7 million local customers, up from 3.1 million a year earlier, handling all areas of phone service for customers, including billing, repair and maintenance. In July the company announced it was shifting its focus away from traditional consumer services such as wireline residential telephone services, and concentrating its growth efforts going forward on business markets and emerging technologies, such as Voice over Internet Protocol (VoIP), that can serve businesses as well as consumers. As of July 2004, T had launched its residential VoIP service in 100 major markets.

In September 2003, T determined that the liability on its balance sheet pertaining to 2001 and 2002 access and other connection expenses was understated by $125 million. It recorded a $77 million after-tax charge ($0.10) in the 2003 third quarter to reflect the liability.

In the 2004 third quarter, the company recorded an asset impairment charge of $8.86 a share, to reduce the carrying value of its long-distance network. In addition, T incurred a restructuring charge of $0.84 a share to reflect ongoing headcount reductions.

Company Financials Fiscal Year ending December 31

Per Share Data ($)

(Year Ended December 31)	2003	2002	2001	2000	1999	1998	1997	1996	1995	1994
Tangible Bk. Val.	10.93	9.11	NM	13.15	47.30	29.20	26.77	22.40	15.63	26.90
Cash Flow	8.53	7.47	2.53	21.07	17.24	18.27	16.97	17.23	10.43	18.87
Earnings	2.36	1.26	-6.65	4.40	8.70	9.70	9.13	11.57	0.30	10.03
S&P Core Earnings	2.09	-0.21	-2.10	NA	NA	NA	NA	NA	NA	NA
Dividends	0.85	0.75	0.75	4.40	4.40	4.40	4.40	4.40	4.40	4.40
Payout Ratio	36%	60%	NM	100%	51%	45%	48%	38%	NM	44%
Prices - High	27.88	96.25	125.75	304.06	333.33	263.33	213.33	229.58	228.33	190.41
- Low	13.45	25.11	73.75	82.50	207.50	161.25	102.50	110.83	158.75	157.50
P/E Ratio - High	12	76	NM	69	38	27	23	20	NM	19
- Low	6	20	NM	19	24	17	11	10	NM	16

Income Statement Analysis (Million $)

	2003	2002	2001	2000	1999	1998	1997	1996	1995	1994
Revs.	34,529	37,827	52,550	65,981	62,391	53,223	51,319	52,184	79,609	75,094
Oper. Inc.	8,728	10,686	15,622	21,573	19,804	14,630	10,795	11,550	13,905	13,137
Depr.	4,870	4,888	9,338	10,267	7,439	4,629	3,827	2,740	4,845	4,136
Int. Exp.	1,158	1,448	3,242	3,183	1,651	427	191	527	859	1,520
Pretax Inc.	2,678	2,436	-8,596	3,891	6,708	8,307	7,205	8,866	935	7,582
Eff. Tax Rate	30.5%	65.1%	NM	NM	48.6%	37.0%	37.8%	36.8%	85.1%	37.0%
Net Inc.	1,863	963	-6,842	4,669	3,428	5,235	4,472	5,608	139	4,710
S&P Core Earnings	1,642	-169	-1,551	NA	NA	NA	NA	NA	NA	NA

Balance Sheet & Other Fin. Data (Million $)

	2003	2002	2001	2000	1999	1998	1997	1996	1995	1994
Cash	4,353	8,014	10,592	126	1,024	3,160	145	134	908	1,208
Curr. Assets	9,848	15,903	22,528	17,087	13,884	14,118	16,179	18,310	39,509	37,611
Total Assets	47,988	55,272	165,282	242,223	169,406	59,550	58,635	55,552	88,884	79,262
Curr. Liab.	8,883	12,024	25,427	50,867	28,207	15,442	16,942	16,318	39,372	30,930
LT Debt	13,066	18,812	45,247	37,802	27,917	5,556	6,826	7,883	11,635	11,358
Common Equity	13,956	12,312	51,680	103,198	78,927	25,522	22,647	20,295	17,274	17,921
Total Cap.	32,417	35,863	128,647	182,596	133,434	36,531	32,184	33,005	35,034	34,517
Cap. Exp.	3,157	3,878	9,300	15,524	14,306	7,817	7,143	6,339	6,411	5,304
Cash Flow	6,733	5,851	1,844	14,936	10,867	9,864	8,299	8,349	4,984	8,846
Curr. Ratio	1.1	1.3	0.9	0.3	0.5	0.9	1.0	1.1	1.0	1.2
% LT Debt of Cap.	40.3	52.5	35.2	20.7	20.9	15.2	21.2	23.9	33.2	32.9
% Net Inc.of Revs.	5.4	2.5	NM	7.1	5.5	9.8	8.7	10.8	0.2	6.3
% Ret. on Assets	3.6	0.9	NM	2.3	3.0	8.9	7.8	9.5	0.2	6.3
% Ret. on Equity	14.2	3.0	NM	5.1	6.6	21.7	20.8	29.9	0.8	27.7

Data as orig reptd.; bef. results of disc opers/spec. items. Per share data adj. for stk. divs.; EPS diluted. E-Estimated. NA-Not Available. NM-Not Meaningful. NR-Not Ranked. UR-Under Review.

Office: 1 Att Way, Bedminster, NJ 07921-2694.
Telephone: 908-221-2000.
Email: attir@att.com
Website: http://www.att.com
Chrmn & CEO: D.W. Dorman.
Pres: W.J. Hannigan.
EVP & General Counsel: J.W. Cicconi.

SVP & CFO: T.W. Horton.
VP & Treas: E.M. Dwyer.
Investor Contact: C. Jones 202-457-3933.
Dirs: W. F. Aldinger, K. T. Derr, D. W. Dorman, M. K. Eickhoff, H. L. Henkel, F. C. Herringer, S. A. Jackson, J. C. Madonna, D. F. McHenry, T. L. White.

Founded: in 1885.
Domicile: New York.
Employees: 61,600.
S&P Analyst: Todd Rosenbluth/PMW/GG

Autodesk, Inc.

Recommendation: **SELL** ★ ☆ ☆ ☆ ☆
SELL | SELL | HOLD | BUY | BUY

12-Month Target Price: **$45.00**
(as of August 25, 2004)

ADSK has an approximate 0.06% weighting in the **S&P 500**

Sector: Information Technology
Sub-Industry: Application Software
Peer Group: Computer Aided Designing

Summary: Autodesk develops, markets and supports computer-aided design and drafting (CAD) software, including its flagship AutoCAD program, for use on desktop computers and workstations.

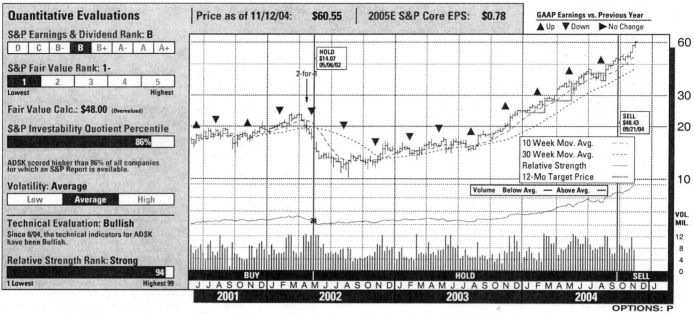

Analyst commentary prepared by Jonathan Rudy, CFA /CB/GG

Highlights September 22, 2004

- We expect revenues to advance about 25% in FY 05 (Jan.), following a 15% increase in FY 04. We believe that revenues are benefiting from an improving global economy, and from a product upgrade cycle for AutoCAD. We anticipate significantly higher AutoCAD sales in FY 05, due to the March 2004 release of AutoCAD 2005.

- We think the company will benefit from diversifying its product line, as we see many of ADSK's newer vertical market solutions selling well. We also expect that revenues will be boosted over time as the company leverages opportunities from the Internet with new product announcements.

- We expect operating margins to widen from the depressed levels of FY 04. Excluding amortization and one-time items, we see EPS advancing to $1.51 in FY 05, from $0.83 in FY 04, and we anticipate $1.82 in FY 06. Our FY 05 Standard & Poor's Core Earnings estimate of $0.78 a share includes the impact of projected stock option expense.

Investment Rationale/Risk September 22, 2004

- We recently downgraded the shares to avoid, from hold, primarily due to ADSK's premium valuation to our fair value estimate, based on relative valuation and our discounted cash flow analysis. In addition to our valuation concerns, we believe that ADSK has a weaker quality of earnings than peers due to restructuring charges recorded in seven of the past 10 quarters, with another restructuring charge anticipated in FY 05. The shares trade at a premium to peers, at an enterprise value to sales ratio of 5.1X, and at 27X our FY 06 EPS estimate of $1.82. However, we believe that ADSK has executed better than our recent expectations, and has a solid balance sheet, with nearly $4.60 a share of net cash/marketable securities.

- Risks to our opinion and target price include better than expected company execution, further market share gains, and an acceleration of global information technology (IT) spending.

- Our 12-month target price of $45 is based on relative enterprise value to sales and our discounted cash flow analysis assuming 15% sustainable cash flow growth over the next five years, a weighted cost of capital of 11.5%, and a terminal growth rate of 3%.

Key Stock Statistics

S&P Oper. EPS 2005E	**1.51**	52-week Range	**$60.85-19.12**
P/E on S&P Oper. EPS 2005E	**40.1**	12 Month P/E	**44.9**
Yield (%)	**0.2%**	Beta	**1.04**
Dividend Rate/Share	**0.12**	Shareholders	**767**
Shares Outstanding (M)	**115.6**	Market Cap (B)	**$ 7.0**

Value of $10,000 invested five years ago: **$ 66,056**

Dividend Data Dividends have been paid since 1989

Amount ($)	Date Decl.	Ex-Div. Date	Stock of Record	Payment Date
0.030	Dec. 16	Dec. 30	Jan. 02	Jan. 16 '04
0.030	Mar. 18	Mar. 31	Apr. 02	Apr. 16 '04
0.030	Jun. 17	Jun. 30	Jul. 02	Jul. 16 '04
0.030	Sep. 09	Sep. 22	Sep. 24	Oct. 08 '04

Revenues/Earnings Data Fiscal year ending January 31

Revenues (Million $)

	2005	2004	2003	2002	2001	2000
1Q	297.9	210.8	229.3	245.7	223.3	194.9
2Q	279.6	211.7	211.4	231.4	226.3	202.9
3Q	—	233.9	188.7	216.4	221.8	202.1
4Q	—	295.3	195.5	254.0	243.1	220.2
Yr.	—	951.6	825.0	947.5	936.3	820.2

Earnings Per Share ($)

	2005	2004	2003	2002	2001	2000
1Q	0.36	0.07	0.15	0.25	0.21	-0.15
2Q	0.31	0.29	0.10	0.17	0.18	0.01
3Q	E0.30	0.20	-0.03	0.19	0.16	0.01
4Q	E0.47	0.48	0.06	0.19	0.26	0.21
Yr.	E1.51	1.04	0.28	0.80	0.80	0.08

Next earnings report expected: late-November Source: S&P, Company Reports
EPS Estimates based on S&P Operating Earnings; historical GAAP earnings are as reported.

Recommendation: **SELL** ★★☆☆☆   12-Month Target Price: **$45.00** (as of August 25, 2004)

Business Summary September 23, 2004

Autodesk makes software products that are used across industries and in the home for architectural design and land development, manufacturing, utilities, telecommunications, and media and entertainment.

ADSK is organized into two segments: the Design Solutions segment and the Discreet segment. The Design Solutions segment includes the following business divisions: Manufacturing Solutions, Building Solutions, Infrastructure Solutions, and Platform Technology and Other.

The Design Solutions segment sells design software for professionals, occasional users, and consumers who design, draft and diagram; and mapping and geographic information systems technology for public and private users. End users of design software products include architects, engineers, construction firms, designers and drafters.

The Manufacturing Solutions division accounted for 17% of Design Solutions segment revenues in FY 04. Autodesk Inventor Series delivers Autodesk Mechanical Desktop, a 3D mechanical design program and Autodesk Inventor software, a 3D mechanical design creation tool, in one solution. AutoCAD Mechanical software, a 2D mechanical design and engineering tool, is also included in this division.

The Building Solutions division accounted for 10% of Design Solutions segment revenues in FY 04. The division's main product lines are Autodesk Architectural Desktop, and Autodesk Revit.

The Infrastructure Solutions division accounted for 14% of Design Solutions revenues in FY 04. The division's main products are Autodesk Map, and Autodesk Land Desktop.

The Platform Technology division and Other accounted for 59% of Design Solutions segment revenues in FY 04. The division includes the company's flagship product, AutoCAD, a leading computer aided design (CAD) tool. It is a general-purpose CAD tool for design, modeling, drafting, mapping, rendering and facility management tasks. The most current version, AutoCAD 2005, was introduced in March 2004. Other products in the division include AutoCAD LT, a low cost CAD package with 2D and basic 3D drafting capabilities; and Autodesk Buzzsaw, an online collaboration service that allows users to store, manage, and share project documents from any Internet connection.

The Discreet segment develops, assembles, markets, sells and supports nonlinear digital systems and software for creating, editing and compositing imagery. Its products are used in film and video post-production, games and multimedia, broadcasters' graphics, programming and on-air event coverage, and by designers and architects for 3D visualization and conceptualization. Products include 3ds max, a 3D modeling and animation software package; flame, a digital system used by professionals to create and edit special visual effects in real-time; and inferno, which provides all the features of flame with film tools, and increased image resolution and color control for digital film work.

Company Financials Fiscal Year ending January 31

Per Share Data ($)

(Year Ended January 31)	2004	2003	2002	2001	2000	1999	1998	1997	1996	1995
Tangible Bk. Val.	4.13	3.68	4.40	3.71	4.45	4.12	3.15	2.70	3.70	3.43
Cash Flow	1.48	0.70	1.36	1.39	0.73	1.57	0.59	0.81	1.14	0.74
Earnings	1.04	0.28	0.80	0.80	0.08	0.93	0.15	0.44	0.88	0.57
S&P Core Earnings	0.65	-0.14	0.17	0.33	NA	NA	NA	NA	NA	NA
Dividends	0.12	0.12	0.12	0.12	0.12	0.12	0.12	0.12	0.12	0.12
Payout Ratio	12%	43%	15%	15%	150%	13%	77%	27%	14%	20%

Cal. Yrs.	2003	2002	2001	2000	1999	1998	1997	1996	1995	1994
Prices - High	24.90	23.68	21.09	28.03	24.71	25.03	25.56	22.12	26.50	20.75
- Low	12.82	10.18	12.09	9.71	8.50	10.81	14.00	9.25	15.62	10.56
P/E Ratio - High	24	85	26	35	NM	27	NM	50	30	36
- Low	12	36	15	12	NM	12	NM	21	18	19

Income Statement Analysis (Million $)

Revs.	952	825	947	936	820	740	632	510	547	465
Oper. Inc.	0.16	100	195	208	115	200	147	99	154	130
Depr.	50.3	48.8	62.9	68.8	79.7	63.2	43.9	34.8	25.2	17.4
Int. Exp.	Nil	Nil	Nil	Nil	Nil	Nil	Nil	Nil	Nil	Nil
Pretax Inc.	117	38.5	55.1	41.7	23.9	147	55.0	66.5	138	89.1
Eff. Tax Rate	NM	17.1%	NM	NM	59.0%	38.2%	72.1%	37.5%	36.6%	36.5%
Net Inc.	120	31.9	90.3	93.2	9.81	90.6	15.4	41.6	87.8	56.6
S&P Core Earnings	74.4	-16.2	19.5	38.5	NA	NA	NA	NA	NA	NA

Balance Sheet & Other Fin. Data (Million $)

Cash	364	247	505	423	359	378	96.1	183	193	240
Curr. Assets	597	450	564	491	545	450	308	311	348	373
Total Assets	1,017	884	902	808	907	694	534	492	518	482
Curr. Liab.	385	310	371	334	299	232	199	150	144	155
LT Debt	Nil	Nil	Nil	Nil	Nil	Nil	Nil	Nil	Nil	Nil
Common Equity	622	569	529	460	602	460	303	244	342	323
Total Cap.	629	571	529	473	607	461	304	247	344	326
Cap. Exp.	25.9	36.1	45.1	32.4	14.9	30.4	15.0	17.4	16.3	20.0
Cash Flow	171	80.7	153	162	89.6	154	59.2	76.4	113	74.0
Curr. Ratio	1.6	1.5	1.5	1.5	1.8	1.9	1.5	2.1	2.4	2.4
% LT Debt of Cap.	Nil	Nil	Nil	Nil	Nil	Nil	Nil	Nil	Nil	Nil
% Net Inc.of Revs.	12.6	3.9	9.5	10.0	1.2	12.2	2.4	8.2	16.1	12.2
% Ret. on Assets	12.7	3.6	10.6	10.9	1.1	14.8	3.0	8.3	17.6	12.8
% Ret. on Equity	20.2	5.8	18.3	17.6	1.7	23.7	5.6	14.2	26.4	18.3

Data as orig reptd.; bef. results of disc opers/spec. items. Per share data adj. for stk. divs.; EPS diluted. E-Estimated. NA-Not Available. NM-Not Meaningful. NR-Not Ranked. UR-Under Review.

Office: 111 McInnis Parkway, San Rafael, CA 94903-2700.
Telephone: 415-507-5000.
Email: investor.relations@autodesk.com
Website: http://www.autodesk.com
Chrmn, Pres & CEO: C.A. Bartz.

COO: C. Bass.
SVP & CFO: A.J. Castino.
SVP, Secy & General Counsel: M.K. Sterling.
Dirs: C. A. Bartz, M. A. Bertelsen, C. W. Beveridge, J. H. Dawson, M. Fister, P. Halvorsen, S. L. Scheid, M. A. Taylor, L. W. Wangberg.

Founded: in 1982.
Domicile: Delaware.
Employees: 3,493.
S&P Analyst: Jonathan Rudy, CFA /CB/GG

Automatic Data Processing

Recommendation: **BUY** ★★★★★   12-Month Target Price: **$54.00**
SELL | SELL | HOLD | BUY | BUY
(as of January 26, 2004)

ADP has an approximate 0.24% weighting in the **S&P 500**

Sector: Information Technology
Sub-Industry: Data Processing & Outsourced Services
Peer Group: Billing & Payroll Services

Summary: ADP, one of the world's largest independent computing services companies, provides a broad range of data processing services.

Quantitative Evaluations

S&P Earnings & Dividend Rank: A+
D | C | B- | B | B+ | A- | A | **A+**

S&P Fair Value Rank: 2+
1 | **2** | 3 | 4 | 5
Lowest | | | | Highest

Fair Value Calc.: $38.50 (Overvalued)

S&P Investability Quotient Percentile
98%
ADP scored higher than 98% of all companies for which an S&P Report is available.

Volatility: Average
Low | **Average** | High

Technical Evaluation: Bullish
Since 10/04, the technical indicators for ADP have been Bullish.

Relative Strength Rank: Moderate
62
1 Lowest | Highest 99

Price as of 11/12/04: $45.37   **2005E S&P Core EPS:** $1.58

GAAP Earnings vs. Previous Year
▲ Up ▼ Down ► No Change

10 Week Mov. Avg.
30 Week Mov. Avg.
Relative Strength
12-Mo Target Price

Volume Below Avg. — Above Avg.

BUY $38.44 10/07/03
HOLD $31.60 07/18/02

BUY | HOLD | BUY
J J A S O N D | J F M A M J J A S O N D | J F M A M J J A S O N D | J F M A M J J A S O N D J
2001 | 2002 | 2003 | 2004

OPTIONS: ASE, CBOE, P, Ph

Analyst commentary prepared by Stephanie S. Crane/MF/JWP

Highlights November 05, 2004

- We see revenues increasing 5.7% in FY 05 (Jun.), to $8.2 billion, compared with 8.5% growth in FY 04. We expect quarterly results to accelerate into the second half of the year, on favorable comparisons for interest rates and investment spending, coupled with a moderate recovery in employer, dealer and brokerage services.

- The employer services segment should grow in the high single digits, aided by recent acquisitions, strong customer retention rates, and upward trending payroll data. We expect brokerage services revenue to grow in the mid-single digits, with 9% growth in transaction processing and 3% in investor communications. Dealer and claims service revenues should each rise in the mid-single digits.

- We think operating margins will widen in FY 05, on benefits from investments made in FY 04. We see FY 05 operating EPS increasing 17%, to $1.82, from $1.56 in FY 04. Our FY 05 Standard & Poor's Core Earnings per share estimate of $1.58 includes pension expense and projected option expense.

Investment Rationale/Risk November 05, 2004

- We have a buy recommendation on the shares, based on valuation, as well as on expected improvement in the job market, which we see aiding payroll providers such as ADP in 2004. We think the market for payroll outsourcing is relatively untapped, providing opportunities for future earnings growth. We view the balance sheet as strong, with $2.2 billion in cash/securities and little debt.

- Risks to our recommendation and target price stem from competition in the business process outsourcing market, an area where ADP is venturing, which could in turn cause downward pressure on pricing and profit margins.

- We would buy the stock, trading at a discount to our 12-month target price of $54 based on our discounted cash flow analysis and relative enterprise to sales valuation. We believe the shares deserve a premium valuation to peers, based on our view of ADP's market share leadership, healthy balance sheet, and strong cash flow generation.

Key Stock Statistics

S&P Oper. EPS 2005E	1.82	52-week Range	$47.31-37.00
P/E on S&P Oper. EPS 2005E	24.9	12 Month P/E	28.5
Yield (%)	1.4%	Beta	1.06
Dividend Rate/Share	0.62	Shareholders	38,331
Shares Outstanding (M)	582.5	Market Cap (B)	$ 26.4

Value of $10,000 invested five years ago: **$ 9,823**

Dividend Data Dividends have been paid since 1974

Amount ($)	Date Decl.	Ex-Div. Date	Stock of Record	Payment Date
0.140	Jan. 29	Mar. 11	Mar. 15	Apr. 01 '04
0.140	May. 11	Jun. 09	Jun. 11	Jul. 01 '04
0.140	Aug. 11	Sep. 08	Sep. 10	Oct. 01 '04
0.155	Nov. 09	Dec. 08	Dec. 10	Jan. 01 '05

Revenues/Earnings Data Fiscal year ending June 30

Revenues (Million $)

	2005	2004	2003	2002	2001	2000
1Q	1,855	1,720	1,648	1,608	1,587	1,351
2Q	—	1,927	1,683	1,681	1,684	1,492
3Q	—	2,121	1,906	1,870	1,894	1,720
4Q	—	2,086	1,912	1,845	1,853	1,724
Yr.	—	7,755	7,147	7,004	7,018	6,288

Earnings Per Share ($)

	2005	2004	2003	2002	2001	2000
1Q	0.35	0.32	0.34	0.31	0.27	0.23
2Q	E0.38	0.38	0.43	0.42	0.32	0.31
3Q	E0.55	0.50	0.54	0.56	0.45	0.42
4Q	E0.54	0.36	0.36	0.46	0.40	0.36
Yr.	E1.82	1.56	1.68	1.75	1.44	1.31

Next earnings report expected: late-January Source: S&P, Company Reports
EPS Estimates based on S&P Operating Earnings; historical GAAP earnings are as reported.

Automatic Data Processing, Inc.

Recommendation: **BUY** ★ ★ ★ ★ ★   12-Month Target Price: **$54.00** (as of January 26, 2004)

Business Summary November 05, 2004

Automatic Data Processing provides a broad range of data processing services in four business segments: employer, brokerage, dealer and claims. ADP is the largest independent computing services company in the U.S.

Employer services, accounting for 62% of revenues in FY 03 (Jun.), provides payroll, human resource, benefits administration, time and attendance, and tax filing and reporting services to more than 460,000 clients in North America, Europe, Australia, Asia and Brazil. The company processes the paychecks of nearly 30 million workers. ADP TotalSource is the third largest professional employer organization (PEO) in the U.S. A PEO provides a comprehensive out-sourcing solution, including payroll, human resources, benefits and workers' compensation. In FY 02, Employer Services acquired Avert, Inc., a leading provider of pre-employment screening and selection services.

Brokerage services (22% of revenues) includes securities processing, desktop productivity applications, and investor communications services to the financial services industry. The company is the largest provider of securities processing services in North America. ADP handled an average of 1.3 million trades per day in FY 03, down about 13% from the level of FY 02. The company also processed more than 750 million shareholder mailings.

Dealer services (11% of revenues) is a leading provider of transaction systems, data products, and professional services to automobile and truck dealers and manufacturers worldwide. More than 16,000 auto and truck dealer clients, and

more than 30 vehicle manufacturers, use the company's on-site systems and communications networks to manage sales and operations.

Claims services (5% of revenues) offers a broad line of products to help clients accurately estimate auto damage, bodily injury and property claims. Clients include most of the major property and casualty insurance carriers and many of the independent adjusting companies, collision repair centers, and auto parts recycling facilities.

In FY 03, revenues grew 5% in employer services, decreased 9% in brokerage services, increased 12% in dealer services, and declined 1% in claims services and other. Overall, revenues rose 2%.

In FY 03, cash flow from operations totaled about $1.6 billion. The company repurchased more than 27 million common shares. ADP also acquired several businesses in FY 03, at an aggregate total cost of $650 million. It made acquisitions totaling $232 million in FY 02, and $75 million in FY 01. Capital spending totaled $134 million in FY 03.

In June 2003, ADP acquired ProBusiness Services, an employee administration outsourcer, for about $500 million in cash. In May, ADP acquired the retirement services recordkeeping operations of Scudder Investments, specifically a 401(k) and defined contribution plan recordkeeping business.

Company Financials Fiscal Year ending June 30

Per Share Data ($)

(Year Ended June 30)	2004	2003	2002	2001	2000	1999	1998	1997	1996	1995
Tangible Bk. Val.	4.23	4.57	5.25	4.97	4.71	3.97	2.90	2.30	1.85	2.41
Cash Flow	2.07	2.13	2.19	1.93	1.74	1.52	1.37	1.27	1.14	0.99
Earnings	1.56	1.68	1.75	1.44	1.31	1.10	0.99	0.88	0.79	0.69
S&P Core Earnings	1.38	1.42	1.49	1.31	NA	NA	NA	NA	NA	NA
Dividends	0.54	0.48	0.45	0.40	0.34	0.30	0.26	0.22	0.20	0.15
Payout Ratio	35%	28%	26%	27%	26%	21%	26%	25%	25%	22%
Prices - High	47.31	40.81	59.53	63.56	69.31	54.81	42.15	31.29	21.68	20.56
- Low	38.60	27.24	31.15	41.00	40.00	36.25	28.78	19.75	17.81	14.37
P/E Ratio - High	30	24	34	44	53	50	43	36	28	30
- Low	25	16	18	28	31	33	29	22	23	21

Income Statement Analysis (Million $)

	2004	2003	2002	2001	2000	1999	1998	1997	1996	1995
Revs.	7,755	7,147	7,004	7,018	6,288	5,540	4,798	4,112	3,567	2,894
Oper. Inc.	1,745	1,793	1,952	1,938	1,904	1,376	1,153	1,005	867	731
Depr.	307	275	279	321	284	273	245	223	202	173
Int. Exp.	Nil	Nil	21.2	14.3	13.1	19.1	24.0	27.8	29.7	24.3
Pretax Inc.	1,495	1,645	1,787	1,525	1,290	1,085	884	724	635	534
Eff. Tax Rate	37.4%	38.1%	38.4%	39.4%	34.8%	35.7%	31.5%	29.1%	28.4%	26.1%
Net Inc.	936	1,018	1,101	925	841	697	605	514	455	395
S&P Core Earnings	824	857	940	842	NA	NA	NA	NA	NA	NA

Balance Sheet & Other Fin. Data (Million $)

	2004	2003	2002	2001	2000	1999	1998	1997	1996	1995
Cash	1,129	2,344	2,750	1,791	1,824	1,092	752	1,025	636	698
Curr. Assets	2,762	3,676	2,817	3,083	3,064	2,194	1,829	1,805	1,454	1,211
Total Assets	21,121	19,834	18,277	17,889	16,851	5,825	5,175	4,383	3,840	3,201
Curr. Liab.	1,768	1,999	1,411	1,336	1,297	1,286	1,221	1,020	836	543
LT Debt	76.2	84.7	90.6	110	132	146	192	401	404	390
Common Equity	5,418	5,371	5,114	4,701	4,583	4,062	3,406	2,661	2,315	2,097
Total Cap.	5,778	5,777	5,442	5,019	4,866	4,346	3,745	3,165	2,832	2,506
Cap. Exp.	8,087	134	146	185	166	178	199	175	164	118
Cash Flow	1,242	1,293	1,380	1,246	1,125	970	850	737	656	567
Curr. Ratio	1.6	1.8	2.0	2.3	2.4	1.7	1.5	1.8	1.7	2.2
% LT Debt of Cap.	1.3	1.5	1.7	2.2	2.7	3.4	5.1	12.7	14.3	15.6
% Net Inc.of Revs.	12.1	14.2	15.7	13.2	13.4	12.6	12.6	12.5	12.7	13.6
% Ret. on Assets	4.6	5.3	6.1	5.3	5.7	12.6	12.7	12.5	12.9	13.4
% Ret. on Equity	17.3	19.4	22.4	19.9	19.6	17.9	20.0	20.6	20.6	20.8

Data as orig reptd.; bef. results of disc opers/spec. items. Per share data adj. for stk. divs.; EPS diluted. E-Estimated. NA-Not Available. NM-Not Meaningful. NR-Not Ranked. UR-Under Review.

Office: 1 Adp Blvd, Roseland, NJ 07068-1728.
Telephone: 973-974-5000.
Website: http://www.adp.com
Chrmn & CEO: A.F. Weinbach.
Pres & COO: G.C. Bulter.

VP, Secy & General Counsel: J.B. Benson.
Dirs: G. D. Brenneman, L. Brun, G. C. Butler, J. A. Califano, Jr., L. G. Cooperman, G. Hubbard, A. D. Jordan, H. M. Krueger, F. V. Malek, H. Taub, A. F. Weinbach.

Founded: in 1949.
Domicile: Delaware.
Employees: 42,000.
S&P Analyst: Stephanie S. Crane/MF/JWP

AutoNation

Recommendation: **HOLD** ★★★☆☆   SELL SELL HOLD BUY BUY   **12-Month Target Price: $18.00**
(as of September 10, 2003)

AN has an approximate 0.04% weighting in the **S&P 500**

Sector: Consumer Discretionary
Sub-Industry: Specialty Stores
Peer Group: Vehicle-related Retailers

Summary: AN is the largest U.S. retail auto dealer.

Quantitative Evaluations

Price as of 11/12/04: $17.61   **2004E S&P Core EPS:** $1.30

S&P Earnings & Dividend Rank: B

D	C	B-	B	B+	A-	A	A+

S&P Fair Value Rank: 5+

1	2	3	4	5
Lowest				Highest

Fair Value Calc.: $19.70 (Slightly Undervalued)

S&P Investability Quotient Percentile

90%

AN scored higher than 90% of all companies for which an S&P Report is available.

Volatility: Low

Low	Average	High

Technical Evaluation: Bullish
Since 11/04, the technical indicators for AN have been Bullish.

Relative Strength Rank: Moderate

50

1 Lowest   Highest 99

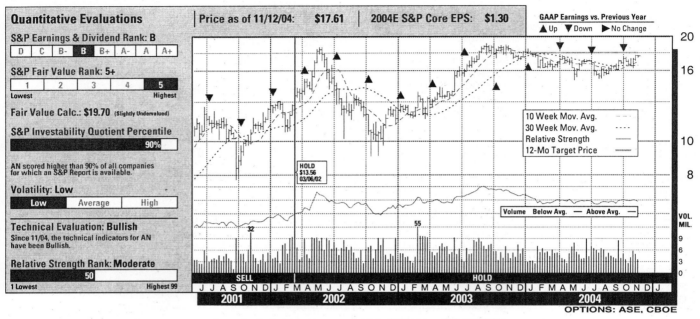

GAAP Earnings vs. Previous Year
▲ Up ▼ Down ▶ No Change

- 10 Week Mov. Avg.
- 30 Week Mov. Avg.
- Relative Strength
- 12-Mo Target Price

HOLD $13.56 03/06/02

Volume Below Avg. — Above Avg. —

SELL   HOLD

J J A S O N D J F M A M J J A S O N D J F M A M J J A S O N D J F M A M J J A S O N D J
2001   2002   2003   2004

OPTIONS: ASE, CBOE

Analyst commentary prepared by Efraim Levy, CFA /PMW/BK

Highlights November 02, 2004

- We expect 2005 revenues to grow 1% to 3%. We expect new vehicle sales to advance, on higher industry demand. We see used vehicle revenues likely to remain weak, due to lower volume and pricing pressures, but we expect gains in parts and service, and in finance and insurance contributions.

- We see margins benefiting from continued cost cutting, partly offset by lower used vehicle pricing and lower sales of U.S. brands. Continued share buybacks should help EPS comparisons. However, we believe macroeconomic factors, such as pressures on car prices and intensifying competition, will continue to weigh on profitability. Second quarter results were hurt by weaker sales at Ford and GM. Third quarter results were hurt by bad weather and increased price competition. After solid improvement during the third quarter, we expect AN to focus on a modest further reduction of vehicle inventories.

- We expect cash flow to be used to repurchase shares, and to expand the business internally and via acquisitions. Excluding tax benefits of $0.44 a share from a settlement with the IRS regarding the treatment of certain past transactions, EPS in 2003 would have been $1.32. We expect 2004 EPS of $1.32, and see $1.49 for 2005.

Investment Rationale/Risk November 02, 2004

- We would hold existing positions. The stock trades at premium P/E multiple and price to free cash flow ratio levels to those of some peers in our coverage universe. Based on S&P Core Earnings methodology, we view earnings quality for 2005 as high, with adjustments for stock option expense expected to reduce EPS by less than 5%.

- Risks to our recommendation and target price include concerns about volatile multiples for automotive retailers, and changes in vehicle demand and pricing for both new and used vehicles.

- Our use of a P/E multiple of about 12X applied to our 2005 EPS estimate reflects peer and historical P/E multiple comparisons. Our discounted cash flow model, which assumes a weighted average cost of capital of 10.3%, a compound annual growth rate of 8.7% over the next 15 years, and a terminal growth rate of 3%, calculates intrinsic value of $18. Based on a combination of our discounted cash flow and P/E multiple analyses, our 12-month target price is $18.

Key Stock Statistics

S&P Core EPS 2005E	1.43	52-week Range	$18.50-15.01
S&P Oper. EPS 2004E	1.32	12 Month P/E	13.9
P/E on S&P Oper. EPS 2004E	13.3	Beta	0.61
S&P Oper. EPS 2005E	1.49	Shareholders	3,000
Yield (%)	Nil	Market Cap (B)	$ 4.7
Dividend Rate/Share	Nil	Shares Outstanding (M)	264.6

Value of $10,000 invested five years ago: **NA**

Dividend Data

No cash dividends have been paid.

Revenues/Earnings Data Fiscal year ending December 31

Revenues (Million $)

	2004	2003	2002	2001	2000	1999
1Q	4,797	4,459	4,751	4,888	5,230	5,354
2Q	4,989	5,069	5,016	4,945	5,340	5,070
3Q	5,097	5,257	5,194	5,011	5,338	5,460
4Q	—	4,596	4,519	5,146	4,702	5,020
Yr.	—	19,381	19,479	19,989	20,610	20,112

Earnings Per Share ($)

	2004	2003	2002	2001	2000	1999
1Q	0.32	0.72	0.28	0.17	0.18	0.11
2Q	0.35	0.37	0.32	0.26	0.27	0.21
3Q	0.35	0.38	0.33	0.24	0.26	0.22
4Q	E0.31	0.28	0.26	0.06	0.21	-0.71
Yr.	E1.32	1.76	1.19	0.73	0.91	-0.07

Next earnings report expected: early-February Source: S&P, Company Reports
EPS Estimates based on S&P Operating Earnings; historical GAAP earnings are as reported.

AutoNation, Inc.

Recommendation: **HOLD** ★ ★ ★ ★ ★   12-Month Target Price: **$18.00** (as of September 10, 2003)

Business Summary November 02, 2004

Car retailing is a very tough business. With razor-thin profit margins and highly leveraged inventories that depreciate rapidly, dealers must generate high volume and fast turnover. However, auto demand itself is driven by volatile factors such as strength of the economy, interest rate levels, and consumer confidence. In addition, dealerships operate with high overhead costs, resulting in a high sales break-even point.

AutoNation (formerly Republic Industries) has changed significantly over the past several years. While expanding revenues through dealer acquisitions, the company divested or eliminated its electronic security, solid waste, and used car businesses. In June 2000, AN spun off to shareholders its car rental business.

The company's vehicle retailing unit operates in saturated markets; about 75% of total U.S. vehicle sales are to replace existing autos.

Due to saturated markets, price sensitivity, and intense competition, dealerships typically post very low profit margins. Average new car gross profits hover around 6%, with total dealer pretax margins of about 1.7%.

AN's new auto retailing operations (61% of 2003 revenues) consist of about 372 dealerships. Although the company is the largest U.S. auto retailer, it controls only about 2% of the nearly $1 trillion U.S. new and used car market.

The sale of used vehicles accounted for 23% of revenues in 2003. Fixed operations provided 13% of sales, while finance and insurance and other accounted for the balance.

The company's rental car business, spun off to shareholders in June 2000, consisted of Alamo, National and CarTemps. AN believed the separation of its rental car business would provide increased capital for and greater management focus on automotive retail operations, while strengthening the company's financial position.

AN has been actively repurchasing shares under recent stock buyback programs. In 2003, the company purchased 39.2 million shares, for $575 million.

In the 1999 fourth quarter, the company recorded pretax charges of about $444 million ($298 million, after tax) for the closure and integration of its used vehicle megastores, corporate work force reduction, and other restructuring activities.

In the 2001 fourth quarter, AN recorded a non-cash pretax charge of about $85.8 million ($52.3 million, after tax) to increase reserves for auto loans and cover costs of exiting that business.

In March 2003, the company reached a settlement with the IRS in connection with IRS objections to past transactions that reduced tax liabilities. The settlement will result in total net payments of about $470 million through March 2007. In July, AN said it planned to prepay a portion of the settlement in order to save interest expense.

Company Financials Fiscal Year ending December 31

Per Share Data ($)

(Year Ended December 31)	2003	2002	2001	2000	1999	1998	1997	1996	1995	1994
Tangible Bk. Val.	3.91	3.14	2.99	2.64	4.72	11.84	4.34	4.93	2.21	1.41
Cash Flow	2.01	1.40	1.18	1.28	0.07	2.94	2.72	2.15	0.21	0.24
Earnings	1.76	1.19	0.73	0.91	-0.07	0.71	0.46	-0.12	0.18	0.15
S&P Core Earnings	1.69	1.12	0.57	NA	NA	NA	NA	NA	NA	NA
Dividends	Nil	Nil	Nil	Nil	Nil	Nil	Nil	Nil	Nil	Nil
Payout Ratio	Nil	Nil	Nil	Nil	Nil	Nil	Nil	Nil	Nil	Nil
Prices - High	19.19	18.73	13.07	10.75	18.37	30.00	44.37	34.62	18.06	2.06
- Low	11.61	9.05	4.93	4.62	7.50	10.00	19.00	13.18	1.50	1.25
P/E Ratio - High	11	16	18	12	NM	42	96	NM	NM	13
- Low	7	8	7	5	NM	14	41	NM	NM	8

Income Statement Analysis (Million $)

	2003	2002	2001	2000	1999	1998	1997	1996	1995	1994
Revs.	19,381	19,479	19,989	20,610	20,112	16,118	10,306	2,365	260	49.0
Oper. Inc.	805	786	667	855	461	1,588	1,350	576	57.6	14.2
Depr.	71.0	69.7	152	134	60.0	1,052	971	540	21.0	4.75
Int. Exp.	143	125	43.7	248	35.0	22.0	17.0	33.4	5.60	1.13
Pretax Inc.	591	618	401	525	-27.0	523	315	-10.2	36.7	8.50
Eff. Tax Rate	14.4%	38.3%	38.9%	37.5%	NM	35.9%	36.5%	NM	36.8%	Nil
Net Inc.	506	382	245	328	-31.0	335	200	-27.9	23.2	8.50
S&P Core Earnings	486	359	192	NA	NA	NA	NA	NA	NA	NA

Balance Sheet & Other Fin. Data (Million $)

	2003	2002	2001	2000	1999	1998	1997	1996	1995	1994
Cash	171	176	128	82.2	369	217	148	63.6	160	2.70
Curr. Assets	3,990	3,629	3,153	4,176	4,301	8,406	6,826	2,584	207	14.2
Total Assets	8,823	8,585	8,065	8,830	9,613	13,926	10,527	3,776	542	132
Curr. Liab.	3,810	2,981	2,578	3,141	3,165	5,540	4,263	2,228	64.0	10.1
LT Debt	809	643	647	850	836	2,316	2,334	170	NM	14.9
Common Equity	3,950	3,910	3,828	3,843	4,601	5,425	3,484	1,276	436	88.0
Total Cap.	4,935	5,500	5,329	5,570	6,241	9,968	5,818	1,447	449	114
Cap. Exp.	133	183	164	148	242	438	460	203	48.9	5.50
Cash Flow	577	451	397	462	29.0	1,387	1,171	513	44.2	13.3
Curr. Ratio	1.0	1.2	1.2	1.3	1.4	1.5	1.6	1.2	3.2	1.4
% LT Debt of Cap.	16.4	11.7	12.1	15.3	13.4	29.1	40.1	11.7	NM	13.1
% Net Inc.of Revs.	2.6	2.0	1.2	1.6	NM	2.1	1.9	NM	8.9	17.4
% Ret. on Assets	5.8	4.6	2.9	3.6	NM	2.8	2.8	NM	5.9	5.9
% Ret. on Equity	12.9	9.9	6.4	7.8	NM	7.5	8.4	NM	8.5	10.3

Data as orig. reptd.; bef. results of disc. opers. and/or spec. items. Per share data adj. for stk. divs.; EPS diluted. E-Estimated. NA-Not Available. NM-Not Meaningful. NR-Not Ranked.

Office: 110 S.E. 6th Street, Ft. Lauderdale, FL 33301-5012.
Telephone: 954-769-6000.
Website: http://www.autonation.com
Chrmn & CEO: M.J. Jackson.
Pres & COO: M.E. Maroone.
SVP & CFO: C.T. Monaghan.

SVP, Secy & General Counsel: J.P. Ferrando.
VP & Investor Contact: J. Zimmerman 954-769-7342.
Dirs: R. J. Brown, J. P. Bryan, R. L. Burdick, W. C. Crowley, A. S. Dawes, H. W. Huizenga, M. A. Jackson, G. D. Johnson, Jr., E. S. Lampert, I. B. Rosenfield.

Founded: in 1991.
Domicile: Delaware.
Employees: 28,000.
S&P Analyst: Efraim Levy, CFA /PMW/BK

The **McGraw·Hill** Companies

AutoZone

Recommendation: **BUY ★★★★** | SELL | SELL | HOLD | BUY | BUY | 12-Month Target Price: **$89.00**
(as of September 22, 2004)

AZO has an approximate 0.06% weighting in the **S&P 500**

Sector: Consumer Discretionary
Sub-Industry: Specialty Stores
Peer Group: Auto Parts Retailers

Summary: This retailer of automotive parts and accessories operates over 3,000 AutoZone stores throughout most of the U.S. and in Mexico.

Quantitative Evaluations

S&P Earnings & Dividend Rank: B+

| D | C | B- | B | B+ | A- | A | A+ |

S&P Fair Value Rank: 3+

| 1 | 2 | 3 | 4 | 5 |
| Lowest | | | | Highest |

Fair Value Calc.: $80.90 (Slightly Overvalued)

S&P Investability Quotient Percentile

99%

AZO scored higher than 99% of all companies for which an S&P Report is available.

Volatility: Average

| Low | Average | High |

Technical Evaluation: Bullish

Since 10/04, the technical indicators for AZO have been Bullish.

Relative Strength Rank: Moderate

62

| 1 Lowest | Highest 99 |

Price as of 11/12/04: **$85.13** | **2005E S&P Core EPS:** **$7.30**

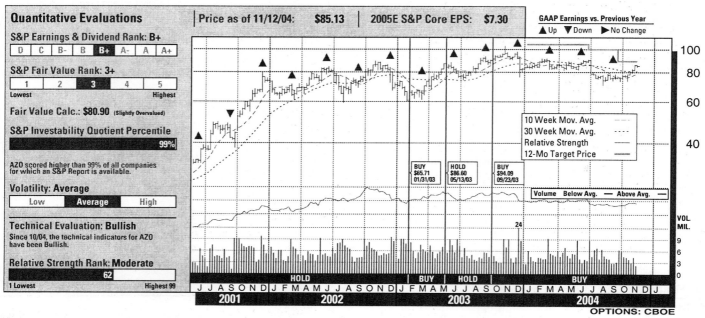

GAAP Earnings vs. Previous Year
▲ Up ▼ Down ▶ No Change

10 Week Mov. Avg. ......
30 Week Mov. Avg. - - - -
Relative Strength ——
12-Mo Target Price - - - -

BUY $65.71 01/31/03
HOLD $86.60 05/13/03
BUY $94.09 09/23/03

Volume Below Avg. — Above Avg.

VOL. MIL.

OPTIONS: CBOE

Analyst commentary prepared by Yogeesh Wagle/MF/JWP

Highlights October 07, 2004

■ We see sales growth in the mid-single digits in FY 05 (Aug.), reflecting the addition of about 200 new stores, representing an increase of 5% to 6% in retail square footage. We project a low single-digit rise in same-store sales, driven mainly by strong gains in commercial sales. We expect do-it-yourself (DIY) sales to improve slightly, after staying level in FY 04, on increased customer traffic and average ticket.

■ We look for operating margins to widen slightly, as leverage from sales growth, well controlled store and payroll costs, and a greater share for wider margin private label products in the retail segment outweigh an increased proportion of lower margin commercial sales in the mix and higher advertising and marketing spending.

■ After projected higher interest expense, on increased debt, taxes estimated at 37.5%, and lower share count, reflecting stock repurchases, we project that FY 05 EPS will grow 16%, to $7.61, from $6.56 in FY 04. With our S&P Core EPS projections only 4% to 6% lower than our operating EPS projections, reflecting estimated stock option expense, we think AZO has a relatively high quality of earnings.

Key Stock Statistics

S&P Oper. EPS 2005E	7.61	52-week Range	$97.90-70.35
P/E on S&P Oper. EPS 2005E	11.2	12 Month P/E	13.0
Yield (%)	Nil	Beta	0.44
Dividend Rate/Share	Nil	Shareholders	3,391
Shares Outstanding (M)	79.8	Market Cap (B)	$ 6.8

Value of $10,000 invested five years ago: **$ 29,469**

Dividend Data

No cash dividends have been paid.

Investment Rationale/Risk October 07, 2004

■ We recommend accumulating the shares. At 9.8X our FY 05 EPS estimate, the shares are trading at a discount to the S&P 500 and to peers. At a P/E to growth ratio of 0.8X, based on our three-year 12% EPS growth projection, the shares are also at a discount to the S&P 500 and peers. In recent quarters, the company trailed competitors in same-store sales growth, a key metric in retail. We believe that AZO and its peers have been affected in 2004 by a relatively mild summer and high gas prices. For the longer term, we see AZO poised to benefit from what we see as favorable vehicle demographic trends, including a rising number of cars older than seven years (the point after which vehicles tend to require more post-warranty repairs) and increasing vehicle usage.

■ Risks to our recommendation and target price include a slowdown in the U.S. economy; a steep hike in oil prices, dampening auto usage; and technological changes that might reduce the need for auto parts. We also see execution risk for AZO as it tries to turn around anemic same-store sales growth.

■ Our 12-month target price of $89, based on our DCF analysis, is equal to 12X our FY 05 EPS estimate, in line with our three-year EPS growth projection.

Revenues/Earnings Data Fiscal year ending August 31

Revenues (Million $)

	2004	2003	2002	2001	2000	1999
1Q	1,282	1,219	1,176	1,064	1,006	901.0
2Q	1,159	1,121	1,081	974.0	924.0	852.5
3Q	1,360	1,288	1,225	1,140	1,059	970.2
4Q	1,836	1,830	1,843	1,641	1,493	1,393
Yr.	5,637	5,457	5,326	4,818	4,483	4,116

Earnings Per Share ($)

	2004	2003	2002	2001	2000	1999
1Q	1.35	1.04	0.76	0.46	0.40	0.34
2Q	1.04	0.79	0.58	0.28	0.28	0.24
3Q	1.68	1.30	0.96	0.56	0.50	0.39
4Q	2.53	2.27	1.73	0.24	0.84	0.67
Yr.	6.56	5.34	4.00	1.54	2.00	1.63

Next earnings report expected: early-December Source: S&P, Company Reports
EPS Estimates based on S&P Operating Earnings; historical GAAP earnings are as reported.

AutoZone, Inc.

Recommendation: **BUY** ★★★★☆   12-Month Target Price: **$89.00** (as of September 22, 2004)

Business Summary October 07, 2004

AutoZone is a leading specialty retailer of automotive parts, chemicals and accessories, focusing primarily on do-it-yourself (DIY) consumers. At August 28, 2004, the company operated 3,420 U.S. AutoZone stores, in 48 states and the District of Columbia, and 63 stores in Mexico. AZO also sells automotive diagnostic equipment and repair software through ALLDATA, diagnostic and repair information through alldatadiy.com, and parts and accessories online at autozone.com.

The company's 3,420 U.S. stores as of August 28, 2004, represented 21.7 million sq. ft., up from 3,219 stores and 20.5 million sq. ft. a year earlier.

Each store's product line includes new and remanufactured automotive hard parts, such as alternators, starters, water pumps, brake shoes and pads, carburetors, clutches and engines; maintenance items, such as oil, antifreeze, transmission, brake and power steering fluids, engine additives, protectants and waxes; and accessories, such as car stereos and floor mats. Parts are carried for domestic and foreign cars, sport utility vehicles, vans and light trucks.

Stores, generally in high-visibility locations, range in size from about 4,000 sq. ft. to 8,100 sq. ft., with new stores increasingly using a larger format. Of the 3,219 stores in operation at August 31, 2003, 277 (9%) were under 4,000 sq. ft., 1,788 (56%) ranged from 4,000 sq. ft. to 7,000 sq. ft., and the remaining stores were over 7,000 sq. ft. There were 387 stores in California, 374 in Texas, 191 in Ohio, 149 in Florida, 155 in Illinois, 120 in Tennessee, 124 in Michigan, 108 in North Carolina, 106 in Georgia, and 105 in Indiana, with the rest in other states.

AZO offers everyday low prices, and attempts to be the price leader in hard parts. Stores generally carry between 21,000 and 23,000 stock-keeping units. In addition to targeting the do-it-yourself customer, the company also has a commercial sales program in the U.S. (AZ Commercial), which provides commercial credit and delivery of parts and other products to local, regional and national repair garages, dealers and service stations. At August 30, 2003, 1,941 stores, supported by 115 hub stores, had commercial sales programs. The hub stores provide fast replenishment of key merchandise to support the DIY and commercial sales businesses. AZO does not perform repairs or installations.

In June 1998, the company acquired Chief Auto Parts, Inc. Chief operated full-line auto parts and accessories retail stores in five states. In December 2001, AZO sold its TruckPro heavy duty truck parts subsidiary.

In FY 01 (Aug.), the company recorded pretax restructuring and impairment charges totaling $156.8 million. Charges were related primarily to asset write-downs (including an expected loss on the sale of TruckPro) and accrual of lease obligations related to store closings and terminated projects under development, plus inventory rationalization charges.

During FY 04, AZO bought back $848 million of common stock. From January 1998 through August 2004, the company repurchased 82 million shares, at a total cost of $3.6 billion, significantly aiding EPS comparisons over the period.

Company Financials Fiscal Year ending August 31

Per Share Data ($)

(Year Ended August 31)	2004	2003	2002	2001	2000	1999	1998	1997	1996	1995
Tangible Bk. Val.	NM	0.90	3.87	5.13	5.49	6.83	7.37	7.00	5.65	4.54
Cash Flow	7.79	6.47	5.10	2.70	2.88	2.44	2.10	1.78	1.52	1.25
Earnings	6.56	5.34	4.00	1.54	2.00	1.63	1.48	1.28	1.11	0.93
S&P Core Earnings	6.40	5.09	3.87	1.45	NA	NA	NA	NA	NA	NA
Dividends	Nil	Nil	Nil	Nil	Nil	Nil	Nil	Nil	Nil	Nil
Payout Ratio	Nil	Nil	Nil	Nil	Nil	Nil	Nil	Nil	Nil	Nil
Prices - High	91.59	103.53	89.34	80.00	32.50	37.31	38.00	32.81	37.62	27.75
- Low	70.35	58.21	59.20	24.37	21.00	22.56	20.50	19.50	22.12	22.00
P/E Ratio - High	14	19	22	52	16	23	26	26	34	30
- Low	11	11	15	16	10	14	14	15	20	24

Income Statement Analysis (Million $)

	2004	2003	2002	2001	2000	1999	1998	1997	1996	1995
Revs.	5,637	5,457	5,326	4,818	4,483	4,116	3,243	2,691	2,243	1,808
Oper. Inc.	1,106	1,028	889	646	630	555	478	399	332	276
Depr.	107	110	118	131	118	122	95.5	77.2	62.9	48.3
Int. Exp.	93.0	84.8	79.9	101	76.8	45.3	18.2	8.84	1.97	Nil
Pretax Inc.	906	833	691	287	435	388	364	313	267	228
Eff. Tax Rate	37.5%	37.9%	38.1%	38.8%	38.5%	36.9%	37.4%	37.6%	37.4%	39.2%
Net Inc.	566	518	428	176	268	245	228	195	167	139
S&P Core Earnings	553	492	415	165	NA	NA	NA	NA	NA	NA

Balance Sheet & Other Fin. Data (Million $)

	2004	2003	2002	2001	2000	1999	1998	1997	1996	1995
Cash	76.9	6.74	6.50	7.29	6.97	5.92	6.63	4.67	3.90	6.40
Curr. Assets	1,756	1,585	1,450	1,329	1,187	1,225	1,117	779	613	448
Total Assets	3,913	3,680	3,478	3,433	3,333	3,285	2,748	1,884	1,498	1,112
Curr. Liab.	1,818	1,676	1,534	1,267	1,035	1,001	860	592	613	418
LT Debt	1,869	1,547	1,195	1,225	1,250	888	545	198	Nil	Nil
Common Equity	171	374	1,378	866	997	1,324	1,302	1,075	866	685
Total Cap.	2,046	1,921	2,573	2,092	2,247	2,212	1,302	1,274	866	686
Cap. Exp.	185	182	117	169	250	428	337	297	288	258
Cash Flow	673	627	546	307	386	367	323	272	230	187
Curr. Ratio	1.0	0.9	0.9	1.0	1.1	1.2	1.3	1.3	1.0	1.1
% LT Debt of Cap.	91.3	80.5	46.4	58.6	55.6	40.2	29.5	15.5	NM	NM
% Net Inc.of Revs.	10.0	9.5	8.0	3.6	6.0	5.9	7.0	7.2	7.5	7.7
% Ret. on Assets	14.7	14.5	12.4	5.2	8.1	8.1	9.8	11.5	20.5	13.9
% Ret. on Equity	207.7	97.4	27.5	18.9	23.1	18.6	19.2	20.1	22.7	22.9

Data as orig reptd.; bef. results of disc opers/spec. items. Per share data adj. for stk. divs. Bold denotes diluted EPS (FASB 128)-prior periods restated. E-Estimated. NA-Not Available. NM-Not Meaningful. NR-Not Ranked. UR-Under Review.

Office: 123 South Front Street, Memphis, TN 38103-3607.
Telephone: 901-495-6500.
Email: investor.relations@autozone.com
Website: http://www.autozone.com
Chrmn, Pres & CEO: S. Odland.

EVP & CFO: M.G. Archbold.
SVP, Secy & General Counsel: H.L. Goldsmith.
Investor Contact: B. Campbell 901-495-7005.
Dirs: C. M. Elson, E. G. Graves, N. G. House, J. R. Hyde III, E. S. Lampert, W. A. McKenna, S. Odland, J. J. Postl.

Founded: in 1986.
Domicile: Nevada.
Employees: 49,000.
S&P Analyst: Yogeesh Wagle/MF/JWP

Avaya Inc.

Recommendation: **BUY** ★★★★☆ SELL SELL HOLD BUY BUY   12-Month Target Price: **$17.00**
(as of October 29, 2004)

AV has an approximate 0.07% weighting in the **S&P 500**

Sector: Information Technology
Sub-Industry: Communications Equipment
Peer Group: Core Network Systems

Summary: This former division of Lucent Technologies was spun off in September 2000; it provides communication systems and software for enterprises worldwide.

Quantitative Evaluations

S&P Earnings & Dividend Rank: NR

D	C	B-	B	B+	A-	A	A+

S&P Fair Value Rank: 5

1	2	3	4	5
Lowest				Highest

Fair Value Calc.: $18.60 (Slightly Undervalued)

S&P Investability Quotient Percentile

74%

AV scored higher than 74% of all companies for which an S&P Report is available.

Volatility: High

Low	Average	High

Technical Evaluation: Bullish
Since 11/04, the technical indicators for AV have been Bullish.

Relative Strength Rank: Strong

87
1 Lowest   Highest 99

Price as of 11/12/04: **$16.28**   2005E S&P Core EPS: **$0.65**

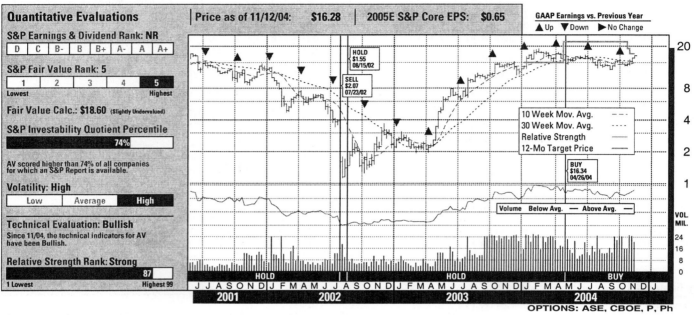

GAAP Earnings vs. Previous Year
▲ Up ▼ Down ▶ No Change

10 Week Mov. Avg.
30 Week Mov. Avg.
Relative Strength
12-Mo Target Price

Volume Below Avg. — Above Avg.

OPTIONS: ASE, CBOE, P, Ph

Analyst commentary prepared by A. Bensinger/MF/BK

Highlights November 01, 2004

- Following a 6% decline in FY 04, we expect sales to increase 8% in FY 05 (Sep.), reflecting what we see as an improved technology spending market and disciplined product pricing. We forecast solid growth for new data solutions such as Internet protocol (IP) convergence products, as both large and small enterprises are accelerating deployments of Internet telephony. Our sales estimate excludes the projected impact of Tenovis, a European enterprise communication systems provider with $1 billion in annual revenue, which AV agreed to acquire in October 2004.

- We expect gross margins to widen about 100 basis points, aided by a gradual product mix shift toward more software-based IP private branch exchange (PBX) sales. We see FY 04 operating profitability improving dramatically, aided by lower SG&A and R&D spending. As a result of aggressive restructuring, AV's cost structure has been substantially reduced.

- After lower interest expense due to continued repurchase of debt, but higher taxes reflecting the reversal of tax allowance deferrals, we forecast FY 05 operating EPS of $0.79, a 52% increase from the $0.52 EPS posted in FY 04.

Investment Rationale/Risk November 01, 2004

- Given its leading market share and largest installed base in the legacy private branch exchange (PBX) arena, we believe that Avaya is well positioned to benefit from the current transition to Internet Protocol (IP) telephony. On both a relative and intrinsic valuation basis, we view the stock's current valuation as attractive, and recommend accumulation of the shares.

- Risks to our recommendation and target price include a weakening enterprise technology spending environment, a slowdown in Internet telephony deployments, and increased acceptance of competing technologies.

- The stock trades below peers on a P/E, P/E-to-growth, and price-to-sales valuation basis. We believe that these discounts are unwarranted, given our view that earnings will ramp up materially over the next two years, as sales growth begins to benefit from what we expect to be the company's successful transition to next generation growth products. Based on the significant operating leverage that we see inherent in AV's business model, we believe that the company's target for 9.5% to 10% operating margins during FY 05 is readily achievable. Applying a blend of peer average P/E and price to sales metrics, we derive a 12-month target price of $17.

Key Stock Statistics

S&P Oper. EPS 2005E	0.79	52-week Range	$19.00-10.59
P/E on S&P Oper. EPS 2005E	20.6	12 Month P/E	25.4
Yield (%)	Nil	Beta	NA
Dividend Rate/Share	Nil	Shareholders	1,035,892
Shares Outstanding (M)	452.6	Market Cap (B)	$ 7.4

Value of $10,000 invested five years ago: **NA**

Dividend Data

No dividends have been paid.

Revenues/Earnings Data Fiscal year ending September 30

Revenues (Million $)

	2004	2003	2002	2001	2000	1999
1Q	971.0	1,067	1,306	1,785	1,845	—
2Q	1,006	1,081	1,279	1,852	1,934	—
3Q	1,016	1,072	1,219	1,714	1,885	—
4Q	1,076	1,118	1,152	1,442	2,016	—
Yr.	4,069	4,338	4,956	6,793	7,680	8,268

Earnings Per Share ($)

	2004	2003	2002	2001	2000	1999
1Q	0.07	-0.33	-0.09	0.03	0.25	—
2Q	0.22	-0.11	-0.63	-0.25	0.24	—
3Q	0.12	0.02	-0.11	0.06	0.12	—
4Q	0.21	0.15	-1.50	-1.17	-1.95	—
Yr.	0.63	-0.23	-2.44	-1.33	-1.39	0.70

Next earnings report expected: late-January Source: S&P, Company Reports
EPS Estimates based on S&P Operating Earnings; historical GAAP earnings are as reported.

Avaya Inc.

Recommendation: **BUY** ★★★★☆   12-Month Target Price: **$17.00** (as of October 29, 2004)

Business Summary November 01, 2004

Avaya (formerly the Network Enterprise Group of Lucent Technologies Inc.) provides communications systems and software for enterprises, including businesses, government agencies and other organizations. The company offers converged voice and data networks, traditional voice communications systems, customer relationship management, and unified communications. AV was spun off by Lucent Technologies to its shareholders in September 2000.

AV reported operations in four segments in FY 03 (Sep.): enterprise communications group, small and medium business solutions, services, and connectivity solutions. The majority of revenue is derived from the U.S. (74% in FY 03).

The enterprise communications group, which accounted for 40% of revenue in FY 03 (Sep.), focuses on the sale of communications solutions to large enterprise customers. Segment products include converged voice and data networks and traditional voice communications systems, customer relationship management offerings, and unified communications solutions. A critical part of the division's strategy focuses on migration from circuit-switched voice communications systems, or traditional voice communications systems, to converged packet-based networks that provide for integration of voice, data, video and other application traffic on a single unified network.

The company's services organization (42%) provides standard and customized solutions to enterprises, including network planning and design, network implementation, management and operations, and maintenance and support. AV believes it is the leading U.S. provider of maintenance services for enterprise voice communications systems.

The small and medium business solutions segment (5%) develops communications solutions, including Internet protocol (IP) telephony, traditional voice systems, unified communication and contact center solutions, for small and medium-sized businesses, and for branch offices of large enterprises.

In early 2004, the company sold substantially all the assets of its connectivity solutions segment to CommScope Inc. (CTV: hold, $18.50) for $250 million in cash, subject to adjustments, plus about 1.8 million CTV common shares. The segment, which develops structured cabling systems for wiring phones, workstations, PCs, local area networks and other communications devices under the SYSTIMAX and ExchangeMAX brand names, accounted for 13% of sales in FY 03.

In November 2003, the company acquired the assets and assumed certain liabilities of Expanets, Inc., a subsidiary of NorthWestern Corporation. Expanets is a nationwide provider of networked communications and data products and services to small and mid-sized businesses and, prior to the acquisition, one of the company's largest dealers.

In connection with its September 2000 spinoff from Lucent, AV engaged in a comprehensive review of operations, aimed at improving profitability and business performance. The company subsequently adopted an aggressive restructuring plan that included outsourcing the manufacture of substantially all communications systems and software to Celestica Inc., decreasing its real estate holdings, and reducing its workforce.

Company Financials Fiscal Year ending September 30

Per Share Data ($)

(Year Ended September 30)	2004	2003	2002	2001	2000	1999	1998	1997	1996	1995
Tangible Bk. Val.	NA	0.13	NM	0.79	1.99	4.63	NA	NA	NA	NA
Cash Flow	NA	0.27	-1.74	-0.28	-0.58	NA	NA	NA	NA	NA
Earnings	0.63	-0.23	-2.44	-1.33	-1.39	0.70	NA	NA	NA	NA
S&P Core Earnings	NA	-0.32	-3.02	-0.90	NA	NA	NA	NA	NA	NA
Dividends	Nil	Nil	Nil	Nil	Nil	NA	NA	NA	NA	NA
Payout Ratio	Nil	Nil	Nil	Nil	Nil	NA	NA	NA	NA	NA
Prices - High	19.00	14.35	12.73	19.24	26.00	NA	NA	NA	NA	NA
- Low	11.95	1.93	1.12	8.50	10.00	NA	NA	NA	NA	NA
P/E Ratio - High	30	NM	NM	NM	NM	NA	NA	NA	NA	NA
- Low	19	NM	NM	NM	NM	NA	NA	NA	NA	NA

Income Statement Analysis (Million $)

	2004	2003	2002	2001	2000	1999	1998	1997	1996	1995
Revs.	NA	4,338	4,956	6,793	7,680	8,268	NA	NA	NA	NA
Oper. Inc.	NA	310	620	6,218	461	NA	NA	NA	NA	NA
Depr.	NA	201	229	273	220	NA	NA	NA	NA	NA
Int. Exp.	NA	78.0	51.0	Nil	76.0	90.0	NA	NA	NA	NA
Pretax Inc.	NA	5.00	-401	-570	-448	307	NA	NA	NA	NA
Eff. Tax Rate	NA	NM	NM	NM	NM	39.4%	NA	NA	NA	NA
Net Inc.	NA	-88.0	-666	-352	-375	186	NA	NA	NA	NA
S&P Core Earnings	NA	-125	-997	-257	NA	NA	NA	NA	NA	NA

Balance Sheet & Other Fin. Data (Million $)

	2004	2003	2002	2001	2000	1999	1998	1997	1996	1995
Cash	NA	1,192	597	250	271	217	NA	NA	NA	NA
Curr. Assets	NA	2,569	2,303	2,769	3,362	2,763	NA	NA	NA	NA
Total Assets	NA	4,057	3,897	4,648	5,037	4,609	NA	NA	NA	NA
Curr. Liab.	NA	1,168	1,324	2,018	2,589	2,233	NA	NA	NA	NA
LT Debt	NA	953	933	1,127	713	Nil	NA	NA	NA	NA
Common Equity	NA	266	170	660	764	1,288	NA	NA	NA	NA
Total Cap.	NA	1,219	1,103	2,182	1,477	1,288	NA	NA	NA	NA
Cap. Exp.	NA	60.0	111	341	499	NA	NA	NA	NA	NA
Cash Flow	NA	113	-574	-79.0	-155	NA	NA	NA	NA	NA
Curr. Ratio	NA	2.2	1.7	1.4	1.3	1.2	NA	NA	NA	NA
% LT Debt of Cap.	NA	78.2	84.6	51.6	48.3	Nil	NA	NA	NA	NA
% Net Inc.of Revs.	NA	NM	NM	NM	NM	2.2	NA	NA	NA	NA
% Ret. on Assets	NA	NM	NM	NM	NM	NA	NA	NA	NA	NA
% Ret. on Equity	NA	NM	NM	NM	NM	NA	NA	NA	NA	NA

Data as orig reptd.; bef. results of disc opers/spec. items. Data for 1999 pro forma. Per share data adj. for stk. divs.; EPS diluted. E-Estimated. NA-Not Available. NM-Not Meaningful. NR-Not Ranked.

Office: 211 Mount Airy Rd, Basking Ridge, NJ 07920.
Telephone: 908-953-6000.
Email: avirsvcs@avaya.com
Website: http://www.avaya.com
Chrmn & CEO: D.K. Peterson.
SVP & CFO: G.K. McGuire, Sr.

SVP, Secy & General Counsel: P.F. Craven.
VP & Investor Contact: M. Booher 908-953-7500.
Treas: P. Hong.
Dirs: B. Bond, J. P. Landy, M. Leslie, P. Odeen, D. K. Peterson, H. S. Runtagh, D. C. Stanzione, P. Stern, A. Terracciano, R. Wallman, R. Zarrella.

Founded: in 2000.
Domicile: Delaware.
Employees: 16,900.
S&P Analyst: A. Bensinger/MF/BK

The **McGraw·Hill** Companies

Avery Dennison

Recommendation: **HOLD** ★ ★ ★ ★ ★
SELL | SELL | HOLD | BUY | BUY

12-Month Target Price: **$60.00**
(as of November 08, 2004)

AVY has an approximate 0.06% weighting in the **S&P 500**

Sector: Industrials
Sub-Industry: Office Services & Supplies
Peer Group: Office Supplies - Forms & Stationary

Summary: AVY is a leading worldwide manufacturer of pressure-sensitive adhesives and materials, office products, labels, retail systems and specialty chemicals.

Quantitative Evaluations

S&P Earnings & Dividend Rank: A

D	C	B-	B	B+	A-	A	A+

S&P Fair Value Rank: 4

1	2	3	4	5
Lowest				Highest

Fair Value Calc.: $55.30 (Slightly Overvalued)

S&P Investability Quotient Percentile

98%

AVY scored higher than 98% of all companies for which an S&P Report is available.

Volatility: Low

Low	Average	High

Technical Evaluation: Bearish

Since 10/04, the technical indicators for AVY have been Bearish.

Relative Strength Rank: Weak

13

1 Lowest   Highest 99

Price as of 11/12/04:	$56.63	2004E S&P Core EPS:	$2.76

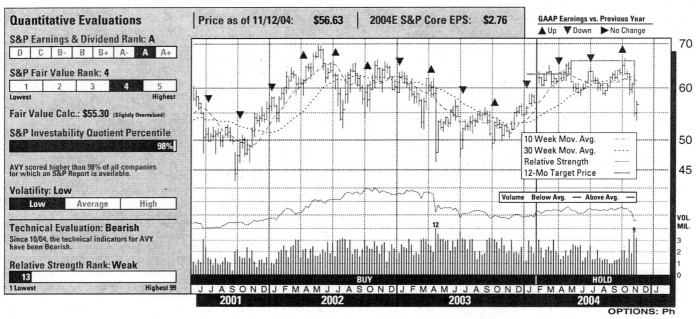

GAAP Earnings vs. Previous Year
▲ Up ▼ Down ► No Change

10 Week Mov. Avg.
30 Week Mov. Avg.
Relative Strength
12-Mo Target Price

Volume Below Avg. — Above Avg. —

Analyst commentary prepared by Richard O'Reilly, CFA /CB/JWP

Highlights November 08, 2004

- We see sales in 2005 increasing about 8%, on top of a projected 10% gain for 2004, which will be aided by one extra week in the fiscal year. We expect volumes at existing businesses to grow about 6% in 2005, led by continued growth in the roll material and retail information services businesses and continued strong gains in Asia and Latin America.

- We expect office products comparisons to improve in 2005, assuming a better back-to-school season, aided by the recovery of lost market shares and new products. The price/mix decline will likely again be less than the typical 2.0% rate, offset by favorable currency rates.

- We see profitability benefiting from the greater volume expected and the completion of actions designed to generate cost savings of up to $30 million in 2004, partly offset by increased raw material costs (annual run rate of about $60 million as of late 2004). AVY expects product development spending for radio frequency identification (RFID) to nearly double in 2005, partly offset by initial sales of about $10 million. We project that the tax rate will remain at 26.0%. Our 2004 EPS estimate excludes pretax restructuring charges of $35.2 million ($0.25 a share) in the first half and any possible anti-trust fines.

Investment Rationale/Risk November 08, 2004

- We have a hold opinion on the shares. We believe fundamentals remain sound, with growth driven by increasing use of non-impact printing systems for computers and for product tracking and information needs. We also see a proliferation of high-quality graphics on packaging and consumer products spurring sales of pressure-sensitive labels.

- Risks to our recommendation and target price include the potentially adverse impact of anti-trust investigations involving AVY, and an inability to introduce new products or raise selling prices in response to higher raw material costs. In November 2004, AVY said that an expected anti-trust fine by the European Commission could well be material in amount. In 2003, the Justice Department began an investigation, which is still ongoing, into competitive practices in the label stock industry.

- Our concerns regarding anti-trust investigations largely offset continued growth in organic sales growth that we project; as a result, we see AVY's P/E multiple below its typical premium to the S&P 500 of about 20%, and have a 12-month target price of $60. We think AVY's record of earnings and dividend growth (Standard & Poor's Earnings/Dividend Ranking of A; 29 consecutive years of dividend growth) provides support for the shares.

Key Stock Statistics

S&P Core EPS 2005E	3.08	52-week Range	$66.60-51.75
S&P Oper. EPS 2004E	2.98	12 Month P/E	22.2
P/E on S&P Oper. EPS 2004E	19.0	Beta	0.67
S&P Oper. EPS 2005E	3.30	Shareholders	11,287
Yield (%)	2.7%	Market Cap (B)	$ 6.3
Dividend Rate/Share	1.52	Shares Outstanding (M)	110.5

Value of $10,000 invested five years ago: **$ 9,770**

Dividend Data Dividends have been paid since 1964

Amount ($)	Date Decl.	Ex-Div. Date	Stock of Record	Payment Date
0.370	Jan. 29	Mar. 01	Mar. 03	Mar. 17 '04
0.370	Apr. 22	May. 28	Jun. 02	Jun. 16 '04
0.370	Jul. 23	Aug. 30	Sep. 01	Sep. 15 '04
0.380	Oct. 28	Nov. 29	Dec. 01	Dec. 15 '04

Revenues/Earnings Data Fiscal year ending December 31

Revenues (Million $)

	2004	2003	2002	2001	2000	1999
1Q	1,247	1,135	930.8	963.2	965.3	933.9
2Q	1,324	1,192	1,056	960.8	993.4	928.5
3Q	1,336	1,204	1,115	966.7	1,002	961.0
4Q	—	1,231	1,105	912.6	933.1	944.8
Yr.	—	4,763	4,207	3,803	3,894	3,768

Earnings Per Share ($)

	2004	2003	2002	2001	2000	1999
1Q	0.52	0.71	0.66	0.65	0.70	0.18
2Q	0.68	0.70	0.74	0.61	0.73	0.63
3Q	0.75	0.65	0.64	0.63	0.73	0.65
4Q	E0.77	0.40	0.56	0.59	0.69	0.67
Yr.	E2.98	2.43	2.59	2.47	2.84	2.13

Next earnings report expected: late-January Source: S&P, Company Reports
EPS Estimates based on S&P Operating Earnings; historical GAAP earnings are as reported.

Avery Dennison Corporation

Recommendation: **HOLD** ★★★☆☆   12-Month Target Price: **$60.00** (as of November 08, 2004)

Business Summary November 09, 2004

Avery Dennison is the leading global manufacturer of pressure-sensitive technology and self-adhesive solutions for consumer products and label systems, including office products, product identification and control systems, and specialty tapes and chemicals. The company believes it is benefiting from increasing demand for more informative labels on products; expanding use of PCs and printers; accelerating use of bar codes; and growth of consumer spending in developing countries. AVY achieved record sales and earnings for nine consecutive years until 2001, despite the cost of investments in new businesses and products. Excluding the impact of currency translation, sales increased 8.6% in 2003, and the company realized a return on equity of 22.3%.

Foreign operations, primarily in Europe, accounted for 50% of sales in 2003. The company has been investing in an effort to build a business base in Asia Pacific, Latin America and Eastern Europe.

The pressure-sensitive adhesives and materials group (61% of sales and 48% of operating profits in 2003) includes Fasson-brand pressure sensitive, self-adhesive coated papers, plastic films and metal foils in roll and sheet form, graphic and decoration films and labels, specialty fastening and bonding tapes, and adhesives, protective coatings and electroconductive resins, for industrial, automotive, aerospace, appliance, electronic, medical and consumer markets. The acquisition of Jackstadt in May 2002 was AVY's largest in more than a decade, and strengthened its business in many developing markets worldwide.

The consumer and converted products group (39% and 52%) consists of consumer and office products such as pressure-sensitive labels, laser and ink-jet print labels and software, notebooks, binders, presentation and organizing systems, marking devices, and many other products sold under the Avery, National and Hi-Liter brands for office, home and school uses.

Converted products include custom labels and application and imprinting machines for the industrial, durable goods, consumer goods and electronic data processing markets; self-adhesive postal stamps; on-battery testing labels; automotive and industrial decoration films and graphics; and retail information products (tags, labels, printers, marking and coding systems, application devices, and plastic fasteners and cable ties) for apparel, retail, distribution, and industrial markets for use in identification, tracking and control applications.

AVY has bought back 37.2 million common shares since 1990, for a total of $1 billion. In November 1999, directors authorized the purchase of up to another 5 million shares. The company has a debt target of 45% to 50% of total capitalization; the ratio was 47% at September 30, 2004. Capital spending for 2004 is projected at $200 million, versus $201.4 million in 2003.

Company Financials Fiscal Year ending December 31

Per Share Data ($)

(Year Ended December 31)	2003	2002	2001	2000	1999	1998	1997	1996	1995	1994
Tangible Bk. Val.	4.08	2.53	4.70	3.94	3.66	5.98	5.91	5.73	6.52	5.54
Cash Flow	4.22	4.12	4.05	4.41	3.61	3.37	3.03	2.76	2.36	1.91
Earnings	2.43	2.59	2.47	2.84	2.13	2.15	1.93	1.68	1.35	0.99
S&P Core Earnings	2.05	2.02	1.81	NA	NA	NA	NA	NA	NA	NA
Dividends	1.45	1.35	1.23	1.11	0.99	0.87	0.72	0.62	0.56	0.50
Payout Ratio	60%	52%	50%	39%	46%	40%	37%	37%	41%	50%
Prices - High	63.75	69.70	60.50	78.50	73.00	62.06	45.75	36.50	25.06	18.00
- Low	46.25	52.06	43.25	41.12	39.37	39.43	33.37	23.75	16.56	13.18
P/E Ratio - High	26	27	24	28	34	29	24	22	19	18
- Low	19	20	18	14	18	18	17	14	12	13

Income Statement Analysis (Million $)

	2003	2002	2001	2000	1999	1998	1997	1996	1995	1994
Revs.	4,763	4,207	3,803	3,894	3,768	3,460	3,346	3,223	3,114	2,857
Oper. Inc.	602	593	566	638	589	499	460	419	375	318
Depr.	179	153	156	157	150	127	117	113	108	103
Int. Exp.	57.7	43.7	50.2	54.6	43.4	34.6	31.7	40.9	47.5	45.7
Pretax Inc.	335	365	360	426	330	337	311	271	225	173
Eff. Tax Rate	27.5%	29.5%	32.4%	33.5%	34.8%	33.7%	34.2%	35.0%	36.0%	36.7%
Net Inc.	243	257	243	284	215	223	205	176	144	109
S&P Core Earnings	205	201	179	NA	NA	NA	NA	NA	NA	NA

Balance Sheet & Other Fin. Data (Million $)

	2003	2002	2001	2000	1999	1998	1997	1996	1995	1994
Cash	29.5	22.8	19.1	11.4	6.90	18.5	3.30	3.80	27.0	3.10
Curr. Assets	1,441	1,216	983	982	956	802	794	805	800	677
Total Assets	4,105	3,652	2,819	2,699	2,593	2,143	2,047	2,037	1,964	1,763
Curr. Liab.	1,496	1,296	951	801	850	664	630	694	673	554
LT Debt	888	837	627	773	701	466	404	371	334	347
Common Equity	1,319	1,056	929	828	810	833	838	832	816	729
Total Cap.	2,274	1,968	1,647	1,695	1,610	1,363	1,292	1,247	1,191	1,116
Cap. Exp.	201	152	135	198	178	160	177	188	190	163
Cash Flow	422	410	399	440	366	351	322	289	252	212
Curr. Ratio	1.0	0.9	1.0	1.2	1.1	1.2	1.3	1.2	1.2	1.2
% LT Debt of Cap.	39.0	42.5	38.0	45.6	43.5	34.2	31.3	29.8	28.0	31.1
% Net Inc.of Revs.	5.1	6.1	6.4	7.3	5.7	6.5	6.1	5.5	4.6	3.8
% Ret. on Assets	6.3	7.8	8.8	10.7	9.1	10.7	10.0	8.8	7.7	6.6
% Ret. on Equity	20.4	25.9	27.7	34.6	26.2	26.7	24.5	21.4	18.2	15.5

Data as orig reptd.; bef. results of disc opers/spec. items. Per share data adj. for stk. divs.; EPS diluted. E-Estimated. NA-Not Available. NM-Not Meaningful. NR-Not Ranked. UR-Under Review.

Office: 150 North Orange Grove Boulevard, Pasadena, CA 91103.
Telephone: 626-304-2000.
Email: investorcom@averydennison.com
Website: http://www.averydennison.com
Chrmn & CEO: P.M. Neal.
Pres & COO: D.A. Scarborough.
EVP, Secy & General Counsel: R.G. van Schoonenberg.

SVP & CFO: D.R. O'Bryant.
VP & Treas: K.E. Rodriguez.
Investor Contact: C.S. Guenther 626-304-2204.
Dirs: P. K. Barker, F. V. Cahouet, J. T. Cardis, R. M. Ferry, B. E. Karatz, K. Kresa, C. D. Miller, P. W. Mullin, P. M. Neal, D. E. Pyott, D. A. Scarborough, J. A. Stewart.

Founded: in 1935.
Domicile: Delaware.
Employees: 20,300.
S&P Analyst: Richard O'Reilly, CFA /CB/JWP

The McGraw·Hill Companies

Avon Products

Recommendation: **HOLD** ★ ★ ★ ☆ ☆
SELL | SELL | HOLD | BUY | BUY

12-Month Target Price: **$42.00**
(as of October 29, 2004)

AVP has an approximate 0.17% weighting in the **S&P 500**

Sector: Consumer Staples
Sub-Industry: Personal Products
Peer Group: Larger Personal Care Cos.

Summary: AVP is the world's leading direct marketer of cosmetics, toiletries, fashion jewelry and fragrances, with more than 3 million sales representatives worldwide.

Quantitative Evaluations

S&P Earnings & Dividend Rank: A

D | C | B- | B | B+ | A- | **A** | A+

S&P Fair Value Rank: 1

1 | 2 | 3 | 4 | 5
Lowest | | | | Highest

Fair Value Calc.: $31.80 (Overvalued)

S&P Investability Quotient Percentile

100%

AVP scored higher than 100% of all companies for which an S&P Report is available.

Volatility: Average

Low | **Average** | High

Technical Evaluation: Bearish

Since 10/04, the technical indicators for AVP have been Bearish.

Relative Strength Rank: Weak

16
1 Lowest | Highest 99

Price as of 11/12/04: $39.75 | **2004E S&P Core EPS:** $1.64

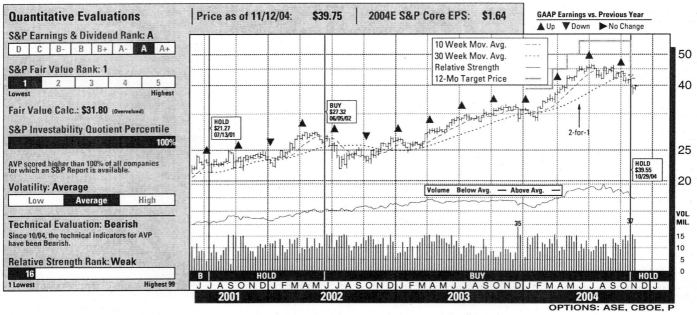

GAAP Earnings vs. Previous Year ▲ Up ▼ Down ► No Change

OPTIONS: ASE, CBOE, P

Analyst commentary prepared by Howard Choe/PMW/BK

Highlights November 02, 2004

- We expect 2004 sales to grow nearly 9%, on solid volume gains in the core direct selling business, fueled by strong sales representative growth and new product introductions. We see a weak outlook for the U.S. dollar and Latin American currencies, and expect AVP to benefit modestly from foreign exchange translations. We believe that regional sales gains will be led by Europe and Asia/Pacific. We expect U.S. sales to rise only slightly, largely due to a less favorable product mix and slow sales representative growth. We see strong consumer demand in Central and Eastern Europe driving European growth. We estimate 8% sales growth for 2005, led again by Europe and Asia/Pacific.

- We project an expansion of about 80 basis point in operating margins, driven by supply chain initiatives and greater sales from higher profit regions, partly offset by higher advertising and R&D spending. We expect a similar widening of margins in 2005.

- We project that 2004 EPS will advance 27%, to $1.77, from $1.39 in 2003 (excluding charges and one-time items). For 2005, we expect 10% growth, to $1.95. We project S&P Core EPS of $1.64 for 2004 and $1.81 for 2005, primarily reflecting estimated stock option expense.

Investment Rationale/Risk November 02, 2004

- We recently downgraded the shares to hold, from buy, reflecting our weaker outlook for the U.S. market. AVP indicated recently that fourth quarter U.S. sales and operating income were likely to decline 3% and in the mid-teens, respectively. We expect weakness in the U.S. market to continue for the near term, in light of what we see as a lack of catalysts. Overall, we see global sales as healthy, due to success in developing markets. However, we believe weakness in the U.S. market has added risk to earnings growth and consistency. Until there are signs indicating stabilization or recovery in the U.S. market, we believe the stock will have difficulty in returning to the high end of its historical range.

- Risks to our recommendation and target price include further deterioration in the U.S. market, political and economic instability in international markets, competition from various sales channels, and unfavorable consumer reception of new products.

- In light of our less robust outlook for AVP, we see the shares as fairly valued at a recent level of 19X our 2005 EPS estimate, slightly above the peer group average, but at a discount to our 12-month target price of $42, which we derived from relative valuation and discounted cash flow analyses.

Key Stock Statistics

S&P Core EPS 2005E	1.81	52-week Range	$46.65-30.67
S&P Oper. EPS 2004E	1.74	12 Month P/E	23.1
P/E on S&P Oper. EPS 2004E	22.8	Beta	0.47
S&P Oper. EPS 2005E	2.00	Shareholders	120,263
Yield (%)	1.4%	Market Cap (B)	$ 18.8
Dividend Rate/Share	0.56	Shares Outstanding (M)	473.0

Value of $10,000 invested five years ago: **$ 29,271**

Dividend Data Dividends have been paid since 1919

Amount ($)	Date Decl.	Ex-Div. Date	Stock of Record	Payment Date
0.280	May. 07	May. 13	May. 17	Jun. 01 '04
0.140	Aug. 05	Aug. 16	Aug. 18	Sep. 01 '04
0.140	Aug. 05	Aug. 16	Aug. 18	Sep. 01 '04
0.140	Nov. 04	Nov. 12	Nov. 16	Dec. 01 '04

Revenues/Earnings Data Fiscal year ending December 31

Revenues (Million $)

	2004	2003	2002	2001	2000	1999
1Q	1,775	1,481	1,384	1,358	1,325	1,214
2Q	1,866	1,656	1,527	1,463	1,378	1,258
3Q	1,806	1,629	1,463	1,423	1,343	1,251
4Q	—	2,109	1,854	1,752	1,648	1,566
Yr.	—	6,876	6,228	5,995	5,674	5,289

Earnings Per Share ($)

	2004	2003	2002	2001	2000	1999
1Q	0.31	0.21	0.20	0.17	0.15	-0.10
2Q	0.49	0.36	0.32	0.29	0.26	0.23
3Q	0.37	0.28	0.19	0.21	0.20	0.17
4Q	E0.60	0.55	0.40	0.23	0.41	0.29
Yr.	E1.74	1.39	1.11	0.90	1.01	0.59

Next earnings report expected: early-February Source: S&P, Company Reports
EPS Estimates based on S&P Operating Earnings; historical GAAP earnings are as reported.

Avon Products, Inc.

Recommendation: **HOLD** ★ ★ ★ ☆ ☆   12-Month Target Price: **$42.00** (as of October 29, 2004)

Business Summary November 02, 2004

Avon Products, which began operations in 1886, is a global manufacturer and marketer of beauty and related products. The company has four product categories: Beauty, which consists of cosmetics, fragrance and toiletries; Beauty Plus, consisting of jewelry, watches and apparel and accessories; Beyond Beauty, which consists of home products, gift and decorative and candles; and Health and Wellness, which consists of vitamins, an aromatherapy line, exercise equipment, as well as stress relief and weight management products. AVP's business is carried out primarily through direct selling, and is conducted in North America, Latin America, the Pacific and Europe. The company's reportable segments are based on geographic operations.

The company has operations in 59 countries, including the U.S., and its products are distributed in 72 additional countries, for coverage in 131 markets. Sales are made to the ultimate customer mainly through a combination of direct selling and marketing by about 4.4 million independent Avon Representatives, about 500,000 of whom are in the U.S. Representatives are independent contractors or independent dealers, and are not agents or employees of the company. Representatives purchase products directly from AVP, and sell them to their customers.

Geographically, 37% of 2003 sales were derived from North America, while Latin America, Asia Pacific and Europe accounted for 26%, 14% and 24% of sales, respectively. Foreign operations accounted for 67% of operating profits in 2003.

In 2001, the company launched the Wellness line globally, to serve the needs of women in the area of health and wellness. The products are sold through a separate catalog and include vitamins and nutrition supplements, exercise and fitness items, and self-care and stress relief products.

In 2001, AVP opened 92 Avon Centers in J.C. Penney stores, to sell a new line of beauty products, as well as a selection of jewelry and accessories and health and wellness products under beComing line. However, after achieving lower than expected results, the two parties agreed to end the venture in January 2003. The beComing brand was designated to be sold by the Avon Beauty Advisors, who are independent sales representatives.

In 2003, the company launched a new global cosmetics brand, mark., focusing on the fast growing market for young women in the 16 to 24 year age group, in an effort to increase share in the worldwide youth market. The mark. brand is sold both by AVP's core direct selling channel of U.S. representatives and by a separate mark. sales force. AVP intends to introduce mark. into additional markets over the next several years.

Company Financials Fiscal Year ending December 31

Per Share Data ($)

(Year Ended December 31)	2003	2002	2001	2000	1999	1998	1997	1996	1995	1994
Tangible Bk. Val.	0.79	NM	NM	NM	NM	0.55	0.54	0.46	0.36	0.32
Cash Flow	1.63	1.34	1.10	1.20	0.74	0.64	0.77	0.72	0.63	0.57
Earnings	1.39	1.11	0.90	1.01	0.59	0.51	0.64	0.59	0.52	0.47
S&P Core Earnings	1.36	0.95	0.77	NA	NA	NA	NA	NA	NA	NA
Dividends	0.42	0.40	0.38	0.37	0.36	0.34	0.32	0.29	0.26	0.24
Payout Ratio	30%	36%	42%	37%	62%	67%	50%	49%	50%	51%
Prices - High	34.87	28.55	25.06	24.87	29.56	23.12	19.50	14.87	9.79	7.95
- Low	24.46	21.74	17.77	12.62	11.65	12.50	12.65	9.07	6.75	6.04
P/E Ratio - High	25	26	28	25	51	45	31	25	19	17
- Low	18	20	20	12	20	25	20	15	13	13

Income Statement Analysis (Million $)

	2003	2002	2001	2000	1999	1998	1997	1996	1995	1994
Revs.	6,876	6,228	5,995	5,715	5,289	5,213	5,079	4,814	4,492	4,267
Oper. Inc.	1,162	1,029	951	886	762	706	616	609	566	551
Depr.	124	125	109	97.1	83.0	72.0	72.1	64.5	58.3	55.7
Int. Exp.	33.3	52.0	71.1	84.7	43.2	41.0	41.8	40.0	41.3	51.0
Pretax Inc.	994	836	666	691	507	456	535	510	465	434
Eff. Tax Rate	32.1%	35.0%	34.7%	29.2%	40.3%	41.9%	37.0%	37.5%	37.9%	37.7%
Net Inc.	665	535	430	485	302	270	339	318	286	265
S&P Core Earnings	652	455	367	NA	NA	NA	NA	NA	NA	NA

Balance Sheet & Other Fin. Data (Million $)

	2003	2002	2001	2000	1999	1998	1997	1996	1995	1994
Cash	694	607	509	123	117	106	142	185	151	215
Curr. Assets	2,226	2,048	1,889	1,546	1,338	1,341	1,344	1,350	1,215	1,150
Total Assets	3,562	3,328	3,193	2,826	2,529	2,434	2,273	2,222	2,053	1,978
Curr. Liab.	1,588	1,976	1,461	1,359	1,713	1,330	1,356	1,391	1,245	1,141
LT Debt	878	767	1,236	1,108	701	201	102	105	114	117
Common Equity	371	-128	-74.6	-216	-406	285	285	242	193	186
Total Cap.	1,300	712	1,192	954	365	559	456	422	387	383
Cap. Exp.	163	127	155	194	203	190	169	104	73.0	100
Cash Flow	788	659	539	582	385	342	411	382	344	321
Curr. Ratio	1.4	1.0	1.3	1.1	0.8	1.0	1.0	1.0	1.0	1.0
% LT Debt of Cap.	67.5	107.8	103.7	116.1	192.3	36.0	22.3	24.9	29.5	30.4
% Net Inc.of Revs.	9.7	8.6	7.2	8.5	5.7	5.2	6.7	6.6	6.4	6.2
% Ret. on Assets	19.3	16.4	14.3	18.1	12.2	11.5	15.1	14.9	14.2	13.7
% Ret. on Equity	545.8	NM	NM	NM	NM	94.7	128.7	146.0	151.3	108.9

Data as orig reptd.; bef. results of disc opers/spec. items. Per share data adj. for stk. divs.; EPS diluted. E-Estimated. NA-Not Available. NM-Not Meaningful. NR-Not Ranked. UR-Under Review.

Office: 1345 Avenue of the Americas, New York, NY 10105-0196.
Telephone: 212-282-5000.
Email: individual.investor@avon.com
Website: http://www.avon.com
Chrmn & CEO: A. Jung.
Pres & COO: S.J. Kropf.

EVP & CFO: R.J. Corti.
SVP, Secy & General Counsel: G.L. Klemann II.
Investor Contact: R. Johansen 212-282-5320.
Dirs: W. D. Cornwell, E. T. Fogarty, S. C. Gault, F. Hassan, A. Jung, S. J. Kropf, M. E. Lagomasino, A. S. Moore, P. Stern, L. A. Weinbach.

Founded: in 1886.
Domicile: New York.
Employees: 45,900.
S&P Analyst: Howard Choe/PMW/BK

The **McGraw·Hill** Companies

Baker Hughes

Recommendation: **HOLD** ★ ★ ★ ☆ ☆
SELL | SELL | HOLD | BUY | BUY

12-Month Target Price: **$44.00**
(as of October 28, 2004)

BHI has an approximate 0.13% weighting in the **S&P 500**

Sector: Energy
Sub-Industry: Oil & Gas Equipment & Services
Peer Group: Oil & Gas - Services & Equipment - Large

Summary: BHI is one of the world's largest providers of oil and gas exploration and production equipment, products and services.

Quantitative Evaluations

Price as of 11/12/04: $42.16   **2004E S&P Core EPS:** $1.34

S&P Earnings & Dividend Rank: B-

| D | C | B- | B | B+ | A- | A | A+ |

S&P Fair Value Rank: 2

| 1 | 2 | 3 | 4 | 5 |
| Lowest | | | | Highest |

Fair Value Calc.: $37.70 (Slightly Overvalued)

S&P Investability Quotient Percentile

96%

BHI scored higher than 96% of all companies for which an S&P Report is available.

Volatility: Low

| Low | Average | High |

Technical Evaluation: Neutral
Since 11/04, the technical indicators for BHI have been Neutral.

Relative Strength Rank: Moderate

35

| 1 Lowest | | Highest 99 |

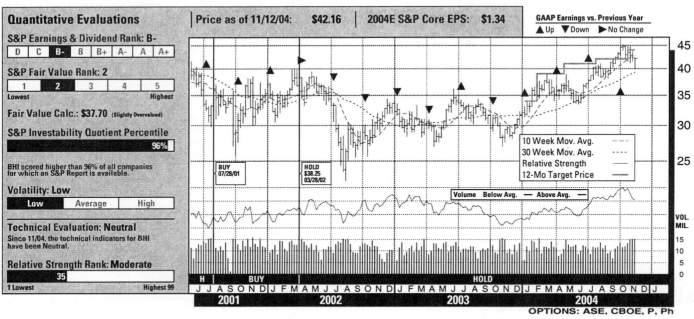

GAAP Earnings vs. Previous Year
▲ Up   ▼ Down   ► No Change

10 Week Mov. Avg.
30 Week Mov. Avg.
Relative Strength
12-Mo Target Price

Volume   Below Avg. — Above Avg. —

BUY 07/28/01
HOLD $38.25 03/28/02

H | BUY | HOLD
J J A S O N D | J F M A M J J A S O N D | J F M A M J J A S O N D | J F M A M J J A S O N D | J
2001 | 2002 | 2003 | 2004

VOL. MIL.

OPTIONS: ASE, CBOE, P, Ph

Analyst commentary prepared by Stewart Glickman/PMW/GG

Highlights August 17, 2004

- In the second quarter, WesternGeco achieved its second consecutive quarterly operating profit, after five consecutive quarters of losses. Through the 2004 first half, WesternGeco contributed $12.8 million in operating profits, versus $9.8 million in losses for all of 2003; we look for about $25 million to $30 million in profits for all of 2004 from this segment. We expect total company revenues to grow in the low double digits in 2004, with most of the increase coming from international markets. We look for operating margins of the core oilfield segment to average in the mid-double digits.

- We project significant free cash flow in 2004. In light of the company's stock repurchase authorization, we expect additional stock buybacks, as well as a reduction in financial leverage. At June 30, 2004, long term debt was about 25% of total capitalization, below the peer group average. In July 2004, BHI agreed to sell Baker Hughes Mining Tools, a product line group in the Hughes Christensen division that makes rotary drill bits; the sale, subject to necessary approvals, was expected to close in the third quarter.

- We look for 2004 EPS of $1.44, followed by $1.63 in 2005. On an S&P Core Earnings basis, we expect respective EPS of $1.34 and $1.53.

Investment Rationale/Risk August 17, 2004

- Through early August, the shares climbed about 24% in 2004, versus an increase of 18% for the S&P Oil & Gas Equipment and Services Index. The shares are trading at a slight premium to peers on several metrics. At an enterprise value of 11.5X our 2005 EBITDA estimate, the stock is slightly above the peer average of 10.8X, and it is at 33X estimated net equity per share, versus a peer level of 31X. In addition, the stock is trading at 24X our 2005 EPS estimate, versus the peer group average of 22X. However, based on strong brand value that we see in the oilfield services space, we think a modest premium is warranted.

- Risks to our recommendation and target price include lower prices for oil and natural gas; reduced drilling activity in international markets; and a return to operating losses at WesternGeco.

- Our 12-month target price of $42 is based on our expectations that the stock will achieve an enterprise value of 12X our 2005 EBITDA estimate. We think that BHI's solid fundamentals and strong growth potential are fairly reflected in the stock price, and would not add to positions.

Key Stock Statistics

S&P Core EPS 2005E	1.53	52-week Range	$45.30-28.01
S&P Oper. EPS 2004E	1.44	12 Month P/E	31.2
P/E on S&P Oper. EPS 2004E	29.3	Beta	0.49
S&P Oper. EPS 2005E	1.63	Shareholders	71,000
Yield (%)	1.1%	Market Cap (B)	$ 14.1
Dividend Rate/Share	0.46	Shares Outstanding (M)	335.5

Value of $10,000 invested five years ago: **$ 19,453**

Dividend Data Dividends have been paid since 1987

Amount ($)	Date Decl.	Ex-Div. Date	Stock of Record	Payment Date
0.115	Jan. 28	Feb. 05	Feb. 09	Feb. 20 '04
0.115	Apr. 28	May. 06	May. 10	May. 21 '04
0.115	Jul. 28	Aug. 05	Aug. 09	Aug. 20 '04
0.115	Oct. 27	Nov. 04	Nov. 08	Nov. 19 '04

Revenues/Earnings Data Fiscal year ending December 31

Revenues (Million $)

	2004	2003	2002	2001	2000	1999
1Q	1,399	1,200	1,203	1,229	1,241	1,325
2Q	1,499	1,315	1,245	1,342	1,256	1,211
3Q	1,538	1,338	1,280	1,436	1,354	1,208
4Q	—	1,440	1,292	1,376	1,384	1,104
Yr.	—	5,293	5,020	5,382	5,234	4,547

Earnings Per Share ($)

	2004	2003	2002	2001	2000	1999
1Q	0.29	0.15	0.21	0.21	0.04	0.13
2Q	0.35	0.24	0.21	0.31	0.19	0.20
3Q	0.41	-0.29	0.19	0.41	0.20	0.04
4Q	E0.43	0.30	-0.01	0.37	-0.12	-0.28
Yr.	E1.44	0.40	0.62	1.31	0.31	0.10

Next earnings report expected: mid-February Source: S&P, Company Reports
EPS Estimates based on S&P Operating Earnings; historical GAAP earnings are as reported.

Baker Hughes Incorporated

Recommendation: **HOLD** ★ ★ ★ ☆ ☆   12-Month Target Price: **$44.00** (as of October 28, 2004)

Business Summary August 17, 2004

Baker Hughes was formed through the 1987 merger of Baker International Corp. and Hughes Tool Co. In 1998, it acquired seismic and wireline logging company Western Atlas, creating the third largest oilfield services company. BHI has operations in 80 countries. The U.S. accounted for 36% of 2003 revenues (35% in 2002), followed by Canada 7% (5%), Norway 6% (6%) and the U.K. 6% (7%).

The Oilfield segment is comprised of seven operating divisions: Baker Atlas, Baker Oil Tools, Baker Petrolite, Centrilift, Hughes Christensen, INTEQ, and Drilling Fluids. These divisions manufacture and sell equipment and provide services used in the drilling, completion, production and maintenance of oil and gas wells and in reservoir measurement and evaluation. The Oilfield segment also includes the company's 30% interest in WesternGeco, a seismic venture between BHI and Schlumberger Ltd.

Baker Atlas provides formation evaluation and perforating services for oil and natural gas wells. Formation evaluation involves measuring and analyzing specific physical properties of the rock in the vicinity of the wellbore, to determine an oil or natural gas reservoir's boundaries, volume of hydrocarbons, and ability to produce fluids to the surface. Perforating services involve puncturing a well's steel casing and cement sheath with explosive charges; this creates a fracture in the formation, and provides a path for the hydrocarbons in the formation to enter the wellbore.

Baker Oil Tools is a leading provider of completion, workover and fishing equipment and services. Well completions are the equipment installed in the well after it is drilled to allow the safe and efficient production of oil or natural gas to the surface. Product lines include packer systems, fishing services, liner hangers,

sand control, service tools, and subsurface safety systems. Workover products and services seek to improve, maintain or restore economical production from an already producing well, and include service tools and inflatable products to repair and stimulate new and existing wells.

Baker Petrolite is a leading provider of oilfield specialty chemicals and integrated chemical technology solutions for petroleum production, transportation and refining. The division provides oilfield chemical programs for drilling, well stimulation, production, pipeline transportation, and maintenance programs. Products and services include hydrate inhibitors, corrosion inhibitors, and emulsion breakers.

Centrilift is a leader in technology for oilfield electric submersible pumping systems, which help raise oil to the surface, as well as progressing cavity pump systems. Hughes Christensen manufactures and markets drill bit products, primarily Tricone roller cone drill bits and polycrystalline diamond compact (PDC) fixed cutter bits for the oil, gas, mining and geothermal industries.

INTEQ supplies directional and horizontal drilling services, coring services, subsurface surveying, logging-while-drilling, and measurement-while-drilling services to the oil and gas industry. The new Drilling Fluids division, created in July 2004, will be responsible for business formerly included in INTEQ, including oilfield drilling fluids, completion fluids, and fluids environmental services businesses.

The company formerly operated a Process segment that manufactured and sold process equipment for separating solids from liquids, and liquids from other liquids. In 2003, BHI agreed to sell BIRD Machine, its last remaining division in this segment; the sale closed in January 2004.

Company Financials Fiscal Year ending December 31

Per Share Data ($)

(Year Ended December 31)	2003	2002	2001	2000	1999	1998	1997	1996	1995	1994
Tangible Bk. Val.	5.87	6.05	5.69	4.64	4.17	3.98	9.16	6.45	5.21	4.56
Cash Flow	1.59	1.56	2.32	2.14	2.52	1.43	1.93	2.32	1.89	1.94
Earnings	0.40	0.66	1.31	0.31	0.16	-0.92	0.71	1.23	0.67	0.85
S&P Core Earnings	0.62	0.55	1.17	NA	NA	NA	NA	NA	NA	NA
Dividends	0.46	0.46	0.46	0.46	0.46	0.46	0.46	0.43	0.46	0.46
Payout Ratio	115%	70%	35%	148%	NM	NM	65%	35%	69%	54%
Prices - High	36.15	39.95	45.29	43.37	36.25	44.12	49.62	38.87	24.87	22.12
- Low	26.90	22.60	25.76	19.62	15.00	15.00	32.62	22.75	16.75	17.00
P/E Ratio - High	90	61	35	NM	NM	NM	70	32	37	26
- Low	67	34	20	NM	NM	NM	46	18	25	20

Income Statement Analysis (Million $)

	2003	2002	2001	2000	1999	1998	1997	1996	1995	1994
Revs.	5,293	5,020	5,382	5,234	4,547	6,312	3,685	3,028	2,637	2,505
Oper. Inc.	957	856	1,077	1,076	992	1,058	616	502	410	361
Depr. Depl. & Amort.	349	302	345	612	778	758	186	156	155	154
Int. Exp.	103	111	126	173	159	149	48.6	55.5	55.6	63.8
Pretax Inc.	328	380	662	236	85.0	-281	213	299	205	226
Eff. Tax Rate	45.1%	41.2%	33.7%	56.7%	37.6%	NM	48.8%	41.0%	41.5%	42.0%
Net Inc.	180	224	439	102	53.0	-297	109	176	120	131
S&P Core Earnings	209	186	393	NA	NA	NA	NA	NA	NA	NA

Balance Sheet & Other Fin. Data (Million $)

	2003	2002	2001	2000	1999	1998	1997	1996	1995	1994
Cash	98.4	144	45.4	34.6	18.0	16.6	8.60	7.71	6.82	69.0
Curr. Assets	2,524	2,556	2,697	2,487	2,330	2,725	2,221	1,717	1,565	1,400
Total Assets	6,302	6,401	6,676	6,453	7,040	7,811	4,756	3,298	3,167	3,000
Curr. Liab.	1,302	1,080	1,212	988	1,000	1,310	936	635	580	545
LT Debt	1,133	1,424	1,682	2,050	2,706	2,726	772	674	798	638
Common Equity	3,350	3,397	3,328	3,047	3,072	3,199	2,605	1,689	1,514	1,438
Total Cap.	4,611	4,988	5,221	5,255	5,813	6,082	3,652	2,513	2,430	2,334
Cap. Exp.	405	317	319	599	634	1,318	343	182	139	109
Cash Flow	529	525	783	714	831	461	295	332	267	273
Curr. Ratio	1.9	2.4	2.2	2.5	2.3	2.1	2.4	2.7	2.7	2.6
% LT Debt of Cap.	24.6	28.6	32.2	39.0	46.6	44.8	21.1	26.8	32.8	27.3
% Ret. on Assets	2.8	3.4	6.7	1.5	0.7	NM	2.7	5.4	3.9	4.3
% Ret. on Equity	5.3	6.7	13.8	3.3	1.7	NM	5.1	11.0	7.1	8.4

Data as orig. reptd.; bef. results of disc. opers. and/or spec. items. Yrs. end Sep. 30 pr. to 1998. Per share data adj. for stk. divs.; EPS diluted (primary prior to 1998). E-Estimated. NA-Not Available. NM-Not Meaningful. NR-Not Ranked.

Office: 3900 Essex Lane, Houston, TX 77027-5177.
Telephone: 713-439-8600.
Website: http://www.bakerhughes.com
Chrmn & CEO: C.C. Deaton.
Pres & COO: J.R. Clark.
SVP & CFO: G.S. Finley.

VP & General Counsel: A.R. Crain.
Investor Contact: G.R. Flaharty 713-439-8039.
Dirs: L. D. Brady, C. P. Cazalot, Jr., E. Djerejian, A. G. Fernandes, C. W. Gargalli, J. A. Lash, J. F. McCall, J. L. Nichols, H. J. Riley Jr., C. C. Watson.

Founded: in 1972.
Domicile: Delaware.
Employees: 26,650.
S&P Analyst: Stewart Glickman/PMW/GG

Recommendation: BUY ★★★★☆   SELL SELL HOLD BUY BUY

12-Month Target Price: **$44.00**
(as of October 28, 2004)

BLL has an approximate 0.04% weighting in the **S&P 500**

Sector: Materials
Sub-Industry: Metal & Glass Containers
Peer Group: Metal, Glass & Plastic Containers and Packaging Products

Summary: BLL, the world's second largest maker of aluminum beverage cans, derives 10% of its revenues from sales of hi-tech equipment to the aerospace industry.

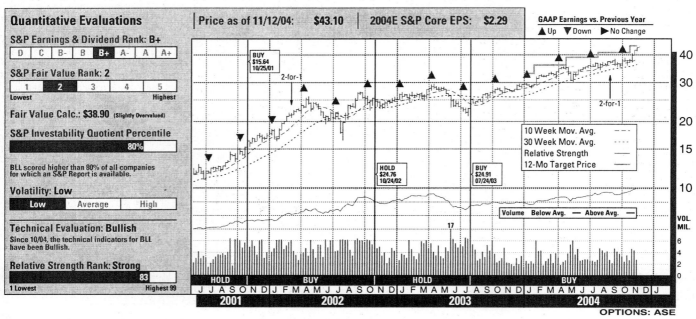

Quantitative Evaluations

S&P Earnings & Dividend Rank: B+

| D | C | B- | B | B+ | A- | A | A+ |

S&P Fair Value Rank: 2

| 1 | 2 | 3 | 4 | 5 |
| Lowest | | | | Highest |

Fair Value Calc.: $38.90 (Slightly Overvalued)

S&P Investability Quotient Percentile   80%

BLL scored higher than 80% of all companies for which an S&P Report is available.

Volatility: Low

| Low | Average | High |

Technical Evaluation: Bullish
Since 10/04, the technical indicators for BLL have been Bullish.

Relative Strength Rank: Strong   83

| 1 Lowest | | Highest 99 |

Price as of 11/12/04: $43.10   **2004E S&P Core EPS:** $2.29

GAAP Earnings vs. Previous Year ▲ Up ▼ Down ▶ No Change

Chart annotations: BUY $15.64 10/25/01; 2-for-1; HOLD $24.76 10/24/02; BUY $24.91 07/24/03; 2-for-1; 10 Week Mov. Avg.; 30 Week Mov. Avg.; Relative Strength; 12-Mo Target Price; Volume Below Avg. — Above Avg.; VOL. MIL.; HOLD; BUY; HOLD; BUY; J J A S O N D J F M A M J J A S O N D J F M A M J J A S O N D J F M A M J J A S O N D J 2001 2002 2003 2004 OPTIONS: ASE

Analyst commentary prepared by Stewart Scharf/PMW/JWP

Highlights November 08, 2004

- We expect 2005 internal sales growth in the high single digits, following our projection of mid-single-digit growth in 2004, on strong beverage can sales in Europe and North America; a recovery in North American food can sales, aided by a recent plant expansion; and strength in plastic containers and aerospace and technologies. We see average price hikes of 1% for U.S. and European beverage cans, with production efficiencies in Europe expected to offset the negative effects of a mandatory deposit on beverage cans in Germany.

- We believe gross margins will widen, as a more favorable product mix and price pass-throughs offset high steel and aluminum costs, as well as higher resin costs. We expect EBITDA margins in 2005 to widen from our projection of 13.5% for 2004, as production efficiencies from a new plant in Belgrade and a line conversion in Colorado, as well as a restructuring at China operations, outweigh higher insurance costs. We project lower interest expense, due to debt refinancings, and expect strong free cash flow generation to continue in 2005, expanding from our 2004 projection of $360 million. We see this used for $200 million of stock buybacks and for debt paydowns of at least $60 million.

- Our 2004 EPS estimate is $2.50, and we see $2.75 for 2005. We forecast S&P Core EPS of $2.29 for 2004 and $2.53 for 2005, reflecting estimated pension expense.

Key Stock Statistics

S&P Core EPS 2005E	2.53	52-week Range	$43.12-27.15
S&P Oper. EPS 2004E	2.50	12 Month P/E	16.7
P/E on S&P Oper. EPS 2004E	17.2	Beta	0.09
S&P Oper. EPS 2005E	2.75	Shareholders	5,520
Yield (%)	0.9%	Market Cap (B)	$ 4.9
Dividend Rate/Share	0.40	Shares Outstanding (M)	112.6

Value of $10,000 invested five years ago: $ 45,057

Dividend Data Dividends have been paid since 1958

Amount ($)	Date Decl.	Ex-Div. Date	Stock of Record	Payment Date
0.150	Apr. 28	May. 27	Jun. 01	Jun. 15 '04
2-for-1	Jul. 28	Aug. 24	Aug. 04	Aug. 23 '04
0.100	Jul. 28	Aug. 30	Sep. 01	Sep. 15 '04
0.100	Oct. 27	Nov. 29	Dec. 01	Dec. 15 '04

Investment Rationale/Risk November 08, 2004

- We continue to recommend accumulating the shares, based on what we view as positive market trends for food and beverage packaging products, as well as valuation. We expect the interest coverage ratio to remain above peer levels; BLL pays 6.87% on its refinanced debt. We also think the stock may be more attractive to investors following a 33% dividend hike in September; the company plans to repurchase more stock, under a recent authorization to buy back 12 million shares.

- Risks to our recommendation and target price include slower than expected demand for beverage cans, a cool and wet summer in 2005, greater negative impact from a mandatory deposit law in Germany, less strength in aerospace, and significant supply shortages for steel.

- With the stock trading at under 15X our 2005 EPS estimate, a discount to the S&P 500 and below peers, we see potential for further gains. Based on our DCF model, which assumes a 3.5% perpetual growth rate and a weighted average cost of capital of 8.3%, BLL is at a 12% discount to intrinsic value. We believe BLL's return on capital should exceed its cost of capital. Based on a peer average forward P/E multiple of 16X applied to our 2005 EPS estimate, our 12-month target price is $44.

Revenues/Earnings Data Fiscal year ending December 31

Revenues (Million $)

	2004	2003	2002	2001	2000	1999
1Q	1,232	1,071	875.9	850.0	817.6	820.3
2Q	1,467	1,353	1,034	992.6	961.0	979.0
3Q	1,479	1,359	1,039	1,001	961.3	991.6
4Q	—	1,194	910.2	843.0	827.7	793.0
Yr.	—	4,977	3,859	3,686	3,665	3,584

Earnings Per Share ($)

	2004	2003	2002	2001	2000	1999
1Q	0.41	0.28	0.24	0.15	0.15	0.12
2Q	0.80	0.65	0.43	-1.48	-0.14	0.24
3Q	0.90	0.60	0.43	0.30	0.36	0.24
4Q	E0.43	0.49	0.28	0.07	0.15	0.15
Yr.	E2.50	2.01	1.38	-0.93	0.54	0.79

Next earnings report expected: late-January Source: S&P, Company Reports
EPS Estimates based on S&P Operating Earnings; historical GAAP earnings are as reported.

Ball Corporation

Recommendation: **BUY** ★★★★   12-Month Target Price: **$44.00** (as of October 28, 2004)

Business Summary November 08, 2004

Ball Corp. primarily manufactures rigid packaging products for beverages and foods. Two beverage concerns account for a substantial part of its packaging sales: in 2003, SABMiller plc accounted for 12% of sales, and PepsiCo. for 10%. BLL is comprised of three segments: North American packaging; international packaging; and aerospace and technologies.

In late 2002, BLL acquired Germany-based Schmalbach-Lubeca AG, the second largest European beverage can manufacturer (31% unit market share, second to Rexam plc's 39%), for $929 million, including the assumption of debt. Schmalbach, which has 2,500 employees, produces 12 billion aluminum and steel cans and can ends annually, with sales exceeding $1 billion. It now operates as Ball Packaging Europe. In connection with the acquisition, the company refinanced $389 million of debt, resulting in a charge of $3.2 million ($0.03 a share, as adjusted). International packaging sales accounted for 23% of 2003 sales ($159 million of pretax earnings), including 20% from Europe and the rest from Asia metal beverage and plastic containers.

The company's packaging products include aluminum and steel two-piece beverage cans, and two- and three-piece steel food cans. North American metal beverage containers and ends are BLL's largest product line, accounting for 46% of 2003 net sales; metal food container sales accounted for 13% and plastic containers 8%. Total North American packaging segment net sales dropped to 67% of the total in 2003 ($283 million pretax earnings), from 84% in 2002, due to the addition of Ball Packaging Europe. BLL estimates that it accounts for over 30% of all North American aluminum beverage can shipments. In 2003, it incurred $13 million of startup costs in its metal food container operations, related to a new line to produce two-piece food cans at its Milwaukee plant. In October 2004, BLL said it would convert a beverage can manufacturing line in its Golden, CO, plant from the production of 12-ounce cans to 24-ounce cans, due to a double-digit growth rate. The conversion, at a cost of $12.5 million, is scheduled for completion in the second quarter of 2005.

BLL entered the plastics business in 1995, when it began to make polyethylene terephthalate (PET) bottles. Its primary competitor in the PET bottle business is Owens-Illinois.

The aerospace and technologies segment (11% of 2003 revenues; $49.5 million operating profits) provides products and services to the defense and commercial markets. U.S. government agencies account for about 95% of segment sales.

In 2003, the company bought back $31 million of common stock. It projected 2004 capital spending of $175 million to $200 million, up from 2003's $137 million, as it began construction of a new beverage can plant in Belgrade. It estimated its normal capital spending run rate at under $150 million. BLL planned to reduce net debt by $250 million in 2004.

In the 2004 fourth quarter, BLL posted a $4.2 million after-tax gain ($0.04 a share), related to proceeds from asset dispositions in China. In the 2003 third quarter, it incurred an after-tax charge of $9.9 million ($0.08 a share, as adjusted) for early debt extinguishment. It also recorded a $2.2 million after-tax gain ($0.02), mainly related to the completion of China capacity consolidations begun in 2001.

The company expected pension expense to stabilize in 2004, after more than doubling in 2003, to over $23 million in the U.S. ($54 million total).

Company Financials Fiscal Year ending December 31

Per Share Data ($)

(Year Ended December 31)	2003	2002	2001	2000	1999	1998	1997	1996	1995	1994
Tangible Bk. Val.	NM	NM	1.27	1.81	1.27	0.32	3.45	4.27	4.16	3.95
Cash Flow	3.81	2.68	0.44	1.81	2.03	1.41	1.34	0.86	0.77	1.61
Earnings	2.01	1.38	-0.93	0.54	0.79	0.23	0.43	0.09	-0.18	0.59
S&P Core Earnings	2.12	1.10	-0.88	NA	NA	NA	NA	NA	NA	NA
Dividends	0.24	0.18	0.15	0.15	0.15	0.15	0.15	0.15	0.15	0.15
Payout Ratio	12%	13%	NM	28%	19%	66%	34%	176%	NM	26%
Prices - High	29.87	27.24	18.03	11.98	14.78	12.23	9.75	8.06	9.68	8.03
- Low	21.15	16.30	9.52	6.50	8.84	7.15	5.93	5.78	6.43	6.09
P/E Ratio - High	15	20	NM	22	19	54	22	95	NM	14
- Low	11	12	NM	12	11	31	14	68	NM	10

Income Statement Analysis (Million $)

	2003	2002	2001	2000	1999	1998	1997	1996	1995	1994
Revs.	4,977	3,859	3,686	3,665	3,584	2,896	2,389	2,184	2,592	2,595
Oper. Inc.	663	458	127	445	442	334	248	177	254	291
Depr.	206	149	153	159	163	155	118	93.5	114	122
Int. Exp.	126	75.6	88.3	95.2	108	78.6	53.5	39.9	41.3	44.5
Pretax Inc.	331	245	-110	110	171	32.9	85.2	20.1	-14.1	122
Eff. Tax Rate	30.2%	34.3%	NM	38.9%	38.0%	26.7%	37.6%	35.8%	NM	36.5%
Net Inc.	230	159	-99	68.2	104	32.0	58.3	13.1	-18.6	73.0
S&P Core Earnings	242	127	-96.0	NA	NA	NA	NA	NA	NA	NA

Balance Sheet & Other Fin. Data (Million $)

	2003	2002	2001	2000	1999	1998	1997	1996	1995	1994
Cash	36.5	259	83.1	25.6	35.8	34.0	25.5	169	5.10	10.4
Curr. Assets	924	1,225	794	969	896	886	798	767	593	698
Total Assets	4,070	4,132	2,314	2,650	2,732	2,855	2,090	1,701	1,613	1,760
Curr. Liab.	861	1,069	575	659	670	688	838	511	498	500
LT Debt	1,579	1,854	949	1,012	1,093	1,230	366	408	320	377
Common Equity	808	493	504	640	635	565	574	587	568	605
Total Cap.	2,393	2,353	1,463	1,709	1,803	1,877	1,113	1,047	937	1,066
Cap. Exp.	137	158	68.5	99	107	84.2	97.7	196	206	95.0
Cash Flow	435	309	51.3	225	264	184	173	104	91.9	192
Curr. Ratio	1.1	1.1	1.4	1.5	1.3	1.3	1.0	1.5	1.2	1.4
% LT Debt of Cap.	66.0	78.8	64.9	59.2	60.6	65.5	32.9	39.0	34.2	35.4
% Net Inc.of Revs.	4.6	4.1	NM	1.9	2.9	1.1	2.4	0.6	NM	2.8
% Ret. on Assets	5.6	4.9	NM	2.5	3.7	1.3	3.1	0.8	NM	4.1
% Ret. on Equity	35.4	32.0	NM	10.1	16.9	5.1	9.9	1.8	NM	12.0

Data as orig reptd.; bef. results of disc opers/spec. items. Per share data adj. for stk. divs.; EPS diluted. E-Estimated. NA-Not Available. NM-Not Meaningful. NR-Not Ranked. UR-Under Review.

Office: 10 Longs Peak Dr, Broomfield, CO 80021-2510.
Telephone: 303-469-3131.
Website: http://www.ball.com
Chrmn, Pres & CEO: R.D. Hoover.
COO & SVP: J.R. Friedery.
SVP & CFO: R.J. Seabrook.

SVP & Secy: D.A. Westerlund.
VP & Treas: S. Morrison.
Investor Contact: A.T. Scott 303-460-2103.
Dirs: H. M. Dean, H. C. Fiedler, R. D. Hoover, J. F. Lehman, J. Nicholson, G. A. Sissel, T. M. Solso, W. P. Stiritz, S. A. Taylor II, E. H. van der Kaay.

Founded: in 1880.
Domicile: Indiana.
Employees: 12,700.
S&P Analyst: Stewart Scharf/PMW/JWP

Recommendation: **BUY** ★★★★★ 12-Month Target Price: **$50.00**
(as of July 14, 2004)

BAC has an approximate 1.75% weighting in the **S&P 500**

Sector: Financials
Sub-Industry: Diversified Banks
Peer Group: Money Center Banks

Summary: This banking company has offices in 21 states, and provides international corporate financial services.

Quantitative Evaluations

S&P Earnings & Dividend Rank: A-

| D | C | B- | B | B+ | A- | A | A+ |

S&P Fair Value Rank: 4-

| 1 | 2 | 3 | 4 | 5 |
| Lowest | | | | Highest |

Fair Value Calc.: $45.90 (Slightly Overvalued)

S&P Investability Quotient Percentile

98%

BAC scored higher than 98% of all companies for which an S&P Report is available.

Volatility: Low

| Low | Average | High |

Technical Evaluation: Bullish

Since 5/04, the technical indicators for BAC have been Bullish.

Relative Strength Rank: Moderate

62

1 Lowest   Highest 99

Price as of 11/12/04: **$47.44**   **2004E S&P Core EPS:** **$3.69**

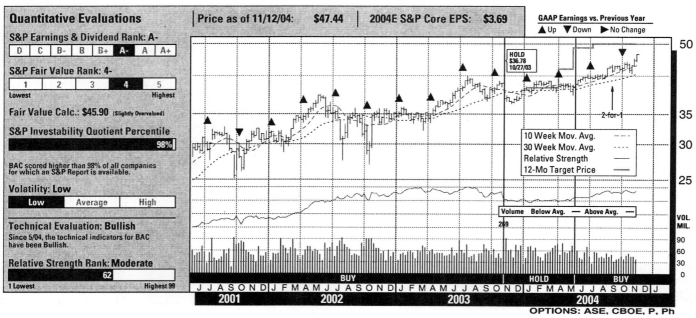

GAAP Earnings vs. Previous Year
▲ Up ▼ Down ▶ No Change

- 10 Week Mov. Avg.
- 30 Week Mov. Avg.
- Relative Strength
- 12-Mo Target Price

Volume Below Avg. Above Avg.

Analyst commentary prepared by Evan M. Momios, CFA /CB/GG

OPTIONS: ASE, CBOE, P, Ph

Highlights August 31, 2004

- We expect strong economic conditions to support revenue growth in consumer and small business lending, offsetting comparatively weak large corporate lending results. We see productivity and efficiency improvements increasing the contribution of the FleetBoston franchise, which was acquired on April 1, 2004.

- We believe the company's balance sheet is positioned for higher interest rates, and project that the net interest margin will widen to 3.35% in the fourth quarter, from the second quarter's 3.29%. Expenses are likely to remain under tight control. BAC expects to derive $1.1 billion to $1.4 billion in total after-tax cost savings from FleetBoston, mainly from personnel-related expenses.

- We see EPS rising to $3.70 in 2004 and $4.00 in 2005. Our 2004 and 2005 Standard & Poor's Core Earnings per share estimates are $3.69 and $3.99, respectively, primarily reflecting our projections of stock option expense.

Investment Rationale/Risk August 31, 2004

- We believe BAC shares offer an attractive risk-reward trade-off at current valuation levels, and an above-peer average dividend yield. BAC recently traded at about 12X our 2004 EPS estimate, in line with the peer average, and at a slight discount to our intrinsic value estimate of $46.

- Risks to our recommendation and target price include litigation costs potentially exceeding our and market expectations, a severe economic downturn in combination with higher short-term interest rates that could result in an inverted yield curve, and a serious geopolitical event that could affect domestic equity markets.

- Our 12-month target price of $50 equates to 12.5X our 2005 EPS estimate, and the shares offer a 4.00% dividend yield. We believe this is a reasonable valuation multiple based on the company's progress thus far in integrating the FleetBoston franchise, our expectation for strong economic conditions, BAC's extensive geographic footprint, and our view of its balanced business model.

Key Stock Statistics

S&P Core EPS 2005E	3.99	52-week Range	$47.47-36.86
S&P Oper. EPS 2004E	3.70	12 Month P/E	12.9
P/E on S&P Oper. EPS 2004E	12.8	Beta	0.65
S&P Oper. EPS 2005E	4.00	Shareholders	226,796
Yield (%)	3.8%	Market Cap (B)	$191.6
Dividend Rate/Share	1.80	Shares Outstanding (M)	4039.2

Value of $10,000 invested five years ago: **$ 17,163**

Dividend Data Dividends have been paid since 1903

Amount ($)	Date Decl.	Ex-Div. Date	Stock of Record	Payment Date
0.800	Apr. 02	Jun. 02	Jun. 04	Jun. 25 '04
2-for-1	Jun. 23	Aug. 30	Aug. 06	Aug. 27 '04
0.450	Jun. 23	Sep. 01	Sep. 03	Sep. 24 '04
0.450	Oct. 27	Dec. 01	Dec. 03	Dec. 22 '04

Revenues/Earnings Data Fiscal year ending December 31

Revenues (Million $)

	2004	2003	2002	2001	2000	1999
1Q	12,289	11,410	11,311	14,021	14,132	12,554
2Q	16,448	12,250	11,465	13,666	14,237	12,780
3Q	16,413	12,294	11,405	12,751	14,910	13,066
4Q	—	12,111	—	—	14,468	13,232
Yr.	—	48,065	45,732	52,641	57,747	51,632

Earnings Per Share ($)

	2004	2003	2002	2001	2000	1999
1Q	0.92	0.80	0.69	0.58	0.67	0.54
2Q	0.93	0.90	0.70	0.62	0.61	0.54
3Q	0.91	0.96	0.73	0.26	0.55	0.61
4Q	E0.95	0.92	0.85	0.64	0.43	0.55
Yr.	E3.70	3.56	2.95	2.09	2.26	2.24

Next earnings report expected: mid-January Source: S&P, Company Reports
EPS Estimates based on S&P Operating Earnings; historical GAAP earnings are as reported.

Bank of America Corporation

Recommendation: **BUY** ★ ★ ★ ★ ★   12-Month Target Price: **$50.00** (as of July 14, 2004)

Business Summary August 31, 2004

Bank of America is a bank holding company that provides a range of banking and financial services and products to 28 million households and 2 million businesses. Its primary market areas encompass the Mid-Atlantic, Midwest, Southeast, Southwest, Northwest and West, as well as selected international markets. Operations are divided into the following main business segments: consumer and commercial banking asset management, global corporate and investment management, and equity investments.

Consumer and commercial banking provides a wide range of products and services to individuals, small businesses, and mid-market companies through delivery channels that include about 4,277 banking centers and 13,241 ATMs, located in 21 states and the District of Columbia. The segment provides specialized services such as the origination and servicing of residential mortgage loans, issuance of credit cards, student lending and certain insurance services, commercial lending, and treasury management services.

Asset management includes the private bank (financial solutions for high net worth clients), capital management (equity, fixed income, cash and alternatives investments), and investment services (full-service and discount brokerage services).

Global corporate and investment banking provides capital-raising products, trade finance, treasury management, capital markets, leasing and financial advisory services to domestic and international corporations, financial institutions, and government entities.

In 2003, average earning assets, from which interest income is derived, amounted to $657.5 million, and consisted mainly of loans and leases (54%) and investment securities (39%). Average sources of funds were: interest-bearing deposits (37%), short-term borrowings (24%), noninterest-bearing deposits (16%), long-term debt (9%), shareholders' equity (6%), and other (7%).

Nonperforming assets, consisting of nonperforming loans and foreclosed properties, totaled $3.0 billion (0.81% of loans and related assets) at December 31, 2003, down from $5.3 billion (1.53%) a year earlier. The allowance for loan losses, which is set aside for possible loan defaults, was $6.6 billion (1.66% of loans and leases) at December 31, 2003, versus $6.9 billion (1.85%) a year earlier. Net chargeoffs in 2003 totaled $3.1 billion (0.87% of average loans), down from $3.7 billion (1.10%) in 2002.

In April 2004, the company acquired FleetBoston Financial (FBF) for a total consideration of $47.2 billion. As of year-end 2003, FBF had total assets of $200.2 billion (including $128.9 billion in loans), and $137.8 billion in deposits.

Company Financials Fiscal Year ending December 31

Per Share Data ($)

(Year Ended December 31)	2003	2002	2001	2000	1999	1998	1997	1996	1995	1994
Tangible Bk. Val.	12.34	12.59	11.65	10.66	9.05	9.01	8.33	9.21	9.55	8.31
Earnings	3.57	2.96	2.09	2.26	2.24	1.45	2.08	2.00	1.78	1.53
S&P Core Earnings	3.54	2.70	1.96	NA	NA	NA	NA	NA	NA	NA
Dividends	1.44	1.22	1.14	1.03	0.93	0.80	0.52	0.60	0.52	0.47
Payout Ratio	40%	41%	55%	46%	41%	55%	25%	30%	29%	31%
Prices - High	42.45	38.54	32.77	30.50	38.18	44.21	35.84	26.31	18.68	14.34
- Low	32.13	26.97	22.50	18.15	23.81	22.00	24.00	16.09	11.15	10.84
P/E Ratio - High	12	13	16	13	17	30	17	13	10	9
- Low	9	9	11	8	11	15	12	8	6	7

Income Statement Analysis (Million $)

	2003	2002	2001	2000	1999	1998	1997	1996	1995	1994
Net Int. Inc.	21,464	20,923	20,290	18,442	18,237	18,298	7,898	6,329	5,447	5,211
Tax Equiv. Adj.	643	588	343	322	215	128	116	94.0	113	94.0
Non Int. Inc.	16,422	13,571	14,348	14,489	14,069	12,189	6,351	3,646	3,078	2,597
Loan Loss Prov.	2,839	3,697	4,287	2,535	182	2,920	800	605	382	310
Exp./Op. Revs.	52.4%	63.1%	59.8%	63.7%	56.9%	67.4%	52.3%	57.4%	60.0%	62.4%
Pretax Inc.	15,861	12,991	10,117	11,788	12,215	8,048	4,796	3,634	2,991	2,555
Eff. Tax Rate	31.8%	28.8%	32.9%	36.2%	35.5%	35.8%	35.8%	34.6%	34.8%	33.9%
Net Inc.	10,810	9,249	6,792	7,517	7,882	5,165	3,077	2,452	1,950	1,690
% Net Int. Marg.	3.36	3.75	3.68	3.22	3.47	3.69	3.79	3.62	3.33	3.58
S&P Core Earnings	10,708	8,452	6,384	NA	NA	NA	NA	NA	NA	NA

Balance Sheet & Other Fin. Data (Million $)

	2003	2002	2001	2000	1999	1998	1997	1996	1995	1994
Money Mkt. Assets	153,090	115,687	81,384	76,544	81,226	73,498	36,095	27,491	26,393	23,212
Inv. Securities	68,240	69,148	85,499	65,838	83,069	80,587	47,203	14,387	23,847	25,825
Com'l Loans	131,384	145,170	163,898	203,542	195,779	196,130	71,442	58,796	52,101	48,109
Other Loans	240,159	197,585	165,255	188,651	174,883	161,198	69,568	61,519	66,919	55,580
Total Assets	736,445	660,458	621,764	642,191	632,574	617,679	264,562	185,794	187,298	169,604
Demand Deposits	121,530	124,359	113,934	100,645	95,469	94,336	34,674	25,738	23,414	21,380
Time Deposits	292,583	262,099	259,561	263,599	251,804	262,974	103,520	80,760	77,277	79,090
LT Debt	75,343	67,176	68,026	72,502	60,441	50,842	27,204	22,985	17,775	8,488
Common Equity	47,926	50,261	48,455	47,556	44,355	45,855	21,243	13,538	12,699	10,900
% Ret. on Assets	1.5	1.4	1.1	1.2	1.3	0.9	1.4	13.0	1.1	1.0
% Ret. on Equity	22.0	18.7	14.1	16.3	17.5	11.5	17.6	18.0	16.5	16.3
% Loan Loss Resv.	1.7	2.0	2.1	1.7	1.8	2.0	1.9	1.9	1.9	2.1
% Loans/Deposits	89.7	88.4	97.8	107.7	106.7	99.4	104.1	113.0	116.2	103.2
% Equity to Assets	7.0	7.7	7.6	7.2	7.2	7.6	7.7	7.0	6.6	6.2

Data as orig. reptd.; bef. results of disc opers. and/or spec. items. Data for 1997 and prior yrs. for NationsBank Corp. before merger with BankAmerica Corp. Per share data adj. for stk. divs.; EPS diluted. E-Estimated. NA-Not Available. NM-Not Meaningful. NR-Not Ranked.

Office: 100 N Tryon St, Charlotte, NC 28255.
Telephone: 704-386-8486.
Website: http://www.bankofamerica.com
Chrmn, Pres & CEO: K.D. Lewis.
Vice Chrmn & CFO: J.H. Hance, Jr.
COO: A.S. Kirsch.
CTO: B. Desoer.

Secy: R.R. Cummings.
Investor Contact: L. McEntire 704-388-6780.
Dirs: J. R. Belk, C. W. Coker, F. Dowd IV, K. F. Feldstein, P. Fulton, D. E. Guinn, J. H. Hance, Jr., K. D. Lewis, W. E. Massey, C. S. McMillan, P. E. Mitchell, E. L. Romero, O. T. Sloan, Jr., M. R. Spangler, R. Townsend, J. M. Ward, V. R. Williams.

Founded: in 1874.
Domicile: Delaware.
Employees: 133,549.
S&P Analyst: Evan M. Momios, CFA /CB/GG

Bank of New York

Recommendation: **HOLD** ★★★☆☆ (SELL SELL HOLD BUY BUY)   12-Month Target Price: **$34.00**
(as of June 29, 2004)

BK has an approximate 0.24% weighting in the **S&P 500**

Sector: Financials
Sub-Industry: Asset Management & Custody Banks
Peer Group: East Super Regional Banks

Summary: BK is a leader in securities processing, and also provides a complete range of banking and other financial services.

Quantitative Evaluations

Price as of 11/12/04: $33.39   **2004E S&P Core EPS:** $1.80

S&P Earnings & Dividend Rank: A-

D	C	B-	B	B+	A-	A	A+

S&P Fair Value Rank: 3

1	2	3	4	5
Lowest				Highest

Fair Value Calc.: $33.30 (Fairly Valued)

S&P Investability Quotient Percentile

93%

BK scored higher than 93% of all companies for which an S&P Report is available.

Volatility: Low

Low	Average	High

Technical Evaluation: Bullish
Since 10/04, the technical indicators for BK have been Bullish.

Relative Strength Rank: Moderate

66

1 Lowest		Highest 99

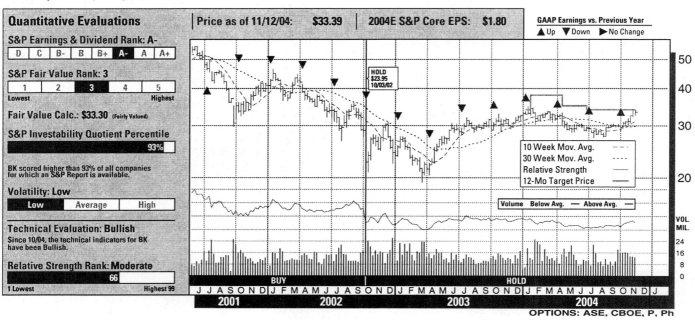

GAAP Earnings vs. Previous Year
▲ Up ▼ Down ▶ No Change

10 Week Mov. Avg.
30 Week Mov. Avg.
Relative Strength
12-Mo Target Price

Volume Below Avg. — Above Avg.

OPTIONS: ASE, CBOE, P, Ph

Analyst commentary prepared by Evan M. Momios, CFA /MF/BK

Highlights November 03, 2004

- We believe improved revenue and earnings growth in the remainder of 2004 and into 2005 will largely depend on an acceleration in capital market activities, particularly trading, securities issuance, and mergers and acquisitions (M&As). For the longer term, we think a trend on the part of investment advisors and brokers toward outsourcing middle and back-office processing will aid earnings growth.

- Based on our view of the company's credit quality as of September 30, 2004, we expect loan loss provision requirements to remain minimal until later in 2005. We see operating expenses remaining under control, as the benefits of completed cost reduction initiatives should moderate some pressure from higher option expenses that we expect.

- We project 2004 operating EPS of $1.90, up from $1.62 (excluding non-recurring items) in 2003. For 2005, we expect EPS to increase to $2.15 in a forecasted stronger economy with rising interest rates. Our respective 2004 and 2005 Standard & Poor's Core Earnings per share estimates of $1.80 and $2.06 reflect modest pension plan and employee stock option expenses.

Investment Rationale/Risk November 03, 2004

- We would not add to positions. BK's results highly correlate with stock market performance, adding uncertainty to our outlook. Year to date, as of early November, the shares have underperformed peers and the S&P 500. We think this is due to investor concerns over broader geo-political issues that have suppressed capital market activity and lingering regulatory issues surrounding the mutual fund industry.

- Risks to our recommendation and target price include a significant decline in economic activity, a serious geopolitical event that could impact equity markets, a rapid and sizable increase in short-term interest rates, and legal and regulatory risks.

- The stock trades at about 15X our 2005 EPS estimate, compared to an average of 19X 12-month forward EPS during the past three years. Our 12-month target price is $34, or approximately 16X our 2005 EPS estimate and at the high end of discounted cash flow intrinsic value estimates. This implies our expectation for only limited P/E multiple expansion in the healthy economic environment we see, below peer levels and below the stock's historical average valuation P/E multiple.

Key Stock Statistics

S&P Core EPS 2005E	2.06	52-week Range	$34.85-27.25
S&P Oper. EPS 2004E	1.90	12 Month P/E	18.7
P/E on S&P Oper. EPS 2004E	17.6	Beta	1.35
S&P Oper. EPS 2005E	2.15	Shareholders	26,951
Yield (%)	2.4%	Market Cap (B)	$ 25.9
Dividend Rate/Share	0.80	Shares Outstanding (M)	776.9

Value of $10,000 invested five years ago: **$ 9,239**

Dividend Data Dividends have been paid since 1785

Amount ($)	Date Decl.	Ex-Div. Date	Stock of Record	Payment Date
0.190	Jan. 13	Jan. 21	Jan. 23	Feb. 05 '04
0.200	Apr. 13	Apr. 22	Apr. 26	May. 06 '04
0.200	Jul. 13	Jul. 21	Jul. 23	Aug. 05 '04
0.200	Oct. 12	Oct. 21	Oct. 25	Nov. 04 '04

Revenues/Earnings Data Fiscal year ending December 31

Revenues (Million $)

	2004	2003	2002	2001	2000	1999
1Q	1,671	1,420	1,480	1,891	1,770	1,482
2Q	1,767	1,591	1,530	1,781	1,887	1,490
3Q	1,739	1,638	1,285	1,745	1,892	2,365
4Q	—	1,686	1,461	1,777	1,934	1,629
Yr.	—	6,336	5,756	7,160	7,486	6,966

Earnings Per Share ($)

	2004	2003	2002	2001	2000	1999
1Q	0.47	0.41	0.50	0.52	0.46	0.41
2Q	0.48	0.39	0.50	0.52	0.48	0.42
3Q	0.46	0.34	0.11	0.33	0.49	1.02
4Q	E0.49	0.40	0.14	0.45	0.50	0.44
Yr.	E1.90	1.52	1.24	1.81	1.92	2.27

Next earnings report expected: late-January Source: S&P, Company Reports
EPS Estimates based on S&P Operating Earnings; historical GAAP earnings are as reported.

The Bank of New York Company, Inc.

Recommendation: **HOLD** ★★★☆☆   12-Month Target Price: **$34.00** (as of June 29, 2004)

Business Summary November 03, 2004

The Bank of New York Company, founded in 1784, is the oldest U.S. bank operating under its original name. Over the past few years, it has derived an increasing percentage of revenues from businesses that provide fee revenues; traditional interest-revenue generating businesses have been de-emphasized. BK has acquired and integrated several corporate trust and custody operations from other large banks that did not have the volume scale to compete successfully in these businesses.

The Servicing and Fiduciary segment (56% of pretax income in 2003) provides a broad range of fee-based services, including securities servicing (global custody, securities clearance, mutual funds, UIT, securities lending, depositary receipts, corporate trust, stock transfer and execution services), global payment services (funds transfer, cash management and trade finance), and private client services and asset management businesses (traditional banking and trust services to affluent clients and asset management to institutional and private clients).

The Corporate Banking segment (16%) focuses on providing lending services, such as term loans, lines of credit, asset based financings, and commercial mortgages, to large public and private corporations, as well as public and private mid-size businesses in the New York metropolitan area. Through BNY Capital Markets, the company provides syndicated loans, bond underwriting, private placements of corporate debt and equity securities, and merger, acquisition, and advisory services.

The Retail Banking segment (11%) includes consumer lending, residential mortgage lending, and retail deposit services through 341 branches. The Financial Markets segment (17%) includes trading of foreign exchange and interest rate products, investing and leasing activities, and treasury services to other segments.

In 2003, average earning assets, from which interest income is derived, totaled $74.2 billion, consisting mainly of loans (48%) and investment securities (33%). Average sources of funds included domestic deposits (24%), foreign deposits (26%), noninterest-bearing deposits (14%), short-term borrowings (6%), long-term debt (7%), shareholders' equity (8%), and other (5%).

At December 31, 2003, nonperforming assets, consisting primarily of non-accrual loans and other real estate, were $349 million (1.2% of loans and related assets), down from $440 million (1.4%) a year earlier. The allowance for loan losses (set aside for possible loan defaults) was $804 million (2.28% of loans), versus $831 million (2.65%) a year earlier. Net chargeoffs (the amount of loans actually written off as uncollectible) were $155 million (0.51% of average loans) in 2003, down from $685 million (1.37%) in 2002.

In May 2003, the company acquired Pershing, a global provider of clearing services for financial institutions for $2 billion.

Company Financials Fiscal Year ending December 31

Per Share Data ($)

(Year Ended December 31)	2003	2002	2001	2000	1999	1998	1997	1996	1995	1994
Tangible Bk. Val.	5.59	5.66	5.79	8.30	6.95	7.05	6.67	6.50	6.46	5.57
Earnings	1.52	1.24	1.81	1.92	2.27	1.53	1.35	1.24	1.14	0.98
S&P Core Earnings	1.46	1.01	1.56	NA	NA	NA	NA	NA	NA	NA
Dividends	0.76	0.76	0.72	0.66	0.58	0.54	0.49	0.42	0.34	0.27
Payout Ratio	50%	61%	40%	34%	26%	35%	36%	34%	30%	28%
Prices - High	33.49	46.50	58.12	59.37	45.18	40.56	29.28	18.06	12.25	8.31
- Low	19.25	20.85	29.75	29.75	31.81	24.00	16.37	10.87	7.12	6.23
P/E Ratio - High	22	37	32	31	20	27	22	15	11	8
- Low	13	17	16	15	14	16	12	9	6	6

Income Statement Analysis (Million $)

	2003	2002	2001	2000	1999	1998	1997	1996	1995	1994
Net Int. Inc.	1,609	1,665	1,681	1,870	1,701	1,651	1,855	1,961	2,029	1,717
Tax Equiv. Adj.	35.0	49.0	60.0	54.0	44.0	58.0	35.0	38.0	39.0	46.0
Non Int. Inc.	3,971	3,261	3,386	2,959	3,294	2,108	2,001	2,033	1,381	1,274
Loan Loss Prov.	155	685	375	105	135	20.0	280	600	330	162
Exp./Op. Revs.	65.9%	55.3%	54.4%	51.4%	44.0%	50.5%	48.6%	45.6%	49.7%	54.0%
Pretax Inc.	1,762	1,372	2,058	2,251	2,840	1,891	1,773	1,656	1,482	1,198
Eff. Tax Rate	34.3%	34.3%	34.7%	36.5%	38.8%	37.0%	37.7%	38.3%	38.3%	37.5%
Net Inc.	1,157	902	1,343	1,429	1,739	1,192	1,104	1,020	914	749
% Net Int. Marg.	2.22	2.62	2.57	2.96	3.11	3.24	3.89	4.35	4.53	4.11
S&P Core Earnings	1,097	728	1,159	NA	NA	NA	NA	NA	NA	NA

Balance Sheet & Other Fin. Data (Million $)

	2003	2002	2001	2000	1999	1998	1997	1996	1995	1994
Money Mkt. Assets	18,521	13,798	19,684	23,178	20,948	9,422	7,562	3,249	2,680	4,951
Inv. Securities	22,903	18,300	12,862	7,401	6,899	6,415	6,628	5,053	4,870	4,651
Com'l Loans	13,646	20,335	19,034	21,327	17,851	16,407	14,429	12,844	14,434	16,085
Other Loans	21,637	11,004	16,713	14,934	21,251	21,979	20,698	24,162	23,253	17,868
Total Assets	92,397	77,564	81,025	77,114	74,756	63,503	59,961	55,765	53,720	48,879
Demand Deposits	14,789	13,301	12,635	13,255	12,162	11,480	12,561	11,812	10,465	8,579
Time Deposits	41,617	42,086	43,076	43,121	43,589	33,152	28,796	27,531	25,453	25,512
LT Debt	Nil	Nil	Nil	4,536	4,311	3,386	1,809	1,816	1,848	1,774
Common Equity	8,428	6,684	6,317	6,151	5,142	5,447	5,001	5,015	5,119	4,177
% Ret. on Assets	1.4	1.1	1.7	1.9	2.5	1.9	1.9	1.9	1.8	1.5
% Ret. on Equity	15.3	13.9	21.5	25.3	32.8	22.8	21.9	20.0	19.4	19.5
% Loan Loss Resv.	1.9	2.7	1.7	1.7	1.6	1.7	1.8	2.4	2.0	2.4
% Loans/Deposits	62.6	56.6	64.2	64.3	67.3	86.0	84.9	94.1	104.9	97.0
% Equity to Assets	8.9	8.2	7.9	7.4	7.7	8.5	8.7	9.3	9.1	7.5

Data as orig reptd.; bef. results of disc opers/spec. items. Per share data adj. for stk. divs. Bold denotes primary EPS - prior periods restated. E-Estimated. NA-Not Available. NM-Not Meaningful. NR-Not Ranked. UR-Under Review.

Office: One Wall Street, New York, NY 10286.
Telephone: 212-495-1784.
Email: shareowner-svcs@bankofny.com
Website: http://www.bankofny.com
Chrmn & CEO: T.A. Renyi.
Pres: G.L. Hassell.
Vice Chrmn: A.R. Griffith.

Sr EVP & CFO: B.W. Van Saun.
EVP, Secy & General Counsel: J.M. Shepherd.
Dirs: F. J. Biondi, Jr., N. M. Donofrio, A. R. Griffith, G. L. Hassell, R. J. Kogan, M. J. Kowalski, J. A. Luke, Jr., J. C. Malone, P. Myners, R. C. Pozen, C. A. Rein, T. A. Renyi, W. C. Richardson, B. L. Roberts, S. C. Scott, III.

Founded: in 1784.
Domicile: New York.
Employees: 22,901.
S&P Analyst: Evan M. Momios, CFA /MF/BK

Recommendation: HOLD ★★★☆☆ SELL SELL HOLD BUY BUY   **12-Month Target Price: $59.00**
(as of April 21, 2004)

BCR has an approximate 0.06% weighting in the **S&P 500**

Sector: Health Care
Sub-Industry: Health Care Equipment
Peer Group: Large Multi-Line Medical Device Manufacturers

Summary: This diversified manufacturer of disposable therapeutic and diagnostic medical devices has exposure to the vascular, urology, oncology and specialty surgical markets.

Quantitative Evaluations

S&P Earnings & Dividend Rank: B+

| D | C | B- | B | B+ | A- | A | A+ |

S&P Fair Value Rank: 3

| 1 | 2 | 3 | 4 | 5 |
| Lowest | | | | Highest |

Fair Value Calc.: $56.50 (Slightly Overvalued)

S&P Investability Quotient Percentile

97%

BCR scored higher than 97% of all companies for which an S&P Report is available.

Volatility: Low

| Low | Average | High |

Technical Evaluation: Bullish
Since 11/04, the technical indicators for BCR have been Bullish.

Relative Strength Rank: Moderate

62

1 Lowest   Highest 99

| **Price as of 11/12/04:** | **$59.70** | **2004E S&P Core EPS:** | **$2.21** |

GAAP Earnings vs. Previous Year
▲ Up ▼ Down ▶ No Change

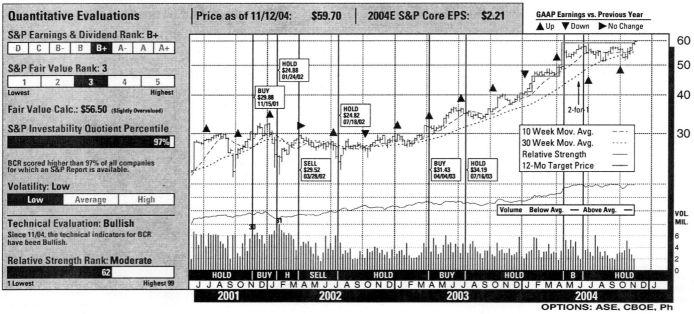

- 10 Week Mov. Avg.
- 30 Week Mov. Avg.
- Relative Strength
- 12-Mo Target Price

Volume Below Avg. — Above Avg.

OPTIONS: ASE, CBOE, Ph

Analyst commentary prepared by Robert M. Gold/PMW/GG

Highlights October 25, 2004

- We see 2004 sales of $1.6 billion, including about $400 million from the vascular segment, $490 million from urology, $390 million from oncology, and $310 million from surgical. Looking to 2005, we believe revenue growth will decelerate somewhat, reflecting more challenging comparisons and reduced foreign currency tailwind expectations. Our 2005 revenue forecast stands at $1.8 billion.

- We believe the consolidation of manufacturing facilities will allow gross margins to reach 60.0% in 2004, with 2005 gross margins estimated at 61.0%. Selling, general and administrative costs, including some patent and litigation expenses and IT spending, consumed about 31.3% of sales in 2003. Despite an expanded sales force and rising performance-based sales compensation, we think the ratio will decline to about 31.0% in 2004 and 30.5% in 2005. We see R&D costs absorbing up to 7.0% of sales in 2004 and 7.5% in 2005.

- After taxes at an estimated effective rate of 26.0% to 26.5%, and assuming some additional common share buybacks, we see 2004 operating EPS of $2.40, up from 2003's operating EPS of $1.94. Looking to 2005, we project operating EPS of $2.70.

Investment Rationale/Risk October 25, 2004

- We believe investments in R&D will drive double-digit EPS growth over the next three years. We view positively newly launched products and those nearing commercialization, such as a dialysis catheter, a diagnostic electrophysiology catheter, and a constant flow pain pump. In the interim, we see continued strength for products such as peripheral angioplasty, stents and grafts, implantable drug ports, and specialty catheters. The 2004 third quarter was the fourth consecutive quarter of double-digit, constant-currency revenue growth. We see some moderation in the fourth quarter, but still expect sales to grow 11% to 13%.

- Risks to our opinion and target price include unfavorable patent litigation outcomes, adverse changes in Medicare reimbursement rates for key product lines, an inability to successfully launch new products, negative foreign currency fluctuations, and continued valuation compression recently evident throughout the medical device subsector.

- The stock has performed strongly in 2004, reducing the valuation gap versus device peers. We see further valuation expansion as difficult in the absence of material upside earnings surprises. With the shares trading near our 12-month target price of $59, derived on the basis of a peer-average PEG ratio of 1.6X, we would hold the shares, which we see performing in line with the S&P 500.

Key Stock Statistics

S&P Oper. EPS 2004E	**2.40**	52-week Range	**$59.98-37.09**
P/E on S&P Oper. EPS 2004E	**24.9**	12 Month P/E	**25.3**
S&P Oper. EPS 2005E	**2.70**	Beta	**0.41**
Yield (%)	**0.8%**	Shareholders	**5,113**
Dividend Rate/Share	**0.48**	Market Cap (B)	**$ 6.2**
Shares Outstanding (M)	**104.7**		

Value of $10,000 invested five years ago: **$ 22,272**

Dividend Data Dividends have been paid since 1960

Amount ($)	Date Decl.	Ex-Div. Date	Stock of Record	Payment Date
0.230	Apr. 21	Apr. 29	May. 03	May. 14 '04
2-for-1	Apr. 21	Jun. 01	May. 17	May. 28 '04
0.120	Jul. 14	Jul. 22	Jul. 26	Aug. 06 '04
0.120	Oct. 13	Oct. 21	Oct. 25	Nov. 05 '04

Revenues/Earnings Data Fiscal year ending December 31

Revenues (Million $)

	2004	2003	2002	2001	2000	1999
1Q	393.8	335.9	301.9	284.8	268.5	248.5
2Q	416.3	354.2	317.5	295.9	274.6	257.8
3Q	421.9	361.8	322.7	297.8	275.4	259.5
4Q	—	381.2	331.7	302.8	280.3	270.7
Yr.	—	1,433	1,274	1,181	1,099	1,037

Earnings Per Share ($)

	2004	2003	2002	2001	2000	1999
1Q	0.68	0.45	0.33	0.33	0.31	0.26
2Q	0.55	0.47	0.42	0.34	0.33	0.28
3Q	0.95	0.49	0.29	0.34	0.33	0.29
4Q	E0.60	0.20	0.45	0.37	0.08	0.32
Yr.	E2.40	1.60	1.47	1.38	1.05	1.14

Next earnings report expected: late-January Source: S&P, Company Reports
EPS Estimates based on S&P Operating Earnings; historical GAAP earnings are as reported.

C. R. Bard, Inc.

Recommendation: HOLD ★ ★ ★ ☆ ☆   12-Month Target Price: $59.00 (as of April 21, 2004)

Business Summary October 25, 2004

Started by Charles Russell Bard in 1907 as a marketer of urethral catheters and other urinary products, C. R. Bard offers a range of medical, surgical, diagnostic and patient care devices. Sales in 2003 came from urology (32%), vascular (21%), oncology (23%), surgery (19%), and other (5%) product lines. By geographic market, about 71% of 2003 sales were derived from the U.S., with 18% from Europe, 5% from Japan, and 6% from other international markets.

The company's line of minimally invasive vascular products includes peripheral angioplasty stents, catheters, guidewires, introducers and accessories, vena cava filters and biopsy devices; electrophysiology products such as cardiac mapping and laboratory systems, and diagnostic and temporary pacing electrode catheters; fabrics and meshes; and implantable vascular grafts.

Bard also offers a complete line of urological diagnosis and intervention products, including the well known Foley catheters, procedure kits and trays, and related urine monitoring and collection systems; urethral stents; and specialty devices for incontinence, endoscopic procedures, and stone removal. Newer products include the Infection Control Foley catheter, which the company believes reduces the rate of urinary tract infections; an innovative collagen implant and sling materials used to treat urinary incontinence, and brachytherapy services, devices, and radioactive seeds to treat prostate cancer.

Oncology products are designed for the detection and treatment of various cancers. Products include specialty access catheters and ports; gastroenterological products (endoscopic accessories, percutaneous feeding devices and stents); biopsy devices; and a suturing system for gastroesophageal reflux disease.

Surgical specialties products include meshes for vessel and hernia repair; irrigation devices for orthopedic, laparoscopic and gynecological procedures; and topical hemostatic devices. In January 2003, Bard introduced the VentralexT hernia patch, a simplified intra-abdominal hernia repair technology characterized by minimal suturing, small incisions, and potentially shorter recovery times.

During 1999, the company entered into an agreement with Endologix Inc. It acquired exclusive distribution rights to Endologix's endoluminal graft, used for minimally invasive treatment of abdominal aortic aneurysms, in Europe and Australia.

In 2003, research and development outlays totaled $87.4 million (6.1% of sales), up from $61.7 million (4.8%) in 2002. For 2004, Bard has estimated R&D spending will equal about 7.5% of sales. New products introduced in 2003 included the Conquest PTA balloon catheter, the Fluency stent graft, the Hemosplit dialysis access catheter, and the Recovery vena cava filter. Clinical trials for the company's AV access stent graft have been completed, and clinical trials on a carotid stent are scheduled to begin in 2004. Also in 2004, Bard plans to launch its Vacora vacuum-assisted breast biopsy device.

Company Financials Fiscal Year ending December 31

Per Share Data ($)

(Year Ended December 31)	2003	2002	2001	2000	1999	1998	1997	1996	1995	1994
Tangible Bk. Val.	5.35	4.83	3.97	2.53	2.33	2.02	1.31	1.35	2.18	1.68
Cash Flow	2.03	1.87	1.89	1.53	1.61	2.78	1.13	1.32	1.21	1.10
Earnings	1.60	1.47	1.38	1.05	1.14	2.25	0.63	0.81	0.77	0.72
S&P Core Earnings	1.72	1.27	1.21	NA	NA	NA	NA	NA	NA	NA
Dividends	0.45	0.43	0.42	0.41	0.39	0.37	0.35	0.33	0.31	0.29
Payout Ratio	28%	29%	31%	39%	34%	16%	56%	41%	41%	40%
Prices - High	40.80	31.97	32.47	27.46	29.93	25.12	19.50	18.68	16.12	15.25
- Low	27.01	22.05	20.43	17.50	20.84	14.25	13.18	12.93	12.75	11.12
P/E Ratio - High	25	22	24	26	26	11	31	23	21	21
- Low	17	15	15	17	18	6	21	16	17	15

Income Statement Analysis (Million $)

	2003	2002	2001	2000	1999	1998	1997	1996	1995	1994
Revs.	1,433	1,274	1,181	1,099	1,037	1,165	1,214	1,194	1,138	1,018
Oper. Inc.	333	295	266	244	239	217	222	227	208	190
Depr.	44.7	42.3	53.2	49.6	49.1	58.7	57.3	57.4	50.6	39.6
Int. Exp.	12.5	12.6	14.2	19.3	19.3	26.4	32.9	26.4	24.2	15.1
Pretax Inc.	223	211	205	154	173	464	105	103	124	103
Eff. Tax Rate	24.5%	26.5%	30.1%	30.6%	31.9%	45.7%	31.1%	10.0%	29.8%	27.3%
Net Inc.	169	155	143	107	118	252	72.3	92.5	86.8	74.9
S&P Core Earnings	181	134	126	NA	NA	NA	NA	NA	NA	NA

Balance Sheet & Other Fin. Data (Million $)

	2003	2002	2001	2000	1999	1998	1997	1996	1995	1994
Cash	417	23.1	30.8	21.3	17.3	25.6	8.00	78.0	51.3	34.2
Curr. Assets	875	758	647	527	529	489	564	577	504	428
Total Assets	1,692	1,417	1,231	1,089	1,126	1,080	1,279	1,333	1,091	958
Curr. Liab.	422	317	235	225	353	303	311	336	273	365
LT Debt	152	152	156	204	158	160	341	343	198	78.3
Common Equity	1,046	880	789	614	574	568	573	602	565	440
Total Cap.	1,197	1,033	945	818	733	728	914	945	763	518
Cap. Exp.	72.1	41.0	27.4	19.4	26.1	43.8	32.8	41.6	39.6	34.2
Cash Flow	213	197	196	157	167	311	130	150	137	115
Curr. Ratio	2.1	2.4	2.8	2.3	1.5	1.6	1.8	1.7	1.8	1.2
% LT Debt of Cap.	12.7	14.7	16.5	25.0	21.6	22.0	37.3	36.3	26.0	15.1
% Net Inc. of Revs.	11.8	12.2	12.1	9.7	11.4	21.7	6.0	7.8	7.6	7.4
% Ret. on Assets	10.8	11.5	12.3	9.6	10.7	21.4	5.5	7.7	8.1	8.5
% Ret. on Equity	17.5	18.6	20.4	18.0	20.7	44.2	12.3	15.9	16.4	18.2

Data as orig reptd.; bef. results of disc opers/spec. items. Per share data adj. for stk. divs.; EPS diluted. E-Estimated. NA-Not Available. NM-Not Meaningful. NR-Not Ranked. UR-Under Review.

Office: 730 Central Avenue, Murray Hill, NJ 07974.
Telephone: 908-277-8000.
Website: http://www.crbard.com
Chrmn & CEO: T.M. Ring.
SVP & CFO: T.C. Schermerhorn.

VP & Treas: S.T. Lowry.
VP, Secy & General Counsel: N.J. Bernstein.
VP & Investor Contact: E.J. Shick .
Dirs: M. C. Breslawsky, T. K. Dunnigan, H. L. Henkel, W. H. Longfield, T. E. Martin, G. K. Naughton, T. M. Ring, A. Welters, T. L. White.

Founded: in 1907.
Domicile: New Jersey.
Employees: 8,300.
S&P Analyst: Robert M. Gold/PMW/GG

STANDARD &POOR'S

Bausch & Lomb

Recommendation: **HOLD** ★ ★ ★ ☆ ☆
SELL SELL HOLD BUY BUY

12-Month Target Price: **$69.00**
(as of April 02, 2004)

BOL has an approximate 0.03% weighting in the **S&P 500**

Sector: Health Care
Sub-Industry: Health Care Supplies
Peer Group: Vision Care Supplies

Summary: BOL, the world's leading maker of contact lenses and related solutions, also produces ophthalmic drugs and consumer items.

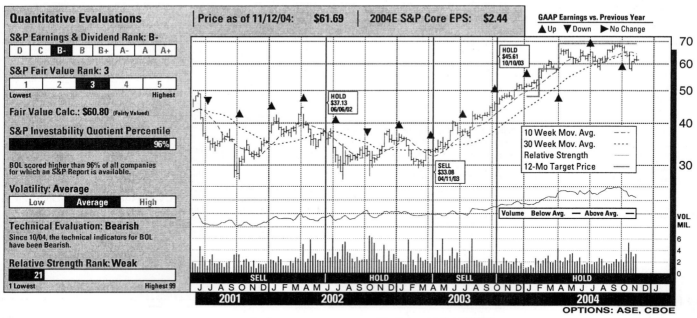

Quantitative Evaluations

S&P Earnings & Dividend Rank: B-

| D | C | B- | B | B+ | A- | A | A+ |

S&P Fair Value Rank: 3

| 1 | 2 | 3 | 4 | 5 |
| Lowest | | | | Highest |

Fair Value Calc.: $60.80 (Fairly Valued)

S&P Investability Quotient Percentile

96%

BOL scored higher than 96% of all companies for which an S&P Report is available.

Volatility: Average

| Low | Average | High |

Technical Evaluation: Bearish

Since 10/04, the technical indicators for BOL have been Bearish.

Relative Strength Rank: Weak

21

| 1 Lowest | | Highest 99 |

Price as of 11/12/04: $61.69 **2004E S&P Core EPS: $2.44**

Chart legend:
- 10 Week Mov. Avg. — — —
- 30 Week Mov. Avg. · · · · ·
- Relative Strength
- 12-Mo Target Price

Chart annotations: HOLD $37.13 06/06/02; SELL $33.08 04/11/03; HOLD $45.61 10/10/03

GAAP Earnings vs. Previous Year: ▲ Up ▼ Down ► No Change

Volume Below Avg. — Above Avg. ■

Timeline: SELL / HOLD / SELL / HOLD — J J A S O N D J F M A M J J A S O N D J F M A M J J A S O N D J F M A M J J A S O N D J 2001 2002 2003 2004

OPTIONS: ASE, CBOE

Analyst commentary prepared by Robert M. Gold/CB/BK

Highlights October 22, 2004

- Our 2004 revenue forecast is $2.2 billion. We believe 2004 sales will benefit from renewed growth in laser vision correction, aided by the launch of the new Zyoptix system. Consumer product sales should benefit from the recent launch of a daily disposable contact lens in Japan. For the longer term, through 2007, we project currency-neutral revenue growth of 6%-8%, below our medical device average, reflecting a mature contact lens business, what we view as a relatively light pharmaceutical R&D pipeline, intense competition in the laser vision correction market, and modest growth in consumer products. For 2005 specifically, we see revenues rising about 6% on a constant-currency basis.

- We expect gross margins to widen by 100 basis points in 2004, reaching an estimated 58.6%, with an estimated gain to 59.0% in 2005. We see 2004 R&D costs of $170 million to $175 million, rising to about $182 million in 2005, and see SG&A consuming 38%-39% of sales in both years.

- We are looking for 2004 EPS of $2.88 and 2005 EPS of $3.30. This excludes the possible dilution associated with a change in accounting for contingent convertible securities that BOL estimates would reduce 2005 EPS by up to $0.10. After adjusting for projected stock option expense and pension plan-related costs, our 2004 Standard & Poor's Core EPS estimate is $2.44. Free cash flow in 2004 is seen at $120 million.

Investment Rationale/Risk October 22, 2004

- Although we think BOL remains behind VISX (EYE: accumulate, $19) and Alcon (ACL: accumulate, $69) in terms of installed vision correction lasers in the U.S., results in recent quarters indicated to us that the company is gaining significant share in the U.S., and we believe it has the potential to capture up to 20% of the U.S. market, aided by the launch of its Zyoptix system. In our opinion, this new revenue stream is important in light of clinical uncertainties in the pharmaceutical area and expected slow growth in consumer products. On a procedure basis, we estimate that BOL had an approximate 18% share of the laser vision correction market at the end of the 2004 third quarter.

Key Stock Statistics

S&P Oper. EPS 2004E	2.88	52-week Range	$69.00-46.87
P/E on S&P Oper. EPS 2004E	21.4	12 Month P/E	21.1
S&P Oper. EPS 2005E	3.30	Beta	0.34
Yield (%)	0.8%	Shareholders	8,000
Dividend Rate/Share	0.52	Market Cap (B)	$ 3.3
Shares Outstanding (M)	53.5		

Value of $10,000 invested five years ago: **$ 11,447**

Dividend Data Dividends have been paid since 1952

Amount ($)	Date Decl.	Ex-Div. Date	Stock of Record	Payment Date
0.130	Feb. 24	Feb. 26	Mar. 01	Apr. 01 '04
0.130	Apr. 27	May. 27	Jun. 01	Jul. 01 '04
0.130	Jul. 20	Aug. 30	Sep. 01	Oct. 01 '04
0.130	Nov. 02	Nov. 29	Dec. 01	Jan. 04 '05

Revenues/Earnings Data Fiscal year ending December 31

Revenues (Million $)

	2004	2003	2002	2001	2000	1999
1Q	510.3	448.0	414.2	412.2	408.9	389.9
2Q	566.5	512.5	458.4	414.0	455.2	453.3
3Q	548.9	508.9	466.7	433.7	443.2	446.3
4Q	—	550.1	477.4	452.0	465.1	466.6
Yr.	—	2,020	1,817	1,712	1,772	1,756

Earnings Per Share ($)

	2004	2003	2002	2001	2000	1999
1Q	0.43	0.31	0.16	-0.02	0.68	0.26
2Q	0.78	0.53	0.40	0.13	0.64	0.49
3Q	0.79	0.60	0.17	0.43	0.27	0.71
4Q	E0.90	0.92	0.60	0.24	-0.09	0.29
Yr.	E2.88	2.36	1.34	0.78	1.49	1.75

Next earnings report expected: late-January Source: S&P, Company Reports
EPS Estimates based on S&P Operating Earnings; historical GAAP earnings are as reported.

STANDARD &POOR'S

Bausch & Lomb Incorporated

Stock Report
November 13, 2004
NYSE Symbol: **BOL**

Recommendation: HOLD ★ ★ ★ ☆ ☆   12-Month Target Price: **$69.00** (as of April 02, 2004)

Business Summary October 25, 2004

Bausch & Lomb, which makes well known contact lenses and contact lens solution brands, also produces ophthalmic pharmaceuticals and equipment used for eye surgery. Sales outside the U.S. accounted for 55% of the total in 2003.

Contact lenses (29%) include daily disposable, continuous wear, planned replacement disposable and rigid gas permeable products. Principal brand names include SofLens, Boston and PureVision. In early 2002, the company introduced SofLens66 toric lenses, which are high performance cast-molded lenses for people with astigmatism. BOL has also obtained an exclusive worldwide license to a patented cast-molded multifocal soft contact lens design from Unilab.

BOL is involved in a patent dispute with Wesley Jessen Vision Care Inc. (a unit of CIBA Vision Corp.), which alleges that the company's PureVision product infringes on intellectual property held by Wesley. In June 2002, a court ruled in favor of Wesley, and a subsequent ruling, which BOL is appealing, ordered it to discontinue U.S. manufacture and sale of the product. In November 2003, the company filed a lawsuit against CIBA Vision for infringement of a BOL patent related to a method of making contact lenses.

The lens care division (25%) includes multi-purpose solutions, enzyme cleaners and saline solutions marketed to licensed eye care professionals, health product retailers, independent pharmacies, drug stores, food stores and mass merchan-

disers. The company's ReNu brand is believed to be the leading U.S. lens care brand. Contact lens care is a relatively mature business in the U.S., but the company sees growth potential overseas, and plans to launch a next-generation product in the U.S. in 2004. In 2001, it introduced a no-rub version of its ReNu MultiPlus multipurpose lens cleaning solution.

Pharmaceuticals (23%) include generic and proprietary prescription and OTC medications, with strategic emphasis on the ophthalmic field and on ocular vitamins and vision accessories. Key products include Lotemax, a steroid to treat inflammation; Alrex, to relieve allergic conjunctivitis; Optipranolol, a beta blocker used to treat ocular hypertension and glaucoma: Muro-128 to treat corneal edema; and Ocuvite, a vitamin/mineral supplement brand. In 2000, BOL acquired Groupe Chauvin, a collection of related ophthalmic pharmaceutical companies based in France. The company's Retisert implant is currently in Phase III trials in the U.S., using the steroid fluocinolone acetonide to treat a potentially blinding condition, posterior uveitis.

The surgical segment (23%) makes products and equipment for cataract, refractive and retinal surgery. In 2000, the company received FDA approval to market its Technolas 217 vision correction laser system. In October 2003, BOL received FDA approval to sell its Technolas 217z Zyoptix system for customized ablation.

Company Financials Fiscal Year ending December 31

Per Share Data ($)

(Year Ended December 31)	2003	2002	2001	2000	1999	1998	1997	1996	1995	1994
Tangible Bk. Val.	5.20	2.87	2.48	4.18	1.10	1.52	7.41	8.86	9.62	8.79
Cash Flow	4.70	3.75	3.65	4.20	4.42	3.35	2.90	3.47	3.62	1.89
Earnings	2.36	1.34	0.78	1.49	1.75	0.45	0.89	1.47	1.94	0.23
S&P Core Earnings	2.26	0.49	-0.07	NA	NA	NA	NA	NA	NA	NA
Dividends	0.52	0.65	1.04	1.04	1.04	1.04	1.04	1.04	1.01	0.96
Payout Ratio	22%	49%	133%	70%	59%	NM	117%	71%	52%	NM
Prices - High	52.66	44.80	54.93	80.87	84.75	60.00	47.87	44.50	44.50	53.87
- Low	36.05	27.16	27.20	33.56	51.37	37.75	32.50	32.50	30.87	30.62
P/E Ratio - High	22	33	70	54	48	NM	54	30	23	NM
- Low	15	20	35	22	29	NM	37	22	16	NM

Income Statement Analysis (Million $)

	2003	2002	2001	2000	1999	1998	1997	1996	1995	1994
Revs.	2,020	1,817	1,712	1,772	1,756	2,363	1,916	1,927	1,933	1,851
Oper. Inc.	354	329	263	371	424	425	332	319	343	268
Depr.	125	130	155	148	156	164	112	113	105	99
Int. Exp.	54.2	53.9	58.3	68.5	88.4	101	56.0	51.7	45.8	41.4
Pretax Inc.	197	137	85.0	161	185	130	118	169	212	90.0
Eff. Tax Rate	34.0%	34.5%	33.8%	40.8%	36.0%	60.9%	38.6%	37.7%	36.9%	58.5%
Net Inc.	126	72.5	42.0	82.0	103	25.2	49.4	83.1	112	13.0
S&P Core Earnings	121	27.0	-3.35	NA	NA	NA	NA	NA	NA	NA

Balance Sheet & Other Fin. Data (Million $)

	2003	2002	2001	2000	1999	1998	1997	1996	1995	1994
Cash	563	465	534	660	827	429	184	168	194	233
Curr. Assets	1,421	1,285	1,397	1,646	1,810	1,587	1,090	948	930	954
Total Assets	3,006	2,908	2,994	3,086	3,274	3,492	2,773	2,603	2,550	2,458
Curr. Liab.	876	829	704	809	620	812	887	929	859	677
LT Debt	652	656	703	763	977	1,281	511	236	191	290
Common Equity	1,203	1,018	975	1,039	1,234	845	818	882	929	914
Total Cap.	1,982	1,950	2,190	2,179	2,554	2,573	1,129	1,550	1,551	1,632
Cap. Exp.	91.5	91.9	96.4	95.0	156	202	126	130	95.0	85.0
Cash Flow	251	203	197	230	259	189	161	196	217	113
Curr. Ratio	1.6	1.5	2.0	2.0	2.9	2.0	1.2	1.0	1.1	1.4
% LT Debt of Cap.	32.9	33.6	32.1	35.0	38.2	49.8	45.3	15.2	12.4	17.7
% Net Inc.of Revs.	6.3	4.0	2.5	4.6	5.8	1.1	2.6	4.3	5.8	0.7
% Ret. on Assets	4.4	2.5	1.3	2.6	3.0	0.8	1.8	3.2	4.5	0.5
% Ret. on Equity	11.4	7.3	4.2	7.2	9.9	3.0	5.8	9.2	12.2	1.5

Data as orig reptd.; bef. results of disc opers/spec. items. Per share data adj. for stk. divs.; EPS diluted. E-Estimated. NA-Not Available. NM-Not Meaningful. NR-Not Ranked. UR-Under Review.

Office: One Bausch & Lomb Place, Rochester, NY 14604-2701.
Telephone: 585-338-6000.
Website: http://www.bausch.com
Chrmn & CEO: R.L. Zarrella.
SVP & CFO: S.C. McCluski.
SVP & CSO: P. Tyle.

SVP & General Counsel: R.B. Stiles.
VP & Treas: A. Resnick.
VP & Investor Contact: B.M. Kelley .
Dirs: A. M. Bennett, D. De Sole, P. A. Friedman, J. S. Linen, R. R. McMullin, J. R. Purcell, L. J. Rice, W. H. Waltrip, B. W. Wilson, K. L. Wolfe, R. L. Zarrella.

Founded: in 1853.
Domicile: New York.
Employees: 11,600.
S&P Analyst: Robert M. Gold/CB/BK

Baxter International

Recommendation: **SELL** ★ ★ ★ ★ ★ 12-Month Target Price: **$26.00**
SELL SELL HOLD BUY BUY
(as of July 22, 2004)

BAX has an approximate 0.18% weighting in the **S&P 500**

Sector: Health Care
Sub-Industry: Health Care Equipment
Peer Group: Large Multi-Line Medical Device Manufacturers

Summary: This global medical products and services company provides critical therapies for people with life-threatening conditions.

Quantitative Evaluations

S&P Earnings & Dividend Rank: B+

| D | C | B- | B | B+ | A- | A | A+ |

S&P Fair Value Rank: 4

| 1 | 2 | 3 | 4 | 5 |
| Lowest | | | | Highest |

Fair Value Calc.: $31.60 (Fairly Valued)

S&P Investability Quotient Percentile

53%

BAX scored higher than 53% of all companies for which an S&P Report is available.

Volatility: Average

| Low | Average | High |

Technical Evaluation: Neutral
Since 11/04, the technical indicators for BAX have been Neutral.

Relative Strength Rank: Moderate

40

1 Lowest   Highest 99

| Price as of 11/12/04: | $32 | 2004E S&P Core EPS: | $1.75 |

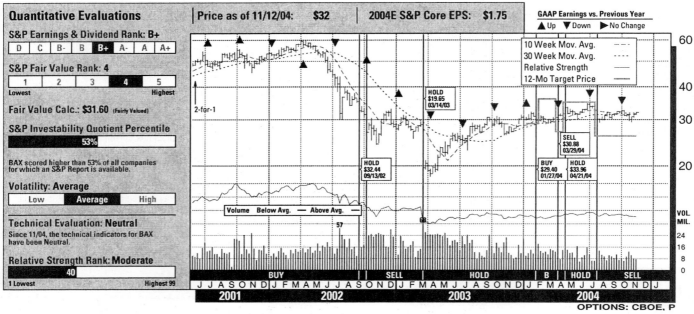

GAAP Earnings vs. Previous Year
▲ Up ▼ Down ► No Change

10 Week Mov. Avg.
30 Week Mov. Avg.
Relative Strength
12-Mo Target Price

Analyst commentary prepared by Robert M. Gold/PMW/BK

OPTIONS: CBOE, P

Highlights October 26, 2004

- We project 2004 revenues of $9.1 billion, excluding potential foreign currency benefits that the company believes will add 3% to 4% to reported sales growth. By segment, excluding currency, we expect medication delivery sales to grow 3%, aided by a new contract with the Premier hospital alliance and improved performance in drug delivery. In renal, we see sales up about 2%. We expect bioscience sales to rise 1% to 2%, as price reductions on Advate drive market conversion in both the U.S. and Europe, helping outweigh moderately lower sales of vaccines and sluggish growth for plasma-based products. Advate sales are currently projected to approximate $250 million in 2004. Looking to 2005, we project constant-currency revenue growth of 4% to 5%.

Investment Rationale/Risk October 26, 2004

- We would avoid the shares. We see near-term operating challenges, including rising competition in the generic anesthesia market, less favorable medication delivery contract pricing, eroding prices in the plasma protein market, and weak vaccine sales. We also think the company will need to continue funding its pension plan in 2005, and believe that costs associated with unwinding foreign currency hedging contracts could exceed $300 million. We are encouraged by steps by new management to improve the balance sheet and increase the transparency of the income statement, but we think weaker business conditions will persist through 2005. We are also concerned about the possibility of additional accounting-related problems, following the July 2004 disclosure that BAX will restate financial results for 2001 through 2003 and for the 2004 first quarter, due to incorrect revenue recognition and inadequate bad debt provisions in Brazil.

- Risks to our recommendation and target price include greater than expected Advate product sales, a meaningful recovery in the renal division, favorable adjustments to Medicare reimbursement rates, and broad-based strength in the health care sector.

- Our 12-month target price of $26 assumes that the 2004 P/E multiple will be moderately discounted to the S&P 500, and is based in part on our discounted free cash flow model.

Key Stock Statistics

S&P Oper. EPS 2004E	1.67	52-week Range	$34.84-26.86
P/E on S&P Oper. EPS 2004E	19.2	12 Month P/E	29.6
S&P Oper. EPS 2005E	1.85	Beta	0.62
Yield (%)	1.8%	Shareholders	63,342
Dividend Rate/Share	0.58	Market Cap (B)	$ 19.7
Shares Outstanding (M)	616.4		

Value of $10,000 invested five years ago: **NA**

Dividend Data Dividends have been paid since 1934

Amount ($)	Date Decl.	Ex-Div. Date	Stock of Record	Payment Date
0.582	Nov. 18	Dec. 10	Dec. 12	Jan. 05 '04

Revenues/Earnings Data Fiscal year ending December 31

Revenues (Million $)

	2004	2003	2002	2001	2000	1999
1Q	2,209	1,997	1,875	1,757	1,583	1,462
2Q	2,379	2,163	1,945	1,870	1,694	1,560
3Q	2,320	2,219	2,029	1,900	1,687	1,589
4Q	—	2,537	2,261	2,136	1,932	1,769
Yr.	—	8,916	8,110	7,663	6,896	6,380

Earnings Per Share ($)

	2004	2003	2002	2001	2000	1999
1Q	0.31	0.36	0.41	0.36	0.33	0.28
2Q	-0.28	0.08	0.32	0.42	0.08	0.32
3Q	0.42	0.47	0.51	0.45	0.39	0.34
4Q	E0.55	0.62	0.42	-0.13	0.45	0.39
Yr.	E1.67	1.52	1.67	1.09	1.24	1.32

Next earnings report expected: late-January Source: S&P, Company Reports
EPS Estimates based on S&P Operating Earnings; historical GAAP earnings are as reported.

Baxter International Inc.

Recommendation: **SELL** ★ ★ ★ ★ ★   12-Month Target Price: **$26.00** (as of July 22, 2004)

Business Summary October 26, 2004

Founded in 1931 as the first producer of commercially prepared IV solutions, Baxter International produces and distributes medical products and equipment, with a focus on the blood and circulatory system. In 2003, international sales accounted for 52% of the total.

The medication delivery unit (43% of 2003 net sales from continuing operations) makes intravenous (IV) solutions and various specialty products such as critical-care generic injectable drugs, anesthetic agents, and nutrition and oncology products. The products work with devices such as drug-reconstitution systems, IV infusion pumps, nutritional compounding equipment and medication management systems to provide fluid replenishment, general anesthesia, parenteral nutrition, pain management, antibiotic therapy and chemotherapy.

The BioSciences unit (37%) produces plasma-based and recombinant clotting factors for hemophilia, as well as biopharmaceuticals for immune deficiencies, cancer and other disorders. It also develops biosurgery products for hemostasis, tissue sealing and tissue regeneration, and vaccines. The company makes blood collection, processing and storage systems used by hospitals, blood banks and plasma collection centers to collect and process blood components for therapeutic use. BAX also sells a meningitis C vaccine, and is developing cell culture-derived vaccines for influenza, smallpox, Severe Acute Respiratory Syndrome and other diseases. In 2003, the company received FDA approval to sell Advate, a recombinant blood clotting agent produced without adding human or animal proteins in the cell culture, purification or final formulation process.

During 2003, BAX acquired Alpha Therapeutic Corp.'s Aralast alpha-1 proteinase inhibitor (A1PI) treatment for hereditary emphysema, and 42 FDA-licensed plasma collection centers in the U.S. In January 2003, Aralast received FDA approval as an augmentation therapy for patients with congenital deficiency of A1PI and clinically evident emphysema. In December 2002, the company acquired most of ESI Lederle, a unit of Wyeth Inc. ESI makes injectable generic drugs and patent-expired branded products.

The company also sells dialysis equipment and other products and services to kidney failure patients (20%). BAX sells products for peritoneal dialysis (PD), including solutions, container systems and automated machines that cleanse patients' blood overnight while they sleep. The company also makes dialyzers and instrumentation for hemodialysis (HD). During 2003, BAX launched its Extraneal (icodextrin) solution in the U.S. and Japan, which offers the potential for increased fluid removal from the bloodstream during dialysis.

In April 2004, BAX began implementing a restructuring plan that included the elimination of about 7% to 8% of its global workforce and a reduction in plasma production. Cost savings equal to $0.05 a share were expected in the second half of 2004, with annual savings of up to $0.25 envisioned in 2005 and up to $0.35 thereafter. A related charge of $0.64 a share was recorded in the 2004 second quarter.

Company Financials Fiscal Year ending December 31

Per Share Data ($)

(Year Ended December 31)	2003	2002	2001	2000	1999	1998	1997	1996	1995	1994
Tangible Bk. Val.	1.74	1.53	3.44	2.43	4.19	1.79	1.78	2.05	4.79	6.59
Cash Flow	2.42	2.38	1.81	1.91	1.95	1.28	1.24	1.70	1.28	1.86
Earnings	1.52	1.67	1.09	1.24	1.32	0.55	0.53	1.06	0.67	1.06
S&P Core Earnings	1.25	1.30	0.53	NA	NA	NA	NA	NA	NA	NA
Dividends	0.58	0.58	0.58	0.15	0.58	0.58	0.57	0.59	0.56	0.51
Payout Ratio	38%	35%	53%	12%	44%	107%	107%	55%	83%	48%
Prices - High	31.32	59.90	55.90	45.12	38.00	33.00	30.12	24.06	22.37	14.43
- Low	18.18	24.07	40.06	25.87	28.40	24.25	19.93	19.87	13.37	10.81
P/E Ratio - High	21	36	51	37	29	61	57	23	33	14
- Low	12	14	37	21	22	44	38	19	20	10

Income Statement Analysis (Million $)

	2003	2002	2001	2000	1999	1998	1997	1996	1995	1994
Revs.	8,916	8,110	7,663	6,896	6,380	6,599	6,138	5,438	5,048	9,324
Oper. Inc.	2,161	2,168	1,934	1,673	1,522	1,545	1,403	1,259	1,150	1,471
Depr.	545	439	441	405	372	426	398	348	336	448
Int. Exp.	118	71.0	108	124	152	193	198	103	96.0	242
Pretax Inc.	1,150	1,397	964	946	1,052	549	523	793	524	810
Eff. Tax Rate	19.8%	26.1%	31.1%	22.0%	26.0%	42.6%	42.6%	27.5%	29.1%	25.3%
Net Inc.	922	1,033	664	738	779	315	300	575	371	596
S&P Core Earnings	756	794	313	NA	NA	NA	NA	NA	NA	NA

Balance Sheet & Other Fin. Data (Million $)

	2003	2002	2001	2000	1999	1998	1997	1996	1995	1994
Cash	927	1,169	582	579	606	709	465	761	476	471
Curr. Assets	5,437	5,160	3,977	3,651	3,819	4,651	3,870	3,480	2,911	4,340
Total Assets	13,779	12,478	10,343	8,733	9,644	10,085	8,707	7,596	9,437	10,002
Curr. Liab.	3,819	3,851	3,294	3,372	2,700	2,988	2,557	2,445	2,154	2,766
LT Debt	4,421	4,398	2,486	1,726	2,601	3,096	2,635	1,695	2,372	2,341
Common Equity	3,323	2,939	3,757	2,659	3,348	2,839	2,619	2,504	3,704	3,720
Total Cap.	7,744	7,366	6,461	4,545	6,260	6,440	5,570	4,454	6,249	6,228
Cap. Exp.	789	734	669	101	529	492	403	318	309	502
Cash Flow	1,467	1,472	1,105	1,143	1,151	741	698	923	707	1,044
Curr. Ratio	1.4	1.3	1.2	1.1	1.4	1.6	1.5	1.4	1.4	1.6
% LT Debt of Cap.	57.1	59.7	38.5	38.0	41.5	48.1	47.3	38.1	38.0	37.6
% Net Inc.of Revs.	10.3	12.7	8.7	10.7	12.2	4.8	4.9	10.6	7.3	6.4
% Ret. on Assets	7.0	9.1	7.0	8.0	8.0	3.4	3.7	6.8	4.0	5.7
% Ret. on Equity	29.4	30.9	20.7	24.6	25.2	11.5	11.7	18.5	10.0	17.1

Data as orig reptd.; bef. results of disc opers/spec. items. Per share data adj. for stk. divs.; EPS diluted. E-Estimated. NA-Not Available. NM-Not Meaningful. NR-Not Ranked. UR-Under Review.

Office: One Baxter Parkway, Deerfield, IL 60015.
Telephone: 847-948-2000.
Website: http://www.baxter.com
Chrmn & CEO: R.L. Parkinson, Jr.
SVP & CFO: J. Greisch.
Treas: S.J. Meyer.

Secy: J.S. Reed.
Investor Contact: M. Ladone 847-948-2000.
Dirs: W. E. Boomer, P. Chia, J. D. Forsyth, G. D. Fosler, J. R. Gavin III, J. B. Martin, R. L. Parkinson, Jr., T. T. Stallkamp, K. J. Storm, A. P. Stroucken, M. E. Trout, F. L. Turner, C. J. Uhrich.

Founded: in 1931.
Domicile: Delaware.
Employees: 51,300.
S&P Analyst: Robert M. Gold/PMW/BK

Recommendation: **HOLD** ★★★★★
SELL SELL HOLD BUY BUY

12-Month Target Price: **$41.00**
(as of October 14, 2004)

BBT has an approximate 0.22% weighting in the **S&P 500**

Sector: Financials
Sub-Industry: Regional Banks
Peer Group: Southeast Major Regional Banks

Summary: This bank holding company, through subsidiaries, operates banking offices in the Carolinas, Georgia, Virginia, West Virginia, Kentucky, Maryland, and Washington, DC.

Quantitative Evaluations

S&P Earnings & Dividend Rank: A-

D	C	B-	B	B+	A-	A	A+

S&P Fair Value Rank: 3

1	2	3	4	5
Lowest				Highest

Fair Value Calc.: $41.00 (Slightly Overvalued)

S&P Investability Quotient Percentile

95%

BBT scored higher than 95% of all companies for which an S&P Report is available.

Volatility: Low

Low	Average	High

Technical Evaluation: Bullish

Since 10/04, the technical indicators for BBT have been Bullish.

Relative Strength Rank: Moderate

63

| 1 Lowest | | Highest 99 |

Price as of 11/12/04: **$43** | 2004E S&P Core EPS: **$2.93**

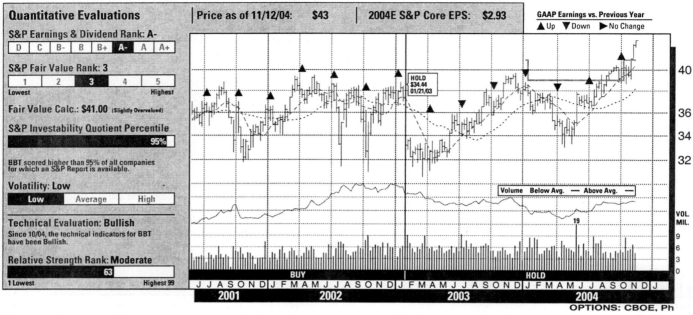

GAAP Earnings vs. Previous Year
▲ Up ▼ Down ► No Change

Analyst commentary prepared by James M. O'Brien/CB/BK

Highlights 15-NOV-04

- Third quarter results for 2004 were driven by a wider net interest margin, improved credit quality, fee income growth and an improved efficiency ratio. We expect the net interest margin to stabilize in the fourth quarter of 2004 and into 2005, following BBT's balance sheet restructuring in the third quarter of 2003. Assuming gradually rising interest rates for the next couple of quarters, we expect the margin to remain at about 4.25%.
- We see loan growth outside the retail market as likely to remain below historical trends, but to accelerate later in 2004 and into the first half of 2005, as the economy continues to improve. Credit quality appears to have stabilized, and our model assumes that chargeoffs remain at 0.45% of average loans in 2004. We see fee income growth remaining strong, boosted by insurance agency fees, trust income, and deposit service charges.
- We believe expenses will show only modest growth, as the integration of First Virginia Bank operations continues. Excluding merger-related charges, we see 2004 EPS growing to $2.74, still at the low end of management's guidance. Our 2005 estimate is $3.10.

Investment Rationale/Risk 15-NOV-04

- The stock came under pressure early in 2003 when BBT first agreed to acquire First Virginia Banks (the transaction was finalized in July). We believe this reflected investor skepticism about the acquisition price (18X EPS and 2.7X book value), the unusually long period expected for the transaction to become accretive to earnings, and aggressive cost cutting proposed. Although the company has a solid track record of merger integrations, this deal was considerably larger and more complex, and we think it could prove more difficult than past acquisitions. BBT laid out its cost savings projections indicating 100% savings captured by the first quarter of 2006; the most recent quarter did show signs of an improved efficiency ratio.
- Risks to our opinion and target price include acquisition integration issues, interest rate risk and tepid loan growth.
- We believe the ongoing merger integration, as well as the lack of any strong near term catalyst in BBT's markets, will likely remain of concern to investors for the near term, and we think the shares will have difficulty outperforming. Our 12-month target price of $41 is equal to about 13.2X our 2005 EPS estimate, in line with the peer average.

Key Stock Statistics

S&P Oper. EPS 2004E	2.74	52-week Range	$43.00-33.02
P/E on S&P Oper. EPS 2004E	15.7	12 Month P/E	16.5
S&P Oper. EPS 2005E	3.10	Beta	0.29
Yield (%)	3.3%	Shareholders	274,000
Dividend Rate/Share	1.40	Market Cap (B)	$ 23.8
Shares Outstanding (M)	552.4		

Value of $10,000 invested five years ago: **$ 13,800**

Dividend Data Dividends have been paid since 1934

Amount ($)	Date Decl.	Ex-Div. Date	Stock of Record	Payment Date
0.320	Dec. 16	Jan. 14	Jan. 16	Feb. 02 '04
0.320	Feb. 24	Apr. 14	Apr. 16	May. 03 '04
0.350	Jun. 22	Jul. 14	Jul. 16	Aug. 02 '04
0.350	Aug. 24	Oct. 13	Oct. 15	Nov. 01 '04

Revenues/Earnings Data Fiscal year ending December 31

Revenues (Million $)

	2004	2003	2002	2001	2000	1999
1Q	1,559	1,500	1,456	1,476	1,121	828.3
2Q	1,693	1,507	1,526	1,487	1,176	886.9
3Q	1,698	1,611	1,549	1,550	1,222	954.7
4Q	—	1,627	1,629	1,500	1,398	1,048
Yr.	—	6,244	6,127	6,228	5,117	3,964

Earnings Per Share ($)

	2004	2003	2002	2001	2000	1999
1Q	0.60	0.69	0.64	0.53	0.46	0.44
2Q	0.72	0.67	0.68	0.60	0.41	0.49
3Q	0.74	0.21	0.68	0.48	0.12	0.44
4Q	E0.72	0.55	0.70	0.61	0.56	0.47
Yr.	E2.74	2.07	2.70	2.12	1.55	1.83

Next earnings report expected: mid-January Source: S&P, Company Reports
EPS Estimates based on S&P Operating Earnings; historical GAAP earnings are as reported.

BB&T Corporation

Recommendation: **HOLD** ★ ★ ★ ☆ ☆   12-Month Target Price: **$41.00** (as of October 14, 2004)

Business Summary 15-NOV-04

BB&T Corp., headquartered in Winston-Salem, NC, operates more than 1,350 banking offices, in North and South Carolina, Georgia, Virginia, West Virginia, Tennessee, Kentucky, Maryland, Alabama, Florida, Indiana, and Washington, DC. Principal subsidiaries include BB&T Leasing Corp., which specializes in lease financing to commercial businesses; BB&T Investment Services, which offers nondeposit investment alternatives including annuities, mutual funds and discount brokerage; and Scott & Stringfellow Financial, an investment banking and full-service brokerage firm.

Operations are divided into six segments. The banking network segment serves individual and business clients by offering a variety of loan and deposit products and other financial services. The mortgage banking segment retains and services mortgages originated by the banking network as well as those purchased from other originators. The trust service segment provides personal trust administration, estate planning, investment counseling, asset management, employee benefits services and corporate trust services. The agency insurance segment provides property and casualty, life and health insurance to businesses and individuals. The investment banking and brokerage segment offers investment alternatives including discount brokerage, annuities and mutual funds. The treasury segment is responsible for the management of the company's securities portfolio, overall balance sheet funding and liquidity, and management of interest rate risk.

Gross loans of $64.9 billion at December 31, 2003, were divided as follows: real estate mortgage 56%; commercial, financial and agricultural 11%; consumer 14%; lease receivables 8%; real estate construction and land development 10%; and other 1%.

Nonperforming assets, consisting of nonaccrual loans and leases, restructured loans and foreclosed property, totaled $447.1 million (0.56% of loans and related assets) at the end of 2003, down from $451.6 million (0.70%) a year earlier. The allowance for loan losses, which is set aside for possible loan defaults, amounted to $784.9 million (1.26% of loans and leases) at December 31, 2003, up from $723.7 million (1.35%) a year earlier. Net chargeoffs, or the amount of loans deemed uncollectible, totaled $247.8 million (0.43% of average loans) in 2003, versus $246.5 million (0.48%) in 2002.

In July 2003, BBT acquired First Virginia Banks via an exchange of stock valued at $3.05 billion. At the time, First Virginia had $11.2 billion in assets, and operated 363 branch offices in Virginia, Maryland and Tennessee. In February 2004, BB&T Insurance Services acquired insurance broker McGriff, Seibels & Williams Inc., based in Birmingham, AL, for $300 million in stock and $50 million in cash, plus possible contingent payments, and in March 2004, acquired Florida-based insurance agency Iler Wall & Shonter Insurance Inc. In April 2004, the bank acquired Republic Bancshares in a $392 million transaction.

Company Financials Fiscal Year ending December 31

Per Share Data ($)

(Year Ended December 31)	2003	2002	2001	2000	1999	1998	1997	1996	1995	1994
Tangible Bk. Val.	11.66	12.04	13.50	11.91	9.66	9.95	8.22	7.91	8.01	6.96
Earnings	2.07	2.70	2.12	1.55	1.83	1.71	1.30	1.28	0.83	1.13
S&P Core Earnings	1.97	2.59	2.02	NA	NA	NA	NA	NA	NA	NA
Dividends	1.22	1.10	0.98	0.86	0.75	0.66	0.58	0.50	0.43	0.37
Payout Ratio	59%	41%	46%	55%	41%	39%	45%	39%	52%	33%
Prices - High	39.69	39.47	38.84	38.25	40.62	40.75	32.50	18.50	14.00	11.00
- Low	30.66	31.03	30.24	21.68	27.18	26.25	17.50	12.87	9.37	8.43
P/E Ratio - High	19	15	18	25	22	24	25	14	17	10
- Low	15	11	14	14	15	15	13	10	11	7

Income Statement Analysis (Million $)

	2003	2002	2001	2000	1999	1998	1997	1996	1995	1994
Net Int. Inc.	3,082	2,747	2,434	2,018	1,582	1,247	1,100	775	742	737
Tax Equiv. Adj.	21.2	151	19.1	130	86.7	64.8	52.9	34.2	32.5	25.5
Non Int. Inc.	1,782	1,522	1,256	996	639	520	473	294	226	226
Loan Loss Prov.	248	264	224	127	92.1	80.3	89.8	53.7	31.4	17.8
Exp./Op. Revs.	63.6%	54.0%	60.1%	56.0%	58.4%	52.5%	59.6%	74.4%	67.2%	58.7%
Pretax Inc.	1,617	1,791	1,360	906	904	734	547	418	264	362
Eff. Tax Rate	34.1%	27.8%	28.4%	30.8%	32.2%	31.6%	34.2%	32.2%	32.6%	34.5%
Net Inc.	1,065	1,293	974	626	613	502	360	284	178	237
% Net Int. Marg.	4.06	4.25	4.17	3.56	4.27	3.75	4.55	4.45	4.05	4.29
S&P Core Earnings	1,012	1,241	927	NA	NA	NA	NA	NA	NA	NA

Balance Sheet & Other Fin. Data (Million $)

	2003	2002	2001	2000	1999	1998	1997	1996	1995	1994
Money Mkt. Assets	604	591	458	379	390	168	178	21.0	120	13.0
Inv. Securities	16,317	17,655	16,662	13,851	10,579	8,099	6,629	5,262	5,355	5,425
Com'l Loans	12,429	7,061	6,551	5,894	4,593	3,444	3,018	2,375	2,098	NA
Other Loans	49,151	44,079	38,985	33,561	24,320	19,932	16,499	12,150	11,783	12,800
Total Assets	90,467	80,217	70,870	59,340	43,481	34,427	29,178	21,247	20,493	19,855
Demand Deposits	11,098	7,864	6,940	5,064	3,908	3,247	2,829	1,990	1,886	1,843
Time Deposits	48,252	43,416	37,794	32,951	23,343	19,800	17,381	12,963	12,798	12,471
LT Debt	10,808	13,588	11,721	8,355	5,492	4,737	3,283	2,052	1,384	911
Common Equity	9,935	7,388	6,150	4,786	3,199	2,759	2,238	1,729	1,670	1,493
% Ret. on Assets	1.2	1.7	1.4	1.1	1.5	1.6	1.4	1.4	0.9	1.3
% Ret. on Equity	12.3	19.1	16.8	14.2	19.2	20.1	18.1	16.5	11.6	16.8
% Loan Loss Resv.	1.3	1.4	1.4	1.3	1.3	1.4	1.3	1.3	1.3	1.3
% Loans/Deposits	105.0	104.4	106.1	106.0	107.1	98.3	97.9	97.2	92.4	85.3
% Equity to Assets	10.1	9.0	8.4	7.9	7.7	7.9	7.9	8.1	7.7	7.7

Data as orig reptd.; bef. results of disc opers/spec. items. Per share data adj. for stk. divs.; EPS diluted. E-Estimated. NA-Not Available. NM-Not Meaningful. NR-Not Ranked. UR-Under Review.

Office: 200 West Second Street, Winston-Salem, NC 27101.
Telephone: 336-733-2000.
Website: http://www.bbandt.com
Chrmn & CEO: J. A. Allison IV.
Pres & COO: K. S. King.
EVP & CFO: S. E. Reed.

Investor Contact: Tom A. Nicholson (336-733-3058).
Dirs: J. A. Allison IV, J. S. Banner, N. R. Chilton, A. E. Cleveland, R. E. Deal, T. D. Efird, B. J. Fitzpatrick, L. V. Hackley, J. P. Helm, J. E. Lathem, J. H. Maynard, A. O. McCauley, J. H. Morrison, R. L. Player, Jr., N. R. Qubein, E. R. Sasser, J. E. Shaw, A. F. Zettlemoyer.

Founded: in 1968.
Domicile: North Carolina.
Employees: 26,300.
S&P Analyst: James M. O'Brien/CB/BK

Bear Stearns

Recommendation: **BUY** ★★★★★
SELL SELL HOLD BUY BUY

12-Month Target Price: $120.00
(as of March 17, 2004)

BSC has an approximate 0.09% weighting in the **S&P 500**

Sector: Financials
Sub-Industry: Investment Banking & Brokerage
Peer Group: Investment Banking/Brokerage - Major

Summary: This company's Bear, Stearns & Co. unit is a leading investment bank and broker, and is ranked as one of the largest NYSE member firms.

Quantitative Evaluations	**Price as of 11/12/04: $98.55** — **2004E S&P Core EPS: $8.88** — **GAAP Earnings vs. Previous Year** ▲ Up ▼ Down ▶ No Change

S&P Earnings & Dividend Rank: A

D	C	B-	B	B+	A-	**A**	A+

S&P Fair Value Rank: 5

1	2	3	4	**5**
Lowest				Highest

Fair Value Calc.: $121.70 (Undervalued)

S&P Investability Quotient Percentile
99%

BSC scored higher than 99% of all companies for which an S&P Report is available.

Volatility: Low

Low	Average	High

Technical Evaluation: Bullish
Since 11/04, the technical indicators for BSC have been Bullish.

Relative Strength Rank: Moderate
67

1 Lowest		Highest 99

10 Week Mov. Avg.
30 Week Mov. Avg.
Relative Strength
12-Mo Target Price

Volume Below Avg. — Above Avg. —

OPTIONS: CBOE, P, Ph, ASE, CBOE, P

Analyst commentary prepared by Robert Hansen, CFA /DC/GG

Highlights October 07, 2004

- We think the company has a strong competitive position, due to the breadth of its fixed income franchise, the stability and consistency of its trading revenues, and the growth of its prime brokerage business. We are impressed with BSC's diversification beyond mortgages and high yield in its fixed income franchise. In FY 03 (Nov.), Fixed Income had 13 businesses (five mortgage-related), each with annual revenue in excess of $100 million, up from two businesses in FY 00.

- We expect revenue growth in Investment Banking, Global Clearing Services and Wealth Management to largely offset a decline that we see for Fixed Income in FY 05. We believe that an increase in ARM originations and relatively stable Alt-A originations will help offset a decline that we see in traditional fixed-rate mortgage originations. We look for a modest recovery in the institutional equity business in FY 05, while margins remain depressed. We forecast strong revenue growth in Global Clearing Services in FY 05, on higher volumes and increased margin loan balances.

- We forecast EPS of $9.30 for FY 04 and $9.00 for FY 05, reflecting what we expect to be continued prudent expense management and modest headcount growth. We think that compensation to net revenue, excluding merchant banking, will trend down slightly through 2005, and remain toward the low end of the company's previous guidance of 48%-52%.

Investment Rationale/Risk October 07, 2004

- We believe the shares are trading at a significant discount to peers due to concerns about a slowing in the company's Capital Markets segment, which generated the majority of revenues in FY 03. However, we believe BSC's fixed income revenue is more sustainable and balanced than is generally accepted. We think significant insider ownership of about 41% on a fully diluted basis also helps merit a higher valuation. Finally, we believe BSC would make an attractive acquisition candidate for several potential acquirers.

- Risks to our recommendation and target price include interest rate volatility and potential trading losses. We view favorably what we regard as BSC's cautious risk management policies and its reluctance to make large proprietary investments, which we think minimizes losses on dealer positions and on hedges covering its origination pipeline.

- Having risen about 17% year to date, the shares recently traded at a P/E multiple of about 10X our FY 05 EPS estimate. Our 12-month target price of $120 is equal to about 13X our FY 05 EPS estimate, which is still at a discount to both the company's peer group and to the S&P 500.

Key Stock Statistics

S&P Core EPS 2005E	8.60	52-week Range	$98.81-70.62
S&P Oper. EPS 2004E	9.30	12 Month P/E	10.6
P/E on S&P Oper. EPS 2004E	10.6	Beta	1.27
S&P Oper. EPS 2005E	9.00	Shareholders	1,859
Yield (%)	1.0%	Market Cap (B)	$ 10.2
Dividend Rate/Share	1.00	Shares Outstanding (M)	103.2

Value of $10,000 invested five years ago: **$ 24,866**

Dividend Data Dividends have been paid since 1986

Amount ($)	Date Decl.	Ex-Div. Date	Stock of Record	Payment Date
0.200	Jan. 07	Jan. 14	Jan. 16	Jan. 30 '04
0.200	Apr. 01	Apr. 14	Apr. 16	Apr. 30 '04
0.200	Jun. 17	Jul. 14	Jul. 16	Jul. 30 '04
0.250	Sep. 22	Oct. 13	Oct. 15	Oct. 29 '04

Revenues/Earnings Data Fiscal year ending November 30

Revenues (Million $)

	2004	2003	2002	2001	2000	1999
1Q	2,081	1,838	1,718	2,136	2,688	1,724
2Q	2,064	1,850	2,070	2,449	2,504	2,003
3Q	1,894	1,842	1,581	2,302	2,416	1,805
4Q	—	1,865	1,521	1,814	2,669	2,351
Yr.	—	7,395	6,891	8,701	10,277	7,882

Earnings Per Share ($)

	2004	2003	2002	2001	2000	1999
1Q	2.57	2.00	2.00	1.10	1.89	0.36
2Q	2.49	2.05	2.59	1.18	0.77	0.80
3Q	2.09	2.30	1.23	0.95	1.32	1.35
4Q	E2.13	2.19	1.36	1.08	1.36	1.76
Yr.	E9.30	8.52	6.47	4.31	5.35	4.27

Next earnings report expected: mid-December Source: S&P, Company Reports
EPS Estimates based on S&P Operating Earnings; historical GAAP earnings are as reported.

Please read the Required Disclosures and Reg. AC certification on the last page of this report.

The McGraw·Hill Companies

The Bear Stearns Companies Inc.

Recommendation: **BUY** ★ ★ ★ ★ ★   12-Month Target Price: **$120.00** (as of March 17, 2004)

Business Summary October 07, 2004

The Bear Stearns Companies is a leading investment banking and securities trading firm serving corporate, government, institutional and individual clients. BSC operates offices in several cities across the U.S., and in international business centers such as London and Hong Kong, among others. The company operates in three segments: Capital Markets, Global Clearing Services, and Wealth Management.

The Capital Markets segment (80% of FY 03 (Nov.) net revenues) is comprised of institutional equities (16%), fixed income (49%) and investment banking (16%). Institutional equities includes sales, trading and research in such areas as block trading, convertible bonds, OTC equities, equity derivatives, and risk arbitrage. Fixed income includes sales, trading and research for institutional clients in a variety of products such as mortgage-backed and asset-backed securities, corporate and government bonds, municipal and high yield products, foreign exchange and fixed income derivatives. Investment banking provides capabilities in capital raising, strategic advice, mergers and acquisitions and merchant banking. Capital raising encompasses BSC's underwriting of equity, investment-grade debt, and high yield debt products. BSC is particularly strong in the asset-backed securities, mortgage-backed securities and municipal bond areas.

The Global Clearing Services segment (13%) provides clearing, margin lending and securities borrowing to facilitate customer short sales, to about 3,000 clearing clients worldwide. Prime brokerage clients include hedge funds and clients of money managers, short sellers, arbitraguers, and other professional investors.

Fully disclosed clients engage in either the retail or institutional brokerage business. BSC held about $204 billion of equity in Global Clearing Services client accounts at the end of FY 03, up from $164 billion at the end of FY 02. In 2003, HedgeWorld ranked BSC as the largest prime broker in the U.S., and the second largest in the world.

The Wealth Management segment (9%) is comprised of Private Client Services (PCS) and Bear Stearns Asset Management (BSAM). PCS, with 513 brokers at the end of FY 03, provides high net worth individuals with an institutional level of service. The asset management area had $27.1 billion in assets under management at the end of FY 03, up from $24.0 billion at the end of FY 02. Asset management serves the diverse investment needs of corporations, municipal governments, multi-employer plans, foundations, endowments, family groups and high net worth individuals.

More than 40% of the fully diluted shares outstanding are held by company employees.

In December 2002, BSC and other leading investment banks entered into a $1.4 billion agreement to settle allegations that their research was tainted with conflicts of interest and misled investors; BSC's share was $80 million. The investment banks also agreed to make organizational changes intended to reduce conflicts of interest in their research departments.

Company Financials Fiscal Year ending November 30

Per Share Data ($)

(Year Ended November 30)	2003	2002	2001	2000	1999	1998	1997	1996	1995	1994
Tangible Bk. Val.	67.58	57.91	45.25	45.49	33.90	27.84	22.69	17.57	14.03	12.17
Cash Flow	7.76	5.75	3.85	4.89	4.64	4.47	4.16	3.27	1.69	2.50
Earnings	8.52	6.47	4.31	5.35	4.27	4.17	3.81	2.96	1.40	2.26
S&P Core Earnings	8.16	6.15	4.09	NA	NA	NA	NA	NA	NA	NA
Dividends	0.74	0.62	0.60	0.55	0.55	0.54	0.53	0.52	0.49	0.44
Payout Ratio	9%	10%	14%	10%	13%	13%	14%	17%	35%	20%
Prices - High	83.12	67.55	64.45	72.50	50.47	58.05	43.99	24.51	19.23	18.46
- Low	57.58	50.50	40.65	36.50	31.90	23.58	23.21	15.73	11.94	12.53
P/E Ratio - High	10	10	15	14	12	14	12	8	14	8
- Low	7	8	9	7	7	6	6	5	9	6

Income Statement Analysis (Million $)

	2003	2002	2001	2000	1999	1998	1997	1996	1995	1994
Commissions	1,078	1,111	1,117	1,207	1,014	903	732	687	547	483
Int. Inc.	1,955	2,232	4,339	5,642	4,009	4,286	3,058	2,393	1,970	1,304
Total Revs.	7,395	6,891	8,701	10,277	7,882	7,980	6,077	4,964	3,754	3,441
Int. Exp.	1,401	1,763	3,794	4,801	3,380	3,639	2,551	1,981	1,679	1,020
Pretax Inc.	1,772	1,311	934	1,172	1,064	1,063	1,014	835	388	643
Eff. Tax Rate	34.8%	33.0%	33.1%	34.0%	36.8%	37.9%	39.5%	41.2%	38.0%	39.8%
Net Inc.	1,156	878	625	773	673	660	613	491	241	387
S&P Core Earnings	1,154	883	622	NA	NA	NA	NA	NA	NA	NA

Balance Sheet & Other Fin. Data (Million $)

	2003	2002	2001	2000	1999	1998	1997	1996	1995	1994
Total Assets	212,168	184,854	185,530	171,166	153,894	154,496	121,434	92,085	74,597	67,392
Cash Items	12,495	12,620	16,620	6,093	5,020	3,357	2,698	1,830	2,010	3,285
Receivables	23,645	19,762	23,702	19,305	18,065	90,537	79,258	63,221	50,372	49,014
Secs. Owned	59,233	53,116	51,911	61,760	41,943	44,620	38,437	26,222	21,509	14,444
Sec. Borrowed	6,648	58,879	63,794	69,036	64,819	59,960	53,848	43,222	38,155	34,847
Due Brokers & Cust.	71,343	62,365	61,470	51,236	43,019	47,175	32,730	23,753	17,404	17,098
Other Liabs.	2,688	2,378	2,660	23,863	25,954	29,423	23,109	16,171	12,475	9,722
Capitalization:										
Debt	29,993	24,244	24,192	17,243	15,147	13,296	8,120	6,044	4,060	3,408
Equity	6,932	5,689	4,829	4,958	4,156	3,499	2,941	2,307	2,000	1,729
Total	37,463	30,626	29,820	22,898	20,103	17,938	11,746	8,789	6,562	5,725
% Return On Revs.	18.3	15.2	8.2	8.5	9.8	8.3	10.1	9.9	6.4	11.2
% Ret. on Assets	0.6	0.5	0.4	0.5	0.4	0.5	0.6	0.6	0.3	0.6
% Ret. on Equity	17.8	16.0	12.1	16.2	16.6	19.5	22.1	25.6	11.3	22.9

Data as orig reptd.; bef. results of disc opers/spec. items. Per share data adj. for stk.; EPS diluted. Prior to 2000, yrs. ended Jun. 30. E-Estimated. NA-Not Available. NM-Not Meaningful. NR-Not Ranked.

Office: 383 Madison Avenue, New York, NY 10179.
Telephone: 212-272-2000.
Email: ir@bear.com
Website: http://www.bearstearns.com
Chrmn & CEO: J.E. Cayne.
Pres & COO: A.D. Schwartz.
Pres & COO: W.J. Spector.

EVP & CFO: S.L. Molinaro, Jr.
Treas: M. Minikes.
Investor Contact: E. Ventura 212-272-9251.
Dirs: H. S. Bienen, J. E. Cayne, C. D. Glickman, A. C. Greenberg, D. J. Harrington, F. T. Nickell, P. A. Novelly, F. V. Salerno, A. D. Schwartz, W. J. Spector, V. Tese.

Founded: in 1923.
Domicile: Delaware.
Employees: 10,532.
S&P Analyst: Robert Hansen, CFA /DC/GG

Becton, Dickinson

Recommendation: **HOLD** ★ ★ ★ ★ ★
SELL | SELL | HOLD | BUY | BUY

12-Month Target Price: **$51.00**
(as of July 23, 2004)

BDX has an approximate 0.12% weighting in the **S&P 500**

Sector: Health Care
Sub-Industry: Health Care Equipment
Peer Group: Large Multi-Line Medical Device Manufacturers

Summary: BDX provides a wide range of medical devices and diagnostic products used in hospitals, doctors' offices, research labs, and other settings.

Quantitative Evaluations

| Price as of 11/12/04: | $54.44 | 2005E S&P Core EPS: | NA |

S&P Earnings & Dividend Rank: A

| D | C | B- | B | B+ | A- | A | A+ |

S&P Fair Value Rank: 4+

| 1 | 2 | 3 | 4 | 5 |
| Lowest | | | | Highest |

Fair Value Calc.: $53.00 (Slightly Overvalued)

S&P Investability Quotient Percentile
98%

BDX scored higher than 98% of all companies for which an S&P Report is available.

Volatility: Low

| Low | Average | High |

Technical Evaluation: Bullish
Since 10/04, the technical indicators for BDX have been Bullish.

Relative Strength Rank: Moderate
62
| 1 Lowest | Highest 99 |

GAAP Earnings vs. Previous Year
▲ Up ▼ Down ▶ No Change

- 10 Week Mov. Avg.
- 30 Week Mov. Avg.
- Relative Strength
- 12-Mo Target Price

Volume Below Avg. — Above Avg. —

VOL. MIL.

HOLD | BUY | HOLD

J J A S O N D J F M A M J J A S O N D J F M A M J J A S O N D J F M A M J J A S O N D J
2001 | 2002 | 2003 | 2004

OPTIONS: CBOE, P, Ph

Analyst commentary prepared by Robert M. Gold/CB/GG

Highlights August 03, 2004

- Including foreign currency benefits, we estimate FY 04 (Sep.) revenues at $5.0 billion, up from $4.5 billion in FY 03. Broken down by segment, we see FY 04 medical systems sales growth of about 9%, with diagnostics rising by an estimated 10% and biosciences gaining roughly 12%. In our opinion, however, the company has not met expectations regarding the launch of a blood glucose monitor, a development we believe reflects the competitive pressures within that product category. We are therefore assuming less robust contributions from this product in our FY 05 model. We currently project that FY 05 revenues will approximate $5.3 billion, representing growth of about 6%, excluding currency.

- In our view, gross margins in the current fiscal year can reach 50%, aided by a more favorable sales mix, and we see gross margins at a similar level in FY 05. With an improving revenue growth outlook, we now look for R&D costs to consume 5.0% of sales in both years, while SG&A outlays account for an estimated 27% of sales in FY 04, and 26.0% of sales in FY 05. We expect interest costs to decrease, due to debt repayments. We estimate operating cash flow in FY 04 at $1.0 billion, and see capital expenditures approximating $300 million.

- After taxes projected at 25%, we see operating EPS of $2.53 in FY 04, rising to $2.75 in FY 05. Our FY 04 Standard & Poor's Core EPS forecast stands at $2.48, as $0.16 of projected stock option expense is partially offset by favorable adjustments to estimated pension plan costs.

Key Stock Statistics

S&P Oper. EPS 2005E	2.75	52-week Range	$54.44-37.07
P/E on S&P Oper. EPS 2005E	19.8	12 Month P/E	30.8
Yield (%)	1.1%	Beta	0.12
Dividend Rate/Share	0.60	Shareholders	9,801
Shares Outstanding (M)	250.5	Market Cap (B)	$ 13.6

Value of $10,000 invested five years ago: **$ 19,833**

Dividend Data Dividends have been paid since 1926

Amount ($)	Date Decl.	Ex-Div. Date	Stock of Record	Payment Date
0.150	Nov. 24	Dec. 10	Dec. 12	Jan. 02 '04
0.150	Jan. 27	Mar. 08	Mar. 10	Mar. 31 '04
0.150	May. 25	Jun. 07	Jun. 09	Jun. 30 '04
0.150	Jul. 27	Sep. 07	Sep. 09	Sep. 30 '04

Investment Rationale/Risk August 03, 2004

- We believe BDX should benefit from improved revenue visibility amid signs of recovering end user demand in the life sciences industry and momentum in the diagnostics and diabetes management areas. On a more cautious note, we think there will be less favorable currency tailwinds in coming quarters, and upcoming quarterly comparisons will be more challenging. Given the recent valuation compression evident throughout the medical device subsector, we believe the shares, having appreciated about 17% year to date through early August 2004, will generate returns close to that of the S&P 500 over the coming 12 months.

- Risks to our recommendation and target price include a slower-than-expected recovery in key life science markets, unfavorable foreign currency fluctuations and additional valuation compression recently evident within the health care sector.

- Recently valued at 18X our FY 05 EPS forecast, BDX was trading at a 15% discount to our medical device coverage universe. In our opinion, this valuation gap is justified by the company's relatively modest sales and earnings growth rates, which we believe reflect a lack of exposure to the more dynamic markets in the industry. Our 12-month target price of $51 assumes an FY 05 P/E of about 19X, which would represent a premium multiple relative to the S&P 500 but a discount to our medical equipment group. On a P/E-to-growth (PEG) basis, our target represents a ratio of 1.6X, in line with our device universe.

Revenues/Earnings Data Fiscal year ending September 30

Revenues (Million $)

	2004	2003	2002	2001	2000	1999
1Q	1,200	1,052	945.0	843.3	859.2	769.0
2Q	1,271	1,134	1,013	961.2	925.1	874.0
3Q	1,258	1,165	998.5	954.2	914.1	873.0
4Q	1,253	1,177	1,077	987.5	919.9	902.5
Yr.	4,935	4,528	4,033	3,754	3,618	3,418

Earnings Per Share ($)

	2004	2003	2002	2001	2000	1999
1Q	0.48	0.43	0.37	0.23	0.29	0.29
2Q	0.62	0.54	0.48	0.44	0.45	0.34
3Q	0.41	0.49	0.44	0.46	0.43	0.12
4Q	0.70	0.61	0.50	0.49	0.32	0.29
Yr.	2.21	2.07	1.79	1.63	1.49	1.04

Next earnings report expected: late-January Source: S&P, Company Reports
EPS Estimates based on S&P Operating Earnings; historical GAAP earnings are as reported.

Becton, Dickinson and Company

Recommendation: **HOLD** ★ ★ ★ ☆ ☆   12-Month Target Price: **$51.00** (as of July 23, 2004)

Business Summary August 03, 2004

Becton, Dickinson traces its roots to a concern started by Maxwell Becton and Fairleigh Dickinson in 1897. One of the first companies to sell U.S.-made glass syringes, BDX was also a pioneer in the production of hypodermic needles. The company now manufactures and sells medical supplies, devices, lab equipment and diagnostic products used by health care institutions, life science researchers, clinical laboratories, industry and the general public. In FY 03 (Sep.), about 49% of sales were generated in foreign markets.

Major products in the core medical systems division (54% of FY 03 revenue, 59% of operating income) include hypodermic syringes and needles for injection, insulin syringes and pen needles and blood glucose monitoring systems for diabetes care, infusion therapy devices, prefillable drug delivery systems and surgical blades and scalpels. The segment also includes specialty blades and cannulas for ophthalmic surgery procedures, anesthesia needles, critical care systems, elastic support products and thermometers.

The diagnostics segment (30%, 32%) sells clinical and industrial microbiology products, sample collection products, specimen management systems, hematology instruments and other diagnostic systems, including immunodiagnostic test kits. The segment also includes consulting services and customized, automated bar-code systems for patient identification and point-of-care data capture.

The biosciences unit (16%, 9%) provides research tools and reagents to clinicians and medical researchers studying genes, proteins and cells in order to better understand disease, improve diagnosis and disease management and facilitate the discovery and development of novel therapeutics. Products include instrument systems for cell sorting and analysis, monoclonal antibody reagents and kits for diagnostic and research use, tools to aid in drug discovery and vaccine development, molecular biology products, fluid handling, cell growth and screening products.

Research and development spending totaled $235 million in FY 03 (5.2% of revenue), compared with $220 million (5.5%) in FY 02. Incremental spending was concentrated primarily in the blood glucose monitoring, ophthalmic systems and advance drug delivery systems projects.

In January 2003, BDX introduced two new FDA-approved blood glucose monitoring systems, the BD Logic Glucose Monitor and the BD Latitude Diabetes Management System. It also entered into strategic relationships with Medtronic's MiniMed division, and with Eli Lilly & Co., under which both companies will co-promote the products.

In January 2004, directors authorized the company to repurchase up to 10 million BDX common shares. This authorization was in addition to the approximately 1.7 million shares remaining under a 10 million share repurchase program authorized in January 2003.

Company Financials Fiscal Year ending September 30

Per Share Data ($)

(Year Ended September 30)	2004	2003	2002	2001	2000	1999	1998	1997	1996	1995
Tangible Bk. Val.	NA	8.82	6.06	5.35	3.80	2.74	3.30	4.11	4.44	4.46
Cash Flow	NA	3.54	2.92	2.76	2.58	2.01	1.77	1.97	1.81	1.66
Earnings	2.21	2.07	1.79	1.63	1.49	1.04	0.90	1.15	1.06	0.90
S&P Core Earnings	NA	2.01	1.57	1.38	NA	NA	NA	NA	NA	NA
Dividends	0.60	0.40	0.39	0.38	0.37	0.34	0.29	0.26	0.23	0.21
Payout Ratio	27%	19%	22%	23%	25%	33%	32%	23%	22%	23%
Prices - High	54.44	41.82	38.60	39.25	35.31	44.18	49.62	27.81	22.75	16.62
- Low	40.90	28.82	24.70	29.96	23.75	22.37	24.37	20.93	17.68	12.00
P/E Ratio - High	25	20	22	24	24	42	55	24	22	19
- Low	19	14	14	18	16	21	27	18	17	13

Income Statement Analysis (Million $)

	2004	2003	2002	2001	2000	1999	1998	1997	1996	1995
Revs.	NA	4,528	4,033	3,754	3,618	3,418	3,117	2,811	2,770	2,713
Oper. Inc.	NA	1,094	1,002	952	861	780	714	661	632	604
Depr.	NA	344	305	306	288	259	229	210	200	208
Int. Exp.	NA	73.1	33.3	47.1	78.3	72.1	64.2	48.6	64.4	58.7
Pretax Inc.	NA	710	629	577	520	373	341	423	394	350
Eff. Tax Rate	NA	22.9%	23.6%	24.0%	24.4%	26.0%	30.6%	29.0%	28.0%	28.0%
Net Inc.	NA	547	480	438	393	276	237	300	283	252
S&P Core Earnings	NA	525	417	364	NA	NA	NA	NA	NA	NA

Balance Sheet & Other Fin. Data (Million $)

	2004	2003	2002	2001	2000	1999	1998	1997	1996	1995
Cash	NA	520	243	82.1	49.2	59.9	83.3	113	165	240
Curr. Assets	NA	2,339	1,929	1,763	1,661	1,684	1,543	1,313	1,277	1,328
Total Assets	NA	5,572	5,040	4,802	4,505	4,437	3,846	3,080	2,890	3,000
Curr. Liab.	NA	1,043	1,252	1,265	1,354	1,329	1,092	678	766	720
LT Debt	NA	1,184	803	1,902	780	954	765	665	468	558
Common Equity	NA	2,863	2,450	2,288	1,912	1,722	1,565	1,334	1,272	1,344
Total Cap.	NA	4,200	3,396	4,321	2,823	2,764	2,428	2,095	1,829	1,935
Cap. Exp.	NA	261	260	371	376	312	181	170	146	124
Cash Flow	NA	889	783	742	679	532	463	507	481	459
Curr. Ratio	NA	2.2	1.5	1.4	1.2	1.3	1.4	1.9	1.7	1.8
% LT Debt of Cap.	NA	28.2	23.6	44.0	27.6	34.5	31.5	31.7	25.6	28.8
% Net Inc.of Revs.	NA	12.1	11.9	11.7	10.9	8.1	7.6	10.7	10.2	9.3
% Ret. on Assets	NA	10.3	9.8	9.4	8.8	6.7	6.8	10.1	9.6	8.2
% Ret. on Equity	NA	20.5	20.2	20.8	21.5	16.6	16.1	22.8	21.5	18.4

Data as orig reptd.; bef. results of disc opers/spec. items. Per share data adj. for stk. divs.; EPS diluted. E-Estimated. NA-Not Available. NM-Not Meaningful. NR-Not Ranked. UR-Under Review.

Office: One Becton Drive, Franklin Lakes, NJ 07417-1880.
Telephone: 201-847-6800.
Email: investor_relations@bdhq.bd.com
Website: http://www.bd.com
Chrmn, Pres & CEO: E.J. Ludwig.
EVP & CFO: J. Considine.

VP & General Counsel: J.S. Sherman.
VP & Investor Contact: W. Tozzi 201-847-6800.
Dirs: B. L. Anderson, H. N. Beaty, H. P. Becton, Jr., E. F. DeGraan, E. J. Ludwig, F. A. Olson, J. F. Orr, W. J. Overlock Jr., J. E. Perrella, B. L. Scott, A. Sommer, M. af Ugglas.

Founded: in 1897.
Domicile: New Jersey.
Employees: 24,783.
S&P Analyst: Robert M. Gold/CB/GG

Bed Bath & Beyond

Recommendation: **BUY** ★★★★☆
SELL | SELL | HOLD | BUY | BUY

12-Month Target Price: **$45.00**
(as of April 28, 2004)

BBBY has an approximate 0.12% weighting in the **S&P 500**

Sector: Consumer Discretionary
Sub-Industry: Specialty Stores
Peer Group: Home Furnishings Retailers

Summary: BBBY operates a nationwide chain of nearly 400 superstores selling better-quality domestics merchandise and home furnishings at prices below those offered by department stores.

Quantitative Evaluations

S&P Earnings & Dividend Rank: A-

| D | C | B- | B | B+ | A- | A | A+ |

S&P Fair Value Rank: 5

| 1 | 2 | 3 | 4 | 5 |
| Lowest | | | | Highest |

Fair Value Calc.: $51.60 (Undervalued)

S&P Investability Quotient Percentile
99%

BBBY scored higher than 99% of all companies for which an S&P Report is available.

Volatility: Average

| Low | Average | High |

Technical Evaluation: Bullish
Since 10/04, the technical indicators for BBBY have been Bullish.

Relative Strength Rank: Strong
78

| 1 Lowest | Highest 99 |

Price as of 11/12/04: $43.49 | **2005E S&P Core EPS:** $1.40

GAAP Earnings vs. Previous Year
▲ Up ▼ Down ► No Change

10 Week Mov. Avg.
30 Week Mov. Avg.
Relative Strength
12-Mo Target Price

Volume Below Avg. — Above Avg. —

BUY

J J A S O N D | J F M A M J J A S O N D | J F M A M J J A S O N D | J F M A M J J A S O N D | J
2001 | 2002 | 2003 | 2004

OPTIONS: ASE, CBOE, Ph

Analyst commentary prepared by Yogeesh Wagle/PMW/JWP

Highlights September 27, 2004

- We expect sales to climb 18% to 20% in FY 05 (Feb.), reflecting the addition of about 91 new stores, representing nearly 2.4 million sq. ft. of store space; same-store sales gains of 4% to 5%; and the June 2003 acquisition of Christmas Tree Shops. We see same-store sales growth as likely to be driven by new product introductions in specialty foods and health and beauty care, and by higher consumer spending spurred by improved economic conditions.

- We project that gross margins will widen slightly, on a more favorable product mix, higher markups, and lower markdowns at Bed Bath & Beyond stores, partly offset by the inclusion of lower margin Christmas Trees stores. With modest SG&A leverage over higher sales, and with level projected store opening and expansion costs, we see operating margins widening 60 to 80 basis points.

- After expected level interest income and taxes at 38.0%, versus 38.5% in FY 04, we see FY 05 EPS of $1.62, up 24% from FY 04's $1.31. For FY 06, we project that mid-teen revenue growth and better cost controls will drive EPS of $1.97.

Key Stock Statistics

S&P Oper. EPS 2005E	1.62	52-week Range	$44.43-33.88
P/E on S&P Oper. EPS 2005E	26.8	12 Month P/E	29.8
S&P Oper. EPS 2006E	1.97	Beta	1.06
Yield (%)	Nil	Shareholders	727
Dividend Rate/Share	Nil	Market Cap (B)	$ 13.1
Shares Outstanding (M)	300.9		

Value of $10,000 invested five years ago: **$ 23,657**

Dividend Data

No cash dividends have been paid.

Investment Rationale/Risk September 27, 2004

- We would accumulate the stock. The shares traded recently at 23X our FY 05 EPS estimate, above the level of peers and the S&P 500, but below their historical P/E multiple. On a P/E to growth (PEG) basis, BBBY's PEG of 1.2X, based on our three-year annual EPS growth projection of 20%, is below the PEG of the S&P 500. We view the P/E multiple premium as warranted and as likely to widen, as we see the company continuing to gain market share in home furnishings with better merchandising and store level execution than that of peers. We believe the Christmas Tree Shops acquisition complements the Bed Bath & Beyond concept, leveraging distribution and buying capabilities, and diversifying the revenue base somewhat.

- Risks to our target price and recommendation include a potential slowdown in the U.S. economy, an unanticipated shift in consumer spending away from home-centered products, and possible miscues in BBBY's store expansion strategy.

- Based on our discounted cash flow analysis, we calculate intrinsic value of $45 to $47 a share. Our 12-month target price of $45 is equal to 23X our FY 06 EPS estimate.

Revenues/Earnings Data Fiscal year ending February 28

Revenues (Million $)

	2005	2004	2003	2002	2001	2000
1Q	1,101	893.9	776.8	575.8	462.7	359.4
2Q	1,274	1,111	903.0	713.6	597.0	457.6
3Q	—	1,175	936.0	759.4	609.5	486.5
4Q	—	1,298	1,049	879.1	746.1	574.5
Yr.	—	4,478	3,665	2,928	2,397	1,878

Earnings Per Share ($)

	2005	2004	2003	2002	2001	2000
1Q	0.27	0.19	0.15	0.10	0.08	0.06
2Q	0.39	0.33	0.25	0.18	0.15	0.12
3Q	E0.40	0.33	0.25	0.18	0.14	0.11
4Q	E0.55	0.47	0.35	0.28	0.22	0.17
Yr.	E1.62	1.31	1.00	0.74	0.59	0.46

Next earnings report expected: mid-December Source: S&P, Company Reports
EPS Estimates based on S&P Operating Earnings; historical GAAP earnings are as reported.

Bed Bath & Beyond Inc.

Stock Report
November 13, 2004
NASDAQ Symbol: **BBBY**

Recommendation: **BUY** ★ ★ ★ ☆   12-Month Target Price: **$45.00** (as of April 28, 2004)

Business Summary September 27, 2004

Bed Bath & Beyond operates one of the largest U.S. chains of superstores selling domestics merchandise and home furnishings. Its goal is to offer a broader selection of better quality, reasonably priced merchandise than do department stores. While most large department stores typically devote about 20,000 sq. ft. to home furnishings, BBBY stores range in size from 20,000 sq. ft. to 50,000 sq. ft., with some exceeding 80,000 sq. ft. The company has grown rapidly, from 38 stores at the end of FY 93 (Feb.) to 575 stores in 44 states and Puerto Rico at FY 04 year end. BBBY plans to increase its total store square footage by about 25% a year. It opened 85 stores in FY 04, after opening 95 stores in FY 03; it expected to open 85 to 90 new stores in FY 05. During FY 04, total square footage of Bed Bath & Beyond stores grew 12%, to 19.4 million sq. ft., from 17.3 million sq. ft.

In March 2002, the company acquired Harmon Stores, Inc., a health and beauty care retailer. The Harmon chain had 30 stores in three states at February 28, 2004. In June 2003, BBBY acquired Christmas Tree Shops, a retailer of home decor, giftware, housewares, food and seasonal items, for $200 million in cash. Christmas Tree Shops, with 23 stores, mostly in the Northeast, had 2002 sales of about $370 million. The company operated 24 Christmas Tree Shops in six states at FY 04 year end.

BBBY believes the breadth and depth of selection that it offers in most product categories gives its customers the convenience of one-stop shopping for most household items. The company sells domestics products such as bed linens, sheets, comforters, bedspreads, draperies, pillows and blankets. Bath accessories include towels, shower curtains, waste baskets, hampers and rugs. Kitchen textiles include tablecloths, placemats, napkins and dish towels. BBBY stores also sell home furnishings: kitchen and tabletop items, such as cookware, cutlery, flatware and glassware; basic housewares, including storage items and closet items; small electric appliances such as blenders, coffee makers, vacuum cleaners, toaster ovens and hair dryers; and miscellaneous gift items, including picture frames, luggage, small toys and seasonal merchandise.

In addition to its broader product selection (a typical store carries about 25,000 stock-keeping units), the company maintains an everyday low price policy, with prices 20% to 40% below those charged by department stores. Despite this pricing strategy, BBBY has been able to post healthy margins by shipping products directly to stores, eliminating the need for warehouses and distribution centers. Inventory is displayed on store floors, and the company maintains consistent in-stock availability of merchandise to build customer loyalty. Advertising costs are kept to a minimum; BBBY relies more on word of mouth than on advertising.

Despite its rapid growth, BBBY holds a very small portion of the home goods market, leaving what it regards as significant opportunities for future growth.

Company Financials Fiscal Year ending February 28

Per Share Data ($)

(Year Ended February 28)	2004	2003	2002	2001	2000	1999	1998	1997	1996	1995
Tangible Bk. Val.	6.14	4.93	3.75	2.84	1.99	1.48	2.14	0.78	0.56	0.40
Cash Flow	1.59	1.25	0.94	0.75	0.57	0.42	0.64	0.24	0.18	0.14
Earnings	1.31	1.00	0.74	0.59	0.46	0.34	0.26	0.20	0.14	0.11
S&P Core Earnings	1.23	0.92	0.67	0.53	NA	NA	NA	NA	NA	NA
Dividends	Nil	NA	Nil	Nil	Nil	Nil	Nil	Nil	Nil	Nil
Payout Ratio	Nil	NA	Nil	Nil	Nil	Nil	Nil	Nil	Nil	Nil

Cal. Yrs.	2003	2002	2001	2000	1999	1998	1997	1996	1995	1994
Prices - High	45.00	37.90	35.70	27.31	19.68	17.59	9.81	7.87	4.95	4.31
- Low	30.18	26.70	18.70	11.00	12.75	8.56	5.71	4.09	2.25	2.84
P/E Ratio - High	34	38	48	46	43	52	38	40	35	40
- Low	23	27	25	19	28	25	22	21	16	26

Income Statement Analysis (Million $)

	2004	2003	2002	2001	2000	1999	1998	1997	1996	1995
Revs.	4,478	3,665	2,928	2,397	1,878	1,397	1,067	823	601	440
Oper. Inc.	724	555	409	319	241	181	137	104	77.5	58.5
Depr.	84.6	74.8	62.5	46.6	31.6	23.2	18.2	13.4	9.90	7.19
Int. Exp.	Nil	Nil	Nil	Nil	Nil	Nil	Nil	Nil	0.70	0.82
Pretax Inc.	650	491	357	282	215	162	121	91.3	66.9	50.9
Eff. Tax Rate	38.5%	38.5%	38.5%	39.0%	39.0%	39.7%	39.8%	39.8%	41.0%	41.0%
Net Inc.	399	302	220	172	131	97.3	73.1	55.0	39.5	30.0
S&P Core Earnings	370	277	200	155	NA	NA	NA	NA	NA	NA

Balance Sheet & Other Fin. Data (Million $)

	2004	2003	2002	2001	2000	1999	1998	1997	1996	1995
Cash	867	516	429	239	144	90.4	53.3	38.8	10.3	6.50
Curr. Assets	1,969	1,594	1,227	886	647	455	326	228	160	118
Total Assets	2,865	2,189	1,648	1,196	866	633	458	330	236	177
Curr. Liab.	770	680	511	353	287	206	150	106	73.0	46.1
LT Debt	Nil	Nil	Nil	Nil	Nil	Nil	Nil	Nil	5.00	16.8
Common Equity	1,991	1,452	1,094	817	559	411	295	214	151	109
Total Cap.	1,991	1,452	1,094	817	559	411	295	214	156	126
Cap. Exp.	113	135	121	140	90.1	62.3	41.2	35.1	24.5	24.5
Cash Flow	484	377	282	219	163	121	91.4	68.5	49.4	37.2
Curr. Ratio	2.6	2.3	2.4	2.5	2.3	2.2	2.2	2.1	2.2	2.6
% LT Debt of Cap.	Nil	Nil	Nil	Nil	Nil	Nil	Nil	Nil	3.2	13.4
% Net Inc.of Revs.	8.9	8.2	7.5	7.2	7.0	7.0	6.9	6.7	6.6	6.8
% Ret. on Assets	15.8	15.8	15.4	16.7	17.5	17.8	18.6	19.5	19.1	20.1
% Ret. on Equity	23.2	23.7	23.0	25.0	27.1	27.6	28.7	30.1	30.3	32.2

Data as orig reptd.; bef. results of disc opers/spec. items. Per share data adj. for stk. divs.; EPS diluted. E-Estimated. NA-Not Available. NM-Not Meaningful. NR-Not Ranked. UR-Under Review.

Office: 650 Liberty Avenue, Union, NJ 07083.
Telephone: 908-688-0888.
Website: http://www.bedbathandbeyond.com
Co-Chrmn: W. Eisenberg.
Co-Chrmn: L. Feinstein.

Pres & CEO: S.H. Temares.
VP, CFO & Chief Acctg Officer: E.A. Castagna.
Investor Contact: R. Curwin 908-688-0888.
Dirs: D. S. Adler, S. Barshay, W. Eisenberg, K. Eppler, L. Feinstein, J. Heller, R. Kaplan, V. A. Morrison, F. Stoller, S. H. Temares.

Founded: in 1971.
Domicile: New York.
Employees: 29,000.
S&P Analyst: Yogeesh Wagle/PMW/JWP

The McGraw·Hill Companies

Recommendation: **SELL** ★ ☆ ☆ ☆ ☆
SELL | SELL | HOLD | BUY | BUY

12-Month Target Price: $24.00
(as of August 27, 2003)

BLS has an approximate 0.47% weighting in the **S&P 500**

Sector: Telecommunication Services
Sub-Industry: Integrated Telecommunication Services
Peer Group: Regional Bell Operating Companies (RBOC's)

Summary: BLS, one of the largest U.S. telephone holding companies, provides local service in nine southeastern states, and also owns significant wireless assets.

Quantitative Evaluations

S&P Earnings & Dividend Rank: A-

| D | C | B- | B | B+ | A- | A | A+ |

S&P Fair Value Rank: 2

| 1 | 2 | 3 | 4 | 5 |
| Lowest | | | | Highest |

Fair Value Calc.: $25.60 (Slightly Overvalued)

S&P Investability Quotient Percentile

64%

BLS scored higher than 64% of all companies for which an S&P Report is available.

Volatility: Low

| Low | Average | High |

Technical Evaluation: Neutral
Since 11/04, the technical indicators for BLS have been Neutral.

Relative Strength Rank: Moderate

49

| 1 Lowest | Highest 99 |

| Price as of 11/12/04: | **$28.28** | 2004E S&P Core EPS: | **$1.68** |

GAAP Earnings vs. Previous Year
▲ Up ▼ Down ▶ No Change

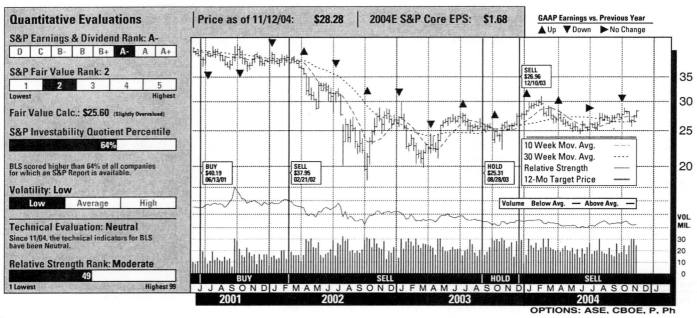

10 Week Mov. Avg.
30 Week Mov. Avg.
Relative Strength
12-Mo Target Price

Volume Below Avg. — Above Avg. —

BUY $40.19 06/13/01
SELL $37.95 02/21/02
HOLD $25.31 08/28/03
SELL $26.96 12/10/03

BUY | SELL | HOLD | SELL

J J A S O N D J F M A M J J A S O N D J F M A M J J A S O N D J F M A M J J A S O N D J
2001 | 2002 | 2003 | 2004

OPTIONS: ASE, CBOE, P, Ph

Analyst commentary prepared by Todd Rosenbluth/CB/BK

Highlights October 26, 2004

- Excluding Latin American operations, which are being sold, we see 2004 revenues up fractionally, with modest gains in wireless and growth in DSL outweighed by declines in total access lines, due to increased wireless substitution. We expect increased pressures from wireless and cable carriers to restrict fourth quarter results, and believe that the recent hurricanes in the Southeast curtailed BLS's service bundle penetration efforts. For 2005, we look for revenue growth to be aided by the acquisition of AT&T Wireless (AWE: hold, $15), though wireline challenges should persist. A large portion of the Latin American deal still awaits necessary approvals.

- Despite workforce and other operational cuts, we see margins at 42% in 2004 and 39% in 2005, as an improvement in collections is counterbalanced by rising marketing costs and expenses to retain customers, and expected AWE integration costs; we see initially higher network and marketing expenses now that the deal has closed. We also project high pension-related expenses, in part due to BLS's new wireline labor agreement.

- We estimate 2004 operating EPS of $1.94, and our S&P Core Earnings estimate is $1.68, due to projected pension adjustments. We expect that 2005 operating EPS will drop to $1.45, in part the result of likely integration and financing charges.

Key Stock Statistics

S&P Core EPS 2005E	1.26	52-week Range	$31.00-24.46
S&P Oper. EPS 2004E	1.94	12 Month P/E	12.4
P/E on S&P Oper. EPS 2004E	14.6	Beta	1.06
S&P Oper. EPS 2005E	1.45	Shareholders	730,185
Yield (%)	3.8%	Market Cap (B)	$ 51.8
Dividend Rate/Share	1.08	Shares Outstanding (M)	1831.8

Value of $10,000 invested five years ago: **$ 6,707**

Dividend Data Dividends have been paid since 1984

Amount ($)	Date Decl.	Ex-Div. Date	Stock of Record	Payment Date
0.250	Nov. 24	Jan. 06	Jan. 08	Feb. 02 '04
0.250	Feb. 23	Apr. 06	Apr. 08	May. 03 '04
0.270	Jun. 28	Jul. 09	Jul. 13	Aug. 02 '04
0.270	Sep. 27	Oct. 07	Oct. 12	Nov. 01 '04

Investment Rationale/Risk October 26, 2004

- As we expected, recent hurricanes in the Southeast hurt BLS. In addition to lost revenues and service repair costs incurred for approximately 6% of BLS's total local access lines, BLS's long distance and DSL penetration efforts were curtailed. We expect additional discounts to be offered to increase customer loyalty. In addition, as Cingular's AWE deal has now been completed, we do not believe BLS stock reflects the integration challenges the parent companies face, particularly related to the company's branding efforts, customer base, and pricing strategy. We believe the recent labor agreement will make it problematic for BLS to reduce operating expenses.

- Risks to our recommendation and target price include reduced competition from wireless, wireline and cable carriers due to consolidation and regulatory changes, and a sustainable recovery for telecom services.

- We think the stock should trade at about 17X our estimated 2005 operating EPS, with a 2004 enterprise value to EBITDA multiple of 5. Our DCF valuation, assuming a WACC of 9%, and little or no cash flow growth from 2004 to 2008, before modest growth in perpetuity, shows the stock as unattractive. Despite its 4% dividend yield, with our 12-month target price of $24, we would sell BLS.

Revenues/Earnings Data Fiscal year ending December 31

Revenues (Million $)

	2004	2003	2002	2001	2000	1999
1Q	4,976	5,523	5,534	5,919	6,487	5,973
2Q	5,083	5,642	5,780	5,985	6,752	6,148
3Q	5,095	5,728	5,434	6,013	6,903	6,422
4Q	—	5,742	5,692	6,213	6,160	6,681
Yr.	—	22,635	22,440	24,130	26,151	25,224

Earnings Per Share ($)

	2004	2003	2002	2001	2000	1999
1Q	0.63	0.49	0.61	0.47	0.53	0.32
2Q	0.51	0.51	0.16	0.47	0.56	0.51
3Q	0.46	0.51	0.35	Nil	0.55	0.53
4Q	E0.46	0.43	0.32	0.42	0.59	0.55
Yr.	E1.94	1.94	1.44	1.36	2.23	1.80

Next earnings report expected: late-January Source: S&P, Company Reports
EPS Estimates based on S&P Operating Earnings; historical GAAP earnings are as reported.

STANDARD & POOR'S

BellSouth Corporation

Standard Report
November 13, 2004
NYSE Symbol: BLS

Recommendation: SELL ★ ☆ ☆ ☆ ☆   12-Month Target Price: **$24.00** (as of August 27, 2003)

Business Summary October 27, 2004

BellSouth Corp. is the third largest Regional Bell Operating Company (behind Verizon and SBC Communications), with 21.6 million local phone lines as of September 2004. The company is the predominant telephone service provider in the Southeast, and owns a 40% interest in Cingular Wireless.

The wireline communications segment (62% of normalized 2003 revenue) includes local services, network access, long-distance, Internet access, and Digital Subscriber Lines (DSL). BLS ended the third quarter of 2004 with 2.8 million UNE-P lines (down from 2.9 million at June 2004) and 1.87 million DSL customers (up from 1.74 million). In May 2002, the company received FCC approval to offer in-region long-distance telephone service to customers in Georgia and Louisiana. In September 2002, BLS received approval to offer long-distance service in Alabama, Kentucky, Mississippi, North Carolina, and South Carolina. In December 2002, it received FCC approval to offer long-distance in Florida and Tennessee, its final two states. At the end of September 2004, BLS had 5.7 million long-distance customers.

In August 2004, BLS agreed to a five-year contract extension with its unionized wireline workforce. Terms of the contract include an increase of base wages of more than 10.5% and an increase to the retiree medical benefit obligation of approximately $3.3 billion, which will be recognized over the average remaining service life of employees.

Cingular Wireless (22%) began operations in October 2000 through the merger of the wireless operations of SBC and BLS. The joint venture launched a nationwide advertising campaign in January 2001 to reinforce brand awareness for the newly created brand. Cingular's net subscriber base increased 657,000 in the third quarter of 2004 bringing it to 25.7 million. Cingular has completely deployed 2.5G GPRS-based services in its GSM markets. In early 2003, Cingular restructured its marketing and sales organizations, and began addressing pricing strategies intended to strengthen its competitive position. In February 2004, Cingular agreed to buy AT&T Wireless (AWE), one of its competitors, for $41 billion in cash. In October, the Justice Department approved the deal, conditional on the sale of assets in 13 mostly Southern and Midwestern markets. The deal was completed in late October 2004, and is expected to be dilutive until 2007.

BLS's Latin America operations (8%) primarily consisted of wireless service providers operating in 11 countries, including Argentina, Colombia and Venezuela. The company's investments represent a controlling interest in most businesses, and provided services to about 9.7 million customers as of December 2003. In March 2004, BLS agreed to sell its remaining Latin American assets to Telefonica for $5.85 billion. The deal, which is subject to approvals, is expected to close in the second half of 2004.

The advertising and publishing unit (7%) publishes, prints and sells advertising in classified telephone directories in both paper and electronic formats. In the 2003 first quarter, BLS changed its method of recognizing revenues and expenses in its directory publishing business to the deferral method, which recognizes them ratably over the life of the directory. This resulted in a charge of $0.27 a share.

Company Financials Fiscal Year ending December 31

Per Share Data ($)

(Year Ended December 31)	2003	2002	2001	2000	1999	1998	1997	1996	1995	1994
Tangible Bk. Val.	9.33	8.05	7.51	6.81	5.86	6.79	6.67	5.98	5.18	6.48
Cash Flow	4.19	3.92	3.90	4.84	4.24	3.97	3.64	3.31	2.52	2.70
Earnings	1.94	1.44	1.36	2.23	1.80	1.78	1.65	1.44	0.79	1.09
S&P Core Earnings	1.95	0.56	1.21	NA	NA	NA	NA	NA	NA	NA
Dividends	0.87	0.78	0.76	0.76	0.76	0.72	0.72	0.72	0.70	0.69
Payout Ratio	45%	54%	56%	34%	42%	40%	44%	50%	89%	63%
Prices - High	30.00	40.90	45.87	53.50	51.31	50.00	29.06	22.93	21.93	15.87
- Low	19.79	18.32	36.26	34.93	39.75	27.06	19.06	17.62	13.40	12.62
P/E Ratio - High	15	28	34	24	29	28	18	16	28	15
- Low	10	13	27	16	22	15	12	12	17	12

Income Statement Analysis (Million $)

	2003	2002	2001	2000	1999	1998	1997	1996	1995	1994
Revs.	22,635	22,440	24,130	26,151	24,224	23,123	20,561	19,040	17,886	16,845
Depr.	4,179	4,643	4,782	4,935	4,671	4,357	3,964	3,719	3,455	3,206
Maint.	NA	NA	NA	NA	NA	NA	NA	NA	NA	NA
Constr. Credits	NA	NA	NA	NA	NA	NA	NA	NA	NA	NA
Eff. Tax Rate	35.9%	40.8%	36.0%	36.0%	37.2%	38.7%	39.4%	37.9%	39.6%	36.5%
Net Inc.	3,589	2,708	2,570	4,220	3,448	3,527	3,270	2,863	1,564	2,160
S&P Core Earnings	3,594	1,045	2,269	NA	NA	NA	NA	NA	NA	NA

Balance Sheet & Other Fin. Data (Million $)

	2003	2002	2001	2000	1999	1998	1997	1996	1995	1994
Gross Prop.	65,715	64,435	64,332	24,157	61,009	57,974	53,828	50,059	46,869	44,199
Net Prop.	23,807	23,445	24,943	24,157	24,631	23,940	22,861	21,825	21,092	25,162
Cap. Exp.	3,200	3,785	5,997	6,995	6,200	5,212	4,858	4,455	4,203	3,600
Total Cap.	36,550	34,641	36,817	32,955	26,759	17,862	25,324	21,365	19,749	25,893
Fxd. Chgs. Cov.	6.3	4.6	3.9	5.9	6.5	7.4	7.1	6.8	6.2	6.1
Capitalization:										
LT Debt	11,489	12,283	15,014	12,463	9,113	8,715	7,348	8,116	7,924	7,435
Pfd.	Nil	Nil	Nil	Nil	Nil	Nil	Nil	Nil	Nil	Nil
Common	19,712	17,686	18,597	16,912	14,815	17,862	15,740	13,249	11,825	14,367
% Return On Revs.	15.9	12.1	10.7	16.1	14.2	15.3	15.9	15.0	8.7	12.8
% Return On Invest. Capital	13.6	13.7	12.2	20.7	17.7	26.0	14.0	12.2	19.1	11.1
% Return On Com. Equity	19.1	14.9	14.5	26.6	22.3	21.0	22.2	22.8	11.9	15.4
% Earn. on Net Prop.	43.6	43.6	46.8	50.9	47.1	43.8	41.8	39.6	33.9	11.3
% LT Debt of Cap.	36.8	41.0	44.7	42.4	38.1	29.8	31.8	37.9	40.1	34.1
Capital. % Pfd.	Nil	Nil	Nil	Nil	Nil	Nil	Nil	Nil	Nil	Nil
Capital. % Common	63.2	59.0	55.3	57.6	61.9	70.2	68.2	66.7	59.9	65.9

Data as orig reptd.; bef. results of disc opers/spec. items. Per share data adj. for stk. divs.; EPS diluted. E-Estimated. NA-Not Available. NM-Not Meaningful. NR-Not Ranked. UR-Under Review.

Office: 1155 Peachtree St NE Rm 15G03, Atlanta, GA 30309-7629.
Telephone: 404-249-2000.
Email: investor@bellsouth.com
Website: http://www.bellsouth.com
Chrmn, Pres & CEO: F.D. Ackerman.
SVP & Secy: R.M. Dunn.
VP & Treas: L. Wentworth.

VP & General Counsel: M. Gary.
CFO: R.M. Dykes.
Investor Contact: J. Battcher 800-241-3419.
Dirs: F. D. Ackerman, R. V. Anderson, J. H. Blanchard, J. H. Brown, A. M. Codina, K. F. Feldstein, J. P. Kelly, L. F. Mullin, R. B. Smith, W. S. Stavropoulos.

Founded: in 1983.
Domicile: Georgia.
Employees: 76,000.
S&P Analyst: Todd Rosenbluth/CB/BK

Source: S&P, Company Reports
Redistribution or reproduction is prohibited without written permission. Copyright © 2004 The McGraw-Hill Companies, Inc.

The McGraw·Hill Companies

Recommendation: **HOLD** ★ ★ ★ ★ ★
SELL SELL HOLD BUY BUY
12-Month Target Price: **$27.00**
(as of October 21, 2004)

BMS has an approximate 0.03% weighting in the **S&P 500**

Sector: Materials
Sub-Industry: Paper Packaging
Peer Group: Containers and Packaging (Paper)

Summary: Bemis is a leading maker of a broad range of flexible packaging and pressure sensitive materials.

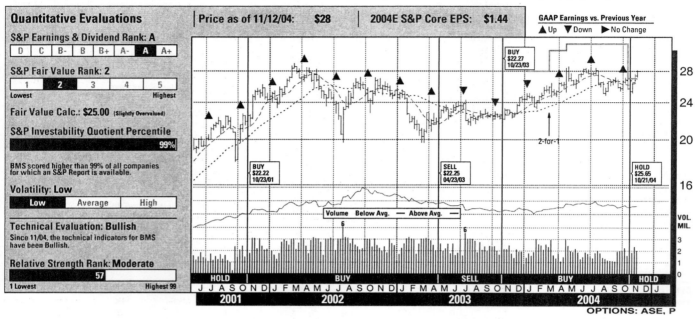

Quantitative Evaluations

S&P Earnings & Dividend Rank: A
D | C | B- | B | B+ | A- | **A** | A+

S&P Fair Value Rank: 2
1 | **2** | 3 | 4 | 5
Lowest — Highest

Fair Value Calc.: $25.00 (Slightly Overvalued)

S&P Investability Quotient Percentile
99%

BMS scored higher than 99% of all companies for which an S&P Report is available.

Volatility: Low
Low | Average | High

Technical Evaluation: Bullish
Since 11/04, the technical indicators for BMS have been Bullish.

Relative Strength Rank: Moderate
57
1 Lowest — Highest 99

Price as of 11/12/04: $28   **2004E S&P Core EPS:** $1.44

GAAP Earnings vs. Previous Year
▲ Up   ▼ Down   ▶ No Change

Analyst commentary prepared by Stewart Scharf/PMW/GG

OPTIONS: ASE, P

Highlights October 22, 2004

- We expect net sales to advance in the high single digits in 2005, following mid-single-digit growth seen for 2004, reflecting strong demand for new high barrier roll label products, positive foreign exchange, and niche acquisitions. We expect volume growth to be driven by innovative flexible and pressure sensitive packaging products.

- We think 2005 gross margins will widen somewhat from our projection of about 21% for 2004, as BMS passes on higher resin prices to customers and tries to adjust its raw material component mix toward less volatile materials. Operating income should benefit from well controlled SG&A expenses (seen under 10% of sales), on annual saving of $10 million from 2003 restructuring efforts in the pressure sensitive materials segment. However, we believe increased pension expense and rising raw material costs will limit margin gains. We see free cash flow being used mainly for debt paydowns, as well as possible acquisitions and share buybacks.

- We project 2004 EPS of $1.65 (before $0.02 of restructuring charges), and see $1.80 for 2005. Our S&P Core EPS estimates are $1.44 for 2004 and $1.59 for 2005, mainly reflecting projected pension costs.

Investment Rationale/Risk October 22, 2004

- We would not add to positions, based on a challenging pricing environment and our valuation models, which indicate that the shares are fairly valued. We think BMS could fall short of its goal of high-single-digit return on sales by 2005, up from our 2004 projection of 6%.

- Risks to our recommendation and target price include further significant increases in resin costs due to rising petrochemicals prices, a slower than expected economic rebound, a negative foreign currency effect, a lag in passing higher resin costs onto customers, and an inability to implement price escalators in the 50% of flexible packaging contracts that do not have them.

- The shares, trading at 14X our 2005 EPS estimate, are at a modest discount to their closest peers, and below the projected P/E multiple of the S&P 500. Based on our discounted cash flow (DCF) analysis, the stock is at a 9% discount to intrinsic value. We assumed a 3% perpetual growth rate and a weighted average cost of capital of 8.5%. Applying a peer-average forward P/E multiple of 15X to our 2005 EPS estimate, our 12-month target price is $27.

Key Stock Statistics

S&P Core EPS 2005E	1.59	52-week Range	$28.65-22.21
S&P Oper. EPS 2004E	1.65	12 Month P/E	17.6
P/E on S&P Oper. EPS 2004E	17.0	Beta	0.66
S&P Oper. EPS 2005E	1.80	Shareholders	4,484
Yield (%)	2.3%	Market Cap (B)	$ 3.0
Dividend Rate/Share	0.64	Shares Outstanding (M)	106.9

Value of $10,000 invested five years ago: **$ 18,140**

Dividend Data Dividends have been paid since 1922

Amount ($)	Date Decl.	Ex-Div. Date	Stock of Record	Payment Date
2-for-1	Jan. 29	Mar. 02	Feb. 17	Mar. 01 '04
0.160	May. 06	May. 14	May. 18	Jun. 01 '04
0.160	Jul. 29	Aug. 16	Aug. 18	Sep. 01 '04
0.160	Oct. 28	Nov. 15	Nov. 17	Dec. 01 '04

Revenues/Earnings Data Fiscal year ending December 31

Revenues (Million $)

	2004	2003	2002	2001	2000	1999
1Q	684.0	638.6	552.7	577.4	512.6	450.6
2Q	712.9	670.2	584.8	581.6	537.3	481.3
3Q	711.9	662.0	601.0	575.6	542.8	492.2
4Q	—	664.3	630.6	558.6	571.9	493.9
Yr.	—	2,635	2,369	2,293	2,165	1,918

Earnings Per Share ($)

	2004	2003	2002	2001	2000	1999
1Q	0.40	0.33	0.33	0.28	0.28	0.18
2Q	0.42	0.36	0.41	0.34	0.33	0.30
3Q	0.41	0.32	0.41	0.34	0.30	0.30
4Q	E0.41	0.35	0.40	0.36	0.32	0.32
Yr.	E1.65	1.37	1.54	1.32	1.22	1.09

Next earnings report expected: late-January Source: S&P, Company Reports
EPS Estimates based on S&P Operating Earnings; historical GAAP earnings are as reported.

Bemis Company, Inc.

Recommendation: **HOLD** ★★★☆☆   12-Month Target Price: **$27.00** (as of October 21, 2004)

Business Summary October 22, 2004

Bemis Co., a leading North American producer of flexible packaging products, as well as pressure sensitive materials, focuses on the food industry. Markets also include the chemicals, agribusiness, pharmaceutical, personal care products, electronics, automotive and graphic industries. The company has 52 manufacturing plants, in nine countries. As of late 2004, the 10 largest customers accounted for 26% of sales.

Although BMS focuses on marketing its products in the U.S. (77% of 2003 net sales), Canada (2.9%) and Europe (18%), it has broadened its reach to Southeast Asia, South America, and Mexico (2.5% combined), due to strong demand for barrier films to extend the shelf life of perishable foods.

The Flexible Packaging Products segment (80% of net sales in 2003; $264 million in operating profits) produces a wide range of consumer and industrial packaging products, including high barrier, polyethylene, and paper products. High barrier products, which comprise more than 50% of net sales, include flexible polymer film structures and barrier laminates for food, medical and personal care products. Polyethylene products include film that has been printed on and converted into bags for bakery products, seed, lawn and garden, ice, fresh and frozen produce, and disposable diapers. Paper products are multiwall and small paper bags for premium pet food, fertilizers, dairy products, chemicals, and sugar. During the 2004 third quarter, BMS completed the installation of a new multilayer film capacity in its European operatons.

The Pressure Sensitive Materials segment (20% of net sales in 2003; $16.3 million in operating profits) produces printing products, decorative and sheet products, and technical products. In July 2003, the company agreed to terminate the planned sale of its global pressure sensitive business (MACtac-Morgan Adhesives Co.) to UPM-Kymmene Corp. for $420 million, as the U.S. Department of Justice was granted an injunction to block the transaction, due to antitrust concerns.

Total debt was 29% of capitalization at September 30, 2004, down from 31% at the end of 2003 and 36% a year earlier.

Flexible packaging competitors include Alcan Packaging, Sealed Air, Rexam plc, Sonoco Products, and Smurfit-Stone Container. Pressure sensitive materials competitors include Avery Dennison, Minnesota Mining and Manufacturing (3M), and Spinnaker Industries.

During 2004, the company contributed $40 million to its defined benefit pension plan, avoiding a required $4 million contribution in late 2004. BMS projected 2004 pension expense of $25 million, up from 2003's $10 million, but saw smaller increases in later years, based on actuarial estimates and assumptions.

BMS expects 2004 fourth quarter earnings to be comparable to those of the third quarter. The company projects 2004 capital spending of $140 million to $145 million, to support its North American and European growth initiatives. The dividend was boosted 14% in early 2004, and a two-for-one stock split was effected in March. The company expects to maintain a payout ratio of 35% to 45%. As of the end of 2003, 4.7 million shares were authorized for repurchase.

EPS of $1.36 in 2003 (as adjusted) included $0.10 of special charges. The company recorded about $3 million of charges ($0.02 a share, after tax) in the first nine months of 2004.

Company Financials Fiscal Year ending December 31

Per Share Data ($)

(Year Ended December 31)	2003	2002	2001	2000	1999	1998	1997	1996	1995	1994
Tangible Bk. Val.	5.81	4.11	4.39	4.76	5.52	4.88	4.62	4.38	4.48	3.79
Cash Flow	2.56	2.65	2.49	2.24	2.02	1.88	1.73	1.57	1.38	1.19
Earnings	1.37	1.54	1.32	1.22	1.09	1.05	1.00	0.95	0.82	0.70
S&P Core Earnings	1.32	1.28	1.02	NA	NA	NA	NA	NA	NA	NA
Dividends	0.56	0.52	0.50	0.48	0.46	0.44	0.40	0.36	0.32	0.27
Payout Ratio	41%	34%	38%	39%	42%	42%	40%	38%	39%	39%
Prices - High	25.58	29.12	26.23	19.65	20.18	23.46	23.96	18.81	15.00	12.87
- Low	19.66	19.70	14.34	11.46	15.09	16.75	16.81	12.81	11.50	10.25
P/E Ratio - High	19	19	20	16	19	22	24	20	18	18
- Low	14	13	11	9	14	16	17	13	14	15

Income Statement Analysis (Million $)

	2003	2002	2001	2000	1999	1998	1997	1996	1995	1994
Revs.	2,635	2,369	2,293	2,165	1,918	1,848	1,877	1,655	1,523	1,390
Oper. Inc.	384	401	384	363	316	297	274	242	206	180
Depr.	128	119	124	108	97.7	88.9	78.9	66.2	58.0	50.9
Int. Exp.	12.6	15.4	30.3	31.6	21.2	21.9	18.9	13.4	11.5	8.40
Pretax Inc.	240	268	228	212	190	186	180	163	136	121
Eff. Tax Rate	38.4%	37.9%	38.2%	38.2%	37.4%	37.8%	37.4%	27.9%	37.4%	37.3%
Net Inc.	147	166	140	131	115	111	108	101	85.2	72.8
S&P Core Earnings	142	137	108	NA	NA	NA	NA	NA	NA	NA

Balance Sheet & Other Fin. Data (Million $)

	2003	2002	2001	2000	1999	1998	1997	1996	1995	1994
Cash	76.5	56.4	35.1	28.9	18.2	23.7	13.8	10.2	22.0	12.7
Curr. Assets	752	722	587	640	584	518	516	467	442	419
Total Assets	2,293	2,257	1,923	1,889	1,532	1,453	1,363	1,169	1,031	923
Curr. Liab.	316	326	238	495	253	243	251	214	219	211
LT Debt	583	718	595	438	372	371	317	241	166	172
Common Equity	1,139	959	886	799	726	671	640	567	513	418
Total Cap.	1,878	1,788	1,606	1,342	1,227	1,156	1,055	865	729	654
Cap. Exp.	106	91.0	117	100	137	140	168	112	93.6	106
Cash Flow	275	285	264	239	212	200	186	167	143	124
Curr. Ratio	2.4	2.2	2.5	1.3	2.3	2.1	2.1	2.2	2.0	2.0
% LT Debt of Cap.	31.1	40.2	37.1	32.6	30.3	32.1	30.0	27.9	22.8	26.3
% Net Inc.of Revs.	5.6	7.0	6.1	6.0	6.0	6.0	5.7	6.1	5.6	5.2
% Ret. on Assets	6.5	7.9	7.4	7.6	7.6	7.9	8.5	9.2	8.7	8.5
% Ret. on Equity	14.0	17.9	16.7	17.1	16.2	17.0	17.8	18.8	18.3	18.5

Data as orig reptd.; bef. results of disc opers/spec. items. Per share data adj. for stk. divs.; EPS diluted. E-Estimated. NA-Not Available. NM-Not Meaningful. NR-Not Ranked. UR-Under Review.

Office: 222 South 9th Street, Minneapolis, MN 55402-4099.
Telephone: 612-376-3000.
Website: http://www.bemis.com
Chrmn: J.H. Roe.
Pres & CEO: J.H. Curler.
COO & EVP: H.J. Theisen.

VP, CFO & Treas: G.C. Wulf.
VP, Secy & General Counsel: J.J. Seifert.
VP & Investor Contact: M.E. Miller 612-376-3030.
Dirs: J. G. Bollinger, W. J. Bolton, W. H. Buxton, J. H. Curler, D. S. Haffner, B. L. Johnson, L. W. Knoblauch, N. P. McDonald, R. D. O'Shaughnessy, E. N. Perry, J. H. Roe, W. J. Scholle.

Founded: in 1858.
Domicile: Missouri.
Employees: 11,500.
S&P Analyst: Stewart Scharf/PMW/GG

Recommendation: **BUY** ★★★★ 12-Month Target Price: **$68.00**
(as of September 16, 2004)

BBY has an approximate 0.18% weighting in the **S&P 500**

Sector: Consumer Discretionary
Sub-Industry: Computer & Electronics Retail
Peer Group: Retailers/Resellers

Summary: This leading retailer of consumer electronics and entertainment software operates more than 700 stores in the U.S. and Canada.

Quantitative Evaluations

S&P Earnings & Dividend Rank: B

| D | C | B- | **B** | B+ | A- | A | A+ |

S&P Fair Value Rank: 4

| 1 | 2 | 3 | **4** | 5 |
| Lowest | | | | Highest |

Fair Value Calc.: $61.70 (Slightly Undervalued)

S&P Investability Quotient Percentile

99%

BBY scored higher than 99% of all companies for which an S&P Report is available.

Volatility: Average

| Low | **Average** | High |

Technical Evaluation: Bullish
Since 9/04, the technical indicators for BBY have been Bullish.

Relative Strength Rank: Moderate

68

| 1 Lowest | Highest 99 |

| Price as of 11/12/04: | **$59.73** | 2005E S&P Core EPS: | **$2.64** |

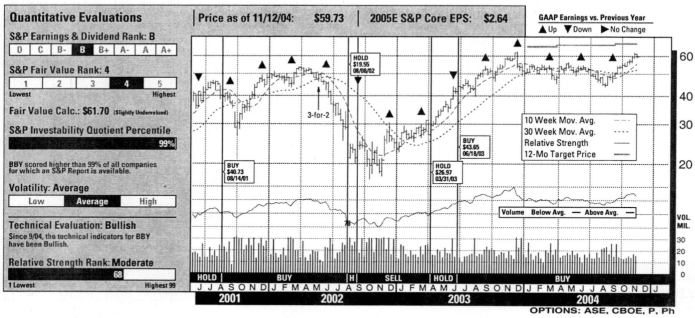

GAAP Earnings vs. Previous Year
▲ Up ▼ Down ▶ No Change

10 Week Mov. Avg.
30 Week Mov. Avg.
Relative Strength
12-Mo Target Price

Volume Below Avg. — Above Avg.

OPTIONS: ASE, CBOE, P, Ph

Analyst commentary prepared by Amy Glynn, CFA /MF/GG

Highlights September 16, 2004

- We view BBY as the best positioned retailer of consumer electronics, based on its digital product focus, knowledgeable sales staff, and use of advertising and marketing campaigns to drive sales. We think BBY's focus on advanced televisions, notebook computers and digital imaging products should help drive revenue growth, as we believe that BBY continues to gain market share in these product categories. Additionally, with average selling prices declining for digital TVs, we think mass adoption will be a key driver of BBY's growth.

- We look for FY 05 (Feb.) sales from continuing operations to advance about 12%, to $27.5 billion, from FY 04's $24.5 billion, spurred by contributions from new stores and mid-single digit comparable-store sales growth at existing stores. We expect operating margins to widen, due to leveraging of some fixed costs and cost reduction initiatives. Additionally, we see BBY continuing to benefit from a more profitable revenue mix. Longer term, BBY's goal is to achieve 7% operating margins by FY 07, with improvements expected to come largely from four key strategic initiatives.

- We estimate FY 05 net income of $974 million ($2.95 a share), up from $800 million ($2.44) posted in FY 04. We see FY 05 Standard & Poor's Core Earnings of $2.64 a share, including $0.32 of estimated stock option expense.

Key Stock Statistics

S&P Oper. EPS 2005E	2.95	52-week Range	$62.70-43.87
P/E on S&P Oper. EPS 2005E	20.2	12 Month P/E	23.0
S&P Oper. EPS 2006E	3.51	Beta	2.19
Yield (%)	0.7%	Shareholders	2,000
Dividend Rate/Share	0.44	Market Cap (B)	$ 19.4
Shares Outstanding (M)	324.4		

Value of $10,000 invested five years ago: **$ 18,428**

Dividend Data Dividends have been paid since 2003

Amount ($)	Date Decl.	Ex-Div. Date	Stock of Record	Payment Date
0.100	Oct. 22	Jan. 05	Jan. 07	Jan. 28 '04
0.100	Apr. 01	Apr. 19	Apr. 21	May. 12 '04
0.100	Jun. 18	Jul. 02	Jul. 07	Jul. 28 '04
0.110	Jun. 24	Oct. 04	Oct. 06	Oct. 27 '04

Investment Rationale/Risk September 16, 2004

- We recommend purchasing the shares, based on our view of BBY's above-average growth prospects and strong market leadership position. We think the company's Reward Zone customer loyalty program will continue to drive customer traffic at stores. Also, we believe BBY's "customer centricity" initiative should enable the company to effectively target and retain its most profitable customers. Of note, the 32 customer centricity lab stores have generated comp-store sales double the company average, and gross margins about 50 basis points wider. BBY expects to convert 70 California stores to this format in the third quarter. With a P/E multiple of 18X our FY 05 EPS estimate, the shares are trading at a premium to the S&P 500, but at a discount to the stock's average historical P/E multiple.

- Risks to our opinion and target price include an adverse shift in the economic climate and consumer confidence, increased competition, and the risk that BBY may be unable to successfully execute its strategic objectives and meet market expectations for sales growth and profitability. In particular, we think the customer centricity store conversion heightens the level of execution risk.

- Our 12-month target price of $68 is based on our historical P/E multiple model, and assumes a P/E multiple of 23X our FY 05 EPS estimate of $2.95.

Revenues/Earnings Data Fiscal year ending February 28

Revenues (Million $)

	2005	2004	2003	2002	2001	2000
1Q	5,475	4,668	4,202	3,697	2,964	2,386
2Q	6,080	5,396	4,624	4,164	3,169	2,688
3Q	—	6,034	5,131	4,756	3,732	3,107
4Q	—	8,449	6,989	6,980	5,462	4,315
Yr.	—	24,547	20,946	19,597	15,327	12,494

Earnings Per Share ($)

	2005	2004	2003	2002	2001	2000
1Q	0.34	0.21	0.24	0.17	0.23	0.15
2Q	0.46	0.42	0.24	0.26	0.24	0.19
3Q	E0.45	0.37	0.27	0.25	0.18	0.25
4Q	E1.63	1.42	1.16	1.08	0.59	0.52
Yr.	E2.95	2.44	1.91	1.77	1.24	1.09

Next earnings report expected: mid-December Source: S&P, Company Reports
EPS Estimates based on S&P Operating Earnings; historical GAAP earnings are as reported.

Please read the Required Disclosures and Reg. AC certification on the last page of this report.

The **McGraw·Hill** Companies

Best Buy Co., Inc.

Recommendation: **BUY** ★★★★★   12-Month Target Price: **$68.00** (as of September 16, 2004)

Business Summary September 17, 2004

As of February 28, 2004, the operations of this leading specialty retailer included 627 Best Buy stores (608 in the U.S. and 19 in Canada), 108 Future Shop stores in Canada, and 22 Magnolia Audio Video stores in the U.S. In June 2003, the company sold its Musicland business, which had been classified as a discontinued operation, to Sun Capital Partners Inc. Sun Capital acquired all of Musicland's liabilities, including lease obligations, and paid no cash consideration. In FY 03 (Feb.), the Musicland business was unprofitable, on revenue of $1.7 billion.

In FY 04, total sales advanced 17%, to $24.5 billion, resulting from a 7.1% comparable store sales gain and the addition of 60 U.S. Best Buy stores, 11 Canadian Best Buy stores, four Future Shop stores, and three Magnolia Audio Video stores. Domestic revenue grew 15%, to $22.2 billion, and international sales were up 41%, to $2.3 billion. Merchandise is also sold via the Internet.

In the consumer electronics category (36% of FY 04 sales at U.S. Best Buy stores), BBY sells products such as televisions, digital video disk players, digital cameras, digital camcorders, digital broadcast satellite systems, and audio components and systems. In the home office category (35%), BBY sells products such as desktop and notebook computers and related peripheral equipment, telephones, cellular telephones, and MP3 players.

In the entertainment software category (23%), Best Buy stores sell such products as compact discs, digital video disk movies, computer software, and video game hardware and software. In the appliance category (6%), the company sells major appliances, vacuums, small electrics, and housewares. BBY gets additional revenue from products and services, such as extended service contracts, blank recording media, furniture, batteries, business cases, and storage products.

In November 2001, the company acquired Canadian retailer Future Shop Ltd. for about US$377 million. In December 2000, it acquired the smaller Magnolia Hi-Fi, Inc. business for $88 million. In FY 04, Magnolia Hi-Fi started doing business as Magnolia Audio Video.

In FY 01, BBY acquired Musicland Stores Corp., for $425 million, including transaction costs, plus long-term debt valued at $271 million. The Musicland business, which was divested in June 2003, included stores operating under the Sam Goody, Suncoast and Media Play names.

In FY 03, the company acquired Geek Squad Inc., a provider of residential consumer customer support, for about $3 million, net of cash acquired, including transaction costs.

Company Financials Fiscal Year ending February 28

Per Share Data ($)

(Year Ended February 28)	2004	2003	2002	2001	2000	1999	1998	1997	1996	1995
Tangible Bk. Val.	8.96	7.04	5.48	4.60	3.65	3.97	2.08	1.69	1.68	1.49
Cash Flow	3.61	2.87	2.86	1.83	1.43	0.96	0.54	0.26	0.39	0.37
Earnings	2.44	1.91	1.77	1.24	1.09	0.71	0.35	0.01	0.18	0.22
S&P Core Earnings	2.17	1.66	1.61	1.14	NA	NA	NA	NA	NA	NA
Dividends	Nil	Nil	Nil	Nil	Nil	Nil	Nil	Nil	Nil	Nil
Payout Ratio	Nil	Nil	Nil	Nil	Nil	Nil	Nil	Nil	Nil	Nil

Cal. Yrs.	2003	2002	2001	2000	1999	1998	1997	1996	1995	1994
Prices - High	62.70	53.74	50.13	59.25	53.66	20.75	6.83	4.37	5.60	7.54
- Low	23.65	16.99	18.54	14.00	20.58	6.00	1.31	1.62	2.66	3.16
P/E Ratio - High	26	28	28	48	49	29	20	NM	31	34
- Low	10	9	10	11	19	8	4	NM	15	14

Income Statement Analysis (Million $)

	2004	2003	2002	2001	2000	1999	1998	1997	1996	1995
Revs.	24,547	20,946	19,597	15,327	12,494	10,078	8,358	7,771	7,217	5,080
Oper. Inc.	1,609	1,320	1,292	793	649	443	255	120	177	160
Depr.	385	310	355	188	110	78.4	68.3	66.8	54.9	38.6
Int. Exp.	31.0	Nil	1.00	7.00	5.00	23.8	33.0	50.3	43.6	27.9
Pretax Inc.	1,296	1,014	936	642	562	365	154	2.87	79.0	94.1
Eff. Tax Rate	38.3%	38.7%	39.1%	38.3%	38.3%	38.5%	38.6%	39.0%	39.2%	38.7%
Net Inc.	800	622	570	396	347	224	94.5	1.75	48.0	57.7
S&P Core Earnings	704	538	512	361	NA	NA	NA	NA	NA	NA

Balance Sheet & Other Fin. Data (Million $)

	2004	2003	2002	2001	2000	1999	1998	1997	1996	1995
Cash	2,600	1,914	1,855	747	751	786	520	89.8	86.0	145
Curr. Assets	5,724	4,867	4,611	2,929	2,238	2,063	1,710	1,385	1,561	1,241
Total Assets	8,652	7,663	7,375	4,840	2,995	2,512	2,056	1,734	1,891	1,507
Curr. Liab.	4,501	3,793	3,730	2,715	1,785	1,387	1,034	818	975	632
LT Debt	482	828	813	181	15.0	30.5	210	217	206	227
Common Equity	3,422	2,703	2,527	1,822	1,096	1,064	558	438	432	376
Total Cap.	3,904	3,531	3,340	2,003	1,111	1,095	775	885	868	833
Cap. Exp.	545	725	627	658	361	166	72.0	87.5	126	118
Cash Flow	1,185	932	925	584	457	303	163	68.5	103	96.2
Curr. Ratio	1.3	1.3	1.2	1.1	1.3	1.5	1.7	1.7	1.6	2.0
% LT Debt of Cap.	12.3	23.4	24.3	9.0	1.4	2.8	27.1	24.5	23.8	27.3
% Net Inc.of Revs.	3.3	3.0	2.9	2.6	2.8	2.2	1.1	Nil	0.7	1.1
% Ret. on Assets	9.8	8.3	9.3	10.1	12.6	9.8	5.0	Nil	2.8	4.7
% Ret. on Equity	26.0	23.8	26.2	27.1	32.6	27.7	19.0	Nil	11.9	16.7

Data as orig reptd.; bef. results of disc opers/spec. items. Per share data adj. for stk. divs.; EPS diluted. E-Estimated. NA-Not Available. NM-Not Meaningful. NR-Not Ranked. UR-Under Review.

Office: 7075 Flying Cloud Drive, Eden Prairie, MN 55344-3538.
Telephone: 952-947-2000.
Email: moneytalk@bestbuy.com
Website: http://www.bestbuy.com
Chrmn: R.M. Schulze.
Pres & COO: A.U. Lenzmeier.
Vice Chrmn & CEO: B.H. Anderson.

EVP & CFO: D.R. Jackson.
SVP & General Counsel: J.M. Joyce.
Investor Contact: J. Driscoll 612-291-6110.
Dirs: B. H. Anderson, R. T. Blanchard, K. J. Higgins Victor, J. James, E. S. Kaplan, A. U. Lenzmeier, M. Paull, R. M. Schulze, M. Tolan, F. D. Trestman, H. A. Tyabji, J. C. Wetherbe.

Auditor: Ernst & Young.
Founded: in 1966.
Domicile: Minnesota.
Employees: 98,000.
S&P Analyst: Amy Glynn, CFA /MF/GG

Recommendation: **HOLD** ★ ★ ★ ★ ★
SELL | SELL | HOLD | BUY | BUY

12-Month Target Price: **$13.00**
(as of July 08, 2004)

BLI has an approximate 0.01% weighting in the **S&P 500**

Sector: Consumer Discretionary
Sub-Industry: General Merchandise Stores
Peer Group: Discounters - General

Summary: BLI is a leading broadline closeout retailer, with more than 1,460 Big Lots and Big Lots Furniture stores in 46 states.

Quantitative Evaluations

S&P Earnings & Dividend Rank: B-

| D | C | B- | B | B+ | A- | A | A+ |

S&P Fair Value Rank: 5+

| 1 | 2 | 3 | 4 | 5 |
| Lowest | | | | Highest |

Fair Value Calc.: $17.10 (Undervalued)

S&P Investability Quotient Percentile

86%

BLI scored higher than 86% of all companies for which an S&P Report is available.

Volatility: Average

| Low | Average | High |

Technical Evaluation: Neutral
Since 10/04, the technical indicators for BLI have been Neutral.

Relative Strength Rank: Moderate

48

| 1 Lowest | | Highest 99 |

| Price as of 11/12/04: | **$12.77** | 2005E S&P Core EPS: | **$0.47** |

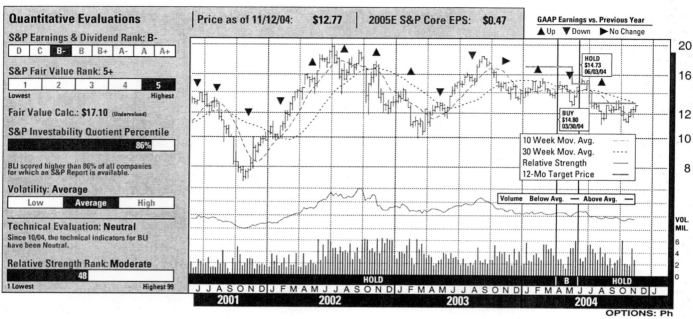

GAAP Earnings vs. Previous Year
▲ Up ▼ Down ▶ No Change

HOLD $14.73 06/03/04
BUY $14.80 03/30/04

10 Week Mov. Avg.
30 Week Mov. Avg.
Relative Strength
12-Mo Target Price

Volume Below Avg. — Above Avg.

HOLD | B | HOLD

J J A S O N D | J F M A M J J A S O N D | J F M A M J J A S O N D | J F M A M J J A S O N D | J
2001 | 2002 | 2003 | 2004

VOL. MIL.

OPTIONS: Ph

Analyst commentary prepared by Jason N. Asaeda/CB/GG

Highlights October 15, 2004

- We expect sales to advance nearly 4% in FY 05 (Jan.), to $4.3 billion, paced by the opening of about 60 net new stores. Store remodels, the addition of more than 200 furniture departments, and aggressive sourcing of branded closeout merchandise in key categories such as home decorative and hardlines should also provide a sales lift. In addition, we look for continued investment in national television ads to raise awareness of the Big Lots brand. However, we anticipate only a modest increase in same-store sales, reflecting a limited improvement in customer spending levels. BLI believes its core customers are not yet benefiting from an improving economy.

- We think EBIT (earnings before interest and taxes) margins will narrow, due to markdowns on summer seasonal items, a shift in the sales mix to more lower margin consumables, reduced expense leverage as a result of weak sales, higher freight costs in the first half of FY 05, and investments in a new merchandise planning and allocation system.

- Factoring share buybacks, we see FY 05 operating EPS of $0.54, and Standard & Poor's Core Earnings of $0.47, with the difference reflecting projected stock option and pension costs.

Key Stock Statistics

S&P Core EPS 2006E	0.73	52-week Range	$15.62-11.05
S&P Oper. EPS 2005E	0.54	12 Month P/E	19.4
P/E on S&P Oper. EPS 2005E	23.6	Beta	0.81
S&P Oper. EPS 2006E	0.80	Shareholders	1,351
Yield (%)	Nil	Market Cap (B)	$ 1.4
Dividend Rate/Share	Nil	Shares Outstanding (M)	112.4

Value of $10,000 invested five years ago: **$ 6,853**

Dividend Data

Proceeds from the sale of rights amounting to $0.01 a share were distributed in 2001.

Investment Rationale/Risk October 15, 2004

- We recommend holding the shares, based mainly on valuation. In our opinion, expanded assortments of everyday basics and home furnishings, including furniture, and better in-stock levels, should support a higher average basket in FY 05. However, our short-term sales outlook remains guarded, as BLI continues to report that economic factors such as high gasoline prices are having a dampening effect on customer traffic. We also think growing competition in the discount sector is hurting the company's top line. As a result, we expect limited sales and earnings growth.

- Risks to our recommendation and target price include a prolonged weak spending trend for core customers, and unexpected delays in new store openings. Both these factors could adversely affect BLI's sales and profit margins.

- We calculate intrinsic value of $11 for the shares using our discounted cash flow (DCF) model, which assumes a cost of capital of 9% and a terminal growth rate of 3%. Our 12-month target price of $13 blends a price to estimated FY 06 sales ratio of 0.4X, the three-year historical average, and our DCF model.

Revenues/Earnings Data Fiscal year ending January 31

Revenues (Million $)

	2005	2004	2003	2002	2001	2000
1Q	1,019	948.4	904.1	773.6	723.1	923.8
2Q	995.0	949.3	879.3	748.4	708.5	929.8
3Q	—	948.1	868.2	773.1	733.5	1,000
4Q	—	1,329	1,217	1,138	1,112	1,847
Yr.	—	4,174	3,869	3,433	3,277	4,700

Earnings Per Share ($)

	2005	2004	2003	2002	2001	2000
1Q	0.06	0.09	0.11	Nil	0.13	-0.03
2Q	-0.06	-0.07	0.03	-0.09	0.08	-0.04
3Q	E-0.14	-0.04	-0.04	-0.14	0.06	-0.14
4Q	E0.68	0.80	0.57	-0.02	0.61	1.06
Yr.	E0.54	0.78	0.66	-0.25	0.87	0.85

Next earnings report expected: mid-November Source: S&P, Company Reports
EPS Estimates based on S&P Operating Earnings; historical GAAP earnings are as reported.

Big Lots, Inc.

Recommendation: **HOLD** ★ ★ ★ ☆ ☆   12-Month Target Price: **$13.00** (as of July 08, 2004)

Business Summary October 15, 2004

Big Lots is one of the largest broadline U.S. closeout retailers. At July 31, 2004, the company operated 1,469 closeout stores, in 46 states, under the Big Lots and Big Lots Furniture names. BLI also conducts wholesale operations through Big Lots Wholesale, Consolidated International and Wisconsin Toy, and with online shopping at biglotswholesale.com. The company seeks to build on its leadership position by expanding its market presence in both existing and new markets.

BLI's stores stock a wide assortment of closeout merchandise. Although the specific brand names offered may change frequently, certain core merchandise categories are carried on a continual basis. The stores also offer a small but consistent line of basic items, seasonal items for each major holiday, and private label merchandise in selected product categories. Furniture, which was expanded to over 60% of the chain, accounted for about 13% of FY 04 (Jan.) sales.

Much of the closeout merchandise provided is likely to be new, name-brand products obtained from manufacturers' excess inventories. Such inventories have generally resulted from production overruns, package changes, discontinued products, and returns.

The company uses a combination of printed advertising circulars and television advertising in all markets. In FY 04, BLI distributed 25 circulars featuring 35-50 products that varied each week. It also ran television promotions in selected markets, each featuring highly recognizable, brand-name products. The company continues to refine its use of television advertising to increase awareness of its stores, strengthen its brand image, and attract new and repeat customers. BLI began a national television campaign in the first quarter of FY 04.

Over the past three years, BLI remodeled 645 stores. In FY 02 and FY 03, the company converted 434 stores to the Big Lots name, including 380 stores that had been operating under the names Odd Lots, Mac Frugal's, and Pic 'N' Save. The sales increases experienced and maintained in these markets were significant enough to generate a payback in less than two years. In FY 04, the company remodeled 211 stores, including some of its more mature existing Big Lots locations. In light of lower than expected financial returns from these remodels, BLI scaled back its remodeling program for FY 05, targeting only 68 stores.

The company purchases merchandise from U.S. and overseas suppliers. About 25% of products are purchased directly from overseas suppliers, and a material amount of U.S.-purchased merchandise is also manufactured abroad. As a result, a substantial portion of BLI's merchandise supply is subject to risks that include increased import duties, work stoppages, and currency fluctuations.

Company Financials Fiscal Year ending January 31

Per Share Data ($)

(Year Ended January 31)	2004	2003	2002	2001	2000	1999	1998	1997	1996	1995
Tangible Bk. Val.	9.54	8.83	8.11	8.28	11.71	10.79	9.60	8.15	5.22	4.31
Cash Flow	1.56	1.35	0.35	1.43	1.74	1.71	1.47	1.93	1.24	1.09
Earnings	0.78	0.66	-0.25	0.87	0.85	0.97	0.77	1.44	0.84	0.74
S&P Core Earnings	0.78	0.60	-0.32	0.83	NA	NA	NA	NA	NA	NA
Dividends	Nil	Nil	Nil	Nil	Nil	Nil	Nil	Nil	Nil	Nil
Payout Ratio	Nil	Nil	Nil	Nil	Nil	Nil	Nil	Nil	Nil	Nil
Cal. Yrs.	2003	2002	2001	2000	1999	1998	1997	1996	1995	1994
Prices - High	18.39	19.90	15.75	16.37	38.12	46.12	50.00	28.32	16.40	12.96
- Low	9.92	9.75	7.15	8.25	13.68	15.50	24.50	12.40	10.08	7.36
P/E Ratio - High	24	30	NM	19	45	48	65	21	19	18
- Low	13	14	NM	9	16	16	32	9	12	10

Income Statement Analysis (Million $)

	2004	2003	2002	2001	2000	1999	1998	1997	1996	1995
Revs.	4,174	3,869	3,433	3,277	4,700	4,194	4,055	2,648	1,512	1,275
Oper. Inc.	222	228	41.7	248	271	288	268	245	142	12.5
Depr.	91.6	81.5	69.0	62.3	100	84.0	79.2	48.4	30.0	26.5
Int. Exp.	16.4	20.1	20.2	22.9	25.3	24.3	25.7	16.8	8.00	8.00
Pretax Inc.	115	127	-47.5	-47.5	145	179	162	180	102	92.0
Eff. Tax Rate	20.9%	39.5%	NM	39.5%	39.5%	39.0%	47.0%	37.0%	37.1%	40.0%
Net Inc.	90.9	76.6	-28.7	98.3	96.1	109	85.9	113	64.4	55.2
S&P Core Earnings	91.6	70.7	-36.7	92.6	NA	NA	NA	NA	NA	NA

Balance Sheet & Other Fin. Data (Million $)

	2004	2003	2002	2001	2000	1999	1998	1997	1996	1995
Cash	191	167	28.8	30.7	96.3	75.9	41.7	30.0	13.0	40.4
Curr. Assets	1,168	1,069	994	1,101	1,420	1,335	1,107	927	452	381
Total Assets	1,785	1,642	1,533	1,585	2,187	2,043	1,746	1,331	640	552
Curr. Liab.	464	411	322	325	711	460	525	457	198	171
LT Debt	204	204	204	268	60.5	296	115	151	25.0	40.0
Common Equity	1,116	1,026	928	928	1,300	1,182	1,035	682	390	315
Total Cap.	1,320	1,230	1,211	1,260	1,468	1,583	1,106	870	434	372
Cap. Exp.	164	102	108	115	147	167	146	93.6	48.1	41.6
Cash Flow	183	158	40.3	161	197	193	165	162	94.5	81.7
Curr. Ratio	2.5	2.6	3.1	3.4	2.0	2.9	2.1	2.0	2.3	2.2
% LT Debt of Cap.	15.5	16.6	16.8	21.3	4.1	18.7	11.1	17.4	5.8	10.7
% Net Inc.of Revs.	2.2	2.0	NM	3.0	2.0	2.6	2.1	4.2	4.3	4.3
% Ret. on Assets	5.3	4.9	NM	5.6	4.5	5.8	5.6	11.5	10.9	10.8
% Ret. on Equity	8.5	7.8	NM	8.8	7.7	9.9	10.0	21.2	18.3	19.2

Data as orig reptd.; bef. results of disc opers/spec. items. Per share data adj. for stk. divs.; EPS diluted. E-Estimated. NA-Not Available. NM-Not Meaningful. NR-Not Ranked. UR-Under Review.

Office: 300 Phillipi Road, Columbus, OH 43228-5311.
Telephone: 614-278-6800.
Website: http://www.biglots.com
Chrmn, Pres & CEO: M.J. Potter.
SVP & CFO: J.R. Cooper.

VP, Secy & General Counsel: C.W. Haubiel II.
VP & Investor Contact: T.A. Johnson 614-278-6622.
Dirs: S. M. Berman, D. T. Kollat, B. J. Lauderback, P. E. Mallott, N. Mansour, M. J. Potter, R. Solt, D. B. Tishkoff.

Founded: in 1983.
Domicile: Ohio.
Employees: 47,249.
S&P Analyst: Jason N. Asaeda/CB/GG

Biogen Idec

Recommendation: **HOLD** ★★★☆☆
SELL | SELL | HOLD | BUY | BUY
12-Month Target Price: **$68.00**
(as of October 08, 2004)

BIIB has an approximate 0.18% weighting in the **S&P 500**

Sector: Health Care
Sub-Industry: Biotechnology
Peer Group: Biotech Therapeutics - Larger Capitalization

Summary: This major biopharmaceutical concern develops and markets targeted therapies for the treatment of multiple sclerosis and non-Hodgkin's lymphoma.

Quantitative Evaluations

S&P Earnings & Dividend Rank: C

| D | **C** | B- | B | B+ | A- | A | A+ |

S&P Fair Value Rank: 1-

| **1** | 2 | 3 | 4 | 5 |
| Lowest | | | | Highest |

Fair Value Calc.: $47.60 (Overvalued)

S&P Investability Quotient Percentile

91%

BIIB scored higher than 91% of all companies for which an S&P Report is available.

Volatility: Average

| Low | **Average** | High |

Technical Evaluation: Bearish

Since 10/04, the technical indicators for BIIB have been Bearish.

Relative Strength Rank: Weak

27

| 1 Lowest | Highest 99 |

Price as of 11/12/04: **$59.04**   2004E S&P Core EPS: **$1.24**

GAAP Earnings vs. Previous Year
▲ Up ▼ Down ► No Change

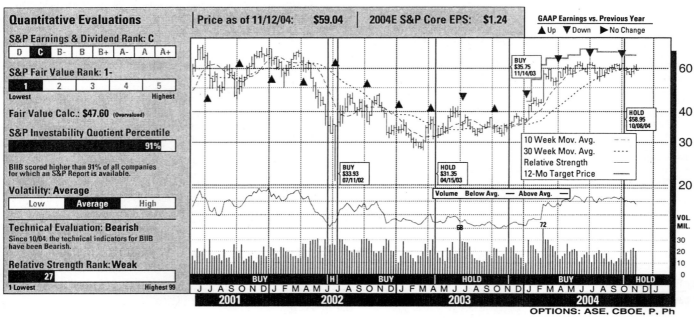

10 Week Mov. Avg. ....
30 Week Mov. Avg. - - - -
Relative Strength ———
12-Mo Target Price ———

Volume Below Avg. — Above Avg. —

OPTIONS: ASE, CBOE, P, Ph

Analyst commentary prepared by Frank DiLorenzo, CFA /PMW/JWP

Highlights November 02, 2004

- Third quarter pro forma EPS of $0.37 was $0.01 above our estimate, and up $0.02, year to year. As already reported by partner Genentech, third quarter U.S. Rituxan sales were $393 million, about $1 million lower than our forecast, but up 11%, year to year. Avonex sales of $346 million were $5 million below our forecast, but up 16%, year to year. BIIB's growth goals include annualized revenue gains of 15% and annualized EPS gains of 20%. To achieve these objectives, we consider approval of Antegren and a strong launch and sales ramp-up to be necessary.

- In May, BIIB submitted a Biologics License Application to the FDA for approval of Antegren to treat multiple sclerosis (MS). The filing was followed in June by a European application for approval to treat MS. In September, the company filed for European approval of Antegren to treat Crohn's disease. We expect FDA approval of Antegren in MS by the end of 2004. We see Antegren cannibalizing some sales of Avonex and other MS therapies. However, we expect limited cannibalization in 2005. Our initial sales estimate for 2005 U.S. Antegren sales is $187 million.

- We project 2004 U.S. Rituxan sales of $1.55 billion, Avonex sales of $1.4 billion, Amevive sales of $48 million, and Zevalin sales of $21 million. We estimate pro forma EPS of $1.48 for 2004 and $1.75 for 2005.

Key Stock Statistics

S&P Oper. EPS 2004E	1.48	52-week Range	$64.00-34.29
P/E on S&P Oper. EPS 2004E	39.9	12 Month P/E	NM
S&P Oper. EPS 2005E	1.75	Beta	0.83
Yield (%)	Nil	Shareholders	1,367
Dividend Rate/Share	Nil	Market Cap (B)	$ 19.7
Shares Outstanding (M)	333.6		

Value of $10,000 invested five years ago: **$ 28,837**

Dividend Data

No cash dividends have been paid.

Investment Rationale/Risk November 02, 2004

- We recommend holding the shares, as we think that Antegren approval and a strong launch are largely reflected in the share price. Our valuation assumes peak annual Antegren sales of $2.3 billion by 2012. We expect BIIB to spend heavily on the Antegren launch, limiting potential for upside for our 2005 EPS estimate. Sales of Rituxan and Avonex continue to rise, but growth has been slowing, and we expect further growth compression in 2005. Antegren profits would be split with partner Elan Corp., but we expect wide margins to drive solid long-term EPS gains. For Antegren, we assume commercial success in MS. The drug is also being developed as a treatment for Crohn's disease and rheumatoid arthritis. Success in one of these areas would potentially provide some upside to our peak revenue forecast.

- Risks to our recommendation and target price include the possibility that Antegren fails to receive approval, or that approval is delayed; lower than expected sales of Rituxan, Avonex and Antegren; and possible negative Medicare reimbursement changes for Rituxan in 2005.

- Our annualized EPS growth rate projection is 20.7% through 2008. Using our 2005 estimates, the stock's forward P/E to growth (PEG) ratio of 1.7X is above our peer average of 1.2X (excluding BIIB). Based on our net present value analysis, our 12-month target price is $68.

Revenues/Earnings Data Fiscal year ending December 31

Revenues (Million $)

	2004	2003	2002	2001	2000	1999
1Q	541.7	117.3	79.74	56.54	25.40	20.51
2Q	538.8	123.6	97.13	64.85	37.39	35.29
3Q	543.3	138.5	103.7	69.62	41.18	30.19
4Q	—	299.9	123.7	81.68	45.84	32.01
Yr.	—	679.2	404.2	272.7	154.7	118.0

Earnings Per Share ($)

	2004	2003	2002	2001	2000	1999
1Q	-0.12	0.24	0.17	0.12	0.02	0.12
2Q	Nil	0.17	0.20	0.15	0.09	0.13
3Q	0.10	0.26	0.22	0.16	0.10	0.07
4Q	E0.37	-4.03	0.26	0.16	0.12	0.05
Yr.	E1.48	-4.92	0.85	0.59	0.36	0.29

Next earnings report expected: early-March Source: S&P, Company Reports
EPS Estimates based on S&P Operating Earnings; historical GAAP earnings are as reported.

Biogen Idec Inc.

Recommendation: **HOLD** ★ ★ ★ ★ ★   12-Month Target Price: **$68.00** (as of October 08, 2004)

Business Summary November 02, 2004

Biogen Idec researches, develops and markets therapeutics to treat cancer and autoimmune diseases. The company was formed through the November 2003 merger of IDEC Pharmaceuticals and Biogen.

The company's largest selling drug is Rituxan, a treatment for relapsed or refractory, low grade or follicular B-cell non-Hodgkin's lymphomas (NHL). There are about 300,000 U.S. patients with various forms of this disease. Rituxan is being marketed and sold in the U.S. under a co-promotion agreement with Genentech; BIIB receives joint business revenues on a percentage of sales. F. Hoffman-La Roche has marketing rights (under the name MabThera) outside the U.S., with BIIB receiving royalties on sales. MabThera received EU marketing approval in June 1998, and Japanese approval in June 2001. U.S. Rituxan sales were $1.36 billion in 2003, up 26% from 2002.

BIIB, Genentech and Roche are conducting Phase III and Phase II trials of Rituxan to treat rheumatoid arthritis. A Phase III trial to treat relapsed chronic lymphocytic leukemia is ongoing. Trials in multiple sclerosis (MS) are planned.

Avonex was approved by the FDA to treat relapsing forms of MS in 1996. European approval was granted in 1997. Avonex sales were $1.17 billion in 2003, up from $1.03 billion in 2002. The company estimates that more than 120,000 patients use Avonex worldwide. It markets Avonex in the U.S. and Europe.

In January 2003, the FDA approved Amevive to treat moderate-to-severe chronic plaque psoriasis. BIIB directly markets the drug in the U.S. Approval has been delayed in Europe, and new trials will be needed to potentially gain European approval.

Zevalin is a radioimmunotherapy for use in combination with Rituxan in a regimen intended for patients with advanced forms of NHL who have not adequately responded to standard treatments. In February 2002, the FDA approved Zevalin to treat NHL patients who are relapsed or refractory to Rituxan-based treatments. The company has rights to Zevalin in the U.S. Zevalin was approved in the EU in January 2004, with Schering AG having marketing rights. It is entitled to royalties on sales from Schering.

BIIB is co-developing Antegren with Elan Corp. to treat MS and Crohn's disease. Two two-year Phase III trials are ongoing in MS. Based on one-year interim data, the companies filed for FDA approval in May 2004; a filing for European approval in MS was submitted in June 2004. Phase III results in inducing a positive response in Crohn's disease have been disappointing, but Phase III results for maintenance of response in Crohn's disease patients have been more encouraging. In September 2004, BIIB and Elan filed for European approval in Crohn's disease. A phase II trial of Antegren for the treatment of rheumatoid arthritis is also ongoing.

In June 2004, the company in-licensed V2006, an antagonist of adenosine A2A receptor, from Vernalis. V2006 is scheduled to begin a Phase II trial in Parkinson's disease in 2005. In October 2003, BIIB licensed a second generation fumarate derivative, BG-12, from Fumapharm AG to treat psoriasis. It has worldwide rights, except for Germany. Phase III trials began in Europe in 2004.

BIIB also receives royalties from licensee sales of hepatitis B vaccines, alpha interferon, and diagnostics. The majority of royalties stem from sales of Schering-Plough's PEG-Intron to treat hepatitis C.

Company Financials Fiscal Year ending December 31

Per Share Data ($)

(Year Ended December 31)	2003	2002	2001	2000	1999	1998	1997	1996	1995	1994
Tangible Bk. Val.	6.89	7.25	6.22	4.63	1.11	0.88	0.53	0.61	0.19	0.34
Cash Flow	-4.57	0.88	0.62	0.39	0.31	0.18	-0.10	-0.02	-0.17	-0.24
Earnings	-4.92	0.85	0.59	0.36	0.29	0.15	-0.14	-0.06	-0.20	-0.28
S&P Core Earnings	-5.13	0.54	0.34	NA	NA	NA	NA	NA	NA	NA
Dividends	Nil	Nil	Nil	Nil	Nil	Nil	Nil	Nil	Nil	Nil
Payout Ratio	Nil	Nil	Nil	Nil	Nil	Nil	Nil	Nil	Nil	Nil
Prices - High	42.15	71.40	75.00	77.64	35.00	8.03	7.70	5.43	3.93	1.12
- Low	27.80	20.76	32.62	18.54	6.60	2.87	2.62	2.31	0.35	0.35
P/E Ratio - High	NM	84	NM	NM	NM	52	NM	NM	NM	NM
- Low	NM	24	NM	NM	NM	19	NM	NM	NM	NM

Income Statement Analysis (Million $)

	2003	2002	2001	2000	1999	1998	1997	1996	1995	1994
Revs.	679	404	273	155	118	87.0	44.6	30.0	23.6	7.44
Oper. Inc.	14.6	285	137	60.6	45.8	23.2	-14.0	-2.79	-2.56	-16.1
Depr.	61.3	10.2	6.31	4.74	4.37	4.28	4.01	2.64	2.40	2.42
Int. Exp.	Nil	16.1	7.30	7.05	6.06	0.63	0.92	2.70	2.28	0.47
Pretax Inc.	-881	232	162	69.3	45.6	21.9	-15.5	-4.96	-17.3	-18.0
Eff. Tax Rate	NM	36.0%	37.1%	17.2%	5.37%	1.93%	NM	NM	NM	NM
Net Inc.	-875	148	102	57.4	43.2	21.5	-15.5	-4.96	-17.3	-18.0
S&P Core Earnings	-914	93.4	61.4	NA	NA	NA	NA	NA	NA	NA

Balance Sheet & Other Fin. Data (Million $)

	2003	2002	2001	2000	1999	1998	1997	1996	1995	1994
Cash	836	373	426	401	61.4	73.5	34.8	25.3	18.8	13.7
Curr. Assets	1,839	978	700	631	279	101	79.2	91.6	27.4	22.6
Total Assets	9,504	2,060	1,141	856	307	125	106	114	47.6	45.5
Curr. Liab.	405	56.2	35.3	23.0	15.6	14.5	19.4	13.7	8.74	9.43
LT Debt	887	866	136	129	123	2.10	2.02	5.00	6.60	7.40
Common Equity	7,053	1,110	956	695	160	106	80.7	66.0	17.1	27.9
Total Cap.	9,049	1,976	1,092	824	283	109	84.4	71.0	23.7	35.3
Cap. Exp.	301	166	0.07	31.4	4.29	1.72	5.88	6.30	1.30	1.60
Cash Flow	-814	158	108	62.1	47.5	25.8	-11.5	-2.31	-14.9	-15.6
Curr. Ratio	4.5	17.4	19.8	27.4	17.8	7.0	4.1	6.7	3.1	2.4
% LT Debt of Cap.	9.8	43.8	12.4	15.7	43.4	1.9	2.4	7.0	27.9	20.9
% Net Inc.of Revs.	NM	36.6	37.3	37.1	36.6	24.7	NM	NM	NM	NM
% Ret. on Assets	NM	9.3	10.2	9.9	20.0	18.6	NM	NM	NM	NM
% Ret. on Equity	NM	14.3	12.3	13.4	32.4	23.0	NM	NM	NM	NM

Data as orig reptd.; bef. results of disc opers/spec. items. Per share data adj. for stk. divs.; EPS diluted. E-Estimated. NA-Not Available. NM-Not Meaningful. NR-Not Ranked. UR-Under Review.

Office: 14 Cambridge Center, Cambridge, MA 02142.
Telephone: 617-679-2000.
Website: http://www.biogenidec.com
Chrmn: W.H. Rastetter.
Pres & CEO: J.C. Mullen.
COO: W.R. Rohn.

EVP & CFO: P.N. Kellogg.
EVP & General Counsel: T.J. Bucknum.
Investor Contact: C. Dillon 617-679-2812.
Dirs: A. Belzer, L. C. Best, A. B. Glassberg, M. L. Good, T. F. Keller, J. C. Mullen, R. W. Pangia, W. H. Rastetter, B. R. Ross, L. Schenk, P. A. Sharp, W. D. Young.

Founded: in 1985.
Domicile: Delaware.
Employees: 3,727.
S&P Analyst: Frank DiLorenzo, CFA /PMW/JWP

Biomet, Inc.

Recommendation: **HOLD** ★ ★ ★ ☆ ☆   12-Month Target Price: **$48.00**
(as of June 14, 2004)

BMET has an approximate 0.11% weighting in the **S&P 500**

Sector: Health Care
Sub-Industry: Health Care Equipment
Peer Group: Orthopedic Products

Summary: Biomet makes surgical implants for replacement of hip and knee joints, orthopedic support items, fracture fixation devices, and other related medical devices.

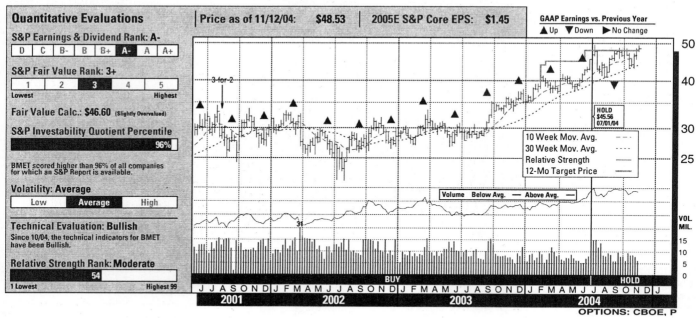

Analyst commentary prepared by Robert M. Gold/CB/BK

Highlights September 21, 2004

- We project FY 05 (May) revenue growth of about 18%, to $1.9 billion. By division, we see a 15% advance in reconstructive knee, hip, shoulder, dental and bone cement/other products; 7% growth in internal/external fixation; and a 60% increase in the spinal area, including the acquisition of Interpore International Inc. In our view, the company's performance in the hip implant area could benefit from the launch of three new products during FY 05. We see currency adding 3% to reported FY 05 revenue growth. In addition, increased pricing could, in our opinion, contribute 2%-3% to reported growth.

- We believe gross margins will approximate 72.0% in FY 05, up from 71.6% in FY 04, and we see operating margin expansion as the company focuses on reducing its SG&A expense ratio. We estimate that research and development costs will approximate 4.0% of sales. Per share earnings will, in our opinion, continue to be supported by an active common share repurchase program.

- After taxes at an estimated 35% rate, we see FY 05 operating EPS of $1.55, and look for FY 06 EPS of $1.80. After removing an estimated $0.10 of projected stock option expense, our Standard & Poor's Core EPS estimate for FY 05 is $1.45. We believe the divergence between S&P Core and operating EPS is modest relative to the company's peers.

Key Stock Statistics

S&P Oper. EPS 2005E	1.55	52-week Range	$49.60-33.19
P/E on S&P Oper. EPS 2005E	31.3	12 Month P/E	40.1
S&P Oper. EPS 2006E	1.80	Beta	0.25
Yield (%)	0.4%	Shareholders	6,319
Dividend Rate/Share	0.20	Market Cap (B)	$ 12.3
Shares Outstanding (M)	253.1		

Value of $10,000 invested five years ago: **$ 33,332**

Dividend Data Dividends have been paid since 1996

Amount ($)	Date Decl.	Ex-Div. Date	Stock of Record	Payment Date
0.200	Jun. 25	Jul. 14	Jul. 16	Jul. 23 '04

Investment Rationale/Risk September 21, 2004

- Biomet remains one of the more consistent generators of revenues, cash flow and EPS in our device universe. We see the company capturing share in the knee implant and spine segments. However, we think Biomet is currently at a competitive disadvantage in the hip implant market, due to the absence of ceramic-on-ceramic and minimally invasive product offerings.

- Risks to our opinion and target price include unfavorable Medicare reimbursement proposals, rising competition in some key orthopedic markets, and adverse outcomes in patent liability lawsuits.

- Recently valued at 31X our FY 05 EPS forecast and 6.6X estimated FY 05 sales, the stock trades at a significant premium to the S&P 500 and its orthopedic device peer group. Our 12-month target price of $48 assumes that the stock generates no meaningful valuation expansion on either a forward P/E or P/E-to-growth basis. We would therefore not recommend that investors add to positions, although we think the company's strong long-term fundamentals support keeping BMET as part of a core group of holdings in a diversified health care portfolio.

Revenues/Earnings Data Fiscal year ending May 31

Revenues (Million $)

	2005	2004	2003	2002	2001	2000
1Q	438.2	370.3	317.6	272.0	230.3	192.2
2Q	—	387.6	341.4	289.4	243.5	202.5
3Q	—	410.2	354.0	304.6	266.7	232.9
4Q	—	447.2	377.2	325.9	288.0	250.2
Yr.	—	1,615	1,390	1,192	1,031	920.6

Earnings Per Share ($)

	2005	2004	2003	2002	2001	2000
1Q	0.24	0.30	0.25	0.21	0.18	0.16
2Q	E0.38	0.32	0.27	0.23	0.19	0.16
3Q	E0.40	0.34	0.28	0.23	0.14	0.17
4Q	E0.41	0.31	0.30	0.23	0.22	0.19
Yr.	E1.55	1.27	1.10	0.88	0.73	0.65

Next earnings report expected: mid-December Source: S&P, Company Reports
EPS Estimates based on S&P Operating Earnings; historical GAAP earnings are as reported.

Biomet, Inc.

Recommendation: **HOLD** ★ ★ ★ ☆ ☆   12-Month Target Price: **$48.00** (as of June 14, 2004)

Business Summary September 21, 2004

Biomet sells a variety of reconstructive orthopedic implants, electrical bone stimulators and related products. Products are used primarily by orthopedic medical specialists in the surgical replacement of hip and knee joints and in fracture fixation procedures as an aid to healing.

Foreign sales contributed 33% of total net sales in FY 04 (May), up from 30% in FY 03. Major international markets for the company's products are Western Europe, Asia-Pacific, Australia, Canada and Latin America. During FY 04, foreign sales were bolstered by $63.7 million from foreign currency translations.

Reconstructive devices (65% of FY 04 sales) are used to replace joints that have deteriorated due to disease (principally osteoarthritis) or injury. These include implants for replacement of hips, knees, shoulders, ankles and elbows. For minimally invasive knee arthroplasty procedures, BMET sells devices including the Repicci II Unicondylar Knee System and the Oxford Phase 3 Unicompartmental Knee and the Vanguard Complete Knee Replacement System. BMET also offers over 20 hip systems in various sizes and configurations, most of which use titanium or cobalt chromium alloy femoral components and the proprietary ARCom polythelene-lined or metal-on-metal acetabular components. BMET also makes instruments used by orthopedic surgeons, and sells dental reconstruction implants and related instrumentation, regenerative products and materials and bone substitute materials.

Fixation products (15%) include electrical stimulation devices to treat recalcitrant bone fractures that have not healed with conventional surgical and/or non-surgical methods; external fixation devices for complicated trauma, limb-lengthening and deformity correction uses, and for fracture repair; craniomaxillofacial fixation systems and neurosurgical titanium implants; internal fixation devices such as nails, plates, screws, pins and wires; and bone substitute materials.

Spinal products (10%) include implantable, direct current electrical stimulation devices that provide an adjunct to surgical intervention in the treatment of nonunions and spinal fusions; and spinal fixation systems that address the inherent drawbacks of traditional rod and plate systems. In July 2004, BMET completed its acquisition of Interpore International Inc., for $280 million in cash. Interpore, which sells products for spinal surgery, including implants, orthobiologics and minimally invasive surgery products, had 2003 revenues of $67.5 million.

Other products (10%) include orthopedic support devices, arthroscopy products, operating room supplies, casting materials, general surgical instruments, wound care and other surgical products.

BMET spent $64.9 million on R&D in FY 04, up from $55.3 million in FY 03, and the company expects that ongoing R&D expenses will continue to increase. Principal research and development efforts relate to reconstructive devices, electrical stimulation, spinal fixation and revision orthopedic reconstructive devices, dental implants, arthroscopy, resorbable technology, biomaterials, gene therapy technologies and image-guided software in the musculoskeletal products field.

Company Financials Fiscal Year ending May 31

Per Share Data ($)

(Year Ended May 31)	2004	2003	2002	2001	2000	1999	1998	1997	1996	1995
Tangible Bk. Val.	4.44	4.46	3.96	3.73	3.28	2.84	2.40	2.11	1.96	1.60
Cash Flow	1.50	1.27	1.06	0.89	0.80	0.57	0.58	0.49	0.44	0.36
Earnings	1.27	1.10	0.88	0.73	0.65	0.46	0.49	0.42	0.36	0.31
S&P Core Earnings	1.23	1.08	0.88	0.72	NA	NA	NA	NA	NA	NA
Dividends	0.10	NA	0.07	0.06	0.06	0.05	0.05	0.04	Nil	Nil
Payout Ratio	8%	NA	8%	9%	10%	12%	10%	11%	Nil	Nil

Cal. Yrs.	2003	2002	2001	2000	1999	1998	1997	1996	1995	1994
Prices - High	38.02	33.26	34.36	27.83	20.33	18.30	12.00	9.16	8.83	6.33
- Low	26.74	21.75	20.45	12.05	10.94	10.50	6.33	5.55	5.83	4.00
P/E Ratio - High	30	38	39	38	31	40	24	22	24	21
- Low	21	25	23	17	17	23	13	13	16	13

Income Statement Analysis (Million $)

	2004	2003	2002	2001	2000	1999	1998	1997	1996	1995
Revs.	1,615	1,390	1,192	1,031	921	757	651	580	535	452
Oper. Inc.	553	472	419	360	315	256	204	178	158	133
Depr.	59.5	45.7	47.8	42.8	39.8	29.5	23.5	18.5	20.8	14.4
Int. Exp.	3.54	4.40	3.38	4.11	3.19	Nil	0.34	0.70	1.12	1.03
Pretax Inc.	509	452	376	311	281	186	204	169	150	125
Eff. Tax Rate	34.6%	34.7%	33.9%	34.1%	35.5%	33.6%	38.8%	37.1%	37.1%	36.6%
Net Inc.	326	287	240	198	174	116	125	106	94.1	79.2
S&P Core Earnings	316	281	240	193	NA	NA	NA	NA	NA	NA

Balance Sheet & Other Fin. Data (Million $)

	2004	2003	2002	2001	2000	1999	1998	1997	1996	1995
Cash	159	226	154	235	214	129	117	123	137	90.0
Curr. Assets	1,116	1,112	953	968	790	682	571	464	463	392
Total Assets	1,788	1,672	1,522	1,489	1,218	1,068	849	628	598	539
Curr. Liab.	313	267	238	242	181	201	98.1	72.9	62.0	89.2
LT Debt	Nil	Nil	Nil	Nil	Nil	Nil	Nil	Nil	Nil	Nil
Common Equity	1,448	1,286	1,176	1,146	943	776	667	553	534	445
Total Cap.	1,474	1,405	1,284	1,247	1,037	866	750	555	536	447
Cap. Exp.	61.3	59.8	62.3	35.3	43.1	51.1	44.1	21.4	14.1	28.9
Cash Flow	385	332	288	240	214	146	148	125	115	93.6
Curr. Ratio	3.6	4.2	4.0	4.0	4.4	3.4	5.8	6.4	7.5	4.4
% LT Debt of Cap.	Nil	Nil	Nil	Nil	Nil	Nil	Nil	Nil	Nil	Nil
% Net Inc.of Revs.	20.2	20.6	20.1	19.2	18.9	15.4	19.1	18.3	17.6	17.5
% Ret. on Assets	18.8	18.0	15.9	14.6	14.9	12.1	16.9	17.4	16.5	16.5
% Ret. on Equity	23.8	23.3	20.6	18.9	20.0	16.1	20.4	19.6	19.2	19.8

Data as orig reptd.; bef. results of disc opers/spec. items. Per share data adj. for stk. divs.; EPS diluted. E-Estimated. NA-Not Available. NM-Not Meaningful. NR-Not Ranked. UR-Under Review.

Office: 56 East Bell Drive, Warsaw, IN 46582.
Telephone: 574-267-6639.
Email: investors@biomet.com
Website: http://www.biomet.com
Chrmn: N.L. Noblitt.
Pres & CEO: D.A. Miller.
Vice Chrmn: J.L. Ferguson.

SVP, CFO & Treas: G.D. Hartman.
SVP, Secy & General Counsel: D.P. Hann.
Investor Contact: B.A. Goslee 574-267-6639.
Dirs: J. L. Ferguson, D. P. Hann, C. S. Harrison, M. R. Harroff, T. F. Kearns, Jr., K. V. Miller, D. A. Miller, J. L. Miller, C. E. Niemier, N. L. Noblitt, M. T. Quayle, L. G. Tanner.

Founded: in 1977.
Domicile: Indiana.
Employees: 3,620.
S&P Analyst: Robert M. Gold/CB/BK

The McGraw·Hill Companies

BJ Services

Recommendation: **BUY** ★★★★
SELL | SELL | HOLD | BUY | BUY
12-Month Target Price: $57.00
(as of November 02, 2004)

BJS has an approximate 0.07% weighting in the **S&P 500**

Sector: Energy
Sub-Industry: Oil & Gas Equipment & Services
Peer Group: Oil & Gas - Services & Equipment - Medium

Summary: BJS provides pressure pumping and other oilfield services to the petroleum industry worldwide.

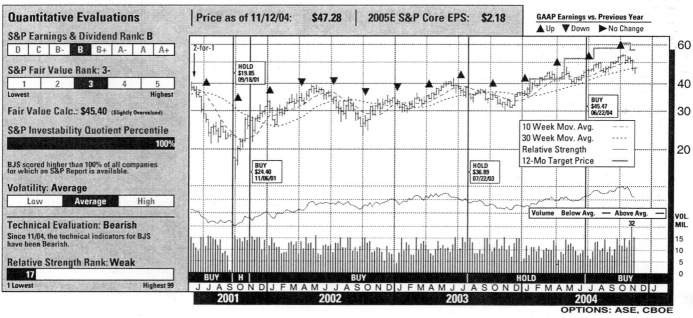

Quantitative Evaluations

S&P Earnings & Dividend Rank: B

| D | C | B- | B | B+ | A- | A | A+ |

S&P Fair Value Rank: 3-

| 1 | 2 | 3 | 4 | 5 |
| Lowest | | | | Highest |

Fair Value Calc.: $45.40 (Slightly Overvalued)

S&P Investability Quotient Percentile
100%

BJS scored higher than 100% of all companies for which an S&P Report is available.

Volatility: Average

| Low | Average | High |

Technical Evaluation: Bearish
Since 11/04, the technical indicators for BJS have been Bearish.

Relative Strength Rank: Weak
17
1 Lowest | Highest 99

Price as of 11/12/04: $47.28 | **2005E S&P Core EPS:** $2.18

GAAP Earnings vs. Previous Year
▲ Up ▼ Down ► No Change

10 Week Mov. Avg.
30 Week Mov. Avg.
Relative Strength
12-Mo Target Price

Analyst commentary prepared by Stewart Glickman/PMW/BK

OPTIONS: ASE, CBOE

Highlights November 05, 2004

- FY 04 (Sep.) fourth quarter results fell short of our expectations, with EPS of $0.52 missing our estimate by $0.06. Results were hurt by hurricane damage in the U.S. Gulf of Mexico, unusually wet weather in Canada, a slowdown in drilling activity by PEMEX (Mexico's national oil company), and unplanned maintenance on a vessel in the North Sea. We expect total revenues to increase about 10% in FY 05, and we see operating margins widening by about 270 basis points.

- We believe the main growth driver continues to be the U.S. market, where we expect rig count to remain at relatively high levels in FY 05. We look for over $180 million in free cash flow in FY 05. However, we think that a current malaise in drilling activity in Mexico may take some time to improve, as we see PEMEX as likely to rein in spending in the near term.

- We expect international operations to continue to provide earnings stability, and see growth markets such as Russia and Brazil offering upside potential, albeit with higher risk. We estimate FY 05 EPS from continuing operations of $2.29, with $2.18 on an S&P Core Earnings basis. For FY 06, we see operating EPS of $2.58.

Investment Rationale/Risk November 05, 2004

- We recommend buying the shares, based on valuation and on expected improving fundamentals for pressure pumping. Through early November, the stock was up about 30% in 2004, versus an increase of 24% for the S&P Oil & Gas Equipment & Services Index. The shares were trading at an enterprise value of 11.0X our calendar 2005 EBITDA estimate, in line with the peer group average of 11.0X. The stock has historically traded at a slight premium, reflecting, in our view, higher growth expectations relative to peers.

- Risks to our recommendation and target price include reduced demand for pressure pumping services, lower-than-expected cash flow from operations, a sharp reduction in oil and natural gas prices, and longer-than-expected slowdown in drilling activity in Mexico.

- We estimate return on capital employed of 13% in FY 05. Our discounted cash flow analysis, which assumes free cash flow growth of 8% to 9% for 10 years and 4% thereafter, indicates that the shares are undervalued. Applying a 13.5X multiple to our calendar 2005 EBITDA projection, blended with our DCF analysis, our 12-month target price is $57.

Key Stock Statistics

S&P Oper. EPS 2005E	2.29	52-week Range	$54.65-30.87
P/E on S&P Oper. EPS 2005E	20.6	12 Month P/E	22.1
S&P Oper. EPS 2006E	2.58	Beta	1.36
Yield (%)	0.7%	Shareholders	3,469
Dividend Rate/Share	0.32	Market Cap (B)	$ 7.6
Shares Outstanding (M)	161.5		

Value of $10,000 invested five years ago: $ 29,760

Dividend Data Dividends have been paid since 2004

Amount ($)	Date Decl.	Ex-Div. Date	Stock of Record	Payment Date
0.080	Jul. 22	Sep. 13	Sep. 15	Oct. 15 '04

Revenues/Earnings Data Fiscal year ending September 30

Revenues (Million $)

	2004	2003	2002	2001	2000	1999
1Q	600.8	473.1	510.1	489.7	354.8	294.4
2Q	647.1	534.6	442.4	549.7	390.8	269.6
3Q	658.7	546.6	439.6	579.8	371.3	253.1
4Q	694.5	588.6	473.7	614.3	438.5	314.2
Yr.	2,601	2,143	1,866	2,234	1,555	1,131

Earnings Per Share ($)

	2004	2003	2002	2001	2000	1999
1Q	0.38	0.21	0.42	0.38	0.13	-0.05
2Q	0.45	0.28	0.24	0.46	0.18	-0.08
3Q	0.79	0.31	0.17	0.63	0.15	-0.12
4Q	0.52	0.37	0.21	0.61	0.25	0.03
Yr.	2.14	1.17	1.04	2.09	0.70	-0.21

Next earnings report expected: mid-January Source: S&P, Company Reports
EPS Estimates based on S&P Operating Earnings; historical GAAP earnings are as reported.

BJ Services Company

Recommendation: **BUY** ★ ★ ★ ★ ★   12-Month Target Price: **$57.00** (as of November 02, 2004)

Business Summary November 05, 2004

BJ Services is a leading provider of pressure pumping and other oilfield services to the petroleum industry worldwide. Demand for its services depends on the number of oil and natural gas wells being drilled, the depth and drilling conditions of the wells, the number of well completions, and the level of workover activity worldwide.

BJS's principal customers consist of major and independent oil and natural gas producing companies. The company operates in more than 50 countries in the major international oil and natural gas producing areas of Canada, Latin America, Europe, Africa, Russia, Asia, the Middle East, Russia and China. In FY 03 (Sep.), 50% of revenues were generated in the U.S., 12% in Canada, and 38% elsewhere. With the June 1999 acquisition of Fracmaster Ltd. (1998 revenues of $209 million) for $78.4 million, Canada became the largest international segment. Other than Canada, the international market tends to be less volatile than the U.S. due to the size and complexity of investment, and projects tend to be managed with a longer-term perspective with regard to commodity prices. In addition, the international market is dominated by major oil and national oil companies, which tend to have different objectives and more operating stability than typical independent producers in the U.S.

Pressure pumping services (83% of FY 03 revenues) are used in the completion of oil and gas wells, both onshore and offshore. Customers are mainly served in the U.S. (50%). Stimulation services (53%) are designed to improve the flow of oil and natural gas from producing formations using fracturing, acidizing, sand control, nitrogen, coiled tubing and downhole tool services. Cementing (28%) is done between the casing pipe and the wellbore during the drilling and completion phase of a well. This is done to isolate fluids that could damage productivity, seal the casing from corrosive fluids and provide structural support for the casing string. Cementing services are also used when recompleting wells from one producing zone to another, and when plugging and abandoning wells.

In May 2002, BJS acquired OSCA, Inc., a provider of oil and gas well completion fluids and services and downhole tools, for about $420 million.

The company estimates that BJS and its two primary competitors, Halliburton and Schlumberger, hold about 90% of the pressure pumping market. Although its major competitors hold the largest market share overall, the company has the largest share in certain areas.

Other oilfield services (17%) include casing and tubular services, process and pipeline services, production chemicals, and, with the acquisition of OSCA, completion tools and completion fluids services in the U.S. and internationally.

Company Financials Fiscal Year ending September 30

Per Share Data ($)

(Year Ended September 30)	2004	2003	2002	2001	2000	1999	1998	1997	1996	1995
Tangible Bk. Val.	NA	4.87	3.48	5.57	4.81	2.72	3.08	5.80	1.80	2.45
Cash Flow	NA	1.91	1.69	2.72	1.30	0.50	1.28	2.40	0.85	0.61
Earnings	2.14	1.17	1.04	2.09	0.70	-0.21	0.72	0.66	0.32	0.12
S&P Core Earnings	NA	1.07	0.89	1.94	NA	NA	NA	NA	NA	NA
Dividends	0.08	Nil	Nil	Nil	Nil	Nil	Nil	Nil	Nil	Nil
Payout Ratio	4%	Nil	Nil	Nil	Nil	Nil	Nil	Nil	Nil	Nil
Prices - High	54.65	42.40	39.49	43.10	38.37	21.71	21.90	22.68	13.12	6.84
- Low	34.85	29.25	23.00	14.55	19.06	6.71	5.93	9.56	6.28	3.87
P/E Ratio - High	26	36	38	21	53	NM	30	35	41	60
- Low	16	25	22	7	26	NM	8	15	19	34

Income Statement Analysis (Million $)

	2004	2003	2002	2001	2000	1999	1998	1997	1996	1995
Revs.	NA	2,143	1,866	2,234	1,555	1,131	1,527	1,467	965	634
Oper. Inc.	NA	414	368	641	297	125	316	273	148	79.6
Depr. Depl. & Amort.	NA	120	105	105	102	100	91.0	90.4	66.1	42.1
Int. Exp.	NA	31.9	8.98	13.3	20.0	31.4	26.0	30.7	26.9	15.2
Pretax Inc.	NA	276	253	529	175	-44.9	175	154	52.6	8.76
Eff. Tax Rate	NA	31.7%	34.1%	34.0%	32.7%	NM	31.1%	30.1%	23.0%	NM
Net Inc.	NA	188	166	349	118	-29.7	117	108	40.5	9.89
S&P Core Earnings	NA	173	142	324	NA	NA	NA	NA	NA	NA

Balance Sheet & Other Fin. Data (Million $)

	2004	2003	2002	2001	2000	1999	1998	1997	1996	1995
Cash	NA	278	84.7	84.1	6.47	3.92	2.00	3.90	2.90	1.84
Curr. Assets	NA	942	649	733	506	439	452	475	418	257
Total Assets	NA	2,786	2,442	1,985	1,785	1,825	1,743	1,727	1,709	990
Curr. Liab.	NA	471	356	390	337	445	513	385	292	204
LT Debt	NA	494	489	79.4	142	423	242	299	523	260
Common Equity	NA	1,651	1,419	1,370	1,170	877	900	960	842	467
Total Cap.	NA	2,152	1,917	1,460	1,320	1,306	1,151	1,314	1,365	738
Cap. Exp.	NA	167	179	183	80.5	111	168	102	54.2	31.0
Cash Flow	NA	308	271	454	220	70.1	208	198	107	52.0
Curr. Ratio	NA	2.0	1.8	1.9	1.5	1.0	0.9	1.2	1.4	1.3
% LT Debt of Cap.	NA	22.9	25.5	5.4	10.8	32.4	21.0	22.7	38.3	35.2
% Ret. on Assets	NA	7.2	7.5	18.5	6.5	NM	6.7	6.3	3.0	1.4
% Ret. on Equity	NA	12.3	11.9	27.5	11.5	NM	12.6	12.0	6.2	3.0

Data as orig reptd.; bef. results of disc opers/spec. items. Per share data adj. for stk. divs.; EPS diluted. E-Estimated. NA-Not Available. NM-Not Meaningful. NR-Not Ranked. UR-Under Review.

Office: 5500 NorthWest Central Drive, Houston, TX 77092.
Telephone: 713-462-4239.
Website: http://www.bjservices.com
Chrmn, Pres & CEO: J.W. Stewart.
VP & CFO: T.M. Wichard, III.

VP, Secy & General Counsel: M.B. Shannon.
Treas: J. Smith.
Investor Contact: R.C. Coons 713-462-4239.
Dirs: L. W. Heiligbrodt, J. R. Huff, D. D. Jordan, M. E. Patrick, J. L. Payne, J. W. Stewart, W. H. White.

Founded: in 1872.
Domicile: Delaware.
Employees: 12,261.
S&P Analyst: Stewart Glickman/PMW/BK

Recommendation: HOLD ★ ★ ★ ★ ★
SELL SELL HOLD BUY BUY

12-Month Target Price: **$91.00**
(as of November 03, 2004)

BDK has an approximate 0.06% weighting in the **S&P 500**

Sector: Consumer Discretionary
Sub-Industry: Household Appliances
Peer Group: Hardware & Tools

Summary: BDK is a leading global producer of power tools, hardware and home improvement products and fastening systems.

Quantitative Evaluations

S&P Earnings & Dividend Rank: B+

| D | C | B- | B | B+ | A- | A | A+ |

S&P Fair Value Rank: 4-

| 1 | 2 | 3 | 4 | 5 |
Lowest | | | | Highest

Fair Value Calc.: $87.00 (Fairly Valued)

S&P Investability Quotient Percentile

96%

BDK scored higher than 96% of all companies for which an S&P Report is available.

Volatility: Average

| Low | Average | High |

Technical Evaluation: Bullish
Since 6/04, the technical indicators for BDK have been Bullish.

Relative Strength Rank: Strong

81

1 Lowest | Highest 99

| Price as of 11/12/04: | $85.60 | 2004E S&P Core EPS: | $5.05 |

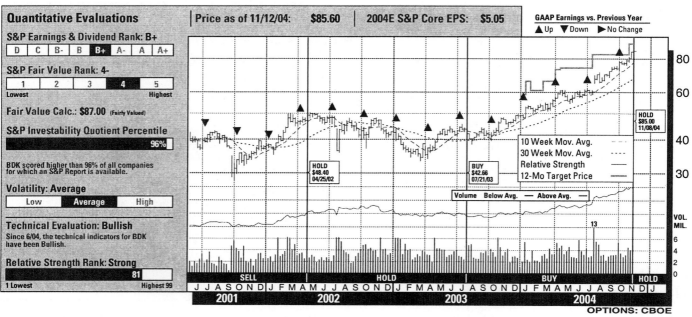

GAAP Earnings vs. Previous Year
▲ Up ▼ Down ▶ No Change

10 Week Mov. Avg.
30 Week Mov. Avg.
Relative Strength
12-Mo Target Price

Volume   Below Avg. — Above Avg. —

HOLD $48.40 04/25/02
BUY $42.66 07/21/03
HOLD $85.00 11/08/04

SELL | HOLD | BUY | HOLD
J J A S O N D J F M A M J J A S O N D J F M A M J J A S O N D J F M A M J J A S O N D J
2001 | 2002 | 2003 | 2004

VOL. MIL.
OPTIONS: CBOE

Analyst commentary prepared by Amy Glynn/PMW

Highlights November 08, 2004

- We forecast 2004 sales growth of 14%, aided by acquisitions and currency benefits. We expect the benefits of volume growth to outweigh modest price deflation. We expect organic revenues to grow in the mid-single digits in 2005. We think BDK will be able to maintain or gain share in key markets via the introduction of new products. Including the full-year inclusion of the Tools Group, acquired from Pentair in October 2004, we see total revenue growth in the high teens.

- We see BDK aided in 2005 by the integration of the Tools Group and previous acquisitions, and by continued benefits from a restructuring plan. We think improved efficiency of operations will be partly offset by increased commodity costs, and higher pension costs and option expense.

- We think the company is focusing on cash flow generation, and should be able to convert at least 90% of net earnings to free cash flow in 2004 and 2005. We project 2004 EPS of $5.36, and see $6.08 for 2005. We forecast 2004 and 2005 S&P Core EPS of $5.05 and $5.90, respectively; BDK expects to begin expensing options in the second half of 2005.

Investment Rationale/Risk November 08, 2004

- In light of recent restructuring and productivity initiatives, we believe BDK is better positioned than most tool manufacturer peers for an industry sales recovery. Margins have widened as a result of these initiatives, but we see limited additional margin upside, as we think cost savings from the restructuring will taper off in 2005. We think the company will continue to execute well on integrating acquisitions, which we think should aid EPS over the next few years. The shares were recently up about 75% in 2004, and are trading at about 14X our 2005 EPS estimate, in line with the historical average. Our 12-month target price of $91 assumes some multiple expansion, but with only about 6% potential upside to our target price, we have downgraded the shares to hold, from buy.

- Risks to our opinion and target price include an unexpected weakening in the company's major markets, a negative change in BDK's relationship with a major customer, poor market acceptance of new products, increased competition, and adverse changes in currency exchange rates or raw material prices.

- Our 12-month target price of $91 is based on our historical P/E multiple model, and applies a P/E multiple of 15X to our 2005 EPS estimate, as we think that the shares will benefit from multiple expansion. Our discounted free cash flow model calculates intrinsic value of $87.

Key Stock Statistics

S&P Core EPS 2005E	5.90	52-week Range	$85.69-44.45
S&P Oper. EPS 2004E	5.36	12 Month P/E	16.4
P/E on S&P Oper. EPS 2004E	16.0	Beta	1.10
S&P Oper. EPS 2005E	6.08	Shareholders	13,497
Yield (%)	1.0%	Market Cap (B)	$ 6.9
Dividend Rate/Share	0.84	Shares Outstanding (M)	80.7

Value of $10,000 invested five years ago: **$ 19,362**

Dividend Data Dividends have been paid since 1937

Amount ($)	Date Decl.	Ex-Div. Date	Stock of Record	Payment Date
0.210	Feb. 12	Mar. 10	Mar. 12	Mar. 26 '04
0.210	Apr. 27	Jun. 09	Jun. 11	Jun. 25 '04
0.210	Jul. 20	Sep. 08	Sep. 10	Sep. 24 '04
0.210	Oct. 27	Dec. 15	Dec. 17	Dec. 31 '04

Revenues/Earnings Data Fiscal year ending December 31

Revenues (Million $)

	2004	2003	2002	2001	2000	1999
1Q	1,093	939.2	951.7	979.0	1,038	978.5
2Q	1,298	1,090	1,125	1,070	1,126	1,084
3Q	1,283	1,116	1,085	1,063	1,133	1,111
4Q	—	1,338	1,232	1,221	1,264	1,347
Yr.	—	4,483	4,394	4,333	4,561	4,521

Earnings Per Share ($)

	2004	2003	2002	2001	2000	1999
1Q	0.93	0.55	0.41	0.40	0.69	0.44
2Q	1.50	0.94	0.81	0.51	0.97	0.80
3Q	1.35	0.95	0.68	0.57	1.01	0.85
4Q	E1.57	1.23	0.94	-0.16	0.64	1.31
Yr.	E5.36	3.68	2.84	1.33	3.34	3.40

Next earnings report expected: late-January Source: S&P, Company Reports
EPS Estimates based on S&P Operating Earnings; historical GAAP earnings are as reported.

The Black & Decker Corporation

Recommendation: **HOLD** ★ ★ ★ ☆ ☆   12-Month Target Price: **$91.00** (as of November 03, 2004)

Business Summary November 08, 2004

Black & Decker, incorporated in 1910, is a global manufacturer and marketer of power tools and accessories, hardware and home improvement products, and technology-based fastening systems. Its products are sold under a number of well known brand names in more than 100 countries. The company has 36 manufacturing facilities, including 18 located outside the U.S., in nine foreign countries.

Operations consist of three segments: Power Tools and Accessories (72% of 2003 sales), Hardware and Home Improvement (16%), and Fastening and Assembly Systems (12%). The U.S. accounted for 63% of sales in 2003, Europe 25%, and other countries 12%.

BDK is one of the world's leading producers of portable electric power tools and electric lawn and garden tools, as well as one of the largest suppliers of power tool accessories and specialized, engineered fastening and assembly systems in the markets it serves. Its plumbing products business is one of the largest North American faucet makers.

The Power Tools and Accessories segment manufactures and sells consumer and professional power tools (such as drills, screwdrivers and saws) and accessories, outdoor products (electric lawn and garden tools), cleaning and lighting products and product services. Products are sold mainly to retailers, wholesalers, jobbers, and distributors, although some discontinued or reconditioned products are sold through company-operated service centers and factory outlets directly to end users. Principal materials used to manufacture products in this segment include plastics, aluminum, copper, steel, certain electronic components, and batteries.

The Hardware and Home Improvement segment (formerly building products)

makes and sells security hardware (locksets and deadbolts) and plumbing products (faucets, shower heads and bath accessories). Products are sold primarily to retailers, wholesalers, distributors, and jobbers. Certain security hardware products are sold to commercial, institutional, and industrial customers. The principal materials used in the manufacture of products in this segment are plastics, aluminum, steel, brass, zamak, and ceramics.

BDK's Fastening and Assembly Systems segment includes a line of metal and plastic fasteners and engineered fastening systems for commercial applications. Products are marketed directly to customers and also through distributors and representatives.

In 2003, two customers, Home Depot and Lowe's Home Improvement Warehouse, each accounted for over 10% of consolidated sales.

In 2001, the company began a restructuring plan to reduce its manufacturing cost base, and to cut selling, general and administrative expenses. The plan, expected to be completed in 2004, has resulted in pre-tax restructuring charges over a three-year period totaling $170.5 million. In addition to the cost savings already realized from the 2001 restructuring plan, BDK expected incremental pretax savings associated with the plan to boost 2004 and 2005 results by $45 million and $10 million, respectively, net of restructuring-related expenses.

In October 2004, BDK acquired the Tools Group from Pentair, Inc., for about $775 million in cash. The Tools Group, which includes the Porter-Cable, Delta, DeVilbiss Air Power, Oldham Saw, and FLEX businesses, had 2003 sales of $1.08 billion, and operating profit of $82 million.

Company Financials Fiscal Year ending December 31

Per Share Data ($)

(Year Ended December 31)	2003	2002	2001	2000	1999	1998	1997	1996	1995	1994
Tangible Bk. Val.	0.96	NM	NM	NM	0.66	NM	NM	NM	NM	NM
Cash Flow	5.40	4.49	3.30	5.28	5.21	-6.52	4.55	4.11	4.34	3.91
Earnings	3.68	2.84	1.33	3.34	3.40	-8.22	2.35	1.64	2.33	1.37
S&P Core Earnings	3.23	1.56	0.11	NA	NA	NA	NA	NA	NA	NA
Dividends	0.57	0.48	0.48	0.48	0.48	0.48	0.48	0.48	0.40	0.40
Payout Ratio	15%	17%	36%	14%	14%	NM	20%	29%	17%	29%
Prices - High	49.90	50.50	46.95	52.37	64.62	65.50	43.43	44.25	38.12	25.75
- Low	33.20	35.00	28.26	27.56	41.00	37.93	29.62	29.00	22.87	17.00
P/E Ratio - High	14	18	35	16	19	NM	18	27	16	19
- Low	9	12	21	8	12	NM	13	18	10	12

Income Statement Analysis (Million $)

	2003	2002	2001	2000	1999	1998	1997	1996	1995	1994
Revs.	4,483	4,394	4,333	4,561	4,521	4,560	4,940	4,914	4,766	5,248
Oper. Inc.	594	549	407	686	696	639	703	572	633	607
Depr.	133	128	159	163	160	155	214	215	207	214
Int. Exp.	60.7	84.3	84.3	104	126	145	133	140	193	195
Pretax Inc.	391	307	155	405	441	-589	349	203	226	190
Eff. Tax Rate	26.5%	25.3%	30.5%	30.3%	32.0%	NM	35.0%	21.6%	4.00%	33.0%
Net Inc.	287	230	108	282	300	-755	227	159	217	127
S&P Core Earnings	251	126	9.48	NA	NA	NA	NA	NA	NA	NA

Balance Sheet & Other Fin. Data (Million $)

	2003	2002	2001	2000	1999	1998	1997	1996	1995	1994
Cash	308	517	245	135	147	88.0	247	142	132	66.0
Curr. Assets	2,203	2,194	1,892	1,962	1,911	1,752	2,079	1,804	2,107	1,833
Total Assets	4,223	4,131	4,014	4,090	4,013	3,853	5,361	5,154	5,545	5,434
Curr. Liab.	1,312	1,453	1,071	1,632	1,573	1,375	1,373	507	1,787	1,880
LT Debt	916	928	1,191	799	847	1,149	1,624	1,416	1,705	1,723
Common Equity	847	600	751	692	801	573	1,791	1,632	1,273	1,019
Total Cap.	1,942	1,739	2,204	1,712	1,892	2,002	3,473	3,116	3,181	2,938
Cap. Exp.	103	96.6	135	200	171	146	203	196	203	199
Cash Flow	421	358	267	445	460	-600	441	374	412	329
Curr. Ratio	1.7	1.5	1.8	1.2	1.2	1.3	1.5	1.2	1.2	1.0
% LT Debt of Cap.	47.1	53.4	54.1	46.6	44.8	57.4	46.8	45.4	53.6	58.7
% Net Inc.of Revs.	6.4	5.2	2.5	6.2	6.6	NM	4.6	3.2	4.6	2.4
% Ret. on Assets	6.9	5.6	2.7	7.0	7.6	NM	4.3	3.0	4.0	2.4
% Ret. on Equity	39.7	34.0	15.0	37.8	43.7	NM	13.3	10.9	15.8	12.0

Data as orig reptd.; bef. results of disc opers/spec. items. Per share data adj. for stk. divs.; EPS diluted. E-Estimated. NA-Not Available. NM-Not Meaningful. NR-Not Ranked. UR-Under Review.

Office: 701 East Joppa Road, Towson, MD 21286.
Telephone: 410-716-3900.
Email: investor.relations@bdk.com
Website: http://www.bdk.com
Chrmn, Pres & CEO: N.D. Archibald.
SVP & CFO: M.D. Mangan.

SVP & Secy: B.B. Lucas.
SVP & General Counsel: C.E. Fenton.
VP, Treas & Investor Contact: M.M. Rothleitner .
Dirs: N. D. Archibald, N. R. Augustine, B. L. Bowles, M. A. Burns, M. Candlish, K. B. Clark, M. A. Fernandez, B. H. Griswold IV, A. Luiso.

Founded: in 1910.
Domicile: Maryland.
Employees: 22,100.
S&P Analyst: Amy Glynn/PMW

Block (H&R)

Recommendation: **HOLD** ★★★☆☆
SELL SELL HOLD BUY BUY

12-Month Target Price: **$51.00**
(as of June 10, 2004)

HRB has an approximate 0.07% weighting in the **S&P 500**

Sector: Industrials
Sub-Industry: Diversified Commercial Services
Peer Group: Personal Consumer Services

Summary: This diversified company provides a wide range of financial products and services, including income tax preparation, mortgage loans and investment services.

Quantitative Evaluations

S&P Earnings & Dividend Rank: A-

| D | C | B- | B | B+ | A- | A | A+ |

S&P Fair Value Rank: 5+

| 1 | 2 | 3 | 4 | 5 |
| Lowest | | | | Highest |

Fair Value Calc.: $61.60 (Undervalued)

S&P Investability Quotient Percentile

72%

HRB scored higher than 72% of all companies for which an S&P Report is available.

Volatility: Average

| Low | Average | High |

Technical Evaluation: Neutral
Since 11/04, the technical indicators for HRB have been Neutral.

Relative Strength Rank: Moderate

49
1 Lowest   Highest 99

Price as of 11/12/04: $50.17   **2005E S&P Core EPS:** $3.88

GAAP Earnings vs. Previous Year
▲ Up ▼ Down ► No Change

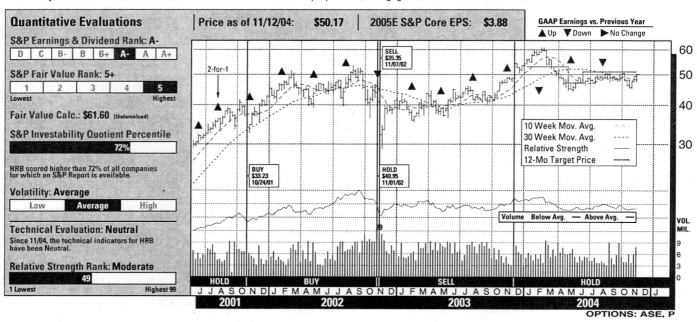

10 Week Mov. Avg.
30 Week Mov. Avg.
Relative Strength
12-Mo Target Price

Volume Below Avg. ── Above Avg.

Analyst commentary prepared by Andrew West, CFA /PMW/BK

Highlights September 01, 2004

- We project a 6% increase in total revenues in FY 05 (Apr.), on higher tax service revenues, driven by office openings and price increases; and growing brokerage and business services activity. Despite a growing number of HRB tax offices and an anticipated employment upturn, we expect client growth to be sluggish.

- We expect tax service margins to be flat, and see less room to raise customer fees or cut costs. We see improving business service and brokerage profitability, but expect a more challenging environment for the mortgage division, reflecting our expectations of rising interest rates and slowing refinancing and cash-out activity.

- We forecast FY 05 EPS of $4.03, up 3% from FY 04's $3.90, with expected gains hampered by declining profits from the mortgage division, but assisted by an expected 7% reduction in shares outstanding. We expect 6% EPS growth in 2006. We project FY 05 S&P Core Earnings of $3.88 a share, after anticipated gains on asset sales.

Investment Rationale/Risk September 01, 2004

- Although the stock appears to have a low valuation, we think the shares are fairly valued, based on our assessment of risks and our expectations of slowing growth following an unusually favorable mortgage environment. We see HRB's value proposition in tax services challenged by competitors and computerized substitutes. Over the next five years, we project sales growth at an annualized rate of 5%, with free cash flow and EPS rising about 3%.

- Risks to our opinion and target price include litigation and regulation issues, tax law changes; unusual interest rate or mortgage default rate scenarios; and the possibility of lower than anticipated demand and spreads, or higher hedging costs, for HRB's subprime, variable rate mortgage, and refinancing business.

- Our discounted cash flow model assumes a 9% cost of capital and 4.5% terminal growth, and calculates value at $48. Our relative value model, which relates historical peer group valuations to profitability and leverage, targets a forward price to sales multiple of 2.1X, and a price of $55. Blending our models, our 12-month target price is $51.

Key Stock Statistics

S&P Core EPS 2006E	4.11	52-week Range	$61.00-44.16
S&P Oper. EPS 2005E	4.03	12 Month P/E	13.9
P/E on S&P Oper. EPS 2005E	12.4	Beta	0.21
S&P Oper. EPS 2006E	4.27	Shareholders	31,063
Yield (%)	1.8%	Market Cap (B)	$ 8.3
Dividend Rate/Share	0.88	Shares Outstanding (M)	164.9

Value of $10,000 invested five years ago: **$ 25,808**

Dividend Data Dividends have been paid since 1962

Amount ($)	Date Decl.	Ex-Div. Date	Stock of Record	Payment Date
0.200	Nov. 25	Dec. 10	Dec. 12	Jan. 02 '04
0.200	Feb. 26	Mar. 09	Mar. 11	Apr. 01 '04
0.200	May. 26	Jun. 08	Jun. 10	Jul. 01 '04
0.220	Jun. 09	Sep. 08	Sep. 10	Oct. 01 '04

Revenues/Earnings Data Fiscal year ending April 30

Revenues (Million $)

	2005	2004	2003	2002	2001	2000
1Q	482.7	494.8	431.4	329.0	320.6	121.6
2Q	—	579.9	471.4	373.9	362.3	209.9
3Q	—	977.2	958.4	733.5	661.4	512.5
4Q	—	2,192	1,919	1,881	1,704	1,608
Yr.	—	4,206	3,780	3,318	3,002	2,452

Earnings Per Share ($)

	2005	2004	2003	2002	2001	2000
1Q	-0.26	0.06	-0.05	-0.17	-0.28	-0.19
2Q	E-0.13	0.06	-0.21	-0.15	-0.27	-0.23
3Q	E0.55	0.59	0.73	0.16	0.03	-0.04
4Q	E3.87	3.23	2.71	2.46	2.00	1.73
Yr.	E4.03	3.90	3.15	2.31	1.52	1.28

Next earnings report expected: late-November Source: S&P, Company Reports
EPS Estimates based on S&P Operating Earnings; historical GAAP earnings are as reported.

H&R Block, Inc.

Recommendation: **HOLD** ★ ★ ★ ☆ ☆   12-Month Target Price: **$51.00** (as of June 10, 2004)

Business Summary September 01, 2004

H&R Block provides various financial products and services. In FY 04 (Apr.), U.S. Tax accounted for 50% of revenues and 54% of profits, International Tax 2% and 1%, Mortgage 30% and 58%, Investment Services 5% and -6%, and Business Services 12% and 2%.

The U.S. Tax division served about 19.2 million clients in FY 04 (19.4 million in FY 03), and an estimated 15.6% of the individual returns filed with the IRS as of April 30, 2004 (15.9% for 2003). U.S. Tax also offers refund anticipation loans (RALs), whereby clients are offered loans up to $7,000 from a designated bank through a contractual relationship with Household Tax Masters, Inc., based on their antici-pated federal income tax refunds. There were 9,851 company-owned and franchised U.S. H&R Block offices at April 30, 2004 (9,301 at April 30, 2003). Offices in shared locations included 742 offices in Sears stores and 553 in Wal-Mart stores. HRB also offered tax preparation services at 405 H&R Block Premium offices (427) for more complex returns. During FY 04, HRB paid $243 million related to acquisitions of assets and stock in the franchise territories of 10 former major franchisees.

The International Tax segment consists of 1,334 company-owned and franchise offices, mostly in Australia, Canada, and the U.K.

HRB offers mortgage services through Option One Mortgage and H&R Block Mortgage. The division originates, services and sells conforming and

non-conforming loans in the U.S. through more than 32,500 brokers. At the end of FY 04, the segment was servicing non-prime loans valued at over $45.3 billion ($31.3 billion at the end of FY 03).

Investment Services provides brokerage services and investment planning prima-rily through H&R Block Financial Advisors, Inc., a registered broker dealer and investment advisor.

The business services segment, mostly through RSM McGladrey Inc., provides accounting, tax and consulting services to business clients (primarily mid-sized firms), and tax, estate planning, and financial planning to individuals in the U.S.

In June 2003, the company received court approval of a settlement of a class action suit related to RALs issued to Texas clients from 1992 through 1996. Under the settlement, HRB and its major Texas franchisee provided a five-year package of coupons that offered class members discounts on various tax preparation and planning services from the company and its units. The suit alleged that HRB had breached a fiduciary duty by not disclosing cash payments from the bank that provided the loans. HRB continues to be a defendant in a number of lawsuits regarding refund anticipation loan programs.

In the FY 05 first quarter, HRB acquired 7.5 million common shares, at a cost of $347 million.

Company Financials Fiscal Year ending April 30

Per Share Data ($)

(Year Ended April 30)	2004	2003	2002	2001	2000	1999	1998	1997	1996	1995
Tangible Bk. Val.	2.81	3.38	1.45	1.33	0.63	3.36	4.92	4.42	4.82	2.90
Cash Flow	4.85	4.03	3.13	5.21	2.02	1.55	1.07	1.02	0.74	0.83
Earnings	3.90	3.15	2.31	1.52	1.28	1.18	0.81	0.68	0.59	0.51
S&P Core Earnings	3.69	2.88	2.13	1.46	NA	NA	NA	NA	NA	NA
Dividends	0.78	0.70	0.59	0.54	0.51	0.43	0.40	0.52	0.64	0.61
Payout Ratio	20%	22%	25%	35%	40%	36%	49%	NM	108%	121%

Cal. Yrs.	2003	2002	2001	2000	1999	1998	1997	1996	1995	1994
Prices - High	55.78	53.50	46.37	24.75	29.75	24.53	22.87	21.06	24.43	24.37
- Low	35.28	29.00	18.31	13.46	19.00	17.65	14.00	11.81	16.68	16.50
P/E Ratio - High	14	17	20	16	23	21	28	94	41	48
- Low	9	9	8	9	15	15	17	52	28	33

Income Statement Analysis (Million $)

	2004	2003	2002	2001	2000	1999	1998	1997	1996	1995
Revs.	4,206	2,707	3,318	3,002	2,452	1,645	1,307	1,916	861	1,326
Oper. Inc.	1,411	240	987	913	704	499	364	171	23.0	258
Depr.	172	162	155	206	147	74.6	55.8	167	32.4	67.7
Int. Exp.	84.6	92.6	116	243	154	69.3	52.3	11.7	5.53	4.10
Pretax Inc.	1,164	987	717	473	412	384	281	62.4	197	220
Eff. Tax Rate	39.5%	41.2%	39.4%	41.5%	38.9%	38.0%	38.0%	23.5%	36.7%	51.2%
Net Inc.	704	580	434	277	252	238	174	47.8	125	107
S&P Core Earnings	665	527	400	268	NA	NA	NA	NA	NA	NA

Balance Sheet & Other Fin. Data (Million $)

	2004	2003	2002	2001	2000	1999	1998	1997	1996	1995
Cash	1,617	1,337	617	326	442	250	901	680	419	353
Curr. Assets	2,961	2,747	2,245	2,271	3,864	1,087	2,143	1,270	1,263	636
Total Assets	5,380	4,604	4,231	4,122	5,699	1,910	2,904	1,906	1,418	1,078
Curr. Liab.	2,472	1,897	1,880	1,988	3,520	554	1,277	713	340	359
LT Debt	546	822	868	871	872	250	250	Nil	NM	Nil
Common Equity	1,897	1,664	1,369	1,174	1,219	1,062	1,342	999	1,040	686
Total Cap.	2,443	2,486	2,238	2,045	2,091	1,312	1,591	1,025	1,040	686
Cap. Exp.	128	151	112	90.0	113	78.8	44.3	165	36.9	173
Cash Flow	876	742	590	482	399	312	230	215	158	175
Curr. Ratio	1.2	1.4	1.2	1.1	1.1	2.0	1.7	1.8	3.7	1.8
% LT Debt of Cap.	22.3	33.1	38.8	42.6	41.7	19.0	15.7	Nil	NM	Nil
% Net Inc.of Revs.	16.7	21.4	13.1	9.2	10.3	14.5	13.3	2.5	14.5	8.1
% Ret. on Assets	13.9	13.1	10.4	5.6	6.6	9.9	7.2	2.6	10.0	10.0
% Ret. on Equity	39.6	38.2	34.2	23.1	22.1	19.8	14.9	4.7	14.4	15.5

Data as orig reptd.; bef. results of disc opers/spec. items. Per share data adj. for stk. divs.; EPS diluted. E-Estimated. NA-Not Available. NM-Not Meaningful. NR-Not Ranked. UR-Under Review.

Office: 4400 Main Street, Kansas City, MO 64111-1812.
Telephone: 816-753-6900.
Email: investorrelations@hrblock.com
Website: http://www.hrblock.com
Chrmn, Pres & CEO: M.A. Ernst.
COO & EVP: J.W. Yabuki.

EVP & CFO: W.L. Trubeck.
SVP & General Counsel: N.J. Spaeth.
VP & Treas: B. Shulman.
Investor Contact: M. Barnett 816-701-4443.
Dirs: G. K. Baum, T. M. Bloch, D. R. Ecton, M. A. Ernst, H. F. Frigon, R. W. Hale, D. B. Lewis, T. D. Seip, L. W. Smith, R. Wilkins, Jr.

Founded: in 1946.
Domicile: Missouri.
Employees: 15,300.
S&P Analyst: Andrew West, CFA /PMW/BK

The McGraw·Hill Companies

Recommendation: **HOLD** ★ ★ ★ ★
SELL SELL HOLD BUY BUY

12-Month Target Price: **$19.00**
(as of November 02, 2004)

BMC has an approximate 0.04% weighting in the **S&P 500**

Sector: Information Technology
Sub-Industry: Systems Software
Peer Group: Systems Software - Larger

Summary: BMC provides systems management software that improves the availability, performance and recovery of applications and data.

Quantitative Evaluations

S&P Earnings & Dividend Rank: C

| D | C | B- | B | B+ | A- | A | A+ |

S&P Fair Value Rank: 3+

| 1 | 2 | 3 | 4 | 5 |
| Lowest | | | | Highest |

Fair Value Calc.: $17.00 (Slightly Overvalued)

S&P Investability Quotient Percentile

80%

BMC scored higher than 80% of all companies for which an S&P Report is available.

Volatility: Average

| Low | Average | High |

Technical Evaluation: Bullish
Since 10/04, the technical indicators for BMC have been Bullish.

Relative Strength Rank: Moderate

60

| 1 Lowest | Highest 99 |

Price as of 11/12/04: $17.95 | **2005E S&P Core EPS:** $-0.13

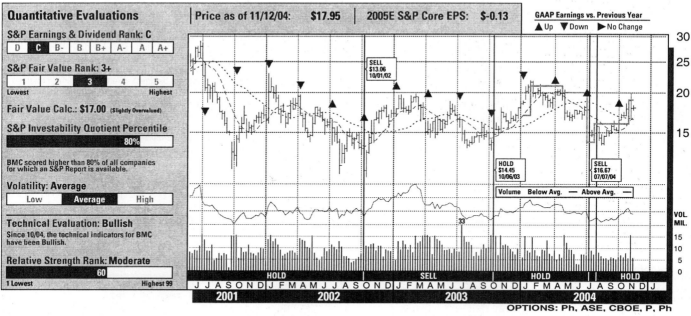

GAAP Earnings vs. Previous Year
▲ Up ▼ Down ► No Change

SELL $13.06 10/01/02
HOLD $14.45 10/06/03
SELL $16.67 07/07/04
Volume Below Avg. — Above Avg.

OPTIONS: Ph, ASE, CBOE, P, Ph

Analyst commentary prepared by Zaineb Bokhar/PMW/JWP

Highlights November 08, 2004

- We expect revenues to increase 5.6% in FY 05 (Mar.) and 7.9% in FY 06, driven by strong growth in Service Management solutions. We expect BMC's distributed business to decrease 6.2% in FY 05, due to reduced sales force emphasis on distributed infrastructure products, with more emphasis on newer service management solutions. We look for sales of distributed solutions to trend higher in FY 06, as new products are introduced and sales force interest is renewed. In the second quarter, maintenance revenue declined sequentially. BMC attributed this to an aggressive focus in prior quarters on signing customers to longer-term prepaid maintenance contracts to thwart competitive replacement. We expect maintenance revenue to resume normal growth patterns in the third quarter, and look for growth of 7.2% and 9.4% in FY 05 and FY 06, respectively.

- We expect operating margins to widen to 11% in FY 05, from 6.1% in FY 04, due to recent cost-cutting efforts. We expect further improvement in FY 06, and look for operating margins of 13%.

- We project operating EPS (excluding one-time charges and amortization) of $0.77 and $0.89 for FY 05 and FY 06, respectively. On an S&P Core Earnings basis, we forecast a loss of $0.13 a share for FY 05 and EPS of $0.26 for FY 06, reflecting estimated stock option expense.

Key Stock Statistics

S&P Core EPS 2006E	0.26	52-week Range	$21.87-13.70
S&P Oper. EPS 2005E	0.77	12 Month P/E	NM
P/E on S&P Oper. EPS 2005E	23.3	Beta	2.21
S&P Oper. EPS 2006E	0.89	Shareholders	1,333
Yield (%)	Nil	Market Cap (B)	$ 4.0
Dividend Rate/Share	Nil	Shares Outstanding (M)	222.0

Value of $10,000 invested five years ago: **$ 3,033**

Dividend Data

No cash dividends have been paid.

Investment Rationale/Risk November 08, 2004

- We remain concerned that independent software vendors such as the company are vulnerable to competition from platform vendors, most notably IBM, particularly in mainframes. We think that BMC's efforts to sign customers to longer-term prepaid maintenance agreements support our view. We also remain cautious about the potential for large deals to slip in the third quarter, due to restricted corporate IT spending. However, we would hold the shares, as the balance sheet shows no debt and over $1 billion in cash and marketable securities. A large portion of cash and marketable securities is invested overseas. Recent tax legislation may allow BMC to repatriate some of this cash to use for additional share repurchases or strategic acquisitions.

- Risks to our recommendation and target price include intense competition from large platform vendors as well as smaller point solution vendors, further deterioration in corporate information technology spending, and pricing pressures.

- The shares are trading at a discount to peers on a relative basis, after a drop following the company's earnings call on November 2. We used an intrinsic value calculation based on discounted cash flow analysis to arrive at our 12-month target price of $19. Our assumptions include a weighted average cost of capital of 15%, and an expected terminal growth rate of 2%.

Revenues/Earnings Data Fiscal year ending March 31

Revenues (Million $)

	2005	2004	2003	2002	2001	2000
1Q	326.0	309.9	305.2	341.0	400.7	400.7
2Q	355.1	333.8	291.2	295.1	323.0	415.7
3Q	—	374.8	349.6	321.0	385.5	426.3
4Q	—	400.2	380.7	311.8	422.8	476.4
Yr.	—	1,419	1,327	1,289	1,504	1,719

Earnings Per Share ($)

	2005	2004	2003	2002	2001	2000
1Q	0.05	-0.03	0.02	-0.14	0.07	0.07
2Q	0.06	-0.06	0.04	-0.22	-0.05	0.23
3Q	E0.22	-0.20	0.05	-0.39	0.09	0.27
4Q	E0.25	0.16	0.09	-0.01	0.09	0.39
Yr.	E0.77	-0.12	0.20	-0.75	0.17	0.96

Next earnings report expected: late-January Source: S&P, Company Reports
EPS Estimates based on S&P Operating Earnings; historical GAAP earnings are as reported.

BMC Software, Inc.

Recommendation: **HOLD** ★★★☆☆   12-Month Target Price: **$19.00** (as of November 02, 2004)

Business Summary November 08, 2004

BMC Software is one of the world's largest independent systems software vendors, delivering comprehensive enterprise management. Using its Business Service Management (BSM) strategy, the company aims to provide solutions that will enable customers to link their information technology (IT) resources tightly to business objectives, and to manage these resources based on business priorities by providing a whole view of their business and IT operations. BMC's software solutions span enterprise systems, applications, databases, and service management.

In FY 04 (Mar.), the company's product solutions fell into the following broad categories: Enterprise Data Management, Enterprise Systems Management, Remedy, and Security and other solutions.

Enterprise Data Management solutions provide intelligent, automated data management tools across all major databases, including IBM's IMS and DB2 for the mainframe environment, and Microsoft's SQL Server, IBM's DB2 UDB and Informix databases, and databases from Oracle and Sybase for distributed computing environments. The segment contributed 37% of license revenues in FY 04, down from 44% in FY 03.

Enterprise Systems Management solutions provide software tools for businesses to pro-actively and centrally manage their IT infrastructure. Solutions include the PATROL product line for distributed computing environments, and MAINVIEW product line for mainframe computing environments, and enterprise job schedul-

ing and output management solutions. The segment contributed 42% of license revenues in FY 04, down from 47% in FY 03.

Remedy, acquired in November 2002, delivers Service Management software solutions that enable organizations to automate and manage internal and external service and support processes. Remedy software solutions contributed 19% of license revenue in FY 04, including two months of Magic Solutions, acquired in February 2004, up from 6% in FY 03.

Security and other software solutions primarily include storage management, security, enterprise application management, subscription services, and Linux management solutions. The segment contributed 2% of license revenues in FY 04, down from 3% in FY 03.

International operations accounted for 46% of total revenues in FY 04, versus 44% in FY 03.

BMC has made a number of acquisitions integral to its strategy in recent years. In November 2002, the company acquired the assets of Remedy from Peregrine Systems, Inc., for $347 million in cash, plus the assumption of certain liabilities of Remedy. In March 2003, BMC acquired IT Masters, for $42.5 million in cash. In February 2004, it acquired Magic Solutions from Network Associates, for $49 million in cash. In July 2004, the company acquired Marimba, Inc., for $239 million in cash.

Company Financials Fiscal Year ending March 31

Per Share Data ($)

(Year Ended March 31)	2004	2003	2002	2001	2000	1999	1998	1997	1996	1995
Tangible Bk. Val.	3.11	3.70	5.49	5.67	5.67	5.64	3.68	2.73	1.92	1.52
Cash Flow	1.03	1.25	0.78	1.42	1.89	1.77	1.03	0.92	0.64	0.46
Earnings	-0.12	0.20	-0.75	0.17	0.96	1.47	0.76	0.77	0.51	0.38
S&P Core Earnings	-0.56	-0.01	-0.94	-0.19	NA	NA	NA	NA	NA	NA
Dividends	Nil	Nil	Nil	Nil	Nil	Nil	Nil	Nil	Nil	Nil
Payout Ratio	Nil	Nil	Nil	Nil	Nil	Nil	Nil	Nil	Nil	Nil

Cal. Yrs.	2003	2002	2001	2000	1999	1998	1997	1996	1995	1994
Prices - High	19.84	23.00	33.00	86.62	84.06	60.25	35.62	23.37	12.87	8.87
- Low	13.18	10.85	11.50	13.00	30.00	29.25	19.81	9.31	6.75	5.03
P/E Ratio - High	NM	NM	NM	NM	88	41	47	31	25	23
- Low	NM	NM	NM	NM	31	20	26	12	13	13

Income Statement Analysis (Million $)

	2004	2003	2002	2001	2000	1999	1998	1997	1996	1995
Revs.	1,419	1,327	1,289	1,504	1,719	1,304	731	563	429	345
Oper. Inc.	162	349	400	336	656	548	357	261	200	127
Depr.	259	248	376	315	236	76.8	58.0	32.5	23.5	18.8
Int. Exp.	1.10	Nil	0.40	11.3	23.4	Nil	Nil	Nil	Nil	Nil
Pretax Inc.	-29.4	69.3	-231	60.4	311	478	257	237	163	120
Eff. Tax Rate	NM	30.7%	NM	29.8%	22.1%	23.8%	35.4%	30.9%	35.2%	35.6%
Net Inc.	-26.8	48.0	-184	42.4	243	364	166	164	106	77.5
S&P Core Earnings	-128	-3.42	-232	-46.6	NA	NA	NA	NA	NA	NA

Balance Sheet & Other Fin. Data (Million $)

	2004	2003	2002	2001	2000	1999	1998	1997	1996	1995
Cash	909	1,015	546	146	152	1,205	72.1	139	122	93.8
Curr. Assets	1,425	1,098	997	903	896	873	374	248	228	183
Total Assets	3,045	2,846	2,676	3,034	2,962	2,283	1,248	844	608	503
Curr. Liab.	987	839	681	829	884	651	336	205	184	148
LT Debt	Nil	Nil	Nil	Nil	Nil	Nil	Nil	Nil	Nil	Nil
Common Equity	1,215	1,383	1,507	1,815	1,781	1,334	759	546	384	306
Total Cap.	1,215	1,383	1,507	1,815	1,781	1,334	803	546	384	306
Cap. Exp.	50.4	23.6	64.3	183	148	116	67.0	26.8	21.5	20.2
Cash Flow	233	296	192	357	478	441	224	196	134	96.3
Curr. Ratio	1.4	1.3	1.5	1.1	1.0	1.3	1.1	1.2	1.3	1.2
% LT Debt of Cap.	Nil	Nil	Nil	Nil	Nil	Nil	Nil	Nil	Nil	Nil
% Net Inc.of Revs.	NM	3.6	NM	2.8	14.1	27.9	22.7	29.1	39.2	22.5
% Ret. on Assets	NM	1.7	NM	1.4	9.2	20.6	15.9	22.6	19.1	16.9
% Ret. on Equity	NM	3.3	NM	2.4	15.6	34.8	25.4	35.2	30.7	27.9

Data as orig reptd.; bef. results of disc opers/spec. items. Per share data adj. for stk. divs.; EPS diluted. E-Estimated. NA-Not Available. NM-Not Meaningful. NR-Not Ranked. UR-Under Review.

Office: 2101 Citywest Boulevard, Houston, TX 77042-2827.
Telephone: 713-918-8800.
Email: investor@bmc.com
Website: http://www.bmc.com
Chrmn: B.G. Cupp.
Pres & CEO: R.E. Beauchamp.
SVP & CFO: G. Harrington.

SVP, Secy & General Counsel: R.H. Whilden, Jr.
VP & Chief Acctg Officer: L.E. Travis.
Investor Contact: N. Yekell 713-918-4233.
Dirs: J. E. Barfield, J. W. Barter, R. E. Beauchamp, B. G. Cupp, M. K. Gafner, L. W. Gray, L. J. Lavigne, Jr., K. A. O'Neill, G. F. Raymond, T. C. Tinsley.

Founded: in 1980.
Domicile: Delaware.
Employees: 6,429.
S&P Analyst: Zaineb Bokhar/PMW/JWP

Boeing Co.

Recommendation: **HOLD** ★★★☆☆
SELL | SELL | HOLD | BUY | BUY

12-Month Target Price: $53.00
(as of September 20, 2004)

BA has an approximate 0.41% weighting in the **S&P 500**

Sector: Industrials
Sub-Industry: Aerospace & Defense
Peer Group: Aircraft Manufacturers

Summary: BA is the world's second-largest commercial jet and military weapons manufacturer.

Quantitative Evaluations

S&P Earnings & Dividend Rank: B

| D | C | B- | **B** | B+ | A- | A | A+ |

S&P Fair Value Rank: 2

| 1 | **2** | 3 | 4 | 5 |
| Lowest | | | | Highest |

Fair Value Calc.: $43.80 (Overvalued)

S&P Investability Quotient Percentile

86%

BA scored higher than 86% of all companies for which an S&P Report is available.

Volatility: Average

| Low | **Average** | High |

Technical Evaluation: Bearish
Since 10/04, the technical indicators for BA have been Bearish.

Relative Strength Rank: Moderate

57

| 1 Lowest | | Highest 99 |

Price as of 11/12/04: **$53.93**   **2004E S&P Core EPS:** **$2.14**

GAAP Earnings vs. Previous Year
▲ Up   ▼ Down   ► No Change

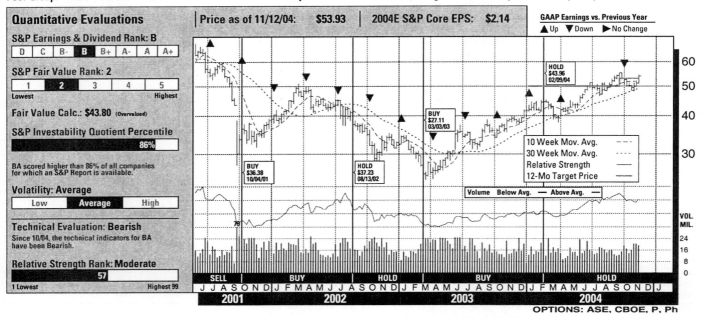

- 10 Week Mov. Avg.
- 30 Week Mov. Avg.
- Relative Strength
- 12-Mo Target Price

Volume Below Avg. — Above Avg.

OPTIONS: ASE, CBOE, P, Ph

Analyst commentary prepared by Robert E. Friedman, CPA /DC/JWP

Highlights September 23, 2004

- We believe that a rise in 2004 orders for BA's commercial jets (40% of sales) and military hardware (50% of sales) should allow the aerospace giant to post a 10%+ rise in 2005 revenues.
- The consequent increase in commercial aircraft and military hardware sales should more than offset a rise in commercial jet-related R&D expense, which in turn, should propel EBIT margins upward toward still-modest 8% levels, in our opinion. Following an expected decline in interest expense, we project that BA will post about a 10% advance in 2005 operating EPS, to $2.72; a 6% increase in 2005 Standard & Poor's Core EPS, to $2.26; and 2005 debt-adjusted ROE of 13%.
- Looking at BA's long-term financial fortunes, we are not overly optimistic about its ability to post sustainable outsized earnings growth and returns. We expect the global airline fleet market to grow at a 3% long-term annual rate, at best. Moreover, we look for severe price discounting to continue far into the future, due to mature markets, substantial pricing power on the part of airlines, and intensifying Airbus competition. Regarding BA's military weapons unit, we expect lackluster long-term growth potential for the U.S. defense budget and the mediocre economics of the military weapons-making business to put downward pressure on long-term EPS growth and returns. Consequently, we project that BA will, at best, post long-term free cash EPS growth of 6% and ROE of 13%.

Investment Rationale/Risk September 23, 2004

- We recommend holding the shares on a total return basis.
- Risks to our recommendation and target price primarily include further deterioration in the structural growth and economics of the civil and military aerospace markets, which, in turn, could depress BA's 10-year free cash EPS growth rate to below our 6% projection and its ROE below our 13% estimate.
- Our DCF model (which values BA by adding the sum of free cash earnings growing at a projected 6% compound annual growth rate (CAGR) over the next 10 years, and at 3.0% thereafter) calculates BA to be worth about $53 a share, which is our 12-month target price.

Key Stock Statistics

S&P Core EPS 2005E	2.26	52-week Range	$55.24-37.60
S&P Oper. EPS 2004E	2.50	12 Month P/E	15.5
P/E on S&P Oper. EPS 2004E	21.6	Beta	0.71
S&P Oper. EPS 2005E	2.60	Shareholders	135,640
Yield (%)	1.5%	Market Cap (B)	$ 45.3
Dividend Rate/Share	0.80	Shares Outstanding (M)	839.6

Value of $10,000 invested five years ago: **$ 12,514**

Dividend Data Dividends have been paid since 1942

Amount ($)	Date Decl.	Ex-Div. Date	Stock of Record	Payment Date
0.170	Dec. 15	Feb. 11	Feb. 13	Mar. 05 '04
0.200	May. 03	May. 19	May. 21	Jun. 11 '04
0.200	Jun. 28	Aug. 11	Aug. 13	Sep. 03 '04
0.200	Oct. 25	Nov. 09	Nov. 12	Dec. 03 '04

Revenues/Earnings Data Fiscal year ending December 31

Revenues (Million $)

	2004	2003	2002	2001	2000	1999
1Q	12,959	12,258	13,821	13,293	9,910	14,392
2Q	13,088	12,772	13,857	15,516	14,841	15,132
3Q	13,152	12,241	12,690	13,687	11,877	13,279
4Q	—	13,214	13,701	15,702	14,893	15,200
Yr.	—	50,485	54,069	58,198	51,321	57,993

Earnings Per Share ($)

	2004	2003	2002	2001	2000	1999
1Q	0.77	-0.60	0.72	1.45	0.48	0.50
2Q	E0.72	-0.24	0.96	0.99	0.71	0.75
3Q	0.54	1.40	0.46	0.80	0.70	0.52
4Q	E0.47	1.40	0.73	0.12	0.55	0.74
Yr.	E2.50	0.89	2.87	3.41	2.44	2.49

Next earnings report expected: late-January Source: S&P, Company Reports
EPS Estimates based on S&P Operating Earnings; historical GAAP earnings are as reported.

STANDARD &POOR'S

The Boeing Company

Stock Report
November 13, 2004
NYSE Symbol: **BA**

Recommendation: **HOLD** ★ ★ ★ ☆ ☆   12-Month Target Price: **$53.00** (as of September 20, 2004)

Business Summary September 23, 2004

This global aerospace giant conducts business through four segments:

Boeing Commercial Aircraft (43% of revenues, 57% of operating profits and 3.2% profit margins in 2003) and EADS's 80%-owned Airbus division are the world's only makers of 100-plus seat passenger jets. Based on 2003 year-end order backlogs, BCA and Airbus control 43% and 57%, respectively, of the global 100-plus seat passenger jet market. Demand for jetliners is driven primarily by growth in the global 100-plus seat commercial aircraft fleet. Based on the latest statistics provided by independent research firm Avitas, Inc., and the International Air Transport Association (IATA), from 1992 through 2002, the global airliner fleet grew at a 2.4% average annual rate.

Integrated Defense Systems (IDS; 53%, 62%, 3.0%; results include $1.6 billion of restructuring and goodwill charges), the world's second-largest military contractor, makes a wide range of military aircraft and missiles, as well as computer-based information networking systems used in everything from missile defense systems to combat vehicles.

IDS conducts business through four divisions: Aircraft and Weapons Systems (mostly fighter, transport and fuel tanker aircraft; 21% of total BA revenues, 115% of operating profits and 13% operating profit margins in 2003); Network Systems (computer-based information systems; 18%, 51%, 6.7%); Support Systems (military weapons servicing; 8%, 38%, 11%) and Launch & Orbital Systems (payload-carrying rocket and satellite manufacturing; 6%, -142%, NA).

Demand for IDS's equipment and systems is primarily driven by growth in the procurement and R&D sectors of the U.S. defense budget, which accounts for about 40% of global military weapons spending. The market for military weapons systems is mature. Based on U.S. Department of Defense statistics, from FY 93 (Oct.) through FY 03, the procurement and R&D sectors of the total U.S. defense budget grew at 1.5% and 1.8% average annual rates, respectively.

To a lesser extent, demand for IDS's products and services is driven by growth in the U.S. Homeland Security and NASA budgets. Since the formulation of the Department of Homeland Security in 2002, the agency's annual budget has been relatively flat, at about $30 billion; NASA's budget growth has also been flat, coming in at about $15 billion.

BA's BCC segment (2%, 12%, 12%) primarily finances commercial aircraft to airlines.

Boeing's Other segment (2%, -31%, NA) primarily consists of the fledgling Connexion by Boeing unit, which provides inflight Internet services.

In recent years, BA has not been very successful in boosting intrinsic value. From 1997 through 2003, growth in per-share equity, a proxy for intrinsic value expansion, fell at a negative CAGR of 6.3%. Over the past seven years, BA stock underperformed the S&P 500, declining at a CAGR of 3.3%, versus a 6.0% rise in the S&P 500.

Based on S&P's Core Earnings methodology, BA's quality of earnings is mediocre. Over the past seven years, the reported earnings-to-S&P Core earnings variance was 59%, primarily due to non-operating gains posted by BA's pension plans.

Company Financials Fiscal Year ending December 31

Per Share Data ($)

(Year Ended December 31)	2003	2002	2001	2000	1999	1998	1997	1996	1995	1994
Tangible Bk. Val.	6.17	4.53	5.23	6.63	10.14	10.25	10.56	11.75	14.39	14.23
Cash Flow	2.68	2.46	5.52	4.14	4.27	2.84	1.32	3.03	2.00	2.94
Earnings	0.89	2.87	3.41	2.44	2.49	1.15	-0.18	1.59	0.58	1.26
S&P Core Earnings	1.33	0.26	-0.06	NA	NA	NA	NA	NA	NA	NA
Dividends	0.68	0.68	0.68	0.56	0.56	0.56	0.56	0.55	0.50	0.50
Payout Ratio	76%	24%	20%	23%	22%	49%	NM	34%	87%	40%
Prices - High	43.37	51.07	69.85	70.93	48.50	56.25	60.50	53.75	40.00	25.06
- Low	24.73	28.53	27.60	32.00	32.56	29.00	43.00	37.06	22.18	21.06
P/E Ratio - High	49	18	20	29	19	49	NM	34	70	20
- Low	28	10	8	13	13	25	NM	23	39	17

Income Statement Analysis (Million $)

	2003	2002	2001	2000	1999	1998	1997	1996	1995	1994
Revs.	50,485	54,069	58,198	51,321	57,993	56,154	45,800	22,681	19,515	21,924
Oper. Inc.	3,198	5,447	6,467	4,996	4,724	3,189	2,503	2,212	1,878	2,293
Depr.	1,450	1,497	1,750	1,479	1,645	1,622	1,458	991	976	1,142
Int. Exp.	800	730	650	445	431	453	513	203	183	217
Pretax Inc.	550	1,353	3,565	2,999	3,324	1,397	-341	1,363	360	1,143
Eff. Tax Rate	NM	63.6%	20.7%	29.0%	30.5%	19.8%	NM	19.7%	NM	25.1%
Net Inc.	718	492	2,827	2,128	2,309	1,120	-178	1,095	393	856
S&P Core Earnings	1,074	203	284	NA	NA	NA	NA	NA	NA	NA

Balance Sheet & Other Fin. Data (Million $)

	2003	2002	2001	2000	1999	1998	1997	1996	1995	1994
Cash	4,633	2,333	633	1,010	3,354	2,462	4,420	5,258	3,730	2,643
Curr. Assets	17,258	16,855	16,206	15,864	15,712	16,375	19,263	15,080	13,178	10,414
Total Assets	53,035	52,342	48,343	42,028	36,147	36,672	38,024	27,254	22,098	21,463
Curr. Liab.	18,448	19,810	20,486	18,289	13,656	13,422	14,152	8,642	7,415	6,827
LT Debt	13,299	12,589	10,866	7,567	5,980	6,103	6,123	3,980	2,344	2,603
Common Equity	8,139	7,696	10,825	11,020	11,462	12,316	12,953	10,941	9,898	9,700
Total Cap.	21,438	20,285	21,868	18,587	17,614	18,419	19,076	14,921	12,242	12,354
Cap. Exp.	741	1,001	1,068	932	1,236	1,584	1,391	726	629	795
Cash Flow	2,168	1,989	4,577	3,607	3,954	2,742	1,280	2,086	1,369	1,998
Curr. Ratio	0.9	0.9	0.8	0.9	1.2	1.2	1.4	1.8	1.8	1.5
% LT Debt of Cap.	62.0	62.1	49.7	40.7	34.0	33.1	47.2	26.7	19.1	21.1
% Net Inc.of Revs.	1.4	0.9	4.9	4.1	4.0	2.0	NM	4.8	2.0	3.9
% Ret. on Assets	1.4	1.0	6.2	5.4	6.3	3.0	NM	4.4	1.8	4.1
% Ret. on Equity	9.1	5.3	25.9	18.9	19.4	8.9	NM	10.5	4.0	9.2

Data as orig reptd.; bef. results of disc opers/spec. items. Per share data adj. for stk. divs.; EPS diluted. E-Estimated. NA-Not Available. NM-Not Meaningful. NR-Not Ranked. UR-Under Review.

Office: 100 N. Riverside, Chicago, IL 60606.
Telephone: 312-544-2000 .
Website: http://www.boeing.com
Chrmn: L. Platt.
Pres & CEO: H. Stonecipher.
EVP & CFO: J.A. Bell.

SVP & General Counsel: D.G. Bain.
Investor Contact: P. Kinscherff 312-544-2140.
Dirs: J. H. Biggs, J. E. Bryson, L. Cook, K. M. Duberstein, P. E. Gray, J. F. McDonnell, W. J. McNerney, Jr., L. E. Platt, R. L. Ridgway, J. M. Shalikashvili, H. C. Stonecipher, M. S. Zafirovski.

Founded: in 1934.
Domicile: Delaware.
Employees: 157,000.
S&P Analyst: Robert E. Friedman, CPA /DC/JWP

Boston Scientific

Recommendation: **BUY** ★★★★☆
SELL | SELL | HOLD | BUY | BUY

12-Month Target Price: **$44.00**
(as of September 08, 2004)

BSX has an approximate 0.26% weighting in the **S&P 500**

Sector: Health Care
Sub-Industry: Health Care Equipment
Peer Group: Large Multi-Line Medical Device Manufacturers

Summary: BSX is a leading manufacturer of minimally invasive medical devices used in interventional cardiology, radiology and other medical applications.

Quantitative Evaluations

Price as of 11/12/04: $34.70 **2004E S&P Core EPS:** $1.46

S&P Earnings & Dividend Rank: B

| D | C | B- | **B** | B+ | A- | A | A+ |

S&P Fair Value Rank: 4-

| 1 | 2 | 3 | **4** | 5 |
| Lowest | | | | Highest |

Fair Value Calc.: $39.40 (Slightly Undervalued)

S&P Investability Quotient Percentile

89%

BSX scored higher than 89% of all companies for which an S&P Report is available.

Volatility: Average

| Low | **Average** | High |

Technical Evaluation: Bearish

Since 10/04, the technical indicators for BSX have been Bearish.

Relative Strength Rank: Weak

14

| 1 Lowest | Highest 99 |

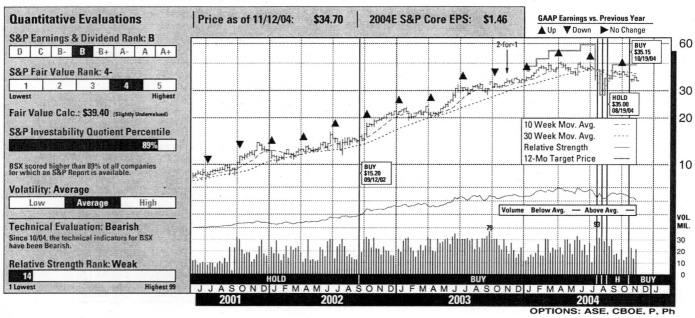

GAAP Earnings vs. Previous Year
▲ Up ▼ Down ► No Change

10 Week Mov. Avg.
30 Week Mov. Avg.
Relative Strength
12-Mo Target Price

Volume Below Avg. — Above Avg. —

OPTIONS: ASE, CBOE, P, Ph

Analyst commentary prepared by Robert M. Gold/PMW/JWP

Highlights October 20, 2004

- In July and August 2004, BSX recalled about 100,000 Taxus coronary stents and 11,000 Express2 stent systems, to address a problem with balloon deployment that occurred in a small percentage of the products. The FDA subsequently validated the manufacturing plants, and no confirmed cases of balloon non-deployment have occurred since the company altered its manufacturing and inspection processes. In our opinion, BSX will remain the leading seller of drug-coated stents in the U.S. through 2006.

- We see 2004 revenues of $5.5 billion, as significant contributions from the Taxus product combine with projected growth in electrophysiology, gastroenterology, neuro-endovascular therapy, urology, and vascular surgery. For Taxus alone, we see 2004 worldwide sales approximating $2.2 billion. We project gross margins of 78.0%. We expect SG&A costs to consume 30% to 32% of revenues, but we see R&D spending rising less rapidly than sales in 2004 and into 2005. Looking to 2005, we believe revenues will approximate $6.6 billion.

Investment Rationale/Risk October 20, 2004

- We expect the stock to be volatile, amid some lingering market concerns regarding the safety of the Taxus stent and uncertainties about the company's growth prospects beyond 2005. However, BSX quickly recaptured coronary stent market share in the 2004 third quarter. In dollar terms, we estimate that the company had a 64% share of the U.S. market and a 47% share of the non-U.S. market at September 30, 2004, for a worldwide market share of about 59%. Although we believe the stock will continue to trade at a discount to cardiovascular device peers until there is greater visibility regarding growth drivers after Taxus, we would accumulate the shares, trading recently at 16.5X our 2005 EPS estimate, nearly a 30% discount to peers.

Key Stock Statistics

S&P Core EPS 2005E	2.00	52-week Range	$46.10-31.25
S&P Oper. EPS 2004E	1.61	12 Month P/E	33.0
P/E on S&P Oper. EPS 2004E	21.6	Beta	0.46
S&P Oper. EPS 2005E	2.20	Shareholders	8,798
Yield (%)	Nil	Market Cap (B)	$ 29.3
Dividend Rate/Share	Nil	Shares Outstanding (M)	844.5

Value of $10,000 invested five years ago: $ 34,596

Dividend Data

Dividends have never been paid.

Revenues/Earnings Data Fiscal year ending December 31

Revenues (Million $)

	2004	2003	2002	2001	2000	1999
1Q	1,082	807.0	675.0	654.0	679.0	708.0
2Q	1,460	854.0	708.0	672.0	695.0	726.0
3Q	1,482	876.0	722.0	670.0	652.0	691.0
4Q	—	939.0	814.0	677.0	638.0	717.0
Yr.	—	3,476	2,919	2,673	2,664	2,842

Earnings Per Share ($)

	2004	2003	2002	2001	2000	1999
1Q	0.23	0.12	0.10	-0.01	0.13	0.13
2Q	0.36	0.14	0.03	-0.21	0.15	0.14
3Q	0.30	0.15	0.20	0.07	0.11	0.07
4Q	E0.47	0.16	0.13	0.08	0.08	0.13
Yr.	E1.61	0.56	0.45	-0.07	0.46	0.45

Next earnings report expected: early-February Source: S&P, Company Reports
EPS Estimates based on S&P Operating Earnings; historical GAAP earnings are as reported.

Boston Scientific Corporation

Recommendation: **BUY** ★★★★☆   12-Month Target Price: **$44.00** (as of September 08, 2004)

Business Summary October 20, 2004

Boston Scientific develops and markets minimally invasive medical devices that are used in a broad range of interventional medical specialties, including interventional cardiology, peripheral intervention, neurovascular, electrophysiology, gastroenterology, gynecology, oncology and urology. About 45% of 2003 sales were derived outside the U.S.

In 2003, 72% of sales came from the cardiovascular business. The company sells products used to treat the coronary vessel disease known as atherosclerosis. The majority of BSX's cardiovascular products are used in percutaneous transluminal coronary angioplasty (PTCA) and percutaneous transluminal coronary rotational atherectomy. These products include PTCA balloon catheters, rotational atherectomy systems, guide wires, guide catheters, and diagnostic catheters and, more recently, a cutting balloon catheter. Other products include thrombectomy catheters, peripheral vascular stents, embolic protection filters, blood clot filter systems, and electrophysiology products such as catheters and systems for use in less-invasive procedures to diagnose abnormally fast heart rhythms.

BSX also markets balloon-expandable and self-expanding coronary stent systems. Stents are tiny mesh tubes that are used in the treatment of coronary artery disease. They are implanted in patients to prop open arteries and facilitate blood flow to the heart. In 2002, the company launched its Express 2 coronary stent system, featuring both the Express stent and the Maverick balloon dilatation catheter. In March 2004, BSX gained FDA approval and subsequently launched TAXUS, which is essentially an Express stent coated with a polymer embedded with the anti-cancer compound paclitaxel. Clinical studies showed that this stent significantly reduced the rate of instent restenosis, or vessel reclosure, that occurs in about one-third of patients who undergo angioplasty and stenting. The Taxus approval covered stent sizes ranging from 2.5 millimeters to 3.5 millimeters in diameter, and 8 millimeters to 32 millimeters in length. BSX believed these sizes would cover 85% to 90% of all potential patients.

The endosurgery product line (28%) includes devices to diagnose, treat and palliate gastrointestinal diseases and conditions such as esophagitis, gastric esophageal reflux disease, peptic ulcers, esophageal cancer, polyps, inflammatory bowel disease, diverticulitis, and colon cancer. BSX also sells products used for benign and malignant structures of the pancreatico-biliary system, and to remove stones found in the common bile duct, as well as devices that address chronic bronchitis and lung cancer, urinary tract infections, prostate cancer, and urinary incontinence and bladder disease.

R&D spending totaled $452 million in 2003, equal to 13.0% of sales, with a focus on development of the Taxus coronary stent.

In June 2004, BSX agreed to acquire privately held Advanced Bionics Corp. for $740 million in cash plus potential milestone payments based on sales targets. Advanced Bionics has developed implantable microelectronics for treating neurological disorders.

Company Financials Fiscal Year ending December 31

Per Share Data ($)

(Year Ended December 31)	2003	2002	2001	2000	1999	1998	1997	1996	1995	1994
Tangible Bk. Val.	0.49	0.12	NM	0.33	NM	NM	0.87	0.85	0.89	0.79
Cash Flow	0.79	0.64	0.22	0.68	0.67	-0.18	0.31	0.32	0.07	0.23
Earnings	0.56	0.45	-0.07	0.46	0.45	-0.34	0.20	0.23	0.01	0.20
S&P Core Earnings	0.50	0.33	-0.10	NA	NA	NA	NA	NA	NA	NA
Dividends	Nil	Nil	Nil	Nil	Nil	Nil	Nil	Nil	Nil	Nil
Payout Ratio	Nil	Nil	Nil	Nil	Nil	Nil	Nil	Nil	Nil	Nil
Prices - High	36.85	22.15	13.94	14.59	23.53	20.42	19.59	15.37	12.34	4.46
- Low	19.10	10.24	6.62	6.09	8.78	10.06	10.25	9.43	4.15	2.96
P/E Ratio - High	66	49	NM	32	52	NM	112	67	NM	22
- Low	34	23	NM	13	20	NM	59	41	NM	15

Income Statement Analysis (Million $)

	2003	2002	2001	2000	1999	1998	1997	1996	1995	1994
Revs.	3,476	2,919	2,673	2,664	2,842	2,234	1,872	1,462	1,107	449
Oper. Inc.	1,451	757	614	819	857	-93.8	502	403	781	139
Depr.	196	161	232	181	178	129	86.7	61.4	39.5	9.10
Int. Exp.	46.0	43.0	59.0	70.0	118	67.6	14.3	11.2	8.20	2.04
Pretax Inc.	643	549	44.0	527	562	-274	259	297	85.8	129
Eff. Tax Rate	26.6%	32.1%	NM	29.2%	34.0%	NM	38.0%	43.7%	90.2%	38.2%
Net Inc.	472	373	-54.0	373	371	-263	160	167	8.40	79.7
S&P Core Earnings	423	269	-77.0	NA	NA	NA	NA	NA	NA	NA

Balance Sheet & Other Fin. Data (Million $)

	2003	2002	2001	2000	1999	1998	1997	1996	1995	1994
Cash	671	277	180	54.0	64.0	70.3	58.0	75.5	115	118
Curr. Assets	1,880	1,208	1,106	992	1,055	1,267	1,064	749	537	264
Total Assets	5,699	4,450	3,974	3,427	3,572	3,893	1,968	1,512	1,075	432
Curr. Liab.	1,393	923	831	819	1,055	1,620	808	464	271	73.7
LT Debt	1,172	847	973	562	678	1,364	46.3	Nil	13.2	8.90
Common Equity	2,854	2,467	2,015	1,935	1,724	821	986	916	752	340
Total Cap.	4,177	3,414	2,988	2,497	2,402	2,185	1,091	976	765	355
Cap. Exp.	188	112	121	76.0	80.0	174	220	135	68.6	35.8
Cash Flow	668	534	178	554	549	-135	247	229	47.9	88.8
Curr. Ratio	1.3	1.3	1.3	1.2	1.0	0.8	1.3	1.6	2.0	3.6
% LT Debt of Cap.	28.1	24.8	32.6	22.5	28.2	62.4	4.2	Nil	1.7	2.5
% Net Inc.of Revs.	13.6	12.8	NM	14.0	13.1	9.6	8.6	11.4	1.0	17.8
% Ret. on Assets	9.3	8.9	NM	10.7	9.9	NM	9.2	12.7	1.0	21.1
% Ret. on Equity	17.8	16.6	NM	20.4	29.2	NM	16.9	19.8	1.1	27.2

Data as orig reptd.; bef. results of disc opers/spec. items. Per share data adj. for stk. divs. Bold denotes primary EPS - prior periods restated. E-Estimated. NA-Not Available. NM-Not Meaningful. NR-Not Ranked. UR-Under Review.

Office: One Boston Scientific Place, Natick, MA 01760-1537.
Telephone: 508-650-8000.
Email: investor_relations@bsci.com
Website: http://www.bsci.com
Chrmn: P.M. Nicholas.
Pres & CEO: J.R. Tobin.

SVP & CFO: L.C. Best.
SVP, Secy & General Counsel: P.W. Sandman.
Investor Contact: M. Kofol 508-650-8569.
Dirs: J. E. Abele, U. M. Burns, J. A. Ciffolillo, J. L. Fleishman, M. A. Fox, R. J. Groves, E. Mario, P. M. Nicholas, N. J. Nicholas, Jr., J. E. Pepper, U. E. Reinhardt, W. B. Rudman, J. R. Tobin.

Founded: in 1979.
Domicile: Delaware.
Employees: 15,000.
S&P Analyst: Robert M. Gold/PMW/JWP

Bristol-Myers Squibb

Recommendation: **SELL** ★ ★ ☆ ☆ ☆
SELL SELL HOLD BUY BUY
(as of July 29, 2004)

12-Month Target Price: $21.00

BMY has an approximate 0.43% weighting in the **S&P 500**

Sector: Health Care
Sub-Industry: Pharmaceuticals
Peer Group: Health Care Diversified

Summary: This leading global drugmaker is strong in both prescription and nonprescription products.

Quantitative Evaluations

S&P Earnings & Dividend Rank: A

| D | C | B- | B | B+ | A- | **A** | A+ |

S&P Fair Value Rank: 1

| **1** | 2 | 3 | 4 | 5 |
| Lowest | | | | Highest |

Fair Value Calc.: $19.60 (Overvalued)

S&P Investability Quotient Percentile
95%

BMY scored higher than 95% of all companies for which an S&P Report is available.

Volatility: Low

| **Low** | Average | High |

Technical Evaluation: Bullish
Since 11/04, the technical indicators for BMY have been Bullish.

Relative Strength Rank: Moderate
41
1 Lowest — Highest 99

Price as of 11/15/04: $24.31 | **2004E S&P Core EPS:** $1.51

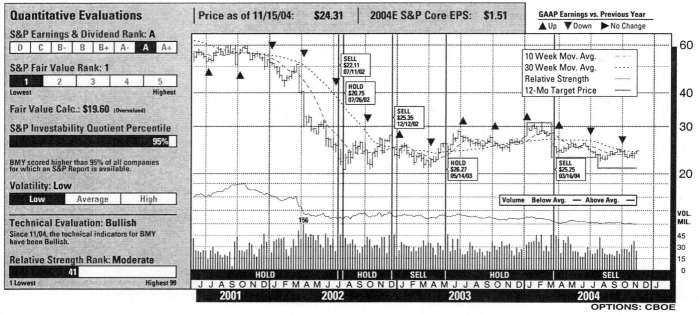

GAAP Earnings vs. Previous Year
▲ Up ▼ Down ► No Change

10 Week Mov. Avg.
30 Week Mov. Avg.
Relative Strength
12-Mo Target Price

Volume Below Avg. — Above Avg.

SELL $22.11 07/11/02
HOLD $20.75 07/26/02
SELL $25.35 12/12/02
HOLD $26.27 05/14/03
SELL $25.25 03/16/04

VOL. MIL.

HOLD | HOLD | SELL | HOLD | SELL
J J A S O N D | J F M A M J J A S O N D | J F M A M J J A S O N D | J F M A M J J A S O N D | J F M A M J J A S O N D | J
2001 | 2002 | 2003 | 2004
OPTIONS: CBOE

Analyst commentary prepared by H. B. Saftlas/PMW/BK

Highlights 16-NOV-04

- Largely reflecting ongoing sales erosion in patent expired drugs, we believe total revenues in 2005 will be little changed from the $21.4 billion that we estimate for 2004. Key drugs being affected by patent expirations either in the U.S. or abroad include Pravachol cholesterol-lowering agent, Paraplatin and Taxol anticancer agents, Monopril heart drug, Zerit HIV treatment, and Glucophage/Glucovance diabetes drugs. On the positive side, we see another year of strong growth for Plavix anti-platelet therapy, as well as growing momentum in newer products such as Abilify anti-psychotic, Reyataz HIV/AIDS therapy, and Erbitux anticancer (sold under license from Imclone Systems). We see sales of distributed oncology products increasing, but expect relatively flat sales for consumer and nutritional products.
- We expect gross margins to narrow in 2005, due to projected declines in sales of older, higher-margin products. Operating results are also likely to remain under pressure from heavy R&D and new product launch costs. We expect other income to decline, but the effective tax rate will probably be modestly lower.
- We project 2005 operating EPS of $1.40, down from $1.60 that we see for 2004. After estimated option and pension expenses, we project 2005 S&P Core EPS of $1.31, down from $1.51 expected in 2004.

Key Stock Statistics

S&P Core EPS 2005E	1.31	52-week Range	$31.30-22.22
S&P Oper. EPS 2004E	1.60	12 Month P/E	17.5
P/E on S&P Oper. EPS 2004E	15.2	Beta	0.43
S&P Oper. EPS 2005E	1.40	Shareholders	96,752
Yield (%)	4.6%	Market Cap (B)	$ 47.3
Dividend Rate/Share	1.12	Shares Outstanding (M)	1945.6

Value of $10,000 invested five years ago: **NA**

Dividend Data Dividends have been paid since 1900

Amount ($)	Date Decl.	Ex-Div. Date	Stock of Record	Payment Date
0.280	Dec. 09	Dec. 30	Jan. 02	Feb. 02 '04
0.280	Mar. 02	Mar. 31	Apr. 02	May. 03 '04
0.280	Jun. 08	Jun. 30	Jul. 02	Aug. 02 '04
0.280	Sep. 15	Sep. 29	Oct. 01	Nov. 01 '04

Investment Rationale/Risk 16-NOV-04

- BMY posted stronger than expected third quarter operating EPS of $0.44, buoyed by favorable foreign exchange, lighter than expected spending on SG&A and R&D, and a lower effective tax rate. Sales of Plavix remained strong, but sales of Pravachol continued to erode, and generic competition grew in other lines. The company faces a generic challenge to Plavix, expected to be litigated in 2005. We believe BMY has surpassed many of its peers on the new product front, with a string of successful launches and what we view as a fairly good R&D pipeline. However, we are concerned that new products may not offset the expected impact from patent expirations of about $1.1 billion annually over the next few years. We see this leading to flat to lower EPS in 2004 to 2007. Although maintenance of the dividend appears to be a high management priority, we are not convinced that a payout over 70% is sustainable. Our recommendation is sell.
- Risks to our opinion and target price include stronger than expected sales and profits from new products, and a possible takeover of the company.
- Our 12-month target price of $21 is based on applying a peer group P/E multiple of 15X to our 2005 EPS estimate. Our DCF model also calculates intrinsic value of about $21, assuming flat cash flows over the next three years and a weighted average cost of capital of 8.3%.

Revenues/Earnings Data Fiscal year ending December 31

Revenues (Million $)

	2004	2003	2002	2001	2000	1999
1Q	5,181	4,728	4,661	4,689	5,260	4,854
2Q	5,430	5,129	4,127	4,709	4,418	4,920
3Q	5,427	5,372	4,537	4,743	4,563	5,050
4Q	—	5,665	4,794	5,282	4,784	5,408
Yr.	—	20,894	18,119	19,423	18,216	20,222

Earnings Per Share ($)

	2004	2003	2002	2001	2000	1999
1Q	0.49	0.41	0.43	0.63	0.56	0.53
2Q	0.27	0.46	0.25	0.56	0.50	0.47
3Q	0.38	0.47	0.17	0.63	0.45	0.54
4Q	E0.35	0.26	0.19	-0.54	0.54	0.52
Yr.	E1.60	1.59	1.05	1.29	2.36	2.06

Next earnings report expected: late-January Source: S&P, Company Reports
EPS Estimates based on S&P Operating Earnings; historical GAAP earnings are as reported.

STANDARD &POOR'S

Bristol-Myers Squibb Company

Stock Report
November 16, 2004
NYSE Symbol: **BMY**

Recommendation: **SELL** ★ ★ ☆ ☆ ☆   12-Month Target Price: **$21.00** (as of July 29, 2004)

Business Summary 16-NOV-04

Bristol-Myers Squibb, which traces its roots to companies formed in the second half of the 19th century, was formed via the merger of Bristol-Myers and Squibb Corp. in 1989. The company ranks among the world's largest pharmaceutical concerns, offering a wide range of prescription and OTC products. In recent years, BMY divested its Clairol beauty care and Zimmer orthopedic device subsidiaries, in an effort to focus on wider margin prescription pharmaceuticals. In October 2001, the company acquired DuPont Pharmaceuticals, for $7.8 billion.

Prescription pharmaceuticals accounted for 83% of sales in 2003, nutritionals 9%, medical devices 6%, and consumer health care 2%.

BMY is a global leader in chemotherapy drugs, and ranks near the top in cardiovasculars and antibiotics. The company's principal cardiovascular product is Pravachol cholesterol-reducing agent (sales of $2.8 billion in 2003). Other heart drugs include Monopril antihypertensive ($470 million) and Coumadin anticoagulant ($303 million). Through a joint venture with Sanofi SA, BMY produces Plavix ($2.5 billion), a platelet aggregation inhibitor for the prevention of stroke, heart attack, and vascular disease; and Avapro ($757 million), an angiotensin II receptor blocker for hypertension. Principal anticancer drugs consist of Paraplatin ($905 million), Taxol ($934 million), VePesid and Platinol. Through its Oncology Therapeutics Network ($2.2 billion), the company distributes specialty anticancer medicines and related products.

The company offers a wide variety of of anti-infective drugs, including Sustiva ($544 million), Videx, Zerit and Reyataz AIDS therapeutics, and Duricef/Ultracef, Cefzil, Tequin, Maxipime and Megace antibiotics; and central nervous system agents, including Serzone antidepressant, Buspar anti-anxiety agent, and Stadol NS analgesic. Other prescription pharmaceuticals include Abilify anti-psychotic agent; Glucophage XR ($395 million), Glucovance ($424 million), Glucophage IR, and Avandia diabetes treatments; Vaniqa topical facial hair remover; and various other dermatological products.

Nutritionals include infant formulas such as Enfamil and ProSobee, vitamins, and nutritional supplements. Consumer medications include OTC analgesics such as Bufferin, Excedrin and Comtrex cough/cold remedies; and skin care items. Convatec offers ostomy and wound care products.

R&D spending totaled $2.3 billion (11% of sales) in 2003. The company has more than 50 drugs in development. Key compounds include Entecavir for hepatitis B, Erbitux anti-cancer therapy, CTLA4-Ig for rheumatoid arthritis and multiple sclerosis, Muraglitazar for type 2 diabetes, as well as treatments for organ transplants, deep vein thrombosis, infectious diseases, migraine, inflammation, pain, and skin problems.

Company Financials Fiscal Year ending December 31

Per Share Data ($)

(Year Ended December 31)	2003	2002	2001	2000	1999	1998	1997	1996	1995	1994
Tangible Bk. Val.	1.62	0.88	1.70	3.96	3.61	3.01	2.81	2.53	2.28	2.34
Cash Flow	1.99	1.43	1.68	2.42	2.39	1.85	1.86	1.68	1.12	1.07
Earnings	1.59	1.05	1.29	2.36	2.06	1.55	1.57	1.42	0.90	0.91
S&P Core Earnings	1.57	1.07	0.67	NA	NA	NA	NA	NA	NA	NA
Dividends	1.12	1.12	1.10	0.98	0.86	0.78	0.77	0.75	0.74	0.73
Payout Ratio	70%	107%	85%	42%	42%	50%	49%	53%	83%	81%
Prices - High	29.21	51.95	73.50	74.87	79.25	67.62	49.09	29.09	21.78	15.25
- Low	21.00	19.49	48.50	42.43	57.25	44.15	26.62	19.50	14.43	12.50
P/E Ratio - High	18	49	57	32	38	44	31	20	24	17
- Low	13	19	38	18	28	29	17	14	16	14

Income Statement Analysis (Million $)

	2003	2002	2001	2000	1999	1998	1997	1996	1995	1994
Revs.	20,894	18,119	19,423	18,216	20,222	18,284	16,701	15,065	13,767	11,984
Oper. Inc.	5,726	4,851	7,034	6,732	6,531	5,746	5,029	4,472	4,063	3,549
Depr.	779	735	781	746	678	625	591	519	448	328
Int. Exp.	277	410	182	108	130	154	118	93.0	112	83.0
Pretax Inc.	4,694	2,647	2,986	5,478	5,767	4,268	4,482	4,013	2,402	2,555
Eff. Tax Rate	25.9%	16.4%	15.4%	25.2%	27.7%	26.4%	28.5%	29.0%	24.6%	27.9%
Net Inc.	3,106	2,034	2,527	4,096	4,167	3,141	3,205	2,850	1,812	1,842
S&P Core Earnings	3,043	2,076	1,321	NA	NA	NA	NA	NA	NA	NA

Balance Sheet & Other Fin. Data (Million $)

	2003	2002	2001	2000	1999	1998	1997	1996	1995	1994
Cash	5,457	3,989	5,654	3,385	2,957	2,529	1,794	2,185	2,178	2,423
Curr. Assets	11,918	9,975	12,349	9,824	9,267	8,782	7,736	7,528	7,018	6,710
Total Assets	27,471	24,874	27,057	17,578	17,114	16,272	14,977	14,685	13,929	12,910
Curr. Liab.	7,530	8,220	8,826	5,632	5,537	5,791	5,032	5,050	4,806	4,274
LT Debt	8,522	6,261	6,237	1,336	1,342	1,364	1,279	966	635	644
Common Equity	19,572	8,967	10,736	9,180	8,645	7,576	7,219	6,570	5,821	5,703
Total Cap.	28,094	15,228	16,973	10,516	9,987	8,940	8,498	7,536	6,457	6,348
Cap. Exp.	937	997	1,023	589	709	788	767	601	513	573
Cash Flow	3,885	2,769	3,308	4,842	4,845	3,766	3,796	3,369	2,260	2,170
Curr. Ratio	1.6	1.2	1.4	1.7	1.7	1.5	1.5	1.5	1.5	1.6
% LT Debt of Cap.	30.3	41.1	36.7	12.7	13.4	15.3	15.1	12.8	9.8	10.1
% Net Inc.of Revs.	14.9	11.2	13.0	22.5	20.6	17.2	19.2	18.9	13.2	15.4
% Ret. on Assets	11.8	7.7	11.3	23.6	25.0	20.1	21.6	19.9	13.5	14.8
% Ret. on Equity	16.8	22.5	25.4	46.0	51.4	42.5	46.5	46.0	31.4	31.8

Data as orig reptd.; bef. results of disc opers/spec. items. Per share data adj. for stk. divs.; EPS diluted. E-Estimated. NA-Not Available. NM-Not Meaningful. NR-Not Ranked. UR-Under Review.

Office: 345 Park Avenue, New York, NY 10154-0037.
Telephone: 212-546-4000.
Website: http://www.bms.com
Chrmn & CEO: P. R. Dolan, Jr.
SVP & CFO: A. R. Bonfield.
EVP & General Counsel: J. L. McGoldrick.

EVP: D. J. Hayden, Jr.
Investor Contact: John Elicker (212-546-3775).
Dirs: R. E. Allen, L. B. Campbell, V. D. Coffman, P. R. Dolan, E. V. Futter, L. V. Gerstner, Jr., L. H. Glimcher, L. Johansson, J. D. Robinson III, L. W. Sullivan.

Founded: in 1887.
Domicile: Delaware.
Employees: 44,000.
S&P Analyst: H. B. Saftlas/PMW/BK

Broadcom Corp.

Recommendation: **HOLD** ★★★★★
SELL SELL HOLD BUY BUY

12-Month Target Price: **$31.00**
(as of September 13, 2004)

BRCM has an approximate 0.09% weighting in the **S&P 500**

Sector: Information Technology
Sub-Industry: Semiconductors
Peer Group: Semiconductors Communications IC

Summary: BRCM provides semiconductors for broadband communications markets, including cable set-top boxes, cable modems, office networks and home networking.

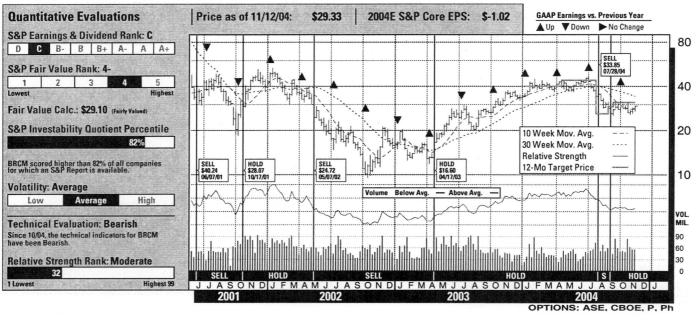

| Quantitative Evaluations | Price as of 11/12/04: $29.33 | 2004E S&P Core EPS: $-1.02 | GAAP Earnings vs. Previous Year ▲ Up ▼ Down ► No Change |

S&P Earnings & Dividend Rank: C
D **C** B- B B+ A- A A+

S&P Fair Value Rank: 4-
1 2 3 **4** 5
Lowest   Highest

Fair Value Calc.: $29.10 (Fairly Valued)

S&P Investability Quotient Percentile
82%

BRCM scored higher than 82% of all companies for which an S&P Report is available.

Volatility: Average
Low **Average** High

Technical Evaluation: Bearish
Since 10/04, the technical indicators for BRCM have been Bearish.

Relative Strength Rank: Moderate
32
1 Lowest   Highest 99

10 Week Mov. Avg. – – –
30 Week Mov. Avg. ·······
Relative Strength ——
12-Mo Target Price ——

Analyst commentary prepared by Amrit Tewary/MF/BK

OPTIONS: ASE, CBOE, P, Ph

Highlights October 28, 2004

■ We expect sales to climb 49% in 2004, and 5.5% in 2005, reflecting a multi-year expansion that we see for the semiconductor industry. BRCM's chips enable broadband digital transmission and networking of voice, video and data signals in home and office environments. We see gross margin widening to 51% in 2004 and 52% in 2005, from 50% in 2003. We expect R&D expenses and SG&A costs to narrow as a percentage of sales during 2004 and 2005.

■ We believe BRCM has succeeded in diversifying its product line via an acquisition campaign over the past few years. On May 10, the company closed on its acquisition of Widcomm, a provider of Bluetooth wireless solutions, for about $49 million in cash.

■ Pro forma EPS (excluding acquisition- and restructuring-related and other special charges) of $0.49 in 2003 contrasted with a reported GAAP loss per share of $3.29. We estimate pro forma EPS of $1.21 (GAAP EPS $0.48) for 2004. We project pro forma EPS of $1.35 (GAAP EPS $0.63) for 2005. We do not expect profitability on a Standard & Poor's Core Earnings basis at least through 2006.

Investment Rationale/Risk October 28, 2004

■ We would hold BRCM shares. Following a significant share price decline in recent months, we believe current price levels appropriately reflect our concerns about the moderating growth we see and our view of the company's relatively low earnings quality, indicated by BRCM's above-peer stock option expense.

■ Risks to our opinion and target price include unanticipated fluctuations in end demand; semiconductor industry cyclicality; competition; and above-average share price volatility.

■ Our 12-month target price of $31 is based on our historical P/E and price-to-sales analyses. Our target price applies a P/E of 26X, below historical norms, to our forward 12-month pro forma EPS estimate of $1.19. Also, our target price applies a price-to-sales ratio of 4.3X, which is well below the stock's three-year average ratio of 6.0X, to our 2005 sales per share estimate. Given our above concerns and noting the past tendency of chip stocks to trade at relatively low multiples during peak or near-peak EPS years, we think BRCM will continue to trade at a discount to historical norms over the next 12 months.

Key Stock Statistics

S&P Core EPS 2005E	-0.87	52-week Range	$47.05-25.25
S&P Oper. EPS 2004E	1.21	12 Month P/E	57.5
P/E on S&P Oper. EPS 2004E	24.2	Beta	NA
S&P Oper. EPS 2005E	1.35	Shareholders	2,187
Yield (%)	Nil	Market Cap (B)	$ 7.9
Dividend Rate/Share	Nil	Shares Outstanding (M)	329.1

Value of $10,000 invested five years ago: **$ 3,772**

Dividend Data

No cash dividends have been paid.

Revenues/Earnings Data Fiscal year ending December 31

Revenues (Million $)

	2004	2003	2002	2001	2000	1999
1Q	573.4	327.5	238.8	310.5	191.6	96.32
2Q	641.3	377.9	258.2	210.9	245.2	116.3
3Q	646.5	425.6	290.0	213.6	319.2	138.3
4Q	—	479.1	295.9	226.8	340.2	160.8
Yr.	—	1,610	1,083	961.8	1,096	518.2

Earnings Per Share ($)

	2004	2003	2002	2001	2000	1999
1Q	0.12	-0.25	-0.63	-1.43	0.15	0.10
2Q	0.18	-3.08	-0.49	-1.73	0.22	0.02
3Q	0.14	-0.02	-0.68	-6.36	-0.06	0.12
4Q	E0.22	0.02	-6.40	-1.27	-3.28	0.15
Yr.	E1.21	-3.29	-8.35	-10.79	-3.13	0.36

Next earnings report expected: late-January Source: S&P, Company Reports
EPS Estimates based on S&P Operating Earnings; historical GAAP earnings are as reported.

STANDARD &POOR'S

Broadcom Corporation

Stock Report
November 13, 2004
NASDAQ Symbol: **BRCM**

Recommendation: **HOLD** ★ ★ ★ ☆ ☆   12-Month Target Price: **$31.00** (as of September 13, 2004)

Business Summary October 28, 2004

Founded in 1991, Broadcom designs, develops and supplies semiconductor products that address business and consumer demand for high-speed access to multimedia information and entertainment content consisting of voice, video and data.

The company's integrated circuits (ICs) address all major broadband communications markets, including digital cable and direct broadcast satellite set-top boxes; cable and DSL modems; high-speed transmission and switching for local, metropolitan, wide area and storage networking; home and wireless networking; wireless communications; Voice over Internet Protocol (VoIP) gateway and telephony systems; broadband network processors; and system I/O server solutions.

Broadband products mainly consist of high-performance digital signal processing ICs working with analog and mixed-signal ICs, along with related software. According to the company, BRCM aims to make highly integrated, comprehensive systems solutions on single chips or chipsets, reducing board space, simplifying the customer's manufacturing process, lowering the customer's system costs, and boosting performance.

In 2003, 57% of sales (65% in 2002) came from the Enterprise Networking segment, 23% (27%) from Broadband Communications, and 20% (8%) from Mobile and Wireless.

Customers include leading communications equipment and computer companies such as 3Com, Cisco Systems, Echostar, Nortel Networks, IBM, and Scientific-Atlanta. BRCM does most of its business with a small number of customers. In 2003, Hewlett-Packard accounted for 15% (15% in 2002) of sales, Dell 12% (11%); in 2002, Motorola represented 12% of sales and Cisco 10%. In 2003, the five leading customers accounted for 52% of total revenue, similar to 2002 and down from 55% in 2001. The international portion of total sales rose to 26% in 2003, from 25% in 2002.

The company contracts out the manufacture of its chips to foundries located mainly in Southeast Asia. Being a fabless design shop eliminates costs associated with the ownership of wafer fabrication facilities, and permits wide gross margins, but creates a reliance on chip foundries. At the end of 2003, only 8% of the workforce was engaged in manufacturing, with 67% in R&D, 13% in sales, and 12% in administration.

In 2000-2002, the company completed 13 acquisitions, for a total equity consideration of $6.35 billion. In 2002, BRCM acquired Mobilink Telecom Inc., a maker of chipsets and designs for cellular phones, cellular modem cards, and wireless PDAs. In January 2001, it acquired ServerWorks Corp., a leading supplier of high performance I/O (input/output) integrated circuits for servers, workstations and storage platforms. Reacting to a semiconductor industry downturn that developed after a boom in 2000, the company booked impairment of goodwill and other intangible assets equivalent to 117% of revenue in 2002, and 123% in 2001.

Company Financials Fiscal Year ending December 31

Per Share Data ($)

(Year Ended December 31)	2003	2002	2001	2000	1999	1998	1997	1996	1995	1994
Tangible Bk. Val.	2.14	1.41	3.28	4.97	2.38	1.17	0.04	NA	NA	NA
Cash Flow	-2.98	-7.80	-7.30	-2.38	0.42	0.23	0.02	NA	NA	NA
Earnings	-3.29	-8.35	-10.79	-3.13	0.36	0.20	-0.04	NA	NA	NA
S&P Core Earnings	-3.46	-7.61	-10.31	NA	NA	NA	NA	NA	NA	NA
Dividends	Nil	Nil	Nil	Nil	Nil	Nil	NA	NA	NA	NA
Payout Ratio	Nil	Nil	Nil	Nil	Nil	Nil	NA	NA	NA	NA
Prices - High	37.65	53.35	139.50	274.75	144.50	33.75	NA	NA	NA	NA
- Low	11.86	9.52	18.40	74.75	23.12	6.00	NA	NA	NA	NA
P/E Ratio - High	NM	NM	NM	NM	NM	NM	NA	NA	NA	NA
- Low	NM	NM	NM	NM	NM	NM	NA	NA	NA	NA

Income Statement Analysis (Million $)

	2003	2002	2001	2000	1999	1998	1997	1996	1995	1994
Revs.	1,610	1,083	962	1,096	518	203	37.0	NA	NA	NA
Oper. Inc.	-121	-442	-573	-169	157	59.7	0.80	NA	NA	NA
Depr.	90.9	147	889	165	14.0	7.50	3.04	NA	NA	NA
Int. Exp.	Nil	Nil	Nil	Nil	Nil	Nil	Nil	NA	NA	NA
Pretax Inc.	-935	-1,939	-2,799	-692	119	56.0	-1.95	NA	NA	NA
Eff. Tax Rate	NM	NM	NM	NM	30.2%	35.0%	NM	NA	NA	NA
Net Inc.	-960	-2,237	-2,742	-688	83.3	36.4	-1.17	NA	NA	NA
S&P Core Earnings	-1,011	-2,039	-2,617	NA	NA	NA	NA	NA	NA	NA

Balance Sheet & Other Fin. Data (Million $)

	2003	2002	2001	2000	1999	1998	1997	1996	1995	1994
Cash	606	543	540	524	174	62.6	22.1	NA	NA	NA
Curr. Assets	996	722	674	876	391	157	36.5	NA	NA	NA
Total Assets	2,018	2,216	3,623	4,678	585	237	45.2	NA	NA	NA
Curr. Liab.	504	534	412	203	86.1	27.1	10.3	NA	NA	NA
LT Debt	Nil	1.21	4.01	Nil	0.55	Nil	1.60	NA	NA	NA
Common Equity	1,490	1,645	3,207	4,475	499	210	4.78	NA	NA	NA
Total Cap.	1,490	1,646	3,211	4,475	499	210	35.0	NA	NA	NA
Cap. Exp.	47.9	75.2	71.4	80.7	29.2	27.3	NA	NA	NA	NA
Cash Flow	-869	-2,090	-1,853	-523	97.3	43.9	1.87	NA	NA	NA
Curr. Ratio	2.0	1.4	1.6	4.3	4.5	5.8	3.6	NA	NA	NA
% LT Debt of Cap.	Nil	0.1	0.1	Nil	0.1	Nil	4.6	NA	NA	NA
% Net Inc.of Revs.	NM	NM	NM	NM	16.1	17.9	NM	NA	NA	NA
% Ret. on Assets	NM	NM	NM	NM	19.7	25.8	NM	NA	NA	NA
% Ret. on Equity	NM	NM	NM	NM	23.3	33.8	NM	NA	NA	NA

Data as orig reptd.; bef. results of disc opers/spec. items. Per share data adj. for stk. divs.; EPS diluted. E-Estimated. NA-Not Available. NM-Not Meaningful. NR-Not Ranked. UR-Under Review.

Office: 16215 Alton Parkway, Irvine, CA 92618-3616.
Telephone: 949-450-8700.
Email: investorinfo@broadcom.com
Website: http://www.broadcom.com
Chrmn: H. Samueli.
Pres & CEO: A.E. Ross.

VP & CFO: W.J. Ruehle.
VP, Secy & General Counsel: D.A. Dull.
Investor Contact: P. Andrew 949-926-5663.
Dirs: G. L. Farinsky, J. E. Major, A. E. Ross, H. Samueli, R. E. Switz, W. F. Wolfen.

Founded: in 1991.
Domicile: California.
Employees: 2,729.
S&P Analyst: Amrit Tewary/MF/BK

Recommendation: **BUY** ★★★★★   SELL | SELL | HOLD | BUY | BUY   12-Month Target Price: **$57.00**
(as of September 24, 2004)

BF.B has an approximate 0.05% weighting in the **S&P 500**

Sector: Consumer Staples
Sub-Industry: Distillers & Vintners
Peer Group: Wine & Spirits

Summary: This leading distiller and importer of alcoholic beverages markets such brands as Jack Daniel's, Southern Comfort, Korbel and Bolla.

Quantitative Evaluations

S&P Earnings & Dividend Rank: A

| D | C | B- | B | B+ | A- | A | A+ |

S&P Fair Value Rank: 1

| 1 | 2 | 3 | 4 | 5 |
| Lowest | | | | Highest |

Fair Value Calc.: $33.30 (Overvalued)

S&P Investability Quotient Percentile

100%

BF.B scored higher than 100% of all companies for which an S&P Report is available.

Volatility: NA

| Low | Average | High |

Technical Evaluation: NA

Relative Strength Rank: Moderate

| | 47 | |
| 1 Lowest | | Highest 99 |

Price as of 11/12/04: $47.65   **2005E S&P Core EPS: $2.35**

GAAP Earnings vs. Previous Year
▲ Up   ▼ Down   ▶ No Change

- - - 10 Week Mov. Avg.
····· 30 Week Mov. Avg.
—— Relative Strength
—— 12-Mo Target Price

2-for-1

Volume   Below Avg. —   Above Avg. ▬

HOLD   BUY

J J A S O N D | J F M A M J J A S O N D | J F M A M J J A S O N D | J F M A M J J A S O N D | J
2001   2002   2003   2004

Analyst commentary prepared by Anishka Clarke/CB/JWP

Highlights September 29, 2004

- We expect net sales (excluding excise taxes) to increase about 9% in FY 05 (Apr.), reflecting 6.5% growth in the wines and spirits segment, and 1% higher sales in the consumer durables business. We believe Jack Daniel's and Southern Comfort will continue to drive robust spirits sales, while new low-carbohydrate introductions should spur the wine segment. Overall, beverage volumes should benefit further from strong advertising and marketing in FY 05.

- We believe that the strong margin expansion seen in the FY 05 first quarter in the core beverage segment will likely continue throughout the year. Margins should benefit from easing grape cost pressures, an improved U.K. distribution arrangement, and cost-cutting efforts in the consumer durables division. However, we see these benefits partly offset by pricing pressures for wine and costs of increased marketing support. We see improvement in consumer durables, in line with continued economic recovery and more focused strategies.

- Excluding unusual items, we see FY 05 EPS advancing 11%, to $2.49, from $2.24 in FY 04. We project FY 05 Standard & Poor's Core Earnings of $2.35 a share, mainly reflecting pension cost adjustments.

Key Stock Statistics

S&P Oper. EPS 2005E	**2.49**	52-week Range	**$50.00-42.63**
P/E on S&P Oper. EPS 2005E	**19.1**	12 Month P/E	**21.0**
Yield (%)	**1.8%**	Beta	**0.34**
Dividend Rate/Share	**0.85**	Shareholders	**4,161**
Shares Outstanding (M)	**121.8**	Market Cap (B)	**$ 3.1**

Value of $10,000 invested five years ago: **$ 15,176**

Dividend Data Dividends have been paid since 1960

Amount ($)	Date Decl.	Ex-Div. Date	Stock of Record	Payment Date
2-for-1	Jan. 24	Jan. 21	Jan. 12	Jan. 20 '04
0.213	Jan. 22	Mar. 04	Mar. 08	Apr. 01 '04
0.213	May. 27	Jun. 03	Jun. 07	Jul. 01 '04
0.213	Jul. 22	Sep. 02	Sep. 07	Oct. 01 '04

Investment Rationale/Risk September 29, 2004

- We recommend buying the shares, based on our expectation of continued industry outperformance. We believe targeted on-premise marketing and increased media advertising will continue to drive strong industry growth trends in the spirits category. We also think spirits will continue to make successful inroads into the 21- to 27-year-old demographic, with innovative line extensions and affordability. We believe that BF can continue to capitalize on what we see as positive industry factors with its strong portfolio of spirits and international reach, particularly with its Jack Daniel's brand. In addition, we believe the company's commitment to improving distribution and brand building should support outperformance.

- Risks to our recommendation and target price include the potential for an unexpected slowdown in the growth of top-performing brands Jack Daniel's and Southern Comfort.

- Based on our discounted cash flow model using an 8.5% cost of capital, we estimate intrinsic value of the stock at $55. We applied a P/E multiple of 20X, lowered from 22X based on anticipated pressures in beverage multiples and slightly above the stock's historical average, to our calendar 2005 EPS estimate of $2.92. Our new 12-month target price of $57 results from a blend of our DCF and P/E analyses.

Revenues/Earnings Data Fiscal year ending April 30

Revenues (Million $)

	2005	2004	2003	2002	2001	2000
1Q	578.0	532.6	479.0	469.7	466.0	437.3
2Q	—	725.2	692.0	644.1	646.8	643.0
3Q	—	697.0	636.0	570.5	559.0	558.0
4Q	—	625.0	571.0	523.9	444.3	497.7
Yr.	—	2,577	2,378	2,208	1,924	1,877

Earnings Per Share ($)

	2005	2004	2003	2002	2001	2000
1Q	0.42	0.26	0.27	0.29	0.31	0.28
2Q	E0.77	0.73	0.59	0.59	0.59	0.53
3Q	E0.73	0.66	0.51	0.42	0.41	0.40
4Q	E0.61	0.47	0.45	0.38	0.40	0.38
Yr.	E2.49	2.11	1.82	1.66	1.70	1.59

Next earnings report expected: late-November Source: S&P, Company Reports
EPS Estimates based on S&P Operating Earnings; historical GAAP earnings are as reported.

Brown-Forman Corporation

Recommendation: **BUY** ★★★★★ 12-Month Target Price: **$57.00** (as of September 24, 2004)

Business Summary September 29, 2004

Brown-Forman Corp., with origins that date back to 1870, is the world's fourth largest producer of distilled spirits. With a portfolio of well known brands, the company is best known for its popular Jack Daniel's Tennessee Whiskey, which continues to be its largest sales and profit producer. BF also makes consumer products, such as Lenox china, crystal and glassware, and Hartmann luggage, which are included in the consumer durables segment. The wines and spirits segment contributed 96% to operating profits in FY 04 (Apr.), and consumer durables the remaining 4%.

Although many alcoholic beverage companies have moved in recent years to reduce their dependence on the highly mature brown spirits market, BF has remained whiskey-oriented. Its product line is stocked with well known whiskies, bourbons, vodkas, tequila, rum, and liqueur. Brands include Jack Daniel's, Canadian Mist, Southern Comfort, and Early Times. Jack Daniel's volume growth in FY 04 was 6%, with the U.S. market accounting for 55% of its sales. Statistics based on case sales rank Jack Daniel's as the largest selling Tennessee whiskey in the U.S., Canadian Mist as the second largest selling Canadian whisky in the U.S., and Southern Comfort as the largest selling domestic proprietary liqueur in the U.S.

The company's other major alcoholic beverage lines include wine brands such as Fetzer and Bolla wines, and Korbel Champagnes. Despite the on-going over-supply of grapes in California, this segment's profitability has suffered due to high cost long-term grape contracts and a competitive pricing environment.

BF has also been aggressive in launching new products, such as One.6 Chardonnay and One.9 Merlot, introduced in 2004 and targeted to diet-conscious individu-

als. The company added Finlandia vodkas and Michel Picard French wines to its U.S. product portfolio in FY 97. BF's strategy to increase the division's reach includes international expansion and continually introducing successful new products.

Consumer durables consist of china, crystal and giftware, marketed under the Lenox and Gorham trademarks, sold through retail outlets, company-operated stores, catalogs, and the internet. The segment also includes Dansk, a producer of tableware and giftware, Gorham, Kirk Steiff, and Hartmann Luggage. Since January 2004, this division has restructured its operations in an effort to restore profitability and competitiveness.

International sales, consisting principally of exports of wines and spirits, increased 29% in FY 04, to about $684 million, accounting for 19% of total net revenues. Beverage growth in recent years has come primarily from international markets for the company's spirits brands. The key export markets for brands include the U.K., Australia, and South Africa.

In FY 03, BF changed its distribution process in the U.K., its second largest market. The company now sells direct to trade via a cost-sharing arrangement with Bacardi, which it believes allows it to focus more on its brands and improve margins.

In March 2003, the company repurchased 7.9 million common shares for $561 million, via a Dutch Auction tender offer, financed by the issuance of $600 million of debt.

Company Financials Fiscal Year ending April 30

Per Share Data ($)

(Year Ended April 30)	2004	2003	2002	2001	2000	1999	1998	1997	1996	1995
Tangible Bk. Val.	4.29	2.41	7.72	6.75	5.68	4.77	4.04	3.37	2.63	1.97
Cash Flow	2.29	2.21	2.05	2.15	2.03	1.87	1.70	1.58	1.49	1.39
Earnings	2.11	1.82	1.66	1.70	1.59	1.47	1.33	1.23	1.16	1.07
S&P Core Earnings	2.07	1.55	1.39	1.52	NA	NA	NA	NA	NA	NA
Dividends	0.73	0.73	0.68	0.64	0.60	0.58	0.55	0.53	0.51	0.48
Payout Ratio	34%	40%	41%	38%	38%	39%	41%	43%	44%	45%

Cal. Yrs.	2003	2002	2001	2000	1999	1998	1997	1996	1995	1994
Prices - High	47.56	40.27	36.00	34.62	38.62	38.43	27.68	23.75	20.37	16.25
- Low	30.12	29.34	28.82	20.93	27.46	25.87	21.00	17.62	14.68	13.06
P/E Ratio - High	23	22	22	20	24	26	21	19	18	15
- Low	14	16	17	12	17	18	16	14	13	12

Income Statement Analysis (Million $)

	2004	2003	2002	2001	2000	1999	1998	1997	1996	1995
Revs.	2,577	2,378	1,958	1,924	1,877	1,776	1,669	1,584	1,544	1,420
Oper. Inc.	473	429	408	438	410	377	358	337	320	311
Depr.	56.0	55.0	55.0	64.0	62.0	55.0	51.0	50.0	46.0	43.5
Int. Exp.	21.0	8.00	8.00	16.0	15.0	10.0	14.0	17.0	20.0	22.6
Pretax Inc.	388	373	348	366	343	318	296	273	257	247
Eff. Tax Rate	33.5%	34.3%	34.5%	36.3%	36.4%	36.5%	37.5%	38.0%	37.7%	39.8%
Net Inc.	258	245	228	233	218	202	185	169	160	149
S&P Core Earnings	252	209	190	208	NA	NA	NA	NA	NA	NA

Balance Sheet & Other Fin. Data (Million $)

	2004	2003	2002	2001	2000	1999	1998	1997	1996	1995
Cash	68.0	72.0	116	86.0	180	171	78.0	58.0	54.0	62.0
Curr. Assets	1,083	1,068	1,029	994	1,020	999	869	802	768	698
Total Assets	2,376	2,264	2,016	1,939	1,802	1,735	1,494	1,428	1,381	1,286
Curr. Liab.	369	548	495	538	522	517	382	399	303	286
LT Debt	630	629	40.0	40.0	41.0	53.0	50.0	63.0	211	247
Common Equity	1,085	840	1,311	1,187	1,048	917	805	718	622	534
Total Cap.	1,837	1,547	1,409	1,289	1,184	1,107	1,005	975	972	907
Cap. Exp.	56.0	119	71.0	96.0	78.0	46.0	44.0	55.0	59.0	51.1
Cash Flow	314	300	283	297	280	257	235	218	205	192
Curr. Ratio	2.9	1.9	2.1	1.8	2.0	1.9	2.3	2.0	2.5	2.4
% LT Debt of Cap.	34.3	40.7	2.8	3.1	3.5	4.8	4.9	6.4	21.7	27.2
% Net Inc.of Revs.	10.0	10.3	11.6	12.1	11.6	11.4	11.1	10.6	10.4	10.5
% Ret. on Assets	11.1	11.4	11.5	12.5	12.3	12.3	12.7	12.0	12.0	11.8
% Ret. on Equity	26.8	22.8	18.3	20.9	22.2	23.5	24.3	25.2	27.5	30.1

Data as orig reptd.; bef. results of disc opers/spec. items. Per share data adj. for stk. divs.; EPS diluted. E-Estimated. NA-Not Available. NM-Not Meaningful. NR-Not Ranked. UR-Under Review.

Office: 850 Dixie Highway, Louisville, KY 40210-1091.
Telephone: 502-585-1100.
Website: http://www.brown-forman.com
Chrmn & CEO: O. Brown, II.
EVP & CFO: P.A. Wood.

SVP, Secy & General Counsel: M.B. Crutcher.
Investor Contact: L. Whiting .
Dirs: I. B. Bond, B. D. Bramley, O. Brown, II, G. G. Brown, III, D. G. Calder, O. B. Frazier, R. P. Mayer, S. E. O'Neil, M. R. Simmons, W. M. Street, D. B. Stubs, P. C. Varga.

Founded: in 1870.
Domicile: Delaware.
Employees: 6,400.
S&P Analyst: Anishka Clarke/CB/JWP

STANDARD &POOR'S

Brunswick Corp.

Recommendation: **BUY** ★★★★☆
SELL SELL HOLD BUY BUY

12-Month Target Price: **$52.00**
(as of October 08, 2004)

BC has an approximate 0.04% weighting in the **S&P 500**

Sector: Consumer Discretionary
Sub-Industry: Leisure Products
Peer Group: Recreation-related Vehicles

Summary: This leading manufacturer of marine engines and boats also has other recreational businesses.

Quantitative Evaluations

S&P Earnings & Dividend Rank: B

| D | C | B- | **B** | B+ | A- | A | A+ |

S&P Fair Value Rank: 4-

| 1 | 2 | 3 | **4** | 5 |
| Lowest | | | | Highest |

Fair Value Calc.: $49.80 (Fairly Valued)

S&P Investability Quotient Percentile

98%

BC scored higher than 98% of all companies for which an S&P Report is available.

Volatility: Average

| Low | **Average** | High |

Technical Evaluation: Bullish

Since 8/04, the technical indicators for BC have been Bullish.

Relative Strength Rank: Strong

81

| 1 Lowest | | Highest 99 |

| Price as of 11/12/04: | **$49.81** | 2004E S&P Core EPS: | **$2.31** |

GAAP Earnings vs. Previous Year
▲ Up ▼ Down ► No Change

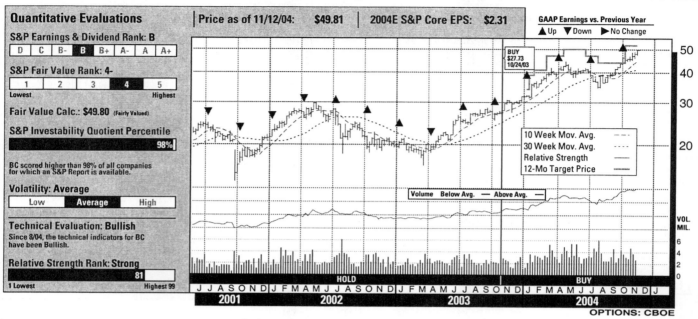

- 10 Week Mov. Avg.
- 30 Week Mov. Avg.
- Relative Strength
- 12-Mo Target Price

Volume Below Avg. — Above Avg.

BUY
$27.73
10/24/03

HOLD   BUY

J J A S O N D | J F M A M J J A S O N D | J F M A M J J A S O N D | J F M A M J J A S O N D | J
2001   2002   2003   2004

OPTIONS: CBOE

Analyst commentary prepared by Jason N. Asaeda/MF/JWP

Highlights November 03, 2004

- In 2005, we expect sales to advance 8% to $5.6 billion, from a projected $5.2 billion in 2004, paced by continued strength in the marine segment that we see supported by recent brand acquisitions, a recovery in marine retail, product enhancements, and improved dealer service. In our view, BC will likely maintain its industry leadership position in 2005 due, in part, to its successful use of differentiated technology to drive product innovation. We also look for fitness revenues and bowling and billiards sales to increase on new product launches and improved marketing support.

- With higher margin boat sales expected to rise, and leveraging of global sourcing and manufacturing to gain greater efficiencies, we look for the gross margin to widen. We expect controls over selling expenses to outweigh higher pension, insurance, and healthcare costs, leading to about a 100 basis point improvement in EBIT (earnings before interest and taxes) margins. Interest expense is likely to increase, due to an additional $150 million of notes issued during the second quarter of 2004.

- Factoring modest share dilution, we see 2004 operating EPS of $2.62 and Standard & Poor's Core Earnings of $2.31, and 2005 operating EPS of $3.30 and S&P Core EPS of $2.99. The annual differences reflect estimated stock option expense and pension costs.

Investment Rationale/Risk November 03, 2004

- We recommend accumulating the shares, based on our favorable opinion of BC's future prospects. Disruptions to the marine marketplace from four hurricanes cost the company an estimated $0.05 in earnings per share in the recent third quarter. The company expects to see some carryover impact of the hurricanes on its sales over the near term. However, it also believes there will be a substantial new boat and repair parts sales opportunity in 2005, as the replacement cycle starts. In our view, BC's continued expansion into more current areas of the marine business should additionally leverage sales and distribution and diversify risk. Combining our strong growth expectations with what we view as effective cost controls, we look for sustained margin expansion over the next several years.

- Risks to our recommendation and target price include weakening in the marine retail environment that could dampen sales, as well as poor execution of key product, manufacturing, sourcing and service initiatives.

- We calculate intrinsic value for the shares of $55 using our DCF model, which assumes a cost of capital of 9.2% and a terminal growth rate of 4%. Our 12-month target price of $52 is based on a blend of our historical forward P/E multiple of 15X applied to our 2005 operating EPS estimate of $3.30, and our DCF analysis.

Key Stock Statistics

S&P Core EPS 2005E	2.99	52-week Range	$49.81-27.20
S&P Oper. EPS 2004E	2.62	12 Month P/E	19.1
P/E on S&P Oper. EPS 2004E	19.0	Beta	0.80
S&P Oper. EPS 2005E	3.30	Shareholders	15,174
Yield (%)	1.2%	Market Cap (B)	$ 4.8
Dividend Rate/Share	0.60	Shares Outstanding (M)	96.2

Value of $10,000 invested five years ago: **$ 22,119**

Dividend Data Dividends have been paid since 1969

Amount ($)	Date Decl.	Ex-Div. Date	Stock of Record	Payment Date
0.500	Oct. 22	Nov. 21	Nov. 23	Dec. 12 '03
0.600	—	Nov. 18	Nov. 22	Dec. 15 '04

Revenues/Earnings Data Fiscal year ending December 31

Revenues (Million $)

	2004	2003	2002	2001	2000	1999
1Q	1,200	934.5	866.7	913.2	955.4	1,083
2Q	1,423	1,071	1,017	928.8	1,041	1,175
3Q	1,273	1,036	900.0	811.0	939.1	1,005
4Q	—	1,087	928.0	717.8	876.6	1,021
Yr.	—	4,129	3,712	3,371	3,812	4,284

Earnings Per Share ($)

	2004	2003	2002	2001	2000	1999
1Q	0.50	0.04	0.15	0.45	0.66	0.62
2Q	0.93	0.59	0.51	0.47	0.93	0.89
3Q	0.75	0.41	0.26	0.07	0.20	0.19
4Q	E0.55	0.43	0.22	-0.03	0.48	-1.30
Yr.	E2.62	1.47	1.14	0.96	2.28	0.41

Next earnings report expected: late-January Source: S&P, Company Reports
EPS Estimates based on S&P Operating Earnings; historical GAAP earnings are as reported.

Brunswick Corporation

Recommendation: **BUY** ★ ★ ★ ★ ☆   12-Month Target Price: **$52.00** (as of October 08, 2004)

Business Summary November 03, 2004

Brunswick Corp. is a major marine products company that also sells fitness equipment, as well as products related to bowling or billiards. In addition, the company operates more than 100 bowling centers.

In 2003, net sales increased 11%, to $4.1 billion, with international sales totaling $1.2 billion. About one-third of sales growth was attributed to the following acquisitions completed in 2003: Valley-Dynamo, L.P., a manufacturer of commercial and consumer billiards, Air Hockey and foosball tables; Land 'N' Sea Corp., a distributor of marine parts and accessories; Navman NZ Ltd., a manufacturer of marine electronics and global positioning systems-based products; Attwood Corp., a manufacturer of marine hardware and accessories; and Protokon LLC, a Hungarian steel fabricator and electronic equipment manufacturer. Cash paid for these acquisitions totaled $177.3 million.

In 2003, the company's marine-related businesses accounted for 79% of net sales, or $3.2 billion; $1.9 billion from the Marine Engine area, $1.6 billion from the Boat segment, and $276 million of eliminations that likely represent intra-company sales. Operating profits totaled $171 million for the Marine Engine segment and $64 million for the Boat segment.

In the Marine Engine segment, BC's brands include Mercury and Mariner outboard engines, and MerCruiser sterndrives and inboard engines. The Boat segment includes Sea Ray, Maxum and Sealine yachts, cruisers and runabouts; Bayliner cruisers and runabouts; Meridian motoryachts; Hatteras luxury sportfish-

ing convertibles and motoryachts; Boston Whaler and Trophy offshore fishing boats; Baja high-performance boats; and Princecraft aluminum fishing, deck and pontoon boats. In April 2004, the company acquired the Crestliner, Lowe and Lund aluminum boat brands from Genmar Industries, Inc., for about $191 million in cash.

The Fitness segment includes cardiovascular fitness equipment (including treadmills, total body cross trainers, stair climbers, and stationary exercise bicycles) and strength-training equipment under the Life Fitness, Hammer Strength, and ParaBody brands. In 2003, the company had Fitness segment sales of $487 million (12% of total net sales), and operating earnings of $30 million. Fitness segment sales are made to both commercial and higher-end consumer markets. Commercial sales are primarily to private health clubs and fitness facilities operated by professional sports teams, the military, governmental agencies, corporations, hotels, and schools. About 10% of 2003 segment sales were made through Omni Fitness, a chain of specialty fitness retail stores owned by BC since 2001. Most other consumer sales in the segment are to other specialty retailers, including some in which the company has ownership interests.

In 2003, BC's Bowling and Billiards segment had net sales of $392 million (9%), and operating earnings of $26 million. The segment includes the production of bowling balls and bowling capital equipment; the operation of more than 100 bowling centers; and the marketing of billiards tables, balls, cues, and related accessories.

Company Financials Fiscal Year ending December 31

Per Share Data ($)

(Year Ended December 31)	2003	2002	2001	2000	1999	1998	1997	1996	1995	1994
Tangible Bk. Val.	6.77	5.90	5.78	6.41	6.98	5.34	4.75	7.02	6.51	5.41
Cash Flow	3.11	2.78	2.78	3.96	2.20	3.42	3.07	3.19	2.58	2.60
Earnings	1.47	1.14	0.96	2.28	0.41	1.80	1.51	1.88	1.39	1.35
S&P Core Earnings	1.77	0.69	0.42	NA	NA	NA	NA	NA	NA	NA
Dividends	0.50	0.50	0.50	0.50	0.50	0.50	0.50	0.50	0.50	0.44
Payout Ratio	34%	44%	52%	22%	122%	28%	33%	27%	36%	33%
Prices - High	32.08	30.01	25.01	22.12	30.00	35.68	37.00	25.87	24.00	25.37
- Low	16.35	18.30	14.03	14.75	18.06	12.00	23.12	17.25	16.25	17.00
P/E Ratio - High	22	26	26	10	73	20	25	14	17	19
- Low	11	16	15	6	44	7	15	9	12	13

Income Statement Analysis (Million $)

	2003	2002	2001	2000	1999	1998	1997	1996	1995	1994
Revs.	4,129	3,712	3,371	3,812	4,284	3,945	3,657	3,160	3,041	2,700
Oper. Inc.	397	345	352	601	544	560	526	435	380	330
Depr.	151	148	160	149	166	160	157	130	121	120
Int. Exp.	41.0	43.3	52.9	67.6	61.0	62.7	51.3	33.4	32.5	28.5
Pretax Inc.	201	162	132	323	55.0	284	236	290	208	198
Eff. Tax Rate	32.8%	36.0%	35.9%	37.5%	31.1%	37.1%	36.0%	36.0%	35.5%	35.0%
Net Inc.	135	104	84.7	202	37.9	179	151	186	127	129
S&P Core Earnings	163	63.7	37.1	NA	NA	NA	NA	NA	NA	NA

Balance Sheet & Other Fin. Data (Million $)

	2003	2002	2001	2000	1999	1998	1997	1996	1995	1994
Cash	346	351	109	125	101	126	85.6	242	356	203
Curr. Assets	1,715	1,660	1,401	1,832	1,578	1,454	1,366	1,242	1,278	1,058
Total Assets	3,603	3,407	3,158	3,397	3,355	3,352	3,241	2,802	2,361	2,122
Curr. Liab.	1,102	1,006	903	1,248	1,088	1,036	948	831	680	621
LT Debt	584	590	600	602	Nil	635	646	455	313	319
Common Equity	1,323	1,102	1,111	1,067	1,300	1,311	1,366	1,198	1,044	911
Total Cap.	1,907	1,691	1,896	1,884	1,432	2,112	2,105	1,809	1,515	1,363
Cap. Exp.	160	113	111	156	198	198	191	170	123	105
Cash Flow	286	252	245	351	204	338	308	316	248	249
Curr. Ratio	1.6	1.7	1.6	1.5	1.4	1.4	1.4	1.5	1.9	1.7
% LT Debt of Cap.	30.6	34.9	31.7	31.9	Nil	30.1	30.7	25.2	20.7	23.4
% Net Inc.of Revs.	3.3	2.8	2.5	5.3	0.9	4.5	4.1	5.9	4.2	4.8
% Ret. on Assets	3.9	3.2	2.7	6.1	1.1	5.4	5.0	7.2	6.0	6.3
% Ret. on Equity	11.2	9.4	7.8	17.1	2.9	13.3	11.7	16.6	13.7	15.0

Data as orig reptd.; bef. results of disc opers/spec. items. Per share data adj. for stk. divs.; EPS diluted. E-Estimated. NA-Not Available. NM-Not Meaningful. NR-Not Ranked. UR-Under Review.

Office: 1 North Field Court, Lake Forest, IL 60045-4811.
Telephone: 847-735-4700.
Website: http://www.brunswickcorp.com
Chrmn & CEO: G.W. Buckley.
Vice Chrmn: P.B. Hamilton.
SVP & CFO: P.G. Leemputte.

VP & Treas: W.L. Metzger.
VP, Secy & General Counsel: M.I. Smith.
VP & Investor Contact: K.J. Chieger 847-735-4700.
Dirs: N. D. Archibald, D. J. Bern, J. L. Bleustein, G. W. Buckley, M. J. Callahan, M. A. Fernandez, P. B. Hamilton, P. Harf, G. H. Phillips, R. W. Schipke, R. Stayer.

Founded: in 1844.
Domicile: Delaware.
Employees: 23,225.
S&P Analyst: Jason N. Asaeda/MF/JWP

Burlington Northern Santa Fe

Recommendation: **BUY** ★★★★ 12-Month Target Price: **$54.00**
(as of November 16, 2004)

SELL | SELL | HOLD | BUY | BUY

BNI has an approximate 0.15% weighting in the **S&P 500**

Sector: Industrials
Sub-Industry: Railroads
Peer Group: Railroads (U.S.) - Major

Summary: Through the Burlington Northern and Santa Fe Railway Company, BNI owns one of the largest railroad networks in the U.S.

Quantitative Evaluations

S&P Earnings & Dividend Rank: A-

| D | C | B- | B | B+ | A- | A | A+ |

S&P Fair Value Rank: 3

| 1 | 2 | 3 | 4 | 5 |
Lowest .... Highest

Fair Value Calc.: $43.30 (Slightly Overvalued)

S&P Investability Quotient Percentile

96%

BNI scored higher than 96% of all companies for which an S&P Report is available.

Volatility: Low

| Low | Average | High |

Technical Evaluation: Bullish
Since 5/04, the technical indicators for BNI have been Bullish.

Relative Strength Rank: Strong

83
1 Lowest .... Highest 99

Price as of 11/16/04: $44.66 | **2004E S&P Core EPS:** $2.53

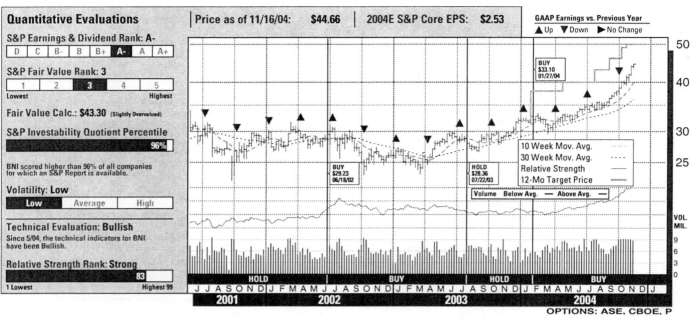

GAAP Earnings vs. Previous Year
▲ Up ▼ Down ► No Change

- 10 Week Mov. Avg.
- 30 Week Mov. Avg.
- Relative Strength
- 12-Mo Target Price

Volume Below Avg. — Above Avg.

BUY $33.10 01/27/04

BUY $29.23 06/18/02

HOLD $28.36 07/22/03

HOLD / BUY / HOLD / BUY
J J A S O N D J F M A M J J A S O N D J F M A M J J A S O N D J F M A M J J A S O N D J
2001 / 2002 / 2003 / 2004

OPTIONS: ASE, CBOE, P

Analyst commentary prepared by Andrew West, CFA /PMW/JWP

Highlights 18-NOV-04

- We forecast 2004 revenue growth of about 14%, as we see an improving economy driving increased manufacturing output and higher retail sales. We think pricing improvements will contribute about 3% to sales growth. We project continued gains for intermodal sales, on expected solid growth from shipping lines and additional volumes from UPS and major truckload carriers. We believe coal traffic will increase, due to greater purchases at power producers and the addition of new customers. We see 2005 revenues up about 6.5%.
- We forecast wider operating margins, as we see the positive impact of fuller and more efficient asset utilization, safety improvements, and cost control initiatives outweighing the impact of higher labor costs and depreciation charges, and increased fuel prices. We expect interest expense to decline, reflecting lower debt levels.
- We forecast 2004 operating EPS of $2.72 (excluding special charges), followed by an increase to $3.16 for 2005. We project S&P Core EPS of $2.53 for 2004 and $2.99 for 2005, reflecting estimated option and pension expenses.

Investment Rationale/Risk 18-NOV-04

- We believe the company will benefit from above-average revenue growth, driven by its outsized exposure to intermodal transport, coal and grain. We are encouraged by BNI's efficiency efforts, and by prospects of wider operating margins in future years. We believe management is skilled at optimizing capital investments, and project 2004 free cash flow of about $1 billion. We forecast 14% annual EPS and free cash flow growth over the next six years.
- Risks to our opinion and target price include unfavorable fuel price moves, weaker than expected economic and freight growth, declines in railroad system fluidity, unfavorable changes in international trade flows, regulatory and legal risks, and a faster than expected rise in interest rates.
- Our discounted cash flow model, which assumes an 8% cost of capital and 3% terminal growth, calculates value of $57 a share. Our relative value model, which relates historical peer group valuations to profitability and leverage, suggests a forward price to sales multiple of 1.7X, and a price of $50. Combining these models, our 12-month target price is $54.

Key Stock Statistics

S&P Core EPS 2005E	2.99	52-week Range	$44.50-28.98
S&P Oper. EPS 2004E	2.72	12 Month P/E	24.8
P/E on S&P Oper. EPS 2004E	16.4	Beta	0.47
S&P Oper. EPS 2005E	3.16	Shareholders	40,000
Yield (%)	1.5%	Market Cap (B)	$ 16.8
Dividend Rate/Share	0.68	Shares Outstanding (M)	375.9

Value of $10,000 invested five years ago: **$ 15,730**

Dividend Data Dividends have been paid since 1940

Amount ($)	Date Decl.	Ex-Div. Date	Stock of Record	Payment Date
0.150	Feb. 12	Mar. 09	Mar. 11	Apr. 01 '04
0.150	Apr. 22	Jun. 08	Jun. 10	Jul. 01 '04
0.170	Jul. 22	Sep. 08	Sep. 10	Oct. 01 '04
0.170	Oct. 21	Dec. 09	Dec. 13	Jan. 03 '05

Revenues/Earnings Data Fiscal year ending December 31

Revenues (Million $)

	2004	2003	2002	2001	2000	1999
1Q	2,490	2,232	2,163	2,293	2,264	2,190
2Q	2,685	2,294	2,207	2,271	2,260	2,194
3Q	2,793	2,395	2,308	2,343	2,342	2,346
4Q	—	2,492	2,301	2,301	2,339	2,378
Yr.	—	9,413	8,979	9,208	9,205	9,100

Earnings Per Share ($)

	2004	2003	2002	2001	2000	1999
1Q	0.52	0.40	0.45	0.36	0.55	0.50
2Q	0.67	0.54	0.51	0.50	0.53	0.50
3Q	0.01	0.55	0.51	0.58	0.64	0.75
4Q	E0.76	0.61	0.54	0.46	0.65	0.69
Yr.	E2.72	2.09	2.00	1.89	2.36	2.45

Next earnings report expected: late-January Source: S&P, Company Reports
EPS Estimates based on S&P Operating Earnings; historical GAAP earnings are as reported.

STANDARD &POOR'S

Burlington Northern Santa Fe Corporation

Stock Report
November 18, 2004
NYSE Symbol: **BNI**

Recommendation: **BUY** ★ ★ ★ ★ ★ 12-Month Target Price: **$54.00** (as of November 16, 2004)

Business Summary 18-NOV-04

Burlington Northern Santa Fe, created in 1995 through the merger of Burlington Northern Inc. and Santa Fe Pacific Corp., operates the second largest U.S. rail system, delivering about 45% of rail traffic in the West. It provides freight service to the consumer, industrial, coal, and agricultural sectors.

The company operates over a 32,500 mile rail system that spans 28 western and midwestern states and two Canadian provinces. About 24,500 miles of its system are owned; the remaining 8,000 route miles consist of trackage rights that permit BNI to operate its trains over other the tracks of other railroads. In 2003, revenue ton miles rose 3.7%, to 508 billion, while freight revenue per thousand ton miles rose 0.9%, to $18.27. At December 31, 2003, the average age of the locomotive fleet was 15 years, while the average age from date of manufacture or remanufacture of the freight car fleet was 16 years.

Consumer freight provided 39% of freight revenues in 2003 (38% in 2002). Consumer freight consisted of seven types of business: international (37% of consumer business), which is primarily container traffic from steamship companies; direct marketing (20%), which centers around intermodal traffic contracted from United Parcel Service and less-than-truckload carriers; truckload (17%), mainly comprised of business through a joint service arrangement with J.B. Hunt, as well as other truckload companies; automotive (8%); intermodal marketing companies (10%), primarily shippers and consolidators; and perishables and dry boxcar (8% of consumer business), which consists of beverages, canned goods and perishable food items.

Industrial products provided 23% of freight revenues in each of 2003 and 2002,

and was comprised of construction products (36% of industrial revenues), including steel; building products (35%), including forest products, chemicals and plastics (16%); and petroleum (13%).

Coal accounted for 22% of 2003 freight revenues (23% in 2002). BNI is a major transporter of low-sulfur coal, with 90% of its coal traffic originating in the Powder River Basin of Wyoming and Montana, primarily delivered to power utilities.

Agricultural products accounted for 16% of 2003 and 2002 freight revenues, including deliveries of grains, ethanol, and fertilizer.

As a condition for the merger of Union Pacific (UP) and Southern Pacific in late 1996, BNI was awarded trackage rights over 4,000 miles of those railroads, and UP sold to the company 335 miles of track in Louisiana, Texas and California, to preserve competition.

In July 2004, the company initiated an arbitration proceeding under its joint service agreement with J.B. Hunt, a major truckload carrier with which BNSF Railway handles substantial joint intermodal movements. BNSF is seeking an increase in its future divisions of joint revenue.

In October, BNI said it would record a non-cash after-tax charge of about $288 million in the 2004 third quarter, to reflect changes in the way it estimates asbestos and environmental remediation liabilities.

In October, BNI forecast double-digit revenue growth and EPS ranging from $0.74 to $0.77 for the 2004 fourth quarter.

Company Financials Fiscal Year ending December 31

Per Share Data ($)

(Year Ended December 31)	2003	2002	2001	2000	1999	1998	1997	1996	1995	1994
Tangible Bk. Val.	22.84	21.10	20.33	19.08	17.96	16.53	14.53	12.95	11.22	7.07
Cash Flow	4.53	4.44	4.21	4.52	4.36	4.17	3.52	3.52	2.24	2.83
Earnings	2.09	2.00	1.89	2.36	2.45	2.43	1.88	1.90	0.55	1.49
S&P Core Earnings	2.01	1.75	1.73	NA	NA	NA	NA	NA	NA	NA
Dividends	0.54	0.48	0.49	0.48	0.48	0.42	0.40	0.40	0.40	0.40
Payout Ratio	26%	24%	26%	20%	20%	17%	21%	21%	72%	27%
Prices - High	32.50	31.75	34.00	29.56	37.93	35.70	33.64	30.04	28.25	22.20
- Low	23.29	23.18	22.40	19.06	22.87	26.87	23.41	24.50	15.16	15.50
P/E Ratio - High	16	16	18	13	15	15	18	16	51	15
- Low	11	12	12	8	9	11	12	13	27	10

Income Statement Analysis (Million $)

	2003	2002	2001	2000	1999	1998	1997	1996	1995	1994
Revs.	9,413	8,979	9,208	9,205	9,100	8,941	8,413	8,187	6,183	4,995
Oper. Inc.	2,575	2,587	2,664	3,003	3,096	2,990	2,630	2,508	1,781	1,215
Depr.	910	931	909	895	897	832	773	760	520	362
Int. Exp.	420	428	463	453	387	354	344	301	220	155
Pretax Inc.	1,231	1,216	1,182	1,585	1,819	1,849	1,404	1,440	334	695
Eff. Tax Rate	36.9%	37.5%	37.6%	38.2%	37.5%	37.5%	37.0%	38.3%	40.7%	38.7%
Net Inc.	777	760	737	980	1,137	1,155	885	889	198	426
S&P Core Earnings	743	667	676	NA	NA	NA	NA	NA	NA	NA

Balance Sheet & Other Fin. Data (Million $)

	2003	2002	2001	2000	1999	1998	1997	1996	1995	1994
Cash	18.0	28.0	26.0	11.0	22.0	25.0	31.0	47.0	50.0	27.0
Curr. Assets	862	791	723	976	1,066	1,206	1,234	1,331	1,264	1,012
Total Assets	26,939	25,767	24,721	24,375	23,700	22,690	21,336	19,846	18,269	7,592
Curr. Liab.	2,346	2,091	2,161	2,186	2,075	2,197	2,060	2,311	2,369	1,447
LT Debt	6,440	6,641	6,363	6,614	5,655	5,188	5,181	4,546	4,153	1,697
Common Equity	8,495	7,932	7,849	7,480	8,172	7,770	6,812	5,981	5,037	1,892
Total Cap.	22,416	21,548	20,943	20,516	19,924	18,620	17,168	15,256	13,423	5,390
Cap. Exp.	1,726	1,358	1,459	1,399	1,788	2,147	2,182	2,234	890	698
Cash Flow	1,687	1,691	1,646	1,875	2,034	1,987	1,658	1,649	718	766
Curr. Ratio	0.4	0.4	0.3	0.4	0.5	0.5	0.6	0.6	0.5	0.7
% LT Debt of Cap.	28.7	30.8	30.4	32.2	28.4	27.9	30.2	29.8	30.9	31.5
% Net Inc.of Revs.	8.3	8.5	8.0	10.6	12.5	12.9	10.5	10.9	3.2	8.5
% Ret. on Assets	2.9	3.0	3.0	4.1	4.9	5.2	4.3	4.7	1.5	5.8
% Ret. on Equity	9.5	9.6	9.6	12.5	14.3	15.8	13.8	16.1	4.9	23.3

Data as orig reptd.; bef. results of disc opers/spec. items. Per share data adj. for stk. divs. Bold denotes primary EPS - prior periods restated. E-Estimated. NA-Not Available. NM-Not Meaningful. NR-Not Ranked. UR-Under Review.

Office: 2650 Lou Menk Drive, Fort Worth, TX 76131-2830.
Telephone: 817-352-1000.
Email: investor.relations@bnsf.com
Website: http://www.bnsf.com
Chrmn, Pres & CEO: M. K. Rose.
EVP & CFO: T. N. Hund.

Secy & EVP: J. R. Moreland.
EVP: C. R. Ice.
Investor Contact: Marsha K. Morgan (817-352-4813).
Dirs: A. L. Boeckman, V. S. Martinez, M. F. Racicot, R. S. Roberts, M. Rose, M. J. Shapiro, J. C. Watts, Jr., R. H. West, J. S. Whisler, E. E. Whitacre, Jr., M. B. Yanney.

Founded: in 1994.
Domicile: Delaware.
Employees: 36,500.
S&P Analyst: Andrew West, CFA /PMW/JWP

Burlington Resources

Recommendation: **BUY** ★★★★☆
SELL SELL HOLD BUY BUY

12-Month Target Price: $48.00
(as of October 06, 2004)

BR has an approximate 0.15% weighting in the **S&P 500**

Sector: Energy
Sub-Industry: Oil & Gas Exploration & Production
Peer Group: Exploration & Production - Large

Summary: This holding company has subsidiaries operating in exploration and production worldwide, and is one of the largest natural gas producers in North America.

Quantitative Evaluations

S&P Earnings & Dividend Rank: B

| D | C | B- | **B** | B+ | A- | A | A+ |

S&P Fair Value Rank: 5+

| 1 | 2 | 3 | 4 | **5** |
| Lowest | | | | Highest |

Fair Value Calc.: $47.50 (Slightly Undervalued)

S&P Investability Quotient Percentile

88%

BR scored higher than 88% of all companies for which an S&P Report is available.

Volatility: Average

| Low | **Average** | High |

Technical Evaluation: Bullish
Since 9/04, the technical indicators for BR have been Bullish.

Relative Strength Rank: Moderate

51

| 1 Lowest | | Highest 99 |

| Price as of 11/12/04: | $41.68 | 2004E S&P Core EPS: | $3.67 |

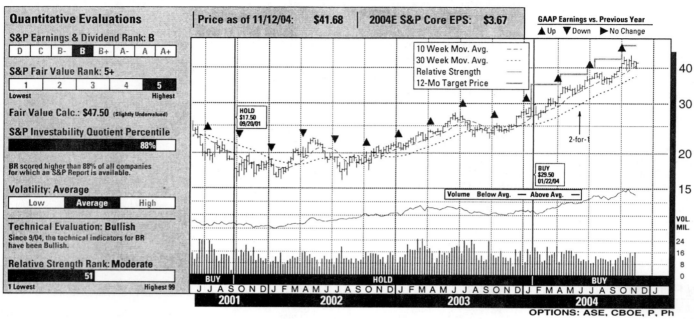

GAAP Earnings vs. Previous Year
▲ Up ▼ Down ▶ No Change

10 Week Mov. Avg.
30 Week Mov. Avg.
Relative Strength
12-Mo Target Price

HOLD $17.50 09/20/01

BUY $29.50 01/22/04

2-for-1

Volume Below Avg. — Above Avg.

VOL. MIL.

OPTIONS: ASE, CBOE, P, Ph

Analyst commentary prepared by Charles LaPorta, CFA /DC/BK

Highlights November 09, 2004

- Third quarter EPS was $0.98 versus $0.67 last year, beating our estimate of $0.95 on better than expected U.S. natural gas volumes and international oil volumes.

- Hydrocarbon production grew 10% during the quarter, and though BR projects production growth of 3% to 8% for 2004 and 2005, international volumes nearly doubled from last year during the quarter, as fields in Algeria, Ecuador, and offshore China continue to ramp up their production. Canadian production declined sequentially due to wet weather, but BR has an aggressive winter development program that is currently being implemented. As a result, we are projecting production growth of 10% in 2004 and 7% in 2005. In the past two years, BR has been realigning its upstream assets, using proceeds to acquire what it views as higher growth properties.

- We expect earnings before interest, taxes, depreciation, amortization and exploration expense (EBITDAX) of $4.16 billion in 2004 to grow about 7% in 2005, to $4.43 billion, in-line with projected volume growth in a likely supportive commodity price environment. Although the company expects per unit production costs to increase 5% to 10% over 2003 levels, BR's unit costs continue to be lower than most peers.

Investment Rationale/Risk November 09, 2004

- We would accumulate the shares. We view BR's low cost, long duration North American natural gas assets as adding value to the stock in a market of tight natural gas supplies and rising demand. BR anticipates generating about $3 billion in cash flow from operations, and its 2004 capital expenditure budget is for $1.7 billion. Consequently, BR has deployed a portion of the resulting free cash flow toward share repurchases that have exceeded 10 million shares year to date. We estimate that BR has $410 million left on its repurchase authorization.

- Risks to our opinion and target price include events that would cause substantial and sustained declines in oil and gas prices; a persistent inability by BR to replace its reserves; and acts of terrorism on BR's production facilities.

- Given our estimates for oil and gas prices and BR's production growth, we arrive at our 12-month target price of $48, which is based on a multiple of 11.6X our 2005 EPS estimate and an enterprise value of 4.8X our 2005 EBITDAX estimate. This valuation suggests a slight premium to peers, which we believe is deserved given BR's 38% debt-to-cap ratio, $1.8 billion in cash and, in our view, strong free cash flow generation ability.

Key Stock Statistics

S&P Core EPS 2005E	3.97	52-week Range	$44.31-24.58
S&P Oper. EPS 2004E	4.00	12 Month P/E	10.9
P/E on S&P Oper. EPS 2004E	10.4	Beta	0.46
S&P Oper. EPS 2005E	4.15	Shareholders	12,631
Yield (%)	0.8%	Market Cap (B)	$ 16.3
Dividend Rate/Share	0.34	Shares Outstanding (M)	391.5

Value of $10,000 invested five years ago: $ 26,850

Dividend Data Dividends have been paid since 1988

Amount ($)	Date Decl.	Ex-Div. Date	Stock of Record	Payment Date
2-for-1	Jan. 21	Jun. 02	May. 05	Jun. 01 '04
0.150	Apr. 21	Jun. 08	Jun. 10	Jul. 09 '04
0.085	Jul. 21	Sep. 08	Sep. 10	Oct. 12 '04
0.085	Oct. 20	Dec. 08	Dec. 10	Jan. 11 '05

Revenues/Earnings Data Fiscal year ending December 31

Revenues (Million $)

	2004	2003	2002	2001	2000	1999
1Q	1,308	1,128	694.0	1,143	708.0	436.0
2Q	1,333	1,059	786.0	917.0	680.0	455.0
3Q	1,419	1,059	651.0	655.0	760.0	547.0
4Q	—	1,065	833.0	611.0	999	627.0
Yr.	—	4,311	2,964	3,326	3,147	2,065

Earnings Per Share ($)

	2004	2003	2002	2001	2000	1999
1Q	0.89	0.81	0.12	0.78	0.18	Nil
2Q	0.96	0.69	0.42	0.55	0.21	0.06
3Q	1.00	0.67	0.20	0.18	0.47	0.14
4Q	E1.16	0.98	0.39	-0.20	0.71	-0.19
Yr.	E4.00	3.15	1.12	1.34	1.56	Nil

Next earnings report expected: late-January Source: S&P, Company Reports
EPS Estimates based on S&P Operating Earnings; historical GAAP earnings are as reported.

Burlington Resources Inc.

Recommendation: **BUY** ★★★★☆   12-Month Target Price: **$48.00** (as of October 06, 2004)

Business Summary November 09, 2004

Burlington Resources is a holding company with operating subsidiaries that are engaged in exploration and production activities: Burlington Oil & Gas Co. LP, The Louisiana Land and Exploration Co. (LL&E), Burlington Resources Canada Ltd. (formerly Poco Petroleum Ltd.), Burlington Resources Canada (Hunter) Ltd. (formerly Canadian Hunter Exploration Ltd.), and their affiliated companies (collectively, the company). The company is one of the largest producers of natural gas in North America, and participates in exploration for, and development, production and marketing of, crude oil, natural gas liquids (NGLs), and natural gas. BR expects to continue to focus on exploring for and producing North American natural gas as its primary business.

BR's assets are concentrated in major producing fields in basins spread along the North American gas fairway that extends from the U.S. Gulf Coast through the U.S. Rocky Mountain regions and Canada. International operations focus on Northwest Europe (assets in the East Irish and the Dutch sector of the North Sea), North Africa (assets in Algeria and Egypt), China (such as the Panyu offshore project in the Pearl River Mouth Basin of the South China Sea, and the onshore Chuanzhong Block in the Sichuan Basin), and South America (assets in Ecuador, Argentina, Peru and Columbia).

The company replaced 142% of its 2003 worldwide production from all sources, at a cost of $1.19 per thousand cubic feet equivalent (Mcfe). Excluding acquisitions, the replacement rate was 118%, at a cost of $1.23 per Mcfe. About 69% of 2003

proved reserves consisted of natural gas, 17% NGLs, and 14% crude oil. Proved oil reserves were 282.1 million barrels (MMBbl; 85% developed; 65% U.S., 6% Canada, and 29% elsewhere) in 2003, versus 287.9 MMBbl (63% developed; 65% U.S., 5% Canada, and 30% elsewhere) in 2002. Proved NGL reserves were 330.9 MMBbl (72% developed; 81% U.S., and 19% Canada) in 2003, versus 300.2 MMBbl (77% developed; 80% U.S., and 20% Canada) in 2002. Proved natural gas reserves were 8.074 trillion cubic feet (Tcf; 73% developed; 60% U.S., 29% Canada, and 11% elsewhere) in 2003, versus 8.074 Tcf (72% developed; 60% U.S., 29% Canada, and 11% elsewhere) in 2002.

Production of natural gas averaged 1.899 billion cubic feet (Bcf) per day (46% U.S., 46% Canada, and 8% elsewhere) in 2003, versus 1.916 Bcf per day (49% U.S., 42% Canada, and 9% elsewhere) in 2002. NGL production averaged 64,800 barrels per day (bpd; 58% U.S., 36% Canada, and 6% elsewhere) in 2003, versus 60,100 bpd (54% U.S. and 46% Canada) in 2002. Crude oil production averaged 46,500 bpd (63% U.S., 11% Canada, and 26% elsewhere) in 2003, versus 49,100 bpd (72% U.S., 16% Canada, and 12% elsewhere) in 2002. The average sales price (including hedging) for natural gas was $4.83 per thousand cubic feet (Mcf) in 2003 ($3.20 in 2002). The average sales price for NGLs was $20.40 per barrel (Bbl) in 2003 ($14.46 in 2002). The average sales price for crude oil was $27.22 per Bbl in 2003 ($24.11 in 2002). Average worldwide production costs were $0.57 per Mcfe in 2003, versus a three-year (2001-2003) average of $0.57.

Company Financials Fiscal Year ending December 31

Per Share Data ($)

(Year Ended December 31)	2003	2002	2001	2000	1999	1998	1997	1996	1995	1994
Tangible Bk. Val.	5.69	7.54	NM	8.72	7.52	8.51	8.54	9.34	8.77	10.15
Cash Flow	5.47	3.19	3.11	3.19	1.46	1.74	2.41	2.38	0.36	1.91
Earnings	3.15	1.12	1.34	1.56	Nil	0.24	0.90	1.01	-1.10	0.60
S&P Core Earnings	3.12	0.97	1.30	NA	NA	NA	NA	NA	NA	NA
Dividends	0.29	0.28	0.28	0.28	0.28	0.28	0.28	0.28	0.28	0.28
Payout Ratio	9%	24%	20%	18%	NM	115%	31%	27%	NM	46%
Prices - High	28.72	22.67	26.81	26.43	23.81	24.81	27.25	26.75	21.12	24.81
- Low	20.37	16.00	15.84	12.87	14.75	14.71	19.87	17.56	16.81	16.56
P/E Ratio - High	9	20	20	17	NM	NM	30	26	NM	41
- Low	6	14	12	8	NM	NM	22	17	NM	28

Income Statement Analysis (Million $)

	2003	2002	2001	2000	1999	1998	1997	1996	1995	1994
Revs.	4,311	2,964	3,419	3,147	2,065	1,637	2,000	1,293	873	1,055
Oper. Inc.	2,825	1,577	2,004	1,895	1,129	752	1,041	764	-94.6	512
Depr. Depl. & Amort.	927	833	735	704	631	534	538	346	373	337
Int. Exp.	260	274	190	197	211	148	142	113	109	90.0
Pretax Inc.	1,570	569	907	967	23.0	95.0	411	307	-577	90.0
Eff. Tax Rate	19.7%	20.2%	38.5%	30.2%	95.7%	9.47%	22.4%	16.9%	NM	NM
Net Inc.	1,260	454	558	675	1.00	86.0	319	255	-280	154
S&P Core Earnings	1,247	389	537	NA	NA	NA	NA	NA	NA	NA

Balance Sheet & Other Fin. Data (Million $)

	2003	2002	2001	2000	1999	1998	1997	1996	1995	1994
Cash	757	443	116	132	89.0	Nil	152	68.0	20.5	20.0
Curr. Assets	1,517	1,061	715	1,011	667	456	678	442	265	266
Total Assets	12,995	10,645	10,582	7,506	7,191	5,917	5,821	4,316	4,165	4,809
Curr. Liab.	891	1,022	711	758	648	494	538	368	322	262
LT Debt	3,873	3,853	Nil	2,301	2,769	1,938	1,748	1,350	1,350	1,309
Common Equity	5,521	3,832	3,525	3,750	3,246	3,018	3,016	2,333	2,220	2,568
Total Cap.	11,342	9,121	9,265	6,317	6,120	5,155	4,967	3,768	3,681	4,358
Cap. Exp.	1,899	1,851	1,293	941	989	1,165	1,245	554	589	882
Cash Flow	2,187	1,287	1,293	1,379	632	620	857	601	93.0	492
Curr. Ratio	1.7	1.0	1.0	1.3	1.0	0.9	1.3	1.2	0.8	1.0
% LT Debt of Cap.	34.1	42.2	Nil	36.4	45.2	37.6	35.2	35.8	36.7	30.0
% Ret. on Assets	10.7	4.3	6.2	9.2	0.0	1.5	6.3	6.0	NM	3.4
% Ret. on Equity	26.9	12.3	15.3	19.3	0.0	2.9	11.9	11.2	NM	6.0

Data as orig reptd.; bef. results of disc opers/spec. items. Per share data adj. for stk. divs. Bold denotes basic EPS (FASB 128)-prior periods restated. E-Estimated. NA-Not Available. NM-Not Meaningful. NR-Not Ranked. UR-Under Review.

Office: 717 Texas Avenue, Houston, TX 77002-2712.
Telephone: 713-624-9500.
Email: info@br-inc.com
Website: http://www.br-inc.com
Chrmn, Pres & CEO: B.S. Shackouls.
COO & EVP: R.L. Limbacher.
EVP & CFO: S.J. Shapiro.

VP & Chief Acctg Officer: J.P. McCoy.
VP & Treas: D.D. Hawk.
VP & Investor Contact: E.R. DeSanctis 713-624-9548.
Dirs: B. T. Alexander, R. V. Anderson, L. I. Grant, R. J. Harding, J. T. LaMacchia, R. L. Limbacher, J. F. McDonald, K. W. Orce, D. M. Roberts, J. A. Runde, J. F. Schwarz, W. Scott, Jr., B. S. Shackouls, S. J. Shapiro, W. E. Wade, Jr.

Founded: in 1988.
Domicile: Delaware.
Employees: 2,111.
S&P Analyst: Charles LaPorta, CFA /DC/BK

Calpine Corp.

Recommendation: **HOLD** ★ ★ ★ ★ ★
SELL | SELL | HOLD | BUY | BUY

12-Month Target Price: **$5.00**
(as of August 23, 2004)

CPN has an approximate 0.02% weighting in the **S&P 500**

Sector: Utilities
Sub-Industry: Multi-Utilities & Unregulated Power
Peer Group: Independent Power Producers

Summary: This company acquires, develops, owns and operates power generation plants, and sells electricity and steam in the U.S. and Canada.

Quantitative Evaluations

S&P Earnings & Dividend Rank: B

| D | C | B- | **B** | B+ | A- | A | A+ |

S&P Fair Value Rank: NR

| 1 | 2 | 3 | 4 | 5 |
| Lowest | | | | Highest |

Fair Value Calc.: NA

S&P Investability Quotient Percentile

26%

CPN scored lower than 74% of all companies for which an S&P Report is available.

Volatility: High

| Low | Average | **High** |

Technical Evaluation: Neutral
Since 11/04, the technical indicators for CPN have been Neutral.

Relative Strength Rank: Moderate

51

| 1 Lowest | | Highest 99 |

Price as of 11/12/04: $3.13   **2004E S&P Core EPS:** $-0.47

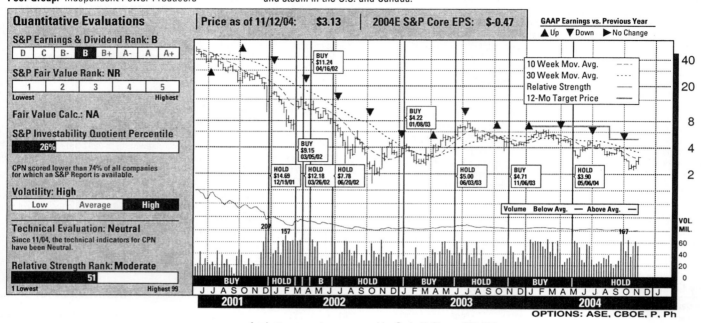

GAAP Earnings vs. Previous Year
▲ Up   ▼ Down   ▶ No Change

10 Week Mov. Avg.
30 Week Mov. Avg.
Relative Strength
12-Mo Target Price

Volume   Below Avg. — Above Avg. —

OPTIONS: ASE, CBOE, P, Ph

Analyst commentary prepared by Craig K. Shere, CFA /GG

Highlights August 24, 2004

- Reported 2003 EPS includes approximately $0.14 in net one-time gains. Our 2004 operating EPS estimate excludes $0.17 of net one-time gains. Excluding one-time items, we look for operating EPS in 2004 to decline $0.53, to a loss of $0.39 per share.

- We see lower 2004 results driven by a more than 25% decline in average power margins and increased depreciation and interest expense stemming from the completed construction of new power plants in 2003 and 2004. Including purchased power (which CPN uses to fulfill supply contracts when it is cheaper to buy power than to run its own plants), we expect CPN's gross margin after fuel costs per megawatt-hour (MWH) will be almost $13 in 2004. Given our projection of improving margins over time, we look for CPN to earn over $15 per delivered MWH in 2005 and almost $17 in 2006. We project CPN will almost have break-even cash flow after capital expenditures in 2006 (versus about a $200 million cash drain in 2005).

- Our 2004 Standard & Poor's Core EPS estimate is $0.08 below our operating EPS projection, due to the exclusion of gains from asset sales, but inclusion of other one-time charges relating to operating businesses.

Key Stock Statistics

S&P Core EPS 2005E	-0.35	52-week Range	$6.42-2.24
S&P Oper. EPS 2004E	-0.39	12 Month P/E	NM
P/E on S&P Oper. EPS 2004E	NM	Beta	2.44
S&P Oper. EPS 2005E	-0.35	Shareholders	2,169
Yield (%)	Nil	Market Cap (B)	$1.7
Dividend Rate/Share	Nil	Shares Outstanding (M)	534.3

Value of $10,000 invested five years ago: **$1,743**

Dividend Data

No cash dividends have been paid. Calpine's ability to pay cash dividends is restricted by its debt agreements.

Investment Rationale/Risk August 24, 2004

- We believe mild summer temperatures and moderating economic growth have restricted 2004 electricity demand and margins. Calpine's share price has fallen over 40% over the six months ended late August, as the company reported significant negative free cash flow after capital expenditures, exacerbating levels of potential dilution associated with the use of common equity to redeem a portion of $1 billion of preferred shares coming due for remarketing. We are impressed by Calpine's success at improving liquidity through the sale of natural gas producing properties and power contracts and securing of project level financing for contracted plants. However, we believe these transactions tend to improve short-term liquidity at the expense of longer-term operating cash flow.

- Risks to our recommendation and target price include the company's inability to sign new long-term power supply agreements as old sales agreements expire, a delayed recovery in wholesale power margins, unusually mild summer weather, and a soft economy.

- With $3 billion of targeted year end 2004 liquidity, we believe CPN can sustain its heavy debt service until power margins ultimately recover. But, given potential near-term share dilution and long-term operating risks, we believe the stock would be fairly priced at about 50% of today's book value. Our 12-month target price is $5.

Revenues/Earnings Data Fiscal year ending December 31

Revenues (Million $)

	2004	2003	2002	2001	2000	1999
1Q	2,043	2,166	1,333	1,340	235.4	145.9
2Q	2,315	2,165	1,766	1,613	363.7	190.7
3Q	2,557	2,668	2,476	2,916	678.9	263.6
4Q	—	1,921	1,889	1,721	1,005	247.5
Yr.		8,920	7,458	7,590	2,283	847.7

Earnings Per Share ($)

	2004	2003	2002	2001	2000	1999
1Q	-0.23	-0.14	-0.25	0.36	0.07	0.02
2Q	-0.07	-0.04	0.16	0.32	0.19	0.08
3Q	-0.11	0.51	0.31	0.88	0.48	0.18
4Q	E-0.15	-0.15	-0.18	0.28	0.34	0.12
Yr.	E-0.39	0.28	0.14	1.85	1.11	0.43

Next earnings report expected: late-February Source: S&P, Company Reports
EPS Estimates based on S&P Operating Earnings; historical GAAP earnings are as reported.

Calpine Corporation

Recommendation: **HOLD** ★★★☆☆   12-Month Target Price: **$5.00** (as of August 23, 2004)

Business Summary August 24, 2004

Calpine is the largest producer of unregulated wholesale power in North America. As of August 2004, CPN had 91 power plants representing 26,199 megawatts of generation in operation (including 1,200 MW in the U.K.). This is expected to grow to over 30,000 MW as the company finishes its plant construction program. Calpine Energy Services, CPN's risk management and energy marketing arm, manages about 3.4% of total U.S. electric consumption and 4% of U.S. natural gas supply. Calpine believes it can garner above-average margins from long term power supply contracts because its clustered power plants allow it to offer premium services (such as guaranteed power delivery and flexible power supplies to meet fluctuating load demand), which cannot be offered from single power plants.

Since the bankruptcy of Enron and the ensuing collapse of power margins (largely due to industry overbuilding), Calpine has sought to improve its financial liquidity. In 2002, it divested oil and gas properties and a 180 MW power plant for aggregate consideration of $447.8 million; deferred development of plants not in construction; and restructured orders for combustion turbines. In 2003, the company sold almost $670 million of assets, monetized $990 million of power contracts, obtained $1.08 billion in project level financings, and issued $5.9 billion of long term debt. These efforts permitted CPN to extend its debt maturities and repurchase $2.04 billion of debt in 2004 at a more than $300 million discount.

Liquidity has been important to Calpine because of the high fixed costs associated with its power plant construction plans. During 2003, the company completed 15 power plants (3,500 MW) and in the first half of 2004 it completed 6 plants (3,400 MW). As of August 2004, 12 plants totaling 5,800 MW remained under construction

(though 3 locations without power sales contracts may be indefinitely delayed). CPN expects to obtain project financing for plants whose output is hedged with long term power sales contracts. Accordingly, the company expects existing liquidity and operating cash flows to fund only $150 million of construction expenditures in the second half of 2004 and $50 million for all of 2005. The remainder of construction capital expenditures (totaling $600 million in the 2004 second half and $525 million in 2005, excluding three discretionary projects) is expected to be funded with project level debt.

As of August 2004, power margins for 97.1 million MWH's in 2005 (about 46% of available capacity) were under contract, and another 81.6 million MWH's in 2006 (35%) were hedged. In dollar terms, the contractually secured gross margin as of August 2004 declined from $2.03 billion in 2005 to $1.6 billion by 2007. Given a glut of electric generation in the U.S., CPN has been unable to sell significant amounts of uncontracted generating capacity in recent periods. The MWH's CPN has been able to sell on the spot market have garnered much lower gross margins than contracted capacity.

CPN has historically hedged a portion of its fuel cost risks through direct ownership of natural gas producing properties. Assuming market prices, this equity gas production contributed $188 million to 2003 gross margin. Given rising natural gas prices, in August 2004, CPN restructured certain power supply contracts to eliminate its fuel cost risk and divested Canadian and Rockies gas producing properties for about $850 million in cash.

Company Financials Fiscal Year ending December 31

Per Share Data ($)

(Year Ended December 31)	2003	2002	2001	2000	1999	1998	1997	1996	1995	1994
Tangible Bk. Val.	10.81	9.78	9.12	7.39	3.61	1.64	1.37	1.28	1.05	NA
Earnings	0.28	0.14	1.85	1.11	0.43	0.27	0.21	0.16	0.11	NA
S&P Core Earnings	0.03	-0.17	1.70	NA	NA	NA	NA	NA	NA	NA
Dividends	Nil	Nil	Nil	Nil	Nil	Nil	Nil	Nil	Nil	NA
Payout Ratio	Nil	Nil	Nil	Nil	Nil	Nil	Nil	Nil	Nil	NA
Prices - High	8.03	17.28	58.04	52.96	16.37	3.45	2.86	2.50	NA	NA
- Low	2.51	1.55	10.00	16.09	3.15	1.59	1.54	2.00	NA	NA
P/E Ratio - High	29	NM	31	48	38	13	14	16	NA	NA
- Low	9	NM	5	14	7	6	7	13	NA	NA

Income Statement Analysis (Million $)

	2003	2002	2001	2000	1999	1998	1997	1996	1995	1994
Revs.	8,996	7,474	7,590	2,283	847	556	276	214	224	NA
Depr.	584	459	370	154	87.2	74.3	46.8	36.6	42.1	NA
Maint.	NA	NA	NA	NA	NA	NA	NA	NA	NA	NA
Fxd. Chgs. Cov.	0.71	1.91	1.89	2.84	1.79	1.71	1.87	NA	1.38	NA
Constr. Credits	NA	NA	NA	NA	NA	NA	NA	NA	Nil	NA
Eff. Tax Rate	NM	NM	35.0%	40.1%	39.2%	36.9%	34.7%	32.7%	40.6%	NA
Net Inc.	110	49.1	641	325	96.2	46.3	34.7	18.6	12.8	NA
S&P Core Earnings	9.36	-61.1	588	NA	NA	NA	NA	NA	NA	NA

Balance Sheet & Other Fin. Data (Million $)

	2003	2002	2001	2000	1999	1998	1997	1996	1995	1994
Gross Prop.	21,916	20,071	16,334	7,788	3,094	1,298	868	732	NA	NA
Cap. Exp.	1,886	4,036	6,172	2,967	930	98.2	107	24.0	NA	NA
Net Prop.	20,081	18,851	15,385	7,459	2,866	1,094	720	631	658	NA
Capitalization:										
LT Debt	17,096	11,548	12,947	5,553	2,277	1,066	743	564	589	NA
% LT Debt	78.7	75.0	81.1	71.3	70.2	78.8	75.6	73.5	78.4	NA
Pfd.	Nil	Nil	Nil	Nil	Nil	Nil	Nil	Nil	Nil	NA
% Pfd.	Nil	Nil	Nil	Nil	Nil	Nil	Nil	Nil	Nil	NA
Common	4,621	3,852	3,011	2,237	965	287	240	203	162	NA
% Common	21.3	25.0	18.9	28.7	29.8	21.2	24.4	26.5	21.6	NA
Total Cap.	23,454	16,709	16,970	8,394	3,595	1,513	1,125	867	851	NA
% Oper. Ratio	93.0	90.0	94.4	83.2	91.0	78.5	71.5	68.8	72.6	NA
% Earn. on Net Prop.	5.8	6.6	12.9	11.6	15.8	24.4	21.0	10.5	NA	NA
% Return On Revs.	1.2	0.7	8.4	14.2	11.4	8.3	12.6	8.7	5.7	NA
% Return On Invest. Capital	4.7	5.5	7.0	7.1	7.4	7.1	7.9	NA	NA	NA
% Return On Com. Equity	2.6	1.4	23.6	20.3	15.4	17.6	15.7	NA	NA	NA

Data as orig. reptd. (pro forma in 1995); bef. results of disc. opers. and/or spec. items. Per share data adj. for stock divs.; EPS diluted. E-Estimated. NA-Not Available. NM-Not Meaningful. NR-Not Ranked.

Office: 50 West San Fernando Street, San Jose, CA 95113.
Telephone: 408-995-5115.
Email: investor-relations@calpine.com
Website: http://www.calpine.com
Chrmn, Pres & CEO: P. Cartwright.
Vice Chrmn & Secy: A.B. Curtis.

EVP & CFO: R.D. Kelly.
EVP & General Counsel: L. Bodensteiner.
SVP & Treas: M.P. Thomas.
SVP & Investor Contact: R. Barraza 408-995-5115.
Dirs: P. Cartwright, A. B. Curtis, K. T. Derr, J. E. Garten, G. Greenwald, S. C. Schwab, G. J. Stathakis, S. Wang, J. O. Wilson.

Founded: in 1984.
Domicile: Delaware.
Employees: 3,418.
S&P Analyst: Craig K. Shere, CFA /GG

Campbell Soup

Recommendation: **HOLD** ★★★★★
SELL SELL HOLD BUY BUY

12-Month Target Price: **$28.00**
(as of June 28, 2004)

CPB has an approximate 0.10% weighting in the **S&P 500**

Sector: Consumer Staples
Sub-Industry: Packaged Foods & Meats
Peer Group: Larger Food Manufacturers

Summary: Campbell Soup is a major producer of branded soups and other grocery food products.

Quantitative Evaluations

S&P Earnings & Dividend Rank: B+

| D | C | B- | B | B+ | A- | A | A+ |

S&P Fair Value Rank: 3

| 1 | 2 | 3 | 4 | 5 |
| Lowest | | | | Highest |

Fair Value Calc.: $26.20 (Slightly Overvalued)

S&P Investability Quotient Percentile

88%

CPB scored higher than 88% of all companies for which an S&P Report is available.

Volatility: Low

| Low | Average | High |

Technical Evaluation: Bullish

Since 10/04, the technical indicators for CPB have been Bullish.

Relative Strength Rank: Moderate

43

| 1 Lowest | Highest 99 |

| Price as of 11/12/04: | **$27.16** | 2005E S&P Core EPS: | **$1.58** |

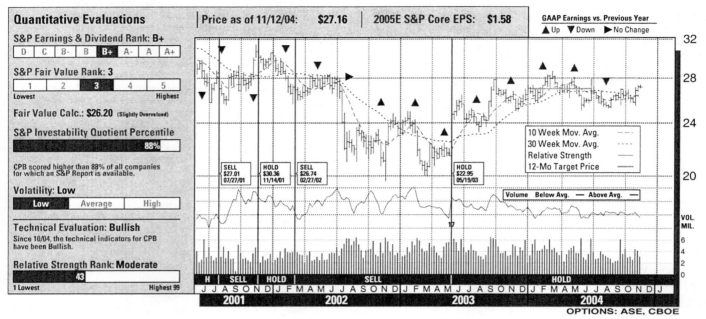

GAAP Earnings vs. Previous Year
▲ Up ▼ Down ► No Change

10 Week Mov. Avg.
30 Week Mov. Avg.
Relative Strength
12-Mo Target Price

Volume Below Avg. — Above Avg. —

SELL $27.01 07/27/01
HOLD $30.36 11/14/01
SELL $26.74 02/27/02
HOLD $22.95 05/19/03

OPTIONS: ASE, CBOE

Analyst commentary prepared by Richard Joy/CB/BK

Highlights October 12, 2004

- We expect CPB's net sales to advance about 5% in FY 05 (Jul.), reflecting low single digit growth for the North American soups and foodservice, sauces and beverages businesses, close to 5% growth for the biscuits and confectionery segment, and nearly 6% growth for the international soup business. Volumes should benefit from new products and packaging, as well as from higher levels of marketing spending. We think margins are likely to remain unchanged, as savings from cost reduction initiatives are offset by commodity cost inflation and increased marketing spending.

- Following a modest reduction in interest expense and no change in shares outstanding, we expect FY 05 operating EPS to rise 5%, to $1.66, from EPS before special items of $1.58 in FY 04. Longer term, we project 5% to 7% operating EPS growth.

- Our FY 05 Standard & Poor's Core Earnings projection, reflecting projected stock option expense of $0.04 per share and adjustments for pension costs, is $1.58.

Investment Rationale/Risk October 12, 2004

- Our hold recommendation primarily reflects mixed results in recent quarters and our belief that the company's turnaround plan will need more time to gain traction. While earnings visibility is improving, in our opinion, CPB recently reduced its long-term annual EPS growth target to 5% to 7%, from its previous 8% EPS growth goal. With the stock recently trading at approximately 15X our calendar 2005 EPS estimate of $1.75, a discount to the P/E multiples of comparable packaged food peers and the multiple for the S&P 500 Index, we believe CPB is worth holding.

- Risks to our recommendation and target price relate to competitive pressures in CPB's businesses, consumer acceptance of new product introductions, weather conditions, and the company's ability to achieve sales and earnings growth forecasts.

- Our 12-month target price of $28 is based on our analyses of comparable peer multiples and discounted cash flows. Our DCF assumptions include a weighted average cost of capital of 9% and an expected terminal growth rate for cash flows of 3%.

Key Stock Statistics

S&P Oper. EPS 2005E	1.66	52-week Range	$28.70-24.92
P/E on S&P Oper. EPS 2005E	16.4	12 Month P/E	17.3
S&P Oper. EPS 2006E	1.76	Beta	0.43
Yield (%)	2.5%	Shareholders	32,299
Dividend Rate/Share	0.68	Market Cap (B)	$ 11.1
Shares Outstanding (M)	408.0		

Value of $10,000 invested five years ago: **$ 6,920**

Dividend Data Dividends have been paid since 1902

Amount ($)	Date Decl.	Ex-Div. Date	Stock of Record	Payment Date
0.158	Nov. 20	Dec. 30	Jan. 02	Feb. 02 '04
0.158	Mar. 25	Apr. 07	Apr. 12	May. 03 '04
0.158	Jun. 24	Jul. 08	Jul. 12	Aug. 02 '04
0.170	Sep. 23	Oct. 06	Oct. 11	Nov. 01 '04

Revenues/Earnings Data Fiscal year ending July 31

Revenues (Million $)

	2004	2003	2002	2001	2000	1999
1Q	1,909	1,705	1,729	1,778	1,768	1,804
2Q	2,100	1,918	1,810	1,958	1,916	1,832
3Q	1,667	1,600	1,371	1,439	1,394	1,492
4Q	1,433	1,455	1,223	1,330	1,189	1,296
Yr.	7,109	6,678	6,133	6,664	6,267	6,424

Earnings Per Share ($)

	2004	2003	2002	2001	2000	1999
1Q	0.51	0.47	0.42	0.47	0.54	0.58
2Q	0.57	0.56	0.49	0.65	0.65	0.49
3Q	0.34	0.31	0.23	0.30	0.32	0.37
4Q	0.14	0.18	0.13	0.13	0.14	0.18
Yr.	1.57	1.52	1.28	1.55	1.65	1.63

Next earnings report expected: late-November Source: S&P, Company Reports
EPS Estimates based on S&P Operating Earnings; historical GAAP earnings are as reported.

Recommendation: **HOLD** ★ ★ ★ ☆ ☆   12-Month Target Price: **$28.00** (as of June 28, 2004)

Business Summary October 12, 2004

Probably known best for its ubiquitous red and white soup cans (elevated to icon status by Andy Warhol), Campbell Soup Co. is a major force in the U.S. packaged foods industry. The company, which traces its origins in the food business as far back as 1869, manufactures and markets a wide array of branded, prepared convenience food products worldwide.

Campbell's operations outside the U.S. accounted for 33% of net sales and 23% of pretax earnings in FY 03 (Jul.), mostly in Europe (14% and 10%) and Australia/Asia Pacific (11% and 7%). Contributions to sales and operating profits by division in FY 03 were: North American Soup and Away From Home (39% and 50%), North American Sauces and Beverages (19%, 23%), Biscuit and Confectionery (26% and 17%) and International Soup and Sauces (16% and 10%).

In March 1998, Campbell completed the spin-off of several non-core businesses, with revenues totaling $1.4 billion, including its Swanson frozen foods and Vlasic pickles units. The spin-off was consistent with the company's initiatives to improve its financial profile. These initiatives have also involved aggressive cost reduction actions, the sale of non-strategic businesses, and share repurchases.

Campbell's major U.S. products include both condensed and ready-to-serve soups (Campbell's, Home Cookin', Chunky, Healthy Request); broth (Swanson); convenience meals (Hungry Man); beans (Homestyle Pork and Beans); juices (Camp-

bell's Tomato, V8, V8 Splash); canned spaghetti and gravies (Franco-American); spaghetti sauce (Prego); and Mexican sauces (Pace). Foodservice operations serve the away-from-home eating market.

The company's Biscuit and Confectionery division products include Pepperidge Farm, Inc. in the U.S., a producer of bread, cakes and related products; and Arnotts Biscuits Ltd. of Australia, a maker of biscuit and bakery products. Godiva Chocolatier (worldwide) and Lamy-Lutti (Europe) serve the candy market.

International businesses consist of soup, grocery and frozen foods units in Canada, Mexico, Argentina, Europe, Australia and Asia. Major brands include Fray Bentos, Betis, Pleybin, Freshbake and Groko.

In May 2001, the company completed the purchase of several market-leading soup and sauces businesses in Europe from Unilever N.V. The businesses, with combined annual sales of more than $400 million, include three instant dry soup brands (Batchelors in the U.K., Royco in France and Belgium, and Heisse Tasse in Germany), and Oxo bouillon cubes in the U.K. The purchase price was 1 billion euros, or approximately $900 million.

The Dorrance family controls more than 50% of the common stock.

Company Financials Fiscal Year ending July 31

Per Share Data ($)

(Year Ended July 31)	2004	2003	2002	2001	2000	1999	1998	1997	1996	1995
Tangible Bk. Val.	NM	NM	NM	NM	NM	NM	NM	NM	1.89	1.51
Cash Flow	2.20	2.11	2.05	2.19	2.23	2.20	2.07	2.21	2.27	1.99
Earnings	1.57	1.52	1.28	1.55	1.65	1.63	1.50	1.51	1.61	1.40
S&P Core Earnings	1.47	1.46	1.00	1.28	NA	NA	NA	NA	NA	NA
Dividends	0.63	0.63	0.63	0.90	0.68	0.89	0.82	0.75	0.67	0.60
Payout Ratio	40%	41%	49%	58%	41%	55%	55%	50%	42%	43%
Prices - High	28.70	27.90	30.00	35.43	39.62	55.75	62.87	59.37	42.12	30.62
- Low	25.03	19.95	19.65	25.52	23.75	37.43	46.68	39.37	28.00	20.50
P/E Ratio - High	18	18	23	23	24	34	42	39	26	22
- Low	16	13	15	16	14	23	31	26	17	15

Income Statement Analysis (Million $)

	2004	2003	2002	2001	2000	1999	1998	1997	1996	1995
Revs.	7,109	6,678	6,133	6,664	6,267	6,424	6,696	7,964	7,678	7,278
Oper. Inc.	1,394	1,376	1,442	1,470	1,516	1,625	1,782	1,950	1,715	1,504
Depr.	260	243	319	266	251	255	261	382	326	294
Int. Exp.	174	186	190	216	192	184	189	167	137	123
Pretax Inc.	947	924	798	987	1,077	1,097	1,079	1,114	1,197	1,042
Eff. Tax Rate	31.7%	32.3%	34.2%	34.2%	33.7%	34.0%	35.6%	35.4%	33.0%	33.0%
Net Inc.	647	626	525	649	714	724	689	713	802	698
S&P Core Earnings	603	604	413	536	NA	NA	NA	NA	NA	NA

Balance Sheet & Other Fin. Data (Million $)

	2004	2003	2002	2001	2000	1999	1998	1997	1996	1995
Cash	32.0	32.0	21.0	24.0	27.0	6.00	16.0	26.0	34.0	53.0
Curr. Assets	1,481	1,290	1,199	1,221	1,168	1,294	1,440	1,583	1,618	1,581
Total Assets	6,675	6,205	5,721	5,927	5,196	5,522	5,633	6,459	6,632	6,315
Curr. Liab.	2,339	2,783	2,678	3,120	3,032	3,146	2,803	2,981	2,229	2,164
LT Debt	2,543	2,249	2,449	2,243	1,218	1,330	1,169	1,153	744	857
Common Equity	874	387	-114	-247	137	275	874	1,420	2,742	2,468
Total Cap.	3,417	2,636	2,335	1,996	1,355	1,564	2,293	2,656	4,028	3,865
Cap. Exp.	288	283	269	200	200	297	256	331	416	391
Cash Flow	907	869	844	915	965	979	950	1,095	1,128	992
Curr. Ratio	0.6	0.5	0.4	0.4	0.4	0.4	0.5	0.5	0.7	0.7
% LT Debt of Cap.	74.4	85.3	104.9	112.4	89.9	85.0	51.0	43.4	18.5	22.2
% Net Inc.of Revs.	9.1	9.4	8.6	9.7	11.4	11.3	10.3	9.0	10.5	9.6
% Ret. on Assets	10.0	10.5	9.0	11.7	13.3	13.0	11.4	10.9	12.4	11.1
% Ret. on Equity	102.6	458.6	NA	NA	383.9	130.6	60.1	34.3	30.8	31.3

Data as orig reptd.; bef. results of disc opers/spec. items. Per share data adj. for stk. divs.; EPS diluted. E-Estimated. NA-Not Available. NM-Not Meaningful. NR-Not Ranked. UR-Under Review.

Office: Campbell Place, Camden, NJ 08103-1799.
Telephone: 856-342-4800.
Website: http://www.campbellsoup.com
Chrmn: G.M. Sherman.
Pres & CEO: D.R. Conant.

SVP, CFO & Investor Contact: R.A. Schiffner 856-342-4800.
Dirs: E. M. Carpenter, P. R. Charron, D. R. Conant, B. Dorrance, K. B. Foster, H. Golub, R. W. Larrimore, P. E. Lippincott, M. A. Malone, D. C. Patterson, C. R. Perrin, G. M. Sherman, D. M. Stewart, G. Strawbridge, Jr., L. C. Vinney, C. C. Weber.

Founded: in 1869.
Domicile: New Jersey.
Employees: 24,000.
S&P Analyst: Richard Joy/CB/BK

Capital One Financial

Recommendation: **BUY** ★★★★ 12-Month Target Price: **$91.00**
(SELL SELL HOLD BUY BUY)
(as of September 10, 2004)

COF has an approximate 0.17% weighting in the **S&P 500**

Sector: Financials
Sub-Industry: Consumer Finance
Peer Group: Consumer Finance - Credit Cards

Summary: This company is one of the largest issuers of Visa and MasterCard credit cards, with 33.8 million cardholders.

Quantitative Evaluations

S&P Earnings & Dividend Rank: A+

D	C	B-	B	B+	A-	A	A+

S&P Fair Value Rank: 5

1	2	3	4	5
Lowest				Highest

Fair Value Calc.: $108.40 (Undervalued)

S&P Investability Quotient Percentile

100%

COF scored higher than 100% of all companies for which an S&P Report is available.

Volatility: Average

Low	Average	High

Technical Evaluation: Bullish
Since 11/04, the technical indicators for COF have been Bullish.

Relative Strength Rank: Strong

74

1 Lowest   Highest 99

Price as of 11/12/04: $79.72   **2004E S&P Core EPS:** $5.61

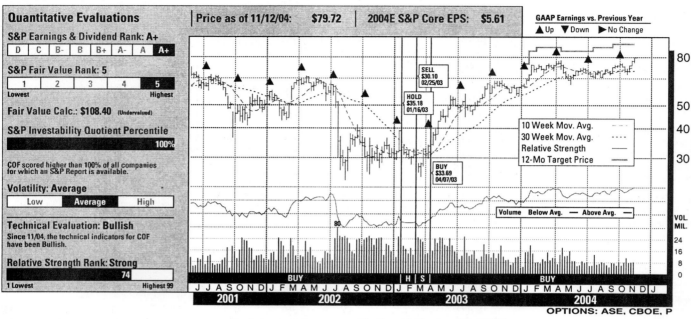

GAAP Earnings vs. Previous Year
▲ Up ▼ Down ► No Change

10 Week Mov. Avg.
30 Week Mov. Avg.
Relative Strength
12-Mo Target Price

Volume Below Avg. — Above Avg. —

SELL $30.10 02/25/03
HOLD $35.18 01/16/03
BUY $33.69 04/07/03

OPTIONS: ASE, CBOE, P

Analyst commentary prepared by Evan M. Momios, CFA /CB/BK

Highlights September 13, 2004

- Year to date results have far exceeded our expectations, as improved delinquencies allowed COF to reduce its loan loss allowance, directly adding to reported EPS. We expect quarterly EPS in the second half of 2004 to be lower than in the first half but continue to compare favorably on a year over year basis. Higher marketing costs related to the introduction of new products and additions to the company's loan loss reserve on loan growth that we anticipate should suppress quarterly EPS from first half levels.

- Our model assumes 15% loan growth, improving credit quality, a declining net interest margin, lower quarterly fee income on a year over year basis, and increasing marketing costs as COF continues to shift its product mix toward higher quality and higher average balance, but lower margin, products.

- We do not think that higher short interest rates pose a meaningful threat to earnings, as COF has an asset sensitive balance sheet that should benefit the bottom line in a rising interest rate environment. We also think COF's smaller size and ability to capture market share should help mitigate this risk. We see EPS advancing to $6.12 in 2004, with a further gain to $6.72 in 2005.

Investment Rationale/Risk September 13, 2004

- We believe investors should buy the shares, based on the company's progress in the implementation of its dual operating strategy of diversification and emphasis on lower loss rate products that, in our view, is likely to generate consistent and above industry-average EPS growth in the years ahead. We believe our expectation is not currently reflected in the stock's valuation.

- Risks to our recommendation and target price include increased competition from larger credit card issuers in the prime segment that may pressure returns over time, a decline in consumer confidence that may suppress consumer spending, and a rise in unemployment that could impact credit quality.

- Our 12-month target price of $91 equates to 13.5X our 2005 EPS estimate, and is equal to the group mean. We believe this is an appropriate valuation multiple given the current stage of the economic expansion and the meaningful progress the company has made in improving its credit risk profile and product mix.

Key Stock Statistics

S&P Core EPS 2005E	6.19	52-week Range	$79.82-55.15
S&P Oper. EPS 2004E	6.35	12 Month P/E	12.2
P/E on S&P Oper. EPS 2004E	12.6	Beta	1.68
S&P Oper. EPS 2005E	6.95	Shareholders	10,227
Yield (%)	0.1%	Market Cap (B)	$ 19.3
Dividend Rate/Share	0.11	Shares Outstanding (M)	242.7

Value of $10,000 invested five years ago: **$ 14,682**

Dividend Data Dividends have been paid since 1995

Amount ($)	Date Decl.	Ex-Div. Date	Stock of Record	Payment Date
0.027	Jan. 30	Feb. 06	Feb. 10	Feb. 20 '04
0.027	May. 03	May. 06	May. 10	May. 20 '04
0.027	Jul. 30	Aug. 06	Aug. 10	Aug. 20 '04
0.027	Oct. 29	Nov. 09	Nov. 12	Nov. 22 '04

Revenues/Earnings Data Fiscal year ending December 31

Revenues (Million $)

	2004	2003	2002	2001	2000	1999
1Q	2,608	2,411	2,133	1,675	1,171	877.7
2Q	2,548	2,381	2,369	1,731	1,247	949.8
3Q	2,768	2,466	2,628	1,867	1,428	1,033
4Q	—	2,525	2,434	1,982	1,578	1,105
Yr.	—	9,784	9,648	7,254	5,424	3,966

Earnings Per Share ($)

	2004	2003	2002	2001	2000	1999
1Q	1.84	1.35	0.83	0.66	0.51	0.39
2Q	1.65	1.23	0.92	0.70	0.54	0.41
3Q	1.97	1.23	1.13	0.75	0.58	0.45
4Q	E0.97	1.11	1.05	0.80	0.61	0.47
Yr.	E6.35	4.92	3.93	2.91	2.24	1.72

Next earnings report expected: late-January Source: S&P, Company Reports
EPS Estimates based on S&P Operating Earnings; historical GAAP earnings are as reported.

Capital One Financial Corporation

Recommendation: **BUY** ★ ★ ★ ★ ★   12-Month Target Price: **$91.00** (as of September 10, 2004)

Business Summary September 14, 2004

Capital One Financial (COF) is one of the largest U.S. issuers of Visa and MasterCard credit cards. At the end of 2003, it had 47.0 million customer accounts and $71.2 billion in total managed loans outstanding, versus 47.3 million customer accounts and $59.7 billion in managed loans a year earlier. COF, which has grown rapidly over the past decade, attributes this growth not only to the favorable dynamics of the credit card industry, but also to the company's information-based strategy (IBS), which it initiated in 1988. Prior to its November 1994 IPO, COF was a wholly owned subsidiary of Signet Banking Corp., which was acquired by First Union Corp. in late 1997.

COF uses IBS to differentiate among customers based on credit risk, card usage and other characteristics. IBS is also used to match customer characteristics with appropriate product offerings, which helps product launches. The company continuously seeks to apply IBS to other financial products and services. In July 1998, it acquired Summit Acceptance Corp., an automobile finance lender that offers loans throughout the U.S. secured by automobiles and marketed mainly through dealer networks. COF used Summit as a platform to test IBS in the auto loan market. In October 2001, the company expanded its auto loan business by acquiring PeopleFirst, Inc., the largest online provider of direct motor vehicle loans in the U.S., in exchange for 3.7 million common shares (valued at about $167.5 million).

The company's credit card products are offered throughout the U.S., as well as internationally, primarily in the U.K. and Canada; about $7.6 billion (11%) of the company's consumer loan portfolio consisted of international loans as of the end of 2003, versus $5.3 billion (9%) at year-end 2002. Credit card products are designed to apply to different consumer preferences and needs by combining different product features such as annual percentage rates, fees and charges, and reward programs.

Marketing is an important part of COF's operations. In 2003, the company spent about $1.12 billion on marketing, slightly more than the $1.07 billion it spent in 2002. Most of COF's accounts are generated through direct mail and telemarketing solicitations, although the company is increasing its efforts to generate accounts through Internet, newspaper, magazine, radio and television advertising.

At the end of 2003, 4.46% of total managed loans were 30 days or more past due, versus 5.60% in 2002. Net chargeoffs include the principal amount of losses less any current period recoveries. Loans that are 180 days past due are charged off. The company's net chargeoff ratio declined to 5.32% during the fourth quarter of 2003, from 6.21% in the fourth quarter of 2002. The company's net interest margin narrowed to 8.24% in the fourth quarter of 2003, from 9.19% in the fourth quarter of 2002.

Company Financials Fiscal Year ending December 31

Per Share Data ($)

(Year Ended December 31)	2003	2002	2001	2000	1999	1998	1997	1996	1995	1994
Tangible Bk. Val.	25.75	20.44	15.33	9.94	7.69	6.45	4.55	3.72	3.02	2.39
Earnings	4.92	3.93	2.91	2.24	1.72	1.32	0.93	0.77	0.63	0.48
S&P Core Earnings	4.41	3.37	2.55	NA	NA	NA	NA	NA	NA	NA
Dividends	0.11	0.11	0.11	0.11	0.11	0.11	0.11	0.11	0.08	Nil
Payout Ratio	2%	3%	4%	5%	6%	8%	11%	14%	13%	Nil
Prices - High	64.25	66.50	72.58	73.25	60.25	43.31	18.10	12.29	9.87	5.54
- Low	24.91	24.05	36.40	32.06	35.81	16.85	10.16	7.25	5.12	4.62
P/E Ratio - High	13	17	25	33	35	33	19	16	16	12
- Low	5	6	13	14	21	13	11	9	8	10

Income Statement Analysis (Million $)

	2003	2002	2001	2000	1999	1998	1997	1996	1995	1994
Net Int. Inc.	2,785	2,719	1,663	1,589	1,053	695	383	365	208	165
Non Int. Inc.	5,416	5,467	4,420	3,034	2,372	1,488	1,069	763	553	397
Loan Loss Prov.	1,517	2,149	990	718	383	267	263	167	65.9	30.7
Non Int. Exp.	4,857	4,586	4,058	3,148	2,465	1,472	884	713	497	384
Exp./Op. Revs.	59.2%	56.0%	66.7%	68.1%	72.0%	67.4%	60.9%	63.2%	65.4%	68.4%
Pretax Inc.	1,827	1,451	1,035	757	577	444	305	248	198	147
Eff. Tax Rate	37.0%	38.0%	38.0%	38.0%	37.1%	38.0%	38.0%	37.5%	36.1%	35.1%
Net Inc.	1,151	900	642	470	363	275	189	155	129	95.3
% Net Int. Marg.	7.45	8.73	8.03	12.0	10.8	9.95	8.86	8.16	6.28	6.90
S&P Core Earnings	1,012	742	545	NA	NA	NA	NA	NA	NA	NA

Balance Sheet & Other Fin. Data (Million $)

	2003	2002	2001	2000	1999	1998	1997	1996	1995	1994
Money Mkt. Assets	1,598	641	352	162	112	284	174	450	465	300
Inv. Securities	5,867	4,424	3,116	1,697	1,856	1,797	1,243	895	769	113
Tot. Loans	32,850	27,854	20,921	14,059	9,914	6,157	4,862	4,225	2,450	2,160
Total Assets	46,284	37,382	28,184	18,889	13,336	9,419	7,078	6,467	4,759	3,092
Demand Deposits	Nil	Nil	Nil	Nil	Nil	Nil	Nil	Nil	Nil	Nil
Time Deposits	22,416	17,326	12,839	8,379	3,784	2,000	1,314	943	696	452
LT Debt	14,813	8,124	Nil	4,051	4,181	3,038	3,633	3,994	2,592	1,376
Common Equity	6,052	4,623	3,324	1,963	1,518	1,270	893	740	599	475
% Ret. on Assets	2.8	2.7	2.7	2.9	3.2	3.3	2.8	2.8	2.9	3.6
% Ret. on Equity	21.6	22.6	24.3	27.0	26.0	25.4	23.2	22.9	23.3	39.8
% Loan Loss Resv.	4.9	6.2	4.0	3.7	3.5	3.8	3.8	2.7	2.9	3.1
% Loans/Deposits	146.5	160.8	162.9	167.8	262.0	307.9	370.1	NM	NM	NM
% Loans/Assets	71.9	74.4	74.3	72.3	70.6	66.8	68.0	77.4	64.3	69.8
% Equity to Assets	12.8	12.1	11.2	10.8	12.3	13.1	12.1	15.7	12.6	15.4

Data as orig reptd.; bef. results of disc opers/spec. items. Per share data adj. for stk. divs.; EPS diluted. E-Estimated. NA-Not Available. NM-Not Meaningful. NR-Not Ranked. UR-Under Review.

Office: 1680 Capital One Drive, McLean, VA 22102-3406.
Telephone: 703-205-1000.
Email: investor.relations@capitalone.com
Website: http://www.capitalone.com
Chrmn, Pres & CEO: R.D. Fairbank.
Vice Chrmn: N.W. Morris.

EVP & CFO: G.L. Perlin.
EVP, Secy & General Counsel: J.G. Finneran, Jr.
VP & Investor Contact: P. Paquin 703-720-2455.
Dirs: W. R. Dietz, R. D. Fairbank, J. A. Flick, Jr., P. W. Gross, L. Hay III, J. V. Kimsey, N. W. Morris, M. A. Shattuck III, S. I. Westreich.

Founded: in 1993.
Domicile: Delaware.
Employees: 17,760.
S&P Analyst: Evan M. Momios, CFA /CB/BK

Cardinal Health

Recommendation: **HOLD** ★ ★ ★
SELL SELL HOLD BUY BUY

12-Month Target Price: $49.00
(as of November 05, 2004)

CAH has an approximate 0.20% weighting in the **S&P 500**

Sector: Health Care
Sub-Industry: Health Care Distributors
Peer Group: Diversified Distributors

Summary: CAH is one of the leading wholesale distributors of pharmaceuticals, medical/surgical supplies and related products to a broad range of health care customers.

Quantitative Evaluations

S&P Earnings & Dividend Rank: A+

D	C	B-	B	B+	A-	A	A+

S&P Fair Value Rank: 5+

1	2	3	4	5
Lowest				Highest

Fair Value Calc.: $53.60 (Slightly Undervalued)

S&P Investability Quotient Percentile

83%

CAH scored higher than 83% of all companies for which an S&P Report is available.

Volatility: High

Low	Average	High

Technical Evaluation: Neutral

Since 10/04, the technical indicators for CAH have been Neutral.

Relative Strength Rank: Strong

81

1 Lowest	Highest 99

Price as of 11/12/04:	$51.94	2005E S&P Core EPS:	$3.17

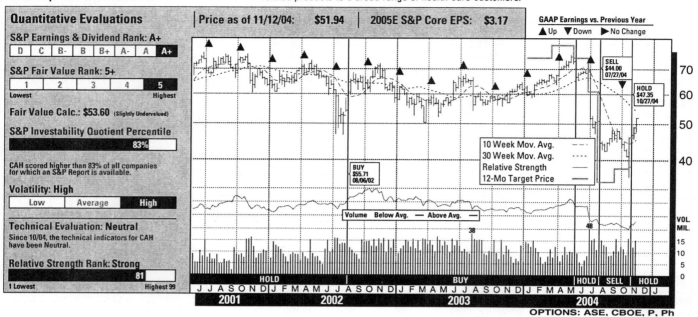

GAAP Earnings vs. Previous Year
▲ Up ▼ Down ▶ No Change

- 10 Week Mov. Avg.
- 30 Week Mov. Avg.
- Relative Strength
- 12-Mo Target Price

Volume Below Avg. — Above Avg.

BUY $55.71 08/06/02

SELL $44.00 07/27/04

HOLD $47.35 10/27/04

OPTIONS: ASE, CBOE, P, Ph

Analyst commentary prepared by Phillip M. Seligman/PMW/BK

Highlights November 01, 2004

- On October 26, CAH released its FY 04 (Jun.) 10-K report, after a long wait during which it restated results for FY 01, FY 02, FY 03, and the first three quarters of FY 04. For FY 05, the company looks for EPS to grow 10%, although it expects first half EPS to be down 10% to 15%, with first quarter EPS down 25%, on drug price hike delays, a continued transition of the distribution segment's business model, margin pressures on medical products, and delays in the startup of new sterile manufacturing projects.

- We do not expect any easing of what we see as greater than normal pharmaceutical supply gross margin pressures at least until FY 06, when we expect drugmaker inventory cutbacks to be at or near an end. We see little visibility that far out, as the transition to the fee-for-service business model is being accepted by small and mid-sized drug makers but so far by few large manufacturers.

- We believe CAH's estimate of FY 05 EPS growth of 10% is optimistic, in light of changing manufacturer-distributor dynamics and difficult EPS comparisons that we see in the first half. However, with cost cuts, we see improvement in the second half. We project FY 05 operating EPS of $3.45, versus FY 04 operating EPS of $3.55. Our FY 05 S&P Core EPS projection, reflecting estimated stock option expense, a modest pension plan adjustment, and a litigation settlement in FY 04, is $3.17.

Key Stock Statistics

S&P Oper. EPS 2005E	3.45	52-week Range	$76.54-36.08
P/E on S&P Oper. EPS 2005E	15.1	12 Month P/E	16.2
S&P Oper. EPS 2006E	4.10	Beta	0.19
Yield (%)	0.2%	Shareholders	19,300
Dividend Rate/Share	0.12	Market Cap (B)	$ 22.4
Shares Outstanding (M)	432.0		

Value of $10,000 invested five years ago: **$ 16,658**

Dividend Data Dividends have been paid since 1983

Amount ($)	Date Decl.	Ex-Div. Date	Stock of Record	Payment Date
0.030	Nov. 05	Dec. 29	Jan. 01	Jan. 15 '04
0.030	Feb. 11	Mar. 30	Apr. 01	Apr. 15 '04
0.030	May. 05	Jun. 29	Jul. 01	Jul. 15 '04
0.030	Aug. 04	Sep. 29	Oct. 01	Oct. 15 '04

Investment Rationale/Risk November 01, 2004

- We are encouraged by the company's filing of its FY 04 10-K report after a long delay, and, more importantly, by its establishment of new controls and procedures and improved transparency. We view these developments as helping management regain credibility with investors. Nothing has been found thus far in SEC and internal probes beyond what was previously announced, and we believe this relieved investors. However, we think that all four segments underperformed in the fourth quarter. Looking ahead, we see the pharmaceutical technologies and services division as best positioned for meaningful growth. We remain concerned about a lack of gross margin visibility related to CAH's transition to a fee-for-service business model.

- Risks to our recommendation and target price include the possibility that probes will find cause for further financial restatements; resistance by the largest drugmakers to the fee-for-service business model; unfavorable changes in healthcare regulations; and negative fundamentals affecting pharmaceutical manufacturers.

- The SEC probe continues, but we think the cloud overhanging the stock is mostly gone, and we believe the shares will trade in line with peer P/E multiples. Our 12-month target price of $46 is equal to 13X our FY 05 EPS estimate. We would not to add to current positions.

Revenues/Earnings Data Fiscal year ending June 30

Revenues (Million $)

	2005	2004	2003	2002	2001	2000
1Q	17,796	15,388	11,417	9,865	8,735	6,784
2Q	—	16,351	12,706	11,222	9,638	7,400
3Q	—	16,392	12,837	11,541	12,580	7,473
4Q	—	16,923	13,506	11,766	12,401	8,214
Yr.	—	65,054	50,468	44,394	47,947	29,871

Earnings Per Share ($)

	2005	2004	2003	2002	2001	2000
1Q	0.50	0.72	0.64	0.53	0.41	0.29
2Q	E0.82	0.85	0.82	0.62	0.49	0.41
3Q	E1.00	0.99	0.74	0.66	0.42	0.45
4Q	E1.06	0.91	0.82	0.64	0.55	0.46
Yr.	E3.45	3.47	3.12	2.45	1.88	1.59

Next earnings report expected: late-January Source: S&P, Company Reports
EPS Estimates based on S&P Operating Earnings; historical GAAP earnings are as reported.

Cardinal Health, Inc.

Recommendation: **HOLD** ★ ★ ★ ☆ ☆   12-Month Target Price: **$49.00** (as of November 05, 2004)

Business Summary November 01, 2004

Cardinal Health provides a broad array of complementary products and services intended to help providers and manufacturers improve the efficiency and quality of health care.

The pharmaceutical distribution and provider services segment (84% of FY 04 (Jun.) operating revenue) is one of the leading U.S. wholesale distributors of pharmaceutical and related healthcare products to independent and chain drug stores, hospitals, alternate care centers, and supermarket and mass merchandiser pharmacies. CAH complements its distribution activities by offering a broad range of value-added services to assist customers and suppliers in maintaining and improving sales volumes. These include online procurement, fulfillment and information through cardinal.com, computerized order entry and order confirmation systems, generic sourcing programs, product movement and management reports, and consultation on store operation and merchandising.

The medical-surgical products and services unit (11%), operating through Allegiance Corp., provides non-pharmaceutical healthcare products and cost saving services for hospitals and other healthcare providers. These products represent more than 2,000 suppliers. Allegiance also makes sterile and non-sterile procedure kits, single-use surgical drapes, gowns and apparel, medical-surgical gloves, fluid suction and collection systems, respiratory therapy products, surgical instruments, and instrument reprocessing products.

The pharmaceutical technologies and services division (4%) provides services to the drug manufacturing industry. These include manufacturing with unique drug delivery systems and related manufacturing capabilities. It also provides custom packaging services, and contract manufacturing and packaging of sterile liquid pharmaceuticals and other healthcare products in topical, oral, inhaled and ophthalmic formulations.

In the automation and information services segment (1%), the company operates businesses focusing on meeting customer needs through automation and information products and services, including Pyxis Corp., which develops, manufactures, leases, sells and services point-of-use pharmacy systems that automate the distribution and management of medications and supplies in hospitals and other healthcare facilities. CAH also provides information systems that analyze clinical outcomes and clinical pharmaceutical utilization information.

In February 2001, CAH acquired Bindley Western Industries Inc., a wholesale distributor of pharmaceuticals and a provider of nuclear pharmacy services, for $2.2 billion in stock. Bindley had annual operating revenues of about $6 billion. In April 2002, the company acquired Magellan Laboratories Inc., a pharmaceutical contract development organization, for $221 million before consideration of tax benefits associated with the transaction. In January 2003, CAH acquired Syncor International Corp., a leading provider of nuclear pharmacy services, in exchange for 12.5 million common shares; in addition, Syncor's options converted into options to purchase 3 million CAH shares.

Company Financials Fiscal Year ending June 30

Per Share Data ($)

(Year Ended June 30)	2004	2003	2002	2001	2000	1999	1998	1997	1996	1995
Tangible Bk. Val.	7.05	12.10	11.50	9.50	7.28	6.13	9.04	4.94	3.88	3.87
Cash Flow	4.15	3.70	2.98	2.50	2.17	1.65	1.86	0.95	0.66	0.74
Earnings	3.47	3.12	2.45	1.88	1.59	1.09	0.97	0.74	0.51	0.60
S&P Core Earnings	3.14	2.78	2.26	1.69	NA	NA	NA	NA	NA	NA
Dividends	0.12	0.11	0.10	0.09	0.05	0.05	0.05	0.04	0.04	0.04
Payout Ratio	3%	4%	4%	5%	3%	5%	5%	6%	7%	6%
Prices - High	76.54	67.96	73.70	77.32	69.95	55.50	50.91	35.00	26.00	17.22
- Low	36.08	50.00	46.60	56.66	24.66	24.66	30.97	22.88	15.53	12.29
P/E Ratio - High	22	22	30	41	44	51	53	47	51	29
- Low	10	16	19	30	15	23	32	31	30	21

Income Statement Analysis (Million $)

	2004	2003	2002	2001	2000	1999	1998	1997	1996	1995
Revs.	65,054	50,467	44,394	47,948	29,871	25,034	15,918	10,968	8,862	7,806
Oper. Inc.	2,694	3,723	2,216	1,893	1,377	1,257	538	443	315	185
Depr.	299	266	244	281	246	234	64.3	51.3	32.0	21.0
Int. Exp.	99	115	133	155	117	99	23.0	28.0	23.9	19.3
Pretax Inc.	2,238	2,127	1,701	1,332	1,078	759	403	312	202	147
Eff. Tax Rate	31.9%	33.6%	33.8%	35.6%	36.9%	39.9%	38.6%	42.0%	44.7%	42.0%
Net Inc.	1,525	1,412	1,126	857	680	456	247	181	112	85.0
S&P Core Earnings	1,369	1,266	1,045	771	NA	NA	NA	NA	NA	NA

Balance Sheet & Other Fin. Data (Million $)

	2004	2003	2002	2001	2000	1999	1998	1997	1996	1995
Cash	1,096	1,724	1,382	934	505	165	305	243	288	41.0
Curr. Assets	13,058	13,250	11,907	10,716	6,871	5,147	3,229	2,504	2,240	1,687
Total Assets	21,369	18,521	16,438	14,642	10,265	8,289	3,961	3,109	2,681	1,842
Curr. Liab.	9,369	7,314	6,810	6,575	4,262	2,959	1,844	1,409	1,386	1,073
LT Debt	2,835	2,472	2,207	1,871	1,486	1,224	273	278	265	209
Common Equity	7,976	7,758	6,393	5,437	3,981	3,463	1,625	1,332	931	548
Total Cap.	12,000	11,207	8,600	7,308	5,467	5,208	1,898	1,610	1,196	757
Cap. Exp.	410	423	285	341	308	320	111	75.2	73.0	43.0
Cash Flow	1,824	1,678	1,370	1,138	926	690	311	232	144	106
Curr. Ratio	1.4	1.8	1.7	1.6	1.6	1.7	1.8	1.8	1.6	1.6
% LT Debt of Cap.	23.6	22.1	25.7	25.6	27.2	23.5	14.4	17.3	22.2	27.6
% Net Inc.of Revs.	2.3	2.8	2.5	1.8	2.3	1.8	1.6	1.7	1.3	1.1
% Ret. on Assets	7.7	8.1	7.2	6.4	7.3	5.8	7.0	6.1	4.7	5.3
% Ret. on Equity	19.5	20.0	19.0	17.4	18.0	14.2	16.7	15.3	13.0	18.5

Data as orig reptd.; bef. results of disc opers/spec. items. Per share data adj. for stk. divs.; EPS diluted. E-Estimated. NA-Not Available. NM-Not Meaningful. NR-Not Ranked. UR-Under Review.

Office: 7000 Cardinal Place, Dublin, OH 43017.
Telephone: 614-757-5000.
Website: http://www.cardinal.com
Chrmn & CEO: R.D. Walter.
Pres & COO: G.L. Fotiades.
EVP, Secy & General Counsel: P.S. Williams.

CFO: J.M. Losh.
Investor Contact: S.T. Fischbach 614-757-7067.
Dirs: D. Bing, G. H. Conrades, J. F. Finn, R. L. Gerbig, J. F. Havens, J. M. Losh, J. B. McCoy, R. C. Notebaert, M. D. O'Halleran, D. Raisbeck, J. G. Spaulding, R. D. Walter, M. D. Walter.

Founded: in 1979.
Domicile: Ohio.
Employees: 55,000.
S&P Analyst: Phillip M. Seligman/PMW/BK

Caremark Rx

Recommendation: **BUY** ★★★★☆
SELL · SELL · HOLD · BUY · BUY

12-Month Target Price: **$42.00**
(as of November 12, 2004)

CMX has an approximate 0.15% weighting in the **S&P 500**

Sector: Health Care
Sub-Industry: Health Care Services

Summary: This pharmacy benefits manager provides drug benefit services to more than 2,000 health plan sponsors holding contracts to serve about 24 million participants throughout the U.S.

Quantitative Evaluations

S&P Earnings & Dividend Rank: B-

| D | C | **B-** | B | B+ | A- | A | A+ |

S&P Fair Value Rank: 5

| 1 | 2 | 3 | 4 | **5** |
Lowest — Highest

Fair Value Calc.: $38.50 (Slightly Undervalued)

S&P Investability Quotient Percentile

95%

CMX scored higher than 95% of all companies for which an S&P Report is available.

Volatility: Average

| Low | **Average** | High |

Technical Evaluation: Bullish

Since 11/04, the technical indicators for CMX have been Bullish.

Relative Strength Rank: Strong

89
1 Lowest — Highest 99

Price as of 11/12/04: **$36.28** | **2004E S&P Core EPS:** **$1.38**

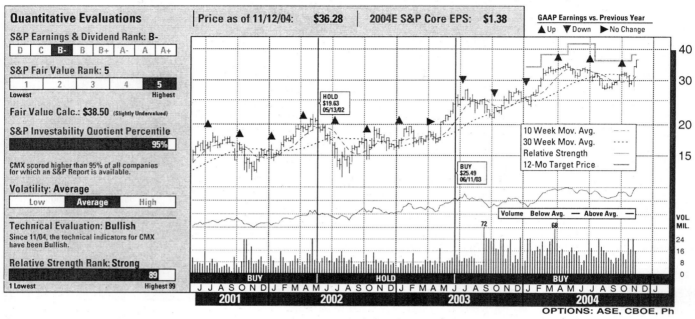

GAAP Earnings vs. Previous Year
▲ Up ▼ Down ► No Change

HOLD $19.63 05/13/02
BUY $25.49 06/11/03

10 Week Mov. Avg.
30 Week Mov. Avg.
Relative Strength
12-Mo Target Price

Volume Below Avg. — Above Avg.

72   68

VOL. MIL.
24
16
8
0

BUY   J J A S O N D   HOLD   BUY
J J A S O N D J F M A M J J A S O N D J F M A M J J A S O N D J F M A M J J A S O N D J
2001 **2002** **2003** **2004**

OPTIONS: ASE, CBOE, Ph

Analyst commentary prepared by Phillip M. Seligman/PMW/JWP

Highlights 15-NOV-04

- We project 2005 revenues of $33.4 billion, up 30% from our 2004 estimate of $25.7 billion, reflecting the March 2004 acquisition of AdvancePCS, expected net new business, drug price inflation, and increased service usage by existing accounts, tempered by a mix shift toward lower-priced but highly profitable generic drugs. On a pro forma basis, if AdvancePCS been acquired prior to 2004, we estimate that 2005 revenue growth would be 8%.
- We expect EBITDA per adjusted claim, which advanced 27% in the third quarter on a pro forma basis, to grow at near that level in the fourth quarter, on the continued integration of AdvancePCS. We think CMX is on track to exceeding its 2004 year-end target of $125 million in cost-saving synergies. The company sees another potential $125 million in synergies to be realized over the next few years. We think these would consist mainly of top-line synergies from cross-selling and new products and services. Other drivers that we see for expanding EBITDA per adjusted claim are continued mail order, generic, and specialty drug penetration.
- We look for 2005 EPS of $1.95, up 35% from our 2004 EPS estimate of $1.44. Our projections of 2004 and 2005 S&P Core EPS are $1.38 and $1.91, respectively, reflecting estimated stock option expense.

Investment Rationale/Risk 15-NOV-04

- Our recommendation is buy. We think that profit prospects have been significantly enhanced by the acquisition of AdvancePCS. We see annual EPS growth exceeding 25% for the next three to five years, aided by cross-selling and new product opportunities, favorable demographics, and improved drug affordability for seniors through the Medicare Modernization Act. However, we note that frequent negative press about the pharmacy benefit management industry, part of which we attribute to lack of transparency of its operations, and frequent state and federal government probes that we think may lead to increased regulatory oversight, have made the shares volatile.
- Risks to our recommendation and target price include greater competition, pressures on margins from clients seeking greater discounts and/or enhanced services, increased government oversight and adverse regulatory changes, loss of key client and provider accounts, and risks due to investigations. CMX is being probed by 25 states and the District of Columbia. A worst-case scenario, in our view, would be a loss of government and other business.
- Based on our view of healthy organic growth, we think the positive factors that we see outweigh investor concern over the state probes. In light of our view of fundamentals, we think the stock merits a forward P/E multiple at a wide premium to the S&P 500. Our target price of $42 is equal to 21.5X our 2005 EPS estimate.

Key Stock Statistics

S&P Core EPS 2005E	1.91	52-week Range	$36.30-23.50	
S&P Oper. EPS 2004E	1.44	12 Month P/E	28.3	
P/E on S&P Oper. EPS 2004E	25.2	Beta	0.35	
S&P Oper. EPS 2005E	1.95	Shareholders	16,218	
Yield (%)	Nil	Market Cap (B)	$ 16.9	
Dividend Rate/Share	Nil	Shares Outstanding (M)	454.6	

Value of $10,000 invested five years ago: **$ 69,104**

Dividend Data

No cash dividends have been paid.

Revenues/Earnings Data Fiscal year ending December 31

Revenues (Million $)

	2004	2003	2002	2001	2000	1999
1Q	3,026	2,164	1,614	1,374	1,053	785.1
2Q	7.30	2,204	1,626	1,373	1,084	796.2
3Q	7,458	2,257	1,713	1,380	1,089	813.0
4Q	—	2,443	1,851	1,486	1,204	913.5
Yr.	—	9,067	6,805	5,614	4,430	3,308

Earnings Per Share ($)

	2004	2003	2002	2001	2000	1999
1Q	0.29	0.24	0.24	0.15	0.09	0.06
2Q	0.30	0.26	0.27	0.16	0.09	0.06
3Q	0.37	0.29	0.31	0.19	0.11	0.07
4Q	E0.44	0.31	2.34	0.23	0.14	0.10
Yr.	E1.44	1.10	3.15	0.73	0.43	-0.74

Next earnings report expected: early-February Source: S&P, Company Reports
EPS Estimates based on S&P Operating Earnings; historical GAAP earnings are as reported.

Caremark Rx, Inc.

Recommendation: **BUY** ★ ★ ★ ★ ☆   12-Month Target Price: **$42.00** (as of November 12, 2004)

Business Summary 15-NOV-04

In March 2004, Caremark Rx acquired AdvancePCS, a formerly publicly traded pharmacy benefit manager, with sales and net income in the nine months ended December 31, 2003, of $11.4 billion and $154 million, respectively. The company believed that the transaction combined two highly complementary organizations, and greatly enhanced the company's ability to offer clients a broader selection of health care products and services to help control drug spending and improve quality of care. The following description applies to CMX prior to the acquisition.

CMX (formerly MedPartners Inc.) provides pharmacy benefit management services and therapeutic pharmaceutical services that assist employers, insurance companies, unions, government employee group, HMOs and other sponsors of health benefit plans and individuals throughout the U.S. in delivering prescription drugs in a cost-effective manner. In 2003, the company managed 114.8 million prescriptions for individuals from more than 1,200 organizations.

Pharmacy benefits management involves the design and administration of programs aimed at reducing costs and improving the safety, effectiveness and convenience of prescription drug use. The company dispenses prescription drugs to patients through a network of more than 55,000 third party retail pharmacies (about 96% of all retail pharmacies in the U.S.), and through three of its own mail service pharmacies. In 2003, CMX processed about 89.9 million retail prescriptions (up from 71.3 million in 2002), and filled 24.9 million (20.2 million) mail order prescriptions.

At December 31, 2003, CMX operated four automated mail service pharmacies, located in Phoenix, AZ; Westin, FL; Mount Prospect, IL; and San Antonio TX. It has an FDA-regulated repackaging facility, located in Vernon Hills, IL. Three regional call centers (two in San Antonio, TX, and one in Kansas City, MO) support participant and retail pharmacist inquiries, and there is a disease management call center in one of the call centers.

Through its Caremark Therapeutic Services (CTS) unit, the company offers specialized home or office delivery of high-cost biotech pharmaceuticals and related therapeutic services, including compliance management, emergency telephone counseling, education programs, and, where necessary, coordination of in-home nursing services. Services generally include provision of injectable and other specialized infusion drugs, and are delivered by express courier from a national network of 19 specialty pharmacies. CTS programs currently serve more than 34,000 patients, delivering more than 322,000 specialized prescriptions annually.

In July 1999, CMX launched RxRequest.com, a fully secure customer Internet website that provides expanded services, including on-line prescription refill order capabilities for company prescription drug plan participants. RxRequest.com also lets users check the status of their prescription refill orders, print order and claim forms, and locate the most appropriate participating retail pharmacies.

Company Financials Fiscal Year ending December 31

Per Share Data ($)

(Year Ended December 31)	2003	2002	2001	2000	1999	1998	1997	1996	1995	1994
Tangible Bk. Val.	2.18	0.75	NM	NM	NM	NM	NA	0.49	1.49	NA
Cash Flow	1.27	3.22	0.78	0.55	-0.62	0.29	-3.09	-0.05	0.68	0.51
Earnings	1.10	3.15	0.73	0.43	-0.74	0.16	-4.25	-0.58	Nil	-0.08
S&P Core Earnings	1.07	3.10	0.66	NA	NA	NA	NA	NA	NA	NA
Dividends	Nil	Nil	Nil	Nil	Nil	Nil	Nil	Nil	Nil	NA
Payout Ratio	Nil	Nil	Nil	Nil	Nil	Nil	Nil	Nil	Nil	NA
Prices - High	27.92	21.95	18.50	13.93	9.00	22.37	32.00	36.00	34.50	NA
- Low	16.20	12.24	10.75	3.75	2.87	1.62	17.87	16.37	13.00	NA
P/E Ratio - High	25	7	25	32	NM	NM	NM	NM	NM	NA
- Low	15	4	15	9	NM	NM	NM	NM	NM	NA

Income Statement Analysis (Million $)

	2003	2002	2001	2000	1999	1998	1997	1996	1995	1994
Revs.	9,067	6,805	5,614	4,430	3,308	2,634	6,331	4,813	1,137	802
Oper. Inc.	576	411	297	236	201	163	110	318	103	34.0
Depr.	45.1	29.9	26.9	25.4	22.1	24.7	120	81.9	29.1	21.9
Int. Exp.	42.5	46.8	77.3	110	120	78.8	55.7	23.9	8.44	5.96
Pretax Inc.	485	334	193	100	-138	49.6	-772	-95.1	-25.5	4.30
Eff. Tax Rate	40.0%	NM	8.01%	8.49%	NM	38.0%	NM	NM	NM	NM
Net Inc.	291	829	177	91.4	-143	30.8	-694	-89.8	-0.18	-3.07
S&P Core Earnings	285	807	159	NA	NA	NA	NA	NA	NA	NA

Balance Sheet & Other Fin. Data (Million $)

	2003	2002	2001	2000	1999	1998	1997	1996	1995	1994
Cash	815	307	159	2.35	6.80	23.1	216	124	90.9	NA
Curr. Assets	1,947	1,226	647	453	535	1,186	1,313	947	269	NA
Total Assets	2,474	1,913	874	686	771	1,862	2,891	2,266	579	NA
Curr. Liab.	1,064	877	679	635	563	1,100	1,237	777	210	NA
LT Debt	693	696	896	933	1,430	1,735	1,471	716	201	NA
Common Equity	641	258	-772	-969	-1,281	-1,144	90.9	739	184	NA
Total Cap.	1,334	953	123	-35.7	149	591	1,562	1,455	385	NA
Cap. Exp.	63.2	48.4	39.9	23.2	20.4	28.7	123	122	NA	NA
Cash Flow	336	849	204	117	-121	55.5	-573	-7.90	28.9	18.8
Curr. Ratio	1.8	1.4	1.0	0.7	0.9	1.1	1.1	1.2	1.3	NA
% LT Debt of Cap.	52.0	73.0	727.2	NM	962.7	293.6	94.1	49.2	52.2	NA
% Net Inc.of Revs.	3.2	12.2	3.2	2.1	NM	1.2	NM	NM	NM	NM
% Ret. on Assets	13.3	59.5	22.7	12.6	NM	1.3	NM	NM	NM	NA
% Ret. on Equity	64.8	NM	NM	NM	NM	NA	NM	NM	NM	NA

Data as orig. reptd. (pro forma prior to 1996); bef. results of disc. opers. and/or spec. items. Per share data adj. for stk. divs.; EPS diluted. E-Estimated. NA-Not Available. NM-Not Meaningful. NR-Not Ranked.

Office: 211 Commerce Street, Nashville, TN 37201-1817.
Telephone: 615-743-6600.
Website: http://www.caremark.com
Chrmn, Pres & CEO: E. M. Crawford.
EVP & CFO: H. A. McLure.
EVP & General Counsel: E. L. Hardin, Jr.

EVP: B. S. Karro.
Investor Contact: John Jennings (615-743-6600).
Dirs: E. M. Banks, C. D. Brown II, C. Conway-Welch, E. M. Crawford, H. Diamond, K. E. Gibney-Williams, E. L. Hardin, Jr., R. L. Headrick, T. H. McCourtney, J. Millon, C. L. Piccolo, G. Poste, M. D. Ware.

Founded: in 1993.
Domicile: Delaware.
Employees: 11,000.
S&P Analyst: Phillip M. Seligman/PMW/JWP

Recommendation: **HOLD** ★ ★ ★ ★ ★
SELL | SELL | HOLD | BUY | BUY

12-Month Target Price: **$54.00**
(as of September 17, 2004)

CCL has an approximate 0.31% weighting in the **S&P 500**

Sector: Consumer Discretionary
Sub-Industry: Hotels, Resorts & Cruise Lines
Peer Group: Cruise Ships, Resorts, Timeshares, etc.

Summary: This expanding company owns and operates businesses that operate more than 70 cruise ships.

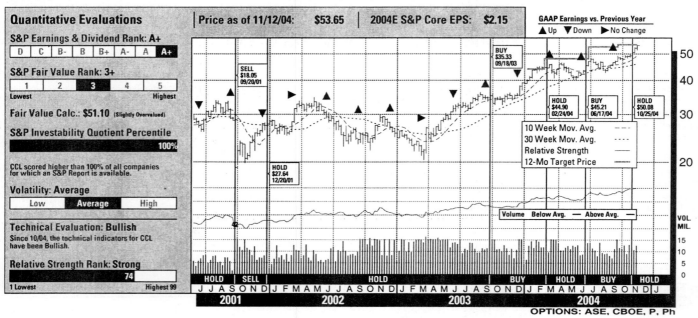

Quantitative Evaluations

S&P Earnings & Dividend Rank: A+
D | C | B- | B | B+ | A- | A | **A+**

S&P Fair Value Rank: 3+
1 | 2 | **3** | 4 | 5
Lowest | | | | Highest

Fair Value Calc.: $51.10 (Slightly Overvalued)

S&P Investability Quotient Percentile
100%
CCL scored higher than 100% of all companies for which an S&P Report is available.

Volatility: Average
Low | **Average** | High

Technical Evaluation: Bullish
Since 10/04, the technical indicators for CCL have been Bullish.

Relative Strength Rank: Strong
74
1 Lowest | Highest 99

Price as of 11/12/04: $53.65 | **2004E S&P Core EPS:** $2.15

GAAP Earnings vs. Previous Year
▲ Up ▼ Down ▶ No Change

Chart annotations: SELL $18.05 09/20/01; HOLD $27.64 12/20/01; BUY $35.33 09/18/03; HOLD $44.90 02/24/04; BUY $45.21 06/17/04; HOLD $50.08 10/25/04

10 Week Mov. Avg.
30 Week Mov. Avg.
Relative Strength
12-Mo Target Price

Volume   Below Avg.   Above Avg.

VOL. MIL.
15
10
5
0

HOLD | SELL | HOLD | BUY | HOLD | BUY | HOLD
J J A S O N D | J F M A M J J A S O N D | J F M A M J J A S O N D | J F M A M J J A S O N D | J
2001 | 2002 | 2003 | 2004

OPTIONS: ASE, CBOE, P, Ph

Analyst commentary prepared by Tom Graves, CFA /PMW/BK

Highlights October 27, 2004

- In April 2003, this leading cruise ship company merged with P&O Princess Cruises plc (renamed Carnival plc), creating a business with operations that include more than 70 ships. In connection with the merger, which was effected via an exchange of stock, CCL's diluted share base increased by about 210 million, to a total of about 800 million shares. With a dual listing format, CCL shares continue to trade on the NYSE, while Carnival plc shares trade on the London Stock Exchange.

- In FY 05 (Nov.), including the addition of new ships and stronger consumer demand for cruise ship travel, we look for the company to have revenue of $10.9 billion, up 13% from the $9.6 billion that we project for FY 04. We estimate FY 05 net income of $2.2 billion ($2.65 per share), up from the $1.8 billion ($2.21) that we project for FY 04.

- Directors have authorized the repurchase of up to $1 billion of Carnival Corp. and Carnival plc shares, and have approved a 20% increase in the quarterly dividend, to $0.15 a share.

Investment Rationale/Risk October 27, 2004

- Our hold opinion on the shares reflects our view that the stock is appropriately priced. We see longer-term demographics for the cruise ship industry as generally favorable, based on the expectation that aging baby boomers will be attracted to cruise vacations. We also think that the company's competitive standing, including its ability to attract more cruise customers, is being helped by the addition of new ships.

- Risks to our recommendation and target price include the possibility that increased terrorism fears could restrict future demand for cruise ship vacations; and what we see as the likely negative impact on profitability that would result from a sharp spike in fuel prices from current levels.

- Our 12-month target price of $54 reflects our view that CCL's P/E multiple premium to the S&P 500 will be largely maintained, as investors focus on prospective benefits to the company from what we expect to be slowing growth in industry capacity and rising free cash flow beyond FY 04.

Key Stock Statistics

S&P Core EPS 2005E	2.66	52-week Range	$53.65-33.77
S&P Oper. EPS 2004E	2.21	12 Month P/E	25.1
P/E on S&P Oper. EPS 2004E	24.3	Beta	0.79
S&P Oper. EPS 2005E	2.65	Shareholders	4,897
Yield (%)	1.1%	Market Cap (B)	$ 34.0
Dividend Rate/Share	0.60	Shares Outstanding (M)	633.3

Value of $10,000 invested five years ago: **$ 12,020**

Dividend Data Dividends have been paid since 1988

Amount ($)	Date Decl.	Ex-Div. Date	Stock of Record	Payment Date
0.125	Jan. 23	Feb. 18	Feb. 20	Mar. 12 '04
0.125	Apr. 21	May. 19	May. 21	Jun. 11 '04
0.125	Jul. 20	Aug. 18	Aug. 20	Sep. 10 '04
0.150	Oct. 25	Nov. 17	Nov. 19	Dec. 10 '04

Revenues/Earnings Data Fiscal year ending November 30

Revenues (Million $)

	2004	2003	2002	2001	2000	1999
1Q	1,980	1,031	905.8	1,008	824.9	748.3
2Q	2,256	1,335	989.2	1,079	875.1	796.1
3Q	3,245	2,524	1,438	1,490	1,228	1,169
4Q	—	1,817	1,036	959.1	850.3	791.2
Yr.	—	6,718	4,368	4,536	3,779	3,498

Earnings Per Share ($)

	2004	2003	2002	2001	2000	1999
1Q	0.25	0.22	0.22	0.22	0.28	0.26
2Q	0.41	0.19	0.33	0.32	0.34	0.33
3Q	1.23	0.90	0.85	0.84	0.67	0.67
4Q	E0.31	0.26	0.33	0.20	0.33	0.40
Yr.	E2.21	1.66	1.73	1.58	1.60	1.66

Next earnings report expected: mid-December   Source: S&P, Company Reports
EPS Estimates based on S&P Operating Earnings; historical GAAP earnings are as reported.

STANDARD &POOR'S

Carnival Corporation

Recommendation: **HOLD** ★ ★ ★ ☆ ☆   12-Month Target Price: **$54.00** (as of September 17, 2004)

Business Summary October 27, 2004

In April 2003, Carnival Corp., a leading cruise ship company, merged with P&O Princess Cruises plc, creating a business that now operates more than 70 ships. In September 2004, the company said that the number of available lower berth days in 2005 and 2006 (likely the fiscal years ending November), primarily from new ships entering service, was expected to be 9.1% and 5.6%, respectively. As of October 2004, CCL had 14 new ships scheduled for delivery between November 2004 and the spring of 2009. Carnival also has tour operations in Alaska and the Canadian Yukon.

The merger with P&O Princess (renamed Carnival plc) was effected through an exchange of stock. With a dual listing company (DLC) format, CCL shares continue to trade on the New York Stock Exchange, while Carnival plc (formerly Princess) shares trade on the London Stock Exchange. According to CCL, on a pro forma basis, in the fiscal year ended November 30, 2003, the combined companies had revenue of $7.6 billion. Pro forma net income, including some unusual costs, was $1.2 billion, with EPS, based on 805 million shares, of $1.45.

Under the DLC structure, the businesses of Carnival Corporation and Carnival plc have been combined principally through a series of contracts. Each company has retained its separate legal identity, but the two share a single senior executive management team, have identical boards of directors, and are run as if they were a single economic enterprise.

At February 15, 2004, Carnival had a combined fleet of 73 cruise ships with passenger capacity of 118,040 (based on two passengers per cabin). This included the following brands: Carnival Cruise Lines (20 ships; 43,446 passenger capacity); Princess Cruises (11 ships; 19,880 capacity); Holland America (12 ships; 16,320 capacity); Costa Cruises (10 ships; 15,570 capacity); P&O Cruises (four ships; 7,724 capacity); AIDA (four ships; 5,314 capacity); and Cunard Line (three ships; 5,078 capacity). Carnival also operates two tour companies, which include 17 hotels or lodges in Alaska and the Canadian Yukon, more than 500 motorcoaches and 20 domed rail cars; and two dayboats.

In FY 03 (Nov.), Carnival's reported revenue of $6.7 billion included $6.5 billion in the cruise category, of which $5.0 billion was from passenger tickets. Also in FY 03, Carnival had depreciation and amortization charges amounting to $585 million, up from $382 million in FY 02.

In 2001, CCL sold, for about $500 million, its 25% equity ownership interest in European tour operator Airtours plc.

In early 2004, the company said it believed that substantially all of its income, with the exception of its U.S. source income from the transportation, hotel and tour businesses of Holland America Tours and Princess Tours, plus some other items that the IRS does not consider incidental to ship operations, was exempt from U.S. federal taxes.

Company Financials Fiscal Year ending November 30

Per Share Data ($)

(Year Ended November 30)	2003	2002	2001	2000	1999	1998	1997	1996	1995	1994
Tangible Bk. Val.	11.83	11.48	10.13	8.84	8.86	6.46	4.82	4.77	3.72	3.00
Cash Flow	2.46	2.38	2.21	2.08	2.06	1.73	1.40	1.23	1.02	0.87
Earnings	1.66	1.73	1.58	1.60	1.66	1.40	1.11	0.98	0.80	0.68
S&P Core Earnings	1.61	1.70	1.45	NA	NA	NA	NA	NA	NA	NA
Dividends	0.44	0.42	0.42	0.42	0.38	0.32	0.24	0.19	0.16	0.15
Payout Ratio	27%	24%	27%	26%	23%	22%	22%	19%	20%	21%
Prices - High	39.84	34.64	34.93	51.25	53.50	48.50	27.93	16.56	13.56	13.06
- Low	20.34	22.07	16.95	18.31	38.12	19.00	15.68	11.62	10.00	9.56
P/E Ratio - High	24	20	22	32	32	35	25	17	17	19
- Low	12	13	11	11	23	14	14	12	13	14

Income Statement Analysis (Million $)

	2003	2002	2001	2000	1999	1998	1997	1996	1995	1994
Revs.	6,718	4,368	4,536	3,779	3,497	3,009	2,447	2,213	1,998	1,806
Oper. Inc.	1,968	1,444	1,448	1,233	1,188	1,020	828	697	618	554
Depr.	585	382	372	288	244	201	167	145	128	111
Int. Exp.	195	111	121	41.4	47.0	57.8	55.9	90.0	81.9	73.0
Pretax Inc.	1,223	959	948	967	1,044	851	672	575	460	392
Eff. Tax Rate	2.37%	NM	2.34%	0.11%	0.27%	0.45%	0.93%	1.56%	2.00%	2.60%
Net Inc.	1,194	1,016	926	965	1,027	836	666	566	451	382
S&P Core Earnings	1,161	996	850	NA	NA	NA	NA	NA	NA	NA

Balance Sheet & Other Fin. Data (Million $)

	2003	2002	2001	2000	1999	1998	1997	1996	1995	1994
Cash	1,070	667	1,421	189	522	137	140	124	104	124
Curr. Assets	2,132	1,132	1,959	549	792	370	336	291	236	240
Total Assets	24,491	12,335	11,564	9,831	8,286	7,179	5,427	5,102	4,105	3,670
Curr. Liab.	3,315	1,620	1,480	1,715	1,405	1,135	786	663	595	565
LT Debt	6,918	3,012	2,955	2,099	868	1,563	1,015	1,317	1,150	1,162
Common Equity	13,793	7,418	6,591	5,871	5,931	4,285	3,605	3,031	2,345	1,929
Total Cap.	20,711	10,430	9,546	7,970	6,799	5,981	4,620	4,348	3,495	3,091
Cap. Exp.	2,516	1,986	827	1,003	873	1,150	498	902	484	595
Cash Flow	1,779	1,398	1,298	1,253	1,271	1,037	833	711	580	492
Curr. Ratio	0.6	0.7	1.3	0.3	0.6	0.3	0.4	0.4	0.4	0.4
% LT Debt of Cap.	33.4	28.9	31.0	26.3	12.8	26.1	22.0	30.3	32.9	37.6
% Net Inc.of Revs.	17.8	23.3	20.4	25.6	29.4	27.8	27.2	25.5	22.6	21.1
% Ret. on Assets	6.5	8.5	8.7	10.7	13.3	13.3	12.7	13.2	11.6	11.1
% Ret. on Equity	11.3	14.5	14.9	16.4	20.1	21.2	20.1	21.1	21.1	21.5

Data as orig reptd.; bef. results of disc opers/spec. items. Per share data adj. for stk. divs.; EPS diluted. E-Estimated. NA-Not Available. NM-Not Meaningful. NR-Not Ranked. UR-Under Review.

Office: 3655 NW 87th Avenue, Doral, FL 33178-2428.
Telephone: 305-599-2600.
Website: http://www.carnivalcorp.com
Chrmn & CEO: M. Arison.
Vice Chrmn & COO: H.S. Frank.
EVP, CFO & Chief Acctg Officer: G.R. Cahill.
SVP, Secy & General Counsel: A. Perez.

Treas: D. Bernstein.
Investor Contact: B. Roberts 1-305-406-4832.
Dirs: M. Arison, R. G. Capen, Jr., R. H. Dickinson, A. W. Donald, P. L. Foschi, H. S. Frank, R. J. Glasier, B. Hogg, A. K. Lanterman, M. A. Maidique, J. McNulty, S. J. Parker, P. Ratcliffe, S. S. Subotnick, U. Zucker.

Founded: in 1974.
Domicile: Panama.
Employees: 66,000.
S&P Analyst: Tom Graves, CFA /PMW/BK

The McGraw·Hill Companies

Caterpillar Inc.

Recommendation: **HOLD** ★ ★ ★ ★ ★   12-Month Target Price: **$86.00**
SELL SELL HOLD BUY BUY (as of September 29, 2004)

CAT has an approximate 0.28% weighting in the **S&P 500**

Sector: Industrials
Sub-Industry: Construction & Farm Machinery & Heavy Trucks
Peer Group: Construction Equipment Manufacturers

Summary: CAT, the world's largest producer of earthmoving equipment, is also a big maker of truck engines and power generators.

Quantitative Evaluations

S&P Earnings & Dividend Rank: B+

| D | C | B- | B | B+ | A- | A | A+ |

S&P Fair Value Rank: 3

| 1 | 2 | 3 | 4 | 5 |
Lowest — Highest

Fair Value Calc.: $85.10 (Slightly Overvalued)

S&P Investability Quotient Percentile
79%

CAT scored higher than 79% of all companies for which an S&P Report is available.

Volatility: Average

| Low | Average | High |

Technical Evaluation: Bullish
Since 9/04, the technical indicators for CAT have been Bullish.

Relative Strength Rank: Strong
83
1 Lowest — Highest 99

Price as of 11/12/04: $89.97   **2004E S&P Core EPS: $4.73**

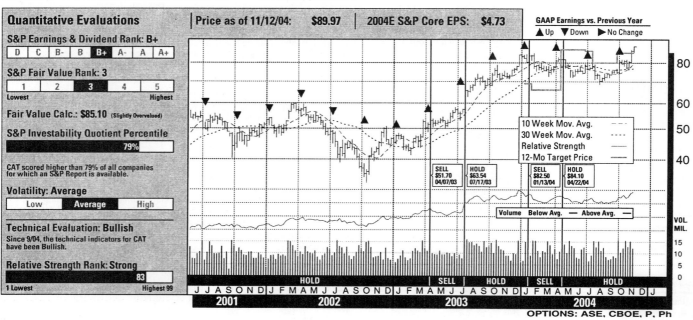

GAAP Earnings vs. Previous Year
▲ Up ▼ Down ► No Change

10 Week Mov. Avg.
30 Week Mov. Avg.
Relative Strength
12-Mo Target Price

SELL $51.70 04/07/03 | HOLD $63.54 07/17/03 | SELL $82.50 01/13/04 | HOLD $84.10 04/22/04

Volume — Below Avg. — Above Avg.

OPTIONS: ASE, CBOE, P, Ph

Analyst commentary prepared by Anthony M. Fiore, CFA /CB/BK

Highlights October 22, 2004

- We expect revenues to rise about 10% in 2005, following a projected advance of close to 30% in 2004. Our outlook is based on our expectation of strong demand for heavy-duty truck engines and machinery as a result of improving commercial construction and mining activity. In addition, we believe that sales will benefit from increased pricing of CAT products and improving market share in the Asia/Pacific region.

- We see a modest expansion of operating margins in 2005, as we expect a combination of increased price realization and benefits from cost control efforts to be partially offset by higher raw material costs and supply constraints. Although we do not expect a return to peak profitability in 2005, we see the company making significant progress toward its longer-term return on sales target of at least 9%.

- Our Standard & Poor's Core Earnings estimates for 2004 and 2005 are $0.92 and $0.74 a share below our respective operating EPS forecasts, with the differences reflecting projected stock option expense and pension and post-retirement cost adjustments.

Investment Rationale/Risk October 22, 2004

- We have a hold recommendation on the shares. While we expect favorable end market conditions to continue over the next 12 months, we believe that our outlook is largely reflected in the price of the stock.

- Risks to our recommendation and target price include an unexpected downturn in the non-residential construction, trucking, and/or mining end markets; continued escalation of raw material costs; and further supply constraints.

- Our discounted cash flow model, which assumes a 7% average annual free cash flow growth rate over the next 10 years, 3.5% growth in perpetuity, and a 7.7% weighted average cost of capital, indicates intrinsic value of about $88. In terms of relative valuation, the shares traded recently at a P/E multiple of about 11X our 2005 EPS estimate. Applying a target P/E multiple of 12X, in line with historical norms, suggests a value of $84 a share. Our 12-month target price of $86 is derived by combining these two methodologies.

Key Stock Statistics

S&P Core EPS 2005E	6.26	52-week Range	$90.00-68.50
S&P Oper. EPS 2004E	5.65	12 Month P/E	17.4
P/E on S&P Oper. EPS 2004E	15.9	Beta	0.92
S&P Oper. EPS 2005E	7.00	Shareholders	38,440
Yield (%)	1.8%	Market Cap (B)	$ 30.7
Dividend Rate/Share	1.64	Shares Outstanding (M)	341.2

Value of $10,000 invested five years ago: **$ 18,295**

Dividend Data Dividends have been paid since 1914

Amount ($)	Date Decl.	Ex-Div. Date	Stock of Record	Payment Date
0.370	Dec. 10	Jan. 15	Jan. 20	Feb. 20 '04
0.370	Apr. 14	Apr. 22	Apr. 26	May. 20 '04
0.410	Jun. 09	Jul. 16	Jul. 20	Aug. 20 '04
0.410	Oct. 13	Oct. 21	Oct. 25	Nov. 20 '04

Revenues/Earnings Data Fiscal year ending December 31

Revenues (Million $)

	2004	2003	2002	2001	2000	1999
1Q	6,467	4,821	4,409	4,810	4,919	4,867
2Q	7,564	5,932	5,291	5,488	5,363	5,101
3Q	7,649	5,545	5,075	5,060	4,779	4,715
4Q	—	6,465	5,377	5,096	5,114	5,019
Yr.	—	22,763	20,152	20,450	20,175	19,702

Earnings Per Share ($)

	2004	2003	2002	2001	2000	1999
1Q	1.16	0.37	0.23	0.47	0.73	0.57
2Q	1.55	1.15	0.58	0.78	0.90	0.78
3Q	1.41	0.62	0.61	0.59	0.62	0.61
4Q	E1.59	0.97	0.88	0.48	0.76	0.67
Yr.	E5.65	3.13	2.30	2.32	3.02	2.63

Next earnings report expected: late-January Source: S&P, Company Reports
EPS Estimates based on S&P Operating Earnings; historical GAAP earnings are as reported.

Caterpillar Inc.

Recommendation: **HOLD** ★★★☆☆   12-Month Target Price: **$86.00** (as of September 29, 2004)

Business Summary October 25, 2004

Caterpillar's distinctive yellow machines are in service in nearly every country in the world; about 48% of the company's revenues are derived from outside of North America. About 71% of CAT's 220 independent dealers are located outside the U.S.

Global 2003 revenue contributions by geographic region were as follows: North America 52%; Europe/Africa/Middle East 27%; Asia/Pacific 13%; and Latin America 8.0%.

The company conducts business through three operating segments: Machinery, Engines, and Financial Products.

CAT's largest operating segment, the Machinery unit (60% of revenues in 2003, and 74% of operating profits; 9.1% operating margin), makes the company's well known earthmoving equipment. Machinery's end-markets include heavy construction, general construction, and mining quarry and aggregate, industrial, waste, forestry and agriculture. End markets are very cyclical and competitive; demand for CAT's earthmoving equipment is driven by many volatile factors, including the health of global economies, commodity prices, and interest rates. Principal competitors include Japan's Komatsu Ltd.; CNH Global NV (Case and NewHolland brands); Deere & Co.; and Sweden's Volvo. Segment profitability has decreased in recent years, due to volatile Asian and Latin American markets, as well as accelerating price competition in maturing North American and European markets.

For decades, the Engine segment (32%, 11%; 2.6%) made diesel engines solely for CAT's own earthmoving equipment. Currently, however, Engine derives about 90% of sales from third-party customers, such as Paccar, Inc., the maker of well known Kenworth and Peterbilt brand tractor/trailer trucks. Engine's major end markets are electric power generation, on-highway truck, oil and gas, industrial/OEM and marine. CAT, Cummins Inc., and DaimlerChrysler's Detroit Diesel division each account for about 30% of the world diesel engine market.

The Financial Products segment (7.5%, 20%; 20%) primarily provides equipment financing to CAT dealers and customers. Financing plans include operating and finance leases, installment sales contracts, working capital loans and wholesale financing plans. At December 31, 2003, total long-term finance-related receivables and long-term finance-related debt stood at $7.8 billion and $11 billion, respectively.

In 2003, 2002 and 2001, research and development spending totaled $669, $656 million and $696 million, respectively. Historically, R&D spending has been equal to about 3.1% of yearly sales.

At December 31, 2003, the fair market value of CAT's pension plan stood at $9.0 billion, with the benefit obligation totaling $10.8 billion. At the same date, the fair market value of the company's other post-retirement benefit plan stood at $867 million, with the benefit obligation totalling $5.0 billion.

Company Financials Fiscal Year ending December 31

Per Share Data ($)

(Year Ended December 31)	2003	2002	2001	2000	1999	1998	1997	1996	1995	1994
Tangible Bk. Val.	12.95	11.01	11.49	11.93	11.11	10.89	11.71	10.17	8.29	6.67
Cash Flow	6.97	5.82	5.69	5.95	5.27	6.46	6.32	5.39	4.59	4.03
Earnings	3.13	2.30	2.32	3.02	2.63	4.11	4.37	3.54	2.86	2.35
S&P Core Earnings	3.00	0.39	0.31	NA	NA	NA	NA	NA	NA	NA
Dividends	1.42	1.40	1.38	1.33	1.25	1.10	0.90	0.75	0.60	0.23
Payout Ratio	45%	61%	59%	44%	48%	27%	21%	21%	21%	10%
Prices - High	84.95	59.99	56.83	55.12	66.43	60.75	61.62	40.50	37.62	30.37
- Low	41.24	33.75	39.75	29.56	42.00	39.06	36.25	27.00	24.12	25.31
P/E Ratio - High	27	26	24	18	25	15	14	11	13	13
- Low	13	15	17	10	16	10	8	8	8	11

Income Statement Analysis (Million $)

	2003	2002	2001	2000	1999	1998	1997	1996	1995	1994
Revs.	22,763	20,152	20,450	20,175	19,702	20,977	18,925	16,522	16,072	14,328
Oper. Inc.	3,505	3,060	3,137	3,447	2,999	3,607	3,529	2,983	2,656	2,321
Depr.	1,347	1,220	1,169	1,022	945	865	738	696	682	680
Int. Exp.	716	800	942	980	829	753	580	510	484	410
Pretax Inc.	1,497	1,110	1,172	1,500	1,401	2,178	2,461	1,974	1,637	1,309
Eff. Tax Rate	26.6%	28.1%	31.3%	29.8%	32.5%	30.5%	32.3%	31.5%	30.6%	27.0%
Net Inc.	1,099	798	805	1,053	946	1,513	1,665	1,361	1,136	955
S&P Core Earnings	1,052	133	99	NA	NA	NA	NA	NA	NA	NA

Balance Sheet & Other Fin. Data (Million $)

	2003	2002	2001	2000	1999	1998	1997	1996	1995	1994
Cash	342	309	400	334	548	360	292	487	638	419
Curr. Assets	16,791	14,628	13,400	12,521	11,734	11,459	9,814	8,783	7,647	7,409
Total Assets	36,465	32,851	30,657	28,464	26,635	25,128	20,756	18,728	16,830	16,250
Curr. Liab.	12,621	11,344	10,273	8,568	8,178	7,945	6,379	7,013	6,049	5,498
LT Debt	14,078	11,596	11,291	11,334	9,928	9,404	6,942	4,532	3,964	4,270
Common Equity	6,078	5,472	5,611	5,600	5,465	5,131	4,679	4,116	3,388	2,911
Total Cap.	20,156	17,068	16,902	16,934	15,393	14,593	11,679	8,696	7,388	7,181
Cap. Exp.	682	1,773	1,968	665	1,280	1,269	968	771	679	694
Cash Flow	2,446	2,018	1,974	2,075	1,891	2,378	2,403	2,057	1,818	1,635
Curr. Ratio	1.3	1.3	1.3	1.5	1.4	1.4	1.5	1.3	1.3	1.3
% LT Debt of Cap.	69.8	67.9	66.8	66.9	64.5	64.4	59.4	52.1	53.7	59.5
% Net Inc.of Revs.	4.8	4.0	3.9	5.2	4.8	7.2	8.8	8.2	7.1	6.7
% Ret. on Assets	3.2	2.5	2.7	3.8	3.7	6.6	8.4	7.7	6.9	6.2
% Ret. on Equity	19.0	14.4	14.4	19.0	17.9	30.8	37.9	36.3	36.1	37.6

Data as orig reptd.; bef. results of disc opers/spec. items. Per share data adj. for stk. divs.; EPS diluted. E-Estimated. NA-Not Available. NM-Not Meaningful. NR-Not Ranked. UR-Under Review.

Office: 100 N.E. Adams Street, Peoria, IL 61629.
Telephone: 309-675-1000.
Email: catir@cat.com
Website: http://www.cat.com
Chrmn & CEO: J. Owens.
VP & CFO: F.L. McPheeters.

VP, Secy & General Counsel: J.B. Buda.
Treas: K.E. Colgan.
Investor Contact: N.L. Snowden 309-675-4549.
Dirs: W. F. Blount, J. R. Brazil, J. T. Dillon, E. Fife, G. D. Fosler, J. Gallardo, D. R. Goode, P. A. Magowan, W. A. Osborn, J. Owens, G. R. Parker, C. D. Powell, E. B. Rust, Jr., J. I. Smith.

Founded: in 1925.
Domicile: Delaware.
Employees: 69,169.
S&P Analyst: Anthony M. Fiore, CFA /CB/BK

Recommendation: **HOLD** ★ ★ ★ ☆ ☆   12-Month Target Price: **$24.00**
(as of September 29, 2004)

CD has an approximate 0.22% weighting in the **S&P 500**

Sector: Industrials
Sub-Industry: Diversified Commercial Services
Peer Group: Business Services

Summary: This travel, lodging and real estate services company has brands that include Avis car rental, Century 21 real estate, and Days Inn hotels.

Quantitative Evaluations

S&P Earnings & Dividend Rank: B-

| D | C | B- | B | B+ | A- | A | A+ |

S&P Fair Value Rank: 5

| 1 | 2 | 3 | 4 | 5 |
| Lowest | | | | Highest |

Fair Value Calc.: $29.80 (Undervalued)

S&P Investability Quotient Percentile

87%

CD scored higher than 87% of all companies for which an S&P Report is available.

Volatility: Average

| Low | Average | High |

Technical Evaluation: Neutral
Since 11/04, the technical indicators for CD have been Neutral.

Relative Strength Rank: Moderate

48

| 1 Lowest | Highest 99 |

Price as of 11/12/04: **$22.90**   **2004E S&P Core EPS:** **$1.60**

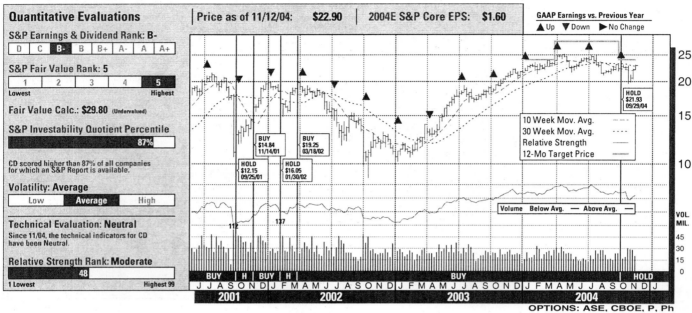

GAAP Earnings vs. Previous Year
▲ Up ▼ Down ► No Change

10 Week Mov. Avg. — — —
30 Week Mov. Avg. ·······
Relative Strength
12-Mo Target Price

BUY $14.84 11/14/01
HOLD $12.15 09/25/01
BUY $19.25 03/18/02
HOLD $16.05 01/30/02
HOLD $21.93 09/29/04

Volume Below Avg. — Above Avg. —

VOL. MIL.

BUY | H | BUY | H | BUY | HOLD
J J A S O N D | J F M A M J J A S O N D | J F M A M J J A S O N D | J F M A M J J A S O N D | J
2001 | 2002 | 2003 | 2004

OPTIONS: ASE, CBOE, P, Ph

Analyst commentary prepared by Tom Graves, CFA /PMW/JWP

Highlights October 14, 2004

- In October 2004, the company said it planned to spin off ownership of its PHH mortgage and fleet management businesses to CD shareholders. The transaction is expected to be a tax-free distribution, to be completed in the 2005 first quarter. Revenues of the businesses to be spun off exceeded $2 billion in the 12 months ended June 30, 2004. In September, the company said it had reached a definitive agreement to acquire travel company Orbitz, Inc., for about $1.25 billion in cash. The transaction, subject to necessary approvals, was expected to be completed in November 2004.

- In 2005, we look for revenue from continuing operations to increase moderately from the $18 billion that we project for 2004. We expect reported earnings growth to be restricted by the absence of a benefit of $0.10 a share benefit (excluded from our 2004 EPS estimate of $1.53) that was reported in the 2004 first quarter. For 2005, we see EPS of $1.70. We look for the expected spinoff of the PHH businesses to reduce CD's EPS from continuing operations by about $0.08 in each of 2004 and 2005, and see the proposed acquisition of Orbitz as relatively neutral to 2005 EPS.

- In mid-2004, there was an IPO of Jackson Hewitt Tax Service Inc. (JTX), which was formerly owned by CD. The company said it would receive about $770 million of net proceeds from the offering, including a special cash dividend of $175 million. CD now classifies JTX as a discontinued operation.

Investment Rationale/Risk October 14, 2004

- Our hold opinion on the stock reflects our view that, based on projected free cash flow and on the stock's P/E multiple discount to the level of the S&P 500, the shares are adequately discounted for business risks, the company's complexity, and what we view as its tarnished past. Accounting irregularities and errors related to Cendant were disclosed in 1998.

- Risks to our recommendation and target price include the potential for heightened terrorism fears, resulting in travel activity being less than currently anticipated; and the possibility that rising interest rates have a greater than expected negative impact on CD's real estate-related businesses.

- We have a favorable view of CD's free cash flow and EPS growth prospects, but we expect these high beta shares to continue to trade at a P/E multiple discount to the S&P 500 (currently about 15%, based on our 2005 EPS estimates). Our 12-month target price of $24 is equal to about 13X estimated 2005 EPS. In March 2004, the company began paying quarterly cash dividends, and a 29% boost in the dividend was approved in July. The stock has an indicated annual dividend yield of about 1.6%.

Key Stock Statistics

S&P Core EPS 2005E	1.80	52-week Range	$25.19-19.63
S&P Oper. EPS 2004E	1.53	12 Month P/E	12.0
P/E on S&P Oper. EPS 2004E	15.0	Beta	1.97
S&P Oper. EPS 2005E	1.70	Shareholders	8,372
Yield (%)	1.6%	Market Cap (B)	$ 24.1
Dividend Rate/Share	0.36	Shares Outstanding (M)	1052.8

Value of $10,000 invested five years ago: **$ 14,705**

Dividend Data Dividends have been paid since 2004

Amount ($)	Date Decl.	Ex-Div. Date	Stock of Record	Payment Date
0.070	Feb. 11	Feb. 19	Feb. 23	Mar. 16 '04
q.07	Apr. 20	May. 20	May. 24	Jun. 15 '04
0.090	Jul. 20	Aug. 12	Aug. 16	Sep. 14 '04
0.090	Oct. 19	Nov. 18	Nov. 22	Dec. 14 '04

Revenues/Earnings Data Fiscal year ending December 31

Revenues (Million $)

	2004	2003	2002	2001	2000	1999
1Q	4,477	4,128	2,616	1,486	945.0	1,318
2Q	5,209	4,617	3,784	2,403	973.0	1,391
3Q	5,363	5,098	3,839	2,481	1,044	1,410
4Q	—	4,349	3,849	2,580	968.0	1,283
Yr.	—	18,192	14,088	8,950	3,930	5,402

Earnings Per Share ($)

	2004	2003	2002	2001	2000	1999
1Q	0.42	0.30	0.31	-0.30	0.15	0.20
2Q	0.47	0.37	0.25	0.27	0.21	1.06
3Q	0.56	0.48	0.24	0.23	0.25	0.27
4Q	E0.31	0.28	0.24	-0.31	0.17	-2.08
Yr.	E1.53	1.41	1.04	0.45	0.78	-0.30

Next earnings report expected: early-February Source: S&P, Company Reports
EPS Estimates based on S&P Operating Earnings; historical GAAP earnings are as reported.

Recommendation: **HOLD** ★ ★ ★ ☆ ☆   12-Month Target Price: **$24.00** (as of September 29, 2004)

Business Summary October 14, 2004

Cendant Corp., a large consumer and business services company, has been reshaped through acquisitions and other transactions. The company, which has also disposed of various businesses in recent years, was formed through the 1997 merger of CUC International (renamed Cendant Corp.) and HFS Inc. Accounting irregularities and errors were disclosed in 1998, and some past earnings were restated downward. In May 2002, the company completed the funding of a stockholder litigation settlement trust, to which CD paid a total of about $2.85 billion.

The Travel Services segment (55% of 2003 revenue) includes operating and franchising of the Avis and Budget vehicle rental businesses, and providing fleet management and fuel card services to corporate clients and government agencies through PHH Arval and Wright Express. Vehicle Services revenue totaled $5.9 billion in 2003. The Hospitality business (2003 revenue of $2.5 billion) includes the operation of various lodging franchise systems, including Days Inn, Ramada (in the U.S. and Canada), Super 8 Motel, Howard Johnson, Wingate Inn, Knights Inn, Travelodge (in North America), Villager Group, and AmeriHost Inn. The segment also includes facilitating the sale and development of vacation ownership intervals through Fairfield Resorts, Inc., and Trendwest Resorts, Inc.; the exchange of vacation ownership intervals through Resort Condominiums International, LLC; and the marketing of vacation rental properties in Europe. The Travel Distribution

business ($1.7 billion segment revenue) includes providing global distribution and computer reservation services to airlines, hotels, car rental companies and other travel suppliers; providing travel agent customers the ability to electronically access information, book reservations and issue tickets through CD's Galileo International business; and providing other travel-related services through other outlets.

Real Estate Services segment (37% of 2003 revenue) operations include franchising the real estate brokerage businesses of the Century 21, Coldwell Banker, and ERA brands; providing real estate brokerage services under its franchise brands through NRT Inc.; providing home buyers with mortgages through Cendant Mortgage Corp.; providing settlement services, including title, appraisal review, and closing services, through Cendant Settlement Services Group; and assisting in employee relocations through Cendant Mobility Services Corp.

CD's Financial Services area (8% of 2003 revenue) includes insurance, the Jackson Hewitt tax preparation business, for which an initial public offering of 100% of CD's ownership interest was held in June 2004; and various membership programs that offer discounted products and services to consumers through a relationship with Trilegiant Corp.

Company Financials Fiscal Year ending December 31

Per Share Data ($)

(Year Ended December 31)	2003	2002	2001	2000	1999	1998	1997	1996	1995	1994
Tangible Bk. Val.	NM	NM	NM	NM	NM	NM	NM	2.28	1.60	1.60
Cash Flow	1.91	1.50	0.94	1.33	0.19	0.55	0.36	0.49	0.49	0.53
Earnings	1.41	1.04	0.45	0.78	-0.30	0.18	0.08	0.39	0.28	0.44
S&P Core Earnings	0.82	0.82	0.21	NA	NA	NA	NA	NA	NA	NA
Dividends	Nil	Nil	Nil	Nil	Nil	Nil	Nil	Nil	Nil	Nil
Payout Ratio	Nil	Nil	Nil	Nil	Nil	Nil	Nil	Nil	Nil	Nil
Prices - High	22.39	20.15	21.53	26.31	26.93	41.68	34.37	27.50	26.16	15.94
- Low	10.40	8.90	9.62	8.12	13.62	6.50	19.25	18.33	14.50	11.11
P/E Ratio - High	16	19	48	34	NM	NM	NM	71	93	36
- Low	7	9	21	10	NM	NM	NM	47	52	25

Income Statement Analysis (Million $)

	2003	2002	2001	2000	1999	1998	1997	1996	1995	1994
Revs.	18,192	14,088	8,950	4,569	5,402	5,284	4,240	2,348	1,415	1,039
Oper. Inc.	3,173	2,761	2,204	1,725	1,919	1,590	1,250	479	286	209
Depr.	518	466	501	352	371	323	238	32.5	15.4	23.3
Int. Exp.	328	303	Nil	148	199	149	51.0	Nil	Nil	NA
Pretax Inc.	2,231	1,659	682	1,106	-574	315	257	276	266	191
Eff. Tax Rate	33.4%	33.5%	34.5%	32.7%	NM	33.3%	74.3%	40.6%	38.7%	38.3%
Net Inc.	1,465	1,081	423	660	-229	160	66.0	164	163	118
S&P Core Earnings	828	831	195	NA	NA	NA	NA	NA	NA	NA

Balance Sheet & Other Fin. Data (Million $)

	2003	2002	2001	2000	1999	1998	1997	1996	1995	1994
Cash	840	433	1,971	944	1,164	1,009	67.0	553	270	181
Curr. Assets	4,478	3,358	6,492	2,728	4,592	4,547	2,590	1,430	768	504
Total Assets	39,037	35,897	33,452	15,072	15,149	20,217	14,073	2,473	1,141	768
Curr. Liab.	7,171	4,997	7,688	2,466	5,610	2,872	2,534	481	150	109
LT Debt	4,373	6,969	6,594	6,046	6,238	4,835	5,603	23.5	14.0	15.0
Common Equity	10,186	9,315	16,986	5,624	2,206	4,836	3,922	1,255	727	443
Total Cap.	14,559	16,284	24,630	12,146	8,754	10,089	9,891	1,279	741	458
Cap. Exp.	463	399	349	246	277	355	155	59.7	30.2	17.6
Cash Flow	1,983	1,547	924	1,012	142	483	304	197	179	141
Curr. Ratio	0.6	0.7	0.8	1.1	0.8	1.6	1.0	3.0	5.1	4.6
% LT Debt of Cap.	30.0	42.8	26.8	49.8	71.3	47.9	56.6	1.8	1.9	3.3
% Net Inc.of Revs.	8.1	7.7	4.7	14.4	NM	3.0	1.6	7.0	11.5	11.3
% Ret. on Assets	3.9	3.1	1.7	4.4	NM	0.9	0.9	9.1	16.2	16.9
% Ret. on Equity	15.0	11.2	3.3	16.9	NM	3.7	2.8	16.6	27.1	32.0

Data bef. results of disc. opers. and/or spec. items. Some data reflect restatements in Sep. 1998. Also, some years likely reflect different fiscal year ends. Per share data adj. for stk. divs.; EPS diluted. E-Estimated. NA-Not Available. NM-Not Meaningful. NR-Not Ranked.

Office: 9 West 57th Street, New York, NY 10019.
Telephone: 212-413-1800.
Website: http://www.cendant.com
Chrmn & CEO: H.R. Silverman.
Pres & CFO: R.L. Nelson.
Vice Chrmn: S.B. Holmes.
Vice Chrmn & General Counsel: J. Buckman.

EVP & Chief Acctg Officer: V. Wilson .
SVP & Investor Contact: S.J. Levenson .
Dirs: M. Biblowit, J. E. Buckman, L. S. Coleman, M. L. Edelman, G. Herrera, S. P. Holmes, C. D. Mills, B. Mulroney, R. E. Nederlander, R. L. Nelson, R. W. Pittman, P. D. Richards, S. Z. Rosenberg, H. R. Silverman, R. F. Smith.

Founded: in 1973.
Domicile: Delaware.
Employees: 87,000.
S&P Analyst: Tom Graves, CFA /PMW/JWP

Recommendation: **HOLD** ★★★☆☆
SELL | SELL | HOLD | BUY | BUY

12-Month Target Price: **$11.00**
(as of September 15, 2004)

CNP has an approximate 0.03% weighting in the **S&P 500**

Sector: Utilities
Sub-Industry: Electric Utilities
Peer Group: Electric & Gas- Larger

Summary: This Houston-based energy company (formerly Reliant Energy) is one of the largest electric and natural gas delivery companies in the U.S.

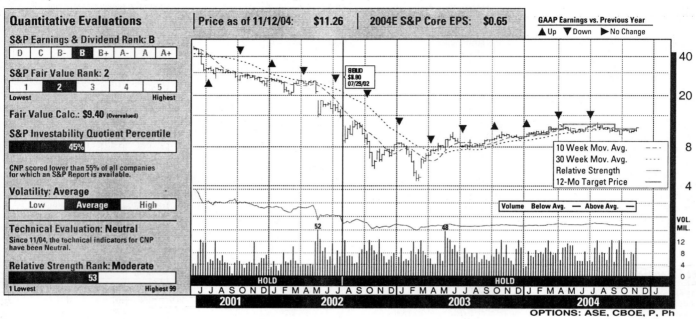

Quantitative Evaluations

S&P Earnings & Dividend Rank: B

D | C | B- | **B** | B+ | A- | A | A+

S&P Fair Value Rank: 2

1 | **2** | 3 | 4 | 5
Lowest | | | | Highest

Fair Value Calc.: $9.40 (Overvalued)

S&P Investability Quotient Percentile

45%

CNP scored lower than 55% of all companies for which an S&P Report is available.

Volatility: Average

Low | **Average** | High

Technical Evaluation: Neutral
Since 11/04, the technical indicators for CNP have been Neutral.

Relative Strength Rank: Moderate

53

1 Lowest | Highest 99

Price as of 11/12/04: $11.26 | **2004E S&P Core EPS:** $0.65

GAAP Earnings vs. Previous Year
▲ Up ▼ Down ► No Change

Chart legend:
- 10 Week Mov. Avg.
- 30 Week Mov. Avg.
- Relative Strength
- 12-Mo Target Price

Volume: Below Avg. ■ — Above Avg. ■

HOLD ... HOLD

J J A S O N D | J F M A M J J A S O N D | J F M A M J J A S O N D | J F M A M J J A S O N D | J
2001 | 2002 | 2003 | 2004

OPTIONS: ASE, CBOE, P, Ph

Analyst commentary prepared by Justin McCann/GG

Highlights August 24, 2004

- We expect 2004 EPS to drop significantly from 2003's EPS from continuing operations of $1.62, which was aided by a strong performance from 81%-owned Texas Genco (TGN) and gas distribution rate increases, helping to offset a sharp rise in interest and pension expenses.

- The drop that we see for 2004 primarily reflects the absence of non-cash income from a generation-related regulatory asset that is expected to be recovered in 2004, and the absence of earnings from TGN, which is to be sold to private equity investors, subject to necessary approvals. CNP, which should receive about $2.9 billion in cash for its 81% interest in TGN, is expected to use the bulk of the proceeds for debt reduction.

- On March 31, 2004, the company filed a "true-up" request with the Texas utility commission to recover $3.8 billion of stranded investments and other regulatory assets. The request, allowed by the state's electric restructuring legislation, would reflect the difference between the book value of formerly regulated power generating units and their market value.

Investment Rationale/Risk August 24, 2004

- The stock is trading at a P/E multiple premium to electric and gas utility peers. We think investors are looking past what we see as a restricted 2004 earnings outlook to what we view as marked improvement in CNP's financial strength. Through financial restructurings, CNP was able to cut its interest rate by about 125 basis points. We would hold the stock.

- Risks to our investment recommendation and target price include a smaller than expected recovery resulting from the company's "true-up" filing, unanticipated problems in completing the sale of TGN, and a potential sharp drop in the average P/E multiple of the stock's industry peers.

- We believe CNP would use much of the proceeds from its "true-up" recovery and the pending sale of Texas Genco to reduce debt, which exceeds $10.5 billion. With the company expected to emerge from this transition period financially stronger, we see the stock trading at a significant premium to the average 13.3X peer P/E multiple on our EPS estimates for 2005. Our 12-month target price is $12.

Key Stock Statistics

S&P Core EPS 2005E	0.63	52-week Range	$12.32-9.03
S&P Oper. EPS 2004E	0.24	12 Month P/E	NM
P/E on S&P Oper. EPS 2004E	46.9	Beta	0.60
S&P Oper. EPS 2005E	0.65	Shareholders	62,981
Yield (%)	3.6%	Market Cap (B)	$ 3.5
Dividend Rate/Share	0.40	Shares Outstanding (M)	307.5

Value of $10,000 invested five years ago: **NA**

Dividend Data Dividends have been paid since 1922

Amount ($)	Date Decl.	Ex-Div. Date	Stock of Record	Payment Date
0.100	Nov. 05	Nov. 13	Nov. 17	Dec. 10 '03
0.100	Jan. 28	Feb. 11	Feb. 16	Mar. 10 '04
0.100	May. 13	May. 20	May. 24	Jun. 10 '04
0.100	Jul. 29	Aug. 12	Aug. 16	Sep. 10 '04

Revenues/Earnings Data Fiscal year ending December 31

Revenues (Million $)

	2004	2003	2002	2001	2000	1999
1Q	2,959	2,900	2,078	13,284	4,213	2,643
2Q	2,241	2,090	1,804	11,991	5,755	3,658
3Q	1,667	2,250	1,923	12,511	9,502	4,947
4Q	—	2,519	2,117	8,440	9,869	4,055
Yr.	—	9,760	7,923	46,226	29,339	15,303

Earnings Per Share ($)

	2004	2003	2002	2001	2000	1999
1Q	0.24	0.27	0.49	0.69	0.47	-0.74
2Q	0.19	0.27	0.29	1.08	0.82	0.26
3Q	—	0.60	0.54	1.21	1.36	5.90
4Q	E-0.07	0.23	-0.03	0.16	0.02	0.38
Yr.	E0.24	1.37	1.29	3.14	2.68	5.82

Next earnings report expected: mid-February Source: S&P, Company Reports
EPS Estimates based on S&P Operating Earnings; historical GAAP earnings are as reported.

CenterPoint Energy, Inc.

Recommendation: **HOLD** ★★★☆☆   12-Month Target Price: **$11.00** (as of September 15, 2004)

Business Summary August 24, 2004

CenterPoint Energy (formerly Reliant Energy) is a Houston-based energy delivery company with operations that include electric transmission and distribution, natural gas distribution, and interstate natural gas pipelines and a gas gathering company.

In September 2002, Reliant Energy completed the spinoff of then 83%-owned Reliant Resources (NYSE: RRI), which had been formed through the transfer of Reliant Energy's unregulated operations. On October 1, CenterPoint Energy began trading under the symbol CNP.

CNP's CenterPoint Energy Houston Electric subsidiary serves about 1.8 million customers in a 5,000 mile territory that includes the cities of Houston and Galveston, TX, and (with the exception of Texas City) nearly all of the Houston/Galveston metropolitan area. With the start of electricity deregulation in Texas on January 1, 2002, wholesale and retail suppliers pay the company to deliver the electricity over its transmission lines.

CNP's natural gas subsidiary, CenterPoint Energy Resources Corp. (CERC), serves about 3 million customers, in six states. CERC's gas distribution companies include CenterPoint Energy Entex, which serves about 1.6 million customers, in Louisiana, Mississippi, and Texas, including a separately managed unit serving the Houston metropolitan area; CenterPoint Energy Minnegasco, which serves about 746,000 customers in Minneapolis and other communities in Minnesota; and CenterPoint Energy Arkla, which serves about 695,000 customers in Arkansas, Louisiana, Oklahoma and Texas.

The company operates two interstate natural gas pipelines: CenterPoint Energy Gas Transmission Company and CenterPoint Energy-Mississippi River Transmission Corp. With over 8,200 miles of combined pipe, they combine to make up one the largest interstate pipelines in the Mid-Continent U.S. CNP's gas gathering company, CenterPoint Energy Field Services, operates 4,300 miles of gathering pipelines, and about 200 natural gas gathering systems, in Arkansas, Oklahoma, Louisiana and Texas.

On July 21, 2004, CNP announced an agreement to sell 81%-owned Texas Genco (TGN) to private equity investors, for $3.65 billion. TGN is an unregulated electric generation business that sells power to wholesale customers and retail providers. Its 12 power plants (including a 30.8% interest in the South Texas Project nuclear unit) combine for over 14,000 megawatts of generating capacity. The other 19% of TGN common stock was distributed to CNP shareholders on January 6, 2003. As the first step in the sale agreement, the publicly owned 19% of TGN's shares are to be repurchased at $47 each. Subject to required regulatory approvals, the transaction is expected to be completed in the first quarter of 2005.

In July 2002, Reliant Energy and RRI filed amended annual reports for 2001 restating their annual financial results, reflecting the fact (announced in May 2002) that RRI had engaged in round-trip electricity trades from 1999 through 2001. The transactions had the effect of increasing revenues about 10% over the three years.

Company Financials Fiscal Year ending December 31

Per Share Data ($)

(Year Ended December 31)	2003	2002	2001	2000	1999	1998	1997	1996	1995	1994
Tangible Bk. Val.	NM	NM	13.05	8.11	7.69	6.77	9.01	14.88	15.08	8.91
Earnings	1.37	1.29	3.14	2.68	5.82	-0.50	1.66	1.66	1.60	1.66
S&P Core Earnings	1.28	2.17	3.00	NA	NA	NA	NA	NA	NA	NA
Dividends	0.40	1.07	1.50	1.50	1.50	1.50	1.50	1.50	1.50	1.50
Payout Ratio	29%	83%	48%	56%	26%	NM	90%	90%	94%	90%
Prices - High	10.49	27.10	50.45	49.00	32.50	33.37	27.25	25.62	24.50	23.87
- Low	4.35	4.24	23.27	19.75	22.75	25.00	18.87	20.50	17.68	15.00
P/E Ratio - High	8	21	16	18	6	NM	16	15	15	14
- Low	3	3	7	7	4	NM	11	12	11	9

Income Statement Analysis (Million $)

	2003	2002	2001	2000	1999	1998	1997	1996	1995	1994
Revs.	9,760	7,922	46,226	29,339	15,303	11,488	6,873	4,095	3,730	4,002
Depr.	625	616	911	906	911	857	652	550	478	484
Maint.	NA	NA	NA	NA	NA	NA	NA	NA	NA	NA
Fxd. Chgs. Cov.	1.37	1.80	3.33	2.60	2.32	1.64	2.56	3.31	2.13	2.49
Constr. Credits	NA	NA	NA	NA	Nil	4.00	3.00	6.72	12.0	10.0
Eff. Tax Rate	35.6%	35.0%	33.3%	32.9%	35.0%	NM	32.9%	33.1%	33.4%	33.1%
Net Inc.	420	386	919	771	1,666	-141	421	405	398	407
S&P Core Earnings	390	642	868	NA	NA	NA	NA	NA	NA	NA

Balance Sheet & Other Fin. Data (Million $)

	2003	2002	2001	2000	1999	1998	1997	1996	1995	1994
Gross Prop.	11,812	11,409	24,214	15,260	20,133	17,030	16,039	13,015	12,781	13,018
Cap. Exp.	648	854	2,053	1,842	1,179	743	329	318	301	418
Net Prop.	11,812	11,409	15,857	15,260	13,267	11,531	11,269	8,756	8,865	9,329
Capitalization:										
LT Debt	10,783	9,194	6,448	5,701	5,666	7,153	5,218	3,026	3,338	4,223
% LT Debt	86.0	71.0	48.4	51.0	51.6	62.4	49.8	43.3	42.5	52.3
Pfd.	Nil	Nil	Nil	10.0	10.0	10.0	10.0	135	402	473
% Pfd.	Nil	Nil	Nil	0.09	0.09	0.01	0.10	1.40	5.10	5.90
Common	1,761	3,756	6,881	5,472	5,296	4,312	4,887	3,828	4,124	3,369
% Common	14.0	29.0	51.6	48.9	48.3	37.6	46.7	39.8	52.4	41.8
Total Cap.	12,934	13,180	16,970	13,998	13,694	14,158	13,619	9,628	10,324	10,560
% Oper. Ratio	85.8	85.8	96.6	94.9	97.8	86.9	87.5	80.7	81.1	80.2
% Earn. on Net Prop.	21.8	17.2	12.8	13.2	10.0	13.0	10.6	4.6	7.9	8.6
% Return On Revs.	4.3	4.9	2.0	2.6	10.9	NM	6.1	9.9	10.7	10.2
% Return On Invest. Capital	11.1	14.7	11.2	10.3	20.5	16.6	7.9	10.3	7.0	7.3
% Return On Com. Equity	26.4	10.3	14.8	14.3	34.7	NM	9.7	10.2	10.6	12.3

Data as orig reptd.; bef. results of disc opers/spec. items. Per share data adj. for stk. divs. Bold denotes primary EPS - prior periods restated. E-Estimated. NA-Not Available. NM-Not Meaningful. NR-Not Ranked. UR-Under Review.

Office: 1111 Louisiana Street, Houston, TX 77002-5200.
Telephone: 713-207-1111.
Email: info@reliantenergy.nl
Website: http://www.centerpointenergy.com
Chrmn: M. Carroll.
Pres & CEO: D.M. McClanahan.

EVP & CFO: G.L. Whitlock.
EVP, Secy & General Counsel: S.E. Rozzell.
SVP & Chief Acctg Officer: J.S. Brian.
Investor Contact: M. Paulsen 713-207-6500.
Dirs: M. Carroll, J. T. Cater, D. Cody, O. H. Crosswell, T. F. Madison, D. M. McClanahan, R. T. O'Connell, M. E. Shannon.

Founded: in 1882.
Domicile: Texas.
Employees: 11,046.
S&P Analyst: Justin McCann/GG

Recommendation: **HOLD** ★★★☆☆
SELL SELL HOLD BUY BUY

12-Month Target Price: **$53.00**
(as of September 22, 2004)

CTX has an approximate 0.06% weighting in the **S&P 500**

Sector: Consumer Discretionary
Sub-Industry: Homebuilding
Peer Group: Homebuilders - National

Summary: This major U.S. homebuilder sells homes in 26 states, and also engages in mortgage banking and general construction contracting.

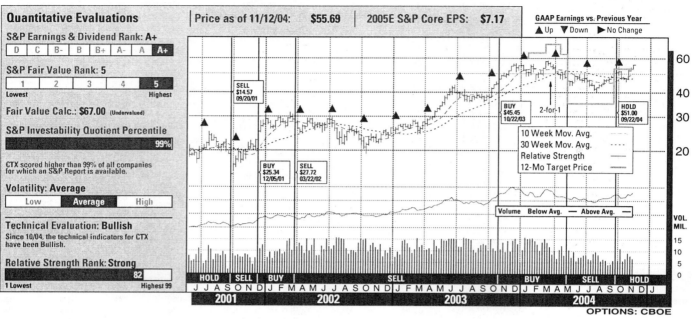

Quantitative Evaluations	Price as of 11/12/04:	$55.69	2005E S&P Core EPS:	$7.17

S&P Earnings & Dividend Rank: A+

| D | C | B- | B | B+ | A- | A | A+ |

S&P Fair Value Rank: 5

| 1 | 2 | 3 | 4 | 5 |
| Lowest | | | | Highest |

Fair Value Calc.: $67.00 (Undervalued)

S&P Investability Quotient Percentile

99%

CTX scored higher than 99% of all companies for which an S&P Report is available.

Volatility: Average

| Low | Average | High |

Technical Evaluation: Bullish
Since 10/04, the technical indicators for CTX have been Bullish.

Relative Strength Rank: Strong

82

| 1 Lowest | | Highest 99 |

GAAP Earnings vs. Previous Year
▲ Up ▼ Down ▶ No Change

10 Week Mov. Avg.
30 Week Mov. Avg.
Relative Strength
12-Mo Target Price

Volume Below Avg. — Above Avg.

OPTIONS: CBOE

Analyst commentary prepared by Michael W. Jaffe/MF/BK

Highlights October 04, 2004

- We see sales from continuing operations growing 16% in FY 05 (Mar.). We expect home sales to be aided by an approximate 8% increase in average neighborhoods, a 5% rise in average home prices that we project, and a small gain in average sales per neighborhood. We also expect a small rise in construction services revenues, as we believe that commercial construction markets finally bottomed in early calendar 2004. We look for these gains to be partly offset by a likely small downturn in financial services revenues, as our forecast of moderately higher interest rates leads us to expect a reduced level of refinancings.

- We project relatively flat net margins in FY 05. We see the higher prices that we forecast, the leveraging of overhead, and cost controls being offset by the negative impact of the downturn in refinancings that we see.

- Our Standard & Poor's Core Earnings estimate for FY 05 falls $0.08 a share below our operating forecast, with the difference reflecting projected option expense.

Investment Rationale/Risk October 04, 2004

- We believe housing markets will stay strong in coming periods. However, in light of our forecast of a modest upturn in mortgage rates over the next few years, and the maturity of the housing cycle, we do not expect substantial appreciation in CTX's shares over the next 12 months. Based on these factors and on valuation, we would not add to positions in CTX.

- A primary risk to our recommendation and target price is a stronger than expected upturn in interest rates.

- The stock traded recently at a little over 7X our FY 05 EPS forecast, well below the S&P 500's valuation, but about in line with CTX's peers. Although we are calling for an ongoing upturn in Centex's profits over the next couple of years, we do not foresee much expansion of its valuation over the next 12 months. This view stems from our belief that the company's valuation will be restricted by CTX's large exposure to first-time buyers, who we believe are most susceptible to any negative impact from the modest rise in mortgage rates that we expect. Our 12-month target price is $53, or a little less than 8X our FY 05 EPS estimate.

Key Stock Statistics

S&P Core EPS 2006E	7.58	52-week Range	$58.40-39.94
S&P Oper. EPS 2005E	7.25	12 Month P/E	8.2
P/E on S&P Oper. EPS 2005E	7.7	Beta	1.05
S&P Oper. EPS 2006E	7.65	Shareholders	3,056
Yield (%)	0.3%	Market Cap (B)	$ 6.9
Dividend Rate/Share	0.16	Shares Outstanding (M)	124.3

Value of $10,000 invested five years ago: **NA**

Dividend Data Dividends have been paid since 1973

Amount ($)	Date Decl.	Ex-Div. Date	Stock of Record	Payment Date
0.080	Feb. 17	Mar. 17	Mar. 19	Apr. 12 '04
0.040	May 27	Jun. 07	Jun. 09	Jul. 07 '04
0.040	Jul. 22	Aug. 02	Aug. 04	Aug. 25 '04
0.040	Oct. 20	Nov. 01	Nov. 03	Nov. 24 '04

Revenues/Earnings Data Fiscal year ending March 31

Revenues (Million $)

	2005	2004	2003	2002	2001	2000
1Q	2,766	2,173	1,844	1,709	1,422	1,372
2Q	2,985	2,428	2,084	1,884	1,601	1,429
3Q	—	2,570	2,305	1,894	1,639	1,429
4Q	—	3,193	2,885	2,261	2,005	1,726
Yr.	—	10,363	9,117	7,748	6,711	5,956

Earnings Per Share ($)

	2005	2004	2003	2002	2001	2000
1Q	1.35	1.04	0.69	0.61	0.41	0.48
2Q	1.61	1.56	0.92	0.75	0.49	0.54
3Q	E1.90	1.43	1.25	0.77	0.56	0.52
4Q	E2.39	2.05	1.56	0.93	0.86	0.59
Yr.	E7.25	6.01	4.41	3.06	2.33	2.11

Next earnings report expected: late-January Source: S&P, Company Reports
EPS Estimates based on S&P Operating Earnings; historical GAAP earnings are as reported.

Centex Corporation

Recommendation: **HOLD** ★ ★ ★   12-Month Target Price: **$53.00** (as of September 22, 2004)

Business Summary October 04, 2004

Centex Corp. constructs site-built homes in 26 states throughout the U.S., and in Washington, DC. It is the only company to rank among the 10 leading U.S. homebuilders in each of the past 35 years. CTX sells homes to first-time and move-up buyers, as well as active adult and second home buyers. It also has operations in various construction and real estate-related businesses.

To reduce exposure to local market volatility, the company built homes in an average of 558 neighborhoods in FY 04 (Mar.), versus 519 in FY 03; and in an average of 570 in the FY 05 first quarter. CTX delivered 30,358 homes in FY 04, up 15% from the FY 03 level, marking its sixth consecutive record year. Sales prices vary widely, with an average of $242,000 in FY 04 (up 10%). Single-family detached homes account for most home sales. Conventional homebuilding operations accounted for 73% of sales and 68% of operating earnings in FY 04.

Unit orders in the FY 05 first quarter were up 7.4%, year to year, to 9,031 homes. Order backlog at June 30, 2004, was $5.0 billion (17,062 units), up 44% (21% in units) from the level a year earlier.

In January 2003, CTX acquired the St. Louis and Indianapolis homebuilding operations of privately held Jones Company. The purchase was expected to add about 950 units to annual home sales in FY 04.

In 1999, the company acquired Fairclough Homes from AMEC, p.l.c., for $220 million, becoming the first U.S. homebuilder to enter the U.K. market.

To aid in the home selling process, the company's financial services business provides mortgage financing and sub-prime home equity lending, and sells title insurance and other insurance coverages. CTX provided financing for 69% of its home closings (other than cash sales) over the past five fiscal years, including 74% in FY 04. The division also originates mortgages on homes sold by others.

CTX also operates a nationwide construction contracting business, and a home services business that provides pest management and termite treatment services.

The company's investment real estate operations acquire, develop and sell land, primarily for industrial, office, multi-family, retail, residential and mixed-use projects. In early 2004, CTX determined that no significant capital would be allocated to this business. Effective April 1, 2004, it began to include its results in its Other Business segment.

In January 2004, CTX spun off its 65% stake in Centex Construction Products, which was renamed Eagle Materials (EXP). For each Centex share held, holders received 0.044 of an EXP common share and 0.149 of a Class B common share. EXP makes and distributes cement, aggregates, readymix concrete, recycled paperboard, and gypsum wallboard; it contributed $0.59 to the company's EPS in FY 03. In June 2003, CTX spun off its Cavco Industries manufactured home business to shareholders.

Company Financials Fiscal Year ending March 31

Per Share Data ($)

(Year Ended March 31)	2004	2003	2002	2001	2000	1999	1998	1997	1996	1995
Tangible Bk. Val.	23.89	19.05	14.49	11.59	10.32	8.78	7.20	6.31	6.36	5.95
Cash Flow	6.79	5.31	3.75	2.65	2.51	2.17	1.39	1.02	0.57	0.81
Earnings	6.01	4.41	3.06	2.33	2.11	1.88	1.18	0.91	0.46	0.76
S&P Core Earnings	5.90	4.25	2.86	2.17	NA	NA	NA	NA	NA	NA
Dividends	0.08	0.08	0.08	0.08	0.08	0.08	0.07	0.05	0.05	0.05
Payout Ratio	1%	2%	3%	3%	4%	4%	6%	6%	11%	7%

Cal. Yrs.	2003	2002	2001	2000	1999	1998	1997	1996	1995	1994
Prices - High	56.54	31.54	29.40	20.00	22.87	22.87	16.50	9.43	9.00	11.43
- Low	24.15	19.15	14.01	8.75	11.18	13.18	8.37	6.31	5.46	5.03
P/E Ratio - High	9	7	10	9	11	12	14	10	20	15
- Low	4	4	5	4	5	7	7	7	12	7

Income Statement Analysis (Million $)

	2004	2003	2002	2001	2000	1999	1998	1997	1996	1995
Revs.	10,363	9,117	7,748	6,711	5,956	5,155	3,975	3,785	3,103	3,278
Oper. Inc.	1,221	1,058	846	608	597	505	334	243	74.7	76.0
Depr.	102	113	91.0	41.0	49.0	36.2	25.6	13.5	12.5	6.40
Int. Exp.	39.9	120	116	99	67.0	41.6	33.3	34.1	40.9	33.0
Pretax Inc.	1,149	825	640	468	481	427	232	164	87.8	146
Eff. Tax Rate	32.4%	29.0%	37.0%	32.9%	33.1%	33.1%	37.5%	34.9%	39.2%	36.7%
Net Inc.	777	556	382	282	257	232	145	107	53.4	92.2
S&P Core Earnings	765	536	358	264	NA	NA	NA	NA	NA	NA

Balance Sheet & Other Fin. Data (Million $)

	2004	2003	2002	2001	2000	1999	1998	1997	1996	1995
Cash	193	644	326	115	140	111	98.3	31.3	14.0	24.0
Curr. Assets	NA	NA	NA	NA	NA	NA	NA	NA	NA	NA
Total Assets	16,069	11,611	8,985	6,649	4,039	4,335	3,416	2,679	2,337	2,050
Curr. Liab.	NA	NA	NA	NA	NA	NA	NA	NA	1,277	1,133
LT Debt	8,616	6,237	4,944	3,041	751	284	238	237	321	221
Common Equity	3,050	2,459	2,116	1,714	1,420	1,198	991	836	723	668
Total Cap.	12,002	8,866	7,214	4,899	2,300	1,623	1,464	1,314	1,060	916
Cap. Exp.	53.8	63.0	60.0	52.0	88.0	52.5	36.9	16.1	7.03	10.6
Cash Flow	879	669	473	323	306	268	170	120	65.9	99
Curr. Ratio	NA	NA	NA	NA	NA	NA	NA	NA	NA	NA
% LT Debt of Cap.	71.8	70.3	68.5	62.1	32.7	17.5	16.2	18.0	30.3	24.2
% Net Inc.of Revs.	7.5	6.1	4.9	4.2	4.3	4.5	3.6	2.8	1.7	2.8
% Ret. on Assets	5.6	5.4	4.9	5.3	6.1	6.0	4.8	4.2	2.4	4.3
% Ret. on Equity	27.2	24.3	19.9	18.0	19.6	21.2	15.9	13.7	7.7	14.6

Data as orig reptd.; bef. results of disc opers/spec. items. Per share data adj. for stk. divs. Bold denotes primary EPS - prior periods restated. E-Estimated. NA-Not Available. NM-Not Meaningful. NR-Not Ranked. UR-Under Review.

Office: 2728 North Harwood, Dallas, TX 75201-1516.
Telephone: 214-981-5000.
Email: ir@centex.com
Website: http://www.centex.com
Chrmn, Pres, CEO & COO: T.R. Eller.

EVP & CFO: L.E. Echols.
EVP, Secy & General Counsel: R. Smerge.
VP & Investor Contact: M.G. Moyer 214-981-5000.
Dirs: B. T. Alexander, D. W. Cook III, J. L. Elek, T. R. Eller, T. J. Falk, C. W. Murchison III, F. M. Poses, J. J. Postl, D. W. Quinn, T. M. Schoewe.

Founded: in 1950.
Domicile: Nevada.
Employees: 16,532.
S&P Analyst: Michael W. Jaffe/MF/BK

CenturyTel

Recommendation: **BUY** ★★★★ | 12-Month Target Price: **$39.00**
(as of September 09, 2004)

CTL has an approximate 0.04% weighting in the **S&P 500**

Sector: Telecommunication Services
Sub-Industry: Integrated Telecommunication Services
Peer Group: Incumbent Local Exchange Carriers (Independent)

Summary: This holding company provides a range of telephone services in 22 states, with operations concentrated in Wisconsin, Louisiana, Michigan and Ohio.

Quantitative Evaluations

S&P Earnings & Dividend Rank: A

| D | C | B- | B | B+ | A- | A | A+ |

S&P Fair Value Rank: 3+

| 1 | 2 | 3 | 4 | 5 |
Lowest — Highest

Fair Value Calc.: $32.30 (Slightly Overvalued)

S&P Investability Quotient Percentile
95%

CTL scored higher than 95% of all companies for which an S&P Report is available.

Volatility: Average

| Low | Average | High |

Technical Evaluation: Neutral
Since 11/04, the technical indicators for CTL have been Neutral.

Relative Strength Rank: Moderate
44
1 Lowest — Highest 99

Price as of 11/12/04: $33.93 | **2004E S&P Core EPS:** $2.24

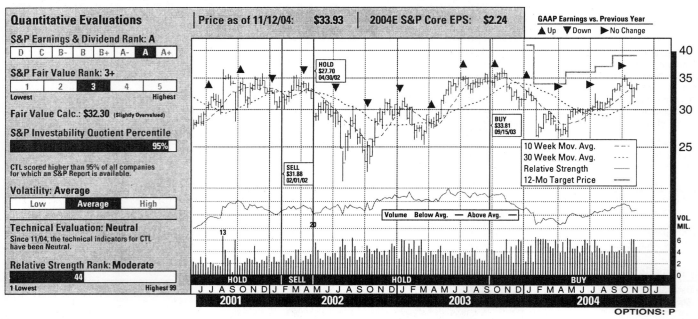

GAAP Earnings vs. Previous Year
▲ Up ▼ Down ▶ No Change

- 10 Week Mov. Avg.
- 30 Week Mov. Avg.
- Relative Strength
- 12-Mo Target Price

Volume Below Avg. — Above Avg.

OPTIONS: P

Analyst commentary prepared by Todd Rosenbluth/CB/JWP

Highlights November 01, 2004

- We see revenues declining 1% in 2005, following a likely 1.5% rise in 2004, with DSL, long-distance and enhanced services penetration gains offset by anticipated 2% fewer access lines and lower universal funding. We expect CTL's bundling of wholesale wireless and satellite offerings with traditional telecom services to help offset some of the pending competitive pressures in its rural markets.

- Despite strong cost cutting efforts in the first nine months of 2004, we see EBITDA margins, among the industry's best, narrowing fractionally in 2005 to about 51% as benefits from the recent billing system integration is counterbalanced by increased selling and marketing costs related to the rollout of new services. We look for interest expense to decline, as proceeds from the prior sale of the company's wireless unit and free cash flow help pay down debt.

- We project operating EPS of $2.36 for 2004 and $2.40 for 2005, aided by recent and likely future share repurchases. We estimate Standard & Poor's Core Earnings of $2.24 a share for 2004, with the modest difference relative to telecom peers accounted for by projected stock option expense and pension adjustments.

Investment Rationale/Risk November 01, 2004

- We would buy the shares. We believe this rural carrier's prospects are more favorable than those of the Baby Bells, based on our view of CTL's limited competitive pressures from wireless and cable carriers, and what we see as higher earnings quality. (We expect about 5% S&P Core Earnings dilution in 2004). Over the next 12 months, we see slight growth derived from vertical service integration and an increase in share buybacks from free cash flow. We believe the company remains conservative in its guidance. We also view positively the stock's high S&P Earnings and Dividend Ranking.

- Risks to our recommendation and target price include adjustments to the universal service fund or access charges, from which CTL receives revenues; and a potential increase in customer migration and wireless substitution.

- Our discounted cash flow model, based on a weighted average cost of capital of 8% and expected cash flow growth of 5% to 8% from 2004 to 2009 and 3% thereafter, indicates a value of $39. Our rural carrier relative P/E multiple and enterprise value/EBITDA ratio analyses also show the stock to be undervalued. Our 12-month target price is $39.

Key Stock Statistics

S&P Core EPS 2005E	2.33	52-week Range	$35.54-26.20
S&P Oper. EPS 2004E	2.36	12 Month P/E	14.3
P/E on S&P Oper. EPS 2004E	14.4	Beta	0.92
S&P Oper. EPS 2005E	2.40	Shareholders	4,530
Yield (%)	0.7%	Market Cap (B)	$ 4.6
Dividend Rate/Share	0.23	Shares Outstanding (M)	135.0

Value of $10,000 invested five years ago: **$ 8,566**

Dividend Data Dividends have been paid since 1974

Amount ($)	Date Decl.	Ex-Div. Date	Stock of Record	Payment Date
0.055	Nov. 20	Nov. 26	Dec. 01	Dec. 12 '03
0.058	Feb. 25	Mar. 04	Mar. 08	Mar. 19 '04
0.058	May. 27	Jun. 03	Jun. 07	Jun. 18 '04
0.058	Aug. 24	Sep. 02	Sep. 07	Sep. 17 '04

Revenues/Earnings Data Fiscal year ending December 31

Revenues (Million $)

	2004	2003	2002	2001	2000	1999
1Q	593.7	580.5	422.9	516.0	412.9	391.4
2Q	603.5	590.1	438.7	367.9	423.2	416.8
3Q	603.9	603.8	524.5	539.4	482.1	419.2
4Q	—	606.3	585.9	543.1	527.2	395.2
Yr.	—	2,381	1,972	2,117	1,846	1,677

Earnings Per Share ($)

	2004	2003	2002	2001	2000	1999
1Q	0.58	0.58	0.30	0.33	0.35	0.43
2Q	0.60	0.60	0.28	1.09	0.41	0.38
3Q	0.63	0.63	0.45	0.65	0.47	0.46
4Q	E0.59	0.57	0.30	0.35	0.40	0.42
Yr.	E2.36	2.38	1.33	2.41	1.63	1.70

Next earnings report expected: late-January Source: S&P, Company Reports
EPS Estimates based on S&P Operating Earnings; historical GAAP earnings are as reported.

CenturyTel Inc.

Recommendation: **BUY** ★ ★ ★ ★ ★   12-Month Target Price: **$39.00** (as of September 09, 2004)

Business Summary November 02, 2004

Following the sale in 2002 of its wireless operations to Alltel (AT) for $1.6 billion in cash, CenturyTel focuses solely on wireline local telecommunications. The company plans to pursue acquisitions of underserved incumbent local exchange carrier (ILEC) markets, to promote efficiencies through synergies with its existing network and drive long-term earnings growth through enhanced service offerings. At September 2004, CTL operated 2.34 million telephone access lines, primarily in rural and suburban areas in 22 states. It is now the eighth largest U.S. local exchange telephone company, based on access lines.

In October 2001, CTL agreed to acquire from Verizon approximately 675,000 access lines in Alabama and Missouri, for $2.159 billion in cash. The Alabama transaction closed in July 2002 and the Missouri properties deal closed in August 2002. To help fund this ILEC expansion, CTL sold its wireless properties, including 780,000 cellular subscribers in portions of Arkansas, Louisiana, Michigan, Mississippi, Texas and Wisconsin, to AT in the 2002 third quarter.

The company's local exchange subsidiaries derive revenue from providing local telephone services, network access services, and other related services including billing and local directory publications. Local access lines declined 2.4% in the 12 months ended September 2004 (they fell 1.6% in all of 2003), due to, in part, the displacement of traditional wireline telephone services by other competitive service providers. According to the company, the installation of digital switches and

high-speed data circuits has been an important component of CTL's growth strategy because it allows the installation of enhanced voice and data services to increase utilization of existing lines. Network access revenues relate to services provided to long-distance and wireless carriers in connection with the use of CTL's facilities to originate and terminate interstate and intrastate long-distance calls. The company also generated revenues by offering long distance service to about 1.1 million customers as of September 2004, as well as by offering DSL, caller ID and call waiting.

In late 2000, CTL began offering competitive local exchange telephone services coupled with long-distance and Internet access to small and medium-sized businesses in Monroe and Shreveport, LA.

In February 2003, a federal bankruptcy court approved CTL's $38 million bid for Digital Teleport, a regional wholesale data transport provider that operates in Missouri and and Kansas. The transaction closed in the 2003 second quarter.

In October 2004, CTL completed the installation of a new billing and customer care system. In addition, the company has partnered with Cingular Wireless and Echostar Communications to offer wholesale wireless and satellite services in CTL's product bundles in 2005.

Company Financials Fiscal Year ending December 31

Per Share Data ($)

(Year Ended December 31)	2003	2002	2001	2000	1999	1998	1997	1996	1995	1994
Tangible Bk. Val.	0.37	NM	NM	NM	1.39	NM	NM	3.60	2.95	1.73
Cash Flow	5.63	4.21	5.73	4.36	4.16	2.65	3.02	1.94	1.75	1.62
Earnings	2.38	1.33	2.41	1.63	1.70	1.63	1.87	0.96	0.88	0.84
S&P Core Earnings	2.35	1.08	1.21	NA	NA	NA	NA	NA	NA	NA
Dividends	0.22	0.21	0.20	0.19	0.09	0.17	0.16	0.16	0.15	0.14
Payout Ratio	9%	16%	8%	12%	5%	11%	9%	17%	17%	17%
Prices - High	36.76	35.50	39.87	47.31	49.00	45.16	22.41	15.77	14.72	14.33
- Low	25.25	21.13	25.45	24.43	35.18	21.55	12.66	12.66	12.00	9.72
P/E Ratio - High	15	27	17	29	29	28	12	17	17	17
- Low	11	16	11	15	21	13	7	13	14	12

Income Statement Analysis (Million $)

	2003	2002	2001	2000	1999	1998	1997	1996	1995	1994
Revs.	2,381	1,972	2,117	1,846	1,677	1,577	902	750	645	540
Depr.	471	412	473	388	349	329	159	132	114	94.4
Maint.	NA	NA	NA	NA	NA	NA	NA	NA	NA	NA
Constr. Credits	NA	NA	NA	NA	NA	NA	NA	NA	NA	NA
Eff. Tax Rate	35.2%	35.3%	37.2%	39.0%	41.5%	39.6%	36.8%	36.6%	37.3%	37.9%
Net Inc.	345	190	343	231	240	229	256	129	115	100
S&P Core Earnings	339	153	171	NA	NA	NA	NA	NA	NA	NA

Balance Sheet & Other Fin. Data (Million $)

	2003	2002	2001	2000	1999	1998	1997	1996	1995	1994
Gross Prop.	3,455	6,668	5,839	5,915	4,194	4,290	3,845	1,686	1,500	1,311
Net Prop.	3,455	3,532	3,000	2,959	2,256	2,351	2,259	1,149	1,048	947
Cap. Exp.	378	386	507	450	390	311	181	223	197	201
Total Cap.	6,588	6,666	4,425	5,082	3,926	4,471	4,237	1,802	1,511	1,169
Fxd. Chgs. Cov.	3.3	2.3	3.3	3.1	3.4	2.8	5.2	5.6	4.7	4.4
Capitalization:										
LT Debt	3,109	3,578	2,088	3,050	2,078	2,558	2,610	626	623	519
Pfd.	7.97	7.97	7.97	7.97	7.97	8.11	8.11	10.0	2.30	2.30
Common	3,471	3,080	2,329	2,024	1,840	1,523	1,292	1,018	886	648
% Return On Revs.	14.5	9.6	16.2	12.5	14.3	14.5	28.4	17.2	17.8	18.6
% Return On Invest. Capital	8.6	7.4	12.2	9.4	10.4	14.1	15.8	10.5	10.9	12.9
% Return On Com. Equity	10.5	7.0	15.7	12.0	14.2	16.2	22.1	13.5	14.9	17.2
% Earn. on Net Prop.	35.0	31.5	34.6	35.0	37.2	35.1	25.1	13.5	13.5	12.2
% LT Debt of Cap.	47.2	53.7	47.2	60.0	52.9	62.6	61.7	37.8	41.2	44.4
Capital. % Pfd.	0.1	0.1	0.2	0.2	0.2	0.2	1.9	0.6	0.1	0.2
Capital. % Common	52.7	46.2	52.6	39.8	46.9	37.3	30.5	61.6	58.6	55.4

Data as orig reptd.; bef. results of disc opers/spec. items. Per share data adj. for stk. divs.; EPS diluted. E-Estimated. NA-Not Available. NM-Not Meaningful. NR-Not Ranked. UR-Under Review.

Office: 100 CenturyTel Drive, Monroe, LA 71203.
Telephone: 318-388-9000.
Website: http://www.centurytel.com
Chrmn & CEO: G.F. Post.
Pres & COO: K.A. Puckett.

EVP & CFO: R.S. Ewing.
SVP, Secy & General Counsel: S.W. Goff.
Dirs: W. R. Boles, Jr., V. Boulet, C. Czeschin, J. B. Gardner, W. B. Hanks, R. L. Hargrove, Jr., J. Hebert, C. G. Melville, Jr., F. Nichols, H. P. Perry, G. F. Post, III, J. D. Reppond, J. Zimmel.

Founded: in 1968.
Domicile: Louisiana.
Employees: 6,720.
S&P Analyst: Todd Rosenbluth/CB/JWP

ChevronTexaco Corp.

Recommendation: **BUY** ★★★★★ 12-Month Target Price: **$65.00**
SELL | SELL | HOLD | BUY | BUY
(as of September 15, 2004)

CVX has an approximate 1.05% weighting in the **S&P 500**

Sector: Energy
Sub-Industry: Integrated Oil & Gas
Peer Group: Supermajor Integrated Oil & Gas

Summary: This global integrated oil company, with interests in exploration, production, refining and marketing and petrochemicals, merged with Texaco in October 2001.

Quantitative Evaluations

S&P Earnings & Dividend Rank: B+

| D | C | B- | B | B+ | A- | A | A+ |

S&P Fair Value Rank: 2

| 1 | 2 | 3 | 4 | 5 |
Lowest | | | | Highest

Fair Value Calc.: $47.70 (Slightly Overvalued)

S&P Investability Quotient Percentile

97%

CVX scored higher than 97% of all companies for which an S&P Report is available.

Volatility: Low

| Low | Average | High |

Technical Evaluation: Bullish
Since 8/04, the technical indicators for CVX have been Bullish.

Relative Strength Rank: Moderate

54

1 Lowest   Highest 99

| Price as of 11/12/04: | $54.57 | 2004E S&P Core EPS: | $5.40 |

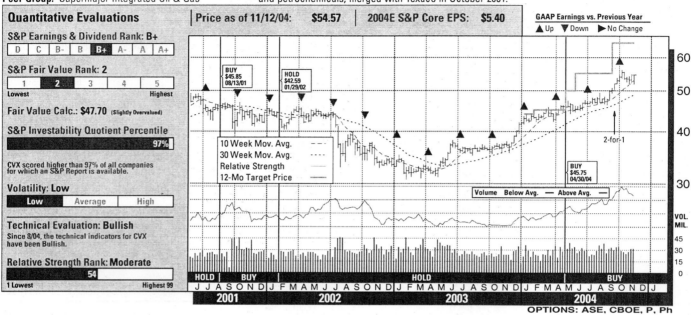

GAAP Earnings vs. Previous Year
▲ Up   ▼ Down   ► No Change

BUY $45.85 08/13/01
HOLD $42.59 01/29/02
10 Week Mov. Avg.
30 Week Mov. Avg.
Relative Strength
12-Mo Target Price
2-for-1
BUY $45.75 04/30/04
Volume Below Avg. — Above Avg.
VOL. MIL.
HOLD | BUY | HOLD | BUY
J J A S O N D J F M A M J J A S O N D J F M A M J J A S O N D J F M A M J J A S O N D J
2001   2002   2003   2004
OPTIONS: ASE, CBOE, P, Ph

Analyst commentary prepared by T. J. Vital/CB/BK

Highlights November 03, 2004

- Third quarter operating earnings climbed 54%, year to year, to $2.936 billion, or $1.38 per share -- $0.03 below our estimate, reflecting a sharper than expected drop in U.S. West Coast refining and marketing margins, and the loss of Gulf of Mexico production due to Hurricane Ivan (25,000 boe/d lost in the third quarter; 50,000-60,000 boe/d loss expected in the fourth quarter and 30,000 boe/d in the 2005 first quarter). Results for the 2004 period included a $234 million ($0.11 per share) after-tax gain on the sale of assets. CVX initiated a $5 billion stock buyback program in April 2004, and repurchased $1.35 billion of common shares during the second and third quarters.

- Restructurings continue, and the company is shifting toward a global functional business model in an effort to boost returns. Thus far in 2004, proceeds from asset sales have totaled more than $3 billion, including the August sale of certain U.S. onshore properties to XTO Energy for about $912 million, and the July sale of its wholly owned subsidiary Muanda International Oil Co. in the Democratic Republic of Congo. On the downstream side, more than 1,100 retail service stations worldwide have been sold since early 2003 as part of a plan to dispose of about 1,500 sites.

- EBITDAX (EBITDA before exploration expenses) climbed 38% in 2003, and we project an increase of 22% in 2004, reflecting strong pricing, before a projected drop of about 3% in 2005 on lower expected volumes and narrower refining and marketing margins.

Key Stock Statistics

S&P Core EPS 2005E	5.42	52-week Range	$56.07-35.57
S&P Oper. EPS 2004E	5.74	12 Month P/E	10.0
P/E on S&P Oper. EPS 2004E	9.5	Beta	0.60
S&P Oper. EPS 2005E	5.48	Shareholders	239,000
Yield (%)	2.9%	Market Cap (B)	$115.6
Dividend Rate/Share	1.60	Shares Outstanding (M)	2118.6

Value of $10,000 invested five years ago: **$15,095**

Dividend Data Dividends have been paid since 1912

Amount ($)	Date Decl.	Ex-Div. Date	Stock of Record	Payment Date
0.730	Apr. 28	May. 17	May. 19	Jun. 10 '04
0.800	Jul. 28	Aug. 17	Aug. 19	Sep. 10 '04
2-for-1	Jul. 28	Sep. 13	Aug. 19	Sep. 10 '04
0.400	Oct. 28	Nov. 16	Nov. 18	Dec. 10 '04

Investment Rationale/Risk November 03, 2004

- As the second largest U.S. oil company, and a top five U.S. refiner focused on the West and Gulf Coasts with the ability to process heavy/sour crude feedstocks, we view CVX as an attractive investment, and would buy the shares. While we see improvement in its earnings and returns, hydrocarbon production declined 5.6% in the third quarter, and we expect a drop of about 8% in 2004 and flat production in 2005, before a recovery in 2006 on new developments. However, CVX's reserve replacement has been strong, and we calculate its 2003 organic rate at 114%. To fund its upstream growth, CVX expects spending to rise 15% in 2004, to $8.5 billion (75% for exploration and production), and over 13% in 2005, to near $9.65 billion.

- Risks to our recommendation and target price include geopolitical risk associated with production growth in Venezuela and Nigeria, sensitivity to oil prices (74% of 2003 upstream production was liquids), and the risks of not achieving expected synergies from the Texaco merger and not improving returns as its businesses expand.

- Based on our upwardly revised oil and gas price projections, using a blend of our discounted cash flows and peer and transaction multiples, our 12-month target price is $65, which represents a forward P/E of 12X our 2005 EPS estimate, slightly below the peer average, reflecting our view of near-term upstream production declines.

Revenues/Earnings Data Fiscal year ending December 31

Revenues (Million $)

	2004	2003	2002	2001	2000	1999
1Q	33,566	30,965	21,155	12,298	11,727	6,399
2Q	38,301	29,361	25,333	13,006	13,224	8,473
3Q	40,715	30,970	25,503	11,563	13,621	10,177
4Q	—	30,465	27,058	19,606	13,557	10,979
Yr.	—	121,761	99,049	106,245	52,129	36,586

Earnings Per Share ($)

	2004	2003	2002	2001	2000	1999
1Q	1.19	0.99	0.34	1.25	0.80	0.25
2Q	1.92	0.75	0.20	1.03	0.86	0.27
3Q	1.38	1.01	-0.43	0.91	1.18	0.44
4Q	E1.34	0.82	0.43	-1.11	1.16	0.61
Yr.	E5.74	3.57	0.54	1.85	3.99	1.57

Next earnings report expected: late-January Source: S&P, Company Reports
EPS Estimates based on S&P Operating Earnings; historical GAAP earnings are as reported.

ChevronTexaco Corporation

Recommendation: **BUY** ★ ★ ★ ★ ★   12-Month Target Price: **$65.00** (as of September 15, 2004)

Business Summary November 04, 2004

In October 2001, Chevron Corp. (CHV) and Texaco Inc. (TX) merged, creating the second largest U.S.-based oil company, ChevronTexaco Corp. (CVX). As of April 2003, CVX expected annual pretax savings of about $2.2 billion (up from a forecast of $1.8 billion in June 2002) from operating efficiencies and the elimination of redundant operations. As a condition to approve the merger, the FTC required the sale of certain TX assets, such as its investments in the Equilon Enterprises LLC (44% ownership) and Motiva Enterprises LLC (31%) joint ventures; these were sold in February 2002 for $3.86 billion.

CVX separately manages its exploration and production (21% of 2003 revenues; 83% of 2003 segment income); refining, marketing and transportation (77%; 16%); chemicals (1%; 1%); and other (including its investment in Dynegy, coal mining, power and gasification, technology investments, insurance, real estate and other corporate functions) businesses.

The exploration and production segment is involved in the production of crude oil and natural gas. In 2003, worldwide net production of crude oil and natural gas liquids averaged 1.808 million b/d, down 4.7% from 2002. Worldwide net production of natural gas declined 1.9%, to 4.292 billion cubic feet (Bcf) per day. Worldwide production costs averaged $4.60 per bbl in 2003, versus $4.29 in 2002. Net proved reserves of crude oil and liquids were 8,599 million bbl. and 8,668 million bbl. at year-end 2003 and 2002, and 20,191 Bcf and 19,335 Bcf of natural gas. In 2003, CVX replaced 116% of net production (including purchases, excluding sales). In 2003, the company combined its existing natural gas focused businesses into a new unit, ChevronTexaco Global Gas.

CVX's refining, marketing, transportation and trading business operates globally under the Chevron, Texaco and Caltex brands. The company owns and is affiliated with 21 refineries located in the Pacific and Atlantic basins, with global refining capacity of 2.068 million b/d (46% North America, 31% Asia Pacific, 16% Europe) at the end of 2003. The company has a worldwide marketing network of more than 18,565 retail sites in 84 countries. CVX is among the four largest marketers of lubricants, with operations in 180 countries; brands include Havoline, Delo, Ursa, Revtex, and Texaco Xpress Lube. ChevronTexaco Shipping manages a company-controlled fleet of 35 vessels, including 22 double-hulled tankers. In 2002, the company combined its Global Trading/Fuel and Marine Marketing groups under one leadership team in an effort to capture synergies between the two businesses. In June 2004, CVX acquired half of BP Singapore Private Ltd's 33% interest in the Singapore Refining Co. to become a 50/50 joint owner with Singapore Petroleum Co. Ltd.

In July 2000, CHV and Phillips Petroleum combined their chemical operations into an equally owned joint venture, Chevron Phillips Chemical Co. LLC (CPChem). CPChem manufactures products at 32 locations in eight countries, and operates six research and technical facilities.

Other activities include CVX's Pittsburg & Midway Coal Mining Co. (P&M) subsidiary, a 20% interest in the Athabasca Oil Sands Project (AOSP), Global Power Generation (GPG), Worldwide Gasification Technology (WGT), and its 50/50 Sasol Chevron Global Joint Venture to develop gas-to-liquids technology.

Company Financials Fiscal Year ending December 31

Per Share Data ($)

(Year Ended December 31)	2003	2002	2001	2000	1999	1998	1997	1996	1995	1994
Tangible Bk. Val.	16.98	14.79	15.92	15.54	13.53	13.04	13.32	11.96	11.01	11.13
Cash Flow	5.99	2.98	5.17	6.17	3.74	2.78	4.22	3.70	3.31	3.17
Earnings	3.57	0.54	1.85	3.99	1.57	1.02	2.48	2.00	0.72	1.30
S&P Core Earnings	3.50	1.22	1.66	NA	NA	NA	NA	NA	NA	NA
Dividends	1.43	1.40	1.32	1.30	1.24	1.22	1.14	1.04	0.96	0.93
Payout Ratio	40%	NM	72%	33%	79%	120%	46%	52%	135%	71%
Prices - High	43.49	45.80	49.24	47.43	52.46	45.09	44.59	34.18	26.81	23.65
- Low	30.65	32.70	39.21	34.96	36.56	33.87	30.87	25.50	21.68	19.93
P/E Ratio - High	12	86	27	12	33	44	18	17	37	18
- Low	9	61	21	9	23	33	12	13	30	15

Income Statement Analysis (Million $)

	2003	2002	2001	2000	1999	1998	1997	1996	1995	1994
Revs.	120,032	98,691	104,409	50,592	35,448	29,943	40,583	42,782	31,322	30,340
Oper. Inc.	49,336	28,848	16,031	15,834	5,848	3,945	6,747	6,209	4,799	4,925
Depr. Depl. & Amort.	5,384	5,231	7,059	2,848	2,866	2,320	2,300	2,216	3,381	2,431
Int. Exp.	474	565	833	460	463	405	312	472	543	419
Pretax Inc.	12,850	4,213	8,412	9,270	3,648	1,834	5,502	4,740	1,789	2,803
Eff. Tax Rate	41.6%	71.8%	51.8%	44.1%	43.3%	27.0%	40.8%	45.0%	48.0%	39.7%
Net Inc.	7,426	1,132	3,931	5,185	2,070	1,339	3,256	2,607	930	1,693
S&P Core Earnings	7,454	2,590	3,518	NA	NA	NA	NA	NA	NA	NA

Balance Sheet & Other Fin. Data (Million $)

	2003	2002	2001	2000	1999	1998	1997	1996	1995	1994
Cash	5,267	3,781	3,150	2,630	2,032	1,413	1,015	1,637	1,384	1,306
Curr. Assets	19,426	17,776	18,327	8,213	8,297	6,297	7,006	7,942	7,867	7,591
Total Assets	81,470	77,359	77,572	41,264	40,668	36,540	35,473	34,854	34,330	34,407
Curr. Liab.	16,111	19,876	20,654	7,674	8,889	7,166	6,946	8,907	9,445	9,392
LT Debt	10,894	10,911	8,989	5,153	5,485	4,393	4,431	3,988	4,521	4,128
Common Equity	40,022	36,176	37,120	21,761	17,749	17,034	17,472	15,623	14,355	14,596
Total Cap.	57,601	53,009	52,524	31,822	28,244	25,072	25,118	22,462	21,309	21,398
Cap. Exp.	5,625	7,597	9,713	3,657	4,366	3,880	3,899	3,424	3,529	3,112
Cash Flow	12,810	6,363	10,990	8,033	4,936	3,659	5,556	4,823	4,311	4,124
Curr. Ratio	1.2	0.9	0.9	1.1	0.9	0.9	1.0	0.9	0.8	0.8
% LT Debt of Cap.	18.9	20.6	17.1	16.2	19.4	17.5	17.6	17.8	21.2	19.3
% Ret. on Assets	9.4	1.5	5.1	12.7	5.4	3.7	9.3	7.6	2.7	4.9
% Ret. on Equity	19.5	3.1	10.7	25.1	11.9	7.8	19.7	17.4	6.4	11.8

Data as orig. reptd.; bef. results of disc. opers. and/or spec. items. Revenues exclude excise taxes and other income. Per share data adj. for stk. divs.; EPS diluted (primary prior to 1998). Qrty. revs. incl. inc. from equity affil. and other inc. E-Estimated. NA-Not Available. NM-Not Meaningful. NR-Not Ranked.

Office: 6001 Bollinger Canyon Road, San Ramon, CA 94583-2324.
Telephone: 925-842-1000.
Email: invest@chevrontexaco.com
Website: http://www.chevrontexaco.com
Chrmn & CEO: D.J. O'Reilly.
Vice Chrmn: P.J. Robertson.
VP & CFO: J.S. Watson.

VP & CTO: D.L. Paul.
VP & Treas: D.M. Krattebol.
Investor Contact: R. Richards 925-842-5690.
Dirs: S. H. Armacost, R. E. Denham, R. J. Eaton, S. L. Ginn, C. A. Hills, F. G. Jenifer, J. B. Johnston, S. Nunn, D. J. O'Reilly, P. J. Robertson, C. R. Shoemate, C. Ware.

Founded: in 1901.
Domicile: Delaware.
Employees: 50,582.
S&P Analyst: T. J. Vital/CB/BK

The McGraw-Hill Companies

Chiron Corp.

Recommendation: **HOLD** ★ ★ ★ ☆ ☆
SELL SELL HOLD BUY BUY

12-Month Target Price: $33.00
(as of October 05, 2004)

CHIR has an approximate 0.05% weighting in the **S&P 500**

Sector: Health Care
Sub-Industry: Biotechnology
Peer Group: Biotech Therapeutics - Larger Capitalization

Summary: This major biotechnology concern, 42% owned by Novartis AG, manufactures biopharmaceuticals, vaccines and blood testing products.

Quantitative Evaluations

S&P Earnings & Dividend Rank: B-

| D | C | B- | B | B+ | A- | A | A+ |

S&P Fair Value Rank: 5

| 1 | 2 | 3 | 4 | 5 |
| Lowest | | | | Highest |

Fair Value Calc.: $35.80 (Slightly Undervalued)

S&P Investability Quotient Percentile

94%

CHIR scored higher than 94% of all companies for which an S&P Report is available.

Volatility: Average

| Low | Average | High |

Technical Evaluation: Bearish
Since 10/04, the technical indicators for CHIR have been Bearish.

Relative Strength Rank: Weak

| 1 Lowest | | Highest 99 |

Price as of 11/12/04: $31.95   **2004E S&P Core EPS:** $0.47

GAAP Earnings vs. Previous Year
▲ Up   ▼ Down   ► No Change

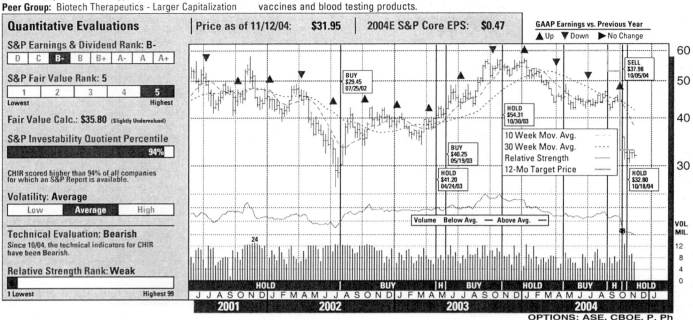

Analyst commentary prepared by Frank DiLorenzo, CFA /PMW/BK

OPTIONS: ASE, CBOE, P, Ph

Highlights November 05, 2004

- Third quarter pro forma EPS was $0.26, versus $0.60 in the 2003 period, reflecting the absence of Fluvirin revenues. Our estimate was for EPS of $0.21. However, a Roche settlement positively affected EPS by about $0.18. Overall, we view earnings quality for the quarter as below average. Procleix sales of $64 million were $3 million below our estimate, but up 19%, year to year. Biopharmaceutical-related revenues of $145 million were $13 million above our projection.

- In October, CHIR said it would not ship its Fluvirin flu vaccine for the 2004/2005 flu season, due to manufacturing problems at its production facility in Liverpool, England. We assume that Fluvirin will be available for the 2005/2006 flu season. However, we believe the company may supply only up to 30 million doses to the U.S. market next year, well below our prior expectations of more than 50 million doses, as we expect potentially higher production from Aventis and MedImmune, as well as the possible entry of GlaxoSmithKline into the U.S. influenza market.

- We project total revenues of $1.76 billion for 2004 and $2.14 billion for 2005. We estimate pro forma EPS of $0.75 for 2004 and $1.90 for 2005. If CHIR is unable to supply Fluvirin to the U.S. market for the 2005/2006 flu season, we think 2005 EPS could be adversely affected by at least $0.30. However, a supply of more than 30 million doses to the U.S. market would provide some upside to our 2005 EPS estimate.

Key Stock Statistics

S&P Oper. EPS 2004E	0.75	52-week Range	$57.29-29.00	
P/E on S&P Oper. EPS 2004E	42.6	12 Month P/E	26.6	
S&P Oper. EPS 2005E	1.90	Beta	0.82	
Yield (%)	Nil	Shareholders	4,159	
Dividend Rate/Share	Nil	Market Cap (B)	$ 6.0	
Shares Outstanding (M)	186.8			

Value of $10,000 invested five years ago: **$ 10,963**

Dividend Data

No cash dividends have been paid.

Investment Rationale/Risk November 05, 2004

- We recommend holding the shares, as we believe a price correction has led to a more reasonable valuation. We see CHIR's longer-term flu vaccine prospects in the U.S. as diminished, but consider its other vaccines to have moderate growth potential. We continue to expect solid growth for the blood testing unit, with recent U.S. and EU submissions for approval of the Ultrio assay that simultaneously tests for HIV-1, hepatitis B, and hepatitis C. We project annualized gains of at least 20% for the division through 2006. Separately, in October, CHIR filed for FDA approval of Pulminiq (inhalable cyclosporine) to prevent lung transplant rejection.

- Risks to our recommendation and target price include lower than expected product sales, potentially strong Betaseron competition from Antegren, and the possibility that CHIR will not be able to supply flu vaccine in time for the 2005/2006 flu season.

- Based on our 2005 EPS estimate of $1.90 and our annualized EPS growth forecast of 12.4%, the stock's 2005 P/E to growth (PEG) ratio of 1.3X is slightly above S&P's biotech peer average of 1.2X. We consider a reasonable PEG range for the biotech group to be 1.4X to 1.6X. With growth prospects that are, in our view, below those of most peers, we think that CHIR should trade at a PEG no higher than the low end of our target range. Based on a PEG of 1.4X, our 12-month target price is $33.

Revenues/Earnings Data Fiscal year ending December 31

Revenues (Million $)

	2004	2003	2002	2001	2000	1999
1Q	379.7	321.0	252.2	259.6	216.8	175.6
2Q	295.1	350.3	299.3	261.2	240.9	189.1
3Q	524.0	540.5	368.5	302.0	221.0	204.4
4Q	—	554.6	356.3	317.9	293.5	193.6
Yr.	—	1,766	1,276	1,141	972.1	762.6

Earnings Per Share ($)

	2004	2003	2002	2001	2000	1999
1Q	0.14	0.32	-0.10	0.23	0.21	0.13
2Q	0.17	0.32	0.26	0.17	0.30	0.18
3Q	0.13	-0.11	0.43	0.26	0.23	0.24
4Q	E0.02	0.59	0.35	0.23	-0.69	0.14
Yr.	E0.75	1.15	0.94	0.90	0.08	0.69

Next earnings report expected: late-January Source: S&P, Company Reports
EPS Estimates based on S&P Operating Earnings; historical GAAP earnings are as reported.

Chiron Corporation

Recommendation: **HOLD** ★ ★ ★ ☆ ☆   12-Month Target Price: **$33.00** (as of October 05, 2004)

Business Summary November 05, 2004

Chiron, a major biotech company, focuses on the development, manufacture and marketing of biopharmaceuticals, vaccines and blood testing products. Biopharmaceutical sales were $439.1 million in 2003 ($408.7 million in 2002), vaccine sales were $678.3 million ($357.3 million), and blood testing product sales were $228.5 million ($148.1 million).

CHIR's Proleukin is a recombinant form of interleukin-2, a protein produced by the body to stimulate the production of infection-fighting white blood cells. Proleukin is approved to treat kidney cancer and melanoma. Betaseron is an interferon beta-1b treatment for relapsing/remitting multiple sclerosis that Chiron manufactures for sale by Berlex Laboratories.

TOBI is an inhalable drug (administered via a nebulizer) approved to treat chronic pseudomonal lung infection in cystic fibrosis patients in the U.S. and Europe. A more convenient hand-held device using a drypowder formulation is being developed. The company has said that a Phase III trial may begin by early 2005.

In July 2003, CHIR acquired U.K.-based PowderJect Pharmaceuticals, for $880 million in cash. PowderJect's primary product is Fluvirin, which was the second leading U.S. flu vaccine. For the 2004/2005 flu season, CHIR does not plan to sell Fluvirin due to manufacturing problems. Menjugate, to prevent meningococcal C, and Fluad, a flu vaccine, are co-marketed by the company and Aventis Pasteur in Europe.

Blood testing operations are conducted through a joint venture with Johnson & Johnson's Ortho unit, and an alliance with Gen-Probe. The Ortho venture produces diagnostic tests for hepatitis and HIV, with Chiron performing certain research and antigen manufacturing functions, and Ortho producing and marketing assays and instrument systems. CHIR and Ortho share equally in the venture's pretax earnings.

The company's collaboration with Gen-Probe has led to products that use a nucleic acid amplification test (NAT) to screen blood and plasma for viral infections, including HIV, hepatitis B and C, and West Nile virus. In February 2002, Procleix, an NAT blood test to detect HIV-1 and hepatitis C, was approved by the FDA. Procleix is marketed by CHIR. A regulatory submission for the Ultrio assay, which simultaneously tests for HIV and hepatitis B and C, was filed with the FDA in September 2004. An FDA filing for approval of an assay that tests for West Nile virus is expected in the 2005 first quarter. In October 2000, the company licensed certain NAT technology rights to Roche for use in blood testing, with CHIR receiving royalties on sales from related products sold by Roche.

In May 2004, CHIR began a Phase III trial of tifacogin in patients with severe community-acquired pneumonia. Separate Phase II trials of Proleukin in combination with Biogen Idec's Rituxan are under way for the treatment of non-Hodgkin's lymphoma patients who failed prior Rituxan therapy and who have not previously received Rituxan therapy, respectively. In October 2004, the company filed for FDA approval of aerosolized cyclosporine to prevent lung transplant rejection. CHIR also expects to file for European approval of daptomycin to treat Gram-positive bacterial infections by the end of 2004.

Company Financials Fiscal Year ending December 31

Per Share Data ($)

(Year Ended December 31)	2003	2002	2001	2000	1999	1998	1997	1996	1995	1994
Tangible Bk. Val.	4.99	7.47	6.72	6.20	8.51	7.58	4.26	3.65	3.12	4.29
Cash Flow	1.89	1.59	1.49	0.51	1.05	1.02	0.86	0.95	-2.54	0.50
Earnings	1.15	0.94	0.90	0.08	0.69	0.42	0.29	0.31	-3.16	0.13
S&P Core Earnings	0.56	0.56	0.61	NA	NA	NA	NA	NA	NA	NA
Dividends	Nil	Nil	Nil	Nil	Nil	Nil	Nil	Nil	Nil	Nil
Payout Ratio	Nil	Nil	Nil	Nil	Nil	Nil	Nil	Nil	Nil	Nil
Prices - High	57.07	49.16	58.05	71.03	44.18	26.62	24.75	29.81	28.43	24.00
- Low	34.02	26.38	35.37	33.06	18.50	13.75	16.50	16.75	11.93	12.68
P/E Ratio - High	50	52	65	NM	64	63	85	96	NM	NM
- Low	30	28	39	NM	27	33	57	54	NM	NM

Income Statement Analysis (Million $)

	2003	2002	2001	2000	1999	1998	1997	1996	1995	1994
Revs.	1,766	1,276	1,056	888	763	737	1,162	1,005	1,020	372
Oper. Inc.	484	402	315	198	151	221	212	203	-59.0	9.00
Depr.	146	124	115	81.4	68.9	108	103	112	99	49.4
Int. Exp.	19.1	12.8	7.51	12.8	23.9	24.7	33.3	30.7	30.4	20.2
Pretax Inc.	311	263	256	104	157	95.0	76.9	80.0	-491	32.0
Eff. Tax Rate	28.5%	31.8%	31.3%	83.8%	18.0%	20.0%	33.9%	31.0%	NM	42.7%
Net Inc.	220	181	175	16.1	128	76.0	50.8	55.0	-512	18.0
S&P Core Earnings	108	108	118	NA	NA	NA	NA	NA	NA	NA

Balance Sheet & Other Fin. Data (Million $)

	2003	2002	2001	2000	1999	1998	1997	1996	1995	1994
Cash	538	248	777	702	364	513	98.5	107	135	222
Curr. Assets	1,258	1,386	1,189	1,103	1,339	1,632	770	697	637	434
Total Assets	4,195	2,960	2,873	2,458	2,459	2,524	1,768	1,689	1,490	1,050
Curr. Liab.	437	299	331	414	613	557	471	473	369	120
LT Debt	1,084	417	409	3.04	97.0	338	397	420	413	338
Common Equity	2,444	2,076	1,932	1,881	1,693	1,546	874	765	672	573
Total Cap.	3,643	2,498	2,404	1,962	1,790	1,884	1,271	1,184	1,086	911
Cap. Exp.	139	106	64.9	54.4	64.6	126	77.5	120	101	106
Cash Flow	366	305	290	97.5	197	184	153	168	-413	68.0
Curr. Ratio	2.9	4.6	3.6	2.7	2.2	2.9	1.6	1.5	1.7	3.6
% LT Debt of Cap.	29.8	16.7	17.0	0.2	5.4	17.9	31.2	35.4	38.1	37.1
% Net Inc.of Revs.	12.5	14.2	16.5	1.8	16.8	10.3	4.4	4.2	NM	4.9
% Ret. on Assets	6.2	6.2	6.6	0.7	5.2	3.5	2.9	3.5	NM	1.8
% Ret. on Equity	9.7	9.0	9.2	0.9	7.9	6.3	6.2	7.7	NM	3.3

Data as orig reptd.; bef. results of disc opers/spec. items. Per share data adj. for stk. divs.; EPS diluted. E-Estimated. NA-Not Available. NM-Not Meaningful. NR-Not Ranked. UR-Under Review.

Office: 4560 Horton Street, Emeryville, CA 94608-2916.
Telephone: 510-655-8730.
Website: http://www.chiron.com
Chrmn: S.P. Lance.
Pres & CEO: H. Pien.
VP & CFO: D. Smith.

VP & General Counsel: U.B. Bartels.
VP & Investor Contact: J.A. Lonergan.
Dirs: R. Breu, V. D. Bryson, L. W. Coleman, P. E. Douaze, J. R. Fredericks, P. L. Herrling, S. P. Lance, D. O'Leary, E. E. Penhoet, H. Pien, P. J. Strijkert, R. Wills.

Founded: in 1981.
Domicile: Delaware.
Employees: 5,332.
S&P Analyst: Frank DiLorenzo, CFA /PMW/BK

The McGraw·Hill Companies

Chubb Corp.

Recommendation: **BUY** ★★★★☆
SELL SELL HOLD BUY BUY

12-Month Target Price: **$82.00**
(as of October 26, 2004)

CB has an approximate 0.13% weighting in the **S&P 500**

Sector: Financials
Sub-Industry: Property & Casualty Insurance
Peer Group: Commercial/Personal Insurers - National

Summary: This company is one of the largest U.S. property-casualty insurance groups.

Quantitative Evaluations	Price as of 11/12/04: **$74.82**	2004E S&P Core EPS: **$5.22**

S&P Earnings & Dividend Rank: B+

D	C	B-	B	B+	A-	A	A+

S&P Fair Value Rank: 4-

1	2	3	4	5
Lowest				Highest

Fair Value Calc.: $75.80 (Fairly Valued)

S&P Investability Quotient Percentile

99%

CB scored higher than 99% of all companies for which an S&P Report is available.

Volatility: Low

Low	Average	High

Technical Evaluation: Bullish
Since 11/04, the technical indicators for CB have been Bullish.

Relative Strength Rank: Moderate

63

1 Lowest — Highest 99

GAAP Earnings vs. Previous Year
▲ Up ▼ Down ► No Change

BUY $57.30 10/30/02

10 Week Mov. Avg.
30 Week Mov. Avg.
Relative Strength
12-Mo Target Price

HOLD $63.05 09/17/01

BUY $76.70 04/30/02

HOLD $54.83 09/30/02

Volume Below Avg. — Above Avg.

VOL. MIL.

OPTIONS: CBOE

Analyst commentary prepared by Catherine A. Seifert/CB/BK

Highlights October 29, 2004

- We anticipate that earned premium growth in 2004 will likely not exceed 10%, largely due to some pricing weakness in the specialty commercial lines area. As a result of what appears to be a softening in certain commercial lines premium pricing, we anticipate that earned premium growth will average 8% to 10% in 2005. Pricing in the personal lines segments appears to be more stable. We also believe terms and conditions on most commercial lines policies have held steady, but may be off a bit from peak levels.
- We see investment income growth as likely to be up by at least 10% in 2004, as relatively low investment yields are being offset by stronger than expected cash flow amid a generally favorable claims environment (despite higher catastrophe losses). Assuming these trends carry into 2005, we think net investment income growth could be in double digits.
- Our operating EPS estimates of $6.80 for 2004 and $7.50 for 2005 assume that the company does not incur any large one-time reserve boosts like those for asbestos reserves. Earnings in 2003 included a $250 million increase to asbestos loss reserves. This followed a 2002 third quarter charge of $625 million ($2.38 a share, after tax) to boost asbestos reserves. Year to date results in 2004 include the impact of higher catastrophe losses (which are masking otherwise improved claim trends, in our view). Operating EPS for the first nine months of 2004 rose to $5.10, from $3.82 in the 2003 interim, despite a 29% increase in catastrophe losses.

Key Stock Statistics

S&P Oper. EPS 2004E	6.80	52-week Range	$75.00-62.48
P/E on S&P Oper. EPS 2004E	11.0	12 Month P/E	12.6
S&P Oper. EPS 2005E	7.50	Beta	0.70
Yield (%)	2.1%	Shareholders	5,800
Dividend Rate/Share	1.56	Market Cap (B)	$ 14.3
Shares Outstanding (M)	191.6		

Value of $10,000 invested five years ago: **$ 13,518**

Dividend Data Dividends have been paid since 1902

Amount ($)	Date Decl.	Ex-Div. Date	Stock of Record	Payment Date
0.360	Dec. 04	Dec. 16	Dec. 18	Jan. 06 '04
0.390	Mar. 05	Mar. 17	Mar. 19	Apr. 06 '04
0.390	Jun. 04	Jun. 22	Jun. 24	Jul. 09 '04
0.390	Sep. 09	Sep. 22	Sep. 24	Oct. 12 '04

Investment Rationale/Risk October 29, 2004

- We view the shares of this property-casualty insurer as modestly undervalued on both a relative and historical basis. We believe the stock deserves a premium-to-peers P/E multiple, based on what we see as CB's superior premium growth prospects and its wider margin mix of business. We were also encouraged to see that in the wake of a record number of hurricanes in the third quarter, CB's catastrophe losses were lower than its market share would indicate. Our outlook is tempered by concerns over a more competitive premium pricing environment and the adequacy of Chubb's loss reserves in certain lines of business.
- Risks to our opinion and target price include a deterioration in claim trends and loss reserves, a significant terrorist attack or catastrophe in the U.S., or a sharp increase in premium price competition. Also, although Chubb has not been implicated in the investigation currently being conducted by several Attorneys General in the wake of New York Attorney General Elliot Spitzer's civil lawsuit against insurance broker Marsh & McLennan that alleges bid rigging (among other improprieties), there is a risk that the investigation could be broadened.
- Our target price of $82 assumes that the stock's forward P/E multiple will increase to put it at a slight premium to the peer group average P/E multiple.

Revenues/Earnings Data Fiscal year ending December 31

Revenues (Million $)

	2004	2003	2002	2001	2000	1999
1Q	3,178	2,616	2,105	1,892	1,767	1,630
2Q	3,206	2,839	2,224	1,915	1,774	1,687
3Q	3,345	2,947	2,364	1,956	1,859	1,709
4Q	—	2,992	2,447	1,992	1,852	1,443
Yr.	—	11,394	9,140	7,754	7,252	5,652

Earnings Per Share ($)

	2004	2003	2002	2001	2000	1999
1Q	1.88	1.31	1.15	0.97	0.87	1.14
2Q	1.85	1.45	1.20	0.83	1.02	1.18
3Q	1.88	1.37	-1.42	-1.40	1.17	0.44
4Q	—	0.38	0.33	0.16	0.95	0.93
Yr.	—	4.46	1.29	0.63	4.01	3.66

Next earnings report expected: early-February Source: S&P, Company Reports
EPS Estimates based on S&P Operating Earnings; historical GAAP earnings are as reported.

The Chubb Corporation

Recommendation: **BUY** ★★★★☆   12-Month Target Price: **$82.00** (as of October 26, 2004)

Business Summary November 01, 2004

Chubb's property-casualty operations, as a group, constitute the 10th largest U.S. property-casualty (p-c) insurer, based on 2003 net written premiums (latest available aggregate data). In 2003, the company wrote $11.07 billion in net property-casualty premiums, up over 22% from $9.05 billion in 2002. Premium growth in 2003 reflected rate increases resulting from an industrywide upturn in premium pricing, coupled with contributions from new business. Underwriting results in 2003 improved, in part due to a lower level of asbestos and toxic waste losses. CB's property-casualty operations are divided into three strategic business units: Personal Lines (23% of net written premiums in 2003); Commercial Insurance (37%); and Specialty Insurance (40%).

The Personal Insurance division offers primarily automobile and homeowners' insurance coverage. The company's products are typically targeted to individuals with upscale homes and automobiles, requiring more coverage choices and higher policy limits than are offered under standard insurance policies. Net written premiums totaled $2.6 billion in 2003 (up 13% from $2.3 billion in 2002), and were divided as follows: homeowners' 57%, automobile 23%, and other (mainly personal article coverage) 20%. The combined loss and expense ratio rose somewhat during 2003, but remained profitable, at 98.2%, versus 97.2% in 2002.

Chubb Commercial Insurance underwrites an array of commercial insurance policies, including those for multiple peril, casualty, workers' compensation, and property and marine coverage. Net written premiums totaled $4.1 billion in 2003 (up 21% from $3.4 billion in 2002) and were divided as follows: commercial casualty 33%, commercial multi-peril 27%, property and marine 25%, and workers' compensation 15%. The combined loss and expense ratio improved substantially in 2003, amid a drop in asbestos claims, to 95.9%, from 118.6% in 2002.

Chubb Specialty Insurance offers a variety of specialized executive protection and professional liability products for privately and publicly owned companies, financial institutions, professional firms, and healthcare organizations. Net written premiums totaled $4.4 billion in 2002 (up 33% from $3.3 billion in 2002) and were divided as follows: executive protection 48%, financial institutions 19%, and other 33%. The combined loss and expense ratio improved significantly in 2003, to 98.0%, from 106.7% in 2002.

Company Financials Fiscal Year ending December 31

Per Share Data ($)

(Year Ended December 31)	2003	2002	2001	2000	1999	1998	1997	1996	1995	1994
Tangible Bk. Val.	43.00	37.34	35.62	37.15	32.85	34.84	33.47	31.24	29.71	24.05
Oper. Earnings	NA	1.16	0.62	3.82	3.33	3.65	4.00	3.58	3.45	2.75
Earnings	4.46	1.29	0.63	4.01	3.66	4.19	4.39	2.75	3.93	2.98
S&P Core Earnings	4.16	0.84	0.37	NA	NA	NA	NA	NA	NA	NA
Dividends	1.44	1.40	1.36	1.32	1.27	1.22	1.16	1.08	0.98	0.92
Payout Ratio	32%	109%	NM	33%	35%	29%	26%	39%	25%	31%
Prices - High	69.29	78.64	86.62	90.25	76.37	88.81	78.50	56.25	50.31	41.56
- Low	41.78	51.91	55.54	43.25	44.00	55.37	51.12	40.87	38.06	34.31
P/E Ratio - High	16	61	NM	23	21	21	18	20	13	14
- Low	9	40	NM	11	12	13	12	15	10	12

Income Statement Analysis (Million $)

	2003	2002	2001	2000	1999	1998	1997	1996	1995	1994
Premium Inc.	10,183	8,035	6,656	6,146	5,652	5,304	5,157	4,569	4,770	4,612
Net Invest. Inc.	1,118	997	983	957	893	822	785	712	901	829
Oth. Revs.	93.2	57.7	115	6,294	184	224	721	400	418	268
Total Revs.	11,394	9,140	7,754	7,252	6,730	6,350	6,664	5,681	6,089	5,710
Pretax Inc.	934	168	-66.0	851	710	850	973	547	900	639
Net Oper. Inc.	NA	201	111	681	565	615	701	434	614	487
Net Inc.	809	223	112	715	621	707	770	486	697	528
S&P Core Earnings	754	146	65.2	NA	NA	NA	NA	NA	NA	NA

Balance Sheet & Other Fin. Data (Million $)

	2003	2002	2001	2000	1999	1998	1997	1996	1995	1994
Cash & Equiv.	1,044	1,644	691	720	735	229	12.0	200	257	221
Premiums Due	2,188	6,112	6,198	3,263	1,235	1,199	1,144	985	873	787
Invest. Assets: Bonds	22,412	18,263	16,117	15,564	14,519	13,319	12,454	11,158	12,603	10,722
Invest. Assets: Stocks	1,514	795	710	831	769	1,092	871	646	588	642
Invest. Assets: Loans	Nil	Nil	Nil	Nil	Nil	Nil	Nil	Nil	212	203
Invest. Assets: Total	26,934	21,279	17,784	17,001	16,019	14,755	14,049	1,281	13,887	12,378
Deferred Policy Costs	1,343	1,150	929	842	780	729	677	601	1,171	1,136
Total Assets	38,361	34,114	29,449	25,027	23,537	20,746	19,616	19,939	22,997	20,723
Debt	2,814	1,959	2,901	754	759	608	399	1,071	1,344	1,439
Common Equity	8,522	6,859	6,525	6,982	6,272	5,644	5,657	5,463	5,263	4,247
Prop. & Cas. Loss Ratio	67.6	75.4	80.8	67.5	70.3	66.3	64.5	66.2	64.7	NA
Prop. & Cas. Expense Ratio	30.4	31.3	32.6	32.9	32.5	33.5	32.4	32.1	32.1	NA
Prop. & Cas. Combined Ratio	98.0	106.7	113.4	100.4	102.8	99.8	96.9	98.3	96.8	NA
% Return On Revs.	7.1	2.4	1.4	9.9	9.2	11.1	11.6	8.6	11.4	9.3
% Ret. on Equity	10.5	3.3	1.7	10.8	10.4	12.5	13.8	9.1	14.7	12.5

Data as orig reptd.; bef. results of disc opers/spec. items. Per share data adj. for stk. divs.; EPS diluted. E-Estimated. NA-Not Available. NM-Not Meaningful. NR-Not Ranked. EPS estimates excl. realized. investment gains/losses; historical EPS data incl. them.

Office: 15 Mountain View Road, Warren, NJ 07061-1615.
Telephone: 908-903-2000.
Email: info@chubb.com
Website: http://www.chubb.com
Chrmn & CEO: J.D. Finnegan.
Vice Chrmn & COO: T.F. Motamed.
Vice Chrmn & CFO: M. O'Reilly.

SVP & General Counsel: J.L. Bober.
SVP & Investor Contact: G.A. Montgomery .
Dirs: Z. Baird, S. P. Burke, J. I. Cash, Jr., J. J. Cohen, J. M. Cornelius, J. Finnegan, D. H. Hoag, K. J. Mangold, W. B. Rudman, D. G. Scholey, R. G. Seitz, L. M. Small, D. E. Somers, K. H. Williams, J. M. Zimmerman, A. W. Zollar.

Founded: in 1966.
Domicile: New Jersey.
Employees: 12,300.
S&P Analyst: Catherine A. Seifert/CB/BK

Ciena Corp.

Recommendation: **HOLD** ★ ★ ★ ☆
SELL SELL HOLD BUY BUY

12-Month Target Price: **$2.00**
(as of August 19, 2004)

CIEN has an approximate 0.01% weighting in the **S&P 500**

Sector: Information Technology
Sub-Industry: Communications Equipment
Peer Group: Core Network Systems

Summary: CIEN manufactures telecommunications equipment used to increase the capacity of fiber optic networks.

Quantitative Evaluations

S&P Earnings & Dividend Rank: NR

D	C	B-	B	B+	A-	A	A+

S&P Fair Value Rank: NR

1	2	3	4	5
Lowest				Highest

Fair Value Calc.: NA

S&P Investability Quotient Percentile

22%

CIEN scored lower than 78% of all companies for which an S&P Report is available.

Volatility: High

Low	Average	High

Technical Evaluation: Bullish
Since 10/04, the technical indicators for CIEN have been Bullish.

Relative Strength Rank: Moderate

56

1 Lowest   Highest 99

Price as of 11/12/04: $2.43 | **2004E S&P Core EPS:** $-0.55

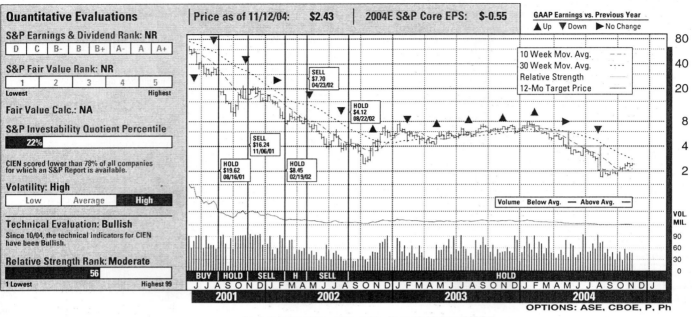

Analyst commentary prepared by Kenneth M. Leon/MF/BK

Highlights August 23, 2004

- We expect total sales to increase sequentially as CIEN's addressable markets begin to stabilize. After a 22% sales decline in FY 03 (Oct.), we project a 3.7% sales increase for FY 04 (Oct.), followed by a 24% increase in FY 05 with sales contributions from recent acquisitions.

- Despite aggressive restructuring to reduce operating costs, we believe CIEN will not be profitable in FY 04 or FY 05, as the company may not attain the $125 million or more in quarterly sales that we think is necessary to break even. We estimate gross margins of 24% in FY 04, improving to 34% in FY 05 on a more favorable product mix.

- Excluding one-time items, we see operating losses of $0.35 a share in FY 04 and $0.15 in FY 05. Our FY 04 and FY 05 Standard & Poor's Core Earnings projections are for per share losses of $0.55 and $0.17, respectively, reflecting the impact of estimated stock option expense and other one-time adjustments.

Investment Rationale/Risk August 23, 2004

- We think greater revenue growth and widening margins are needed for the company to reach breakeven. CIEN has been seeking to diversify its customer base with a greater proportion of international sales, but domestic sales actually rose to 81% of the total in the third quarter of FY 04, from 63% in FY 03. We estimate that the recent acquisitions of Catena Networks and Internet Photonics, two private companies, may increase shares outstanding by approximately 20% in FY 04.

- Risks to our opinion and target price include disappointment with sales growth in FY 05 for the company's core optical products and poor execution in realizing higher sales from four acquisitions made in the past year; higher operating expenses than the company's guidance of $65 million to $70 million per quarter in FY 05; and the possibility that management may use CIEN's $1.3 billion in cash and cash equivalents for more acquisitions.

- We view the stock, trading at 0.7X book value, well below the peer average of 2.6X, and backed by $2.30 a share in cash, as worth holding for a potential sale of the company. We believe a fundamental turnaround may take longer than FY 05 to realize profitability. To be conservative, we apply an assumed price to sales ratio of 3.1X our FY 05 estimate and an enterprise value of 6.3X our FY 05 EBITDA estimate to arrive at our 12-month target price of $2.

Key Stock Statistics

S&P Core EPS 2005E	-0.17	52-week Range	$8.14-1.67
S&P Oper. EPS 2004E	-0.35	12 Month P/E	NM
P/E on S&P Oper. EPS 2004E	NM	Beta	NA
S&P Oper. EPS 2005E	-0.15	Shareholders	2,473
Yield (%)	Nil	Market Cap (B)	$ 1.4
Dividend Rate/Share	Nil	Shares Outstanding (M)	569.2

Value of $10,000 invested five years ago: **$ 1,065**

Dividend Data

No cash dividends have been paid.

Revenues/Earnings Data Fiscal year ending October 31

Revenues (Million $)

	2004	2003	2002	2001	2000	1999
1Q	66.41	70.47	162.2	352.0	152.2	100.4
2Q	73.54	73.54	87.05	425.4	185.7	111.5
3Q	75.59	68.48	50.03	458.1	233.3	128.8
4Q	—	70.64	61.92	367.8	287.6	141.3
Yr.	—	283.1	361.2	1,603	858.8	482.1

Earnings Per Share ($)

	2004	2003	2002	2001	2000	1999
1Q	-0.16	-0.25	-0.22	-0.22	0.03	0.01
2Q	-0.17	-0.17	-1.86	-0.17	0.06	0.01
3Q	-0.25	-0.20	-0.42	0.02	0.10	-0.02
4Q	E-0.06	-0.24	-1.75	-5.51	0.09	0.02
Yr.	E-0.35	-0.87	-4.37	-5.75	0.27	-0.02

Next earnings report expected: mid-December Source: S&P, Company Reports
EPS Estimates based on S&P Operating Earnings; historical GAAP earnings are as reported.

Ciena Corporation

Recommendation: **HOLD** ★ ★ ★ ☆ ☆   12-Month Target Price: **$2.00** (as of August 19, 2004)

Business Summary August 23, 2004

Ciena Corp. offers network solutions that enable service providers and enterprises to provision, manage and deliver economic, high-bandwidth services. Its customer base includes long-distance carriers, local exchange carriers, Internet service providers, wireless and wholesale carriers, systems integrators, governments, large businesses, and non-profit institutions.

CoreDirector, the company's intelligent optical core switch offering, is designed to enable carriers to manage network bandwidth more efficiently. It helps carriers solve the challenges of network scalability and escalating operating costs by using software to run multiple network elements into a single element with switching and bandwidth management capabilities. MetroDirector K2 is CIEN's next-generation multi-service access and switching platform, designed for service providers.

CIEN's long-distance optical transport products, CoreStream, MultiWave Sentry 1600 and 4000, and short-distance products, MultiWave Metro, MultiWave Metro One, and ONLINE Metro and Edge, use dense wave division multiplexing (DWDM) technology that enables carriers to add critical network bandwidth cost-effectively when and where they need it.

Revenue from switching products exceeded revenue from long-distance transport equipment in FY 03 (Oct.), and domestic revenues were equal to 63% of total revenues, with international equal to 37%. Product sales provided 85% of total revenues, and service revenues 15%; two customers, AT&T and Qwest, accounted for 25% of total revenues. Service activities include network deployment, maintenance, training and documentation services.

In June 2003, the company acquired privately held Wavesmith Networks, Inc., a supplier of multiservice switching. Wavesmith shareholders received 36 million CIEN common shares in exchange for their common and preferred stock.

In August 2003, CIEN acquired privately held Akara Corp. for $46.2 million, consisting of $31 million in cash and $15.2 million in common stock. The company said Akara is an emerging leader in SONET/SDH-based extended storage area networking (SAN), or storage-over-distance solutions for enterprises and carriers.

In April 2004, the company announced plans to close its San Jose, CA, facility on September 30, 2004, affecting 425 employees, or 25% of CIEN's current workforce. The company said it expects to record total restructuring charges of $75 million to $85 million tied to the timing of specific actions over the next several fiscal quarters.

In May 2004, CIEN completed the acquisition of two private companies: Catena Networks Inc., a supplier of broadband access, and Internet Photonics, a supplier of carrier-grade optical Ethernet transport and switching solutions. CIEN views optical Ethernet as the new triple play of bundled services -- video on demand, Voice over IP and HDTV. CIEN agreed to issue 24.1 million common shares for Internet Photonics and 75.9 million common shares for Catena Networks. CIEN sees these two acquisitions as expanding the company beyond optical systems to a full networking and service delivery capability for its customers.

Company Financials Fiscal Year ending October 31

Per Share Data ($)

(Year Ended October 31)	2003	2002	2001	2000	1999	1998	1997	1996	1995	1994
Tangible Bk. Val.	1.87	2.89	2.80	2.79	3.94	2.22	1.83	0.82	NA	NA
Cash Flow	-0.66	-4.21	0.16	0.48	0.35	0.40	0.62	0.08	NA	NA
Earnings	-0.87	-4.37	-5.75	0.27	-0.02	0.25	0.55	0.08	NA	NA
S&P Core Earnings	-0.87	-3.36	-3.21	NA	NA	NA	NA	NA	NA	NA
Dividends	Nil	Nil	Nil	Nil	Nil	Nil	Nil	NA	NA	NA
Payout Ratio	Nil	Nil	Nil	Nil	Nil	Nil	Nil	NA	NA	NA
Prices - High	7.74	17.30	108.00	151.00	37.28	46.18	31.81	NA	NA	NA
- Low	4.19	2.41	9.20	22.68	6.81	4.06	11.12	NA	NA	NA
P/E Ratio - High	NM	NM	NM	NM	NM	NM	58	NA	NA	NA
- Low	NM	NM	NM	NM	NM	NM	20	NA	NA	NA

Income Statement Analysis (Million $)

	2003	2002	2001	2000	1999	1998	1997	1996	1995	1994
Revs.	283	361	482	859	482	508	374	54.8	Nil	Nil
Oper. Inc.	-209	-640	43.8	163	43.5	157	187	0.88	-7.38	-2.34
Depr.	93.7	60.0	46.8	63.6	50.4	33.3	10.2	1.01	0.36	0.03
Int. Exp.	36.3	45.3	0.50	0.34	0.50	0.26	0.34	0.30	0.09	NM
Pretax Inc.	-385	-1,487	-5.99	121	-5.99	93.4	184	17.0	-7.60	-2.40
Eff. Tax Rate	NM	NM	NM	32.5%	NM	43.1%	38.6%	13.2%	Nil	Nil
Net Inc.	-387	-1,597	-3.92	81.4	-3.92	53.2	113	14.7	-7.60	-2.40
S&P Core Earnings	-386	-1,225	-1,001	NA	NA	NA	NA	NA	NA	NA

Balance Sheet & Other Fin. Data (Million $)

	2003	2002	2001	2000	1999	1998	1997	1996	1995	1994
Cash	1,106	377	143	238	262	243	263	129	NA	NA
Curr. Assets	1,229	1,638	813	813	533	428	379	NA	NA	NA
Total Assets	2,378	2,751	1,027	1,027	678	572	447	174	NA	NA
Curr. Liab.	186	224	173	173	106	61.9	53.6	NA	NA	NA
LT Debt	794	914	Nil	Nil	Nil	Nil	Nil	2.67	NA	NA
Common Equity	1,331	1,527	810	810	530	475	364	152	NA	NA
Total Cap.	2,125	2,441	849	810	567	509	364	155	NA	NA
Cap. Exp.	29.5	66.3	124	124	46.8	86.4	66.6	NA	NA	NA
Cash Flow	-293	-1,538	42.9	145	46.5	86.5	123	15.7	NA	NA
Curr. Ratio	6.6	7.3	4.7	4.7	5.1	6.9	7.1	NA	NA	NA
% LT Debt of Cap.	37.4	37.4	Nil	Nil	Nil	Nil	Nil	1.7	NA	NA
% Net Inc.of Revs.	NM	NM	NM	9.5	NM	10.5	30.2	26.8	NM	NM
% Ret. on Assets	NM	NM	NM	9.5	NM	10.4	43.9	NA	NA	NA
% Ret. on Equity	NM	NM	NM	12.1	NM	12.7	61.3	NA	NA	NA

Data as orig reptd.; bef. results of disc opers/spec. items. Per share data adj. for stk. divs.; EPS diluted. E-Estimated. NA-Not Available. NM-Not Meaningful. NR-Not Ranked. UR-Under Review.

Office: 1201 Winterson Road, Linthicum, MD 21090-2205.
Telephone: 410-865-8500.
Website: http://www.ciena.com
Chrmn: P.H. Nettles.
Pres & CEO: G. Smith.
SVP & CFO: J.R. Chinnici.

SVP, Secy & General Counsel: R.B. Stevenson, Jr.
VP & Treas: A.C. Petrik.
Investor Contact: S. DuLong 888-243-6223.
Dirs: S. P. Bradley, H. B. Cash, D. H. Davis, Jr., J. R. Dillon, L. W. Fitt, P. H. Nettles, J. M. O'Brien, M. J. Rowny, G. B. Smith, G. H. Taylor.

Founded: in 1992.
Domicile: Delaware.
Employees: 1,816.
S&P Analyst: Kenneth M. Leon/MF/BK

CIGNA Corp.

Recommendation: **HOLD** ★★★★★ SELL SELL HOLD BUY BUY

12-Month Target Price: $68.00
(as of August 04, 2004)

CI has an approximate 0.09% weighting in the **S&P 500**

Sector: Health Care
Sub-Industry: Managed Health Care
Peer Group: Managed Care - Large

Summary: CIGNA is one of the largest investor-owned employee benefits organizations in the U.S. Its subsidiaries are major providers of employee benefits offered through the workplace.

Quantitative Evaluations

S&P Earnings & Dividend Rank: B+

| D | C | B- | B | B+ | A- | A | A+ |

S&P Fair Value Rank: 3+

| 1 | 2 | 3 | 4 | 5 |
| Lowest | | | | Highest |

Fair Value Calc.: $64.00 (Slightly Overvalued)

S&P Investability Quotient Percentile

96%

CI scored higher than 96% of all companies for which an S&P Report is available.

Volatility: Average

| Low | Average | High |

Technical Evaluation: Bearish

Since 10/04, the technical indicators for CI have been Bearish.

Relative Strength Rank: Moderate

57

1 Lowest   Highest 99

Price as of 11/12/04: $69.93   **2004E S&P Core EPS:** $4.31

GAAP Earnings vs. Previous Year
▲ Up   ▼ Down   ► No Change

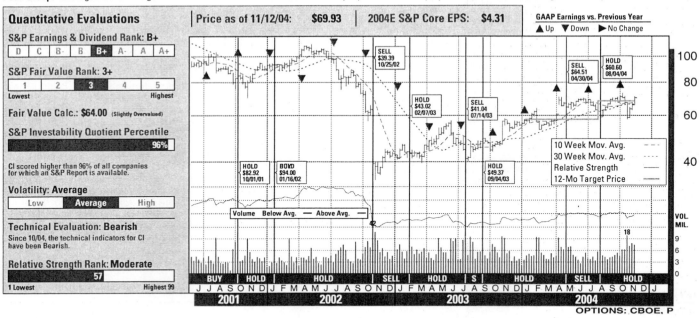

- - - 10 Week Mov. Avg.
...... 30 Week Mov. Avg.
——— Relative Strength
——— 12-Mo Target Price

OPTIONS: CBOE, P

Analyst commentary prepared by Phillip M. Seligman/CB/JWP

Highlights November 11, 2004

- We expect 2005 premium and fee revenues to decline about 10%, as CI's outlook for 9% to 10% higher premium yields (rates minus buydowns) are outweighed by a further loss of members. Following its expectation of a 15% to 16% decline in membership during 2004, CI sees enrollment down another 8% to 9% in the first quarter, with national accounts comprising the largest decline. Assuming middle-market retention rates improve, CI expects overall enrollment to be stable for the rest of 2005.

- We think Health Care's operating profit will stabilize. Assuming the commercial HMO medical cost trend is 100 to 150 basis points below 2004's estimated 10.5%, we believe the medical cost ratio will be flat or modestly below 2004's estimated 85.0%. The commercial administrative expense ratio should continue to decline, as CI targets a 5% to 6% decline in operating expenses via restructurings and other cost reductions.

- Assuming improving financial discipline in health care and gains in related operations, we look for 2005 EPS of $6.20, modestly above our 2004 operating EPS estimate of $6.00, before favorable prior period reserve development. Our 2004 and 2005 Standard & Poor's Core Earnings estimates of $4.31 and $5.18 a share, which include projected stock option expense, pension-related and post-retirement benefit costs, and net nonrecurring gains in 2004, are, respectively, 29% and 16% below our operating EPS estimates.

Key Stock Statistics

S&P Core EPS 2005E	5.18	52-week Range	$72.78-52.03
S&P Oper. EPS 2004E	6.00	12 Month P/E	7.3
P/E on S&P Oper. EPS 2004E	11.7	Beta	0.39
S&P Oper. EPS 2005E	6.20	Shareholders	9,608
Yield (%)	0.1%	Market Cap (B)	$ 9.4
Dividend Rate/Share	0.10	Shares Outstanding (M)	134.3

Value of $10,000 invested five years ago: **$ 8,654**

Dividend Data Dividends have been paid since 1867

Amount ($)	Date Decl.	Ex-Div. Date	Stock of Record	Payment Date
0.330	Feb. 25	Mar. 11	Mar. 15	Apr. 12 '04
0.025	Apr. 28	Jun. 10	Jun. 14	Jul. 12 '04
0.025	Jul. 28	Sep. 09	Sep. 13	Oct. 08 '04
0.025	Oct. 27	Dec. 09	Dec. 13	Jan. 10 '05

Investment Rationale/Risk November 11, 2004

- We are encouraged by CI's improved underwriting discipline, and service and cost reduction initiatives. The company sold its retirement unit effective April 1, 2004, enabling it to focus more on health care and related areas. However, we remain concerned about competition and continued enrollment declines.

- Risks to our recommendation and target price include enrollment continuing to decline well past the 2005 first quarter, a further reduction of CI's more profitable accounts as a percentage of the total, and an inability to moderate its medical cost trend.

- We see little, if any, earnings visibility over the next two years. We think management exhibited reasonably good execution so far in 2004 and look for the same in 2005. However, given continued enrollment declines, our estimated forward P/E is a below-peer 11X, and our 12-month target price is $68, based on our 2005 EPS estimate. We have a hold opinion as we look for signs of a turnaround on the enrollment front.

Revenues/Earnings Data Fiscal year ending December 31

Revenues (Million $)

	2004	2003	2002	2001	2000	1999
1Q	4,722	4,900	4,690	4,732	4,891	5,400
2Q	4,633	4,634	4,877	4,663	4,971	4,697
3Q	4,479	4,773	5,083	4,778	5,026	4,689
4Q	—	4,501	4,748	4,942	5,106	4,898
Yr.	—	18,808	19,348	19,115	19,994	18,781

Earnings Per Share ($)

	2004	2003	2002	2001	2000	1999
1Q	1.54	1.34	1.52	1.78	1.60	1.34
2Q	3.71	-0.38	1.50	1.66	0.99	1.48
3Q	2.34	1.39	-6.27	1.81	1.74	-0.68
4Q	E1.44	2.06	0.33	1.32	1.76	1.63
Yr.	E6.00	4.41	-2.83	6.59	6.08	3.54

Next earnings report expected: early-February Source: S&P, Company Reports
EPS Estimates based on S&P Operating Earnings; historical GAAP earnings are as reported.

STANDARD
&POOR'S

CIGNA Corporation

Recommendation: **HOLD** ★ ★ ★ ☆ ☆   12-Month Target Price: **$68.00** (as of August 04, 2004)

Business Summary November 12, 2004

CIGNA Corp. is one of the largest investor-owned U.S. employee benefits organizations. The company provides health care products and services, group life, accident and disability insurance, and investment management. The retirement benefits business was sold April 1, 2004.

Segment contributions to operating income in recent years: Employee Health Care, $468 million in 2003 and $600 million in 2002; Disability and Life, $137 million and $124 million; Employee Retirement and Investment Management, $227 million and $231 million; International, $50 million and $31 million; run-off reinsurance operations, losses of $73 million and $38 million; and other, $73 million and $74 million.

CIGNA Health Care offers a complete range of group medical, dental and life insurance products, and designs benefit plans to meet the needs of employers of all sizes and their employees. It is a leading provider of employee benefits, with programs in all 50 states, the District of Columbia and Puerto Rico. Medical covered lives at December 31, 2003, totaled 11.5 million: 6.0 million managed care members, and 5.5 million medical indemnity lives. At the end of 2003, company HMO networks included 275,000 physicians and 2,700 hospitals. The company also offers dental, behavioral health and employee assistance services.

CIGNA Group Insurance provides employer-paid and voluntary life, accident and disability products, and designs disability management services to meet specific company needs. Based on earned premiums, it is a leading U.S. provider of group accident insurance and among the largest providers of group long-term disability

insurance. At December 31, 2003, CI held group life insurance policies covering 18.3 million lives.

CIGNA Retirement and Investment Services businesses, as of 2003 year end, provided investment products, including its proprietary Charter Funds, and professional services primarily to sponsors of qualified pension, profit sharing and retirement savings plans. These operations were sold April 1, 2004, for $2.1 billion. It still offers corporate life insurance, principally to Fortune 1000 companies. At December 31, 2003, assets under management totaled $57.5 billion, down from $53.8 billion a year earlier.

CIGNA International Life, Health and Employee Benefits operates in selected markets outside the U.S., providing individual and group life, accident and health, health care and pension products. In November 2001, CI sold its remaining interest in its Japanese life operation.

Until June 2000, the company offered reinsurance coverage for part or all of the risks written by other insurance companies under life and annuity policies (both group and individual); accident policies (personal accident, catastrophe, and workers' compensation coverages) and health policies. In June 2000, CI sold its U.S. individual life, group life and accidental death reinsurance business and placed its remaining reinsurance businesses (including accident, domestic health, international life and health, and specialty life reinsurance) into run-off, and stopped underwriting new reinsurance business.

Company Financials Fiscal Year ending December 31

Per Share Data ($)

(Year Ended December 31)	2003	2002	2001	2000	1999	1998	1997	1996	1995	1994
Tangible Bk. Val.	20.56	8.23	22.87	23.26	24.67	28.07	24.95	27.66	26.49	21.44
Oper. Earnings	NA	NA	7.34	6.05	3.52	4.63	4.72	4.38	0.23	2.42
Earnings	4.41	-2.83	6.59	6.08	3.54	6.05	4.88	4.62	0.95	2.55
S&P Core Earnings	3.63	-0.71	5.31	NA	NA	NA	NA	NA	NA	NA
Dividends	1.32	1.32	1.28	1.24	1.19	1.14	1.11	1.07	1.01	1.01
Relative Payout	30%	NM	19%	20%	34%	19%	23%	23%	106%	40%
Prices - High	58.58	111.00	134.95	136.75	98.62	82.37	66.91	47.79	38.33	24.66
- Low	39.10	34.15	69.86	60.75	63.43	56.00	44.70	33.58	20.75	19.00
P/E Ratio - High	13	NM	20	22	28	14	14	10	40	10
- Low	9	NM	11	10	18	9	9	7	22	7

Income Statement Analysis (Million $)

	2003	2002	2001	2000	1999	1998	1997	1996	1995	1994
Life Ins. In Force	459,995	516,661	609,970	647,464	662,693	670,667	695,272	NA	NA	NA
Prem. Inc.: Life A & H	15,441	15,737	15,367	16,328	15,079	13,913	12,251	9,518	9,272	8,869
Prem. Inc.: Cas./Prop.	Nil	Nil	Nil	Nil	Nil	2,500	2,684	4,398	4,640	5,043
Net Invest. Inc.	2,594	2,716	2,843	2,942	2,959	3,705	4,245	4,333	4,296	3,946
Total Revs.	18,808	19,348	19,115	19,994	18,781	21,437	20,038	18,950	18,955	18,392
Pretax Inc.	903	-569	1,497	1,497	1,219	2,010	1,650	1,601	251	805
Net Oper. Inc.	NA	NA	1,101	983	695	1,190	971	1,000	50.0	526
Net Inc.	620	-397	989	987	699	1,292	1,086	1,056	211	554
S&P Core Earnings	509	-99	794	NA	NA	NA	NA	NA	NA	NA

Balance Sheet & Other Fin. Data (Million $)

	2003	2002	2001	2000	1999	1998	1997	1996	1995	1994
Cash & Equiv.	1,860	2,079	2,455	2,739	2,732	3,797	2,625	2,177	2,467	2,528
Premiums Due	9,421	9,981	2,832	2,814	2,475	4,469	4,265	4,229	4,268	3,986
Invest. Assets: Bonds	17,121	27,803	23,401	24,776	22,944	32,634	36,358	36,253	37,354	31,670
Invest. Assets: Stocks	11,300	295	404	569	585	1,043	854	701	661	1,860
Invest. Assets: Loans	10,227	11,134	12,694	12,755	12,816	15,784	18,112	18,223	18,117	15,325
Invest. Assets: Total	39,658	40,362	38,261	41,516	38,295	50,707	37,697	56,534	57,710	50,919
Deferred Policy Costs	580	494	448	1,052	927	1,069	1,542	1,230	1,109	1,128
Total Assets	90,953	88,950	91,589	95,088	95,333	114,612	108,199	98,932	95,903	86,102
Debt	1,500	1,500	1,627	1,163	1,359	1,431	2,155	1,021	1,066	1,389
Common Equity	4,465	3,665	5,055	5,634	6,149	8,277	7,932	7,208	7,157	5,811
Comb. Loss-Exp. Ratio	NA	NA	NA	NA	NA	107.1	NA	132.0	144.5	123.9
% Return On Revs.	3.3	NM	5.2	4.9	3.7	6.0	5.4	5.6	1.1	3.0
% Ret. on Equity	15.3	NM	18.9	16.5	9.1	15.9	14.3	14.7	3.3	8.9
% Invest. Yield	6.5	6.9	7.3	7.1	7.4	8.4	7.5	7.6	15.2	7.8

Data as orig reptd.; bef. results of disc opers/spec. items. Per share data adj. for stk. divs.; EPS diluted. E-Estimated. NA-Not Available. NM-Not Meaningful. NR-Not Ranked. UR-Under Review.

Office: One Liberty Place, Philadelphia, PA 19192-0004.
Telephone: 215-761-1000.
Website: http://www.cigna.com
Chrmn, Pres & CEO: H.E. Hanway.
EVP & CFO: M.W. Bell.

EVP & General Counsel: J.E. Soltz.
VP & Investor Contact: G. Deavens 215-761-6128.
Dirs: R. H. Campbell, H. E. Hanway, J. E. Henney, P. N. Larson, J. Neubauer, C. R. Shoemate, L. W. Sullivan, H. A. Wagner, C. C. Wait, M. Ware.

Founded: in 1792.
Domicile: Delaware.
Employees: 32,700.
S&P Analyst: Phillip M. Seligman/CB/JWP

Recommendation: **SELL** ★ ★ ☆ ☆ ☆

12-Month Target Price: **$37.00**
(as of October 21, 2004)

CINF has an approximate 0.07% weighting in the **S&P 500**

Sector: Financials
Sub-Industry: Property & Casualty Insurance
Peer Group: Commercial/Personal Insurers - National

Summary: This insurance holding company markets primarily property and casualty coverage; it also conducts life insurance and asset management operations.

Quantitative Evaluations

S&P Earnings & Dividend Rank: A-

| D | C | B- | B | B+ | A- | A | A+ |

S&P Fair Value Rank: 1

| **1** | 2 | 3 | 4 | 5 |
| Lowest | | | | Highest |

Fair Value Calc.: $34.50 (Overvalued)

S&P Investability Quotient Percentile

97%

CINF scored higher than 97% of all companies for which an S&P Report is available.

Volatility: Low

| Low | Average | High |

Technical Evaluation: Bullish

Since 11/04, the technical indicators for CINF have been Bullish.

Relative Strength Rank: Moderate

56

1 Lowest — Highest 99

Price as of 11/12/04: $43.45 | **2004E S&P Core EPS:** $2.10

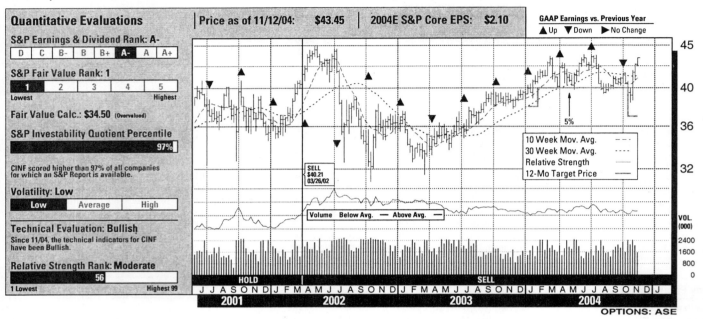

Analyst commentary prepared by C. A. Seifert/MF/GG

Highlights August 26, 2004

- We anticipate earned premium growth of 10% to 12% in 2004. We believe CINF's strategy of leveraging its core network of independent agents has enabled the company to expand, both geographically and by product line. We see underwriting results in 2004 continuing to show benefits from CINF's concerted efforts at tightening its underwriting standards. Partly offsetting this could be an uptick in catastrophe and weather related claims, particularly in the homeowners' and certain commercial lines. However, we believe the company does not have any significant exposure either to mold or asbestos claims.

- Net investment income growth will likely be modest in 2004 (less than 5%), as positive cash flow is partly offset by the impact of relatively lower investment yields.

- We see operating EPS of $2.60 in 2004 and $2.90 in 2005. These estimates assume a normal level of catastrophe and weather related losses.

Investment Rationale/Risk August 26, 2004

- Despite the shares' rather steady ascent since early 2003, we do not see them outperforming their peers in coming periods. We acknowledge CINF's healthy rate of net written premium growth and lack of exposure to any meaningful asbestos or mold claims. However, at recent levels, the stock's P/E multiple and its P/E to growth (PEG) ratio were at premiums to those of equities in CINF's peer group. In addition, the company has among the lowest returns on equity (under 7%) in its peer group. We are also concerned that CINF's mix of commercial lines business is too heavily exposed to the contractor market.

- Risks to our opinion and target price include a significantly better than expected rate of premium growth and a sharp improvement in the company's underwriting results and profitability.

- Our 12-month target price of $40 assumes a modest contraction in the shares' forward P/E multiple.

Key Stock Statistics

S&P Oper. EPS 2004E	2.60	52-week Range	$43.87-37.77
P/E on S&P Oper. EPS 2004E	16.7	12 Month P/E	14.2
S&P Oper. EPS 2005E	2.90	Beta	0.37
Yield (%)	2.5%	Shareholders	11,616
Dividend Rate/Share	1.10	Market Cap (B)	$ 7.3
Shares Outstanding (M)	168.0		

Value of $10,000 invested five years ago: **$ 13,984**

Dividend Data Dividends have been paid since 1954

Amount ($)	Date Decl.	Ex-Div. Date	Stock of Record	Payment Date
0.275	Feb. 02	Mar. 22	Mar. 24	Apr. 15 '04
5%	Feb. 02	Apr. 28	Apr. 30	Jun. 15 '04
0.275	May. 21	Jun. 23	Jun. 25	Jul. 15 '04
0.275	Aug. 16	Sep. 22	Sep. 24	Oct. 15 '04

Revenues/Earnings Data Fiscal year ending December 31

Revenues (Million $)

	2004	2003	2002	2001	2000	1999
1Q	870.0	707.0	687.0	618.0	571.3	536.7
2Q	923.0	798.0	703.0	645.0	578.8	541.3
3Q	879.0	836.0	731.0	644.0	600.0	538.0
4Q	—	840.0	722.0	654.0	581.1	511.9
Yr.	—	3,181	2,843	2,561	2,331	2,128

Earnings Per Share ($)

	2004	2003	2002	2001	2000	1999
1Q	0.86	0.33	0.44	0.43	0.46	0.36
2Q	0.91	0.50	0.20	0.29	0.43	0.50
3Q	0.53	0.61	0.42	0.21	0.03	0.32
4Q	—	0.76	0.33	0.21	-0.25	0.27
Yr.	—	2.20	1.39	1.13	0.70	1.45

Next earnings report expected: early-February Source: S&P, Company Reports
EPS Estimates based on S&P Operating Earnings; historical GAAP earnings are as reported.

STANDARD &POOR'S

Cincinnati Financial Corporation

Recommendation: **SELL** ★ ★ ☆ ☆ ☆   12-Month Target Price: **$37.00** (as of October 21, 2004)

Business Summary August 26, 2004

Cincinnati Financial Corp. underwrites and sells property-casualty insurance primarily in the Midwest and Southeast, through a network of independent agents. In recent years, the company's strategy has focused on leveraging the strength of its independent agency network to expand geographically. Revenues totaled $3.2 billion in 2003, with property-casualty insurance premiums accounting for 83%, life and accident/health insurance premiums for 3%, and investment income and other for 14%.

The company's principal property-casualty subsidiary, Cincinnati Insurance Co. (CIC), underwrites and sells a broad array of personal and commercial insurance. Operations as of 2003 year end were conducted in 31 states, through a network of 963 independent insurance agents, many of whom own stock in the company. CIC is licensed in all 50 states, the District of Columbia, and Puerto Rico. An ongoing geographical expansion plan is being implemented. Property-casualty net earned premiums totaled $2.7 billion in 2003, with commercial lines accounting for 72% and personal lines for 28%. Commercial lines net earned premiums increased nearly 11% in 2003, while personal lines earned premium growth was more than 11%. Four lines of business (commercial multi-peril, workers compensation, commercial auto and other liability) accounted for 90.5% of commercial lines earned

premiums in 2003. Personal auto and homeowners coverage accounted for over 89% of personal lines earned premiums in 2003.

Underwriting results improved in 2003, despite an absolute increase in the level of catastrophe losses. The loss ratio in 2003 equaled 67.7% (including 3.6 points of catastrophe losses), versus 72.9% (including 3.6 points of catastrophe losses). The expense ratio inched upward, to 27.0%, from 26.8%. Taken together, the GAAP combined ratio equaled 94.7% in 2003, an improvement from 2002's combined ratio of 99.7%.

Life, accident and health insurance is marketed through property-casualty agents and independent life insurance agents. This unit has been expanding its worksite marketing activities, introducing a new product line and exploring expansion opportunities.

Total invested assets of more than $12.5 billion at December 31, 2003, were divided as follows: fixed maturities 31%, equity securities 68%, and other invested assets 1%. CinFin Capital Management offers asset management services to institutions and high net worth individuals. Assets under management totaled $762 million at December 31, 2003.

Company Financials Fiscal Year ending December 31

Per Share Data ($)

(Year Ended December 31)	2003	2002	2001	2000	1999	1998	1997	1996	1995	1994
Tangible Bk. Val.	36.93	32.90	35.30	35.49	31.87	32.11	27.00	18.05	15.14	11.08
Oper. Earnings	NA	1.75	1.23	0.86	1.45	1.13	1.46	1.07	1.22	1.06
Earnings	2.20	1.39	1.13	0.70	1.45	1.34	1.69	1.24	1.33	1.12
S&P Core Earnings	2.19	1.63	1.11	NA	NA	NA	NA	NA	NA	NA
Dividends	0.95	0.85	0.80	0.72	0.63	0.57	0.52	0.47	0.43	0.37
Relative Payout	43%	61%	71%	104%	44%	42%	31%	38%	31%	33%
Prices - High	39.91	45.04	40.88	41.25	40.47	44.68	44.92	20.79	20.19	16.77
- Low	31.49	30.88	32.38	24.94	28.69	29.04	19.68	16.90	14.60	13.24
P/E Ratio - High	18	32	36	59	28	33	27	17	15	14
- Low	14	22	29	36	20	22	12	14	11	11

Income Statement Analysis (Million $)

	2003	2002	2001	2000	1999	1998	1997	1996	1995	1994
Life Ins. In Force	38,486	32,480	27,526	23,525	17,890	13,048	10,845	9,776	8,329	7,474
Prem. Inc.: Life A & H	95.0	87.0	81.0	79.3	75.0	70.1	62.9	56.0	50.9	49.1
Prem. Inc.: Cas./Prop.	2,653	2,391	2,071	1,828	1,657	1,543	1,454	1,367	1,263	1,170
Net Invest. Inc.	465	445	421	415	387	368	349	327	300	263
Total Revs.	3,181	2,843	2,586	2,331	2,128	2,054	1,942	1,809	1,656	1,513
Pretax Inc.	480	279	221	109	322	307	395	282	295	249
Net Oper. Inc.	NA	300	210	120	255	199	254	193	207	189
Net Inc.	374	238	193	118	255	242	299	224	227	201
S&P Core Earnings	372	279	189	NA	NA	NA	NA	NA	NA	NA

Balance Sheet & Other Fin. Data (Million $)

	2003	2002	2001	2000	1999	1998	1997	1996	1995	1994
Cash & Equiv.	91.0	112	93.0	60.3	420	135	80.2	130	85.1	104
Premiums Due	1,677	1,483	732	652	192	164	159	162	161	142
Invest. Assets: Bonds	3,925	3,305	3,010	2,721	2,617	2,812	2,751	2,562	2,447	1,943
Invest. Assets: Stocks	8,524	7,884	8,495	8,526	7,511	7,455	5,999	3,740	3,042	2,231
Invest. Assets: Loans	Nil	Nil	Nil	Nil	Nil	Nil	Nil	Nil	Nil	Nil
Invest. Assets: Total	12,527	11,257	11,571	11,316	10,194	10,325	8,797	6,344	5,529	4,212
Deferred Policy Costs	372	343	286	259	154	143	135	128	120	110
Total Assets	15,509	14,059	13,959	13,287	11,380	11,087	9,493	7,046	6,109	4,734
Debt	603	420	609	449	457	472	339	342	301	209
Common Equity	7,229	6,452	5,998	11,990	5,420	5,621	4,717	3,163	2,658	1,940
Comb. Loss-Exp. Ratio	94.7	98.4	104.9	112.5	100.0	103.6	97.7	103.0	NA	NA
% Return On Revs.	11.8	8.4	7.5	5.1	12.0	11.8	15.4	12.4	13.7	13.3
% Ret. on Equity	5.4	3.6	3.2	1.0	4.6	4.7	7.6	7.7	9.9	10.3
% Invest. Yield	3.9	3.9	3.7	3.9	3.8	3.8	4.6	5.5	6.2	6.3

Data as orig reptd.; bef. results of disc opers/spec. items. Per share data adj. for stk. divs.; EPS diluted (primary prior to 1998). E-Estimated. NA-Not Available. NM-Not Meaningful. NR-Not Ranked. Oper. EPS est. excl. real. inv. gains/losses; historical EPS data incl. them.

Office: 6200 South Gilmore Road, Fairfield, OH 45014-5141.
Telephone: 513-870-2000.
Email: investor_inquiries@cinfin.com
Website: http://www.cinfin.com
Chrmn, Pres & CEO: J.J. Schiff, Jr.
Vice Chrmn: J.E. Benoski.

SVP, CFO, Treas & Secy: K.W. Stecher.
Investor Contact: H.J. Wietzel 513-603-5236.
Dirs: W. F. Bahl, J. E. Benoski, M. Brown, D. J. Debbink, K. C. Lichtendahl, W. R. McMullen, G. W. Price, R. C. Schiff, T. R. Schiff, J. J. Schiff, Jr., F. J. Schultheis, J. M. Shepherd, D. S. Skidmore, L. R. Webb, E. A. Woods.

Founded: in 1968.
Domicile: Ohio.
Employees: 3,720.
S&P Analyst: C. A. Seifert/MF/GG

Cinergy Corp.

Recommendation: **HOLD** ★★★☆☆
SELL SELL HOLD BUY BUY

12-Month Target Price: **$40.00**
(as of September 08, 2004)

CIN has an approximate 0.07% weighting in the **S&P 500**

Sector: Utilities
Sub-Industry: Electric Utilities
Peer Group: Electric & Gas- Larger

Summary: CIN is the holding company for Cincinnati Gas & Electric Co. and PSI Energy, serving more than 1.5 million electric and 495,000 gas customers in Indiana, Ohio and Kentucky.

Quantitative Evaluations

S&P Earnings & Dividend Rank: B+

D	C	B-	B	B+	A-	A	A+

S&P Fair Value Rank: 3-

1	2	3	4	5
Lowest				Highest

Fair Value Calc.: $39.40 (Slightly Overvalued)

S&P Investability Quotient Percentile

77%

CIN scored higher than 77% of all companies for which an S&P Report is available.

Volatility: Low

Low	Average	High

Technical Evaluation: Bullish
Since 11/04, the technical indicators for CIN have been Bullish.

Relative Strength Rank: Moderate

56

1 Lowest	Highest 99

Price as of 11/12/04:	**$41.80**	2004E S&P Core EPS:	**$2.38**

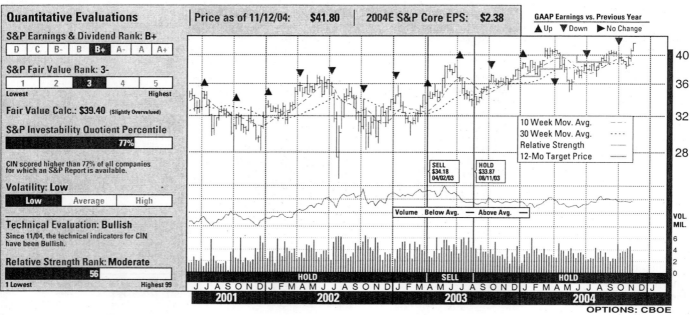

GAAP Earnings vs. Previous Year
▲ Up ▼ Down ► No Change

- 10 Week Mov. Avg.
- 30 Week Mov. Avg.
- Relative Strength
- 12-Mo Target Price

SELL $34.18 04/02/03
HOLD $33.87 08/11/03

Volume Below Avg. — Above Avg.

VOL. MIL.

HOLD 2001 | 2002 | SELL 2003 | HOLD 2004

OPTIONS: CBOE

Analyst commentary prepared by Justin McCann/CB/JWP

Highlights September 09, 2004

- Following an anticipated 11% increase in 2004 (from 2003's operating EPS of $2.43), we expect operating EPS to increase approximately 7% in 2005. Our outlook for 2004 and 2005 includes the expected impact from the average 8.36% PSI rate increase approved by the Indiana Utility Commission that went into effect in late May 2004. In an agreement reached with the staff of the Ohio Utility Commission (which must still approve it), CG&E would freeze residential rates until 2006, but could defer certain costs for future recovery.

- Operating earnings in the 2004 first half were hurt by higher fuel and emission allowance expenses for the non-regulated commercial businesses during the second quarter, as well as the first quarter impact of milder weather on the regulated businesses, and a decline in margins at the non-regulated wholesale gas business (reflecting the strong performance in the year-ago period).

- In September 2004, CIN announced that it will begin a new two-phase environmental construction program aimed at reducing power plant emissions. The company, which has already spent $1.7 billion on emission reductions since 1990, estimates that it will invest more than $2 billion for the new program.

Investment Rationale/Risk September 09, 2004

- With a dividend yield (recently around 4.7%) slightly above the industry average, we believe the stock is fairly valued at a modest premium to the average 14X peer P/E on our EPS estimates for 2005. While we don't expect a major near-term increase in the share price, investors should note that with the tax rate on dividends having been cut to a 15% rate, the recent after-tax yield was approximately 4%. We would hold the shares on a total return basis.

- Risks to our investment recommendation and target price include significantly lower than expected earnings from the non-regulated operations, and a major shift in the average P/E multiple of the group as a whole.

- The dividend was increased 2.2% with the February 2004 payment, and with the dividend payout ratio (72% of our 2004 EPS estimate) within the company's target level of 68% to 75%, we expect similar annual increases over the next few years. Based on our assumption that CIN shares will continue to trade at a similar, if relatively stagnant, premium-to-peers P/E multiple on our 2005 EPS estimate of $2.90, we have a 12-month target price of $40.

Key Stock Statistics

S&P Core EPS 2005E	2.80	52-week Range	$41.80-34.92
S&P Oper. EPS 2004E	2.50	12 Month P/E	21.1
P/E on S&P Oper. EPS 2004E	16.7	Beta	0.04
S&P Oper. EPS 2005E	2.90	Shareholders	52,506
Yield (%)	4.5%	Market Cap (B)	$ 7.5
Dividend Rate/Share	1.88	Shares Outstanding (M)	180.6

Value of $10,000 invested five years ago: **$ 19,856**

Dividend Data Dividends have been paid since 1853

Amount ($)	Date Decl.	Ex-Div. Date	Stock of Record	Payment Date
0.470	Jan. 15	Jan. 28	Jan. 30	Feb. 15 '04
0.470	Apr. 22	Apr. 29	May. 03	May. 15 '04
0.470	Jul. 22	Jul. 29	Aug. 02	Aug. 15 '04
0.470	Oct. 01	Oct. 07	Oct. 12	Nov. 15 '04

Revenues/Earnings Data Fiscal year ending December 31

Revenues (Million $)

	2004	2003	2002	2001	2000	1999
1Q	1,289	1,282	2,204	3,707	1,583	1,402
2Q	1,054	933.9	2,480	3,642	1,770	1,275
3Q	1,129	1,092	3,886	3,324	2,300	1,782
4Q	—	1,122	3,417	2,250	2,770	1,478
Yr.	—	4,416	11,960	12,923	8,422	5,938

Earnings Per Share ($)

	2004	2003	2002	2001	2000	1999
1Q	0.57	0.80	0.58	0.75	0.87	0.80
2Q	0.32	0.42	0.26	0.51	0.47	0.37
3Q	0.50	0.62	0.77	0.80	0.58	0.76
4Q	E0.77	0.59	0.58	0.69	0.58	0.60
Yr.	E2.50	2.43	2.34	2.75	2.50	2.53

Next earnings report expected: late-January Source: S&P, Company Reports
EPS Estimates based on S&P Operating Earnings; historical GAAP earnings are as reported.

Cinergy Corp.

Recommendation: **HOLD** ★ ★ ★ ☆ ☆   12-Month Target Price: **$40.00** (as of September 08, 2004)

Business Summary September 09, 2004

Cinergy Corp. is a holding company serving about 1.5 million electric customers and 505,000 gas customers in a 25,000 square mile area of Ohio, Indiana and Kentucky. It was formed through the 1994 merger of Cincinnati Gas & Electric Co. and PSI Resources, Inc.,

Contributions to revenues by business segment in 2003 were: electric, 76.6% (82.2% in 2002, 81.4% in 2001); gas, 18.9% (14.5%, 16.6%), and other, 4.5% (3.1%, 2.0%).

In its order approving the merger, the SEC reserved jurisdiction over the company's ownership of Cincinnati Gas & Electric's (CG&E) gas operations for three years. At the end of the three years, CIN was required to state how its retention of the gas properties met all relevant standards of the Public Utility Holding Company Act (PUHCA) of 1935. In February 1998, the company filed with the SEC its rationale of how its retention of the gas operations met PUHCA requirements. In November 1998, the SEC approved Cinergy's retention of the CG&E gas operations.

Cincinnati Gas & Electric (CG&E) and its subsidiaries supply electricity and natural gas to a population of nearly 2.1 million in the southwestern portion of Ohio and adjacent areas in Kentucky and Indiana. The primary subsidiary of PSI Resources (formerly PSI Holdings) is PSI Energy (formerly Public Service Company of Indiana), which is the largest electric utility in Indiana, serving a population approaching 2.3 million.

CG&E and PSI purchase over 25 million tons of coal annually, with a substantial portion through long-term contracts, and the rest through the spot market or short-term supply agreements. The coal is primarily received from mines located in Indiana, West Virginia, Ohio, Kentucky, Pennsylvania and Illinois.

Consolidated construction and other capital expenditures for 2003 were about $1.5 billion. For the period from 2004 though 2008, CIN has projected consolidated capital and investment spending of about $7.9 billion. The forecast includes capital expenditures (estimated at approximately $1.2 billion) required to comply with proposed nitrogen oxide (NOx) limits.

In July 1999, CIN sold its 50% interest in Midlands Electricity plc, a British regional electric company serving more than 2 million customers in England, to GPU for about $700 million. Including CIN's share of liabilities assumed by GPU, the transaction was valued at $1.55 billion. CIN retained Midlands' London-based gas trading operations. It also maintained its U.K.-based Cinergy Global Power Services, which was involved in the development of international energy projects.

The company's other principal subsidiaries include Cinergy Wholesale Energy, the holding company for Cinergy Power Generation Services, which provides electric production-related construction, operation and maintenance services; Cinergy Services, which provides the subsidiaries with centralized administrative, management and support services; and Cinergy Investments, which holds most of the company's domestic non-regulated, energy-related businesses and investments.

Company Financials Fiscal Year ending December 31

Per Share Data ($)

(Year Ended December 31)	2003	2002	2001	2000	1999	1998	1997	1996	1995	1994
Tangible Bk. Val.	20.50	19.14	18.02	17.54	16.69	15.91	16.00	16.26	16.17	15.40
Earnings	2.43	2.34	2.75	2.50	2.53	1.65	2.28	2.00	2.22	1.30
S&P Core Earnings	2.56	2.11	2.41	NA	NA	NA	NA	NA	NA	NA
Dividends	1.84	1.80	1.80	1.80	1.80	1.80	1.80	1.74	1.72	1.39
Payout Ratio	76%	77%	65%	72%	71%	109%	10%	87%	77%	107%
Prices - High	38.86	37.19	35.60	35.25	34.87	39.87	39.12	34.25	31.12	27.75
- Low	29.77	25.40	28.00	20.00	23.43	30.81	32.00	27.50	23.37	20.75
P/E Ratio - High	16	16	13	14	14	24	17	17	14	21
- Low	12	11	10	8	9	19	14	14	11	16

Income Statement Analysis (Million $)

	2003	2002	2001	2000	1999	1998	1997	1996	1995	1994
Revs.	4,416	11,960	12,923	8,422	5,938	5,876	4,353	3,243	3,031	2,924
Depr.	419	414	378	374	354	326	289	283	280	294
Maint.	NA	NA	NA	205	206	192	176	194	182	201
Fxd. Chgs. Cov.	2.98	2.95	3.56	3.82	2.90	2.30	3.13	3.43	2.33	2.31
Constr. Credits	NA	NA	NA	NA	NA	NA	7.41	7.41	10.0	18.5
Eff. Tax Rate	24.9%	28.2%	36.7%	38.7%	34.0%	31.0%	37.0%	39.5%	38.7%	44.3%
Net Inc.	434	397	442	399	404	261	363	335	347	191
S&P Core Earnings	457	360	388	NA	NA	NA	NA	NA	NA	NA

Balance Sheet & Other Fin. Data (Million $)

	2003	2002	2001	2000	1999	1998	1997	1996	1995	1994
Gross Prop.	14,536	13,816	13,083	11,186	10,677	10,195	9,914	9,881	9,619	9,363
Cap. Exp.	704	857	846	520	386	369	328	323	325	480
Net Prop.	9,628	8,649	8,237	6,630	6,417	6,155	6,114	6,290	6,251	6,199
Capitalization:										
LT Debt	4,195	4,452	3,966	2,939	3,082	2,604	2,166	2,535	2,531	2,715
% LT Debt	53.1	57.5	57.4	51.3	53.7	49.7	44.4	47.7	46.3	48.4
Pfd.	Nil	Nil	Nil	Nil	Nil	92.6	178	194	388	478
% Pfd.	Nil	Nil	Nil	Nil	Nil	1.80	3.60	3.70	7.10	8.50
Common	3,701	3,293	2,942	2,789	2,654	2,541	2,539	2,584	2,549	2,414
% Common	46.9	42.5	42.6	48.7	46.3	48.5	52.0	48.6	46.6	43.1
Total Cap.	9,563	9,217	8,209	6,914	5,736	6,486	6,283	6,636	6,774	6,874
% Oper. Ratio	84.9	93.3	94.7	92.8	91.8	89.1	86.4	82.8	80.8	84.9
% Earn. on Net Prop.	8.6	9.5	12.5	13.2	10.9	9.2	8.8	8.9	9.4	7.2
% Return On Revs.	9.8	3.3	3.4	4.7	6.8	4.4	8.3	10.3	11.5	6.5
% Return On Invest. Capital	7.6	7.7	9.4	9.1	11.7	9.0	11.9	8.6	8.9	6.7
% Return On Com. Equity	12.4	12.7	15.4	14.7	15.6	10.3	14.2	13.0	14.0	8.2

Data as orig reptd.; bef. results of disc opers/spec. items. Per share data adj. for stk. divs.; EPS diluted. E-Estimated. NA-Not Available. NM-Not Meaningful. NR-Not Ranked. UR-Under Review.

Office: 139 East Fourth Street, Cincinnati, OH 45202-4003.
Telephone: 513-421-9500.
Email: shareholders@cinergy.com
Website: http://www.cinergy.com
Chrmn, Pres & CEO: J.E. Rogers.
EVP & CFO: R.F. Duncan.

Treas: W.L. Aumiller.
Secy: J.S. Janson.
Investor Contact: B.C. Arnett 513-287-3024.
Dirs: M. G. Browning, P. R. Cox, G. C. Juilfs, T. E. Petry, J. E. Rogers, M. L. Schapiro, J. J. Schiff, Jr., P. R. Sharp, D. S. Taft.

Founded: in 1993.
Domicile: Delaware.
Employees: 7,693.
S&P Analyst: Justin McCann/CB/JWP

Cintas Corp.

Recommendation: **BUY** ★★★★☆
SELL | SELL | HOLD | BUY | BUY

12-Month Target Price: $56.00
(as of December 18, 2003)

CTAS has an approximate 0.07% weighting in the **S&P 500**

Sector: Industrials
Sub-Industry: Diversified Commercial Services
Peer Group: Rental & Leasing Services

Summary: CTAS, a leader in the corporate identity uniform business, also provides outsourcing services, including entrance mats, sanitation supplies, and first aid products and services.

Quantitative Evaluations

S&P Earnings & Dividend Rank: A+

| D | C | B- | B | B+ | A- | A | A+ |

S&P Fair Value Rank: 4

| 1 | 2 | 3 | 4 | 5 |
| Lowest | | | | Highest |

Fair Value Calc.: $44.20 (Slightly Overvalued)

S&P Investability Quotient Percentile 98%

CTAS scored higher than 98% of all companies for which an S&P Report is available.

Volatility: Average

| Low | Average | High |

Technical Evaluation: Neutral
Since 10/04, the technical indicators for CTAS have been Neutral.

Relative Strength Rank: Moderate 56

| 1 Lowest | | Highest 99 |

| Price as of 11/12/04: | $45.34 | 2005E S&P Core EPS: | $1.78 |

GAAP Earnings vs. Previous Year
▲ Up ▼ Down ► No Change

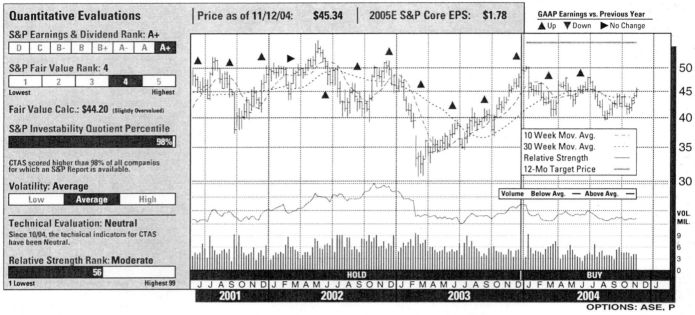

- - - 10 Week Mov. Avg.
······ 30 Week Mov. Avg.
—— Relative Strength
—— 12-Mo Target Price

Volume   Below Avg. —   Above Avg. —

HOLD   BUY

| J J A S O N D | J F M A M J J A S O N D | J F M A M J J A S O N D | J F M A M J J A S O N D | J |
| **2001** | **2002** | **2003** | **2004** |

OPTIONS: ASE, P

Analyst commentary prepared by Bryon J. Korutz/PMW/JWP

Highlights September 23, 2004

- We expect total revenues to increase 8.9% in FY 05 (May), and anticipate 10% growth for FY 06. We think that rental revenues have started to show signs of firming, and see an expanded sales force resulting in increased new business. We expect these trends to continue.

- S&P projects that real GDP will grow 4.3% in calendar 2004. We see this eventually supporting improved uniform rentals and purchases, as we believe that a firming economy will boost employment levels and subsequently stimulate demand for uniforms. We expect selling expenses to rise, as the company seeks to capture market share and launches new marketing programs. We expect higher revenues, coupled with cost cuts, to help boost gross margins. We see gross margins widening to 43.0% and 43.5% in FY 05 and FY 06, respectively, from 42.2% in FY 04. We also expect CTAS to continue to pay down debt.

- With FY 05 Standard & Poor's Core Earnings estimated at $1.78 a share, versus our operating EPS projection of $1.80, we view the company's quality of earnings as high.

Investment Rationale/Risk September 23, 2004

- We would accumulate the shares. We expect firming uniform rentals as the economy improves, and view CTAS's prospects favorably.

- Risks to our recommendation and target price include a slower than anticipated recovery in employment levels and uniform rentals.

- Our discounted cash flow model calculates intrinsic value of $56 a share, which is our 12-month target price. We assume an 8.9% weighted average cost of capital and 3.0% growth in perpetuity. In addition, we assume 11.5% compound average annual free cash flow growth rate over our 15-year forecast period. We see this growth rate supported by our expectations that CTAS will continue to make acquisitions, and will capture a greater portion of the fragmented uniform rental market. The company estimates that it holds less than 10% of the $31 billion uniform rental market.

Key Stock Statistics

S&P Oper. EPS 2005E	1.80	52-week Range	$50.68-39.51
P/E on S&P Oper. EPS 2005E	25.2	12 Month P/E	27.8
S&P Oper. EPS 2006E	2.00	Beta	1.15
Yield (%)	0.6%	Shareholders	65,000
Dividend Rate/Share	0.29	Market Cap (B)	$7.8
Shares Outstanding (M)	171.7		

Value of $10,000 invested five years ago: **$ 12,027**

Dividend Data Dividends have been paid since 1984

Amount ($)	Date Decl.	Ex-Div. Date	Stock of Record	Payment Date
0.290	Jan. 30	Feb. 06	Feb. 10	Mar. 16 '04

Revenues/Earnings Data Fiscal year ending May 31

Revenues (Million $)

	2005	2004	2003	2002	2001	2000
1Q	746.0	677.7	665.7	564.6	522.0	457.4
2Q	—	701.3	681.0	557.1	539.0	465.9
3Q	—	696.9	663.8	545.5	536.7	473.9
4Q	—	738.1	676.1	603.8	563.0	504.8
Yr.	—	2,814	2,687	2,271	2,161	1,902

Earnings Per Share ($)

	2005	2004	2003	2002	2001	2000
1Q	—	0.37	0.36	0.33	0.30	0.25
2Q	E0.43	0.40	0.37	0.34	0.33	0.29
3Q	E0.46	0.39	0.34	0.32	0.32	0.29
4Q	E0.49	0.42	0.38	0.37	0.35	0.31
Yr.	E1.80	1.58	1.45	1.36	1.30	1.14

Next earnings report expected: mid-December Source: S&P, Company Reports
EPS Estimates based on S&P Operating Earnings; historical GAAP earnings are as reported.

STANDARD &POOR'S

Cintas Corporation

Stock Report
November 13, 2004
NASDAQ Symbol: **CTAS**

Recommendation: **BUY** ★★★★☆   12-Month Target Price: **$56.00** (as of December 18, 2003)

Business Summary September 23, 2004

FY 03 (May) marked Cintas Corp.'s 34th consecutive year of sales and profit growth. The company constantly seeks to increase its market share of the uniform rental and sales business in North America, to penetrate the customer base with all products and services offered, and to identify additional product and service opportunities.

CTAS offers a full service program, including the design, manufacture and implementation of corporate identity uniform programs. The company classifies its business into two operating segments: Rental and Other Services. In FY 04, 78% of total revenues were derived from Rental (78% in FY 03), while the remaining 22% (22%) of revenues came from the Other Services operating segment.

The Rentals operating segment designs and manufactures corporate uniforms that it rents, together with other items, to its customers. Services provided to the rental markets by the company also include cleaning of uniforms, as well as the provision of ongoing replacements as required by each customer. CTAS rents uniforms to a variety of industries, including airlines, hotels and grocery stores. The company also offers ancillary products, including the rental or sale of entrance mats, fender covers, towels, mops, and linen products.

The Other Services segment involves the design, manufacture and direct sale of uniforms to CTAS's customers. The company's design team has created uniforms for Chicago's Peninsula Hotel, Ritz-Carlton's Reynolds Plantation, Alamo, Culver's, and The Inn at Spanish Bay. In addition, the segment sells ancillary products, including sanitation supplies and services and cleanroom supplies, as well as entrance mats, fender covers, towels, mops, and linen products.

Through Xpect, the company offers first aid, safety and emergency care supplies and training. These services are available through local distributors in 42 major U.S. cities.

At May 31, 2003, CTAS had 161 processing plants, 77 branch offices, 34 first aid business facilities, 11 cleanroom facilities, 13 garment manufacturing plants, 20 direct sales offices, and seven distribution centers.

In May 2002, the company acquired Omni Services, Inc., for about $656 million. Omni had annual revenues of about $300 million. In April 2002, CTAS acquired the non-health care portion of Angelica Corp.'s manufacturing and marketing segment, for about $22 million.

Company Financials Fiscal Year ending May 31

Per Share Data ($)

(Year Ended May 31)	2004	2003	2002	2001	2000	1999	1998	1997	1996	1995
Tangible Bk. Val.	6.32	5.42	4.39	6.08	4.91	4.03	3.38	3.54	3.03	2.14
Cash Flow	2.42	2.12	1.95	1.82	1.74	1.23	1.16	0.97	0.84	0.71
Earnings	1.58	1.45	1.36	1.30	1.14	0.82	0.79	0.64	0.53	0.45
S&P Core Earnings	1.54	1.43	1.33	1.27	NA	NA	NA	NA	NA	NA
Dividends	0.29	0.27	0.25	0.22	0.19	0.15	0.12	0.10	0.08	0.07
Payout Ratio	18%	19%	18%	17%	17%	18%	15%	16%	17%	15%

Cal. Yrs.	2003	2002	2001	2000	1999	1998	1997	1996	1995	1994
Prices - High	50.68	56.62	53.25	54.00	52.25	47.50	28.33	21.16	16.00	12.08
- Low	30.60	39.15	33.75	23.16	26.00	26.00	17.00	13.91	11.16	9.91
P/E Ratio - High	32	42	39	42	46	58	36	33	30	27
- Low	19	29	25	18	23	32	21	22	21	22

Income Statement Analysis (Million $)

	2004	2003	2002	2001	2000	1999	1998	1997	1996	1995
Revs.	2,814	2,687	2,271	2,161	1,902	1,752	1,198	840	730	615
Oper. Inc.	602	539	478	459	423	338	258	198	172	144
Depr.	143	115	101	90.2	100	68.8	57.2	47.8	43.1	37.7
Int. Exp.	25.1	30.9	11.0	15.1	15.9	16.4	9.07	7.97	9.07	7.35
Pretax Inc.	432	396	372	356	312	224	179	147	122	101
Eff. Tax Rate	37.0%	37.0%	37.0%	37.6%	38.0%	38.0%	31.5%	38.0%	38.5%	37.9%
Net Inc.	272	249	234	222	193	139	123	90.8	75.2	62.7
S&P Core Earnings	265	245	229	219	NA	NA	NA	NA	NA	NA

Balance Sheet & Other Fin. Data (Million $)

	2004	2003	2002	2001	2000	1999	1998	1997	1996	1995
Cash	254	57.7	85.1	110	110	88.1	12.7	103	82.5	45.5
Curr. Assets	1,034	878	853	820	721	634	509	365	298	241
Total Assets	2,810	2,583	2,519	1,752	1,581	1,408	1,018	762	669	596
Curr. Liab.	326	305	313	251	235	212	159	116	103	95.0
LT Debt	474	535	703	221	254	284	180	111	118	120
Common Equity	1,888	1,646	1,424	1,231	1,043	871	654	512	429	364
Total Cap.	2,485	2,278	2,207	1,501	1,346	1,196	858	646	566	501
Cap. Exp.	113	115	170	147	161	171	97.0	67.8	56.8	58.9
Cash Flow	415	365	335	313	293	208	180	139	118	100
Curr. Ratio	3.2	2.9	2.7	3.3	3.1	3.0	3.2	3.1	2.9	2.5
% LT Debt of Cap.	19.1	23.5	31.9	14.7	18.9	23.7	21.0	17.3	20.8	24.0
% Net Inc.of Revs.	44.4	9.3	10.3	10.3	10.3	7.9	10.3	10.8	10.3	10.2
% Ret. on Assets	10.1	9.8	11.0	13.3	12.9	10.2	13.8	12.7	11.9	11.4
% Ret. on Equity	15.4	16.2	17.6	19.6	20.2	17.1	21.1	19.3	18.9	18.6

Data as orig reptd.; bef. results of disc opers/spec. items. Per share data adj. for stk. divs.; EPS diluted. E-Estimated. NA-Not Available. NM-Not Meaningful. NR-Not Ranked. UR-Under Review.

Office: 6800 Cintas Boulevard, Cincinnati, OH 45262-5737.
Telephone: 513-459-1200.
Website: http://www.cintas.com
Chrmn: R.T. Farmer.
Pres & CEO: S.D. Farmer.

Vice Chrmn: R.J. Kohlhepp.
SVP, CFO & Investor Contact: W.C. Gale 513-459-1200.
VP & Treas: K.L. Carnahan.
Dirs: P. R. Carter, G. V. Dirvin, R. T. Farmer, S. D. Farmer, R. J. Herbold, J. Hergenhan, R. L. Howe, R. J. Kohlhepp, D. C. Phillips.

Founded: in 1968.
Domicile: Washington.
Employees: 28,300.
S&P Analyst: Bryon J. Korutz/PMW/JWP

Circuit City Stores

Recommendation: **BUY** ★★★★☆
SELL · SELL · HOLD · BUY · BUY

12-Month Target Price: **$20.00**
(as of November 12, 2004)

CC has an approximate 0.03% weighting in the **S&P 500**

Sector: Consumer Discretionary
Sub-Industry: Computer & Electronics Retail
Peer Group: Retailers/Resellers

Summary: Circuit City is a large retailer of brand-name consumer electronics, personal computers, and entertainment software.

Quantitative Evaluations

S&P Earnings & Dividend Rank: B-

| D | C | B- | B | B+ | A- | A | A+ |

S&P Fair Value Rank: 2+

| 1 | 2 | 3 | 4 | 5 |
Lowest · Highest

Fair Value Calc.: $15.60 (Slightly Overvalued)

S&P Investability Quotient Percentile
95%
CC scored higher than 95% of all companies for which an S&P Report is available.

Volatility: High

| Low | Average | High |

Technical Evaluation: Bullish
Since 8/04, the technical indicators for CC have been Bullish.

Relative Strength Rank: Strong
87
1 Lowest · Highest 99

| Price as of 11/12/04: | $17.45 | 2005E S&P Core EPS: | $0.31 |

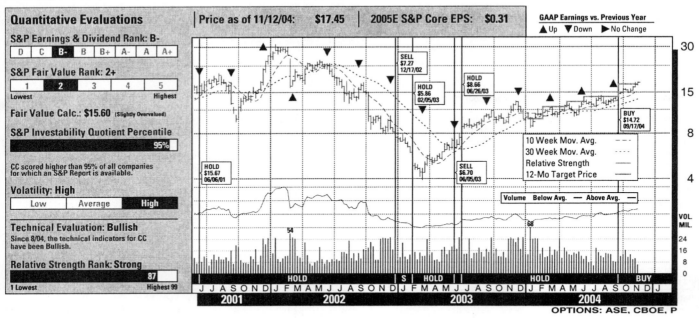

GAAP Earnings vs. Previous Year
▲ Up ▼ Down ► No Change

10 Week Mov. Avg.
30 Week Mov. Avg.
Relative Strength
12-Mo Target Price

Volume Below Avg. — Above Avg. —

OPTIONS: ASE, CBOE, P

Analyst commentary prepared by Amy Glynn, CFA /CB/BK

Highlights 15-NOV-04

- We expect FY 05 (Feb.) revenues from continuing operations to grow in the mid-single digits from FY 04's $9.7 billion. We expect sales to be boosted by improved merchandising layouts at remodeled stores, a focus on selling extended warranties (which carry higher margins), and new marketing initiatives. As for the consumer electronics industry in general, we think that CC, as well as peer companies, will benefit from stronger consumer demand for advanced TVs, as price points in this product category are expected to decline.
- We expect margins to widen in FY 05, aided by cost cutting and an improved sales mix. We forecast additional remodeling and relocation costs, as CC continues a multi-year store renovation program. We estimate FY 05 and FY 06 earnings per share of $0.39 and $0.59, respectively.
- CC has about $5 per share in cash on its balance sheet. With this cash, we expect CC to continue to invest in its store revitalization program, in addition to its ongoing stock repurchase program.

Investment Rationale/Risk 15-NOV-04

- At about 0.3X our estimate of FY 05 sales per share, CC trades about in line with its three-year historical average price to sales ratio. By this price to sales metric, CC trades at a significant, and we think warranted, discount to Best Buy (BBY: strong buy, $59.80), which we view as the leader in consumer electronics retailing. However, strong second quarter results lead us to believe that CC is executing on its strategies to improve store level performance, adhere to cost controls, and revitalize its store base. In addition, new marketing programs and the expected October launch of a rewards program should help increase customer traffic. Lastly, we think that some higher margin products are gaining favor with consumers due to lower price points, which should drive industry growth. We believe these factors could serve as a catalyst for CC's stock price.
- Risks to our opinion and target price include an adverse shift in the economic climate and consumer confidence, increased competition, and the possibility that CC will fail to achieve its strategic objectives and meet sales growth and profitability expectations.
- Our 12-month target price of $20 assigns CC a price to sales ratio of 0.35X estimated FY 06 sales, slightly above the company's three-year historical average, but we think warranted by our view of improving fundamentals.

Key Stock Statistics

S&P Oper. EPS 2005E	0.39	52-week Range	$17.58-8.69
P/E on S&P Oper. EPS 2005E	44.7	12 Month P/E	51.3
S&P Oper. EPS 2006E	0.59	Beta	1.82
Yield (%)	0.4%	Shareholders	5,819
Dividend Rate/Share	0.07	Market Cap (B)	$ 3.4
Shares Outstanding (M)	195.4		

Value of $10,000 invested five years ago: **NA**

Dividend Data Dividends have been paid since 1979

Amount ($)	Date Decl.	Ex-Div. Date	Stock of Record	Payment Date
0.018	Dec. 15	Dec. 29	Dec. 31	Jan. 15 '04
0.018	Mar. 15	Mar. 29	Mar. 31	Apr. 15 '04
0.018	Jun. 16	Jun. 28	Jun. 30	Jul. 15 '04
0.018	Sep. 15	Sep. 28	Sep. 30	Oct. 15 '04

Revenues/Earnings Data Fiscal year ending February 28

Revenues (Million $)

	2005	2004	2003	2002	2001	2000
1Q	2,067	1,933	2,118	2,678	3,075	2,691
2Q	2,345	2,156	2,221	2,888	3,180	2,958
3Q	—	2,407	2,422	3,054	2,888	2,985
4Q	—	3,249	3,192	4,171	3,817	3,980
Yr.	—	9,745	9,954	12,791	12,959	12,614

Earnings Per Share ($)

	2005	2004	2003	2002	2001	2000
1Q	-0.03	-0.14	-0.01	0.05	0.28	0.21
2Q	-0.06	-0.19	-0.05	0.03	0.27	0.36
3Q	E-0.04	-0.14	-0.10	0.10	-0.32	0.26
4Q	E0.52	0.46	0.36	0.73	0.49	0.78
Yr.	E0.39	Nil	0.20	0.92	0.73	1.60

Next earnings report expected: mid-December Source: S&P, Company Reports
EPS Estimates based on S&P Operating Earnings; historical GAAP earnings are as reported.

STANDARD &POOR'S

Circuit City Stores, Inc.

Recommendation: **BUY** ★ ★ ★ ★ ☆   12-Month Target Price: **$20.00** (as of November 12, 2004)

Stock Report
November 15, 2004
NYSE Symbol: **CC**

Business Summary 15-NOV-04

Circuit City Stores is a large retailer of brand-name consumer electronics, PCs, and entertainment software. It sells video equipment, audio equipment, mobile electronics, home office products, entertainment software, and other consumer electronics products. At the end of FY 04 (Feb.), the company operated 604 retail locations, including 599 superstores and five mall-based stores.

Total revenues amounted to $9.75 billion in FY 04, down 2% from FY 03's $9.95 billion. The FY 04 total sales decrease reflected a 3% decline in comparable-store sales, partly offset by the net addition of eight superstores.

Products sold at Circuit City retail stores typically include televisions, VCRs, audio equipment, and computers. In 2000, the company discontinued selling major appliances, which accounted for about $1.5 billion of FY 00 sales. CC also undertook partial remodels of many of its stores, to expand the selection of computer software, peripherals, and accessories, videogame hardware and software, movie titles, and digital cameras; and to add 35 mm cameras and accessories. As of April 2004, 22% of its superstores had been fully remodeled, relocated, or newly constructed since the start of FY 01.

In FY 05, CC plans to open 60 to 70 superstores, with a relatively even split between new stores and relocations. In February 2004, the company closed 19 underperforming superstores. As of June 2004, CC expected FY 05 net capital spending, net of sale-leasebacks and tenant improvement allowances, to total about $165 million. It anticipated that expenses related to relocations and one remodel would total about $52 million in FY 05.

In the company's consumer electronics business, the video and information technology categories accounted for 41% and 32% of FY 04 revenues, respectively. The audio and entertainment categories accounted for 13% and 14%, respectively.

In May 2004, CC acquired Ontario-based consumer electronics retailer InterTAN for $14 a share in cash. Also in May, CC sold its private-label credit card operation to Bank One Corp. In November 2003, the company completed the sale of its bankcard operation to FleetBoston Financial.

In October 2002, the CarMax vehicle retail business was separated from CC, becoming part of an independent, separately traded public company, CarMax, Inc. (KMX). CarMax Group common stock had been about 64%-owned by CC. As of September 2002, the CarMax Auto Superstores included 40 CarMax retail units at 38 locations. In FY 02, CarMax had total revenues of $3.2 billion, and CC's ownership of KMX contributed $0.30 a share to EPS, versus $0.17 in FY 01.

Company Financials Fiscal Year ending February 28

Per Share Data ($)

(Year Ended February 28)	2004	2003	2002	2001	2000	1999	1998	1997	1996	1995
Tangible Bk. Val.	10.91	11.15	11.13	10.13	9.33	7.69	7.12	6.73	5.46	4.55
Cash Flow	0.96	0.95	1.78	1.53	2.33	1.41	1.11	1.18	1.32	1.21
Earnings	Nil	0.20	0.92	0.73	1.60	0.74	0.57	0.69	0.91	0.86
S&P Core Earnings	0.01	0.08	0.80	0.63	NA	NA	NA	NA	NA	NA
Dividends	0.07	0.07	0.07	0.07	0.07	0.07	0.07	0.07	0.06	0.05
Payout Ratio	NM	35%	8%	10%	4%	9%	8%	9%	6%	6%

Cal. Yrs.	2003	2002	2001	2000	1999	1998	1997	1996	1995	1994
Prices - High	13.21	31.40	26.65	65.18	53.87	27.25	22.75	19.37	19.00	13.50
- Low	3.91	6.95	9.55	8.68	23.68	14.40	14.31	12.50	10.50	8.25
P/E Ratio - High	NM	NM	29	89	34	37	33	28	21	16
- Low	NM	NM	10	12	15	19	21	18	12	10

Income Statement Analysis (Million $)

	2004	2003	2002	2001	2000	1999	1998	1997	1996	1995
Revs.	9,745	9,954	12,791	12,959	12,614	10,804	8,871	7,664	7,029	5,583
Oper. Inc.	166	163	519	462	701	399	311	-8.00	392	345
Depr.	198	157	151	153	148	140	116	99	79.8	66.9
Int. Exp.	1.80	1.09	5.84	19.4	24.2	28.3	36.5	6.28	32.2	13.9
Pretax Inc.	-1.24	67.0	353	259	529	231	168	15.9	287	269
Eff. Tax Rate	NM	38.0%	38.0%	38.0%	38.0%	38.0%	38.0%	41.5%	37.5%	37.5%
Net Inc.	-0.79	41.6	219	161	328	143	104	136	179	168
S&P Core Earnings	0.83	16.3	166	129	NA	NA	NA	NA	NA	NA

Balance Sheet & Other Fin. Data (Million $)

	2004	2003	2002	2001	2000	1999	1998	1997	1996	1995
Cash	783	885	1,252	446	644	266	117	203	43.7	47.0
Curr. Assets	2,919	3,103	3,653	2,847	2,943	2,395	2,146	2,163	1,736	1,387
Total Assets	3,633	3,799	4,539	3,871	3,955	3,445	3,232	3,081	2,526	2,004
Curr. Liab.	1,177	1,280	1,641	1,292	1,406	964	906	837	831	706
LT Debt	22.7	11.3	14.1	116	249	427	424	430	399	179
Common Equity	2,224	2,342	2,734	2,356	2,142	1,905	1,730	1,615	1,064	877
Total Cap.	2,247	2,353	2,749	2,488	2,419	2,369	2,181	2,078	1,481	1,056
Cap. Exp.	176	151	214	286	222	367	588	542	518	375
Cash Flow	197	199	370	314	476	283	221	235	259	235
Curr. Ratio	2.5	2.4	2.2	2.2	2.1	2.5	2.4	2.6	2.1	2.0
% LT Debt of Cap.	1.0	0.5	0.5	4.7	10.3	18.0	24.5	20.7	27.0	16.9
% Net Inc.of Revs.	NM	0.4	1.7	1.2	2.6	1.3	1.2	1.8	2.6	3.0
% Ret. on Assets	NM	1.0	5.2	4.1	8.9	4.3	3.3	4.9	18.5	9.4
% Ret. on Equity	NM	1.6	8.6	7.1	16.2	7.9	6.2	10.2	21.4	21.1

Data as orig reptd.; bef. results of disc opers/spec. items. Per share data adj. for stk. divs.; EPS diluted. E-Estimated. NA-Not Available. NM-Not Meaningful. NR-Not Ranked. UR-Under Review.

Office: 9950 Mayland Drive, Richmond, VA 23233-1464.
Telephone: 804-527-4000.
Website: http://www.circuitcity.com
Chrmn, Pres & CEO: W. A. McCollough.
EVP & COO: J. W. Froman.

EVP: P. J. Schoonover.
SVP: D. J. Bowman.
Investor Contact: Ann M. Collier (804-527-4058).
Dirs: R. Brill, C. H. Byrd, B. S. Feigin, J. F. Hardymon, A. Kane, A. B. King, W. A. McCollough, M. Salovaara, J. P. Spainhour, C. Y. Woo.

Founded: in 1949.
Domicile: Virginia.
Employees: 43,211.
S&P Analyst: Amy Glynn, CFA /CB/BK

Cisco Systems

Recommendation: **BUY** ★★★★☆
SELL | SELL | HOLD | BUY | BUY

12-Month Target Price: $23.00
(as of November 02, 2004)

CSCO has an approximate 1.18% weighting in the **S&P 500**

Sector: Information Technology
Sub-Industry: Communications Equipment
Peer Group: Data Networking

Summary: CSCO offers a complete line of routers and switching products that connect and manage communications among local and wide area computer networks employing a variety of protocols.

Quantitative Evaluations

S&P Earnings & Dividend Rank: B+

D	C	B-	B	B+	A-	A	A+

S&P Fair Value Rank: 5+

1	2	3	4	5
Lowest				Highest

Fair Value Calc.: $22.40 (Slightly Undervalued)

S&P Investability Quotient Percentile
95%

CSCO scored higher than 95% of all companies for which an S&P Report is available.

Volatility: Average

Low	Average	High

Technical Evaluation: Neutral
Since 10/04, the technical indicators for CSCO have been Neutral.

Relative Strength Rank: Weak
28

1 Lowest		Highest 99

Price as of 11/12/04:	$19.26	2005E S&P Core EPS:	$0.68

GAAP Earnings vs. Previous Year
▲ Up ▼ Down ▶ No Change

- 10 Week Mov. Avg.
- 30 Week Mov. Avg.
- Relative Strength
- 12-Mo Target Price

BUY $15.24 11/21/02

Volume   Below Avg.   — Above Avg.

HOLD | BUY

2001 | 2002 | 2003 | 2004

OPTIONS: ASE, CBOE, P, Ph

Analyst commentary prepared by A. Bensinger/PMW/JWP

Highlights November 03, 2004

- Following a 17% increase in FY 04 (Jul.), we project a revenue advance of 15% in FY 05, reflecting a continuing recovery after a period of weakness due to a downturn in networking equipment demand. We see double-digit sales growth for the company's core routing and switching divisions (65% of total sales). The new advanced technologies division (15%), which includes home networking, Internet Protocol (IP) telephony, optical networking, security, storage area networking, and wireless technology, should grow at the mid-20% level.

- We expect gross margins to narrow to 67.6% in FY 05, from 68.6% in FY 04, as cost saving efforts are outweighed by the impact of pricing pressures and a less favorable product mix. Product gross margins are being restricted, in our view, by an increasing proportion of lower margin advanced technologies products. Service gross margins should continue to fluctuate, due to a shift in mix between technical and advanced services.

- Aided by anticipated higher sales volume, we believe CSCO can meet its target of reducing operating expenses to 35% of total revenue by the beginning of FY 06. After lower interest income and a stable tax rate of 28%, we forecast FY 05 operating EPS of $0.90, versus $0.76 posted in FY 04. Our FY 05 S&P Core EPS forecast of $0.68 reflects estimated stock option expense of $0.22 a share.

Key Stock Statistics

S&P Core EPS 2006E	0.79	52-week Range	$29.39-17.53
S&P Oper. EPS 2005E	0.90	12 Month P/E	25.3
P/E on S&P Oper. EPS 2005E	21.4	Beta	2.21
S&P Oper. EPS 2006E	1.05	Shareholders	84,686
Yield (%)	Nil	Market Cap (B)	$128.1
Dividend Rate/Share	Nil	Shares Outstanding (M)	6650.4

Value of $10,000 invested five years ago: $ 5,438

Dividend Data

No cash dividends have been paid.

Investment Rationale/Risk November 03, 2004

- We would accumulate the shares. In our view, CSCO is maintaining its dominant market position in the large network routing and switching markets, while successfully positioning itself in attractive sub-segments. Its balance sheet is one of the best in the industry, with over $20 billion in cash and no long term debt, and we see strong cash flow generation. We view CSCO as a core holding for investors seeking exposure to what we view as an improving networking equipment environment.

- Risks to our opinion and target price include a slowing of momentum in the recovery in the data networking industry, potential market share losses as peers increasingly target CSCO's dominant share in the enterprise market, and narrowing margins, due to intensifying pricing pressures.

- The stock trades at a P/E multiple of 18X our 2005 EPS estimate, slightly below the peer mean. Using our five-year earnings growth rate projection of 13%, the shares trade at a forward P/E to growth (PEG) ratio of 1.4X, well below the industry average of 2X. We believe these discounts are unwarranted, as we expect the company's sales mix to shift gradually to faster-growing advanced technology markets. Our discounted cash flow model, which assumes a weighted average cost of capital of 11.5%, indicates intrinsic value over $21. Applying a blend of relative and intrinsic analyses, our 12-month target price is $23.

Revenues/Earnings Data Fiscal year ending July 31

Revenues (Million $)

	2005	2004	2003	2002	2001	2000
1Q	5,971	5,101	4,845	4,448	6,519	3,918
2Q	—	5,398	4,713	4,816	6,748	4,357
3Q	—	5,620	4,618	4,822	4,728	4,933
4Q	—	5,926	4,702	4,829	4,298	5,720
Yr.	—	22,045	18,878	18,915	22,293	18,928

Earnings Per Share ($)

	2005	2004	2003	2002	2001	2000
1Q	0.21	0.15	0.08	-0.04	0.11	0.06
2Q	E0.22	0.18	0.14	0.09	0.12	0.11
3Q	E0.23	0.17	0.14	0.10	-0.37	0.08
4Q	E0.24	0.20	0.14	0.10	Nil	0.11
Yr.	E0.90	0.70	0.50	0.25	-0.14	0.36

Next earnings report expected: early-February Source: S&P, Company Reports
EPS Estimates based on S&P Operating Earnings; historical GAAP earnings are as reported.

Cisco Systems, Inc.

Recommendation: **BUY** ★ ★ ★ ★ ☆   12-Month Target Price: **$23.00** (as of November 02, 2004)

Business Summary November 04, 2004

Cisco Systems, which supplies the majority of networking gear used for the Internet, is the world's largest supplier of high-performance computer internetworking systems. Its routers and other communication products connect and manage local and wide area networks (LANs and WANs) that employ various protocols, media interfaces, network topologies and cabling systems, enabling customers to connect different computer networks using different hardware and software.

The company offers the industry's broadest line of networking products. CSCO asserts that this is critical, as customers prefer complete end-to-end networking solutions. Demand for the company's equipment is driven by the adoption of the Internet and web-based applications and services to boost productivity. Products are categorized into four segments; switches, routers, advanced technologies, and other. Other products primarily consist of access and network management software.

Switches are devices that filter and forward packets of data between LANs (local area networks). CSCO's switching products support various technologies, including Ethernet, Gigabit Ethernet, Token Ring and asynchronous transfer mode (ATM). Cisco's LAN switching products include the Catalyst Family, and its WAN switching products include the Cisco IGX, Cisco BPX and Cisco MGX Families. During FY 04 (Jul.), the switches segment provided 48% of total sales; sales increased 15%, to $8.9 billion.

Routers move information from one network to another and are considered to be intelligent devices. The company offers a broad range of routers, from core

backbone infrastructure at service providers to home network deployments, with features designed to increase the intelligence, security, reliability, and level of performance in the transmission of information. In FY 04, the router segment accounted for 29% of total sales, and sales increased 11%, to $5.4 billion.

In May 2004, CSCO introduced its new, high-end core router, the Carrier Routing System-1 (CRS-1), with capacity for 640 Gbps. The product offers large customers a clear migration path for higher-speed, large capacity routing functionality for next generation services.

The company currently identifies six advanced technologies for particular focus: home networking, Internet Protocol (IP) telephony, optical networking, security, storage area networking, and wireless technology. In FY 04, the advanced technologies segment provided 19% of total sales, and increased 71%, to $3.4 billion.

Company products support multiprotocol multiple media connectivity in multivendor environments. CSCO's Internetwork Operating System (IOS) provides a common software platform across networks.

The company has been active in making acquisitions, gaining key technologies. CSCO is increasingly making acquisitions that boost its technologies in the area of voice/video/data integration on a single network and optical networking. In 1999, it purchased Cerent Corp., for about $7 billion in stock, and Monterey Networks ($500 million). It bought Pirelli Optical Systems in early 2000, for $2 billion. In March 2003, the company acquired The Linksys Group, Inc., a maker of wireless LANs, for an aggregate value of $500 million in stock.

Company Financials Fiscal Year ending July 31

Per Share Data ($)

(Year Ended July 31)	2004	2003	2002	2001	2000	1999	1998	1997	1996	1995
Tangible Bk. Val.	3.16	3.35	3.33	3.07	3.14	3.57	1.14	1.06	0.48	0.28
Cash Flow	0.91	0.72	0.52	0.17	0.47	0.76	0.26	0.30	0.18	0.10
Earnings	0.70	0.50	0.25	-0.14	0.36	0.31	0.21	0.17	0.15	0.08
S&P Core Earnings	0.52	0.28	0.12	-0.37	NA	NA	NA	NA	NA	NA
Dividends	Nil	Nil	Nil	Nil	Nil	Nil	Nil	Nil	Nil	Nil
Payout Ratio	Nil	Nil	Nil	Nil	Nil	Nil	Nil	Nil	Nil	Nil
Prices - High	29.39	24.60	21.84	44.50	82.00	53.59	24.43	10.10	7.68	4.95
- Low	17.53	12.33	12.24	11.04	35.15	22.46	8.58	5.02	3.54	1.79
P/E Ratio - High	42	49	87	NM	NM	NM	NM	60	50	60
- Low	25	25	49	NM	98	72	41	30	23	21

Income Statement Analysis (Million $)

	2004	2003	2002	2001	2000	1999	1998	1997	1996	1995
Revs.	22,045	18,878	18,915	22,293	18,928	12,154	8,459	6,440	4,096	1,979
Oper. Inc.	7,738	6,477	4,941	2,257	4,098	3,470	2,432	1,839	1,533	701
Depr.	1,443	1,591	1,957	2,236	863	486	327	212	133	58.5
Int. Exp.	Nil	Nil	Nil	Nil	Nil	Nil	Nil	Nil	Nil	Nil
Pretax Inc.	6,992	5,013	2,710	-874	4,343	3,316	2,302	1,889	1,465	679
Eff. Tax Rate	28.9%	28.6%	30.1%	NM	38.6%	36.8%	41.4%	44.5%	37.7%	38.0%
Net Inc.	4,968	3,578	1,893	-1,014	2,668	2,096	1,350	1,049	913	421
S&P Core Earnings	3,652	2,051	931	-2,641	NA	NA	NA	NA	NA	NA

Balance Sheet & Other Fin. Data (Million $)

	2004	2003	2002	2001	2000	1999	1998	1997	1996	1995
Cash	3,722	8,485	9,484	4,873	4,234	2,016	535	270	1,038	440
Curr. Assets	14,343	13,415	17,433	12,835	11,110	4,615	3,762	3,101	2,160	996
Total Assets	35,594	37,107	37,795	35,238	32,870	14,725	8,917	5,452	3,630	1,757
Curr. Liab.	8,703	8,294	8,375	8,096	5,196	3,003	1,767	1,120	769	338
LT Debt	Nil	Nil	Nil	Nil	Nil	Nil	Nil	Nil	Nil	Nil
Common Equity	25,826	28,029	28,656	27,120	26,497	11,678	7,107	4,290	2,820	1,379
Total Cap.	25,916	28,039	28,671	27,142	27,674	11,722	7,150	4,332	2,852	1,420
Cap. Exp.	613	717	2,641	2,271	1,086	584	415	330	283	112
Cash Flow	6,411	5,169	3,850	1,222	3,531	2,582	1,677	1,261	1,046	480
Curr. Ratio	1.6	1.6	2.1	1.6	2.1	1.5	2.1	2.8	2.8	2.9
% LT Debt of Cap.	Nil	Nil	Nil	Nil	Nil	Nil	Nil	Nil	NM	Nil
% Net Inc.of Revs.	22.5	19.0	10.0	NM	14.1	17.2	16.0	16.3	22.3	21.3
% Ret. on Assets	13.7	9.6	5.2	NM	11.2	17.7	18.8	23.1	32.5	30.0
% Ret. on Equity	18.4	12.6	6.8	NM	13.9	22.3	23.7	29.5	41.7	37.8

Data as orig reptd.; bef. results of disc opers/spec. items. Per share data adj. for stk. divs. Bold denotes primary EPS - prior periods restated. E-Estimated. NA-Not Available. NM-Not Meaningful. NR-Not Ranked. UR-Under Review.

Office: 170 West Tasman Drive, San Jose, CA 95134-1706.
Telephone: 408-526-4000.
Email: investor-relations@cisco.com
Website: http://www.cisco.com
Chrmn: J.P. Morgridge.
Pres & CEO: J.T. Chambers.

Vice Chrmn: D.T. Valentine.
SVP & CFO: D. Powell.
SVP & CTO: C.H. Giancarlo.
Dirs: C. A. Bartz, M. M. Burns, L. R. Carter, J. T. Chambers, J. F. Gibbons, J. L. Hennessy, R. McGeary, J. C. Morgan, J. P. Morgridge, D. T. Valentine, S. M. West, J. Yang.

Founded: in 1984.
Domicile: California.
Employees: 34,000.
S&P Analyst: A. Bensinger/PMW/JWP

The McGraw·Hill Companies

Citigroup Inc.

Recommendation: **BUY** ★★★★★   12-Month Target Price: **$57.00**

SELL | SELL | HOLD | BUY | BUY
(as of September 17, 2004)

C has an approximate 2.21% weighting in the **S&P 500**

Sector: Financials
Sub-Industry: Other Diversified Financial Services
Peer Group: Financial Cos. - Major Diversified

Summary: This diversified financial services company provides a wide range of financial services to consumers and corporate customers in more than 100 countries and territories.

Quantitative Evaluations

S&P Earnings & Dividend Rank: A+

D	C	B-	B	B+	A-	A	A+

S&P Fair Value Rank: 2

1	2	3	4	5
Lowest				Highest

Fair Value Calc.: $42.90 (Slightly Overvalued)

S&P Investability Quotient Percentile

100%

C scored higher than 100% of all companies for which an S&P Report is available.

Volatility: Low

Low	Average	High

Technical Evaluation: Neutral
Since 11/04, the technical indicators for C have been Neutral.

Relative Strength Rank: Moderate

51

1 Lowest		Highest 99

Price as of 11/12/04:	**$47.07**	2004E S&P Core EPS:	**$4.01**

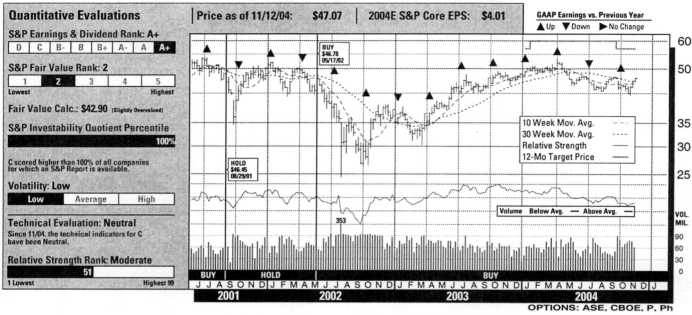

GAAP Earnings vs. Previous Year
▲ Up ▼ Down ► No Change

- 10 Week Mov. Avg.
- 30 Week Mov. Avg.
- Relative Strength
- 12-Mo Target Price

Volume Below Avg. — Above Avg.

OPTIONS: ASE, CBOE, P, Ph

Analyst commentary prepared by Evan M. Momios, CFA /PMW/BK

Highlights October 18, 2004

- We think that the company's business mix of high growth consumer businesses, combined with a recovering corporate lending and investment banking market, should benefit from improving global economies.

- C's consumer businesses performed well during the recent economic down cycle, and continued to support operating results in the first nine months of 2004. In the quarters ahead, we expect the company's corporate and investment banking businesses to make an increasing contribution to earnings. We believe earnings from consumer businesses, such as credit cards, consumer finance, and retail banking, will continue to be driven by a mixture of market growth and acquisitions. We look for revenues to increase 12% in 2004, followed by 9% growth in 2005.

- We see 2004 operating EPS of $4.10, up from 2003's $3.42, and expect a further increase in 2005, to $4.50, as we see U.S. economic conditions remaining strong and capital market activities accelerating. Our respective 2004 and 2005 S&P Core EPS estimates are $4.01 and $4.43, mainly reflecting projected stock option expense and a modest pension plan adjustment.

Investment Rationale/Risk October 18, 2004

- We recommend buying the shares, based on the company's geographic and product diversity, and on what we view as above-peer-average revenue growth and profitability prospects that we believe are not reflected in the stock's current valuation. The shares traded recently at about 10X our 2005 operating EPS estimate, versus about 15X on average over the past five years.

- Risks to our recommendation and target price include a severe downturn in global economic conditions, a significant rise in credit losses, legal and regulatory risks, and a serious geopolitical event that could affect global capital markets.

- We expect the stock's valuation to trend toward its historical average as global economic activity increases, although over the next year, we think that increased regulatory scrutiny and litigation risk surrounding capital markets businesses could limit P/E multiple expansion somewhat. Our 12-month target price of $57 is equal to 12.7X our 2005 EPS estimate, reflecting a 15% discount to the stock's historical average multiple.

Key Stock Statistics

S&P Core EPS 2005E	4.43	52-week Range	$52.88-42.10
S&P Oper. EPS 2004E	4.10	12 Month P/E	14.9
P/E on S&P Oper. EPS 2004E	11.5	Beta	1.36
S&P Oper. EPS 2005E	4.50	Shareholders	211,100
Yield (%)	3.4%	Market Cap (B)	$243.8
Dividend Rate/Share	1.60	Shares Outstanding (M)	5180.3

Value of $10,000 invested five years ago: **NA**

Dividend Data Dividends have been paid since 1986

Amount ($)	Date Decl.	Ex-Div. Date	Stock of Record	Payment Date
0.400	Jan. 20	Jan. 29	Feb. 02	Feb. 27 '04
0.400	Apr. 20	Apr. 29	May. 03	May. 28 '04
0.400	Jul. 20	Jul. 29	Aug. 02	Aug. 27 '04
0.400	Oct. 19	Oct. 28	Nov. 01	Nov. 24 '04

Revenues/Earnings Data Fiscal year ending December 31

Revenues (Million $)

	2004	2003	2002	2001	2000	1999
1Q	25,976	23,199	22,654	29,804	26,815	20,521
2Q	27,287	23,840	23,601	27,854	27,059	20,436
3Q	—	23,334	23,505	27,714	28,624	14,021
4Q	—	24,340	22,796	26,650	29,328	27,027
Yr.	—	94,713	92,556	112,022	111,826	82,005

Earnings Per Share ($)

	2004	2003	2002	2001	2000	1999
1Q	1.01	0.79	0.66	0.70	0.78	0.51
2Q	0.22	0.83	0.73	0.71	0.65	0.53
3Q	1.02	0.90	0.72	0.61	0.67	0.53
4Q	E1.04	0.91	0.47	0.74	0.55	0.56
Yr.	E4.10	3.42	2.59	2.75	2.62	2.12

Next earnings report expected: mid-January Source: S&P, Company Reports
EPS Estimates based on S&P Operating Earnings; historical GAAP earnings are as reported.

Citigroup Inc.

Recommendation: **BUY** ★ ★ ★ ★ ★   12-Month Target Price: **$57.00** (as of September 17, 2004)

Business Summary October 18, 2004

Citigroup is a diversified global financial services company. It operates in more than 100 countries and territories. Subsidiaries include familiar names such as Citicorp, Smith Barney, Travelers Life and Annuity, and Student Loan Corp. C spun off all but 9.9% of its Travelers Property Casualty unit in August 2002. Operations are in four segments: Global Consumer, Global Corporate and Investment Bank, Global Investment Management, and Private Client Services.

The Global Consumer segment (54% of net income in 2003) delivers banking, lending, insurance and investment services. Global consumer includes Cards, which provides MasterCard, VISA and private label products ($164 billion in managed loans); Consumer Finance, which offers real estate-secured loans, personal loans, auto loans and loans to finance consumer goods through 2,328 offices in the U.S. and Canada and 875 offices internationally; and Retail Banking, which provides banking, lending, investment and insurance to customers through retail branches and electronic delivery systems.

The Global Corporate and Investment Bank (30%) includes Capital Markets and Banking (investment banking, institutional brokerage, advisory services, foreign exchange, structured products, derivatives, loans, leasing and equipment finance); and Transaction Services (cash management, trade finance and e-commerce services, custody services and clearing services to broker-dealers, and depository and agency and trust services to corporations and governments).

The Global Investment Management segment (10%) includes Travelers Life and Annuity, Private Bank and Citigroup Asset Management. These businesses provide life insurance, annuities, asset management and personalized wealth management products and services to institutions, high net worth and retail clients. The Private Client Services segment (4%) provides investment advice, financial planning and brokerage services to affluent individuals, small and mid-size businesses, non-profits and large corporations.

North America accounted for 60% of net income in 2002, Asia 10%, Mexico 9%, Japan 8%, Western Europe 7%, and Central/Eastern Europe, Middle East and Africa 6%.

In November 2002, C acquired Golden State Bancorp, for $2.3 billion in cash and 79.5 million common shares. With $54 billion in assets, GSB was the second largest U.S. thrift and the eighth largest mortgage servicer, and operated 352 branches in California and Nevada. In November 2003, the company acquired the Sears' Credit Card and Financial products business, for $2.9 billion, plus annual performance payments over 10 years based on new accounts. In January 2004, C acquired Washington Mutual Finance Corp., the consumer finance subsidiary of Washington Mutual Inc., for $1.25 billion in cash.

Company Financials Fiscal Year ending December 31

Per Share Data ($)

(Year Ended December 31)	2003	2002	2001	2000	1999	1998	1997	1996	1995	1994
Tangible Bk. Val.	10.75	9.70	15.49	12.84	10.64	8.95	6.99	4.97	4.08	3.07
Earnings	3.42	2.59	2.75	2.62	2.12	1.22	1.27	1.17	0.81	0.64
S&P Core Earnings	3.35	2.33	2.51	NA	NA	NA	NA	NA	NA	NA
Dividends	1.10	0.70	0.60	0.52	0.41	0.28	0.20	0.15	0.13	0.10
Payout Ratio	32%	27%	22%	20%	19%	23%	16%	13%	16%	15%
Prices - High	49.15	52.20	57.37	59.12	43.68	36.75	28.68	15.83	10.64	7.18
- Low	30.25	24.48	34.51	35.34	24.50	14.25	14.58	9.41	5.39	5.06
P/E Ratio - High	14	20	21	23	21	30	23	14	11	11
- Low	9	9	13	13	12	12	11	8	7	8

Income Statement Analysis (Million $)

	2003	2002	2001	2000	1999	1998	1997	1996	1995	1994
Premium Inc.	3,749	3,410	13,460	12,429	10,441	9,850	8,995	7,633	4,977	7,590
Invest. Inc.	18,937	21,036	26,949	27,562	21,971	23,696	16,214	5,549	4,355	3,637
Oth. Revs.	72,027	68,110	71,613	71,835	49,593	42,885	12,400	8,163	7,251	7,238
Total Revs.	94,713	92,556	112,022	111,826	82,005	76,431	37,609	21,345	16,583	18,465
Int. Exp.	17,271	21,248	31,965	36,638	24,768	27,495	11,443	2,259	1,956	1,284
Exp./Op. Revs.	66.4%	80.8%	80.5%	81.1%	80.6%	87.9%	86.7%	85.9%	84.7%	89.7%
Pretax Inc.	26,333	20,537	21,897	21,143	15,948	9,269	5,012	3,398	2,521	2,149
Eff. Tax Rate	31.1%	34.1%	34.4%	35.6%	35.8%	34.9%	33.8%	30.9%	35.4%	38.3%
Net Inc.	17,853	13,448	14,284	13,519	9,994	5,807	3,104	2,300	1,628	1,326
S&P Core Earnings	17,424	12,000	12,943	NA	NA	NA	NA	NA	NA	NA

Balance Sheet & Other Fin. Data (Million $)

	2003	2002	2001	2000	1999	1998	1997	1996	1995	1994
Receivables	26,476	25,358	47,528	36,237	32,677	21,413	16,549	12,174	10,123	12,256
Cash & Invest.	204,041	186,839	179,352	134,743	127,284	129,152	65,867	56,745	42,831	40,347
Loans	478,006	447,805	391,933	367,022	244,206	215,431	10,816	5,722	5,936	6,746
Total Assets	1,264,032	1,097,190	1,051,450	902,210	716,937	668,641	386,555	151,067	114,475	115,297
Capitalization:										
Debt	168,762	133,079	128,756	116,698	49,392	52,991	28,352	12,884	10,658	9,555
Equity	114,367	85,318	79,722	64,461	47,761	40,395	19,533	12,460	10,910	7,840
Total	284,254	219,797	210,003	182,904	99,078	95,839	51,906	25,294	21,568	18,333
Price Times Bk. Val.: High	4.6	5.4	3.7	4.6	4.1	4.1	4.1	3.2	2.6	2.3
Price Times Bk. Val.: Low	2.8	2.5	2.2	2.7	2.3	1.6	2.1	1.9	1.3	1.6
% Return On Revs.	18.8	14.5	12.8	12.9	12.2	7.6	8.3	10.8	9.8	7.2
% Ret. on Assets	1.5	1.3	1.5	1.6	1.4	1.1	1.2	1.7	1.4	1.2
% Ret. on Equity	16.5	11.6	19.7	22.2	22.3	14.2	18.6	18.9	16.4	15.2
Loans/Equity	4.3	3.6	5.3	5.6	5.3	516.9	51.7	50.0	54.4	0.8

Data as orig. reptd. (for Travelers prior to 1998); bef. results of disc. opers. and/or spec. items. Per share data adj. for stk. divs. as of ex-div. date. Bold denotes primary EPS. E-Estimated. NA-Not Available. NM-Not Meaningful. NR-Not Ranked.

Office: 399 Park Avenue, New York, NY 10043.
Telephone: 212-559-1000.
Website: http://www.citigroup.com
Chrmn: S.I. Weill.
Pres & COO: R.B. Willumstad.
Vice Chrmn: D.C. Maughan.

Vice Chrmn: S. Fischer.
Vice Chrmn: V.J. Menezes.
Dirs: C. M. Armstrong, A. J. Belda, G. David, K. T. Derr, J. M. Deutch, G. R. Ford, R. Hernandez Ramirez, A. D. Jordan, D. C. Mecum, A. Mulcahy, R. D. Parsons, A. E. Pearson, C. Prince, J. Rodin, R. E. Rubin, F. A. Thomas, S. I. Weill, R. B. Willumstad, A. Zankel.

Founded: in 1901.
Domicile: Delaware.
Employees: 259,000.
S&P Analyst: Evan M. Momios, CFA /PMW/BK

Citizens Communications

Recommendation: **HOLD** ★ ★ ★ ★ ★   12-Month Target Price: **$14.00**
(as of May 06, 2004)

CZN has an approximate 0.04% weighting in the **S&P 500**

Sector: Telecommunication Services
Sub-Industry: Integrated Telecommunication Services
Peer Group: Incumbent Local Exchange Carriers (Independent)

Summary: This telecommunications company provides wireline communications services in rural areas and small and medium-sized towns and cities.

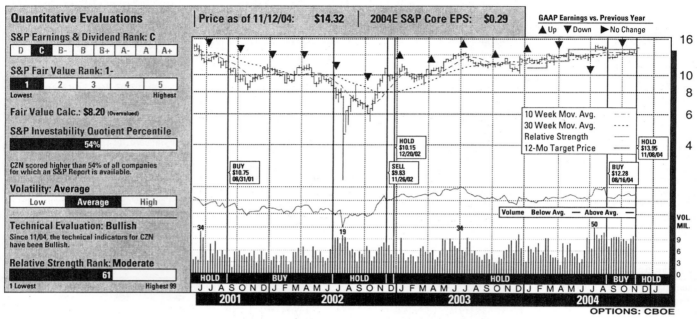

Quantitative Evaluations

S&P Earnings & Dividend Rank: C

| D | C | B- | B | B+ | A- | A | A+ |

S&P Fair Value Rank: 1-

| 1 | 2 | 3 | 4 | 5 |
Lowest   Highest

Fair Value Calc.: $8.20 (Overvalued)

S&P Investability Quotient Percentile
54%

CZN scored higher than 54% of all companies for which an S&P Report is available.

Volatility: Average

| Low | Average | High |

Technical Evaluation: Bullish
Since 11/04, the technical indicators for CZN have been Bullish.

Relative Strength Rank: Moderate
61
1 Lowest   Highest 99

Price as of 11/12/04: $14.32 | **2004E S&P Core EPS:** $0.29

GAAP Earnings vs. Previous Year
▲ Up ▼ Down ► No Change

- 10 Week Mov. Avg.
- 30 Week Mov. Avg.
- Relative Strength
- 12-Mo Target Price

Volume Below Avg. ▬ Above Avg. ▬

BUY $10.75 08/31/01
HOLD $10.15 12/20/02
SELL $9.83 11/26/02
BUY $12.28 08/16/04
HOLD $13.95 11/08/04

HOLD | BUY | HOLD | HOLD | BUY | HOLD
J J A S O N D J F M A M J J A S O N D J F M A M J J A S O N D J F M A M J J A S O N D J
2001   2002   2003   2004

OPTIONS: CBOE

Analyst commentary prepared by Todd Rosenbluth/PMW/BK

Highlights November 09, 2004

- We expect revenues to be down fractionally in 2005, after a similar decrease that we project for 2004, as long-distance and enhanced services penetration is offset by lower access charges due to a decline in federal universal service support, and total access line weakness, due to moderate competition and the lingering effects of macroeconomic weakness.

- Excluding restructuring charges, we believe margins should widen fractionally, as we see the company benefiting from workforce cuts and continued deployment of higher margin calling services. After capital spending cuts, we look for depreciation charges to decrease modestly. Interest expense should drop, as proceeds from the sale of utility properties (completed in April 2004) are used to reduce and refinance debt. However, interest income should also fall, as cash is used for dividend payouts.

- We see 2004 operating EPS of $0.42, with S&P Core EPS estimated at $0.29. We see operating EPS of $0.45 for 2005. Results thus far in 2004 include a gain of $0.05 a share from a liability expiration, and a charge of $0.31 for CZN's strategic alternative review and management succession.

Investment Rationale/Risk November 09, 2004

- We would hold the shares, based on valuation. We consider CZN less vulnerable to pricing pressures than its national telecom peers, as we believe that only the Rochester market faces somewhat sizable competition. The company's customer retention rate is similar to CZN's rural peer average, but stronger than that of the Baby Bells, which had declines of 4% in their bases amid increased competition. We also view favorably the stock's above-peer dividend yield.

- Risks to our opinion and target price include a balance sheet that appears more leveraged than those of most telecom peers; a potential shift in direction with the hiring of a new CEO; and changes to the universal service fund, from which CZN receives revenues.

- Our 12-month target price of $14 is based on a slightly above-average EBITDA multiple relative to our rural telecom peer group. We believe the recent initiation of a quarterly dividend adds to potential total return. CZN paid a $2 special dividend to shareholders of record August 18, 2004.

Key Stock Statistics

S&P Core EPS 2005E	0.24	52-week Range	$14.80-10.23
S&P Oper. EPS 2004E	0.42	12 Month P/E	62.3
P/E on S&P Oper. EPS 2004E	34.1	Beta	NA
S&P Oper. EPS 2005E	0.45	Shareholders	29,698
Yield (%)	7.0%	Market Cap (B)	$ 4.8
Dividend Rate/Share	1.00	Shares Outstanding (M)	335.5

Value of $10,000 invested five years ago: **$ 14,341**

Dividend Data Dividends have been paid since 2004

Amount ($)	Date Decl.	Ex-Div. Date	Stock of Record	Payment Date
0.250	Jul. 11	Aug. 16	Aug. 18	Sep. 02 '04
0.250	Nov. 01	Dec. 08	Dec. 10	Dec. 31 '04

Revenues/Earnings Data Fiscal year ending December 31

Revenues (Million $)

	2004	2003	2002	2001	2000	1999
1Q	558.5	651.9	679.3	624.3	282.4	437.5
2Q	544.1	644.0	662.4	505.7	287.3	414.9
3Q	545.4	595.0	668.8	661.1	389.9	271.5
4Q	—	554.1	658.7	665.9	482.3	277.2
Yr.	—	2,445	2,669	2,457	1,802	1,087

Earnings Per Share ($)

	2004	2003	2002	2001	2000	1999
1Q	0.15	0.22	-0.16	0.07	-0.02	0.21
2Q	0.08	0.12	-0.15	-0.06	Nil	0.03
3Q	-0.04	0.04	-2.49	-0.11	-0.02	0.03
4Q	E0.10	0.05	-0.13	-0.41	-0.16	0.24
Yr.	E0.42	0.42	-2.93	-0.28	-0.15	0.45

Next earnings report expected: early-March Source: S&P, Company Reports
EPS Estimates based on S&P Operating Earnings; historical GAAP earnings are as reported.

Citizens Communications Company

Recommendation: **HOLD** ★ ★ ★ ☆ ☆   12-Month Target Price: **$14.00** (as of May 06, 2004)

Business Summary November 09, 2004

Citizens Communications focuses on telecommunications. It provides wireline services to rural areas and small and medium-sized towns and cities, including the Rochester, NY, metropolitan area, as an incumbent local exchange carrier (ILEC). In addition, it provides competitive local exchange carrier (CLEC) services to business customers and to other communications carriers in the West through Electric Lightwave (ELI). CZN ended 2003 with about 2.4 million telephone access lines (down 2%, year to year), in 24 states, including Arizona, California, Minnesota, New York, and Illinois.

In June 2001, the company acquired Global Crossing's ILEC subsidiary, Frontier Communications. The acquisition (involving about 1.1 million telephone access lines) cost about $3.4 billion in cash. In July, CZN sold its Louisiana Gas utility for $363 million in cash, plus the assumption of certain liabilities. In January 2002, it sold its water and wastewater treatment operations for $859 million in cash and $120 million in assumed debt. In October 2002, the company agreed to sell its Arizona Electric and Gas division for $230 million in cash. Closing was in the 2003 third quarter. In December 2002, CZN sold its Hawaiian gas division for $115 million in cash.

Not all of CZN's acquisition and divestiture plans have gone smoothly. In August 2000, Hawaiian regulators rejected a $270 million cash sale agreement for the company's Kauai electric division, citing concerns regarding the overall price and financing plans for the acquirer. A new agreement to sell Kauai Electric for $215 million was reached in March 2002, and the sale was completed in November

2002. In July 2001, CZN canceled its acquisition of 556,800 telephone access lines from Qwest Communications. In December 2001, it canceled its acquisition of 63,000 California and Arizona access lines from Verizon Communications.

The ILEC services business (which accounted for 93% of total revenues in 2003) is primarily with retail customers. The company believes it can generate value added returns from acquired ILEC properties by providing rural local residential phone customers with enhanced services. The penetration rates for enhanced services in the acquired service territories are currently far below the national average. CZN also offers long-distance and DSL service for its ILEC customers. In addition, it provides network access services to long-distance carriers in connection with the use of its facilities to originate and terminate interstate and intrastate long-distance calls.

With a facilities-based network consisting of optical fiber and voice and data switches, ELI, which accounted for 7% of revenues in 2003, provides a broad range of wireline products in the western U.S.

In December 2003, CZN said directors had decided to explore strategic alternatives, and to retain a financial adviser to assist in the process. In July 2004, the company announced a $2 special dividend and the initiation of a $0.25 quarterly dividend, to be paid out of existing and expected cash, beginning in September. CZN also announced the resignation of chairman L. Tow as CEO.

Company Financials Fiscal Year ending December 31

Per Share Data ($)

(Year Ended December 31)	2003	2002	2001	2000	1999	1998	1997	1996	1995	1994
Tangible Bk. Val.	NM	NM	NM	4.09	7.36	7.27	6.93	6.90	6.02	5.17
Cash Flow	2.37	-0.24	2.08	1.30	1.45	1.22	NA	NA	NA	NA
Earnings	0.42	-2.93	-0.28	-0.15	0.45	0.23	0.04	0.72	0.64	0.64
S&P Core Earnings	0.67	-2.83	-0.58	NA	NA	NA	NA	NA	NA	NA
Dividends	Nil	Nil	Nil	Nil	Nil	Nil	Nil	Nil	Nil	Nil
Payout Ratio	Nil	Nil	Nil	Nil	Nil	Nil	Nil	Nil	Nil	Nil
Prices - High	13.40	11.52	15.88	19.00	14.31	11.18	11.70	11.22	11.79	14.03
- Low	8.81	2.51	8.20	12.50	7.25	6.88	7.61	9.44	8.97	10.26
P/E Ratio - High	32	NM	NM	NM	32	51	NM	16	18	22
- Low	21	NM	NM	NM	16	31	NM	13	14	16

Income Statement Analysis (Million $)

	2003	2002	2001	2000	1999	1998	1997	1996	1995	1994
Revs.	2,445	2,669	2,457	1,802	1,087	1,542	1,394	1,307	1,069	916
Oper. Inc.	1,173	1,179	927	549	8.07	178	15.8	296	254	NA
Depr.	595	756	632	388	262	258	236	194	159	115
Int. Exp.	423	478	386	194	93.2	112	114	96.1	87.8	NA
Pretax Inc.	189	-1,238	-78.7	-44.0	158	73.9	23.5	269	226	NA
Eff. Tax Rate	35.5%	NM	NM	NM	40.8%	25.4%	41.5%	31.5%	29.5%	30.9%
Net Inc.	122	-823	-63.9	-40.1	117	59.6	16.3	185	160	144
S&P Core Earnings	194	-794	-164	NA	NA	NA	NA	NA	NA	NA

Balance Sheet & Other Fin. Data (Million $)

	2003	2002	2001	2000	1999	1998	1997	1996	1995	1994
Cash	584	393	57.7	31.2	37.1	31.9	35.1	24.2	17.9	NA
Curr. Assets	896	1,201	2,533	2,263	309	414	377	370	253	NA
Total Assets	7,689	8,147	10,554	6,955	5,772	5,293	4,873	4,523	3,918	NA
Curr. Liab.	536	771	1,567	992	467	508	418	409	504	NA
LT Debt	4,397	5,159	5,736	3,264	2,309	1,900	1,707	1,510	1,187	994
Common Equity	1,415	1,172	1,946	1,720	1,920	1,793	1,679	1,678	1,560	1,157
Total Cap.	6,259	6,468	8,112	5,474	4,700	4,669	4,305	3,536	3,135	2,471
Cap. Exp.	278	469	531	537	485	483	531	348	257	14.4
Cash Flow	717	-67.5	568	348	380	318	252	379	319	288
Curr. Ratio	1.7	1.6	1.6	2.3	0.7	0.8	0.9	0.9	0.5	NA
% LT Debt of Cap.	70.2	79.8	70.7	59.6	49.1	52.0	50.0	47.0	43.0	46.0
% Net Inc.of Revs.	5.0	NM	NM	NM	10.8	3.9	1.2	14.1	14.9	15.7
% Ret. on Assets	1.5	NM	NM	NM	2.1	1.2	0.3	4.4	4.3	NA
% Ret. on Equity	9.4	NM	NM	NM	6.5	3.4	3.4	11.1	11.7	13.5

Data as orig reptd.; bef. results of disc opers/spec. items. Per share data adj. for stk. divs.; EPS diluted. E-Estimated. NA-Not Available. NM-Not Meaningful. NR-Not Ranked. UR-Under Review.

Office: 3 High Ridge Park, Stamford, CT 06905-1337.
Telephone: 203-614-5600.
Email: citizens@cnz.com
Website: http://www.czn.net
Chrmn: R.J. Graf.
Pres & CEO: M. Wilderrotter.
EVP & CFO: J. Elliott.

SVP & Chief Acctg Officer: R.J. Larson.
SVP & Treas: D.B. Armour.
VP & Investor Contact: M. Zarrella 203-614-5179.
Dirs: J. Elliott, A. I. Fleischman, R. J. Graf, S. Harfenist, A. N. Heine, W. Kraus, S. N. Schneider, J. L. Schroeder, R. A. Stanger, E. Tornberg, D. H. Ward, M. Wilderotter.

Founded: in 1927.
Domicile: Delaware.
Employees: 6,708.
S&P Analyst: Todd Rosenbluth/PMW/BK

CIT Group

Recommendation: **BUY** ★★★★☆   12-Month Target Price: **$44.00**
(SELL | SELL | HOLD | BUY | BUY)   (as of October 21, 2004)

CIT has an approximate 0.08% weighting in the **S&P 500**

Sector: Financials
Sub-Industry: Specialized Finance
Peer Group: Equipment Financing Companies

Summary: This diversified finance company engages in vendor, equipment, commercial, consumer and structured financing as well as leasing activities.

Quantitative Evaluations

S&P Earnings & Dividend Rank: NR

| D | C | B- | B | B+ | A- | A | A+ |

S&P Fair Value Rank: NR

| 1 | 2 | 3 | 4 | 5 |
| Lowest | | | | Highest |

Fair Value Calc.: NA

S&P Investability Quotient Percentile

93%

CIT scored higher than 93% of all companies for which an S&P Report is available.

Volatility: Average

| Low | Average | High |

Technical Evaluation: Bullish
Since 10/04, the technical indicators for CIT have been Bullish.

Relative Strength Rank: Moderate

59

| 1 Lowest | | Highest 99 |

| Price as of 11/12/04: | $40.38 | 2004E S&P Core EPS: | $3.22 |

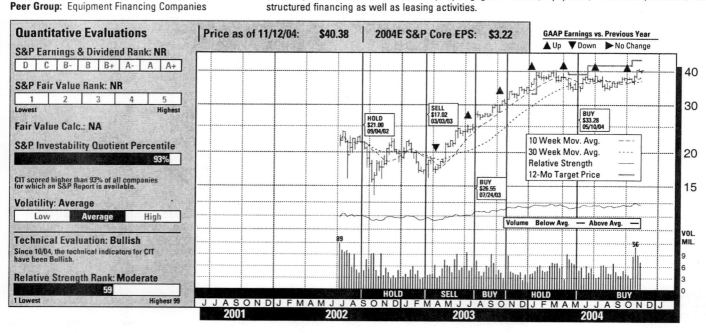

GAAP Earnings vs. Previous Year
▲ Up ▼ Down ► No Change

10 Week Mov. Avg.
30 Week Mov. Avg.
Relative Strength
12-Mo Target Price

Analyst commentary prepared by Robert Hansen, CFA /DC/BK

Highlights 15-NOV-04

- CIT Group continues to benefit from an improvement in utilization, lease rates and credit quality thus far in 2004, due to, we believe, a strengthening in the domestic economy, in CIT's Argentine portfolio, and among its telecommunications and airline borrowers. However, we think CIT's target markets will remain highly competitive in 2004 and 2005 as customers increasingly access the bank and high yield markets.

- Third quarter EPS of $0.86, up from $0.69 in the year-earlier period, matched our estimate, aided by 5% sequential growth in managed assets, higher risk adjusted margins, and improved credit quality, as well as a lower loan loss provision and prudent compensation growth. We see credit quality improving in 2005 given declines in delinquencies and non-performing assets throughout 2004.

- We expect a modest rise in loan demand, origination volume and factoring commissions in 2005, as business conditions in the company's target markets gradually improve. We estimate EPS of $3.25 in 2004 and $3.70 in 2005, driven by higher total managed assets, a wider net finance margin, and well controlled growth in operating expenses.

Investment Rationale/Risk 15-NOV-04

- We view CIT as a well managed company with an established brand and disciplined risk management policies. We think improvements in the company's loan demand, credit quality and net finance margin are sustainable and merit a higher valuation. We are impressed with the company's commitment to sound corporate governance policies, such as the high proportion of independent directors on the board, which we view as favorable to shareholder interests.

- Risks to our recommendation and target price include potential further increases in interest rates, competition, and credit losses. However, we expect that net interest margins will remain relatively stable, based on the company's matched-funding strategy and improved credit spreads.

- Having risen about 10% thus far in 2004, the shares recently traded at a P/E multiple of nearly 11X our 2005 EPS estimate, a significant discount to the S&P 500 and peers. Our 12-month target price of $44 represents a multiple of nearly 12X our 2005 EPS estimate, comparable to peers. Although we forecast only modest growth in managed assets, we have a buy opinion on the shares based on our view of their valuation, which we find attractive.

Key Stock Statistics

S&P Core EPS 2005E	3.65	52-week Range	$41.00-31.66
S&P Oper. EPS 2004E	3.25	12 Month P/E	12.3
P/E on S&P Oper. EPS 2004E	12.4	Beta	NA
S&P Oper. EPS 2005E	3.70	Shareholders	86,541
Yield (%)	1.3%	Market Cap (B)	$ 8.5
Dividend Rate/Share	0.52	Shares Outstanding (M)	210.2

Value of $10,000 invested five years ago: **NA**

Dividend Data Dividends have been paid since 2002

Amount ($)	Date Decl.	Ex-Div. Date	Stock of Record	Payment Date
0.130	Jan. 21	Feb. 11	Feb. 15	Feb. 27 '04
0.130	Apr. 21	May. 12	May. 14	May. 28 '04
0.130	Jul. 21	Aug. 11	Aug. 13	Aug. 30 '04
0.130	Oct. 20	Nov. 10	Nov. 15	Nov. 30 '04

Revenues/Earnings Data Fiscal year ending December 31

Revenues (Million $)

	2004	2003	2002	2001	2000	1999
1Q	1,134	1,175	1,199	—	—	—
2Q	1,149	1,161	1,107	—	—	—
3Q	1,180	1,142	1,022	—	—	—
4Q	—	1,172	—	—	—	—
Yr.	—	4,678	5,275	3,975	—	—

Earnings Per Share ($)

	2004	2003	2002	2001	2000	1999
1Q	0.88	0.60	0.87	—	—	—
2Q	0.82	0.65	-21.84	—	—	—
3Q	0.86	0.69	-11.33	—	—	—
4Q	E0.89	0.72	0.64	—	—	—
Yr.	E3.25	2.66	-31.66	—	—	—

Next earnings report expected: late-January Source: S&P, Company Reports
EPS Estimates based on S&P Operating Earnings; historical GAAP earnings are as reported.

CIT Group Inc.

Recommendation: **BUY** ★★★★☆   12-Month Target Price: **$44.00** (as of October 21, 2004)

Business Summary 15-NOV-04

CIT Group is a leading global commercial and consumer finance company that has provided financing and leasing capital since 1908. In 2001, the company was acquired by Tyco International and renamed Tyco Capital Corporation; it was subsequently spun off in July 2002. CIT had total managed assets of $49.7 billion at December 31, 2003. The company intends to maintain its competitive position by expanding its existing markets, industries and products, improving overall efficiency and flexibility, and restoring debt credit ratings to higher levels.

Transactions are generated through direct calling efforts with borrowers, lessees, equipment end-users, vendors, manufacturers and distributors and through referral sources and other intermediaries. In addition, the company's business units jointly structure certain transactions and refer transactions to other CIT units to meet overall customer financing needs. The company also buys and sells participations in, and syndications of, finance receivables and/or lines of credit.

Specialty finance (37.8% of total managed assets at the end of 2003) consists of the vendor financing and consumer finance businesses. Assets include certain small ticket commercial financing and leasing assets, vendor programs and consumer home equity. The primary focus of the consumer business is home equity lending. To improve overall profitability, the specialty finance group sells individual loans and portfolios of loans to banks, thrifts and other investors.

CIT's equipment financing and leasing operations (35.1%) conduct business through two units. The equipment financing unit offers secured equipment financing and leasing, and focuses on the distribution of its products through manufacturers, dealers/distributors, intermediaries and direct calling efforts primarily in manufacturing, construction, transportation and other industries. The capital finance unit offers secured equipment financing and leasing by directly marketing customized transactions of commercial aircraft and rail equipment.

The commercial finance segment (20.8%) conducts commercial finance operations through two business units, both of which focus on accounts receivable and inventories as the primary source of security for their loans. Commercial services provides traditional secured commercial financing, as well as factoring and receivable/collection management. The business credit unit provides traditional secured commercial financing for working capital business expansion and turnaround needs.

The structured finance segment (6.3%) provides specialized investment banking services by providing asset-based financing for large ticket asset acquisitions and project financing and related advisory services to equipment manufacturers, corporate clients, regional airlines, governments and public sector agencies.

In September 2003, CIT purchased $446 million of factoring receivables from GE Commercial Services, and in December 2003, acquired $1 billion in U.S. factoring assets from HSBC.

Company Financials Fiscal Year ending December 31

Per Share Data ($)

(Year Ended December 31)	2003	2002	2001	2000	1999	1998	1997	1996	1995	1994
Tangible Bk. Val.	23.14	20.67	NA	NA	NA	NA	NA	NA	NA	NA
Cash Flow	7.61	-25.75	NA	NA	NA	NA	NA	NA	NA	NA
Earnings	2.66	-31.66	NA	NA	NA	NA	NA	NA	NA	NA
S&P Core Earnings	2.58	-1.03	NA	NA	NA	NA	NA	NA	NA	NA
Dividends	48.00	Nil	NA	NA	NA	NA	NA	NA	NA	NA
Payout Ratio	18%	Nil	NA	NA	NA	NA	NA	NA	NA	NA
Prices - High	36.20	24.05	NA	NA	NA	NA	NA	NA	NA	NA
- Low	16.08	13.80	NA	NA	NA	NA	NA	NA	NA	NA
P/E Ratio - High	14	NM	NA	NA	NA	NA	NA	NA	NA	NA
- Low	6	NM	NA	NA	NA	NA	NA	NA	NA	NA

Income Statement Analysis (Million $)

	2003	2002	2001	2000	1999	1998	1997	1996	1995	1994
Revs.	4,589	5,275	4,548	NA	NA	NA	NA	NA	NA	NA
Oper. Inc.	3,270	2,299	2,394	NA	NA	NA	NA	NA	NA	NA
Depr.	1,053	1,241	1,037	NA	NA	NA	NA	NA	NA	NA
Int. Exp.	1,319	2,102	1,620	NA	NA	NA	NA	NA	NA	NA
Pretax Inc.	937	-6,314	622	NA	NA	NA	NA	NA	NA	NA
Eff. Tax Rate	38.9%	NM	45.0%	NA	NA	NA	NA	NA	NA	NA
Net Inc.	567	-6,699	334	NA	NA	NA	NA	NA	NA	NA
S&P Core Earnings	549	NA	NA	NA	NA	NA	NA	NA	NA	NA

Balance Sheet & Other Fin. Data (Million $)

	2003	2002	2001	2000	1999	1998	1997	1996	1995	1994
Cash	1,974	2,274	808	NA	NA	NA	NA	NA	NA	NA
Accounts Receivable	31,575	27,681	31,387	NA	NA	NA	NA	NA	NA	NA
Accounts Payable	3,895	2,514	2,393	NA	NA	NA	NA	NA	NA	NA
Total Assets	46,343	42,710	51,090	NA	NA	NA	NA	NA	NA	NA
LT Debt	20,758	17,327	18,907	NA	NA	NA	NA	NA	NA	NA
Lease Obligations	NA	NA	NA	NA	NA	NA	NA	NA	NA	NA
Common Equity	5,394	4,758	10,598	NA	NA	NA	NA	NA	NA	NA
Total Cap.	26,191	22,085	29,505	NA	NA	NA	NA	NA	NA	NA
Cap. Exp.	2,096	1,877	1,451	NA	NA	NA	NA	NA	NA	NA
Cash Flow	1,620	-5,458	1,371	NA	NA	NA	NA	NA	NA	NA
% LT Debt of Cap.	79.3	78.5	64.1	NA	NA	NA	NA	NA	NA	NA
% Net Inc.of Revs.	12.4	NM	7.3	NA	NA	NA	NA	NA	NA	NA
% Ret. on Assets	1.3	NM	NM	NA	NA	NA	NA	NA	NA	NA
% Ret. on Equity	11.2	NM	NM	NA	NA	NA	NA	NA	NA	NA

Data as orig reptd.; bef. results of disc opers/spec. items. Per share data adj. for stk. divs.; EPS diluted. E-Estimated. NA-Not Available. NM-Not Meaningful. NR-Not Ranked. Prior to 2003, fiscal yr. ended Sep. 30. Results for 2001 are for 9 mos.

Office: 1 CIT Drive, Livingston, NJ 07039.
Telephone: 973-740-5000.
Email: investor.relations@cit.com
Website: http://www.citgroup.com
Chrmn: A. R. Gamper, Jr.
EVP, CFO & Vice Chrmn: J. M. Leone.

Vice Chrmn: T. B. Hallman.
Vice Chrmn: L. A. Marsiello.
Investor Contact: Valerie L. Gerard (973-422-3284).
Dirs: G. C. Butler, W. A. Farlinger, W. M. Freeman, A. R. Gamper, Jr., T. H. Kean, E. J. Kelly III, M. M. Parrs, J. M. Peek, J. R. Ryan, P. J. Tobin, L. M. Van Deusen.

Auditor: PricewaterhouseCoopers.
Founded: in 1908.
Domicile: Delaware.
Employees: 5,835.
S&P Analyst: Robert Hansen, CFA /DC/BK

Recommendation: **BUY** ★★★★☆   12-Month Target Price: **$28.00**
(as of October 21, 2004)

CTXS has an approximate 0.04% weighting in the **S&P 500**

Sector: Information Technology
Sub-Industry: Application Software
Peer Group: Application Software - Larger Cos.

Summary: This company is a leading developer and supplier of access infrastructure software and services.

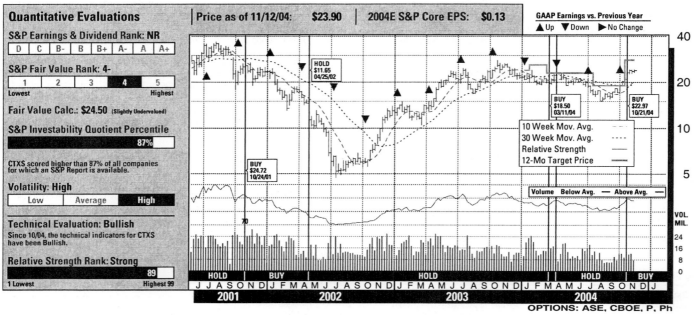

Quantitative Evaluations

S&P Earnings & Dividend Rank: NR

D	C	B-	B	B+	A-	A	A+

S&P Fair Value Rank: 4-

1	2	3	4	5
Lowest				Highest

Fair Value Calc.: $24.50 (Slightly Undervalued)

S&P Investability Quotient Percentile

87%

CTXS scored higher than 87% of all companies for which an S&P Report is available.

Volatility: High

Low	Average	High

Technical Evaluation: Bullish
Since 10/04, the technical indicators for CTXS have been Bullish.

Relative Strength Rank: Strong

89
| 1 Lowest | | Highest 99 |

Price as of 11/12/04: **$23.90**   2004E S&P Core EPS: **$0.13**

Analyst commentary prepared by Scott H. Kessler/CB/BK

OPTIONS: ASE, CBOE, P, Ph

Highlights October 25, 2004

- We expect weakness in corporate technology spending to dissipate somewhat in the 2004 fourth quarter, and we project 2004 revenue growth of about 23%, including Expertcity.com (the private company developer of the GoToMyPC remote access software that CTXS acquired in February 2004 for up to $237 million in cash and stock). We expect revenues to increase 14% in 2005. Despite somewhat sluggish overall demand for technology offerings, we still believe large organizations will continue to look to the company for efficient and cost-effective software deployment, remote access, and business continuity solutions.

- We believe gross and operating margins will continue to benefit from a favorable revenue mix, and from what we view as well controlled variable costs and expenses. Net interest and other income has been aided by the March 2004 repurchase of convertible debt valued at $355.7 million.

- We expect EPS to continue to be positively affected by an active share repurchase program. The discrepancies between our annual operating EPS and Standard & Poor's Core Earnings estimates reflect notable projected stock option expenses.

Investment Rationale/Risk October 25, 2004

- We recommend investors accumulate the shares. CTXS has won a number of high profile customers in recent quarters, with particular success with international companies and government entities (including the General Services Administration). The GSA contract provides a vehicle by which federal agencies can directly purchase CTXS products. Federal agency customers include the Air Force, Army and Navy; the Department of Transportation; and the Department of Veterans Affairs. We view positively CTXS's recent efforts to diversify its revenues and strengthen its balance sheet.

- Risks to our opinion and target price include slowing demand for the company's access infrastructure offerings, increased competition from Microsoft (MSFT: buy, $28), and issues related to the integration and performance of the former Expertcity businesses.

- Based on relative P/E-to-growth rate (PEG) analysis, where CTXS's PEG multiple was recently about 8% below that of the S&P 500 Software Industry, our 12-month target price is $28. The stock's recent P/E was somewhat above those of its peers.

Key Stock Statistics

S&P Core EPS 2005E	0.33	52-week Range	$25.21-15.02
S&P Oper. EPS 2004E	0.89	12 Month P/E	35.7
P/E on S&P Oper. EPS 2004E	26.9	Beta	2.06
S&P Oper. EPS 2005E	1.05	Shareholders	1,293
Yield (%)	Nil	Market Cap (B)	$ 4.0
Dividend Rate/Share	Nil	Shares Outstanding (M)	169.4

Value of $10,000 invested five years ago: **$ 6,169**

Dividend Data

No cash dividends have been paid.

Revenues/Earnings Data Fiscal year ending December 31

Revenues (Million $)

	2004	2003	2002	2001	2000	1999
1Q	161.3	143.5	142.3	132.8	127.5	85.04
2Q	178.3	143.1	117.5	147.3	106.1	94.42
3Q	187.6	144.3	118.9	153.5	113.5	105.8
4Q	—	157.7	148.8	158.1	123.3	118.0
Yr.	—	588.6	527.5	591.6	470.4	403.3

Earnings Per Share ($)

	2004	2003	2002	2001	2000	1999
1Q	0.05	0.18	0.14	0.15	0.19	0.14
2Q	0.18	0.17	0.06	0.12	0.07	0.15
3Q	0.22	0.18	0.10	0.14	0.11	0.15
4Q	E0.26	0.21	0.23	0.13	0.10	0.17
Yr.	E0.89	0.74	0.52	0.54	0.47	0.61

Next earnings report expected: late-January Source: S&P, Company Reports
EPS Estimates based on S&P Operating Earnings; historical GAAP earnings are as reported.

Citrix Systems, Inc.

Recommendation: **BUY** ★ ★ ★ ★ ☆   12-Month Target Price: **$28.00** (as of October 21, 2004)

Business Summary October 26, 2004

Citrix Systems supplies access infrastructure software and services that enable enterprise-wide deployment and management of applications and information that are found on Windows, UNIX and/or Internet platforms. The company's MetaFrame products permit organizations to access software and data regardless of location, network connection, or hardware.

Historically, information technology (IT) has not been created, sold or deployed with the entire IT environment, from the enterprise perspective, in mind. In most organizations, these environments have expanded incrementally over time, with new waves of computing to some extent being added to existing systems. At the same time, the users of IT have grown more dynamic and unpredictable. People often change roles and locations, use multiple access devices, and switch network connections. These conditions, together with mixed application environments, the extension of enterprise systems to external users (such as suppliers, distributors and customers), and Internet business initiatives, have contributed to notable challenges in providing users with fast and simple access to applications and information.

CTXS seeks to address these issues by trying to make it easy for people to access information on demand. Its mission is to make every organization an on-demand enterprise where information is securely, easily and instantly accessible from virtually anywhere using any device. The vehicle for fulfilling this goal is access infrastructure.

CTXS access infrastructure is sold as the MetaFrame Access Suite, which

enables organizations to provide a secure, single point of access to enterprise applications and information on demand. The Access Suite consists of MetaFrame Presentation Server (the foundation for the suite that centrally manages heterogeneous applications and delivers the functionality as a service to workers, wherever they may be), MetaFrame Secure Access Manager (provides secure, single-point access via the Internet to any enterprise resource), MetaFrame Password Manager (provides password security and single sign-on access to applications running in the suite environment), and MetaFrame Conferencing Manager (adds application conferencing capabilities). These offerings accounted for 63% of net revenues in 2003 (69% in 2002).

To provide customers with an easy and convenient way to keep their CTXS software current, Subscription Advantage is available for an additional fee. It constitutes post-contract support that includes automatic delivery of software upgrades, enhancements and maintenance releases. This offering accounted for 29% of net revenues in 2003 (20% in 2002).

In February 2004, the company acquired Expertcity.com, a market leader in Web-based desktop access and Web-based training and customer assistance. The new Citrix Online division largely reflects the purchase of Expertcity.com.

Services, which consist of Citrix Consulting Services (for product implementation), Citrix Technical Support Services, and Product Training & Certification, accounted for 8% of net revenues in 2003 (7%).

Company Financials Fiscal Year ending December 31

Per Share Data ($)

(Year Ended December 31)	2003	2002	2001	2000	1999	1998	1997	1996	1995	1994
Tangible Bk. Val.	3.24	2.57	2.48	2.94	2.59	2.92	1.19	0.89	0.30	NA
Cash Flow	0.94	0.75	0.95	0.72	0.75	0.84	0.25	0.12	0.02	0.00
Earnings	0.74	0.52	0.54	0.47	0.61	0.34	0.24	0.11	0.02	0.00
S&P Core Earnings	0.23	-0.34	-0.19	NA	NA	NA	NA	NA	NA	NA
Dividends	Nil	Nil	Nil	Nil	Nil	Nil	Nil	Nil	Nil	NA
Payout Ratio	Nil	Nil	Nil	Nil	Nil	Nil	Nil	Nil	Nil	NA
Prices - High	27.86	24.70	37.18	122.31	65.00	24.43	14.08	9.45	2.91	NA
- Low	10.48	4.70	16.87	14.25	13.25	9.09	1.62	1.95	1.25	NA
P/E Ratio - High	38	47	69	NM	NM	73	59	83	NM	NA
- Low	14	9	31	NM	NM	27	7	17	NM	NA

Income Statement Analysis (Million $)

	2003	2002	2001	2000	1999	1998	1997	1996	1995	1994
Revs.	589	527	592	941	403	249	124	44.5	14.6	10.1
Oper. Inc.	189	145	216	172	201	119	60.4	18.1	2.00	0.25
Depr.	34.3	41.4	79.6	50.2	27.6	15.2	1.71	0.38	0.18	0.06
Int. Exp.	18.3	18.2	20.6	17.0	12.6	Nil	NA	Nil	0.04	0.01
Pretax Inc.	161	113	153	135	183	95.5	64.6	22.3	1.99	0.24
Eff. Tax Rate	21.0%	17.0%	31.0%	30.0%	36.0%	36.0%	36.0%	16.0%	4.68%	NA
Net Inc.	127	93.9	105	94.5	117	61.1	41.4	18.7	1.90	0.24
S&P Core Earnings	39.3	-60.5	-36.2	NA	NA	NA	NA	NA	NA	NA

Balance Sheet & Other Fin. Data (Million $)

	2003	2002	2001	2000	1999	1998	1997	1996	1995	1994
Cash	359	143	140	375	216	128	140	99	43.5	1.91
Curr. Assets	809	375	346	587	570	244	258	147	46.4	3.72
Total Assets	1,345	1,162	1,208	1,113	1,038	431	283	150	46.7	3.93
Curr. Liab.	626	189	193	159	137	85.1	35.4	7.72	3.67	1.73
LT Debt	Nil	334	346	330	314	Nil	Nil	Nil	Nil	NA
Common Equity	707	622	647	593	533	297	197	142	42.9	-16.5
Total Cap.	707	955	994	923	847	297	197	142	42.9	NA
Cap. Exp.	11.1	19.1	60.6	43.5	26.3	11.4	6.10	2.16	0.06	0.08
Cash Flow	161	135	185	145	145	76.3	43.1	19.1	2.08	0.30
Curr. Ratio	1.3	2.0	1.8	3.7	4.2	2.9	7.3	19.1	12.6	2.2
% LT Debt of Cap.	Nil	34.9	34.8	35.8	37.1	Nil	Nil	NA	NA	NA
% Net Inc.of Revs.	21.6	17.8	17.8	10.0	29.0	24.6	33.4	42.0	13.0	2.4
% Ret. on Assets	10.1	7.9	9.1	8.8	15.9	17.1	19.1	19.1	7.5	NA
% Ret. on Equity	19.1	14.6	17.0	16.8	28.2	24.7	24.4	20.2	14.3	NA

Data as orig reptd.; bef. results of disc opers/spec. items. Per share data adj. for stk. divs.; EPS diluted. E-Estimated. NA-Not Available. NM-Not Meaningful. NR-Not Ranked. UR-Under Review.

Office: 851 West Cypress Creek Road, Fort Lauderdale, FL 33309.
Telephone: 954-267-3000.
Email: investor@citrix.com
Website: http://www.citrix.com
Chrmn: S.M. Dow.
Pres & CEO: M.B. Templeton.

VP & CFO: D.J. Henshall.
VP, Secy & General Counsel: D.R. Friedman.
Investor Contact: J. Lilly 954-267-2886.
Dirs: T. Bogan, K. R. Compton, S. M. Dow, G. Morin, T. F. Pike, M. B. Templeton, J. W. White.

Founded: in 1989.
Domicile: Delaware.
Employees: 1,885.
S&P Analyst: Scott H. Kessler/CB/BK

The **McGraw·Hill** Companies

STANDARD &POOR'S

Clear Channel Communications

Recommendation: HOLD ★ ★ ★ ★
SELL SELL HOLD BUY BUY

12-Month Target Price: $40.00
(as of July 23, 2004)

CCU has an approximate 0.18% weighting in the **S&P 500**

Sector: Consumer Discretionary
Sub-Industry: Broadcasting & Cable TV
Peer Group: Radio Broadcasting - Larger

Summary: CCU has radio and televisions stations, outdoor advertising displays and live entertainment productions and venues throughout the U.S. and in 65 other countries.

Quantitative Evaluations

Price as of 11/12/04: $34.23 | **2004E S&P Core EPS:** $1.26

S&P Earnings & Dividend Rank: B-

| D | C | B- | B | B+ | A- | A | A+ |

S&P Fair Value Rank: 4+

| 1 | 2 | 3 | 4 | 5 |
| Lowest | | | | Highest |

Fair Value Calc.: $33.70 (Fairly Valued)

S&P Investability Quotient Percentile

49%

CCU scored lower than 51% of all companies for which an S&P Report is available.

Volatility: Average

| Low | Average | High |

Technical Evaluation: Bullish
Since 11/04, the technical indicators for CCU have been Bullish.

Relative Strength Rank: Moderate

44

| 1 Lowest | Highest 99 |

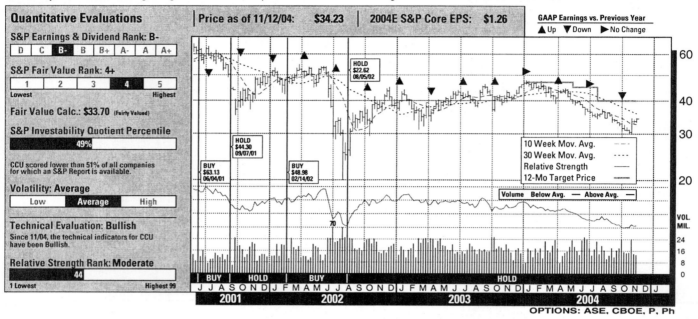

GAAP Earnings vs. Previous Year
▲ Up ▼ Down ▶ No Change

- 10 Week Mov. Avg.
- 30 Week Mov. Avg.
- Relative Strength
- 12-Mo Target Price

Volume Below Avg. — Above Avg.

OPTIONS: ASE, CBOE, P, Ph

Analyst commentary prepared by Tuna N. Amobi, CFA, CPA /CB/JWP

Highlights November 03, 2004

- We forecast consolidated revenue growth of approximately 7% in 2004, moderating to 5% in 2005. Our cautious outlook for low to mid-single digit growth at the core radio division is predicated on some lingering near-term concerns of an apparent supply/demand imbalance in the radio industry. In addition, recent data point to continued softness in national advertising, compared with more encouraging trends for local advertising, traffic and network revenues. Notably weak radio categories have recently included automotive and telecom. However, we expect continued strong high single digit to low double digit advertising growth at the outdoor segment, as rates and occupancies continue to firm. We assume a flat to modest decline in live entertainment attendance in 2005. We anticipate modest growth in other revenues, reflecting the absence of incremental TV political advertising at the local stations.

- We anticipate modest margin expansion in 2005, benefiting from improved operating leverage at the outdoor unit. Radio expenses are projected to remain essentially flat. We estimate consolidated EBITDA growing about 6% in 2004, to about $2.4 billion, and another 8% in 2005, to approximately $2.6 billion.

- After a modest decline in interest expense and outstanding shares, we forecast EPS of $1.42 in 2004 ($1.26 S&P Core, after projected stock option expenses), and $1.57 in 2005 ($1.39 S&P Core).

Key Stock Statistics

S&P Core EPS 2005E	1.39	52-week Range	$47.76-29.96
S&P Oper. EPS 2004E	1.42	12 Month P/E	25.5
P/E on S&P Oper. EPS 2004E	24.1	Beta	1.53
S&P Oper. EPS 2005E	1.57	Shareholders	3,350
Yield (%)	1.5%	Market Cap (B)	$ 20.2
Dividend Rate/Share	0.50	Shares Outstanding (M)	590.0

Value of $10,000 invested five years ago: **$ 4,054**

Dividend Data Dividends have been paid since 2003

Amount ($)	Date Decl.	Ex-Div. Date	Stock of Record	Payment Date
0.100	Feb. 19	Mar. 29	Mar. 31	Apr. 15 '04
0.100	May. 04	Jun. 28	Jun. 30	Jul. 15 '04
0.125	Jul. 21	Sep. 28	Sep. 30	Oct. 15 '04
0.125	Oct. 20	Dec. 29	Dec. 31	Jan. 15 '05

Investment Rationale/Risk November 03, 2004

- We recommend holding the shares. As by far the largest radio group in the U.S., we believe CCU is well positioned to benefit from an eventual recovery in radio ad spending to drive growth in free cash flow, which we project at $1.4 billion for 2004 and $1.6 billion for 2005. In addition, early management reports on the company's new "Less Is More" radio inventory strategy have been quite positive. However, we remain cautious on the potential impact of "Less Is More" on our 2005 outlook. Meanwhile, the global outdoor industry seems to be in the early stages of a renaissance. Separately, we believe that the company recently enhanced its balance sheet flexibility through continued debt reduction, as leverage ratios continue to support an investment grade credit rating. Free cash flow should support a modest share buyback, while the company maintains or modestly increases the stock's current dividend yield of 1.5%.

- The primary risk we see to our opinion and target price relates to uncertainty surrounding the "Less is More" strategy, and the radio advertising recovery at large. We also see some regulatory risk exposure.

- Our 12-month target price of $40 is based on an analysis of discounted cash flows (DCF). On a relative basis, this target implies about 15.5X estimated 2005 free cash flow, or 11.8X enterprise value to projected 2005 EBITDA. While these multiples are below historical norms, we think they adequately offer a fair risk/reward.

Revenues/Earnings Data Fiscal year ending December 31

Revenues (Million $)

	2004	2003	2002	2001	2000	1999
1Q	1,970	1,779	1,698	1,628	782.5	376.8
2Q	2,485	2,317	2,173	2,179	965.9	617.7
3Q	2,649	2,544	2,340	2,300	1,577	887.9
4Q	—	2,290	2,210	1,862	2,020	888.0
Yr.	—	8,931	8,421	7,970	5,345	2,678

Earnings Per Share ($)

	2004	2003	2002	2001	2000	1999
1Q	0.19	0.12	0.15	-0.53	-0.12	-0.02
2Q	0.41	0.41	0.39	-0.40	0.09	0.33
3Q	0.44	1.03	0.34	-0.39	0.96	Nil
4Q	E0.41	0.30	0.30	-0.61	-0.33	-0.03
Yr.	E1.42	1.85	1.18	-1.93	0.57	0.26

Next earnings report expected: late-February Source: S&P, Company Reports
EPS Estimates based on S&P Operating Earnings; historical GAAP earnings are as reported.

STANDARD &POOR'S

Clear Channel Communications, Inc.

Stock Report
November 13, 2004
NYSE Symbol: **CCU**

Recommendation: **HOLD** ★ ★ ★ ☆ ☆   12-Month Target Price: **$40.00** (as of July 23, 2004)

Business Summary November 03, 2004

Clear Channel Communications is a major diversified media company with three business segments: radio broadcasting, outdoor advertising, and live entertainment. At December 31, 2003, the company owned or operated 1,182 U.S. radio stations and 39 U.S. television stations. CCU is also one of the world's largest outdoor advertising companies.

At December 31, 2003, the radio segment (41% of 2003 revenues) owned, programmed, or sold air time for 366 AM and 816 FM U.S. radio stations, of which 492 were in the 100 markets leading according to the Arbitron fall 2003 rankings. In August 2000, CCU acquired AMFM Inc. for stock and debt valued at $23.8 billion, combining the two largest U.S. radio station owners. The company also owns a leading national radio networks, with a weekly audience of more than 180 million listeners.

In June 2004, aiming to stimulate demand, improve pricing and enhance the experience of its listeners and advertisers, Clear Channel Radio unveiled a new "Less Is More" inventory management strategy. Billed to be implemented by mid-December 2004, this strategy entails a company-wide reduction in commercial/promotional clutter by nearly 20% of the entire inventory, with reduced spot breaks and lower average commercial length, as CCU plans to migrate a portion of its traditional 60-second spots to 30 seconds. Local managers would retain wide implementation autonomy in their respective markets.

The outdoor advertising division (24%) operates in more than 40 U.S. markets and 63 foreign countries. CCU's display faces (145,895 U.S., 641,680 international) include billboards of various sizes, wallscapes, transit displays, and street furniture displays. Segment revenues are mostly derived from local sales.

The live entertainment segment (30%) was significantly expanded with the August 2000 acquisition of SFX Entertainment, one of the world's largest producers, promoters and marketers of live entertainment. The company reached 69 million people at 103 owned and operated venues in 2003 (74 U.S., 29 international), and promoted or produced more than 32,000 events, including live music concerts, theatrical shows, and specialized sports events. In addition, CCU is a leading fully integrated sports marketing and management company, representing several hundred professional athletes. Revenues from this segment are derived primarily from ticket sales, rental income, corporate sponsorships and advertising, concessions and merchandise.

The other segment (5%) included 39 company-owned or operated television stations, affiliated with various television networks, including FOX, UPN, ABC, NBC and CBS, and Katz Media, a media representation firm, and a sports representation business.

In January 2004, CCU sold its remaining non-voting equity stake in Spanish media operator Univision for about $599 million in net proceeds. Earlier in 2003, it sold a portion of its UVN stake for $344 million. In 2003, the company entered into a five-year secured contract regarding its investment in XM Satellite Radio, and received $83.5 million at inception.

In 2003, the company acquired 16 radio stations in 10 markets, for about $46 million in cash; and 727 outdoor display faces in four international markets, for about $28 million in cash. In 2002, it acquired The Ackerley Group, Inc., a diversified media company, for $493 million in stock, plus the assumption of $319 million in debt. Also in 2002, CCU acquired 27 radio stations in 17 markets, for about $80 million in cash; as well as 225 outdoor display faces in 22 U.S markets and 9,050 display faces in six international markets, for about $124 million in cash.

Company Financials Fiscal Year ending December 31

Per Share Data ($)

(Year Ended December 31)	2003	2002	2001	2000	1999	1998	1997	1996	1995	1994
Tangible Bk. Val.	NM	NM	NM	NM	NM	0.35	NM	NM	-1.00	-0.56
Cash Flow	2.93	2.19	2.40	2.82	2.49	1.44	0.97	0.56	0.47	0.34
Earnings	1.85	1.18	-1.93	0.57	0.26	0.22	0.34	0.25	0.23	0.16
S&P Core Earnings	1.06	1.04	-2.00	NA	NA	NA	NA	NA	NA	NA
Dividends	0.20	Nil	Nil	Nil	Nil	Nil	Nil	Nil	Nil	Nil
Payout Ratio	11%	Nil	Nil	Nil	Nil	Nil	Nil	Nil	Nil	Nil
Prices - High	47.48	54.90	68.08	95.50	91.50	62.31	39.93	22.62	11.06	6.50
- Low	31.00	20.00	35.20	43.87	52.00	31.00	16.81	10.18	6.26	3.92
P/E Ratio - High	26	47	NM	NM	NM	NM	NM	90	49	41
- Low	17	17	NM	NM	NM	NM	NM	41	28	25

Income Statement Analysis (Million $)

	2003	2002	2001	2000	1999	1998	1997	1996	1995	1994
Revs.	8,931	8,421	7,970	5,345	2,678	1,351	697	352	244	173
Oper. Inc.	2,263	2,186	1,899	1,722	976	546	282	145	105	67.6
Depr.	671	621	2,562	1,401	722	305	114	45.8	33.8	24.7
Int. Exp.	388	433	560	383	192	136	75.1	30.1	20.8	7.67
Pretax Inc.	1,925	1,218	-1,249	714	236	126	111	76.4	52.7	36.4
Eff. Tax Rate	40.5%	40.5%	NM	65.1%	63.8%	57.2%	42.6%	37.2%	39.3%	39.5%
Net Inc.	1,146	725	-1,144	249	85.7	54.0	63.6	37.7	32.0	22.0
S&P Core Earnings	653	635	-1,181	NA	NA	NA	NA	NA	NA	NA

Balance Sheet & Other Fin. Data (Million $)

	2003	2002	2001	2000	1999	1998	1997	1996	1995	1994
Cash	123	170	159	825	81.1	36.5	24.7	16.7	5.39	6.82
Curr. Assets	2,186	2,123	1,941	2,343	925	410	199	113	70.5	53.9
Total Assets	28,353	27,672	47,603	50,056	16,822	7,540	3,456	1,325	563	412
Curr. Liab.	1,893	3,011	2,960	2,129	686	258	86.9	43.5	36.0	27.7
LT Debt	7,075	7,382	7,968	1,597	4,584	2,324	1,540	725	334	238
Common Equity	15,554	14,210	29,736	30,347	10,084	4,483	1,747	513	164	131
Total Cap.	25,736	24,109	44,269	38,777	15,987	7,206	3,318	1,256	510	371
Cap. Exp.	378	549	598	496	239	142	31.0	19.7	15.1	5.70
Cash Flow	1,817	1,346	1,418	1,650	808	359	178	83.5	65.8	46.7
Curr. Ratio	1.2	0.7	0.7	1.1	1.3	1.6	2.3	2.6	2.0	1.9
% LT Debt of Cap.	27.5	30.6	18.0	4.1	28.7	32.2	46.4	57.7	65.5	64.1
% Net Inc.of Revs.	12.8	8.6	NM	4.7	3.2	4.0	9.1	10.7	13.2	12.7
% Ret. on Assets	4.1	1.9	NM	0.7	0.7	1.0	2.7	4.0	6.6	6.9
% Ret. on Equity	7.7	3.3	NM	1.2	1.2	1.7	5.6	11.1	21.8	19.1

Data as orig. reptd.; bef. results of disc. opers. and/or spec. items. Per share data adj. for stk. divs.; EPS diluted (primary prior to 1998). E-Estimated. NA-Not Available. NM-Not Meaningful. NR-Not Ranked.

Office: 200 East Basse Road , San Antonio, TX 78209-8328.
Telephone: 210-822-2828.
Website: http://www.clearchannel.com
Chrmn: L.L. Mays.
Pres, CEO & COO: M.P. Mays.
EVP, CFO & Secy: R.T. Mays.

SVP & Chief Acctg Officer: H.W. Hill, Jr.
SVP & General Counsel: K.E. Wyker.
VP & Investor Contact: R. Palmer 210-832-3315.
Dirs: A. D. Feld, T. O. Hicks, P. J. Lewis, L. L. Mays, R. T. Mays, M. P. Mays, B. J. McCombs, P. B. Riggins, T. H. Strauss, J. Watts, J. H. Williams.

Founded: in 1974.
Domicile: Texas.
Employees: 61,500.
S&P Analyst: Tuna N. Amobi, CFA, CPA /CB/JWP

Recommendation: **HOLD** ★★★★★
SELL | SELL | HOLD | BUY | BUY

12-Month Target Price: **$59.00**
(as of November 02, 2004)

CLX has an approximate 0.11% weighting in the **S&P 500**

Sector: Consumer Staples
Sub-Industry: Household Products
Peer Group: Household Products

Summary: CLX is a diversified producer of household cleaning, grocery and specialty food products.

Quantitative Evaluations

S&P Earnings & Dividend Rank: A

| D | C | B- | B | B+ | A- | A | A+ |

S&P Fair Value Rank: 3

| 1 | 2 | 3 | 4 | 5 |
| Lowest | | | | Highest |

Fair Value Calc.: $54.90 (Fairly Valued)

S&P Investability Quotient Percentile

98%

CLX scored higher than 98% of all companies for which an S&P Report is available.

Volatility: Low

| Low | Average | High |

Technical Evaluation: Bullish

Since 8/04, the technical indicators for CLX have been Bullish.

Relative Strength Rank: Moderate

44

1 Lowest | Highest 99

Price as of 11/12/04: $55.75 | **2005E S&P Core EPS:** $2.50

GAAP Earnings vs. Previous Year
▲ Up ▼ Down ► No Change

HOLD $39.05 01/07/02
BUY $37.48 11/01/01
BUY $38.40 08/07/02

10 Week Mov. Avg.
30 Week Mov. Avg.
Relative Strength
12-Mo Target Price

Volume Below Avg. — Above Avg.

HOLD | BUY | HOLD | BUY | HOLD
J J A S O N D | J F M A M J J A S O N D | J F M A M J J A S O N D | J F M A M J J A S O N D | J
2001 | 2002 | 2003 | 2004

OPTIONS: CBOE, P, Ph

Analyst commentary prepared by Howard Choe/PMW/JWP

Highlights September 29, 2004

- We expect the company's sales to rise about 4% in FY 05 (Jun.), reflecting modest volume gains driven by new product introductions. We see the household products division benefiting from new product introductions such as the Toiletwand, a toilet bowl cleaning apparatus with a disposable cleaning head, and other new products. We expect the specialty products and international divisions to experience nearly 4% sales growth.

- We expect operating margins to expand by 60 basis points, driven by cost savings derived from more efficient manufacturing, promotional spending, sourcing and distribution. In light of what we see as a need to support new product introductions, advertising as a percentage of sales should be similar to the 10% of FY 04.

- We see FY 05 EPS advancing 4%, to $2.65, from FY 04's $2.55. We project FY 05 Standard & Poor's Core Earnings of $2.50 a share, mainly reflecting estimated stock option expense.

Investment Rationale/Risk September 29, 2004

- We are maintaining our hold opinion on the stock, reflecting the impact of a share overhang created by The Henkel Group's potential sale of 29% of CLX's stock, and our concerns about earnings volatility and profitability. We believe the pattern of CLX's new product cycle has caused erratic earnings growth. We do not expect this trend to change in the near term. However, we have a favorable view of the company's strong brands, solid balance sheet, and the stock's dividend yield.

- Risks to our recommendation and target price include increased competition and promotional activity that would impact profitability, low consumer acceptance of new products, unfavorable foreign exchange, and potential challenges in the implementation of new enterprise resource planning system software.

- The shares traded recently at a slight discount to peers, at 19X our calendar 2005 EPS estimate, but we view them as fairly valued, in light of the share overhang and their modest discount to our 12-month target price of $55 (derived from our relative and DCF analyses).

Key Stock Statistics

S&P Oper. EPS 2005E	2.65	52-week Range	$56.50-46.29
P/E on S&P Oper. EPS 2005E	21.0	12 Month P/E	22.0
Yield (%)	1.9%	Beta	0.20
Dividend Rate/Share	1.08	Shareholders	14,256
Shares Outstanding (M)	213.4	Market Cap (B)	$ 11.9

Value of $10,000 invested five years ago: **$ 15,382**

Dividend Data Dividends have been paid since 1968

Amount ($)	Date Decl.	Ex-Div. Date	Stock of Record	Payment Date
0.270	Nov. 19	Jan. 27	Jan. 29	Feb. 13 '04
0.270	Mar. 17	Apr. 26	Apr. 28	May. 14 '04
0.270	May. 19	Jul. 26	Jul. 28	Aug. 13 '04
0.270	Sep. 15	Oct. 27	Oct. 29	Nov. 15 '04

Revenues/Earnings Data Fiscal year ending June 30

Revenues (Million $)

	2005	2004	2003	2002	2001	2000
1Q	1,090	1,048	1,047	991.0	985.0	942.0
2Q	—	947.0	926.0	901.0	899.0	954.0
3Q	—	1,086	1,019	1,033	989.0	1,034
4Q	—	1,243	1,152	1,136	1,102	1,153
Yr.	—	4,324	4,144	4,061	3,903	4,083

Earnings Per Share ($)

	2005	2004	2003	2002	2001	2000
1Q	0.57	0.60	0.71	0.33	0.42	0.36
2Q	E0.55	0.52	0.39	0.22	0.27	0.32
3Q	E0.64	0.59	0.51	0.20	0.33	0.44
4Q	E0.91	0.83	0.72	0.63	0.34	0.52
Yr.	E2.65	2.55	2.33	1.37	1.36	1.64

Next earnings report expected: early-February Source: S&P, Company Reports
EPS Estimates based on S&P Operating Earnings; historical GAAP earnings are as reported.

The Clorox Company

Recommendation: **HOLD** ★ ★ ★ ☆ ☆   12-Month Target Price: **$59.00** (as of November 02, 2004)

Business Summary September 29, 2004

From its divestiture from The Procter & Gamble Company in 1969 through its January 1999 acquisition of First Brands, Clorox grew into a company with over $4 billion in annual sales. Over that time, the name Clorox became nearly synonymous with household bleach.

Many of the company's objectives for FY 04 (Jun.) were similar to those of FY 03. CLX planned to drive growth through innovation and investing in its brands. It also planned to cut costs, become more customer focused, and improve its competitiveness through executional excellence, aided by Project Delta, a systems and processes upgrade.

Sales contributions in FY 03 were as follows: Household Products - North America 55%; Specialty Products 33%, and Household Products - Latin America/Other 12%. In FY 03, Wal-Mart Stores and its affiliated companies accounted for 25% consolidated net sales, up from 23% in FY 02.

The company's Household Products - North America segment includes household cleaning, bleach and other home care products, water filtration products, food storage and trash disposal categories marketed in the U.S. and Canada. Its Household Products - Latin America/Other segment includes operations outside the U.S. and Canada, exports and Puerto Rico, primarily focusing on the laundry, household cleaning, automotive care, insecticides (Brazil and Korea), and food storage and trash disposal categories. The Specialty Products segment includes

charcoal, U.S. and European automotive care, cat litter, insecticides, dressings and sauces, and professional products categories.

Most non-durable household consumer products are nationally advertised and sold in the U.S. to grocery stores through a network of brokers and sold to mass merchandisers, warehouse clubs, and military and other retail stores primarily through a direct sales force. Within the U.S., Clorox also sells institutional versions of specialty food and non-food products. Outside the U.S., the company sells consumer products through subsidiaries, licensees, distributors and joint-venture arrangements with local partners.

In the FY 03 first quarter, CLX said it intended to sell its Brazilian business, due to deteriorating economic and market conditions and lack of scale. The company divested its Jonny Cat litter business and Black Flag insecticides business in FY 03. Sales proceeds totaled $14 million.

On January 31, 2003, CLX entered into an agreement with Procter & Gamble (PG) to form a venture related to the company's Glad plastic bags, wraps and containers business. PG contributed certain production and R&D equipment, licenses to use certain trademarks, and other proprietary technologies to CLX, in exchange for an interest in the profits, losses and cash flows of the Glad business. The agreement's initial term was for 20 years, subject to renewal options. For the first five years, PG had an option to purchase an additional 10% interest.

Company Financials Fiscal Year ending June 30

Per Share Data ($)

(Year Ended June 30)	2004	2003	2002	2001	2000	1999	1998	1997	1996	1995
Tangible Bk. Val.	0.77	NM	0.24	1.38	1.10	0.31	NM	NM	1.11	1.68
Cash Flow	3.47	3.19	2.18	2.30	2.48	1.87	2.27	1.82	1.63	1.43
Earnings	2.55	2.33	1.37	1.36	1.64	1.03	1.41	1.21	1.07	0.95
S&P Core Earnings	2.43	2.26	1.63	1.11	NA	NA	NA	NA	NA	NA
Dividends	1.08	0.88	0.84	0.84	0.61	0.76	0.64	0.58	0.53	0.48
Payout Ratio	42%	38%	61%	62%	37%	74%	45%	48%	50%	51%
Prices - High	56.50	49.16	47.95	40.85	56.37	66.46	58.75	40.18	27.56	19.81
- Low	46.50	37.40	31.92	29.95	28.37	37.50	37.18	24.31	17.50	13.81
P/E Ratio - High	22	21	35	30	34	65	42	33	23	21
- Low	18	16	23	22	17	36	26	20	16	15

Income Statement Analysis (Million $)

	2004	2003	2002	2001	2000	1999	1998	1997	1996	1995
Revs.	4,324	4,144	4,061	3,903	4,083	4,003	2,741	2,533	2,218	1,984
Oper. Inc.	1,069	1,046	942	895	981	933	676	593	532	463
Depr.	197	191	190	225	201	202	137	126	117	104
Int. Exp.	30.0	28.0	39.0	88.0	98.0	97.0	69.7	55.6	38.3	25.1
Pretax Inc.	840	802	498	487	622	430	472	416	370	338
Eff. Tax Rate	35.0%	35.9%	35.3%	33.3%	36.7%	42.8%	36.9%	40.0%	40.0%	40.6%
Net Inc.	546	514	322	325	394	246	298	249	222	201
S&P Core Earnings	521	496	383	266	NA	NA	NA	NA	NA	NA

Balance Sheet & Other Fin. Data (Million $)

	2004	2003	2002	2001	2000	1999	1998	1997	1996	1995
Cash	232	172	177	251	245	132	89.7	101	90.8	137
Curr. Assets	1,043	951	1,002	1,103	1,454	1,116	799	673	574	600
Total Assets	3,834	3,652	3,630	3,995	4,353	4,132	3,030	2,778	2,179	1,907
Curr. Liab.	1,268	1,451	1,225	1,069	1,541	1,368	1,225	893	624	479
LT Debt	475	495	678	685	590	702	316	566	356	253
Common Equity	1,540	1,215	1,354	1,900	1,794	1,178	1,085	1,036	933	944
Total Cap.	2,189	1,825	2,174	2,732	2,608	2,117	1,401	1,773	1,438	1,342
Cap. Exp.	172	205	177	192	158	176	99	95.2	84.8	62.9
Cash Flow	743	705	512	550	595	448	480	376	339	305
Curr. Ratio	0.8	0.7	0.8	1.0	0.9	0.8	0.7	0.8	0.9	1.3
% LT Debt of Cap.	21.7	27.1	31.2	25.1	22.6	33.2	22.6	31.9	24.8	18.9
% Net Inc.of Revs.	12.6	12.4	7.9	8.3	9.6	6.1	10.9	9.8	10.0	10.1
% Ret. on Assets	14.6	14.3	8.4	7.8	9.3	6.0	10.3	10.1	10.9	11.1
% Ret. on Equity	39.6	39.8	19.8	17.6	23.4	19.6	28.1	25.1	23.7	21.7

Data as orig reptd.; bef. results of disc opers/spec. items. Per share data adj. for stk. divs. Bold denotes primary EPS - prior periods restated. E-Estimated. NA-Not Available. NM-Not Meaningful. NR-Not Ranked. UR-Under Review.

Office: 1221 Broadway, Oakland, CA 94612.
Telephone: 510-271-7000.
Email: investor_relations@clorox.com
Website: http://www.clorox.com
Chrmn: R.W. Matschullat.
Pres & CEO: G.E. Johnston.
SVP & CFO: D.J. Heinrich.

SVP & General Counsel: P.D. Bewley.
VP & Treas: G.S. Frank.
VP & Investor Contact: S. Austenfeld 510-271-2270.
Dirs: D. Boggan, Jr., T. M. Friedman, C. Henkel, W. R. Johnson, G. E. Johnston, R. W. Matschullat, G. Michael, K. Morwind, J. Murley, L. R. Scott, M. E. Shannon.

Founded: in 1913.
Domicile: Delaware.
Employees: 8,600.
S&P Analyst: Howard Choe/PMW/JWP

CMS Energy

Recommendation: **SELL** ★ ★ ☆ ☆ ☆
SELL SELL HOLD BUY BUY

12-Month Target Price: **$8.50**
(as of September 15, 2004)

CMS has an approximate 0.02% weighting in the **S&P 500**

Sector: Utilities
Sub-Industry: Multi-Utilities & Unregulated Power

Summary: This energy holding company's principal subsidiary is Consumers Energy, the largest utility in Michigan and the sixth largest gas and 13th largest electric utility in the U.S.

Quantitative Evaluations

S&P Earnings & Dividend Rank: B

| D | C | B- | B | B+ | A- | A | A+ |

S&P Fair Value Rank: 4-

| 1 | 2 | 3 | 4 | 5 |
Lowest | | | | Highest

Fair Value Calc.: $10.10 (Fairly Valued)

S&P Investability Quotient Percentile

51%

CMS scored higher than 51% of all companies for which an S&P Report is available.

Volatility: Average

| Low | Average | High |

Technical Evaluation: Bullish

Since 11/04, the technical indicators for CMS have been Bullish.

Relative Strength Rank: Strong

72

1 Lowest | Highest 99

Price as of 11/12/04: $10.27 | **2004E S&P Core EPS:** $0.72

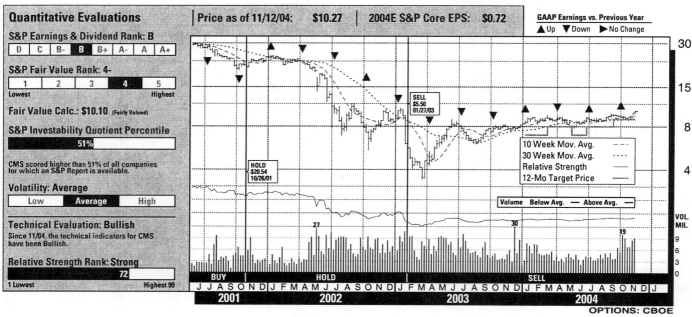

GAAP Earnings vs. Previous Year
▲ Up ▼ Down ▶ No Change

- 10 Week Mov. Avg.
- 30 Week Mov. Avg.
- Relative Strength
- 12-Mo Target Price

Volume   Below Avg. — Above Avg.

HOLD $20.54 10/26/01

SELL $5.50 01/27/03

VOL. MIL.

OPTIONS: CBOE

Analyst commentary prepared by Justin McCann/MF/GG

Highlights October 04, 2004

- After an anticipated 5% increase in 2004 from 2003's EPS from ongoing operations of $0.81 (which excludes a net loss of $1.11 from asset writedowns and other one-time charges), we expect EPS from ongoing operations to decline about 2% in 2005. We now expect CMS's reported results in 2004 to be around breakeven, compared to the previously projected loss of about $0.35 a share. This is due to the company's announcement of more favorable timing and projected proceeds from the planned sale of some of its international assets.

- We expect operating results in 2004 to benefit from a sharp decline in interest expense, reflecting lower average debt, as well as a drop of 84 basis points in the average interest rate, to 7.8%. Although we expect the utilities to benefit from an improved economy in Michigan, we think this will be largely offset by a continuing loss of electric customers to other suppliers.

- We also see earnings restricted by costs of upgrading CMS's generating plants in connection with compliance with the Clean Air Act. We do not expect to see the dividend restored in 2004. The dividend was suspended in January 2003, and has resulted in annual savings of over $100 million.

Investment Rationale/Risk October 04, 2004

- While the stock has rebounded from its 2003 low, we view it as an unattractive investment and would avoid the shares. In addition to the suspension of the dividend and what we view as a weak earnings outlook for 2004 and 2005, we think the stock will be restricted by what we see as CMS's higher than average financing costs, below investment grade credit rating, and the residual impact from negative events of the past four years.

- Risks to our investment recommendation and target price include the company making much sooner than anticipated progress in the strengthening of its balance sheet and the restoration of its dividend, as well as a sharp increase in the average P/E multiple of the group as a whole.

- The company's debt was over 84% of total capitalization at the end of 2003, as a new accounting standard shifted $664 million of trust preferred stock from equity to debt. In the absence of a dividend, we believe the stock should trade at a significant discount to the average peer P/E multiple of about 13.3X our EPS estimates for 2005. Our 12-month target price of $8.50 is approximately 10X our operating EPS estimate for 2005.

Key Stock Statistics

S&P Core EPS 2005E	0.66	52-week Range	$10.31-7.41
S&P Oper. EPS 2004E	0.85	12 Month P/E	22.3
P/E on S&P Oper. EPS 2004E	12.1	Beta	1.56
S&P Oper. EPS 2005E	0.75	Shareholders	60,791
Yield (%)	Nil	Market Cap (B)	$ 2.0
Dividend Rate/Share	Nil	Shares Outstanding (M)	194.7

Value of $10,000 invested five years ago: **$ 3,308**

Dividend Data

Dividend payments were suspended in January 2003.

Revenues/Earnings Data Fiscal year ending December 31

Revenues (Million $)

	2004	2003	2002	2001	2000	1999
1Q	1,754	1,968	2,263	2,859	1,825	1,538
2Q	1,093	1,126	2,137	2,237	1,595	1,353
3Q	1,063	1,047	2,579	2,150	2,391	1,488
4Q	—	1,372	1,708	2,351	3,187	1,768
Yr.	—	5,513	8,687	9,597	8,998	6,103

Earnings Per Share ($)

	2004	2003	2002	2001	2000	1999
1Q	-0.06	0.47	0.70	0.85	0.65	0.80
2Q	0.10	-0.08	0.27	0.40	0.71	0.67
3Q	0.29	-0.47	0.07	-2.89	0.49	0.78
4Q	E0.18	-0.22	-3.78	-1.03	-1.44	0.17
Yr.	E0.85	-0.30	-2.99	-2.53	0.36	2.17

Next earnings report expected: early-March Source: S&P, Company Reports
EPS Estimates based on S&P Operating Earnings; historical GAAP earnings are as reported.

CMS Energy Corporation

Recommendation: **SELL** ★ ★ ☆ ☆ ☆   12-Month Target Price: **$8.50** (as of September 15, 2004)

Business Summary October 04, 2004

CMS Energy is the holding company for Consumers Energy (formerly Consumers Power Co.), an electric and gas utility serving Michigan's lower peninsula; and for CMS Enterprises, which is engaged in U.S. and international energy-related businesses.

Contributions by segment in 2003 were: electric utility 46.8% of revenues (30.5% of 2002 revenues, as restated), $419 million operating income ($512 million); gas utility 33.5% (17.5%) and $126 million ($127 million); enterprises 19.7% (52.0%) and $18 million (a loss of $574 million); and other $32 million of operating income ($10 million).

Consumers Energy provides electricity to about 1.75 million customers in 61 of the 68 counties in the lower peninsula of Michigan, and gas to about 1.67 million customers in 54 counties. It has four generating plants, using coal as a fuel source, that accounted for 76.0% of its power generation in 2003 (73.6% in 2002, 85.7% in 2003). The utility owns two nuclear plants: Big Rock, which ceased operating in 1997; and Palisades, which produced 23.2% of its power generation in 2003 (24.2% in 2002, 10.4% in 2001). In May 2001, Consumers transferred its authority to operate Palisades to the Nuclear Management Company, which acts as an agent for the utility.

In May 2002, the company announced that its CMS Marketing and Trading (MST) unit had entered into "round trip" electricity trades involving simultaneous

purchases and sales with the same counterparties at the same price from May 2000 through mid-January 2002. The trades were not recorded for the 2001 fourth quarter, and revenues and expenses for the first three quarters of 2001 were restated to eliminate $3.4 billion of previously reported revenues and expenses. In 2000, the trades represented $1 billion of revenues and expenses.

In February 2004, CMS MST changed its name to CMS Energy Resource Management (ERM). During 2003, the unit sold its wholesale electric power business, a major portion of its wholesale natural gas trading book, and its energy management services businesses. CMS EMR intends to focus on the purchase and sale of energy commodities in support of the CMS Energy's generating facilities.

In 1999, the company acquired Panhandle Eastern Pipeline Co., Trunkline Gas Co., and the Trunkline LNG Co. terminal from Duke Energy, for $2.2 billion, including $300 million of Panhandle debt. In June 2003, CMS sold its Panhandle Cos. and its interstate natural gas pipeline business to Southern Union Panhandle in return for $582 million in cash, the purchaser's assumption of $1.17 billion of debt, and 3 million Southern Union common shares.

Other businesses include CMS Generation, an independent power production company that is reducing its ownership interests to operating projects located in the U.S., the Middle East, and North Africa. In October 2002, CMS sold its CMS Oil and Gas Co. assets for about $232 million.

Company Financials Fiscal Year ending December 31

Per Share Data ($)

(Year Ended December 31)	2003	2002	2001	2000	1999	1998	1997	1996	1995	1994
Tangible Bk. Val.	9.69	7.47	8.11	12.15	13.23	20.30	19.49	17.86	15.94	12.40
Earnings	-0.30	-2.99	-2.53	0.36	2.17	2.22	2.61	2.45	2.27	2.09
S&P Core Earnings	0.25	-3.75	-3.29	NA	NA	NA	NA	NA	NA	NA
Dividends	Nil	1.09	1.46	1.46	1.39	1.26	1.14	1.02	0.90	0.78
Payout Ratio	Nil	NM	NM	NM	64%	57%	44%	42%	40%	37%
Prices - High	10.74	24.80	31.80	32.25	48.43	50.12	44.06	33.75	30.00	25.00
- Low	3.41	5.45	19.49	16.06	30.31	38.75	31.12	27.81	22.62	19.62
P/E Ratio - High	NM	NM	NM	NM	22	23	17	14	13	12
- Low	NM	NM	NM	NM	14	17	12	11	10	9

Income Statement Analysis (Million $)

	2003	2002	2001	2000	1999	1998	1997	1996	1995	1994
Revs.	5,513	8,687	9,597	8,998	6,103	5,141	4,787	4,333	3,890	3,619
Depr.	428	403	530	637	595	484	477	441	416	379
Maint.	226	211	263	298	216	176	174	178	186	192
Fxd. Chgs. Cov.	1.23	0.12	1.26	1.63	1.73	1.75	2.28	2.32	2.13	2.13
Constr. Credits	NA	NA	NA	NA	Nil	Nil	16.0	8.00	8.00	6.00
Eff. Tax Rate	NM	NM	NM	57.7%	18.8%	29.2%	30.4%	36.7%	36.6%	31.2%
Net Inc.	-43.0	-416	-331	41.0	277	242	268	240	204	179
S&P Core Earnings	40.6	-522	-431	NA	NA	NA	NA	NA	NA	NA

Balance Sheet & Other Fin. Data (Million $)

	2003	2002	2001	2000	1999	1998	1997	1996	1995	1994
Gross Prop.	11,790	11,344	15,195	14,087	14,278	11,253	10,705	10,147	9,701	9,125
Cap. Exp.	535	747	1,262	1,032	1,124	1,295	711	659	535	575
Net Prop.	6,944	5,234	8,362	7,835	8,121	6,040	5,435	5,280	5,074	4,826
Capitalization:										
LT Debt	8,652	6,399	6,983	7,913	7,075	5,486	3,347	2,945	3,012	2,817
% LT Debt	84.5	85.0	78.7	77.0	74.2	71.2	60.1	58.9	62.3	65.8
Pfd.	Nil	Nil	Nil	Nil	Nil	Nil	238	356	356	356
% Pfd.	Nil	Nil	Nil	Nil	Nil	Nil	4.28	7.10	7.30	8.30
Common	1,585	1,133	1,890	2,361	2,456	2,216	1,977	1,702	1,469	1,107
% Common	15.5	15.0	21.3	23.0	25.8	28.8	35.5	34.0	30.4	25.9
Total Cap.	11,010	8,058	9,834	11,221	10,359	8,486	6,456	5,962	5,648	5,043
% Oper. Ratio	91.5	92.1	89.6	88.9	84.7	86.9	86.9	87.6	87.8	88.9
% Earn. on Net Prop.	8.1	1.8	3.7	9.1	12.9	13.5	13.9	13.1	9.6	8.5
% Return On Revs.	NM	NM	NM	0.5	4.5	4.7	5.6	5.5	5.2	4.9
% Return On Invest. Capital	6.7	7.9	9.4	9.5	10.0	12.0	9.9	11.5	8.9	8.7
% Return On Com. Equity	NM	NM	NM	1.7	11.9	11.5	14.6	15.1	15.8	17.3

Data as orig reptd.; bef. results of disc opers/spec. items. Per share data adj. for stk. divs. Bold denotes primary EPS - prior periods restated. E-Estimated. NA-Not Available. NM-Not Meaningful. NR-Not Ranked. UR-Under Review.

Office: 1 Energy Plaza Dr, Jackson, MI 49201-2357.
Telephone: 517-788-0550.
Email: invest@cmsenergy.com
Website: http://www.cmsenergy.com
Chrmn & CEO: K. Whipple.
Pres & COO: D.W. Joos.
Vice Chrmn & General Counsel: S.K. Smith, Jr.

EVP & CFO: T.J. Webb.
VP & Chief Acctg Officer: G.P. Barba.
VP, Treas & Investor Contact: L.L. Mountcastle 517-788-2590.
Dirs: M. S. Ayres, J. J. Duderstadt, K. R. Flaherty, E. D. Holton, D. W. Joos, M. T. Monahan, J. F. Paquette, Jr., W. U. Parfet, P. A. Pierre, S. K. Smith, Jr., K. L. Way, K. Whipple, J. B. Yasinsky.

Auditor: Ernst & Young.
Founded: in 1987.
Domicile: Michigan.
Employees: 8,411.
S&P Analyst: Justin McCann/MF/GG

Recommendation: **BUY** ★★★★☆
SELL SELL HOLD BUY BUY

12-Month Target Price: **$50.00**
(as of August 03, 2004)

COH has an approximate 0.08% weighting in the **S&P 500**

Sector: Consumer Discretionary
Sub-Industry: Apparel, Accessories & Luxury Goods
Peer Group: Leather Goods and Accessories

Summary: COH designs, makes and markets accessories for men and women, including handbags, luggage and travel accessories, leather outerwear, gloves and scarves.

Quantitative Evaluations

S&P Earnings & Dividend Rank: NR

D	C	B-	B	B+	A-	A	A+

S&P Fair Value Rank: 5

1	2	3	4	5
Lowest				Highest

Fair Value Calc.: $62.30 (Undervalued)

S&P Investability Quotient Percentile

95%

COH scored higher than 95% of all companies for which an S&P Report is available.

Volatility: Average

Low	Average	High

Technical Evaluation: Bullish
Since 10/04, the technical indicators for COH have been Bullish.

Relative Strength Rank: Strong

78

1 Lowest		Highest 99

Price as of 11/12/04: $48.35 | **2005E S&P Core EPS: $1.54**

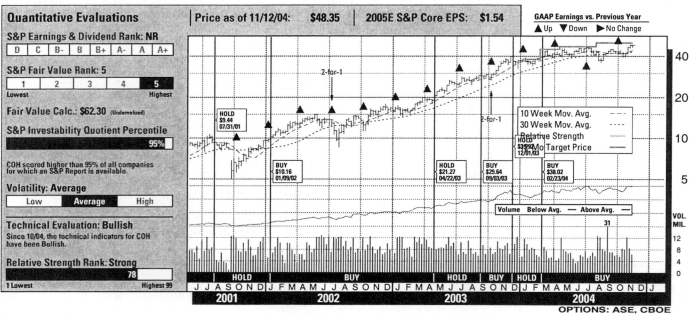

Analyst commentary prepared by Marie Driscoll, CFA /CB/GG

OPTIONS: ASE, CBOE

Highlights August 13, 2004

- We continue to see ample opportunities for Coach as it further penetrates the estimated $3.8 billion domestic market for luxury handbags and small leather goods with its emphasis on frequent new product flow and new usage occasions. Potential abounds with the Japanese luxury consumer as well, where we see Coach doubling its share of the market from about 6% at present to about 12% by 2010. We see FY 05 (Jun.) net sales growing about 23%, to $1.6 billion, driven by store expansion, a high single digit increase in same-store sales for U.S. retail locations, a slightly slower same-store sales gain in Japan, reflecting increased travel by this demographic, and product diversification.

- We expect EBIT (earnings before interest and taxes) margins to widen, on continued diversification into mixed-material collections, sold at the same price levels as all-leather items; introduction of more sophisticated styles at higher price points; sourcing cost initiatives; a favorable channel mix; and improved expense leverage.

- With modest share dilution expected, we see FY 05 operating EPS climbing 25%, to $1.70, from $1.36. We project Standard & Poor's Core Earnings of $1.54 a share for FY 05, reflecting $0.16 of projected option expense.

Key Stock Statistics

S&P Oper. EPS 2005E	**1.80**	52-week Range	**$48.80-32.50**
P/E on S&P Oper. EPS 2005E	**26.9**	12 Month P/E	**32.5**
Yield (%)	**Nil**	Beta	**NA**
Dividend Rate/Share	**Nil**	Shareholders	**NA**
Shares Outstanding (M)	**188.6**	Market Cap (B)	**$ 9.1**

Value of $10,000 invested five years ago: **NA**

Dividend Data

No cash dividends have been paid.

Investment Rationale/Risk August 13, 2004

- We would accumulate the stock. We see favorable sales and earnings prospects, and think the stock warrants a premium valuation to peers. Same-store sales were up 16.9% in FY 04, with retail ahead 21.9% and factory stores 10.3% higher. We see continued momentum in autumn 2004, as we expect product diversification to draw new customers to Coach stores, while also appealing to loyal consumers. We think increased store traffic and purchases at higher average price points will support growing sales and earnings momentum. We expect EPS to increase at a five-year compound annual rate of 25%.

- Risks to our recommendation and target price include changes in consumer spending, access to sourcing, fashions, and inventory risk.

- The stock traded recently at 19X our calendar 2005 operating EPS estimate of $2.00, a 36% premium to specialty apparel retail peers, and a 32% premium to the S&P MidCap 400. We applied a P/E multiple of 25X, which is our three- to five-year projected EPS growth rate, to our calendar 2005 EPS estimate of $2.00 to arrive at our 12-month target price of $50.

Revenues/Earnings Data Fiscal year ending June 30

Revenues (Million $)

	2005	2004	2003	2002	2001	2000
1Q	344.1	258.4	192.8	150.7	134.6	—
2Q	—	411.5	308.5	235.8	214.2	—
3Q	—	313.1	220.4	161.6	130.6	—
4Q	—	338.1	231.5	171.4	136.8	—
Yr.	—	1,321	953.2	719.4	616.1	548.9

Earnings Per Share ($)

	2005	2004	2003	2002	2001	2000
1Q	0.35	0.22	0.12	0.07	0.04	—
2Q	E0.65	0.50	0.34	0.25	0.22	—
3Q	E0.37	0.30	0.17	0.07	0.05	—
4Q	E0.43	0.34	0.16	0.10	0.05	—
Yr.	E1.80	1.36	0.79	0.47	0.38	0.21

Next earnings report expected: late-January Source: S&P, Company Reports
EPS Estimates based on S&P Operating Earnings; historical GAAP earnings are as reported.

Coach, Inc.

Recommendation: **BUY** ★★★★☆   12-Month Target Price: **$50.00** (as of August 03, 2004)

Business Summary August 17, 2004

Over the past several years, Coach has transformed the Coach brand, building on its popular core categories by introducing new products in a broader array of materials, styles and categories. The company has also implemented a flexible sourcing and manufacturing model, enabling it to bring a broader range of products to market more rapidly and efficiently.

Primary product offerings include handbags, men's and women's accessories, business cases, luggage and travel accessories, personal planning products, leather outerwear, gloves and scarves. The company also offers watches, foot-wear, home and office furniture, and eyewear under its brand name through licensing agreements. COH launches new handbags and accessories in the fall and spring.

COH sells its products through direct to consumer and indirect channels, with the former accounting for 59% of total sales in FY 03 (Jun.), down from 62% in FY 02. At June 30, 2003, direct to consumer channels included 156 U.S. retail stores, direct mail catalogs, the company's online store, and 76 U.S. factory stores. Indirect channels included 1,400 U.S. department store and specialty retailer locations; 107 international department store, retail store and duty free shop locations in 18 countries; 93 retail and department store locations operated by Coach Japan, Inc.; and corporate sales programs.

International wholesale revenues accounted for 6% of revenue in FY 03. In June 2001, the company and Sumitomo Corp. formed a joint venture, Coach Japan, Inc. (CJI), to manage the Coach business in Japan. CJI acquired 63 Coach retail and department store locations from the Mitsukoshi Department Store Group in July 2001, for $9.0 million, and an additional 13 locations from J. Osawa and Co., Ltd. in January 2002 for $5.8 million. CJI accounted for about 18% of FY 03 net sales.

In July 2002, COH signed an agreement with Case London Ltd. for the exclusive distribution of Coach products in the U.K. and Ireland. Case also assumed the responsibility of operating the existing Coach store on Sloane Street, and the Coach shop in Harrods in London.

The company is pursuing five strategies aimed at strengthening its leadership position and building lasting market share. COH is modernizing retail presentation (including store remodels); opening at least 20 new U.S. stores a year in each of FY 04 and FY 05, bringing its retail store base to 156; expanding its presence in international markets; improving operational efficiencies; and emphasizing new usage occasions for its products.

In September 2001, directors authorized the repurchase of up to $80 million of common stock through September 2004. In January 2003, directors authorized the purchase of up to an additional $100 million of stock through January 2006, and the existing program was also extended through January 2006. At March 27, 2004, about $65 million remained available under the program.

Company Financials Fiscal Year ending June 30

Per Share Data ($)

(Year Ended June 30)	2004	2003	2002	2001	2000	1999	1998	1997	1996	1995
Tangible Bk. Val.	4.00	2.21	1.33	0.85	0.71	NA	NA	NA	NA	NA
Cash Flow	1.58	0.95	0.61	0.49	0.33	NA	NA	NA	NA	NA
Earnings	1.36	0.79	0.47	0.38	0.21	NA	NA	NA	NA	NA
S&P Core Earnings	1.22	0.70	0.41	0.35	NA	NA	NA	NA	NA	NA
Dividends	Nil	Nil	Nil	Nil	Nil	NA	NA	NA	NA	NA
Payout Ratio	Nil	Nil	Nil	Nil	Nil	NA	NA	NA	NA	NA
Prices - High	48.80	40.84	17.85	10.68	7.34	NA	NA	NA	NA	NA
- Low	33.75	14.51	8.59	5.00	4.00	NA	NA	NA	NA	NA
P/E Ratio - High	36	52	38	28	36	NA	NA	NA	NA	NA
- Low	25	18	18	13	20	NA	NA	NA	NA	NA

Income Statement Analysis (Million $)

	2004	2003	2002	2001	2000	1999	1998	1997	1996	1995
Revs.	1,321	953	719	616	549	NA	NA	NA	NA	NA
Oper. Inc.	487	274	163	130	77.0	NA	NA	NA	NA	NA
Depr.	42.9	30.2	25.5	24.1	22.6	NA	NA	NA	NA	NA
Int. Exp.	0.81	0.69	1.12	2.26	6.00	NA	NA	NA	NA	NA
Pretax Inc.	448	245	133	99	49.9	NA	NA	NA	NA	NA
Eff. Tax Rate	37.5%	37.0%	35.5%	35.6%	29.5%	NA	NA	NA	NA	NA
Net Inc.	262	147	85.8	64.0	35.2	NA	NA	NA	NA	NA
S&P Core Earnings	236	129	74.9	58.3	NA	NA	NA	NA	NA	NA

Balance Sheet & Other Fin. Data (Million $)

	2004	2003	2002	2001	2000	1999	1998	1997	1996	1995
Cash	263	229	94.0	3.69	Nil	NA	NA	NA	NA	NA
Curr. Assets	706	449	288	152	154	NA	NA	NA	NA	NA
Total Assets	1,029	618	441	259	252	NA	NA	NA	NA	NA
Curr. Liab.	182	161	159	104	104	NA	NA	NA	NA	NA
LT Debt	3.42	Nil	3.62	3.69	17.8	NA	NA	NA	NA	NA
Common Equity	782	427	260	148	128	NA	NA	NA	NA	NA
Total Cap.	842	449	279	152	146	NA	NA	NA	NA	NA
Cap. Exp.	67.7	57.1	42.8	31.9	NA	NA	NA	NA	NA	NA
Cash Flow	305	177	111	88.2	57.7	NA	NA	NA	NA	NA
Curr. Ratio	3.9	2.8	1.8	1.5	1.5	NA	NA	NA	NA	NA
% LT Debt of Cap.	0.4	Nil	1.3	2.4	12.2	NA	NA	NA	NA	NA
% Net Inc.of Revs.	19.8	15.4	11.9	10.4	6.4	NA	NA	NA	NA	NA
% Ret. on Assets	31.8	27.7	24.5	23.1	NA	NA	NA	NA	NA	NA
% Ret. on Equity	43.3	42.7	42.0	35.5	NA	NA	NA	NA	NA	NA

Data as orig reptd.; bef. results of disc opers/spec. items. Per share data adj. for stk. divs.; EPS diluted. Pro forma data in 2000, balance sheet & book value as of Dec. 20, 2000. E-Estimated. NA-Not Available. NM-Not Meaningful. NR-Not Ranked.

Office: 516 West 34th Street, New York, NY 10001-1394.
Telephone: 212-594-1850.
Email: info@coach.com
Website: http://www.coach.com
Chrmn & CEO: L. Frankfort.
Pres & COO: K. Monda.

SVP, CFO & Chief Acctg Officer: M. Devine.
SVP, Secy & General Counsel: C. Sadler.
Investor Contact: A. Shaw Resnick 212-629-2618.
Dirs: J. Ellis, L. Frankfort, S. F. Kasaks, G. Loveman, I. Miller, K. Monda, M. Murphy.

Founded: in 1941.
Domicile: Maryland.
Employees: 4,200.
S&P Analyst: Marie Driscoll, CFA /CB/GG

Recommendation: **HOLD** ★ ★ ★ ★
SELL SELL HOLD BUY BUY
12-Month Target Price: **$44.00**
(as of September 15, 2004)

KO has an approximate 0.90% weighting in the **S&P 500**

Sector: Consumer Staples
Sub-Industry: Soft Drinks
Peer Group: Soft Drinks

Summary: Coca-Cola is the world's largest soft drink company and has a sizable fruit juice business. Its bottling interests include a 40% stake in NYSE-listed Coca-Cola Enterprises.

Quantitative Evaluations

S&P Earnings & Dividend Rank: B+

D	C	B-	B	B+	A-	A	A+

S&P Fair Value Rank: 2+

1	2	3	4	5
Lowest				Highest

Fair Value Calc.: $37.60 (Slightly Overvalued)

S&P Investability Quotient Percentile

91%

KO scored higher than 91% of all companies for which an S&P Report is available.

Volatility: Low

Low	Average	High

Technical Evaluation: Neutral

Since 10/04, the technical indicators for KO have been Neutral.

Relative Strength Rank: Weak

20

1 Lowest	Highest 99

Price as of 11/12/04: $40.79 | **2004E S&P Core EPS:** $1.99

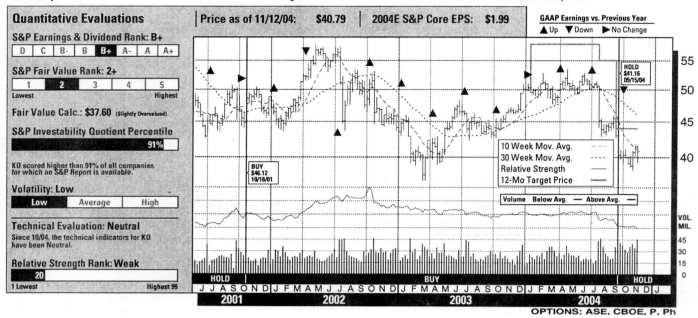

GAAP Earnings vs. Previous Year
▲ Up ▼ Down ▶ No Change

- 10 Week Mov. Avg.
- 30 Week Mov. Avg.
- Relative Strength
- 12-Mo Target Price

Volume Below Avg. — Above Avg.

OPTIONS: ASE, CBOE, P, Ph

Analyst commentary prepared by Richard Joy/CB/BK

Highlights September 24, 2004

- We see net sales rising about 5% in 2004, reflecting 1% to 2% higher worldwide volumes, higher concentrate prices, and favorable foreign currency exchange. Volume growth is expected to be restricted by poor weather in Europe and higher retail prices in the U.S. Operating profits should benefit from operating efficiencies and a focus on more profitable products and packaging, but increased promotional spending could be an offset. We believe equity income will decline moderately, reflecting sluggish operating results at Coca-Cola Enterprises and other bottlers. Strong free cash flows should allow the company to continue to aggressively repurchase shares.

- Based on our estimate for an increase in the effective tax rate and a 1% to 2% reduction in KO's shares outstanding, we expect EPS of $2.00 in 2004, up 3% from operating EPS of $1.95 in 2003. Our EPS estimate for 2004 includes an estimated $0.13 for stock option expense, but excludes a $0.10 to $0.11 impairment charge that KO plans to take in the third quarter. For 2005, we project a 10% rise to $2.20. Longer term, we expect annual EPS growth of 8%-10%.

- Our 2004 and 2005 Standard & Poor's Core Earnings per share projections, reflecting a modest pension plan adjustment, are $1.99 and $2.19, respectively.

Key Stock Statistics

S&P Core EPS 2005E	2.19	52-week Range	$53.50-38.30	
S&P Oper. EPS 2004E	2.00	12 Month P/E	21.7	
P/E on S&P Oper. EPS 2004E	20.4	Beta	0.29	
S&P Oper. EPS 2005E	2.08	Shareholders	348,768	
Yield (%)	2.5%	Market Cap (B)	$ 98.7	
Dividend Rate/Share	1.00	Shares Outstanding (M)	2419.4	

Value of $10,000 invested five years ago: **$ 7,735**

Dividend Data Dividends have been paid since 1893

Amount ($)	Date Decl.	Ex-Div. Date	Stock of Record	Payment Date
0.250	Feb. 19	Mar. 11	Mar. 15	Apr. 01 '04
0.250	Apr. 21	Jun. 14	Jun. 15	Jul. 01 '04
0.250	Jul. 22	Sep. 13	Sep. 15	Oct. 01 '04
0.250	Oct. 21	Nov. 29	Dec. 01	Dec. 15 '04

Investment Rationale/Risk September 24, 2004

- We recently lowered our recommendation on the shares to hold, from accumulate, reflecting challenging conditions in several key markets. We believe the challenges facing Coca-Cola's global businesses will take longer than we originally expected to fix, and the company is likely to reduce its long-term growth targets when it presents its new growth strategy in mid-November. Even with lowered operating income growth targets, we believe the company will continue to generate strong free cash flows. Despite trading recently at more than 18X our 2005 EPS estimate, a premium to the S&P 500, we view the shares as a worthwhile holding, given our view of KO's strong free cash flow generation and long-term growth potential.

- Risks to our recommendation and target price include a rise in competitive pressures for KO's beverage businesses, an inability to meet volume and revenue growth targets, and unfavorable weather conditions in the company's markets.

- Our analysis of discounted free cash flows, using a weighted average cost of capital of 9%, suggests an intrinsic value for the shares in the high $40s to low $50s. However, we believe near-term share price appreciation will be limited until evidence emerges that the company can generate sustainable volume and earnings growth. We have a 12-month target price of $44, which we derive from our analysis of discounted free cash flow and relative P/E multiples.

Revenues/Earnings Data Fiscal year ending December 31

Revenues (Million $)

	2004	2003	2002	2001	2000	1999
1Q	5,078	4,502	4,079	4,479	4,391	4,428
2Q	5,965	5,695	5,368	5,293	5,621	5,379
3Q	5,662	5,671	5,322	5,397	5,543	5,195
4Q	—	5,176	4,795	4,923	4,903	4,931
Yr.	—	21,044	19,564	20,092	20,458	19,805

Earnings Per Share ($)

	2004	2003	2002	2001	2000	1999
1Q	0.46	0.34	0.32	0.35	-0.02	0.30
2Q	0.65	0.55	0.52	0.45	0.37	0.38
3Q	0.39	0.50	0.47	0.43	0.43	0.32
4Q	E0.40	0.38	0.38	0.37	0.10	-0.02
Yr.	E2.00	1.77	1.60	1.60	0.88	0.98

Next earnings report expected: mid-February Source: S&P, Company Reports
EPS Estimates based on S&P Operating Earnings; historical GAAP earnings are as reported.

Recommendation: **HOLD** ★ ★ ★ ☆ ☆   12-Month Target Price: **$44.00** (as of September 15, 2004)

Business Summary September 24, 2004

The Coca-Cola Company is the world's largest producer of soft drink concentrates and syrups, as well as the world's largest producer of juice and juice-related products. Finished soft drink products bearing the company's trademarks have been sold in the U.S. since 1886, and are now sold in nearly 200 countries. Sales and operating profit (before accounting for intercompany sales and corporate overhead) in 2003 by geographic region were distributed as follows: North America (30.5% of revenues, 20% of profits); Europe, Eurasia and Middle East (31.5%, 32%); Latin America (10%, 16%); Asia (24%, 28%); and Africa (4%, 4%).

The company's business, which is extremely focused, encompasses the production and sale of soft drink and non-carbonated beverage concentrates and syrups. These products are sold to the company's authorized independent and company-owned bottling/canning operations, and fountain wholesalers. These customers then either combine the syrup with carbonated water, or combine the concentrate with sweetener, water and carbonated water to produce finished soft drinks. The finished soft drinks are packaged in authorized containers bearing the company's well-known trademarks, which include Coca-Cola (best-selling soft drink in the world, including Coca-Cola classic), caffeine free Coca-Cola (classic), diet Coke (sold as Coke light in many markets outside the U.S.), Cherry Coke, diet Cherry Coke, diet Coke with lemon, Vanilla Coke, diet Vanilla Coke, Fanta, Sprite, diet Sprite, Barq's, Surge, Mr. PiBB, Mello Yello, TAB, Fresca, PowerAde, Minute Maid, Hi-C, Fruitopia, and other products developed for specific markets, including

Georgia ready-to-drink coffees. The company also markets the Schweppes and Canada Dry mixer (such as tonic water, club soda and ginger ale), Crush and Dr. Pepper brands in more than 160 countries outside of the U.S. KO has equity positions in approximately 52 unconsolidated bottling, canning and distribution operations for its products worldwide, including bottlers that accounted for approximately 58% of the company's worldwide unit case volume in 2003.

In June 2002, KO entered into a partnership agreement with Groupe Danone for the production, marketing and distribution of Danone's retail bottled spring and source water business in the U.S. In addition to a $128 million cash payment for a 51% interest in the partnership, KO will provide marketing, distribution and management expertise.

KO typically enters into forward exchange contracts, and purchases currency options (principally European currencies and Japanese yen) to reduce the risk that its eventual dollar net cash inflows resulting from sales outside the U.S. will be adversely affected by changes in exchange rates. Foreign currency exposures are managed on a consolidated basis, which allows the company to net certain exposures and take advantage of natural offsets. With approximately 76% of 2003 operating income before corporate expenses generated outside of North America, weakness in one particular currency is often offset by strength in others over time.

Company Financials Fiscal Year ending December 31

Per Share Data ($)

(Year Ended December 31)	2003	2002	2001	2000	1999	1998	1997	1996	1995	1994
Tangible Bk. Val.	4.14	3.34	3.53	2.98	3.06	3.19	2.67	2.18	1.78	1.80
Cash Flow	2.11	1.93	1.92	1.19	1.30	1.67	1.89	1.59	1.36	1.14
Earnings	1.77	1.60	1.60	0.88	0.98	1.42	1.64	1.40	1.19	0.99
S&P Core Earnings	1.77	1.62	1.46	NA	NA	NA	NA	NA	NA	NA
Dividends	0.88	0.80	0.72	0.68	0.64	0.60	0.56	0.50	0.44	0.39
Payout Ratio	50%	50%	45%	77%	65%	42%	34%	36%	37%	39%
Prices - High	50.90	57.91	62.18	66.87	70.87	88.93	72.62	54.25	40.18	26.75
- Low	37.01	42.90	42.37	42.87	47.31	53.62	51.12	36.06	24.37	19.43
P/E Ratio - High	29	36	39	76	72	63	44	39	34	27
- Low	21	27	26	49	48	38	31	26	21	20

Income Statement Analysis (Million $)

	2003	2002	2001	2000	1999	1998	1997	1996	1995	1994
Revs.	21,044	19,564	20,092	20,458	19,805	18,813	18,868	18,546	18,018	16,172
Oper. Inc.	6,071	6,264	6,155	8,155	4,774	5,612	5,627	4,394	4,546	4,090
Depr.	850	806	803	773	792	645	626	479	454	382
Int. Exp.	178	199	289	447	337	277	258	286	272	199
Pretax Inc.	5,495	5,499	5,670	3,399	3,819	5,198	6,055	4,596	4,328	3,728
Eff. Tax Rate	20.9%	27.7%	29.8%	36.0%	36.3%	32.0%	31.8%	24.0%	31.0%	31.5%
Net Inc.	4,347	3,976	3,979	2,177	2,431	3,533	4,129	3,492	2,986	2,554
S&P Core Earnings	4,350	4,021	3,654	NA	NA	NA	NA	NA	NA	NA

Balance Sheet & Other Fin. Data (Million $)

	2003	2002	2001	2000	1999	1998	1997	1996	1995	1994
Cash	3,482	2,345	1,934	1,892	1,812	1,807	1,737	1,658	1,315	1,531
Curr. Assets	8,396	7,352	7,171	6,620	6,480	6,380	5,969	5,910	5,450	5,205
Total Assets	27,342	24,501	22,417	20,834	21,623	19,145	16,940	16,161	15,041	13,873
Curr. Liab.	7,886	7,341	8,429	9,321	9,856	8,640	7,379	7,416	7,348	6,177
LT Debt	2,517	2,701	1,219	835	854	687	801	1,116	1,141	1,426
Common Equity	14,090	11,800	11,366	9,316	9,513	8,403	7,311	6,156	5,392	5,235
Total Cap.	16,944	14,900	13,027	10,509	10,865	9,514	8,560	7,573	6,727	6,841
Cap. Exp.	812	851	769	733	1,069	863	1,093	990	937	878
Cash Flow	5,197	4,782	4,782	2,950	3,223	4,178	4,755	3,971	3,440	2,936
Curr. Ratio	1.1	1.0	0.9	0.7	0.7	0.7	0.8	0.8	0.7	0.8
% LT Debt of Cap.	14.9	18.1	9.4	7.9	7.9	7.2	9.4	14.7	17.0	20.8
% Net Inc.of Revs.	20.7	20.3	19.8	10.6	12.3	18.8	21.9	18.8	16.6	15.8
% Ret. on Assets	16.8	16.9	18.4	10.3	11.9	19.6	24.9	22.4	20.7	19.9
% Ret. on Equity	33.6	34.3	38.5	23.1	27.1	45.0	61.3	60.5	56.2	52.4

Data as orig reptd.; bef. results of disc opers/spec. items. Per share data adj. for stk. divs.; EPS diluted. E-Estimated. NA-Not Available. NM-Not Meaningful. NR-Not Ranked. UR-Under Review.

Office: One Coca-Cola Plaza NW, Atlanta, GA 30313-2499.
Telephone: 404-676-2121.
Website: http://www.coca-cola.com
Chrmn & CEO: E.N. Isdell.
Pres & COO: S.J. Heyer.
EVP & CFO: G.P. Fayard.

EVP, Secy & General Counsel: D.L. Patrick.
Investor Contact: B. Deutsch 404-676-2121.
Dirs: R. W. Allen, H. A. Allen, C. P. Black, W. E. Buffett, B. Diller, E. N. Isdell, D. Keogh, S. B. King, M. E. Lagomasino, D. F. McHenry, R. L. Nardelli, S. Nunn, J. P. Reinhard, J. D. Robinson III, P. V. Ueberroth, J. B. Williams.

Founded: in 1886.
Domicile: Delaware.
Employees: 49,000.
S&P Analyst: Richard Joy/CB/BK

Coca-Cola Enterprises

Recommendation: **HOLD** ★ ★ ★ ☆ ☆
SELL SELL HOLD BUY BUY

12-Month Target Price: $21.00
(as of September 08, 2004)

CCE has an approximate 0.09% weighting in the **S&P 500**

Sector: Consumer Staples
Sub-Industry: Soft Drinks
Peer Group: Soft Drink Bottlers

Summary: This company is the world's largest bottler of Coca-Cola beverage products, distributing to about 79% of the North American market. Coca-Cola Co. holds 37% of CCE's common stock.

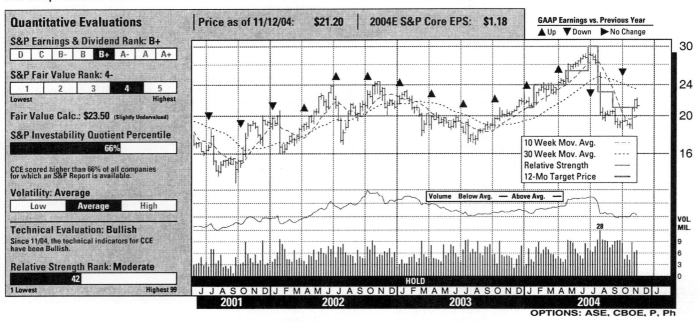

Price as of 11/12/04: $21.20 | **2004E S&P Core EPS:** $1.18

Quantitative Evaluations

S&P Earnings & Dividend Rank: B+
D | C | B- | B | B+ | A- | A | A+

S&P Fair Value Rank: 4-
1 | 2 | 3 | 4 | 5
Lowest | | | | Highest

Fair Value Calc.: $23.50 (Slightly Undervalued)

S&P Investability Quotient Percentile
66%
CCE scored higher than 66% of all companies for which an S&P Report is available.

Volatility: Average
Low | Average | High

Technical Evaluation: Bullish
Since 11/04, the technical indicators for CCE have been Bullish.

Relative Strength Rank: Moderate
42
1 Lowest | Highest 99

GAAP Earnings vs. Previous Year
▲ Up ▼ Down ▶ No Change

10 Week Mov. Avg.
30 Week Mov. Avg.
Relative Strength
12-Mo Target Price

Volume Below Avg. — Above Avg. —

OPTIONS: ASE, CBOE, P, Ph

Analyst commentary prepared by Richard Joy/MF/JWP

Highlights August 19, 2004

- We expect net revenues in 2004 to advance 6% to 7%, reflecting consolidated bottle and can unit case volume growth of less than 1%, a 2% to 3% increase in net revenues per case, and a positive impact from foreign currency translations. We expect North American volumes to gain 1% to 2%, while European volumes will likely decline at a low single digit rate. Operating margins could see some benefit from a continued product mix shift toward "cold channel" sales, modestly higher pricing, and restructuring savings, with modestly higher sweetener and packaging costs as offsets. SG&A expenses will likely increase as a percentage of sales, due to higher pension and fuel costs.

- Following modestly lower interest expense, due to lower interest rates and debt levels, we estimate that 2004 EPS will advance 7%, to $1.39, from operating EPS of $1.30 in 2003. For 2005, we expect an 11.5% increase to $1.55. We see EBITDA rising to $2.75 billion in 2004, from $2.6 billion in 2003.

- Our 2004 and 2005 Standard & Poor's Core Earnings per share projections, reflecting estimated stock option expense of $0.13 per share and an adjustment for estimated pension costs, are $1.18 and $1.36, respectively.

Investment Rationale/Risk August 19, 2004

- We have a hold recommendation on the shares, as our outlook for pricing gains and near-term profit improvement are balanced by our expectation for sluggish volume trends in 2004. In addition to pricing gains, near-term profitability should benefit from a relatively weak U.S. dollar and low interest rates. The shares were recently trading at 13X our 2005 EPS estimate, a discount to the S&P 500 and comparable peers. However, given the poor volume trends for CCE's North American and European businesses, we believe the stock is likely to continue to trade with this discount until volume and earnings growth trends improve. The company's debt load is relatively high, but we believe CCE's finances are sound, reflecting strong cash generation capability and implicit credit backing by The Coca-Cola Co.

- Risks to our recommendation and target price relate to competitive pressures in CCE's markets, consumer acceptance of new product introductions, and the company's ability to achieve sales and earnings growth forecasts.

- Our 12-month target price of $23 is based on our analysis of peer P/E and EV/EBITDA multiples, and our discounted cash flow model, which assumes a weighed average cost of capital of 8.5% and a terminal growth rate of 3%.

Key Stock Statistics

S&P Core EPS 2005E	1.36	52-week Range	$29.34-18.45
S&P Oper. EPS 2004E	1.28	12 Month P/E	15.4
P/E on S&P Oper. EPS 2004E	16.6	Beta	0.03
S&P Oper. EPS 2005E	1.40	Shareholders	15,257
Yield (%)	0.8%	Market Cap (B)	$ 9.9
Dividend Rate/Share	0.16	Shares Outstanding (M)	469.2

Value of $10,000 invested five years ago: **$ 9,933**

Dividend Data Dividends have been paid since 1986

Amount ($)	Date Decl.	Ex-Div. Date	Stock of Record	Payment Date
0.040	Feb. 17	Mar. 17	Mar. 19	Apr. 01 '04
0.040	Apr. 27	Jun. 16	Jun. 18	Jul. 01 '04
0.040	Jul. 27	Sep. 16	Sep. 20	Oct. 01 '04
0.040	Oct. 26	Dec. 01	Dec. 03	Dec. 15 '04

Revenues/Earnings Data Fiscal year ending December 31

Revenues (Million $)

	2004	2003	2002	2001	2000	1999
1Q	4,240	3,667	3,642	3,352	3,293	3,269
2Q	4,844	4,617	4,448	4,105	4,027	3,797
3Q	4,670	4,734	4,549	4,276	3,868	3,831
4Q	—	4,312	4,249	3,967	3,561	3,509
Yr.	—	17,330	16,889	15,700	14,750	14,406

Earnings Per Share ($)

	2004	2003	2002	2001	2000	1999
1Q	0.22	0.06	0.02	-0.24	-0.08	-0.15
2Q	0.43	0.56	0.47	0.24	0.29	0.08
3Q	0.44	0.56	0.42	0.02	0.30	0.24
4Q	E0.14	0.28	0.17	-0.08	0.04	-0.04
Yr.	E1.28	1.48	1.07	-0.05	0.54	0.13

Next earnings report expected: late-January Source: S&P, Company Reports
EPS Estimates based on S&P Operating Earnings; historical GAAP earnings are as reported.

Coca-Cola Enterprises Inc.

Recommendation: **HOLD** ★ ★ ★ ☆ ☆   12-Month Target Price: **$21.00** (as of September 08, 2004)

Business Summary August 19, 2004

Coca-Cola Enterprises is the world's largest bottler of Coca-Cola beverage products, distributing approximately 79% of all bottle/can volume of carbonated soft-drink products of The Coca-Cola Co. (KO) in North America. KO owns approximately 37% of the company's common stock. CCE's product line also includes other nonalcoholic beverages, such as still and sparkling waters, juices, isotonics and teas. In 2003, the company sold approximately 43 billion bottles and cans throughout its territories, representing approximately 21% of The Coca-Cola Company's worldwide volume. About 93% of this volume consisted of beverages produced and sold under licenses from The Coca-Cola Company. CCE also distributes Dr Pepper and several other beverage brands.

Based on net operating revenues in 2003, North America accounted for 73% of total revenues, and Europe for 27%. CCE operates in parts of 46 states in the U.S., the District of Columbia, all 10 Canadian provinces, and portions of Europe including Belgium, France, the U.K., Luxembourg, Monaco and the Netherlands. As of December 31, 2003, CCE bottling territories encompassed a population of 405 million people. The company's top five brands in North America in 2003 were Coca-Cola classic, caffeine free diet Coke, Dasani, Diet Coke and Sprite, while the top five brands in Europe were Coca-Cola, diet Coke/Coke light, Fanta, Schweppes and Sprite.

The company conducts its business primarily under bottle contracts with KO. CCE

has the exclusive right to produce and market Coca-Cola soft drinks in authorized containers in specified territories; KO has the ability, in its sole discretion, to set prices for concentrates and syrups. At 2003 year end, CCE operated 440 production and distribution facilities, 54,000 vehicles, and approximately 2.5 million coolers, beverage dispensers and vending machines used to market, distribute and produce the company's products.

The company continues to aggressively pursue independently owned bottling operations, facilitating the rapid consolidation of the Coca-Cola bottling system. In July 2001, the company acquired Hondo Inc. and Herbco Enterprises, Inc. (collectively known as Herb Coca-Cola), for total consideration of $1.4 billion. The company also acquired Southwest Dr. Pepper Bottling Company in August 2001, and Tarpon Springs Coca-Cola Bottling Company in October 2001. The total cost of all the company's acquisitions since 1986 is approximately $14.6 billion (including assumed and issued debt).

The company expects capital spending to be approximately $1.15 billion in 2004, within its targeted range of 6% of anticipated revenues. Capital spending in 2003 totaled $1.1 billion. The company intends to use the majority of excess operating cash flow for debt reduction purposes.

Company Financials Fiscal Year ending December 31

Per Share Data ($)

(Year Ended December 31)	2003	2002	2001	2000	1999	1998	1997	1996	1995	1994
Tangible Bk. Val.	NM	NM	6.25	6.67	6.83	6.08	4.61	3.75	3.64	3.38
Cash Flow	3.88	3.35	3.08	3.48	3.22	3.11	2.82	1.98	1.58	1.35
Earnings	1.48	1.07	-0.05	0.54	0.13	0.35	0.43	0.28	0.21	0.17
S&P Core Earnings	1.22	0.78	-0.34	NA	NA	NA	NA	NA	NA	NA
Dividends	0.16	0.16	0.12	0.16	0.16	0.15	0.08	0.03	0.02	0.02
Payout Ratio	11%	15%	NM	30%	123%	41%	19%	12%	8%	10%
Prices - High	23.30	24.50	23.90	30.25	37.50	41.56	36.00	16.37	9.95	6.50
- Low	16.85	15.94	13.46	14.00	16.81	22.87	15.70	8.00	5.91	4.66
P/E Ratio - High	16	23	NM	56	NM	NM	84	58	48	37
- Low	11	15	NM	26	NM	NM	37	28	29	27

Income Statement Analysis (Million $)

	2003	2002	2001	2000	1999	1998	1997	1996	1995	1994
Revs.	17,330	16,889	15,700	14,750	14,406	13,414	11,278	7,921	6,773	6,011
Oper. Inc.	2,674	2,409	1,954	2,387	2,187	1,989	1,666	1,172	997	901
Depr.	1,097	1,045	1,353	1,261	1,348	1,120	946	627	529	461
Int. Exp.	607	662	753	791	751	703	538	353	333	310
Pretax Inc.	972	705	-150	333	88.0	169	178	194	145	127
Eff. Tax Rate	30.5%	29.9%	NM	29.1%	33.0%	16.0%	3.90%	41.2%	43.4%	45.7%
Net Inc.	676	494	-19.0	236	59.0	142	171	114	82.0	69.0
S&P Core Earnings	563	356	-147	NA	NA	NA	NA	NA	NA	NA

Balance Sheet & Other Fin. Data (Million $)

	2003	2002	2001	2000	1999	1998	1997	1996	1995	1994
Cash	80.0	68.0	284	294	141	68.0	45.0	47.0	8.00	22.0
Curr. Assets	3,000	2,844	2,876	2,631	2,581	2,285	1,813	1,319	982	810
Total Assets	25,700	24,375	23,719	22,162	22,730	21,132	17,487	11,234	9,064	8,738
Curr. Liab.	3,941	3,455	4,522	3,094	3,614	3,397	3,032	1,690	859	1,089
LT Debt	10,552	11,236	10,365	10,348	10,153	9,605	7,760	4,814	4,138	3,896
Common Equity	4,365	3,310	2,783	2,790	2,877	2,389	1,782	1,416	1,405	1,310
Total Cap.	19,882	19,122	17,521	17,956	18,028	16,758	13,538	6,230	7,605	7,119
Cap. Exp.	1,099	1,029	972	1,181	1,480	1,551	967	622	501	366
Cash Flow	1,771	1,536	1,331	1,494	1,404	1,262	1,115	741	611	528
Curr. Ratio	0.8	0.8	0.6	0.9	0.7	0.7	0.6	0.8	1.1	0.7
% LT Debt of Cap.	53.1	58.8	59.2	57.6	56.3	57.3	57.3	77.2	54.4	54.7
% Net Inc.of Revs.	3.9	2.9	NM	1.6	0.4	1.1	1.5	1.4	1.2	1.1
% Ret. on Assets	2.7	2.1	NM	1.1	0.3	0.7	1.2	1.1	0.9	0.8
% Ret. on Equity	17.6	16.1	NM	8.2	2.1	6.8	10.6	8.1	5.9	5.3

Data as orig reptd.; bef. results of disc opers/spec. items. Per share data adj. for stk. divs.; EPS diluted. E-Estimated. NA-Not Available. NM-Not Meaningful. NR-Not Ranked. UR-Under Review.

Office: 2500 Windy Ridge Parkway , Atlanta, GA 30339.
Telephone: 770-989-3000.
Website: http://www.cokecce.com
Chrmn: L.F. Kline.
Pres & CEO: J.R. Alm.
COO & EVP: G.D. Van Houten, Jr.

SVP & General Counsel: J.J. Culhane.
VP & Chief Acctg Officer: R.L. Engum.
VP & Investor Contact: S. Anthony 770-989-3246.
Dirs: J. R. Alm, J. L. Clendenin, J. Copeland, C. Darden, J. T. Eyton, G. P. Fayard, M. J. Herb, S. J. Heyer, J. E. Jacob, S. K. Johnston, Jr., J. Killy, L. F. Kline, D. L. Patrick, P. G. Rosput.

Founded: in 1944.
Domicile: Delaware.
Employees: 74,000.
S&P Analyst: Richard Joy/MF/JWP

Colgate-Palmolive

Recommendation: **HOLD** ★ ★ ★ ☆ ☆
SELL | SELL | HOLD | BUY | BUY

12-Month Target Price: $49.00
(as of October 21, 2004)

CL has an approximate 0.23% weighting in the **S&P 500**

Sector: Consumer Staples
Sub-Industry: Household Products
Peer Group: Household Products

Summary: This major consumer products company markets oral, personal and household care and pet nutrition products in more than 200 countries and territories.

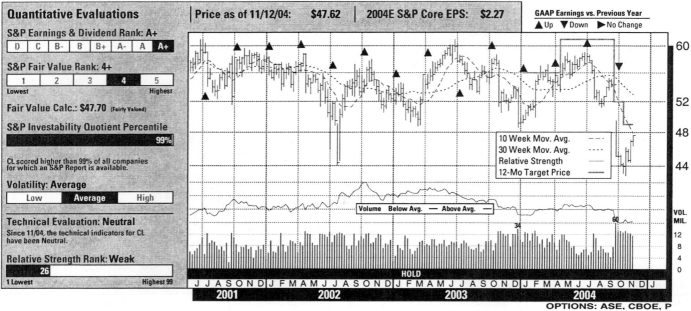

Quantitative Evaluations

Price as of 11/12/04: $47.62 | **2004E S&P Core EPS:** $2.27

S&P Earnings & Dividend Rank: A+

| D | C | B- | B | B+ | A- | A | A+ |

S&P Fair Value Rank: 4+

| 1 | 2 | 3 | 4 | 5 |
| Lowest | | | | Highest |

Fair Value Calc.: $47.70 (Fairly Valued)

S&P Investability Quotient Percentile 99%

CL scored higher than 99% of all companies for which an S&P Report is available.

Volatility: Average

| Low | Average | High |

Technical Evaluation: Neutral
Since 11/04, the technical indicators for CL have been Neutral.

Relative Strength Rank: Weak
26
1 Lowest | Highest 99

GAAP Earnings vs. Previous Year: ▲ Up ▼ Down ► No Change

10 Week Mov. Avg.
30 Week Mov. Avg.
Relative Strength
12-Mo Target Price

Volume Below Avg. — Above Avg.

VOL. MIL.

OPTIONS: ASE, CBOE, P

Analyst commentary prepared by Howard Choe/PMW/GG

Highlights October 28, 2004

- Third quarter results were in line with lower guidance provided by CL in September. We view these results as weak, in light of a higher level of marketing spending to defend market share. We think that the outlook remains weak for the remainder of 2004. The company projected 2005 EPS growth of 6% to 10%, assuming a slower rise in raw material costs and marketing spending.

- We estimate 2004 sales growth of about 6%, reflecting expected solid volume gains driven by new product introductions and lower prices to the consumer. We see the company posting solid volume gains in most operating regions, with the strongest gains expected in Asia/Africa and Europe. We believe volume growth will be aided in part by increased advertising and promotional efforts. With higher promotions partly negating gains from more efficient manufacturing and purchasing, we project modest gross margin expansion of 50 basis points. In light of higher expected marketing spending in North America, we expect operating margins to narrow by over one percentage point. We expect sales in 2005 to increase 5%.

- We expect 2004 EPS to decline 2%, to $2.42, from $2.46 in 2003. We see 2005 EPS up 7%. We project 2004 and 2005 S&P Core EPS of $2.27 and $2.45, respectively, largely reflecting estimated stock option expense.

Key Stock Statistics

S&P Core EPS 2005E	2.45	52-week Range	$59.04-42.89
S&P Oper. EPS 2004E	2.42	12 Month P/E	19.2
P/E on S&P Oper. EPS 2004E	19.7	Beta	0.43
S&P Oper. EPS 2005E	2.60	Shareholders	37,700
Yield (%)	2.0%	Market Cap (B)	$ 25.3
Dividend Rate/Share	0.96	Shares Outstanding (M)	530.3

Value of $10,000 invested five years ago: **$ 8,740**

Dividend Data Dividends have been paid since 1895

Amount ($)	Date Decl.	Ex-Div. Date	Stock of Record	Payment Date
0.240	Jan. 08	Jan. 22	Jan. 26	Feb. 13 '04
0.240	Mar. 11	Apr. 22	Apr. 26	May. 14 '04
0.240	Jul. 08	Jul. 22	Jul. 26	Aug. 16 '04
0.240	Oct. 07	Oct. 21	Oct. 25	Nov. 15 '04

Investment Rationale/Risk October 28, 2004

- We are maintaining our hold opinion on the shares, reflecting our belief that CL's solid sales but declining profitability are fairly reflected in the share price. We are concerned about prospects of an increasingly competitive landscape in the global and oral and household care categories, principally due to more aggressive marketing and pricing strategies on the part of Procter & Gamble (PG: buy, $54) and Unilever (UN:, hold, $57). CL believes it is taking an appropriate longer-term approach to preserving market share with a higher level of marketing spending. However, we believe investor enthusiasm will be restrained pending the adoption of measures to offset the spending and boost profitability.

- Risks to our recommendation and target price include intensified competition in the global oral care market, unfavorable currency translations, and low consumer acceptance of new products.

- The stock traded recently at a 10% discount to the level of its large-cap peers, but at a premium to the S&P 500, at 18X our 2005 EPS estimate. We view the shares as fairly valued, in light of strong market share positions and wide profit margins, balanced against increased competition. In light of our weaker profit outlook, we reduced our 12-month target price to $49, applying a P/E multiple of 19X to our 2005 EPS estimate.

Revenues/Earnings Data Fiscal year ending December 31

Revenues (Million $)

	2004	2003	2002	2001	2000	1999
1Q	2,514	2,348	2,195	2,293	2,242	2,175
2Q	2,572	2,459	2,297	2,330	2,337	2,285
3Q	2,696	2,524	2,382	2,391	2,367	2,314
4Q	—	2,573	2,420	2,414	2,413	2,344
Yr.	—	9,903	9,294	9,428	9,358	9,118

Earnings Per Share ($)

	2004	2003	2002	2001	2000	1999
1Q	0.59	0.56	0.49	0.44	0.38	0.33
2Q	0.66	0.62	0.55	0.47	0.42	0.36
3Q	0.58	0.63	0.57	0.49	0.44	0.38
4Q	E0.59	0.65	0.59	0.49	0.46	0.41
Yr.	E2.42	2.46	2.19	1.89	1.70	1.47

Next earnings report expected: early-February Source: S&P, Company Reports
EPS Estimates based on S&P Operating Earnings; historical GAAP earnings are as reported.

Colgate-Palmolive Company

Recommendation: **HOLD** ★ ★ ★ ☆ ☆   12-Month Target Price: **$49.00** (as of October 21, 2004)

Business Summary October 28, 2004

With nearly 67% of its sales derived from from international markets, Colgate-Palmolive Co. is a leading global consumer products company in oral, personal and household care, and pet food markets. Its products are marketed in more than 200 countries and territories worldwide, under such internationally recognized brand names as Colgate, Palmolive, Mennen, Ajax, Fab, Suavitel and Soupline, as well as Hill's Science Diet and Hill's Prescription Diet.

Following what it viewed as a successful 2002, the company planned to focus its resources on its most profitable categories: oral care, personal care, and pet nutrition. CL believed it would realize additional benefits from its information technology and regional manufacturing investments in 2003 and beyond. The company has set a long-term gross profit margin goal of 61% by 2008.

Sales of oral, personal, household, fabric care, and pet nutrition products accounted respectively for 34%, 24%, 16%, 13% and 13% of total worldwide sales in 2002.

The company's oral care products include toothbrushes, toothpaste, mouth rinses, and dental floss, and pharmaceutical products for dentists and other oral health professionals. Significant recent product launches included Colgate Fresh Confidence, Colgate 2in1 toothpaste and mouthwash, Colgate Total Plus Whitening toothpastes, and the Colgate Actibrush and Motion battery-powered toothbrushes.

CL's personal care products include bar and liquid soaps, shampoos, conditioners, deodorants and antiperspirants and shave products. The company is the U.S. market leader in liquid soaps, and the global market leader in male deodorant sticks. Significant CL brands in this segment include Softsoap, Palmolive and Mennen.

The household care division produces major brands such as Palmolive and Ajax dishwashing liquid and hand soaps. The company also markets other brands, such as Fab, Ajax and Murphy's oil soap (North America's leading wood floor cleaner). Outside the U.S., CL has leading fabric softener brands, with Suavitel in Latin America, Soupline in Europe and Softlan in Asia.

Oral, personal and household care sales outside of North America accounted for 62% of total sales in 2002. Sales in Latin America, Europe and Asia/Africa accounted for 27%, 25% and 19% of segment sales, respectively. Economic uncertainty in certain Latin American countries and fluctuations in the euro may affect overall results in those regions.

With its Hill's Pet Nutrition subsidiary, CL regards itself as the world leader in specialty pet nutrition products for dogs and cats. Hill's markets pet foods mainly under two trademarks: Science Diet, which is sold through pet supply retailers, breeders and veterinarians, and Prescription Diet, for dogs and cats with disease conditions. Hill's sells its products in 86 countries, and leads the premium pet food segment in Japan, North America, and South Africa. Sales of Hill's accounted for 13% of total worldwide sales in 2002.

Company Financials Fiscal Year ending December 31

Per Share Data ($)

(Year Ended December 31)	2003	2002	2001	2000	1999	1998	1997	1996	1995	1994
Tangible Bk. Val.	NM	NM	NM	NM	NM	NM	NM	NM	NM	0.22
Cash Flow	3.15	2.65	2.40	2.32	1.96	1.69	1.60	1.58	0.82	1.36
Earnings	2.46	2.19	1.89	1.70	1.47	1.31	1.14	1.05	0.26	0.96
S&P Core Earnings	2.31	2.00	1.71	NA	NA	NA	NA	NA	NA	NA
Dividends	0.90	0.72	0.68	0.63	0.59	0.55	0.53	0.47	0.44	0.39
Payout Ratio	37%	33%	36%	37%	40%	42%	47%	45%	169%	40%
Prices - High	60.99	58.86	64.75	66.75	65.00	49.43	39.34	24.12	19.34	16.34
- Low	48.56	44.05	48.50	40.50	36.56	32.53	22.50	17.21	14.50	12.37
P/E Ratio - High	25	27	34	39	44	38	35	23	74	17
- Low	20	20	26	24	25	25	20	16	56	13

Income Statement Analysis (Million $)

	2003	2002	2001	2000	1999	1998	1997	1996	1995	1994
Revs.	9,903	9,294	9,428	9,358	9,118	8,972	9,057	8,749	8,358	7,588
Oper. Inc.	2,467	2,333	2,198	2,132	1,904	1,733	1,591	1,470	1,337	1,228
Depr.	316	297	336	410	340	330	320	316	300	235
Int. Exp.	124	151	192	200	212	205	232	244	251	131
Pretax Inc.	2,042	1,870	1,709	1,600	1,425	1,278	1,131	955	364	918
Eff. Tax Rate	30.4%	31.1%	30.6%	31.4%	32.1%	31.4%	32.0%	33.5%	52.7%	32.7%
Net Inc.	1,421	1,288	1,147	1,064	937	849	740	635	172	580
S&P Core Earnings	1,309	1,152	1,011	NA	NA	NA	NA	NA	NA	NA

Balance Sheet & Other Fin. Data (Million $)

	2003	2002	2001	2000	1999	1998	1997	1996	1995	1994
Cash	265	168	173	213	235	182	183	308	257	218
Curr. Assets	2,497	2,228	2,203	2,347	2,355	2,245	2,196	2,372	2,360	2,178
Total Assets	7,479	7,087	6,985	7,252	7,423	7,685	7,539	7,902	7,642	6,142
Curr. Liab.	2,445	2,149	2,124	2,244	2,274	2,114	1,959	1,904	1,753	1,529
LT Debt	2,685	3,211	2,812	2,537	2,243	2,301	2,341	2,787	2,992	1,752
Common Equity	594	27.3	505	1,115	1,467	1,709	1,793	1,641	1,272	1,799
Total Cap.	4,028	4,050	4,139	4,453	4,701	4,834	4,805	5,055	4,909	3,870
Cap. Exp.	302	344	340	367	373	390	479	459	432	401
Cash Flow	1,736	1,563	1,461	1,453	1,255	1,158	1,039	930	472	794
Curr. Ratio	1.0	1.0	1.0	1.0	1.0	1.1	1.1	1.3	1.3	1.4
% LT Debt of Cap.	66.7	79.3	67.9	57.0	47.7	47.6	48.7	55.2	60.9	45.3
% Net Inc.of Revs.	14.4	13.9	12.2	11.4	10.3	9.5	8.2	7.3	2.1	7.6
% Ret. on Assets	19.5	18.3	16.1	14.5	12.4	11.2	9.6	7.9	2.5	9.9
% Ret. on Equity	457.2	475.7	139.0	80.8	57.6	47.3	41.9	42.1	11.2	31.1

Data as orig reptd.; bef. results of disc opers/spec. items. Per share data adj. for stk. divs. Bold denotes primary EPS - prior periods restated. E-Estimated. NA-Not Available. NM-Not Meaningful. NR-Not Ranked. UR-Under Review.

Office: 300 Park Avenue, New York, NY 10022.
Telephone: 212-310-2000.
Email: investor_relations@colpal.com
Website: http://www.colgate.com
Chrmn & CEO: R. Mark.
Pres: W.S. Shanahan.

Vice Chrmn: J. Teruel.
Vice Chrmn: L. Juliber.
COO: I. Cook.
VP & Investor Contact: D.H. Thompson 212-310-3072.
Dirs: J. K. Conway, R. E. Ferguson, C. M. Gutierrez, E. M. Hancock, D. W. Johnson, R. J. Kogan, D. E. Lewis, R. Mark, E. A. Monrad.

Founded: in 1806.
Domicile: Delaware.
Employees: 36,600.
S&P Analyst: Howard Choe/PMW/GG

The McGraw·Hill Companies

Comcast Corp. Class 'A'

Recommendation: **HOLD** ★ ★ ★ ★ ★   12-Month Target Price: **$32.00**
SELL | SELL | HOLD | BUY | BUY
(as of September 01, 2004)

CMCSA has an approximate 0.61% weighting in the **S&P 500**

Sector: Consumer Discretionary
Sub-Industry: Broadcasting & Cable TV
Peer Group: Cable Television - U.S.

Summary: With the November 2002 acquisition of AT&T Broadband (ATTB), Comcast became the largest cable TV system operator in the U.S., with 21.5 million subscribers.

Quantitative Evaluations

S&P Earnings & Dividend Rank: C

| D | C | B- | B | B+ | A- | A | A+ |

S&P Fair Value Rank: 1

| 1 | 2 | 3 | 4 | 5 |
| Lowest | | | | Highest |

Fair Value Calc.: $19.70 (Overvalued)

S&P Investability Quotient Percentile

56%

CMCSA scored higher than 56% of all companies for which an S&P Report is available.

Volatility: Average

| Low | Average | High |

Technical Evaluation: Bullish
Since 11/04, the technical indicators for CMCSA have been Bullish.

Relative Strength Rank: Moderate

48

1 Lowest   Highest 99

Price as of 11/12/04: $29.83   **2004E S&P Core EPS:** $0.23

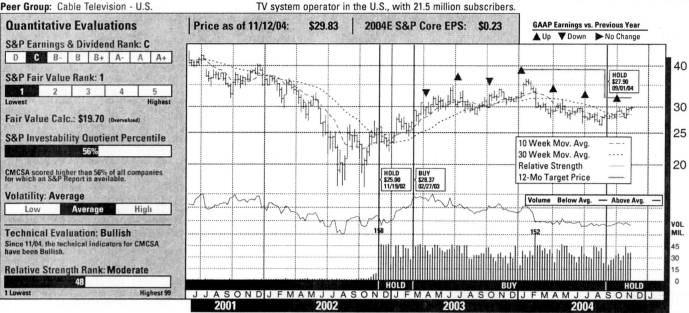

GAAP Earnings vs. Previous Year
▲ Up   ▼ Down   ▶ No Change

- 10 Week Mov. Avg.
- 30 Week Mov. Avg.
- Relative Strength
- 12-Mo Target Price

Volume   Below Avg. ━ Above Avg.

HOLD $27.90 09/01/04
HOLD $25.00 11/19/02
BUY $28.37 02/27/03

OPTIONS: Ph

Analyst commentary prepared by Tuna N. Amobi, CFA, CPA /CB/BK

Highlights November 04, 2004

- We estimate that core cable division revenues will increase about 10% each in 2004 and 2005, mainly driven by continued penetration of high-speed data revenues, although we could start to see some data pricing pressure in 2005. Our model calls for a modest increase in video revenues, as the impact of at best a flat basic subscriber base is offset by basic rate increases and continued penetration of digital cable with the further deployment of advanced video services. We anticipate a continued contraction of the telephony business in 2004, but we expect this to start abating in 2005, as the company begins an earnest transition to VoIP. We see an improved infrastructure of regional systems interconnects, which should drive increased contributions from local cable advertising. Also, a broad advertising recovery and higher distribution revenues should fuel continued good growth at the content division.

- We expect combined cable margins for the historical and acquired systems to exceed 40% by the first quarter of 2005, as annual programming expense growth moderates at 5% to 6%, well below industry averages. In addition, personnel expenses are sharply down, but higher marketing expenses should support the rollout of advanced services. We project consolidated EBITDA growth of 17% and 19% in 2004 and 2005, respectively.

- With a modest decline in outstanding shares expected as a result of a buyback, we forecast EPS of $0.35 in 2004 ($0.23 S&P Core EPS, after employee stock option expense), and $0.67 in 2005 ($0.54 S&P Core).

Key Stock Statistics

S&P Core EPS 2005E	0.54	52-week Range	$36.50-26.25	
S&P Oper. EPS 2004E	0.35	12 Month P/E	72.8	
P/E on S&P Oper. EPS 2004E	85.2	Beta	0.78	
S&P Oper. EPS 2005E	0.67	Shareholders	1,160,769	
Yield (%)	Nil	Market Cap (B)	$ 40.5	
Dividend Rate/Share	Nil	Shares Outstanding (M)	2219.9	

Value of $10,000 invested five years ago: **$ 8,043**

Dividend Data

No cash dividends have been paid.

Investment Rationale/Risk November 04, 2004

- We recommend holding the shares, and believe that the company is well positioned to leverage its infrastructure upgrades and significant scale economies arising from its acquisition of the former AT&T Broadband systems to drive advanced services deployment and accelerating free cash flow, which we estimate at $2.1 billion in 2004 and $3.6 billion in 2005. With its recently enhanced balance sheet flexibility, the company could further grow its scale via an acquisition of some of Adelphia Communications' cable systems, which we think could be financed through non-strategic equity holdings potentially worth over $10 billion. In addition, improved penetration of bundled services and churn should reflect the continued deployment of advanced digital offerings such as VOD, HDTV and PVRs. We believe that VoIP telephony could start to contribute meaningfully to operating cash flow in 2006.

- Risks to our recommendation and target price include increased competitive pressures and potentially aggressive price discounting in "triple-play" services from DBS and Bell companies; likely near-term overhang from any new acquisition; near-term uncertainties with the telephony business and strategy; cable regulatory exposure; and macroeconomic factors.

- Our 12-month target price of $32 is derived from an analysis of discounted cash flows (DCF), adjusted for off balance sheet assets and certain content minority interests. This implies an enterprise value of 8.4X estimated 2005 cable-only EBITDA, or nearly $3,400 per subscriber, which we view as fair market value.

Revenues/Earnings Data Fiscal year ending December 31

Revenues (Million $)

	2004	2003	2002	2001	2000	1999
1Q	4,908	4,466	2,672	—	1,939	1,374
2Q	5,066	4,594	2,709	—	1,912	1,479
3Q	5,098	4,546	2,705	—	1,960	1,525
4Q	—	4,742	4,374	—	2,408	1,832
Yr.	—	18,348	12,460	19,697	8,219	6,209

Earnings Per Share ($)

	2004	2003	2002	2001	2000	1999
1Q	0.03	-0.16	-0.09	—	-0.23	0.12
2Q	0.12	-0.01	-0.22	—	0.20	1.10
3Q	0.10	-0.07	0.08	—	1.29	0.07
4Q	E0.10	0.17	-0.03	—	0.81	-0.23
Yr.	E0.35	-0.10	-0.25	-1.34	2.16	0.95

Next earnings report expected: mid-February   Source: S&P, Company Reports
EPS Estimates based on S&P Operating Earnings; historical GAAP earnings are as reported.

Comcast Corporation Class 'A'

Recommendation: **HOLD** ★ ★ ★ ☆ ☆   12-Month Target Price: **$32.00** (as of September 01, 2004)

Business Summary November 05, 2004

Comcast Corp. was formed through the November 2002 merger of Comcast Corp. with the AT&T Broadband (ATTB) business of AT&T Corp. The $50.78 billion purchase consideration consisted of $25.5 billion in Comcast stock and options, and $24.86 billion in assumed ATTB debt. Comcast and ATTB became wholly owned subsidiaries of Comcast Corp. Common shares consist of Class A (voting rights), Class A Special (non-voting), and Class B (super-voting) shares.

Comcast is involved in two key lines of business: cable - through the development, management and operation of broadband communications networks; and content - through consolidated subsidiaries including Comcast Spectacor, Comcast SportsNet, Comcast Sports Net Mid-Atlantic, Comcast Sports Southeast, E! Entertainment Television, The Golf Channel, Outdoor Life Network and G4 Media, and through other programming investments. In May 2004, the company acquired the Tech TV cable channel from Vulcan Programming and combined it with its G4 channel.

As of September 30, 2004, Comcast served 21.5 million subscribers in 35 states, passed 40.5 million homes, and provided digital cable to 8.4 million subscribers, high-speed Internet service to 6.6 million subscribers, and phone service to 1.2 million subscribers.

In September 2004, the company committed to an investment of $300 million as part of a consortium led by Sony Corp. (SNE, $35), which agreed to acquire film studio Metro-Goldwyn-Mayer (MGM: hold; $12) for $12 in cash. As part of the agreement, Comcast, Sony Pictures Entertainment and the equity partners in the MGM transaction have agreed to a broad programming and distribution arrangement that will allow for the distribution of Sony Pictures' and MGM content on

Comcast's VOD platform, and for the creation of a joint venture, to be managed by Comcast, establishing new cable channels featuring Sony Pictures and MGM content.

In July 2004, the company unwound its holding of 120.3 million Liberty Media (L: hold; $9) Series A shares in exchange for 100% of Encore ICCP, Inc. (an L subsidiary which notably held L's 10.4% interest in the E! network, raising Comcast's stake in E! to 60.5%) and about $545 million in cash.

In April 2004, Comcast withdrew its offer to merge with Walt Disney Co. (DIS: $24), citing Disney's lack of interest in its offer after an earlier rejection.

In September 2003, the company sold its 57% interest in the electronic retailer QVC, Inc. to its partner, Liberty Media (L: $11) for about $7.7 billion, comprising $4.0 billion of three-year unsecured floating rate notes, 218 million Liberty Class A shares valued at $2.34 billion, and cash of $1.35 billion.

In March 2003, the Time Warner Entertainment (TWE) partnership with AOL Time Warner, in which Comcast held a 27.6% interest acquired from AT&T, was restructured. Comcast received $2.1 billion in cash, $1.5 billion in AOL stock, and a 21% interest in Time Warner Cable (TWC); in September 2004, the company acquired an option, exercisable between December 1, 2004 and April 1, 2005, to reduce this TWC stake to 17%, in exchange for acquiring cable systems serving about 90,000 subcribers, plus $750 million in cash. Also in March, the company transferred to Bresnan Communications certain cable systems acquired from AT&T serving about 317,000 subscribers in exchange for $525 million in cash, plus preferred and common equity.

Company Financials Fiscal Year ending December 31

Per Share Data ($)

(Year Ended December 31)	2003	2002	2001	2000	1999	1998	1997	1996	1995	1994
Tangible Bk. Val.	NM	NM	NM	NM	NM	NM	NM	NM	NM	NM
Cash Flow	0.36	1.58	1.48	4.90	2.40	2.38	1.05	1.30	1.36	0.55
Earnings	-0.10	-0.25	-1.34	2.16	0.95	1.25	-0.33	-0.11	-0.08	-0.16
S&P Core Earnings	-0.45	0.71	-1.54	NA	NA	NA	NA	NA	NA	NA
Dividends	Nil	Nil	Nil	Nil	0.01	0.05	0.05	0.05	0.05	0.05
Payout Ratio	Nil	Nil	Nil	Nil	1%	4%	NM	NM	NM	NM
Prices - High	34.85	37.55	45.81	52.37	54.62	29.50	16.56	10.56	11.25	12.12
- Low	23.42	17.05	31.85	27.93	28.06	14.75	7.18	6.87	6.87	6.87
P/E Ratio - High	NM	NM	NM	24	57	24	NM	NM	NM	NM
- Low	NM	NM	NM	13	30	12	NM	NM	NM	NM

Income Statement Analysis (Million $)

	2003	2002	2001	2000	1999	1998	1997	1996	1995	1994
Revs.	18,348	12,460	19,697	8,219	6,209	5,145	4,913	4,038	3,363	1,375
Oper. Inc.	6,392	3,691	1,576	2,470	1,880	1,497	1,469	1,207	1,019	576
Depr.	4,438	2,032	6,345	2,631	1,216	940	936	698	689	336
Int. Exp.	2,018	884	2,341	691	538	467	565	541	525	313
Pretax Inc.	-137	70.0	-5,927	3,602	1,500	1,557	-229	-16.1	-45.4	-84.6
Eff. Tax Rate	NM	NM	NM	40.0%	48.2%	38.1%	NM	NM	NM	NM
Net Inc.	-218	-276	-3,021	2,045	781	1,008	-209	-52.5	-37.8	-75.3
S&P Core Earnings	-979	792	-1,482	NA	NA	NA	NA	NA	NA	NA

Balance Sheet & Other Fin. Data (Million $)

	2003	2002	2001	2000	1999	1998	1997	1996	1995	1994
Cash	1,550	781	558	652	922	871	414	331	539	335
Curr. Assets	5,403	7,076	4,944	5,144	9,759	5,624	1,560	1,406	1,654	609
Total Assets	109,159	113,105	109,319	35,745	28,686	14,817	12,804	12,089	9,580	6,763
Curr. Liab.	9,654	15,383	12,489	4,042	5,527	3,093	1,418	1,365	1,122	661
LT Debt	23,835	27,957	27,528	10,517	8,707	5,464	6,559	7,103	6,944	4,811
Common Equity	41,662	38,329	38,451	28,113	9,772	3,243	1,101	520	-828	-727
Total Cap.	91,689	92,070	94,758	45,734	23,159	10,780	10,317	9,796	7,634	5,475
Cap. Exp.	4,161	1,975	NA	1,637	894	899	926	670	623	270
Cash Flow	4,220	1,756	3,324	4,653	1,967	1,918	713	646	651	261
Curr. Ratio	0.6	0.5	0.4	1.3	1.8	1.8	1.1	1.0	1.5	0.9
% LT Debt of Cap.	26.0	30.4	29.1	23.0	37.6	50.7	63.6	72.5	91.0	87.9
% Net Inc.of Revs.	NM	NM	NM	24.9	12.6	19.6	NM	NM	NM	NM
% Ret. on Assets	NM	NM	NM	6.3	3.6	7.3	NM	NM	NM	NM
% Ret. on Equity	NM	NM	NM	8.4	11.5	45.1	NM	NM	NM	NM

Data as orig reptd.; bef. results of disc opers/spec. items. Per share data adj. for stk. divs.; EPS diluted (primary prior to 1998). Pro forma data in 2001, balance sheet & book value as of Jun. 30, 2002. E-Estimated. NA-Not Available. NM-Not Meaningful. NR-Not Ranked.

Office: 1500 Market Street, Philadelphia, PA 19102-2148.
Telephone: 215-665-1700.
Website: http://www.comcast.com
Chrmn: C.M. Armstrong.
Pres & CEO: B.L. Roberts.
Vice Chrmn: J.A. Brodsky.

COO: S. Burke.
EVP & CFO: L.S. Smith.
VP & Investor Contact: M. Dooner 215-981-7392.
Dirs: D. Anstrom, C. M. Armstrong, K. J. Bacon, S. M. Bonovitz, J. A. Brodsky, J. L. Castle II, J. J. Collins, J. M. Cook, R. J. Roberts, B. L. Roberts, J. Rodin, M. I. Sovern.

Founded: in 1969.
Domicile: Pennsylvania.
Employees: 68,000.
S&P Analyst: Tuna N. Amobi, CFA, CPA /CB/BK

Comerica Inc.

Recommendation: HOLD ★★★☆☆
SELL · SELL · HOLD · BUY · BUY
(as of October 19, 2004)

12-Month Target Price: $66.00

CMA has an approximate 0.10% weighting in the **S&P 500**

Sector: Financials
Sub-Industry: Diversified Banks
Peer Group: Midwest/West Major Regionals

Summary: This Detroit-based bank holding company operates banking affiliates in Michigan, Texas, California and Florida.

Quantitative Evaluations

S&P Earnings & Dividend Rank: A

D	C	B-	B	B+	A-	A	A+

S&P Fair Value Rank: 3+

1	2	3	4	5
Lowest				Highest

Fair Value Calc.: $59.60 (Slightly Overvalued)

S&P Investability Quotient Percentile

99%

CMA scored higher than 99% of all companies for which an S&P Report is available.

Volatility: Low

Low	Average	High

Technical Evaluation: Neutral

Since 10/04, the technical indicators for CMA have been Neutral.

Relative Strength Rank: Moderate

54

1 Lowest · Highest 99

Price as of 11/12/04: $63.46 | **2004E S&P Core EPS:** $4.02

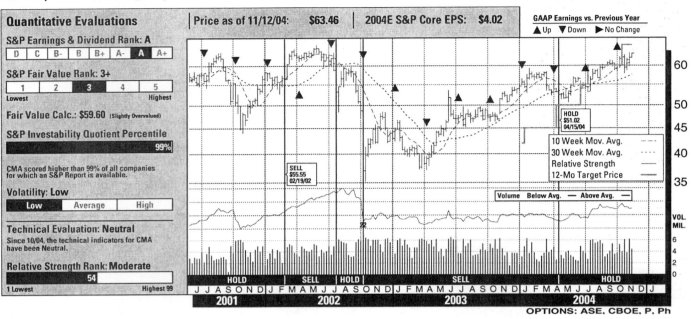

GAAP Earnings vs. Previous Year — ▲ Up ▼ Down ► No Change

10 Week Mov. Avg.
30 Week Mov. Avg.
Relative Strength
12-Mo Target Price

Volume Below Avg. — Above Avg. —

HOLD | SELL | HOLD | SELL | HOLD
J J A S O N D | J F M A M J J A S O N D | J F M A M J J A S O N D | J F M A M J J A S O N D | J
2001 | 2002 | 2003 | 2004

OPTIONS: ASE, CBOE, P, Ph

Analyst commentary prepared by Evan M. Momios, CFA /MF/GG

Highlights August 19, 2004

- We see net interest income declining about 4% year over year in 2004, based on our expectation of lower levels of average loans and an average net interest margin of 3.80%. We think fee income should remain in the $220 million to $230 million range for the remainder of the year, on improving investment advisory fees and fiduciary income, assuming that the equity market environment remains favorable. Year over year, we expect recurring fee income growth of less than 5% over 2003 levels.

- In recent quarters, CMA has reduced its level of nonperforming loans, net chargeoffs, and delinquencies. We believe net chargeoffs are likely to improve at a slower pace in the quarters ahead, and we assume a net chargeoff to average loan ratio of 0.59% in 2004, versus 0.87% reported for 2003. We see operating expenses likely to remain flat compared to 2003 levels.

- Assuming additional share repurchases, we estimate 2004 EPS of $4.17, with an increase to $4.44 seen for 2005. Our respective 2004 and 2005 S&P Core EPS estimates of $4.02 and $4.32 reflect our estimates of stock option expense and modest pension plan adjustments.

Investment Rationale/Risk August 19, 2004

- We advise investors to maintain positions based on our view of the company's progress in improving the credit quality of its loan portfolio in recent quarters, which we think is fully reflected in the stock's valuation. The stock, as of early August, was trading at approximately 14.3X our 2004 EPS estimate, compared to about 13X forward 12-month EPS on average over the past three and five years.

- Risks to our recommendation and target price include a severe economic downturn in combination with higher short term interest rates that could result in an inverted yield curve, legal and regulatory risks, a decline in business spending, and a serious geopolitical event that could impact domestic equity markets.

- Our 12-month target price of $60 is based on a P/E multiple of 13.5X our 2005 EPS estimate, slightly above the stock's average historical P/E multiple but at the mid-point of our discounted cash flow-derived valuation estimates 12 months from now. We believe that the stock's indicated dividend yield of about 3.5% offers support to the shares.

Key Stock Statistics

S&P Core EPS 2005E	4.32	52-week Range	$63.71-50.45
S&P Oper. EPS 2004E	4.25	12 Month P/E	15.7
P/E on S&P Oper. EPS 2004E	14.9	Beta	0.61
S&P Oper. EPS 2005E	4.60	Shareholders	16,010
Yield (%)	3.3%	Market Cap (B)	$ 10.8
Dividend Rate/Share	2.08	Shares Outstanding (M)	170.6

Value of $10,000 invested five years ago: **$ 12,262**

Dividend Data Dividends have been paid since 1936

Amount ($)	Date Decl.	Ex-Div. Date	Stock of Record	Payment Date
0.500	Nov. 25	Dec. 11	Dec. 15	Jan. 01 '04
0.520	Jan. 27	Mar. 11	Mar. 15	Apr. 01 '04
0.520	May. 18	Jun. 14	Jun. 15	Jul. 01 '04
0.520	Jul. 27	Sep. 13	Sep. 15	Oct. 01 '04

Revenues/Earnings Data Fiscal year ending December 31

Revenues (Million $)

	2004	2003	2002	2001	2000	1999
1Q	763.0	866.0	920.0	1,110	980.6	786.3
2Q	773.0	853.0	927.0	1,078	1,002	836.1
3Q	764.0	800.0	910.0	1,039	1,040	842.0
4Q	—	780.0	940.0	970.3	1,065	924.7
Yr.	—	3,299	3,697	4,197	4,088	3,390

Earnings Per Share ($)

	2004	2003	2002	2001	2000	1999
1Q	0.92	1.00	1.20	0.50	1.10	0.98
2Q	1.10	0.97	0.88	1.13	1.15	1.03
3Q	1.13	0.89	0.14	1.14	1.18	1.05
4Q	E1.10	0.89	1.18	1.11	1.20	1.08
Yr.	E4.25	3.75	3.40	3.88	4.63	4.14

Next earnings report expected: mid-January Source: S&P, Company Reports
EPS Estimates based on S&P Operating Earnings; historical GAAP earnings are as reported.

Comerica Incorporated

Recommendation: **HOLD** ★ ★ ★ ☆ ☆   12-Month Target Price: **$66.00** (as of October 19, 2004)

Business Summary August 19, 2004

The owner of one of Michigan's oldest banks, Comerica is a Detroit-based bank holding company that operates banking units in Michigan, California, Texas and Florida. It also has banking subsidiaries in Canada and Mexico. With about $53 billion in assets at December 31, 2003, CMA is one of the 20 largest U.S. bank holding companies.

Operations are divided into three major lines of business: the Business Bank, Small Business and Personal Financial Services, and Wealth and Institutional Management. The Business Bank consists of mid-market lending, asset-based lending, large corporate banking, and international financial services. Products include commercial loans and lines of credit, deposits, cash management, capital markets products, trade finance and loan syndication services. Small Business and Personal Financial Services includes consumer lending and deposit gathering, mortgage loan origination, small business banking and a range of financial services provided to small businesses and municipalities. Wealth and Institutional Management includes private banking, personal and institutional trust, retirement plans and asset management, as well as CMA's securities brokerage and insurance business. In addition, the company has a finance segment that focuses on CMA's securities portfolio and asset and liability management activities.

In 2003, average earning assets, from which interest income is derived, totaled

$48.8 billion, consisting of loans and leases (87%), investment securities (9%), and short term investments (4%). Average sources of funds, used in the lending business, included interest-bearing deposits (52%), noninterest-bearing deposits (26%), short-term borrowings (1%), medium- and long-term debt (10%), shareholders' equity (9%) and other (2%).

At the end of 2003, nonperforming assets, mainly nonaccrual loans and other real estate owned, totaled $538 million (1.26% of total loans), down from $579 million (1.34%) a year earlier. The allowance for loan losses, set aside for possible loan defaults, was $803 million (1.99% of loans), versus $791 million (1.87%) a year earlier. Net chargeoffs, or the amount of loans actually written off as uncollectible, were $365 million (0.86% of average loans) in 2003, versus $481 million (1.14%) in 2002.

In January 2001, the company acquired Los Angeles-based Imperial Bancorp (assets of $7.4 billion), via an exchange of stock valued at $1.3 billion.

In 2003, CMA opened 10 new branches. It plans to open 50 more over the next three years, including about 15 in 2004, with a focus on the California and Texas markets.

Company Financials Fiscal Year ending December 31

Per Share Data ($)

(Year Ended December 31)	2003	2002	2001	2000	1999	1998	1997	1996	1995	1994
Tangible Bk. Val.	29.20	28.31	27.15	23.94	20.60	17.94	16.02	14.70	15.17	12.21
Earnings	3.75	3.40	3.88	4.63	4.14	3.72	3.19	2.37	2.36	2.19
S&P Core Earnings	3.72	3.30	3.27	NA	NA	NA	NA	NA	NA	NA
Dividends	2.00	1.92	1.76	1.60	1.40	1.25	1.15	1.01	0.91	0.83
Payout Ratio	53%	56%	45%	35%	34%	34%	36%	43%	39%	38%
Prices - High	56.34	66.09	65.15	61.12	70.00	73.00	61.87	39.58	28.50	20.83
- Low	37.10	35.20	44.02	32.93	44.00	46.50	34.16	24.16	16.08	16.08
P/E Ratio - High	15	19	17	13	17	20	19	17	12	10
- Low	10	10	11	7	11	12	11	10	7	7

Income Statement Analysis (Million $)

	2003	2002	2001	2000	1999	1998	1997	1996	1995	1994
Net Int. Inc.	1,926	2,132	2,102	1,659	1,547	1,461	1,443	1,412	1,300	1,230
Tax Equiv. Adj.	3.00	4.00	4.00	4.00	5.00	7.00	9.00	15.0	21.0	24.1
Non Int. Inc.	837	819	784	827	711	597	522	493	487	463
Loan Loss Prov.	377	635	236	145	114	113	146	114	86.5	56.0
Exp./Op. Revs.	53.6%	51.3%	53.9%	53.6%	49.3%	49.4%	51.3%	55.7%	59.7%	61.6%
Pretax Inc.	953	882	1,111	1,151	1,033	931	817	646	626	582
Eff. Tax Rate	30.6%	31.9%	36.1%	34.9%	34.9%	34.8%	35.0%	35.4%	33.9%	33.5%
Net Inc.	661	601	710	749	673	607	530	417	413	387
% Net Int. Marg.	3.95	4.55	4.61	4.54	4.55	4.57	4.53	4.54	4.19	4.32
S&P Core Earnings	657	584	587	NA	NA	NA	NA	NA	NA	NA

Balance Sheet & Other Fin. Data (Million $)

	2003	2002	2001	2000	1999	1998	1997	1996	1995	1994
Money Mkt. Assets	4,013	2,446	1,079	165	613	110	203	65.5	238	429
Inv. Securities	8,502	5,499	5,370	2,843	2,739	2,822	4,006	4,800	6,859	7,876
Com'l Loans	32,153	33,732	32,660	28,001	25,429	23,266	16,323	13,926	12,371	10,892
Other Loans	7,274	8,549	8,536	8,060	7,265	7,339	12,572	12,281	12,071	11,408
Total Assets	52,592	53,301	50,732	41,985	38,653	36,601	36,292	34,206	35,470	33,430
Demand Deposits	14,104	16,335	12,596	6,815	6,136	6,999	6,761	6,713	5,580	5,257
Time Deposits	27,359	25,440	24,974	20,353	17,155	17,314	15,825	15,654	17,587	17,175
LT Debt	4,801	5,216	5,503	8,089	8,580	5,282	7,286	4,242	4,644	1,742
Common Equity	5,110	4,947	4,807	3,757	3,225	2,797	2,512	2,366	2,608	2,392
% Ret. on Assets	1.2	1.2	1.4	1.9	1.8	1.7	1.5	1.2	1.2	1.2
% Ret. on Equity	13.1	12.3	15.4	21.0	21.8	22.2	21.1	16.4	16.5	16.7
% Loan Loss Resv.	2.0	1.9	-1.6	1.5	1.5	1.5	1.5	1.4	1.4	1.5
% Loans/Deposits	99.3	101.2	109.7	132.7	140.4	125.9	127.9	117.2	105.5	99.4
% Equity to Assets	9.5	9.4	9.0	8.7	8.0	7.3	6.9	7.1	7.3	7.4

Data as orig reptd.; bef. results of disc opers/spec. items. Per share data adj. for stk. divs. Bold denotes diluted EPS (FASB 128)-prior periods restated. E-Estimated. NA-Not Available. NM-Not Meaningful. NR-Not Ranked.

Office: 500 Woodward Avenue, Detroit, MI 48226.
Telephone: 800-521-1190.
Website: http://www.comerica.com
Chrmn, Pres & CEO: R.W. Babb, Jr.
Vice Chrmn: J.D. Lewis.
Vice Chrmn: J.J. Buttigieg III.

EVP & CFO: E.S. Acton.
SVP & Investor Contact: J.S. Love 313-222-2840.
Dirs: R. W. Babb, Jr., L. Bauder, J. J. Buttigieg III, J. F. Cordes, P. D. Cummings, J. P. DiNapoli, A. F. Earley, Jr., M. M. Fisher, R. Fridholm, T. W. Herrick, A. A. Piergallini, R. S. Taubman, W. P. Vititoe, P. M. Wallington, G. L. Warden, K. L. Way.

Founded: in 1849.
Domicile: Delaware.
Employees: 11,282.
S&P Analyst: Evan M. Momios, CFA /MF/GG

Computer Associates Int'l

Recommendation: **HOLD** ★★★☆☆
SELL | SELL | HOLD | BUY | BUY

12-Month Target Price: **$30.00**
(as of May 26, 2004)

CA has an approximate 0.16% weighting in the **S&P 500**

Sector: Information Technology
Sub-Industry: Systems Software
Peer Group: Systems Software - Larger

Summary: CA develops systems software, database management systems, and applications software.

Quantitative Evaluations

S&P Earnings & Dividend Rank: B-

| D | C | B- | B | B+ | A- | A | A+ |

S&P Fair Value Rank: 2-

| 1 | 2 | 3 | 4 | 5 |
| Lowest | | | | Highest |

Fair Value Calc.: $25.10 (Overvalued)

S&P Investability Quotient Percentile

57%

CA scored higher than 57% of all companies for which an S&P Report is available.

Volatility: Average

| Low | Average | High |

Technical Evaluation: Bullish
Since 9/04, the technical indicators for CA have been Bullish.

Relative Strength Rank: Strong

78

| 1 Lowest | | Highest 99 |

Price as of 11/12/04: $29.70 | **2005E S&P Core EPS:** $0.77

GAAP Earnings vs. Previous Year
▲ Up ▼ Down ▶ No Change

- 10 Week Mov. Avg. (dashed)
- 30 Week Mov. Avg. (dotted)
- Relative Strength (solid)
- 12-Mo Target Price (solid)

Volume Below Avg. — Above Avg.

HOLD

| J J A S O N D | J F M A M J J A S O N D | J F M A M J J A S O N D | J F M A M J J A S O N D | J |
| 2001 | 2002 | 2003 | 2004 |

OPTIONS: ASE, CBOE, P, Ph

Analyst commentary prepared by Jonathan Rudy, CFA /MF/BK

Highlights October 26, 2004

- We project that FY 05 (Mar.) revenues will increase about 6%. We see the company attempting to put controversy behind it and focusing on execution. In recent years, in our view, CA has struggled with its mainframe software business, market concerns over a change to a new business model, and, more recently, a settlement with the SEC relating to revenue recognition practices prior to the change in its business model.

- We expect revenues to be driven by the company's e-business initiatives over the longer term. We believe that recent results were boosted by strength in security and storage software offerings. We also see CA benefiting from solid demand for its flagship system management software product, Unicenter.

- We estimate FY 05 operating EPS of $0.81, up from $0.64 for FY 04, excluding amortization and one-time charges. Our FY 05 Standard & Poor's Core Earnings projection of $0.77 a share reflects potential stock option expense.

Investment Rationale/Risk October 26, 2004

- We have a hold recommendation on the shares, primarily due to what we see as an improvement in the company's business fundamentals. CA has been surrounded by controversy in recent years, which culminated in a recent settlement with the SEC and Department of Justice. Operationally, the company has exceeded our revenue and earnings expectations over the past couple of quarters, and has improved its balance sheet by paying down debt. The shares trade at a slight premium to peers, with a price to sales multiple of 4.6X.

- Risks to our opinion and target price include a rapidly changing technology landscape, and ongoing supervision by the SEC and DOJ stemming from revenue recognition practices at CA prior to the company's adoption of a new business model. Although the investigations are mainly historical in nature, we see risk that penalties could potentially be more substantial than a possible fine.

- Our 12-month target price of $30 is based on a blend of relative P/E multiple to growth and price to sales metrics.

Key Stock Statistics

S&P Oper. EPS 2005E	0.81	52-week Range	$29.71-22.10
P/E on S&P Oper. EPS 2005E	36.7	12 Month P/E	NM
S&P Oper. EPS 2006E	0.88	Beta	2.38
Yield (%)	0.3%	Shareholders	8,000
Dividend Rate/Share	0.08	Market Cap (B)	$ 17.4
Shares Outstanding (M)	585.6		

Value of $10,000 invested five years ago: $ 4,975

Dividend Data Dividends have been paid since 1990

Amount ($)	Date Decl.	Ex-Div. Date	Stock of Record	Payment Date
0.040	Oct. 21	Dec. 18	Dec. 22	Jan. 07 '04
0.040	Jun. 16	Jun. 28	Jun. 30	Jul. 15 '04
0.040	Oct. 18	Dec. 16	Dec. 20	Jan. 05 '05

Revenues/Earnings Data Fiscal year ending March 31

Revenues (Million $)

	2005	2004	2003	2002	2001	2000
1Q	860.0	813.0	765.0	712.0	1,137	1,222
2Q	855.0	833.0	772.0	733.0	1,545	1,605
3Q	—	844.0	778.0	747.0	783.0	1,812
4Q	—	850.0	801.0	772.0	733.0	2,127
Yr.	—	3,276	3,116	2,964	4,198	6,766

Earnings Per Share ($)

	2005	2004	2003	2002	2001	2000
1Q	0.09	0.02	-0.11	-0.59	0.04	-0.80
2Q	-0.16	-0.15	-0.09	-0.50	0.23	0.60
3Q	E0.19	0.04	-0.08	-0.40	-0.59	0.72
4Q	E0.23	0.05	-0.18	-0.41	-0.71	0.70
Yr.	E0.81	-0.06	-0.46	-1.91	-1.02	1.25

Next earnings report expected: late-January Source: S&P, Company Reports
EPS Estimates based on S&P Operating Earnings; historical GAAP earnings are as reported.

Computer Associates International, Inc.

Recommendation: **HOLD** ★ ★ ★ ☆ ☆   12-Month Target Price: **$30.00** (as of May 26, 2004)

Business Summary October 26, 2004

Computer Associates International is one of the leading enterprise software companies. The company's solutions address all areas of process management, information management, and infrastructure management. Built on a common infrastructure, CA's solutions are available for use on a variety of mainframe and distributed systems.

CA offers solutions in six focus areas under seven brand names: Unicenter for Enterprise Management, eTrust for Security, BrightStor for Storage, CleverPath for Portal and Business Intelligence, Allfusion for Application Life Cycle Management, and Advantage and Jasmine for Data Management and Application Development.

Enterprise management solutions address the primary focus areas of IT professionals, including network and systems management, automated operations, IT resource management, database management, web infrastructure management, and application management. The company's Unicenter family is designed to enable IT professionals to manage complex and heterogeneous infrastructures from a centralized perspective.

BrightStor is CA's storage management solution. This suite of technology is intended to help customers protect and manage data, from an application perspective, across all major platforms and storage architectures.

eTrust is designed to safeguard resources across the enterprise. Solutions include intrusion detection, administration authentication, PKI, access control, and Virtual Private Networks.

The company's CleverPath family includes unified Portal and Business Intelligence solutions that deliver portal, knowledge management, predictive analysis and visualization capabilities.

CA also offers Allfusion, a family of comprehensive solutions for end-to-end application life-cycle management designed to enable customers to control the costs of developing, maintaining and managing business applications across the enterprise.

The company's Advantage family of application development solutions offers a range of design, creation and delivery options. These solutions include the following cross-platform technologies: database management systems, application development tools, application integration, and data transformation tools.

During FY 04, CA made several acquisitions to complement certain company product lines. These acquisitions included eSecurity Online, a maker of security and security-related software; Silent Runner, a maker of network security software that safeguards electronic property; and Miramar Systems, a leading provider of desktop migration tools. The aggregate purchase price for all the acquisitions was approximately $53 million.

In March 2004, CA sold its approximate 90% in ACCPAC International, Inc., to The Sage Group, plc. CA's proceeds totaled $104 million, with $90 million received in FY 04, and the remainder in FY 05.

International revenue comprised approximately 48% of total revenue in FY 04, up from 43% in FY 03.

Company Financials Fiscal Year ending March 31

Per Share Data ($)

(Year Ended March 31)	2004	2003	2002	2001	2000	1999	1998	1997	1996	1995
Tangible Bk. Val.	8.09	NM	NM	0.66	1.71	2.06	2.53	0.95	1.28	2.36
Cash Flow	0.17	0.60	-0.01	0.89	2.32	1.69	2.68	2.08	0.64	1.18
Earnings	-0.06	-0.46	-1.91	-1.02	1.25	1.11	2.06	0.65	-0.10	0.76
S&P Core Earnings	0.02	-0.53	-2.05	-1.18	NA	NA	NA	NA	NA	NA
Dividends	0.08	0.08	0.08	0.08	0.08	0.08	0.07	0.06	0.06	0.04
Payout Ratio	NM	NM	NM	NM	6%	7%	3%	10%	NM	5%

Cal. Yrs.	2003	2002	2001	2000	1999	1998	1997	1996	1995	1994
Prices - High	29.29	38.74	39.03	79.43	70.62	61.93	57.50	45.25	31.33	15.07
- Low	12.39	7.47	18.31	18.12	32.12	26.00	24.83	22.55	13.88	8.11
P/E Ratio - High	NM	NM	NM	NM	56	56	28	70	NM	20
- Low	NM	NM	NM	NM	26	23	12	35	NM	11

Income Statement Analysis (Million $)

	2004	2003	2002	2001	2000	1999	1998	1997	1996	1995
Revs.	3,276	3,116	2,964	4,198	6,103	5,253	4,719	4,040	3,505	2,623
Oper. Inc.	417	421	-62.0	604	3,318	2,529	2,366	2,056	1,678	1,190
Depr.	134	612	1,096	1,110	594	325	349	424	404	236
Int. Exp.	Nil	172	227	344	339	154	147	104	81.0	23.6
Pretax Inc.	-54.0	-363	-1,385	-666	1,590	1,010	1,874	932	-101	697
Eff. Tax Rate	NM	NM	NM	NM	56.2%	38.0%	37.6%	60.7%	NM	38.0%
Net Inc.	-36.0	-267	-1,102	-591	696	626	1,169	366	-56.0	432
S&P Core Earnings	7.10	-301	-1,185	-688	NA	NA	NA	NA	NA	NA

Balance Sheet & Other Fin. Data (Million $)

	2004	2003	2002	2001	2000	1999	1998	1997	1996	1995
Cash	1,902	1,512	1,180	850	1,387	536	251	143	201	301
Curr. Assets	3,358	3,565	3,061	2,643	3,992	2,631	2,255	1,780	1,448	1,148
Total Assets	10,679	11,054	12,226	14,143	17,493	8,070	6,706	6,084	5,016	3,269
Curr. Liab.	2,455	2,974	2,321	2,286	3,004	1,863	1,876	1,727	1,501	848
LT Debt	2,298	2,298	3,334	3,639	4,527	2,032	1,027	1,663	945	50.0
Common Equity	4,718	4,363	4,617	5,780	7,037	2,729	2,481	1,503	1,482	1,578
Total Cap.	7,634	7,525	9,218	11,319	13,929	5,795	4,460	4,019	3,148	2,089
Cap. Exp.	30.0	30.0	25.0	89.0	198	222	84.0	41.4	21.0	35.0
Cash Flow	98.0	345	-6.00	519	1,290	951	1,518	790	348	668
Curr. Ratio	1.4	1.2	1.3	1.2	1.3	1.4	1.2	1.0	1.0	1.4
% LT Debt of Cap.	30.1	30.5	36.2	32.1	32.5	35.1	23.0	43.0	30.0	2.4
% Net Inc.of Revs.	NM	NM	NM	NM	11.4	11.9	24.8	9.1	NM	16.5
% Ret. on Assets	NM	NM	NM	NM	5.4	8.5	18.3	6.6	NM	15.1
% Ret. on Equity	NM	NM	NM	NM	14.3	24.0	58.7	24.5	NM	30.9

Data as orig reptd.; bef. results of disc opers/spec. items. Per share data adj. for stk. divs. Bold denotes primary EPS - prior periods restated. E-Estimated. NA-Not Available. NM-Not Meaningful. NR-Not Ranked. UR-Under Review.

Office: One Computer Associates Plaza, Islandia, NY 11749-7001.
Telephone: 631-342-6000.
Email: cainvestor@ca.com
Website: http://www.ca.com
Chrmn: L.S. Ranieri.
CEO: K.D. Cron.

COO & CFO: J. Clarke.
EVP & General Counsel: K.V. Handal.
SVP & CTO: Y. Gupta.
Investor Contact: M. May 631-342-6193.
Dirs: R. M. Artzt, K. D. Cron, A. M. D'Amato, G. J. Fernandes, R. E. La Blanc, J. W. Lorsch, L. S. Ranieri, W. P. Schuetze, L. S. Unger.

Founded: in 1974.
Domicile: Delaware.
Employees: 15,300.
S&P Analyst: Jonathan Rudy, CFA /MF/BK

The **McGraw·Hill** Companies

Computer Sciences

Recommendation: **BUY** ★★★★
SELL | SELL | HOLD | BUY | BUY

12-Month Target Price: $63.00
(as of November 10, 2004)

CSC has an approximate 0.09% weighting in the **S&P 500**

Sector: Information Technology
Sub-Industry: Data Processing & Outsourced Services
Peer Group: Outsourced Services - Larger Sales

Summary: This leading computer services company provides consulting, systems integration and outsourcing services.

Quantitative Evaluations

S&P Earnings & Dividend Rank: B+

| D | C | B- | B | B+ | A- | A | A+ |

S&P Fair Value Rank: 5

| 1 | 2 | 3 | 4 | 5 |
| Lowest | | | | Highest |

Fair Value Calc.: $87.40 (Undervalued)

S&P Investability Quotient Percentile

100%

CSC scored higher than 100% of all companies for which an S&P Report is available.

Volatility: Average

| Low | Average | High |

Technical Evaluation: Bullish
Since 8/04, the technical indicators for CSC have been Bullish.

Relative Strength Rank: Strong

83

| 1 Lowest | | Highest 99 |

Price as of 11/15/04: $54.90 | **2005E S&P Core EPS:** $2.93

GAAP Earnings vs. Previous Year
▲ Up ▼ Down ► No Change

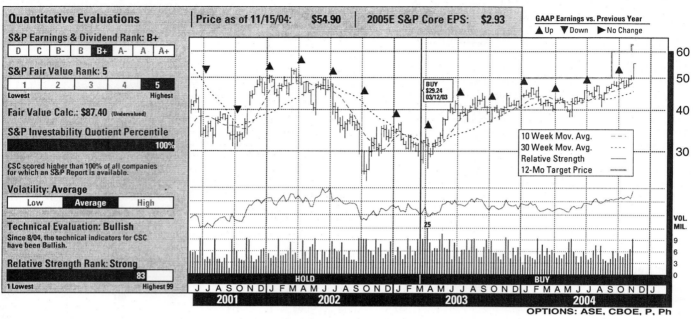

10 Week Mov. Avg.
30 Week Mov. Avg.
Relative Strength
12-Mo Target Price

BUY $29.24 03/12/03

HOLD | BUY

J J A S O N D | J F M A M J J A S O N D | J F M A M J J A S O N D | J F M A M J J A S O N D | J
2001 | 2002 | 2003 | 2004

OPTIONS: ASE, CBOE, P, Ph

Analyst commentary prepared by Stephanie S. Crane/MF/BK

Highlights 16-NOV-04

- We see revenues increasing about 8% in FY 05 (Mar.), following an advance of 30% in FY 04. We expect slower growth, due to more difficult comparisons, as FY 04 results included the acquisition of DynCorp. We anticipate improving demand for global outsourcing services, with particular strength in the U.S. federal government segment, outweighing consulting and systems integration projects.

- CSC sees its addressable federal market pipeline of opportunities consisting of $37 billion in awards that are expected to be allocated over the next 20 months, with nearly $15 billion to be awarded in FY 05. Revenues related to the Department of Defense climbed 70% in FY 04, due to the DynCorp acquisition.

- We think that the company's gross margins should widen, as results benefit from higher volumes. We estimate FY 05 EPS of $3.19, up 16% from FY 04 EPS of $2.75. For FY 06, we project EPS of $3.64. Our FY 05 Standard & Poor's Core Earnings estimate is $2.93, reflecting estimated stock option expense.

Investment Rationale/Risk 16-NOV-04

- We have a strong buy recommendation on CSC. We believe the stock's recent gains reflect new contract announcements, strength from a shift in focus toward outsourcing, improving earnings as well as return on investment, and the acquisition of DynCorp, which we think helped expand CSC's opportunities in the federal government marketplace. Furthermore, we consider recent management comments about stability in IT consulting, as well as a continued upward momentum in outsourcing, noteworthy.

- Risks to our recommendation and target price stem from increased competition for large and long term contracts in the IT infrastructure and outsourcing arena. In turn, this could cause pressure on pricing, which would adversely affect profit margins.

- Our 12-month target price of $63 compares our analysis of the stock's P/E multiple relative to that of the S&P 500. We use a P/E multiple of 20X our FY 05 EPS estimate of $3.19. This multiple is based on a peer average, and is slightly higher than the market multiple. CSC currently trades at 16X our FY 05 estimate, and 14X our FY 06 estimate.

Key Stock Statistics

S&P Oper. EPS 2005E	3.19	52-week Range	$55.29-38.07
P/E on S&P Oper. EPS 2005E	17.3	12 Month P/E	18.6
S&P Oper. EPS 2006E	3.64	Beta	1.66
Yield (%)	Nil	Shareholders	12,174
Dividend Rate/Share	Nil	Market Cap (B)	$10.4
Shares Outstanding (M)	189.3		

Value of $10,000 invested five years ago: **$ 8,689**

Dividend Data

No regular cash dividends have been paid since 1969.

Revenues/Earnings Data Fiscal year ending March 31

Revenues (Million $)

	2005	2004	2003	2002	2001	2000
1Q	3,736	3,555	2,754	2,714	2,463	2,063
2Q	3,935	3,591	2,720	2,765	2,499	2,126
3Q	—	3,621	2,794	2,901	2,665	2,360
4Q	—	4,000	3,079	3,046	2,897	2,575
Yr.	—	14,768	11,347	11,426	10,524	9,371

Earnings Per Share ($)

	2005	2004	2003	2002	2001	2000
1Q	0.58	0.49	0.46	0.28	0.56	0.48
2Q	0.68	0.57	0.54	0.40	0.64	0.55
3Q	E0.87	0.68	0.61	0.51	0.38	0.48
4Q	E1.06	1.01	0.93	0.82	-0.22	0.84
Yr.	E3.19	2.75	2.54	2.01	1.37	2.37

Next earnings report expected: mid-February Source: S&P, Company Reports
EPS Estimates based on S&P Operating Earnings; historical GAAP earnings are as reported.

Computer Sciences Corporation

Recommendation: **BUY** ★★★★★   12-Month Target Price: **$63.00** (as of November 10, 2004)

Business Summary 16-NOV-04

Computer Sciences offers a broad array of services to clients in the global commercial and government markets. The company specializes in the application of complex information technology (IT) to achieve the strategic objectives of its customers. Offerings include IT and business process outsourcing, and IT and professional services.

Outsourcing (45% of revenue in FY 04 (Mar.) versus 53% in FY 03) involves operating all or a portion of a customer's technology infrastructure, including systems analysis, applications development, network operations, desktop computing, and data center management. CSC also provides business process outsourcing, which involves managing key functions for clients such as claims processing, credit checking, logistics, and customer call centers.

IT and professional services (55%, 47%) includes systems integration, consulting and professional services. Systems integration encompasses designing, developing, implementing and integrating complete information systems. Consulting and professional services includes advising clients on the strategic acquisition and utilization of IT, and on business strategy, security, modeling, engineering, and business process re-engineering. CSC also licenses sophisticated software systems for healthcare and financial services markets, and provides a broad array of end-to-end e-business solutions to meet the needs of large commercial and government clients.

The company provides services to clients in global commercial industries, and to the U.S. federal government. In the global commercial segment (59%, 71%), offerings are marketed to clients in a wide variety of industries, including aerospace/defense, automotive, and consumer goods. CSC's largest commercial award in FY 04 was a 10-year, $2.4 billion deal to manage the IT operations of Royal Mail, the post office in the U.K.

In the U.S. federal government market (41%; 29%), CSC provides traditional systems integration and outsourcing for complex project management and technical services. The company has extensive experience in the development of software for mission-critical systems for defense and civil agency applications, and also provides systems engineering and technical assistance in network management, satellite communications, aerospace and related high-technology fields. As a result of the 2003 DynCorp acquisition, CSC also offers various technical functions, such as aircraft maintenance and marine services.

In March 2003, CSC acquired DynCorp, a provider of systems, services, outsourcing, and electronic business solutions to the U.S. government, for $918 million, including the assumption of debt. The acquisition has significantly strengthened CSC's position in the U.S. federal marketplace, and provides an opportunity for diversification into new markets.

In FY 04, revenues by region were: U.S. 67% (versus 64% in FY 03), Europe 25% (26%), and other international 8% (11%).

Company Financials Fiscal Year ending March 31

Per Share Data ($)

(Year Ended March 31)	2004	2003	2002	2001	2000	1999	1998	1997	1996	1995
Tangible Bk. Val.	15.44	11.78	11.58	9.26	12.78	10.98	9.32	7.23	7.68	6.18
Cash Flow	8.29	6.95	7.02	5.17	5.59	4.85	4.08	3.36	3.58	2.68
Earnings	2.75	2.54	2.01	1.37	2.37	2.11	1.64	1.23	1.24	1.05
S&P Core Earnings	2.68	1.84	1.48	0.80	NA	NA	NA	NA	NA	NA
Dividends	Nil	Nil	Nil	Nil	Nil	Nil	Nil	Nil	Nil	Nil
Payout Ratio	Nil	Nil	Nil	Nil	Nil	Nil	Nil	Nil	Nil	Nil

Cal. Yrs.	2003	2002	2001	2000	1999	1998	1997	1996	1995	1994
Prices - High	44.99	53.47	66.71	99.87	94.62	74.87	43.87	43.25	37.62	26.31
- Low	26.52	24.30	28.99	58.25	52.37	39.96	28.93	32.06	23.25	15.81
P/E Ratio - High	16	21	33	73	40	35	27	35	30	25
- Low	10	10	14	43	22	19	18	26	19	15

Income Statement Analysis (Million $)

	2004	2003	2002	2001	2000	1999	1998	1997	1996	1995
Revs.	14,768	11,347	11,426	10,524	9,371	7,660	6,601	5,616	4,242	3,373
Oper. Inc.	1,968	1,609	1,497	1,302	1,239	990	849	718	514	376
Depr.	1,038	858	858	649	546	445	387	333	252	173
Int. Exp.	170	143	155	106	58.1	48.5	51.0	40.3	35.0	28.8
Pretax Inc.	747	612	497	330	611	511	191	303	231	174
Eff. Tax Rate	30.5%	28.0%	30.7%	29.4%	34.1%	33.3%	NM	36.7%	38.8%	36.3%
Net Inc.	519	440	344	233	403	341	260	192	142	111
S&P Core Earnings	507	319	254	137	NA	NA	NA	NA	NA	NA

Balance Sheet & Other Fin. Data (Million $)

	2004	2003	2002	2001	2000	1999	1998	1997	1996	1995
Cash	610	300	149	185	260	603	275	110	105	155
Curr. Assets	4,867	4,088	3,304	3,204	2,766	2,669	1,983	1,612	1,144	1,082
Total Assets	11,804	10,433	8,611	8,175	5,874	5,008	4,047	3,581	2,596	2,334
Curr. Liab.	3,253	2,987	2,708	3,589	1,984	2,081	1,215	1,087	760	778
LT Debt	2,306	2,205	1,873	1,029	652	398	736	631	405	310
Common Equity	5,504	4,606	3,624	3,215	3,044	2,400	2,001	1,670	1,306	1,149
Total Cap.	7,810	6,811	5,497	4,245	3,780	2,798	2,737	2,416	1,783	1,511
Cap. Exp.	725	639	672	897	586	426	349	322	260	193
Cash Flow	1,558	1,298	1,202	883	949	786	647	526	394	283
Curr. Ratio	1.5	1.4	1.2	0.9	1.4	1.3	1.6	1.5	1.5	1.4
% LT Debt of Cap.	29.5	32.4	34.1	24.3	17.3	14.2	26.9	26.1	22.7	20.5
% Net Inc.of Revs.	3.5	3.9	3.0	2.2	4.3	4.5	3.9	3.4	3.3	3.3
% Ret. on Assets	4.7	4.6	4.1	3.3	7.2	7.5	6.8	5.9	5.7	5.1
% Ret. on Equity	10.3	10.7	10.1	7.5	14.3	15.5	14.2	12.5	11.5	10.9

Data as orig reptd.; bef. results of disc opers/spec. items. Per share data adj. for stk. divs. Bold denotes primary EPS - prior periods restated. E-Estimated. NA-Not Available. NM-Not Meaningful. NR-Not Ranked. UR-Under Review.

Office: 2100 East Grand Avenue, El Segundo, CA 90245.
Telephone: 310-615-0311.
Email: investorrelations@csc.com
Website: http://www.csc.com
Chrmn & CEO: V. B. Honeycutt.
Pres & COO: M. W. Laphen.

VP & CFO: L. J. Level.
VP, Secy & General Counsel: H. D. Fisk.
Dirs: I. W. Bailey II, S. L. Baum, R. F. Chase, V. B. Honeycutt, W. R. Hoover, T. A. McDonnell, F. W. McFarlan, J. R. Mellor, T. H. Patrick, W. P. Rutledge.

Founded: in 1959.
Domicile: Nevada.
Employees: 90,000.
S&P Analyst: Stephanie S. Crane/MF/BK

Compuware

Recommendation: **HOLD** ★ ★ ★ ★ ★
SELL SELL HOLD BUY BUY

12-Month Target Price: $6.00
(as of July 13, 2004)

CPWR has an approximate 0.02% weighting in the **S&P 500**

Sector: Information Technology
Sub-Industry: Application Software
Peer Group: Application Software - Larger Cos.

Summary: CPWR provides software products and professional services designed to increase productivity of information systems departments.

Quantitative Evaluations

S&P Earnings & Dividend Rank: NR

D	C	B-	B	B+	A-	A	A+

S&P Fair Value Rank: 3

1	2	3	4	5
Lowest				Highest

Fair Value Calc.: $5.70 (Slightly Overvalued)

S&P Investability Quotient Percentile

19%

CPWR scored lower than 81% of all companies for which an S&P Report is available.

Volatility: High

Low	Average	High

Technical Evaluation: Bullish
Since 10/04, the technical indicators for CPWR have been Bullish.

Relative Strength Rank: Moderate

	65	
1 Lowest		Highest 99

Price as of 11/12/04: $5.86 | **2005E S&P Core EPS: $0.06**

GAAP Earnings vs. Previous Year
▲ Up ▼ Down ► No Change

- 10 Week Mov. Avg.
- 30 Week Mov. Avg.
- Relative Strength
- 12-Mo Target Price

Volume Below Avg. — Above Avg. —

HOLD

J J A S O N D | J F M A M J J A S O N D | J F M A M J J A S O N D | J F M A M J J A S O N D | J
2001 | 2002 | 2003 | 2004

OPTIONS: ASE, CBOE, P

Analyst commentary prepared by Zaineb Bokhari/PMW/MGH

Highlights November 02, 2004

- CPWR has struggled in recent years amid notably weak demand for mainframe products and services that we attribute to excessive purchases in preparation for Y2K. Overcapacity in the mainframe industry was expected to last for only a quarter or two, but has persisted into FY 05 (Mar.). Despite the release of multiple versions of IBM's latest mainframe operating system, z/OS, and CPWR's continuing transition to build up its distributed computing offerings, we believe the company has been negatively affected by restrictions on corporate spending on technology.

- We expect flat to slightly lower FY 05 revenue, followed by an increase of 4.6% in FY 06, driven by improving traction in distributed testing solutions. With tight cost controls, we anticipate that operating margins will widen in FY 05 and again in FY 06. We also look for improving professional service margins, as CPWR continues to focus on higher-margin IT professional services rather than low-margin IT staff augmentation services.

- We expect FY EPS of $0.19, up from $0.13 in FY 04. We see an increase to $0.22 in FY 06. Our respective S&P Core EPS projections of $0.06 and $0.07 reflect estimated stock option expense.

Investment Rationale/Risk November 02, 2004

- We would not add to positions, despite the stock's discount to peer valuation, mainly due to our view of the company's operational struggles and inconsistent financial results. We also see significant competition from companies such as IBM as likely to continue to hurt CPWR's financial performance. At 1.6X sales, the stock's valuation on a price to sales basis is at a discount to peers. We view the balance sheet as strong, with nearly $700 million (about $1.80 a share) in cash and investments, and no debt. However, we see concerns about the company's ability to generate steady revenue gains and improved profitability.

- Risks to our opinion and target price include slower than IT expected spending, related to softness in the broader economy; and heightened competition in the systems management software segment both from traditional software vendors, and, increasingly, from large hardware vendors looking to capture additional revenue from sales of their platforms.

- Our 12-month target price of $6 is based on our analysis, using a blend of relative price to sales and P/E multiple to growth metrics.

Key Stock Statistics

S&P Core EPS 2006E	0.07	52-week Range	$8.95-4.35
S&P Oper. EPS 2005E	0.19	12 Month P/E	34.5
P/E on S&P Oper. EPS 2005E	30.8	Beta	NA
S&P Oper. EPS 2006E	0.22	Shareholders	6,710
Yield (%)	Nil	Market Cap (B)	$ 2.3
Dividend Rate/Share	Nil	Shares Outstanding (M)	387.2

Value of $10,000 invested five years ago: **$ 2,028**

Dividend Data

No cash dividends have been paid.

Revenues/Earnings Data Fiscal year ending March 31

Revenues (Million $)

	2005	2004	2003	2002	2001	2000
1Q	287.1	306.0	346.6	446.8	513.9	443.1
2Q	295.5	302.8	358.0	424.0	486.3	568.1
3Q	—	318.2	333.1	450.6	495.4	637.4
4Q	—	337.7	337.6	407.2	514.5	582.1
Yr.	—	1,265	1,375	1,729	2,010	2,231

Earnings Per Share ($)

	2005	2004	2003	2002	2001	2000
1Q	Nil	0.01	0.06	0.09	0.06	0.24
2Q	0.02	-0.02	0.09	0.07	0.03	0.24
3Q	E0.07	0.06	0.07	0.08	0.10	0.34
4Q	E0.11	0.09	0.06	-0.90	0.12	0.12
Yr.	E0.19	0.13	0.27	-0.66	0.32	0.91

Next earnings report expected: late-January Source: S&P, Company Reports
EPS Estimates based on S&P Operating Earnings; historical GAAP earnings are as reported.

Compuware Corporation

Recommendation: **HOLD** ★ ★ ★ ☆ ☆   12-Month Target Price: **$6.00** (as of July 13, 2004)

Business Summary November 02, 2004

Compuware provides products and professional services intended to improve productivity in a number of information technology (IT) areas: mainframes, distributed and web development, testing, and operations. CPWR targets companies with IT departments, because it believes they invest substantial resources to build and maintain large, complex and mission-critical applications.

Each of CPRW's markets includes four primary categories: the application development environment in which application software is initially constructed; the testing and implementation environment in which application software is executed, debugged, tested and maintained in a series of repetitive, ongoing cycles for the life of the application; the performance testing phase, when an application is tested under simulated production conditions to ensure it will function well once implemented; and the production environment in which the performance of operating systems, databases, servers, applications and networks is monitored and managed.

Revenues in FY 04 (Mar.) and FY 03 were derived from software license fees (24% and 21%, respectively), maintenance fees (32%, 30%), and professional service fees (44%, 49%).

Mainframe testing and implementation software products improve application testing productivity, test data preparation, error analysis and system maintenance for IBM-compatible mainframes. Products are used for file and data management (File-AID), fault management (Abend-AID), interactive analysis and debugging (XPEDITER), automated testing (QA Center Mainframe), and resource conservation (STROBE). Mainframe revenue was 42% of total revenue in FY 04, up from 40% in FY 03.

CPWR's distributed systems application development toolset (UNIFACE and Optimal) is designed to assist software developers to create, deploy and maintain complex applications. Distributed and Internet testing products are used for file and data management (File-AID/Client Server); for detection, diagnosis and resolution of software errors and performance problems (DevPartner); automated testing (QA Center Distributed); management, analysis and performance improvement (Vantage). Distributed revenue was 14% of total revenue in FY 04, up from 11% in FY 03.

Professional services include IT staffing and project assistance, e-business and wireless development, and electronic resource planning (ERP) implementation. The company also offers application lifecycle management assistance and services related to its products.

In FY 03, Ford Motor accounted for 12% of total revenues. In FY 04 and 02, no customer accounted for over 10% of total revenues.

In recent years, CPWR has focused on strengthening its balance sheet, which now shows no debt.

Company Financials Fiscal Year ending March 31

Per Share Data ($)

(Year Ended March 31)	2004	2003	2002	2001	2000	1999	1998	1997	1996	1995
Tangible Bk. Val.	3.11	2.93	2.60	2.02	1.51	2.70	1.81	4.54	0.94	0.91
Cash Flow	0.27	0.41	-0.40	0.60	1.10	0.97	0.59	0.63	0.15	0.19
Earnings	0.13	0.27	-0.66	0.32	0.91	0.87	0.50	0.27	0.12	0.16
S&P Core Earnings	0.03	0.14	-0.15	0.17	NA	NA	NA	NA	NA	NA
Dividends	Nil	Nil	Nil	Nil	Nil	Nil	Nil	Nil	Nil	Nil
Payout Ratio	Nil	Nil	Nil	Nil	Nil	Nil	Nil	Nil	Nil	Nil

Cal. Yrs.	2003	2002	2001	2000	1999	1998	1997	1996	1995	1994
Prices - High	6.52	14.00	14.50	37.81	40.00	39.90	19.75	7.78	5.37	6.15
- Low	3.22	2.35	6.25	5.62	16.37	15.56	6.03	1.93	2.18	3.06
P/E Ratio - High	50	52	NM	NM	44	46	39	29	43	38
- Low	25	9	NM	NM	18	18	12	7	18	19

Income Statement Analysis (Million $)

	2004	2003	2002	2001	2000	1999	1998	1997	1996	1995
Revs.	1,265	1,375	1,729	2,010	2,231	1,638	1,139	813	614	534
Oper. Inc.	90.5	188	264	296	641	547	317	181	116	129
Depr.	55.2	53.8	98.2	104	71.5	41.5	36.5	15.5	8.57	8.86
Int. Exp.	Nil	6.10	7.43	31.3	24.5	Nil	Nil	Nil	Nil	0.38
Pretax Inc.	56.0	156	-245	192	562	530	291	149	78.8	95.2
Eff. Tax Rate	11.0%	34.0%	NM	38.0%	37.3%	34.0%	33.3%	34.8%	43.8%	34.8%
Net Inc.	49.8	103	-245	119	352	350	194	97.4	44.2	62.1
S&P Core Earnings	9.71	51.2	-55.3	62.2	NA	NA	NA	NA	NA	NA

Balance Sheet & Other Fin. Data (Million $)

	2004	2003	2002	2001	2000	1999	1998	1997	1996	1995
Cash	455	319	233	53.3	30.5	193	206	107	108	165
Curr. Assets	1,143	1,050	1,063	1,004	988	1,072	676	452	362	370
Total Assets	2,234	2,123	1,994	2,279	2,416	1,677	1,073	755	556	524
Curr. Liab.	493	469	556	569	596	522	314	272	220	180
LT Debt	Nil	Nil	Nil	140	450	Nil	6.96	6.07	Nil	Nil
Common Equity	1,414	1,332	1,170	1,377	1,204	1,080	708	446	319	336
Total Cap.	1,418	1,332	1,170	1,538	1,667	1,080	715	452	320	344
Cap. Exp.	74.6	225	90.4	39.8	34.9	26.4	28.0	23.4	15.8	33.5
Cash Flow	105	157	-147	223	423	391	230	113	52.8	71.0
Curr. Ratio	2.3	2.2	1.9	1.8	1.7	2.1	2.2	1.7	1.6	2.1
% LT Debt of Cap.	Nil	Nil	Nil	9.1	27.0	Nil	1.0	1.3	NM	NM
% Net Inc.of Revs.	3.9	7.5	NM	5.9	15.8	21.4	17.0	12.0	7.2	11.6
% Ret. on Assets	2.3	5.0	NM	5.1	17.2	25.5	21.2	14.9	8.2	12.8
% Ret. on Equity	3.6	8.2	NM	9.2	30.8	39.1	33.6	25.5	13.5	19.8

Data as orig reptd.; bef. results of disc opers/spec. items. Per share data adj. for stk. divs. Bold denotes primary EPS - prior periods restated. E-Estimated. NA-Not Available. NM-Not Meaningful. NR-Not Ranked. UR-Under Review.

Office: 1 Campus Martius, Detroit, MI 48226-5099.
Telephone: 313-227-7300.
Email: investor.relations@compuware.com
Website: http://www.compuware.com
Chrmn & CEO: P. Karmanos, Jr.
COO: T.A. White.

SVP, CFO & Treas: L. Fournier.
SVP, Secy & General Counsel: T. Costello, Jr.
Investor Contact: L. Elkin 248-737-7345.
Dirs: D. W. Archer, G. S. Bedi, E. Chappell, E. Didier, W. O. Grabe, W. Halling, P. Karmanos, Jr., F. A. Nelson, G. D. Price, W. J. Prowse, G. S. Romney, L. Weicker, Jr.

Founded: in 1973.
Domicile: Michigan.
Employees: 8,660.
S&P Analyst: Zaineb Bokhari/PMW/MGH

Comverse Technology

Recommendation: **HOLD** ★ ★ ★ ★ ★
SELL SELL HOLD BUY BUY

12-Month Target Price: $25.00
(as of November 09, 2004)

CMVT has an approximate 0.04% weighting in the **S&P 500**

Sector: Information Technology
Sub-Industry: Communications Equipment
Peer Group: Communications Equip. - Enhanced Services

Summary: This company manufactures computer and telecommunications systems and software for communications and information processing applications.

Quantitative Evaluations

S&P Earnings & Dividend Rank: B-

| D | C | B- | B | B+ | A- | A | A+ |

S&P Fair Value Rank: 1-

| 1 | 2 | 3 | 4 | 5 |
| Lowest | | | | Highest |

Fair Value Calc.: $18.60 (Overvalued)

S&P Investability Quotient Percentile
96%

CMVT scored higher than 96% of all companies for which an S&P Report is available.

Volatility: Average

| Low | Average | High |

Technical Evaluation: Bullish
Since 9/04, the technical indicators for CMVT have been Bullish.

Relative Strength Rank: Strong
90
1 Lowest — Highest 99

Price as of 11/15/04: $23.10 **2005E S&P Core EPS:** $-0.60

GAAP Earnings vs. Previous Year
▲ Up ▼ Down ► No Change

10 Week Mov. Avg.
30 Week Mov. Avg.
Relative Strength
12-Mo Target Price

Volume Below Avg. — Above Avg.

OPTIONS: ASE, CBOE, P, Ph

Analyst commentary prepared by Kenneth M. Leon/CB/BK

Highlights 16-NOV-04

- We expect sales to advance 23% in FY 05 (Jan.), following a 4% increase in FY 04, and see 20% growth in FY 06, reflecting our view of an improved wireless telecom spending market. Despite the maturity of CMVT's voice mail products, we are encouraged by positive growth in its software for wireless short messaging services, wireless prepaid services, and enterprise security and surveillance applications.

- We expect the gross margin to approach 60% in FY 05 and FY 06, compared to 57.2% in FY 04, as cost saving efforts, an improving product mix and volume increases outweigh any pricing pressures. The company enjoys a low tax rate as a result of the location of its manufacturing facilities in Israel, which provides significant tax incentives.

- All told, reflecting lower cost of sales as a percentage of total sales, we see operating EPS of $0.27 in FY 05, compared with an operating loss of $0.03 in FY 04. We project operating EPS of $0.46 for FY 06. Our Standard & Poor's Core Earnings estimates are a loss of $0.60 in FY 05 and a loss of $0.27 in FY 06, reflecting the projected impact of stock option expense, to which we believe CMVT has more exposure than its peers.

Investment Rationale/Risk 16-NOV-04

- Following a nearly 45% rise since mid-August, we have lowered our recommendation from buy to hold. While we believe CMVT is well positioned for wireless software applications, we think further upside in the shares is limited near term, based on valuation and our caution on wireless carrier spending for the next four to six months. We recently lowered the S&P Communications Equipment Sub-Industry to neutral from positive on concerns about carrier spending in the fist half of 2005. Should there be a recovery, we think CMVT is poised to take advantage of demand for enhanced wireless service applications around the globe.

- Risks to our recommendation and target price include political risks in Israel, where a substantial portion of CMVT's research and development and manufacturing facilities are located, market conditions in the telecommunications industry, and potential operational problems with its software applications. The company may be at risk for potential delays in realizing sales from its order backlog.

- We are encouraged by the company's steady execution, which helped it realize better than expected revenue and earnings in the second quarter of FY 05, and an order backlog of $437 million at the end of July. We see the balance sheet remaining strong, with about $12 a share in cash and cash equivalents. Applying an assumed price to sales ratio of 4.4X to our FY 06 sales estimate and a price to book value of 2.9X, we arrive at our 12-month target price of $25.

Key Stock Statistics

S&P Core EPS 2006E	-0.27	52-week Range	$23.00-15.25
S&P Oper. EPS 2005E	0.27	12 Month P/E	NM
P/E on S&P Oper. EPS 2005E	85.2	Beta	1.95
S&P Oper. EPS 2006E	0.46	Shareholders	37,500
Yield (%)	Nil	Market Cap (B)	$ 4.5
Dividend Rate/Share	Nil	Shares Outstanding (M)	196.0

Value of $10,000 invested five years ago: **$ 3,793**

Dividend Data

No cash dividends have been paid.

Revenues/Earnings Data Fiscal year ending January 31

Revenues (Million $)

	2005	2004	2003	2002	2001	2000
1Q	221.4	180.6	211.2	365.0	261.3	200.5
2Q	233.4	188.5	181.2	345.1	292.1	209.3
3Q	—	193.8	167.5	295.0	318.0	221.8
4Q	—	203.0	176.0	265.1	346.6	240.6
Yr.	—	765.9	735.9	1,270	1,225	872.2

Earnings Per Share ($)

	2005	2004	2003	2002	2001	2000
1Q	0.03	-0.03	-0.13	0.43	0.33	0.24
2Q	0.06	-0.01	0.02	0.15	0.30	0.26
3Q	E0.08	-0.02	-0.43	0.01	0.35	0.28
4Q	E0.09	0.02	-0.16	-0.29	0.41	0.30
Yr.	E0.27	-0.03	-0.69	0.29	1.39	1.07

Next earnings report expected: early-December Source: S&P, Company Reports
EPS Estimates based on S&P Operating Earnings; historical GAAP earnings are as reported.

Comverse Technology, Inc.

Recommendation: **HOLD** ★ ★ ★ ☆ ☆   12-Month Target Price: **$25.00** (as of November 09, 2004)

Business Summary 16-NOV-04

Comverse Technology's multimedia communications and information processing technology and products cover four primary categories: call completion and call management solutions; advanced messaging solutions; management and delivery of data and content-based services; and real-time billing and account management.

Enhanced Services Solutions (69% of FY 04 (Jan.) sales) include enhanced service platforms (ESP) for telecommunications carriers. These platforms enable the provision of revenue generating value added services, including call answering, unified messaging, short text messaging, one-touch call return and other personal communications services. CMVT customers benefit from receiving service subscription fees and from traffic revenue generated by the increase in completed calls. In addition, the services help reduce overall network traffic due to repeated busy or no-answer calls.

More than 400 wireless and wireline network operators use CMVT's ESP systems in more than 110 countries. Users include a majority of the world's largest telephone companies. Major customers include AT&T (U.S.), Deutsche Telekom (Germany), KDDI (Japan), MCI Worldcom (U.S.), O2 (Germany and U.K.), NTT (Japan), Orange (several countries), SBC Communications (U.S.), SFR (France), Sprint PCS (U.S.), Telecom Italia (Italy), Telmex (Mexico), Telstra (Australia), Verizon (USA), and Vodafone (multiple countries).

Digital Security and Surveillance and Enterprise Business Intelligence Products (25% of FY 04 sales), offered through 61.8%-owned Verint, include analytic software-based solutions for communications interception, digital video security and surveillance, and enterprise business intelligence. Verint's software generates intelligence through the collection, retention and analysis of voice, fax, video, e-mail, Internet and data transmission from multiple types of communications networks.

Service Enabling Signaling Software Products (5% of FY 04 sales), offered through 70.2%-owned Ulticom, include service enabling software for wireline, wireless and Internet communications. Ulticom's Signalware family of products are used by equipment manufacturers, application developers and service providers to deploy revenue generating infrastructure, enhanced and mandated services such as mobility, messaging, payment and location-based services.

Other Products and Services (1% of FY 04 sales) include automatic call distribution and messaging systems for telephone answering service bureaus and other organizations, and intelligent IP gateways for wireless roaming. In FY 04, sales by country, based on end-user location, were: U.S. 34%, Germany 6%, and other 60%. A substantial portion of CMVT's research and development, manufacturing and other operations are located in Israel and, accordingly, may be affected by economic, political and military conditions in that country.

Company Financials Fiscal Year ending January 31

Per Share Data ($)

(Year Ended January 31)	2004	2003	2002	2001	2000	1999	1998	1997	1996	1995
Tangible Bk. Val.	8.60	8.25	8.63	7.24	4.62	2.71	3.46	2.84	1.86	1.66
Cash Flow	0.35	-0.33	0.64	1.59	1.15	0.92	0.65	0.44	0.34	0.26
Earnings	-0.03	-0.69	0.29	1.39	1.07	0.78	0.54	0.39	0.25	0.19
S&P Core Earnings	-0.68	-1.35	-0.54	0.92	NA	NA	NA	NA	NA	NA
Dividends	Nil	Nil	Nil	Nil	Nil	Nil	Nil	Nil	Nil	Nil
Payout Ratio	Nil	Nil	Nil	Nil	Nil	Nil	Nil	Nil	Nil	Nil

Cal. Yrs.	2003	2002	2001	2000	1999	1998	1997	1996	1995	1994
Prices - High	19.65	28.28	124.75	123.87	72.50	23.83	18.29	13.95	8.66	5.20
- Low	8.50	6.65	15.03	61.81	21.66	9.79	10.45	5.37	3.66	2.66
P/E Ratio - High	NM	NM	NM	89	68	31	34	36	35	27
- Low	NM	NM	NM	44	20	13	19	14	15	14

Income Statement Analysis (Million $)

	2004	2003	2002	2001	2000	1999	1998	1997	1996	1995
Revs.	766	736	1,270	1,225	872	696	280	207	137	93.0
Oper. Inc.	39.3	-48.7	192	304	205	136	51.5	34.8	20.5	15.5
Depr.	71.8	67.4	63.8	53.2	33.5	20.9	9.70	7.13	5.87	4.19
Int. Exp.	6.98	Nil	Nil	18.0	19.3	15.2	9.77	7.10	4.40	3.75
Pretax Inc.	8.58	-126	59.1	268	186	123	48.3	31.3	19.1	13.5
Eff. Tax Rate	NM	NM	7.51%	7.03%	8.38%	9.56%	9.96%	10.7%	10.8%	12.7%
Net Inc.	-5.39	-129	54.6	249	170	112	43.5	28.0	17.1	11.8
S&P Core Earnings	-129	-252	-94.8	162	NA	NA	NA	NA	NA	NA

Balance Sheet & Other Fin. Data (Million $)

	2004	2003	2002	2001	2000	1999	1998	1997	1996	1995
Cash	1,531	1,403	1,362	1,275	339	584	174	236	123	128
Curr. Assets	2,462	2,127	2,397	2,276	1,176	933	405	351	190	167
Total Assets	2,728	2,404	2,704	2,625	1,352	1,031	458	391	221	188
Curr. Liab.	321	360	367	415	327	225	75.2	58.7	35.2	22.7
LT Debt	Nil	391	600	900	300	415	115	115	60.0	60.0
Common Equity	1,673	1,550	1,616	1,236	711	382	261	212	122	103
Total Cap.	1,834	2,024	2,278	2,190	1,011	797	377	327	182	163
Cap. Exp.	35.4	34.1	54.6	97.3	84.8	24.7	12.6	9.75	5.56	4.24
Cash Flow	66.4	-62.1	118	302	204	132	53.2	35.1	22.9	16.0
Curr. Ratio	7.7	5.9	6.5	5.5	3.6	4.1	5.4	6.0	5.4	7.4
% LT Debt of Cap.	Nil	19.3	26.3	41.1	29.7	52.1	30.5	35.1	33.0	36.8
% Net Inc.of Revs.	NM	NM	4.3	20.3	19.5	16.0	15.5	25.9	12.4	12.6
% Ret. on Assets	NM	NM	2.0	12.5	14.3	15.0	15.0	9.2	8.2	6.6
% Ret. on Equity	NM	NM	3.8	25.4	31.2	34.8	34.7	16.8	15.3	12.2

Data as orig. reptd.; bef. results of disc. opers. and/or spec. items. Per share data adj. for stk. divs.; EPS diluted (primary prior to 1998). Prior to 1999, yr. ended Dec. 31 of the prior cal. yr. E-Estimated. NA-Not Available. NM-Not Meaningful. NR-Not Ranked.

Office: 170 Crossways Park Drive, Woodbury, NY 11797-2029.
Telephone: 516-677-7200.
Email: info@comverse.com
Website: http://www.cmvt.com
Chrmn & CEO: K. Alexander.
Pres: I. Danziger.

EVP & CFO: D. Kreinberg.
Secy: W. F. Sorin.
Investor Contact: Paul D. Baker (516-677-7226).
Dirs: K. Alexander, R. Alon, I. Danziger, J. H. Friedman, R. Hiram, S. Oolie, W. F. Sorin.

Founded: in 1984.
Domicile: New York.
Employees: 4,663.
S&P Analyst: Kenneth M. Leon/CB/BK

STANDARD &POOR'S

ConAgra Foods

Recommendation: **HOLD** ★ ★ ★ ★ ☆   12-Month Target Price: **$29.00**
SELL | SELL | HOLD | BUY | BUY
(as of June 24, 2004)

CAG has an approximate 0.13% weighting in the **S&P 500**

Sector: Consumer Staples
Sub-Industry: Packaged Foods & Meats
Peer Group: Very Large Food Manufacturers

Summary: CAG is one of the largest U.S. packaged food processors.

Quantitative Evaluations

S&P Earnings & Dividend Rank: A

D	C	B-	B	B+	A-	A	A+

S&P Fair Value Rank: 4+

1	2	3	4	5
Lowest				Highest

Fair Value Calc.: $27.20 (Slightly Overvalued)

S&P Investability Quotient Percentile

90%

CAG scored higher than 90% of all companies for which an S&P Report is available.

Volatility: Low

Low	Average	High

Technical Evaluation: Bullish
Since 11/04, the technical indicators for CAG have been Bullish.

Relative Strength Rank: Moderate

58

1 Lowest   Highest 99

Price as of 11/12/04: $28.13   **2005E S&P Core EPS:** $1.57

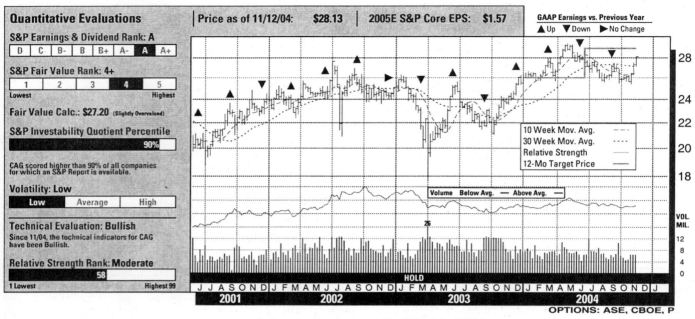

GAAP Earnings vs. Previous Year
▲ Up   ▼ Down   ► No Change

- 10 Week Mov. Avg.
- 30 Week Mov. Avg.
- Relative Strength
- 12-Mo Target Price

Volume   Below Avg. — Above Avg. —

HOLD

J J A S O N D | J F M A M J J A S O N D | J F M A M J J A S O N D | J F M A M J J A S O N D | J
2001   2002   2003   2004

OPTIONS: ASE, CBOE, P

Analyst commentary prepared by Richard Joy/MF/GG

Highlights July 15, 2004

- We expect net sales to edge up at a low single digit rate in FY 05 (May), as modest growth for the packaged foods and ingredients segments outweighs the November 2003 divestiture of the agricultural products business. We see the packaged food segment generating 3% to 5% operating profit growth, as volume gains and mix improvements are partly offset by higher marketing spending. We expect profits of the food ingredients segment to advance 2% to 3%. We expect free cash flows to grow in line with revenue growth.

- Aided by a 3% to 4% reduction in shares outstanding, we estimate FY 05 EPS of $1.60, up 7% from EPS of $1.50 for FY 04. For the longer term, we expect annual EPS growth of 6% to 8%.

- Our FY 04 and FY 05 Standard and Poor's Core Earnings projections, reflecting estimated stock options expense of $0.04 a share and pension adjustments in each year, are $1.47 and $1.57 a share, respectively.

Investment Rationale/Risk July 15, 2004

- Our hold recommendation on the stock primarily reflects mixed operating results in recent quarters, and our view that moves by CAG to become more of a branded food company are reflected in the current valuation. The divestitures of the fresh beef, pork and chicken processing businesses, together with the agricultural products segment, should reduce earnings volatility, but we expect results to continue to be affected by high energy and raw material costs. With the stock recently trading at 17.5X our calendar 2005 EPS estimate of $1.57, in line with the P/E multiples of comparable packaged food peers, we view the shares as fairly valued.

- Risks to our recommendation and target price include competitive pressures in CAG's businesses, commodity cost inflation, and the company's inability to achieve cost savings and efficiency targets.

- Our DCF analysis, which assumes a weighted average cost of capital of 8.5%, calculates intrinsic value in the high $20 area. Our 12-month target price of $29 is derived from an analysis of comparable peer multiples and our DCF model.

Key Stock Statistics

S&P Oper. EPS 2005E	1.60	52-week Range	$29.53-23.88
P/E on S&P Oper. EPS 2005E	17.6	12 Month P/E	18.2
S&P Oper. EPS 2006E	1.70	Beta	0.25
Yield (%)	3.9%	Shareholders	271,000
Dividend Rate/Share	1.09	Market Cap (B)	$ 14.5
Shares Outstanding (M)	514.3		

Value of $10,000 invested five years ago: **$ 13,784**

Dividend Data Dividends have been paid since 1976

Amount ($)	Date Decl.	Ex-Div. Date	Stock of Record	Payment Date
0.260	Apr. 09	Apr. 29	May. 03	Jun. 01 '04
0.260	Jul. 09	Jul. 29	Aug. 02	Sep. 01 '04
0.273	Sep. 23	Oct. 28	Nov. 01	Dec. 01 '04

Revenues/Earnings Data Fiscal year ending May 31

Revenues (Million $)

	2005	2004	2003	2002	2001	2000
1Q	3,496	4,394	6,529	7,608	6,802	6,594
2Q	—	3,873	5,438	7,364	7,206	6,603
3Q	—	3,598	3,963	6,245	6,429	5,798
4Q	—	3,962	3,910	6,414	6,437	6,392
Yr.	—	14,522	19,839	27,630	27,194	25,386

Earnings Per Share ($)

	2005	2004	2003	2002	2001	2000
1Q	0.26	0.38	0.42	0.36	0.30	0.21
2Q	E0.50	0.45	0.44	0.44	0.58	0.39
3Q	E0.42	0.36	0.30	0.31	0.19	0.30
4Q	E0.40	0.37	0.42	0.36	0.23	-0.04
Yr.	E1.60	1.50	1.58	1.47	1.33	0.86

Next earnings report expected: late-December   Source: S&P, Company Reports
EPS Estimates based on S&P Operating Earnings; historical GAAP earnings are as reported.

ConAgra Foods, Inc.

Recommendation: **HOLD** ★★★☆☆   12-Month Target Price: **$29.00** (as of June 24, 2004)

Business Summary July 15, 2004

ConAgra Foods (formerly ConAgra, Inc.) is one of the largest food companies in North America. Following the divestiture of the company's fresh beef and pork business in FY 03 (May), and the sale of its chicken processing and agricultural products businesses in early FY 04, CAG's businesses are divided into two main segments: packaged foods, which provided 62% of total sales in FY 03 (May); and food ingredients (11%). The remaining 27% of sales came from divested businesses.

Packaged foods consists of branded shelf-stable, frozen and refrigerated food products. Major shelf-stable grocery brands include Hunt's and Healthy Choice tomato products; Wesson oils; Healthy Choice soups; Orville Redenbacher's and Act II popcorn; Peter Pan peanut butter; and Van Camp's canned beans. Major frozen grocery brands include Healthy Choice, Banquet, Marie Callender's, Kid Cuisine, Morton, Chun King, and La Choy. Diversified products businesses include Lamb-Weston (frozen potatoes) and Arrow Industries (private label products). Refrigerated products include cheeses (County Line) and refrigerated dessert toppings (Reddi-Wip).

The food ingredients segment includes the company's food ingredient, spice and grain processing (flour, oat and dry corn milling) operations. CAG sold its agricultural products business, which included crop protection chemicals and fertilizers, to Apollo Management L.P. in November 2003, for total consideration of $610 million.

In August 2000, CAG acquired International Home Foods (IHF), for $2.9 billion, including the assumption of $1.3 billion of debt. IHF manufactures, distributes and markets food products with established brands, including Chef Boyardee pasta products, PAM cooking spray, Bumble Bee seafood, and Gulden's mustard.

In May 2001, the company said it would restate revenues and earnings for FY 98 to FY 00, due to the discovery of accounting improprieties at its United Agri Products Companies subsidiary. Revenue and diluted EPS reductions were as follows: for FY 98, $42 million and $0.02; for FY 99, $84 million and $0.06; and for FY 00, $161 million and $0.06. For FY 01, the restatement would have the effect of increasing revenues by $324 million, and diluted EPS by $0.16.

In September 2002, the company sold its fresh beef and pork processing business to a joint venture led by Hicks, Muse, Tate & Furst Inc., for $1.36 billion, leaving CAG with a 46% stake in the new venture. In November 2003, the company sold its chicken business to Pilgrim's Pride Corp., for $590 million. The transaction included all of CAG's fresh chicken business, representing over $2 billion in annual sales, but did not include the Butterball turkey brand or the company's prepared chicken products, sold in retail channels under brands such as Banquet, Healthy Choice, and Marie Callender's.

Company Financials Fiscal Year ending May 31

Per Share Data ($)

(Year Ended May 31)	2004	2003	2002	2001	2000	1999	1998	1997	1996	1995
Tangible Bk. Val.	0.41	NM	NM	NM	1.22	1.02	0.81	0.08	NM	0.15
Cash Flow	2.16	2.30	2.39	2.30	1.98	1.80	2.33	2.24	1.30	1.85
Earnings	1.50	1.58	1.47	1.33	0.86	0.75	1.36	1.34	0.40	1.03
S&P Core Earnings	1.53	1.42	1.27	1.20	NA	NA	NA	NA	NA	NA
Dividends	0.98	NA	0.88	0.79	0.74	0.65	0.60	0.53	0.46	0.39
Payout Ratio	65%	NA	60%	59%	86%	86%	44%	39%	116%	38%

Cal. Yrs.	2003	2002	2001	2000	1999	1998	1997	1996	1995	1994
Prices - High	26.41	27.65	26.00	26.18	34.37	33.62	38.75	27.37	20.87	16.56
- Low	17.75	20.90	17.50	15.06	20.62	22.56	24.50	18.81	14.87	12.75
P/E Ratio - High	18	18	18	20	40	45	28	20	53	16
- Low	12	14	12	11	24	30	18	14	38	12

Income Statement Analysis (Million $)

	2004	2003	2002	2001	2000	1999	1998	1997	1996	1995
Revs.	14,522	19,839	27,630	27,194	25,386	24,594	23,841	24,022	24,822	24,109
Oper. Inc.	1,735	1,123	2,144	2,026	1,828	1,940	1,767	1,709	1,629	1,476
Depr.	352	392	474	499	537	500	446	414	408	376
Int. Exp.	275	276	402	423	303	354	338	332	352	311
Pretax Inc.	1,151	1,276	1,268	1,104	666	682	1,021	1,081	409	826
Eff. Tax Rate	30.9%	34.2%	38.1%	38.2%	38.0%	47.5%	38.5%	39.6%	53.8%	40.0%
Net Inc.	796	840	785	683	413	358	628	615	189	496
S&P Core Earnings	811	750	668	612	NA	NA	NA	NA	NA	NA

Balance Sheet & Other Fin. Data (Million $)

	2004	2003	2002	2001	2000	1999	1998	1997	1996	1995
Cash	589	629	158	198	158	62.8	95.0	106	114	60.0
Curr. Assets	5,145	6,060	6,434	7,363	5,967	5,656	5,487	5,205	5,567	5,140
Total Assets	14,230	15,071	15,496	16,481	12,296	12,146	11,703	11,277	11,197	10,801
Curr. Liab.	3,002	3,803	4,313	6,936	5,489	5,386	5,070	4,990	5,194	3,965
LT Debt	5,281	5,570	5,919	4,635	3,092	3,068	3,028	2,356	2,263	2,520
Common Equity	4,840	4,622	4,308	3,983	2,964	2,909	2,780	2,472	2,256	2,495
Total Cap.	10,120	10,192	10,227	8,618	6,056	5,977	5,808	5,352	5,044	5,895
Cap. Exp.	352	390	531	560	539	662	569	670	669	428
Cash Flow	1,148	1,232	1,259	1,181	950	858	1,074	1,029	597	847
Curr. Ratio	1.7	1.6	1.5	1.1	1.1	1.1	1.1	1.0	1.1	1.3
% LT Debt of Cap.	52.2	54.7	57.9	53.8	51.1	51.3	52.1	44.0	44.9	42.7
% Net Inc.of Revs.	5.5	4.2	2.8	2.5	1.6	1.5	2.6	2.6	0.8	2.1
% Ret. on Assets	5.4	5.5	4.9	4.8	3.4	3.0	5.5	5.5	1.7	4.6
% Ret. on Equity	16.8	18.8	18.9	19.9	14.1	12.5	23.9	26.0	7.6	20.0

Data as orig reptd.; bef. results of disc opers/spec. items. Per share data adj. for stk. divs. Bold denotes primary EPS - prior periods restated. E-Estimated. NA-Not Available. NM-Not Meaningful. NR-Not Ranked. UR-Under Review.

Office: One Conagra Dr, Omaha, NE 68102-5001.
Telephone: 402-595-4000.
Website: http://www.conagra.com
Chrmn, Pres & CEO: B.C. Rohde.
EVP & Secy: O.C. Johnson.

VP & Investor Contact: C.W. Klinefelter 402-595-4154.
Dirs: D. Batchelder, M. Bay, H. G. Buffett, S. G. Butler, J. T. Chain, Jr., S. F. Goldstone, A. B. Hayes, W. Jurgensen, M. H. Rauenhorst, C. E. Reichardt, B. Rohde, R. W. Roskens, K. E. Stinson.

Founded: in 1919.
Domicile: Delaware.
Employees: 39,000.
S&P Analyst: Richard Joy/MF/GG

ConocoPhillips

Recommendation: **HOLD** ★★★☆☆
SELL · SELL · HOLD · BUY · BUY

12-Month Target Price: $85.00
(as of September 29, 2004)

COP has an approximate 0.55% weighting in the **S&P 500**

Sector: Energy
Sub-Industry: Integrated Oil & Gas
Peer Group: Major Integrated Oil & Gas

Summary: This integrated oil and gas company (formerly Phillips Petroleum) acquired Tosco Corp. in September 2001, and merged with Conoco Inc. in August 2002.

Quantitative Evaluations

S&P Earnings & Dividend Rank: B

| D | C | B- | **B** | B+ | A- | A | A+ |

S&P Fair Value Rank: 4-

| 1 | 2 | 3 | **4** | 5 |
| Lowest | | | | Highest |

Fair Value Calc.: $94.20 (Slightly Undervalued)

S&P Investability Quotient Percentile

85%

COP scored higher than 85% of all companies for which an S&P Report is available.

Volatility: Low

| **Low** | Average | High |

Technical Evaluation: Bullish
Since 9/04, the technical indicators for COP have been Bullish.

Relative Strength Rank: Moderate

62

1 Lowest — Highest 99

Price as of 11/12/04: $87.89 | **2004E S&P Core EPS:** $9.93

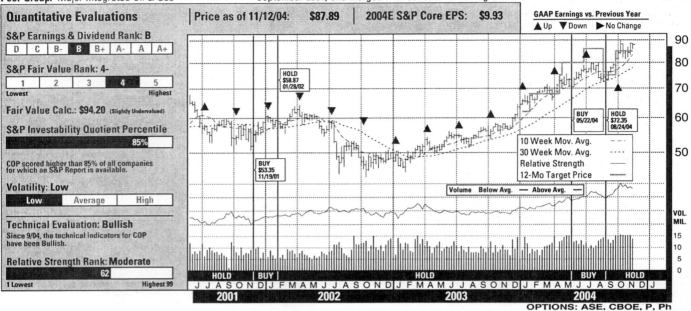

GAAP Earnings vs. Previous Year
▲ Up ▼ Down ► No Change

Legend:
- - - 10 Week Mov. Avg.
······ 30 Week Mov. Avg.
—— Relative Strength
—— 12-Mo Target Price

Volume — Below Avg. — Above Avg.

VOL. MIL.

OPTIONS: ASE, CBOE, P, Ph

Analyst commentary prepared by T. J. Vital/MF/BK

Highlights October 01, 2004

- Strong oil and gas prices and refining margins boosted second quarter operating earnings 77%, year to year, to $2.01 billion, or $2.88 per share, $0.19 above our estimate.

- Second quarter hydrocarbon production fell 4.8%, year to year, on scheduled maintenance, seasonal declines, and asset sales. COP expects third quarter production to decline sequentially, but ramp up in the fourth quarter; 2004 production is expected to average 1.56 million boe/d, a 3% drop from 2003 levels. With large development projects under way and an active exploration program, COP projects 3% annual growth through 2008. However, with natural gas production slowing, we expect a production decline in 2005, before a rebound of about 4% in 2006, on improved liquids volumes. We view organic reserve replacement as strong; we calculate a rate of 132% for 2003. In August, COP and BP announced plans to increase West Sak heavy oil production by 45,000 b/d by 2007, and COP agreed to supply about 2.3 Tcf of natural gas over 17 years (beginning in the 2007) to the industrial market in West Java and Jakarta.

- EBITDA climbed 154% in 2003, reflecting the Conoco merger and strong pricing. We expect a rise of 26% in 2004, on continued strong projected pricing and refining margins, followed by a drop of 20% in 2005, on anticipated lower pricing and reduced volumes.

Key Stock Statistics

S&P Core EPS 2005E	7.55	52-week Range	$89.75-56.41
S&P Oper. EPS 2004E	10.36	12 Month P/E	9.1
P/E on S&P Oper. EPS 2004E	8.5	Beta	0.75
S&P Oper. EPS 2005E	8.30	Shareholders	59,165
Yield (%)	2.3%	Market Cap (B)	$ 60.7
Dividend Rate/Share	2.00	Shares Outstanding (M)	690.2

Value of $10,000 invested five years ago: **$ 22,411**

Dividend Data Dividends have been paid since 1934

Amount ($)	Date Decl.	Ex-Div. Date	Stock of Record	Payment Date
0.430	Feb. 09	Feb. 18	Feb. 20	Mar. 01 '04
0.430	May. 06	May. 13	May. 17	Jun. 01 '04
0.430	Jul. 15	Jul. 28	Jul. 31	Sep. 01 '04
0.500	Sep. 22	Oct. 27	Oct. 29	Dec. 01 '04

Investment Rationale/Risk October 01, 2004

- On September 29, 2004, COP announced it was the successful bidder in an auction for 7.59% of the integrated oil Lukoil's shares held by the Russian government, at a price of $1.988 billion. COP plans to increase its stake by 2.4% in the open market, and will have an option to raise its stake to a maximum 20%. We like the deal, which values Lukoil proved reserves (on an SEC basis) at $3.74 per boe compared with a three-year reserve replacement cost of $5.24 per boe for COP. COP will also pay more than $370 million for 30% of a venture with Lukoil to develop northern Russian reserves, and will seek to develop Iraq's West Qurna oil field. With Lukoil's proved reserves estimated at about 8 billion to 11 billion boe, and 5% oil production growth projected for 2003-2008, we see the deal as opening new growth opportunities for COP in some low-cost regions of the world. COP has been reshaping its portfolio to focus on higher growth assets; its divestment program was completed in the 2004 first half. Funds have been used for dividends and to reduce debt. Capital spending for 2004 is projected to remain near 2003 levels of $6.2 billion.

- Risks to our opinion and target price include geopolitical risk associated with the company's international operations, its ability to achieve upstream production targets, and operational risk from several large development projects.

- Based on a blend of DCF analysis and market and peer valuations, our 12-month target price is $85, or 11X our 2005 EPS estimate, in line with peer levels. With the stock yielding 2.4%, we maintain our hold opinion.

Revenues/Earnings Data Fiscal year ending December 31

Revenues (Million $)

	2004	2003	2002	2001	2000	1999
1Q	29,800	27,077	8,431	4,904	4,768	2,500
2Q	31,886	25,347	10,414	5,000	5,400	3,200
3Q	34,741	26,493	14,557	6,159	5,200	3,800
4Q	—	25,830	23,346	9,964	5,800	4,300
Yr.	—	105,097	57,224	26,868	21,227	13,900

Earnings Per Share ($)

	2004	2003	2002	2001	2000	1999
1Q	2.31	1.86	-0.27	1.91	0.98	0.28
2Q	2.88	1.58	0.95	2.40	1.73	0.27
3Q	2.87	1.82	-0.11	1.34	1.66	0.87
4Q	E2.62	1.48	0.85	0.42	2.88	0.98
Yr.	E10.36	6.75	1.47	5.57	7.26	2.39

Next earnings report expected: late-January Source: S&P, Company Reports
EPS Estimates based on S&P Operating Earnings; historical GAAP earnings are as reported.

STANDARD &POOR'S

ConocoPhillips

Recommendation: **HOLD** ★ ★ ★ ☆ ☆   12-Month Target Price: **$85.00** (as of September 29, 2004)

Business Summary October 01, 2004

On August 30, 2002, Phillips Petroleum (P) and Conoco (COC) merged, creating ConocoPhillips (COP), the third largest integrated U.S. energy company, based on market capitalization, oil and gas reserves, and production. Targeted synergy capture from the merger (both cost and income enhancements) of $1.75 billion (pretax) was achieved by the first quarter 2004. COP operates in exploration and production (E&P; 25% of 2003 sales, $4.3 billion of 2003 segment net income), refining and marketing (R&M; 72%, $1.3 billion), midstream (3%, $130 million), chemicals (less than 1%, $7 million), and emerging business (less than 1%, and a loss of $99 million). It operates in more than 40 countries, including the U.S. (72% of 2003 sales), the U.K. (11%), Norway (3%), Canada (2%) and elsewhere (12%).

COP explores for and produces crude oil, natural gas and natural gas liquids (NGLs), and mines oil sands to produce Syncrude. In 2003, the company replaced 106% of production; excluding sales and acquisitions, the replacement ratio was 133%. Proved crude oil reserves were 4,667 million bbl. (60% developed) in 2003, versus 4,632 million bbl. (63%) in 2002. Proved natural gas reserved were 16.06 trillion cubic feet (Tcf; 78% developed) in 2003, versus 16.02 Tcf (80%) in 2002. Crude oil production averaged 934,000 bbl. per day (b/d; 44% North America) in 2003, versus 682,000 b/d (56%) in 2002. Syncrude production averaged 19,000 b/d in 2003, versus 8,000 b/d in 2002. NGL production averaged 69,000 b/d (84%) in 2003, versus 46,000 b/d (78%) in 2002. Natural gas production averaged 3.522 Bcf per day (54%) in 2003, versus 2.047 Bcf (62%) in 2002. Three-year (2001-2003) average finding and development costs were $4.29. Production costs were $4.98 per BOE in 2003, versus a three-year average of $4.83.

The company is the largest U.S. refiner, and the fifth largest refiner in the world. At the end of 2003, COP owned or had interests in 12 U.S. refineries, five European refineries, and one refinery in Malaysia, with total capacity of 2.61 million b/d. Crude throughput averaged 2.459 million b/d in 2003, versus 1.813 million b/d in 2002. Product sales averaged 3.046 million b/d (86% U.S.) in 2003, versus 2.451 million b/d (93%) in 2002. During 2003, the company made significant changes to its marketing business, and agreed to sell nearly $1.5 billion in assets. It completed the program in the first half of 2004, with $1.4 billion of divestments. COP will retain 300 to 350 retail outlets in the U.S. (under the Phillips 66, 76 and Conoco brands).

COP is reshaping its midstream segment to focus on its 30% interest in Duke Energy Field Services, LLC (DEFS), one of the largest U.S. natural gas and NGL gathering, processing and marketing companies.

The company participates in the chemicals sector through an equally owned joint venture partnership in Chevron Phillips Chemical Co. LLC (CPChem), one of the world's largest producers of ethylene, polyethylene, styrene, alpha olefins, and one of the largest marketers of cyclohexane.

COP has four emerging businesses under development: fuels technology (including the S Zorb technology), gas-to-liquids (GTL), power generation, and other technologies (such as renewable energy).

Company Financials Fiscal Year ending December 31

Per Share Data ($)

(Year Ended December 31)	2003	2002	2001	2000	1999	1998	1997	1996	1995	1994
Tangible Bk. Val.	25.70	19.81	28.13	21.53	16.13	15.01	16.49	14.56	10.96	11.29
Cash Flow	11.79	10.62	10.28	11.88	5.95	5.92	6.88	8.53	5.12	4.89
Earnings	6.75	1.47	5.57	7.26	2.39	0.91	3.61	4.96	1.79	1.85
S&P Core Earnings	6.85	1.27	5.20	NA	NA	NA	NA	NA	NA	NA
Dividends	1.63	1.48	1.40	1.36	1.36	1.36	1.34	1.25	1.20	1.12
Payout Ratio	24%	101%	25%	19%	57%	149%	37%	25%	67%	61%
Prices - High	66.04	64.10	68.00	70.00	57.25	53.25	52.25	45.87	37.12	37.25
- Low	53.60	44.03	50.00	35.93	37.68	40.18	37.37	31.12	29.87	25.50
P/E Ratio - High	10	44	12	10	24	59	14	9	21	20
- Low	8	30	9	5	16	44	10	6	17	14

Income Statement Analysis (Million $)

	2003	2002	2001	2000	1999	1998	1997	1996	1995	1994
Revs.	104,196	56,748	26,868	21,113	13,751	11,545	15,210	15,731	13,368	12,211
Oper. Inc.	11,866	4,571	8,393	5,528	2,452	1,630	2,748	2,730	2,079	1,752
Depr. Depl. & Amort.	3,485	4,446	1,391	1,179	902	1,302	863	941	871	794
Int. Exp.	864	614	391	422	332	253	280	250	295	265
Pretax Inc.	8,337	2,164	3,302	3,769	1,185	421	1,900	2,172	1,064	852
Eff. Tax Rate	44.9%	67.0%	50.2%	50.6%	48.6%	43.7%	49.5%	40.0%	56.0%	43.2%
Net Inc.	4,593	714	1,643	1,862	609	237	959	1,303	469	484
S&P Core Earnings	4,697	619	1,533	NA	NA	NA	NA	NA	NA	NA

Balance Sheet & Other Fin. Data (Million $)

	2003	2002	2001	2000	1999	1998	1997	1996	1995	1994
Cash	490	307	142	149	138	97.0	163	615	67.0	193
Curr. Assets	11,192	10,903	4,363	2,606	2,773	2,349	2,648	3,306	2,409	2,465
Total Assets	82,455	76,836	35,217	20,509	15,201	14,216	13,860	13,548	11,978	11,436
Curr. Liab.	14,011	12,816	4,542	3,492	2,520	2,132	2,445	3,137	2,815	2,441
LT Debt	16,340	19,267	9,295	7,272	4,921	4,756	2,775	2,555	3,097	3,106
Common Equity	34,366	29,517	14,340	6,093	4,549	4,219	4,814	4,251	3,188	2,953
Total Cap.	60,113	57,796	27,650	15,259	10,950	10,292	9,497	9,286	7,584	7,354
Cap. Exp.	6,169	4,388	3,085	2,022	1,690	2,052	2,043	1,544	1,456	1,154
Cash Flow	8,078	5,160	3,034	3,041	1,511	1,539	1,822	2,244	1,340	1,278
Curr. Ratio	0.8	0.9	1.0	0.7	1.1	1.1	1.1	1.1	0.9	1.0
% LT Debt of Cap.	27.2	33.3	33.6	47.7	44.9	46.2	29.2	27.5	40.9	42.2
% Ret. on Assets	5.8	1.3	5.9	10.4	4.1	1.7	7.0	10.2	4.0	4.3
% Ret. on Equity	14.4	3.3	16.1	35.0	13.9	5.2	21.2	35.0	15.3	17.2

Data as orig reptd.; bef. results of disc opers/spec. items. Per share data adj. for stk. divs.; EPS diluted. E-Estimated. NA-Not Available. NM-Not Meaningful. NR-Not Ranked. UR-Under Review.

Office: 600 North Dairy Ashford, Houston, TX 77079-1175.
Telephone: 281-293-1000.
Website: http://www.conocophillips.com
Chrmn, Pres & CEO: J.J. Mulva.
EVP & CFO: J.A. Carrig.

SVP & General Counsel: S.F. Gates.
Dirs: N. H. Auchinleck, N. R. Augustine, D. L. Boren, J. Copeland, K. M. Duberstein, R. R. Harkin, L. D. Horner, C. C. Krulak, F. A. McPherson, J. J. Mulva, W. K. Reilly, W. R. Rhodes, J. S. Roy, R. L. Tobias, V. J. Tschinkel, K. C. Turner.

Founded: in 1917.
Domicile: Delaware.
Employees: 39,000.
S&P Analyst: T. J. Vital/MF/BK

Consolidated Edison

Recommendation: **SELL** ★ ☆ ☆ ☆ ☆
SELL SELL HOLD BUY BUY

12-Month Target Price: $39.00
(as of October 22, 2004)

ED has an approximate 0.10% weighting in the **S&P 500**

Sector: Utilities
Sub-Industry: Electric Utilities
Peer Group: Electric & Gas- Larger

Summary: This electric and gas utility holding company serves parts of New York, New Jersey and Pennsylvania.

Quantitative Evaluations

S&P Earnings & Dividend Rank: B+

| D | C | B- | B | B+ | A- | A | A+ |

S&P Fair Value Rank: 3-

| 1 | 2 | 3 | 4 | 5 |
| Lowest | | | | Highest |

Fair Value Calc.: $43.30 (Slightly Overvalued)

S&P Investability Quotient Percentile

84%

ED scored higher than 84% of all companies for which an S&P Report is available.

Volatility: Low

| Low | Average | High |

Technical Evaluation: Bullish

Since 7/04, the technical indicators for ED have been Bullish.

Relative Strength Rank: Moderate

61

| 1 Lowest | | Highest 99 |

Price as of 11/12/04: $45.59 | **2004E S&P Core EPS:** $1.24

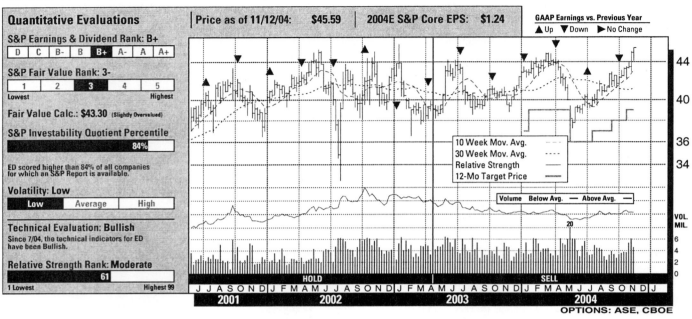

GAAP Earnings vs. Previous Year
▲ Up ▼ Down ▶ No Change

- 10 Week Mov. Avg.
- 30 Week Mov. Avg.
- Relative Strength
- 12-Mo Target Price

Volume Below Avg. — Above Avg.

OPTIONS: ASE, CBOE

Analyst commentary prepared by Justin McCann/CB/GG

Highlights July 29, 2004

- We expect 2004 EPS to decline about 8%, to $2.60, from 2003's EPS from continuing operations of $2.83. A 9.6% decrease in 2003 operating EPS reflected increased benefit costs, and higher depreciation and tax payments, which reduced EPS by $0.24 and $0.12, respectively.

- While the stronger than expected second quarter was aided by a full quarter of two new power plants, we expect the second half of 2004 to be restricted by an increase in pension and other post-retirement benefit costs, higher insurance premiums and depreciation charges, and more shares outstanding. In May 2004, the company issued 14 million new shares; this is expected to dilute 2004 EPS by about $0.10. ED is now in the fourth year of a five-year, $2.4 billion program to upgrade its electric delivery system.

- In the summer of 2004, the New York Public Service Commission (PSC) is expected to issue a ruling on rate increase requests by Con Edison of New York (ConED) for its gas (9.8%) and steam (14.6%) operations. If approved, the three-year rate plan would go into effect October 1, 2004. In April 2004, ConED filed a request for a 6.7% electric rate increase. If approved (a PSC ruling is expected in March 2005), the three-year rate plan would become effective on April 1, 2005.

Key Stock Statistics

S&P Core EPS 2005E	1.58	52-week Range	$45.59-37.23
S&P Oper. EPS 2004E	2.60	12 Month P/E	20.1
P/E on S&P Oper. EPS 2004E	17.5	Beta	-0.11
S&P Oper. EPS 2005E	2.75	Shareholders	93,760
Yield (%)	5.0%	Market Cap (B)	$ 11.0
Dividend Rate/Share	2.26	Shares Outstanding (M)	242.0

Value of $10,000 invested five years ago: $ 15,823

Dividend Data Dividends have been paid since 1885

Amount ($)	Date Decl.	Ex-Div. Date	Stock of Record	Payment Date
0.565	Jan. 22	Feb. 09	Feb. 11	Mar. 15 '04
0.565	Apr. 23	May. 10	May. 12	Jun. 15 '04
0.565	Jul. 22	Aug. 09	Aug. 11	Sep. 15 '04
0.565	Oct. 22	Nov. 08	Nov. 10	Dec. 15 '04

Investment Rationale/Risk July 29, 2004

- We expect ED to post a third consecutive year of lower earnings in 2004. With the shares trading at a P/E multiple on our EPS estimate for 2004 at about a 13% premium to peers, we expect the stock to continue to underperform ED's electric and gas utility peers. We think that one of the company's strengths has been its conservative approach to the development of its non-regulated business, which enabled it to avoid the huge debt and related liquidity and credit problems experienced by other utility holding companies.

- Risks to our investment recommendation and target price include a significantly greater than anticipated economic recovery in the utility's service territory and a sharp increase in the average P/E multiple of the peer group as a whole.

- While ED's stable A credit rating is among the best in its peer group, we believe the stock's performance will be restricted by reduced earnings expectations for 2004 and 2005. Although the shares have benefited from an above-peer dividend yield (recently 5.7%) from what we consider to be a secure dividend, we expect the stock price to decline over the next 12 months. Assuming some contraction in the stock's current P/E multiple premium to peers, based on our 2005 EPS estimate, our 12-month target price is $37.

Revenues/Earnings Data Fiscal year ending December 31

Revenues (Million $)

	2004	2003	2002	2001	2000	1999
1Q	2,685	2,570	2,099	2,886	2,319	1,777
2Q	2,169	2,175	1,900	2,112	2,034	1,479
3Q	2,743	2,801	2,539	2,693	2,821	2,346
4Q	—	2,279	2,057	1,943	2,277	1,889
Yr.	—	9,827	8,482	9,634	9,431	7,491

Earnings Per Share ($)

	2004	2003	2002	2001	2000	1999
1Q	0.68	0.72	0.78	0.84	0.88	0.76
2Q	0.37	0.29	0.46	0.48	0.33	0.30
3Q	1.01	1.16	1.33	1.30	1.32	1.50
4Q	E0.54	0.19	0.56	0.59	0.30	0.57
Yr.	E2.60	2.36	3.13	3.21	2.74	3.13

Next earnings report expected: late-January Source: S&P, Company Reports
EPS Estimates based on S&P Operating Earnings; historical GAAP earnings are as reported.

Consolidated Edison, Inc.

Recommendation: **SELL** ★ ★ ☆ ☆ ☆   12-Month Target Price: **$39.00** (as of October 22, 2004)

Business Summary August 03, 2004

Consolidated Edison is a holding company with electric and gas utilities serving a territory that includes New York City (except part of Queens), most of Westchester County, southeastern New York state, northern New Jersey, and northeastern Pennsylvania.

In 1999, the company acquired Orange and Rockland Utilities (O&R) for $790 million. At December 31, 2003, O&R served 288,746 electric customers and 122,565 gas customers in an area of 1,350 sq. mi. Combined with Consolidated Edison Company of New York, ED provides electricity to around 3,426,000 customers and natural gas to 1,176,500 customers. It also provides steam service to around 1,825 customers in parts of Manhattan.

At December 31, 2003, the distribution system of Consolidated Edison Company of New York had about 32,840 miles of overhead distribution lines and around 90,218 miles of underground distribution lines. The distribution system of O&R had about 5,120 miles of overhead distribution lines, and about 2,688 miles of underground distribution lines.

Electric revenues accounted for 69.8% of consolidated sales in 2003 (73.7% in 2002, 71.5% in 2001); gas revenues 15.2% (14.2%, 15.2%); non-utility revenues 9.5% (7.3%, 8.1%); and steam revenues 5.5% (4.8%, 5.2%).

Consolidated Edison has four unregulated subsidiaries: Consolidated Edison Solutions, which sells electricity and gas to delivery customers of utilities; Consoli-

dated Edison Development, which acquires, develops and operates generating projects; Consolidated Edison Energy, which enters into financial and commodity instruments as part of its wholesale energy trading activities; and Con Edison Communications, which builds and operates fiber optic networks to provide wholesale telecommunications services.

In September 2001, ED sold its Indian Point nuclear facility for $602 million. The sale included the Indian Point 2 unit, which returned to operation in January 2001 after an 11-month shutdown.

In September 1997, the New York Public Service Commission approved an agreement implementing a five-year rate plan that immediately reduced base rates 25% for ED's largest industrial customers and, by the fifth year of the transition, 10% for industrial, residential and commercial customers. In November 2000, the agreement was extended three years, to 2005, and included an additional two-stage, $379 million rate reduction (to be fully implemented as of April 1, 2001), resulting in a combined rate reduction of 16.8%. In August 1999, ED sold fossil-fuel electric generating stations that it was required to sell under the 1997 agreement.

In October 1999, ED agreed to acquire Northeast Utilities System (NU), a holding company with utilities serving 1.7 million customers. However, in March 2001, NU said it considered the merger agreement terminated.

Company Financials Fiscal Year ending December 31

Per Share Data ($)

(Year Ended December 31)	2003	2002	2001	2000	1999	1998	1997	1996	1995	1994
Tangible Bk. Val.	29.09	25.40	24.23	23.50	22.41	25.19	24.52	23.69	22.81	21.90
Earnings	2.36	3.13	3.21	2.74	3.13	3.04	2.95	2.93	2.93	2.98
S&P Core Earnings	1.66	0.50	0.66	NA	NA	NA	NA	NA	NA	NA
Dividends	2.24	2.22	2.20	2.18	2.14	2.12	2.10	2.08	2.04	2.00
Payout Ratio	95%	71%	69%	80%	68%	70%	71%	71%	70%	67%
Prices - High	46.02	45.40	43.37	39.50	53.43	56.12	41.50	34.75	32.25	32.37
- Low	36.55	32.65	31.43	26.18	33.56	39.06	27.00	25.87	25.50	23.00
P/E Ratio - High	20	15	14	14	17	18	14	12	11	11
- Low	15	10	10	10	11	13	9	9	9	8

Income Statement Analysis (Million $)

	2003	2002	2001	2000	1999	1998	1997	1996	1995	1994
Revs.	9,827	8,482	9,634	9,431	7,491	7,093	7,121	6,960	6,537	6,373
Depr.	529	495	526	586	526	519	503	496	456	422
Maint.	353	387	430	458	438	477	475	459	512	506
Fxd. Chgs. Cov.	3.13	3.25	3.46	3.06	4.03	4.24	4.05	4.25	3.95	4.25
Constr. Credits	27.0	14.0	9.00	8.00	6.00	4.00	7.00	5.00	5.59	18.9
Eff. Tax Rate	37.5%	35.6%	38.9%	34.0%	34.3%	35.7%	34.8%	36.4%	35.4%	37.4%
Net Inc.	525	680	696	596	715	730	713	694	724	734
S&P Core Earnings	370	106	141	NA	NA	NA	NA	NA	NA	NA

Balance Sheet & Other Fin. Data (Million $)

	2003	2002	2001	2000	1999	1998	1997	1996	1995	1994
Gross Prop.	19,294	18,000	16,630	17,021	16,088	16,132	15,659	15,352	14,851	14,390
Cap. Exp.	1,292	1,216	1,104	986	695	626	669	724	706	805
Net Prop.	15,225	13,330	12,136	11,786	11,354	11,406	11,267	11,067	10,814	10,561
Capitalization:										
LT Debt	6,769	6,206	5,542	5,447	4,560	4,087	4,229	4,281	3,962	4,078
% LT Debt	51.3	50.3	48.3	48.8	44.5	39.4	40.4	41.4	39.1	40.6
Pfd.	Nil	Nil	250	250	250	250	233	323	640	640
% Pfd.	Nil	Nil	2.18	2.24	2.44	2.41	3.00	3.10	6.30	6.40
Common	6,423	5,921	5,690	5,471	5,448	6,026	5,930	5,728	5,523	5,313
% Common	48.7	48.0	49.6	49.0	53.1	58.1	56.6	55.4	54.5	53.0
Total Cap.	16,406	15,037	13,835	13,602	12,666	12,911	12,949	12,793	12,603	12,562
% Oper. Ratio	88.8	74.1	88.1	117.8	86.0	85.1	85.3	85.4	84.1	83.7
% Earn. on Net Prop.	6.4	8.3	9.4	8.8	9.0	9.3	9.4	9.3	51.4	10.0
% Return On Revs.	5.3	8.0	7.2	6.3	9.5	10.3	10.0	10.0	11.1	11.5
% Return On Invest. Capital	7.3	7.8	8.3	7.7	8.2	11.1	8.1	8.0	11.5	8.5
% Return On Com. Equity	8.5	11.5	12.2	10.7	12.2	11.9	11.9	12.2	12.7	13.5

Data as orig reptd.; bef. results of disc opers/spec. items. Per share data adj. for stk. divs.; EPS diluted. E-Estimated. NA-Not Available. NM-Not Meaningful. NR-Not Ranked. UR-Under Review.

Office: 4 Irving Place, New York, NY 10003.
Telephone: 212-460-4600.
Email: corpcom@coned.com
Website: http://www.coned.com
Chrmn, Pres & CEO: E.R. McGrath.
EVP & CFO: J.S. Freilich.

VP & Treas: R.P. Stelben.
General Counsel: C.E. McTiernan.
Dirs: V. A. Calarco, G. Campbell, G. J. Davis, M. J. Del Giudice, J. S. Freilich, E. V. Futter, S. Hernandez-Pinero, P. W. Likins, E. R. McGrath, F. V. Salerno, R. A. Voell, S. R. Volk.

Founded: in 1884.
Domicile: New York.
Employees: 14,079.
S&P Analyst: Justin McCann/CB/GG

Recommendation: **BUY** ★★★★★ 12-Month Target Price: **$48.00**
SELL | SPIL | HOLD | BUY | BUY
(as of October 29, 2004)

CEG has an approximate 0.07% weighting in the **S&P 500**

Sector: Utilities
Sub-Industry: Multi-Utilities & Unregulated Power
Peer Group: Integrated Gas & Electric distribution

Summary: This holding company owns energy-related businesses, including a North American wholesale power marketing and merchant generation business, and Baltimore Gas and Electric Co.

Quantitative Evaluations

S&P Earnings & Dividend Rank: B

| D | C | B- | **B** | B+ | A- | A | A+ |

S&P Fair Value Rank: 2-

| 1 | **2** | 3 | 4 | 5 |
| Lowest | | | | Highest |

Fair Value Calc.: $38.70 (Slightly Overvalued)

S&P Investability Quotient Percentile

95%

CEG scored higher than 95% of all companies for which an S&P Report is available.

Volatility: Low

| **Low** | Average | High |

Technical Evaluation: Neutral

Since 9/04, the technical indicators for CEG have been Neutral.

Relative Strength Rank: Moderate

68

| 1 Lowest | | Highest 99 |

Price as of 11/12/04: $44.11   **2004E S&P Core EPS: $3.26**

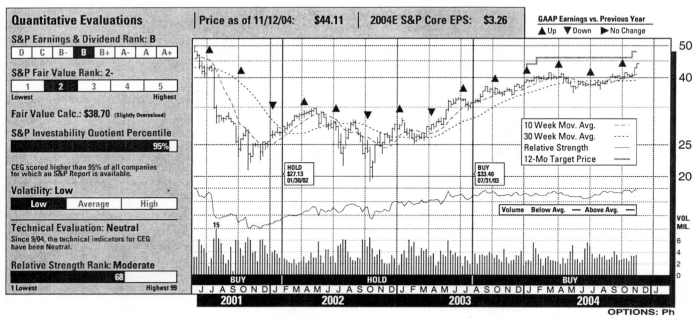

GAAP Earnings vs. Previous Year
▲ Up ▼ Down ► No Change

10 Week Mov. Avg.
30 Week Mov. Avg.
Relative Strength
12-Mo Target Price

HOLD $27.13 01/30/02
BUY $33.40 07/31/03

Volume Below Avg. — Above Avg.

BUY | HOLD | BUY
J J A S O N D J F M A M J J A S O N D J F M A M J J A S O N D J F M A M J J A S O N D J
2001 | 2002 | 2003 | 2004

VOL. MIL.

OPTIONS: Ph

Analyst commentary prepared by Craig K. Shere, CFA /PMW/BK

Highlights August 23, 2004

- Our 2004 operating EPS estimate excludes one-time gains for prior period tax credits ($0.21), the reversal of a prior period writedown of a receivable ($0.04), and asset sale gains ($0.02). Reported 2003 results include $0.02 in one-time hurricane expense net of asset sale gains.

- We look for operating EPS to increase nearly 13% in 2004, driven by growth in commercial and industrial supply operations, full-year contributions from a new California power plant, the June 2004 Ginna acquisition, tax benefits from a new synfuel investment, and shorter plant outages. We see CEG posting strong earnings growth through 2008, driven by the ability to sell power to its Maryland utility at higher market rates (versus current fixed rates) over time, increasing commercial and industrial competitive power supply market share, increased power plant output, and the allocation of free cash flow toward share repurchases and debt reduction. We expect the loss of utility competitive transition charges (CTCs) and synfuel tax credits over time to slow the rate of EPS growth (which we project at 8% between 2005 and 2008).

- Our projected 2005 S&P Core EPS is $0.12 below our operating EPS estimate, primarily due to negative adjustments for pension accounting. Negative pension adjustments are exacerbated by our projection for 2005 pension returns below long-term average returns, due to rising interest rates.

Key Stock Statistics

S&P Core EPS 2005E	3.43	52-week Range	$44.11-35.20
S&P Oper. EPS 2004E	3.25	12 Month P/E	14.4
P/E on S&P Oper. EPS 2004E	13.6	Beta	0.42
S&P Oper. EPS 2005E	3.55	Shareholders	48,287
Yield (%)	2.6%	Market Cap (B)	$ 7.8
Dividend Rate/Share	1.14	Shares Outstanding (M)	175.9

Value of $10,000 invested five years ago: **$ 16,693**

Dividend Data Dividends have been paid since 1910

Amount ($)	Date Decl.	Ex-Div. Date	Stock of Record	Payment Date
0.285	Jan. 23	Mar. 08	Mar. 10	Apr. 01 '04
0.285	Apr. 23	Jun. 08	Jun. 10	Jul. 01 '04
0.285	Jul. 23	Sep. 08	Sep. 10	Oct. 01 '04
0.285	Oct. 25	Dec. 08	Dec. 10	Jan. 03 '05

Investment Rationale/Risk August 23, 2004

- CEG's energy merchant model involves predominantly low cost, baseload generation; an absence of short-term speculative trading; and significantly hedged commodity price risks. This model is, in our opinion, distinguished from and an improvement over the historically speculative energy merchant models that relied on peaking generation, speculative trading, and aggressive accounting. Assuming the the company continues to post steady EPS growth, we expect the market to acknowledge its sustainable business model and afford the stock a valuation at least in line with that of slower growth utility peers.

- Risks to our recommendation and target price include the company's need to hedge contracted electric load obligations, increased competition in wholesale power and competitive commercial and industrial markets, a need to meet targeted increases in plant output, and a potential narrowing of power margins.

- In light of a dividend payout ratio of 35%, well below the peer group average, we believe CEG has ample room to continue its string of annual dividend increases begun in 2002. We believe the stock would be fairly valued at a 2005 P/E multiple closer to the diversified multi-utility average of 12.8X, versus its recent multiple of 11X. Based on a P/E multiple of 12X applied to our 2005 EPS estimate, and assuming appreciation in line with expected longer-term EPS growth, our 12-month target price is $46.

Revenues/Earnings Data Fiscal year ending December 31

Revenues (Million $)

	2004	2003	2002	2001	2000	1999
1Q	3,037	2,330	1,046	1,147	992.2	932.3
2Q	2,793	2,271	1,021	843.2	868.0	820.0
3Q	3,435	2,604	1,270	1,036	981.6	970.5
4Q	—	2,498	1,372	901.9	1,036	1,064
Yr.	—	9,703	4,703	3,928	3,879	3,785

Earnings Per Share ($)

	2004	2003	2002	2001	2000	1999
1Q	0.66	0.40	1.40	0.68	0.48	0.55
2Q	0.77	0.58	0.50	0.46	0.26	0.45
3Q	1.19	1.15	0.92	1.00	0.98	0.91
4Q	E0.80	0.71	0.39	-1.59	0.57	0.26
Yr.	E3.25	2.85	3.20	0.52	2.30	2.18

Next earnings report expected: late-January Source: S&P, Company Reports
EPS Estimates based on S&P Operating Earnings; historical GAAP earnings are as reported.

STANDARD &POOR'S

Constellation Energy Group, Inc.

Stock Report
November 13, 2004
NYSE Symbol: CEG

Recommendation: **BUY** ★★★★★   12-Month Target Price: **$48.00** (as of October 29, 2004)

Business Summary August 23, 2004

In recent periods, Constellation Energy Group has made strategic acquisitions from distressed energy merchants and utilities, while divesting non-core operations. In September 2002, the company acquired NewEnergy, a competitive energy supplier for large commercial and industrial customers, from AES Corp., for $250 million in cash. In 2003, it acquired competitive energy supply and management businesses from Dynegy, CMS Energy Corp., Nicor Energy, Allegheny Energy and Wisconsin Energy for over $84 million. In June 2004, CEG acquired the 495 MW Ginna nuclear power plant from Rochester Gas and Electric for about $408 million.

CEG's operating segments include its Merchant Energy business, accounting for 67% of segment operating income in 2003 (64% in 2002); Regulated Electric Utility operations 23% (28%); Regulated Gas Utility operations 10% (8%). Other Nonregulated businesses posted losses in 2003 and 2002.

Merchant Energy operations include wholesale power generation, energy marketing and risk management services for wholesale customers, competitive retail supply services for commercial and industrial customers and consulting services. Including the April 2003 completion of a new 830 MW California power plant, Merchant Energy ended 2003 with 12,028 MW of owned generating capacity. In 2003, 86% of Energy Merchants generation output was derived from nuclear and coal fired power plants.

Merchant Energy also houses energy marketing and risk management operations, which had about 27,300 MW of 2004 customer load serving requirements as of

April 2004. These operations are conducted by NewEnergy, serving the commercial and industrial (C&I) market, and Power Source, serving the wholesale market. CEG contracts for power from third parties to meet customer power supply obligations in excess of owned generating capacity.

Regulated utility operations are performed by Baltimore Gas and Electric (BGE), which served nearly 1.18 million electric customers and 617,500 gas customers at the end of 2003. BGE currently derives 100% of its electric supply from Merchant Energy's Mid-Atlantic Fleet. Residential ratepayer bills (including delivery fees, commodity costs and competitive transition charges - CTCs) will not change until July 2006, when CTCs will end and competitive bids will set electric commodity costs.

Other Nonregulated businesses include Energy Products and Services for commercial and industrial customers, residential HVAC (heating, ventilation and air-conditioning) and competitive retail energy supply services, and district cooling services for Baltimore commercial customers.

During 2003 and 2002, CEG divested assets for total cash consideration of $149 million and $838 million, respectively. Asset sales in 2003 included real estate, an oil tanker and financial investments. Asset sales in 2002 included shares of Orion Power (sold for $454 million to Reliant Resources), an IPO of Corporate Office Properties Trust (raising $101.3 million), a South American generation project, 18 senior living facilities, and about 800 acres of land holdings.

Company Financials Fiscal Year ending December 31

Per Share Data ($)

(Year Ended December 31)	2003	2002	2001	2000	1999	1998	1997	1996	1995	1994
Tangible Bk. Val.	23.81	22.71	23.44	20.88	19.95	19.98	19.44	19.25	18.96	18.42
Earnings	2.85	3.20	0.52	2.30	2.18	2.06	1.72	1.85	2.02	1.93
S&P Core Earnings	2.66	1.75	0.34	NA	NA	NA	NA	NA	NA	NA
Dividends	1.04	0.96	0.48	1.68	1.68	1.66	1.63	1.59	1.55	1.51
Payout Ratio	36%	30%	92%	73%	77%	81%	95%	86%	77%	78%
Prices - High	39.61	32.38	50.14	52.06	31.50	35.25	34.31	29.50	29.00	25.50
- Low	25.17	19.30	20.90	27.06	24.68	29.25	24.75	25.00	22.00	20.50
P/E Ratio - High	14	10	96	23	14	17	20	16	14	13
- Low	9	6	40	12	11	14	14	14	11	11

Income Statement Analysis (Million $)

	2003	2002	2001	2000	1999	1998	1997	1996	1995	1994
Revs.	9,703	4,703	3,928	3,879	3,787	3,358	3,308	3,153	2,935	2,783
Depr.	479	481	419	470	450	377	343	330	317	296
Maint.	NA	NA	NA	NA	186	178	179	174	168	165
Fxd. Chgs. Cov.	3.12	2.90	3.01	3.12	2.98	2.81	2.92	2.59	2.63	2.63
Constr. Credits	NA	NA	NA	NA	NA	9.70	5.30	10.0	21.8	33.5
Eff. Tax Rate	36.2%	37.1%	31.5%	40.0%	36.3%	35.2%	35.8%	34.9%	33.4%	32.2%
Net Inc.	476	526	82.4	345	326	328	283	311	338	324
S&P Core Earnings	444	290	54.9	NA	NA	NA	NA	NA	NA	NA

Balance Sheet & Other Fin. Data (Million $)

	2003	2002	2001	2000	1999	1998	1997	1996	1995	1994
Gross Prop.	13,580	12,354	11,862	10,442	8,989	8,744	8,495	8,196	7,979	7,722
Cap. Exp.	658	850	1,318	1,079	436	339	373	361	458	483
Net Prop.	9,602	7,957	7,700	6,644	5,523	5,657	5,652	5,582	5,498	5,417
Capitalization:										
LT Debt	5,229	4,804	2,903	3,349	2,765	3,128	2,989	2,759	2,598	2,585
% LT Debt	55.8	55.4	43.0	51.5	48.0	51.3	48.5	46.3	43.9	44.6
Pfd.	Nil	Nil	Nil	Nil	Nil	-7.00	23.0	345	511	489
% Pfd.	Nil	Nil	Nil	Nil	Nil	NM	4.87	5.80	8.60	8.40
Common	4,141	3,862	3,844	3,153	2,993	2,982	2,870	2,857	2,813	2,718
% Common	44.2	44.6	57.0	48.5	52.0	48.9	46.6	48.0	47.5	46.9
Total Cap.	10,833	10,083	8,271	7,943	7,157	7,727	7,432	7,261	7,234	7,097
% Oper. Ratio	91.6	87.2	78.3	84.3	84.8	82.5	75.4	84.1	82.1	82.7
% Earn. on Net Prop.	17.1	17.8	5.0	13.3	13.6	13.1	11.9	12.1	12.7	9.1
% Return On Revs.	4.9	11.2	2.1	8.9	8.6	9.8	8.6	9.9	11.5	11.6
% Return On Invest. Capital	8.2	9.8	10.5	8.2	7.8	11.0	8.6	9.2	9.6	7.2
% Return On Com. Equity	11.9	13.6	2.3	11.2	10.9	10.5	8.9	9.6	10.8	10.6

Data as orig reptd (for Baltimore G&E pr. to 4/30/99); bef. results of disc opers/spec. items. Per share data adj. for stk. divs.; EPS diluted (primary prior to 1998). E-Estimated. NA-Not Available. NM-Not Meaningful. NR-Not Ranked.

Office: 750 E Pratt St, Baltimore, MD 21202-3106.
Telephone: 410-783-2800.
Website: http://www.constellationenergy.com
Chrmn, Pres & CEO: M.A. Shattuck III.
EVP & CFO: E.F. Smith.
SVP, Secy & General Counsel: K. Chagnon.

Investor Contact: J.W. Thayer 410-783-3647.
Dirs: D. L. Becker, J. T. Brady, F. P. Bramble, Sr., E. A. Crooke, J. R. Curtiss, R. W. Gale, F. A. Hrabowski III, E. J. Kelly III, N. Lampton, R. J. Lawless, L. M. Martin, M. A. Shattuck III, M. D. Sullivan, Y. de Balmann.

Founded: in 1906.
Domicile: Maryland.
Employees: 8,650.
S&P Analyst: Craig K. Shere, CFA /PMW/BK

Convergys Corp.

Recommendation: HOLD ★★★☆☆
SELL SELL HOLD BUY BUY

12-Month Target Price: **$14.00**
(as of October 20, 2004)

CVG has an approximate 0.02% weighting in the **S&P 500**

Sector: Information Technology
Sub-Industry: Data Processing & Outsourced Services
Peer Group: Billing & Payroll Services

Summary: This company is a leading provider of outsourced billing and customer management solutions.

Quantitative Evaluations

S&P Earnings & Dividend Rank: NR

D	C	B-	B	B+	A-	A	A+

S&P Fair Value Rank: 5

1	2	3	4	5
Lowest				Highest

Fair Value Calc.: $16.20 (Slightly Undervalued)

S&P Investability Quotient Percentile

81%

CVG scored higher than 81% of all companies for which an S&P Report is available.

Volatility: Average

Low	Average	High

Technical Evaluation: Neutral
Since 11/04, the technical indicators for CVG have been Neutral.

Relative Strength Rank: Moderate

61

1 Lowest	Highest 99

Price as of 11/12/04: $14.39 | **2004E S&P Core EPS:** $0.68

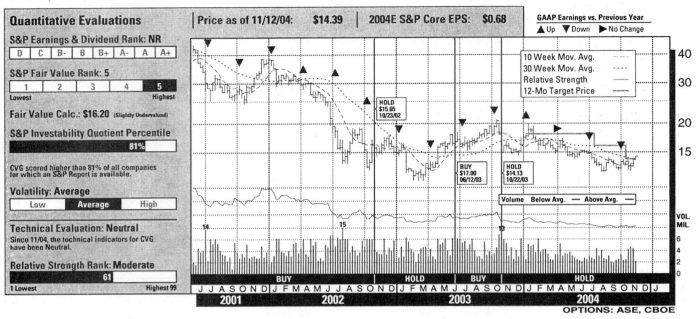

GAAP Earnings vs. Previous Year
▲ Up ▼ Down ► No Change

10 Week Mov. Avg.
30 Week Mov. Avg.
Relative Strength
12-Mo Target Price

Volume Below Avg. — Above Avg.

OPTIONS: ASE, CBOE

Analyst commentary prepared by Todd Rosenbluth/CB/GG

Highlights October 25, 2004

- We expect revenues to rise 8% in 2005, following an estimated 9% climb in 2004, as gains of 14% at CMG are likely to be somewhat offset by sluggish revenue growth at IMG. We see IMG being negatively affected by slowing subscriber growth rates and overall pricing pressures related to the Sprint PCS and AT&T Wireless contracts. We believe CMG will be aided by recent client wins such as the U.S. Postal Service and financial institutions, and recent acquisitions.

- We expect EBITDA margins in 2005 to widen fractionally to 14.6%, from a likely 14.3% in 2003, as high fixed costs are offset by a reduction in employees and increased volumes. In the 2004 fourth quarter, the company is expected to take a restructuring charge of $15 to $20 million related to a workforce reduction. We expect cash to be used more for capital spending than share repurchases.

- We forecast 2004 operating EPS of $0.89. We see EPS of $1.03 in 2005, with results stronger in the second half of the year. Our 2004 Standard & Poor's Core Earnings estimate is $0.68, with the difference due to projected option expense. In April, CVG said it will have expenses of $0.01 a share in each quarter for restricted stock expenses.

Investment Rationale/Risk October 25, 2004

- Third quarter results were slightly below our expectations, hurt by investments in new business opportunities in the CMG segment. While we see strength in CMG as outsourcing by financial companies continues, we are concerned that CVG will eventually lose business from top customer AT&T Wireless (AWE) when the company is acquired by Cingular. We believe this pending merger will serve as an overhang on CVG shares over the next few months.

- Risks to our recommendation and target price include potential consolidation among wireless customer care clients, pricing pressure on margins, and currency risk for international operations.

- CVG shares trade below data processing and outsourcing peers on both a forward P/E and an enterprise value to EBITDA basis. However, we believe a discount is warranted given what we view as sizable customer migration risk related to AWE. Our 12-month target price is $14.

Key Stock Statistics

S&P Oper. EPS 2004E	0.89	52-week Range	$19.96-12.30
P/E on S&P Oper. EPS 2004E	16.2	12 Month P/E	15.0
S&P Oper. EPS 2005E	1.03	Beta	1.26
Yield (%)	Nil	Shareholders	15,537
Dividend Rate/Share	Nil	Market Cap (B)	$ 2.1
Shares Outstanding (M)	142.5		

Value of $10,000 invested five years ago: **$ 7,701**

Dividend Data

No cash dividends have been paid.

Revenues/Earnings Data Fiscal year ending December 31

Revenues (Million $)

	2004	2003	2002	2001	2000	1999
1Q	573.9	560.4	587.5	577.8	513.6	399.8
2Q	601.7	563.2	572.7	571.2	521.9	426.2
3Q	639.9	570.7	561.2	567.2	544.5	450.2
4Q	—	594.5	564.8	590.7	582.5	486.7
Yr.	—	2,289	2,286	2,321	2,163	1,763

Earnings Per Share ($)

	2004	2003	2002	2001	2000	1999
1Q	0.22	0.22	0.35	0.34	0.28	0.21
2Q	0.20	0.29	0.35	0.16	0.29	0.21
3Q	0.21	0.31	0.34	0.02	0.32	0.26
4Q	E0.26	0.33	-0.18	0.33	0.34	0.21
Yr.	E0.89	1.15	0.88	0.80	1.23	0.89

Next earnings report expected: late-January Source: S&P, Company Reports
EPS Estimates based on S&P Operating Earnings; historical GAAP earnings are as reported.

STANDARD &POOR'S

Convergys Corporation

Stock Report
November 13, 2004
NYSE Symbol: **CVG**

Recommendation: **HOLD** ★ ★ ★ ★ ★   12-Month Target Price: **$14.00** (as of October 20, 2004)

Business Summary October 25, 2004

Convergys Corp.'s strategy for growth includes leveraging its industry leadership position, pursuing international growth, deploying aggressive sales and marketing efforts, and entering into strategic acquisitions and alliances. The company is a leading provider of outsourced, integrated billing, and employee and customer care software and services. CVG focuses on developing long-term strategic relationships with clients in employee- and customer-intensive industries including telecommunications, cable, broadband, direct satellite broadcasting, financial services and government. The company serves clients through two segments: the Information Management Group (IMG) and the Customer Management Group (CMG).

IMG (34% of 2003 revenues, down from 39% in 2002) serves clients principally by providing and managing complex billing and information software that addresses all segments of the communications industry. IMG's component-based, next-generation framework supports the creation of billing and customer care solutions ranging from a single module to the combination of modules put into application suites to a complete, end-to-end billing system. Its global, three-tiered billing product portfolio is designed to give clients a flexible migration path to expand their billing and customer care systems without the loss of their initial investment. In 2003, 58% of IMG's revenues came from data processing services from recurring monthly payments from clients. Professional and consulting services accounted for 8% of IMG's revenues; remaining revenues came primarily from software license arrangements and international sales. In December 2003,

CVG acquired billing and customer care assets from Alltel Communications for $37 million, including new customers such as Cingular Wireless. In the first quarter of 2004, CVG acquired DigitalThink, a custom e-learning outsourcer.

CMG (66%, 61%) provides outsourced customer management and employee care services for clients, utilizing its advanced information systems capabilities, human resource management skills, and industry experience. CMG handles customer contacts ranging from initial product information requests to customer retention initiatives, answers technical support inquiries for customers, and manages the entire customer relationship. Clients include the U.S. Postal Service, the State of Florida, and a number of financial institutions.

The company has a 45% limited partnership interest in the Cellular Partnership, which operates a cellular telecommunications business in central and southwestern Ohio and northern Kentucky.

During 2003, 2002 and 2001, CVG's three largest customers, AT&T Wireless, Sprint PCS and DirecTV, together accounted for 31.1%, 34.9% and 21.7% of CVG's accounts receivable for these years. Major clients also included ALLTEL, Comcast, SBC and Sprint PCS. In June 2003, CVG said it was supporting the migration of Sprint PCS to an in-house billing system; in December 2003, CVG signed a seven-year agreement with Sprint PCS to provide continued outsourced billing support.

Company Financials Fiscal Year ending December 31

Per Share Data ($)

(Year Ended December 31)	2003	2002	2001	2000	1999	1998	1997	1996	1995	1994
Tangible Bk. Val.	2.60	2.54	3.08	2.41	1.13	0.29	-0.09	NA	NA	NA
Cash Flow	1.99	1.70	1.81	2.25	1.73	1.28	1.07	NA	NA	NA
Earnings	1.15	0.88	0.80	1.23	0.89	0.57	0.54	NA	NA	NA
S&P Core Earnings	0.91	0.54	0.51	NA	NA	NA	NA	NA	NA	NA
Dividends	Nil	Nil	Nil	Nil	Nil	Nil	NA	NA	NA	NA
Payout Ratio	Nil	Nil	Nil	Nil	Nil	Nil	NA	NA	NA	NA
Prices - High	20.80	37.98	50.25	55.43	31.75	23.75	NA	NA	NA	NA
- Low	11.30	12.50	24.46	26.62	14.50	9.62	NA	NA	NA	NA
P/E Ratio - High	18	43	63	45	36	42	NA	NA	NA	NA
- Low	10	14	31	22	16	17	NA	NA	NA	NA

Income Statement Analysis (Million $)

	2003	2002	2001	2000	1999	1998	1997	1996	1995	1994
Revs.	2,289	2,286	2,321	2,163	1,763	1,447	988	NA	NA	NA
Oper. Inc.	415	498	543	489	388	313	220	NA	NA	NA
Depr.	124	137	176	161	130	101	61.0	NA	NA	NA
Int. Exp.	6.90	11.0	20.0	32.9	32.5	33.9	5.40	NA	NA	NA
Pretax Inc.	272	244	255	317	223	131	131	NA	NA	NA
Eff. Tax Rate	36.8%	40.3%	45.5%	38.6%	38.4%	38.0%	33.7%	NA	NA	NA
Net Inc.	172	146	139	195	137	81.0	86.6	NA	NA	NA
S&P Core Earnings	133	88.9	91.3	NA	NA	NA	NA	NA	NA	NA

Balance Sheet & Other Fin. Data (Million $)

	2003	2002	2001	2000	1999	1998	1997	1996	1995	1994
Cash	37.2	12.2	41.1	28.2	30.8	3.80	2.10	NA	NA	NA
Curr. Assets	420	418	523	481	298	361	266	NA	NA	NA
Total Assets	1,810	1,620	1,743	1,780	1,580	1,451	654	NA	NA	NA
Curr. Liab.	543	462	492	359	387	698	217	NA	NA	NA
LT Debt	58.8	4.60	3.60	291	250	Nil	430	NA	NA	NA
Common Equity	1,144	1,126	1,227	1,113	927	732	431	NA	NA	NA
Total Cap.	1,202	1,131	1,230	1,403	1,178	732	NA	NA	NA	NA
Cap. Exp.	174	90.8	114	175	155	93.5	NA	NA	NA	NA
Cash Flow	296	283	315	356	267	182	148	NA	NA	NA
Curr. Ratio	0.8	0.9	1.1	1.3	0.8	0.5	1.2	NA	NA	NA
% LT Debt of Cap.	4.9	0.4	0.3	20.7	21.3	Nil	NA	NA	NA	NA
% Net Inc.of Revs.	7.5	6.4	6.0	9.0	7.8	5.6	8.8	NA	NA	NA
% Ret. on Assets	10.0	8.7	7.8	11.6	9.0	7.7	NA	NA	NA	NA
% Ret. on Equity	15.1	12.4	11.8	19.1	16.5	13.9	NA	NA	NA	NA

Data as orig reptd.; bef. results of disc opers/spec. items. Per share data adj. for stk. divs.; EPS diluted. E-Estimated. NA-Not Available. NM-Not Meaningful. NR-Not Ranked. UR-Under Review.

Office: 201 East Fourth Street, Cincinnati, OH 45202.
Telephone: 513-723-7000.
Email: investor@convergys.com
Website: http://www.convergys.com
Chrmn, Pres & CEO: J.F. Orr.
SVP, Secy & General Counsel: W.H. Hawkins II.

CFO: E. Shanks.
Investor Contact: T. Greenwald 513-723-7000.
Dirs: Z. Baird, J. F. Barrett, G. C. Butler, D. B. Dillon, E. C. Fast, J. E. Gibbs, R. L. Howe, S. C. Mason, P. A. Odeen, J. F. Orr, S. A. Ribeau, B. H. Rowe, D. R. Whitwam, J. M. Zimmerman.

Founded: in 1998.
Domicile: Ohio.
Employees: 56,500.
S&P Analyst: Todd Rosenbluth/CB/GG

Cooper Industries

Recommendation: **HOLD** ★★★☆☆
SELL SELL HOLD BUY BUY

12-Month Target Price: $66.00
(as of October 21, 2004)

CBE has an approximate 0.06% weighting in the **S&P 500**

Sector: Industrials
Sub-Industry: Electrical Components & Equipment
Peer Group: Electrical Equipment - Diversified

Summary: Cooper Industries is a diversified worldwide manufacturer of electrical products, tools and hardware.

Quantitative Evaluations

S&P Earnings & Dividend Rank: B+

| D | C | B- | B | B+ | A- | A | A+ |

S&P Fair Value Rank: 1

| 1 | 2 | 3 | 4 | 5 |
| Lowest | | | | Highest |

Fair Value Calc.: $45.40 (Overvalued)

S&P Investability Quotient Percentile
97%

CBE scored higher than 97% of all companies for which an S&P Report is available.

Volatility: Low

| Low | Average | High |

Technical Evaluation: Bullish
Since 9/04, the technical indicators for CBE have been Bullish.

Relative Strength Rank: Strong
76
1 Lowest   Highest 99

| Price as of 11/12/04: | **$66.94** | 2004E S&P Core EPS: | **$3.35** |

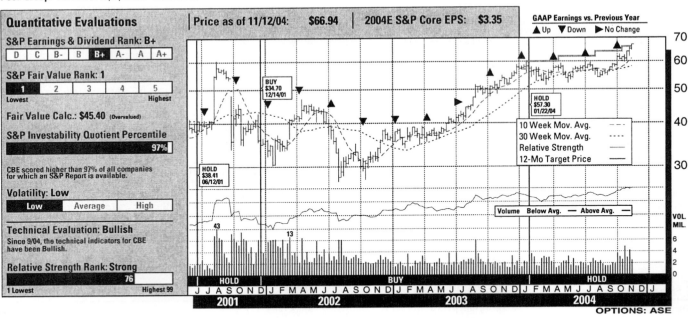

GAAP Earnings vs. Previous Year
▲ Up ▼ Down ► No Change

BUY $34.70 12/14/01
HOLD $38.41 06/12/01
HOLD $57.30 01/22/04

10 Week Mov. Avg.
30 Week Mov. Avg.
Relative Strength
12-Mo Target Price

Volume   Below Avg. — Above Avg.

43   13

HOLD   BUY   HOLD
J J A S O N D J F M A M J J A S O N D J F M A M J J A S O N D J F M A M J J A S O N D J
2001   2002   2003   2004

VOL. MIL.
6
4
2
0

OPTIONS: ASE

Analyst commentary prepared by Efraim Levy, CFA /PMW/JWP

Highlights October 27, 2004

- Based on our expectations of improving economic conditions, we see net sales increasing 5% to 6% in 2005. We think that market conditions should improve for most of the company's products. We see expense reduction required to offset pressures on selling prices and higher raw material costs. We expect negative pension fund returns of recent years, combined with changes in pension-related accounting, to boost pension and post-retirement expenses. Our earnings estimates for CBE reflect the lower tax rates it enjoys as a Bermuda corporation.

- Our 2004 EPS estimate of $3.55 is equal to company guidance, which was raised from prior guidance of $3.40 to $3.55. We forecast that EPS will increase to $3.95 in 2005.

- We think that a focus on cash generation should help boost cash flows and allow for share repurchases and debt reduction. Long term debt was 39% of total capitalization at the end of 2003, and has declined since then.

Investment Rationale/Risk October 27, 2004

- In our view, based on P/E multiple and on price to free cash and P/E to expected EPS growth rate ratios, the shares are within the range of key peers. The shares provide an above-average yield of 2.3%.

- Risks to our target price include possible exposure to asbestos liabilities stemming from the October 2001 Federal-Mogul (FMO) bankruptcy filing; FMO has said it may not fulfill an agreement to indemnify CBE for asbestos claims stemming from Pneumo-Abex product lines that it bought from CBE.

- Our use of a P/E multiple of about 16X applied to our 2005 EPS estimate reflects peer and historical P/E multiple comparisons. Our discounted cash flow model, which assumes a weighted average cost of capital of 10.2%, a compound annual growth rate of 5.6% over the next 15 years, and a terminal growth rate of 3.4%, calculates intrinsic value of $68. Based on a combination of our P/E multiple and DCF analyses, our 12-month target price is $66. We would hold existing positions.

Key Stock Statistics

S&P Core EPS 2005E	3.76	52-week Range	$66.94-51.34
S&P Oper. EPS 2004E	3.55	12 Month P/E	35.1
P/E on S&P Oper. EPS 2004E	18.9	Beta	0.86
S&P Oper. EPS 2005E	3.95	Shareholders	25,974
Yield (%)	2.1%	Market Cap (B)	$ 6.1
Dividend Rate/Share	1.40	Shares Outstanding (M)	91.8

Value of $10,000 invested five years ago: **$ 17,970**

Dividend Data Dividends have been paid since 1947

Amount ($)	Date Decl.	Ex-Div. Date	Stock of Record	Payment Date
0.350	Feb. 11	Feb. 26	Mar. 01	Apr. 01 '04
0.350	Apr. 27	Jun. 03	Jun. 07	Jul. 01 '04
0.350	Aug. 03	Sep. 08	Sep. 10	Oct. 01 '04
0.350	Nov. 02	Nov. 29	Dec. 01	Jan. 03 '05

Revenues/Earnings Data Fiscal year ending December 31

Revenues (Million $)

	2004	2003	2002	2001	2000	1999
1Q	1,065	957.8	975.0	1,095	1,039	924.7
2Q	1,109	1,011	1,001	1,073	1,168	957.5
3Q	1,140	1,049	999	1,052	1,146	982.2
4Q	—	1,044	985.0	1,000	1,107	1,005
Yr.	—	4,061	3,961	4,210	4,460	3,869

Earnings Per Share ($)

	2004	2003	2002	2001	2000	1999
1Q	0.81	0.61	0.52	0.60	0.89	0.80
2Q	0.89	0.78	0.78	0.72	0.99	0.92
3Q	0.95	0.75	0.68	0.78	0.97	0.89
4Q	E0.90	0.78	0.30	0.66	0.95	0.89
Yr.	E3.55	2.92	2.28	2.75	3.80	3.50

Next earnings report expected: late-January Source: S&P, Company Reports
EPS Estimates based on S&P Operating Earnings; historical GAAP earnings are as reported.

Cooper Industries, Inc.

Recommendation: **HOLD** ★ ★ ★ ★ ★   12-Month Target Price: **$66.00** (as of October 21, 2004)

Business Summary October 27, 2004

Cooper Industries, a diversified, worldwide manufacturer of electrical products, tools and hardware, is focusing on leveraging its strong brand name recognition by broadening its product line; strengthening its manufacturing and distribution systems to lower costs and improve customer service; expanding globally via acquisitions and joint ventures to participate in growing economies; and improving working capital efficiency and increasing cash flow to fuel future growth.

Electrical products contributed 83% of revenues in 2003, and tools and hardware provided 17%.

The electrical products segment makes electrical and electronic distribution and circuit protection products and lighting fixtures for use in residential, commercial and industrial construction, maintenance and repair. It also makes products for use by utilities and industries for primary power distribution and control. Products are marketed under the Arrow Hart, Buss, Edison, Crouse-Hinds, CEAG, Mc-Graw-Edison, Fail-Safe, halo, Kyle, Metalux and RTE names. About 27% of electrical products shipments in 2003 were international.

Tools and hardware items are made for use in residential, commercial and industrial construction, maintenance and repair, and for general industrial and consumer use. Product lines include a variety of hand and power tool brands as well as chain and fittings. The company generally believes business risks associated with international markets do not differ significantly from those of U.S. operations.

The countries that generate the most international revenues for CBE are Canada, Germany, Mexico, and the U.K. The company has several small joint ventures with operations in China.

In October 1998, the company sold its automotive operations ($1.9 billion in annual revenues) to Federal-Mogul Corp., for $1.9 billion in cash.

Cash flow from operations in 2003 was $445 million, down from $480 million in 2002.

In the four years through 2000, CBE completed 33 acquisitions: 23 in the electrical products group and 10 in the tools and hardware segment. Six acquisitions in 2000 cost about $578 million. The company did not make any acquisitions in 2001 through 2003, but completed a $10 million acquisition in the first quarter of 2004.

Reflecting slowing demand, the company reduced 2001 capital spending to $115 million, from 2000's $175 million. A further reduction was seen in 2002, to $74 million. Capital spending in 2003 totaled $80 million, but the company expected 2004 spending to increase to $100 million to $110 million, as it planned to invest in new products, new business systems, and cost reduction programs.

At December 31, 2003, long term debt totaled $1.34 billion, up from $1.28 billion at December 31, 2002.

Company Financials Fiscal Year ending December 31

Per Share Data ($)

(Year Ended December 31)	2003	2002	2001	2000	1999	1998	1997	1996	1995	1994
Tangible Bk. Val.	0.66	0.07	1.25	NM	0.04	0.91	1.60	NM	-4.71	5.02
Cash Flow	4.22	3.58	4.72	5.69	5.05	4.19	5.26	5.08	4.46	4.31
Earnings	2.92	2.28	2.75	3.80	3.50	2.93	3.26	2.93	2.51	2.10
S&P Core Earnings	2.83	1.82	2.29	NA	NA	NA	NA	NA	NA	NA
Dividends	1.40	1.40	1.40	1.40	1.32	1.32	1.32	1.32	1.32	1.32
Payout Ratio	48%	61%	51%	37%	38%	45%	40%	45%	53%	63%
Prices - High	58.85	47.01	60.45	47.00	56.75	70.37	58.62	44.62	40.50	52.25
- Low	33.86	27.14	31.61	29.37	39.62	36.87	40.00	34.12	32.87	31.62
P/E Ratio - High	20	21	22	12	16	24	18	15	16	25
- Low	12	12	11	8	11	13	12	12	13	15

Income Statement Analysis (Million $)

	2003	2002	2001	2000	1999	1998	1997	1996	1995	1994
Revs.	4,061	3,961	4,210	4,460	3,869	3,651	5,289	5,284	4,886	4,588
Oper. Inc.	516	516	662	825	725	683	939	869	848	777
Depr.	121	122	186	174	148	138	220	234	219	199
Int. Exp.	74.1	74.5	84.7	100	55.2	102	90.0	142	151	73.0
Pretax Inc.	347	280	316	550	519	524	627	558	478	505
Eff. Tax Rate	20.8%	23.7%	17.4%	35.0%	36.0%	35.9%	37.0%	43.5%	41.2%	42.0%
Net Inc.	274	214	261	357	332	336	395	315	281	293
S&P Core Earnings	265	169	217	NA	NA	NA	NA	NA	NA	NA

Balance Sheet & Other Fin. Data (Million $)

	2003	2002	2001	2000	1999	1998	1997	1996	1995	1994
Cash	464	302	11.5	26.4	26.9	21.0	30.0	16.0	18.0	25.3
Curr. Assets	1,961	1,689	1,651	1,735	1,467	1,417	2,137	2,098	2,127	2,100
Total Assets	4,965	4,688	4,611	4,789	4,143	3,779	6,053	6,053	6,064	6,401
Curr. Liab.	1,022	960	1,106	1,174	1,086	971	1,385	1,381	1,382	1,333
LT Debt	1,337	1,281	1,107	1,301	895	775	1,272	1,738	1,865	1,362
Common Equity	2,118	2,002	2,023	1,904	1,743	1,563	2,577	1,890	1,717	2,741
Total Cap.	3,455	3,283	3,130	3,205	2,638	2,338	3,849	3,628	3,582	4,103
Cap. Exp.	79.9	73.8	115	175	166	142	196	202	188	209
Cash Flow	396	335	448	532	480	474	615	549	500	492
Curr. Ratio	1.9	1.8	1.5	1.5	1.4	1.5	1.5	1.5	1.5	1.6
% LT Debt of Cap.	38.7	39.0	35.4	40.6	33.9	33.1	33.0	47.9	52.1	33.2
% Net Inc.of Revs.	6.8	5.4	6.2	8.0	8.6	9.2	7.5	6.0	5.8	6.4
% Ret. on Assets	5.7	4.6	5.6	8.0	8.4	6.8	6.6	5.2	4.5	4.6
% Ret. on Equity	13.3	10.6	13.3	19.6	20.1	16.2	17.7	17.5	12.6	10.2

Data as orig reptd.; bef. results of disc opers/spec. items. Per share data adj. for stk. divs.; EPS diluted. E-Estimated. NA-Not Available. NM-Not Meaningful. NR-Not Ranked. UR-Under Review.

Office: 600 Travis, Houston, TX 77002-1001.
Telephone: 713-209-8400.
Email: info@cooperindustries.com
Website: http://www.cooperindustries.com
Chrmn & CEO: H.J. Riley, Jr.
Pres & COO: K.S. Hachigian.
SVP & CFO: T.A. Klebe.

SVP & General Counsel: D.K. Schumacher.
VP & Treas: A.J. Hill.
VP & Investor Contact: R.J. Bajenski 713-209-8610.
Dirs: S. G. Butler, R. M. Devlin, I. J. Evans, C. J. Grum, K. S. Hachigian, L. A. Hill, J. J. Postl, H. J. Riley, Jr., G. B. Smith, D. F. Smith, J. R. Wilson.

Founded: in 1833.
Domicile: Bermuda.
Employees: 27,188.
S&P Analyst: Efraim Levy, CFA /PMW/JWP

Recommendation: **HOLD** ★★★☆☆
SELL SELL HOLD BUY BUY

12-Month Target Price: **$26.00**
(as of July 22, 2004)

CTB has an approximate 0.01% weighting in the **S&P 500**

Sector: Consumer Discretionary
Sub-Industry: Tires & Rubber
Peer Group: Tire Companies

Summary: CTB, the fourth largest U.S. tire maker, supplies tires exclusively for the replacement market. It also manufactures original equipment automotive components.

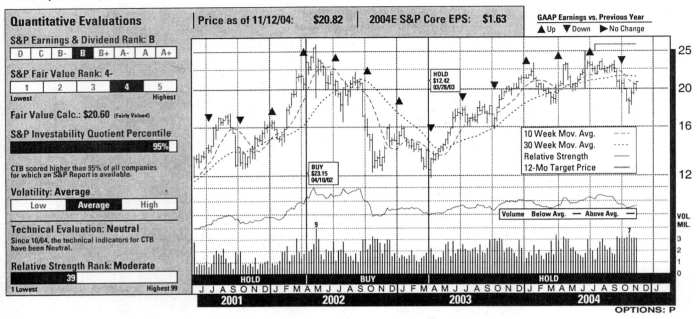

Quantitative Evaluations

S&P Earnings & Dividend Rank: B
D · C · B- · **B** · B+ · A- · A · A+

S&P Fair Value Rank: 4-
1 · 2 · 3 · **4** · 5
Lowest — Highest

Fair Value Calc.: $20.60 (Fairly Valued)

S&P Investability Quotient Percentile
95%
CTB scored higher than 95% of all companies for which an S&P Report is available.

Volatility: Average
Low · **Average** · High

Technical Evaluation: Neutral
Since 10/04, the technical indicators for CTB have been Neutral.

Relative Strength Rank: Moderate
39
1 Lowest — Highest 99

Price as of 11/12/04: **$20.82** | 2004E S&P Core EPS: **$1.63**

GAAP Earnings vs. Previous Year
▲ Up ▼ Down ► No Change

10 Week Mov. Avg.
30 Week Mov. Avg.
Relative Strength
12-Mo Target Price

Volume Below Avg. — Above Avg.

HOLD $12.42 03/28/03

BUY $23.15 04/10/02

HOLD | BUY | HOLD

J J A S O N D J F M A M J J A S O N D J F M A M J J A S O N D J F M A M J J A S O N D J
2001 · 2002 · 2003 · 2004

VOL. MIL.

OPTIONS: P

Analyst commentary prepared by Efraim Levy, CFA /MF/GG

Highlights August 17, 2004

- We expect 2005 sales to grow 4% to 6%, on improved industry replacement tire demand, market share gains and a more favorable sales mix. We see contributions from price increases and new engineered product contracts, but margins are likely to be hurt by higher raw material costs in the tire segment if current trends continue. Restructuring should help margins, but we expect pension and healthcare costs to rise. Interest expense should benefit from lower debt levels.

- The company has been capacity-restrained in the tire segment. We expect CTB to announce restructuring initiatives and to raise the volume of Asia-sourced production.

- The acquisitions of Standard Products and the fluid handling division of Incensys expanded the company's global reach and provided greater product balance, in our opinion, between the tire and other automotive parts segments. However, CTB is considering the sale of its automotive segment to focus on tire operations.

Investment Rationale/Risk August 17, 2004

- We would hold existing positions in CTB, which is trading at a discount to the S&P 500. The balance sheet has become more leveraged with the addition of merger-related debt, but we see positive operating cash flows and the potential sale of automotive parts operations allowing for debt reduction. The company has said it intends to continue to operate the automotive business if a satisfactory bid is not received. We view the quality of earnings as high; Standard & Poor's Core Earnings adjustments for option and pension expenses are estimated to add $0.09 to our 2005 operating EPS forecast of $1.89, with pension credits outweighing option expense. CTB has been gaining tire market share.

- Risks to our recommendation and target price include rising Asian tire imports, increases in raw material costs, and pressures on tire prices.

- Based on historical and peer P/E ratios, our 12-month target price is $26, equal to 14X our 2005 EPS forecast of $1.89.

Key Stock Statistics

Yield (%)	2.0%	52-week Range	$23.89-17.20	
Dividend Rate/Share	0.42	12 Month P/E	16.3	
Shares Outstanding (M)	74.9	Beta	1.09	
Market Cap (B)	$1.6	Shareholders	3,729	

Value of $10,000 invested five years ago: **$14,280**

Dividend Data Dividends have been paid since 1950

Amount ($)	Date Decl.	Ex-Div. Date	Stock of Record	Payment Date
0.105	Nov. 14	Nov. 26	Dec. 01	Dec. 26 '03
0.105	Feb. 04	Mar. 03	Mar. 05	Mar. 31 '04
0.105	May. 04	Jun. 02	Jun. 04	Jun. 30 '04
0.105	Jul. 21	Sep. 01	Sep. 03	Sep. 30 '04

Revenues/Earnings Data Fiscal year ending December 31

Revenues (Million $)

	2004	2003	2002	2001	2000	1999
1Q	974.5	794.8	813.0	757.6	922.3	467.9
2Q	991.8	839.6	836.1	829.0	886.6	495.4
3Q	551.5	913.2	839.3	791.5	843.6	532.3
4Q	—	966.8	841.6	776.6	819.9	701.2
Yr.	—	3,514	3,330	3,155	3,472	2,196

Earnings Per Share ($)

	2004	2003	2002	2001	2000	1999
1Q	0.32	0.21	0.36	0.05	0.42	0.41
2Q	0.44	0.17	0.52	0.25	0.48	0.50
3Q	0.17	0.24	0.31	-0.27	0.32	0.46
4Q	—	0.38	0.32	0.22	0.09	0.42
Yr.	—	1.00	1.51	0.25	1.31	1.79

Next earnings report expected: early-February Source: S&P, Company Reports
EPS Estimates based on S&P Operating Earnings; historical GAAP earnings are as reported.

Cooper Tire & Rubber Company

Recommendation: **HOLD** ★ ★ ★ ☆ ☆   12-Month Target Price: **$26.00** (as of July 22, 2004)

Business Summary August 17, 2004

Acquisitions since early 1999 have nearly doubled Cooper Tire & Rubber's revenues, and have broadened its product and geographic ranges. The company, the fourth largest U.S. producer of tires, and the world's eighth largest, diversified its auto parts operations in 1999 by purchasing Standard Products Co. for $757 million, including assumed debt. In 2000, CTB acquired for $244.5 million Siebe Automotive, Invensys plc's automotive fluid handling division.

In 1997, CTB acquired the tire operations of Avon Rubber p.l.c. of the U.K., for $97 million. The company markets its products in more than 100 countries worldwide, and the acquisition gave CTB manufacturing and distribution facilities located closer to its overseas customers. The acquisition included a manufacturing plant in England, as well as tire distribution companies and facilities in France, Germany and Switzerland.

CTB, founded in 1914 and based in Findlay, OH, sells tires exclusively to the replacement market. It also makes rubber-based and other automotive components for OEMs.

The company makes both automobile and truck tires, which are sold through independent dealers and distributors under the Cooper, Mastercraft, Starfire and Cooper-Avon brand names, and under private label brands. Independent tire dealers account for about 72% of the replacement tires sold in the U.S.

CTB supplies engineered rubber products to nearly every automobile maker in the U.S. and Canada. The company makes vibration control products for increased riding comfort and to reduce vehicle noise; rubber seals for doors, trunks, windows and hoods; and reinforced hoses used mainly to transport fluids, fuels and gases.

The company has an alliance with Pirelli Tyres. CTB distributes Pirelli automotive tires in North America, and Pirelli shares technology with the company, and distributes Cooper brand tires in South America.

The automotive segment produces sealing systems, hose and hose assemblies, active and passive vibration control systems, and exterior trim products primarily for the global automotive OEMs.

In 2003, tire operations accounted for 53% of revenues, with automotive products provided the remaining 47%. North America accounted for 80% of 2003 sales.

In October 2000, CTB announced a restructuring plan that resulted in the closure or downsizing of 21 facilities; the program was completed in 2002. The plan resulted in $39 million of restructuring charges, mostly in the 2000 fourth quarter. Some of the charges were reversed in 2001 and 2002.

Company Financials Fiscal Year ending December 31

Per Share Data ($)

(Year Ended December 31)	2003	2002	2001	2000	1999	1998	1997	1996	1995	1994
Tangible Bk. Val.	7.48	3.91	4.19	4.79	7.15	11.45	10.22	9.67	8.95	7.65
Cash Flow	3.55	3.94	2.87	3.88	3.48	2.95	2.74	2.22	2.11	2.20
Earnings	1.00	1.51	0.25	1.31	1.79	1.64	1.55	1.30	1.35	1.54
S&P Core Earnings	1.09	1.00	0.23	NA	NA	NA	NA	NA	NA	NA
Dividends	0.42	0.42	0.42	0.42	0.42	0.39	0.35	0.31	0.27	0.23
Payout Ratio	42%	28%	168%	32%	23%	24%	23%	24%	20%	15%
Prices - High	21.80	26.10	17.43	16.00	25.00	26.25	28.43	27.37	29.62	29.50
- Low	11.84	12.25	10.55	9.18	13.25	15.43	18.00	17.87	22.25	21.62
P/E Ratio - High	22	17	70	12	14	16	18	21	22	19
- Low	12	8	42	7	7	9	12	14	16	14

Income Statement Analysis (Million $)

	2003	2002	2001	2000	1999	1998	1997	1996	1995	1994
Revs.	3,514	3,330	3,155	3,472	2,196	1,876	1,813	1,619	1,494	1,403
Oper. Inc.	378	431	377	480	365	312	304	250	240	264
Depr.	190	178	190	189	128	102	94.5	76.8	63.6	55.6
Int. Exp.	67.9	75.6	90.7	97.5	24.4	15.2	15.7	6.00	3.39	3.85
Pretax Inc.	114	177	29.2	160	215	198	195	172	180	208
Eff. Tax Rate	35.3%	36.9%	37.7%	39.6%	37.1%	35.9%	37.2%	37.4%	37.4%	38.2%
Net Inc.	73.8	112	18.2	96.7	135	127	122	108	113	129
S&P Core Earnings	80.6	74.3	16.5	NA	NA	NA	NA	NA	NA	NA

Balance Sheet & Other Fin. Data (Million $)

	2003	2002	2001	2000	1999	1998	1997	1996	1995	1994
Cash	66.4	44.7	71.8	45.8	71.1	42.0	52.9	19.0	23.0	103
Curr. Assets	1,024	859	952	1,031	945	569	555	444	431	455
Total Assets	2,869	2,711	2,764	2,922	2,758	1,541	1,496	1,273	1,144	1,040
Curr. Liab.	477	433	648	607	396	193	200	187	158	152
LT Debt	872	875	882	1,037	1,046	205	206	69.5	28.6	33.6
Common Equity	1,030	942	910	953	976	1,178	834	787	749	662
Total Cap.	1,916	1,831	1,812	2,052	2,119	1,459	1,047	909	814	725
Cap. Exp.	155	143	136	201	150	132	108	194	194	78.0
Cash Flow	264	290	208	286	264	229	217	185	176	184
Curr. Ratio	2.1	2.0	1.5	1.7	2.4	3.0	2.8	2.4	2.7	3.0
% LT Debt of Cap.	45.5	47.8	48.7	50.5	49.4	14.1	19.6	7.7	3.5	4.6
% Net Inc.of Revs.	2.1	3.4	0.6	2.8	6.2	6.8	6.8	6.7	7.6	9.2
% Ret. on Assets	2.6	4.1	0.6	3.4	6.3	8.4	8.8	9.0	10.3	13.3
% Ret. on Equity	7.5	12.1	2.0	10.0	14.7	12.6	15.1	14.1	16.0	21.2

Data as orig reptd.; bef. results of disc opers/spec. items. Per share data adj. for stk. divs. Bold denotes primary EPS - prior periods restated. E-Estimated. NA-Not Available. NM-Not Meaningful. NR-Not Ranked. UR-Under Review.

Office: 701 Lima Avenue, Findlay, OH 45840.
Telephone: 419-423-1321.
Email: cooperinfo@coopertire.com
Website: http://www.coopertire.com
Chrmn, Pres & CEO: T.A. Dattilo.

VP & CFO: P.G. Weaver.
VP, Secy & General Counsel: J.E. Kline.
Investor Contact: R.S. Hendriksen 419-427-4768.
Dirs: A. H. Aronson, L. B. Breininger, T. A. Dattilo, D. J. Gormley, J. J. Holland, J. F. Meier, B. O. Pond, J. H. Shuey, R. Wambold.

Founded: in 1913.
Domicile: Delaware.
Employees: 22,899.
S&P Analyst: Efraim Levy, CFA /MF/GG

Coors (Adolph) Co.

Recommendation: **HOLD** ★★★★ | SELL | SELL | HOLD | BUY | BUY |

12-Month Target Price: **$73.00**
(as of October 28, 2004)

RKY has an approximate 0.02% weighting in the **S&P 500**

Sector: Consumer Staples
Sub-Industry: Brewers
Peer Group: Beer Companies

Summary: RKY is the parent company of the third largest U.S. brewer, with an approximate 10% market share.

Quantitative Evaluations

S&P Earnings & Dividend Rank: A

| D | C | B- | B | B+ | A- | **A** | A+ |

S&P Fair Value Rank: 4-

| 1 | 2 | 3 | **4** | 5 |
| Lowest | | | | Highest |

Fair Value Calc.: $69.80 (Slightly Overvalued)

S&P Investability Quotient Percentile

81%

RKY scored higher than 81% of all companies for which an S&P Report is available.

Volatility: Low

| **Low** | Average | High |

Technical Evaluation: Bullish

Since 11/04, the technical indicators for RKY have been Bullish.

Relative Strength Rank: Moderate

58

| 1 Lowest | | Highest 99 |

| Price as of 11/12/04: | **$71.88** | 2004E S&P Core EPS: | **$4.44** |

GAAP Earnings vs. Previous Year
▲ Up ▼ Down ► No Change

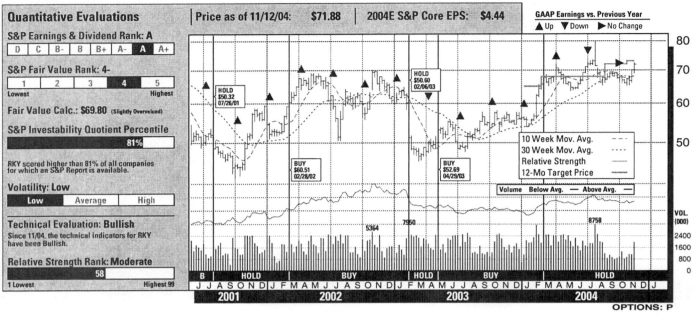

10 Week Mov. Avg. — — —
30 Week Mov. Avg. ....
Relative Strength ———
12-Mo Target Price

Volume Below Avg. ——— Above Avg.

OPTIONS: P

Analyst commentary prepared by Anishka Clarke/MF/BK

Highlights November 12, 2004

- We see net sales (after excise taxes) increasing 4% in 2005, following an anticipated 7% rise in 2004. We believe domestic volumes will benefit from strong performance from the new low-carbohydrate product, Aspen Edge, but we remain wary of any potential growth in major brand Coors Light. However, we do see continued strength in the Canadian market aiding top-line growth. European volumes should advance, driven by strong U.K. growth in the on- and off-premise trades and anticipated improvement in distribution and execution.

- We see modest net revenue per barrel growth in 2005, given our expectations for a continued favorable U.S. pricing environment. In addition, we look for greater efficiencies from supply chain improvements, increased productivity, and possible volume growth to offset cost pressures in transportation, packaging and marketing.

- We see operating margins widening about 70 basis points, on an improving mix. We project 2005 EPS of $5.29, before special items, up 11% from our $4.77 2004 estimate. We estimate Standard & Poor's Core EPS for 2004 at $4.44, reflecting projected option and pension adjustments.

Investment Rationale/Risk November 12, 2004

- We maintain our hold opinion on the stock, based on valuation and what we see as easy 2005 earnings comparisons in the Americas and effective cost-cutting efforts over the longer term. We also look for new products and international growth to aid the top line over the next few years. Further, we think the potential merger with Molson, Canada, could provide certain cost synergies and expand RKY's geographic footprint. However, we remain wary of any significant top-line growth potential.

- Risks to our opinion and target price include RKY's ability to compete effectively against rivals Anheuser-Busch (BUD: accumulate, $51) and SAB Miller. In addition, we believe the planned Molson merger has near-term operational risks.

- Our discounted cash flow model suggests an intrinsic value of $66 a share, based on a projected 5% annual growth rate in revenues for the next five years, and further debt repayments. Our 12-month target price of $73 combines our DCF estimate with a projected P/E multiple of about 15X applied to our 2005 EPS estimate of $5.29.

Key Stock Statistics

S&P Core EPS 2005E	4.74	52-week Range	$80.11-53.73
S&P Oper. EPS 2004E	4.77	12 Month P/E	15.2
P/E on S&P Oper. EPS 2004E	15.1	Beta	0.44
S&P Oper. EPS 2004E	15.1	Shareholders	2,985
S&P Oper. EPS 2005E	5.29	Market Cap (B)	$ 2.6
Yield (%)	1.1%	Shares Outstanding (M)	37.4
Dividend Rate/Share	0.82		

Value of $10,000 invested five years ago: **$ 13,376**

Dividend Data Dividends have been paid since 1970

Amount ($)	Date Decl.	Ex-Div. Date	Stock of Record	Payment Date
0.205	Feb. 13	Feb. 25	Feb. 27	Mar. 15 '04
0.205	May. 14	May. 26	May. 28	Jun. 15 '04
0.205	Aug. 18	Aug. 27	Aug. 31	Sep. 15 '04
0.205	Nov. 12	Nov. 26	Nov. 30	Dec. 15 '04

Revenues/Earnings Data Fiscal year ending December 31

Revenues (Million $)

	2004	2003	2002	2001	2000	1999
1Q	923.5	828.1	745.8	543.7	505.4	439.9
2Q	1,151	1,100	1,048	692.7	669.8	575.6
3Q	1,104	1,049	1,002	634.7	657.1	544.0
4Q	—	1,023	981.1	558.4	582.1	497.2
Yr.	—	4,000	3,776	2,429	2,414	2,057

Earnings Per Share ($)

	2004	2003	2002	2001	2000	1999
1Q	0.13	0.02	0.75	0.49	0.40	0.32
2Q	1.90	2.09	1.84	1.33	1.29	1.23
3Q	1.68	1.68	1.28	1.05	0.92	0.58
4Q	E1.05	0.98	0.55	0.44	0.32	0.33
Yr.	E4.77	4.77	4.42	3.31	2.93	2.46

Next earnings report expected: early-February Source: S&P, Company Reports
EPS Estimates based on S&P Operating Earnings; historical GAAP earnings are as reported.

Adolph Coors Company

Recommendation: **HOLD** ★ ★ ★ ☆ ☆   12-Month Target Price: **$73.00** (as of October 28, 2004)

Business Summary November 12, 2004

Founded in 1873, Adolph Coors Co., through its Coors Brewing Co. subsidiary, is the third largest U.S. brewer. In 2003, the company held an 11% share of the U.S. beer market, selling 32.7 million barrels of beer and other malt beverage products, up 3% from the level of 2002.

The company's stable of well known U.S. brands, sold in all 50 states and the District of Columbia, includes Coors Light (51% of total sales volume), Original Coors, and Coors Non-Alcoholic premium beers; above-premium brews such as George Killian's Irish Red and Blue Moon Belgian White Ale; and lower-priced beers, including Extra Gold, Keystone Premium, Keystone Light, and Keystone Ice. RKY also produces Zima and Zima Citrus malt-based beverages. In early 2004, the company introduced a new low-carbohydrate beer, Aspen Edge, to the U.S. market.

RKY has three U.S. production facilities. The first, the world's largest single-site brewery, is in Golden, CO. The second, a packaging and brewing facility, is in Memphis, TN. The third facility, which currently operates as a packaging plant and distribution facility, is located near Elkton, VA. Significant portions of the company's aluminum can, glass bottle and malt requirements are produced in its own facilities. In 2001, RKY added a third bottling line at the Elkton, VA, plant, and also added brewing capacity to the Memphis facility. The company believes its facilities provide sufficient brewing and packaging capacity to meet near-term consumer demand.

In February 2002, the company completed the acquisition of the Carling Brewers business from Interbrew S.A., for about $1.7 billion, and subsequently renamed it Coors Brewers Ltd. (CBL). With 20% of the U.K. beer market, CBL is the second largest beer company in the U.K. CBL's brand portfolio consists of 20 U.K. beer brands, including Carling (about 22% of 2003 sales volumes), Worthington and Caffreys, the U.K. distribution rights to Grolsch, and four flavored alcoholic beverage brands. CBL also supplies other companies' brands in the on-premise channel to provide a full range of products. In 2003, the company introduced two new products to the on- and off-trade channels in the U.K.: Carling Extra Cold and Coors Fine Light. The international market accounted for 32% of total 2003 sales volume.

Through its U.S. and foreign production facilities, RKY markets its products to about 30 international markets, and to U.S. military bases worldwide. Original Coors and Coors Light are brewed and distributed by Molson Breweries of Canada Ltd. under a partnership agreement in which RKY owns 50.1%. In 2003, Coors Light held an 8.7% share of the Canadian beer market. The company also imports, markets, sells and distributes Molson's brands of beer in the U.S.

On July 22, 2004, Coors announced its intention to merge with Canadian brewer Molson Inc., to create a new company with estimated combined sales of about 61 million hectoliters, making it the fifth largest brewer in the world. The company anticipates synergies upwards of $175 million by 2007, with accretion to earnings within the first full year of combined operations. Under the proposed plan, each Molson Class B voting shares will convert into shares with 0.126 voting rights and 0.234 non-voting rights of Molson Coors stock, and each Molson Class A will convert into shares with 0.360 non-voting share of Molson Coors. The transaction is expected to close at the end of 2004, pending necessary approvals.

Company Financials Fiscal Year ending December 31

Per Share Data ($)

(Year Ended December 31)	2003	2002	2001	2000	1999	1998	1997	1996	1995	1994
Tangible Bk. Val.	NM	NM	24.06	24.32	22.06	20.51	19.36	18.30	17.59	17.06
Cash Flow	11.43	10.72	6.56	6.38	5.77	4.89	5.24	4.33	4.30	4.67
Earnings	4.77	4.42	3.31	2.93	2.46	1.81	2.16	1.14	1.13	1.52
S&P Core Earnings	4.20	1.53	1.36	NA	NA	NA	NA	NA	NA	NA
Dividends	0.82	0.82	0.80	0.72	0.65	0.60	0.55	0.50	0.50	0.50
Payout Ratio	17%	19%	24%	25%	26%	33%	25%	44%	44%	33%
Prices - High	64.81	70.15	81.18	82.31	65.81	56.75	41.25	24.25	23.25	20.87
- Low	45.85	50.50	42.65	37.37	45.25	29.25	17.50	16.75	15.12	14.75
P/E Ratio - High	14	16	25	28	27	31	19	21	21	14
- Low	10	11	13	13	18	16	8	15	13	10

Income Statement Analysis (Million $)

	2003	2002	2001	2000	1999	1998	1997	1996	1995	1994
Revs.	4,000	3,776	2,429	2,414	2,057	1,900	1,822	1,732	1,675	1,663
Oper. Inc.	551	535	296	295	271	239	233	208	188	215
Depr.	244	230	121	129	124	116	117	121	123	121
Int. Exp.	81.2	70.9	2.01	6.41	4.36	9.80	13.6	17.1	18.4	17.8
Pretax Inc.	254	257	198	170	151	111	147	75.0	73.0	104
Eff. Tax Rate	31.2%	37.0%	37.9%	35.3%	38.7%	39.0%	44.0%	42.1%	41.1%	44.2%
Net Inc.	175	162	123	110	92.3	67.8	82.3	43.4	43.2	58.1
S&P Core Earnings	154	56.1	50.7	NA	NA	NA	NA	NA	NA	NA

Balance Sheet & Other Fin. Data (Million $)

	2003	2002	2001	2000	1999	1998	1997	1996	1995	1994
Cash	19.4	59.2	310	120	164	256	169	111	32.4	27.0
Curr. Assets	1,079	1,054	607	498	613	549	517	417	363	355
Total Assets	4,486	4,297	1,740	1,629	1,546	1,461	1,412	1,363	1,387	1,372
Curr. Liab.	1,134	1,148	518	379	393	384	359	292	324	380
LT Debt	1,160	1,383	20.0	105	105	105	145	176	195	131
Common Equity	1,267	982	951	932	842	775	737	715	695	674
Total Cap.	2,623	2,522	1,033	1,127	1,025	946	958	968	960	872
Cap. Exp.	240	240	245	154	134	105	60.3	65.0	146	160
Cash Flow	418	392	244	239	216	184	199	165	166	179
Curr. Ratio	1.0	0.9	1.2	1.3	1.6	1.4	1.4	1.4	1.1	0.9
% LT Debt of Cap.	44.2	54.9	1.9	9.3	10.2	11.1	15.1	18.2	20.3	14.9
% Net Inc.of Revs.	4.4	4.3	5.1	4.5	4.5	3.6	4.5	2.5	2.6	3.5
% Ret. on Assets	4.0	5.4	7.3	6.9	6.1	4.7	5.9	3.2	3.1	4.3
% Ret. on Equity	15.5	16.7	13.1	12.4	11.4	9.0	11.3	6.2	6.3	8.9

Data as orig reptd.; bef. results of disc opers/spec. items. Per share data adj. for stk. divs.; EPS diluted. E-Estimated. NA-Not Available. NM-Not Meaningful. NR-Not Ranked. UR-Under Review.

Office: 311 10th St, Golden, CO 80401-5811.
Telephone: 303-279-6565.
Website: http://www.coors.com
Chrmn: P.H. Coors.
CEO: W.L. Kiely III.
VP & CFO: T.V. Wolf.

VP & Treas: M.J. Gannon.
VP & General Counsel: R.M. Reese.
Investor Contact: D. Dunnewald 303-279-6565.
Dirs: P. H. Coors, C. M. Herington, F. W. Hobbs, W. L. Kiely III, R. Oliphant, P. H. Patsley, W. R. Sanders, A. C. Yates.

Founded: in 1873.
Domicile: Delaware.
Employees: 8,500.
S&P Analyst: Anishka Clarke/MF/BK

Recommendation: **HOLD** ★★★☆
SELL | SELL | HOLD | BUY | BUY

12-Month Target Price: $12.00
(as of September 07, 2004)

GLW has an approximate 0.15% weighting in the **S&P 500**

Sector: Information Technology
Sub-Industry: Communications Equipment
Peer Group: Optical Components & Subsystems

Summary: GLW, once an old-line housewares company, is now a leading maker of fiber optics and semiconductor components for the fast growing telecommunications and electronics industries.

Quantitative Evaluations

S&P Earnings & Dividend Rank: C

D	C	B-	B	B+	A-	A	A+

S&P Fair Value Rank: 1-

1	2	3	4	5
Lowest				Highest

Fair Value Calc.: $10.50 (Overvalued)

S&P Investability Quotient Percentile

41%

GLW scored lower than 59% of all companies for which an S&P Report is available.

Volatility: High

Low	Average	High

Technical Evaluation: Bullish
Since 11/04, the technical indicators for GLW have been Bullish.

Relative Strength Rank: Moderate

70

1 Lowest	Highest 99

Price as of 11/12/04:	**$12.24**	**2004E S&P Core EPS:**	**$0.28**

GAAP Earnings vs. Previous Year
▲ Up ▼ Down ► No Change

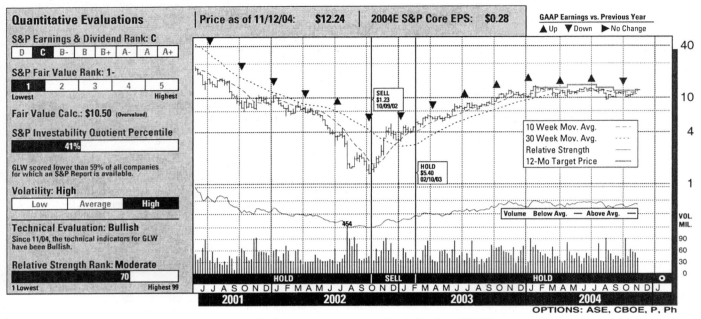

10 Week Mov. Avg. – – –
30 Week Mov. Avg. · · · ·
Relative Strength ———
12-Mo Target Price ———

Volume Below Avg. — Above Avg.

OPTIONS: ASE, CBOE, P, Ph

Analyst commentary prepared by A. Bensinger/CB/BK

Highlights September 07, 2004

- After an estimated 25% increase in 2004, we see sales advancing 15% in 2005, reflecting an improved telecom spending environment. Demand for the company's liquid crystal display and automotive and diesel emissions products remains strong. We think sales growth could accelerate faster than expected if the fiber optic market begins to rebound, on new fiber to the premise (FTTP) initiatives.

- Operationally, we believe the disposal of the struggling photonics and conventional TV glass units should help improve profitability markedly. In light of aggressive cost cutting efforts, we expect 2005 gross margins to widen toward the 38% level; this would still be below historical margins of 40%. We expect operating expenses as a percentage of sales to drop from the 2004 level.

- Factoring in higher equity earnings expected from Dow Corning and Samsung Corning, we project 2005 EPS (excluding charges) of $0.54, up 26% from our 2004 estimate of $0.43. Our 2004 Standard & Poor's Core Earnings estimate of $0.28 a share reflects projected stock option expense of $0.13.

Investment Rationale/Risk September 07, 2004

- In our view, GLW has made significant progress in improving its balance sheet and cost structure. While we believe that fiber to the premise (FTTP) initiatives present an attractive long-term growth opportunity for the company, the exact timing of FTTP revenue contribution remains uncertain. Based on our valuation analysis, we think the stock is fairly valued, and expect it to perform in line with the S&P 500 over the next 12 months.

- Risks to our recommendation and target price include lower telecom spending, prolonged anti-dumping fiber tariffs in China, a slowdown in the demand for display glass, and increased fiber product pricing pressure.

- The shares are trading at 19X our 2005 EPS estimate of $0.54, below the peer average, and at 3X our 2005 sales estimate, above the peer average. Based on our view that earnings and sales are greatly depressed, we believe book value is a more appropriate valuation metric. Largely on that basis, applying a group average book value ratio, our 12-month target price is $12.

Key Stock Statistics

S&P Core EPS 2005E	0.37	52-week Range	$13.89-9.29
S&P Oper. EPS 2004E	0.43	12 Month P/E	NM
P/E on S&P Oper. EPS 2004E	28.5	Beta	NA
S&P Oper. EPS 2005E	0.54	Shareholders	700,000
Yield (%)	Nil	Market Cap (B)	$ 17.2
Dividend Rate/Share	Nil	Shares Outstanding (M)	1402.2

Value of $10,000 invested five years ago: **$ 4,646**

Dividend Data

Dividends were omitted in July 2001.

Revenues/Earnings Data Fiscal year ending December 31

Revenues (Million $)

	2004	2003	2002	2001	2000	1999
1Q	844.0	746.0	839.0	1,921	1,351	892.2
2Q	971.0	752.0	827.0	1,868	1,803	1,031
3Q	1,006	772.0	762.0	1,509	1,944	1,137
4Q	—	820.0	736.0	974.0	2,145	1,260
Yr.	—	3,090	3,164	6,272	7,273	4,368

Earnings Per Share ($)

	2004	2003	2002	2001	2000	1999
1Q	0.04	-0.17	-0.10	0.14	0.09	0.12
2Q	0.07	-0.02	-0.41	-5.13	0.17	0.16
3Q	-1.79	0.02	-0.27	-0.24	0.28	0.18
4Q	E0.12	-0.02	-0.96	-0.69	-0.08	0.18
Yr.	E0.43	-0.18	-1.85	-5.89	0.46	0.65

Next earnings report expected: late-January Source: S&P, Company Reports
EPS Estimates based on S&P Operating Earnings; historical GAAP earnings are as reported.

Corning Incorporated

Recommendation: **HOLD** ★ ★ ★ ☆ ☆   12-Month Target Price: **$12.00** (as of September 07, 2004)

Business Summary September 08, 2004

Corning has completed a transformation from an old line, slow growing housewares company into a leading maker of high technology fiber optics and high performance glass components for the global telecommunications and personal computer industries. Starting in the 2002 fourth quarter, it began reporting in two operating segments: telecommunications (46% of 2003 revenues) and technologies (53%).

The telecommunications segment produces optical fiber and cable, optical hardware and equipment, and photonic modules and components for the worldwide telecommunications industry. Service providers install the company's optical fiber and cable products to help boost capacity.

GLW is the largest producer of optical fiber and cable products, but faces significant competition, due to continued excess capacity in the market place, price pressures, and new product innovations. The company obtained the first significant optical fiber patents and believes its large scale manufacturing experience, fiber process, technology leadership and intellectual property assets yield cost advantages relative to several of its competitors.

The technologies segment manufactures specialized products with unique properties, for customer applications using glass, glass ceramic, and polymer technologies. Businesses in this segment include liquid crystal display glass for flat panel displays, environmental products, life science products, and glass panels and funnels for televisions.

GLW is the largest worldwide producer of advanced liquid crystal display glass substrate products. The company believes it has competitive advantages in liquid crystal display glass substrate products by using its proprietary fusion manufacturing process that delivers thinner, lighter weight and larger size products.

The company's conventional glass television business includes a 50% interest in Samsung Corning Company, Ltd., a producer of glass panels and funnels for cathode ray tubes for televisions and computer monitors, with manufacturing facilities in Korea, Germany and Malaysia. Samsung Electronics Company, Ltd., owns the remaining 50% interest in Samsung Corning. In 2003, the company ceased production of Corning Asahi Video (CAV), a 51%-owned, consolidated venture that produced glass panels and funnels for cathode ray television tubes.

GLW holds a 50% interest in Dow Corning Corp. (DC), which filed for Chapter 11 bankruptcy protection as a result of charges that DC's silicone breast implants were injuring women. DC has filed a plan of reorganization that needs to be approved by many classes of creditors, and by the bankruptcy court. GLW has concluded that the emergence of DC from bankruptcy protection is probable, and resumed recognizing equity earnings in DC in the 2003 first quarter.

In 2003, the company completed equity offerings of about 90 million common shares, realizing net proceeds of about $630 million.

Company Financials Fiscal Year ending December 31

Per Share Data ($)

(Year Ended December 31)	2003	2002	2001	2000	1999	1998	1997	1996	1995	1994
Tangible Bk. Val.	2.65	2.14	3.39	3.56	2.60	1.72	1.28	0.92	1.00	1.25
Cash Flow	0.22	-1.04	-4.74	0.46	1.15	0.85	1.03	0.92	-0.48	0.97
Earnings	-0.18	-1.85	-5.89	0.46	0.65	0.46	0.62	0.50	-0.08	0.44
S&P Core Earnings	-0.16	-2.14	-3.11	NA	NA	NA	NA	NA	NA	NA
Dividends	Nil	Nil	0.12	0.30	0.24	0.24	0.24	0.24	0.24	0.23
Payout Ratio	Nil	Nil	NM	65%	37%	52%	39%	48%	NM	52%
Prices - High	12.34	11.15	72.18	113.29	43.02	15.22	21.70	15.41	12.45	11.68
- Low	3.34	1.10	6.92	34.33	14.91	7.62	11.25	9.29	8.04	9.20
P/E Ratio - High	NM	NM	NM	NM	66	33	35	31	NM	27
- Low	NM	NM	NM	NM	23	16	18	19	NM	21

Income Statement Analysis (Million $)

	2003	2002	2001	2000	1999	1998	1997	1996	1995	1994
Revs.	3,090	3,164	6,272	7,273	4,297	3,484	4,090	3,652	5,313	4,799
Oper. Inc.	386	21.0	805	2,075	1,053	762	1,084	850	1,032	1,028
Depr.	517	661	1,080	765	381	298	322	288	377	338
Int. Exp.	154	179	153	107	77.6	70.0	99	87.0	128	122
Pretax Inc.	-550	-2,604	-5,963	840	599	522	743	559	183	508
Eff. Tax Rate	NM	NM	NM	48.4%	31.5%	25.5%	30.6%	29.2%	84.7%	33.5%
Net Inc.	-223	-1,780	-5,498	410	477	328	440	343	-51.0	281
S&P Core Earnings	-200	-2,207	-2,908	NA	NA	NA	NA	NA	NA	NA

Balance Sheet & Other Fin. Data (Million $)

	2003	2002	2001	2000	1999	1998	1997	1996	1995	1994
Cash	833	1,553	1,037	138	116	12.0	65.0	223	215	161
Curr. Assets	2,694	3,825	4,107	4,634	1,783	1,310	1,424	1,419	1,834	1,726
Total Assets	10,752	11,548	12,793	17,526	6,012	4,982	4,811	4,321	5,987	6,023
Curr. Liab.	1,553	1,680	1,994	1,949	1,488	1,075	1,018	808	1,165	1,074
LT Debt	2,668	3,963	4,461	3,966	1,289	998	1,134	1,208	1,393	1,406
Common Equity	5,379	4,536	5,414	10,633	2,227	1,506	1,246	961	2,103	2,263
Total Cap.	8,168	8,713	10,001	14,808	3,814	3,233	3,016	2,867	3,768	4,305
Cap. Exp.	366	357	1,800	1,525	733	714	775	598	495	387
Cash Flow	294	-1,247	-4,418	409	856	624	760	629	-324	618
Curr. Ratio	1.7	2.3	2.1	2.4	1.2	1.2	1.4	1.8	1.6	1.6
% LT Debt of Cap.	32.7	45.5	44.6	26.8	33.8	30.9	37.6	42.1	66.2	32.7
% Net Inc.of Revs.	NM	NM	NM	5.6	11.1	9.4	10.8	9.4	Nil	5.9
% Ret. on Assets	NM	NM	NM	3.4	8.7	6.7	9.6	7.0	Nil	4.7
% Ret. on Equity	NM	NM	NM	6.2	25.5	23.7	39.7	22.3	Nil	13.4

Data as orig reptd.; bef. results of disc opers/spec. items. Per share data adj. for stk. divs.; EPS diluted. E-Estimated. NA-Not Available. NM-Not Meaningful. NR-Not Ranked. UR-Under Review.

Office: One Riverfront Plaza, Corning, NY 14831-0001.
Telephone: 607-974-9000.
Email: info@corning.com
Website: http://www.corning.com
Chrmn & CEO: J.R. Houghton.
Pres & COO: W.P. Weeks.
Vice Chrmn & CFO: J.B. Flaws.

SVP & Treas: M.S. Rogus.
SVP & General Counsel: W.D. Eggers.
VP & Investor Contact: K.M. Dietz 607-974-8217.
Dirs: J. S. Brown, J. B. Flaws, G. Gund, J. M. Hennessy, J. R. Houghton, J. Knowles, J. J. O'Connor, D. D. Rieman, H. O. Ruding, E. C. Sit, W. D. Smithburg, H. E. Tookes II, P. F. Volanakis, W. P. Weeks.

Founded: in 1851.
Domicile: New York.
Employees: 20,600.
S&P Analyst: A. Bensinger/CB/BK

Costco Wholesale

Recommendation: **HOLD** ★ ★ ★ ☆ ☆
SELL SELL HOLD BUY BUY

12-Month Target Price: $51.00
(as of November 10, 2004)

COST has an approximate 0.21% weighting in the **S&P 500**

Sector: Consumer Staples
Sub-Industry: Hypermarkets & Super Centers
Peer Group: Retail - General Merchandise

Summary: Costco Wholesale operates more than 430 membership warehouses in the U.S., Puerto Rico, Canada, the U.K., Taiwan, Japan, Korea and Mexico.

Quantitative Evaluations

S&P Earnings & Dividend Rank: B+

D	C	B-	B	B+	A-	A	A+

S&P Fair Value Rank: 3

1	2	3	4	5
Lowest				Highest

Fair Value Calc.: $48.70 (Fairly Valued)

S&P Investability Quotient Percentile
98%

COST scored higher than 98% of all companies for which an S&P Report is available.

Volatility: Low

Low	Average	High

Technical Evaluation: Bullish
Since 9/04, the technical indicators for COST have been Bullish.

Relative Strength Rank: Strong
74
1 Lowest   Highest 99

Price as of 11/12/04: $49.12   **2005E S&P Core EPS:** $2.05

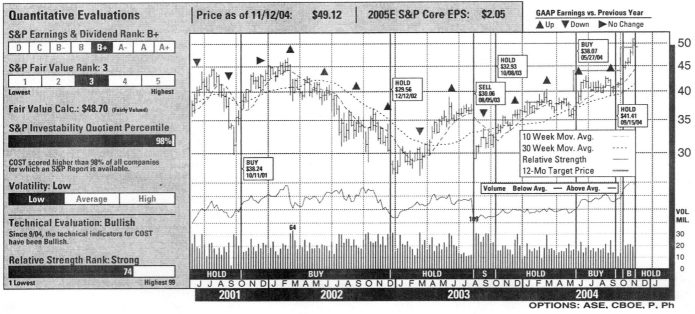

GAAP Earnings vs. Previous Year ▲ Up ▼ Down ▶ No Change

Legend: 10 Week Mov. Avg. / 30 Week Mov. Avg. / Relative Strength / 12-Mo Target Price
Volume Below Avg. — Above Avg.

Analyst commentary prepared by Joseph Agnese/PMW/BK

OPTIONS: ASE, CBOE, P, Ph

Highlights November 10, 2004

- We see net sales advancing 10% to 12% in FY 05 (Aug.), to exceed $53 billion, reflecting same-store sales gains in the mid-single digits and the addition of about 7% to 8% to square footage (about 27 to 30 new clubs). We expect sales growth in double digits for fresh foods, gasoline, and other ancillary business categories. We look for membership fees to equal about 2.0% of sales, or $1.1 billion.

- We expect gross margins on sales to remain level, at about 10.7%, as the benefits of wider margins on food and sundries, soft and hard lines, and fresh foods are likely to be offset by narrower ancillary business margins (due to difficult gasoline margin comparisons) and the impact of a 2% reward on executive memberships and new accounting for vendor allowances. We look for EBIT (earnings before interest and taxes) margins to widen modestly, on expected healthcare cost reductions and lower workers' compensation costs due to new legislation in California.

- After modest share dilution, we project that FY 05 EPS will increase to $2.15, from $1.85 in FY 04.

Investment Rationale/Risk November 10, 2004

- We believe the shares are a worthwhile holding, as we believe valuation will benefit from continued positive sales and margin trends. We expect COST to maintain or capture additional market share in FY 05, reflecting what we view as a strong value proposition and a relatively upscale product mix that appeals to a more affluent customer base. Based on FY 04 results, we think the company appears to have a better handle on expenses, which grew faster than sales over the past few years. With workers' compensation and healthcare cost controls in place, we expect earnings growth to outpace sales gains in FY 05.

- Risks to our recommendation and target price include a slowdown in the economy and increased pricing competition.

- Our 12-month target price of $51 is derived from our analysis of relative P/E multiples, as well as our discounted cash flow model. We assume that the stock will trade at a P/E multiple of 23X our calendar 2005 EPS estimate of $2.23, maintaining its P/E multiple premium to the S&P 500, and calculate value of about $51. Our DCF assumptions include a weighted average cost of capital of 9% and an expected terminal growth rate of 3.5%.

Key Stock Statistics

S&P Oper. EPS 2005E	2.15	52-week Range	$50.46-33.27
P/E on S&P Oper. EPS 2005E	22.8	12 Month P/E	26.6
Yield (%)	0.8%	Beta	0.80
Dividend Rate/Share	0.40	Shareholders	7,805
Shares Outstanding (M)	461.2	Market Cap (B)	$ 22.7

Value of $10,000 invested five years ago: **$ 11,674**

Dividend Data Dividends have been paid since 2004

Amount ($)	Date Decl.	Ex-Div. Date	Stock of Record	Payment Date
0.100	Apr. 28	May. 06	May. 10	May. 31 '04
0.100	Jul. 12	Jul. 21	Jul. 23	Aug. 27 '04
0.100	Oct. 26	Nov. 03	Nov. 05	Nov. 26 '04

Revenues/Earnings Data Fiscal year ending August 31

Revenues (Million $)

	2004	2003	2002	2001	2000	1999
1Q	10,521	9,199	8,467	7,637	6,944	5,998
2Q	11,549	10,114	9,383	8,306	7,737	6,592
3Q	10,897	9,543	8,617	7,719	6,769	6,054
4Q	15,139	13,690	12,296	11,135	10,589	8,812
Yr.	48,107	42,546	38,763	34,797	32,164	27,456

Earnings Per Share ($)

	2004	2003	2002	2001	2000	1999
1Q	0.34	0.31	0.28	0.28	0.28	0.23
2Q	0.48	0.39	0.41	0.38	0.39	0.33
3Q	0.42	0.33	0.28	0.23	0.26	0.23
4Q	0.62	0.51	0.52	0.41	0.42	0.33
Yr.	1.85	1.53	1.48	1.29	1.35	1.11

Next earnings report expected: early-December Source: S&P, Company Reports
EPS Estimates based on S&P Operating Earnings; historical GAAP earnings are as reported.

Costco Wholesale Corporation

Recommendation: **HOLD** ★ ★ ★ ☆ ☆   12-Month Target Price: **$51.00** (as of November 10, 2004)

Business Summary November 10, 2004

Costco Wholesale (formerly Costco Companies, Inc., and prior to that, Price/Costco, Inc.) began the pioneering "I can get it for you wholesale" membership warehouse concept in 1976, in San Diego, CA. The company operated about 431 warehouses worldwide as of March 3, 2004, mainly in the U.S. and Canada. COST also operates an e-commerce Web site, costco.com.

Low prices on a limited selection of national brand merchandise and selected private-label products in a wide range of merchandise categories produce high sales volume and rapid inventory turnover. High levels of turnover, combined with operating efficiencies achieved by volume purchasing in a no-frills, self-service warehouse facility, enable the company to operate profitably at significantly narrower gross margins than traditional retailers and even discounters and supermarkets. COST buys virtually all of its merchandise directly from manufacturers, for shipment either directly to warehouse clubs or to a consolidation point (depot), at which shipments are combined in order to minimize freight and handling costs. The company generally receives cash from the sale of a substantial portion of its inventory at mature warehouse operations before it is required to pay vendors, even though COST often pays early to obtain payment discounts.

COST has two primary types of memberships: Business and Gold Star (individual) members. Individual memberships are available to employees of federal, state and local governments; financial institutions; corporations; utility and transportation

companies; public and private educational institutions; and other organizations. Gold Star membership is $45 annually. There were 15 million Gold Star memberships as of August 31, 2003.

Businesses, including individuals with retail sales or business licenses, may become Business members by paying an annual $45 fee, with add-on membership cards available for an annual fee of $35. As of August 31, 2003, there were 4.6 million Business memberships. Executive memberships, available for a $100 annual fee, offer business and individual members savings on services such as merchant credit card processing and small business loans, as well as a 2% reward, up to a maximum of $500 annually, on qualified purchases.

A typical warehouse format averages about 139,000 sq. ft. Floor plans are designed for economy and efficiency in the use of selling space, in the handling of merchandise, and in the control of inventory. Merchandise is generally stored on racks above the sales floor, and is displayed on pallets containing large quantities of each item, reducing the labor required for handling and stocking. Specific items in each product line are limited to fast selling models, sizes and colors. COST carries only an average of about 3,700 to 4,500 stockkeeping units (SKUs) per warehouse, well below the 40,000 to 60,000 SKUs of a typical discount store or supermarket.

Company Financials Fiscal Year ending August 31

Per Share Data ($)

(Year Ended August 31)	2004	2003	2002	2001	2000	1999	1998	1997	1996	1995
Tangible Bk. Val.	NA	14.33	12.51	10.71	9.37	7.98	6.71	5.66	4.54	3.92
Cash Flow	NA	2.32	2.17	1.90	1.86	1.57	1.41	1.16	1.00	0.86
Earnings	1.85	1.53	1.48	1.29	1.35	1.11	1.02	0.73	0.62	0.53
S&P Core Earnings	NA	1.40	1.32	1.12	NA	NA	NA	NA	NA	NA
Dividends	0.20	Nil	Nil	Nil	Nil	Nil	Nil	Nil	Nil	Nil
Payout Ratio	11%	Nil	Nil	Nil	Nil	Nil	Nil	Nil	Nil	Nil
Prices - High	50.46	39.02	46.90	46.37	60.50	49.37	38.06	22.56	13.00	9.37
- Low	35.05	27.00	27.09	29.83	25.93	32.68	20.62	11.87	7.31	6.00
P/E Ratio - High	27	26	32	36	45	44	38	31	21	18
- Low	19	18	18	23	19	29	20	16	12	11

Income Statement Analysis (Million $)

	2004	2003	2002	2001	2000	1999	1998	1997	1996	1995
Revs.	NA	42,546	38,763	34,797	32,164	27,456	24,270	21,874	19,567	17,906
Oper. Inc.	NA	1,567	1,494	1,312	1,299	1,141	989	838	663	582
Depr.	NA	391	342	301	254	225	196	182	162	142
Int. Exp.	NA	36.9	29.1	32.0	39.3	45.5	48.0	76.0	78.0	67.9
Pretax Inc.	NA	1,158	1,138	1,003	1,052	859	766	520	423	368
Eff. Tax Rate	NA	37.8%	38.5%	40.0%	40.0%	40.0%	39.9%	40.0%	41.2%	41.0%
Net Inc.	NA	721	700	602	631	515	460	312	249	217
S&P Core Earnings	NA	660	624	525	NA	NA	NA	NA	NA	NA

Balance Sheet & Other Fin. Data (Million $)

	2004	2003	2002	2001	2000	1999	1998	1997	1996	1995
Cash	NA	1,545	806	603	525	441	362	176	102	45.7
Curr. Assets	NA	5,712	4,631	3,882	3,470	3,316	2,628	2,110	1,828	1,702
Total Assets	NA	13,192	11,620	10,090	8,634	7,505	6,260	5,476	4,912	4,437
Curr. Liab.	NA	5,011	4,450	4,112	3,404	2,866	2,197	1,964	1,772	1,693
LT Debt	NA	1,290	1,211	859	790	919	930	917	1,229	1,095
Common Equity	NA	6,555	5,694	4,883	4,240	3,532	2,966	2,468	1,778	1,531
Total Cap.	NA	8,181	7,025	5,858	5,139	4,572	3,896	3,507	3,136	2,690
Cap. Exp.	NA	811	1,039	1,448	1,228	788	572	553	507	531
Cash Flow	NA	1,112	1,042	903	886	740	656	494	411	359
Curr. Ratio	NA	1.1	1.0	0.9	1.0	1.2	1.2	1.1	1.0	1.0
% LT Debt of Cap.	NA	15.8	17.2	14.7	15.4	20.1	23.9	26.1	39.2	40.1
% Net Inc.of Revs.	NA	1.7	1.8	1.7	2.0	1.9	1.9	1.4	1.3	1.2
% Ret. on Assets	NA	5.8	6.4	6.4	7.8	7.5	7.8	6.0	5.3	5.0
% Ret. on Equity	NA	11.8	13.2	13.2	16.2	15.9	16.9	14.7	15.1	13.5

Data as orig reptd.; bef. results of disc opers/spec. items. Per share data adj. for stk. divs. Bold denotes primary EPS - prior periods restated. E-Estimated. NA-Not Available. NM-Not Meaningful. NR-Not Ranked. UR-Under Review.

Office: 999 Lake Drive, Issaquah, WA 98027.
Telephone: 425-313-8100.
Email: investor@costco.com
Website: http://www.costco.com
Chrmn: J.H. Brotman.
Pres & CEO: J.D. Sinegal.

COO & EVP: R.D. DiCerchio.
EVP, CFO & Investor Contact: R.A. Galanti 425-313-8203.
SVP & Secy: J. Benoliel.
Dirs: J. H. Brotman, B. S. Carson, Sr., R. D. DiCerchio, D. J. Evans, R. A. Galanti, W. H. Gates II, H. E. James, R. M. Libenson, J. W. Meisenbach, C. T. Munger, J. S. Ruckelshaus, J. D. Sinegal.

Founded: in 1976.
Domicile: Washington.
Employees: 103,000.
S&P Analyst: Joseph Agnese/PMW/BK

Countrywide Financial

Recommendation: HOLD ★★★☆☆ | 12-Month Target Price: **$35.00**
(as of November 04, 2004)

CFC has an approximate 0.16% weighting in the **S&P 500**

Sector: Financials
Sub-Industry: Thrifts & Mortgage Finance
Peer Group: Consumer Finance - Mortgage - Larger

Summary: This leading mortgage banker (formerly Countrywide Credit Industries) originates, purchases, sells and services mortgage loans.

Quantitative Evaluations

S&P Earnings & Dividend Rank: A

| D | C | B- | B | B+ | A- | A | A+ |

S&P Fair Value Rank: 3-

| 1 | 2 | 3 | 4 | 5 |
Lowest | | | | Highest

Fair Value Calc.: $30.50 (Fairly Valued)

S&P Investability Quotient Percentile

92%

CFC scored higher than 92% of all companies for which an S&P Report is available.

Volatility: Average

| Low | Average | High |

Technical Evaluation: Bearish

Since 10/04, the technical indicators for CFC have been Bearish.

Relative Strength Rank: Weak

10

1 Lowest | Highest 99

| Price as of 11/12/04: | $31.10 | 2004E S&P Core EPS: | $3.86 |

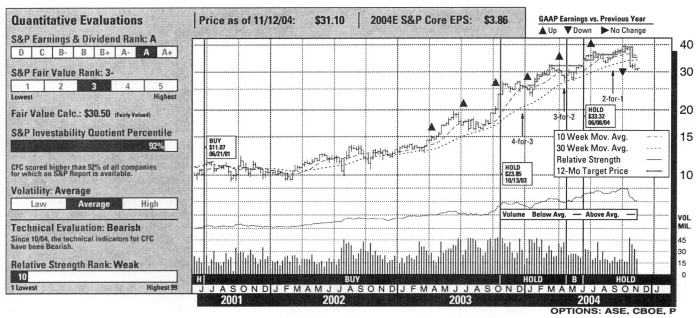

GAAP Earnings vs. Previous Year
▲ Up ▼ Down ▶ No Change

Analyst commentary prepared by Erik J. Eisenstein/PMW/BK

OPTIONS: ASE, CBOE, P

Highlights November 09, 2004

- We expect mortgage origination and application activity to be less robust in 2005 than in 2004, reflecting somewhat higher mortgage rates and some exhaustion of refinancing candidates. Based on our expectations, we believe that CFC's loan production revenue will drop 42% in 2005. We see a 13% increase in net interest earned, with projected higher inventories of loans held for investment outweighing forecasted lower average balances of loans held for sale.

- With expected lower impairment and amortization of loan servicing rights, amid reduced expected refinancing activity, we forecast an improvement in net loan administration results. Aided by a larger contribution we anticipate from CFC's insurance services providers, we forecast that net revenues will decrease only 13%. We expect expenses to decline 23%, reflecting some projected variable cost savings stemming from lower forecasted production volume.

- We estimate that 2005 EPS will slide 1%, to $3.85, from $3.90 projected for 2004. Our 2004 and 2005 S&P Core EPS projections are $3.86 and $3.81, respectively, reflecting estimated stock-based compensation expense.

Investment Rationale/Risk November 09, 2004

- Although we believe the refinancing boom will taper off amid higher rates in the coming year, we continue to think that the company will generate solid fundamental results. In addition to what we view as excellent loan production, CFC has posted strong gains in its insurance, capital markets, global and banking businesses in recent quarters. After seeing third quarter results, our concerns about operating expense control during periods of lower mortgage volume increased somewhat. Nevertheless, we believe that the company's efforts to diversify its earnings base will serve it well as it navigates the ebb and flow of the cyclical mortgage business. While we continue to view CFC as interest-rate sensitive in comparison to other financial institutions, we see it as less so than in the past.

- Risks to our opinion and target price include the possibility that fixed mortgage rates will rise higher or faster than expected.

- Our 12-month target price of $35 is derived by applying a P/E multiple of 9.1X to our 2005 EPS estimate. This is significantly higher than the historical average, but well below the multiple awarded the shares of most other financial institutions.

Key Stock Statistics

S&P Core EPS 2005E	3.81	52-week Range	$39.93-23.01
S&P Oper. EPS 2004E	3.90	12 Month P/E	7.6
P/E on S&P Oper. EPS 2004E	8.0	Beta	0.29
S&P Oper. EPS 2005E	3.85	Shareholders	1,966
Yield (%)	1.5%	Market Cap (B)	$ 18.1
Dividend Rate/Share	0.48	Shares Outstanding (M)	580.4

Value of $10,000 invested five years ago: **$ 42,350**

Dividend Data Dividends have been paid since 1979

Amount ($)	Date Decl.	Ex-Div. Date	Stock of Record	Payment Date
0.150	Apr. 30	May. 11	May. 13	Jun. 01 '04
0.200	Jul. 23	Aug. 11	Aug. 13	Aug. 31 '04
2-for-1	Jun. 25	Aug. 31	Aug. 25	Aug. 30 '04
0.120	Oct. 22	Nov. 08	Nov. 10	Nov. 30 '04

Revenues/Earnings Data Fiscal year ending December 31

Revenues (Million $)

	2004	2003	2002	2001	2000	1999
1Q	2,215	1,451	913.8	—	474.6	537.0
2Q	2,333	1,636	998.3	—	512.3	537.0
3Q	2,246	2,934	1,211	—	520.6	491.8
4Q	—	2,006	1,397	—	548.8	452.9
Yr.	—	8,027	4,519	2,636	2,056	2,019

Earnings Per Share ($)

	2004	2003	2002	2001	2000	1999
1Q	1.11	0.61	0.33	—	0.18	0.22
2Q	1.12	0.68	0.37	—	0.19	0.23
3Q	0.94	1.93	0.43	—	0.20	0.22
4Q	E0.74	0.91	0.49	—	0.21	0.22
Yr.	E3.90	4.15	1.62	0.97	0.79	0.88

Next earnings report expected: late-January Source: S&P, Company Reports
EPS Estimates based on S&P Operating Earnings; historical GAAP earnings are as reported.

Countrywide Financial Corporation

Recommendation: **HOLD** ★ ★ ★ ☆ ☆   12-Month Target Price: **$35.00** (as of November 04, 2004)

Business Summary November 09, 2004

Countrywide Financial (formerly Countrywide Credit Industries) is the largest independent U.S. residential mortgage banker. Its mortgage banking business involves originating, purchasing, selling and servicing mortgage loans, as well as loan closing services. In 2003, mortgage banking provided 77% of pretax earnings. CFC has undertaken a diversification initiative to reduce earnings cyclicality. It plans to leverage its mortgage platform to develop its other businesses, which include insurance and insurance agency, mortgage-related capital markets, global mortgage processing, and, with the May 2001 acquisition of Treasury Bank, banking. Its goal is for diversification businesses to contribute 50% of consolidated pretax earnings by 2008.

In 2003, CFC produced (through origination and purchase) $435 billion in mortgage loans, an increase of 73% from the level of 2002. About 91% of the loans were prime, first mortgage loans, including conventional mortgage loans, Federal Housing Administration-insured mortgage loans, and Veterans Administration-guaranteed mortgage loans. The majority of the conventional loans qualify for inclusion in guarantee programs sponsored by Fannie Mae or Freddie Mac. Some conventional loans were non-conforming loans that either had original balances in excess of $333,700 or did not meet Fannie Mae or Freddie Mac guidelines. Remaining loan production included sub-prime loans (4.6%) and prime home equity loans (4.2%). As a mortgage banker, the company sells most of the loans that it produces.

The company services substantially all mortgage loans that it produces. Servicing activities include collecting loan payments, responding to borrower inquiries, counseling delinquent borrowers and supervising foreclosures and property dispositions. At December 31, 2003, CFC serviced $645 billion of mortgage loans, up 42% from the level a year earlier. The net value of its mortgage servicing rights was $6.9 billion.

In 2003, according to an industry trade publication, CFC was the third largest mortgage originator and the third largest servicer, trailing Wells Fargo Home Mortgage and Washington Mutual in both categories. Its mortgage origination market share grew to 12% in 2003, from 9.4% in 2002. Its servicing market share rose to 8.8%, from 7.0%. The company has a strategic goal of becoming the leading mortgage originator (with at least 30% market share) and servicer by 2008.

The company's income statement includes certain fairly complex items necessary to account for its servicing business. Amortization and impairment/recovery of mortgage servicing rights refers to the noncash writedown or writeup CFC makes to its loan servicing portfolio in response to such things as increased prepayments, or runoff. The servicing hedge gain or loss derives from price changes in the various financial instruments that the company holds to offset changes in the value of its mortgage servicing portfolio.

Company Financials Fiscal Year ending December 31

Per Share Data ($)

(Year Ended December 31)	2003	2002	2001	2000	1999	1998	1997	1996	1995	1994
Tangible Bk. Val.	14.61	10.20	8.33	7.56	6.36	5.59	4.78	3.80	3.23	2.58
Cash Flow	4.15	1.62	3.42	2.08	0.88	0.93	0.88	0.71	0.57	0.57
Earnings	4.15	1.62	0.97	0.79	0.88	0.82	0.77	0.61	0.49	0.24
S&P Core Earnings	4.12	1.59	0.93	NA	NA	NA	NA	NA	NA	NA
Dividends	0.15	0.11	0.10	0.10	0.10	0.08	0.08	0.08	0.08	0.08
Payout Ratio	4%	7%	10%	13%	11%	10%	10%	13%	16%	33%
Prices - High	27.27	13.75	13.00	12.62	12.85	14.06	10.81	7.56	6.68	4.78
- Low	12.62	9.40	9.34	5.57	6.15	7.15	6.09	4.93	3.12	3.09
P/E Ratio - High	7	8	13	16	15	17	14	12	14	20
- Low	3	6	10	7	7	9	8	8	6	13

Income Statement Analysis (Million $)

	2003	2002	2001	2000	1999	1998	1997	1996	1995	1994
Loan Fees	2,804	2,029	2,048	1,600	1,599	1,647	1,209	967	632	471
Int. Inc.	3,342	2,253	1,822	1,341	999	999	440	350	354	343
Total Revs.	10,430	10,663	5,331	4,022	3,394	3,676	2,495	1,656	1,485	1,032
Int. Exp.	1,940	1,461	1,475	1,348	930	984	424	317	282	268
Exp./Op. Revs.	78.5%	58.5%	70.1%	82.6%	131.6%	205.3%	119.4%	164.0%	71.5%	83.1%
Pretax Inc.	3,846	1,343	789	586	631	632	566	422	326	147
Eff. Tax Rate	38.3%	37.3%	38.4%	36.2%	35.0%	39.0%	39.0%	39.0%	40.0%	40.0%
Net Inc.	2,373	842	486	374	410	385	345	257	196	88.4
S&P Core Earnings	2,351	826	462	NA	NA	NA	NA	NA	NA	NA

Balance Sheet & Other Fin. Data (Million $)

	2003	2002	2001	2000	1999	1998	1997	1996	1995	1994
Net Prop.	755	577	447	397	411	312	226	274	141	146
Cash & Secs.	58,962	41,388	9,876	8,337	2,044	1,519	5,303	18.3	16.4	17.6
Loans	24,104	15,026	10,369	1,964	2,653	6,231	5,292	2,580	4,740	2,899
Total Assets	97,950	58,031	37,217	22,956	15,822	15,648	12,219	8,089	8,658	5,580
Capitalization:										
Debt	20,104	14,117	11,309	8,144	7,753	6,453	7,975	2,368	1,912	1,499
Equity	8,085	5,161	4,088	3,559	2,888	2,519	2,088	1,612	1,320	943
Total	28,188	19,278	17,212	13,273	10,641	8,972	6,284	3,980	3,145	2,442
Price Times Bk. Val.: High	1.9	1.3	1.6	1.7	2.0	2.5	2.3	2.0	2.1	1.9
Price Times Bk. Val.: Low	0.9	0.9	1.1	0.7	1.0	1.3	1.3	1.6	1.0	1.2
Cash Flow	2,373	842	1,706	991	476	435	390	298	227	210
% Return On Revs.	22.8	8.3	9.1	9.3	12.1	10.5	13.8	15.6	13.2	8.6
% Ret. on Assets	3.0	1.8	1.6	1.9	2.6	2.9	3.4	3.1	2.8	1.6
% Ret. on Equity	35.8	18.2	12.7	11.6	14.2	16.7	18.7	17.6	17.3	9.7

Data as orig reptd.; bef. results of disc opers/spec. items. Per share data adj. for stk. divs.; EPS diluted (primary prior to 1998). Quarterly revenues are net of interest expense and amortization and impairment/recovery of mortgage servicing rights. E-Estimated. NA-Not Available. NM-Not Meaningful. NR-Not Ranked. Prior to 2001 (10 mos.), years ended Feb. 28 of following cal. yr.

Office: 4500 Park Granada, Calabasas, CA 91302-7137.
Telephone: 818-225-3000.
Email: ir@countrywide.com
Website: http://www.countrywide.com
Chrmn & CEO: A.R. Mozilo.
Pres & COO: S.L. Kurland.
CFO: T.K. McLaughlin.

Chief Admin: T.H. Boone.
Chief Acctg Officer: L.K. Milleman.
Investor Contact: L. Riodan 818-225-3550.
Dirs: H. G. Cisneros, J. M. Cunningham, R. J. Donato, M. E. Dougherty, B. M. Enis, E. Heller, G. S. King, S. S. Kurland, M. R. Melone, A. R. Mozilo, R. T. Parry, O. P. Robertson, K. P. Russell, H. W. Snyder.

Founded: in 1969.
Domicile: Delaware.
Employees: 34,298.
S&P Analyst: Erik J. Eisenstein/PMW/BK

Crane Co.

Recommendation: **HOLD** ★★★☆☆
SELL SELL HOLD BUY BUY

12-Month Target Price: $36.00
(as of December 01, 2003)

CR has an approximate 0.02% weighting in the **S&P 500**

Sector: Industrials
Sub-Industry: Industrial Machinery
Peer Group: Engineered Products

Summary: CR is a diversified manufacturer and distributor of engineered products for the fluid handling, aerospace, construction and automatic merchandising industries.

Quantitative Evaluations

Price as of 11/12/04: $29.58 | **2004E S&P Core EPS:** $1.78

S&P Earnings & Dividend Rank: B+

| D | C | B- | B | B+ | A- | A | A+ |

S&P Fair Value Rank: 3

| 1 | 2 | 3 | 4 | 5 |
Lowest ... Highest

Fair Value Calc.: $27.80 (Slightly Overvalued)

S&P Investability Quotient Percentile

95%

CR scored higher than 95% of all companies for which an S&P Report is available.

Volatility: Average

| Low | Average | High |

Technical Evaluation: Neutral
Since 11/04, the technical indicators for CR have been Neutral.

Relative Strength Rank: Moderate

48

1 Lowest ... Highest 99

GAAP Earnings vs. Previous Year
▲ Up ▼ Down ▶ No Change

10 Week Mov. Avg.
30 Week Mov. Avg.
Relative Strength
12-Mo Target Price

Volume Below Avg. — Above Avg.

VOL. (000)

SELL | HOLD | SELL | HOLD
J J A S O N D | J F M A M J J A S O N D | J F M A M J J A S O N D | J F M A M J J A S O N D | J
2001 | 2002 | 2003 | 2004

OPTIONS: Ph

Analyst commentary prepared by L. J. Larkin/CB/JWP

Highlights August 18, 2004

- Based on S&P's forecast of 4.6% GDP growth in 2004, versus 2003's 3.1% growth, an expected cyclical upturn in aerospace, and acquisitions, we see 2004 sales up 18% to 20%. We anticipate gains in all business units, with the largest increases coming from aerospace, engineered materials and fluid handling segments. We expect a rebound in commercial aerospace to boost the aerospace segment, while anticipated strong economic growth should help sales in engineered materials, fluid handling, and controls.

- Aided by workforce reductions and general cost cutting, we see operating income likely to rise in all units. Aided further by flat to lower interest expense, we believe EPS should grow at least 14% in 2004. In addition, we think aggressive working capital management should enable CR to achieve 2004 free cash flow of about $120 million ($2.00 a share), versus 2003's $110.8 million ($1.87).

- Assuming GDP growth of 3.9% in 2005, together with further acceleration in aerospace, fluid handling and engineered materials, we project another advance in sales, EPS and free cash flow.

Investment Rationale/Risk August 18, 2004

- We would hold existing positions. The stock traded recently at 13X our 2005 EPS estimate, versus 15X and 16X for rivals Harsco Corp. (HSC: hold, $42) and Pentair (PNR: accumulate, $31), respectively. We believe CR deserves a higher P/E relative to peers, as its rate of return on equity and assets exceeds those of HSC and PNR by a wide margin, and it has a higher projected earnings growth rate. However, asbestos claims temper our view. At the end of the 2003 and 2004 second quarters, claims totaled 63,651 and 75,428, respectively. An increase in claims both sequentially and year over year may explain the recent pressure on the stock price. Ultimately, we think Congress may provide legislative relief for the problem. We believe such relief would result in a higher stock price and a P/E above that of peers. However, we doubt that any legislative relief will occur in an election year.

- Risks to our recommendation and target price include uncertainty regarding asbestos liabilities and unexpected weakness in the aerospace industry.

- Based on our view that CR's P/E is too low relative to that of its peers, even given asbestos concerns, we project that CR will sell at 17X our 2005 EPS estimate, leading to our 12-month target price of $36.

Key Stock Statistics

S&P Core EPS 2005E	2.01	52-week Range	$34.40-25.83
S&P Oper. EPS 2004E	1.99	12 Month P/E	NM
P/E on S&P Oper. EPS 2004E	14.9	Beta	1.08
S&P Oper. EPS 2005E	2.15	Shareholders	4,198
Yield (%)	1.4%	Market Cap (B)	$ 1.7
Dividend Rate/Share	0.40	Shares Outstanding (M)	59.1

Value of $10,000 invested five years ago: **$ 16,609**

Dividend Data Dividends have been paid since 1939

Amount ($)	Date Decl.	Ex-Div. Date	Stock of Record	Payment Date
0.100	Jan. 26	Mar. 01	Mar. 03	Mar. 12 '04
0.100	May. 24	Jun. 01	Jun. 03	Jun. 11 '04
0.100	Jul. 26	Aug. 31	Sep. 02	Sep. 10 '04
0.100	Oct. 25	Nov. 29	Dec. 01	Dec. 10 '04

Revenues/Earnings Data Fiscal year ending December 31

Revenues (Million $)

	2004	2003	2002	2001	2000	1999
1Q	448.3	376.5	371.6	379.3	383.8	400.1
2Q	479.1	406.0	391.6	409.0	387.9	405.3
3Q	477.3	425.3	386.0	426.2	363.2	384.2
4Q	—	428.3	367.2	372.6	356.3	364.1
Yr.	—	1,636	1,516	1,587	1,491	1,554

Earnings Per Share ($)

	2004	2003	2002	2001	2000	1999
1Q	0.37	0.28	0.35	0.33	0.45	0.47
2Q	0.52	0.44	0.44	0.54	0.78	0.53
3Q	-3.48	0.47	0.34	0.30	0.35	0.27
4Q	E0.57	0.56	-0.86	0.30	0.44	0.22
Yr.	E1.99	1.75	0.28	1.47	2.02	1.50

Next earnings report expected: late-January Source: S&P, Company Reports
EPS Estimates based on S&P Operating Earnings; historical GAAP earnings are as reported.

Recommendation: **HOLD** ★★★☆☆   12-Month Target Price: **$36.00** (as of December 01, 2003)

Business Summary August 19, 2004

Founded in 1855, Crane is a diversified manufacturer of engineered industrial products, conducting operations through five main segments: Fluid Handling (46% of 2003 sales), Aerospace & Electronics (26%), Engineered Materials (15%), Crane Controls (4%), and Merchandising Systems (9%).

EPS for the 2003 fourth quarter totaled $0.56, versus a loss of $0.86 a share in the 2002 period. Excluding a non-cash charge of $1.23 for asbestos related claims, 2002 fourth quarter EPS was $0.37. The increase in 2003 reflected margin improvement in all segments except fluid handling.

The Fluid Handling segment consists of Engineered Valves, Commercial Valves, Valve Services, and Crane Supply, as well as pump and water treatment businesses. The unit sells a wide variety of commodity and special purpose valves and fluid control products for the chemical and hydrocarbon processing, power generation, marine, general industrial, and commercial construction industries.

The Aerospace & Electronics segment consists of two groups. Aerospace includes products made under the brand names ELDEC, Hydro-Aire, Lear Romec and Resistoflex-Aerospace. ELDEC manufactures custom position indication and control systems, proximity sensors, pressure sensors and power conversion systems for general aviation. Hydro-Aire makes aircraft brake control and anti-skid systems for the commercial and military aerospace markets. Lear Romec manufactures lubrication and fuel pumps and radar cooling systems for the aerospace industry. Resistoflex makes high-performance, separable fittings for aerospace.

Electronics includes products made under the brand names Interpoint, General Technology, STC Microwave Systems, Keltec, Olektron, Eldec, and Advanced Integrated Systems. Interpoint makes standard and custom miniature DC-to-DC power converters and custom miniature electronic circuits for applications in aerospace, fiber optic, and medical technology applications. STC manufactures power management products and sophisticated electronic radio frequency (RF) components and subsystems. GTC is provides customized contract manufacturing services, focusing on military and defense applications.

The Engineered Materials segment consists of Kemlite and Polyflon. Kemlite manufactures fiberglass reinforced plastic panels for sale to the recreational vehicles, truck trailer, and commercial construction markets. Polyflon manufactures microwave laminates, high-voltage RF capacitors, radomes, and circuit processing.

The Crane Controls segment consists of businesses involved in the design, manufacture and marketing of products that control flow and processes in the petroleum, chemical, construction, food and beverage, power generation, and transportation industries.

The Merchandising Systems segment manufactures food and beverage vending machines and electronic coin validators for automated merchandising and gambling/amusement markets in Europe.

In its second quarter 2004 report, the company said it expects third quarter 2004 earnings per share of $0.50 to $0.55, and added that it was maintaining its full year 2004 earnings per share guidance of $1.90 to $2.05.

Company Financials Fiscal Year ending December 31

Per Share Data ($)

(Year Ended December 31)	2003	2002	2001	2000	1999	1998	1997	1996	1995	1994
Tangible Bk. Val.	3.24	3.24	3.87	4.11	3.10	3.53	3.81	2.95	2.14	1.38
Cash Flow	2.65	1.11	2.70	2.92	2.40	2.88	2.42	2.05	1.82	1.35
Earnings	1.75	0.28	1.47	2.02	1.50	2.00	1.63	1.34	1.11	0.83
S&P Core Earnings	1.58	1.10	1.10	NA	NA	NA	NA	NA	NA	NA
Dividends	0.40	0.40	0.40	0.40	0.40	0.27	0.33	0.33	0.33	0.33
Payout Ratio	23%	143%	27%	20%	27%	13%	20%	25%	30%	40%
Prices - High	30.81	28.99	32.25	29.50	32.75	37.58	31.50	21.00	17.55	13.11
- Low	15.19	17.72	19.95	18.62	16.06	21.75	18.33	16.00	11.50	10.72
P/E Ratio - High	18	NM	22	15	22	19	19	16	16	16
- Low	9	NM	14	9	11	11	11	12	10	13

Income Statement Analysis (Million $)

	2003	2002	2001	2000	1999	1998	1997	1996	1995	1994
Revs.	1,636	1,516	1,587	1,491	1,554	2,269	2,037	1,848	1,782	1,653
Oper. Inc.	223	89.5	246	239	266	300	252	216	192	145
Depr.	54.0	49.8	149	55.3	61.3	61.5	55.4	49.4	48.8	35.5
Int. Exp.	20.0	16.9	21.2	21.6	27.9	27.8	23.8	23.4	26.9	24.2
Pretax Inc.	151	24.5	136	190	156	215	176	145	122	91.0
Eff. Tax Rate	31.0%	32.0%	34.8%	35.0%	35.2%	35.5%	35.9%	36.5%	37.2%	38.7%
Net Inc.	104	16.6	88.6	124	101	138	113	92.1	76.3	55.9
S&P Core Earnings	94.3	65.8	66.2	NA	NA	NA	NA	NA	NA	NA

Balance Sheet & Other Fin. Data (Million $)

	2003	2002	2001	2000	1999	1998	1997	1996	1995	1994
Cash	143	36.6	21.2	10.9	3.25	15.9	6.98	11.6	5.50	2.10
Curr. Assets	662	509	523	500	505	699	608	540	498	480
Total Assets	1,812	1,414	1,292	1,144	1,175	1,455	1,186	1,089	998	1,008
Curr. Liab.	419	288	249	232	234	351	296	254	241	244
LT Debt	296	205	302	214	287	359	261	268	281	331
Common Equity	786	649	651	607	568	643	533	463	375	328
Total Cap.	1,140	863	953	849	881	1,028	816	760	684	692
Cap. Exp.	28.1	25.5	32.1	30.0	29.0	54.3	40.6	50.5	26.6	28.0
Cash Flow	158	66.4	238	179	162	200	168	142	125	91.4
Curr. Ratio	1.6	1.8	2.1	2.2	2.2	2.0	2.1	2.1	2.1	2.0
% LT Debt of Cap.	26.0	23.8	31.7	25.2	32.6	34.9	31.9	35.2	41.1	47.9
% Net Inc.of Revs.	6.4	1.1	5.6	8.3	6.5	6.1	5.5	5.0	4.3	3.4
% Ret. on Assets	6.5	1.2	7.3	10.6	7.9	10.5	9.9	8.8	7.6	6.4
% Ret. on Equity	14.5	2.6	14.1	21.1	16.7	23.5	22.7	22.0	21.7	18.0

Data as orig reptd.; bef. results of disc opers/spec. items. Per share data adj. for stk. divs.; EPS diluted. E-Estimated. NA-Not Available. NM-Not Meaningful. NR-Not Ranked. UR-Under Review.

Office: 100 First Stamford Place, Stamford, CT 06902.
Telephone: 203-363-7300.
Email: investors@craneco.com
Website: http://www.craneco.com
Chrmn: R.S. Evans.
Pres & CEO: E.C. Fast.
VP & CFO: G.S. Scimone.

VP, Secy & General Counsel: A.I. duPont.
Treas: G.A. Dickoff.
Investor Contact: P.J. Styles 203-363-7300.
Dirs: E. T. Bigelow, Jr., K. E. Dykstra, R. S. Evans, E. C. Fast, R. S. Forte, D. R. Gardner, J. Gaulin, W. E. Lipner, D. C. Minton, C. J. Queenan, Jr., J. L. Tullis.

Founded: in 1865.
Domicile: Delaware.
Employees: 10,136.
S&P Analyst: L. J. Larkin/CB/JWP

CSX Corp.

Recommendation: **HOLD** ★ ★ ★ ☆ ☆
SELL SELL HOLD BUY BUY

12-Month Target Price: $37.00
(as of October 28, 2004)

CSX has an approximate 0.07% weighting in the **S&P 500**

Sector: Industrials
Sub-Industry: Railroads
Peer Group: Railroads (U.S.) - Major

Summary: CSX operates a major U.S. rail network, and provides intermodal and U.S. container shipping services.

Quantitative Evaluations

S&P Earnings & Dividend Rank: B-

| D | C | B- | B | B+ | A- | A | A+ |

S&P Fair Value Rank: 3

| 1 | 2 | 3 | 4 | 5 |
| Lowest | | | | Highest |

Fair Value Calc.: $36.40 (Slightly Overvalued)

S&P Investability Quotient Percentile

70%

CSX scored higher than 70% of all companies for which an S&P Report is available.

Volatility: Low

| Low | Average | High |

Technical Evaluation: Bullish
Since 9/04, the technical indicators for CSX have been Bullish.

Relative Strength Rank: Strong

76

| 1 Lowest | | Highest 99 |

Price as of 11/12/04: $37.95   **2004E S&P Core EPS:** $1.56

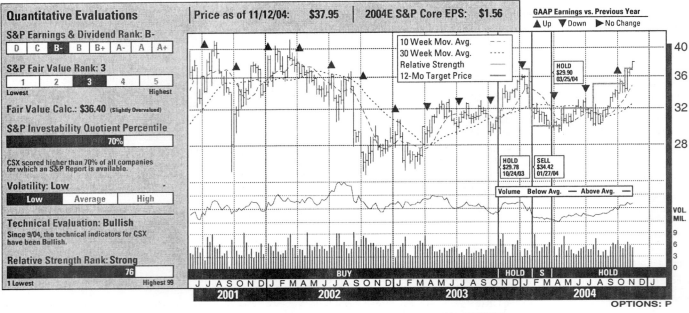

GAAP Earnings vs. Previous Year
▲ Up ▼ Down ► No Change

Analyst commentary prepared by Andrew West, CFA /PMW/BK

Highlights November 01, 2004

- We project 2004 revenue growth of about 3%, with intermodal and metals aided by economic growth and below-average stockpiles at power producers boosting coal shipments. We see automotive traffic lagging, due to plant closings. We see total ton miles increasing about 2%, while prices per car rise modestly. We expect revenues to grow about 5% in 2005, on rising freight rates, fuel surcharges, and stronger volumes.

- We see margins widening somewhat, as increasing labor costs and reduced efficiencies from slower train speeds and deteriorating service are outweighed by higher prices per carload and reduced administrative costs. We expect recent managerial-level personnel cuts to reduce costs by about $90 million annually. We think weak operational safety and efficiency metrics in 2004 could affect customer relationships and require further expenditures, but we expect recovering system performance in 2005 to boost profitability.

- We forecast 2004 operating EPS of $1.88, up from 2003's EPS of $0.88. CSX incurred a $232 million charge in the 2003 third quarter to accrue for potential asbestos liabilities, and a $108 million charge for disputes related to the 1999 sale of its international container unit. We project 2004 S&P Core EPS of $1.56, reflecting estimated option and pension expenses.

Investment Rationale/Risk November 01, 2004

- We regard the shares as fairly valued, in light of the company's below-peer-average performance in terms of revenues, margins, and operational performance over the past four quarters. CSX has engaged consultants and managers in an effort to improve operations, and we believe near-term performance will benefit from these efforts. We forecast some earnings recovery in 2004, with free cash flow of $580 million, followed by five-year annual growth of 14% for EPS and 6% for free cash flow.

- Risks to our opinion and target price include unfavorable fuel and interest rate moves, failure to improve operating efficiency, weather, weaker than expected economic and freight growth, and declining railroad system fluidity.

- Our discounted cash flow model, which assumes an 8% cost of capital and 3% terminal growth, calculates intrinsic value of $35. Our relative value model relates historical peer group valuations to profitability and leverage, and uses a forward price to sales multiple of 1.0X to yield a price of $38. Blending these models, we arrive at our 12-month target price of $37.

Key Stock Statistics

S&P Core EPS 2005E	2.23	52-week Range	$38.00-28.80
S&P Oper. EPS 2004E	1.88	12 Month P/E	20.7
P/E on S&P Oper. EPS 2004E	20.2	Beta	0.59
S&P Oper. EPS 2005E	2.50	Shareholders	56,331
Yield (%)	1.1%	Market Cap (B)	$ 8.2
Dividend Rate/Share	0.40	Shares Outstanding (M)	214.8

Value of $10,000 invested five years ago: **$ 10,615**

Dividend Data Dividends have been paid since 1922

Amount ($)	Date Decl.	Ex-Div. Date	Stock of Record	Payment Date
0.100	Feb. 12	Feb. 23	Feb. 25	Mar. 15 '04
0.100	May. 05	May. 21	May. 25	Jun. 15 '04
0.100	Jul. 14	Aug. 23	Aug. 25	Sep. 15 '04
0.100	Oct. 20	Nov. 22	Nov. 24	Dec. 15 '04

Revenues/Earnings Data Fiscal year ending December 31

Revenues (Million $)

	2004	2003	2002	2001	2000	1999
1Q	1,963	2,016	1,964	2,025	2,147	2,541
2Q	2,033	1,942	2,073	2,057	2,190	2,616
3Q	1,980	1,882	2,055	2,019	2,039	2,906
4Q	—	1,953	2,060	2,009	2,047	2,748
Yr.	—	7,793	8,152	8,110	8,191	10,811

Earnings Per Share ($)

	2004	2003	2002	2001	2000	1999
1Q	0.14	0.20	0.32	0.10	0.14	0.36
2Q	0.55	0.59	0.63	0.51	0.26	0.53
3Q	0.57	-0.48	0.60	0.47	0.28	-0.54
4Q	E0.62	0.57	0.64	0.31	0.26	-0.12
Yr.	E1.88	0.88	2.19	1.38	0.88	0.24

Next earnings report expected: late-January Source: S&P, Company Reports
EPS Estimates based on S&P Operating Earnings; historical GAAP earnings are as reported.

CSX Corporation

Recommendation: **HOLD** ★ ★ ★ ☆ ☆   12-Month Target Price: **$37.00** (as of October 28, 2004)

Business Summary November 01, 2004

CSX operates the largest rail network in the eastern U.S. In 1997, it purchased a 42% stake in Conrail for $4.3 billion. The routes acquired brought CSX's system into New York City, Boston, Philadelphia and Buffalo. With these routes, the company was able to offer shippers broader geographic coverage, access more ports, and expand its share of north-south traffic.

In June 2003, CSX and NSC together petitioned the Surface Transportation Board to establish direct ownership of the Conrail assets operated by the respective companies, and argued that this would let them make decisions about their respective assets without each other's consent, and would increase efficiencies, as well as transparency of financial reporting. A corporate reorganization of Conrail was completed in August 2004, with direct ownership and control of Conrail's New York Central Lines transferred to CSX, and Pennsylvania Lines assets transferred to NSC. In 2003, Conrail Inc. reported net income of $203 million.

The company has disposed of much of its non-rail holdings. Barge assets were conveyed to Vectura Group in 1998. In 1999, CSX sold Sea-Land's international routes for $750 million; in 2000, it sold its logistics unit for $650 million. In February 2003, the company sold most of its interest in CSX Lines LLC, to a new venture formed with the Carlyle Group, for about $300 million, made up of $240 million in cash and $60 million in securities. CSX Lines was subsequently renamed Horizon Lines LLC.

When it began operations on the Conrail lines, CSX encountered significant problems in keeping its system fluid. As a result, in 2000, management defined a series of 18 critical operating metrics, including safety standards, train velocity, locomotive productivity and on-time performance. In 2003, CSX saw a decline in certain performance measures, including personal injury frequency, train accident frequency, train velocity, train recrews, and on-time originations and arrivals.

CSX Transportation (79% of revenues and 86% of operating income in 2003) operates the largest rail network in the eastern U.S. The integration of Conrail in June 1999 expanded CSX's system by over 25%, to 23,400 miles, in 23 states, Washington, DC, and two Canadian provinces. In 2003, shipments of coal, coke and iron ore accounted for 26% of rail revenues, agriculture/food 11%, phosphates 5%, metals 7%, chemicals 16%, automotive 14%, and forest/industrial products 13%.

CSX World Terminals (3% and 11%), formed in 1999, operates container-freight terminal facilities in Asia, Europe, Australia, Latin America and the U.S. CSX expects the loss of a significant customer in Hong Kong to reduce the division's 2004 operating income by about $29 million.

CSX Intermodal (16% and 18%) provides transcontinental intermodal services, employing most national railroads, and running about 450 dedicated trains between its 45 terminals weekly.

Company Financials Fiscal Year ending December 31

Per Share Data ($)

(Year Ended December 31)	2003	2002	2001	2000	1999	1998	1997	1996	1995	1994
Tangible Bk. Val.	30.01	29.03	28.64	28.25	26.40	27.10	26.45	23.02	20.15	16.61
Cash Flow	3.89	5.24	4.32	5.52	2.92	5.45	6.73	6.89	5.80	5.87
Earnings	0.88	2.19	1.38	0.88	0.24	2.51	3.62	4.00	2.94	3.12
S&P Core Earnings	1.31	1.69	1.18	NA	NA	NA	NA	NA	NA	NA
Dividends	0.40	0.40	0.80	1.20	1.20	1.20	1.08	1.04	0.92	0.88
Payout Ratio	45%	18%	58%	136%	NM	48%	30%	26%	31%	28%
Prices - High	36.29	41.40	41.30	33.43	53.93	60.75	62.43	53.12	46.12	46.18
- Low	25.50	25.09	24.81	19.50	28.81	36.50	41.25	42.12	34.68	31.56
P/E Ratio - High	41	19	30	38	NM	24	17	13	16	15
- Low	29	11	18	22	NM	15	11	11	12	10

Income Statement Analysis (Million $)

	2003	2002	2001	2000	1999	1998	1997	1996	1995	1994
Revs.	7,793	8,152	8,110	8,191	10,811	9,898	10,621	10,536	10,504	9,608
Oper. Inc.	1,269	1,776	1,579	1,405	1,685	1,790	2,271	2,142	2,029	1,809
Depr.	643	649	622	600	621	630	688	620	600	577
Int. Exp.	418	445	518	543	521	506	451	249	270	310
Pretax Inc.	265	723	448	656	130	808	1,224	1,316	974	1,027
Eff. Tax Rate	28.7%	35.4%	34.6%	13.9%	67.7%	29.2%	31.4%	35.0%	36.6%	34.5%
Net Inc.	189	467	293	565	51.0	537	799	855	618	652
S&P Core Earnings	280	363	249	NA	NA	NA	NA	NA	NA	NA

Balance Sheet & Other Fin. Data (Million $)

	2003	2002	2001	2000	1999	1998	1997	1996	1995	1994
Cash	368	264	618	684	974	533	690	682	660	535
Curr. Assets	1,903	1,789	2,074	2,046	2,563	1,984	2,175	2,072	1,935	1,665
Total Assets	21,760	20,951	20,801	20,491	20,720	20,427	19,957	19,957	14,282	13,724
Curr. Liab.	2,210	2,454	3,303	3,280	3,473	2,600	2,707	2,757	2,991	2,505
LT Debt	6,886	6,519	5,839	5,810	6,196	6,432	6,416	4,331	2,222	2,618
Common Equity	7,569	7,091	7,060	6,017	5,756	5,880	5,766	4,995	4,242	3,731
Total Cap.	18,207	17,177	16,520	15,211	15,179	15,485	15,121	12,046	9,024	8,919
Cap. Exp.	1,059	1,080	930	913	1,517	1,479	1,125	1,223	1,156	875
Cash Flow	832	1,116	915	1,165	623	1,167	1,487	1,475	1,218	1,229
Curr. Ratio	0.9	0.7	0.6	0.6	0.7	0.8	0.8	0.8	0.6	0.7
% LT Debt of Cap.	37.8	38.0	35.3	38.2	40.8	41.5	42.4	36.0	24.6	29.4
% Net Inc.of Revs.	2.4	5.7	3.6	6.9	0.5	5.4	7.5	8.1	5.9	6.8
% Ret. on Assets	0.9	2.2	1.4	2.7	0.2	2.7	4.3	5.5	4.4	4.8
% Ret. on Equity	2.6	6.6	4.2	9.6	0.9	9.2	14.8	18.5	15.5	18.8

Data as orig reptd.; bef. results of disc opers/spec. items. Per share data adj. for stk. divs.; EPS diluted. E-Estimated. NA-Not Available. NM-Not Meaningful. NR-Not Ranked. UR-Under Review.

Office: 500 Water Street , Jacksonville , FL 32202.
Telephone: 904-359-3200.
Website: http://www.csx.com
Chrmn, Pres & CEO: M.J. Ward.
EVP & CFO: O. Munoz.

Dirs: E. E. Bailey, R. L. Burrus, Jr., B. C. Gottwald, J. R. Hall, E. J. Kelly, R. D. Kunisch, J. W. McGlothlin, S. J. Morcott, D. M. Ratcliffe, C. E. Rice, W. C. Richardson, F. S. Royal, D. J. Shepard, J. W. Snow, M. J. Ward.

Founded: in 1978.
Domicile: Virginia.
Employees: 37,516.
S&P Analyst: Andrew West, CFA /PMW/BK

Recommendation: **HOLD** ★★★☆☆
SELL · SELL · HOLD · BUY · BUY

12-Month Target Price: **$80.00**
(as of October 20, 2004)

CMI has an approximate 0.03% weighting in the **S&P 500**

Sector: Industrials
Sub-Industry: Construction & Farm Machinery & Heavy Trucks
Peer Group: Trailers/Engines/Related Equipment

Summary: This leading manufacturer of truck engines also makes stand-by power equipment and industrial filters.

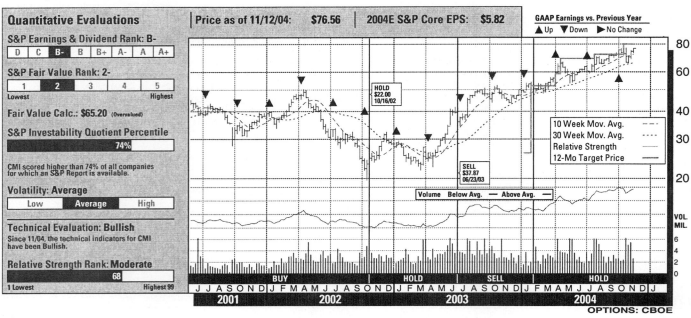

Quantitative Evaluations

Price as of 11/12/04: **$76.56** | 2004E S&P Core EPS: **$5.82**

S&P Earnings & Dividend Rank: B-
D · C · **B-** · B · B+ · A- · A · A+

S&P Fair Value Rank: 2-
1 · **2** · 3 · 4 · 5
Lowest · · · · Highest

Fair Value Calc.: $65.20 (Overvalued)

S&P Investability Quotient Percentile
74%
CMI scored higher than 74% of all companies for which an S&P Report is available.

Volatility: Average
Low · **Average** · High

Technical Evaluation: Bullish
Since 11/04, the technical indicators for CMI have been Bullish.

Relative Strength Rank: Moderate
68
1 Lowest · · Highest 99

GAAP Earnings vs. Previous Year
▲ Up ▼ Down ▶ No Change

HOLD $22.00 10/16/02
SELL $37.87 06/23/03

10 Week Mov. Avg.
30 Week Mov. Avg.
Relative Strength
12-Mo Target Price

Volume Below Avg. — Above Avg. —

VOL. MIL.

BUY | HOLD | SELL | HOLD
J J A S O N D | J F M A M J J A S O N D | J F M A M J J A S O N D | J F M A M J J A S O N D | J
2001 | 2002 | 2003 | 2004
OPTIONS: CBOE

Analyst commentary prepared by Anthony M. Fiore, CFA /CB/BK

Highlights October 25, 2004

- We expect revenues to rise about 10% in 2005, following a projected advance of about 35% in 2004. We believe improved carrier profitability, combined with an aging motor fleet, should drive strong replacement demand for heavy-duty truck engines in 2005. In addition, we see sales benefiting from expected strength in power generation end-markets, due to pent-up demand and global capacity issues.

- We anticipate a further expansion of operating margins in 2005, based on our outlook for higher volumes combined with the benefits of cost reduction actions implemented over the past few years. In addition, we expect higher joint venture income from further international expansion, most notably in China.

- Our Standard & Poor's Core Earnings estimates for 2004 and 2005 are $0.48 and $0.35 a share below our respective operating EPS forecasts. Most of the difference reflects pension and other post-retirement cost adjustments and projected stock option expense.

Investment Rationale/Risk October 25, 2004

- We have a hold recommendation on the shares. While we expect favorable conditions in the truck market to continue over the next 12 months, we believe that our positive outlook is largely reflected in the price of the stock.

- Risks to our recommendation and target price include an unexpected downturn in the truck manufacturing and/or power generation markets; potential for supply disruptions; and continued escalation of raw material costs.

- Our 12-month target price of $80 combines two separate valuation metrics. Our discounted cash flow model, which assumes an 8% to 9% average annual free cash flow growth rate over the next 10 years, 3.5% growth in perpetuity, and an 8% weighted average cost of capital, indicates intrinsic value of about $76. In terms of relative valuation, the shares traded recently at a P/E multiple of about 8.5X our 2005 EPS estimate. Applying a target P/E multiple of 10X-11X, in line with historical norms, suggests a value of about $84 a share.

Key Stock Statistics

S&P Core EPS 2005E	7.65	52-week Range	$76.95-43.55
S&P Oper. EPS 2004E	6.30	12 Month P/E	12.5
P/E on S&P Oper. EPS 2004E	12.2	Beta	1.34
S&P Oper. EPS 2005E	8.00	Shareholders	4,200
Yield (%)	1.6%	Market Cap (B)	$ 3.5
Dividend Rate/Share	1.20	Shares Outstanding (M)	45.5

Value of $10,000 invested five years ago: **$ 19,790**

Dividend Data Dividends have been paid since 1948

Amount ($)	Date Decl.	Ex-Div. Date	Stock of Record	Payment Date
0.300	Feb. 10	Feb. 13	Feb. 18	Mar. 01 '04
0.300	Apr. 06	May. 12	May. 14	Jun. 01 '04
0.300	Jul. 13	Aug. 16	Aug. 18	Sep. 01 '04
0.300	Oct. 12	Nov. 12	Nov. 16	Dec. 01 '04

Revenues/Earnings Data Fiscal year ending December 31

Revenues (Million $)

	2004	2003	2002	2001	2000	1999
1Q	1,771	1,387	1,333	1,349	1,648	1,505
2Q	2,124	1,539	1,458	1,461	1,769	1,667
3Q	2,194	1,634	1,648	1,408	1,572	1,631
4Q	—	1,736	1,414	1,463	1,608	1,836
Yr.	—	6,296	5,853	5,681	6,597	6,639

Earnings Per Share ($)

	2004	2003	2002	2001	2000	1999
1Q	0.76	-0.79	-0.69	-0.68	1.09	0.63
2Q	1.76	0.34	0.40	-2.14	1.62	1.50
3Q	2.40	0.60	1.06	0.08	0.66	1.35
4Q	E1.99	1.07	1.10	0.08	-3.16	0.65
Yr.	E6.30	1.36	2.06	-2.66	-0.20	4.13

Next earnings report expected: late-January Source: S&P, Company Reports
EPS Estimates based on S&P Operating Earnings; historical GAAP earnings are as reported.

STANDARD &POOR'S

Cummins, Inc.

Stock Report
November 13, 2004
NYSE Symbol: **CMI**

Recommendation: HOLD ★ ★ ★ ★ ★  12-Month Target Price: **$80.00** (as of October 20, 2004)

Business Summary October 25, 2004

Truck engine makers such as Cummins continue to contend with price wars, highly cyclical markets, and an overabundance of global engine-making capacity. In addition, engine makers are constantly plowing back profits into engine development and plant and machinery, just to maintain market share. Over the past 10 years, research and development expenses and capital spending averaged 4.1% and 3.8% of revenues, respectively.

Strong, consistent earnings growth and return on equity (ROE) have been hard to achieve in the truck engine-making business. Over the past 10 years, earnings were very erratic. During this period, CMI reported EPS as high as $6.11, and losses per share of as much as $2.66. ROE over the past 10 years averaged only 12%, versus an estimated 14% for the S&P 500 Index.

In an effort to reduce earnings cyclicality and enter markets with better long-term growth potential, the company has been expanding into the power generation equipment and industrial filter arenas. As a result, these segments have been accounting for an increasing proportion of CMI's total sales and profits.

CMI's diesel engine making segment (58% and 39% of revenues and operating profits in 2003; 1.9% operating margin) consists of heavy, medium and small truck/bus engines (71% of the engine segments sales), and machinery engines (29%).

Major competitors include Caterpillar's truck engine operations and Daimler-Chrysler's Detroit Diesel subsidiary.

The power generation segment (21%; $17 million operating loss) primarily makes back-up power generators for homes, offices and hospitals. Increasing unreliability of power utility authorities, improving technology, and the need to prevent computer and Internet systems from power outages are driving consumer and institutional demand for the company's stand-by power generators. Primary competitors include Caterpillar, Emerson Electric, Ingersoll Rand, and Honeywell International.

The company's most profitable unit, the filtration segment (17% and 48%; 8.1% margins), makes various industrial filter and exhaust systems. New products include filters and exhaust systems for small equipment.

In the 2001 fourth quarter, CMI realigned its reporting structure and created a new business segment, International Distributors (11% and 22%; 5.9% margin). The segment consists of 17 wholly owned and three joint venture distributors that are engaged in selling engines and generator sets, and service parts and provide repair services on company products at 111 locations, in 50 countries and territories.

Company Financials Fiscal Year ending December 31

Per Share Data ($)

(Year Ended December 31)	2003	2002	2001	2000	1999	1998	1997	1996	1995	1994
Tangible Bk. Val.	11.15	9.66	16.24	20.20	25.66	13.26	29.57	28.12	24.73	25.78
Cash Flow	7.01	7.16	3.39	6.49	10.08	4.56	9.49	7.92	9.18	9.19
Earnings	1.36	2.06	-2.66	-0.20	4.13	-0.55	5.48	4.01	5.52	6.11
S&P Core Earnings	1.59	-1.56	-5.75	NA	NA	NA	NA	NA	NA	NA
Dividends	1.20	1.20	1.20	1.20	1.13	1.10	1.07	1.00	1.00	0.63
Payout Ratio	88%	58%	NM	NM	27%	NM	20%	25%	18%	10%
Prices - High	52.31	50.29	45.50	50.00	65.68	62.75	83.00	47.75	48.62	57.62
- Low	21.72	19.60	28.00	27.06	34.56	28.31	44.25	34.50	34.00	35.87
P/E Ratio - High	38	24	NM	NM	16	NM	15	12	9	9
- Low	16	10	NM	NM	8	NM	8	9	6	6

Income Statement Analysis (Million $)

	2003	2002	2001	2000	1999	1998	1997	1996	1995	1994
Revs.	6,296	5,853	5,681	6,597	6,639	6,266	5,625	5,257	5,245	4,737
Oper. Inc.	316	327	304	479	625	498	434	357	459	435
Depr.	223	219	231	240	233	199	158	149	143	128
Int. Exp.	101	82.0	87.0	86.0	75.0	71.0	26.0	18.0	13.0	17.5
Pretax Inc.	80.0	57.0	-129	3.00	221	-6.00	286	214	177	294
Eff. Tax Rate	15.0%	NM	NM	NM	24.9%	NM	25.9%	25.2%	NM	13.8%
Net Inc.	54.0	79.0	-102	8.00	160	-21.0	212	160	224	253
S&P Core Earnings	62.8	-61.4	-221	NA	NA	NA	NA	NA	NA	NA

Balance Sheet & Other Fin. Data (Million $)

	2003	2002	2001	2000	1999	1998	1997	1996	1995	1994
Cash	195	298	92.0	62.0	74.0	38.0	49.0	108	60.0	147
Curr. Assets	2,130	1,982	1,635	1,830	2,180	1,876	1,710	1,553	1,388	1,298
Total Assets	5,126	4,837	4,335	4,500	4,697	4,542	3,765	3,369	3,056	2,706
Curr. Liab.	1,391	1,329	970	1,223	1,314	1,071	1,055	1,021	1,053	840
LT Debt	1,380	1,290	1,206	1,032	1,092	1,137	522	283	117	155
Common Equity	949	841	1,025	1,336	1,429	1,272	1,422	1,312	1,183	1,073
Total Cap.	2,452	2,223	2,314	2,440	2,595	2,471	1,997	1,595	1,300	1,248
Cap. Exp.	111	90.0	206	228	215	271	405	304	223	238
Cash Flow	277	298	129	248	393	178	370	309	367	381
Curr. Ratio	1.5	1.5	1.7	1.5	1.7	1.8	1.6	1.5	1.3	1.5
% LT Debt of Cap.	56.3	58.0	52.1	42.3	42.1	46.0	26.1	17.7	9.0	12.4
% Net Inc.of Revs.	0.9	1.3	NM	0.1	2.4	NM	3.8	3.0	4.3	5.3
% Ret. on Assets	1.1	1.7	NM	0.2	3.5	NM	5.9	5.0	7.8	9.6
% Ret. on Equity	6.0	8.7	NM	0.6	11.8	NM	15.5	12.8	19.9	27.5

Data as orig reptd.; bef. results of disc opers/spec. items. Per share data adj. for stk. divs.; EPS diluted. E-Estimated. NA-Not Available. NM-Not Meaningful. NR-Not Ranked. UR-Under Review.

Office: 500 Jackson Street, Columbus, IN 47202-3005.
Telephone: 812-377-5000.
Email: investor_relations@cummins.com
Website: http://www.cummins.com
Chrmn & CEO: T.M. Solso.
VP & CFO: J.S. Blackwell.

VP & Treas: R. Harris.
VP, Secy & General Counsel: M.M. Rose.
Investor Contact: K.A. Battin 812-377-3121.
Dirs: R. J. Darnall, J. M. Deutch, A. M. Herman, W. I. Miller, G. Nelson, W. D. Ruckelshaus, T. M. Solso, J. L. Wilson.

Founded: in 1919.
Domicile: Indiana.
Employees: 24,200.
S&P Analyst: Anthony M. Fiore, CFA /CB/BK

CVS Corp.

Recommendation: **BUY ★★★★**☆
SELL · SELL · HOLD · BUY · BUY

12-Month Target Price: **$51.00**
(as of November 04, 2004)

CVS has an approximate 0.17% weighting in the **S&P 500**

Sector: Consumer Staples
Sub-Industry: Drug Retail
Peer Group: Drug Stores

Summary: CVS, the largest U.S. retail drug store chain, purchased 1,260 Eckerd drugstores from J.C. Penney in July 2004.

Quantitative Evaluations

S&P Earnings & Dividend Rank: B

| D | C | B- | **B** | B+ | A- | A | A+ |

S&P Fair Value Rank: 4-

| 1 | 2 | 3 | **4** | 5 |
| Lowest | | | | Highest |

Fair Value Calc.: $47.30 (Slightly Undervalued)

S&P Investability Quotient Percentile

97%

CVS scored higher than 97% of all companies for which an S&P Report is available.

Volatility: Low

| **Low** | Average | High |

Technical Evaluation: Bullish

Since 9/04, the technical indicators for CVS have been Bullish.

Relative Strength Rank: Moderate

67

| 1 Lowest | | Highest 99 |

| Price as of 11/12/04: | **$46.35** | 2004E S&P Core EPS: | **$2.05** |

GAAP Earnings vs. Previous Year
▲ Up ▼ Down ► No Change

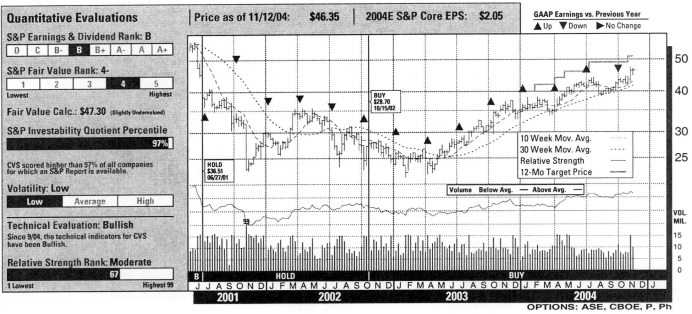

- 10 Week Mov. Avg.
- 30 Week Mov. Avg.
- Relative Strength
- 12-Mo Target Price

Volume Below Avg. — Above Avg. ―

BUY $28.70 10/15/02

HOLD $36.51 06/27/01

B · HOLD · BUY

J J A S O N D J F M A M J J A S O N D J F M A M J J A S O N D J F M A M J J A S O N D J
2001 · 2002 · 2003 · 2004

OPTIONS: ASE, CBOE, P, Ph

Analyst commentary prepared by Joseph Agnese/MF/BK

Highlights 15-NOV-04

- We expect total sales to grow about 20% in 2005, to over $37.5 billion, reflecting approximately $7 billion in revenues from Eckerd stores acquired in July 2004. We see sales growth aided by the planned addition of 105 net new stores, which should result in about 2% square footage growth. We project same-store sales growth in the mid-single digits, reflecting low to mid-single-digit non-pharmacy sales growth and upper single-digit pharmacy sales growth. We look for pharmacy sales growth to be restricted by an increased proportion of sales of lower priced generic drugs, but non-prescription sales should benefit from a stronger economy and improved in-stock positions.

- We expect margins to widen, as the company realizes acquisition synergies resulting from increased sales leverage, improved purchasing power and larger market scale. Additional margin benefits we see include an increased propor-tion of sales of wider margin generic drugs and improved cost management, due to inventory and pharmacy efficiency programs. Margin gains may be restricted by a shift in sales mix, reflecting a rise in the proportion of lower margin pharmacy sales and higher employee benefit costs due to rising health-care costs.

- We estimate 2005 operating EPS of $2.65, up significantly from our estimate of $2.14 in 2004.

Investment Rationale/Risk 15-NOV-04

- We have a buy recommendation on CVS shares, based on our view of the potential for significant earnings benefits following the acquisition of 1,260 Eckerd drug stores in July. We incorporated a benefit of $0.15 to $0.20 in our 2005 EPS estimate of $2.65. We expect significant synergies to be generated through the elimination of corporate personnel and purchasing efficiencies.

- Risks to our recommendation and target price include potential problems that may arise in implementing and managing the acquisition of Eckerd's drug stores, and increasing competition.

- Assuming that the shares trade at a P/E ratio of 18X, a 15% premium to our estimate for the S&P 500 but below its historical average of 20X, and applying that ratio to our 2005 EPS estimate of $2.65, results in a share value of $48. Our analysis of discounted cash flows, using a weighted average cost of capital of 9.0%, suggests an intrinsic value of $52 to $54. Using a blend of both valuation metrics, our 12-month target price is $51.

Key Stock Statistics

S&P Oper. EPS 2004E	2.14	52-week Range	$47.34-32.90
P/E on S&P Oper. EPS 2004E	21.7	12 Month P/E	20.8
S&P Oper. EPS 2005E	2.65	Beta	0.51
Yield (%)	0.6%	Shareholders	9,300
Dividend Rate/Share	0.27	Market Cap (B)	$ 18.5
Shares Outstanding (M)	400.1		

Value of $10,000 invested five years ago: **$ 13,298**

Dividend Data Dividends have been paid since 1916

Amount ($)	Date Decl.	Ex-Div. Date	Stock of Record	Payment Date
0.066	Oct. 29	Jan. 20	Jan. 22	Feb. 03 '04
0.066	Mar. 03	Apr. 21	Apr. 23	May. 03 '04
0.066	Jul. 07	Jul. 20	Jul. 22	Aug. 02 '04
0.066	Sep. 14	Oct. 20	Oct. 22	Nov. 01 '04

Revenues/Earnings Data Fiscal year ending December 31

Revenues (Million $)

	2004	2003	2002	2001	2000	1999
1Q	6,819	6,313	5,971	5,386	4,740	4,241
2Q	6,943	6,445	5,990	5,494	4,943	4,362
3Q	7,909	6,378	5,876	5,411	4,916	4,312
4Q	—	7,452	6,345	5,951	5,489	5,184
Yr.	—	26,588	24,182	22,241	20,088	18,098

Earnings Per Share ($)

	2004	2003	2002	2001	2000	1999
1Q	0.59	0.48	0.43	0.54	0.47	0.40
2Q	0.56	0.49	0.43	0.48	0.46	0.40
3Q	0.44	0.46	0.40	0.30	0.39	0.30
4Q	E0.55	0.64	0.49	-0.34	0.51	0.46
Yr.	E2.14	2.06	1.75	1.00	1.83	1.55

Next earnings report expected: mid-February Source: S&P, Company Reports
EPS Estimates based on S&P Operating Earnings; historical GAAP earnings are as reported.

STANDARD &POOR'S

CVS Corporation

Stock Report
November 15, 2004
NYSE Symbol: **CVS**

Recommendation: **BUY** ★ ★ ★ ★ ☆   12-Month Target Price: **$51.00** (as of November 04, 2004)

Business Summary 15-NOV-04

CVS Corp. has grown to become one of the largest U.S. drug store chains, based on sales and store count, with over $26 billion in sales in 2003, and 4,179 stores as of January 2004, in 32 states and the District of Columbia. The company holds the leading market share in 32 of the 100 largest U.S. drug store markets, more markets than any other retail drug store chain. It filled more than 334 million prescriptions in 2003, accounting for about 10% of the U.S. retail market.

Pharmacy operations are critical to CVS's success; pharmacy operations accounted for 69% of sales in 2003. Payments by third party managed care providers under prescription drug plans accounted for over 93% of total pharmacy sales in 2003. The company expects its pharmacy operations to continue to be a key focus, reflecting its ability to succeed in the rapidly growing managed care arena, and its ongoing purchase of prescription files from independent pharmacies.

Front-end operations benefit directly from the success of pharmacy operations; shoppers who come in to have a prescription filled often make a front-end purchase. In 2003, front-end store sales accounted for 31% of total sales; these sales typically provide wider gross margins than pharmacy sales. CVS offers a broad array of general merchandise, including OTC drugs, greeting cards, film and photofinishing services, beauty aids and cosmetics, seasonal merchandise, and convenience foods.

Stores are located primarily in strip shopping centers or free-standing locations, with a typical store ranging in size from 8,000 sq. ft. to 12,000 sq. ft. Most new stores being built are based on either a 10,000 sq. ft. or 12,000 sq. ft. prototype building that typically includes a drive-thru pharmacy. The company believes that about half of its store base was opened or remodeled over the past five years. As of December 2003, net selling space for its retail and specialty pharmacy drugstores was 32.6 million sq. ft.

The company has grown in large part through acquisitions. In July 2004, CVS acquired 1,260 Eckerd drug stores, as well as Eckerd's mail order, specialty pharmacy, and pharmacy benefits management businesses, from J.C. Penney for $2.15 billion. Following completion of the acquisition, the company became the largest U.S. drugstore chain, based on store count and sales. In 1997, CVS completed a merger with Revco, D.S. Inc., doubling its sales at the time, and making it the leading drugstore chain in terms of store count. The merger enabled the company to penetrate fast growing drugstore markets in the Mid-Atlantic, Southeast and Midwest. In 1998, CVS acquired Arbor Drugs Inc., the leading regional drug store chain in southern Michigan, with 207 stores, and annual revenues of nearly $1 billion. This provided an entry into Detroit, the fourth largest U.S. drug store market.

Company Financials Fiscal Year ending December 31

Per Share Data ($)

(Year Ended December 31)	2003	2002	2001	2000	1999	1998	1997	1996	1995	1994
Tangible Bk. Val.	11.96	10.09	8.90	8.21	6.88	5.40	3.97	3.93	4.79	9.09
Cash Flow	2.92	2.50	1.76	2.52	2.20	1.56	0.71	1.43	2.00	2.35
Earnings	2.06	1.75	1.00	1.83	1.55	0.98	0.07	1.06	-3.01	1.38
S&P Core Earnings	1.96	1.59	0.82	NA	NA	NA	NA	NA	NA	NA
Dividends	0.23	0.23	0.23	0.23	0.23	0.28	0.22	0.22	0.76	0.76
Payout Ratio	11%	13%	23%	13%	15%	29%	NM	21%	NM	55%
Prices - High	37.55	35.70	63.75	60.43	58.37	56.00	35.00	23.00	19.93	20.81
- Low	21.84	23.03	22.89	27.75	30.00	30.43	19.50	13.62	14.31	14.75
P/E Ratio - High	18	20	64	33	38	57	NM	22	NM	15
- Low	11	13	23	15	19	31	NM	13	NM	11

Income Statement Analysis (Million $)

	2003	2002	2001	2000	1999	1998	1997	1996	1995	1994
Revs.	26,588	24,182	22,241	20,088	18,098	15,274	12,738	5,528	8,689	11,286
Oper. Inc.	1,765	1,517	1,091	1,619	1,413	1,181	864	376	391	817
Depr.	342	310	321	297	278	250	222	76.0	197	206
Int. Exp.	48.0	50.4	61.0	79.3	59.1	61.0	45.0	31.0	55.0	34.1
Pretax Inc.	1,376	1,156	710	1,243	1,076	711	155	403	-798	578
Eff. Tax Rate	38.4%	38.0%	41.8%	40.0%	41.0%	44.3%	76.1%	40.6%	NM	37.8%
Net Inc.	847	717	413	746	635	396	37.0	239	-616	307
S&P Core Earnings	785	635	323	NA	NA	NA	NA	NA	NA	NA

Balance Sheet & Other Fin. Data (Million $)

	2003	2002	2001	2000	1999	1998	1997	1996	1995	1994
Cash	843	700	236	337	230	181	169	424	130	117
Curr. Assets	6,497	5,982	5,454	4,937	4,608	4,349	3,685	1,973	2,560	2,650
Total Assets	10,543	9,645	8,628	7,950	7,275	6,736	5,637	2,832	3,962	4,735
Curr. Liab.	3,489	3,106	3,066	2,964	2,890	3,183	2,855	1,182	1,798	1,643
LT Debt	753	1,076	810	537	559	276	273	304	328	350
Common Equity	6,022	4,991	4,306	4,037	3,404	2,830	2,077	946	1,212	2,369
Total Cap.	6,817	6,318	12,706	4,869	4,265	3,386	2,634	1,569	1,644	2,924
Cap. Exp.	1,122	1,109	714	695	494	502	312	224	395	421
Cash Flow	1,189	1,012	719	1,028	898	632	245	301	-419	497
Curr. Ratio	1.9	1.9	1.8	1.7	1.6	1.4	1.3	1.7	1.4	1.6
% LT Debt of Cap.	11.0	17.0	63.8	11.0	13.1	8.2	10.4	19.4	20.0	12.0
% Net Inc.of Revs.	3.2	3.0	1.9	3.7	3.5	2.6	0.3	4.3	NM	2.7
% Ret. on Assets	8.4	7.8	5.0	9.8	9.1	6.4	0.9	7.1	NM	6.8
% Ret. on Equity	15.4	15.1	9.6	19.7	19.9	15.6	1.5	20.8	NM	12.6

Data as orig reptd.; bef. results of disc opers/spec. items. Per share data adj. for stk. divs. Bold denotes primary EPS - prior periods restated. E-Estimated. NA-Not Available. NM-Not Meaningful. NR-Not Ranked. UR-Under Review.

Office: One CVS Drive, Woonsocket, RI 02895.
Telephone: 401-765-1500.
Email: investorinfo@cvs.com
Website: http://www.cvs.com
Chrmn, Pres & CEO: T. M. Ryan.
EVP & CFO: D. B. Rickard.

EVP: C. Bodine.
EVP: L. J. Merlo.
Investor Contact: Nancy R. Christal (914-722-4704).
Dirs: W. D. Cornwell, T. B. Gerrity, S. P. Goldstein, M. Heard, W. H. Joyce, T. Murray, D. Rickard, S. Z. Rosenberg, T. M. Ryan, L. D. Solberg, A. J. Verrecchia.

Founded: in 1892.
Domicile: Delaware.
Employees: 110,000.
S&P Analyst: Joseph Agnese/MF/BK

Danaher Corp.

Recommendation: HOLD ★ ★ ★ ★
SELL | SELL | HOLD | BUY | BUY

12-Month Target Price: **$55.00**
(as of October 21, 2004)

DHR has an approximate 0.16% weighting in the **S&P 500**

Sector: Industrials
Sub-Industry: Industrial Machinery
Peer Group: Engines, Auto and Machine Parts

Summary: DHR is a leading maker of tools, including Sears Craftsman hand tools, and of process/environmental controls and telecommunications equipment.

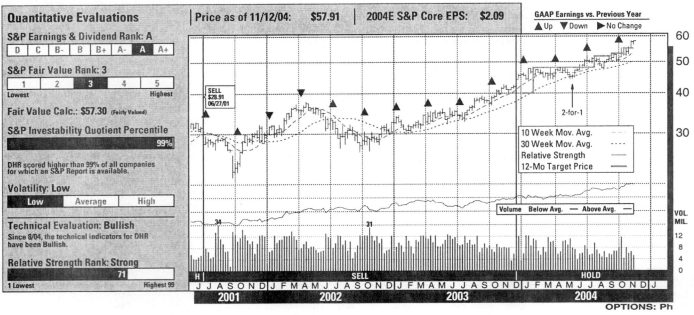

Quantitative Evaluations	Price as of 11/12/04: $57.91	2004E S&P Core EPS: $2.09

S&P Earnings & Dividend Rank: A
D | C | B- | B | B+ | A- | **A** | A+

S&P Fair Value Rank: 3
1 | 2 | **3** | 4 | 5
Lowest — Highest

Fair Value Calc.: $57.30 (Fairly Valued)

S&P Investability Quotient Percentile — 99%

DHR scored higher than 99% of all companies for which an S&P Report is available.

Volatility: Low
Low | Average | High

Technical Evaluation: Bullish
Since 8/04, the technical indicators for DHR have been Bullish.

Relative Strength Rank: Strong — 71
1 Lowest — Highest 99

GAAP Earnings vs. Previous Year
▲ Up ▼ Down ▶ No Change

SELL $28.91 06/27/01

2-for-1

10 Week Mov. Avg.
30 Week Mov. Avg.
Relative Strength
12-Mo Target Price

Volume Below Avg. — Above Avg.

VOL. MIL.

Analyst commentary prepared by Efraim Levy, CFA /PMW/BK

Highlights October 26, 2004

- After projected sales gains of 25% to 30% in 2004, we expect revenues to increase 12% to 16% in 2005, driven by a combination of U.S. and foreign economic growth, acquisitions made in 2004, and acquisitions that we anticipate for 2005.

- We see 2005 margins benefiting from employment reductions and other streamlining activities, partly offset by narrower margins at some acquired businesses. DHR expects two acquisitions made in the first quarter of 2004 to be accretive to EPS for the full year by $0.14 to $0.17. We expect EPS of $2.27 for 2004 and $2.60 for 2005.

- For the longer term, we see sales increases driven by internal growth (5% to 7% a year), supplemented by acquisitions. We look for a steady flow of new and enhanced products, as well as greater sales of traditional tool lines, to aid comparisons. We expect margins to widen over time, as DHR consolidates acquisitions and benefits from higher capacity utilization, productivity gains, and cost-cutting efforts.

Investment Rationale/Risk October 26, 2004

- We would hold existing positions. With long term debt under 30% of capitalization, the balance sheet appears healthy to us. Based on several valuation measures, the stock is at a premium to that of some peers. However, we believe this reflects DHR's wider net margins and faster growth. Quality of earnings appears high to us, as we expect free cash flow in 2005 to exceed net income, and we think that S&P Core Earnings adjustments are likely to reduce expected 2005 operating EPS by less than 7%.

- Risks to our opinion and target price include slowing demand for the company's products, increased competition, and unfavorable changes in foreign exchange rates.

- We used a P/E multiple of about 22X our 2005 EPS estimate in our target price calculation, reflecting peer and historical P/E multiples. Our DCF model, which assumes a weighted average cost of capital of 9.9%, a compound annual growth rate of 6.2% over the next 15 years, and a terminal growth rate of 4%, calculates intrinsic value of about $52. Based on a combination of our P/E multiple and DCF analyses, our 12-month target price is $55.

Key Stock Statistics

S&P Core EPS 2005E	2.44	52-week Range	$58.12-39.89
S&P Oper. EPS 2004E	2.27	12 Month P/E	26.9
P/E on S&P Oper. EPS 2004E	25.5	Beta	0.79
S&P Oper. EPS 2005E	2.60	Shareholders	3,000
Yield (%)	0.1%	Market Cap (B)	$ 17.9
Dividend Rate/Share	0.06	Shares Outstanding (M)	308.6

Value of $10,000 invested five years ago: **$ 24,332**

Dividend Data Dividends have been paid since 1993

Amount ($)	Date Decl.	Ex-Div. Date	Stock of Record	Payment Date
0.025	Mar. 17	Mar. 24	Mar. 26	Apr. 30 '04
2-for-1	Apr. 22	May. 21	May. 06	May. 20 '04
0.015	Jun. 18	Jun. 23	Jun. 25	Jul. 30 '04
0.015	Sep. 17	Sep. 22	Sep. 24	Oct. 29 '04

Revenues/Earnings Data Fiscal year ending December 31

Revenues (Million $)

	2004	2003	2002	2001	2000	1999
1Q	1,543	1,196	1,004	1,005	867.9	754.4
2Q	1,621	1,299	1,146	956.6	890.8	741.8
3Q	1,745	1,309	1,152	901.6	986.8	781.9
4Q	—	1,489	1,275	918.9	1,032	848.2
Yr.	—	5,294	4,577	3,782	3,778	3,197

Earnings Per Share ($)

	2004	2003	2002	2001	2000	1999
1Q	0.45	0.33	0.28	0.28	0.25	0.20
2Q	0.56	0.40	0.33	0.32	0.28	0.23
3Q	0.62	0.43	0.37	0.30	0.29	0.21
4Q	E0.63	0.53	0.52	0.12	0.30	0.26
Yr.	E2.27	1.69	1.49	1.01	1.11	0.90

Next earnings report expected: late-January Source: S&P, Company Reports
EPS Estimates based on S&P Operating Earnings; historical GAAP earnings are as reported.

STANDARD &POOR'S

Danaher Corporation

Stock Report
November 13, 2004
NYSE Symbol: **DHR**

Recommendation: **HOLD** ★ ★ ★ ☆ ☆   12-Month Target Price: **$55.00** (as of October 21, 2004)

Business Summary October 26, 2004

Danaher Corp. is a leading maker of hand tools and process and environmental controls.

The process/environmental controls segment (77% of sales and 80% of profits in 2003) makes a broad range of monitoring, sensing, controlling, measuring, counting, electrical power quality and telecommunications products, systems, instruments and components. Operating companies include Cyberex, Current Technology, Danaher Controls, Hach, Fluke, Gulton Graphic Instruments, Hengstler, A. L. Hyde, Jennings, the controls product line business of Joslyn Electronics, Joslyn Hi-Voltage, Joslyn Sunbank, Kollmorgen, Partlow/West Anderson, QualiTROI, Mc-Crometer, Veeder-Root, Pacific Scientific, United Power Corp., and West Instruments; and the operating units of Acme-Cleveland Corp. (Namco Controls, M&M Precision Systems, Communications Technology, and TxPort).

The tools and components segment (23%, 20%) makes and distributes hand tools, tool holders, storage containers, hardware, wheel service equipment, fasteners and components for consumer, industrial and professional markets. DHR is one of the largest U.S. producers and distributors of general-purpose mechanics' hand tools and automotive specialty tools. The segment consists of Danaher Hand Tool Group, Matco Tools, Jacobs Chuck Manufacturing, Delta Consolidated, Jacobs Vehicle Systems, Hennessy Industries, and Joslyn Manufacturing hardware and electrical apparatus lines.

Products are sold under the Sears Craftsman, NAPA, Allen, Ammco, Coats, Jacobs, Matco, Delta, Armstrong, K-D and Holo-Krome names. DHR has been the main supplier of Sears Craftsman mechanics' hand tools for more than 60 years. Sears is DHR's largest customer. Matco professional mechanics' tools are distributed by independent mobile distributors. Components, primarily sold to OEMs, include keyless chucks for portable drills and heavy-duty diesel engine retarders.

In the process/environmental controls segment, the company seeks rapid expansion of its environmental controls measuring, leak and detection products, especially for underground petroleum storage tanks and fuel lines.

In 2000, as part of its acquisition strategy, DHR acquired Kollmorgen Corp., a provider of high performance electronic motion control equipment; American Precision Industries, a diversified U.S. and European motion control supplier; and the motion control businesses of Warner Electric Co. In early 2001, it acquired United Power Corp.

In early 2002, the company acquired Marconi Data Systems (formerly known as Videojet Technologies), with about $300 million in annual revenues, for about $400 million. DHR also purchased Marconi Commerce Systems (formerly Gilbarco), with $500 million in sales, for about $325 million.

Company Financials Fiscal Year ending December 31

Per Share Data ($)

(Year Ended December 31)	2003	2002	2001	2000	1999	1998	1997	1996	1995	1994
Tangible Bk. Val.	0.99	0.01	NM	0.28	1.46	0.25	0.27	0.03	NM	0.14
Cash Flow	2.07	1.87	1.57	1.63	1.33	1.05	0.96	0.82	0.70	0.54
Earnings	1.69	1.49	1.01	1.11	0.90	0.66	0.64	0.53	0.44	0.35
S&P Core Earnings	1.55	1.20	0.85	NA	NA	NA	NA	NA	NA	NA
Dividends	0.06	0.05	0.04	0.04	0.03	0.03	0.03	0.02	0.02	0.02
Payout Ratio	4%	3%	4%	3%	3%	4%	4%	4%	5%	5%
Prices - High	46.17	37.73	34.34	34.90	34.50	27.62	16.00	11.65	8.59	6.64
- Low	29.77	26.30	21.95	18.21	21.37	14.00	9.75	7.31	6.06	4.50
P/E Ratio - High	27	25	34	31	39	42	25	22	19	19
- Low	18	18	22	16	24	21	15	14	14	13

Income Statement Analysis (Million $)

	2003	2002	2001	2000	1999	1998	1997	1996	1995	1994
Revs.	5,294	4,577	3,782	3,778	3,197	2,910	2,051	1,812	1,487	1,289
Oper. Inc.	957	824	750	702	584	475	343	295	239	190
Depr.	133	130	178	150	126	109	76.1	68.6	58.5	44.6
Int. Exp.	59.0	43.7	25.7	29.2	16.7	24.9	13.1	16.4	7.20	9.30
Pretax Inc.	797	657	476	523	430	301	254	210	173	137
Eff. Tax Rate	32.6%	29.4%	37.5%	38.0%	39.1%	39.2%	39.0%	39.0%	38.9%	40.2%
Net Inc.	537	464	298	324	262	183	155	128	108	81.7
S&P Core Earnings	491	373	249	NA	NA	NA	NA	NA	NA	NA

Balance Sheet & Other Fin. Data (Million $)

	2003	2002	2001	2000	1999	1998	1997	1996	1995	1994
Cash	1,230	810	707	177	260	41.9	33.3	26.4	7.90	2.00
Curr. Assets	2,942	2,387	1,875	1,474	1,202	887	618	547	466	389
Total Assets	6,890	6,029	4,820	4,032	3,047	2,739	1,880	1,765	1,486	1,135
Curr. Liab.	1,380	1,265	1,017	1,019	709	689	524	475	404	396
LT Debt	1,284	1,197	1,119	714	341	413	163	220	269	117
Common Equity	3,647	3,010	2,229	1,942	1,709	1,352	917	800	586	476
Total Cap.	4,931	4,207	3,348	2,656	2,050	1,765	1,080	1,020	855	593
Cap. Exp.	80.3	65.4	80.6	88.5	88.9	90.3	62.8	51.3	59.2	54.5
Cash Flow	670	594	476	474	388	292	231	197	167	126
Curr. Ratio	2.1	1.9	1.8	1.4	1.7	1.3	1.2	1.2	1.2	1.0
% LT Debt of Cap.	26.0	28.5	33.4	26.9	16.6	23.4	15.1	21.5	31.4	19.7
% Net Inc.of Revs.	10.1	10.1	7.9	8.6	8.2	6.3	7.5	7.1	7.3	6.3
% Ret. on Assets	8.3	8.6	6.7	9.2	8.9	7.4	8.5	7.9	8.4	8.0
% Ret. on Equity	16.1	17.7	14.3	17.8	16.8	14.7	18.0	18.5	34.2	19.2

Data as orig reptd.; bef. results of disc opers/spec. items. Per share data adj. for stk. divs. Bold denotes primary EPS - prior periods restated. E-Estimated. NA-Not Available. NM-Not Meaningful. NR-Not Ranked. UR-Under Review.

Office: 2099 Pennsylvania Avenue NW, Washington, DC 20006-1813.
Telephone: 202-828-0850.
Email: ir@danaher.com
Website: http://www.danaher.com
Chrmn: S.M. Rales.

Pres & CEO: H.L. Culp.
EVP, CFO & Secy: P.W. Allender.
Dirs: M. M. Caplin, H. L. Culp, Jr., D. J. Ehrlich, W. G. Lohr, Jr., M. P. Rales, S. M. Rales, J. T. Schwieters, A. G. Spoon, A. E. Stephenson, Jr.

Founded: in 1969.
Domicile: Delaware.
Employees: 30,000.
S&P Analyst: Efraim Levy, CFA /PMW/BK

Dana Corp.

Recommendation: HOLD ★★★★★
SELL SELL HOLD BUY BUY

12-Month Target Price: **$17.00**
(as of October 20, 2004)

DCN has an approximate 0.02% weighting in the **S&P 500**

Sector: Consumer Discretionary
Sub-Industry: Auto Parts & Equipment
Peer Group: Automobile Original Equipment - Larger Cos.

Summary: This company manufactures truck and car components, as well as parts, both for OEMs and for distribution in the automotive aftermarket.

Quantitative Evaluations

S&P Earnings & Dividend Rank: B-

| D | C | B- | B | B+ | A- | A | A+ |

S&P Fair Value Rank: 3

| 1 | 2 | 3 | 4 | 5 |
| Lowest | | | | Highest |

Fair Value Calc.: $16.00 (Fairly Valued)

S&P Investability Quotient Percentile

54%

DCN scored higher than 54% of all companies for which an S&P Report is available.

Volatility: High

| Low | Average | High |

Technical Evaluation: Neutral
Since 11/04, the technical indicators for DCN have been Neutral.

Relative Strength Rank: Weak

20

| 1 Lowest | Highest 99 |

Price as of 11/12/04: $16.25 | **2004E S&P Core EPS: $1.22**

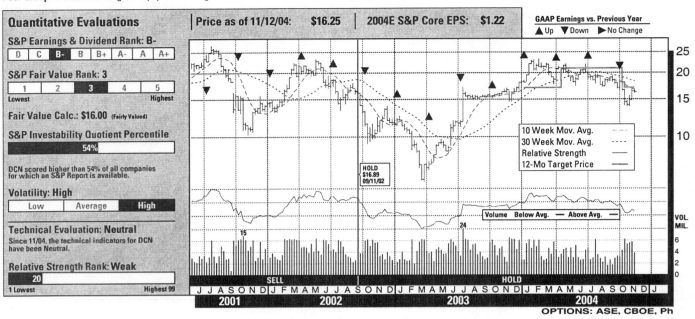

GAAP Earnings vs. Previous Year
▲ Up ▼ Down ► No Change

- 10 Week Mov. Avg.
- 30 Week Mov. Avg.
- Relative Strength
- 12-Mo Target Price

HOLD $16.89 09/11/02

Volume Below Avg. — Above Avg. —

OPTIONS: ASE, CBOE, Ph

Analyst commentary prepared by Efraim Levy, CFA /DC/GG

Highlights October 22, 2004

- We estimate that 2005 revenues from continuing operations will rise 3% to 5%. We expect DCN to benefit from new business, stable to modestly higher light vehicle production, and increased heavy duty vehicle production. An anticipated stronger euro versus the dollar should help reported revenues, in our opinion. We look for operating margins to benefit from savings due to restructuring activities, including cutting personnel and closing plants, and from higher volume and reduced startup costs. However, increased steel and other raw materials costs are likely to put pressure on margins. Continued debt reduction should help reduce interest expense.

- In July, the company agreed to sell its automotive aftermarket business for about $1.1 billion in cash. We think that the transaction fits with DCN's renewed focus on its core business and on generating cash for debt reduction. The company expects the transaction to close in November. The segment is not included in our operating forecast.

- We think the planned sale of the credit division (DCC) and other assets, exclusive of the aftermarket assets, could net about $300 million in proceeds.

Investment Rationale/Risk October 22, 2004

- We would hold existing positions. The stock's P/E multiple, based on our 2005 EPS estimate, is below that of the S&P 500, and in the middle of DCN's historical and peer ranges. The stock is also within the peer range based on our free cash flow forecast. Due to net debits, we estimate that pension accounting adjustments, including total post-retirement costs, will result in 2005 S&P Core EPS of $1.50, which is about 14% below our 2005 EPS estimate.

- Risks to our recommendation and target price include reduced demand for vehicles, in general, and for products with high DCN parts content, in particular. Also, higher steel and commodity prices could hurt the stock's performance.

Key Stock Statistics

S&P Core EPS 2005E	1.50	52-week Range	$23.20-13.86
S&P Oper. EPS 2004E	1.60	12 Month P/E	8.6
P/E on S&P Oper. EPS 2004E	10.2	Beta	1.73
S&P Oper. EPS 2005E	1.75	Shareholders	37,000
Yield (%)	3.0%	Market Cap (B)	$ 2.4
Dividend Rate/Share	0.48	Shares Outstanding (M)	149.3

Value of $10,000 invested five years ago: **$ 6,692**

Dividend Data Dividends have been paid since 1936

Amount ($)	Date Decl.	Ex-Div. Date	Stock of Record	Payment Date
0.120	Feb. 10	Feb. 26	Mar. 01	Mar. 15 '04
0.120	Apr. 20	May. 27	Jun. 01	Jun. 15 '04
0.120	Jul. 20	Aug. 30	Sep. 01	Sep. 15 '04
0.120	Oct. 19	Nov. 29	Dec. 01	Dec. 15 '04

Revenues/Earnings Data Fiscal year ending December 31

Revenues (Million $)

	2004	2003	2002	2001	2000	1999
1Q	2,311	2,472	2,321	2,731	3,468	3,381
2Q	2,331	2,581	2,576	2,768	3,296	3,408
3Q	2,114	2,452	2,356	2,399	2,865	3,127
4Q	—	2,050	2,251	2,373	2,688	3,243
Yr.	—	8,067	9,504	10,271	12,317	13,270

Earnings Per Share ($)

	2004	2003	2002	2001	2000	1999
1Q	0.33	0.31	-0.09	-0.18	1.54	0.97
2Q	0.49	0.38	0.39	0.10	0.95	1.14
3Q	0.34	0.41	-0.01	0.08	0.19	0.97
4Q	E0.37	0.37	0.09	-2.01	-0.57	Nil
Yr.	E1.60	1.17	0.39	-2.01	2.18	3.08

Next earnings report expected: mid-February Source: S&P, Company Reports
EPS Estimates based on S&P Operating Earnings; historical GAAP earnings are as reported.

Recommendation: **HOLD** ★ ★ ★ ★ ★   12-Month Target Price: **$17.00** (as of October 20, 2004)

Business Summary October 22, 2004

In an effort to secure its place in a rapidly consolidating group of automotive component manufacturers, Dana Corp. is attempting to build critical mass by focusing on its core businesses, while divesting units that do not meet its goals. The company defines a core business as one with leading or second place market share, global sales in excess of $500 million, at least 10% annual sales growth, and a net return on sales of 6% or better (unleveraged). In 1998, DCN purchased Echlin Inc. for about $3.9 billion.

Operations are organized into three market-focused strategic business units: automotive systems (48% of 2003 sales from continuing operations); engine and fluid management (27%); heavy vehicle technologies and systems group (24%); and other (1%). Dana Credit Corp. and the automotive aftermarket group have been classified as discontinued.

Consolidated non-U.S. sales were 40% of consolidated sales in 2003. Including U.S. exports, non-U.S. sales were 45% of consolidated sales.

DCN makes components and systems for the worldwide vehicular, industrial and off-highway OE markets, and is a major supplier to related aftermarkets.

During 2002, the company combined the former commercial vehicle systems and off-highway systems groups to form the heavy vehicle technologies and systems group.

The company plans to sell its Dana Commercial Credit (DCC) operations, which provide leasing and financial services through subsidiaries. In July, DCN reached an agreement to sell most of its automotive aftermarket group.

The automotive systems group's products consist of drivetrain modules, systems and components such as axles and driveshafts, structures and chassis products for the automotive light vehicle markets, as well as driveshafts for the commercial vehicle market.

The engine and fluid management group produces and sells sealing, thermal management, fluid transfer and engine power products for the automotive, light and commercial vehicle and leisure and outdoor power equipment markets.

The heavy vehicle technologies and systems group manufactures and sells axles, brakes, driveshafts, chassis and suspension modules, ride controls and related modules and systems for the commercial and off-highway vehicle markets, and transaxles, transmissions and electronic controls for the off-highway market.

Ford and DaimlerChrysler are DCN's two largest customers. Ford accounted for 27% of sales in 2003, and DaimlerChrysler for 10%.

During 2000, the company recorded restructuring charges aggregating $87 million for the closure of facilities, and for workforce reductions, in the U.S., the U.K., France and Argentina.

In October 2001, DCN announced plans to accelerate the restructuring of operations. After-tax charges recorded for the restructuring aggregated about $442 million.

Company Financials Fiscal Year ending December 31

Per Share Data ($)

(Year Ended December 31)	2003	2002	2001	2000	1999	1998	1997	1996	1995	1994
Tangible Bk. Val.	10.04	6.13	7.50	11.21	12.02	11.30	10.99	11.11	8.08	6.77
Cash Flow	3.82	3.90	1.69	5.60	6.22	6.12	6.77	5.73	5.27	4.45
Earnings	1.17	0.39	-2.01	2.18	3.08	3.20	3.49	3.01	2.84	2.31
S&P Core Earnings	0.83	-0.61	-3.18	NA	NA	NA	NA	NA	NA	NA
Dividends	0.09	0.04	0.94	1.24	1.24	1.14	1.04	0.98	0.90	0.83
Payout Ratio	8%	10%	NM	57%	40%	36%	30%	33%	32%	36%
Prices - High	18.40	23.22	26.90	33.25	54.06	61.50	54.37	35.50	32.62	30.68
- Low	6.15	9.28	10.25	12.81	26.00	31.31	30.62	27.25	21.37	19.62
P/E Ratio - High	16	60	NM	15	18	19	16	12	11	13
- Low	5	24	NM	6	8	10	9	9	8	8

Income Statement Analysis (Million $)

	2003	2002	2001	2000	1999	1998	1997	1996	1995	1994
Revs.	7,918	9,589	10,386	12,317	13,270	12,637	8,291	7,686	7,598	6,763
Oper. Inc.	593	863	681	1,252	1,633	1,553	705	725	709	738
Depr.	394	523	548	523	519	488	335	278	246	211
Int. Exp.	221	260	309	323	279	280	196	159	146	113
Pretax Inc.	119	100	-451	518	777	857	686	416	509	416
Eff. Tax Rate	NM	27.0%	NM	33.0%	32.3%	36.8%	42.9%	32.2%	35.5%	37.9%
Net Inc.	175	58.0	-298	334	513	534	369	306	288	228
S&P Core Earnings	124	-91.0	-471	NA	NA	NA	NA	NA	NA	NA

Balance Sheet & Other Fin. Data (Million $)

	2003	2002	2001	2000	1999	1998	1997	1996	1995	1994
Cash	731	571	199	179	111	230	93.0	228	66.0	48.2
Curr. Assets	4,533	4,118	3,797	4,323	4,801	4,337	NA	NA	NA	NA
Total Assets	9,617	9,553	10,207	11,236	11,123	10,138	7,119	7,119	5,694	5,111
Curr. Liab.	2,965	2,824	3,489	4,331	3,888	3,987	NA	NA	NA	NA
LT Debt	2,605	3,215	3,008	2,649	2,732	1,718	2,178	1,698	1,315	870
Common Equity	2,050	1,482	1,958	2,628	2,957	2,940	1,701	1,429	1,165	940
Total Cap.	4,751	4,804	5,078	5,398	5,837	4,950	4,033	3,127	2,634	1,962
Cap. Exp.	305	662	425	662	807	661	426	357	204	337
Cash Flow	569	581	250	857	1,032	1,022	704	584	534	439
Curr. Ratio	1.5	1.5	1.1	1.0	1.2	1.1	NA	NA	NA	NA
% LT Debt of Cap.	54.8	66.9	59.2	49.1	46.8	34.7	54.0	54.3	49.9	44.3
% Net Inc.of Revs.	2.2	0.6	NM	2.7	3.9	4.2	4.5	4.0	3.8	3.4
% Ret. on Assets	1.8	0.6	NM	3.0	4.8	6.2	5.6	5.2	5.3	4.7
% Ret. on Equity	9.9	3.4	NM	12.0	17.4	23.0	23.6	23.6	27.4	26.2

Data as orig reptd.; bef. results of disc opers/spec. items. Per share data adj. for stk. divs.; EPS diluted. E-Estimated. NA-Not Available. NM-Not Meaningful. NR-Not Ranked. UR-Under Review.

Office: 4500 Dorr Street, Toledo, OH 43615-4040.
Telephone: 419-535-4500.
Website: http://www.dana.com
Chrmn: G. Hiner.
Pres & CEO: M.J. Burns.

VP & CFO: R.C. Richter.
Chief Acctg Officer: R.J. Westerheide.
Dirs: B. F. Bailar, A. C. Baillie, M. J. Burns, E. M. Carpenter, E. Clark, C. W. Grise, G. H. Hiner, J. P. Kelly, M. R. Marks, R. B. Priory, F. M. Senderos.

Founded: in 1904.
Domicile: Virginia.
Employees: 59,000.
S&P Analyst: Efraim Levy, CFA /DC/GG

Recommendation: **HOLD** ★ ★ ★ ☆ ☆
SELL · SELL · HOLD · BUY · BUY

12-Month Target Price: **$25.00**
(as of September 27, 2004)

DRI has an approximate 0.04% weighting in the **S&P 500**

Sector: Consumer Discretionary
Sub-Industry: Restaurants
Peer Group: Casual Dining - Larger

Summary: This restaurant company operates the Red Lobster and Olive Garden chains.

Quantitative Evaluations

S&P Earnings & Dividend Rank: A-

| D | C | B- | B | B+ | **A-** | A | A+ |

S&P Fair Value Rank: 3+

| 1 | 2 | **3** | 4 | 5 |
| Lowest | | | | Highest |

Fair Value Calc.: $26.50 (Slightly Overvalued)

S&P Investability Quotient Percentile

93%

DRI scored higher than 93% of all companies for which an S&P Report is available.

Volatility: Average

| Low | **Average** | High |

Technical Evaluation: Bullish

Since 11/04, the technical indicators for DRI have been Bullish.

Relative Strength Rank: Strong

86

| 1 Lowest | | Highest 99 |

Price as of 11/12/04: **$27.08** | 2005E S&P Core EPS: **$1.50**

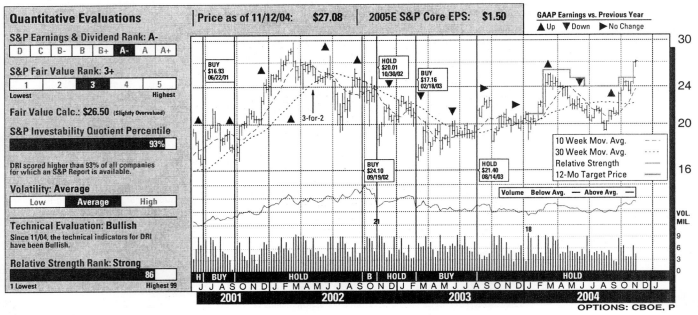

Analyst commentary prepared by Dennis Milton/CB/DRJ

Highlights September 28, 2004

- The company in June revised its long-term annual EPS growth target to "the double-digit range," from 12% to 15%. The company set its target for FY 05 (May) at 8% to 12% EPS growth, based on 1% to 3% same-store sales growth at Red Lobster and Olive Garden, the opening of 50 to 60 new restaurants, and a 52-week fiscal year, versus 53 weeks in FY 04.

- We expect revenues to grow at a 6% to 7% compound annual rate over the next five to seven years, primarily due to expansion and blended same-store sales growth of 2% to 3%. Results should benefit from leveraging fixed corporate costs over an expanding sales base.

- For FY 05, we see revenue growth of only 2.5%, reflecting a 52-week fiscal year, same-store sales growth of approximately 3% at Olive Garden, and flat same-store sales at Red Lobster. However, we expect results to benefit from improved cost controls at Red Lobster and from significant share repurchases, partly offset by higher food prices. We project FY 05 EPS of $1.60, up 7%, excluding one-time items. Our FY 05 Standard & Poor's Core Earnings estimate, including $0.10 in projected stock option and pension-related expenses, is $1.50.

Investment Rationale/Risk September 28, 2004

- The stock traded recently at 15X our calendar 2004 EPS estimate of $1.54, a slight discount to peers. We believe that DRI will benefit from strong demographic and economic trends that we think will sustain strong demand growth for the casual dining industry over the next decade. However, we believe the stock's valuation fairly reflects the company's growth potential, given the maturity of its flagship Red Lobster and Olive Garden chains relative to industry competitors. Our discounted cash flow model, which assumes that DRI will be able to boost revenues about 7% annually for the next several years, yields intrinsic value for the shares near recent levels.

- Risks to our opinion and target price include declining traffic, especially at Red Lobster units, and lack of customer acceptance of the company's smaller, but growing, Smokey Bones and Bahama Breeze concepts.

- We have based our 12-month target price of $25 on a P/E multiple of 15X, slightly below the current industry average, and our calendar 2005 EPS estimate of $1.68.

Key Stock Statistics

S&P Core EPS 2006E	1.70	52-week Range	$27.24-18.48
S&P Oper. EPS 2005E	1.60	12 Month P/E	19.3
P/E on S&P Oper. EPS 2005E	16.9	Beta	0.42
S&P Oper. EPS 2006E	1.81	Shareholders	37,501
Yield (%)	0.3%	Market Cap (B)	$ 4.3
Dividend Rate/Share	0.08	Shares Outstanding (M)	157.2

Value of $10,000 invested five years ago: **$ 20,869**

Dividend Data Dividends have been paid since 1995

Amount ($)	Date Decl.	Ex-Div. Date	Stock of Record	Payment Date
0.040	Mar. 26	Apr. 06	Apr. 09	May. 01 '04
0.040	Sep. 28	Oct. 06	Oct. 08	Nov. 01 '04

Revenues/Earnings Data Fiscal year ending May 31

Revenues (Million $)

	2005	2004	2003	2002	2001	2000
1Q	1,279	1,260	1,175	1,074	1,018	929.4
2Q	—	1,143	1,143	1,007	932.0	848.2
3Q	—	1,242	1,181	1,125	988.6	917.5
4Q	—	1,359	1,227	1,162	1,082	1,006
Yr.	—	5,003	4,655	4,369	4,021	3,701

Earnings Per Share ($)

	2005	2004	2003	2002	2001	2000
1Q	0.44	0.40	0.40	0.34	0.31	0.23
2Q	E0.18	0.18	0.18	0.20	0.16	0.12
3Q	E0.49	0.46	0.35	0.36	0.27	0.24
4Q	E0.49	0.32	0.35	0.40	0.33	0.31
Yr.	E1.60	1.36	1.31	1.30	1.06	0.89

Next earnings report expected: mid-December Source: S&P, Company Reports
EPS Estimates based on S&P Operating Earnings; historical GAAP earnings are as reported.

Darden Restaurants, Inc.

Recommendation: **HOLD**  12-Month Target Price: **$25.00** (as of September 27, 2004)

Business Summary September 28, 2004

Darden Restaurants is the world's largest publicly held casual dining restaurant chain. At August 29, 2004, it operated 1,335 restaurants in the U.S. and Canada, including 681 Red Lobster units, 545 Olive Garden units, 76 Smokey Bones BBQ Sports Bar units, and 32 Bahama Breeze restaurants.

Red Lobster, founded by William Darden in 1968, is the largest U.S. casual dining, seafood-specialty restaurant operator. System sales totaled $2.4 billion in FY 04 (May), unchanged from the level of FY 03. Average restaurant sales were $3.6 million in both FY 04 and FY 03, and $3.7 million in FY 02. Same-store sales declined 3.5% in FY 04, after a 2.7% rise in FY 03 and a 6.2% increase in FY 02. The restaurants feature fresh fish, shrimp, crab, lobster, scallops, and other seafood, served in a casual atmosphere. DRI maintains about 105 different menus to reflect geographic differences in consumer preferences, prices and selections in its trade areas. The average check per person in FY 04 was $16.50 to $17.50, with alcoholic beverages accounting for 8.4% of sales.

Olive Garden is the U.S. market share leader among casual dining Italian-food restaurants. FY 04 system-wide sales grew 11%, to $2.2 billion. Same-restaurant sales were up 4.6%, after rising 2.2% in FY 03 and 6.3% in FY 02, and average restaurant sales were $4.1 million. The Olive Garden menu includes a variety of authentic Italian foods featuring fresh ingredients, and an expanded wine list that includes a broad selection of wines imported from Italy. Dinner entree prices at Olive Garden restaurants range from about $7.95 to $17.95, and lunch entree prices range from about $5.95 to $9.50.

The company's other concepts, Bahama Breeze and Smokey Bones, are relatively new, and have not yet gained enough scale to contribute meaningfully to profits. Bahama Breeze, first opened in 1996, is a Caribbean-themed restaurant that offers a distinctive island dining experience. Smokey Bones, first opened in 1999, combines barbecue with a relaxed sports bar atmosphere. The company expected the concepts to contribute only slightly to profits in FY 05, due to high operating costs and expansion-related expenses. It is currently experimenting with a new prototype for the Bahama Breeze chain in an attempt to closely match its cost structure with expected revenues.

DRI plans to grow by increasing the number of restaurants in each of its existing concepts, and by developing or acquiring additional concepts that can be expanded profitably. The company plans to open 49 to 65 new restaurants in FY 05, with growth focused on the Olive Garden and Smokey Bones concepts. The company intends to focus on improving operational returns at Olive Garden and Red Lobster, and will limit new unit expansion of those concepts to high potential sites that it believes will generate significant returns on investment.

The company repurchased about 2.9 million common shares in the first three months of FY 05, and 10.7 million common shares in FY 04. Since the start of a buyback program in December 1995, it has acquired about 112.2 million shares.

DRI does not currently expense its stock option grants. Had they been expensed, EPS would have been lower by $0.08, $0.09 and $0.09 in FY 04, FY 03 and FY 02, respectively.

Company Financials Fiscal Year ending May 31

Per Share Data ($)

(Year Ended May 31)	2004	2003	2002	2001	2000	1999	1998	1997	1996	1995
Tangible Bk. Val.	7.86	7.03	6.56	5.66	5.09	4.81	4.69	4.81	5.05	4.91
Cash Flow	2.60	2.43	2.20	1.85	1.55	1.34	1.00	0.20	0.88	0.78
Earnings	1.36	1.31	1.30	1.06	0.89	0.66	0.45	0.23	0.31	0.21
S&P Core Earnings	1.29	1.18	1.16	0.97	NA	NA	NA	NA	NA	NA
Dividends	0.08	0.05	0.05	0.05	0.05	0.05	0.05	0.05	0.05	Nil
Payout Ratio	6%	4%	4%	5%	6%	8%	12%	23%	17%	Nil

Cal. Yrs.	2003	2002	2001	2000	1999	1998	1997	1996	1995	1994
Prices - High	23.01	29.76	24.98	18.00	15.58	12.62	8.33	9.33	8.08	NA
- Low	16.50	18.00	12.66	8.29	10.41	7.83	4.50	5.00	6.08	NA
P/E Ratio - High	17	23	19	17	17	19	19	40	26	NA
- Low	12	14	10	8	12	12	10	21	19	NA

Income Statement Analysis (Million $)

	2004	2003	2002	2001	2000	1999	1998	1997	1996	1995
Revs.	5,003	4,655	4,369	4,021	3,701	3,458	3,287	3,172	3,192	3,163
Oper. Inc.	636	588	563	479	421	352	300	235	345	316
Depr.	210	198	166	147	130	125	126	137	135	135
Int. Exp.	43.7	44.1	37.8	31.5	23.1	40.6	20.5	23.3	24.9	26.1
Pretax Inc.	340	348	363	301	274	216	154	27.6	114	59.8
Eff. Tax Rate	31.9%	33.2%	34.5%	34.6%	35.5%	34.9%	33.8%	NM	34.6%	17.7%
Net Inc.	231	232	238	197	177	141	102	-91.0	74.4	49.2
S&P Core Earnings	218	208	212	181	NA	NA	NA	NA	NA	NA

Balance Sheet & Other Fin. Data (Million $)

	2004	2003	2002	2001	2000	1999	1998	1997	1996	1995
Cash	36.7	48.6	153	61.8	26.1	41.0	33.5	25.5	30.3	20.1
Curr. Assets	346	326	450	328	290	328	398	337	288	308
Total Assets	2,780	2,665	2,530	2,218	1,971	1,906	1,985	1,964	2,089	2,113
Curr. Liab.	683	640	601	554	607	534	559	481	445	517
LT Debt	653	658	663	518	304	314	311	313	301	304
Common Equity	1,246	1,196	1,129	1,035	960	964	1,020	1,081	1,223	1,174
Total Cap.	2,075	2,005	1,909	1,644	1,344	1,350	1,408	1,464	1,625	1,580
Cap. Exp.	354	423	318	355	269	124	112	160	214	358
Cash Flow	441	430	404	344	307	266	228	45.8	209	185
Curr. Ratio	0.5	0.5	0.7	0.6	0.5	0.6	0.7	0.7	0.6	0.6
% LT Debt of Cap.	31.5	32.8	34.7	31.5	22.6	23.3	22.0	21.4	18.5	19.2
% Net Inc.of Revs.	4.6	5.0	5.4	4.9	4.8	4.1	3.1	NM	2.3	1.6
% Ret. on Assets	8.5	8.9	10.0	9.4	9.2	7.2	5.2	NM	3.5	NA
% Ret. on Equity	19.0	20.0	22.0	19.7	18.4	14.2	9.7	NM	6.2	NA

Data as orig reptd.; bef. results of disc opers/spec. items. Per share data adj. for stk. divs.; EPS diluted. E-Estimated. NA-Not Available. NM-Not Meaningful. NR-Not Ranked. UR-Under Review.

Office: 5900 Lake Ellenor Drive, Orlando, FL 32809-4634.
Telephone: 407-245-4000.
Email: irinfo@darden.com
Website: http://www.darden.com
Chrmn & CEO: J.R. Lee.
Pres & COO: A.H. Madsen.

CEO: C. Otis, Jr.
SVP, Secy & General Counsel: P.J. Shives.
Dirs: L. L. Berry, O. C. Donald, D. Hughes, J. R. Lee, A. H. Madsen, C. McGillicuddy III, C. Otis, Jr., M. D. Rose, M. A. Sastre, J. A. Smith, B. Sweatt III, R. P. Wilson.

Founded: in 1968.
Domicile: Florida.
Employees: 141,300.
S&P Analyst: Dennis Milton/CB/DRJ

Deere & Co.

Recommendation: **BUY** ★★★★ ☆
SELL SELL HOLD BUY BUY

12-Month Target Price: **$76.00**
(as of September 09, 2004)

DE has an approximate 0.16% weighting in the **S&P 500**

Sector: Industrials
Sub-Industry: Construction & Farm Machinery & Heavy Trucks
Peer Group: Farm Equipment Manufacturers

Summary: DE, the world's largest producer of farm equipment, is also a large maker of construction machinery and lawn and garden equipment.

Quantitative Evaluations

S&P Earnings & Dividend Rank: B

| D | C | B- | **B** | B+ | A- | A | A+ |

S&P Fair Value Rank: 4-

| 1 | 2 | 3 | **4** | 5 |
| Lowest | | | | Highest |

Fair Value Calc.: $65.10 (Slightly Overvalued)

S&P Investability Quotient Percentile

96%

DE scored higher than 96% of all companies for which an S&P Report is available.

Volatility: Average

| Low | **Average** | High |

Technical Evaluation: Neutral

Since 11/04, the technical indicators for DE have been Neutral.

Relative Strength Rank: Strong

73

| 1 Lowest | | Highest 99 |

| Price as of 11/12/04: | **$68.92** | 2004E S&P Core EPS: | **$5.00** |

GAAP Earnings vs. Previous Year
▲ Up ▼ Down ▶ No Change

- 10 Week Mov. Avg.
- 30 Week Mov. Avg.
- Relative Strength
- 12-Mo Target Price

Volume Below Avg. — Above Avg.

VOL. MIL.

HOLD | BUY

J J A S O N D J F M A M J J A S O N D J F M A M J J A S O N D J F M A M J J A S O N D J
2001 | **2002** | **2003** | **2004**

OPTIONS: ASE, CBOE, Ph

Analyst commentary prepared by Anthony M. Fiore, CFA /PMW/JWP

Highlights September 10, 2004

- We expect revenue growth of about 7% in FY 05 (Oct.), based on our outlook for continued strength in U.S. farm cash receipts, combined with new products and projected improving end markets outside the U.S. We anticipate that payments made to farmers as a result of the current farm bill will continue to provide support for farm equipment sales in FY 05. However, for the longer term we believe that these subsidies could stimulate excess production and exert downward pressure on prices of agricultural commodities.

- We expect a modest expansion of operating margins in FY 05, based on our outlook for continued strength in unit volumes and further benefits from previously implemented business-improvement initiatives. We see these factors outweighing the likely negative impact of continued high steel costs that we anticipate. All told, we project mid-teens EPS growth for FY 05. For the longer term, we believe that earnings will continue to exhibit large swings, due to the extreme cyclicality of the farm and construction industries in which the company operates.

- Our Standard & Poor's Core Earnings estimate for FY 05 is $0.09 a share below our operating EPS forecast of $5.75, with the majority of the difference reflecting projected stock option expense.

Investment Rationale/Risk September 10, 2004

- We recommend accumulating the shares. We anticipate that favorable conditions will continue over the next 12 months for many of the end markets that DE serves. In addition, we expect support from farm programs, new products, and continued international expansion to have a positive impact on results.

- Risks to our recommendation and target price include the potential for lower crop prices to negatively affect spending on farm equipment; sales being pulled from future periods into FY 04 due to the expiration of depreciation allowances; continued raw material cost escalation; and an unexpected slowdown in end markets.

- Our 12-month target price of $76 combines two valuation metrics. Our discounted cash flow model, which assumes a 5.5% average annual free cash flow growth rate over the next 10 years, 3.5% growth in perpetuity, and a 7.5% weighted average cost of capital, indicates intrinsic value of about $82. Based on P/E multiple, the shares traded recently at 11X our FY 05 EPS estimate. Applying a P/E multiple of about 12X, in line with historical norms, to our FY 05 EPS estimate suggests a value of $69. As in prior industry cycles, we expect the stock to trade at lower multiples during peak or near-peak EPS years.

Key Stock Statistics

S&P Core EPS 2005E	**5.66**	52-week Range	**$74.93-56.72**
S&P Oper. EPS 2004E	**5.08**	12 Month P/E	**15.6**
P/E on S&P Oper. EPS 2004E	**13.6**	Beta	**0.52**
S&P Oper. EPS 2005E	**5.75**	Shareholders	**31,089**
Yield (%)	**1.6%**	Market Cap (B)	**$ 17.1**
Dividend Rate/Share	**1.12**	Shares Outstanding (M)	**248.2**

Value of $10,000 invested five years ago: **$ 18,424**

Dividend Data Dividends have been paid since 1937

Amount ($)	Date Decl.	Ex-Div. Date	Stock of Record	Payment Date
0.220	Dec. 03	Dec. 29	Dec. 31	Feb. 02 '04
0.280	Feb. 25	Mar. 29	Mar. 31	May. 03 '04
0.280	May. 26	Jun. 28	Jun. 30	Aug. 02 '04
0.280	Aug. 25	Sep. 28	Sep. 30	Nov. 01 '04

Revenues/Earnings Data Fiscal year ending October 31

Revenues (Million $)

	2004	2003	2002	2001	2000	1999
1Q	2,912	2,794	2,522	2,680	2,339	2,459
2Q	5,877	4,400	3,987	3,776	3,790	2,957
3Q	5,418	4,402	3,969	3,584	3,632	3,036
4Q	—	3,939	3,469	3,161	3,376	2,788
Yr.	—	15,535	13,947	13,293	13,137	11,751

Earnings Per Share ($)

	2004	2003	2002	2001	2000	1999
1Q	0.68	0.28	-0.16	0.24	0.16	0.21
2Q	1.88	1.07	0.59	0.54	0.87	0.65
3Q	1.58	1.02	0.61	0.30	0.72	0.29
4Q	E0.94	0.27	0.28	-1.36	0.30	-0.13
Yr.	E5.08	2.64	1.33	-0.27	2.06	1.02

Next earnings report expected: late-November Source: S&P, Company Reports
EPS Estimates based on S&P Operating Earnings; historical GAAP earnings are as reported.

Deere & Company

Recommendation: **BUY** ★ ★ ★ ★ ☆ 12-Month Target Price: **$76.00** (as of September 09, 2004)

Business Summary September 10, 2004

With revenues exceeding $15 billion, Deere & Co. is the world's largest maker of farm tractors and combines, and a leading maker of construction equipment. Its largest competitors include construction equipment behemoth Caterpillar Inc. ($20 billion in revenues); Netherlands-based CNH Global N.V. ($9.7 billion), a worldwide maker of both farm and construction equipment; and AGCO Corp. ($2.5 billion), the world's third largest global farm equipment maker.

The farm equipment segment (47% of FY 03 (Oct.) revenues; 4.6% margin) primarily makes tractors; combine, cotton and sugar cane harvesters; tillage, seeding and soil preparation machinery; hay and forage equipment; material handling equipment; and integrated agricultural management systems technology for the global farming industry. Over the past five years, segment margins averaged about 4.9%.

The commercial and consumer equipment segment (C&CE; 21%; 7.0%) manufactures and distributes equipment and service parts for commercial uses. Products include small tractors for lawn, garden, commercial and utility purposes; riding and walk-behind mowers; golf course equipment; utility vehicles; landscape and irrigation equipment; and other outdoor products. In addition, this division also includes John Deere Landscapes, Inc., a distributor of irrigation equipment, nursery products and landscape products. Over the past four years, segment margins averaged 4.5%.

The construction and forestry segment (18%; 5.6%) manufactures and distributes a broad range of machines and service parts used in construction, earth-moving,

material handling and timber harvesting. Products include backhoe loaders; crawler dozers and loaders; four-wheel-drive loaders; excavators; motor graders; articulated dump trucks; landscape loaders; skid-steer loaders; and log skidders, feller bunchers, loaders, forwarders, harvesters and related attachments. Over the past four years, margins for this segment averaged 3.5%.

The credit segment (9%; 35%) finances sales and leases by John Deere dealers of new and used agricultural, commercial and consumer, and construction and forestry equipment. In addition, this division provides wholesale financing to dealers, provides operating loans and finances retail revolving charge accounts. Credit operations had receivables under management of $9.5 billion at October 31, 2003. Over the past four years, margins for the segment averaged about 22%.

DE makes large expenditures for engineering and research to improve the quality and performance of its products. R&D in FY 03, FY 02 and FY 01 totaled approximately $577 million (3.8% of sales), $528 million (3.9% of sales) and $590 million (4.1%), respectively.

In North America, the company sells equipment to about 3,167 primarily independently owned dealers. Of these, approximately 1,600 sell agricultural equipment, while 576 sell construction, earth-moving, material handling and/or forestry equipment. Outside North America, DE sells equipment to distributors and dealers in more than 160 countries.

Company Financials Fiscal Year ending October 31

Per Share Data ($)

(Year Ended October 31)	2003	2002	2001	2000	1999	1998	1997	1996	1995	1994
Tangible Bk. Val.	11.82	9.49	13.14	15.56	16.24	16.65	15.96	12.72	10.61	8.77
Cash Flow	5.24	4.34	2.78	4.80	3.21	5.85	5.30	4.39	3.79	3.35
Earnings	2.64	1.33	-0.27	2.06	1.02	4.16	3.78	3.14	2.71	2.34
S&P Core Earnings	3.07	-0.38	-1.63	NA	NA	NA	NA	NA	NA	NA
Dividends	0.88	0.88	0.88	0.88	0.88	0.88	0.80	0.80	0.75	0.68
Payout Ratio	33%	66%	NM	43%	86%	21%	21%	25%	28%	29%
Prices - High	67.41	51.60	46.12	49.62	45.93	64.12	60.50	47.12	36.00	30.29
- Low	37.56	37.50	33.50	30.31	31.56	28.37	39.87	33.00	21.62	20.41
P/E Ratio - High	26	39	NM	24	45	15	16	15	12	13
- Low	14	28	NM	15	31	7	11	11	8	9

Income Statement Analysis (Million $)

	2003	2002	2001	2000	1999	1998	1997	1996	1995	1994
Revs.	15,535	13,947	13,108	13,137	11,751	13,749	12,791	11,229	10,291	8,934
Oper. Inc.	2,231	1,696	1,274	2,102	1,435	2,497	2,295	1,999	1,768	1,390
Depr.	631	725	718	648	513	418	366	311	283	262
Int. Exp.	1,257	637	766	677	557	519	422	402	392	303
Pretax Inc.	980	578	-46.3	779	374	1,575	1,511	1,298	1,104	936
Eff. Tax Rate	34.4%	44.7%	NM	37.7%	36.1%	35.2%	36.5%	37.0%	36.1%	35.5%
Net Inc.	643	319	-64.0	486	239	1,021	960	817	706	604
S&P Core Earnings	743	-94.8	-385	NA	NA	NA	NA	NA	NA	NA

Balance Sheet & Other Fin. Data (Million $)

	2003	2002	2001	2000	1999	1998	1997	1996	1995	1994
Cash	4,616	3,004	1,206	419	612	1,177	330	1,161	364	245
Curr. Assets	NA	NA	NA	NA	NA	NA	NA	NA	NA	NA
Total Assets	26,258	23,768	22,663	20,469	17,578	18,002	16,320	14,653	13,847	12,781
Curr. Liab.	NA	NA	NA	NA	NA	NA	NA	NA	NA	NA
LT Debt	10,404	8,950	6,561	4,764	3,806	2,792	2,623	2,425	2,176	2,054
Common Equity	2,834	1,797	3,992	4,302	4,094	4,080	4,148	3,557	3,085	2,558
Total Cap.	13,238	10,772	10,566	9,141	7,963	6,892	6,792	5,991	5,277	4,625
Cap. Exp.	310	359	491	427	316	435	485	687	383	331
Cash Flow	1,275	1,045	654	1,133	752	1,439	1,326	1,128	989	866
Curr. Ratio	NA	NA	NA	NA	NA	NA	NA	NA	NA	NA
% LT Debt of Cap.	78.6	83.1	62.1	52.1	47.8	40.5	38.6	40.5	41.2	44.4
% Net Inc.of Revs.	4.2	2.4	NM	3.8	2.0	7.4	7.5	7.3	6.9	6.8
% Ret. on Assets	2.6	1.4	NM	2.6	1.3	5.9	6.2	5.7	5.3	5.0
% Ret. on Equity	27.8	11.8	NM	11.6	5.8	24.8	24.9	24.6	25.0	25.9

Data as orig reptd.; bef. results of disc opers/spec. items. Per share data adj. for stk. divs.; EPS diluted. E-Estimated. NA-Not Available. NM-Not Meaningful. NR-Not Ranked. UR-Under Review.

Office: One John Deere Place, Moline, IL 61265.
Telephone: 309-765-8000.
Email: stockholder@deere.com
Website: http://www.deere.com
Chrmn, Pres & CEO: R.W. Lane.
SVP & CFO: N.J. Jones.

SVP & General Counsel: J.R. Jenkins.
VP & Treas: J.R. Jabanoski.
VP & Investor Contact: M. Ziegler 309-765-4491.
Dirs: J. R. Block, C. C. Bowles, T. K. Dunnigan, L. A. Hadley, D. C. Jain, A. L. Kelly, R. W. Lane, A. Madero, J. Milberg, T. H. Patrick, A. L. Peters, J. R. Walter.

Founded: in 1837.
Domicile: Delaware.
Employees: 43,221.
S&P Analyst: Anthony M. Fiore, CFA /PMW/JWP

Dell, Inc.

Recommendation: **HOLD** ★ ★ ★ ★ ★
SELL SELL HOLD BUY BUY

12-Month Target Price: **$38.00**
(as of November 12, 2004)

DELL has an approximate 0.92% weighting in the **S&P 500**

Sector: Information Technology
Sub-Industry: Computer Hardware
Peer Group: Computer Hardware - Large System Vendors

Summary: Dell (formerly Dell Computer Corp.) is the leading direct marketer and one of the world's 10 leading manufacturers of PCs compatible with industry standards established by IBM.

Quantitative Evaluations

S&P Earnings & Dividend Rank: B+

| D | C | B- | B | **B+** | A- | A | A+ |

S&P Fair Value Rank: 5+

| 1 | 2 | 3 | 4 | **5** |
| Lowest | | | | Highest |

Fair Value Calc.: $45.20 (Slightly Undervalued)

S&P Investability Quotient Percentile

98%

DELL scored higher than 98% of all companies for which an S&P Report is available.

Volatility: Low

| **Low** | Average | High |

Technical Evaluation: Bullish
Since 11/04, the technical indicators for DELL have been Bullish.

Relative Strength Rank: Strong

84
1 Lowest   Highest 99

Price as of 11/12/04: $40.44 | **2005E S&P Core EPS:** $0.92

GAAP Earnings vs. Previous Year
▲ Up ▼ Down ► No Change

- 10 Week Mov. Avg. — — —
- 30 Week Mov. Avg. ....
- Relative Strength
- 12-Mo Target Price

BUY $33.76 03/25/04
HOLD $33.57 08/11/04

Volume Below Avg. —— Above Avg. ——

HOLD   BUY   HOLD

J J A S O N D | J F M A M J J A S O N D | J F M A M J J A S O N D | J F M A M J J A S O N D | J
2001   2002   2003   2004

OPTIONS: ASE, CBOE, P, Ph

Analyst commentary prepared by Megan Graham-Hackett/MF/BK

Highlights 15-NOV-04

- We forecast revenue growth of 19% for FY 05 (Jan.), following a 17% advance in FY 04. Results in FY 04 reflected a recovery in demand for PCs, but we believe the industry continues to experience an aggressive pricing environment. We see Dell's ability to boost its penetration of the corporate sales market for servers, together with expected sustained growth in notebooks, servers and storage, offsetting these pressures and enabling it to fare better than its peers. We see 17% revenue growth for FY 06.
- We believe that gross margins should remain about flat in FY 05, at 18.2%, as we see contributions from wider margin products offsetting pricing pressures. We expect sales and marketing expenses to increase less rapidly than revenues in FY 05, as Dell benefits from several strategies aimed at improving cost efficiency. However, we expect some acceleration in spending in FY 06 as Dell reinvests in its business to support potential future revenue growth.
- We estimate FY 05 EPS of $1.28 on an operating basis. Our FY 05 Standard & Poor's Core Earnings per share estimate is $0.92, reflecting our projection of stock option expense. Our FY 06 operating EPS estimate is $1.50.

Investment Rationale/Risk 15-NOV-04

- We continue to recommend holding the shares. We believe Dell sets the standard for the computer industry, reflecting the strength of its direct sales model and what we see as its superior cash flow management, but we think that the company faces tough year-over-year comparisons next year. Nevertheless, Dell has generated strong cash flow from operations, including over $3.6 billion in FY 04, and has succeeded in offsetting the negative impact of a weak pricing environment in computer hardware by gaining market share; we believe that it should continue to do so, given its low cost structure.
- Risks to our opinion and target price include market share losses by Dell as its peers improve their cost position in PCs, a slowdown in technology spending, and adverse geopolitical events.
- Our 12-month target price of $38 is based on our discounted cash flow (DCF) and price to sales (P/S) analyses. Our DCF model assumes free cash flow growth of 12% for the next 15 years and a weighted average cost of capital of 10.6%. Our P/S analysis assumes that the shares will trade at a multiple of 1.7X our calendar 2005 revenue estimate, based on the stock's historical range.

Key Stock Statistics

S&P Core EPS 2006E	1.14	52-week Range	$40.53-31.14
S&P Oper. EPS 2005E	1.28	12 Month P/E	33.4
P/E on S&P Oper. EPS 2005E	31.6	Beta	1.66
S&P Oper. EPS 2006E	1.50	Shareholders	46,495
Yield (%)	Nil	Market Cap (B)	$101.0
Dividend Rate/Share	Nil	Shares Outstanding (M)	2496.6

Value of $10,000 invested five years ago: **$ 9,686**

Dividend Data

No cash dividends have been paid.

Revenues/Earnings Data Fiscal year ending January 31

Revenues (Million $)

	2005	2004	2003	2002	2001	2000
1Q	11,540	9,532	8,066	8,028	7,280	5,537
2Q	11,706	9,778	8,459	7,611	7,670	6,142
3Q	12,502	10,622	9,144	7,468	8,264	6,784
4Q	—	11,512	9,735	8,061	8,674	6,801
Yr.	—	41,444	35,404	31,168	31,888	25,265

Earnings Per Share ($)

	2005	2004	2003	2002	2001	2000
1Q	0.28	0.23	0.17	0.17	0.19	0.16
2Q	0.31	0.24	0.19	-0.04	0.22	0.19
3Q	—	0.26	0.21	0.16	0.25	0.11
4Q	E0.36	0.29	0.23	0.17	0.16	0.16
Yr.	E1.28	1.01	0.80	0.46	0.81	0.61

Next earnings report expected: mid-February Source: S&P, Company Reports
EPS Estimates based on S&P Operating Earnings; historical GAAP earnings are as reported.

Dell, Inc.

Recommendation: **HOLD** ★ ★ ★ ☆ ☆   12-Month Target Price: **$38.00** (as of November 12, 2004)

Business Summary 15-NOV-04

In 1994, Dell (formerly Dell Computer Corp.) discontinued retail channel sales to focus exclusively on its direct business. Since then, it has posted rapid growth. As of the first quarter of calendar 2004, according to market research firm International Data Corp., Dell was the world's largest PC maker. It regained the top spot from Hewlett Packard Co., which via its May 2002 acquisition of Compaq Computer has become a larger rival to Dell. The company adopted its current name in July 2003.

The company is a direct marketer of PCs, including desktops, notebooks, servers and workstations. In addition, Dell entered the storage market in FY 00 (Jan.); and the printer, handheld and portable projector markets in FY 03.

Dell's strategy is to leverage its competitive advantages via its direct sales model to increase penetration of corporate accounts with its higher margin notebooks and servers, and internationally. Its strategy includes giving customers the ability to electronically design, price and purchase computer systems, and to obtain online support through its Internet site. Most sales to consumers and small businesses are made online.

The company's enterprise systems (22% of FY 04 total net revenues; 20% in FY 03) include workstations, servers, and storage and network switches. Dell's Power-Edge servers are used in networked environments to distribute files, database information, applications and communication products. Its PowerApp Servers are new appliance servers aimed at Web-related workloads. After entering the market for Windows-based workstations in 1997, the company quickly became the world's leading supplier. In 2002, Dell and EMC announced a strategic alliance under which Dell resells EMC's CLARiiON line.

Desktop computer systems, which remain the largest segment (51%; 53%), include the OptiPlex line, targeted at corporate and other major account customers, and offering advanced features and high reliability; and Dell Dimension, targeted at small to medium-sized businesses and individual users. Dell ranked first worldwide in desktop shipments in calendar 2003.

The company's higher margin notebooks, or portables (28%; 27%), include the Latitude product lines, for corporate users; and the Inspiron line for consumers and small businesses. Dell ranked second worldwide in notebook computer shipments in calendar 2003.

Dell also offers services that include professional consulting, custom hardware and software integration, and network installation and support.

Manufacturing sites, among others, include Austin, TX; Limerick, Ireland; Penang, Malaysia; and Xiamen, China.

Had stock option expenses been included in FY 04 results, EPS would have been reduced by $0.33, or 33%.

Company Financials Fiscal Year ending January 31

Per Share Data ($)

(Year Ended January 31)	2004	2003	2002	2001	2000	1999	1998	1997	1996	1995
Tangible Bk. Val.	2.46	1.89	1.80	2.16	1.94	0.91	0.50	0.29	0.32	0.21
Cash Flow	1.11	0.88	0.54	0.90	0.67	0.56	0.34	0.19	0.10	0.07
Earnings	1.01	0.80	0.46	0.81	0.61	0.53	0.32	0.17	0.08	0.05
S&P Core Earnings	0.68	0.49	0.28	0.58	NA	NA	NA	NA	NA	NA
Dividends	Nil	Nil	Nil	Nil	Nil	Nil	Nil	Nil	Nil	Nil
Payout Ratio	Nil	Nil	Nil	Nil	Nil	Nil	Nil	Nil	Nil	Nil

Cal. Yrs.	2003	2002	2001	2000	1999	1998	1997	1996	1995	1994
Prices - High	37.18	31.06	31.32	59.68	55.00	37.90	12.98	4.02	1.54	0.74
- Low	22.59	21.90	16.01	16.25	31.37	9.92	3.11	0.71	0.61	0.29
P/E Ratio - High	37	39	68	74	90	73	41	23	18	14
- Low	22	27	35	20	51	19	10	4	7	6

Income Statement Analysis (Million $)

	2004	2003	2002	2001	2000	1999	1998	1997	1996	1995
Revs.	41,444	35,404	31,168	31,888	25,265	18,243	12,327	7,759	5,296	3,475
Oper. Inc.	3,807	3,055	2,510	3,008	2,419	2,149	1,383	761	415	282
Depr.	263	211	239	240	156	103	67.0	47.0	38.0	33.1
Int. Exp.	14.0	17.0	29.0	47.0	34.0	Nil	3.00	7.00	15.0	12.2
Pretax Inc.	3,724	3,027	1,731	3,194	2,451	2,084	1,368	747	383	213
Eff. Tax Rate	29.0%	29.9%	28.0%	30.0%	32.0%	29.9%	31.0%	28.9%	28.9%	30.0%
Net Inc.	2,645	2,122	1,246	2,236	1,666	1,460	944	531	272	149
S&P Core Earnings	1,806	1,356	781	1,602	NA	NA	NA	NA	NA	NA

Balance Sheet & Other Fin. Data (Million $)

	2004	2003	2002	2001	2000	1999	1998	1997	1996	1995
Cash	4,317	4,232	3,641	4,910	3,809	3,181	1,844	1,352	646	527
Curr. Assets	10,633	8,924	7,877	9,491	7,681	6,339	3,912	2,747	1,957	1,470
Total Assets	19,311	15,470	13,535	13,435	11,471	6,877	4,268	2,993	2,148	1,594
Curr. Liab.	10,896	8,933	7,519	6,543	5,192	3,695	2,697	1,658	939	751
LT Debt	505	506	520	509	508	512	17.0	18.0	113	113
Common Equity	6,280	4,873	4,694	5,622	5,308	2,321	1,293	806	967	527
Total Cap.	6,785	5,379	5,214	6,131	5,816	2,833	1,310	824	1,080	765
Cap. Exp.	329	305	303	482	397	296	187	114	101	63.7
Cash Flow	2,908	2,333	1,485	2,476	1,822	1,563	1,011	578	310	174
Curr. Ratio	1.0	1.0	1.0	1.5	1.5	1.7	1.5	1.7	2.1	2.0
% LT Debt of Cap.	7.4	9.4	10.0	8.3	8.7	18.1	1.3	2.2	10.5	14.8
% Net Inc.of Revs.	6.4	6.0	4.0	7.0	6.6	8.0	7.7	6.8	5.1	4.3
% Ret. on Assets	15.2	14.6	9.2	18.0	18.2	26.2	26.0	20.7	14.5	10.9
% Ret. on Equity	47.4	44.4	24.2	40.9	43.7	80.8	89.9	59.9	36.3	32.2

Data as orig reptd.; bef. results of disc opers/spec. items. Per share data adj. for stk. divs.; EPS diluted. E-Estimated. NA-Not Available. NM-Not Meaningful. NR-Not Ranked. UR-Under Review.

Office: One Dell Way, Round Rock, TX 78682.
Telephone: 512-338-4400.
Email: investor_relations_fulfillment@dell.com
Website: http://www.dell.com
Chrmn: M. S. Dell.
Pres & CEO: K. B. Rollins.

SVP & CFO: J. M. Schneider.
SVP & General Counsel: L. Tu.
Investor Contact: Brenda Everett (512-728-7800).
Dirs: D. J. Carty, M. S. Dell, W. H. Gray III, J. C. Lewent, T. W. Luce III, K. S. Luft, A. J. Mandl, M. A. Miles, S. S. Nunn, Jr., K. B. Rollins.

Founded: in 1984.
Domicile: Delaware.
Employees: 46,000.
S&P Analyst: Megan Graham-Hackett/MF/BK

Delphi Corp.

Recommendation: SELL ★☆☆☆☆
SELL SELL HOLD BUY BUY

12-Month Target Price: $8.00
(as of November 07, 2003)

DPH has an approximate 0.05% weighting in the **S&P 500**

Sector: Consumer Discretionary
Sub-Industry: Auto Parts & Equipment
Peer Group: Automobile Original Equipment - Larger Cos.

Summary: DPH (formerly Delphi Automotive Systems), which makes a wide variety of automotive components and systems, was spun off from GM in 1999.

Quantitative Evaluations

S&P Earnings & Dividend Rank: NR

D	C	B-	B	B+	A-	A	A+

S&P Fair Value Rank: 1

1	2	3	4	5
Lowest				Highest

Fair Value Calc.: $7.10 (Overvalued)

S&P Investability Quotient Percentile

22%

DPH scored lower than 78% of all companies for which an S&P Report is available.

Volatility: Average

Low	Average	High

Technical Evaluation: Neutral
Since 11/04, the technical indicators for DPH have been Neutral.

Relative Strength Rank: Moderate

41

| 1 Lowest | | Highest 99 |

Price as of 11/12/04: $9.14   **2004E S&P Core EPS:** $0.21

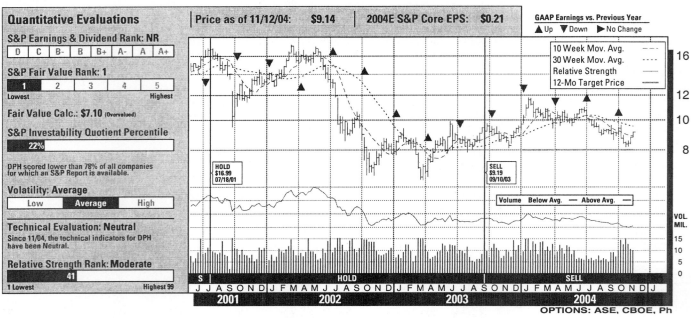

GAAP Earnings vs. Previous Year
▲ Up   ▼ Down   ▶ No Change

- 10 Week Mov. Avg.
- 30 Week Mov. Avg.
- Relative Strength
- 12-Mo Target Price

HOLD $16.99 07/18/01

SELL $9.19 09/10/03

Volume   Below Avg.   — Above Avg.

VOL. MIL.

OPTIONS: ASE, CBOE, Ph

Analyst commentary prepared by Efraim Levy, CFA /PMW/BK

Highlights October 19, 2004

- Revenues are highly dependent on production volume in the cyclical automobile industry. With GM vehicle inventory above what we see as optimum levels, we think that if sales do not strengthen, GM may announce additional production cuts later in 2004 or in early 2005. We believe this would negatively affect DPH's sales and profits. We expect 2004 revenues to rise 2% to 3%, led by growth in non-GM revenues, but we expect sales to GM to decline, due to lower production and a reduced level of business. We believe results could be hurt by a less favorable content mix and higher costs. Assuming that GM reduces its vehicle inventory toward historical levels by the end of 2004, we expect 2005 revenues to grow 4% to 6%, on 14% higher non-GM revenues, partly offset by 3% lower sales to GM. We see sales to GM accounting for 53% of total revenues in 2004 and 49% in 2005 (with the percentage likely to continue to decline over time).

- We see margins benefiting from lower overhead and employee attrition, but we expect pricing pressures to remain intense and raw materials costs to rise.

- We believe DPH may have to subsidize certain financially weak suppliers. We also see earnings being hurt by pension and health care costs.

Investment Rationale/Risk October 19, 2004

- We recommend selling the shares. The stock's P/E multiple is near the upper end of its peer range, and we see our estimates vulnerable to possible additional production cuts at GM. In addition, the company's pension plans and other post-retirement benefit (OPEB) plans were underfunded by $4.0 billion and $8.5 billion, respectively, at the end of 2003. Based on Standard & Poor's Core Earnings methodology, after estimated pension income and option expense, S&P Core EPS would be $0.19 and $0.10, respectively, below our 2004 and 2005 operating EPS forecasts.

- Risks to our recommendation and target price include stronger that expected demand for automobile parts, especially from former parent company GM; and potential growing demand in China, where DPH is a leading parts supplier.

- We use a P/E multiple of about 7X applied to our 2006 EPS estimate of $1.05 to determine a 12-month target price, reflecting peer and historical P/E multiple comparisons. Our DCF model, which assumes a weighted cost of capital of 9.6%, compound annual growth of 10.5% over the next 14 years, and a terminal growth rate of 1%, calculates intrinsic value of $9. Based on a combination of our P/E multiple and DCF analyses, our 12-month target price is $8.

Key Stock Statistics

S&P Core EPS 2005E	0.58	52-week Range	$11.78-8.10
S&P Oper. EPS 2004E	0.40	12 Month P/E	33.9
P/E on S&P Oper. EPS 2004E	22.9	Beta	0.96
S&P Oper. EPS 2005E	0.68	Shareholders	353,633
Yield (%)	3.1%	Market Cap (B)	$ 5.1
Dividend Rate/Share	0.28	Shares Outstanding (M)	561.2

Value of $10,000 invested five years ago: **$ 6,292**

Dividend Data Dividends have been paid since 1999

Amount ($)	Date Decl.	Ex-Div. Date	Stock of Record	Payment Date
0.070	Dec. 03	Dec. 11	Dec. 15	Jan. 14 '04
0.070	Mar. 01	Mar. 11	Mar. 15	Apr. 12 '04
0.070	Jun. 22	Jul. 01	Jul. 06	Aug. 03 '04
0.070	Sep. 09	Sep. 16	Sep. 20	Oct. 19 '04

Revenues/Earnings Data Fiscal year ending December 31

Revenues (Million $)

	2004	2003	2002	2001	2000	1999
1Q	7,411	7,182	6,688	6,535	7,804	7,469
2Q	7,549	7,094	7,322	6,944	7,778	7,683
3Q	6,650	6,563	6,446	6,229	6,648	6,790
4Q	—	7,257	6,971	6,380	6,909	7,250
Yr.	—	28,096	27,427	26,088	29,139	29,192

Earnings Per Share ($)

	2004	2003	2002	2001	2000	1999
1Q	0.10	0.23	-0.09	-0.77	0.51	0.55
2Q	0.23	0.16	0.39	0.29	0.75	0.69
3Q	-0.20	-0.63	0.10	0.05	0.26	0.24
4Q	E0.02	0.15	0.21	-0.23	0.36	0.48
Yr.	E0.40	-0.10	0.61	-0.66	1.88	1.95

Next earnings report expected: mid-January Source: S&P, Company Reports
EPS Estimates based on S&P Operating Earnings; historical GAAP earnings are as reported.

Delphi Corporation

Recommendation: **SELL** ★ ☆ ☆ ☆ ☆   12-Month Target Price: **$8.00** (as of November 07, 2003)

Business Summary October 19, 2004

Delphi Corp. (formerly Delphi Automotive Systems), a wholly owned subsidiary of GM prior to February 1999, is the world's largest and most diversified supplier of components, integrated systems and modules to the automotive industry. The company's spinoff from GM was completed in May 1999, and it adopted its current name in March 2002.

The company believes it has become a leader in the global automotive parts industry by capitalizing on extensive experience gained as the principal supplier of automotive parts to GM, the world's largest manufacturer of automotive vehicles. DPH is primarily a Tier 1 supplier, meaning that it generally provides products directly to automotive vehicle manufacturers (VMs). It also sells products to the worldwide aftermarket for replacement parts, and to non-VM customers. Sales to customers other than GM grew from 13% of the total in 1993 to 39% in 2003 (including sales from joint venture and other non-consolidated minority interest holdings).

Major elements of DPH's business strategy are to supply customers with innovative components, systems and modules; leverage its global presence to meet customer needs; improve operating performance; and complete strategic acquisitions, joint ventures, and alliances.

In November 2003, the company reorganized its segment structure into three parts. Revenues in 2003 were attributable to the following sectors: electrical,

electronics, safety & interior (48%); dynamics, propulsion & thermal (42%): and the automotive holdings group (10%).

The dynamics, propulsion & thermal sector offers electronic energy and engine management systems designed to optimize engine performance and emissions control through management of vehicle air intake, fuel delivery, combustion and exhaust after-treatment. It also provides all major electronic chassis control systems (steering, braking, suspension and engine), as well as selected thermal management products.

The electrical, electronics, safety & interior sector produces connectors, wiring harnesses, switches and sensors for electrical/electronic systems. It also offers various products related to vehicle safety systems.

The automotive holdings group is comprised of plant sites and product lines that do not meet DPH's targets for net income or other financial metrics. The principal product lines in this segment include: halfshafts, condensers, batteries, filters, spark plugs, generators and compressors. The group recently had 11 sites, and was working to consolidate four plants.

Excluding $262 million in net pretax restructuring and product line charges, 2002 EPS would have been $0.92.

Company Financials Fiscal Year ending December 31

Per Share Data ($)

(Year Ended December 31)	2003	2002	2001	2000	1999	1998	1997	1996	1995	1994
Tangible Bk. Val.	1.42	1.04	4.13	6.72	5.69	5.61	NA	NA	NA	NA
Cash Flow	1.88	2.37	1.39	3.55	3.49	1.91	4.24	NA	NA	NA
Earnings	-0.10	0.61	-0.66	1.88	1.95	-0.04	0.75	NA	NA	NA
S&P Core Earnings	0.25	-0.13	-1.37	NA	NA	NA	NA	NA	NA	NA
Dividends	0.28	0.28	0.28	0.28	0.14	Nil	Nil	NA	NA	NA
Payout Ratio	NM	46%	NM	15%	7%	Nil	Nil	NA	NA	NA
Prices - High	10.30	17.40	17.50	21.12	22.25	NA	NA	NA	NA	NA
- Low	6.39	6.60	9.50	10.50	14.00	NA	NA	NA	NA	NA
P/E Ratio - High	NM	29	NM	11	11	NA	NA	NA	NA	NA
- Low	NM	11	NM	6	7	NA	NA	NA	NA	NA

Income Statement Analysis (Million $)

	2003	2002	2001	2000	1999	1998	1997	1996	1995	1994
Revs.	28,096	27,427	26,088	29,139	29,192	28,479	31,447	NA	NA	NA
Oper. Inc.	1,132	1,903	1,402	2,680	2,538	992	2,657	NA	NA	NA
Depr.	1,110	988	1,150	936	856	1,102	1,970	NA	NA	NA
Int. Exp.	198	191	222	183	132	277	287	NA	NA	NA
Pretax Inc.	-142	531	-528	1,667	1,721	-155	594	NA	NA	NA
Eff. Tax Rate	NM	35.4%	NM	36.3%	37.1%	NM	28.8%	NA	NA	NA
Net Inc.	-56.0	343	-370	1,062	1,083	-24.0	423	NA	NA	NA
S&P Core Earnings	142	-72.5	-766	NA	NA	NA	NA	NA	NA	NA

Balance Sheet & Other Fin. Data (Million $)

	2003	2002	2001	2000	1999	1998	1997	1996	1995	1994
Cash	880	1,014	757	760	1,556	2,062	1,973	NA	NA	NA
Curr. Assets	8,046	7,542	7,498	8,603	9,811	4,567	9,432	NA	NA	NA
Total Assets	20,904	19,316	18,602	18,521	18,350	18,668	18,003	NA	NA	NA
Curr. Liab.	6,191	5,860	5,850	6,243	6,737	4,061	3,831	NA	NA	NA
LT Debt	2,434	2,084	2,083	1,623	1,640	3,137	2,294	NA	NA	NA
Common Equity	1,570	1,279	2,312	3,766	3,200	3,171	3,034	NA	NA	NA
Total Cap.	4,004	3,363	4,395	5,389	4,840	6,380	5,328	NA	NA	NA
Cap. Exp.	1,005	1,035	1,057	1,272	1,200	NA	NA	NA	NA	NA
Cash Flow	1,054	1,331	780	1,998	1,939	1,078	2,393	NA	NA	NA
Curr. Ratio	1.3	1.3	1.3	1.4	1.5	2.4	2.5	NA	NA	NA
% LT Debt of Cap.	60.8	62.0	47.4	30.1	33.9	49.2	52.1	NA	NA	NA
% Net Inc.of Revs.	NM	1.3	NM	3.6	3.7	NM	1.3	NA	NA	NA
% Ret. on Assets	NM	1.8	NM	5.8	6.4	NM	NA	NA	NA	NA
% Ret. on Equity	NM	19.1	NM	30.5	67.5	NM	NA	NA	NA	NA

Data as orig reptd.; certain data pro forma -- assuming the company's IPO had occurred on Jan. 1, 1998; bef. results of disc opers/spec. items. Per share data adj. for stk. divs.; EPS diluted. E-Estimated. NA-Not Available. NM-Not Meaningful. NR-Not Ranked.

Office: 5725 Delphi Drive, Troy, MI 48098-2815.
Telephone: 248-813-2000.
Website: http://www.delphi.com
Chrmn, Pres & CEO: J.T. Battenberg III.
Vice Chrmn & CFO: A.S. Dawes.
VP & Treas: J.G. Blahnik.

VP & General Counsel: L.G. Robinson.
Chief Acctg Officer: J. Sheehan.
Investor Contact: C.E. Marentette IV 248-813-2495.
Dirs: J. T. Battenberg III, O. D. Bernardes Neto, R. Brust, V. W. Colbert, A. S. Dawes, D. Farr, B. Gottschalk, S. Irimajiri, C. A. Niekamp, J. D. Opie, D. L. Runkle.

Founded: in 1998.
Domicile: Delaware.
Employees: 190,000.
S&P Analyst: Efraim Levy, CFA /PMW/BK

Delta Air Lines

Recommendation: **SELL** ★ ★ ☆ ☆ ☆
SELL · SELL · HOLD · BUY · BUY

12-Month Target Price: **$2.00**
(as of October 20, 2004)

DAL has an approximate 0.01% weighting in the **S&P 500**

Sector: Industrials
Sub-Industry: Airlines
Peer Group: Airlines (U.S.) - Major

Summary: DAL, the third largest U.S. airline, said recently that a bankruptcy was possible if it was not successful in implementing its business transformation plan.

Quantitative Evaluations

S&P Earnings & Dividend Rank: C

| D | C | B- | B | B+ | A- | A | A+ |

S&P Fair Value Rank: NR

| 1 | 2 | 3 | 4 | 5 |
| Lowest | | | | Highest |

Fair Value Calc.: NA

S&P Investability Quotient Percentile

10

DAL scored lower than 90% of all companies for which an S&P Report is available.

Volatility: High

| Low | Average | High |

Technical Evaluation: Bullish
Since 10/04, the technical indicators for DAL have been Bullish.

Relative Strength Rank: Strong

98

1 Lowest   Highest 99

| Price as of 11/12/04: | **$6.84** | 2004E S&P Core EPS: | **$-16.34** |

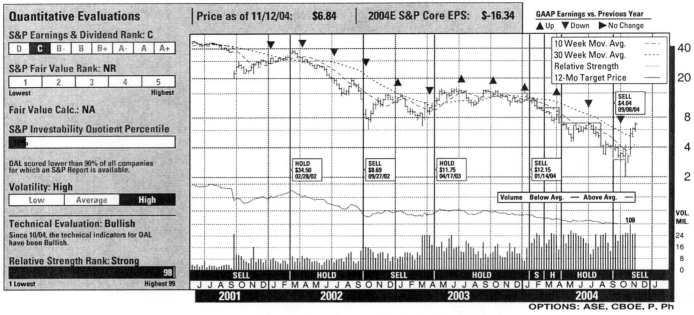

GAAP Earnings vs. Previous Year
▲ Up   ▼ Down   ► No Change

- - - 10 Week Mov. Avg.
······ 30 Week Mov. Avg.
Relative Strength
12-Mo Target Price

HOLD $34.50 02/28/02
SELL $8.69 09/27/02
HOLD $11.75 04/17/03
SELL $12.15 01/14/04
SELL $4.04 09/08/04

Volume   Below Avg. — Above Avg.

109

VOL. MIL.
24
16
8
0

SELL | HOLD | SELL | HOLD | S | H | HOLD | SELL
J J A S O N D | J F M A M J J A S O N D | J F M A M J J A S O N D | J F M A M J J A S O N D | J F M A M J J A S O N D | J
2001 | 2002 | 2003 | 2004

OPTIONS: ASE, CBOE, P, Ph

Analyst commentary prepared by Jim Corridore/DC/GG

Highlights October 25, 2004

- We forecast that 2005 revenues will grow 8% to 10%, on about a 5% increase in capacity and higher passenger load factors, aided by some pent-up travel demand and stimulation in demand from lower fares. We see airfares as likely to remain under pressure due to price competition on transcontinental routes as well as aggressive growth by discount carriers, whose airfares DAL has been forced to match in many markets.

- Margins should benefit from the roll out of the company's business transformation plan that it announced in September 2004, in our opinion. Key components of the plan include cutting 6,000-7,000 jobs, eliminating the use of Dallas/Ft. Worth as a hub and obtaining cost concessions from pilots, suppliers and debtholders. We expect operating margins to remain solidly negative until DAL is able to reach an agreement with its pilots union to reduce its labor costs, which the company has been seeking for some time. We think that fuel costs are likely to rise about 50%, on near-record oil prices. We see no signs that oil prices will back off of near-record highs. DAL currently is totally unhedged against oil prices.

- We forecast a loss of $7.00 a share for 2005, an improvement from our 2004 estimate of a $15.42 loss, excluding unusual items. On a Standard & Poor's Core Earnings basis, we project a 2005 loss of $8.07, with the difference from our operating earnings estimate largely due to estimated pension expense.

Investment Rationale/Risk October 25, 2004

- We have an avoid opinion on the shares based on what we see as increased bankruptcy risk. We are concerned that DAL's restructuring may wind up taking place through the Chapter 11 bankruptcy process. On September 8, 2004, the company said that if it did not see results quickly from its new plan, a bankruptcy filing was possible. In addition, the balance sheet has been weakened by increased debt and major asset writedowns over the past two years. We think this will make it difficult for DAL to access capital markets, and some major debt repayments are coming up this year.

- Risks to our recommendation and target price include the possibility that DAL will be able to get the concessions from its employees that it is seeking, and the possibility that if oil prices back off sharply or industry capacity shrinks enough to allow for airfare increases, the profit outlook could be better than we expect.

- Our 12-month target price of $2 values the stock at an enterprise value to EBITDA multiple of 4X our 2006 EBITDA estimate, below the level of peers and the stock's historical range on this metric, due to what we see as an elevated risk of bankruptcy. We do not expect positive earnings or EBITDA in 2004 or 2005.

Key Stock Statistics

S&P Core EPS 2005E	**-8.07**	52-week Range	**$13.20-2.75**
S&P Oper. EPS 2004E	**-15.42**	12 Month P/E	**NM**
P/E on S&P Oper. EPS 2004E	**NM**	Beta	**2.03**
S&P Oper. EPS 2005E	**-7.00**	Shareholders	**22,401**
Yield (%)	**Nil**	Market Cap (B)	**$0.859**
Dividend Rate/Share	**Nil**	Shares Outstanding (M)	**125.6**

Value of $10,000 invested five years ago: **$ 1,205**

Dividend Data Dividends have been paid since 1949

Amount ($)	Date Decl.	Ex-Div. Date	Stock of Record	Payment Date

Revenues/Earnings Data Fiscal year ending December 31

Revenues (Million $)

	2004	2003	2002	2001	2000	1999
1Q	3,292	3,155	3,103	3,842	3,911	3,877
2Q	3,961	3,307	3,474	3,776	4,469	3,713
3Q	3,871	3,443	3,420	3,398	—	3,960
4Q	—	3,398	3,308	2,863	4,016	4,469
Yr.	—	13,303	13,305	13,879	16,741	15,888

Earnings Per Share ($)

	2004	2003	2002	2001	2000	1999
1Q	-3.12	-3.81	-3.25	-1.11	—	2.38
2Q	-15.79	1.40	-1.54	-0.76	—	2.50
3Q	-5.16	-1.36	-2.67	-2.13	—	1.67
4Q	E-4.75	-2.69	-2.98	-5.98	0.12	3.51
Yr.	E-15.42	-6.40	-10.44	-9.98	7.05	9.90

Next earnings report expected: mid-January Source: S&P, Company Reports
EPS Estimates based on S&P Operating Earnings; historical GAAP earnings are as reported.

Delta Air Lines, Inc.

Recommendation: **SELL** ★ ★ ☆ ☆ ☆   12-Month Target Price: **$2.00** (as of October 20, 2004)

Business Summary October 25, 2004

Delta Air Lines is the third largest U.S. airline in terms of operating revenues and revenue passenger miles. Its labor force is 82% non-union, but its pilots are unionized. DAL established Delta Express in 1996 in a competitive response to low-cost carriers. However, in January 2003, the company said it would discontinue Delta Express in favor of a new low-cost operator named Song. Song was launched April 15, 2003. As of March 1, 2004, Song offered 144 daily flights, using 36 Boeing 757 aircraft.

In September 2004, DAL announced a business turnaround plan that the company said would result in annual cash savings of $5 billion from the level of 2002. Key parts of the plan included eliminating 6,000 to 7,000 jobs over 18 months, closing the Dallas/Ft. Worth hub, and increasing utilization and flights at the Atlanta hub. The company is seeking $1 billion in annual cost cuts from pilots, and expects to seek other concessions from lessors, lenders and vendors.

DAL derived 82% of its 2003 revenues from U.S. operations,. Including regional affiliates, it offers service to 206 U.S. cities in 47 states, the District of Columbia, Puerto Rico, and the U.S. Virgin Islands. Short-haul traffic is fed to company hubs by Delta Connection carriers, which include Atlantic Southeast Airlines (100% owned), COMAIR (100%) and SkyWest (13%).

The route system is structured around DAL's Atlanta Worldport. U.S. hubs are in Cincinnati, Dallas/Ft. Worth, and Salt Lake City. JFK serves as DAL's European gateway.

International passenger operations accounted for 18% of 2003 revenues (13% from the Atlantic region, 4% from the Pacific, and 1% from Latin America). DAL directly serves 48 cities in 32 nations. In June 2000, it launched the SkyTeam alliance with Air France, Korean Air Lines and AeroMexico. Alitalia and CSA Czech Airlines joined SkyTeam in March 2001. With these and other partners, DAL is able to serve 230 cities in 84 countries.

In August 2002, the company entered into a marketing alliance with Continental Airlines and Northwest Airlines; this included mutual codesharing and reciprocal frequent flyer and airport lounge access arrangements. The alliance was approved by the Department of Transportation in March 2003.

In June 2001, DAL ratified a new contract with its pilots, calling for 24% to 34% wage hikes over five years. In February 2003, the pilots' union declined a company request to renegotiate its contract. Talks between DAL and the pilots have been ongoing, but as of September 2004, no concessions had been made by the pilots.

On July 24, 2003, the company said it was discontinuing the payment of common stock dividends. It had paid cash dividends on its common stock continuously since 1949. DAL said it expected to realize a resulting annual cash flow benefit of $12 million. In June 2003, the company sold its 40% interest in WorldSpan, L.P., which operated a computer reservation system, for $330 million. In December 2003, DAL sold a portion of its stake in Orbitz, an online travel agency, for $33 million. As of March 1, 2004, DAL owned 13% of Orbitz.

In 2001, DAL received $650 million from the federal government through the U.S. Airline Industry Stabilization Act. In 2003, the company received an additional $398 million under the Emergency Wartime Supplemental Appropriations Act, intended to compensate airlines for costs associated with security and the war in Iraq.

Company Financials Fiscal Year ending December 31

Per Share Data ($)

(Year Ended December 31)	2003	2002	2001	2000	1999	1998	1997	1996	1995	1994
Tangible Bk. Val.	NM	NM	12.87	25.14	21.20	25.56	25.05	17.75	10.60	NM
Cash Flow	3.32	-1.13	0.43	16.05	20.61	13.49	11.72	10.37	7.67	8.98
Earnings	-6.40	-10.44	-9.98	7.05	9.90	7.20	6.34	5.65	0.71	2.04
S&P Core Earnings	-6.16	-15.90	-16.74	NA	NA	NA	NA	NA	NA	NA
Dividends	0.05	0.10	0.13	0.10	0.10	0.10	0.10	0.10	0.10	0.10
Payout Ratio	NM	NM	NM	1%	1%	1%	2%	2%	14%	5%
Prices - High	16.05	38.69	52.93	58.31	58.31	72.00	71.81	60.31	43.50	40.62
- Low	6.56	6.10	20.00	39.62	39.62	45.68	40.87	34.62	33.43	25.12
P/E Ratio - High	NM	NM	NM	8	6	10	11	11	61	20
- Low	NM	NM	NM	6	4	6	6	6	47	12

Income Statement Analysis (Million $)

	2003	2002	2001	2000	1999	1998	1997	1996	1995	1994
Revs.	13,303	13,305	13,879	16,741	15,455	14,711	14,138	13,590	12,455	12,194
Oper. Inc.	907	244	800	2,932	3,365	2,831	2,554	2,292	1,926	1,283
Depr.	1,202	1,148	1,283	1,187	1,146	961	861	710	634	622
Int. Exp.	732	646	410	381	305	153	186	207	269	292
Pretax Inc.	-1,189	-2,002	-1,864	1,549	2,283	1,826	1,648	1,415	276	494
Eff. Tax Rate	NM	NM	NM	40.1%	40.0%	39.7%	39.3%	39.6%	43.5%	NM
Net Inc.	-773	-1,272	-1,216	928	1,369	1,101	1,001	854	156	294
S&P Core Earnings	-762	-1,960	-2,062	NA	NA	NA	NA	NA	NA	NA

Balance Sheet & Other Fin. Data (Million $)

	2003	2002	2001	2000	1999	1998	1997	1996	1995	1994
Cash	2,710	2,103	2,210	1,364	1,648	1,647	1,634	1,170	1,652	1,233
Curr. Assets	4,967	3,902	3,567	3,205	3,346	2,672	3,362	2,867	3,282	3,014
Total Assets	26,356	24,720	23,605	21,931	20,566	16,544	14,603	12,741	12,226	12,143
Curr. Liab.	6,624	6,455	6,403	5,245	5,940	5,327	4,577	4,083	3,638	3,441
LT Debt	11,538	10,174	8,347	5,896	4,525	1,952	1,782	1,797	2,175	3,121
Common Equity	-659	893	3,769	5,343	4,873	4,172	3,723	3,007	2,540	1,827
Total Cap.	11,154	11,504	12,836	12,693	10,732	7,415	6,242	4,804	4,715	5,068
Cap. Exp.	744	1,286	2,793	4,060	3,289	2,819	2,291	1,948	936	626
Cash Flow	412	-139	53.0	2,102	2,515	2,051	1,851	1,555	790	916
Curr. Ratio	0.7	0.6	0.6	0.6	0.6	0.5	0.7	0.7	0.9	0.9
% LT Debt of Cap.	103.4	88.4	65.0	46.5	42.2	26.3	28.5	37.4	46.1	61.5
% Net Inc.of Revs.	NM	NM	NM	5.5	8.9	7.5	7.1	6.3	1.3	2.4
% Ret. on Assets	NM	NM	NM	4.4	7.3	7.1	7.3	6.8	12.8	2.4
% Ret. on Equity	NM	NM	NM	17.9	29.4	27.6	30.9	30.5	71.4	17.8

Data as orig reptd.; bef. results of disc opers/spec. items. Per share data adj. for stk. divs.; EPS diluted. E-Estimated. NA-Not Available. NM-Not Meaningful. NR-Not Ranked. UR-Under Review.

Office: Hartsfield Atlanta International Airport, Atlanta, GA 30320-6001.
Telephone: 404-715-2600.
Website: http://www.delta-air.com
CEO: G. Grinstein.
EVP & CFO: M.J. Palumbo.

SVP & Treas: T. Helvie.
SVP & General Counsel: G. Briggs.
Dirs: E. H. Budd, G. M. Fisher, C., D. R. Goode, G. Grinstein, P. G. Rosput, J. F. Smith, Jr., J. E. Spero, L. D. Thompson.

Founded: in 1930.
Domicile: Delaware.
Employees: 70,600.
S&P Analyst: Jim Corridore/DC/GG

Recommendation: **BUY** ★★★★ ☆
SELL SELL HOLD BUY BUY

12-Month Target Price: **$46.00**
(as of October 28, 2004)

DLX has an approximate 0.02% weighting in the **S&P 500**

Sector: Industrials
Sub-Industry: Diversified Commercial Services
Peer Group: Document & Communications Services

Summary: This major printer of bank checks also produces computer forms, provides software and services to financial institutions, and is a direct marketer of consumer products.

Quantitative Evaluations

S&P Earnings & Dividend Rank: B+

| D | C | B- | B | B+ | A- | A | A+ |

S&P Fair Value Rank: NR

| 1 | 2 | 3 | 4 | 5 |
| Lowest | | | | Highest |

Fair Value Calc.: NA

S&P Investability Quotient Percentile

97%

DLX scored higher than 97% of all companies for which an S&P Report is available.

Volatility: Low

| Low | Average | High |

Technical Evaluation: Bearish
Since 8/04, the technical indicators for DLX have been Bearish.

Relative Strength Rank: Weak

17
1 Lowest   Highest 99

| Price as of 11/12/04: | **$39.17** | 2004E S&P Core EPS: | **$3.80** |

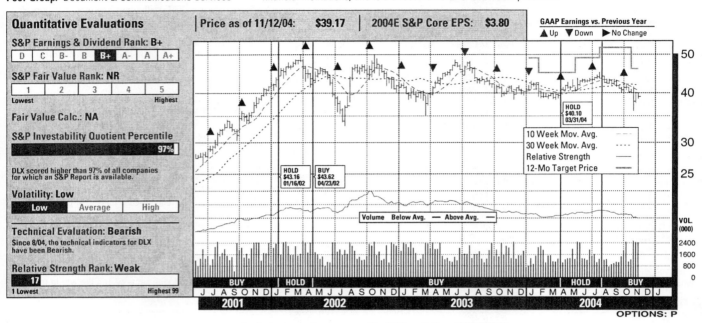

GAAP Earnings vs. Previous Year
▲ Up   ▼ Down   ► No Change

HOLD $40.10 03/31/04

10 Week Mov. Avg.
30 Week Mov. Avg.
Relative Strength
12-Mo Target Price

HOLD $43.16 01/16/02   BUY $43.62 04/23/02

Volume   Below Avg. — Above Avg.

VOL. (000)
2400 1600 800 0

BUY | HOLD | BUY | HOLD | BUY
J J A S O N D J F M A M J J A S O N D J F M A M J J A S O N D J F M A M J J A S O N D J
2001   2002   2003   2004

OPTIONS: P

Analyst commentary prepared by William H. Donald/PMW/GG

Highlights August 12, 2004

- We expect revenues in 2004 and 2005 to climb by over 25%, reflecting the acquisition of New England Business Service (NEBS) in June 2004. We believe the acquisition of NEBS considerably enhances the company's competitive position in the growing small business segment. NEBS serves more than 6 million small business customers with a broad range of products and services. We also see NEBS helping DLX to diversify away from the check printing business, in which unit volume is slowly declining each year due to increased use of electronic payments.

- DLX reported stronger earnings gains in the second quarter than it expected, due to aggressive cost management measures. The company raised its guidance for the third quarter and full year, based on an improved outlook for operating margins. We also see results aided by efforts to drive increased revenue per check order, and expect operating margins of about 25%.

- After nonoperating items, including sharply higher net interest expense due to the $643 million purchase of NEBS and the assumption of $166 million of debt, we expect 2004 net income to rise 2%, to $196.8 million, and EPS to gain 7%, to $3.73. Aided by an estimated $0.35 to $0.45 contribution from NEBS, we project 2005 EPS of $4.40, up 18%.

Investment Rationale/Risk August 12, 2004

- We recently upgraded the shares to accumulate, from hold, reflecting the fact that the stock is at a substantial discount to our 12-month target price. In addition, the shares are trading at 12X our 2004 EPS estimate of $3.73, and at about 10X our 2005 EPS estimate of $4.40, below respective peer averages of 14X and 12X. We believe the recent acquisition of NEBS will eventually boost the organic revenue and earnings growth prospects

Key Stock Statistics

S&P Oper. EPS 2004E	3.85	52-week Range	$45.09-36.02	
P/E on S&P Oper. EPS 2004E	10.2	12 Month P/E	10.4	
S&P Oper. EPS 2005E	4.40	Beta	0.19	
Yield (%)	3.8%	Shareholders	9,901	
Dividend Rate/Share	1.48	Market Cap (B)	$ 2.0	
Shares Outstanding (M)	50.2			

Value of $10,000 invested five years ago: **NA**

Dividend Data Dividends have been paid since 1921

Amount ($)	Date Decl.	Ex-Div. Date	Stock of Record	Payment Date
0.370	Jan. 28	Feb. 12	Feb. 17	Mar. 01 '04
0.370	May. 04	May. 20	May. 24	Jun. 07 '04
0.370	Aug. 10	Aug. 19	Aug. 23	Sep. 07 '04
0.370	Oct. 26	Nov. 18	Nov. 22	Dec. 06 '04

Revenues/Earnings Data Fiscal year ending December 31

Revenues (Million $)

	2004	2003	2002	2001	2000	1999
1Q	308.8	317.2	328.9	316.7	321.6	414.1
2Q	309.4	309.6	328.5	318.6	322.3	407.8
3Q	485.0	314.9	319.8	324.3	316.1	417.1
4Q	—	300.6	306.8	318.7	302.8	412.0
Yr.	—	1,242	1,284	1,278	1,263	1,651

Earnings Per Share ($)

	2004	2003	2002	2001	2000	1999
1Q	0.94	0.83	0.84	0.59	0.58	0.59
2Q	0.91	0.80	0.85	0.63	0.59	0.61
3Q	1.14	1.09	0.83	0.75	0.65	0.65
4Q	E0.86	0.77	0.84	0.73	0.52	0.79
Yr.	E3.85	3.49	3.36	2.69	2.34	2.64

Next earnings report expected: late-January   Source: S&P, Company Reports
EPS Estimates based on S&P Operating Earnings; historical GAAP earnings are as reported.

Deluxe Corporation

Recommendation: **BUY** ★★★★☆   12-Month Target Price: **$46.00** (as of October 28, 2004)

Business Summary August 12, 2004

Deluxe Corp. (formerly Deluxe Check Printers), the largest provider of checks in the U.S., accounts for about 50% of the U.S. check printing market. The company produces business forms, including continuous forms, deposit tickets, invoices, statements, tax forms, and labels. DLX also sells accessories such as checkbook covers, deskbooks, and rubber stamps. In addition, the company offers products and services to financial institution clients and consumers, including protection from check order fraud. Products and services are sold entirely in the U.S.

Payment systems and methods have changed in the U.S. in recent decades, as the banking and other industries introduced alternatives to traditional checks, including ATMs, charge cards, credit cards, debit cards, and electronic payment systems, such as electronic bill presentment and payment. Check sales and prices have also been under pressure from increased competition. In addition, the direct mail segment of the check market has grown as a lower-priced alternative to financial institution checks, and now accounts for about 20% of the personal check market. According to a recently released Federal Reserve Bank Payment Study, checks remain the most preferred method of non-cash payment by consumers. However, the number of checks written has declined slightly each year since 1997. In response to this trend, DLX has implemented measures to reduce production costs, and has taken other cost management measures. It has also instituted a number of strategies to boost revenues and gain market share.

Deluxe Financial Services (DFS) provides check printing, direct marketing, customer database management, and related services. It also provides payment systems protection services, including check authorization, account verification, and collection services. Its major customers are financial institutions and retailers. Small businesses also rely on DFS for short-run computer and business forms. DFS also sells personalized ATM cards and credit and debit cards to financial institutions and retailers, and driver's licenses and other identification cards to government agencies.

Deluxe Electronic Payment Systems provides electronic funds transfer processing and software. It also provides electronic benefit transfer and retail point-of-sale (POS) transaction processing. These programs use ATM and POS terminals to deliver food stamps and welfare assistance in nine states. Medicaid verification services are provided in New York State. Deluxe Direct markets specialty papers and other products to small businesses, tax forms and electronic tax filing services to tax preparers, and direct mail greeting cards, gift wrap and related products to consumers.

In August 2002, DLX announced a five-year strategic plan to boost its debt level to about $700 million. It is using the added cash, augmented by $400 million of annual cash flow, to repurchase up to 12 million common shares (about 12% of the shares outstanding).

Company Financials Fiscal Year ending December 31

Per Share Data ($)

(Year Ended December 31)	2003	2002	2001	2000	1999	1998	1997	1996	1995	1994
Tangible Bk. Val.	NM	NM	NM	0.55	2.89	7.16	6.36	6.54	4.96	5.90
Cash Flow	4.57	4.43	3.76	3.29	3.73	2.87	1.71	2.09	2.40	2.76
Earnings	3.49	3.36	2.69	2.34	2.64	1.80	0.55	0.80	1.15	1.71
S&P Core Earnings	3.51	3.28	2.29	NA	NA	NA	NA	NA	NA	NA
Dividends	1.48	1.48	1.48	1.48	1.48	1.48	1.48	1.48	1.48	1.46
Payout Ratio	42%	44%	55%	63%	56%	82%	NM	185%	129%	85%
Prices - High	48.46	50.13	42.65	29.00	40.50	38.18	37.00	39.75	34.00	38.00
- Low	35.14	33.02	18.85	19.62	24.43	26.06	29.75	27.00	25.75	25.62
P/E Ratio - High	14	15	16	12	15	21	67	50	30	22
- Low	10	10	7	8	9	14	54	34	22	15

Income Statement Analysis (Million $)

	2003	2002	2001	2000	1999	1998	1997	1996	1995	1994
Revs.	1,242	1,284	1,278	1,263	1,651	1,932	1,919	1,896	1,858	1,748
Oper. Inc.	384	403	378	346	386	332	253	306	287	320
Depr.	60.1	58.2	74.0	68.6	83.9	85.8	97.0	107	103	86.4
Int. Exp.	19.2	5.08	5.58	10.8	8.51	8.27	8.80	10.6	13.1	11.3
Pretax Inc.	299	341	298	273	325	247	115	119	169	241
Eff. Tax Rate	35.7%	37.1%	37.5%	38.0%	37.5%	41.0%	61.2%	44.9%	44.2%	41.5%
Net Inc.	192	214	186	169	203	145	44.7	65.5	94.4	141
S&P Core Earnings	193	208	159	NA	NA	NA	NA	NA	NA	NA

Balance Sheet & Other Fin. Data (Million $)

	2003	2002	2001	2000	1999	1998	1997	1996	1995	1994
Cash	2.97	125	9.57	88.2	199	310	179	143	19.9	78.0
Curr. Assets	78.9	200	84.0	209	419	619	513	450	381	421
Total Assets	563	669	538	649	993	1,203	1,148	1,176	1,295	1,256
Curr. Liab.	388	215	367	305	405	451	382	341	369	290
LT Debt	381	307	10.1	10.2	116	106	110	109	111	111
Common Equity	-298	64.3	78.7	263	417	609	610	713	780	814
Total Cap.	125	425	134	334	579	751	726	835	926	966
Cap. Exp.	22.0	40.7	28.8	48.5	115	121	110	92.0	125	126
Cash Flow	253	272	260	238	287	231	142	172	198	227
Curr. Ratio	0.2	0.9	0.2	0.7	1.0	1.4	1.3	1.3	1.0	1.4
% LT Debt of Cap.	304.0	72.1	7.5	3.1	19.9	14.2	15.2	13.1	12.0	11.5
% Net Inc.of Revs.	15.5	16.7	14.5	13.4	12.3	7.5	2.3	3.5	5.1	8.1
% Ret. on Assets	31.2	35.5	31.1	21.8	18.8	12.4	3.8	9.3	7.4	11.2
% Ret. on Equity	NM	299.8	108.9	49.8	39.7	23.9	6.8	8.8	11.8	17.5

Data as orig reptd.; bef. results of disc opers/spec. items. Per share data adj. for stk. divs. Bold denotes basic EPS (FASB 128)-prior periods restated. E-Estimated. NA-Not Available. NM-Not Meaningful. NR-Not Ranked. UR-Under Review.

Office: 3680 Victoria Street North, Shoreview, MN 55126-2966.
Telephone: 651-483-7111.
Website: http://www.deluxe.com
Chrmn & CEO: L.J. Mosner.
Pres & COO: R.E. Eilers.
SVP & CFO: D.S. Treff.

SVP, Secy & General Counsel: A.C. Scarfone.
VP & Investor Contact: S. Alexander 612-483-7355.
Dirs: R. E. Eilers, T. M. Glenn, B. B. Grogan, C. A. Haggerty, I. Harris, Jr., C. E. Mayberry-McKissack, L. J. Mosner, S. Nachtsheim, M. O'Dwyer, M. R. Redgrave, R. C. Salipante.

Founded: in 1915.
Domicile: Minnesota.
Employees: 5,805.
S&P Analyst: William H. Donald/PMW/GG

Devon Energy

Recommendation: **BUY** ★ ★ ★ ★ ★
SELL SELL HOLD BUY BUY

12-Month Target Price: $44.00
(as of October 12, 2004)

DVN has an approximate 0.17% weighting in the **S&P 500**

Sector: Energy
Sub-Industry: Oil & Gas Exploration & Production
Peer Group: Exploration & Production - Large

Summary: This independent oil and gas exploration and production company has grown through its acquisitions of Ocean Energy, Mitchell Energy, and Anderson Exploration.

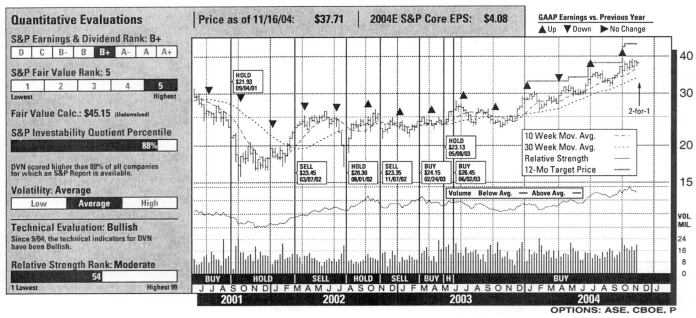

Quantitative Evaluations	Price as of 11/16/04: $37.71	2004E S&P Core EPS: $4.08

S&P Earnings & Dividend Rank: B+
D | C | B- | B | **B+** | A- | A | A+

S&P Fair Value Rank: 5
1 | 2 | 3 | 4 | **5**
Lowest — Highest

Fair Value Calc.: $45.15 (Undervalued)

S&P Investability Quotient Percentile
88%

DVN scored higher than 88% of all companies for which an S&P Report is available.

Volatility: Average
Low | **Average** | High

Technical Evaluation: Bullish
Since 9/04, the technical indicators for DVN have been Bullish.

Relative Strength Rank: Moderate
54
1 Lowest — Highest 99

GAAP Earnings vs. Previous Year
▲ Up ▼ Down ▶ No Change

Analyst commentary prepared by Charles LaPorta, CFA /MF/GG

Highlights October 11, 2004

- Second quarter EPS was $0.17 above our $1.85 estimate, on higher international oil and Canadian gas production. Given the rampup of production at several new projects, plus a full-year of volume from the Ocean properties, we expect double-digit production growth for 2004. We are modeling 5% production growth in 2005.

- On a per unit basis, lease operating expenses increased 2% in the second quarter, and transportation expense declined 5%; production taxes showed a 26% increase. Since production taxes are based on a percentage of revenues, the 18% increase in DVN's realized hydrocarbon price drove the increase in production costs. We believe DVN's first half performance supports our projection of unit operating costs increasing at a slower rate than peers, due to expected cost savings resulting from the Ocean merger.

- Based on our respective 2004 and 2005 projections for WTI crude oil and Henry Hub natural gas prices, our EBITDAX (earnings before interest, taxes, depreciation, amortization, and exploration expense) expectations are $6.0 billion and $5.9 billion. For 2004, our S&P Core EPS estimate is only 1.1% lower than our operating forecast, which suggests to us good earnings quality.

Investment Rationale/Risk October 11, 2004

- We believe DVN's recently announced divestiture of non-core acreage will help drive its relatively high finding and development costs down to more reasonable levels; significant high-impact exploration programs in the deepwater Gulf of Mexico and international geographies should meaningfully add to production in the 2006-08 timeframe. Meanwhile, the substantial excess cash generated from operations as well as divestiture proceeds will be used to accelerate balance sheet improvements and repurchase 10% of shares outstanding over the next 18 months.

- Risks to our recommendation and target price include events that would cause substantial and sustained declines in oil and gas prices; a persistent inability of the company to replace its reserves; and acts of terrorism on DVN's production facilities.

- Both on an earnings and cash flow basis, DVN is currently among the least expensive stocks in our universe. The company has stated a strategy to address its weaknesses, and we believe it has the financial resources to implement them. Our 12-month target price of $85 is based on 10.4X earnings and 4.3X times discretionary cash flow, both discounts to peers due to DVN's higher finding and discovery costs and our expectation of flat production growth for 2004 and 2005.

Key Stock Statistics

S&P Core EPS 2005E	4.06	52-week Range	$39.10-23.96
S&P Oper. EPS 2004E	4.13	12 Month P/E	9.0
P/E on S&P Oper. EPS 2004E	9.2	Beta	0.61
S&P Oper. EPS 2005E	4.10	Shareholders	30,431
Yield (%)	0.5%	Market Cap (B)	$ 18.3
Dividend Rate/Share	0.20	Shares Outstanding (M)	486.0

Value of $10,000 invested five years ago: **$ 19,595**

Dividend Data Dividends have been paid since 1993

Amount ($)	Date Decl.	Ex-Div. Date	Stock of Record	Payment Date
0.100	Feb. 26	Mar. 11	Mar. 15	Mar. 31 '04
0.100	Jun. 02	Jun. 14	Jun. 15	Jun. 30 '04
0.100	Sep. 01	Sep. 13	Sep. 15	Sep. 30 '04
2-for-1 Stk.	Sep. 27	Nov. 16	Oct. 29	Nov. 15 '04

Revenues/Earnings Data Fiscal year ending December 31

Revenues (Million $)

	2004	2003	2002	2001	2000	1999
1Q	2,238	1,671	903.0	1,024	560.4	87.27
2Q	2,219	1,813	1,149	725.2	648.5	104.3
3Q	2,267	1,948	1,031	586.7	725.1	219.8
4Q	—	1,921	1,233	740.0	850.1	323.1
Yr.	—	7,352	4,316	3,075	2,784	734.5

Earnings Per Share ($)

	2004	2003	2002	2001	2000	1999
1Q	1.00	1.29	0.20	1.30	0.40	0.06
2Q	1.01	0.81	-0.65	0.51	0.59	0.17
3Q	1.04	0.86	0.35	0.32	0.61	0.19
4Q	E1.08	1.13	0.25	-2.06	1.14	0.26
Yr.	E4.13	4.00	0.16	0.17	2.75	0.73

Next earnings report expected: early-February Source: S&P, Company Reports
EPS Estimates based on S&P Operating Earnings; historical GAAP earnings are as reported.

STANDARD &POOR'S

Devon Energy Corporation

Stock Report
November 16, 2004
NYSE Symbol: **DVN**

Recommendation: **BUY** ★★★★★   12-Month Target Price: **$44.00** (as of October 12, 2004)

Business Summary October 11, 2004

Following the April 2003 merger of Devon Energy Corp. with Ocean Energy Inc. (OEI), DVN shareholders held a 68% equity interest in the new company. The transaction made DVN the largest U.S.-based independent producer of oil and natural gas, with barrel of oil equivalent (BOE) proved reserves of about 2.1 billion (58% natural gas, 42% liquids; 85% North America). The combined company holds over 27 million net undeveloped acres worldwide, including the largest lease position of any independent in the deepwater Gulf of Mexico (GOM). The Ocean merger boosted expenses in most categories. The company is focusing on increasing its upstream reserves and production, and on controlling costs.

During the past four years, the company completed four major mergers: Ocean Energy, Mitchell Energy & Development Corp., Anderson Exploration Ltd., and Santa Fe Snyder. The January 2002 acquisition of Mitchell Energy acquisition added about 404 million BOE (MMBOE) to proved reserves. DVN issued about 30 million common shares and paid $1.6 billion in cash to Mitchell shareholders. In October 2001, the company acquired Anderson Exploration Ltd., for about $3.5 billion in cash, adding about 534 MMBOE to proved reserves. In August 2000, DVN merged with Santa Fe Snyder Corp., adding about 386 MMBOE to proved reserves.

DVN is an independent energy company, engaged primarily in oil and natural gas exploration, development, production, acquisition of producing properties, transportation of oil, natural gas, and natural gas liquids (NGLs), and processing of natural gas. The company operates oil and gas properties in the U.S., Canada, and internationally. U.S. operations focus on the Permian Basin, the Mid-Continent, the

Rocky Mountains, and onshore and offshore Gulf of Mexico. Canadian operations focus on the Western Canadian Sedimentary Basin in Alberta and British Columbia. Operations outside North America currently include Azerbaijan, Brazil, China, Egypt, and West Africa (including Equatorial Guinea).

Including 556 million BOE of proved reserves that were acquired (predominately through its merger with Ocean Energy), the company replaced 321% of its production in 2003. This resulted in unit finding and development costs (all-in cost of $10.62 per BOE, drill-bit cost of $15 per BOE) that were higher than for DVN alone, and higher than the industry average. Proved BOE reserves totaled 2,089 MMBOE (58% natural gas, 32% oil, 10% NGL) at December 31, 2003, up from 1,609 MMBOE (60%, 28%, 12%) a year earlier. The present value of pre-tax future net revenues discounted at 10% per annum assuming essentially constant prices of such reserves was $22.7 billion in 2003; after taxes, the present value was $15.9 billion. Production grew 21% in 2003, to 228 MMBOE (63% natural gas, 27% oil, and 10% NGLs), versus 188 MMBOE (68% natural gas, 22% oil, and 10% NGLs) in 2002. Average price realizations in 2003 were $25.63 per bbl. of oil, $4.51 per Mcf of natural gas, and $18.65 per bbl. of NGL, versus $21.71 per bbl., $2.80 per Mcf, and $14.05 per bbl. in 2002, respectively. Total production and operating expenses were $5.63 per BOE in 2003, versus $4.71 in 2002.

The Marketing and Midstream division operates pipelines, and markets natural gas, oil and NGLs. The division also includes the construction and operation of pipelines, storage and treating facilities, and gas processing plants.

Company Financials Fiscal Year ending December 31

Per Share Data ($)

(Year Ended December 31)	2003	2002	2001	2000	1999	1998	1997	1996	1995	1994
Tangible Bk. Val.	11.50	3.20	4.32	11.03	16.03	5.40	8.41	7.35	4.96	4.68
Cash Flow	8.10	4.04	3.54	5.37	2.65	0.66	2.49	1.77	1.19	1.10
Earnings	4.00	0.16	0.17	2.75	0.73	-0.63	1.08	0.79	0.33	0.32
S&P Core Earnings	3.99	0.47	0.09	NA	NA	NA	NA	NA	NA	NA
Dividends	0.10	0.10	0.10	0.10	0.10	0.10	0.10	0.07	0.06	0.06
Payout Ratio	3%	63%	59%	4%	14%	NM	9%	9%	18%	19%
Prices - High	29.40	26.55	33.37	32.37	22.46	20.56	24.56	18.50	13.00	13.25
- Low	21.22	16.93	15.27	15.68	10.06	13.06	13.68	9.93	8.37	8.00
P/E Ratio - High	7	NM	NM	12	31	NM	23	24	39	41
- Low	5	NM	NM	6	14	NM	13	13	25	25

Income Statement Analysis (Million $)

	2003	2002	2001	2000	1999	1998	1997	1996	1995	1994
Revs.	7,352	4,316	3,075	2,784	734	388	306	163	112	101
Oper. Inc.	4,589	2,403	2,350	2,094	491	237	209	111	69.9	60.5
Depr. Depl. & Amort.	1,793	1,211	876	693	254	124	85.3	43.4	38.1	33.7
Int. Exp.	504	533	220	154	66.9	22.6	0.27	5.28	7.05	5.44
Pretax Inc.	2,245	-134	84.0	1,142	160	-75.8	121	59.3	25.6	21.4
Eff. Tax Rate	22.9%	NM	35.7%	36.0%	40.8%	NM	38.0%	41.4%	43.4%	35.6%
Net Inc.	1,731	59.0	54.0	730	94.6	-60.3	75.3	34.8	14.5	13.7
S&P Core Earnings	1,715	147	22.9	NA	NA	NA	NA	NA	NA	NA

Balance Sheet & Other Fin. Data (Million $)

	2003	2002	2001	2000	1999	1998	1997	1996	1995	1994
Cash	1,273	292	193	228	167	19.2	42.1	9.40	8.90	8.30
Curr. Assets	2,364	1,064	1,081	934	417	111	93.2	43.4	24.9	25.3
Total Assets	27,162	16,225	13,184	6,860	4,623	1,226	846	746	422	351
Curr. Liab.	2,071	1,042	919	629	227	80.7	30.8	23.6	15.6	17.0
LT Debt	8,635	7,562	6,589	2,049	1,787	555	Nil	8.00	143	98.0
Common Equity	11,055	4,652	3,258	3,276	2,024	523	544	472	219	206
Total Cap.	24,061	14,842	11,990	5,953	4,204	1,111	795	711	396	332
Cap. Exp.	2,587	3,426	5,326	1,280	315	376	130	99	118	36.0
Cash Flow	3,514	1,260	920	1,414	345	63.6	161	78.2	52.6	47.5
Curr. Ratio	1.1	1.0	1.2	1.5	1.8	1.4	3.0	1.8	1.6	1.5
% LT Debt of Cap.	35.9	51.0	55.0	34.4	42.5	49.9	Nil	1.2	36.1	29.5
% Ret. on Assets	8.0	NM	0.5	11.3	3.2	NM	9.5	6.0	3.8	4.2
% Ret. on Equity	21.9	NM	1.3	24.9	7.1	NM	14.8	10.1	6.8	7.1

Data as orig reptd.; bef. results of disc opers/spec. items. Per share data adj. for stk. divs.; EPS diluted. E-Estimated. NA-Not Available. NM-Not Meaningful. NR-Not Ranked. UR-Under Review.

Office: 20 North Broadway, Oklahoma City, OK 73102-8260.
Telephone: 405-235-3611.
Website: http://www.devonenergy.com
Chrmn & CEO: J.L. Nichols.
Pres: J. Richels.
SVP & CFO: B.J. Jennings.

SVP & General Counsel: D.R. Ligon.
Secy: J.A. Dobbs.
Investor Contact: Z. Hager 405-552-4526.
Dirs: M. Carroll, T. F. Ferguson, P. J. Fluor, D. M. Gavrin, M. E. Gellert, J. A. Hill, R. L. Howard, W. J. Johnson, M. M. Kanovsky, J. T. Mitchell, C. F. Mitchell, R. A. Mosbacher, Jr., J. L. Nichols, J. W. Nichols.

Founded: in 1988.
Domicile: Delaware.
Employees: 3,924.
S&P Analyst: Charles LaPorta, CFA /MF/GG

Recommendation: **SELL** ★ ☆ ☆ ☆ **12-Month Target Price: $18.00**
SELL SELL HOLD BUY BUY
(as of September 03, 2004)

DDS has an approximate 0.02% weighting in the **S&P 500**

Sector: Consumer Discretionary
Sub-Industry: Department Stores
Peer Group: Department Store Cos. - Larger

Summary: Dillard's operates about 330 department stores, located primarily in the South and the Midwest.

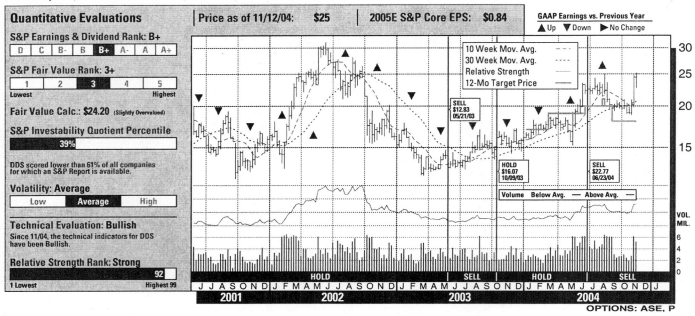

Quantitative Evaluations

S&P Earnings & Dividend Rank: B+

| D | C | B- | B | B+ | A- | A | A+ |

S&P Fair Value Rank: 3+

| 1 | 2 | 3 | 4 | 5 |
Lowest ——— Highest

Fair Value Calc.: $24.20 (Slightly Overvalued)

S&P Investability Quotient Percentile
39%

DDS scored lower than 61% of all companies for which an S&P Report is available.

Volatility: Average

| Low | Average | High |

Technical Evaluation: Bullish
Since 11/04, the technical indicators for DDS have been Bullish.

Relative Strength Rank: Strong
92
1 Lowest ——— Highest 99

Price as of 11/12/04: $25 | **2005E S&P Core EPS:** $0.84

GAAP Earnings vs. Previous Year
▲ Up ▼ Down ► No Change

Chart legend: 10 Week Mov. Avg. / 30 Week Mov. Avg. / Relative Strength / 12-Mo Target Price

SELL $12.83 05/21/03
HOLD $16.07 10/09/03
SELL $22.77 06/23/04

Volume Below Avg. — Above Avg.

HOLD | SELL | HOLD | SELL

2001 | 2002 | 2003 | 2004
J J A S O N D | J F M A M J J A S O N D | J F M A M J J A S O N D | J F M A M J J A S O N D | J

OPTIONS: ASE, P

Analyst commentary prepared by Jason N. Asaeda/PMW/JWP

Highlights November 04, 2004

- We see FY 05 (Jan.) revenues of $7.7 billion, including $7.5 billion of net sales and $240 million of interest and service charges, net of writeoffs, related to DDS's proprietary credit card sales. On November 1, 2004, the company sold its credit card subsidiary, Dillard National Bank, to GE Consumer Finance, for about $1.1 billion and payments from a credit marketing and servicing alliance. DDS anticipates that income over the initial 10-year alliance could approximate earnings previously derived from Dillard National Bank.

- Balancing our view of better assortments against increased competition from department store peers and specialty retailers, we see same-store sales down in the low single digits in FY 05. DDS plans to open eight new stores, including four replacement stores, for a total of about 1.1 million sq. ft. We look for wider EBIT (earnings before interest and taxes) margins, aided by improved levels of markups and cost controls, partly offset by lack of expense leverage on weak sales. We expect lower interest and debt expense, due to the recent redemption of preferred securities and notes, and an improvement in credit granting operations.

- Factoring in share buybacks, we estimate FY 05 operating EPS of $0.90. Our FY 05 S&P Core EPS forecast is $0.84; the difference from our operating projection mainly reflects one-time charges and estimated option expense.

Key Stock Statistics

S&P Core EPS 2006E	1.03	52-week Range	$25.20-14.39
S&P Oper. EPS 2005E	0.90	12 Month P/E	33.3
P/E on S&P Oper. EPS 2005E	27.8	Beta	0.36
S&P Oper. EPS 2006E	1.05	Shareholders	4,827
Yield (%)	0.6%	Market Cap (B)	$ 2.0
Dividend Rate/Share	0.16	Shares Outstanding (M)	84.0

Value of $10,000 invested five years ago: **$ 13,759**

Dividend Data Dividends have been paid since 1969

Amount ($)	Date Decl.	Ex-Div. Date	Stock of Record	Payment Date
0.040	Dec. 04	Dec. 29	Dec. 31	Feb. 02 '04
0.040	Mar. 15	Mar. 29	Mar. 31	May. 03 '04
0.040	May. 25	Jun. 28	Jun. 30	Aug. 02 '04
0.040	Sep. 07	Sep. 28	Sep. 30	Nov. 01 '04

Investment Rationale/Risk November 04, 2004

- We would avoid the stock, based mainly on valuation considerations. In our view, the sale of DDS's credit card operations should boost shareholder value, as we expect proceeds to be used for debt reduction and share buybacks. Combined with marketing and service alliance payments from GE Consumer Finance, the company expects the transaction to be accretive to FY 06 earnings. We view favorably DDS's focused full-price sales effort on differentiated and exclusive brand assortments, and the expansion of "better" categories. However, we see challenges remaining for this struggling retailer, and what we see as a record of disappointing sales and earnings leads us to question whether margin gains can be sustained and profitability can be restored over the longer term.

- Risks to our recommendation and target price include better than expected sales growth and profit margin expansion due to DDS's turnaround efforts.

- Balancing a potential payoff of turnaround efforts with what we view as DDS's weak operating history, we think the stock is overvalued at 22X our FY 05 operating EPS estimate, above the levels of more profitable peers. Our 12-month target price of $18 blends a forward P/E multiple of 19X applied to our FY 06 EPS estimate of $1.05, a price to estimated FY 06 sales per share ratio of 0.2X, and 6.2X enterprise value to estimated FY 05 EBITDA, the five-year historical averages.

Revenues/Earnings Data Fiscal year ending January 31

Revenues (Million $)

	2005	2004	2003	2002	2001	2000
1Q	1,912	1,814	1,911	1,920	2,146	2,192
2Q	1,730	1,721	1,818	1,828	1,902	1,897
3Q	—	1,764	1,794	1,872	2,047	2,132
4Q	—	2,299	2,388	2,534	2,472	2,659
Yr.	—	7,599	7,911	8,155	8,567	8,921

Earnings Per Share ($)

	2005	2004	2003	2002	2001	2000
1Q	0.64	0.29	0.68	0.30	0.48	0.63
2Q	-0.31	-0.60	0.15	-0.24	0.10	0.34
3Q	E-0.22	-0.19	-0.07	-0.48	-0.10	0.33
4Q	E0.76	0.61	0.85	1.20	0.58	0.26
Yr.	E0.90	0.11	1.60	0.35	1.06	1.55

Next earnings report expected: late-November Source: S&P, Company Reports
EPS Estimates based on S&P Operating Earnings; historical GAAP earnings are as reported.

STANDARD &POOR'S

Dillard's, Inc.

Recommendation: **SELL**  12-Month Target Price: **$18.00** (as of September 03, 2004)

Business Summary November 04, 2004

Dillard's, an outgrowth of a department store originally founded in 1938 by William Dillard, capped more than a decade of expansion through acquisitions with the purchase of Mercantile Stores Company, Inc., in 1998. At November 2, 2004, the company operated 329 traditional department stores in 29 states. The heaviest concentrations of stores were in the Southwest, the Southeast and the Midwest.

In light of a highly competitive retail environment, DDS has adopted a number of strategies intended to improve its profitability and balance sheet. The company has streamlined its assortment of merchandise in stores, and is replacing underperforming national brands with high margin, private label products. It currently has a number of private label products in home and children's, men's and women's wear categories. Private brand merchandise accounted for 20.9% of sales in FY 04 (Jan.), up from 18.2% in FY 03. Gross margins on exclusive brand merchandise exceeded gross margins on national brand merchandise in FY 04, with particular strength in the juniors', shoes, and home areas.

DDS is continuing a strategy of entering or further penetrating markets in which it believes it can become the dominant conventional department store operator. It has focused on stores with low occupancy costs and that present an opportunity to generate higher profits on lower volumes. The company opened five new stores, including one replacement store in FY 04, and closed 10 locations. Total capital spending was $227 million. For FY 05, capital spending was expected to approximate $240 million, including about eight new stores. Since announcing a policy in late 2000 of closing underperforming stores as conditions permitted, DDS has closed 36 locations.

The company is continuing its efforts to improve and expand its Web site, www.dillards.com, not only to offer customers the convenience of online shopping but also to create excitement about its stores and drive store traffic. In FY 04, DDS launched brand-specific Web sites to promote recognition and online shopping of its exclusive Antonio Melani, Gianni Bini, and Michelle D merchandise lines.

DDS's assets include investments in joint ventures, which consist of malls and a general contracting company that constructs company stores and other commercial buildings. The malls are located in Crestview Hills, KY, Toledo, OH, and Denver, CO, with two currently under construction, in Bonita Springs, FL, and Yuma, AZ. In FY 04, the company recorded earnings from joint ventures of $8.1 million, and a $15.6 million pretax gain from the sale of its interest in Sunrise Mall and its associated center in Brownsville, TX, for $80.7 million.

In November 2004, DDS sold its private-label credit card subsidiary, Dillard National Bank, to GE Consumer Finance, for about $1.1 billion, including the assumption of $400 million of securitization liabilities, the purchase of owned accounts receivable, and an undisclosed premium. As part of the transaction, the two companies entered into a marketing and servicing alliance with an initial term of 10 years. DDS planned to use net proceeds for debt reduction, share buybacks and general corporate purposes.

In May 2000, directors authorized the repurchase of up to $200 million of common stock. The company purchased about 1.5 million shares in FY 04, for $18.9 million. About $56 million remained available at January 31, 2004.

Company Financials Fiscal Year ending January 31

Per Share Data ($)

(Year Ended January 31)	2004	2003	2002	2001	2000	1999	1998	1997	1996	1995
Tangible Bk. Val.	26.35	26.25	25.02	25.06	22.68	20.39	25.76	23.83	21.93	20.55
Cash Flow	3.67	5.21	4.49	4.40	4.31	3.47	4.09	3.80	3.18	3.91
Earnings	0.11	1.60	0.35	1.06	1.55	1.26	2.31	2.09	1.48	2.23
S&P Core Earnings	-0.03	1.01	0.71	0.92	NA	NA	NA	NA	NA	NA
Dividends	0.16	0.16	0.16	0.16	0.16	0.16	0.16	0.14	0.12	0.12
Payout Ratio	145%	10%	46%	15%	10%	13%	7%	7%	8%	5%

Cal. Yrs.	2003	2002	2001	2000	1999	1998	1997	1996	1995	1994
Prices - High	17.80	31.20	22.50	20.81	37.43	44.50	44.75	41.75	33.87	37.62
- Low	12.32	12.94	11.43	9.43	17.75	26.50	28.00	27.12	24.00	25.50
P/E Ratio - High	NM	20	64	20	24	35	19	20	23	17
- Low	NM	8	33	9	11	21	12	13	16	11

Income Statement Analysis (Million $)

	2004	2003	2002	2001	2000	1999	1998	1997	1996	1995
Revs.	7,663	7,911	8,155	8,567	8,677	7,797	6,632	6,228	6,097	5,729
Oper. Inc.	273	429	386	469	640	441	554	511	529	721
Depr.	297	306	314	303	293	240	200	194	192	190
Int. Exp.	181	183	190	224	237	197	129	121	120	124
Pretax Inc.	16.0	211	112	141	284	219	410	380	270	406
Eff. Tax Rate	41.6%	35.4%	41.0%	31.2%	42.3%	38.4%	37.1%	37.1%	37.8%	38.0%
Net Inc.	9.34	136	65.8	97.0	164	135	258	239	167	252
S&P Core Earnings	-2.90	85.8	60.1	83.8	NA	NA	NA	NA	NA	NA

Balance Sheet & Other Fin. Data (Million $)

	2004	2003	2002	2001	2000	1999	1998	1997	1996	1995
Cash	161	142	153	194	199	72.0	42.0	64.0	58.4	51.1
Curr. Assets	3,024	3,130	2,815	2,843	3,424	3,438	2,998	2,761	2,658	2,525
Total Assets	6,411	6,676	7,075	7,199	7,918	8,178	5,592	5,060	4,779	4,578
Curr. Liab.	1,336	886	928	877	811	1,094	1,099	895	870	759
LT Debt	2,073	2,743	2,677	2,906	3,452	3,562	1,378	1,187	1,179	1,201
Common Equity	2,237	2,264	2,668	2,630	2,832	2,840	2,807	2,716	2,478	2,323
Total Cap.	4,927	5,007	5,989	6,175	6,986	7,084	4,493	4,165	3,909	3,819
Cap. Exp.	227	233	271	226	247	248	509	350	347	253
Cash Flow	307	442	379	400	457	375	458	433	359	442
Curr. Ratio	2.3	3.5	3.0	3.2	4.2	3.1	2.7	3.1	3.1	3.3
% LT Debt of Cap.	42.1	54.8	44.7	47.1	49.4	50.3	30.6	28.5	30.2	31.4
% Net Inc.of Revs.	0.1	1.7	0.8	1.1	1.9	1.7	3.9	3.8	2.8	4.4
% Ret. on Assets	0.1	2.0	0.9	1.3	2.0	2.0	4.8	4.9	3.6	5.6
% Ret. on Equity	0.4	5.5	2.5	3.6	5.8	4.8	9.3	9.2	7.0	11.4

Data as orig. reptd.; bef. results of disc. opers. and/or spec. items. Per share data adj. for stk. divs.; EPS diluted. E-Estimated. NA-Not Available. NM-Not Meaningful. NR-Not Ranked.

Office: 1600 Cantrell Rd, Little Rock, AR 72201-1145.
Telephone: 501-376-5200.
Website: http://www.dillards.com
Chrmn & CEO: W. Dillard II.
Pres: A. Dillard.

SVP, CFO & Investor Contact: J.I. Freeman .
Investor Contact: J.J. Bull 501-376-5965.
Dirs: R. C. Connor, D. Corbusier, W. D. Davis, A. Dillard, M. J. Dillard, W. Dillard II, J. I. Freeman, J. P. Hammerschmidt, B. L. Martin, W. A. Stephens, W. H. Sutton, J. C. Watts, Jr.

Founded: in 1938.
Domicile: Delaware.
Employees: 53,598.
S&P Analyst: Jason N. Asaeda/PMW/JWP

The **McGraw·Hill** Companies

Disney (Walt)

Recommendation: **HOLD** ★ ★ ★ ★ ★
SELL SELL HOLD BUY BUY

12-Month Target Price: **$26.00**
(as of August 11, 2004)

DIS has an approximate 0.50% weighting in the **S&P 500**

Sector: Consumer Discretionary
Sub-Industry: Movies & Entertainment
Peer Group: Entertainment Content Providers - Larger

Summary: The operations of this major filmed entertainment and theme park company include the ABC television network.

Quantitative Evaluations

S&P Earnings & Dividend Rank: B

| D | C | B- | **B** | B+ | A- | A | A+ |

S&P Fair Value Rank: 3

| 1 | 2 | **3** | 4 | 5 |
| Lowest | | | | Highest |

Fair Value Calc.: $26.00 (Slightly Overvalued)

S&P Investability Quotient Percentile

76%

DIS scored higher than 76% of all companies for which an S&P Report is available.

Volatility: Average

| Low | **Average** | High |

Technical Evaluation: Bullish
Since 10/04, the technical indicators for DIS have been Bullish.

Relative Strength Rank: Strong

73

1 Lowest   Highest 99

Price as of 11/12/04: $26.80   **2004E S&P Core EPS:** $0.97

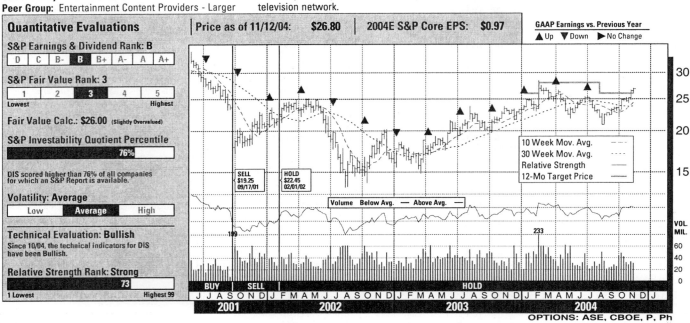

GAAP Earnings vs. Previous Year
▲ Up   ▼ Down   ► No Change

- SELL $19.25 09/17/01
- HOLD $22.45 02/01/02
- Volume Below Avg. — Above Avg.
- 10 Week Mov. Avg.
- 30 Week Mov. Avg.
- Relative Strength
- 12-Mo Target Price

BUY | SELL | HOLD
J J A S O N D J F M A M J J A S O N D J F M A M J J A S O N D J F M A M J J A S O N D J
2001   2002   2003   2004

VOL. MIL.
60 40 20 0
30 25 20 15

OPTIONS: ASE, CBOE, P, Ph

Analyst commentary prepared by Tuna N. Amobi, CFA, CPA /PMW/JWP

Highlights August 20, 2004

- Reflecting a recent consolidation of variable interest entities and prior year restatement, we see consolidated revenue growth in the high teens for FY 04 (Sep.) and low double digits for FY 05. Primary growth drivers will likely include cable networks advertising and affiliate revenues (chiefly the ESPN networks, but with greater contributions from ABC Family), and continued recovery in theme park attendances, hotel occupancies and guest spending at the Walt Disney World and Disneyland resorts. Other expected catalysts include continued growth in home video entertainment fueled by DVD sales, incremental political advertising at the owned and operated TV stations, and increased licensing revenues from direct-to-retail alliances (as Disney Stores undergo restructuring).

- We see margins benefiting from greater contributions from high-margin advertising and merchandise licensing businesses. However, results will likely reflect higher employee-related costs at theme parks, and could be hurt by a high level of film writeoffs. We are encouraged that prime-time programming costs at the ABC broadcast network have recently started to moderate. From $3.6 billion in FY 03, we see consolidated EBITDA growing to $5.4 billion in FY 04 and $6.1 billion in FY 05.

- With a likely decline in interest expenses, we forecast operating EPS of $1.17 for FY 04 (S&P Core Earnings of $1.04, after estimated stock option expense), and $1.34 in FY 05 ($1.20).

Key Stock Statistics

S&P Core EPS 2005E	1.12	52-week Range	$28.41-20.88
S&P Oper. EPS 2004E	1.10	12 Month P/E	24.6
P/E on S&P Oper. EPS 2004E	24.4	Beta	1.11
S&P Oper. EPS 2005E	1.26	Shareholders	1,026,000
Yield (%)	0.8%	Market Cap (B)	$ 55.1
Dividend Rate/Share	0.21	Shares Outstanding (M)	2054.6

Value of $10,000 invested five years ago: **$ 11,387**

Dividend Data Dividends have been paid since 1957

Amount ($)	Date Decl.	Ex-Div. Date	Stock of Record	Payment Date
0.210	Dec. 03	Dec. 10	Dec. 12	Jan. 06 '04

Investment Rationale/Risk August 20, 2004

- We would hold the shares, which have given back most of the gains made in the wake of an aborted merger bid in February 2004 from Comcast (CMCSA: $28). Our fundamental outlook is based on recent signs of improvement in travel and tourism, the potential draw of new park attractions (Mission:SPACE and Mickey's PhilharMagic) and hotels (Disney's Pop Century Resort), expected cross-platform benefits from new franchises, and continued international expansion of the Disney Channel. We also think the balance sheet is strong, with likely further improvement in leverage ratios helping to solidify an investment grade debt rating. With declining capital spending, we project free cash flow of about $2.4 billion for FY 04 and $2.9 billion for FY 05, which could be used in part for a dividend increase or stock buyback.

- Risks to our recommendation and target price include pending corporate governance issues, geopolitical anxieties, ABC ratings declines, film volatility, ESPN regulatory exposure and margin compression, uncertainties with Euro Disney debt restructuring, piracy threats, Disney Stores strategic challenges, and macroeconomic factors.

- Our 12-month target price of $26 is based on our DCF analysis. At about 19X projected 2005 free cash flow, or 12X enterprise value to 2005 EBITDA, we view the stock as fairly valued relative to the media and entertainment group.

Revenues/Earnings Data Fiscal year ending September 30

Revenues (Million $)

	2004	2003	2002	2001	2000	1999
1Q	8,549	7,170	7,016	7,433	6,932	6,589
2Q	7,189	6,500	5,856	6,049	6,303	5,510
3Q	7,471	6,377	5,795	5,975	6,051	5,522
4Q	—	7,014	6,662	5,812	6,116	5,781
Yr.	—	27,061	25,329	25,269	25,402	23,402

Earnings Per Share ($)

	2004	2003	2002	2001	2000	1999
1Q	0.33	0.06	0.21	0.16	0.17	0.30
2Q	0.26	0.15	0.13	-0.26	0.08	0.11
3Q	0.29	0.24	0.18	0.19	0.21	0.18
4Q	E0.20	0.20	0.09	0.03	0.11	0.04
Yr.	E1.10	0.65	0.60	0.11	0.57	0.62

Next earnings report expected: late-November Source: S&P, Company Reports
EPS Estimates based on S&P Operating Earnings; historical GAAP earnings are as reported.

The Walt Disney Company

Recommendation: **HOLD** ★ ★ ★ ☆ ☆   12-Month Target Price: **$26.00** (as of August 11, 2004)

Business Summary August 20, 2004

The Walt Disney Co., with operations ranging from theme parks and retail stores to movies and broadcasting, aims to combine imaginative material with masterful marketing, as it delivers popular culture worldwide. In October 2001, DIS acquired Fox Family Worldwide, Inc., which had assets that included the Fox Family Channel in the U.S. and interests in some international channels, for $2.9 billion in cash, plus the assumption of $2.3 billion in debt.

The company's filmed entertainment operations include production and distribution of theatrical motion pictures, television shows and home videos. DIS also owns and operates 10 television stations, the ABC TV network, and various radio stations. In cable television, the company owns and operates The Disney Channel, has 80% ownership of various ESPN cable channels, and has an equity interest of 50% or less in various cable networks, including the Lifetime cable channel (50%), the E! Entertainment cable channel (39.6%), and the Arts & Entertainment cable network (37.5%).

Theme park and resorts mainly comprises the Walt Disney World and Disneyland complexes in Orlando, FL, and Anaheim, CA (with a total of six theme parks and at least 16 hotels), respectively, as well as the Disney Cruise Line. Theme park attractions include the Magic Kingdom, Epcot Center, the Disney-MGM Studio Theme Park, the Animal Kingdom, Disney's California Adventure and, most recently, Mission:SPACE, Mickey's PhilharMagic, and Disney's Pop Century Resort. In Japan, Tokyo Disneyland is owned and operated by Oriental Land Co., Ltd., under a licensing agreement. In Europe, DIS owns about 39% of Euro Disney S.C.A., a French company that operates the Disneyland Paris theme park busi-

ness. In Hong Kong, the company plans to open a Hong Kong Disneyland by 2006, in a joint venture with the Hong Kong government in which DIS would hold an initial 43% equity stake. The company plans to open another international park location in mainland China by 2010.

The consumer products business mainly comprises the worldwide merchandise licensing operations, as well as a chain of about 481 primarily mall-based Disney retail stores in North America and Europe (369 U.S., 112 international) as of September 30, 2003. In 2001, the company sold its Disney retail stores in Japan under a licensing arrangement.

In August 2004, DIS said it had signed a non-binding letter of intent with specialty apparel retailer Children's Place in regard to its plan to sell the Disney Stores chain in North America. The company said certain issues were still being negotiated, but it thought that a sale agreement could be completed in the FY 05 (Sep.) first quarter.

In March 2004, DIS separated the positions of chairman and CEO, both formerly held by CEO Michael Eisner, after 45% of shareholders withheld their vote for Mr. Eisner at the company's annual meeting.

In March 2001, the company discontinued its Go.com Internet portal, converting each Go.com share into 0.19353 of a DIS share; however, the company continues to focus on other Internet sites, including those related to entertainment, sports and news.

Company Financials Fiscal Year ending September 30

Per Share Data ($)

(Year Ended September 30)	2003	2002	2001	2000	1999	1998	1997	1996	1995	1994
Tangible Bk. Val.	2.01	1.78	3.99	2.24	2.59	1.75	0.63	NM	4.23	3.31
Cash Flow	1.18	1.11	0.89	1.48	2.22	2.70	3.36	2.78	2.03	1.66
Earnings	0.65	0.60	0.11	0.57	0.62	0.89	0.95	0.65	0.87	0.68
S&P Core Earnings	0.49	0.29	0.21	NA	NA	NA	NA	NA	NA	NA
Dividends	0.21	0.21	0.21	0.21	0.21	0.19	0.16	0.13	0.11	0.09
Payout Ratio	32%	35%	191%	37%	34%	21%	17%	20%	13%	13%
Prices - High	23.80	25.17	34.80	43.87	38.68	42.79	33.41	25.75	21.41	16.20
- Low	14.84	13.48	15.50	26.00	23.37	22.50	22.12	17.75	15.00	12.58
P/E Ratio - High	37	42	NM	77	62	48	35	39	25	24
- Low	23	22	NM	46	38	25	23	27	17	19

Income Statement Analysis (Million $)

	2003	2002	2001	2000	1999	1998	1997	1996	1995	1994
Revs.	27,061	25,329	25,269	25,402	23,402	22,976	22,473	18,739	12,112	10,055
Oper. Inc.	3,790	3,426	4,586	5,043	7,010	7,533	8,903	6,968	4,115	3,412
Depr.	1,077	1,042	1,754	2,195	3,323	3,754	4,958	3,944	1,853	1,608
Int. Exp.	Nil	453	417	558	717	685	741	545	236	172
Pretax Inc.	2,254	2,190	1,283	2,633	2,314	3,157	3,387	2,061	2,117	1,703
Eff. Tax Rate	35.0%	38.9%	82.5%	61.0%	43.8%	41.4%	42.0%	41.1%	34.8%	34.8%
Net Inc.	1,338	1,236	120	920	1,300	1,850	1,966	1,214	1,380	1,110
S&P Core Earnings	1,006	606	458	NA	NA	NA	NA	NA	NA	NA

Balance Sheet & Other Fin. Data (Million $)

	2003	2002	2001	2000	1999	1998	1997	1996	1995	1994
Cash	1,583	1,239	618	842	414	127	317	732	1,943	187
Curr. Assets	8,314	7,849	7,029	10,007	10,200	9,375	NA	NA	NA	NA
Total Assets	49,988	50,045	43,699	45,027	43,679	41,378	37,776	37,777	14,606	12,826
Curr. Liab.	8,669	7,819	6,219	8,402	7,707	7,525	NA	NA	NA	NA
LT Debt	10,643	12,467	8,940	6,959	9,278	9,562	11,068	12,342	2,984	2,107
Common Equity	23,791	23,445	22,672	24,100	20,975	19,388	17,285	16,086	6,651	5,508
Total Cap.	37,574	38,943	34,724	34,248	32,913	31,438	30,032	29,172	10,702	8,554
Cap. Exp.	1,049	1,086	1,795	2,013	2,134	2,314	1,922	1,745	897	1,026
Cash Flow	2,415	2,278	1,874	3,115	4,623	5,604	6,924	5,158	3,233	2,719
Curr. Ratio	1.0	1.0	1.1	1.2	1.3	1.2	NA	NA	NA	NA
% LT Debt of Cap.	28.3	32.0	25.7	20.3	28.2	30.4	36.9	42.3	27.9	24.6
% Net Inc.of Revs.	4.9	4.9	0.5	3.6	5.6	8.1	8.7	6.5	11.4	11.0
% Ret. on Assets	2.7	2.6	0.3	2.1	3.1	4.7	5.2	4.7	10.1	9.1
% Ret. on Equity	5.7	5.4	0.5	4.1	6.4	10.1	11.8	10.7	22.7	21.3

Data as orig. reptd.; bef. results of disc. opers. and/or spec. items. Per share data adj. for stk. divs. as of ex-div. date. Bold denotes primary EPS. E-Estimated. NA-Not Available. NM-Not Meaningful. NR-Not Ranked.

Office: 500 South Buena Vista Street, Burbank, CA 91521.
Telephone: 818-560-1000.
Website: http://www.disney.com
Chrmn: G.J. Mitchell.
Pres & COO: R.A. Iger.
CEO: M.D. Eisner.

EVP & CFO: T.O. Staggs.
EVP & General Counsel: A. Braverman.
Investor Contact: W. Webb 818-560-5758.
Dirs: J. E. Bryson, J. Chen, M. D. Eisner, J. L. Estrin, R. A. Iger, A. Lewis, M. C. Lozano, R. W. Matschullat, G. J. Mitchell, T. S. Murphy, L. J. O'Donovan, R. L. Watson, G. L. Wilson.

Founded: in 1936.
Domicile: Delaware.
Employees: 112,000.
S&P Analyst: Tuna N. Amobi, CFA, CPA /PMW/JWP

Dollar General

Recommendation: HOLD ★ ★ ★ ★ ★
SELL | SELL | HOLD | BUY | BUY

12-Month Target Price: $21.00
(as of December 04, 2003)

DG has an approximate 0.06% weighting in the **S&P 500**

Sector: Consumer Discretionary
Sub-Industry: General Merchandise Stores
Peer Group: Discounters - General

Summary: This discount retailer sells inexpensive soft and hard goods to low-, middle- and fixed-income families through more than 7,000 stores in 27 states.

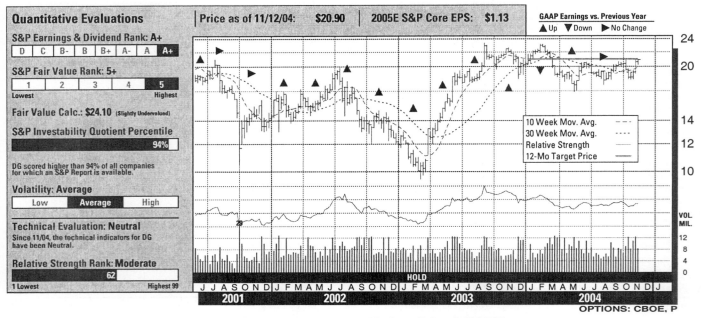

Quantitative Evaluations

S&P Earnings & Dividend Rank: A+

| D | C | B- | B | B+ | A- | A | A+ |

S&P Fair Value Rank: 5+

| 1 | 2 | 3 | 4 | 5 |
| Lowest | | | | Highest |

Fair Value Calc.: $24.10 (Slightly Undervalued)

S&P Investability Quotient Percentile
94%

DG scored higher than 94% of all companies for which an S&P Report is available.

Volatility: Average

| Low | Average | High |

Technical Evaluation: Neutral
Since 11/04, the technical indicators for DG have been Neutral.

Relative Strength Rank: Moderate
62
1 Lowest — Highest 99

Price as of 11/12/04: **$20.90**   2005E S&P Core EPS: **$1.13**

GAAP Earnings vs. Previous Year
▲ Up ▼ Down ► No Change

- - - 10 Week Mov. Avg.
····· 30 Week Mov. Avg.
Relative Strength
—— 12-Mo Target Price

HOLD

J J A S O N D J F M A M J J A S O N D J F M A M J J A S O N D J F M A M J J A S O N D J
2001   2002   2003   2004

OPTIONS: CBOE, P

Analyst commentary prepared by Jason N. Asaeda/PMW/GG

Highlights August 31, 2004

- We look for sales to advance 11% in FY 05 (Jan.), to $7.6 billion, on a 3% to 5% same-store sales increase, and the opening of nearly 700 new stores. As of July 30, 2004, DG had opened 418 Dollar General stores and two General Market stores. In our view, the company's planned installation of coolers for perishables in about 3,500 stores should boost sales, as cooler stores show, on average, higher customer and sales levels than non-cooler stores. We also see a sales lift from an improved in-stock position, due to chain-wide rollout of DG's automated inventory replenishment system, and from chain-wide acceptance of debit/check cards (via PIN entry) and DiscoverCard, and an accelerated pace of Electronics Benefit Transfer (EBT) card acceptance in stores with coolers.

- EBIT (earnings before interest and taxes) margins should narrow, as expected increases in store occupancy, store labor, and workers' compensation costs, as well as fees associated with debit card acceptance and professional fees related to a store work-flow study, are likely to offset the benefits of higher initial merchandise markups due to a focus on opportunistic buys.

- Factoring in share buybacks under a 12 million share repurchase authorization, we expect FY 05 operating EPS and Standard & Poor's Core Earnings per share of $1.01.

Investment Rationale/Risk August 31, 2004

- We recommend holding the shares, mainly based on valuation. Despite difficult industry conditions, DG posted a 3.1% same-store sales increase in the first half of FY 05, well ahead of its closest dollar store peers. These results, in our view, attest to favorable customer response to the company's improving value proposition and sales mix. However, we see rising fuel prices potentially having a dampening effect on sales, as well as raising DG's markdown exposure over the next few months, as most of the company's customers fall into the lower income brackets. DG is also implementing a number of changes to store operations in FY 05; while aimed at improving merchandise flow and raising sales productivity, this somewhat clouds our sales and earnings outlook.

- Risks to our recommendation and target price include a decline in consumer spending due to economic and geopolitical uncertainties, and delays in new store openings. Investors should also note that although past performance is not an indicator of future results, in the early stages of a period of rising interest rates retail stocks have historically tended to underperform.

- Our 12-month target price of $21 is based on a blend of a forward P/E multiple of 19X applied to our FY 06 EPS estimate of $1.15, and a price to estimated FY 06 sales ratio of 0.8X, the three-year historical averages.

Key Stock Statistics

S&P Oper. EPS 2005E	1.01	52-week Range	$23.19-16.91
P/E on S&P Oper. EPS 2005E	20.7	12 Month P/E	22.0
S&P Oper. EPS 2006E	1.15	Beta	1.05
Yield (%)	0.8%	Shareholders	12,777
Dividend Rate/Share	0.16	Market Cap (B)	$6.9
Shares Outstanding (M)	328.4		

Value of $10,000 invested five years ago: **$ 9,871**

Dividend Data Dividends have been paid since 1975

Amount ($)	Date Decl.	Ex-Div. Date	Stock of Record	Payment Date
0.035	Dec. 03	Dec. 30	Jan. 02	Jan. 16 '04
0.040	Mar. 15	Mar. 30	Apr. 01	Apr. 15 '04
0.040	May. 25	Jun. 29	Jul. 01	Jul. 15 '04
0.040	Aug. 24	Sep. 28	Sep. 30	Oct. 14 '04

Revenues/Earnings Data Fiscal year ending January 31

Revenues (Million $)

	2005	2004	2003	2002	2001	2000
1Q	1,748	1,569	1,389	1,203	997.1	844.6
2Q	1,836	1,836	1,454	1,225	1,017	915.2
3Q	—	1,685	1,498	1,309	1,094	950.4
4Q	—	1,966	1,760	1,586	1,442	1,178
Yr.	—	6,872	6,100	5,323	4,551	3,888

Earnings Per Share ($)

	2005	2004	2003	2002	2001	2000
1Q	0.20	0.18	0.14	0.11	0.09	0.10
2Q	0.22	0.22	0.13	0.08	0.08	0.10
3Q	E0.25	0.23	0.20	0.14	0.14	0.13
4Q	E0.37	0.30	0.32	0.29	-0.10	0.23
Yr.	E1.01	0.89	0.79	0.62	0.21	0.55

Next earnings report expected: early-December Source: S&P, Company Reports
EPS Estimates based on S&P Operating Earnings; historical GAAP earnings are as reported.

Dollar General Corporation

Recommendation: **HOLD** ★ ★ ★ ☆ ☆   12-Month Target Price: **$21.00** (as of December 04, 2003)

Business Summary August 31, 2004

Dollar General Corp. focuses on customers that most other retailers ignore. The company serves the consumable basics needs of customers mainly in the low- and middle-income brackets, and of customers on fixed incomes. Its merchandise assortment includes health and beauty aids, packaged food products, cleaning supplies, housewares, stationery, seasonal goods, basic apparel, and domestics. About 48% of customers live in households with incomes under $30,000, and about 26% earn under $20,000.

DG's stores are located in 29 states, mainly in the South, East and Midwest. About 56% are located in strip shopping centers, 41% in freestanding buildings, and 3% in downtown buildings. The average Dollar General store has about 6,800 sq. ft. of selling space, and serves customers living within a five mile radius. More than 50% of the stores are located in communities with populations below 20,000. The company believes its customers prefer the convenience of small, neighborhood stores.

Store expansion has been rapid, from 3,687 at January 29, 1999, to 7,079 at July 30, 2004. The company opened 673 stores in FY 04 (Jan.), including two 16,000 sq. ft. Dollar General Market concept stores carrying an expanded assortment of grocery products and perishable items. In FY 05, DG expected to open 695 new stores.

DG limits its stockkeeping units to 4,250 items per store. In FY 04, the average customer transaction was about $8.56 ($8.50 in FY 03). The average number of items in each customer purchase was 5.8 (5.7), and the average price of each purchased item was $1.49 ($1.48). The majority of items are priced at $10 or less, with about 33% at $1 or less.

In FY 04, 61.2% of sales consisted of highly consumable items (60.2% in FY 03), 16.8% (16.3%) seasonal items, 12.5% (13.3%) home products, and 9.5% (10.2%) basic clothing. In recent years, the company has increased its emphasis on the highly consumable category by adding items in the food, paper, household chemicals, and health and beauty care categories. DG has reduced emphasis on the home products division by eliminating certain items. In FY 02, it began offering perishable products, including a selection of dairy products, luncheon meats, frozen foods, and ice cream. The perishable program was expanded from 411 stores at the end of FY 02 to 2,445 stores at the end of FY 04.

Store investment and infrastructure upgrades continue to be a priority. Recent investments in technology included improvements to automated distribution center replenishment systems, establishment of perpetual inventories in all stores, a new order processing system, and systems to enable automated store replenishment.

In March 2003, directors authorized the repurchase of up to 12 million common shares through March 13, 2005. DG purchased about 1.5 million shares in FY 04, at a total cost of $29.7 million.

Company Financials Fiscal Year ending January 31

Per Share Data ($)

(Year Ended January 31)	2004	2003	2002	2001	2000	1999	1998	1997	1996	1995
Tangible Bk. Val.	4.69	3.86	3.13	2.60	3.50	2.61	2.65	1.78	1.52	1.20
Cash Flow	1.34	1.19	0.99	0.55	1.05	0.69	0.67	0.53	0.41	0.27
Earnings	0.89	0.79	0.62	0.21	0.55	0.45	0.43	0.34	0.26	0.22
S&P Core Earnings	NA	0.69	0.59	0.45	NA	NA	NA	NA	NA	NA
Dividends	0.13	0.13	0.13	0.12	0.10	0.08	0.07	0.06	0.05	0.03
Payout Ratio	14%	16%	21%	57%	18%	17%	15%	18%	19%	14%

Cal. Yrs.	2003	2002	2001	2000	1999	1998	1997	1996	1995	1994
Prices - High	23.40	19.95	24.05	23.18	26.10	24.19	16.38	9.14	7.13	5.11
- Low	9.50	11.70	10.50	13.43	15.07	12.80	7.79	4.03	4.08	3.28
P/E Ratio - High	26	25	39	NM	47	54	38	27	27	23
- Low	11	15	17	NM	27	28	18	12	16	15

Income Statement Analysis (Million $)

	2004	2003	2002	2001	2000	1999	1998	1997	1996	1995
Revs.	6,872	6,100	5,323	4,551	3,888	3,221	2,627	2,134	1,765	1,449
Oper. Inc.	674	563	497	427	413	342	274	221	174	138
Depr.	152	135	123	111	63.9	53.1	38.7	31.0	25.2	17.3
Int. Exp.	31.5	42.6	45.8	45.4	5.16	8.35	3.76	4.70	7.40	2.80
Pretax Inc.	480	415	328	109	344	281	232	185	142	118
Eff. Tax Rate	37.3%	36.1%	36.7%	35.0%	36.2%	35.2%	37.6%	37.8%	38.0%	37.8%
Net Inc.	301	265	208	70.6	219	182	145	115	87.8	73.6
S&P Core Earnings	NA	231	196	150	NA	NA	NA	NA	NA	NA

Balance Sheet & Other Fin. Data (Million $)

	2004	2003	2002	2001	2000	1999	1998	1997	1996	1995
Cash	398	121	262	262	58.8	22.3	7.13	6.60	4.30	33.0
Curr. Assets	1,652	1,324	1,556	1,125	1,096	879	667	505	516	410
Total Assets	2,653	2,333	2,552	2,282	1,451	1,212	915	718	680	541
Curr. Liab.	744	665	1,134	538	472	455	308	224	254	209
LT Debt	265	330	339	721	1.20	0.79	1.30	2.60	3.30	4.80
Common Equity	1,577	557	1,042	862	926	725	583	485	419	323
Total Cap.	1,909	938	1,419	1,583	979	757	607	494	426	332
Cap. Exp.	149	134	125	217	153	140	108	84.4	60.5	65.8
Cash Flow	453	400	330	182	282	232	180	144	111	90.1
Curr. Ratio	2.2	2.0	1.4	2.1	2.3	1.9	2.2	2.2	2.0	2.0
% LT Debt of Cap.	13.9	35.2	23.9	45.5	0.1	0.1	0.2	0.5	0.8	1.4
% Net Inc.of Revs.	4.4	4.3	3.9	1.6	5.6	5.7	5.5	5.4	5.0	5.1
% Ret. on Assets	12.1	10.8	8.6	3.4	16.5	17.1	17.7	16.5	14.4	16.7
% Ret. on Equity	21.0	33.1	21.8	8.3	26.4	27.3	26.5	24.9	23.1	27.5

Data as orig reptd.; bef. results of disc opers/spec. items. Per share data adj. for stk. divs. Bold denotes primary EPS - prior periods restated. E-Estimated. NA-Not Available. NM-Not Meaningful. NR-Not Ranked. UR-Under Review.

Office: 100 Mission Ridge, Goodlettsville, TN 37072.
Telephone: 615-855-4000.
Website: http://www.dollargeneral.com
Chrmn & CEO: D.A. Perdue.
Pres & COO: L.V. Jackson.
EVP & CFO: D.M. Tehle.

SVP, Secy & General Counsel: S.S. Lanigan.
Investor Contact: E.J. Kaufman 615-855-5525.
Dirs: D. L. Bere, D. C. Bottorff, B. L. Bowles, J. L. Clayton, R. D. Dickson, E. G. Gee, J. B. Holland, B. M. Knuckles, D. A. Perdue, J. D. Robbins, D. M. Wilds, W. S. Wire II.

Founded: in 1939.
Domicile: Tennessee.
Employees: 57,800.
S&P Analyst: Jason N. Asaeda/PMW/GG

Recommendation: **HOLD** ★★★☆☆
SELL SELL HOLD BUY BUY

12-Month Target Price: **$66.00**
(as of July 27, 2004)

D has an approximate 0.20% weighting in the **S&P 500**

Sector: Utilities
Sub-Industry: Multi-Utilities & Unregulated Power

Summary: This energy holding company's principal subsidiaries are Virginia Electric & Power Co. and Consolidated Natural Gas.

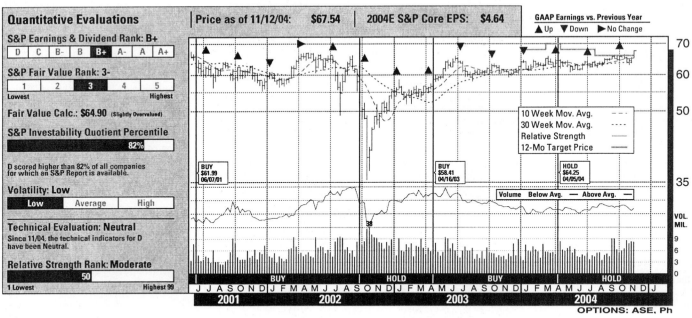

Quantitative Evaluations

S&P Earnings & Dividend Rank: B+
D C B- B **B+** A- A A+

S&P Fair Value Rank: 3-
1 2 **3** 4 5
Lowest   Highest

Fair Value Calc.: $64.90 (Slightly Overvalued)

S&P Investability Quotient Percentile
82%
D scored higher than 82% of all companies for which an S&P Report is available.

Volatility: Low
Low Average High

Technical Evaluation: Neutral
Since 11/04, the technical indicators for D have been Neutral.

Relative Strength Rank: Moderate
50
1 Lowest   Highest 99

Price as of 11/12/04: $67.54 | **2004E S&P Core EPS:** $4.64

GAAP Earnings vs. Previous Year
▲ Up ▼ Down ▶ No Change

10 Week Mov. Avg. – – –
30 Week Mov. Avg. ·····
Relative Strength ——
12-Mo Target Price ——

BUY $61.99 06/07/01
BUY $58.41 04/16/03
HOLD $64.25 04/05/04

Volume Below Avg. — Above Avg.

BUY | HOLD | BUY | HOLD
J J A S O N D | J F M A M J J A S O N D | J F M A M J J A S O N D | J F M A M J J A S O N D | J
2001 | 2002 | 2003 | 2004

OPTIONS: ASE, Ph

Analyst commentary prepared by Craig K. Shere, CFA /PMW/GG

Highlights August 18, 2004

- Reported EPS for 2003 included impairment, contract termination, and severance charges totaling $1.38. Our 2004 EPS estimate excludes $0.03 of net one-time charges in the first half. Excluding one-time items, we look for 2004 operating EPS growth of about 8%.

- We see 2004 EPS growth driven by normal weather (including the absence of Hurricane Isabel), contributions from new deepwater E&P projects, full-year contributions from the Cove Point LNG terminal, and increased sales from nuclear power plants. We project lower interest expense, due to debt reduction. We see 2005 EPS growth driven by a planned expansion of Cove Point storage capacity, full-year contributions from the pending 2004 Kewaunee nuclear power plant acquisition, subject to approvals, new 2004 deepwater E&P projects, and the absence of a one-time fuel expense charge.

- Our 2004 S&P Core EPS estimate is $0.24 below our operating EPS estimate, due to pension accounting adjustments, the expensing of employee stock options, and the inclusion of one-time items effecting depreciable assets and operating businesses.

Investment Rationale/Risk August 18, 2004

- The shares trade about in line with the average 2005 P/E multiple for peer multi-utilities. The stock's price to book value multiple is at a slight premium to the average, but in line with a handful of specific peers. We see the stock's premium price to trailing operating cash flow multiple justified by our expectations of above-average free cash flow growth, due to a $1 billion decrease in capital expenditures in 2004 and improving operating cash flows.

- Risks to our recommendation and target price include potential delays or cost overruns related to the Frontrunner deepwater E&P project and expansion of the Cove Point LNG terminal; a prolonged decline in natural gas prices; potential complications with the Kewaunee nuclear plant acquisition; higher than expected interest rates; and a weaker economy.

- In light of the stock's valuation multiples relative to peers, we view the shares as slightly overvalued. However, from a modestly lower fair value, we believe the shares should appreciate in line with the company's guidance of 5% to 7% average annual EPS growth through 2008. Our 12-month target price is $66.

Key Stock Statistics

S&P Core EPS 2005E	4.94	52-week Range	$67.61-59.27
S&P Oper. EPS 2004E	4.75	12 Month P/E	65.6
P/E on S&P Oper. EPS 2004E	14.2	Beta	0.24
S&P Oper. EPS 2005E	5.15	Shareholders	188,000
Yield (%)	4.0%	Market Cap (B)	$ 22.4
Dividend Rate/Share	2.68	Shares Outstanding (M)	331.4

Value of $10,000 invested five years ago: **$ 16,831**

Dividend Data Dividends have been paid since 1925

Amount ($)	Date Decl.	Ex-Div. Date	Stock of Record	Payment Date
0.645	Feb. 03	Feb. 25	Feb. 27	Mar. 20 '04
0.645	Apr. 23	May. 26	May. 28	Jun. 20 '04
0.645	Jul. 13	Aug. 25	Aug. 27	Sep. 20 '04
0.665	Oct. 15	Nov. 24	Nov. 29	Dec. 20 '04

Revenues/Earnings Data Fiscal year ending December 31

Revenues (Million $)

	2004	2003	2002	2001	2000	1999
1Q	3,879	3,579	2,634	3,198	2,005	1,293
2Q	3,040	2,630	2,332	2,309	2,056	1,315
3Q	3,292	2,853	2,545	2,544	2,351	1,663
4Q	—	3,016	2,707	2,507	2,781	1,250
Yr.	—	12,078	10,218	10,558	9,260	5,520

Earnings Per Share ($)

	2004	2003	2002	2001	2000	1999
1Q	1.36	1.32	1.20	1.20	0.63	—
2Q	0.79	0.78	0.97	0.62	-0.44	—
3Q	1.02	1.01	1.54	1.37	1.07	—
4Q	E1.33	-0.10	1.12	-0.45	0.49	0.33
Yr.	E4.75	2.98	4.82	2.15	1.76	2.81

Next earnings report expected: late-January Source: S&P, Company Reports
EPS Estimates based on S&P Operating Earnings; historical GAAP earnings are as reported.

Dominion Resources, Inc.

Recommendation: **HOLD** ★ ★ ★ ☆ ☆   12-Month Target Price: **$66.00** (as of July 27, 2004)

Business Summary August 18, 2004

As of the 2004 first quarter, Dominion Resources was the third largest U.S. utility company (in terms of equity market capitalization) and the eighth largest owner of natural gas pipelines (in miles). The company's operating segments are Generation (30% of 2003 operating income), Energy (20%), Delivery (26%), and Exploration & Production (24%).

As of the end of 2003, Generation included 14,840 MW of utility and 5,873 MW of unregulated generating capacity. Due to a Virginia regulatory electric rate freeze through 2007, the company is allowed to retain cost savings in this jurisdiction. Unregulated plants included nuclear (33% of capacity), coal (29%), and natural gas (37%) fueled generating capacity. In November 2003, D agreed to acquire 545 MW of fully contracted unregulated nuclear capacity in Wisconsin. The $220 million acquisition was expected to close in the fall of 2004. The company plans to complete the construction of an unregulated 1,180 MW natural gas-fired plant in Pennsylvania in 2004.

In April 2003, D agreed with the EPA and five states to install about $1.2 billion in new pollution control equipment at the company's coal-fired power plants.

The Energy division includes about 6,000 miles of electric transmission wires, 7,900 miles of gas transmission, gathering and storage pipelines, 26 underground gas storage fields (net 717 Bcf), certain Appalachian gas production properties, Dominion Clearinghouse (the energy trading arm), and a Maryland liquefied natural gas (LNG) terminal. In 2003, Clearinghouse was the 11th largest U.S. wholesale marketer of power (it does not report natural gas volumes). D bought the mothballed Maryland LNG terminal in September 2002, and brought the facility back to commercial service in August 2003. By early 2005, it plans to expand the LNG terminal's storage capacity to 7.8 Bcf, from 5 Bcf currently. Another LNG expansion is planned for 2008, bringing storage to 14.6 Bcf, and expanding daily output capacity to 1.8 Bcf/day (from 1 Bcf/day currently).

The Delivery segment includes electric and gas utility service and competitive retail energy marketing. Delivery serves a total of 3.9 million electric and gas utility customers in five states, and has 1.4 million competitive retail marketing customers in eight states.

The Exploration and Production (E&P) unit owned 6.4 Tcfe of proved reserves at the end of 2003 (84% natural gas and 16% oil) and produced 449 Bcfe during the year (88% gas and 12% oil). In 2003, the company participated in 922 net wells, and it expects to drill more in 2004.

D normally emphasizes longer-lived onshore E& P. By May 2004 and October 2004, respectively, it expects two major deepwater projects (Devil's Tower and Frontrunner) to come on line. The projects are expected to contribute 20% of total 2005 production, and to generate $1.8 billion to $2.6 billion in free cash flow over the 10 years beginning in 2005.

Company Financials Fiscal Year ending December 31

Per Share Data ($)

(Year Ended December 31)	2003	2002	2001	2000	1999	1998	1997	1996	1995	1994
Tangible Bk. Val.	19.19	18.18	15.69	14.20	24.80	26.56	16.55	27.21	26.73	26.51
Earnings	2.98	4.82	2.15	1.76	2.81	2.75	2.15	2.65	2.45	2.81
S&P Core Earnings	3.15	3.84	1.31	NA	NA	NA	NA	NA	NA	NA
Dividends	2.58	2.58	2.58	2.58	2.58	2.58	2.58	2.58	2.58	2.55
Payout Ratio	87%	54%	120%	147%	92%	94%	120%	97%	105%	91%
Prices - High	65.95	67.06	69.99	67.93	49.37	48.93	42.87	44.37	41.62	45.37
- Low	51.74	35.40	55.13	34.81	36.56	37.81	33.25	36.87	34.87	34.87
P/E Ratio - High	22	14	33	39	18	18	20	17	17	16
- Low	17	7	26	20	13	14	15	14	14	12

Income Statement Analysis (Million $)

	2003	2002	2001	2000	1999	1998	1997	1996	1995	1994
Revs.	12,078	10,218	10,558	9,260	5,520	6,086	7,678	4,842	4,652	4,491
Depr.	1,216	1,258	1,245	1,176	716	734	819	615	551	533
Maint.	NA	NA	NA	NA	NA	NA	NA	251	261	263
Fxd. Chgs. Cov.	2.63	3.15	2.02	1.99	2.44	1.83	2.38	3.12	2.35	2.61
Constr. Credits	NA	NA	Nil	Nil	Nil	Nil	Nil	Nil	6.70	6.40
Eff. Tax Rate	38.6%	33.3%	40.5%	30.5%	31.3%	35.2%	34.3%	31.1%	30.0%	26.3%
Net Inc.	949	1,362	544	415	551	536	399	472	425	478
S&P Core Earnings	1,004	1,088	331	NA	NA	NA	NA	NA	NA	NA

Balance Sheet & Other Fin. Data (Million $)

	2003	2002	2001	2000	1999	1998	1997	1996	1995	1994
Gross Prop.	37,107	32,631	33,105	31,011	18,646	18,106	19,520	16,816	15,977	15,415
Cap. Exp.	2,138	2,828	1,224	1,385	737	755	649	484	578	721
Net Prop.	25,850	20,257	18,681	14,849	10,764	10,637	12,533	10,509	10,322	10,245
Capitalization:										
LT Debt	16,033	13,714	12,119	10,486	7,321	5,071	7,196	4,728	4,612	4,711
% LT Debt	60.3	57.3	58.1	58.3	58.2	44.2	49.1	45.2	45.3	46.6
Pfd.	Nil	Nil	Nil	509	509	1,074	1,074	824	824	816
% Pfd.	Nil	Nil	Nil	2.83	4.05	9.40	7.30	7.90	8.10	8.10
Common	10,538	10,213	8,368	6,992	4,752	5,315	5,040	4,924	4,742	4,586
% Common	39.7	42.7	40.1	38.9	37.8	46.4	34.4	47.0	46.6	45.3
Total Cap.	31,134	28,136	24,811	20,955	14,427	13,475	14,658	12,474	12,111	12,016
% Oper. Ratio	83.7	78.5	85.6	80.5	80.9	64.4	83.6	81.6	80.0	76.9
% Earn. on Net Prop.	10.6	21.4	10.6	11.9	9.7	9.4	13.0	11.5	11.2	10.2
% Return On Revs.	7.9	13.3	5.2	4.5	10.0	8.8	5.2	9.8	9.1	10.6
% Return On Invest. Capital	6.5	8.5	7.2	10.7	7.9	8.4	7.6	9.8	8.6	8.8
% Return On Com. Equity	9.1	14.7	7.1	7.1	10.9	10.4	8.0	9.8	9.1	10.6

Data as orig reptd.; bef. results of disc opers/spec. items. Per share data adj. for stk. divs.; EPS diluted. E-Estimated. NA-Not Available. NM-Not Meaningful. NR-Not Ranked. UR-Under Review.

Office: 120 Tredegar Street, Richmond, VA 23219.
Telephone: 804-819-2000.
Email: investor_relations@domres.com
Website: http://www.dom.com
Chrmn & CEO: T.E. Capps.
Pres & COO: T.F. Farrell II.
EVP & CFO: T.N. Chewning.

SVP & Treas: G.S. Hetzer.
Investor Contact: T. Wohlfarth 804-819-2150.
Dirs: S. B. Allen, P. W. Brown, R. J. Calise, T. E. Capps, G. A. Davidson, Jr., J. W. Harris, R. S. Jepson, Jr., B. J. Lambert III, R. L. Leatherwood, M. A. McKenna, K. A. Randall, F. S. Royal, S. D. Simmons, R. H. Spilman, D. A. Wollard.

Auditor: Deloitte & Touche.
Founded: in 1909.
Domicile: Virginia.
Employees: 16,700.
S&P Analyst: Craig K. Shere, CFA /PMW/GG

Donnelley (R.R.)

Recommendation: **HOLD** ★ ★ ★ ★ ★
SELL | SELL | HOLD | BUY | BUY

12-Month Target Price: $37.00
(as of November 04, 2004)

RRD has an approximate 0.07% weighting in the **S&P 500**

Sector: Industrials
Sub-Industry: Commercial Printing
Peer Group: Printing - Specialty

Summary: The largest U.S. commercial printer, Donnelley specializes in the production of catalogs, inserts, magazines, books, directories, and financial and computer documentation.

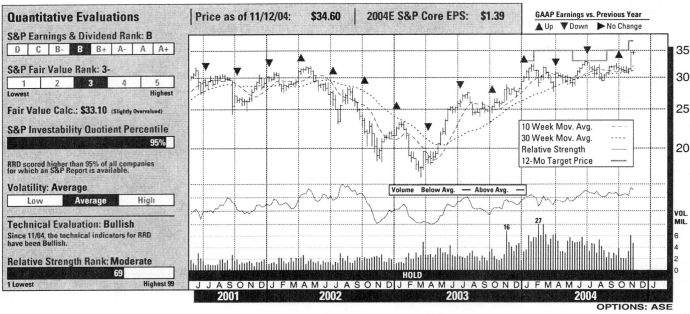

Quantitative Evaluations

| Price as of 11/12/04: | **$34.60** | 2004E S&P Core EPS: | **$1.39** |

S&P Earnings & Dividend Rank: B

| D | C | B- | **B** | B+ | A- | A | A+ |

S&P Fair Value Rank: 3-

| 1 | 2 | **3** | 4 | 5 |
| Lowest | | | | Highest |

Fair Value Calc.: $33.10 (Slightly Overvalued)

S&P Investability Quotient Percentile

95%

RRD scored higher than 95% of all companies for which an S&P Report is available.

Volatility: Average

| Low | **Average** | High |

Technical Evaluation: Bullish
Since 11/04, the technical indicators for RRD have been Bullish.

Relative Strength Rank: Moderate

69

| 1 Lowest | Highest 99 |

GAAP Earnings vs. Previous Year
▲ Up ▼ Down ▶ No Change

10 Week Mov. Avg.
30 Week Mov. Avg.
Relative Strength
12-Mo Target Price

Volume Below Avg. — Above Avg.

Analyst commentary prepared by W. Donald/PMW/GG

OPTIONS: ASE

Highlights August 31, 2004

- Largely due to the company's February 2004 acquisition of Moore Wallace, we expect 2004 revenues to climb nearly 66%, to about $7.94 billion. We see little incremental growth from the combination. However, largely reflecting our expectations of continued economic growth, higher paper prices, and the likelihood of a stronger market for book printing for 2005, we project a 5.7% increase in total revenues in 2005, to about $8.40 billion.

- The company now believes it will achieve its stated goal of at least $100 million in cost savings within 12 months of the Moore Wallace acquisition, rather than in 12 to 24 months as expected at the time of the acquisition on February 27, 2004. For 2004, we expect (non-GAAP) EBITDA margins to widen by 180 basis points, to 7.46%, from 5.66%, before unusual charges. We expect profitability to continue to improve in 2005, and project 9.03% EBITDA margins.

- We project 2004 earnings of $332.4 million ($1.55 a share), versus $176.5 million ($1.54, on 47% fewer shares) reported for 2003. Our non-GAAP 2004 earnings estimate excludes over $250 million in pretax restructuring, asset impairment, and integration charges. For 2005, we estimate net income of $418.6 million ($1.97).

Key Stock Statistics

S&P Oper. EPS 2004E	**1.60**	52-week Range	**$34.89-26.75**
P/E on S&P Oper. EPS 2004E	**21.6**	12 Month P/E	**31.7**
S&P Oper. EPS 2005E	**1.97**	Beta	**0.59**
Yield (%)	**3.0%**	Shareholders	**8,260**
Dividend Rate/Share	**1.04**	Market Cap (B)	**$ 7.6**
Shares Outstanding (M)	**219.6**		

Value of $10,000 invested five years ago: **$ 17,160**

Dividend Data Dividends have been paid since 1911

Amount ($)	Date Decl.	Ex-Div. Date	Stock of Record	Payment Date
0.260	Jan. 22	Feb. 02	Feb. 04	Feb. 28 '04
0.260	Mar. 26	May. 06	May. 10	Jun. 02 '04
0.260	Jul. 22	Aug. 05	Aug. 09	Sep. 01 '04
0.260	Sep. 30	Nov. 04	Nov. 08	Dec. 01 '04

Investment Rationale/Risk August 31, 2004

- We would not add to positions, despite operating benefits that we foresee from the Moore Wallace acquisition, based on difficulties that we see in boosting revenue growth over the next several years, as well as a number of risks and uncertainties. The stock has traded historically at a P/E multiple above the peer average, and we think that a premium continues to be warranted by the company's industry-leading position.

- Risks to our recommendation and target price include those related to Moore Wallace, including the elimination of duplicate overhead without excessive cost or adverse effects on the business, potential loss of clients and key employees as a result of the acquisition, and RRD's ability to complete the integration in a timely and successful way; and the company's ability to meet our revenue projections. In addition to economic risk, we believe that RRD operates in a highly competitive industry that faces inroads in demand for print services from the rapid growth of electronic dissemination of information.

- Our 12-month target price of $35 assumes that the stock will trade at a P/E multiple of 18X applied to our 2005 EPS estimate, maintaining its premium to peers. Based our DCF model, which assumes a weighted average cost of capital of 9.71% and 4% average cash flow growth for 15 years, we calculate intrinsic value of about $33.

Revenues/Earnings Data Fiscal year ending December 31

Revenues (Million $)

	2004	2003	2002	2001	2000	1999
1Q	1,446	1,074	1,094	1,303	1,343	1,180
2Q	2,029	1,142	1,149	1,292	1,389	1,195
3Q	1,969	1,194	1,177	1,288	1,433	1,340
4Q	—	1,377	1,335	1,415	1,600	1,468
Yr.	—	4,787	4,755	5,298	5,764	5,183

Earnings Per Share ($)

	2004	2003	2002	2001	2000	1999
1Q	-0.35	0.05	0.20	0.12	0.38	0.33
2Q	-0.06	0.17	0.22	0.05	0.46	0.40
3Q	0.52	0.47	0.42	0.36	0.75	0.67
4Q	E0.60	0.85	0.42	-0.33	0.58	1.01
Yr.	E1.60	1.54	1.24	0.21	2.17	2.40

Next earnings report expected: early-February Source: S&P, Company Reports
EPS Estimates based on S&P Operating Earnings; historical GAAP earnings are as reported.

R.R. Donnelley & Sons Company

Recommendation: **HOLD** ★ ★ ★ ☆ ☆   12-Month Target Price: **$37.00** (as of November 04, 2004)

Business Summary August 31, 2004

On February 27, 2004, R.R. Donnelley acquired Moore Wallace Inc. (MWI), for $2.8 billion in stock (about 100,000 common shares), plus the assumption of $900 million in debt. MWI was created in May 2003 via the merger of Moore Corp. and Wallace Computer Services. The combined company provides customers with a broad array of long- and short-run print products and solutions, ranging from magazines, telephone directories, books, catalogs, inserts and financial documents to billing statements, outsourced customer communications, highly personalized direct mail, premedia, print fulfillment, labels, collateral materials, forms, and logistics services.

The commercial print industry, which is large and fragmented, generates over $150 billion in annual revenue. The company has leading positions in five categories of the market served by its business units: Merchandise Media, which serves the catalog, retail insert and direct-mail markets; Magazine Publishing Services, which serves the consumer and the trade and specialty magazine markets; Book Publishing Services, which serves the trade and educational book markets; Telecommunications, which serves the domestic and international directory markets; and Financial Services, which serves the communication needs of the capital markets and the mutual fund and healthcare industries.

Geographically, RRD's business is concentrated in the U.S., where it has 46 manufacturing plants dedicated to commercial printing, and 24 logistics facilities that, combined, generated over $4.2 billion (88%) in net sales in 2003. The company also operates 12 commercial print plants in Mexico, South America, Europe and China. International operations generated about $583 million in revenue in 2003. RRD plans to extend its core competencies into new geographic markets that have a need for high-quality print and related services with no local solution.

At the end of 2003, about 70% of total sales were under contracts with customers, with the remainder on a single-order basis. Contracts with larger customers normally run for three to five years, with some longer contracts that require significant capital investment. These sales contracts generally provide for price adjustments to reflect price changes for material, wages and utilities. In 2003 no single customer accounted for over 10% of revenues.

In 2003, print operations accounted for 60% of total revenues. Logistics provided 19%, financial services 9%, direct mail 2%, and all other 8%.

Company Financials Fiscal Year ending December 31

Per Share Data ($)

(Year Ended December 31)	2003	2002	2001	2000	1999	1998	1997	1996	1995	1994
Tangible Bk. Val.	5.14	4.51	3.92	5.89	6.01	6.85	8.31	7.22	7.46	7.13
Cash Flow	4.43	4.32	3.41	5.34	5.29	4.66	3.91	1.53	4.53	3.78
Earnings	1.54	1.24	0.21	2.17	2.40	2.08	1.40	-1.04	1.95	1.75
S&P Core Earnings	1.18	0.18	-0.65	NA	NA	NA	NA	NA	NA	NA
Dividends	1.02	0.98	0.94	0.90	0.86	0.82	0.78	0.74	0.68	0.60
Payout Ratio	66%	79%	NM	41%	36%	39%	56%	NM	35%	34%
Prices - High	30.15	32.10	31.90	27.50	44.75	48.00	41.75	39.87	41.25	32.50
- Low	16.94	18.50	24.30	19.00	21.50	33.75	29.50	29.37	28.87	26.87
P/E Ratio - High	20	26	NM	13	19	23	30	NM	21	19
- Low	11	15	NM	9	9	16	21	NM	15	15

Income Statement Analysis (Million $)

	2003	2002	2001	2000	1999	1998	1997	1996	1995	1994
Revs.	4,787	4,755	5,298	5,764	5,183	5,018	4,850	6,599	6,512	4,889
Oper. Inc.	617	686	722	891	905	856	811	813	958	773
Depr.	329	352	379	390	374	367	371	389	398	313
Int. Exp.	50.4	62.8	71.2	89.6	88.2	78.0	91.0	95.0	121	63.7
Pretax Inc.	208	176	74.9	434	507	510	304	-110	440	39.5
Eff. Tax Rate	15.3%	19.1%	66.6%	38.5%	38.5%	42.2%	31.9%	NM	32.0%	32.0%
Net Inc.	177	142	25.0	267	312	295	207	-158	299	269
S&P Core Earnings	136	21.3	-78.3	NA	NA	NA	NA	NA	NA	NA

Balance Sheet & Other Fin. Data (Million $)

	2003	2002	2001	2000	1999	1998	1997	1996	1995	1994
Cash	60.8	60.5	48.6	60.9	41.9	66.0	48.0	31.1	33.0	21.0
Curr. Assets	1,000	866	940	1,206	1,230	1,145	1,147	1,753	1,908	1,353
Total Assets	3,189	3,152	3,400	3,914	3,853	3,788	4,134	4,849	5,385	4,452
Curr. Liab.	884	955	984	1,191	1,203	898	813	1,148	1,130	802
LT Debt	752	753	881	739	748	999	1,153	1,431	1,561	1,212
Common Equity	983	915	888	1,233	1,138	1,301	1,592	1,631	2,173	1,978
Total Cap.	1,970	1,882	1,982	2,205	2,140	2,585	2,974	3,316	4,035	3,478
Cap. Exp.	203	242	273	237	276	225	360	403	456	425
Cash Flow	506	495	404	657	686	662	578	232	697	582
Curr. Ratio	1.1	0.9	1.0	1.0	1.0	1.3	1.4	1.5	1.7	1.7
% LT Debt of Cap.	38.2	40.0	44.5	33.5	35.0	38.6	38.8	43.1	38.7	34.9
% Net Inc.of Revs.	3.7	3.0	0.5	4.6	6.0	5.9	4.3	NM	4.6	5.5
% Ret. on Assets	5.5	4.4	0.7	6.9	8.1	7.4	4.6	NM	6.1	6.6
% Ret. on Equity	18.6	15.8	2.4	22.5	25.5	20.4	12.8	NM	14.4	14.1

Data as orig reptd.; bef. results of disc opers/spec. items. Per share data adj. for stk. divs. Bold denotes primary EPS - prior periods restated. E-Estimated. NA-Not Available. NM-Not Meaningful. NR-Not Ranked. UR-Under Review.

Office: 77 West Wacker Drive, Chicago, IL 60601-1696.
Telephone: 312-326-8000.
Email: investor.info@rrd.com
Website: http://www.rrdonnelley.com
Chrmn, Pres & CEO: M.A. Angelson.
EVP & CFO: K.J. Smith.
SVP, Secy & General Counsel: M.M. Fohrman.

VP & Treas: A. Robertson.
VP & Investor Contact: D.N. Leib 312-326-8000.
Dirs: M. A. Angelson, G. Q. Brown, R. F. Cummings, Jr., J. R. Donnelley, A. C. Eckert III, J. H. Hamilton, T. S. Johnson, J. D. Manley, J. C. Pope, M. T. Riordan, L. H. Schipper, O. R. Sockwell, B. L. Thomas, N. Wesley, S. M. Wolf.

Founded: in 1864.
Domicile: Delaware.
Employees: 30,000.
S&P Analyst: W. Donald/PMW/GG

Dover Corp.

Recommendation: **BUY** ★★★★☆
SELL SELL HOLD BUY BUY

12-Month Target Price: **$42.00**
(as of October 20, 2004)

DOV has an approximate 0.08% weighting in the **S&P 500**

Sector: Industrials
Sub-Industry: Industrial Machinery
Peer Group: Components and Systems

Summary: This company makes equipment and components, mostly for electronics manufacturers and for oil and gas drillers, as well as for auto makers and repair shops.

Quantitative Evaluations

S&P Earnings & Dividend Rank: A-

| D | C | B- | B | B+ | A- | A | A+ |

S&P Fair Value Rank: 3

| 1 | 2 | 3 | 4 | 5 |
| Lowest | | | | Highest |

Fair Value Calc.: $38.90 (Slightly Overvalued)

S&P Investability Quotient Percentile

99%

DOV scored higher than 99% of all companies for which an S&P Report is available.

Volatility: Average

| Low | Average | High |

Technical Evaluation: Bullish
Since 11/04, the technical indicators for DOV have been Bullish.

Relative Strength Rank: Moderate

64

| 1 Lowest | | Highest 99 |

| Price as of 11/12/04: | **$41.68** | 2004E S&P Core EPS: | **$1.87** |

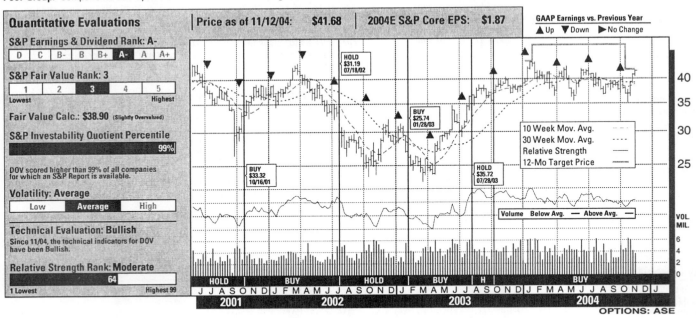

GAAP Earnings vs. Previous Year
▲ Up ▼ Down ► No Change

HOLD $31.19 07/18/02
BUY $25.74 01/28/03
BUY $33.32 10/16/01
HOLD $35.72 07/28/03

10 Week Mov. Avg.
30 Week Mov. Avg.
Relative Strength
12-Mo Target Price

Volume Below Avg. — Above Avg.

HOLD | BUY | HOLD | BUY | H | BUY
J J A S O N D J F M A M J J A S O N D J F M A M J J A S O N D J F M A M J J A S O N D J
2001 | 2002 | 2003 | 2004

OPTIONS: ASE

Analyst commentary prepared by John F. Hingher, CFA /CB/GG

Highlights October 22, 2004

- Based on recent macroeconomic trends, we believe industrial and technology related equipment spending will rise significantly in 2004. Combined with our view of rising replacement demand in the electronics end markets, higher capital spending, and possible contributions from bolt-on acquisitions, we believe DOV's revenues will advance about 23% in 2004. For 2005, we forecast 9% revenue growth, as softness in the circuit board assembly and test businesses somewhat offsets continued robust growth in the remaining businesses.

- We expect margins to widen in 2004 and 2005, as increasing material prices are more than offset by improved pricing and productivity.

- All told, we expect earnings from continuing operations to advance 43% in 2004 and 18% in 2005. For the longer term, we have confidence in management's ability to control costs and maintain a strong balance sheet, as shown by the most recent 10-year CAGR for book value (which we view as a good proxy for long-term shareholder returns) of 11%, versus a growth rate of 5.6% in book value for the S&P 500 over the same period.

Investment Rationale/Risk October 22, 2004

- Despite an expected slowdown in the Technologies segment, we recommend accumulating DOV shares based on our view of management's ability to generate strong free cash flow, expected continuing solid growth in the industrial economy, inherent operating leverage of DOV's businesses, consistent dividend payments that have grown at a 10-year CAGR of about 9%, and an average yield of 1.7%.

- Risks to our opinion and target price include reduced industrial capital spending in a rising interest rate environment; deterioration in demand for technology products should the semiconductor cycle peak; and rising raw material costs.

- Our discounted cash flow model, which values the stock by adding future free cash flows growing at our estimated CAGR of 8% to 9% for 10 years, and at 4.0% thereafter, indicates that the stock is undervalued. The shares traded recently at 17X our forward 12-month EPS estimate of $2.24, in line with the peer level of 17X, but below the stock's 10-year historical average. Blending these methodologies leads to our 12-month target price of $42.

Key Stock Statistics

S&P Core EPS 2005E	2.23	52-week Range	$44.13-35.12
S&P Oper. EPS 2004E	2.00	12 Month P/E	21.8
P/E on S&P Oper. EPS 2004E	20.8	Beta	1.26
S&P Oper. EPS 2005E	2.35	Shareholders	14,000
Yield (%)	1.5%	Market Cap (B)	$ 8.5
Dividend Rate/Share	0.64	Shares Outstanding (M)	203.4

Value of $10,000 invested five years ago: **$ 10,015**

Dividend Data Dividends have been paid since 1947

Amount ($)	Date Decl.	Ex-Div. Date	Stock of Record	Payment Date
0.150	Feb. 12	Feb. 25	Feb. 27	Mar. 15 '04
0.150	May. 06	May. 26	May. 28	Jun. 15 '04
0.160	Aug. 05	Aug. 27	Aug. 31	Sep. 15 '04
0.160	Nov. 04	Nov. 26	Nov. 30	Dec. 15 '04

Revenues/Earnings Data Fiscal year ending December 31

Revenues (Million $)

	2004	2003	2002	2001	2000	1999
1Q	1,242	1,028	994.6	1,210	1,251	969.8
2Q	1,380	1,124	1,082	1,115	1,379	1,078
3Q	1,444	1,154	1,062	1,085	1,390	1,151
4Q	—	1,198	1,045	1,050	1,380	1,248
Yr.	—	4,413	4,184	4,460	5,401	4,446

Earnings Per Share ($)

	2004	2003	2002	2001	2000	1999
1Q	0.41	0.29	0.22	0.38	0.57	0.32
2Q	0.53	0.36	0.31	0.24	0.67	0.44
3Q	0.58	0.37	0.29	0.02	0.71	0.58
4Q	E0.48	0.39	0.19	0.18	0.66	0.58
Yr.	E2.00	1.40	1.04	0.82	2.61	1.92

Next earnings report expected: late-January Source: S&P, Company Reports
EPS Estimates based on S&P Operating Earnings; historical GAAP earnings are as reported.

Dover Corporation

Recommendation: **BUY** ★★★★☆   12-Month Target Price: **$42.00** (as of October 20, 2004)

Business Summary October 22, 2004

Dover Corp.'s overall strategy is to acquire and develop platform businesses, marked by growth, innovation, and higher than average profit margin. Traditionally, the company focused on purchasing entities that could operate independently (stand-alones). However, over the past 10 years, DOV has put increased emphasis on also acquiring businesses that can be added to existing operations (add-ons).

Dover Diversified (DD; 26% and 28% of 2003 sales and segment operating earnings, respectively; 11.3% operating margin) has 11 stand-alone operating companies that manufacture equipment and components for industrial, commercial and defense applications. Major units include Hill Phoenix, Tranter, Mark Andy, Crenlo, Waukesha Bearings Corp., Graphics Microsystems, Belvac and Sargent. Over the past 10 years, average segment margin was about 14%.

Dover Industries (DI; 24% and 26%; 11.7%) is comprised of 12 stand-alone operating companies that manufacture a diverse mix of equipment and components for use in the waste handling, bulk transport, automotive service, commercial food service, packaging and construction equipment industries. Major units include PDQ Manufacturing, Heil Environmental, Rotary Lift, Heil Trailer International, Tipper Tie, Marathon Equipment, Triton Systems, DI Foodservice, and Texas Hydraulics. Over the past 10 years, average margin for the segment was about 13%.

Dover Resources (DR; 22% and 29%; 13.9%) has 12 stand-alone operating companies that manufacture components primarily for the oil and gas production

industry, the petroleum retailing industry, the process industries, the automotive industries, and select commercial markets. Major DR units include OPW Fueling Components, The Petroleum Equipment Group, De-Sta-Co Industries, Blackmer, OPW Fluid Transfer Group, Wilden Pump & Engineering Company, and C. Lee Cook. In October 2003, DR acquired high performance winch maker Warn Industries, Inc. (annual sales of $150 million) for about $325 million. Over the past 10 years, DR's average margin was about 15%.

Dover Technologies (DT; 28% and 18%; 6.9%) is comprised of 13 stand-alone operating companies that manufacture products in three broad groupings: Circuit Board Assembly and Test equipment (CBAT), Specialized Electronic Components (SEC), and Marking and Imaging systems. Major units of CBAT include Universal Instruments, Everett Charles Technologies, DEK, OK International, Vitronics-Soltec, Alphasem, and recently acquired Hover-Davis. SEC's major units include Quadrant Technologies, K&L Microwave, Novacap, Dow-Key Microwave and Dielectric Laboratories. Marking and Imaging's major unit is Imaje. Over the past 10 years, average margin for the segment was about 11%.

At December 31, 2003, DOV had cash and cash equivalents of $370 million, up from $294 million a year earlier. Capital spending totaled $96.4 million in 2003, flat with 2002 spending. The company spent $362 million on acquisitions in 2003, up from $100 million in 2002.

Company Financials Fiscal Year ending December 31

Per Share Data ($)

(Year Ended December 31)	2003	2002	2001	2000	1999	1998	1997	1996	1995	1994
Tangible Bk. Val.	2.71	2.66	1.97	1.79	1.08	2.11	2.81	2.29	1.79	1.85
Cash Flow	2.14	1.83	1.89	3.60	2.79	2.20	2.54	2.27	1.70	1.30
Earnings	1.40	1.04	0.82	2.61	1.92	1.45	1.79	1.73	1.23	0.89
S&P Core Earnings	1.31	0.90	0.68	NA	NA	NA	NA	NA	NA	NA
Dividends	0.57	0.54	0.52	0.48	0.44	0.40	0.36	0.32	0.29	0.25
Payout Ratio	41%	52%	63%	18%	23%	28%	20%	19%	24%	28%
Prices - High	40.45	43.55	43.55	54.37	47.93	39.93	36.68	27.56	20.84	16.71
- Low	22.85	23.54	26.40	34.12	29.31	25.50	24.12	18.31	12.90	12.43
P/E Ratio - High	29	42	53	21	25	28	20	16	17	19
- Low	16	23	32	13	15	18	13	11	11	14

Income Statement Analysis (Million $)

	2003	2002	2001	2000	1999	1998	1997	1996	1995	1994
Revs.	4,413	4,184	4,460	5,401	4,446	3,978	4,548	4,076	3,746	3,085
Oper. Inc.	595	503	518	1,047	819	700	783	664	546	421
Depr.	151	161	219	203	183	168	171	125	108	95.8
Int. Exp.	62.2	70.0	91.2	97.5	53.4	60.7	46.9	42.0	40.1	36.5
Pretax Inc.	372	270	238	772	615	489	617	589	417	307
Eff. Tax Rate	23.3%	21.7%	30.0%	31.0%	34.1%	33.2%	34.3%	33.7%	33.3%	34.1%
Net Inc.	285	211	167	533	405	326	405	390	278	202
S&P Core Earnings	267	182	138	NA	NA	NA	NA	NA	NA	NA

Balance Sheet & Other Fin. Data (Million $)

	2003	2002	2001	2000	1999	1998	1997	1996	1995	1994
Cash	370	295	177	187	138	96.8	125	218	149	145
Curr. Assets	1,850	1,658	1,655	1,975	1,612	1,305	1,591	1,490	1,384	1,133
Total Assets	5,134	4,437	4,602	4,892	4,132	3,627	3,278	2,993	2,667	2,071
Curr. Liab.	911	697	819	1,605	1,345	990	1,197	1,139	95.0	772
LT Debt	1,004	1,030	1,033	632	608	610	263	253	256	254
Common Equity	2,743	2,395	2,520	2,442	2,039	1,911	1,778	1,490	1,228	996
Total Cap.	3,980	3,561	3,656	3,141	2,689	2,571	2,007	1,797	1,530	1,252
Cap. Exp.	96.4	102	167	198	130	126	146	126	104	84.9
Cash Flow	437	372	386	737	588	494	576	515	386	298
Curr. Ratio	2.0	2.4	2.0	1.2	1.2	1.3	1.3	1.3	2.1	1.5
% LT Debt of Cap.	25.2	28.9	28.3	20.1	22.6	23.7	13.1	14.1	16.8	20.3
% Net Inc.of Revs.	6.5	5.0	3.7	9.9	9.1	8.2	8.9	9.6	7.5	6.6
% Ret. on Assets	6.0	4.7	3.5	11.8	10.4	9.5	12.9	13.8	11.8	10.6
% Ret. on Equity	11.1	8.6	6.7	23.8	20.5	17.7	24.4	28.7	25.1	21.8

Data as orig reptd.; bef. results of disc opers/spec. items. Per share data adj. for stk. divs.; EPS diluted. E-Estimated. NA-Not Available. NM-Not Meaningful. NR-Not Ranked. UR-Under Review.

Office: 280 Park Avenue, New York, NY 10017-1215.
Telephone: 212-922-1640.
Website: http://www.dovercorporation.com
Chrmn, Pres & CEO: T.L. Reece.
Pres & COO: R.L. Hoffman.

VP, CFO, Treas & Investor Contact: R.G. Kuhbach .
VP, Secy & General Counsel: J.W. Schmidt.
Dirs: D. H. Benson, J. M. Ergas, K. C. Graham, R. L. Hoffman, J. L. Koley, R. K. Lochridge, T. L. Reece, B. G. Rethore, G. L. Roubos, M. B. Stubbs.

Founded: in 1947.
Domicile: Delaware.
Employees: 25,700.
S&P Analyst: John F. Hingher, CFA /CB/GG

Recommendation: **BUY** ★★★★★   12-Month Target Price: **$55.00**
(as of January 29, 2004)

DOW has an approximate 0.42% weighting in the **S&P 500**

Sector: Materials
Sub-Industry: Diversified Chemicals
Peer Group: Major Diversified Companies

Summary: The largest U.S. chemical company, DOW provides innovative chemical, plastic and agricultural products and services to many essential consumer markets.

Quantitative Evaluations

S&P Earnings & Dividend Rank: B

| D | C | B- | **B** | B+ | A- | A | A+ |

S&P Fair Value Rank: 1-

| **1** | 2 | 3 | 4 | 5 |
| Lowest | | | | Highest |

Fair Value Calc.: $36.20 (Overvalued)

S&P Investability Quotient Percentile

93%

DOW scored higher than 93% of all companies for which an S&P Report is available.

Volatility: Average

| Low | **Average** | High |

Technical Evaluation: Bullish
Since 10/04, the technical indicators for DOW have been Bullish.

Relative Strength Rank: Strong

81

| 1 Lowest | Highest 99 |

| Price as of 11/12/04: | **$49.36** | 2004E S&P Core EPS: | **$2.23** |

GAAP Earnings vs. Previous Year
▲ Up ▼ Down ► No Change

- 10 Week Mov. Avg.
- 30 Week Mov. Avg.
- Relative Strength
- 12-Mo Target Price

Volume Below Avg. ░ Above Avg. ▬

VOL. MIL.

HOLD   BUY

J J A S O N D | J F M A M J J A S O N D | J F M A M J J A S O N D | J F M A M J J A S O N D | J
2001   2002   2003   2004

OPTIONS: CBOE, P

Analyst commentary prepared by Richard O'Reilly, CFA /CB/BK

Highlights August 15, 2004

- We expect the company to post favorable operating EPS comparisons for the rest of 2004 and into 2005, driven by improved industry fundamentals and lower overhead costs. DOW reduced overhead costs by over $600 million in 2003, and is implementing plans for an additional $350 million of annual savings by 2005.

- Feedstock costs rose substantially in the 2004 first half, on top of a 33% climb in 2003, and we see further cost increases for the rest of the year. As a result, we expect margins for many of the company's basic plastics and chemicals to remain under pressure, largely offsetting price hikes that are being implemented for commodity plastics and chemicals.

- We expect volumes to continue to grow with improving economic conditions, but at a slower pace than the 9% gain in 2004's first half. We project that the agricultural segment in 2004 will have another record performance, driven by strong first half results. We see the joint ventures in low cost feedstock locations continuing to perform well, and interest expense declining due to debt reduction. We expect the tax rate to rise to about 29%, from 21% in 2003.

Investment Rationale/Risk August 15, 2004

- We have a buy recommendation on the shares. We believe the chemical industry's supply/demand fundamentals will continue to show cyclical improvement over the next two years. DOW plans additional overhead cost reductions and a continued focus on capital discipline, as capital spending in 2004 should be well below depreciation. We view the dividend, which provides a yield well above the market average, as secure.

- Risks to our recommendation and target price include unexpected softening of the U.S. economy and higher than expected energy costs. We remain somewhat concerned about the long-term adverse impact of high energy costs on the U.S. chemicals industry, and about possible additional asbestos liabilities for DOW, largely related to the Union Carbide unit, which once made products containing asbestos.

- Our 12-month target price of $55 is based on a historical peak-of-cycle P/E multiple of 10X and annualized earnings of more than $5.00 a share that we believe DOW can be earning some time in the 2005 to 2006 period.

Key Stock Statistics

S&P Core EPS 2005E	2.93	52-week Range	$49.45-36.16
S&P Oper. EPS 2004E	2.50	12 Month P/E	17.2
P/E on S&P Oper. EPS 2004E	19.7	Beta	0.88
S&P Oper. EPS 2005E	3.00	Shareholders	114,409
Yield (%)	2.7%	Market Cap (B)	$ 46.5
Dividend Rate/Share	1.34	Shares Outstanding (M)	943.0

Value of $10,000 invested five years ago: **$ 14,613**

Dividend Data Dividends have been paid since 1911

Amount ($)	Date Decl.	Ex-Div. Date	Stock of Record	Payment Date
0.335	Dec. 11	Dec. 29	Dec. 31	Jan. 30 '04
0.335	Feb. 12	Mar. 29	Mar. 31	Apr. 30 '04
0.335	May. 13	Jun. 28	Jun. 30	Jul. 30 '04
0.335	Sep. 09	Sep. 28	Sep. 30	Oct. 29 '04

Revenues/Earnings Data Fiscal year ending December 31

Revenues (Million $)

	2004	2003	2002	2001	2000	1999
1Q	9,309	8,081	6,305	7,386	5,652	4,417
2Q	9,844	8,242	7,259	7,344	5,912	4,619
3Q	10,072	7,977	7,084	6,729	5,811	4,693
4Q	—	8,332	6,961	6,346	5,633	5,200
Yr.	—	32,632	27,609	27,805	23,008	18,929

Earnings Per Share ($)

	2004	2003	2002	2001	2000	1999
1Q	0.50	0.09	0.04	-0.80	0.61	0.49
2Q	0.72	0.43	0.26	0.31	0.77	0.61
3Q	0.65	0.36	0.14	0.06	0.48	0.48
4Q	E0.63	0.99	-0.89	-0.04	0.36	0.40
Yr.	E2.50	1.88	-0.44	-0.46	2.22	1.98

Next earnings report expected: late-January   Source: S&P, Company Reports
EPS Estimates based on S&P Operating Earnings; historical GAAP earnings are as reported.

The Dow Chemical Company

Recommendation: **BUY** ★ ★ ★ ★ ★   12-Month Target Price: **$55.00** (as of January 29, 2004)

Business Summary August 16, 2004

In the late 1990s, DOW ended an effort to diversify, and refocused on its chemical-related businesses. Businesses sold in those years included pharmaceuticals, personal care and household products units. At the same time, the company expanded geographically in Latin America, Eastern Europe and Asia, and entered new businesses, such as polypropylene, PET polyester and elastomers. DOW also expanded its agricultural biotechnology business. The 2001 purchase of Union Carbide Corp., a leading producer of polyethylene, ethylene glycol, solvents and specialty chemicals made DOW the largest U.S. chemical company. Capital spending for 2004 is budgeted at $1.3 billion, below estimated depreciation charges of $1.9 billion.

Foreign operations accounted for 61% of 2003 sales.

Chemicals (14% of sales and 12% of profits in 2003) include inorganics (chlorine, caustic soda, chlorinated solvents, ethylene dichloride and vinyl chloride), ethylene oxide/glycol and vinyl acetate monomer, used primarily as raw materials in the manufacture of customer products. DOW is the world's largest maker of chlorine, caustic soda, vinyl chloride and ethylene oxide/glycol. Performance chemicals (17%, 24%) consist of latex coatings and binders, water-based emulsions (acrylic latexes), water soluble polymers, cellulose ethers and resins, custom manufacturing, fine chemicals, superabsorbent polymers, ion exchange resins, membranes, glycine, glycols, amines, surfactants, heat transfer and de-icing fluids, lubricants, and solvents.

Dow AgroSciences (9%, 16%) is a leading global maker of herbicides (Clincher, Starane), insecticides (Dursban, Lorsban, Sentricon termite colony elimination system, Tracer) and fungicides for crop protection and industrial/commercial pest control. It is also building a plant genetics and biotechnology business in crop seeds (Mycogen), traits (Herculex) and value-added grains.

The company, a major producer of plastics (24%, 23%), is the world's largest producer of polyethylene and polystyrene resins, which are used in a broad variety of applications. It also makes polypropylene and PET polyester plastics, and rubbers. Performance plastics (24%, 25%) consist of engineering plastics (polycarbonates, ABS), adhesives and sealants, polyurethanes, polyols, isocyanates, propylene oxide/glycol, epoxy resins and intermediates (phenol and acetone), fabricated products (foams and films), polyolefins for wire and cable insulation, and technology licensing (UNIPOL for polyethylene and polypropylene, Meteor for ethylene oxide/glycol) and catalysts (the UOP partnership).

DOW is also a world leader in the production of olefins and styrene, hydrocarbons and energy (12%, nil); it produces ethylene, propylene, aromatics, styrene, and power and steam. The company closed two U.S. ethylene plants in 2003 with total capacity of 2.5 billion lbs. Other businesses include advanced electronic materials and industrial biotechnology.

Company Financials Fiscal Year ending December 31

Per Share Data ($)

(Year Ended December 31)	2003	2002	2001	2000	1999	1998	1997	1996	1995	1994
Tangible Bk. Val.	5.79	4.19	7.59	10.78	9.59	8.77	8.69	9.73	8.84	4.57
Cash Flow	3.93	4.57	1.55	4.14	3.91	3.83	4.46	4.33	4.31	2.92
Earnings	1.88	-0.44	-0.46	2.22	1.98	1.91	2.57	2.57	2.34	1.12
S&P Core Earnings	1.58	-1.41	-1.43	NA	NA	NA	NA	NA	NA	NA
Dividends	1.34	1.34	1.30	1.16	1.16	1.16	1.12	1.00	0.97	0.87
Payout Ratio	71%	NM	NM	52%	59%	61%	44%	39%	41%	77%
Prices - High	42.00	37.00	39.67	47.16	46.00	33.81	34.20	30.83	26.00	26.41
- Low	24.83	23.66	25.06	23.00	28.50	24.89	25.45	22.75	20.45	18.83
P/E Ratio - High	22	NM	NM	21	23	18	13	12	11	24
- Low	13	NM	NM	10	14	13	10	9	9	17

Income Statement Analysis (Million $)

	2003	2002	2001	2000	1999	1998	1997	1996	1995	1994
Revs.	32,632	27,609	27,805	23,008	18,929	18,441	20,018	20,053	20,200	20,015
Oper. Inc.	3,922	2,925	2,953	3,462	3,407	3,498	4,013	4,385	5,333	3,795
Depr.	1,903	1,825	1,815	1,315	1,301	1,305	1,287	1,298	1,442	1,490
Int. Exp.	828	774	733	460	431	493	471	529	462	603
Pretax Inc.	1,751	-622	-613	2,401	2,166	2,012	2,948	3,288	3,529	2,052
Eff. Tax Rate	NM	NM	NM	34.3%	35.4%	34.0%	35.3%	36.1%	40.9%	38.0%
Net Inc.	1,739	-405	-417	1,513	1,331	1,310	1,808	1,907	2,078	938
S&P Core Earnings	1,462	-1,295	-1,303	NA	NA	NA	NA	NA	NA	NA

Balance Sheet & Other Fin. Data (Million $)

	2003	2002	2001	2000	1999	1998	1997	1996	1995	1994
Cash	2,434	1,573	264	304	1,212	390	235	2,302	3,450	1,134
Curr. Assets	13,002	11,681	10,308	9,260	8,847	8,040	8,640	9,830	10,554	8,693
Total Assets	41,891	39,562	35,515	27,645	25,499	23,830	24,040	24,673	23,582	26,545
Curr. Liab.	9,534	8,856	8,125	7,873	6,295	6,842	7,340	6,004	5,601	6,618
LT Debt	12,763	12,659	10,266	5,365	5,022	4,051	4,196	4,196	4,705	5,303
Common Equity	9,175	7,626	9,993	9,186	8,323	7,429	7,626	7,954	7,361	8,212
Total Cap.	23,438	21,645	21,376	15,848	14,642	12,802	13,196	15,280	14,841	16,687
Cap. Exp.	1,100	1,623	1,587	1,349	1,412	1,546	1,198	1,344	1,417	1,183
Cash Flow	3,642	1,420	1,398	2,828	2,627	2,609	3,089	3,198	3,520	2,421
Curr. Ratio	1.4	1.3	1.3	1.2	1.4	1.2	1.2	1.6	1.9	1.3
% LT Debt of Cap.	54.5	58.5	48.0	33.9	34.3	31.6	31.7	15.0	31.7	31.8
% Net Inc.of Revs.	5.3	NM	NM	6.6	7.0	7.1	9.0	9.5	10.3	4.7
% Ret. on Assets	4.3	NM	NM	5.7	5.4	5.5	7.4	7.9	8.3	5.6
% Ret. on Equity	20.7	NM	NM	17.3	16.8	17.3	23.1	24.8	26.7	11.4

Data as orig reptd.; bef. results of disc opers/spec. items. Per share data adj. for stk. divs.; EPS diluted. E-Estimated. NA-Not Available. NM-Not Meaningful. NR-Not Ranked. UR-Under Review.

Office: 2030 Dow Center, Midland, MI 48674-0001.
Telephone: 989-636-1000.
Website: http://www.dow.com
Chrmn & CEO: W.S. Stavropoulos.
Pres & COO: A.N. Liveris.
Vice Chrmn: A.J. Carbone.
EVP & CFO: J.P. Reinhard.

VP & Treas: F. Ruiz.
Investor Contact: K.C. Fothergill 989-636-2876.
Dirs: A. A. Allemang, J. K. Barton, A. J. Carbone, J. M. Cook, J. C. Danforth, W. D. Davis, J. M. Fettig, B. H. Franklin, A. N. Liveris, K. R. McKennon, J. P. Reinhard, J. M. Ringler, H. T. Shapiro, W. S. Stavropoulos, P. G. Stern.

Founded: in 1897.
Domicile: Delaware.
Employees: 46,372.
S&P Analyst: Richard O'Reilly, CFA /CB/BK

Dow Jones & Co.

Recommendation: **BUY** ★★★★
SELL SELL HOLD BUY BUY

12-Month Target Price: **$49.00**
(as of November 11, 2004)

DJ has an approximate 0.03% weighting in the **S&P 500**

Sector: Consumer Discretionary
Sub-Industry: Publishing
Peer Group: Newspaper Cos. - Large

Summary: Dow Jones publishes The Wall Street Journal and Barron's, provides newswire, news retrieval and financial information services, and publishes general circulation newspapers.

Quantitative Evaluations

S&P Earnings & Dividend Rank: B

| D | C | B- | B | B+ | A- | A | A+ |

S&P Fair Value Rank: 1

| 1 | 2 | 3 | 4 | 5 |
| Lowest | | | | Highest |

Fair Value Calc.: $31.00 (Overvalued)

S&P Investability Quotient Percentile

97%

DJ scored higher than 97% of all companies for which an S&P Report is available.

Volatility: Low

| Low | Average | High |

Technical Evaluation: Bullish
Since 10/04, the technical indicators for DJ have been Bullish.

Relative Strength Rank: Moderate

| 53 | |
| 1 Lowest | Highest 99 |

Price as of 11/12/04: $45 | **2004E S&P Core EPS:** $0.74

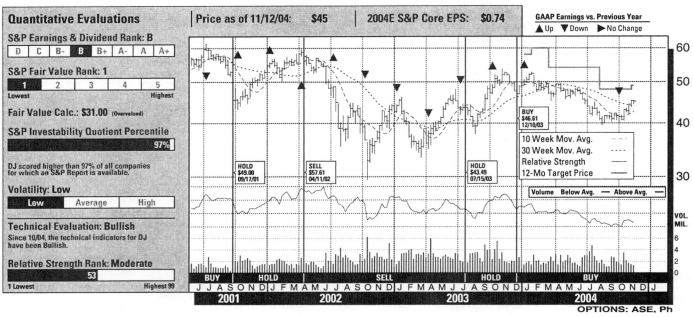

Analyst commentary prepared by William H. Donald/PMW/JWP

Highlights August 30, 2004

- We forecast an 11% increase in advertising revenues in 2005, to $1.04 billion, and a 9.6% gain in total revenues, to $1.80 billion. We look for continued strong recoveries in financial and classified ad linage, modest improvement in general advertising, and a turnaround in technology advertising. Despite an uneven recovery, we look for a 6% rise in total revenues in 2004, to $1.64 billion, including a 7.5% increase in advertising revenues, to about $937 million. The gain that we see for 2004 mostly reflects comparisons with a weak 2003 first half.

- We believe that revenue growth and recent restructuring efforts, combined with ongoing cost controls, should contribute to margin improvement in 2005 and beyond. We expect 2005 operating earnings to advance 33%, to $192.5 million, and EBITDA to grow 21%, to $305.5 million. EBITDA margins should widen to 17.0%, from 15.4% that we estimate for 2004.

- After other items, we project a 29% advance in pretax earnings in 2005, and a 28% gain in net operating earnings, to $141.6 million ($1.75 a share), from $110.3 million ($1.35) that we estimate for 2004.

Investment Rationale/Risk August 30, 2004

- We would accumulate the shares. The stock trailed peers and the S&P 500 in 2004 through late August, due, we believe, to concerns about the impact on advertising demand of volatile business confidence and spending commitments. However, we expect investor sentiment toward the stock to improve, on a projected strengthening of advertising in coming months. We see EPS advances averaging about 30% in the three years through 2006, in line with a three-year average P/E multiple in the low 30s. The stock's P/E multiple has typically been higher than the peer average.

- Risks to our opinion and target price include a slower than expected recovery in business-to-business advertising demand; inconsistent trends across major advertising categories, such as technology and finance; and the possibility that, after extensive cost-cutting and in light of planned growth initiatives, the company may not be able to limit or control expense growth.

- Based on discounted cash flow analysis, our 12-month target price is $48. We assume that the stock will trade at 27X our 2005 EPS estimate, toward the middle of its historical range, but above peer levels.

Key Stock Statistics

S&P Core EPS 2005E	1.10	52-week Range	$52.74-39.50
S&P Oper. EPS 2004E	1.25	12 Month P/E	34.1
P/E on S&P Oper. EPS 2004E	36.0	Beta	1.05
S&P Oper. EPS 2005E	1.65	Shareholders	11,995
Yield (%)	2.2%	Market Cap (B)	$ 2.8
Dividend Rate/Share	1.00	Shares Outstanding (M)	81.9

Value of $10,000 invested five years ago: **$ 7,954**

Dividend Data Dividends have been paid since 1906

Amount ($)	Date Decl.	Ex-Div. Date	Stock of Record	Payment Date
0.250	Jan. 21	Jan. 29	Feb. 02	Mar. 01 '04
0.250	Apr. 21	Apr. 29	May. 03	Jun. 01 '04
0.250	Jun. 16	Jul. 29	Aug. 02	Sep. 01 '04
0.250	Sep. 15	Oct. 28	Nov. 01	Dec. 01 '04

Revenues/Earnings Data Fiscal year ending December 31

Revenues (Million $)

	2004	2003	2002	2001	2000	1999
1Q	401.6	358.2	392.9	459.9	550.8	462.1
2Q	437.8	393.6	417.0	484.1	621.6	510.6
3Q	394.9	375.9	352.4	397.6	500.3	469.8
4Q	—	420.7	396.9	431.5	558.4	559.4
Yr.	—	1,548	1,559	1,773	2,203	2,002

Earnings Per Share ($)

	2004	2003	2002	2001	2000	1999
1Q	E0.22	0.82	1.53	0.07	0.98	0.56
2Q	E0.41	0.38	0.64	0.50	1.13	0.62
3Q	0.15	0.35	0.03	0.19	-0.39	1.13
4Q	E0.48	0.54	0.18	0.38	-0.22	0.67
Yr.	E1.25	2.08	2.40	1.14	-1.35	2.99

Next earnings report expected: late-January Source: S&P, Company Reports
EPS Estimates based on S&P Operating Earnings; historical GAAP earnings are as reported.

Dow Jones & Company, Inc.

Recommendation: **BUY** ★★★★☆   12-Month Target Price: **$49.00** (as of November 11, 2004)

Business Summary   August 30, 2004

Dow Jones & Co., a global provider of business and financial news and information, is the parent of The Wall Street Journal and Barron's National Business and Financial Weekly. Its operations are divided into three operating segments: print publishing (59% of revenues and 5% of operating income in 2003), electronic publishing (21% and 43%), and general interest community newspapers (20% and 52%).

The Wall Street Journal, a financial and business daily, is the largest circulation daily newspaper in the U.S., with average daily circulation in 2003 of 1,792,000. DJ publishes two international editions. The Asian Wall Street Journal, with daily circulation of more than 76,000, is the leader in its market. It is headquartered and published in Hong Kong and is transmitted by satellite to additional printing sites throughout Asia. The Wall Street Journal/Europe, with daily circulation of more than 95,000, is the second largest business daily in Europe. It is headquartered and published in Brussels, and printed in Belgium, Switzerland, the U.K., Italy, Spain and Germany. DJ has expanded its readership by introducing Wall Street Journal news content in the form of special editions to 36 newspapers in 33 countries.

The company also publishes Barron's, a weekly magazine with 297,000 average circulation, covering business and finance. The Far Eastern Economic Review, published weekly in Hong Kong, is Asia's leading English-language business magazine, with circulation of about 90,000. Ottaway Newspapers publishes 15 daily newspapers in nine states with combined circulation of 444,000. In June

2003, Ottaway acquired The Record of Stockton, CA, and affiliated publications from Omaha World-Herald Co., for $144 million cash, plus working capital. The Record Group had revenues of $37 million in 2002, and EBITDA of $10.6 million. DJ also holds equity or other interests in international business and financial wire services, newspapers, and other publications.

Electronic publishing includes the operations of WSJ.com, Dow Jones Newswires, Factiva, and Dow Jones Indexes. The Wall Street Journal Interactive Edition (WSJ.com) is the largest paid-subscription site on the World Wide Web, with more than 689,000 subscribers as of December 31, 2003. Dow Jones Newswires delivers a spectrum of real-time global business and financial news across five asset classes to financial professionals around the world. Factiva was formed in 1999 from the combination of Dow Jones Interactive and Reuters Business Briefing. Factiva is an online, customizable research product that provides business and professional users with online access to the contents of more than 8,500 business, trade and local publications, including information sources in 22 languages.

In February 2004, DJ acquired Alternative Investor from Wicks Business Information for about $85 million. Alternative Investor is a provider of newsletters, databases and industry conferences for the venture capital and private equity markets. The acquisition was combined into the company's Dow Jones Newswires business.

Company Financials   Fiscal Year ending December 31

Per Share Data ($)

(Year Ended December 31)	2003	2002	2001	2000	1999	1998	1997	1996	1995	1994
Tangible Bk. Val.	NM	NM	NM	0.98	5.24	4.60	4.07	3.89	3.01	1.83
Cash Flow	3.38	3.71	2.36	-0.13	4.13	1.56	-5.74	4.22	4.08	3.90
Earnings	2.08	2.40	1.14	-1.35	2.99	0.09	-8.36	1.96	1.96	1.83
S&P Core Earnings	0.91	0.16	1.09	NA	NA	NA	NA	NA	NA	NA
Dividends	1.00	1.00	1.00	1.00	0.96	0.96	0.96	0.96	0.92	0.84
Payout Ratio	48%	42%	88%	NM	32%	NM	NM	49%	47%	46%
Prices - High	53.62	60.20	64.30	77.31	71.37	59.00	55.87	41.87	40.12	41.87
- Low	33.25	29.50	43.05	51.37	43.62	41.56	33.37	31.87	30.62	28.12
P/E Ratio - High	26	25	56	NM	24	NM	NM	21	20	23
- Low	16	12	38	NM	15	NM	NM	16	16	15

Income Statement Analysis (Million $)

	2003	2002	2001	2000	1999	1998	1997	1996	1995	1994
Revs.	1,548	1,559	1,773	2,203	2,002	2,158	2,573	2,482	2,284	2,091
Oper. Inc.	231	209	289	606	496	437	510	555	510	564
Depr.	106	110	106	108	104	142	251	218	206	205
Int. Exp.	2.83	3.08	0.50	2.04	5.27	7.19	19.4	18.8	18.3	16.9
Pretax Inc.	221	258	100	76.4	418	71.7	-764	331	323	339
Eff. Tax Rate	23.4%	24.8%	98.5%	NM	34.8%	88.0%	NM	44.6%	43.3%	46.5%
Net Inc.	171	202	98.2	-119	272	8.36	-802	190	190	181
S&P Core Earnings	74.9	12.3	93.2	NA	NA	NA	NA	NA	NA	NA

Balance Sheet & Other Fin. Data (Million $)

	2003	2002	2001	2000	1999	1998	1997	1996	1995	1994
Cash	23.5	39.3	21.0	49.3	86.4	143	23.8	6.77	14.0	11.0
Curr. Assets	246	251	246	368	456	442	507	404	371	310
Total Assets	1,304	1,208	1,298	1,362	1,531	1,491	1,920	2,760	2,599	2,446
Curr. Liab.	614	622	602	587	579	600	672	601	582	531
LT Debt	153	92.9	174	151	150	150	229	332	254	296
Common Equity	2,270	40.5	41.8	159	553	509	781	1,644	1,602	1,482
Total Cap.	2,430	134	220	318	703	659	1,010	1,976	1,856	1,777
Cap. Exp.	55.9	77.7	129	187	191	226	348	232	219	222
Cash Flow	277	311	204	-11.1	376	151	-551	408	396	386
Curr. Ratio	0.4	0.4	0.4	0.6	0.8	0.7	0.8	0.7	0.6	0.6
% LT Debt of Cap.	6.3	69.3	79.2	47.4	21.3	22.7	22.7	16.8	13.7	16.6
% Net Inc.of Revs.	11.0	12.9	5.5	NM	13.6	0.4	NM	7.7	8.3	8.7
% Ret. on Assets	13.6	16.1	7.4	NM	18.1	0.5	NM	7.1	7.5	7.7
% Ret. on Equity	7.7	489.5	98.0	NM	51.3	1.3	NM	11.7	12.3	12.4

Data as orig reptd.; bef. results of disc opers/spec. items. Per share data adj. for stk. divs.; EPS diluted. E-Estimated. NA-Not Available. NM-Not Meaningful. NR-Not Ranked. UR-Under Review.

Office: 200 Liberty Street, New York, NY 10281.
Telephone: 212-416-2000.
Email: investorrelations@dowjones.com
Website: http://www.dowjones.com
Chrmn & CEO: P.R. Kann.
COO: R.F. Zannino.
EVP, Secy & General Counsel: P.G. Skinner.

VP & CFO: C.W. Vieth.
Treas: T.W. McGuirl.
Investor Contact: M. Donohue 609-520-5660.
Dirs: C. Bancroft, L. B. Campbell, H. Golub, R. Hammer, L. Hill, I. O. Hockaday, Jr., V. E. Jordan, Jr., P. R. Kann, D. K. Li, M. P. McPherson, F. N. Newman, J. H. Ottaway, Jr., E. Steele, W. C. Steere, Jr., D. von Holtzbrinck.

Founded: in 1882.
Domicile: Delaware.
Employees: 6,975.
S&P Analyst: William H. Donald/PMW/JWP

DTE Energy

Recommendation: **HOLD** ★★★☆☆
SELL | SELL | HOLD | BUY | BUY

12-Month Target Price: **$42.00**
(as of June 25, 2004)

DTE has an approximate 0.07% weighting in the **S&P 500**

Sector: Utilities
Sub-Industry: Electric Utilities
Peer Group: Electric Cos. (Domestic) - Large

Summary: This Detroit-based diversified energy company is involved in the development and management of energy-related businesses and services nationwide.

Quantitative Evaluations

S&P Earnings & Dividend Rank: B+

| D | C | B- | B | B+ | A- | A | A+ |

S&P Fair Value Rank: 3-

| 1 | 2 | 3 | 4 | 5 |
| Lowest | | | | Highest |

Fair Value Calc.: $43.30 (Slightly Overvalued)

S&P Investability Quotient Percentile

73%

DTE scored higher than 73% of all companies for which an S&P Report is available.

Volatility: Low

| Low | Average | High |

Technical Evaluation: Bullish
Since 8/04, the technical indicators for DTE have been Bullish.

Relative Strength Rank: Moderate

61

1 Lowest   Highest 99

Price as of 11/12/04: $44.72 | **2004E S&P Core EPS:** $2.12

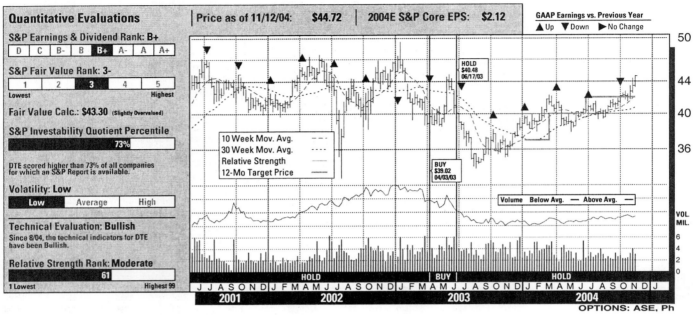

GAAP Earnings vs. Previous Year
▲ Up   ▼ Down   ► No Change

10 Week Mov. Avg.
30 Week Mov. Avg.
Relative Strength
12-Mo Target Price

HOLD $40.48 06/17/03
BUY $39.02 04/03/03

Volume   Below Avg. — Above Avg.

VOL. MIL.

OPTIONS: ASE, Ph

Analyst commentary prepared by Justin McCann/CB/GG

Highlights June 29, 2004

- We expect EPS in 2004 to increase about 5% from 2003's operating EPS of $3.09, which was hurt by the impact of customers switching to other power suppliers, as well as milder weather, lost margins related to the August power blackout, and increased pension, health care and insurance costs.

- Earnings in 2004 will depend upon rate increase requests pending before the Michigan Public Service Commission (MPSC). On February 20, 2004, the MPSC granted Detroit Edison annualized interim rate relief of $82 million. However, with the increase not effective until February 21, and after a related $20 million refund, there would only be a $51 million net increase.

- DTE believes the MPSC will grant further relief in its final order, which is expected in September. It is also working with Michigan legislators to reform the June 2000 legislation related to the electric choice program, which has resulted in a large migration of customers to other suppliers. With the IRS decision to renew tax credits related to DTE's synthetic fuel production, the company plans to resume the sale of interests in its synthetic fuel facilities.

Investment Rationale/Risk June 29, 2004

- We expect the shares to stabilize at around their current level. The shares had benefited from what we viewed as an encouraging MPSC interim order related to the pending rate proceedings. However, the shares will also reflect the outlook for proposed legislative changes to Michigan's electric customer choice program.

- Risks to our investment recommendation and target price include smaller than expected electric and natural gas rate increases, inadequate reform of the electric choice program, and a significant decline in the average P/E multiple of the peer group as a whole.

- With the yield (recently around 5.1%) from what we consider a secure dividend above the industry average, we would hold the shares. However, given the uncertainties related the electric choice program, we expect the stock to trade at about a 10% discount to the average 13.3X peer P/E multiple on our EPS estimates for 2005. Our 12-month target price is $42.

Key Stock Statistics

S&P Core EPS 2005E	3.22	52-week Range	$44.75-35.90
S&P Oper. EPS 2004E	2.90	12 Month P/E	14.0
P/E on S&P Oper. EPS 2004E	15.4	Beta	0.01
S&P Oper. EPS 2005E	3.50	Shareholders	105,173
Yield (%)	4.6%	Market Cap (B)	$ 7.8
Dividend Rate/Share	2.06	Shares Outstanding (M)	174.0

Value of $10,000 invested five years ago: **$ 16,223**

Dividend Data Dividends have been paid since 1909

Amount ($)	Date Decl.	Ex-Div. Date	Stock of Record	Payment Date
0.515	Dec. 08	Dec. 18	Dec. 22	Jan. 15 '04
0.515	Mar. 09	Mar. 18	Mar. 22	Apr. 15 '04
0.515	May. 14	Jun. 17	Jun. 21	Jul. 15 '04
0.515	Jul. 14	Sep. 17	Sep. 21	Oct. 15 '04

Revenues/Earnings Data Fiscal year ending December 31

Revenues (Million $)

	2004	2003	2002	2001	2000	1999
1Q	2,093	2,095	1,896	1,842	1,182	1,024
2Q	1,501	1,600	1,478	1,790	1,428	1,150
3Q	1,594	1,654	1,636	2,081	1,547	1,440
4Q	—	1,692	1,739	2,136	1,440	1,114
Yr.	—	7,041	6,749	7,849	5,597	4,728

Earnings Per Share ($)

	2004	2003	2002	2001	2000	1999
1Q	1.13	0.64	1.24	0.95	0.81	0.79
2Q	0.20	-0.22	0.42	-0.60	0.76	0.76
3Q	0.54	1.06	0.96	0.38	0.73	1.11
4Q	E1.18	1.36	1.21	1.34	0.97	0.67
Yr.	E2.90	2.85	3.83	2.14	3.27	3.33

Next earnings report expected: early-February Source: S&P, Company Reports
EPS Estimates based on S&P Operating Earnings; historical GAAP earnings are as reported.

STANDARD &POOR'S

DTE Energy Company

Stock Report
November 13, 2004
NYSE Symbol: **DTE**

Recommendation: **HOLD** ★ ★ ★ ☆ ☆   12-Month Target Price: **$42.00** (as of June 25, 2004)

Business Summary June 30, 2004

DTE Energy, formed on January 1, 1996, is the holding company for Detroit Edison Co., the largest electric utility in Michigan, serving 2.1 million customers in the southeastern part of the state.

On May 31, 2001, the company acquired Detroit-based MCN Energy Group, Inc. (MCN), the holding company for Michigan Consolidated Gas Co. (MichCon). The transaction, under a February 2001 revision of an October 1999 agreement, was for cash (55%) and stock (45%) valued at $2.34 billion (versus $2.6 billion in the original agreement), plus the assumption of $1.5 billion of debt and preferred securities. MichCon distributes gas to 1.2 million customers throughout Michigan.

DTE Energy's regulated electric and gas businesses accounted for 73.8% of operating revenues in 2003 (80.7% in 2002) and 58.5% of net income from continuing operations (72.8%). DTE's non-regulated businesses accounted for 26.3% of operating revenues in 2003 (19.3% in 2001) and 41.5% of net income from continuing operations (27.2%).

The company's non-regulated businesses include DTE Energy Marketing and Trading Company, which is involved in the trading and marketing of electricity, gas and coal; Energy Services, which consists of businesses that develop and manage energy-related assets and services such as coke and synfuels production, independent power plants, on-site powerhouses and cogeneration facilities, coal services and landfill gas recovery; and DTE Energy Technologies, which markets distributed generation products and monitors and manages system operations.

DTE's other non-regulated businesses include operations acquired in the merger with MCN Energy: the gas and oil exploration and production business, and the gas storage, pipelines and processing business.

The company's consolidated capital spending in 2003 totaled $751 million. This was down 23.7% from $984 million in 2002, which was down 10.2% from $1.096 billion in 2001.

In December 1998, the Michigan Public Service Commission (MPSC) authorized accelerated amortization of the Fermi 2 nuclear assets, providing for complete recovery of assets by December 31, 2007.

In June 2000, Michigan enacted legislation that established January 1, 2002, as the date for full implementation of the MPSC's program providing for full customer choice of electricity supplier. The legislation also required the MPSC to reduce residential electric rates by 5%, and provided Detroit Edison with the right to recover stranded costs.

In January 2002, transmission assets owned by Detroit Edison were transferred to wholly owned ITC. In December 2002, DTE agreed to sell ITC for about $610 million; the sale was completed February 28, 2003.

Company Financials Fiscal Year ending December 31

Per Share Data ($)

(Year Ended December 31)	2003	2002	2001	2000	1999	1998	1997	1996	1995	1994
Tangible Bk. Val.	19.05	14.61	16.06	28.15	26.96	25.49	24.55	23.41	23.40	22.66
Earnings	2.85	3.83	2.14	3.27	3.33	3.05	2.88	2.13	2.80	2.67
S&P Core Earnings	3.22	2.80	2.09	NA	NA	NA	NA	NA	NA	NA
Dividends	2.06	2.06	2.06	2.06	2.06	2.06	2.06	2.06	2.06	2.06
Payout Ratio	72%	54%	96%	63%	62%	68%	72%	97%	74%	77%
Prices - High	49.50	47.70	47.13	41.31	44.68	49.25	34.75	37.25	34.87	30.25
- Low	34.00	33.05	33.12	28.43	31.06	33.43	26.12	27.62	25.75	24.25
P/E Ratio - High	17	12	22	13	13	16	12	17	12	11
- Low	12	9	15	9	9	11	9	13	9	9

Income Statement Analysis (Million $)

	2003	2002	2001	2000	1999	1998	1997	1996	1995	1994
Revs.	7,041	6,749	7,849	5,597	4,728	4,221	3,764	3,645	3,635	3,519
Depr.	687	759	795	758	735	661	660	527	501	476
Maint.	NA	NA	NA	NA	NA	NA	NA	278	240	262
Fxd. Chgs. Cov.	1.49	2.00	2.04	2.42	2.60	2.84	3.21	3.19	3.24	3.04
Constr. Credits	NA	NA	NA	NA	NA	Nil	Nil	5.36	3.70	3.70
Eff. Tax Rate	24.0%	NM	NM	1.89%	11.0%	25.8%	38.1%	41.9%	41.1%	38.9%
Net Inc.	480	632	329	468	483	443	417	309	406	420
S&P Core Earnings	542	463	322	NA	NA	NA	NA	NA	NA	NA

Balance Sheet & Other Fin. Data (Million $)

	2003	2002	2001	2000	1999	1998	1997	1996	1995	1994
Gross Prop.	17,679	17,862	17,067	13,162	12,746	12,178	14,495	13,777	13,304	13,046
Cap. Exp.	751	984	1,096	749	739	555	456	531	454	378
Net Prop.	10,324	9,813	9,543	7,387	7,148	6,943	8,934	8,501	8,519	8,586
Capitalization:										
LT Debt	7,669	7,785	7,928	4,062	4,052	4,323	3,914	3,895	3,756	3,951
% LT Debt	59.2	63.0	63.0	50.3	50.9	53.9	51.3	52.1	50.0	52.5
Pfd.	Nil	Nil	Nil	Nil	Nil	Nil	144	144	327	380
% Pfd.	Nil	Nil	Nil	Nil	Nil	Nil	1.80	1.90	4.30	5.00
Common	5,287	4,565	4,657	4,015	3,909	3,698	3,562	3,444	3,436	3,326
% Common	40.8	37.0	37.0	49.7	49.1	46.1	46.7	46.0	45.7	44.2
Total Cap.	14,256	13,434	14,063	9,878	9,886	9,909	9,904	9,822	9,902	10,019
% Oper. Ratio	91.1	82.8	86.3	85.3	82.2	81.4	80.2	79.1	79.7	79.6
% Earn. on Net Prop.	7.2	11.4	8.2	11.4	12.8	11.8	8.4	7.2	8.6	8.3
% Return On Revs.	6.8	9.4	4.2	8.4	10.2	10.5	11.1	8.5	11.2	11.9
% Return On Invest. Capital	7.5	9.1	8.9	8.1	8.3	6.2	9.9	6.2	7.4	7.1
% Return On Com. Equity	9.7	13.8	7.6	11.8	12.7	12.2	11.9	8.9	12.0	11.8

Data as orig reptd.; bef. results of disc opers/spec. items. Per share data adj. for stk. divs.; EPS diluted. E-Estimated. NA-Not Available. NM-Not Meaningful. NR-Not Ranked. UR-Under Review.

Office: 2000 2nd Ave, Detroit, MI 48226-1279.
Telephone: 313-235-4000.
Email: shareholdersvcs@dteenergy.com
Website: http://www.dteenergy.com
Chrmn, Pres, CEO & COO: A.F. Earley, Jr.
SVP & CFO: D.E. Meador.
SVP & General Counsel: E.H. Peterson.

VP & Secy: S.M. Beale.
Investor Contact: P.J. Pintar 313-235-8030.
Dirs: T. E. Adderley, L. Bauder, D. E. Bing, A. F. Earley, Jr., A. D. Gillmour, A. R. Glancy III, F. M. Hennessey, T. S. Leipprandt, J. E. Lobbia, G. McGovern, E. A. Miller, C. W. Pryor, Jr., J. Robles, Jr., H. F. Sims.

Founded: in 1995.
Domicile: Michigan.
Employees: 11,099.
S&P Analyst: Justin McCann/CB/GG

Duke Energy

Recommendation: **HOLD** ★★★☆☆
SELL | SELL | HOLD | BUY | BUY

12-Month Target Price: $24.00
(as of November 03, 2004)

DUK has an approximate 0.22% weighting in the **S&P 500**

Sector: Utilities
Sub-Industry: Multi-Utilities & Unregulated Power
Peer Group: Integrated Gas & Electric distribution

Summary: DUK provides electric service to about 2 million customers in North and South Carolina, and is one of the largest U.S. transporters and marketers of natural gas.

Quantitative Evaluations

S&P Earnings & Dividend Rank: B+

| D | C | B- | B | B+ | A- | A | A+ |

S&P Fair Value Rank: 3-

| 1 | 2 | 3 | 4 | 5 |
| Lowest | | | | Highest |

Fair Value Calc.: $24.30 (Slightly Overvalued)

S&P Investability Quotient Percentile

82%

DUK scored higher than 82% of all companies for which an S&P Report is available.

Volatility: Low

| Low | Average | High |

Technical Evaluation: Bullish
Since 9/04, the technical indicators for DUK have been Bullish.

Relative Strength Rank: Strong

73

1 Lowest | Highest 99

Price as of 11/12/04: $25.54 | **2004E S&P Core EPS:** $1.29

GAAP Earnings vs. Previous Year
▲ Up ▼ Down ► No Change

10 Week Mov. Avg.
30 Week Mov. Avg.
Relative Strength
12-Mo Target Price

Volume Below Avg. — Above Avg.

OPTIONS: ASE, CBOE, P, Ph

Analyst commentary prepared by Yogeesh Wagle/MF/JWP

Highlights October 07, 2004

- Reported EPS for 2003 includes $2.41 in net one-time charges related to DUK's exit from certain Duke Energy North America and Duke Energy International operations and severance charges, partly offset by asset sale gains. Results for the first half of 2004 include about $48 million after-tax in net one-time gains and asset sales. DUK's second quarter results were better than expected.

- Excluding one-time items, we see flat 2004 operating EPS as much higher contributions from Field Services (due to higher commodity prices), growth in Crescent real estate, reduced pension expense, one-time tax benefits and cost cutting are offset by the loss of earnings associated with divested operations and the expiration of more favorable wholesale power supply contracts, and over 3% more shares. We see 2005 EPS increasing 19%, as narrowing DENA losses and declining interest expense outweigh a higher tax rate and over 5% more shares projected.

- Our 2004 Standard and Poor's Core Earnings projection is a penny below our operating EPS estimate, with the full expensing of stock options and negative accounting adjustments for pension expense slightly exceeding positive adjustments to post-retirement expense.

Key Stock Statistics

S&P Core EPS 2005E	1.30	52-week Range	$25.54-17.08
S&P Oper. EPS 2004E	1.34	12 Month P/E	NM
P/E on S&P Oper. EPS 2004E	19.1	Beta	0.58
S&P Oper. EPS 2005E	1.55	Shareholders	147,900
Yield (%)	4.3%	Market Cap (B)	$ 24.0
Dividend Rate/Share	1.10	Shares Outstanding (M)	937.8

Value of $10,000 invested five years ago: **$ 11,309**

Dividend Data Dividends have been paid since 1926

Amount ($)	Date Decl.	Ex-Div. Date	Stock of Record	Payment Date
0.275	Jan. 07	Feb. 11	Feb. 13	Mar. 16 '04
0.275	Apr. 22	May. 12	May. 14	Jun. 16 '04
0.275	Jun. 22	Aug. 11	Aug. 13	Sep. 16 '04
0.275	Oct. 26	Nov. 09	Nov. 12	Dec. 16 '04

Investment Rationale/Risk October 07, 2004

- Using our 2006 EPS estimate of $1.70, the shares appear to trade with a long-term P/E in line with utility peers, but its EPS growth rate is, in our opinion, below its peer average. The stock's price to book and price to trailing cash flow multiples are at discounts to peers. In our opinion, DUK's goodwill balance and positive changes in working capital explain some of these significant valuation discounts, but not all.

- Risks to our recommendation and target price include a prolonged period of low electric margins, a slow southeastern real estate market, rapid increases in interest rates, and slower than expected economic growth.

- We are concerned that DUK is more susceptible to rising interest rates than peers given a dividend payout ratio of almost 85% and our expectation for below average EPS growth. However, given what we see as DUK's stabilizing earnings outlook and valuation discounts, we believe the stock can sustain current levels over the coming year, in addition to distributing a $1.10 annual dividend. Our 12-month target price is $23. We would hold the shares, currently yielding 4.6%, on a total return basis.

Revenues/Earnings Data Fiscal year ending December 31

Revenues (Million $)

	2004	2003	2002	2001	2000	1999
1Q	5,845	6,228	3,227	16,491	7,236	4,160
2Q	5,360	5,235	3,698	15,580	10,926	4,691
3Q	5,507	5,609	3,982	16,718	15,691	6,694
4Q	—	5,457	4,756	10,714	15,411	6,197
Yr.	—	22,529	15,663	59,503	49,318	21,742

Earnings Per Share ($)

	2004	2003	2002	2001	2000	1999
1Q	0.07	0.43	0.48	0.73	0.53	0.42
2Q	0.43	0.46	0.56	0.53	0.44	0.39
3Q	0.42	0.05	0.27	1.01	1.04	0.59
4Q	E0.21	-1.99	-0.06	0.28	0.38	-0.27
Yr.	E1.34	-1.13	1.22	2.56	2.38	1.13

Next earnings report expected: late-January Source: S&P, Company Reports
EPS Estimates based on S&P Operating Earnings; historical GAAP earnings are as reported.

Duke Energy Corporation

Recommendation: **HOLD** ★ ★ ★ ☆ ☆   12-Month Target Price: **$24.00** (as of November 03, 2004)

Business Summary October 07, 2004

At the end of 2003, Duke Energy was the sixth largest U.S. owner of interstate natural gas pipelines (by route miles) and the largest producer of natural gas liquids. The company also provides electric utility services in North Carolina and South Carolina, and gas utility services in Ontario, and owns a fleet of unregulated wholesale power plants.

Driven by weak unregulated energy merchant operations, most credit ratings for company operations were reduced to levels one or two notches above junk status. In an attempt to stabilize its credit, DUK has reduced capital spending and pursued asset sales. In 2003, it ceased construction activities on three partially completed power plants, with the intent of ultimately divesting the units or obtaining a partner to help fund completion. In 2003, capital expenditures were nearly $2.5 billion (with an equal amount planned for 2004), down from over $4.9 billion in 2002. In 2003, the company raised nearly $2.0 billion in cash from asset sales, up from over $500 million in 2002. DUK expected to raise just over $1 billion in net cash from asset sales that had closed or been announced through mid-May 2004. It expected to reduce debt by $3.5 billion to $4 billion during 2004.

DUK has also sought to enhance its earnings stability and credit rating by exiting speculative energy trading activities. In 2003, it largely unwound its speculative energy trading positions at Duke Energy Merchants, and began the process of exiting its European trading business. In January 2004, the company announced plans to wind down Duke Energy Trading & Marketing, an energy trading joint venture 40%-owned by Exxon Mobil.

Operating segments include Franchise Electric (30.6% of assets at the end of 2003), Natural Gas Transmission (31.1%), Duke Energy Field Services (DEFS; 12.2%), Duke Energy North America (DENA; 17.5%), Duke Energy International (DEI; 8.6%). Franchise Electric served about 2.2 million electric utility customers and owned 17,873 net megawatts of power as of May 2004. Transmission operations consist of 16,800 miles of gas pipelines in the U.S. and Canada. Franchise Electric and Natural Gas Transmission together represent DUK's regulated operations; they contributed nearly 83% of 2003 segment earnings before interest and taxes (excluding losses from DENA).

DEFS is a joint venture 69.7%-owned by DUK and 30.3%-owned by ConocoPhillips. It gathers natural gas, processes it (separating out natural gas liquids, or NGLs), transports gas and NGLs, fractionates NGLs (dividing them into component parts), and serves as the general partner for the TEPPCO Partners MLP. DENA is DUK's wholesale power generation and marketing unit, with 10,336 net MW of unregulated generation as of May 2004, excluding southeast plants (5,325 MW) that DUK has agreed to sell, and western plants in deferred construction (2,402 MW).

DEI primarily consists of power generation (4,121 net MW) in Central and South America. In April 2004, the company sold its Australian pipeline assets, for $1.24 billion (including $900 million of assumed debt).

Company Financials Fiscal Year ending December 31

Per Share Data ($)

(Year Ended December 31)	2003	2002	2001	2000	1999	1998	1997	1996	1995	1994
Tangible Bk. Val.	10.74	12.51	14.11	11.21	10.69	10.09	9.36	11.57	11.09	10.46
Earnings	-1.13	1.22	2.56	2.38	1.13	1.71	1.25	1.69	1.63	1.44
S&P Core Earnings	-1.10	1.01	2.29	NA	NA	NA	NA	NA	NA	NA
Dividends	1.10	1.10	1.10	1.10	1.10	1.10	1.08	1.04	1.00	0.96
Payout Ratio	NM	90%	43%	46%	98%	64%	86%	62%	62%	67%
Prices - High	21.57	40.00	47.74	45.21	32.65	35.50	28.28	26.50	23.93	21.50
- Low	12.21	16.42	32.22	22.87	23.37	26.56	20.93	21.68	18.68	16.43
P/E Ratio - High	NM	33	19	19	29	21	23	16	15	15
- Low	NM	13	13	10	21	16	17	13	11	11

Income Statement Analysis (Million $)

	2003	2002	2001	2000	1999	1998	1997	1996	1995	1994
Revs.	22,529	15,663	59,503	49,318	21,742	17,610	16,309	4,758	4,677	4,489
Depr.	1,803	1,571	1,336	1,167	968	909	841	492	458	460
Maint.	NA	NA	NA	NA	NA	NA	NA	NA	416	430
Fxd. Chgs. Cov.	1.96	2.46	5.33	4.25	3.16	4.78	3.67	4.20	4.35	4.08
Constr. Credits	NA	NA	53.0	63.0	82.0	88.0	109	112	23.1	27.4
Eff. Tax Rate	NM	35.1%	33.1%	32.9%	31.4%	36.4%	39.1%	40.0%	39.5%	38.3%
Net Inc.	-1,005	1,034	1,994	1,776	847	1,260	974	730	715	639
S&P Core Earnings	-994	908	1,777	NA	NA	NA	NA	NA	NA	NA

Balance Sheet & Other Fin. Data (Million $)

	2003	2002	2001	2000	1999	1998	1997	1996	1995	1994
Gross Prop.	47,157	48,677	39,464	34,615	30,436	27,128	25,448	14,946	14,937	14,489
Cap. Exp.	2,470	4,924	5,930	5,634	NA	2,159	1,323	646	713	772
Net Prop.	34,986	36,219	28,415	24,469	20,995	16,875	15,736	9,386	9,361	9,264
Capitalization:										
LT Debt	20,622	21,629	13,728	12,425	10,087	7,191	6,530	3,538	3,711	3,567
% LT Debt	59.8	58.9	51.5	54.7	52.0	45.9	44.8	39.0	40.4	40.2
Pfd.	134	157	234	247	313	313	489	684	684	780
% Pfd.	0.39	0.43	0.88	1.09	1.61	2.00	3.40	7.50	7.50	8.80
Common	13,748	14,944	12,689	10,056	8,998	8,150	7,540	4,889	4,785	4,533
% Common	39.8	40.7	47.6	44.2	46.4	52.1	51.8	54.3	52.1	51.0
Total Cap.	40,490	43,644	33,393	29,225	24,225	19,882	18,673	11,737	11,824	11,501
% Oper. Ratio	85.4	87.1	95.0	94.3	93.8	90.6	91.8	81.4	91.1	82.6
% Earn. on Net Prop.	NM	7.6	15.5	16.8	9.5	14.9	15.4	14.5	14.5	8.6
% Return On Revs.	NM	6.6	3.4	3.6	3.9	7.2	6.0	15.3	15.3	14.2
% Return On Invest. Capital	8.7	6.3	10.5	11.2	7.6	13.2	11.2	16.9	12.6	7.9
% Return On Com. Equity	NM	7.4	17.4	18.4	9.6	15.5	14.1	14.2	14.3	13.3

Data as orig reptd.; bef. results of disc opers/spec. items. Per share data adj. for stk. divs. Bold denotes primary EPS - prior periods restated. E-Estimated. NA-Not Available. NM-Not Meaningful. NR-Not Ranked. UR-Under Review.

Office: 526 South Church Street, Charlotte, NC 28202-1904.
Telephone: 704-594-6200.
Website: http://www.duke-energy.com
Chrmn & CEO: P. Anderson.
Pres & COO: F. Fowler.
EVP & CFO: D. Hauser.

EVP, Secy & General Counsel: M.B. Wyrsch.
Investor Contact: G. Ebel 704-382-8118.
Dirs: R. Agnelli, P. M. Anderson, G. A. Bernhardt, Sr., R. J. Brown, W. T. Esrey, A. M. Gray, G. D. Johnson, Jr., M. Lennon, L. E. Linbeck, Jr., J. G. Martin, M. Phelps, J. T. Rhodes.

Founded: in 1916.
Domicile: North Carolina.
Employees: 23,800.
S&P Analyst: Yogeesh Wagle/MF/JWP

du Pont (E.I.) de Nemours

Recommendation: **SELL** ★ ☆ ☆ ☆ ☆
SELL | SELL | HOLD | BUY | BUY

12-Month Target Price: $38.00
(as of September 18, 2003)

DD has an approximate 0.40% weighting in the **S&P 500**

Sector: Materials
Sub-Industry: Diversified Chemicals
Peer Group: Major Diversified Companies

Summary: This broadly diversified company is the second largest U.S. chemicals manufacturer.

Quantitative Evaluations

S&P Earnings & Dividend Rank: B

| D | C | B- | **B** | B+ | A- | A | A+ |

S&P Fair Value Rank: 2

| 1 | **2** | 3 | 4 | 5 |
| Lowest | | | | Highest |

Fair Value Calc.: $38.80 (Slightly Overvalued)

S&P Investability Quotient Percentile

76%

DD scored higher than 76% of all companies for which an S&P Report is available.

Volatility: Low

| **Low** | Average | High |

Technical Evaluation: Bullish
Since 11/04, the technical indicators for DD have been Bullish.

Relative Strength Rank: Moderate

47

| 1 Lowest | | Highest 99 |

| Price as of 11/12/04: | $44.50 | 2004E S&P Core EPS: | $1.72 |

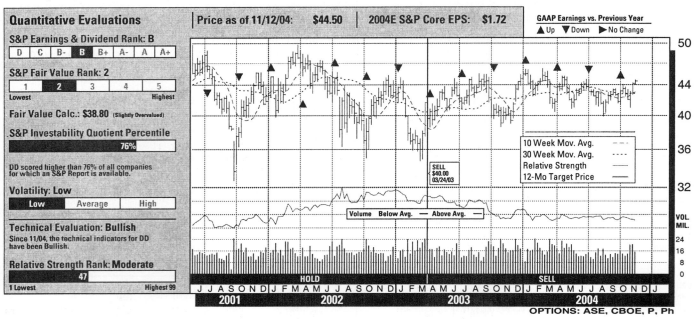

GAAP Earnings vs. Previous Year
▲ Up ▼ Down ► No Change

- 10 Week Mov. Avg.
- 30 Week Mov. Avg.
- Relative Strength
- 12-Mo Target Price

SELL $40.00 03/24/03

Volume Below Avg. — Above Avg.

HOLD | SELL

J J A S O N D J F M A M J J A S O N D J F M A M J J A S O N D J F M A M J J A S O N D J
2001 | 2002 | 2003 | 2004

OPTIONS: ASE, CBOE, P, Ph

Analyst commentary prepared by Richard O'Reilly, CFA /CB/JWP

Highlights September 24, 2004

- In April 2004, the company sold its INVISTA (Textile and Interiors) unit, for $4.2 billion; it expected the transaction to be neutral to accretive to 2004 EPS. DD used most of the net proceeds of $4.1 billion to repay debt. The company is also implementing a $900 million cost reduction plan, including a 6% workforce reduction, with the full amount to be achieved in 2005.

- We expect 2004 operating EPS of $2.30 (before special charges of about $0.60), with $2.55 projected for 2005. We expect combined profits of the chemicals and materials segments to continue to improve, assuming a continued pickup in volumes along with industrial activity. We think selling prices will rise moderately, helping to offset projected higher raw material costs in 2005 after a nearly $0.40 a share increase expected for 2004. Pension expense will likely be unchanged in both years, after climbing nearly $0.40 in 2003.

- We see the agriculture segment posting a record year in 2004, as both pesticides and seeds are benefiting from higher U.S. corn acreage and growth in biotech products. We also expect increased pharmaceutical profits in 2004, due to projected 8% to 16% higher sales of Cozaar/Hyzaar. We project an effective tax rate of 25% for the second half of 2004, versus credits in the comparable 2003 period, with a possible slightly higher rate for 2005.

Investment Rationale/Risk September 24, 2004

- We would avoid the stock, trading recently at what we view as an excessive premium to the P/E multiple of the S&P 500. While sales volumes should continue to advance into 2005, we see high raw material costs continuing to put pressure on chemicals margins. We view positively the 2004 sale of the fiber businesses, reducing about 50% of DD's exposure to raw material cost changes, but are disappointed that the company does not plan to use any of the proceeds to buy back common stock.

- Risks to our recommendation and target price include stronger than expected industrial activity, and lower raw material costs than we currently assume.

- The stock is trading at a premium P/E multiple to the S&P 500 at 16.5X our 2005 EPS estimate of $2.30, and is modestly above our intrinsic value calculation, which assumes average annual free cash flow growth of 10%, and a discount rate of 10.5%. Our 12-month target price is $38.

Key Stock Statistics

S&P Core EPS 2005E	2.59	52-week Range	$46.25-39.00
S&P Oper. EPS 2004E	2.30	12 Month P/E	21.0
P/E on S&P Oper. EPS 2004E	19.3	Beta	0.88
S&P Oper. EPS 2005E	2.55	Shareholders	110,676
Yield (%)	3.1%	Market Cap (B)	$ 44.2
Dividend Rate/Share	1.40	Shares Outstanding (M)	993.7

Value of $10,000 invested five years ago: **$ 8,263**

Dividend Data Dividends have been paid since 1904

Amount ($)	Date Decl.	Ex-Div. Date	Stock of Record	Payment Date
0.350	Jan. 28	Feb. 11	Feb. 13	Mar. 13 '04
0.350	Apr. 28	May. 12	May. 14	Jun. 12 '04
0.350	Jul. 28	Aug. 11	Aug. 13	Sep. 11 '04
0.350	Oct. 27	Nov. 10	Nov. 15	Dec. 14 '04

Revenues/Earnings Data Fiscal year ending December 31

Revenues (Million $)

	2004	2003	2002	2001	2000	1999
1Q	8,205	7,008	6,142	6,859	7,941	6,313
2Q	7,732	7,369	6,700	6,997	8,132	6,994
3Q	5,740	6,142	5,482	5,641	6,865	6,640
4Q	—	6,477	5,682	5,229	6,316	7,140
Yr.	—	26,996	24,006	24,726	29,202	26,918

Earnings Per Share ($)

	2004	2003	2002	2001	2000	1999
1Q	0.66	0.56	0.48	0.46	0.76	0.55
2Q	0.50	0.67	0.54	-0.21	0.65	0.74
3Q	0.33	-0.88	0.47	0.13	0.53	0.17
4Q	E0.29	0.64	0.35	3.82	0.25	1.38
Yr.	E2.30	0.99	1.84	4.15	2.19	0.19

Next earnings report expected: late-January Source: S&P, Company Reports
EPS Estimates based on S&P Operating Earnings; historical GAAP earnings are as reported.

STANDARD &POOR'S

E.I. du Pont de Nemours and Company

Stock Report
November 13, 2004
NYSE Symbol: **DD**

Recommendation: **SELL** ★ ★ ☆ ☆ ☆   12-Month Target Price: **$38.00** (as of September 18, 2003)

Business Summary September 24, 2004

E.I. du Pont de Nemours and Company, the second largest domestic chemicals producer, has made several major changes in recent years, including divesting its Conoco energy business in 1999, and expanding its life sciences businesses (now crop pesticides and nutrition). As part of its strategy, in October 1999, the company acquired the remaining 80% stake in Pioneer Hi-Bred International, for a total of $7.7 billion, including 68.6 million common shares. In October 2001, DD sold its pharmaceuticals unit to Bristol-Myers Squibb, for $7.8 billion; the company used a portion of the proceeds to repurchase common stock. In early 2002, DD realigned its businesses, and said it would consider all options for its new Textile and Interiors unit (consisting of nylon, polyester and Lycra fibers, with total annual sales of $6.3 billion). In April 2004, it sold the Textile and Interiors unit for $4.2 billion.

Foreign sales accounted for 55% of the total in 2003.

The Agricultural and Nutrition segment (18% of sales in 2003, and $540 million of after-tax operating income) consists of crop pesticides, nutrition and health (including the Protein Technology soy business, microbial diagnostic testing products, and Liqui-Box food packaging products), and Pioneer Hi-Bred, the world's largest seed company, including corn (75% of sales) and soybeans. The Pharmaceutical segment (nil, $355 million) consists of DD's interest in the financial results of Cozaar and Hyzaar antihypertensive products (sales in 2003 of $2.5 billion), marketed by Merck & Co.

The Coatings and Color Technologies unit (18%, $477 million) is the largest global auto paint supplier and maker of titanium pigments (33% of segment sales). The segment also includes industrial and powder coatings and inks. The Electronic and Communication Technologies segment (10%, $147 million) includes electronic materials and display products, and printing and proofing systems. DD is the world's largest maker of fluorochemicals (refrigerants, blowing agents, aerosols) and fluoropolymers (Teflon resins and coatings). Performance Materials (18%, $262 million) includes engineering polymers for auto, electrical, consumer and industrial uses; packaging and industrial polymers and films; and joint ventures in elastomers and polyester films. Safety & Protection (13%, $536 million) consists of Kevlar and Nomex aramid fibers and Tyvek nonwovens for industrial, packaging and textile uses; specialty and intermediate chemicals; Corian fabricated products; and safety consulting services.

Textiles & Interiors (23%, loss of $1.34 billion, including special charges of $1.36 billion) is the world's largest maker of fibers. It is the global leader in nylon intermediates and fibers for carpeting (Stainmaster and Antron brand), and industrial and apparel uses; and Lycra spandex used in apparel. It is also a leading global maker of polyester fibers (Dacron), films, resins and intermediates.

Company Financials Fiscal Year ending December 31

Per Share Data ($)

(Year Ended December 31)	2003	2002	2001	2000	1999	1998	1997	1996	1995	1994
Tangible Bk. Val.	4.63	4.54	7.30	4.50	3.72	9.78	8.66	8.85	6.59	9.08
Cash Flow	2.58	3.35	5.83	3.99	1.73	2.70	4.16	5.58	5.14	4.19
Earnings	0.99	1.84	4.15	2.19	0.19	1.43	2.08	3.24	2.81	2.00
S&P Core Earnings	1.14	0.40	-1.04	NA	NA	NA	NA	NA	NA	NA
Dividends	1.40	1.40	1.40	1.40	1.40	1.36	1.23	1.11	1.02	0.91
Payout Ratio	141%	76%	34%	64%	NM	96%	59%	34%	36%	45%
Prices - High	46.00	49.80	49.88	74.00	75.18	84.43	69.75	49.68	36.50	31.18
- Low	38.60	35.02	32.64	38.18	50.06	51.68	46.37	34.81	26.31	24.12
P/E Ratio - High	46	27	12	34	NM	59	34	15	13	16
- Low	39	19	8	17	NM	36	22	11	9	12

Income Statement Analysis (Million $)

	2003	2002	2001	2000	1999	1998	1997	1996	1995	1994
Revs.	26,996	24,006	24,726	28,268	26,918	24,767	45,079	43,810	42,163	39,333
Oper. Inc.	3,910	4,263	3,486	5,244	5,469	5,860	8,118	7,975	7,675	6,944
Depr.	1,584	1,515	1,754	1,860	1,690	1,452	2,385	2,621	2,722	2,976
Int. Exp.	347	359	590	810	535	640	642	857	929	702
Pretax Inc.	143	2,124	6,844	3,447	1,690	2,613	4,680	5,981	5,390	4,382
Eff. Tax Rate	NM	8.71%	36.0%	31.1%	83.4%	36.0%	48.6%	39.2%	38.9%	37.8%
Net Inc.	1,002	1,841	4,328	2,314	219	1,648	2,405	3,636	3,293	2,727
S&P Core Earnings	1,132	398	-1,087	NA	NA	NA	NA	NA	NA	NA

Balance Sheet & Other Fin. Data (Million $)

	2003	2002	2001	2000	1999	1998	1997	1996	1995	1994
Cash	3,298	4,143	5,848	1,617	1,582	1,059	1,004	1,319	1,455	1,109
Curr. Assets	18,462	13,459	14,801	11,656	12,653	9,236	11,874	11,103	10,955	11,108
Total Assets	37,039	34,621	40,319	39,426	40,777	38,536	42,942	37,987	37,312	36,892
Curr. Liab.	13,043	7,096	8,067	9,255	11,228	11,610	14,070	10,987	12,731	7,565
LT Debt	4,301	5,647	5,350	6,658	6,625	4,495	5,929	5,087	5,678	6,376
Common Equity	9,544	8,826	14,215	13,062	12,638	13,717	11,033	10,472	8,199	12,585
Total Cap.	15,087	18,755	24,916	22,442	21,677	19,286	19,953	17,929	15,897	20,889
Cap. Exp.	1,713	1,280	1,494	1,925	2,055	2,240	4,768	3,303	3,240	3,050
Cash Flow	2,576	3,346	6,072	4,164	1,899	3,090	4,780	6,257	6,015	5,693
Curr. Ratio	1.4	1.9	1.8	1.3	1.1	0.8	0.8	1.0	0.9	1.5
% LT Debt of Cap.	28.5	30.1	21.5	29.7	30.6	23.3	29.7	28.4	35.7	30.5
% Net Inc.of Revs.	3.7	7.7	17.5	8.2	0.8	6.7	5.3	8.3	7.8	8.0
% Ret. on Assets	2.8	4.9	10.9	5.8	0.6	4.4	5.9	9.7	8.9	7.4
% Ret. on Equity	10.8	15.9	31.7	17.9	1.6	13.3	22.3	38.8	31.6	23.0

Data as orig reptd.; bef. results of disc opers/spec. items. Per share data adj. for stk. divs.; EPS diluted. E-Estimated. NA-Not Available. NM-Not Meaningful. NR-Not Ranked. UR-Under Review.

Office: 1007 Market Street, Wilmington, DE 19898.
Telephone: 302-774-1000.
Email: info@dupont.com
Website: http://www.dupont.com
Chrmn & CEO: C.O. Holliday, Jr.
COO & EVP: R.R. Goodmanson.
SVP & CFO: G.M. Pfeiffer.

SVP, Chief Admin & General Counsel: S.J. Mobley.
VP & Treas: J.P. Jessup.
VP & Investor Contact: C.J. Lukach 800-441-7515.
Dirs: A. J. Belda, R. H. Brown, C. J. Crawford, J. T. Dillon, L. C. Duemling, C. O. Holliday, Jr., D. C. Hopkins, L. D. Juliber, M. Naitoh, W. K. Reilly, H. R. Sharp III, C. M. Vest.

Founded: in 1802.
Domicile: Delaware.
Employees: 81,000.
S&P Analyst: Richard O'Reilly, CFA /CB/JWP

Dynegy Inc.

Recommendation: HOLD ★★★☆☆
SELL SELL HOLD BUY BUY

12-Month Target Price: $6.00
(as of October 28, 2004)

DYN has an approximate 0.02% weighting in the **S&P 500**

Sector: Utilities
Sub-Industry: Multi-Utilities & Unregulated Power
Peer Group: Independent Power Producers

Summary: This company provides electricity, natural gas and natural gas liquids to customers throughout the U.S.

Quantitative Evaluations

S&P Earnings & Dividend Rank: C

| D | C | B- | B | B+ | A- | A | A+ |

S&P Fair Value Rank: NR

| 1 | 2 | 3 | 4 | 5 |
| Lowest | | | | Highest |

Fair Value Calc.: NA

S&P Investability Quotient Percentile

83%

DYN scored higher than 83% of all companies for which an S&P Report is available.

Volatility: Average

| Low | Average | High |

Technical Evaluation: Bullish
Since 8/04, the technical indicators for DYN have been Bullish.

Relative Strength Rank: Strong

77

| 1 Lowest | | Highest 99 |

| Price as of 11/12/04: | **$5.17** | 2004E S&P Core EPS: | **$-0.17** |

GAAP Earnings vs. Previous Year
▲ Up   ▼ Down   ▶ No Change

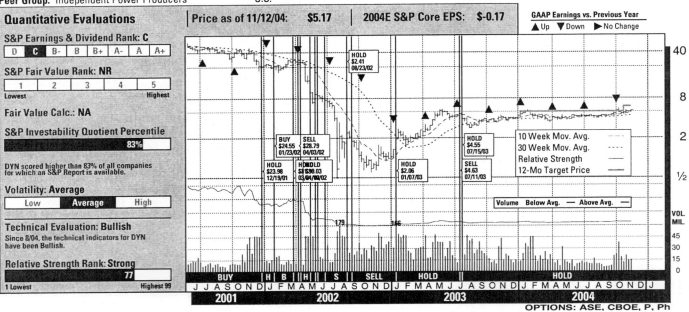

- 10 Week Mov. Avg.
- 30 Week Mov. Avg.
- Relative Strength
- 12-Mo Target Price

Volume   Below Avg. ─ Above Avg.

OPTIONS: ASE, CBOE, P, Ph

Analyst commentary prepared by Craig K. Shere, CFA /CB/GG

Highlights August 04, 2004

- Our 2004 EPS estimate incorporates results from Illinois Power (including $75 million after tax for normal depreciation, which the company discontinued in February), which DYN has agreed to sell, subject to necessary approvals. We exclude an estimated $220 million after tax of net one-time items for asset sale gains, asset and goodwill writedowns, legal costs and settlement charges, tax benefits and finance charges.

- We see 2004 operating earnings increasing, driven by widening midstream liquids margins (due to high commodity prices and frac spreads), the absence of some money-losing tolling contracts, and lower corporate overhead. We see narrowing generation margins (from higher transportation costs for coal fuel) offsetting increased volumes. In 2005, we expect operating earnings to fall, as much lower equity income (due to the expiration of a profitable California power contract) and less favorable liquids margins outweigh the July 2005 expiration of another power tolling contract, wider power margins, and lower interest expense.

- Reported 2003 EPS included a non-cash restructuring gain of $2.71 for maturing convertible preferred stock that DYN had insufficient funds to redeem. Our 2004 Standard & Poor's Core Earnings per share projection is $0.12 less than our operating EPS estimate, primarily due to the expensing of employee stock options and the inclusion of one-time asset impairments, financing costs and tax benefits.

Key Stock Statistics

S&P Core EPS 2005E	-0.14	52-week Range	$5.58-3.40
S&P Oper. EPS 2004E	0.20	12 Month P/E	NM
P/E on S&P Oper. EPS 2004E	25.8	Beta	1.81
S&P Oper. EPS 2005E	-0.05	Shareholders	22,308
Yield (%)	Nil	Market Cap (B)	$ 1.5
Dividend Rate/Share	Nil	Shares Outstanding (M)	379.5

Value of $10,000 invested five years ago: **$ 2,939**

Dividend Data

Dividends were paid from 1994 to mid-2002.

Investment Rationale/Risk August 04, 2004

- We think Dynegy has made good progress in stabilizing its credit profile and resolving regulatory and legal disputes. In May, Moody's Investors Service changed its ratings outlook for DYN to positive, from developing. Assuming DYN can continue to pay down debt and ultimately exit its four remaining money-losing tolling contracts, we would expect continuing improvement in its credit outlook and collateral postings. However, DYN is still relying on asset sales to help meet its debt retirement and capital spending obligations in 2004. Furthermore, we believe DYN's 2005 operating results will be subject to a number of unhedged commodity price risks.

- Risks to our opinion and target price include DYN's ability to obtain new long-term power sales agreements to replace profitable contracts expiring in 2004, successful closing of various asset sales, closure of remaining money-losing power tolling contracts, lower NGL and natural gas prices, higher coal transportation costs, and reductions in weather-driven electricity demand.

- Despite cash flow challenges, we believe DYN now has sufficient liquidity to avoid financial distress. However, we expect the company will issue new equity and pay down debt once cash flows and its share price begin to recover. Given risks and potential dilution from new equity, we believe the shares would be fairly valued at 1.2X book value (versus 1.0X recently, and regulated utilities at 1.7X). Our 12-month target price is $5.

Revenues/Earnings Data Fiscal year ending December 31

Revenues (Million $)

	2004	2003	2002	2001	2000	1999
1Q	1,657	1,879	1,444	14,168	5,349	3,045
2Q	1,440	1,067	1,380	10,812	5,720	3,161
3Q	1,650	1,385	1,407	8,519	8,366	4,585
4Q	—	1,456	1,322	8,743	10,010	4,639
Yr.	—	5,787	5,553	42,242	29,445	15,430

Earnings Per Share ($)

	2004	2003	2002	2001	2000	1999
1Q	0.12	-0.03	-0.26	0.42	0.23	0.12
2Q	-0.06	-0.99	-1.76	0.43	0.19	0.12
3Q	0.16	2.65	-4.71	0.85	0.73	0.22
4Q	E0.10	-0.54	-0.98	0.21	0.32	0.19
Yr.	E0.20	1.30	-6.24	1.89	1.48	0.65

Next earnings report expected: early-February Source: S&P, Company Reports
EPS Estimates based on S&P Operating Earnings; historical GAAP earnings are as reported.

Dynegy Incorporated

Stock Report
November 13, 2004
NYSE Symbol: DYN

Recommendation: **HOLD** ★ ★ ★    12-Month Target Price: **$6.00** (as of October 28, 2004)

Business Summary August 05, 2004

Dynegy has sought to strengthen its balance sheet in the wake of credit, accounting, regulatory and operating difficulties that negatively affected the energy merchant industry in 2002 and 2003. In the course of 2002, Standard & Poor's Credit Services reduced DYN's corporate credit rating from BBB+ to B, where it remained as of May 2004. As of April 2004, the company expected to raise $640 million to $655 million in cash from the sale of businesses and investments in 2004, versus $72 million in 2003 and $1.58 billion in 2002. The company projected 2004 capital spending of $375 million, versus $333 million in 2003, $947 million in 2002, and $2.55 billion in 2001.

In May 2004, the company obtained a new $1.3 billion credit facility, which it used to refinance $1.1 billion of higher cost bank debt maturing in February 2005. In 2003, DYN issued $225 million of debt convertible into stock at $4.12 a share, and exchanged $1.5 billion of convertible preferred stock for $850 million in cash, notes, and new convertible preferred shares.

In January and April 2004, DYN and its 50%-owned California power operations reached initial settlement agreements (definitive agreements were expected in the third quarter) with the FERC and California with regard to trading strategies, power refunds, and unpaid electricity bills relating to the 2000-01 energy crisis. In April and May 2003, the company filed amended financial statements for the periods from 1999 through 2001.

The company operates in four business segments: Power Generation (GEN), Natural Gas Liquids (NGL), Regulated Energy Delivery (REG), and Customer Risk Management (CRM). At the end of 2003, GEN owned 12,713 net MW of capacity. During 2004, GEN planned to pursue the sale of certain partly owned plants. GEN has profitable power sales agreements with California and DYN's Illinois utility, both of which expire at the end of 2004.

REG represents DYN's Illinois utility operations. In February 2004, DYN agreed to sell REG and a 20% interest in a 1,086 MW coal-fired plant to Ameren Corp., for $400 million in cash, $1.8 billion in assumed debt, and $100 million in contingent payments. The transaction, expected to close in the fourth quarter, subject to necessary approvals, includes a power purchase agreement that would aid GEN's operations.

NGL includes mid-stream natural gas gathering and processing, NGL fractionation, and NGL marketing. NGL's assets are principally in Texas, Louisiana, and New Mexico.

The CRM business consists largely of four remaining power tolling contracts, with capacity payment obligations of $160 million in 2004 and $154 million in 2005, and gas transportation contracts. DYN has sought to exit its CRM operations since October 2002, and has already exited five power tolling contracts and speculative energy trading activities. In January 2003, the company agreed to end its natural gas marketing relationship with ChevronTexaco. The exit from trading activities helped reduce collateral requirements for DYN. At the end of March 2004, collateral posted by DYN was $512 million, down from $1.1 billion a year earlier.

Company Financials Fiscal Year ending December 31

Per Share Data ($)

(Year Ended December 31)	2003	2002	2001	2000	1999	1998	1997	1996	1995	1994
Tangible Bk. Val.	5.04	4.57	8.85	6.49	4.03	3.15	4.52	2.67	3.81	3.36
Cash Flow	-0.05	-4.00	3.23	2.71	1.22	0.93	1.41	0.55	0.58	0.93
Earnings	1.30	-6.24	1.89	1.48	0.65	0.48	-0.42	0.60	0.29	0.15
S&P Core Earnings	2.10	-1.96	0.73	NA	NA	NA	NA	NA	NA	NA
Dividends	Nil	0.15	0.30	0.32	0.04	0.04	0.04	0.05	0.03	0.04
Payout Ratio	Nil	NM	16%	22%	5%	8%	NM	6%	13%	50%
Prices - High	5.43	32.19	59.00	59.87	17.93	12.68	17.48	17.93	8.51	8.87
- Low	1.13	0.49	20.00	17.11	7.33	6.79	10.66	6.25	6.06	5.79
P/E Ratio - High	4	NM	31	40	27	27	NM	30	29	NM
- Low	1	NM	11	12	11	14	NM	10	21	NM

Income Statement Analysis (Million $)

	2003	2002	2001	2000	1999	1998	1997	1996	1995	1994
Revs.	5,787	5,553	42,242	29,445	15,430	14,258	13,378	7,280	3,666	584
Oper. Inc.	367	327	1,424	1,130	343	225	490	Nil	127	73.3
Depr.	454	613	454	389	129	103	379	0.50	44.9	33.8
Int. Exp.	509	374	259	251	78.2	75.0	63.5	28.1	32.4	35.8
Pretax Inc.	-675	-2,546	977	791	243	175	-140	170	65.2	5.50
Eff. Tax Rate	NM	NM	27.5%	33.0%	30.7%	28.7%	NM	33.2%	31.3%	49.7%
Net Inc.	-474	-1,955	646	501	152	108	-87.7	113	44.8	2.77
S&P Core Earnings	879	-711	246	NA	NA	NA	NA	NA	NA	NA

Balance Sheet & Other Fin. Data (Million $)

	2003	2002	2001	2000	1999	1998	1997	1996	1995	1994
Cash	496	774	218	86.0	45.2	28.4	23.0	NM	16.3	1.59
Curr. Assets	3,030	7,586	9,507	10,150	2,805	2,117	2,019	456	763	118
Total Assets	13,293	20,030	24,874	21,406	6,525	5,264	4,517	1,278	1,875	757
Curr. Liab.	2,576	6,748	8,555	9,405	2,539	2,026	1,753	393	706	102
LT Debt	5,893	5,666	3,854	3,174	1,499	1,247	1,202	333	523	372
Common Equity	2,045	2,087	4,719	3,613	1,234	1,053	944	552	552	235
Total Cap.	9,221	10,062	12,694	8,214	3,144	2,692	2,475	885	1,118	635
Cap. Exp.	333	947	1,845	769	365	299	220	Nil	129	26.6
Cash Flow	-20.0	-1,672	1,097	855	281	211	291	114	89.7	36.6
Curr. Ratio	1.2	1.1	1.1	1.1	1.1	1.0	1.2	1.2	1.1	1.2
% LT Debt of Cap.	63.9	56.3	30.4	38.6	47.7	46.3	40.5	37.6	46.8	58.6
% Net Inc.of Revs.	NM	NM	1.5	1.7	1.0	0.8	NM	1.6	1.2	0.5
% Ret. on Assets	NM	NM	2.8	3.6	2.6	2.2	NM	7.3	3.4	0.4
% Ret. on Equity	NM	NM	15.5	19.2	13.2	10.8	NM	13.6	11.4	1.2

Data as orig reptd.; bef. results of disc opers/spec. items. Per share data adj. for stk. divs.; EPS diluted. E-Estimated. NA-Not Available. NM-Not Meaningful. NR-Not Ranked. UR-Under Review.

Office: 1000 Louisiana Street, Houston, TX 77002-5050.
Telephone: 713-507-6400.
Email: ir@dynegy.com
Website: http://www.dynegy.com
Chrmn: D. Dienstbier.
Pres & CEO: B.A. Williamson.
EVP & CFO: N.J. Caruso.

EVP & General Counsel: C.F. Graebner.
SVP & Treas: H.C. Nichols.
VP & Investor Contact: J. Sousa 713-507-6466.
Dirs: C. E. Bayless, D. W. Biegler, L. W. Bynoe, T. D. Clark, D. L. Dienstbier, B. J. Galt, P. A. Hammick, J. L. Johnson, R. Oelkers, H. B. Sheppard, J. J. Stewart, W. L. Trubeck, J. S. Watson, R. I. Wilcox, B. A. Williamson.

Founded: in 1985.
Domicile: Illinois.
Employees: 4,103.
S&P Analyst: Craig K. Shere, CFA /CB/GG

Eastman Chemical

Recommendation: **HOLD** ★★★ ☆ ☆
SELL | SELL | HOLD | BUY | BUY

12-Month Target Price: $52.00
(as of November 02, 2004)

EMN has an approximate 0.04% weighting in the **S&P 500**

Sector: Materials
Sub-Industry: Diversified Chemicals
Peer Group: Major Diversified Companies

Summary: This global company, based in Tennessee, manufactures and markets more than 1,200 chemicals, fibers and plastics products.

Quantitative Evaluations

S&P Earnings & Dividend Rank: B-

| D | C | B- | B | B+ | A- | A | A+ |

S&P Fair Value Rank: 3

| 1 | 2 | 3 | 4 | 5 |
Lowest | | | | Highest

Fair Value Calc.: $46.90 (Slightly Overvalued)

S&P Investability Quotient Percentile

77%

EMN scored higher than 77% of all companies for which an S&P Report is available.

Volatility: Low

| Low | Average | High |

Technical Evaluation: Bullish

Since 10/04, the technical indicators for EMN have been Bullish.

Relative Strength Rank: Strong

72

1 Lowest | Highest 99

Price as of 11/12/04: $51.04 | **2004E S&P Core EPS:** $2.08

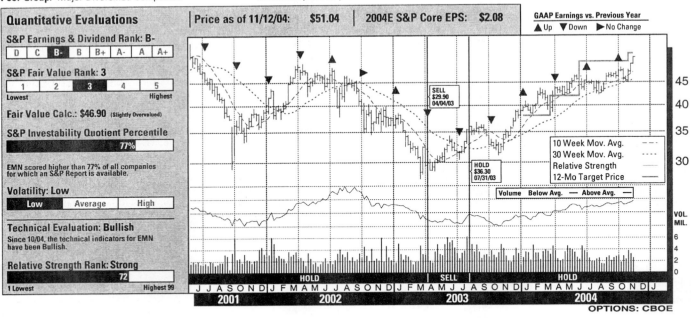

GAAP Earnings vs. Previous Year
▲ Up ▼ Down ▶ No Change

SELL $29.90 04/04/03
HOLD $36.30 07/31/03

10 Week Mov. Avg.
30 Week Mov. Avg.
Relative Strength
12-Mo Target Price

Volume Below Avg. — Above Avg.

45
40
35
30

VOL. MIL.
6
4
2
0

HOLD | SELL | HOLD
J J A S O N D|J F M A M J J A S O N D|J F M A M J J A S O N D|J F M A M J J A S O N D|J
2001 | **2002** | **2003** | **2004**

OPTIONS: CBOE

Analyst commentary prepared by Richard O'Reilly, CFA /DC/BK

Highlights September 20, 2004

- We expect 2004 sales to gain about 10%, reflecting increased volume growth in the high-single digit range in response to strengthening global economies as well as selling price increases implemented in response to higher raw material costs. We look for demand for polyester resins (the company is the world's largest producer) to return to a longer-term growth trend of nearly 10%. The industry has achieved price hikes, after some erosion in late 2003. We see the filter tow unit having relatively stable revenues and profits in 2004, after modest declines in 2003.

- We believe margins will remain under pressure from high raw material costs, despite overhead cost controls. EMN has sold portions of its coatings and adhesives segment, which posted an operating loss of about $75 million in 2003; it has also implemented actions that we think together will boost profits by more than $100 million in 2004. We expect sales for the developing segment to increase in 2004 as a result of new Cendian contracts signed in 2003, although margins have been hurt by spending on new projects; Cendian will not pursue new customers or renew existing contracts and EMN expects segment losses to decline in 2005.

- Interest expense should decrease, on lower debt. We project that the effective tax rate will rise to a normal level of 30%. Our 2004 EPS estimate excludes a first half net charge of $0.34.

Investment Rationale/Risk September 20, 2004

- We would hold the shares. Based on our 2005 EPS estimate, the shares are trading at what we view as a justified P/E multiple premium to those of other major chemical company equities, and to that of the S&P 500. We expect polyester resin over the next few years to grow near its long term annual growth rate of 10%. In 2004, the company has, in our view, successfully implemented steps to improve results in its coatings and adhesives segment, including the sales of unprofitable product lines.

- Risks to our recommendation and target price include the cyclical character of polyester resins, potential asbestos liabilities, and higher than expected raw material costs.

- Based on EPS gains that we expect through 2005, and assuming a premium P/E multiple of 18X our 2005 EPS estimate, our 12-month target price is $50. We believe the dividend, which provides an above-average yield of about 3.8%, is secure. We believe that capital spending may only slightly exceed depreciation expense in 2005.

Key Stock Statistics

S&P Core EPS 2005E	2.72	52-week Range	$51.08-33.97
S&P Oper. EPS 2004E	2.60	12 Month P/E	31.7
P/E on S&P Oper. EPS 2004E	19.6	Beta	0.89
S&P Oper. EPS 2005E	3.00	Shareholders	36,265
Yield (%)	3.4%	Market Cap (B)	$ 4.0
Dividend Rate/Share	1.76	Shares Outstanding (M)	77.8

Value of $10,000 invested five years ago: **$ 16,141**

Dividend Data Dividends have been paid since 1994

Amount ($)	Date Decl.	Ex-Div. Date	Stock of Record	Payment Date
0.440	Dec. 04	Dec. 11	Dec. 15	Jan. 02 '04
0.440	Mar. 04	Mar. 11	Mar. 15	Apr. 01 '04
0.440	May. 06	Jun. 14	Jun. 15	Jul. 01 '04
0.440	Aug. 05	Sep. 13	Sep. 15	Oct. 01 '04

Revenues/Earnings Data Fiscal year ending December 31

Revenues (Million $)

	2004	2003	2002	2001	2000	1999
1Q	1,597	1,441	1,236	1,344	1,217	1,023
2Q	1,676	1,481	1,395	1,402	1,316	1,122
3Q	1,649	1,444	1,374	1,367	1,387	1,190
4Q	—	1,434	1,315	1,271	1,372	1,255
Yr.	—	5,800	5,320	5,384	5,292	4,590

Earnings Per Share ($)

	2004	2003	2002	2001	2000	1999
1Q	-0.07	0.23	0.30	0.48	0.88	0.31
2Q	1.07	0.46	0.58	-1.92	1.12	0.54
3Q	0.49	-4.35	0.31	0.31	1.27	0.42
4Q	E0.47	0.13	-0.16	-1.20	0.68	-0.67
Yr.	E2.60	-3.54	1.02	-2.33	3.94	0.61

Next earnings report expected: late-January Source: S&P, Company Reports
EPS Estimates based on S&P Operating Earnings; historical GAAP earnings are as reported.

STANDARD &POOR'S

Eastman Chemical Company

Stock Report
November 13, 2004
NYSE Symbol: **EMN**

Recommendation: **HOLD** ★ ★ ★ ☆ ☆   12-Month Target Price: **$52.00** (as of November 02, 2004)

Business Summary September 20, 2004

Eastman Chemical Co. is a large global maker of a broad range of chemicals, plastics and fibers. In 2003, EMN implemented a number of initiatives aimed at boosting profitability and cash flows, including a profitability revaluation, restructuring, divestiture and consolidation actions in its coatings and adhesives segment, and efforts related to costs and working capital reduction. In early 2003, the company added a new developing business segment. EMN is narrowing the focus of this segment.

International operations accounted for 47% of sales in 2003.

The Eastman chemicals division consists of three segments. The coatings, adhesive, specialty polymers, and inks segment (28% of 2003 sales, an operating loss of $358 million, including $407 million of special charges) is a leading supplier of binders, resins, solvents, alcohols, pigment concentrates, unsaturated polyester resins, and emulsions. EMN made several acquisitions between 1998 and 2000 in order to expand this segment. Despite efforts to improve the financial performance of these product lines, they continued to experience operating losses. In 2003, the company decided to undertake steps to restructure or divest these product lines and assets. In August 2004, EMN sold certain product lines with annual sales of about $600 million for $215 million. Performance chemicals and intermediates (20%, loss of $89 million) includes additives for food and beverage ingredients, oxo chemicals, acetyls, plasticizers used for polymers, photographic and home care products, agricultural chemicals, and pharmaceutical intermediates. Volume growth of these chemicals tends to follow world economic growth. Specialty plastics (10%, profits of $63 million) includes modified copolyesters and cellulosic plastics for consumer, medical, packaging, sheeting, films and specialty applications.

The Voridian division consists of plastics (30%, profit of $62 million) and acetate fibers (11%, $125 million). EMN is the world's largest producer of polyester plastics, including polyethylene terephthalate (PET), used for packaging applications and containers such as soft-drink bottles; it also makes polyethylene resins used for packaging, films and containers. In the latter half of the 1990s, the company increased its PET capacity to 3 billion lbs. In September 2004, EMN announced plans to build a new plant with annual capacity of 770 million lbs. using new technology, with the start-up expected in late 2006. The polyethylene business is a U.S.-based business, and has a relatively small market share. EMN is one of the world's two largest suppliers of acetate cigarette filter tow and acetate yarn. The fibers unit posted a 6% decline in profits in 2003, reflecting a 1% decrease in revenues, and a less favorable product mix.

Developing businesses (1%, loss of $65 million) consists of less capital-intensive service businesses. In recent years, the company has invested about 1% to 1.5% of sales in non-traditional growth opportunities. The segment includes Cendian Corp., a marketer of logistics solutions to chemical companies; Ariel Research Corp., a provider of regulatory information and software products; and a gasification services business. In July 2004, EMN said that the segment had narrowed its focus to four projects from 10 to 15 projects and that Cendian would not pursue new customers and renew existing contracts.

Company Financials Fiscal Year ending December 31

Per Share Data ($)

(Year Ended December 31)	2003	2002	2001	2000	1999	1998	1997	1996	1995	1994
Tangible Bk. Val.	9.00	9.06	9.92	15.64	16.81	24.45	22.40	21.28	19.10	15.59
Cash Flow	1.22	6.18	3.33	9.36	5.46	7.59	7.86	9.01	10.52	8.04
Earnings	-3.54	1.02	-2.33	3.94	0.61	3.13	3.63	4.80	6.78	4.05
S&P Core Earnings	-3.45	0.26	-3.06	NA	NA	NA	NA	NA	NA	NA
Dividends	1.76	1.76	1.76	1.76	1.76	1.76	1.76	1.72	1.64	1.60
Payout Ratio	NM	173%	NM	45%	NM	56%	48%	36%	24%	40%
Prices - High	39.57	49.55	55.65	54.75	60.31	72.93	65.37	76.25	69.50	56.00
- Low	27.56	34.53	29.03	33.62	36.00	43.50	50.75	50.75	48.50	39.50
P/E Ratio - High	NM	49	NM	14	99	23	18	16	10	14
- Low	NM	34	NM	9	59	14	14	11	7	10

Income Statement Analysis (Million $)

	2003	2002	2001	2000	1999	1998	1997	1996	1995	1994
Revs.	5,800	5,320	5,384	5,292	4,590	4,481	4,678	4,782	5,040	4,329
Oper. Inc.	590	610	755	989	663	785	895	977	1,272	965
Depr.	367	397	435	418	383	351	327	314	308	329
Int. Exp.	124	128	140	135	126	96.0	87.0	67.0	79.0	98.0
Pretax Inc.	-381	84.0	-297	452	72.0	360	446	607	899	550
Eff. Tax Rate	NM	5.95%	NM	33.0%	33.3%	30.8%	35.9%	37.3%	37.8%	38.9%
Net Inc.	-273	79.0	-179	303	48.0	249	286	380	559	336
S&P Core Earnings	-266	20.4	-236	NA	NA	NA	NA	NA	NA	NA

Balance Sheet & Other Fin. Data (Million $)

	2003	2002	2001	2000	1999	1998	1997	1996	1995	1994
Cash	558	77.0	66.0	101	186	29.0	29.0	24.0	100	90.0
Curr. Assets	2,010	1,529	1,458	1,523	1,489	1,415	1,490	1,345	1,469	1,273
Total Assets	6,230	6,273	6,086	6,550	6,303	5,876	5,778	5,266	4,854	4,375
Curr. Liab.	1,477	1,224	958	1,258	1,608	985	954	787	873	800
LT Debt	2,089	2,054	2,143	1,914	1,506	1,649	1,714	1,523	1,217	1,195
Common Equity	1,913	1,271	1,378	1,812	2,521	1,934	1,753	1,639	1,528	1,295
Total Cap.	4,318	3,809	3,973	4,333	4,512	3,998	3,864	3,510	3,075	2,815
Cap. Exp.	230	427	234	226	292	500	749	789	446	281
Cash Flow	94.0	476	256	721	431	600	613	694	867	665
Curr. Ratio	1.4	1.2	1.5	1.2	0.9	1.4	1.6	1.7	1.7	1.6
% LT Debt of Cap.	48.4	53.9	53.9	44.2	33.4	41.2	44.4	43.3	39.6	42.5
% Net Inc.of Revs.	NM	1.5	NM	5.7	1.0	5.6	6.1	7.9	11.1	7.8
% Ret. on Assets	NM	1.3	NM	4.7	0.8	4.3	5.6	7.5	12.1	7.7
% Ret. on Equity	NM	6.0	NM	17.0	1.9	13.5	16.9	24.0	39.6	28.5

Data as orig. reptd.; pro forma prior to 1994, bef. results of disc. opers. and/or spec. items. Per share data adj. for stk. divs. as of ex-div. date. Bold denotes primary EPS. E-Estimated. NA-Not Available. NM-Not Meaningful. NR-Not Ranked.

Office: 100 North Eastman Road, Kingsport, TN 37660.
Telephone: 423-229-2000.
Website: http://www.eastman.com
Chrmn & CEO: J.B. Ferguson.
SVP & CFO: R.A. Lorraine.

SVP, Secy & General Counsel: T.K. Lee.
Investor Contact: G. Riddle 423-229-8692.
Dirs: H. J. Arnelle, C. A. Campbell, Jr., S. R. Demeritt, J. B. Ferguson, D. W. Griffin, R. M. Hernandez, R. J. Hornbaker, T. H. McLain, D. W. Raisbeck, J. A. White, P. M. Wood.

Founded: in 1993.
Domicile: Delaware.
Employees: 15,000.
S&P Analyst: Richard O'Reilly, CFA /DC/BK

Eastman Kodak

Recommendation: **SELL** ★ ☆ ☆ ☆   12-Month Target Price: **$25.00**
(SELL | SELL | HOLD | BUY | BUY)   (as of August 31, 2004)

EK has an approximate 0.08% weighting in the **S&P 500**

Sector: Consumer Discretionary
Sub-Industry: Photographic Products
Peer Group: Photography/Imaging Products

Summary: This multinational company has a large presence in consumer, professional and health imaging.

Quantitative Evaluations

S&P Earnings & Dividend Rank: B-

D	C	B-	B	B+	A-	A	A+

S&P Fair Value Rank: 4

1	2	3	4	5
Lowest				Highest

Fair Value Calc.: $33.40 (Slightly Undervalued)

S&P Investability Quotient Percentile

65%

EK scored higher than 65% of all companies
for which an S&P Report is available.

Volatility: Average

Low	Average	High

Technical Evaluation: Neutral
Since 11/04, the technical indicators for EK
have been Neutral.

Relative Strength Rank: Moderate

54

1 Lowest   Highest 99

Price as of 11/12/04:	**$32.31**	2004E S&P Core EPS:	**$0.62**

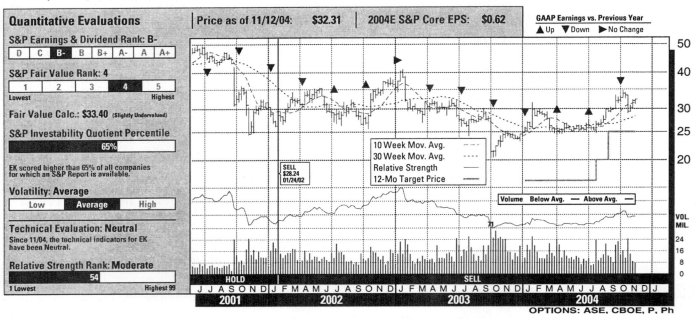

GAAP Earnings vs. Previous Year
▲ Up ▼ Down ► No Change

10 Week Mov. Avg.
30 Week Mov. Avg.
Relative Strength
12-Mo Target Price

SELL
$28.24
01/24/02

Volume Below Avg. — Above Avg. —

VOL.
MIL.

HOLD   SELL
J J A S O N D J F M A M J J A S O N D J F M A M J J A S O N D J F M A M J J A S O N D J
  2001   2002   2003   2004

OPTIONS: ASE, CBOE, P, Ph

Analyst commentary prepared by Richard N. Stice, CFA /CB/JWP

Highlights October 25, 2004

- We are forecasting 4% revenue growth in 2005, following our expectation of a similar increase in 2004. We believe an improving domestic economy and an expected resulting increase in demand for photographic products will likely aid results. However, we see these factors being somewhat offset by the impact of the expansion of the digital photography market, which is cannibalizing sales of traditional film offerings, as well as a less favorable currency impact.

- We anticipate that gross margins will narrow as a result of pricing pressures and ongoing digital substitution. We see SG&A expenses declining as a percentage of revenue, as we think the benefits of cost structure improvements will be realized.

- We expect 2005 operating EPS of $2.40, a 6% decline from our 2004 projection of $2.55 (excluding special items that add $0.46 to EPS). Our Standard & Poor's Core Earnings per share estimates for 2005 and 2004 are $1.76 and $0.62, respectively, reflecting projected costs associated with pensions and stock options, as well as the exclusion of an August 2004 asset sale.

Investment Rationale/Risk October 25, 2004

- Our avoid opinion is based on our view of EK's uncertain future in the digital marketplace. We see the company struggling to maintain its market share, and think pricing pressures are cutting into margins. In addition, while EK's digital operations have performed well, in our view, we believe they are cannibalizing sales from traditional film.

- Risks to our recommendation and target price include faster than expected integration of acquisitions, a slower than expected decline in demand for traditional film product offerings, improved margins, and gains in market share.

- Our 12-month target price of $25 is based on a combination of relative P/E-to-growth and our intrinsic value calculation using discounted cash flow analysis. Our assumptions include a weighted average cost of capital of 10.6% and an expected terminal growth rate of 3%. In light of the risk factors and excessive valuation that we perceive, we expect the shares to underperform the S&P 500 over the next 12 months.

Key Stock Statistics

S&P Core EPS 2005E	1.76	52-week Range	$34.74-23.19
S&P Oper. EPS 2004E	2.55	12 Month P/E	13.6
P/E on S&P Oper. EPS 2004E	12.7	Beta	1.01
S&P Oper. EPS 2005E	2.40	Shareholders	85,712
Yield (%)	1.5%	Market Cap (B)	$ 9.3
Dividend Rate/Share	0.50	Shares Outstanding (M)	286.6

Value of $10,000 invested five years ago: **$ 5,645**

Dividend Data Dividends have been paid since 1902

Amount ($)	Date Decl.	Ex-Div. Date	Stock of Record	Payment Date
0.250	Sep. 25	Oct. 30	Nov. 03	Dec. 23 '03
0.250	May. 12	May. 27	Jun. 01	Jul. 15 '04
0.250	Oct. 19	Oct. 28	Nov. 01	Dec. 14 '04

Revenues/Earnings Data Fiscal year ending December 31

Revenues (Million $)

	2004	2003	2002	2001	2000	1999
1Q	2,919	2,740	2,707	2,975	3,095	3,100
2Q	3,469	3,352	3,339	3,592	3,749	3,610
3Q	3,364	3,447	3,354	3,308	3,590	3,580
4Q	—	3,778	3,441	3,441	3,560	3,799
Yr.	—	13,317	12,835	13,234	13,994	14,089

Earnings Per Share ($)

	2004	2003	2002	2001	2000	1999
1Q	0.06	-0.01	0.13	0.52	0.93	0.59
2Q	0.50	0.39	0.97	0.12	1.63	1.52
3Q	0.16	0.42	1.15	0.33	1.36	0.73
4Q	E0.70	0.03	0.39	0.39	0.66	1.50
Yr.	E2.55	0.83	2.72	0.26	4.59	4.33

Next earnings report expected: late-January Source: S&P, Company Reports
EPS Estimates based on S&P Operating Earnings; historical GAAP earnings are as reported.

Eastman Kodak Company

Stock Report
November 13, 2004
NYSE Symbol: EK

Recommendation: **SELL** ★ ★ ☆ ☆ ☆   12-Month Target Price: **$25.00** (as of August 31, 2004)

Business Summary October 26, 2004

Eastman Kodak is a major participant in infoimaging, a $385 billion industry composed of devices (digital cameras and flat-panel displays), infrastructure (online networks and delivery systems for images), and services and media (software, film and paper), designed to enable people to access, analyze and print images. As of the end of 2003, EK had three reportable business units: Photography, Health Imaging, and Commercial Imaging. However, following an announced realignment in August 2003, EK instituted a new reporting structure that was implemented in the first quarter of 2004.

The Photography segment (69% of 2003 revenues) includes traditional and digital product offerings for consumers, professional photographers and the entertainment industry. The unit manufactures and/or markets films, photographic papers, processing services, photofinishing equipment and cameras. The company has also developed products that bridge traditional silver halide and digital offerings, including kiosks, printer docks, consumer digital services and inkjet media. In addition, other digitization options have been created to stimulate more pictures in use, adding to the consumption of film and paper. Digital product offerings are substituting for some of the traditional film and output products at varying rates. For 2004, the company estimates that consumer film industry volumes will decline in the U.S. by 10%-12% and worldwide by 7%-9%, primarily due to digital substitution.

The Health Imaging segment (18%) enables health care customers (hospitals, imaging centers, etc.) to capture, process, integrate, archive and display images and information in a variety of forms. Products include medical films, chemicals and processing equipment. The segment serves the general radiology market and specialty health markets, including dental, mammography and oncology. The unit also provides molecular imaging for the biotechnology research market.

Commercial Imaging (12%) encompasses EK's expertise in imaging solutions, providing image capture, analysis, printing and archiving. Markets for the segment include commercial printing and industrial, banking and insurance applications. Products offered consist of aerial, industrial, graphic and micrographic films, inkjet printers, high speed production document scanners and digital printing equipment. The company also provides maintenance and professional services for EK and other manufacturers' products.

Customers outside the U.S. accounted for 56% of sales in 2003, up from 53% in 2002. Europe, the Middle East and Africa accounted for the largest portion, providing 28% and 26% of total sales in 2003 and 2002, respectively.

In September 2003, EK announced a new strategy to address the digital marketplace. As a result, the company planned to spend up to $3 billion on acquisitions over the next three years, and targeted revenues of $16 billion by 2006 and $20 billion by 2010. In January 2004, EK announced plans to develop and execute a new cost reduction program throughout the 2004 to 2006 period. As a result, the company expects total charges of $1.3-$1.7 billion over the three year period and cost savings of $800 million to $1 billion for full year 2007.

Company Financials Fiscal Year ending December 31

Per Share Data ($)

(Year Ended December 31)	2003	2002	2001	2000	1999	1998	1997	1996	1995	1994
Tangible Bk. Val.	5.53	6.27	6.71	8.56	9.45	8.54	8.09	12.51	13.25	10.01
Cash Flow	3.72	5.52	3.42	7.48	7.19	6.84	2.51	5.68	6.34	4.28
Earnings	0.83	2.72	0.26	4.59	4.33	4.24	0.01	3.00	3.67	1.65
S&P Core Earnings	0.48	0.44	-1.86	NA	NA	NA	NA	NA	NA	NA
Dividends	1.15	1.80	1.77	1.76	1.76	1.76	1.76	1.60	1.60	1.60
Payout Ratio	139%	68%	NM	38%	41%	42%	NM	53%	44%	97%
Prices - High	41.08	38.48	49.95	67.50	80.37	88.93	94.75	85.00	70.37	56.37
- Low	20.39	25.58	24.40	35.31	56.62	57.93	53.31	65.12	47.12	40.68
P/E Ratio - High	49	15	19	15	19	21	NM	28	19	34
- Low	25	10	9	8	13	14	NM	22	13	25

Income Statement Analysis (Million $)

	2003	2002	2001	2000	1999	1998	1997	1996	1995	1994
Revs.	13,317	12,835	13,234	13,994	14,089	13,406	14,538	15,967	14,980	13,557
Oper. Inc.	1,685	2,898	1,923	3,103	2,908	2,783	2,431	3,107	2,841	2,545
Depr.	830	818	919	889	918	853	828	903	916	883
Int. Exp.	148	173	219	178	142	110	98.0	83.0	78.0	177
Pretax Inc.	196	946	97.0	2,132	2,109	2,106	53.0	1,556	1,926	1,002
Eff. Tax Rate	NM	16.1%	33.0%	34.0%	34.0%	34.0%	90.6%	35.1%	35.0%	44.7%
Net Inc.	238	793	76.0	1,407	1,392	1,390	5.00	1,011	1,252	554
S&P Core Earnings	133	127	-541	NA	NA	NA	NA	NA	NA	NA

Balance Sheet & Other Fin. Data (Million $)

	2003	2002	2001	2000	1999	1998	1997	1996	1995	1994
Cash	1,250	569	448	251	393	500	728	1,796	1,811	2,068
Curr. Assets	5,455	4,534	4,683	5,491	5,444	5,599	5,475	6,965	7,309	7,683
Total Assets	14,818	13,369	13,362	14,212	14,370	14,733	13,145	14,438	14,477	14,968
Curr. Liab.	5,307	5,377	5,354	6,215	5,769	6,178	5,177	5,417	4,643	5,735
LT Debt	2,302	1,164	1,666	1,166	Nil	504	585	559	665	660
Common Equity	3,264	2,777	2,894	3,428	3,912	3,988	3,161	4,734	5,121	4,017
Total Cap.	5,566	3,941	4,560	4,655	3,971	1,108	3,746	5,395	5,812	4,772
Cap. Exp.	506	577	743	945	1,127	4,561	1,485	1,341	1,034	1,153
Cash Flow	1,068	1,611	995	2,296	2,310	2,243	833	1,914	2,168	1,437
Curr. Ratio	1.0	0.8	0.9	0.9	0.9	0.9	1.1	1.3	1.6	1.3
% LT Debt of Cap.	41.4	29.5	36.5	25.0	Nil	11.1	15.6	10.4	11.5	13.8
% Net Inc.of Revs.	1.8	6.2	0.6	10.1	9.9	10.4	0.0	6.4	8.4	4.1
% Ret. on Assets	1.7	5.9	0.6	9.8	9.6	10.0	0.0	7.0	8.5	3.1
% Ret. on Equity	7.9	27.9	2.4	38.3	35.2	38.9	0.1	20.6	27.4	14.8

Data as orig reptd.; bef. results of disc opers/spec. items. Per share data adj. for stk. divs.; EPS diluted. E-Estimated. NA-Not Available. NM-Not Meaningful. NR-Not Ranked. UR-Under Review.

Office: 343 State Street, Rochester, NY 14650.
Telephone: 585-724-4000.
Website: http://www.kodak.com
: R.G. Brown, Jr.
Chrmn & CEO: D.A. Carp.
Pres & COO: A.M. Perez.

EVP & CFO: R.H. Brust.
SVP & Chief Admin: C.S. Brown, Jr.
Investor Contact: D. Flick 585-724-4352.
Dirs: R. S. Braddock, W. W. Bradley, D. A. Carp, M. L. Collins, T. M. Donahue, W. H. Hernandez, D. I. Jager, D. L. Lee, D. E. Lewis, P. H. O'Neill, A. M. Perez, H. d. Ruiz, L. D. Tyson.

Founded: in 1880.
Domicile: New Jersey.
Employees: 63,900.
S&P Analyst: Richard N. Stice, CFA /CB/JWP

Eaton Corp.

Recommendation: **SELL** ★★☆☆☆ 12-Month Target Price: **$50.00**
(SELL SELL HOLD BUY BUY) (as of July 15, 2004)

ETN has an approximate 0.09% weighting in the **S&P 500**

Sector: Industrials
Sub-Industry: Industrial Machinery
Peer Group: Control and/or Filter Products-- Specialized

Summary: This industrial conglomerate is the world's largest maker of truck transmissions and the second largest maker of hydraulics.

Quantitative Evaluations

S&P Earnings & Dividend Rank: B+

| D | C | B- | B | B+ | A- | A | A+ |

S&P Fair Value Rank: 2

| 1 | 2 | 3 | 4 | 5 |
| Lowest | | | | Highest |

Fair Value Calc.: $61.40 (Slightly Overvalued)

S&P Investability Quotient Percentile

97%

ETN scored higher than 97% of all companies for which an S&P Report is available.

Volatility: Average

| Low | Average | High |

Technical Evaluation: Bullish
Since 11/04, the technical indicators for ETN have been Bullish.

Relative Strength Rank: Moderate

64

1 Lowest   Highest 99

| Price as of 11/12/04: | **$68** | 2004E S&P Core EPS: | **$3.76** |

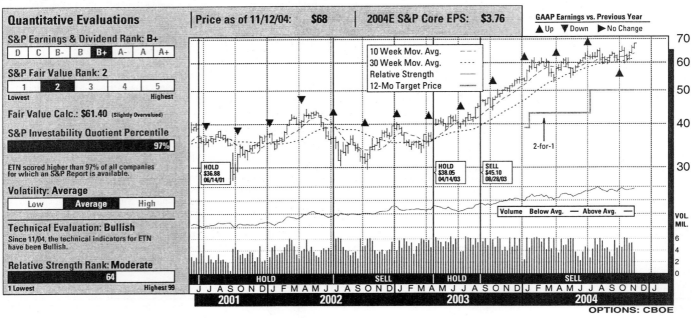

GAAP Earnings vs. Previous Year
▲ Up ▼ Down ▶ No Change

- 10 Week Mov. Avg.
- 30 Week Mov. Avg.
- Relative Strength
- 12-Mo Target Price

HOLD $36.88 06/14/01
HOLD $38.05 04/14/03
SELL $45.10 08/28/03
2-for-1

Volume Below Avg. — Above Avg.

VOL. MIL.

HOLD   SELL   HOLD   SELL

J J A S O N D | J F M A M J J A S O N D | J F M A M J J A S O N D | J F M A M J J A S O N D | J
2001   2002   2003   2004

OPTIONS: CBOE

Analyst commentary prepared by Robert E. Friedman, CPA /CB/GG

Highlights August 23, 2004

- We predict that revenues will rise about 15% in 2004, as we expect that recovering global economies and favorable exchange rates should drive increased demand for ETN's truck and auto components. Near-term sales growth should also be augmented by higher defense-related hydraulics sales, as well as by acquisitions. However, we believe global production overcapacity will continue to prevent ETN from raising prices materially.

- Nevertheless, the volume sales increase and ongoing cost cutting initiatives should allow EBIT (earnings before interest and taxes) margins to rise above 10%. Consequently, we look for ETN to post a 50%-plus increase in 2004 EPS, to $4.00, and generate 2004 ROE of 16%.

- As for ETN's long-term prospects, we are forecasting that the company will be able to grow per-share free cash flow at a 7%+ CAGR and post ROE of about 15%. Currently, ETN generates a majority of revenues from sales to the mature North American and European markets, which we estimate will grow at 3%-4% CAGRs. However, we believe ETN's ongoing efforts to boost international (especially Asian) sales as a percentage of revenues, as well as its ongoing migration to higher-margin niche industrial components and services, will be the impetus behind our expectations of 10-year, 7%+ free cash flow CAGR performance.

Investment Rationale/Risk August 23, 2004

- We are maintaining our avoid opinion on ETN, as the stock is trading at a material premium to our DCF-based 12-month target price of $50 a share.

- Risks to our recommendation and target price include any unexpected improvements to the structural growth prospects of ETN's main end-markets, and/or structural improvements to the underlying economics of ETN's primary manufacturing businesses.

- Our free cash flow model (which adds the discounted sum of projected 10-year free cash flow growing at our projected 7% CAGR) values ETN at about $50 a share, which is our 12-month target price. Another intrinsic valuation, which incorporates our projected 15% ROE estimate, a 9% hurdle rate (projected 7% normalized 10-year U.S. bond yield plus a 2% risk premium) and per share equity value of $21, values ETN at $35 a share.

Key Stock Statistics

S&P Oper. EPS 2004E	**4.00**	52-week Range	**$68.00-49.40**
P/E on S&P Oper. EPS 2004E	**17.0**	12 Month P/E	**18.4**
S&P Oper. EPS 2005E	**4.50**	Beta	**0.60**
Yield (%)	**1.6%**	Shareholders	**10,107**
Dividend Rate/Share	**1.08**	Market Cap (B)	**$ 10.3**
Shares Outstanding (M)	**151.9**		

Value of $10,000 invested five years ago: **NA**

Dividend Data Dividends have been paid since 1923

Amount ($)	Date Decl.	Ex-Div. Date	Stock of Record	Payment Date
0.540	Jan. 21	Feb. 05	Feb. 09	Feb. 27 '04
0.270	Apr. 28	May. 06	May. 10	May. 28 '04
0.270	Jul. 28	Aug. 05	Aug. 09	Aug. 27 '04
0.270	Oct. 27	Nov. 04	Nov. 08	Nov. 26 '04

Revenues/Earnings Data Fiscal year ending December 31

Revenues (Million $)

	2004	2003	2002	2001	2000	1999
1Q	2,238	1,925	1,723	1,983	2,325	1,661
2Q	2,403	2,027	1,881	1,871	2,335	2,300
3Q	2,543	2,026	1,830	1,750	2,191	2,227
4Q	—	2,083	1,775	1,695	1,948	2,214
Yr.	—	8,061	7,209	7,299	8,309	8,402

Earnings Per Share ($)

	2004	2003	2002	2001	2000	1999
1Q	0.85	0.50	0.24	0.36	0.89	0.59
2Q	1.03	0.64	0.60	0.35	0.98	0.86
3Q	1.09	0.70	0.65	0.29	0.64	1.23
4Q	E1.07	0.72	0.47	0.21	0.42	1.49
Yr.	E4.00	2.56	1.96	1.20	2.50	4.18

Next earnings report expected: late-January Source: S&P, Company Reports
EPS Estimates based on S&P Operating Earnings; historical GAAP earnings are as reported.

Eaton Corporation

Recommendation: **SELL** ★ ★ ☆ ☆ ☆   12-Month Target Price: **$50.00** (as of July 15, 2004)

Business Summary August 25, 2004

This $9 billion-revenue industrial equipment and parts manufacturer conducts business through four business segments:

The Fluid Power segment (35% of revenues, 45% of operating earnings and 8.9% profit margins in 2003) makes hydraulics for everything from jet planes to farm tractors. FP sells its hydraulics equipment to three market channels: Mobile (primarily earthmovers and farm tractors; about 38% of FP sales); stationary (primarily machine tools; 37%); and aerospace (mainly commercial and military aircraft; 25%).

Parker Hannifin, the world's largest hydraulics equipment maker, Eaton (second largest), Germany-based Sauer Danfoss (third), and Germany-based Mannesmann (fourth) account for about 40% of the $50 billion revenue global hydraulics equipment industry. The 60% balance is comprised of hundreds of small hydraulics equipment makers.

ETN's growing Electrical segment (29%; 29%; 6.8%) makes a wide range of electrical distribution equipment, such as switchboards, circuit boards and circuit breakers. The segment also makes electronic sensors that control industrial machinery, as well as electricity quality-monitoring systems. The unit's primary competitors include GE, Germany-based Siemens and Schneider Electric.

Demand for ETN's electrical equipment and components is primarily driven by the health of the residential and commercial construction industry. Based on U.S. Census Bureau statistics, from 1993 through 2003, total residential and commercial construction spending grew at a 6.3% average annual rate.

ETN's Automotive Components segment (21%; 41%; 13%) is the world's largest maker of engine valves, which are used to control the air flow of internal combustion engines of cars and small trucks. TRW Automotive and Ger-

many-based INA are the world's second- and third-largest engine valve makers. The segment also makes safety- and environmental-related automotive components, and actuators that move certain auto components (such as side-view mirrors). Demand for ETN's automotive components is primarily driven by the health of the auto and light-truck market. Based on U.S. Census Bureau statistics, from 1993 through 2003, the combined auto and light-truck manufacturing industries grew at a 4.7% average annual rate.

With about 85% of the global truck transmission market, ETN's Truck Component unit (16%; 31%; 13%) is the world's largest maker of medium- and heavy-duty truck transmissions. The segment's primary competitor is Germany-based ZedF. ETN is also a major manufacturer of brake clutches. The segment's primary competitor in this segment is Wabco. Other truck transmission and clutch makers include European truck manufacturers, which primarily make transmissions and clutches for their own trucks.

Demand for ETN's truck components is primarily driven by the health of the medium- and heavy-duty truck market. Based on U.S. Census Bureau statistics, from 1993 through 2003, the truck manufacturing industry grew at a 4.2% average annual rate.

Looking at ETN's historical financial performance, from 1993 through 2003, reported net operating EPS rose at a compound annual growth rate (CAGR) of 7.3%; per-share equity growth (a proxy for growth in intrinsic value) grew at a 10% CAGR. In addition, debt-adjusted ROE averaged 14%. Based on Standard & Poor's Core Earnings methodology, 10-year average S&P Core EPS variance stood at -27%, primarily due to reversals of non-operating pension income and the inclusion of employee stock option expense.

Company Financials Fiscal Year ending December 31

Per Share Data ($)

(Year Ended December 31)	2003	2002	2001	2000	1999	1998	1997	1996	1995	1994
Tangible Bk. Val.	3.14	NM	0.29	NM	0.64	7.17	7.37	7.16	6.33	5.25
Cash Flow	5.18	4.49	3.78	5.05	7.25	4.66	5.17	4.35	4.36	3.63
Earnings	2.56	1.96	1.20	2.50	4.18	2.40	2.97	2.25	2.56	2.20
S&P Core Earnings	2.43	0.99	-0.18	NA	NA	NA	NA	NA	NA	NA
Dividends	0.92	0.88	0.88	0.88	0.88	0.88	0.86	0.80	0.75	0.60
Payout Ratio	36%	45%	74%	35%	21%	37%	29%	36%	29%	27%
Prices - High	54.70	44.34	40.71	43.28	51.75	49.81	51.68	35.43	31.25	31.06
- Low	33.01	29.55	27.56	28.75	31.00	28.75	33.62	25.18	22.62	21.93
P/E Ratio - High	21	23	34	17	12	21	17	16	12	14
- Low	13	15	23	11	7	12	11	11	9	10

Income Statement Analysis (Million $)

	2003	2002	2001	2000	1999	1998	1997	1996	1995	1994
Revs.	8,061	7,209	7,299	8,309	8,402	6,625	7,563	6,961	6,822	6,052
Oper. Inc.	984	870	703	1,013	1,170	813	1,042	854	921	776
Depr.	394	353	355	364	441	331	342	320	281	216
Int. Exp.	87.0	104	142	177	152	88.0	86.0	93.0	96.0	101
Pretax Inc.	508	399	278	552	963	485	668	485	592	488
Eff. Tax Rate	24.0%	29.6%	39.2%	34.2%	35.9%	28.0%	30.5%	28.1%	32.6%	31.8%
Net Inc.	386	281	169	363	617	349	464	349	399	333
S&P Core Earnings	367	141	-25.0	NA	NA	NA	NA	NA	NA	NA

Balance Sheet & Other Fin. Data (Million $)

	2003	2002	2001	2000	1999	1998	1997	1996	1995	1994
Cash	61.0	75.0	112	82.0	81.0	80.0	53.0	60.0	84.0	41.0
Curr. Assets	3,093	2,457	2,387	2,571	2,782	1,982	2,055	2,017	1,967	1,846
Total Assets	8,223	7,138	7,646	8,180	8,437	5,665	5,465	5,307	5,053	4,682
Curr. Liab.	2,126	1,734	1,669	2,107	2,649	1,516	1,357	1,230	1,145	1,102
LT Debt	1,651	1,887	2,252	2,447	1,915	1,191	1,272	1,062	1,084	1,053
Common Equity	3,117	2,302	2,475	2,410	2,624	2,057	2,071	2,160	1,975	1,680
Total Cap.	4,768	4,752	5,307	4,857	4,539	3,248	3,343	3,222	3,059	2,733
Cap. Exp.	2,733	228	295	386	496	483	438	347	399	267
Cash Flow	780	634	524	727	1,058	680	806	669	680	549
Curr. Ratio	1.5	1.4	1.4	1.2	1.1	1.3	1.5	1.6	1.7	1.7
% LT Debt of Cap.	34.6	39.7	42.4	50.4	42.2	36.7	38.0	33.0	35.5	38.5
% Net Inc.of Revs.	4.8	3.9	2.3	4.4	7.3	5.3	6.1	5.1	5.9	5.5
% Ret. on Assets	5.0	3.8	2.1	4.4	8.8	6.3	8.6	6.8	8.2	8.1
% Ret. on Equity	14.2	11.8	6.9	14.4	26.4	16.9	21.9	16.9	21.9	23.1

Data as orig reptd.; bef. results of disc opers/spec. items. Per share data adj. for stk. divs.; EPS diluted. E-Estimated. NA-Not Available. NM-Not Meaningful. NR-Not Ranked. UR-Under Review.

Office: 1111 Superior Ave E, Cleveland, OH 44114-2535.
Telephone: 216-523-5000.
Website: http://www.eaton.com
Chrmn, Pres & CEO: A.M. Cutler.
EVP & CFO: R.H. Fearon.
VP & Treas: R.E. Parmenter.

VP & Secy: E.R. Franklin.
VP & General Counsel: J.R. Horst.
VP & Investor Contact: W. Hartman 216-523-4501.
Dirs: M. J. Critelli, A. M. Cutler, E. Green, N. C. Lautenbach, D. L. McCoy, J. R. Miller, G. R. Page, K. M. Patel, V. A. Pelson, G. L. Tooker.

Founded: in 1916.
Domicile: Ohio.
Employees: 51,000.
S&P Analyst: Robert E. Friedman, CPA /CB/GG

The McGraw-Hill Companies

Recommendation: **BUY** ★ ★ ★ ★ ☆
SELL | SELL | HOLD | BUY | BUY

12-Month Target Price: $111.00
(as of October 20, 2004)

EBAY has an approximate 0.66% weighting in the **S&P 500**

Sector: Consumer Discretionary
Sub-Industry: Internet Retail
Peer Group: Internet Retail - Large

Summary: EBAY operates one of the Internet's most popular e-commerce destinations, as well as PayPal, an online payments company.

Quantitative Evaluations

S&P Earnings & Dividend Rank: NR

D	C	B-	B	B+	A-	A	A+

S&P Fair Value Rank: 2-

1	2	3	4	5
Lowest				Highest

Fair Value Calc.: $88.30 (Overvalued)

S&P Investability Quotient Percentile

92%

EBAY scored higher than 92% of all companies for which an S&P Report is available.

Volatility: Average

Low	Average	High

Technical Evaluation: Bullish
Since 8/04, the technical indicators for EBAY have been Bullish.

Relative Strength Rank: Strong

90

1 Lowest   Highest 99

Price as of 11/12/04: **$109.89** | 2004E S&P Core EPS: **$0.92**

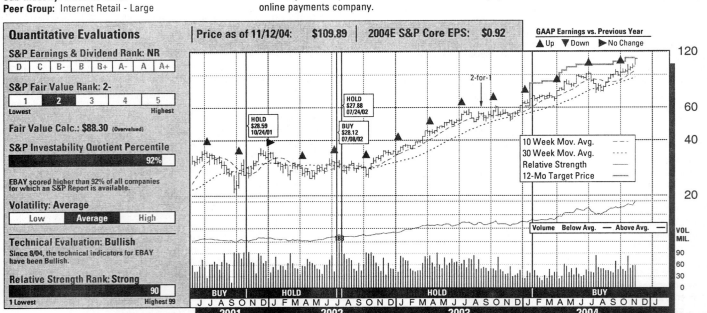

GAAP Earnings vs. Previous Year
▲ Up   ▼ Down   ► No Change

- 10 Week Mov. Avg.
- 30 Week Mov. Avg.
- Relative Strength
- 12-Mo Target Price

Volume   Below Avg. — Above Avg.

OPTIONS: ASE, CBOE, P, Ph

Analyst commentary prepared by Scott H. Kessler/MF/JWP

Highlights October 27, 2004

- We expect sales to climb 50% in 2004 and 31% in 2005, reflecting growth in registered users, listings, gross merchandise sales, and payment accounts and activity. We expect international operations (42% of 2004 third quarter revenues) to continue to contribute significant additional listing and transaction fees, and to account for an increasing percentage of revenues. We believe that continued expansion in fixed-price capabilities and online payments have also contributed to greater user activity and revenue growth.

- We project that EBAY's annual pro forma operating margin will widen from 33% in 2003 to over 36% in 2004 and 37% in 2005, reflecting increased scale and efficiencies. However, we expect margins to be somewhat restricted by costs of investment in PayPal, sales and marketing, and technology.

- Our financial projections exclude payroll expenses related to employee stock options, amortization of acquired intangibles, impairment of certain equity investments, and one-time items. The differences between our annual forecasts for per-share operating earnings and Standard & Poor's Core Earnings reflect material projected stock option expenses.

Investment Rationale/Risk October 27, 2004

- We recommend accumulating the shares. We see EBAY as the clear leader in the online auction segment, a mainstream Internet retail destination, a major facilitator of large transactions involving cars and real estate, a growing international presence, and the owner of the world's leading purely online payment platform. We are optimistic about the company's core businesses and emerging growth vehicles, including its international and payment segments.

- Risks to our recommendation and target price include potential greater regulation and taxation of the company's businesses in the U.S. and abroad, and increasing international competition, particularly in Asia.

- Although the stock's recent P/E multiple of 79X our projected 2004 EPS was well above that of the S&P 500, its recent P/E multiple to growth ratio was only modestly above that of the S&P 500. Based on our discounted cash flow model, with assumptions that include a weighted average cost of capital of 10.5%, and projected average annual free cash flow growth of 46% over the next five years, our 12-month target price is $111.

Key Stock Statistics

S&P Core EPS 2005E	1.29	52-week Range	$110.25-50.63
S&P Oper. EPS 2004E	1.22	12 Month P/E	NM
P/E on S&P Oper. EPS 2004E	90.1	Beta	1.68
S&P Oper. EPS 2005E	1.59	Shareholders	2,400
Yield (%)	Nil	Market Cap (B)	$ 72.8
Dividend Rate/Share	Nil	Shares Outstanding (M)	662.9

Value of $10,000 invested five years ago: **$ 29,922**

Dividend Data

No cash dividends have been paid.

Revenues/Earnings Data Fiscal year ending December 31

Revenues (Million $)

	2004	2003	2002	2001	2000	1999
1Q	756.2	476.5	245.1	154.1	85.89	34.01
2Q	773.4	509.3	266.3	180.9	98.15	49.48
3Q	805.9	530.9	288.8	194.4	113.4	58.53
4Q	—	648.4	413.9	219.4	134.0	73.92
Yr.	—	2,165	1,214	748.8	431.4	224.7

Earnings Per Share ($)

	2004	2003	2002	2001	2000	1999
1Q	0.30	0.16	0.09	0.04	0.01	0.01
2Q	0.28	0.14	0.10	0.05	0.02	0.00
3Q	0.27	0.17	0.11	0.04	0.03	0.00
4Q	E0.33	0.21	0.14	0.05	0.05	0.01
Yr.	E1.22	0.68	0.43	0.16	0.09	0.03

Next earnings report expected: late-January Source: S&P, Company Reports
EPS Estimates based on S&P Operating Earnings; historical GAAP earnings are as reported.

eBay Inc.

Recommendation: **BUY** ★★★★☆   12-Month Target Price: **$111.00** (as of October 20, 2004)

Business Summary October 27, 2004

eBay operates the world's largest online trading community. As of September 2004, EBAY had 125.0 million confirmed registered users (up from 85.5 million a year earlier). In the 2004 third quarter, the company hosted 348.0 million listings (up from 234.6 million in the 2003 quarter). Items are listed in thousands of specific categories; primary categories are Antiques; Art; Books; Business & Industrial; Cameras & Photo; Cars, Parts & Vehicles; Clothing, Shoes & Accessories; Coins; Collectibles; Computers & Networking; Consumer Electronics; Crafts; Dolls & Bears; DVDs & Movies; Entertainment Memorabilia; Health & Beauty; Home & Garden; Jewelry & Watches; Music; Musical Instruments; Pottery & Glass; Real Estate; Specialty Services; Sporting Goods & Fan Shop; Sports Cards & Memorabilia; Stamps; Tickets; Toys & Hobbies; Travel; Video Games; and Everything Else. Specialty sites include eBay Motors, eBay Stores, Half.com by eBay (fixed pricing), and PayPal.

The eBay service was introduced in 1995, and was intended to establish an efficient marketplace for individuals to trade goods with one another. EBAY enables users to list items for sale, browse through listed items using a 24-hour-a-day service organized by topics, and bid on items of interest. Users can search online auction listings for specific items by keyword(s), price range, category, pricing format, location, currency or payment method. The company aims to become the world's most efficient and abundant marketplace by expanding its community of users (by delivering value to buyers and sellers and creating a global marketplace); and by providing a faster, easier and safer trading experience (through efforts such as category growth and payment services).

The company and its affiliates have websites directed toward the following geographies: Argentina, Australia, Austria, Belgium, Brazil, Canada, China, France, Germany, Hong Kong, Ireland, Italy, Mexico, the Netherlands, New Zealand, Singapore, South Korea, Spain, Sweden, Switzerland, Taiwan, and the U.K. It discontinued its Japanese website in early 2002.

In May 2001, EBAY acquired iBazar, an online auction company with marketplaces in Belgium, Brazil, France, Italy, the Netherlands, Portugal, Spain and Sweden, for cash and stock valued at about $126 million. In April 2002, the company purchased NeoCom Technology Co., Ltd., Taiwan's leading operator of auction-style websites, for about $11 million. In March 2002, EBAY paid $30 million for a 33% stake in EachNet, the leading online trading community in China. In July 2003, it acquired the remainder of EachNet, for $150 million. In April 2004, EBAY purchased mobile.de, one of Germany's leading online classifieds websites for vehicles, for about $149 million. In August 2004, EBAY acquired Baazee.com, an online marketplace in India, for some $50 million.

The company acquired online payments company PayPal in October 2002, for about $1.5 billion in stock. PayPal enables any business or consumer with e-mail to send and receive online payments. PayPal's system, which builds on the legacy financial infrastructure of bank accounts and credit cards to create an online payment network, was available in 38 countries as of December 2003.

Company Financials Fiscal Year ending December 31

Per Share Data ($)

(Year Ended December 31)	2003	2002	2001	2000	1999	1998	1997	1996	1995	1994
Tangible Bk. Val.	4.47	2.93	2.22	1.86	1.63	0.17	0.00	NA	NA	NA
Cash Flow	0.92	0.56	0.32	0.15	0.06	0.01	0.00	NA	NA	NA
Earnings	0.68	0.43	0.16	0.09	0.03	0.01	0.00	NA	NA	NA
S&P Core Earnings	0.41	0.09	-0.01	NA	NA	NA	NA	NA	NA	NA
Dividends	Nil	Nil	Nil	Nil	Nil	Nil	Nil	NA	NA	NA
Payout Ratio	Nil	Nil	Nil	NM	Nil	Nil	Nil	NA	NA	NA
Prices - High	64.80	35.42	36.37	63.75	58.50	25.93	NA	NA	NA	NA
- Low	33.75	24.42	14.21	13.37	13.83	1.50	NA	NA	NA	NA
P/E Ratio - High	95	83	NM	NM	NM	NM	NA	NA	NA	NA
- Low	50	57	NM	NM	NM	NM	NA	NA	NA	NA

Income Statement Analysis (Million $)

	2003	2002	2001	2000	1999	1998	1997	1996	1995	1994
Revs.	2,165	1,214	749	431	225	47.4	5.74	NA	NA	NA
Oper. Inc.	828	431	227	74.6	23.8	8.65	1.56	NA	NA	NA
Depr.	159	76.6	86.6	38.0	20.6	2.49	0.07	NA	NA	NA
Int. Exp.	4.31	1.49	2.85	3.37	1.94	0.04	Nil	NA	NA	NA
Pretax Inc.	662	398	163	78.0	20.5	7.03	1.54	NA	NA	NA
Eff. Tax Rate	31.3%	36.7%	49.1%	42.0%	45.8%	65.9%	43.4%	NA	NA	NA
Net Inc.	447	250	90.4	48.3	10.8	2.40	0.87	NA	NA	NA
S&P Core Earnings	270	52.2	-4.04	NA	NA	NA	NA	NA	NA	NA

Balance Sheet & Other Fin. Data (Million $)

	2003	2002	2001	2000	1999	1998	1997	1996	1995	1994
Cash	1,382	1,244	654	328	220	31.8	3.72	NA	NA	NA
Curr. Assets	2,146	1,468	884	675	460	83.4	4.97	NA	NA	NA
Total Assets	5,820	4,124	1,679	1,182	964	92.5	5.62	NA	NA	NA
Curr. Liab.	647	386	180	137	88.8	8.04	1.12	NA	NA	NA
LT Debt	124	13.8	12.0	11.4	15.0	Nil	0.31	NA	NA	NA
Common Equity	4,896	3,556	1,429	1,014	852	84.4	1.01	NA	NA	NA
Total Cap.	5,139	3,715	1,479	1,038	867	84.4	4.52	NA	NA	NA
Cap. Exp.	365	139	57.4	49.8	141	8.86	NA	NA	NA	NA
Cash Flow	606	326	177	86.3	31.5	4.89	0.68	NA	NA	NA
Curr. Ratio	3.3	3.8	4.9	4.9	5.2	10.4	4.4	NA	NA	NA
% LT Debt of Cap.	2.4	0.4	0.8	1.1	1.7	Nil	6.9	NA	NA	NA
% Net Inc.of Revs.	20.7	20.6	12.1	11.2	4.8	5.1	15.2	NA	NA	NA
% Ret. on Assets	9.1	8.6	6.3	4.5	1.9	4.9	NA	NA	NA	NA
% Ret. on Equity	10.6	10.0	7.4	5.2	2.3	5.6	NA	NA	NA	NA

Data as orig reptd.; bef. results of disc opers/spec. items. Per share data adj. for stk. divs. Bold denotes primary EPS - prior periods restated. E-Estimated. NA-Not Available. NM-Not Meaningful. NR-Not Ranked. UR-Under Review.

Office: 2145 Hamilton Avenue, San Jose, CA 95125-6123.
Telephone: 408-376-7400.
Email: investor_relations@ebay.com
Website: http://www.ebay.com
Chrmn: P.M. Omidyar.
Pres & CEO: M.C. Whitman.

COO: M. Webb, Jr.
SVP & CFO: R. Dutta.
SVP, Secy & General Counsel: M.R. Jacobson.
Investor Contact: K. Pursglove 408-376-7458.
Dirs: F. D. Anderson, P. Bourguignon, S. D. Cook, R. C. Kagle, D. G. Lepore, P. M. Omidyar, R. T. Schlosberg III, T. Tierney, M. C. Whitman.

Founded: in 1995.
Domicile: Delaware.
Employees: 5,700.
S&P Analyst: Scott H. Kessler/MF/JWP

The McGraw·Hill Companies

Ecolab Inc.

Recommendation: **BUY** ★★★★☆
SELL | SELL | HOLD | BUY | BUY

12-Month Target Price: $36.00
(as of October 21, 2004)

ECL has an approximate 0.08% weighting in the **S&P 500**

Sector: Materials
Sub-Industry: Specialty Chemicals
Peer Group: Specialty Chemicals (Larger)

Summary: This company is the leading worldwide marketer of cleaning, sanitizing and maintenance products and services for the hospitality, institutional and industrial markets.

Quantitative Evaluations

S&P Earnings & Dividend Rank: A

| D | C | B- | B | B+ | A- | A | A+ |

S&P Fair Value Rank: 2

| 1 | 2 | 3 | 4 | 5 |
Lowest — Highest

Fair Value Calc.: $31.90 (Slightly Overvalued)

S&P Investability Quotient Percentile
99%

ECL scored higher than 99% of all companies for which an S&P Report is available.

Volatility: Low

| Low | Average | High |

Technical Evaluation: Bullish
Since 10/04, the technical indicators for ECL have been Bullish.

Relative Strength Rank: Moderate
67
1 Lowest — Highest 99

| Price as of 11/12/04: | $34.95 | 2004E S&P Core EPS: | $1.12 |

GAAP Earnings vs. Previous Year
▲ Up ▼ Down ► No Change

10 Week Mov. Avg.
30 Week Mov. Avg.
Relative Strength
12-Mo Target Price

2-for-1

Volume Below Avg. — Above Avg.

BUY
J J A S O N D | J F M A M J J A S O N D | J F M A M J J A S O N D | J F M A M J J A S O N D | J
2001 | 2002 | 2003 | 2004

OPTIONS: CBOE

Analyst commentary prepared by Richard O'Reilly, CFA /CB/BK

Highlights September 13, 2004

- We expect sales for 2004 and in 2005 to increase about 10%, aided by favorable currency exchange rates. We see organic sales growth from existing businesses similar to 2003's gain of about 4%, aided by expected healthy conditions in the domestic food service, travel and lodging industries, and continued benefits from new products and customers, aggressive sales efforts, and sales force expansion.

- We expect the domestic institutional, Kay, janitorial, health care and pest elimination units to continue to grow. We also see growth for newer businesses, such as vehicle care and water treatment. We see international sales increasing in most parts of the world, boosted by a weaker U.S. dollar. Margins will likely widen on the sales growth, despite higher selling expenses. We expect an effective tax rate of 37.2% for 2004, down from 38.1% in 2003, reflecting a better geographic mix of profits.

- We project 2004 Standard & Poor's Core Earnings of $1.12 a share, including projected stock option expense of about $0.07. Henkel has said it may sell a portion of its 28% stake in ECL to help finance the purchase of another company.

Investment Rationale/Risk September 13, 2004

- We recommend accumulating the stock, despite its P/E multiple premium to the S&P 500. We view the premium as justified, based on what we regard as the company's attractive EPS record. We view ECL as a strong company, with attractive longer-term growth prospects and cash flow, and believe the travel and hotel sectors will continue to show improved trends. We believe a possible repurchase of a portion of Henkel's 28% interest would be accretive to EPS.

- Risks to our recommendation and target price include unexpected slowdowns in the hospitality and foodservice industries, and an inability to continue to successfully introduce new products and services.

- Assuming that the stock continues to trade at its current P/E multiple of 25.5X, and applying it to our 2005 EPS estimate of $1.33, our 12-month target price is $34. We expect annual increases in the dividend, which has been boosted for 12 consecutive years.

Key Stock Statistics

S&P Core EPS 2005E	1.27	52-week Range	$35.34-25.30
S&P Oper. EPS 2004E	1.19	12 Month P/E	29.6
P/E on S&P Oper. EPS 2004E	29.4	Beta	0.62
S&P Oper. EPS 2005E	1.33	Shareholders	4,725
Yield (%)	0.9%	Market Cap (B)	$ 9.0
Dividend Rate/Share	0.32	Shares Outstanding (M)	257.7

Value of $10,000 invested five years ago: **$ 21,970**

Dividend Data Dividends have been paid since 1936

Amount ($)	Date Decl.	Ex-Div. Date	Stock of Record	Payment Date
0.080	Dec. 11	Dec. 19	Dec. 23	Jan. 15 '04
0.080	Mar. 01	Mar. 12	Mar. 16	Apr. 15 '04
0.080	May. 07	Jun. 14	Jun. 15	Jul. 15 '04
0.080	Aug. 13	Sep. 17	Sep. 21	Oct. 15 '04

Revenues/Earnings Data Fiscal year ending December 31

Revenues (Million $)

	2004	2003	2002	2001	2000	1999
1Q	979.4	875.9	786.1	580.9	526.3	489.3
2Q	1,043	946.7	839.2	595.8	570.7	520.4
3Q	1,090	982.8	894.9	616.2	600.7	554.5
4Q	—	956.5	883.4	561.8	566.7	515.8
Yr.	—	3,762	3,404	2,355	2,264	2,080

Earnings Per Share ($)

	2004	2003	2002	2001	2000	1999
1Q	0.25	0.21	0.14	0.17	0.16	0.13
2Q	0.30	0.25	0.20	0.18	0.18	0.16
3Q	0.36	0.33	0.28	0.23	0.23	0.21
4Q	E0.29	0.26	0.20	0.15	0.22	0.16
Yr.	E1.19	1.06	0.81	0.73	0.79	0.66

Next earnings report expected: early-February Source: S&P, Company Reports
EPS Estimates based on S&P Operating Earnings; historical GAAP earnings are as reported.

Ecolab Inc.

Recommendation: **BUY** ★★★★☆   12-Month Target Price: **$36.00** (as of October 21, 2004)

Business Summary September 13, 2004

Using its Circle the Customer-Circle the Globe strategy, Ecolab, a global supplier of cleaning, sanitizing and maintenance products and services for hospitality, institutional and industrial markets, believes it has leveraged its customer base by providing all services and products to meet their needs, and expanded its products and services worldwide. It achieved record net income and share earnings for nine consecutive years until 2001, when a slowdown in key markets restricted results.

In the U.S. cleaning and sanitizing business (47% of 2003 sales, 61% of profits), the institutional division (28% of 2003 total sales) is the leading provider of cleaners and sanitizers for warewashing, laundry, kitchen cleaning and general house-keeping, product dispensing equipment and dishwashing racks and related kitchen sundries to the foodservice, lodging and health care industries. It also provides products and services for pool and spa treatment. The Kay division (4%) is the largest supplier of cleaning and sanitizing products for the quick-service restaurant, convenience store and food retail markets. The Food and Beverage division (8%) offers cleaning and sanitizing products and services to farms, dairy plants, food and beverage processors, and pharmaceutical plants. ECL also sells professional janitorial and health care products (detergents, floor care, disinfectants, odor control, hand care, and sterilants; 3%) under the Airkem and Huntington brand names; textile care products (1%) for large institutional and commercial

laundries; vehicle care products (soaps, polishes, wheel treatments) for rental, fleet and retail car washes (2%); and water treatment products (1%) to institutional, laundry and food processing markets for boilers, cooling and waste treatment systems.

Other U.S. services (9%, 5%) include institutional and commercial pest elimination and prevention services (6%) and GCS Services, a provider of commercial kitchen equipment repair and maintenance services (3%). ECL bought GCS Service in 1998, and has added to this business through small acquisitions.

International business (44%, 34%) provides services similar to those offered in the U.S. to Canada (3%) and about 70 countries in Europe (30%), Latin America (3%), the Asia/Pacific region (7%), and other (1%).

In November 2001, the company acquired for $430 million the remaining 50% interest in the Henkel-Ecolab joint venture, which provides cleaning and sanitizing services for European institutional and industrial markets. Sales in 2001 were $869 million; equity income in the venture was $15.8 million. Henkel KGaA owns a 28% stake in ECL. ECL expanded its pest elimination business to Europe through acquisitions in the U.K. in September 2002 (annual sales of $65 million), and in France in January 2004 ($55 million).

Company Financials Fiscal Year ending December 31

Per Share Data ($)

(Year Ended December 31)	2003	2002	2001	2000	1999	1998	1997	1996	1995	1994
Tangible Bk. Val.	1.14	0.83	0.41	1.77	1.98	1.76	1.30	1.63	1.57	1.57
Cash Flow	1.93	1.67	1.35	1.35	1.15	1.03	0.88	0.79	0.67	0.56
Earnings	1.06	0.81	0.73	0.79	0.66	0.58	0.50	0.44	0.38	0.31
S&P Core Earnings	0.98	0.64	0.61	NA	NA	NA	NA	NA	NA	NA
Dividends	0.30	0.28	0.26	0.25	0.21	0.19	0.17	0.15	0.13	0.11
Payout Ratio	28%	34%	36%	31%	32%	33%	34%	33%	34%	36%
Prices - High	27.91	25.20	22.09	22.84	22.21	19.00	14.00	9.87	7.93	5.87
- Low	23.07	18.26	14.25	14.00	15.84	13.06	9.06	7.28	5.00	4.81
P/E Ratio - High	26	31	30	29	34	33	28	23	21	19
- Low	22	23	20	18	24	23	18	17	13	15

Income Statement Analysis (Million $)

	2003	2002	2001	2000	1999	1998	1997	1996	1995	1994
Revs.	3,762	3,404	2,355	2,264	2,080	1,888	1,640	1,490	1,341	1,208
Oper. Inc.	713	656	482	471	714	384	319	275	239	212
Depr.	230	223	163	148	135	122	101	89.5	76.3	66.9
Int. Exp.	45.3	43.9	28.4	24.6	22.7	25.0	12.6	14.4	11.5	16.2
Pretax Inc.	448	354	306	338	286	256	219	184	159	135
Eff. Tax Rate	38.1%	39.6%	38.4%	38.3%	38.4%	39.7%	38.9%	38.5%	37.6%	37.4%
Net Inc.	277	214	188	209	176	155	134	113	99	84.6
S&P Core Earnings	260	167	157	NA	NA	NA	NA	NA	NA	NA

Balance Sheet & Other Fin. Data (Million $)

	2003	2002	2001	2000	1999	1998	1997	1996	1995	1994
Cash	85.6	49.2	41.8	44.0	47.7	28.4	61.2	69.3	24.7	98.0
Curr. Assets	1,150	1,016	930	601	577	504	510	436	358	401
Total Assets	3,229	2,878	2,525	1,714	1,586	1,471	1,416	1,208	1,061	1,020
Curr. Liab.	851	866	828	532	471	400	404	328	311	254
LT Debt	604	540	512	234	169	227	259	149	89.4	105
Common Equity	1,295	1,100	880	757	929	691	552	520	457	462
Total Cap.	1,900	1,639	1,393	991	1,098	918	811	669	546	567
Cap. Exp.	212	213	158	150	146	148	122	112	110	88.0
Cash Flow	507	437	351	357	310	276	235	203	175	151
Curr. Ratio	1.4	1.2	1.1	1.1	1.2	1.3	1.3	1.3	1.2	1.6
% LT Debt of Cap.	31.8	32.9	36.8	23.6	15.4	24.7	31.9	22.2	16.4	18.6
% Net Inc.of Revs.	7.4	6.3	8.0	9.2	8.5	8.2	8.2	7.6	7.4	7.0
% Ret. on Assets	9.1	7.9	8.9	12.6	11.5	10.7	10.2	10.0	9.6	8.7
% Ret. on Equity	23.2	21.6	23.0	27.5	18.9	24.9	25.0	23.2	21.6	19.6

Data as orig reptd.; bef. results of disc opers/spec. items. Per share data adj. for stk. divs.; EPS diluted. E-Estimated. NA-Not Available. NM-Not Meaningful. NR-Not Ranked. UR-Under Review.

Office: 370 North Wabasha Street, St. Paul, MN 55102-2233.
Telephone: 651-293-2233.
Email: investor.info@ecolab.com
Website: http://www.ecolab.com
Chrmn: A.L. Schuman.
Pres & CEO: D.M. Baker.

EVP & CFO: S.L. Fritze.
SVP, Secy & General Counsel: L.T. Bell.
Investor Contact: M.J. Monahan 651-293-2809.
Dirs: D. M. Baker, Jr., L. S. Biller, R. U. De Schutter, J. A. Grundhofer, S. Hamelmann, J. J. Howard, W. L. Jews, J. W. Johnson, J. Krautter, U. Lehner, J. W. Levin, R. L. Lumpkins, B. M. Pritchard, A. L. Schuman.

Founded: in 1924.
Domicile: Delaware.
Employees: 20,826.
S&P Analyst: Richard O'Reilly, CFA /CB/BK

Recommendation: **HOLD** ★★★☆☆
SELL SELL HOLD BUY BUY

12-Month Target Price: **$31.00**
(as of November 05, 2004)

EIX has an approximate 0.09% weighting in the **S&P 500**

Sector: Utilities
Sub-Industry: Electric Utilities
Peer Group: Electric Cos. (Domestic) - Very Large

Summary: EIX is the holding company for Southern California Edison. Other businesses include electric power generation, financial investments, and real estate development.

Quantitative Evaluations

S&P Earnings & Dividend Rank: B

| D | C | B- | **B** | B+ | A- | A | A+ |

S&P Fair Value Rank: 1

| **1** | 2 | 3 | 4 | 5 |
| Lowest | | | | Highest |

Fair Value Calc.: $24.10 (Overvalued)

S&P Investability Quotient Percentile

59%

EIX scored higher than 59% of all companies for which an S&P Report is available.

Volatility: Low

| **Low** | Average | High |

Technical Evaluation: Bullish
Since 10/04, the technical indicators for EIX have been Bullish.

Relative Strength Rank: Strong

83
1 Lowest   Highest 99

| Price as of 11/12/04: | **$32.09** | 2004E S&P Core EPS: | **$1.21** |

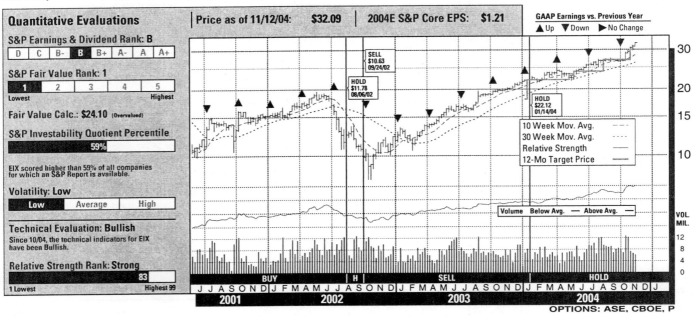

GAAP Earnings vs. Previous Year
▲ Up ▼ Down ▶ No Change

SELL $10.63 09/24/02
HOLD $11.78 08/06/02
HOLD $22.12 01/14/04

10 Week Mov. Avg.
30 Week Mov. Avg.
Relative Strength
12-Mo Target Price

Volume ▫ Below Avg. — Above Avg.

VOL. MIL.

BUY | H | SELL | HOLD

J J A S O N D | J F M A M J J A S O N D | J F M A M J J A S O N D | J F M A M J J A S O N D | J
2001 | 2002 | 2003 | 2004

OPTIONS: ASE, CBOE, P

Analyst commentary prepared by Justin McCann/DC/JWP

Highlights August 19, 2004

- We expect EPS in 2005 to grow about 4% from projected results in 2004. We look for EPS in 2004 to decline sharply from 2003 results, which benefited from the recovery of purchased power costs, and the regulatory allocation of certain costs. EPS in 2004 will also reflect the expiration of an Incentive Cost in Pricing mechanism related to a nuclear facility, which lifted 2003 EPS by $0.38.

- The debt restructuring plan of EIX's Edison Mission Energy (EME) unit will not require any investment from the parent company. It is expected to be funded from the proceeds of the pending sales (announced in July 2004) of all of EME's non-U.S. power facilities. EME hopes to complete the sales by the end of 2004.

- In December 2003, a federal appeals court upheld the Southern California Edison (SCE) October 2001 settlement with the California Public Utility Commission, which had authorized SCE to recover about $3.6 billion of uncollected purchased power costs (the final recovery was completed in July 2003). Also in December 2003, Standard & Poor's Rating Services raised SCE's credit rating to an investment grade BBB.

Investment Rationale/Risk August 19, 2004

- We think that EIX has passed a critical stage in its financial recovery. We expect the stock to perform more in line with peers. Dividends, suspended in October 2000, were resumed in January 2004, after the company obtained favorable court rulings and an upgrade to an investment grade credit rating for SCE. We would hold the shares on a total return basis.

- Risks to our opinion and target price include the potential for unfavorable regulatory or legislative acts that could strain the company's recently recovered financial and credit strength, and a significant market-related change in the P/E multiple of the electric utility group as a whole.

- Based on what we view as favorable developments for SCE, as well as an expected improvement at EME, we believe the shares will continue to trade at a modest premium to the approximate 13.3X peer P/E multiple on our EPS estimate for 2005. However, we expect the multiple to remain relatively flat in 2005. Our 12-month target price is $27.

Key Stock Statistics

S&P Core EPS 2005E	1.75	52-week Range	$32.22-19.74
S&P Oper. EPS 2004E	1.74	12 Month P/E	14.3
P/E on S&P Oper. EPS 2004E	18.4	Beta	0.13
S&P Oper. EPS 2005E	2.13	Shareholders	68,203
Yield (%)	2.5%	Market Cap (B)	$ 10.5
Dividend Rate/Share	0.80	Shares Outstanding (M)	325.8

Value of $10,000 invested five years ago: **$ 11,672**

Dividend Data Dividends have been paid since 2004

Amount ($)	Date Decl.	Ex-Div. Date	Stock of Record	Payment Date
0.200	Dec. 11	Jan. 02	Jan. 06	Jan. 31 '04
0.200	Mar. 18	Mar. 29	Mar. 31	Apr. 30 '04
0.200	May. 20	Jun. 28	Jun. 30	Jul. 31 '04
0.200	Sep. 16	Sep. 28	Sep. 30	Oct. 31 '04

Revenues/Earnings Data Fiscal year ending December 31

Revenues (Million $)

	2004	2003	2002	2001	2000	1999
1Q	2,510	2,532	2,488	2,196	2,723	2,088
2Q	2,919	3,133	2,824	2,446	2,749	2,116
3Q	3,188	3,833	3,707	3,882	3,653	2,957
4Q	—	2,655	2,469	2,912	2,590	2,509
Yr.	—	12,135	11,488	11,437	11,717	9,670

Earnings Per Share ($)

	2004	2003	2002	2001	2000	1999
1Q	0.30	0.20	0.24	-1.93	0.32	0.40
2Q	-1.13	0.08	1.99	0.18	0.40	0.37
3Q	0.95	1.52	1.05	2.46	1.10	0.73
4Q	E0.24	0.59	0.17	6.67	-7.83	0.28
Yr.	E1.74	2.37	3.46	7.36	-5.84	1.79

Next earnings report expected: late-February Source: S&P, Company Reports
EPS Estimates based on S&P Operating Earnings; historical GAAP earnings are as reported.

Edison International

Recommendation: **HOLD** ★ ★ ★ ☆ ☆   12-Month Target Price: **$31.00** (as of November 05, 2004)

Business Summary October 06, 2004

Edison International is the holding company for the regulated Southern California Edison (SCE) utility, and for several non-regulated subsidiaries.

In 2003, SCE accounted for 73.0% of EIX's consolidated revenues; the nonutility power generation business 26.2%; and financial services and other operations 0.8%.

SCE provides electricity to a service territory with a population of more than 12 million people in a 50,000 square mile area of central, coastal and southern California (excluding Los Angeles and several other cities).

Commercial customers accounted for 42% of SCE's operating revenues in 2003; residential customers 33%; industrial customers 8%; public authorities 6%; agricultural and other customers 6%; and other electric revenue 5%.

In October 2001, SCE and the California Public Utility Commission (CPUC) announced an agreement enabling SCE to recover in retail electric rates previously uncollected power procurement costs and repay outstanding overdue obligations. The CPUC agreed to maintain rates until December 31, 2003, or until SCE recovered about $3.6 billion of procurement-related liabilities that occurred in July 2003. In August 2003, the California Supreme Court, in response to an order by a federal appeals court, determined that the agreement did not violate state law. EIX, which agreed not to declare dividends until the liabilities were recovered (or until January 1, 2005), resumed dividend payments in January 2004.

In 2003, SCE's sources of power were: purchased 40.5%; the California Department of Water Resources (CDWR) 22.9%; and SCE-owned generation 36.6% (consisting of 19.8% nuclear; 12.2% coal; and 4.6% hydro).

On January 1, 2003, SCE resumed responsibility for all of its power purchases, following a two-year period beginning January 2001 during which CDWR made power purchases needed to cover SCE's net short position.

Non-regulated operations include Edison Mission Energy (EME), which develops, owns and operates independent power facilities; Edison Capital, which has investments in worldwide energy and infrastructure projects, and U.S. affordable housing projects; and Mission Energy Holding Company (MEHC), which holds the common stock of EME.

At December 31, 2003, EME owned or leased interests in 80 operating plants worldwide, with a net physical capacity of 14,066 megawatts (mw) in the Americas region (with EME's pro rata capacity of 12,581 mw), and 9,705 mw in the Europe and Asia-Pacific regions (6,152 mw). On July 20, 2004, EME agreed to sell its 51.2% interest in the New Zealand-based Contact Energy for about $750 million. On July 30, 2004, EME agreed to sell its remaining 5,381 mw international generation portfolio for approximately $2.2 billion. Both transactions are expected to close, pending regulatory approvals, by the end of 2004. In December 2001, EME sold two U.K. electric power plants for about $960 million.

In 1998, choice of electric supplier was provided to all California customers, under legislation passed in 1996. The legislation included a 10% rate reduction (implemented in 1998) for residential and small commercial customers; a rate freeze for industrial, agricultural, and large commercial customers through March 31, 2002; and the formation of a power exchange and an independent system operator to manage and control the transmission system.

Company Financials Fiscal Year ending December 31

Per Share Data ($)

(Year Ended December 31)	2003	2002	2001	2000	1999	1998	1997	1996	1995	1994
Tangible Bk. Val.	13.86	11.59	8.10	7.43	14.04	13.55	13.65	14.12	13.40	12.76
Earnings	2.37	3.46	7.36	-5.84	1.79	1.84	1.73	1.64	1.66	1.52
S&P Core Earnings	2.45	2.81	6.78	NA	NA	NA	NA	NA	NA	NA
Dividends	Nil	Nil	Nil	1.11	1.07	1.04	1.00	1.25	1.00	1.10
Payout Ratio	Nil	Nil	Nil	NM	60%	56%	58%	76%	60%	73%
Prices - High	22.07	19.60	16.12	30.00	29.62	31.00	27.81	20.37	18.00	20.50
- Low	10.57	7.80	6.25	14.12	21.62	25.12	19.37	15.00	14.37	12.37
P/E Ratio - High	9	6	2	NM	17	17	16	12	11	13
- Low	4	2	1	NM	12	14	11	9	9	8

Income Statement Analysis (Million $)

	2003	2002	2001	2000	1999	1998	1997	1996	1995	1994
Revs.	12,135	11,488	11,436	11,717	9,670	10,208	9,235	8,545	8,405	8,345
Depr.	1,184	1,030	973	1,933	1,794	1,662	1,362	1,173	1,014	945
Maint.	NA	NA	NA	NA	NA	411	406	331	359	332
Fxd. Chgs. Cov.	1.73	1.91	3.38	-0.98	1.96	1.71	2.27	3.20	3.34	2.87
Constr. Credits	NA	NA	NA	NA	Nil	12.0	17.0	26.0	33.0	28.0
Eff. Tax Rate	21.5%	25.6%	40.7%	NM	32.0%	40.4%	40.3%	44.0%	41.7%	39.5%
Net Inc.	779	1,135	2,402	-1,943	623	668	700	717	739	681
S&P Core Earnings	808	921	2,211	NA	NA	NA	NA	NA	NA	NA

Balance Sheet & Other Fin. Data (Million $)

	2003	2002	2001	2000	1999	1998	1997	1996	1995	1994
Gross Prop.	24,674	23,264	22,396	25,737	27,203	17,223	24,661	21,134	20,717	20,127
Cap. Exp.	1,288	1,590	933	1,488	1,231	963	783	744	NA	1,137
Net Prop.	20,288	15,170	14,427	17,903	19,683	10,326	14,117	11,703	12,148	12,417
Capitalization:										
LT Debt	12,221	12,915	14,007	13,660	15,050	8,543	8,871	7,475	7,195	6,347
% LT Debt	69.4	74.4	81.1	85.0	74.3	62.6	59.1	51.3	50.4	48.0
Pfd.	9.00	Nil	Nil	Nil	Nil	Nil	609	709	709	721
% Pfd.	0.05	Nil	Nil	Nil	Nil	Nil	4.05	4.80	5.00	5.50
Common	5,383	4,437	3,272	2,420	5,211	5,099	5,527	6,397	6,360	6,144
% Common	30.6	25.6	18.9	15.0	25.7	37.4	36.8	43.9	44.6	46.5
Total Cap.	24,246	23,786	24,163	21,609	26,252	18,520	19,452	19,943	19,638	18,305
% Oper. Ratio	75.2	82.8	93.2	86.4	92.9	96.9	87.8	82.7	83.6	84.4
% Earn. on Net Prop.	9.1	16.0	36.9	NM	11.6	6.4	10.2	12.4	11.2	10.5
% Return On Revs.	6.4	9.9	21.0	NM	6.4	6.5	7.6	8.4	8.8	8.2
% Return On Invest. Capital	14.9	10.9	4.8	7.8	3.6	7.9	10.5	7.1	7.9	7.0
% Return On Com. Equity	15.9	29.4	84.4	NM	12.1	12.6	11.7	11.2	11.8	11.3

Data as orig reptd.; bef. results of disc opers/spec. items. Per share data adj. for stk. divs. Bold denotes primary EPS - prior periods restated. E-Estimated. NA-Not Available. NM-Not Meaningful. NR-Not Ranked. UR-Under Review.

Office: 2244 Walnut Grove Avenue, Rosemead, CA 91770-3714.
Telephone: 626-302-2222.
Website: http://www.edison.com
Chrmn, Pres & CEO: J.E. Bryson.
EVP, CFO & Treas: T.F. Craver, Jr.

EVP & General Counsel: B.C. Danner.
VP & Secy: B.P. Ryder.
Dirs: J. E. Bryson, F. A. Cordova, A. J. Fohrer, B. M. Freeman, B. Karatz, L. G. Nogales, R. L. Olson, J. M. Rosser, R. T. Schlosberg III, R. H. Smith, T. C. Sutton, D. M. Tellep.

Founded: in 1987.
Domicile: California.
Employees: 15,407.
S&P Analyst: Justin McCann/DC/JWP

Electronic Arts

Recommendation: **BUY** ★ ★ ★ ★ ☆
(SELL SELL HOLD BUY BUY)

12-Month Target Price: **$56.00**
(as of October 20, 2004)

ERTS has an approximate 0.13% weighting in the **S&P 500**

Sector: Information Technology
Sub-Industry: Home Entertainment Software
Peer Group: Entertainment/Multimedia Software

Summary: ERTS produces entertainment software for PCs, as well as for hardware console entertainment systems.

Quantitative Evaluations

S&P Earnings & Dividend Rank: B+

D	C	B-	B	B+	A-	A	A+

S&P Fair Value Rank: 4-

1	2	3	4	5
Lowest				Highest

Fair Value Calc.: $47.90 (Fairly Valued)

S&P Investability Quotient Percentile

98%

ERTS scored higher than 98% of all companies for which an S&P Report is available.

Volatility: Average

Low	Average	High

Technical Evaluation: Neutral
Since 11/04, the technical indicators for ERTS have been Neutral.

Relative Strength Rank: Moderate

33

1 Lowest		Highest 99

Price as of 11/12/04: $47.59 | **2005E S&P Core EPS: $1.74**

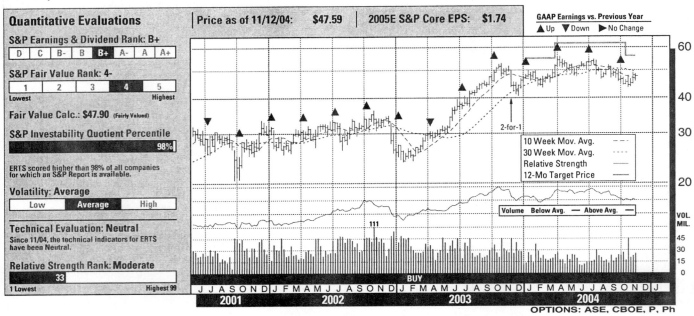

GAAP Earnings vs. Previous Year
▲ Up   ▼ Down   ► No Change

Legend:
- 10 Week Mov. Avg.
- 30 Week Mov. Avg.
- Relative Strength
- 12-Mo Target Price

2-for-1

Volume   Below Avg. — Above Avg.

VOL. MIL.

J J A S O N D | J F M A M J J A S O N D | J F M A M J J A S O N D | J F M A M J J A S O N D | J F M A M J J A S O N D | J
2001 | 2002 | 2003 | 2004

BUY

OPTIONS: ASE, CBOE, P, Ph

Analyst commentary prepared by Jonathan Rudy, CFA /MF/GG

Highlights October 21, 2004

- We believe FY 05 (Mar.) revenues will increase about 11%, benefiting from a further buildout of the installed base of current generation hardware consoles. We see increasing production and lower price points for PlayStation 2, Microsoft's X-Box, and Nintendo's GameCube driving further growth in the industry during this current hardware cycle. We also expect ERTS to benefit from the consolidation of its Internet initiatives, which have been a drag on results.

- We see operating margins narrowing slightly in FY 05, as ERTS begins to increase its spending on research and development in preparation for the next generation of hardware consoles. Despite more shares outstanding and a higher effective tax rate, we expect FY 05 operating EPS to advance about 10%, to $2.05, from $1.86 in FY 04, excluding one-time and restructuring charges. We see EPS of $2.20 in FY 06.

- Our FY 05 Standard & Poor's Core Earnings projection of $1.74 a share reflects estimated stock option expense.

Investment Rationale/Risk October 21, 2004

- We recommend accumulating the shares of this market leader. We believe ERTS has a strong, well diversified brand library, and should continue to benefit from a growing installed base of current generation hardware consoles. We see the company as a prime beneficiary of recent price cuts for PlayStation 2 and X-Box. We view the balance sheet as strong, with approximately $2.5 billion in cash and short-term investments (about $7.90 a share), and no debt. With the stock trading at a discount to peers on a P/E to growth basis, and what we view as ERTS's industry leading position and strong financials, we regard the shares as attractive.

- Risks to our recommendation and target price include a potential slowdown in the video game industry as the next generation hardware cycle approaches, lower prices for high end titles, and a potential slowdown in consumer spending.

- Based on a blend of our relative P/E multiple to growth ratio and discounted cash flow analyses, our 12-month target price is $56.

Key Stock Statistics

S&P Oper. EPS 2005E	2.05	52-week Range	$55.91-40.60
P/E on S&P Oper. EPS 2005E	23.2	12 Month P/E	24.5
S&P Oper. EPS 2006E	2.20	Beta	0.65
Yield (%)	Nil	Shareholders	1,686
Dividend Rate/Share	Nil	Market Cap (B)	$14.5
Shares Outstanding (M)	305.3		

Value of $10,000 invested five years ago: **$ 23,393**

Dividend Data

Amount ($)	Date Decl.	Ex-Div. Date	Stock of Record	Payment Date
2-for-1	Oct. 22	Nov. 18	Nov. 03	Nov. 17 '03

Revenues/Earnings Data Fiscal year ending March 31

Revenues (Million $)

	2005	2004	2003	2002	2001	2000
1Q	431.6	353.4	331.9	181.9	154.8	186.1
2Q	715.7	530.0	453.5	240.2	219.9	338.9
3Q	—	1,475	1,234	832.9	640.3	600.7
4Q	—	598.4	463.1	469.7	307.3	294.3
Yr.	—	2,957	2,482	1,725	1,322	1,420

Earnings Per Share ($)

	2005	2004	2003	2002	2001	2000
1Q	0.08	0.06	0.03	-0.17	-0.16	0.01
2Q	0.31	0.25	0.17	-0.12	-0.15	0.07
3Q	E1.32	1.32	0.85	0.46	0.32	0.35
4Q	E0.34	0.29	0.03	0.17	-0.07	0.01
Yr.	E2.05	1.87	1.09	0.36	-0.04	0.44

Next earnings report expected: late-January Source: S&P, Company Reports
EPS Estimates based on S&P Operating Earnings; historical GAAP earnings are as reported.

Electronic Arts Inc.

Recommendation: **BUY** ★★★★☆   12-Month Target Price: **$56.00** (as of October 20, 2004)

Business Summary October 21, 2004

Electronic Arts creates, markets and distributes interactive entertainment software for various platforms, including the Sony PlayStation and PlayStation 2, Microsoft X-Box, Nintendo 64, and GameCube entertainment systems, and for CD-ROM-based systems, including IBM PCs and compatibles.

Several current generation hardware platforms have been released in recent years. Sony introduced PlayStation II in Japan in March 2000, and in North America in October 2000. Microsoft released its first video game system, X-Box, in North America in November 2001. Nintendo also launched GameCube in North America in November 2001.

Revenues by platform in FY 04 (Mar.) included PlayStation (1%, versus 4% in FY 03), PlayStation 2 (44%; 37%), PC-CD (16%; 20%), Affiliated Labels (13%; 15%), X-Box (13%; 9%), Game Boy Advance/Game Boy Color (3%; 3%), Subscription services (2%; 2%), Nintendo GameCube (7%; 7%), and other (1%; 3%). As of March 31, 2004, the company was developing or publishing products for 10 different hardware platforms.

ERTS introduced more than 32 EA Studios titles in FY 04, versus 31 in FY 03. In FY 04, no single title accounted for over 10% of revenues. In FY 03, one title, Harry Potter and the Chamber of Secrets, accounted for about 10% of revenues. In FY 04, 27 titles sold more than 1 million units, versus 22 in FY 03. In FY 04, six franchises sold more than 5 million units: The Sims, Need for Speed, Medal of Honor, FIFA Soccer, The Lord of the Rings, and Madden NFL Football.

About 69% of FY 04 revenues were derived from EA Studio-produced products released during the year. Products are distributed through a direct sales force in the U.S., and primarily through third-party distributors in Europe and Asia, to more than 58,000 retail locations worldwide.

In FY 04, international markets accounted for 45% of revenues, up from 42% in FY 03, and 37% in FY 02.

In February 2000, the company acquired Kesmai Corp., for $22.5 million in cash, plus about $8.7 million in stock. Kesmai specializes in design and development of multiplayer games delivered directly to consumers over the Internet.

In February 2001, ERTS acquired Pogo Corp., for about $43 million. Pogo's Internet-based family games focus on easy-to-play card, board and puzzle games.

In March 2000, shareholders approved a proposal to authorize the issuance of a tracking stock, intended to reflect the performance of the company's online and e-commerce division (EA.com). In October 2000, EA.com was launched on the Worldwide web and AOL Games Channel. On April 1, 2003, ERTS consolidated reporting related to the online products into the core EA business, and therefore discontinued separate reporting of the tracking stock.

Company Financials Fiscal Year ending March 31

Per Share Data ($)

(Year Ended March 31)	2004	2003	2002	2001	2000	1999	1998	1997	1996	1995
Tangible Bk. Val.	8.52	11.62	3.92	3.33	2.86	2.38	2.34	1.80	1.53	1.17
Cash Flow	2.12	2.79	0.74	0.22	0.62	0.47	0.41	0.34	0.26	0.32
Earnings	1.87	1.09	0.36	-0.04	0.44	0.29	0.30	0.24	0.19	0.27
S&P Core Earnings	1.59	0.82	0.10	-0.25	NA	NA	NA	NA	NA	NA
Dividends	Nil	Nil	Nil	Nil	Nil	Nil	Nil	Nil	Nil	Nil
Payout Ratio	Nil	Nil	Nil	Nil	Nil	Nil	Nil	Nil	Nil	Nil

Cal. Yrs.	2003	2002	2001	2000	1999	1998	1997	1996	1995	1994
Prices - High	52.88	36.22	33.46	28.96	31.10	14.28	10.06	9.96	10.56	8.37
- Low	23.75	24.73	17.25	12.25	9.50	8.31	4.81	5.28	3.84	3.18
P/E Ratio - High	28	33	94	NM	71	50	34	42	56	31
- Low	13	23	49	NM	22	29	16	22	20	12

Income Statement Analysis (Million $)

	2004	2003	2002	2001	2000	1999	1998	1997	1996	1995
Revs.	2,957	2,482	1,725	1,322	1,420	1,222	909	625	532	493
Oper. Inc.	863	629	267	42.1	219	196	123	88.8	69.4	74.2
Depr.	77.5	91.6	111	69.7	46.7	46.3	26.9	21.5	15.9	9.34
Int. Exp.	Nil	Nil	Nil	Nil	Nil	Nil	Nil	0.01	0.14	0.05
Pretax Inc.	797	316	147	-13.4	169	118	108	79.0	59.6	78.1
Eff. Tax Rate	27.5%	NM	31.3%	NM	31.2%	38.3%	33.0%	34.5%	31.5%	32.0%
Net Inc.	577	317	102	-11.1	117	72.9	72.6	53.0	40.5	55.7
S&P Core Earnings	482	239	28.0	-68.2	NA	NA	NA	NA	NA	NA

Balance Sheet & Other Fin. Data (Million $)

	2004	2003	2002	2001	2000	1999	1998	1997	1996	1995
Cash	2,150	1,589	804	477	340	318	375	236	186	185
Curr. Assets	2,911	1,911	1,153	819	705	569	590	369	300	272
Total Assets	3,401	2,360	1,699	1,379	1,192	902	746	517	424	341
Curr. Liab.	722	571	453	340	265	236	182	127	101	103
LT Debt	Nil	Nil	Nil	Nil	Nil	Nil	Nil	Nil	Nil	Nil
Common Equity	2,678	1,785	1,243	1,034	923	663	564	389	322	237
Total Cap.	2,678	1,789	1,246	1,039	927	666	564	389	323	238
Cap. Exp.	89.6	59.1	51.5	120	135	116	45.2	36.2	56.8	16.5
Cash Flow	655	409	212	58.6	163	119	99	74.5	56.3	65.1
Curr. Ratio	4.0	3.3	2.5	2.4	2.7	2.4	3.2	2.9	3.0	2.6
% LT Debt of Cap.	Nil	Nil	Nil	Nil	Nil	Nil	Nil	Nil	Nil	Nil
% Net Inc.of Revs.	19.5	12.8	5.9	NM	8.2	6.0	8.0	8.5	7.7	11.3
% Ret. on Assets	20.0	15.6	6.6	NM	11.2	8.8	11.5	11.3	10.6	17.6
% Ret. on Equity	25.9	20.9	8.9	NM	14.7	11.9	15.2	14.9	14.5	26.5

Data as orig reptd.; bef. results of disc opers/spec. items. Per share data adj. for stk. divs. Bold denotes primary EPS - prior periods restated. E-Estimated. NA-Not Available. NM-Not Meaningful. NR-Not Ranked. UR-Under Review.

Office: 209 Redwood Shores Parkway, Redwood City, CA 94065-1175.
Telephone: 650-628-1500.
Email: investorrelations@ea.com
Website: http://www.ea.com
Chrmn & CEO: L.F. Probst III.
COO & EVP: V.P. Lee.

EVP & CFO: W. Jenson.
VP & Chief Acctg Officer: K. Barker.
Investor Contact: K. Sansot 650-628-5597.
Dirs: M. R. Asher, W. J. Byron, L. S. Coleman, G. M. Kusin, G. Maffei, T. Mott, R. W. Pittman, L. F. Probst III, L. J. Srere.

Founded: in 1982.
Domicile: Delaware.
Employees: 4,800.
S&P Analyst: Jonathan Rudy, CFA /MF/GG

Electronic Data Systems

Recommendation: **HOLD** ★★★☆ | 12-Month Target Price: **$22.00**
SELL SELL HOLD BUY BUY
(as of November 16, 2004)

EDS has an approximate 0.11% weighting in the **S&P 500**

Sector: Information Technology
Sub-Industry: Data Processing & Outsourced Services
Peer Group: Outsourced Services - Larger Sales

Summary: EDS, which split off from GM in 1996, is a leading provider of a full range of information technology services.

Quantitative Evaluations	Price as of 11/16/04: $22.56	2004E S&P Core EPS: $0.13

S&P Earnings & Dividend Rank: B+
D C B- B **B+** A- A A+

S&P Fair Value Rank: 2-
1 **2** 3 4 5
Lowest / Highest

Fair Value Calc.: $20.00 (Slightly Overvalued)

S&P Investability Quotient Percentile
49%

EDS scored lower than 51% of all companies for which an S&P Report is available.

Volatility: Average
Low / **Average** / High

Technical Evaluation: Bullish
Since 10/04, the technical indicators for EDS have been Bullish.

Relative Strength Rank: Strong
84
1 Lowest / Highest 99

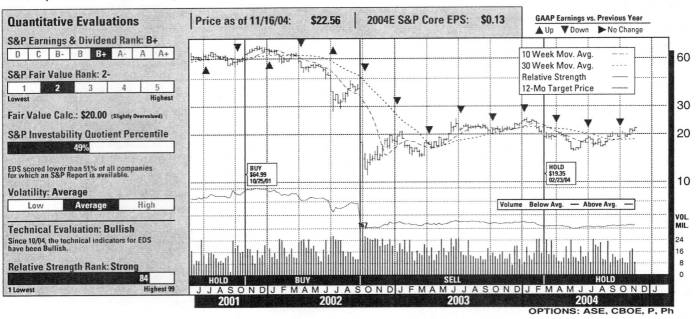

GAAP Earnings vs. Previous Year
▲ Up ▼ Down ► No Change

10 Week Mov. Avg.
30 Week Mov. Avg.
Relative Strength
12-Mo Target Price

BUY $64.99 10/25/01

HOLD $19.35 02/23/04

Volume Below Avg. — Above Avg.

VOL. MIL. 24 16 8 0

HOLD | BUY | SELL | HOLD
J J A S O N D | J F M A M J J A S O N D | J F M A M J J A S O N D | J F M A M J J A S O N D | J
2001 | 2002 | 2003 | 2004

OPTIONS: ASE, CBOE, P, Ph

Analyst commentary prepared by Stephanie S. Crane/CB/JWP

Highlights September 20, 2004

- We expect revenues to decline 1.8% in 2004. Although we believe that the company's backlog of opportunities remains strong, we think that a lack of discretionary spending on the part of clients, lengthening sales cycles, and ongoing delays in implementing new business are likely to restrict revenues. However, we expect EDS's shifting business mix, which is increasingly focusing on the business process outsourcing market, to help to offset these factors. The company signed $4.0 billion of new business in the 2004 second quarter, up 25% from the $3.2 billion signed in the 2003 period.

- We see operating margins widening, as benefits resulting from restructuring efforts, together with more favorable comparisons, should outweigh the impact of continued pricing pressures and the possibility of further renegotiation of contracts.

- The company lowered guidance for the third quarter after setting aside a reserve on a loss from a contract with US Airways, which filed Chapter 11 protection. EDS has $27 million in receivables and $16 million in other assets at risk. We forecast 2004 EPS of $0.22, down from $0.49 in 2003 (excluding special charges of $1.02). We project Standard & Poor's Core Earnings of $0.13 a share for 2004, reflecting projected option expense.

Investment Rationale/Risk September 20, 2004

- We recommend holding the shares. We see recent efforts by the company to realign its leadership team, refocus its business strategy, reduce its net debt, increase liquidity and focus on productivity initiatives as positive. However, we still think EDS faces several challenges in coming months as it seeks to deal with poorly performing contracts and attempts to address intensifying competition.

- Risks to our recommendation and target price come from accelerating competition in the outsourcing market, which could cause pricing pressures and negatively affect profit margins. Moody's recent downgrade of company debt to below investment grade status could also negatively affect its ability to win business.

- Our 12-month target price of $20 is based on a combination of relative P/E multiple and discounted cash flow (DCF) analyses. Our DCF assumptions include a weighted average cost of capital of 8.9% and an expected terminal growth rate of 3%.

Key Stock Statistics

S&P Oper. EPS 2004E	0.22	52-week Range	$25.44-15.62
P/E on S&P Oper. EPS 2004E	99.4	12 Month P/E	NM
Yield (%)	0.9%	Beta	1.27
Dividend Rate/Share	0.20	Shareholders	129,000
Shares Outstanding (M)	513.9	Market Cap (B)	$ 11.6

Value of $10,000 invested five years ago: **$ 3,786**

Dividend Data Dividends have been paid since 1984

Amount ($)	Date Decl.	Ex-Div. Date	Stock of Record	Payment Date
0.150	Feb. 04	Feb. 11	Feb. 13	Mar. 10 '04
0.150	Apr. 23	May. 12	May. 14	Jun. 10 '04
0.050	Jul. 27	Aug. 11	Aug. 13	Sep. 10 '04
0.050	Oct. 21	Nov. 10	Nov. 15	Dec. 10 '04

Revenues/Earnings Data Fiscal year ending December 31

Revenues (Million $)

	2004	2003	2002	2001	2000	1999
1Q	5,198	5,221	5,266	4,987	4,576	4,326
2Q	5,238	5,273	5,395	5,091	4,656	4,616
3Q	4,945	5,220	5,334	5,559	4,793	4,715
4Q	—	5,762	5,507	5,906	5,202	4,877
Yr.	—	21,476	21,502	21,543	19,227	18,534

Earnings Per Share ($)

	2004	2003	2002	2001	2000	1999
1Q	-0.07	0.01	0.70	0.98	0.60	-0.04
2Q	-0.27	0.19	0.63	0.62	0.53	0.48
3Q	-0.33	Nil	0.21	0.44	0.59	0.31
4Q	E0.21	-0.73	0.52	0.82	0.68	0.09
Yr.	E0.22	-0.53	2.06	2.86	2.40	0.85

Next earnings report expected: early-February Source: S&P, Company Reports
EPS Estimates based on S&P Operating Earnings; historical GAAP earnings are as reported.

STANDARD &POOR'S

Electronic Data Systems Corporation

Stock Report
November 16, 2004
NYSE Symbol: **EDS**

Recommendation: **HOLD** ★ ★ ★ ☆ ☆   12-Month Target Price: **$22.00** (as of November 16, 2004)

Business Summary September 21, 2004

Electronic Data Systems is a leading provider of professional information technology (IT) services. The company split off from GM in 1996. In 2003, as part of efforts to manage costs and boost efficiencies, EDS combined Operations Solutions and Solutions Consulting into a single segment, Outsourcing. The transition was to be completed by end of 2004, with more than 5,000 employees terminated. In March 2004, the company agreed to sell its UGS Product Lifecycle Management Solutions business.

Operations Solutions manages IT and business process solutions to help companies and governments worldwide in reducing complexity, creating efficiencies, and managing risk. EDS also provides hosting and communications services, as well as business process outsourcing.

Solutions Consulting encompasses a continuum of innovative and scalable solutions from enterprise strategy through application design, development and deployment. This business focuses on planning, developing and managing custom applications, packaged software and industry specific solutions.

Product Lifecycle Management Solutions enables all of the participants involved in a company's product lifecycle to work in concert to bring products to market and support its customer base by combining the capabilities and advantages of digital product design, simulation, manufacturing and collaboration technologies.

A.T. Kearney provides clients with management consulting services, including strategy and organization consulting and executive search services. The segment serves clients in various industries, and works in collaboration with other EDS business units.

EDS signed $14 billion of new contracts in 2003, down 43% from $24.4 billion of new business signed in 2002; $31.4 billion of new business was signed in 2001.

Revenues derived from contracts with GM provided 12% of the total in 2002, down from 15% in 2001. In 1996, the company entered into a 10-year agreement to continue as GM's principal provider of information technology services. Other than GM, no client accounted for over 10% of revenues in any of the past three years.

In October 2000, EDS was awarded a contract by the U.S. Navy and Marine Corps to provide end-to-end IT infrastructure on a seat management basis. The contract had a base period of five years, extended in October 2002 to seven years, with a minimum aggregate order obligation of $6 billion.

In the 2003 first quarter, the company recorded a $334 million pretax loss associated with its Navy Marine Corps Intranet contract. The loss was related to an adjustment to the average seat price and deployment schedule. EDS does not expect the contract to turn cash flow positive until 2005.

Company Financials Fiscal Year ending December 31

Per Share Data ($)

(Year Ended December 31)	2003	2002	2001	2000	1999	1998	1997	1996	1995	1994
Tangible Bk. Val.	NM	3.22	3.05	4.53	6.04	11.06	8.15	7.54	7.87	7.01
Cash Flow	4.73	5.01	5.93	5.40	3.73	4.31	3.95	3.32	3.65	2.91
Earnings	-0.53	2.06	2.86	2.40	0.85	1.50	1.48	0.89	1.96	1.71
S&P Core Earnings	-0.97	1.16	1.64	NA	NA	NA	NA	NA	NA	NA
Dividends	0.60	0.60	0.60	0.60	0.60	0.60	0.60	0.60	0.52	0.48
Payout Ratio	NM	29%	21%	25%	71%	40%	41%	67%	27%	28%
Prices - High	25.03	68.55	72.45	76.68	70.00	51.31	49.62	63.37	52.62	39.50
- Low	19.85	10.09	50.90	38.37	44.12	30.43	25.50	40.75	36.87	27.50
P/E Ratio - High	NM	33	25	32	82	34	34	71	27	23
- Low	NM	5	18	16	52	20	17	46	19	16

Income Statement Analysis (Million $)

	2003	2002	2001	2000	1999	1998	1997	1996	1995	1994
Revs.	21,476	21,502	21,543	19,227	18,534	16,891	15,236	14,441	12,422	9,960
Oper. Inc.	2,601	3,312	3,707	3,252	1,909	2,509	2,753	2,767	2,337	1,821
Depr.	2,529	1,443	1,482	1,431	1,436	1,394	1,210	1,181	808	578
Int. Exp.	266	258	247	210	150	131	176	153	121	52.9
Pretax Inc.	-389	1,525	2,199	1,800	658	1,133	1,142	674	1,467	1,284
Eff. Tax Rate	NM	34.0%	36.9%	36.5%	36.0%	34.4%	36.0%	36.0%	36.0%	36.1%
Net Inc.	-252	1,007	1,387	1,143	421	743	731	432	939	822
S&P Core Earnings	-461	560	795	NA	NA	NA	NA	NA	NA	NA

Balance Sheet & Other Fin. Data (Million $)

	2003	2002	2001	2000	1999	1998	1997	1996	1995	1994
Cash	2,313	1,890	839	693	729	1,312	677	963	639	758
Curr. Assets	6,823	9,385	7,374	6,167	5,878	5,633	5,169	5,008	4,382	3,354
Total Assets	18,280	18,880	16,353	12,700	12,522	11,526	11,174	11,174	10,832	8,787
Curr. Liab.	7,473	6,129	4,367	4,318	4,996	3,657	3,258	3,163	3,261	2,873
LT Debt	3,488	4,148	4,692	2,586	2,391	1,184	1,791	2,324	1,853	1,021
Common Equity	5,714	7,022	6,446	5,139	4,535	5,917	5,310	4,783	4,979	4,232
Total Cap.	9,686	11,221	11,986	8,382	7,194	7,869	7,575	8,030	7,571	5,913
Cap. Exp.	703	973	1,285	768	685	870	769	1,158	1,262	1,121
Cash Flow	2,277	2,450	2,869	2,575	1,857	2,137	1,941	1,613	1,747	1,399
Curr. Ratio	0.9	1.5	1.7	1.4	1.2	1.5	1.6	1.6	1.3	1.2
% LT Debt of Cap.	36.0	37.0	39.1	30.8	33.2	15.0	23.6	28.9	24.5	17.3
% Net Inc.of Revs.	NM	4.7	6.4	5.9	2.3	4.4	4.8	3.0	7.6	8.3
% Ret. on Assets	NM	5.7	9.6	9.1	3.5	6.5	6.5	3.9	9.6	10.4
% Ret. on Equity	NM	15.0	23.9	23.6	8.1	13.2	14.5	8.9	20.4	20.9

Data as orig reptd.; bef. results of disc opers/spec. items. Per share data adj. for stk. divs.; EPS diluted. E-Estimated. NA-Not Available. NM-Not Meaningful. NR-Not Ranked. UR-Under Review.

Office: 5400 Legacy Drive, Plano, TX 75024-3199.
Telephone: 972-605-6000.
Email: invest@eds.com
Website: http://www.eds.com
Chrmn & CEO: M.H. Jordan.
EVP & CFO: R.H. Swan.

EVP, Secy & General Counsel: B.N. Hawthorne.
VP & Treas: S.J. Krenz.
Investor Contact: M. Paludan 256-705-2544.
Dirs: R. A. Enrico, R. Fisher, R. J. Groves, E. M. Hancock, J. M. Heller, R. L. Hunt, M. H. Jordan, E. Kangas, C. R. Kidder, J. Rodin.

Founded: in 1962.
Domicile: Delaware.
Employees: 132,000.
S&P Analyst: Stephanie S. Crane/CB/JWP

El Paso Corp.

Recommendation: HOLD ★★★☆☆   12-Month Target Price: **$9.00**
SELL SELL HOLD BUY BUY   (as of August 23, 2004)

EP has an approximate 0.06% weighting in the **S&P 500**

Sector: Energy
Sub-Industry: Oil & Gas Refining, Marketing & Transportation

Summary: EP provides natural gas and related energy products. It owns North America's largest natural gas pipeline system and one of its largest independent natural gas producers.

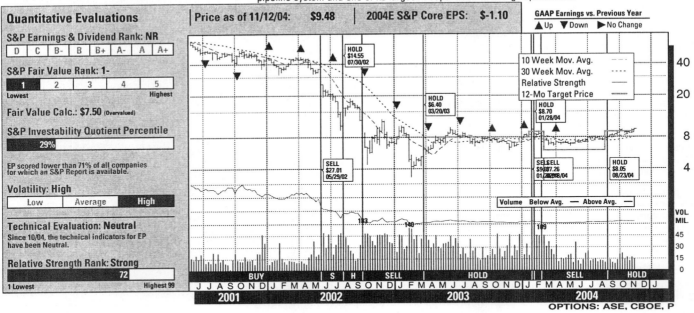

Quantitative Evaluations

Price as of 11/12/04: $9.48   **2004E S&P Core EPS:** $-1.10

S&P Earnings & Dividend Rank: NR

| D | C | B- | B | B+ | A- | A | A+ |

S&P Fair Value Rank: 1-

| 1 | 2 | 3 | 4 | 5 |
| Lowest | | | | Highest |

Fair Value Calc.: $7.50 (Overvalued)

S&P Investability Quotient Percentile

29%

EP scored lower than 71% of all companies for which an S&P Report is available.

Volatility: High

| Low | Average | High |

Technical Evaluation: Neutral
Since 10/04, the technical indicators for EP have been Neutral.

Relative Strength Rank: Strong
72
1 Lowest   Highest 99

GAAP Earnings vs. Previous Year
▲ Up ▼ Down ► No Change

- 10 Week Mov. Avg. ---
- 30 Week Mov. Avg. ····
- Relative Strength ——
- 12-Mo Target Price ——

OPTIONS: ASE, CBOE, P

Analyst commentary prepared by Craig K. Shere, CFA /PMW/GG

Highlights August 24, 2004

- By the end of the 2004 third quarter, EP expects to complete the restatement of reported earnings for the period from 1999 through 2002, and to issue final audited 2003 results. The restatements are related primarily to a negative 1.8 Tcfe oil and natural gas reserve revision announced in February 2004, and to the accounting treatment of offsetting natural gas price contracts (disclosed in August 2004) which were originally presented as price hedges for oil and gas production.

- We see mark to market trading losses and one-time operating charges depressing 2004 earnings. However, in light of the late August announcement that EP's natural gas price hedges for Production operations were much lower than previously reported, we see 2005 and 2006 results benefiting from a recovery in Production volumes and much higher realized commodity prices. As a result of more extensive writedowns of oil and gas production properties in 1999-2002, we see ongoing amortization of production finding costs 30% to 40% lower than EP's guidance prior to August 2004. Earnings growth, in our opinion, should also benefit from the completion of a number of pipeline expansion projects between the second half of 2004 and early 2006.

- We look for 2004 S&P Core EPS to be well below our operating EPS estimate, primarily due to the exclusion of gains from asset sales and inclusion of writedowns for depreciable assets and other one-time charges related to ongoing businesses.

Investment Rationale/Risk August 24, 2004

- In light of the company's August statement that its exploration and production (E&P) operations were far less hedged (at commodity prices below current market prices) than previously reported, we see EP in the enviable position of being able to substantially hedge future gas and oil volumes at prices well in excess of production costs. We expect the company to announce updated hedging plans before the end of 2004. To achieve production growth, following a substantial negative February reserve revision, we believe the E&P division will need to pursue more acquisitions and relatively larger capital expenditures than peer E&P companies.

- Risks to our recommendation and target price include the financial inability to lock in currently high futures prices for future natural gas production, a prolonged decline in natural gas prices, the inability to wind down remaining energy trading positions (and related collateral postings), a slowing economy, and warmer than normal winter weather.

- Based on our belief that EP will have proportionately larger capital expenditures (including acquisitions) than most peers, we believe the shares should trade at a discount to the price to operating cash flow (OCF) multiple of energy merchant peers. We look for the shares to trade at 3X annualized 2004 first half 2004, versus a peer group average of about 4X trailing 12-month OCF. Our 12-month target price is $9.

Key Stock Statistics

S&P Oper. EPS 2004E	Nil	52-week Range	$9.88-5.97
P/E on S&P Oper. EPS 2004E	NM	12 Month P/E	NM
S&P Oper. EPS 2005E	0.50	Beta	1.40
Yield (%)	1.7%	Shareholders	68,070
Dividend Rate/Share	0.16	Market Cap (B)	$ 6.1
Shares Outstanding (M)	643.2		

Value of $10,000 invested five years ago: **$ 2,671**

Dividend Data Dividends have been paid since 1992

Amount ($)	Date Decl.	Ex-Div. Date	Stock of Record	Payment Date
0.040	Oct. 30	Dec. 03	Dec. 05	Jan. 05 '04
0.040	Feb. 04	Mar. 03	Mar. 05	Apr. 05 '04
0.040	Apr. 29	Jun. 02	Jun. 04	Jul. 06 '04
0.040	Jul. 16	Sep. 01	Sep. 03	Oct. 04 '04

Revenues/Earnings Data Fiscal year ending December 31

Revenues (Million $)

	2004	2003	2002	2001	2000	1999
1Q	1,585	1,844	3,755	17,754	3,106	2,275
2Q	—	1,574	2,987	13,363	4,227	2,600
3Q	—	1,724	2,656	13,845	6,987	3,263
4Q	—	1,569	2,796	12,115	7,543	2,443
Yr.	—	6,711	12,194	57,475	21,950	10,581

Earnings Per Share ($)

	2004	2003	2002	2001	2000	1999
1Q	-0.23	-0.33	0.43	-0.78	0.70	-0.62
2Q	E Nil	-0.53	0.02	-0.26	0.56	0.17
3Q	E Nil	0.12	-0.06	0.42	0.57	0.17
4Q	E Nil	-0.28	-2.54	0.72	0.61	-0.78
Yr.	E Nil	-1.03	-2.30	0.13	2.44	-1.06

Next earnings report expected: NA Source: S&P, Company Reports
EPS Estimates based on S&P Operating Earnings; historical GAAP earnings are as reported.

STANDARD &POOR'S

El Paso Corporation

Stock Report
November 13, 2004
NYSE Symbol: **EP**

Recommendation: **HOLD** ★ ★ ★ ☆ ☆   12-Month Target Price: **$9.00** (as of August 23, 2004)

Business Summary August 24, 2004

As a result of accounting delays related to a 40% downward revision in El Paso Corp.'s exploration and production reserves in mid-February 2004, the company had not made its 2003 full year or 2004 first quarter SEC filings as of early June. In 2002, the company experienced significant liquidity constraints prompted by regulatory disputes, weak energy trading markets, low power prices, credit downgrades, collateral calls, and significant capital spending. As a result, Standard & Poor's Credit Market Services lowered EP's rating to BB (below investment grade) as of December 2002. In 2003 and early 2004, the company incurred additional credit downgrades, with S&P rating it B- with a negative outlook as of early June 2004.

EP has sought to improve liquidity, reduce risk and resolve regulatory disputes. Year to date through May 2004, the company had sold or had pending asset sales totaling $3.5 billion. As of February 2003, EP expected to reduce 2003 capital spending to $2.6 billion, from $3.7 billion in 2002. In May 2003, EP announced cost reduction initiatives intended to reduce annual expenses by $400 million by the end of 2004.

In March 2003, the company agreed to a settlement with California and other western states in response to a September 2002 administrative law judge's decision that the company manipulated natural gas prices in California, and renegotiated long-term power supply contracts. The settlement resulted in after-tax charges of over $750 million in 2002 and 2003.

Core operating segments include Pipelines, which provided 50% of 2002 core segment earnings before interest and taxes (EBIT), Production (33%), and Field Services (17%). The company is liquidating its Merchant Energy segment (which incurred a 2002 EBIT loss of $1.6 billion), including power, petroleum and energy trading assets.

The Pipeline unit is the largest U.S. owner of interstate natural gas pipelines, transporting about 25% of the natural gas used in the U.S. along its 51,588 net route miles of pipeline. The division also has 440 Bcf of natural gas storage capacity, a liquefied natural gas terminal in Georgia, and international pipeline operations.

The Production segment produces natural gas (84% of reserves) and oil primarily in the U.S. In 2002, EP was the most active U.S. production company, drilling 557 development and exploratory wells, with a 96.5% success rate. Worldwide, the company produced 592 Bcfe in 2002 and had 4.9 Tcfe of reserves at December 31, 2002.

Field Services is the second largest U.S. natural gas gatherer. The unit includes natural gas gathering and natural gas liquids pipelines, and treating, processing and fractionation facilities. As of March 2003, Field Services owned 11,674,245 common units of GulfTerra Energy Partners, and was its general partner.

Company Financials Fiscal Year ending December 31

Per Share Data ($)

(Year Ended December 31)	2003	2002	2001	2000	1999	1998	1997	1996	1995	1994
Tangible Bk. Val.	5.36	11.70	17.65	15.25	10.47	13.06	15.39	13.77	9.71	9.98
Cash Flow	0.99	0.21	2.76	4.82	1.61	3.92	3.60	1.93	2.28	2.11
Earnings	-1.03	-2.30	0.13	2.44	-1.06	1.85	1.59	0.53	1.24	1.23
S&P Core Earnings	-0.68	-1.95	-0.37	NA	NA	NA	NA	NA	NA	NA
Dividends	0.16	0.87	0.85	0.82	0.79	0.76	0.73	0.70	0.66	0.60
Payout Ratio	NM	NM	NM	34%	NM	41%	46%	131%	53%	49%
Prices - High	10.30	46.89	75.30	74.25	43.43	38.93	33.75	26.62	16.25	20.93
- Low	3.33	4.39	36.00	30.31	30.68	24.68	24.43	14.31	12.37	14.81
P/E Ratio - High	NM	NM	NM	30	NM	21	21	50	13	17
- Low	NM	NM	NM	12	NM	13	15	27	10	12

Income Statement Analysis (Million $)

	2003	2002	2001	2000	1999	1998	1997	1996	1995	1994
Revs.	6,711	12,194	57,475	21,950	10,581	5,782	5,638	3,010	1,038	870
Oper. Inc.	2,907	2,872	4,391	2,155	1,482	775	757	370	284	302
Depr.	1,207	1,405	1,359	589	609	269	236	101	72.1	65.0
Int. Exp.	1,839	1,400	1,155	538	453	267	238	110	86.3	78.8
Pretax Inc.	-1,200	-1,567	466	1,012	-287	377	340	65.0	133	148
Eff. Tax Rate	NM	NM	39.1%	28.3%	NM	33.7%	37.9%	38.5%	36.0%	39.5%
Net Inc.	-616	-1,289	67.0	582	-242	225	186	38.0	85.4	90.0
S&P Core Earnings	-401	-1,096	-194	NA	NA	NA	NA	NA	NA	NA

Balance Sheet & Other Fin. Data (Million $)

	2003	2002	2001	2000	1999	1998	1997	1996	1995	1994
Cash	1,429	1,591	1,139	688	545	90.0	116	200	39.0	28.0
Curr. Assets	8,922	11,924	12,659	10,076	2,911	1,209	1,629	1,965	369	299
Total Assets	37,084	46,224	48,171	27,445	16,657	10,069	9,532	9,532	2,535	2,332
Curr. Liab.	7,074	10,350	13,565	10,467	3,702	2,162	2,464	2,712	643	452
LT Debt	20,722	19,727	14,109	6,574	5,548	3,177	2,119	2,215	772	779
Common Equity	4,474	8,377	9,356	3,569	2,947	2,108	1,959	1,638	712	710
Total Cap.	25,196	31,680	31,012	14,623	11,601	6,914	5,993	5,280	1,798	1,794
Cap. Exp.	2,452	3,716	4,079	1,336	1,086	406	293	119	166	173
Cash Flow	591	116	1,426	1,171	367	494	422	139	157	155
Curr. Ratio	1.3	1.2	0.9	1.0	0.8	0.6	0.7	0.7	0.6	0.7
% LT Debt of Cap.	82.2	62.3	45.5	45.0	47.8	46.0	35.4	42.0	42.9	43.4
% Net Inc.of Revs.	NM	NM	0.1	2.7	NM	3.9	3.3	1.3	8.2	10.3
% Ret. on Assets	NM	NM	0.1	2.6	NM	2.3	2.0	0.7	3.5	4.0
% Ret. on Equity	NM	NM	0.8	17.9	NM	11.1	10.3	3.2	12.0	12.9

Data as orig reptd.; bef. results of disc opers/spec. items. Per share data adj. for stk. divs.; EPS diluted. E-Estimated. NA-Not Available. NM-Not Meaningful. NR-Not Ranked. UR-Under Review.

Office: El Paso Energy Building, Houston, TX 77002-5089.
Telephone: 713-420-2600.
Email: investorrelations@epenergy.com
Website: http://www.elpaso.com
Pres & CEO: D.L. Foshee.
EVP & CFO: D.D. Scott.
EVP & Treas: J.W. Somerhalder II.

EVP & General Counsel: P. Heeg.
Secy: D.L. Siddall.
Investor Contact: C. Jones 713-420-4136.
Dirs: J. Bissell, J. C. Braniff, J. Dunlap, D. L. Foshee, R. W. Goldman, A. W. Hall, Jr., T. R. Hix, W. H. Joyce, R. L. Kuehn, M. Talbert, J. L. Whitmire, J. B. Wyatt.

Founded: in 1928.
Domicile: Delaware.
Employees: 7,574.
S&P Analyst: Craig K. Shere, CFA /PMW/GG

EMC Corp.

Recommendation: **BUY** ★★★★
SELL | SELL | HOLD | BUY | BUY

12-Month Target Price: $17.00
(as of April 15, 2004)

EMC has an approximate 0.29% weighting in the **S&P 500**

Sector: Information Technology
Sub-Industry: Computer Storage & Peripherals
Peer Group: Computer Peripherals - Storage (Large)

Summary: This company is the leading supplier of enterprise data storage systems and software.

Quantitative Evaluations

S&P Earnings & Dividend Rank: B

| D | C | B- | **B** | B+ | A- | A | A+ |

S&P Fair Value Rank: 5

| 1 | 2 | 3 | 4 | **5** |
| Lowest | | | | Highest |

Fair Value Calc.: $14.70 (Slightly Undervalued)

S&P Investability Quotient Percentile
97%

EMC scored higher than 97% of all companies for which an S&P Report is available.

Volatility: Average

| Low | **Average** | High |

Technical Evaluation: Bullish
Since 9/04, the technical indicators for EMC have been Bullish.

Relative Strength Rank: Strong
78
1 Lowest .... Highest 99

Price as of 11/12/04: $13.24   **2004E S&P Core EPS:** $0.18

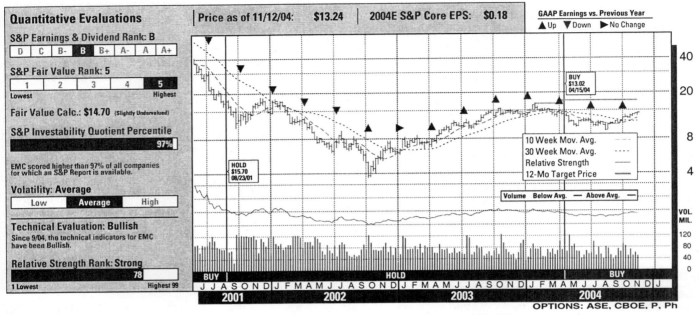

GAAP Earnings vs. Previous Year
▲ Up ▼ Down ▶ No Change

- 10 Week Mov. Avg.
- 30 Week Mov. Avg.
- Relative Strength
- 12-Mo Target Price

Volume   Below Avg. — Above Avg.

BUY $13.02 04/15/04
HOLD $15.70 08/23/01

BUY | HOLD | BUY
J J A S O N D | J F M A M J J A S O N D | J F M A M J J A S O N D | J F M A M J J A S O N D J
2001 | 2002 | 2003 | 2004

OPTIONS: ASE, CBOE, P, Ph

Analyst commentary prepared by Richard N. Stice, CFA /CB/BK

Highlights October 19, 2004

- We see 2005 revenues increasing about 17%, following an expected 30% rise in 2004. We see sales being aided by a modest pickup in IT spending, acquisition benefits, market share gains, and international expansion. We believe companies continue to view data storage, particularly data management, as a high level priority.

- We expect gross margins to widen, benefiting from projected volume increases and a more favorable product mix. We see operating expenses declining modestly, as a percentage of revenues, due to acquisition-related synergies. Results should also benefit from a sizable amount of investment income, as cash and investments exceeded $7 billion at the end of the 2004 third quarter.

- We are forecasting 2005 operating EPS of $0.48, a 37% increase from 2004's anticipated $0.35 (excluding a $0.01 restructuring charge). Our 2005 and 2004 Standard & Poor's Core Earnings per share estimates are $0.31 and $0.18, respectively, reflecting projected stock option expense.

Investment Rationale/Risk October 19, 2004

- We believe EMC will continue to benefit from what we view as a more favorable IT spending environment, given its industry leading position in the enterprise data storage sector. Moreover, we think the expansion of its product portfolio, resulting from recent acquisition activity, should also have a positive impact.

- Risks to our recommendation and target price include increasing competitive threats in the enterprise market, a delay in the integration of recent acquisitions, and inability to bring new products to market in a timely manner.

- Our 12-month target price of $17 combines three separate valuation metrics. The first is an historical average price/sales measure that comprises a 25% weighting of the overall target price. The second, also at 25%, equates EMC's P/E-to-growth ratio with that of the S&P 500. The third, at 50%, is an intrinsic value calculation based on discounted cash flow analysis. Our assumptions include a weighted average cost of capital of 13.9% and an expected terminal growth rate of 3%.

Key Stock Statistics

S&P Core EPS 2005E	0.31	52-week Range	$15.80-9.24
S&P Oper. EPS 2004E	0.35	12 Month P/E	40.1
P/E on S&P Oper. EPS 2004E	37.8	Beta	NA
S&P Oper. EPS 2005E	0.48	Shareholders	18,011
Yield (%)	Nil	Market Cap (B)	$ 31.7
Dividend Rate/Share	Nil	Shares Outstanding (M)	2396.3

Value of $10,000 invested five years ago: **NA**

Dividend Data

No cash dividends have been paid.

Revenues/Earnings Data Fiscal year ending December 31

Revenues (Million $)

	2004	2003	2002	2001	2000	1999
1Q	1,872	1,384	1,302	2,345	1,823	1,128
2Q	1,971	1,479	1,388	2,021	2,146	1,292
3Q	2,029	1,511	1,259	1,212	2,283	1,334
4Q	—	1,863	1,489	1,513	2,621	1,876
Yr.	—	6,237	5,438	7,091	8,873	6,716

Earnings Per Share ($)

	2004	2003	2002	2001	2000	1999
1Q	0.06	0.02	-0.03	0.18	0.15	0.10
2Q	0.08	0.04	Nil	0.05	0.19	0.14
3Q	0.09	0.07	0.01	-0.43	0.20	0.15
4Q	E0.11	0.09	-0.03	-0.03	0.25	0.10
Yr.	E0.35	0.22	-0.05	-0.23	0.79	0.46

Next earnings report expected: late-January Source: S&P, Company Reports
EPS Estimates based on S&P Operating Earnings; historical GAAP earnings are as reported.

EMC Corporation

Recommendation: **BUY** ★ ★ ★ ★ ★   12-Month Target Price: **$17.00** (as of April 15, 2004)

Business Summary October 20, 2004

EMC's strategy is to focus on the management of information across its entire lifecycle, from creation and use to archive and disposal. The company's goal is to help customers improve the utilization of their information technology (IT) assets, simplify and automate the management of their information, provide cost effective business continuity and ensure easier compliance with government and industry regulations.

EMC's customers are located worldwide and represent a cross section of industries and government agencies. The company's products and services are used in conjunction with a variety of computing platforms, storage systems and software applications that support key business processes including transaction processing, data warehousing, electronic commerce, and content management.

EMC offers a wide range of information storage systems designed to meet the specific needs of its customers in terms of performance, functionality, availability and cost. In 2003, the company introduced a complete new line of Symmetrix systems, the Symmetrix DMX series. This series includes the DMX800, a modular high-end storage model, which enables customers to purchase Symmetrix storage capabilities in smaller increments and deploy the systems outside data centers, thereby reducing acquisition costs, environmental costs and total cost of ownership.

Another product offering, Centera, addresses the requirements of "fixed content." The company defines fixed content as information whose value lies in part on its unchanging nature, such as digital X-rays and other medical records, movies,

check images and e-mail correspondence. Centera eliminates the need for applications to be aware of the physical location of information, regardless of scale, thereby simplifying the task of having applications access and manage huge numbers of objects.

In 2003, revenues from information storage systems (including Symmetrix, CLARiiON, Celerra, Connectrix and Centera) accounted for 53% of the total, down from 55% in 2002.

During 2001, EMC announced a significant new software strategy, AutoIS (Automated Information Storage), focused on the automation, simplification and openness of heterogeneous storage infrastructures. This offering is designed to enable customers to centralize the management of their entire storage infrastructure in a single, unified and consistent manner. Software provided 22% of revenues in 2003, down from 23% in 2002. These numbers exclude revenues from LEGATO and Documentum.

In July 2003, EMC agreed to acquire LEGATO Systems for about $1.3 billion in stock. EMC expects the acquisition, which was completed during the fourth quarter of 2003, to be slightly accretive to 2004 EPS. In October 2003, EMC agreed to acquire Documentum for $1.7 billion in stock. EMC expects the acquisition, which was completed in December 2003, to become accretive to EPS by 2005. In December 2003, EMC agreed to acquire VMware, Inc. for $635 million in cash. The company expects the transaction, which was consummated in January 2004, to be neutral to 2004 EPS.

Company Financials Fiscal Year ending December 31

Per Share Data ($)

(Year Ended December 31)	2003	2002	2001	2000	1999	1998	1997	1996	1995	1994
Tangible Bk. Val.	3.19	3.05	3.31	3.72	2.38	1.60	1.19	0.83	0.62	0.45
Cash Flow	0.45	0.24	0.07	1.02	0.66	0.46	0.32	0.24	0.19	0.16
Earnings	0.22	-0.05	-0.23	0.79	0.46	0.37	0.26	0.20	0.17	0.15
S&P Core Earnings	0.04	-0.23	-0.33	NA	NA	NA	NA	NA	NA	NA
Dividends	Nil	Nil	Nil	Nil	Nil	Nil	Nil	Nil	Nil	Nil
Payout Ratio	Nil	Nil	Nil	Nil	Nil	Nil	Nil	Nil	Nil	Nil
Prices - High	14.66	17.97	82.00	104.93	55.50	21.65	8.14	4.54	3.42	3.00
- Low	5.98	3.67	10.01	47.50	21.00	6.00	3.96	1.89	1.62	1.56
P/E Ratio - High	67	NM	NM	NM	NM	58	31	23	20	20
- Low	27	NM	NM	NM	NM	16	15	10	10	11

Income Statement Analysis (Million $)

	2003	2002	2001	2000	1999	1998	1997	1996	1995	1994
Revs.	6,237	5,438	7,091	8,873	6,716	3,974	2,938	2,274	1,878	1,377
Oper. Inc.	988	310	355	2,774	3,138	1,185	798	583	489	383
Depr.	521	654	655	517	447	203	136	86.9	53.6	32.7
Int. Exp.	3.03	11.4	11.3	14.6	33.5	20.2	15.5	12.0	12.9	15.3
Pretax Inc.	571	-296	-577	2,441	1,357	1,058	718	519	451	355
Eff. Tax Rate	13.1%	NM	NM	27.0%	25.5%	25.0%	25.0%	25.6%	27.5%	29.5%
Net Inc.	496	-119	-508	1,782	1,011	793	539	386	327	251
S&P Core Earnings	84.2	-477	-720	NA	NA	NA	NA	NA	NA	NA

Balance Sheet & Other Fin. Data (Million $)

	2003	2002	2001	2000	1999	1998	1997	1996	1995	1994
Cash	1,869	1,687	2,129	1,983	1,109	1,530	955	727	380	241
Curr. Assets	4,687	4,217	4,923	6,100	4,320	3,105	2,627	1,754	1,319	902
Total Assets	14,093	9,590	9,890	10,628	7,173	4,569	3,490	2,294	1,746	1,318
Curr. Liab.	2,547	2,042	2,179	2,114	1,398	653	506	418	359	301
LT Debt	130	Nil	Nil	14.5	687	539	559	191	246	286
Common Equity	10,885	7,226	7,601	8,177	4,952	3,324	2,376	1,637	1,140	728
Total Cap.	11,015	7,226	7,601	8,494	5,764	3,914	2,980	1,874	1,386	1,014
Cap. Exp.	369	391	889	858	524	373	211	126	92.0	109
Cash Flow	1,017	535	147	2,299	1,458	997	675	473	380	283
Curr. Ratio	1.8	2.1	2.3	2.9	3.1	4.8	5.2	4.2	3.7	3.0
% LT Debt of Cap.	1.2	Nil	Nil	0.2	11.9	13.8	18.8	10.2	17.7	28.2
% Net Inc.of Revs.	8.0	NM	NM	20.1	15.0	20.0	18.3	17.0	17.4	18.2
% Ret. on Assets	4.2	NM	NM	20.0	15.8	19.7	18.6	19.1	21.3	22.8
% Ret. on Equity	5.5	NM	NM	27.1	34.4	27.8	26.8	27.8	35.0	42.7

Data as orig reptd.; bef. results of disc opers/spec. items. Per share data adj. for stk. divs.; EPS diluted. E-Estimated. NA-Not Available. NM-Not Meaningful. NR-Not Ranked. UR-Under Review.

Office: 176 South Street, Hopkinton, MA 01748-2230.
Telephone: 508-435-1000.
Email: emc_ir@emc.com
Website: http://www.emc.com
Chrmn: M.C. Ruettgers.
Pres & CEO: J.M. Tucci.
EVP & CFO: W.J. Teuber.

SVP & CTO: J.M. Nick.
SVP & Treas: I. Simmons.
Investor Contact: P. Cooley 508-435-1000.
Dirs: M. J. Cronin, G. Deegan, J. R. Egan, W. P. Fitzgerald, O. Kallasvuo, W. B. Priem, M. C. Ruettgers, D. N. Strohm, J. M. Tucci, A. M. Zeien.

Founded: in 1979.
Domicile: Massachusetts.
Employees: 20,000.
S&P Analyst: Richard N. Stice, CFA /CB/BK

The *McGraw-Hill* Companies

Emerson Electric

Recommendation: **HOLD** ★★★☆☆
SELL SELL HOLD BUY BUY

12-Month Target Price: **$70.00**
(as of November 02, 2004)

EMR has an approximate 0.26% weighting in the **S&P 500**

Sector: Industrials
Sub-Industry: Electrical Components & Equipment
Peer Group: Electrical Equipment - Diversified

Summary: Emerson primarily makes backup power equipment for telecom and Internet providers and users; climate control components; and electric motors.

Quantitative Evaluations

S&P Earnings & Dividend Rank: A

| D | C | B- | B | B+ | A- | **A** | A+ |

S&P Fair Value Rank: 4

| 1 | 2 | 3 | **4** | 5 |
| Lowest | | | | Highest |

Fair Value Calc.: $71.50 (Slightly Undervalued)

S&P Investability Quotient Percentile

99%

EMR scored higher than 99% of all companies for which an S&P Report is available.

Volatility: Low

| **Low** | Average | High |

Technical Evaluation: Bullish
Since 10/04, the technical indicators for EMR have been Bullish.

Relative Strength Rank: Moderate

67

| 1 Lowest | | Highest 99 |

Price as of 11/12/04: **$68.62**   **2005E S&P Core EPS:** **$3.30**

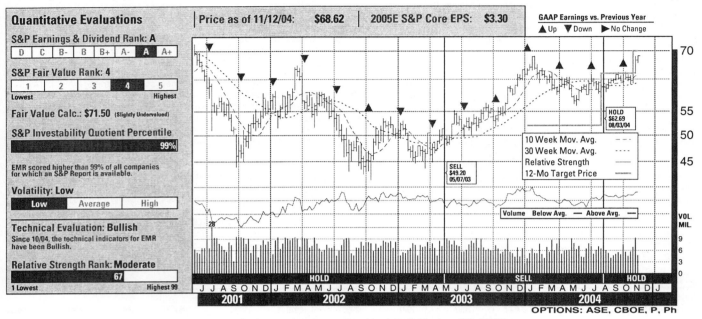

GAAP Earnings vs. Previous Year
▲ Up ▼ Down ► No Change

10 Week Mov. Avg.
30 Week Mov. Avg.
Relative Strength
12-Mo Target Price

Volume Below Avg. — Above Avg.

HOLD $62.69 08/03/04
SELL $49.20 05/07/03

HOLD   SELL   HOLD
J J A S O N D J F M A M J J A S O N D J F M A M J J A S O N D J F M A M J J A S O N D J
2001   2002   2003   2004

OPTIONS: ASE, CBOE, P, Ph

Analyst commentary prepared by John F. Hingher, CFA /CB/SB

Highlights November 04, 2004

- We see pent-up replacement demand for capital equipment in a number of segments and anticipated price increases driving revenue growth of 8% to 9% in FY 05 (Sep.). We think EMR will aim for price increases to offset rising raw material costs, particularly for metals such as copper and steel.

- We expect margins to widen in FY 05, aided by the anticipated greater volumes, a shift to low-cost manufacturing, improved productivity, and increased operating leverage resulting from a continued focus on cost control.

- All told, we see EPS growing about 16% in FY 05, to $3.35, from $2.98 in FY 04. On an S&P Core Earnings basis, we see FY 05 EPS of $3.30, mainly reflecting adjustments for pension gains and option expense. For the longer term, we have confidence in management's ability to continue to control costs and maintain a strong balance sheet. We see our view supported by the company's 10-year historical average ROE of about 19%, versus an average of 14% achieved by the S&P 500 over the same time frame.

Investment Rationale/Risk November 04, 2004

- We project an uptick in some of the company's important end markets, and believe that strong growth in emerging markets, particularly in Asia, Latin America and Eastern Europe, will continue. We are optimistic regarding the short-term outlook and the company's solid cash flow generating ability. Based on valuation, though, we would not add to positions.

- Risks to our opinion and target price include slowing customer capital spending; slower than anticipated growth in Asia; deceleration in demand at the telecom and electronics business; and rising prices for key inputs.

- Our discounted cash flow model (which values EMR by adding the sum of free cash flows growing at a projected 9% compound annual rate over the next 10 years, and at 3.5% thereafter) indicates that the shares are undervalued. In terms of relative valuation, the stock is trading at 20X our forward 12-month EPS estimate of $3.27, a modest premium to its historical average P/E; and above peers' 17X average multiple. Blending these methodologies leads to our 12-month target price of $70.

Key Stock Statistics

S&P Oper. EPS 2005E	3.35	52-week Range	$68.65-56.22
P/E on S&P Oper. EPS 2005E	20.5	12 Month P/E	23.0
Yield (%)	2.4%	Beta	0.96
Dividend Rate/Share	1.66	Shareholders	31,800
Shares Outstanding (M)	420.1	Market Cap (B)	$ 28.8

Value of $10,000 invested five years ago: **$ 13,508**

Dividend Data Dividends have been paid since 1947

Amount ($)	Date Decl.	Ex-Div. Date	Stock of Record	Payment Date
0.400	Feb. 03	Feb. 11	Feb. 13	Mar. 10 '04
0.400	May. 04	May. 12	May. 14	Jun. 10 '04
0.400	Aug. 03	Aug. 11	Aug. 13	Sep. 10 '04
0.415	Nov. 02	Nov. 09	Nov. 12	Dec. 10 '04

Revenues/Earnings Data Fiscal year ending September 30

Revenues (Million $)

	2004	2003	2002	2001	2000	1999
1Q	3,600	3,226	3,295	3,920	3,543	3,427
2Q	3,859	3,465	3,421	4,103	3,895	3,589
3Q	4,036	3,573	3,571	3,905	4,042	3,634
4Q	4,120	3,694	3,538	3,552	3,966	3,620
Yr.	15,615	13,958	13,824	15,480	15,545	14,270

Earnings Per Share ($)

	2004	2003	2002	2001	2000	1999
1Q	0.58	0.52	0.61	0.83	0.75	0.69
2Q	0.75	0.56	0.65	0.83	0.82	0.74
3Q	0.81	0.66	0.67	0.77	0.87	0.79
4Q	0.84	0.66	0.59	-0.03	0.86	0.78
Yr.	2.98	2.41	2.52	2.40	3.30	3.00

Next earnings report expected: early-February Source: S&P, Company Reports
EPS Estimates based on S&P Operating Earnings; historical GAAP earnings are as reported.

Emerson Electric Co.

Recommendation: **HOLD** ★ ★ ★ ☆ ☆   12-Month Target Price: **$70.00** (as of November 02, 2004)

Business Summary November 09, 2004

Emerson had been well known for posting 43 years of uninterrupted annual EPS growth and dividend hikes. However, in the late 1990s, the stock price languished. In response, the company embarked on an uncharacteristically aggressive acquisition spree in 1999, as part of management's aim to boost average annual EPS growth to 10% to 15% levels. In short order, EMR purchased several leading makers of back-up power equipment for telecom, Internet and computer network users.

The company's Process Control segment, which accounted for 24% of FY 03 (Sep.) total revenues, 22% of profits, and had 11% margins, produces analytical instrumentation, valves, and control systems for measurement and control of fluid flow, and integrated solutions for process and industrial applications. Segment brand names include Emerson Process Management, Bettis, Brooks, CSI, Daniel, Delta V, El-o-matic, Fisher, Fisher-Rosemount Systems, Micro Motion, PlantWeb, En-Tech, Kenonic Controls, Rosemount, SAAB Marine, and Emerson Process Management Power and Water Solutions. Over the past seven years, segment margins averaged 11%.

The Industrial Automation segment (19%, 19%, 13%) primarily makes industrial motors, drives, controls and equipment for automated equipment. Brand names of this segment include Emerson Industrial Automation, AMTECH, Appleton, ASCO, Branson, Browning, Buehler, Control Techniques, Emerson Motion Control, Jouco-

matic, Kato Engineering, Kop-Flex, KVT, Leroy Somer, McGill, Morse, O-Z/Gedney, Rollway and SIRAI. Over the past seven years, margins averaged 13%.

The Electronics and Telecommunications segment (17%, 9.6%, 7.0%) primarily makes back-up power equipment used in computer, telecommunications and Internet infrastructure. Brand names include Emerson Network Power, ASCO, Astec, Emerson Energy Systems, HIROSS, Liebert and Liebert Global Services. Over the past seven years, margins averaged 9%.

EMR's Heating, Ventilating and Air Conditioning (HVAC) segment (19%, 22%, 15%) mostly makes home and building thermostats and compressors. Compressors are cooling components used in air conditioning units and refrigerators. Brand names of this segment include Emerson Climate Technologies, Alco Controls, Copeland, Fusite, Thermo-O-Disc and White-Rodgers. Over the past seven years, margins averaged 15%.

The Appliance & Tools segment (25%, 27%, 14%) primarily makes various household appliances, electric motors and controls for appliances, and hand-held tools. Brand names include Emerson, ClosetMaid, Digital Appliance Controls, In-Sink-Erator, Knaack, Mallory, METRO, RIDGID, Stack-a-Shelf, U.S. Electrical Motors and Weatherguard. Over the past seven years, margins averaged 15%.

Company Financials Fiscal Year ending September 30

Per Share Data ($)

(Year Ended September 30)	2004	2003	2002	2001	2000	1999	1998	1997	1996	1995
Tangible Bk. Val.	NA	3.61	1.98	2.22	2.53	4.43	4.79	5.23	5.77	5.54
Cash Flow	NA	3.67	3.80	4.15	4.87	4.45	4.04	3.67	3.31	2.99
Earnings	2.98	2.41	2.52	2.40	3.30	3.00	2.77	2.52	2.27	2.03
S&P Core Earnings	NA	2.26	1.87	1.76	NA	NA	NA	NA	NA	NA
Dividends	1.60	1.57	1.55	1.53	1.45	1.33	1.18	1.08	0.98	0.89
Payout Ratio	54%	65%	62%	64%	44%	44%	43%	43%	43%	44%
Prices - High	68.65	65.00	66.09	79.25	79.75	71.43	67.43	60.37	51.75	40.87
- Low	56.22	43.78	41.74	44.04	40.50	51.43	54.50	45.00	38.75	30.75
P/E Ratio - High	23	27	26	33	24	24	24	24	23	20
- Low	19	18	17	18	12	17	20	18	17	15

Income Statement Analysis (Million $)

	2004	2003	2002	2001	2000	1999	1998	1997	1996	1995
Revs.	NA	13,958	13,824	15,480	15,545	14,270	13,447	12,298	11,150	10,013
Oper. Inc.	NA	2,497	2,443	2,988	3,219	2,943	2,738	2,494	2,259	2,009
Depr.	NA	534	541	709	679	638	563	512	465	409
Int. Exp.	NA	246	250	304	288	190	152	121	127	111
Pretax Inc.	NA	1,414	1,565	1,589	2,178	2,021	1,924	1,784	1,609	1,460
Eff. Tax Rate	NA	28.4%	32.3%	35.0%	34.7%	35.0%	36.1%	37.1%	36.7%	36.3%
Net Inc.	NA	1,013	1,060	1,032	1,422	1,314	1,229	1,122	1,019	929
S&P Core Earnings	NA	951	785	753	NA	NA	NA	NA	NA	NA

Balance Sheet & Other Fin. Data (Million $)

	2004	2003	2002	2001	2000	1999	1998	1997	1996	1995
Cash	NA	696	381	356	281	266	210	221	149	117
Curr. Assets	NA	5,500	4,961	5,320	5,483	5,124	5,001	4,717	4,187	3,784
Total Assets	NA	15,194	14,545	15,046	15,164	13,624	12,660	11,463	10,481	9,399
Curr. Liab.	NA	3,417	4,400	5,379	5,219	4,590	4,022	3,842	3,021	3,281
LT Debt	NA	3,733	2,990	2,256	2,248	1,317	1,057	571	773	209
Common Equity	NA	6,460	5,741	6,114	10,248	6,181	5,803	5,420	5,353	4,871
Total Cap.	NA	10,193	8,731	8,370	12,496	7,498	6,860	5,992	6,126	5,080
Cap. Exp.	NA	337	384	554	692	592	603	575	514	421
Cash Flow	NA	1,547	1,601	1,740	2,101	1,951	1,792	1,634	1,484	1,338
Curr. Ratio	NA	1.6	1.1	1.0	1.1	1.1	1.2	1.2	1.4	1.2
% LT Debt of Cap.	NA	36.6	34.2	26.9	18.0	17.6	15.4	9.6	12.6	4.1
% Net Inc.of Revs.	NA	7.3	7.7	6.7	9.2	9.2	9.1	9.1	9.1	9.2
% Ret. on Assets	NA	6.8	7.2	6.8	9.9	10.0	10.2	10.2	10.3	10.5
% Ret. on Equity	NA	16.6	17.9	16.5	14.5	21.9	21.9	20.8	19.9	20.1

Data as orig reptd.; bef. results of disc opers/spec. items. Per share data adj. for stk. divs.; EPS diluted. E-Estimated. NA-Not Available. NM-Not Meaningful. NR-Not Ranked. UR-Under Review.

Office: 8000 West Florissant Avenue, St. Louis, MO 63136.
Telephone: 314-553-2000.
Website: http://www.gotoemerson.com
Chrmn & CEO: D.N. Farr.
Pres: J.G. Berges.
COO: E.L. Monser.
EVP & CFO: W.J. Galvin.

SVP, Secy & General Counsel: W.W. Withers.
Investor Contact: R.T. Sharp 314-553-2197.
Dirs: J. G. Berges, L. L. Browning, Jr., A. A. Busch III, D. N. Farr, D. C. Farrell, C. G. Fernandez, W. J. Galvin, A. F. Golden, R. B. Horton, G. A. Lodge, V. R. Loucks, Jr., R. B. Loynd, J. B. Menzer, C. A. Peters, J. W. Prueher, R. L. Ridgway, W. M. Van Cleve, E. E. Whitacre, Jr.

Founded: in 1890.
Domicile: Missouri.
Employees: 106,700.
S&P Analyst: John F. Hingher, CFA /CB/SB

Engelhard Corp.

Recommendation: HOLD ★ ★ ★ ★   12-Month Target Price: $32.00
SELL SELL HOLD BUY BUY   (as of September 09, 2003)

EC has an approximate 0.03% weighting in the **S&P 500**

Sector: Materials
Sub-Industry: Diversified Chemicals
Peer Group: Diversified Companies

Summary: This leading producer of catalysts, pigments and additives and engineered materials also provides precious and base metals management services.

Quantitative Evaluations

| Price as of 11/12/04: | $30.27 | 2004E S&P Core EPS: | $1.86 |

S&P Earnings & Dividend Rank: B+

| D | C | B- | B | B+ | A- | A | A+ |

S&P Fair Value Rank: 4+

| 1 | 2 | 3 | 4 | 5 |
| Lowest | | | | Highest |

Fair Value Calc.: $31.30 (Slightly Undervalued)

S&P Investability Quotient Percentile
94%

EC scored higher than 94% of all companies for which an S&P Report is available.

Volatility: Low

| Low | Average | High |

Technical Evaluation: Bullish
Since 11/04, the technical indicators for EC have been Bullish.

Relative Strength Rank: Moderate
60
1 Lowest   Highest 99

GAAP Earnings vs. Previous Year
▲ Up ▼ Down ▶ No Change

10 Week Mov. Avg.
30 Week Mov. Avg.
Relative Strength
12-Mo Target Price

HOLD

J J A S O N D J F M A M J J A S O N D J F M A M J J A S O N D J F M A M J J A S O N D J
2001   2002   2003   2004

VOL.
MIL.

OPTIONS: CBOE

Analyst commentary prepared by Richard O'Reilly, CFA /CB/JWP

Highlights September 21, 2004

- We expect sales to continue to grow in 2005, partly reflecting pass-throughs of higher platinum prices. We project that EPS will advance after expected flat operating results in 2004; 2003 EPS included unusual income and special gains totaling $0.20. We expect the environmental technologies segment to face difficult comparisons for the rest of 2004 and in early 2005 until new regulations begin to aid the auto OEM product mix in late 2005. We also see sales of medium-duty diesel engine emission catalysts continuing to increase.

- The process catalysts unit should continue to grow, as we expect chemical catalysts to begin to turn up in 2005, while the appearance and performance technologies segment should improve, assuming stronger paper markets. We expect materials services profits to remain in the low single digit million dollar area until industrial activity picks up for the recycling business.

- Equity income should be much lower in 2004, in the absence of $0.15 a share of income related to the liquidation of a joint venture. We see post-retirement expenses increasing in 2004 by an amount similar to 2003's $0.06 a share. We expect the effective tax rate to return to 22%; second quarter 2004 EPS included a $0.06 one-time tax benefit. Comparisons should benefit from a decrease in the number of shares outstanding.

Investment Rationale/Risk September 21, 2004

- We have a hold recommendation on the stock. We anticipate flat EPS in 2004, with some upturn in 2005 with a more favorable product mix in auto catalysts for use in 2006 model year vehicles. We believe the volatility of the materials services business is likely to continue to restrict the stock's P/E multiple relative to the multiples accorded the shares of other specialty chemical companies, but we see the discount narrowing, as EC's technologies units continue to grow.

- Risks to our recommendation and target price include unexpected delays or changes in environmental regulations, and EC's ability to successfully introduce new products.

- Our 12-month target price of $32 is based on our 2005 EPS estimate of $2.05 and using a P/E multiple of 16X that is closer to the average for peer industry companies. The company has accelerated its stock repurchase program. In 2003, EC raised its dividend 10%, marking the first increase since 1997.

Key Stock Statistics

S&P Core EPS 2005E	1.99	52-week Range	$32.72-26.49
S&P Oper. EPS 2004E	1.88	12 Month P/E	15.8
P/E on S&P Oper. EPS 2004E	16.1	Beta	0.74
S&P Oper. EPS 2005E	2.05	Shareholders	4,876
Yield (%)	1.5%	Market Cap (B)	$ 3.8
Dividend Rate/Share	0.44	Shares Outstanding (M)	124.4

Value of $10,000 invested five years ago: $ 18,304

Dividend Data Dividends have been paid since 1981

Amount ($)	Date Decl.	Ex-Div. Date	Stock of Record	Payment Date
0.110	Feb. 12	Mar. 11	Mar. 15	Mar. 31 '04
0.110	May. 06	Jun. 14	Jun. 15	Jun. 30 '04
0.110	Aug. 05	Sep. 13	Sep. 15	Sep. 30 '04
0.110	Oct. 07	Dec. 13	Dec. 15	Dec. 31 '04

Revenues/Earnings Data Fiscal year ending December 31

Revenues (Million $)

	2004	2003	2002	2001	2000	1999
1Q	1,040	830.4	1,002	1,611	1,165	1,073
2Q	1,108	929.4	982.3	1,472	1,398	1,203
3Q	1,002	915.4	858.6	1,143	374.4	1,016
4Q	—	1,039	910.9	871.0	1,542	1,113
Yr.	—	3,714	3,754	5,097	5,543	4,405

Earnings Per Share ($)

	2004	2003	2002	2001	2000	1999
1Q	0.40	0.46	0.40	0.37	0.45	0.28
2Q	0.54	0.43	0.46	0.45	0.47	0.41
3Q	0.47	0.47	0.02	0.43	0.40	0.40
4Q	E0.47	0.50	0.44	0.46	-0.01	0.39
Yr.	E1.88	1.86	1.31	1.71	1.31	1.47

Next earnings report expected: early-February Source: S&P, Company Reports
EPS Estimates based on S&P Operating Earnings; historical GAAP earnings are as reported.

Engelhard Corporation

Recommendation: **HOLD** ★ ★ ★ ☆ ☆   12-Month Target Price: **$32.00** (as of September 09, 2003)

Business Summary September 21, 2004

Since commercializing the first automotive catalyst (for emission control) in the mid-1970s, Engelhard has been a leader in catalyst development for environmental, transportation and industrial applications, and in pigments and colorants for paper and other materials. International operations accounted for 50% of sales in 2003.

Environmental technologies (23% of sales and 40% of profits in 2003) consists of emission control and ozone abatement catalysts and systems for automobile, truck, aircraft, power generation and process industries. In 2000, the company started up its first auto emission catalyst plants in South America and in China. In early 2000, Volvo began equipping a new car model with radiators coated with EC's PremAir catalyst system which converts ozone into oxygen. Volvo was also to use PremAir on a line of station wagons. EC is expanding its non-auto catalyst businesses such as emission control systems for gas turbines and advanced catalytic converters for diesel engines used in bus retrofits. In 2001, the EPA approved the company's DPX emission control technology for buses and trucks.

Process technologies (15%, 33%) consists of catalysts for chemical, petrochemical, polymers, pharmaceutical, and food processing, and for petroleum refining (fluid catalytic cracking, reforming, hydrotreating and hydrogenations). The 1998 acquisition of Mallinckrodt's catalyst business ($100 million in annual sales) expanded operations into polymerization catalysts. EC further expanded its polymer catalysts business through the October 2000 purchase of a plant located in Spain. In October 2001, it acquired the fats and oils catalyst business of Sud-Chemie AG, broadening its product offering to the olechemical market.

The appearance and performance technologies segment (18%, 24%), formed in 2001, provides pigments and additives. It consists of paper pigments and additives (kaolin-based coatings and extender pigments for a wide variety of papers, including printing, writing, newsprint and paperboard) and specialty pigments and additives (color and pearlescent pigments, dispersions, colorants, extender pigments, thickeners and absorbents used in coatings, plastics, rubbers, inks, and cosmetics). It also provides iridescent and specialty films used in decorative, packaging and textile applications.

The materials services group (44%, 3%) purchases and sells precious metals and base metals, providing a full array of services to EC's technology businesses and their customers. EC is also engaged in the secondary refining and storage of precious metals.

EC recorded a charge of $57.7 million ($0.44 a share) in the 2002 third quarter related to a plan to liquidate the Engelhard-CLAL joint venture. The company received liquidation distributions of cash and assets totaling $42 million, including $26 million in 2003. At the end of 2003, the venture had been substantially liquidated. In 1995, the majority of EC's engineered materials business (fabricated precious metal (platinum, gold and silver) products and coatings for industrial markets) was transferred to Engelhard-CLAL.

Company Financials Fiscal Year ending December 31

Per Share Data ($)

(Year Ended December 31)	2003	2002	2001	2000	1999	1998	1997	1996	1995	1994
Tangible Bk. Val.	6.31	6.32	5.44	4.52	3.49	4.02	3.95	5.79	5.13	4.31
Cash Flow	2.86	2.16	2.53	2.23	2.20	1.98	0.66	1.57	1.41	1.30
Earnings	1.86	1.31	1.71	1.31	1.47	1.29	0.33	1.05	0.96	0.82
S&P Core Earnings	1.68	1.51	1.48	NA	NA	NA	NA	NA	NA	NA
Dividends	0.41	0.40	0.40	0.40	0.40	0.40	0.38	0.36	0.32	0.31
Payout Ratio	22%	31%	23%	31%	27%	31%	115%	34%	33%	37%
Prices - High	30.58	33.00	29.20	21.50	23.68	22.81	23.75	26.12	32.50	21.00
- Low	19.02	21.18	18.20	12.56	16.25	15.75	17.06	17.87	14.91	13.91
P/E Ratio - High	16	25	17	16	16	18	72	25	34	26
- Low	10	16	11	10	11	12	52	17	16	17

Income Statement Analysis (Million $)

	2003	2002	2001	2000	1999	1998	1997	1996	1995	1994
Revs.	3,714	3,754	5,097	5,543	4,405	4,175	3,631	3,184	2,840	2,385
Oper. Inc.	397	414	436	465	414	410	320	332	281	247
Depr.	128	111	109	117	98.3	101	47.8	74.8	65.5	69.1
Int. Exp.	24.3	27.4	44.0	62.6	56.6	58.9	52.8	45.0	31.3	22.0
Pretax Inc.	301	238	305	246	284	261	85.8	210	185	157
Eff. Tax Rate	21.3%	28.0%	26.1%	31.5%	30.5%	28.2%	44.3%	28.3%	25.8%	25.0%
Net Inc.	236	171	226	168	197	187	47.8	150	138	118
S&P Core Earnings	215	197	196	NA	NA	NA	NA	NA	NA	NA

Balance Sheet & Other Fin. Data (Million $)

	2003	2002	2001	2000	1999	1998	1997	1996	1995	1994
Cash	87.9	48.2	33.0	33.5	54.4	22.3	28.8	39.6	40.0	26.0
Curr. Assets	1,394	1,566	1,494	1,742	1,388	1,360	1,255	1,184	601	574
Total Assets	2,933	3,021	2,996	3,167	2,904	2,866	2,586	2,495	1,646	1,441
Curr. Liab.	948	1,386	1,501	1,827	1,456	1,270	1,240	1,069	495	549
LT Debt	391	248	238	249	499	497	374	375	212	112
Common Equity	1,285	1,056	1,004	875	764	902	785	833	738	615
Total Cap.	1,676	1,304	1,241	1,123	1,264	1,399	1,159	1,208	950	726
Cap. Exp.	114	113	169	137	102	116	137	128	148	98.0
Cash Flow	364	282	334	285	296	288	95.6	225	203	187
Curr. Ratio	1.5	1.1	1.0	1.0	1.0	1.1	1.0	1.1	1.2	1.0
% LT Debt of Cap.	23.3	19.0	19.2	22.1	39.5	35.6	32.2	31.0	22.4	15.4
% Net Inc.of Revs.	6.4	4.6	4.4	3.0	4.5	4.5	1.3	4.7	4.9	4.9
% Ret. on Assets	7.9	5.7	7.3	5.5	6.8	6.9	1.9	6.8	9.0	8.7
% Ret. on Equity	20.0	16.6	24.0	20.5	23.6	22.2	5.9	19.1	20.4	20.7

Data as orig reptd.; bef. results of disc opers/spec. items. Per share data adj. for stk. divs.; EPS diluted. E-Estimated. NA-Not Available. NM-Not Meaningful. NR-Not Ranked. UR-Under Review.

Office: 101 Wood Ave S, Iselin, NJ 08830-0770.
Telephone: 732-205-5000.
Email: investor.relations@engelhard.com
Website: http://www.engelhard.com
Chrmn & CEO: B.W. Perry.
VP & CFO: M.A. Sperduto.

VP, Secy & General Counsel: A.A. Dornbusch II.
VP & Investor Contact: G.A. Bell 732-205-6313.
Treas: M.C. Mak.
Dirs: M. H. Antonini, D. L. Burner, J. V. Napier, N. T. Pace, B. W. Perry, H. R. Slack, D. G. Watson.

Founded: in 1938.
Domicile: Delaware.
Employees: 5,839.
S&P Analyst: Richard O'Reilly, CFA /CB/JWP

Entergy Corp.

Recommendation: HOLD ★★★☆☆
SELL | SELL | HOLD | BUY | BUY

12-Month Target Price: **$65.00**
(as of October 21, 2004)

ETR has an approximate 0.14% weighting in the **S&P 500**

Sector: Utilities
Sub-Industry: Electric Utilities
Peer Group: Electric Cos. (Domestic) - Large

Summary: This electric utility holding company serves customers in Arkansas, Louisiana, Mississippi and Texas.

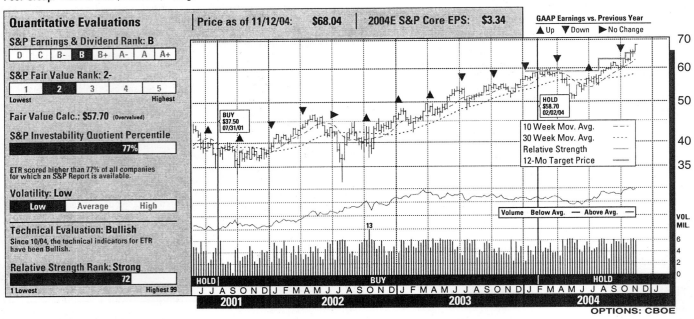

Quantitative Evaluations

S&P Earnings & Dividend Rank: B

| D | C | B- | B | B+ | A- | A | A+ |

S&P Fair Value Rank: 2-

| 1 | 2 | 3 | 4 | 5 |
| Lowest | | | | Highest |

Fair Value Calc.: $57.70 (Overvalued)

S&P Investability Quotient Percentile

77%

ETR scored higher than 77% of all companies for which an S&P Report is available.

Volatility: Low

| Low | Average | High |

Technical Evaluation: Bullish
Since 10/04, the technical indicators for ETR have been Bullish.

Relative Strength Rank: Strong

72

1 Lowest   Highest 99

Price as of 11/12/04: $68.04   **2004E S&P Core EPS:** $3.34

GAAP Earnings vs. Previous Year
▲ Up   ▼ Down   ► No Change

BUY $37.50 07/31/01

HOLD $58.70 02/02/04

- 10 Week Mov. Avg.
- 30 Week Mov. Avg.
- Relative Strength
- 12-Mo Target Price

Volume   Below Avg. — Above Avg.

VOL. MIL.

HOLD | BUY | HOLD

J J A S O N D J F M A M J J A S O N D J F M A M J J A S O N D J F M A M J J A S O N D J
2001 | 2002 | 2003 | 2004

OPTIONS: CBOE

Analyst commentary prepared by Justin McCann/PMW/BK

Highlights September 07, 2004

- After an anticipated 10% decline in 2004 from 2003 operating EPS of $4.25, we expect operating EPS to increase more than 20% in 2005. The projected decline in 2004 reflects the absence of earnings (including $0.13 already reported) from the Entergy-Koch partnership, which ETR has agreed to sell, subject to necessary approvals. In 2003, the company received a higher proportion of income ($0.88) from the trading unit of the Entergy-Koch partnership, while income from the unit was to be divided evenly in 2004.

- We expect the utilities and the holding company (which had operating EPS of $2.62 in 2003) to earn about $2.75 a share in 2004, aided by lower interest expense; the nuclear operations ($0.85) about $1.15, aided by higher contract prices and reduced operation and maintenance expenses; and a loss of about $0.10 from the commodity services segment ($0.78), reflecting the absence of Entergy-Koch, a decline in commodity trading results, and lower prices in the non-nuclear wholesale business.

- We expect 2005 EPS to benefit from higher earnings from the nuclear business, reduced interest expense, and accretion from a new stock buyback program through which the company intends to purchase up to $1.5 billion of common stock through the end of 2006.

Investment Rationale/Risk September 07, 2004

- In light of what we see as a strong balance sheet, a stable BBB investment grade credit rating, and a dividend payout ratio (43%) well below the industry average, we think that ETR has the financial flexibility to pursue either share buybacks or additional acquisitions. With its current share repurchase program, we believe it can realize about 12% EPS growth in 2005 and 9% in 2006. Thereafter, we believe ETR can realize (excluding the impact of future acquisitions) an organic growth rate of 5% to 6% over the longer term, at the upper end of the industry range.

- Risks to our recommendation and target price include the possibility of a sharp narrowing of the margins of ETR's non-regulated operations, and a potential decline in the average P/E multiple of the group as a whole.

- Although the dividend yield (recently about 3.0%) remains below the industry average, we think that a 29% increase in the September 2003 dividend payment enhanced the appeal of what we regard a growth-oriented utility holding company. However, in light of what we see as higher risks for the wholesale energy business, we expect the shares to trade at a modest discount to the approximate 13.3X peer P/E multiple based on our 2005 EPS estimates. Our 12-month target price is $63.

Key Stock Statistics

S&P Core EPS 2005E	4.47	52-week Range	$68.14-50.64
S&P Oper. EPS 2004E	3.75	12 Month P/E	22.0
P/E on S&P Oper. EPS 2004E	18.1	Beta	-0.04
S&P Oper. EPS 2005E	4.70	Shareholders	54,304
Yield (%)	3.2%	Market Cap (B)	$ 15.4
Dividend Rate/Share	2.16	Shares Outstanding (M)	226.9

Value of $10,000 invested five years ago: **$ 26,543**

Dividend Data Dividends have been paid since 1988

Amount ($)	Date Decl.	Ex-Div. Date	Stock of Record	Payment Date
0.450	Jan. 30	Feb. 09	Feb. 11	Mar. 01 '04
0.450	Apr. 07	May. 10	May. 12	Jun. 01 '04
0.450	Aug. 02	Aug. 10	Aug. 12	Sep. 01 '04
0.540	Oct. 21	Nov. 15	Nov. 17	Dec. 01 '04

Revenues/Earnings Data Fiscal year ending December 31

Revenues (Million $)

	2004	2003	2002	2001	2000	1999
1Q	2,252	2,038	1,861	2,653	1,811	1,640
2Q	2,485	2,354	2,097	2,495	2,138	2,316
3Q	2,964	2,700	2,469	2,576	3,432	3,065
4Q	—	2,103	1,879	1,885	2,635	1,752
Yr.	—	9,195	8,305	9,621	10,016	8,773

Earnings Per Share ($)

	2004	2003	2002	2001	2000	1999
1Q	0.88	1.10	-0.36	0.69	0.42	0.25
2Q	1.14	0.89	1.06	1.06	1.04	0.81
3Q	1.22	1.57	1.59	1.39	1.34	1.16
4Q	E0.37	-0.14	0.35	-0.01	0.19	-0.02
Yr.	E3.75	3.42	2.64	3.13	2.97	2.25

Next earnings report expected: early-February Source: S&P, Company Reports
EPS Estimates based on S&P Operating Earnings; historical GAAP earnings are as reported.

STANDARD &POOR'S

Entergy Corporation

Stock Report
November 13, 2004
NYSE Symbol: **ETR**

Recommendation: **HOLD** ★ ★ ★ ☆ ☆   12-Month Target Price: **$65.00** (as of October 21, 2004)

Business Summary September 07, 2004

As the holding company for Entergy Arkansas, Entergy Gulf States, Entergy Louisiana, Entergy Mississippi, and Entergy New Orleans, Entergy Corp. provides electricity to 2.6 million U.S. retail customers. ETR also owns System Energy Resources, which has a 90% interest in the Grand Gulf 1 nuclear plant.

In 2003, the utility segment accounted for 82% of revenues (82% in 2002, 77% in 2001), 52% of net income (97%, 77%), and 79% of assets (79%, 78%); the domestic non-utility nuclear segment accounted for 14% of revenues (14%, 8%), 32% of net income (32%, 17%), and 15% of assets (16%, 13%); the energy commodity services segment accounted for 2% of revenues (4%, 14%), 19% of net income (-23%, 14%), and 7% of assets (8%, 9%); and other segments, 2% of revenues (nil, 1%), -3% of net income (-6%, -8%), and 0% of assets (0%, 0%).

Fuel sources for the five utilities and System Energy Resources in 2003 were: nuclear, 52% (46% in 2002, 43% in 2001); natural gas, 26% (39%, 34%); coal, 18% (15%, 15%); and fuel oil, 4% (nil, 8%).

The company owns and operates power plants with about 30,000 megawatts of generating capacity, and is the second largest nuclear generator in the U.S.

ETR's non-utility nuclear business owns five plants and provides power to whole-sale customers as well as services to nuclear facilities owned by other utilities. In July 2002, the company completed the purchase of the Vermont Yankee Nuclear

Plant for $180 million. In September 2001, it acquired, in a transaction valued at $602 million, the Indian Point 1 and 2 nuclear units in New York. (Unit 1 was shut down and placed in storage in the 1970s.) Earlier, in November 2000, ETR acquired for $967 million the New York-based Indian Point 3 and James A. FitzPatrick nuclear facilities. In July 1999, the company acquired the Pilgrim nuclear station in Massachusetts, for $81 million.

The company's Energy Commodity Services segment was formed in the third quarter of 2001 through the integration of Entergy-Koch (an energy trading joint venture formed in January 2001) and Entergy Wholesale Operations. Prior to the first quarter of 2001, ETR had operated and reported its power marketing and trading segment separately.

Entergy-Koch gathers, transmits and stores natural gas in the Gulf Coast region of the U.S., through its Gulf South Pipeline subsidiary. It is involved in physical and financial natural gas and power trading, and weather derivatives trading in the U.S., Canada, the U.K., and Western Europe. Entergy-Koch also provides energy management services to its customers. On September 2, 2004, the company agreed to sell the Entergy-Koch trading business, in a transaction that was expected to close in the 2004 fourth quarter, subject to regulatory approvals. ETR said it would now pursue a sale of Gulf South Pipeline.

Company Financials Fiscal Year ending December 31

Per Share Data ($)

(Year Ended December 31)	2003	2002	2001	2000	1999	1998	1997	1996	1995	1994
Tangible Bk. Val.	36.38	33.61	33.74	31.83	29.71	28.82	19.72	25.77	28.25	27.74
Earnings	3.42	2.64	3.13	2.97	2.25	3.00	1.03	1.83	2.13	1.49
S&P Core Earnings	3.70	2.14	2.21	NA	NA	NA	NA	NA	NA	NA
Dividends	1.60	1.34	1.28	1.22	1.20	1.50	1.80	1.80	1.80	1.80
Payout Ratio	47%	51%	41%	41%	53%	50%	175%	98%	85%	121%
Prices - High	57.24	46.85	44.67	43.87	33.50	32.43	30.25	30.37	29.25	37.37
- Low	42.26	32.12	32.56	15.93	23.68	23.25	22.37	24.87	20.00	21.25
P/E Ratio - High	17	18	14	15	15	11	29	17	14	25
- Low	12	12	10	5	11	8	22	14	9	14

Income Statement Analysis (Million $)

	2003	2002	2001	2000	1999	1998	1997	1996	1995	1994
Revs.	9,195	8,304	9,621	10,016	8,773	11,495	9,562	7,164	6,274	5,963
Depr.	851	839	721	785	745	985	980	791	691	657
Maint.	NA	NA	NA	NA	NA	NA	NA	NA	NA	410
Fxd. Chgs. Cov.	2.66	2.23	2.25	2.83	2.34	1.91	1.87	2.51	2.32	1.62
Constr. Credits	75.9	57.0	48.0	56.0	52.0	23.0	18.0	18.3	18.0	21.8
Eff. Tax Rate	37.6%	32.1%	38.5%	40.3%	37.5%	24.4%	59.4%	50.1%	41.0%	23.7%
Net Inc.	813	623	727	711	595	786	301	420	485	342
S&P Core Earnings	856	487	495	NA	NA	NA	NA	NA	NA	NA

Balance Sheet & Other Fin. Data (Million $)

	2003	2002	2001	2000	1999	1998	1997	1996	1995	1994
Gross Prop.	31,181	32,964	32,403	29,865	28,178	26,892	29,102	25,109	24,080	23,557
Cap. Exp.	1,569	1,580	1,380	1,494	1,196	1,144	847	572	618	676
Net Prop.	18,561	20,657	20,597	18,501	17,279	16,816	19,517	16,223	15,821	15,917
Capitalization:										
LT Debt	7,498	7,458	7,536	8,014	7,253	7,349	9,304	7,838	7,081	7,367
% LT Debt	45.2	47.6	49.1	52.2	49.3	49.7	54.7	50.9	48.8	49.1
Pfd.	334	359	361	335	338	338	1,003	928	954	1,001
% Pfd.	2.01	2.29	2.35	2.18	2.30	2.28	5.80	6.00	6.60	6.90
Common	8,773	7,839	7,456	7,003	7,118	7,107	6,693	6,641	6,472	6,351
% Common	52.8	50.1	48.6	45.6	48.4	48.0	39.3	43.1	44.6	44.0
Total Cap.	21,805	20,355	19,399	19,095	18,539	18,942	22,156	19,876	18,897	19,959
% Oper. Ratio	89.4	85.8	88.6	89.0	88.3	86.8	81.3	82.4	80.6	82.1
% Earn. on Net Prop.	8.1	5.8	8.1	8.6	7.3	8.3	10.1	7.9	7.7	6.7
% Return On Revs.	8.8	7.5	7.6	7.1	6.8	6.8	3.1	5.9	7.7	5.7
% Return On Invest. Capital	2.4	7.7	7.6	7.1	7.0	14.8	7.7	6.2	6.3	5.5
% Return On Com. Equity	9.5	7.8	9.7	9.6	7.8	10.7	3.7	6.3	7.6	5.3

Data as orig reptd.; bef. results of disc opers/spec. items. Per share data adj. for stk. divs.; EPS diluted. E-Estimated. NA-Not Available. NM-Not Meaningful. NR-Not Ranked. UR-Under Review.

Office: 639 Loyola Avenue, New Orleans, LA 70113.
Telephone: 504-576-4000.
Website: http://www.entergy.com
Pres: D.C. Hintz.
CEO: J.W. Leonard.
EVP & CFO: L. Denault.
EVP, Secy & General Counsel: R.D. Sloan.

SVP & Chief Acctg Officer: N.E. Langston.
VP & Investor Contact: N. Morovich 504-576-5506.
Dirs: M. S. Bateman, W. F. Blount, G. W. Davis, C. P. Deming, A. M. Herman, D. C. Hintz, J. W. Leonard, R. V. Luft, K. A. Murphy, P. W. Murrill, J. R. Nichols, W. A. Percy II, D. H. Reilley, W. C. Smith, B. A. Steinhagen, S. V. Wilkinson, S. D. deBree.

Founded: in 1989.
Domicile: Delaware.
Employees: 14,773.
S&P Analyst: Justin McCann/PMW/BK

EOG Resources

Recommendation: **HOLD** ★★★☆☆
SELL SELL HOLD BUY BUY

12-Month Target Price: $70.00
(as of October 27, 2004)

EOG has an approximate 0.07% weighting in the **S&P 500**

Sector: Energy
Sub-Industry: Oil & Gas Exploration & Production
Peer Group: Exploration & Production - Large

Summary: EOG explores for, develops, produces and markets natural gas and crude oil in the U.S., Trinidad and Canada.

Quantitative Evaluations

S&P Earnings & Dividend Rank: B

| D | C | B- | B | B+ | A- | A | A+ |

S&P Fair Value Rank: 2-

| 1 | 2 | 3 | 4 | 5 |
| Lowest | | | | Highest |

Fair Value Calc.: $62.50 (Slightly Overvalued)

S&P Investability Quotient Percentile

95%

EOG scored higher than 95% of all companies for which an S&P Report is available.

Volatility: Average

| Low | Average | High |

Technical Evaluation: Bullish
Since 9/04, the technical indicators for EOG have been Bullish.

Relative Strength Rank: Moderate

59

| 1 Lowest | | Highest 99 |

Price as of 11/12/04: **$68.37** | **2004E S&P Core EPS:** **$4.78**

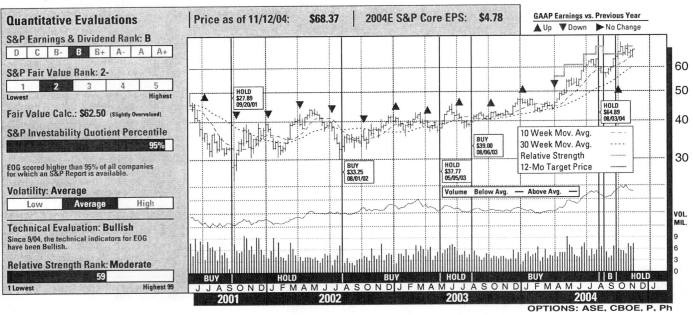

GAAP Earnings vs. Previous Year
▲ Up ▼ Down ▶ No Change

OPTIONS: ASE, CBOE, P, Ph

Analyst commentary prepared by Charles LaPorta, CFA /CB/JWP

Highlights September 28, 2004

- EOG reported lower than expected production volume for the second quarter. However, the company continues to note development drilling success in its Barnett Shale play, North Sea and Trinidad properties, which has resulted in EOG's reiterating its 2004 production growth estimate of 8%.

- The success of these developments has also caused EOG to lower its depreciation, depletion, exploration and impairment cost guidance. Based on estimated usage, the company has also locked in its steel costs through 2005. In the past few weeks, we have increased our 2005 oil and gas price estimates from $34.83 per bbl. and $5.13 per Mcf, respectively, to $39.33 and $5.83.

- Our 2004 and 2005 EBITDAX (earnings before interest, taxes, depreciation, amortization and exploration expense) estimates are $1.63 billion and $1.7 billion, respectively. With EOG's debt to capitalization ratio of 31% as of June 30, 2004, we expect interest expense to trend lower through the year.

Investment Rationale/Risk September 28, 2004

- We think EOG is one of the best managed among the independent oil and gas exploration and production companies, and we think a premium valuation is warranted because EOG's cost structure is among the lowest versus peers, and its five-year ROCE of 17.1% is among the highest.

- Risks to our recommendation and target price include events that would cause substantial and sustained declines in oil and gas prices; a persistent inability by EOG to replace its reserves; and acts of terrorism against EOG's production facilities.

- We believe EOG's shares currently reflect the company's superior financial performance, as the stock trades at 14.4X our 2005 EPS estimate and its enterprise value is over 5X our 2005 EBITDAX estimate -- well above peer group averages. Given current healthy heating oil inventories, and above average natural gas storage injections, we believe there is limited short-term upside to natural gas prices. Natural gas represents 85% of EOG's total production. With the stock trading near our 12-month target price of $66, we would hold positions.

Key Stock Statistics

S&P Core EPS 2005E	5.08	52-week Range	$72.48-41.60
S&P Oper. EPS 2004E	4.90	12 Month P/E	16.8
P/E on S&P Oper. EPS 2004E	14.0	Beta	0.71
S&P Oper. EPS 2005E	5.20	Shareholders	75,000
Yield (%)	0.4%	Market Cap (B)	$ 8.1
Dividend Rate/Share	0.24	Shares Outstanding (M)	118.6

Value of $10,000 invested five years ago: **$ 37,741**

Dividend Data Dividends have been paid since 1990

Amount ($)	Date Decl.	Ex-Div. Date	Stock of Record	Payment Date
0.050	Nov. 06	Jan. 14	Jan. 16	Jan. 30 '04
0.060	Feb. 04	Apr. 14	Apr. 16	Apr. 30 '04
0.060	May. 04	Jul. 14	Jul. 16	Jul. 30 '04
0.060	Sep. 16	Oct. 13	Oct. 15	Oct. 29 '04

Revenues/Earnings Data Fiscal year ending December 31

Revenues (Million $)

	2004	2003	2002	2001	2000	1999
1Q	464.3	464.7	186.5	597.3	259.9	158.9
2Q	519.0	424.8	290.5	466.1	322.7	187.2
3Q	594.2	458.7	279.9	354.2	402.1	226.8
4Q	—	396.5	338.2	237.4	505.1	228.5
Yr.	—	1,745	1,095	1,655	1,490	801.4

Earnings Per Share ($)

	2004	2003	2002	2001	2000	1999
1Q	0.83	1.15	-0.23	1.79	0.33	0.03
2Q	E1.04	0.91	0.30	1.13	0.63	0.13
3Q	1.42	0.99	0.22	0.59	0.95	3.75
4Q	E1.61	0.61	0.36	-0.24	1.33	0.25
Yr.	E4.90	3.66	0.65	3.30	2.24	3.99

Next earnings report expected: early-February Source: S&P, Company Reports
EPS Estimates based on S&P Operating Earnings; historical GAAP earnings are as reported.

The McGraw-Hill Companies

EOG Resources, Inc.

Recommendation: **HOLD** ★ ★ ★ ☆ ☆   12-Month Target Price: **$70.00** (as of October 27, 2004)

Business Summary September 28, 2004

In August 1999, Enron Corp. exchanged 62.3 million of its 82.3 million shares of EOG Resources, Inc. (formerly Enron Oil & Gas) for EOG's China and India operations, plus $600 million in cash. Following the exchange, which also included a series of equity offerings, EOG Resources was transformed from a 54%-owned subsidiary of Enron into an independent exploration and production company with operations primarily in North America. Subsequent to the transaction, Enron essentially liquidated its remaining position in the company.

EOG's operations are all related to natural gas and crude oil exploration and production. Its North American operations are organized into eight operating divisions, each focusing on several basins: Midland, TX (2003 net natural gas production of 100 million cubic feet (MMcf) per day, net crude oil production of 7.8 thousand barrels (MBbl) per day); Denver, CO (117 MMcf per day, 5.5 MBbl per day); Oklahoma City/Mid-Continent (79 MMcf per day, 1.5 MBbl per day); Tyler, TX (96 MMcf per day, 3.1 MBbl per day); Corpus Christi, TX (169 MMcf per day, 2.2 MBbl per day); Pittsburgh, PA (22 MMcf per day); Houston, TX/Offshore (55 MMcf per day, 1.3 MBbl per day); and Calgary, AB (165 MMcf per day, 3MBbl per day). The company also has producing operations offshore Trinidad, and is evaluating exploration, exploitation and development opportunities in selected other international areas. At the end of 2003, 49% of EOG's reserves were located in the U.S., 24% in Canada, and 27% in Trinidad. At December 31, 2003, 87% of proven reserves in North America were natural gas, with 13% crude oil, condensate, and natural gas liquids (NGLs).

In 2003, the company established a new venue outside North America with two natural gas discoveries in the Southern Gas Basin of the U.K. North Sea. The wells were farm-in opportunities from major oil companies. EOG expects net production of about 40 Mmcf per day by the end of 2004. It is reviewing other farm-in opportunities in the area.

Estimated net proved natural gas reserves increased 14% in 2003, to 4.66 trillion cubic feet (Tcf) at December 31, 2003. Estimated net proved crude oil, condensate, and NGL reserves grew 12%, to 95 million bbl. From all sources, EOG replaced 249% of 2003 production, at a finding cost of $1.28 per thousand cubic feet equivalent (Mcfe). Reserve replacement in North America was 259%, with a total all-in finding cost of $1.36 per Mcfe. From drilling alone, the company replaced 183% of production, at a finding cost of $1.21 per Mcfe.

Natural gas production averaged 978 MMcf a day in 2003, versus 963 MMcf a day in 2002. Crude oil and condensate production averaged 25.2 MBbl a day (23.1 MBbl). NGL production averaged 4.4 MBbl a day (3.0 MBbl). Average price realizations were $4.00 per Mcf of natural gas ($3.09); $25.20 per bbl. of crude oil ($23.10); and $22.02 per bbl. of NGLs ($17.97).

Capital spending (including acquisitions) increased to $1.32 billion in 2003, from $821 million in 2002; $405 million of the 2003 total was for acquisitions. Of the drilling programs, 29% were exploration spending and 71% were development; 95% of 2003 net exploration and development spending was in North America. The 2004 capital spending budget (excluding acquisitions) is $1.1 billion.

Company Financials Fiscal Year ending December 31

Per Share Data ($)

(Year Ended December 31)	2003	2002	2001	2000	1999	1998	1997	1996	1995	1994
Tangible Bk. Val.	17.89	13.27	12.93	10.53	8.22	8.33	8.26	7.92	7.28	6.52
Cash Flow	7.45	4.04	6.64	6.35	7.22	2.39	2.53	2.45	2.39	2.60
Earnings	3.66	0.65	3.30	2.24	3.99	0.36	0.77	0.88	0.89	0.93
S&P Core Earnings	3.54	0.53	3.20	NA	NA	NA	NA	NA	NA	NA
Dividends	0.18	0.16	0.15	0.13	0.12	0.12	0.12	0.12	0.12	0.18
Payout Ratio	5%	25%	5%	6%	3%	33%	15%	14%	13%	19%
Prices - High	47.52	44.15	55.50	56.68	25.37	24.50	27.00	30.62	25.37	24.62
- Low	35.70	30.02	25.80	13.68	14.37	11.75	17.50	22.37	17.12	17.37
P/E Ratio - High	13	68	17	25	6	68	35	35	29	26
- Low	10	46	8	6	4	33	22	25	19	19

Income Statement Analysis (Million $)

	2003	2002	2001	2000	1999	1998	1997	1996	1995	1994
Revs.	1,745	1,095	1,655	1,490	801	769	774	731	649	572
Oper. Inc.	697	648	1,181	697	18.2	114	193	209	195	373
Depr. Depl. & Amort.	442	398	392	370	460	315	278	251	240	267
Int. Exp.	58.7	59.7	45.1	61.0	61.8	48.6	27.7	22.0	18.4	14.6
Pretax Inc.	654	120	631	634	568	60.3	163	191	184	154
Eff. Tax Rate	33.1%	27.2%	36.9%	37.3%	NM	6.82%	25.4%	26.7%	22.8%	3.90%
Net Inc.	437	87.2	399	397	569	56.2	122	140	142	148
S&P Core Earnings	412	62.4	376	NA	NA	NA	NA	NA	NA	NA

Balance Sheet & Other Fin. Data (Million $)

	2003	2002	2001	2000	1999	1998	1997	1996	1995	1994
Cash	4.44	9.85	2.51	20.2	24.8	6.30	9.33	7.64	23.0	6.00
Curr. Assets	396	395	272	394	201	246	282	326	218	156
Total Assets	4,749	3,814	3,414	3,001	2,611	3,018	2,723	2,458	2,147	1,862
Curr. Liab.	477	276	311	370	219	263	291	317	169	165
LT Debt	1,109	1,145	856	859	990	1,143	741	466	289	190
Common Equity	2,098	1,524	1,495	1,234	982	1,280	1,281	1,265	1,164	1,043
Total Cap.	4,125	3,478	3,050	2,580	2,346	2,683	2,310	2,040	1,761	1,503
Cap. Exp.	1,204	714	974	603	403	690	626	539	445	442
Cash Flow	868	474	780	756	1,028	371	400	391	382	415
Curr. Ratio	0.8	1.4	0.9	1.1	0.9	0.9	1.0	1.0	1.3	1.0
% LT Debt of Cap.	26.9	32.9	28.1	33.3	42.2	42.6	32.1	22.8	16.4	12.7
% Ret. on Assets	10.2	2.4	12.4	14.1	20.2	2.0	4.7	6.1	7.1	8.1
% Ret. on Equity	23.4	5.0	28.4	34.8	50.3	4.4	9.6	11.5	12.9	15.0

Data as orig reptd.; bef. results of disc opers/spec. items. Per share data adj. for stk. divs.; EPS diluted. E-Estimated. NA-Not Available. NM-Not Meaningful. NR-Not Ranked. UR-Under Review.

Office: 333 Clay Street, Houston, TX 77002-7361.
Telephone: 877-363-3647.
Email: ir@eogresources.com
Website: http://www.eogresources.com
Chrmn & CEO: M.G. Papa.
Pres: E.P. Segner III.

SVP & General Counsel: B. Hunsaker, Jr.
VP & Chief Acctg Officer: T.K. Driggers.
VP & Treas: D.R. Looney.
VP & Investor Contact: M.A. Baldwin 713-651-6364.
Dirs: G. A. Alcorn, C. R. Crisp, M. G. Papa, E. P. Segner III, D. F. Textor, F. G. Wisner.

Founded: in 1985.
Domicile: Delaware.
Employees: 1,100.
S&P Analyst: Charles LaPorta, CFA /CB/JWP

E*TRADE Financial

Recommendation: **BUY** ★★★★☆
SELL SELL HOLD BUY BUY

12-Month Target Price: $18.00
(as of November 15, 2004)

ET has an approximate 0.05% weighting in the **S&P 500**

Sector: Financials
Sub-Industry: Investment Banking & Brokerage
Peer Group: Discount/Online Brokers

Summary: E*TRADE provides online discount brokerage, mortgage and banking services, primarily to retail customers.

Quantitative Evaluations

S&P Earnings & Dividend Rank: B-
| D | C | B- | B | B+ | A- | A | A+ |

S&P Fair Value Rank: 4-
| 1 | 2 | 3 | 4 | 5 |
Lowest — Highest

Fair Value Calc.: $15.20 (Slightly Undervalued)

S&P Investability Quotient Percentile
97%
ET scored higher than 97% of all companies for which an S&P Report is available.

Volatility: Average
| Low | Average | High |

Technical Evaluation: Bullish
Since 10/04, the technical indicators for ET have been Bullish.

Relative Strength Rank: Strong
89
1 Lowest — Highest 99

Price as of 11/15/04: $14.19   **2004E S&P Core EPS: $0.87**

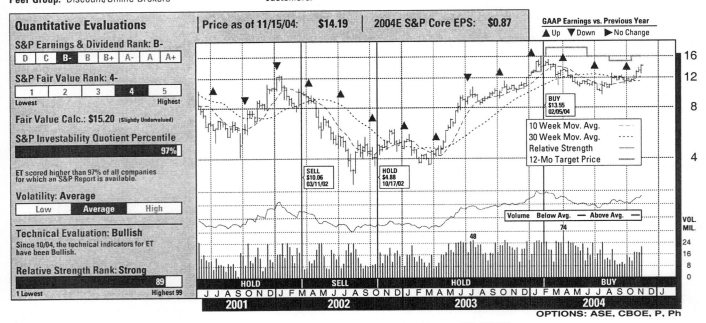

GAAP Earnings vs. Previous Year
▲ Up ▼ Down ► No Change

BUY $13.55 02/05/04

10 Week Mov. Avg.
30 Week Mov. Avg.
Relative Strength
12-Mo Target Price

SELL $10.06 03/11/02
HOLD $4.88 10/17/02

Volume Below Avg. — Above Avg.

| HOLD | SELL | HOLD | BUY |
J J A S O N D | J F M A M J J A S O N D | J F M A M J J A S O N D | J F M A M J J A S O N D | J
2001 | 2002 | 2003 | 2004

OPTIONS: ASE, CBOE, P, Ph

Analyst commentary prepared by Robert Hansen, CFA /CB/BK

Highlights October 21, 2004

- We like ET's diversification between its retail brokerage and mortgage businesses, which provides synergies and has resulted in more stable operating earnings, in our view. We think the company is gaining market share among active investors based on growth in brokerage accounts and impressive growth in total client assets in investing accounts, which stood at $71.4 billion at the end of the third quarter. We think new branches and the two-second execution ad campaign will drive additional market share gains.

- Daily average revenue trades declined 24% sequentially in the third quarter following a 19% sequential decline in the second quarter from record levels in the first quarter. We expect banking profits to rebound in 2004 from the depressed levels of the first quarter, due to growth in banking assets, lower funding costs resulting from ET's Sweep Deposit Account program introduced in 2003, and a rebound in the mortgage pipeline.

- We forecast operating EPS of $0.90 in 2004 (excluding a $0.07 gain on asset sales), driven, we believe, by a rebound in trading activity from depressed levels in the third quarter and continued increases in margin loan balances. We see EPS of $1.00 in 2005.

Investment Rationale/Risk October 21, 2004

- We think the company is gaining market share and maintains a strong competitive position, which we believe helps support its valuation. We think continued industry consolidation could help justify a higher P/E multiple for the shares. We also view favorably the company's $20 million stock buyback in the third quarter. We expect the multiple to expand as investors begin to focus on 2005 and the company's diversified business model, which we view as a competitive advantage.

- Risks to our recommendation and target price include interest rate volatility, increasing price competition, various regulatory issues, and equity market volatility, notably in the Nasdaq.

- Having declined about 5% thus far in 2004, the shares recently traded at a P/E multiple of nearly 12X our 2005 EPS estimate, a discount to peers. Our 12-month target price of $16 is 16X our 2005 EPS estimate. We think the shares should trade at a discount to focused brokerage competitors, largely due to the company's banking segment, which we think merits a lower multiple.

Key Stock Statistics

S&P Core EPS 2005E	1.00	52-week Range	$15.40-9.51
S&P Oper. EPS 2004E	0.92	12 Month P/E	13.6
P/E on S&P Oper. EPS 2004E	15.3	Beta	NA
S&P Oper. EPS 2005E	1.05	Shareholders	2,462
Yield (%)	Nil	Market Cap (B)	$ 5.3
Dividend Rate/Share	Nil	Shares Outstanding (M)	373.3

Value of $10,000 invested five years ago: **$ 3,836**

Dividend Data

No cash dividends have been paid.

Revenues/Earnings Data Fiscal year ending December 31

Revenues (Million $)

	2004	2003	2002	2001	2000	1999
1Q	410.9	322.2	554.6	550.1	246.0	115.9
2Q	380.9	381.1	531.2	516.0	555.3	155.3
3Q	337.1	397.7	468.6	481.4	496.2	177.0
4Q	—	382.8	484.7	514.6	536.6	173.2
Yr.	—	1,484	2,302	2,062	1,973	621.4

Earnings Per Share ($)

	2004	2003	2002	2001	2000	1999
1Q	0.23	0.06	0.05	-0.02	-0.02	-0.05
2Q	0.24	0.03	0.09	-0.04	-0.08	0.03
3Q	0.21	0.17	0.06	-0.77	-0.02	-0.10
4Q	E0.24	0.27	0.08	0.02	0.15	-0.11
Yr.	E0.92	0.55	0.30	-0.81	-0.06	-0.23

Next earnings report expected: late-January Source: S&P, Company Reports
EPS Estimates based on S&P Operating Earnings; historical GAAP earnings are as reported.

E*TRADE Financial Corp.

Recommendation: **BUY** ★★★★★   12-Month Target Price: **$18.00** (as of November 15, 2004)

Business Summary October 21, 2004

E*TRADE Financial (ET) is one of the industry's leading online financial services concerns. The company provides online discount brokerage and banking services, primarily to retail customers. Although most of the company's business is done over the Internet, ET also serves customers through branches, automated and live telephone service, and Internet-enabled wireless devices. Retail customers can move money electronically between brokerage, banking, and lending accounts.

Through its Brokerage segment, ET's customers can buy and sell stocks, bonds, options, futures, and nearly 5,000 mutual funds. Customers can also obtain streaming quotes and charts, access real-time market commentary and research reports, and perform personalized portfolio tracking. Brokerage customers can also obtain margin loans collateralized by their securities. The company uses sophisticated proprietary transaction-enabling technology to automate tradition- ally labor-intensive transactions. The brokerage business continues to be the primary point of introduction for the majority of ET's customers, who are typically self-directed investors. At the end of 2003, ET had about 2.85 million active brokerage accounts and total assets in investing accounts of $70.8 billion.

Through its Banking segment, the company offers residential mortgage products, home equity loans and home equity lines of credit (HELOC). The segment also offers credit card, automobile, recreational vehicle (RV), marine and other con- sumer loans. During 2003, the Banking segment lowered its cost of funds by

sweeping Brokerage customer money market balances into an FDIC-insured Sweep Deposit Account product. At the end of 2003, ET had about 638,345 active banking accounts and total deposits in banking accounts of $12.5 billion. In 2003, ET shifted its loan portfolio toward adjustable-rate mortgages and higher-yielding HELOC and RV loans and away from fixed-rate mortgages and automobile loans. However, ET's total allowance for loan losses as a percentage of total nonperforming loans increased to 154% at the end of 2003 from 104% at the end of 2002 due to a significant increase in the loan loss provision.

ET has completed several acquisitions aimed at diversifying its earnings and strengthening existing businesses. In December 2002, it purchased Ganis Credit Corp., the motor home and boat lending division of Deutsche Bank, for about $100 million in cash. Also in December, the company acquired Engelman Securities, a privately held, Chicago Stock Exchange member and registered broker-dealer, for about $7.5 million, plus up to $14 million in contingent stock consideration. In June 2002, ET purchased Tradescape.Com, an on-site professional trading platform, for $100 million in stock. In October 2001, the company acquired Dempsey & Com- pany, a Chicago-based specialist and market-maker, for $173.5 million in cash and stock. The acquisition was part of ET's efforts to establish a market-making capability, deliver added value to customers, and diversify its revenue streams.

Company Financials Fiscal Year ending December 31

Per Share Data ($)

(Year Ended December 31)	2003	2002	2001	2000	1999	1998	1997	1996	1995	1994
Tangible Bk. Val.	3.73	2.68	2.54	4.43	3.81	3.14	1.82	0.59	NA	NA
Cash Flow	0.55	1.20	-0.28	0.37	-0.09	0.07	0.13	0.00	0.03	NA
Earnings	0.55	0.30	-0.81	-0.06	-0.23	-0.01	0.10	-0.01	0.03	0.01
S&P Core Earnings	0.27	0.27	-0.86	NA	NA	NA	NA	NA	NA	NA
Dividends	Nil	Nil	Nil	Nil	Nil	Nil	Nil	Nil	Nil	NA
Payout Ratio	Nil	Nil	Nil	Nil	Nil	Nil	Nil	Nil	Nil	NA
Prices - High	12.91	12.64	15.37	34.25	72.25	16.25	11.96	3.46	NA	NA
- Low	3.65	2.81	4.07	6.65	12.73	2.50	2.75	2.06	NA	NA
P/E Ratio - High	23	42	NM	NM	NM	NM	119	NM	NA	NA
- Low	7	9	NM	NM	NM	NM	27	NM	NA	NA

Income Statement Analysis (Million $)

	2003	2002	2001	2000	1999	1998	1997	1996	1995	1994
Commissions	337	302	407	739	356	162	110	44.2	20.8	9.50
Int. Inc.	6.54	12.7	22.2	17.2	196	95.7	40.2	7.00	1.00	0.30
Total Revs.	1,719	2,302	2,062	1,973	695	285	158	58.6	23.3	10.9
Int. Exp.	532	609	832	630	73.4	39.7	14.9	2.22	Nil	Nil
Pretax Inc.	310	194	-310	104	-91.5	-1.67	23.3	-1.38	4.31	0.24
Eff. Tax Rate	36.2%	43.9%	NM	81.8%	NM	NM	40.4%	NM	40.1%	NM
Net Inc.	203	107	-271	19.2	-54.4	-0.71	13.9	-0.83	2.58	0.79
S&P Core Earnings	101	96.1	-291	NA	NA	NA	NA	NA	NA	NA

Balance Sheet & Other Fin. Data (Million $)

	2003	2002	2001	2000	1999	1998	1997	1996	1995	1994
Total Assets	26,049	21,534	18,172	17,317	3,927	1,969	990	990	14.2	NA
Cash Items	921	2,223	1,601	301	189	26.8	36.8	50.1	9.62	NA
Receivables	2,298	1,500	2,139	6,543	2,913	1,310	728	193	2.05	NA
Secs. Owned	9,876	8,702	4,726	985	189	503	191	35.0	NA	NA
Sec. Borrowed	Nil	Nil	Nil	NA	NA	NA	NA	NA	NA	NA
Due Brokers & Cust.	3,691	2,792	2,700	6,056	2,824	1,185	681	0.22	NA	NA
Other Liabs.	79.3	775	818	471	189	73.8	18.1	6.10	NA	NA
Capitalization:										
Debt	695	907	605	3,336	Nil	Nil	9.40	0.02	0.07	NA
Equity	1,918	1,506	1,571	1,857	914	710	281	69.3	11.1	NA
Total	2,614	2,412	2,175	5,192	914	710	291	69.3	11.2	NA
% Return On Revs.	11.8	5.4	NM	1.6	NM	NM	8.8	NM	11.6	8.3
% Ret. on Assets	0.9	0.5	NM	0.2	NM	NM	2.2	NM	NA	NA
% Ret. on Equity	11.9	7.0	NM	1.2	NM	NM	7.9	NM	NA	NA

Data as orig reptd.; bef. results of disc opers/spec. items. Per share data adj. for stk. divs.; EPS diluted. E-Estimated. NA-Not Available. NM-Not Meaningful. NR-Not Ranked. Prior to 2001, yrs. ended Sep. 30.

Office: 135 E 57th St , New York, NY 10022.
Telephone: 646-521-4300.
Email: ir@etrade.com
Website: http://www.etrade.com
Chrmn: G. Hayter.
Pres & COO: R.J. Lilien.

CEO: M. Caplan.
CFO: R.J. Simmons.
Secy & General Counsel: R.S. Elmer.
Investor Contact: C. Dotson 650-331-6000.
Dirs: M. H. Caplan, R. D. Fisher, W. E. Ford, G. Hayter, M. K. Parks, W. A. Porter, C. C. Raffaeli, L. E. Randall, L. C. Thurow, D. L. Weaver.

Founded: in 1982.
Domicile: Delaware.
Employees: 3,500.
S&P Analyst: Robert Hansen, CFA /CB/BK

Equifax

Recommendation: **HOLD** ★★★☆☆
SELL SELL HOLD BUY BUY

12-Month Target Price: **$29.00**
(as of November 01, 2004)

EFX has an approximate 0.03% weighting in the **S&P 500**

Sector: Industrials
Sub-Industry: Diversified Commercial Services
Peer Group: Business Services

Summary: This company is a leading worldwide source of consumer and commercial credit information.

Quantitative Evaluations

S&P Earnings & Dividend Rank: B+

D	C	B-	B	B+	A-	A	A+

S&P Fair Value Rank: 5+

1	2	3	4	5
Lowest				Highest

Fair Value Calc.: $29.50 (Slightly Undervalued)

S&P Investability Quotient Percentile

95%

EFX scored higher than 95% of all companies for which an S&P Report is available.

Volatility: Low

Low	Average	High

Technical Evaluation: Bullish
Since 10/04, the technical indicators for EFX have been Bullish.

Relative Strength Rank: Moderate

54

1 Lowest   Highest 99

Price as of 11/12/04: $27.29   **2004E S&P Core EPS:** $1.46

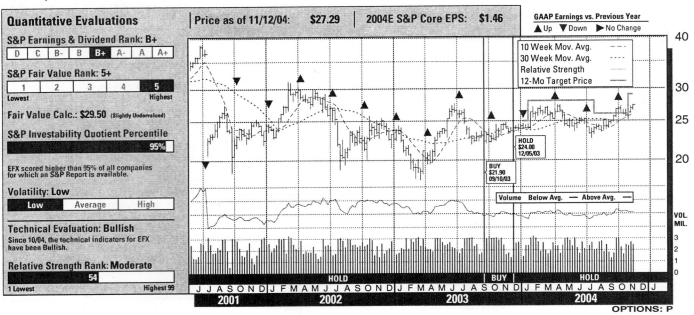

GAAP Earnings vs. Previous Year
▲ Up ▼ Down ▶ No Change

- 10 Week Mov. Avg.
- 30 Week Mov. Avg.
- Relative Strength
- 12-Mo Target Price

HOLD $24.00 12/05/03
BUY $21.90 09/10/03

Volume Below Avg. — Above Avg.

VOL. MIL.

HOLD | BUY | HOLD
J J A S O N D J F M A M J J A S O N D J F M A M J J A S O N D J F M A M J J A S O N D J
2001 | 2002 | 2003 | 2004

OPTIONS: P

Analyst commentary prepared by Zaineb Bokhari/CB/JWP

Highlights November 01, 2004

- We expect revenue growth of 5% and 4% in 2004 and 2005, respectively, reflecting a gradual economic recovery. However, we believe that December 2003 changes to the Fair Credit Report Act (FCRA) making free EFX credit reports available to consumers (effective December 1, 2004) could restrict revenues and margins. Due to a lower rate of investment in new initiatives, we expect capital spending to decline in 2004 and 2005, aiding free cash flow.

- Although we view EFX's traditional operations as relatively mature, we are positive on its Consumer Direct (credit profile and privacy protection) offerings. We see promise in the Business Exchange initiative, whereby the company has begun to aggregate, analyze and sell credit data on small businesses. We also see notable potential for EFX's homeland defense and security business, which hosts and manages the primary domestic database used to identify potential high-risk individuals, groups and companies.

- We expect operating EPS of $1.63 in 2004 (adjusted for gains and asset impairment charges of $0.14 per share, after tax), and $1.73 in 2005. Our Standard & Poor's Core EPS estimates for 2004 and 2005 of $1.46 and $1.56, respectively, reflect projected stock-based compensation and pension expense.

Investment Rationale/Risk November 01, 2004

- We believe the mid-2001 spin-off of the payment services business (now known as Certegy) has made EFX easier to understand and more appealing to investors, and has enabled its management to focus on remaining operations. We are encouraged by the performance of the North American Information Services segment (55% of 2004 third quarter revenues), the largest contributor to sales, and anticipate continued improvement at international units, where revenues declined in 2001, 2002, and through the first half of 2003, after which they began to improve.

- Risks to our opinion and target price include negatives associated with the FCRA, and increasing competition from other major credit bureaus Experian and TransUnion.

- Our $29 target price is based on a relative value analysis using blended P/E and P/E-to-growth multiples on our 2005 estimate of $1.73. A rising interest rate environment has limited revenue and earnings growth for EFX, and we think there is a potential for further dampening from the implementation of changes to FCRA. However, EFX is currently trading at a 31% discount to peers on a P/E basis, and it continues to show cash flows we view as strong. As a result, we believe 20% is a more appropriate discount for EFX shares.

Key Stock Statistics

S&P Core EPS 2005E	1.56	52-week Range	$27.37-22.60
S&P Oper. EPS 2004E	1.63	12 Month P/E	17.8
P/E on S&P Oper. EPS 2004E	16.7	Beta	0.79
S&P Oper. EPS 2005E	1.73	Shareholders	9,458
Yield (%)	0.4%	Market Cap (B)	$ 3.7
Dividend Rate/Share	0.12	Shares Outstanding (M)	135.1

Value of $10,000 invested five years ago: **NA**

Dividend Data Dividends have been paid since 1914

Amount ($)	Date Decl.	Ex-Div. Date	Stock of Record	Payment Date
0.020	Jan. 30	Feb. 19	Feb. 23	Mar. 15 '04
0.030	Apr. 28	May. 21	May. 25	Jun. 15 '04
0.030	Aug. 09	Aug. 23	Aug. 25	Sep. 15 '04
0.030	Nov. 11	Nov. 22	Nov. 24	Dec. 15 '04

Revenues/Earnings Data Fiscal year ending December 31

Revenues (Million $)

	2004	2003	2002	2001	2000	1999
1Q	313.6	301.6	259.0	285.2	451.1	421.5
2Q	318.9	317.0	268.0	289.6	498.2	442.6
3Q	323.0	309.8	289.7	282.4	517.9	444.4
4Q	—	297.0	292.6	281.9	498.7	464.2
Yr.	—	1,225	1,109	1,139	1,966	1,773

Earnings Per Share ($)

	2004	2003	2002	2001	2000	1999
1Q	0.38	0.33	0.30	0.24	0.31	0.31
2Q	0.55	0.36	0.34	0.28	0.39	0.37
3Q	0.40	0.39	0.36	0.26	0.47	0.42
4Q	E0.44	0.23	0.38	0.07	0.50	0.45
Yr.	E1.63	1.31	1.39	0.84	1.68	1.55

Next earnings report expected: late-January Source: S&P, Company Reports
EPS Estimates based on S&P Operating Earnings; historical GAAP earnings are as reported.

Equifax Inc.

Recommendation: **HOLD** ★ ★ ★ ★ ★   12-Month Target Price: **$29.00** (as of November 01, 2004)

Business Summary November 01, 2004

Equifax collects, organizes and manages credit, financial, demographic, and marketing information regarding individuals and businesses, which the company collects from various sources. These sources include financial or credit granting institutions (which provide accounts receivable information), public records of bankruptcies, liens and judgments, and surveys and warranty cards. The company maintains information in proprietary databases regarding approximately 400 million consumers and businesses worldwide. EFX amasses and processes this data using proprietary systems, and makes the data available to customers in various formats.

Products and services include consumer credit information, information database management, marketing information, business credit information, decisioning and analytical tools, and identity verification services that enable businesses to make informed decisions about extending credit or providing service(s), managing portfolio risk, and developing marketing strategies. According to the company, EFX allows consumers to manage and protect their financial affairs through products the company sells directly to individuals using the Internet.

The North American Information Services segment (83% and 89% of 2003 and 2002 revenues, respectively) includes Consumer Services (credit information regarding individuals), Commercial Services (credit information regarding businesses), Mortgage Services (loan origination information), Canadian Operations (commercial credit reporting), Credit Marketing offerings (pre-screening, portfolio review, database and other marketing products), Direct Marketing Services (consumer demographic and lifestyle information), and Consumer Direct (credit reporting and monitoring services provided to individuals over the Internet).

Equifax Europe (11%, 11%) provides credit reporting and scoring, risk management, fraud detection, and modeling services. Operations are located in the U.K. (which contributed 78% of unit revenue in 2003), Ireland, Spain, Italy and Portugal. During the 2002 third quarter, EFX decided to exit its commercial services business in Spain, whose purchase was agreed to in January 2004. Equifax Latin America (6%, 7%) provides credit reporting and scoring, risk management, identity verification, and fraud detection services. EFX has a presence in Brazil (which accounted for 58% of segment revenue in 2003), Argentina, Chile, El Salvador, Peru and Uruguay.

In August 2002, EFX acquired Naviant, an e-mail marketing company, for $135 million in cash. Naviant's solutions enable marketers to identify, target, and build consumer relationships through e-mail marketing. Naviant had a database of more than 100 million permission-based e-mail addresses as of August 2002. In 2003, EFX renamed the company Naviant Equifax eMarketing Solutions, and restructured the business, recording related charges of $26 million for asset impairment, reduced headcount, and facilities and product consolidation.

In July 2001, EFX spun off its payments operations to shareholders as a new publicly traded company, Certegy, Inc. (NYSE: CEY). In 2000, the primary operating units were Information Services (60%, 75%) and Payment Services (40%, 34%). On August 9, 2004 EFX announced that its directors had approved an increase of $250 million to its existing share repurchase program, under which EFX had remaining authorization to buy back $62.3 million of its shares at June 30, 2004.

Company Financials Fiscal Year ending December 31

Per Share Data ($)

(Year Ended December 31)	2003	2002	2001	2000	1999	1998	1997	1996	1995	1994
Tangible Bk. Val.	NM	NM	NM	NM	NM	NM	NM	NM	NM	0.20
Cash Flow	2.00	1.96	1.61	2.77	2.44	2.06	1.78	1.81	1.48	1.26
Earnings	1.31	1.39	0.84	1.68	1.55	1.34	1.25	1.03	0.98	0.81
S&P Core Earnings	1.18	1.04	0.52	NA	NA	NA	NA	NA	NA	NA
Dividends	0.08	0.08	0.25	0.37	0.36	0.35	0.35	0.33	0.32	0.30
Payout Ratio	6%	6%	29%	22%	23%	26%	28%	32%	32%	37%
Prices - High	27.59	31.30	38.76	36.50	39.87	45.00	37.18	34.50	21.75	15.25
- Low	17.84	18.95	18.60	19.87	20.12	29.75	26.50	17.75	12.62	10.93
P/E Ratio - High	21	23	46	22	26	34	30	33	22	19
- Low	14	14	22	12	13	22	21	17	13	14

Income Statement Analysis (Million $)

	2003	2002	2001	2000	1999	1998	1997	1996	1995	1994
Revs.	1,225	1,109	1,139	1,966	1,773	1,621	1,366	1,811	1,623	1,422
Oper. Inc.	438	432	420	604	540	469	401	401	340	281
Depr.	95.3	80.5	106	149	125	104	77.1	85.9	77.0	66.5
Int. Exp.	39.6	41.2	47.8	76.0	61.0	42.7	20.8	23.0	21.0	15.6
Pretax Inc.	286	317	205	385	366	327	323	304	249	207
Eff. Tax Rate	36.5%	39.0%	41.7%	40.8%	41.0%	40.9%	42.6%	41.5%	40.8%	42.0%
Net Inc.	179	191	117	228	216	193	186	178	148	120
S&P Core Earnings	162	146	73.6	NA	NA	NA	NA	NA	NA	NA

Balance Sheet & Other Fin. Data (Million $)

	2003	2002	2001	2000	1999	1998	1997	1996	1995	1994
Cash	39.3	30.5	33.2	89.4	137	90.6	52.3	49.9	26.0	79.0
Curr. Assets	286	286	358	605	609	520	401	437	367	376
Total Assets	1,553	1,507	1,423	2,070	1,840	1,829	1,177	1,303	1,054	1,021
Curr. Liab.	355	428	276	426	505	419	328	375	251	300
LT Debt	663	691	694	994	934	869	339	306	303	212
Common Equity	372	221	244	384	393	366	349	425	353	362
Total Cap.	1,079	938	1,026	1,467	1,400	1,286	688	731	656	581
Cap. Exp.	14.6	12.8	13.0	37.1	39.0	44.9	34.5	56.0	31.7	20.2
Cash Flow	274	272	224	377	341	297	263	264	225	187
Curr. Ratio	0.8	0.7	1.3	1.4	1.2	1.2	1.2	1.2	1.5	1.3
% LT Debt of Cap.	61.5	73.7	67.6	67.7	66.7	67.6	49.2	41.9	46.1	36.5
% Net Inc.of Revs.	14.6	17.2	10.3	11.6	12.2	11.9	13.6	9.8	9.1	8.5
% Ret. on Assets	11.7	13.1	7.1	11.7	11.8	12.9	15.0	15.1	14.2	13.7
% Ret. on Equity	60.3	82.4	37.4	76.1	49.7	54.0	47.9	45.6	41.3	38.8

Data as orig reptd.; bef. results of disc opers/spec. items. Per share data adj. for stk. divs.; EPS diluted. E-Estimated. NA-Not Available. NM-Not Meaningful. NR-Not Ranked. UR-Under Review.

Office: 1550 Peachtree Street NW, Atlanta, GA 30309.
Telephone: 404-885-8000.
Email: investor@equifax.com
Website: http://www.equifax.com
Chrmn & CEO: T.F. Chapman.
SVP & Investor Contact: J. Dodge .

VP & CFO: D.T. Heroman.
VP & Treas: M.G. Schirk.
VP, Secy & General Counsel: K.E. Mast.
Dirs: L. A. Ault III, T. F. Chapman, J. L. Clendenin, J. E. Copeland Jr., A. W. Dahlberg, L. P. Humann, L. A. Kennedy, L. L. Prince, D. R. Riddle, L. W. Sullivan, J. M. Ward.

Founded: in 1913.
Domicile: Georgia.
Employees: 4,600.
S&P Analyst: Zaineb Bokhari/CB/JWP

Equity Office Properties Trust

Recommendation: **SELL** ★ ★ ★ ★ ★
SELL SELL HOLD BUY BUY
(as of September 09, 2003)

12-Month Target Price: **$25.00**

EOP has an approximate 0.10% weighting in the **S&P 500**

Sector: Financials
Sub-Industry: Real Estate Investment Trusts
Peer Group: REITs - Office

Summary: This REIT is the largest publicly held owner and manager of office properties in the U.S.

Quantitative Evaluations

S&P Earnings & Dividend Rank: NR

D	C	B-	B	B+	A-	A	A+

S&P Fair Value Rank: 2+

1	2	3	4	5
Lowest				Highest

Fair Value Calc.: $25.40 (Slightly Overvalued)

S&P Investability Quotient Percentile

56%

EOP scored higher than 56% of all companies for which an S&P Report is available.

Volatility: Low

Low	Average	High

Technical Evaluation: Neutral
Since 11/04, the technical indicators for EOP have been Neutral.

Relative Strength Rank: Moderate

38	
1 Lowest	Highest 99

Price as of 11/12/04: **$28.25**   **2004E S&P Core EPS:** **$0.95**

GAAP Earnings vs. Previous Year
▲ Up ▼ Down ▶ No Change

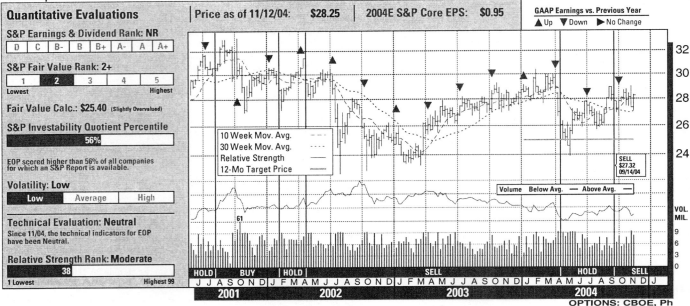

10 Week Mov. Avg.
30 Week Mov. Avg.
Relative Strength
12-Mo Target Price

SELL $27.32 09/14/04

Volume Below Avg. — Above Avg.

OPTIONS: CBOE, Ph

Analyst commentary prepared by Raymond Mathis/PMW/BK

Highlights September 15, 2004

- We see the trust's occupancy stagnating, with rental rates remaining weak. Although nationwide net absorption of office space has turned positive, we expect EOP to be affected by weak fundamentals that we see in some of its major markets. Northern California markets in particular, which account for 16% of the trust's portfolio and 22% of net operating income, have suffered the sharpest downturns in employment and, thus, occupancy and rent. They also represent EOP's highest concentration of lease expirations through 2005. Average rent on new and renewed leases of $23.25 per sq. ft. is lower than that of both expiring and terminated leases, at $26.05 and $31.72, respectively. The trust is beginning to aggressively address its concentration in weaker markets, particularly the Silicon Valley portfolio. It recently accelerated its planned disposition of non-core assets, most of which were located in San Jose. We approve of the strategy, but believe the timing is late.
- Property tax and insurance expenses have risen sharply, offsetting the benefits of lease termination fees, gains on dispositions, and share repurchases. As conditions firm, we expect declining lease termination fee income and rising tenant installation capital spending to put pressure on cash flows and the dividend.
- We see 2004 operating EPS declining to $0.94, with FFO projected at $2.20 a share. In 2005, we see flattish results, with improving occupancy offset by dilution from net property dispositions.

Investment Rationale/Risk September 15, 2004

- We recently downgraded the shares to avoid, from hold. We do not expect operating earnings to bottom until late 2004, and we view EOP's stock buyback authorization as inadequate to support the share price. We estimate that funds available for distribution will be insufficient over the next several quarters to cover the common dividend. We do not believe that a dividend cut is imminent, because the trust has been generating cash through asset sales, but we think the risk is growing.
- Risks to our recommendation and target price include the possibility that national employment growth exceeds expectations; and the possibility that a major geographic market will experience an economic surge.
- A high and rising payout ratio leads us to expect no dividend growth at least until 2006, and see longer-term dividend growth remaining well below the historical average. Assuming no dividend cut, we calculate intrinsic value at $26, based on our dividend discount model. Our estimate of net asset value per share is $24. At 10.9X estimated FFO, the shares traded recently at a modest discount to the peer average. Although strong execution in redeployment of capital from dispositions could bolster results, until we see evidence of this, we believe the stock should continue to trade at a discount to peers, due to what we see as operational underperformance. Our blended 12-month target price is $25.

Key Stock Statistics

S&P Core EPS 2005E	0.96	52-week Range	$30.40-23.90
S&P Oper. EPS 2004E	0.94	12 Month P/E	42.8
P/E on S&P Oper. EPS 2004E	30.1	Beta	0.26
S&P Oper. EPS 2005E	0.96	Shareholders	3,363
Yield (%)	7.1%	Market Cap (B)	$ 11.4
Dividend Rate/Share	2.00	Shares Outstanding (M)	402.9

Value of $10,000 invested five years ago: **$ 16,822**

Dividend Data Dividends have been paid since 1997

Amount ($)	Date Decl.	Ex-Div. Date	Stock of Record	Payment Date
0.500	Dec. 04	Dec. 11	Dec. 15	Dec. 31 '03
0.500	Mar. 15	Mar. 29	Mar. 31	Apr. 15 '04
0.500	Jun. 15	Jun. 28	Jun. 30	Jul. 15 '04
0.500	Sep. 15	Sep. 28	Sep. 30	Oct. 15 '04

Revenues/Earnings Data Fiscal year ending December 31

Revenues (Million $)

	2004	2003	2002	2001	2000	1999
1Q	796.2	829.3	873.4	666.2	468.7	475.1
2Q	795.5	811.0	872.9	668.9	496.9	481.2
3Q	790.7	806.2	875.2	893.7	641.3	491.4
4Q	—	828.8	884.5	901.4	657.2	494.5
Yr.	—	3,196	3,506	3,130	2,264	1,942

Earnings Per Share ($)

	2004	2003	2002	2001	2000	1999
1Q	0.23	0.33	0.51	0.39	0.37	0.30
2Q	0.24	0.30	0.41	0.40	0.48	0.36
3Q	-0.33	0.28	0.41	0.49	0.34	0.32
4Q	E0.24	0.45	0.42	0.30	0.35	0.68
Yr.	E0.94	1.26	1.75	1.58	1.53	1.52

Next earnings report expected: early-February Source: S&P, Company Reports
EPS Estimates based on S&P Operating Earnings; historical GAAP earnings are as reported.

STANDARD &POOR'S

Equity Office Properties Trust

Stock Report
November 13, 2004
NYSE Symbol: **EOP**

Recommendation: **SELL** ★ ★ ☆ ☆ ☆   12-Month Target Price: **$25.00** (as of September 09, 2003)

Business Summary September 15, 2004

Equity Office Properties Trust is the largest publicly held owner and operator of U.S. office buildings, in terms both of market capitalization and square footage. The trust's strategy is to achieve sustainable long-term growth in cash flow and portfolio value.

At December 31, 2003, EOP owned or had interests in 684 office properties, with 122.3 million rentable sq. ft. of space; and in 75 industrial properties; with 5.8 million sq. ft. The office properties, by rentable sq. ft., were about 42.3% in central business districts and 57.7% in suburban markets. Occupancy levels at EOP's office properties have trended down in recent years, from 95% at the end of 1998 to 93.7% at year-end 1999, 94.6% at year-end 2000, 91.8% at December 31, 2001, 89.9% at year-end 2002, and 86.6% at year-end 2003.

The trust owns a geographically diversified portfolio, with properties in 18 states and the District of Columbia. At year-end 2003, EOP's largest markets for its office properties were San Francisco (9.0% of rentable sq. ft., 10.7% of annualized rent), San Jose (7.1%, 8.5%), Boston (10.3%, 13.9%), Seattle (8.2%, 7.4%), New York (4.1%, 7.9%), Chicago (9.2%, 8.1%), Los Angeles (5.6%, 5.6%), and Washington, DC (4.9%, 5.6%). No city accounted for over 5% of annualized rent.

EOP believes internal growth in future periods will come from leasing of vacant space, reinvesting capital gains from disposition of non-core assets, completion and lease-up of development properties, and achieving economies of scale. At December 31, 2003, 13.4% of the trust's office space was vacant, and 0.4 million sq. ft. of projects were under development. In addition, EOP owns undeveloped land on which it could develop office space if market conditions warrant, assuming that it could obtain needed permits and licenses.

The trust plans to concentrate its capital in 15 or 20 core markets with prospects for employment growth, and it believes it can best position itself to outperform its competition. To that end, in 2003, it disposed of 53 office properties, two industrial properties, and four land parcels for about $922.1 million. In 2002, EOP disposed of 45 office properties, four parking facilities, two industrial properties and three land parcels in various transactions, for a total of about $508.3 million.

EOP acquired two office properties in 2003, for about $183.2 million. In 2002, it acquired two office buildings containing 3.1 million sq. ft., for about $92.3 million. The trust significantly expanded its operations with the $7.3 billion July 2001 acquisition of Spieker Properties, adding 391 office properties and 98 industrial properties. In 1997, the acquisition of Beacon Properties for $4.3 billion added 130 properties and 21 million sq. ft. In 2000, the trust acquired Cornerstone Properties, for $2.7 billion. Cornerstone, an office REIT, owned 86 U.S. office properties, totaling over 18.5 million sq. ft.

Company Financials Fiscal Year ending December 31

Per Share Data ($)

(Year Ended December 31)	2003	2002	2001	2000	1999	1998	1997	1996	1995	1994
Tangible Bk. Val.	24.96	24.67	27.09	24.01	26.91	24.56	24.80	14.28	NA	NA
Earnings	1.26	1.75	1.58	1.53	1.52	1.24	1.11	0.91	NA	NA
S&P Core Earnings	1.24	1.59	1.77	NA	NA	NA	NA	NA	NA	NA
Dividends	2.00	2.00	1.90	1.71	1.58	1.38	0.56	NA	NA	NA
Payout Ratio	159%	114%	120%	112%	61%	111%	50%	NA	NA	NA
Prices - High	29.30	31.36	33.19	33.50	29.37	32.00	34.68	NA	NA	NA
- Low	23.31	22.78	26.20	22.87	20.81	20.18	21.00	NA	NA	NA
P/E Ratio - High	23	18	21	22	11	26	31	NA	NA	NA
- Low	18	13	17	15	8	16	19	NA	NA	NA

Income Statement Analysis (Million $)

	2003	2002	2001	2000	1999	1998	1997	1996	1995	1994
Rental Income	2,537	2,715	2,426	1,733	1,493	1,538	1,127	503	NA	NA
Mortgage Income	Nil	Nil	Nil	36.2	14.2	11.7	23.1	9.85	NA	NA
Total Income	3,196	3,506	3,130	2,228	1,942	1,680	1,451	670	NA	NA
General Exp.	858	137	767	865	751	664	838	422	NA	NA
Interest Exp.	820	815	734	526	414	339	275	111	NA	NA
Prov. for Losses	Nil	Nil	Nil	Nil	Nil	Nil	Nil	Nil	NA	NA
Depr.	716	684	575	427	359	306	253	135	NA	NA
Net Inc.	549	732	630	473	442	357	282	134	NA	NA
S&P Core Earnings	490	660	654	NA	NA	NA	NA	NA	NA	NA

Balance Sheet & Other Fin. Data (Million $)

	2003	2002	2001	2000	1999	1998	1997	1996	1995	1994
Cash	69.4	58.5	61.1	53.3	2.30	67.0	229	31.5	NA	NA
Total Assets	24,189	25,247	25,808	18,794	14,046	14,261	11,752	5,009	NA	NA
Real Estate Invest.	25,439	25,164	24,816	17,619	13,203	13,684	11,041	NA	NA	NA
Loss Reserve	Nil	Nil	Nil	Nil	Nil	Nil	Nil	NA	NA	NA
Net Invest.	22,861	23,086	23,322	16,641	13,438	13,332	10,976	4,843	NA	NA
ST Debt	334	1,008	130	159	187	1,332	2,041	240	NA	NA
Capitalization:										
Debt	11,479	11,743	11,859	8,644	5,665	4,693	2,243	1,358	NA	NA
Equity	9,733	10,209	10,445	7,453	6,211	7,052	6,205	3,059	NA	NA
Total	23,214	24,261	24,772	17,930	13,375	13,077	9,403	4,662	NA	NA
% Earn & Depr/Assets	5.1	5.5	5.4	5.4	5.7	5.1	6.4	NA	NA	NA
Price Times Book Value:										
Hi	1.2	1.3	1.2	1.4	1.1	1.3	1.4	NA	NA	NA
Low	0.9	0.9	1.0	0.9	0.8	0.8	0.9	NA	NA	NA

Data as orig. reptd. (pro forma in 1996); bef. results of disc. opers. and/or spec. items. Per share data adj. for stk. divs.; EPS diluted (primary prior to 1998). E-Estimated. NA-Not Available. NM-Not Meaningful. NR-Not Ranked.

Office: Two North Riverside Plaza, Chicago, IL 60606-2621.
Telephone: 312-466-3300.
Website: http://www.equityoffice.com
Chrmn: S. Zell.
Pres & CEO: R. Kincaid.
COO & EVP: P. Owen, Jr.

EVP & CFO: M.C. Williams.
EVP, Secy & General Counsel: S.M. Stevens.
Investor Contact: C. Shipstead 312-466-4336.
Trustees: T. E. Dobrowski, W. M. Goodyear, J. D. Harper, Jr., R. D. Kincaid, D. K. McKown, S. Z. Rosenberg, E. N. Sidman, S. Zell, J. H. van der Vlist.

Founded: in 1996.
Domicile: Maryland.
Employees: 2,400.
S&P Analyst: Raymond Mathis/PMW/BK

Equity Residential

Recommendation: **SELL** ★ ★ ★ ★ ★
SELL | SELL | HOLD | BUY | BUY

12-Month Target Price: $28.00
(as of November 02, 2004)

EQR has an approximate 0.09% weighting in the **S&P 500**

Sector: Financials
Sub-Industry: Real Estate Investment Trusts
Peer Group: REITs - Residential

Summary: This equity REIT (formerly Equity Residential Properties Trust) owns and operates a nationally diversified portfolio of apartment properties.

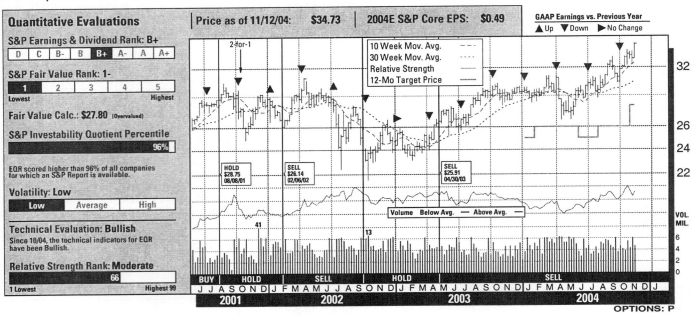

Quantitative Evaluations

S&P Earnings & Dividend Rank: B+

| D | C | B- | B | B+ | A- | A | A+ |

S&P Fair Value Rank: 1-

| 1 | 2 | 3 | 4 | 5 |
Lowest — Highest

Fair Value Calc.: $27.80 (Overvalued)

S&P Investability Quotient Percentile 96%

EQR scored higher than 96% of all companies for which an S&P Report is available.

Volatility: Low

| Low | Average | High |

Technical Evaluation: Bullish
Since 10/04, the technical indicators for EQR have been Bullish.

Relative Strength Rank: Moderate
66
1 Lowest — Highest 99

Price as of 11/12/04: $34.73   **2004E S&P Core EPS:** $0.49

Price chart legend:
- 10 Week Mov. Avg.
- 30 Week Mov. Avg.
- Relative Strength
- 12-Mo Target Price

GAAP Earnings vs. Previous Year ▲ Up ▼ Down ▶ No Change

Chart annotations:
HOLD $28.75 08/08/01
SELL $26.14 02/06/02
SELL $25.91 04/30/03

Volume Below Avg. — Above Avg.

BUY | HOLD | SELL | HOLD | SELL

2001 | 2002 | 2003 | 2004

OPTIONS: P

Analyst commentary prepared by Raymond Mathis/CB/GG

Highlights September 10, 2004

- Home ownership is at an all-time high, while low mortgage rates have continued to persuade many apartment tenants to buy homes at a near record pace. Relatively high property prices, coupled with historically inexpensive construction loans, should provide a solid foundation for new residential construction, potentially leading to oversupply in many areas. We think employment growth will be insufficient to raise household formations to levels needed to match robust housing unit construction. Thus, we see a supply/demand disequilibrium leading to only a modest improvement in net effective rents, as the trust seeks to stabilize occupancy.

- With strong condo demand boosting the value of apartments suitable for conversion, EQR has been able to divest several properties at what we consider premium prices, but has found limited opportunity to redeploy proceeds. Although this strategy could potentially produce big one-time gains, it could have a dilutive impact on per share results in subsequent periods.

- With operating expenses projected to rise, we forecast 2004 EPS from property operations of $0.47, with funds from operations (FFO) per share of $2.18. For 2005, we see improvement to operating EPS of $0.55, with FFO of $2.26.

Investment Rationale/Risk September 10, 2004

- We believe the shares are trading at a premium to their intrinsic value, and think declining operating earnings and worrisome industry fundamentals could lead investors to reassess long-term growth expectations for the trust. Our model predicts EQR will have difficulty covering its common dividend consistently until mid-2005 at the earliest.

- Risks to our recommendation and target price include the potential for faster than expected increases in interest rates to abruptly curtail single-family home sales and/or new housing construction. Also, higher than expected levels of household formation could boost demand.

- Our dividend discount model assumes dividend growth resuming in 2006, and gradually ratcheting up to historical levels, leading to our intrinsic value calculation of $26 a share. We also calculate net asset value at about $26 a share, assuming EQR could liquidate its properties in an orderly fashion. Using these two metrics, our 12-month target price is $26, and we would avoid the shares.

Key Stock Statistics

S&P Core EPS 2005E	0.55	52-week Range	$34.83-26.65
S&P Oper. EPS 2004E	0.47	12 Month P/E	26.3
P/E on S&P Oper. EPS 2004E	73.9	Beta	0.31
S&P Oper. EPS 2005E	0.55	Shareholders	55,000
Yield (%)	5.0%	Market Cap (B)	$ 9.8
Dividend Rate/Share	1.73	Shares Outstanding (M)	282.8

Value of $10,000 invested five years ago: **$ 21,676**

Dividend Data Dividends have been paid since 1993

Amount ($)	Date Decl.	Ex-Div. Date	Stock of Record	Payment Date
0.432	Nov. 25	Dec. 17	Dec. 19	Jan. 09 '04
0.432	Feb. 19	Mar. 17	Mar. 19	Apr. 09 '04
0.432	May. 19	Jun. 16	Jun. 18	Jul. 09 '04
0.432	Aug. 23	Sep. 15	Sep. 17	Oct. 08 '04

Revenues/Earnings Data Fiscal year ending December 31

Revenues (Million $)

	2004	2003	2002	2001	2000	1999
1Q	462.7	448.5	498.8	537.9	485.4	416.2
2Q	488.6	455.9	502.7	544.4	493.1	422.3
3Q	491.5	459.4	499.6	552.4	537.0	435.2
4Q	—	459.5	492.9	536.5	532.2	479.6
Yr.	—	1,823	1,994	2,171	2,030	1,753

Earnings Per Share ($)

	2004	2003	2002	2001	2000	1999
1Q	0.12	0.13	0.28	0.40	0.29	0.27
2Q	0.13	0.17	0.32	0.28	0.48	0.29
3Q	0.07	0.15	0.23	0.26	0.53	0.28
4Q	E0.12	0.02	0.43	0.43	0.37	0.32
Yr.	E0.47	0.43	0.78	1.36	1.67	1.15

Next earnings report expected: early-February Source: S&P, Company Reports
EPS Estimates based on S&P Operating Earnings; historical GAAP earnings are as reported.

Recommendation: **SELL** ★ ★ ☆ ☆ ☆   12-Month Target Price: **$28.00** (as of November 02, 2004)

Business Summary September 10, 2004

Equity Residential (formerly Equity Residential Properties Trust) acquires, owns, manages and operates multifamily residential properties through its 92.7% interest in its operating limited partnership. It is the largest publicly traded U.S. REIT owner of multifamily properties. At December 31, 2003, EQR owned or had interests in 968 multifamily properties with 207,506 units in 34 states. The trust adopted its current name in May 2002.

EQR's properties fall into three categories: garden, mid/high-rise, and ranch. Garden-style properties have two or three floors, while mid-rise/high-rise properties have more than three floors. The two types typically provide residents with amenities such as clubhouses, swimming pools, laundry facilities, and cable television access. Ranch-style properties, defined as single-story properties, generally do not provide additional amenities for residents. EQR also owned one military housing property.

At the end of 2003, the trust's 614 garden-style properties each had an average of 265 units, and an average occupancy rate of 92.4%. The 44 mid/high-rise properties had an average of 291 units, and an average occupancy rate of 86.4%. The 309 ranch properties had an average of 91 units, and an occupancy rate of 91.1%.

The company seeks to maximize both current income and long-term growth in income, thereby increasing: the value of its properties; distributions to common shares; and shareholder value. EQR's strategies for accomplishing these objectives are: maintaining and increasing property occupancy while increasing rental rates; controlling expenses; maintaining a ratio of debt to total market cap of less than 50%; strategically acquiring and disposing of properties; co-investing in the development of multifamily properties; entering into joint ventures to own properties; and strategically investing in various businesses that will enhance services for the properties.

Acquisitions have played an integral part in EQR's growth. The trust uses a market database to evaluate acquisition opportunities, letting it review the primary economic indicators of various markets in which it currently operates, and in which it plans to expand. In 2003, EQR acquired 17 properties containing 5,200 units.

The trust continually reviews its property portfolio, disposing of properties located in markets that it believes will be unable to deliver long-term growth. Factors that influence a decision to dispose of a property include potential increases in new construction, and areas in which the economy is expected to decline substantially. In 2003, it sold 96 properties containing 23,486 units.

With apartment tenants on relatively short leases compared to those of commercial and industrial properties, apartment REITs are generally more sensitive to changes in market conditions than REITs in other property categories. Results could be hurt by new construction that adds new space in excess of actual demand. Trends in home price affordability also affect both rent levels and the level of new construction, since the relative price attractiveness of owning versus renting is an important factor in consumer decision making.

Company Financials Fiscal Year ending December 31

Per Share Data ($)

(Year Ended December 31)	2003	2002	2001	2000	1999	1998	1997	1996	1995	1994
Tangible Bk. Val.	15.43	15.57	16.20	20.82	16.32	16.46	14.74	10.28	8.48	8.80
Earnings	0.43	0.78	1.36	1.67	1.15	0.82	0.88	0.85	0.84	0.67
S&P Core Earnings	0.41	0.72	1.38	NA	NA	NA	NA	NA	NA	NA
Dividends	1.73	1.73	1.68	1.58	1.47	1.36	1.27	1.20	1.09	1.01
Payout Ratio	NM	222%	124%	94%	128%	167%	145%	169%	130%	150%
Prices - High	30.30	30.96	30.45	28.62	24.18	26.28	27.50	21.75	15.93	17.56
- Low	23.12	21.55	24.80	19.34	19.06	17.34	19.87	14.12	12.43	12.87
P/E Ratio - High	70	40	22	17	21	32	31	26	19	26
- Low	54	28	18	12	17	21	23	17	15	19

Income Statement Analysis (Million $)

	2003	2002	2001	2000	1999	1998	1997	1996	1995	1994
Rental Income	1,809	1,970	2,075	1,960	1,712	1,296	708	454	372	221
Mortgage Income	Nil	Nil	8.79	11.2	12.6	18.6	20.4	12.8	9.40	5.57
Total Income	1,823	1,994	2,171	2,030	1,753	1,337	747	478	389	231
General Exp.	802	841	924	812	673	833	291	288	251	146
Interest Exp.	333	343	361	388	341	249	124	85.6	82.0	39.0
Prov. for Losses	Nil	Nil	Nil	Nil	Nil	Nil	Nil	Nil	Nil	Nil
Depr.	444	462	457	450	409	302	157	93.3	72.4	37.3
Net Inc.	212	302	474	555	394	258	177	102	67.6	34.4
S&P Core Earnings	86.4	194	374	NA	NA	NA	NA	NA	NA	NA

Balance Sheet & Other Fin. Data (Million $)

	2003	2002	2001	2000	1999	1998	1997	1996	1995	1994
Cash	524	540	449	417	114	4.00	209	147	13.0	20.0
Total Assets	11,467	11,811	12,236	12,264	11,716	10,700	7,095	2,986	2,141	1,848
Real Estate Invest.	12,874	13,046	13,016	12,591	12,239	10,942	7,121	2,984	2,187	1,963
Loss Reserve	Nil	Nil	Nil	Nil	Nil	Nil	Nil	Nil	Nil	Nil
Net Invest.	10,578	10,934	11,297	11,239	11,168	10,224	6,677	2,682	2,057	1,771
ST Debt	Nil	334	699	Nil	250	151	61.1	28.2	38.4	32.8
Capitalization:										
Debt	4,836	5,050	5,044	5,706	5,224	4,530	2,887	1,226	975	966
Equity	4,345	4,251	4,447	4,436	4,195	5,330	3,690	1,459	885	610
Total	10,452	10,858	11,094	11,938	11,186	9,860	6,851	2,685	1,860	1,753
% Earn & Depr/Assets	5.6	6.4	7.6	8.3	7.2	6.3	6.6	7.6	7.0	6.0
Price Times Book Value:										
Hi	2.0	2.0	1.9	1.4	1.5	1.6	1.9	2.1	1.9	2.0
Low	1.5	1.4	1.5	0.9	1.2	1.1	1.3	1.4	1.5	1.5

Data as orig reptd.; bef. results of disc opers/spec. items. Per share data adj. for stk. divs.; EPS diluted. E-Estimated. NA-Not Available. NM-Not Meaningful. NR-Not Ranked. UR-Under Review.

Office: Two North Riverside Plaza, Chicago, IL 60606.
Telephone: 312-474-1300.
Email: investorrelations@eqrworld.com
Website: http://www.equityapartments.com
Chrmn: S. Zell.
Pres & CEO: B.W. Duncan.
COO & EVP: G.A. Spector.

EVP & CFO: D. Brandin.
EVP, Chief Acctg Officer & Treas: M.J. McHugh.
Investor Contact: M. McKenna 888-879-6356.
Trustees: J. W. Alexander, C. L. Atwood, B. W. Duncan, S. O. Evans, J. D. Harper, Jr., B. A. Knox, D. Rogers, S. Z. Rosenberg, G. A. Spector, B. J. White, S. Zell.

Founded: in 1993.
Domicile: Maryland.
Employees: 6,000.
S&P Analyst: Raymond Mathis/CB/GG

Exelon

Recommendation: **HOLD** ★ ★ ★ ☆ ☆
SELL | SELL | HOLD | BUY | BUY

12-Month Target Price: $42.00
(as of November 17, 2004)

EXC has an approximate 0.25% weighting in the **S&P 500**

Sector: Utilities
Sub-Industry: Electric Utilities
Peer Group: Electric & Gas- Larger

Summary: This Chicago-based holding company was formed in October 2000 via the merger of Philadelphia-based PECO Energy and Chicago-based Unicom.

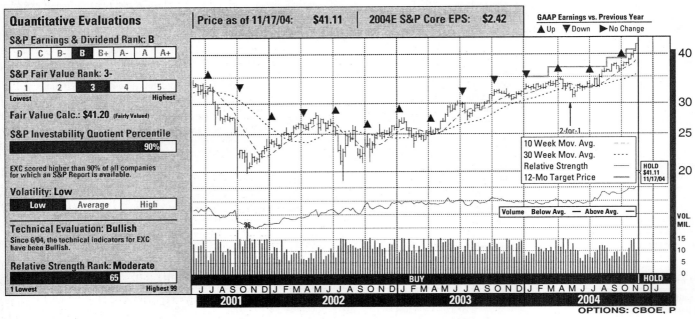

Quantitative Evaluations

S&P Earnings & Dividend Rank: B
D | C | B- | **B** | B+ | A- | A | A+

S&P Fair Value Rank: 3-
1 | 2 | **3** | 4 | 5
Lowest | | | | Highest

Fair Value Calc.: $41.20 (Fairly Valued)

S&P Investability Quotient Percentile 90%

EXC scored higher than 90% of all companies for which an S&P Report is available.

Volatility: Low
Low | Average | High

Technical Evaluation: Bullish
Since 6/04, the technical indicators for EXC have been Bullish.

Relative Strength Rank: Moderate 65
1 Lowest | Highest 99

Price as of 11/17/04: $41.11 **2004E S&P Core EPS:** $2.42

GAAP Earnings vs. Previous Year
▲ Up ▼ Down ▶ No Change

10 Week Mov. Avg.
30 Week Mov. Avg.
Relative Strength
12-Mo Target Price

HOLD $41.11 11/17/04

Volume   Below Avg. — Above Avg.

VOL. MIL.

2-for-1

BUY | HOLD

J J A S O N D | J F M A M J J A S O N D | J F M A M J J A S O N D | J F M A M J J A S O N D | J
2001 | 2002 | 2003 | 2004

OPTIONS: CBOE, P

Analyst commentary prepared by Justin McCann/PMW/GG

Highlights 17-NOV-04

- The STARS recommendation for Exelon Corporation (EXC) has recently been changed to 3 from 4. The Highlights section of this Stock Report will be updated accordingly.

Investment Rationale/Risk 17-NOV-04

- The Investment Rationale/Risk section of this Stock Report will be updated shortly. For the latest news story on Exelon Corporation (EXC) from Market-Scope, see below.

11/17/04 03:22 pm EST... S&P DOWNGRADES SHARES OF EXELON CORP TO HOLD FROM BUY (EXC 41.13***): Following their recent rise, we believe EXC's shares are fairly valued now at an approximate peer-P/E multiple. We expect the company's proposed 2005 contribution of $2B to its underfunded pension plan (which requires board approval) would be funded by $1.4B in new debt, taking into account the tax benefit of the contribution. We calculate the action would increase annual free cash flow by about $160M and could add about $0.05 to annual EPS. We are raising our 12-month target price by $1 to $42, but our EPS estimates remain $2.83 for '04 and $2.95 for '04. /J.McCann

Key Stock Statistics

S&P Core EPS 2005E	2.60	52-week Range	$42.42-30.48
S&P Oper. EPS 2004E	2.83	12 Month P/E	15.7
P/E on S&P Oper. EPS 2004E	15.0	Beta	0.05
S&P Oper. EPS 2005E	2.95	Shareholders	180,059
Yield (%)	3.9%	Market Cap (B)	$ 27.2
Dividend Rate/Share	1.60	Shares Outstanding (M)	662.5

Value of $10,000 invested five years ago: **$ 27,394**

Dividend Data Dividends have been paid since 1902

Amount ($)	Date Decl.	Ex-Div. Date	Stock of Record	Payment Date
2-for-1	Jan. 27	May. 06	Apr. 19	May. 05 '04
0.550	Apr. 27	May. 12	May. 15	Jun. 10 '04
0.305	Jul. 29	Aug. 11	Aug. 15	Sep. 10 '04
0.400	Oct. 21	Nov. 10	Nov. 15	Dec. 10 '04

Revenues/Earnings Data Fiscal year ending December 31

Revenues (Million $)

	2004	2003	2002	2001	2000	1999
1Q	3,722	4,074	3,357	3,823	1,352	1,256
2Q	3.55	3,721	3,519	3,651	1,385	1,194
3Q	3,865	4,441	4,370	4,285	1,629	1,732
4Q	—	3,577	3,709	3,381	3,133	1,254
Yr.	—	15,812	14,955	15,140	7,499	5,437

Earnings Per Share ($)

	2004	2003	2002	2001	2000	1999
1Q	0.57	0.39	0.36	0.59	0.45	0.33
2Q	0.78	0.57	0.75	0.49	0.35	0.22
3Q	0.86	-0.15	0.85	0.58	0.69	0.61
4Q	E0.64	0.42	0.61	0.53	0.08	0.40
Yr.	E2.83	1.20	2.58	2.20	1.44	1.58

Next earnings report expected: late-January Source: S&P, Company Reports
EPS Estimates based on S&P Operating Earnings; historical GAAP earnings are as reported.

STANDARD &POOR'S

Exelon Corporation

Stock Report
November 17, 2004
NYSE Symbol: **EXC**

Recommendation: **HOLD** ★ ★ ★ ☆ ☆   12-Month Target Price: **$42.00** (as of November 17, 2004)

Business Summary August 31, 2004

Exelon Corp. was formed in October 2000, through the acquisition by Philadelphia-based PECO Energy of Chicago-based Unicom Corp. The company is head-quartered in Chicago.

EXC operates in three business segments: Energy Delivery, which consists of the retail operations of PECO Energy and ComEd; Generation, which includes the equity interests and power generation and marketing operations of Sithe Energies and AmerGen Energy; and Enterprises, which combined the competitive businesses held by PECO Energy and Unicom.

Segment contributions to net income in 2003 were: Energy Delivery, $1,170 billion ($1,268 billion in 2002); Generation, a loss of $241 million (net income of $387 million); Enterprises, a loss of $135 million (net income of $65 million); and Corporate, a loss of $1 million (a loss of $50 million).

PECO Energy provides electric service to about 1.5 million customers and gas service to about 460,000 customers in southeastern Pennsylvania, and, through a subsidiary, to two northeastern Maryland counties. ComEd provides electricity to about 3.6 million customers in Chicago and northern Illinois.

In May 1998, the Pennsylvania Public Utility Commission authorized PECO to recover $5.26 billion in stranded costs from January 1, 1999, through 2010. It also phased in the implementation of customer choice of supplier that was completed January 2, 2000. In 1997, Illinois enacted legislation requiring a phased-implementation of customer choice of supplier; this was completed May 1, 2002.

The generation segment includes Exelon Nuclear, which has direct ownership interests in 11 nuclear generating stations, consisting of 19 units (with 16,959 megawatts of generating capacity), located in Illinois, Pennsylvania, and New Jersey. In 2003, it accounted for over 50% of the generation segment's power supply. In December 2003, EXC purchased the remaining 50% of its joint venture interest in the nuclear operating company AmerGen from British Energy, for $276.5 million.

In May 2003, the Nuclear Regulatory Commission approved a 20-year extension of the operating licenses for Peach Bottom Unit 2 (to 2033) and Unit 3 (to 2034).

The generation segment, which has a 50% interest in Sithe Energies (an independent power producer), also owns 9,925 megawatts of fossil generation assets and 1,608 megawatts of hydroelectric assets, located in the Midwest (40% of capacity), the Mid-Atlantic (39%), the Northeast (12%), and Texas (9%). In November 2002, EXC acquired from Sithe, in a transaction valued at nearly $1.7 billion, power plants with 4,400 megawatts of combined generating capacity. The Exelon Power Team is a major wholesale marketer of energy. It supplies load requirements of ComEd and PECO, and markets the remainder in the wholesale and spot markets.

In November 2003, the company and Dynegy terminated an agreement (announced earlier in the month) for EXC to acquire Illinois Power from Dynegy for $2.225 billion, including the assumption of $1.8 billion of debt. The termination reflected a failure to obtain legislation required to meet the terms of the agreement.

Company Financials Fiscal Year ending December 31

Per Share Data ($)

(Year Ended December 31)	2003	2002	2001	2000	1999	1998	1997	1996	1995	1994
Tangible Bk. Val.	5.77	4.25	4.51	3.18	4.57	6.81	6.13	10.44	10.20	9.71
Earnings	1.21	2.58	2.20	1.44	1.58	1.16	0.72	1.12	1.32	0.88
S&P Core Earnings	1.74	1.64	1.49	NA	NA	NA	NA	NA	NA	NA
Dividends	0.96	0.88	0.91	0.46	0.50	0.50	0.90	0.88	0.83	0.77
Payout Ratio	80%	34%	41%	32%	32%	43%	125%	78%	62%	88%
Prices - High	33.31	28.49	35.13	35.50	25.25	21.09	13.18	16.25	15.12	15.00
- Low	23.04	18.92	19.37	16.50	15.37	9.43	9.37	11.50	12.12	11.81
P/E Ratio - High	28	11	16	25	16	18	18	15	11	17
- Low	19	7	9	11	10	8	13	10	9	13

Income Statement Analysis (Million $)

	2003	2002	2001	2000	1999	1998	1997	1996	1995	1994
Revs.	15,812	14,955	15,140	7,499	5,437	5,210	4,618	4,284	4,186	4,041
Depr.	1,126	1,340	1,449	458	237	643	581	489	457	442
Maint.	NA	NA	NA	NA	NA	NA	NA	325	308	328
Fxd. Chgs. Cov.	2.19	3.56	2.98	2.94	3.24	3.52	2.41	3.05	3.15	2.33
Constr. Credits	NA	NA	NA	Nil	4.00	3.52	21.8	19.9	27.1	22.2
Eff. Tax Rate	29.4%	37.4%	39.7%	27.3%	36.6%	37.5%	46.5%	39.7%	39.4%	36.9%
Net Inc.	793	1,670	1,416	907	619	532	337	517	610	427
S&P Core Earnings	1,142	1,062	962	NA	NA	NA	NA	NA	NA	NA

Balance Sheet & Other Fin. Data (Million $)

	2003	2002	2001	2000	1999	1998	1997	1996	1995	1994
Gross Prop.	27,578	25,904	21,526	19,886	9,412	7,228	6,574	14,945	14,696	15,247
Cap. Exp.	1,954	2,150	2,041	752	491	415	490	549	578	571
Net Prop.	20,630	17,134	13,742	12,936	5,045	4,337	3,884	9,898	10,072	11,003
Capitalization:										
LT Debt	13,576	14,580	13,492	14,398	6,098	3,269	4,325	4,371	4,626	4,900
% LT Debt	61.5	65.3	62.1	66.6	75.6	49.9	59.4	47.0	48.9	50.6
Pfd.	Nil	Nil	Nil	Nil	193	230	230	292	292	370
% Pfd.	Nil	Nil	Nil	Nil	2.39	3.51	3.20	3.10	3.10	3.80
Common	8,503	7,742	8,230	7,215	1,773	3,057	3,079	4,646	4,531	4,303
% Common	38.5	34.7	37.9	33.4	22.0	46.6	37.4	49.9	48.0	44.4
Total Cap.	26,724	26,325	26,341	26,352	10,760	9,233	9,897	13,390	13,481	13,394
% Oper. Ratio	82.2	73.1	83.9	80.5	80.7	81.5	84.6	78.9	76.0	79.5
% Earn. on Net Prop.	11.4	21.3	25.2	17.0	28.6	31.2	14.4	9.1	9.9	7.6
% Return On Revs.	5.0	11.2	9.4	12.1	11.4	10.2	7.3	12.1	14.6	10.6
% Return On Invest. Capital	10.2	10.2	9.8	9.8	10.3	14.3	6.3	6.8	3.4	6.3
% Return On Com. Equity	9.8	21.1	18.3	20.2	25.1	16.9	8.0	10.9	13.3	9.1

Data as orig reptd.; bef. results of disc opers/spec. items. Per share data adj. for stk. divs. Bold denotes basic EPS (FASB 128)-prior periods restated. E-Estimated. NA-Not Available. NM-Not Meaningful. NR-Not Ranked. UR-Under Review.

Office: 10 South Dearborn Street, Chicago, IL 60680-5379.
Telephone: 312-394-7398.
Website: http://www.exeloncorp.com
Chrmn & CEO: J.W. Rowe.
Pres & COO: O.D. Kingsley.
EVP & CFO: R.S. Shapard.

EVP & Chief Admin: P.B. Strobel.
EVP & General Counsel: R.E. Mehrberg.
Dirs: C. H. Cantu, S. W. Catherwood, D. L. Cooper, N. DeBenedictis, B. DeMars, S. L. Gin, R. H. Glanton, R. B. Greco, E. D. Jannotta, J. M. Palms, J. Rowe, R. Rubin.

Founded: in 1887.
Domicile: Pennsylvania.
Employees: 20,000.
S&P Analyst: Justin McCann/PMW/GG

Express Scripts

Recommendation: **HOLD** ★★★ ★ ★
SELL SELL HOLD BUY BUY
(as of November 15, 2004)

12-Month Target Price: $81.00

ESRX has an approximate 0.05% weighting in the **S&P 500**

Sector: Health Care
Sub-Industry: Health Care Services
Peer Group: Pharmacy Benefits Management

Summary: ESRX offers prescription benefits, vision care, and disease state management services.

Quantitative Evaluations

S&P Earnings & Dividend Rank: B+

D	C	B-	B	B+	A-	A	A+

S&P Fair Value Rank: 3+

1	2	3	4	5
Lowest				Highest

Fair Value Calc.: $73.40 (Slightly Overvalued)

S&P Investability Quotient Percentile

91%

ESRX scored higher than 91% of all companies for which an S&P Report is available.

Volatility: Average

Low	Average	High

Technical Evaluation: Bullish

Since 11/04, the technical indicators for ESRX have been Bullish.

Relative Strength Rank: Strong

82

1 Lowest		Highest 99

Price as of 11/15/04: $75.05 | **2004E S&P Core EPS:** $3.57

GAAP Earnings vs. Previous Year
▲ Up ▼ Down ► No Change

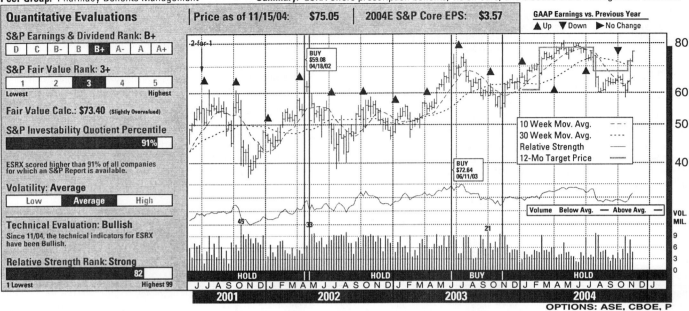

10 Week Mov. Avg. ‑ ‑ ‑
30 Week Mov. Avg. ·······
Relative Strength
12-Mo Target Price

Volume Below Avg. — Above Avg. ▬

OPTIONS: ASE, CBOE, P

Analyst commentary prepared by Phillip M. Seligman/PMW/JWP

Highlights November 15, 2004

- We look for 2005 revenue to grow about 11%, to $16.7 billion, from our 2004 estimate of $15.1 billion, based on drug price inflation, new drugs, assuming benefits from the company's participation in the new Medicare drug discount card program, and new business wins. We think another revenue driver, to a lesser extent, may be increased drug utilization among customers with the company in 2004.

Investment Rationale/Risk November 15, 2004

- We see ESRX continuing to benefit from a desire on the part of health benefit plan sponsors to restrain the rapid growth of pharmaceutical costs, and from favorable demographic trends and the Medicare Modernization Act. We expect EBITDA per script and cash flow growth to be supported by growth in members and utilization, new value-added services, and other productivity gains. However, we note that frequent negative press about the pharmacy benefit management industry, part of which we think is due to the lack of transparency of operations, and frequent government probes, which we believe may lead to increased regulatory oversight, make the shares volatile.

- Risks to our recommendation and target price include intensifying competition, pressures on margins from clients seeking greater discounts and/or enhanced services, increased government oversight and adverse regulatory changes, potential loss of key client and provider accounts, and risks due to investigations. If ESRX were to be found guilty of defrauding New York State or if probes by 22 other states and the District of Columbia were to find improper practices, we think it could lose government and business accounts.

- ESRX's new business wins suggest to us that the positive factors that we see outweigh investor concerns about litigation by New York State and probes under way. Based on our view of fundamentals, our forward P/E multiple is on a par with that forecast for the S&P 500. Our 12-month target price of $81 is equal to 17.5X our 2005 EPS estimate.

Key Stock Statistics

S&P Core EPS 2005E	4.53	52-week Range	$81.20-58.30
S&P Oper. EPS 2004E	3.90	12 Month P/E	22.1
P/E on S&P Oper. EPS 2004E	19.5	Beta	0.05
S&P Oper. EPS 2005E	4.65	Shareholders	53,797
Yield (%)	Nil	Market Cap (B)	$ 5.7
Dividend Rate/Share	Nil	Shares Outstanding (M)	76.0

Value of $10,000 invested five years ago: $ 27,657

Dividend Data

No cash dividends have been paid.

Revenues/Earnings Data Fiscal year ending December 31

Revenues (Million $)

	2004	2003	2002	2001	2000	1999
1Q	3,628	3,224	2,540	2,091	1,476	899.1
2Q	3,780	3,334	3,178	2,247	1,653	996.8
3Q	3,768	3,249	3,177	2,381	1,736	1,084
4Q	—	3,488	3,366	2,610	1,922	1,309
Yr.	—	13,295	12,261	9,329	6,787	4,288

Earnings Per Share ($)

	2004	2003	2002	2001	2000	1999
1Q	0.89	0.75	0.55	0.35	0.28	0.20
2Q	0.83	0.74	0.61	0.38	-0.98	0.10
3Q	0.80	0.81	0.68	0.40	0.32	0.23
4Q	E1.08	0.86	0.72	0.43	0.26	1.52
Yr.	E3.90	3.17	2.56	1.56	-0.11	2.13

Next earnings report expected: late-February Source: S&P, Company Reports
EPS Estimates based on S&P Operating Earnings; historical GAAP earnings are as reported.

Express Scripts, Inc.

Recommendation: **HOLD** ★ ★ ★ ☆ ☆   12-Month Target Price: **$81.00** (as of November 15, 2004)

Business Summary November 15, 2004

Express Scripts is one of the largest U.S. pharmacy benefits managers (PBM). The company provides a full range of pharmacy benefit management services, including retail drug card programs, mail pharmacy services, drug formulary management programs and other clinical management programs for thousands of client groups that include HMOs, health insurers, third-party administrators, employers, union-sponsored benefit plans and government health programs. The five largest clients accounted for 18% of revenues in 2003.

The company's PBM services (98.5% of 2003 revenues) involve management of outpatient prescription drug usage through the application of managed care principles and advanced information technologies. Core services include retail pharmacy network administration, mail pharmacy services, benefit plan design, formulary administration, electronic point-of-sale claims processing, and drug utilization review. Advanced PBM services include development of formulary compliance and therapeutic substitution programs, therapy management services such as prior authorization, therapy guidelines, step therapy protocols and formulary interventions, management information reporting and analytic capabilities, provider profiling, and outcomes assessments.

ESRX's PBM net revenues generally include administrative fees, dispensing fees, and ingredient costs of pharmaceuticals dispensed from retail pharmacies included in one of its networks or from one of its mail pharmacies. The company records the associated costs in the cost of revenues. In cases in which ESRX only administers the contracts between clients and client retail pharmacy networks, net revenues include only administrative fees.

In 2003, the company processed 378.9 million network pharmacy claims, 32.3 million mail pharmacy prescriptions, and 3.6 million specialty distribution prescriptions.

As of April 2003, ESRX operated nine mail pharmacies, located in Missouri, Arizona, New Mexico, Pennsylvania, New Jersey, and New York.

Non-PBM services (1.5%) include outpatient infusion therapy, specialty distribution, and vision care services. In June 2001, the company entered into an agreement to sell its infusion services branch offices, and discontinued its acute home infusion services.

Company Financials Fiscal Year ending December 31

Per Share Data ($)

(Year Ended December 31)	2003	2002	2001	2000	1999	1998	1997	1996	1995	1994
Tangible Bk. Val.	NM	NM	NM	NM	NM	NM	3.08	2.52	1.29	0.89
Cash Flow	3.86	3.59	2.57	0.92	3.12	1.03	0.66	0.50	0.37	0.27
Earnings	3.17	2.56	1.56	-0.11	2.13	0.64	0.51	0.40	0.30	0.21
S&P Core Earnings	3.01	2.40	1.44	NA	NA	NA	NA	NA	NA	NA
Dividends	Nil	Nil	Nil	Nil	Nil	Nil	Nil	Nil	Nil	Nil
Payout Ratio	Nil	Nil	Nil	Nil	Nil	Nil	Nil	Nil	Nil	Nil
Prices - High	75.45	65.90	61.45	53.50	52.75	34.50	16.18	14.50	13.75	9.56
- Low	46.33	38.65	34.84	14.25	22.18	13.50	7.81	6.62	6.25	5.50
P/E Ratio - High	24	26	39	NM	25	54	32	36	46	46
- Low	15	15	22	NM	10	21	15	17	21	26

Income Statement Analysis (Million $)

	2003	2002	2001	2000	1999	1998	1997	1996	1995	1994
Revs.	13,295	12,261	9,329	6,787	4,288	2,825	1,231	774	544	385
Oper. Inc.	503	454	317	279	241	116	59.3	46.3	33.3	23.8
Depr.	54.0	82.0	80.1	78.6	74.0	27.0	10.5	6.71	4.38	3.32
Int. Exp.	41.4	42.2	34.2	47.9	60.0	20.2	0.23	0.06	0.09	0.07
Pretax Inc.	405	330	208	-4.47	265	76.2	54.7	43.1	29.6	20.8
Eff. Tax Rate	38.2%	38.2%	39.9%	NM	40.7%	44.0%	38.9%	39.3%	38.2%	38.8%
Net Inc.	251	204	125	-8.02	157	42.7	33.4	26.1	18.3	17.7
S&P Core Earnings	239	192	115	NA	NA	NA	NA	NA	NA	NA

Balance Sheet & Other Fin. Data (Million $)

	2003	2002	2001	2000	1999	1998	1997	1996	1995	1994
Cash	396	191	178	53.2	283	123	64.2	79.6	11.5	5.70
Curr. Assets	1,560	1,394	1,213	998	1,066	657	364	263	144	92.8
Total Assets	3,409	3,207	2,500	2,277	2,487	1,095	403	300	164	108
Curr. Liab.	1,626	1,544	1,246	1,116	1,100	539	198	135	86.0	55.9
LT Debt	455	563	346	396	636	306	Nil	Nil	Nil	Nil
Common Equity	1,194	1,003	832	705	699	250	204	164	77.4	52.5
Total Cap.	1,649	1,565	1,178	1,102	1,335	556	204	166	78.3	52.5
Cap. Exp.	53.1	61.3	57.3	80.2	37.0	23.9	13.0	9.48	8.05	6.35
Cash Flow	305	286	205	70.6	231	69.7	43.9	32.9	22.7	16.0
Curr. Ratio	1.0	0.9	1.0	0.9	1.0	1.2	1.8	2.0	1.7	1.7
% LT Debt of Cap.	27.6	35.9	29.4	36.0	47.6	55.1	Nil	Nil	Nil	Nil
% Net Inc.of Revs.	1.9	1.7	1.3	NM	3.7	1.5	2.7	3.4	3.4	3.3
% Ret. on Assets	7.6	7.1	5.2	NM	8.8	5.7	9.5	11.3	13.4	13.8
% Ret. on Equity	22.8	22.2	16.3	NM	33.2	18.8	18.2	21.7	28.2	28.0

Data as orig reptd.; bef. results of disc opers/spec. items. Per share data adj. for stk. divs.; EPS diluted. E-Estimated. NA-Not Available. NM-Not Meaningful. NR-Not Ranked. UR-Under Review.

Office: 13900 Riverport Drive, Maryland Heights, MO 63043-4804.
Telephone: 314-770-1666.
Email: investor.relations@express-scripts.com
Website: http://www.express-scripts.com
Chrmn & CEO: B.A. Toan.
Pres: G. Paz.
COO: D.A. Lowenberg.

SVP & CFO: E.J. Stiften.
SVP, Secy & General Counsel: T.M. Boudreau.
Investor Contact: D. Myers 314-702-7173.
Dirs: S. L. Bascomb, F. J. Borelli, M. C. Breen, T. P. Mac Mahon, J. O. Parker, Jr., S. K. Skinner, S. Sternberg, B. A. Toan, H. L. Waltman, N. Zachary.

Founded: in 1986.
Domicile: Delaware.
Employees: 8,575.
S&P Analyst: Phillip M. Seligman/PMW/JWP

Exxon Mobil

Recommendation: **BUY** ★★★★★ 12-Month Target Price: $57.00
SELL SELL HOLD BUY BUY
(as of October 10, 2004)

XOM has an approximate 2.97% weighting in the **S&P 500**

Sector: Energy
Sub-Industry: Integrated Oil & Gas
Peer Group: Supermajor Integrated Oil & Gas

Summary: XOM, formed through the merger of Exxon and Mobil in late 1999, is the world's largest publicly owned integrated oil company.

Quantitative Evaluations

| Price as of 11/12/04: | $50.42 | 2004E S&P Core EPS: | $3.68 |

S&P Earnings & Dividend Rank: A-

| D | C | B- | B | B+ | A- | A | A+ |

S&P Fair Value Rank: 1+

| 1 | 2 | 3 | 4 | 5 |
| Lowest | | | | Highest |

Fair Value Calc.: $41.20 (Overvalued)

S&P Investability Quotient Percentile

100%

XOM scored higher than 100% of all companies for which an S&P Report is available.

Volatility: Low

| Low | Average | High |

Technical Evaluation: Bullish
Since 8/04, the technical indicators for XOM have been Bullish.

Relative Strength Rank: Moderate

52

| 1 Lowest | Highest 99 |

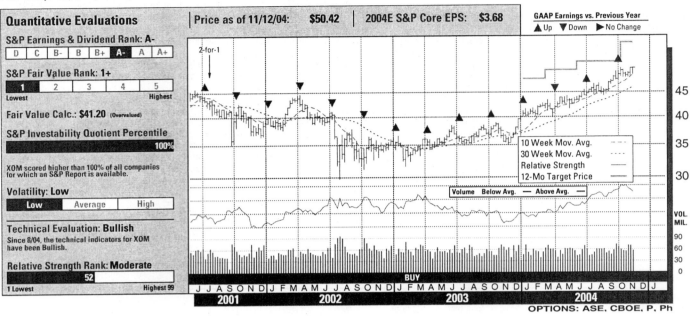

GAAP Earnings vs. Previous Year
▲ Up ▼ Down ► No Change

- 10 Week Mov. Avg.
- 30 Week Mov. Avg.
- Relative Strength
- 12-Mo Target Price

Volume Below Avg. — Above Avg. —

OPTIONS: ASE, CBOE, P, Ph

Analyst commentary prepared by T. J. Vital/PMW/DRJ

Highlights November 01, 2004

- Improved refining and chemical margins and throughputs, aided by XOM's ability to refine lower quality feedstocks (about 85% of its crude oil feedstocks are sour), boosted third quarter operating earnings 71%, to $6.23 billion ($0.96 a share, $0.11 above our estimate). Exploration & production earnings climbed 45%, but were slightly below our estimate, reflecting Gulf of Mexico volume losses due to Hurricane Ivan, and increased exploration expenses.

- Hydrocarbon production rose about 1% in the third quarter, slightly below our estimate, reflecting natural field declines, increased maintenance, asset sales, and weather-related problems in the Gulf of Mexico. We expect upstream production to be relatively flat in 2004 and 2005, but to increase over 3% annually thereafter, on contributions from developments in the U.S. and Canada, the Middle East, Russia and Africa.

- EBITDAX (EBITDA minus exploration expense) climbed 63% in 2003, on higher prices. We expect EBITDAX to grow 31% in 2004 and 6% in 2005, reflecting on strong oil and gas prices and XOM's ability to refine lower cost heavy/sour crude feedstocks.

Investment Rationale/Risk November 01, 2004

- We would buy the shares. We believe XOM's diversified, high quality asset base should help mitigate commodity price and geopolitical risk, while benefiting from improved demand as economies rebound. The shares have outperformed the S&P 500 on a total return basis over the past 20 years. We view reserve replacement as strong; we estimate the 2003 organic rate at 107%. To fund growth, the company boosted 2003 spending by $1.6 billion, to $15.5 billion (77% for E&P), and projected 2004 and 2005 spending at $15 billion to $16 billion.

- Risks to our recommendation and target price include XOM's ability to replace its reserves through the drillbit, geopolitical risk associated with upstream developments, and contingent liabilities (such as the Valdez incident).

- Our 12-month target price of $57, derived from a blend of DCF, market and peer multiple valuations, represents a P/E multiple of 15X applied our 2005 EPS estimate, a premium to peers that we think is justified by what we regard as XOM's high earnings quality and stability.

Key Stock Statistics

S&P Core EPS 2005E	3.84	52-week Range	$50.50-35.05
S&P Oper. EPS 2004E	3.66	12 Month P/E	14.0
P/E on S&P Oper. EPS 2004E	13.8	Beta	0.37
S&P Oper. EPS 2005E	3.80	Shareholders	658,249
Yield (%)	2.1%	Market Cap (B)	$325.3
Dividend Rate/Share	1.08	Shares Outstanding (M)	6451.3

Value of $10,000 invested five years ago: **$ 16,087**

Dividend Data Dividends have been paid since 1882

Amount ($)	Date Decl.	Ex-Div. Date	Stock of Record	Payment Date
0.250	Jan. 28	Feb. 09	Feb. 11	Mar. 10 '04
0.270	Apr. 28	May. 11	May. 13	Jun. 10 '04
0.270	Jul. 28	Aug. 11	Aug. 13	Sep. 10 '04
0.270	Oct. 27	Nov. 09	Nov. 12	Dec. 10 '04

Revenues/Earnings Data Fiscal year ending December 31

Revenues (Million $)

	2004	2003	2002	2001	2000	1999
1Q	67,602	63,780	43,531	57,278	54,081	26,884
2Q	70,693	57,165	50,909	56,184	55,956	29,422
3Q	76,375	59,841	54,182	52,113	58,568	33,072
4Q	—	65,952	56,211	47,300	64,132	55,961
Yr.	—	246,738	204,506	212,900	232,737	185,527

Earnings Per Share ($)

	2004	2003	2002	2001	2000	1999
1Q	0.83	0.97	0.30	0.72	0.43	0.21
2Q	0.88	0.62	0.39	0.63	0.57	0.25
3Q	0.88	0.55	0.39	0.46	0.58	0.30
4Q	E0.99	1.01	0.54	0.39	0.70	0.33
Yr.	E3.66	3.15	1.61	2.21	2.27	1.13

Next earnings report expected: late-January Source: S&P, Company Reports
EPS Estimates based on S&P Operating Earnings; historical GAAP earnings are as reported.

STANDARD &POOR'S

Exxon Mobil Corporation

Stock Report
November 13, 2004
NYSE Symbol: **XOM**

Recommendation: **BUY** ★★★★★   12-Month Target Price: **$57.00** (as of October 10, 2004)

Business Summary November 01, 2004

In late 1999, in a corporate family reunion 88 years in the making, the FTC allowed Exxon and Mobil to reunite, in one of the largest mergers in history. In 1911, the Supreme Court ordered the break-up of John D. Rockefeller's Standard Oil Trust, resulting in a spinoff of 34 companies, two of which were Standard Oil Co. of New Jersey (later Exxon) and Standard Oil Co. of New York (later Mobil). As of March 2004, XOM estimated that it had achieved about $10 billion in synergies and efficiencies from the merger.

XOM serves customers in more than 200 countries worldwide, with the U.S. contributing 30% of 2003 sales, Japan 9%, the U.K. 8%, Canada 8%, Germany 7%, and Italy 6%, and other areas 32%. Company activities include oil and natural gas exploration and production (9% of 2003 sales; 72% of 2003 segment earnings, excluding merger effects and special items); refining and marketing (83%; 20%); chemicals (8%; 8%); and other operations, such as electric power generation, coal and minerals. Through wholly owned ExxonMobil Canada Ltd. and its 69.6%-owned affiliate, Imperial Oil, XOM is the largest crude oil producer in Canada.

The company maintains the largest portfolio of proved reserves and production in North America, and is the largest net producer of oil and gas in Europe. Proved liquids reserves totaled 12.075 billion bbl. at the end of 2003, versus 11.823 billion bbl. a year earlier. Proved natural gas reserves totaled 54.769 Tcf (55.718 Tcf). Liquids production averaged 2.516 million b/d, up 0.8%. Natural gas production available for sale averaged 10.119 Bcf/d, down 3.2%. In 2003, XOM added 1.7

billion barrel oil equivalent (BOE), replacing 108% of production, excluding tar sands and property sales. Finding costs averaged $0.58 per BOE, versus $0.61 per BOE in 2002. Development costs were estimated at $3.15 per BOE in 2003 ($3.25). Finding and development costs over the past five years averaged $4.77 per BOE.

XOM is the world's largest refiner, and the second largest refiner in the U.S. At the end of 2003, the company had an ownership interest in 46 refineries in 25 countries, with 6.3 million b/d of distillation capacity (U.S. 31%, Europe 28%, SouthEast Asia 16%, Japan 12%, Canada 8%, and other 5%), and lubricant basestock capacity of 0.145 million b/d. Refinery throughput averaged 5.51 million b/d in 2003, versus 5.44 million b/d in 2002, reflecting increased runs in Europe and Asia-Pacific, on improved industry economics. Operating in more than 100 countries, the Exxon, Mobil and Esso brands served motorists at about 39,488 retail sites (36% owned/leased, 64% distributors/resellers) in 2003. Petroleum product sales averaged 7.957 million b/d in 2003 (43% motor gasoline, 31% heating oils, 10% aviation fuels, 7% heavy fuels, and 9% lubricants), versus 7.757 million b/d in 2002 (41% motor gasoline, 29% heating oils, 9% aviation fuels, 8% heavy fuels, and 13% lubricants).

The company is also a major manufacturer and marketer of basic petrochemicals, including olefins, aromatics, polyethylene and polypropylene plastics, and a wide variety of specialty products. Prime product sales totaled 26.567 million tonnes in 2003, versus 26.606 million tonnes in 2002.

Company Financials Fiscal Year ending December 31

Per Share Data ($)

(Year Ended December 31)	2003	2002	2001	2000	1999	1998	1997	1996	1995	1994
Tangible Bk. Val.	13.69	11.13	10.74	10.21	9.13	8.83	8.69	8.32	7.66	7.42
Cash Flow	4.50	2.84	3.32	3.43	2.30	2.38	2.81	2.58	2.38	2.03
Earnings	3.15	1.61	2.21	2.27	1.13	1.31	1.69	1.51	1.30	1.02
S&P Core Earnings	3.03	1.52	2.03	NA	NA	NA	NA	NA	NA	NA
Dividends	0.98	0.92	0.90	0.88	0.84	0.82	0.82	0.78	0.75	0.73
Payout Ratio	31%	57%	41%	39%	74%	63%	48%	52%	58%	71%
Prices - High	41.13	44.57	45.83	47.71	43.62	38.65	33.62	25.31	21.50	16.84
- Low	31.58	29.75	35.01	34.93	32.15	28.31	24.12	19.40	15.03	14.03
P/E Ratio - High	13	28	21	21	39	30	20	17	17	17
- Low	10	18	16	15	29	22	14	13	12	14

Income Statement Analysis (Million $)

	2003	2002	2001	2000	1999	1998	1997	1996	1995	1994
Revs.	237,054	200,949	209,417	228,439	185,527	115,417	135,142	131,543	121,804	99,683
Oper. Inc.	93,730	23,280	84,886	33,309	42,565	12,326	16,993	15,387	14,584	11,942
Depr. Depl. & Amort.	9,047	8,310	7,944	8,130	8,304	5,340	5,474	5,329	5,386	5,015
Int. Exp.	207	398	293	589	695	100	415	984	1,104	1,178
Pretax Inc.	32,660	17,719	24,688	27,493	11,295	9,241	13,204	11,916	10,442	8,037
Eff. Tax Rate	33.7%	36.7%	36.5%	40.3%	28.7%	28.3%	32.9%	37.0%	38.0%	33.6%
Net Inc.	20,960	11,011	15,105	15,990	7,910	6,440	8,460	7,510	6,470	5,100
S&P Core Earnings	20,214	10,418	14,042	NA	NA	NA	NA	NA	NA	NA

Balance Sheet & Other Fin. Data (Million $)

	2003	2002	2001	2000	1999	1998	1997	1996	1995	1994
Cash	10,626	7,229	6,547	7,080	1,761	1,461	4,047	2,969	1,789	1,775
Curr. Assets	45,960	38,291	35,681	40,399	31,141	17,593	21,192	19,910	17,318	16,460
Total Assets	174,278	152,644	143,174	149,000	144,521	92,630	96,064	95,527	91,296	87,862
Curr. Liab.	38,386	33,175	30,114	38,191	38,733	19,412	19,654	19,505	18,736	19,493
LT Debt	4,756	6,655	7,099	7,280	8,402	4,530	7,050	7,236	7,778	8,831
Common Equity	94,498	74,597	73,161	70,757	63,466	43,645	43,470	43,239	39,982	36,861
Total Cap.	119,372	100,522	99,444	97,709	91,807	63,229	66,533	66,167	62,815	59,849
Cap. Exp.	12,859	11,437	9,989	8,446	10,849	8,359	7,393	7,209	7,128	6,643
Cash Flow	30,007	19,321	23,049	24,120	16,178	11,770	13,915	12,812	11,818	10,069
Curr. Ratio	1.2	1.2	1.2	1.1	0.8	0.9	1.1	2.1	0.9	0.8
% LT Debt of Cap.	4.0	6.6	7.1	7.5	9.2	7.2	10.6	10.9	12.4	14.8
% Ret. on Assets	12.8	7.4	10.3	10.9	5.6	6.8	8.8	8.0	7.2	5.9
% Ret. on Equity	22.9	14.9	21.0	23.8	12.6	14.8	19.5	18.0	16.8	14.1

Data as orig reptd. for Exxon; bef. results of disc opers/spec. items. Per share data adj. for stk. divs.; EPS diluted (primary prior to 1998). E-Estimated. NA-Not Available. NM-Not Meaningful. NR-Not Ranked.

Office: 5959 Las Colinas Boulevard, Irving, TX 75039-2298.
Telephone: 972-444-1000.
Website: http://www.exxonmobil.com
Chrmn & CEO: L.R. Raymond.
Pres: R.W. Tillerson.

VP, Secy & Investor Contact: P.T. Mulva 972-444-1538.
VP & General Counsel: C.W. Matthews.
Dirs: M. J. Boskin, J. R. Houghton, W. R. Howell, R. C. King, P. E. Lippincott, H. J. Longwell, H. A. McKinnell, Jr., M. C. Nelson, L. R. Raymond, W. V. Shipley, R. W. Tillerson.

Founded: in 1870.
Domicile: New Jersey.
Employees: 88,300.
S&P Analyst: T. J. Vital/PMW/DRJ

Family Dollar Stores

Recommendation: **SELL** ★☆☆☆☆
SELL SELL HOLD BUY BUY

12-Month Target Price: $25.00
(as of September 30, 2004)

FDO has an approximate 0.05% weighting in the **S&P 500**

Sector: Consumer Discretionary
Sub-Industry: General Merchandise Stores
Peer Group: Discounters - General

Summary: FDO operates a chain of more than 5,000 retail discount stores in 43 states across the U.S.

Price as of 11/12/04: $31.26	**2005E S&P Core EPS:** $1.56

Quantitative Evaluations

S&P Earnings & Dividend Rank: A+

D	C	B-	B	B+	A-	A	A+

S&P Fair Value Rank: 2+

1	2	3	4	5
Lowest				Highest

Fair Value Calc.: $27.90 (Slightly Overvalued)

S&P Investability Quotient Percentile

70%

FDO scored higher than 70% of all companies
for which an S&P Report is available.

Volatility: Average

Low	Average	High

Technical Evaluation: Bullish
Since 10/04, the technical indicators for FDO
have been Bullish.

Relative Strength Rank: Strong

76

1 Lowest   Highest 99

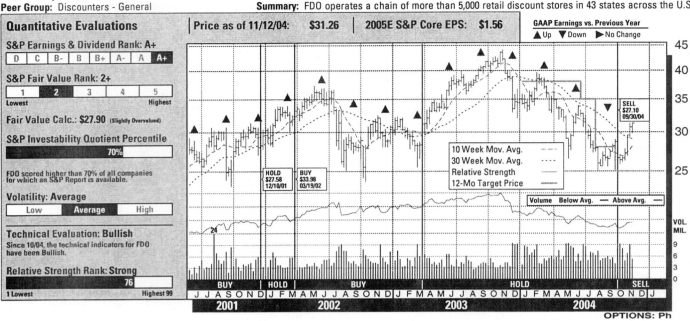

GAAP Earnings vs. Previous Year
▲ Up   ▼ Down   ► No Change

- 10 Week Mov. Avg.
- 30 Week Mov. Avg.
- Relative Strength
- 12-Mo Target Price

Volume   Below Avg. ▬ Above Avg. ▬

OPTIONS: Ph

Analyst commentary prepared by Jason N. Asaeda/MF/JWP

Highlights October 05, 2004

- We expect FY 05 (Aug.) sales to advance about 10%, to $5.8 billion. FDO plans to focus on four key initiatives to drive top-line growth: improving productivity in over 1,000 high-volume urban stores; adding excitement to the sales mix with "treasure hunt" items; installing coolers and food stamps acceptance capability in about 500 stores; and opening 500 to 560 stores (9% to 10% net square footage growth). The company expects to open 60% to 65% of its new stores in urban markets, where lead times for opening stores have historically been less predictable. Reflecting easier historical comparisons, we look for same-store sales to rise 3% to 4%. FDO believes its core low to low-middle income customers have cut back on more discretionary purchases in recent months, as many remain financially strapped despite an improved economy. As such, we expect the company to continue to emphasize consumables in its sales mix and to plan inventory of apparel and seasonal items conservatively.

- With the shift in FDO's merchandise mix toward lower margin consumables, higher shrinkage in urban market stores, rising insurance and occupancy costs, and investment costs of growth initiatives, we look for EBIT (earnings before interest and taxes) margins to narrow. The company expects the opening of its eighth distribution center this winter to mitigate anticipated increases in freight costs due to higher fuel costs.

- We see FY 05 EPS of $1.60 and S&P Core EPS of $1.56. The difference reflects estimated stock option expense.

Key Stock Statistics

S&P Oper. EPS 2005E	1.60	52-week Range	$39.90-25.09
P/E on S&P Oper. EPS 2005E	19.5	12 Month P/E	20.4
Yield (%)	1.1%	Beta	0.52
Dividend Rate/Share	0.34	Shareholders	2,305
Shares Outstanding (M)	168.3	Market Cap (B)	$ 5.3

Value of $10,000 invested five years ago: **$ 17,726**

Dividend Data Dividends have been paid since 1976

Amount ($)	Date Decl.	Ex-Div. Date	Stock of Record	Payment Date
0.085	Jan. 15	Mar. 11	Mar. 15	Apr. 15 '04
0.085	May. 14	Jun. 14	Jun. 15	Jul. 15 '04
0.085	Aug. 17	Sep. 13	Sep. 15	Oct. 15 '04
0.085	Nov. 03	Dec. 13	Dec. 15	Jan. 14 '05

Investment Rationale/Risk October 05, 2004

- With FDO's growing focus on consumables and name brands, we see an opportunity for the company to improve its share of wallet with core customers. However, our outlook is tempered by challenges seen in opening and operating urban stores. While we view favorably the company's report that urban stores have the highest levels of sales and return on investment, lead times for opening stores have historically been less predictable, and shrinkage and staffing remain widespread problems. To create a more consistent opening plan, FDO has devoted additional real estate resources to focus on small town and rural markets. It is also making changes in hiring and training practices, but results of these efforts remain to be seen. Based on uncertain payoff of turnaround initiatives over the next 12 months, we would avoid the shares.

- Risks to our recommendation and target price include a faster than expected recovery in discretionary spending by core customers, due to declining energy prices and a pickup in employment rates; gross margin expansion due to opportunistic buys; and a marked improvement in urban store shrinkage rates.

- We calculate intrinsic value of $20 based on our DCF model, which assumes a cost of capital of 8% and a terminal growth rate of 3%. Our 12-month target price of $25 blends a forward P/E multiple of 18X, a 10% discount to the stock's five-year historical average, which we see as warranted given FDO's weakened fundamentals, applied to our FY 05 EPS estimate with our DCF analysis.

Revenues/Earnings Data Fiscal year ending August 31

Revenues (Million $)

	2004	2003	2002	2001	2000	1999
1Q	1,245	1,109	977.1	820.1	713.5	628.0
2Q	1,403	1,256	1,105	1,037	858.5	752.2
3Q	1,310	1,177	1,022	887.0	770.8	678.9
4Q	1,324	1,208	1,058	920.8	789.8	692.1
Yr.	5,282	4,750	4,163	3,665	3,133	2,751

Earnings Per Share ($)

	2004	2003	2002	2001	2000	1999
1Q	0.37	0.33	0.29	0.24	0.21	0.17
2Q	0.47	0.42	0.37	0.35	0.32	0.24
3Q	0.43	0.40	0.35	0.31	0.29	0.24
4Q	0.26	0.28	0.24	0.20	0.18	0.16
Yr.	1.53	1.43	1.25	1.10	1.00	0.81

Next earnings report expected: mid-December Source: S&P, Company Reports
EPS Estimates based on S&P Operating Earnings; historical GAAP earnings are as reported.

Family Dollar Stores, Inc.

Recommendation: **SELL** ★ ★ ☆ ☆ ☆   12-Month Target Price: **$25.00** (as of September 30, 2004)

Business Summary October 05, 2004

The predecessor of Family Dollar Stores was organized in 1959 to operate a self-service retail store in Charlotte, NC. In subsequent years, the company opened additional stores, and separate corporations were established to operate them. Today, indirect subsidiaries and related entities provide distribution, trucking, operations, merchandising, marketing and other services to FDO.

At August 28, 2004, there were 5,466 self-service retail discount stores, in 44 states and the District of Columbia, operating under the Family Dollar or Family Dollar Stores names. The stores were highly concentrated, with 20 states having 100 or more stores.

FDO opened 500 stores and closed 61 locations in FY 04 (Aug.). For FY 05, the company plans to open 500 to 560 new stores, and to close 60 to 70 stores.

A typical store has about 7,500 sq. ft. to 9,500 sq. ft. of total area. The relatively small store size enables the company to open new units in rural areas and small towns, as well as in large urban areas, in locations convenient to its low and low-middle income customer base. In recent years, the company has increased its focus on urban areas with populations exceeding 75,000. In FY 05, FDO expects to open 60% to 65% of its new stores in urban markets.

The stores offer both hardlines and softlines merchandise. The former includes mainly household chemical and paper products, candy, snack and other food, health and beauty aids, electronics, housewares, toys, stationery and school supplies, seasonal items, hardware and automotive supplies. Softlines include

men's, women's, children's and infants' clothing, shoes, and domestic items such as blankets, sheets and towels. Most items of merchandise are priced under $10.

FDO does not accept credit cards or extend credit. However, following testing in selected stores during FY 03, the company began accepting PIN-based debit cards and electronic benefits in about 95% of its stores during the FY 04 first quarter.

In FY 03, hardlines accounted for 76.7% of sales. The balance of sales was softlines, with hanging apparel and shoes representing 12.4%, basic apparel 4.4%, and domestics 6.5%. Nationally advertised brand merchandise accounted for 35% of sales, Family Dollar label merchandise 4%, and merchandise sold under other labels, or which was unlabeled, the balance of sales. Irregular merchandise accounted for less than one-quarter of 1% of sales.

The company purchases its merchandise from about 1,500 suppliers. About 60% of merchandise is manufactured in the U.S., with substantially all such goods purchased directly from the manufacturer. Imported merchandise is purchased directly from the manufacturer or from importers.

In October 2002, directors authorized the repurchase of up to 5 million common shares. As of August 30, 2003, FDO had purchased 2,202,200 shares, for $65,851,000. In April 2004, directors authorized the purchase of up to an additional 5 million shares. In FY 04, the company acquired about 5.6 million shares, at a cost of $176.7 million.

Company Financials Fiscal Year ending August 31

Per Share Data ($)

(Year Ended August 31)	2004	2003	2002	2001	2000	1999	1998	1997	1996	1995
Tangible Bk. Val.	8.13	7.61	6.66	5.57	4.66	4.00	3.36	2.92	2.61	2.40
Cash Flow	2.10	1.94	1.69	1.49	1.31	1.06	0.80	0.60	0.50	0.47
Earnings	1.53	1.43	1.25	1.10	1.00	0.81	0.60	0.43	0.36	0.34
S&P Core Earnings	NA	1.39	1.22	1.08	NA	NA	NA	NA	NA	NA
Dividends	0.32	0.28	0.25	0.23	0.21	0.20	0.17	0.15	0.14	0.12
Payout Ratio	21%	20%	20%	21%	21%	24%	28%	35%	39%	36%
Prices - High	39.66	44.13	37.25	31.35	24.50	26.75	22.43	15.06	7.00	6.58
- Low	25.09	25.46	23.75	18.37	14.25	14.00	11.50	6.25	3.66	3.62
P/E Ratio - High	26	31	30	29	25	33	37	35	20	19
- Low	16	18	19	17	14	17	19	14	10	11

Income Statement Analysis (Million $)

	2004	2003	2002	2001	2000	1999	1998	1997	1996	1995
Revs.	5,282	4,750	4,163	3,665	3,133	2,751	2,362	1,995	1,715	1,547
Oper. Inc.	-4,356	478	419	366	325	266	201	151	123	117
Depr.	97.9	88.3	77.0	67.7	54.5	43.8	34.8	29.1	24.6	22.2
Int. Exp.	Nil	Nil	Nil	Nil	Nil	Nil	0.01	0.31	Nil	Nil
Pretax Inc.	414	390	342	298	271	223	166	121	99	94.0
Eff. Tax Rate	36.6%	36.5%	36.5%	36.5%	36.5%	37.1%	37.8%	38.5%	38.7%	38.5%
Net Inc.	263	247	217	190	172	140	103	74.7	60.6	58.0
S&P Core Earnings	NA	241	213	186	NA	NA	NA	NA	NA	NA

Balance Sheet & Other Fin. Data (Million $)

	2004	2003	2002	2001	2000	1999	1998	1997	1996	1995
Cash	150	207	220	21.8	43.6	95.3	134	42.5	18.8	8.90
Curr. Assets	1,225	1,156	1,056	807	751	720	647	545	508	475
Total Assets	2,167	1,986	1,755	1,400	1,244	1,095	942	780	697	636
Curr. Liab.	714	595	531	390	412	379	343	261	234	210
LT Debt	Nil	Nil	Nil	Nil	Nil	Nil	Nil	Nil	Nil	Nil
Common Equity	1,360	1,533	1,245	959	798	691	578	500	445	408
Total Cap.	1,454	1,612	1,314	1,009	832	717	599	519	463	426
Cap. Exp.	218	220	187	163	172	125	96.4	77.1	54.3	27.7
Cash Flow	361	336	294	257	227	184	138	104	85.2	80.3
Curr. Ratio	1.7	1.9	2.0	2.1	1.8	1.9	1.9	2.1	2.2	2.3
% LT Debt of Cap.	Nil	Nil	Nil	Nil	Nil	Nil	Nil	Nil	Nil	Nil
% Net Inc.of Revs.	5.0	5.2	5.2	5.2	5.5	5.1	4.4	3.7	3.6	3.8
% Ret. on Assets	12.7	13.2	13.8	14.3	14.7	13.7	12.0	10.1	9.1	9.5
% Ret. on Equity	19.7	17.8	18.9	21.6	23.1	22.1	19.2	15.8	14.3	15.0

Data as orig reptd.; bef. results of disc opers/spec. items. Per share data adj. for stk. divs.; EPS diluted. E-Estimated. NA-Not Available. NM-Not Meaningful. NR-Not Ranked. UR-Under Review.

Office: 10401 Old Monroe Road, Matthews, NC 28105.
Telephone: 704-847-6961.
Website: http://www.familydollar.com
Chrmn & CEO: H.R. Levine.
Pres & COO: R.D. Alexander, Jr.

Vice Chrmn & CFO: R.J. Kelly.
EVP, Secy & General Counsel: G.R. Mahoney, Jr.
SVP & Investor Contact: C.M. Sowers 704-847-6961.
Dirs: M. R. Bernstein, S. A. Decker, E. C. Dolby, G. A. Eisenberg, R. J. Kelly, H. R. Levine, G. R. Mahoney, Jr., J. G. Martin.

Founded: in 1959.
Domicile: Delaware.
Employees: 37,000.
S&P Analyst: Jason N. Asaeda/MF/JWP

Federal Home Loan Mortgage

Recommendation: **SELL** ★ ☆ ☆ ☆ ☆
SELL | SELL | HOLD | BUY | BUY

12-Month Target Price: $57.00
(as of November 03, 2004)

FRE has an approximate 0.43% weighting in the **S&P 500**

Sector: Financials
Sub-Industry: Thrifts & Mortgage Finance
Peer Group: Financial Cos. - Major Diversified

Summary: Federal Home Loan Mortgage (Freddie Mac), a U.S. government-sponsored enterprise (GSE), buys mortgages from lenders to increase the supply of funds for housing.

Quantitative Evaluations

S&P Earnings & Dividend Rank: A+

| D | C | B- | B | B+ | A- | A | **A+** |

S&P Fair Value Rank: 5

| 1 | 2 | 3 | 4 | **5** |
| Lowest | | | | Highest |

Fair Value Calc.: $95.70 (Undervalued)

S&P Investability Quotient Percentile

91%

FRE scored higher than 91% of all companies for which an S&P Report is available.

Volatility: Low

| **Low** | Average | High |

Technical Evaluation: Neutral

Since 11/04, the technical indicators for FRE have been Neutral.

Relative Strength Rank: Moderate

52

1 Lowest | Highest 99

Price as of 11/12/04: $69.30 | **2004E S&P Core EPS:** $4.84

Analyst commentary prepared by Erik J. Eisenstein/MF/BK

OPTIONS: ASE, CBOE, P, Ph

Highlights November 05, 2004

- For 2005, we see about 7% retained mortgage portfolio growth, reflecting more attractive investment opportunities amid higher mortgage to debt spreads. We forecast a narrower net interest yield, leading to a 9% decline in net interest income. We expect credit-related expenses to be moderate, with the housing market performing well.

- The company's derivative results are difficult to predict. We estimate that 2004 derivative results will be a drag on earnings, reflecting a much higher interest rate environment. We estimate somewhat more favorable outcomes for 2005 than for 2004, with more stable long-term interest rates expected. As a result, we see $1.1 billion in noninterest income in 2005, versus a $1.2 billion noninterest loss in 2004.

- With a forecasted 11% rise in noninterest expenses, we expect 2005 EPS to grow 40%, to $6.78, from a depressed $4.85 seen for 2004. Our 2004 and 2005 Standard & Poor's Core Earnings estimates are $4.84 and $6.77, a share, respectively.

Key Stock Statistics

S&P Core EPS 2005E	6.77	52-week Range	$69.50-53.25
S&P Oper. EPS 2004E	4.85	12 Month P/E	10.2
P/E on S&P Oper. EPS 2004E	14.3	Beta	0.16
S&P Oper. EPS 2005E	6.78	Shareholders	250,000
Yield (%)	1.7%	Market Cap (B)	$ 47.6
Dividend Rate/Share	1.20	Shares Outstanding (M)	687.0

Value of $10,000 invested five years ago: **$ 13,884**

Dividend Data Dividends have been paid since 1989

Amount ($)	Date Decl.	Ex-Div. Date	Stock of Record	Payment Date
0.260	Dec. 05	Dec. 11	Dec. 15	Dec. 31 '03
0.300	Mar. 05	Mar. 11	Mar. 15	Mar. 31 '04
0.300	Jun. 04	Jun. 10	Jun. 14	Jun. 30 '04
0.300	Sep. 10	Sep. 16	Sep. 20	Sep. 30 '04

Investment Rationale/Risk November 05, 2004

- We would avoid the shares. For several reasons, our target price discounts the shares relative to their historical trading range. First, we think that FRE's earnings restatement, together with its 2003 results, shows a volatile earnings profile. Combined with the fact that we are still awaiting 2004 quarterly results, this reduces visibility in our estimates. Second, we remain concerned about the events that precipitated FRE's management changes, about what ongoing regulatory investigations may uncover surrounding these events, and about potential political fallout. The latter concern was elevated in September, in our view, with findings of GAAP violations at fellow GSE Fannie Mae (FNM: avoid, $70). We also see significant hurdles remaining in remedying what we view as weak corporate governance that helped give rise to the controversy, despite what we see as some positive steps in recent months.

- Risks to our recommendation and target price include P/E multiple expansion if various issues are resolved favorably for FRE.

- Our 12-month target price of $57 is derived by applying a P/E multiple of 8.3X to our 2005 EPS estimate, near the low end of the stock's historical trading range.

Revenues/Earnings Data Fiscal year ending December 31

Revenues (Million $)

	2003	2002	2001	2000	1999	1998
1Q	—	9,799	8,528	6,930	5,627	3,985
2Q	—	9,268	8,876	7,323	5,818	4,318
3Q	—	9,650	9,108	7,652	6,269	4,502
4Q	—	10,704	9,661	8,064	6,554	5,243
Yr.	36,839	46,258	36,173	29,969	24,268	18,048

Earnings Per Share ($)

	2003	2002	2001	2000	1999	1998
1Q	—	2.07	1.12	0.81	0.69	0.54
2Q	—	1.50	1.29	0.83	0.74	0.56
3Q	—	1.90	1.49	0.86	0.74	0.58
4Q	—	2.38	2.06	0.89	0.79	0.62
Yr.	6.79	14.18	5.96	3.39	2.95	2.31

Next earnings report expected: NA Source: S&P, Company Reports
EPS Estimates based on S&P Operating Earnings; historical GAAP earnings are as reported.

Federal Home Loan Mortgage Corporation

Recommendation: **SELL** ★ ★ ☆ ☆ ☆ 12-Month Target Price: **$57.00** (as of November 03, 2004)

Business Summary November 05, 2004

The Federal Home Loan Mortgage Corp., better known as Freddie Mac, is one of two public government-sponsored enterprises (the other is rival Fannie Mae) formed to promote home ownership by increasing the availability of mortgage financing. The company was originally part of the Federal Home Loan Bank Board, which was dismantled under the S&L bailout law of 1989. Of its 18 directors, 13 are elected by stockholders and five are picked by the President of the U.S. Freddie Mac has two principal business segments.

In its portfolio business, Freddie Mac functions in a manner similar to a savings and loan that originates home mortgage loans to hold for its own account. The major differences are that Freddie Mac uses capital market borrowings to finance its mortgage purchases, whereas thrifts use retail savings; and that Freddie Mac purchases mortgages from various lenders, while thrifts actually issue mortgages to homebuyers.

The term retained mortgage portfolio is intended to indicate that these mortgages are warehoused (held) as a long-term investment for their valuable interest income. This business is quite profitable for Freddie Mac, because its cost of funds is in one sense subsidized by its quasi-agency status. The retained portfolio business generates the majority of the company's profits.

The company's mortgage backed securities (MBS) operation is best illustrated by an example. Typically, a bank or thrift decides that it prefers to hold MBSs, as opposed to originated loans. The institution then turns over the loan, or more often a pool of loans, to Freddie Mac, which gives the lender MBSs in return. The

transaction helps both parties. Freddie Mac receives a fee of about one-fifth of 1% to guarantee the principal and interest on the MBSs. Meanwhile, the lender has a nearly risk-free instrument on which it receives principal and interest payments. Freddie Mac makes money in this business because its loss rate is very low: people will default on all sorts of bills, but the basic need for shelter provides a powerful incentive to keep the mortgage more or less current.

In April 2001, Freddie Mac completed implementation of the six voluntary commitments made in October 2000 to enhance its risk management, capital and disclosure practices.

In January 2003, the company announced that it expected to restate its financial results for 2002, 2001 and possibly 2000. In June, directors elected a new chairman, CEO and president, and COO, and appointed a new CFO. FRE had noted serious questions regarding the cooperation and candor of its former president and COO in connection with its review of accounting errors identified in the restatement process. Also in June 2003, the SEC began a formal investigation into the company's accounting. In November, FRE restated its results for 2000, 2001 and 2002, with a net cumulative effect of increasing its net income by $5.0 billion, including $0.6 billion related to periods prior to 2000. In February 2004, the company released its annual report for 2002. In June, FRE announced preliminary 2003 results. In November, it announced a timetable for reporting 2004 and 2005 financial results culminating with the registration of its common stock under the Securities and Exchange Act of 1934 in the second quarter of 2006.

Company Financials Fiscal Year ending December 31

Per Share Data ($)

(Year Ended December 31)	2003	2002	2001	2000	1999	1998	1997	1996	1995	1994
Tangible Bk. Val.	NA	45.58	15.51	16.80	11.99	11.55	8.74	9.63	7.38	6.45
Earnings	6.79	14.18	5.96	3.39	2.95	2.31	1.88	1.67	1.42	1.33
S&P Core Earnings	NA	14.22	5.91	NA	NA	NA	NA	NA	NA	NA
Dividends	1.04	0.88	0.80	0.68	0.60	0.48	0.40	0.35	0.30	0.26
Payout Ratio	15%	6%	13%	20%	20%	21%	21%	21%	21%	20%
Prices - High	64.78	69.50	71.25	70.12	65.25	66.37	44.56	29.25	20.90	15.71
- Low	46.48	52.60	58.75	36.87	45.37	38.68	26.68	19.06	12.46	11.75
P/E Ratio - High	10	5	12	21	22	29	24	18	15	12
- Low	7	4	10	11	15	17	14	11	9	9

Income Statement Analysis (Million $)

	2003	2002	2001	2000	1999	1998	1997	1996	1995	1994
Interest On: Mtges.	NA	34,239	30,180	23,989	19,714	14,269	11,030	9,038	6,505	4,528
Interest On: Invest.	NA	4,147	4,180	4,361	3,039	2,369	1,971	1,745	1,888	1,287
Int. Exp.	NA	26,564	28,808	25,512	20,213	14,711	11,119	8,241	6,997	4,703
Guaranty Fees	NA	NA	1,639	1,489	1,405	1,307	1,298	1,249	1,087	1,108
Loan Loss Prov.	NA	128	45.0	40.0	60.0	190	310	320	255	200
Admin. Exp.	NA	1,553	1,020	883	655	578	495	440	395	379
Pretax Inc.	NA	14,987	6,300	3,534	3,161	2,356	2,215	1,797	1,586	1,482
Eff. Tax Rate	NA	31.4%	30.6%	28.2%	29.8%	27.8%	25.7%	30.0%	31.2%	30.7%
Net Inc.	NA	10,090	4,373	2,539	2,218	1,700	1,395	1,243	1,091	1,027
S&P Core Earnings	NA	9,881	4,121	NA	NA	NA	NA	NA	NA	NA

Balance Sheet & Other Fin. Data (Million $)

	2003	2002	2001	2000	1999	1998	1997	1996	1995	1994
Mtges.	NA	589,722	494,585	385,117	322,569	255,348	164,250	137,520	107,411	72,295
Invest.	NA	124,245	75,894	40,718	31,747	44,753	13,402	16,331	13,962	17,808
Cash & Equiv.	NA	10,792	1,508	366	5,144	2,565	438	9,141	7,483	11,442
Total Assets	NA	752,249	617,340	459,297	386,684	321,421	194,597	173,866	137,181	106,199
ST Debt	NA	NA	250,338	183,576	175,525	193,871	85,128	80,105	62,141	47,303
LT Debt	NA	421,267	311,608	243,178	185,056	Nil	83,446	76,386	57,820	48,984
Equity	NA	24,381	10,777	11,642	8,330	8,028	5,934	6,685	5,000	4,300
% Ret. on Assets	NA	1.4	0.8	0.6	0.6	0.7	0.8	0.8	0.9	1.1
% Ret. on Equity	NA	49.3	37.1	23.6	25.2	22.6	20.6	18.5	22.1	24.4
Equity/Assets Ratio	NA	34.9	2.1	2.4	2.3	2.7	3.1	4.0	3.8	4.2
Price Times Book Value:										
Hi	NA	1.5	4.6	4.2	5.4	5.7	5.1	3.0	2.8	2.4
Low	NA	1.2	3.8	2.2	3.8	3.3	4.1	2.0	1.7	1.8

Data as orig reptd.; bef. results of disc opers/spec. items. Per share data adj. for stk. divs.; EPS diluted. E-Estimated. NA-Not Available. NM-Not Meaningful. NR-Not Ranked. UR-Under Review.

Office: 8200 Jones Branch Drive, McLean, VA 22102-3107.
Telephone: 703-903-2000.
Website: http://www.freddiemac.com
Chrmn & CEO: R.F. Syron.
Pres & COO: E.M. McQuade.
EVP & CFO: M.F. Baumann.

EVP & General Counsel: R. Boyd, Jr.
Dirs: B. Alexander, G. Boisi, C. B. Cabrera, M. Engler, R. K. Goeltz, D. J. Gribbin, III, T. S. Johnson, W. Lewis, Jr., J. B. McCoy, E. McQuade, S. F. O'Malley, R. F. Poe, S. A. Ross, D. J. Schuenke, C. Stepp, R. F. Syron, W. J. Turner.

Auditor: PricewaterhouseCoopers, McLean, VA.
Founded: in 1970.
Domicile: United States.
Employees: 3,800.
S&P Analyst: Erik J. Eisenstein/MF/BK

Federal National Mortgage Assoc.

Recommendation: **SELL** ★ ★ ☆ ☆ ☆
SELL STRS HOLD BUY BUY

12-Month Target Price: **$56.00**
(as of November 15, 2004)

FNM has an approximate 0.62% weighting in the **S&P 500**

Sector: Financials
Sub-Industry: Thrifts & Mortgage Finance
Peer Group: Financial Cos. - Major Diversified

Summary: FNM (Fannie Mae), a U.S. government-sponsored enterprise (GSE), uses mostly borrowed funds to buy a variety of mortgages, thereby creating a secondary market for mortgage lenders.

Quantitative Evaluations

S&P Earnings & Dividend Rank: A+

D	C	B-	B	B+	A-	A	A+

S&P Fair Value Rank: 4+

1	2	3	4	5
Lowest				Highest

Fair Value Calc.: $73.20 (Slightly Undervalued)

S&P Investability Quotient Percentile

90%

FNM scored higher than 90% of all companies for which an S&P Report is available.

Volatility: Average

Low	Average	High

Technical Evaluation: Bullish
Since 11/04, the technical indicators for FNM have been Bullish.

Relative Strength Rank: Weak

25

1 Lowest   Highest 99

Price as of 11/16/04: $69.40   **2004E S&P Core EPS:** $7.70

GAAP Earnings vs. Previous Year
▲ Up   ▼ Down   ► No Change

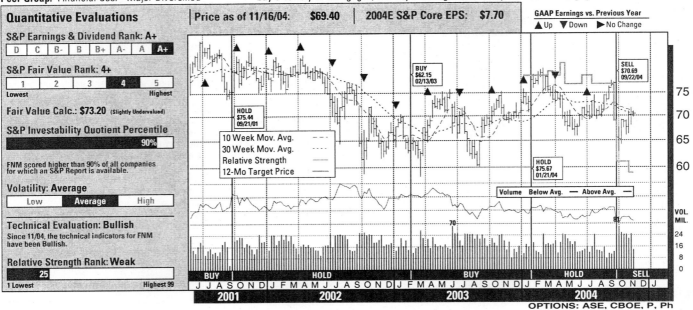

10 Week Mov. Avg.
30 Week Mov. Avg.
Relative Strength
12-Mo Target Price

Volume   Below Avg. —   Above Avg. —

OPTIONS: ASE, CBOE, P, Ph

Analyst commentary prepared by Erik J. Eisenstein/CB/JWP

Highlights 17-NOV-04

- In September, FNM agreed with the Office of Federal Housing Enterprise and Oversight (OFHEO), its safety and soundness regulator, to change several accounting practices and maintain a capital surplus of 30% over the minimum capital requirement in the interim. In light of this agreement, coupled with the prospect of a $9 billion loss in the event of restatement, we think our EPS projections lack visibility. With that caveat, we expect a 9% reduction in the mortgage portfolio in 2005, reflecting our view of FNM's need to raise capital. We see a much narrower net interest margin than in 2004, and forecast that net interest income will decline 25%.

- We project an 11% advance in guarantee fee income, reflecting continued growth in mortgage-backed securities outstanding. However, new business volume should be down in a slower overall mortgage origination market, and, with it, technology and transaction fees. Comparisons will benefit from the absence of a second quarter 2004 impairment charge of $278.2 million on debt securities, including manufactured housing securities. As a result, we see improved fee and other income. Overall, we expect operating revenues to drop 18%.

- We see credit-related expenses as moderate, reflecting a stable housing market. With administrative expenses projected to rise 10%, and reduced losses expected on early extinguishment of debt, we see a fractional decline in 2005 EPS, to $7.73, from $7.74 projected for 2004.

Key Stock Statistics

S&P Core EPS 2005E	7.71	52-week Range		$80.82-62.95
S&P Oper. EPS 2004E	7.74	12 Month P/E		9.0
P/E on S&P Oper. EPS 2004E	9.1	Beta		0.20
S&P Oper. EPS 2005E	7.73	Shareholders		410,000
Yield (%)	3.0%	Market Cap (B)		$ 67.2
Dividend Rate/Share	2.08	Shares Outstanding (M)		967.9

Value of $10,000 invested five years ago: **$ 11,127**

Dividend Data Dividends have been paid since 1956

Amount ($)	Date Decl.	Ex-Div. Date	Stock of Record	Payment Date
0.520	Jan. 23	Jan. 28	Jan. 31	Feb. 25 '04
0.520	Apr. 20	Apr. 28	Apr. 30	May. 25 '04
0.520	Jul. 20	Jul. 28	Jul. 30	Aug. 25 '04
0.520	Oct. 19	Oct. 27	Oct. 31	Nov. 25 '04

Investment Rationale/Risk 17-NOV-04

- In September, OFHEO, while examining the company's accounting practices, found the company in violation of GAAP. In October, FNM announced that it was the subject of a formal SEC investigation. We see these events bolstering the regulatory reform movement, seemingly spawned by an accounting controversy surrounding fellow GSE Freddie Mac (FRE: sell, $68). We think that movement will likely gain significant traction in 2005, especially following the re-election of President Bush, whose administration we view as being critical of the GSEs. The movement would further strengthen, in our view, should the SEC agree with OFHEO's findings of GAAP violations, necessitating a restatement. As a result, we now view political risk at a historical high. In addition, we think this risk could increase further still, should the economy become more vibrant and less dependent on home lending. We also view interest rate risk as above average, with rates forecast to rise across the yield curve.

- Risks to our recommendation and target price include P/E multiple expansion if various issues are resolved favorably for FNM.

- Our 12-month target price of $56 is derived by applying a P/E multiple of 7.2X to our 2005 EPS estimate. This multiple, which is below the low end of the stock's historical range, reflects our view of historically high political risk, as well as possible remedial hurdles and lack of visibility caused by events surrounding the regulatory investigations. With FNM trading above our target price, we have a sell recommendation on the shares.

Revenues/Earnings Data Fiscal year ending December 31

Revenues (Million $)

	2004	2003	2002	2001	2000	1999
1Q	13,083	13,557	12,988	12,366	10,305	8,658
2Q	12,542	13,456	13,211	12,560	10,658	8,938
3Q	—	13,275	13,319	12,880	11,204	9,433
4Q	—	13,480	13,383	12,958	11,921	9,939
Yr.	—	53,768	52,901	50,803	44,088	36,968

Earnings Per Share ($)

	2004	2003	2002	2001	2000	1999
1Q	1.90	1.93	1.17	1.14	1.02	0.88
2Q	1.10	1.09	1.44	1.45	1.02	0.92
3Q	E2.45	2.50	0.98	1.32	1.09	0.94
4Q	E2.28	2.21	0.94	1.98	1.13	0.99
Yr.	E7.74	7.72	4.53	5.89	4.26	3.73

Next earnings report expected: NA   Source: S&P, Company Reports
EPS Estimates based on S&P Operating Earnings; historical GAAP earnings are as reported.

The Federal National Mortgage Association

Recommendation: **SELL** ★ ★ ☆ ☆ ☆   12-Month Target Price: **$56.00** (as of November 15, 2004)

Business Summary 17-NOV-04

The Federal National Mortgage Association (known as Fannie Mae) is a government-sponsored enterprise, chartered by Congress to increase the availability of mortgage credit for homebuyers. Its mission is essentially to increase the rate of home ownership, making American society more stable. The company's predecessor was formed during the Great Depression, in an effort to make home ownership possible at a time when it was nearly impossible for people in certain parts of the U.S. to obtain a mortgage. FNM basically operates in two business segments.

In its retained mortgage portfolio business, which accounts for most of its profits, the company buys mortgages from lenders such as thrifts, banks and mortgage bankers, and holds them on account. It funds mortgage purchases with debt of various maturities, earning a spread on the difference between the yield on the mortgages and the cost of the debt. FNM purchased $573 billion of mortgages in 2003, versus $371 billion in 2002 and $271 billion in 2001.

In securitization operations, which account for much of FNM's remaining profits, the company swaps mortgage-backed securities (MBSs) for mortgages with various lending institutions, and in the process earns a fee of about 0.20%. One reason that lenders swap loans for MBSs is that the latter add to liquidity. FNM functions as a mortgage insurer in that it accepts the risk of default on the mortgage in exchange for a fee or a premium. In 2003, it issued $850 billion in MBSs for other investors, versus $478 billion in 2002 and $345 billion in 2001.

Congress is constantly concerned about the government's risk exposure on over $1 trillion of mortgages and mortgage-backed securities outstanding, since the U.S. government might ultimately have to make good on large-scale defaults. Congress has therefore established capital standards, which the company meets.

In October 2000, FNM agreed to a number of voluntary measures to enhance disclosure, capital and market discipline. The company put these initiatives in place in the 2001 first quarter.

During 2003, several bills were introduced in Congress proposing to alter the regulatory regime under which Fannie Mae operates. The bills sought to transfer regulatory responsibility for overseeing Fannie Mae's safety and soundness from its current regulator, the Office of Federal Housing Enterprise Oversight. Several bills sought to provide additional or expanded powers to the proposed new regulator, including the power to set capital levels, currently set by Act of Congress.

In January 2003, directors authorized the repurchase of up to 49.4 million common shares (5% of the shares outstanding at December 31, 2002). After purchasing 2.8 million shares in the 2004 second quarter, FNM had acquired 20.9 million shares under the plan.

Company Financials Fiscal Year ending December 31

Per Share Data ($)

(Year Ended December 31)	2003	2002	2001	2000	1999	1998	1997	1996	1995	1994
Tangible Bk. Val.	18.73	13.76	15.86	18.58	16.03	13.95	12.34	11.10	10.04	8.74
Earnings	7.72	4.53	5.89	4.26	3.73	3.26	2.84	2.50	1.94	1.95
S&P Core Earnings	7.66	4.45	5.65	NA	NA	NA	NA	NA	NA	NA
Dividends	1.68	1.32	1.20	1.12	1.08	0.96	0.84	0.76	0.68	0.60
Payout Ratio	22%	29%	20%	26%	29%	29%	30%	30%	35%	31%
Prices - High	75.95	84.10	87.93	89.37	75.87	76.18	57.31	41.62	31.50	22.59
- Low	58.40	58.85	72.08	47.87	58.56	49.56	36.12	27.50	17.18	17.03
P/E Ratio - High	10	19	15	21	20	23	20	17	16	12
- Low	8	13	12	11	16	15	13	11	9	9

Income Statement Analysis (Million $)

	2003	2002	2001	2000	1999	1998	1997	1996	1995	1994
Interest On: Mtges.	49,754	49,265	46,478	39,403	32,672	25,676	22,716	20,560	18,154	15,851
Interest On: Invest.	1,166	1,588	2,692	3,378	2,823	4,319	3,662	3,212	2,917	1,496
Int. Exp.	37,351	40,287	41,080	37,107	30,601	25,885	22,429	20,180	18,024	14,524
Guaranty Fees	2,411	1,816	1,482	1,351	1,282	1,229	1,274	1,196	1,086	1,083
Loan Loss Prov.	100	128	Nil	Nil	-120	50.0	100	195	140	155
Admin. Exp.	1,575	1,219	1,017	905	800	708	636	560	546	525
Pretax Inc.	10,413	6,048	8,291	5,982	5,440	4,645	4,337	3,905	2,995	3,146
Eff. Tax Rate	25.9%	23.6%	26.8%	26.2%	27.9%	25.9%	29.3%	29.5%	28.0%	31.9%
Net Inc.	7,720	4,619	6,067	4,416	3,921	3,444	3,068	2,754	2,155	2,141
S&P Core Earnings	7,518	4,440	5,688	NA	NA	NA	NA	NA	NA	NA

Balance Sheet & Other Fin. Data (Million $)

	2003	2002	2001	2000	1999	1998	1997	1996	1995	1994
Mtges.	901,795	797,693	705,167	607,399	522,780	415,223	313,316	286,259	252,588	220,525
Invest.	59,293	59,844	74,554	54,968	39,751	58,213	64,596	56,606	57,273	46,335
Cash & Equiv.	1,415	1,710	1,518	617	2,099	743	2,205	850	318	231
Total Assets	1,009,569	887,515	799,791	675,072	575,167	485,014	391,673	351,041	316,550	272,508
ST Debt	483,193	382,412	343,492	280,322	226,582	205,413	175,400	159,900	146,153	112,602
LT Debt	478,539	468,570	419,975	362,360	321,037	254,878	194,374	171,370	153,021	144,628
Equity	18,265	13,610	15,815	18,560	16,329	14,303	12,793	12,773	10,959	9,541
% Ret. on Assets	0.8	1.0	0.8	0.7	0.7	0.8	0.8	0.8	0.7	0.9
% Ret. on Equity	47.5	30.7	34.5	24.6	25.1	25.4	24.4	23.9	21.0	24.3
Equity/Assets Ratio	59.5	1.7	2.3	3.6	2.9	3.1	3.6	3.4	3.5	3.6
Price Times Book Value:										
Hi	4.1	6.1	5.5	4.8	4.7	5.5	4.6	3.8	3.1	2.6
Low	3.1	4.3	4.5	2.6	3.7	3.6	2.9	2.5	1.7	1.9

Data as orig reptd.; bef. results of disc opers/spec. items. Per share data adj. for stk. divs.; EPS diluted. E-Estimated. NA-Not Available. NM-Not Meaningful. NR-Not Ranked. UR-Under Review.

Office: 3900 Wisconsin Avenue NW, Washington, DC 20016-2892.
Telephone: 202-752-7000.
Email: investor_relations1@fanniemae.com
Website: http://www.fanniemae.com
Chrmn & CEO: F. D. Raines.
COO & Vice Chrmn: D. H. Mudd.

CFO & Vice Chrmn: T. Howard.
Secy & EVP: T. E. Donilon.
Dirs: V. Ashe, S. B. Ashley, M. H. Bordonaro, K. M. Duberstein, T. P. Gerrity, W. R. Harvey, T. Howard, M. J. Justiz, A. M. Korologos, F. V. Malek, D. B. Marron, D. H. Mudd, A. M. Mulcahy, J. K. Pickett, L. Rahl, F. D. Raines, T. C. Segue III, H. P. Swygert.

Founded: in 1938.
Domicile: United States.
Employees: 5,055.
S&P Analyst: Erik J. Eisenstein/CB/JWP

Federated Department Stores

Recommendation: **HOLD** ★ ★ ★ ★ ★
SELL SELL HOLD BUY BUY

12-Month Target Price: **$56.00**
(as of November 10, 2004)

FD has an approximate 0.09% weighting in the **S&P 500**

Sector: Consumer Discretionary
Sub-Industry: Department Stores
Peer Group: Department Store Cos. - Larger

Summary: This company operates more than 450 department stores in 34 states, under names that include Macy's, Bloomingdale's, Burdines-Macy's and Rich's-Macy's.

Quantitative Evaluations

S&P Earnings & Dividend Rank: B

| D | C | B- | **B** | B+ | A- | A | A+ |

S&P Fair Value Rank: 5+

| 1 | 2 | 3 | 4 | **5** |
| Lowest | | | | Highest |

Fair Value Calc.: $64.10 (Slightly Undervalued)

S&P Investability Quotient Percentile

88%

FD scored higher than 88% of all companies for which an S&P Report is available.

Volatility: Average

| Low | **Average** | High |

Technical Evaluation: Bullish

Since 10/04, the technical indicators for FD have been Bullish.

Relative Strength Rank: Strong

84

| 1 Lowest | | Highest 99 |

Price as of 11/12/04: $54.73 | **2005E S&P Core EPS:** $3.24

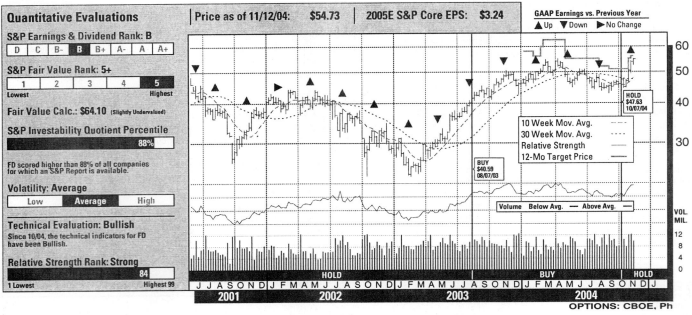

GAAP Earnings vs. Previous Year
▲ Up ▼ Down ► No Change

10 Week Mov. Avg.
30 Week Mov. Avg.
Relative Strength
12-Mo Target Price

HOLD $47.63 10/07/04

BUY $40.59 08/07/03

Volume Below Avg. — Above Avg.

VOL. MIL.
12
8
4
0

HOLD   BUY   HOLD

J J A S O N D J F M A M J J A S O N D J F M A M J J A S O N D J F M A M J J A S O N D J
2001   2002   2003   2004

OPTIONS: CBOE, Ph

Analyst commentary prepared by Jason N. Asaeda/DC/BK

Highlights 16-NOV-04

- We see net sales of $16.2 billion in FY 06 (Jan.), up from a projected $15.7 billion in FY 05, with growth driven by positive customer response to FD's mix of fashion and differentiated merchandise. We think that the company's increased focus on "better" apparel and accessory assortments has resonated well with customers. In our view, this reflects improved customer perceptions of fair value in less discounted prices, increased accessibility of luxury items, and the desire to express individual styles. We also believe FD has improved its national competitive position by extending the Macy's brand to its regional markets.
- We expect earnings before interest and taxes (EBIT) margins to widen, in the anticipated absence of expenses related to the FY 05 Rich's-Macy's and Burdines-Macy's consolidation and the formation of a centralized Macy's home store business and marketing function. We also look for initial cost savings and improved operating efficiencies from these actions in FY 06.
- We estimate FY 05 operating EPS of $4.09 and Standard & Poor's Core EPS of $3.24, and FY 06 operating EPS of $4.53 and S&P Core EPS of $3.87. The differences reflect one-time costs for debt redemption, and estimated stock option and pension costs.

Investment Rationale/Risk 16-NOV-04

- We have a hold recommendation on the shares, based on valuation. We think FD has raised the bar for its competition by adding freshness to its merchandise assortments, enhancing its in-store shopping experiences, and better leveraging its strong Macy's brand. We also see expected benefits of consolidation and centralization steps aiding longer-term sales prospects. Based on October sales trends, we have a favorable outlook for the upcoming holiday selling season, although we expect it to be highly competitive. While we look for the company to drive sales, in part, by taking markdowns early in the season, we think light inventories will help it to maintain gross margins.
- Risks to our recommendation and target price include potential sales downturns due to merchandising mistakes or unexpected shifts in fashion trends, and increased promotional activity to drive sales.
- We calculate intrinsic value of $72, based on our DCF model, which assumes a 10.5% cost of capital and a terminal growth rate of 4%. Our 12-month target price of $56 is based on a blend of our DCF model, along with a forward P/E multiple of 12X applied to our FY 06 EPS estimate of $4.53, and a price to estimated FY 06 sales ratio of 0.5X, both of which are in line with three-year historical averages.

Key Stock Statistics

S&P Core EPS 2006E	3.87	52-week Range	$55.06-42.54
S&P Oper. EPS 2005E	4.09	12 Month P/E	14.6
P/E on S&P Oper. EPS 2005E	13.4	Beta	1.36
S&P Oper. EPS 2006E	4.53	Shareholders	12,207
Yield (%)	1.0%	Market Cap (B)	$ 9.7
Dividend Rate/Share	0.54	Shares Outstanding (M)	172.7

Value of $10,000 invested five years ago: **$ 13,043**

Dividend Data Dividends have been paid since 2003

Amount ($)	Date Decl.	Ex-Div. Date	Stock of Record	Payment Date
0.125	Feb. 27	Mar. 11	Mar. 15	Apr. 01 '04
0.135	May. 21	Jun. 14	Jun. 15	Jul. 01 '04
0.135	Aug. 27	Sep. 13	Sep. 15	Oct. 01 '04
0.135	Oct. 21	Dec. 13	Dec. 15	Jan. 03 '05

Revenues/Earnings Data Fiscal year ending January 31

Revenues (Million $)

	2005	2004	2003	2002	2001	2000
1Q	3,517	3,291	3,453	3,556	4,032	3,707
2Q	3,548	3,434	3,486	3,488	4,065	4,111
3Q	3,491	3,486	3,479	3,475	4,195	4,242
4Q	—	5,053	5,017	5,132	6,115	6,157
Yr.	—	15,264	15,435	15,651	18,407	18,217

Earnings Per Share ($)

	2005	2004	2003	2002	2001	2000
1Q	0.52	0.24	0.43	0.29	0.41	0.40
2Q	0.43	0.64	0.66	0.62	0.30	0.61
3Q	0.42	0.36	0.38	0.13	-3.32	0.56
4Q	E2.52	2.50	1.78	1.55	1.55	2.04
Yr.	E4.09	3.71	3.21	2.59	-0.90	3.62

Next earnings report expected: late-February Source: S&P, Company Reports
EPS Estimates based on S&P Operating Earnings; historical GAAP earnings are as reported.

Federated Department Stores, Inc.

Recommendation: **HOLD** ★ ★ ★ ☆ ☆   12-Month Target Price: **$56.00** (as of November 10, 2004)

Business Summary 16-NOV-04

Federated Department Stores and its predecessors have been operating department stores in the U.S. since 1830. The company operates more than 450 stores in 34 states, under the Macy's and Bloomingdale's national nameplates, and The Bon-Macy's, Burdines-Macy's, Goldsmith's-Macy's, Lazarus-Macy's and Rich's-Macy's regional nameplates. Each division is well established in its trade area, and sells a wide variety of merchandise, including women's, men's and children's apparel, cosmetics, home furnishings and other consumer goods.

The company also operates direct-to-customer retail business via the Macys.com e-commerce site, and a national catalog, Bloomingdale's By Mail. In addition, it offers customers online bridal registry and gift purchase facilities.

FD entered 2003 strategically focused on four key priorities for improving the business over the longer term: differentiating merchandise assortments; simplifying pricing; enriching the overall shopping experience; and communicating better with customers through more effective marketing. The company believes that recent results indicated that these strategies are working and that customers are responding favorably.

In 2004, the company took a further step in re-inventing its department stores, with the creation of a centralized organization that is responsible for the overall strategy, merchandising and marketing of home-related categories of business in all Macy's-branded stores. The centralized operation is expected to accelerate sales, largely by improving and further differentiating assortments. In FY 04 (Jan.),

home-related categories, which include textiles, tabletop, housewares and furniture, accounted for $2.6 billion of FD's sales (19% of total sales in the Macy's-named divisions).

As a step toward fulfilling its vision of Macy's as "America's department store," FD plans to convert all of its regional department stores to the Macy's nameplate in January 2005. With the name change, the company intends to offer customers a new national Macy's customer loyalty program, access to an enhanced national Macy's gift and bridal registry, and an accelerated 2005 rollout of its re-invention initiatives in local stores.

FD provides a number of support functions to its retail operating divisions. For example, Federated Merchandising Group (FMG) develops and executes merchandising strategies that, while consistent companywide, can be tailored to the particular character and customer base of each retail operating division. FMG is also responsible for all of the private label development for FD's Macy's-branded stores. In FY 04, sales of the company's private label brands continued to outperform national brands, and accounted for 17.1% of sales in Macy's-branded stores, up from 16.4% in FY 03.

Capital spending totaled $568 million in FY 04, as FD opened 12 new stores and closed eight stores nationally. For FY 05, the company plans to open seven new stores, including four department stores and three furniture stores, and to close two stores.

Company Financials Fiscal Year ending January 31

Per Share Data ($)

(Year Ended January 31)	2004	2003	2002	2001	2000	1999	1998	1997	1996	1995
Tangible Bk. Val.	NM	26.93	24.31	24.93	22.51	24.30	21.74	19.00	17.38	14.39
Cash Flow	7.84	6.61	5.89	2.65	6.99	5.82	5.22	3.91	3.07	3.54
Earnings	3.71	3.21	2.59	-0.90	3.62	3.06	2.58	1.24	0.39	1.41
S&P Core Earnings	3.38	2.47	1.82	0.49	NA	NA	NA	NA	NA	NA
Dividends	Nil	Nil	Nil	Nil	Nil	Nil	Nil	Nil	Nil	Nil
Payout Ratio	Nil	Nil	Nil	Nil	Nil	Nil	Nil	Nil	Nil	Nil
Cal. Yrs.	2003	2002	2001	2000	1999	1998	1997	1996	1995	1994
Prices - High	50.60	44.26	49.90	53.87	57.06	56.18	48.87	37.00	30.12	25.25
- Low	23.51	23.59	26.05	21.00	36.43	32.81	30.00	25.00	17.87	18.00
P/E Ratio - High	14	14	19	NM	16	18	19	29	77	18
- Low	6	7	10	NM	10	11	12	20	46	13

Income Statement Analysis (Million $)

	2004	2003	2002	2001	2000	1999	1998	1997	1996	1995
Revs.	15,264	15,435	15,651	18,407	17,716	15,833	15,668	15,229	15,049	8,636
Oper. Inc.	2,047	2,019	1,923	2,239	2,443	2,085	1,951	1,760	1,498	919
Depr.	706	676	657	727	742	630	610	558	515	283
Int. Exp.	266	311	331	444	368	304	418	499	509	263
Pretax Inc.	1,084	1,048	780	113	1,346	1,163	958	441	202	331
Eff. Tax Rate	36.1%	39.1%	33.6%	NM	40.9%	41.1%	40.0%	39.9%	62.9%	43.4%
Net Inc.	693	638	518	-184	795	685	575	266	75.0	188
S&P Core Earnings	628	490	364	102	NA	NA	NA	NA	NA	NA

Balance Sheet & Other Fin. Data (Million $)

	2004	2003	2002	2001	2000	1999	1998	1997	1996	1995
Cash	925	716	636	322	218	307	142	149	173	206
Curr. Assets	7,452	7,154	7,280	8,700	8,522	5,972	6,194	6,429	6,360	5,190
Total Assets	14,550	14,441	15,044	17,012	17,692	13,464	13,738	14,264	14,295	12,380
Curr. Liab.	3,883	3,601	3,714	4,869	4,552	3,068	3,060	3,596	3,098	2,712
LT Debt	3,151	3,408	3,859	4,374	4,589	3,057	3,919	4,606	5,632	4,529
Common Equity	5,940	5,762	5,564	5,822	6,552	5,709	5,256	4,669	4,274	3,640
Total Cap.	10,089	10,168	10,768	11,589	12,585	9,826	10,114	10,106	10,639	9,162
Cap. Exp.	508	568	615	742	770	695	696	846	696	387
Cash Flow	1,399	1,314	1,175	543	1,537	1,315	1,185	824	590	471
Curr. Ratio	1.9	2.0	2.0	1.8	1.9	1.9	2.0	1.8	2.0	1.9
% LT Debt of Cap.	31.2	33.5	35.8	37.7	36.5	31.1	38.7	45.6	52.9	49.4
% Net Inc.of Revs.	4.5	4.1	3.3	NM	4.5	4.3	3.7	1.8	0.5	2.2
% Ret. on Assets	4.8	4.2	3.4	NM	5.1	5.0	4.1	1.9	0.6	1.6
% Ret. on Equity	11.8	11.3	9.1	NM	13.0	12.5	11.6	6.0	1.9	5.4

Data as orig reptd.; bef. results of disc opers/spec. items. Per share data adj. for stk. divs.; EPS diluted. E-Estimated. NA-Not Available. NM-Not Meaningful. NR-Not Ranked. UR-Under Review.

Office: 7 W Seventh St, Cincinnati, OH 45202.
Telephone: 513-579-7000.
Website: http://www.fds.com
Chrmn, Pres & CEO: T. J. Lundgren.
Vice Chrmn: T. G. Cody.
Vice Chrmn: T. Cole.

Vice Chrmn: J. Grove.
Investor Contact: Susan Robinson.
Dirs: M. Feldberg, E. G. Graves, Sr., S. Levinson, T. J. Lundgren, J. Neubauer, J. A. Pichler, R. W. Tysoe, K. M. Von der Heyden, C. E. Weatherup, M. C. Whittington.

Founded: in 1858.
Domicile: Delaware.
Employees: 111,000.
S&P Analyst: Jason N. Asaeda/DC/BK

Federated Investors

Recommendation: **HOLD** ★★★☆☆ SELL SELL HOLD BUY BUY **12-Month Target Price: $29.00**
(as of July 27, 2004)

FII has an approximate 0.03% weighting in the **S&P 500**

Sector: Financials
Sub-Industry: Asset Management & Custody Banks
Peer Group: Investment Management Cos. - Larger

Summary: Federated is a leading U.S. investment management company, with a strong market share in money market products.

Quantitative Evaluations

S&P Earnings & Dividend Rank: B
D | C | B- | **B** | B+ | A- | A | A+

S&P Fair Value Rank: 3
1 | 2 | **3** | 4 | 5
Lowest | | | | Highest

Fair Value Calc.: $28.70 (Slightly Overvalued)

S&P Investability Quotient Percentile
72%

FII scored higher than 72% of all companies for which an S&P Report is available.

Volatility: Low
Low | Average | High

Technical Evaluation: Neutral
Since 10/04, the technical indicators for FII have been Neutral.

Relative Strength Rank: Moderate
48
1 Lowest | | Highest 99

Price as of 11/12/04: **$29.80** | 2004E S&P Core EPS: **$1.70**

GAAP Earnings vs. Previous Year
▲ Up ▼ Down ► No Change

Analyst commentary prepared by Robert Hansen, CFA /MF/JWP

Highlights November 03, 2004

- Federated has experienced declines in total managed assets throughout 2004 thus far, due, we think, to concerns about potentially higher interest rates. Unlike at other large fund companies, we think Federated's customers will not necessarily reallocate money market assets to its fixed income and equity products. However, we believe the company's direct sales force and strong relationships with wholesalers and intermediaries will help generate demand for its higher margin equity and fixed income products in 2005.

- Results in the third quarter were hurt by a 3% sequential decline in total managed assets to $178 billion, partially offset by lower expenses for professional services. Federated is aggressively expanding its equity product portfolio in an attempt, we believe, to offset a decline in its money market business, which experienced a peak in managed assets in the second quarter of 2003. We expect FII's acquisition of Alliance's cash management business to close in phases in early 2005 and be accretive to EPS.

- We see continued net outflows from money market products, which account for 71% of managed assets, and from fixed income products. However, we expect net inflows into equity products, notably at the Kaufman Fund, which was acquired in 2001. We forecast EPS of $1.77 in 2004 and $1.75 in 2005, based on lower managed assets, offset by reduced compensation earnouts at Kaufman.

Investment Rationale/Risk November 03, 2004

- We believe the shares should trade at a discount to peers, given the potential for money market redemptions and ongoing regulatory issues. We expect investors to increasingly seek higher returns in 2005 and exit the company's money market products. However, we think the company's common share repurchase program, which was increased by 5 million shares in October, should help support the valuation.

- Risks to our investment recommendation and target price include competition, potential increases in interest rates, and the ongoing SEC and NASD investigations into allegations of improper mutual fund trading.

- The shares recently traded at nearly 17X our 2005 EPS estimate and have underperformed peers thus far in 2004. Our 12-month target price of $29 is nearly 17X our 2005 EPS estimate, a discount to the current peer group average of about 18X. We would not add to positions, as we view the valuation as appropriate and see competitive challenges from larger, more diversified fund management companies.

Key Stock Statistics

S&P Core EPS 2005E	1.66	52-week Range	$33.79-26.72
S&P Oper. EPS 2004E	1.77	12 Month P/E	17.1
P/E on S&P Oper. EPS 2004E	16.8	Beta	0.50
S&P Oper. EPS 2005E	1.75	Shareholders	16,538
Yield (%)	1.7%	Market Cap (B)	$ 3.2
Dividend Rate/Share	0.50	Shares Outstanding (M)	107.5

Value of $10,000 invested five years ago: **$ 24,341**

Dividend Data Dividends have been paid since 1998

Amount ($)	Date Decl.	Ex-Div. Date	Stock of Record	Payment Date
0.085	Feb. 09	Feb. 18	Feb. 20	Feb. 27 '04
0.102	Apr. 20	May. 05	May. 07	May. 14 '04
0.102	Jul. 26	Aug. 04	Aug. 06	Aug. 13 '04
0.125	Oct. 28	Nov. 04	Nov. 08	Nov. 15 '04

Revenues/Earnings Data Fiscal year ending December 31

Revenues (Million $)

	2004	2003	2002	2001	2000	1999
1Q	227.1	194.1	181.6	171.4	168.9	141.3
2Q	213.1	202.5	182.4	180.9	168.3	150.2
3Q	205.2	210.0	173.2	181.2	173.1	152.2
4Q	—	216.8	173.8	182.3	170.5	157.5
Yr.	—	823.3	711.1	715.8	680.8	601.1

Earnings Per Share ($)

	2004	2003	2002	2001	2000	1999
1Q	0.46	0.43	0.44	0.35	0.30	0.21
2Q	0.44	0.44	0.45	0.36	0.30	0.23
3Q	0.43	0.46	0.43	0.36	0.33	0.24
4Q	E0.43	0.38	0.42	0.38	0.34	0.28
Yr.	E1.77	1.71	1.74	1.44	1.27	0.96

Next earnings report expected: early-February Source: S&P, Company Reports
EPS Estimates based on S&P Operating Earnings; historical GAAP earnings are as reported.

Federated Investors, Inc.

Recommendation: **HOLD** ★ ★ ★ ☆ ☆   12-Month Target Price: **$29.00** (as of July 27, 2004)

Business Summary November 04, 2004

A leading provider of investment management products and related financial services, Federated Investors (FII) has been in the mutual fund business for more than 40 years. The company is one of the largest mutual fund managers in the United States, based on assets under management. Assets under management at December 31, 2003, totaled $198 billion, up from $195 billion at the end of 2002.

Federated manages assets across a wide range of asset categories, including substantial participation in fast growing areas such as equity and international investments. It is among the industry leaders in money market and fixed income funds, based on assets under management, and offers one of the industry's most comprehensive product lines. Assets under management by class include money market (72% of total), fixed income (15%), and equity (13%). By product type, mutual funds represented about 89% of total assets under management, with the balance held in separately managed accounts.

Federated strengthened its equity and fixed-income product portfolio in 2003. The company added 16 investment professionals in 2003 to its investment team, which includes about 150 portfolio managers, analysts and traders. The company ended the year with 136 equity, fixed-income and money market mutual funds. The company has managed institutional separate accounts since 1973, and is focused on growing its managed account business for high-net-worth individuals with investable equity assets of $100,000 or more.

Federated believes that it benefits from a developing industry trend toward intermediary assisted sales (sales of mutual fund products through a financial intermediary), driven by the wide array of options now available to investors, and by a need for financial planning advice that has resulted from a recent increase in the average household's financial assets.

Federated's distribution strategy is to provide products geared to financial intermediaries, primarily banks, broker/dealers, investment advisers, and directly to institutions such as corporations and government entities. Federated has developed relationships with more than 5,000 intermediaries, and sells products directly to corporations and government entities through its trained sales force of 190 representatives and managers across the U.S. The company offers a wide array of pricing options for its load funds, sold by more than 2,000 national, regional and bank broker/dealers. No-load products are sold primarily to and through bank trust departments, insurance companies, investment advisers, government entities, and corporate and advisory firms.

In September 2003, Federated announced that it had received a subpoena from the office of the New York State Attorney General in connection with a continuing investigation into illegal trading practices in the mutual fund industry.

Company Financials Fiscal Year ending December 31

Per Share Data ($)

(Year Ended December 31)	2003	2002	2001	2000	1999	1998	1997	1996	1995	1994
Tangible Bk. Val.	2.05	1.46	0.79	0.86	0.62	0.28	NM	-5.57	NA	NA
Cash Flow	1.95	1.90	1.65	1.40	1.10	0.88	0.70	0.77	NA	NA
Earnings	1.71	1.74	1.44	1.27	0.96	0.71	0.61	0.13	0.16	-0.35
S&P Core Earnings	1.67	1.69	1.46	NA	NA	NA	NA	NA	NA	NA
Dividends	0.30	0.22	0.22	0.14	0.11	0.05	0.07	0.13	NA	NA
Payout Ratio	17%	12%	15%	11%	11%	7%	Nil	34%	NA	NA
Prices - High	31.90	36.18	32.80	31.68	14.12	13.45	NA	NA	NA	NA
- Low	23.85	23.43	23.31	12.45	10.04	7.33	NA	NA	NA	NA
P/E Ratio - High	19	21	23	25	15	19	NA	NA	NA	NA
- Low	14	13	16	10	10	10	NA	NA	NA	NA

Income Statement Analysis (Million $)

	2003	2002	2001	2000	1999	1998	1997	1996	1995	1994
Income Int.	2.15	2.40	9.74	19.0	13.9	8.88	3.03	2.16	1.11	NA
Income Other	0.00	2.27	706	662	587	513	401	320	279	NA
Total Income	823	711	716	681	601	522	401	322	280	271
General Exp.	531	399	388	394	364	340	294	272	217	NA
Interest Exp.	4.71	4.79	29.7	34.2	31.8	27.6	20.1	18.6	9.40	NA
Depr.	20.6	19.2	26.0	15.8	18.1	22.9	22.4	18.3	15.6	NA
Net Inc.	191	204	173	155	124	92.4	51.0	13.6	28.5	-39.3
S&P Core Earnings	187	199	175	NA	NA	NA	NA	NA	NA	NA

Balance Sheet & Other Fin. Data (Million $)

	2003	2002	2001	2000	1999	1998	1997	1996	1995	1994
Cash	234	151	73.5	150	171	186	NA	NA	NA	NA
Receivables	38.3	31.2	32.6	36.9	35.2	31.0	NA	NA	NA	NA
Cost of Investments	1.53	1.00	4.60	85.3	66.4	13.4	NA	NA	NA	NA
Total Assets	879	530	432	705	673	580	NA	NA	NA	NA
Loss Reserve	Nil	Nil	0.32	0.09	0.18	1.27	NA	NA	NA	NA
ST Debt	Nil	Nil	Nil	14.3	14.3	0.24	0.28	NA	NA	NA
Capitalization:										
Debt	328	59.2	55.0	394	394	372	284	NA	NA	NA
Equity	396	341	237	148	119	88.7	-41.1	NA	NA	NA
Total	744	416	299	583	551	491	244	NA	NA	NA
Price Times Bk. Val.: High	15.6	24.8	41.5	36.7	22.0	49.0	NA	NA	NA	NA
Price Times Bk. Val.: Low	11.6	16.0	29.5	14.5	16.0	27.0	NA	NA	NA	NA
Cash Flow	212	223	199	171	142	115	73.4	25.9	44.1	NA
% Exp./Op. Revs.	65.1	56.7	58.4	62.9	65.9	70.4	78.3	84.0	77.5	NA
% Earn & Depr/Assets	25.3	46.4	35.0	24.8	22.7	NA	NA	NA	NA	NA

Data as orig. reptd.; bef. results of disc opers. and/or spec. items. Bk. val & bal. sheet data in 1997 are pro forma. Per share data adj. for stk. divs.; EPS diluted (primary prior to 1998). E-Estimated. NA-Not Available. NM-Not Meaningful. NR-Not Ranked.

Office: 1001 Liberty Avenue, Pittsburgh, PA 15222-3779.
Telephone: 800-341-7400.
Email: investors@federatedinv.com
Website: http://www.federatedinvestors.com
Chrmn: J.F. Donahue.
Pres & CEO: J.C. Donahue.

CFO & Treas: T.R. Donahue.
Secy & Chief Lgl Officer: J.W. McGonigle.
Investor Contact: J.T. Tuskan 412-288-7895.
Dirs: J. C. Donahue, J. F. Donahue, M. J. Farrell, D. M. Kelly, J. W. McGonigle, J. L. Murdy, E. G. O'Connor.

Founded: in 1955.
Domicile: Pennsylvania.
Employees: 1,643.
S&P Analyst: Robert Hansen, CFA /MF/JWP

FedEx Corp.

Recommendation: **BUY** ★ ★ ★ ★ ★
SELL · SELL · HOLD · BUY · BUY

12-Month Target Price: **$106.00**
(as of June 10, 2004)

FDX has an approximate 0.26% weighting in the **S&P 500**

Sector: Industrials
Sub-Industry: Air Freight & Logistics

Summary: FDX provides guaranteed domestic and international air express, residential and business ground package delivery, heavy freight and logistics services.

Quantitative Evaluations

| Price as of 11/12/04: | $95.37 | 2005E S&P Core EPS: | $3.77 |

S&P Earnings & Dividend Rank: B+

| D | C | B- | B | **B+** | A- | A | A+ |

S&P Fair Value Rank: 3

| 1 | 2 | **3** | 4 | 5 |
| Lowest | | | | Highest |

Fair Value Calc.: $87.80 (Slightly Overvalued)

S&P Investability Quotient Percentile
97%

FDX scored higher than 97% of all companies for which an S&P Report is available.

Volatility: Low

| **Low** | Average | High |

Technical Evaluation: Bullish
Since 8/04, the technical indicators for FDX have been Bullish.

Relative Strength Rank: Strong
75

| 1 Lowest | Highest 99 |

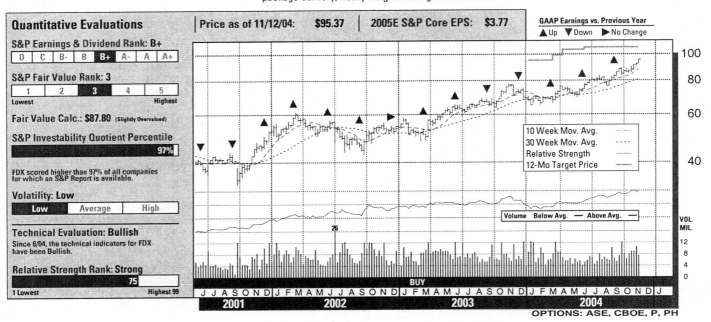

GAAP Earnings vs. Previous Year
▲ Up ▼ Down ► No Change

10 Week Mov. Avg.
30 Week Mov. Avg.
Relative Strength
12-Mo Target Price

Volume Below Avg. — Above Avg.

VOL.
MIL.
12
8
4
0

BUY

J J A S O N D J F M A M J J A S O N D J F M A M J J A S O N D J F M A M J J A S O N D J
2001 2002 2003 2004

OPTIONS: ASE, CBOE, P, PH

Analyst commentary prepared by Jim Corridore/PMW/JWP

Highlights October 28, 2004

- We see FY 05 (May) revenues growing 15%. We expect the acquisition of Kinko's to add about $2 billion to FY 05 revenues. We expect increased U.S. package volumes at ground and express as a result of improved U.S. business and economic activity. We also see rate increases for air, ground and freight services contributing to revenue growth. We expect international revenues to grow in the double digits, driven by increasing export activity out of China, a trend that we expect to continue for several years. Export volumes out of the rest of Asia and In Europe should also remain strong.

Investment Rationale/Risk October 28, 2004

- The shares traded recently below the level of key peer UPS (UPS: buy, $77), based on P/E multiple and P/E to growth and price to sales ratios. FDX has long lagged UPS in a number of financial metrics, such as return on assets and return on invested capital. We see much of the company's future growth coming from less asset-intensive ground and freight operations, and from Kinko's, which has proved more accretive than we initially expected. We see the company closing the gap somewhat on these metrics. In our view, this argues for a valuation more closely rivaling that of UPS. We would buy the shares.

- Risks to our recommendation and target price include integration risk for Kinko's, and the possibility that improvement in the U.S. economy and international strength will be less than expected. In addition, although the company passes on rising fuel costs to its customers in the form of a fuel surcharge, rising oil prices could eventually hurt the economy, in turn putting pressure on shipping volumes.

- Our 12-month target price of $106 values the stock at 23X our FY 05 EPS estimate and at 21X our FY 06 estimate, in line with the historical P/E multiple range, but still at a modest discount to the valuation of UPS.

Key Stock Statistics

S&P Core EPS 2006E	4.52	52-week Range	$95.40-64.84
S&P Oper. EPS 2005E	4.55	12 Month P/E	27.9
P/E on S&P Oper. EPS 2005E	21.0	Beta	0.57
S&P Oper. EPS 2006E	5.15	Shareholders	17,901
Yield (%)	0.3%	Market Cap (B)	$ 28.7
Dividend Rate/Share	0.28	Shares Outstanding (M)	300.6

Value of $10,000 invested five years ago: **$ 22,151**

Dividend Data Dividends have been paid since 2002

Amount ($)	Date Decl.	Ex-Div. Date	Stock of Record	Payment Date
0.060	Dec. 02	Dec. 10	Dec. 12	Jan. 02 '04
0.060	Feb. 19	Mar. 09	Mar. 11	Apr. 01 '04
0.070	May. 28	Jun. 08	Jun. 10	Jul. 01 '04
0.070	Aug. 20	Sep. 08	Sep. 10	Oct. 01 '04

Revenues/Earnings Data Fiscal year ending May 31

Revenues (Million $)

	2005	2004	2003	2002	2001	2000
1Q	6,975	5,687	5,445	5,037	4,779	4,320
2Q	—	5,920	5,667	5,135	4,895	4,570
3Q	—	6,062	5,545	5,019	4,839	4,518
4Q	—	7,041	5,830	5,416	5,117	4,849
Yr.	—	24,710	22,487	20,607	19,629	18,257

Earnings Per Share ($)

	2005	2004	2003	2002	2001	2000
1Q	1.08	0.42	0.52	0.41	0.58	0.52
2Q	E1.15	0.30	0.81	0.81	0.67	0.57
3Q	E0.87	0.68	0.49	0.39	0.37	0.39
4Q	E1.45	1.36	0.92	0.78	0.38	0.85
Yr.	E4.55	2.76	2.74	2.39	1.99	2.32

Next earnings report expected: mid-December Source: S&P, Company Reports
EPS Estimates based on S&P Operating Earnings; historical GAAP earnings are as reported.

FedEx Corporation

Recommendation: **BUY** ★ ★ ★ ★ ★   12-Month Target Price: **$106.00** (as of June 10, 2004)

Business Summary October 28, 2004

FedEx Corp. provides global time-definite air express services for packages, documents and freight in 215 countries, and provides ground-based delivery of small packages in North America. In addition, the company provides expedited critical shipment delivery, customs brokerage solutions, less-than-truckload (LTL) freight transportation, and customized logistics. In February 2004, FDX paid $2.4 billion in cash for Kinko's, which operates about 1,200 copy centers that also provide business services. Kinko's has annual revenues of about $2 billion. Kinko joined three other FedEx companies: Express, Ground and Freight.

Federal Express Corp. (dba FedEx Express) is the company's original business. Formed in 1973, FedEx Express is the world's leading provider of guaranteed express delivery services. It provides same-day, overnight and deferred delivery services for documents, packages and freight, using a network of 47,000 ground vehicles, 645 aircraft, and 52,000 drop-off boxes. In FY 04 (May), FedEx Express accounted for 71% of revenues, versus 73% in FY 03. About 68% of FedEx Express's revenues in FY 04 were from U.S. services, with 59% express delivery and 41% deferred delivery and other revenue. In January 2001, FDX entered into two service contracts with the U.S. Postal Service: one for domestic air transportation of postal express shipments, and the other for placement of FedEx drop boxes at U.S. post offices.

International business (32% of FedEx Express revenues in FY 03; latest available) provides package and document delivery to 215 countries. FDX is active in Asian markets. It is one of four U.S. air carriers with rights to serve China. In FY 04,

FedEx Express increased capacity on flights between Europe and Asia, expanded its network in Europe and Asia, and increased its presence in China. In China, FDX plans to establish a new regional headquarters in Shanghai, and to expand service from 220 Chinese cities to 320 cities over the next five years. FDX launched express service to Iraq in FY 04.

FedEx Ground (16% of total revenue in FY 04) is North America's second largest ground package delivery company. In FY 04, FedEx Ground continued a six-year, $1.8 billion expansion plan aimed at doubling daily package volume capacity to 5.1 million by the end of 2009. FedEx Ground operations are conducted with 16,200 owner-operated vehicles and 18,700 company-owned trailers.

FedEx Freight (11% of total revenue in FY 04) was established in 2002, to serve as the holding company for American Freightways (rebranded FedEx Freight East) and Viking Freight (rebranded FedEx Freight West). The two companies provide LTL freight service throughout the U.S. Kinko's, acquired in February 2004, accounted for the remaining 2% of FY 04 revenues. In 2005, FedEx Kinkos plans to open about 70 new locations, including many internationally.

In June 2003, FDX announced a voluntary early retirement and severance program at FedEx Express. The company has said that the program saved $150 million in FY 04, and was expected to save an additional $230 million to $240 million in FY 05. FDX incurred a related pretax charge of $435 million ($270 million, after tax) in FY 04.

Company Financials Fiscal Year ending May 31

Per Share Data ($)

(Year Ended May 31)	2004	2003	2002	2001	2000	1999	1998	1997	1996	1995
Tangible Bk. Val.	17.62	21.03	18.38	16.20	14.33	14.50	12.26	11.29	9.63	8.26
Cash Flow	7.45	7.20	6.89	6.35	6.23	5.55	4.91	4.91	4.51	4.20
Earnings	2.76	2.74	2.39	1.99	2.32	2.10	1.68	1.56	1.35	1.32
S&P Core Earnings	2.61	1.38	0.95	0.44	NA	NA	NA	NA	NA	NA
Dividends	0.20	Nil	Nil	Nil	Nil	Nil	Nil	Nil	Nil	Nil
Payout Ratio	7%	Nil	Nil	Nil	Nil	Nil	Nil	Nil	Nil	Nil

Cal. Yrs.	2003	2002	2001	2000	1999	1998	1997	1996	1995	1994
Prices - High	78.05	61.35	53.48	49.85	61.87	46.56	42.25	22.50	21.50	20.18
- Low	47.70	42.75	33.15	30.56	34.87	21.81	21.00	16.71	14.62	13.37
P/E Ratio - High	28	22	22	25	27	22	25	14	16	15
- Low	17	16	14	15	15	10	12	11	11	10

Income Statement Analysis (Million $)

	2004	2003	2002	2001	2000	1999	1998	1997	1996	1995
Revs.	24,710	22,487	20,607	19,629	18,257	16,773	15,873	11,520	10,274	9,392
Oper. Inc.	4,338	2,822	5,563	2,347	2,376	2,198	2,047	1,477	1,344	1,244
Depr.	1,375	1,351	1,364	1,276	1,155	1,034	964	778	720	652
Int. Exp.	136	118	139	144	106	98.0	124	91.0	135	142
Pretax Inc.	1,319	1,338	1,160	928	1,138	106	899	628	540	522
Eff. Tax Rate	36.5%	38.0%	37.5%	37.0%	39.5%	40.5%	44.6%	42.5%	43.0%	42.9%
Net Inc.	838	830	725	584	688	631	498	361	308	298
S&P Core Earnings	790	415	286	130	NA	NA	NA	NA	NA	NA

Balance Sheet & Other Fin. Data (Million $)

	2004	2003	2002	2001	2000	1999	1998	1997	1996	1995
Cash	1,046	538	331	121	68.0	325	230	122	93.0	358
Curr. Assets	4,970	3,941	3,665	3,449	3,285	3,141	2,880	2,133	1,728	1,869
Total Assets	19,134	15,385	13,812	13,340	11,527	10,648	9,686	7,625	6,699	6,433
Curr. Liab.	4,732	3,335	2,942	3,250	2,891	2,785	2,804	1,963	1,618	1,779
LT Debt	2,837	1,709	1,800	1,900	1,776	1,360	1,385	1,398	1,325	1,325
Common Equity	8,036	7,388	6,545	5,900	4,785	4,663	3,961	2,962	2,576	2,246
Total Cap.	12,054	9,979	8,944	8,256	6,906	6,316	5,620	4,520	3,965	3,627
Cap. Exp.	1,271	1,511	1,615	1,893	1,627	1,550	1,880	1,471	1,412	1,061
Cash Flow	2,213	2,181	2,089	1,860	1,843	1,665	1,462	1,139	1,028	950
Curr. Ratio	1.1	1.2	1.2	1.1	1.1	1.1	1.0	1.1	1.1	1.1
% LT Debt of Cap.	23.5	17.1	20.1	23.0	25.7	21.5	24.6	31.0	33.4	36.5
% Net Inc.of Revs.	3.4	3.7	3.5	3.0	3.8	3.8	3.1	3.1	3.0	3.2
% Ret. on Assets	4.9	5.7	5.3	4.7	6.2	6.2	5.8	5.0	4.7	4.8
% Ret. on Equity	10.9	11.8	11.7	10.9	14.6	14.6	14.4	13.0	12.8	14.3

Data as orig reptd.; bef. results of disc opers/spec. items. Per share data adj. for stk. divs.; EPS diluted. E-Estimated. NA-Not Available. NM-Not Meaningful. NR-Not Ranked. UR-Under Review.

Office: 942 South Shady Grove Road, Memphis, TN 38120-4117.
Telephone: 901-818-7500.
Website: http://www.fedex.com
Chrmn, Pres & CEO: F.W. Smith.
EVP & CFO: A.B. Graf, Jr.

EVP, Secy & General Counsel: K.R. Masterson.
Investor Contact: J. Clippard 901-818-7200.
Dirs: J. L. Barksdale, A. A. Busch IV, J. A. Edwardson, J. L. Estrin, J. K. Glass, P. Greer, J. R. Hyde III, S. A. Jackson, C. T. Manatt, F. W. Smith, J. I. Smith, P. S. Walsh, P. S. Willmott.

Founded: in 1971.
Domicile: Delaware.
Employees: 238,650.
S&P Analyst: Jim Corridore/PMW/JWP

Fifth Third Bancorp

Recommendation: **BUY** ★★★★
(SELL SELL HOLD BUY BUY)

12-Month Target Price: **$60.00**
(as of October 15, 2004)

FITB has an approximate 0.27% weighting in the **S&P 500**

Sector: Financials
Sub-Industry: Regional Banks
Peer Group: Midwest/West Major Regional Banks

Summary: This regional bank holding company operates about 1,000 full service banking centers, in Ohio, Kentucky, Indiana, Michigan, Illinois, Florida, and West Virginia.

Quantitative Evaluations

Price as of 11/12/04: $51.47 | **2004E S&P Core EPS:** $3.05

S&P Earnings & Dividend Rank: A+
D | C | B- | B | B+ | A- | A | **A+**

S&P Fair Value Rank: 3+
1 | 2 | **3** | 4 | 5
Lowest | | | | Highest

Fair Value Calc.: $50.80 (Fairly Valued)

S&P Investability Quotient Percentile
99%
FITB scored higher than 99% of all companies for which an S&P Report is available.

Volatility: Low
Low | Average | High

Technical Evaluation: Neutral
Since 11/04, the technical indicators for FITB have been Neutral.

Relative Strength Rank: Moderate
46
1 Lowest | Highest 99

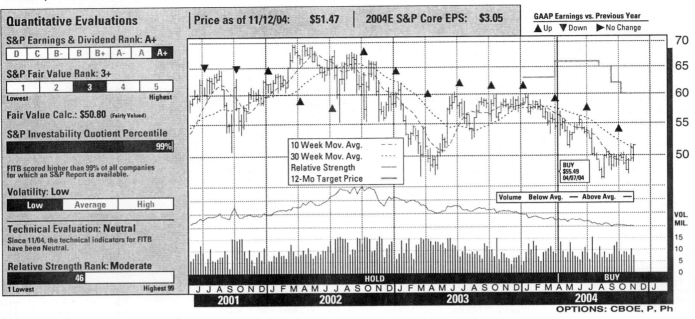

GAAP Earnings vs. Previous Year ▲ Up ▼ Down ▶ No Change

10 Week Mov. Avg.
30 Week Mov. Avg.
Relative Strength
12-Mo Target Price

BUY $55.49 04/07/04

Volume Below Avg. — Above Avg.

HOLD | BUY

J J A S O N D | J F M A M J J A S O N D | J F M A M J J A S O N D | J F M A M J J A S O N D | J
2001 | 2002 | 2003 | 2004

OPTIONS: CBOE, P, Ph

Analyst commentary prepared by Evan Momios, CFA /PMW

Highlights October 18, 2004

- We expect loan growth to continue at above industry-average levels in the fourth quarter, and to accelerate in 2005. We see results being aided by strong momentum in commercial lending in an improving economy. We believe the net interest margin is likely to remain under pressure for the rest of 2004, and project an average level of about 3.48% for the year, followed by a modest expansion to 3.55% on average for 2005. We think loan losses are likely to trend lower, reflecting improving economic conditions and reduced levels of nonperformers in recent quarters.

- We project double-digit growth in fee-based income, supported by particularly healthy gains that we see in coming quarters for deposit service charges and payment processing income, on electronic funds transfer and merchant processing activities. Benign equity market conditions that we expect, combined with anticipated new business gains, should boost investment advisory fees. We expect expense growth to remain well controlled, based on the company's performance in recent quarters.

- Assuming an average effective tax rate of 32.9%, we estimate 2004 EPS of $3.20, aided by share repurchases, up from $2.97 in 2003. We expect 2005 EPS of $3.55, assuming continued economic growth and measured increases in short-term interest rates.

Investment Rationale/Risk October 18, 2004

- We recommend buying the shares, based on our view of the company's proven ability to generate peer-leading revenue growth, ROE and ROA while keeping expenses under control.

- Risks to our recommendation and target price include a severe economic downturn combined with higher short-term interest rates that could result in an inverted yield curve; deterioration of consumer confidence that could affect consumer spending levels; legal and regulatory risks; and a geopolitical event that could affect U.S. equity markets.

- Over the past three and five years, the shares traded, on average, at what we view as respective multiples of 20X and 21X 12-month forward EPS. We believe that FITB remains one of the bank industry's most profitable institutions, with strong fundamentals. As a result, we think the shares can command a premium multiple to those of peers. Our 12-month target price of $60 is equal to about 17X our 2005 EPS estimate.

Key Stock Statistics

S&P Core EPS 2005E	3.39	52-week Range	$60.00-46.59
S&P Oper. EPS 2004E	3.20	12 Month P/E	15.6
P/E on S&P Oper. EPS 2004E	16.1	Beta	0.51
S&P Oper. EPS 2005E	3.55	Shareholders	53,900
Yield (%)	2.5%	Market Cap (B)	$ 28.9
Dividend Rate/Share	1.28	Shares Outstanding (M)	561.3

Value of $10,000 invested five years ago: **$ 11,549**

Dividend Data Dividends have been paid since 1952

Amount ($)	Date Decl.	Ex-Div. Date	Stock of Record	Payment Date
0.290	Dec. 16	Dec. 29	Dec. 31	Jan. 15 '04
0.320	Mar. 16	Mar. 29	Mar. 31	Apr. 15 '04
0.320	Jun. 15	Jun. 28	Jun. 30	Jul. 15 '04
0.320	Sep. 21	Sep. 28	Sep. 30	Oct. 14 '04

Revenues/Earnings Data Fiscal year ending December 31

Revenues (Million $)

	2004	2003	2002	2001	2000	1999
1Q	1,617	1,588	1,514	1,110	1,007	847.4
2Q	1,749	1,641	1,554	1,653	1,066	889.8
3Q	1,654	1,666	1,644	1,621	1,097	924.9
4Q	—	1,587	1,611	1,560	—	953.7
Yr.	—	6,474	6,324	6,506	4,276	3,616

Earnings Per Share ($)

	2004	2003	2002	2001	2000	1999
1Q	0.75	0.72	0.66	0.51	0.44	0.38
2Q	0.79	0.75	0.68	0.22	0.41	0.39
3Q	0.83	0.78	0.70	0.47	0.48	0.42
4Q	E0.83	0.73	0.72	0.65	0.50	0.25
Yr.	E3.20	2.97	2.76	1.86	1.83	1.43

Next earnings report expected: mid-January Source: S&P, Company Reports
EPS Estimates based on S&P Operating Earnings; historical GAAP earnings are as reported.

Fifth Third Bancorp

Recommendation: **BUY** ★ ★ ★ ★ ★   12-Month Target Price: **$60.00** (as of October 15, 2004)

Business Summary October 18, 2004

Cincinnati-based Fifth Third Bancorp has a track record of 30 consecutive years of higher earnings through 2003, a feat that few companies have accomplished. At the end of 2003, FITB operated 17 affiliates, with about 950 branches, located throughout Ohio, Kentucky, Indiana, Michigan, Illinois, Florida, West Virginia, and Tennessee. The company has consistently been ranked as one of the most efficient large U.S. banks, as measured by the efficiency ratio (noninterest expense to operating revenue). FITB's loan and lease portfolio of $54.2 billion at the end of 2003 was nearly evenly divided between commercial (51%) and consumer (49%).

Operations are divided into the Retail Banking, Commercial Banking, Investment Advisory Services and Electronic Payment Processing segments. Retail Banking (44% of net income in 2003) provides a full range of deposit products and consumer loans and leases. Commercial Banking (35%) offers banking, cash management and financial services to business, government and professional customers. Investment Advisory Services (6%) provides a full range of investment alternatives for individuals, companies, and not-for-profit organizations. Fifth Third Processing Solutions, its Electronic Payment Processing subsidiary (9%), provides electronic funds transfer services, merchant transaction processing, and other data processing.

In 2003, average earning assets, from which interest income is derived, amounted to $81.4 billion and consisted mainly of loans (62%) and investment securities (35%). Average sources of funds included interest, savings and money market deposits (34%), other time and certificates of deposit (12%), foreign deposits (4%), short-term borrowings (14%), long-term debt (10%), non-interest bearing demand deposits (12%), stockholders' equity (10%), and other (4%).

At December 31, 2003, nonperforming assets, consisting primarily of non-accrual loans, renegotiated loans and other real estate owned, were $319 million (0.61% of total loans and related assets), up from $273 million (0.59%) a year earlier. The allowance for loan losses, which is set aside for possible loan defaults, was $770.4 million (1.47% of total loans), versus $683.2 million (1.49%). Net chargeoffs, or the amount actually written off as uncollectible, were $312.2 million (0.63% of average loans) in 2003, versus $186.8 million (0.43%) in 2002.

In March 2003, directors authorized the repurchase of up to 20 million common shares in open market or private transactions. In 2003, the company bought back about 11.5 million shares, at an average price of $57 a share, under the March 2003 and previous authorizations. At the end of 2003, about 14.1 million shares remained authorized for purchase.

Company Financials Fiscal Year ending December 31

Per Share Data ($)

(Year Ended December 31)	2003	2002	2001	2000	1999	1998	1997	1996	1995	1994
Tangible Bk. Val.	13.46	13.12	13.09	10.50	8.79	7.04	8.47	5.19	4.79	4.18
Earnings	2.97	2.76	1.86	1.83	1.43	1.17	1.13	0.95	0.86	0.75
S&P Core Earnings	2.84	2.56	1.63	NA	NA	NA	NA	NA	NA	NA
Dividends	1.13	0.98	0.83	0.70	0.56	0.44	0.38	0.33	0.28	0.24
Payout Ratio	38%	36%	45%	38%	39%	37%	33%	34%	33%	32%
Prices - High	62.15	69.70	64.77	60.87	50.29	49.41	37.11	22.00	15.11	10.86
- Low	47.05	55.26	45.68	29.33	38.58	31.66	18.00	12.88	9.28	8.88
P/E Ratio - High	21	25	35	33	35	42	33	23	18	14
- Low	16	20	25	16	27	27	16	14	11	12

Income Statement Analysis (Million $)

	2003	2002	2001	2000	1999	1998	1997	1996	1995	1994
Net Int. Inc.	2,905	2,700	2,433	1,470	1,405	1,003	745	689	563	517
Tax Equiv. Adj.	39.0	39.5	45.5	93.0	73.0	49.2	43.0	39.0	33.0	24.6
Non Int. Inc.	2,399	2,047	1,626	1,013	876	626	439	364	301	256
Loan Loss Prov.	399	247	236	89.0	134	109	80.3	64.0	43.0	35.8
Exp./Op. Revs.	46.0%	51.9%	57.7%	45.1%	47.7%	47.9%	42.7%	45.0%	44.1%	46.6%
Pretax Inc.	2,547	2,432	1,653	1,275	1,026	726	604	500	431	365
Eff. Tax Rate	31.6%	31.2%	33.3%	32.3%	34.9%	34.4%	33.6%	33.0%	33.2%	33.1%
Net Inc.	1,722	1,635	1,101	863	668	476	401	335	288	244
% Net Int. Marg.	3.62	3.96	3.82	3.77	3.99	3.94	4.11	3.99	3.90	4.16
S&P Core Earnings	1,650	1,513	965	NA	NA	NA	NA	NA	NA	NA

Balance Sheet & Other Fin. Data (Million $)

	2003	2002	2001	2000	1999	1998	1997	1996	1995	1994
Money Mkt. Assets	55.0	312	225	198	355	119	29.4	44.6	6.80	23.8
Inv. Securities	29,402	25,828	20,748	15,827	12,817	8,539	6,469	6,401	4,338	2,531
Com'l Loans	28,242	22,614	10,839	12,382	11,141	9,093	5,684	5,903	5,209	4,345
Other Loans	25,493	23,314	30,709	13,570	14,746	9,375	7,555	7,060	6,808	5,586
Total Assets	91,143	80,894	71,026	45,857	41,589	28,922	21,375	20,549	17,053	14,957
Demand Deposits	31,899	11,139	10,595	5,604	8,011	6,355	2,426	2,496	6,103	1,680
Time Deposits	25,196	41,069	35,259	25,344	18,072	12,425	12,488	11,879	6,383	8,951
LT Debt	9,063	8,179	7,030	4,034	1,977	2,288	458	278	425	179
Common Equity	8,516	8,466	7,630	4,891	4,306	3,179	2,277	2,144	1,725	1,399
% Ret. on Assets	2.0	2.2	1.6	2.0	1.7	1.9	1.9	1.8	1.8	1.8
% Ret. on Equity	20.3	20.3	15.4	19.2	16.6	17.5	18.1	17.3	18.4	18.6
% Loan Loss Resv.	1.4	1.4	1.4	1.4	4.9	1.5	1.5	1.5	1.5	1.5
% Loans/Deposits	94.9	94.4	95.4	85.6	100.4	94.7	90.1	87.1	93.6	95.3
% Equity to Assets	9.9	10.6	10.2	10.3	10.3	10.8	10.5	10.3	7.5	9.5

Data as orig reptd.; bef. results of disc opers/spec. items. Per share data adj. for stk. divs. Bold denotes primary EPS - prior periods restated. E-Estimated. NA-Not Available. NM-Not Meaningful. NR-Not Ranked. UR-Under Review.

Office: 38 Fountain Square Plaza, Cincinnati, OH 45263.
Telephone: 513-534-5300.
Website: http://www.53.com
Pres & CEO: G.A. Schaefer, Jr.
EVP & CFO: N.E. Arnold.
EVP, Secy & General Counsel: P.L. Reynolds.

SVP & Treas: R.M. Graf.
VP & Investor Contact: B.S. Adams 513-534-0983.
Dirs: D. F. Allen, J. F. Barrett, R. T. Farmer, J. P. Hackett, J. H. Head, Jr., J. R. Herschede, A. M. Hill, R. L. Koch II, M. D. Livingston, K. W. Lowe, H. G. Meijer, R. B. Morgan, J. E. Rogers, G. A. Schaefer, Jr., J. J. Schiff, Jr., D. S. Taft, T. W. Traylor.

Founded: in 1862.
Domicile: Ohio.
Employees: 18,899.
S&P Analyst: Evan Momios, CFA /PMW

FirstEnergy Corp.

Recommendation: **HOLD** ★★★☆☆ SELL | SELL | HOLD | BUY | BUY

12-Month Target Price: **$41.00**
(as of October 22, 2004)

FE has an approximate 0.13% weighting in the **S&P 500**

Sector: Utilities
Sub-Industry: Electric Utilities
Peer Group: Electric Cos. (Domestic) - Very Large

Summary: This electric utility holding company serves about 4.3 million customers in portions of Ohio, Pennsylvania and New Jersey.

Quantitative Evaluations

S&P Earnings & Dividend Rank: B+

| D | C | B- | B | B+ | A- | A | A+ |

S&P Fair Value Rank: 2-

| 1 | 2 | 3 | 4 | 5 |
| Lowest | | | | Highest |

Fair Value Calc.: $38.50 (Slightly Overvalued)

S&P Investability Quotient Percentile

82%

FE scored higher than 82% of all companies for which an S&P Report is available.

Volatility: Low

| Low | Average | High |

Technical Evaluation: Bullish
Since 7/04, the technical indicators for FE have been Bullish.

Relative Strength Rank: Moderate

56

1 Lowest   Highest 99

Price as of 11/12/04: $43.15 | **2004E S&P Core EPS:** $2.51

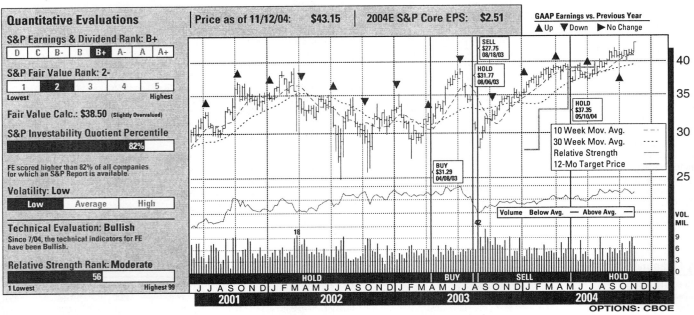

GAAP Earnings vs. Previous Year
▲ Up ▼ Down ► No Change

- 10 Week Mov. Avg.
- 30 Week Mov. Avg.
- Relative Strength
- 12-Mo Target Price

SELL $27.75 08/18/03
HOLD $31.77 08/06/03
HOLD $37.35 05/10/04
BUY $31.29 04/08/03

Volume Below Avg. — Above Avg.

VOL. MIL.

OPTIONS: CBOE

Analyst commentary prepared by Justin McCann/PMW/GG

Highlights August 30, 2004

- We expect 2004 EPS to advance over 45% from 2003's operating EPS of $1.86. With the Davis-Besse nuclear unit back in operation as of early April, FE no longer faces outage-related costs that cut 2003 EPS by $0.56. We expect 2004 results to benefit from a drop in interest expense and a lower level of pension and other benefit costs.

- In April 2004, a U.S./Canadian task force issued a final report that cited FE (as did a November 2003 interim report) as being largely responsible for the power blackout of August 14, 2003, due to what the task force called inadequate situational awareness following the automatic shutdown of one of its power plants, and its failure to manage tree growth along its transmission lines. However, the Department of Energy said it did not plan to take any action against the company.

- In August 2004, the Public Utilities Commission of Ohio issued an order that would maintain current generation prices for customers of the company's Ohio-based utilities through 2008. However, the utilities would be allowed to seek approval for the recovery of increased fuel costs from 2006 through 2008. In August 2003, FE said that, due to accounting changes, it had restated its earnings from 2000 to the first quarter of 2003.

Investment Rationale/Risk August 30, 2004

- The return to operation of the Davis-Besse nuclear unit is expected to improve and stabilize the earnings outlook, as should lower interests costs that have resulted from redemptions and refinancings that helped FE reduce its long term debt by over $1.8 billion in 2003, and reduced debt to 53% of total capitalization. We also think that risks were reduced in July 2004, when the company agreed to pay $89.9 million to settle shareholder lawsuits related to the blackout, the extended Davis-Besse outage, and restatements of financial results.

- Risks to our recommendation and target price include the possibility of a sharp reduction in the average P/E multiple of the Electric Utility group as a whole, as well as potential fallout (unrelated to the shareholder settlement) that could emerge from the U.S./Canadian task force findings related to FE's contribution to the August 2003 power blackout.

- With FE's projected annual EPS growth of about 5% above the industry average, we believe the shares are fairly valued, at a modest premium to the approximate peer P/E multiple of 13.3X on 2005 EPS estimates. Applying a P/E multiple of 13.5X to our 2005 EPS estimate of $2.95, our 12-month target price is $40.

Key Stock Statistics

S&P Core EPS 2005E	2.72	52-week Range	$43.15-32.61
S&P Oper. EPS 2004E	2.80	12 Month P/E	17.8
P/E on S&P Oper. EPS 2004E	15.4	Beta	0.06
S&P Oper. EPS 2005E	2.95	Shareholders	153,020
Yield (%)	3.5%	Market Cap (B)	$ 14.2
Dividend Rate/Share	1.50	Shares Outstanding (M)	329.8

Value of $10,000 invested five years ago: **$ 20,801**

Dividend Data Dividends have been paid since 1930

Amount ($)	Date Decl.	Ex-Div. Date	Stock of Record	Payment Date
0.375	Jan. 20	Feb. 04	Feb. 06	Mar. 01 '04
0.375	Apr. 20	May. 05	May. 07	Jun. 01 '04
0.375	Jul. 20	Aug. 04	Aug. 06	Sep. 01 '04
0.375	Oct. 19	Nov. 03	Nov. 05	Dec. 01 '04

Revenues/Earnings Data Fiscal year ending December 31

Revenues (Million $)

	2004	2003	2002	2001	2000	1999
1Q	3,183	3,221	2,762	2,000	1,608	1,418
2Q	3,150	2,853	2,899	1,804	1,702	1,524
3Q	3,536	3,434	3,451	1,952	1,892	1,732
4Q	—	2,799	3,040	2,300	1,827	1,646
Yr.	—	12,307	12,150	7,999	7,029	6,320

Earnings Per Share ($)

	2004	2003	2002	2001	2000	1999
1Q	0.53	0.39	0.29	0.49	0.63	0.60
2Q	0.62	0.03	0.79	0.67	0.60	0.55
3Q	0.91	0.51	1.05	1.06	0.89	0.82
4Q	E0.63	0.44	0.20	0.64	0.57	0.53
Yr.	E2.80	1.39	2.33	2.84	2.69	2.50

Next earnings report expected: mid-February Source: S&P, Company Reports
EPS Estimates based on S&P Operating Earnings; historical GAAP earnings are as reported.

FirstEnergy Corp.

Recommendation: **HOLD** ★ ★ ★ ☆ ☆   12-Month Target Price: **$41.00** (as of October 22, 2004)

Business Summary August 30, 2004

In November 2001, FirstEnergy acquired GPU, Inc. (GPU), a New Jersey-based holding company, for about $4.5 billion in cash and stock. It also assumed about $7.4 billion of GPU debt.

Three electric utilities were acquired in the GPU transaction: Jersey Central Power & Light (JCP&L), Metropolitan Edison (Met-Ed), and Pennsylvania Electric (Penelec). In 1996, the utilities were combined into a single subsidiary that now serves a population of about 5.4 million, in New Jersey and Pennsylvania.

FE was formed in November 1997, through the merger of Ohio Edison and Centerior Energy. Ohio Edison (OE) and its wholly owned Pennsylvania Power Co. unit serve a population of about 3 million in the highly industrialized areas of central and northeastern Ohio and western Pennsylvania. Centerior Energy, formed through the 1986 merger of Cleveland Electric Illuminating (CEI) and Toledo Edison (TE), supplies electricity to a population of about 2.7 million in northern Ohio.

FE's consolidated sources of fuel supply in 2003 were: coal, 68.4% (65.6% in 2002); and nuclear, 31.6% (34.4%).

In July 2000, the Public Utility Commission of Ohio approved the company's transition plan. The plan continues a freeze on the distribution rates of OE, TE and CEI through 2007, but enables FE to recover transition costs, including regulatory

assets (utility-related costs that can be recovered from customers), through 2006 for OE, mid-2007 for TE, and 2008 for CEI.

In 1996, GPU and Cinergy formed a joint venture to acquire Midlands Electricity plc, one of the 12 British regional electric companies, for about $2.6 billion. In 1999, GPU acquired Cinergy's 50% interest in Midlands for $700 million. Including GPU's assumption of CIN's share of liabilities, the transaction was valued at $1.55 billion. In May 2002, FE sold a 79.9% interest in the holding company for Midlands to Aquila, Inc. (formerly UtiliCorp), for about $264 million, plus the assumption of $1.7 billion of Midlands debt. In January 2004, the company sold its remaining 20.1% interest in Midlands to a subsidiary of PowerGen UK plc. Terms were not disclosed. In February 2004, FE said it had sold all remaining international assets that were acquired in the GPU transaction, and no longer had ownership interests in international operating assets.

In March 2002, the company found corrosion at a nozzle on the reactor head at its Davis-Besse nuclear plant. After receiving approval from the Nuclear Regulatory Commission, the unit was returned to operation on April 4, 2004. With the GPU acquisition, FE now owns the Three Mile Island Unit 2 nuclear plant, which is in a post-defueling monitored storage condition. In December 1999, GPU sold the Three Mile Island Unit 1 plant to AmerGen Energy for $100 million, with payments to be made over five years.

Company Financials Fiscal Year ending December 31

Per Share Data ($)

(Year Ended December 31)	2003	2002	2001	2000	1999	1998	1997	1996	1995	1994
Tangible Bk. Val.	6.55	4.11	6.04	11.42	10.47	9.62	8.91	16.41	15.78	15.13
Earnings	1.39	2.33	2.84	2.69	2.50	1.95	1.94	2.10	2.05	1.97
S&P Core Earnings	1.61	1.69	2.36	NA	NA	NA	NA	NA	NA	NA
Dividends	1.50	1.50	1.13	1.50	1.50	1.50	1.50	1.50	1.50	1.50
Payout Ratio	108%	64%	40%	56%	60%	77%	77%	71%	73%	76%
Prices - High	38.90	39.12	36.98	32.12	33.18	34.06	29.00	24.87	23.75	22.75
- Low	25.82	24.85	25.10	18.00	22.12	27.06	19.25	19.25	18.50	16.50
P/E Ratio - High	28	17	13	12	13	17	15	12	12	12
- Low	19	11	9	7	9	14	10	9	9	8

Income Statement Analysis (Million $)

	2003	2002	2001	2000	1999	1998	1997	1996	1995	1994
Revs.	12,307	12,152	7,999	7,029	6,320	5,861	2,821	2,470	2,466	2,368
Depr.	1,282	1,106	890	934	938	741	475	356	256	221
Maint.	NA	NA	NA	NA	NA	NA	NA	NA	192	185
Fxd. Chgs. Cov.	1.88	2.25	2.85	2.71	2.62	2.21	2.64	2.87	2.68	2.54
Constr. Credits	NA	24.5	35.5	27.1	13.4	7.64	3.50	3.10	5.70	5.20
Eff. Tax Rate	49.0%	44.5%	42.0%	38.6%	41.0%	42.2%	40.5%	39.0%	38.6%	38.4%
Net Inc.	422	686	655	599	568	441	306	315	317	304
S&P Core Earnings	492	496	546	NA	NA	NA	NA	NA	NA	NA

Balance Sheet & Other Fin. Data (Million $)

	2003	2002	2001	2000	1999	1998	1997	1996	1995	1994
Gross Prop.	22,374	21,231	20,589	12,839	15,013	15,255	17,516	8,733	8,747	8,745
Cap. Exp.	856	998	852	588	625	653	204	148	198	258
Net Prop.	13,269	12,680	12,428	7,575	9,093	9,243	11,880	5,418	5,695	5,835
Capitalization:										
LT Debt	9,789	11,636	12,508	6,552	6,906	7,307	6,970	2,713	2,786	3,167
% LT Debt	53.1	62.0	62.8	58.5	60.2	62.2	57.5	48.6	50.1	54.1
Pfd.	352	Nil	Nil	Nil	Nil	Nil	995	367	372	368
% Pfd.	1.91	Nil	Nil	Nil	Nil	Nil	8.20	6.60	6.70	6.30
Common	8,289	7,120	7,399	4,653	4,564	4,449	4,160	2,503	2,408	2,317
% Common	45.0	38.0	37.2	41.5	39.8	37.8	34.3	44.8	43.2	39.6
Total Cap.	20,608	21,360	22,852	13,540	13,970	14,325	14,754	7,560	7,552	7,875
% Oper. Ratio	90.4	86.6	50.8	37.8	82.0	82.2	81.2	78.5	77.0	76.5
% Earn. on Net Prop.	11.2	17.4	16.8	18.1	16.7	NA	6.0	9.5	9.8	9.5
% Return On Revs.	3.4	5.6	8.2	8.5	9.0	7.5	10.8	12.8	12.9	12.8
% Return On Invest. Capital	6.5	7.4	21.8	32.0	7.8	NA	5.5	7.5	7.5	7.4
% Return On Com. Equity	5.5	9.5	10.9	13.0	12.6	NA	9.2	12.3	12.5	12.4

Data as orig. reptd.; bef. results of disc. opers. and/or spec. items. Data pr. to Nov. 7, 1997 are for Ohio Edison before the merger. Per share data adj. for stk. divs. as of ex-div. date. Bold denotes basic EPS (FASB 128). E-Estimated. NA-Not Available. NM-Not Meaningful. NR-Not Ranked.

Office: 76 South Main Street, Akron, OH 44308-1890.
Telephone: 330-384-5100.
Website: http://www.firstenergycorp.com
Chrmn: G.M. Smart.
Pres & CEO: A.J. Alexander.
COO & EVP: R.R. Grigg.
SVP & CFO: R.H. Marsh.

SVP & General Counsel: L.L. Vespoli.
Investor Contact: K.E. Turosky 330-384-5500.
Dirs: P. T. Addison, A. J. Alexander, C. A. Cartwright, W. T. Cottle, R. W. Maier, E. J. Novak, Jr., R. N. Pokelwaldt, P. J. Powers, C. A. Rein, R. C. Savage, G. M. Smart, W. M. Taylor, J. T. Williams, Sr., P. K. Woolf.

Founded: in 1996.
Domicile: Ohio.
Employees: 15,905.
S&P Analyst: Justin McCann/PMW/GG

First Data

Recommendation: **HOLD** ★ ★ ★ ★ ★
SELL SELL HOLD BUY BUY

12-Month Target Price: $46.00
(as of October 14, 2004)

FDC has an approximate 0.34% weighting in the **S&P 500**

Sector: Information Technology
Sub-Industry: Data Processing & Outsourced Services
Peer Group: Payment Processors & Services

Summary: FDC provides credit and debit card issuing and processing services; e-commerce solutions; wire transfers and money orders; and check processing and verification services.

Quantitative Evaluations

S&P Earnings & Dividend Rank: A-

| D | C | B- | B | B+ | A- | A | A+ |

S&P Fair Value Rank: 4-

| 1 | 2 | 3 | 4 | 5 |
| Lowest | | | | Highest |

Fair Value Calc.: $45.50 (Slightly Undervalued)

S&P Investability Quotient Percentile

90%

FDC scored higher than 90% of all companies for which an S&P Report is available.

Volatility: Low

| Low | Average | High |

Technical Evaluation: Neutral
Since 11/04, the technical indicators for FDC have been Neutral.

Relative Strength Rank: Moderate

44

| 1 Lowest | Highest 99 |

Price as of 11/12/04: **$43.34** | 2004E S&P Core EPS: **$2.28**

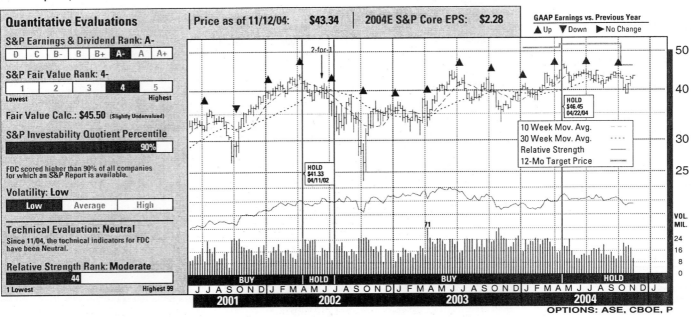

Analyst commentary prepared by Scott H. Kessler/PMW/BK

Highlights October 20, 2004

- We expect EPS to grow nearly 15% annually over the next three years. We see results continuing to be paced by the Payment Services segment (40% of 2004 third quarter revenues), driven by Western Union, particularly its international operations. Western Union has made progress in expanding its money transfer services throughout what we view as the extremely attractive markets of China and India. The business had 14% of its agent locations based in those two countries as of June 2004; FDC entered those markets in 2001.

- We see the Merchant Services segment (39%) and Card Issuing Services unit (24%) bolstered by the acquisition of Concord EFS, which was completed in February 2004.

- EPS has been aided by share repurchases that led to sequential reductions in the number of shares outstanding in 2002 and 2003. In October 2004, directors increased FDC's buyback authorization by $1.5 billion. Year to date into October 2004, the company had purchased 63 million shares for $2.7 billion (about $42.86 a share). Our EPS projections include the acquisition of Concord EFS, but exclude certain one-item items such as associated integration expenses.

Investment Rationale/Risk October 20, 2004

- We believe the acquisition of Concord EFS (valued at $6.7 billion in stock) will strengthen FDC's merchant payment processing, electronic payments, and debit card businesses. However, the purchase was allowed based on the company's indication that it would sell its majority stake in NYCE. In September 2004, FDC sold this stake, for $610 million. We believe NYCE was an attractive strategic asset for FDC.

- Risks to our opinion and target price include competitive threats to the Western Union business in the U.S. and abroad (particularly from large banks such as Citibank and Bank America), pricing pressures in the card Issuing segment (especially following the announcement of the impending loss of JPMorgan Chase as a major card processing customer in July 2004), and issues associated with recent and pending transactions.

- Based on relative P/E multiple and P/E to growth ratio analyses (the shares traded recently at a modest discount to the levels of the S&P 500 Data Processing & Outsourced Services Sub-Industry) and our DCF model, which assumes a discount rate of 11.3% and annual free cash flow growth averaging 15% over the next five years, our 12-month target price is $46.

Key Stock Statistics

S&P Core EPS 2005E	2.26	52-week Range	$46.80-35.80
S&P Oper. EPS 2004E	2.22	12 Month P/E	19.5
P/E on S&P Oper. EPS 2004E	19.5	Beta	0.83
S&P Oper. EPS 2005E	2.60	Shareholders	3,028
Yield (%)	0.2%	Market Cap (B)	$ 36.0
Dividend Rate/Share	0.08	Shares Outstanding (M)	829.8

Value of $10,000 invested five years ago: **$ 18,574**

Dividend Data Dividends have been paid since 1992

Amount ($)	Date Decl.	Ex-Div. Date	Stock of Record	Payment Date
0.020	Dec. 10	Dec. 30	Jan. 02	Jan. 12 '04
0.020	Mar. 10	Mar. 30	Apr. 01	Apr. 12 '04
0.020	May. 19	Jun. 29	Jul. 01	Jul. 12 '04
0.020	Jul. 14	Sep. 29	Oct. 01	Oct. 11 '04

Revenues/Earnings Data Fiscal year ending December 31

Revenues (Million $)

	2004	2003	2002	2001	2000	1999
1Q	2,258	2,009	1,740	1,509	1,318	1,270
2Q	2,529	2,114	1,890	1,608	1,384	1,398
3Q	2,536	2,140	1,948	1,652	1,440	1,400
4Q	—	2,244	2,059	1,682	1,508	1,472
Yr.	—	8,400	7,636	6,451	5,705	5,540

Earnings Per Share ($)

	2004	2003	2002	2001	2000	1999
1Q	0.61	0.39	0.32	0.24	0.20	0.16
2Q	0.53	0.47	0.39	0.30	0.26	0.22
3Q	0.54	0.49	0.45	0.19	0.38	0.24
4Q	E0.62	0.55	0.46	0.37	0.30	0.78
Yr.	E2.22	1.86	1.61	1.10	1.13	1.38

Next earnings report expected: early-February Source: S&P, Company Reports
EPS Estimates based on S&P Operating Earnings; historical GAAP earnings are as reported.

Recommendation: **HOLD** ★ ★ ★ ☆ ☆   12-Month Target Price: **$46.00** (as of October 14, 2004)

Business Summary October 20, 2004

In 2003, First Data had more than 348 million card accounts on file, processed 12.2 billion North American merchant transactions, and operated more than 182,000 Western Union agent locations. FDC has transformed itself from a small credit card processing operation (part of American Express) into one of the world's largest independent data services companies.

The Payment Services segment, which accounted for 41% of 2003 total revenues (40% in 2002), includes Western Union, and provides money transfer services to consumers and businesses from one location to another, or through the issuance of an official check or money order from a bank or other institution. Offerings include consumer-to-consumer money transfers (for emergency situations or to send funds to family/friends in other locations), consumer-to-business bill payment services (for payments to utility companies, collection agencies, finance companies, mortgage lenders, and other billers), official checks and money orders (which are alternatives to cashier's or bank checks), and prepaid services (development, implementation and management of pre-paid stored-value card issuance and processing services for retailers).

Merchant Services (34%, 33%) facilitates the acceptance of consumer transactions at the point of sale, whether that is a physical merchant location, the Internet, or an ATM. Services include merchant acquiring (facilitation of credit and debit card acceptance by merchants), check verification and guarantee services, ATM- and PIN-based processing (operation of ATM network and provision of transaction processing services including authorization and settlement to

issuers of PIN-based debit cards), and gaming services (ownership and management of ATMs in gaming establishments, provision of credit card cash advance and debit card cash access services to customers of gaming establishments, and guarantee or verification of check transactions for such establishments).

Card Issuing Services (23%, 24%) provides U.S. and international card processing for card issuers. Offerings include card processing (credit, debit, and private label card processing services for financial institutions and other issuers of cards, including account maintenance, transaction authorization and posting, statement generation and printing, card embossing, fraud and risk management services, and settlement) and card processing software (VisionPLUS card processing software to financial institutions, retailers, and third-party processors primarily in international markets).

The Emerging Payments segment (1.6%, 1.8%) consists of a 75% stake in eOne Global, which focuses on identifying, developing, commercializing, and operating emerging payment systems and related technologies in three areas: government payments (electronic tax payments to government entities), mobile payments (software and services for wireless payments and transaction processing for mobile phone carriers), and enterprise payments (accounts receivable and payable systems and processing services and commercial tax compliance systems). In April 2004, FDC announced that the Emerging Payments segment would be included in All Other and Corporate revenue.

Company Financials Fiscal Year ending December 31

Per Share Data ($)

(Year Ended December 31)	2003	2002	2001	2000	1999	1998	1997	1996	1995	1994
Tangible Bk. Val.	NM	NM	NM	0.20	0.51	NM	NM	NM	NM	2.36
Cash Flow	2.62	2.30	1.90	1.83	2.09	1.18	0.95	1.11	0.29	0.79
Earnings	1.86	1.61	1.10	1.13	1.38	0.52	0.40	0.69	-0.10	0.47
S&P Core Earnings	1.71	1.44	1.07	NA	NA	NA	NA	NA	NA	NA
Dividends	0.08	0.07	0.04	0.04	0.04	0.04	0.04	0.04	0.03	0.03
Payout Ratio	4%	4%	4%	4%	3%	8%	10%	5%	NM	6%
Prices - High	44.90	45.07	40.10	28.84	25.75	18.03	23.06	22.00	17.81	12.65
- Low	30.90	23.75	24.87	18.50	15.65	9.84	12.50	15.18	11.50	10.12
P/E Ratio - High	24	28	36	26	19	35	58	32	NM	27
- Low	17	15	23	16	11	19	32	22	NM	22

Income Statement Analysis (Million $)

	2003	2002	2001	2000	1999	1998	1997	1996	1995	1994
Revs.	8,400	7,636	6,451	5,705	5,540	5,118	5,235	4,934	4,081	1,652
Oper. Inc.	2,519	2,374	2,154	1,925	1,831	1,726	1,726	1,548	1,162	526
Depr.	569	539	638	589	618	591	534	424	347	144
Int. Exp.	107	117	120	99	104	104	117	110	106	41.3
Pretax Inc.	1,978	1,773	1,211	1,308	1,825	712	706	1,032	168	356
Eff. Tax Rate	23.5%	24.4%	27.8%	28.9%	34.3%	34.6%	49.5%	38.3%	NM	41.6%
Net Inc.	1,394	1,238	875	930	1,200	466	357	637	-84.0	208
S&P Core Earnings	1,285	1,118	854	NA	NA	NA	NA	NA	NA	NA

Balance Sheet & Other Fin. Data (Million $)

	2003	2002	2001	2000	1999	1998	1997	1996	1995	1994
Cash	840	819	918	853	3,324	460	411	272	231	1,188
Curr. Assets	NA	NA	NA	NA	NA	NA	NA	NA	NA	NA
Total Assets	25,586	26,591	21,912	17,295	17,005	16,587	15,315	14,340	12,218	5,419
Curr. Liab.	NA	NA	NA	NA	NA	NA	NA	NA	NA	NA
LT Debt	2,916	2,562	2,685	975	1,072	1,129	1,134	1,709	886	429
Common Equity	4,047	6,691	3,520	6,025	3,908	3,756	3,657	3,710	3,145	1,015
Total Cap.	6,963	9,253	6,205	7,000	4,980	4,885	5,408	5,417	4,031	1,444
Cap. Exp.	162	212	187	149	244	326	297	393	262	155
Cash Flow	1,963	1,776	1,513	1,518	1,818	1,057	891	106	263	352
Curr. Ratio	NA	NA	NA	NA	NA	NA	NA	NA	NA	NA
% LT Debt of Cap.	41.9	27.7	43.3	13.9	21.5	23.1	32.4	31.5	22.0	29.7
% Net Inc.of Revs.	16.6	16.2	13.6	16.3	21.7	9.1	6.8	12.9	NM	12.6
% Ret. on Assets	5.3	5.1	4.5	5.4	7.1	2.9	2.4	4.8	NM	4.4
% Ret. on Equity	34.0	19.6	24.1	15.3	20.0	12.6	9.7	18.6	NM	21.4

Data as orig reptd.; bef. results of disc opers/spec. items. Per share data adj. for stk. divs.; EPS diluted. E-Estimated. NA-Not Available. NM-Not Meaningful. NR-Not Ranked. UR-Under Review.

Office: 6200 South Quebec Street, Greenwood Village, CO 80111-4729.
Telephone: 303-967-8000.
Email: fdc.ir@firstdatacorp.com
Website: http://www.firstdata.com
Chrmn, Pres & CEO: C.T. Fote.
EVP & CFO: K.S. Patmore.

EVP, Secy & General Counsel: M.T. Whealy.
Investor Contact: D. Banks 303-967-6756.
Dirs: D. Burnham, A. Davis, H. Duques, C. T. Fote, J. Greenberg, C. F. Jones, R. P. Kiphart, J. D. Robinson, III, C. T. Russell, B. L. Schwartz, J. E. Spero, A. F. Weinbach.

Founded: in 1989.
Domicile: Delaware.
Employees: 29,000.
S&P Analyst: Scott H. Kessler/PMW/BK

First Horizon National

Recommendation: **SELL** ★ ★ ★ ★ ★
SELL · SELL · HOLD · BUY · BUY

12-Month Target Price: **$38.00**
(as of October 04, 2004)

FHN has an approximate 0.05% weighting in the **S&P 500**

Sector: Financials
Sub-Industry: Regional Banks
Peer Group: South Larger Regional Banks

Summary: FHN (formerly First Tennessee National) owns First Tennessee Bank and First Horizon Home Loan Corporation.

Quantitative Evaluations		Price as of 11/12/04: **$44.23**	2004E S&P Core EPS: **$3.48**

S&P Earnings & Dividend Rank: A+

D	C	B-	B	B+	A-	A	**A+**

S&P Fair Value Rank: 4+

1	2	3	**4**	5
Lowest				Highest

Fair Value Calc.: $43.30 (Slightly Overvalued)

S&P Investability Quotient Percentile

95%

FHN scored higher than 95% of all companies for which an S&P Report is available.

Volatility: Low

Low	Average	High

Technical Evaluation: Neutral
Since 11/04, the technical indicators for FHN have been Neutral.

Relative Strength Rank: Moderate

38	
1 Lowest	Highest 99

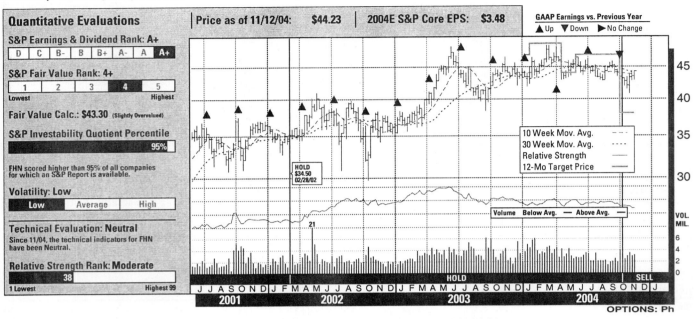

GAAP Earnings vs. Previous Year
▲ Up ▼ Down ► No Change

- - - 10 Week Mov. Avg.
····· 30 Week Mov. Avg.
—— Relative Strength
—— 12-Mo Target Price

Volume Below Avg. — Above Avg. —

HOLD $34.50 02/28/02

HOLD   SELL

VOL. MIL.

J J A S O N D J F M A M J J A S O N D J F M A M J J A S O N D J F M A M J J A S O N D J
2001   2002   2003   2004

OPTIONS: Ph

Analyst commentary prepared by Richard Tortoriello/DC/GG

Highlights October 07, 2004

- We continue to expect that higher mortgage rates, along with a dearth of refinancing candidates, will have a negative impact on mortgage banking revenue. Mortgage origination volume fell 41%, year to year, in the second quarter, as refinancing volume declined 76%. Even with our belief that an acceleration of economic activity should aid the rest of FHN's national product lines, we still expect noninterest income to drop 14% in 2004. We see net interest income rising 7%, on more robust demand for commercial credit in an improving economy. As a result, we project that total revenue will decline 6% for the year.

- We expect asset quality to improve as the company continues to focus on its risk profile, and see loan loss provisioning down 38%. We project that operating expenses will decline 9%, on the forecast decline in mortgage originations that we project.

- All told, we expect EPS to rise 3% in 2004, to $3.74, from $3.62 in 2003, with a rise to $4.00 in 2005. Our 2004 Standard & Poor's Core Earnings projection is $3.57, reflecting our view of average earnings quality for a regional bank.

Investment Rationale/Risk October 07, 2004

- We believe FHN is significantly more dependent on mortgage banking income for its profit growth than most of its South Eastern regional banking peers. Given our expectation that mortgage rate volatility will increase in late 2004 and into 2005, negatively affecting FHN's interest-rate hedging strategy, we have recently become more negative on FHN and recommend avoiding the shares. We also note that FHN announced in September that third quarter earnings would be negatively affected by unusually low fixed income demand, and we are concerned such low demand could continue for the foreseeable future.

- Risks to our recommendation and target price include better than anticipated mortgage banking results, as well as better than expected results from FHN's capital markets division.

- Our 12-month target price is $38, derived by applying a 1.20X P/E to growth (PEG) multiple using our 2004 EPS estimate and our five-year EPS growth projection. This is a discount to the 1.30-1.35 multiple afforded comparable regional banks, reflecting our view of relatively high interest rate sensitivity stemming from FHN's reliance on mortgage banking.

Key Stock Statistics

S&P Core EPS 2005E	3.59	52-week Range	$48.65-40.79
S&P Oper. EPS 2004E	3.65	12 Month P/E	12.2
P/E on S&P Oper. EPS 2004E	12.1	Beta	0.54
S&P Oper. EPS 2005E	3.80	Shareholders	8,579
Yield (%)	3.9%	Market Cap (B)	$ 5.4
Dividend Rate/Share	1.72	Shares Outstanding (M)	123.1

Value of $10,000 invested five years ago: **$ 12,459**

Dividend Data Dividends have been paid since 1895

Amount ($)	Date Decl.	Ex-Div. Date	Stock of Record	Payment Date
0.400	Jan. 21	Mar. 10	Mar. 12	Apr. 01 '04
0.400	Apr. 20	Jun. 09	Jun. 11	Jul. 01 '04
0.400	Jul. 20	Sep. 08	Sep. 10	Oct. 01 '04
0.430	Oct. 20	Dec. 15	Dec. 17	Jan. 01 '05

Revenues/Earnings Data Fiscal year ending December 31

Revenues (Million $)

	2004	2003	2002	2001	2000	1999
1Q	624.1	773.1	582.9	643.3	541.7	586.8
2Q	630.1	814.4	585.3	693.1	595.0	587.4
3Q	627.8	801.8	652.5	664.5	613.8	589.5
4Q	—	639.7	759.4	633.2	676.0	578.9
Yr.	—	2,693	2,580	2,515	2,426	2,343

Earnings Per Share ($)

	2004	2003	2002	2001	2000	1999
1Q	0.92	0.91	0.67	0.47	0.30	0.40
2Q	0.92	0.90	0.69	0.68	0.42	0.45
3Q	0.89	0.91	0.73	0.68	0.50	0.52
4Q	E0.92	0.90	0.80	0.68	0.55	0.54
Yr.	E3.65	3.62	2.89	2.51	1.77	1.91

Next earnings report expected: late-January Source: S&P, Company Reports
EPS Estimates based on S&P Operating Earnings; historical GAAP earnings are as reported.

STANDARD &POOR'S

First Horizon National Corporation

Stock Report
November 13, 2004
NYSE Symbol: **FHN**

Recommendation: **SELL** ★ ★ ☆ ☆ ☆   12-Month Target Price: **$38.00** (as of October 04, 2004)

Business Summary October 07, 2004

First Horizon National (formerly First Tennessee National) is a Memphis, TN-based regional bank holding company with $25.1 billion in assets at December 31, 2003. Its principal subsidiary is First Tennessee Bank. During 2003, 67% of revenues came from fee income and 33% from net interest income. This contrasts with the average regional bank, which derives about 30% of its revenues from fee income sources. The present corporate title was adopted in April 2004.

Income from mortgage banking operations was the largest contributor to fee income, accounting for 38% of fee income in 2003, up from 33% in 2002. FHN provides mortgage banking services through its subsidiary, First Horizon Home Loan Corporation. At December 31, 2003, First Horizon Home Loan had 301 offices in 39 states, and ranked among the 15 U.S. leaders in mortgage loan originations and mortgage loan servicing, as reported by Inside Mortgage Finance.

Unlike many of its competitors, the company has generally not grown through an aggressive acquisition strategy, swallowing up neighboring banks, but has focused on expanding its nationally ranked specialty lines of business. In addition to traditional banking activities such as lending, key operations include mortgage banking (origination and servicing), bond underwriting and sales, check clearing (First Express), and merchant processing of credit card transactions.

Traditional retail/commercial banking activities are still an important profit driver for the bank. The primary indicator, net interest income (the interest income received on loans and other investments less the interest expense it pays for the use of those funds), increased 6.8% in 2003, even with the net interest margin narrowing to 3.78%, from 4.35% in 2002, after average earning assets increased 23%.

FHN's loan portfolio totaled $14.0 billion at December 31, 2003, up from $11.3 billion a year earlier. Commercial, financial and industrial loans comprised 33% of the portfolio, and residential real estate loans accounted for 49%.

A key benchmark for assessing a bank's loan quality is the ratio of nonperforming loans to total loans. Nonperforming loans decreased to 0.30% of the total at December 31, 2003, from 0.49% a year earlier. Net chargeoffs dropped to 0.54% of average loans in 2003, from 0.93% in 2002. The allowance for loan losses was reduced to 1.15% of loans at year-end 2003, from 1.27% a year earlier.

In June 2001, the company sold its interest in Check Solutions Co., recording a divestiture gain of $44.9 million. In April 2001, FHN sold its subsidiary, Peoples & Union Bank of Lewisburg, TN. Also in April, it sold its existing portfolio of educational loans. The bank planned to continue to make loans to students and their families under the First Tennessee brand. FHN expected the sales to boost its long-term growth rate by enhancing its overall business mix.

In April 2004, the corporation's name was changed to First Horizon National Corporation. FHN believes the name better reflects its national presence, rather than the regional focus suggested by the First Tennessee name.

Company Financials Fiscal Year ending December 31

Per Share Data ($)

(Year Ended December 31)	2003	2002	2001	2000	1999	1998	1997	1996	1995	1994
Tangible Bk. Val.	13.43	11.92	10.27	9.81	8.53	2.34	3.38	4.25	4.43	4.61
Earnings	3.62	2.89	2.51	1.77	1.91	1.72	1.50	1.34	1.21	1.14
S&P Core Earnings	3.32	2.59	1.88	NA	NA	NA	NA	NA	NA	NA
Dividends	1.30	1.05	0.91	0.88	0.76	0.66	0.61	0.55	0.49	0.43
Payout Ratio	36%	36%	36%	50%	40%	38%	41%	41%	40%	38%
Prices - High	48.50	41.00	37.49	29.31	45.37	38.37	34.81	19.43	15.43	11.93
- Low	35.58	29.76	27.12	15.93	27.37	23.37	18.37	14.25	9.81	9.25
P/E Ratio - High	13	14	15	17	24	22	23	15	13	10
- Low	10	10	11	9	14	14	12	11	8	8

Income Statement Analysis (Million $)

	2003	2002	2001	2000	1999	1998	1997	1996	1995	1994
Net Int. Inc.	806	753	686	598	590	541	483	451	391	381
Tax Equiv. Adj.	NA	1.50	2.10	2.60	3.00	NA	NA	5.40	5.00	4.86
Non Int. Inc.	1,638	1,550	1,321	1,068	1,121	982	669	574	494	369
Loan Loss Prov.	86.7	92.2	93.5	67.4	57.9	51.4	51.1	35.7	20.6	16.7
Exp./Op. Revs.	67.1%	71.3%	67.7%	75.5%	74.4%	73.7%	68.1%	68.7%	69.0%	72.4%
Pretax Inc.	719	558	494	337	379	353	315	282	253	207
Eff. Tax Rate	34.2%	32.5%	33.2%	31.0%	34.8%	36.0%	37.3%	36.2%	34.8%	29.4%
Net Inc.	473	376	330	233	248	226	197	180	165	146
% Net Int. Marg.	3.78	4.33	4.27	3.73	3.80	3.80	4.23	4.13	3.92	4.28
S&P Core Earnings	434	337	248	NA	NA	NA	NA	NA	NA	NA

Balance Sheet & Other Fin. Data (Million $)

	2003	2002	2001	2000	1999	1998	1997	1996	1995	1994
Money Mkt. Assets	1,182	1,157	877	380	430	484	482	291	250	440
Inv. Securities	2,470	2,700	2,526	2,839	3,101	2,426	2,186	2,240	2,111	2,094
Com'l Loans	6,904	5,723	5,598	5,327	4,431	4,117	3,769	3,522	3,331	2,889
Other Loans	7,087	5,622	4,685	4,912	4,933	4,440	4,416	4,088	4,792	3,829
Total Assets	24,507	23,823	20,617	18,555	18,373	18,734	14,388	13,059	12,077	10,522
Demand Deposits	4,540	5,149	4,010	2,847	2,798	3,058	2,536	2,123	1,984	1,702
Time Deposits	11,140	10,564	9,596	9,342	8,560	8,665	7,136	6,910	6,598	5,987
LT Debt	1,117	1,074	3,066	3,119	459	514	169	175	260	92.4
Common Equity	1,850	1,691	1,478	1,384	1,241	1,100	954	955	873	749
% Ret. on Assets	2.0	1.7	1.7	1.3	1.3	1.4	1.4	1.4	1.4	1.4
% Ret. on Equity	26.7	23.8	23.0	17.7	21.1	23.0	20.7	20.1	20.0	20.0
% Loan Loss Resv.	0.9	0.9	1.1	1.2	1.2	1.6	1.5	1.5	1.4	1.6
% Loans/Deposits	108.2	102.7	100.6	98.2	100.5	78.3	85.9	84.3	94.6	87.4
% Equity to Assets	7.3	7.1	7.3	7.1	6.3	6.2	7.0	7.1	7.2	7.2

Data as orig reptd.; bef. results of disc opers/spec. items. Per share data adj. for stk. divs.; EPS diluted. E-Estimated. NA-Not Available. NM-Not Meaningful. NR-Not Ranked. UR-Under Review.

Office: 165 Madison Avenue, Memphis, TN 38103.
Telephone: 901-523-4444.
Website: http://www.firsttennessee.com
Chrmn, Pres & CEO: J.K. Glass.
EVP & CFO: M.L. Mosby III.
EVP & Chief Acctg Officer: J.F. Keen.

EVP & General Counsel: H.A. Johnson III.
SVP & Secy: C.A. Billings, Jr.
Investor Contact: M. Yates 901-523-4068.
Dirs: R. C. Blattberg, G. E. Cates, J. K. Glass, J. A. Haslam III, R. B. Martin, V. R. Palmer, M. D. Rose, M. F. Sammons, W. B. Sansom, J. P. Ward, L. Yancy III.

Founded: in 1968.
Domicile: Tennessee.
Employees: 11,494.
S&P Analyst: Richard Tortoriello/DC/GG

Recommendation: **BUY** ★★★★☆
SELL SELL HOLD BUY BUY

12-Month Target Price: $42.00
(as of July 22, 2004)

FISV has an approximate 0.07% weighting in the **S&P 500**

Sector: Information Technology
Sub-Industry: Data Processing & Outsourced Services
Peer Group: Financial Services Processors & Services

Summary: This company is a full-service provider of computerized account processing and integrated information management systems for financial institutions.

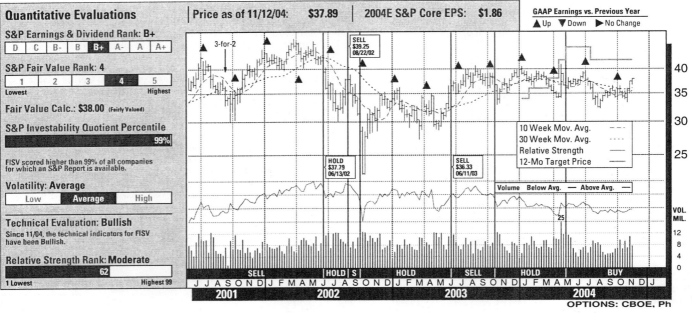

Quantitative Evaluations

S&P Earnings & Dividend Rank: B+

| D | C | B- | B | B+ | A- | A | A+ |

S&P Fair Value Rank: 4

| 1 | 2 | 3 | 4 | 5 |
| Lowest | | | | Highest |

Fair Value Calc.: $38.00 (Fairly Valued)

S&P Investability Quotient Percentile

99%

FISV scored higher than 99% of all companies for which an S&P Report is available.

Volatility: Average

| Low | Average | High |

Technical Evaluation: Bullish
Since 11/04, the technical indicators for FISV have been Bullish.

Relative Strength Rank: Moderate

62

1 Lowest   Highest 99

Price as of 11/12/04: $37.89 | **2004E S&P Core EPS:** $1.86

Analyst commentary prepared by Scott H. Kessler/CB/JWP

Highlights October 28, 2004

- We expect operating revenues to increase about 30% in 2004, 16% in 2005, and roughly 13% to 15% annually over the next three years, reflecting internal growth and completed acquisitions, with particular strength in the relatively new health plan management services business (26% of 2004 third quarter revenues) and the financial institution outsourcing, systems and services segment (65%).

- FISV generally uses free cash flow to make strategic acquisitions that broaden its offerings and customer base. We see the remainder of 2004 and 2005 marked by heightened efforts related to, and expected success in, cross-selling software and services. Acquired companies and businesses have historically accounted for about 50% of annual revenue growth. In 2003, FISV completed 12 purchases, but there has been less transactional activity in 2004.

- We expect a combination of organic and acquisition-related growth to enable FISV to post annual EPS gains averaging about 15% to 16% over the next three years. FISV completed three acquisitions recently, one in August 2004 (Results International, a provider of insurance solutions), one in September (Pharmacy Fulfillment, which provides mail-order prescription services), and one in October (CheckAGAIN, which converts into electronic transactions paper and imaged checks returned for insufficient funds).

Key Stock Statistics

S&P Core EPS 2005E	2.11	52-week Range	$41.00-32.20
S&P Oper. EPS 2004E	1.95	12 Month P/E	20.6
P/E on S&P Oper. EPS 2004E	19.4	Beta	1.04
S&P Oper. EPS 2005E	2.20	Shareholders	55,513
Yield (%)	Nil	Market Cap (B)	$ 7.4
Dividend Rate/Share	Nil	Shares Outstanding (M)	195.6

Value of $10,000 invested five years ago: **$ 17,376**

Dividend Data

No cash dividends have been paid.

Investment Rationale/Risk October 28, 2004

- We recommend that investors buy the shares. We expect FISV to benefit from greater employment, increased securities processing transaction volumes, and higher margin balances. Although FISV uses acquisitions to contribute to growth, internal revenue increases have been trending higher. From January to September 2004, internal growth was what we consider a healthy 9%, compared with the 4% generated in the comparable 2003 period.

- Risks to our opinion and target price include internal growth deceleration, and negatives associated with FISV potentially being linked to improper securities transactions.

- FISV has historically traded at a premium to the S&P 500 Data Processing & Outsourced Services sub-Industry, based on P/E and P/E-to-growth rate ratios. We attribute this to what we see as a record of consistently high-quality results. FISV's S&P Quality Ranking, which measures the growth and stability of earnings and dividends, is the highest possible for a company that does not pay a dividend. Based largely on our analysis of FISV's peers (its P/E was recently some 16% below and its P/E-to-growth rate about 27% below those of its peers), and our discounted cash flow model (including inputs of a 12.3% discount rate and average growth of 17% over the next five years), our 12-month target price is $42.

Revenues/Earnings Data Fiscal year ending December 31

Revenues (Million $)

	2004	2003	2002	2001	2000	1999
1Q	937.5	707.5	631.9	453.9	396.4	337.1
2Q	946.0	738.6	632.4	472.6	416.4	343.3
3Q	958.1	796.0	635.7	467.2	406.2	352.7
4Q	—	837.3	668.9	496.7	434.6	374.5
Yr.	—	3,034	2,569	1,890	1,654	1,408

Earnings Per Share ($)

	2004	2003	2002	2001	2000	1999
1Q	0.47	0.38	0.33	0.27	0.23	0.17
2Q	0.48	0.40	0.34	0.27	0.24	0.18
3Q	0.47	0.41	0.34	0.27	0.23	0.19
4Q	E0.52	0.42	0.35	0.27	0.23	0.19
Yr.	E1.95	1.61	1.37	1.09	0.93	0.73

Next earnings report expected: late-January Source: S&P, Company Reports
EPS Estimates based on S&P Operating Earnings; historical GAAP earnings are as reported.

Fiserv, Inc.

Recommendation: **BUY** ★ ★ ★ ★ ★ 12-Month Target Price: **$42.00** (as of July 22, 2004)

Business Summary October 29, 2004

The market for products and services offered by financial institutions continues to change. The financial industry continues to develop and introduce new alternative lending and investment products. Moreover, distinctions among financial services provided by banking and thrift organizations and securities and insurance companies are narrowing. As financial institutions diversify and consolidate, the number of industry participants may decline, but the number of customers and financial accounts served should not drop to the same extent. To stay competitive in a changing marketplace, financial institutions seek to meet customer needs for products that are transaction-oriented and fee-based. The growing volume and types of financial services transactions and accounts have increased the data processing requirements of these institutions. Fiserv believes it stands to benefit, as the financial services industry requires more specialized systems and development, maintenance and enhancement of applications software.

FISV's Financial Institution Outsourcing, Systems and Services segment, which accounted for 73% of 2003 revenues (76% in 2002) provides solutions to financial institutions, including banks, credit unions, leasing companies, mortgage lenders and savings institutions. Offerings include account and transactions processing services, item processing, loan servicing, and lending systems.

The Health Plan Management Services segment (15%, 10%) provides solutions for the administration of health plans to customers nationwide, including claim adjudication and payment, customer services, and other related offerings. These offerings are provided to employers that self-fund their health plans, and to insurance companies and HMOs.

The company also offers integrated securities clearing, execution, margin and stock lending, mutual fund and customer account processing, and facilitation of traditional and Internet brokerage services through its Securities Processing and Trust Services businesses (8%, 10%). Through TradeStar Investments, FISV offers retail brokerage services at discount commission rates. In addition, the company provides self-directed retirement plan administration services and mutual fund custody trading services, and is the largest independent U.S. trust company, in terms of revenues.

FISV has a history of making acquisitions. It completed 105 deals from 1984 to 2002. In 2003, 12 transactions were consummated, bolstering the company's offerings in data processing (Electronic Data Systems' Credit Union Industry Group business), health plan management (AVIDYN, MedPay, and WBI Holdings), insurance data processing (Insurance Management Solutions Group, MI-Assistant Software, ReliaQuote, and Unisure), and lending services (Chase Credit Systems and Chase Credit Research, and GAC Holdings).

Company Financials Fiscal Year ending December 31

Per Share Data ($)

(Year Ended December 31)	2003	2002	2001	2000	1999	1998	1997	1996	1995	1994
Tangible Bk. Val.	NM	2.60	2.60	2.18	1.57	1.57	1.50	1.08	0.50	2.65
Cash Flow	2.48	2.09	1.86	1.33	1.18	1.00	0.64	0.67	-0.15	0.50
Earnings	1.61	1.37	1.09	0.93	0.73	0.60	0.50	0.40	-0.40	0.28
S&P Core Earnings	1.47	1.26	1.00	NA	NA	NA	NA	NA	NA	NA
Dividends	Nil	Nil	Nil	Nil	Nil	Nil	Nil	Nil	Nil	Nil
Payout Ratio	Nil	Nil	Nil	Nil	Nil	Nil	Nil	Nil	Nil	Nil
Prices - High	40.77	47.24	44.61	42.75	27.16	23.83	15.25	11.96	9.18	7.03
- Low	27.23	22.50	29.08	16.20	16.08	13.33	9.62	7.40	6.22	5.33
P/E Ratio - High	25	34	41	46	37	40	30	30	NM	25
- Low	17	16	27	17	22	22	19	19	NM	19

Income Statement Analysis (Million $)

	2003	2002	2001	2000	1999	1998	1997	1996	1995	1994
Revs.	3,034	2,569	1,890	1,654	1,408	1,234	974	798	703	564
Oper. Inc.	704	734	501	429	347	282	229	191	-21.7	99
Depr.	172	141	148	70.1	86.3	76.5	63.2	42.2	38.5	30.0
Int. Exp.	22.9	17.8	12.1	22.1	19.4	16.0	11.9	19.1	18.8	8.71
Pretax Inc.	516	436	347	300	234	194	154	105	-99	62.8
Eff. Tax Rate	39.0%	39.0%	40.0%	41.0%	41.0%	41.0%	41.0%	41.0%	NM	40.0%
Net Inc.	315	266	208	177	138	114	90.8	61.7	-59.9	37.7
S&P Core Earnings	288	246	191	NA	NA	NA	NA	NA	NA	NA

Balance Sheet & Other Fin. Data (Million $)

	2003	2002	2001	2000	1999	1998	1997	1996	1995	1994
Cash	203	227	136	99	80.6	71.6	89.4	80.8	59.7	28.0
Curr. Assets	NA	NA	NA	NA	NA	NA	NA	NA	NA	NA
Total Assets	7,214	6,439	5,322	5,586	5,308	3,958	3,636	1,909	1,885	1,418
Curr. Liab.	NA	NA	NA	NA	NA	NA	NA	NA	NA	NA
LT Debt	699	483	343	335	326	390	252	273	383	132
Common Equity	2,200	1,828	1,605	1,252	1,091	886	769	507	434	351
Total Cap.	2,990	2,357	1,948	1,622	1,477	1,276	1,021	780	818	505
Cap. Exp.	143	142	68.0	73.0	69.7	77.5	39.8	36.2	45.0	52.8
Cash Flow	487	407	356	247	224	191	154	104	-21.4	67.7
Curr. Ratio	NA	NA	NA	NA	NA	NA	NA	NA	NA	NA
% LT Debt of Cap.	23.4	20.5	17.6	20.7	22.1	30.6	24.7	35.0	46.9	26.0
% Net Inc.of Revs.	10.4	10.4	11.0	10.7	9.8	9.3	9.3	7.7	NM	6.7
% Ret. on Assets	4.6	4.5	3.8	3.2	3.0	3.0	3.3	3.3	NM	2.9
% Ret. on Equity	15.6	15.5	14.6	15.1	13.9	13.8	14.2	13.1	NM	11.4

Data as orig. reptd.; bef. results of disc. opers. and/or spec. items. Per share data adj. for stk. divs.; EPS diluted. Book value incl. intangibles. E-Estimated. NA-Not Available. NM-Not Meaningful. NR-Not Ranked.

Office: 255 Fiserv Drive, Brookfield, WI 53045.
Telephone: 262-879-5000.
Email: general_info@fiserv.com
Website: http://www.fiserv.com
Chrmn: D.F. Dillon.
Pres, CEO & Investor Contact: L.M. Muma .

COO & SVP: N.J. Balthasar.
EVP, Secy & General Counsel: C.W. Sprague.
SVP, CFO & Treas: K.R. Jensen.
Dirs: D. F. Dillon, K. R. Jensen, D. P. Kearney, G. J. Levy, L. M. Muma,
G. M. Renwick, K. M. Robak, L. W. Seidman, T. R. Shackelford, T. C.
Wertheimer.

Founded: in 1984.
Domicile: Wisconsin.
Employees: 21,700.
S&P Analyst: Scott H. Kessler/CB/JWP

Fisher Scientific Intl.

Recommendation: **BUY** ★★★★☆
SELL SELL HOLD BUY BUY

12-Month Target Price: **$66.00**
(as of November 05, 2004)

FSH has an approximate 0.06% weighting in the **S&P 500**

Sector: Health Care
Sub-Industry: Health Care Equipment

Summary: FSH serves as a one-stop source of products, services and global solutions for the scientific research, clinical laboratory and industrial safety markets.

Quantitative Evaluations

S&P Earnings & Dividend Rank: B-

D	C	B-	B	B+	A-	A	A+

S&P Fair Value Rank: 5

1	2	3	4	5
Lowest				Highest

Fair Value Calc.: $70.40 (Undervalued)

S&P Investability Quotient Percentile

87%

FSH scored higher than 87% of all companies for which an S&P Report is available.

Volatility: Average

Low	Average	High

Technical Evaluation: Bearish
Since 10/04, the technical indicators for FSH have been Bearish.

Relative Strength Rank: Weak

23

1 Lowest	Highest 99

Price as of 11/12/04: $55.92 | **2004E S&P Core EPS:** $2.57

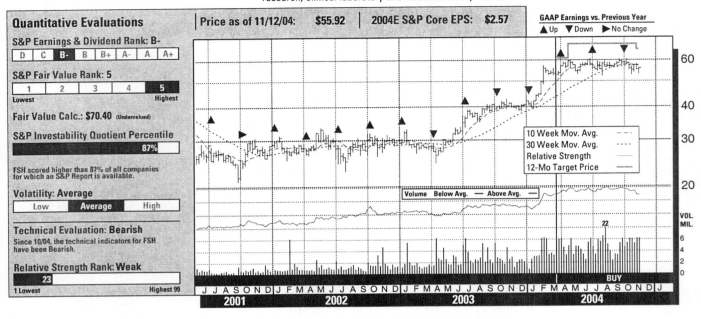

GAAP Earnings vs. Previous Year
▲ Up ▼ Down ► No Change

10 Week Mov. Avg.
30 Week Mov. Avg.
Relative Strength
12-Mo Target Price

Volume Below Avg. — Above Avg.

Analyst commentary prepared by Jeffrey Loo, CFA /DC/JWP

Highlights November 09, 2004

- In August 2004, FSH completed its $3.7 billion acquisition of Apogent Technologies, forming a company with sales exceeding $5 billion, including $1.1 billion in the higher margin life sciences segment. We believe this acquisition improves FSH's competitive position and will enable it to effectively enter new markets. We estimate sales of $4.6 billion in 2004, and increasing about 20%, to $5.5 billion in 2005. We expect the higher margin products, cost saving synergies, and fixed costs leverage to improve operating margins to 10.2% and 13.2% in 2004 and 2005, respectively. We believe it is still too early to determine the full impact of the Apogent transaction but we expect some sales cannibalization and integration issues to partially offset some revenue and cost savings synergies.

- We view positively FSH's recent acquisitions of Perbio, Oxoid, Dharmacon, and Apogent. We believe these transactions improve FSH's operating margins by transforming it predominantly from a distribution company to one with significant manufacturing capabilities. We expect FSH's higher margin proprietary products sales, which consist of self-manufactured products and exclusive provider products, to approach 60% of sales.

- Our 2004 and 2005 operating EPS forecasts are $2.84 and $3.57, respectively, utilizing an estimated tax rate of 30%. After estimated stock option expense, our 2005 Standard & Poor's Core Earnings estimate is $3.15.

Key Stock Statistics

S&P Core EPS 2005E	3.15	52-week Range	$60.77-38.40
S&P Oper. EPS 2004E	2.84	12 Month P/E	40.5
P/E on S&P Oper. EPS 2004E	19.7	Beta	-0.20
S&P Oper. EPS 2005E	3.57	Shareholders	112
Yield (%)	Nil	Market Cap (B)	$ 6.4
Dividend Rate/Share	Nil	Shares Outstanding (M)	114.9

Value of $10,000 invested five years ago: **$ 22,195**

Dividend Data

No cash dividends have been paid since 1997.

Investment Rationale/Risk November 09, 2004

- We would accumulate the shares, as we think increased R&D spending in the pharmaceutical and health care markets will drive organic growth, while strategic acquisitions provide additional revenue and profitability and solidify FSH's presence in the higher margin life science market. Although the company is highly leveraged, with net debt of about $2.3 billion as of September 30, 2004, we believe its forecast free cash flow of about $360 million in 2005, along with management's stated commitment to reduce debt, should alleviate some concerns.

- Risks to our recommendation and target price include a slowdown in research spending, the failure to achieve projected revenue and cost savings synergies from its acquisitions and its high debt level, and increasing interest rates, which may pressure margins.

- Our 12-month target price of $66 is based on our discounted cash flow and relative value analyses, which value FSH at about 19X our forward 2005 EPS estimate, at the mid-point of its P/E multiple over the past several years. We see additional potential upside if FSH successfully integrates the operations of Apogent with minimal problems, realizes projected cost savings, and is able to limit sales cannibalization while increasing sales through synergistic product bundling.

Revenues/Earnings Data Fiscal year ending December 31

Revenues (Million $)

	2004	2003	2002	2001	2000	1999
1Q	1,011	833.4	775.5	687.0	653.2	600.9
2Q	1,058	864.5	809.9	708.8	662.1	615.0
3Q	1,263	890.0	830.9	729.5	662.3	631.6
4Q	—	976.5	822.1	754.7	644.7	621.7
Yr.	—	3,564	3,238	2,880	2,622	2,470

Earnings Per Share ($)

	2004	2003	2002	2001	2000	1999
1Q	0.51	-0.02	0.34	-0.59	0.19	0.08
2Q	0.65	0.57	0.35	0.23	0.21	0.13
3Q	0.10	0.47	0.52	0.30	0.30	0.20
4Q	E0.75	0.28	0.46	0.19	-0.21	0.13
Yr.	E2.84	1.29	1.67	0.31	0.51	0.55

Next earnings report expected: early-February Source: S&P, Company Reports
EPS Estimates based on S&P Operating Earnings; historical GAAP earnings are as reported.

STANDARD &POOR'S

Fisher Scientific International Inc.

Stock Report
November 13, 2004
NYSE Symbol: **FSH**

Recommendation: **BUY** ★★★★☆   12-Month Target Price: **$66.00** (as of November 05, 2004)

Business Summary November 11, 2004

Fisher Scientific is a provider of products and services to the global scientific research and U.S. clinical laboratory markets. Customers include pharmaceutical and biotechnology companies; colleges and universities; medical research institutions; hospitals and reference labs; and quality control, process control and research and development laboratories. FSH provides a broad range of product offerings, including more than 600,000 products and services to more than 350,000 customers located in 145 countries. Approximately 80% of FSH's revenues are from the sale of consumable products.

The company operates through three segments: scientific products and services, which accounted for 70% of sales in 2003 (70% in 2002); health care products and services, 25% (25%); and laboratory workstations, 6% (6%).

The scientific segment provides products and services to entities conducting scientific research, including quality control and basic research and development, drug discovery and development. This segment manufactures and distributes a broad range of biochemicals and bioreagents, custom peptide, organic and inorganic chemicals, sera, cell culture media, sterile liquid-handling systems, safety products and other consumable products. This segment also provides services to pharmaceutical and biotechnology companies engaged in clinical trials, including specialized packaging, over-encapsulation, and labeling and distribution for Phase III and Phase IV clinical trials.

The health care segment manufactures and distributes diagnostic kits and reagents, consumable supplies, equipment, instruments and medical devices to

hospitals and group purchasing organizations, clinical labs, reference labs and physician offices in the U.S., as well as ear, nose and throat products outside of the U.S. This segment also provides outsourced manufacturing services for diagnostic reagents, calibrators and controls to the health care and pharmaceutical industries.

The laboratory workstations segment manufactures and sells workstations and fume hoods for laboratories. Products include steel, wood and plastic laminate casework systems, adaptable furniture systems, airflow products and other laboratory fixtures and accessories.

FSH has developed an integrated global logistics network to deliver its products. Its domestic network consists of 21 distribution facilities, and its international network consists of 19 facilities in 10 countries and is augmented with network sales offices in 22 countries with independent dealers in more than 100 countries. Products are distributed through third party carriers and through its own fleet of delivery vehicles. United Parcel Service handles approximately 65% of FSH's domestic product deliveries.

In August 2004, FSH acquired Apogent Technologies for $3.7 billion. The company also acquired Dharmacon, Inc. for $80 million in April 2004 and Oxoid Group Holdings for $330 million in March 2004. In late 2003, FSH acquired Perbio Science AB, a Swedish public company, for $689 million in cash plus the assumption of $44 million of net debt.

Company Financials Fiscal Year ending December 31

Per Share Data ($)

(Year Ended December 31)	2003	2002	2001	2000	1999	1998	1997	1996	1995	1994
Tangible Bk. Val.	NM	NM	NM	NM	NM	NM	0.71	0.69	NM	0.70
Cash Flow	2.66	2.96	1.86	1.94	2.00	0.09	0.16	0.87	0.39	0.67
Earnings	1.29	1.67	0.31	0.51	0.55	-1.24	-0.30	0.39	0.04	0.44
S&P Core Earnings	0.93	1.23	-0.04	NA	NA	NA	NA	NA	NA	NA
Dividends	Nil	Nil	Nil	Nil	Nil	Nil	0.01	0.02	0.02	0.02
Payout Ratio	Nil	Nil	Nil	Nil	Nil	Nil	NM	4%	42%	4%
Prices - High	42.80	33.43	40.00	51.00	44.00	22.50	10.25	9.55	6.95	7.75
- Low	24.55	22.85	21.00	19.87	16.12	9.52	7.02	6.65	4.92	4.57
P/E Ratio - High	33	20	NM	NM	80	NM	NM	24	NM	18
- Low	19	14	NM	NM	29	NM	NM	17	NM	10

Income Statement Analysis (Million $)

	2003	2002	2001	2000	1999	1998	1997	1996	1995	1994
Revs.	3,564	3,238	2,880	2,622	2,470	2,252	2,175	2,144	1,436	1,127
Oper. Inc.	341	318	213	218	219	186	120	139	82.0	83.3
Depr.	82.8	74.9	82.0	63.6	62.4	53.0	47.0	44.6	28.9	19.4
Int. Exp.	84.8	91.3	100	99	104	90.3	23.0	27.1	15.0	9.00
Pretax Inc.	96.1	142	30.3	37.8	57.8	-60.3	-5.10	67.6	4.30	63.0
Eff. Tax Rate	18.4%	31.7%	45.9%	39.9%	59.5%	NM	NM	45.6%	25.6%	43.1%
Net Inc.	78.4	96.7	16.4	22.7	23.4	-49.5	-30.5	36.8	3.20	36.0
S&P Core Earnings	56.4	70.4	-2.38	NA	NA	NA	NA	NA	NA	NA

Balance Sheet & Other Fin. Data (Million $)

	2003	2002	2001	2000	1999	1998	1997	1996	1995	1994
Cash	83.8	38.8	75.1	66.0	50.3	65.6	18.2	24.7	63.7	45.0
Curr. Assets	1,011	769	758	651	635	561	592	653	674	358
Total Assets	2,859	1,871	1,839	1,386	1,403	1,358	1,177	1,263	1,271	723
Curr. Liab.	649	583	638	508	520	453	355	877	390	195
LT Debt	1,386	922	956	991	1,011	1,022	268	282	446	128
Common Equity	575	134	23.3	-312	-331	-325	347	386	226	219
Total Cap.	1,962	1,055	979	679	681	697	615	668	672	347
Cap. Exp.	80.2	43.9	40.1	23.1	41.1	67.2	59.2	40.7	24.6	17.7
Cash Flow	161	172	98.4	86.3	85.8	3.50	16.5	81.4	32.1	55.0
Curr. Ratio	1.6	1.3	1.2	1.3	1.2	1.2	1.7	0.7	1.7	1.8
% LT Debt of Cap.	70.7	87.3	97.6	145.9	148.6	146.6	43.5	42.2	66.4	37.0
% Net Inc.of Revs.	2.2	3.0	0.6	0.9	0.9	NM	NM	1.7	1.0	3.2
% Ret. on Assets	3.3	5.2	1.0	1.6	1.7	NM	NM	2.9	1.0	5.1
% Ret. on Equity	22.1	123.3	NM	NM	NM	NM	NM	12.0	14.3	17.9

Data as orig reptd.; bef. results of disc opers/spec. items. Per share data adj. for stk. divs.; EPS diluted. E-Estimated. NA-Not Available. NM-Not Meaningful. NR-Not Ranked. UR-Under Review.

Office: One Liberty Lane, Hampton, NH 03842.
Telephone: 603-926-5911.
Website: http://www.fishersci.com
Chrmn & CEO: P.M. Montrone.
Pres & COO: D.D. Della Penta.

Vice Chrmn: P.M. Meister.
VP & CFO: K.P. Clark.
VP, Secy & General Counsel: T.M. DuChene.
Dirs: A. J. DiNovi, M. D. Dingman, P. M. Meister, P. M. Montrone, C. A. Sanders, S. M. Sperling, W. C. Stephens.

Founded: in 1991.
Domicile: Delaware.
Employees: 10,200.
S&P Analyst: Jeffrey Loo, CFA /DC/JWP

The **McGraw·Hill** Companies

Fluor Corp.

Recommendation: **HOLD** ★★★☆☆
SELL · SELL · HOLD · BUY · BUY

12-Month Target Price: $50.00
(as of October 27, 2004)

FLR has an approximate 0.04% weighting in the **S&P 500**

Sector: Industrials
Sub-Industry: Construction & Engineering
Peer Group: Engineering & Construction- Larger

Summary: FLR is one of the world's largest engineering, procurement and construction companies.

Quantitative Evaluations

S&P Earnings & Dividend Rank: B

| D | C | B- | **B** | B+ | A- | A | A+ |

S&P Fair Value Rank: 3-

| 1 | 2 | **3** | 4 | 5 |
| Lowest | | | | Highest |

Fair Value Calc.: $42.10 (Slightly Overvalued)

S&P Investability Quotient Percentile

95%

FLR scored higher than 95% of all companies for which an S&P Report is available.

Volatility: Average

| Low | **Average** | High |

Technical Evaluation: Neutral
Since 10/04, the technical indicators for FLR have been Neutral.

Relative Strength Rank: Moderate

61

| 1 Lowest | | Highest 99 |

Price as of 11/12/04: **$47.33**
2004E S&P Core EPS: **$2.33**

GAAP Earnings vs. Previous Year
▲ Up ▼ Down ▶ No Change

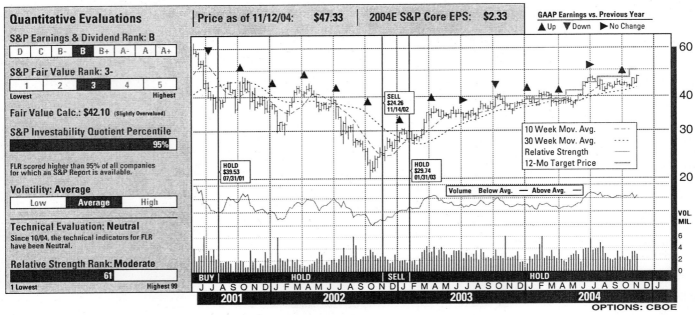

- 10 Week Mov. Avg.
- 30 Week Mov. Avg.
- Relative Strength
- 12-Mo Target Price

Volume Below Avg. — Above Avg.

SELL $24.26 11/14/02
HOLD $39.53 07/31/01
HOLD $29.74 01/31/03

OPTIONS: CBOE

Analyst commentary prepared by Stewart Scharf/CB/BK

Highlights November 01, 2004

- We expect revenues to advance close to 10% in 2005, following modest growth seen for 2004, reflecting strength in oil and gas projects, growth in the government segment, and a pickup in industrial and infrastructure work. However, projects to rebuild Iraq have slowed in recent months, and the amount of new awards from that region is uncertain. We see FLR focusing on clean fuels projects and downstream chemical work, as it diversifies into new regions and markets, such as life sciences and transportation.

- We think 2005 gross margins may narrow somewhat from our projection of just over 4% for 2004, as the company moves from completion of higher-margin power projects to lower-margin oil and gas projects. We expect a lag in the recognition of earnings in the early stages of a project, while the timing of new bookings remains uncertain. However, we believe margins should widen sequentially during 2005, as the pace of earnings from new awards picks up. EBITDA margins should widen in 2005, on contributions from new projects and well controlled SG&A expenses.

- We project 2004 operating EPS of $2.20 (before $0.06 from asset sales), and see 16% growth in 2005, to $2.55. We view earnings quality as good; our Standard & Poor's Core Earnings projections of $2.33 and $2.56 a share for 2004 and 2005 exceed our respective operating estimates.

Investment Rationale/Risk November 01, 2004

- Third quarter EPS in 2004 matched our estimate, but, based on uncertain markets and our valuation models, we believe investors should not add to their positions. We think the timing of new awards is unclear, as FLR shifts toward what we view as riskier projects in diverse and unstable regions of the world.

- Risks to our recommendation and target price include greater than expected pressures on margins due to a shift to oil and gas projects, geopolitical unrest in the Middle East and uncertainties regarding reconstruction projects in Iraq, possible delays in projects and the timing of executing new awards, and lower than expected capital spending.

- Although new project awards suggest that results should improve during 2005, following what we view as a transition year in 2004, we caution investors regarding the uncertainties that exist due to the lag time in converting backlog into earnings. The stock is trading near 18X our 2005 EPS estimate, a premium to our projected P/E for the S&P 500 and FLR's peers. However, our DCF model indicates that the shares are at a 10% discount to intrinsic value, assuming a terminal growth rate of 3% and a weighted average cost of capital of 8.5%. Based on historically high P/E multiples, we believe the stock deserves a P/E of 19.5X our 2005 EPS estimate, and our 12-month target price is $50.

Key Stock Statistics

S&P Core EPS 2005E	**2.56**	52-week Range	**$48.15-34.29**	
S&P Oper. EPS 2004E	**2.20**	12 Month P/E	**20.3**	
P/E on S&P Oper. EPS 2004E	**21.5**	Beta	**0.47**	
S&P Oper. EPS 2005E	**2.55**	Shareholders	**6,456**	
Yield (%)	**1.4%**	Market Cap (B)	**$ 3.9**	
Dividend Rate/Share	**0.64**	Shares Outstanding (M)	**83.4**	

Value of $10,000 invested five years ago: **NA**

Dividend Data Dividends have been paid since 1974

Amount ($)	Date Decl.	Ex-Div. Date	Stock of Record	Payment Date
0.160	Feb. 04	Mar. 05	Mar. 09	Apr. 01 '04
0.160	Apr. 28	Jun. 04	Jun. 08	Jul. 01 '04
0.160	Jul. 29	Sep. 03	Sep. 08	Oct. 01 '04
0.160	Oct. 27	Dec. 06	Dec. 08	Jan. 03 '05

Revenues/Earnings Data Fiscal year ending December 31

Revenues (Million $)

	2004	2003	2002	2001	2000	1999
1Q	2,063	2,077	2,507	1,911	2,999	3,384
2Q	2,214	2,243	2,536	2,227	2,558	3,091
3Q	2,363	2,121	2,451	2,199	2,903	3,069
4Q	—	2,365	2,465	2,635	2,309	2,873
Yr.	—	8,806	9,959	8,972	9,970	12,417

Earnings Per Share ($)

	2004	2003	2002	2001	2000	1999
1Q	0.57	0.51	0.45	0.21	0.69	0.68
2Q	0.54	0.54	0.54	0.44	0.66	-0.97
3Q	0.57	0.55	0.58	0.56	0.44	0.66
4Q	E0.58	0.63	0.56	0.39	0.22	1.00
Yr.	E2.20	2.23	2.13	1.61	1.31	1.37

Next earnings report expected: early-February Source: S&P, Company Reports
EPS Estimates based on S&P Operating Earnings; historical GAAP earnings are as reported.

Recommendation: **HOLD** ★ ★ ★ ☆ ☆   12-Month Target Price: **$50.00** (as of October 27, 2004)

Business Summary November 02, 2004

Fluor Corp., which completed a reverse spinoff of its Massey Coal operations in late 2000, is one of the world's largest engineering, procurement, construction and maintenance companies. The company realigned itself into five principal operating segments, exiting non-strategic businesses.

The Oil & Gas segment provides design, engineering, procurement and construction (EPC) services to oil, gas, refining, chemical, polymer and petrochemical customers. Industrial & Infrastructure provides EPC services to businesses that include industrial, commercial, institutional, telecommunications, mining and technology clients. Global Services provides operations and maintenance support, temporary staffing, equipment and outsourcing, and asset management solutions to company projects and to third party clients through TRS Staffing Solutions. Government Services provides administrative and support services to the federal government and other government parties.

In February 2004, the U.S. Army Corps of Engineers awarded FLR three task orders worth $154 million for electrical power restoration in Iraq. The contract has a potential value $500 million in the first year, with four one-year options having a maximum value of $250 million each. Also in February, the company was awarded a $100 million contract to build a U.S. Army camp near Baghdad.

Contributions to revenues and operating profits in 2003 were as follows: Oil and Gas, 30% of revenues and 30% of segment operating profit ($121 million); Industrial & Infrastructure, 29% and 16% ($63 million); Power, 8.6% and 19% ($77 million); Global Services, 13% and 24% ($97 million); and Government Services, 19% and 12% ($48 million).

Backlog by geographic region at the end of 2003 was: U.S. 48%; the Americas

11%; Europe, Africa and the Middle East 36%; and Asia/Pacific 5%. At June 30, 2004, backlog was: U.S. 36%; the Americas 24%; Europe, Africa and the Middle East 33%; and Asia/Pacific 7%.

Total backlog of $10.6 billion at December 31, 2003, was divided by segment as follows: Oil & Gas $3.4 billion, up 46%, year to year; Industrial & Infrastructure $3.3 billion, down 22%; Power, $0.6 billion, down 28%; Global Services $1.8 billion, up 17%; and Government Services $1.5 billion, up 87%. Total backlog of $13.7 billion at September 30, 2004, was up 33% from $10.3 billion a year earlier. New awards in the third quarter of 2004 totaled $3.2 billion, up from $2.7 billion a year earlier. At September 30, 2004, segment backlog was: Oil & Gas $4.8 billion, up 43%; Industrial & Infrastructure $5.2 billion, up 52%; Power $78 million, down 86%; Government Services $1.7 billion, up 28%; Global Services $1.9 billion, up 20%.

At the end of 2003, gross margin in backlog was 6.1%, up from 6.0% a year earlier. New awards amounted to nearly $10.0 billion, up 16%; new awards gross margins were 6.6%, down from 7.0%.

At September 30, 2004, total debt was equal to 22% of capitalization, below FLR's 30% target level; depreciation in the third quarter totaled nearly $21 million; and capital spending exceeded $26 million (nearly $69 million through the first nine months).

In February 2004, FLR sold $300 million of senior notes due 2024, convertible into common stock at $55.94 a share beginning February 15, 2005. It expected proceeds of $323 million to be used mainly for debt paydowns and working capital.

Company Financials Fiscal Year ending December 31

Per Share Data ($)

(Year Ended December 31)	2003	2002	2001	2000	1999	1998	1997	1996	1995	1994
Tangible Bk. Val.	12.51	10.76	9.57	19.96	19.27	18.35	18.84	18.86	16.80	14.79
Cash Flow	6.54	3.11	2.52	5.39	5.56	6.63	4.64	5.46	4.57	3.70
Earnings	2.23	2.13	1.61	1.31	1.37	2.97	1.73	3.17	2.78	2.32
S&P Core Earnings	2.33	1.79	1.13	NA	NA	NA	NA	NA	NA	NA
Dividends	0.64	0.64	0.64	1.00	0.80	0.80	0.76	0.68	0.60	0.52
Payout Ratio	29%	30%	40%	76%	58%	27%	44%	21%	22%	22%
Prices - High	40.82	44.95	63.20	48.50	46.50	52.50	75.87	71.87	68.00	56.25
- Low	26.65	20.06	31.20	23.93	26.18	34.12	33.50	57.75	42.75	40.12
P/E Ratio - High	18	21	39	37	34	18	44	23	24	24
- Low	12	9	19	18	19	11	19	18	15	17

Income Statement Analysis (Million $)

	2003	2002	2001	2000	1999	1998	1997	1996	1995	1994
Revs.	8,806	9,959	8,972	9,970	12,417	13,505	14,299	11,015	9,301	8,485
Oper. Inc.	344	492	258	451	654	675	511	596	489	413
Depr.	79.7	78.0	71.9	312	318	289	248	194	147	114
Int. Exp.	10.1	8.93	25.0	26.3	50.9	45.0	31.0	16.0	13.0	17.0
Pretax Inc.	536	261	185	142	186	362	255	413	362	303
Eff. Tax Rate	16.5%	34.8%	31.1%	29.8%	44.0%	35.1%	42.7%	35.1%	35.9%	36.6%
Net Inc.	447	170	128	100	104	235	146	268	232	192
S&P Core Earnings	188	143	90.2	NA	NA	NA	NA	NA	NA	NA

Balance Sheet & Other Fin. Data (Million $)

	2003	2002	2001	2000	1999	1998	1997	1996	1995	1994
Cash	497	753	573	69.4	210	341	299	316	292	492
Curr. Assets	2,214	1,941	1,851	1,448	1,910	2,277	2,226	1,797	1,412	1,258
Total Assets	3,449	3,142	3,091	3,653	4,886	5,019	4,698	3,952	3,229	2,825
Curr. Liab.	1,829	1,756	1,811	1,620	2,204	2,496	1,991	1,646	1,239	1,021
LT Debt	44.7	17.6	17.6	17.6	318	300	301	3.00	3.00	30.0
Common Equity	1,082	884	789	1,609	1,581	1,525	1,741	1,670	1,430	1,220
Total Cap.	1,126	901	807	1,627	2,061	1,931	2,108	1,713	1,477	1,296
Cap. Exp.	79.2	63.0	148	284	504	601	647	392	319	237
Cash Flow	527	248	200	412	422	524	394	462	379	307
Curr. Ratio	1.2	1.1	1.0	0.9	0.9	0.9	1.1	1.1	1.1	1.2
% LT Debt of Cap.	4.0	2.0	2.2	1.1	15.4	15.5	14.3	0.2	0.2	2.3
% Net Inc.of Revs.	5.1	1.7	1.4	1.0	0.8	1.7	1.0	2.4	2.4	2.3
% Ret. on Assets	13.6	5.4	4.4	2.3	2.1	4.8	3.4	7.5	7.7	7.1
% Ret. on Equity	45.5	20.3	18.0	6.3	6.7	14.4	8.6	17.3	NA	17.0

Data as orig reptd. (fiscal years ended Oct. 31 prior to 2001); bef. results of disc opers/spec. items. Per share data adj. for stk. divs.; EPS diluted. E-Estimated. NA-Not Available. NM-Not Meaningful. NR-Not Ranked.

Office: One Enterprise Drive, Aliso Viejo, CA 92656-2606.
Telephone: 949-349-2000.
Email: investor@fluor.com
Website: http://www.fluor.com
Chrmn & CEO: A.L. Boeckmann.
SVP & CFO: D.M. Steuert.

SVP, Secy & General Counsel: L.N. Fisher.
VP & Investor Contact: L.J. Churney 949-349-6788.
Dirs: A. L. Boeckmann, P. J. Fluor, D. P. Gardner, J. T. Hackett, K. Kresa, V. S. Martinez, D. R. O'Hare, J. W. Prueher, R. W. Renwick, M. R. Seger, S. H. Woolsey.

Founded: in 1924.
Domicile: Delaware.
Employees: 29,011.
S&P Analyst: Stewart Scharf/CB/BK

Ford Motor

Recommendation: HOLD ★★★☆☆
SELL | SEL | HOLD | BSY | CUY

12-Month Target Price: $14.00
(as of October 19, 2004)

F has an approximate 0.24% weighting in the **S&P 500**

Sector: Consumer Discretionary
Sub-Industry: Automobile Manufacturers
Peer Group: Automakers

Summary: Ford, the world's second largest producer of cars and trucks, has a rapidly growing financial services operation.

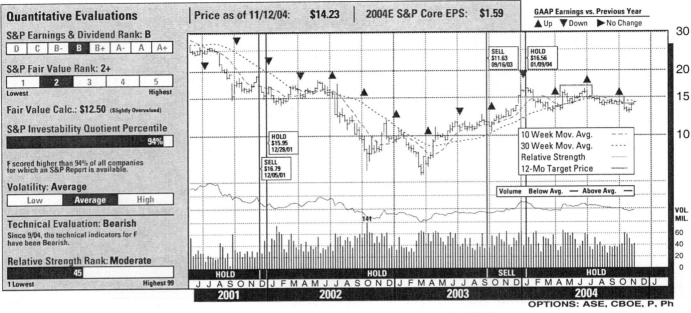

Quantitative Evaluations

S&P Earnings & Dividend Rank: B
D | C | B- | B | B+ | A- | A | A+

S&P Fair Value Rank: 2+
1 (Lowest) | 2 | 3 | 4 | 5 (Highest)

Fair Value Calc.: $12.50 (Slightly Overvalued)

S&P Investability Quotient Percentile
94%

F scored higher than 94% of all companies for which an S&P Report is available.

Volatility: Average
Low | Average | High

Technical Evaluation: Bearish
Since 9/04, the technical indicators for F have been Bearish.

Relative Strength Rank: Moderate
45
1 Lowest | Highest 99

Price as of 11/12/04: **$14.23** | 2004E S&P Core EPS: **$1.59**

Analyst commentary prepared by Efraim Levy, CFA /CB/BK

OPTIONS: ASE, CBOE, P, Ph

Highlights October 20, 2004

- We see 2004 North American industry light vehicle sales of 16.6 million units, even with 2003's levels. Our estimates for 2005 assume a rise in industry volume to 17.0 million units. We expect Ford's 2005 automotive revenues to grow 2% to 4%, on the introduction of new products and a better vehicle mix, despite pricing pressures; financial services revenues should decline 1% to 4%, as expected higher interest rates should hurt demand. Financial services has been an important contributor to recent sales and earnings at Ford.

- Pensions and other retiree benefit expenses, excluding $1.6 billion in expenses assumed in 2003 through an agreement with Visteon, should increase in 2004, but F does not anticipate required pension fund payments before 2009. We believe that a new contract with the UAW will enhance productivity by allowing the company to close several production plants that it views as unnecessary.

- We expect results to benefit from cost cutting and the launch of several new products. We project 2004 operating EPS of $2.12, compared with 2003 EPS from continuing operations of $1.14. For 2005, we expect operating EPS of $1.88.

Investment Rationale/Risk October 20, 2004

- We would hold existing positions. While the company should benefit from the introduction of several new and updated vehicles in 2004, followed by additional new vehicles in 2005, it continued to lose market share in the first nine months of 2004. However, profitability has been better than we expected, and with their above-average dividend yield, we would hold Ford shares.

- Risks to our opinion and target price include increased competitive challenges, and lower production in the remainder of 2004 or early 2005, due to what we believe are high inventory levels. We are also concerned about the company's dependence on financial services income in a rising interest rate environment.

- We expect multiples on auto stocks to narrow in the rising interest rate environment that we anticipate and amid rising oil and gasoline prices. The stock recently traded at a premium to the P/E multiple of General Motors (GM: hold, $38), but at a discount to the S&P 500. We think the premium should narrow. Based on historical and peer comparative P/E multiples, our 12-month target price is $14 (about 7.5X our 2005 EPS estimate).

Key Stock Statistics

S&P Core EPS 2005E	1.49	52-week Range	$17.34-12.17
S&P Oper. EPS 2004E	2.12	12 Month P/E	11.3
P/E on S&P Oper. EPS 2004E	6.7	Beta	1.30
S&P Oper. EPS 2005E	1.88	Shareholders	219,400
Yield (%)	2.8%	Market Cap (B)	$ 25.0
Dividend Rate/Share	0.40	Shares Outstanding (M)	1829.8

Value of $10,000 invested five years ago: **NA**

Dividend Data Dividends have been paid since 1983

Amount ($)	Date Decl.	Ex-Div. Date	Stock of Record	Payment Date
0.100	Dec. 11	Jan. 28	Jan. 30	Mar. 01 '04
0.100	Apr. 08	Apr. 28	Apr. 30	Jun. 01 '04
0.100	Jul. 08	Jul. 28	Jul. 30	Sep. 01 '04
0.100	Oct. 13	Oct. 28	Nov. 01	Dec. 01 '04

Revenues/Earnings Data Fiscal year ending December 31

Revenues (Million $)

	2004	2003	2002	2001	2000	1999
1Q	44,691	40,815	39,541	42,446	42,894	37,885
2Q	42,802	40,582	42,127	42,314	44,519	42,282
3Q	38,996	36,791	39,338	36,502	40,064	37,973
4Q	—	46,008	41,580	41,150	42,587	44,418
Yr.	—	164,196	163,420	162,412	170,064	162,558

Earnings Per Share ($)

	2004	2003	2002	2001	2000	1999
1Q	0.95	0.45	-0.05	0.56	1.58	1.60
2Q	0.57	0.22	0.31	-0.42	1.24	1.89
3Q	0.25	0.13	-0.14	-0.39	0.53	0.90
4Q	E0.27	-0.35	0.01	-2.81	0.57	1.47
Yr.	E2.12	0.50	0.15	-3.02	3.59	5.86

Next earnings report expected: late-January Source: S&P, Company Reports
EPS Estimates based on S&P Operating Earnings; historical GAAP earnings are as reported.

Ford Motor Company

Recommendation: **HOLD** ★ ★ ★ ☆ ☆   12-Month Target Price: **$14.00** (as of October 19, 2004)

Business Summary October 20, 2004

Ford is the world's second largest motor vehicle manufacturer. It produces cars and trucks, many of the vehicles' plastic, glass and electronic components, and replacement parts. It also owns a 33% stake in Mazda Motor Corp. Financial services include Ford Motor Credit (automotive financing and insurance), American Road Insurance Co., Hertz Corp. (car rental) and Granite Management. Granite manages a portfolio of real estate loans.

In March 2001, Ford purchased the shares of Hertz that it did not already own for about $750 million. In 1997, it had spun off 18.5% of Hertz Corp. via a public offering. In 1998, it distributed its 81% interest in Associates First Capital Corp. to Ford common and Class B shareholders, and recorded a related gain of $12.90 a share.

In 1999, the company acquired the car operations of AB Volvo for $6.45 billion.

In 2000, Ford acquired Land Rover from BMW Group. About two-thirds of the $1.9 billion price was paid at closing.

In August 2000, the company completed a financial restructuring. As part of the plan, stockholders exchanged existing common and class B shares for new F common and Class B shares. In addition, shareholders had the option of receiving either $20 in cash per share, or the equivalent value in new F common shares, or a combination of cash and stock worth $20 a share. Nearly $6 billion in cash was distributed to shareholders. The company also distributed ownership of its Visteon parts subsidiary to Ford stockholders.

In a reversal from an earlier strategic plan to be involved in all stages of the automobile life cycle, Ford plans to sell Kwik-Fit, Europe's largest vehicle maintenance and light repair chain, which it acquired in 1999 for about $1.6 billion. In addition, it plans to sell other non-core assets.

The company, together with GM, DaimlerChrysler and others, owns a founding equity stake in Covisint LLC. Covisint is a business-to-business Internet-based supplier exchange.

Ford, Mercury, Lincoln, Volvo (since 1999) and Jaguar models accounted for about 15.4% of cars sold in U.S. markets (including foreign-built) in 2003, versus 16.4% in 2002, 17.7% in 2001, 19.1% in 2000, and 19.9% in 1999. Comparable respective figures for trucks were 24.7%, 25.5%, 27.5%, 28.2%, and 28.6%. Vehicle unit sales totaled 6,720,000 in 2003, including 3,811,000 in North America, versus 6,973,000 (4,341,000) in 2002.

In January 2002, the company said that, including earlier initiatives since January 2001, it planned to eliminate up to 35,000 employees worldwide as part of a restructuring. It recorded a related charge of $4.1 billion ($2.27 a share) in 2001 for asset impairment, restructuring and other costs. Ford plans significant new or freshened products in the U.S. annually, and capacity reduction of about 1 million vehicles per year by mid-decade. It will focus on material cost reduction, discontinuance of low margin-models, and divestiture of non-core assets.

In December 2003, Ford assumed about $1.65 billion in post-retirement health care and insurance obligations from Visteon Corp., its former subsidiary.

Company Financials Fiscal Year ending December 31

Per Share Data ($)

(Year Ended December 31)	2003	2002	2001	2000	1999	1998	1997	1996	1995	1994
Tangible Bk. Val.	2.30	NM	NM	6.10	16.60	16.80	21.01	17.52	15.53	17.85
Cash Flow	8.31	8.45	5.78	13.46	13.36	24.70	11.86	9.60	9.93	14.21
Earnings	0.50	0.15	-3.02	3.59	5.86	17.76	5.62	3.72	3.58	4.97
S&P Core Earnings	1.03	-1.16	-4.56	NA	NA	NA	NA	NA	NA	NA
Dividends	0.40	0.40	1.05	2.30	1.88	2.18	1.65	1.47	1.23	0.91
Payout Ratio	80%	NM	NM	64%	32%	12%	29%	40%	34%	18%
Prices - High	17.33	18.23	31.42	57.25	67.87	65.93	50.25	37.25	32.87	35.06
- Low	6.58	6.90	14.70	21.68	46.25	37.50	30.00	27.25	24.62	25.62
P/E Ratio - High	35	NM	NM	16	12	4	9	10	9	7
- Low	13	NM	NM	6	8	2	5	7	7	5

Income Statement Analysis (Million $)

	2003	2002	2001	2000	1999	1998	1997	1996	1995	1994
Revs.	165,066	163,420	162,412	170,064	162,558	144,416	153,731	146,991	137,137	128,439
Oper. Inc.	23,283	25,034	22,941	34,530	29,311	27,400	31,017	25,267	24,423	25,408
Depr.	14,297	15,177	15,922	14,849	9,254	8,589	7,645	6,875	6,500	9,336
Int. Exp.	7,690	8,824	10,848	10,902	9,076	8,865	10,500	10,399	10,046	7,744
Pretax Inc.	1,370	953	-7,584	8,234	11,026	25,396	10,939	6,793	6,705	8,789
Eff. Tax Rate	9.85%	31.7%	NM	32.9%	33.3%	12.5%	34.2%	31.9%	35.5%	37.9%
Net Inc.	921	284	-5,453	5,410	7,237	22,071	6,920	4,446	4,139	5,308
S&P Core Earnings	1,905	-2,202	-8,266	NA	NA	NA	NA	NA	NA	NA

Balance Sheet & Other Fin. Data (Million $)

	2003	2002	2001	2000	1999	1998	1997	1996	1995	1994
Cash	33,642	30,521	15,028	16,490	23,585	23,805	20,835	15,414	12,406	13,822
Total Assets	304,594	289,357	276,543	284,421	276,229	237,545	279,097	262,867	243,283	219,354
LT Debt	148,126	125,806	121,430	99,560	78,734	64,898	80,245	77,136	73,734	65,207
Total Debt	148,126	167,892	168,009	166,229	152,738	132,835	168,925	150,239	141,354	123,868
Common Equity	12,065	5,590	7,786	18,610	27,537	23,409	30,734	26,068	23,547	18,259
Cap. Exp.	7,749	7,278	7,008	8,348	8,535	8,617	8,717	8,651	8,997	9,470
Cash Flow	15,218	15,446	10,454	20,244	16,476	30,553	14,511	11,321	10,639	14,357
% Ret. on Assets	0.3	0.1	NM	2.0	2.8	8.5	2.6	1.8	1.8	2.5
% Ret. on Equity	7.6	4.0	NM	23.3	28.4	81.1	23.9	17.7	16.6	32.7
% LT Debt of Cap.	87.5	87.8	87.2	78.3	68.6	73.5	68.5	71.3	72.1	70.3

Data as orig reptd.; bef. results of disc opers/spec. items. Per share data adj. for stk. divs.; EPS diluted. E-Estimated. NA-Not Available. NM-Not Meaningful. NR-Not Ranked. UR-Under Review.

Office: 1 American Rd, Dearborn, MI 48126-2798.
Telephone: 313-322-3000.
Website: http://www.ford.com
Chrmn & CEO: W.C. Ford, Jr.
Pres & COO: N.V. Scheele.
Vice Chrmn: A.D. Gilmour.

VP & General Counsel: D.E. Ross.
CFO: D.R. Leclair.
Dirs: J. R. Bond, S. G. Butler, K. Casiano, W. C. Ford, E. B. Ford II, W. C. Ford, Jr., I. O. Hockaday, Jr., M. Kravis, R. A. Manoogian, E. R. Marram, H. A. Neal, J. Ollila, C. E. Reichardt, R. E. Rubin, N. V. Scheele, J. L. Thornton.

Founded: in 1903.
Domicile: Delaware.
Employees: 327,531.
S&P Analyst: Efraim Levy, CFA /CB/BK

Forest Laboratories

Recommendation: HOLD ★★★☆☆
SELL SELL HOLD BUY BUY

12-Month Target Price: **$53.00**
(as of August 31, 2004)

FRX has an approximate 0.15% weighting in the **S&P 500**

Sector: Health Care
Sub-Industry: Pharmaceuticals
Peer Group: Ethical Pharmaceuticals - Major

Summary: FRX develops and makes branded and generic ethical drug products, sold primarily in the U.S., Puerto Rico, and Western and Eastern Europe.

Quantitative Evaluations

S&P Earnings & Dividend Rank: B+

| D | C | B- | B | B+ | A- | A | A+ |

S&P Fair Value Rank: 4-

| 1 | 2 | 3 | 4 | 5 |
| Lowest | | | | Highest |

Fair Value Calc.: $45.00 (Slightly Undervalued)

S&P Investability Quotient Percentile

94%

FRX scored higher than 94% of all companies for which an S&P Report is available.

Volatility: Average

| Low | Average | High |

Technical Evaluation: Bearish

Since 10/04, the technical indicators for FRX have been Bearish.

Relative Strength Rank: Weak

16

1 Lowest   Highest 99

Price as of 11/12/04: $43.64 | **2005E S&P Core EPS: $2.40**

GAAP Earnings vs. Previous Year
▲ Up ▼ Down ▶ No Change

BUY $39.10 07/17/01
HOLD $34.75 06/21/02
BUY $38.09 09/10/02
BUY $53.03 01/03/03
HOLD $51.48 06/04/03
BUY $73.00 01/20/04

2-for-1

10 Week Mov. Avg.
30 Week Mov. Avg.
Relative Strength
12-Mo Target Price

Volume Below Avg. — Above Avg. —

H | BUY | HOLD | BUY | H | BUY | HOLD | BUY | HOLD
J J A S O N D J F M A M J J A S O N D J F M A M J J A S O N D J F M A M J J A S O N D J
2001   2002   2003   2004

VOL. MIL.
24
16
8
0

OPTIONS: ASE, CBOE, Ph

Analyst commentary prepared by H. B. Saftlas/PMW/BK

Highlights November 11, 2004

- We expect revenues to advance about 17% in FY 05 (Mar.), boosted by continued robust demand for the company's new Lexapro antidepressant and projected strong sales growth for recently launched Namenda for Alzheimer's disease. We think that FRX has successfully shifted patients from its older Celexa antidepressant, for which marketing exclusivity expired in late October 2004, to its enhanced Lexapro therapy. We project a 40% drop in sales of Celexa, reflecting the recent entry of generic competition in that line.

- Although we believe that reduced Celexa sales will restrict gross margins, we expect overall profitability to benefit from tight cost controls, with SG&A spending expected to decline as a percentage of sales. Other income should be higher, boosted by initial profit contributions from Benicar, a cardiovascular drug marketed through a joint venture with Sankyo.

- Our FY 05 EPS forecast is $2.50, up 28% from the level of FY 04. We project only single-digit growth in FY 06, to $2.65, largely reflecting significantly lower Celexa sales. After subtracting estimated stock option expense, we project S&P Core EPS of $2.40 for FY 05 and $2.55 for FY 06.

Key Stock Statistics

S&P Core EPS 2006E	2.55	52-week Range	$78.81-40.70	
S&P Oper. EPS 2005E	2.50	12 Month P/E	18.4	
P/E on S&P Oper. EPS 2005E	17.5	Beta	0.42	
S&P Oper. EPS 2006E	2.65	Shareholders	1,876	
Yield (%)	Nil	Market Cap (B)	$ 16.2	
Dividend Rate/Share	Nil	Shares Outstanding (M)	370.3	

Value of $10,000 invested five years ago: **$ 36,650**

Dividend Data

No cash dividends have been paid.

Investment Rationale/Risk November 11, 2004

- We are maintaining our hold opinion on the shares. We think that FRX has successfully extended its antidepressant franchise with Lexapro, which accounted for about 12% of the U.S. prescription market in September 2004. We are also encouraged by initial market reception for recently launched Namenda Alzheimer's treatment. However, we see this balanced by expected generic erosion for Celexa, which started in late October, versus the company's forecast of January 2005. In addition, FRX recently released disappointing Phase II clinical results on its experimental lercanidipine treatment for hypertension. In early November, the company reduced its EPS guidance for FY 05 to $2.50, from $2.70, reflecting generic competition in the Celexa line, as well as anticipated marketing expenses associated with the launch of Campral for alcohol dependence, and a possible launch of Combunox pain treatment.

- Risks to our opinion and target price include greater than expected competitive pressures in the antidepression area, and a failure to successfully develop and commercialize pipeline products.

- Our 12-month target price of $53 applies a P/E multiple of 20X to our FY 06 EPS estimate of $2.65. We believe a premium multiple relative to peers is justified by what we see as FRX's impressive new drug pipeline.

Revenues/Earnings Data Fiscal year ending March 31

Revenues (Million $)

	2005	2004	2003	2002	2001	2000
1Q	792.8	614.4	467.2	350.5	265.9	186.9
2Q	881.2	625.5	531.6	376.3	287.6	206.3
3Q	—	707.2	586.8	403.1	317.7	240.8
4Q	—	733.1	621.1	436.8	333.9	265.3
Yr.	—	2,680	2,207	1,602	1,205	899.3

Earnings Per Share ($)

	2005	2004	2003	2002	2001	2000
1Q	0.60	0.48	0.34	0.20	0.08	0.07
2Q	0.79	0.49	0.39	0.21	0.14	0.08
3Q	E0.56	0.60	0.47	0.24	0.18	0.09
4Q	E0.55	0.38	0.48	0.26	0.19	0.08
Yr.	E2.50	1.95	1.66	0.91	0.59	0.32

Next earnings report expected: mid-January Source: S&P, Company Reports
EPS Estimates based on S&P Operating Earnings; historical GAAP earnings are as reported.

Forest Laboratories, Inc.

Recommendation: **HOLD** ★ ★ ★ ☆ ☆   12-Month Target Price: **$53.00** (as of August 31, 2004)

Business Summary November 11, 2004

Forest Laboratories produces niche-oriented branded and generic prescription pharmaceuticals, as well as a line of OTC medications. Most of the company's key products were developed in collaboration with licensing partners. FRX's most important products are Celexa and Lexapro antidepressants, which accounted for a combined total of 82% of net sales in FY 04 (Mar.).

With the loss of marketing exclusivity on Celexa antidepressant (generically known as citalopram HBr) in late October 2004, Lexapro (escitalopram oxalate) has become the company's principal antidepressant. Lexapro is an advanced selective serotonin reuptake inhibitor (SSRI) indicated for the treatment of both depression and generalized anxiety disorder. Both Lexapro and Celexa had sales of about $1.1 billion in FY 04. Based on data from IMS Health, Lexapro and Celexa accounted respectively for 12.4% and 5.3% of the U.S. prescription antidepressant market in September 2004. Celexa and Lexapro were both licensed from H. Lundbeck A/S, a privately held drug company based in Copenhagen, Denmark.

Other products include Tiazac, a once daily diltiazem calcium channel blocker for the treatment of hypertension; Aerobid, a metered-dose inhaled steroid to treat asthma; the Lorcet line of potent analgesics; Aerochamber, a spacer device used to improve the delivery of aerosol products; Levothroid, a thyroid product; Infasurf, a treatment for respiratory conditions in premature infants; Cervidil, used to aid in cervical dilation; Monurol, a treatment for urinary tract infections; Aerospan, an inhalation treatment for asthma; and Benicar antihypertensive. FRX also receives royalties from Climara, a transdermal estrogen patch marketed by Berlex Laboratories. In October 2003, the FDA approved Namenda (licensed from Merz Pharmaceuticals of Germany) for moderate to severe Alzheimer's disease. FRX also plans an FDA submission to market Nemanda for the treatment of mild to moderate Alzheimer's disease.

The generic product line, marketed in the U.S. by the Inwood Laboratories unit, specializes in controlled-release pharmaceuticals. These include Propranolol E.R., a beta blocker used to treat hypertension; Indomethacin E.R., an antiarthritic; and Theochron, an asthma drug. The company's U.K. and Ireland subsidiaries offer various prescription and OTC drugs.

R&D spending totaled $246 million in FY 04, equal to 9.2% of total revenues. Key products in the R&D pipeline include oxycodone/ibuprofen for pain; and various other treatments for osteoarthritis, central nervous system disorders, irritable bowel syndrome, and other conditions. Lexapro is also being studied for relapsed depression and panic disorder.

Company Financials Fiscal Year ending March 31

Per Share Data ($)

(Year Ended March 31)	2004	2003	2002	2001	2000	1999	1998	1997	1996	1995
Tangible Bk. Val.	8.03	5.66	3.75	2.60	1.79	1.60	1.25	1.22	1.58	1.43
Cash Flow	2.01	1.80	1.06	0.71	0.44	0.29	0.17	-0.01	0.32	0.31
Earnings	1.95	1.66	0.91	0.59	0.32	0.23	0.11	-0.07	0.28	0.27
S&P Core Earnings	1.85	1.58	0.73	0.47	NA	NA	NA	NA	NA	NA
Dividends	Nil	Nil	Nil	Nil	Nil	Nil	Nil	Nil	Nil	Nil
Payout Ratio	Nil	Nil	Nil	Nil	Nil	Nil	Nil	Nil	Nil	Nil

Cal. Yrs.	2003	2002	2001	2000	1999	1998	1997	1996	1995	1994
Prices - High	63.23	54.99	41.59	35.32	15.43	13.31	6.16	6.96	6.53	6.56
- Low	41.85	32.12	23.25	14.34	10.31	6.07	3.95	3.53	5.04	5.00
P/E Ratio - High	32	33	46	60	48	59	56	NM	24	24
- Low	21	19	26	24	32	27	36	NM	18	19

Income Statement Analysis (Million $)

	2004	2003	2002	2001	2000	1999	1998	1997	1996	1995
Revs.	2,650	2,207	1,567	1,181	882	546	427	281	447	393
Oper. Inc.	929	833	490	318	181	54.3	27.2	-48.1	164	159
Depr.	22.2	51.6	54.6	43.3	40.6	21.3	20.1	19.2	16.5	14.1
Int. Exp.	Nil	Nil	Nil	Nil	Nil	Nil	Nil	Nil	Nil	Nil
Pretax Inc.	937	821	470	299	157	111	54.8	-39.0	162	156
Eff. Tax Rate	21.4%	24.2%	28.1%	28.0%	28.4%	30.4%	33.0%	NM	35.8%	35.9%
Net Inc.	736	622	338	215	113	77.2	36.7	-23.5	104	100
S&P Core Earnings	697	589	272	170	NA	NA	NA	NA	NA	NA

Balance Sheet & Other Fin. Data (Million $)

	2004	2003	2002	2001	2000	1999	1998	1997	1996	1995
Cash	2,131	1,556	893	506	355	279	150	172	124	142
Curr. Assets	2,916	2,255	1,195	884	645	502	372	360	471	349
Total Assets	3,863	2,918	1,952	1,447	1,098	875	744	700	899	757
Curr. Liab.	605	564	325	224	211	130	130	73.5	89.5	57.6
LT Debt	Nil	Nil	Nil	Nil	Nil	Nil	Nil	Nil	Nil	Nil
Common Equity	3,256	2,352	1,625	1,222	885	744	614	626	810	699
Total Cap.	3,258	2,354	1,627	1,223	887	745	614	626	810	700
Cap. Exp.	102	79.6	36.4	30.9	35.3	17.2	6.89	9.66	11.6	22.2
Cash Flow	758	674	393	258	153	98.4	56.8	-4.36	121	114
Curr. Ratio	4.8	4.0	3.7	4.0	3.1	3.9	2.9	4.9	5.3	6.1
% LT Debt of Cap.	Nil	Nil	Nil	Nil	Nil	Nil	Nil	Nil	Nil	Nil
% Net Inc.of Revs.	27.8	28.2	21.6	18.2	12.8	14.1	8.6	NM	23.3	25.5
% Ret. on Assets	21.7	25.5	19.9	16.7	11.4	9.5	5.1	NM	12.6	14.3
% Ret. on Equity	26.2	31.3	23.7	20.4	13.8	11.4	5.9	NM	13.8	15.6

Data as orig reptd.; bef. results of disc opers/spec. items. Per share data adj. for stk. divs. Bold denotes primary EPS - prior periods restated. E-Estimated. NA-Not Available. NM-Not Meaningful. NR-Not Ranked. UR-Under Review.

Office: 909 Third Avenue, New York, NY 10022-4731.
Telephone: 212-421-7850.
Email: investor.relations@frx.com
Website: http://www.frx.com
Chrmn & CEO: H. Solomon.
Pres & COO: K.E. Goodman.

CFO: F.I. Pierier, Jr.
Secy: W.J. Candee III.
Investor Contact: C. Triano 212-224-6713.
Dirs: W. J. Candee III, G. S. Cohan, D. L. Goldwasser, K. E. Goodman, L. B. Salans, P. M. Satow, H. Solomon.

Founded: in 1956.
Domicile: Delaware.
Employees: 4,967.
S&P Analyst: H. B. Saftlas/PMW/BK

Fortune Brands

Recommendation: **BUY** ★★★★☆
SELL | SELL | HOLD | BUY | BUY

12-Month Target Price: **$86.00**
(as of October 11, 2004)

FO has an approximate 0.10% weighting in the **S&P 500**

Sector: Consumer Discretionary
Sub-Industry: Housewares & Specialties
Peer Group: Houseware Products

Summary: This diversified holding company has interests in consumer businesses that include home improvement, spirits and wine, office products, and golf-related products.

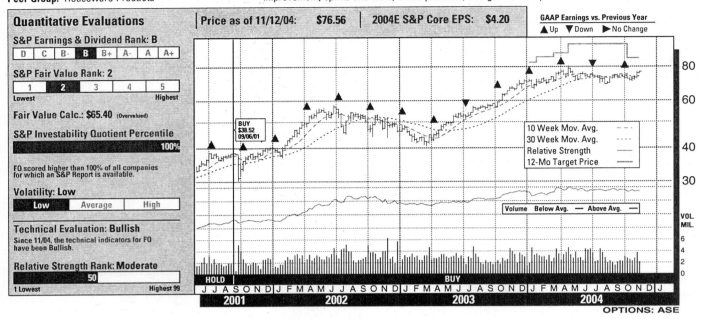

Quantitative Evaluations

S&P Earnings & Dividend Rank: B

| D | C | B- | **B** | B+ | A- | A | A+ |

S&P Fair Value Rank: 2

| 1 | **2** | 3 | 4 | 5 |
| Lowest | | | | Highest |

Fair Value Calc.: $65.40 (Overvalued)

S&P Investability Quotient Percentile

100%

FO scored higher than 100% of all companies for which an S&P Report is available.

Volatility: Low

| **Low** | Average | High |

Technical Evaluation: Bullish

Since 11/04, the technical indicators for FO have been Bullish.

Relative Strength Rank: Moderate

50

1 Lowest — Highest 99

Price as of 11/12/04: **$76.56** | 2004E S&P Core EPS: **$4.20**

GAAP Earnings vs. Previous Year
▲ Up ▼ Down ► No Change

- 10 Week Mov. Avg. ---
- 30 Week Mov. Avg. ····
- Relative Strength
- 12-Mo Target Price

BUY $38.52 09/06/01

Volume   Below Avg. — Above Avg. —

VOL. MIL.

HOLD | BUY

J J A S O N D J F M A M J J A S O N D J F M A M J J A S O N D J F M A M J J A S O N D J
2001   2002   2003   2004

OPTIONS: ASE

Analyst commentary prepared by Howard Choe/DC/BK

Highlights October 26, 2004

- We expect sales to increase approximately 15% in 2004, reflecting acquisitions, increased product presence in retail stores and new product introductions. We expect home product sales growth to be driven by a resilient market for home repairs and remodeling. We look for continued strength in the golf division, driven by new products and brand strength. Solid demand for Jim Beam products and premium brands, in addition to price increases, should drive spirits and wine division sales up modestly, in our opinion. The office products division should benefit from strong demand for Kensington computer accessories and modest category growth, in our view. We expect sales to increase 5% in 2005, given difficult comparisons and no assumption of acquisitions.

- We think profitability will improve modestly, due to savings from consolidation and the relocation of manufacturing facilities. We believe operating margin expansion will be greater than gross margin expansion due to higher commodity costs and well controlled SG&A expenses.

- We project that operating EPS will advance to $4.57 in 2004, from $3.79 in 2003. In 2005, we estimate EPS will increase 13%, to $5.15. Our Standard & Poor's Core Earnings estimates of $4.20 in 2004 and $4.75 in 2005 mainly reflect adjustments related to estimated stock option expense.

Key Stock Statistics

S&P Core EPS 2005E	4.75	52-week Range	$80.50-65.37
S&P Oper. EPS 2004E	4.57	12 Month P/E	16.6
P/E on S&P Oper. EPS 2004E	16.8	Beta	0.57
S&P Oper. EPS 2005E	5.15	Shareholders	26,212
Yield (%)	1.7%	Market Cap (B)	$ 11.0
Dividend Rate/Share	1.32	Shares Outstanding (M)	144.0

Value of $10,000 invested five years ago: **$ 24,883**

Dividend Data Dividends have been paid since 1905

Amount ($)	Date Decl.	Ex-Div. Date	Stock of Record	Payment Date
0.300	Jan. 27	Feb. 09	Feb. 11	Mar. 01 '04
0.300	Apr. 27	May. 10	May. 12	Jun. 01 '04
0.330	Jul. 27	Aug. 09	Aug. 11	Sep. 01 '04
0.330	Sep. 28	Nov. 08	Nov. 10	Dec. 01 '04

Investment Rationale/Risk October 26, 2004

- We are maintaining our buy opinion on the stock, given our view of the high growth profile of the company and attractive valuation. We believe consumers will continue to invest in new homes and remodel existing homes, aiding FO's home and hardware division, which markets the popular Moen faucet lines and various kitchen cabinet lines. In addition, we believe the company's other operating segments of golf, wine and spirits and office products provide diversification benefits. We believe management will continue to focus on bolstering the balance sheet as well as cash flows. Free cash flow is likely to be strong again in 2004, in our opinion.

- Risks to our recommendation and target price include a deterioration in the economy, a rapid increase in interest rates, and low consumer acceptance of new products.

- FO has a strong record of generating earnings growth at a higher level than peers and the S&P 500 and yet the shares trade below that of the S&P 500. Given FO's strong track record of operating performance and healthy near term growth prospects that we see, we believe the shares should trade at a premium to that of the S&P 500. Consequently, we view the shares as undervalued, recently trading at a forward P/E of 14X, a 7% discount to the level of the S&P 500, and well below our 12-month target price of $86, which assumes a 17X forward P/E.

Revenues/Earnings Data Fiscal year ending December 31

Revenues (Million $)

	2004	2003	2002	2001	2000	1999
1Q	1,708	1,392	1,271	1,301	1,364	1,292
2Q	1,890	1,582	1,513	1,433	1,501	1,421
3Q	1,812	1,584	1,463	1,472	1,403	1,339
4Q	—	1,657	1,432	1,472	1,527	1,472
Yr.	—	6,215	5,678	5,679	5,845	5,525

Earnings Per Share ($)

	2004	2003	2002	2001	2000	1999
1Q	0.92	0.66	0.55	0.39	0.39	0.32
2Q	1.11	1.18	1.27	0.66	0.64	-6.56
3Q	1.52	0.98	0.73	0.60	0.46	0.28
4Q	E1.18	1.04	0.86	0.84	-2.41	0.68
Yr.	E4.57	3.86	3.41	2.49	-0.88	-5.35

Next earnings report expected: late-January Source: S&P, Company Reports
EPS Estimates based on S&P Operating Earnings; historical GAAP earnings are as reported.

Fortune Brands, Inc.

Recommendation: **BUY** ★ ★ ★ ★ ★ 12-Month Target Price: **$86.00** (as of October 11, 2004)

Business Summary October 26, 2004

Fortune Brands (formerly American Brands, Inc.) is a holding company with subsidiaries that operate several consumer-related businesses. In May 1997, the company divested its remaining tobacco operations to shareholders via a tax free spinoff of the shares of Gallaher Group Plc, a newly formed U.K. company. FO's remaining operating companies have some of the world's best known consumer brands.

Home and hardware products are sold through the MasterBrand Industries subsidiary. Major units include MasterBrand Cabinets, Moen, Master Lock, Waterloo and Therma-Tru. Moen is a leading producer of faucets, sinks, and plumbing accessories in the U.S. and Asia. Master Lock makes key-controlled and combination locks, and door locksets and related hardware. MasterBrand Cabinets manufactures stock and semi-custom kitchen cabinets and vanities and ready-to-assemble kitchen cabinets and bathroom vanities under the Aristokraft, Schrock, Omega, Kemper, Decora and Diamond names. Waterloo makes tool storage products for Sears Craftsman and other private labels. Therma-Tru (acquired in November 2003) is the leading U.S. manufacturer of fiberglass and steel residential entry doors. In 2003, hardware and home improvement products accounted for 47% of total sales and 49% of operating company contributions (before corporate expenses).

Office products (18%, 15%) are sold through the ACCO World Corp. unit. ACCO sells a wide variety of traditional and computer-related office products and supplies, PC accessory products, time management products, and labels and presentation aids. After considering the divestiture of this division since October 1999, the company said in April 2001 that it would not divest the unit due to unfavorable economic and industry conditions.

Golf products (18%, 15%) operations are conducted through Acushnet, a leading producer of golf balls (Titleist, Pinnacle), golf shoes (FootJoy), golf clubs (Cobra, Titleist), and golf gloves. Other products include bags, carts, dress and athletic shoes, socks and accessories.

Spirits and wine (17%, 33%) are sold through the JBB Worldwide subsidiary. Leading brands include Jim Beam Bourbon whiskey, DeKuyper cordials, Gilbey's gin, Kamchatka vodka, and Geyser Peak wine. Principal markets are the U.S., the U.K., and Australia. About 20% to 25% of the division's sales come from international markets. In 1999, the Jim Beam unit entered into a joint venture (Maxxium) with Highland Distillers and Remy-Cointreau to establish an international distribution company. In 2001, the company entered into certain transactions with Sweden's Vin & Spirit, which was to create a U.S. distribution joint venture designed to expand the distribution of various brands, buy a 10% interest in Jim Beam Brands, and purchase an equal equity stake in Maxxium.

Company Financials Fiscal Year ending December 31

Per Share Data ($)

(Year Ended December 31)	2003	2002	2001	2000	1999	1998	1997	1996	1995	1994
Tangible Bk. Val.	NM	NM	2.06	0.89	0.83	1.91	1.93	-1.55	3.13	5.33
Cash Flow	5.14	4.57	3.89	0.63	-3.96	3.09	1.64	4.46	4.28	5.94
Earnings	3.86	3.41	2.49	-0.88	-5.35	1.67	0.23	2.86	2.90	4.38
S&P Core Earnings	3.79	3.14	2.38	NA	NA	NA	NA	NA	NA	NA
Dividends	1.14	1.02	0.97	0.93	0.89	0.85	1.41	2.00	2.00	1.99
Payout Ratio	30%	30%	39%	NM	NM	51%	NM	70%	69%	45%
Prices - High	71.80	57.86	40.54	33.25	45.87	42.25	56.00	50.12	47.25	38.37
- Low	40.60	36.85	28.37	19.18	29.37	25.25	30.25	39.87	36.62	29.37
P/E Ratio - High	19	17	16	NM	NM	25	NM	18	16	9
- Low	11	11	11	NM	NM	15	NM	14	13	7

Income Statement Analysis (Million $)

	2003	2002	2001	2000	1999	1998	1997	1996	1995	1994
Revs.	6,215	5,678	5,679	5,845	5,525	5,241	4,845	5,776	5,355	7,490
Oper. Inc.	1,142	1,011	870	938	853	871	723	1,363	1,293	1,557
Depr.	193	179	219	237	231	251	243	275	258	314
Int. Exp.	73.8	74.1	96.8	134	107	103	117	179	160	212
Pretax Inc.	884	756	492	38.9	-721	512	140	824	894	1,351
Eff. Tax Rate	32.7%	28.3%	19.2%	NM	NM	42.6%	70.0%	39.8%	39.3%	34.5%
Net Inc.	579	526	386	-138	-891	294	42.0	497	543	885
S&P Core Earnings	567	484	367	NA	NA	NA	NA	NA	NA	NA

Balance Sheet & Other Fin. Data (Million $)

	2003	2002	2001	2000	1999	1998	1997	1996	1995	1994
Cash	105	15.4	48.7	20.9	72.0	40.0	54.0	120	140	110
Curr. Assets	2,282	1,903	1,970	2,265	2,313	2,265	2,096	3,873	3,164	4,671
Total Assets	7,445	5,822	5,301	5,764	6,417	7,360	6,943	9,504	8,021	9,794
Curr. Liab.	2,134	1,515	1,258	2,040	2,003	1,845	1,769	3,695	2,411	3,116
LT Debt	1,243	200	950	1,152	1,205	982	739	1,598	1,155	1,512
Common Equity	2,712	2,305	2,094	2,127	2,728	4,087	4,006	3,671	3,863	4,622
Total Cap.	4,664	2,983	3,444	3,343	3,991	5,080	4,795	5,402	5,160	6,283
Cap. Exp.	194	194	207	227	241	252	197	240	208	201
Cash Flow	772	704	605	99	-661	544	284	771	800	1,198
Curr. Ratio	1.1	1.3	1.6	1.1	1.2	1.2	1.2	1.1	1.3	1.5
% LT Debt of Cap.	26.6	6.7	27.6	34.5	30.2	19.3	15.4	29.6	22.4	24.1
% Net Inc.of Revs.	9.3	9.3	6.8	NM	NM	5.6	0.9	8.6	10.1	11.8
% Ret. on Assets	8.7	9.5	7.0	NM	NM	4.1	0.5	5.7	6.1	6.8
% Ret. on Equity	23.1	23.9	18.3	NM	NM	7.2	1.1	13.2	12.8	19.9

Data as orig reptd.; bef. results of disc opers/spec. items. Per share data adj. for stk. divs.; EPS diluted (primary prior to 1998). E-Estimated. NA-Not Available. NM-Not Meaningful. NR-Not Ranked. UR-Under Review.

Office: 300 Tower Parkway, Lincolnshire, IL 60069-3640.
Telephone: 847-484-4400.
Email: investorrelations@fortunebrands.com
Website: http://www.fortunebrands.com
Chrmn & CEO: N.H. Wesley.
SVP & CFO: C.P. Omtvedt.

SVP & Treas: M. Hausberg.
SVP, Secy & General Counsel: M.A. Roche.
VP & Investor Contact: T. Diaz 847-484-4410.
Dirs: P. O. Ewers, T. C. Hays, P. E. Leroy, G. R. Lohman, E. A. Renna, J. C. Reyes, A. M. Tatlock, D. M. Thomas, N. H. Wesley, P. M. Wilson.

Founded: in 1904.
Domicile: Delaware.
Employees: 30,988.
S&P Analyst: Howard Choe/DC/BK

FPL Group

Recommendation: **HOLD** ★★★☆☆
SELL · STRONG SELL · HOLD · BUY · STRONG BUY

12-Month Target Price: $71.00
(as of September 15, 2004)

FPL has an approximate 0.12% weighting in the **S&P 500**

Sector: Utilities
Sub-Industry: Electric Utilities
Peer Group: Electric Cos. (Domestic) - Large

Summary: Through its Florida Power & Light subsidiary, FPL serves more than 4,000,000 customer accounts; through FPL Energy, it produces electricity from clean and renewable fuels.

Quantitative Evaluations

S&P Earnings & Dividend Rank: A-

| D | C | B- | B | B+ | A- | A | A+ |

S&P Fair Value Rank: 3

| 1 | 2 | 3 | 4 | 5 |
| Lowest | | | | Highest |

Fair Value Calc.: $66.80 (Slightly Overvalued)

S&P Investability Quotient Percentile

93%

FPL scored higher than 93% of all companies for which an S&P Report is available.

Volatility: Low

| Low | Average | High |

Technical Evaluation: Bullish

Since 10/04, the technical indicators for FPL have been Bullish.

Relative Strength Rank: Moderate

58

| 1 Lowest | Highest 99 |

Price as of 11/12/04: $72.56 | **2004E S&P Core EPS:** $4.29

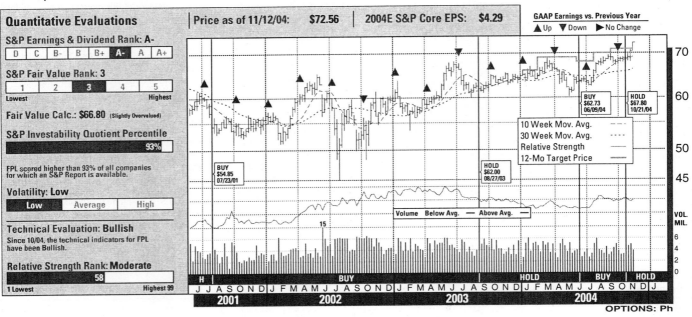

GAAP Earnings vs. Previous Year
▲ Up ▼ Down ► No Change

- 10 Week Mov. Avg.
- 30 Week Mov. Avg.
- Relative Strength
- 12-Mo Target Price

BUY $54.85 07/23/01
HOLD $62.00 08/27/03
BUY $62.73 06/09/04
HOLD $67.80 10/21/04

Volume Below Avg. — Above Avg.

VOL. MIL.

OPTIONS: Ph

Analyst commentary prepared by Justin McCann/CB/GG

Highlights October 25, 2004

- After an anticipated flat performance in 2004, compared with 2003's operating EPS of $4.89, we expect operating EPS to increase about 5% in 2005. In the wake of the three major hurricanes that struck the territory of Florida Power & Light (FP&L) during the third quarter and created some 5.4 million customer outages, the company has estimated that the lost revenues and other impacts from the storms will reduce 2004 EPS by about $0.15.

- For 2005, we expect FP&L to contribute operating EPS of about $4.05, and FPL Energy about $1.40, while corporate and other operations are expected to record a loss of about $0.30, with increased losses due to a higher level of debt related to FPL Energy's projects. For 2005, FPL Energy has already hedged a large percentage of its portfolio at higher prices than in 2004. We also expect FP&L to continue to benefit from strong customer growth.

- On June 2, 2004, the Florida Public Service Commission approved FP&L's proposed $600 million expansion of its Turkey Point power plant facility. The utility hopes to receive all state and federal approvals required by mid-2005, with the proposed plant slated to go into operation in 2007.

Investment Rationale/Risk October 25, 2004

- Given the recent rise in the shares, we have lowered our investment recommendation to hold from accumulate. The shares had benefited from the nearly 10% increase in the dividend that became effective with the September 2004 payment, and the improved outlook for 2005. We believe the stock is now fairly valued at the approximate average peer P/E multiple of about 13.4X our 2005 EPS estimate.

- Risks to our investment recommendation and target price include lower than expected results from the unregulated FPL Energy business, and a reduction in the average P/E multiple of the group as a whole.

- While the increase in the dividend raised the payout ratio on our EPS estimate for 2004 from 49% to 53%, this is still well below the industry average. We would not expect annual increases in the dividend to be continued at the level of the recent one, but we do expect to see future annual increases at around the 3% level of previous increases. Expecting the shares to trade at a similar peer P/E multiple of about 13.4X our preliminary 2006 EPS estimate of $5.30, our 12-month target price is $71.

Key Stock Statistics

S&P Core EPS 2005E	4.54	52-week Range	$72.60-60.20
S&P Oper. EPS 2004E	4.90	12 Month P/E	15.2
P/E on S&P Oper. EPS 2004E	14.8	Beta	0.22
S&P Oper. EPS 2005E	5.15	Shareholders	35,076
Yield (%)	3.7%	Market Cap (B)	$ 13.5
Dividend Rate/Share	2.72	Shares Outstanding (M)	185.6

Value of $10,000 invested five years ago: **$ 17,581**

Dividend Data Dividends have been paid since 1944

Amount ($)	Date Decl.	Ex-Div. Date	Stock of Record	Payment Date
0.620	Feb. 13	Feb. 25	Feb. 27	Mar. 15 '04
0.620	May. 21	Jun. 02	Jun. 04	Jun. 15 '04
0.680	Jul. 26	Aug. 25	Aug. 27	Sep. 15 '04
0.680	Oct. 15	Nov. 23	Nov. 26	Dec. 15 '04

Revenues/Earnings Data Fiscal year ending December 31

Revenues (Million $)

	2004	2003	2002	2001	2000	1999
1Q	2,331	2,082	1,843	1,941	1,468	1,412
2Q	2,619	2,339	2,248	2,166	1,670	1,614
3Q	2,983	2,775	2,353	2,529	2,087	1,892
4Q	—	2,435	2,029	1,839	1,857	1,520
Yr.	—	9,630	8,311	8,475	7,082	6,438

Earnings Per Share ($)

	2004	2003	2002	2001	2000	1999
1Q	0.77	0.99	0.98	0.65	0.71	1.22
2Q	1.43	1.34	1.46	1.30	1.20	0.45
3Q	1.76	1.88	0.85	1.98	1.84	1.70
4Q	E0.94	0.81	0.73	0.70	0.38	0.71
Yr.	E4.90	5.02	4.01	4.62	4.14	4.07

Next earnings report expected: late-January Source: S&P, Company Reports
EPS Estimates based on S&P Operating Earnings; historical GAAP earnings are as reported.

Recommendation: **HOLD** ★ ★ ★ ☆ ☆   12-Month Target Price: **$71.00** (as of September 15, 2004)

Business Summary October 25, 2004

FPL Group is the holding company for Florida Power & Light Company and FPL Group Capital.

Florida Power & Light Company provides electricity to about 4.1 million customer accounts in an area covering nearly all of Florida's eastern seaboard, as well as the southern part of the state. The utility's electric revenues by customer class in 2003 were: residential 56% (55% in 2002, 56% in 2001); commercial 37% (36%, 38%); industrial 3% (3%, 3%); and other 4% (6%, 3%). The company owns and operates four nuclear units: two at Turkey Point and two at St. Lucie.

Capital spending for Florida Power & Light in 2003 totaled about $1.4 billion, versus $1.3 billion in 2002. The company projected capital spending of about $1.65 billion for 2004, $1.65 billion for 2005, and $1.57 billion for 2006.

In March 2002, the Florida Public Service Commission approved a new retail rate agreement (effective April 15, 2002, through 2005) that provided for an annual $250 million (7%) rate reduction in Florida Power & Light's customer base rates and service charges.

Wholly owned FPL Group Capital owns and funds FPL's non-utility operations. In January 1998, it formed FPL Energy, to manage existing non-regulated investments and to pursue new investments in the domestic energy markets.

In November 2002, an FPL Energy subsidiary purchased an 88% interest in the Seabrook nuclear facility, located in New Hampshire. FPL's ownership interest consists of 1,024 megawatts of nuclear generated capacity.

At December 31, 2003, FPL Energy had ownership interest in operating independent power projects with a net generating capacity of 11,041 megawatts (all of which consisted of ownership interests in operating independent power projects). Fuel sources for these projects in 2003 were: natural gas 55% (44% in 2002); wind 25% (24%); nuclear 9% (14%); oil 6% (11%); hydro 3% (5%); and other 2% (2%).

FPL Energy's capital spending in 2003 was about $1.6 billion, versus $2.1 billion in 2002 and $1.98 billion in 2001. Pending the enactment of legislation reestablishing production tax credits for new wind facilities, the subsidiary has projected a sharp drop in capital expenditures to $225 million in 2004, $40 million in 2005, and $60 million in 2006. The unit expected a new gas-fired power plant, with a total capacity of about 744 megawatts (mw), to start operations in the second half of 2004. PMI, a subsidiary of FPL Energy, is involved in energy marketing and trading.

In January 2000, FPL formed FPL FiberNet through the transfer of its existing 1,600 miles of fiber-optic lines. At December 31, 2003, the network consisted of about 2,500 route miles. The unit sells its capacity to FPL, and to telephone, cable television, and Internet customers, and other telecommunications companies.

In April 2001, the company agreed to terminate a merger agreement (announced in July 2000) with Entergy Corp. (ETR), a New Orleans-based energy holding company.

Company Financials Fiscal Year ending December 31

Per Share Data ($)

(Year Ended December 31)	2003	2002	2001	2000	1999	1998	1997	1996	1995	1994
Tangible Bk. Val.	37.86	34.92	34.18	31.78	30.00	28.32	26.62	24.61	24.06	22.50
Earnings	5.02	4.01	4.62	4.14	4.07	3.85	3.57	3.33	3.16	2.91
S&P Core Earnings	4.42	3.04	3.65	NA	NA	NA	NA	NA	NA	NA
Dividends	2.40	2.32	2.24	2.16	2.08	2.00	1.92	1.84	1.76	1.88
Payout Ratio	48%	58%	48%	52%	51%	52%	54%	55%	56%	65%
Prices - High	68.07	65.31	71.62	73.00	61.93	72.56	60.00	48.12	46.50	39.12
- Low	53.55	45.00	51.21	36.37	41.12	56.06	42.62	41.50	34.00	26.87
P/E Ratio - High	14	16	16	18	15	19	17	14	15	13
- Low	11	11	11	9	10	15	12	12	11	9

Income Statement Analysis (Million $)

	2003	2002	2001	2000	1999	1998	1997	1996	1995	1994
Revs.	9,630	8,311	8,475	7,082	6,438	6,661	6,369	6,037	5,592	5,423
Depr.	1,105	952	983	1,032	1,040	1,284	1,061	960	918	724
Maint.	NA	NA	NA	NA	NA	NA	NA	NA	NA	NA
Fxd. Chgs. Cov.	3.95	4.52	4.51	4.55	4.96	NA	3.97	4.01	3.64	3.20
Constr. Credits	NA	NA	NA	Nil	Nil	Nil	Nil	2.00	15.0	24.0
Eff. Tax Rate	29.2%	26.0%	32.7%	32.3%	31.7%	29.6%	33.0%	33.6%	37.3%	37.2%
Net Inc.	893	695	781	704	697	664	618	579	553	519
S&P Core Earnings	786	527	616	NA	NA	NA	NA	NA	NA	NA

Balance Sheet & Other Fin. Data (Million $)

	2003	2002	2001	2000	1999	1998	1997	1996	1995	1994
Gross Prop.	30,272	26,505	23,388	21,022	19,554	17,952	17,820	17,034	16,725	16,390
Cap. Exp.	1,383	1,277	1,544	1,299	861	617	551	488	671	906
Net Prop.	20,297	14,304	11,662	9,934	9,264	8,555	9,354	9,384	9,852	10,203
Capitalization:										
LT Debt	8,728	6,016	5,084	4,202	3,704	2,347	2,949	3,144	3,377	4,050
% LT Debt	55.6	47.4	45.8	42.9	40.8	30.5	36.8	39.0	41.6	47.1
Pfd.	Nil	Nil	Nil	Nil	Nil	226	226	332	340	545
% Pfd.	Nil	Nil	Nil	Nil	Nil	2.90	2.80	4.10	4.20	6.30
Common	6,967	6,688	6,015	5,593	5,370	5,126	4,845	4,592	4,392	4,197
% Common	44.4	52.6	54.2	57.1	59.2	66.6	60.4	56.9	54.2	48.8
Total Cap.	17,850	14,444	12,629	11,442	10,337	9,159	9,493	10,201	10,299	10,917
% Oper. Ratio	87.9	85.7	87.6	86.3	88.0	85.4	85.5	85.5	84.5	84.5
% Earn. on Net Prop.	8.1	9.5	10.3	12.9	18.2	14.0	13.1	9.1	11.9	8.2
% Return On Revs.	9.3	8.4	9.2	9.9	10.8	10.0	9.7	9.6	9.9	9.6
% Return On Invest. Capital	8.1	9.0	9.6	9.7	11.4	10.7	9.4	8.5	NM	7.8
% Return On Com. Equity	13.4	10.7	13.5	12.8	13.3	13.3	13.1	12.9	12.9	12.5

Data as orig reptd.; bef. results of disc opers/spec. items. Per share data adj. for stk. divs.; EPS diluted. E-Estimated. NA-Not Available. NM-Not Meaningful. NR-Not Ranked. UR-Under Review.

Office: 700 Universe Boulevard, Juno Beach, FL 33408-0420.
Telephone: 561-694-4000.
Website: http://www.fplgroup.com
Chrmn, Pres & CEO: L. Hay III.
VP & CFO: M.P. Dewhurst.
Chief Acctg Officer: K.M. Davis.

Treas: P. Cutler.
Secy & General Counsel: D.P. Coyle.
Investor Contact: M. Haggerty 800-222-4511.
Dirs: H. J. Arnelle, S. S. Barrat, R. M. Beall II, J. H. Brown, J. L. Camaren, A. W. Dreyfoos, Jr., L. Hay III, F. V. Malek, M. Thaman, P. R. Tregurtha, F. G. Zarb.

Founded: in 1984.
Domicile: Florida.
Employees: 11,500.
S&P Analyst: Justin McCann/CB/GG

Franklin Resources

Recommendation: **BUY** ★★★★
SELL SELL HOLD BUY BUY

12-Month Target Price: **$77.00**
(as of November 09, 2004)

BEN has an approximate 0.15% weighting in the **S&P 500**

Sector: Financials
Sub-Industry: Asset Management & Custody Banks
Peer Group: Investment Management Cos. - Larger

Summary: Franklin Resources is one of the world's largest asset managers, serving retail, institutional, and high-net-worth clients.

Quantitative Evaluations

S&P Earnings & Dividend Rank: A-

| D | C | B- | B | B+ | A- | A | A+ |

S&P Fair Value Rank: 3

| 1 | 2 | 3 | 4 | 5 |
| Lowest | | | | Highest |

Fair Value Calc.: $60.40 (Slightly Overvalued)

S&P Investability Quotient Percentile

99%

BEN scored higher than 99% of all companies for which an S&P Report is available.

Volatility: Average

| Low | Average | High |

Technical Evaluation: Bullish
Since 8/04, the technical indicators for BEN have been Bullish.

Relative Strength Rank: Strong

83
1 Lowest | Highest 99

| Price as of 11/12/04: | **$64.50** | 2005E S&P Core EPS: | **$3.15** |

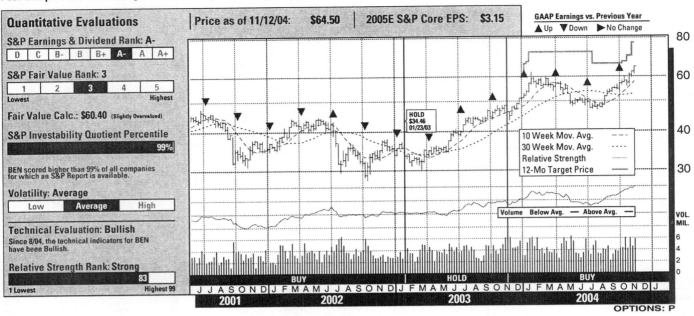

GAAP Earnings vs. Previous Year
▲ Up ▼ Down ► No Change

- 10 Week Mov. Avg.
- 30 Week Mov. Avg.
- Relative Strength
- 12-Mo Target Price

Volume Below Avg. — Above Avg.

VOL. MIL.

HOLD $34.46 01/23/03

BUY | HOLD | BUY

J J A S O N D | J F M A M J J A S O N D | J F M A M J J A S O N D | J F M A M J J A S O N D | J
2001 | 2002 | 2003 | 2004

OPTIONS: P

Analyst commentary prepared by Robert Hansen, CFA /MF/BK

Highlights November 11, 2004

- We believe that BEN's broad product offerings and strong relative track record will continue to attract investors in FY 05 (Sep.), as we see investors reallocating assets toward large fund companies. We see a continued shift by investors toward higher-margin equity and global funds helping EPS in FY 05, partly offset by higher regulatory and compensation expenses.

- In our view, the company generated impressive earnings growth in FY 04, largely due to a 20% increase in assets under management, to $362 billion. Assets under management increased due to continued net client inflows (sales minus redemptions) and market appreciation. However, results were hurt by $86.5 million in charges, primarily for ongoing governmental investigations, proceedings and actions related to market timing allegations.

- We forecast EPS of $3.50 for FY 05, driven by increased assets under management, prudent expense growth, and a mix shift toward higher-margin equity and global funds. We think that a potential further decline in the dollar would aid BEN, as we estimate that nearly 41% of client assets are in global products.

Investment Rationale/Risk November 11, 2004

- We believe the shares deserve to trade at a premium to peers, based on our view of the company's consistent net client inflows, strong relative fund performance, and considerable operating leverage. In addition, we think the stock's P/E multiple should expand, based on impressive EPS growth that we see, a continued shift toward higher-margin equity and global funds, and reduced concerns over regulatory issues.

- Risks to our recommendation and target price include increased competition, regulatory issues, and volatility in global equity, bond, and currency markets that can materially affect assets under management and net investor flows.

- The shares, which recently traded at nearly 18X our FY 05 EPS estimate, have outperformed their peer group thus far in 2004. Our 12-month target price of $77 is equal to 22X our FY 05 EPS estimate, a premium to peers that we believe is warranted. We would buy the shares, as we expect investors to reallocate assets toward large fund companies with solid track records and broad product offerings, and see BEN gaining market share.

Key Stock Statistics

S&P Oper. EPS 2005E	3.50	52-week Range	$64.61-43.39
P/E on S&P Oper. EPS 2005E	18.4	12 Month P/E	22.8
Yield (%)	0.5%	Beta	1.16
Dividend Rate/Share	0.34	Shareholders	4,900
Shares Outstanding (M)	249.4	Market Cap (B)	$ 16.1

Value of $10,000 invested five years ago: **$ 19,443**

Dividend Data Dividends have been paid since 1981

Amount ($)	Date Decl.	Ex-Div. Date	Stock of Record	Payment Date
0.085	Dec. 11	Dec. 29	Dec. 31	Jan. 15 '04
0.085	Mar. 17	Mar. 29	Mar. 31	Apr. 15 '04
0.085	Jun. 23	Jul. 01	Jul. 06	Jul. 16 '04
0.085	Sep. 24	Sep. 30	Oct. 04	Oct. 15 '04

Revenues/Earnings Data Fiscal year ending September 30

Revenues (Million $)

	2004	2003	2002	2001	2000	1999
1Q	806.2	605.5	618.2	564.1	565.7	567.7
2Q	874.6	613.1	626.0	577.4	612.5	554.1
3Q	862.8	683.9	666.0	609.5	568.9	566.8
4Q	881.7	722.0	608.3	603.9	593.0	574.0
Yr.	3,438	2,624	2,519	2,355	2,340	2,263

Earnings Per Share ($)

	2004	2003	2002	2001	2000	1999
1Q	0.67	0.43	0.45	0.61	0.55	0.27
2Q	0.68	0.43	0.46	0.54	0.09	0.41
3Q	0.69	0.52	0.48	0.46	0.58	0.49
4Q	0.79	0.61	0.26	0.32	0.58	0.52
Yr.	2.83	1.97	1.65	1.91	2.28	1.69

Next earnings report expected: late-January Source: S&P, Company Reports
EPS Estimates based on S&P Operating Earnings; historical GAAP earnings are as reported.

Franklin Resources, Inc.

Recommendation: **BUY** ★★★★★   12-Month Target Price: **$77.00** (as of November 09, 2004)

Business Summary November 11, 2004

Franklin Resources is one of the largest U.S. money managers, with $301.9 billion in assets under management at the end of FY 03 (Sep.), up from $247.8 billion at the end of FY 02. At the end of FY 03, equity-based investments accounted for 51% of assets under management, fixed income investments 32%, hybrid funds 15%, and money funds 2%. Global equity and fixed income accounted for 37% of assets under management. U.S. investors owned about 79% of BEN's assets under management. Employee headcount was 6,504, versus 6,711 at the end of FY 02.

Operating revenues come primarily from investment management fees, which include investment advisory and administration fees. Many factors affect the value of assets under management, including the level of sales of shares of funds compared to redemptions, and the increase or decrease in market value of securities owned by the funds. Through acquisitions, BEN has shifted its asset mix from predominantly fixed-income securities to a majority of equity-based investments.

The company's sponsored investment products are distributed under five distinct names: Franklin, Templeton, Mutual Series, Bisset and Fiduciary. Using its broad range of sponsored investment products, BEN covers key market segments: retail, high net-worth, separate accounts, and institutional. At the end of FY 03, assets

under management by distribution included retail 67%, institutional 30%, and high net-worth 3%. Although the company advertises significantly, and engages in sales promotion through media sources, fund shares are still sold primarily through a large network of independent securities dealers.

In October 2003, BEN acquired Darby Overseas Investments, Ltd., and Darby Overseas Partners, L.P., for $75.9 million. In July 2002, 75%-owned Templeton Asset Management (India) Private Ltd. acquired Pioneer ITI AMC Ltd., for about $55.4 million. In April 2001, BEN acquired Fiduciary Trust Co. International, another investment management company catering to high net worth and institutional clients, for about $776 million at closing. The Templeton funds were acquired in 1992, with the purchase of Templeton, Galbraith & Hansberger, which was run by legendary investor Sir John Templeton, known for international investing.

The company's mutual funds have a multi-class share structure to meet investor varied demands. Class A shares have a traditional fee structure whereby investors pay a commission to a broker at the time of purchase. Class B shares have a declining schedule of sales charges if the investor redeems within the first six years. Class C shares are a hybrid, combining front-end sales charges, back-end sales charges, and level load pricing.

Company Financials Fiscal Year ending September 30

Per Share Data ($)

(Year Ended September 30)	2004	2003	2002	2001	2000	1999	1998	1997	1996	1995
Tangible Bk. Val.	NA	9.31	8.69	7.23	7.37	5.79	4.08	5.00	3.15	2.06
Cash Flow	NA	2.67	2.35	2.79	3.13	2.48	2.74	4.40	1.42	1.27
Earnings	2.83	1.97	1.65	1.91	2.28	1.69	1.98	1.72	1.26	1.08
S&P Core Earnings	NA	1.70	1.56	1.61	NA	NA	NA	NA	NA	NA
Dividends	0.33	0.30	0.28	0.26	0.24	0.22	0.20	0.17	0.15	0.13
Payout Ratio	12%	15%	17%	14%	11%	13%	10%	10%	12%	12%
Prices - High	64.61	52.25	44.48	48.30	45.62	45.00	57.87	51.90	24.87	19.33
- Low	46.85	29.99	27.90	30.85	24.62	27.00	25.75	22.08	15.45	11.00
P/E Ratio - High	23	27	27	25	20	27	29	30	20	18
- Low	17	15	17	16	11	16	13	13	12	10

Income Statement Analysis (Million $)

	2004	2003	2002	2001	2000	1999	1998	1997	1996	1995
Income Int.	NA	NA	NA	NA	NA	NA	NA	NA	NA	NA
Income Other	NA	NA	NA	NA	NA	NA	NA	NA	NA	NA
Total Income	NA	2,624	2,519	2,355	2,340	2,262	2,577	2,163	1,523	874
General Exp.	NA	NA	NA	NA	NA	NA	NA	NA	NA	NA
Interest Exp.	NA	19.9	12.3	10.6	14.0	21.0	22.5	25.3	36.9	39.8
Depr.	NA	NA	NA	NA	200	200	191	124	40.0	41.0
Net Inc.	NA	503	433	485	562	427	500	434	315	269
S&P Core Earnings	NA	432	410	407	NA	NA	NA	NA	NA	NA

Balance Sheet & Other Fin. Data (Million $)

	2004	2003	2002	2001	2000	1999	1998	1997	1996	1995
Cash	NA	1,054	981	569	746	819	537	435	502	246
Receivables	NA	441	393	603	693	552	318	438	188	149
Cost of Investments	NA	NA	NA	NA	NA	NA	NA	NA	NA	NA
Total Assets	NA	6,971	6,423	6,266	4,042	3,667	3,480	3,095	2,374	2,245
Loss Reserve	NA	NA	NA	NA	NA	NA	NA	NA	NA	NA
ST Debt	NA	0.29	7.80	NA	NA	NA	NA	NA	NA	NA
Capitalization:										
Debt	NA	1,109	595	566	294	294	612	493	400	382
Equity	NA	4,310	4,267	3,978	2,965	2,657	2,281	1,854	1,401	1,161
Total	NA	5,622	5,037	4,544	3,260	2,951	2,775	2,347	1,800	1,543
Price Times Bk. Val.: High	NA	5.5	5.1	NA	NA	NA	NA	NA	NA	NA
Price Times Bk. Val.: Low	NA	3.2	3.2	NA	NA	NA	NA	NA	NA	NA
Cash Flow	NA	NA	NA	NA	762	627	691	558	496	428
% Exp./Op. Revs.	NA	NA	NA	NA	NA	NA	NA	NA	71.4	54.7
% Earn & Depr/Assets	NA	NA	NA	NA	NA	NA	NA	NA	NA	NA

Data as orig reptd.; bef. results of disc opers/spec. items. Per share data adj. for stk. divs. Bold denotes primary EPS - prior periods restated. E-Estimated. NA-Not Available. NM-Not Meaningful. NR-Not Ranked. UR-Under Review.

Office: One Franklin Parkway, San Mateo, CA 94403.
Telephone: 650-312-2000.
Website: http://www.franklintempleton.com
Chrmn: C.B. Johnson.
Pres & CEO: G.E. Johnson.
Pres, CEO & COO: M.L. Flanagan.

EVP & General Counsel: M.L. Simpson.
SVP & CFO: J. Baio.
Investor Contact: A. Weinfeld 650-525-7584.
Dirs: H. E. Burns, C. Crocker, R. Joffe, C. B. Johnson, R. H. Johnson, Jr., T. Kean, J. A. McCarthy, C. Ratnathicam, P. M. Sacerdote, A. M. Tatlock, L. E. Woodworth.

Founded: in 1947.
Domicile: Delaware.
Employees: 6,500.
S&P Analyst: Robert Hansen, CFA /MF/BK

Freeport-McM. Copper & Gold

Recommendation: **HOLD** ★ ★ ★ ★ ★
SELL SELL HOLD BUY BUY

12-Month Target Price: $35.00
(as of May 10, 2004)

FCX has an approximate 0.06% weighting in the **S&P 500**

Sector: Materials
Sub-Industry: Diversified Metals & Mining
Peer Group: Copper Mining

Summary: FCX explores for, mines and mills copper, gold and silver in Indonesia, and has a copper smelting and refining operation in Spain.

Quantitative Evaluations

S&P Earnings & Dividend Rank: B

| D | C | B- | B | B+ | A- | A | A+ |

S&P Fair Value Rank: 2-

| 1 | 2 | 3 | 4 | 5 |
| Lowest | | | | Highest |

Fair Value Calc.: $32.90 (Overvalued)

S&P Investability Quotient Percentile
73%

FCX scored higher than 73% of all companies for which an S&P Report is available.

Volatility: High

| Low | Average | High |

Technical Evaluation: Neutral
Since 10/04, the technical indicators for FCX have been Neutral.

Relative Strength Rank: Moderate
70
1 Lowest   Highest 99

Price as of 11/12/04: $40.38   **2004E S&P Core EPS:** $0.42

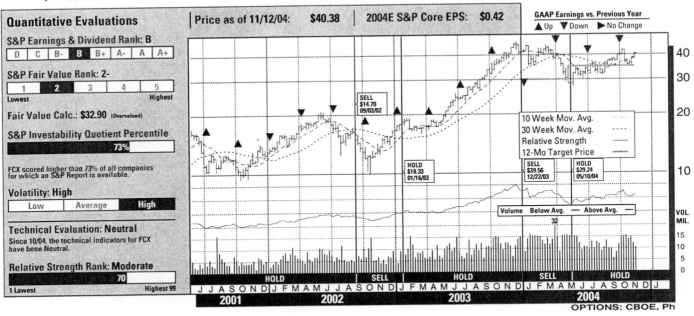

GAAP Earnings vs. Previous Year
▲ Up ▼ Down ▶ No Change

SELL $14.70 09/03/02
HOLD $18.33 01/16/03
SELL $39.56 12/22/03
HOLD $29.24 05/10/04

10 Week Mov. Avg.
30 Week Mov. Avg.
Relative Strength
12-Mo Target Price

Volume Below Avg. — Above Avg.
32

VOL. MIL.

OPTIONS: CBOE, Ph

Analyst commentary prepared by Leo J. Larkin/CB/BK

Highlights August 18, 2004

- We see 2004 revenues rising 2% to 3%, as a projected decline in production partly offsets much higher prices for copper and gold. As a result of rock slides in the 2003 fourth quarter, we believe mining of ore in 2004 will be limited to the Deep Ore Zone underground mine, and to low grade material from the Grasberg open pit. Consequently, higher grade ore that was expected to be mined in 2004 will likely not be mined until 2005. Thus, FCX sees a decline in production from 2003's levels. Penalized by rising unit costs and scheduled maintenance outages at Atlantic Copper and PT Smelting, we look for EPS to decline in 2004.

- Assuming no more rock slides, FCX projects production of 1.5 billion lb. of copper and 2.9 million oz. of gold in 2005, versus estimated copper production of 1.0 billion lb. and gold production of 1.5 million oz. in 2004. Aided by lower expected unit costs stemming from higher volume and a higher gold price, we see a sharp rebound in EPS in 2005.

- According to data compiled by the World Bureau of Metal Statistics, there was a deficit of refined copper consumption over refined copper production of 509,000 metric tons in the first four months of 2004, versus a deficit of 81,000 metric in the first four months of 2003.

Investment Rationale/Risk August 18, 2004

- We recommend holding FCX shares. Aided by a steady increase in sales and EPS from 2000 through 2003 and a decline in capital spending, FCX reinstated the dividend and extended the maturity of its debt. Based on our expectation for generally higher EPS and free cash flow in the years ahead, we believe FCX will be able to increase its dividend, reduce debt further or repurchase shares.

- Risks to our opinion and target price include the possibility that rock slides may become a recurring problem in the Grasberg open pit, impairing FCX's ability to resume higher levels of production. Also, there is the risk posed by the concentration of all of FCX's mining assets in Indonesia.

- Although FCX's P/E multiple on projected 2005 EPS appears lofty compared with a P/E of 10X 2005 estimated EPS for copper rival Phelps Dodge (PD: avoid, $79), we think PD's lack of meaningful exposure to gold explains the disparity. We think FCX is more likely to have a P/E more in line with gold producer Newmont Mining (NEM: accumulate, $41), which has a P/E multiple of 23X. On that basis, using a P/E of 18X our 2005 estimate, we have a 12-month target price of $35.

Key Stock Statistics

S&P Core EPS 2005E	1.88	52-week Range	$46.74-27.76
S&P Oper. EPS 2004E	0.45	12 Month P/E	NM
P/E on S&P Oper. EPS 2004E	89.7	Beta	1.10
S&P Oper. EPS 2005E	2.15	Shareholders	9,769
Yield (%)	2.5%	Market Cap (B)	$ 7.1
Dividend Rate/Share	1.00	Shares Outstanding (M)	177.1

Value of $10,000 invested five years ago: **$ 23,539**

Dividend Data Dividends have been paid since 2003

Amount ($)	Date Decl.	Ex-Div. Date	Stock of Record	Payment Date
0.200	Jan. 05	Jan. 13	Jan. 15	Feb. 01 '04
0.200	Apr. 01	Apr. 13	Apr. 15	May. 01 '04
0.200	Jul. 01	Jul. 13	Jul. 15	Aug. 01 '04
0.250	Oct. 07	Oct. 13	Oct. 15	Nov. 01 '04

Revenues/Earnings Data Fiscal year ending December 31

Revenues (Million $)

	2004	2003	2002	2001	2000	1999
1Q	360.2	524.6	392.7	447.1	467.6	415.8
2Q	486.3	609.5	408.0	538.3	397.4	470.3
3Q	600.6	632.0	538.7	441.2	473.8	473.7
4Q	—	446.1	571.0	412.3	529.8	527.5
Yr.	—	2,212	1,910	1,839	1,869	1,887

Earnings Per Share ($)

	2004	2003	2002	2001	2000	1999
1Q	-0.10	0.28	-0.01	0.26	0.06	0.11
2Q	-0.30	0.37	0.04	0.25	-0.12	0.12
3Q	0.10	0.41	0.39	0.03	-0.06	0.16
4Q	E0.63	Nil	0.41	-0.01	0.40	0.23
Yr.	E0.45	1.07	0.89	0.53	0.26	0.61

Next earnings report expected: mid-January Source: S&P, Company Reports
EPS Estimates based on S&P Operating Earnings; historical GAAP earnings are as reported.

Freeport-McMoRan Copper & Gold Inc.

Recommendation: **HOLD** ★ ★ ★ ★ ★   12-Month Target Price: **$35.00** (as of May 10, 2004)

Business Summary August 19, 2004

Freeport-McMoRan Copper & Gold is one of the world's largest and lowest cost copper and gold producers. The company conducts mining operations in Indonesia through majority-owned subsidiaries PT Freeport Indonesia Co. (PT-FI) and PT IRJA Eastern Minerals Corp. FCX is also engaged in copper smelting and refining through Atlantic Copper Holding, S.A., and PT Smelting.

Mill throughput was 203,000 metric tons in 2003, versus 235,600 metric tons in 2002. Copper cash production costs were a negative $0.02 a lb. in 2003, versus $0.08 a lb. in 2002. Total production costs were $0.14 a lb. in 2003, versus $0.23 a lb. in 2002.

Copper sales amounted to 1,295,600 lb. in 2003 at an average price of $0.82 a lb., versus 1,522,300 lb., at an average price of $0.71 in 2002.

Gold sales totaled 2,469,800 oz in 2003 at an average price of $366.60 an oz., versus 2,293,200 oz. in 2002, at an average price of $311.97 an oz.

Silver sales totaled 4,126,700 oz. in 2003 at an average price of $5.15 an oz., versus 4,116,100 oz. in 2002, at an average price of $4.66 an oz.

At the end of 2003, FCX's equity interest in proven and probable reserves was 36.0 billion lb. of copper, 42.2 million oz. of gold and 105.9 million oz. of silver.

FCX conducts most of its exploration at its Grasberg property. The Grasberg deposit contains extensive gold reserves, and has one of the three largest open-pit copper reserves of any mine in the world.

The company's main competitors in copper include Phelps Dodge, Chile's state-owned Corporacion Nacional del Cobre de Chile (Codelco), Grupo Mexico, and Southern Peru Copper. Copper is used mostly in the construction, electrical and electronic industries.

According to the World Bureau of Metal Statistics, there was a deficit of supply over demand for copper in 2003 of 231,000 metric tons, versus a surplus of 345,000 metric tons in 2002.

In April 2003, the company said directors had authorized a new common stock dividend policy of $0.36 annually. An initial dividend of $0.09 was paid May 1, 2003.

In 2004's second quarter, FCX completed several transactions designed to strengthen its balance sheet. The company repurchased $9.7 million of its 6 7/8% senior notes due 2014 for $8.8 million, and prepaid $66.2 million of equipment notes. During the quarter, FCX purchased 3.4 million of its common shares at an average price of $29.39 a share under its 20 million share repurchase program. As of July 19, 2004, 16.6 million shares remained available for repurchase.

On August 2, 2004, FCX announced the completion of the call for redemption of its 8 % senior convertible notes due 2006, resulting in the conversion of all $66.5 million of notes into some 4.7 million FCX common shares. Following this transaction, there were approximately 178.5 million FCX common shares outstanding.

Company Financials Fiscal Year ending December 31

Per Share Data ($)

(Year Ended December 31)	2003	2002	2001	2000	1999	1998	1997	1996	1995	1994
Tangible Bk. Val.	4.23	NM	NM	NM	NM	NM	NM	1.61	1.55	1.68
Cash Flow	2.52	2.67	2.49	2.09	2.39	2.25	2.32	2.03	1.84	0.75
Earnings	1.07	0.89	0.53	0.26	0.61	0.67	1.06	0.89	0.98	0.38
S&P Core Earnings	1.03	0.84	0.49	NA	NA	NA	NA	NA	NA	NA
Dividends	0.27	Nil	Nil	Nil	Nil	0.20	0.90	0.90	0.68	0.60
Payout Ratio	25%	Nil	Nil	Nil	Nil	30%	85%	101%	69%	158%
Prices - High	46.74	20.83	17.15	21.43	21.37	21.43	34.87	36.12	30.75	NA
- Low	16.01	9.95	8.31	6.75	9.12	9.81	14.93	27.37	22.62	NA
P/E Ratio - High	44	23	32	82	35	32	33	41	31	NA
- Low	15	11	16	26	15	15	14	31	23	NA

Income Statement Analysis (Million $)

	2003	2002	2001	2000	1999	1998	1997	1996	1995	1994
Revs.	2,212	1,910	1,839	1,869	1,887	1,757	2,001	1,905	1,834	1,212
Oper. Inc.	1,054	901	827	778	876	852	878	812	718	323
Depr.	231	260	284	284	293	277	214	174	124	75.1
Int. Exp.	197	171	174	205	194	225	175	140	97.7	35.1
Pretax Inc.	584	450	359	273	381	361	517	522	545	279
Eff. Tax Rate	57.9%	54.6%	56.6%	58.4%	51.4%	47.2%	44.8%	47.3%	43.0%	44.2%
Net Inc.	197	168	113	77.0	136	154	245	226	254	130
S&P Core Earnings	167	123	70.8	NA	NA	NA	NA	NA	NA	NA

Balance Sheet & Other Fin. Data (Million $)

	2003	2002	2001	2000	1999	1998	1997	1996	1995	1994
Cash	464	7.84	7.59	7.97	6.70	5.90	9.00	37.1	26.9	44.0
Curr. Assets	1,100	638	548	569	564	46.0	463	661	653	603
Total Assets	4,718	4,192	4,212	3,951	4,083	4,193	4,152	3,866	3,582	3,040
Curr. Liab.	632	538	628	634	515	518	476	598	527	432
LT Debt	2,076	1,961	2,133	1,988	2,033	2,329	2,308	1,426	1,080	526
Common Equity	776	-83.2	-246	-312	-153	-247	-71.1	325	882	346
Total Cap.	3,925	3,514	3,464	3,204	3,453	3,599	3,551	3,066	2,267	2,396
Cap. Exp.	139	188	167	292	161	292	595	490	308	743
Cash Flow	401	391	360	323	394	395	459	400	378	154
Curr. Ratio	1.7	1.2	0.9	0.9	1.1	1.1	1.0	1.1	1.2	1.4
% LT Debt of Cap.	52.9	55.8	61.6	62.0	58.9	64.7	65.0	46.5	47.6	21.9
% Net Inc.of Revs.	8.9	8.8	6.1	4.1	7.2	8.8	12.2	11.9	13.8	10.7
% Ret. on Assets	4.4	4.0	2.8	1.9	3.3	3.7	6.1	7.1	7.7	5.0
% Ret. on Equity	49.0	NM	NM	NA	NM	NM	NM	56.7	27.0	21.5

Data as orig reptd.; bef. results of disc opers/spec. items. Per share data adj. for stk. divs.; EPS diluted. E-Estimated. NA-Not Available. NM-Not Meaningful. NR-Not Ranked. UR-Under Review.

Office: 1615 Poydras Street, New Orleans, LA 70112-1254.
Telephone: 504-582-4000.
Email: ir@fmi.com
Website: http://www.fcx.com
Chrmn: J.R. Moffett.
Pres, CEO & Investor Contact: R.C. Adkerson .

COO & SVP: M.J. Johnson.
SVP, CFO & Treas: K.L. Quirk.
Dirs: R. J. Allison, Jr., R. L. Clifford, R. A. Day, G. J. Ford, H. D. Graham, Jr., O. Y. Groeneveld, J. B. Johnston, B. L. Lackey, J. R. Moffett, B. M. Rankin, Jr., J. T. Wharton.

Founded: in 1987.
Domicile: Delaware.
Employees: 8,749.
S&P Analyst: Leo J. Larkin/CB/BK

Gannett Co.

Recommendation: **BUY** ★★★★☆
SELL SELL HOLD BUY BUY

12-Month Target Price: $96.00
(as of November 12, 2004)

GCI has an approximate 0.20% weighting in the **S&P 500**

Sector: Consumer Discretionary
Sub-Industry: Publishing
Peer Group: Newspaper Cos. - Large

Summary: GCI publishes 100 daily and nearly 500 non-daily newspapers in the U.S., and more than 300 in Great Britain, and operates 22 TV stations in the U.S.

Quantitative Evaluations

S&P Earnings & Dividend Rank: A

| D | C | B- | B | B+ | A- | **A** | A+ |

S&P Fair Value Rank: 4+

| 1 | 2 | 3 | **4** | 5 |
| Lowest | | | | Highest |

Fair Value Calc.: $85.20 (Slightly Undervalued)

S&P Investability Quotient Percentile

99%

GCI scored higher than 99% of all companies for which an S&P Report is available.

Volatility: Low

| **Low** | Average | High |

Technical Evaluation: Neutral
Since 11/04, the technical indicators for GCI have been Neutral.

Relative Strength Rank: Weak

27
1 Lowest   Highest 99

| Price as of 11/12/04: | **$83.14** | 2004E S&P Core EPS: | **$5.14** |

GAAP Earnings vs. Previous Year
▲ Up ▼ Down ► No Change

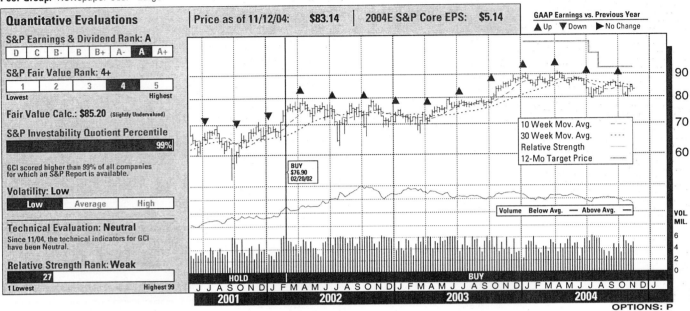

- 10 Week Mov. Avg.
- 30 Week Mov. Avg.
- Relative Strength
- 12-Mo Target Price

BUY
$76.90
02/20/02

Volume   Below Avg. — Above Avg. —

VOL.
MIL.

HOLD   BUY
J J A S O N D J F M A M J J A S O N D J F M A M J J A S O N D J F M A M J J A S O N D J
2001   **2002**   **2003**   **2004**

OPTIONS: P

Analyst commentary prepared by William H. Donald/PMW/BK

Highlights August 16, 2004

- We recently became more cautious regarding the outlook for advertising in general, in light of uncertainty surrounding business and consumer spending amid uneven economic signals and oil price concerns. We reduced our 2004 revenue estimate for GCI, and now see an 8.4% gain, to $7.27 billion, from $6.71 billion in 2003. We expect an 8.8% gain in newspaper advertising revenue, led by double-digit growth at USA TODAY. We see a 17% advance in broadcasting. We expect both segments to benefit from improving advertising demand, and think that TV in particular will get an additional boost from political and Olympics-related advertising.

- Aided by ongoing operating efficiencies, despite higher newsprint costs, we see operating profits up 11% in 2004, to $2.20 billion. We expect 2004 earnings before interest, depreciation, taxes, and amortization (EBIDTA) to grow 11%, to $2.45 billion, with EBITDA margins widening to 33.7%, from 33.0%.

- After nonoperating items, including taxes, we expect 2004 net operating profits to advance 12%, to $1.36 billion, from $1.21 billion in 2003. We were encouraged by news of a $1 billion addition to the share buyback program. We recently cut our 2004 EPS estimate to $5.00, up 12% from 2003's $4.46. We also reduced our 2005 EPS estimate to $5.40, to reflect a more cautious view of revenue gains, which we project at about 7.5%, instead of 8.0%. We see margins being maintained, despite expected lower revenue gains.

Investment Rationale/Risk August 16, 2004

- We recently downgraded the shares to accumulate, from buy. Reflecting our more cautious stance on the outlook for consumer and business spending, we have reduced our earnings and stock market performance expectations for publishing media stocks. On a P/E multiple basis, GCI is trading at a discount to peers, at a recent level of about 16X our 2004 EPS estimate and 15X our 2005 EPS estimate, versus respective peer averages of 20X and 17X.

- Risks to our recommendation and target price include the impact on results if advertising demand and/or advertising prices in the U.S. or Great Britain suddenly weakened; the possibility of an earnings shortfall due to a sharp runup in newsprint costs; an escalation in programming expenses; unexpected drops in audience ratings at network-affiliated TV stations; a sharp fall in newspaper readership and/or circulation; and a sharp rise in interest rates. The company is also exposed to foreign exchange rate risk due to its ownership of Newsquest.

- We recently cut our 12-month target price to $93, to reflect our reduced EPS growth expectations for 2005. Our target price is based on a valuation of about 17X our 2005 EPS estimate of $5.40. Based on our discounted cash flow calculations, the shares traded recently at a discount of about 15% to intrinsic value.

Key Stock Statistics

S&P Oper. EPS 2004E	5.00	52-week Range	$91.38-79.43
P/E on S&P Oper. EPS 2004E	16.6	12 Month P/E	17.4
S&P Oper. EPS 2005E	5.40	Beta	0.69
Yield (%)	1.3%	Shareholders	12,800
Dividend Rate/Share	1.08	Market Cap (B)	$ 21.2
Shares Outstanding (M)	255.3		

Value of $10,000 invested five years ago: **$ 12,311**

Dividend Data Dividends have been paid since 1929

Amount ($)	Date Decl.	Ex-Div. Date	Stock of Record	Payment Date
0.250	Feb. 24	Mar. 03	Mar. 05	Apr. 01 '04
0.250	May. 04	Jun. 02	Jun. 04	Jul. 01 '04
0.270	Aug. 04	Sep. 08	Sep. 10	Oct. 01 '04
0.270	Oct. 26	Dec. 15	Dec. 17	Jan. 03 '05

Revenues/Earnings Data Fiscal year ending December 31

Revenues (Million $)

	2004	2003	2002	2001	2000	1999
1Q	1,730	1,552	1,513	1,575	1,321	1,248
2Q	1,873	1,705	1,613	1,627	1,448	1,343
3Q	1,816	1,631	1,570	1,518	1,559	1,358
4Q	—	1,822	1,726	1,624	1,895	1,501
Yr.	—	6,711	6,422	6,344	6,222	5,260

Earnings Per Share ($)

	2004	2003	2002	2001	2000	1999
1Q	1.00	0.93	0.91	0.66	0.74	0.64
2Q	1.30	1.20	1.13	0.88	1.00	0.98
3Q	1.18	1.03	0.99	0.66	0.79	0.74
4Q	E1.59	1.31	1.29	0.93	1.11	1.01
Yr.	E5.00	4.46	4.31	3.12	3.63	3.26

Next earnings report expected: early-February Source: S&P, Company Reports
EPS Estimates based on S&P Operating Earnings; historical GAAP earnings are as reported.

Recommendation: **BUY** ★ ★ ★ ★ ☆   12-Month Target Price: **$96.00** (as of November 12, 2004)

Business Summary August 16, 2004

Gannett Co. publishes more than 100 daily and more than 500 non-daily newspapers in the U.S., including USA TODAY, and operates 22 television stations. Operations are conducted in 45 states, the District of Columbia, and Guam, and were expanded to the U.K. with the 1999 purchase of Newsquest, a publisher of more than 300 newspapers, including 17 dailies.

GCI significantly bolstered its position as the largest U.S. newspaper group in terms of circulation with the August 2000 purchase of Central Newspapers for about $2.6 billion, and the July 2000 purchase of 19 newspapers from Thomson Newspapers Inc. for about $1.04 billion. The Newsquest unit operates the second largest regional newspaper network in the U.K. It significantly expanded its U.K. presence with the June 2000 purchase of Newscom, which at that time was the eighth largest U.K. regional newspaper publisher. U.K. holdings expanded into Scotland in March 2003, with the purchase of the Herald Group, consisting of three newspapers and 11 consumer and business magazines, from Scottish Media Group Plc, for $344 million. Also in March 2003, Newsquest agreed to purchase 45 Greater London regional newspapers from Independent News and Media Ltd., for $94 million.

Major U.S. holdings include USA TODAY and USA WEEKEND. USA WEEKEND, a weekend newspaper magazine with weekly circulation of 21.2 million, is distributed with 526 newspapers nationwide. Other major newspapers include The News Journal (Wilmington, DE); FLORIDA TODAY; News-Press (Fort Myers); The San Bernardino County Sun; The Honolulu Advertiser; The Journal News (Westchester, Rockland and Putnam counties, New York); The Des Moines Register; The Courier-Journal (Louisville); The Detroit News; The Detroit News and Free Press; The Clarion-Ledger (Jackson, MS); Asbury Park Press (New Jersey); Rochester Democrat and Chronicle; The Arizona Republic; The Indianapolis Star; The Cincinnati Enquirer; The Greenville News (South Carolina); and The Tennessean (Nashville). In 2003, newspaper publishing contributed 90% of consolidated revenues and 84% of operating profits.

Broadcasting (10% of revenues, 16% of operating EPS) consists of 22 network-affiliated TV stations. GCI owns three stations in Arizona (Flagstaff, Kingman and Phoenix); three in Florida (Jacksonville (two) and Tampa-St. Petersburg); two in Georgia (Atlanta and Macon); and two in Maine (Bangor and Portland). It also owns one station each in Little Rock, AR; Sacramento, CA; Denver, CO; Washington, DC; Grand Rapids, MI; Minneapolis-St. Paul, MN; St. Louis, MO; Buffalo, NY; Greensboro, NC; Cleveland, OH; Columbia, SC; and Knoxville, TN. GCI sold its cable TV operations to Cox Communications in January 2000, for $2.7 billion.

The company's media properties maintain more than 50 Web sites. GCI also owns Nursing Spectrum, a bi-weekly periodical; Army Times, the publisher of military and defense newspapers; and the 101 Things to Do series of four quarterly tourist magazines in Hawaii.

Company Financials Fiscal Year ending December 31

Per Share Data ($)

(Year Ended December 31)	2003	2002	2001	2000	1999	1998	1997	1996	1995	1994
Tangible Bk. Val.	NM	NM	NM	NM	NM	0.66	NM	NM	NM	1.26
Cash Flow	5.30	5.13	4.78	4.99	3.87	4.59	3.55	4.37	2.45	2.33
Earnings	4.46	4.31	3.12	3.63	3.26	3.50	2.50	2.22	1.71	1.61
S&P Core Earnings	4.23	3.70	2.39	NA	NA	NA	NA	NA	NA	NA
Dividends	0.98	0.94	0.90	0.86	0.81	0.78	0.74	0.71	0.69	0.67
Payout Ratio	22%	22%	29%	24%	25%	22%	30%	32%	40%	41%
Prices - High	89.63	79.90	71.14	81.56	83.62	75.12	61.81	39.37	32.43	29.50
- Low	66.70	62.76	53.00	48.37	60.62	47.62	35.68	29.50	24.75	23.06
P/E Ratio - High	20	19	23	22	26	21	25	18	19	18
- Low	15	15	17	13	19	14	14	13	15	14

Income Statement Analysis (Million $)

	2003	2002	2001	2000	1999	1998	1997	1996	1995	1994
Revs.	6,711	6,422	6,344	6,222	5,260	5,121	4,729	4,421	4,007	3,825
Oper. Inc.	2,213	2,149	2,034	2,190	1,843	1,754	1,617	1,354	1,062	1,022
Depr.	232	215	444	376	169	310	301	193	210	209
Int. Exp.	139	146	222	219	94.6	79.4	98.2	136	52.2	46.2
Pretax Inc.	1,840	1,765	1,371	1,609	1,527	1,669	1,209	1,087	803	782
Eff. Tax Rate	34.2%	34.3%	39.4%	39.6%	39.8%	40.1%	41.1%	42.6%	40.6%	46.5%
Net Inc.	1,211	1,160	831	972	919	1,000	713	624	477	465
S&P Core Earnings	1,150	998	638	NA	NA	NA	NA	NA	NA	NA

Balance Sheet & Other Fin. Data (Million $)

	2003	2002	2001	2000	1999	1998	1997	1996	1995	1994
Cash	67.2	90.4	141	193	46.2	66.2	52.8	27.0	47.0	44.3
Curr. Assets	1,223	1,133	1,178	1,302	1,075	906	885	767	854	651
Total Assets	14,706	13,733	13,096	12,980	9,006	6,979	6,890	6,350	6,504	3,707
Curr. Liab.	962	959	1,128	1,174	884	728	768	719	813	527
LT Debt	3,835	4,547	5,080	5,748	2,463	1,307	1,741	1,880	2,768	767
Common Equity	8,423	6,912	5,736	5,103	4,630	3,980	3,480	2,931	2,146	1,822
Total Cap.	13,094	12,138	11,319	11,126	7,572	5,709	5,623	4,811	5,241	2,754
Cap. Exp.	281	275	325	351	258	244	221	260	184	151
Cash Flow	1,443	1,375	1,275	1,348	1,089	1,310	1,014	1,230	687	674
Curr. Ratio	1.3	1.2	1.0	1.1	1.2	1.2	1.2	1.1	1.1	1.2
% LT Debt of Cap.	29.3	37.5	44.9	51.7	32.5	22.8	30.9	39.0	52.8	27.9
% Net Inc.of Revs.	18.0	18.1	13.1	15.6	17.5	19.5	15.1	14.1	11.9	12.2
% Ret. on Assets	8.5	8.6	6.4	8.8	11.5	14.4	10.8	9.7	9.3	12.7
% Ret. on Equity	15.8	18.3	15.3	20.0	21.4	26.8	22.2	24.6	24.1	25.6

Data as orig reptd.; bef. results of disc opers/spec. items. Per share data adj. for stk. divs. Bold denotes diluted EPS (FASB 128)-prior periods restated. E-Estimated. NA-Not Available. NM-Not Meaningful. NR-Not Ranked.

Office: 7950 Jones Branch Drive, McLean, VA 22107-0910.
Telephone: 703-854-6000.
Email: gcishare@gannett.com
Website: http://www.gannett.com
Chrmn, Pres & CEO: D.H. McCorkindale.
SVP & CFO: G.C. Martore.

SVP & General Counsel: T.L. Chapple.
Secy: T.A. Mayman.
Investor Contact: J. Heinz 703-854-6917.
Dirs: L. D. Boccardi, M. A. Brokaw, J. A. Johnson, D. H. McCorkindale, D. M. McFarland, S. P. Munn, D. Shalala, S. D. Trujillo, K. H. Williams.

Founded: in 1923.
Domicile: Delaware.
Employees: 53,000.
S&P Analyst: William H. Donald/PMW/BK

Gap, Inc.

Recommendation: BUY ★★★★ ☆   **12-Month Target Price: $25.00**
(as of August 20, 2004)

GPS has an approximate 0.19% weighting in the **S&P 500**

Sector: Consumer Discretionary
Sub-Industry: Apparel Retail
Peer Group: Women's Apparel Retailers

Summary: This specialty apparel retailer operates Gap, Banana Republic and Old Navy stores, offering casual clothing to upper, moderate and value-oriented market segments.

Quantitative Evaluations

S&P Earnings & Dividend Rank: A

D	C	B-	B	B+	A-	A	A+

S&P Fair Value Rank: 4-

1	2	3	4	5
Lowest				Highest

Fair Value Calc.: $22.50 (Slightly Overvalued)

S&P Investability Quotient Percentile

89%

GPS scored higher than 89% of all companies for which an S&P Report is available.

Volatility: Average

Low	Average	High

Technical Evaluation: Bullish
Since 11/04, the technical indicators for GPS have been Bullish.

Relative Strength Rank: Strong

83

| 1 Lowest | | Highest 99 |

Price as of 11/12/04: $23.24 | **2005E S&P Core EPS:** $1.23

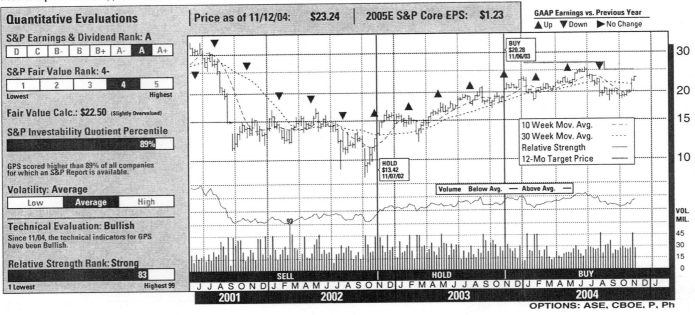

GAAP Earnings vs. Previous Year ▲ Up ▼ Down ► No Change

Analyst commentary prepared by Marie Driscoll, CFA /PMW/JWP

Highlights August 30, 2004

- Sales momentum slowed across all retail concepts in the second quarter: Old Navy, Gap, and Banana Republic. However we expect a new marketing campaign at Gap brand, featuring Sara Parker, and Old Navy's further market segmentation to Hispanics, larger sizes, and maternity to expand target audiences. In October, the company is launching a combination credit card for all three brands that we think could enable it to capture an increased share of spending by existing customers. We see sales up about 5% in FY 05 (Jan.). We expect square footage to remain constant. Regular priced sales and improved traffic should generate same-store sales gains in the low to mid-single digits.

- We believe customer-centric merchandise and marketing strategies, strict attention to cost cuts via labor scheduling, inventory flows, and store rationalization will likely boost profitability. We think refocused assortments and more brand appropriate styles should yield significant earnings gains. We project about 280 basis points of gross margin expansion from increased full-price sales, improved inventory management and sourcing, and continued leverage of occupancy costs. We look for operating margins to widen about 150 basis points, to 13.4%.

- We estimate that FY 05 EPS will grow 20%, to $1.31. For FY 06, we see an advance to $1.55. Our FY 05 Standard & Poor's Core Earnings projection of $1.23 a share includes estimated stock option expense.

Investment Rationale/Risk August 30, 2004

- We would accumulate the stock. We view GPS as undervalued, trading recently at 12.4X our FY 06 EPS estimate, a discount to the S&P 500 and peers. We believe the company's new management team has restored credibility to GPS's business model. We think market segmentation is deepening customer relationships, improving merchandise buying and design, generating more profitable sales, and creating potential for increased brand equity. For the longer term, management is looking at expanding the company's international presence and is considering a fourth retail concept as sources of growth.

- Risks to our opinion and target price include fashion, markdown and inventory risk, dependence on key personnel, and geopolitical risk. In addition, although past performance is not an indicator of future results, rising interest rates have historically adversely affected shares of specialty apparel retailers.

- Our 12-month target price of $25 incorporates a peer group P/E multiple of 19X applied to our FY 05 EPS estimate. Historically, the stock has traded at a modest premium to peers, in contrast to its current 20% discount.

Key Stock Statistics

S&P Core EPS 2006E	1.47	52-week Range	$25.72-18.12
S&P Oper. EPS 2005E	1.27	12 Month P/E	19.7
P/E on S&P Oper. EPS 2005E	18.3	Beta	1.57
S&P Oper. EPS 2006E	1.51	Shareholders	10,575
Yield (%)	0.4%	Market Cap (B)	$ 21.0
Dividend Rate/Share	0.09	Shares Outstanding (M)	903.8

Value of $10,000 invested five years ago: **$ 6,989**

Dividend Data Dividends have been paid since 1976

Amount ($)	Date Decl.	Ex-Div. Date	Stock of Record	Payment Date
0.022	Jan. 27	Feb. 25	Feb. 27	Mar. 15 '04
0.022	Mar. 23	May. 19	May. 21	Jun. 07 '04
0.022	Jul. 27	Aug. 25	Aug. 27	Sep. 20 '04
0.022	Sep. 28	Nov. 17	Nov. 19	Dec. 13 '04

Revenues/Earnings Data Fiscal year ending January 31

Revenues (Million $)

	2005	2004	2003	2002	2001	2000
1Q	3,668	3,353	2,891	3,180	2,732	2,278
2Q	3,721	3,685	3,268	3,245	2,948	2,453
3Q	—	3,929	3,645	3,333	3,415	3,045
4Q	—	4,886	4,651	4,089	4,579	3,859
Yr.	—	15,854	14,455	13,848	13,674	11,635

Earnings Per Share ($)

	2005	2004	2003	2002	2001	2000
1Q	0.32	0.22	0.04	0.13	0.27	0.23
2Q	0.21	0.22	0.06	0.10	0.21	0.22
3Q	E0.28	0.28	0.15	-0.21	0.21	0.35
4Q	E0.44	0.37	0.27	-0.04	0.31	0.47
Yr.	E1.27	1.09	0.54	-0.01	1.00	1.26

Next earnings report expected: late-November Source: S&P, Company Reports
EPS Estimates based on S&P Operating Earnings; historical GAAP earnings are as reported.

Recommendation: **BUY ★★★★**☆   12-Month Target Price: **$25.00** (as of August 20, 2004)

Business Summary August 30, 2004

Gap is a global specialty retailer operating stores selling casual apparel, accessories and personal care products for men, women and children under the Gap, Banana Republic and Old Navy brands. On January 31, 2004, it operated 3,022 stores (1,747 Gap, 435 Banana Republic, and 840 Old Navy) in the U.S., Canada, the U.K., France, Germany and Japan, with 36.5 million sq. ft. of retail space. In FY 04 (Jan.), international sales accounted for 13% of the total.

In FY 04, led by a new management team, GPS's financial health improved. According to management, disciplined inventory management, better product assortments, and selective store closures were effected. The Gap reported positive monthly same-store sales growth, as well as improved margins, earnings and returns on capital. Cash rose to $4.3 billion at the end of FY 04, from $1.3 billion a year earlier.

The Gap brand (46% of FY 04 sales) continued a turnaround in FY 04, with a focus on deepening its relationships with two primary customer segments identified for men and women: "style conscious" and "updated classics." Iconic products, compelling marketing, and convenient service remain the brand's key goals, and improved store associate training and streamlining product development as well as real estate optimization also remain priorities for FY 05. The Gap format is the company's original concept, conceived in 1969 in San Francisco, when jeans dominated the stores. GapKids and babyGap were subsequently introduced.

Banana Republic (13% of FY 04 sales) aims to offer sophisticated styling and quality casual and luxury items for men and women at competitive prices versus national brands and private labels at better department stores. In FY 04, petites and B. Republic, a new line of active sport-inspired weekend wear, were introduced. In FY 05, GPS is focusing on further refinement of Banana Republic's brand positioning and marketing.

Old Navy's strategy is to sell clothing for the entire family in a casual environment at value prices, targeting low-income customers in stores nearly double the size of Gap stores (15,000 sq. ft.). Old Navy, launched in 1994, accounted for 41% of FY 04 net sales. In FY 05, GPS is focusing on new product extensions and existing categories, such as extended sizes, to drive growth at Old Navy.

FY 05 capital spending was projected at $500 million: about $155 million for information technology; $120 million for new stores and $200 million for existing stores; and $25 million for headquarters and distribution centers. GPS expected to open 125 store locations and to close 135 store locations, with openings weighted toward Old Navy, and Gap U.S. stores accounting for the majority of closures. Since 2002, more than 220 underperforming stores have been closed. In August 2004, the company planned to exit the German market, closing 10 Gap stores, to focus on other international growth opportunities that it views as stronger. GPS spent $509 million in FY 04 to advertise its brands.

Company Financials Fiscal Year ending January 31

Per Share Data ($)

(Year Ended January 31)	2004	2003	2002	2001	2000	1999	1998	1997	1996	1995
Tangible Bk. Val.	5.33	4.12	3.48	3.43	2.63	1.83	1.79	1.79	1.69	1.41
Cash Flow	1.71	1.43	0.93	1.67	1.75	1.25	0.87	0.70	0.57	0.50
Earnings	1.09	0.54	-0.01	1.00	1.26	0.91	0.58	0.47	0.36	0.33
S&P Core Earnings	1.03	0.50	-0.10	0.86	NA	NA	NA	NA	NA	NA
Dividends	0.09	0.09	0.09	0.09	0.09	0.09	0.09	0.09	0.07	0.07
Payout Ratio	8%	17%	NM	9%	7%	9%	15%	19%	20%	21%

Cal. Yrs.	2003	2002	2001	2000	1999	1998	1997	1996	1995	1994
Prices - High	23.47	17.14	34.98	53.75	52.68	40.91	17.14	10.81	7.55	7.31
- Low	12.01	8.35	11.12	18.50	30.81	15.30	8.25	6.22	4.40	4.27
P/E Ratio - High	22	32	NM	54	42	45	30	23	21	22
- Low	11	15	NM	18	24	17	14	13	12	13

Income Statement Analysis (Million $)

	2004	2003	2002	2001	2000	1999	1998	1997	1996	1995
Revs.	15,854	14,455	13,848	13,673	11,635	9,054	6,508	5,284	4,395	3,723
Oper. Inc.	2,543	1,794	1,148	2,035	2,253	1,659	1,121	944	767	687
Depr.	664	781	810	590	436	326	270	215	197	168
Int. Exp.	234	249	109	74.9	31.8	13.6	Nil	NA	NA	NA
Pretax Inc.	1,683	801	242	1,382	1,785	1,319	854	749	585	529
Eff. Tax Rate	38.8%	40.4%	NM	36.5%	36.9%	37.5%	37.5%	39.4%	39.5%	39.5%
Net Inc.	1,030	477	-7.76	877	1,127	825	534	453	354	320
S&P Core Earnings	978	439	-89.1	760	NA	NA	NA	NA	NA	NA

Balance Sheet & Other Fin. Data (Million $)

	2004	2003	2002	2001	2000	1999	1998	1997	1996	1995
Cash	2,261	3,389	1,036	409	450	565	913	622	669	588
Curr. Assets	6,689	5,740	3,045	2,648	2,198	1,872	1,831	1,329	1,280	1,056
Total Assets	10,343	9,902	7,591	7,013	5,189	3,964	3,338	2,627	2,343	2,004
Curr. Liab.	2,492	2,727	2,056	2,799	1,753	1,553	992	775	552	500
LT Debt	2,487	2,896	1,961	780	785	496	496	Nil	Nil	Nil
Common Equity	4,783	3,658	3,010	2,928	2,233	1,574	1,584	1,654	1,640	1,375
Total Cap.	7,270	6,554	4,971	3,708	3,018	2,070	2,080	1,654	1,640	1,375
Cap. Exp.	272	303	940	1,859	1,239	798	466	372	302	233
Cash Flow	1,694	1,258	803	1,468	1,563	1,151	804	668	551	488
Curr. Ratio	2.7	2.1	1.5	0.9	1.3	1.2	1.8	1.7	2.3	2.1
% LT Debt of Cap.	34.2	44.2	39.5	21.0	26.0	24.0	23.8	Nil	Nil	Nil
% Net Inc.of Revs.	6.5	3.3	NM	6.4	9.7	9.1	8.2	8.6	8.1	8.6
% Ret. on Assets	10.2	5.4	NM	14.4	24.6	22.6	17.9	18.2	16.3	17.0
% Ret. on Equity	24.4	14.3	NM	34.0	59.2	52.2	33.0	27.5	23.5	25.6

Data as orig reptd.; bef. results of disc opers/spec. items. Per share data adj. for stk. divs.; EPS diluted (primary prior to 1998). E-Estimated. NA-Not Available. NM-Not Meaningful. NR-Not Ranked. UR-Under Review.

Office: 2 Folsom St, San Francisco, CA 94105-1205.
Telephone: 650-952-4400.
Email: investor_relations@gap.com
Website: http://www.gapinc.com
Chrmn: D.G. Fisher.
Pres & CEO: P. Pressler.

EVP & CFO: B.H. Pollitt, Jr.
Investor Contact: M. Webb 415-427-2161.
Dirs: H. Behar, A. D. Bellamy, D. G. Fisher, D. F. Fisher, R. J. Fisher, P. Huges, B. Martin, P. Pressler, J. Schneider, C. R. Schwab, M. A. Shattuck, M. Whitman.

Founded: in 1969.
Domicile: Delaware.
Employees: 153,000.
S&P Analyst: Marie Driscoll, CFA /PMW/JWP

Gateway

Recommendation: **HOLD** ★ ★ ★ ☆ ☆
SELL SELL HOLD BUY BUY

12-Month Target Price: **$6.00**
(as of October 27, 2003)

GTW has an approximate 0.02% weighting in the **S&P 500**

Sector: Information Technology
Sub-Industry: Computer Hardware
Peer Group: Computer Hardware - Large System Vendors

Summary: Gateway is a leading supplier of personal computers worldwide.

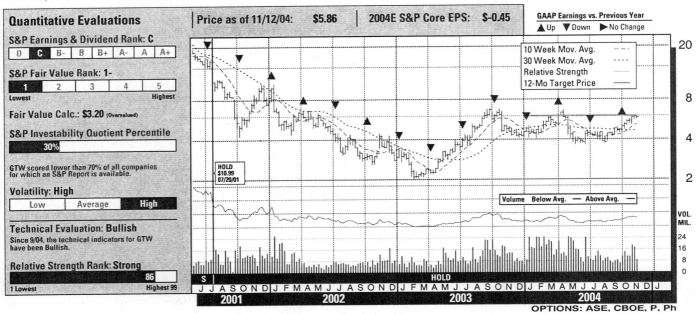

Quantitative Evaluations

S&P Earnings & Dividend Rank: C

| D | C | B- | B | B+ | A- | A | A+ |

S&P Fair Value Rank: 1-

| 1 | 2 | 3 | 4 | 5 |
| Lowest | | | | Highest |

Fair Value Calc.: $3.20 (Overvalued)

S&P Investability Quotient Percentile

30%

GTW scored lower than 70% of all companies for which an S&P Report is available.

Volatility: High

| Low | Average | **High** |

Technical Evaluation: Bullish
Since 9/04, the technical indicators for GTW have been Bullish.

Relative Strength Rank: Strong

86

1 Lowest   Highest 99

Price as of 11/12/04: $5.86   **2004E S&P Core EPS: $-0.45**

GAAP Earnings vs. Previous Year
▲ Up   ▼ Down   ▶ No Change

10 Week Mov. Avg. ---
30 Week Mov. Avg. ····
Relative Strength
12-Mo Target Price

HOLD
$10.99
07/20/01

Volume Below Avg. —— Above Avg.

VOL. MIL.

S | HOLD

J J A S O N D J F M A M J J A S O N D J F M A M J J A S O N D J F M A M J J A S O N D J
2001   **2002**   **2003**   **2004**

OPTIONS: ASE, CBOE, P, Ph

Analyst commentary prepared by Megan Graham-Hackett/MF/BK

Highlights November 02, 2004

- After an estimated 6.6% increase in revenues in 2004, including revenues from eMachines, Inc., which Gateway acquired in March 2004, we project a 12% rise in 2005 revenues. In connection with GTW's acquisition of eMachines it exited its own retail store strategy. We believe 2005 revenues should benefit from the company's greater participation in retail superstores such as Best Buy. We note that over the past few years, GTW's sales have been pressured by price competition in PCs, exacerbated, we believe, by some execution issues. GTW has struggled to position itself profitably as a niche vendor in the PC industry, including exiting international markets and entering new digital consumer markets. In its latest attempt, the eMachines acquisition is intended to add new distribution channels for GTW, which we expect to contribute to revenue growth.

- Gross margins should narrow to 11.2% in 2004, from 15.5% in 2003, due to the lower margin profile of eMachine's desktops, partly offset by higher margin contributions from GTW's non-PC sales and cost reduction efforts. We project modest gross margin expansion in 2005, to 11.5%, based on these efforts.

- We see a 2004 operating loss of $0.33 a share. Our Standard & Poor's Core Earnings per share estimate is for a loss of $0.45, reflecting our projection of the impact of stock option expense. Our 2005 operating estimate is for EPS of $0.15.

Investment Rationale/Risk November 02, 2004

- GTW continues, in our opinion, to struggle to obtain a business model that will enable it to compete profitably against peers. GTW has shifted its strategy to one of becoming a "branded integrator," and in March 2004, it announced the acquisition of eMachines to help broaden its distribution.

- Risks to our recommendation and target price include integration risk related to the acquisition of eMachines and a highly competitive market. If GTW sustains market share losses, we believe the loss of volume will challenge the company's ability to achieve profitability.

- We have a 12-month target price for GTW of $6, based on our price to sales analysis. Based on peer averages and GTW's historical P/S multiple, we believe the shares should trade at nearly 0.6X our 2005 sales per share estimate. While the shares are currently trading below this level, we would not add to positions, given our view of the risks to GTW achieving sustained profitability.

Key Stock Statistics

S&P Oper. EPS 2004E	-0.33	52-week Range	$6.62-3.64
P/E on S&P Oper. EPS 2004E	NM	12 Month P/E	NM
S&P Oper. EPS 2005E	0.15	Beta	NA
Yield (%)	Nil	Shareholders	5,128
Dividend Rate/Share	Nil	Market Cap (B)	$ 2.2
Shares Outstanding (M)	372.7		

Value of $10,000 invested five years ago: $ 817

Dividend Data

No cash dividends have been paid.

Revenues/Earnings Data Fiscal year ending December 31

Revenues (Million $)

	2004	2003	2002	2001	2000	1999
1Q	868.4	844.5	992.2	2,034	2,338	2,103
2Q	837.6	799.6	1,005	1,501	2,142	1,912
3Q	0.92	883.1	1,118	1,410	2,530	2,179
4Q	—	875.1	1,056	1,135	2,446	2,452
Yr.	—	3,402	4,171	6,080	9,601	8,646

Earnings Per Share ($)

	2004	2003	2002	2001	2000	1999
1Q	-0.51	-0.62	-0.39	-1.48	0.41	0.31
2Q	-0.91	-0.22	-0.19	-0.06	0.37	0.28
3Q	-0.16	-0.43	-0.15	-1.61	0.46	0.35
4Q	E0.01	-0.35	-0.22	0.02	-0.40	0.38
Yr.	E-0.33	-1.62	-0.95	-3.14	0.76	1.32

Next earnings report expected: late-January   Source: S&P, Company Reports
EPS Estimates based on S&P Operating Earnings; historical GAAP earnings are as reported.

STANDARD
&POOR'S

Gateway, Inc.

Recommendation: **HOLD** ★ ★ ★ ☆ ☆   12-Month Target Price: **$6.00** (as of October 27, 2003)

Business Summary November 02, 2004

Gateway (formerly Gateway 2000) is a direct seller of personal computers (PCs). However, the company's Gateway Country stores (now closed) enabled it to address a broader consumer market for PCs. GTW has also introduced digital technology products, including the Gateway Plasma TV, to diversify the company's revenue base and improve its margin profile. Still, desktop PCs generated 48% of the company's net sales in 2003, while notebooks contributed 22%.

Until the second half of 2000, GTW was gaining market share in the PC industry, as its shipments grew faster than the overall industry. Its growth has since reversed, but the company still believes it has a strong presence in the U.S. consumer market. In early 2001, management reviewed GTW's operations, and the company discontinued certain unprofitable revenue streams, beginning in the second quarter of 2001, of roughly $200 million per quarter, exited its international operations in the third quarter, and took other actions to reduce its cost structure. In March 2003, in another restructuring effort, GTW planned to save $400 million annually from workforce cuts, cost programs and a reduction in the number of its stores. Following the March 2004 acquisition of privately-held eMachines Inc. (for 50 million shares of GTW and $30 million in cash), GTW announced it would incur $400-$450 million in restructuring and transformation costs, beyond the $25 million of costs associated with prior actions.

In 1997 Gateway introduced an extension of its traditional business model. Instead of relying on customers willing to buy PCs unseen, by the end of 1997, GTW had opened 37 Gateway Country stores in which customers could test drive PCs in the store. After years of expansion, the company started closing stores. As of December 31, 2002, Gateway had 272 retail stores in the U.S., down from 327 at the end of 2000. During 2003, the company closed 82 stores, and in April 2004, closed the remainder of its stores.

Gateway.net, an Internet service, was also launched in 1997. However, in October 1999, the company announced a strategic alliance with America Online, calling for GTW to package AOL service into all computers it makes and sells. AOL was to invest $800 million in GTW over two years, including $150 million in AOL stock. In December 2001, GTW extinguished its convertible note to AOL through the issuance of 50,000 shares of Series C redeemable convertible preferred stock, resulting in an extraordinary gain of $4.3 million, net of tax. The third and final funding of GTW's investment agreement with AOL occurred in December 2001, when GTW issued $200 million of Series A convertible preferred stock.

The company was among the first major PC vendors to emphasize growth in what it calls beyond the box revenues. These revenues had included software and peripherals, financing, and warranty and training revenue, and in recent years have grown to include consumer electronics, such as plasma TVs and digital cameras. This category represented 28% of GTW's net sales in 2003.

Gateway's reported net loss of $1.62 in 2003 excluded an estimated $0.09 in stock option expense.

Company Financials Fiscal Year ending December 31

Per Share Data ($)

(Year Ended December 31)	2003	2002	2001	2000	1999	1998	1997	1996	1995	1994
Tangible Bk. Val.	1.57	3.16	4.72	6.85	6.15	4.08	2.75	2.66	1.86	1.30
Cash Flow	-1.12	-0.46	-2.52	1.34	1.73	1.42	0.63	1.00	0.67	0.36
Earnings	-1.62	-0.95	-3.14	0.76	1.32	1.09	0.35	0.80	0.55	0.30
S&P Core Earnings	-1.71	-1.00	-2.77	NA	NA	NA	NA	NA	NA	NA
Dividends	Nil	Nil	Nil	Nil	Nil	Nil	Nil	Nil	Nil	Nil
Payout Ratio	Nil	Nil	Nil	Nil	Nil	Nil	Nil	Nil	Nil	Nil
Prices - High	6.85	10.60	24.21	75.12	84.00	34.37	23.12	16.56	9.37	6.18
- Low	2.02	2.61	4.24	16.43	25.59	15.50	11.78	4.50	4.00	2.31
P/E Ratio - High	NM	NM	NM	99	64	32	66	21	17	20
- Low	NM	NM	NM	22	19	14	34	6	7	8

Income Statement Analysis (Million $)

	2003	2002	2001	2000	1999	1998	1997	1996	1995	1994
Revs.	3,402	4,171	6,080	9,601	8,646	7,468	6,294	5,035	3,676	2,701
Oper. Inc.	-347	-352	-984	700	730	600	377	418	287	159
Depr.	164	159	200	189	134	106	86.8	61.8	38.1	18.0
Int. Exp.	Nil	Nil	Nil	Nil	Nil	Nil	Nil	Nil	Nil	NA
Pretax Inc.	-491	-476	-1,290	409	663	541	204	383	262	146
Eff. Tax Rate	NM	NM	NM	38.0%	35.5%	36.0%	46.1%	34.5%	34.0%	34.3%
Net Inc.	-515	-298	-1,014	253	428	346	110	251	173	96.0
S&P Core Earnings	-553	-325	-896	NA	NA	NA	NA	NA	NA	NA

Balance Sheet & Other Fin. Data (Million $)

	2003	2002	2001	2000	1999	1998	1997	1996	1995	1994
Cash	1,089	1,067	1,166	614	1,336	1,328	594	516	169	244
Curr. Assets	1,663	1,955	2,123	2,267	2,697	2,228	1,545	1,318	866	659
Total Assets	2,028	2,509	2,987	4,153	3,955	2,890	2,039	1,673	1,124	771
Curr. Liab.	999	940	1,146	1,631	1,810	1,430	1,004	800	525	349
LT Debt	Nil	Nil	Nil	Nil	3.00	3.36	7.24	7.24	10.8	27.1
Common Equity	522	1,047	1,365	2,380	2,017	1,344	930	816	555	376
Total Cap.	920	1,442	1,758	2,380	2,020	1,348	937	823	573	410
Cap. Exp.	73.0	78.5	199	315	338	235	162	86.0	77.5	29.0
Cash Flow	-362	-150	-814	442	562	452	197	312	211	114
Curr. Ratio	1.7	2.1	1.9	1.4	1.5	1.6	1.5	1.6	1.6	1.9
% LT Debt of Cap.	Nil	Nil	Nil	Nil	0.1	0.2	0.8	0.9	1.9	6.7
% Net Inc.of Revs.	NM	NM	NM	2.6	4.9	4.6	1.7	5.0	4.7	3.6
% Ret. on Assets	NM	NM	NM	6.2	12.5	14.1	5.9	17.9	18.3	14.4
% Ret. on Equity	NM	NM	NM	11.5	25.5	30.5	12.6	36.6	37.2	29.3

Data as orig reptd.; bef. results of disc opers/spec. items. Per share data adj. for stk. divs.; EPS diluted. E-Estimated. NA-Not Available. NM-Not Meaningful. NR-Not Ranked. UR-Under Review.

Office: 14303 Gateway Place , Poway, CA 92064-7140.
Telephone: 858-848-3401.
Email: investorrelations@gateway.com
Website: http://www.gateway.com
Chrmn: T.W. Waitt.
Pres & CEO: W. Inouye.

EVP & CFO: R. Sherwood.
SVP, Secy & General Counsel: M.R. Tyler.
Investor Contact: M. Johnson 800-846-4503.
Dirs: C. G. Carey, G. H. Krauss, D. L. Lacey, J. F. McCann, R. D. Snyder, T. W. Waitt.

Founded: in 1985.
Domicile: Delaware.
Employees: 7,407.
S&P Analyst: Megan Graham-Hackett/MF/BK

The McGraw·Hill Companies

General Dynamics

Recommendation: HOLD ★★★☆☆
SELL SELL HOLD BUY BUY

12-Month Target Price: **$110.00**
(as of November 04, 2004)

GD has an approximate 0.20% weighting in the **S&P 500**

Sector: Industrials
Sub-Industry: Aerospace & Defense
Peer Group: Aero/Def. Equipment Manuf. - Larger

Summary: GD, a major military contractor, is also one of the world's largest makers of corporate jets.

Quantitative Evaluations

S&P Earnings & Dividend Rank: B+

| D | C | B- | B | B+ | A- | A | A+ |

S&P Fair Value Rank: 4-

| 1 | 2 | 3 | 4 | 5 |
| Lowest | | | | Highest |

Fair Value Calc.: $107.20 (Fairly Valued)

S&P Investability Quotient Percentile

97%

GD scored higher than 97% of all companies
for which an S&P Report is available.

Volatility: Low

| Low | Average | High |

Technical Evaluation: Bullish
Since 11/04, the technical indicators for GD
have been Bullish.

Relative Strength Rank: Moderate

63

1 Lowest — Highest 99

| Price as of 11/12/04: | **$108.03** | 2004E S&P Core EPS: | **$5.10** |

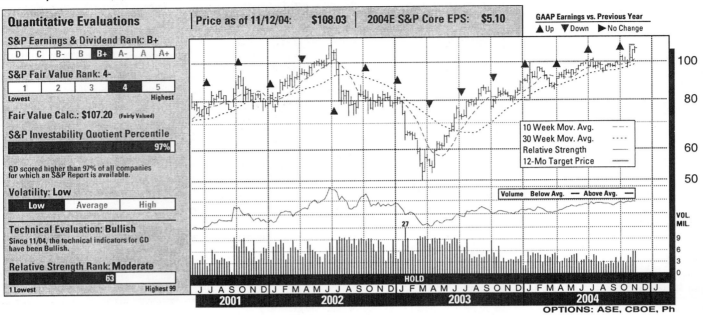

GAAP Earnings vs. Previous Year
▲ Up ▼ Down ► No Change

10 Week Mov. Avg. ----
30 Week Mov. Avg. ·····
Relative Strength ——
12-Mo Target Price ——

Volume Below Avg. — Above Avg.

HOLD

J J A S O N D J F M A M J J A S O N D J F M A M J J A S O N D J F M A M J J A S O N D J
2001 / 2002 / 2003 / 2004

OPTIONS: ASE, CBOE, Ph

Analyst commentary prepared by Robert E. Friedman, CPA /MF/JWP

Highlights November 08, 2004

- We see GD posting annual revenue growth of 3% to 5% over the company's operating cycle, driven primarily by the Gulfstream segment (20% of sales), the world's largest maker of long-range business jets. We believe new demand drivers, primarily increasing corporate affordability of business jets (via fractional share ownership), will spur sustainable, healthy demand for Gulfstream planes. GD's growing presence in the military and government information technologies business should also augment short- and long-term revenue growth.

- However, despite recent U.S. military actions, we are not as sanguine about sustainable growth prospects for GD's other military weapons businesses. We see tight global defense budgets and fundamental changes in global warfare tempering outsized demand for traditional military hardware, such as tanks, destroyers and submarines (50% of total revenues).

- Nevertheless, we believe a combination of higher margin Gulfstream jet sales growth and GD's history of good cost controls will enable the company to generate what we view as respectable operating profit margins and return on equity (ROE) of 12% to 15% and 17% to 20%, respectively.

Investment Rationale/Risk November 08, 2004

- We are maintaining our hold opinion on GD, as the stock is trading slightly below our revised DCF-based 12-month target price.

- Risks to our recommendation and target price primarily include any unexpected structural deterioration of GD's military and corporate jet end-markets, and/or structural deterioration of the economics of the military weapons and corporate jet manufacturing businesses.

- We have a 12-month target price of $110 for GD shares. Our free cash flow model, which values the stock by adding the discounted sum of annual free cash flow rising at an estimated CAGR of 8.5% to 10% over the next 10 years, and matching 3% GDP growth thereafter, calculates a value of $110 a share. We calculated our free cash CAGR by multiplying our 17% to 20% long-term average ROE estimates by our projected 50% long-term annual earnings retention rate. Our relative valuation model, which compares a company's earnings yield (EPS divided by current stock price) with 10-year AAA-rated corporate bond yields, supports our contention that GD is only trading at a modest discount. Based on our projected 2005 S&P Core EPS of $5.65, the stock is sporting an earnings yield of 5.3%, versus a 4.7% yield for 10-year AAA corporate bonds.

Key Stock Statistics

S&P Core EPS 2005E	5.65	52-week Range	$109.00-78.82
S&P Oper. EPS 2004E	6.00	12 Month P/E	18.5
P/E on S&P Oper. EPS 2004E	18.0	Beta	0.48
S&P Oper. EPS 2005E	6.55	Shareholders	117,800
Yield (%)	1.3%	Market Cap (B)	$ 21.6
Dividend Rate/Share	1.44	Shares Outstanding (M)	200.3

Value of $10,000 invested five years ago: **$ 21,380**

Dividend Data Dividends have been paid since 1979

Amount ($)	Date Decl.	Ex-Div. Date	Stock of Record	Payment Date
0.320	Dec. 03	Jan. 14	Jan. 16	Feb. 06 '04
0.360	Mar. 03	Apr. 06	Apr. 08	May. 07 '04
0.360	Jun. 02	Jun. 30	Jul. 02	Aug. 06 '04
0.360	Aug. 04	Oct. 06	Oct. 08	Nov. 12 '04

Revenues/Earnings Data Fiscal year ending December 31

Revenues (Million $)

	2004	2003	2002	2001	2000	1999
1Q	4,760	3,421	3,102	2,673	2,546	2,002
2Q	4,761	3,935	3,506	2,962	2,617	2,087
3Q	4,754	4,427	3,284	3,020	2,502	2,215
4Q	—	4,834	3,937	3,508	2,691	2,655
Yr.	—	16,617	13,829	12,163	10,356	8,959

Earnings Per Share ($)

	2004	2003	2002	2001	2000	1999
1Q	1.34	1.11	1.13	1.19	0.91	1.60
2Q	1.47	1.22	1.34	1.12	1.01	0.86
3Q	1.60	1.28	1.37	1.13	1.02	0.91
4Q	E1.59	1.40	1.33	1.21	1.09	0.98
Yr.	E6.00	5.00	5.18	4.65	4.48	4.36

Next earnings report expected: late-January Source: S&P, Company Reports
EPS Estimates based on S&P Operating Earnings; historical GAAP earnings are as reported.

General Dynamics Corporation

Recommendation: **HOLD** ★ ★ ★ ☆ ☆ 12-Month Target Price: **$110.00** (as of November 04, 2004)

Business Summary November 08, 2004

General Dynamics is a $17+ billion-revenue defense contractor and corporate jet maker that conducts business through five operating segments.

The Information Systems & Technology segment (30% of revenues; 37% of operating earnings; 11% profit margins in 2003) primarily makes sophisticated electronics for land-, sea- and air-based weapons systems. IST also provides computer hardware and software for the U.S. military and federal government. We believe the $60 billion U.S. government IT market is fragmented; IS&T's main competitors are the IT divisions of Northrop Grumman, Lockheed Martin and Boeing.

The Marine Systems (MS) segment (26%; 15%; 5%) is the Pentagon's second largest military shipbuilder (Northrop Grumman is the largest). Although the U.S. military shipbuilding industry operates as a duopoly, profit margins are relatively low, primarily reflecting industrywide gluts in production capacity.

The Combat Systems (CS) segment (25%; 32%; 11%) makes wheeled armored vehicles and munitions. GD is also the only U.S. tank maker. Reflecting the U.S. Army's desire to transform itself into a highly agile fighting force, demand is expected to slow for GD's tanks, but to accelerate for its various wheeled combat vehicles. CS's main competitor is United Defense Industries.

Demand for GD's military weapons systems is driven mainly by growth in the procurement and R&D sectors of the U.S. military budget (40% of world military spending, according to independent aerospace and defense researcher Teal Group). Based on Pentagon statistics, from FY 93 (Oct.) through FY 03, procurement and R&D spending grew at 8.6% and 2.9% average annual rates, respectively.

The Aerospace segment (18%; 15%; 7.4%) makes the well known Gulfstream business jet. Based on revenues, Gulfstream is the world's second-largest corporate jet maker. Canada-based Bombardier, Textron's Cessna division, France's Dassault and Raytheon's aircraft-making unit are the world's first-, third-, fourth- and fifth-largest corporate aircraft makers, respectively. The $9 billion global corporate jet market is oligopolistic; based on statistics provided by independent aviation research firm Teal Group, the five largest corporate jet makers account for 99% of global corporate jet sales.

Demand for small planes, especially business jets, is primarily driven by the health of corporate budgets. Demand for corporate jets is also driven by the health of the fractional (or time-share) market. Based on statistics provided by trade group General Aviation Manufacturers Association, from 1994 through 2003, the U.S. small plane (corporate jet and piston) market (in unit sales) grew at a 9% average annual rate.

GD also mines and sells stone, sand and gravel for highway, commercial and residential construction companies (2%; 2%; 13%).

We believe GD is one of the most profitable global defense contractors. From 1993 through 2003, debt-adjusted return on equity (ROE) averaged 22%, reported net operating EPS grew at an 8.9% compound annual growth rate (CAGR), per-share free cash flow expanded at a 19% CAGR, and per-share equity (a proxy for intrinsic value growth) grew at a 12% CAGR.

Company Financials Fiscal Year ending December 31

Per Share Data ($)

(Year Ended December 31)	2003	2002	2001	2000	1999	1998	1997	1996	1995	1994
Tangible Bk. Val.	NM	5.62	3.83	6.43	3.27	5.48	5.65	13.58	12.39	10.45
Cash Flow	6.40	6.29	5.98	5.61	5.31	3.86	1.61	2.67	2.26	2.06
Earnings	5.00	5.18	4.65	4.48	4.36	2.86	2.50	2.14	1.96	1.76
S&P Core Earnings	4.67	3.24	3.13	NA	NA	NA	NA	NA	NA	NA
Dividends	1.26	1.18	1.10	1.02	0.94	0.86	0.82	0.80	0.74	0.68
Payout Ratio	25%	23%	24%	23%	22%	30%	33%	38%	38%	38%
Prices - High	90.80	111.18	96.00	79.00	75.43	62.00	45.75	37.75	31.50	23.81
- Low	50.00	73.25	60.50	36.25	46.18	40.25	31.56	28.50	21.18	19.00
P/E Ratio - High	18	21	21	18	17	22	18	18	16	14
- Low	10	14	13	8	11	14	13	13	11	11

Income Statement Analysis (Million $)

	2003	2002	2001	2000	1999	1998	1997	1996	1995	1994
Revs.	16,617	13,829	12,163	10,356	8,959	4,970	4,062	3,581	3,067	3,058
Oper. Inc.	1,744	1,795	1,756	1,555	1,396	668	549	434	353	360
Depr.	277	213	271	226	193	126	91.0	67.0	38.0	39.0
Int. Exp.	98.0	45.0	56.0	60.0	34.0	12.0	12.0	14.0	4.00	5.00
Pretax Inc.	1,372	1,584	1,424	1,262	1,126	549	479	409	375	343
Eff. Tax Rate	27.3%	33.6%	33.8%	28.6%	21.8%	33.7%	34.0%	34.0%	34.2%	35.0%
Net Inc.	997	1,051	943	901	880	364	316	270	247	223
S&P Core Earnings	931	658	636	NA	NA	NA	NA	NA	NA	NA

Balance Sheet & Other Fin. Data (Million $)

	2003	2002	2001	2000	1999	1998	1997	1996	1995	1994
Cash	860	328	442	177	270	220	336	894	1,095	1,059
Curr. Assets	6,394	5,098	4,893	3,551	3,491	1,873	1,689	1,858	2,013	1,797
Total Assets	16,183	11,731	11,069	7,987	7,774	4,572	4,091	3,299	3,164	2,673
Curr. Liab.	5,616	4,582	4,579	2,901	3,453	1,461	1,291	833	859	626
LT Debt	3,296	718	724	162	169	249	257	156	170	196
Common Equity	5,921	5,199	4,528	3,820	3,171	2,219	1,915	1,714	1,567	1,316
Total Cap.	9,217	5,917	5,252	3,982	3,340	2,468	2,172	1,870	1,737	1,512
Cap. Exp.	224	264	356	288	197	158	83.0	75.0	32.0	23.0
Cash Flow	1,274	1,264	1,214	1,127	1,073	490	407	337	285	262
Curr. Ratio	1.1	1.1	1.1	1.2	1.0	1.3	1.3	2.2	2.3	2.9
% LT Debt of Cap.	35.8	12.1	13.8	4.1	5.1	10.1	11.8	8.3	9.8	13.0
% Net Inc.of Revs.	6.0	7.6	7.8	8.7	9.8	7.3	7.8	7.5	8.1	7.3
% Ret. on Assets	7.1	9.2	9.9	11.4	12.6	8.4	8.6	8.3	8.5	8.4
% Ret. on Equity	17.9	21.6	22.6	25.8	31.5	17.6	17.4	16.5	17.2	17.8

Data as orig reptd.; bef. results of disc opers/spec. items. Per share data adj. for stk. divs.; EPS diluted. E-Estimated. NA-Not Available. NM-Not Meaningful. NR-Not Ranked. UR-Under Review.

Office: 3190 Fairview Park Drive, Falls Church, VA 22042-4523.
Telephone: 703-876-3000.
Website: http://www.generaldynamics.com
Chrmn & CEO: N.D. Chabraja.
SVP & CFO: M.J. Mancuso.
SVP, Secy & General Counsel: D.A. Savner.

VP & Treas: D.H. Fogg.
VP & Investor Contact: R. Lewis 703-876-3195.
Dirs: N. D. Chabraja, J. S. Crown, L. Crown, W. P. Fricks, C. H. Goodman, J. L. Johnson, G. A. Joulwan, P. G. Kaminski, J. M. Keane, L. L. Lyles, C. E. Mundy, Jr., R. Walmsley.

Founded: in 1899.
Domicile: Delaware.
Employees: 67,600.
S&P Analyst: Robert E. Friedman, CPA /MF/JWP

General Electric

Recommendation: **HOLD** ★★★☆☆
SELL SELL HOLD BUY BUY

12-Month Target Price: **$34.00**
(as of October 08, 2004)

GE has an approximate 3.47% weighting in the **S&P 500**

Sector: Industrials
Sub-Industry: Industrial Conglomerates
Peer Group: Conglomerates - Domestic

Summary: This industrial and media behemoth is also one of the world's largest providers of financing and insurance.

Quantitative Evaluations

S&P Earnings & Dividend Rank: A+

| D | C | B- | B | B+ | A- | A | **A+** |

S&P Fair Value Rank: 2-

| 1 | **2** | 3 | 4 | 5 |
| Lowest | | | | Highest |

Fair Value Calc.: $32.40 (Slightly Overvalued)

S&P Investability Quotient Percentile

97%

GE scored higher than 97% of all companies for which an S&P Report is available.

Volatility: Low

| **Low** | Average | High |

Technical Evaluation: Bullish

Since 10/04, the technical indicators for GE have been Bullish.

Relative Strength Rank: Moderate

65

| 1 Lowest | | Highest 99 |

| Price as of 11/12/04: | **$36.25** | 2004E S&P Core EPS: | **$1.50** |

GAAP Earnings vs. Previous Year
▲ Up ▼ Down ▶ No Change

- 10 Week Mov. Avg.
- 30 Week Mov. Avg.
- Relative Strength
- 12-Mo Target Price

Volume Below Avg. — Above Avg. —

HOLD

J J A S O N D J F M A M J J A S O N D J F M A M J J A S O N D J F M A M J J A S O N D J
2001   2002   2003   2004

OPTIONS: ASE, CBOE, P, Ph

Analyst commentary prepared by Robert E. Friedman, CPA /MF/JWP

Highlights September 27, 2004

- Reflecting our expectations of a tepid global economic recovery and modest dilution from 2% more shares, due to acquisitions, we believe 2004 EPS will rise only 4%, to $1.61.

- We see sales hikes in the medical equipment and media segments, and ongoing cost-containment initiatives, outweighing expected weak near-term aerospace, electric utility, industrial and consumer demand for jet engines, power turbines, plastics and appliances. We project that 2004 Standard & Poor's Core Earnings per share will grow 7%, to $1.50, due to a decline in pension income reversals.

- Looking at GE's longer-term financial prospects, we do not think the company will be able to show EPS growth at better than an 8.5% compound annual growth rate (CAGR), and see debt-adjusted ROE of 17%. We believe GE's sheer size will make it very difficult to match historical revenue and EPS growth rates, and ROE. Ironically, we think increasing sales contributions from the financing and leasing segment (45% of revenues) could restrict long-term profitability, leading to a narrowing of the stock's P/E multiple. With profit margins over 8%, GE Capital is one of the least profitable GE operating units.

Investment Rationale/Risk September 27, 2004

- We recommend holding the shares on a total return basis.

- Risks to our recommendation and target price primarily include any unexpected, concurrent structural deterioration of demand for at least three of GE's primary product/service offerings, and/or concurrent structural deterioration of business fundamentals of at least three of GE's primary businesses.

- Our free cash flow models (which value the stock by adding the sum of free cash income expanding at a projected 8.5% CAGR over the next 10 years, and at 3.0% thereafter) indicate a value of $32 a share (our projected 8.5% free cash EPS CAGR is much lower than the 15% consensus CAGR).

Key Stock Statistics

S&P Core EPS 2005E	1.63	52-week Range	$36.25-27.37
S&P Oper. EPS 2004E	1.61	12 Month P/E	23.7
P/E on S&P Oper. EPS 2004E	22.5	Beta	1.10
S&P Oper. EPS 2005E	1.76	Shareholders	670,000
Yield (%)	2.2%	Market Cap (B)	$382.7
Dividend Rate/Share	0.80	Shares Outstanding (M)	10558.2

Value of $10,000 invested five years ago: **$ 8,724**

Dividend Data Dividends have been paid since 1899

Amount ($)	Date Decl.	Ex-Div. Date	Stock of Record	Payment Date
0.200	Feb. 13	Feb. 26	Mar. 01	Apr. 26 '04
0.200	Jun. 11	Jun. 24	Jun. 28	Jul. 26 '04
0.200	Sep. 17	Sep. 23	Sep. 27	Oct. 25 '04

Revenues/Earnings Data Fiscal year ending December 31

Revenues (Million $)

	2004	2003	2002	2001	2000	1999
1Q	33,350	30,319	30,521	30,493	29,996	24,165
2Q	37,035	33,373	33,214	31,977	32,862	27,410
3Q	38,272	33,394	32,585	29,468	32,014	27,200
4Q	—	36,964	35,378	33,975	34,981	32,855
Yr.	—	134,187	131,698	125,913	129,853	111,630

Earnings Per Share ($)

	2004	2003	2002	2001	2000	1999
1Q	0.32	0.32	0.35	0.30	0.26	0.22
2Q	0.38	0.38	0.44	0.39	0.34	0.28
3Q	0.38	0.40	0.41	0.33	0.32	0.27
4Q	E0.53	0.45	0.31	0.39	0.36	0.31
Yr.	E1.61	1.55	1.51	1.41	1.27	1.07

Next earnings report expected: mid-January Source: S&P, Company Reports
EPS Estimates based on S&P Operating Earnings; historical GAAP earnings are as reported.

General Electric Company

Recommendation: **HOLD** ★ ★ ★ ☆ ☆   12-Month Target Price: **$34.00** (as of October 08, 2004)

Business Summary September 27, 2004

This multi-industry, media and financing giant does business through two segments: GE Industrial and GE Capital.

The company's Industrial segment (53% of revenues, 61% of operating profits, and 17% operating profit margins in 2003) is comprised of nine operating divisions: Power Systems (power utility generator-making and servicing; 13% of total revenues, 20% of total operating profits, and 22% operating profit margins); Aircraft Engines (jet engine-making and servicing; 8%, 11%, 20%); Medical Systems (primarily medical diagnostics equipment-making and servicing; 7%, 8%, 17%); Consumer Products (appliances and lighting; 6%, 3%, 7%); Industrial Systems (mostly electric motors and electrical component-making; 6%, 3%, 8%); NBC (broadcasting, cable; 5%, 10%, 29%); Plastics (4%, 2%, 8%); Specialty Materials (silicones, additives, industrial diamonds; 2%, 2%, 12%); and Transportation Systems (primarily locomotive and railroad equipment-making and servicing; 2%, 2%, 18%).

The GE Capital (GEC) segment (47% of revenues, 39% of operating profits, and 12% operating profit margins) consists of Insurance (19% of total revenues, 10% of total operating profits, and 8% total operating profit margins in 2003); Commercial Finance (14%, 19%, 20%); Consumer Finance (9%, 11%, 17%); Equipment Leasing (3%, 1%, 4%); and Other (1%, -2%, -27%).

We calculate that over the past seven years (1995 through 2003), revenues, reported EPS and per-share free cash flow expanded at 7.8%, 11% and 12% compound annual growth rates (CAGRs), respectively. During this period, debt-adjusted return on equity averaged about 18%. Global economic expansion

and debt-fueled growth of GEC were primarily behind GE's seven-year financial performance.

A material portion of GEC debt is used to fund its portfolio of financing receivables. GEC's financing receivables is the parent company's largest asset category, and one of GE's primary sources of revenues. GEC's portfolio of financing receivables primarily consists of commercial financing receivables (equipment loans and leased equipment) and consumer financing receivables (credit card receivables, installment loans, auto loans and residential mortgages). At year-end 2003, financing receivables stood at $226 billion (including estimated loss allowance of $6.3 billion), a 14% increase from $198 billion ($5.5 billion) at year-end 2002.

As a consequence of debt-fueled growth at GEC, GE's total debt levels rose from $1 billion in 1981 (11% debt/equity) to $305 billion (432%) at the end of 2003. Short-term debt (primarily GE Capital commercial paper) accounted for 27% of total debt at 2003 year end.

In analyzing GE's quality of earnings, the company's seven-year average reported-to-S&P Core earnings variance stood at 14%. We attribute most of the variance to non-operating pension gains, which accounted for about 10% of reported EPS in 2003. GE also has a history of fully or partly offsetting non-operating gains from asset disposals with operating charges from restructurings and asset writedowns. From 1996 through 2003, S&P Core Earnings grew at a seven-year CAGR of 10%, versus 11% on a reported EPS basis.

Company Financials Fiscal Year ending December 31

Per Share Data ($)

(Year Ended December 31)	2003	2002	2001	2000	1999	1998	1997	1996	1995	1994
Tangible Bk. Val.	2.40	1.76	2.34	2.32	1.68	1.55	1.56	1.36	1.63	1.47
Cash Flow	2.24	2.12	2.11	2.04	1.74	1.52	1.22	1.12	1.01	0.89
Earnings	1.55	1.51	1.41	1.27	1.07	0.93	0.82	0.73	0.65	0.58
S&P Core Earnings	1.41	1.10	0.98	NA	NA	NA	NA	NA	NA	NA
Dividends	0.77	0.73	0.66	0.57	0.47	0.40	0.36	0.32	0.28	0.25
Payout Ratio	50%	48%	47%	45%	43%	43%	44%	43%	43%	43%
Prices - High	32.42	41.84	53.55	60.50	53.16	34.64	25.52	17.68	12.18	9.14
- Low	21.30	21.40	28.50	41.64	31.35	23.00	15.97	11.58	8.31	7.50
P/E Ratio - High	21	28	38	48	50	37	31	24	19	16
- Low	14	14	20	33	29	25	19	16	13	13

Income Statement Analysis (Million $)

	2003	2002	2001	2000	1999	1998	1997	1996	1995	1994
Revs.	134,187	131,698	125,679	129,853	111,630	100,469	90,840	79,179	70,028	59,316
Oper. Inc.	38,089	35,431	37,966	38,329	32,646	29,355	25,072	22,764	20,821	16,194
Depr.	6,956	5,998	7,089	7,736	6,691	5,860	4,082	3,785	3,594	3,207
Int. Exp.	10,432	10,216	11,062	11,720	10,013	9,753	8,384	7,904	7,327	5,024
Pretax Inc.	20,194	19,217	20,049	18,873	15,577	13,742	11,419	10,806	9,737	8,831
Eff. Tax Rate	21.4%	19.6%	27.8%	30.3%	31.1%	30.4%	26.1%	32.6%	32.5%	31.1%
Net Inc.	15,589	15,133	14,128	12,735	10,717	9,296	8,203	7,280	6,573	5,915
S&P Core Earnings	14,195	11,038	9,889	NA	NA	NA	NA	NA	NA	NA

Balance Sheet & Other Fin. Data (Million $)

	2003	2002	2001	2000	1999	1998	1997	1996	1995	1994
Cash	12,664	125,772	110,099	99,534	90,312	83,034	76,482	64,080	43,890	33,556
Curr. Assets	NA	NA	NA	NA	NA	NA	NA	NA	NA	NA
Total Assets	647,483	575,244	495,023	437,006	405,200	355,935	304,012	272,402	228,035	194,484
Curr. Liab.	NA	NA	NA	NA	NA	NA	NA	NA	82,001	72,854
LT Debt	170,004	140,632	79,806	82,132	71,427	59,663	46,603	49,246	51,027	36,979
Common Equity	79,180	63,706	54,824	50,492	42,557	38,880	34,438	31,125	29,609	26,387
Total Cap.	267,611	222,328	148,975	146,250	128,436	112,158	93,374	91,651	90,972	70,418
Cap. Exp.	9,767	13,351	15,520	13,967	15,502	8,982	8,388	7,760	6,447	7,492
Cash Flow	22,545	21,131	21,217	20,471	17,408	15,156	12,285	11,065	10,162	9,122
Curr. Ratio	NA	NA	NA	NA	NA	NA	NA	NA	NA	NA
% LT Debt of Cap.	63.5	63.3	53.6	56.2	55.6	53.2	50.0	53.7	56.1	52.5
% Net Inc.of Revs.	11.6	11.5	11.2	9.8	9.6	9.3	9.0	9.2	9.4	10.0
% Ret. on Assets	2.5	2.8	3.0	3.0	2.8	2.8	2.8	2.9	3.2	2.7
% Ret. on Equity	21.8	25.5	26.8	27.4	26.3	25.4	25.0	24.0	23.5	22.7

Data as orig reptd.; bef. results of disc opers/spec. items. Per share data adj. for stk. divs.; EPS diluted. E-Estimated. NA-Not Available. NM-Not Meaningful. NR-Not Ranked. UR-Under Review.

Office: 3135 Easton Tpke, Fairfield, CT 06828-0001.
Telephone: 203-373-2211.
Website: http://www.ge.com
Chrmn & CEO: J.R. Immelt.
Vice Chrmn: D.D. Dammerman.
Vice Chrmn: R.C. Wright.

SVP & CFO: K.S. Sherin.
VP & Treas: K.A. Cassidy.
Dirs: J. I. Cash, Jr., D. D. Dammerman, A. M. Fudge, C. X. Gonzalez, J. R. Immelt, A. Jung, A. G. Lafley, K. G. Langone, R. S. Larsen, R. B. Lazarus, S. Nunn, R. S. Penske, A. C. Sigler, R. J. Swieringa, D. A. Warner III, R. C. Wright.

Founded: in 1892.
Domicile: New York.
Employees: 305,000.
S&P Analyst: Robert E. Friedman, CPA /MF/JWP

Recommendation: **BUY** ★★★★☆
SELL | SELL | HOLD | BUY | BUY

12-Month Target Price: $53.00
(as of September 15, 2003)

GIS has an approximate 0.16% weighting in the **S&P 500**

Sector: Consumer Staples
Sub-Industry: Packaged Foods & Meats
Peer Group: Larger Food Manufacturers

Summary: GIS is a major producer of packaged consumer food products, including Big G cereals and Betty Crocker desserts/baking mixes.

Quantitative Evaluations

S&P Earnings & Dividend Rank: A-

| D | C | B- | B | B+ | A- | A | A+ |

S&P Fair Value Rank: 5

| 1 | 2 | 3 | 4 | 5 |
| Lowest | | | | Highest |

Fair Value Calc.: $52.40 (Slightly Undervalued)

S&P Investability Quotient Percentile

85%

GIS scored higher than 85% of all companies for which an S&P Report is available.

Volatility: Low

| Low | Average | High |

Technical Evaluation: Neutral
Since 11/04, the technical indicators for GIS have been Neutral.

Relative Strength Rank: Moderate

38

1 Lowest   Highest 99

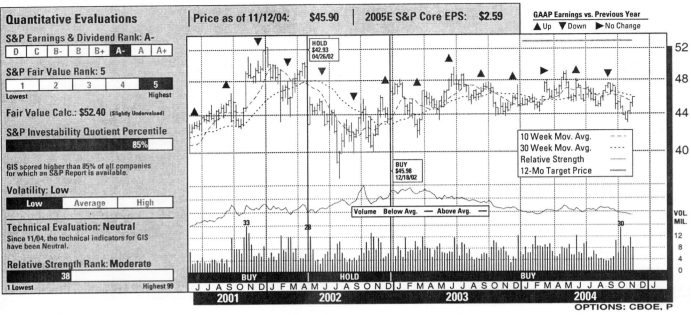

Price as of 11/12/04: $45.90   **2005E S&P Core EPS:** $2.59

GAAP Earnings vs. Previous Year
▲ Up ▼ Down ► No Change

10 Week Mov. Avg.
30 Week Mov. Avg.
Relative Strength
12-Mo Target Price

Volume Below Avg. — Above Avg.

HOLD $42.93 04/26/02
BUY $45.98 12/18/02

VOL. MIL.

BUY | HOLD | BUY
J J A S O N D J F M A M J J A S O N D J F M A M J J A S O N D J F M A M J J A S O N D J
2001 | 2002 | 2003 | 2004

OPTIONS: CBOE, P

Analyst commentary prepared by Richard Joy/MF/GG

Highlights August 02, 2004

- We see sales advancing 2% to 3% in FY 05 (May), led by 3% unit volume growth and higher prices, partially offset by one less shipping week compared to FY 04. We expect operating margins to benefit from a combination of productivity gains and volume-based efficiencies arising from the streamlining of manufacturing and distribution activities, incremental merger synergies, and continued improvement in profits from international joint venture operations. However, expected higher marketing and promotional spending to support new product introductions and an estimated $165 million increase in commodity costs will likely result in modest margin erosion. We expect interest costs to decline 5% to 6%, on lower debt levels and interest rates.

- With the effective tax rate expected to remain at 35%, and with an expected modest increase in shares outstanding, we see FY 05 operating EPS increasing to $2.90, from $2.85 in FY 04. For FY 06, we expect EPS to advance 9%, to $3.15. For the longer term, we see EPS growth of 8% to 10%.

- Our FY 05 and FY 06 Standard & Poor's Core Earnings per share projections, reflecting projected option expense of $0.13 per share and pension adjustments in each year, are $2.59 and $2.84, respectively.

Key Stock Statistics

S&P Core EPS 2006E	2.84	52-week Range	$49.17-43.01
S&P Oper. EPS 2005E	2.90	12 Month P/E	17.4
P/E on S&P Oper. EPS 2005E	15.8	Beta	0.02
S&P Oper. EPS 2006E	3.15	Shareholders	37,013
Yield (%)	2.7%	Market Cap (B)	$ 17.5
Dividend Rate/Share	1.24	Shares Outstanding (M)	380.9

Value of $10,000 invested five years ago: **$ 12,433**

Dividend Data Dividends have been paid since 1898

Amount ($)	Date Decl.	Ex-Div. Date	Stock of Record	Payment Date
0.275	Dec. 15	Jan. 08	Jan. 12	Feb. 02 '04
0.275	Feb. 23	Apr. 07	Apr. 12	May. 03 '04
0.310	Jun. 30	Jul. 08	Jul. 12	Aug. 02 '04
0.310	Sep. 27	Oct. 06	Oct. 11	Nov. 01 '04

Investment Rationale/Risk August 02, 2004

- Our accumulate recommendation on the shares reflects our expectation of continuing improvement in volume growth trends and earnings visibility in coming quarters. The company's non-cold cereal businesses have resumed their strong growth trends, and we think results will benefit from new product introductions and productivity gains. Our discounted cash flow analysis, using a weighted average cost of capital of 9%, yields an intrinsic value for the stock in the low to mid-$50s. We view the shares, recently trading at about 15X our calendar 2005 EPS estimate of $3.01, in line with peer levels and at a modest discount to the S&P 500 Index, as attractive.

- Risks to our recommendation and target price relate to competitive pressures in General Mills' businesses, consumer acceptance of new product introductions, weather conditions, and the company's ability to achieve sales and earnings growth forecasts.

- We have a 12-month target price of $53, which is based upon an analysis of peer P/E and EV/EBITDA multiples, and our discounted free cash flow model, which assumes a weighted average cost of capital of 9% and a terminal growth rate of 3%.

Revenues/Earnings Data Fiscal year ending May 31

Revenues (Million $)

	2005	2004	2003	2002	2001	2000
1Q	2,585	2,518	2,362	1,404	1,675	1,573
2Q	—	3,060	2,953	1,842	1,895	1,817
3Q	—	2,703	2,645	2,379	1,702	1,620
4Q	—	2,789	2,546	2,324	1,806	1,690
Yr.	—	11,070	10,506	7,949	7,078	6,700

Earnings Per Share ($)

	2005	2004	2003	2002	2001	2000
1Q	0.47	0.59	0.47	0.65	0.55	0.50
2Q	E0.88	0.81	0.73	0.41	0.70	0.62
3Q	E0.70	0.63	0.63	0.22	0.54	0.50
4Q	E0.72	0.72	0.59	0.15	0.50	0.38
Yr.	E2.90	2.75	2.43	1.35	2.28	2.00

Next earnings report expected: mid-December Source: S&P, Company Reports
EPS Estimates based on S&P Operating Earnings; historical GAAP earnings are as reported.

General Mills, Inc.

Recommendation: **BUY** ★ ★ ★ ★ ☆   12-Month Target Price: **$53.00** (as of September 15, 2003)

Business Summary August 02, 2004

General Mills (GIS) is the second largest U.S. producer of ready-to-eat breakfast cereals, and a leading producer of other well known packaged consumer foods. Following the company's October 2001 acquisition of The Pillsbury Company, GIS organizes its businesses into three reportable segments: U.S. Retail (71% of FY 03 (May) sales, 88% of operating income); Bakeries and Foodservice (17%, 8%); and International (12%, 4%).

Major cereal brands, most of which bear the Big G label, include Cheerios, Wheaties, Lucky Charms, Total and Chex cereals. Other consumer packaged food products include baking mixes (Betty Crocker, Bisquick); meals (Betty Crocker dry packaged dinner mixes, Progresso soups, Green Giant canned and frozen vegetables); snacks (Pop Secret microwave popcorn, Bugles snacks, grain and fruit snack products); Pillsbury refrigerated and frozen dough products, frozen breakfast products and frozen pizza and snack products; organic foods and other products, including Yoplait and Colombo yogurt. The company also engages in grain merchandising, produces its own ingredient flour requirements, and sells flour to bakeries. Products are also made and sold in Canada and Europe, Japan, Korea, and Latin America.

Joint ventures include a 50% equity interest in Cereal Partners Worldwide, a joint venture with Nestle that manufactures and markets breakfast cereals in more than 130 countries outside North America, including France, Spain, Portugal, Italy, Ireland, Germany, the U.K., Mexico and the Philippines; a 40.5% equity interest in Snack Ventures Europe, a joint venture with PepsiCo that manufactures and markets snack foods in continental Europe; a 50% interest in joint ventures for the manufacture, distribution and marketing of Haagen-Dazs frozen ice cream products and novelties in Japan, Korea, Thailand, and the Philippines; a 50% interest in Seretram, a joint venture with Co-op de Pau for the production of Green Giant canned corn in France; and a 50% equity interest in 8th Continent, LLC, a joint venture with DuPont to develop and market soy foods and beverages. The joint ventures, which are reflected in GIS's financial statements on an equity accounting basis, contributed an aggregate of $61 million in after-tax income in FY 03, up from $33 million in FY 02.

In October 2001, the company acquired the worldwide operations of Pillsbury from Diageo plc, for $9.7 billion. Payment in the transaction included 134 million GIS common shares, as well as cash paid and assumed debt of Pillsbury totaling $3.8 billion. In addition to these payments, the company was required to pay Diageo $273 million on April 30, 2003, under terms of the purchase agreement.

Company Financials Fiscal Year ending May 31

Per Share Data ($)

(Year Ended May 31)	2004	2003	2002	2001	2000	1999	1998	1997	1996	1995
Tangible Bk. Val.	NM	NM	NM	NM	NM	NM	NM	NM	0.62	0.07
Cash Flow	3.79	3.39	2.21	3.04	2.68	4.63	1.90	1.99	2.08	1.43
Earnings	2.75	2.43	1.35	2.28	2.00	1.70	1.30	1.41	1.50	0.82
S&P Core Earnings	2.43	1.74	0.55	1.79	NA	NA	NA	NA	NA	NA
Dividends	1.10	1.10	1.10	1.10	1.10	1.08	1.06	1.02	0.96	0.94
Payout Ratio	40%	45%	81%	48%	55%	64%	82%	72%	64%	115%

Cal. Yrs.	2003	2002	2001	2000	1999	1998	1997	1996	1995	1994
Prices - High	49.66	51.73	52.86	45.31	43.93	39.84	39.12	33.75	32.31	31.12
- Low	41.43	37.38	37.26	29.37	32.50	29.59	28.87	26.00	23.62	24.68
P/E Ratio - High	18	21	39	20	22	23	30	24	22	38
- Low	15	15	28	13	16	17	22	18	16	30

Income Statement Analysis (Million $)

	2004	2003	2002	2001	2000	1999	1998	1997	1996	1995
Revs.	11,070	10,506	7,949	7,078	6,700	6,246	6,033	5,609	5,416	5,027
Oper. Inc.	2,442	2,290	1,569	1,392	1,308	1,212	1,145	1,042	1,046	881
Depr.	399	365	296	223	209	194	195	183	187	191
Int. Exp.	529	547	416	221	166	131	129	117	117	126
Pretax Inc.	1,583	1,377	700	1,015	950	839	664	703	756	405
Eff. Tax Rate	33.4%	33.4%	34.1%	34.5%	35.3%	36.3%	36.4%	36.7%	37.0%	35.8%
Net Inc.	1,055	917	461	665	614	535	422	445	476	260
S&P Core Earnings	931	652	189	512	NA	NA	NA	NA	NA	NA

Balance Sheet & Other Fin. Data (Million $)

	2004	2003	2002	2001	2000	1999	1998	1997	1996	1995
Cash	751	703	975	64.1	25.6	3.90	6.00	13.0	21.0	13.0
Curr. Assets	3,215	3,179	3,437	1,408	1,190	1,103	1,035	1,011	100	897
Total Assets	18,448	18,227	16,540	5,091	4,574	4,141	3,861	3,902	3,295	3,358
Curr. Liab.	2,757	3,444	5,747	2,209	2,529	1,700	1,444	1,293	1,192	1,221
LT Debt	7,410	7,516	5,591	2,221	1,760	1,702	1,640	1,530	1,221	1,401
Common Equity	5,248	4,175	3,576	52.2	-289	164	191	495	308	141
Total Cap.	14,730	13,652	9,727	2,696	1,859	2,156	2,244	2,441	1,936	1,960
Cap. Exp.	628	711	506	308	268	281	184	163	129	157
Cash Flow	1,454	1,282	757	888	823	729	617	628	663	451
Curr. Ratio	1.2	0.9	0.6	0.6	0.5	0.6	0.7	0.8	0.8	0.7
% LT Debt of Cap.	50.3	55.1	57.5	82.4	94.7	79.0	73.1	62.7	63.1	71.5
% Net Inc.of Revs.	9.5	8.7	5.8	9.4	9.2	8.6	7.0	8.0	8.8	5.2
% Ret. on Assets	5.8	5.3	4.3	13.8	14.1	13.4	10.9	12.4	14.3	6.4
% Ret. on Equity	22.4	23.7	25.4	NM	NM	301.6	123.2	110.7	212.0	40.2

Data as orig reptd.; bef. results of disc opers/spec. items. Per share data adj. for stk. divs. Bold denotes primary EPS - prior periods restated. E-Estimated. NA-Not Available. NM-Not Meaningful. NR-Not Ranked. UR-Under Review.

Office: Number One General Mills Blvd, Minneapolis, MN 55426.
Telephone: 763-764-7600.
Website: http://www.generalmills.com
Chrmn & CEO: S.W. Sanger.
Vice Chrmn: S.R. Demeritt.
EVP & CFO: J.A. Lawrence.

SVP, Secy & General Counsel: S.S. Marshall.
Investor Contact: G. Zimprich 763-764-7780.
Dirs: L. D. DeSimone, S. R. Demeritt, W. T. Esrey, R. V. Gilmartin, J. R. Hope, H. G. Miller, H. Ochoa-Brillembourg, S. Odland, M. D. Rose, S. W. Sanger, A. M. Spence, D. A. Terrell.

Founded: in 1928.
Domicile: Delaware.
Employees: 27,580.
S&P Analyst: Richard Joy/MF/GG

General Motors

Recommendation: HOLD ★★★☆☆
SELL SELL HOLD BUY BUY

12-Month Target Price: $41.00
(as of October 14, 2004)

GM has an approximate 0.21% weighting in the **S&P 500**

Sector: Consumer Discretionary
Sub-Industry: Automobile Manufacturers
Peer Group: Automakers

Summary: GM is the world's largest producer of cars and trucks, and has significant finance, aerospace, defense and electronics operations.

Quantitative Evaluations

S&P Earnings & Dividend Rank: B

| D | C | B- | **B** | B+ | A- | A | A+ |

S&P Fair Value Rank: 4

| 1 | 2 | 3 | **4** | 5 |
| Lowest | | | | Highest |

Fair Value Calc.: $39.90 (Fairly Valued)

S&P Investability Quotient Percentile

91%

GM scored higher than 91% of all companies for which an S&P Report is available.

Volatility: Average

| Low | **Average** | High |

Technical Evaluation: Bearish

Since 10/04, the technical indicators for GM have been Bearish.

Relative Strength Rank: Weak

24

| 1 Lowest | Highest 99 |

Price as of 11/12/04: $40.21 | **2004E S&P Core EPS:** $2.35

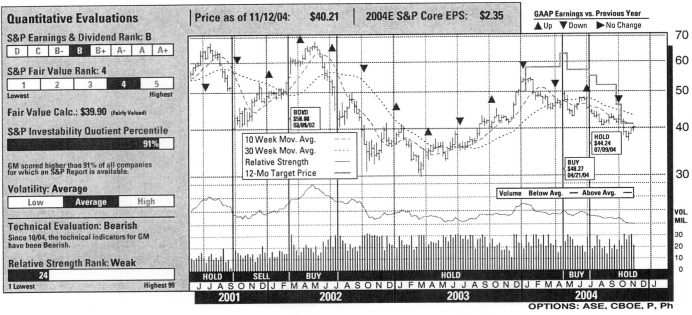

GAAP Earnings vs. Previous Year
▲ Up ▼ Down ► No Change

10 Week Mov. Avg. ·– – –
30 Week Mov. Avg. ·······
Relative Strength
12-Mo Target Price

Volume Below Avg. — Above Avg.

BOYD $56.66 03/05/02
HOLD $44.24 07/09/04
BUY $48.27 04/21/04

HOLD | SELL | BUY | HOLD | BUY | HOLD
J J A S O N D J F M A M J J A S O N D J F M A M J J A S O N D J F M A M J J A S O N D J
2001 | 2002 | 2003 | 2004

OPTIONS: ASE, CBOE, P, Ph

Analyst commentary prepared by Efraim Levy, CFA /CB/GG

Highlights October 15, 2004

- We expect U.S. car and light truck sales of 16.6 million in 2004, slightly above 2003 levels. We project an increase in 2005 to 17.0 million. We expect demand in 2004 and 2005 to continue to benefit from an improving economy and high incentive levels. The introduction of 17 new products should also aid sales. We expect GM to maintain strength in trucks, but see competition remaining intense, as Asian and European manufacturers add to their vehicle offerings. We think that a more favorable mix and cost cutting initiatives will help offset price competition, increased steel prices and high marketing expenses.

- We are concerned that high inventory could lead to reduced production or increased incentives later this year and early 2005, and have lowered our 2004 EPS estimate to $6.21 and our 2005 estimate to $6.20. We expect the income improvement from financial services to slow from 2003's pace, reflecting a likely bottom in interest rates. We see China contributing to profits, even as Europe continues its losses. We do not expect certain likely changes in accounting rules for contingent convertible debt to result in dilution of 2004 or 2005 EPS or restatement of past earnings.

- After $18.5 billion in pension contributions and positive investment returns in 2003, we expect pension-related expenses to be lower in 2004 and 2005.

Investment Rationale/Risk October 15, 2004

- Based on our 2005 EPS estimate, the stock recently traded at the low end of its historical P/E multiple range, and below the levels of Ford, DaimlerChrysler and the S&P 500. In 2003, GM contributed about $18.5 billion to its pension fund. We expect reduced U.S. pension and retirement obligations to help the stock's valuation.

- Risks to our opinion and target price include our concern about future pension and health care costs and the impact of costly sales incentives, as well as high inventory levels, increased gasoline and steel prices and greater competition in China.

- Based on our concerns about what we view as excessive inventories and despite the discount to our target price and the stock's lower P/E versus peers and the S&P 500, we would not add to positions. Our projection of a P/E of about 7X our 2005 EPS estimate reflects peer and historical P/E comparisons. However, our DCF model, which assumes a WACC of 7.3%, a compound annual growth rate of 6% over the next 15 years, and a terminal growth rate of 0.5%, generates an intrinsic value approaching $39. Based on a combination of historical and comparative P/E multiples and DCF, we have a 12-month target price of $41.

Key Stock Statistics

S&P Core EPS 2005E	3.85	52-week Range	$55.55-36.90
S&P Oper. EPS 2004E	6.21	12 Month P/E	5.4
P/E on S&P Oper. EPS 2004E	6.5	Beta	1.21
S&P Oper. EPS 2005E	6.20	Shareholders	418,540
Yield (%)	5.0%	Market Cap (B)	$ 22.7
Dividend Rate/Share	2.00	Shares Outstanding (M)	564.8

Value of $10,000 invested five years ago: **$ 7,171**

Dividend Data Dividends have been paid since 1915

Amount ($)	Date Decl.	Ex-Div. Date	Stock of Record	Payment Date
0.500	Feb. 03	Feb. 11	Feb. 13	Mar. 10 '04
0.500	May. 04	May. 12	May. 14	Jun. 10 '04
0.500	Aug. 03	Aug. 11	Aug. 13	Sep. 10 '04
0.500	Oct. 29	Nov. 04	Nov. 08	Dec. 10 '04

Revenues/Earnings Data Fiscal year ending December 31

Revenues (Million $)

	2004	2003	2002	2001	2000	1999
1Q	47,779	47,146	46,264	42,615	46,858	42,455
2Q	49,148	45,944	48,265	46,220	48,743	45,067
3Q	44,858	43,351	43,578	42,475	42,690	42,794
4Q	—	49,084	48,656	45,950	46,341	46,262
Yr.	—	185,524	182,108	177,268	184,632	176,558

Earnings Per Share ($)

	2004	2003	2002	2001	2000	1999
1Q	2.25	2.74	0.57	0.53	2.80	2.68
2Q	2.36	1.57	2.43	1.03	2.93	2.66
3Q	0.78	0.80	-1.42	-0.41	1.55	1.33
4Q	E0.82	Nil	1.71	0.60	-1.16	1.86
Yr.	E6.21	5.03	3.35	1.77	6.68	8.53

Next earnings report expected: mid-January Source: S&P, Company Reports
EPS Estimates based on S&P Operating Earnings; historical GAAP earnings are as reported.

General Motors Corporation

Recommendation: **HOLD** ★ ★ ★ ☆ ☆   12-Month Target Price: **$41.00** (as of October 14, 2004)

Business Summary October 15, 2004

General Motors is the world's largest manufacturer of cars and trucks. The majority of its business is derived from the automotive and electronics industries, but it also has financing and insurance operations, and produces products and provides services in other industries. General Motors Automotive (GMA) designs, manufactures and markets vehicles.

In December 2003, GM sold its approximate 19.8% economic interest in Hughes Electronics (GMH) to News Corp., for about $4.1 billion. The company received about $3.1 billion in cash, with the balance in News Corp. ADSs. Concurrent with the transaction, GM split off GMH, and News Corp. purchased an additional 14.2% of GMH's shares.

In the 2000 second quarter, the company retired about 86.4 million common shares, in exchange for about 92 million GMH shares, issuing 1.065 GMH shares for each GM share accepted for tender. GM also contributed $5.6 billion in GMH stock to its pension fund and other company benefit programs. Upon completion of the transactions, GM's economic interest in Hughes was reduced to 30%, from 62%.

In February 1999, GM completed an IPO of 100 million Delphi Automotive Systems common shares. The remaining 82.3% of the shares were distributed to GM shareholders in May 1999.

Chevrolet, Buick, Cadillac, Oldsmobile, Pontiac, Saturn and GEO models accounted for 25.7% of total new U.S. car registrations (including imports) in 2003,

versus 25.4% in 2002, 26.9% in 2001, and 28.6% in 2000. Comparable figures for Chevrolet, GMC, Pontiac and Oldsmobile trucks were 29.9%, 31.0%, 29.2%, and 26.9%, respectively. Worldwide wholesale sales were 8,098,000 vehicles in 2003 and 8,411,000 in 2002. GM's market share in Europe was 9.4% in 2003 and 9.1% in 2002.

General Motors Acceptance Corp. provides vehicle financing, insurance and other financial services.

In December 1997, Hughes defense operations were spun off to shareholders and merged into Raytheon Co. in a $9.8 billion transaction. GM Class H common stock was recapitalized into a new class of GM common stock that tracks the Hughes telecommunications and space business (Hughes Telecom).

In October 1999, the United Auto Workers ratified a four-year agreement with GM, calling for annual increases of 3%, plus cost of living adjustments, and a $1,350 signing bonus. In return, GM obtained greater flexibility to increase productivity. A work stoppage in mid-1998 cost the company about $2 billion in lost profits.

During the 2000 second quarter, the company acquired an equity ownership interest in Fuji Heavy Industries of Japan, the maker of Subaru cars.

In October 2002, GM invested $251 million for a 42.1% controlling stake in a new company that owns selected assets of South Korea's Daewoo Motor Co. GM partners own 24.9%, and Daewoo creditors own the remaining 33%.

Company Financials Fiscal Year ending December 31

Per Share Data ($)

(Year Ended December 31)	2003	2002	2001	2000	1999	1998	1997	1996	1995	1994
Tangible Bk. Val.	35.28	NM	1.93	13.60	16.03	6.25	5.80	7.30	7.68	12.14
Cash Flow	29.60	25.84	24.30	30.04	27.20	22.39	31.97	22.11	24.99	20.72
Earnings	5.03	3.35	1.77	6.68	8.53	4.18	8.62	6.07	7.28	6.20
S&P Core Earnings	7.91	-1.49	-5.77	NA	NA	NA	NA	NA	NA	NA
Dividends	2.00	2.00	2.00	2.00	2.00	2.00	2.00	1.60	1.10	0.80
Payout Ratio	40%	60%	113%	30%	23%	48%	23%	26%	15%	13%
Prices - High	54.39	68.17	67.80	94.62	94.87	76.68	72.43	59.37	53.12	65.37
- Low	29.75	30.80	39.17	48.43	59.75	47.06	52.25	45.75	37.25	36.12
P/E Ratio - High	11	20	38	14	11	18	8	10	7	11
- Low	6	9	22	7	7	11	6	8	5	6

Income Statement Analysis (Million $)

	2003	2002	2001	2000	1999	1998	1997	1996	1995	1994
Revs.	185,524	182,108	169,054	175,332	170,111	155,854	167,970	158,015	163,861	152,172
Oper. Inc.	26,423	18,078	12,853	19,310	21,715	18,715	20,225	19,513	23,811	21,565
Depr.	13,978	12,938	12,908	13,411	12,318	12,201	16,616	11,840	12,022	10,025
Int. Exp.	9,464	7,715	8,590	9,552	7,750	6,893	6,113	5,744	5,352	5,466
Pretax Inc.	3,593	2,080	1,518	7,164	8,722	4,428	7,714	6,676	9,776	8,353
Eff. Tax Rate	20.3%	25.6%	50.6%	33.4%	35.7%	33.0%	13.9%	25.8%	29.1%	32.3%
Net Inc.	2,862	1,736	601	4,452	5,576	2,956	6,698	4,953	6,933	5,659
S&P Core Earnings	4,510	-838	-3,209	NA	NA	NA	NA	NA	NA	NA

Balance Sheet & Other Fin. Data (Million $)

	2003	2002	2001	2000	1999	1998	1997	1996	1995	1994
Cash	32,554	38,274	9,222	10,280	11,428	20,024	11,262	22,262	16,643	10,939
Total Assets	448,507	370,782	323,969	303,100	274,730	257,389	228,888	222,142	217,123	198,598
LT Debt	193,946	135,788	104,638	65,704	62,745	52,574	41,472	39,040	36,675	38,123
Total Debt	271,756	201,940	166,314	144,655	131,688	114,372	93,249	86,266	83,324	73,730
Common Equity	21,662	6,814	19,707	30,175	20,644	14,983	17,505	23,168	2,961	9,155
Cap. Exp.	7,330	7,443	8,631	9,722	7,384	9,618	10,320	9,949	10,077	17,465
Cash Flow	16,840	14,627	13,509	17,753	17,814	15,094	23,242	16,712	18,745	15,363
% Ret. on Assets	0.7	0.5	0.2	1.5	2.1	1.2	3.0	2.3	3.3	2.9
% Ret. on Equity	216.5	12.7	2.0	17.1	30.8	17.8	32.4	21.1	38.3	102.6
% LT Debt of Cap.	85.4	89.1	68.5	68.1	74.8	70.7	69.5	59.7	61.1	74.2

Data as orig reptd.; bef. results of disc opers/spec. items. Per share data adj. for stk. divs.; EPS diluted. E-Estimated. NA-Not Available. NM-Not Meaningful. NR-Not Ranked. UR-Under Review.

Office: 300 Renaissance Center, Detroit, MI 48265-3000.
Telephone: 313-556-5000.
Website: http://www.gm.com
Chrmn & CEO: G.R. Wagoner, Jr.
Vice Chrmn: R.A. Lutz.

Vice Chrmn & CFO: J.M. Devine.
EVP & General Counsel: T.A. Gottschalk.
Chief Acctg Officer: P.R. Bible.
Dirs: P. N. Barnevik, J. H. Bryan, A. M. Codina, G. M. Fisher, K. Katen, K. Kresa, A. G. Lafley, P. A. Laskawy, E. S. O'Neal, E. Pfeiffer.

Founded: in 1908.
Domicile: Delaware.
Employees: 326,000.
S&P Analyst: Efraim Levy, CFA /CB/GG

Genuine Parts

Recommendation: **SELL** ★ ★ ☆ ☆ ☆
SELL SELL HOLD BUY BUY

12-Month Target Price: $37.00
(as of October 15, 2004)

GPC has an approximate 0.07% weighting in the **S&P 500**

Sector: Consumer Discretionary
Sub-Industry: Distributors
Peer Group: Distributors - Larger (Sales)

Summary: GPC is a leading wholesale distributor of automotive replacement parts, industrial parts and supplies, and office products.

Quantitative Evaluations

S&P Earnings & Dividend Rank: A

| D | C | B- | B | B+ | A- | A | A+ |

S&P Fair Value Rank: 1

| **1** | 2 | 3 | 4 | 5 |
| Lowest | | | | Highest |

Fair Value Calc.: $34.10 (Overvalued)

S&P Investability Quotient Percentile

93%

GPC scored higher than 93% of all companies for which an S&P Report is available.

Volatility: Low

| Low | Average | High |

Technical Evaluation: Bullish

Since 10/04, the technical indicators for GPC have been Bullish.

Relative Strength Rank: Strong

75

| 1 Lowest | Highest 99 |

| Price as of 11/12/04: | **$43.08** | 2004E S&P Core EPS: | **$2.10** |

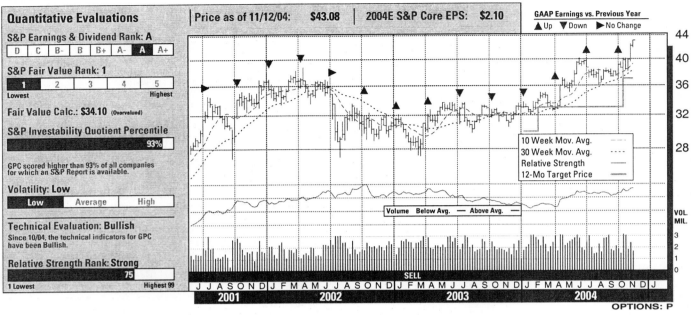

GAAP Earnings vs. Previous Year
▲ Up   ▼ Down   ▶ No Change

10 Week Mov. Avg.
30 Week Mov. Avg.
Relative Strength
12-Mo Target Price

Volume   Below Avg. —   Above Avg. —

SELL

J J A S O N D | J F M A M J J A S O N D | J F M A M J J A S O N D | J F M A M J J A S O N D | J
2001 | **2002** | **2003** | **2004**

OPTIONS: P

Analyst commentary prepared by Efraim Levy, CFA /PMW/BK

Highlights October 18, 2004

- We expect revenues to increase 7% in 2004 and 5% in 2005. Based on our outlook for economic growth, we see sales gains in all four segments: automotive, industrial, office products, and electrical/electronic materials. We expect pricing to remain competitive, and see gross margins as likely to narrow, as lower margin businesses grow more rapidly than higher margin segments. We estimate that a lower effective tax rate will add $0.03 to $0.04 to our 2004 EPS forecast.

- We see longer-term prospects for GPC's auto parts segment enhanced by the rising number and increasing complexity of vehicles. The average vehicle in the U.S. is currently more than eight years old. We expect the company to benefit from an expanding market share, as long-term industry consolidation drives out smaller participants. We also see GPC as likely to use its distribution strength to leverage sales of acquired parts companies.

- What we view as GPC's solid balance sheet, low debt and strong cash flow are resources that could potentially be used to accelerate earnings growth in the longer term.

Investment Rationale/Risk October 18, 2004

- We would avoid the shares, which we view as overvalued, based on our projected price to free cash flow ratio; the shares traded recently at about 16X our 2005 EPS projection and our free cash flow projection. Earnings quality appears high to us, and we expect only minor adjustments to reported EPS using Standard & Poor's Core Earnings methodology. We also believe that an above-average dividend yield will provide some downside for the shares.

- Risks to our recommendation and target price include stronger than expected demand for the company's products, especially in industrial and electric and electronics

- Based on our 2005 estimates, the stock's P/E multiple of 16X and its price to free cash flow ratio of 16X are above the respective averages for key peers of 9X and 10X. Our use of a projected P/E multiple of about 15X applied to our 2005 EPS estimate reflects historical P/E multiple comparisons, and leads to our 12-month target price of $37. Despite what we believe is an above-average, secure and growing dividend payout, we would avoid the shares.

Key Stock Statistics

S&P Core EPS 2005E	**2.34**	52-week Range	**$43.08-30.51**
S&P Oper. EPS 2004E	**2.24**	12 Month P/E	**19.5**
P/E on S&P Oper. EPS 2004E	**19.2**	Beta	**0.42**
S&P Oper. EPS 2005E	**2.46**	Shareholders	**7,719**
Yield (%)	**2.8%**	Market Cap (B)	**$ 7.5**
Dividend Rate/Share	**1.20**	Shares Outstanding (M)	**174.6**

Value of $10,000 invested five years ago: **$ 19,279**

Dividend Data Dividends have been paid since 1948

Amount ($)	Date Decl.	Ex-Div. Date	Stock of Record	Payment Date
0.295	Nov. 17	Dec. 03	Dec. 05	Jan. 02 '04
0.300	Feb. 17	Mar. 03	Mar. 05	Apr. 01 '04
0.300	Apr. 19	Jun. 09	Jun. 11	Jul. 01 '04
0.300	Aug. 16	Sep. 08	Sep. 10	Oct. 01 '04

Revenues/Earnings Data Fiscal year ending December 31

Revenues (Million $)

	2004	2003	2002	2001	2000	1999
1Q	2,197	2,022	1,978	2,055	2,078	1,901
2Q	2,298	2,153	2,131	2,119	2,136	2,023
3Q	2,349	2,189	2,157	2,099	2,160	2,082
4Q	—	2,085	1,994	1,948	2,019	1,975
Yr.	—	8,449	8,259	8,221	8,370	7,982

Earnings Per Share ($)

	2004	2003	2002	2001	2000	1999
1Q	0.57	0.51	0.50	0.52	0.52	0.48
2Q	0.58	0.52	0.55	0.55	0.55	0.52
3Q	0.56	0.51	0.54	0.51	0.53	0.51
4Q	E0.53	0.50	0.52	0.14	0.61	0.61
Yr.	E2.24	2.03	2.10	1.71	2.20	2.11

Next earnings report expected: mid-February Source: S&P, Company Reports
EPS Estimates based on S&P Operating Earnings; historical GAAP earnings are as reported.

STANDARD
&POOR'S

Genuine Parts Company

Recommendation: **SELL** ★ ★ ☆ ☆ ☆   12-Month Target Price: **$37.00** (as of October 15, 2004)

Business Summary October 18, 2004

Genuine Parts is the leading independent U.S. distributor of automotive replacement parts. As of December 2003, it operated 58 NAPA warehouse distribution centers in the U.S., about 900 company-owned jobbing stores, six Rayloc auto parts rebuilding plants, four Balkamp distribution centers, and 12 Johnson Industries facilities. The company has been expanding via a combination of internal growth and acquisitions.

In 2001, GPC ended a streak of 51 consecutive years of higher sales and 40 years of record profits. Revenues increased in 2002 and 2003, and in 2003, the cash dividend was increased for the 48th consecutive year.

The automotive parts segment (53% of 2003 revenues, 55% of profits) serves about 5,000 NAPA Auto Parts jobbing stores, including about 900 company-owned stores, selling to garages, service stations, car and truck dealers, fleet operators, leasing companies, bus and truck lines, etc. It stocks more than 300,000 items. Rebuilt parts are distributed under the Rayloc brand name. Majority-owned Balkamp distributes service and supply items to NAPA distribution centers. UAP Inc. is Canada's leading automotive parts distributor.

The industrial parts segment (27%, 23%) distributes more than 200,000 parts and related supply items, including bearings, power transmission equipment replacement parts including hydraulic and pneumatic products, material handling compo-

nents, agricultural and irrigation equipment, and related items from locations in 48 states and nine Canadian provinces, with approximately 420 branches, 32 service centers, and nine distribution centers.

Through S. P. Richards Co., the office products group (17%, 22%) distributes more than 30,000 office product items, including information processing supplies and office furniture, machines and supplies to office suppliers, from 43 facilities in the U.S. and Canada.

The EIS electrical/electronics materials group (3%, 1%) was formed via the 1998 acquisition of EIS, Inc., for $200 million. EIS is a wholesale distributor of material and supplies to the electrical and electronic industries. The group was expanded in January 1999 through the acquisitions of H. A. Holden, Inc., and Summit Insulation Supply.

In 2003, auto parts sales grew 3%, while industrial parts revenues rose 0.3%, office products sales increased 4%, and the EIS electrical/electronics materials group fell 6%. Sales overall were up 2.3%.

In early 2000, GPC acquired a 15% interest in Mitchell Repair Information, the leading U.S. electronic repair information source in the automotive aftermarket.

Company Financials Fiscal Year ending December 31

Per Share Data ($)

(Year Ended December 31)	2003	2002	2001	2000	1999	1998	1997	1996	1995	1994
Tangible Bk. Val.	12.95	11.88	10.97	10.50	9.80	9.52	10.39	6.41	6.02	8.30
Cash Flow	2.42	2.50	2.21	2.72	2.61	2.36	2.23	2.09	1.91	1.75
Earnings	2.03	2.10	1.71	2.20	2.11	1.98	1.90	1.82	1.68	1.55
S&P Core Earnings	1.95	1.80	1.53	NA	NA	NA	NA	NA	NA	NA
Dividends	1.18	1.16	1.14	1.10	1.03	0.99	0.96	0.89	0.84	0.77
Payout Ratio	58%	55%	67%	50%	49%	50%	51%	49%	50%	49%
Prices - High	33.75	38.80	37.94	26.68	35.75	38.25	35.87	31.66	28.00	26.25
- Low	27.20	27.10	23.91	18.25	22.25	28.25	28.66	26.66	23.66	22.41
P/E Ratio - High	17	18	22	12	17	19	19	17	17	17
- Low	13	13	14	8	11	14	15	15	14	14

Income Statement Analysis (Million $)

	2003	2002	2001	2000	1999	1998	1997	1996	1995	1994
Revs.	8,449	8,259	8,221	8,370	7,982	6,614	6,005	5,720	5,262	4,858
Oper. Inc.	641	676	656	739	718	658	624	596	554	502
Depr.	69.0	70.2	85.8	92.3	90.0	69.3	58.9	50.4	43.2	37.4
Int. Exp.	Nil	Nil	Nil	Nil	Nil	Nil	Nil	NM	NM	1.32
Pretax Inc.	572	606	496	647	628	589	566	545	511	477
Eff. Tax Rate	38.1%	39.3%	40.1%	40.4%	39.9%	39.6%	39.5%	39.5%	39.5%	39.0%
Net Inc.	354	368	297	385	378	356	342	330	309	289
S&P Core Earnings	339	316	265	NA	NA	NA	NA	NA	NA	NA

Balance Sheet & Other Fin. Data (Million $)

	2003	2002	2001	2000	1999	1998	1997	1996	1995	1994
Cash	15.4	20.0	85.8	27.7	45.7	85.0	72.8	67.4	44.3	82.0
Curr. Assets	3,418	3,336	3,146	3,019	2,895	2,683	2,094	1,938	1,764	1,596
Total Assets	4,116	4,020	4,207	4,142	3,930	3,600	2,754	2,522	2,274	2,029
Curr. Liab.	1,017	1,070	919	988	916	818	557	568	476	422
LT Debt	625	675	836	771	702	589	210	110	60.6	11.4
Common Equity	2,312	2,130	2,345	2,261	2,178	2,053	1,859	1,732	1,651	1,526
Total Cap.	3,100	2,950	3,287	3,154	3,014	2,782	2,198	1,953	1,770	1,607
Cap. Exp.	73.9	64.8	41.9	71.1	88.3	88.2	90.4	95.2	91.0	66.0
Cash Flow	423	438	383	478	468	425	401	380	352	326
Curr. Ratio	3.4	3.1	3.4	3.1	3.2	3.3	3.8	3.4	3.7	3.8
% LT Debt of Cap.	20.2	22.9	25.4	24.4	23.3	21.1	9.5	5.6	3.4	0.7
% Net Inc.of Revs.	4.2	4.4	3.6	4.6	4.7	5.4	5.7	5.8	5.9	5.9
% Ret. on Assets	8.6	8.9	7.1	9.5	10.0	11.2	13.0	13.8	14.4	14.9
% Ret. on Equity	15.9	16.4	12.9	17.4	17.9	18.2	19.1	19.5	19.5	19.5

Data as orig reptd.; bef. results of disc opers/spec. items. Per share data adj. for stk. divs.; EPS diluted. E-Estimated. NA-Not Available. NM-Not Meaningful. NR-Not Ranked. UR-Under Review.

Office: 2999 Circle 75 Parkway, Atlanta, GA 30339.
Telephone: 770-953-1700.
Website: http://www.genpt.com
Chrmn: L.L. Prince.
Pres & CEO: T.C. Gallagher.
EVP, CFO & Investor Contact: J.W. Nix 770-953-1700.

SVP & Treas: F.M. Howard.
VP & Secy: C.B. Yancey.
Dirs: M. B. Bullock, R. W. Courts II, J. Douville, R. P. Forrestal, T. C. Gallagher, M. M. Johns, J. D. Johns, J. H. Lanier, W. B. Needham, L. L. Prince, L. G. Steiner, J. B. Williams.

Founded: in 1928.
Domicile: Georgia.
Employees: 30,800.
S&P Analyst: Efraim Levy, CFA /PMW/BK

Recommendation: **BUY** ★★★★☆
SELL SELL HOLD BUY BUY

12-Month Target Price: $61.00
(as of May 05, 2004)

GENZ has an approximate 0.12% weighting in the **S&P 500**

Sector: Health Care
Sub-Industry: Biotechnology
Peer Group: Biotech Therapeutics - Larger Capitalization

Summary: This biopharmaceutical concern makes and markets human therapeutic and diagnostic products. Its largest selling product is Cerezyme, a drug to treat Gaucher disease.

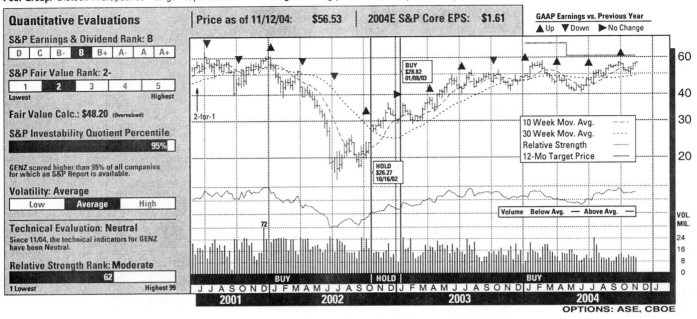

Quantitative Evaluations

S&P Earnings & Dividend Rank: B

| D | C | B- | B | B+ | A- | A | A+ |

S&P Fair Value Rank: 2-

| 1 | 2 | 3 | 4 | 5 |
| Lowest | | | | Highest |

Fair Value Calc.: $48.20 (Overvalued)

S&P Investability Quotient Percentile

95%

GENZ scored higher than 95% of all companies for which an S&P Report is available.

Volatility: Average

| Low | Average | High |

Technical Evaluation: Neutral
Since 11/04, the technical indicators for GENZ have been Neutral.

Relative Strength Rank: Moderate

62

| 1 Lowest | | Highest 99 |

Price as of 11/12/04: $56.53 | **2004E S&P Core EPS:** $1.61

Analyst commentary prepared by Frank DiLorenzo, CFA /PMW/GG

Highlights October 22, 2004

- Third quarter pro forma EPS of $0.49, versus $0.37 in the 2003 period, was $0.06 above our estimate, largely due to solid sales and lower than expected R&D and SG&A spending. Renagel sales of $93.3 million were $4.1 million above our forecast. Cerezyme sales of $208.4 million were $7.8 million above our view, while Fabrazyme revenues of $58.0 million were $11.2 million better than our projection. Aldurazyme sales of $10.3 million were $2.2 million below our estimate, while Synvisc sales of $24.6 million were $6.6 million below our projection.

- The company expects its planned acquisition of ILEX Oncology (ILXO: $25), valued at about $1 billion, to close in the fourth quarter, delayed from previous expectations of a summer closing. We think ILEX could provide slight upside to our 2006 EPS estimate if its clofarabine is approved, and if Campath, a treatment for chronic lymphocytic leukemia (CLL), expands into earlier stage use in CLL. Clofarabine, a treatment for relapsed or refractory acute leukemia in children, is under FDA review, with an advisory panel meeting scheduled for December 1, 2004.

- We project total operating revenues of $2.2 billion for 2004 and $2.5 billion for 2005. Due to a stronger than expected third quarter, we increased our estimate for 2004 pro forma EPS to $1.75, from $1.69. We raised our 2005 EPS estimate to $2.10, from $2.06; and see $2.56 for 2006 ($2.53).

Key Stock Statistics

S&P Oper. EPS 2004E	1.75	52-week Range	$58.08-40.67
P/E on S&P Oper. EPS 2004E	32.3	12 Month P/E	43.5
S&P Oper. EPS 2005E	2.10	Beta	0.67
Yield (%)	Nil	Shareholders	2,364
Dividend Rate/Share	Nil	Market Cap (B)	$ 12.9
Shares Outstanding (M)	228.0		

Value of $10,000 invested five years ago: $ 26,272

Dividend Data

Dividends, paid since 1984, were omitted in 1987.

Investment Rationale/Risk October 22, 2004

- We continue to recommend accumulating the shares, based on what we view as strong financial performance, good growth prospects, and a reasonable valuation. GENZ does not have any blockbuster products, but we regard its product portfolio as well diversified, offering predictable growth. Looking to 2005, we project Renagel sales of $421 million, up 17%. We expect Cerezyme revenues to rise 3%, to $853 million, with Fabrazyme sales of $260 million, versus $206 million seen for 2004. GENZ continues to expect to file for European approval of Myozyme, a treatment for Pompe disease, by the end of 2004. Filings in the U.S. and Japan are planned for mid-2005. We forecast Myozyme sales exceeding $500 million on an annual basis by 2012.

- Risks to our recommendation and target price include increased competition for Renagel and Synvisc, disappointing sales of GENZ's other products, rejection of Myozyme by regulatory authorities, and potential decreases in Medicare reimbursement for certain drugs in 2005.

- The stock's recent forward P/E multiple to growth (PEG) ratio, based on our 2005 EPS estimate, was 1.2X, in line with the weighted average PEG for S&P's biotech peer group, excluding GENZ. Our annualized projected EPS growth rate for GENZ is 21%, versus 23.3% for its peer group. Based on our DCF analysis, our 12-month target price is $61.

Revenues/Earnings Data Fiscal year ending December 31

Revenues (Million $)

	2004	2003	2002	2001	2000	1999
1Q	491.3	314.1	242.2	222.7	170.6	150.8
2Q	549.6	347.7	267.2	239.0	186.7	154.2
3Q	569.2	437.0	272.8	255.1	192.2	157.7
4Q	—	481.2	298.1	265.2	203.0	272.9
Yr.	—	1,714	1,080	981.9	752.5	635.4

Earnings Per Share ($)

	2004	2003	2002	2001	2000	1999
1Q	0.29	0.28	0.14	0.18	0.28	0.25
2Q	0.34	0.32	0.23	0.31	0.39	0.23
3Q	0.42	-0.43	0.25	-0.37	0.32	0.21
4Q	E0.45	0.29	0.20	0.20	-0.34	0.31
Yr.	E1.75	0.42	0.81	0.19	0.68	1.00

Next earnings report expected: mid-February Source: S&P, Company Reports
EPS Estimates based on S&P Operating Earnings; historical GAAP earnings are as reported.

Genzyme Corporation

Recommendation: **BUY** ★★★☆   12-Month Target Price: **$61.00** (as of May 05, 2004)

Business Summary October 22, 2004

Genzyme Corp. develops, manufactures and markets therapeutic and diagnostic products. In July 2003, the company eliminated its tracking stock structure. Shares of Genzyme Biosurgery, which markets biomaterial-based products for treating osteoarthritis and preventing surgical adhesions, and Genzyme Molecular Oncology, which focuses on experimental cancer vaccines, were exchanged for GENZ shares.

The company's lead therapeutic product is Cerezyme, an enzyme replacement therapy for Gaucher disease. Cerezyme sales totaled $739 million in 2003 ($619 million in 2002). An injectable drug, Cerezyme is a recombinant form of the enzyme glucocerbrosidase made in mammalian cell culture. Gaucher disease is a debilitating genetic disease that causes fatigue, anemia, and bone erosion. About 4,100 patients worldwide are treated with Cerezyme.

In 2000, GENZ acquired GelTex Pharmaceuticals, for about $1 billion. GelTex was the company's co-marketing partner for Renagel, a drug used to reduce elevated serum phosphorus in patients on kidney dialysis; 2003 sales were $281 million ($157 million). GENZ markets Renagel in the U.S. and Europe.

Enzyme replacement therapy Fabrazyme was approved in Europe in August 2001 and in the U.S. in April 2003 for the treatment of Fabry disease, a rare genetic disorder. Aldurazyme, an enzyme replacement therapy for MPS-I, was approved by the FDA in April 2003, and by the EU in June 2003. Aldurazyme is partnered with BioMarin through a 50%-owned joint venture. GENZ is developing Myozyme, an enzyme replacement therapy for Pompe disease. An FDA filing for approval is planned by mid-2005. The company is also developing tolevamer to treat clostrid-

ium difficile colitis, with a Phase III trial planned for early 2005. Preliminary results from a Phase I/II trial of CAT-192 to treat scleroderma were released in early 2004. GENZ is evaluating the possibility of a Phase II trial. It is also collaborating with Dyax in developing DX-88 (Phase II) to treat hereditary angioedema, a condition that results in temporary uncontrolled swelling.

Synvisc is an injectable hyaluronan-based biomaterial that is used to treat osteoarthritis of the knee by improving joint lubrication. Seprafilm is used to reduce cellular adhesion in patients undergoing abdominal and pelvic surgery.

GENZ markets Thyrogen as an adjunctive diagnostic for thyroid cancer patients. It also produces active drug substances, intermediates, synthetic phospholipids and other items sold to life sciences concerns.

Diagnostic products include diagnostic components (enzymes, substrates, antibodies and antigens); bulk reagents and devices (including test kits for infectious diseases, cholesterol, pregnancy, etc.); and related items. Genetic diagnostic services include prenatal, postnatal and cancer cytogenetics, fluorescence in situ hybridization, flow cytometry, and molecular (DNA) analysis. In 2004, GENZ acquired IMPATH Inc.'s cancer diagnostic business, for about $215 million in cash.

In September 2003, GENZ acquired SangStat Medical, for about $640 million cash. SangStat's Thymoglobulin is approved by the FDA to treat kidney transplant rejection. In April 2004, RDP58, an experimental SangStat agent, was licensed to Proctor & Gamble in exchange for upfront fees, milestones, and royalties. P&G will initially focus its clinical development of RDP58 in ulcerative colitis.

Company Financials Fiscal Year ending December 31

Per Share Data ($)

(Year Ended December 31)	2003	2002	2001	2000	1999	1998	1997	1996	1995	1994
Tangible Bk. Val.	6.31	NM	6.10	4.05	5.54	5.56	4.75	4.22	5.04	NA
Cash Flow	0.41	1.16	0.75	0.91	1.27	1.02	0.77	-0.01	0.55	NA
Earnings	0.46	0.81	0.19	0.68	1.00	0.74	0.49	-0.23	0.36	NA
S&P Core Earnings	-0.26	0.59	0.02	NA	NA	NA	NA	NA	NA	NA
Dividends	Nil	Nil	Nil	Nil	Nil	0.01	Nil	Nil	Nil	NA
Payout Ratio	Nil	Nil	Nil	Nil	Nil	1%	Nil	Nil	Nil	NA
Prices - High	52.45	58.55	64.00	51.87	31.56	25.00	16.50	19.25	17.51	NA
- Low	28.45	15.64	34.34	19.84	15.37	11.75	10.37	9.87	6.81	NA
P/E Ratio - High	NM	72	NM	77	32	34	34	NM	48	NA
- Low	NM	19	NM	29	15	16	21	NM	19	NA

Income Statement Analysis (Million $)

	2003	2002	2001	2000	1999	1998	1997	1996	1995	1994
Revs.	1,714	1,080	982	753	635	673	597	511	379	NA
Oper. Inc.	463	318	380	-185	280	185	140	128	81.2	NA
Depr.	160	96.0	118	41.2	50.2	45.8	43.7	29.3	22.0	NA
Int. Exp.	26.6	17.8	23.2	14.2	19.9	17.1	8.11	6.84	1.07	NA
Pretax Inc.	2.82	207	56.5	-179	226	164	90.6	-27.3	65.3	NA
Eff. Tax Rate	NM	27.3%	93.1%	51.9%	37.3%	38.2%	37.1%	NM	46.7%	NA
Net Inc.	-67.6	151	3.88	85.9	142	101	57.0	-47.5	34.8	NA
S&P Core Earnings	-61.0	125	5.25	NA	NA	NA	NA	NA	NA	NA

Balance Sheet & Other Fin. Data (Million $)

	2003	2002	2001	2000	1999	1998	1997	1996	1995	1994
Cash	293	373	167	136	94.5	100	66.3	77.2	104	NA
Curr. Assets	1,323	1,100	721	605	605	610	406	491	371	NA
Total Assets	5,005	3,556	3,225	2,499	1,400	1,646	1,203	1,230	855	NA
Curr. Liab.	392	275	243	167	117	197	97.5	110	62.6	NA
LT Debt	Nil	600	600	454	273	275	118	224	124	NA
Common Equity	2,936	2,586	2,280	1,750	1,008	1,167	981	884	659	NA
Total Cap.	3,142	3,268	2,961	2,329	1,280	1,442	1,099	1,108	784	NA
Cap. Exp.	260	220	171	72.6	52.9	55.3	28.5	42.5	48.7	NA
Cash Flow	92.9	247	122	127	192	147	101	-18.2	56.8	NA
Curr. Ratio	3.4	4.0	3.0	3.6	5.2	3.1	4.2	4.5	5.9	NA
% LT Debt of Cap.	Nil	18.4	20.3	19.5	21.3	19.1	10.7	20.2	15.9	NA
% Net Inc.of Revs.	NM	14.0	0.4	11.4	22.4	15.0	9.5	NM	9.2	NA
% Ret. on Assets	NM	4.4	0.2	4.0	10.1	7.1	4.7	NM	4.7	NA
% Ret. on Equity	NM	6.2	0.1	5.5	14.6	9.4	6.1	NM	6.6	NA

Data as orig reptd.; bef. results of disc opers/spec. items. Per share data adj. for stk. divs.; EPS diluted. E-Estimated. NA-Not Available. NM-Not Meaningful. NR-Not Ranked. UR-Under Review.

Office: 500 Kendall St, Cambridge, MA 02142-1108.
Telephone: 617-252-7570.
Email: information@genzyme.com
Website: http://www.genzyme.com
Chrmn, Pres & CEO: H.A. Termeer.
EVP, CFO & Chief Acctg Officer: M.S. Wyzga.

SVP & General Counsel: T.J. DesRosier.
VP & Treas: E.M. Lebson.
Investor Contact: S. Curley 617-768-6140.
Dirs: C. E. Anagnostopoulos, D. A. Berthiaume, H. E. Blair, R. J. Carpenter, C. L. Cooney, V. J. Dzau, C. Mack III, H. A. Termeer.

Founded: in 1991.
Domicile: Massachusetts.
Employees: 5,625.
S&P Analyst: Frank DiLorenzo, CFA /PMW/GG

Georgia-Pacific

Recommendation: **SELL** ★★★★★ 12-Month Target Price: **$24.00**
SELL SELL HOLD BUY BUY (as of May 12, 2004)

GP has an approximate 0.08% weighting in the **S&P 500**

Sector: Materials
Sub-Industry: Paper Products
Peer Group: Paper Products - Larger

Summary: GP, which formerly focused on commodity paper and wood products, became the world's leading tissue maker through the November 2000 takeover of Fort James.

Quantitative Evaluations

Price as of 11/12/04: $36.02 **2004E S&P Core EPS:** $3.25

S&P Earnings & Dividend Rank: B-

| D | C | B- | B | B+ | A- | A | A+ |

S&P Fair Value Rank: 1-

| 1 | 2 | 3 | 4 | 5 |
| Lowest | | | | Highest |

Fair Value Calc.: $26.70 (Overvalued)

S&P Investability Quotient Percentile

42%

GP scored lower than 58% of all companies for which an S&P Report is available.

Volatility: Average

| Low | Average | High |

Technical Evaluation: Neutral

Since 10/04, the technical indicators for GP have been Neutral.

Relative Strength Rank: Moderate

50

| 1 Lowest | | Highest 99 |

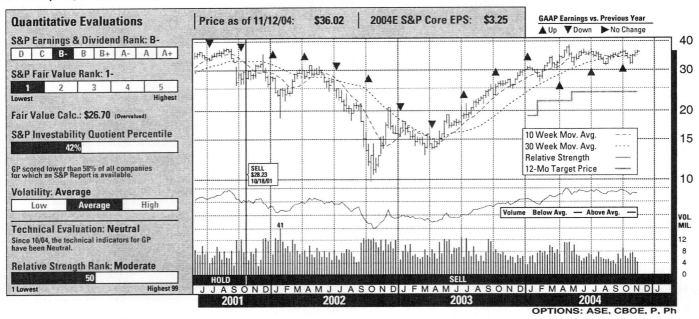

GAAP Earnings vs. Previous Year
▲ Up ▼ Down ▶ No Change

- 10 Week Mov. Avg.
- 30 Week Mov. Avg.
- Relative Strength
- 12-Mo Target Price

SELL $28.23 10/18/01

41

Volume Below Avg. — Above Avg.

VOL. MIL.

HOLD   SELL

2001 2002 2003 2004

OPTIONS: ASE, CBOE, P, Ph

Analyst commentary prepared by Bryon J. Korutz/DC/JWP

Highlights November 11, 2004

- After an expected 4.6% decline in revenues in 2004, we see a 5.7% drop in 2005. The projected drop in 2004 is related to the sales of its building products distribution units, partly offset by greater volumes and prices for paper, packaging, and wood products. We estimate that margins will be pressured by higher raw material and energy costs. In 2005, we see sales pressured by our projected drop in wood products prices.

- Standard & Poor's projects that real GDP will grow 4.5% and 3.5% in 2004 and 2005, respectively. We see this growth supporting improved demand and pricing for GP's paper and packaging products. For consumer products, we see demand and pricing firming, and look for margins to benefit from improved cost structures. We expect that average wood products prices in 2004 will be above 2003 levels. However, we see lumber and structural panels prices coming under pressure, based on our projection that housing starts will have slowed in the latter part of 2004. We see most year-over-year declines occurring in 2005, based on our estimation that housing starts will drop 7% in that year.

- We estimate 2004 Standard & Poor's Core Earnings of $3.25, due to net credits stemming primarily from lower pension assets. The net pension gain, estimated at $0.21, should be partly offset by projected post-retirement expense.

Investment Rationale/Risk November 11, 2004

- We look for wood products supply to outpace demand in late 2004 and into 2005. We are also concerned about higher raw material costs in the consumer products segment. We view favorably GP's debt reduction, but with long term debt of $8.9 billion (49% of total capital), we still view debt levels as elevated. In light of our concerns about the company's potential asbestos liability and high debt levels, we would avoid the shares.

- Risks to our recommendation and target price include a smaller than expected drop in wood products prices.

- Applying a forward peer average P/E of 14.4X to our 2005 EPS estimate, we value the stock at $33. Our second valuation metric, which applies an historical price to sales ratio of 0.19X to our 2005 revenue estimate, values the stock at $16. Our 12-month target price of $24 is a weighted average of these valuation metrics. Although we see an improved pricing and demand environment for GP's consumer products and packaging units, we would avoid the shares given our expected drop in wood products prices in 2005 and uncertainty surrounding its asbestos liability.

Key Stock Statistics

S&P Core EPS 2005E	2.87	52-week Range	$38.60-24.82
S&P Oper. EPS 2004E	3.08	12 Month P/E	14.8
P/E on S&P Oper. EPS 2004E	11.7	Beta	1.81
S&P Oper. EPS 2005E	2.70	Shareholders	39,075
Yield (%)	1.4%	Market Cap (B)	$ 9.3
Dividend Rate/Share	0.50	Shares Outstanding (M)	258.2

Value of $10,000 invested five years ago: **$ 9,568**

Dividend Data Dividends have been paid since 1927

Amount ($)	Date Decl.	Ex-Div. Date	Stock of Record	Payment Date
0.125	Feb. 02	Feb. 10	Feb. 12	Feb. 23 '04
0.125	May. 04	May. 12	May. 14	May. 24 '04
0.125	Jul. 30	Aug. 05	Aug. 09	Aug. 19 '04
0.125	Nov. 05	Nov. 17	Nov. 19	Nov. 29 '04

Revenues/Earnings Data Fiscal year ending December 31

Revenues (Million $)

	2004	2003	2002	2001	2000	1999
1Q	5,222	4,567	5,796	6,317	5,421	3,354
2Q	5,188	5,048	6,222	6,603	5,451	3,809
3Q	4,741	5,278	6,152	6,306	5,310	5,483
4Q	—	5,362	5,101	5,790	5,515	5,151
Yr.	—	20,255	23,271	25,016	22,076	17,796

Earnings Per Share ($)

	2004	2003	2002	2001	2000	1999
1Q	0.55	-0.22	0.26	-0.60	1.11	0.57
2Q	0.88	0.25	-0.36	0.13	1.20	1.20
3Q	0.91	0.75	0.27	-0.80	0.76	1.31
4Q	E0.65	0.12	-0.94	-0.81	-0.98	1.00
Yr.	E3.08	0.90	-0.80	-2.09	1.94	4.07

Next earnings report expected: early-February Source: S&P, Company Reports
EPS Estimates based on S&P Operating Earnings; historical GAAP earnings are as reported.

Georgia-Pacific Corporation

Recommendation: **SELL** ★ ★ ☆ ☆ ☆   12-Month Target Price: **$24.00** (as of May 12, 2004)

Business Summary November 11, 2004

Georgia-Pacific Corp., which produces a wide variety of paper and building products, has undergone a major business transformation over the past few years, from a commodity-based business to a consumer products-based business, through its November 2000 acquisition of Fort James Corp.

The company's consumer products segment (32% of 2003 sales) offers an array of branded and private label bath and facial tissue products, paper towels and napkins to retail and commercial customers in the U.S. and Europe. Leading retail brands include Mardi Gras, Vanity Fair, Quilted Northern, Sparkle, Brawny and Dixie. Through its Dixie business, GP is the largest producer of disposable tableware in North America. The company also supplies disposable tabletop products to the warehouse club channel and to the foodservice industry. GP operates 25 tissue mills in Europe and the U.S., and 12 disposable tableware mills in North America. At December 31, 2003, it had 4.1 million tons of tissue capacity worldwide.

Through the building products segment (25%), GP manufactures wood panels (plywood, oriented strand board and industrial panels), lumber, gypsum products, chemicals and other products. At December 31, 2003, the company had 8.7 billion square feet of structural panels capacity, 1.1 billion square feet of particleboard capacity, 2.4 billion board feet of lumber capacity, and 6.5 billion square feet of gypsum capacity. At December 31, 2003, the company had 127 building products manufacturing facilities in the U.S., seven plants in Canada, four plants in South America, and a joint venture in South Africa.

The company's building products distribution business (19%) sold products made by GP and by third parties to independent dealers, industrial customers, and large home improvement centers throughout the U.S. In May 2004, GP sold its building products distribution business to Ceberus Capital Management L.P., a New York-based investment firm, for $810 million, subject to working capital adjustments.

In packaging (12%), GP holds fourth place in the North American containerboard market, with 3.7 million tons of production capacity. The company's 54 packaging plants use about 70% of the segment's containerboard production. The remaining 30% is sold to independent box converters in the U.S.

The bleached pulp and paper segment (12%) makes market and fluff pulp, communications paper, uncoated free-sheet and bleached board. At December 31, 2003, the company had an annual production capacity of uncoated free-sheet of 1.1 million tons, 1.7 million tons of market pulp, 0.6 million tons of bleached board, 0.85 million tons of fluff pulp, and 0.3 million tons of kraft paper. In November 2002, GP sold a 60% controlling interest in Unisource, its distribution business, to Bain Capital. Starting in November 2002, the remaining 40% equity investment was included in the bleached pulp and paper segment.

Company Financials Fiscal Year ending December 31

Per Share Data ($)

(Year Ended December 31)	2003	2002	2001	2000	1999	1998	1997	1996	1995	1994
Tangible Bk. Val.	NM	NM	NM	NM	6.12	8.24	10.43	10.19	9.88	4.52
Cash Flow	5.06	3.53	3.80	7.08	8.75	7.26	4.53	6.04	9.89	6.35
Earnings	0.90	-0.80	-2.09	1.94	4.07	0.61	-0.47	0.89	5.65	1.83
S&P Core Earnings	0.96	0.48	-3.47	NA	NA	NA	NA	NA	NA	NA
Dividends	0.50	0.50	0.50	0.50	0.50	0.50	1.00	1.00	0.95	0.80
Payout Ratio	56%	NM	NM	26%	12%	82%	NM	112%	17%	44%
Prices - High	31.11	31.60	37.65	51.93	54.12	40.50	54.28	40.50	47.87	39.50
- Low	12.77	9.81	25.39	19.31	29.34	18.68	28.00	31.50	32.87	28.37
P/E Ratio - High	35	NM	NM	27	13	66	NM	46	8	22
- Low	14	NM	NM	10	7	31	NM	35	6	16

Income Statement Analysis (Million $)

	2003	2002	2001	2000	1999	1998	1997	1996	1995	1994
Revs.	20,255	23,271	25,016	22,076	17,796	13,223	12,968	13,024	14,292	12,738
Oper. Inc.	2,234	2,233	2,541	2,262	2,793	1,781	1,159	1,672	2,854	1,773
Depr.	1,045	1,030	1,343	910	815	1,211	910	937	762	805
Int. Exp.	833	841	1,080	595	426	372	381	470	434	460
Pretax Inc.	335	-508	-295	553	1,164	198	-118	296	1,697	572
Eff. Tax Rate	32.5%	NM	NM	38.0%	38.5%	43.9%	45.1%	45.6%	40.1%	43.0%
Net Inc.	226	-190	-476	343	716	111	-86.0	161	1,018	326
S&P Core Earnings	242	123	-791	NA	NA	NA	NA	NA	NA	NA

Balance Sheet & Other Fin. Data (Million $)

	2003	2002	2001	2000	1999	1998	1997	1996	1995	1994
Cash	51.0	35.0	31.0	40.0	25.0	5.00	8.00	10.0	11.0	53.0
Curr. Assets	4,598	4,706	5,460	6,262	4,536	2,640	2,911	2,615	2,595	1,862
Total Assets	24,405	24,629	26,364	29,273	15,380	11,538	11,779	12,818	12,335	10,728
Curr. Liab.	4,423	4,045	5,810	5,676	3,821	2,381	2,698	2,490	1,762	2,325
LT Debt	9,170	10,185	10,221	13,218	4,846	3,395	3,057	4,371	4,704	3,904
Common Equity	5,394	4,560	4,905	5,577	3,750	-3,209	3,523	3,521	3,519	2,620
Total Cap.	16,150	16,187	16,972	20,950	9,756	7,591	7,539	9,053	9,370	7,578
Cap. Exp.	710	693	739	906	721	632	731	1,059	1,339	894
Cash Flow	1,271	840	867	1,253	1,531	1,322	824	1,098	1,780	1,131
Curr. Ratio	1.0	1.2	0.9	1.1	1.2	1.1	1.1	1.1	1.5	0.8
% LT Debt of Cap.	56.8	62.9	60.2	63.1	49.7	44.7	40.5	48.3	50.2	51.5
% Net Inc.of Revs.	1.1	NM	NM	1.6	4.0	0.8	1.0	1.2	7.2	2.6
% Ret. on Assets	0.9	NM	NM	1.5	5.3	1.0	1.0	1.3	8.8	3.1
% Ret. on Equity	4.5	NM	NM	7.4	20.6	3.3	3.7	4.6	33.2	13.0

Data as orig reptd.; bef. results of disc opers/spec. items. Per share data adj. for stk. divs.; EPS diluted. E-Estimated. NA-Not Available. NM-Not Meaningful. NR-Not Ranked. UR-Under Review.

Office: 133 Peachtree Street, N.E., Atlanta, GA 30303-1847.
Telephone: 404-652-4000.
Website: http://www.gp.com
Chrmn & CEO: A.D. Correll.
Pres & COO: L. Thomas.
EVP & CFO: D.W. Huff.

EVP & General Counsel: J. Kelley.
VP & Investor Contact: M. Nollen 404-652-4720.
Dirs: J. S. Balloun, B. L. Bowles, W. H. Clark, Jr., A. D. Correll, D. V. Fites, R. V. Giordano, D. R. Goode, M. D. Ivester, L. W. Sullivan, L. M. Thomas, J. B. Williams, J. D. Zeglis.

Founded: in 1927.
Domicile: Georgia.
Employees: 61,000.
S&P Analyst: Bryon J. Korutz/DC/JWP

Gilead Sciences

Recommendation: **HOLD** ★ ★ ★ ☆ ☆
SELL SELL HOLD BUY BUY

12-Month Target Price: **$37.00**
(as of October 22, 2004)

GILD has an approximate 0.14% weighting in the **S&P 500**

Sector: Health Care
Sub-Industry: Biotechnology
Peer Group: Biotech Therapeutics - Larger Capitalization

Summary: This biopharmaceutical company is engaged in the discovery, development and commercialization of treatments to fight bacterial, fungal and viral infections.

Quantitative Evaluations

S&P Earnings & Dividend Rank: B-

D	C	B-	B	B+	A-	A	A+

S&P Fair Value Rank: 1-

1	2	3	4	5
Lowest				Highest

Fair Value Calc.: $29.40 (Overvalued)

S&P Investability Quotient Percentile

80%

GILD scored higher than 80% of all companies for which an S&P Report is available.

Volatility: Average

Low	Average	High

Technical Evaluation: Bullish
Since 11/04, the technical indicators for GILD have been Bullish.

Relative Strength Rank: Moderate

49

1 Lowest   Highest 99

Price as of 11/12/04:	$36.94	2004E S&P Core EPS:	$0.72

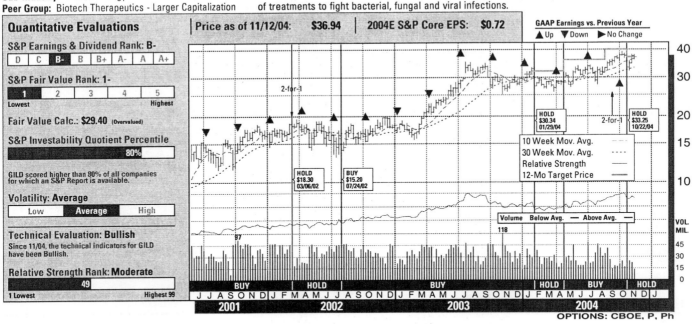

GAAP Earnings vs. Previous Year
▲ Up ▼ Down ▶ No Change

10 Week Mov. Avg.
30 Week Mov. Avg.
Relative Strength
12-Mo Target Price

Volume Below Avg. — Above Avg.

OPTIONS: CBOE, P, Ph

Analyst commentary prepared by Frank DiLorenzo, CFA /CB/BK

Highlights October 25, 2004

- GILD reported third quarter EPS of $0.25, which was $0.04 above our estimate, largely due to lower than expected costs. Combined sales of HIV products Viread, Truvada and Emtriva of $228.1 million were $4 million above our forecast. Hepsera sales of $29.7 million met our view, while AmBisome sales of $49.8 million were $3.4 million above our estimate. Truvada, a once-daily tablet that combines Viread and Emtriva, was approved by the FDA in August. GILD continues to work with Bristol-Myers Squibb (BMY: hold, $24) on a potential single-tablet triple formulation drug combining Viread, Emtriva and BMY's Sustiva. However, a deal has not been finalized.

- In October, GILD announced it would stop development on anti-HIV treatments GS 7340, which was in Phase I/II studies, and GS 9005, which was in Phase I testing. GS 7340 is a nucleotide reverse transcriptase inhibitor, while GS 9005 is a protease inhibitor. GILD does not have any new investigational candidates in Phase II or Phase III trials. The company continues to focus its research efforts on anti-infective therapeutics.

- We project combined sales of Viread, Emtriva and Truvada of $897 million for 2004 and $1.07 billion for 2005. We forecast Hepsera revenues of $108 million for 2004 and $144 million for 2005. We project AmBisome sales of $203 million for 2004, and see revenues essentially flat in 2005. We estimate 2004 EPS of $0.94, up from our prior $0.89 view. For 2005, we are looking for EPS of $1.10, boosted from our prior $1.05 estimate.

Key Stock Statistics

S&P Oper. EPS 2004E	0.94	52-week Range	$39.10-25.75
P/E on S&P Oper. EPS 2004E	39.3	12 Month P/E	30.3
S&P Oper. EPS 2005E	1.10	Beta	0.85
Yield (%)	Nil	Shareholders	511
Dividend Rate/Share	Nil	Market Cap (B)	$ 16.0
Shares Outstanding (M)	432.9		

Value of $10,000 invested five years ago: **$ 64,120**

Dividend Data

Amount ($)	Date Decl.	Ex-Div. Date	Stock of Record	Payment Date
2-for-1	Jul. 28	Sep. 07	Aug. 12	Sep. 03 '04

Investment Rationale/Risk October 25, 2004

- Following release of third quarter results, we downgraded our recommendation to hold, from accumulate, as a result of our concerns over GILD's pipeline and its long-term implications for growth. We view the discontinuations of GS 9005 and GS 7340 as a disappointment, since GILD's pipeline now lacks any new investigational compounds. Since GILD acquired Triangle Pharmaceuticals in January 2003, there has been a relative lack of M&A activity by the firm to shore up its late stage pipeline. We believe that an acquisition or partnership for a later stage clinical candidate is likely by 2005. However, GILD is entitled to royalties from Macugen, an eye treatment from Pfizer and Eyetech. The FDA is reviewing this medication, and we are assuming that it will garner approval. On balance, we are concerned that the gap in the firm's pipeline could result in a sharp moderation in growth by 2007 unless new products are added to the fold.

- Risks to our recommendation and target price include uncertainty over Viread inventory changes that could result in an inaccurate picture of demand for the drug, disappointing sales of GILD's other drugs, increased competition, and a continued lack of progress in the pipeline.

- We project annualized EPS growth of 20.5% through 2007, resulting in a PEG ratio of 1.5X, based on our 2005 EPS estimate of $1.10. This compares with S&P's biotech peer average PEG of 1.2X, exclusive of GILD. Based on our DCF model, our 12-month target price is $37.

Revenues/Earnings Data Fiscal year ending December 31

Revenues (Million $)

	2004	2003	2002	2001	2000	1999
1Q	309.1	165.1	78.42	57.84	47.71	4.94
2Q	319.7	238.9	109.4	50.69	50.13	8.68
3Q	326.2	200.4	134.0	50.92	45.24	38.39
4Q	—	263.5	145.0	74.33	52.48	48.78
Yr.	—	867.9	466.8	233.8	195.6	169.0

Earnings Per Share ($)

	2004	2003	2002	2001	2000	1999
1Q	0.25	-1.10	-0.01	-0.06	-0.01	-0.06
2Q	0.25	0.23	0.05	-0.09	-0.01	-0.06
3Q	0.25	0.17	0.05	-0.07	-0.05	-0.09
4Q	E0.22	0.43	0.09	0.31	-0.05	-0.03
Yr.	E0.94	-0.18	0.17	0.13	-0.12	-0.19

Next earnings report expected: late-January Source: S&P, Company Reports
EPS Estimates based on S&P Operating Earnings; historical GAAP earnings are as reported.

Gilead Sciences, Inc.

Recommendation:  **HOLD** ★★★☆☆   12-Month Target Price: **$37.00** (as of October 22, 2004)

Business Summary October 25, 2004

Gilead Sciences focuses on the research, development, and marketing of anti-infective medications, with a primary focus on treatments for HIV.

In October 2001, the FDA approved Viread (tenofovir) to treat HIV patients. In addition to being used on patients who have become resistant to other reverse transcriptase inhibitors, clinical data on Viread's use in treating naive patients was expected to drive sales in the frontline treatment setting. EU approval was granted in February 2002. Viread sales grew to $566 million in 2003, from $226 million in 2002, and provided 68% of total product revenues.

In January 2003, GILD acquired Triangle Pharmaceuticals (VIRS) for about $464 million in cash. VIRS's lead product was Emtriva (emtricitabine), an anti-HIV medication. Emtriva was approved by the FDA in July 2003, and in Europe in October 2003. In August 2004, the FDA approved Truvada, a once-daily combination tablet formulated with Viread and Emtriva. Separately, emtricitabine is undergoing Phase III trials to treat hepatitis B.

In September 2002, Hepsera (adefovir dipivoxil) was approved by the FDA. In March 2003, Hepsera was approved in the EU. GILD directly markets Viread and Hepsera in the U.S. and the EU. The company out-licensed rights to adefovir for Asia and Latin America to GlaxoSmithKline (GSK) in exchange for milestones and royalties. A Phase II/III trial of adefovir was begun by GSK in China in December 2002.

AmBisome is a liposomal formulation of amphotericin B, an antifungal agent that can attack and kill a broad variety of life-threatening fungal infections. Amphotericin B also has serious side effects. By delivering amphotericin B in a proprietary liposomal formulation, studies have shown it to be effective in reducing the rate and severity of kidney toxicity and injection-related reactions. AmBisome is co-marketed in the U.S. with Fujisawa Healthcare, and is also approved by the FDA to treat cryptococcal meningitis in AIDS patients. Sales were $198 million in 2003, up from $186 million in 2002.

Through a partnership with F. Hoffmann-La Roche of Switzerland, GILD has developed Tamiflu, an orally administered treatment for influenza A and B, approved by the FDA in 1999. Japanese approval was granted in December 2000, as was FDA approval for pediatric use. F. Hoffmann-La Roche markets the drug, paying royalties to the company. In November 2000, Tamiflu was approved by the FDA to prevent influenza; EU approval came in June 2002.

The company also markets Vistide, a treatment for cytomegalovirus (CMV) retinitis in AIDS patients, and DaunoXome, a liposomal formulation of the anticancer agent daunorubicin, for treating AIDS-related Kaposi's sarcoma.

In October 2004, GILD announced that it was discontinuing development of anti-HIV drug GS 7340, which was in a Phase I/II trial. The company will also stop developing protease inhibitor GS 9005, another anti-HIV agent that recently completed a Phase I/II trial. GILD is working with Genelabs Technologies, Inc. on research into compounds that may treat hepatitis C by inhibiting HCV polymerase.

In July 2003, GILD outlicensed Japanese rights to Viread, Emtriva, and the coformulated tablet of the two drugs to Japan Tobacco (JT). It is entitled to an up-front fee, milestones, and royalties. In April 2004, Viread was approved in Japan.

Company Financials Fiscal Year ending December 31

Per Share Data ($)

(Year Ended December 31)	2003	2002	2001	2000	1999	1998	1997	1996	1995	1994
Tangible Bk. Val.	2.35	1.45	1.17	0.93	0.84	0.94	1.15	1.27	0.80	0.56
Cash Flow	-0.13	0.21	0.16	-0.09	-0.16	-0.22	0.13	-0.08	-0.14	-0.15
Earnings	-0.18	0.17	0.13	-0.12	-0.19	-0.23	-0.12	-0.10	-0.21	-0.17
S&P Core Earnings	-0.33	0.02	-0.27	NA	NA	NA	NA	NA	NA	NA
Dividends	Nil	Nil	Nil	Nil	Nil	Nil	Nil	Nil	Nil	Nil
Payout Ratio	Nil	Nil	Nil	Nil	Nil	Nil	Nil	Nil	Nil	Nil
Prices - High	35.30	20.00	18.41	14.76	11.93	5.53	5.90	5.31	4.28	1.78
- Low	15.62	13.04	6.21	5.40	4.40	2.25	2.64	2.03	1.15	0.82
P/E Ratio - High	NM	NM	NM	NM	NM	NM	NM	NM	NM	NM
- Low	NM	NM	NM	NM	NM	NM	NM	NM	NM	NM

Income Statement Analysis (Million $)

	2003	2002	2001	2000	1999	1998	1997	1996	1995	1994
Revs.	868	467	234	196	169	32.6	40.0	33.4	2.70	4.08
Oper. Inc.	361	95.4	-106	-40.3	-39.2	-71.6	-42.8	-31.6	-28.8	-26.8
Depr.	20.9	14.4	14.7	12.0	12.6	2.76	2.98	4.48	3.25	2.77
Int. Exp.	21.9	13.9	14.0	Nil	6.52	0.19	0.49	0.71	0.61	0.30
Pretax Inc.	-168	73.4	55.3	-41.9	-65.6	-56.1	28.0	-21.7	-27.4	-25.7
Eff. Tax Rate	NM	1.77%	7.48%	NM	NM	NM	NM	NM	NM	NM
Net Inc.	-72.0	72.1	51.2	-43.1	-66.5	-56.1	28.0	-21.7	-27.4	-25.7
S&P Core Earnings	-133	8.55	-108	NA	NA	NA	NA	NA	NA	NA

Balance Sheet & Other Fin. Data (Million $)

	2003	2002	2001	2000	1999	1998	1997	1996	1995	1994
Cash	707	942	583	513	294	32.5	32.0	132	27.4	13.0
Curr. Assets	1,266	1,184	708	594	372	288	340	300	157	117
Total Assets	1,555	1,288	795	678	437	303	352	311	167	127
Curr. Liab.	186	105	80.1	58.2	47.9	31.8	33.4	16.1	11.7	8.84
LT Debt	345	595	250	252	84.8	0.56	1.33	2.91	3.48	5.45
Common Equity	1,003	571	452	351	297	271	317	292	151	115
Total Cap.	1,348	1,166	703	603	382	271	318	295	154	91.2
Cap. Exp.	38.6	17.6	26.3	15.6	12.5	2.50	3.86	3.72	0.57	NA
Cash Flow	-51.1	86.5	65.9	-31.1	-53.9	-53.3	31.0	-17.3	-24.2	-22.9
Curr. Ratio	6.8	11.3	8.8	10.2	7.8	9.1	10.2	18.7	13.5	13.2
% LT Debt of Cap.	25.6	51.0	35.6	41.8	22.2	0.2	0.0	1.0	2.3	6.0
% Net Inc.of Revs.	NM	15.4	21.9	NM	NM	NM	69.9	NM	NM	NM
% Ret. on Assets	NM	6.9	6.9	NM	NM	NM	8.4	NM	NM	NM
% Ret. on Equity	NM	14.1	12.7	NM	NM	NM	9.2	NM	NM	NM

Data as orig. reptd.; bef. results of disc. opers. and/or spec. items. Prior to 1995 (nine mos.), yrs. ended Mar. 31 of fol cal. yr. Per share data adj. for stk. divs.; EPS diluted (primary prior to 1998). E-Estimated. NA-Not Available. NM-Not Meaningful. NR-Not Ranked.

Office: 333 Lakeside Drive, Foster City, CA 94404.
Telephone: 650-574-3000.
Email: investor_relations@gilead.com
Website: http://www.gilead.com
Chrmn: J.M. Denny.

Pres & CEO: J.C. Martin.
EVP & CFO: J.F. Milligan.
Investor Contact: S. Hubbard (650) 522-5715.
Dirs: P. Berg, E. F. Davignon, J. M. Denny, J. C. Martin, G. E. Moore, N. G. Moore, G. P. Schultz, G. E. Wilson.

Founded: in 1987.
Domicile: Delaware.
Employees: 1,425.
S&P Analyst: Frank DiLorenzo,CFA /CB/BK

Gillette Co.

Recommendation: **HOLD** ★★★☆☆
SELL | SELL | HOLD | BUY | BUY

12-Month Target Price: **$43.00**
(as of July 27, 2004)

G has an approximate 0.40% weighting in the **S&P 500**

Sector: Consumer Staples
Sub-Industry: Personal Products
Peer Group: Larger Personal Care Cos.

Summary: This company is a global manufacturer of razors and blades, hair care products, toiletries, writing instruments, small appliances and alkaline batteries.

Quantitative Evaluations

S&P Earnings & Dividend Rank: A-

| D | C | B- | B | B+ | **A-** | A | A+ |

S&P Fair Value Rank: 3+

| 1 | 2 | **3** | 4 | 5 |
| Lowest | | | | Highest |

Fair Value Calc.: $42.50 (Slightly Overvalued)

S&P Investability Quotient Percentile

99%

G scored higher than 99% of all companies for which an S&P Report is available.

Volatility: Low

| **Low** | Average | High |

Technical Evaluation: Bullish
Since 11/04, the technical indicators for G have been Bullish.

Relative Strength Rank: Moderate

62

1 Lowest   Highest 99

Price as of 11/12/04: $44.35 | **2004E S&P Core EPS: $1.51**

GAAP Earnings vs. Previous Year
▲ Up ▼ Down ► No Change

- 10 Week Mov. Avg.
- 30 Week Mov. Avg.
- Relative Strength
- 12-Mo Target Price

Volume Below Avg. — Above Avg.

OPTIONS: ASE, CBOE, P, Ph

Analyst commentary prepared by Howard Choe/BK

Highlights August 24, 2004

- We expect 2004 revenues to increase approximately 8%, reflecting solid volume growth and modest foreign exchange gains. We see volume growth led by the blade and razor division, driven by new product introductions. We expect high-single digit sales growth in the Braun, oral care and personal care divisions, also largely driven by new product introductions. Duracell sales gains are likely to be modest due to intense domestic competition for Duracell and difficult sales comparisons.

- We expect gross margins to widen approximately 50 basis points, mainly reflecting cost savings from G's Functional Excellence efficiency program, partially offset by higher raw material costs. Operating margins should widen considerably, mainly on benefits of cost cutting and lower general and administrative expenses.

- We expect margin expansion to lead to a 21% increase in 2004 EPS, to $1.62, from $1.34 in 2003. We estimate 2004 Standard & Poor's Core Earnings per share of $1.51, mainly reflecting adjustments related to projected stock option expense.

Investment Rationale/Risk August 24, 2004

- We maintain our hold opinion on the shares, reflecting our view of solid execution, partially offset by concerns over industry competition and valuation. G continues to bolster its financial condition, market position, and infrastructure. However, we believe G's qualities and growth potential are adequately reflected in its current valuation. In addition, the financially attractive categories of wet shaving and batteries have become increasingly competitive with companies such as Energizer and Rayovac.

- Risks to our recommendation and target price include a potential decline in product pricing in the shaving and battery categories due to competitive activity, and low acceptance of new products by consumers.

- G recently traded at a 25X current P/E, a 14% premium to the large cap companies in our household and personal care coverage universe. Given an earnings outlook that is just slightly ahead of the pack, we do not believe such a large premium is warranted. We view the shares as fairly valued at a modest discount to our 12-month target price of $43.

Key Stock Statistics

S&P Core EPS 2005E	1.69	52-week Range	$44.35-32.55
S&P Oper. EPS 2004E	1.66	12 Month P/E	27.4
P/E on S&P Oper. EPS 2004E	26.7	Beta	0.31
S&P Oper. EPS 2005E	1.85	Shareholders	43,106
Yield (%)	1.5%	Market Cap (B)	$ 44.0
Dividend Rate/Share	0.65	Shares Outstanding (M)	992.8

Value of $10,000 invested five years ago: **$ 13,747**

Dividend Data Dividends have been paid since 1906

Amount ($)	Date Decl.	Ex-Div. Date	Stock of Record	Payment Date
0.163	Dec. 10	Jan. 29	Feb. 02	Mar. 05 '04
0.163	Mar. 25	Apr. 29	May. 03	Jun. 04 '04
0.163	Jun. 17	Jul. 29	Aug. 02	Sep. 03 '04
0.163	Oct. 21	Oct. 28	Nov. 01	Dec. 03 '04

Revenues/Earnings Data Fiscal year ending December 31

Revenues (Million $)

	2004	2003	2002	2001	2000	1999
1Q	2,235	1,971	1,732	1,763	1,907	1,939
2Q	2,443	2,254	2,024	2,118	2,249	2,414
3Q	2,691	2,405	2,168	2,362	2,321	2,509
4Q	—	2,622	2,529	2,718	2,818	3,035
Yr.	—	9,252	8,453	8,961	9,295	9,897

Earnings Per Share ($)

	2004	2003	2002	2001	2000	1999
1Q	0.37	0.25	0.21	0.17	0.24	0.24
2Q	0.42	0.33	0.28	0.22	0.28	0.26
3Q	0.47	0.41	0.33	0.28	0.33	0.32
4Q	E0.40	0.35	0.32	0.19	-0.08	0.32
Yr.	E1.66	1.34	1.14	0.86	0.77	1.14

Next earnings report expected: late-January Source: S&P, Company Reports
EPS Estimates based on S&P Operating Earnings; historical GAAP earnings are as reported.

The Gillette Company

Recommendation: **HOLD** ★ ★ ★ ☆ ☆   12-Month Target Price: **$43.00** (as of July 27, 2004)

Business Summary August 24, 2004

Founded in 1901, Gillette is a world leader in personal grooming, alkaline batteries, toothbrushes and oral care supplies. In addition to its core MACH3 blades and razors, the company holds a leading market share in most of its businesses, which include Duracell batteries, toiletries and cosmetics (Right Guard and Soft & Dri), Braun electric shavers and appliances, and Oral-B dental products.

G's blade and razor business is its bread and butter, accounting for 41% of sales in 2002, and 69% of operating profits, up from 38% and 65%, respectively, in 2001. The company is the world leader in blades and razors, selling systems under the Mach3Turbo, Mach3, SensorExcel, Sensor, Atra and Trac II brands, and disposable razors under the Custom Plus and Good News brands. In November 2002, G introduced Sensor 3, a premium triple blade disposable razor for men and women. Female shaving systems are sold under the Venus, SensorExcel for Women and Sensor for Women brands, as well as disposable brands, Agility and Daisy.

The company also sells electric shavers and electric hair epilators as part of the Braun products division. These products include the world's most popular foil electric shaver for men and women. The Toiletries segment includes shave preparations, after-shave products, deodorants, and antiperspirants, including the Gillette series, Satin Care, Right Guard, Soft & Dri and Dry Idea brands.

G holds the global leadership position in manual and power toothbrushes under the Oral-B brand. The company also offers power toothbrushes under the Braun brand.

In September 1996, the company acquired Duracell International Inc., the world's leading manufacturer and marketer of high-performance alkaline batteries, with a 40% market share. In 2002, Duracell products accounted for 22% of total sales and 12% of operating profits, versus 26% and 12%, respectively, in 2001. In January 2003, G announced a price-deal alignment program in the U.S., designed to restore brand value to Duracell. The program's goal is to simplify product offerings to the consumer, with fewer SKUs and price points; improve everyday pricing; and engage in more efficient trade and consumer promotion, as well as increase investment in category and brand-building activities.

G believes that geographic expansion has played an important role in the company's success, with businesses in developing markets showing especially significant growth. Manufacturing operations are conducted at 32 facilities in 15 countries, and products are distributed through wholesalers, retailers and agents in more than 200 countries and territories.

Company Financials Fiscal Year ending December 31

Per Share Data ($)

(Year Ended December 31)	2003	2002	2001	2000	1999	1998	1997	1996	1995	1994
Tangible Bk. Val.	0.70	0.86	0.74	0.33	0.58	1.82	2.08	1.57	1.34	1.22
Cash Flow	1.91	1.61	1.34	1.28	1.58	1.34	1.61	1.20	1.21	1.03
Earnings	1.34	1.14	0.86	0.77	1.14	0.95	1.25	0.86	0.93	0.79
S&P Core Earnings	1.31	0.95	0.72	NA	NA	NA	NA	NA	NA	NA
Dividends	0.65	0.65	0.65	0.64	0.57	0.49	0.41	0.35	0.29	0.24
Payout Ratio	49%	57%	76%	82%	50%	52%	33%	40%	31%	31%
Prices - High	36.78	37.30	36.37	43.00	64.37	62.65	53.18	38.87	27.68	19.12
- Low	28.00	27.57	24.50	27.12	33.06	35.31	36.00	24.12	17.68	14.43
P/E Ratio - High	27	33	42	56	56	66	43	45	30	24
- Low	21	24	28	35	29	37	29	28	19	18

Income Statement Analysis (Million $)

	2003	2002	2001	2000	1999	1998	1997	1996	1995	1994
Revs.	9,252	8,453	8,961	9,295	9,897	10,056	10,062	9,698	6,795	6,070
Oper. Inc.	2,581	2,270	2,179	2,619	2,605	2,783	2,746	2,431	1,620	1,442
Depr.	578	500	509	535	500	459	422	381	249	215
Int. Exp.	54.0	84.0	145	223	136	94.0	78.0	77.0	59.0	61.0
Pretax Inc.	1,964	1,752	1,342	1,288	1,930	1,669	2,221	1,525	1,297	1,104
Eff. Tax Rate	30.0%	31.0%	32.2%	36.3%	34.7%	35.2%	35.7%	37.8%	36.5%	36.8%
Net Inc.	1,375	1,209	910	821	1,260	1,081	1,427	949	824	698
S&P Core Earnings	1,331	991	763	NA	NA	NA	NA	NA	NA	NA

Balance Sheet & Other Fin. Data (Million $)

	2003	2002	2001	2000	1999	1998	1997	1996	1995	1994
Cash	681	801	947	62.0	80.0	102	105	84.0	48.0	46.0
Curr. Assets	3,650	3,797	4,455	4,682	5,132	5,440	4,690	4,732	3,105	2,747
Total Assets	9,955	9,863	9,969	10,402	11,786	11,902	10,864	10,435	6,340	5,494
Curr. Liab.	3,658	3,488	4,838	5,471	4,180	3,478	2,641	2,935	2,124	1,783
LT Debt	2,453	2,457	1,654	1,650	2,931	2,256	1,476	1,490	691	715
Common Equity	2,224	2,260	2,137	2,023	2,975	4,453	4,748	4,396	2,416	1,963
Total Cap.	5,368	5,455	4,292	4,164	6,452	7,249	6,715	6,310	3,296	2,937
Cap. Exp.	408	405	624	793	932	1,000	973	830	471	400
Cash Flow	1,953	1,709	1,419	1,356	1,756	1,540	1,849	1,330	1,068	909
Curr. Ratio	1.0	1.1	0.9	0.9	1.2	1.6	1.8	1.6	1.5	1.5
% LT Debt of Cap.	45.7	45.0	38.5	39.6	45.4	31.1	22.0	23.6	21.0	24.4
% Net Inc.of Revs.	14.9	14.3	10.2	8.8	12.7	10.7	14.2	9.8	12.1	11.5
% Ret. on Assets	13.9	12.2	8.9	7.4	10.6	9.5	13.4	9.8	14.1	13.2
% Ret. on Equity	61.3	54.6	44.8	30.7	33.8	23.4	31.2	23.0	37.6	40.8

Data as orig reptd.; bef. results of disc opers/spec. items. Per share data adj. for stk. divs. Bold denotes primary EPS - prior periods restated. E-Estimated. NA-Not Available. NM-Not Meaningful. NR-Not Ranked. UR-Under Review.

Office: Prudential Tower Building, Boston, MA 02199.
Telephone: 617-421-7000.
Email: investorrelations@gillette.com
Website: http://www.gillette.com
Chrmn, Pres & CEO: J.M. Kilts.
Vice Chrmn: E.F. DeGraan.
SVP & CFO: C.W. Cramb.

SVP & General Counsel: R.K. Willard.
VP & Chief Acctg Officer: J.J. Schena.
Investor Contact: L. Barrett 617-421-7968.
Dirs: E. F. DeGraan, R. K. Deromedi, W. H. Gantz, M. B. Gifford, R. J. Groves, D. F. Hightower, H. H. Jacobi, N. J. Karch, J. M. Kilts, F. H. Langhammer, J. P. Lemann, M. M. Yang.

Founded: in 1901.
Domicile: Delaware.
Employees: 29,400.
S&P Analyst: Howard Choe/BK

Golden West Financial

Recommendation: **SELL** ★☆☆☆☆
SELL SELL HOLD BUY BUY

12-Month Target Price: $104.00
(as of November 17, 2004)

GDW has an approximate 0.17% weighting in the **S&P 500**

Sector: Financials
Sub-Industry: Thrifts & Mortgage Finance
Peer Group: Major Savings & Loan Companies

Summary: GDW is the holding company for World Savings Bank, one of the largest U.S. savings institutions.

Quantitative Evaluations

S&P Earnings & Dividend Rank: A+

D	C	B-	B	B+	A-	A	A+

S&P Fair Value Rank: 1

1	2	3	4	5
Lowest				Highest

Fair Value Calc.: $81.10 (Overvalued)

S&P Investability Quotient Percentile

98%

GDW scored higher than 98% of all companies for which an S&P Report is available.

Volatility: Low

Low	Average	High

Technical Evaluation: Bullish
Since 10/04, the technical indicators for GDW have been Bullish.

Relative Strength Rank: Moderate

63

1 Lowest	Highest 99

Price as of 11/17/04:	$120.97	2004E S&P Core EPS:	$8.09

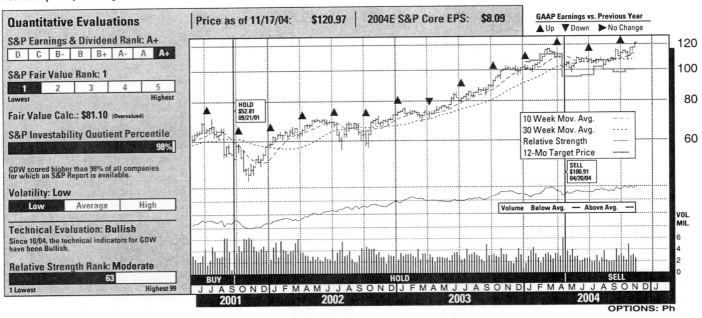

Analyst commentary prepared by Erik J. Eisenstein/MF/TV

Highlights November 09, 2004

- Thus far in 2004, GDW has originated a considerable volume of its specialty, the adjustable rate mortgage (ARM), aided, in our view, by low short-term interest rates. We see a decline in such originations in the coming year, amid a projected rising interest rate environment. Nevertheless, we forecast 28% average earning asset growth in 2005, aided by the full-year effects of loans originated in the latter part of 2004, as well as an anticipated decline in refinancing-induced loan prepayments. We expect significant net interest margin contraction in 2005, reflecting anticipated higher borrowing costs. As a result, we expect the increase in net interest income to be about 18%. We are not concerned about GDW's credit quality, and expect low loan loss provisions in 2004.

- We forecast a 10% decline in non-interest income, on lower gains on sales of loans and securities. We see noninterest expenses up 29%, a bit above average earning asset growth. All told, we expect 2005 EPS to grow about 7%, to $8.68, from $8.15 projected for 2004.

- Our 2004 and 2005 Standard & Poor's Core Earnings projections are $8.09 and $8.62, respectively, reflecting our estimate of employee stock option expense.

Investment Rationale/Risk November 09, 2004

- We would avoid the shares, based on valuation. We view GDW as a well managed S&L, with one of the lowest cost structures in the industry. This is an important advantage, in our view, in light of the commodity-like characteristics of the thrift business. The company has resisted the temptation to venture into higher risk lending; we believe this has led to consistently strong relative asset quality. We also view GDW's earnings quality as above average compared to other thrifts, reflecting our view of less stock option expense and relatively simple financial statements. However, we believe these positive attributes are more than fully reflected in the stock's current valuation, which we believe is likely to contract in a forecast higher interest rate environment in coming periods.

- Risks to our recommendation and target price include the possibility that short-term interest rates will rise less than we expect, resulting in greater demand for ARMs loans and/or a wider net interest margin than we project.

- Our 12-month target price of $100 is derived by applying a P/E multiple of 11.5X to our 2005 EPS estimate, a bit above the five-year historical average.

Key Stock Statistics

S&P Core EPS 2005E	8.62	52-week Range	$121.31-96.06
S&P Oper. EPS 2004E	8.15	12 Month P/E	15.2
P/E on S&P Oper. EPS 2004E	14.9	Beta	0.10
S&P Oper. EPS 2005E	8.68	Shareholders	1,098
Yield (%)	0.4%	Market Cap (B)	$ 18.5
Dividend Rate/Share	0.48	Shares Outstanding (M)	153.1

Value of $10,000 invested five years ago: **$ 33,347**

Dividend Data Dividends have been paid since 1977

Amount ($)	Date Decl.	Ex-Div. Date	Stock of Record	Payment Date
0.100	Apr. 28	May. 12	May. 15	Jun. 10 '04
0.100	Jul. 27	Aug. 11	Aug. 15	Sep. 10 '04
0.060	Oct. 21	Nov. 10	Nov. 15	Dec. 10 '04
2-for-1	Oct. 21	Dec. 13	Nov. 15	Dec. 10 '04

Revenues/Earnings Data Fiscal year ending December 31

Revenues (Million $)

	2004	2003	2002	2001	2000	1999
1Q	1,000	944.5	938.2	1,178	826.0	730.3
2Q	1,059	954.3	905.1	1,165	932.3	727.9
3Q	1,145	967.6	946.3	1,085	1,056	733.7
4Q	—	975.3	954.4	1,020	1,143	777.4
Yr.	—	3,842	3,744	4,446	3,957	2,969

Earnings Per Share ($)

	2004	2003	2002	2001	2000	1999
1Q	1.93	1.44	1.51	1.10	0.78	0.70
2Q	2.04	1.76	1.44	1.30	0.84	0.72
3Q	2.09	1.83	1.56	1.28	0.86	0.71
4Q	E2.08	1.88	1.60	1.44	0.93	0.73
Yr.	E8.15	7.14	6.12	5.11	3.41	2.87

Next earnings report expected: late-January Source: S&P, Company Reports
EPS Estimates based on S&P Operating Earnings; historical GAAP earnings are as reported.

Golden West Financial Corporation

Recommendation: **SELL ★★**   12-Month Target Price: **$104.00** (as of November 17, 2004)

Business Summary November 09, 2004

Golden West Financial Corp., the holding company for World Savings Bank, is the second largest U.S. savings institution, with assets of over $100 billion at September 30, 2004. The company had 276 savings branches in 10 states and lending offices in 38 states at October 21, 2004. GDW believes it operates a straightforward, focused, and highly profitable business model. It originates adjustable rate mortgages (ARMs), keeps them in its portfolio, and funds them with consumer deposits and capital market borrowings. Savings branch operations are concentrated in California. GDW also owns Atlas Advisers, Inc., an investment adviser to its Atlas family of mutual funds; and Atlas Securities, Inc., the distributor of Atlas funds and annuities.

In 2003, GDW originated a record $36.0 billion of mortgage loans, up 35% from the previous record level of 2002. ARMs accounted for more than 93% of all originations; virtually all had interest rates that adjust monthly. The thrift believes its focus on ARM loans minimizes its sensitivity to changes in interest rates over longer terms. However, because GDW's adjustable rate mortgages are tied to indexes that lag changes in market rates, its primary spread (the difference in percentage terms between yield earned on loans and involvements and the rate paid on deposits and borrowings) tends to widen temporarily in falling rate environments, and to narrow when rates rise. Over the course of the interest rate cycle, these fluctuations tend to offset each other. In 2003, the primary spread averaged 2.94%, versus 2.99% in 2002.

The company's strategy includes rigorous control of its general and administrative

(G&A) expenses. This is reflected in the ratio of G&A expenses to average assets. In 2003, the thrift's G&A ratio was 0.98%, up from 0.96% in 2002, reflecting additional costs associated with higher mortgage origination levels. The thrift believes its low expense base gives it pricing flexibility, an important advantage in the commodity-like home loan and deposit markets. GDW believes that leadership also enables it to remain profitable in that market, without turning to wider margin but higher risk lending.

To reduce credit risk, the company focuses on mortgages secured by moderately priced single-family homes in geographically diverse areas, and in cases in which borrowers have a meaningful equity stake in their property. In 2003, the average loan to value ratio for new mortgages was 71%. The ratio of nonperforming assets to total assets fell in 2003 to 0.51%, from 0.62% in 2002, indicating improving asset quality.

In 2003, GDW accumulated $5.7 billion in deposits, down from the record level of $6.6 billion in 2002. At December 31, 2003, deposits accounted for 61% of total liabilities, down from 65% a year earlier.

Since 1993, through five separate actions, directors authorized the buyback of up to 60.6 million common shares. As of December 31, 2003, 51.3 million shares had been repurchased, including 2.0 million in 2003.

Company Financials Fiscal Year ending December 31

Per Share Data ($)

(Year Ended December 31)	2003	2002	2001	2000	1999	1998	1997	1996	1995	1994
Tangible Bk. Val.	39.10	32.73	27.55	23.28	19.80	18.30	15.73	13.63	12.07	10.60
Earnings	7.14	6.12	5.11	3.41	2.87	2.58	2.04	2.11	1.33	1.24
S&P Core Earnings	7.10	6.09	5.08	NA	NA	NA	NA	NA	NA	NA
Dividends	0.36	0.30	0.26	0.22	0.19	0.17	0.15	0.13	0.12	0.10
Payout Ratio	5%	5%	5%	6%	7%	7%	7%	6%	9%	8%
Prices - High	103.95	73.75	70.90	70.50	38.41	38.16	32.64	22.91	19.16	15.33
- Low	68.64	56.20	45.02	26.87	28.91	23.27	19.62	16.33	11.58	11.41
P/E Ratio - High	15	12	14	21	13	15	16	11	14	12
- Low	10	9	9	8	10	9	10	8	9	9

Income Statement Analysis (Million $)

	2003	2002	2001	2000	1999	1998	1997	1996	1995	1994
Net Int. Inc.	2,208	1,930	1,631	1,151	1,006	967	890	831	723	721
Loan Loss Prov.	11.9	21.2	22.3	9.20	-2.09	11.3	57.6	84.3	61.0	63.0
Non Int. Inc.	313	202	194	150	121	99	73.1	74.9	43.0	37.5
Non Int. Exp.	721	601	514	425	386	355	327	453	319	303
Pretax Inc.	1,789	1,555	1,332	878	763	739	587	368	385	390
Eff. Tax Rate	38.2%	38.4%	38.5%	37.8%	37.1%	39.5%	39.7%	NM	39.1%	41.0%
Net Inc.	1,106	958	819	546	480	447	354	370	235	230
% Net Int. Marg.	2.96	3.05	2.81	2.31	2.48	2.46	2.32	2.39	2.13	2.43
S&P Core Earnings	1,098	955	814	NA	NA	NA	NA	NA	NA	NA

Balance Sheet & Other Fin. Data (Million $)

	2003	2002	2001	2000	1999	1998	1997	1996	1995	1994
Total Assets	82,550	68,406	58,586	55,704	42,142	38,469	39,590	37,731	35,118	31,684
Loans	74,081	58,269	41,065	33,763	27,920	25,721	33,261	34,179	34,380	28,265
Deposits	46,727	41,039	34,473	30,048	27,715	26,219	24,110	22,100	20,848	19,219
Capitalization:										
Debt	19,094	12,786	18,834	15,898	7,213	7,713	9,737	10,712	9,367	8,874
Equity	5,947	5,025	4,284	3,687	3,195	3,124	2,698	2,350	2,278	2,000
Total	25,042	17,811	23,118	19,585	10,408	10,838	12,435	13,062	11,645	10,874
% Ret. on Assets	1.5	1.5	1.4	1.1	1.2	1.1	0.9	1.1	0.7	0.8
% Ret. on Equity	20.2	20.6	20.5	15.9	15.2	15.4	14.0	16.0	11.0	11.1
% Loan Loss Resv.	0.4	0.5	0.6	0.7	0.8	0.9	0.7	0.1	0.1	0.4
% Risk Based Capital	22.9	24.1	25.1	12.4	11.9	12.9	12.8	10.0	13.4	13.5
Price Times Book Value:										
Hi	2.7	2.2	2.6	3.0	1.9	2.1	2.1	1.7	1.6	1.4
Low	1.8	1.7	1.6	1.2	1.5	1.3	1.2	1.2	1.0	1.1

Data as orig reptd.; bef. results of disc opers/spec. items. Per share data adj. for stk. divs.; EPS diluted. E-Estimated. NA-Not Available. NM-Not Meaningful. NR-Not Ranked. UR-Under Review.

Office: 1901 Harrison St, Oakland, CA 94612.
Telephone: 510-446-3420.
Website: http://www.gdw.com
Chrmn & CEO: H.M. Sandler.
Chrmn & CEO: M.O. Sandler.

Pres & CFO: R.W. Kettell.
EVP, Secy & General Counsel: M. Roster.
SVP, Chief Acctg Officer & Investor Contact: W.C. Nunan .
Dirs: L. J. Galen, A. Hernandez, M. C. Herringer, P. A. King, B. A. Osher, K. T. Rosen, H. M. Sandler, M. O. Sandler, L. T. Schilling.

Founded: in 1959.
Domicile: Delaware.
Employees: 9,440.
S&P Analyst: Erik J. Eisenstein/MF/TV

Goldman Sachs Group

Stock Report
November 13, 2004
NYSE Symbol: **GS**

Recommendation: **BUY** ★ ★ ★ ★ ★
SELL | SELL | HOLD | BUY | BUY

12-Month Target Price: **$116.00**
(as of September 21, 2004)

GS has an approximate 0.46% weighting in the **S&P 500**

Sector: Financials
Sub-Industry: Investment Banking & Brokerage
Peer Group: Investment Banking/Brokerage - Major

Summary: Goldman Sachs is one of the world's leading investment banking and securities companies.

Quantitative Evaluations

S&P Earnings & Dividend Rank: NR

| D | C | B- | B | B+ | A- | A | A+ |

S&P Fair Value Rank: 5

| 1 | 2 | 3 | 4 | 5 |
| Lowest | | | | Highest |

Fair Value Calc.: $123.20 (Undervalued)

S&P Investability Quotient Percentile

96%

GS scored higher than 96% of all companies for which an S&P Report is available.

Volatility: Low

| Low | Average | High |

Technical Evaluation: Bullish

Since 10/04, the technical indicators for GS have been Bullish.

Relative Strength Rank: Strong

77

| 1 Lowest | | Highest 99 |

| Price as of 11/12/04: | $104.66 | 2004E S&P Core EPS: | $7.72 |

GAAP Earnings vs. Previous Year
▲ Up ▼ Down ▶ No Change

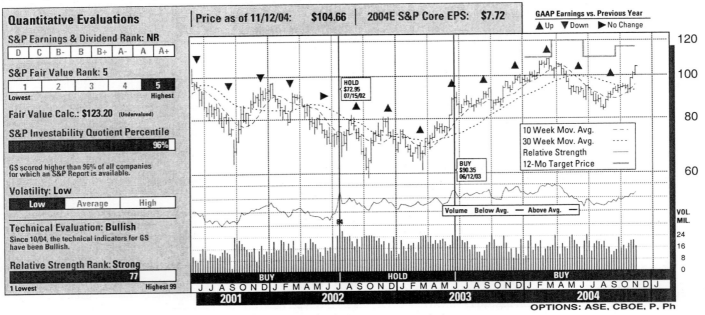

HOLD $72.95 07/15/02
BUY $90.35 06/12/03

10 Week Mov. Avg.
30 Week Mov. Avg.
Relative Strength
12-Mo Target Price

Volume Below Avg. — Above Avg.

VOL. MIL.

BUY | HOLD | BUY

J J A S O N D | J F M A M J J A S O N D | J F M A M J J A S O N D | J F M A M J J A S O N D | J
2001 | 2002 | 2003 | 2004

OPTIONS: ASE, CBOE, P, Ph

Analyst commentary prepared by Robert Hansen, CFA /CB/JWP

Highlights September 22, 2004

- We think Goldman maintains a strong competitive position across its segments, notably in its sales and trading, principal investments and asset management businesses. The company, in our view, is benefiting from tight corporate credit spreads, improving global equity markets, and a pickup in merger and acquisition activity. We are impressed by the 17% year over year gain in assets under management, to $426 billion, at the end of August.

- We expect strong growth in equity underwriting, asset management and advisory fees in FY 05 (Nov.), partially offset by a decline we see in sales and trading revenue from record levels. We think the fixed income business will remain relatively strong in FY 05, despite a flattening yield curve, given the segment's breadth of revenues. We expect growth in investment banking fees in FY 05, helped by a rebound in equity underwriting activity. We expect strong results in the securities services business in FY 05, driven by higher margin balances and a greater mix of electronic trading activity.

- We forecast EPS of $8.35 in FY 04 and $7.75 in FY 05, boosted by significantly higher gains on principal investments.

Investment Rationale/Risk September 22, 2004

- We think GS shares should trade at a modest premium to peers based on our view of the company's global footprint, significant operating leverage, and strong competitive position. We also view positively the prudent growth in headcount and stable compensation ratios, which we think should benefit the multiple. Finally, we think the company's stock buyback should support the valuation.

- Risks to our recommendation and target price include interest rate increases, the company's proprietary investments, and enhanced regulatory scrutiny. The company often makes large proprietary investments in its fixed income and equity trading businesses to facilitate customer trades, which can increase the volatility of reported results.

- Having declined nearly 5% thus far in 2004, the shares recently traded at a P/E multiple of about 12X our FY 05 EPS estimate, comparable to peers, but a significant discount to their historical average of 17X. Our 12-month target price is $116 a share, which represents a P/E multiple of 15X our FY 05 EPS estimate and is a modest premium to the peer group average of nearly 13X.

Key Stock Statistics

S&P Core EPS 2005E	7.17	52-week Range	$109.29-83.29
S&P Oper. EPS 2004E	8.35	12 Month P/E	12.4
P/E on S&P Oper. EPS 2004E	12.5	Beta	1.73
S&P Oper. EPS 2005E	7.75	Shareholders	6,038
Yield (%)	1.0%	Market Cap (B)	$ 50.7
Dividend Rate/Share	1.00	Shares Outstanding (M)	484.2

Value of $10,000 invested five years ago: **$ 14,189**

Dividend Data Dividends have been paid since 1999

Amount ($)	Date Decl.	Ex-Div. Date	Stock of Record	Payment Date
0.250	Dec. 18	Jan. 23	Jan. 27	Feb. 26 '04
0.250	Mar. 23	Apr. 23	Apr. 27	May. 27 '04
0.250	Jun. 22	Jul. 23	Jul. 27	Aug. 26 '04
0.250	Sep. 22	Oct. 21	Oct. 25	Nov. 22 '04

Revenues/Earnings Data Fiscal year ending November 30

Revenues (Million $)

	2004	2003	2002	2001	2000	1999
1Q	7,905	6,094	5,700	9,502	7,964	5,856
2Q	7,676	5,985	6,234	8,158	8,196	6,355
3Q	6,803	5,715	5,872	7,360	8,851	6,440
4Q	—	5,829	5,048	6,118	7,989	6,712
Yr.	—	23,623	22,854	31,138	33,000	25,363

Earnings Per Share ($)

	2004	2003	2002	2001	2000	1999
1Q	2.50	1.29	0.98	1.40	1.76	0.06
2Q	2.31	1.36	1.06	1.06	1.48	0.69
3Q	1.74	1.32	1.00	0.87	1.62	1.31
4Q	E1.79	1.89	0.98	0.93	1.16	1.54
Yr.	E8.35	5.87	4.03	4.26	6.00	5.27

Next earnings report expected: mid-December Source: S&P, Company Reports
EPS Estimates based on S&P Operating Earnings; historical GAAP earnings are as reported.

The Goldman Sachs Group, Inc.

Recommendation: **BUY** ★ ★ ★ ★ ★   12-Month Target Price: **$116.00** (as of September 21, 2004)

Business Summary September 23, 2004

Goldman Sachs is one of the world's leading investment banking and securities companies. Its activities are divided into the three following segments: investment banking, trading and principal investments, and asset management and securities services. Despite its diversification, the company notes that its business, by its nature, doesn't lend itself to predictable recurring earnings.

Trading and principal investments accounted for 65% of net revenues in FY 03 (Nov.). Goldman makes markets in equity and fixed income products, currencies and commodities. The company also enters into derivative transactions such as swaps, and engages in proprietary trading and arbitrage. The company's Fixed Income, Currency and Commodities (FICC) segment consists of the following five major areas: interest rates, credit, mortgages, currencies, and commodities. In its principal investments business, Goldman invests in private equity deals as well as real estate. Merchant banking activities account for most of the net revenues in principal investments.

Goldman considers risk management to be one of its most vital functions. Risk management begins at the top of the firm with the establishment of risk limits for major business units. In FY 03, the company's average daily Value at Risk (VaR), one principal tool used to measure market risk in trading positions, was $58 million. Goldman believes that its willingness to take significant trading risk for appropriate reward is a distinguishing feature of the firm that provides it with a competitive advantage.

As an investment bank, the company helps clients raise capital by issuing various debt and equity securities. The investment banking business has two components: financial advisory and underwriting. In the underwriting business, Goldman underwrites a wide variety of securities and other instruments. In the financial advisory business, the company advises clients on corporate takeovers, defenses, mergers and acquisitions; Goldman also provides acquisition financing, currency hedging and cross border structuring expertise. The company has consistently ranked among the world's leading financial advisers and underwriters. Investment banking revenues accounted for 17% of net revenues in FY 03.

The asset management and securities services business accounted for 18% of net revenues in FY 03. Assets under management grew from $94 billion at the end of FY 96 to $373 billion at the end of FY 03. Goldman experienced net client inflows of $15 billion in FY 03 across non-money market asset classes, offset by $19 billion of outflows in money market assets. Securities services benefited in FY 03 from the creation and growth of new and existing hedge funds, as well as the rally in equity markets.

In December 2002, the company and other leading investment banks entered into a $1.4 billion agreement to settle allegations that their research was tainted with conflicts of interest and misled investors; Goldman's share of the settlement was $110 million. The banks also agreed to make organizational changes to reduce conflicts of interest in their research departments.

Company Financials Fiscal Year ending November 30

Per Share Data ($)

(Year Ended November 30)	2003	2002	2001	2000	1999	1998	1997	1996	1995	1994
Tangible Bk. Val.	45.73	40.18	38.30	34.15	22.65	NA	NA	NA	NA	NA
Cash Flow	6.97	5.20	5.39	6.94	6.27	NA	NA	NA	NA	NA
Earnings	5.87	4.03	4.26	6.00	5.27	2.62	NA	NA	NA	NA
S&P Core Earnings	5.26	3.30	3.60	NA	NA	NA	NA	NA	NA	NA
Dividends	0.74	0.48	0.48	0.48	0.24	NA	NA	NA	NA	NA
Payout Ratio	13%	12%	11%	8%	4%	NA	NA	NA	NA	NA
Prices - High	100.78	97.25	120.00	133.62	94.81	NA	NA	NA	NA	NA
- Low	61.02	58.57	63.27	65.50	53.00	NA	NA	NA	NA	NA
P/E Ratio - High	17	24	28	22	17	NA	NA	NA	NA	NA
- Low	10	15	15	11	10	NA	NA	NA	NA	NA

Income Statement Analysis (Million $)

	2003	2002	2001	2000	1999	1998	1997	1996	1995	1994
Commissions	4,317	3,273	3,020	2,307	Nil	NA	NA	NA	NA	NA
Int. Inc.	10,751	11,269	16,620	17,396	12,722	NA	NA	NA	NA	NA
Total Revs.	23,623	22,854	31,138	33,000	25,363	22,478	NA	NA	NA	NA
Int. Exp.	7,600	8,868	15,327	16,410	12,018	13,986	NA	NA	NA	NA
Pretax Inc.	4,445	3,253	3,696	5,020	1,992	2,129	NA	NA	NA	NA
Eff. Tax Rate	32.4%	35.0%	37.5%	38.9%	NM	41.0%	NA	NA	NA	NA
Net Inc.	3,005	2,114	2,310	3,067	2,708	1,256	NA	NA	NA	NA
S&P Core Earnings	NA	1,737	1,949	NA	NA	NA	NA	NA	NA	NA

Balance Sheet & Other Fin. Data (Million $)

	2003	2002	2001	2000	1999	1998	1997	1996	1995	1994
Total Assets	403,799	355,574	312,218	289,760	250,491	231,796	NA	NA	NA	NA
Cash Items	36,802	25,211	29,043	21,002	12,190	2,702	NA	NA	NA	NA
Receivables	36,377	28,938	33,463	159,019	150,154	NA	NA	NA	NA	NA
Secs. Owned	160,719	129,775	108,885	95,260	81,809	NA	NA	NA	NA	NA
Sec. Borrowed	17,528	12,238	81,579	40,211	49,352	NA	NA	NA	NA	NA
Due Brokers & Cust.	109,028	95,590	97,297	82,148	59,534	NA	NA	NA	NA	NA
Other Liabs.	8,144	6,002	7,129	11,116	110,508	NA	NA	NA	NA	NA
Capitalization:										
Debt	57,482	38,711	31,016	31,395	20,952	20,776	NA	NA	NA	NA
Equity	21,632	19,003	18,231	16,530	10,145	7,627	NA	NA	NA	NA
Total	79,114	57,714	49,247	47,925	31,097	28,403	NA	NA	NA	NA
% Return On Revs.	12.7	9.3	7.4	9.3	10.7	5.6	NA	NA	NA	NA
% Ret. on Assets	0.8	0.6	0.8	1.1	1.2	NA	NA	NA	NA	NA
% Ret. on Equity	14.8	11.4	13.3	23.0	30.4	NA	NA	NA	NA	NA

Data as orig reptd.; bef. results of disc opers/spec. items. Per share data adj. for stk. divs.; EPS diluted. E-Estimated. NA-Not Available. NM-Not Meaningful. NR-Not Ranked. UR-Under Review.

Office: 85 Broad Street, New York, NY 10004.
Telephone: 212-902-1000.
Email: gs-investor-relations@gs.com
Website: http://www.gs.com
Chrmn & CEO: H.M. Paulson, Jr.
Pres & COO: L.C. Blankfein.

Vice Chrmn: R.S. Kaplan.
EVP & CFO: D.A. Viniar.
EVP & General Counsel: G.K. Palm.
Dirs: L. C. Blankfein, J. H. Bryan, C. Dahlback, W. George, J. A. Johnson, L. D. Juliber, E. M. Liddy, B. o. Madingley, H. M. Paulson, Jr., J. F. Rodgers, R. J. Simmons.

Founded: in 1869.
Domicile: Delaware.
Employees: 19,476.
S&P Analyst: Robert Hansen, CFA /CB/JWP

Goodrich Corp.

Recommendation: **BUY** ★★★★ ☆
SELL | SELL | HOLD | BUY | BUY

12-Month Target Price: $40.00
(as of October 31, 2003)

GR has an approximate 0.04% weighting in the **S&P 500**

Sector: Industrials
Sub-Industry: Aerospace & Defense
Peer Group: Aerospace/Defense - Parts

Summary: GR is one of the world's largest providers of commercial jet equipment, parts and services.

Quantitative Evaluations

S&P Earnings & Dividend Rank: B

| D | C | B- | **B** | B+ | A- | A | A+ |

S&P Fair Value Rank: 3

| 1 | 2 | **3** | 4 | 5 |
| Lowest | | | | Highest |

Fair Value Calc.: $32.40 (Fairly Valued)

S&P Investability Quotient Percentile

82%

GR scored higher than 82% of all companies for which an S&P Report is available.

Volatility: Average

| Low | **Average** | High |

Technical Evaluation: Bullish
Since 11/04, the technical indicators for GR have been Bullish.

Relative Strength Rank: Moderate

51

| 1 Lowest | | Highest 99 |

| Price as of 11/12/04: | $32.66 | 2004E S&P Core EPS: | $0.70 |

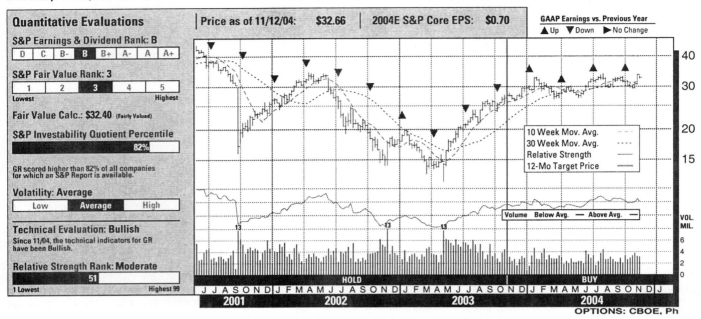

GAAP Earnings vs. Previous Year
▲ Up ▼ Down ▶ No Change

10 Week Mov. Avg.
30 Week Mov. Avg.
Relative Strength
12-Mo Target Price

Volume Below Avg. — Above Avg.

VOL. MIL.

HOLD | BUY
J J A S O N D J F M A M J J A S O N D J F M A M J J A S O N D J F M A M J J A S O N D J
2001 | 2002 | 2003 | 2004

OPTIONS: CBOE, Ph

Analyst commentary prepared by Robert E. Friedman, CPA /PMW/BK

Highlights October 19, 2004

- We expect revenues to rise about 5% in 2005, primarily on modest volume sales hikes in GR's military/space and commercial aircraft component-making segments. However, we believe pricing will remain about flat, due to intense competitive environments.

- We believe modest hikes in volume sales, ongoing cost-cutting initiatives, and the absence of large restructuring charges should allow near-term EBIT (earnings before interest and taxes) margins to widen fractionally, from 8.4% in 2004 to 8.7% in 2005. Based on our expectations of controlled interest and non-operating expenses, we project that 2005 EPS will advance about 14% from our 2004 estimate, to $1.54. We also see S&P Core EPS up about 14%, to $0.80, from a projected $0.70 for 2004. We expect GR to generate what we view as subpar near-term debt-adjusted return on equity (ROE) of somewhat over 6%.

- Looking at the company's longer-term prospects, we project that GR's free cash flow will increase at a 5% to 6.5% compound annual growth rate (CAGR), with average ROE of 10% to 13%. We believe mature markets and intense competitive environments will prevent the company from posting outsized sustainable EPS growth and return on capital.

Investment Rationale/Risk October 19, 2004

- We believe GR has what we view as mediocre business economics and caters to mature end-markets, but we still recommend accumulating the shares, which are at a substantial discount to our 12-month target price of $40.

- Risks to our recommendation and target price include unexpected structural deterioration of GR's primary commercial and military aerospace endmarkets; and structural deterioration of the economics of the aerospace components making and servicing businesses.

- Our free cash flow model (which values the stock by adding the sum of projected cash earnings with an estimated CAGR of 5% to 6.5% over the first 10 years and 3% thereafter) indicates a vaue ot $40, which is our 12-month target price. Our CAGR projection for free cash folow is based on multiplying our 10% to 13% longer-term average ROE estimates by one minus our 50% earnings retention forecast. In addition, we used a $380 million free cash earnings starting point, representing the latest seven-year average free cash earnings generated by GR's aerospace operations, and a discount rate of 10%.

Key Stock Statistics

S&P Core EPS 2005E	0.80	52-week Range	$33.90-26.32
S&P Oper. EPS 2004E	1.45	12 Month P/E	27.4
P/E on S&P Oper. EPS 2004E	22.5	Beta	1.13
S&P Oper. EPS 2005E	1.60	Shareholders	10,406
Yield (%)	2.4%	Market Cap (B)	$ 3.9
Dividend Rate/Share	0.80	Shares Outstanding (M)	118.9

Value of $10,000 invested five years ago: **NA**

Dividend Data Dividends have been paid since 1939

Amount ($)	Date Decl.	Ex-Div. Date	Stock of Record	Payment Date
0.200	Feb. 17	Mar. 04	Mar. 08	Apr. 01 '04
0.200	Apr. 27	Jun. 03	Jun. 07	Jul. 01 '04
0.200	Jul. 28	Sep. 02	Sep. 07	Oct. 01 '04
0.200	Oct. 19	Dec. 02	Dec. 06	Jan. 03 '05

Revenues/Earnings Data Fiscal year ending December 31

Revenues (Million $)

	2004	2003	2002	2001	2000	1999
1Q	1,162	1,094	921.2	1,008	1,378	1,036
2Q	1,134	1,095	925.5	1,072	1,380	1,082
3Q	1,167	1,064	882.1	1,052	1,378	1,332
4Q	—	1,130	1,181	1,053	1,117	1,330
Yr.	—	4,383	3,910	4,185	4,364	5,538

Earnings Per Share ($)

	2004	2003	2002	2001	2000	1999
1Q	0.25	-0.28	0.47	0.66	0.78	0.66
2Q	0.32	0.12	0.56	0.70	0.75	0.82
3Q	0.41	0.29	0.45	0.76	0.77	-0.74
4Q	E0.45	0.19	0.11	-0.50	0.68	0.60
Yr.	E1.45	0.33	1.57	1.65	2.68	1.53

Next earnings report expected: early-February Source: S&P, Company Reports
EPS Estimates based on S&P Operating Earnings; historical GAAP earnings are as reported.

Goodrich Corporation

Recommendation: **BUY** ★★★★☆   12-Month Target Price: **$40.00** (as of October 31, 2003)

Business Summary October 19, 2004

Goodrich Corp. conducts business through three segments:

The largest segment, Airframe Systems (AS; 41% of revenues and 25% of operating profits in 2003; 4.4% operating profit margins) primarily makes landing gear, wheels and brakes for passenger jets with at least 100 seats. AS and Messier-Dowty (a division of France-based SNECMA) each control 50% of the global landing gear market. The unit is also a major global provider of aircraft maintenance, repair and overhaul (MRO) services. AS's MRO customers mostly comprise the world's major airlines. Primary aircraft maintenance competitors include TIMCO Aviation Services, SIA Engineering Co., Singapore Technologies and Lufthansa Technik.

GR's Engine Systems segment (36%; 31%; 6.3%) is a global maker of various jet engine components and parts. Its largest customers include Airbus, Boeing, Rolls-Royce and global airlines. Primary competitors in this market include United Technologies, BAE Systems and Honeywell.

Electronic Systems (24%; 44%; 13%) mostly makes equipment that either controls or monitors the performance of aircraft. Primary offerings include sensor equipment for military and commercial rockets and satellites, flight and jet engine controls equipment, and electrical power equipment for civil and military aircraft. In addition, it is a major maker of inflatable evacuation slides and ice detection equipment. Primary competitors include Smiths Group, Parker Hannifin, and Honeywell.

The company derives a material amount of revenues from sales to Boeing, Airbus, and the U.S. government (primarily the Department of Defense). In 2003, Boeing,

Airbus, and the U.S. government accounted for 17%, 14% and 19% of total revenues, respectively.

Although GR maintains dominant shares in several key aircraft component markets, most of its markets are mature.

Demand for the company's commercial aircraft equipment offerings is driven by growth of the global commercial jetliner fleet for planes with more than 100 seats. Based on the latest statistics provided by independent research firm Avitas, Inc., and the International Air Transport Association (IATA), from 1992 through 2002, the global 100+ seat passenger aircraft fleet grew at a 2.4% average annual rate. Growth in the worldwide jetliner fleet is driven by airline industry profitability and passenger air traffic growth.

Demand for GR's MRO services is also driven by airline industry profitability, air traffic growth, and the age of the global airline fleet. Based on statistics from the Aerospace Industries Association, from 1993 through 2003, the MRO industry grew at a 2.6% average annual rate.

Following several large multi-year acquisitions and divestitures, the company completed a transformation to a pure-play aviation equipment and service provider in mid-2002. However, acquisition-related long term debt grew from 60% of equity in 1998 to 240% in 2002. In an effort to cut debt to manageable levels, GR sold 15 million common shares in late 2002, potentially diluting EPS by 15%. As a result of the stock offering, long term debt fell to 179% of equity at the end of 2003.

Company Financials Fiscal Year ending December 31

Per Share Data ($)

(Year Ended December 31)	2003	2002	2001	2000	1999	1998	1997	1996	1995	1994
Tangible Bk. Val.	NM	NM	4.66	3.48	1.41	9.63	11.35	8.53	6.58	4.14
Cash Flow	2.18	3.31	3.28	4.39	3.62	5.25	3.38	4.16	4.42	3.30
Earnings	0.33	1.57	1.65	2.68	1.53	3.04	1.53	1.97	2.15	1.12
S&P Core Earnings	0.42	0.42	0.41	NA	NA	NA	NA	NA	NA	NA
Dividends	0.80	0.88	1.10	1.10	1.10	1.10	1.10	1.10	1.10	1.10
Payout Ratio	242%	56%	67%	41%	72%	36%	72%	56%	51%	98%
Prices - High	30.30	34.45	44.50	43.12	45.68	56.00	48.25	45.87	36.31	24.18
- Low	12.20	14.17	15.91	21.56	21.00	26.50	35.12	33.37	20.81	19.50
P/E Ratio - High	92	22	27	16	30	18	32	23	17	22
- Low	37	9	10	8	14	9	23	17	10	17

Income Statement Analysis (Million $)

	2003	2002	2001	2000	1999	1998	1997	1996	1995	1994
Revs.	4,383	3,910	4,185	4,364	5,538	3,951	3,373	2,239	2,409	2,199
Oper. Inc.	515	586	666	830	973	653	501	361	357	292
Depr.	219	184	174	193	231	165	139	118	114	112
Int. Exp.	163	117	118	129	138	79.0	73.0	40.4	58.0	48.0
Pretax Inc.	61.3	259	271	443	316	374	207	178	198	109
Eff. Tax Rate	37.2%	36.0%	34.8%	35.4%	46.3%	39.1%	45.4%	34.5%	38.0%	39.5%
Net Inc.	38.5	166	177	286	170	228	113	106	118	66.0
S&P Core Earnings	48.6	44.9	44.7	NA	NA	NA	NA	NA	NA	NA

Balance Sheet & Other Fin. Data (Million $)

	2003	2002	2001	2000	1999	1998	1997	1996	1995	1994
Cash	378	150	85.8	77.5	66.4	31.7	47.0	48.7	60.0	36.0
Curr. Assets	2,087	2,008	1,921	3,080	2,101	1,615	1,401	912	950	879
Total Assets	5,890	5,990	4,638	5,718	5,456	4,193	3,494	2,663	2,490	2,469
Curr. Liab.	1,401	1,554	1,159	2,147	1,511	991	935	663	601	638
LT Debt	2,137	2,254	1,432	1,590	1,788	995	564	400	422	427
Common Equity	1,194	933	1,361	1,227	1,293	1,600	1,423	1,050	879	813
Total Cap.	3,330	3,187	2,808	2,819	3,208	2,718	2,110	1,573	1,423	1,350
Cap. Exp.	125	107	191	148	246	209	160	184	148	129
Cash Flow	258	349	351	479	400	394	252	225	232	170
Curr. Ratio	1.5	1.3	1.7	1.4	1.4	1.6	1.5	1.4	1.6	1.4
% LT Debt of Cap.	64.2	70.7	51.0	56.4	55.7	36.6	26.7	25.5	29.7	31.6
% Net Inc.of Revs.	0.9	4.2	4.2	6.6	3.1	5.8	3.4	4.8	4.9	3.0
% Ret. on Assets	0.6	3.0	3.6	5.3	3.2	5.9	3.7	4.2	4.8	2.7
% Ret. on Equity	3.6	14.5	13.7	22.7	13.4	15.1	9.2	11.1	14.0	7.2

Data as orig reptd.; bef. results of disc opers/spec. items. Per share data adj. for stk. divs.; EPS diluted. E-Estimated. NA-Not Available. NM-Not Meaningful. NR-Not Ranked.

Office: Four Coliseum Centre, Charlotte, NC 28217-4578.
Telephone: 704-423-7000.
Website: http://www.goodrich.com
Chrmn, Pres & CEO: M.O. Larsen.
EVP & CFO: U.R. Schmidt.
EVP & General Counsel: T.G. Linnert.

VP & Treas: S.E. Kuechle.
VP, Secy & General Counsel: A.C. Schoch.
Investor Contact: P. Gifford 704-423-5517.
Dirs: D. C. Creel, G. A. Davidson, Jr., H. E. DeLoach, Jr., J. J. Glasser, J. W. Griffith, W. R. Holland, M. O. Larsen, D. E. Olesen, R. d. Osborne, A. M. Rankin, Jr., J. R. Wilson, A. T. Young.

Founded: in 1912.
Domicile: New York.
Employees: 20,600.
S&P Analyst: Robert E. Friedman, CPA /PMW/BK

Goodyear Tire & Rubber

Recommendation: **SELL** ★ ☆ ☆ ☆ ☆
SELL | SELL | HOLD | BUY | BUY

12-Month Target Price: $9.00
(as of November 10, 2004)

GT has an approximate 0.02% weighting in the **S&P 500**

Sector: Consumer Discretionary
Sub-Industry: Tires & Rubber
Peer Group: Tire Companies

Summary: GT is the largest U.S. manufacturer of tires, and one of the largest worldwide. Operations also include rubber and plastic products and chemicals.

Quantitative Evaluations

S&P Earnings & Dividend Rank: B-

| D | C | B- | B | B+ | A- | A | A+ |

S&P Fair Value Rank: 1

| 1 | 2 | 3 | 4 | 5 |
Lowest ... Highest

Fair Value Calc.: $6.40 (Overvalued)

S&P Investability Quotient Percentile

89%

GT scored higher than 89% of all companies for which an S&P Report is available.

Volatility: High

| Low | Average | High |

Technical Evaluation: Neutral
Since 10/04, the technical indicators for GT have been Neutral.

Relative Strength Rank: Strong

79

1 Lowest ... Highest 99

| Price as of 11/12/04: | $11.66 | 2004E S&P Core EPS: | $-0.06 |

GAAP Earnings vs. Previous Year
▲ Up ▼ Down ► No Change

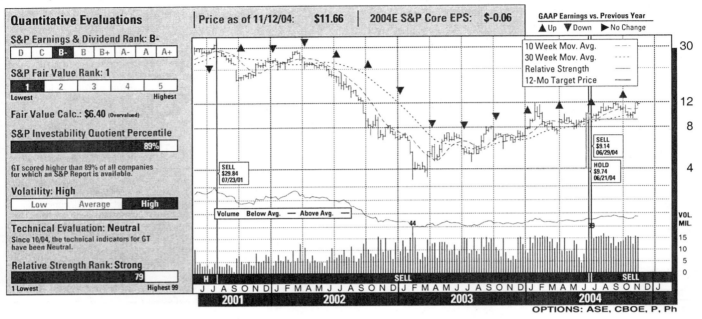

- 10 Week Mov. Avg.
- 30 Week Mov. Avg.
- Relative Strength
- 12-Mo Target Price

SELL $29.84 07/23/01

SELL $9.14 06/29/04

HOLD $9.74 06/21/04

Volume Below Avg. — Above Avg.

VOL. MIL.

J J A S O N D | J F M A M J J A S O N D | J F M A M J J A S O N D | J F M A M J J A S O N D | J F M A M J J A S O N D | J
2001 | 2002 | 2003 | 2004

OPTIONS: ASE, CBOE, P, Ph

Analyst commentary prepared by Efraim Levy, CFA /CB/JWP

Highlights November 10, 2004

- We expect 2005 revenues to increase 3% to 5%, following a 19% to 20% advance that we expect for 2004. We see higher light and heavy vehicle production boosting U.S. original equipment tire shipments in 2005. We also see European and other international sales as likely to increase, due to a weaker dollar and greater tire demand. Consolidation of certain joint ventures into the financial statements should also boost sales in 2004. Pension costs should rise in both years. Although we expect margins to benefit from expense reduction due to past and ongoing restructuring activities, we think they will likely suffer from the impact of higher raw material prices. Revenue gains and restructuring savings should help reduce the loss in 2004.

- The elimination of the quarterly dividend is saving the company about $84 million in cash annually. Reductions in employee benefits should provide additional savings. However, the company has significant debt obligations coming due that must be paid or refinanced during 2005 and 2006, as well as obligations due to retirees that must be paid.

- We expect the restructuring of its credit facilities to give GT more time and flexibility to make operating improvements in the key North American market.

Key Stock Statistics

S&P Core EPS 2005E	0.75	52-week Range	$12.00-6.15
S&P Oper. EPS 2004E	-0.04	12 Month P/E	NM
P/E on S&P Oper. EPS 2004E	NM	Beta	1.22
S&P Oper. EPS 2005E	0.61	Shareholders	28,443
Yield (%)	Nil	Market Cap (B)	$ 2.0
Dividend Rate/Share	Nil	Shares Outstanding (M)	175.3

Value of $10,000 invested five years ago: **$ 3,696**

Dividend Data

Dividends were paid from 1937 to 2002.

Investment Rationale/Risk November 10, 2004

- We would avoid the shares. Based on our projections, the stock's price to EBITDA ratio is below those of peers. We think the discount reflects GT's higher debt levels. The potential sale of certain assets would provide cash to repay some debt, and the company is looking to extend its debt maturities. We see a $350 million convertible debt offering helping liquidity, but it would be dilutive to shareholders. We regard liquidity challenges from debt and employee retirement obligations as matters of concern for the longer term.

- Risks to our recommendation and target price include a reduction in GT's need for and improvement in the availability of cash; stronger than anticipated demand for tires; more favorable selling prices; greater than expected cost savings; and easing of raw material prices.

- Based on company guidance, we sharply increased our outlook for capital expenditures for 2004 and 2005, and have reduced our free cash flow outlook. Based on our DCF model, which assumes a weighted average cost of capital of 10.2%, a compound annual growth rate of 3.2% over the next 14 years, and a terminal growth rate of 1%, we derive our 12-month target price of $9.

Revenues/Earnings Data Fiscal year ending December 31

Revenues (Million $)

	2004	2003	2002	2001	2000	1999
1Q	4,291	3,546	3,311	3,414	3,537	2,991
2Q	4,509	3,753	3,479	3,583	3,475	3,049
3Q	4,714	3,906	3,530	3,678	3,482	3,289
4Q	—	3,914	3,530	3,473	3,526	3,552
Yr.	—	15,119	13,850	14,147	14,417	12,881

Earnings Per Share ($)

	2004	2003	2002	2001	2000	1999
1Q	-0.44	-1.12	-0.39	-0.30	0.40	0.16
2Q	0.14	-0.30	0.18	0.05	0.38	0.41
3Q	0.21	-0.67	0.20	0.06	-0.04	0.69
4Q	E0.04	-2.49	-6.30	-1.07	-0.65	0.26
Yr.	E-0.04	-4.58	-6.62	-1.27	0.26	1.52

Next earnings report expected: NA Source: S&P, Company Reports
EPS Estimates based on S&P Operating Earnings; historical GAAP earnings are as reported.

STANDARD &POOR'S

The Goodyear Tire & Rubber Company

Stock Report
November 13, 2004
NYSE Symbol: **GT**

Recommendation: **SELL** ★ ★ ☆ ☆ ☆   12-Month Target Price: **$9.00** (as of November 10, 2004)

Business Summary November 11, 2004

In the consolidating global rubber fabrication and tire industry, Goodyear Tire & Rubber aims to emerge as one of a handful of clear winners. Despite efforts to rationalize operations, divest non-core operations, and explore international growth opportunities, the company has posted losses in recent years. GT holds the leading market share in North America, Latin America, China and India.

In early 2003, new management articulated its targets for 2005: tire market share gains of two percentage points in North America and one percentage point in the rest of the world; 4% higher revenue per tire; $1 billion to $1.5 billion in cost reductions; return on sales of 6.0%; and 15% to 20% return on invested capital.

In 1999, the company and Sumitomo Rubber Industries (SRI) completed a global alliance that again made GT the world's leading tire manufacturer. The company paid SRI $916 million, and recorded a $138 million gain from the creation of a European joint venture with SRI. GT and SRI own 75% and 25%, respectively, of both the North American and European joint ventures. In Japan, the ownership ratio is reversed. In April 2003, GT sold 20.83 million SRI shares to SRI, for about $83.4 million, reducing its 10% ownership interest in SRI to about 1.5%.

In 2003, 85% of segment sales (86% in 2002) and 68% of profits (69%) came from tire products. Engineered and chemical products together accounted for 15% (14%) and 32% (31%) of revenues and profits, respectively.

Tires and related products include new tires and inner tubes, retreads, repair/ maintenance items, and auto repairs and services. Replacement volume is significantly higher than sales to the original equipment market.

General products include automotive and industrial belts and hoses, molded products, foam cushioning accessories, tank track, organic chemicals for rubber and plastic processing, synthetic rubber, and rubber lattices.

GT and Pacific Dunlop Ltd. participate in equally owned joint ventures in South Pacific Tyres, an Australian partnership, and South Pacific Tyres N.Z. Ltd., a New Zealand company (together SPT).

In October 2003, the company determined that it was appropriate to restate previously issued financial statements. GT restated financial statements for 1998 through 2002, and for parts of 2003.

In February 2004, the SEC initiated a formal order of investigation into the company's accounting restatements.

A net loss of $1.23 billion (as restated) was recorded in 2002, primarily reflecting a non-cash charge of $1.2 billion to establish a valuation allowance against net federal and state deferred tax assets.

GT is obligated to make pension plan contributions of about $160 million in 2004 and $425 million to $450 million in 2005.

Company Financials Fiscal Year ending December 31

Per Share Data ($)

(Year Ended December 31)	2003	2002	2001	2000	1999	1998	1997	1996	1995	1994
Tangible Bk. Val.	NM	NM	14.06	18.49	19.87	24.01	21.68	21.03	21.38	16.44
Cash Flow	-0.62	-3.01	2.71	4.22	5.18	7.63	6.51	3.63	6.88	6.46
Earnings	-4.58	-6.62	-1.27	0.26	1.52	4.53	3.53	0.66	4.02	3.75
S&P Core Earnings	-3.32	-8.16	-3.09	NA	NA	NA	NA	NA	NA	NA
Dividends	Nil	0.48	1.02	1.20	1.20	1.20	1.14	1.03	0.95	0.75
Payout Ratio	Nil	NM	NM	NM	79%	26%	32%	156%	24%	20%
Prices - High	8.19	28.85	32.10	31.62	66.75	76.75	71.25	53.00	45.37	49.25
- Low	3.35	6.50	17.37	15.60	25.50	45.87	49.25	41.50	33.00	31.62
P/E Ratio - High	NM	NM	NM	NM	44	17	20	80	11	13
- Low	NM	NM	NM	NM	17	10	14	63	8	8

Income Statement Analysis (Million $)

	2003	2002	2001	2000	1999	1998	1997	1996	1995	1994
Revs.	15,119	13,850	14,147	14,417	12,881	12,626	13,155	13,113	13,166	12,288
Oper. Inc.	-549	915	916	1,173	1,094	1,560	1,689	1,657	1,570	1,492
Depr.	693	603	637	630	582	488	469	461	435	410
Int. Exp.	296	241	292	283	179	147	119	134	140	135
Pretax Inc.	-655	37.9	-273	92.3	337	1,035	845	122	926	890
Eff. Tax Rate	NM	NM	NM	20.0%	16.5%	27.6%	28.5%	16.8%	34.0%	33.6%
Net Inc.	-802	-1,106	-204	40.3	241	717	559	102	611	567
S&P Core Earnings	-584	-1,362	-495	NA	NA	NA	NA	NA	NA	NA

Balance Sheet & Other Fin. Data (Million $)

	2003	2002	2001	2000	1999	1998	1997	1996	1995	1994
Cash	1,565	947	959	253	241	239	259	239	268	266
Curr. Assets	6,988	5,227	5,255	5,467	5,261	4,529	4,164	4,025	3,842	3,623
Total Assets	15,006	13,147	13,513	13,568	13,103	10,589	9,917	9,672	9,790	9,123
Curr. Liab.	3,686	4,071	3,327	4,226	3,960	3,277	3,251	2,766	2,736	2,572
LT Debt	4,826	2,989	3,204	2,350	2,348	1,187	845	1,132	1,320	1,109
Common Equity	-13.1	651	2,864	3,503	3,617	3,746	3,395	3,279	3,282	2,803
Total Cap.	5,639	4,380	6,855	6,698	6,856	5,192	4,240	4,652	4,765	4,056
Cap. Exp.	375	458	435	615	805	838	699	618	616	523
Cash Flow	-109	-503	433	671	823	1,205	1,028	563	1,046	977
Curr. Ratio	1.9	1.3	1.6	1.3	1.3	1.4	1.3	1.5	1.4	1.4
% LT Debt of Cap.	85.6	68.2	46.7	35.1	34.2	22.9	19.9	24.3	27.7	27.3
% Net Inc.of Revs.	NM	NM	NM	0.3	1.9	5.7	4.2	0.8	4.6	4.6
% Ret. on Assets	NM	NM	NM	0.3	2.0	7.0	5.7	1.0	6.5	6.4
% Ret. on Equity	NM	NM	NM	1.1	6.5	20.1	16.7	3.1	20.1	22.2

Data as orig reptd.; bef. results of disc opers/spec. items. Per share data adj. for stk. divs.; EPS diluted. E-Estimated. NA-Not Available. NM-Not Meaningful. NR-Not Ranked. UR-Under Review.

Office: 1144 East Market Street, Akron, OH 44316-0002.
Telephone: 330-796-2121.
Email: goodyear.investor.relations@goodyear.com
Website: http://www.goodyear.com
Chrmn, Pres & CEO: R.J. Keegan.
EVP & CFO: R.W. Tieken.

SVP, Secy & General Counsel: C.T. Harvie.
VP & Treas: D. Wells.
Investor Contact: B. Gold 330-796-8576.
Dirs: S. E. Arnold, J. C. Boland, J. G. Breen, G. D. Forsee, W. J. Hudson, Jr., R. J. Keegan, S. A. Minter, R. O'Neal, S. D. Peterson, J. M. Zimmerman.

Founded: in 1898.
Domicile: Ohio.
Employees: 86,000.
S&P Analyst: Efraim Levy, CFA /CB/JWP

Grainger (W.W.)

Recommendation: **BUY** ★ ★ ★ ★
SELL · SELL · HOLD · BUY · BUY

12-Month Target Price: **$67.00**
(as of September 29, 2004)

GWW has an approximate 0.05% weighting in the **S&P 500**

Sector: Industrials
Sub-Industry: Trading Companies & Distributors
Peer Group: Trading Companies & Distributors

Summary: Grainger is the largest global distributor of industrial and commercial supplies, such as hand tools, electric motors, light bulbs and janitorial items.

Quantitative Evaluations

S&P Earnings & Dividend Rank: A-

| D | C | B- | B | B+ | A- | A | A+ |

S&P Fair Value Rank: 4+

| 1 | 2 | 3 | 4 | 5 |
| Lowest | | | | Highest |

Fair Value Calc.: $62.20 (Slightly Undervalued)

S&P Investability Quotient Percentile

100%

GWW scored higher than 100% of all companies for which an S&P Report is available.

Volatility: Average

| Low | **Average** | High |

Technical Evaluation: Bullish

Since 9/04, the technical indicators for GWW have been Bullish.

Relative Strength Rank: Moderate

57

1 Lowest ——— Highest 99

Price as of 11/12/04: $60.06 | **2004E S&P Core EPS:** $2.75

GAAP Earnings vs. Previous Year
▲ Up   ▼ Down   ► No Change

- - - 10 Week Mov. Avg.
······ 30 Week Mov. Avg.
——— Relative Strength
~~~~ 12-Mo Target Price

Volume   Below Avg. —— Above Avg.

HOLD ··· BUY

J J A S O N D J F M A M J J A S O N D J F M A M J J A S O N D J F M A M J J A S O N D J
2001 ···· 2002 ···· 2003 ···· 2004

OPTIONS: ASE

Analyst commentary prepared by Stewart Scharf/DC/GG

Highlights October 20, 2004

- We expect sales to advance close to 10% for 2005, following our projection of high single digit growth in 2004, as North American markets gradually recover and sales in Mexico remain strong due to branch expansions and better economic conditions. We see expanding market share aiding the lab safety and branch-based distribution units.

- We look for the gross margin to widen further in 2005, to above 37%, following a 100-basis point gain, to 36%, seen for 2004, reflecting price hikes and a more favorable product mix. We expect wider EBITDA margins on supply chain cost savings, which should add $10 million to earnings in 2004 and $20 million in 2005, while other technology programs (SAP and telephony) save $15 million on an annualized basis going forward. Working capital should improve, in our opinion, and we see free cash flow being used for internal investments, more share buybacks, dividend hikes, and bolt-on lab safety acquisitions.

- We think that a 2% drop in the effective tax rate will add $0.08 to EPS in 2004. Third quarter EPS was $0.04 above our estimate, and we now project operating EPS of $2.90 for the year, at the high end of GWW's new projected range; we estimate 17% growth, to $3.40, for 2005. We see S&P Core EPS of $2.75 for 2004 and $3.25 for 2005, primarily reflecting estimated stock option expense.

Investment Rationale/Risk October 20, 2004

- Based on favorable market trends and valuations, we believe that investors should purchase the shares on a total return basis. We think the company's strategic initiatives, which include new plants, additional branches and a new billing system, will enhance the distribution network and aid operating results.

- Risks to our recommendation and target price include a slower than expected economic recovery, difficulties in fully implementing new technology programs, and an inability to pass through higher costs to customers.

- We see return on invested capital (ROIC) exceeding 20%, slightly above the measure for GWW's peers. At about 17X our 2005 EPS estimate, the stock is at a 15% discount to the company's peer group. Based on our discounted cash flow model, applying a 3.5% terminal growth rate and an 8.75% weighted average cost of capital, the shares are trading 20% below intrinsic value. We believe the stock warrants a forward P/E multiple of about 20X our 2005 EPS projection, on par with the stock's historical forward P/E levels and our projected P/E relative to peers. Our 12-month target price remains at $67.

Key Stock Statistics

S&P Core EPS 2005E	3.25	52-week Range	$60.10-44.24
S&P Oper. EPS 2004E	2.90	12 Month P/E	21.3
P/E on S&P Oper. EPS 2004E	20.7	Beta	0.70
S&P Oper. EPS 2005E	3.40	Shareholders	1,400
Yield (%)	1.3%	Market Cap (B)	$ 5.4
Dividend Rate/Share	0.80	Shares Outstanding (M)	90.1

Value of $10,000 invested five years ago: **$ 15,478**

Dividend Data Dividends have been paid since 1965

Amount ($)	Date Decl.	Ex-Div. Date	Stock of Record	Payment Date
0.185	Jan. 29	Feb. 05	Feb. 09	Mar. 01 '04
0.200	Apr. 28	May. 06	May. 10	Jun. 01 '04
0.200	Jul. 28	Aug. 05	Aug. 09	Sep. 01 '04
0.200	Oct. 27	Nov. 04	Nov. 08	Dec. 01 '04

Revenues/Earnings Data Fiscal year ending December 31

Revenues (Million $)

	2004	2003	2002	2001	2000	1999
1Q	1,228	1,139	1,125	1,219	1,222	1,091
2Q	1,256	1,173	1,195	1,225	1,272	1,146
3Q	1,301	1,201	1,203	1,199	1,273	1,175
4Q	—	1,154	1,120	1,111	1,210	1,121
Yr.	—	4,667	4,644	4,754	4,977	4,534

Earnings Per Share ($)

	2004	2003	2002	2001	2000	1999
1Q	0.69	0.57	0.61	0.45	0.44	0.60
2Q	0.72	0.60	0.57	0.15	0.59	0.53
3Q	0.74	0.62	0.64	0.59	0.51	0.49
4Q	E0.75	0.67	0.67	0.65	0.51	0.30
Yr.	E2.90	2.46	2.50	1.84	2.05	1.92

Next earnings report expected: late-January Source: S&P, Company Reports
EPS Estimates based on S&P Operating Earnings; historical GAAP earnings are as reported.

W.W. Grainger, Inc.

Recommendation: **BUY** ★ ★ ★ ★ ★   12-Month Target Price: **$67.00** (as of September 29, 2004)

Business Summary October 20, 2004

In recent years, W.W. Grainger has invested significantly in expanding its Web businesses, anticipating positive growth trends for Web-based industrial supplies procurement and outsourcing. GWW has nearly 600 branches and 17 distribution centers. The company completed its new logistics network in March 2004, which it expects will lead to a headcount reduction of 1,000 between 1999 and the end of 2005. GWW plans to replace its legacy systems in 2005, while it has already met its goal of eliminating $100 million in inventory. The company has opened 11 distribution centers since early 2003, while closing 12 branches in Canada (two in the 2004 second quarter) and three in the U.S.

GWW sees several trends in its business. The first is increasing use of the Internet by buyers of industrial supplies. Accelerating Internet-based supplies procurement is being driven primarily by expectations of lower procurement processing and management costs. Sales processed through the Internet (Grainger.com) increased 14% in 2003, to $479 million. In July 2004, the company raised its 2004 projection for Web-based sales to a range of $575 million to $625 million, from $500 million to $550 million.

A second trend is the outsourcing of supplies procurement operations to third-party contractors such as the company. Since supplies procurement and inventory management can be complex and costly, companies are focusing on their core operations and on improving cash flow. It is estimated that the U.S. outsourcing market totals about $200 billion.

The Branch Distribution segment (89% of revenues, $390 million operating earnings and nearly 23% ROIC in 2003) mainly consists of GWW's 396 U.S. bricks and mortar branch stores (two in Puerto Rico), as well as 174 in Canada and five in

Mexico. These branches sell both company-made and third-party industrial supplies, via in-store catalogs and Internet services.

The company's Lab Safety Supply segment (6.5%, $42 million, 13.7% and 37% ROIC) is a direct marketer of safety and other industrial products to U.S. and Canadian businesses. It acquired Gempler Inc. in April 2003.

Grainger Integrated Supply (4.4%, $3.2 million, 1.5% and nearly 21% ROIC) primarily consists of GWW's industrial supply outsourcing services, and offers consulting and inventory and information management services.

In the 2003 fourth quarter, the company incurred a pretax restructuring charge of $564,000 and a $1.9 million writedown of investments in two Asian joint ventures.

In 2003, U.S. customers by category were: heavy manufacturing 17%; commercial 19%; contractor 14%; government 17%; light manufacturing 11%; reseller 8%; retail 7%; transportation 4%; and other 3%.

GWW projects that annual sales will reach $7 billion by late 2008, with operating margins (after depreciation and amortization) of 9.5% to 10%, up from 8% to 8.4% forecast for 2004. The company repurchased 908,100 shares in the third quarter of 2004, and nearly 1.9 million through the first nine months of the year, with 7.2 million shares still authorized for repurchase. In October 2004, GWW revised its capital expenditure projection for 2004 to a range of $130 million to $140 million, from $150 million to $175 million, due to lower spending for the market expansion and other programs. It projects capital expenditures of $50 million to $55 million for the SAP system and $15 million to $20 million for the telephony program.

Company Financials Fiscal Year ending December 31

Per Share Data ($)

(Year Ended December 31)	2003	2002	2001	2000	1999	1998	1997	1996	1995	1994
Tangible Bk. Val.	18.43	16.92	15.51	14.67	14.00	11.74	11.13	11.65	10.87	9.33
Cash Flow	3.28	3.30	2.73	3.01	2.85	3.20	3.05	2.74	2.52	1.90
Earnings	2.46	2.50	1.84	2.05	1.92	2.44	2.27	2.02	1.82	1.25
S&P Core Earnings	2.36	2.29	1.87	NA	NA	NA	NA	NA	NA	NA
Dividends	0.73	0.72	0.70	0.67	0.63	0.59	0.53	0.49	0.45	0.39
Payout Ratio	30%	29%	38%	33%	33%	24%	23%	24%	24%	31%
Prices - High	53.30	59.40	48.99	56.87	58.12	54.71	49.87	40.75	33.81	34.56
- Low	41.40	39.20	29.51	24.31	36.87	36.43	35.25	31.31	27.75	25.75
P/E Ratio - High	22	24	27	28	30	22	22	20	19	28
- Low	17	16	16	12	19	15	16	16	15	21

Income Statement Analysis (Million $)

	2003	2002	2001	2000	1999	1998	1997	1996	1995	1994
Revs.	4,667	4,644	4,754	4,977	4,534	4,341	4,137	3,537	3,277	3,023
Oper. Inc.	463	467	461	426	406	482	473	420	387	368
Depr.	76.1	75.9	83.7	90.6	88.4	74.2	79.7	74.3	70.9	66.7
Int. Exp.	6.01	6.16	10.7	24.4	15.6	6.65	5.46	3.00	6.40	3.80
Pretax Inc.	381	398	297	332	304	401	390	349	312	229
Eff. Tax Rate	40.4%	40.8%	41.3%	41.8%	40.5%	40.5%	40.5%	40.2%	40.2%	44.1%
Net Inc.	227	235	175	193	181	239	232	209	187	128
S&P Core Earnings	217	213	177	NA	NA	NA	NA	NA	NA	NA

Balance Sheet & Other Fin. Data (Million $)

	2003	2002	2001	2000	1999	1998	1997	1996	1995	1994
Cash	403	209	169	63.4	62.7	43.1	46.9	127	11.4	15.0
Curr. Assets	1,633	1,485	1,393	1,483	1,471	1,206	1,183	1,320	1,063	964
Total Assets	2,625	2,437	2,331	2,460	2,565	2,104	1,998	2,119	1,669	1,535
Curr. Liab.	707	586	554	747	871	664	534	616	444	459
LT Debt	4.89	120	118	125	125	123	131	6.15	8.71	1.00
Common Equity	1,845	1,668	1,603	1,537	1,481	1,279	1,295	1,463	1,179	1,033
Total Cap.	1,850	1,787	1,723	1,663	1,654	1,402	1,429	1,471	1,188	1,049
Cap. Exp.	74.1	134	100	65.5	114	130	108	62.1	112	120
Cash Flow	303	311	258	284	269	313	311	283	258	195
Curr. Ratio	2.3	2.5	2.5	2.0	1.7	1.8	2.2	2.1	2.4	2.1
% LT Debt of Cap.	0.3	6.7	6.9	7.5	7.6	8.8	9.2	0.4	0.7	0.1
% Net Inc.of Revs.	4.9	5.1	3.7	3.9	4.0	5.5	5.6	5.9	5.7	4.2
% Ret. on Assets	9.0	9.9	7.3	7.7	7.7	11.6	11.3	11.0	11.7	8.8
% Ret. on Equity	12.9	14.4	11.1	12.8	13.1	18.5	16.8	15.8	16.9	12.9

Data as orig reptd.; bef. results of disc opers/spec. items. Per share data adj. for stk. divs.; EPS diluted. E-Estimated. NA-Not Available. NM-Not Meaningful. NR-Not Ranked. UR-Under Review.

Office: 100 Grainger Pkwy, Lake Forest, IL 60045.
Telephone: 847-535-1000.
Website: http://www.grainger.com
Chrmn & CEO: R.L. Keyser.
Pres & COO: W.M. Clark.
SVP & CFO: P.O. Loux.

SVP & General Counsel: J.L. Howard.
SVP & Investor Contact: N.A. Hobor 847-535-0065.
Dirs: B. P. Anderson, W. M. Clark, W. H. Gantz, D. W. Grainger, R. L. Keyser, F. A. Krehbiel, J. W. McCarter, Jr., N. S. Novich, J. D. Slavik, H. B. Smith, J. S. Webb.

Founded: in 1927.
Domicile: Illinois.
Employees: 14,701.
S&P Analyst: Stewart Scharf/DC/GG

Great Lakes Chemical

Recommendation: **BUY** ★★★★☆
SELL · SELL · HOLD · BUY · BUY

12-Month Target Price: **$32.00**
(as of January 14, 2004)

GLK has an approximate 0.01% weighting in the **S&P 500**

Sector: Materials
Sub-Industry: Specialty Chemicals
Peer Group: Specialty Chemicals (Larger)

Summary: GLK is the world's leading producer of certain specialty chemicals for applications such as water treatment, household cleaners, flame retardants and polymer stabilizers.

Quantitative Evaluations

S&P Earnings & Dividend Rank: B

| D | C | B- | B | B+ | A- | A | A+ |

S&P Fair Value Rank: 1

| 1 | 2 | 3 | 4 | 5 |
| Lowest | | | | Highest |

Fair Value Calc.: $21.90 (Overvalued)

S&P Investability Quotient Percentile — 94%

GLK scored higher than 94% of all companies for which an S&P Report is available.

Volatility: Average

| Low | Average | High |

Technical Evaluation: Bullish
Since 11/04, the technical indicators for GLK have been Bullish.

Relative Strength Rank: Moderate — 65

| 1 Lowest | Highest 99 |

Price as of 11/12/04: $27.54 | **2004E S&P Core EPS:** $0.98

GAAP Earnings vs. Previous Year
▲ Up ▼ Down ▶ No Change

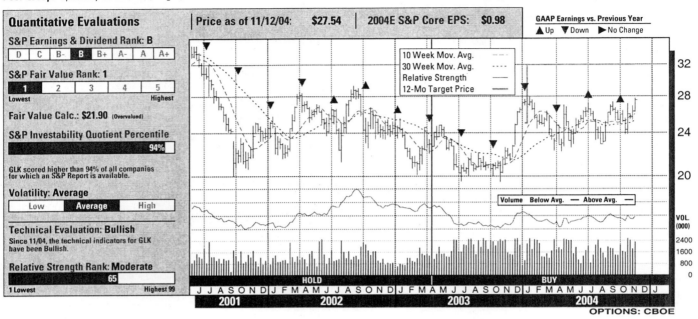

- 10 Week Mov. Avg.
- 30 Week Mov. Avg.
- Relative Strength
- 12-Mo Target Price

Volume Below Avg. — Above Avg. —

VOL. (000): 2400, 1600, 800, 0

HOLD · BUY
J J A S O N D | J F M A M J J A S O N D | J F M A M J J A S O N D | J F M A M J J A S O N D | J
2001 · 2002 · 2003 · 2004

OPTIONS: CBOE

Analyst commentary prepared by Richard O'Reilly/PMW/JWP

Highlights September 27, 2004

- We expect GLK to post 10% higher sales in 2004, aided by favorable exchange rates and the acquisition of two consumer products companies in 2003. We see a further gain in 2005. We expect operating results to be aided by restructuring actions announced in late 2003, designed to generate savings of $32 million by 2005. The company expects to record related pretax charges through 2004 totaling $140 million, including $137 million ($1.98 a share) to date.

- We expect polymer additives volumes to rebound, on better conditions in the plastics industry; price increases for both flame retardants and stabilizers should continue to take hold over the rest of 2004. We also look for recreational water chemical sales to improve in 2004, on more normal weather, after unusually cool and wet conditions in 2003. Despite expected competitive price erosion of about $0.12 a share and lost sales (up to $20 million) and costs related to a warehouse fire in late May, we believe the water care business continues to be well positioned with mass merchandisers.

- We expect the house cleaning products businesses to grow in 2005, and see fluorine chemicals sales showing some recovery. Higher raw material costs reduced 2003 EPS by about $0.32; we see material costs being modestly higher in 2004. Results in the 2004 second quarter include a tax benefit of $0.34 a share tax; the ongoing tax rate should remain at about 31%.

Investment Rationale/Risk September 27, 2004

- We recommend accumulating the shares, based on our belief that earnings will rebound. We think selling prices of polymer additives are improving, and see the water care business with a record of steady growth. What we see as a strong balance sheet (net debt was 31% of capitalization as of June 2004) should allow GLK to make additional acquisitions.

- Risks to our recommendation and target price include the impact of unfavorable summer weather on the pool chemicals business, inability to successfully introduce new products, and unexpected competitive pressures.

- The shares are trading at a 2004 P/E multiple that is modestly above the average P/E multiple for a group of leading specialty chemicals companies. Our 12-month target price of $32, using our 2005 EPS estimate, assumes that the P/E multiple will move closer to that of the company's peer group, as GLK experiences an EPS rebound.

Key Stock Statistics

S&P Core EPS 2005E	1.38	52-week Range	$28.00-21.31
S&P Oper. EPS 2004E	0.85	12 Month P/E	74.4
P/E on S&P Oper. EPS 2004E	32.4	Beta	1.13
S&P Oper. EPS 2005E	1.30	Shareholders	2,006
Yield (%)	1.4%	Market Cap (B)	$ 1.4
Dividend Rate/Share	0.38	Shares Outstanding (M)	51.1

Value of $10,000 invested five years ago: **$ 7,905**

Dividend Data Dividends have been paid since 1973

Amount ($)	Date Decl.	Ex-Div. Date	Stock of Record	Payment Date
0.095	Dec. 04	Dec. 29	Jan. 01	Jan. 30 '04
0.095	Feb. 17	Mar. 30	Apr. 01	Apr. 30 '04
0.095	May. 06	Jun. 29	Jul. 01	Jul. 30 '04
0.095	Sep. 09	Sep. 29	Oct. 01	Oct. 29 '04

Revenues/Earnings Data Fiscal year ending December 31

Revenues (Million $)

	2004	2003	2002	2001	2000	1999
1Q	368.1	334.0	305.0	410.3	404.5	334.2
2Q	454.0	416.7	408.5	461.4	442.6	374.8
3Q	391.9	375.3	360.6	380.5	418.2	374.4
4Q	—	338.6	327.4	342.5	405.2	369.9
Yr.	—	1,465	1,402	1,595	1,671	1,453

Earnings Per Share ($)

	2004	2003	2002	2001	2000	1999
1Q	-0.08	0.02	0.10	0.40	0.52	0.53
2Q	0.55	0.33	0.44	-3.06	0.75	0.73
3Q	-0.03	-0.31	0.27	-0.02	0.67	0.59
4Q	E0.15	-0.71	0.15	-0.98	0.48	0.57
Yr.	E0.85	-0.67	0.95	-5.76	2.42	2.41

Next earnings report expected: late-January Source: S&P, Company Reports
EPS Estimates based on S&P Operating Earnings; historical GAAP earnings are as reported.

STANDARD
&POOR'S

Great Lakes Chemical Corporation

Stock Report
November 13, 2004
NYSE Symbol: **GLK**

Recommendation: **BUY** ★★★★☆   12-Month Target Price: **$32.00** (as of January 14, 2004)

Business Summary September 27, 2004

Great Lakes Chemical Corp. is a leading global supplier of plastics additives and consumer pool chemicals. In 2003, the company entered the consumer household cleaning products market by acquiring two makers of specialty cleaning products. At the end of May 2002, it sold its remaining 53% interest in its OSCA, Inc., oil services unit to BJ Services Co., receiving after-tax proceeds of about $200 million. In June 2000, GLK sold a 43% interest in OSCA through an IPO; total proceeds to the company were $91 million. The company plans to divest its remaining unprofitable fine chemicals business (2003 sales of $46 million; reported as discontinued operations in 2002).

Foreign operations accounted for 38% of sales in 2003.

Polymer additives accounted for 51% of sales and had a operating loss of $89.5 million in 2003. GLK is a leading worldwide producer of brominated, antimony and phosphate based flame retardants, which together with polymer stabilizers (anti-oxidants, UV absorbers, light stabilizers) are used to enhance the performance of a wide variety of polymer systems. It also makes lubricant additives for use in industrial applications. The segment also produces bromine and derivative products used in electronics, rubber compounds, and detergents; clear brine fluids for oil well drilling; and methyl bromide fumigants for agricultural and food applications. In addition, the company makes optical monomers used in eyewear, photographic filters, and safety shields and goggles.

Performance chemicals (7%, profits of $13.8 million) consist of fluorine chemicals for use in electronics, refrigerants and medical propellants; fire suppressants (FM 200); and WIL Laboratories toxicological testing and bioanalytical services. GLK plans to divest its unprofitable fine chemicals business.

Specialty Products (42%, $72.7 million) includes the BioLab unit, the world's leading supplier of bromine and chlorine-based specialty sanitizers, biocides and oxidizers for recreational pool and spa water treatment, sold under the BioGuard, OMNI, Hydrotech and AquaChem brand names. It also supplies water additives (corrosion inhibitors, dispersants, antifoams, scale control and desalination solutions) for industrial water and wastewater treatment, paper production and desalination industries. In 2003, GLK acquired two makers of consumer cleaning products, for a total of $106 million. In February 2003, the company acquired Lime-O-Sol Co., a maker of household cleaning products (bathroom cleaners, glass and surface cleaners, and drain openers) sold under the brand name The Works, with annual sales of about $45 million. In July, GLK acquired A&M Cleaning Products, a maker of multi-purpose cleaners sold under the names Greased Lighting and Orange Blast, with 2002 sales of $30 million.

The company has repurchased about 22.6 million common shares since 1993, for about $1.04 billion. About 2.8 million shares remain available for purchase under existing plans, including 2 million shares authorized by directors in October 2000.

Company Financials Fiscal Year ending December 31

Per Share Data ($)

(Year Ended December 31)	2003	2002	2001	2000	1999	1998	1997	1996	1995	1994
Tangible Bk. Val.	9.38	11.34	9.44	13.38	13.72	16.07	20.23	17.07	15.52	13.37
Cash Flow	1.20	2.53	-3.76	4.51	3.95	2.36	2.41	5.89	5.80	5.47
Earnings	-0.67	0.95	-5.76	2.42	2.41	0.95	1.19	3.94	4.52	4.00
S&P Core Earnings	-0.50	0.60	-4.43	NA	NA	NA	NA	NA	NA	NA
Dividends	0.36	0.33	0.32	0.32	0.32	0.48	0.63	0.57	0.44	0.39
Payout Ratio	NM	35%	NM	13%	13%	51%	53%	14%	10%	10%
Prices - High	27.60	29.31	37.62	40.50	50.00	54.18	54.87	78.62	74.62	82.00
- Low	19.51	21.24	20.00	26.50	33.18	36.68	41.50	44.25	55.75	48.75
P/E Ratio - High	NM	31	NM	17	21	57	46	20	17	20
- Low	NM	22	NM	11	14	39	35	11	12	12

Income Statement Analysis (Million $)

	2003	2002	2001	2000	1999	1998	1997	1996	1995	1994
Revs.	1,465	1,402	1,595	1,671	1,453	1,394	1,311	2,212	2,361	2,065
Oper. Inc.	112	196	90.5	304	270	274	265	570	581	541
Depr.	94.7	80.1	101	100	89.5	83.5	73.7	124	83.4	102
Int. Exp.	25.8	27.6	43.9	72.8	31.0	44.7	56.3	26.0	21.2	11.9
Pretax Inc.	-89.0	68.7	-357	165	175	66.2	117	379	438	436
Eff. Tax Rate	NM	31.0%	NM	23.0%	20.4%	14.8%	38.7%	33.9%	32.4%	28.4%
Net Inc.	-33.9	47.4	-290	127	140	56.4	71.8	250	296	279
S&P Core Earnings	-25.1	29.8	-222	NA	NA	NA	NA	NA	NA	NA

Balance Sheet & Other Fin. Data (Million $)

	2003	2002	2001	2000	1999	1998	1997	1996	1995	1994
Cash	171	259	71.6	223	478	412	73.7	202	181	145
Curr. Assets	760	847	681	1,008	1,168	996	669	1,177	1,125	980
Total Assets	1,693	1,718	1,688	2,134	2,261	2,005	2,270	2,661	2,469	2,111
Curr. Liab.	403	418	453	385	311	347	304	434	465	428
LT Debt	428	433	528	688	883	515	561	504	340	144
Common Equity	744	746	613	1,899	994	1,054	1,307	1,487	1,416	1,311
Total Cap.	1,178	1,184	1,184	2,670	1,915	1,621	1,936	2,119	1,876	1,557
Cap. Exp.	62.7	64.8	166	157	119	161	133	237	247	123
Cash Flow	60.8	128	-189	227	229	140	145	375	379	381
Curr. Ratio	1.9	2.0	1.5	2.6	3.8	2.9	2.2	2.7	2.4	2.3
% LT Debt of Cap.	36.3	36.5	44.6	25.8	46.1	31.8	29.0	23.7	18.1	9.2
% Net Inc.of Revs.	NM	3.4	NM	7.6	9.6	4.0	5.5	11.3	12.5	13.5
% Ret. on Assets	NM	2.8	NM	5.8	6.5	2.6	2.9	4.8	12.9	14.3
% Ret. on Equity	NM	7.0	NM	6.5	13.6	4.8	5.1	17.2	21.7	22.3

Data as orig reptd.; bef. results of disc opers/spec. items. Per share data adj. for stk. divs. Bold denotes primary EPS - prior periods restated. E-Estimated. NA-Not Available. NM-Not Meaningful. NR-Not Ranked. UR-Under Review.

Office: 9025 N River Rd Ste 400, Indianapolis, IN 46240-6436.
Telephone: 317-715-3000.
Email: investorinfo@glcc.com
Website: http://www.greatlakeschem.com
Chrmn, Pres & CEO: M.P. Bulriss.

SVP & CFO: J.J. Gallagher III.
SVP, Secy & General Counsel: J.M. Lipshaw.
Investor Contact: J. Potrzebowski 317-715-3027.
Dirs: N. G. Andrews, M. P. Bulriss, J. Crownover, T. M. Fulton, M. M. Hale, L. E. Lataif, J. C. Lechleiter, M. G. Nichols, J. D. Proops.

Founded: in 1933.
Domicile: Delaware.
Employees: 4,200.
S&P Analyst: Richard O'Reilly/PMW/JWP

Guidant Corp.

Recommendation: HOLD ★★★☆☆   12-Month Target Price: **$70.00**
(as of September 29, 2004)

GDT has an approximate 0.19% weighting in the **S&P 500**

Sector: Health Care
Sub-Industry: Health Care Equipment
Peer Group: Large Multi-Line Medical Device Manufacturers

Summary: Guidant, which designs and markets medical devices, has leadership positions in the interventional cardiology, cardiac rhythm management, and cardiac and vascular surgery markets.

Quantitative Evaluations

S&P Earnings & Dividend Rank: B

| D | C | B- | **B** | B+ | A- | A | A+ |

S&P Fair Value Rank: 2-

| 1 | **2** | 3 | 4 | 5 |
| Lowest | | | | Highest |

Fair Value Calc.: $61.60 (Slightly Overvalued)

S&P Investability Quotient Percentile

86%

GDT scored higher than 86% of all companies for which an S&P Report is available.

Volatility: Average

| Low | **Average** | High |

Technical Evaluation: Bullish
Since 8/04, the technical indicators for GDT have been Bullish.

Relative Strength Rank: Moderate

47

| 1 Lowest | | Highest 99 |

Price as of 11/12/04: $65.37   **2004E S&P Core EPS: $2.08**

GAAP Earnings vs. Previous Year
▲ Up ▼ Down ► No Change

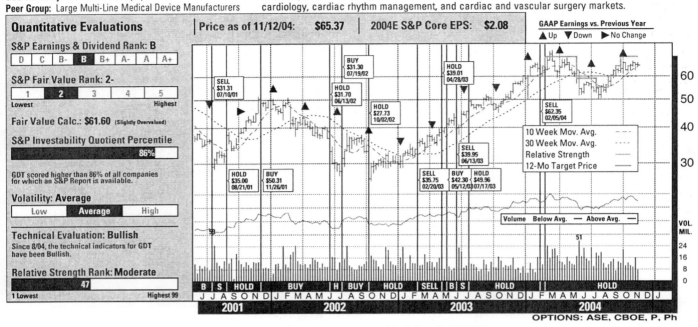

- 10 Week Mov. Avg.
- 30 Week Mov. Avg.
- Relative Strength
- 12-Mo Target Price

Volume Below Avg. — Above Avg.

VOL. MIL.

OPTIONS: ASE, CBOE, P, Ph

Analyst commentary prepared by Robert Gold/CB/GG

Highlights October 26, 2004

- We look for 2004 revenues of $3.7 billion, as a strong performance for implantable defibrillators (ICDs, including the Contak CD for congestive heart failure), and contributions from cardiac surgery offset projected lower sales from interventional cardiology. Looking at 2005, we believe low single digit revenue growth is likely, as 10% growth in defibrillator sales helps mitigate declining sales of interventional vascular products and flat pacemaker revenues.
- In our view, GDT will continue to face challenges in coronary stents as the U.S. and European markets convert to drug-coated devices, and we do not believe the company will participate in the U.S. drug-coated stent market prior to 2007 at the earliest. The company is capturing some drug-coated stent revenue through a deal to co-promote Johnson & Johnson's (JNJ: buy, $57) Cypher device, and we think quarterly revenues will be boosted by upwards of $30 million as a result of this alliance.
- To streamline its cost structure amid weakened sales growth, GDT has pursued a restructuring focused on the declining vascular intervention division. We see 2004 gross margins of 75%, falling to 74% in 2005. We think SG&A costs will consume about 31% of sales in 2004 and 2005, with the R&D ratio declining from 14% to 13%. Excluding restructuring charges, costs tied to a change in stock-based compensation, and charges for in-process R&D, our 2004 operating EPS estimate is $2.42. We project 2005 EPS of $2.65. Our S&P Core EPS estimate for 2004 is $2.08.

Investment Rationale/Risk October 26, 2004

- We believe the company's participation in ICD markets will enable it to offset expected weakness in the vascular intervention business in coming quarters, but do not envision material sales growth prior to the end of 2005. We believe ICD market growth will exceed 20% for the forseeable future. However, the company appears to have lost ICD market share in the third quarter of 2004, following the launch of a new ICD by St. Jude Medical (STJ: hold, $73). We do not think Guidant can compete in the U.S. drug-coated coronary stent market prior to 2007, although it participates indirectly through its agreement with JNJ. We would not recommend that investors add to holdings, but think the possibility of a takeover will provide near-term support to the stock.

Key Stock Statistics

S&P Oper. EPS 2004E	2.42	52-week Range	$73.70-49.95
P/E on S&P Oper. EPS 2004E	27.0	12 Month P/E	33.2
S&P Oper. EPS 2005E	2.65	Beta	0.16
Yield (%)	0.6%	Shareholders	5,356
Dividend Rate/Share	0.40	Market Cap (B)	$ 20.8
Shares Outstanding (M)	318.6		

Value of $10,000 invested five years ago: **$ 12,542**

Dividend Data Dividends have been paid since 2003

Amount ($)	Date Decl.	Ex-Div. Date	Stock of Record	Payment Date
0.100	Feb. 17	Feb. 26	Mar. 01	Mar. 15 '04
0.100	May. 17	May. 27	Jun. 01	Jun. 15 '04
0.100	Aug. 17	Aug. 30	Sep. 01	Sep. 15 '04
0.100	Oct. 18	Nov. 29	Dec. 01	Dec. 15 '04

Revenues/Earnings Data Fiscal year ending December 31

Revenues (Million $)

	2004	2003	2002	2001	2000	1999
1Q	934.1	885.4	709.7	671.0	630.7	590.1
2Q	938.8	944.9	807.0	656.3	688.4	603.5
3Q	924.5	937.8	827.4	661.6	600.8	560.9
4Q	—	951.4	895.5	718.7	648.8	576.0
Yr.	—	3,699	3,240	2,708	2,549	2,352

Earnings Per Share ($)

	2004	2003	2002	2001	2000	1999
1Q	0.48	0.30	0.45	0.36	0.38	0.18
2Q	0.42	-0.26	0.67	0.38	0.40	0.31
3Q	0.50	0.47	0.57	0.40	0.40	0.32
4Q	E0.65	0.63	0.31	0.44	0.03	0.31
Yr.	E2.42	1.36	2.00	1.58	1.21	1.11

Next earnings report expected: early-February Source: S&P, Company Reports
EPS Estimates based on S&P Operating Earnings; historical GAAP earnings are as reported.

STANDARD &POOR'S

Guidant Corporation

Stock Report
November 13, 2004
NYSE Symbol: GDT

Recommendation: HOLD ★ ★ ★ ☆ ☆   12-Month Target Price: **$70.00** (as of September 29, 2004)

Business Summary October 27, 2004

Guidant Corp., created in 1994 via a combination of five medical device units of Eli Lilly, holds leadership positions in interventional cardiology, cardiac rhythm management (CRM), and cardiac and vascular surgery markets.

CRM products include implantable cardioverter defibrillator (ICD) systems (40% of 2003 revenues) that are used to detect and treat potentially fatal, abnormally fast heart rhythms by delivering electrical energy to the heart and restoring normal rhythm. The key product line is the Ventak defibrillator family. Cardiac pacemakers (19%) are used to manage a slow or irregular heartbeat caused by disorders that disrupt the heart's normal electrical conduction system. GDT's primary brady products include the Pulsar Max and Insignia lines.

The company has created device solutions for heart failure, a condition that affects nearly five million Americans yearly. In May 2002, GDT received FDA approval for its Contak CD/Easytrak system, which combines an implantable defibrillator with cardiac resynchronization therapy that uses wires implanted in different spots in the heart to make the chambers pump together. In January 2004, the FDA approved the company's Contak Renewal TR cardiac resynchronization therapy pacemaker. Sales from Contak are included in those of ICDs and pacemakers, as deemed appropriate by GDT.

More than 6 million Americans have been diagnosed with coronary artery disease (CAD), a potentially fatal restriction of blood flow in coronary arteries due to the formation of atherosclerotic lesions. The company offers various products to treat CAD. Its coronary stent systems (23% of 2003 sales) are metal tubes or coils mounted on coronary dilatation catheters and permanently deployed at a blockage in a coronary artery. The Multi-Link stent family includes the Penta, the Vision and the Pixel. GDT is studying stents coated with drugs that can prevent excessive cell re-growth at the site of stent placement, and hopes to enter the U.S. market during 2006.

In February 2004, GDT entered into an alliance with Johnson & Johnson (JNJ) under which it will co-promote JNJ's Cypher drug-coated coronary stent in the U.S. and possibly in Japan, in return for commissions based on unit sales. The agreement will terminate in 2011 or earlier if GDT gains FDA approval to sell its own drug-coated stent.

The company also sells angioplasty systems and accessories, including dilatation catheters, guide wires, guiding catheters, atherectomy catheters and related products (13%).

Non-coronary products (5%) include non-coronary stent systems, together with guidewires, guiding catheters, dilatation catheters and other peripheral vascular stents, and products for minimally invasive, beating heart surgery. In peripheral disease, GDT gained FDA approval in August 2004 for the Rx Acculink Carotid Stent System and Rx Accunet Embolic Protection system for the minimally invasive treatment of carotid artery disease. In 2003, the company discontinued its abdominal aortic aneurysm graft product line.

Company Financials Fiscal Year ending December 31

Per Share Data ($)

(Year Ended December 31)	2003	2002	2001	2000	1999	1998	1997	1996	1995	1994
Tangible Bk. Val.	6.60	5.58	3.05	1.76	0.65	1.02	1.31	0.84	0.30	-0.14
Cash Flow	1.91	2.42	2.05	1.64	1.49	0.24	0.72	0.46	0.59	0.55
Earnings	1.36	2.00	1.58	1.21	1.11	-0.01	0.50	0.23	0.35	0.32
S&P Core Earnings	2.03	1.46	1.17	NA	NA	NA	NA	NA	NA	NA
Dividends	0.24	Nil	Nil	Nil	Nil	0.03	0.03	0.03	0.01	Nil
Payout Ratio	18%	Nil	Nil	Nil	Nil	NM	5%	11%	4%	Nil
Prices - High	60.53	51.00	55.12	75.37	69.87	56.50	34.75	15.34	10.65	4.03
- Low	28.89	24.75	26.90	44.00	41.00	25.50	13.40	9.87	3.87	3.62
P/E Ratio - High	45	25	35	62	63	NM	70	67	30	15
- Low	21	12	17	36	37	NM	27	43	11	14

Income Statement Analysis (Million $)

	2003	2002	2001	2000	1999	1998	1997	1996	1995	1994
Revs.	3,699	3,240	2,708	2,549	2,352	1,897	1,328	1,049	931	862
Oper. Inc.	1,060	1,032	955	921	757	576	353	301	266	236
Depr.	172	128	141	133	120	72.9	66.0	66.2	67.8	64.4
Int. Exp.	17.2	23.9	31.5	55.0	56.0	15.3	19.5	24.2	33.1	18.8
Pretax Inc.	485	839	667	596	527	128	249	150	170	156
Eff. Tax Rate	12.3%	27.1%	27.5%	37.2%	34.7%	NM	39.7%	56.0%	40.5%	40.9%
Net Inc.	426	612	484	374	344	-2.20	150	65.8	101	92.1
S&P Core Earnings	637	446	357	NA	NA	NA	NA	NA	NA	NA

Balance Sheet & Other Fin. Data (Million $)

	2003	2002	2001	2000	1999	1998	1997	1996	1995	1994
Cash	1,468	1,015	438	163	28.0	15.6	17.7	1.50	3.00	113
Curr. Assets	3,080	2,303	1,548	1,162	916	764	625	419	389	458
Total Assets	4,640	3,716	2,917	2,521	2,250	1,570	1,225	1,004	1,057	1,104
Curr. Liab.	1,062	866	789	709	739	587	541	308	279	341
LT Debt	698	362	460	509	528	390	80.0	234	385	473
Common Equity	2,713	2,322	1,546	1,185	866	554	582	448	384	264
Total Cap.	3,412	2,684	2,006	1,694	1,394	944	662	682	769	737
Cap. Exp.	141	141	149	160	175	116	76.8	62.1	64.7	51.1
Cash Flow	597	739	625	507	464	70.7	216	132	169	157
Curr. Ratio	2.9	2.7	2.0	1.6	1.2	1.3	1.2	1.4	1.4	1.3
% LT Debt of Cap.	20.5	13.5	22.9	30.0	37.9	41.3	13.7	34.3	50.1	64.1
% Net Inc.of Revs.	11.5	18.9	17.9	14.7	14.6	NM	11.3	6.3	10.9	10.7
% Ret. on Assets	10.2	18.4	17.8	15.7	17.8	NM	13.5	6.4	9.4	NM
% Ret. on Equity	16.9	31.6	35.5	36.5	47.2	NM	29.1	15.8	31.2	NM

Data as orig reptd.; bef. results of disc opers/spec. items. Per share data adj. for stk. divs.; EPS diluted. E-Estimated. NA-Not Available. NM-Not Meaningful. NR-Not Ranked. UR-Under Review.

Office: 111 Monument Circle, Indianapolis, IN 46204-5100.
Telephone: 317-971-2000.
Website: http://www.guidant.com
Chrmn: J.M. Cornelius.
Pres & CEO: R.W. Dollens.
VP & CFO: K.E. Brauer.
VP & Secy: D.F. Minott.

VP & General Counsel: B.E. Kury.
Investor Contact: A. Rieth 317-971-2061.
Dirs: J. M. Cornelius, M. A. Cox, Jr., N. M. DeParle, R. W. Dollens, E. C. Falla, M. Grobstein, K. M. Johnson, J. B. King, S. B. King, J. K. Moore, M. Novitch, J. A. Shaw, E. L. Step, R. E. Wager, A. M. Watanabe.

Founded: in 1994.
Domicile: Indiana.
Employees: 12,000.
S&P Analyst: Robert Gold/CB/GG

Halliburton Co.

Recommendation: **HOLD** ★ ★ ★ ★   **12-Month Target Price: $38.00**
(as of October 26, 2004)

HAL has an approximate 0.15% weighting in the **S&P 500**

Sector: Energy
Sub-Industry: Oil & Gas Equipment & Services
Peer Group: Oil & Gas - Services & Equipment - Large

Summary: HAL provides services, equipment, maintenance, and engineering and construction to energy, industrial and governmental customers.

Quantitative Evaluations

S&P Earnings & Dividend Rank: B

| D | C | B- | **B** | B+ | A- | A | A+ |

S&P Fair Value Rank: 1

| **1** | 2 | 3 | 4 | 5 |
| Lowest | | | | Highest |

Fair Value Calc.: $25.00 (Overvalued)

S&P Investability Quotient Percentile

60%

HAL scored higher than 60% of all companies for which an S&P Report is available.

Volatility: Average

| Low | **Average** | High |

Technical Evaluation: Bullish

Since 9/04, the technical indicators for HAL have been Bullish.

Relative Strength Rank: Strong

82

| 1 Lowest | | Highest 99 |

Price as of 11/12/04: $38   2004E S&P Core EPS: $1.20

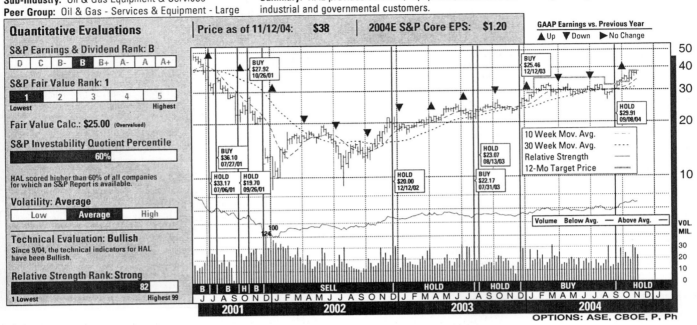

GAAP Earnings vs. Previous Year
▲ Up ▼ Down ► No Change

- 10 Week Mov. Avg.
- 30 Week Mov. Avg.
- Relative Strength
- 12-Mo Target Price

Volume   Below Avg. — Above Avg.

OPTIONS: ASE, CBOE, P, Ph

Analyst commentary prepared by Stewart Glickman/MF/DRJ

Highlights November 01, 2004

- In the Energy Services Group, we look for low double-digit revenue growth and a widening of operating margins in 2004, followed by 15% revenue growth in 2005, albeit with slightly narrower margins. In the Engineering and Construction Group, we had expected 2004 revenues to advance over 50%, reflecting a strong backlog as well as additional Iraq-related contracts awarded to KBR in January 2004. However, in early September, the U.S. Army announced plans to re-bid about $13 billion of such contracts, opening the possibility that HAL will lose these contracts. We see operating margins in the group remaining in the low single digits, well below both historical and projected levels for the Energy Services Group.

- In July 2004, a U.S. district court approved HAL's plans for a $4.2 billion asbestos settlement and restructuring to bring DII, KBR and other affected subsidiaries out of bankruptcy. Recent issues regarding KBR's methodology of cost accounting have raised the possibility that the Army Materiel Command may withhold 15% of future payments to KBR until the dispute is resolved. However, since the company would likely withhold 15% of its own payments to subcontractors, we do not see an immediate financial impact if the Army withholding occurs.

- For 2004, we estimate EPS of $1.41, excluding discontinued operations and special charges, and see an advance to $1.70 in 2005. On an S&P Core Earnings basis, we expect respective EPS of $1.20 and $1.56.

Investment Rationale/Risk November 01, 2004

- We have a hold recommendation on the shares, based largely on valuation. Through late October, the stock was up 41% in 2004, versus an increase of 32% for the S&P Oil & Gas Equipment & Services Index. In terms of relative valuation, the shares recently traded at an enterprise value of 9.0X our 2005 EBITDA estimate, below the 11.3X peer group average, and also at a discount on a price to cash flow basis, but were at a premium to peers on a price to net equity basis.

- Risks to our recommendation and target price include potential delays in completing planned restructurings; reduced oil and gas drilling activity; lower than expected oil and natural gas prices; and the possible loss of KBR contract work for the U.S. Army.

- Our discounted cash flow model, which assumes free cash flow growth of about 8% to 9% per year for 10 years and 3.5% thereafter, calculates intrinsic value of $35 a share. We expect asbestos claims to be settled according to global settlement terms toward the end of 2004. As a result, we expect the shares to trade closer to peer levels. Our 12-month target price of $38 is derived by blending the results of our enterprise value to 2005 EBITDA valuation, our price to net equity valuation, price to cash flow metrics, and our DCF model.

Key Stock Statistics

S&P Core EPS 2005E	1.56	52-week Range	$38.17-22.23	
S&P Oper. EPS 2004E	1.41	12 Month P/E	NM	
P/E on S&P Oper. EPS 2004E	27.0	Beta	1.31	
S&P Oper. EPS 2005E	1.70	Shareholders	24,143	
Yield (%)	1.3%	Market Cap (B)	$ 16.8	
Dividend Rate/Share	0.50	Shares Outstanding (M)	442.0	

Value of $10,000 invested five years ago: **$ 11,423**

Dividend Data Dividends have been paid since 1947

Amount ($)	Date Decl.	Ex-Div. Date	Stock of Record	Payment Date
0.125	Feb. 18	Mar. 02	Mar. 04	Mar. 25 '04
0.125	May. 19	Jun. 01	Jun. 03	Jun. 24 '04
0.125	Jul. 15	Aug. 31	Sep. 02	Sep. 23 '04
0.125	Oct. 21	Nov. 29	Dec. 01	Dec. 22 '04

Revenues/Earnings Data Fiscal year ending December 31

Revenues (Million $)

	2004	2003	2002	2001	2000	1999
1Q	5,519	3,060	3,007	3,144	2,859	3,924
2Q	4,956	3,599	3,235	3,339	2,868	3,670
3Q	4,790	4,148	2,982	3,391	3,024	3,533
4Q	—	5,464	3,348	3,172	3,193	3,771
Yr.	—	16,271	12,572	13,046	11,944	14,898

Earnings Per Share ($)

	2004	2003	2002	2001	2000	1999
1Q	-0.17	0.14	0.12	0.20	0.06	0.18
2Q	-0.13	0.09	-0.83	0.33	0.12	0.19
3Q	0.42	0.21	0.22	0.42	0.29	0.13
4Q	E0.34	0.34	-0.30	0.33	-0.05	0.17
Yr.	E1.41	0.78	-0.80	1.28	0.42	0.67

Next earnings report expected: early-February Source: S&P, Company Reports
EPS Estimates based on S&P Operating Earnings; historical GAAP earnings are as reported.

Recommendation: **HOLD** ★ ★ ★ ☆ ☆   12-Month Target Price: **$38.00** (as of October 26, 2004)

Business Summary November 01, 2004

In 1998, Halliburton and Dresser Industries merged to form the world's largest oilfield services company, Halliburton Co. HAL is a global provider of services, products, maintenance, engineering and construction to energy, industrial and governmental customers. In 2003, about 27% of total revenues were generated from the U.S., and an additional 15% of total revenues were derived from Iraq, mainly through work for the U.S. government. No other country accounted for over 10% of total revenues in 2003. Sales of services and products to the energy industry provided 66% of 2003 revenues (86% in 2002).

The Energy Services Group (ESG; 43% of total revenues in 2003, versus 54% in 2002) provides a wide range of products and services for the exploration, development and production of oil and gas. Early in 2003, the company reorganized the group into four segments: Drilling and Formation Evaluation, Fluids, Production Optimization, and Landmark and Other Services.

The Drilling and Formation Evaluation segment (23% of ESG revenues in 2003, and 21% of ESG operating profits) is primarily involved in drilling and evaluating formations related to bore-hole construction and initial oil and gas formation evaluation. Products and services include drilling systems, drill bits, and logging.

The Fluids segment (29%, 30%) focuses on fluid management and technologies to assist in the drilling and construction of oil and gas wells, and also offers cementing services.

The Production Optimization segment (40%, 51%) primarily tests, measures and provides means to manage well production once a well has been drilled. Services include production enhancement, where the company will optimize oil and gas reservoirs through a variety of pressure pumping services; completion products,

including sub-surface safety valves, flow control equipment, and production automation; and tools and testing services.

The Landmark and Other Services segment (8%, -2%) provides integrated exploration and development software information systems, consulting services, real-time information, and other integrated solutions.

The Engineering and Construction Group (ECG: 57% of total revenues in 2003; 46% in 2002) provides engineering, procurement, construction, project management, and facilities operation and maintenance for oil and gas and other industrial and governmental customers. During the 2001 first quarter, ECG was restructured, and the engineering, construction, fabrication and project management capabilities are now part of Halliburton Kellogg Brown & Root (KBR). ECG, operating as KBR, includes the following five product lines: onshore operations (engineering and construction activities), offshore operations (specialty offshore deepwater engineering, marine technology, fabrication), government operations (operations, maintenance and logistics), operations and maintenance (mainly industrial, hydrocarbon and commercial applications for private sector customers), and infrastructure (which provides civil engineering, consulting and project management services).

In 2003, the company disposed of a number of non-core businesses. Among these were the Mono Pumps business, sold in January 2003 to National Oilwell Inc.; assets related to HAL's Wellstream business, a provider of flexible pipe products, sold in March 2003 to Candover Partners Ltd.; and certain assets of Halliburton Measurement Systems, which provides flow measurement and sampling systems, sold in May 2003 to NuFlo Technologies.

Company Financials Fiscal Year ending December 31

Per Share Data ($)

(Year Ended December 31)	2003	2002	2001	2000	1999	1998	1997	1996	1995	1994
Tangible Bk. Val.	4.28	6.50	9.29	7.80	7.96	7.48	8.63	7.70	6.76	7.58
Cash Flow	1.96	0.37	2.52	1.55	3.06	1.30	2.94	2.25	2.08	1.93
Earnings	0.78	-0.80	1.28	0.42	0.67	-0.03	1.75	1.19	1.02	0.78
S&P Core Earnings	0.68	-1.03	0.65	NA	NA	NA	NA	NA	NA	NA
Dividends	0.50	0.50	0.50	0.50	0.50	0.50	0.50	0.50	0.50	0.50
Payout Ratio	64%	NM	39%	119%	75%	NM	29%	42%	49%	64%
Prices - High	27.20	21.65	49.25	55.18	51.75	57.25	63.25	31.81	25.43	18.62
- Low	17.20	8.60	10.94	32.25	28.12	25.00	29.68	22.37	16.43	13.93
P/E Ratio - High	35	NM	38	NM	77	NM	36	27	25	24
- Low	22	NM	9	NM	42	NM	17	19	16	18

Income Statement Analysis (Million $)

	2003	2002	2001	2000	1999	1998	1997	1996	1995	1994
Revs.	16,246	12,498	13,046	11,856	14,765	17,159	8,819	7,385	5,699	5,648
Oper. Inc.	1,166	289	1,615	789	1,069	1,769	1,117	772	627	446
Depr. Depl. & Amort.	518	505	531	503	599	587	310	269	244	262
Int. Exp.	139	113	147	146	144	137	43.0	24.0	46.0	47.0
Pretax Inc.	612	-228	954	335	1,012	278	766	404	367	291
Eff. Tax Rate	38.2%	NM	40.3%	38.5%	21.1%	NM	39.2%	25.5%	36.0%	38.8%
Net Inc.	339	-346	551	188	755	-15.0	454	300	234	178
S&P Core Earnings	299	-445	287	NA	NA	NA	NA	NA	NA	NA

Balance Sheet & Other Fin. Data (Million $)

	2003	2002	2001	2000	1999	1998	1997	1996	1995	1994
Cash	1,815	1,107	290	231	466	203	221	214	175	507
Curr. Assets	7,919	5,560	5,573	5,568	6,022	6,083	2,972	2,398	2,050	NA
Total Assets	15,463	12,844	10,966	10,103	10,728	11,112	5,603	4,437	3,647	5,268
Curr. Liab.	6,542	3,272	2,908	3,826	3,693	4,004	1,773	1,505	1,156	950
LT Debt	3,415	1,181	1,403	1,049	1,056	1,370	539	200	200	623
Common Equity	2,547	3,558	4,752	5,618	4,287	4,061	2,585	2,159	1,750	1,942
Total Cap.	6,062	4,810	6,196	6,705	5,496	5,601	3,144	2,359	1,950	2,570
Cap. Exp.	515	764	797	578	593	914	577	396	289	235
Cash Flow	857	159	1,082	691	1,354	572	764	568	478	439
Curr. Ratio	1.2	1.7	1.9	1.5	1.6	1.5	1.7	1.6	1.8	NA
% LT Debt of Cap.	56.3	24.6	22.6	15.6	19.2	24.5	17.1	8.5	10.3	24.2
% Ret. on Assets	2.4	NM	5.2	1.9	6.9	NM	9.0	7.3	6.1	3.3
% Ret. on Equity	11.1	NM	12.7	3.7	18.1	NM	19.1	14.7	12.7	9.3

Data as orig reptd.; bef. results of disc opers/spec. items. Per share data adj. for stk. divs.; EPS diluted. E-Estimated. NA-Not Available. NM-Not Meaningful. NR-Not Ranked. UR-Under Review.

Office: 1401 McKinney St Ste 2400, Houston, TX 77010-4040.
Telephone: 713-759-2600.
Email: investors@halliburton.com
Website: http://www.halliburton.com
Chrmn, Pres & CEO: D.J. Lesar.
EVP & CFO: C.C. Gaut.
EVP & General Counsel: A.O. Cornelison, Jr.

SVP & Chief Acctg Officer: M. McCollum.
VP & Treas: P. Holsinger.
VP & Investor Contact: P. Koeller 713-759-2600.
Dirs: R. L. Crandall, K. T. Derr, C. J. DiBona, W. R. Howell, R. L. Hunt, D. J. Lesar, A. B. Lewis, J. L. Martin, J. A. Precourt, D. L. Reed, C. J. Silas.

Founded: in 1919.
Domicile: Delaware.
Employees: 101,000.
S&P Analyst: Stewart Glickman/MF/DRJ

The McGraw·Hill Companies

Harley-Davidson

Recommendation: **HOLD** ★ ★ ★ ☆ ☆
SELL SELL HOLD BUY BUY

12-Month Target Price: **$66.00**
(as of July 14, 2004)

HDI has an approximate 0.16% weighting in the **S&P 500**

Sector: Consumer Discretionary
Sub-Industry: Motorcycle Manufacturers
Peer Group: Motorcycles

Summary: This leading maker of heavyweight motorcycles also produces a line of motorcycle parts and accessories.

Quantitative Evaluations

S&P Earnings & Dividend Rank: A+

D	C	B-	B	B+	A-	A	**A+**

S&P Fair Value Rank: 4+

1	2	3	**4**	5
Lowest				Highest

Fair Value Calc.: $60.70 (Slightly Undervalued)

S&P Investability Quotient Percentile

99%

HDI scored higher than 99% of all companies for which an S&P Report is available.

Volatility: Average

Low	**Average**	High

Technical Evaluation: Bearish
Since 10/04, the technical indicators for HDI have been Bearish.

Relative Strength Rank: Weak

28

1 Lowest   Highest 99

Price as of 11/12/04:	**$58.85**	2004E S&P Core EPS:	**$2.98**

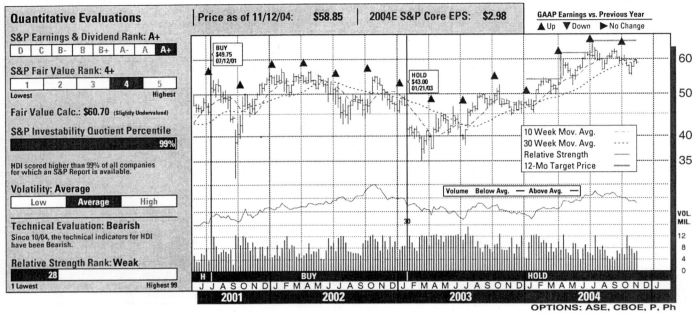

GAAP Earnings vs. Previous Year
▲ Up   ▼ Down   ► No Change

- 10 Week Mov. Avg.
- 30 Week Mov. Avg.
- Relative Strength
- 12-Mo Target Price

Volume Below Avg. — Above Avg. —

VOL. MIL.
12
8
4
0

OPTIONS: ASE, CBOE, P, Ph

Analyst commentary prepared by Tom Graves, CFA /BK

Highlights August 11, 2004

- We look for revenues to increase about 9% in 2005, to $5.6 billion, from the $5.1 billion that we project for 2004. In both years, we expect sales of Harley-Davidson brand bikes to again account for close to 80% of HDI's total revenues. In 2005, we project net income of $972 million ($3.40 a share, on 3.1% fewer shares), up 10% from $885 million ($3.00) that we estimate for 2004.

- In June 2004, HDI said that its line of 2005 Sportster bikes would include a new model (the XL Sportster 883L, and an update to the rear axle of all Sportster models. We look for the company's efforts with the Sportster line, which included a redesign for the 2004 models, to help attract younger buyers for Harley-Davidson brand bikes. However, a change in the product mix, toward lower-priced bikes, would limit the average price that the company charges for its entire line of Harley brand bikes.

- In June 2004, HDI announced the signing of a memo of understanding with the Zongshen Motorcycle Group, which HDI said could facilitate Harley-Davidson's entry into the Chinese motorcycle market. Separately, in April 2004, HDI announced that its Board of Directors had approved a 25% increase in HDI's quarterly dividend, and had authorized the repurchase of up to 20 million shares of HDI's stock.

Investment Rationale/Risk August 11, 2004

- Our hold opinion on the stock reflects our view that the shares will be bolstered by expectations of annual mid-teens EPS growth of during at least the next few years, and generation of free cash flow. In the future, we expect HDI to make further stock repurchases, as well as increase the dividend.

- Risks to our recommendation and target price include the possibility that soft economic conditions will restrict demand for HDI bikes and that company will have increased difficulty attracting new owners or riders to its motorcycles. Also, a sharp rise in interest rates could make financing costs for consumers more difficult.

- We believe that the growth and free cash flow prospects that we see for the company justify a premium P/E multiple for the stock relative to the multiple of the S&P 500. Our 12-month target price for the stock is $66, reflecting our view that the current P/E multiple premium of about 15% (based on 2005 EPS estimates) will largely be maintained. The current indicated dividend yield is 0.7%. As of June 27, 2004, the company had cash equivalents and marketable securities totaling $1.3 billion.

Key Stock Statistics

S&P Core EPS 2005E	**3.38**	52-week Range	**$63.75-44.57**
S&P Oper. EPS 2004E	**3.00**	12 Month P/E	**20.4**
P/E on S&P Oper. EPS 2004E	**19.6**	Beta	**1.12**
S&P Oper. EPS 2005E	**3.40**	Shareholders	**84,909**
Yield (%)	**0.7%**	Market Cap (B)	**$ 17.3**
Dividend Rate/Share	**0.40**	Shares Outstanding (M)	**293.8**

Value of $10,000 invested five years ago: **$ 20,191**

Dividend Data Dividends have been paid since 1993

Amount ($)	Date Decl.	Ex-Div. Date	Stock of Record	Payment Date
0.080	Dec. 05	Dec. 11	Dec. 15	Dec. 29 '03
0.080	Feb. 11	Mar. 09	Mar. 11	Mar. 25 '04
0.100	Apr. 26	Jun. 01	Jun. 03	Jun. 24 '04
0.100	Aug. 04	Sep. 13	Sep. 15	Sep. 29 '04

Revenues/Earnings Data Fiscal year ending December 31

Revenues (Million $)

	2004	2003	2002	2001	2000	1999
1Q	1,166	1,114	927.9	767.3	681.1	558.6
2Q	1,328	1,219	1,001	850.9	755.0	608.7
3Q	1,301	1,134	1,136	850.8	714.1	623.2
4Q	—	1,158	1,027	894.4	756.2	662.5
Yr.	—	4,624	4,091	3,363	2,906	2,453

Earnings Per Share ($)

	2004	2003	2002	2001	2000	1999
1Q	0.68	0.61	0.39	0.30	0.26	0.19
2Q	0.83	0.66	0.47	0.38	0.29	0.22
3Q	0.77	0.62	0.54	0.36	0.27	0.21
4Q	E0.72	0.60	0.49	0.39	0.31	0.24
Yr.	E3.00	2.50	1.90	1.43	1.13	0.86

Next earnings report expected: late-January Source: S&P, Company Reports
EPS Estimates based on S&P Operating Earnings; historical GAAP earnings are as reported.

STANDARD &POOR'S

Harley-Davidson, Inc.

Stock Report
November 13, 2004
NYSE Symbol: **HDI**

Recommendation: **HOLD** ★ ★ ★ ☆ ☆   12-Month Target Price: **$66.00** (as of July 14, 2004)

Business Summary August 11, 2004

Harley-Davidson is a leading supplier of heavyweight motorcycles. The company believes that it benefits from having one of the world's most recognized and respected brand names.

The company primarily manufactures and sells heavyweight (engine displacement of 651cc or more) motorcycles, along with a broad range of related products that include motorcycle parts, accessories, riding apparel, and collectibles. HDI's operating profit from motorcycles and related products (excluding income from related financial services) totaled $997 million in 2003, up 26% from the level of 2002.

HDI has held the largest share of the U.S. heavyweight (651c and up) motorcycle market since 1986. Based on data provided by the Motorcycle Industry Council, Harley-Davidson model bikes accounted for about 50% of new U.S. heavyweight motorcycle retail registrations in 2003. Including overseas markets, competitors include Honda, Suzuki, Kawasaki and Yamaha.

The company manufactures and sells about 25 models of Harley-Davidson touring and custom heavyweight motorcycles, with suggested U.S. retail prices ranging from about $6,495 to $28,595. HDI believes that about 9% of its Harley-Davidson U.S. retail motorcycle sales are to female buyers. The touring segment of the heavyweight market includes motorcycles equipped for long distance riding, including fairings, windshields and saddlebags. Custom motorcycles are differentiated through the use of trim and accessories.

In the past, despite continuous production increases, U.S. consumers often had to wait to purchase a new Harley-Davidson brand bike at list price. Studies by HDI have indicated that the average U.S. Harley-Davidson purchaser is a married male in his mid-40s, with household income of about $79,500, who purchases a motorcycle for recreational purposes. HDI believes it has a strong brand name, and offers 100 years of heritage, something other companies cannot match.

In 2003, $3.7 billion (80%) of net revenue came from motorcycles. About $713 million came from parts and accessories, and $211 million came from general merchandise. HDI's licensing activity has included T-shirts, jewelry, small leather goods, toys, and two cafes. Royalty revenues from licensing totaled about $38 million in 2003.

In 2003, shipments of Harley-Davidson brand motorcycles totaled 291,147 units, including 237,656 for the U.S. and 53,491 for export. This compared with 263,653 units in 2002 (212,833 U.S.; 50,820 export).

In February 1998, the company acquired substantially all of the remaining common stock of Buell Motorcycle Co., in which it had held a 49% equity interest since 1993. In 2003, company shipments of Buell motorcycles totaled 9,974 units, down from 10,943 in 2002. In 2003, HDI expanded its Buell motorcycle line with the introduction of the Firebolt XB12R and the Lightning XB12S models. Other Buell motorcycles include the XB9 models and the Buell Blast. As of early 2004, HDI's XB bikes had domestic suggested retail prices of $9,195 to $10,995; the suggested retail price for the Blast was $4,595.

The company's financial services segment includes the financing and servicing of wholesale inventory receivables and consumer retail loans. In 2003, HDI had financial services operating profit of $167.9 million, up 61% from the level of 2002.

Company Financials Fiscal Year ending December 31

Per Share Data ($)

(Year Ended December 31)	2003	2002	2001	2000	1999	1998	1997	1996	1995	1994
Tangible Bk. Val.	9.63	7.21	5.64	4.47	3.65	3.20	2.58	2.06	1.51	1.40
Cash Flow	3.18	2.48	1.93	1.56	1.23	0.97	0.79	0.66	0.51	0.46
Earnings	2.50	1.90	1.43	1.13	0.86	0.69	0.57	0.48	0.37	0.34
S&P Core Earnings	2.51	1.85	1.34	NA	NA	NA	NA	NA	NA	NA
Dividends	0.20	0.14	0.12	0.10	0.09	0.08	0.07	0.06	0.05	0.06
Payout Ratio	8%	7%	8%	9%	10%	11%	12%	12%	12%	18%
Prices - High	52.51	57.25	55.99	50.62	32.03	23.75	15.62	12.37	7.53	7.46
- Low	35.01	42.60	32.00	29.53	21.37	12.46	8.34	6.59	5.50	5.40
P/E Ratio - High	21	30	39	45	37	34	28	26	20	22
- Low	14	22	22	26	25	18	15	14	15	16

Income Statement Analysis (Million $)

	2003	2002	2001	2000	1999	1998	1997	1996	1995	1994
Revs.	4,624	4,091	3,363	2,906	2,453	2,064	1,763	1,531	1,351	1,542
Oper. Inc.	1,067	850	754	611	502	401	328	258	220	197
Depr.	197	176	153	133	114	87.4	70.2	55.2	42.3	36.9
Int. Exp.	Nil	Nil	Nil	Nil	Nil	Nil	Nil	Nil	1.40	2.40
Pretax Inc.	1,166	886	673	549	421	336	276	228	176	162
Eff. Tax Rate	34.7%	34.5%	35.0%	36.6%	36.5%	36.5%	37.0%	36.9%	36.9%	35.7%
Net Inc.	761	580	438	348	267	214	174	143	111	104
S&P Core Earnings	763	564	411	NA	NA	NA	NA	NA	NA	NA

Balance Sheet & Other Fin. Data (Million $)

	2003	2002	2001	2000	1999	1998	1997	1996	1995	1994
Cash	1,323	796	635	420	183	165	147	142	31.5	59.3
Total Assets	4,923	3,861	3,118	2,436	2,112	1,920	1,599	1,320	1,001	739
LT Debt	670	380	380	355	280	280	280	258	164	9.40
Total Debt	670	380	380	355	280	427	371	258	167	27.7
Common Equity	2,958	2,233	1,756	1,406	1,161	1,080	827	663	495	433
Cap. Exp.	227	324	204	204	166	183	186	179	113	94.7
Cash Flow	958	756	591	481	381	301	244	199	153	141
% Ret. on Assets	17.3	16.6	15.8	15.3	13.3	12.2	11.9	12.3	13.4	15.5
% Ret. on Equity	29.3	29.1	27.7	27.1	24.4	23.0	23.4	24.6	23.9	27.5
% LT Debt of Cap.	17.8	14.4	17.6	20.2	19.4	21.4	25.3	NM	24.9	2.1

Data as orig reptd.; bef. results of disc opers/spec. items. Per share data adj. for stk. divs. Bold denotes primary EPS - prior periods restated. E-Estimated. NA-Not Available. NM-Not Meaningful. NR-Not Ranked. UR-Under Review.

Office: 3700 West Juneau Avenue, Milwaukee, WI 53208.
Telephone: 414-342-4680.
Email: investor_relations@harley-davidson.com
Website: http://www.harley-davidson.com
Chrmn & CEO: J.L. Bleustein.
VP, CFO & Investor Contact: J.L. Ziemer .

VP & Treas: J.M. Brostowitz.
VP, Secy & General Counsel: G.A. Lione.
Investor Contact: P. Davidson 414-343-4782.
Dirs: B. K. Allen, R. I. Beattie, J. L. Bleustein, G. H. Conrades, D. A. James, S. L. Levinson, G. L. Miles, J. A. Norling, R. F. Teerlink.

Founded: in 1903.
Domicile: Wisconsin.
Employees: 9,460.
S&P Analyst: Tom Graves, CFA /BK

Harrah's Entertainment

Stock Report
November 13, 2004
NYSE Symbol: **HET**

Recommendation: HOLD ★★★ ☆ ☆
SELL · SELL · HOLD · BUY · BUY

12-Month Target Price: $61.00
(as of October 27, 2004)

HET has an approximate 0.06% weighting in the **S&P 500**

Sector: Consumer Discretionary
Sub-Industry: Casinos & Gaming
Peer Group: Casino/Hotel Companies - Larger

Summary: This geographically diverse company operates and/or has ownership interests in more than 20 gaming properties, mostly operating under the Harrah's, Showboat and Rio brand names.

Quantitative Evaluations

S&P Earnings & Dividend Rank: B

| D | C | B- | B | B+ | A- | A | A+ |

S&P Fair Value Rank: 3-

| 1 | 2 | 3 | 4 | 5 |
| Lowest | | | | Highest |

Fair Value Calc.: $57.60 (Slightly Overvalued)

S&P Investability Quotient Percentile

80%

HET scored higher than 80% of all companies for which an S&P Report is available.

Volatility: Average

| Low | Average | High |

Technical Evaluation: Bullish

Since 9/04, the technical indicators for HET have been Bullish.

Relative Strength Rank: Strong

74

| 1 Lowest | | Highest 99 |

Price as of 11/12/04: $59.80 | **2004E S&P Core EPS:** $3.08

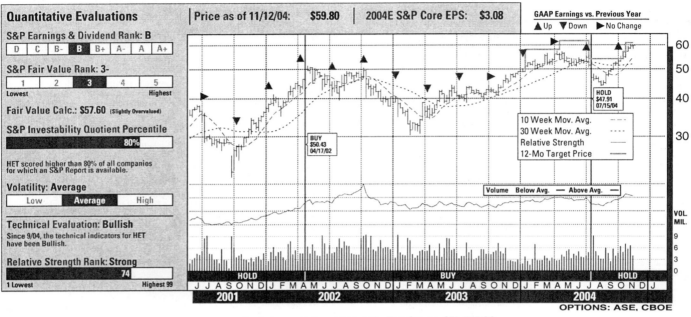

GAAP Earnings vs. Previous Year
▲ Up   ▼ Down   ▶ No Change

10 Week Mov. Avg.
30 Week Mov. Avg.
Relative Strength
12-Mo Target Price

Volume   Below Avg. — Above Avg.

VOL. MIL.

OPTIONS: ASE, CBOE

Analyst commentary prepared by Tom Graves, CFA /MF/GG

Highlights September 17, 2004

- On July 15, HET said it had signed a definitive agreement to acquire Caesars Entertainment, Inc. (CZR: $16), in a transaction through which CZR shareholders would receive 66.3 million HET common shares and $1.8 billion in cash. We look for the deal, which is subject to various approvals, to be completed around mid-2005. We expect that approval of the deal will require the divestiture of one or more casinos currently operated by HET or CZR. In August 2004, HET and CZR said that they have been discussing the sale of Harrah's East Chicago, Harrah's Tunica, the Atlantic City Hilton and Bally's Tunica with potential purchasers, including an affiliate of Colony Capital, LLC.

Investment Rationale/Risk September 17, 2004

- Our hold opinion on the stock reflects our view that the company's growth prospects, including the mid-2004 acquisition of Horseshoe Gaming Holding Corp. and the pending acquisition of CZR, are adequately represented in HET's share price. We have some concern about the prospect of a larger HET presence in Atlantic City and a potentially modest dilutive impact of prospective asset sales. However, we view the CZR deal as offering some strategic value, including a bigger HET casino/hotel presence in the important Las Vegas market.

- Risks to our recommendation and target price include prospective threats of new competition, and the possibility that acquisitions by HET will be less successful than anticipated. Also, if terrorism fears increase in the future, this could reduce customer levels and be a negative for HET shares.

- Our 12-month target price of $54 reflects our view that the stock will continue to trade at a discount to the S&P 500, largely due to concerns about competition and levels of consumer spending, and uncertainty about the outcome of acquisition-related activity. The stock has an indicated dividend yield of about 2.6%.

Key Stock Statistics

S&P Core EPS 2005E	3.26	52-week Range	$60.46-43.94
S&P Oper. EPS 2004E	3.28	12 Month P/E	20.6
P/E on S&P Oper. EPS 2004E	18.2	Beta	0.42
S&P Oper. EPS 2005E	3.50	Shareholders	8,690
Yield (%)	2.2%	Market Cap (B)	$ 6.7
Dividend Rate/Share	1.32	Shares Outstanding (M)	112.1

Value of $10,000 invested five years ago: **$ 21,262**

Dividend Data Dividends have been paid since 2003

Amount ($)	Date Decl.	Ex-Div. Date	Stock of Record	Payment Date
0.300	Feb. 04	Feb. 09	Feb. 11	Feb. 25 '04
0.300	Apr. 30	May. 10	May. 12	May. 26 '04
0.330	Jul. 15	Aug. 09	Aug. 11	Aug. 25 '04
0.330	Oct. 20	Nov. 08	Nov. 10	Nov. 24 '04

Revenues/Earnings Data Fiscal year ending December 31

Revenues (Million $)

	2004	2003	2002	2001	2000	1999
1Q	1,109	1,059	974.7	867.2	783.6	711.7
2Q	1,129	1,080	1,021	873.5	879.2	751.1
3Q	1,310	1,139	1,124	1,008	953.4	814.0
4Q	—	1,044	1,016	960.6	854.9	748.0
Yr.	—	4,323	4,136	3,709	3,471	3,024

Earnings Per Share ($)

	2004	2003	2002	2001	2000	1999
1Q	0.73	0.73	0.75	0.38	0.25	0.30
2Q	0.79	0.70	0.75	0.40	0.40	0.37
3Q	0.99	0.89	0.89	0.55	0.61	0.58
4Q	E0.64	0.32	0.48	0.49	-1.41	0.45
Yr.	E3.28	2.64	2.86	1.81	-0.09	1.71

Next earnings report expected: early-February Source: S&P, Company Reports
EPS Estimates based on S&P Operating Earnings; historical GAAP earnings are as reported.

Harrah's Entertainment, Inc.

Recommendation: **HOLD** ★ ★ ★ ☆ ☆   12-Month Target Price: **$61.00** (as of October 27, 2004)

Business Summary September 17, 2004

Harrah's Entertainment is the most geographically diversified casino company in North America. It operates and/or has ownership interests in about 28 gaming properties, including seven in Nevada and two in Atlantic City. In July 2004, HET said it had signed a definitive agreement to acquire Caesars Entertainment, Inc. (CZR), in a transaction through which CZR shareholders would receive 66.3 million HET common shares and $1.8 billion in cash. We look for the deal, which is subject to various approvals, to be completed around mid-2005. As of July 2004, CZR was operating 28 casinos, including a significant presence in Las Vegas, Atlantic City and Mississippi. We expect that approval of the CZR acquisition will require the divestiture of one or more casinos currently operated by HET or CZR. In mid-2004, HET acquired privately owned Horseshoe Gaming Holding Corp. for about $1.45 billion, including assumption of debt. Horseshoe's operations included three casinos in Indiana, Mississippi and Louisiana. In recent years, other HET acquisitions have included Harveys Casino Resorts (2001), Players International (2000), Rio Hotel and Casino Inc. (1999), and Showboat Inc. (1998).

In southern Nevada, HET operates Harrah's Las Vegas, the Rio facility, and Harrah's Laughlin. The three facilities have a total of about 6,640 hotel rooms or suites, and 241,700 sq. ft. of casino space. For 2003, the company reported revenue and operating profit from southern Nevada of about $900 million and $165 million, respectively. All operating profit figures in this section include depreciation and/or amortization charges, but exclude certain non-recurring items such as project opening costs. In northern Nevada, operations include Harrah's Reno, Harrah's Lake Tahoe, Harveys Lake Tahoe, and Bill's Lake Tahoe Casino. The four

facilities have about 2,200 rooms or suites and 196,300 sq. ft. of casino space. Another gaming property, Harvey's Wagon Wheel in Central City, CO, was sold in May 2003. HET's 2003 revenue and profit from northern Nevada totaled $447 million and $55 million, respectively. In Atlantic City, the company operates casino/hotels under the Harrah's and Showboat names. Following the debut of a new hotel tower at the Showboat property, the two facilities have about 2,930 rooms or suites, and 242,700 sq. ft. of casino space. HET's 2003 revenue and profit from Atlantic City totaled $781 million and $217 million, respectively.

HET operates casinos on boats or barges in locations that include Joliet and Metropolis, IL; Tunica, MS; Lake Charles and Bossier City, LA; North Kansas City, MO; Maryland Heights, MO; and East Chicago and Hammond, IN. Some projects or markets include at least two HET casinos. As of 2003 year end (prior to the Horseshoe acquisition and the divestiture of a Shreveport, LA, property, HET's water-based operations had about 494,300 sq. ft. of gaming space. In addition, the company now has a 100% ownership interest in and manages a land-based New Orleans casino, and operates about 900 slot machines at the majority-owned Louisiana Downs racetrack facility in Bossier City, LA. In 2003, HET had consolidated revenue and profit from casino boat (or barge) projects, plus the New Orleans casino and some other facilities in Louisiana and Iowa, of about $2.1 billion and $329 million, respectively. The company's operations also include management of Native American casinos in Arizona, North Carolina, Kansas and California. In June 2003, HET and Gala Group signed a letter of intent to develop up to eight regional casinos in the U.K. in an equally owned joint venture.

Company Financials Fiscal Year ending December 31

Per Share Data ($)

(Year Ended December 31)	2003	2002	2001	2000	1999	1998	1997	1996	1995	1994
Tangible Bk. Val.	4.41	2.50	2.26	5.04	6.43	2.41	6.79	6.43	5.11	6.09
Cash Flow	5.75	5.55	4.68	2.30	3.40	2.77	2.27	1.94	1.69	1.17
Earnings	2.64	2.86	1.81	-0.09	1.71	1.19	1.06	0.95	0.76	0.49
S&P Core Earnings	2.51	2.66	1.62	NA	NA	NA	NA	NA	NA	NA
Dividends	0.60	Nil	Nil	Nil	Nil	Nil	Nil	Nil	Nil	Nil
Payout Ratio	23%	Nil	Nil	Nil	Nil	Nil	Nil	Nil	Nil	Nil
Prices - High	49.94	51.35	38.29	30.06	30.75	26.37	23.06	38.87	45.87	55.25
- Low	30.30	34.95	22.00	17.00	14.18	11.06	15.50	16.37	22.12	25.87
P/E Ratio - High	19	18	21	NM	18	22	22	41	60	NM
- Low	11	12	12	NM	8	9	15	17	29	NM

Income Statement Analysis (Million $)

	2003	2002	2001	2000	1999	1998	1997	1996	1995	1994
Revs.	4,323	4,136	3,709	3,471	3,024	2,004	1,619	1,588	1,550	1,339
Oper. Inc.	1,081	1,100	939	1,088	755	484	385	392	419	340
Depr.	343	306	333	282	218	159	122	102	95.4	70.6
Int. Exp.	234	240	256	227	193	117	79.1	70.9	98.0	82.0
Pretax Inc.	476	536	348	17.8	79.4	203	184	172	152	139
Eff. Tax Rate	36.2%	36.8%	36.4%	NM	NM	36.7%	37.4%	39.1%	40.0%	54.1%
Net Inc.	292	325	209	-11.3	220	122	108	99	78.8	50.0
S&P Core Earnings	277	303	187	NA	NA	NA	NA	NA	NA	NA

Balance Sheet & Other Fin. Data (Million $)

	2003	2002	2001	2000	1999	1998	1997	1996	1995	1994
Cash	410	416	361	299	234	159	116	105	96.3	85.0
Curr. Assets	685	686	618	583	487	279	212	202	189	172
Total Assets	6,579	6,350	6,129	5,166	4,767	3,286	2,006	1,974	1,637	1,738
Curr. Liab.	583	626	569	778	372	233	211	205	202	295
LT Debt	3,672	3,763	3,719	2,836	2,540	1,999	924	889	754	727
Common Equity	1,738	1,471	1,374	12,853	1,486	851	736	720	586	623
Total Cap.	5,791	5,538	5,386	15,794	4,274	2,941	1,696	1,654	1,363	1,376
Cap. Exp.	405	369	530	421	340	140	230	314	186	219
Cash Flow	635	631	542	270	438	281	230	201	174	121
Curr. Ratio	1.2	1.1	1.1	0.7	1.3	1.2	1.0	1.0	0.9	0.6
% LT Debt of Cap.	63.4	68.0	69.1	17.9	59.4	68.0	54.5	53.7	55.3	52.9
% Net Inc.of Revs.	6.8	7.8	5.6	NM	7.3	6.1	6.6	6.2	5.1	3.7
% Ret. on Assets	4.5	5.2	3.7	NM	5.5	4.6	5.4	9.1	4.7	2.8
% Ret. on Equity	18.2	22.8	15.8	NM	18.8	15.3	14.8	15.1	13.0	8.6

Data as orig reptd.; bef. results of disc opers/spec. items. Per share data adj. for stk. divs. Bold denotes primary EPS - prior periods restated. E-Estimated. NA-Not Available. NM-Not Meaningful. NR-Not Ranked. UR-Under Review.

Office: One Harrah's Court, Las Vegas, NV 89119.
Telephone: 702-407-6000.
Email: investors@harrahs.com
Website: http://www.harrahs.com
Chrmn: P.G. Satre.
Pres & CEO: G.W. Loveman.

COO: T.J. Wilmott.
SVP & CFO: C.L. Atwood.
SVP & General Counsel: S.H. Brammell.
Dirs: B. T. Alexander, F. J. Biondi, Jr., J. M. Henson, R. Horn, G. W. Loveman, R. B. Martin, G. G. Michael, R. G. Miller, P. G. Satre, B. A. Sells, C. J. Williams.

Founded: in 1989.
Domicile: Delaware.
Employees: 41,000.
S&P Analyst: Tom Graves, CFA /MF/GG

Hartford Financial Services Group

Recommendation: **BUY** ★★★★☆
SELL SELL HOLD BUY BUY

12-Month Target Price: $72.00
(as of November 11, 2004)

HIG has an approximate 0.16% weighting in the **S&P 500**

Sector: Financials
Sub-Industry: Multi-line Insurance
Peer Group: Insurers - Multi-Line - Larger

Summary: HIG is one of the largest U.S. multi-line insurance holding companies, and a leading writer of individual variable annuities in the U.S.

Quantitative Evaluations

S&P Earnings & Dividend Rank: B

| D | C | B- | **B** | B+ | A- | A | A+ |

S&P Fair Value Rank: 4-

| 1 | 2 | 3 | **4** | 5 |
Lowest — Highest

Fair Value Calc.: $65.90 (Slightly Undervalued)

S&P Investability Quotient Percentile

95%

HIG scored higher than 95% of all companies for which an S&P Report is available.

Volatility: Average

| Low | **Average** | High |

Technical Evaluation: Neutral
Since 11/04, the technical indicators for HIG have been Neutral.

Relative Strength Rank: Moderate

38
1 Lowest — Highest 99

Price as of 11/12/04: $62 **2004E S&P Core EPS:** $5.03

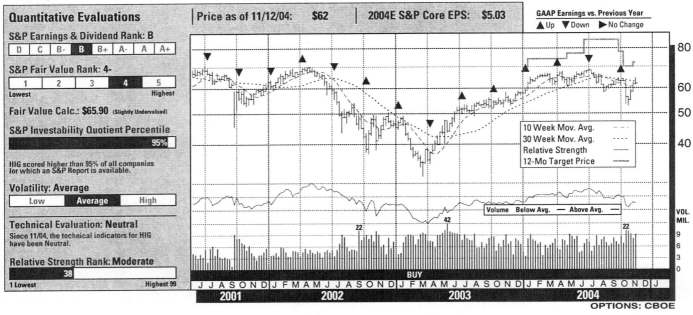

GAAP Earnings vs. Previous Year
▲ Up ▼ Down ► No Change

- 10 Week Mov. Avg.
- 30 Week Mov. Avg.
- Relative Strength
- 12-Mo Target Price

Volume Below Avg. — Above Avg. —

VOL. MIL.

OPTIONS: CBOE

Analyst commentary prepared by Catherine A. Seifert/CB/JWP

Highlights November 12, 2004

■ A rebound in operating earnings that we forecast for 2004 is skewed by 2003 first quarter after-tax charges of $1.7 billion that led to a 2003 operating loss of $0.93 a share. The charges were incurred to cover a $2.6 billion increase in asbestos reserves that boosted HIG's total asbestos reserves to nearly $3.8 billion at December 31, 2003. Third quarter 2004 results included $263 million of catastrophe losses from the four Florida hurricanes, but operating earnings of $1.57 a share (versus $1.18 a year ago) were aided by favorable non-catastrophe claim trends.

■ To replenish its capital base, HIG raised $1.95 billion in additional capital in early 2004 by selling 24.2 million common shares at $45.50 each, for total proceeds of $1.1 billion; and $600 million of equity-linked securities and $250 million of fixed income securities.

■ We view these actions positively, and view HIG shares as modestly undervalued in light of the company's two franchises: property-casualty insurance and variable annuities. However, our near-term outlook is tempered by our concern over the ongoing investigation into certain insurance industry marketing practices that is being conducted by a number of state attorneys general. We see operating earnings of $5.70 a share in 2004 and $7.15 a share in 2005.

Key Stock Statistics

S&P Oper. EPS 2004E	5.70	52-week Range	$69.12-52.73
P/E on S&P Oper. EPS 2004E	10.9	12 Month P/E	9.1
S&P Oper. EPS 2005E	7.15	Beta	1.47
Yield (%)	1.9%	Shareholders	126,000
Dividend Rate/Share	1.16	Market Cap (B)	$ 18.2
Shares Outstanding (M)	293.7		

Value of $10,000 invested five years ago: **$ 12,700**

Dividend Data Dividends have been paid since 1996

Amount ($)	Date Decl.	Ex-Div. Date	Stock of Record	Payment Date
0.280	Feb. 19	Feb. 26	Mar. 01	Apr. 01 '04
0.280	May. 20	May. 27	Jun. 01	Jul. 01 '04
0.280	Jul. 22	Aug. 30	Sep. 01	Oct. 01 '04
0.290	Oct. 21	Nov. 29	Dec. 01	Jan. 03 '05

Investment Rationale/Risk November 12, 2004

■ We lowered our opinion on the shares to buy, from strong buy, in the wake of news that HIG was implicated in a lawsuit filed by the New York Attorney General against insurance broker Marsh & McLennan Companies that alleges fraud and certain antitrust violations. HIG has not been charged with any wrongdoing, but we believe the uncertainty related to this ongoing investigation merits a more cautious stance toward the shares of many insurers, including HIG. We continue to view HIG shares as modestly undervalued (versus peers) based on their fundamentals and the franchise value we see in HIG as a leading variable annuity writer. Our outlook is also tempered by concerns that HIG may have to add to reserves for minimum guaranteed death benefits embedded in many variable annuity contracts.

■ Risks to our opinion and target price include a deterioration in claim trends, a sharp increase in premium price competition, and a sharp downturn in the equity markets. There is also a risk that the attorneys general investigations into certain insurance marketing practices will widen. The SEC and the New York Attorney General are also investigating the timing of a stock sale by an HIG executive.

■ Our 12-month target price of $72 assumes a modest expansion in the shares' forward price/earnings multiple to about 10X our 2005 estimate, which remains discounted to peers.

Revenues/Earnings Data Fiscal year ending December 31

Revenues (Million $)

	2004	2003	2002	2001	2000	1999
1Q	5,732	4,331	3,900	3,722	3,499	3,299
2Q	5,444	4,682	3,885	3,847	3,514	3,349
3Q	5,416	4,947	3,961	3,722	3,791	3,444
4Q	—	4,773	4,161	3,856	3,899	3,436
Yr.	—	18,733	15,907	15,147	14,703	13,528

Earnings Per Share ($)

	2004	2003	2002	2001	2000	1999
1Q	2.01	-5.33	1.17	1.12	1.10	1.04
2Q	1.46	1.88	0.74	0.94	0.97	0.93
3Q	1.66	1.20	1.06	-0.43	1.09	0.82
4Q	—	1.59	1.01	0.58	1.12	1.00
Yr.	—	-0.33	3.97	2.27	4.36	3.79

Next earnings report expected: late-January Source: S&P, Company Reports
EPS Estimates based on S&P Operating Earnings; historical GAAP earnings are as reported.

The Hartford Financial Services Group

Recommendation: **BUY** ★★★★☆   12-Month Target Price: **$72.00** (as of November 11, 2004)

Business Summary November 12, 2004

Hartford Financial Services Group was a subsidiary of ITT Corp. until its December 1995 spin-off. From its founding in 1810 as a local fire insurance company, HIG has grown to become one of the largest insurers in both the property-casualty and life insurance industries. In 2003, segment revenues totaled $18.7 billion, with worldwide life insurance operations accounting for 43% and worldwide property and casualty insurance for 57%. In 2003, there was an operating loss of about $204 million (before corporate and other allocations), versus operating income of $1.3 billion in 2002. Results in 2003 included life insurance operating income of $760 million and a property-casualty operating loss of $964 million (mainly due to a $1.7 billion after-tax asbestos reserve boost).

The worldwide property-casualty operation provides a wide range of commercial, personal, specialty and reinsurance coverages. It constitutes one of the largest U.S. property-casualty insurance organizations, and is the endorsed provider of automobile and homeowners coverages to members of the American Association of Retired Persons (AARP). Written premiums approached $9.1 billion in 2003, up from more than $8.5 billion in 2002, with business insurance accounting for 43%, personal lines 36%, specialty commercial lines 18%, and reinsurance 2%. The combined ratio improved to 98.0% in 2003, from 99.8% in 2002, despite higher catastrophe losses (which added 3.0 and 1.3 points to the respective combined ratios). In May 2003, the company announced plans to exit the reinsurance

business by selling most of that unit's policy renewal rights to Bermuda-based Endurance Specialty Holdings. On September 1, 2003, the company sold a wholly owned subsidiary, Trumbull Associates, LLC.

HIG's life insurance operations are conducted primarily by Hartford Life, Inc. This unit sells an array of variable annuities, mutual funds, individual and corporate-owned life insurance (COLI), a number of employee benefits products, and assorted other retirement savings and investment products. The unit has established a strategy that uses a number of distribution channels, including broker-dealers, other financial institutions (such as banks), and insurance agents and brokers. Growth in recent years has been fueled to a large degree by robust sales of variable annuities; Hartford Life was a leading writer of individual variable annuities in 2003. Net segment operating profits (before other items) in 2003 equaled $819 million, up from $736 million in 2002, with individual annuities accounting for 46%, other investment products (including mutual funds) 14%, individual life insurance 17%, group benefits 18%, and corporate owned life insurance 5%. Assets under management at December 31, 2003, totaled $210.1 billion, up from $165.1 billion at December 31, 2002, with separate account assets accounting for 65%, general account assets 24%, and mutual fund assets 11%. On December 31, 2003, HIG acquired from CNA Financial Corp. that company's group life, accident and disability businesses, for about $485 million in cash.

Company Financials Fiscal Year ending December 31

Per Share Data ($)

(Year Ended December 31)	2003	2002	2001	2000	1999	1998	1997	1996	1995	1994
Tangible Bk. Val.	34.80	35.31	29.87	32.88	25.07	28.17	25.79	19.23	20.07	13.38
Oper. Earnings	-0.93	4.96	3.00	4.29	3.68	3.45	4.70	-1.35	3.17	2.91
Earnings	-0.33	3.97	2.27	4.36	3.79	4.30	5.58	-0.42	2.39	2.66
S&P Core Earnings	-1.15	4.27	2.22	NA	NA	NA	NA	NA	NA	NA
Dividends	1.09	1.05	1.01	0.97	0.90	0.85	0.80	0.80	Nil	NA
Relative Payout	NM	26%	44%	22%	24%	20%	14%	NM	Nil	NA
Prices - High	59.27	70.24	71.15	80.00	66.43	60.00	47.25	34.93	25.06	NA
- Low	31.64	37.25	45.50	29.37	36.50	37.62	32.43	22.25	23.68	NA
P/E Ratio - High	NM	18	31	18	18	14	8	NM	11	NA
- Low	NM	9	20	7	10	9	6	NM	10	NA

Income Statement Analysis (Million $)

	2003	2002	2001	2000	1999	1998	1997	1996	1995	1994
Life Ins. In Force	704,369	629,028	534,489	585,582	527,285	528,608	407,860	312,176	339,291	246,138
Prem. Inc.: Life A & H	11,891	4,884	4,903	4,565	4,069	4,371	3,323	3,185	2,738	2,173
Prem. Inc.: Cas./Prop.	8,805	8,114	7,266	6,975	6,488	7,245	7,000	6,891	6,890	6,580
Net Invest. Inc.	3,233	2,953	2,850	2,674	2,627	3,102	2,655	2,523	2,420	2,259
Total Revs.	18,733	15,907	15,147	14,703	13,528	15,022	13,305	12,473	12,150	11,102
Pretax Inc.	-550	1,068	354	1,418	1,235	1,475	1,703	-318	742	852
Net Oper. Inc.	-253	1,250	724	962	837	816	1,117	-318	742	691
Net Inc.	-91.0	1,000	549	974	862	1,015	1,332	-99	559	632
S&P Core Earnings	-315	1,078	538	NA	NA	NA	NA	NA	NA	NA

Balance Sheet & Other Fin. Data (Million $)

	2003	2002	2001	2000	1999	1998	1997	1996	1995	1994
Cash & Equiv.	462	377	353	227	182	123	140	112	95.0	55.0
Premiums Due	9,043	7,706	2,432	6,874	2,071	1,833	1,873	1,797	1,890	2,000
Invest. Assets: Bonds	61,263	48,889	40,046	34,492	32,875	35,331	35,053	31,449	31,168	27,418
Invest. Assets: Stocks	565	917	1,349	1,056	1,286	1,066	1,922	1,865	1,342	1,350
Invest. Assets: Loans	2,512	2,934	3,317	3,610	4,222	6,687	3,759	3,839	3,380	2,614
Invest. Assets: Total	65,847	54,530	46,689	40,669	39,141	43,696	37,363	33,800	36,675	32,453
Deferred Policy Costs	7,599	6,689	6,420	5,305	5,038	4,579	4,181	3,535	2,945	2,525
Total Assets	225,853	182,043	181,238	171,532	167,051	150,632	131,743	108,840	93,855	76,765
Debt	4,613	4,064	3,377	3,105	2,798	2,798	1,773	1,532	1,022	596
Common Equity	11,639	10,734	9,013	7,464	5,466	6,423	6,085	4,520	4,702	3,184
Comb. Loss-Exp. Ratio	98.0	99.2	112.4	102.4	103.3	102.9	102.3	105.2	104.5	102.8
% Return On Revs.	NM	6.3	3.6	6.6	6.4	6.8	10.0	NM	4.6	5.7
% Ret. on Equity	NM	10.1	6.7	15.1	14.5	16.2	25.1	NM	14.2	15.4
% Invest. Yield	5.4	5.8	6.5	6.7	6.3	7.7	6.7	6.8	7.0	7.0

Data as orig reptd.; bef. results of disc opers/spec. items. Per share data adj. for stk. divs.; EPS diluted. E-Estimated. NA-Not Available. NM-Not Meaningful. NR-Not Ranked. UR-Under Review.

Office: Hartford Plaza, Hartford, CT 06115.
Telephone: 860-547-5000.
Website: http://www.thehartford.com
Chrmn, Pres & CEO: R. Ayer.
EVP & CFO: D.M. Johnson.

EVP & General Counsel: N.S. Wolin.
Investor Contact: H. Miller 860-547-2751.
Dirs: R. V. Araskog, R. Ayer, R. E. Ferguson, D. R. Frahm, E. J. Kelly, III, P. G. Kirk, Jr., T. M. Marra, G. J. McGovern, R. W. Selander, C. B. Strauss, H. P. Swygert, G. I. Ulmer, D. K. Zwiener.

Founded: in 1810.
Domicile: Delaware.
Employees: 30,000.
S&P Analyst: Catherine A. Seifert/CB/JWP

Hasbro Inc.

Recommendation: **HOLD** ★★★☆☆
SELL SELL HOLD BUY BUY

12-Month Target Price: **$19.00**
(as of October 18, 2004)

HAS has an approximate 0.03% weighting in the **S&P 500**

Sector: Consumer Discretionary
Sub-Industry: Leisure Products
Peer Group: Toy-related Companies

Summary: Hasbro, a large toy company, has brands that include Monopoly, Playskool and Tonka, as well as various items related to categories such as Star Wars and Pokemon.

Quantitative Evaluations

S&P Earnings & Dividend Rank: B

| D | C | B- | **B** | B+ | A- | A | A+ |

S&P Fair Value Rank: 1-

| **1** | 2 | 3 | 4 | 5 |
| Lowest | | | | Highest |

Fair Value Calc.: $15.40 (Overvalued)

S&P Investability Quotient Percentile

86%

HAS scored higher than 86% of all companies for which an S&P Report is available.

Volatility: Average

| Low | **Average** | High |

Technical Evaluation: Neutral

Since 11/04, the technical indicators for HAS have been Neutral.

Relative Strength Rank: Moderate

49

| 1 Lowest | Highest 99 |

| Price as of 11/12/04: | **$19** | 2004E S&P Core EPS: | **$1.05** |

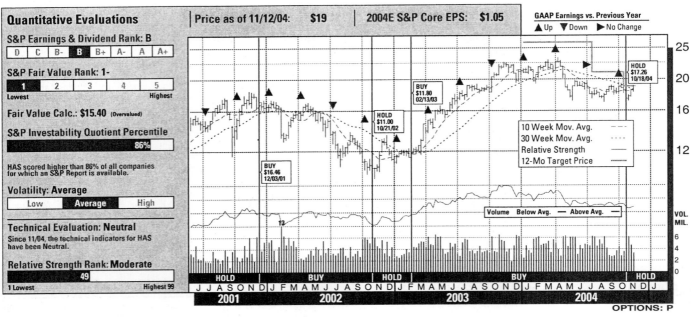

GAAP Earnings vs. Previous Year
▲ Up ▼ Down ► No Change

- 10 Week Mov. Avg.
- 30 Week Mov. Avg.
- Relative Strength
- 12-Mo Target Price

Volume Below Avg. — Above Avg.

BUY $16.46 12/03/01
HOLD $11.00 10/21/02
BUY $11.80 02/13/03
HOLD $17.26 10/18/04

HOLD BUY HOLD BUY HOLD
J J A S O N D J F M A M J J A S O N D J F M A M J J A S O N D J F M A M J J A S O N D J
2001 2002 2003 2004

OPTIONS: P

Analyst commentary prepared by Amy Glynn, CFA /PMW/GG

Highlights October 18, 2004

- We look for a slight decline in revenues in 2004, due in part to an uncertain retail environment that reflects factors such as rising fuel costs that affect consumer spending. In addition, HAS has seen recent softness in the boys business, and we expect this to persist. The company also faces difficult revenue comparisons for Beyblade, which was a strong performer in 2003. We see a strong pipeline of product launches serving to partly offset overall weakness. For 2005, we see revenues up in the low single digits.

- We think gross margins will narrow for 2004, due to the anticipated decline in the higher margin Beyblade product. We think HAS remains sharply focused on controlling costs, but expect operating margins to narrow slightly in 2004. Nevertheless, in October, the company said it remained on target to increase its operating margin to 12% by 2005.

- We see 2004 and 2005 EPS of $1.14 and $1.35, respectively. After estimated stock option expense and pension adjustments, we project 2004 and 2005 S&P Core EPS of $1.05 and $.120, respectively.

Investment Rationale/Risk October 18, 2004

- We continue to view the industry as challenging, particularly in light of what we view as an uncertain retail environment and lackluster top-line growth. We do not see a near-term catalyst for the stock to outperform, and would not add to positions. However, we think that positive factors such as HAS's focused cost cutting initiatives, continued investments in core brands and new products, and improving balance sheet merit holding the shares.

- Risks to our recommendation and target price include more store closings and tight inventory management at toy retailers, increased competitive pressures, and/or a weak holiday season due to lack of consumer demand for HAS product offerings.

- Our 12-month target price of $19 applies a P/E multiple of 14X to our 2005 EPS estimate, in line with our target multiple for close peer Mattel (MAT; hold, $17). We think that the lack of a near-term catalyst warrants a discount to the multiple of the S&P 500.

Key Stock Statistics

S&P Core EPS 2005E	1.20	52-week Range	$23.33-16.90
S&P Oper. EPS 2004E	1.14	12 Month P/E	19.6
P/E on S&P Oper. EPS 2004E	16.7	Beta	0.73
S&P Oper. EPS 2005E	1.35	Shareholders	9,500
Yield (%)	1.3%	Market Cap (B)	$ 3.4
Dividend Rate/Share	0.24	Shares Outstanding (M)	177.0

Value of $10,000 invested five years ago: **$ 8,475**

Dividend Data Dividends have been paid since 1981

Amount ($)	Date Decl.	Ex-Div. Date	Stock of Record	Payment Date
0.030	Dec. 11	Jan. 29	Feb. 02	Feb. 16 '04
0.060	Mar. 04	Apr. 29	May. 03	May. 17 '04
0.060	May. 20	Jul. 29	Aug. 02	Aug. 16 '04
0.060	Jul. 28	Oct. 28	Nov. 01	Nov. 15 '04

Revenues/Earnings Data Fiscal year ending December 31

Revenues (Million $)

	2004	2003	2002	2001	2000	1999
1Q	474.3	461.8	452.3	463.3	773.5	668.4
2Q	516.4	581.5	546.0	511.0	778.4	874.6
3Q	947.3	581.5	820.5	893.4	1,073	1,098
4Q	—	1,124	997.4	988.7	1,163	1,591
Yr.	—	3,139	2,816	2,856	3,787	4,232

Earnings Per Share ($)

	2004	2003	2002	2001	2000	1999
1Q	0.03	0.01	-0.10	-0.14	0.08	0.07
2Q	0.06	0.06	-0.15	-0.11	0.04	0.16
3Q	0.45	0.06	0.32	0.29	0.08	0.43
4Q	E0.60	0.43	0.36	0.30	-1.05	0.29
Yr.	E1.14	0.98	0.43	0.35	-0.82	0.93

Next earnings report expected: early-February Source: S&P, Company Reports
EPS Estimates based on S&P Operating Earnings; historical GAAP earnings are as reported.

STANDARD &POOR'S

Hasbro Inc.

Recommendation: **HOLD** ★ ★ ★ ☆ ☆   12-Month Target Price: **$19.00** (as of October 18, 2004)

Business Summary October 18, 2004

Hasbro is a worldwide leader in children's and family leisure time and entertainment products and services, including the design, manufacture and marketing of games and toys ranging from traditional to high-tech. The company's business strategies include expanding its core brands, developing new and innovative toy and game products, and boosting operating margins by optimizing efficiencies. HAS has a longer-term revenue growth target of 3% to 5% a year, and an operating margin goal of at least 12% by 2005.

In managing its business, HAS focuses on two major areas: toys and games. Organizationally, the company's principal segments are U.S. Toys, Games and International. In the game category, HAS markets products under the Milton Bradley, Parker Brothers, Tiger Games, Avalon Hill, and Wizards of the Coast brand names. Core games include Monopoly, Battleship, The Game of Life, Scrabble, Trivial Pursuit, and trading card and role-playing games related to Pokemon and to Dungeons and Dragons. In 2002 and 2003, the company successfully expanded the Trivial Pursuit brand through the introduction of several new editions. In 2004, HAS planned to introduce new products related to the respective 55th, 70th and 30th anniversaries of Candy Land, Sorry!, and Dungeons and Dragons.

In boys' toys, the company offers a range of products, some of which are licensed and tied to entertainment properties, such as Star Wars, and other licensed products, such as Beyblade. Major boys' toys include G.I. Joe, Transformers, and the Tonka line of trucks and vehicles. Girls' toys include My Little Pony, which was expected to be supported by new product launches in 2004.

In the preschool area, core products are primarily marketed under the Playskool trademark. Creative play items for both boys and girls include Play-Doh, Easy Bake Oven, Lite-Brite and Spirograph.

In addition to the U.S., HAS operates in more than 25 countries, selling a representative range of toy and game products marketed in the U.S., together with some items sold only internationally. Key international brands in 2003 included Action Man, Play-Doh, Magic: The Gathering, Beyblade, and Monopoly. The company also acts as the distributor for Bratz Dolls in certain European markets. In 2003, international operations accounted for 38% of consolidated net revenues. In 2003, products were manufactured in third party facilities in the Far East, and in three owned facilities, in the U.S., Ireland and Spain. In the 2003 fourth quarter, HAS ceased manufacturing at its Valencia, Spain, plant, to take advantage of lower cost production alternatives.

In December 2003, the company announced the closure of all of its remaining retail shops, which had operated under the names Wizards of the Coast and Game Keeper. In 2003, Wal-Mart Stores and Toys R Us accounted for 21% and 16% of consolidated revenues, respectively. The five largest customers accounted for 52% of revenues.

Company Financials Fiscal Year ending December 31

Per Share Data ($)

(Year Ended December 31)	2003	2002	2001	2000	1999	1998	1997	1996	1995	1994
Tangible Bk. Val.	1.32	0.08	NM	NM	0.64	2.05	4.36	4.27	3.60	3.15
Cash Flow	2.37	0.95	1.66	0.69	2.31	1.48	1.20	1.51	1.24	1.32
Earnings	0.98	0.43	0.35	-0.82	0.93	1.01	0.68	1.01	0.78	0.89
S&P Core Earnings	0.93	0.44	0.19	NA	NA	NA	NA	NA	NA	NA
Dividends	0.12	0.12	0.12	0.24	0.23	0.21	0.23	0.25	0.14	0.12
Payout Ratio	12%	28%	34%	NM	25%	21%	33%	25%	18%	13%
Prices - High	22.63	17.30	18.44	18.93	37.00	27.29	24.33	20.77	15.66	16.27
- Low	11.23	9.87	10.31	8.37	16.87	18.66	15.25	12.83	12.61	12.38
P/E Ratio - High	23	40	53	NM	40	27	36	21	20	18
- Low	11	23	29	NM	18	18	22	13	16	14

Income Statement Analysis (Million $)

	2003	2002	2001	2000	1999	1998	1997	1996	1995	1994
Revs.	3,139	2,816	2,856	3,787	4,232	3,304	3,189	3,002	2,858	2,670
Oper. Inc.	509	309	435	268	669	442	473	430	365	394
Depr.	240	89.3	226	264	277	97.0	113	98.2	91.4	85.4
Int. Exp.	52.5	77.5	104	114	69.3	36.1	27.5	31.5	37.6	30.8
Pretax Inc.	244	104	96.2	-226	274	303	205	307	253	292
Eff. Tax Rate	28.3%	27.9%	36.8%	NM	31.0%	32.0%	34.0%	34.9%	38.3%	38.5%
Net Inc.	175	75.1	60.8	-145	189	206	135	200	156	179
S&P Core Earnings	166	79.1	33.8	NA	NA	NA	NA	NA	NA	NA

Balance Sheet & Other Fin. Data (Million $)

	2003	2002	2001	2000	1999	1998	1997	1996	1995	1994
Cash	521	495	233	127	280	178	362	219	161	137
Curr. Assets	1,509	1,432	1,369	1,580	2,132	1,790	1,574	1,487	1,425	1,252
Total Assets	3,163	3,143	3,369	3,828	4,463	3,794	2,900	2,702	2,616	2,378
Curr. Liab.	930	967	759	1,240	2,071	1,366	1,004	831	870	764
LT Debt	687	857	1,166	1,168	421	407	Nil	149	150	150
Common Equity	1,405	1,191	1,353	1,327	1,879	1,945	1,838	1,652	1,526	1,395
Total Cap.	2,092	2,049	2,519	2,495	2,300	2,352	1,838	1,801	1,747	1,545
Cap. Exp.	63.1	58.7	50.0	125	107	142	99	102	101	111
Cash Flow	415	164	287	120	466	303	248	298	247	265
Curr. Ratio	1.6	1.5	1.8	1.3	1.0	1.3	1.6	1.8	1.6	1.6
% LT Debt of Cap.	32.8	41.8	46.3	46.8	18.3	17.3	Nil	8.3	8.6	9.7
% Net Inc.of Revs.	5.6	2.7	2.1	NM	4.5	6.2	4.2	6.7	5.5	6.7
% Ret. on Assets	5.6	2.3	1.7	NM	4.6	6.2	4.8	7.5	6.3	7.7
% Ret. on Equity	13.5	5.9	4.5	NM	9.9	10.9	7.7	12.6	10.7	13.4

Data as orig reptd.; bef. results of disc opers/spec. items. Per share data adj. for stk. divs.; EPS diluted. E-Estimated. NA-Not Available. NM-Not Meaningful. NR-Not Ranked. UR-Under Review.

Office: 1027 Newport Ave, Pawtucket, RI 02861-2500.
Telephone: 401-431-8697.
Website: http://www.hasbro.com
Chrmn & CEO: A.G. Hassenfeld.
Pres & COO: A.J. Verrecchia.
SVP & CFO: D.D. Hargreaves.
SVP & Treas: M.R. Trueb.

SVP, Secy & General Counsel: B. Nagler.
Investor Contact: K.A. Warren 401-727-5401.
Dirs: B. L. Anderson, A. R. Batkin, F. J. Biondi, J. Connors, Jr., E. G. Gee, J. M. Greenberg, A. G. Hassenfeld, C. B. Malone, E. M. Philip, T. Philip, E. J. Rosenwald, Jr., E. J. Segal, C. Spielvogel, C. Spielvogel, P. Stern, A. J. Verrecchia.

Founded: in 1926.
Domicile: Rhode Island.
Employees: 6,900.
S&P Analyst: Amy Glynn, CFA /PMW/GG

Recommendation: SELL ★ ☆ ☆ ☆ ☆   **12-Month Target Price: $33.00**
(as of October 13, 2004)

HCA has an approximate 0.15% weighting in the **S&P 500**

Sector: Health Care
Sub-Industry: Health Care Facilities
Peer Group: Hospital Management

Summary: HCA (formerly HCA-The Healthcare Company) owns and operates the largest U.S. chain of acute care hospitals, and some outpatient surgery centers and psychiatric facilities.

Quantitative Evaluations

S&P Earnings & Dividend Rank: B

| D | C | B- | **B** | B+ | A- | A | A+ |

S&P Fair Value Rank: 4+

| 1 | 2 | 3 | **4** | 5 |
| Lowest | | | | Highest |

Fair Value Calc.: $41.20 (Slightly Undervalued)

S&P Investability Quotient Percentile

89%

HCA scored higher than 89% of all companies for which an S&P Report is available.

Volatility: Average

| Low | **Average** | High |

Technical Evaluation: Neutral
Since 11/04, the technical indicators for HCA have been Neutral.

Relative Strength Rank: Moderate

49

| 1 Lowest | | Highest 99 |

Price as of 11/12/04: $39.40   **2004E S&P Core EPS:** $2.28

GAAP Earnings vs. Previous Year
▲ Up   ▼ Down   ► No Change

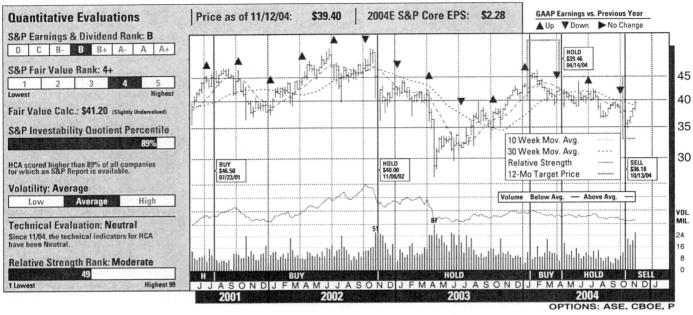

Analyst commentary prepared by C. Lavey/PMW/BK

OPTIONS: ASE, CBOE, P

Highlights 15-NOV-04

- We see 2005 operating revenues increasing about 4%, after growth of 8% expected for 2004. We anticipate price rises of about 7% in 2005, with 2% to 3% volume growth. However, we expect HCA's exposure to self-pay revenue to continue to increase throughout the year, on the impact of higher co-pays and premiums for the insured and a rising uninsured population.

- We forecast 2005 bad-debt expense equal to 11.5% of revenue, in anticipation of higher self-pay revenue. This is below our 2004 forecast of 11.7%, but it is still historically high. Despite a more favorable reimbursement rate environment seen for 2005, we anticipate slightly narrower EBITDA margins, due to higher bad debt expense, increased supply and labor costs, and a shift toward lower-paying managed care plans.

- We see 2005 operating EPS of $2.75, up from $2.44 projected for 2004. Our 2005 forecast includes an estimated positive impact of $0.17 a share due to a recently announced share repurchase program.

Investment Rationale/Risk 15-NOV-04

- We recently downgraded the shares to strong sell, from sell, based on valuation. We believe a recent rise in share price reflects HCA's Dutch auction share repurchase, but we expect future valuations to reflect underlying business trends, which we think are negative. These trends include what we see as slower growth in revenue per adjusted admission, weak volumes, and ongoing problems with bad debt. We believe these trends are likely to continue into 2005, as the number of uninsured continues to rise and demand for services remains soft.

- Risks to our recommendation and target price include a decline in bad debt expense, higher volumes, increased pricing power, faster than anticipated recovery from hurricane damage, and higher collections from uninsured patients.

- Our 12-month target price of $33 is based on a blend of our discounted cash flow model and relative value analyses. Our DCF model assumes a weighted average cost of capital of 7.5%, five-year growth of 12%, and perpetual growth of 3%. Our target price assumes that the shares will trade at 12X our 2005 EPS estimate of $2.75, slightly below the peer P/E multiple, in light of our view of HCA's weak operating performance.

Key Stock Statistics

S&P Core EPS 2005E	2.57	52-week Range	$46.60-34.70
S&P Oper. EPS 2004E	2.44	12 Month P/E	15.7
P/E on S&P Oper. EPS 2004E	16.1	Beta	0.05
S&P Oper. EPS 2005E	2.75	Shareholders	16,100
Yield (%)	1.3%	Market Cap (B)	$ 18.2
Dividend Rate/Share	0.52	Shares Outstanding (M)	482.7

Value of $10,000 invested five years ago: **$ 15,943**

Dividend Data Dividends have been paid since 1993

Amount ($)	Date Decl.	Ex-Div. Date	Stock of Record	Payment Date
0.020	Nov. 20	Jan. 28	Feb. 01	Mar. 01 '04
0.130	Feb. 03	Apr. 28	May. 01	Jun. 01 '04
0.130	May. 27	Jul. 28	Aug. 01	Sep. 01 '04
0.130	Sep. 23	Oct. 28	Nov. 01	Dec. 01 '04

Revenues/Earnings Data Fiscal year ending December 31

Revenues (Million $)

	2004	2003	2002	2001	2000	1999
1Q	5,937	5,273	4,873	4,501	4,271	4,655
2Q	5,833	5,467	4,903	4,476	4,133	4,161
3Q	5,792	5,471	4,929	4,438	4,093	3,899
4Q	—	5,597	5,024	4,538	4,173	3,942
Yr.	—	21,808	19,729	17,953	16,670	16,657

Earnings Per Share ($)

	2004	2003	2002	2001	2000	1999
1Q	0.69	0.90	0.74	0.59	0.52	0.43
2Q	0.72	0.47	0.66	0.48	-0.49	0.31
3Q	0.47	0.61	0.38	0.48	0.31	0.24
4Q	E0.55	0.63	-0.20	0.11	0.04	0.16
Yr.	E2.44	2.61	1.59	1.68	0.39	1.11

Next earnings report expected: early-February Source: S&P, Company Reports
EPS Estimates based on S&P Operating Earnings; historical GAAP earnings are as reported.

HCA Inc.

Recommendation: **SELL** ★ ☆ ☆ ☆ ☆   12-Month Target Price: **$33.00** (as of October 13, 2004)

Business Summary 15-NOV-04

HCA (formerly HCA-The Healthcare Co.; and prior to that Columbia/HCA) operates the largest U.S. chain of acute care hospitals, as well as an extensive network of outpatient surgery centers and some psychiatric hospitals. At the end of 2003, it owned and/or operated 191 hospitals, including six hospitals in joint ventures. In addition, HCA operated 83 freestanding surgery centers. The facilities were located in 23 U.S. states, England (six) and Switzerland (two).

Most of HCA's acute care hospitals provide a full range of medical and surgical services, including inpatient care, intensive care, cardiac care, diagnostic services and emergency services. They also provide outpatient services such as surgery, laboratory, radiology, respiratory therapy, cardiology and physical therapy.

At September 30, 2004, the company owned 183 hospitals (excluding seven jointly owned facilities) with 42,044 licensed beds, and 91 freestanding surgery centers. On a same-store basis, including facilities in operation for the full year, 2003 admissions rose 3.3%, and equivalent admissions advanced 2.8%. The average length of stay remained at 5.0 days, and the occupancy rate also held at 2002 levels, or 54%. Emergency room visits increased 6.8%, to 5.1 million, in 2003.

The seven psychiatric hospitals, containing 680 licensed beds, provide therapeutic programs, including child, adolescent and adult psychiatric care, and adult and adolescent alcohol and drug abuse treatment and counseling.

Patient revenues in 2003 were generated from managed care (54%), Medicare (28%), Medicaid and other (18%) sources.

Capital spending, excluding acquisitions, totaled $1.8 billion in 2003, and was expected to approximate $1.8 billion again in 2004, with $1.6 billion budgeted for 2005. In April 2003, HCA acquired the Health Midwest system in Kansas City, MO. Aggregate cash paid at closing was about $855 million. The company expects to finance capital expenditures with internally generated and borrowed funds. Total capital expenditures for the first nine months of 2004 were $1.125 billion.

In May 2000, the company reached an understanding with the Department of Justice (DOJ). It agreed to settle, subject to certain conditions, civil claims against it concerning DRG (diagnosis related group) coding, outpatient laboratory billing, and home health care issues. The understanding included a payment to the government of $745 million ($498 million, after tax), plus 6.5% interest, which began accruing May 18, 2000.

In March 2002, an appellate court reversed fraud convictions against two former HCA executives, the only criminal charges brought against current or former employees. In December 2002, the company reached an understanding with attorneys for the Department of Justice to recommend an agreement to settle litigation brought by the DOJ. In exchange for releases by the DOJ, HCA has paid the DOJ $631 million. The company also reached an agreement in principle with states with similar claims against it; HCA has paid $17.5 million to state Medicaid agencies.

Company Financials Fiscal Year ending December 31

Per Share Data ($)

(Year Ended December 31)	2003	2002	2001	2000	1999	1998	1997	1996	1995	1994
Tangible Bk. Val.	7.44	7.08	5.33	4.14	5.85	7.26	5.81	7.30	5.43	5.07
Cash Flow	4.98	3.51	3.63	2.20	2.96	2.75	2.14	3.92	3.03	2.58
Earnings	2.61	1.59	1.68	0.39	1.11	0.82	0.27	2.22	1.58	1.42
S&P Core Earnings	2.28	2.32	1.66	NA	NA	NA	NA	NA	NA	NA
Dividends	0.08	0.08	0.08	0.08	0.08	0.08	0.07	0.08	0.08	0.06
Payout Ratio	3%	5%	5%	21%	7%	10%	26%	4%	5%	4%
Prices - High	44.45	52.05	47.28	45.25	29.43	34.62	44.87	41.87	36.00	30.16
- Low	34.50	36.21	33.93	18.75	17.25	17.00	25.75	31.66	23.58	22.16
P/E Ratio - High	17	33	28	NM	27	42	NM	19	23	21
- Low	13	23	20	NM	16	21	NM	14	15	16

Income Statement Analysis (Million $)

	2003	2002	2001	2000	1999	1998	1997	1996	1995	1994
Revs.	21,808	19,729	17,953	16,670	16,657	18,681	18,819	19,909	17,695	11,132
Oper. Inc.	3,721	3,697	3,200	3,051	2,798	2,756	2,783	4,136	3,620	2,214
Depr.	1,112	1,010	1,048	1,033	1,094	1,247	1,238	1,155	981	609
Int. Exp.	491	446	536	559	471	561	493	498	460	260
Pretax Inc.	2,306	1,603	1,624	600	1,284	1,151	538	2,656	1,892	12.6
Eff. Tax Rate	35.7%	38.8%	37.1%	49.5%	44.4%	47.7%	38.3%	38.0%	37.8%	38.6%
Net Inc.	1,332	833	903	219	657	532	182	1,505	1,064	745
S&P Core Earnings	1,169	1,207	894	NA	NA	NA	NA	NA	NA	NA

Balance Sheet & Other Fin. Data (Million $)

	2003	2002	2001	2000	1999	1998	1997	1996	1995	1994
Cash	115	161	85.0	314	190	297	110	113	232	13.0
Curr. Assets	4,822	4,505	4,141	4,453	3,597	3,863	4,423	4,413	4,200	2,550
Total Assets	21,063	18,741	17,730	17,568	16,885	19,429	22,022	21,272	19,892	12,339
Curr. Liab.	3,168	3,739	3,184	4,141	3,332	3,559	2,773	2,946	2,738	1,767
LT Debt	8,042	6,497	6,953	5,631	5,284	5,685	9,276	6,781	7,137	3,853
Common Equity	6,209	5,702	4,762	4,405	5,617	7,581	7,250	8,609	7,129	5,022
Total Cap.	16,581	12,810	12,278	10,608	11,664	14,031	17,362	17,490	16,247	9,612
Cap. Exp.	1,838	1,718	1,370	1,155	1,287	1,255	1,422	1,400	1,527	975
Cash Flow	2,444	1,843	1,951	1,252	1,751	1,779	1,420	2,660	2,045	1,354
Curr. Ratio	1.5	1.2	1.3	1.1	1.1	1.1	1.6	1.5	1.5	1.4
% LT Debt of Cap.	48.5	50.7	56.6	53.1	45.3	40.5	53.4	38.8	43.9	40.1
% Net Inc.of Revs.	6.1	4.2	5.0	1.3	3.9	2.8	1.0	7.6	6.0	6.7
% Ret. on Assets	6.7	4.6	5.1	1.3	3.6	2.6	0.8	7.3	5.9	6.4
% Ret. on Equity	22.4	15.9	19.7	4.4	10.0	7.2	2.3	19.0	16.1	17.0

Data as orig reptd.; bef. results of disc opers/spec. items. Per share data adj. for stk. divs.; EPS diluted. E-Estimated. NA-Not Available. NM-Not Meaningful. NR-Not Ranked. UR-Under Review.

Office: One Park Plaza, Nashville, TN 37203.
Telephone: 615-344-9551.
Website: http://www.hcahealthcare.com
Chrmn & CEO: J. O. Bovender, Jr.
Pres & COO: R. M. Bracken.
EVP & CFO: R. M. Johnson.

SVP & General Counsel: R. A. Waterman.
Dirs: C. M. Armstrong, M. H. Averhoff, J. O. Bovender, Jr., R. M. Bracken, J. M. Cook, M. Feldstein, T. F. Frist, Jr., F. W. Gluck, G. A. Hatchett, C. O. Holliday, Jr., T. M. Long, J. H. McArthur, T. S. Murphy, K. C. Nelson, C. E. Reichardt, F. S. Royal, H. T. Shapiro.

Founded: in 1990.
Domicile: Delaware.
Employees: 188,000.
S&P Analyst: C. Lavey/PMW/BK

Health Management Associates

Recommendation: **SELL** ★ ★ ☆ ☆ ☆
SELL | SELL | HOLD | BUY | BUY

12-Month Target Price: **$17.00**
(as of October 15, 2004)

HMA has an approximate 0.05% weighting in the **S&P 500**

Sector: Health Care
Sub-Industry: Health Care Facilities
Peer Group: Hospital Management

Summary: HMA operates a rapidly growing network of general acute care hospitals located primarily in nonurban areas in the Southeast and Southwest.

Quantitative Evaluations

S&P Earnings & Dividend Rank: B+

| D | C | B- | B | B+ | A- | A | A+ |

S&P Fair Value Rank: 5

| 1 | 2 | 3 | 4 | 5 |
| Lowest | | | | Highest |

Fair Value Calc.: $23.60 (Slightly Undervalued)

S&P Investability Quotient Percentile

94%

HMA scored higher than 94% of all companies for which an S&P Report is available.

Volatility: Average

| Low | Average | High |

Technical Evaluation: Bullish

Since 11/04, the technical indicators for HMA have been Bullish.

Relative Strength Rank: Strong

77

1 Lowest — Highest 99

| Price as of 11/12/04: | **$22.66** | | 2005E S&P Core EPS: | **$1.47** |

GAAP Earnings vs. Previous Year
▲ Up ▼ Down ▶ No Change

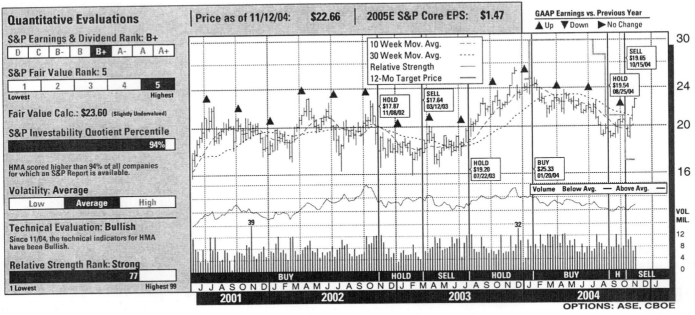

Analyst commentary prepared by Cameron Lavey/CB/BK

OPTIONS: ASE, CBOE

Highlights October 27, 2004

- We expect HMA to generate revenue growth of 13% in FY 05 (Sep.), including organic growth of 6%, on same-facility admissions gains of 3% and high single digit price increases; we look for acquisitions to supply the rest of our forecasted revenue growth. We expect increased discounts for the uninsured and higher levels of charity care to partially offset revenue gains.

- We expect the company to generate FY 05 EBITDA of about $790 million, implying same-hospital EBITDA margins of 22%, down slightly from the level of FY 04, due to higher labor and supply costs, increased bad debt expense, and acquisition integration expenses. HMA's practice of writing off higher levels of charity care distorts EBITDA margins relative to peers, in our view.

- We see share buybacks helping the company meet our earnings growth expectations in FY 05. We look for FY 05 EPS to advance about 14%, to $1.50, from FY 04's $1.32.

Investment Rationale/Risk October 27, 2004

- We believe that several unfavorable industry trends are likely to continue through the rest of 2004 and into 2005. These trends include rising labor and supply costs, higher bad debt expenses, increases in uninsured receivables, and higher physician recruitment expenses. In addition, HMA's total uncompensated care as a percentage of revenue was 22.5% in FY 04, up from 20.0% in FY 03. We expect this number to rise slightly in FY 05 as consumers' share of health care costs rises.

- Risks to our recommendation and target price include lower levels of bad debt, greater pricing power, and unanticipated favorable changes in Medicare and Medicaid reimbursement rates.

- On the basis of a P/E to growth (PEG) ratio of about 1.2X, based on our FY 05 estimates, versus a peer group average PEG of 1.1X, we believe the shares are slightly overvalued. Our 12-month target price of $17 is based on a P/E multiple of about 11X applied to our FY 05 EPS estimate, slightly below peer levels, due to what we see as HMA's slower growth prospects.

Key Stock Statistics

S&P Oper. EPS 2005E	1.50	52-week Range	$26.45-18.80
P/E on S&P Oper. EPS 2005E	15.1	12 Month P/E	17.2
Yield (%)	0.7%	Beta	0.19
Dividend Rate/Share	0.16	Shareholders	1,500
Shares Outstanding (M)	243.4	Market Cap (B)	$ 5.5

Value of $10,000 invested five years ago: **$ 24,404**

Dividend Data Dividends have been paid since 2002

Amount ($)	Date Decl.	Ex-Div. Date	Stock of Record	Payment Date
0.020	Jan. 27	Feb. 04	Feb. 06	Mar. 01 '04
0.020	Apr. 27	May. 05	May. 07	Jun. 01 '04
0.020	Jul. 27	Aug. 05	Aug. 09	Aug. 31 '04
0.040	Sep. 23	Nov. 03	Nov. 05	Nov. 29 '04

Revenues/Earnings Data Fiscal year ending September 30

Revenues (Million $)

	2004	2003	2002	2001	2000	1999
1Q	756.5	609.4	495.8	434.2	370.1	305.5
2Q	833.9	646.5	580.0	481.1	408.7	339.8
3Q	817.3	647.1	592.5	473.2	391.1	352.5
4Q	798.1	657.6	594.4	491.2	407.9	358.0
Yr.	3,206	2,561	2,263	1,880	1,578	1,356

Earnings Per Share ($)

	2004	2003	2002	2001	2000	1999
1Q	0.29	0.24	0.20	0.16	0.14	0.12
2Q	0.37	0.31	0.27	0.19	0.21	0.18
3Q	0.36	0.30	0.26	0.21	0.18	0.13
4Q	0.30	0.28	0.24	0.20	0.16	0.13
Yr.	1.32	1.13	0.97	0.76	0.68	0.59

Next earnings report expected: mid-January Source: S&P, Company Reports
EPS Estimates based on S&P Operating Earnings; historical GAAP earnings are as reported.

Health Management Associates, Inc.

Recommendation: **SELL** ★ ★ ★ ★ ★   12-Month Target Price: **$17.00** (as of October 15, 2004)

Business Summary October 28, 2004

Health Management Associates operates general acute care hospitals in nonurban and rural areas of the U.S., with a primary focus on markets in the Southeast and Southwest. At September 30, 2004, the company operated 53 hospitals in 15 states, with a total of 7,526 licensed beds. The company focuses on acquiring underperforming hospitals, with the goal of upgrading the quality of care and improving operating performance.

HMA seeks to efficiently and profitably operate its existing hospitals, while acquiring underperforming hospitals, in high-growth, nonurban areas with populations of 30,000 to 400,000, and with established physician bases. Many facilities are unprofitable at the time of acquisition, and the company immediately employs an executive director and controller, implements its proprietary management information system, recruits physicians, introduces strict cost control measures with respect to hospital staffing and volume purchasing, and spends the required capital to upgrade the facility and equipment. HMA aims to achieve significant improvement in the operating performance of newly acquired facilities within 12 to 24 months of acquisition, and seeks to recover its cash investment in four years or less.

The company's acute care hospitals offer a broad range of services, including internal medicine, obstetrics, emergency room care, radiology, oncology, diagnostic care, coronary care, pediatrics, behavioral health, psychiatric care, and, in several hospitals, specialized services such as open heart surgery and neurosurgery. HMA seeks to provide at least 90% of the acute care needs of each community in its service areas, reducing out-migration of potential patients to hospitals in larger urban areas.

In FY 04 (Sep.), HMA's acute care hospitals generated total admissions of 237,494 (232,816 in FY 03); patient days reached 1,025,992 (1,014,645). The average length of hospital stay was 4.3 days (4.4); and the occupancy rate was 48.9% (47.5%). Outpatient revenues accounted for 47.9% (45.7%) of total revenue, with inpatient revenue accounting for the rest.

In November 2003, the company acquired five hospitals from subsidiaries of Tenet Healthcare Corp., for about $515 million. In October 2003, HMA received approval from the State of Florida Agency for Health Care Administration to construct a 100-bed facility in southeast Collier County, FL, at an expected cost of about $75 million. In September 2003, it acquired Walton Medical Center, a 135-bed hospital located in Monroe, GA, for about $40 million. In August 2003, the company acquired Providence Yakima Medical Center and Providence Toppenish Hospital, a 289-bed acute care hospital system in Washington, for $82.7 million. In January, HMA acquired the Madison County Medical Center, a 67-bed acute care hospital in Canton, MS, for $9.7 million. In October, HMA acquired an 82-bed hospital in Chester, SC, its first acquisition in FY 05.

HMA expects to spend about $220 million to $240 million on capital equipment, renovations, and replacement hospitals in FY 05.

Company Financials Fiscal Year ending September 30

Per Share Data ($)

(Year Ended September 30)	2004	2003	2002	2001	2000	1999	1998	1997	1996	1995
Tangible Bk. Val.	NA	5.16	4.24	4.08	3.44	2.98	2.82	2.29	1.76	1.36
Cash Flow	NA	1.54	1.31	1.08	0.98	0.83	0.73	0.58	0.45	0.34
Earnings	1.32	1.13	0.97	0.76	0.68	0.59	0.54	0.43	0.34	0.26
S&P Core Earnings	NA	1.08	0.93	0.72	NA	NA	NA	NA	NA	NA
Dividends	0.08	0.08	Nil	Nil	Nil	Nil	Nil	Nil	Nil	Nil
Payout Ratio	6%	7%	Nil	Nil	Nil	Nil	Nil	Nil	Nil	Nil
Prices - High	25.55	26.45	22.99	22.22	22.75	21.62	25.75	17.66	11.11	6.93
- Low	18.80	15.89	16.24	13.42	9.62	7.00	14.91	9.50	7.44	4.64
P/E Ratio - High	19	23	24	29	33	37	48	41	33	27
- Low	14	14	17	18	14	12	28	22	22	18

Income Statement Analysis (Million $)

	2004	2003	2002	2001	2000	1999	1998	1997	1996	1995
Revs.	NA	2,561	2,263	1,880	1,578	1,356	1,139	895	714	531
Oper. Inc.	NA	593	518	432	376	316	280	219	169	128
Depr.	NA	110	95.3	90.6	74.5	61.3	50.4	36.6	27.2	20.6
Int. Exp.	NA	30.4	15.5	20.0	25.4	8.38	4.76	3.71	3.52	3.62
Pretax Inc.	NA	463	407	321	276	247	225	178	138	104
Eff. Tax Rate	NA	37.9%	39.2%	39.2%	39.3%	39.2%	39.3%	39.3%	39.3%	39.3%
Net Inc.	NA	283	246	195	168	150	137	108	84.1	63.3
S&P Core Earnings	NA	273	235	185	NA	NA	NA	NA	NA	NA

Balance Sheet & Other Fin. Data (Million $)

	2004	2003	2002	2001	2000	1999	1998	1997	1996	1995
Cash	NA	395	124	70.3	16.5	12.9	12.7	67.4	31.2	75.3
Curr. Assets	NA	1,093	696	565	487	425	309	236	178	173
Total Assets	NA	2,979	2,364	1,942	1,772	1,517	1,112	728	592	467
Curr. Liab.	NA	273	274	188	170	175	121	82.9	70.9	50.6
LT Debt	NA	925	650	429	520	402	177	49.7	68.7	67.7
Common Equity	NA	1,637	1,347	1,254	1,030	891	757	560	418	318
Total Cap.	NA	2,648	2,048	1,717	1,585	1,325	974	629	505	404
Cap. Exp.	NA	166	116	73.5	121	159	237	111	41.2	22.9
Cash Flow	NA	393	342	286	242	211	187	145	111	83.9
Curr. Ratio	NA	4.0	2.5	3.0	2.9	2.4	2.6	2.8	2.5	3.4
% LT Debt of Cap.	NA	34.9	31.7	25.0	32.8	30.3	18.2	7.9	13.6	16.8
% Net Inc.of Revs.	NA	11.1	10.9	10.4	10.6	11.1	12.0	12.1	11.8	11.9
% Ret. on Assets	NA	10.6	11.4	10.5	10.2	11.4	14.9	16.4	15.9	14.6
% Ret. on Equity	NA	19.0	19.0	17.1	17.5	18.2	20.8	22.2	22.9	22.2

Data as orig reptd.; bef. results of disc opers/spec. items. Per share data adj. for stk. divs.; EPS diluted. E-Estimated. NA-Not Available. NM-Not Meaningful. NR-Not Ranked. UR-Under Review.

Office: 5811 Pelican Bay Boulevard, Naples, FL 34108-2711.
Telephone: 239-598-3131.
Website: http://www.hma-corp.com
Chrmn: W.J. Schoen.
Pres & CEO: J.V. Vumbacco.

SVP & CFO: R.E. Farnham.
SVP, Secy & General Counsel: T.R. Parry.
Investor Contact: J.C. Merriwether 239-598-3104.
Dirs: K. P. Dauten, D. E. Kiernan, R. A. Knox, W. E. Mayberry, W. J. Schoen, W. C. Steere, Jr., J. V. Vumbacco, R. W. Westerfield.

Founded: in 1977.
Domicile: Delaware.
Employees: 24,000.
S&P Analyst: Cameron Lavey/CB/BK

Heinz (H.J.)

Recommendation: HOLD ★ ★ ★ ★ ★
SELL SELL HOLD BUY BUY

12-Month Target Price: **$40.00**
(as of July 07, 2004)

HNZ has an approximate 0.12% weighting in the **S&P 500**

Sector: Consumer Staples
Sub-Industry: Packaged Foods & Meats
Peer Group: Larger Food Manufacturers

Summary: HNZ produces a wide variety of food products worldwide, with major presence in the U.S. in condiments, frozen potatoes, and convenience meals.

Quantitative Evaluations

S&P Earnings & Dividend Rank: B+

| D | C | B- | B | B+ | A- | A | A+ |

S&P Fair Value Rank: 4

| 1 | 2 | 3 | 4 | 5 |
Lowest — Highest

Fair Value Calc.: $40.40 (Slightly Undervalued)

S&P Investability Quotient Percentile

96%

HNZ scored higher than 96% of all companies for which an S&P Report is available.

Volatility: Low

| Low | Average | High |

Technical Evaluation: Bullish
Since 11/04, the technical indicators for HNZ have been Bullish.

Relative Strength Rank: Moderate

58

1 Lowest — Highest 99

Price as of 11/12/04: $38.81 | **2005E S&P Core EPS:** $2.33

GAAP Earnings vs. Previous Year
▲ Up ▼ Down ► No Change

10 Week Mov. Avg.
30 Week Mov. Avg.
Relative Strength
12-Mo Target Price

Volume Below Avg. —— Above Avg.

HOLD

J J A S O N D | J F M A M J J A S O N D | J F M A M J J A S O N D | J F M A M J J A S O N D | J
2001 | 2002 | 2003 | 2004

OPTIONS: ASE, CBOE, P

Analyst commentary prepared by Richard Joy/PMW/GG

Highlights July 08, 2004

- We expect net sales to advance 2% to 3% in FY 05 (Apr.), primarily reflecting strength in U.S. foodservice operations and strong international sales growth. We see foodservice sales gaining 4% to 6%, with Asia/Pacific sales advancing 7% to 9%. We expect operating margins to benefit from an improved sales mix, SKU rationalizations, better working capital management, and cost savings from past restructuring programs. However, we think that higher levels of advertising and marketing spending could limit operating profit growth to 4% to 5%.

- After expected lower interest expense, a lower estimated effective tax rate, and no change in shares outstanding, we project FY 05 EPS of $2.38, up 8% from FY 04's $2.20. We expect EPS of $2.55 for FY 06. For the longer term, we see annual EPS growth of 8% to 9%.

- Our respective FY 05 and FY 06 Standard & Poor's Core Earnings projections, reflecting estimated stock option expense of $0.07 a share and $0.02 a share for pension and post-retirement benefits adjustment, are $2.33 and $2.50 a share.

Investment Rationale/Risk July 08, 2004

- Our hold opinion on the shares primarily reflects mixed results in recent quarters for HNZ's U.S. food businesses. We think that the balance sheet has shown substantial improvement, as the company continues to use free cash flow for debt reduction. We see profitability benefiting from a more favorable product mix, cost structure improvements, and investments in new products. We view the shares as a worthwhile holding at a recent level of 16.5X our calendar 2004 EPS estimate of $2.35, a modest discount to the average P/E multiple for other leading packaged foods companies and the S&P 500.

- Risks to our recommendation and target price include competitive product and pricing pressures in HNZ's markets, raw material cost inflation, consumer acceptance of new product introductions, foreign currency impact, and the company's ability to achieve sales and earnings growth forecasts.

- Our analysis of free cash flows, using a weighted average cost of capital of 9%, suggests that the stock is trading in line with our estimate of intrinsic value. Our 12-month target price of $40 is derived from our analysis of discounted free cash flow and relative P/E multiples.

Key Stock Statistics

S&P Core EPS 2006E	2.50	52-week Range	$39.41-34.53
S&P Oper. EPS 2005E	2.38	12 Month P/E	17.5
P/E on S&P Oper. EPS 2005E	16.3	Beta	0.31
S&P Oper. EPS 2006E	2.55	Shareholders	47,600
Yield (%)	2.9%	Market Cap (B)	$ 13.6
Dividend Rate/Share	1.14	Shares Outstanding (M)	349.4

Value of $10,000 invested five years ago: **NA**

Dividend Data Dividends have been paid since 1911

Amount ($)	Date Decl.	Ex-Div. Date	Stock of Record	Payment Date
0.285	Mar. 10	Mar. 22	Mar. 24	Apr. 10 '04
0.285	Jun. 09	Jun. 22	Jun. 24	Jul. 10 '04
0.285	Sep. 08	Sep. 21	Sep. 23	Oct. 10 '04
0.285	Nov. 10	Dec. 21	Dec. 23	Jan. 10 '05

Revenues/Earnings Data Fiscal year ending April 30

Revenues (Million $)

	2005	2004	2003	2002	2001	2000
1Q	2,003	1,896	1,839	2,077	2,153	2,181
2Q	—	2,090	2,099	2,414	2,296	2,344
3Q	—	2,097	2,105	2,365	2,270	2,295
4Q	—	2,331	2,193	2,574	2,693	2,588
Yr.	—	8,415	8,237	9,431	9,430	9,408

Earnings Per Share ($)

	2005	2004	2003	2002	2001	2000
1Q	0.55	0.60	0.50	0.57	0.57	0.57
2Q	E0.59	0.54	0.60	0.59	0.54	1.14
3Q	E0.61	0.57	0.37	0.57	0.77	0.47
4Q	E0.62	0.56	0.29	0.37	0.49	0.27
Yr.	E2.38	2.20	1.57	2.36	1.41	2.47

Next earnings report expected: late-November Source: S&P, Company Reports
EPS Estimates based on S&P Operating Earnings; historical GAAP earnings are as reported.

H.J. Heinz Company

Recommendation: **HOLD** ★ ★ ★ ☆ ☆   12-Month Target Price: **$40.00** (as of July 07, 2004)

Business Summary July 08, 2004

Although largely known for its familiar ketchup, H.J. Heinz boasts many other branded food products, ranging from Ore-Ida frozen potatoes to Weight Watchers frozen dinners, that are consumed by millions of people daily. The company's current operating strategy rests on three pillars: renewed focus on core competencies, niche acquisitions, and cost control. Sales are broadly based geographically, with contributions by major region in FY 04 (Apr.) as follows: North America (41.5% of sales), Europe (39%), Asia/Pacific (15%), and other (4.5%).

The company's revenues are generated via the manufacture and sale of products in the following categories: ketchup, condiments and sauces (36% of FY 04 sales), such as Heinz and Classico; frozen foods (23%), which include items such as Boston Market HomeStyle Meals, Ore-Ida potatoes, and Smart Ones; convenience meals (22%); infant foods (11%) and other products (8%). Advertising expenses (including production and communication costs) for FY 04 and FY 03 were $360.4 million and $370.9 million, respectively, and are recorded either as a reduction of revenue or as a component of SG&A expenses.

In December 2002, HNZ completed the spinoff of its North American Pet Food and Pet Snacks, U.S. Tuna, U.S. Private Label Soup, College Inn Broth, and U.S. Infant Feeding businesses, merging them with the Del Monte Foods Co. At the close of the transaction, HNZ shareholders owned about 74.5% and Del Monte shareholders about 25.5% of the fully diluted share capital of the new Del Monte. As a result of the merger, HNZ received $1.1 billion in cash, which was used to retire debt.

The strategic rationale behind the Del Monte transaction was to make HNZ a more focused and faster growing business, leveraging the global strategic platforms of Meal Enhancers (ketchup, condiments and sauces) and Meals & Snacks (frozen and ambient). Upon completion of the transaction, HNZ reduced its annual dividend rate to $1.08 a share beginning in April 2003, from an annual rate of $1.62 a share.

In 1999, the company acquired for nearly $100 million a 19.5% interest in The Hain Food Group, Inc., forming a strategic alliance for global production and marketing of natural and organic foods and soy-based beverages. Hain is the leading U.S. natural and organic food company, with more than 3,500 products sold under brands such as Health Valley cereal, bakery and soups; Terra Chip snacks; and Westsoy, the largest soy beverage marketer. As part of the alliance, HNZ was to provide procurement, manufacturing and logistic expertise, with Hain providing marketing, sales and distribution services.

Company Financials Fiscal Year ending April 30

Per Share Data ($)

(Year Ended April 30)	2004	2003	2002	2001	2000	1999	1998	1997	1996	1995
Tangible Bk. Val.	NM	NM	NM	NM	NM	NM	NM	0.02	0.87	0.34
Cash Flow	2.86	2.17	3.22	2.26	3.32	2.11	2.99	1.72	2.66	2.43
Earnings	2.20	1.57	2.36	1.41	2.47	1.29	2.15	0.81	1.75	1.59
S&P Core Earnings	2.11	1.43	1.99	1.31	NA	NA	NA	NA	NA	NA
Dividends	1.08	1.61	1.55	1.45	1.40	1.34	1.24	1.14	1.04	0.94
Payout Ratio	49%	88%	65%	102%	56%	104%	57%	140%	59%	59%

Cal. Yrs.	2003	2002	2001	2000	1999	1998	1997	1996	1995	1994
Prices - High	36.82	43.48	47.93	48.00	58.81	61.75	56.68	38.37	34.87	26.00
- Low	28.90	29.60	36.90	30.81	39.50	48.50	35.25	29.75	24.25	20.50
P/E Ratio - High	17	24	20	34	24	48	26	47	20	16
- Low	13	16	16	22	16	38	16	37	14	13

Income Statement Analysis (Million $)

	2004	2003	2002	2001	2000	1999	1998	1997	1996	1995
Revs.	8,415	8,237	9,431	9,430	9,408	9,300	9,209	9,357	9,112	8,087
Oper. Inc.	1,613	1,389	1,892	1,282	1,575	1,412	1,834	1,096	1,631	1,471
Depr.	234	215	302	299	306	302	314	340	344	315
Int. Exp.	212	224	294	333	270	259	259	274	278	211
Pretax Inc.	1,169	869	1,279	673	1,464	835	1,255	479	1,024	938
Eff. Tax Rate	33.3%	36.1%	34.8%	26.5%	39.2%	43.2%	36.1%	37.0%	35.6%	37.0%
Net Inc.	779	555	834	495	891	474	802	302	659	591
S&P Core Earnings	747	500	702	458	NA	NA	NA	NA	NA	NA

Balance Sheet & Other Fin. Data (Million $)

	2004	2003	2002	2001	2000	1999	1998	1997	1996	1995
Cash	1,180	802	207	139	138	116	96.0	189	108	207
Curr. Assets	3,611	3,284	3,374	3,117	3,170	2,887	2,687	3,013	3,047	2,823
Total Assets	9,877	9,225	10,278	9,035	8,851	8,054	8,023	8,438	8,624	8,247
Curr. Liab.	2,469	1,926	2,509	3,655	2,126	2,786	2,164	2,880	2,715	2,564
LT Debt	4,538	4,776	4,643	3,015	3,936	2,472	2,769	2,284	2,282	2,327
Common Equity	8,841	2,876	1,719	1,374	1,596	1,804	2,216	2,440	2,707	2,472
Total Cap.	13,797	8,252	7,197	4,642	5,804	4,587	5,276	4,989	5,308	5,148
Cap. Exp.	232	154	213	411	452	317	374	377	335	342
Cash Flow	1,013	770	1,136	794	1,197	776	1,116	642	1,003	906
Curr. Ratio	1.5	1.7	1.3	0.9	1.5	1.0	1.2	1.1	1.1	1.1
% LT Debt of Cap.	32.9	57.9	64.5	64.9	67.8	53.9	52.5	45.8	43.0	45.2
% Net Inc.of Revs.	9.3	6.7	8.8	5.2	9.5	5.1	8.7	3.2	7.2	7.3
% Ret. on Assets	8.2	5.7	8.6	5.5	10.5	5.9	9.7	3.5	7.8	8.1
% Ret. on Equity	8.9	17.9	53.9	33.3	52.4	23.6	34.5	11.7	25.4	24.6

Data as orig reptd.; bef. results of disc opers/spec. items. Per share data adj. for stk. divs. Bold denotes primary EPS - prior periods restated. E-Estimated. NA-Not Available. NM-Not Meaningful. NR-Not Ranked. UR-Under Review.

Office: 600 Grant Street, Pittsburgh, PA 15219.
Telephone: 412-456-5700.
Website: http://www.heinz.com
Chrmn, Pres & CEO: W.R. Johnson.
EVP & CFO: A. Winkleblack.
SVP & General Counsel: L. Stein.

VP & Investor Contact: J. Runkle 412-456-5700.
Treas: L.A. Cullo, Jr.
Dirs: C. E. Bunch, M. C. Choksi, L. S. Coleman, Jr., P. H. Coors, E. E. Holiday, W. R. Johnson, C. Kendle, D. R. O'Hare, L. C. Swann, T. J. Usher, J. M. Zimmerman.

Founded: in 1869.
Domicile: Pennsylvania.
Employees: 37,500.
S&P Analyst: Richard Joy/PMW/GG

Hercules Inc.

Recommendation: **HOLD** ★ ★ ★ ★ ★
SELL | SELL | HOLD | BUY | BUY

12-Month Target Price: $16.00
(as of November 10, 2004)

HPC has an approximate 0.01% weighting in the **S&P 500**

Sector: Materials
Sub-Industry: Diversified Chemicals
Peer Group: Diversified Companies

Summary: This specialty chemicals company sold its water treatment business in 2002; the business had accounted for about 36% of sales.

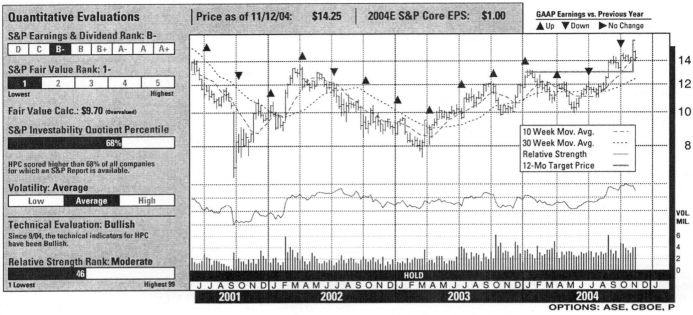

Quantitative Evaluations

S&P Earnings & Dividend Rank: B-
D | C | **B-** | B | B+ | A- | A | A+

S&P Fair Value Rank: 1-
1 | 2 | 3 | 4 | 5
Lowest | | | | Highest

Fair Value Calc.: $9.70 (Overvalued)

S&P Investability Quotient Percentile
68%

HPC scored higher than 68% of all companies for which an S&P Report is available.

Volatility: Average
Low | **Average** | High

Technical Evaluation: Bullish
Since 9/04, the technical indicators for HPC have been Bullish.

Relative Strength Rank: Moderate
46
1 Lowest | Highest 99

Price as of 11/12/04: $14.25 | **2004E S&P Core EPS: $1.00**

GAAP Earnings vs. Previous Year
▲ Up ▼ Down ► No Change

- - - 10 Week Mov. Avg.
· · · 30 Week Mov. Avg.
— Relative Strength
12-Mo Target Price

VOL. MIL.

HOLD

J J A S O N D | J F M A M J J A S O N D | J F M A M J J A S O N D | J F M A M J J A S O N D | J
2001 | **2002** | **2003** | **2004**

OPTIONS: ASE, CBOE, P

Analyst commentary prepared by Richard O'Reilly/DC/GG

Highlights September 23, 2004

- We believe sales for the rest of 2004 and in 2005 will likely continue to grow in the mid-single digits, benefiting from favorable currency rates and stronger demand in several segments. The North American paper industry has been reporting volume growth, together with the overall manufacturing sector. We think selling price comparisons may turn favorable as the company implements price increases for paper chemicals and polypropylene fibers.

- We see overall operating profits improving, as HPC continues to achieve productivity gains. We expect higher raw material costs, including higher polypropylene resins costs for the FiberVisions unit, as well as increased pension expense (up about $16 million) and insurance costs.

- We project interest expense to be modestly lower in 2004, largely as a result of the May redemption of $363 million of debt, which should provide annual interest savings of $10 million; a related $9 million after-tax charge was recorded during the second quarter of 2004. We estimate that the effective tax rate for 2004 will be 41%. We expect capital expenditures to be about $70 million in 2004, but we look for asbestos spending to be much lower than 2003's $33 million as a result of a recent agreement with one insurance carrier. Our S&P Core Earnings estimate of $1.00 for 2004 includes a positive pension expense adjustment.

Key Stock Statistics

S&P Core EPS 2005E	1.12	52-week Range	$15.17-9.93
S&P Oper. EPS 2004E	0.88	12 Month P/E	43.2
P/E on S&P Oper. EPS 2004E	16.2	Beta	0.73
S&P Oper. EPS 2005E	1.00	Shareholders	16,289
Yield (%)	Nil	Market Cap (B)	$ 1.6
Dividend Rate/Share	Nil	Shares Outstanding (M)	111.8

Value of $10,000 invested five years ago: **$ 6,408**

Dividend Data

The quarterly dividend was suspended in November 2000. The last payment of $0.08 a share was in September 2000.

Investment Rationale/Risk September 23, 2004

- We are maintaining our hold recommendation on the stock, which has climbed 13% year to date. We expect continued positive operating EPS comparisons for the rest of 2004 and in 2005, driven by modest sales growth and lower interest expense. In our view, the end of a proxy fight by Samuel Heyman in July 2003 and the appointment in late 2003 of a new CEO from inside the company have added a sense of stability. Although HPC indicated in early 2001 that it might engage in a two-part sale of the company, with BetzDearborn to be sold first, management subsequently publicly backed away from the idea of selling the rest of HPC.

- Risks to our recommendation and target price include the company's high debt-to-capital ratio (94% at June 30, 2004) and the possibility that any increase in asbestos-related legal exposure could dampen interest in the shares. HPC anticipates that asbestos-related costs in 2004 should decline from $33 million in 2003.

- We expect HPC to have free cash flow in 2004. Assuming a multiple of 7X EBITDA for the company's units, equal to the multiple for which its water chemicals unit was sold in 2002, we think that the stock is fairly valued. Our 12-month target price is $13.

Revenues/Earnings Data Fiscal year ending December 31

Revenues (Million $)

	2004	2003	2002	2001	2000	1999
1Q	475.0	447.0	402.0	702.0	785.0	791.0
2Q	510.0	478.0	437.0	670.0	822.0	820.0
3Q	501.0	463.0	443.0	637.0	815.0	813.0
4Q	—	458.0	423.0	611.0	717.0	827.0
Yr.	—	1,846	1,705	2,620	3,152	3,248

Earnings Per Share ($)

	2004	2003	2002	2001	2000	1999
1Q	0.24	0.13	-0.03	-0.09	0.34	0.37
2Q	0.04	0.30	-0.19	0.21	0.15	0.56
3Q	-0.47	0.16	-0.32	-0.66	0.70	0.54
4Q	E0.22	0.10	0.09	Nil	-0.28	0.16
Yr.	E0.88	0.69	-0.45	-0.54	0.91	1.62

Next earnings report expected: mid-February Source: S&P, Company Reports
EPS Estimates based on S&P Operating Earnings; historical GAAP earnings are as reported.

Hercules Incorporated

Recommendation: **HOLD** ★ ★ ★ ★ ★   12-Month Target Price: **$16.00** (as of November 10, 2004)

Business Summary September 23, 2004

Hercules makes specialty chemicals that are used in a broad range of consumer and industrial markets. Key markets for the company's products include pulp and paper (49%), food, pharmaceutical and personal care (20%), industrial (12%), paints and adhesives (10%), and construction materials (9%). In April 2002, HPC sold its BetzDearborn water chemicals business (annual sales of nearly $1 billion) for $1.8 billion, to a unit of GE. The company retained the paper process chemicals business, accounting for about one-third of BetzDearborn, which had been purchased in 1998. Net proceeds of $1.67 billion were used to repay debt, bringing total debt and preferred securities to about $1.5 billion at December 31, 2002.

The company's strategy now focuses on continued productivity gains, improvements in sales, earnings and capital employed, maximization of free cash flow through working capital improvements, reductions in interest expense, restructuring of the capital structure to reduce leverage and interest expense, and growth through product extensions, new products, and bolt-on acquisitions.

International operations contributed 52% of sales in 2003.

Performance products (80% of sales and 97% of profits in 2003) consist of pulp and paper chemicals (48% of sales: sizing agents, coatings, emulsions, defoamers, deposition, corrosion and foam control, de-inking, felt conditioning, and water treatment for utility systems, cooling water and water clarification), and Aqualon (33%), the global leader in water-soluble polymers and coatings used in paints, adhesives, paper, personal care products, drugs, foods and beverages, inks, and oil well drilling.

Engineered materials and additives (20%, 3%) include FiberVisions (15%), one of the world's largest producers of thermal-bond polypropylene staple fiber used in disposable hygiene products and wipes, as well as olefin textile fibers and yarn for use in wipes, upholstery fabrics, geotextiles, and filtration, and the Pinova resins unit (5%), a maker of rosin and terpene resins and aroma chemicals for flavors and fragrances, adhesives and disinfectants for use in consumer and industrial products. In March 2004, HPC said it would not acquire Meraklon S.p. A., an Italy-based maker of polypropylene fiber with 2002 sales of about 65 million euros, as a result of difficulties encountered in obtaining regulatory approval. In May 2001, the company sold a majority of its resins division, including hydrocarbon resins, peroxy chemicals, and portions of the rosin resins business.

In February 2004, HPC sold its minority ownership interest in CP Kelco for $27 million. In late 2000, the company formed CP Kelco, a joint venture combining its food gums division with the Kelco Biogums unit of Pharmacia Corp. HPC received $400 million and a 29% interest in the venture.

At June 30, 2004, there were about 34,490 asbestos-related claims against the company, including 1,040 premises claims; the rest were product claims. Based on the findings of a commissioned study, HPC estimated its possible financial exposure at $225 million to $675 million. At the end of 2003, the company had accruals of $221 million, before insurance recovery. In August 2004, HPC reached an agreement with one insurance company in which HPC will receive $30 million and $67 million will be put into a trust to reimburse HPC for future asbestos costs.

Company Financials Fiscal Year ending December 31

Per Share Data ($)

(Year Ended December 31)	2003	2002	2001	2000	1999	1998	1997	1996	1995	1994
Tangible Bk. Val.	NM	NM	NM	NM	NM	NM	7.18	8.75	9.97	11.10
Cash Flow	1.61	0.47	1.43	3.22	2.94	1.20	3.88	4.03	3.98	3.52
Earnings	0.69	-0.45	-0.54	0.91	1.62	0.10	3.18	3.04	2.93	2.29
S&P Core Earnings	0.70	-0.58	-1.96	NA	NA	NA	NA	NA	NA	NA
Dividends	Nil	Nil	Nil	0.62	1.08	1.08	1.00	0.92	0.84	0.75
Payout Ratio	Nil	Nil	Nil	68%	67%	NM	31%	30%	29%	32%
Prices - High	12.50	13.70	20.00	28.00	40.68	51.37	54.50	66.25	62.25	40.50
- Low	7.40	8.45	6.50	11.37	22.37	24.62	37.75	42.75	38.25	32.12
P/E Ratio - High	18	NM	NM	31	25	NM	17	22	21	18
- Low	11	NM	NM	12	14	NM	12	14	13	14

Income Statement Analysis (Million $)

	2003	2002	2001	2000	1999	1998	1997	1996	1995	1994
Revs.	1,846	1,705	2,620	3,152	3,248	2,145	1,866	2,060	2,427	2,813
Oper. Inc.	355	-323	482	598	624	506	466	528	531	578
Depr.	100	100	212	246	144	108	73.0	106	133	148
Int. Exp.	131	154	254	260	236	103	39.0	40.0	33.0	36.0
Pretax Inc.	95.0	-53.0	14.0	164	243	77.0	593	485	505	408
Eff. Tax Rate	22.1%	NM	NM	40.2%	30.9%	88.3%	45.4%	32.9%	34.1%	32.9%
Net Inc.	74.0	-49.0	-58.0	98.0	168	9.00	324	325	333	274
S&P Core Earnings	76.1	-62.8	-212	NA	NA	NA	NA	NA	NA	NA

Balance Sheet & Other Fin. Data (Million $)

	2003	2002	2001	2000	1999	1998	1997	1996	1995	1994
Cash	125	334	76.0	54.0	63.0	68.0	17.0	30.0	73.0	112
Curr. Assets	820	907	842	1,022	1,338	1,240	689	739	867	1,152
Total Assets	2,766	2,693	5,049	5,309	5,896	5,833	2,411	2,386	2,493	2,941
Curr. Liab.	457	616	917	922	1,559	1,317	799	694	687	767
LT Debt	1,326	1,362	2,583	2,964	2,769	3,296	799	345	298	307
Common Equity	66.0	-123	4,402	4,600	4,733	559	690	887	1,082	1,295
Total Cap.	1,470	1,319	7,319	7,751	7,789	4,080	1,649	1,361	1,475	1,731
Cap. Exp.	48.0	43.0	63.0	187	196	157	119	120	117	164
Cash Flow	174	51.0	154	344	312	117	397	431	466	422
Curr. Ratio	1.8	1.5	0.9	1.1	0.9	0.9	0.9	1.1	1.3	1.5
% LT Debt of Cap.	90.2	103.3	35.3	38.2	35.6	80.8	48.5	25.3	20.2	17.7
% Net Inc.of Revs.	4.0	NM	NM	3.1	5.2	0.4	17.4	15.8	13.7	9.7
% Ret. on Assets	2.7	NM	NM	1.7	2.9	0.2	13.5	13.3	12.3	9.2
% Ret. on Equity	NA	NM	NM	2.1	3.7	1.4	41.1	32.9	28.0	21.1

Data as orig reptd.; bef. results of disc opers/spec. items. Per share data adj. for stk. divs. Bold denotes primary EPS - prior periods restated. E-Estimated. NA-Not Available. NM-Not Meaningful. NR-Not Ranked. UR-Under Review.

Office: 1313 N Market St, Wilmington, DE 19894-0001.
Telephone: 302-594-5000 .
Website: http://www.herc.com
Chrmn: J.K. Wulff.
Pres & CEO: C.A. Rogerson.
VP & CFO: A.A. Spizzo.

VP & Chief Acctg Officer: F.G. Aanonsen.
VP & Treas: S.C. Shears.
Investor Contact: S.L. Fornoff 302-594-7151.
Dirs: P. Duff, T. P. Gerrity, J. C. Hunter III, R. D. Kennedy, J. M. Lipton, C. A. Rogerson, J. K. Wulff, J. B. Wyatt.

Founded: in 1912.
Domicile: Delaware.
Employees: 5,116.
S&P Analyst: Richard O'Reilly/DC/GG

Hershey Foods

Recommendation: **BUY** ★★★★★ SELL · SELL · HOLD · BUY · BUY

12-Month Target Price: **$53.00**
(as of October 21, 2004)

HSY has an approximate 0.12% weighting in the **S&P 500**

Sector: Consumer Staples
Sub-Industry: Packaged Foods & Meats
Peer Group: Larger Food Manufacturers

Summary: Hershey is the leading U.S. producer of chocolate and confectionery products.

Quantitative Evaluations

S&P Earnings & Dividend Rank: A-

| D | C | B- | B | B+ | A- | A | A+ |

S&P Fair Value Rank: 2+

| 1 | 2 | 3 | 4 | 5 |
| Lowest | | | | Highest |

Fair Value Calc.: $46.40 (Slightly Overvalued)

S&P Investability Quotient Percentile

99%

HSY scored higher than 99% of all companies for which an S&P Report is available.

Volatility: Low

| Low | Average | High |

Technical Evaluation: Bullish
Since 10/04, the technical indicators for HSY have been Bullish.

Relative Strength Rank: Moderate

63

| 1 Lowest | | Highest 99 |

| Price as of 11/12/04: | **$51.93** | 2004E S&P Core EPS: | **$1.95** |

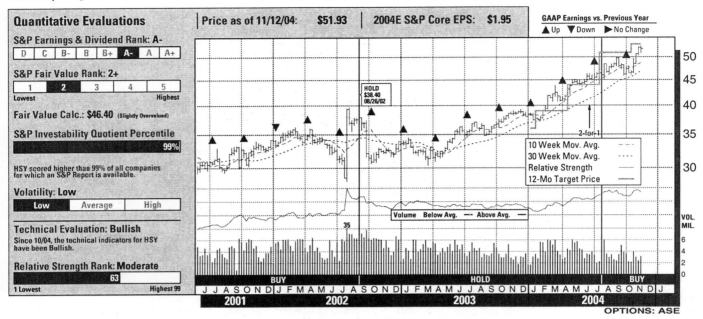

GAAP Earnings vs. Previous Year ▲ Up ▼ Down ▶ No Change

Analyst commentary prepared by Richard Joy/CB/BK

Highlights July 26, 2004

- We expect net sales to rise 3% to 4% in 2004, as growth in core domestic brands, new product introductions, improved product mix, and gains for HSY's international export business outweigh SKU (stock keeping units) reductions. We expect the company to continue to eliminate less profitable products in 2004, with the potential elimination of 100-200 SKUs from the 1,600 at the beginning of the year. We see margins benefiting from facility closures, a sales force reorganization, improved logistics and supply chain costs, and an improved product mix and price realization. The company is targeting annual cost savings of $65 million from its strategic restructuring plan. Advertising and marketing spending will likely increase, and should continue to focus on core brands.

- Following our expectation for lower interest expense and a modest reduction in shares outstanding, we project 2004 operating EPS of $2.01, up 12% from 2003's $1.80. For 2005, we project a further 10% rise to $2.22. For the longer term, we believe 9% to 11% annual EPS growth is possible.

- Our 2004 and 2005 Standard & Poor's Core Earnings per share estimates, reflecting projected stock option expense of $0.06 per share, are $1.95 and $2.16, respectively.

Investment Rationale/Risk July 26, 2004

- We recently raised our recommendation on the shares to accumulate, from hold, reflecting what we view as solid core brand momentum, improving earnings visibility and better than expected results for the first half of 2004. The shares were recently trading at a P/E multiple of more than 23X our 2004 EPS estimate, a premium to the P/E multiple for the S&P 500 and for HSY's food industry peers. We think the premium is well deserved and the shares are attractive, in light of our view of HSY's strong balance sheet, improving cost structure, and dominant position in the fast growing and relatively high margin U.S. confectionery market.

- Risks to our recommendation and target price relate to competitive pressures in HSY's businesses, consumer acceptance of new product introductions, commodity cost inflation, and the company's ability to achieve sales and earnings growth forecasts.

- Our analysis of discounted cash flows, using a weighted average cost of capital of 9%, suggests an intrinsic value for the stock in the low $50s. We have a 12-month target price of $51, derived from our discounted free cash flow and relative P/E multiple analyses.

Key Stock Statistics

S&P Core EPS 2005E	2.16	52-week Range	$52.54-37.28
S&P Oper. EPS 2004E	2.05	12 Month P/E	23.9
P/E on S&P Oper. EPS 2004E	25.3	Beta	-0.24
S&P Oper. EPS 2005E	2.25	Shareholders	39,000
Yield (%)	1.7%	Market Cap (B)	$ 9.6
Dividend Rate/Share	0.88	Shares Outstanding (M)	246.1

Value of $10,000 invested five years ago: **$ 22,903**

Dividend Data Dividends have been paid since 1930

Amount ($)	Date Decl.	Ex-Div. Date	Stock of Record	Payment Date
0.395	Apr. 28	May. 21	May. 25	Jun. 15 '04
2-for-1	Apr. 22	Jun. 16	May. 25	Jun. 15 '04
0.220	Jul. 22	Aug. 23	Aug. 25	Sep. 15 '04
0.220	Oct. 05	Nov. 22	Nov. 24	Dec. 15 '04

Revenues/Earnings Data Fiscal year ending December 31

Revenues (Million $)

	2004	2003	2002	2001	2000	1999
1Q	1,013	953.2	988.5	1,080	993.1	945.1
2Q	893.7	849.1	823.5	898.9	836.0	853.2
3Q	1,255	1,191	1,152	1,304	1,197	1,067
4Q	—	1,179	1,156	1,274	1,195	1,106
Yr.	—	4,173	4,120	4,557	4,221	3,971

Earnings Per Share ($)

	2004	2003	2002	2001	2000	1999
1Q	0.41	0.36	0.32	0.29	0.26	0.79
2Q	0.56	0.27	0.23	0.19	0.15	0.18
3Q	0.66	0.58	0.45	0.44	0.38	0.31
4Q	E0.65	0.55	0.48	-0.17	0.42	0.35
Yr.	E2.05	1.76	1.46	0.75	1.21	1.63

Next earnings report expected: late-January Source: S&P, Company Reports
EPS Estimates based on S&P Operating Earnings; historical GAAP earnings are as reported.

Hershey Foods Corporation

Recommendation: **BUY** ★★★★☆   12-Month Target Price: **$53.00** (as of October 21, 2004)

Business Summary July 26, 2004

Hershey Foods, primarily through its Hershey Chocolate U.S.A., Hershey International and Hershey Canada Inc. units, produces and distributes a broad line of chocolate, confectionery and grocery products. Financial results have strengthened over the past few years, driven mainly by a rationalization of product lines that offered subpar investment returns, the integration of a number of complementary acquisitions, and a high rate of new product success.

The company makes chocolate and confectionery products in various packaged forms, and markets them under more than 50 brands. Principal chocolate and confectionery products in the U.S. are: Hershey's, Hershey's with almonds, and Cookies 'N' Mint bars; Hugs and Kisses (both also with almonds) chocolates; Kit Kat wafer bars; Mr. Goodbar chocolate bars; Reese's Pieces candies; Rolo caramels in milk chocolate; Skor toffee bars; Y&S Twizzlers licorice; and Amazin' Fruit gummy bears fruit candy. HSY significantly increased its participation in the non-chocolate side of the confectionery industry through its 1996 acquisition of Leaf North America, with major brands that included Jolly Rancher, Whoppers, Milk Duds, and Good & Plenty. Grocery products include Hershey's chocolate chips, cocoa and syrup; and Reese's peanut butter and peanut butter chips. Hershey's chocolate milk is produced and sold under license by independent dairies throughout the U.S., using a chocolate milk mix manufactured by HSY. The

most significant raw material used in the production of the company's chocolate and confectionery products is cocoa beans.

In January 1999, the company sold 94% of its U.S. pasta business to New World Pasta, for $450 million in cash. The transaction resulted in an after-tax gain of about $1.17 a share in the 1999 first quarter. HSY had marketed its products on a regional basis, under brand names that included San Giorgio, Ronzoni, Skinner, P&R, Light 'n Fluffy, and American Beauty.

HSY has various international arrangements, the investment in which changes from time to time, but which in the aggregate are not material to the company.

In August 2003, directors increased the dividend 21%, marking the 29th consecutive annual increase.

In December 2000, the company purchased the intense and breath freshener mints and gum businesses of Nabisco, for $135 million. The acquired brands included Breath Savers mints, and Ice Breakers, Carefree, Stickfree, Bubble Yum and Fruit Stripe gums. The businesses had 1999 sales of about $270 million.

Company Financials Fiscal Year ending December 31

Per Share Data ($)

(Year Ended December 31)	2003	2002	2001	2000	1999	1998	1997	1996	1995	1994
Tangible Bk. Val.	3.29	3.55	2.65	2.57	2.34	1.79	1.06	1.95	2.12	2.85
Cash Flow	2.44	2.17	1.44	1.84	2.21	1.71	1.62	1.32	1.26	0.90
Earnings	1.76	1.46	0.75	1.21	1.63	1.17	1.11	0.89	0.85	0.53
S&P Core Earnings	1.73	1.36	0.94	NA	NA	NA	NA	NA	NA	NA
Dividends	0.72	0.63	0.58	0.54	0.50	0.46	0.42	0.38	0.34	0.31
Payout Ratio	41%	43%	78%	45%	31%	39%	38%	43%	40%	59%
Prices - High	39.32	39.74	35.07	33.21	32.43	38.18	31.93	25.87	16.96	13.37
- Low	30.34	28.22	27.56	18.87	22.87	29.84	21.06	15.96	12.00	10.28
P/E Ratio - High	22	27	47	27	20	33	29	29	20	25
- Low	17	19	37	16	14	26	19	18	14	19

Income Statement Analysis (Million $)

	2003	2002	2001	2000	1999	1998	1997	1996	1995	1994
Revs.	4,173	4,120	4,557	4,221	3,971	4,436	4,302	3,989	3,691	3,606
Oper. Inc.	992	904	812	799	722	801	783	697	645	604
Depr.	181	178	190	176	163	158	153	133	134	129
Int. Exp.	63.5	60.7	71.5	81.0	77.3	88.6	79.1	53.6	50.0	40.3
Pretax Inc.	733	638	344	547	728	557	554	480	466	333
Eff. Tax Rate	36.6%	36.7%	39.7%	38.8%	36.8%	38.8%	39.3%	43.1%	39.5%	44.7%
Net Inc.	465	404	207	335	460	341	336	273	282	184
S&P Core Earnings	455	377	258	NA	NA	NA	NA	NA	NA	NA

Balance Sheet & Other Fin. Data (Million $)

	2003	2002	2001	2000	1999	1998	1997	1996	1995	1994
Cash	115	298	134	32.0	118	39.0	54.2	61.4	32.0	27.0
Curr. Assets	1,132	1,264	1,168	1,295	1,280	1,134	1,035	986	922	949
Total Assets	3,583	3,481	3,247	3,448	3,347	3,404	3,291	3,185	2,831	2,891
Curr. Liab.	586	547	606	767	713	815	796	817	864	796
LT Debt	968	852	877	878	878	879	1,029	655	357	157
Common Equity	1,280	1,372	1,147	1,175	1,099	1,042	853	1,161	1,083	1,441
Total Cap.	2,626	2,572	2,280	2,353	2,303	2,243	2,149	2,040	1,632	1,792
Cap. Exp.	219	133	160	138	115	161	173	159	141	139
Cash Flow	646	581	398	511	624	499	489	407	416	313
Curr. Ratio	1.9	2.3	1.9	1.7	1.8	1.4	1.3	1.2	1.1	1.2
% LT Debt of Cap.	36.9	33.1	38.5	37.3	38.1	39.2	47.9	32.1	21.9	8.8
% Net Inc.of Revs.	11.1	9.8	4.5	7.9	11.6	7.7	7.8	6.9	7.6	5.1
% Ret. on Assets	13.2	12.0	6.2	9.8	13.6	10.2	10.4	9.1	9.9	6.4
% Ret. on Equity	35.1	32.0	17.8	29.4	43.0	36.0	33.4	24.4	22.3	13.0

Data as orig reptd.; bef. results of disc opers/spec. items. Per share data adj. for stk. divs.; EPS diluted. E-Estimated. NA-Not Available. NM-Not Meaningful. NR-Not Ranked. UR-Under Review.

Office: 100 Crystal A Drive, Hershey, PA 17033-0810.
Telephone: 717-534-4000.
Website: http://www.hersheys.com
Chrmn, Pres & CEO: R.H. Lenny.
SVP & CFO: F. Cerminara.

SVP, Secy & General Counsel: B.H. Snyder.
VP & Chief Acctg Officer: D.W. Tacka.
Dirs: J. A. Boscia, R. H. Campbell, R. F. Cavanaugh, G. P. Coughlan, H. Edelman, B. G. Hill, R. H. Lenny, M. J. McDonald, M. J. Toulantis.

Founded: in 1893.
Domicile: Delaware.
Employees: 14,800.
S&P Analyst: Richard Joy/CB/BK

Hewlett-Packard

Recommendation: **HOLD** ★ ★ ★ ★ ★
SELL SELL HOLD BUY BUY

12-Month Target Price: **$19.00**
(as of August 13, 2004)

HPQ has an approximate 0.53% weighting in the **S&P 500**

Sector: Information Technology
Sub-Industry: Computer Hardware
Peer Group: Computer Hardware - Large System Vendors

Summary: This leading maker of computer products, including printers, servers, workstations and PCs, has a large service and support network. It acquired Compaq Computer in May 2002.

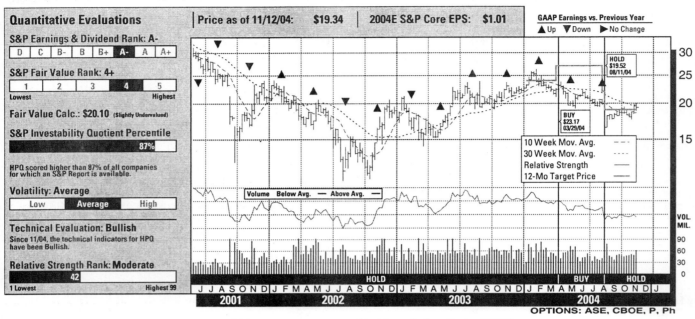

Quantitative Evaluations	Price as of 11/12/04: **$19.34**	2004E S&P Core EPS: **$1.01**

S&P Earnings & Dividend Rank: A-

| D | C | B- | B | B+ | **A-** | A | A+ |

S&P Fair Value Rank: 4+

| 1 | 2 | 3 | **4** | 5 |
| Lowest | | | | Highest |

Fair Value Calc.: $20.10 (Slightly Undervalued)

S&P Investability Quotient Percentile

| | **87%** |

HPQ scored higher than 87% of all companies for which an S&P Report is available.

Volatility: Average

| Low | **Average** | High |

Technical Evaluation: Bullish
Since 11/04, the technical indicators for HPQ have been Bullish.

Relative Strength Rank: Moderate

| | 42 | |
| 1 Lowest | | Highest 99 |

GAAP Earnings vs. Previous Year
▲ Up ▼ Down ▶ No Change

10 Week Mov. Avg. ----
30 Week Mov. Avg. ·····
Relative Strength ——
12-Mo Target Price ——

Volume ▬ Below Avg. — Above Avg. ▬

OPTIONS: ASE, CBOE, P, Ph

Analyst commentary prepared by Megan Graham-Hackett/MF/GG

Highlights August 18, 2004

- We project 8% revenue growth for FY 04 (Oct.), following a rise of 1% in FY 03. Weak technology spending dampened results in servers and PCs in FY 03, while the printing and imaging business held up well. We believe a slightly improved economic backdrop bolstered FY 04's first half results; however execution issues and an uneven economic growth currently have depressed revenues in the third quarter and could impact the fourth quarter. For FY 05, we expect revenues to be up 8%.

- We expect gross margins to narrow to 25.1% in FY 04, from 26.3% in FY 03, as efforts to control costs (including in the areas of supply chain management and procurement) are likely outweighed by continued pricing pressures and adverse business mix. For FY 05, we expect gross margins to widen to over 26%, on further cost efficiencies.

- Based on these assumptions, our FY 04 EPS operating estimate is $1.28. Our FY 04 Standard & Poor's Core Earnings projection is $1.01 a share, reflecting our estimate of stock option and pension expenses. Our operating EPS estimate for FY 05 is $1.57. We continue to monitor the company's exposure to stock option and pension expenses as they relate to quality of earnings.

Investment Rationale/Risk August 18, 2004

- We recently downgraded the shares to hold, from accumulate. We had believed that IT (information technology) spending would gain momentum in the second half of calendar 2004, and that HPQ, with its broad product and customer base, would benefit from this trend. However, recent signals that economic growth could be slowing have caused us to become more cautious, and we view a more prudent stance as warranted, given the level of uncertainty. Nevertheless, we consider the stock to be fairly valued. The shares trade at less than 1X sales, below the level of peers.

- Risks to our opinion and target price include what we view as HPQ's need to augment its capabilities in software and services to offer a more compelling long-term competitive position; potential market share losses if the company is unable to differentiate its products; and a slowdown in technology spending.

- Our 12-month target price of $19 is based on our price to sales analysis and our DCF model, which assumes a weighted average cost of capital 11.2% and 15-year free cash flow growth of 5%.

Key Stock Statistics

S&P Oper. EPS 2004E	1.28	52-week Range	$26.28-16.08
P/E on S&P Oper. EPS 2004E	15.1	12 Month P/E	18.3
S&P Oper. EPS 2005E	1.57	Beta	1.71
Yield (%)	1.7%	Shareholders	162,900
Dividend Rate/Share	0.32	Market Cap (B)	$ 58.4
Shares Outstanding (M)	3019.9		

Value of $10,000 invested five years ago: **NA**

Dividend Data Dividends have been paid since 1965

Amount ($)	Date Decl.	Ex-Div. Date	Stock of Record	Payment Date
0.080	Nov. 21	Dec. 15	Dec. 17	Jan. 07 '04
0.080	Jan. 20	Mar. 15	Mar. 17	Apr. 07 '04
0.080	May. 28	Jun. 14	Jun. 16	Jul. 07 '04
0.080	Jul. 16	Sep. 13	Sep. 15	Oct. 06 '04

Revenues/Earnings Data Fiscal year ending October 31

Revenues (Million $)

	2004	2003	2002	2001	2000	1999
1Q	19,514	17,877	11,383	12,398	11,673	11,937
2Q	20,113	17,983	10,621	11,668	12,028	12,419
3Q	18,889	17,348	16,536	10,284	11,818	10,318
4Q	—	19,853	18,048	10,876	13,263	11,362
Yr.	—	73,061	56,588	45,226	48,782	42,370

Earnings Per Share ($)

	2004	2003	2002	2001	2000	1999
1Q	0.30	0.24	0.25	0.20	0.39	0.46
2Q	0.29	0.22	0.12	0.02	0.40	0.44
3Q	0.19	0.10	-0.67	0.06	0.51	0.33
4Q	E0.35	0.28	0.13	0.04	0.45	0.36
Yr.	E1.28	0.83	-0.37	0.32	1.73	1.49

Next earnings report expected: NA Source: S&P, Company Reports
EPS Estimates based on S&P Operating Earnings; historical GAAP earnings are as reported.

Hewlett-Packard Company

Recommendation: **HOLD** ★ ★ ★ ☆ ☆   12-Month Target Price: **$19.00** (as of August 13, 2004)

Business Summary August 18, 2004

In May 2002, Hewlett-Packard purchased Compaq Computer Corp. (CPQ) in the largest acquisition in computer industry history, exchanging 0.6325 of a Hewlett-Packard share for each CPQ share; the deal was valued at $25 billion when announced in September 2001, but at $19 billion upon completion. Battling several years of disappointing results, the companies sought to reduce capacity in the computer industry, as the outlook for computer sales came under pressure due to a weak global economy. The new HPQ is second to IBM in the computer industry.

Imaging and printing systems contributed 31% of total revenues in FY 03 (Oct.), and continued to account for the bulk of operating profits (74% of total operating profits in FY 03). The segment contributed 22% of the combined companies' revenues, on a pro forma basis, in FY 02. In FY 01, these revenues were over 40% of HPQ's total, and represented over 100% of operating earnings (due to losses recorded by other segments). Segment products include the well known HP LaserJet and DeskJet printer families, scanners, copiers, fax machines, and supplies.

Enterprise Systems sales (servers, storage, etc.) accounted for 20% of total revenues for the company before the merger, and for 18% in FY 02. In FY 03, these sales increased to pre-merger levels, at 21%. HPQ's computers have included the HP9000 family of workstations and multi-user systems for both technical and commercial users, based on HP-UX and the Precision Architecture reduced

instruction set computing (PA-RISC) chip; and HP Netserver PC servers. In January 2001, the company began volume shipments of its high-end Superdome server. In 1999, it ended a reselling agreement for high-end storage with EMC; it now purchases Hitachi's high-end 256 storage equipment. The acquisition of CPQ added that company's leading share position in PC servers, AlphaServer product line and assets in storage. The division was unprofitable in FY 03, but achieved a profit in the fourth quarter.

In PCs, the company commands a 17% share of the worldwide market. HPQ had been more profitable in its consumer line of PCs than CPQ, but CPQ had been more profitable in its commercial line, due to successful leveraging of its direct sales capabilities. In total, Personal Systems (PCs and handheld devices) accounted for 24% of sales for the combined company in FY 02, up from a 20% contribution for the area (known as embedded and personal systems) for Hewlett-Packard alone in FY 01. In FY 03, the division's contribution increased to nearly 29% of total revenues, and the division posted a small profit.

IT services (including maintenance and support services) contributed 13% of Hewlett-Packard's sales in FY 01. Including financing, these services contributed nearly 17% of sales, and for the new company 13%. HPQ has recently focused on the area of consulting, and has aggressively added to its staff. In FY 03, HP services contributed 17% of total sales.

Company Financials Fiscal Year ending October 31

Per Share Data ($)

(Year Ended October 31)	2003	2002	2001	2000	1999	1998	1997	1996	1995	1994
Tangible Bk. Val.	6.08	5.35	7.20	7.30	9.10	8.33	7.76	6.63	5.81	4.61
Cash Flow	1.65	0.48	1.01	2.37	2.10	2.25	2.21	1.85	1.70	1.25
Earnings	0.83	-0.37	0.32	1.73	1.49	1.39	1.48	1.23	1.16	0.77
S&P Core Earnings	0.64	-0.65	0.16	NA	NA	NA	NA	NA	NA	NA
Dividends	0.32	0.32	0.32	0.32	0.32	0.30	0.26	0.23	0.19	0.14
Payout Ratio	39%	NM	100%	18%	22%	22%	18%	19%	16%	18%
Prices - High	23.90	24.12	37.95	77.75	59.21	41.18	36.46	28.84	24.15	12.81
- Low	14.18	10.75	12.50	29.12	31.68	23.53	24.06	18.40	12.25	8.98
P/E Ratio - High	29	NM	NM	45	40	30	25	23	21	17
- Low	17	NM	NM	17	21	17	16	15	11	12

Income Statement Analysis (Million $)

	2003	2002	2001	2000	1999	1998	1997	1996	1995	1994
Revs.	73,061	56,588	45,226	48,782	42,370	47,061	42,895	38,420	31,519	24,991
Oper. Inc.	6,713	4,570	3,192	5,257	5,004	5,730	5,895	5,023	4,707	3,555
Depr.	2,527	2,119	1,369	1,368	1,316	1,869	1,556	1,297	1,139	1,006
Int. Exp.	418	189	285	257	202	235	215	327	206	155
Pretax Inc.	2,888	-1,052	702	4,625	4,194	4,091	4,445	3,694	3,632	2,423
Eff. Tax Rate	12.1%	NM	11.1%	23.0%	26.0%	28.0%	30.0%	30.0%	33.0%	34.0%
Net Inc.	2,539	-923	624	3,561	3,104	2,945	3,119	2,586	2,433	1,599
S&P Core Earnings	1,958	-1,635	285	NA	NA	NA	NA	NA	NA	NA

Balance Sheet & Other Fin. Data (Million $)

	2003	2002	2001	2000	1999	1998	1997	1996	1995	1994
Cash	14,188	11,192	4,197	3,415	5,411	4,046	4,569	3,327	2,616	2,478
Curr. Assets	40,996	36,075	21,305	23,244	21,642	21,584	20,947	17,991	16,239	12,509
Total Assets	74,708	70,710	32,584	34,009	35,297	33,673	31,749	27,699	24,427	19,567
Curr. Liab.	26,630	24,310	13,964	15,197	14,321	13,473	11,219	10,623	10,944	8,230
LT Debt	6,494	6,035	3,729	3,402	1,764	2,063	3,158	2,579	663	547
Common Equity	37,746	36,262	13,953	14,209	18,295	16,919	16,155	13,438	11,839	9,926
Total Cap.	44,240	42,297	17,682	17,611	20,059	18,982	19,313	16,017	12,502	10,473
Cap. Exp.	1,995	1,710	1,527	1,737	1,134	1,997	2,338	2,201	1,601	1,257
Cash Flow	5,066	1,196	1,993	4,929	4,420	4,814	4,675	3,883	3,572	2,605
Curr. Ratio	1.5	1.5	1.5	1.5	1.5	1.6	1.9	1.7	1.5	1.5
% LT Debt of Cap.	14.7	14.3	21.1	19.3	8.8	10.9	16.4	16.1	5.3	5.2
% Net Inc.of Revs.	3.5	NM	1.4	7.3	7.3	6.3	7.3	6.7	7.7	6.4
% Ret. on Assets	3.5	NM	1.9	10.3	9.3	9.0	10.5	9.9	11.1	8.8
% Ret. on Equity	6.9	NM	4.4	21.9	17.6	17.8	14.5	20.5	22.4	17.3

Data as orig reptd.; bef. results of disc opers/spec. items. Per share data adj. for stk. divs.; EPS diluted. E-Estimated. NA-Not Available. NM-Not Meaningful. NR-Not Ranked. UR-Under Review.

Office: 3000 Hanover Street, Palo Alto, CA 94304-1112.
Telephone: 650-857-1501.
Website: http://www.hp.com
Chrmn & CEO: C.S. Fiorina.
EVP & CFO: R.P. Wayman.
SVP & Treas: C.A. Lesjak.

SVP, Secy & General Counsel: A.O. Baskins.
VP & Investor Contact: S. Pavlovich .
Dirs: L. T. Babbio, Jr., P. M. Condit, P. C. Dunn, C. S. Fiorina, S. Ginn, R. A. Hackborn, G. A. Keyworth II, R. E. Knowling, Jr., S. M. Litvack, T. J. Perkins, L. S. Salhany, R. P. Wayman.

Founded: in 1939.
Domicile: Delaware.
Employees: 142,000.
S&P Analyst: Megan Graham-Hackett/MF/GG

Hilton Hotels

Recommendation: HOLD ★ ★ ★ ★ ★
SELL SELL HOLD BUY BUY

12-Month Target Price: $20.00
(as of October 25, 2004)

HLT has an approximate 0.07% weighting in the **S&P 500**

Sector: Consumer Discretionary
Sub-Industry: Hotels, Resorts & Cruise Lines
Peer Group: Hotel Companies - Larger

Summary: This leading hospitality company owns, manages or franchises more than 2,000 hotels, resorts and vacation ownership properties.

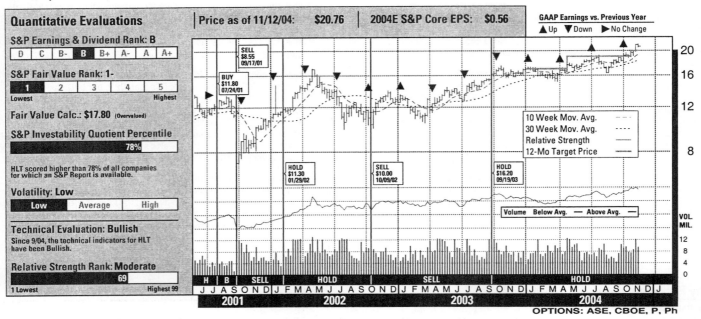

Quantitative Evaluations

S&P Earnings & Dividend Rank: B

| D | C | B- | B | B+ | A- | A | A+ |

S&P Fair Value Rank: 1-

| 1 | 2 | 3 | 4 | 5 |
| Lowest | | | | Highest |

Fair Value Calc.: $17.80 (Overvalued)

S&P Investability Quotient Percentile
78%

HLT scored higher than 78% of all companies for which an S&P Report is available.

Volatility: Low

| Low | Average | High |

Technical Evaluation: Bullish
Since 9/04, the technical indicators for HLT have been Bullish.

Relative Strength Rank: Moderate
69
1 Lowest   Highest 99

Price as of 11/12/04: $20.76 | **2004E S&P Core EPS:** $0.56

Analyst commentary prepared by Tom Graves, CFA /CB/BK

Highlights September 13, 2004

- We look for the company's revenue to increase about 8% in 2005, to $4.5 billion, from the $4.2 billion estimated for 2004. In both years, we expect that owned hotels will account for about half of total revenue.

- In 2005, we estimate that HLT's overall operating profit before special items will be up 14%, to $744 million, from the $654 million projected for 2004. In both years, this is after about $330 million of non-cash depreciation and amortization charges. We estimate net income of $271 million ($0.71 a share) for 2005, up from the $225 million ($0.59) projected for 2004.

- In 2005, we estimate that the company's RevPAR growth will increasingly come from higher average room rates, which we expect will help profit margins improve. We look for HLT's capital spending in 2005 to increase at least moderately from the $275 million projected for 2004, which includes about $155 million for what the company considers to be routine improvements and technology, $60 million for timeshare projects, and $60 million for hotel special projects.

Investment Rationale/Risk September 13, 2004

- Our hold opinion on the stock reflects our view that the shares will be bolstered by prospects of increasing business travel in the latter part of 2004 and in 2005, and by expectations of improving EPS and cash flow for the company. Near term, we expect more debt reduction to be a top priority use for HLT's free cash flow (FCF). In 2005, we expect hotel or timeshare investments to be a preferred use of FCF, but see a dividend boost and/or share repurchases as possibilities.

- Risks to our recommendation and target price include the possibility of heightened terrorism fears, which could cause leisure travelers and businesses to defer or cancel trips.

- We have a 12-month target price for the stock of $19, which reflects our expectation that it will keep much of its P/E premium (based on 2005 EPS estimates) to the S&P 500. Currently at about 25X our 2005 EPS estimate, the shares are at a 64% P/E premium to the S&P 500.

Key Stock Statistics

S&P Core EPS 2005E	0.68	52-week Range	$21.25-15.10
S&P Oper. EPS 2004E	0.60	12 Month P/E	33.5
P/E on S&P Oper. EPS 2004E	34.6	Beta	0.84
S&P Oper. EPS 2005E	0.73	Shareholders	14,000
Yield (%)	0.4%	Market Cap (B)	$ 8.0
Dividend Rate/Share	0.08	Shares Outstanding (M)	386.0

Value of $10,000 invested five years ago: $ 23,434

Dividend Data Dividends have been paid since 1946

Amount ($)	Date Decl.	Ex-Div. Date	Stock of Record	Payment Date
0.020	Jan. 29	Mar. 03	Mar. 05	Mar. 19 '04
0.020	May. 27	Jun. 09	Jun. 11	Jun. 25 '04
0.020	Jul. 22	Sep. 01	Sep. 03	Sep. 10 '04
0.020	Nov. 12	Dec. 01	Dec. 03	Dec. 17 '04

Revenues/Earnings Data Fiscal year ending December 31

Revenues (Million $)

	2004	2003	2002	2001	2000	1999
1Q	994.0	909.0	921.0	833.0	793.0	494.0
2Q	1,065	976.0	782.0	844.0	916.0	539.0
3Q	1,033	952.0	942.0	711.0	867.0	498.0
4Q	—	982.0	957.0	662.0	875.0	816.0
Yr.	—	3,819	3,847	3,050	3,451	3,161

Earnings Per Share ($)

	2004	2003	2002	2001	2000	1999
1Q	0.10	0.02	0.09	0.15	0.16	0.16
2Q	0.19	0.14	0.20	0.23	0.23	0.25
3Q	0.16	0.09	0.13	0.06	0.17	0.16
4Q	E0.16	0.17	0.11	0.01	0.17	0.07
Yr.	E0.60	0.43	0.53	0.45	0.73	0.58

Next earnings report expected: late-January Source: S&P, Company Reports
EPS Estimates based on S&P Operating Earnings; historical GAAP earnings are as reported.

Hilton Hotels Corporation

Stock Report
November 13, 2004
NYSE Symbol: HLT

Recommendation: **HOLD** ★ ★ ★ ☆ ☆   12-Month Target Price: **$20.00** (as of October 25, 2004)

Business Summary September 13, 2004

This hotel company includes about 2,200 properties, operating under various brands. Most of the hotels are franchises operated by others, but Hilton Hotels Corp. owns or manages certain lodging properties. Owned hotels include the Waldorf-Astoria in New York City and the Palmer House Hilton in Chicago. HLT expanded significantly through the 1999 acquisition of Promus Hotel Corp., with brands that included Hampton Inn, Embassy Suites and Doubletree.

In 2003, HLT's revenue from owned hotels totaled $2.03 billion, down from $2.10 billion in 2002. Revenue per available room from comparable owned hotels declined 2.9%, with most of the drop due to a 2.1% decline in the average room rate.

As of December 31, 2003, the company owned, leased, managed or franchised 2,173 hotels or timeshare properties with 348,483 rooms or units, most of which were in the U.S. This included 55 hotels (32,526 rooms) in which HLT had a majority or controlling financial interest, including some of its largest and most profitable hotels; seven leased and managed properties (2,643); 67 hotels (20,556) in which HLT had a minority or non-controlling ownership interest and managed; 206 hotels (52,088) that the company managed but that were wholly owned by others; and 1,808 franchised properties (237,026) owned and operated by third parties. Also, at year-end 2003, the company managed or franchised 30 timeshare properties. Overall in 2003, HLT had a net increase of 89 hotel or timeshare properties (11,367 rooms or units), primarily from an increase in the number of hotel franchise properties.

Based on the number of properties (1,255) and rooms (127,543), HLT's largest brand at the end of 2003 was the Hampton business; however, the vast majority of these hotels were franchises. Another 230 hotels (89,012 rooms) were Hilton Hotels, and 183 hotels (25,010) were Hilton Garden Inn properties. HLT's Doubletree brand included 155 hotels (40,614 rooms), the Embassy Suites chain had 174 properties (42,553), and the Homewood Suites by Hilton business included 130 properties (14,760). Other hotels included 16 hotels with 5,347 rooms. In December 2001, HLT sold its Red Lion Hotels business, which included a portfolio of 43 hotels (nine owned, 12 leased, 22 franchised).

The company has entered into agreements with British company Hilton Group Plc (formerly known as Ladbroke Group PLC), which owns rights to the Hilton name outside of the U.S. The agreements provided for a reunification of the Hilton brand worldwide through a strategic alliance between the two companies, including cooperation on sales and marketing, loyalty programs, and other operational matters.

In November 1999, HLT acquired Promus Hotel Corp. (PRH) for cash and stock valued at about $2.9 billion (excluding assumption of debt). In December 1998, the company spun off to shareholders ownership of most of its gaming assets through a tax-free distribution of equity in Park Place Entertainment (PPE), subsequently renamed Caesars Entertainment (CZR).

Company Financials Fiscal Year ending December 31

Per Share Data ($)

(Year Ended December 31)	2003	2002	2001	2000	1999	1998	1997	1996	1995	1994
Tangible Bk. Val.	0.08	NM	NM	NM	NM	0.72	8.25	7.63	6.49	5.86
Cash Flow	1.30	1.39	1.41	1.67	1.25	1.09	2.21	1.34	1.62	1.29
Earnings	0.43	0.53	0.45	0.73	0.58	0.71	0.94	0.79	0.89	0.63
S&P Core Earnings	0.44	0.50	0.48	NA	NA	NA	NA	NA	NA	NA
Dividends	0.08	0.08	0.08	0.08	0.08	0.32	0.32	0.30	0.30	0.30
Payout Ratio	19%	15%	18%	11%	14%	45%	34%	39%	34%	48%
Prices - High	17.50	17.09	13.57	12.12	17.12	35.50	35.81	31.75	19.93	18.50
- Low	10.38	9.56	6.15	6.37	8.37	12.00	24.00	15.28	15.09	12.43
P/E Ratio - High	41	32	30	17	30	50	38	40	22	29
- Low	24	18	14	9	14	17	26	19	17	20

Income Statement Analysis (Million $)

	2003	2002	2001	2000	1999	1998	1997	1996	1995	1994
Revs.	3,819	3,847	3,050	3,451	2,150	1,769	5,316	3,940	1,649	1,456
Oper. Inc.	850	972	1,023	1,212	682	589	896	507	496	354
Depr.	347	348	391	382	187	125	300	178	142	127
Int. Exp.	315	347	402	462	239	141	190	106	113	92.7
Pretax Inc.	223	285	250	479	313	336	448	267	280	201
Eff. Tax Rate	23.8%	28.4%	30.8%	41.7%	41.5%	40.5%	41.7%	39.7%	36.6%	38.6%
Net Inc.	164	198	166	272	176	188	250	156	173	122
S&P Core Earnings	165	187	179	NA	NA	NA	NA	NA	NA	NA

Balance Sheet & Other Fin. Data (Million $)

	2003	2002	2001	2000	1999	1998	1997	1996	1995	1994
Cash	82.0	54.0	35.0	47.0	104	47.0	330	438	409	393
Curr. Assets	1,020	630	996	840	763	469	1,011	1,151	717	674
Total Assets	8,178	8,348	8,785	9,140	9,253	3,944	7,826	7,577	3,060	2,926
Curr. Liab.	895	575	902	646	629	506	941	998	535	328
LT Debt	3,801	4,554	4,950	5,693	6,085	3,037	2,709	2,606	1,070	1,252
Common Equity	2,239	2,053	1,783	3,284	3,252	187	3,368	3,196	1,254	1,128
Total Cap.	6,815	7,432	7,604	9,879	10,216	3,289	6,695	6,415	2,447	2,504
Cap. Exp.	202	245	370	458	254	171	531	242	187	254
Cash Flow	511	546	557	654	363	303	550	334	315	249
Curr. Ratio	1.1	1.1	1.1	1.3	1.2	0.9	1.1	1.2	1.3	2.1
% LT Debt of Cap.	55.8	61.3	65.1	57.6	59.6	92.3	40.5	40.6	43.8	50.0
% Net Inc.of Revs.	4.3	5.1	5.4	7.8	8.2	10.6	4.7	3.9	10.5	8.4
% Ret. on Assets	2.0	2.3	1.9	2.9	2.7	3.2	3.2	2.8	5.8	4.3
% Ret. on Equity	7.6	10.3	9.7	17.8	9.1	10.0	7.6	7.0	14.6	11.1

Data as orig reptd.; bef. results of disc opers/spec. items. Per share data adj. for stk. divs.; EPS diluted. E-Estimated. NA-Not Available. NM-Not Meaningful. NR-Not Ranked. UR-Under Review.

Office: 9336 Civic Center Drive, Beverly Hills, CA 90210.
Telephone: 310-278-4321.
Website: http://www.hilton.com
Chrmn: B. Hilton.
Chrmn & CEO: S.F. Bollenbach.
Pres & COO: M.J. Hart.

EVP, Secy & General Counsel: M. Kleiner.
SVP & CFO: R.M. La Forgia.
SVP & Investor Contact: M.A. Grossman 310-205-4030.
Dirs: S. F. Bollenbach, A. S. Crown, P. M. George, B. Hilton, D. H. Huckestein, R. L. Johnson, B. V. Lambert, D. Michels, J. H. Myers, J. L. Notter, D. F. Tuttle, P. V. Ueberroth, S. D. Young.

Founded: in 1946.
Domicile: Delaware.
Employees: 70,000.
S&P Analyst: Tom Graves, CFA /CB/BK

Home Depot

Recommendation: BUY ★★★★☆
SELL · SELL · HOLD · BUY · BUY

12-Month Target Price: $48.00
(as of November 16, 2004)

HD has an approximate 0.86% weighting in the **S&P 500**

Sector: Consumer Discretionary
Sub-Industry: Home Improvement Retail
Peer Group: Retail (Building Supplies)

Summary: HD operates a chain of more than 1,700 retail warehouse-type stores, selling a wide variety of home improvement products for the do-it-yourself and home remodeling markets.

Quantitative Evaluations

S&P Earnings & Dividend Rank: A+

D	C	B-	B	B+	A-	A	A+

S&P Fair Value Rank: 5+

1	2	3	4	5
Lowest				Highest

Fair Value Calc.: $50.20 (Slightly Undervalued)

S&P Investability Quotient Percentile
100%

HD scored higher than 100% of all companies for which an S&P Report is available.

Volatility: Low

Low	Average	High

Technical Evaluation: Bullish
Since 10/04, the technical indicators for HD have been Bullish.

Relative Strength Rank: Strong
75

1 Lowest	Highest 99

Price as of 11/16/04: $43 | **2005E S&P Core EPS:** $2.19

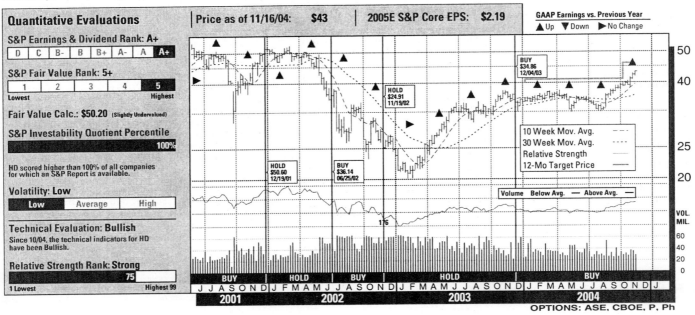

GAAP Earnings vs. Previous Year
▲ Up   ▼ Down   ► No Change

BUY $34.86 12/04/03
HOLD $24.91 11/19/02
HOLD $50.60 12/19/01
BUY $36.14 06/25/02

10 Week Mov. Avg.
30 Week Mov. Avg.
Relative Strength
12-Mo Target Price

Volume   Below Avg. — Above Avg. —

BUY   HOLD   BUY   HOLD   BUY
J J A S O N D | J F M A M J J A S O N D | J F M A M J J A S O N D | J F M A M J J A S O N D | J F M A M J J A S O N D | J
2001   2002   2003   2004

OPTIONS: ASE, CBOE, P, Ph

Analyst commentary prepared by Yogeesh Wagle/PMW/BK

Highlights October 13, 2004

- We expect 10% to 11% sales growth in FY 06 (Jan.), driven by about 170 to 190 new store additions, including international store openings, selected acquisitions, and same-store sales gains in the low single digits. We see same-store sales growth likely to be aided by continued penetration of appliance programs, new product launches in the fast growing lawn and garden category, an expanding installation business, improvements in the merchandise mix and customer service, and higher marketing spending.

- We see FY 06 margins widening slightly, benefiting from a greater proportion of sales mix of higher margin private label brands and more upscale merchandise, and from firmer pricing, partly offset by higher marketing, healthcare and insurance costs. We expect slightly lower interest expense, and a level effective tax rate.

- We project FY 06 EPS of $2.55, up 13% from our $2.25 FY 05 estimate. Our FY 05 EPS outlook excludes an expected one-time, non-cash charge of about $0.05 a share related to an accounting change. Our FY 05 S&P Core EPS estimate of $2.19 reflects projected stock option expense.

Investment Rationale/Risk October 13, 2004

- We recommend accumulating the shares. We think that recent and likely additional acquisitions in the fast growing do-it-for-me segment should help maintain positive earnings momentum. We also see high consumer interest in home makeovers, healthy economic trends, and improved merchandise and customer service as positive for the stock.

- Risks to our recommendation and target price include a potential slowdown in the economy; a faster than expected rise in interest rates, restricting home improvement related spending; and increasing competition from Lowe's (LOW: accumulate, $55).

- Our DCF analysis yields intrinsic value of $44 to $46. The shares are trading at 16X our FY 06 EPS estimate, on a par with the level of the S&P 500, but below those of key peer LOW. Based on our three-year annual EPS growth projection of 15%, the shares trade at a P/E to growth multiple of 1.15X, above that of LOW, but below the S&P 500. Our 12-month target price of $46 is based on a blend of intrinsic and relative valuation.

Key Stock Statistics

S&P Core EPS 2006E	2.51	52-week Range	$43.25-32.34
S&P Oper. EPS 2005E	2.26	12 Month P/E	19.6
P/E on S&P Oper. EPS 2005E	19.1	Beta	1.44
S&P Oper. EPS 2006E	2.58	Shareholders	204,032
Yield (%)	0.8%	Market Cap (B)	$ 94.4
Dividend Rate/Share	0.34	Shares Outstanding (M)	2195.4

Value of $10,000 invested five years ago: **$ 8,300**

Dividend Data Dividends have been paid since 1987

Amount ($)	Date Decl.	Ex-Div. Date	Stock of Record	Payment Date
0.070	Nov. 20	Dec. 02	Dec. 04	Dec. 18 '03
0.070	Feb. 27	Mar. 09	Mar. 11	Mar. 22 '04
0.085	May. 26	Jun. 08	Jun. 10	Jun. 24 '04
0.085	Aug. 06	Aug. 31	Sep. 02	Sep. 16 '04

Revenues/Earnings Data Fiscal year ending January 31

Revenues (Million $)

	2005	2004	2003	2002	2001	2000
1Q	17,550	15,104	14,282	12,200	11,112	8,952
2Q	19,960	17,989	16,277	14,576	12,618	10,431
3Q	18,772	16,598	14,475	13,289	11,545	9,877
4Q	—	15,125	13,213	13,488	10,463	9,174
Yr.	—	64,816	58,247	53,553	45,738	38,434

Earnings Per Share ($)

	2005	2004	2003	2002	2001	2000
1Q	0.49	0.39	0.36	0.27	0.27	0.21
2Q	0.70	0.56	0.50	0.39	0.36	0.29
3Q	0.60	0.50	0.40	0.33	0.28	0.25
4Q	E0.49	0.42	0.30	0.30	0.20	0.25
Yr.	E2.26	1.88	1.56	1.25	1.10	1.00

Next earnings report expected: late-February Source: S&P, Company Reports
EPS Estimates based on S&P Operating Earnings; historical GAAP earnings are as reported.

STANDARD &POOR'S

The Home Depot, Inc.

Stock Report
November 16, 2004
NYSE Symbol: **HD**

Recommendation: **BUY** ★★★★☆   12-Month Target Price: **$48.00** (as of November 16, 2004)

Business Summary October 13, 2004

With revenues exceeding $72 billion, Home Depot, founded in 1978, is the world's largest home improvement retailer, and the second largest U.S. retailer. The company mainly operates retail warehouse-type stores that sell a wide assortment of building materials and home improvement and lawn and garden products, primarily to the do-it-yourself and home remodeling markets. At July 31, 2004, HD operated 1,788 stores, including 1,716 Home Depot stores (105 in Canada and 42 in Mexico), 54 EXPO Design Centers, five Home Depot Supply stores, 11 Home Depot Landscape Supply stores, and two Home Depot Floor stores.

Home Depot stores average 107,000 sq. ft., plus 22,000 sq. ft. of garden center and storage space. They stock 40,000 to 50,000 items, including brand name and proprietary items. HD aims to provide a broad range of merchandise, consisting of many different kinds of building and home improvement materials, at competitive prices. The company trains employees to be knowledgeable about the products in the stores; employees may also have trade skills or direct experience in using the products. HD also offers installation services for do-it-for-me customers, typically homeowners who purchase materials themselves and hire third parties to complete the project and/or installation. In FY 04, the company acquired Installed Products U.S.A., a roofing and fencing installed services business; and RMA Home Services, a replacement windows and siding installed services business.

Home Depot Landscape Supply stores are designed to extend the reach of Home Depot's garden departments, by focusing on professional landscapers and avid do-it-yourself garden enthusiasts.

EXPO Design Centers, which average about 100,000 sq. ft., sell more upscale products and services primarily for home decorating and remodeling projects. Unlike Home Depot stores, they do not sell building materials and lumber.

In late FY 04, under The Home Depot Supply brand, the company combined three wholesale businesses: Maintenance Warehouse, a distributor of maintenance, repair and operations supplies to the multi-family housing, hospitality and lodging industries; Apex Supply Company, a distributor of plumbing, HVAC, appliances and other related products primarily to trade and mechanical contractors; and HD Builder Solutions Group, which provides professional homebuilders with flooring, countertops and window treatments. HD's e-commerce site, homedepot.com, sells about 10,000 products over the Internet. In FY 04, the site was enhanced to allow customers to sign up for in-home consultations for HD's installation services.

During FY 05, HD acquired White Cap Construction Supply, Inc., which now operates 74 Pro distribution branches across the U.S. The company also purchased 20 Home Mart stores in Mexico, bringing the total to 42.

Company Financials Fiscal Year ending January 31

Per Share Data ($)

(Year Ended January 31)	2004	2003	2002	2001	2000	1999	1998	1997	1996	1995
Tangible Bk. Val.	9.56	8.39	7.53	6.32	5.22	3.83	3.17	2.71	2.28	1.64
Cash Flow	2.35	1.95	1.62	1.35	1.19	0.86	0.63	0.53	0.42	0.34
Earnings	1.88	1.56	1.25	1.10	1.00	0.71	0.52	0.43	0.34	0.29
S&P Core Earnings	1.78	1.46	1.18	1.01	NA	NA	NA	NA	NA	NA
Dividends	0.26	0.21	0.17	0.16	0.13	0.07	0.06	0.05	0.04	0.03
Payout Ratio	14%	13%	14%	15%	13%	10%	12%	12%	12%	11%

Cal. Yrs.	2003	2002	2001	2000	1999	1998	1997	1996	1995	1994
Prices - High	37.89	52.60	53.73	70.00	69.75	41.33	20.16	13.22	11.11	10.72
- Low	20.10	23.01	30.30	34.68	34.58	18.43	10.61	9.22	8.13	8.11
P/E Ratio - High	20	34	43	64	70	58	39	31	32	48
- Low	11	15	24	32	35	26	21	21	24	36

Income Statement Analysis (Million $)

	2004	2003	2002	2001	2000	1999	1998	1997	1996	1995
Revs.	64,816	58,247	53,553	45,738	38,434	30,219	24,156	19,536	15,470	12,477
Oper. Inc.	7,922	6,733	5,696	4,792	4,258	3,034	2,299	1,766	1,361	1,117
Depr.	1,076	903	764	601	463	373	283	232	181	130
Int. Exp.	62.0	37.0	22.0	21.0	28.0	37.0	42.0	39.0	25.0	53.5
Pretax Inc.	6,843	5,872	4,957	4,217	3,804	2,654	1,914	1,543	1,195	980
Eff. Tax Rate	37.1%	37.6%	38.6%	38.8%	39.0%	39.2%	38.6%	38.7%	38.8%	38.3%
Net Inc.	4,304	3,664	3,044	2,581	2,320	1,614	1,160	938	732	605
S&P Core Earnings	4,067	3,414	2,780	2,364	NA	NA	NA	NA	NA	NA

Balance Sheet & Other Fin. Data (Million $)

	2004	2003	2002	2001	2000	1999	1998	1997	1996	1995
Cash	2,826	2,253	2,546	167	168	62.0	172	558	108	58.0
Curr. Assets	13,328	11,917	10,361	7,777	6,390	4,933	4,460	3,709	2,672	2,133
Total Assets	34,437	30,011	26,394	21,385	17,081	13,465	11,229	9,342	7,354	5,778
Curr. Liab.	9,554	8,035	6,501	4,385	3,656	2,857	2,456	1,842	1,416	1,214
LT Debt	856	1,321	1,250	1,545	750	1,566	1,303	1,247	720	983
Common Equity	22,407	19,802	18,134	15,004	12,341	8,740	7,098	5,955	4,988	3,442
Total Cap.	24,230	21,485	19,573	16,755	13,188	10,400	8,595	7,366	5,822	4,496
Cap. Exp.	3,508	2,749	3,393	3,558	2,581	2,059	1,525	1,194	1,278	1,101
Cash Flow	5,380	4,567	3,808	3,182	2,783	1,987	1,443	1,170	913	734
Curr. Ratio	1.4	1.5	1.6	1.8	1.7	1.7	1.8	2.0	1.9	1.8
% LT Debt of Cap.	3.5	6.1	6.4	9.2	5.7	15.1	15.2	16.9	16.9	21.9
% Net Inc.of Revs.	6.6	6.3	5.7	5.6	6.0	5.3	4.8	4.8	4.7	4.8
% Ret. on Assets	13.4	13.0	12.7	13.4	15.2	13.1	11.3	11.2	11.1	11.5
% Ret. on Equity	20.4	19.3	18.4	18.9	22.0	20.4	17.8	17.1	17.4	19.2

Data as orig reptd.; bef. results of disc opers/spec. items. Per share data adj. for stk. divs. Bold denotes primary EPS - prior periods restated. E-Estimated. NA-Not Available. NM-Not Meaningful. NR-Not Ranked. UR-Under Review.

Office: 2455 Paces Ferry Road, Atlanta, GA 30339-1834.
Telephone: 770-433-8211.
Website: www.homedepot.com
Chrmn, Pres & CEO: R.L. Nardelli.
EVP & CFO: C.B. Tome.

EVP, Secy & General Counsel: F.L. Fernandez.
VP & Investor Contact: D. Dayhoff 770-384-2666.
Dirs: G. D. Brenneman, R. H. Brown, J. L. Clendenin, B. R. Cox, C. X. Gonzalez, M. A. Hart III, B. G. Hill, L. P. Jackson, Jr., L. R. Johnston, K. G. Langone, R. L. Nardelli, R. S. Penske.

Founded: in 1978.
Domicile: Delaware.
Employees: 299,000.
S&P Analyst: Yogeesh Wagle/PMW/BK

Recommendation: **SELL** ★★★★★
SELL SELL HOLD BUY BUY

12-Month Target Price: **$30.00**
(as of January 29, 2004)

HON has an approximate 0.29% weighting in the **S&P 500**

Sector: Industrials
Sub-Industry: Aerospace & Defense
Peer Group: Aerospace/Transportation/Defense

Summary: HON, the world's largest maker of cockpit controls, small jet engines and climate control equipment, also makes industrial materials and consumer automotive products.

Quantitative Evaluations

S&P Earnings & Dividend Rank: B

| D | C | B- | **B** | B+ | A- | A | A+ |

S&P Fair Value Rank: 2

| 1 | **2** | 3 | 4 | 5 |
| Lowest | | | | Highest |

Fair Value Calc.: $31.10 (Overvalued)

S&P Investability Quotient Percentile

93%

HON scored higher than 93% of all companies for which an S&P Report is available.

Volatility: Average

| Low | **Average** | High |

Technical Evaluation: Neutral
Since 11/04, the technical indicators for HON have been Neutral.

Relative Strength Rank: Moderate

47

| 1 Lowest | | Highest 99 |

Price as of 11/12/04: $36.62 | **2004E S&P Core EPS:** $1.20

GAAP Earnings vs. Previous Year
▲ Up ▼ Down ► No Change

10 Week Mov. Avg. – – –
30 Week Mov. Avg. ·········
Relative Strength ———
12-Mo Target Price ———

Volume Below Avg. — Above Avg. —

Analyst commentary prepared by Robert E. Friedman, CPA /MF/BK

OPTIONS: ASE, CBOE, P, Ph

Highlights November 09, 2004

- We expect recovering airline industry fundamentals and a rebounding global economy to drive solid volume sales growth. We see ongoing gluts in worldwide industrial and automaking capacity likely to continue to put pressure on near-term pricing power. Nevertheless, we expect favorable exchange rates, as well as growth in volume sales, to propel a 10% increase in 2005 revenues.

- Although we anticipate EBIT (earnings before interest and taxes) margins to remain in the 11%, range, the 10% revenue advance should drive a 12% increase in projected 2005 EPS, to $1.65. On a Standard & Poor's Core Earnings basis, we believe EPS will rise about 15%, to about $1.40. Regarding the profitability side of the ledger, we are forecasting average ROE of 13% for 2005.

- Looking at HON's long-term financial prospects, we believe rapidly maturing commercial aircraft, construction and automotive markets, as well as increasingly competitive landscapes we see, will limit outsized volume growth and pricing power. Nevertheless, we believe the company will be able to boost sustainable free cash flow at an 8.5% compound annual growth rate (CAGR) and post ROE of 17% over an operating cycle.

Investment Rationale/Risk November 09, 2004

- We continue to recommend avoiding the shares, as the stock is still trading at a premium to our discounted free cash flow-based 12-month target price.

- Risks to our recommendation and target price include potential structural improvement in the company's primary end markets, and possible structural improvement of underlying business economics.

- Our 12-month target price is $30. Our free cash flow model, which values the stock by adding the discounted sum of projected 10-year cash earnings streams growing at our projected CAGR of 8.5%, and matching 3% GDP growth thereafter, suggests that the stock is worth about $30 a share. We calculated our free cash flow CAGR by multiplying our 17% long-term ROE estimate by our projected 50% long-term annual earnings retention rate. Our relative valuation model, which compares a company's earnings yield (EPS divided by current stock price) with 10-year AAA-rated corporate bond yields, supports our avoid recommendation. Based on our 2005 S&P Core EPS estimate of $1.40, the stock is generating an earnings yield of 4.1%, below the 4.7% for 10-year AAA-rated corporate bonds.

Key Stock Statistics

S&P Core EPS 2005E	1.40	52-week Range	$38.46-28.60
S&P Oper. EPS 2004E	1.65	12 Month P/E	22.1
P/E on S&P Oper. EPS 2004E	22.2	Beta	1.33
S&P Oper. EPS 2005E	1.85	Shareholders	88,454
Yield (%)	2.0%	Market Cap (B)	$ 31.5
Dividend Rate/Share	0.75	Shares Outstanding (M)	860.2

Value of $10,000 invested five years ago: **$ 7,201**

Dividend Data Dividends have been paid since 1887

Amount ($)	Date Decl.	Ex-Div. Date	Stock of Record	Payment Date
0.188	Feb. 05	Feb. 18	Feb. 20	Mar. 10 '04
0.188	Apr. 26	May. 18	May. 20	Jun. 10 '04
0.188	Jul. 30	Aug. 18	Aug. 20	Sep. 10 '04
0.188	Oct. 29	Nov. 17	Nov. 19	Dec. 10 '04

Revenues/Earnings Data Fiscal year ending December 31

Revenues (Million $)

	2004	2003	2002	2001	2000	1999
1Q	6,178	5,399	5,199	5,944	6,044	3,596
2Q	6,388	5,749	5,651	6,066	6,309	3,818
3Q	6,395	5,768	5,569	5,789	6,216	3,838
4Q	—	6,187	5,855	5,853	6,454	6,159
Yr.	—	23,103	22,274	23,652	25,023	23,735

Earnings Per Share ($)

	2004	2003	2002	2001	2000	1999
1Q	0.34	0.32	0.46	0.05	0.63	0.59
2Q	0.42	0.37	0.56	0.06	0.76	0.57
3Q	0.43	0.40	0.50	-0.38	0.35	0.69
4Q	E0.46	0.47	-1.78	0.14	0.31	0.01
Yr.	E1.65	1.56	-0.27	-0.12	2.05	1.90

Next earnings report expected: late-January Source: S&P, Company Reports
EPS Estimates based on S&P Operating Earnings; historical GAAP earnings are as reported.

Honeywell International Inc.

Recommendation: **SELL** ★ ★ ☆ ☆ ☆   12-Month Target Price: **$30.00** (as of January 29, 2004)

Business Summary November 09, 2004

Honeywell conducts business through four operating segments.

The Aerospace segment (38% of 2003 revenues, and 46% of operating profits; 14% profit margins) primarily makes cockpit controls, power generation equipment, and wheels and brakes for commercial and military aircraft. It is also a leading maker of jet engines for regional and business jet manufacturers. Major cockpit controls competitors include Rockwell Collins and France's Thales. Primary aircraft wheel and brake competitors include Goodrich and France's Messier-Bugatti. Major small jet engine competitors include the Pratt & Whitney division of United Technologies and GE's Jet Engine segment.

Demand for HON's aircraft equipment is driven primarily by growth in the global 100+ seat jetliner fleet. Based on statistics provided by independent research firm Avitas, Inc., from 1993 through 2003, the global airliner fleet grew at a 3.0% average annual rate.

The Aerospace segment is also a major player in the $35 billion global aircraft maintenance, repair and overhaul (MRO) industry. Primary competitors include the MRO operations of several global airlines, Goodrich, GE, Boeing, and several small, pure-play MRO companies. The worldwide airline industry is by far the largest customer for MRO services and spare parts. Based on statistics provided by aviation trade group Aerospace Industries Association, from 1993 through 2003, the MRO market grew at a 2.6% average annual rate.

HON's Automation and Control segment (32%; 32%; 11%) is best known as a

global maker of home and office climate controls equipment. The unit also makes home automation systems, energy-efficient lighting controls, and security and fire alarms. With more than 20,000 providers, the $110 billion security systems industry is fragmented (based on statistics provided by trade group Security Industry Association). Primary security systems competitors include Tyco's ADT unit, U.K.-based Kidde PLC, the United Technologies Chubb division, and Sweden-based Securitas AB.

The Specialty Materials segment (14%; 5%; 4.3%) makes specialty chemicals and fibers. HON sells its industrial materials primarily to the food, pharmaceutical, and electronic packaging industries.

The Power & Transportation segment (16%; 17%; 13%) consists of a portfolio of brand name car care products, such as FRAM filters, Prestone antifreeze, Autolite spark plugs, and Simonize car waxes. The unit is also a large truck brake maker.

From 1993 through 2003, reported EPS showed a compound annual growth rate (CAGR) of 3.0%; free cash flow per share posted a 12% CAGR; and equity per share (a proxy for intrinsic value growth) increased at an 11% CAGR. Debt-adjusted ROE averaged 13%. Based on Standard & Poor's Core Earnings methodology, S&P Core EPS variance averaged -91% over the last 10 years, primarily due to the reversal of non-operating gains generated by HON's historically overfunded pension plan.

Company Financials Fiscal Year ending December 31

Per Share Data ($)

(Year Ended December 31)	2003	2002	2001	2000	1999	1998	1997	1996	1995	1994
Tangible Bk. Val.	4.46	2.52	3.45	4.71	4.95	4.12	3.47	4.89	3.57	2.89
Cash Flow	2.25	0.53	1.02	3.28	2.99	3.38	3.07	2.87	2.63	2.26
Earnings	1.56	-0.27	-0.12	2.05	1.90	2.32	2.02	1.81	1.55	1.34
S&P Core Earnings	1.57	0.15	-0.26	NA	NA	NA	NA	NA	NA	NA
Dividends	0.75	0.75	0.75	0.75	0.68	0.60	0.52	0.45	0.39	0.34
Payout Ratio	48%	NM	NM	37%	36%	26%	26%	25%	25%	25%
Prices - High	33.50	40.95	53.90	60.50	68.62	47.56	47.12	37.18	24.93	20.34
- Low	20.20	18.77	22.15	32.12	37.81	32.62	31.62	23.56	16.68	15.18
P/E Ratio - High	21	NM	NM	30	36	21	23	21	16	15
- Low	13	NM	NM	16	20	14	16	13	11	11

Income Statement Analysis (Million $)

	2003	2002	2001	2000	1999	1998	1997	1996	1995	1994
Revs.	23,103	22,274	23,652	25,023	23,735	15,128	14,472	13,971	14,346	12,817
Oper. Inc.	2,513	2,573	1,085	3,794	2,905	2,571	2,019	1,456	1,916	1,675
Depr.	595	671	926	995	881	609	609	602	612	523
Int. Exp.	335	344	405	481	265	162	175	186	189	166
Pretax Inc.	1,647	-945	-422	2,398	2,248	1,980	1,761	1,553	1,261	1,141
Eff. Tax Rate	18.0%	NM	NM	30.8%	31.5%	30.9%	31.0%	34.3%	30.6%	30.9%
Net Inc.	1,344	-220	-99	1,659	1,541	1,331	1,170	1,020	875	759
S&P Core Earnings	1,363	119	-207	NA	NA	NA	NA	NA	NA	NA

Balance Sheet & Other Fin. Data (Million $)

	2003	2002	2001	2000	1999	1998	1997	1996	1995	1994
Cash	2,950	2,021	1,393	1,196	1,991	712	611	1,766	540	508
Curr. Assets	11,523	10,195	9,894	10,661	10,422	5,593	5,573	5,839	4,890	4,585
Total Assets	29,344	27,559	24,226	25,175	23,527	15,560	13,707	12,829	12,465	11,321
Curr. Liab.	6,783	6,574	6,220	7,214	8,272	5,185	4,436	3,696	3,804	3,391
LT Debt	4,961	4,719	4,731	3,941	2,457	1,476	1,215	1,317	1,367	1,424
Common Equity	7,243	8,925	9,170	9,707	8,599	5,297	4,205	4,180	3,592	2,982
Total Cap.	12,520	14,063	14,776	14,821	11,920	7,568	6,114	6,107	5,509	4,812
Cap. Exp.	655	671	876	853	986	684	717	755	746	639
Cash Flow	1,939	451	827	2,654	2,422	1,940	1,779	1,622	1,487	1,282
Curr. Ratio	1.7	1.6	1.6	1.5	1.3	1.1	1.3	1.6	1.3	1.4
% LT Debt of Cap.	39.6	33.6	32.0	26.6	20.6	19.5	19.3	21.6	24.8	29.6
% Net Inc.of Revs.	5.8	NM	NM	6.6	6.5	8.8	8.1	7.3	6.1	5.9
% Ret. on Assets	4.7	NM	NM	6.8	6.7	9.1	8.8	8.1	7.4	6.9
% Ret. on Equity	21.1	NM	NM	18.1	18.5	28.0	27.9	26.2	26.6	28.3

Data as orig reptd.; bef. results of disc opers/spec. items. Per share data adj. for stk. divs.; EPS diluted (primary prior to 1998). E-Estimated. NA-Not Available. NM-Not Meaningful. NR-Not Ranked. UR-Under Review.

Office: 101 Columbia Rd, Morristown, NJ 07960-4640.
Telephone: 973-455-2000.
Website: http://www.honeywell.com
Chrmn, Pres & CEO: D.M. Cote.
SVP & CFO: D.J. Anderson.
SVP & General Counsel: P.M. Kreindler.

Investor Contact: D. Gallagher 973-455-2222.
Dirs: H. W. Becherer, G. M. Bethune, M. N. Carter, D. M. Cote, C. Hollick, J. J. Howard, B. Karatz, R. P. Luciano, R. E. Palmer, J. C. Pardo, I. G. Seidenberg, B. T. Sheares, E. K. Shinseki, J. R. Stafford, M. W. Wright.

Founded: in 1920.
Domicile: Delaware.
Employees: 108,000.
S&P Analyst: Robert E. Friedman, CPA /MF/BK

Hospira Inc.

Recommendation: SELL ★ ☆ ☆ ☆ ☆
SELL | SELL | HOLD | BUY | BUY

12-Month Target Price: **$29.00**
(as of August 12, 2004)

HSP has an approximate 0.05% weighting in the **S&P 500**

Sector: Health Care
Sub-Industry: Health Care Equipment

Summary: Spun off from Abbott Laboratories in May 2004, this new entity provides a variety of hospital products including injectable generic drugs, pumps and syringes.

Quantitative Evaluations

S&P Earnings & Dividend Rank: NR

D	C	B-	B	B+	A-	A	A+

S&P Fair Value Rank: NR

1	2	3	4	5
Lowest				Highest

Fair Value Calc.: NA

S&P Investability Quotient Percentile

94%

HSP scored higher than 94% of all companies for which an S&P Report is available.

Volatility: NA

Low	Average	High

Technical Evaluation: NA

Relative Strength Rank: Moderate

64

1 Lowest	Highest 99

Price as of 11/12/04:	**$32.15**	2004E S&P Core EPS:	**$1.48**

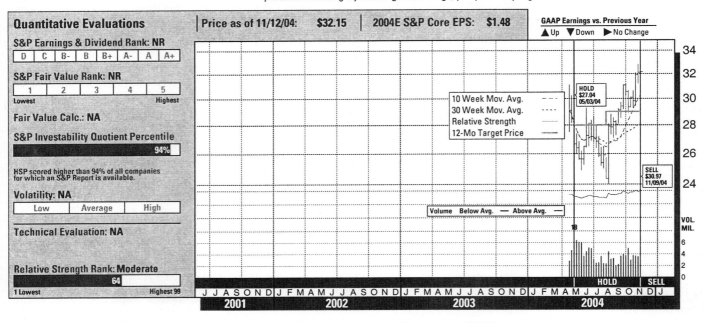

GAAP Earnings vs. Previous Year
▲ Up ▼ Down ► No Change

- - - 10 Week Mov. Avg.
- - - 30 Week Mov. Avg.
Relative Strength
12-Mo Target Price

HOLD $27.04 05/03/04
SELL $30.97 11/09/04

Volume Below Avg. — Above Avg. —

VOL. MIL.

HOLD | SELL

J J A S O N D | J F M A M J J A S O N D | J F M A M J J A S O N D | J F M A M J J A S O N D | J
2001 | 2002 | 2003 | 2004

Analyst commentary prepared by Cameron Lavey/CB/BK

Highlights November 10, 2004

- HSP's third quarter GAAP EPS were $0.39, versus $0.43 in the prior year period. Results included a $0.05 charge for infrastructure transition costs related to the spin-off from Abbott Labs. EPS in the fourth quarter of 2004 are expected to decline significantly due to higher SG&A and R&D expenses, as well as additional transition costs. We expect sales to rise fractionally in 2005, to $2.6 billion.

- We expect gross margins to narrow in the fourth quarter of 2004 due to a product mix shift; we see wider margins in 2005 as HSP transitions to higher margin products. We expect higher SG&A and R&D expenses to restrict profitability in 2005.

- We forecast 2004 pro forma sales of $2.6 billion, up slightly from $2.5 billion in 2003. We estimate 2004 pro forma EPS of $1.67, with no change seen in 2005.

Investment Rationale/Risk November 10, 2004

- We recently downgraded the shares to avoid, from hold, due primarily to valuation. We think that a fair price-to-sales range for HSP is 1.5X to 1.7X, below the current level of almost 2X. In addition, we expect its long-term annualized EPS growth rate to be below that of its competitors. We estimate annualized EPS growth of 7% to 8% over the next four years, and we believe that EPS gains will largely come from operational efficiencies. We think that sales and EPS will remain flat in 2005 as the company continues its transition to a stand-alone entity.

- Risks to our recommendation and target price include higher than expected sales and lower than anticipated operating costs. In addition, HSP could complete the organizational transition to a stand-alone company faster and more cheaply than we project.

- We believe an appropriate price to sales range for HSP would be 1.5X to 1.7X our 2005 sales forecast, considering our expectation for low growth. Combined with our DCF analysis, our 12-month target price is $29.

Key Stock Statistics

S&P Core EPS 2005E	1.49	52-week Range	$34.32-24.02
S&P Oper. EPS 2004E	1.67	12 Month P/E	16.3
P/E on S&P Oper. EPS 2004E	19.3	Beta	NA
S&P Oper. EPS 2005E	1.67	Shareholders	NA
Yield (%)	Nil	Market Cap (B)	$ 5.0
Dividend Rate/Share	Nil	Shares Outstanding (M)	156.1

Value of $10,000 invested five years ago: **NA**

Dividend Data

No cash dividends have been paid.

Revenues/Earnings Data Fiscal year ending December 31

Revenues (Million $)

	2004	2003	2002	2001	2000	1999
1Q	609.0	—	—	—	—	—
2Q	667.4	—	—	—	—	—
3Q	656.1	—	—	—	—	—
4Q	—	—	—	—	—	—
Yr.	—	2,545	—	—	—	—

Earnings Per Share ($)

	2004	2003	2002	2001	2000	1999
1Q	0.43	—	—	—	—	—
2Q	0.80	—	—	—	—	—
3Q	0.39	—	—	—	—	—
4Q	E0.24	—	—	—	—	—
Yr.	E1.67	1.65	—	—	—	—

Next earnings report expected: NA Source: S&P, Company Reports
EPS Estimates based on S&P Operating Earnings; historical GAAP earnings are as reported.

Hospira, Inc.

Recommendation: **SELL** ★ ★ ☆ ☆ ☆   12-Month Target Price: **$29.00** (as of August 12, 2004)

Business Summary November 10, 2004

Hospira (HSP) was created on May 3, 2004, as a spin-off from Abbott Laboratories. Abbott shareholders received one share of Hospira for every 10 shares of Abbott. The new entity primarily provides hospital supplies and related products and services to hospitals, clinics and physicians.

Hospira has an international presence, with operations in close to 70 countries. In 2003, companywide revenues were $2.5 billion. International sales accounted for 15% of total revenues. No individual product accounted for more than 6% of total sales. The company operates 15 manufacturing facilities domestically and internationally.

Operating segments include specialty injectable pharmaceuticals (2003 domestic sales of $858 million), medication delivery systems and critical care devices ($823 million), and injectable pharmaceutical contract manufacturing services ($168 million). Sales to Abbott Laboratories totaled $183 million in 2003. Major competitors include Baxter International, Becton Dickinson, Edwards Lifesciences, Fresenius AG, Patheon, and Sicor.

The specialty injectable pharmaceuticals division provides over 130 generic injectable drugs available in a wide array of dosages and formulations. Therapeutic areas of focus include cardiovascular, pain, infectious disease, and anesthesia. Therapeutic offerings include Precedex for sedation and Corlopam for severe, in-hospital hypertension. Some other products include Carpuject prefilled syringes; First Choice premixed drug formulations, which help decrease preparation and delivery time to patients; and the ADD-Vantage System, which aids in the preparation of drug solutions from prepackaged powders or concentration.

The medication delivery systems unit markets pumps for delivering drugs intravenously and analgesia for patient-controlled management of pain. It also provides infusion therapy products, which include pre-mixed drug solutions, intravenous

(I.V.) nutritionals, and other I.V. supplies. In addition, the delivery systems group sells hemodynamic monitoring systems that are used to measure blood flow and cardiac output in hospital critical care and intensive care units. Another product offering is Hospira MedNet, which provides software-based solutions for the management of drug dosing information and hospital decision support. This software provides data on approximately 1,200 medications.

The injectable pharmaceutical contract manufacturing services segment provides formulation, fill and finish of drugs for leading biotechnology and pharmaceutical companies, including Abbott. HSP's One 2 One manufacturing services group provides custom manufacturing for parenteral products and medical components. HSP estimates that One 2 One is the largest provider of formulation development, filling and finishing of injectable drugs in North America.

In June 2004, HSP acquired a 100,000 square foot manufacturing facility in Clayton, N.C. This facility will be used to produce injectable drugs and intravenous solutions. Generic deferoxamine mesylate, used to treat iron overload, was launched in the second quarter of 2004. In July 2004, the company launched Fluconazole, a generic version of Pfizer's Diflucan, an antifungal agent. In the third quarter of 2004, HSP added four new drug compounds to the injectables pipeline, scheduled for launch in 2007 and beyond.

As part of the terms of the spin-off, Hospira incurred debt-related obligations of approximately $700 million, largely in the form of a credit facility. HSP is largely funding this obligation through the issuance of $700 million in long-term debt. HSP also plans to purchase approximately $236 million of assets from Abbott over a two-year period. In addition, HSP may enter into additional credit facility agreements for at least $300 million to fund operations.

Company Financials Fiscal Year ending December 31

Per Share Data ($)

(Year Ended December 31)	2003	2002	2001	2000	1999	1998	1997	1996	1995	1994
Tangible Bk. Val.	NM	NA	NA	NA	NA	NA	NA	NA	NA	NA
Cash Flow	NA	NA	NA	NA	NA	NA	NA	NA	NA	NA
Earnings	1.65	NA	NA	NA	NA	NA	NA	NA	NA	NA
Dividends	NA	NA	NA	NA	NA	NA	NA	NA	NA	NA
Payout Ratio	NA	NA	NA	NA	NA	NA	NA	NA	NA	NA
Prices - High	NA	NA	NA	NA	NA	NA	NA	NA	NA	NA
- Low	NA	NA	NA	NA	NA	NA	NA	NA	NA	NA
P/E Ratio - High	NA	NA	NA	NA	NA	NA	NA	NA	NA	NA
- Low	NA	NA	NA	NA	NA	NA	NA	NA	NA	NA

Income Statement Analysis (Million $)

	2003	2002	2001	2000	1999	1998	1997	1996	1995	1994
Revs.	2,624	NA	NA	NA	NA	NA	NA	NA	NA	NA
Oper. Inc.	506	NA	NA	NA	NA	NA	NA	NA	NA	NA
Depr.	146	NA	NA	NA	NA	NA	NA	NA	NA	NA
Int. Exp.	Nil	NA	NA	NA	NA	NA	NA	NA	NA	NA
Pretax Inc.	359	NA	NA	NA	NA	NA	NA	NA	NA	NA
Eff. Tax Rate	27.5%	NA	NA	NA	NA	NA	NA	NA	NA	NA
Net Inc.	260	NA	NA	NA	NA	NA	NA	NA	NA	NA

Balance Sheet & Other Fin. Data (Million $)

	2003	2002	2001	2000	1999	1998	1997	1996	1995	1994
Cash	Nil	NA	NA	NA	NA	NA	NA	NA	NA	NA
Curr. Assets	1,075	NA	NA	NA	NA	NA	NA	NA	NA	NA
Total Assets	2,250	NA	NA	NA	NA	NA	NA	NA	NA	NA
Curr. Liab.	360	NA	NA	NA	NA	NA	NA	NA	NA	NA
LT Debt	Nil	NA	NA	NA	NA	NA	NA	NA	NA	NA
Common Equity	1,453	NA	NA	NA	NA	NA	NA	NA	NA	NA
Total Cap.	1,453	NA	NA	NA	NA	NA	NA	NA	NA	NA
Cap. Exp.	197	NA	NA	NA	NA	NA	NA	NA	NA	NA
Cash Flow	406	NA	NA	NA	NA	NA	NA	NA	NA	NA
Curr. Ratio	3.0	NA	NA	NA	NA	NA	NA	NA	NA	NA
% LT Debt of Cap.	Nil	NA	NA	NA	NA	NA	NA	NA	NA	NA
% Net Inc.of Revs.	9.9	NA	NA	NA	NA	NA	NA	NA	NA	NA
% Ret. on Assets	11.8	NA	NA	NA	NA	NA	NA	NA	NA	NA
% Ret. on Equity	18.7	NA	NA	NA	NA	NA	NA	NA	NA	NA

Data as orig reptd.; bef. results of disc opers/spec. items. Per share data adj. for stk. divs.; EPS diluted. E-Estimated. NA-Not Available. NM-Not Meaningful. NR-Not Ranked. UR-Under Review.

Office: 275 North Field Drive, Lake Forest, IL 60045.
Telephone: 847-937-6100.
Chrmn: D.A. Jones.
CEO: C.B. Begley.
SVP & CFO: T.C. Kearney.

SVP, Secy, General Counsel & Investor Contact: B.J. Smith
847-937-6100.
Dirs: J. T. Allison, I. W. Bailey II, C. B. Begley, C. R. Curran, D. A. Jones, J. J. Sokolov, J. C. Staley, W. L. Weiss.
Auditor: Ernst & Young, Chicago, IL.

Founded: in 2003.
Domicile: Delaware.
Employees: 14,000.
S&P Analyst: Cameron Lavey/CB/BK

Humana

Recommendation: **HOLD** ★★★☆☆
SELL · SELL · HOLD · BUY · BUY
12-Month Target Price: **$23.00**
(as of November 01, 2004)

HUM has an approximate 0.03% weighting in the **S&P 500**

Sector: Health Care
Sub-Industry: Managed Health Care
Peer Group: Managed Care - Large

Summary: Humana provides a broad range of managed health care services to about 6.0 million individuals in 18 states and Puerto Rico.

Quantitative Evaluations

S&P Earnings & Dividend Rank: B

D	C	B-	**B**	B+	A-	A	A+

S&P Fair Value Rank: 5+

1	2	3	4	**5**
Lowest				Highest

Fair Value Calc.: $28.00 (Undervalued)

S&P Investability Quotient Percentile

99%

HUM scored higher than 99% of all companies for which an S&P Report is available.

Volatility: Average

Low	**Average**	High

Technical Evaluation: Bullish

Since 11/04, the technical indicators for HUM have been Bullish.

Relative Strength Rank: Strong

90

1 Lowest	Highest 99

Price as of 11/12/04:	**$23**	2004E S&P Core EPS:	**$1.63**

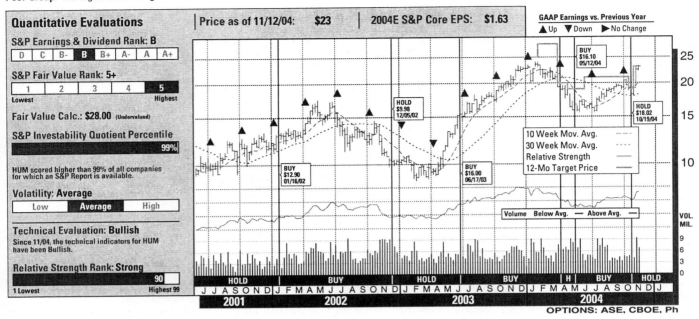

GAAP Earnings vs. Previous Year — ▲ Up ▼ Down ▶ No Change

10 Week Mov. Avg.
30 Week Mov. Avg.
Relative Strength
12-Mo Target Price

Volume Below Avg. — Above Avg.

OPTIONS: ASE, CBOE, Ph

Analyst commentary prepared by Phillip M. Seligman/PMW/JWP

Highlights November 12, 2004

- We see 2005 consolidated revenues up over 6%, to about $14 billion. We look for modestly higher organic commercial enrollment, in light of the lapse of underperforming accounts with a total of 94,000 members and a continued shift of risk-based accounts to ASO (self-funded) status. We see increased enrollment in the MedicareAdvantage (formerly known as Medicare+Choice) program, assuming that HUM's applications to expand into more communities receive a favorable response by the federal government. HUM has not provided guidance on commercial premium rate hikes for 2005, but has said it has been pricing each account in line with its prior experience.

- We believe the medical cost ratio (MCR) will benefit from a transition of all large group accounts to self-funded status, as profitability has tended to be highest among individual and small-to mid-sized accounts. We believe the departure of underperforming accounts will aid the commercial medical loss ratio. We see a further decline in the commercial SG&A cost ratio, on technology gains. Government (Medicare, Medicaid and TRICARE) MCR and SG&A cost ratios are benefiting somewhat from the Medicare Modernization Act.

- We project 2005 EPS of $1.95, up from our 2004 estimate of $1.70. Our respective projections for 2004 and 2005 S&P Core EPS are $1.63 and $1.83, reflecting estimated stock option expense.

Key Stock Statistics

S&P Core EPS 2005E	**1.83**	52-week Range	**$24.02-15.20**
S&P Oper. EPS 2004E	**1.70**	12 Month P/E	**12.6**
P/E on S&P Oper. EPS 2004E	**13.5**	Beta	**0.31**
S&P Oper. EPS 2005E	**1.95**	Shareholders	**6,300**
Yield (%)	**Nil**	Market Cap (B)	**$ 3.7**
Dividend Rate/Share	**Nil**	Shares Outstanding (M)	**159.4**

Value of $10,000 invested five years ago: **$ 27,784**

Dividend Data

Cash dividend payments were suspended in 1993.

Investment Rationale/Risk November 12, 2004

- We believe the company has demonstrated good cost control in several areas. The ASO business is attracting new accounts to Smartsuite; the Medicare business is thriving; and we see HUM's plans to drop unprofitable accounts aiding 2005 EPS. Nevertheless, we do not see the shares outperforming the S&P 500 over the next 12 months, in part due to what we see as market concerns about a possible probe of the managed care industry by New York State Attorney General Spitzer and other state attorneys general.

- Risks to our recommendation and target price include a potential government probe of the managed care industry, intensifying competition, higher than expected medical costs, lower than expected premium yields, and a weaker job market.

- Our 12-month target price of $23 is based on a peer-average forward P/E multiple of 12X applied to our 2005 EPS estimate of $1.95.

Revenues/Earnings Data Fiscal year ending December 31

Revenues (Million $)

	2004	2003	2002	2001	2000	1999
1Q	3,287	2,932	2,733	2,464	2,642	2,477
2Q	3,431	3,030	2,832	2,497	2,696	2,461
3Q	3,176	3,112	2,842	2,611	2,616	2,557
4Q	—	3,153	2,855	2,623	2,560	2,574
Yr.	—	12,226	11,261	10,195	10,395	10,113

Earnings Per Share ($)

	2004	2003	2002	2001	2000	1999
1Q	0.41	0.19	0.28	0.16	0.13	-0.10
2Q	0.50	0.43	0.27	0.15	0.11	0.17
3Q	0.52	0.38	0.31	0.18	0.14	0.13
4Q	E0.27	0.41	Nil	0.21	0.16	-2.48
Yr.	E1.70	1.41	0.85	0.70	0.54	-2.28

Next earnings report expected: early-February Source: S&P, Company Reports
EPS Estimates based on S&P Operating Earnings; historical GAAP earnings are as reported.

Humana Inc.

Recommendation: **HOLD** ★ ★ ★ ☆ ☆   12-Month Target Price: **$23.00** (as of November 01, 2004)

Business Summary November 12, 2004

Humana ranks among the largest U.S. providers of managed health care services, offering a wide range of products to employer groups, as well as to Medicare- and Medicaid-eligible individuals. At December 31, 2003, medical membership totaled 6,769,600, comprised of commercial fully insured (2,352,800), commercial administrative services (712,400), Medicare risk (328,600), TRICARE (formerly CHAMPUS; 1,849,700), TRICARE administrative services (1,057,200) and Medicaid (468,900). Enrollment centers on Florida and Illinois, which, as of December 31, 2003, accounted for 24.9% of total enrollment. Texas, Puerto Rico, Ohio, Wisconsin and Kentucky together accounted for another 33.7%.

HUM manages its business with two segments: Commercial and Government. The Commercial segment consists of members enrolled in products marketed to employer groups and individuals, and includes three lines of business: fully insured medical, administrative services only, or ASO, and specialty. The Government segment consists of members enrolled in government-sponsored programs, and includes three lines of business: Medicare+Choice, Medicaid, and TRICARE.

The company offers a full range of healthcare products in virtually all of its markets. Its principal product is the HMO (health maintenance organization), in which HUM charges members a fixed annual premium in return for an agreement to use only those doctors included in its network. Its other managed care plan, the preferred provider organization (PPO), also offers a fixed annual premium but allows the member the option of going to physicians outside of the network. In return, the member may be required to pay a portion of the provider's fees.

HUM's HMO plans (23.7% of total premium revenues at December 31, 2003) generally reimburse providers on a capitated basis, under an actuarially determined, fixed, per-member-per-month fee. This fee does not vary with the nature or extent of services provided to the member, and is generally designed to shift a portion of the HMO's financial risk to the primary care physician or hospital group. Providers participating in the company's PPO plans (27.9%) are generally reimbursed on a negotiated fee-for-service basis. The company had about 463,300 contracts with healthcare providers participating in its networks, which consists of about 294,400 physicians, 3,300 hospitals, and 165,500 ancillary providers and dentists.

Specialty and administrative service products (ASO) include dental, group life, and short-term disability. Specialty product membership at December 31, 2003, totaled 1,668,100 members.

Company Financials Fiscal Year ending December 31

Per Share Data ($)

(Year Ended December 31)	2003	2002	2001	2000	1999	1998	1997	1996	1995	1994
Tangible Bk. Val.	6.54	5.09	4.33	3.43	2.75	2.98	1.68	4.93	4.64	5.60
Cash Flow	2.20	1.57	1.67	1.42	-1.53	1.53	1.69	0.68	1.60	1.40
Earnings	1.41	0.85	0.70	0.54	-2.28	0.77	1.05	0.07	1.17	1.10
S&P Core Earnings	1.23	0.87	0.63	NA	NA	NA	NA	NA	NA	NA
Dividends	Nil	Nil	Nil	Nil	Nil	Nil	Nil	Nil	Nil	Nil
Payout Ratio	Nil	Nil	Nil	Nil	Nil	Nil	Nil	Nil	Nil	Nil
Prices - High	23.39	17.45	15.62	15.81	20.75	32.12	25.31	28.87	28.00	25.37
- Low	8.68	9.78	8.38	4.75	5.87	12.25	17.37	15.00	17.00	15.87
P/E Ratio - High	17	21	22	29	NM	42	24	NM	24	23
- Low	6	12	12	9	NM	16	17	NM	15	14

Income Statement Analysis (Million $)

	2003	2002	2001	2000	1999	1998	1997	1996	1995	1994
Revs.	12,226	11,261	9,939	10,395	9,959	9,597	7,880	6,677	4,605	3,654
Oper. Inc.	489	384	114	171	59.0	228	242	112	272	300
Depr.	127	121	162	147	124	128	108	98.0	70.0	50.0
Int. Exp.	17.4	17.0	25.0	29.0	33.0	47.0	20.0	11.0	11.0	4.00
Pretax Inc.	345	210	183	114	-404	203	270	18.0	288	257
Eff. Tax Rate	33.6%	32.0%	36.1%	21.1%	NM	36.5%	35.9%	33.3%	23.6%	31.5%
Net Inc.	229	143	117	90.0	-382	129	173	12.0	190	176
S&P Core Earnings	200	145	104	NA	NA	NA	NA	NA	NA	NA

Balance Sheet & Other Fin. Data (Million $)

	2003	2002	2001	2000	1999	1998	1997	1996	1995	1994
Cash	931	721	651	2,067	2,485	2,812	627	1,584	1,338	881
Curr. Assets	3,321	2,795	2,623	2,499	3,064	3,119	2,750	2,002	1,593	1,038
Total Assets	5,293	4,600	4,404	4,167	4,900	5,496	5,418	3,153	2,878	1,957
Curr. Liab.	2,265	2,390	2,307	2,665	3,164	2,643	2,263	1,500	1,192	816
LT Debt	643	340	315	Nil	324	1,011	1,486	225	250	Nil
Common Equity	1,836	1,606	1,508	1,374	1,268	1,688	1,501	1,292	1,287	1,058
Total Cap.	2,479	1,946	1,823	1,374	1,592	2,699	2,987	1,517	1,537	1,058
Cap. Exp.	101	112	115	135	89.0	104	73.0	72.0	54.0	39.0
Cash Flow	356	264	279	237	-258	257	281	110	260	226
Curr. Ratio	1.5	1.2	1.1	0.9	1.0	1.2	1.2	1.3	1.4	1.3
% LT Debt of Cap.	25.9	17.5	17.3	Nil	20.4	37.5	49.7	14.8	16.3	Nil
% Net Inc.of Revs.	1.9	1.3	1.2	0.9	NM	1.3	2.2	0.2	4.1	4.8
% Ret. on Assets	4.5	3.2	2.7	2.0	NM	2.4	4.0	0.4	7.9	9.5
% Ret. on Equity	13.3	9.2	8.2	6.8	NM	8.1	12.4	1.0	16.2	18.0

Data as orig. reptd.; bef. results of disc. opers. and/or spec. items. Per share data adj. for stk. divs. Slight variances betw. revs. as stated in qtrly. table. and Inc. table are due to variances in inclusion of other inc. EPS diluted. E-Estimated. NA-Not Available. NM-Not Meaningful. NR-Not Ranked.

Office: 500 West Main Street, Louisville, KY 40202-4268.
Telephone: 502-580-1000.
Website: http://www.humana.com
Chrmn: D.A. Jones.
Pres & CEO: M.B. McCallister.
Vice Chrmn: D.A. Jones.

COO: J.E. Murray.
SVP, CFO & Treas: J.H. Bloem.
Dirs: C. M. Brewer, F. A. D'Amelio, M. E. Gellert, J. R. Hall, K. J. Hilzinger, D. A. Jones, D. A. Jones, Jr., I. Lerner, M. B. McCallister, W. A. Reynolds.

Founded: in 1964.
Domicile: Delaware.
Employees: 13,700.
S&P Analyst: Phillip M. Seligman/PMW/JWP

Huntington Bancshares

Recommendation: **SELL** ★ ☆ ☆ ☆ ☆
SPEC · SELL · HOLD · BUY · BUY

12-Month Target Price: **$19.00**
(as of August 09, 2004)

HBAN has an approximate 0.05% weighting in the **S&P 500**

Sector: Financials
Sub-Industry: Regional Banks
Peer Group: Midwest/West Major Regional Banks

Summary: This $32 billion regional bank holding company has a network of branches throughout the Midwest.

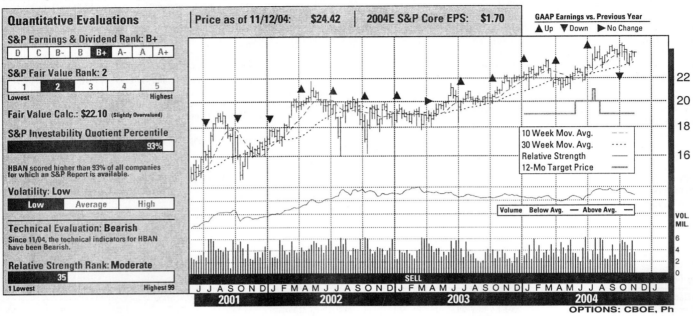

Price as of 11/12/04: $24.42	**2004E S&P Core EPS:** $1.70

Quantitative Evaluations

S&P Earnings & Dividend Rank: B+
D · C · B- · B · **B+** · A- · A · A+

S&P Fair Value Rank: 2
1 · **2** · 3 · 4 · 5
Lowest · · · · Highest

Fair Value Calc.: $22.10 (Slightly Overvalued)

S&P Investability Quotient Percentile
93%
HBAN scored higher than 93% of all companies for which an S&P Report is available.

Volatility: Low
Low · Average · High

Technical Evaluation: Bearish
Since 11/04, the technical indicators for HBAN have been Bearish.

Relative Strength Rank: Moderate
35
1 Lowest · Highest 99

GAAP Earnings vs. Previous Year
▲ Up ▼ Down ► No Change

10 Week Mov. Avg.
30 Week Mov. Avg.
Relative Strength
12-Mo Target Price

Volume   Below Avg. — Above Avg. —

SELL

2001   2002   2003   2004

OPTIONS: CBOE, Ph

Analyst commentary prepared by Erik J. Eisenstein/CB/GG

Highlights October 18, 2004

- Not including the planned acquisition of Unizan Financial Corp. (UNIZ), which is subject to approvals, we expect average earning assets to grow about 14% in 2005, aided by projected stronger demand for commercial credit. We are forecasting a flat net interest margin, and also expect a 14% increase in net interest income. Reflecting expected economic improvement, we project a 32% reduction in loan loss provisions.

- In 2005, we expect automobile leases originated prior to May 2002 to continue to run off. Reflecting projected reduced operating lease income, reduced gains from the sale of auto loans, and lower mortgage banking income, we expect noninterest income to drop 9%, despite higher expected deposit fees. We see operating expenses up 2%, despite the operating lease runoff, reflecting the projected larger asset and deposit bases.

- We forecast a 5% increase in 2005 EPS, to $1.85, from $1.77 seen in 2004. Our 2005 and 2004 Standard & Poor's Core EPS estimates are $1.80 and $1.70, reflecting our view of projected stock-based compensation expense.

Investment Rationale/Risk October 18, 2004

- We think that since announcing a restructuring in July 2001, HBAN has shown some success in increasing its fee income streams and asset quality. However, for the longer term, we view its growth prospects as below average, in light of what we see as relatively unattractive geographic positioning. We project average EPS growth of 8% in the five years beyond 2005, below anticipated peer levels of about 10%. Moreover, we still have concerns about an ongoing SEC investigation, which recently delayed the completion of HBAN's agreed-upon acquisition of Unizan Financial. These concerns were exacerbated in August, after HBAN replaced its CFO and controller, notwithstanding that it also reported settlement negotiations with the SEC.

- Risks to our recommendation and target price include the possibility that the net interest margin will be wider than we forecast, and that HBAN or a comparable regional bank will agree to be acquired at a valuation above that contemplated by our target price.

- Our 12-month target price of $19 is derived by applying a P/E to growth multiple of 1.28 to our five-year EPS growth and 2005 EPS projections, a bit below that of its regional banking peers.

Key Stock Statistics

S&P Core EPS 2005E	1.80	52-week Range	$25.38-20.89	
S&P Oper. EPS 2004E	1.77	12 Month P/E	14.1	
P/E on S&P Oper. EPS 2004E	13.8	Beta	0.43	
S&P Oper. EPS 2005E	1.85	Shareholders	27,764	
Yield (%)	3.3%	Market Cap (B)	$ 5.6	
Dividend Rate/Share	0.80	Shares Outstanding (M)	231.1	

Value of $10,000 invested five years ago: **$ 10,622**

Dividend Data Dividends have been paid since 1912

Amount ($)	Date Decl.	Ex-Div. Date	Stock of Record	Payment Date
0.175	Jan. 14	Mar. 17	Mar. 19	Apr. 01 '04
0.175	Apr. 27	Jun. 16	Jun. 18	Jul. 01 '04
0.200	Jul. 14	Sep. 15	Sep. 17	Oct. 01 '04
0.200	Oct. 13	Dec. 15	Dec. 17	Jan. 03 '05

Revenues/Earnings Data Fiscal year ending December 31

Revenues (Million $)

	2004	2003	2002	2001	2000	1999
1Q	553.6	599.5	695.0	635.7	626.7	605.6
2Q	542.0	604.7	491.8	627.2	635.2	616.0
3Q	527.9	606.1	522.7	609.3	657.4	632.0
4Q	—	564.6	506.9	576.9	668.2	637.8
Yr.	—	2,375	2,216	2,449	2,602	2,491

Earnings Per Share ($)

	2004	2003	2002	2001	2000	1999
1Q	0.45	0.39	0.39	0.27	0.42	0.38
2Q	0.47	0.42	0.33	0.01	0.40	0.41
3Q	0.40	0.45	0.41	0.17	0.20	0.42
4Q	E0.43	0.40	0.36	0.26	0.30	0.45
Yr.	E1.77	1.67	1.49	0.71	1.32	1.65

Next earnings report expected: mid-January Source: S&P, Company Reports
EPS Estimates based on S&P Operating Earnings; historical GAAP earnings are as reported.

STANDARD
&POOR'S

Huntington Bancshares Incorporated

Recommendation: **SELL** ★ ☆ ☆ ☆ ☆   12-Month Target Price: **$19.00** (as of August 09, 2004)

Business Summary October 18, 2004

Huntington Bancshares has been serving the needs of customers for more than 137 years. The $32 billion asset regional bank holding company, headquartered in Columbus, OH, with more than 300 regional banking offices in Indiana, Kentucky, Michigan, Ohio and West Virginia, offers a full line of commercial and consumer banking services. It also offers selected financial services in Florida, Georgia, Tennessee, Pennsylvania, Maryland, Arizona, and New Jersey, and international banking services in the Cayman Islands and Hong Kong. The company seeks to strategically position itself as a local bank with nationwide resources, able to provide a broad of array of financial solutions to its individual, business, corporate and institutional customers.

In July 2001, the company announced a strategic and financial restructuring aimed at focusing on core Midwest markets, streamlining operations and reducing costs, and redeploying capital. In February 2002, as part of the restructuring, it sold its Florida operations to SunTrust Banks.

In September 2002, HBAN acquired LeaseNet Group, an Ohio-based equipment leasing company specializing in high-technology equipment. In April, it acquired Haberer Registered Investment Advisory, Inc., a Cincinnati, OH-based registered investment adviser with $500 million in assets under management. HBAN believed the acquisitions would bolster its growth prospects and customer service capabilities.

Operations are divided into four segments: regional banking, dealer sales, private financial group, and treasury/other. The regional banking segment serves retail and commercial customers with various personal and business loan and deposit products, as well as sales of investment and insurance services. Dealer sales serves the automotive sector, mainly with indirect consumer loans and leases and floor plan financing. The private financial group meets the needs of higher wealth customers with personal trust, asset management, investment advisory, and other wealth management services. Treasury/other includes the results of the investment securities portfolio, as well as other unallocated assets, liabilities, revenues and expenses. Contributions to earnings by segment in 2003, before releases of restructuring charges, gains and losses on disposed assets and a long term-debt extinguishment, were: regional banking 48%, dealer sales 17%, private financial 7%, and treasury/other 27%.

In June 2003, HBAN said it was the subject of an SEC formal investigation into certain accounting practices. It voluntarily restated earnings three times in 2003, with most of the impact related to years prior to 2001.

In January 2004, the company agreed to acquire Canton, OH-based Unizan Financial Corp., with $2.7 billion in assets, in exchange for stock valued at $587 million. In June, HBAN said the Federal Reserve Board was extending its review period to coordinate with the SEC investigation. The transaction is subject to regulatory approvals.

In April 2004, directors authorized the repurchase of up to 7.5 million company common shares (3% of the total).

Company Financials Fiscal Year ending December 31

Per Share Data ($)

(Year Ended December 31)	2003	2002	2001	2000	1999	1998	1997	1996	1995	1994
Tangible Bk. Val.	8.99	8.95	6.77	9.43	8.66	8.43	7.93	7.24	7.09	6.41
Earnings	1.67	1.49	0.71	1.32	1.65	1.17	1.14	1.23	1.11	1.11
S&P Core Earnings	1.56	0.96	0.60	NA	NA	NA	NA	NA	NA	NA
Dividends	0.67	0.64	0.72	0.74	0.68	0.62	0.57	0.52	0.48	0.43
Payout Ratio	40%	43%	101%	56%	41%	53%	50%	42%	44%	39%
Prices - High	22.55	21.77	19.28	21.81	30.88	28.55	29.20	19.72	15.75	13.12
- Low	17.78	16.00	12.62	12.51	19.48	18.18	17.07	13.97	9.97	9.83
P/E Ratio - High	14	15	27	17	19	25	26	16	14	12
- Low	11	11	18	9	12	16	15	11	9	9

Income Statement Analysis (Million $)

	2003	2002	2001	2000	1999	1998	1997	1996	1995	1994
Net Int. Inc.	849	984	996	942	1,042	1,021	1,027	759	725	756
Tax Equiv. Adj.	9.68	5.21	6.35	8.31	9.42	10.3	11.9	5.10	6.80	9.50
Non Int. Inc.	1,064	680	509	494	561	408	335	255	248	233
Loan Loss Prov.	164	227	309	90.5	88.4	105	108	65.0	28.7	15.3
Exp./Op. Revs.	64.3%	50.6%	67.4%	61.7%	56.6%	63.9%	59.0%	55.7%	57.7%	61.1%
Pretax Inc.	524	589	173	460	615	440	459	399	378	366
Eff. Tax Rate	26.4%	38.4%	NM	28.6%	31.3%	31.4%	36.3%	34.3%	35.4%	33.8%
Net Inc.	386	363	179	328	422	302	293	262	244	243
% Net Int. Marg.	3.49	4.19	4.02	3.73	4.11	4.28	4.44	4.11	4.15	4.96
S&P Core Earnings	360	234	152	NA	NA	NA	NA	NA	NA	NA

Balance Sheet & Other Fin. Data (Million $)

	2003	2002	2001	2000	1999	1998	1997	1996	1995	1994
Money Mkt. Assets	138	86.6	118	143	28.9	243	556	12.0	495	18.0
Inv. Securities	4,929	3,411	2,862	4,107	4,889	4,806	5,743	4,804	4,789	3,780
Com'l Loans	9,486	9,336	10,415	8,887	8,452	6,027	5,271	4,463	4,190	4,257
Other Loans	11,590	11,619	11,187	11,723	12,216	13,428	12,468	9,798	9,072	8,146
Total Assets	30,484	27,579	28,500	28,599	29,037	28,296	26,731	20,852	20,255	17,771
Demand Deposits	2,987	3,074	3,741	3,505	7,594	7,771	2,550	5,050	4,861	4,816
Time Deposits	15,500	14,425	16,446	16,272	11,613	11,951	3,768	8,336	7,776	7,149
LT Debt	6,808	3,304	3,039	3,338	4,269	3,247	2,886	1,556	2,103	1,023
Common Equity	2,275	2,304	2,416	2,366	2,182	2,149	2,025	1,512	1,519	1,412
% Ret. on Assets	1.3	1.3	0.6	1.1	1.5	1.1	1.2	1.3	1.3	1.4
% Ret. on Equity	17.3	15.4	7.5	14.4	19.5	14.5	16.5	17.3	16.7	17.3
% Loan Loss Resv.	1.6	1.7	1.8	1.4	-1.4	1.5	1.5	1.4	1.5	1.6
% Loans/Deposits	115.2	122.8	110.1	105.0	NA	98.6	98.6	106.5	104.9	103.7
% Equity to Assets	7.7	8.4	8.4	7.9	7.6	7.6	7.4	7.4	7.7	8.4

Data as orig reptd.; bef. results of disc opers/spec. items. Per share data adj. for stk. divs.; EPS diluted. E-Estimated. NA-Not Available. NM-Not Meaningful. NR-Not Ranked. UR-Under Review.

Office: Huntington Center, Columbus, OH 43287.
Telephone: 614-480-8300.
Website: http://www.huntington.com
Chrmn, Pres & CEO: T.E. Hoaglin.
Vice Chrmn & Treas: M.J. McMennamin.

EVP & CFO: D. Kimble.
SVP & Investor Contact: J.S. Gould 614-480-4060.
Dirs: R. Biggs, D. M. Casto III, M. J. Endres, J. B. Gerlach, Jr., T. E. Hoaglin, K. A. Holbrook, D. P. Lauer, W. J. Lhota, D. L. Porteous, K. H. Ransier, R. H. Schottenstein.

Founded: in 1966.
Domicile: Maryland.
Employees: 7,983.
S&P Analyst: Erik J. Eisenstein/CB/GG

The McGraw·Hill Companies

Illinois Tool Works

Recommendation: **HOLD** ★ ★ ★ ★
SELL | SELL | HOLD | BUY | BUY

12-Month Target Price: **$92.00**
(as of August 25, 2004)

ITW has an approximate 0.26% weighting in the **S&P 500**

Sector: Industrials
Sub-Industry: Industrial Machinery
Peer Group: Industrial Parts

Summary: This diversified manufacturer operates a portfolio of more than 600 industrial and consumer businesses located throughout the world.

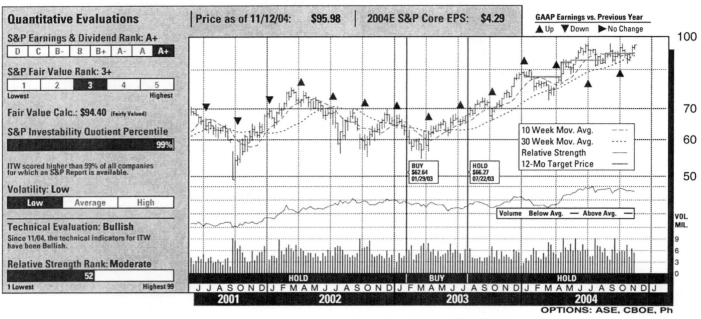

Quantitative Evaluations

S&P Earnings & Dividend Rank: A+

D	C	B-	B	B+	A-	A	A+

S&P Fair Value Rank: 3+

1	2	3	4	5
Lowest				Highest

Fair Value Calc.: $94.40 (Fairly Valued)

S&P Investability Quotient Percentile

99%

ITW scored higher than 99% of all companies for which an S&P Report is available.

Volatility: Low

Low	Average	High

Technical Evaluation: Bullish
Since 11/04, the technical indicators for ITW have been Bullish.

Relative Strength Rank: Moderate

52

1 Lowest | Highest 99

Price as of 11/12/04: **$95.98**   2004E S&P Core EPS: **$4.29**

GAAP Earnings vs. Previous Year
▲ Up ▼ Down ► No Change

10 Week Mov. Avg.
30 Week Mov. Avg.
Relative Strength
12-Mo Target Price

BUY $62.64 01/29/03
HOLD $66.27 07/22/03

Volume Below Avg. — Above Avg.

HOLD | BUY | HOLD
J J A S O N D J F M A M J J A S O N D J F M A M J J A S O N D J F M A M J J A S O N D J
2001 | 2002 | 2003 | 2004

OPTIONS: ASE, CBOE, Ph

Analyst commentary prepared by Anthony M. Fiore, CFA /CB/JWP

Highlights October 20, 2004

- We see revenues increasing about 10% in 2005, following a projected advance of about 16% in 2004. We expect top-line growth in 2005 to be driven by contributions from acquisitions, combined with expected improvement in commercial construction and industrial activity in many of the company's North American and international end markets.

- We see a modest expansion of operating margins in 2005, due to expected benefits from ongoing cost cutting measures, combined with improving volumes. In addition, we see return on equity and EPS benefiting from lower share counts in 2004 and 2005, as we expect the company to continue its share repurchase program.

- Our Standard & Poor's Core Earnings estimates for 2004 and 2005 are $0.05 and $0.04 a share below our respective operating EPS forecasts, with the difference reflecting projected stock option expense and pension and post-retirement cost adjustments.

Investment Rationale/Risk October 20, 2004

- We have a hold recommendation on the shares. While we expect favorable end market conditions to continue over the next 12 months, we believe that our outlook is largely reflected in the price of the stock.

- Risks to our recommendation and target price include an unexpected downturn in industrial activity and/or capital spending; execution risk associated with acquisitions; continued escalation of raw material costs; and a greater than anticipated slowing of the residential housing and/or automotive markets.

- Our discounted cash flow model, which assumes an 8% average annual free cash flow growth rate over the next 10 years, 3.5% growth in perpetuity, and an 8% weighted average cost of capital, indicates intrinsic value of about $88. In terms of relative valuation, applying a target P/E multiple of 19X, in line with historical norms, suggests a value of about $95 a share. We arrive at our 12-month target price of $92 using a blend of these valuation metrics.

Key Stock Statistics

S&P Core EPS 2005E	4.96	52-week Range	$96.70-72.92
S&P Oper. EPS 2004E	4.34	12 Month P/E	23.4
P/E on S&P Oper. EPS 2004E	22.1	Beta	0.82
S&P Oper. EPS 2005E	5.00	Shareholders	12,948
Yield (%)	1.2%	Market Cap (B)	$ 28.4
Dividend Rate/Share	1.12	Shares Outstanding (M)	295.7

Value of $10,000 invested five years ago: **$ 15,269**

Dividend Data Dividends have been paid since 1933

Amount ($)	Date Decl.	Ex-Div. Date	Stock of Record	Payment Date
0.240	Feb. 11	Mar. 29	Mar. 31	Apr. 19 '04
0.240	May. 07	Jun. 28	Jun. 30	Jul. 19 '04
0.280	Aug. 06	Sep. 28	Sep. 30	Oct. 18 '04
0.280	Oct. 29	Dec. 29	Dec. 31	Jan. 24 '05

Revenues/Earnings Data Fiscal year ending December 31

Revenues (Million $)

	2004	2003	2002	2001	2000	1999
1Q	2,710	2,314	2,205	2,296	2,405	1,474
2Q	3,002	2,564	2,435	2,420	2,577	1,624
3Q	2,967	2,532	2,401	2,301	2,472	1,594
4Q	—	2,626	2,427	2,278	2,529	2,487
Yr.	—	10,036	9,468	9,293	9,984	9,333

Earnings Per Share ($)

	2004	2003	2002	2001	2000	1999
1Q	0.93	0.65	0.63	0.60	0.72	0.65
2Q	1.16	0.92	0.86	0.76	0.90	0.79
3Q	1.09	0.87	0.79	0.65	0.87	0.74
4Q	E1.16	0.93	0.74	0.61	0.66	0.59
Yr.	E4.34	3.37	3.02	2.62	3.15	2.76

Next earnings report expected: late-January Source: S&P, Company Reports
EPS Estimates based on S&P Operating Earnings; historical GAAP earnings are as reported.

Illinois Tool Works Inc.

Recommendation: HOLD ★ ★ ★ ☆ ☆   12-Month Target Price: **$92.00** (as of August 25, 2004)

Business Summary October 20, 2004

A key strategy of Illinois Tool Works, a worldwide manufacturer of highly engineered products and specialty systems, is its continuous focus on an 80/20 simplification process. The basic concept of this philosophy is to emphasize what is most important (the 20% of the items that account for 80% of value) and to spend less time and resources on the less important (the 80% of items that account for 20% of value).

ITW operates more than 600 small industrial businesses in a highly decentralized structure that places responsibility on managers at the lowest level possible, in order to focus each business unit on the needs of its particular customers. Each business unit manager is responsible, and is held strictly accountable, for the results of his or her individual business.

The company grows by developing new products, and has made a number of acquisitions of small to mid-sized businesses. Since 1999, ITW has completed 127 acquisitions, totaling nearly $5.6 billion of acquired revenues.

ITW is diversified not only by customer and industry, but also by geographic region, with about 35% of revenues and 25% of operating profits derived overseas.

The Specialty Systems segment (50% of revenues in 2003, and 47% of operating income; 14% operating profit margins) produces longer lead time systems and related consumables for consumer and industrial packaging; marking, labeling and identification systems; industrial spray coating equipment and systems; and quality assurance equipment and systems. Important markets are food retail and service, general industrial, food and beverage, construction, and industrial capital goods. International sales and profits accounted for 37% and 28% of 2003 Specialty Systems revenues and earnings, respectively.

The Engineered Products segment (48%, 46%; 16% operating profit margins in 2003) produces short lead time plastic and metal components, fasteners and assemblies, industrial fluids and adhesives, fastening tools, and welding products. The largest markets served are construction, automotive, general industrial, consumer durables and electronics. International sales and profits accounted for 38% and 35% of 2003 Engineered Products revenues and earnings, respectively.

The company's small leasing and investment segment accounted for 2% of revenues and 7% of operating profits in 2003. The unit is highly profitable; in 2003, it generated 77% profit margins. The segment's investment portfolio consists of about $1.3 billion worth of primarily commercial mortgage loans and real estate, equipment leasing, affordable housing and property development. In 2001, the segment entered the aircraft leasing business, with the purchase and subsequent leasing of a Boeing 777 to a major airline.

In late 2001, ITW classified its Consumer Products (CP) division as discontinued. The segment was made up of companies that make small electric appliances, physical fitness equipment, and ceramic tile. At the end of 2003, the tile business was the only remaining entity that needed to be divested.

Company Financials Fiscal Year ending December 31

Per Share Data ($)

(Year Ended December 31)	2003	2002	2001	2000	1999	1998	1997	1996	1995	1994
Tangible Bk. Val.	16.43	13.79	10.83	9.64	9.27	8.59	8.14	6.80	5.66	4.73
Cash Flow	4.36	4.02	3.88	4.50	3.89	3.50	3.07	2.69	2.29	1.81
Earnings	3.37	3.02	2.62	3.15	2.76	2.67	2.33	1.97	1.65	1.23
S&P Core Earnings	3.26	2.76	2.25	NA	NA	NA	NA	NA	NA	NA
Dividends	0.94	0.90	0.84	0.76	0.68	0.51	0.46	0.36	0.32	0.35
Payout Ratio	28%	30%	32%	24%	25%	19%	20%	18%	19%	28%
Prices - High	84.70	77.80	71.99	69.00	82.00	73.18	60.12	43.62	32.75	22.75
- Low	54.56	55.03	49.15	49.50	58.12	45.18	37.37	25.93	19.87	18.50
P/E Ratio - High	25	26	27	22	30	27	26	22	20	19
- Low	16	18	19	16	21	17	16	13	12	15

Income Statement Analysis (Million $)

	2003	2002	2001	2000	1999	1998	1997	1996	1995	1994
Revs.	10,036	9,468	9,293	9,984	9,333	5,648	5,220	4,997	4,152	3,461
Oper. Inc.	1,940	1,812	1,692	1,977	1,830	1,291	1,113	979	785	624
Depr.	307	306	386	413	343	212	185	178	152	132
Int. Exp.	70.7	68.5	68.1	72.4	67.5	14.2	19.4	27.8	31.6	26.9
Pretax Inc.	1,576	1,434	1,231	1,478	1,353	1,060	924	770	624	450
Eff. Tax Rate	34.0%	35.0%	34.8%	35.2%	37.8%	36.5%	36.5%	36.8%	37.9%	38.3%
Net Inc.	1,040	932	802	958	841	673	587	486	388	278
S&P Core Earnings	1,009	851	691	NA	NA	NA	NA	NA	NA	NA

Balance Sheet & Other Fin. Data (Million $)

	2003	2002	2001	2000	1999	1998	1997	1996	1995	1994
Cash	1,684	1,058	282	151	233	93.5	186	138	117	76.9
Curr. Assets	4,783	3,879	3,163	3,329	3,273	1,834	1,859	1,701	1,532	1,263
Total Assets	11,193	10,623	9,822	9,603	9,060	6,118	5,395	4,806	3,613	2,580
Curr. Liab.	1,489	1,567	1,518	1,818	2,045	1,222	1,158	1,219	851	628
LT Debt	920	1,460	1,267	1,549	1,361	947	854	819	616	273
Common Equity	7,874	6,649	6,041	5,401	4,815	3,338	2,806	2,396	1,924	1,542
Total Cap.	8,795	8,109	7,308	6,950	6,176	4,285	3,660	3,215	2,540	1,884
Cap. Exp.	258	271	257	314	336	208	179	169	150	131
Cash Flow	1,347	1,238	1,189	1,371	1,184	885	772	665	540	410
Curr. Ratio	3.2	2.5	2.1	1.8	1.6	1.5	1.6	1.4	1.8	2.0
% LT Debt of Cap.	10.5	18.0	17.3	22.3	22.0	22.1	23.3	25.4	24.2	14.5
% Net Inc.of Revs.	10.4	9.8	8.6	9.6	9.0	11.9	11.3	9.7	9.3	8.0
% Ret. on Assets	9.5	9.1	8.3	10.3	9.7	11.7	11.5	11.6	12.5	11.3
% Ret. on Equity	14.3	14.7	14.0	18.8	18.6	21.9	22.6	22.5	22.4	19.8

Data as orig reptd.; bef. results of disc opers/spec. items. Per share data adj. for stk. divs.; EPS diluted. E-Estimated. NA-Not Available. NM-Not Meaningful. NR-Not Ranked. UR-Under Review.

Office: 3600 W. Lake Avenue, Glenview, IL 60025-5811.
Telephone: 847-724-7500.
Website: http://www.itwinc.com
Chrmn & CEO: W.J. Farrell.
SVP & CFO: J.C. Kinney.

SVP, Secy & General Counsel: S.S. Hudnut.
VP & Investor Contact: J. Brooklier 847-657-4104.
Dirs: W. F. Aldinger, M. J. Birck, M. D. Brailsford, J. R. Cantalupo, S. Crown, D. H. Davis, W. J. Farrell, R. C. McCormack, R. S. Morrison, H. B. Smith.

Founded: in 1912.
Domicile: Delaware.
Employees: 47,500.
S&P Analyst: Anthony M. Fiore, CFA /CB/JWP

Recommendation: SELL ★ ★ ★ ★ ★
SELL SELL HOLD BUY BUY

12-Month Target Price: $18.00
(as of October 20, 2004)

RX has an approximate 0.05% weighting in the **S&P 500**

Sector: Health Care
Sub-Industry: Health Care Services
Peer Group: Information Technology

Summary: RX integrates information systems, technology and services for the pharmaceutical and health care industries.

Quantitative Evaluations

Price as of 11/12/04: $22.71 | **2004E S&P Core EPS:** $1.06

S&P Earnings & Dividend Rank: NR

D	C	B-	B	B+	A-	A	A+

S&P Fair Value Rank: 4+

1	2	3	4	5
Lowest				Highest

Fair Value Calc.: $24.10 (Slightly Undervalued)

S&P Investability Quotient Percentile

80%

RX scored higher than 80% of all companies for which an S&P Report is available.

Volatility: Average

Low	Average	High

Technical Evaluation: Bearish

Since 10/04, the technical indicators for RX have been Bearish.

Relative Strength Rank: Weak

26

1 Lowest	Highest 99

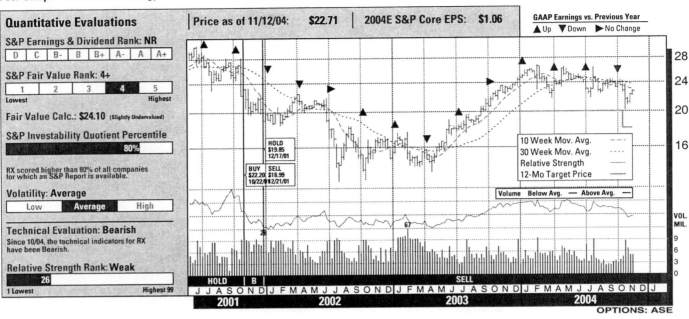

GAAP Earnings vs. Previous Year
▲ Up ▼ Down ▶ No Change

- 10 Week Mov. Avg. — —
- 30 Week Mov. Avg. ....
- Relative Strength
- 12-Mo Target Price

Volume Below Avg. — Above Avg.

HOLD $19.85 12/17/01
BUY $22.20 10/22/01 SELL $18.99 12/21/01

OPTIONS: ASE

Analyst commentary prepared by Michael W. Jaffe/PMW/JWP

Highlights September 15, 2004

- We expect revenues to increase 10% in 2004, from a base that reflects the absence of revenues from Cognizant Technology Solutions. We see a gain of 8% in 2005. We expect revenues in each year to benefit from a small pickup in demand. We think RX's aggressive program of new product introductions will aid revenues, despite sluggish industry conditions. In our view, many large U.S. drug companies need to hold down spending because of patent protection losses and weak pipelines. Nevertheless, we think RX will experience additional demand, as it seeks to design new products to boost the performance of its client base. We also expect revenues to benefit from positive foreign exchange effects in 2004.

- We project flat net margins in 2004 and 2005. We expect the modest pickup in demand that we forecast for RX's services, together with cost-cutting initiatives, to be offset by new product introduction costs. EPS before one-time items totaled $1.05 in 2003; our forecast of $1.15 for 2004 excludes $0.07 a share of net one-time credits included in the Earnings Per Share table.

- Our 2004 and 2005 S&P Core Earnings forecasts are $0.09 and $0.12 a share, respectively, below our operating estimates, reflecting our projections of stock option and pension expenses, and investment transactions.

Investment Rationale/Risk September 15, 2004

- We would avoid the shares. We think that RX has been facing weaker business trends in its client base, as sales growth has slowed at many pharmaceutical companies. We view favorably its efforts to develop new products to address current issues in the pharmaceutical area, but we see the drug sector's likely need to hold down spending as a significant negative factor. We think these conditions will persist at least for a few years. Combined with our relative P/E analysis, we believe the shares are overvalued.

- Risks to our recommendation and target price include stronger than anticipated pharmaceutical trends, with resulting higher spending by the industry.

- The stock traded recently at over 19X our 2005 EPS forecast, below its historical norm, but well above the level of the S&P 500. Based on our expectations of limited EPS growth for the next few years, we think the shares deserve a P/E multiple no higher than that of the S&P 500. Our 12-month target price of $20 is equal to 16X our 2005 EPS forecast.

Key Stock Statistics

S&P Core EPS 2005E	1.13	52-week Range	$26.80-20.16
S&P Oper. EPS 2004E	1.15	12 Month P/E	19.4
P/E on S&P Oper. EPS 2004E	19.7	Beta	0.55
S&P Oper. EPS 2005E	1.25	Shareholders	5,800
Yield (%)	0.4%	Market Cap (B)	$ 5.3
Dividend Rate/Share	0.08	Shares Outstanding (M)	232.0

Value of $10,000 invested five years ago: **NA**

Dividend Data Dividends have been paid since 1997

Amount ($)	Date Decl.	Ex-Div. Date	Stock of Record	Payment Date
0.020	Feb. 10	Feb. 20	Feb. 24	Mar. 30 '04
0.020	Apr. 20	Apr. 30	May. 04	Jun. 11 '04
0.020	Jul. 20	Jul. 30	Aug. 03	Sep. 10 '04
0.020	Oct. 19	Oct. 29	Nov. 02	Dec. 10 '04

Revenues/Earnings Data Fiscal year ending December 31

Revenues (Million $)

	2004	2003	2002	2001	2000	1999
1Q	361.6	313.9	331.6	329.6	352.5	313.2
2Q	379.6	337.8	353.1	334.4	369.4	332.6
3Q	384.2	346.0	361.8	328.1	355.9	348.4
4Q	—	384.1	381.9	340.9	346.5	403.7
Yr.	—	1,382	1,428	1,333	1,424	1,398

Earnings Per Share ($)

	2004	2003	2002	2001	2000	1999
1Q	0.34	-0.20	0.20	0.22	0.27	0.13
2Q	0.27	0.23	0.21	0.21	0.17	0.15
3Q	0.28	0.29	0.29	0.14	-0.20	0.22
4Q	E0.31	0.28	0.22	-0.11	0.14	0.28
Yr.	E1.15	0.56	0.93	0.46	0.39	0.78

Next earnings report expected: mid-February Source: S&P, Company Reports
EPS Estimates based on S&P Operating Earnings; historical GAAP earnings are as reported.

IMS Health Inc.

Recommendation: **SELL**    12-Month Target Price: **$18.00** (as of October 20, 2004)

Business Summary September 15, 2004

IMS Health is a leading provider of information solutions to the pharmaceutical and health care industries, with operations in more than 100 countries. The company was spun off in 1998 from Cognizant Corp. (now Nielsen Media Research). RX derived 61% of its revenues in 2003 from foreign operations; no single customer accounted for over 10% of revenues in any of the past three years. In February 2003, the company completed an exchange offer to distribute its majority interest in Cognizant Technologies Solutions, and began to operate solely through its IMS segment.

IMS provides information and decision support services to the pharmaceutical and health care industry worldwide, including sales management services (60% of revenues in 2003), market research services (36%), and professional consulting and research and development services (4%). The company also has a venture capital unit, Enterprise Associates, that invests in emerging businesses, primarily in the areas of information technology and health care information; and a 26% interest in TriZetto Group, an information technology and services company that focuses on health care.

The company's sales management services are used principally by pharmaceutical manufacturers to measure and forecast the effectiveness and efficiency of sales representatives, and to focus sales and marketing efforts. They include sales territory reports, prescription tracking reports, and self-medication services. RX's principal market research services consist of multinational integrated analytical tools, and syndicated pharmaceutical, medical, hospital, promotional and prescription audits. Clients use these services for strategic purposes that include

market share analysis, therapeutic prescribing trends, and price movements. The information reported in RX's market research services is generated or derived from data collected primarily from pharmaceutical manufacturers, pharmaceutical wholesalers, pharmacies, hospitals and doctors.

In February 2003, RX accepted 36.5 million shares tendered under an exchange offer for its 55% interest in Cognizant Technologies Solutions (CTS; 15% of revenues in 2002). It recognized a net gain from discontinued operations of $496.9 million ($2.01 a share) in the 2003 first quarter. CTS provides software development and maintenance services for companies making a transition to e-business. A major part of CTS's revenues are derived from services performed for RX.

In the 2003 first quarter, the company recorded $44.6 million of pretax charges, related primarily to severance, impairment, and other items, and a $14.8 million after-tax impairment charge on its equity investment in TriZetto Group.

In the 2002 fourth quarter, RX recorded a net charge of $26.3 million, for impairment charges and equity losses related to its 26% interest in TriZetto Group. It also recorded $19.1 million of pretax gains for the year (net of charges) for other unusual items.

RX repurchased 8.1 million common shares for a total of $204.3 million in the 2004 first half. It bought back 9.6 million shares in 2003, for $184.2 million; and 14.2 million shares in 2002, for $267.4 million.

Company Financials Fiscal Year ending December 31

Per Share Data ($)

(Year Ended December 31)	2003	2002	2001	2000	1999	1998	1997	1996	1995	1994
Tangible Bk. Val.	NM	0.13	0.24	NM	0.51	1.45	2.21	1.84	1.72	NA
Cash Flow	0.87	1.14	0.69	0.69	1.10	0.82	1.28	0.97	0.66	NA
Earnings	0.56	0.93	0.46	0.39	0.78	0.53	1.40	0.74	0.26	NA
S&P Core Earnings	0.47	0.82	0.52	NA	NA	NA	NA	NA	NA	NA
Dividends	0.08	0.08	0.08	0.08	0.08	0.06	0.06	Nil	NA	NA
Payout Ratio	14%	9%	17%	21%	10%	11%	4%	Nil	NA	NA
Prices - High	25.07	22.59	30.50	28.68	39.18	38.46	22.75	19.00	NA	NA
- Low	13.68	12.90	17.30	14.25	21.50	21.34	14.00	15.25	NA	NA
P/E Ratio - High	45	24	66	74	50	73	16	26	NA	NA
- Low	24	14	38	37	28	40	10	21	NA	NA

Income Statement Analysis (Million $)

	2003	2002	2001	2000	1999	1998	1997	1996	1995	1994
Revs.	1,382	1,428	1,333	1,424	1,398	1,187	1,418	1,731	1,542	NA
Oper. Inc.	437	510	494	459	439	310	453	477	300	NA
Depr.	75.1	61.8	69.2	92.0	100	96.4	117	134	133	NA
Int. Exp.	15.4	14.4	18.1	17.6	7.59	1.17	2.29	1.34	0.54	NA
Pretax Inc.	305	397	177	257	152	271	430	349	163	NA
Eff. Tax Rate	54.4%	32.9%	21.7%	54.7%	NM	34.1%	27.4%	44.0%	45.3%	NA
Net Inc.	139	266	138	116	250	178	312	195	88.9	NA
S&P Core Earnings	116	236	155	NA	NA	NA	NA	NA	NA	NA

Balance Sheet & Other Fin. Data (Million $)

	2003	2002	2001	2000	1999	1998	1997	1996	1995	1994
Cash	385	415	268	119	116	206	318	429	545	NA
Curr. Assets	779	827	657	569	607	634	694	994	NA	NA
Total Assets	1,644	1,619	1,368	1,243	1,451	1,732	1,580	1,875	NA	NA
Curr. Liab.	837	679	635	827	723	550	441	680	NA	NA
LT Debt	152	325	150	Nil	Nil	Nil	Nil	Nil	65.5	NA
Common Equity	190	222	218	147	494	825	802	873	799	NA
Total Cap.	443	727	513	282	619	972	915	978	865	NA
Cap. Exp.	23.7	44.4	34.3	33.4	33.0	30.9	72.0	75.0	77.0	NA
Cash Flow	214	328	208	208	351	275	430	329	221	NA
Curr. Ratio	0.9	1.2	1.0	0.7	0.8	1.2	1.6	1.5	NA	NA
% LT Debt of Cap.	34.3	44.7	29.2	Nil	Nil	Nil	Nil	Nil	7.6	NA
% Net Inc.of Revs.	10.1	18.6	10.4	8.2	17.9	15.0	22.0	11.3	5.8	NA
% Ret. on Assets	8.5	17.8	10.3	8.7	15.8	11.0	18.1	11.8	NA	NA
% Ret. on Equity	67.6	120.8	86.0	34.7	38.0	21.9	37.3	26.5	NA	NA

Data as orig reptd.; bef. results of disc opers/spec. items. Per share data adj. for stk. divs.; EPS diluted. E-Estimated. NA-Not Available. NM-Not Meaningful. NR-Not Ranked. UR-Under Review.

Office: 1499 Post Road, Fairfield, CT 06430.
Telephone: 203-319-4700.
Website: http://www.imshealth.com
Chrmn & CEO: D.M. Thomas.
Pres & COO: D.R. Carlucci.
SVP & CFO: N. Cooper.

SVP, Secy & General Counsel: R.H. Steinfeld.
VP & Chief Acctg Officer: L.G. Katz.
VP & Investor Contact: D.R. Peck 203-319-4766.
Dirs: C. Clemente, J. D. Edwards, K. E. Giusti, J. P. Imlay, Jr., R. Kamerschen, H. E. Lockhart, M. B. Puckett, D. M. Thomas, W. C. Van Faasen.

Founded: in 1998.
Domicile: Delaware.
Employees: 6,000.
S&P Analyst: Michael W. Jaffe/PMW/JWP

Ingersoll-Rand

Recommendation: **BUY** ★★★★
SELL SELL HOLD BUY BUY

12-Month Target Price: **$90.00**
(as of October 21, 2004)

IR has an approximate 0.12% weighting in the **S&P 500**

Sector: Industrials
Sub-Industry: Industrial Machinery
Peer Group: Industrial Equipment

Summary: This industrial conglomerate primarily makes a wide range of construction and commercial refrigeration equipment.

Quantitative Evaluations

S&P Earnings & Dividend Rank: A

| D | C | B- | B | B+ | A- | A | A+ |

S&P Fair Value Rank: 3-

| 1 | 2 | 3 | 4 | 5 |
Lowest — Highest

Fair Value Calc.: $71.40 (Slightly Overvalued)

S&P Investability Quotient Percentile

100%

IR scored higher than 100% of all companies for which an S&P Report is available.

Volatility: Average

| Low | Average | High |

Technical Evaluation: Bullish
Since 9/04, the technical indicators for IR have been Bullish.

Relative Strength Rank: Strong

72

1 Lowest — Highest 99

| Price as of 11/12/04: | $74.58 | 2004E S&P Core EPS: | $4.32 |

GAAP Earnings vs. Previous Year
▲ Up ▼ Down ▶ No Change

BUY
$71.47
01/26/04

10 Week Mov. Avg.
30 Week Mov. Avg.
Relative Strength
12-Mo Target Price

Volume Below Avg. — Above Avg. —

VOL. MIL.

J J A S O N D J F M A M J J A S O N D J F M A M J J A S O N D J F M A M J J A S O N D J
2001 2002 2003 2004

HOLD BUY

OPTIONS: ASE, CBOE, Ph

Analyst commentary prepared by John F. Hingher, CFA /PMW/BK

Highlights October 22, 2004

- We think a combination of new product introductions, continued strong growth in the security and safety business, solid demand from construction equipment and truck markets, and expansion of IR's services businesses will lead to organic revenue growth of 4% to 6% in each of 2004 and 2005. We see total revenue growth from continued operations likely to be boosted by acquisitions, with advances of 12% in 2004 and 8% to 10% in 2005.

- Combining expected increased sales with benefits anticipated from restructuring actions implemented in 2001 and 2002, we see operating margins, which dropped to a 10-year low of 7.2% in 2001, continuing to rebound. Interest expense should decline, due to lower overall debt levels, although a rising interest rate environment could partially offset this.

- We expect EPS to grow about 45% in 2004, to $4.85, and another 13% in 2005, to $5.50, excluding one-time items. On a Standard & Poor's Core Earnings basis, we see 2004 EPS of $4.32, 11% below our operating EPS projection, reflecting adjustments for pension gains and stock option expense. Our 2005 S&P Core EPS estimate is $5.06.

Investment Rationale/Risk October 22, 2004

- We continue to recommend buying the shares, based in part on what we see as an improving macroeconomic environment, our expectations of further growth in several key end markets, and valuation. In our view, recent momentum in capital spending should accelerate in 2004 and 2005, particularly in construction equipment, and we see this boding well for the company's business prospects.

- Risks to our opinion and target price include slower than expected growth due to a rising interest rate environment; a deceleration in capital spending in construction equipment; and rising prices for key inputs, including steel, oil, and natural gas.

- Our discounted cash flow model, which values the stock by adding the sum of estimated free cash flow growing at 9% a year for the next 10 years and at 3.5% thereafter, suggests that the stock is undervalued. In addition, the shares recently traded at 13X our forward 12-month EPS estimate of $5.12, below their historical 10-year average, and below the peer average of 16X. Blending these methods leads to our 12-month target price of $90.

Key Stock Statistics

S&P Core EPS 2005E	5.06	52-week Range	$74.73-57.50
S&P Oper. EPS 2004E	4.85	12 Month P/E	14.5
P/E on S&P Oper. EPS 2004E	15.4	Beta	1.36
S&P Oper. EPS 2005E	5.50	Shareholders	7,971
Yield (%)	1.3%	Market Cap (B)	$ 12.9
Dividend Rate/Share	1.00	Shares Outstanding (M)	173.3

Value of $10,000 invested five years ago: **$ 16,983**

Dividend Data Dividends have been paid since 1910

Amount ($)	Date Decl.	Ex-Div. Date	Stock of Record	Payment Date
0.190	Feb. 05	Feb. 12	Feb. 17	Mar. 01 '04
0.190	Apr. 08	May. 13	May. 17	Jun. 01 '04
0.250	Aug. 04	Aug. 13	Aug. 17	Sep. 01 '04
0.250	Oct. 04	Nov. 10	Nov. 15	Dec. 01 '04

Revenues/Earnings Data Fiscal year ending December 31

Revenues (Million $)

	2004	2003	2002	2001	2000	1999
1Q	2,292	2,182	2,017	2,120	2,020	2,083
2Q	2,714	2,509	2,666	2,286	2,232	2,249
3Q	2,368	2,520	2,223	2,383	2,301	1,846
4Q	—	2,666	2,245	2,557	2,244	1,888
Yr.	—	9,876	8,951	9,682	8,798	7,661

Earnings Per Share ($)

	2004	2003	2002	2001	2000	1999
1Q	0.94	0.55	0.26	0.31	0.85	0.73
2Q	1.43	0.89	0.63	0.38	1.13	0.99
3Q	1.18	0.88	0.53	0.20	0.80	0.80
4Q	E1.18	1.11	0.74	0.59	0.66	0.86
Yr.	E4.85	3.44	2.16	1.48	3.36	3.29

Next earnings report expected: late-January Source: S&P, Company Reports
EPS Estimates based on S&P Operating Earnings; historical GAAP earnings are as reported.

Ingersoll-Rand Company Limited

Recommendation: **BUY** ★★★★★   12-Month Target Price: **$90.00** (as of October 21, 2004)

Business Summary October 25, 2004

Ingersoll-Rand traces its roots to the merger of the Ingersoll-Sergeant Drill Co. and the Rand Drill Co. in the early 1870s. The company has grown over the years, becoming a leading global provider of climate control, industrial solutions, infrastructure development, and security and safety products. Revenues by geographic region in 2003 were as follows: North America 62%; Europe 25%; Asia Pacific 10%; and Latin America 3%.

The Climate Control segment (27% of 2003 revenue; 22% of operating profit; 8.3% margin) makes transport temperature control units, HVAC systems, refrigerated display merchandisers, beverage coolers, and walk-in storage coolers and freezers. Its brand names include Hussmann and Thermo-King, and Zexel brand industrial refrigeration equipment. Thermo-King is the world's largest maker of commercial refrigeration equipment used in truck trailers, seagoing containers, and railcars. Hussmann is one of the world's largest makers of refrigerated supermarket displays.

The Industrial Solutions segment (27%; 15%; 5.5%) comprises a diverse group of businesses that focus on providing solutions to enhance customer industrial efficiency. The segment includes two divisions: Air and Productivity Solutions, and Dresser-Rand. Air and Productivity Solutions (14% of sales and 10% of operating profits in 2003; 7.6% margins) makes air compressors, fluid products, microturbines, and industrial tools. Dresser-Rand (14%; 4%; 3.3%) makes gas compressors, gas and steam turbines, and generators. A third division that had been included in the Industrial Solutions segment, Engineered Solutions, was sold to The Timken Co. in February 2003, for $840 million.

The Infrastructure segment (30%; 32%; 10.8%) primarily makes skid steer loaders, mini-excavators, electric and gasoline powered golf and utility vehicles, portable compressors and light towers, road construction and repair equipment, and a broad line of drills and drill accessories.

The Security and Safety segment (16%; 32%; 20%) makes doors and locks for the commercial and do-it-yourself markets. The segment makes products that include Schlage locks, door control hardware, and steel and power-operated doors.

In 2002, the company acquired 10 entities, for a total of about $113 million in cash. Also in 2002, IR expanded its Industrial Solutions segment to include Dresser-Rand; aggregated its tools and related production equipment operations (formerly part of the Industrial Products segment) in the Air and Productivity Solutions segment; and added Club Car to the Infrastructure segment.

In February 2004, IR agreed to sell its Drilling Solutions business to Atlas Copco AB of Sweden, for about $225 million, subject to government regulatory approvals. The Drilling Solutions business generated sales of about $300 million in 2003.

Company Financials Fiscal Year ending December 31

Per Share Data ($)

(Year Ended December 31)	2003	2002	2001	2000	1999	1998	1997	1996	1995	1994
Tangible Bk. Val.	NM	NM	NM	NM	NM	NM	NM	5.56	3.32	8.89
Cash Flow	4.57	3.37	3.66	5.19	4.93	4.78	3.60	3.48	2.83	2.17
Earnings	3.44	2.16	1.48	3.36	3.29	3.08	2.31	2.22	1.70	1.33
S&P Core Earnings	3.37	1.24	0.48	NA	NA	NA	NA	NA	NA	NA
Dividends	0.72	0.68	0.68	0.68	0.64	0.60	0.57	0.52	0.49	0.48
Payout Ratio	21%	31%	46%	20%	19%	19%	25%	23%	29%	36%
Prices - High	68.19	54.40	50.28	57.75	73.81	54.00	46.25	31.75	28.25	27.75
- Low	34.52	29.69	30.40	29.50	44.62	34.00	27.83	23.41	18.91	19.66
P/E Ratio - High	20	25	34	17	22	18	20	14	17	21
- Low	10	14	21	9	14	11	12	11	11	15

Income Statement Analysis (Million $)

	2003	2002	2001	2000	1999	1998	1997	1996	1995	1994
Revs.	9,876	8,951	9,682	8,798	7,667	8,292	7,103	6,703	5,729	4,507
Oper. Inc.	1,061	891	979	1,488	1,372	1,327	973	886	676	510
Depr.	194	206	363	297	272	283	212	203	179	133
Int. Exp.	177	230	253	254	203	226	140	120	90.0	47.0
Pretax Inc.	703	402	263	869	874	843	614	568	429	343
Eff. Tax Rate	13.4%	5.05%	NM	32.6%	34.3%	33.2%	38.0%	37.0%	37.0%	34.6%
Net Inc.	594	367	246	546	545	509	381	358	270	211
S&P Core Earnings	583	213	78.0	NA	NA	NA	NA	NA	NA	NA

Balance Sheet & Other Fin. Data (Million $)

	2003	2002	2001	2000	1999	1998	1997	1996	1995	1994
Cash	460	342	121	200	223	77.6	112	192	147	211
Curr. Assets	3,539	4,112	3,188	3,323	2,868	2,428	2,545	2,536	2,346	2,003
Total Assets	10,665	10,810	11,064	10,529	8,400	8,310	8,416	5,622	5,563	3,597
Curr. Liab.	3,053	3,798	2,851	3,967	1,739	1,849	2,328	1,290	1,329	1,040
LT Debt	1,519	2,092	2,901	1,943	2,516	2,569	2,528	1,164	1,304	316
Common Equity	4,493	3,478	3,917	3,495	3,083	2,708	2,341	2,091	1,796	1,531
Total Cap.	6,133	5,685	7,098	5,548	5,695	5,410	4,997	3,368	3,271	2,001
Cap. Exp.	108	123	201	187	191	14.5	186	195	212	159
Cash Flow	788	573	609	843	817	792	593	561	450	344
Curr. Ratio	1.2	1.1	1.1	0.8	1.6	1.3	1.1	2.0	1.8	1.9
% LT Debt of Cap.	24.8	36.8	40.9	35.0	44.2	47.5	50.5	34.5	39.9	15.8
% Net Inc.of Revs.	6.0	4.1	2.5	6.2	7.1	6.1	5.4	5.3	4.7	4.7
% Ret. on Assets	5.5	3.3	2.2	5.8	6.7	6.1	5.4	6.4	5.9	6.1
% Ret. on Equity	14.9	9.9	6.7	16.6	18.7	20.2	17.2	18.4	16.2	14.6

Data as orig reptd.; bef. results of disc opers/spec. items. Per share data adj. for stk. divs. Bold denotes primary EPS - prior periods restated. E-Estimated. NA-Not Available. NM-Not Meaningful. NR-Not Ranked. UR-Under Review.

Office: Clarendon House, Hamilton HM 11, Bermuda.
Telephone: 441-295-2838.
Email: seekinfo@irco.com
Website: http://www.irco.com
Chrmn, Pres & CEO: H.L. Henkel.
SVP & CFO: T.R. McLevish.
SVP & General Counsel: P. Nachtigal.

VP & Treas: B.L. Brasier.
VP & Secy: R.G. Heller.
Investor Contact: J. Fimbianti 201-573-3113.
Dirs: A. C. Berzin, G. W. Buckley, P. C. Godsoe, H. L. Henkel, C. J. Horner, H. W. Lichtenberger, T. E. Martin, P. Nachtigal, O. R. Smith, R. J. Swift, T. L. White.

Founded: in 1905.
Domicile: Bermuda.
Employees: 42,000.
S&P Analyst: John F. Hingher, CFA /PMW/BK

Intel Corp.

Recommendation: **HOLD** ★★★☆☆
SELL | SELL | HOLD | BUY | BUY

12-Month Target Price: **$27.00**
(as of November 18, 2004)

INTC has an approximate 1.42% weighting in the **S&P 500**

Sector: Information Technology
Sub-Industry: Semiconductors
Peer Group: Semiconductors - Logic - Larger Cos.

Summary: INTC is the world's largest manufacturer of microprocessors, the central processing units of PCs, and also produces other products that enhance PC capabilities.

Quantitative Evaluations

S&P Earnings & Dividend Rank: A

D | C | B- | B | B+ | A- | **A** | A+

S&P Fair Value Rank: 3+

1 | 2 | **3** | 4 | 5
Lowest | | | | Highest

Fair Value Calc.: $22.90 (Slightly Overvalued)

S&P Investability Quotient Percentile

97%

INTC scored higher than 97% of all companies for which an S&P Report is available.

Volatility: Average

Low | **Average** | High

Technical Evaluation: Bullish
Since 10/04, the technical indicators for INTC have been Bullish.

Relative Strength Rank: Strong

73

1 Lowest | Highest 99

Price as of 11/17/04: $24.32 | **2004E S&P Core EPS:** $0.93

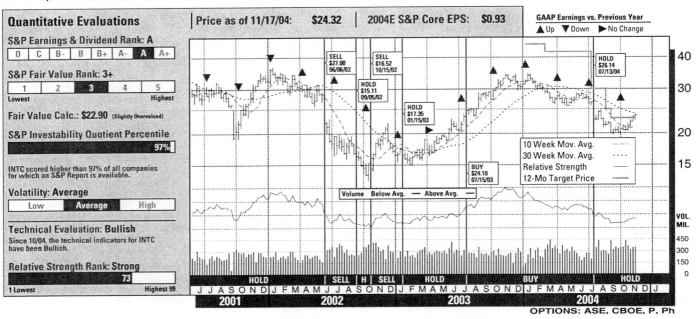

GAAP Earnings vs. Previous Year
▲ Up ▼ Down ► No Change

- 10 Week Mov. Avg.
- 30 Week Mov. Avg.
- Relative Strength
- 12-Mo Target Price

Volume Below Avg. — Above Avg.

OPTIONS: ASE, CBOE, P, Ph

Analyst commentary prepared by Amrit Tewary/PMW/GG

Highlights October 14, 2004

- We expect revenues to increase 11% in 2004 and about 7% in 2005. Processor unit shipments have been solid since last summer, and we believe the company is recapturing market share in flash memory that it lost in early 2003 after it raised prices.

- We see efforts to establish wireless functionality as a standard feature for notebook computers promoting a shift to higher-end semiconductor products that carry wide margins. We also see aggressive adoption of modern 300 mm wafer fabrication plants and leading edge 90 nanometer linewidth production techniques contributing to lower production costs per chip. However, we are concerned about a weaker gross margin outlook in recent months, as growing chip inventories, resulting from higher than expected factory yields of good die per wafer, prompted a slowing of production. In addition, flash memories have narrower margins than processors, so that rapid growth in that segment may dilute overall margins. We expect gross margins to widen to 57.8% in 2004 and 59.0% in 2005, from 56.7% in 2003, as higher volume runs lead to greater plant efficiency.

- We estimate EPS of $1.10 for 2004 and $1.25 for 2005. We forecast S&P Core EPS of $0.93 for 2004 and $1.07 for 2005, reflecting estimated stock option expense.

Investment Rationale/Risk October 14, 2004

- We believe INTC's scale-based strengths in R&D, manufacturing and marketing should help it prosper in a multi-year semiconductor industry expansion that we expect to gain traction in 2004 and endure through 2005. Ironically, strength in production execution in the 2004 first half has led to high die yields and an inventory buildup that we think will take a quarter or two to clear up.

- Risks to our recommendation and target price include fluctuations in demand for PCs; semiconductor industry cyclicality; increased competition; risks of financing, maintaining and managing wafer fabrication plants; and above-average share price volatility.

- Our 12-month target price of $23 is based on our P/E multiple model, and applies a below-historical-norm P/E multiple of 18X to our 2005 EPS estimate of $1.25. Our target price implies a price to sales ratio of 4.2X based on our 2005 sales per share estimate, also below historical norms. Historically, chip stocks have traded at discount multiples during peak or near-peak EPS years.

Key Stock Statistics

S&P Core EPS 2005E	1.07	52-week Range	$34.60-19.64
S&P Oper. EPS 2004E	1.10	12 Month P/E	21.3
P/E on S&P Oper. EPS 2004E	21.5	Beta	2.16
S&P Oper. EPS 2005E	1.25	Shareholders	235,000
Yield (%)	1.3%	Market Cap (B)	$156.0
Dividend Rate/Share	0.32	Shares Outstanding (M)	6415.0

Value of $10,000 invested five years ago: **$ 6,329**

Dividend Data Dividends have been paid since 1992

Amount ($)	Date Decl.	Ex-Div. Date	Stock of Record	Payment Date
0.040	Mar. 25	May. 05	May. 07	Jun. 01 '04
0.040	Jul. 21	Aug. 04	Aug. 07	Sep. 01 '04
0.040	Sep. 09	Nov. 03	Nov. 07	Dec. 01 '04
0.080	Nov. 10	Feb. 03	Feb. 07	Mar. 01 '05

Revenues/Earnings Data Fiscal year ending December 31

Revenues (Million $)

	2004	2003	2002	2001	2000	1999
1Q	8,091	6,751	6,781	6,677	7,993	7,103
2Q	8,049	6,816	6,319	6,334	8,300	6,746
3Q	8,471	7,833	6,504	6,545	8,731	7,328
4Q	—	8,741	7,160	6,983	8,702	8,212
Yr.	—	30,141	26,764	26,539	33,726	29,389

Earnings Per Share ($)

	2004	2003	2002	2001	2000	1999
1Q	0.26	0.14	0.14	0.07	0.39	0.29
2Q	0.27	0.14	0.07	0.03	0.45	0.21
3Q	0.30	0.25	0.10	0.02	0.36	0.21
4Q	E0.28	0.33	0.16	0.07	0.32	0.30
Yr.	E1.10	0.85	0.46	0.19	1.51	1.06

Next earnings report expected: mid-January Source: S&P, Company Reports
EPS Estimates based on S&P Operating Earnings; historical GAAP earnings are as reported.

STANDARD &POOR'S

Intel Corporation

Stock Report
November 18, 2004
NASDAQ Symbol: **INTC**

Recommendation: **HOLD** ★ ★ ★ ☆ ☆   12-Month Target Price: **$27.00** (as of November 18, 2004)

Business Summary October 14, 2004

Intel is the world's largest semiconductor chip maker. It is well known for its dominant market share, estimated at about 80%, in microprocessors for personal computers (PCs). Although the PC processor is a mainstay, INTC has expanded its product lines to serve the networking and communications markets. The company's stated mission is to be the preeminent building block supplier to the worldwide Internet economy, indicating ambitions beyond PCs.

The company's main operating groups are Intel Architecture Business (87% of total sales in 2003), Intel Communications (7%), and Wireless Communications and Computing (6%). In early 2004, the two communications groups were combined into a single segment, known as the Intel Communications Group.

The Intel Architecture Business Group works on microprocessor and chipset products for the desktop and mobile computing platforms, as well as high-performance microprocessors for servers and workstations. Intel introduced the first microprocessor in 1971, and has been the technology leader ever since.

INTC's highest volume desktop processor in 2003 was the Pentium 4 processor, running at speeds ranging from 2.4 GHZ to 3.2 GHZ. For the value PC market segment, the company offers the Celeron processor; several new versions offered in 2003 ran at 2.3 GHZ to 2.8 GHZ. Intel introduced over 30 new mobile processors in 2003. Centrino mobile technology, launched in March 2003, is a product set that combines the Pentium M processor, a chipset, and a wireless network connection

based on industry standard 802.11 wireless local area network (WLAN) technology. For the server and workstation segments, INTC offers the Xeon processor line. For high-end servers and workstations, the company offers the Itanium processor family.

The Communications Group makes wired Ethernet products, wireless connectivity products, and communications infrastructure products such as optical components, network processing components, and embedded control chips.

The Wireless Communications and Computing Group produces flash memory based on the NOR architecture, baseband chipsets, and processors for cellular handsets and handheld computing devices.

Sales are becoming more global. In 2003, revenues were derived 28% from North America, 40% from Asia-Pacific, 23% from Europe, and 9% from Japan. Dell accounted for 19% of 2003 sales, and Hewlett-Packard for 15%.

U.S. manufacturing and test facilities are located in New Mexico, Arizona, Oregon, Colorado, California and Massachusetts. Facilities in Israel and Ireland performed nearly 25% of wafer fabrication in 2003. INTC planned 2004 capital spending of $3.6 billion to $4 billion, versus $3.7 billion in 2003, and below the $4.7 billion spent in 2002 and $7.3 billion in 2001, a year that saw a commitment to next generation 300 mm wafer plants that aim to deliver 30% cost savings per die.

Company Financials Fiscal Year ending December 31

Per Share Data ($)

(Year Ended December 31)	2003	2002	2001	2000	1999	1998	1997	1996	1995	1994
Tangible Bk. Val.	5.26	4.74	4.59	4.67	4.14	3.53	2.96	2.57	1.85	1.40
Cash Flow	1.62	1.25	1.13	2.20	1.57	0.63	1.27	0.99	0.70	0.47
Earnings	0.85	0.46	0.19	1.51	1.06	0.87	0.97	0.73	0.50	0.33
S&P Core Earnings	0.83	0.35	0.11	NA	NA	NA	NA	NA	NA	NA
Dividends	0.08	0.08	0.08	0.07	0.07	0.03	0.03	0.02	0.02	0.01
Payout Ratio	9%	17%	42%	4%	7%	4%	3%	3%	3%	4%
Prices - High	34.51	36.78	38.59	75.81	44.75	31.54	25.50	17.68	9.79	4.59
- Low	14.88	12.95	18.96	29.81	25.06	16.41	15.71	6.22	3.93	3.50
P/E Ratio - High	41	80	NM	50	42	37	26	24	19	14
- Low	18	28	NM	20	24	19	16	9	8	11

Income Statement Analysis (Million $)

	2003	2002	2001	2000	1999	1998	1997	1996	1995	1994
Revs.	30,141	26,764	26,539	33,726	29,389	26,273	25,070	20,847	16,202	11,521
Oper. Inc.	13,220	9,726	8,923	15,339	13,756	11,351	12,079	9,441	6,623	4,863
Depr.	5,070	5,344	6,469	4,835	3,597	2,807	2,192	1,888	1,371	1,028
Int. Exp.	62.0	84.0	56.0	35.0	36.0	34.0	27.0	58.0	75.0	84.0
Pretax Inc.	7,442	4,204	2,183	15,141	11,228	9,137	10,659	7,934	5,638	3,603
Eff. Tax Rate	24.2%	25.9%	40.9%	30.4%	34.9%	33.6%	34.8%	35.0%	36.8%	36.5%
Net Inc.	5,641	3,117	1,291	10,535	7,314	6,068	6,945	5,157	3,566	2,288
S&P Core Earnings	5,467	2,332	740	NA	NA	NA	NA	NA	NA	NA

Balance Sheet & Other Fin. Data (Million $)

	2003	2002	2001	2000	1999	1998	1997	1996	1995	1994
Cash	8,485	7,404	7,970	2,976	3,695	2,038	4,102	7,907	2,458	2,410
Curr. Assets	22,882	18,925	17,633	21,150	17,819	13,475	15,867	13,684	8,097	6,167
Total Assets	47,143	44,224	44,395	47,945	43,849	31,471	28,880	23,765	17,504	13,816
Curr. Liab.	6,879	6,595	6,570	8,650	7,099	5,804	6,020	4,863	3,619	3,024
LT Debt	936	929	1,050	707	955	702	448	728	400	392
Common Equity	37,846	35,468	35,830	37,322	32,665	23,578	21,336	16,872	12,140	9,267
Total Cap.	40,264	37,629	37,825	39,295	36,750	25,667	20,819	18,597	13,160	10,048
Cap. Exp.	3,656	4,703	7,309	6,674	3,403	3,557	4,501	3,024	3,550	2,441
Cash Flow	10,711	8,461	7,760	15,370	10,911	8,875	9,137	7,045	4,937	3,316
Curr. Ratio	3.3	2.9	2.7	2.4	2.5	2.3	2.6	2.8	2.2	2.0
% LT Debt of Cap.	2.3	2.5	2.8	1.8	2.6	2.7	2.2	3.9	3.0	3.9
% Net Inc.of Revs.	18.7	11.6	4.9	31.2	24.9	23.1	27.7	24.7	22.0	19.9
% Ret. on Assets	12.3	7.0	2.8	23.0	19.4	20.1	26.4	25.0	22.8	18.3
% Ret. on Equity	15.4	8.7	3.5	30.1	26.0	27.0	36.1	35.6	33.3	27.4

Data as orig reptd.; bef. results of disc opers/spec. items. Per share data adj. for stk. divs.; EPS diluted. E-Estimated. NA-Not Available. NM-Not Meaningful. NR-Not Ranked. UR-Under Review.

Office: 2200 Mission College Boulevard, Santa Clara, CA 95054-1549.
Telephone: 408-765-8080.
Website: http://www.intc.com
Chrmn: A.S. Grove.
Pres & COO: P.S. Otellini.
CEO: C.R. Barrett.

EVP & CFO: A.D. Bryant.
VP & Treas: A. Sodhani.
Investor Contact: A. Lenke 408-765-1480.
Dirs: C. R. Barrett, C. Barshefsky, J. P. Browne, A. S. Grove, D. J. Guzy, R. E. Hundt, P. S. Otellini, D. S. Pottruck, J. E. Shaw, J. L. Thornton, D. B. Yoffie.

Founded: in 1968.
Domicile: Delaware.
Employees: 80,500.
S&P Analyst: Amrit Tewary/PMW/GG

The McGraw-Hill Companies

Recommendation: **BUY** ★★★★★
SELL | SELL | HOLD | BUY | BUY

12-Month Target Price: **$105.00**
(as of August 11, 2004)

IBM has an approximate 1.45% weighting in the **S&P 500**

Sector: Information Technology
Sub-Industry: Computer Hardware
Peer Group: Computer Hardware - Large System Vendors

Summary: The world's largest technology company, IBM offers a diversified line of computer hardware equipment, application and system software, and related services.

Quantitative Evaluations

S&P Earnings & Dividend Rank: B+

| D | C | B- | B | B+ | A- | A | A+ |

S&P Fair Value Rank: 4+

| 1 | 2 | 3 | 4 | 5 |
| Lowest | | | | Highest |

Fair Value Calc.: $94.10 (Fairly Valued)

S&P Investability Quotient Percentile
97%

IBM scored higher than 97% of all companies for which an S&P Report is available.

Volatility: Low

| Low | Average | High |

Technical Evaluation: Bullish
Since 10/04, the technical indicators for IBM have been Bullish.

Relative Strength Rank: Moderate
67
1 Lowest — Highest 99

| Price as of 11/12/04: | **$95.32** | 2004E S&P Core EPS: | **$2.65** |

GAAP Earnings vs. Previous Year
▲ Up ▼ Down ► No Change

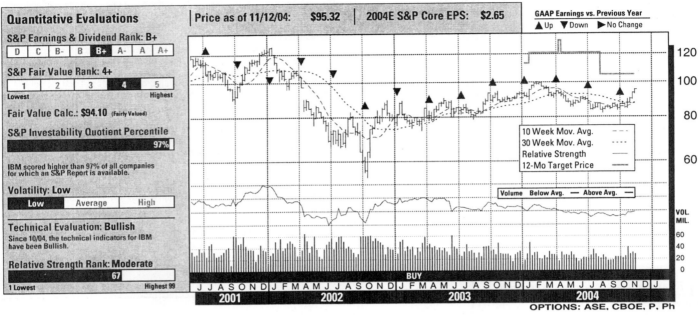

- 10 Week Mov. Avg.
- 30 Week Mov. Avg.
- Relative Strength
- 12-Mo Target Price

Volume Below Avg. — Above Avg.

VOL. MIL.

BUY

J J A S O N D J F M A M J J A S O N D J F M A M J J A S O N D J F M A M J J A S O N D J
2001   2002   2003   2004

OPTIONS: ASE, CBOE, P, Ph

Analyst commentary prepared by M. Graham-Hackett/MF/BK

Highlights November 02, 2004

- We estimate that 2004 revenues will increase 6.3%, excluding discontinued operations. Our forecast is based on our projection of a steady increase in IT (information technology) spending during the year, although slightly more muted than we had expected at the beginning of the year, due to signs of a somewhat slower economic recovery. We also expect results to benefit from market share gains. We think hardware sales comparisons will be easier in 2004, as the company has restructured its microelectronics operations and gained market share in servers. In addition, we believe software and services will grow 5% and 8%, respectively. Our revenue growth expectation for 2005 is for growth of 6.6%.

- We expect 2004 gross margins to remain flat at about 37%, as investments in Global Services offset cost reduction efforts. However, we expect recent improvements in operating results in the company's microelectronics segment to continue, partly offsetting the adverse impact on gross margins related to sales mix, as software sales growth has been somewhat slower than in other business segments.

- We project 2004 EPS of $4.96. Our 2004 Standard & Poor's Core Earnings estimate of $2.65 a share incorporates our projections of stock option expense and pension costs. Our 2005 EPS estimate is $5.80.

Investment Rationale/Risk November 02, 2004

- We recently raised our opinion on the shares to buy, from accumulate. We think IBM's recent third quarter results reflected some of the benefits the company can accrue with its broad solutions-focused product portfolio even in a moderately growing technology demand environment. We believe IBM has gained market share throughout the technology spending downturn, and that these gains in services, software and hardware, as well as an improved operating performance in microelectronics, should strengthen results during this year and next. We believe the stock will outpace the S&P 500, as the company leverages this market position and its competitive strengths.

- Risks to our opinion and target price include a deterioration in technology spending, adverse geopolitical events, and competitive pricing pressures.

- Our 12-month target price of $105 is based on our discounted cash flow (DCF) and price-to-sales analyses. The assumptions in our DCF model include a weighted average cost of capital of 11.0% and compound annual free cash flow growth of 6% for the next 15 years.

Key Stock Statistics

S&P Oper. EPS 2004E	4.96	52-week Range	$100.43-81.90
P/E on S&P Oper. EPS 2004E	19.2	12 Month P/E	20.3
S&P Oper. EPS 2005E	5.80	Beta	1.44
Yield (%)	0.8%	Shareholders	673,607
Dividend Rate/Share	0.72	Market Cap (B)	$158.7
Shares Outstanding (M)	1664.7		

Value of $10,000 invested five years ago: **$ 10,663**

Dividend Data Dividends have been paid since 1916

Amount ($)	Date Decl.	Ex-Div. Date	Stock of Record	Payment Date
0.160	Jan. 27	Feb. 06	Feb. 10	Mar. 10 '04
0.180	Apr. 27	May. 06	May. 10	Jun. 10 '04
0.180	Jul. 27	Aug. 06	Aug. 10	Sep. 10 '04
0.180	Oct. 26	Nov. 08	Nov. 10	Dec. 10 '04

Revenues/Earnings Data Fiscal year ending December 31

Revenues (Million $)

	2004	2003	2002	2001	2000	1999
1Q	22,250	20,065	18,030	21,044	19,348	20,317
2Q	23,153	21,631	19,651	21,568	21,651	21,905
3Q	23,429	21,522	19,821	20,428	21,781	21,144
4Q	—	25,913	23,684	22,826	25,616	24,182
Yr.	—	89,131	81,186	85,866	88,396	87,548

Earnings Per Share ($)

	2004	2003	2002	2001	2000	1999
1Q	0.93	0.79	0.73	0.98	0.83	0.78
2Q	1.16	0.98	0.25	1.15	1.06	1.28
3Q	1.06	1.02	0.99	0.90	1.08	0.93
4Q	E1.70	1.55	1.11	1.33	1.48	1.12
Yr.	E4.96	4.34	3.07	4.35	4.44	4.12

Next earnings report expected: mid-January Source: S&P, Company Reports
EPS Estimates based on S&P Operating Earnings; historical GAAP earnings are as reported.

International Business Machines Corporation

Recommendation: **BUY** ★ ★ ★ ★ ★   12-Month Target Price: **$105.00** (as of August 11, 2004)

Business Summary November 02, 2004

International Business Machines, still the world's largest computer concern, is no longer just a computer vendor. Computer hardware (and related areas, included in the Systems & Technology Group and Personal Systems Group) accounts for about 31% of sales, but IBM has focused on key areas such as services (which provides nearly 49% of sales, versus 15% in 1994), and software (about 16%). Software and services contributed 76% of 2003 pretax profits. Considered key growth engines, services and software have gained momentum as IBM's goal has been to leverage its capabilities in offering e-business (electronic business) solutions in light of the Internet's emergence as a business tool in streamlining everything from supply chain management to customer service.

The Systems group, once thought of principally as mainframes (System/390, now known as zSeries) and minicomputers (AS/400), has made a transition to more open systems. The company, a leader in UNIX systems (with its RS6000, or pSeries), also offers entry level servers and workstations that use Intel microprocessors and run Microsoft operating systems. In its PC business, it has introduced new manufacturing and distribution strategies aimed at maintaining low inventories.

The Systems & Technology group includes IBM's Shark storage offering, and its semiconductor unit (custom logic and communications). In December 2002, the company sold its hard disk drive business to Hitachi, for about $2 billion.

IBM Global Services has been growing at an average double-digit rate over the past several years. The unit has a strong position in emerging e-business services, and had a services backlog of $118 billion as of June 30, 2004, as estimated by the company. In 1999, IBM sold its Global Network Services unit to AT&T for $5 billion in cash.

The software unit's sales growth has recovered on the strength of IBM's middleware and database offerings. To energize the slower growth of host-based software, IBM acquired software pioneer Lotus in 1995 and Tivoli Systems in 1996. In February 2003, IBM acquired Rational Software for $2.1 billion in cash.

Global Financing (4.7% of sales) is primarily used to leverage IBM's financial structuring, portfolio management, etc., to expand its customer base.

IBM was a leader in U.S. patents in 2003; its semiconductor technology innovations include silicon-on-insulator and the use of copper in making chips.

In October 2002, the company acquired the PricewaterhouseCoopers consulting unit for $3.9 billion in cash and stock. The unit comprises 30,000 employees, and had estimated revenues of $4.9 billion. IBM reported that the transaction was dilutive to 2002 fourth quarter EPS, but was neutral to 2003 EPS.

Company Financials Fiscal Year ending December 31

Per Share Data ($)

(Year Ended December 31)	2003	2002	2001	2000	1999	1998	1997	1996	1995	1994
Tangible Bk. Val.	12.36	10.84	12.96	11.08	10.65	9.84	9.62	10.00	9.72	9.30
Cash Flow	7.01	5.21	7.08	6.95	7.40	5.64	4.99	4.30	3.57	3.05
Earnings	4.34	3.07	4.35	4.44	4.12	3.28	3.01	2.56	1.81	1.26
S&P Core Earnings	3.00	0.08	1.33	NA	NA	NA	NA	NA	NA	NA
Dividends	0.63	0.59	0.55	0.51	0.47	0.44	0.39	0.33	0.25	0.25
Payout Ratio	15%	19%	13%	11%	11%	13%	13%	13%	14%	20%
Prices - High	94.54	126.39	124.70	134.93	139.18	94.96	56.75	41.50	28.65	19.09
- Low	73.17	54.01	83.75	80.06	80.87	47.81	31.78	20.78	17.56	12.84
P/E Ratio - High	22	41	29	30	34	29	19	16	16	15
- Low	17	18	19	18	20	15	11	8	10	10

Income Statement Analysis (Million $)

	2003	2002	2001	2000	1999	1998	1997	1996	1995	1994
Revs.	89,131	81,186	85,866	88,396	87,548	81,667	78,508	75,947	71,940	64,052
Oper. Inc.	19,867	10,487	14,115	16,147	18,086	13,639	13,116	12,272	11,546	9,202
Depr.	4,701	3,691	4,820	4,513	6,159	4,475	4,018	3,676	3,955	4,197
Int. Exp.	145	145	238	717	727	713	760	747	748	1,247
Pretax Inc.	10,874	7,524	10,953	11,534	11,757	9,040	9,027	8,587	7,813	5,155
Eff. Tax Rate	30.0%	29.1%	29.5%	29.8%	34.4%	30.0%	32.5%	36.8%	46.5%	41.4%
Net Inc.	7,613	5,334	7,723	8,093	7,712	6,328	6,093	5,429	4,178	3,021
S&P Core Earnings	5,254	111	2,302	NA	NA	NA	NA	NA	NA	NA

Balance Sheet & Other Fin. Data (Million $)

	2003	2002	2001	2000	1999	1998	1997	1996	1995	1994
Cash	7,647	5,975	6,393	3,722	5,831	5,768	7,553	8,137	7,701	10,554
Curr. Assets	44,998	41,652	42,461	43,880	43,155	42,360	40,418	40,695	40,691	41,338
Total Assets	104,457	96,484	88,313	88,349	87,495	86,100	81,499	81,132	80,292	81,091
Curr. Liab.	37,900	34,550	35,119	36,406	39,578	36,827	33,507	34,000	31,648	29,226
LT Debt	16,986	19,986	15,963	18,371	14,124	15,508	13,696	9,872	10,060	12,548
Common Equity	27,864	22,782	23,614	20,377	20,264	19,186	19,564	21,375	22,170	22,288
Total Cap.	44,850	42,768	39,577	38,995	35,989	36,455	34,999	33,127	34,290	37,842
Cap. Exp.	4,393	4,753	5,660	5,616	5,959	6,520	6,793	5,883	4,744	3,078
Cash Flow	12,314	9,025	12,533	12,586	13,851	10,783	10,091	9,085	8,133	7,134
Curr. Ratio	1.2	1.2	1.2	1.2	1.1	1.2	1.2	1.2	1.3	1.4
% LT Debt of Cap.	37.9	46.7	40.3	47.1	39.2	42.5	39.1	29.8	29.3	53.2
% Net Inc.of Revs.	8.5	6.6	9.0	9.2	8.8	7.7	7.8	7.2	5.8	4.7
% Ret. on Assets	7.6	5.7	8.7	9.2	8.9	7.6	7.5	6.8	5.2	3.7
% Ret. on Equity	30.1	23.1	35.1	39.7	39.0	32.7	29.8	24.9	18.5	14.3

Data as orig reptd.; bef. results of disc opers/spec. items. Per share data adj. for stk. divs.; EPS diluted. E-Estimated. NA-Not Available. NM-Not Meaningful. NR-Not Ranked. UR-Under Review.

Office: New Orchard Road, Armonk, NY 10504.
Telephone: 914-499-1900.
Website: http://www.ibm.com
Chrmn, Pres & CEO: S.J. Palmisano.
SVP & CFO: J.R. Joyce.
SVP & General Counsel: E.M. Lineen.

VP & Secy: D.E. O'Donnell.
Treas: J.J. Greene, Jr.
Investor Contact: H. Parke III .
Dirs: C. Black, K. I. Chenault, C. Ghosn, N. O. Keohane, C. F. Knight, M. Makihara, L. A. Noto, S. J. Palmisano, J. B. Slaughter, J. E. Spero, S. Taurel, C. M. Vest, L. H. Zambrano.

Founded: in 1910.
Domicile: New York.
Employees: 319,273.
S&P Analyst: M. Graham-Hackett/MF/BK

Int'l Flavors & Fragrances

Recommendation: **BUY** ★★★★☆
SELL | SELL | HOLD | BUY | BUY

12-Month Target Price: $42.00
(as of January 28, 2004)

IFF has an approximate 0.04% weighting in the **S&P 500**

Sector: Materials
Sub-Industry: Specialty Chemicals
Peer Group: Specialty Chemicals (Larger)

Summary: This leading producer of flavors and fragrances used in a wide variety of consumer goods derives over two-thirds of sales and earnings from operations outside the U.S.

Quantitative Evaluations

S&P Earnings & Dividend Rank: B

| D | C | B- | **B** | B+ | A- | A | A+ |

S&P Fair Value Rank: NR

| 1 | 2 | 3 | 4 | 5 |
| Lowest | | | | Highest |

Fair Value Calc.: NA

S&P Investability Quotient Percentile — 97%

IFF scored higher than 97% of all companies for which an S&P Report is available.

Volatility: Low

| **Low** | Average | High |

Technical Evaluation: Bullish
Since 10/04, the technical indicators for IFF have been Bullish.

Relative Strength Rank: Moderate — 64
1 Lowest — Highest 99

Price as of 11/12/04: $41.05 | **2004E S&P Core EPS:** $2.15

GAAP Earnings vs. Previous Year
▲ Up ▼ Down ► No Change

- 10 Week Mov. Avg.
- 30 Week Mov. Avg.
- Relative Strength
- 12-Mo Target Price

BUY
$31.10
09/23/02

Volume Below Avg. — Above Avg.

VOL. (000)
2400
1600
800
0

HOLD | BUY

J J A S O N D J F M A M J J A S O N D J F M A M J J A S O N D J F M A M J J A S O N D J
2001 | 2002 | 2003 | 2004

OPTIONS: CBOE

Analyst commentary prepared by Richard O'Reilly, CFA /PMW/JWP

Highlights September 10, 2004

- We expect 2004 sales to grow about 8%, boosted by favorable currency exchange rates. We project that sales in local currencies will rise in the low to mid-single digits, after a 2% decline in 2003 that was largely due to the impact of a slowdown in customer orders for fine fragrances in North America. We expect a rebound in sales in North America and Europe, and continued growth in Asia and India, with gains in both fragrances and flavors, reflecting a large number of new product introductions.

- We see margins benefiting from a rebound in sales of fine fragrance sales, and from continuing cost reductions. The company implemented restructuring steps that were aimed at producing savings of $30 million in 2003. IFF expects to record $4.5 million to $6.0 million in new equity compensation expense in 2004. Interest expense will likely be lower in 2004, as IFF reduced debt by $145 million in 2003; we expect a further $100 million reduction in 2004. We project an effective tax rate of about 31.5%, versus 32.0% in 2003.

- Our 2004 operating EPS estimate excludes about $0.13 of expected restructuring charges; reported EPS in 2003 had special charges of $0.29. We estimate Standard & Poor's Core Earnings per share for 2004 of $2.15, which includes stock option expense of about $0.16.

Key Stock Statistics

S&P Core EPS 2005E	2.49	52-week Range	$41.10-31.01
S&P Oper. EPS 2004E	2.27	12 Month P/E	20.1
P/E on S&P Oper. EPS 2004E	18.1	Beta	0.58
S&P Oper. EPS 2005E	2.55	Shareholders	3,655
Yield (%)	1.7%	Market Cap (B)	$ 3.9
Dividend Rate/Share	0.70	Shares Outstanding (M)	94.2

Value of $10,000 invested five years ago: **$ 12,005**

Dividend Data Dividends have been paid since 1956

Amount ($)	Date Decl.	Ex-Div. Date	Stock of Record	Payment Date
0.160	Dec. 16	Dec. 19	Dec. 23	Jan. 09 '04
0.160	Mar. 08	Mar. 19	Mar. 23	Apr. 08 '04
0.175	May. 11	Jun. 22	Jun. 24	Jul. 08 '04
0.175	Sep. 08	Sep. 21	Sep. 23	Oct. 07 '04

Investment Rationale/Risk September 10, 2004

- We recommend accumulating the shares on a total return basis. We think that IFF is renewing sales growth with an improved win rate of new business, especially in North American flavors and fine fragrances. Directors in 2004 again both extended the company's stock repurchase program and raised the dividend. Despite what we view as disappointing sales in 2003, we do not believe that there was any deterioration in IFF's competitive position, and we expect stronger sales growth in 2004.

- Risks to our recommendation and target price include economic uncertainties in global markets, currency fluctuations, and the ability to maintain close relationships with customers.

- We regard the shares, currently yielding 1.8%, as attractive at their recent P/E multiple, which is somewhat below those accorded shares of other major specialty chemical concerns, based on our 2004 EPS estimates. Assuming a further narrowing of the stock's P/E multiple discount to the S&P 500, our 12-month target price is $42.

Revenues/Earnings Data Fiscal year ending December 31

Revenues (Million $)

	2004	2003	2002	2001	2000	1999
1Q	535.0	466.2	445.8	483.7	369.9	367.8
2Q	524.2	482.6	476.3	478.2	368.8	371.1
3Q	506.2	480.9	462.8	462.7	339.6	364.7
4Q	—	471.8	424.3	419.2	384.5	336.0
Yr.	—	1,902	1,809	1,844	1,463	1,440

Earnings Per Share ($)

	2004	2003	2002	2001	2000	1999
1Q	0.59	0.34	0.44	0.21	0.42	0.46
2Q	0.59	0.54	0.47	0.34	0.48	0.26
3Q	0.44	0.54	0.52	0.35	0.29	0.46
4Q	E0.45	0.40	0.41	0.30	0.01	0.35
Yr.	E2.27	1.83	1.84	1.20	1.22	1.53

Next earnings report expected: late-January Source: S&P, Company Reports
EPS Estimates based on S&P Operating Earnings; historical GAAP earnings are as reported.

International Flavors & Fragrances Inc.

Recommendation: **BUY** ★ ★ ★ ★   12-Month Target Price: **$42.00** (as of January 28, 2004)

Business Summary September 10, 2004

International Flavors & Fragrances, founded in 1909, is the leading maker of products used by other manufacturers to enhance the aromas and tastes of consumer products. The November 2000 purchase of Bush Boake Allen Inc. (BOA) for $970 million boosted annual sales to nearly $2 billion. With the purchase, IFF became the world's leading flavors company. The company has been reorganizing into a new global structure, and anticipates annual cost savings of up to $30 million; it recorded related pretax charges of $116.1 million through December 2003, versus earlier projections of about $110 million.

IFF gets about 70% of sales from outside the U.S. The company believes that future opportunities for growth include markets in Asia, Latin America and Eastern Europe, where rising consumer incomes appear likely to boost demand for manufactured products that use ingredients provided by IFF.

In 2003, North America contributed 29% of sales and 18% of operating profits; Europe 40% and 56%; India 3% and 3%; Latin America 12% and 9%; and Asia-Pacific 16% and 14%.

Fragrance products accounted for 54% of sales in 2003. Fragrances are used in the manufacture of soaps, detergents, cosmetic creams, lotions and powders, lipsticks, aftershave lotions, deodorants, hair preparations, air fresheners, perfumes and colognes and other consumer products. Most major U.S. companies in these industries are IFF customers. Cosmetics (including perfumes and toiletries) and household products (soaps and detergents) form the two largest customer groups.

Flavor products account for IFF's remaining sales. Flavors are sold principally to the food, beverage and other industries for use in consumer products such as soft drinks, candies, cake mixes, desserts, prepared foods, dietary foods, dairy products, drink powders, pharmaceuticals, oral care products, alcoholic beverages and tobacco. Two of the largest customers for flavor products are major U.S. producers of prepared foods and beverages.

By category, 40% of sales in 2003 were from flavor compounds, 27% from functional fragrances, 15% from fine fragrances and toiletries, 13% from ingredients, and 5% from fruit.

The company uses both synthetic and natural ingredients in its compounds. IFF manufactures most of the synthetic ingredients, of which a substantial portion is sold to others. It has had a consistent commitment to R&D spending, and anticipates that R&D expense will approximate 8% to 8.5% of annual sales over the next several years. R&D is conducted in 35 laboratories in 24 countries.

The cash dividend was increased for 39 consecutive years until 1999. In late 2002, IFF completed a $100 million stock repurchase program approved in September 2000, and directors authorized a new $100 million plan. About $15 million remained authorized under that program at June 30, 2004. In July 2004, directors approved a new $100 million program, to be completed over the next 18 to 24 months.

Company Financials Fiscal Year ending December 31

Per Share Data ($)

(Year Ended December 31)	2003	2002	2001	2000	1999	1998	1997	1996	1995	1994
Tangible Bk. Val.	NM	NM	NM	NM	8.19	8.91	9.17	9.79	10.06	9.04
Cash Flow	2.77	2.72	2.47	1.90	2.06	2.35	2.45	2.15	2.61	2.35
Earnings	1.83	1.84	1.20	1.22	1.53	1.90	1.99	1.71	2.24	2.03
S&P Core Earnings	1.70	1.37	0.70	NA	NA	NA	NA	NA	NA	NA
Dividends	0.63	0.60	0.60	1.52	1.52	1.48	1.45	1.38	1.27	1.12
Payout Ratio	34%	33%	50%	125%	99%	78%	73%	81%	57%	55%
Prices - High	36.61	37.45	31.69	37.93	48.50	51.87	53.43	51.87	55.87	47.87
- Low	29.18	26.05	19.75	14.68	33.62	32.06	39.87	40.75	45.12	35.62
P/E Ratio - High	20	20	26	31	32	27	27	30	25	24
- Low	16	14	16	12	22	17	20	24	20	18

Income Statement Analysis (Million $)

	2003	2002	2001	2000	1999	1998	1997	1996	1995	1994
Revs.	1,902	1,809	1,844	1,463	1,439	1,407	1,427	1,436	1,439	1,315
Oper. Inc.	415	396	409	322	338	356	382	388	425	385
Depr.	86.7	84.5	123	69.3	56.4	49.0	50.3	47.7	40.7	36.4
Int. Exp.	28.5	37.0	70.4	25.1	5.15	2.04	2.42	2.74	3.16	13.5
Pretax Inc.	252	266	188	184	243	311	340	299	394	360
Eff. Tax Rate	31.5%	34.0%	38.2%	33.2%	33.5%	34.5%	35.9%	36.5%	35.3%	37.3%
Net Inc.	173	176	116	123	162	204	218	190	249	226
S&P Core Earnings	161	131	68.5	NA	NA	NA	NA	NA	NA	NA

Balance Sheet & Other Fin. Data (Million $)

	2003	2002	2001	2000	1999	1998	1997	1996	1995	1994
Cash	12.1	14.9	48.5	129	62.1	116	217	318	297	302
Curr. Assets	903	867	896	1,019	835	848	935	1,006	1,036	964
Total Assets	2,307	2,233	2,268	2,489	1,401	1,388	1,422	1,507	1,534	1,400
Curr. Liab.	526	359	560	1,179	370	273	265	280	276	260
LT Debt	690	1,007	939	417	3.83	4.34	5.11	8.29	11.6	14.3
Common Equity	743	575	524	631	858	945	1,000	1,077	1,117	1,008
Total Cap.	1,433	1,582	1,508	1,152	895	1,084	1,029	1,102	1,142	1,037
Cap. Exp.	6.40	81.8	52.0	60.7	102	89.7	58.2	79.4	94.4	101
Cash Flow	259	260	239	192	218	253	269	238	290	262
Curr. Ratio	1.7	2.4	1.6	0.9	2.3	3.1	3.5	3.6	3.8	3.7
% LT Debt of Cap.	48.2	63.7	62.3	36.2	0.4	0.4	0.5	0.8	1.0	1.4
% Net Inc.of Revs.	9.1	9.7	6.3	8.4	11.3	14.5	15.3	13.2	17.3	17.2
% Ret. on Assets	7.6	7.8	4.9	6.3	11.6	14.5	14.9	12.5	17.0	17.3
% Ret. on Equity	26.2	32.0	20.1	16.5	18.0	20.9	21.0	17.3	23.4	23.9

Data as orig reptd.; bef. results of disc opers/spec. items. Per share data adj. for stk. divs.; EPS diluted. E-Estimated. NA-Not Available. NM-Not Meaningful. NR-Not Ranked. UR-Under Review.

Office: 521 W 57th St, New York, NY 10019-2901.
Telephone: 212-765-5500.
Email: investor.relations@iff.com
Website: http://www.iff.com
Chrmn & CEO: R.A. Goldstein.
COO: J.H. Dunsdon.

SVP, CFO & Investor Contact: D.J. Wetmore .
SVP, Secy & General Counsel: D.M. Meany.
VP & Investor Contact: G.S. Belmuth 212-708-7208.
Dirs: M. H. Adame, G. Blobel, J. M. Cook, P. A. Georgescu, R. A. Goldstein, A. A. Herzan, H. W. Howell, Jr., A. C. Martinez, B. M. Tansky.

Founded: in 1909.
Domicile: New York.
Employees: 5,454.
S&P Analyst: Richard O'Reilly, CFA /PMW/JWP

Recommendation: **HOLD** ★ ★ ★ ☆ ☆
SELL · SELL · HOLD · BUY · BUY

12-Month Target Price: **$37.00**
(as of November 02, 2004)

IGT has an approximate 0.11% weighting in the **S&P 500**

Sector: Consumer Discretionary
Sub-Industry: Casinos & Gaming
Peer Group: Gambling Equipment or Services

Summary: This company is a leading maker of gaming machines and proprietary software systems for gaming machine networks.

Quantitative Evaluations

S&P Earnings & Dividend Rank: B+

| D | C | B- | B | B+ | A- | A | A+ |

S&P Fair Value Rank: 1

| 1 | 2 | 3 | 4 | 5 |
Lowest ... Highest

Fair Value Calc.: $27.90 (Overvalued)

S&P Investability Quotient Percentile
96%

IGT scored higher than 96% of all companies for which an S&P Report is available.

Volatility: Average

| Low | Average | High |

Technical Evaluation: Bullish
Since 11/04, the technical indicators for IGT have been Bullish.

Relative Strength Rank: Moderate
64
1 Lowest ... Highest 99

| Price as of 11/12/04: | **$35.70** | 2005E S&P Core EPS: | **$1.47** |

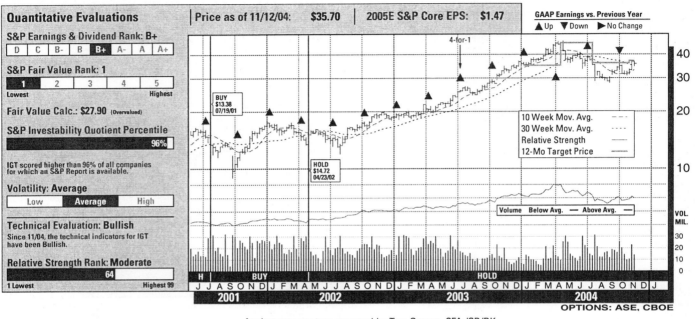

GAAP Earnings vs. Previous Year
▲ Up ▼ Down ▶ No Change

4-for-1

BUY
$13.38
07/19/01

HOLD
$14.72
04/23/02

10 Week Mov. Avg.
30 Week Mov. Avg.
Relative Strength
12-Mo Target Price

Volume Below Avg. — Above Avg.

VOL. MIL.

H | BUY | HOLD
J J A S O N D J F M A M J J A S O N D J F M A M J J A S O N D J F M A M J J A S O N D J
2001 2002 2003 2004

OPTIONS: ASE, CBOE

Analyst commentary prepared by Tom Graves, CFA /CB/BK

Highlights August 12, 2004

- In FY 05 (Sep.), we look for revenues from continuing operations to rise moderately from the $2.5 billion that we project for FY 04. We expect that IGT's already strong position in the U.S. gaming machine market will be bolstered by new game introductions and sales of EZ Pay machines that let gamblers use tickets. We look for IGT's product sales in FY 05 to be weighted toward the second half of the fiscal year, when we expect larger contributions from new or expanded gaming markets, including possibly Pennsylvania, where legislation allowing slot machines was signed in July 2004.

- We see FY 05 net income of $560 million ($1.51 a share), up from the $493 million ($1.34) we project for FY 04, which excludes a $0.03 a share third quarter benefit from utilization of prior year foreign income tax credits.

- IGT initiated a $0.075 a share quarterly dividend in July 2003, and boosted it to $0.10 with the October 2003 payment. We look for IGT's directors to approve another dividend increase within the next few months. As of June 30, 2004, the company had cash equivalents totaling $1.2 billion.

Investment Rationale/Risk August 12, 2004

- We have a hold opinion on the stock, which reflects our view that the shares offer a somewhat appealing opportunity to participate in the prospective growth of the gaming industry in the U.S. and other countries, and to benefit from IGT's skill in developing new games and machines. Prospective expansion in the U.S. includes further placement of gaming machines at U.S. racetracks.

- Risks to our recommendation and target price include the possibility that terrorism threats will increase, leading to reduced consumer spending at casinos. Also, new or expanded gaming markets may take longer to develop than currently anticipated.

- Based on calendar 2004 and calendar 2005 EPS estimates, the stock is at a P/E premium to the S&P 500 of about 39% and 30%, respectively, which we believe limits year-ahead upside prospects for the stock. Also, we look for relatively modest EPS growth in the first half of FY 05. However, we expect the shares to be bolstered by expectations of sizable future free cash flow from the company and prospective future growth of the gaming industry. We look for this to bring some P/E expansion for the stock, leading to our 12-month target price of $36.

Key Stock Statistics

S&P Oper. EPS 2005E	1.55	52-week Range	$47.12-28.22
P/E on S&P Oper. EPS 2005E	23.0	12 Month P/E	26.6
Yield (%)	1.3%	Beta	0.51
Dividend Rate/Share	0.48	Shareholders	2,934
Shares Outstanding (M)	344.6	Market Cap (B)	$ 12.3

Value of $10,000 invested five years ago: **$ 76,593**

Dividend Data Dividends have been paid since 2003

Amount ($)	Date Decl.	Ex-Div. Date	Stock of Record	Payment Date
0.100	Dec. 04	Dec. 12	Dec. 16	Dec. 30 '03
0.100	Mar. 02	Mar. 12	Mar. 16	Mar. 30 '04
0.100	Jun. 16	Jun. 25	Jun. 29	Jul. 13 '04
0.120	Sep. 29	Oct. 07	Oct. 12	Oct. 26 '04

Revenues/Earnings Data Fiscal year ending September 30

Revenues (Million $)

	2004	2003	2002	2001	2000	1999
1Q	608.1	489.6	301.5	301.7	206.5	221.7
2Q	636.1	529.1	500.9	346.9	218.1	220.9
3Q	618.9	561.9	522.4	320.1	263.7	258.9
4Q	621.7	547.5	522.8	295.9	316.2	228.2
Yr.	2,485	2,128	1,848	1,199	1,004	929.7

Earnings Per Share ($)

	2004	2003	2002	2001	2000	1999
1Q	0.33	0.25	0.18	0.16	0.12	0.08
2Q	0.32	0.27	0.20	0.18	0.08	0.08
3Q	0.38	0.30	0.23	0.18	0.13	0.10
4Q	0.15	0.29	0.20	0.18	0.18	-0.11
Yr.	1.18	1.07	0.80	0.70	0.50	0.16

Next earnings report expected: late-January Source: S&P, Company Reports
EPS Estimates based on S&P Operating Earnings; historical GAAP earnings are as reported.

STANDARD &POOR'S

International Game Technology

Stock Report
November 13, 2004
NYSE Symbol: **IGT**

Recommendation: **HOLD**  ★ ★ ★ ★ ★   12-Month Target Price: **$37.00** (as of November 02, 2004)

Business Summary August 12, 2004

International Game Technology (IGT) is a leading maker of gaming machines. In addition to selling machines, IGT's business includes the leasing of gaming machines and equipment, with customer participation agreements.

In October 2003, IGT acquired Acres Gaming Inc. in a transaction valued at about $130 million. Acres specialized in the development of gaming systems technology that may enable casino operators to increase patron loyalty. Earlier, in December 2001, IGT acquired Anchor Gaming, with the purchase price of $987 million largely representing an exchange of stock. IGT also assumed more than $300 million of Anchor debt. Anchor had been a joint venture partner with IGT in a portion of IGT's gaming operations business; other Anchor-related operations included on-line lottery systems. IGT has since sold some assets that were part of the Anchor acquisition, including two Colorado casinos.

In FY 03 (Sep.), 50% of IGT revenues came from product sales, and the remainder were from gaming operations, including progressive systems. In November 2003, IGT sold its online lottery systems provider business to Scientific Games for $143 million. This business had been treated as a discontinued operation.

Product sales in FY 03 included the sale of 134,800 machines, up from 123,900 in FY 02. FY 03 sales included 83,900 machines for the domestic market (likely including Canada), versus 63,500 in FY 02. Shipments to international markets totaled 50,900 in FY 03, down from 60,400 machines in FY 02. International sales

may include some lower-priced machines with relatively low value prizes. In addition to machines for casinos, IGT has made video gaming terminals (VGTs) for government-sponsored programs, including lotteries.

IGT's gaming operations segment includes the placement of games in both casinos and government sponsored gaming markets, under a variety of recurring revenue pricing arrangements, including wide area progressive systems, standalone participation and flat fee, equipment leasing and rental, as well as hybrid pricing or premium products that include a product sale and a recurring fee.

In FY 03, research and development spending totaled $94 million (4.5% of revenues). The company's ability to develop successful machines, with features that appeal to gamblers and casinos, is expected to be a significant factor in the level of "replacement" machines it sells. The company's EZ Pay Ticket System enables gaming machines to print and receive tickets, rather than coins.

Transactions by IGT in 2003 included the sale of assets related to a slot route business, two Colorado casinos operations, and a pari-mutuel systems business. These businesses were treated as discontinued operations.

In FY 02, EPS (adjusted for a subsequent 4-for-1 stock split) included about $0.04 of costs related to litigation accruals.

Company Financials Fiscal Year ending September 30

Per Share Data ($)

(Year Ended September 30)	2004	2003	2002	2001	2000	1999	1998	1997	1996	1995
Tangible Bk. Val.	NA	1.42	0.55	0.40	NM	0.26	0.94	1.14	1.24	1.07
Cash Flow	NA	1.45	1.23	0.91	0.67	0.29	0.42	0.35	0.29	0.23
Earnings	1.18	1.07	0.80	0.70	0.50	0.16	0.33	0.28	0.23	0.18
S&P Core Earnings	NA	1.02	0.79	0.67	NA	NA	NA	NA	NA	NA
Dividends	0.30	0.18	Nil	Nil	Nil	0.03	0.03	0.03	0.03	0.03
Payout Ratio	25%	16%	Nil	Nil	Nil	18%	9%	11%	13%	17%
Prices - High	47.12	37.00	20.02	17.98	12.34	6.03	7.17	6.71	5.87	4.25
- Low	28.21	18.05	11.93	8.92	4.35	3.53	4.03	3.81	2.68	2.68
P/E Ratio - High	40	35	25	26	25	37	22	24	25	24
- Low	24	17	15	13	9	22	12	13	12	15

Income Statement Analysis (Million $)

	2004	2003	2002	2001	2000	1999	1998	1997	1996	1995
Revs.	NA	2,128	1,848	1,199	1,004	930	824	744	733	621
Oper. Inc.	NA	801	646	315	343	267	260	226	200	167
Depr.	NA	134	146	63.3	54.4	52.3	41.5	35.0	30.5	27.9
Int. Exp.	NA	117	117	102	102	72.8	41.0	30.4	23.5	20.4
Pretax Inc.	NA	599	110	339	245	101	235	213	184	145
Eff. Tax Rate	NA	37.3%	NM	37.0%	36.0%	35.6%	35.0%	35.5%	36.0%	36.0%
Net Inc.	NA	375	277	214	157	65.3	152	137	118	92.6
S&P Core Earnings	NA	357	273	204	NA	NA	NA	NA	NA	NA

Balance Sheet & Other Fin. Data (Million $)

	2004	2003	2002	2001	2000	1999	1998	1997	1996	1995
Cash	NA	1,316	424	364	245	426	175	152	231	289
Curr. Assets	NA	2,078	1,195	968	814	975	671	572	616	607
Total Assets	NA	4,185	3,316	1,923	1,624	1,765	1,544	1,215	1,154	972
Curr. Liab.	NA	945	511	371	259	213	201	165	127	97.7
LT Debt	NA	1,146	971	985	992	990	323	141	107	108
Common Equity	NA	1,687	1,433	296	96.6	242	541	520	623	554
Total Cap.	NA	2,833	2,413	1,281	1,088	1,233	865	661	730	662
Cap. Exp.	NA	30.8	33.8	34.7	18.5	17.8	16.8	33.1	71.6	43.5
Cash Flow	NA	509	423	277	211	118	194	172	149	121
Curr. Ratio	NA	2.2	2.3	2.6	3.1	4.6	3.3	3.5	4.9	6.2
% LT Debt of Cap.	NA	40.4	40.3	76.9	91.1	80.3	37.3	21.3	14.7	16.3
% Net Inc.of Revs.	NA	17.6	15.0	17.8	15.6	7.0	18.5	18.4	16.1	14.9
% Ret. on Assets	NA	10.0	10.6	12.1	9.3	3.9	11.1	11.6	11.1	10.1
% Ret. on Equity	NA	24.1	32.0	109.0	92.6	16.7	28.7	24.0	42.1	17.2

Data as orig reptd.; bef. results of disc opers/spec. items. Per share data adj. for stk. divs.; EPS diluted. E-Estimated. NA-Not Available. NM-Not Meaningful. NR-Not Ranked. UR-Under Review.

Office: 9295 Prototype Drive, Reno, NV 89521.
Telephone: 775-448-7777.
Website: http://www.igt.com
Chrmn: G.T. Baker.
Pres, CEO & COO: T.J. Matthews.

EVP, CFO & Treas: M.T. Mullarkey.
SVP, Secy & General Counsel: D.D. Johnson.
Investor Contact: R. Baldwin 866-296-4232.
Dirs: G. T. Baker, N. Barsky, R. A. Bittman, R. R. Burt, L. S. Heisz, R. A. Mathewson, T. J. Matthews, R. Miller, F. B. Rentschler.

Founded: in 1980.
Domicile: Nevada.
Employees: 4,600.
S&P Analyst: Tom Graves, CFA /CB/BK

International Paper

Recommendation: **HOLD** ★ ★ ★ ☆ ☆
SELL SELL HOLD BUY BUY

12-Month Target Price: **$43.00**
(as of October 26, 2004)

IP has an approximate 0.18% weighting in the **S&P 500**

Sector: Materials
Sub-Industry: Paper Products
Peer Group: Paper Products - Larger

Summary: IP is a leading worldwide producer and distributor of printing papers and packaging products.

Quantitative Evaluations

Price as of 11/12/04:	**$40.81**	2004E S&P Core EPS:	**$1.37**

S&P Earnings & Dividend Rank: B-

D	C	B-	B	B+	A-	A	A+

S&P Fair Value Rank: 1-

1	2	3	4	5
Lowest				Highest

Fair Value Calc.: $28.30 (Overvalued)

S&P Investability Quotient Percentile

76%

IP scored higher than 76% of all companies for which an S&P Report is available.

Volatility: Low

Low	Average	High

Technical Evaluation: Bearish
Since 10/04, the technical indicators for IP have been Bearish.

Relative Strength Rank: Moderate

38

1 Lowest   Highest 99

GAAP Earnings vs. Previous Year
▲ Up ▼ Down ▶ No Change

10 Week Mov. Avg. - - -
30 Week Mov. Avg. ·····
Relative Strength ——
12-Mo Target Price ——

Volume Below Avg. — Above Avg.

HOLD

J J A S O N D | J F M A M J J A S O N D | J F M A M J J A S O N D | J F M A M J J A S O N D | J
2001   **2002**   **2003**   **2004**

OPTIONS: ASE, CBOE, P, Ph

Analyst commentary prepared by Bryon J. Korutz/PMW/BK

Highlights November 03, 2004

- We project that revenues will rise 3.8% in 2004, followed by an expected gain of 9.0% in 2005, driven by a firming in uncoated papers and packaging materials.

- Standard & Poor's projects real GDP growth of about 4.5% for 2004 and 3.5% for 2005, and we expect to see price increases and continued strengthening in demand in the uncoated papers and packaging market into 2005. We see average wood products prices in 2004 up from levels reached in 2003. Looking to 2005, we expect prices to fall, as supply outpaces demand. We see IP benefiting from lower interest costs, stemming from projected debt reduction initiatives, and from an improved cost structure.

- We project 2004 operating EPS of $1.47, and expect a sharp rise in 2005, to $3.30, based on our expectations of improved paper and packaging prices and operating leverage as demand firms. We see 2004 S&P Core EPS of $1.37, with the difference from our operating EPS estimate mainly due to projected option expense.

Investment Rationale/Risk November 03, 2004

- We see business trends improving for IP's packaging and uncoated paper grades, but with the shares near our 12-month target price, we would not add to positions.

- Risks to our recommendation and target price include slower than anticipated recovery in paper and packaging prices and demand.

- Our DCF model values the stock at $50 a share, assuming a weighted average cost of capital of 7.8%. It also assumes compound average annual free cash flow growth of 6.5% over the next 10 years, below the historical rate of 8.3%, due to what we view as continued maturation of the paper and packaging industry, and a less aggressive acquisition environment. In addition, our model assumes 3.5% growth in perpetuity. Our second valuation metric, which applies a historical peak P/E multiple of 10X to our 2005 EPS estimate, values the stock at $33. Blending our valuation models, we arrive at our 12-month target price of $43.

Key Stock Statistics

S&P Core EPS 2005E	**3.20**	52-week Range	**$45.01-36.57**
S&P Oper. EPS 2004E	**1.47**	12 Month P/E	**NM**
P/E on S&P Oper. EPS 2004E	**27.8**	Beta	**0.97**
S&P Oper. EPS 2005E	**3.30**	Shareholders	**29,478**
Yield (%)	**2.5%**	Market Cap (B)	**$ 19.8**
Dividend Rate/Share	**1.00**	Shares Outstanding (M)	**486.3**

Value of $10,000 invested five years ago: **$ 8,337**

Dividend Data Dividends have been paid since 1946

Amount ($)	Date Decl.	Ex-Div. Date	Stock of Record	Payment Date
0.250	Feb. 10	Feb. 18	Feb. 20	Mar. 15 '04
0.250	May. 11	May. 19	May. 21	Jun. 15 '04
0.250	Jul. 13	Aug. 18	Aug. 20	Sep. 15 '04
0.250	Oct. 12	Nov. 17	Nov. 19	Dec. 15 '04

Revenues/Earnings Data Fiscal year ending December 31

Revenues (Million $)

	2004	2003	2002	2001	2000	1999
1Q	6,364	6,075	6,038	6,894	6,371	6,032
2Q	6,486	6,264	6,305	6,686	6,780	5,996
3Q	6,600	6,373	6,343	6,529	7,801	6,251
4Q	—	6,500	6,290	6,254	7,228	6,294
Yr.	—	25,179	24,976	26,363	28,180	24,573

Earnings Per Share ($)

	2004	2003	2002	2001	2000	1999
1Q	0.14	0.11	0.13	0.04	0.59	0.08
2Q	0.21	0.19	0.45	-0.65	0.64	-0.14
3Q	0.43	0.25	0.30	-0.57	0.36	0.35
4Q	E0.47	0.11	-0.27	-1.19	-0.67	0.19
Yr.	E1.47	0.66	0.61	-2.37	0.82	0.48

Next earnings report expected: early-February Source: S&P, Company Reports
EPS Estimates based on S&P Operating Earnings; historical GAAP earnings are as reported.

International Paper Company

Recommendation: HOLD ★ ★ ★ ☆ ☆   12-Month Target Price: **$43.00** (as of October 26, 2004)

Business Summary November 03, 2004

The world's largest paper, paperboard and packaging maker, International Paper expanded through the $10.2 billion purchase of Champion International in 2000 and the $7.9 billion takeover of Union Camp in 1999. The two acquisitions added major positions in uncoated papers and substantial timber resources. IP derived 30% of 2002 sales from outside the U.S., including exports.

The printing papers division (28% of 2003 sales) produces various uncoated papers, coated papers, bristols and pulp. At December 31, 2003, the company had 5.2 million tons of uncoated papers capacity, 2.0 million tons of coated papers capacity, and 2.3 million tons of market pulp capacity. Its Brazilian operations had an annual production capacity of 675,000 tons of coated and uncoated papers. IP also owns or manages 1.5 million acres of forestland in Brazil.

The industrial and consumer packaging sector (23%) produces containerboard (used to make corrugated boxes) and corrugated boxes. At December 31, 2003, IP had 4.5 million tons of industrial packaging capacity (65% was used internally for the domestic production of boxes and other forms of packaging). The company's consumer packaging products are used by the cosmetics, food, beverage and pharmaceuticals industries. At December 31, 2003, IP had 2.0 million tons of bleached packaging board capacity (40% was used internally for the production of packaging products).

Through its distribution division, xpedx (24%), the company supplies industry wholesalers and end users with printing, packaging, graphic arts, facility supplies and industrial supply products, mostly made by others (largely in the U.S.).

The forest products division (12%) controls about 8.3 million acres of U.S. timberland, and sells lumber and panels. IP operates 25 plants in the U.S. that produce southern pine lumber (2.4 billion board feet of annual production), plywood (1.6 billion square feet of annual production), engineered wood products and utility poles. Weldwood of Canada Ltd., a wholly owned subsidiary, typically produces 1.2 billion board feet of lumber and 450 million square feet of plywood annually. IP also controls 795,000 acres of New Zealand timberland through a 50.5% stake in Carter Holt Harvey (8% of sales).

Over the recent past, the company took additional steps to focus on its three core businesses of paper, packaging, and forest products. In 2003, IP announced plans to sell 1.5 million acres of southern forestlands over the next five years. In 2002, It sold its oriented strand board facilities, Decorative Products operations, and Arizona Chemical and Industrial Papers business. It also moved to reduce costs, internal capacity, and headcount. The Consumer Packaging business began a reorganizational plan, and divested overlapping facilities. The company also consolidated facilities and started to streamline the transaction process at xpedx, and continued to realign its administrative and support staff and reduce overhead costs.

Other businesses (5% of 2003 sales) include chemicals, decorative products and industrial papers.

Company Financials Fiscal Year ending December 31

Per Share Data ($)

(Year Ended December 31)	2003	2002	2001	2000	1999	1998	1997	1996	1995	1994
Tangible Bk. Val.	6.01	4.31	7.78	11.89	18.65	20.45	20.36	21.99	24.68	22.84
Cash Flow	4.07	3.90	1.51	4.28	4.16	4.65	3.68	5.12	8.50	5.27
Earnings	0.66	0.61	-2.37	0.82	0.48	0.77	-0.50	1.04	4.50	1.73
S&P Core Earnings	0.51	0.92	-2.25	NA	NA	NA	NA	NA	NA	NA
Dividends	1.00	1.00	1.00	1.00	1.00	1.00	1.00	1.00	0.92	0.84
Payout Ratio	152%	164%	NM	122%	NM	130%	NM	96%	20%	49%
Prices - High	43.32	46.20	43.31	60.00	59.50	55.25	61.00	44.62	45.68	40.25
- Low	33.09	31.35	30.70	26.31	39.50	35.50	38.62	35.62	34.12	30.31
P/E Ratio - High	66	76	NM	73	NM	72	NM	43	10	23
- Low	50	51	NM	32	NM	46	NM	34	8	18

Income Statement Analysis (Million $)

	2003	2002	2001	2000	1999	1998	1997	1996	1995	1994
Revs.	25,179	24,976	26,363	28,180	24,573	19,541	20,096	20,143	19,797	14,966
Oper. Inc.	3,293	3,576	3,305	5,432	3,061	2,202	2,404	2,614	3,552	1,898
Depr.	1,644	1,587	1,870	1,916	1,520	1,186	1,258	1,194	1,031	885
Int. Exp.	766	783	929	791	541	496	490	530	551	367
Pretax Inc.	346	371	-1,265	497	448	392	16.0	802	1,872	664
Eff. Tax Rate	NM	NM	NM	23.5%	19.2%	20.4%	237.5%	41.1%	35.5%	34.9%
Net Inc.	315	295	-1,142	142	199	236	-151	303	1,153	432
S&P Core Earnings	242	444	-1,091	NA	NA	NA	NA	NA	NA	NA

Balance Sheet & Other Fin. Data (Million $)

	2003	2002	2001	2000	1999	1998	1997	1996	1995	1994
Cash	2,363	1,074	1,224	1,198	453	477	398	352	312	270
Curr. Assets	9,337	7,738	8,312	10,455	7,241	6,010	5,945	5,998	5,873	4,830
Total Assets	35,525	33,792	37,158	42,109	30,268	26,356	26,754	28,252	23,977	17,836
Curr. Liab.	6,803	4,579	5,374	7,413	4,382	3,636	4,880	5,894	4,863	4,034
LT Debt	13,450	13,042	14,262	14,453	9,325	8,212	7,154	6,691	5,946	4,464
Common Equity	8,237	7,374	10,291	12,034	10,304	8,902	8,710	9,344	7,797	6,514
Total Cap.	25,085	25,435	29,804	32,541	24,554	21,582	20,188	20,668	15,717	12,590
Cap. Exp.	1,166	1,009	1,049	1,352	1,139	1,049	1,111	1,394	1,518	1,114
Cash Flow	1,959	1,882	728	2,058	1,719	1,422	1,107	1,497	2,184	1,317
Curr. Ratio	1.4	1.7	1.5	1.4	1.7	1.7	1.2	1.0	1.2	1.2
% LT Debt of Cap.	53.6	51.3	47.9	44.4	38.0	38.1	35.4	32.3	37.8	35.5
% Net Inc.of Revs.	1.3	1.2	NM	0.5	0.8	1.2	NM	1.5	5.8	2.9
% Ret. on Assets	0.9	0.8	NM	0.4	0.6	0.9	NM	1.2	5.5	2.5
% Ret. on Equity	4.0	3.3	NM	1.3	1.9	2.7	NM	3.5	16.1	6.7

Data as orig reptd.; bef. results of disc opers/spec. items. Per share data adj. for stk. divs.; EPS diluted. E-Estimated. NA-Not Available. NM-Not Meaningful. NR-Not Ranked. UR-Under Review.

Office: 400 Atlantic Street, Stamford, CT 06921.
Telephone: 203-541-8000.
Email: comm@ipaper.com
Website: http://www.internationalpaper.com
Chrmn & CEO: J.V. Faraci.
Pres: R.M. Amen.

SVP & CFO: C.P. Liddell.
SVP, Secy & General Counsel: M.A. Smith.
VP & Investor Contact: D. Sneed 203-541-8541.
Dirs: R. Amen, M. F. Brooks, J. T. Dillon, R. J. Eaton, J. V. Faraci, S. G. Gibara, J. A. Henderson, R. D. Kennedy, W. C. McClelland, D. F. McHenry, J. C. Pfeiffer, C. R. Shoemate.

Founded: in 1898.
Domicile: New York.
Employees: 83,000.
S&P Analyst: Bryon J. Korutz/PMW/BK

Interpublic Group

Recommendation: **HOLD** ★★★☆☆
SELL | SELL | HOLD | BUY | BUY

12-Month Target Price: $15.00
(as of June 25, 2004)

IPG has an approximate 0.05% weighting in the **S&P 500**

Sector: Consumer Discretionary
Sub-Industry: Advertising
Peer Group: Advertising Agencies

Summary: IPG is one of the world's largest organizations of advertising agencies and marketing communications companies.

Quantitative Evaluations

S&P Earnings & Dividend Rank: C

| D | C | B- | B | B+ | A- | A | A+ |

S&P Fair Value Rank: 3-

| 1 | 2 | 3 | 4 | 5 |
| Lowest | | | | Highest |

Fair Value Calc.: $12.10 (Fairly Valued)

S&P Investability Quotient Percentile

28%

IPG scored lower than 72% of all companies for which an S&P Report is available.

Volatility: Average

| Low | Average | High |

Technical Evaluation: Bullish
Since 10/04, the technical indicators for IPG have been Bullish.

Relative Strength Rank: Moderate

44

1 Lowest   Highest 99

Price as of 11/12/04: $12.06 | **2004E S&P Core EPS:** $0.51

GAAP Earnings vs. Previous Year
▲ Up   ▼ Down   ▶ No Change

- 10 Week Mov. Avg.
- 30 Week Mov. Avg.
- Relative Strength
- 12-Mo Target Price

BUY $29.14 11/14/01
HOLD $17.06 08/14/02
BUY $14.13 10/28/03
HOLD $15.35 05/07/04

Volume Below Avg. — Above Avg.

VOL. MIL.

HOLD | BUY | H | SELL | BUY | HOLD
J J A S O N D | J F M A M J J A S O N D | J F M A M J J A S O N D | J F M A M J J A S O N D | J
2001 | 2002 | 2003 | 2004

OPTIONS: CBOE, Ph

Analyst commentary prepared by William H. Donald/PMW/GG

Highlights July 16, 2004

- We project an increase of about 7% in commissions and fees in 2004, largely due to foreign exchange translation gains. Organic revenue, excluding foreign exchange and acquisitions, is likely to be relatively flat to up 1%. Although we see signs of strengthening, organic business continues to be affected by problems stemming in part from recent restructurings and downsizings. For 2005, we project 8% revenue growth, including 3% from organic business.

- Aided by the restructurings, downsizings and efficiency measures throughout IPG's operations, we see wider operating margins and sharply lower restructuring costs contributing to a 37% advance in 2004 EBITDA, and an EBITDA margin of 12.1%, versus 9.5% in 2003. We project a 15.3% EBITDA margin for 2005.

- We look for 2004 net income from continuing operations of about $150 million ($0.40 a share). We project a further earnings recovery, to $330 million ($0.87 for 2005, aided by stronger revenue generation and operating efficiencies.

Investment Rationale/Risk July 16, 2004

- We think that the company's turnaround efforts have begun to pay off, as shown by what we see as an improving operating outlook, and the balance sheet position has been strengthened through debt restructurings. Nevertheless, we would not add to position, due to our concerns that IPG may not be able to show organic revenue growth over the next 12 months. We are encouraged by plans for executive turnover at the corporate level at the end of 2004, but we believe this adds uncertainty at this point in the company's turnaround.

Key Stock Statistics

S&P Oper. EPS 2004E	0.10	52-week Range	$17.31-10.47
P/E on S&P Oper. EPS 2004E	NM	12 Month P/E	NM
S&P Oper. EPS 2005E	0.60	Beta	1.66
Yield (%)	Nil	Shareholders	17,674
Dividend Rate/Share	Nil	Market Cap (B)	$ 5.1
Shares Outstanding (M)	422.1		

Value of $10,000 invested five years ago: **$ 3,346**

Dividend Data

The most recent dividend payment was $0.095 a share in December 2002.

Revenues/Earnings Data Fiscal year ending December 31

Revenues (Million $)

	2004	2003	2002	2001	2000	1999
1Q	1,395	1,316	1,420	1,658	1,090	925.1
2Q	1,544	1,499	1,613	1,743	1,418	1,134
3Q	1,509	1,419	1,502	1,606	1,320	1,044
4Q	—	1,629	1,669	1,720	1,601	1,458
Yr.	—	5,863	6,204	6,727	5,626	4,562

Earnings Per Share ($)

	2004	2003	2002	2001	2000	1999
1Q	-0.05	-0.03	0.16	-0.08	0.13	0.16
2Q	-0.03	-0.06	0.29	-0.30	0.45	0.49
3Q	-1.42	-1.08	-0.24	-1.29	0.20	0.20
4Q	E-0.12	-0.26	0.05	0.30	0.33	0.27
Yr.	E0.10	-1.43	0.26	-1.37	1.15	1.11

Next earnings report expected: early-March Source: S&P, Company Reports
EPS Estimates based on S&P Operating Earnings; historical GAAP earnings are as reported.

The Interpublic Group of Companies, Inc.

Recommendation:  **HOLD** ★ ★ ★ ★ ★   12-Month Target Price: **$15.00** (as of June 25, 2004)

Business Summary July 16, 2004

The Interpublic Group of Companies is one of the world's largest organizations of advertising agencies and marketing communications companies.

In 2001, IPG paid $85 million in cash and issued 58.7 million common shares to acquire 20 companies, including Chicago-based True North Communications. True North was acquired in a pooling, common stock acquisition valued at about $2.1 billion. IPG issued about 58.2 million shares in the transaction. True North, which earned $97 million in 2000, on $1.5 billion of revenues, has three major global brands: FCB Worldwide, advertising; BSMG Worldwide, public relations; and Marketing Drive Worldwide, marketing services. Its other major brands include Bozell Group, New America Strategies Group, Temerlin McClain, R/GA, Tierney Communications and TN Media. The acquisition increased the size of IPG's operations by about 25%. The acquisition precipitated a major reorganization and restructuring, and resulted in some one-time revenue losses, as client conflicts materialized.

In addition to the True North companies, advertising, public relations, and marketing functions are conducted in more than 100 countries, through Mc-Cann-Erickson WorldGroup, The FCB Group, The Partnership, The Interpublic Sports & Entertainment Group and a number of leading independent agencies. The independent agencies include such firms as Campbell Ewald; Deutsch; Hill Holiday; The Martin Agency; Carmichael-Lynch; Gotham; MAGNA Global; Weber Shandwick Worldwide; Holin/Harris International; DeVries Public Relations; Jack Morton Worldwide; Initiative Media; and FutureBrand.

The company generates revenue from planning, creating and placing advertising in various media and from planning and executing other communications or marketing programs. IPG also receives commissions from clients for planning and supervising work done by outside contractors in the physical preparation of finished print advertisements and the production of TV and radio commercials and other forms of advertising. It also derives revenue in a number of other ways, including the planning and placement in media of advertising produced by unrelated advertising agencies; the maintenance of specialized media placement facilities; the creation and publication of brochures, billboards, point of sale materials and direct marketing pieces for clients; the planning and carrying out of specialized marketing research; public relations campaigns; creating and managing special events at which client products are featured; and designing and carrying out interactive programs for special uses.

Operations outside the U.S. accounted for 44% of income from commissions and fees in 2003. By region, the U.K. accounted for 10%, the remainder of Europe 19%, Asia Pacific 7%, Latin America 4%, and all other 4%.

The company's five largest clients combined accounted for 17.4% of total revenues in 2003; the 20 largest clients accounted for 29.8%. The largest client, GM, accounted for 8.3%. Other major clients were Johnson & Johnson, Microsoft, Nestle and Unilever.

Company Financials Fiscal Year ending December 31

Per Share Data ($)

(Year Ended December 31)	2003	2002	2001	2000	1999	1998	1997	1996	1995	1994
Tangible Bk. Val.	NM	NM	NM	NM	NM	NM	0.32	0.50	0.47	0.21
Cash Flow	-0.90	0.83	-0.36	1.99	1.77	1.67	1.21	1.10	0.88	0.79
Earnings	-1.43	0.26	-1.37	1.15	1.11	1.11	0.95	0.85	0.55	0.51
S&P Core Earnings	-0.84	0.36	-0.60	NA	NA	NA	NA	NA	NA	NA
Dividends	Nil	0.38	0.38	0.37	0.33	0.29	0.25	0.22	0.20	0.18
Payout Ratio	Nil	146%	NM	32%	30%	26%	26%	26%	36%	36%
Prices - High	16.50	34.98	47.43	57.68	58.37	40.31	26.50	16.75	14.45	11.95
- Low	7.20	9.85	18.25	32.68	34.40	22.56	15.66	13.20	10.58	9.16
P/E Ratio - High	NM	NM	NM	50	53	36	28	20	26	23
- Low	NM	NM	NM	28	31	20	16	15	19	18

Income Statement Analysis (Million $)

	2003	2002	2001	2000	1999	1998	1997	1996	1995	1994
Revs.	5,863	6,204	6,727	5,626	4,427	3,844	2,997	2,431	2,094	1,916
Oper. Inc.	719	763	1,113	1,096	791	656	437	351	322	278
Depr.	204	218	372	263	190	159	75.0	60.5	77.6	63.9
Int. Exp.	173	146	165	109	66.4	58.7	49.4	40.7	38.0	32.9
Pretax Inc.	-330	271	-519	672	592	570	448	370	260	205
Eff. Tax Rate	NM	51.8%	NM	40.7%	39.9%	40.7%	41.3%	40.5%	47.2%	42.1%
Net Inc.	-553	100	-505	359	322	310	239	205	130	115
S&P Core Earnings	-325	136	-217	NA	NA	NA	NA	NA	NA	NA

Balance Sheet & Other Fin. Data (Million $)

	2003	2002	2001	2000	1999	1998	1997	1996	1995	1994
Cash	2,006	933	935	748	1,018	841	715	504	457	442
Curr. Assets	7,350	6,322	6,467	6,026	5,768	4,777	4,026	3,353	2,974	2,675
Total Assets	12,235	11,794	11,515	10,238	8,727	6,943	5,703	4,765	4,260	3,793
Curr. Liab.	6,625	7,090	6,434	6,106	5,637	4,658	3,752	3,199	2,827	2,595
LT Debt	2,192	1,818	2,481	1,505	867	507	453	346	284	242
Common Equity	2,721	2,100	2,384	2,046	2,407	1,265	1,355	872	750	649
Total Cap.	5,356	3,988	4,953	3,637	3,394	1,828	1,592	1,241	1,048	904
Cap. Exp.	160	183	268	202	150	137	96.9	79.1	69.6	55.9
Cash Flow	-349	317	-133	622	512	469	314	266	207	179
Curr. Ratio	1.1	0.9	1.0	1.0	1.0	1.0	1.1	1.1	1.0	1.0
% LT Debt of Cap.	40.9	45.6	50.1	41.4	25.5	27.7	28.4	27.9	27.1	26.8
% Net Inc.of Revs.	NM	1.6	NM	6.4	7.3	8.1	8.0	8.4	6.2	6.0
% Ret. on Assets	NM	0.9	NM	3.7	4.1	4.9	4.6	4.5	3.2	3.4
% Ret. on Equity	NM	5.1	NM	18.8	14.7	23.7	19.6	25.3	31.8	18.7

Data as orig reptd.; bef. results of disc opers/spec. items. Per share data adj. for stk. divs. Bold denotes primary EPS - prior periods restated. E-Estimated. NA-Not Available. NM-Not Meaningful. NR-Not Ranked. UR-Under Review.

Office: 1271 Avenue of the Americas, New York, NY 10020.
Telephone: 212-399-8000.
Website: http://www.interpublic.com
Chrmn: M. Roth.
Pres & CEO: D. Bell.
EVP & CFO: R.G. Thompson.

SVP & Treas: E. Johnson.
SVP, Secy & General Counsel: N.J. Camera.
VP & Investor Contact: J.L. Lehsne 212-445-8433.
Dirs: D. Bell, F. J. Borelli, R. K. Brack, J. M. Considine, C. J. Coughlin, J. J. Dooner, Jr., R. A. Goldstein, H. J. Greeniaus, M. I. Roth, J. P. Samper.

Founded: in 1902.
Domicile: Delaware.
Employees: 43,400.
S&P Analyst: William H. Donald/PMW/GG

Intuit

Recommendation: **HOLD** ★★★☆☆
SELL | SELL | HOLD | BUY | BUY

12-Month Target Price: **$51.00**
(as of September 30, 2004)

INTU has an approximate 0.08% weighting in the **S&P 500**

Sector: Information Technology
Sub-Industry: Application Software
Peer Group: Accounting & Financial Software

Summary: This company develops and markets small business accounting and management, tax preparation, and personal finance software.

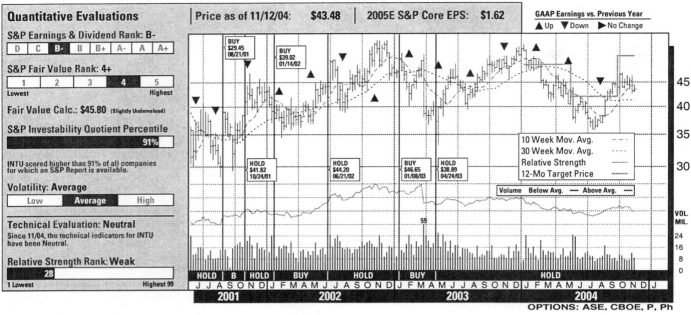

Quantitative Evaluations

S&P Earnings & Dividend Rank: B-

| D | C | B- | B | B+ | A- | A | A+ |

S&P Fair Value Rank: 4+

| 1 | 2 | 3 | 4 | 5 |
| Lowest | | | | Highest |

Fair Value Calc.: $45.80 (Slightly Undervalued)

S&P Investability Quotient Percentile
91%

INTU scored higher than 91% of all companies for which an S&P Report is available.

Volatility: Average

| Low | Average | High |

Technical Evaluation: Neutral
Since 11/04, the technical indicators for INTU have been Neutral.

Relative Strength Rank: Weak
28
1 Lowest — Highest 99

Price as of 11/12/04: **$43.48** | 2005E S&P Core EPS: **$1.62**

GAAP Earnings vs. Previous Year
▲ Up ▼ Down ► No Change

- 10 Week Mov. Avg.
- 30 Week Mov. Avg.
- Relative Strength
- 12-Mo Target Price

Volume Below Avg. — Above Avg. —

BUY $29.45 08/21/01
BUY $39.02 01/14/02
HOLD $41.82 10/24/01
HOLD $44.20 06/21/02
BUY $46.65 01/08/03
HOLD $38.89 04/24/03

HOLD | B | HOLD | BUY | HOLD | BUY | HOLD

J J A S O N D | J F M A M J J A S O N D | J F M A M J J A S O N D | J F M A M J J A S O N D | J
2001 | 2002 | 2003 | 2004

VOL. MIL.
45 40 35 30
24 16 8 0

OPTIONS: ASE, CBOE, P, Ph

Analyst commentary prepared by Scott H. Kessler/CB/BK

Highlights October 11, 2004

- We expect revenues to increase approximately 11% in FY 05 (Jul.), paced by growth in small business and TurboTax offerings. INTU has been increasingly emphasizing the medium-sized small business market (organizations with 20 to 250 employees) by offering more robust and specialized solutions, as well as ancillary services, and we look for the company to introduce several new related offerings and enhancements throughout FY 05.

- Annual pro forma operating margins (which exclude the impact of acquisition-related charges) expanded notably in FY 02 and FY 03, and we expect a further widening through FY 05, reflecting improved business processes and a more disciplined and effective allocation of resources. In August 2004, INTU announced the proposed sale of its public sector business management solutions segment, which contributed $13 million to FY 04 revenues; we expect this transaction to be completed by the end of 2004, subject to necessary approvals.

- We believe that a new $500 million stock repurchase program announced in May 2004 will bolster EPS comparisons. Our EPS estimates exclude amortization of purchased software and charges for purchased R&D, as well as one-time items.

Investment Rationale/Risk October 11, 2004

- Since CEO Steve Bennett joined INTU in 2001, its profitability has improved notably, in our opinion. Despite market share leadership in multiple areas, we believe re-accelerating revenue growth remains INTU's biggest challenge.

- Risks to our opinion and target price include increasing competition in the small-business market from the likes of Microsoft (MSFT: buy, $28) and potential execution issues with respect to anticipated new product enhancements and introductions.

- INTU's recent calendar year 2004 P/E of 26X was modestly higher than that of the S&P 500 Software Industry, but its 2004 P/E-to-growth rate of 1.7X was somewhat below the level of the industry group. Based on our discounted cash flow model (which assumes a weighted average cost of capital of 12.5% and compound annual free cash flow growth of 17% from FY 05 through FY 07, trending gradually lower thereafter), INTU shares trade modestly below our estimate of their intrinsic value. INTU had $1.0 billion in cash, cash equivalents and short-term investments, and no debt, as of June 2004. Based on intrinsic value calculations, our 12-month target price for the stock is $51.

Key Stock Statistics

S&P Oper. EPS 2005E	1.96	52-week Range	$53.89-35.84
P/E on S&P Oper. EPS 2005E	22.2	12 Month P/E	27.5
Yield (%)	Nil	Beta	1.34
Dividend Rate/Share	Nil	Shareholders	108,000
Shares Outstanding (M)	189.1	Market Cap (B)	$ 8.2

Value of $10,000 invested five years ago: **$ 13,507**

Dividend Data

No cash dividends have been paid.

Revenues/Earnings Data Fiscal year ending July 31

Revenues (Million $)

	2004	2003	2002	2001	2000	1999
1Q	242.5	223.3	168.7	187.5	163.1	112.0
2Q	636.3	558.1	490.8	457.6	373.7	345.9
3Q	713.0	634.7	501.7	425.2	329.1	239.7
4Q	275.9	245.1	197.2	191.2	162.3	149.9
Yr.	1,868	1,651	1,358	1,261	1,094	847.6

Earnings Per Share ($)

	2004	2003	2002	2001	2000	1999
1Q	-0.27	-0.26	-0.48	-0.23	-0.33	-0.28
2Q	0.73	0.59	0.47	0.12	0.47	0.47
3Q	1.33	1.06	0.62	-0.07	1.39	0.37
4Q	-0.22	-0.12	-0.31	-0.29	0.08	1.35
Yr.	1.58	1.63	0.32	-0.47	1.45	1.97

Next earnings report expected: NA Source: S&P, Company Reports
EPS Estimates based on S&P Operating Earnings; historical GAAP earnings are as reported.

STANDARD &POOR'S

Intuit Inc.

Recommendation: HOLD ★ ★ ★ ☆ ☆   12-Month Target Price: **$51.00** (as of September 30, 2004)

Business Summary October 11, 2004

Intuit aims to transform the way people run their businesses and manage their finances. Its growth strategy entails pursuing large and underpenetrated markets where it can sustain competitive advantages, providing customer-driven innovation to address consumer needs, and using operational rigor and process excellence to execute effectively.

QuickBooks offerings (which accounted for 35% of total net revenues in FY 04 (Jul.) and 33% of total net revenues in FY 03) provide bookkeeping capabilities and business management tools. Products include QuickBooks Basic, QuickBooks Pro (for up to five simultaneous users), QuickBooks Premier (for small businesses needing more advanced accounting functionality), and QuickBooks Enterprise Solutions Business Management Software (for businesses with up to 250 employees). Premier and Enterprise offerings are also available in a variety of industry specific editions. Additional products are QuickBooks Point of Sale (for retail businesses) and QuickBooks Do-It-Yourself Payroll (for small business to prepare their own payrolls).

Intuit-Branded Small Business offerings (15% and 15%) consist of miscellaneous business management solutions. Outsourced payroll services include QuickBooks Assisted Payroll Service, Intuit Payroll Services Complete Payroll, Complete Payroll, and Premiere Payroll Service. INTU also offers Information Technology Solutions (to track and support technology assets and resources), Distribution Management Solutions (for wholesale durable goods companies), Real Estate Solutions (for residential, commercial and corporate property managers), Con-

struction Business Solutions (for construction companies), and Public Sector Solutions (for non-profit organizations, universities and government agencies).

The Consumer Tax segment (26% and 26%) is centered on TurboTax. TurboTax software enables individuals and small businesses to prepare and file income tax returns using computers. TurboTax for the Web allows individuals to prepare tax returns online. Versions of TurboTax Premier software are designed to address the special income tax needs of different types of users, including investors, those planning for retirement, and rental property owners. Electronic tax filing services are also provided.

The Professional Tax area (13% and 15%) provides software and services for accountants in public practice who serve multiple clients. The two primary products are ProSeries Basic Edition (for smaller tax practices) and ProSeries Express Edition (for tax practices focused on helping taxpayers obtain their tax refunds quickly).

Other Businesses (11% and 11%) consist of Quicken desktop software (used to help organize, understand and manage personal finances); Quicken.com (INTU's primary personal finance Web site); bill payment and online banking services; a Quicken credit card; and operations in Canada, the U.K., Australia, New Zealand and Singapore.

Company Financials Fiscal Year ending July 31

Per Share Data ($)

(Year Ended July 31)	2004	2003	2002	2001	2000	1999	1998	1997	1996	1995
Tangible Bk. Val.	5.50	6.88	8.04	8.29	7.99	5.49	4.03	2.62	1.95	1.57
Cash Flow	2.07	1.61	0.59	-0.18	2.46	2.71	0.28	0.39	0.40	0.15
Earnings	1.58	1.63	0.32	-0.47	1.45	1.97	-0.08	-0.02	-0.11	-0.37
S&P Core Earnings	1.21	0.82	NA	-0.63	NA	NA	NA	NA	NA	NA
Dividends	Nil	Nil	Nil	Nil	Nil	Nil	Nil	Nil	Nil	Nil
Payout Ratio	Nil	Nil	Nil	Nil	Nil	Nil	Nil	Nil	Nil	Nil
Prices - High	53.26	53.89	55.04	47.37	90.00	64.00	24.45	13.72	26.00	29.75
- Low	35.84	33.30	34.52	22.62	25.75	22.50	11.29	6.95	9.08	9.91
P/E Ratio - High	34	33	NM	NM	62	32	NM	NM	NM	NM
- Low	23	20	NM	NM	18	11	NM	NM	NM	NM

Income Statement Analysis (Million $)

	2004	2003	2002	2001	2000	1999	1998	1997	1996	1995
Revs.	1,868	1,651	1,358	1,261	1,094	848	593	599	539	395
Oper. Inc.	561	461	343	265	200	254	70.5	107	70.6	51.9
Depr.	97.0	76.5	59.9	59.9	213	141	53.2	58.7	68.3	64.0
Int. Exp.	Nil	Nil	Nil	Nil	Nil	Nil	Nil	Nil	Nil	0.20
Pretax Inc.	453	393	84.9	-96.5	513	617	-19.8	9.81	1.87	-21.1
Eff. Tax Rate	30.0%	33.0%	17.9%	NM	40.4%	39.0%	NM	129.9%	8.67%	NM
Net Inc.	317	263	69.8	-97.1	306	377	-12.2	-2.93	-14.3	-45.4
S&P Core Earnings	245	172	-0.77	-129	NA	NA	NA	NA	NA	NA

Balance Sheet & Other Fin. Data (Million $)

	2004	2003	2002	2001	2000	1999	1998	1997	1996	1995
Cash	27.2	1,207	452	535	643	950	138	46.8	198	70.0
Curr. Assets	1,517	1,669	1,995	2,148	2,129	1,586	980	455	280	259
Total Assets	2,696	2,790	2,963	2,962	2,879	2,328	1,499	664	418	384
Curr. Liab.	857	796	733	788	807	781	375	212	111	98.1
LT Debt	5.77	29.3	14.6	12.4	0.54	36.3	35.6	36.4	5.58	4.40
Common Equity	1,822	1,965	2,216	2,170	4,143	1,511	1,088	415	762	281
Total Cap.	1,828	1,994	2,230	2,182	4,143	1,547	1,124	452	770	286
Cap. Exp.	52.3	50.4	42.6	77.1	94.9	80.0	69.3	27.6	69.3	4.86
Cash Flow	414	340	130	-37.2	519	518	41.1	55.7	54.0	18.6
Curr. Ratio	1.8	2.1	2.7	2.7	2.6	2.0	2.6	2.1	2.5	2.6
% LT Debt of Cap.	0.3	1.5	0.7	0.6	0.0	2.3	NA	8.1	Nil	1.5
% Net Inc.of Revs.	17.0	15.9	5.1	NM	27.9	44.4	NM	NM	NM	NM
% Ret. on Assets	11.6	9.2	2.4	NM	11.4	19.7	NM	NM	NM	NM
% Ret. on Equity	16.7	12.6	3.2	NM	8.4	29.0	NM	NM	NM	NM

Data as orig reptd.; bef. results of disc opers/spec. items. Per share data adj. for stk. divs.; EPS diluted. E-Estimated. NA-Not Available. NM-Not Meaningful. NR-Not Ranked. UR-Under Review.

Office: 2700 Coast Ave, Mountain View, CA 94043-1140.
Telephone: 650-944-6000.
Email: investor_relations@intuit.com
Website: http://www.intuit.com
Chrmn: W.V. Campbell.
Pres & CEO: S.M. Bennett.

SVP & CFO: R. Henske.
SVP & CTO: R.W. Ihrie.
VP, Secy & General Counsel: L.A. Fennell.
Dirs: S. M. Bennett, C. W. Brody, W. V. Campbell, S. D. Cook, L. J. Doerr, D. L. Dubinsky, M. R. Hallman, D. Powell, S. D. Sclavos.

Founded: in 1984.
Domicile: Delaware.
Employees: 6,700.
S&P Analyst: Scott H. Kessler/CB/BK

Recommendation: **HOLD** ★★★★★
SELL SELL HOLD BUY BUY

12-Month Target Price: $89.00
(as of October 21, 2004)

ITT has an approximate 0.07% weighting in the **S&P 500**

Sector: Industrials
Sub-Industry: Industrial Machinery
Peer Group: Industrial Equipment

Summary: This diversified industrial manufacturer is the legal successor to the old ITT Corp.

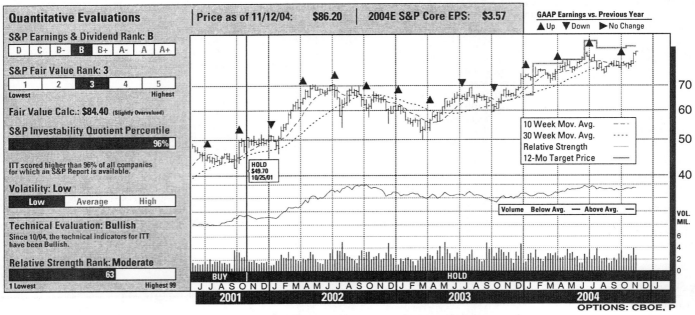

Quantitative Evaluations

S&P Earnings & Dividend Rank: B
D | C | B- | **B** | B+ | A- | A | A+

S&P Fair Value Rank: 3
1 | 2 | **3** | 4 | 5
Lowest ... Highest

Fair Value Calc.: $84.40 (Slightly Overvalued)

S&P Investability Quotient Percentile
96%
ITT scored higher than 96% of all companies for which an S&P Report is available.

Volatility: Low
Low | Average | High

Technical Evaluation: Bullish
Since 10/04, the technical indicators for ITT have been Bullish.

Relative Strength Rank: Moderate
63
1 Lowest ... Highest 99

Price as of 11/12/04: $86.20 | **2004E S&P Core EPS:** $3.57

GAAP Earnings vs. Previous Year
▲ Up ▼ Down ► No Change

10 Week Mov. Avg.
30 Week Mov. Avg.
Relative Strength
12-Mo Target Price

HOLD $49.70 10/25/01

Volume Below Avg. — Above Avg.

VOL. MIL.

BUY | HOLD
J J A S O N D J F M A M J J A S O N D J F M A M J J A S O N D J F M A M J J A S O N D J
2001 | 2002 | 2003 | 2004

OPTIONS: CBOE, P

Analyst commentary prepared by Efraim Levy, CFA /PMW/MWJ

Highlights November 01, 2004

- We expect economic growth through 2005. Against this backdrop, we see ITT's revenues increasing about 7% to 8% in 2005. With an expanding backlog, the defense business should produce 8% to 10% gains. We see fluid technology segment sales also advancing 8% to 10%, aided by improving water and wastewater demand. We look for electronic components to be 6% to 8% higher. We see motion and flow control up about 1% to 3%.

- Aided by an improved cost structure, operating margins before research and development costs should widen. We forecast 2005 EPS of $5.10, after $4.50 that we see for 2004, versus adjusted EPS from continuing operations of $3.72 in 2003. Our 2004 forecast includes a second quarter benefit of $0.12 from several tax items, mostly offset by other special items, including restructuring items, aggregating $0.11.

- For the longer term, we expect revenues to post 8% to 10% average annual growth, reflecting new products, expanded markets, and likely acquisitions.

Investment Rationale/Risk November 01, 2004

- We believe strong cash flow should support a modest cash dividend, debt reduction, and strategic acquisitions. Based on our adjustments for estimated option and pension expense, our 2005 S&P Core EPS forecast is about 13% below our operating EPS estimate. With long term debt at about 20% of capitalization, below that of most peers, the balance sheet appears healthy to us.

- Risks to our opinion and target price include reduced demand at the company's operating segments, and competitive price pressures.

- Our use of a P/E multiple of about 14X applied to our 2005 EPS estimate reflects peer and historical P/E comparisons. Our discounted cash flow model, which assumes a weighted average cost of capital of 10.63%, compound annual growth of 7.7% over the next 15 years, and a terminal growth rate of 4%, generates intrinsic value of about $106. Based on an equal weighting of our P/E multiple and DCF analyses, our 12-month target price is $89.

Key Stock Statistics

S&P Core EPS 2005E	4.44	52-week Range	$86.20-65.20
S&P Oper. EPS 2004E	4.50	12 Month P/E	19.4
P/E on S&P Oper. EPS 2004E	19.2	Beta	0.63
S&P Oper. EPS 2005E	5.10	Shareholders	30,553
Yield (%)	0.8%	Market Cap (B)	$ 8.0
Dividend Rate/Share	0.68	Shares Outstanding (M)	92.3

Value of $10,000 invested five years ago: **$ 27,525**

Dividend Data Dividends have been paid since 1996

Amount ($)	Date Decl.	Ex-Div. Date	Stock of Record	Payment Date
0.170	Feb. 03	Mar. 10	Mar. 12	Apr. 01 '04
0.170	May. 11	May. 19	May. 21	Jul. 01 '04
0.170	Jul. 13	Aug. 25	Aug. 27	Oct. 01 '04
0.170	Oct. 05	Nov. 17	Nov. 19	Jan. 01 '05

Revenues/Earnings Data Fiscal year ending December 31

Revenues (Million $)

	2004	2003	2002	2001	2000	1999
1Q	1,516	1,296	1,186	1,186	1,205	1,092
2Q	1,653	1,438	1,320	1,184	1,224	1,192
3Q	1,668	1,375	1,235	1,124	1,173	1,106
4Q	—	1,517	1,244	1,182	1,215	1,242
Yr.	—	5,627	4,985	4,676	4,829	4,632

Earnings Per Share ($)

	2004	2003	2002	2001	2000	1999
1Q	0.93	0.92	0.77	0.65	0.57	0.45
2Q	1.19	0.98	0.99	0.84	0.78	0.70
3Q	1.16	1.09	1.28	0.75	0.72	0.60
4Q	E1.23	1.16	1.01	0.15	0.87	0.80
Yr.	E4.50	4.15	4.06	2.39	2.94	2.53

Next earnings report expected: late-January Source: S&P, Company Reports
EPS Estimates based on S&P Operating Earnings; historical GAAP earnings are as reported.

ITT Industries, Inc.

Recommendation: **HOLD ★ ★ ★ ★ ★**   12-Month Target Price: **$89.00** (as of October 21, 2004)

Business Summary November 01, 2004

ITT Industries (formerly ITT Corp.) is the legal successor to the old ITT Corp. In a restructuring completed in December 1995, old ITT was divided into three separate, publicly owned entities. ITT Industries retained old ITT's industrial units, and two companies were spun off: ITT Hartford Group (insurance), and New ITT Corp. (hotels, gaming, entertainment and education). Old ITT shares were converted into ITT Industries shares on a one-for-one basis. One share each of New ITT and ITT Hartford were distributed to shareholders for each ITT share. After the discontinuation and spinoff of ITT Hartford Group and New ITT Corp., ITT now produces mostly defense electronics and fluid technology products.

Fluid technology products (40% of 2003 sales) include pumps, valves, heat exchangers, mixers and fluid measuring instruments and controls for residential, agricultural, commercial, municipal and industrial applications. Fluid Technology became the world's largest pump manufacturer (formerly third largest) following its 1997 acquisition of Goulds Pumps, Inc.

Defense electronics and services (32%) are sold to the military and government agencies. Products include traffic control systems, jamming devices that guard military planes against radar guided missiles, digit combat radios, night vision devices, radar, satellite instruments and other. About 81% of segment sales are to the U.S. government.

Motion and flow control (17%) products include switches and valves for industrial and aerospace applications, products for the marine and leisure markets, and fluid handling materials, such as tubing systems and connectors for various automotive and industrial markets for the transportation industry.

Electronic components (11%) are marketed under the Cannon brand. These products include connectors, switches and cabling used in communications, computing, aerospace and industrial applications, as well as network services.

Revenues increased in 2003, with Defense, Fluid Technology, Motion and Flow Control and Electronic Components all posting higher sales.

Excluding a net positive impact of $0.43 a share from special items, 2003 EPS would have been $3.86 (including $0.14 from discontinued operations), versus an adjusted $3.70 in 2002.

In October 2004, ITT projected 2004 EPS at the high end of its prior guidance of $4.45 to $4.50 on a GAAP basis. The company reiterated its forecast of free cash flow of $425 million to $475 million for 2004, and saw 2004 revenues of $6.6 billion to $6.66 billion.

Company Financials Fiscal Year ending December 31

Per Share Data ($)

(Year Ended December 31)	2003	2002	2001	2000	1999	1998	1997	1996	1995	1994
Tangible Bk. Val.	1.56	NM	NM	NM	NM	4.53	NM	3.81	2.26	50.41
Cash Flow	6.15	5.89	4.74	5.18	4.50	0.87	4.07	5.66	3.83	12.30
Earnings	4.15	4.06	2.39	2.94	2.53	-0.86	0.94	1.85	0.03	7.10
S&P Core Earnings	3.87	1.37	-0.35	NA	NA	NA	NA	NA	NA	NA
Dividends	0.64	0.60	0.60	0.60	0.60	0.60	0.60	0.60	0.99	1.98
Payout Ratio	15%	15%	25%	20%	24%	NM	64%	32%	NM	28%
Prices - High	75.40	70.85	52.00	39.62	41.50	40.87	33.68	28.62	24.25	104.25
- Low	50.11	45.80	35.55	22.37	30.50	28.12	22.12	21.50	21.25	77.00
P/E Ratio - High	18	17	22	13	16	NM	36	15	NM	15
- Low	12	11	15	8	12	NM	24	12	NM	11

Income Statement Analysis (Million $)

	2003	2002	2001	2000	1999	1998	1997	1996	1995	1994
Revs.	5,627	4,985	4,676	4,829	4,632	4,493	8,777	8,718	8,884	23,620
Oper. Inc.	559	706	707	695	592	525	904	941	869	2,678
Depr.	188	171	213	202	181	196	378	433	423	592
Int. Exp.	Nil	68.8	85.5	93.1	84.8	126	133	169	175	413
Pretax Inc.	531	509	333	420	370	-160	187	371	71.0	1,259
Eff. Tax Rate	26.3%	25.3%	35.0%	37.0%	37.0%	NM	39.0%	40.0%	70.5%	30.9%
Net Inc.	391	380	217	265	233	-98.0	114	223	21.0	852
S&P Core Earnings	364	129	-31.7	NA	NA	NA	NA	NA	NA	NA

Balance Sheet & Other Fin. Data (Million $)

	2003	2002	2001	2000	1999	1998	1997	1996	1995	1994
Cash	414	202	121	88.7	182	880	192	122	94.0	4,816
Curr. Assets	2,106	1,701	1,459	1,506	1,628	2,382	2,377	2,289	2,502	NA
Total Assets	5,938	5,390	4,508	4,611	4,530	5,049	6,221	5,491	5,879	100,854
Curr. Liab.	1,687	1,730	1,897	2,233	2,110	2,151	3,545	2,538	2,661	NA
LT Debt	461	492	456	408	479	516	532	583	961	3,340
Common Equity	1,848	1,137	1,376	1,211	1,099	1,299	822	799	627	5,326
Total Cap.	2,309	1,630	1,832	1,620	1,578	1,815	1,386	1,492	1,709	8,979
Cap. Exp.	154	153	174	181	228	213	460	406	450	727
Cash Flow	579	551	430	466	414	98.0	492	656	429	1,414
Curr. Ratio	1.2	1.0	0.8	0.7	0.8	1.1	0.7	0.9	0.9	NA
% LT Debt of Cap.	20.0	30.2	24.9	25.2	30.3	28.4	38.4	39.1	56.3	37.2
% Net Inc.of Revs.	6.9	7.6	4.6	5.5	5.0	NM	1.3	2.6	0.3	3.6
% Ret. on Assets	6.9	7.7	4.8	5.8	4.9	NM	1.9	3.9	0.3	1.0
% Ret. on Equity	26.2	30.2	16.8	22.9	19.4	NM	14.1	31.3	0.2	13.5

Data as orig reptd.; bef. results of disc opers/spec. items. Per share data adj. for stk. divs.; EPS diluted. E-Estimated. NA-Not Available. NM-Not Meaningful. NR-Not Ranked. UR-Under Review.

Office: 4 West Red Oak Lane, White Plains, NY 10604-3617.
Telephone: 914-641-2000.
Website: http://www.itt.com
Chrmn: L.J. Guiliano.
Pres & CEO: S.R. Loranger.
SVP & CFO: E.W. Williams.

SVP & Treas: D.E. Foley.
SVP & General Counsel: V.A. Maffeo.
VP & Investor Contact: R. Powers 914-641-2030.
Dirs: R. V. Araskog, C. J. Crawford, L. J. Giuliano, C. A. Gold, R. F. Hake, J. J. Hamre, R. W. LeBoeuf, S. R. Loranger, F. T. MacInnis, L. S. Sanford, M. I. Tambakeras.

Founded: in 1920.
Domicile: Indiana.
Employees: 39,000.
S&P Analyst: Efraim Levy, CFA /PMW/MWJ

Jabil Circuit

Recommendation: HOLD ★★★☆☆
SELL SELL HOLD BUY BUY

12-Month Target Price: $25.00
(as of August 11, 2004)

JBL has an approximate 0.05% weighting in the **S&P 500**

Sector: Information Technology
Sub-Industry: Electronic Manufacturing Services
Peer Group: Circuit Boards/Microelectronics - Larger Sales

Summary: JBL manufactures circuit board assemblies for international OEMs in the PC, peripheral, communications and automotive markets.

Quantitative Evaluations

S&P Earnings & Dividend Rank: B

| D | C | B- | **B** | B+ | A- | A | A+ |

S&P Fair Value Rank: 5

| 1 | 2 | 3 | 4 | **5** |
| Lowest | | | | Highest |

Fair Value Calc.: $29.80 (Slightly Undervalued)

S&P Investability Quotient Percentile
84%

JBL scored higher than 84% of all companies for which an S&P Report is available.

Volatility: Average

| Low | **Average** | High |

Technical Evaluation: Bullish
Since 9/04, the technical indicators for JBL have been Bullish.

Relative Strength Rank: Moderate
67
1 Lowest   Highest 99

Price as of 11/12/04: **$25.55**   **2005E S&P Core EPS:** **$1.10**

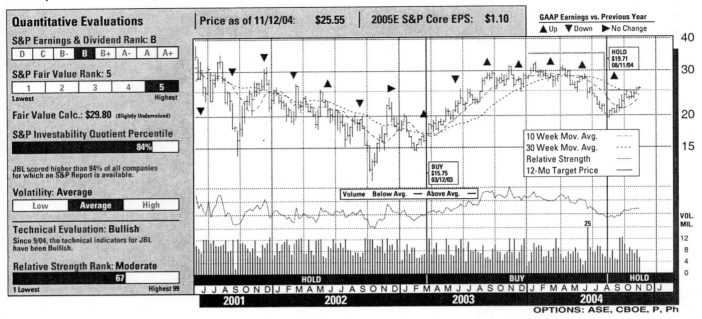

GAAP Earnings vs. Previous Year
▲ Up ▼ Down ► No Change

HOLD $19.71 08/11/04

10 Week Mov. Avg.
30 Week Mov. Avg.
Relative Strength
12-Mo Target Price

BUY $15.75 03/12/03

Volume Below Avg. — Above Avg.

VOL. MIL.

HOLD   BUY   HOLD
J J A S O N D J F M A M J J A S O N D J F M A M J J A S O N D J F M A M J J A S O N D J
2001   2002   2003   2004

OPTIONS: ASE, CBOE, P, Ph

Analyst commentary prepared by Richard N. Stice, CFA /PMW/BK

Highlights September 23, 2004

- We forecast an 18% increase in FY 05 (Aug.) revenue, following growth of 32% in FY 04. We anticipate that gains will be driven by new business wins, a continued pickup in end markets (particularly the consumer and instrumentation segments), and an ongoing trend on the part of customers to outsource more of their production to primary industry participants such as JBL.

- We anticipate that gross margins will narrow, as higher volumes are out-weighed by a less favorable business mix. We expect R&D expenses to increase, due to a pickup in design-related programs. We think that interest income will grow, based on our expectations of increasing free cash flow generation and a rising interest rate environment.

- We project FY 05 EPS of $1.30, up 27% from FY 04's $1.02 (excluding special charges of $0.21). Our Standard & Poor's Core Earnings estimate for FY 05 is $1.10, with the difference reflecting projected stock option expense.

Investment Rationale/Risk September 23, 2004

- We believe the outlook for the electronics manufacturing services industry remains favorable, and we expect the company to benefit from increased penetration of the outsourcing model. However, following a less robust IT spending outlook given by Cisco Systems (CSCO: accumulate, $19), which was one of JBL's two largest customer in FY 04, we would not add to positions in these high beta shares.

- Risks to our recommendation and target price include potential market share losses, a protracted slowdown in demand for telecom products, delays in the implementation of new contracts and facilities, and instability in overseas locations.

- Our 12-month target price of $25 is based on a combination of valuation metrics. The first is a relative price to sales measure based on JBL's peer group; the second is intrinsic value calculated from our discounted cash flow analysis. Our assumptions include a weighted average cost of capital of 12.1% and an expected terminal growth rate of 3%.

Key Stock Statistics

S&P Oper. EPS 2005E	1.30	52-week Range	$32.40-19.18
P/E on S&P Oper. EPS 2005E	19.7	12 Month P/E	31.5
S&P Oper. EPS 2006E	1.60	Beta	NA
Yield (%)	Nil	Shareholders	3,628
Dividend Rate/Share	Nil	Market Cap (B)	$ 5.1
Shares Outstanding (M)	201.0		

Value of $10,000 invested five years ago: **$ 8,211**

Dividend Data

No cash dividends have been paid.

Revenues/Earnings Data Fiscal year ending August 31

Revenues (Million $)

	2004	2003	2002	2001	2000	1999
1Q	1,509	1,068	884.6	1,129	689.8	447.9
2Q	1,492	1,146	822.1	1,211	837.6	493.4
3Q	1,626	1,219	850.6	1,046	965.9	522.5
4Q	1,626	1,296	988.2	944.1	1,065	536.5
Yr.	6,253	4,729	3,545	4,331	3,558	2,000

Earnings Per Share ($)

	2004	2003	2002	2001	2000	1999
1Q	0.20	0.04	0.04	0.24	0.21	0.13
2Q	0.19	0.05	0.02	0.21	0.18	0.14
3Q	0.19	0.02	0.10	0.09	0.21	0.15
4Q	0.22	0.10	0.01	0.06	0.24	0.15
Yr.	0.81	0.21	0.17	0.59	0.78	0.56

Next earnings report expected: mid-December Source: S&P, Company Reports
EPS Estimates based on S&P Operating Earnings; historical GAAP earnings are as reported.

Jabil Circuit, Inc.

Recommendation: **HOLD** ★ ★ ★ ☆ ☆   12-Month Target Price: **$25.00** (as of August 11, 2004)

Business Summary September 23, 2004

Jabil Circuit aims to expand its position as one of the leading global providers of electronic manufacturing services (EMS) to major original equipment manufacturers (OEMs). Its strategies to achieve this goal include establishing and maintaining long-term relationships with electronics companies in expanding industries, using work cell business units (divisions dedicated to one customer, operating with a high level of autonomy), expanding parallel global production, and pursuing selected acquisition opportunities.

JBL designs and manufactures electronic circuit board assemblies and systems for major OEMs in the automotive, computing and storage, consumer products, instrumentation and medical, networking, peripherals and telecom industries. The company serves customers with dedicated work cell business units that combine high volume, highly automated continuous flow manufacturing with advanced electronic design technologies. FY 03 (Aug.) industry revenues were derived as follows: networking 23% (30% in FY 02), consumer 20% (8%), computing and storage 15% (13%), telecom 14% (23%), automotive 9% (7%), peripherals 8% (10%), instrumentation and medical 7% (5%), and other 4% (4%).

The company offers a wide spectrum of value-added design services for products that it manufactures for customers. These services are provided to enhance JBL's current customer affiliations and help develop relationships with new customers. Offerings include electronic, industrial, mechanical and computer assisted design, as well as applied R&D.

JBL conducts operations worldwide, with facilities in the U.S., Brazil, China, England, India, Italy, Japan, Malaysia, Mexico, Poland and Singapore. The company's parallel global production strategy offers customers improved supply-chain management, reduced inventory obsolescence, lower transportation costs, and reduced product fulfillment time. Operations outside North America accounted for 79% of net revenue in FY 03, up from 58% in FY 02.

In FY 03, 32 customers accounted collectively for over 95% of net revenues. Cisco Systems accounted for 16% of FY 03 net revenues, Royal Philips Electronics 15%, and Hewlett-Packard 11%.

In the FY 03 first quarter, the company purchased certain operations of Philips Electronics in Austria, Brazil, Hong Kong/China, Hungary, Poland and Singapore. It completed the purchase of three additional sites in Belgium and India during the FY 03 second quarter. Concurrent with the purchase, it entered into a four-year agreement with Philips to provide design and engineering services, new product introduction, procurement, and to manufacture of a wide range of consumer products. Total consideration was about $198 million.

In the FY 03 second quarter, JBL bought facilities from Quantum Corp. in Penang, Malaysia, broadening its base of manufacturing for the computing and storage sector in Asia, expanding its mechanical assemble capabilities, and strengthening its relationship with Quantum. Together with the acquisition, the company entered into a three-year supply agreement with Quantum to manufacture internal tape drives. Total consideration was about $17 million.

Company Financials Fiscal Year ending August 31

Per Share Data ($)

(Year Ended August 31)	2004	2003	2002	2001	2000	1999	1998	1997	1996	1995
Tangible Bk. Val.	7.29	6.06	6.63	6.43	6.68	3.32	1.67	1.23	0.87	0.50
Cash Flow	1.89	1.32	1.11	1.35	1.31	0.90	0.60	0.51	0.29	0.16
Earnings	0.81	0.21	0.17	0.59	0.78	0.56	0.37	0.34	0.17	0.06
S&P Core Earnings	0.59	0.04	NA	0.46	NA	NA	NA	NA	NA	NA
Dividends	Nil	Nil	Nil	Nil	Nil	Nil	Nil	Nil	Nil	Nil
Payout Ratio	Nil	Nil	Nil	Nil	Nil	Nil	Nil	Nil	Nil	Nil
Prices - High	32.40	31.66	26.79	40.99	68.00	38.96	18.71	18.00	5.32	2.87
- Low	19.18	21.20	11.13	14.00	18.62	14.25	5.75	3.84	0.64	0.46
P/E Ratio - High	40	NM	NM	69	87	70	51	53	16	17
- Low	24	NM	65	24	24	25	16	11	2	3

Income Statement Analysis (Million $)

	2004	2003	2002	2001	2000	1999	1998	1997	1996	1995
Revs.	6,253	4,729	3,545	4,331	3,558	2,000	1,277	978	863	559
Oper. Inc.	439	369	296	508	317	197	142	107	63.6	28.4
Depr.	222	224	188	155	99	56.0	35.7	24.9	18.2	12.0
Int. Exp.	19.4	17.0	13.1	5.86	7.61	1.69	3.12	1.61	7.30	6.35
Pretax Inc.	198	37.0	44.8	166	213	140	82.0	80.2	38.1	10.1
Eff. Tax Rate	15.5%	NM	22.4%	28.7%	31.5%	34.4%	30.6%	34.6%	36.0%	27.7%
Net Inc.	167	43.0	34.7	119	146	91.5	56.9	52.5	24.3	7.28
S&P Core Earnings	122	8.12	-0.11	93.4	NA	NA	NA	NA	NA	NA

Balance Sheet & Other Fin. Data (Million $)

	2004	2003	2002	2001	2000	1999	1998	1997	1996	1995
Cash	621	700	641	431	338	114	23.1	45.5	73.3	5.49
Curr. Assets	2,183	2,094	1,588	1,447	1,387	588	290	266	227	218
Total Assets	3,329	3,245	2,548	2,358	2,018	921	527	406	300	281
Curr. Liab.	1,159	1,263	593	505	692	331	187	169	112	185
LT Debt	305	297	355	362	25.0	33.3	81.7	50.0	58.4	27.9
Common Equity	1,819	1,588	1,507	1,414	1,270	546	248	181	124	59.6
Total Cap.	2,125	1,905	1,903	1,813	1,323	588	338	235	186	91.2
Cap. Exp.	218	117	85.5	309	333	150	100	93.8	27.3	25.8
Cash Flow	389	267	223	274	245	147	92.6	77.4	42.6	19.3
Curr. Ratio	1.9	1.7	2.7	2.9	2.0	1.8	1.6	1.6	2.0	1.2
% LT Debt of Cap.	14.4	15.6	18.6	20.0	1.9	5.7	24.2	21.3	31.5	30.6
% Net Inc.of Revs.	2.7	0.9	1.0	2.7	4.1	4.6	4.5	5.4	2.8	1.3
% Ret. on Assets	5.1	1.5	1.4	5.4	9.5	12.7	12.2	14.9	8.4	3.2
% Ret. on Equity	9.8	2.8	2.4	8.8	15.8	23.0	26.5	34.3	26.5	13.1

Data as orig reptd.; bef. results of disc opers/spec. items. Per share data adj. for stk. divs.; EPS diluted. E-Estimated. NA-Not Available. NM-Not Meaningful. NR-Not Ranked. UR-Under Review.

Office: 10560 Dr. Martin Luther King Jr. Street North, St. Petersburg, FL 33716.
Telephone: 727-577-9749.
Email: investor_relations@jabil.com
Website: http://www.jabil.com
Chrmn: W.D. Morean.

Pres & CEO: T.L. Main.
Vice Chrmn: T.A. Sansone.
COO: M. Mondello.
VP & Investor Contact: B. Walters 727-803-3349.
Dirs: L. S. Grafstein, M. S. Lavitt, T. L. Main, W. D. Morean, L. J. Murphy, F. A. Newman, S. A. Raymund, T. A. Sansone.

Founded: in 1969.
Domicile: Delaware.
Employees: 34,000.
S&P Analyst: Richard N. Stice, CFA /PMW/BK

The McGraw·Hill Companies

Janus Capital Group

Recommendation: **SELL** ★ ☆ ☆ ☆ ☆
SELL SELL HOLD BUY BUY

12-Month Target Price: **$11.00**
(as of July 30, 2004)

JNS has an approximate 0.03% weighting in the **S&P 500**

Sector: Financials
Sub-Industry: Asset Management & Custody Banks
Peer Group: Investment Management Cos. - Larger

Summary: Janus is a U.S.-based investment management company that focuses on growth equity strategies.

Quantitative Evaluations

Price as of 11/12/04:	$15.76	2004E S&P Core EPS:	$0.60

S&P Earnings & Dividend Rank: NR

D	C	B-	B	B+	A-	A	A+

S&P Fair Value Rank: 2

1	2	3	4	5
Lowest				Highest

Fair Value Calc.: $14.70 (Slightly Overvalued)

S&P Investability Quotient Percentile

37%

JNS scored lower than 63% of all companies for which an S&P Report is available.

Volatility: Average

Low	Average	High

Technical Evaluation: Bullish
Since 10/04, the technical indicators for JNS have been Bullish.

Relative Strength Rank: Moderate

66

1 Lowest	Highest 99

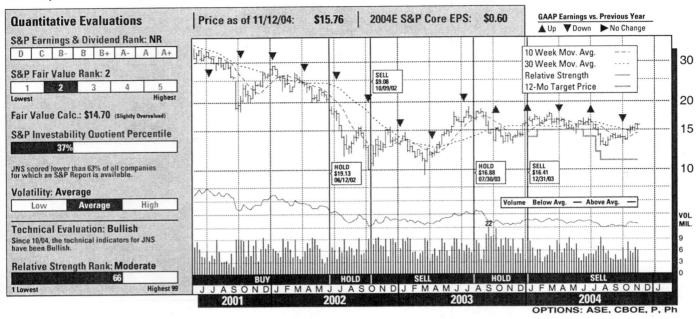

GAAP Earnings vs. Previous Year
▲ Up ▼ Down ► No Change

- 10 Week Mov. Avg. ---
- 30 Week Mov. Avg. ····
- Relative Strength
- 12-Mo Target Price

SELL $9.08 10/09/02
HOLD $19.13 06/12/02
HOLD $16.88 07/30/03
SELL $16.41 12/31/03

Volume Below Avg. — Above Avg. —

VOL. MIL.

BUY | HOLD | SELL | HOLD | SELL
J J A S O N D | J F M A M J J A S O N D | J F M A M J J A S O N D | J F M A M J J A S O N D | J F M A M J J A S O N D J
2001 | 2002 | 2003 | 2004

OPTIONS: ASE, CBOE, P, Ph

Analyst commentary prepared by Robert Hansen, CFA /MF/BK

Highlights October 26, 2004

- We see the company continuing to struggle, based on our view that investors and financial advisors have lost confidence in its funds. We believe weak fund performance, limited product breadth, and regulatory concerns have significantly hurt Janus' competitive position. Despite the company's efforts to diversify into quantitative and value products, reaching agreements with regulators, and hiring a new chief investment officer (CIO), we forecast continued net outflows through 2005.

- Third quarter results were hurt by net redemptions of $1.6 billion, versus $9.9 billion in the second quarter and $10.5 billion in the first quarter. Assets under management were down nearly 4% sequentially, to about $130 billion. We expect Janus to reduce its fees by about $25 million a year for the next five years, and to establish a $100 million fund to compensate investors pursuant to agreements in principle with regulators.

- We forecast operating EPS of $0.64 for 2004 and $0.55 for 2005, hurt by fee reductions, lower equity in earnings of unconsolidated subsidiaries, increased compensation for existing portfolio managers and a new chief investment officer, increased amortization charges, and lower soft dollar reimbursements. We think potential civil settlements could result in additional charges in 2004.

Investment Rationale/Risk October 26, 2004

- With the majority of client assets invested in aggressive growth equity products, we think that a lack of product diversification has contributed to a loss of investor confidence and assets. We remain concerned about net redemptions, our view of weak fund performance, turnover of investment personnel, and legal and regulatory matters. We think these concerns will persist through 2004 and into 2005.

- Risks to our recommendation and target price include stronger equity and bond markets, reduced competition, and the resolution of various regulatory issues.

- Having declined about 7% thus far in 2004, the shares recently traded at nearly 28X our 2005 EPS estimate. Our 12-month target price of $11 is equal to 20X our 2005 EPS estimate. We would sell the shares, given what we see as their premium valuation and our belief that turnarounds are extremely difficult to achieve in the fund management industry.

Key Stock Statistics

S&P Core EPS 2005E	0.51	52-week Range		$17.90-12.60
S&P Oper. EPS 2004E	0.64	12 Month P/E		3.7
P/E on S&P Oper. EPS 2004E	24.6	Beta		NA
S&P Oper. EPS 2005E	0.55	Shareholders		4,330
Yield (%)	0.3%	Market Cap (B)		$ 3.7
Dividend Rate/Share	0.04	Shares Outstanding (M)		236.3

Value of $10,000 invested five years ago: **NA**

Dividend Data Dividends have been paid since 2000

Amount ($)	Date Decl.	Ex-Div. Date	Stock of Record	Payment Date
0.040	May. 13	Jul. 13	Jul. 15	Jul. 30 '04

Revenues/Earnings Data Fiscal year ending December 31

Revenues (Million $)

	2004	2003	2002	2001	2000	1999
1Q	274.4	231.2	328.3	448.5	—	—
2Q	258.8	245.5	310.4	411.5	563.0	—
3Q	237.8	256.6	257.8	361.6	609.5	—
4Q	—	261.4	248.3	334.1	530.5	—
Yr.	—	994.7	1,145	1,556	2,248	1,212

Earnings Per Share ($)

	2004	2003	2002	2001	2000	1999
1Q	-0.08	0.17	0.42	0.48	—	—
2Q	0.56	0.22	0.30	0.39	0.67	—
3Q	0.22	0.24	-0.60	0.11	0.73	—
4Q	E0.13	3.51	0.20	0.32	0.66	—
Yr.	E0.64	4.17	1.31	2.90	1.31

Next earnings report expected: early-February Source: S&P, Company Reports
EPS Estimates based on S&P Operating Earnings; historical GAAP earnings are as reported.

Janus Capital Group Inc.

Recommendation: **SELL** ★ ☆ ☆ ☆ ☆　　12-Month Target Price: **$11.00** (as of July 30, 2004)

Business Summary October 26, 2004

Janus Capital Group, a single-branded global asset management company, was created through the January 1, 2003, merger of Janus Capital Corp. into its parent company, Stilwell Financial Inc., which had been spun off from Kansas City Southern Industries in July 2000 via a stock offering. The company had total assets under management of nearly $152 billion at the end of 2003, up from $138 billion at the end of 2002, but down from $193 billion at the end of 2001.

JNS has diversified its product line, and distributes its products through one global distribution network. The company's products are sold directly to investors, and through advisers and financial intermediaries. By product strategy, assets under management at the end of 2003 consisted of 56% in growth equity, 9% in mathematical/quantitative, 5% in fixed income, 14% in core/blend, 6% in value, and 10% in money market.

Wholly owned Janus Capital Management managed $129 billion at the end of 2003. The subsidiary focuses on growth equities, and uses both fundamental and quantitative investment research. It also offers core, international, specialty fixed-income, and money market products. Its largest funds include Janus Fund (JANSX), Janus Worldwide (JAWWX), and Janus Twenty (JAVLX).

The company owns about 78% of Enhanced Investment Technologies, LLC (IN-TECH), which focuses on mathematically driven equity investing strategies. IN-

TECH's assets under management totaled $14.3 billion at the end of 2003, up from $7.3 billion a year earlier. INTECH, which manages assets for large institutions and endowments, seeks to achieve long-term returns that outperform a passive index, while controlling risks and trading costs.

JNS owns about 30% of Perkins, Wolf, McDonnell and Co., which focuses on value investing, and managed about $7.2 billion at the end of 2003, invested largely in REIT and value equities, through mutual funds and separate accounts. Bay Isle employs a bottom-up analysis with a focus on what it believes to be quality companies that trade at discounts to their fair market value. Vontobel Asset Management is a sub-advisor for several Janus mutual funds and products, which focuses on value equities.

The company owns about 9% of DST Systems, Inc., which provides information processing, printing and mailing, and computer software services and products to mutual funds, investment managers, communications concerns and other service providers. In December 2003, JNS exchanged 32.3 million DST Systems shares for all shares of a DST unit, referred to as JCG Partners, that owns a commercial printing business worth about $115 million, and has $999 million in cash. In December 2003, JNS said it would no longer use the equity method to account for its remaining investment.

Company Financials Fiscal Year ending December 31

Per Share Data ($)

(Year Ended December 31)	2003	2002	2001	2000	1999	1998	1997	1996	1995	1994
Tangible Bk. Val.	1.00	NM	NM	3.50	NA	NA	NA	NA	NA	NA
Cash Flow	4.46	0.70	1.93	3.30	1.51	NA	NA	NA	NA	NA
Earnings	4.17	0.38	1.31	2.90	1.31	NA	NA	NA	NA	NA
S&P Core Earnings	1.60	0.42	1.18	NA	NA	NA	NA	NA	NA	NA
Dividends	0.04	0.05	0.04	0.01	NA	NA	NA	NA	NA	NA
Payout Ratio	1%	13%	3%	NM	NA	NA	NA	NA	NA	NA
Prices - High	19.00	29.24	46.62	54.50	NA	NA	NA	NA	NA	NA
- Low	9.46	8.97	18.20	30.75	NA	NA	NA	NA	NA	NA
P/E Ratio - High	5	77	36	19	NA	NA	NA	NA	NA	NA
- Low	2	24	14	11	NA	NA	NA	NA	NA	NA

Income Statement Analysis (Million $)

	2003	2002	2001	2000	1999	1998	1997	1996	1995	1994
Revs.	995	1,145	1,556	2,248	1,212	671	485	NA	NA	NA
Oper. Inc.	396	441	872	1,118	554	297	212	NA	NA	NA
Depr.	67.6	72.3	131	81.2	35.4	16.8	13.1	NA	NA	NA
Int. Exp.	60.5	57.8	34.8	7.70	5.90	6.50	10.4	NA	NA	NA
Pretax Inc.	895	320	620	1,202	587	289	230	NA	NA	NA
Eff. Tax Rate	NM	72.6%	35.1%	35.5%	36.8%	35.8%	37.8%	NA	NA	NA
Net Inc.	956	84.7	302	664	313	152	118	NA	NA	NA
S&P Core Earnings	367	92.4	276	NA	NA	NA	NA	NA	NA	NA

Balance Sheet & Other Fin. Data (Million $)

	2003	2002	2001	2000	1999	1998	1997	1996	1995	1994
Cash	1,223	161	237	364	324	139	NA	NA	NA	NA
Curr. Assets	1,466	346	478	641	525	259	NA	NA	NA	NA
Total Assets	4,332	3,322	3,392	1,581	1,232	823	NA	NA	NA	NA
Curr. Liab.	301	185	881	196	163	71.1	NA	NA	NA	NA
LT Debt	769	856	400	Nil	Nil	16.6	NA	NA	NA	NA
Common Equity	2,661	1,508	1,363	1,058	815	540	NA	NA	NA	NA
Total Cap.	3,997	3,097	2,466	1,342	1,024	710	NA	NA	NA	NA
Cap. Exp.	23.9	16.3	34.3	107	50.5	35.0	NA	NA	NA	NA
Cash Flow	1,023	157	433	745	348	169	NA	NA	NA	NA
Curr. Ratio	4.9	1.9	0.5	3.3	3.2	3.6	NA	NA	NA	NA
% LT Debt of Cap.	19.2	27.6	16.2	Nil	Nil	2.3	NA	NA	NA	NA
% Net Inc.of Revs.	96.1	7.4	19.4	29.5	25.8	22.7	NA	NA	NA	NA
% Ret. on Assets	25.0	2.5	12.2	47.2	30.5	NA	NA	NA	NA	NA
% Ret. on Equity	45.9	5.9	25.0	70.9	46.2	NA	NA	NA	NA	NA

Data as orig reptd.; bef. results of disc opers/spec. items. Per share data adj. for stk. divs. Bold denotes primary EPS - prior periods restated. E-Estimated. NA-Not Available. NM-Not Meaningful. NR-Not Ranked. UR-Under Review.

Office: 151 Detroit St, Denver, CO 80206-4805.
Telephone: 303-333-3863.
Website: http://www.janus.com
Chrmn & CEO: S. Scheid.
Pres: G.D. Black.
COO & EVP: G.C. Miller.

SVP & CFO: L.M. Starr.
SVP & General Counsel: J. Bluher.
VP, Treas & Investor Contact: S. Belgrad 303-394-7706.
Dirs: P. F. Balser, M. D. Bills, G. D. Black, R. Burt, A. Cox, J. P. Craig, III, D. R. Gatzek, L. H. Rowland, S. Scheid, R. Skidelsky, M. Whiston.

Founded: in 1998.
Domicile: Delaware.
Employees: 1,048.
S&P Analyst: Robert Hansen, CFA /MF/BK

The McGraw·Hill Companies

JDS Uniphase

Recommendation: **HOLD** ★ ★ ★ ☆
SELL SELL HOLD BUY BUY

12-Month Target Price: **$3.50**
(as of October 28, 2004)

JDSU has an approximate 0.04% weighting in the **S&P 500**

Sector: Information Technology
Sub-Industry: Communications Equipment
Peer Group: Optical Components & Subsystems

Summary: This company designs, develops and manufactures components for fiber optic communications systems.

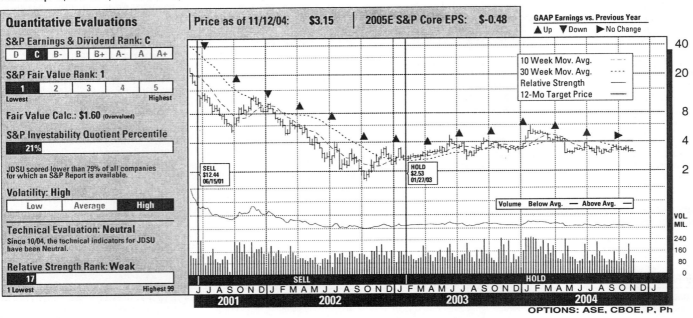

Quantitative Evaluations

S&P Earnings & Dividend Rank: C

D	C	B-	B	B+	A-	A	A+

S&P Fair Value Rank: 1

1	2	3	4	5
Lowest				Highest

Fair Value Calc.: $1.60 (Overvalued)

S&P Investability Quotient Percentile

21%

JDSU scored lower than 79% of all companies for which an S&P Report is available.

Volatility: High

Low	Average	High

Technical Evaluation: Neutral
Since 10/04, the technical indicators for JDSU have been Neutral.

Relative Strength Rank: Weak

17

1 Lowest   Highest 99

Price as of 11/12/04: **$3.15**   2005E S&P Core EPS: **$-0.48**

GAAP Earnings vs. Previous Year
▲ Up ▼ Down ► No Change

10 Week Mov. Avg.
30 Week Mov. Avg.
Relative Strength
12-Mo Target Price

SELL $12.44 06/15/01

HOLD $2.53 01/27/03

Volume Below Avg. — Above Avg.

SELL   HOLD

J J A S O N D J F M A M J J A S O N D J F M A M J J A S O N D J F M A M J J A S O N D J
   2001   2002   2003   2004

OPTIONS: ASE, CBOE, P, Ph

Analyst commentary prepared by A. Bensinger/MF/JWP

Highlights August 18, 2004

- We see sales, following a 5% drop in FY 04 (Jun.), advancing 26% in FY 05, reflecting an improved telecom spending environment. We believe JDSU is leveraging its optical science capabilities to focus on non-communications applications, including currency security and product brand authentication.

- The company is in the midst of a major restructuring program that has already reduced annual expenses by over $1.3 billion. In light of manufacturing efficiencies, we believe FY 05 gross margins will widen about 300 basis points, to the 27% area, albeit still well below JDSU's historical margins of 50%. We expect operating expenses as a percentage of sales to drop significantly from the level of FY 04.

- After higher interest income, we forecast breakeven earnings (excluding special charges) in FY 05, compared to the $0.05 loss posted in FY 04. On a Standard & Poor's Core Earnings basis, we project a FY 04 loss of $0.48, reflecting employee stock option expense of $0.48 a share.

Investment Rationale/Risk August 18, 2004

- We view the company's balance sheet, with $1.6 billion in cash, as much stronger than those of its rivals. Based on our view of its strong market position, we see JDSU as one of the few optical component survivors, and would therefore hold existing positions for their recovery potential.

- Risks to our recommendation and target price include continued reduction in telecom operator inventory levels, continued excess fiber and channel optical capacity, and the loss of a major customer.

- Even when telecom spending begins to rebound, we believe that JDSU's large outstanding share base of 1.4 billion will make it extremely difficult for the company to achieve any significant operating leverage. For FY 06, we see negligible operating earnings of $0.05. Our 12-month target price of $4 is based on 4X book value, a premium to the industry average. We believe this premium is justified by JDSU's market-leading optical technologies and strong liquidity.

Key Stock Statistics

S&P Oper. EPS 2005E	**Nil**	52-week Range	**$5.89-2.84**
P/E on S&P Oper. EPS 2005E	**NM**	12 Month P/E	**NM**
S&P Oper. EPS 2006E	**0.05**	Beta	**NA**
Yield (%)	**Nil**	Shareholders	**8,770**
Dividend Rate/Share	**Nil**	Market Cap (B)	**$ 4.5**
Shares Outstanding (M)	**1440.2**		

Value of $10,000 invested five years ago: **$ 641**

Dividend Data

No cash dividends have been paid.

Revenues/Earnings Data Fiscal year ending June 30

Revenues (Million $)

	2005	2004	2003	2002	2001	2000
1Q	194.5	147.4	193.0	328.6	786.5	230.1
2Q	—	152.6	156.6	286.1	925.1	281.7
3Q	—	161.4	165.7	261.8	920.1	394.6
4Q	—	174.5	160.6	221.7	601.1	524.0
Yr.	—	635.9	675.9	1,098	3,233	1,430

Earnings Per Share ($)

	2005	2004	2003	2002	2001	2000
1Q	-0.02	-0.02	-0.37	-0.93	-1.07	-0.17
2Q	E Nil	-0.04	-0.15	-1.60	-0.93	-0.19
3Q	E Nil	-0.01	-0.10	-3.19	-36.63	-0.32
4Q	E0.01	-0.02	-0.04	-0.76	-9.39	-0.54
Yr.	E Nil	-0.08	-0.66	-6.50	-51.40	-1.26

Next earnings report expected: late-January Source: S&P, Company Reports
EPS Estimates based on S&P Operating Earnings; historical GAAP earnings are as reported.

JDS Uniphase Corporation

Recommendation: **HOLD** ★ ★ ★ ★ ★   12-Month Target Price: **$3.50** (as of October 28, 2004)

Business Summary August 18, 2004

As the world's leading provider of optical components and modules, JDS Uniphase supplies the basic building blocks for fiber optic networks, which in turn enable the rapid transmission of large amounts of data over long distances via light waves. Its fiber optic components and modules are deployed by system manufacturers for the telecommunications, data communications and cable television industries. The company also offers products for display, security, medical environmental instrumentation, decorative, aerospace and defense applications. Products are grouped into two principal segments: communications and thin film products.

The communications product group (49% of total sales in FY 03 (Jun.)) provides fiber optic components and modules, including source lasers, photodetectors and receivers, modulators, transmitters, transceivers, amplifiers, and add-drop multiplexers. Division sales in FY 03 fell 58%, reflecting reduced demand for telecommunications products and lower average selling prices.

The thin film products segment consists primarily of the company's non-telecommunications businesses for display, security, medical/environmental instrumentation, decorative, aerospace and defense applications. As a result of the downturn in the telecommunications industry, revenue from the thin film product group has become increasingly significant, accounting for 51% of total sales in FY 03 as compared to 27% and 13% in FY 02 and FY 01, respectively.

In April 2001, reacting to a dramatic downturn in network deployment and capital spending by the telecommunications carriers, JDSU initiated a global realignment program aimed at restructuring its business. Specific actions under the program included reducing employment by 19,000 and closing 29 facilities.

The company has employed an aggressive acquisition strategy in seeking to realize its strategic vision. In February 2000, it acquired Optical Coating Laboratory Inc., a leader in optical thin film coating. In June 2000, JDSU acquired E-TEK Dynamics, a leader in the design and manufacture of passive components for optical networks, for $18 billion. In February 2001, the company acquired rival component maker SDL Inc., for approximately $41 billion. Subsequently, as a result of a dramatic industry and economic downturn, as well as a general decline of technology valuations, JDSU recorded reductions of over $56 billion in goodwill and other intangible assets, primarily to adjust the carrying value of these acquisitions.

Net sales to customers in North America accounted for 70% of total sales in FY 03. During FY 03, Texas Instruments, a customer of the thin film products group, accounted for 12% of sales. No single customer accounted for over 10% of sales in FY 02.

Company Financials Fiscal Year ending June 30

Per Share Data ($)

(Year Ended June 30)	2004	2003	2002	2001	2000	1999	1998	1997	1996	1995
Tangible Bk. Val.	0.89	0.99	1.43	2.78	2.61	0.27	0.57	1.03	0.56	0.14
Cash Flow	-0.04	-0.60	-5.28	-46.32	0.06	-0.44	-0.26	-0.11	0.02	0.02
Earnings	-0.08	-0.66	-6.50	-51.40	-1.26	-0.54	-0.29	-0.07	0.01	0.00
S&P Core Earnings	-0.32	-0.98	-4.11	-21.95	NA	NA	NA	NA	NA	NA
Dividends	Nil	Nil	Nil	Nil	Nil	Nil	Nil	Nil	Nil	Nil
Payout Ratio	Nil	Nil	Nil	Nil	Nil	Nil	Nil	Nil	Nil	Nil
Prices - High	5.88	4.71	10.34	64.93	153.42	88.75	8.93	5.93	3.78	1.19
- Low	2.84	2.48	1.58	5.12	37.00	7.40	3.90	1.95	0.92	0.39
P/E Ratio - High	NM	NM	NM	NM	NM	NM	NM	NM	185	272
- Low	NM	NM	NM	NM	NM	NM	NM	NM	70	91

Income Statement Analysis (Million $)

	2004	2003	2002	2001	2000	1999	1998	1997	1996	1995
Revs.	636	676	1,098	3,233	1,430	283	176	107	69.1	42.3
Oper. Inc.	-58.5	-306	-374	-62.5	446	94.6	36.7	21.2	15.0	7.09
Depr.	55.9	79.2	1,645	5,542	951	30.7	10.1	4.70	2.08	1.15
Int. Exp.	Nil	Nil	Nil	Nil	0.50	0.02	0.07	0.42	0.08	0.03
Pretax Inc.	-128	-920	-8,501	-56,494	-830	-151	-69.8	-13.4	6.83	1.13
Eff. Tax Rate	NM	NM	NM	NM	NM	NM	NM	NM	59.1%	35.0%
Net Inc.	-113	-934	-8,738	-56,122	-905	-171	-81.1	-18.9	2.79	0.73
S&P Core Earnings	-446	-1,399	-5,534	-23,966	NA	NA	NA	NA	NA	NA

Balance Sheet & Other Fin. Data (Million $)

	2004	2003	2002	2001	2000	1999	1998	1997	1996	1995
Cash	328	242	412	763	319	75.4	39.8	29.2	52.5	2.88
Curr. Assets	1,866	1,515	1,857	3,036	1,973	928	165	134	127	24.2
Total Assets	2,422	2,138	3,005	12,245	26,389	8,192	269	178	174	31.9
Curr. Liab.	350	423	483	849	647	298	45.8	25.3	13.6	6.88
LT Debt	465	Nil	5.50	12.8	41.0	Nil	Nil	Nil	6.10	Nil
Common Equity	1,571	1,671	2,471	10,706	24,779	3,619	218	150	153	24.8
Total Cap.	2,063	1,699	2,519	11,392	25,722	3,937	218	150	160	24.8
Cap. Exp.	66.4	47.2	133	733	280	46.6	24.0	12.0	17.8	17.1
Cash Flow	-56.7	-855	-7,093	-50,580	46.0	-140	-71.0	-14.2	4.87	1.89
Curr. Ratio	5.3	3.6	3.8	3.6	3.0	3.1	3.6	5.3	9.4	3.5
% LT Debt of Cap.	22.5	Nil	0.2	0.1	0.2	Nil	Nil	Nil	3.8	Nil
% Net Inc.of Revs.	NM	NM	NM	NM	NM	NM	NM	NM	4.0	1.7
% Ret. on Assets	NM	NM	NM	NM	NM	NM	NM	NM	2.7	2.5
% Ret. on Equity	NM	NM	NM	NM	NM	NM	NM	NM	3.1	3.2

Data as orig reptd.; bef. results of disc opers/spec. items. Per share data adj. for stk. divs. Bold denotes primary EPS - prior periods restated. E-Estimated. NA-Not Available. NM-Not Meaningful. NR-Not Ranked. UR-Under Review.

Office: 1768 Automation Parkway, San Jose, CA 95131-1873.
Telephone: 408-546-5000.
Email: investor.relations@jdsu.com
Website: http://www.jdsu.com
Chrmn: M.A. Kaplan.

CEO: K. Kennedy.
EVP & CFO: R.C. Foster.
Dirs: B. D. Day, R. E. Enos, P. A. Guglielmi, M. A. Kaplan, K. Kennedy, R. T. Liebhaber, C. S. Skrzypczak.

Founded: in 1979.
Domicile: Delaware.
Employees: 6,041.
S&P Analyst: A. Bensinger/MF/JWP

Jefferson-Pilot

Recommendation: HOLD ★★★☆☆
SELL SELL HOLD BUY BUY

12-Month Target Price: **$54.00**
(as of February 03, 2004)

JP has an approximate 0.06% weighting in the **S&P 500**

Sector: Financials
Sub-Industry: Life & Health Insurance
Peer Group: Life Insurance/Annuities - Larger

Summary: Jefferson-Pilot provides an array of insurance and communications products and services. The bulk of revenues and income is derived from life insurance operations.

Quantitative Evaluations

Price as of 11/16/04: $49.95 | **2004E S&P Core EPS:** $3.74

S&P Earnings & Dividend Rank: A+

D	C	B-	B	B+	A-	A	A+

S&P Fair Value Rank: 1+

1	2	3	4	5
Lowest				Highest

Fair Value Calc.: $41.00 (Overvalued)

S&P Investability Quotient Percentile
98%

JP scored higher than 98% of all companies
for which an S&P Report is available.

Volatility: Low

Low	Average	High

Technical Evaluation: Bullish
Since 11/04, the technical indicators for JP have been Bullish.

Relative Strength Rank: Moderate
41
1 Lowest ..... Highest 99

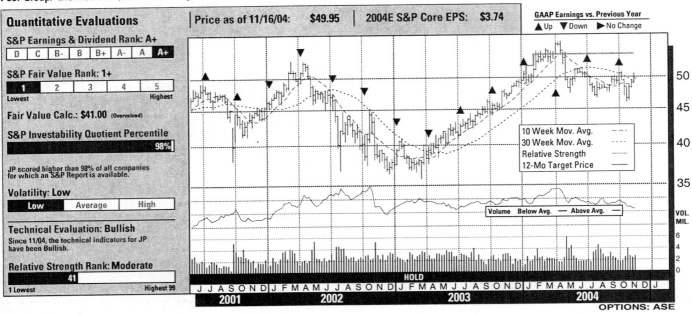

GAAP Earnings vs. Previous Year
▲ Up ▼ Down ► No Change

10 Week Mov. Avg.
30 Week Mov. Avg.
Relative Strength
12-Mo Target Price

Volume Below Avg. Above Avg.

VOL. MIL.

HOLD
J J A S O N D J F M A M J J A S O N D J F M A M J J A S O N D J F M A M J J A S O N D J
2001 2002 2003 2004

OPTIONS: ASE

Analyst commentary prepared by Gregory Simcik, CFA /CB/BK

Highlights 17-NOV-04

- We expect operating earnings to decline modestly in 2004 for the individual products segment on lower revenues, offset somewhat by lower benefits and continued good expense control. We see operating earnings increasing only marginally in 2005, on low single digit revenue growth. We believe operating earnings will decline roughly 10% in 2004 for the annuity segment, primarily on lower net investment income. We expect operating earnings for this segment to remain effectively unchanged in 2005.
- We expect operating earnings in the group benefits segment to grow 40% in 2004, helped by the recent Canada Life transaction, and we expect growth exceeding 20% in 2005. We forecast operating earnings and EBITDA for the communications segment to increase over 20% in 2004, on improvements in advertising due to the Olympics, national elections, and a better economy. We estimate operating earnings and EBITDA for this segment rising in low double digits in 2005.
- We are forecasting 2004 operating EPS to rise 4.9%, to $3.84, excluding $0.18 from realized investment gains and a loss of $0.12 from the cumulative effect of an accounting change. We believe operating EPS will rise at a faster 8.6% rate, to $4.17, in 2005. Our Standard & Poor's Core Earnings per share estimates for 2004 and 2005 are $3.74 and $4.13, respectively, and include adjustments for projected stock option and pension expense.

Key Stock Statistics

S&P Core EPS 2005E	4.13	52-week Range	$56.39-46.00
S&P Oper. EPS 2004E	3.84	12 Month P/E	13.1
P/E on S&P Oper. EPS 2004E	12.9	Beta	0.49
S&P Oper. EPS 2005E	4.17	Shareholders	8,848
Yield (%)	3.0%	Market Cap (B)	$ 6.8
Dividend Rate/Share	1.52	Shares Outstanding (M)	136.5

Value of $10,000 invested five years ago: **$ 10,941**

Dividend Data Dividends have been paid since 1913

Amount ($)	Date Decl.	Ex-Div. Date	Stock of Record	Payment Date
0.380	May. 03	Aug. 18	Aug. 20	Sep. 05 '04
0.380	Feb. 09	May. 19	May. 21	Jun. 09 '04
0.380	Aug. 02	Nov. 17	Nov. 19	Dec. 05 '04
0.380	Nov. 01	Feb. 16	Feb. 18	Mar. 05 '05

Investment Rationale/Risk 17-NOV-04

- We advise investors to hold current positions. Despite strong growth in the communications and employee benefits segments, we believe JP still faces a challenging environment for its individual life and annuity segments, on a combination of low interest rates and competition. As a result, we believe only moderate earnings growth will continue into 2005. Our outlook for moderate earnings growth is mitigated somewhat by our view of JP's attractive dividend yield.
- Risks to our recommendation and target price include competition from other investment vehicles for fixed rate guaranteed income investment products, ongoing investigations of practices and relationships between group life writers and insurance brokers by numerous attorneys general and regulators, sensitivity of broadcast revenues to cyclical changes in the general and local economies as well as political activities and special events, a high concentration of broadcast advertisers in the automotive industry, and sensitivity of insurance, annuity and investment product results to changes in the equity and fixed income markets.
- Our 12-month target price of $54 is based on a P/E multiple of 13X our 2005 operating EPS estimate, below the peer group average of 14X due to our view of relatively slower growth over the next year.

Revenues/Earnings Data Fiscal year ending December 31

Revenues (Million $)

	2004	2003	2002	2001	2000	1999
1Q	985.0	868.0	885.0	854.0	820.0	670.0
2Q	1,047	917.0	878.0	829.0	803.0	639.0
3Q	1,002	906.0	881.0	845.0	807.0	636.0
4Q	—	882.0	836.0	802.0	808.0	616.0
Yr.	—	3,573	3,480	3,330	3,239	2,561

Earnings Per Share ($)

	2004	2003	2002	2001	2000	1999
1Q	0.99	0.76	0.92	0.95	0.89	0.79
2Q	1.02	0.98	0.83	0.87	0.83	0.73
3Q	0.97	0.88	0.81	0.87	0.83	0.73
4Q	E1.03	0.82	0.46	0.64	0.73	0.69
Yr.	E3.84	3.44	3.04	3.34	3.28	2.95

Next earnings report expected: early-February Source: S&P, Company Reports
EPS Estimates based on S&P Operating Earnings; historical GAAP earnings are as reported.

Jefferson-Pilot Corporation

Recommendation: **HOLD** ★ ★ ★ ☆ ☆   12-Month Target Price: **$54.00** (as of February 03, 2004)

Business Summary 17-NOV-04

Jefferson-Pilot is primarily engaged in writing life, dental and disability income insurance and annuity products, selling investment products, operating radio and TV stations and producing sports programming. As of April 1, 1999, JP ceased offering group medical policies. Insurance, annuity and investment products are marketed through independent general agents, independent national account marketing firms, agency building general agents, JP's district agency network, broker/dealers, banks, strategic alliances, investment professionals, annuity marketing organizations, and regional group offices.

JP reports results in five segments: individual products (49% of revenues before investment losses and gains and cumulative effect of change in accounting in 2003; 51% in 2002), annuity and investment products (19%; 20%), benefit partners (23%; 20%), communications (5.9%; 6.1%), and corporate and other (3.3%; 2.9%). The individual products segment includes individual life insurance policies, including universal life and variable universal life, along with other benefits including accidental death, disability, and 401(k) riders. The annuity and investment segment primarily offers proprietary fixed annuity income products, mutual funds, and other investment products.

The benefit partners segment offers group term life, disability income and dental insurance, primarily marketing to employers with fewer than 500 employees through employee benefit brokers, third-party administrators and employee benefit firms. The corporate and other segment includes the activities of the parent company and passive investment affiliates, surplus of the life insurance subsidiaries not allocated to other segments, financing expenses on corporate debt, federal and state income taxes not allocated to other segments, and strategic initiatives intended to benefit the entire company.

As of year-end 2003, Jefferson-Pilot Communication Co. owned and operated three television and 17 AM and FM radio stations in North Carolina, South Carolina, Virginia, Georgia, Florida, Colorado and California. Other operations include Jefferson-Pilot Sports, a sports production company that produces and syndicates broadcasts of Altantic Coast Conference and Southeastern Conference college football and basketball events.

JP has capitalized on opportunities from time to time to add to its core life insurance business through acquisitions. Some of its more recent significant acquisitions included the 1997 purchase of the life insurance unit of Chubb Corp. for $875 million, and the 1999 purchase of The Guarantee Life Companies Inc. for $298 million in cash plus the assumption of $123 million of debt and certain other expenses. In March 2004, JP acquired via a reinsurance transaction Canada Life's group life, disability and dental units.

At December 31, 2003, 92.9% of JP's debt security portfolio based on carrying value was rated investment grade.

Company Financials Fiscal Year ending December 31

Per Share Data ($)

(Year Ended December 31)	2003	2002	2001	2000	1999	1998	1997	1996	1995	1994
Tangible Bk. Val.	24.78	22.57	20.53	18.18	15.81	17.77	15.71	13.89	13.02	10.26
Oper. Earnings	NA	3.14	3.06	2.85	2.53	2.25	1.85	1.63	1.37	1.16
Earnings	3.44	3.04	3.34	3.28	2.95	2.61	2.31	1.82	1.58	1.40
S&P Core Earnings	3.57	2.91	2.83	NA	NA	NA	NA	NA	NA	NA
Dividends	1.29	1.18	1.07	0.96	0.85	0.77	0.69	0.62	0.56	0.50
Payout Ratio	38%	39%	32%	29%	29%	29%	30%	34%	35%	36%
Prices - High	50.72	53.00	49.66	50.58	53.08	52.25	38.55	26.50	21.44	16.33
- Low	35.75	36.35	38.00	33.25	40.78	32.44	22.88	20.05	14.96	12.85
P/E Ratio - High	15	17	15	15	18	20	17	15	14	12
- Low	10	12	11	10	14	12	10	11	9	9

Income Statement Analysis (Million $)

	2003	2002	2001	2000	1999	1998	1997	1996	1995	1994
Life Ins. In Force	266,931	254,199	212,652	218,520	214,225	163,561	162,096	109,407	111,383	45,049
Prem. Inc.: Life	NA	1,564	1,424	NA	NA	NA	NA	NA	NA	NA
Prem. Inc.: A & H	NA	NA	NA	NA	NA	NA	NA	NA	NA	NA
Net Invest. Inc.	1,657	1,623	1,533	1,430	1,272	1,202	1,103	893	541	375
Total Revs.	3,613	3,480	3,330	3,238	2,561	2,610	2,578	2,125	1,569	1,269
Pretax Inc.	738	710	800	814	751	670	591	443	381	348
Net Oper. Inc.	NA	465	468	445	430	386	323	263	222	190
Net Inc.	492	475	537	537	495	444	396	294	255	230
S&P Core Earnings	509	432	435	NA	NA	NA	NA	NA	NA	NA

Balance Sheet & Other Fin. Data (Million $)

	2003	2002	2001	2000	1999	1998	1997	1996	1995	1994
Cash & Equiv.	398	369	420	298	328	262	9.00	271	279	90.0
Premiums Due	1,340	1,375	1,433	1,450	NA	1,342	Nil	96.0	134	64.2
Invest. Assets: Bonds	20,458	19,501	17,467	16,108	15,182	14,503	13,945	10,550	9,986	3,547
Invest. Assets: Stocks	756	409	511	551	NA	949	893	929	863	718
Invest. Assets: Loans	4,341	4,203	4,005	3,694	3,449	3,408	3,138	2,535	2,201	887
Invest. Assets: Total	25,752	24,279	22,135	20,499	19,704	18,978	14,881	14,143	13,168	5,220
Deferred Policy Costs	2,230	2,027	2,070	1,959	2,040	1,412	1,364	934	835	329
Total Assets	32,696	30,609	28,996	27,321	26,446	24,338	23,131	17,562	16,478	6,140
Debt	963	753	747	844	951	916	916	370	137	Nil
Common Equity	3,806	3,540	3,391	3,159	2,753	3,052	2,732	2,297	2,156	1,733
% Return On Revs.	13.6	13.6	16.1	16.6	19.3	17.0	15.4	13.8	16.3	18.1
% Ret. on Assets	1.6	1.6	1.9	2.0	1.9	1.9	1.9	1.7	2.3	3.9
% Ret. on Equity	13.4	13.0	15.6	17.3	16.2	14.5	14.7	13.2	13.1	13.3
% Invest. Yield	7.1	7.0	7.2	7.1	6.6	7.1	6.8	6.5	5.9	7.4

Data as orig reptd.; bef. results of disc opers/spec. items. Per share data adj. for stk. divs.; EPS diluted. E-Estimated. NA-Not Available. NM-Not Meaningful. NR-Not Ranked. UR-Under Review.

Office: 100 North Greene Street, Greensboro, NC 27401-2545.
Telephone: 336-691-3000.
Email: investor.relations@jpfinancial.com
Website: http://www.jpfinancial.com
Chrmn: D. A. Stonecipher.
Pres & CEO: D. R. Glass.

Treas & CFO: T. M. Stone.
EVP: W. H. May.
Dirs: E. B. Borden, W. H. Cunningham, D. R. Glass, R. G. Greer, G. W. Henderson, III, E. V. Long, E. S. Melvin, W. P. Payne, P. S. Pittard, D. S. Russell, Jr., D. A. Stonecipher.

Founded: in 1903.
Domicile: North Carolina.
Employees: 3,365.
S&P Analyst: Gregory Simcik, CFA /CB/BK

Johnson Controls

Recommendation: **BUY** ★★★★☆
SELL SELL HOLD BUY BUY

12-Month Target Price: **$64.00**
(as of October 26, 2004)

JCI has an approximate 0.11% weighting in the **S&P 500**

Sector: Consumer Discretionary
Sub-Industry: Auto Parts & Equipment
Peer Group: Auto Parts - Safety Equipment/Wheels

Summary: JCI supplies building controls and energy management systems, automotive seating, and batteries.

Quantitative Evaluations

Price as of 11/12/04: $61.70 **2005E S&P Core EPS:** $4.28

S&P Earnings & Dividend Rank: A+

| D | C | B- | B | B+ | A- | A | A+ |

S&P Fair Value Rank: 4-

| 1 | 2 | 3 | 4 | 5 |
| Lowest | | | | Highest |

Fair Value Calc.: $60.00 (Slightly Overvalued)

S&P Investability Quotient Percentile
99%

JCI scored higher than 99% of all companies for which an S&P Report is available.

Volatility: Low

| Low | Average | High |

Technical Evaluation: Neutral
Since 10/04, the technical indicators for JCI have been Neutral.

Relative Strength Rank: Moderate
70
1 Lowest   Highest 99

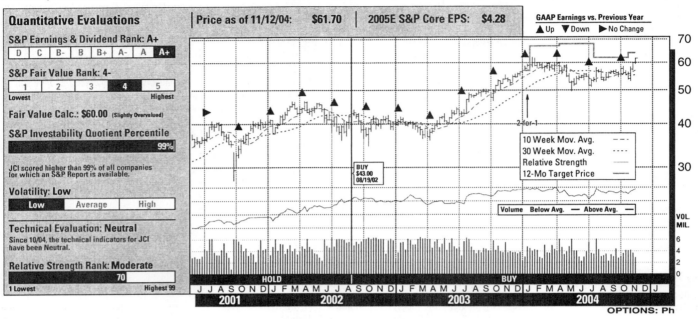

GAAP Earnings vs. Previous Year
▲ Up ▼ Down ► No Change

Legend:
10 Week Mov. Avg. - - -
30 Week Mov. Avg. ·····
Relative Strength ——
12-Mo Target Price ——

2-for-1

BUY $43.00 08/19/02

Volume Below Avg. --- Above Avg. ——

VOL. MIL.

HOLD   BUY
J J A S O N D J F M A M J J A S O N D J F M A M J J A S O N D J F M A M J J A S O N D J
2001   2002   2003   2004

OPTIONS: Ph

Analyst commentary prepared by Efraim Levy/PMW/JWP

Highlights October 28, 2004

- We expect FY 05 (Sep.) sales to advance in the upper single digits, reflecting expansion of the facilities management business, expected new automotive business, higher auto production and acquisitions. We see facility management benefiting from new customers as outsourcing trends continue and the backlog of orders for installed systems continues to grow. Automotive revenues will likely benefit from new contracts and expanding business with Asian and European vehicle makers.

- We see operating margins widening, as the company should realize the benefits of the higher revenues that we see, plus restructuring activities, especially in Europe, and fewer planned new product launches. We see a partial offset in higher healthcare expenses and pricing pressures from customers.

- We expect excess cash to be used to reduce debt and increase the dividend. We see FY 05 S&P Core Earnings adjustments for projected increased option and pension expenses reducing reported earnings by about 10%. We expect JCI's acquisition of the remaining 51% interest in an automotive battery joint venture to be accretive to EPS beginning in FY 05. We see FY 05 EPS of $4.75.

Investment Rationale/Risk October 28, 2004

- We would accumulate the shares on a total return basis. We expect growth to exceed that of peers, with greater earnings stability, and see the stock's P/E multiple widening. The stock trades at a discount to the P/E multiple of the S&P 500. The company has a track record of consistently meeting or exceeding analyst forecasts. We view the balance sheet as strong, with long term debt generally at 28% to 36% of capitalization over the past decade. We regard the shares as attractive, based on our view of steady dividend growth and capital appreciation potential.

- Risks to our recommendation and target price include changes in cyclical demand, especially for automotive parts.

- We applied a P/E multiple of 12X to our FY 05 EPS estimate, reflecting peer and historical comparisons. Our DCF model, which assumes a weighted average cost of capital of 10%, compound annual growth of 9.1% over the next 14 years, and a terminal growth rate of 3%, leads to intrinsic value of nearly $72. Based on an equal weighting of our P/E multiple and DCF analyses, our 12-month target price is $64. The cash dividend adds to total return.

Key Stock Statistics

S&P Oper. EPS 2005E	4.75	52-week Range	$62.32-49.57
P/E on S&P Oper. EPS 2005E	13.0	12 Month P/E	14.6
Yield (%)	1.5%	Beta	0.70
Dividend Rate/Share	0.90	Shareholders	55,499
Shares Outstanding (M)	190.3	Market Cap (B)	$ 11.7

Value of $10,000 invested five years ago: **$ 21,601**

Dividend Data Dividends have been paid since 1887

Amount ($)	Date Decl.	Ex-Div. Date	Stock of Record	Payment Date
2-for-1	Nov. 19	Jan. 05	Dec. 12	Jan. 02 '04
0.225	Jan. 28	Mar. 10	Mar. 12	Mar. 31 '04
0.225	May. 26	Jun. 09	Jun. 11	Jun. 30 '04
0.225	Jul. 28	Sep. 08	Sep. 10	Sep. 30 '04

Revenues/Earnings Data Fiscal year ending September 30

Revenues (Million $)

	2004	2003	2002	2001	2000	1999
1Q	6,384	5,183	4,818	4,454	4,318	3,873
2Q	6,620	5,503	4,811	4,602	4,358	3,880
3Q	6,792	5,960	5,257	4,722	4,389	4,191
4Q	6,757	6,000	5,218	4,649	4,089	4,195
Yr.	26,553	22,646	20,103	18,427	17,155	16,139

Earnings Per Share ($)

	2004	2003	2002	2001	2000	1999
1Q	0.86	0.74	0.64	0.55	0.53	0.43
2Q	0.82	0.70	0.60	0.45	0.48	0.53
3Q	1.15	1.00	0.93	0.73	0.73	0.59
4Q	1.41	1.16	1.01	0.84	0.82	0.69
Yr.	4.24	3.60	3.18	2.56	2.54	2.24

Next earnings report expected: late-January Source: S&P, Company Reports
EPS Estimates based on S&P Operating Earnings; historical GAAP earnings are as reported.

Johnson Controls, Inc.

Recommendation: **BUY** ★★★★☆ 12-Month Target Price: **$64.00** (as of October 26, 2004)

Business Summary October 28, 2004

Johnson Controls, founded in 1885, is a leading manufacturer of automotive interior systems, automotive batteries and automated building control systems. It also provides facility management services for commercial buildings. In FY 03 (Sep.), the automotive segment accounted for 75% of sales and 76% of income, with the balance coming from controls and facility management.

The automotive segment manufactures complete seats and seating components for North American and European car and light-truck manufacturers. The company offers customers complete design, manufacturing and just-in-time delivery capabilities. The segment has grown rapidly in recent years, gaining contracts to produce seats formerly manufactured in-house by automakers, and expanding in Europe. Seating accounted for 89% of segment sales in FY 03. The battery unit, the largest automotive battery operation in North America, makes lead-acid batteries primarily for the automotive replacement market and for OEMs.

The former Big Three U.S. auto manufacturers, GM, DaimlerChrysler and Ford, accounted respectively for 15%, 11% and 11% of FY 03 total sales.

The controls segment manufactures, installs and services controls and control systems, principally for nonresidential buildings, that are used for temperature and energy management, and fire safety and security maintenance. The segment also includes custom engineering, installation and servicing of process control systems and a growing facilities management business. At September 30, 2003, JCI had an unearned backlog of building systems and services contracts totaling $1.9 billion.

The company believes current government building trends promoting facility management outsourcing and energy efficiency programs have created additional opportunities.

In 1997, JCI sold its Plastic Container division to Schmalbach-Lubeca AG/Continental Can Europe (a member of the VIAG Group), for about $650 million. The transaction allowed the company to avoid a stock offering that it had been considering to partially finance the $1.35 billion acquisition of Prince Automotive. Prince supplies overhead systems and consoles, door panels, and floor consoles.

In 1998, the company acquired Becker Group, Inc., a leading supplier of automotive door systems and instrument panels, for $920 million, including the assumption of $372 million of debt. The integration of Prince and Becker provided a new platform for growth in the global interior systems market.

In September 2000, JCI acquired Japan's Ikeda Bussan Co., Ltd.

Company Financials Fiscal Year ending September 30

Per Share Data ($)

(Year Ended September 30)	2004	2003	2002	2001	2000	1999	1998	1997	1996	1995
Tangible Bk. Val.	NA	3.80	2.23	3.52	1.83	0.23	NM	NM	4.69	4.24
Cash Flow	NA	6.52	5.90	5.30	5.37	4.65	3.87	3.33	3.31	2.96
Earnings	4.24	3.60	3.18	2.56	2.54	2.24	1.82	1.19	1.35	1.13
S&P Core Earnings	NA	3.47	2.67	2.10	NA	NA	NA	NA	NA	NA
Dividends	0.90	0.72	0.66	0.62	0.56	0.50	0.46	0.43	0.41	0.39
Payout Ratio	21%	20%	21%	24%	22%	22%	25%	36%	30%	34%
Prices - High	62.32	58.12	46.60	41.35	32.56	38.34	30.93	25.50	21.34	17.43
- Low	49.57	35.87	34.55	25.96	22.90	24.50	20.25	17.68	15.62	11.43
P/E Ratio - High	15	16	15	16	13	17	17	22	16	15
- Low	12	10	11	10	9	11	11	15	12	10

Income Statement Analysis (Million $)

	2004	2003	2002	2001	2000	1999	1998	1997	1996	1995
Revs.	NA	22,646	20,103	18,427	17,155	16,139	12,587	11,145	10,009	8,330
Oper. Inc.	NA	1,720	1,639	1,477	1,427	1,300	1,048	951	830	737
Depr.	NA	558	517	516	462	446	384	355	330	289
Int. Exp.	NA	114	122	129	128	153	134	122	85.0	68.0
Pretax Inc.	NA	1,058	1,006	867	856	770	617	425	443	388
Eff. Tax Rate	NA	31.0%	34.6%	38.7%	39.6%	40.5%	41.5%	42.4%	41.1%	42.0%
Net Inc.	NA	683	601	478	472	420	338	221	235	196
S&P Core Earnings	NA	650	497	385	NA	NA	NA	NA	NA	NA

Balance Sheet & Other Fin. Data (Million $)

	2004	2003	2002	2001	2000	1999	1998	1997	1996	1995
Cash	NA	136	262	375	276	276	134	112	164	104
Curr. Assets	NA	5,620	4,946	4,544	4,277	3,849	3,404	2,529	2,594	2,064
Total Assets	NA	13,127	11,165	9,912	9,428	8,614	7,942	6,049	5,123	4,321
Curr. Liab.	NA	5,584	4,806	4,580	4,510	4,267	4,288	2,973	2,302	1,910
LT Debt	NA	1,777	1,827	1,395	1,315	1,283	998	806	757	630
Common Equity	NA	4,164	3,396	2,862	2,447	2,135	1,801	1,545	1,353	1,180
Total Cap.	NA	6,260	5,515	4,588	3,891	3,553	2,939	2,494	2,264	1,970
Cap. Exp.	NA	664	496	622	547	514	468	371	370	451
Cash Flow	NA	1,234	1,110	985	924	856	712	566	556	485
Curr. Ratio	NA	1.0	1.0	1.0	0.9	0.9	0.8	0.9	1.1	1.1
% LT Debt of Cap.	NA	28.4	33.1	30.4	33.8	36.1	34.0	32.3	33.5	31.9
% Net Inc.of Revs.	NA	3.0	3.0	2.6	2.8	2.6	2.7	2.0	2.4	2.3
% Ret. on Assets	NA	5.6	5.7	4.9	5.2	5.1	4.8	4.0	5.0	4.8
% Ret. on Equity	NA	17.9	18.9	17.7	20.2	20.8	19.6	14.6	16.5	16.8

Data as orig reptd.; bef. results of disc opers/spec. items. Per share data adj. for stk. divs. Bold denotes primary EPS - prior periods restated. E-Estimated. NA-Not Available. NM-Not Meaningful. NR-Not Ranked. UR-Under Review.

Office: 5757 N. Green Bay Avenue, Milwaukee, WI 53201-0591.
Telephone: 414-524-1200.
Website: http://www.johnsoncontrols.com
Chrmn, Pres & CEO: J.M. Barth.
SVP & CFO: S.A. Roell.
SVP, Secy & General Counsel: J.P. Kennedy.

VP & Treas: F.A. Voltolina.
VP & Investor Contact: D.M. Zutz .
Dirs: D. Archer, R. L. Barnett, J. M. Barth, N. A. Black, P. A. Brunner, R. A. Cornog, W. D. Davis, J. A. Joerres, J. H. Keyes, W. H. Lacy, S. J. Morcott, R. F. Teerlink.

Founded: in 1900.
Domicile: Wisconsin.
Employees: 118,000.
S&P Analyst: Efraim Levy/PMW/JWP

Johnson & Johnson

Recommendation: **BUY** ★★★★★
SELL SELL HOLD BUY BUY

12-Month Target Price: $70.00
(as of July 16, 2004)

JNJ has an approximate 1.64% weighting in the **S&P 500**

Sector: Health Care
Sub-Industry: Pharmaceuticals
Peer Group: Health Care Diversified

Summary: The world's largest and most comprehensive health care company, JNJ offers a broad line of drugs, consumer products, and other medical and dental items.

Quantitative Evaluations

S&P Earnings & Dividend Rank: A+

D	C	B-	B	B+	A-	A	**A+**

S&P Fair Value Rank: 4

1	2	3	**4**	5
Lowest				Highest

Fair Value Calc.: $63.40 (Slightly Undervalued)

S&P Investability Quotient Percentile

100%

JNJ scored higher than 100% of all companies for which an S&P Report is available.

Volatility: Low

Low	Average	High

Technical Evaluation: Bullish

Since 10/04, the technical indicators for JNJ have been Bullish.

Relative Strength Rank: Moderate

58

1 Lowest		Highest 99

Price as of 11/12/04: **$61**   **2004E S&P Core EPS:** **$3.11**

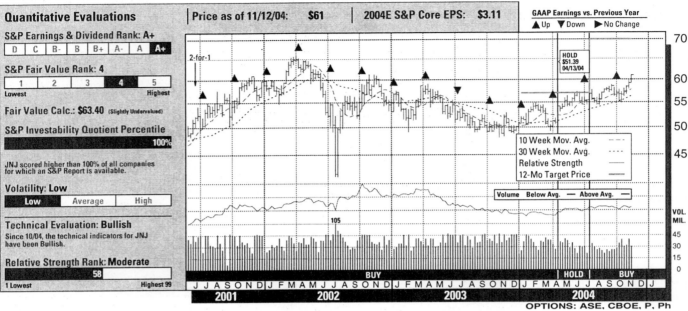

GAAP Earnings vs. Previous Year
▲ Up ▼ Down ► No Change

2-for-1
HOLD $51.39 04/13/04

10 Week Mov. Avg.
30 Week Mov. Avg.
Relative Strength
12-Mo Target Price

Volume Below Avg. — Above Avg.

BUY | HOLD | BUY

J J A S O N D J F M A M J J A S O N D J F M A M J J A S O N D J F M A M J J A S O N D J
2001   2002   2003   2004

VOL. MIL.

OPTIONS: ASE, CBOE, P, Ph

Analyst commentary prepared by Robert M. Gold/CB/GG

Highlights October 14, 2004

- We see 2005 revenues of $50 billion, up from expected 2004 revenues of $46.8 billion. By segment, we see revenue growth of about 5% in pharmaceuticals (versus a projected 11% to 12% advance seen in 2004), 11% in medical devices and diagnostics (12%), and 8% in consumer products (10%). In our opinion, there could be some upside in the medical device segment as the company boosts manufacturing capacity to meet higher global demand for its Cypher device. We think the launch of several drugs currently in the pipeline can drive segment sales growth back into the double-digit range by 2007.

- We project 2005 gross margins of 71.6%, about flat versus our 2004 projection, with R&D costs consuming 11.5% of sales versus 10.7%, and SG&A expenses at 33.4% of sales versus 33.0%. We see 2004 free cash flow of $8.9 billion, and believe JNJ has the ability to generate sustained annual free cash flow growth of 5% to 8%. We look for a 2005 tax rate of 28.3%, up from 28.1% projected for 2004.

- Our 2004 operating EPS estimate is $3.06. After projected stock option expense and the reversal of prior-year expenses associated with JNJ's pension plans, we see 2004 Standard & Poor's Core EPS of $3.11. Looking to 2005, we anticipate that the repatriation of between $350 million and $500 million of foreign earnings could boost EPS by up to $0.01. We recently raised our 2005 EPS estimate by $0.05, to $3.35.

Key Stock Statistics

S&P Core EPS 2005E	3.34	52-week Range	$61.00-48.79
S&P Oper. EPS 2004E	3.06	12 Month P/E	20.0
P/E on S&P Oper. EPS 2004E	19.9	Beta	0.17
S&P Oper. EPS 2005E	3.35	Shareholders	187,708
Yield (%)	1.9%	Market Cap (B)	$181.0
Dividend Rate/Share	1.14	Shares Outstanding (M)	2967.7

Value of $10,000 invested five years ago: **$ 12,101**

Dividend Data   Dividends have been paid since 1944

Amount ($)	Date Decl.	Ex-Div. Date	Stock of Record	Payment Date
0.240	Jan. 05	Feb. 12	Feb. 17	Mar. 09 '04
0.285	Apr. 22	May. 14	May. 18	Jun. 08 '04
0.285	Jul. 20	Aug. 13	Aug. 17	Sep. 07 '04
0.285	Oct. 22	Nov. 12	Nov. 16	Dec. 07 '04

Investment Rationale/Risk October 14, 2004

- In our opinion, the shares of this diversified, well managed health care and consumer products company offer compelling, relatively defensive investment characteristics with a reasonable valuation. We do anticipate some challenging conditions within the pharmaceutical segment through the end of 2005. However, we believe this will be partly offset by momentum in the consumer products segment, and by market share gains in both the drug-coated and bare-metal coronary stent areas. Despite the pharmaceutical pressures, we see currency-neutral revenue growth surpassing the pharmaceutical group average over the coming three years, aided by a development pipeline that includes several potentially significant new drugs that could begin to contribute to revenues by the end of 2006 and into 2007.

- Risks to our opinion and target price include faster than expected loss of branded pharmaceutical sales due to generic competition, unfavorable patent litigation outcomes, and prolonged broad weakness in the health care sector.

- Our 12-month target price of $70 assumes that the shares will trade at 21X our 2005 EPS estimate of $3.35. At that level, the stock would be priced above the S&P 500, but in line with the blended average 2005 P/E for our medical device and pharmaceutical coverage universe. We see our target price further supported by our DCF and sum-of-the-parts valuation models.

Revenues/Earnings Data   Fiscal year ending December 31

Revenues (Million $)

	2004	2003	2002	2001	2000	1999
1Q	11,559	9,821	8,743	7,791	7,319	6,638
2Q	11,484	10,332	9,073	8,342	7,508	6,854
3Q	11,553	10,455	9,079	8,238	7,204	6,749
4Q	—	11,254	9,403	8,403	7,108	6,877
Yr.	—	41,862	36,298	33,004	29,139	27,471

Earnings Per Share ($)

	2004	2003	2002	2001	2000	1999
1Q	0.83	0.69	0.59	0.53	0.47	0.41
2Q	0.82	0.40	0.54	0.48	0.47	0.42
3Q	0.78	0.69	0.57	0.49	0.45	0.40
4Q	E0.63	0.62	0.46	0.36	0.32	0.27
Yr.	E3.06	2.40	2.16	1.84	1.70	1.47

Next earnings report expected: late-January Source: S&P, Company Reports
EPS Estimates based on S&P Operating Earnings; historical GAAP earnings are as reported.

Johnson & Johnson

Recommendation: **BUY** ★ ★ ★ ★ ★ 12-Month Target Price: **$70.00** (as of July 16, 2004)

Business Summary October 15, 2004

Well known for household names such as Tylenol and Band-Aid adhesive bandages, Johnson & Johnson ranks among the world's largest and most diversified health care companies. JNJ traces its roots to James Johnson and Edward Mead Johnson, who formed the company more than 110 years ago. JNJ currently offers a broad list of prescription drugs, medical devices and health-related consumer products.

The pharmaceutical segment (47% of 2003 sales) focuses on the antifungal, anti-infective, cardiovascular, contraceptive, dermatology, gastrointestinal, hematology, immunology, neurology, oncology, pain management, central nervous system, and urology fields. The pharmaceutical division was enlarged in recent years through the acquisitions of ALZA, a leading drug delivery concern; and Centocor, a leading biotechnology company. In 2003, the company had seven products that each generated over $1 billion of sales, including Procrit/Eprex ($4.0 billion), Risperdal ($2.5 billion), Remicade ($1.7 billion), Duragesic ($1.6 billion), hormonal contraceptives ($1.2 billion), Levaquin/Floxin ($1.1 billion) and Topamax ($1.0 billion).

In April 2003, JNJ acquired Scios Inc., a biopharmaceutical company with a commercialized product for cardiovascular disease and research projects focused on autoimmune diseases, for net cash of $2.4 billion. In June 2003, the company entered into an agreement with Millenium Pharmaceuticals Inc. under which JNJ would have rights to sell Velcade, an FDA-approved protease inhibitor to treat multiple myeloma, in markets outside the U.S. if the compound gains regulatory approval in those markets.

The medical devices and diagnostics segment (35%) sells a wide range of products used by physicians, nurses, therapists, hospitals, diagnostic labs and clinics. These include Ethicon's wound care, surgical sports medicine and women's healthcare products; Cordis's circulatory disease management products; Lifescan's blood glucose monitoring products; Ortho-Clinical Diagnostic's professional diagnostic products; Depuy's orthopaedic joint reconstruction and spinal products; and Vistakon's disposable contact lenses.

In April 2003, JNJ received FDA approval to market the Cypher Sirolimus-eluting coronary stent, making it the first U.S. approved drug coated stent intended to help reduce restenosis, or the reblockage of a treated coronary artery. Shipments of the product began in the 2003 second quarter. The company believes that more than 350,000 U.S. patients received the device through the end of 2003.

The consumer segment (18%) primarily sells personal care products, including nonprescription drugs, adult skin and hair care products, baby care products, oral care products, first aid products, women's health products and nutritional products. Major brands include Band-Aid Brand Adhesive Bandages, Imodium A-D anti-diarrheal, Johnson's Baby line of products; Neutrogena skin and hair care products, and Tylenol pain reliever.

The company spent $4.7 billion (11.2% of sales) on R&D in 2003, up from $4.0 billion (10.9%) in 2002.

Company Financials Fiscal Year ending December 31

Per Share Data ($)

(Year Ended December 31)	2003	2002	2001	2000	1999	1998	1997	1996	1995	1994
Tangible Bk. Val.	5.17	4.53	4.97	4.15	3.11	2.38	3.38	2.90	2.35	1.84
Cash Flow	3.01	2.67	2.35	2.23	1.98	1.57	1.59	1.47	1.26	1.06
Earnings	2.40	2.16	1.84	1.70	1.47	1.11	1.21	1.08	0.93	0.78
S&P Core Earnings	2.26	1.99	1.66	NA	NA	NA	NA	NA	NA	NA
Dividends	0.93	0.80	0.70	0.62	0.55	0.49	0.43	0.37	0.32	0.28
Payout Ratio	39%	37%	38%	36%	37%	43%	35%	34%	34%	36%
Prices - High	59.08	65.89	60.97	52.96	53.43	44.87	33.65	27.00	23.09	14.12
- Low	48.05	41.40	40.25	33.06	38.50	31.68	24.31	20.78	13.40	9.00
P/E Ratio - High	25	31	33	31	36	40	28	25	25	18
- Low	20	19	22	19	26	28	20	19	14	12

Income Statement Analysis (Million $)

	2003	2002	2001	2000	1999	1998	1997	1996	1995	1994
Revs.	41,862	36,298	33,004	29,139	27,471	23,657	22,629	21,620	18,842	15,734
Oper. Inc.	12,740	11,340	9,490	7,992	7,370	6,291	5,689	5,312	6,002	3,531
Depr.	1,869	1,662	1,605	1,515	1,444	1,246	1,067	1,009	857	724
Int. Exp.	207	160	153	146	197	110	120	180	213	186
Pretax Inc.	10,308	9,291	7,898	6,622	5,753	4,269	4,576	4,033	3,317	2,681
Eff. Tax Rate	30.2%	29.0%	28.2%	27.5%	27.6%	28.3%	27.8%	28.4%	27.6%	25.2%
Net Inc.	7,197	6,597	5,668	4,800	4,167	3,059	3,303	2,887	2,403	2,006
S&P Core Earnings	6,785	6,052	5,090	NA	NA	NA	NA	NA	NA	NA

Balance Sheet & Other Fin. Data (Million $)

	2003	2002	2001	2000	1999	1998	1997	1996	1995	1994
Cash	9,523	7,596	8,941	6,013	4,320	2,994	2,753	2,136	1,364	704
Curr. Assets	22,995	19,266	18,473	15,450	13,200	11,132	10,563	9,370	7,938	6,680
Total Assets	48,263	40,556	38,488	31,321	29,163	26,211	21,453	20,010	17,873	15,668
Curr. Liab.	13,448	11,449	8,044	7,140	7,454	8,162	5,283	5,184	4,388	4,266
LT Debt	2,955	2,022	2,217	2,037	2,450	1,269	1,126	1,410	2,107	2,199
Common Equity	26,869	22,697	24,233	18,808	16,213	13,590	12,359	10,836	9,045	7,122
Total Cap.	30,604	25,362	26,943	21,100	18,950	15,437	13,660	12,416	11,308	9,451
Cap. Exp.	2,262	2,099	1,731	1,646	1,728	1,460	1,391	1,373	1,256	937
Cash Flow	9,066	8,259	7,273	6,315	5,611	4,305	4,370	3,896	3,260	2,730
Curr. Ratio	1.7	1.7	2.3	2.2	1.8	1.4	2.0	1.8	1.8	1.6
% LT Debt of Cap.	9.7	8.0	8.2	9.7	12.9	8.2	8.2	11.4	18.6	23.3
% Net Inc.of Revs.	17.2	18.2	17.2	16.5	15.2	12.9	14.6	13.3	12.8	12.7
% Ret. on Assets	16.2	16.7	15.6	15.9	14.8	12.8	15.9	15.2	14.3	14.4
% Ret. on Equity	29.0	28.1	25.4	27.4	27.5	23.6	28.5	29.0	29.7	31.6

Data as orig reptd.; bef. results of disc opers/spec. items. Per share data adj. for stk. divs.; EPS diluted. E-Estimated. NA-Not Available. NM-Not Meaningful. NR-Not Ranked. UR-Under Review.

Office: One Johnson & Johnson Plaza, New Brunswick, NJ 08933.
Telephone: 732-524-0400.
Website: http://www.jnj.com
Chrmn & CEO: W.C. Weldon.
Vice Chrmn & CFO: R.J. Darretta.
VP & General Counsel: R.S. Fine.

VP & Investor Contact: H.E. Short 800-950-5089.
Secy: M.H. Ullmann.
Dirs: G. N. Burrow, M. S. Coleman, J. G. Cullen, R. J. Darretta, M. J. Folkman, A. D. Jordan, A. G. Langbo, S. Lindquist, L. F. Mullin, S. S. Reinemund, D. Satcher, H. B. Schacht, W. C. Weldon.

Founded: in 1887.
Domicile: New Jersey.
Employees: 110,600.
S&P Analyst: Robert M. Gold/CB/GG

Jones Apparel Group

Recommendation: **BUY** ★★★★☆
SELL · SELL · HOLD · BUY · BUY

12-Month Target Price: **$39.00**
(as of October 13, 2004)

JNY has an approximate 0.04% weighting in the **S&P 500**

Sector: Consumer Discretionary
Sub-Industry: Apparel, Accessories & Luxury Goods
Peer Group: Designer Mens/Womens Apparel

Summary: JNY is the world's largest manufacturer of women's apparel, footwear and accessories, with brands that include Jones New York, Nine West and Evan-Picone.

Quantitative Evaluations

S&P Earnings & Dividend Rank: B+

| D | C | B- | B | **B+** | A- | A | A+ |

S&P Fair Value Rank: 4+

| 1 | 2 | 3 | **4** | 5 |
| Lowest | | | | Highest |

Fair Value Calc.: $39.00 (Slightly Undervalued)

S&P Investability Quotient Percentile
98%

JNY scored higher than 98% of all companies for which an S&P Report is available.

Volatility: Low

| **Low** | Average | High |

Technical Evaluation: Neutral
Since 11/04, the technical indicators for JNY have been Neutral.

Relative Strength Rank: Weak
22
1 Lowest   Highest 99

Price as of 11/12/04: **$34.95**   2004E S&P Core EPS: **$2.40**

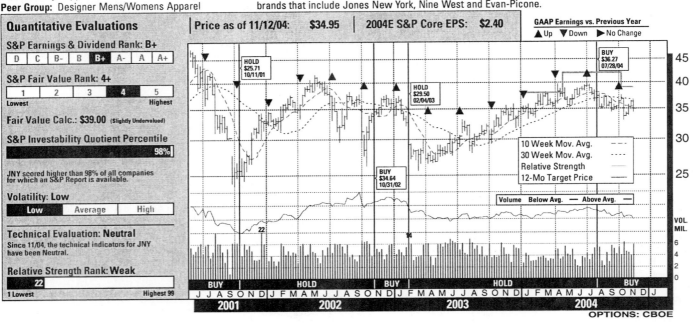

GAAP Earnings vs. Previous Year
▲ Up   ▼ Down   ▶ No Change

10 Week Mov. Avg.
30 Week Mov. Avg.
Relative Strength
12-Mo Target Price

Volume   Below Avg. —   Above Avg. —

OPTIONS: CBOE

Analyst commentary prepared by Marie Driscoll, CFA /PMW/JWP

Highlights October 29, 2004

- JNY is moving ahead with its diversification strategy. The loss of the Lauren license in 2003 appears to be behind the company, with two recent acquisitions and the Signature launch. In better wholesale, Anne Klein (acquired with Kasper) brings JNY into the upscale bridge apparel category, while offering what we view as lucrative line extension and licensing potential. We look for 2005 revenue growth in the mid-single digits, following a 6% increase that we project for 2004. We estimate 2004 revenues of $4.6 billion, as recently acquired Maxwell Shoe is expected to add about $115 million, and Kasper and Signature replace business lost with the Lauren license. We project low-single-digit retail same-store sales gains in 2004 and 2005. We look for the accessories and footwear businesses to continue to strengthen.

- We expect modest gross margin expansion, offset by increased SG&A expenses related to new launches and a number of brand repositionings that should restrict 2004 operating margins, which we project at 12%. We think that 2005 margins should reflect the absence of purchase accounting adjustments, and expected leverage on growing brands.

- With lower interest expense expected, and about $0.10 a share of accretion related to debt refinancing, offset by an estimated $0.15 a share of noncash charges related to the Maxwell acquisition, we project 2004 EPS of $2.52, and see $3.10 for 2005. Our respective S&P Core EPS projections are $2.40 and $2.98, with the difference due to estimated stock option expense.

Investment Rationale/Risk October 29, 2004

- We recommend accumulating the shares on a total return basis. We see JNY as having a significant opportunity to rebuild market share in the better apparel segment. For the longer term, we expect it to make further inroads into bridge apparel with multiple lines acquired with Kasper. We think the Maxwell Shoe acquisition provides opportunities for growth via increased market penetration and potential line extensions for the acquired Mootsie Tootsie, Sam & Libby, and Joan & David brands. We view the stock as undervalued at 11X our 2005 EPS estimate, about a discount of 10% to peers and 20% to the S&P 500.

- Risks to our opinion and target price include changes in consumer spending, fashion and inventory risk, and management's ability to integrate recent acquisitions.

- Our 12-month target price of $39 is derived by combining a 5% discount to JNY's 13.1X historical forward multiple with our 2005 EPS estimate of $3.10, and reflects our expectations of modest P/E multiple expansion in light of operating challenges that we see facing the company: the loss of the Lauren and Ralph brands; the 2004 Signature line launch at slightly lower price points; and the recent Kasper and Maxwell Shoe acquisitions. Our DCF analysis generates an intrinsic value of $46, assuming a 10% decline in free cash flow in 2004, to $415 million, followed by three years of low-double-digit growth, with 4% growth in perpetuity.

Key Stock Statistics

S&P Core EPS 2005E	2.98	52-week Range	$40.00-31.75
S&P Oper. EPS 2004E	2.52	12 Month P/E	14.3
P/E on S&P Oper. EPS 2004E	13.9	Beta	1.16
S&P Oper. EPS 2005E	3.10	Shareholders	457
Yield (%)	1.1%	Market Cap (B)	$ 4.3
Dividend Rate/Share	0.40	Shares Outstanding (M)	122.2

Value of $10,000 invested five years ago: **$ 11,511**

Dividend Data Dividends have been paid since 2003

Amount ($)	Date Decl.	Ex-Div. Date	Stock of Record	Payment Date
0.080	Feb. 18	Feb. 26	Mar. 01	Mar. 12 '04
q.08	Apr. 27	May. 05	May. 07	May. 21 '04
0.100	Jul. 27	Aug. 11	Aug. 13	Aug. 27 '04
0.100	Oct. 27	Nov. 08	Nov. 10	Nov. 24 '04

Revenues/Earnings Data Fiscal year ending December 31

Revenues (Million $)

	2004	2003	2002	2001	2000	1999
1Q	1,218	1,234	1,127	1,071	1,082	579.1
2Q	1,053	980.4	972.1	879.9	906.6	510.4
3Q	1,296	1,181	1,278	1,236	1,192	1,147
4Q	—	980.2	964.5	887.1	962.2	914.5
Yr.	—	4,375	4,341	4,073	4,143	3,151

Earnings Per Share ($)

	2004	2003	2002	2001	2000	1999
1Q	0.73	0.90	0.63	0.75	0.58	0.51
2Q	0.61	0.54	0.49	0.43	0.46	0.28
3Q	0.77	0.71	0.95	0.41	0.93	0.59
4Q	E0.43	0.33	0.39	0.25	0.52	0.22
Yr.	E2.52	2.48	2.46	1.82	2.48	1.60

Next earnings report expected: mid-February Source: S&P, Company Reports
EPS Estimates based on S&P Operating Earnings; historical GAAP earnings are as reported.

STANDARD &POOR'S

Jones Apparel Group, Inc.

Recommendation: **BUY** ★ ★ ★ ★   12-Month Target Price: **$39.00** (as of October 13, 2004)

Business Summary October 29, 2004

Jones Apparel Group is a leading designer and marketer of branded apparel, footwear and accessories in multiple distribution channels. Its brand are differentiated by style, pricing strategy, distribution channel, and target customer. JNY primarily contracts for the manufacture of its broad range of women's career apparel, dresses, shoes, accessories, and men's and women's sportswear through a worldwide network of manufacturers.

The wholesale better apparel segment (34% of 2003 revenues) includes career and casual sportswear, jeanswear, dresses, suits and lifestyle collections. Career and casual sportswear are marketed as individual items or a collection, which, while sold as separates, are coordinated regarding styles, color schemes and fabrics, and are designed to be worn together. Products are sold under brand names such as Jones New York, Nine West, Anne Klein, Easy Spirit, and Signature.

The wholesale moderate apparel segment (30%) targets women's, juniors and girls markets. Labels include Jones Wear, Jones Wear Sport, Evan-Picone, Nine & Company, Bandolino, Norton McNaughton, Gloria Vanderbilt, Energie, Erika and l.e.i.

Wholesale footwear and accessories operations (20%) sell brand name and private label footwear and/or accessories under the Nine West, Bandolino, Easy Spirit, Enzo Angiolini, Napier, and Judith Jack brands. Products include shoes, handbags, small leather goods, belts, wristwatches, and costume and fashion jewelry. JNY also has licenses to produce footwear and accessories under the ESPIRIT brand, and accessories under the Tommy Hilfiger and Givenchy brands.

JNY markets apparel, footwear and accessories directly to consumers through its specialty retail stores (16%) operating in malls and urban retail centers and through company outlet stores. At December 31, 2003, it operated 413 specialty retail stores, primarily under the Nine West, Easy Spirit, Bandolino and Enzo Angiolini names, offering selections of products not marketed to its wholesale customers. Some stores also sell products licensed by the company, including belts, jewelry, legwear, outerwear, watches and sunglasses. At December 31, 2003, the company also operated 577 outlet stores in the U.S. and Canada.

Effective in 2004, JNY ceded its Ralph and Lauren licenses to Polo Ralph Lauren Corp., after failing to agree on terms to restructure the license agreements in 2003. Net sales in 2003 of the Lauren and Ralph brands were $476.4 million and $30.7 million, respectively. JNY retained the Polo Jeans license. The Maxwell Shoe acquisition closed in July 2004, for about $346 million. Kasper was acquired in December 2003, for $259 million. In August 2002, JNY acquired l.e.i., a maker of girls' and young women's moderately priced jeanswear, for $310 million. In April 2002, the company acquired Gloria Vanderbilt for $101 million in cash and stock and the assumption of $44 million of debt.

Federated Department Stores and May Department Stores accounted for 13% and 12% of 2003 sales, respectively. Net advertising expenses of $74.2 million were incurred in 2003. Capital expenditures were $53.3 million in 2003, and were projected at $50 million to $55 million for 2004.

Company Financials Fiscal Year ending December 31

Per Share Data ($)

(Year Ended December 31)	2003	2002	2001	2000	1999	1998	1997	1996	1995	1994
Tangible Bk. Val.	0.98	0.66	0.03	0.16	NM	2.33	3.98	3.41	2.81	2.13
Cash Flow	3.04	3.03	1.96	3.37	2.05	1.68	1.26	0.84	0.66	0.56
Earnings	2.48	2.46	1.82	2.48	1.60	1.47	1.13	0.75	0.60	0.52
S&P Core Earnings	2.40	2.35	1.63	NA	NA	NA	NA	NA	NA	NA
Dividends	0.16	Nil	Nil	Nil	Nil	Nil	Nil	Nil	Nil	Nil
Payout Ratio	6%	Nil	Nil	Nil	Nil	Nil	Nil	Nil	Nil	Nil
Prices - High	37.44	41.68	47.43	35.00	35.87	37.75	28.71	18.68	9.90	8.93
- Low	25.61	26.18	23.75	20.12	21.50	15.87	16.06	8.90	5.65	5.50
P/E Ratio - High	15	17	26	14	22	26	25	25	17	17
- Low	10	11	13	8	13	11	14	12	9	11

Income Statement Analysis (Million $)

	2003	2002	2001	2000	1999	1998	1997	1996	1995	1994
Revs.	4,375	4,341	4,073	4,143	3,151	1,685	1,387	1,034	787	642
Oper. Inc.	664	679	506	714	431	283	211	139	107	92.1
Depr.	84.3	88.8	25.7	109	53.1	21.2	14.6	8.90	6.72	4.19
Int. Exp.	58.8	62.7	84.6	104	66.9	11.8	3.58	3.04	1.91	1.21
Pretax Inc.	529	534	400	503	315	252	195	128	100	87.3
Eff. Tax Rate	37.5%	37.7%	40.9%	40.0%	40.1%	38.5%	37.5%	36.7%	36.3%	37.1%
Net Inc.	331	332	236	302	188	155	122	80.8	63.5	54.9
S&P Core Earnings	318	318	210	NA	NA	NA	NA	NA	NA	NA

Balance Sheet & Other Fin. Data (Million $)

	2003	2002	2001	2000	1999	1998	1997	1996	1995	1994
Cash	350	283	76.5	60.5	47.0	129	51.3	30.1	16.9	21.1
Curr. Assets	1,456	1,318	1,141	1,182	1,131	632	441	390	331	261
Total Assets	4,188	3,853	3,374	2,979	2,792	1,189	581	488	401	318
Curr. Liab.	629	427	378	887	661	174	110	96.0	71.0	54.4
LT Debt	835	978	977	576	834	415	27.3	12.1	10.1	8.03
Common Equity	2,538	2,304	1,905	1,477	1,241	594	436	377	315	249
Total Cap.	3,503	3,380	2,963	2,053	2,075	1,009	463	389	325	257
Cap. Exp.	53.3	52.6	56.4	46.8	29.7	48.5	32.1	34.1	16.0	9.50
Cash Flow	415	421	262	411	242	176	136	89.8	70.2	59.1
Curr. Ratio	2.3	3.1	3.0	1.3	1.7	3.6	4.0	4.1	4.7	4.8
% LT Debt of Cap.	23.8	28.9	33.0	28.1	40.2	41.1	5.9	3.1	3.1	3.1
% Net Inc.of Revs.	7.6	7.7	5.8	7.3	6.0	9.2	8.8	7.8	8.1	8.6
% Ret. on Assets	8.2	9.2	7.4	10.5	9.5	17.5	22.8	18.2	17.7	18.7
% Ret. on Equity	13.7	15.8	14.0	22.2	20.5	30.1	30.0	23.4	22.5	24.9

Data as orig reptd.; bef. results of disc opers/spec. items. Per share data adj. for stk. divs.; EPS diluted. E-Estimated. NA-Not Available. NM-Not Meaningful. NR-Not Ranked. UR-Under Review.

Office: 250 Rittenhouse Circle, Bristol, PA 19007.
Telephone: 215-785-4000.
Website: http://www.jny.com
Chrmn: S. Kimmel.
Pres & CEO: P. Boneparth.

COO & CFO: W.R. Card.
EVP, Secy & General Counsel: I.M. Dansky.
EVP & Investor Contact: A. Britt .
Dirs: P. Boneparth, H. Gittis, M. H. Kamens, J. Kerrey, S. Kimmel, A. N. Reese, A. F. Scarpa, G. Stutz, M. L. Tarnopol.

Founded: in 1975.
Domicile: Pennsylvania.
Employees: 21,845.
S&P Analyst: Marie Driscoll, CFA /PMW/JWP

The **McGraw·Hill** Companies

JPMorgan Chase

Recommendation: **BUY** ★★★★☆
SELL | SELL | HOLD | BUY | BUY

12-Month Target Price: **$44.00**
(as of October 20, 2004)

JPM has an approximate 1.26% weighting in the **S&P 500**

Sector: Financials
Sub-Industry: Other Diversified Financial Services
Peer Group: Financial Cos. - Major Diversified

Summary: JPMorgan Chase is a leading global financial services firm with assets of $1.1 trillion and operations in more than 50 countries.

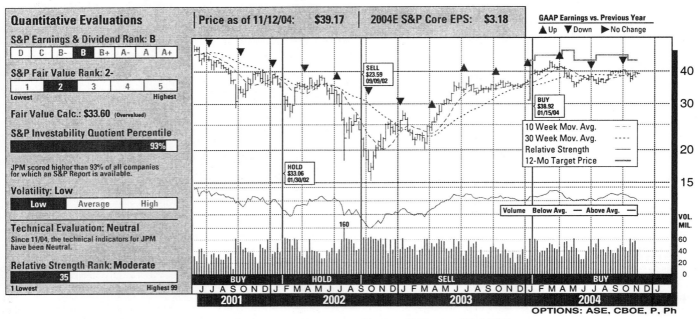

Quantitative Evaluations

S&P Earnings & Dividend Rank: B
D | C | B- | **B** | B+ | A- | A | A+

S&P Fair Value Rank: 2-
1 | **2** | 3 | 4 | 5
Lowest | | | | Highest

Fair Value Calc.: $33.60 (Overvalued)

S&P Investability Quotient Percentile
93%

JPM scored higher than 93% of all companies for which an S&P Report is available.

Volatility: Low
Low | Average | High

Technical Evaluation: Neutral
Since 11/04, the technical indicators for JPM have been Neutral.

Relative Strength Rank: Moderate
35
1 Lowest | Highest 99

Price as of 11/12/04: $39.17 | **2004E S&P Core EPS: $3.18**

GAAP Earnings vs. Previous Year
▲ Up ▼ Down ▶ No Change

SELL $23.59 09/09/02
BUY $38.92 01/15/04
HOLD $33.06 01/30/02
160

10 Week Mov. Avg.
30 Week Mov. Avg.
Relative Strength
12-Mo Target Price

Volume Below Avg. — Above Avg.

BUY | HOLD | SELL | BUY
J J A S O N D | J F M A M J J A S O N D | J F M A M J J A S O N D | J F M A M J J A S O N D | J
2001 | 2002 | 2003 | 2004

OPTIONS: ASE, CBOE, P, Ph

Analyst commentary prepared by Evan M. Momios, CFA /MF/BK

Highlights August 09, 2004

- We believe the recently completed acquisition of Bank One will lead to a more balanced business mix, with higher earnings quality and consistency. Specifically, we think the addition of Bank One's large retail banking and credit card businesses should mitigate the earnings volatility of JPM's trading and capital markets businesses.

- Credit quality improvements in commercial lending at both J.P. Morgan and Bank One, stronger growth seen for retail banking and credit card lending at both institutions, and strengthening capital markets activity should position the company to show accelerating earnings in the 2004 second half and in 2005, in our view.

- Our 2004 operating EPS estimate of $3.30 assumes dilution from the issuance of about 1.61 million new shares, partly offset by $3.0 billion in share repurchases and 17% of an expected $3.0 billion in annual cost savings ($322 million after tax). For 2005, our operating EPS estimate is $3.65; we assume that JPM will realize another 63% of projected annual cost savings ($907 million after tax), and we project another $3.0 billion in share buybacks.

Investment Rationale/Risk August 09, 2004

- We would accumulate the stock. The shares have performed about in line with most peers and the S&P 500 in 2004. The stock traded recently at 11.3X our 2004 EPS estimate, versus forward 12-month multiples of 12.9X over the past three years and 16.7X over the past five years, and offer a 3.7% dividend yield.

- Risks to our recommendation and target price include litigation costs that exceed our expectations; a failure to realize projected cost savings; merger related costs in excess of our expectation; a severe economic downturn in combination with higher short-term interest rates that could result in an inverted yield curve; and a serious geopolitical event that could affect equity markets.

- Our 12-month target price of $46 is equal to approximately 12.5X our 2005 operating EPS estimate. We think this is a fair multiple, reflecting our view that JPM's earnings will become less volatile following its acquisition of Bank One.

Key Stock Statistics

S&P Core EPS 2005E	3.54	52-week Range	$43.84-34.45
S&P Oper. EPS 2004E	3.20	12 Month P/E	20.1
P/E on S&P Oper. EPS 2004E	12.2	Beta	1.71
S&P Oper. EPS 2005E	3.50	Shareholders	126,759
Yield (%)	3.5%	Market Cap (B)	$139.6
Dividend Rate/Share	1.36	Shares Outstanding (M)	3563.3

Value of $10,000 invested five years ago: **$ 8,243**

Dividend Data Dividends have been paid since 1827

Amount ($)	Date Decl.	Ex-Div. Date	Stock of Record	Payment Date
0.340	Nov. 18	Jan. 02	Jan. 06	Jan. 31 '04
0.340	Mar. 16	Apr. 02	Apr. 06	Apr. 30 '04
0.340	Apr. 20	Jul. 01	Jul. 06	Jul. 31 '04
0.340	Sep. 21	Oct. 04	Oct. 06	Oct. 31 '04

Revenues/Earnings Data Fiscal year ending December 31

Revenues (Million $)

	2004	2003	2002	2001	2000	1999
1Q	11,625	11,454	10,957	15,015	—	7,967
2Q	11,227	11,842	11,190	12,559	—	8,344
3Q	16,546	10,396	7,301	12,399	—	8,017
4Q	—	10,671	—	—	16,004	9,382
Yr.	—	44,363	43,372	50,429	60,065	33,710

Earnings Per Share ($)

	2004	2003	2002	2001	2000	1999
1Q	0.92	0.69	0.48	0.59	0.85	0.88
2Q	-0.27	0.89	0.50	0.18	0.79	1.07
3Q	0.39	0.78	0.01	0.22	0.77	0.91
4Q	E0.83	0.89	-0.20	-0.18	0.44	1.32
Yr.	E3.20	3.24	0.80	0.81	2.86	4.18

Next earnings report expected: late-January Source: S&P, Company Reports
EPS Estimates based on S&P Operating Earnings; historical GAAP earnings are as reported.

JPMorgan Chase & Co.

Recommendation: **BUY** ★ ★ ★ ★ ☆   12-Month Target Price: **$44.00** (as of October 20, 2004)

Business Summary August 09, 2004

Formed through the December 2000 merger between J.P. Morgan and Chase Manhattan, J.P. Morgan Chase & Co. is now the second largest U.S. bank holding company, with assets of $771 billion at the end of 2003.

Operations are divided into five major business lines. The investment bank advises on corporate strategy and structure, raises capital, makes markets in financial instruments and offers risk management services. The company is the U.S. leader in syndicated lending, and the second largest in U.S. investment grade bond underwriting.

Chase financial services includes cardmember services (fourth largest credit card issuer in U.S.), Chase auto finance, regional banking (serving consumers and small businesses in New York, New Jersey, Connecticut and Texas), home finance (mortgages and related products), home finance (the fourth largest U.S. mortgage originator), and middle markets (corporate finance, cash management and inter-national finance to middle market companies).

Investment management and private banking provides investment management services to private and public sector institutional investors, high net worth individ-uals and retail customers, and provide personalized advice and solutions to wealthy individuals and families. The investment bank derives about 40% of its revenues from outside the U.S.

Treasury and securities services include fiduciary services to debt and equity issuers and broker-dealers, securities custody and lending and investment analyt-

ics, and cash management services, liquidity management and trade finance services. The company had $7.6 trillion in assets under custody at the end of 2003. JPMorgan Partners provides equity and mezzanine capital financing to private companies. At 2003 year end, JPMorgan Partners' investment portfolio carrying value totaled $8.3 billion.

In 2003, average earning assets, from which interest income is derived, amounted to $589.8 billion, and consisted mainly of loans (38%), trading assets (25%), and securities (13%). Average sources of funds included interest-bearing deposits (29%), noninterest-bearing deposits (26%), short-term borrowings (23%), long-term debt (6%), shareholders' equity (6%) and other (9%).

At December 31, 2003, nonperforming assets, consisting primarily of nonaccrual loans, were $3.09 billion (1.44% of net loans), down from $4.78 billion (2.27%) a year earlier. The allowance for loan losses, which is set aside for possible loan defaults, was $4.52 billion (2.06% of loans), versus $5.35 billion (2.47%) a year earlier. Net chargeoffs, or the amount of loans actually written off as uncollecti-ble, were $2.27 billion (1.00% of average loans) in 2003, versus $3.68 billion (1.74%) in 2002.

In July 2004, the company acquired Bank One, exchanging 1.32 JPM shares for each Bank One share. At that time, JPM expected $2.2 billion in cost savings, and $3.5 billion in share repurchases in 2004 and 2005.

Company Financials Fiscal Year ending December 31

Per Share Data ($)

(Year Ended December 31)	2003	2002	2001	2000	1999	1998	1997	1996	1995	1994
Tangible Bk. Val.	14.77	15.82	12.54	12.95	18.59	17.93	15.84	14.16	13.94	12.63
Earnings	3.24	0.80	0.81	2.86	4.18	2.83	2.68	1.67	2.08	1.55
S&P Core Earnings	3.12	0.65	0.34	NA	NA	NA	NA	NA	NA	NA
Dividends	1.36	1.36	1.34	1.23	1.06	0.93	0.81	0.73	0.63	0.55
Payout Ratio	42%	170%	165%	43%	25%	33%	30%	43%	30%	35%
Prices - High	38.26	39.68	57.33	67.16	60.75	51.70	42.18	31.95	21.58	14.04
- Low	20.13	15.26	29.04	32.37	43.87	23.70	28.20	17.37	11.91	11.20
P/E Ratio - High	12	50	71	23	15	18	16	19	10	9
- Low	6	19	36	11	10	8	11	10	6	7

Income Statement Analysis (Million $)

	2003	2002	2001	2000	1999	1998	1997	1996	1995	1994
Net Int. Inc.	12,337	11,526	10,802	9,512	8,744	8,566	8,158	8,340	8,202	4,674
Tax Equiv. Adj.	NA	NA	NA	NA	NA	NA	NA	NA	45.0	24.0
Non Int. Inc.	19,473	16,525	17,382	23,193	13,372	9,692	8,313	7,377	6,626	35.3
Loan Loss Prov.	NA	4,331	3,185	1,377	1,621	1,343	804	897	758	550
Exp./Op. Revs.	73.0%	81.2%	82.7%	69.8%	55.3%	63.5%	61.1%	59.4%	63.1%	67.0%
Pretax Inc.	10,028	2,519	2,566	8,733	8,375	5,930	5,910	3,811	4,812	2,212
Eff. Tax Rate	33.0%	34.0%	33.0%	34.4%	35.0%	36.2%	37.6%	35.4%	38.3%	41.5%
Net Inc.	6,719	1,663	1,719	5,727	5,446	3,782	3,708	2,461	2,970	1,294
% Net Int. Marg.	NA	2.09	1.99	1.87	2.98	2.89	2.86	3.21	3.37	3.61
S&P Core Earnings	6,439	1,290	698	NA	NA	NA	NA	NA	NA	NA

Balance Sheet & Other Fin. Data (Million $)

	2003	2002	2001	2000	1999	1998	1997	1996	1995	1994
Money Mkt. Assets	329,739	314,110	265,875	293,429	115,168	83,391	106,207	97,266	77,966	29,539
Inv. Securities	109,328	126,834	105,537	117,494	61,513	64,490	52,738	48,546	41,769	26,997
Com'l Loans	83,097	91,548	104,864	119,460	88,120	88,056	88,906	70,245	38,738	24,972
Other Loans	136,421	124,816	112,580	96,590	88,039	83,756	79,548	84,847	112,542	54,255
Total Assets	770,912	758,800	693,575	715,348	406,105	365,875	365,521	336,099	303,989	171,423
Demand Deposits	79,465	82,029	76,974	62,713	55,529	51,623	49,808	47,057	39,116	21,399
Time Deposits	247,027	222,724	216,676	216,652	186,216	160,814	143,880	133,864	132,418	75,107
LT Debt	54,782	45,190	44,172	47,788	20,690	18,375	15,127	13,314	12,825	6,753
Common Equity	45,145	41,297	40,090	40,818	22,689	22,810	20,002	20,444	18,186	9,262
% Ret. on Assets	0.9	0.2	0.2	0.8	1.4	1.0	1.1	0.8	1.0	0.8
% Ret. on Equity	15.4	4.0	4.1	15.2	23.6	17.2	18.4	12.3	16.0	14.8
% Loan Loss Resv.	2.1	2.5	2.1	1.7	2.0	2.1	2.2	2.3	2.5	3.1
% Loans/Deposits	67.2	71.0	74.0	77.3	72.9	84.0	87.0	85.7	87.6	81.6
% Equity to Assets	5.7	5.6	5.7	5.4	5.9	5.9	5.5	5.7	5.8	4.7

Data as orig reptd.; bef. results of disc opers/spec. items. Per share data adj. for stk. divs. Bold denotes primary EPS - prior periods restated. E-Estimated. NA-Not Available. NM-Not Meaningful. NR-Not Ranked. UR-Under Review.

Office: 270 Park Ave, New York, NY 10017-2070.
Telephone: 212-270-6000.
Website: http://www.jpmorganchase.com
Chrmn & CEO: W.B. Harrison, Jr.
CFO: M. Cavanagh.
Secy: A.J. Horan.

General Counsel: W.H. McDavid.
Investor Contact: J. Borden 212-270-7318.
Dirs: H. W. Becherer, R. P. Bechtel, F. A. Bennack, Jr., J. H. Biggs, L. A. Bossidy, M. A. Burns, E. V. Futter, W. H. Gray III, W. B. Harrison, Jr., H. L. Kaplan, L. R. Raymond, J. R. Stafford.

Founded: in 1823.
Domicile: Delaware.
Employees: 93,453.
S&P Analyst: Evan M. Momios, CFA /MF/BK

KB Home

Recommendation: **HOLD** ★★★☆☆
SELL | SELL | HOLD | BUY | BUY

12-Month Target Price: **$86.00**
(as of September 22, 2004)

KBH has an approximate 0.04% weighting in the **S&P 500**

Sector: Consumer Discretionary
Sub-Industry: Homebuilding
Peer Group: Homebuilders - National

Summary: This major homebuilder, which built virtually all of its homes in California and Paris, France, until the early 1990s, has expanded throughout the U.S. since that time.

Quantitative Evaluations

S&P Earnings & Dividend Rank: A-

| D | C | B- | B | B+ | A- | A | A+ |

S&P Fair Value Rank: 5

| 1 | 2 | 3 | 4 | 5 |
| Lowest | | | | Highest |

Fair Value Calc.: $155.90 (Undervalued)

S&P Investability Quotient Percentile

99%

KBH scored higher than 99% of all companies for which an S&P Report is available.

Volatility: Average

| Low | Average | High |

Technical Evaluation: Bullish

Since 10/04, the technical indicators for KBH have been Bullish.

Relative Strength Rank: Strong

85
1 Lowest — Highest 99

Price as of 11/12/04: $89.46 | **2004E S&P Core EPS:** $10.88

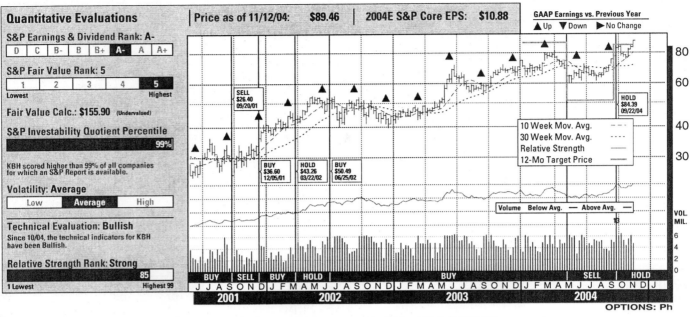

GAAP Earnings vs. Previous Year
▲ Up ▼ Down ► No Change

10 Week Mov. Avg.
30 Week Mov. Avg.
Relative Strength
12-Mo Target Price

Volume Below Avg. — Above Avg.

VOL. MIL.

OPTIONS: Ph

Analyst commentary prepared by Michael W. Jaffe/MF/JWP

Highlights October 01, 2004

- We expect revenues to advance 17% in FY 05 (Nov.). We see this forecasted gain driven mostly by a projected increase in the number of active communities, plus the full-year inclusion of recent acquisitions. In light of our forecast of a modest upturn in mortgage rates in the coming year, we are only anticipating a low-single-digit rise in average home prices for the year. We also see the average home price in FY 05 limited somewhat by our belief that the high-priced California market will likely account for a somewhat smaller proportion of sales.

- We see net margins widening slightly in FY 05, on the strong sales trends that we expect, plus our outlook for ongoing productivity improvements and some likely economies of scale from KBH's recent expansion of operations in the Southeast. We see these factors mostly offset by higher costs related to the projected ramp-up of new communities and what we expect to be still high materials prices.

- Our FY 04 and FY 05 Standard & Poor's Core Earnings estimates fall $0.12 and $0.13 a share, respectively, below our operating forecasts, with the differences reflecting projected stock option expense.

Investment Rationale/Risk October 01, 2004

- We expect housing markets to remain strong through FY 05, as we see higher, but still accommodative, mortgage rates, and economic growth. We also like KBH's business model, as it operates in what we view as strong demographic regions, and uses a pre-selling strategy designed to sell more options, hold down production and overhead costs, and eliminate speculative building. Yet, we see the maturity of the current housing cycle and what we expect to be somewhat higher rates limiting the valuation of KB Home, and would not add to positions.

- The primary risk to our recommendation and target price is a strong upturn in mortgage rates.

- The shares recently traded at around 6X our FY 05 EPS estimate, which was well below the S&P 500, and slightly beneath KBH's peers. However, the company serves a large amount of first-time buyers. Because we believe they are most susceptible to the modest rise in mortgage rates that we expect in FY 05, we think KBH's valuation will remain relatively unchanged over the next year. Our 12-month target price is $86, or 6.4X our FY 05 EPS estimate.

Key Stock Statistics

S&P Core EPS 2005E	13.22	52-week Range	$89.58-60.27
S&P Oper. EPS 2004E	11.00	12 Month P/E	8.7
P/E on S&P Oper. EPS 2004E	8.1	Beta	0.57
S&P Oper. EPS 2005E	13.35	Shareholders	1,018
Yield (%)	1.1%	Market Cap (B)	$ 4.1
Dividend Rate/Share	1.00	Shares Outstanding (M)	46.3

Value of $10,000 invested five years ago: **$ 37,277**

Dividend Data Dividends have been paid since 1986

Amount ($)	Date Decl.	Ex-Div. Date	Stock of Record	Payment Date
0.250	Dec. 08	Feb. 09	Feb. 11	Feb. 25 '04
0.250	Apr. 01	May. 11	May. 13	May. 27 '04
0.250	Jul. 01	Aug. 10	Aug. 12	Aug. 26 '04
0.250	Oct. 07	Nov. 08	Nov. 11	Nov. 25 '04

Revenues/Earnings Data Fiscal year ending November 30

Revenues (Million $)

	2004	2003	2002	2001	2000	1999
1Q	1,353	1,095	915.7	821.1	799.6	694.1
2Q	1,570	1,440	1,140	1,067	906.2	862.3
3Q	1,748	1,442	1,293	1,235	981.0	1,057
4Q	—	1,873	1,683	1,451	1,244	1,223
Yr.	—	5,851	5,031	4,574	3,931	3,836

Earnings Per Share ($)

	2004	2003	2002	2001	2000	1999
1Q	1.75	1.25	0.95	0.70	1.47	0.35
2Q	2.40	1.94	1.42	1.07	0.68	0.58
3Q	2.84	2.33	1.95	1.58	1.14	0.78
4Q	E4.02	3.31	2.92	2.03	2.00	1.36
Yr.	E11.00	8.80	7.15	5.50	5.24	3.08

Next earnings report expected: mid-December Source: S&P, Company Reports
EPS Estimates based on S&P Operating Earnings; historical GAAP earnings are as reported.

KB Home

Recommendation: **HOLD** ★ ★ ★ ☆ ☆   12-Month Target Price: **$86.00** (as of September 22, 2004)

Business Summary October 01, 2004

KB Home (formerly Kaufman & Broad Home) has been one of the largest single-family homebuilders in California for some time. Since 1993, it has expanded into Nevada, Arizona, Colorado, New Mexico, Texas, Florida, Georgia, North Carolina, South Carolina, Illinois and Indiana. It entered Georgia and North Carolina in March 2003, through the acquisition of Colony Homes; Illinois through the September 2003 takeover of Zale Homes; South Carolina through the January 2004, purchase of Palmetto Traditional Homes; and Indiana through the June 2004, purchase of Dura Builders. The company is also one of the largest builders in Paris, France.

In FY 03 (Nov.), KBH derived 35% of homebuilding sales (on a dollar basis) in California, 21% in the Southwest, 20% in the Central U.S., 10% in the Southeast, and 14% in France.

The company delivered 27,331 homes in FY 03, at an average price of $206,500, versus 25,452 in FY 02 ($190,800); the average FY 03 price was $353,900 in California and $168,900 in other U.S. areas and France.

Unit orders rose 23%, year to year, to 8,982 homes, in FY 04's third quarter. Order backlog at August 31, 2004, was $4.8 billion (21,928 homes), up 42% from the year-earlier level (32% in units); all totals exclude joint ventures.

The company mostly sells single-family detached homes. It generally constructs homes in medium-sized developments, close to major metropolitan areas, catering to first time and first move-up buyers. Like most major builders, it acts as general contractor for its communities, and hires subcontractors for all production work.

KBH also provides mortgage banking services to domestic home buyers.

The company expanded into Georgia and North Carolina in March 2003, when it bought Colony Homes (sales of $244 million in 2002), which delivered a total of 1,872 homes in 2002, in Atlanta, GA, and Raleigh and Charlotte, NC. In September 2003, KBH entered the Midwest through the $33 million purchase of Zale Homes (2002 revenues of $106 million), which delivered 302 homes in Chicago in 2002; in January 2004, the company entered South Carolina through the purchase of Palmetto Traditional Homes ($90 million in revenues in 2003); and in June 2004, KBH expanded into Indiana, through its acquisition of Dura Builders, which delivered about 500 homes in 2003 ($75 million in revenues).

In August 2001, KBH's Feline Prides stock purchase contracts were mandatorily converted into a total of 5,977,109 common shares. The company had been making quarterly payments of $3.8 million on the Feline Prides.

KBH repurchased one million of its common shares in the second quarter of FY 04, for a sum of $66.1 million. This followed its buyback of two million shares, for $108.3 million in FY 04; and four million shares, for $190.8 million, in FY 02.

Company Financials Fiscal Year ending November 30

Per Share Data ($)

(Year Ended November 30)	2003	2002	2001	2000	1999	1998	1997	1996	1995	1994
Tangible Bk. Val.	29.25	22.50	17.90	13.25	10.70	10.73	9.02	7.75	12.37	12.46
Cash Flow	8.80	7.54	6.63	6.27	3.90	2.76	1.75	-1.27	0.89	1.00
Earnings	8.80	7.15	5.50	5.24	3.08	2.32	1.45	-1.54	0.73	1.16
S&P Core Earnings	8.48	7.00	5.32	NA	NA	NA	NA	NA	NA	NA
Dividends	0.30	0.30	0.30	0.30	0.30	0.30	0.30	0.30	0.30	0.30
Payout Ratio	3%	4%	5%	6%	10%	13%	21%	NM	41%	26%
Prices - High	74.96	54.39	41.44	38.31	30.25	35.00	23.12	16.87	16.00	25.50
- Low	42.55	37.13	24.67	16.81	16.75	17.12	12.75	11.25	10.87	12.12
P/E Ratio - High	9	8	8	7	10	15	16	NM	22	22
- Low	5	5	4	3	5	7	9	NM	15	10

Income Statement Analysis (Million $)

	2003	2002	2001	2000	1999	1998	1997	1996	1995	1994
Revs.	5,851	5,031	4,574	3,931	3,836	2,449	1,876	1,787	1,397	1,336
Oper. Inc.	584	539	448	373	333	203	141	136	96.0	115
Depr.	21.5	17.2	43.9	41.3	40.0	18.1	11.9	10.8	6.30	3.41
Int. Exp.	30.2	44.2	59.5	50.9	45.0	38.4	42.5	77.1	79.5	62.6
Pretax Inc.	580	486	352	329	257	154	91.5	-95.8	45.5	75.0
Eff. Tax Rate	31.5%	31.9%	31.3%	26.6%	30.7%	33.4%	35.9%	NM	36.1%	36.5%
Net Inc.	371	314	214	210	147	95.3	58.2	-61.2	29.0	46.6
S&P Core Earnings	357	302	207	NA	NA	NA	NA	NA	NA	NA

Balance Sheet & Other Fin. Data (Million $)

	2003	2002	2001	2000	1999	1998	1997	1996	1995	1994
Cash	138	330	281	33.1	28.0	63.4	68.2	9.78	43.4	55.0
Curr. Assets	NA	NA	NA	NA	NA	NA	NA	NA	NA	NA
Total Assets	4,236	4,026	3,693	2,829	2,664	1,860	1,419	1,243	1,574	1,454
Curr. Liab.	NA	NA	NA	NA	NA	NA	NA	NA	NA	NA
LT Debt	1,393	1,181	1,111	1,208	1,308	800	698	578	791	677
Common Equity	1,593	1,274	1,092	655	676	475	383	340	414	403
Total Cap.	3,075	2,530	2,267	1,919	1,994	1,472	1,083	919	1,233	1,115
Cap. Exp.	13.1	31.1	12.2	18.5	19.0	Nil	Nil	Nil	Nil	Nil
Cash Flow	371	332	258	251	187	113	70.1	-50.4	35.3	40.1
Curr. Ratio	NA	NA	NA	NA	NA	NA	NA	NA	NA	NA
% LT Debt of Cap.	45.3	46.7	49.0	62.9	65.6	54.3	64.5	62.9	64.1	60.7
% Net Inc.of Revs.	6.3	6.2	4.7	5.3	3.8	3.9	3.1	NM	2.1	3.5
% Ret. on Assets	9.0	8.1	6.6	7.6	6.5	5.8	4.4	NM	2.0	3.4
% Ret. on Equity	25.9	26.6	24.5	31.6	25.6	22.2	16.1	NM	4.7	9.0

Data as orig reptd.; bef. results of disc opers/spec. items. Per share data adj. for stk. divs.; EPS diluted. E-Estimated. NA-Not Available. NM-Not Meaningful. NR-Not Ranked. UR-Under Review.

Office: 10990 Wilshire Boulevard, Los Angeles, CA 90024.
Telephone: 310-231-4000.
Website: http://www.kbhome.com
Chrmn & CEO: B. Karatz.
COO & EVP: J.T. Mezger.
EVP & General Counsel: B. Hirst.

SVP & CFO: D. Cecere.
VP, Treas & Investor Contact: K. Masuda .
Dirs: R. W. Burkle, R. R. Irani, K. M. Jastrow II, J. A. Johnson, B. Karatz, J. T. Lanni, M. Lora, M. G. McCaffery, L. Moonves, B. Munitz, L. G. Nogales.

Founded: in 1957.
Domicile: Delaware.
Employees: 5,100.
S&P Analyst: Michael W. Jaffe/MF/JWP

Kellogg Co.

Recommendation: HOLD ★★★☆☆
SELL SELL HOLD BUY BUY

12-Month Target Price: **$45.00**
(as of October 25, 2004)

K has an approximate 0.17% weighting in the **S&P 500**

Sector: Consumer Staples
Sub-Industry: Packaged Foods & Meats
Peer Group: Larger Food Manufacturers

Summary: Kellogg is the world's leading producer of ready-to-eat cereal products, with a dominant 40% global volume share.

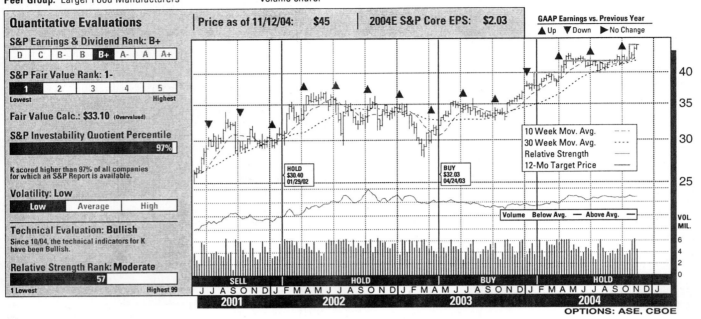

Quantitative Evaluations							

S&P Earnings & Dividend Rank: B+

| D | C | B- | B | B+ | A- | A | A+ |

S&P Fair Value Rank: 1-

| 1 | 2 | 3 | 4 | 5 |
| Lowest | | | | Highest |

Fair Value Calc.: $33.10 (Overvalued)

S&P Investability Quotient Percentile
97%

K scored higher than 97% of all companies for which an S&P Report is available.

Volatility: Low

| Low | Average | High |

Technical Evaluation: Bullish
Since 10/04, the technical indicators for K have been Bullish.

Relative Strength Rank: Moderate
57
| 1 Lowest | | Highest 99 |

Price as of 11/12/04: **$45** | 2004E S&P Core EPS: **$2.03**

GAAP Earnings vs. Previous Year ▲ Up ▼ Down ▶ No Change

- - - 10 Week Mov. Avg.
····· 30 Week Mov. Avg.
Relative Strength
12-Mo Target Price

HOLD $30.40 01/29/02
BUY $32.03 04/24/03

Volume Below Avg. — Above Avg.

SELL | HOLD | BUY | HOLD
J J A S O N D | J F M A M J J A S O N D | J F M A M J J A S O N D | J F M A M J J A S O N D J
2001 | 2002 | 2003 | 2004

OPTIONS: ASE, CBOE

Analyst commentary prepared by Richard Joy/PTW/GG

Highlights July 29, 2004

- We expect net sales to rise 4% to 5% in 2004, as low single digit volume growth, modest pricing and product mix improvements outweigh SKU rationalizations and weakness in the cookie business. Near-term results should be tempered by increased marketing and promotional activity to support new products, higher employee benefit expenses, and increased commodity and fuel costs. A combination of operating leverage, product mix improvement and productivity savings should help offset these higher costs, and allow operating profits to advance at a mid-single digit rate.

- Following lower interest expense and a higher effective tax rate, we project 2004 EPS of $2.14, up 11% from $1.92 in 2003. For 2005, we expect a further 9% rise to $2.33. Longer term, we expect EPS growth of 7% to 9%. Free cash flow, which we think will exceed $900 million in 2004, is expected to be used for debt reduction and share repurchases.

- Our 2004 and 2005 Standard and Poor's Core Earnings per share projections, reflecting estimated stock option expense of $0.07 a share and a $0.04 per share pension adjustment, are $2.03 and $2.22, respectively.

Investment Rationale/Risk July 29, 2004

- Our hold recommendation reflects our belief that improving trends for K's cereal and snack products and strong free cash flow growth will be balanced by rising costs and competitive pressures. While competition in K's core ready-to-eat cereal business remains strong, the company appears to be making solid dollar share gains, and the addition of Keebler has provided diversification and helped reduce its dependence on cereal. The company appears to be more focused on improving profitability over volume growth, and improvements in margins and cash flow trends are materializing. We like the company's longer-term prospects, and think the shares are a worthwhile holding based on our projections of solid earnings growth, strong free cash flows and improving returns.

- Risks to our recommendation and target price relate to competitive pressures in K's businesses, consumer acceptance of new product introductions, commodity cost inflation and the company's ability to achieve sales and earnings growth forecasts.

- The shares were recently trading at 19X our 2004 EPS estimate, a premium to K's packaged food industry peers and to the P/E multiple of the S&P 500 Index. We believe upside is limited given our expectation for rising costs and increasing competitive pressures in 2004. Our 12-month target price of $42 is derived in part from our discounted cash flow model and an analysis of relative comparables.

Key Stock Statistics

S&P Core EPS 2005E	2.22	52-week Range	$45.00-35.00
S&P Oper. EPS 2004E	2.14	12 Month P/E	20.9
P/E on S&P Oper. EPS 2004E	21.0	Beta	-0.05
S&P Oper. EPS 2005E	2.35	Shareholders	44,635
Yield (%)	2.2%	Market Cap (B)	$ 18.6
Dividend Rate/Share	1.01	Shares Outstanding (M)	412.9

Value of $10,000 invested five years ago: **$ 14,696**

Dividend Data Dividends have been paid since 1923

Amount ($)	Date Decl.	Ex-Div. Date	Stock of Record	Payment Date
0.253	Feb. 23	Mar. 02	Mar. 04	Mar. 15 '04
0.253	Apr. 27	May. 27	Jun. 01	Jun. 15 '04
0.253	Jul. 16	Aug. 27	Aug. 31	Sep. 15 '04
0.253	Oct. 22	Nov. 23	Nov. 26	Dec. 15 '04

Revenues/Earnings Data Fiscal year ending December 31

Revenues (Million $)

	2004	2003	2002	2001	2000	1999
1Q	2,391	2,148	2,062	1,707	1,751	1,745
2Q	2,387	2,247	2,125	2,343	1,801	1,784
3Q	2,445	2,282	2,137	2,590	1,846	1,868
4Q	—	2,135	1,981	2,213	1,556	1,586
Yr.	—	8,812	8,304	8,853	6,955	6,984

Earnings Per Share ($)

	2004	2003	2002	2001	2000	1999
1Q	0.53	0.40	0.37	0.23	0.40	0.29
2Q	0.57	0.50	0.42	0.28	0.37	0.38
3Q	0.59	0.56	0.49	0.37	0.45	-0.08
4Q	E0.45	0.46	0.47	0.31	0.23	0.25
Yr.	E2.14	1.92	1.75	1.18	1.45	0.83

Next earnings report expected: late-January Source: S&P, Company Reports
EPS Estimates based on S&P Operating Earnings; historical GAAP earnings are as reported.

Kellogg Company

Recommendation: **HOLD** ★ ★ ★ ☆ ☆  12-Month Target Price: **$45.00** (as of October 25, 2004)

Business Summary July 29, 2004

Kellogg Co., incorporated in 1922, is the world's leading producer of ready-to-eat cereal products, with an approximate 33% dollar market share in North America and nearly 40% globally. In recent years, the company has expanded its operations from ready-to-eat cereals to also include other grain-based convenience food products, such as Pop-Tarts toaster pastries, Eggo frozen waffles, Nutri-Grain cereal bars, and Rice Krispies Treats squares.

With the March 2001 acquisition of the Keebler Foods Company, Kellogg's also markets cookies, crackers and other convenience food products under brand names such as Keebler, Cheez-It, Murray and Famous Amos, and manufactures private label cookies, crackers and other products. These branded products will continue to be marketed through Keebler's direct store door (DSD) delivery system. K is also now marketing some of its other convenience foods products in the U.S. through this DSD system.

Products are manufactured in 17 countries and distributed in more than 180. Ready-to-eat cereals include Corn Flakes, Rice Krispies, Special K, Frosted Flakes, All-Bran, Corn Pops, Raisin Bran, Frosted Mini-Wheats, and Low Fat Granola. Cereals are generally marketed under the Kellogg's name and are sold principally to the grocery trade through direct sales forces for resale to consumers and through broker and distribution arrangements in less developed market areas.

Sales by product category in 2003 were: U.S. cereal 24%, U.S. snacks 24%, all other U.S. (Pop-Tarts, Kashi, Eggo, Morningstar Farms) 16%, International cereal 32%, and International convenience foods 4%. Sales contributions by geographic region in 2003 were: United States 64%, Europe 20%, Latin America 7%, and all other (including Canada, Australia and Asia) 9%.

Kellogg's acquisition activity in 2000 included the purchases of Kashi Company, a leading natural cereal company in the U.S., two convenience foods businesses in Australia, and Mondo Baking Company, a U.S. manufacturer of convenience foods. In November 1999, the company acquired Worthington Foods Inc., a leading manufacturer and marketer of vegetarian and other healthful foods, with brands including Morningstar Farms, Natural Touch, Worthington and Loma Linda.

The company operated, as of December 31, 2003, manufacturing plants and warehouses totaling more than 20 million square feet of building area in the U.S. and other countries. The principal ingredients in K's products include corn grits, oats, rice, soybeans, various fruits, sweeteners, wheat and wheat derivatives. In producing convenience foods products, the company may use flour, shortening, sweeteners, dairy products, eggs, fruit, chocolate and other filling ingredients.

The W. K. Kellogg Foundation Trust holds 34% of the common shares.

Company Financials Fiscal Year ending December 31

Per Share Data ($)

(Year Ended December 31)	2003	2002	2001	2000	1999	1998	1997	1996	1995	1994
Tangible Bk. Val.	NM	NM	NM	1.21	1.28	1.26	2.42	2.15	3.67	4.07
Cash Flow	2.83	2.60	2.26	2.16	1.54	1.91	2.07	1.86	1.72	2.15
Earnings	1.92	1.75	1.18	1.45	0.83	1.23	1.32	1.25	1.12	1.58
S&P Core Earnings	1.86	1.24	0.77	NA	NA	NA	NA	NA	NA	NA
Dividends	1.01	1.01	1.01	0.99	0.96	0.92	0.87	0.81	0.75	0.70
Payout Ratio	53%	58%	86%	69%	116%	75%	66%	65%	67%	44%
Prices - High	38.57	37.00	34.00	32.00	42.25	50.18	50.50	40.31	39.75	30.37
- Low	27.85	29.02	24.25	20.75	30.00	28.50	32.00	31.00	26.25	23.68
P/E Ratio - High	20	21	29	22	51	41	38	32	35	19
- Low	15	17	21	14	36	23	24	25	23	15

Income Statement Analysis (Million $)

	2003	2002	2001	2000	1999	1998	1997	1996	1995	1994
Revs.	8,812	8,304	8,853	6,955	6,984	6,762	6,830	6,677	7,004	6,562
Oper. Inc.	1,917	1,857	1,640	1,367	1,361	1,243	1,480	1,347	1,519	1,419
Depr.	373	348	439	291	288	278	287	252	259	256
Int. Exp.	371	391	352	138	119	119	108	70.0	70.0	52.3
Pretax Inc.	1,170	1,144	804	868	537	783	905	860	796	1,130
Eff. Tax Rate	32.7%	37.0%	40.1%	32.3%	37.0%	35.8%	37.7%	38.3%	38.4%	37.6%
Net Inc.	787	721	482	588	338	503	564	531	490	705
S&P Core Earnings	763	510	312	NA	NA	NA	NA	NA	NA	NA

Balance Sheet & Other Fin. Data (Million $)

	2003	2002	2001	2000	1999	1998	1997	1996	1995	1994
Cash	141	101	2,318	204	151	136	173	244	222	266
Curr. Assets	1,797	1,763	1,902	1,607	1,569	1,497	1,467	1,529	1,429	1,434
Total Assets	10,231	10,219	10,369	4,896	4,809	5,052	4,877	5,051	4,415	4,467
Curr. Liab.	2,766	3,015	2,208	2,493	1,588	1,719	1,657	2,199	1,265	1,185
LT Debt	4,265	4,519	5,619	709	1,613	1,614	1,416	727	718	719
Common Equity	1,443	895	871	898	813	890	998	1,282	1,591	1,808
Total Cap.	5,709	5,415	6,491	1,607	2,426	2,504	2,414	2,235	2,511	2,725
Cap. Exp.	247	254	277	231	266	344	312	307	316	354
Cash Flow	1,160	1,069	921	878	626	781	851	783	749	962
Curr. Ratio	0.6	0.6	0.9	0.6	1.0	0.9	0.9	0.7	1.1	1.2
% LT Debt of Cap.	74.7	83.5	86.6	44.1	66.5	64.5	58.7	32.5	28.6	26.4
% Net Inc.of Revs.	8.9	8.7	5.4	8.5	4.8	7.4	8.3	8.0	7.0	10.7
% Ret. on Assets	7.7	7.0	6.3	12.1	6.9	10.1	11.4	11.2	11.1	16.4
% Ret. on Equity	67.3	81.6	54.5	68.7	39.7	53.3	49.5	37.0	28.8	40.6

Data as orig reptd.; bef. results of disc opers/spec. items. Per share data adj. for stk. divs. Bold denotes primary EPS - prior periods restated. E-Estimated. NA-Not Available. NM-Not Meaningful. NR-Not Ranked. UR-Under Review.

Office: One Kellogg Square, Battle Creek, MI 49016-3599.
Telephone: 616-961-2000.
Website: http://www.kelloggcompany.com
Chrmn & CEO: C.M. Gutierrez.
Pres & COO: D. Mackay.
VP, Secy & General Counsel: G. Pilnick.

CFO: J.M. Boromisa.
Investor Contact: J. Encochson 269-961-2800.
Dirs: B. S. Carson, J. T. Dillon, C. X. Gonzalez, G. Gund, C. M. Gutierrez, J. M. Jenness, D. A. Johnson, L. D. Jorndt, A. M. Korologos, W. D. Perez, W. C. Richardson, J. L. Zabriskie.

Founded: in 1906.
Domicile: Delaware.
Employees: 25,250.
S&P Analyst: Richard Joy/PTW/GG

Kerr-McGee

Recommendation: **BUY** ★★★★ ☆
SELL | SELL | HOLD | BUY | BUY

12-Month Target Price: $66.00
(as of October 27, 2004)

KMG has an approximate 0.08% weighting in the **S&P 500**

Sector: Energy
Sub-Industry: Oil & Gas Exploration & Production
Peer Group: Exploration & Production - Large

Summary: This energy and inorganic chemical holding company has subsidiaries engaged in exploration and production (E&P), and the production and marketing of titanium dioxide pigment.

Quantitative Evaluations

S&P Earnings & Dividend Rank: B

D	C	B-	**B**	B+	A-	A	A+

S&P Fair Value Rank: 1-

1	2	3	4	5
Lowest				Highest

Fair Value Calc.: $49.50 (Overvalued)

S&P Investability Quotient Percentile

87%

KMG scored higher than 87% of all companies for which an S&P Report is available.

Volatility: Low

Low	Average	High

Technical Evaluation: Bullish

Since 10/04, the technical indicators for KMG have been Bullish.

Relative Strength Rank: Moderate

52

1 Lowest   Highest 99

Price as of 11/12/04:	**$59.29**	2004E S&P Core EPS:	**$4.54**

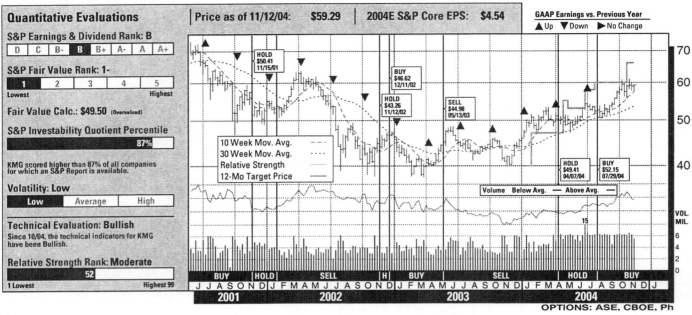

Analyst commentary prepared by Charles LaPorta, CFA /CB/BK

Highlights August 16, 2004

- Second quarter operating EPS was $1.06, versus $1.07 last year and below our estimate of $1.15, reflecting lower-than expected price realizations. KMG completed its merger with Westport Resources on June 25, 2004, which has led to increased production guidance of roughly 80,000 BOE per day.

- KMG expects to utilize best of breed operating procedures to lower Westport Resources' relatively high operating costs, as the company said it now feels comfortable it will exceed its original $40 million estimate in synergy savings beginning in 2005. We forecast 2004 EBITDAX (earnings before interest, taxes, depreciation, amortization and exploration expenses) of $2.4 billion, up about 20% from the 2003 level.

- Asset sales have helped cut debt, and refinancing transactions late in the second quarter should help further lower interest expense. Our 2004 EPS estimate is $4.70. KMG issued 48.9 million shares to purchase Westport Resources, which contributed to a reduction in our 2004 EPS estimate to $4.25 from $4.70. With production from acquired assets, deepwater Gulf of Mexico discoveries and China properties ramping up, we expect at least 25% production growth in 2005, which drives our initial 2005 EPS estimate of $4.80.

Investment Rationale/Risk August 16, 2004

- KMG closed its acquisition of Westport Resources (WRC) on June 25, valuing its proved reserves at about $11 per BOE, but KMG sees potential reserve additions from the properties. Capital spending in 2004 is expected to go to $1.1 billion from $900 million, but the all-stock deal is expected to help KMG bring its total debt down to 42% of capitalization by year end, from 46% as of mid-year.

- Risks to our recommendation and target price include events that would cause substantial and sustained declines in oil and gas prices; a persistent inability by KMG to replace its reserves; and acts of terrorism against KMG's production facilities.

- Given the current elevated price levels for energy commodities, it appears that KMG effectively used its stock currency to acquire attractive reserves. Our 2005 expectations for WTI crude oil and Henry Hub natural gas are $34.83 and $5.32, respectively, lower than 2004 expectations. Despite lower price expectations next year, KMG is one of the few companies in our universe expected to grow its earnings. Our $60 target price is based on what we see as a conservative multiple of 12.5X our 2005 EPS estimate, and an enterprise value to EBITDAX multiple of 5X, which is more in line with peers.

Key Stock Statistics

S&P Core EPS 2005E	4.93	52-week Range	$61.12-40.26
S&P Oper. EPS 2004E	4.92	12 Month P/E	21.9
P/E on S&P Oper. EPS 2004E	12.1	Beta	0.93
S&P Oper. EPS 2005E	5.20	Shareholders	26,500
Yield (%)	3.0%	Market Cap (B)	$ 9.0
Dividend Rate/Share	1.80	Shares Outstanding (M)	151.0

Value of $10,000 invested five years ago: **$ 13,266**

Dividend Data Dividends have been paid since 1941

Amount ($)	Date Decl.	Ex-Div. Date	Stock of Record	Payment Date
0.450	Jan. 13	Mar. 03	Mar. 05	Apr. 01 '04
0.450	May. 11	Jun. 02	Jun. 04	Jul. 01 '04
0.450	Jul. 13	Sep. 01	Sep. 03	Oct. 01 '04
0.450	Nov. 09	Dec. 01	Dec. 03	Jan. 03 '05

Revenues/Earnings Data Fiscal year ending December 31

Revenues (Million $)

	2004	2003	2002	2001	2000	1999
1Q	1,116	1,100	799.0	1,058	856.0	485.9
2Q	1,097	1,052	932.0	939.0	995.0	657.2
3Q	1,366	1,006	984.4	884.0	1,089	725.5
4Q	—	1,027	985.1	757.0	1,118	800.5
Yr.	—	4,185	3,700	3,638	4,121	2,696

Earnings Per Share ($)

	2004	2003	2002	2001	2000	1999
1Q	1.41	0.99	-0.02	3.40	1.94	-1.23
2Q	1.01	0.68	-1.77	1.71	1.11	0.52
3Q	E0.95	0.29	-0.86	0.27	2.57	1.13
4Q	E1.50	0.50	-3.43	-0.50	2.73	1.27
Yr.	E4.92	2.48	-6.09	4.93	8.37	1.69

Next earnings report expected: late-January Source: S&P, Company Reports
EPS Estimates based on S&P Operating Earnings; historical GAAP earnings are as reported.

Kerr-McGee Corporation

Recommendation: **BUY** ★★★★☆   12-Month Target Price: **$66.00** (as of October 27, 2004)

Business Summary August 17, 2004

Kerr-McGee is an energy and inorganic chemical holding company with consolidated operating subsidiaries engaged in oil and gas exploration and production (E&P; 70% of 2003 sales, 2003 segment operating profit of $1.0 billion), and chemical operations that produce and market titanium dioxide pigment (26%, operating loss of $13 million) and other chemicals (4%, operating loss of $35 million). The U.S. accounted for 68% of total sales in 2003.

In August 2001, the company acquired HS Resources, an independent oil and gas exploration and production company. KMG reorganized, forming a new holding company, Kerr-McGee Holdco, which later changed its name to Kerr-McGee Corp. All shares of the former Kerr-McGee were exchanged for an equal number of shares of the new company. The former Kerr-McGee Corp. was renamed, and is now a wholly owned subsidiary.

The exploration and production unit produces and explores for oil and gas in the U.S., the North Sea, and China. Exploration efforts extend to Australia, Benin, Brazil, Gabon, Morocco, Western Sahara, Canada, Yemen, and the Bahamas. Proved reserves of crude oil, condensate and natural gas liquids (NGL) totaled 496 million barrels (MMBbl) in 2003, versus 487 MMBbl in 2002. Proved natural gas reserves totaled 3.181 trillion cubic feet (Tcf) in 2003, versus 3.275 Tcf in 2002. Net production of crude oil and condensate averaged 150,200 barrels per day (bpd; 51% U.S., 48% North Sea, and 1% elsewhere) in 2003, versus 191,300 bpd (42% U.S., 54% North Sea, and 4% elsewhere) in 2002. Natural gas sales averaged 726

million cubic feet (MMcf) per day in 2003, versus 760 MMcf per day in 2002. Production costs averaged $3.90 per barrel oil equivalent (BOE) in 2003, versus $4.45 in 2002. The average price of crude oil sold was $26.04 per barrel (Bbl) in 2003, versus $22.04 in 2002. The average price of natural gas sold was $4.37 per thousand cubic feet (Mcf) in 2003, versus $2.95 in 2002. The standardized measure of discounted future net cash flows was $8.906 billion in 2003, versus $7.062 billion in 2002.

The chemical unit produces and markets titanium dioxide (TiO2), an inorganic white pigment used in paint, plastics, paper and many other products. Chemical production facilities are located in the U.S., Australia, Germany, and the Netherlands. Four of KMG's five wood treatment facilities were closed in 2003, and the fifth was to close by the end of 2004. The chloride process produces a pigment with optical properties preferred by the paint and plastics industries. In 2003, chloride technology accounted for 76% of KMG's pigment production capacity. Remaining capacity is sulfate-process production. Titanium dioxide pigment production averaged 532,000 tonnes in 2003, versus 508,000 tonnes in 2002.

On June 25, 2004, KMG completed its merger with Westport Resources (WRC) via an exchange of stock valued at $3.4 billion. As of December 2003, WRC had 1.8 Tcfe of proved reserves, with 76% natural gas, primarily located in the Rocky Mountain and Texas Gulf Coast areas.

Company Financials Fiscal Year ending December 31

Per Share Data ($)

(Year Ended December 31)	2003	2002	2001	2000	1999	1998	1997	1996	1995	1994
Tangible Bk. Val.	33.00	21.80	28.18	27.87	17.07	26.13	27.93	26.01	27.72	29.73
Cash Flow	26.28	2.33	12.01	15.13	8.76	0.88	9.52	10.41	6.13	8.41
Earnings	2.48	-6.09	4.93	8.37	1.69	-4.78	4.04	4.43	-0.47	1.74
S&P Core Earnings	1.98	-7.09	2.90	NA	NA	NA	NA	NA	NA	NA
Dividends	1.80	1.80	1.80	1.80	1.80	1.80	1.80	1.64	1.55	1.52
Payout Ratio	73%	NM	37%	22%	107%	NM	45%	37%	NM	87%
Prices - High	48.59	63.58	74.10	71.18	62.00	73.18	75.00	74.12	64.00	51.00
- Low	37.82	38.02	46.94	39.87	28.50	36.18	55.50	55.75	44.00	40.00
P/E Ratio - High	20	NM	15	9	37	NM	19	17	NM	29
- Low	15	NM	10	5	17	NM	14	13	NM	23

Income Statement Analysis (Million $)

	2003	2002	2001	2000	1999	1998	1997	1996	1995	1994
Revs.	4,185	3,700	3,638	4,121	2,696	1,396	1,711	1,931	1,801	3,353
Oper. Inc.	2,006	1,405	1,640	2,213	1,177	300	496	565	600	513
Depr.	1,559	844	779	732	607	269	263	297	341	345
Int. Exp.	251	275	192	208	190	58.0	46.0	61.0	72.0	69.0
Pretax Inc.	443	-565	804	1,299	257	-375	277	323	-67.0	132
Eff. Tax Rate	42.7%	NM	37.1%	35.2%	43.1%	NM	30.0%	32.0%	NM	38.0%
Net Inc.	254	-611	506	842	146	-237	194	220	-24.0	90.0
S&P Core Earnings	197	-711	288	NA	NA	NA	NA	NA	NA	NA

Balance Sheet & Other Fin. Data (Million $)

	2003	2002	2001	2000	1999	1998	1997	1996	1995	1994
Cash	142	90.0	91.0	144	267	114	183	121	87.0	82.0
Curr. Assets	1,757	1,290	1,367	1,315	1,161	751	689	805	766	963
Total Assets	10,174	9,909	10,961	7,666	5,899	3,341	3,096	3,124	3,232	3,698
Curr. Liab.	2,232	1,610	1,174	1,349	840	536	523	485	580	890
LT Debt	3,081	3,798	4,540	2,244	2,496	901	660	737	745	673
Common Equity	2,636	2,536	3,174	2,633	1,492	1,333	1,440	1,367	1,416	1,543
Total Cap.	5,717	7,479	8,989	5,581	4,389	2,423	2,259	2,508	2,266	2,395
Cap. Exp.	981	1,159	1,792	774	543	550	341	392	485	411
Cash Flow	1,813	233	1,285	1,574	753	42.0	457	517	317	435
Curr. Ratio	0.8	0.8	1.2	1.0	1.4	1.4	1.3	1.7	1.3	1.1
% LT Debt of Cap.	53.9	50.8	50.5	40.2	56.8	37.2	29.2	29.4	32.8	28.1
% Net Inc.of Revs.	6.1	NM	13.9	20.4	5.4	NM	11.3	11.4	NM	2.7
% Ret. on Assets	2.5	NM	5.4	12.4	3.1	NM	6.2	6.9	NM	2.5
% Ret. on Equity	9.8	NM	17.4	40.8	10.3	NM	13.9	15.8	NM	5.9

Data as orig reptd.; bef. results of disc opers/spec. items. Per share data adj. for stk. divs.; EPS diluted. E-Estimated. NA-Not Available. NM-Not Meaningful. NR-Not Ranked. UR-Under Review.

Office: Kerr-McGee Center, Oklahoma City, OK 73125.
Telephone: 405-270-1313.
Website: http://www.kerr-mcgee.com
Chrmn & CEO: L.R. Corbett.
SVP & CFO: R.M. Wohleber.
SVP, Secy & General Counsel: G.F. Pilcher.

VP & Treas: T. Poos.
Investor Contact: R.C. Buterbaugh 405-270-3561.
Dirs: W. E. Bradford, L. R. Corbett, S. A. Earle, D. C. Genever-Watling, M. C. Jischke, L. C. Richie, M. R. Simmons, W. F. Wallace, F. M. Walters, I. L. White-Thomson.

Founded: in 1932.
Domicile: Delaware.
Employees: 3,915.
S&P Analyst: Charles LaPorta, CFA /CB/BK

Recommendation: **HOLD** ★★★☆☆
SELL | SELL | HOLD | BUY | BUY

12-Month Target Price: **$32.00**
(as of November 04, 2004)

KEY has an approximate 0.13% weighting in the **S&P 500**

Sector: Financials
Sub-Industry: Regional Banks
Peer Group: Midwest/West Major Regional Banks

Summary: This multiregional bank holding company, headquartered in Cleveland, operates more than 900 branch offices.

Quantitative Evaluations

S&P Earnings & Dividend Rank: A-

| D | C | B- | B | B+ | A- | A | A+ |

S&P Fair Value Rank: 3+

| 1 | 2 | 3 | 4 | 5 |
| Lowest | | | | Highest |

Fair Value Calc.: $33.40 (Slightly Overvalued)

S&P Investability Quotient Percentile

97%

KEY scored higher than 97% of all companies for which an S&P Report is available.

Volatility: Low

| Low | Average | High |

Technical Evaluation: Bullish

Since 8/04, the technical indicators for KEY have been Bullish.

Relative Strength Rank: Moderate

60

1 Lowest — Highest 99

| Price as of 11/12/04: | **$34.24** | 2004E S&P Core EPS: | **$2.20** |

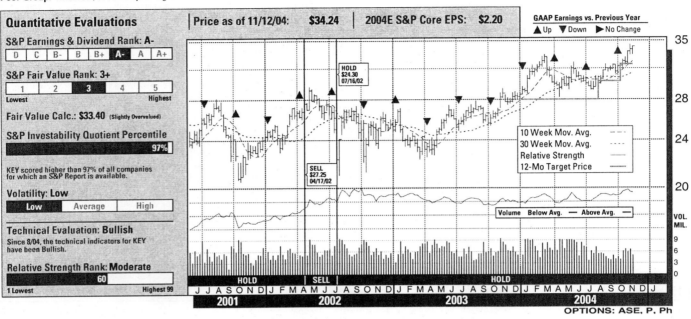

GAAP Earnings vs. Previous Year
▲ Up ▼ Down ▶ No Change

HOLD $24.30 07/16/02

SELL $27.25 04/17/02

- 10 Week Mov. Avg.
- 30 Week Mov. Avg.
- Relative Strength
- 12-Mo Target Price

Volume Below Avg. — Above Avg.

HOLD | SELL | HOLD

J J A S O N D J F M A M J J A S O N D J F M A M J J A S O N D J F M A M J J A S O N D J
2001 | 2002 | 2003 | 2004

OPTIONS: ASE, P, Ph

Analyst commentary prepared by James M. O'Brien/MF/BK

Highlights August 17, 2004

- We expect KEY to continue to focus on expense controls and asset quality improvement. We expect relatively weak large commercial loan demand to hold earning asset growth below historical levels. We see the net interest margin as likely to stabilize, assuming that short-term interest rates rise gradually, as expected, throughout the remainder of 2004. We think asset quality has stabilized in recent quarters, aided by the disposition of low-spread loans and the downsizing of the auto lending business.

- With economic conditions and commercial credit trends improving in recent quarters, we think KEY is likely to continue reducing drawing down its loan loss reserves in 2004. We see noninterest income growth in the low single digits, reflecting a sluggish environment for most fee-based income lines, the negative impact of the Wal-Mart settlement with Mastercard and Visa, and uncertain investment banking and capital markets conditions.

- We see expenses remaining under control. Assuming an effective tax rate of 29.0%, we project 2004 EPS of $2.32, up from $2.12 in 2003. Our 2005 EPS is $2.45.

Investment Rationale/Risk August 17, 2004

- At recent levels, the shares were trading at about 12X our 2005 EPS estimate, versus about 12X on average for large cap peers. We do not anticipate significant P/E multiple expansion until expense control and balance sheet repositioning efforts show a clear impact on the bottom line. In addition, in the absence of improvement in the large commercial sector, which we think is keeping revenue growth sluggish, we do not see earnings growth keeping pace with that of the upper tier of large bank peers. However, we believe the current P/E multiple is sustainable, based on our view that KEY has a geographically attractive franchise that could interest a buyer.

- Risks to our recommendation and target price include general economic risks, interest rate risk, and earnings quality issues.

- With a 4.1% dividend yield, and with the company viewed as a potential acquisition target, we believe the shares are worth holding at current levels. Our 12-month target price is $30, equal to approximately 12X our 2005 EPS estimate.

Key Stock Statistics

S&P Oper. EPS 2004E	2.36	52-week Range	$34.50-27.43
P/E on S&P Oper. EPS 2004E	14.5	12 Month P/E	14.7
S&P Oper. EPS 2005E	2.45	Beta	0.31
Yield (%)	3.6%	Shareholders	40,166
Dividend Rate/Share	1.24	Market Cap (B)	$ 13.9
Shares Outstanding (M)	406.6		

Value of $10,000 invested five years ago: **$ 14,743**

Dividend Data Dividends have been paid since 1963

Amount ($)	Date Decl.	Ex-Div. Date	Stock of Record	Payment Date
0.305	Nov. 21	Nov. 28	Dec. 02	Dec. 12 '03
0.310	Jan. 16	Feb. 27	Mar. 02	Mar. 15 '04
0.310	May. 14	May. 27	Jun. 01	Jun. 15 '04
0.310	Jul. 23	Aug. 27	Aug. 31	Sep. 15 '04

Revenues/Earnings Data Fiscal year ending December 31

Revenues (Million $)

	2004	2003	2002	2001	2000	1999
1Q	1,370	1,418	1,535	2,025	2,295	1,990
2Q	1,358	1,456	1,550	1,865	2,015	1,918
3Q	1,388	1,434	1,527	1,834	2,001	1,922
4Q	—	1,422	1,523	1,628	2,160	2,159
Yr.	—	5,730	6,135	7,352	8,471	7,989

Earnings Per Share ($)

	2004	2003	2002	2001	2000	1999
1Q	0.59	0.51	0.56	0.51	0.83	0.65
2Q	0.58	0.53	0.57	-0.32	0.57	0.62
3Q	0.61	0.53	0.57	0.58	0.28	0.60
4Q	E0.60	0.55	0.57	-0.41	0.62	0.59
Yr.	E2.36	2.12	2.27	0.37	2.30	2.45

Next earnings report expected: mid-January Source: S&P, Company Reports
EPS Estimates based on S&P Operating Earnings; historical GAAP earnings are as reported.

STANDARD &POOR'S

KeyCorp

Stock Report
November 13, 2004
NYSE Symbol: **KEY**

Recommendation: **HOLD** ★ ★ ★ ☆ ☆   12-Month Target Price: **$32.00** (as of November 04, 2004)

Business Summary August 17, 2004

KeyCorp, headquartered in Cleveland, classifies itself as an integrated, multiline financial services company, with operations divided into three lines of business: consumer banking, corporate finance, and capital partners. In May 2001, the company announced a major new strategic focus, designed to accelerate revenue growth, achieve savings through competitiveness initiatives, emphasize relationship-based activities, and increase fee-based revenues. The plan included exiting the auto lease business, reducing indirect lending activities, and eliminating syndicated and leveraged credits. KEY intended to focus on higher return, higher growth businesses, such as asset management, and to diversify its revenues by emphasizing the growth of fee income.

Consumer banking (47% of net income in 2003) includes retail banking, offering branch-based deposit, investment and credit products and personal financial services to consumers; and consumer finance products such as education loans, home equity loans, automobile loans, and marine loans. Corporate finance (44%) offers financing, as well as financial advisory services related to transaction processing, corporate electronic commerce and equipment leasing, and also serves small business clients. Capital partners (11%) offers specialized services to high net worth clients through wealth management and private banking businesses, and also provides asset management, investment banking and capital markets services such as brokerage, employee benefits and insurance.

In 2003, average earning assets, from which interest income is derived, were $73.5 billion, and consisted mainly of loans (86%) and investment securities (14%). Average sources of funds included interest-bearing deposits (45%), short-term borrowings (9%), long-term debt (19%), shareholders' equity (8%), noninterest-bearing deposits (12%), and other (7%).

At December 31, 2003, nonperforming assets, including mainly non-accrual loans, were $753 million (1.20% of loans and other real estate owned), down from $993 million (1.59%) a year earlier. The allowance for loan losses, which is held in anticipation of loan losses, amounted to $1.40 billion (2.24% of loans) at the end of 2003, down from $1.45 billion (2.32%) a year earlier. Net chargeoffs, or the amount of loans actually written off as uncollectible, were $548 million (0.87% of average loans) in 2003, down from $780 million (1.23%) in 2002.

In April 2004, KEY signed a purchase and assumption agreement to acquire the 11 Michigan offices and deposits of Sterling Bank & Trust FSB, a federally chartered savings bank headquartered in Southfield, Michigan. The transaction is expected to close in the 2004 third quarter, subject to necessary approvals.

Company Financials Fiscal Year ending December 31

Per Share Data ($)

(Year Ended December 31)	2003	2002	2001	2000	1999	1998	1997	1996	1995	1994
Tangible Bk. Val.	13.87	13.34	11.85	12.39	11.13	10.28	9.14	8.95	8.39	7.62
Earnings	2.12	2.27	0.37	2.30	2.45	2.23	2.07	1.69	1.65	1.73
S&P Core Earnings	2.12	2.10	0.43	NA	NA	NA	NA	NA	NA	NA
Dividends	1.22	1.20	1.18	1.12	1.04	0.94	0.84	0.76	0.72	0.64
Payout Ratio	58%	53%	NM	49%	42%	42%	41%	45%	44%	37%
Prices - High	29.41	29.40	29.25	28.50	38.12	44.87	36.59	27.12	18.62	16.87
- Low	22.31	20.98	20.49	15.56	21.00	23.37	23.93	16.68	12.37	11.81
P/E Ratio - High	14	13	79	12	16	20	18	16	11	10
- Low	11	9	55	7	9	10	12	10	7	7

Income Statement Analysis (Million $)

	2003	2002	2001	2000	1999	1998	1997	1996	1995	1994
Net Int. Inc.	2,725	2,749	2,825	2,730	2,787	2,749	2,794	2,717	2,637	2,693
Tax Equiv. Adj.	71.0	120	45.0	28.0	32.0	34.0	44.0	50.0	57.3	58.8
Non Int. Inc.	1,749	1,763	1,690	2,222	2,265	1,566	1,305	1,086	974	897
Loan Loss Prov.	501	553	1,350	490	348	297	320	197	101	125
Exp./Op. Revs.	60.3%	57.3%	64.5%	58.6%	60.0%	58.6%	59.4%	71.7%	63.0%	59.4%
Pretax Inc.	1,242	1,312	259	1,517	1,684	1,479	1,345	1,143	1,158	1,283
Eff. Tax Rate	27.3%	25.6%	39.4%	33.9%	34.3%	32.7%	31.7%	31.4%	31.8%	33.5%
Net Inc.	903	976	157	1,002	1,107	996	919	783	789	853
% Net Int. Marg.	3.80	3.97	3.81	3.69	3.93	4.18	4.62	4.78	4.47	4.84
S&P Core Earnings	898	896	179	NA	NA	NA	NA	NA	NA	NA

Balance Sheet & Other Fin. Data (Million $)

	2003	2002	2001	2000	1999	1998	1997	1996	1995	1994
Money Mkt. Assets	NA	NA	NA	NA	NA	NA	NA	NA	NA	NA
Inv. Securities	12,944	13,592	10,676	12,626	9,511	6,254	8,938	9,329	9,748	12,797
Com'l Loans	36,189	36,612	38,063	39,610	36,672	22,685	18,013	14,980	14,422	12,498
Other Loans	26,522	25,845	25,246	27,295	27,550	39,327	35,367	34,255	33,270	34,082
Total Assets	84,487	85,202	80,938	87,270	83,395	80,020	73,699	67,621	66,339	66,798
Demand Deposits	11,175	10,630	23,128	9,076	8,607	9,540	9,368	9,524	9,281	9,136
Time Deposits	39,683	38,716	21,667	39,573	34,626	33,043	35,705	35,793	38,001	39,428
LT Debt	15,294	16,865	15,842	15,404	17,124	13,964	7,446	4,213	4,004	3,570
Common Equity	6,969	6,835	6,155	6,623	6,389	6,167	5,223	4,881	4,993	4,538
% Ret. on Assets	1.1	1.2	0.2	1.2	1.4	1.3	1.3	1.2	1.2	1.4
% Ret. on Equity	13.1	15.0	2.5	15.4	17.6	17.5	18.1	15.6	16.2	19.6
% Loan Loss Resv.	2.2	2.3	2.7	1.5	1.4	1.5	1.7	1.8	1.8	1.8
% Loans/Deposits	123.3	126.6	138.0	137.5	148.5	145.6	118.4	94.9	100.9	95.9
% Equity to Assets	8.1	7.8	7.6	7.6	7.7	7.4	7.2	7.5	7.2	6.8

Data as orig reptd.; bef. results of disc opers/spec. items. Per share data adj. for stk. divs. Bold denotes primary EPS - prior periods restated. E-Estimated. NA-Not Available. NM-Not Meaningful. NR-Not Ranked. UR-Under Review.

Office: 127 Public Square, Cleveland, OH 44114-1306.
Telephone: 216-689-6300.
Website: http://www.key.com
Chrmn, Pres & CEO: H.L. Meyer III.
Vice Chrmn & Secy: T.C. Stevens.
EVP & CFO: J.B. Weeden.

EVP & Chief Acctg Officer: L.G. Irving.
EVP & Investor Contact: V. Patterson 216-689-0520.
Dirs: C. D. Andrus, W. G. Bares, E. P. Campbell, C. A. Cartwright, A. M. Cutler, H. S. Hemingway, C. R. Hogan, S. A. Jackson, D. J. McGregor, E. R. Menasce, H. L. Meyer III, S. A. Minter, T. C. Stevens, D. W. Sullivan, P. G. Ten Eyck II.

Founded: in 1849.
Domicile: Ohio.
Employees: 20,034.
S&P Analyst: James M. O'Brien/MF/BK

KeySpan Corp.

Recommendation: **HOLD** ★★★☆☆
SELL SELL HOLD BUY BUY

12-Month Target Price: $42.00
(as of November 04, 2004)

KSE has an approximate 0.06% weighting in the **S&P 500**

Sector: Utilities
Sub-Industry: Gas Utilities
Peer Group: Distributors - Larger

Summary: KSE is the fifth largest gas utility in the U.S., and has a number of electric and exploration and production (E&P) operations.

Quantitative Evaluations

S&P Earnings & Dividend Rank: B

| D | C | B- | **B** | B+ | A- | A | A+ |

S&P Fair Value Rank: 3

| 1 | 2 | **3** | 4 | 5 |
| Lowest | | | | Highest |

Fair Value Calc.: $40.50 (Slightly Overvalued)

S&P Investability Quotient Percentile

87%

KSE scored higher than 87% of all companies for which an S&P Report is available.

Volatility: Low

| **Low** | Average | High |

Technical Evaluation: Bullish

Since 8/04, the technical indicators for KSE have been Bullish.

Relative Strength Rank: Moderate

58

| 1 Lowest | | Highest 99 |

Price as of 11/12/04: $41.34 | **2004E S&P Core EPS:** $2.20

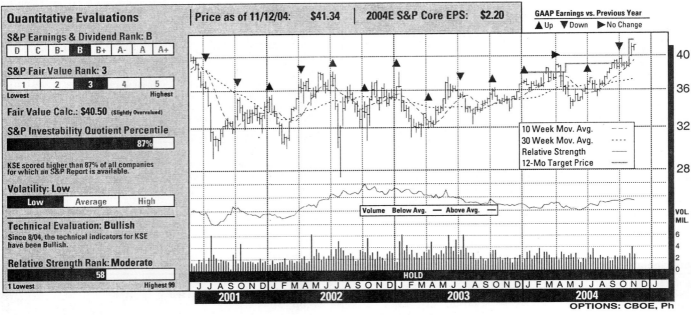

GAAP Earnings vs. Previous Year
▲ Up ▼ Down ▶ No Change

10 Week Mov. Avg.
30 Week Mov. Avg.
Relative Strength
12-Mo Target Price

Volume Below Avg. — Above Avg.

HOLD

J J A S O N D | J F M A M J J A S O N D | J F M A M J J A S O N D | J F M A M J J A S O N D | J
2001 | 2002 | 2003 | 2004

OPTIONS: CBOE, Ph

Analyst commentary prepared by Craig K. Shere, CFA /BK

Highlights August 19, 2004

- In April and June 2004, KSE reduced its ownership interests in Houston Exploration (THX: $50) and Keyspan Energy Canada Partnership, and will no longer consolidate the results of these businesses. As a result, we expect reported revenue and expense to decline, minority interest expense to be eliminated, and equity income to increase.

- We expect 2% operating EPS growth in 2004, as benefits from a Boston utility rate increase, higher natural gas production and commodity prices, cost cuts, and gas utility customer growth are largely offset by higher expenses (including pension, post-retirement, bad debt and interest) and about 2% more shares. We see lower 2005 results, as less favorable weather, lower production contributions and higher utility expense offset growth in gas utility customers.

- Reported 2003 EPS included a net charge of about $0.01 for early retirement of debt, less net gains on the sale of land, International Businesses, and THX shares. Our 2004 operating EPS estimate excludes net gains of $0.53 for asset sale gains less other one-time charges. Our 2005 Standard & Poor's Core Earnings projection exceeds our operating EPS estimate by $0.11, due to positive adjustments to pension income accounting.

Investment Rationale/Risk August 19, 2004

- In light of KSE's interest in continuing to reduce debt, we expect the company to use proceeds from the eventual sale of its remaining THX interests for debt reduction. We expect the associated interest expense reduction to be less than net earnings contributions from THX in 2004. We believe KSE may begin to implement annual dividend increases by the end of 2005, after its debt reduction goals have been achieved.

- Risks to our recommendation and target price include lower long term prices received for natural gas production, potentially higher levels of bad debt expense and healthcare costs, declining returns on pension assets, smaller and costlier levels of new gas utility customer conversions, and higher interest rates.

- KSE is currently trading in line with peer utilities based on its 2005 P/E, but at a discount based on price-to-book and price to trailing cash flow. Given our projection of below average EPS growth in 2005, we believe some discounted valuations are appropriate. We view the shares as fairly valued and look for appreciation in line with our expected 5% long term EPS growth rate. Our 12-month target price is $39.

Key Stock Statistics

S&P Core EPS 2005E	2.76	52-week Range	$41.53-33.64
S&P Oper. EPS 2004E	2.67	12 Month P/E	15.5
P/E on S&P Oper. EPS 2004E	15.5	Beta	0.36
S&P Oper. EPS 2005E	2.75	Shareholders	75,070
Yield (%)	4.4%	Market Cap (B)	$ 6.6
Dividend Rate/Share	1.82	Shares Outstanding (M)	160.6

Value of $10,000 invested five years ago: **$ 19,455**

Dividend Data Dividends have been paid since 1989

Amount ($)	Date Decl.	Ex-Div. Date	Stock of Record	Payment Date
0.445	Dec. 18	Jan. 12	Jan. 14	Feb. 01 '04
0.445	Mar. 10	Apr. 14	Apr. 16	May. 01 '04
0.445	Jun. 30	Jul. 12	Jul. 14	Aug. 01 '04
0.445	Sep. 15	Oct. 08	Oct. 13	Nov. 01 '04

Revenues/Earnings Data Fiscal year ending December 31

Revenues (Million $)

	2004	2003	2002	2001	2000	1999
1Q	2,596	2,513	1,871	2,575	1,317	955.9
2Q	1,366	1,408	1,216	1,339	947.6	539.4
3Q	1,050	1,132	1,076	1,102	947.1	538.5
4Q	—	1,863	1,807	1,616	1,910	911.5
Yr.	—	6,915	5,971	6,633	5,121	2,955

Earnings Per Share ($)

	2004	2003	2002	2001	2000	1999
1Q	1.53	1.53	1.51	1.61	1.22	0.94
2Q	0.80	-0.05	0.20	-0.09	0.35	0.10
3Q	-0.73	0.07	0.02	-0.28	0.10	Nil
4Q	E0.82	1.08	1.03	0.48	0.44	0.56
Yr.	E2.67	2.62	2.75	1.70	2.10	1.62

Next earnings report expected: early-February Source: S&P, Company Reports
EPS Estimates based on S&P Operating Earnings; historical GAAP earnings are as reported.

KeySpan Corporation

Recommendation: **HOLD** ★ ★ ★ ☆ ☆   12-Month Target Price: **$42.00** (as of November 04, 2004)

Business Summary August 19, 2004

KeySpan Corp., which serves 2.5 million natural gas customers in New York City, Long Island, and New England, is the fifth largest U.S. gas utility, and the largest gas distribution company in the Northeast. Its gas utility operations are conducted through six regulated gas utilities, in New York, Massachusetts, and New Hampshire. The company intends to fuel growth by converting new customers to gas heating, building or acquiring new power plants, and investing in new liquefied natural gas plants and gas pipelines.

In 2003, 54.5% of segment operating profit (including equity income, but excluding asset sale gains and Energy Services operations) was 52.4% derived from Gas Distribution operations (55.2% in 2002), 25.2% from Electric Services (29.9%), 18.5% from Gas Exploration and Production (11.5%), and 3.9% from Other Investments (3.4%). Energy Services operations incurred losses in each year.

With low Northeast residential gas-heating penetration, KSE estimates it has 1 million residential and 150,000 business customer prospects for conversion to gas heating. It believes it can convert over 60% of these prospects with limited capital spending, adding $600 million in additional gross profit margin over the longer term. In 2003, the company completed more than 57,000 gas installations, adding about $55 million in new gross profit margin. In 2004, KSE anticipated adding $55 million of new gross profit margin from customer additions.

At the end of 2003, the Electric Services segment owned nearly 6,400 megawatts

of gas and oil-fired electric generation in Long Island and New York City. The division also manages the electrical transmission and distribution system for the Long Island Power Authority (serving 1.1 million electric customers). In the 2004 first quarter, KSE brought another 250 MW of newly built generating capacity into commercial operation. In late 2003, the company and a joint venture partner obtained siting approvals for two additional Long Island power plants (a total 500 MW). However, through mid-2004, they had been unable to obtain a long-term power purchase agreement with the Power Authority.

The company is engaged in E&P operations primarily through its ownership interest in Houston Exploration (ASE: THX). In June 2004, KSE reduced its interest in THX to 24%, from 55%, in exchange for ownership of a THX subsidiary. It intends to divest its THX interests over time.

Other Investments include natural gas pipelines, midstream natural gas processing and gathering, gas storage facilities. Energy Services operations include a unit providing service contracts and plumbing for residential and commercial customers and a business offering engineering, mechanical contracting and facility services to large commercial, industrial and institutional clients.

In 2003, KSE sold non-core assets (including THX stock, a 24.5% interest in an Ireland gas utility, and 39% of KSE's Canadian midstream gas operations), for $360 million in cash and assumed debt.

Company Financials Fiscal Year ending December 31

Per Share Data ($)

(Year Ended December 31)	2003	2002	2001	2000	1999	1998	1997	1996	1995	1994
Tangible Bk. Val.	11.60	8.11	7.95	7.09	22.79	19.50	20.45	19.16	18.51	17.42
Earnings	2.62	2.75	1.70	2.10	1.62	-1.34	2.56	2.20	2.10	2.15
S&P Core Earnings	3.15	1.85	0.32	NA	NA	NA	NA	NA	NA	NA
Dividends	1.78	1.78	1.78	1.78	1.78	1.19	1.78	1.78	1.78	1.78
Payout Ratio	68%	65%	105%	85%	110%	NM	70%	81%	85%	83%
Prices - High	38.14	38.20	41.93	43.62	31.31	34.18	30.50	17.75	24.25	29.62
- Low	31.02	27.41	29.10	20.18	22.50	25.37	21.75	13.25	15.00	23.25
P/E Ratio - High	15	14	25	21	19	NM	12	8	11	14
- Low	12	10	17	10	14	NM	8	6	7	11

Income Statement Analysis (Million $)

	2003	2002	2001	2000	1999	1998	1997	1996	1995	1994
Revs.	6,915	5,971	6,633	5,121	2,955	1,722	3,124	3,151	3,075	3,067
Depr.	574	515	559	335	253	255	159	154	145	131
Maint.	NA	NA	NA	NA	NA	114	NA	NA	54.8	54.3
Fxd. Chgs. Cov.	3.35	3.04	2.33	3.58	3.23	-0.29	2.14	1.95	2.02	1.78
Constr. Credits	NA	NA	NA	NA	NA	Nil	8.44	6.59	6.80	7.00
Eff. Tax Rate	36.2%	34.8%	42.5%	39.8%	33.6%	NM	39.1%	39.9%	40.4%	36.9%
Net Inc.	424	397	244	301	259	-167	362	316	303	302
S&P Core Earnings	502	263	46.2	NA	NA	NA	NA	NA	NA	NA

Balance Sheet & Other Fin. Data (Million $)

	2003	2002	2001	2000	1999	1998	1997	1996	1995	1994
Gross Prop.	12,673	8,191	9,936	6,974	4,761	5,706	5,692	5,425	5,234	5,037
Cap. Exp.	1,223	1,134	1,060	925	726	677	257	240	244	277
Net Prop.	8,894	7,218	6,606	6,358	4,240	3,778	3,814	3,695	3,595	3,498
Capitalization:										
LT Debt	5,611	5,224	4,698	4,275	1,683	1,619	4,396	4,457	4,707	5,145
% LT Debt	54.4	63.3	61.2	59.6	37.5	31.8	57.7	58.0	59.9	62.4
Pfd.	83.6	83.8	84.1	84.2	84.3	448	563	702	703	708
% Pfd.	0.81	1.02	1.10	1.17	1.88	8.80	7.40	9.10	8.90	8.60
Common	4,624	2,945	2,891	2,816	2,724	3,023	2,662	2,523	2,453	2,394
% Common	44.8	35.7	37.7	39.2	60.7	59.4	34.9	32.8	31.2	29.0
Total Cap.	12,102	9,360	8,463	7,752	4,757	5,231	10,160	10,125	10,201	11,189
% Oper. Ratio	89.4	88.6	91.1	88.7	88.3	99.2	75.4	76.6	76.2	75.7
% Earn. on Net Prop.	12.6	13.1	12.7	13.8	8.6	0.3	20.4	20.2	20.7	21.8
% Return On Revs.	6.1	6.7	3.7	5.9	8.8	NM	11.6	10.0	9.9	9.8
% Return On Invest. Capital	7.4	8.1	8.0	9.5	7.9	NM	7.6	9.6	7.5	7.3
% Return On Com. Equity	10.0	13.4	8.3	10.2	7.8	NM	11.9	10.6	10.3	10.8

Data as orig. reptd. (for LILCO only pr. to May 29, 1998); bef. results of disc opers. and/or spec. items. Per share data adj. for stk. divs. as of ex-div. date. Data for 1998 represents 9 mos. transition period ended Dec. 31, 1998; data for 1997 represents yr. ended Mar. 31, 1998; yrs. end. Dec. 31 prior to 1997. Bold denotes primary EPS (FASB 128). E-Estimated. NA-Not Available. NM-Not Meaningful. NR-Not Ranked.

Office: One MetroTech Center, Brooklyn, NY 11201-3850.
Telephone: 718-403-1000.
Email: shareowner-svcs@email.bony.com
Website: http://www.keyspanenergy.com
Chrmn & CEO: R.B. Catell.
Pres & COO: R.J. Fani.
EVP & CFO: G. Luterman.

SVP & Chief Acctg Officer: J.F. Bodanza, Jr.
SVP, Secy & General Counsel: J.J. Bishar, Jr.
VP, Treas & Investor Contact: M.J. Taunton 718-403-3265.
Dirs: R. B. Catell, A. S. Christensen, A. H. Fishman, J. A. Ives, J. R. Jones, J. L. Larocca, G. C. Larson, S. W. McKessy, E. D. Miller, V. L. Pryor.

Founded: in 1895.
Domicile: New York.
Employees: 11,300.
S&P Analyst: Craig K. Shere, CFA /BK

Kimberly-Clark

Recommendation: **SELL** ★ ☆ ☆ ☆ ☆
SELL SELL HOLD BUY BUY

12-Month Target Price: $55.00
(as of October 25, 2004)

KMB has an approximate 0.28% weighting in the **S&P 500**

Sector: Consumer Staples
Sub-Industry: Household Products
Peer Group: Household Products

Summary: This leading consumer products company's global tissue, personal care and health care brands include Huggies, Pull-Ups, Kotex, Depend, Kleenex, Scott and Kimberly-Clark.

Quantitative Evaluations

S&P Earnings & Dividend Rank: A-

| D | C | B- | B | B+ | A- | A | A+ |

S&P Fair Value Rank: 4+

| 1 | 2 | 3 | 4 | 5 |
| Lowest | | | | Highest |

Fair Value Calc.: $62.80 (Fairly Valued)

S&P Investability Quotient Percentile

98%

KMB scored higher than 98% of all companies for which an S&P Report is available.

Volatility: Low

| Low | Average | High |

Technical Evaluation: Bearish
Since 10/04, the technical indicators for KMB have been Bearish.

Relative Strength Rank: Weak

29

1 Lowest — Highest 99

Price as of 11/12/04: $63.25 | **2004E S&P Core EPS: $3.40**

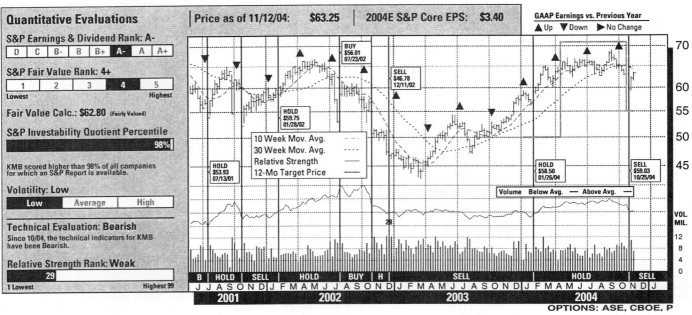

GAAP Earnings vs. Previous Year
▲ Up ▼ Down ► No Change

10 Week Mov. Avg.
30 Week Mov. Avg.
Relative Strength
12-Mo Target Price

Volume Below Avg. — Above Avg. —

OPTIONS: ASE, CBOE, P

Analyst commentary prepared by Howard Choe/PMW/BK

Highlights October 25, 2004

- We project sales growth of about 6% for 2004, reflecting modest volume growth, acquisitions, and favorable currency translations, but negative pricing. We expect personal care division revenues to advance over 6%, due in part to easier comparisons and strength in North America. We see consumer tissue segment sales up nearly 4%, primarily due to an acquisition and foreign exchange. We expect business to business sales to gain 11%, reflecting strength in the healthcare business and increased travel. We see 2005 total sales growing at least 3%.

- Based on our expectations of higher commodities and energy costs and no pricing power in 2004, we expect gross margins to narrow slightly. We project that SG&A costs will rise, on higher marketing costs; we see operating margins narrowing slightly. Based on our expectations of a moderate increase in commodity costs in 2005, we see operating margins narrowing further.

- We project that 2004 operating EPS will increase 8%, to $3.65, from $3.38 in 2003. EPS in 2005 should reach $3.95. We project respective S&P Core EPS of $3.40 and $3.75, reflecting estimated stock option and pension costs.

Investment Rationale/Risk October 25, 2004

- We recently downgraded KMB to sell, from hold, reflecting our reduced outlook for sales and profit growth. We see intense competition in consumer tissues and personal care, difficult comparisons in 2005, and high commodity costs, and believe KMB is likely to deliver results at the low end of its respective sales and EPS targets of 3% to 5% and 6% to 9%. We believe it would need to perform at the high end of these ranges for the shares to gain support. We do not expect a decrease in competition from Procter & Gamble (PG: buy, $52), paper companies, and private label products in the foreseeable future.

- Risks to our recommendation and target price include reduced promotional activity in the consumer paper category, lower commodity and energy costs, improvement in the company's product innovation, and increased consumer acceptance of KMB's products.

- Based on our 2005 outlook, we think the stock is overvalued. The shares trade at a discount to peers on the basis of P/E multiple. However, on a P/E to growth (PEG) basis, their forward PEG is 1.9X, versus 1.8X for peers. We believe the shares should trade at a discount to the S&P 500, for which we project 2005 EPS growth of 10%, versus 8% seen for KMB. We apply a forward P/E multiple of 14X to our 2005 EPS estimate to arrive at our 12-month target price of $55.

Key Stock Statistics

S&P Core EPS 2005E	3.75	52-week Range	$69.00-52.93
S&P Oper. EPS 2004E	3.65	12 Month P/E	17.5
P/E on S&P Oper. EPS 2004E	17.3	Beta	0.22
S&P Oper. EPS 2005E	3.95	Shareholders	36,870
Yield (%)	2.5%	Market Cap (B)	$ 31.3
Dividend Rate/Share	1.60	Shares Outstanding (M)	494.5

Value of $10,000 invested five years ago: **NA**

Dividend Data Dividends have been paid since 1935

Amount ($)	Date Decl.	Ex-Div. Date	Stock of Record	Payment Date
0.400	Feb. 24	Mar. 03	Mar. 05	Apr. 02 '04
0.400	May. 03	Jun. 02	Jun. 04	Jul. 02 '04
0.400	Aug. 02	Sep. 08	Sep. 10	Oct. 04 '04
Stk.	—	Dec. 01	Nov. 19	Nov. 30 '04

Revenues/Earnings Data Fiscal year ending December 31

Revenues (Million $)

	2004	2003	2002	2001	2000	1999
1Q	3,799	3,460	3,331	3,608	3,387	3,125
2Q	3,776	3,545	3,409	3,534	3,465	3,149
3Q	3,866	3,642	3,487	3,710	3,530	3,308
4Q	—	3,702	3,340	3,672	3,601	3,426
Yr.	—	14,348	13,566	14,524	13,982	13,007

Earnings Per Share ($)

	2004	2003	2002	2001	2000	1999
1Q	0.91	0.78	0.86	0.81	0.86	0.69
2Q	0.90	0.82	0.81	0.78	0.79	0.73
3Q	0.89	0.83	0.85	0.79	0.81	0.89
4Q	E0.95	0.91	0.72	0.65	0.85	0.77
Yr.	E3.65	3.33	3.24	3.02	3.34	3.09

Next earnings report expected: late-January   Source: S&P, Company Reports
EPS Estimates based on S&P Operating Earnings; historical GAAP earnings are as reported.

STANDARD &POOR'S

Kimberly-Clark Corporation

Stock Report
November 13, 2004
NYSE Symbol: **KMB**

Recommendation: **SELL** ★ ★ ★ ★ ★   12-Month Target Price: **$55.00** (as of October 25, 2004)

Business Summary November 10, 2004

Kimberly-Clark, best known for brand names such as Kleenex, Scott, Huggies and Kotex, sells consumer products in more than 150 countries. After operating as a broadly diversified enterprise, KMB made a major transition since the early 1990s, transforming itself into a global consumer products company. The company further developed its its health care business through the acquisitions of Technol Medical Products, Ballard Medical Products, and Safeskin Corp. Reflecting more than 30 strategic acquisitions and 20 strategic divestitures since 1992, KMB has become a leading global manufacturer of tissue, personal care and healthcare products, manufacturing in 42 countries.

KMB classifies its business into three segments: consumer tissue, personal care, and business-to-business. The consumer tissue segment includes facial and bathroom tissue, paper towels and napkins for household use; wet wipes; and related products. Products are sold under brand names that include Kleenex, Scott, Cottonelle, Viva, Andrex, Scottex, Page, Huggies and others.

The personal care segment includes disposable diapers, training and youth pants, and swimpants; feminine and incontinence care products; and related products. Products, primarily for household use, are sold under well known brand names that include Huggies, Pull-Ups, Little Swimmers, GoodNites, Kotex, Lightdays, Depend, Poise and others.

The business-to-business segment includes paper tissues, towels, napkins and wipers for away-from-home use; healthcare products, consisting of surgical gowns, drapes, infection control products, sterilization wraps, disposable face masks and exam gloves, respiratory products and other disposable medical products; specialty and technical papers; and other products. Products are sold under the Kimberly-Clark, Kimwipes, Wypall, Safeskin, Ballard and other brand names.

Products for household use are sold directly and through wholesalers to supermarkets, mass merchandisers, drugstores, warehouse clubs, variety and department stores and other retail outlets. Products for away from home use are sold through distributors and directly to manufacturing, lodging, office building, food service and healthcare establishments and other high volume public facilities. Paper products are sold directly to users, converters, manufacturers, publishers and printers, and through paper merchants, brokers, sales agents and other resale agencies. Healthcare products are sold to distributors, converters and end users.

In June 2002, KMB acquired the remaining 45% equity interest in its Australian affiliate, Kimberly-Clark Australia Pty Ltd., from Amcor Ltd.

Company Financials Fiscal Year ending December 31

Per Share Data ($)

(Year Ended December 31)	2003	2002	2001	2000	1999	1998	1997	1996	1995	1994
Tangible Bk. Val.	8.21	6.65	7.10	7.04	7.12	6.12	6.35	7.96	6.50	8.10
Cash Flow	4.80	4.60	1.39	4.55	4.17	3.11	2.46	3.49	1.10	2.69
Earnings	3.33	3.24	3.02	3.34	3.09	2.13	1.58	2.49	0.06	1.67
S&P Core Earnings	3.35	2.74	2.49	NA	NA	NA	NA	NA	NA	NA
Dividends	1.36	1.20	1.12	1.08	1.03	0.99	0.96	0.92	0.90	0.88
Payout Ratio	41%	37%	37%	32%	33%	46%	61%	37%	NM	53%
Prices - High	59.30	66.79	72.19	73.25	69.56	59.43	56.87	49.81	41.50	30.00
- Low	42.92	45.30	52.06	42.00	44.81	35.87	43.25	34.31	23.62	23.50
P/E Ratio - High	18	21	24	22	23	28	36	20	NM	18
- Low	13	14	17	13	15	17	27	14	NM	14

Income Statement Analysis (Million $)

	2003	2002	2001	2000	1999	1998	1997	1996	1995	1994
Revs.	14,348	13,566	14,524	13,982	13,007	12,298	12,547	13,149	13,789	7,364
Oper. Inc.	3,158	3,170	3,162	3,203	2,815	2,320	2,276	2,615	2,235	1,149
Depr.	746	707	740	673	586	542	491	561	582	330
Int. Exp.	168	182	192	222	213	199	165	201	254	139
Pretax Inc.	2,153	2,411	2,319	2,622	2,441	1,763	1,345	2,154	186	828
Eff. Tax Rate	23.9%	27.7%	27.8%	28.9%	29.9%	31.9%	32.2%	32.5%	17.7%	33.4%
Net Inc.	1,694	1,686	1,610	1,801	1,668	1,177	884	1,404	33.0	535
S&P Core Earnings	1,708	1,424	1,329	NA	NA	NA	NA	NA	NA	NA

Balance Sheet & Other Fin. Data (Million $)

	2003	2002	2001	2000	1999	1998	1997	1996	1995	1994
Cash	291	495	405	207	323	144	91.0	83.0	222	24.0
Curr. Assets	4,438	4,274	3,922	3,790	3,562	3,367	3,489	3,539	3,814	1,810
Total Assets	16,780	15,586	15,008	14,480	12,816	11,510	11,266	11,846	11,439	6,716
Curr. Liab.	3,919	4,038	4,168	4,574	3,846	3,791	3,706	3,687	3,870	2,059
LT Debt	3,301	3,398	2,962	Nil	1,927	2,068	1,804	1,739	1,985	930
Common Equity	6,766	5,650	5,647	5,767	5,093	3,887	4,125	4,483	3,650	2,596
Total Cap.	10,366	10,158	9,923	7,036	8,101	6,819	6,673	7,233	6,594	4,218
Cap. Exp.	878	871	1,100	1,170	786	670	944	884	818	485
Cash Flow	2,440	2,393	740	2,474	2,254	1,719	1,375	1,965	615	865
Curr. Ratio	1.1	1.1	0.9	0.8	0.9	0.9	0.9	1.0	1.0	0.9
% LT Debt of Cap.	31.8	33.4	29.9	Nil	23.8	30.3	27.0	24.0	30.1	22.0
% Net Inc.of Revs.	11.8	12.4	11.1	12.9	12.8	9.6	7.0	10.7	1.0	7.3
% Ret. on Assets	10.5	11.0	10.9	13.2	13.6	10.3	7.6	12.1	1.0	8.2
% Ret. on Equity	27.3	29.8	28.2	33.2	37.1	29.4	20.5	34.5	1.0	21.2

Data as orig reptd.; bef. results of disc opers/spec. items. Per share data adj. for stk. divs. Bold denotes primary EPS - prior periods restated. E-Estimated. NA-Not Available. NM-Not Meaningful. NR-Not Ranked. UR-Under Review.

Office: P.O. Box 619100, Dallas, TX 75261-9100.
Telephone: 972-281-1200.
Website: http://www.kimberly-clark.com
Chrmn, Pres & CEO: T.J. Falk.
SVP & CFO: M.A. Buthman.
VPeas: L.R. Turner.

VPvestor Contact: M.B. Szeinbaum.
VP & Treas: W.A. Gamron.
VP & Investor Contact: M.D. Masseth 972-281-1478.
Dirs: D. R. Beresford, J. F. Bergstrom, P. S. Cafferty, P. J. Collins, R. W. Decherd, T. J. Falk, C. X. Gonzalez, M. C. Jemison, L. J. Rice, M. J. Shapiro, R. L. Tobias.

Founded: in 1872.
Domicile: Delaware.
Employees: 62,000.
S&P Analyst: Howard Choe/PMW/BK

Kinder Morgan

Recommendation: **HOLD** ★ ★ ★ ☆ ☆
SELL SELL HOLD BUY BUY

12-Month Target Price: **$68.00**
(as of October 21, 2004)

KMI has an approximate 0.08% weighting in the **S&P 500**

Sector: Energy
Sub-Industry: Oil & Gas Refining, Marketing & Transportation

Summary: KMI (formed through the 1999 merger of KN Energy and privately held Kinder Morgan) is one of the largest midstream energy companies in the U.S.

Quantitative Evaluations

S&P Earnings & Dividend Rank: B

| D | C | B- | **B** | B+ | A- | A | A+ |

S&P Fair Value Rank: 3

| 1 | 2 | **3** | 4 | 5 |
| Lowest | | | | Highest |

Fair Value Calc.: $64.10 (Slightly Overvalued)

S&P Investability Quotient Percentile

76%

KMI scored higher than 76% of all companies for which an S&P Report is available.

Volatility: Low

| **Low** | Average | High |

Technical Evaluation: Bullish

Since 11/04, the technical indicators for KMI have been Bullish.

Relative Strength Rank: Moderate

60

| 1 Lowest | Highest 99 |

| Price as of 11/12/04: | **$67.15** | 2004E S&P Core EPS: | **$3.60** |

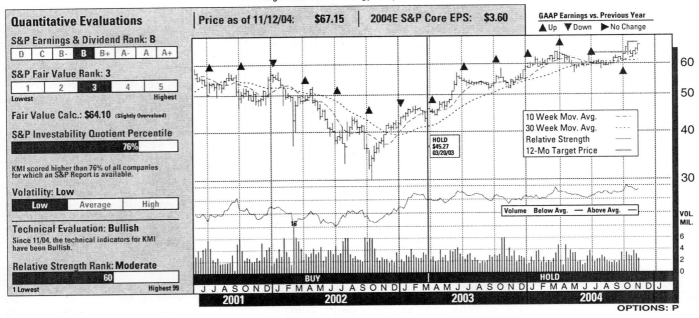

GAAP Earnings vs. Previous Year
▲ Up ▼ Down ► No Change

10 Week Mov. Avg. ----
30 Week Mov. Avg. ----
Relative Strength ......
12-Mo Target Price ——

HOLD $45.27 03/20/03

Volume Below Avg. — Above Avg. —

VOL. MIL.

BUY | HOLD

J J A S O N D J F M A M J J A S O N D J F M A M J J A S O N D J F M A M J J A S O N D J
2001 | 2002 | 2003 | 2004

OPTIONS: P

Analyst commentary prepared by Charles LaPorta, CFA /PMW/BK

Highlights November 10, 2004

- KMI posted third quarter EPS of $0.90, up from $0.77 in 2003 and above our estimate of $0.81, largely due to better than expected performance for the Kinder Morgan Energy Partners (KMP), Natural Gas Pipeline, and TransColorado segments.

- KMP's contribution to KMI in the quarter (including both KMI's general partner and limited partner interests) grew 23%, year to year. The Natural Gas Pipeline Company of America subsidiary's storage facilities are fully subscribed through April 2005, and its firm, long-haul transportation capacity is 99% subscribed through the 2005 first quarter. We expect KMP to account for slightly over 50% of KMI's segment income, and about 75% of free cash flow after maintenance capital spending.

- We anticipate a 13% increase in segment earnings from the TransColorado pipeline, driven by the completion of expansion projects in 2004. KMI is ahead of schedule on its 2004 commitments for debt reduction ($95 million, year to date, versus a goal of $100 million) and share repurchases ($55 million, year to date, versus a commitment of $60 million). The divergence between our operating and S&P Core EPS estimates continues to narrow, suggesting to us that earnings quality is improving.

Key Stock Statistics

S&P Core EPS 2005E	4.10	52-week Range	$67.15-52.71
S&P Oper. EPS 2004E	3.75	12 Month P/E	19.8
P/E on S&P Oper. EPS 2004E	17.9	Beta	0.48
S&P Oper. EPS 2005E	4.25	Shareholders	38,000
Yield (%)	3.4%	Market Cap (B)	$ 8.3
Dividend Rate/Share	2.25	Shares Outstanding (M)	123.9

Value of $10,000 invested five years ago: **$ 35,141**

Dividend Data Dividends have been paid since 1937

Amount ($)	Date Decl.	Ex-Div. Date	Stock of Record	Payment Date
0.563	Jan. 21	Jan. 28	Jan. 30	Feb. 13 '04
0.563	Apr. 21	Apr. 28	Apr. 30	May. 14 '04
0.563	Jul. 21	Jul. 28	Jul. 30	Aug. 13 '04
0.563	Oct. 20	Oct. 27	Oct. 29	Nov. 12 '04

Investment Rationale/Risk November 10, 2004

- We believe performance will increasingly be driven by KMP's performance via KMI's general partner incentive participation and unit ownership. KMI is expected to "drop" its TransColorado assets into KMP before the end of 2004, with cash proceeds to be used to further reduce debt. KMP's increasing contributions to KMI have allowed KMI to increase cash distributions to shareholders. Based on the free cash flow anticipated to be generated by the KMI/KMP relationship, we expect KMI to increase the dividend in the first quarter. We estimate that it could comfortably raise the dividend by 20% to 25%.

- Risks to our recommendation and target price include higher interest rate expectations; an inability to sufficiently pass on increasing power costs and wages and benefits expense; a decline in economic activity that reduces demand for energy commodities reducing pipeline volumes; or the prospect of a large dilutive acquisition.

- We believe the shares would be fairly valued at 16X our 2005 EPS projection and 10X our EBITDA estimate, both premiums to other energy transportation companies, because of the equity structure that allows KMI to reap the majority of the financial rewards while offloading capital intensity to KMP. Based on our view that EPS growth will slow from over 20% in recent years to high single digits into 2005, and on our expected earnings and cash flow multiples, our 12-month target price is $68.

Revenues/Earnings Data Fiscal year ending December 31

Revenues (Million $)

	2004	2003	2002	2001	2000	1999
1Q	352.6	318.9	291.4	325.2	480.5	406.7
2Q	236.9	251.9	213.7	218.8	549.8	408.2
3Q	249.6	247.0	225.1	227.0	749.1	471.1
4Q	—	280.2	285.0	283.8	931.7	459.5
Yr.	—	1,098	1,015	1,055	2,714	1,745

Earnings Per Share ($)

	2004	2003	2002	2001	2000	1999
1Q	1.02	0.90	0.71	0.47	0.41	0.34
2Q	0.84	0.76	0.59	0.41	0.22	0.17
3Q	0.90	0.77	0.66	0.49	0.23	0.08
4Q	E0.99	0.65	0.55	0.60	0.73	1.02
Yr.	E3.75	3.08	2.50	1.97	1.60	1.92

Next earnings report expected: late-January Source: S&P, Company Reports
EPS Estimates based on S&P Operating Earnings; historical GAAP earnings are as reported.

Kinder Morgan, Inc.

Recommendation: **HOLD** ★ ★ ★ ☆ ☆   12-Month Target Price: **$68.00** (as of October 21, 2004)

Business Summary November 10, 2004

Kinder Morgan is one of the largest U.S. natural gas and oil storage and transportation companies. It operates 30,000 miles of gas and oil pipelines for itself or on behalf of Kinder Morgan Energy Partners (KMP), for which it acts as general partner. In addition to pipeline interests, KMI also engages in natural gas utility and unregulated power generation.

In 2003, wholly owned Natural Gas Pipeline Company of America (NGPCA) contributed 42.2% of segment operating earnings (including equity income). NGPCA is comprised of two major interconnected transmission pipelines terminating in the Chicago metropolitan area. The Amarillo Line (consisting of 4,400 miles of pipeline) originates in the West Texas and New Mexico producing areas. The Gulf Coast Line (4,700 miles) originates in the Gulf Coast areas of Texas and Louisiana. Both Amarillo and Gulf Coast are connected at points in Texas and Oklahoma by an 800-mile pipeline.

KMP contributed 45.2% of KMI's 2003 segment earnings. KMP is the largest publicly traded U.S. pipeline master limited partnership, in terms of market capitalization, and owns the largest independent refined petroleum products pipeline system in the U.S. As of December 2003, KMI owned a total 19% equity interest in KMP through the ownership of 32.8 million limited partner units, and 100% of the general partner (GP). In 2003, KMI received about 51% of all quarterly cash distributions from KMP; distributions to KMI are enhanced by extra GP incentive distributions. Incentive distributions are earned when quarterly partnership distributions exceed specified targets (reaching a maximum of 50% of interests in quarterly distributions above $0.23375 per limited partner share).

During 2003, Kinder Morgan Retail contributed 7.5% of segment earnings, Power & Other 2.5%, and the TransColorado pipeline 2.6%. At the end of 2003, Retail operations served about 241,000 gas utility customers in Colorado, Nebraska and Wyoming. Power & Other segment contributions fell significantly in 2003, due to a weak operating environment for power. In October 2002, the TransColorado pipeline became wholly owned, as KMI acquired the 50% interest that it did not already own. About 90% of TransColorado's pipeline capacity is committed under firm transportation contracts that extend through 2007 year end. In September 2003, TransColorado signed a 10-year firm contract with a shipper that will allow for the construction of about a 25% expansion of its capacity, which is expected to be completed in the third quarter of 2004. KMI is considering the transfer of TransColorado to KMP for fair market value.

In April 2004, KMI announced the expansion of a share repurchase program to $550 million, from $50 million that remained from a previous authorization, and said it intended to pay down $100 million in debt during 2004.

Company Financials Fiscal Year ending December 31

Per Share Data ($)

(Year Ended December 31)	2003	2002	2001	2000	1999	1998	1997	1996	1995	1994
Tangible Bk. Val.	13.73	11.21	18.24	15.70	14.79	17.65	12.63	11.42	10.11	9.52
Earnings	3.08	2.50	1.97	1.60	1.92	0.92	1.63	1.43	1.22	0.35
S&P Core Earnings	3.01	2.21	1.68	NA	NA	NA	NA	NA	NA	NA
Dividends	1.10	0.30	0.20	0.20	0.65	0.76	0.73	0.70	0.67	0.65
Payout Ratio	36%	12%	10%	13%	34%	83%	44%	49%	55%	187%
Prices - High	59.27	57.50	60.00	54.25	24.68	40.33	36.00	27.50	20.16	17.91
- Low	42.25	30.05	42.87	19.87	12.18	22.33	24.08	18.00	13.50	13.83
P/E Ratio - High	19	23	30	34	13	44	22	19	17	52
- Low	14	12	22	12	6	24	15	13	11	40

Income Statement Analysis (Million $)

	2003	2002	2001	2000	1999	1998	1997	1996	1995	1994
Revs.	1,098	1,015	1,055	2,714	1,745	4,388	2,145	1,443	1,103	1,084
Depr.	118	106	108	108	144	196	56.0	51.2	49.9	50.3
Maint.	NA	NA	NA	NA	NA	NA	NA	NA	NA	NA
Fxd. Chgs. Cov.	2.78	2.42	1.89	1.92	1.36	1.41	3.80	3.81	3.36	1.77
Constr. Credits	NA	NA	NA	NA	Nil	Nil	Nil	NA	NA	NA
Eff. Tax Rate	36.0%	27.1%	38.0%	37.1%	33.5%	33.4%	31.5%	36.0%	35.6%	38.3%
Net Inc.	382	309	239	184	155	60.0	77.5	63.8	52.5	15.3
S&P Core Earnings	373	273	204	NA	NA	NA	NA	NA	NA	NA

Balance Sheet & Other Fin. Data (Million $)

	2003	2002	2001	2000	1999	1998	1997	1996	1995	1994
Gross Prop.	6,682	6,544	6,079	6,137	6,167	7,767	1,972	1,548	1,353	1,312
Cap. Exp.	161	175	124	137	94.3	257	311	120	79.4	70.6
Net Prop.	6,084	6,048	5,704	5,725	5,790	7,023	1,421	1,029	863	851
Capitalization:										
LT Debt	3,209	2,922	2,680	Nil	3,568	3,306	554	424	316	335
% LT Debt	54.6	55.4	54.2	Nil	68.2	73.0	47.4	44.6	42.1	45.4
Pfd.	Nil	Nil	Nil	Nil	Nil	7.00	7.00	7.00	7.60	8.70
% Pfd.	Nil	Nil	Nil	Nil	Nil	0.20	0.50	0.70	1.00	1.20
Common	2,666	2,355	2,265	1,797	1,666	1,217	606	520	427	394
% Common	45.4	44.6	45.8	100.0	31.8	26.8	51.9	54.7	56.9	53.4
Total Cap.	9,363	8,680	8,191	4,082	7,472	6,567	1,383	1,099	876	846
% Oper. Ratio	85.8	76.8	79.6	90.0	85.6	92.9	93.4	93.1	92.3	96.0
% Earn. on Net Prop.	8.5	8.1	8.7	9.2	4.8	8.3	6.3	14.3	13.3	6.4
% Return On Revs.	34.8	30.5	22.6	6.8	8.9	1.4	3.6	4.4	4.8	1.4
% Return On Invest. Capital	6.7	7.7	6.9	12.0	5.9	10.3	13.2	15.9	13.5	5.6
% Return On Com. Equity	15.2	13.4	11.7	10.6	10.7	6.5	13.8	13.4	12.7	3.7

Data as orig reptd.; bef. results of disc opers/spec. items. Per share data adj. for stk. divs.; EPS diluted. E-Estimated. NA-Not Available. NM-Not Meaningful. NR-Not Ranked. UR-Under Review.

Office: 500 Dallas , Houston, TX 77002.
Telephone: 713-369-9000.
Email: ir@kindermorgan.com
Website: http://www.kindermorgan.com
Chrmn & CEO: R.D. Kinder.
Pres: M.C. Morgan.
EVP & CFO: C.P. Shaper.

VP & General Counsel: J. Listengart.
Treas: K.J. Allen.
Investor Contact: D. Sanders 713-369-9103.
Dirs: E. H. Austin, Jr., C. W. Battey, S. A. Bliss, T. A. Gardner, W. J. Hybl, R. D. Kinder, M. C. Morgan, E. Randall III, F. S. Sarofim, H. A. True III.

Founded: in 1927.
Domicile: Kansas.
Employees: 5,530.
S&P Analyst: Charles LaPorta, CFA /PMW/BK

King Pharmaceuticals

Recommendation: **HOLD** ★★★☆☆
SELL | SELL | HOLD | BUY | BUY

12-Month Target Price: **$12.00**
(as of October 28, 2004)

KG has an approximate 0.03% weighting in the **S&P 500**

Sector: Health Care
Sub-Industry: Pharmaceuticals
Peer Group: Pharmaceuticals - Specialty

Summary: This pharmaceutical company has agreed to be acquired by Mylan Laboratories.

Quantitative Evaluations

S&P Earnings & Dividend Rank: NR

D	C	B-	B	B+	A-	A	A+

S&P Fair Value Rank: 5

1	2	3	4	5
Lowest				Highest

Fair Value Calc.: $12.00 (Fairly Valued)

S&P Investability Quotient Percentile

31%

KG scored lower than 69% of all companies for which an S&P Report is available.

Volatility: High

Low	Average	High

Technical Evaluation: Bearish
Since 10/04, the technical indicators for KG have been Bearish.

Relative Strength Rank: Moderate

33

1 Lowest — Highest 99

Price as of 11/12/04: $11.85 | **2004E S&P Core EPS:** $0.17

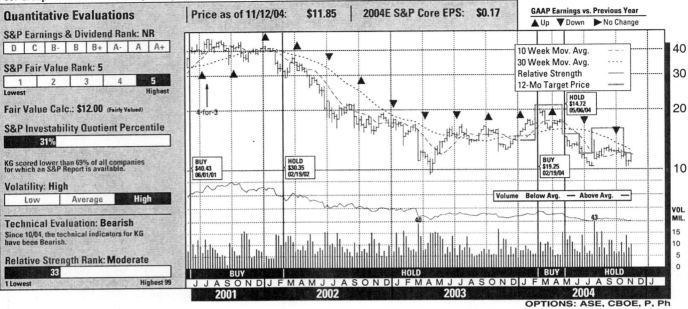

GAAP Earnings vs. Previous Year
▲ Up   ▼ Down   ► No Change

- – – 10 Week Mov. Avg.
- ···· 30 Week Mov. Avg.
- —— Relative Strength
- —— 12-Mo Target Price

Volume Below Avg. — Above Avg.

OPTIONS: ASE, CBOE, P, Ph

Analyst commentary prepared by Phillip M. Seligman/CB/JWP

Highlights 15-NOV-04

- On July 26, 2004, KG and Mylan Laboratories (MYL: hold, $15) announced a definitive agreement for MYL to acquire KG via an exchange of stock. The companies expected the transaction to close by 2004 year end, subject to regulatory and shareholder approvals. However, should KG restate its financials, we believe the pending deal will be jeopardized. For now, our earnings model reflects KG as an ongoing entity.
- An average 2.1-month supply of KG's four key drugs with distributors as of September 30, based on IMS and distributor data, compared to a 2.4-month supply in late August, suggests to us that demand for its products is low. Moreover, the level of returns has been significant enough for KG to mull whether its returns reserve was adequate and, if not, to consider restating prior financials. Assuming distributors start to restock in February, we look for 2005 revenues to rise only 15%, to $1.5 billion, from our 2004 estimate of $1.3 billion. We also expect margin pressure from higher sales, marketing and R&D spending.
- Expecting more destocking, competition, and other problems, we have little visibility. Our 2004 EPS estimate, which we lowered in September, remains $0.66. Anticipating a return to more normalized sales, we estimate 2005 EPS of $0.90. After projected modest option expense, and including one-time charges in the first half, our 2004 Standard & Poor's Core Earnings projection is $0.17 a share. For 2005, our S&P Core EPS estimate is $1.09.

Key Stock Statistics

S&P Core EPS 2005E	1.09	52-week Range	$20.62-10.26
S&P Oper. EPS 2004E	0.66	12 Month P/E	NM
P/E on S&P Oper. EPS 2004E	18.0	Beta	0.50
S&P Oper. EPS 2005E	0.90	Shareholders	1,260
Yield (%)	Nil	Market Cap (B)	$ 2.9
Dividend Rate/Share	Nil	Shares Outstanding (M)	241.6

Value of $10,000 invested five years ago: **$ 5,251**

Dividend Data

No cash dividends have been paid.

Investment Rationale/Risk 15-NOV-04

- We would hold the shares, as we believe that most of KG's sales decline reflects implementation of IMAs (inventory management agreements). We see 2004 as a transition year, and think sales and EPS should be more normalized in 2005. However, we are concerned that IMS data suggest weak demand for some key drugs. We think the pending merger with MYL would give the shares above-average appreciation potential, but recognize a strong risk that the merger will not be consummated.
- Risks to our recommendation and target price include the length of the transition period, demand weakness, potential generic competition, and potential failure of the merger with MYL. We also see uncertainties surrounding an ongoing SEC probe.
- Restatements would end MYL's obligation to acquire KG, and MYL is reevaluating the deal. In addition, KG requested an extension for filing its third quarter 10-Q. Given these developments and little visibility for KG as a standalone entity, our 12-month target price is $12, which represents a below-peer 13X our 2005 EPS estimate. We would not add to positions.

Revenues/Earnings Data Fiscal year ending December 31

Revenues (Million $)

	2004	2003	2002	2001	2000	1999
1Q	290.6	343.8	258.1	181.3	135.2	60.00
2Q	275.1	370.7	282.5	206.5	143.4	76.00
3Q	353.4	424.2	315.7	230.1	165.5	104.9
4Q	—	382.6	272.0	254.3	176.1	107.4
Yr.	—	1,521	1,128	872.3	620.2	348.3

Earnings Per Share ($)

	2004	2003	2002	2001	2000	1999
1Q	-0.01	-0.03	0.29	0.19	0.05	0.07
2Q	-0.27	-0.15	0.24	0.25	0.17	0.11
3Q	0.11	0.44	0.35	0.27	0.03	0.16
4Q	E0.24	0.17	-0.13	0.29	0.24	0.15
Yr.	E0.66	0.44	0.74	0.99	0.47	0.47

Next earnings report expected: mid-February Source: S&P, Company Reports
EPS Estimates based on S&P Operating Earnings; historical GAAP earnings are as reported.

King Pharmaceuticals, Inc.

Recommendation: **HOLD** ★ ★ ★ ☆ ☆   12-Month Target Price: **$12.00** (as of October 28, 2004)

Business Summary 15-NOV-04

On July 26, 2004, King Pharmaceuticals and Mylan Laboratories (MYL) announced an agreement for MYL to acquire KG via an exchange of stock. The companies said they expect the transaction to close by the end of 2004, subject to necessary regulatory and shareholder approvals.

King Pharmaceuticals was formed by the Gregory family in 1994, with the purchase of a plant in Bristol, TN, to manufacture drug products under contract for major pharmaceutical companies such as SmithKline Beecham and Novartis. A key part of its business strategy consists of the acquisition of branded prescription drugs being divested by large global pharmaceutical companies. To date, the company has successfully acquired and commercialized more than 35 branded products, and has introduced several product line extensions. Sales of branded pharmaceuticals accounted for 86% of total net revenues in 2003, Meridian Medical Technologies (a maker of autoinjectors acquired in January 2003) for 8%, royalties from licensed drugs for 4%, and contract manufacturing and other 2%.

The company's most important product is Altace, a heart drug acquired together with two other products from Hoechst Marion Rousell in 1998, for $363 million. An angiotensin converting enzyme (ACE) inhibitor indicated for the treatment of hypertension and congestive heart failure, Altace had 2003 sales of $527 million, up from $481 million in 2002. Altace has benefited from a co-marketing agreement with Wyeth, and from a broader product label. Other cardiovascular drugs include Procanbid treatment for arrythmia, and Thalitone diuretic.

Other drugs include anti-infectives such as Lorabid, Cortisporin, Neosporin, Virop-tic, Septra and Coly-Mycin; women's health products, including Pitocin, a hormone used to initiate labor, and Menest, an estrogen to alleviate menopausal symptoms; and vaccines and biologicals such as Aplisol used in the diagnosis of tuberculosis. King also provides contract manufacturing for leading drug companies such as Amgen, Pfizer, Johnson & Johnson, and Hoffmann-La Roche.

With its purchase of Jones Pharma in mid-2000, KG acquired Levoxyl thyroid hormone replacement treatment (2003 sales of $134 million); Tapazol and Cytomel treatments for thyroid disorders; and Thrombin JMI and Brevital critical care drugs. In February 2000, the company acquired Medco Research, which derives royalties from two cardiovascular drugs, Adenocard and Adenoscan. Product acquisitions in recent years also included Corzide/Corgard heart drugs, Delestrogen injectable estrogen, Florinef corticosteriod, Intal and Tilade asthma treatments, and Synercid injectable antibiotic.

In June 2003, the company acquired Elan Corp.'s primary care business in the U.S. and Puerto Rico, including Sonata anti-insomnia treatment and Skelaxin muscle relaxant, as well as Elan's 350-person primary care field sales force. The acquisition was completed in exchange for $750 million, including $40 million in inventory transfers. Net sales of Sonata and Skelaxin in the U.S. and Puerto Rico totaled about $252 million in 2003, following their acquisition on June 12, 2003. With the added personnel from Elan, KG's total sales force grew to approximately 1,300. The company markets its branded drugs to general/family practitioners, internal medicine physicians, cardiologists and hospitals across the U.S.

Company Financials Fiscal Year ending December 31

Per Share Data ($)

(Year Ended December 31)	2003	2002	2001	2000	1999	1998	1997	1996	1995	1994
Tangible Bk. Val.	0.68	2.90	3.47	0.85	NM	NM	NM	NA	NA	NA
Cash Flow	0.95	0.98	1.20	0.66	1.12	0.86	0.20	NA	NA	NA
Earnings	0.44	0.74	0.99	0.47	0.47	0.28	0.09	NA	NA	NA
S&P Core Earnings	0.41	0.71	0.94	NA	NA	NA	NA	NA	NA	NA
Dividends	Nil	Nil	Nil	Nil	Nil	Nil	NA	NA	NA	NA
Payout Ratio	Nil	Nil	Nil	Nil	Nil	Nil	NA	NA	NA	NA
Prices - High	18.13	42.13	46.05	41.62	34.00	9.58	NA	NA	NA	NA
- Low	9.46	15.00	24.78	14.81	6.45	3.54	NA	NA	NA	NA
P/E Ratio - High	41	57	47	88	72	34	NA	NA	NA	NA
- Low	22	20	25	31	14	13	NA	NA	NA	NA

Income Statement Analysis (Million $)

	2003	2002	2001	2000	1999	1998	1997	1996	1995	1994
Revs.	1,521	1,128	872	620	348	163	123	NA	NA	NA
Oper. Inc.	403	426	429	326	155	64.7	35.4	NA	NA	NA
Depr.	125	59.3	48.0	41.9	26.9	9.30	9.80	NA	NA	NA
Int. Exp.	13.4	12.4	12.7	37.0	55.4	14.9	12.4	NA	NA	NA
Pretax Inc.	177	268	371	192	73.0	40.7	13.1	NA	NA	NA
Eff. Tax Rate	40.2%	31.8%	37.2%	45.4%	37.5%	37.8%	38.1%	NA	NA	NA
Net Inc.	106	183	233	105	45.7	25.3	8.10	NA	NA	NA
S&P Core Earnings	98.4	175	222	NA	NA	NA	NA	NA	NA	NA

Balance Sheet & Other Fin. Data (Million $)

	2003	2002	2001	2000	1999	1998	1997	1996	1995	1994
Cash	146	815	924	76.4	8.50	1.16	12.5	NA	NA	NA
Curr. Assets	946	1,262	1,238	317	131	75.6	NA	NA	NA	NA
Total Assets	3,178	2,751	2,507	1,282	806	668	280	NA	NA	NA
Curr. Liab.	669	370	151	105	89.8	44.5	NA	NA	NA	NA
LT Debt	345	345	346	99	553	514	150	NA	NA	NA
Common Equity	2,042	1,931	1,908	988	148	101	83.3	NA	NA	NA
Total Cap.	2,387	2,310	2,292	1,104	716	623	NA	NA	NA	NA
Cap. Exp.	51.2	73.6	40.2	25.1	8.80	81.1	NA	NA	NA	NA
Cash Flow	230	242	281	147	22.6	34.6	17.9	NA	NA	NA
Curr. Ratio	1.4	3.4	8.2	3.0	1.5	1.7	NA	NA	NA	NA
% LT Debt of Cap.	14.5	14.9	15.1	9.0	77.2	82.5	NA	NA	NA	NA
% Net Inc.of Revs.	7.0	16.2	26.7	16.9	13.1	15.5	6.6	NA	NA	NA
% Ret. on Assets	3.6	6.9	12.3	8.5	6.2	6.5	NA	NA	NA	NA
% Ret. on Equity	5.3	9.5	16.1	14.1	36.7	38.9	NA	NA	NA	NA

Data as orig reptd.; bef. results of disc opers/spec. items. Per share data adj. for stk. divs.; EPS diluted. E-Estimated. NA-Not Available. NM-Not Meaningful. NR-Not Ranked. UR-Under Review.

Office: 501 Fifth Street, Bristol, TN 37620-2304.
Telephone: 423-989-8000.
Email: investorrelations@kingpharm.com
Website: http://www.kingpharm.com
Chrmn: T. G. Wood.
Pres & CEO: B. A. Markison.
COO: B. A. Markison.

CFO: J. R. Lattanzi.
EVP & General Counsel: J. A. Bellamy.
Investor Contact: James E. Green (423-989-8125).
Dirs: E. W. Deavenport, Jr., E. M. Greetham, G. D. Jordan, J. R. Lattanzi, B. A. Markison, R. C. Moyer, P. M. Pfeffer, D. G. Rooker, T. G. Wood.

Founded: in 1993.
Domicile: Tennessee.
Employees: 3,003.
S&P Analyst: Phillip M. Seligman/CB/JWP

The McGraw·Hill Companies

KLA-Tencor Corp.

Recommendation: **BUY** ★★★★☆
SELL SELL HOLD BUY BUY

12-Month Target Price: $50.00
(as of October 22, 2004)

KLAC has an approximate 0.08% weighting in the **S&P 500**

Sector: Information Technology
Sub-Industry: Semiconductor Equipment
Peer Group: Semiconductor Equipment - Larger Front-end

Summary: KLAC is the world's leading manufacturer of yield monitoring and process control systems for the semiconductor industry.

Quantitative Evaluations

S&P Earnings & Dividend Rank: B

D	C	B-	B	B+	A-	A	A+

S&P Fair Value Rank: 4

1	2	3	4	5
Lowest				Highest

Fair Value Calc.: $49.30 (Slightly Undervalued)

S&P Investability Quotient Percentile

92%

KLAC scored higher than 92% of all companies for which an S&P Report is available.

Volatility: Average

Low	Average	High

Technical Evaluation: Bullish
Since 10/04, the technical indicators for KLAC have been Bullish.

Relative Strength Rank: Moderate

52

1 Lowest		Highest 99

Price as of 11/12/04: **$44.42** | **2005E S&P Core EPS:** **$1.34**

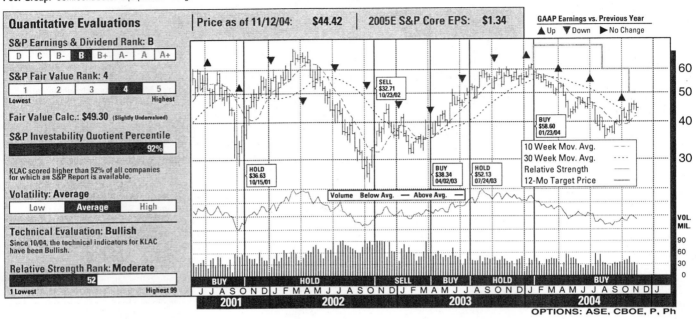

GAAP Earnings vs. Previous Year
▲ Up ▼ Down ► No Change

SELL $32.71 10/23/02

BUY $58.60 01/23/04

HOLD $36.63 10/15/01

BUY $38.34 04/02/03

HOLD $52.13 07/24/03

- - - 10 Week Mov. Avg.
······ 30 Week Mov. Avg.
— Relative Strength
— 12-Mo Target Price

Volume ─ Below Avg. — Above Avg. ─

BUY | HOLD | SELL | BUY | HOLD | BUY
J J A S O N D | J F M A M J J A S O N D | J F M A M J J A S O N D | J F M A M J J A S O N D | J
2001 | 2002 | 2003 | 2004

VOL. MIL. 90 60 30 0

60 50 40 30

OPTIONS: ASE, CBOE, P, Ph

Analyst commentary prepared by Colin McArdle/PMW/BK

Highlights October 28, 2004

■ We expect worldwide semiconductor equipment sales to climb 30% to 40% in calendar 2004, despite a second half slowdown due to higher inventories. For 2005, we expect growth to slow to 10% to 15%. After a 13% sales gain in FY 04 (Jun.), we project a 42% advance in FY 05. Despite slowing orders for the industry and KLAC's indication that orders would be down 10% sequentially in the second quarter, we believe the slowdown will be temporary and see calendar 2005 remaining a growth year.

Investment Rationale/Risk October 28, 2004

■ We recommend accumulating the shares. We believe the semiconductor equipment industry will experience near-term demand weakness in the second half of 2004, but we expect this to be followed by an upturn in 2005. KLAC was one of a very few chip equipment companies to remain profitable in each quarter of the last downturn.

Key Stock Statistics

S&P Oper. EPS 2005E	2.40	52-week Range	$62.82-35.02
P/E on S&P Oper. EPS 2005E	18.5	12 Month P/E	27.6
Yield (%)	Nil	Beta	NA
Dividend Rate/Share	Nil	Shareholders	975
Shares Outstanding (M)	195.5	Market Cap (B)	$ 8.7

Value of $10,000 invested five years ago: **$ 10,368**

Dividend Data

No cash has been paid.

Revenues/Earnings Data Fiscal year ending June 30

Revenues (Million $)

	2005	2004	2003	2002	2001	2000
1Q	518.8	318.0	375.5	502.8	382.8	273.0
2Q	—	338.5	334.9	404.1	500.8	330.8
3Q	—	389.8	304.3	357.1	612.6	413.0
4Q	—	450.4	308.3	373.2	602.6	482.1
Yr.	—	1,497	1,323	1,637	2,104	1,499

Earnings Per Share ($)

	2005	2004	2003	2002	2001	2000
1Q	0.58	0.18	0.26	0.44	0.15	0.21
2Q	E0.58	0.22	0.15	0.25	0.41	0.26
3Q	E0.60	0.33	0.14	0.17	0.71	0.38
4Q	E0.63	0.48	0.15	0.23	0.67	0.47
Yr.	E2.40	1.21	0.70	1.10	1.93	1.32

Next earnings report expected: late-January Source: S&P, Company Reports
EPS Estimates based on S&P Operating Earnings; historical GAAP earnings are as reported.

KLA-Tencor Corporation

Recommendation: **BUY** ★★★★☆   12-Month Target Price: **$50.00** (as of October 22, 2004)

Business Summary October 28, 2004

KLA-Tencor, is the world's leading manufacturer of yield management and process monitoring systems for the semiconductor industry. Overall semiconductor equipment sales fell 60% from calendar 2000 to 2002, but KLAC's sales dropped only 19%, as chipmakers continued to purchase equipment to improve yields for new processes.

Maximizing yields, or the number of good die per wafer, is a key goal in manufacturing integrated circuits (ICs). Higher yields increase revenues obtained for each semiconductor wafer processed. As IC linewidths decrease, yields become more sensitive to the size and density of defects. KLAC's systems are used to improve yields by identifying defects, analyzing them to determine process problems, and, after corrective action has been taken, monitoring subsequent results to ensure that problems have been contained. With in-line systems, corrections can be made while the wafer is still in the production line, rather than waiting days for end-of-process testing and feedback.

The company's wafer inspection systems include unpatterned and patterned wafer inspection tools used to find, count and characterize particles and pattern defects on wafers both in engineering applications and in-line at various stages during the semiconductor manufacturing process.

Reticle inspection systems look for defects on the quartz plates used in copying circuit designs onto an IC during the photolithography process.

Film measurement products measure a variety of optical and electrical properties of thin films. In early FY 04 (Jun.), KLAC introduced the MetriX 100 in-line, non-contact metal films metrology system.

Scanning electron beam microscopes (SEMs) can measure the critical dimensions (CDs) of tiny semiconductor features. In May 2003, the company introduced the eS30 e-beam inspection tool for high-volume production line monitoring of electrical defects.

KLAC sells systems to virtually all of the world's semiconductor manufacturers. In FY 04, international sales accounted for 77% of the total, up from 69% in FY 03. Orders from Japan, Taiwan and the Asia Pacific region accounted for 61% of the total (54%). Order backlog totaled $880 million as of September 2004, up from $550 million a year earlier.

Company Financials Fiscal Year ending June 30

Per Share Data ($)

(Year Ended June 30)	2004	2003	2002	2001	2000	1999	1998	1997	1996	1995
Tangible Bk. Val.	13.34	11.56	10.70	9.38	9.11	6.95	6.85	6.05	5.28	4.04
Cash Flow	1.62	1.07	1.45	2.22	1.65	0.48	0.98	0.93	1.31	0.71
Earnings	1.21	0.70	1.10	1.93	1.32	0.21	0.76	0.62	1.16	0.60
S&P Core Earnings	0.77	0.12	0.49	1.45	NA	NA	NA	NA	NA	NA
Dividends	Nil	Nil	Nil	Nil	Nil	Nil	Nil	Nil	Nil	Nil
Payout Ratio	Nil	Nil	Nil	Nil	Nil	Nil	Nil	Nil	Nil	Nil
Prices - High	62.82	61.25	70.58	61.00	97.75	56.56	24.00	38.43	20.00	24.37
- Low	35.02	31.20	25.16	28.61	25.50	21.18	10.37	16.81	8.75	11.62
P/E Ratio - High	52	88	64	32	74	NM	32	62	17	41
- Low	29	45	23	15	19	99	14	27	8	19

Income Statement Analysis (Million $)

	2004	2003	2002	2001	2000	1999	1998	1997	1996	1995
Revs.	1,497	1,323	1,637	2,103	1,499	843	1,166	1,032	695	442
Oper. Inc.	380	201	314	512	370	80.6	226	259	194	118
Depr.	82.9	71.4	69.6	55.6	63.3	48.2	38.9	52.3	16.3	10.6
Int. Exp.	Nil	0.39	Nil	Nil	Nil	Nil	Nil	Nil	1.36	2.40
Pretax Inc.	325	181	287	513	353	50.3	206	174	189	88.8
Eff. Tax Rate	24.9%	24.0%	24.8%	27.2%	28.1%	22.1%	35.0%	39.4%	36.0%	33.9%
Net Inc.	244	137	216	373	254	39.2	134	105	121	58.6
S&P Core Earnings	156	22.4	96.5	281	NA	NA	NA	NA	NA	NA

Balance Sheet & Other Fin. Data (Million $)

	2004	2003	2002	2001	2000	1999	1998	1997	1996	1995
Cash	1,876	1,488	1,334	697	844	696	216	349	124	119
Curr. Assets	2,192	1,806	1,619	1,897	1,552	942	956	860	494	361
Total Assets	3,539	2,867	2,718	2,745	2,204	1,585	1,548	1,343	713	546
Curr. Liab.	912	651	687	984	495	352	351	325	169	133
LT Debt	Nil	Nil	Nil	Nil	Nil	Nil	Nil	Nil	Nil	Nil
Common Equity	2,628	2,216	2,030	1,760	1,709	1,233	1,198	1,015	537	404
Total Cap.	2,628	2,216	2,030	1,760	1,709	1,233	1,198	1,019	544	413
Cap. Exp.	55.5	134	68.7	162	78.7	56.8	64.4	56.8	39.1	19.0
Cash Flow	327	209	286	429	317	87.4	173	158	137	69.3
Curr. Ratio	2.4	2.8	2.4	1.9	3.1	2.7	2.7	2.6	2.9	2.7
% LT Debt of Cap.	Nil	Nil	Nil	Nil	Nil	Nil	Nil	Nil	Nil	Nil
% Net Inc.of Revs.	16.3	10.4	13.2	17.7	16.9	4.7	11.5	10.2	17.5	13.2
% Ret. on Assets	7.6	4.9	7.9	15.1	13.4	2.5	9.3	11.5	19.2	13.5
% Ret. on Equity	10.1	6.5	11.4	21.5	17.3	3.2	12.1	15.3	25.7	18.5

Data as orig reptd.; bef. results of disc opers/spec. items. Per share data adj. for stk. divs. Bold denotes primary EPS - prior periods restated. E-Estimated. NA-Not Available. NM-Not Meaningful. NR-Not Ranked. UR-Under Review.

Office: 160 Rio Robles, San Jose, CA 95134.
Telephone: 408-875-3000.
Website: http://www.tencor.com
Chrmn: K. Levy.
Pres & CEO: K.L. Schroeder.

EVP & CFO: J.H. Kispert.
Investor Contact: A. Huang 408-875-3600.
Dirs: E. W. Barnholt, H. R. Bingham, R. T. Bond, R. J. Elkus, Jr., S. Kaufman, K. Levy, M. Marks, K. L. Schroeder, J. D. Tompkins, L. Urbanek.

Founded: in 1975.
Domicile: Delaware.
Employees: 5,200.
S&P Analyst: Colin McArdle/PMW/BK

Knight Ridder

Recommendation: **HOLD** ★★★☆☆
SELL | SELL | HOLD | BUY | BUY

12-Month Target Price: $74.00
(as of August 20, 2004)

KRI has an approximate 0.05% weighting in the **S&P 500**

Sector: Consumer Discretionary
Sub-Industry: Publishing
Peer Group: Newspaper Cos. - Large

Summary: KRI is the second largest U.S. newspaper publisher, with products in print and online, and has equity holdings in newsprint mills.

Quantitative Evaluations

S&P Earnings & Dividend Rank: A-

D | C | B- | B | B+ | **A-** | A | A+

S&P Fair Value Rank: 1+

1 | 2 | 3 | 4 | 5
Lowest | | | | Highest

Fair Value Calc.: $52.40 (Overvalued)

S&P Investability Quotient Percentile

96%

KRI scored higher than 96% of all companies for which an S&P Report is available.

Volatility: Low

Low | Average | High

Technical Evaluation: Bullish
Since 10/04, the technical indicators for KRI have been Bullish.

Relative Strength Rank: Moderate

47

1 Lowest | Highest 99

| Price as of 11/12/04: | $70.15 | 2004E S&P Core EPS: | $3.46 |

GAAP Earnings vs. Previous Year
▲ Up ▼ Down ▶ No Change

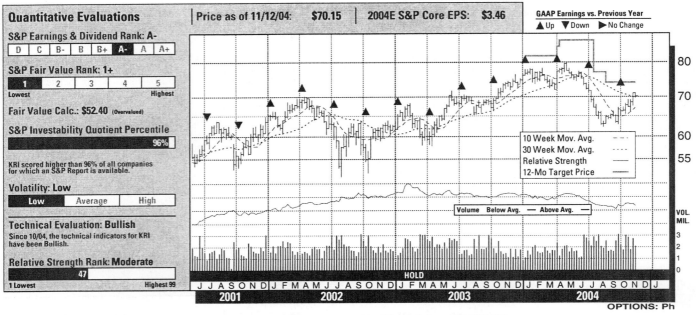

- 10 Week Mov. Avg.
- 30 Week Mov. Avg.
- Relative Strength
- 12-Mo Target Price

Volume ▪ Below Avg. — Above Avg.

HOLD

J J A S O N D J F M A M J J A S O N D J F M A M J J A S O N D J F M A M J J A S O N D J
2001 | 2002 | 2003 | 2004

VOL. MIL.
3
2
1
0

OPTIONS: Ph

Analyst commentary prepared by William H. Donald/PMW/JWP

Highlights August 27, 2004

- We expect total revenues to increase about 7% in 2005, to $3.20 billion, after projected 4.7% growth in 2004, to $3.0 billion. We see gains in each year reflecting increases in all business areas. We expect the strongest growth in each year to come from classifieds, which we think are recovering from a multi-year slump, and which have been hurt most recently by softness in help-wanteds. We look for general advertising revenues to advance about 8.3% in 2005, after a 3.3% rise that we see for 2004. We see retail advertising up 5.7% in 2005, after a gain of 2.5% that we see for 2004.

- We project that operating expenses will rise less rapidly than revenues, despite higher paper and employee benefits costs. We expect operating income to rise 13% and 5.5% in 2005 and 2004, respectively, and project EBITDA margins of 24.4% for 2005, up from 23.7% that we see for 2004.

- After nonoperating charges, including double-digit declines in interest expense in each year, we project a 14% increase in pretax earnings for 2005 after a 7.8% rise for 2004. After taxes projected at 38.4%, versus 36.2% seen for 2004, we estimate that net operating earnings will increase 10% in 2005, to $351.3 million ($4.40 a share), from $318.4 million ($3.97) that we project for 2004.

Investment Rationale/Risk August 27, 2004

- We expect the newspaper publishing group to perform in line with the S&P Super 1500 over the next 12 months, as we believe the group's advertising recovery will gain steam as the general economy grows through the remainder of 2004 and during 2005. The stock's recent P/E multiples based on our 2004 and 2005 EPS estimates were below peer averages, but we see slower EPS growth than the level that we project for peers.

- Risks to our recommendation and target price include a slowdown in U.S. economic growth, a sharp increase in newsprint costs, and a shift in customer preference from newspaper advertising to other media. We also see risk that inconsistent trends across major advertising categories will continue.

- Our 12-month target price of $74 assumes that the shares will trade at a forward P/E multiple of 17X our 2005 EPS projection of $4.40, a discount to the peer average that we calculate at 20X. Our target price is supported by our discounted cash flow analysis, which assumes a 9.87% weighted average cost of capital, and yields intrinsic value of $75.

Key Stock Statistics

S&P Oper. EPS 2004E	3.95	52-week Range	$80.00-62.24
P/E on S&P Oper. EPS 2004E	17.8	12 Month P/E	17.6
S&P Oper. EPS 2005E	4.40	Beta	0.70
Yield (%)	2.0%	Shareholders	7,784
Dividend Rate/Share	1.38	Market Cap (B)	$ 5.4
Shares Outstanding (M)	77.0		

Value of $10,000 invested five years ago: **$ 12,758**

Dividend Data Dividends have been paid since 1941

Amount ($)	Date Decl.	Ex-Div. Date	Stock of Record	Payment Date
0.320	May. 04	May. 17	May. 19	Jun. 01 '04
0.345	Jul. 27	Aug. 09	Aug. 11	Aug. 23 '04
0.345	Jul. 27	Aug. 09	Aug. 11	Aug. 23 '04
0.345	Oct. 26	Nov. 08	Nov. 10	Nov. 22 '04

Revenues/Earnings Data Fiscal year ending December 31

Revenues (Million $)

	2004	2003	2002	2001	2000	1999
1Q	712.3	677.4	678.2	735.4	758.6	770.8
2Q	760.2	721.6	715.1	738.4	806.2	809.7
3Q	722.2	685.3	689.0	693.1	769.2	784.7
4Q	—	772.9	759.3	733.3	877.8	863.0
Yr.	—	2,857	2,842	2,900	3,212	3,228

Earnings Per Share ($)

	2004	2003	2002	2001	2000	1999
1Q	0.70	0.62	0.60	0.47	1.74	0.65
2Q	1.08	0.95	0.90	0.15	1.08	0.88
3Q	0.99	0.85	0.67	0.65	0.87	0.78
4Q	E1.29	1.22	1.16	0.88	-0.29	1.18
Yr.	E3.95	3.63	3.33	2.16	3.53	3.49

Next earnings report expected: late-January Source: S&P, Company Reports
EPS Estimates based on S&P Operating Earnings; historical GAAP earnings are as reported.

Recommendation: **HOLD** ★ ★ ★ ☆ ☆   12-Month Target Price: **$74.00** (as of August 20, 2004)

Business Summary August 27, 2004

Knight Ridder was formed in 1974 by the merger of Knight Newspapers, Inc., and Ridder Publications, Inc. At a time when most newspaper publishers sought to diversify, the company narrowed its focus in 1997 and 1998, selling all non-newspaper businesses, and making a major purchase of four newspapers from Walt Disney Co. With these moves, KRI became the largest publicly owned, pure-play newspaper publisher in the U.S.

Based on circulation, KRI is the second largest U.S. newspaper publisher. The company publishes 32 daily newspapers in 28 U.S. markets, with a readership of 8.4 million daily and 12.3 million on Sunday. It also owns 25 non-daily newspapers, maintains 45 associated websites, and has investments in two newsprint mills. Its larger papers include the Miami Herald, Philadelphia Inquirer, Philadelphia Daily News, Detroit Free Press, Kansas City Star, Fort Worth Star-Telegram, San Jose Mercury, and San Jose News. KnightRidder.com operates and manages an emerging national network of 36 regional information hubs, RealCities.com.

The company sold most of its Business Information Services (BIS) division to M.A.I.D plc in November 1997, for $420 million. In 1998, KRI moved its headquarters from Miami, FL, to San Jose, CA. It also sold its remaining BIS unit, Technimetrics, Inc., its global diversified information subsidiary.

In 1997, KRI acquired four newspapers from Walt Disney Co., for $1.65 billion, comprised of 1,754,930 Series B convertible preferred shares, and the assumption of $990 million of bank debt. Combined circulation of the papers, located in Kansas City, Fort Worth, Belleville, IL, and Wilkes-Barre, PA, was about 630,000 daily and 898,000 Sunday. KRI acquired three additional newspapers during 1997.

EPS of $3.33 in 2002 included a second-quarter charge of $0.29 for the writedown of goodwill. EPS of $2.16 in 2001 included a first quarter loss of $0.08 on the sale of certain Internet investments, and a second quarter charge of $0.55 for buyouts and severance costs. EPS of $3.53 in 2000 included $1.03 of gains on the sale of investments, $1.15 in writedowns of investments, a $0.06 gain on the sale of a building, and a $0.12 charge for severance payments. EPS of $3.49 in 1999 included $0.21 of gains on the sale of stock in Zip2 Corp. and AT&T, as well as $0.03 in severance costs. EPS of $3.11 in 1998 included a one-time gain of $0.48 from the sale of the balance of the company's jointly owned cable systems, a newspaper in Gary, IN, and net settlement adjustments on newspapers sold in 1997; results also included a charge of $0.15 for costs associated with the relocation of the corporate headquarters from Miami to San Jose, and other newspaper severance costs recorded in the fourth quarter.

Company Financials Fiscal Year ending December 31

Per Share Data ($)

(Year Ended December 31)	2003	2002	2001	2000	1999	1998	1997	1996	1995	1994
Tangible Bk. Val.	NM	NM	NM	NM	NM	NM	NM	2.29	1.52	4.79
Cash Flow	5.01	4.80	4.31	5.63	5.43	5.03	5.46	4.45	3.18	2.75
Earnings	3.63	3.33	2.16	3.53	3.49	3.11	3.91	2.75	1.67	1.58
S&P Core Earnings	3.32	2.28	1.32	NA	NA	NA	NA	NA	NA	NA
Dividends	1.18	1.02	1.00	0.92	0.89	0.80	0.80	0.79	0.74	0.73
Payout Ratio	33%	31%	46%	26%	26%	26%	20%	29%	44%	46%
Prices - High	77.42	70.20	65.50	59.75	65.00	59.62	57.12	42.00	33.31	30.50
- Low	57.83	51.35	50.20	44.12	46.00	40.50	35.75	29.87	25.25	23.25
P/E Ratio - High	21	21	30	17	19	19	15	15	20	19
- Low	16	15	23	12	13	13	9	11	15	15

Income Statement Analysis (Million $)

	2003	2002	2001	2000	1999	1998	1997	1996	1995	1994
Revs.	2,946	2,842	2,900	3,212	3,228	3,092	2,877	2,775	2,752	2,649
Oper. Inc.	680	730	646	856	814	693	663	501	391	459
Depr.	112	125	185	188	189	188	157	166	152	128
Int. Exp.	68.7	74.3	99	114	92.2	101	97.3	73.2	60.0	44.6
Pretax Inc.	473	460	317	538	580	519	705	467	288	300
Eff. Tax Rate	35.3%	36.3%	38.7%	39.2%	39.3%	39.0%	42.2%	42.6%	41.7%	39.8%
Net Inc.	296	282	185	314	340	306	397	268	167	171
S&P Core Earnings	271	193	106	NA	NA	NA	NA	NA	NA	NA

Balance Sheet & Other Fin. Data (Million $)

	2003	2002	2001	2000	1999	1998	1997	1996	1995	1994
Cash	33.5	39.3	37.3	41.7	34.1	26.8	160	22.9	26.0	9.30
Curr. Assets	526	539	536	576	570	526	641	566	503	423
Total Assets	4,097	4,165	4,213	4,244	4,192	4,257	4,355	2,900	3,006	2,447
Curr. Liab.	455	467	480	508	497	654	599	555	438	421
LT Debt	1,434	1,521	1,573	1,592	1,261	1,329	1,599	771	1,001	412
Common Equity	1,489	1,461	1,560	1,540	1,779	1,661	1,550	1,132	1,111	1,225
Total Cap.	3,220	3,281	3,390	3,406	3,353	3,287	3,432	2,079	2,278	1,776
Cap. Exp.	73.2	70.0	94.6	108	92.6	132	107	127	121	67.0
Cash Flow	409	406	369	502	529	494	553	434	319	299
Curr. Ratio	1.2	1.2	1.1	1.1	1.1	0.8	1.1	1.0	1.2	1.0
% LT Debt of Cap.	44.5	46.4	46.4	46.7	37.6	40.4	46.6	37.9	43.9	23.2
% Net Inc.of Revs.	10.1	9.9	6.4	9.8	10.5	9.9	13.8	9.7	6.1	6.5
% Ret. on Assets	7.2	6.7	4.4	7.5	8.0	7.1	10.9	9.1	6.1	7.1
% Ret. on Equity	20.1	18.6	11.9	18.9	19.8	19.0	29.6	23.9	14.3	14.1

Data as orig reptd.; bef. results of disc opers/spec. items. Per share data adj. for stk. divs. Bold denotes diluted EPS (FASB 128)-prior periods restated. E-Estimated. NA-Not Available. NM-Not Meaningful. NR-Not Ranked.

Office: 50 W.San Fernando Street, San Jose , CA 95113.
Telephone: 408-938-7700.
Email: plaffoon@knightridder.com
Website: http://www.kri.com
Chrmn & CEO: P.A. Ridder.
Pres: S.B. Rossi.

SVP & CFO: G.R. Effren.
VP, Secy & Investor Contact: P. Laffoon, IV .
VP & General Counsel: G. Yamate.
Dirs: M. A. Ernst, K. F. Feldstein, T. P. Gerrity, R. D. McCray, P. Mitchell, M. K. Oshman, V. Prabhu, P. A. Ridder, G. F. Valdes-Fauli, J. E. Warnock.

Founded: in 1915.
Domicile: Florida.
Employees: 18,000.
S&P Analyst: William H. Donald/PMW/JWP

Kohl's Corp.

Recommendation: HOLD ★ ★ ★ ★ ★
SELL | SELL | HOLD | BUY | BUY

12-Month Target Price: $55.00
(as of November 12, 2004)

KSS has an approximate 0.16% weighting in the **S&P 500**

Sector: Consumer Discretionary
Sub-Industry: Department Stores
Peer Group: Department Store Cos. - Larger

Summary: KSS operates more than 580 specialty department stores in 38 states, featuring moderately priced apparel, shoes, accessories, and products for the home.

Quantitative Evaluations

S&P Earnings & Dividend Rank: B+

| D | C | B- | B | B+ | A- | A | A+ |

S&P Fair Value Rank: 5

| 1 | 2 | 3 | 4 | 5 |
| Lowest | | | | Highest |

Fair Value Calc.: $70.10 (Undervalued)

S&P Investability Quotient Percentile

96%

KSS scored higher than 96% of all companies for which an S&P Report is available.

Volatility: Average

| Low | Average | High |

Technical Evaluation: Bullish
Since 10/04, the technical indicators for KSS have been Bullish.

Relative Strength Rank: Moderate

57

| 1 Lowest | | Highest 99 |

Price as of 11/15/04: **$52.58**   2005E S&P Core EPS: **$2.05**

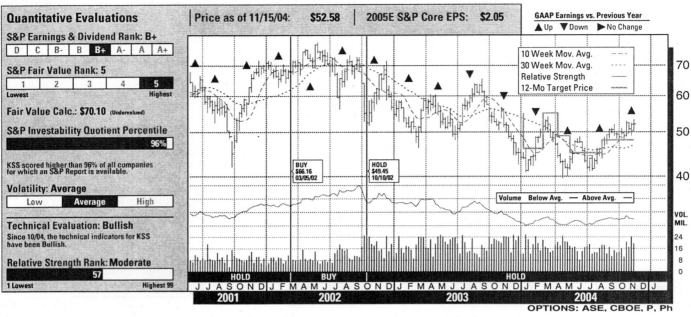

GAAP Earnings vs. Previous Year
▲ Up   ▼ Down   ► No Change

10 Week Mov. Avg.
30 Week Mov. Avg.
Relative Strength
12-Mo Target Price

BUY $66.16 03/05/02
HOLD $49.45 10/10/02

Volume   Below Avg. — Above Avg.

VOL. MIL.

HOLD | BUY | HOLD
J J A S O N D | J F M A M J J A S O N D | J F M A M J J A S O N D | J F M A M J J A S O N D | J
2001 | 2002 | 2003 | 2004

OPTIONS: ASE, CBOE, P, Ph

Analyst commentary prepared by Jason N. Asaeda/PMW/JWP

Highlights November 15, 2004

- From a projected $11.7 billion in FY 05 (Jan.), we see net sales up 14% in FY 06, to $13.4 billion, on a 3% to 5% increase in same-store sales and 15% growth in square footage, with the planned addition of 95 new stores. KSS plans to open 33 stores in the FY 06 first quarter; no additional store openings are scheduled for FY 05. We believe KSS's off-mall growth strategy and easy-to-shop store layouts remain competitive advantages. In response to a strong fashion trend in apparel, KSS has been seeking to improve its assortments with new contemporary brands such as Daisy Fuentes and apt. 9, and with updates to the axcess and Nine & Company lines. The company is also attempting to be conservative in planning women's apparel and seasonal assortments in an effort to reduce its markdown exposure. We see these efforts paying off, with clearance unit inventory per store at the end of October down about 30%, year to year.

- We expect EBIT (earnings before interest and taxes) margins to widen, on improved inventory turns, reflecting changes in merchandise buying and allocation; and well controlled store, distribution center, credit and corporate office expenses.

- We see FY 05 operating EPS of $2.15 and S&P Core EPS of $2.05, followed by FY 06 operating EPS of $2.58 and S&P Core EPS of $2.48. The annual differences reflect estimated stock option expense.

Key Stock Statistics

S&P Core EPS 2006E	2.48	52-week Range	$54.10-39.59
S&P Oper. EPS 2005E	2.15	12 Month P/E	27.4
P/E on S&P Oper. EPS 2005E	24.2	Beta	1.00
S&P Oper. EPS 2006E	2.58	Shareholders	5,655
Yield (%)	Nil	Market Cap (B)	$ 18.0
Dividend Rate/Share	Nil	Shares Outstanding (M)	341.7

Value of $10,000 invested five years ago: **$ 14,828**

Dividend Data

No cash dividends have been paid.

Investment Rationale/Risk November 15, 2004

- Our recommendation is hold. We view KSS as a mature retail concept that has been playing catch-up with competitors that have been better at delivering newness sought by customers. However, we believe that the company's corrective actions have started to pay off, and we expect to see more measurable results in FY 06. In particular, we look for KSS's upcoming store receipts, such as Chaps in men's, Royal Velvet in bath, and Daisy Fuentes and apt. 9 in petites and womens, as well as expected chain-wide rollout of the company's three exclusive beauty brands (American Beauty, Flirt, and Good Skin) to boost sales momentum and sustain gross margin recovery. However, with the shares trading at a premium to peer P/E multiples, we believe KSS's favorable prospects are fairly reflected in its valuation.

- Risks to our recommendation and target price include a possible decline in consumer spending due to geopolitical and economic uncertainties, as well as a failure by KSS to deliver compelling merchandise to customers.

- We calculate intrinsic value of $43 based on our DCF model, which assumes a cost of capital of 10.5% and a terminal growth rate of 4%. Our 12-month target price of $55 is based on a blend of our DCF model, a forward P/E multiple of 28X applied to our FY 06 operating EPS estimate of $2.58, and a price to estimated FY 06 sales ratio of 1.5X, both in line with the one-year historical averages.

Revenues/Earnings Data Fiscal year ending January 31

Revenues (Million $)

	2005	2004	2003	2002	2001	2000
1Q	2,380	2,118	1,871	1,488	1,229	910.3
2Q	2,498	2,208	1,922	1,516	1,255	939.5
3Q	2,744	2,394	2,143	1,760	1,445	1,100
4Q	—	3,562	3,184	2,724	2,223	1,608
Yr.	—	10,282	9,120	7,489	6,152	4,557

Earnings Per Share ($)

	2005	2004	2003	2002	2001	2000
1Q	0.33	0.32	0.31	0.22	0.16	0.12
2Q	0.45	0.33	0.36	0.25	0.19	0.14
3Q	0.42	0.35	0.39	0.29	0.23	0.16
4Q	E0.95	0.72	0.81	0.68	0.52	0.36
Yr.	E2.15	1.72	1.87	1.35	1.10	0.78

Next earnings report expected: late-February Source: S&P, Company Reports
EPS Estimates based on S&P Operating Earnings; historical GAAP earnings are as reported.

Kohl's Corporation

Recommendation: **HOLD** ★ ★ ★ ☆ ☆   12-Month Target Price: **$55.00** (as of November 12, 2004)

Business Summary November 16, 2004

Kohl's Corp. is one of the fastest growing family-oriented U.S. department store chains. Since 1992, the company has boosted square footage at an average of 21.9% a year, expanding from 79 stores in the Midwest to 637 stores nationwide as of October 2004. The stores feature moderately priced, national brand merchandise targeted to middle-income customers.

The company's overall expansion strategy is to open additional stores in existing markets in which it can leverage advertising, purchasing, transportation and other regional overhead expenses, and in contiguous markets in which it can extend regional operating efficiencies. Most stores are located in strip shopping centers, but KSS also operates stores in malls as well as freestanding units.

KSS opened a total of 85 stores in FY 04 (Jan.), including its entry into the Los Angeles, CA, San Antonio, TX, Las Vegas, NV, and Phoenix, Tucson and Flagstaff, AZ, markets. The average opening cost per store was about $550,000. In FY 05, the company planned to open about 95 new stores, evenly divided between new and existing markets. A total of 47 stores opened in the first quarter, including entries into Bakersfield, Fresno, Sacramento, and San Diego, CA, and Memphis, TN. An additional 48 stores opened during the third quarter, including new market entries into San Francisco, CA, Salt Lake City, UT, Rochester, NY, Portland, ME, Reno, NV, and Montgomery, AL. In FY 06, the company plans to open another 95 new stores.

Kohl's stores, which are designed to help customers shop without assistance, emphasize apparel and shoes for women, men and children, soft home products, such as towels, sheets and pillows, and housewares. The company's central merchandising organization and market solution teams tailor assortments to reflect regional climates and preferences. As a complement to its national brands, KSS offers private-label merchandise under several names. It plans to increase private-label sales to about 20% of the total.

The company planned to introduce several new product assortments in FY 05, including a new missy sportswear apparel line from Daisy Fuentes, and a new girls' clothing line created by Nickelodeon, called everGirl. KSS also expected to enter an entirely new category in the fall of 2004, with the introduction of exclusive beauty products developed by Beauty Bank, a new division of Estee Lauder.

KSS seeks to maintain a low cost structure, enabling it to keep prices low and boost profitability. Central to its low cost structure are lean staffing levels, sophisticated management systems, and operating efficiencies resulting from centralized buying, advertising and distribution.

Capital spending totaled about $830 million in FY 04, up from $716 million in FY 03. For FY 05, capital expenditures were expected to approximate $950 million, including new store and remodel spending and base capital needs. Total cash outlay required for newly constructed leased and owned stores are about $5.5 million and $13.5 million, respectively.

Company Financials Fiscal Year ending January 31

Per Share Data ($)

(Year Ended January 31)	2004	2003	2002	2001	2000	1999	1998	1997	1996	1995
Tangible Bk. Val.	11.60	9.85	7.78	6.21	4.70	3.55	2.88	1.57	1.19	0.90
Cash Flow	2.43	2.41	1.93	1.48	1.05	0.81	0.64	0.50	0.36	0.33
Earnings	1.72	1.87	1.35	1.10	0.78	0.59	0.46	0.35	0.25	0.23
S&P Core Earnings	1.62	1.78	1.38	1.04	NA	NA	NA	NA	NA	NA
Dividends	Nil	Nil	Nil	Nil	Nil	Nil	Nil	Nil	Nil	Nil
Payout Ratio	Nil	Nil	Nil	Nil	Nil	Nil	Nil	Nil	Nil	Nil

Cal. Yrs.	2003	2002	2001	2000	1999	1998	1997	1996	1995	1994
Prices - High	65.44	78.83	72.24	66.50	40.62	30.75	18.84	10.50	6.89	6.90
- Low	42.40	44.00	41.95	33.50	28.62	16.20	9.06	6.32	4.75	4.89
P/E Ratio - High	38	42	54	60	52	52	42	30	28	30
- Low	25	24	31	30	37	27	20	18	19	21

Income Statement Analysis (Million $)

	2004	2003	2002	2001	2000	1999	1998	1997	1996	1995
Revs.	10,282	9,120	7,489	6,152	4,557	3,682	3,060	2,388	1,926	1,554
Oper. Inc.	1,260	1,282	1,002	779	537	408	316	233	184	151
Depr.	237	191	152	128	83.3	70.0	57.4	44.0	34.0	27.4
Int. Exp.	75.2	59.4	57.4	Nil	29.5	22.9	24.6	17.9	13.5	7.40
Pretax Inc.	950	1,034	800	605	421	317	235	171	123	117
Eff. Tax Rate	37.8%	37.8%	38.0%	38.5%	38.7%	39.3%	39.9%	40.2%	40.8%	41.7%
Net Inc.	591	643	496	372	258	192	141	102	72.7	68.5
S&P Core Earnings	557	608	471	349	NA	NA	NA	NA	NA	NA

Balance Sheet & Other Fin. Data (Million $)

	2004	2003	2002	2001	2000	1999	1998	1997	1996	1995
Cash	113	90.1	107	124	12.6	29.6	44.2	8.90	2.80	30.4
Curr. Assets	3,025	3,284	2,464	1,922	1,367	939	811	465	300	286
Total Assets	6,698	6,316	4,930	3,855	2,915	1,936	1,620	1,122	805	659
Curr. Liab.	1,122	1,508	880	723	634	380	286	236	155	172
LT Debt	1,076	1,059	1,095	803	495	311	310	312	188	109
Common Equity	4,191	3,512	2,791	2,203	1,686	1,163	955	517	411	334
Total Cap.	5,504	4,743	4,001	3,090	2,247	1,527	1,310	868	629	463
Cap. Exp.	832	716	662	481	625	249	203	223	132	108
Cash Flow	828	835	648	500	341	262	199	146	107	95.9
Curr. Ratio	2.7	2.2	2.8	2.7	2.2	2.5	2.8	2.0	1.9	1.7
% LT Debt of Cap.	19.5	22.3	27.4	26.0	22.0	20.4	23.6	35.9	29.8	23.5
% Net Inc.of Revs.	5.7	7.1	6.6	6.0	5.7	5.2	4.6	4.3	3.8	4.4
% Ret. on Assets	9.1	11.4	11.3	10.9	10.6	10.8	10.3	10.6	9.9	12.1
% Ret. on Equity	15.3	20.4	19.9	19.1	18.1	18.2	19.2	23.0	19.5	22.9

Data as orig reptd.; bef. results of disc opers/spec. items. Per share data adj. for stk. divs.; EPS diluted. E-Estimated. NA-Not Available. NM-Not Meaningful. NR-Not Ranked. UR-Under Review.

Office: N56W17000 Ridgewood Dr, Menomonee Falls, WI 53051-5660.
Telephone: 262-703-7000.
Website: http://www.kohls.com
Chrmn & CEO: L. Montgomery.
Pres: K. Mansell.

Treas & COO: A. Meier.
EVP & CFO: W. McDonald.
Dirs: J. H. Baker, S. A. Burd, W. Embry, J. Ericson, J. F. Herma, W. S. Kellogg, K. Mansell, A. Meier, L. Montgomery, F. V. Sica, P. M. Sommerhauser, J. Sprieser, R. E. White.

Founded: in 1986.
Domicile: Wisconsin.
Employees: 85,500.
S&P Analyst: Jason N. Asaeda/PMW/JWP

Kroger Co.

Recommendation: HOLD ★★★☆☆
SELL | SELL | HOLD | BUY | BUY

12-Month Target Price: **$16.00**
(as of September 14, 2004)

KR has an approximate 0.11% weighting in the **S&P 500**

Sector: Consumer Staples
Sub-Industry: Food Retail
Peer Group: Food Chain Cos. - Large

Summary: This supermarket operator, with more than 2,500 stores in 32 states, also operates convenience stores, jewelry stores, supermarket fuel centers, and food processing plants.

Quantitative Evaluations

S&P Earnings & Dividend Rank: B+

| D | C | B- | B | B+ | A- | A | A+ |

S&P Fair Value Rank: 1+

| 1 | 2 | 3 | 4 | 5 |
| Lowest | | | | Highest |

Fair Value Calc.: $12.40 (Overvalued)

S&P Investability Quotient Percentile

80%

KR scored higher than 80% of all companies for which an S&P Report is available.

Volatility: Average

| Low | **Average** | High |

Technical Evaluation: Neutral
Since 11/04, the technical indicators for KR have been Neutral.

Relative Strength Rank: Moderate

47

| 1 Lowest | | Highest 99 |

| Price as of 11/12/04: | **$16.30** | 2005E S&P Core EPS: | **$1.44** |

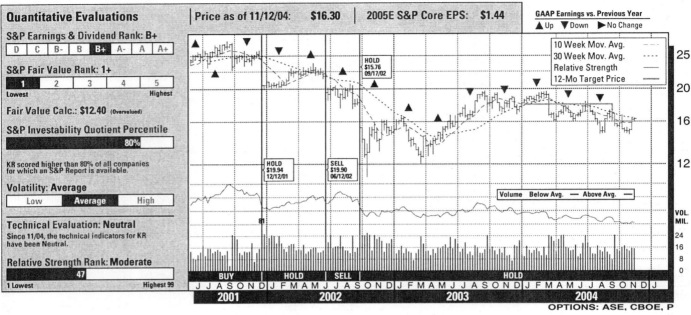

GAAP Earnings vs. Previous Year
▲ Up ▼ Down ▶ No Change

10 Week Mov. Avg.
30 Week Mov. Avg.
Relative Strength
12-Mo Target Price

HOLD $15.76 09/17/02
HOLD $19.94 12/12/01
SELL $19.90 06/12/02

Volume Below Avg. — Above Avg. —

BUY | HOLD | SELL | HOLD
J J A S O N D | J F M A M J J A S O N D | J F M A M J J A S O N D | J F M A M J J A S O N D | J
2001 | 2002 | 2003 | 2004

VOL. MIL.
24
16
8
0

OPTIONS: ASE, CBOE, P

Analyst commentary prepared by Joseph Agnese/PMW/GG

Highlights September 15, 2004

- We expect sales growth in the low to mid-single digits in FY 05 (Jan.), reflecting an increase of 2% to 3% in square footage and low single-digit compara-ble-store sales gains. Total sales should benefit from higher gas prices, and from food cost inflation in the low single digits.

- Despite cost-saving opportunities that we see in areas such as administration, labor, shrinkage, warehousing and transportation, we expect operating margins to narrow, on significant gross margin investments in pricing, promotions and advertising. We believe these investments are needed not only to lure back customers lost during a grocery union strike in Southern California, but also to help the company better compete against lower priced mass merchants.

- Despite the benefits of a share buyback program, we expect operating FY 05 EPS to drop 15%, to $1.26, from FY 04's EPS of $1.48, excluding a negative impact of $1.06 a share from labor disputes and one-time items.

Investment Rationale/Risk September 15, 2004

- We would hold the shares, which we see as having limited downside risk, despite continued intense competition in the food/retail industry. We believe sales and earnings will continue under pressure, as the company increases its focus on reducing prices, improving customer service levels, and increasing product offerings.

- Risks to our recommendation and price target include potential weakness in the economy that would cause consumers to become more price conscious, and increased pricing competition from competitors.

- Our discounted cash flow analysis, which assumes a weighted average cost of capital of 8.5%, leads to intrinsic value of $16 to $18 a share. Based on our expectations of a slow economic recovery, combined with our belief that the current intense competitive environment will continue, we think the shares should trade at 11X our calendar 2005 EPS estimate of $1.42, near the low end of their historical range, leading to an estimated value of $15. Using a blend of our two valuation metrics, we arrive at our 12-month target price of $16.

Key Stock Statistics

S&P Oper. EPS 2005E	1.26	52-week Range	$19.67-14.65
P/E on S&P Oper. EPS 2005E	12.9	12 Month P/E	65.2
S&P Oper. EPS 2006E	1.40	Beta	0.46
Yield (%)	Nil	Shareholders	51,455
Dividend Rate/Share	Nil	Market Cap (B)	$ 12.0
Shares Outstanding (M)	739.1		

Value of $10,000 invested five years ago: **$ 7,164**

Dividend Data

No cash dividends have been paid since 1988.

Revenues/Earnings Data Fiscal year ending January 31

Revenues (Million $)

	2005	2004	2003	2002	2001	2000
1Q	16,905	16,266	15,667	15,102	14,329	13,493
2Q	12,980	12,351	11,927	11,485	11,017	10,289
3Q	—	12,141	11,696	11,382	10,962	10,329
4Q	—	13,034	12,470	12,129	12,692	11,240
Yr.	—	53,791	51,760	50,098	49,000	45,352

Earnings Per Share ($)

	2005	2004	2003	2002	2001	2000
1Q	0.35	0.46	0.40	0.36	0.12	0.24
2Q	0.19	0.25	0.34	0.31	0.25	0.06
3Q	E0.25	0.15	0.33	0.16	0.24	0.15
4Q	E0.43	-0.45	0.50	0.43	0.44	0.29
Yr.	E1.26	0.42	1.56	1.26	1.04	0.74

Next earnings report expected: early-December Source: S&P, Company Reports
EPS Estimates based on S&P Operating Earnings; historical GAAP earnings are as reported.

The Kroger Co.

Recommendation: **HOLD** ★ ★ ★ ☆ ☆   12-Month Target Price: **$16.00** (as of September 14, 2004)

Business Summary September 15, 2004

Kroger is one of the largest U.S. supermarket chains, with 2,532 supermarkets in 32 states as of January 2004. The company's principal operating format is combination food and drug stores (combo stores). In addition to combo stores, KR also operates multi-department stores, price-impact warehouses, convenience stores, fuel centers, jewelry stores, and food processing plants. Total food store square footage exceeded 140 million at the end of FY 04 (Jan.).

Retail food stores are operated under three formats: combination food and drug stores, multi-department stores, and price-impact warehouse stores. Combo stores are considered neighborhood stores, and include many specialty departments, such as whole health sections, pharmacies, general merchandise, pet centers, and perishables, such as fresh seafood and organic produce. Combo banners include Kroger, Ralphs, King Soopers, City Market, Dillons, Smith's, Fry's, QFC, Hilander, Owen's, Jay C, Cala Foods/Bell Markets, Kessel Food Markets, Pay Less, Baker's and Gerbes.

Multi-department stores offer one-stop shopping, are significantly larger in size than combo stores, and sell a wider selection of general merchandise items, including apparel, home fashion and furnishings, electronics, automotive, toys, and fine jewelry. Multi-department formats include Fred Meyer and Fry's Marketplace. Many combination and multi-department stores include a fuel center.

Price-impact warehouse stores offer everyday low prices, plus promotions for a wide selection of grocery and health and beauty care items. Price-impact warehouse stores include Food 4 Less and Foods Co.

KR also operates convenience stores, jewelry stores, and food processing plants. The company's 802 convenience stores offer a limited assortment of staple food items and general merchandise, and, in most cases, sell gasoline. Convenience stores banners include Kwik Shop, Loaf N' Jug Mini Mart, Quik Stop markets, Tom Thumb Food Stores, and Turkey Hill Minit Markets. With 440 jewelry stores, the company is one of the largest U.S. jewelry retailers. Jewelry stores operate banners such as Barclay Jewelers, Fred Meyer Jewelers, Fox's Jewelers, and Littman Jewelers. In addition, KR operates 42 manufacturing plants, consisting of 18 dairies, 11 deli or bakery plants, five grocery products plants, two ice cream plants, three beverage plants, three meat plants, and two cheese plants.

KR offers about 7,800 private label items as an important part of its merchandising strategy. Products are sold in three tiers. Private Selection is a premium quality brand, designed to meet or beat the gourmet or upscale national or regional brands. The banner brand (Kroger, Ralphs, King Soopers, etc.) represents the majority of KR's private label items, and is designed to be equal to or better than the national brand. The FMV (For Maximum Value) brand is the value brand, designed to deliver good quality at an affordable price. About 55% of corporate brand volume is manufactured in the company's plants.

Company Financials Fiscal Year ending January 31

Per Share Data ($)

(Year Ended January 31)	2004	2003	2002	2001	2000	1999	1998	1997	1996	1995
Tangible Bk. Val.	1.18	0.36	NM	NM	NM	NM	NM	NM	NM	-4.98
Cash Flow	2.02	2.93	2.44	2.11	1.86	1.66	1.57	1.33	1.10	1.20
Earnings	0.42	1.56	1.26	1.04	0.74	0.85	0.85	0.67	0.66	0.59
S&P Core Earnings	0.99	1.40	1.12	0.96	NA	NA	NA	NA	NA	NA
Dividends	Nil	Nil	Nil	Nil	Nil	Nil	Nil	Nil	Nil	Nil
Payout Ratio	Nil	Nil	Nil	Nil	Nil	Nil	Nil	Nil	Nil	Nil

Cal. Yrs.	2003	2002	2001	2000	1999	1998	1997	1996	1995	1994
Prices - High	19.70	23.81	27.66	27.93	34.90	18.65	11.87	9.43	6.71	5.43
- Low	12.05	11.00	19.60	14.06	14.87	11.34	8.37	5.84	4.84	3.50
P/E Ratio - High	47	15	22	27	47	22	18	14	11	14
- Low	29	7	16	14	20	13	12	9	8	9

Income Statement Analysis (Million $)

	2004	2003	2002	2001	2000	1999	1998	1997	1996	1995
Revs.	53,791	51,760	50,098	49,000	45,352	28,203	26,567	25,171	23,938	22,959
Oper. Inc.	3,147	3,676	3,567	3,397	3,125	1,410	1,377	1,212	1,134	1,027
Depr.	1,209	1,087	973	907	961	430	380	344	311	278
Int. Exp.	604	600	648	675	652	267	285	300	313	331
Pretax Inc.	770	1,973	1,711	1,508	1,129	713	712	568	510	421
Eff. Tax Rate	59.1%	37.5%	39.0%	41.6%	43.5%	36.9%	37.6%	37.9%	37.4%	36.2%
Net Inc.	315	1,233	1,043	880	638	450	444	353	319	269
S&P Core Earnings	748	1,105	914	816	NA	NA	NA	NA	NA	NA

Balance Sheet & Other Fin. Data (Million $)

	2004	2003	2002	2001	2000	1999	1998	1997	1996	1995
Cash	159	171	161	161	281	122	65.0	Nil	Nil	27.0
Curr. Assets	5,619	5,566	5,512	5,416	5,531	2,673	2,641	2,353	2,107	2,152
Total Assets	20,184	20,102	19,087	18,190	17,966	6,700	6,301	5,825	5,045	4,708
Curr. Liab.	5,586	5,608	5,485	5,591	5,728	3,192	2,944	2,713	2,565	2,395
LT Debt	8,116	8,222	8,412	8,210	8,045	3,229	3,493	3,479	3,490	3,889
Common Equity	4,011	3,850	3,502	3,089	2,683	-388	-784	-1,182	-1,603	-2,154
Total Cap.	13,117	12,072	11,914	11,299	10,728	3,042	2,874	2,629	2,040	1,908
Cap. Exp.	2,000	1,891	2,139	1,623	1,701	923	612	734	726	534
Cash Flow	1,524	2,320	2,016	1,787	1,599	880	824	697	614	547
Curr. Ratio	1.0	1.0	1.0	1.0	1.0	0.8	0.9	0.9	0.8	0.9
% LT Debt of Cap.	61.9	68.1	70.6	72.7	75.0	106.1	121.5	103.2	171.1	203.8
% Net Inc.of Revs.	0.6	2.4	2.1	1.8	1.4	1.6	1.7	1.4	1.3	1.2
% Ret. on Assets	1.6	6.3	5.6	4.9	3.7	6.9	7.3	6.5	6.2	5.8
% Ret. on Equity	8.0	33.5	31.6	30.5	27.7	NM	NM	NM	NM	NM

Data as orig reptd.; bef. results of disc opers/spec. items. Prior to 2000, yrs. ended Dec. 31 of the preceding cal. yr. Per share data adj. for stk. divs. Bold denotes basic EPS (FASB 128)–prior periods restated. E-Estimated. NA-Not Available. NM-Not Meaningful. NR-Not Ranked.

Office: 1014 Vine Street, Cincinnati, OH 45202.
Telephone: 513-762-4000.
Email: investors@kroger.com
Website: http://www.kroger.com
Chrmn & CEO: D.B. Dillon.
Pres & COO: D.W. McGeorge.
Vice Chrmn: W.R. McMullen.

SVP & CFO: J.M. Schlotman.
VP & Treas: S.M. Henderson.
Investor Contact: K. Kelly 513-762-4808.
Dirs: R. V. Anderson, R. D. Beyer, J. L. Clendenin, D. B. Dillon, J. T. LaMacchia, E. M. Liddy, D. W. McGeorge, W. R. McMullen, C. R. Moore, K. D. Ortega, S. M. Phillips, S. R. Rogel.

Founded: in 1883.
Domicile: Ohio.
Employees: 290,000.
S&P Analyst: Joseph Agnese/PMW/GG

Laboratory Corp. of America

Recommendation: **HOLD** ★★★☆☆
SELL SELL HOLD BUY BUY

12-Month Target Price: $48.00
(as of November 15, 2004)

LH has an approximate 0.06% weighting in the **S&P 500**

Sector: Health Care
Sub-Industry: Health Care Services
Peer Group: Diagnostic Test Services

Summary: This clinical laboratory organization offers more than 4,000 different clinical tests through a national network of laboratories.

Quantitative Evaluations

S&P Earnings & Dividend Rank: B-

| D | C | B- | B | B+ | A- | A | A+ |

S&P Fair Value Rank: 4+

| 1 | 2 | 3 | 4 | 5 |
| Lowest | | | | Highest |

Fair Value Calc.: $50.10 (Slightly Undervalued)

S&P Investability Quotient Percentile

91%

LH scored higher than 91% of all companies for which an S&P Report is available.

Volatility: Low

| Low | Average | High |

Technical Evaluation: Bullish
Since 10/04, the technical indicators for LH have been Bullish.

Relative Strength Rank: Strong

71

| 1 Lowest | | Highest 99 |

Price as of 11/15/04: $47.30 | **2004E S&P Core EPS:** $2.38

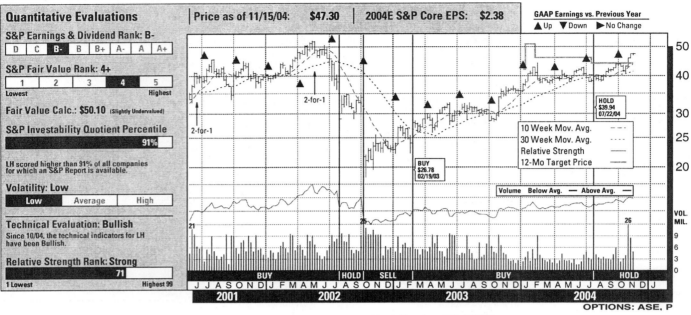

GAAP Earnings vs. Previous Year
▲ Up ▼ Down ► No Change

Analyst commentary prepared by Jeffrey Loo, CFA /CB/BK

OPTIONS: ASE, P

Highlights August 03, 2004

- We expect revenues to increase 6% in 2004, to approximately $3.1 billion, reflecting approximately 1% higher prices, a combined 4% to 5% increase from organic volume growth, a continued shift to more genetic and esoteric tests, and contributions from small acquisitions. We believe the recent Wellpoint contract win in mid-2004 will contribute to revenue growth in 2005, but only moderately in 2004. We also do not expect any significant margin improvement from that contract as it consists of both capitated and fee-for-service volume.

- We see operating margins widening by 140 basis points, to 19.6%, due to improving gross margins and continued improvement in bad debt expense, to 6.25%, as LH further consolidates its billings into a uniform system and aggressively pursues outstanding bills. We expect EBITDA, including income from equity investments, to increase to about 25.7% of net sales.

- We expect 2004 EPS to advance 16%, to $2.58, based on an expected effective tax rate of 41% and taking into account LH's share repurchase program. Our 2005 EPS estimate of $2.77 is based on anticipated mid-single digit sales growth balanced against continued pricing pressures from third-party payers, and modest gross margin and operational improvements. After $0.20 of projected stock option and pension expenses, our 2004 Standard & Poor's Core Earnings estimate is $2.38 a share.

Key Stock Statistics

S&P Oper. EPS 2004E	2.58	52-week Range	$47.48-34.75
P/E on S&P Oper. EPS 2004E	18.3	12 Month P/E	18.8
S&P Oper. EPS 2005E	2.77	Beta	0.13
Yield (%)	Nil	Shareholders	696
Dividend Rate/Share	Nil	Market Cap (B)	$ 6.5
Shares Outstanding (M)	138.3		

Value of $10,000 invested five years ago: **$ 63,120**

Dividend Data

The company's senior credit facilities place certain limits on the payment of dividends.

Investment Rationale/Risk August 03, 2004

- We believe LH's fundamentals are solid, and that it will benefit from an aging population, a better sales mix that includes more genomic and esoteric tests, and increasing awareness of lab testing as a diagnostic tool for the early detection of a multitude of diseases and reducing the overall costs of health care. We see esoteric tests accounting for 31% to 32% of its mix, but we believe LH will continue to face pricing pressure and increased competition for older esoteric tests from regional laboratories. Average revenue per requisition for esoteric tests is currently about $61, more than double the $28 LH receives for routine tests, but we expect esoteric pricing to decline 3% to 4% over the next 18 months. Still, we believe the strong test mix will aid LH as it also continues to face pricing pressures from third-party payers, including Medicare, which imposed a five-year price freeze beginning January 1, 2004.

- Risks to our recommendation and target price include greater than expected pricing pressure from third-party payers, particularly managed care organizations, and prolonged weakness in the job market, which could weigh on utilization.

- Our 12-month target price of $44 is based on our discounted cash flow and relative value analyses, and represents a P/E multiple of 16X our 2005 EPS estimate, in line with the stock's recent valuation, and at a slight discount to the S&P 500. We would hold, but not add to, positions.

Revenues/Earnings Data Fiscal year ending December 31

Revenues (Million $)

	2004	2003	2002	2001	2000	1999
1Q	752.5	712.2	590.0	525.4	462.7	417.9
2Q	784.3	743.7	612.4	549.7	482.4	429.5
3Q	781.5	752.0	655.2	560.9	448.1	428.6
4Q	—	731.5	650.1	563.8	486.1	422.7
Yr.	—	2,939	2,508	2,200	1,919	1,699

Earnings Per Share ($)

	2004	2003	2002	2001	2000	1999
1Q	0.61	0.51	0.47	0.31	0.19	0.06
2Q	0.70	0.60	0.55	0.37	0.24	0.06
3Q	0.66	0.58	0.39	0.30	0.24	0.08
4Q	E0.61	0.54	0.36	0.29	0.15	0.02
Yr.	E2.58	2.22	1.77	1.29	0.81	0.29

Next earnings report expected: mid-February Source: S&P, Company Reports
EPS Estimates based on S&P Operating Earnings; historical GAAP earnings are as reported.

Laboratory Corporation of America Holdings

Recommendation: **HOLD** ★ ★ ★ ☆ ☆   12-Month Target Price: **$48.00** (as of November 15, 2004)

Business Summary August 03, 2004

Laboratory Corporation of America Holdings is the second largest independent U.S. clinical laboratory. Clinical laboratory tests are used by medical professionals in routine testing, patient diagnosis, and in the monitoring and treatment of disease. As of December 2003, LH had 31 primary testing facilities and more than 1,200 service sites consisting of branches, patient service centers, and STAT laboratories that have the ability to perform certain routine tests quickly and report results to the physician immediately.

The company's laboratory services involve the testing of both bodily fluids and human tissues. LH offers more than 4,400 different tests, which consist of routine tests and specialty and niche testing (esoteric). The most frequently administered routine tests include blood chemistry analyses, urinalysis, blood cell counts, pap tests, HIV tests, microbiology cultures and procedures, and alcohol and other substance abuse tests. The company's esoteric tests include testing for infectious diseases, allergies, diagnostic genetics, identity, and oncology. An average of 340,000 specimens were being processed daily as of December 2003, with routine testing results generally available within 24 hours.

One of LH's primary growth strategies is to continue to expand its estoric testing capabilities, which are generally more profitable than routine tests. A component of this strategy is to partner with and enter into various agreements with diagnos-

tic companies that develop esoteric diagnostic tests. The company's esoteric labs include The Center for Molecular Biology and Pathology, located in Research Triangle, N.C.; National Genetics Institute (Los Angeles, CA); Viro-Med Labs (Minneapolis, MN); and DIANON Systems (Stratford, CT).

The company provides testing services to a broad range of health care providers including independent physicians, hospitals, HMOs and other managed care groups, and governmental and other institutions. During 2003, no client accounted for over 4% of net sales. Most testing services are billed to a party other than the physician or other authorized person who ordered the test. Payers other than the direct patient include insurance companies, managed care organizations, Medicare and Medicaid. Commercial clients accounted for 36.0% of requisition volume (37.4% in 2002) and generated an average of $27.07 ($26.27 in 2002) revenue per requisition; managed care clients 40.6% (41.0% in 2002) and $32.47 ($30.45 in 2002); Medicare, Medicaid and Insurance 20.6% (18.7% in 2002) and $34.25 ($31.87 in 2002); and private patients 2.8% (2.9% in 2002) and $118.48 ($119.93).

In March 2004, LH acquired laboratory operations in Poughkeepsie, NY, and Atlanta, GA, from MDS Diagnostic Services. In January 2003, the company acquired DIANON Systems, Inc., for $604.5 million. In July 2002, LH acquired Dynacare Inc., for $496.4 million.

Company Financials Fiscal Year ending December 31

Per Share Data ($)

(Year Ended December 31)	2003	2002	2001	2000	1999	1998	1997	1996	1995	1994
Tangible Bk. Val.	0.27	2.67	0.83	0.09	NM	NM	NM	-12.88	-10.28	-11.38
Cash Flow	3.18	2.47	2.03	1.74	0.19	2.17	-0.89	-1.40	1.55	2.20
Earnings	2.22	1.77	1.29	0.81	0.29	0.50	-2.65	-3.13	-0.08	0.90
S&P Core Earnings	2.04	1.56	1.15	NA	NA	NA	NA	NA	NA	NA
Dividends	Nil	Nil	Nil	Nil	Nil	Nil	Nil	Nil	Nil	0.20
Payout Ratio	Nil	Nil	Nil	Nil	Nil	Nil	Nil	Nil	Nil	22%
Prices - High	37.72	52.37	45.67	45.75	9.68	6.87	10.00	23.43	38.75	39.37
- Low	22.21	18.51	24.87	7.81	3.12	2.81	3.28	5.93	20.31	26.56
P/E Ratio - High	17	30	35	57	33	14	NM	NM	NM	44
- Low	10	10	19	10	11	6	NM	NM	NM	30

Income Statement Analysis (Million $)

	2003	2002	2001	2000	1999	1998	1997	1996	1995	1994
Revs.	2,939	2,508	2,200	1,919	1,699	1,613	1,519	1,608	1,432	873
Oper. Inc.	671	554	472	340	234	212	17.5	174	215	158
Depr.	136	102	104	89.6	84.5	84.2	86.8	84.5	72.4	44.4
Int. Exp.	40.9	19.2	27.0	38.5	41.6	48.7	71.7	71.7	65.5	34.5
Pretax Inc.	540	432	332	208	106	81.5	-161	-188	3.00	55.0
Eff. Tax Rate	40.6%	41.1%	45.0%	46.0%	38.0%	15.6%	NM	NM	NM	45.7%
Net Inc.	321	255	183	112	65.4	68.8	-107	-154	-4.00	30.0
S&P Core Earnings	295	226	162	NA	NA	NA	NA	NA	NA	NA

Balance Sheet & Other Fin. Data (Million $)

	2003	2002	2001	2000	1999	1998	1997	1996	1995	1994
Cash	123	56.4	149	48.8	40.3	22.7	23.3	29.3	16.4	26.8
Curr. Assets	658	597	625	512	500	519	528	722	600	293
Total Assets	3,415	2,612	1,930	1,667	1,590	1,641	1,659	1,917	1,837	1,013
Curr. Liab.	758	229	201	312	246	251	197	253	351	203
LT Debt	361	522	509	354	483	576	650	704	940	564
Common Equity	1,896	1,612	1,085	877	176	154	129	258	412	166
Total Cap.	2,530	2,133	1,594	1,231	1,217	1,257	779	962	1,352	750
Cap. Exp.	83.6	74.3	88.1	55.5	69.4	58.7	34.5	54.1	75.4	48.9
Cash Flow	457	356	287	167	100	109	-44.0	-69.0	68.4	75.0
Curr. Ratio	0.9	2.6	3.1	1.6	2.0	2.1	2.7	2.9	1.7	1.4
% LT Debt of Cap.	14.3	24.4	31.9	28.7	39.7	45.8	83.4	73.2	69.6	75.1
% Net Inc.of Revs.	10.9	10.2	8.3	5.8	3.9	4.3	NM	NM	NM	3.4
% Ret. on Assets	10.7	11.2	10.2	6.9	4.0	4.2	NM	NM	NM	3.8
% Ret. on Equity	18.3	18.9	18.6	14.8	9.1	17.2	NM	NM	NM	19.6

Data as orig. reptd.; bef. results of disc. opers. and/or spec. items. Per share data adj. for stk. divs.; EPS diluted (primary prior to 1998). Prior to 1995, data for National Health Laboratories only. E-Estimated. NA-Not Available. NM-Not Meaningful. NR-Not Ranked.

Office: 358 South Main Street, Burlington, NC 27215.
Telephone: 336-229-1127.
Website: http://www.labcorp.com
Chrmn, Pres & CEO: T.P. Mac Mahon.
COO & EVP: R.L. Novak.

EVP, CFO & Treas: W.R. Elingburg.
EVP & Secy: B.T. Smith.
Dirs: J. Belingard, W. E. Lane, T. P. Mac Mahon, R. E. Mittelstaedt, Jr., J. B. Powell, A. H. Rubenstein, A. G. Wallace, M. K. Weikel.

Founded: in 1971.
Domicile: Delaware.
Employees: 23,000.
S&P Analyst: Jeffrey Loo, CFA /CB/BK

Leggett & Platt

Recommendation: **HOLD** ★ ★ ★ ☆ ☆
SELL | SELL | HOLD | BUY | BUY

12-Month Target Price: $30.00
(as of September 15, 2004)

LEG has an approximate 0.05% weighting in the **S&P 500**

Sector: Consumer Discretionary
Sub-Industry: Home Furnishings
Peer Group: Household Furnishings- Larger (Sales)

Summary: LEG makes a broad line of bedding and furniture components and other home, office and commercial furnishings, as well as diversified products for non-furnishings markets.

Quantitative Evaluations

S&P Earnings & Dividend Rank: B+

| D | C | B- | B | B+ | A- | A | A+ |

S&P Fair Value Rank: 4

| 1 | 2 | 3 | 4 | 5 |
| Lowest | | | | Highest |

Fair Value Calc.: $31.20 (Slightly Undervalued)

S&P Investability Quotient Percentile
97%

LEG scored higher than 97% of all companies for which an S&P Report is available.

Volatility: Average

| Low | Average | High |

Technical Evaluation: Bullish
Since 10/04, the technical indicators for LEG have been Bullish.

Relative Strength Rank: Moderate
62
1 Lowest | Highest 99

| Price as of 11/12/04: | $29.49 | 2004E S&P Core EPS: | $1.38 |

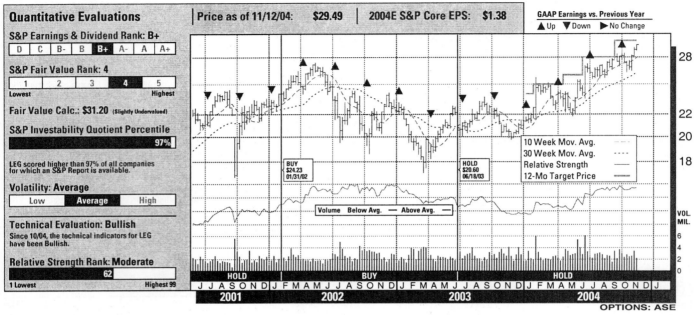

GAAP Earnings vs. Previous Year
▲ Up ▼ Down ► No Change

10 Week Mov. Avg.
30 Week Mov. Avg.
Relative Strength
12-Mo Target Price

Volume Below Avg. — Above Avg.

BUY $24.23 01/31/02
HOLD $20.60 06/18/03

HOLD | BUY | HOLD
J J A S O N D | J F M A M J J A S O N D | J F M A M J J A S O N D | J F M A M J J A S O N D J
2001 | 2002 | 2003 | 2004

OPTIONS: ASE

Analyst commentary prepared by Amy Glynn, CFA /CB/MJ

Highlights November 04, 2004

- We see 2004 revenue growth of approximately 15%, on contributions from acquisitions, combined with comparable-location sales growth in the high single digits. Price increases implemented in early October should also help boost the top line. In 2005, we see organic revenue growth in the mid-single digits. Including our expectations for additional acquisitions in 2005, we see total 2005 revenue growth near 10%.

- Despite rising steel prices, we see operating margins widening in 2004, largely due to the company's productivity initiatives. We see benefits continuing into 2005, especially as LEG focuses on restoring margins in fixtures and displays. We forecast that 2004 EPS will advance about 35%, to $1.42, from $1.05 in 2003. We see 13% EPS growth, to $1.60, in 2005. We believe earnings quality is high. Using Standard & Poor's Core Earnings methodology, we estimate that expensing options and making adjustments for pension accounting would reduce projected 2004 and 2005 EPS by only about $0.04 per year.

- We think LEG will continue to focus on improving cash flow through effective working capital management. We believe restrained capital spending will enhance cash flow and help finance acquisitions, dividends and share repurchases.

Investment Rationale/Risk November 04, 2004

- At almost 18X our 2005 EPS estimate, the stock trades at a premium to most peers. However, based on our expectations for a low to mid-teens long-term growth rate, we think the stock is fairly valued versus peers on a P/E to growth ratio basis. We believe our view of strong free cash flow generation should support the company's average EPS growth goal of 15%, as it affords LEG the flexibility to pursue acquisitions and fund the company's share buyback program. A steadily rising cash dividend, currently yielding 2.1%, boosts the total return. However, with rising raw material costs and our view that a recovery in some of LEG's segments is not yet imminent, we do not see a near-term catalyst, and recommend holding shares.

- Risks to our opinion and target price include an unanticipated change in economic and market conditions; increased competition; fluctuations in raw material, fuel and energy costs and wage rates; litigation risks; and management execution risk.

- Our 12-month target price of $30 is based on our historical P/E multiple model, and is derived by applying a P/E multiple of 19X to our 2005 operating EPS estimate of $1.60. Historically, the stock has traded in a P/E multiple range of 11X to 26X.

Key Stock Statistics

S&P Core EPS 2005E	1.56	52-week Range	$29.49-19.74
S&P Oper. EPS 2004E	1.42	12 Month P/E	20.8
P/E on S&P Oper. EPS 2004E	20.8	Beta	1.03
S&P Oper. EPS 2005E	1.60	Shareholders	13,989
Yield (%)	2.0%	Market Cap (B)	$ 5.6
Dividend Rate/Share	0.60	Shares Outstanding (M)	190.9

Value of $10,000 invested five years ago: **$ 14,262**

Dividend Data Dividends have been paid since 1939

Amount ($)	Date Decl.	Ex-Div. Date	Stock of Record	Payment Date
0.140	Feb. 11	Mar. 11	Mar. 15	Apr. 15 '04
0.140	May. 05	Jun. 14	Jun. 15	Jul. 15 '04
0.150	Aug. 04	Sep. 13	Sep. 15	Oct. 15 '04
0.150	Nov. 04	Dec. 13	Dec. 15	Jan. 14 '05

Revenues/Earnings Data Fiscal year ending December 31

Revenues (Million $)

	2004	2003	2002	2001	2000	1999
1Q	1,187	1,038	1,023	1,053	1,044	887.6
2Q	1,278	1,053	1,115	1,035	1,096	935.2
3Q	1,338	1,157	1,121	1,057	1,130	991.1
4Q	—	1,141	1,013	968.5	1,008	965.1
Yr.	—	4,388	4,272	4,114	4,276	3,779

Earnings Per Share ($)

	2004	2003	2002	2001	2000	1999
1Q	0.32	0.25	0.28	0.23	0.37	0.33
2Q	0.39	0.24	0.35	0.25	0.38	0.36
3Q	0.41	0.26	0.29	0.28	0.34	0.39
4Q	E0.31	0.30	0.25	0.18	0.23	0.37
Yr.	E1.42	1.05	1.17	0.94	1.32	1.45

Next earnings report expected: late-January Source: S&P, Company Reports
EPS Estimates based on S&P Operating Earnings; historical GAAP earnings are as reported.

Leggett & Platt, Incorporated

Recommendation: HOLD ★ ★ ★ ☆ ☆   **12-Month Target Price: $30.00** (as of September 15, 2004)

Business Summary November 05, 2004

Leggett & Platt, founded in 1883, has been known traditionally for designing and making proprietary components and other related products for bedding, furniture, and other furnishings (including commercial fixtures, store displays and shelving) purchased by household, office, institutional and commercial furnishings customers. Non-proprietary products are also produced on company-designed and company-built proprietary machinery.

Residential furnishings accounted for 50.3% of 2003 sales, commercial furnishings 21.8%, aluminum products 10.3%, industrial materials 8.4%, and specialized 9.1%.

Finished products for the home furnishings industry include sleep-related finished furniture and carpet cushioning materials. Some finished furniture products are sold to bedding and furniture makers, which resell the furniture under their own labels to wholesalers or retailers; other finished furniture is sold directly to retailers. Carpet cushioning materials are sold primarily to floor covering distributors, with some direct contract sales.

Outside the home furnishings area, LEG produces a diversified line of components and other products for home, industrial and commercial uses.

In the past 20 years, about two-thirds of the company's sales growth has come through acquisitions. LEG tends to purchase small, private and profitable companies that are usually either complementary to existing businesses, or that allow LEG to secure raw material supply. Over the past 10 years, the average acquisi-

tion target had revenues of $15 million to $20 million. The company has completed only four acquisitions of businesses with annual sales exceeding $100 million.

LEG purchased 10 companies in 2001, with combined annual revenues of about $160 million; and seven companies in 2002, with combined yearly sales of about $70 million. In 2002, it divested three concerns, with annual revenues aggregating about $40 million.

In July 2003, the company purchased the assets of RHC Spacemaster, one of its store fixture competitors. In total, it acquired 15 businesses in 2003, representing about $220 million in combined annualized sales. In addition, the company sold two businesses in 2003: a lumber company and a tubing fabrication facility. Annualized sales associated with the divested businesses were about $23 million.

Additions to property, plant and equipment totaled about $137 million in 2003, and $124 million in 2002. LEG projected 2004 capital spending of about $135 million, primarily for maintaining and expanding production capacity.

The company intends to maintain long-term debt at 30% to 40% of total capital.

In July 2004, LEG projected 2004 organic sales growth of 8% to 11% and full-year sales of $4.8 billion to $5.1 billion. The company forecast 2004 EPS of $1.35 to $1.45.

Company Financials Fiscal Year ending December 31

Per Share Data ($)

(Year Ended December 31)	2003	2002	2001	2000	1999	1998	1997	1996	1995	1994
Tangible Bk. Val.	5.62	5.36	4.81	4.61	4.50	4.59	7.77	3.37	3.46	2.90
Cash Flow	1.89	1.99	1.92	2.18	2.19	1.87	3.25	1.33	1.19	0.99
Earnings	1.05	1.17	0.94	1.32	1.45	1.24	1.08	0.84	0.80	0.70
S&P Core Earnings	1.02	1.11	0.85	NA	NA	NA	NA	NA	NA	NA
Dividends	0.54	0.50	0.48	0.42	0.35	0.31	0.27	0.23	0.19	0.15
Payout Ratio	51%	43%	51%	32%	24%	25%	25%	28%	24%	22%
Prices - High	23.69	27.40	24.45	22.56	28.31	28.75	23.87	17.37	13.43	12.37
- Low	17.16	18.60	16.85	14.18	18.62	16.87	15.75	10.31	8.50	8.31
P/E Ratio - High	23	23	26	17	20	23	22	21	17	18
- Low	16	16	18	11	13	14	15	12	11	12

Income Statement Analysis (Million $)

	2003	2002	2001	2000	1999	1998	1997	1996	1995	1994
Revs.	4,388	4,272	4,114	4,276	3,779	3,370	2,909	2,466	2,059	1,858
Oper. Inc.	520	582	558	660	650	555	467	396	303	251
Depr.	167	165	197	173	149	128	106	92.2	67.1	48.8
Int. Exp.	46.9	42.1	58.8	66.3	43.0	38.5	31.8	30.0	11.5	9.80
Pretax Inc.	315	364	297	419	463	396	333	250	221	190
Eff. Tax Rate	34.7%	35.9%	36.9%	36.9%	37.2%	37.3%	37.5%	38.7%	38.9%	39.1%
Net Inc.	206	233	188	264	291	248	208	153	135	115
S&P Core Earnings	202	221	169	NA	NA	NA	NA	NA	NA	NA

Balance Sheet & Other Fin. Data (Million $)

	2003	2002	2001	2000	1999	1998	1997	1996	1995	1994
Cash	444	225	187	37.3	20.6	83.5	7.70	3.70	6.70	2.70
Curr. Assets	1,819	1,488	1,422	1,405	1,256	1,137	945	763	572	545
Total Assets	3,890	3,501	3,413	3,373	2,978	2,535	2,106	1,713	1,218	1,120
Curr. Liab.	626	598	457	477	432	401	373	293	227	233
LT Debt	1,012	809	978	988	787	574	466	389	192	205
Common Equity	2,114	1,977	1,867	1,794	1,646	1,437	1,174	941	734	625
Total Cap.	3,221	2,865	2,909	2,854	2,502	2,086	1,693	1,384	974	872
Cap. Exp.	137	124	128	170	159	148	119	96.2	93.9	88.5
Cash Flow	373	398	384	437	440	376	314	245	202	164
Curr. Ratio	2.9	2.5	3.1	2.9	2.9	2.8	2.5	2.6	2.5	2.3
% LT Debt of Cap.	31.4	28.2	33.6	34.6	31.5	27.5	27.5	28.1	19.8	23.5
% Net Inc.of Revs.	4.7	5.5	4.6	6.2	7.7	7.4	7.2	6.2	6.6	6.2
% Ret. on Assets	5.6	6.7	5.5	8.3	10.5	10.7	10.9	9.6	11.6	11.3
% Ret. on Equity	10.1	12.1	10.3	15.4	18.8	19.0	19.7	18.1	19.9	19.9

Data as orig reptd.; bef. results of disc opers/spec. items. Per share data adj. for stk. divs.; EPS diluted. E-Estimated. NA-Not Available. NM-Not Meaningful. NR-Not Ranked. UR-Under Review.

Office: No. 1 Leggett Road, Carthage, MO 64836-9649.
Telephone: 417-358-8131.
Email: invest@leggett.com
Website: http://www.leggett.com
Chrmn & CEO: F.E. Wright.
Pres & COO: D.S. Haffner.
VP & CFO: M.C. Flanigan.

VP & Chief Acctg Officer: W.S. Weil.
VP, Secy & General Counsel: E.C. Jett.
Investor Contact: S.R. McCoy 417-358-8131.
Dirs: R. F. Bentele, R. W. Clark, H. M. Cornell, Jr., R. T. Enloe III, R. T. Fisher, K. G. Glassman, D. S. Haffner, J. C. Odom, M. E. Purnell, Jr., F. E. Wright.

Founded: in 1883.
Domicile: Missouri.
Employees: 33,000.
S&P Analyst: Amy Glynn, CFA /CB/MJ

Lehman Brothers Holdings

Recommendation: **BUY** ★★★★
SELL SELL HOLD BUY BUY

12-Month Target Price: $110.00
(as of November 15, 2004)

LEH has an approximate 0.21% weighting in the **S&P 500**

Sector: Financials
Sub-Industry: Investment Banking & Brokerage
Peer Group: Investment Banking/Brokerage - Major

Summary: This major global investment bank serves institutional, corporate and government clients and high net worth individuals.

Quantitative Evaluations

S&P Earnings & Dividend Rank: A-

| D | C | B- | B | B+ | **A-** | A | A+ |

S&P Fair Value Rank: 1-

| **1** | 2 | 3 | 4 | 5 |
| Lowest | | | | Highest |

Fair Value Calc.: $59.30 (Overvalued)

S&P Investability Quotient Percentile

98%

LEH scored higher than 98% of all companies for which an S&P Report is available.

Volatility: Low

| **Low** | Average | High |

Technical Evaluation: Bullish
Since 10/04, the technical indicators for LEH have been Bullish.

Relative Strength Rank: Moderate

60

| 1 Lowest | | Highest 99 |

| Price as of 11/15/04: | **$84.47** | 2004E S&P Core EPS: | **$7.14** |

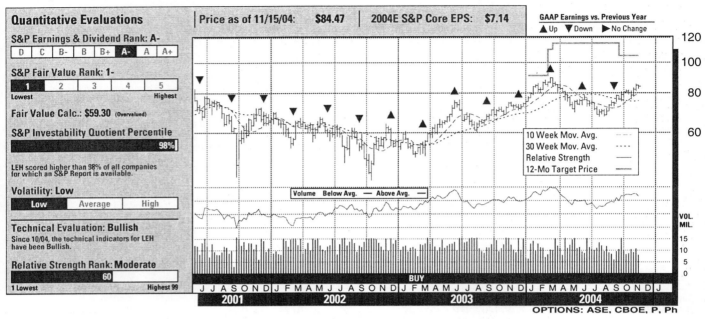

GAAP Earnings vs. Previous Year
▲ Up ▼ Down ► No Change

10 Week Mov. Avg.
30 Week Mov. Avg.
Relative Strength
12-Mo Target Price

Volume Below Avg. — Above Avg.

VOL. MIL.

BUY

J J A S O N D | J F M A M J J A S O N D | J F M A M J J A S O N D | J F M A M J J A S O N D | J
2001 **2002** **2003** **2004**

OPTIONS: ASE, CBOE, P, Ph

Analyst commentary prepared by Robert Hansen, CFA /PMW/GG

Highlights October 15, 2004

- Since its 1994 IPO, the company has expanded aggressively beyond its core fixed income business through organic growth and a focus on employees and clients. We think that LEH is benefiting from strength in its capital markets, equity underwriting, and merger advisory businesses, aided by interest rate volatility, a relatively steep yield curve, and rebounding equity markets.

- Despite a sequential decline in the third quarter of FY 04 (Nov.), we expect continued revenue growth in Investment Banking, Capital Markets, and Client Services in FY 05 (Nov.). We think LEH's recent purchases of several mortgage companies will help securitization margins in FY 05; we estimate that the company originates about 60% of its mortgages internally. In asset management, we see improving fund performance, and think that LEH will seek additional synergies at Neuberger in FY 05.

- We expect strong FY 05 growth in investment banking, equity capital markets and asset management to more than offset a modest decline we see in fixed income. We see Neuberger as slightly accretive in FY 05. We forecast EPS of $7.75 for FY 04 and $7.50 for FY 05, with results in the latter year restricted by higher compensation expenses.

Investment Rationale/Risk October 15, 2004

- We would buy the shares, based on our view of the company's strong competitive position, improving business momentum, and market share gains. In addition, we expect LEH to demonstrate earnings consistency, despite an adverse fixed income cycle, due to what we view as its successful efforts to diversify in this area. We think significant insider ownership (about 30%) contributes to a higher valuation. Finally, we believe that the growing asset management business should also aid valuation.

- Risks to our investment recommendation and target price include increased competition, higher interest rates, and stock and bond market volatility. We note that trading revenues can be highly volatile on a quarterly basis.

- The shares traded recently at nearly 11X our FY 05 EPS estimate, a discount to peers, the S&P 500, and the stock's average multiple of nearly 12X over the past 10 years. Our 12-month target price of $105 is equal to 14X our FY 05 EPS estimate, comparable to peer levels.

Key Stock Statistics

S&P Core EPS 2005E	6.89	52-week Range	$89.72-67.25
S&P Oper. EPS 2004E	7.75	12 Month P/E	11.0
P/E on S&P Oper. EPS 2004E	10.8	Beta	1.84
S&P Oper. EPS 2005E	7.50	Shareholders	22,630
Yield (%)	0.8%	Market Cap (B)	$ 22.8
Dividend Rate/Share	0.64	Shares Outstanding (M)	269.4

Value of $10,000 invested five years ago: **$ 21,929**

Dividend Data Dividends have been paid since 1994

Amount ($)	Date Decl.	Ex-Div. Date	Stock of Record	Payment Date
0.160	Jan. 27	Feb. 11	Feb. 13	Feb. 27 '04
0.160	May. 04	May. 12	May. 14	May. 24 '04
0.160	Aug. 02	Aug. 11	Aug. 13	Aug. 25 '04
0.160	Nov. 03	Nov. 10	Nov. 15	Nov. 23 '04

Revenues/Earnings Data Fiscal year ending November 30

Revenues (Million $)

	2004	2003	2002	2001	2000	1999
1Q	5,125	4,100	4,226	6,752	6,340	4,591
2Q	5,228	4,470	4,347	6,284	6,334	4,932
3Q	5,051	4,463	4,075	5,057	7,359	4,765
4Q	—	4,254	4,133	4,300	6,414	4,701
Yr.	—	17,287	16,781	22,392	26,447	18,989

Earnings Per Share ($)

	2004	2003	2002	2001	2000	1999
1Q	2.21	1.15	0.99	1.39	1.85	0.79
2Q	2.01	1.67	1.08	1.38	1.39	1.05
3Q	1.71	1.81	0.70	1.14	1.69	1.10
4Q	E1.81	1.71	0.69	0.46	1.46	1.14
Yr.	E7.75	6.35	3.47	4.38	6.38	4.08

Next earnings report expected: mid-December Source: S&P, Company Reports
EPS Estimates based on S&P Operating Earnings; historical GAAP earnings are as reported.

Lehman Brothers Holdings Inc.

Recommendation: **BUY** ★★★★★   12-Month Target Price: **$110.00** (as of November 15, 2004)

Business Summary October 18, 2004

Lehman Brothers is an investment bank with operations worldwide. The company generated 68%, 22% and 10% of its FY 03 (Nov.) net revenues in the U.S., Europe, and the Asia Pacific region, respectively. LEH serves institutional, corporate, government and high net worth individual clients through its world headquarters in New York, and regional headquarters in London and Tokyo. The company divides its operations into three segments: Investment Banking; Capital Markets; and Client Services. In FY 03, Investment Banking accounted for 20% of net revenues, Capital Markets accounted for 70%, and Client Services accounted for 10%.

As an investment banker, LEH raises debt and/or equity capital for corporations, governments and other organizations, typically earning a fee representing the difference between what the company buys the offering for from the issuer and what it sells the securities for in the open market. At the end of 2003, LEH increased its share of announced global mergers and acquisitions to 11%.

The Capital Markets segment combines the efforts of the company's sales, trading and research professionals. Results in the Capital Markets segment reflect institutional flow activities and secondary trading and financing activities related to a broad spectrum of equity and fixed income products. In FY 03, LEH expanded its prime brokerage and global equity derivatives businesses. In FY 03, it acquired several mortgage originators, including Aurora Loan Services, allowing for further vertical integration in the company's mortgage platform business. We estimate that LEH originated about 50% of its mortgages internally at the end of FY 03, versus 20% at the end of FY 02.

The Client Services segment encompasses LEH's Private Client Services Group and Asset Management divisions. The Private Client Services Group includes brokers who serve the investment needs of high net worth individuals and mid-sized institutional accounts worldwide. The Asset Management division has grown to over $116 billion in assets under management at the end of FY 03 from $9 billion at the end of FY 02. In October 2003, the company acquired Neuberger Berman Inc., an asset manager, for about $2.8 billion, adding about $67.7 billion in assets. Also in FY 03, LEH acquired Lincoln Capital Management, a manager of $29 billion in fixed income assets, and The Crossroads Group, a manager of about $2 billion in private equity fund-of-funds.

The company seeks to reduce risk through the diversification of its businesses, counterparties and activities in geographic regions by allocating the usage of capital to each of its businesses, establishing trading limits, and setting credit limits for individual counterparties, including regional concentrations.

In December 2002, LEH and other leading investment banks entered into a $1.4 billion agreement to settle allegations that their research was tainted with conflicts of interest and misled investors; the company's share was $80 million. The investment banks also agreed to make organizational changes to reduce conflicts of interest in their research departments.

Company Financials Fiscal Year ending November 30

Per Share Data ($)

(Year Ended November 30)	2003	2002	2001	2000	1999	1998	1997	1996	1995	1994
Tangible Bk. Val.	32.09	34.76	31.90	29.19	25.63	19.10	16.51	15.81	13.44	11.96
Cash Flow	6.18	3.92	4.89	7.08	4.02	2.96	2.72	NA	NA	NA
Earnings	6.35	3.47	4.38	6.38	4.08	2.60	2.36	1.62	0.88	0.41
S&P Core Earnings	5.81	2.13	3.87	NA	NA	NA	NA	NA	NA	NA
Dividends	0.48	0.36	0.28	0.22	0.18	0.15	0.12	0.10	0.10	0.09
Payout Ratio	8%	10%	6%	3%	4%	6%	5%	6%	11%	22%
Prices - High	77.70	69.90	86.20	80.12	42.78	42.50	28.25	16.25	12.31	10.43
- Low	50.15	42.47	43.50	30.31	21.90	11.31	14.25	10.31	7.25	6.87
P/E Ratio - High	12	20	20	13	10	16	12	10	14	26
- Low	8	12	10	5	5	4	6	6	8	17

Income Statement Analysis (Million $)

	2003	2002	2001	2000	1999	1998	1997	1996	1995	1994
Commissions	1,210	1,286	1,091	944	651	513	423	362	450	445
Int. Inc.	9,942	11,728	16,470	19,440	14,251	16,542	13,635	11,298	10,788	6,761
Total Revs.	17,287	16,781	22,392	26,447	18,989	19,894	16,883	14,260	13,476	9,190
Int. Exp.	8,712	10,682	15,712	18,796	13,691	15,781	13,010	10,816	10,405	6,452
Pretax Inc.	2,464	1,343	1,692	2,523	1,589	1,052	937	637	369	193
Eff. Tax Rate	31.0%	27.4%	25.8%	29.6%	28.8%	30.0%	30.9%	34.7%	34.4%	34.7%
Net Inc.	1,699	975	1,255	1,775	1,132	736	647	416	242	126

Balance Sheet & Other Fin. Data (Million $)

	2003	2002	2001	2000	1999	1998	1997	1996	1995	1994
Total Assets	312,061	260,336	247,816	224,720	192,244	153,890	151,705	128,596	115,303	109,947
Cash Items	11,022	6,502	5,850	7,594	7,175	4,238	2,834	2,837	1,819	2,384
Receivables	15,310	13,964	17,057	10,382	12,360	11,965	12,838	9,944	60,694	58,597
Secs. Owned	137,040	119,278	119,362	105,207	89,059	77,000	76,862	61,453	51,322	47,473
Sec. Borrowed	89,870	8,137	12,541	7,242	127,693	96,533	93,284	82,483	67,236	69,853
Due Brokers & Cust.	30,733	11,844	16,636	13,559	16,723	13,690	21,703	14,882	8,824	5,657
Other Liabs.	9,266	6,633	9,895	8,735	10,144	10,913	11,934	11,435	22,780	19,721
Capitalization:										
Debt	44,839	39,388	38,301	36,093	31,401	27,341	20,261	15,922	12,765	11,321
Equity	12,129	8,242	16,218	14,862	5,595	4,505	4,015	3,366	2,990	2,687
Total	58,013	48,330	55,219	51,655	37,684	32,754	24,276	19,796	16,463	14,716
% Return On Revs.	10.6	25.9	26.0	29.3	27.7	3.7	4.3	3.0	1.8	1.4
% Ret. on Assets	0.6	0.4	0.5	0.9	0.7	0.5	0.5	0.3	0.2	NA
% Ret. on Equity	16.2	11.3	7.5	12.6	20.5	15.2	15.5	11.9	7.0	NA

Data as orig. reptd.; bef. results of disc. opers. and/or spec. items. Per share data adj. for stk. divs.; EPS diluted. Pro forma pr. to 1995. E-Estimated. NA-Not Available. NM-Not Meaningful. NR-Not Ranked.

Office: 745 Seventh Avenue, New York, NY 10019.
Telephone: 212-526-7000.
Email: inquiry@lehman.com
Website: http://www.lehman.com
Chrmn & CEO: R.S. Fuld, Jr.
COO: J.M. Gregory.

COO: B.H. Jack.
CFO: D. Goldfarb.
Investor Contact: S.K. Butler 212-526-8381.
Dirs: M. L. Ainslie, J. F. Akers, R. S. Berlind, T. H. Cruikshank, M. J. Evans, R. S. Fuld, Jr., C. Gent, C. Gent, H. Kaufman, J. D. Macomber, D. Merrill.

Founded: in 1983.
Domicile: Delaware.
Employees: 16,188.
S&P Analyst: Robert Hansen, CFA /PMW/GG

Lexmark International

Recommendation: **BUY** ★ ★ ★ ★ ☆
SELL SELL HOLD BUY BUY

12-Month Target Price: $109.00
(as of April 12, 2004)

LXK has an approximate 0.10% weighting in the **S&P 500**

Sector: Information Technology
Sub-Industry: Computer Storage & Peripherals
Peer Group: Printers & Keyboards

Summary: Lexmark develops, manufactures and supplies laser and inkjet printers and associated consumable supplies for the office and home markets.

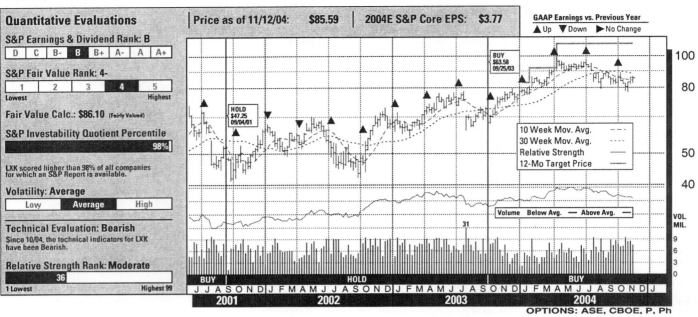

Quantitative Evaluations

S&P Earnings & Dividend Rank: B

| D | C | B- | **B** | B+ | A- | A | A+ |

S&P Fair Value Rank: 4-

| 1 | 2 | 3 | **4** | 5 |
| Lowest | | | | Highest |

Fair Value Calc.: $86.10 (Fairly Valued)

S&P Investability Quotient Percentile
98%

LXK scored higher than 98% of all companies for which an S&P Report is available.

Volatility: Average

| Low | **Average** | High |

Technical Evaluation: Bearish
Since 10/04, the technical indicators for LXK have been Bearish.

Relative Strength Rank: Moderate
36
1 Lowest   Highest 99

Price as of 11/12/04: **$85.59**   2004E S&P Core EPS: **$3.77**

GAAP Earnings vs. Previous Year
▲ Up ▼ Down ► No Change

10 Week Mov. Avg. ---
30 Week Mov. Avg. ·····
Relative Strength ——
12-Mo Target Price ——

Volume Below Avg. · Above Avg. —

VOL. MIL.

OPTIONS: ASE, CBOE, P, Ph

Analyst commentary prepared by Megan Graham-Hackett/CB/GG

Highlights October 19, 2004

- We project that revenues will rise nearly 11% in 2004, following a gain of 9% in 2003. We expect growth in 2004 to continue to be restricted by the impact of a difficult pricing environment, but we see this offset by strong unit growth in new printers, such as All-In-One printer devices, and by higher sales of supplies, aided by growth in LXK's installed base. New photo printers should also aid sales growth in the fourth quarter, as well as in 2005, a year in which we expect revenues to grow 8%.

- We look for gross margins to widen in 2004 to 33.9%, from 32.5% in 2003, as cost improvements offset the effects of continued aggressive pricing in printers. We expect operating margins of about 13.9% in 2004, representing a widening from 2003's 12.5%, on better volumes and despite higher spending in the fourth quarter of 2004 to fund development in new market areas and build brand awareness.

- We project 2004 EPS of $4.21, up from $3.34 in 2003, excluding special items, aided by a lower effective tax rate of 24.0%, versus 26.0% in 2003. Our Standard & Poor's Core Earnings estimate for 2004 is $3.77, reflecting our projection of the impact of stock option and pension expenses.

Key Stock Statistics

S&P Oper. EPS 2004E	4.21	52-week Range	$97.50-71.51
P/E on S&P Oper. EPS 2004E	20.3	12 Month P/E	20.6
S&P Oper. EPS 2005E	4.58	Beta	1.41
Yield (%)	Nil	Shareholders	1,636
Dividend Rate/Share	Nil	Market Cap (B)	$ 11.0
Shares Outstanding (M)	129.1		

Value of $10,000 invested five years ago: **$ 10,494**

Dividend Data

No cash dividends have been paid.

Investment Rationale/Risk October 19, 2004

- We would accumulate the shares. We consider LXK to be the low-cost producer in the printer market. Although we believe the company faces considerable challenges from leading printer maker Hewlett-Packard (HPQ: hold, $20), LXK has been innovative in its product line and owns some important intellectual property, in our view. In addition, we believe LXK could benefit from a joint development agreement with Dell to make printers and cartridges.

- However, although we think that the company has executed well, we see it facing more of a threat from HPQ than in the past. HPQ has reduced its cost structure in its printer unit and introduced a broad range of products. Other risks to our opinion and target price include a deterioration in technology-related spending and competitive pricing pressures.

- Our 12-month target price is $109, based on our discounted cash flow model (which assumes a weighted average cost of capital of 11.4% and five-year free cash flow growth of 10%).

Revenues/Earnings Data Fiscal year ending December 31

Revenues (Million $)

	2004	2003	2002	2001	2000	1999
1Q	1,256	1,108	1,050	999	891.7	787.0
2Q	1,248	1,120	1,058	987.9	893.0	817.3
3Q	1,266	1,157	1,041	1,004	926.6	845.0
4Q	—	1,370	1,207	1,152	1,096	1,003
Yr.	—	4,755	4,356	4,143	3,807	3,452

Earnings Per Share ($)

	2004	2003	2002	2001	2000	1999
1Q	0.91	0.73	0.53	0.60	0.59	0.48
2Q	1.02	0.77	0.67	0.65	0.62	0.55
3Q	1.17	0.79	0.70	0.52	0.50	0.56
4Q	E1.10	1.05	0.90	0.27	0.42	0.73
Yr.	E4.21	3.34	2.79	2.05	2.13	2.32

Next earnings report expected: late-January Source: S&P, Company Reports
EPS Estimates based on S&P Operating Earnings; historical GAAP earnings are as reported.

Lexmark International, Inc.

Recommendation: **BUY** ★★★★☆   12-Month Target Price: **$109.00** (as of April 12, 2004)

Business Summary October 20, 2004

Lexmark International focuses on the monochrome and color workgroup laser printer market; it is a major supplier of these printers, second to Hewlett-Packard (H-P). The overall printer market is estimated by industry analysts to have exceeded $40 billion in 2003, but including multifunction products, Lexmark management estimates this market was $80 billion in 2003, and expects it to grow annually in the low-to-mid-single digits through 2006. LXK has concentrated on the faster growing markets in the printer market, including color inkjet printers and color laser printers. The company (formerly Lexmark International Group), spun off from IBM in 1991, has been trading publicly since November 1995.

Laser printers consist of two main markets: shared workgroup printers, which are typically directly attached to networks; and lower priced desktop printers. In the shared workgroup market, LXK believes it is second in worldwide market share, behind H-P. In the lower priced desktop laser printer market, LXK is one of three leading vendors. Overall, H-P dominates the laser printer market, with about a 50% share.

Growth prospects are believed to be strong for inkjet printers, but pricing is intensely competitive. In the color inkjet printer market, LXK's primary competitors are H-P, Epson and Canon, which together account for about 80% of the worldwide inkjet market. Based on industry data, the company doubled its unit market share over the past several years in this category, to slightly under 20%. It introduced the first desktop color printer priced under $100 with its November 1997 launch of the $99 color inkjet printer, aimed at building brand awareness and installed base.

Expansion of its installed base allows growth in LXK's high margin consumable supplies, helping to protect operating performance in a price competitive marketplace. Consumable supplies are replaced one to three times a year, depending on the type of printer and usage; as a result, demand for laser and inkjet print cartridges grows faster than overall printer shipments. LXK estimates its installed base of laser printers at 5.2 million as of the end of 2003, and 47 million units for inkjet products.

In addition to its core printer business, the company makes supplies for IBM branded printers, after-market supplies for OEM products, and typewriters and typewriter supplies sold under the IBM trademark.

LXK spent heavily to add capacity in the past few years: it completed a new facility in the Philippines in 1999, and built a new inkjet plant in Mexico; existing plants in Scotland and Mexico were also expanded. Capital spending in 2000 was $297 million, followed by a drop to $214 million in 2001. For 2002, the company had capital expenditures of only $112 million and just $94 million in 2003, but plans to spend $200 million in 2004.

International sales, including exports from the U.S., account for over 50% of LXK's sales, with Europe accounting for two-thirds of total international sales.

LXK's 2003 EPS would have been $3.04 instead of the $3.34 reported, if results had included the impact of estimated stock option expense.

Company Financials Fiscal Year ending December 31

Per Share Data ($)

(Year Ended December 31)	2003	2002	2001	2000	1999	1998	1997	1996	1995	1994
Tangible Bk. Val.	17.46	NM	8.25	6.11	6.24	5.21	4.07	3.72	2.74	2.29
Cash Flow	4.48	3.84	2.98	2.80	2.89	2.23	1.60	1.29	0.98	0.81
Earnings	3.34	2.79	2.05	2.13	2.32	1.70	1.08	0.85	0.32	-0.23
S&P Core Earnings	3.04	2.27	1.57	NA	NA	NA	NA	NA	NA	NA
Dividends	Nil	Nil	Nil	Nil	Nil	Nil	Nil	Nil	Nil	NA
Payout Ratio	Nil	Nil	Nil	Nil	Nil	Nil	Nil	Nil	Nil	NA
Prices - High	79.65	69.50	70.75	135.87	104.00	51.00	19.00	13.87	11.18	NA
- Low	56.57	41.94	40.81	28.75	42.09	17.50	9.56	6.68	7.75	NA
P/E Ratio - High	24	25	35	64	45	30	18	16	35	NA
- Low	17	15	20	13	18	10	9	8	24	NA

Income Statement Analysis (Million $)

	2003	2002	2001	2000	1999	1998	1997	1996	1995	1994
Revs.	4,755	4,356	4,143	3,807	3,452	3,021	2,494	2,378	2,158	1,852
Oper. Inc.	743	643	525	548	557	458	352	300	268	242
Depr.	149	138	126	91.2	80.1	75.6	77.5	69.2	99	127
Int. Exp.	12.5	9.00	14.8	12.8	10.7	11.0	10.8	20.9	35.1	61.4
Pretax Inc.	594	496	318	396	459	365	255	202	63.3	50.7
Eff. Tax Rate	26.0%	26.0%	13.9%	28.0%	30.6%	33.5%	36.0%	36.6%	24.0%	12.0%
Net Inc.	439	367	274	285	319	243	163	128	48.1	44.6
S&P Core Earnings	399	298	210	NA	NA	NA	NA	NA	NA	NA

Balance Sheet & Other Fin. Data (Million $)

	2003	2002	2001	2000	1999	1998	1997	1996	1995	1994
Cash	1,196	498	90.7	68.5	93.9	149	43.0	119	151	37.3
Curr. Assets	2,444	1,799	1,493	1,244	1,089	1,020	776	765	716	NA
Total Assets	3,450	2,808	2,450	2,073	1,703	1,483	1,208	1,222	1,143	NA
Curr. Liab.	1,183	1,099	931	979	736	606	548	421	488	NA
LT Debt	149	149	149	149	149	149	57.0	163	175	215
Common Equity	1,643	1,082	1,076	777	659	578	501	540	390	330
Total Cap.	1,792	1,231	1,225	926	808	727	558	704	565	545
Cap. Exp.	93.8	112	214	297	220	102	69.5	145	107	58.1
Cash Flow	588	505	399	377	399	319	241	197	147	99
Curr. Ratio	2.1	1.6	1.6	1.3	1.5	1.7	1.4	1.8	1.5	NA
% LT Debt of Cap.	8.3	12.1	12.2	16.1	18.4	20.5	10.2	23.2	47.9	39.5
% Net Inc.of Revs.	9.2	8.4	6.6	7.5	9.2	8.0	6.5	5.4	2.2	2.4
% Ret. on Assets	14.0	13.9	12.1	15.1	20.0	18.1	13.4	10.8	4.6	NA
% Ret. on Equity	32.2	34.0	29.5	39.7	51.5	45.1	31.3	27.5	7.0	NA

Data as orig reptd.; bef. results of disc opers/spec. items. Per share data adj. for stk. divs.; EPS diluted. E-Estimated. NA-Not Available. NM-Not Meaningful. NR-Not Ranked. UR-Under Review.

Office: 740 West New Circle Road, Lexington, KY 40550.
Telephone: 859-232-2000.
Website: http://www.lexmark.com
Chrmn & CEO: P.J. Curlander.
EVP & CFO: G.E. Morin.
VP & Treas: R.A. Pelini.

VP, Secy & General Counsel: V.J. Cole.
Investor Contact: J. Morgan 859-232-2000.
Dirs: B. C. Ames, T. Beck, F. T. Cary, P. J. Curlander, W. R. Fields, R. E. Gomory, S. R. Hardis, J. F. Hardymon, R. Holland, Jr., M. L. Mann, M. J. Maples, M. D. Walker.

Founded: in 1990.
Domicile: Delaware.
Employees: 11,800.
S&P Analyst: Megan Graham-Hackett/CB/GG

Recommendation: HOLD ★★★ 12-Month Target Price: **$60.00**
(as of October 26, 2004)

LLY has an approximate 0.58% weighting in the **S&P 500**

Sector: Health Care
Sub-Industry: Pharmaceuticals
Peer Group: Ethical Pharmaceuticals - Major

Summary: This major worldwide maker of prescription drugs produces Prozac antidepressant, Zyprexa antipsychotic, diabetic care items, antibiotics, and animal health products.

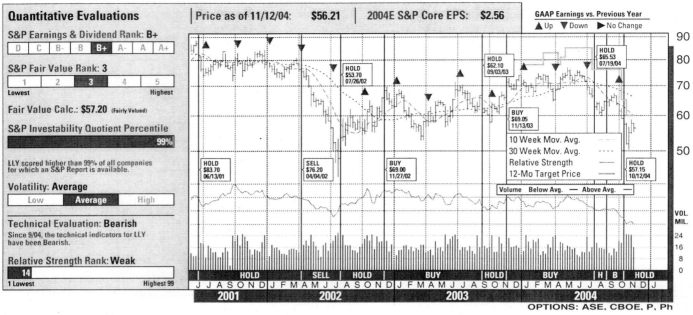

Quantitative Evaluations

S&P Earnings & Dividend Rank: B+

| D | C | B- | B | **B+** | A- | A | A+ |

S&P Fair Value Rank: 3

| 1 | 2 | **3** | 4 | 5 |
| Lowest | | | | Highest |

Fair Value Calc.: $57.20 (Fairly Valued)

S&P Investability Quotient Percentile
99%

LLY scored higher than 99% of all companies for which an S&P Report is available.

Volatility: Average

| Low | **Average** | High |

Technical Evaluation: Bearish
Since 9/04, the technical indicators for LLY have been Bearish.

Relative Strength Rank: Weak
14
1 Lowest   Highest 99

Price as of 11/12/04: **$56.21** | **2004E S&P Core EPS:** **$2.56**

Analyst commentary prepared by H. B. Saftlas/MF/JWP

OPTIONS: ASE, CBOE, P, Ph

Highlights November 01, 2004

- We expect revenues to grow about 12% in 2005, bolstered by gains in key drugs such as Gemzar anticancer, Humalog insulin, Straterra for attention deficit hyperactivity disorder, and Evista osteoporosis treatment. Volume should also be augmented by new products such as Forteo for severe osteoporosis, Yentreve for incontinence, and recently launched Cymbalta antidepressant. We believe Cymbalta has the potential to become a best in class therapy, based on its proven efficacy and favorable side effect profile.

- Despite anticipated heavy new product launch costs and continued aggressive R&D spending, we expect margins to be relatively well maintained, on the anticipated higher volume, productivity enhancements, and cost efficiencies. Boosted by greater contributions from Cialis for erectile dysfunction, other income should be sharply higher.

- We project 2005 operating EPS of $3.15, up from $2.80 expected for 2004. After adjustments from option and pension expenses, we estimate S&P Core EPS of $2.95 for 2005 and $2.56 for 2004.

Investment Rationale/Risk November 01, 2004

- We maintain our hold recommendation, with anticipated benefits from what we consider to be one of the most promising new drug pipelines in the industry balanced against eroding sales of Zyprexa anti-psychotic agent, and uncertainty regarding ongoing Zyprexa patent litigation. Zyprexa, which accounts for an estimated 40% of LLY's profits, has come under considerable competitive pressure from new rivals such as Bristol-Myers Squibb's Abilify and AstraZeneca's Seroquel. Based on IMS data, Zyprexa's share of the new anti-psychotic Rx market shrank to 18% in September 2004, from 25% in November 2003. We also believe that slowing trends in the pharmaceutical industry, partly due to tougher pricing conditions in principal managed care markets and uncertainties with respect to the new Medicare drug benefit, have led to multiple compression in the sector.

- Risks to our recommendation and target price include a possible loss in patent litigation against Zyprexa, growing competitive threats in other lines, and failure to develop and commercialize pipeline products.

- Our 12-month target price of $60 applies a P/E multiple of 19X to our 2005 EPS estimate of $3.15. We think the stock's P/E multiple premium relative to peers is justified by what we see as above-average potential for LLY's new drug pipeline.

Key Stock Statistics

S&P Core EPS 2005E	2.95	52-week Range	$76.95-50.34
S&P Oper. EPS 2004E	2.80	12 Month P/E	23.9
P/E on S&P Oper. EPS 2004E	20.1	Beta	0.36
S&P Oper. EPS 2005E	3.15	Shareholders	54,600
Yield (%)	2.5%	Market Cap (B)	$ 63.6
Dividend Rate/Share	1.42	Shares Outstanding (M)	1131.6

Value of $10,000 invested five years ago: **$ 8,160**

Dividend Data Dividends have been paid since 1885

Amount ($)	Date Decl.	Ex-Div. Date	Stock of Record	Payment Date
0.355	Dec. 15	Feb. 11	Feb. 13	Mar. 10 '04
0.355	Apr. 19	May. 12	May. 14	Jun. 10 '04
0.355	Jun. 28	Aug. 11	Aug. 13	Sep. 10 '04
0.355	Oct. 18	Nov. 10	Nov. 15	Dec. 10 '04

Revenues/Earnings Data Fiscal year ending December 31

Revenues (Million $)

	2004	2003	2002	2001	2000	1999
1Q	3,377	2,889	2,561	2,806	2,451	2,256
2Q	3,556	3,088	2,775	3,034	2,622	2,342
3Q	3,180	3,139	2,786	2,874	2,812	2,585
4Q	—	3,466	2,956	2,829	2,978	2,821
Yr.	—	12,583	11,078	11,543	10,862	10,003

Earnings Per Share ($)

	2004	2003	2002	2001	2000	1999
1Q	0.37	0.38	0.58	0.74	0.77	0.56
2Q	0.60	0.64	0.61	0.76	0.61	0.52
3Q	0.69	0.66	0.63	0.54	0.71	0.67
4Q	E0.73	0.69	0.68	0.54	0.70	0.71
Yr.	E2.80	2.37	2.50	2.58	2.79	2.30

Next earnings report expected: late-January Source: S&P, Company Reports
EPS Estimates based on S&P Operating Earnings; historical GAAP earnings are as reported.

Eli Lilly and Company

Recommendation: **HOLD** ★ ★ ★ ☆ ☆   12-Month Target Price: **$60.00** (as of October 26, 2004)

Business Summary November 01, 2004

Eli Lilly and Co., a leading maker of prescription drugs, is well known for its popular Prozac antidepressant drug. It also produces a wide variety of other ethical drugs and animal health products. The company traces its history to Colonel Eli Lilly, a Union officer in the Civil War, who invented a process for coating pills with gelatin. Foreign operations accounted for 43% of sales in 2003.

LLY's largest selling drug is Zyprexa, a breakthrough treatment for schizophrenia and bipolar disorder that offers clinical advantages over older antipsychotic drugs. Sales of Zyprexa increased 16% in 2003, to $4.3 billion. Zyprexa accounted for 18% of new U.S. antipsychotic prescriptions in September 2004, based on IMS data. Sales of Prozac products ($645 million in 2003) have fallen sharply in recent years, following the loss of patent protection on that drug in August 2001. LLY also offers Symbyax, a combination of Zyprexa and Prozac, to treat bipolar depression. In August 2004, the company launched Cymbalta, a potent antidepressant. Cymbalta works on two body chemicals involved in depression, serotonin and norepinephrine, while most conventional antidepressants affect only serotonin.

Diabetes care products (sales of $2.6 billion in 2003) include Humulin, a human insulin produced through recombinant DNA technology; Humalog, a rapid-acting injectable human insulin analog; Iletin, an animal-source insulin; and Actos, an oral agent for Type 2 diabetes that is manufactured by Takeda Chemical Industries of Japan and co-marketed by Lilly and Takeda.

Other important drugs are Gemzar, a treatment for lung cancer and pancreatic cancer (sales of $1.0 billion); Evista, a drug used to prevent and treat osteoporosis in postmenopausal women ($922 million); and ReoPro, a drug used to prevent adverse effects from angioplasty procedures ($364 million).

LLY also produces anti-infectives such as Ceclor/cefaclor, Vancocin HCI, Keflex and Keftab, and Lorabid; Humatrope, a recombinant human growth hormone; Axid, a medication that reduces excess stomach acid; and Dobutrex for congestive heart failure. Newer lines include Strattera for attention deficit hyperactivity disorder (sales of $370 million), Xigris for sepsis ($160 million), Cialis for erectile dysfunction ($74 million), and Forteo for severe osteoporosis. Animal health products ($727 million) include cattle feed additives, antibiotics and related items.

Research and development spending totaled $2.4 billion in 2003, equal to about 19% of sales, one of the highest R&D to sales ratios in the drug industry. Clinical trials are under way studying new uses and formulations of existing LLY drugs, as well as entirely new compounds. Drugs in the R&D pipeline include Yentreve for urinary incontinence, Exenatide for type II diabetes, ruboxistaurin for diabetic peripheral neuropathy, and Pasrugel oral platelet aggregation inhibitor. The company has R&D alliances with Takeda Pharmaceuticals, Boehringer Ingelheim, ICOS Corp., and others.

Company Financials Fiscal Year ending December 31

Per Share Data ($)

(Year Ended December 31)	2003	2002	2001	2000	1999	1998	1997	1996	1995	1994
Tangible Bk. Val.	8.69	7.37	6.32	5.37	4.49	2.66	2.83	1.87	1.21	0.81
Cash Flow	2.87	2.85	2.91	3.18	2.70	2.31	0.11	1.89	1.64	1.40
Earnings	2.37	2.50	2.58	2.79	2.30	1.87	-0.35	1.39	1.15	1.03
S&P Core Earnings	2.09	1.96	2.17	NA	NA	NA	NA	NA	NA	NA
Dividends	1.34	1.24	1.12	1.04	0.92	0.80	0.74	0.69	0.66	0.63
Payout Ratio	57%	50%	43%	37%	40%	43%	NM	49%	57%	61%
Prices - High	73.89	81.09	95.00	109.00	97.75	91.31	70.43	40.18	28.50	16.56
- Low	52.77	43.75	70.01	54.00	60.56	57.68	35.56	24.68	15.62	11.78
P/E Ratio - High	31	32	37	39	42	49	NM	29	25	16
- Low	22	17	27	19	26	31	NM	18	14	11

Income Statement Analysis (Million $)

	2003	2002	2001	2000	1999	1998	1997	1996	1995	1994
Revs.	12,583	11,078	11,543	10,862	10,003	9,237	8,518	7,347	6,764	5,712
Oper. Inc.	4,050	3,821	4,185	3,996	3,803	3,315	2,968	2,591	2,536	2,227
Depr.	549	493	455	436	440	490	510	544	554	432
Int. Exp.	61.0	79.7	147	182	242	181	234	325	324	129
Pretax Inc.	3,262	3,458	3,552	3,859	3,245	2,665	510	2,032	1,756	1,699
Eff. Tax Rate	21.5%	21.7%	20.9%	20.8%	21.5%	21.4%	175.5%	25.0%	26.1%	30.2%
Net Inc.	2,561	2,708	2,809	3,058	2,547	2,096	-385	1,524	1,307	1,185
S&P Core Earnings	2,261	2,128	2,359	NA	NA	NA	NA	NA	NA	NA

Balance Sheet & Other Fin. Data (Million $)

	2003	2002	2001	2000	1999	1998	1997	1996	1995	1994
Cash	2,756	1,946	2,702	4,115	3,700	1,496	1,948	955	1,084	747
Curr. Assets	8,759	7,804	6,939	7,943	7,056	5,407	5,321	3,891	4,139	3,962
Total Assets	21,678	19,042	16,434	14,691	12,825	12,596	12,577	14,307	14,413	14,507
Curr. Liab.	5,551	5,064	5,203	4,961	3,935	4,607	4,192	4,222	4,967	5,670
LT Debt	4,688	4,358	3,132	2,634	2,812	2,186	2,326	2,517	2,593	2,126
Common Equity	9,765	8,274	7,104	8,682	5,013	4,430	4,645	6,100	5,433	5,356
Total Cap.	14,453	12,632	10,236	11,407	7,962	6,864	7,187	8,993	8,321	7,670
Cap. Exp.	1,707	1,131	884	678	528	420	366	444	551	577
Cash Flow	3,109	3,201	3,264	3,494	2,986	2,586	125	2,068	1,861	1,617
Curr. Ratio	1.6	1.5	1.3	1.6	1.8	1.2	1.3	0.9	0.8	0.7
% LT Debt of Cap.	32.4	34.5	30.6	23.1	35.3	31.8	32.4	28.0	31.2	27.7
% Net Inc.of Revs.	20.4	24.4	24.3	28.2	25.5	22.7	NM	20.7	19.3	20.7
% Ret. on Assets	12.6	15.3	18.1	22.2	20.0	16.7	NM	10.6	9.0	9.8
% Ret. on Equity	28.4	35.2	42.7	44.7	53.9	46.2	NM	26.4	24.2	23.9

Data as orig reptd.; bef. results of disc opers/spec. items. Per share data adj. for stk. divs. Bold denotes primary EPS - prior periods restated. E-Estimated. NA-Not Available. NM-Not Meaningful. NR-Not Ranked. UR-Under Review.

Office: Lilly Corporate Center, Indianapolis, IN 46285.
Telephone: 317-276-2000.
Website: http://www.lilly.com
Chrmn, Pres & CEO: S. Taurel.
EVP & CFO: C.E. Golden.

SVP & General Counsel: R.A. Armitage.
Investor Contact: R. Smith 317-277-1302.
Dirs: S. C. Beering, W. F. Bischoff, M. S. Feldstein, G. M. Fisher, A. G. Gilman, C. E. Golden, K. N. Horn, E. R. Marram, F. G. Prendergast, J. Rose, K. P. Seifert, S. Taurel.

Founded: in 1876.
Domicile: Indiana.
Employees: 46,100.
S&P Analyst: H. B. Saftlas/MF/JWP

Limited Brands

Recommendation: **HOLD** ★★★☆☆
SELL SELL HOLD BUY BUY
(as of October 12, 2004)

12-Month Target Price: $25.00

LTD has an approximate 0.12% weighting in the **S&P 500**

Sector: Consumer Discretionary
Sub-Industry: Apparel Retail
Peer Group: Women's Apparel Retailers

Summary: This specialty retailer of women's apparel (formerly The Limited) operates nearly 4,000 apparel and specialty stores.

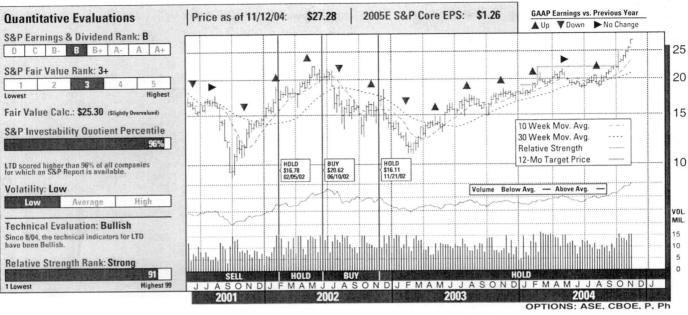

Quantitative Evaluations

| Price as of 11/12/04: | **$27.28** | 2005E S&P Core EPS: | **$1.26** |

S&P Earnings & Dividend Rank: B
D C B- **B** B+ A- A A+

S&P Fair Value Rank: 3+
1 2 **3** 4 5
Lowest   Highest

Fair Value Calc.: $25.30 (Slightly Overvalued)

S&P Investability Quotient Percentile
96%

LTD scored higher than 96% of all companies for which an S&P Report is available.

Volatility: Low
Low Average High

Technical Evaluation: Bullish
Since 8/04, the technical indicators for LTD have been Bullish.

Relative Strength Rank: Strong
91
1 Lowest   Highest 99

GAAP Earnings vs. Previous Year
▲ Up ▼ Down ► No Change

HOLD $16.78 02/05/02
BUY $20.62 06/10/02
HOLD $16.11 11/21/02

10 Week Mov. Avg.
30 Week Mov. Avg.
Relative Strength
12-Mo Target Price

Volume Below Avg. — Above Avg. —

VOL. MIL.

SELL | HOLD | BUY | HOLD
J J A S O N D J F M A M J J A S O N D J F M A M J J A S O N D J F M A M J J A S O N D J
2001   2002   2003   2004

OPTIONS: ASE, CBOE, P, Ph

Analyst commentary prepared by Marie Driscoll, CFA /CB/BK

Highlights October 18, 2004

- We forecast that sales will grow in the mid-single digits in FY 05 (Jan.), mostly due to same-store sales gains; we expect little change in selling space. We look for weak apparel sales at Express and Limited to be outweighed by increases at Victoria's Secret and Bath & Body Works.

- A repositioning in apparel that began in September 2003 includes key item promotions, and the adoption of brand-like behavior. We expect flat apparel sales, due to easy comparisons, with modestly improving profitability. However, we see LTD's future lying in its non-apparel brands. We think a turnaround at Bath & Body Works is in its early stages, and will gain traction; we see productivity and profitability being restored in FY 05 and FY 06. We view Victoria's Secret as the jewel in LTD's portfolio, and we believe the brand will continue to provide growth opportunities via line extensions, sub-brands such as the Pink product line, and additional fragrance launches.

- We project widening gross margins, as we see the non-apparel (higher margin) business growing faster than apparel, and expect a slight leveraging of SG&A costs with productivity gains. Our FY 05 EPS estimate is $1.35, up from FY 04 operating EPS of $1.11.

Investment Rationale/Risk October 18, 2004

- We regard the shares as fairly valued. The stock is trading at about a 5% discount to the S&P 500, based on our FY 06 EPS estimate of $1.65. We expect the discount to continue, due to what we see as the maturity of LTD's store base. We expect improved profitability and store productivity, but we see no near-term catalyst for stock outperformance. We believe the Express Design Studio and a new wear-to-work assortment at Express are attempts to elevate and reposition the Express brand. While we are encouraged by these efforts, we think that a turnaround in apparel will take a number of years. The dividend was boosted 20% earlier this year, and provides about a 2.1% yield.

- Risks to our recommendation and target price include fashion and inventory risk, trends in consumer spending, and same-store sales trends.

- LTD's historical forward P/E multiple of 15.7X implies a $26 target price, as does the peer forward multiple of 15.4X. Our DCF valuation, assuming a double digit decline in free cash flow in FY 05, followed by modest growth in FY 06 and beyond, derives a $17 intrinsic value for LTD shares. Our 12-month target price of $25 is derived from a blend of historical, relative and intrinsic valuation methodologies.

Key Stock Statistics

S&P Core EPS 2006E	1.57	52-week Range	$27.32-16.68
S&P Oper. EPS 2005E	1.35	12 Month P/E	18.6
P/E on S&P Oper. EPS 2005E	20.2	Beta	1.47
S&P Oper. EPS 2006E	1.65	Shareholders	77,000
Yield (%)	1.8%	Market Cap (B)	$ 12.8
Dividend Rate/Share	0.48	Shares Outstanding (M)	469.4

Value of $10,000 invested five years ago: **$ 15,082**

Dividend Data Dividends have been paid since 1970

Amount ($)	Date Decl.	Ex-Div. Date	Stock of Record	Payment Date
0.100	Nov. 10	Dec. 03	Dec. 05	Dec. 16 '03
0.120	Feb. 26	Mar. 03	Mar. 05	Mar. 16 '04
0.120	May. 17	Jun. 02	Jun. 04	Jun. 15 '04
0.120	Aug. 19	Sep. 01	Sep. 03	Sep. 14 '04

Revenues/Earnings Data Fiscal year ending January 31

Revenues (Million $)

	2005	2004	2003	2002	2001	2000
1Q	1,978	1,842	2,027	2,127	2,108	2,105
2Q	2,211	2,014	2,113	2,192	2,263	2,268
3Q	—	1,847	1,983	1,906	2,169	2,064
4Q	—	3,231	2,966	3,138	3,522	3,287
Yr.	—	8,934	8,445	9,363	10,105	9,723

Earnings Per Share ($)

	2005	2004	2003	2002	2001	2000
1Q	0.19	0.19	0.10	0.07	0.14	0.07
2Q	0.31	0.19	0.16	0.17	0.17	0.11
3Q	E0.05	0.25	0.03	-0.21	0.11	0.09
4Q	E1.02	0.74	0.66	0.75	0.54	0.71
Yr.	E1.35	1.36	0.95	0.94	0.96	1.00

Next earnings report expected: mid-November Source: S&P, Company Reports
EPS Estimates based on S&P Operating Earnings; historical GAAP earnings are as reported.

Limited Brands

Recommendation: **HOLD** ★ ★ ★ ☆ ☆   12-Month Target Price: **$25.00** (as of October 12, 2004)

Business Summary October 18, 2004

Limited Brands (formerly The Limited) is a specialty retailer that conducts its business in three primary segments: Victoria's Secret, a women's intimate apparel, personal care products and accessories retail brand; Bath & Body Works, a personal care and home fragrance products retail brand; and the Apparel segment, which operates Express and Limited Stores. At January 31, 2004, the store base consisted of 562 Express Women, 290 Express Men, 104 Express Dual Gender, 341 The Limited, 1,009 Victoria's Secret, and 1,604 Bath & Body Works locations. LTD also operates one Henri Bendel store in New York City, featuring fashions for sophisticated, higher-income women. The company adopted its current name in May 2002.

The Apparel businesses accounted for 30% of total sales in FY 04 (Jan.), Victoria's Secret 43%, and Bath & Body Works 22%.

Victoria's Secret is the leading specialty retailer of women's intimate apparel and related products. Victoria's Secret Beauty, with FY 04 sales of $512 million, retails high quality beauty products through 87 stand-alone stores, as well as 414 side-by-side locations and niches in Victoria's Secret lingerie stores. It also sells products directly through its catalog and website. Bath & Body Works is the leading specialty retailer of personal care products.

Express, launched in 1980, seeks to offer cutting edge style for casual, profes-

sional and urban customer, both men and women. Limited stores focus on sophisticated sportswear for modern American women.

The company also owns Mast Industries, Inc., a contract manufacturer and apparel importer that purchases merchandise for LTD's retail brands and certain third parties. In FY 04, about 35% of merchandise purchases were sourced through Mast. Mast had external sales of $445 million in 2003.

LTD has moved to boost shareholder value and rebuild a franchise in its women's businesses. It spun off and sold various businesses, including Abercrombie & Fitch (ANF); Limited Too (TOO); and a 77% interest in Galyan's Trading Co., Lane Bryant, and Lerner, New York. LTD has also downsized its underperforming women's apparel units, closing more than 1,000 stores in the past five years. In March FY 05, the company repurchased 51 million common shares via a modified Dutch Auction at a $19.75 purchase price.

The company has projected FY 05 capital spending of $500 million to $550 million, with the majority related to remodeling and improving existing stores. LTD is focusing on optimizing its real estate in the 160 leading U.S. malls, the introduction of the Pink line at Victoria's Secret and the Express Design Studio, and a new wear-to-work assortment at Express.

Company Financials Fiscal Year ending January 31

Per Share Data ($)

(Year Ended January 31)	2004	2003	2002	2001	2000	1999	1998	1997	1996	1995
Tangible Bk. Val.	6.78	5.93	6.40	5.43	5.00	4.92	3.75	3.55	4.50	3.86
Cash Flow	1.90	1.48	1.83	1.58	1.61	4.76	0.97	1.29	1.74	1.00
Earnings	1.36	0.95	0.94	0.96	1.00	4.16	0.40	0.77	1.34	0.63
S&P Core Earnings	1.03	0.94	0.80	0.91	NA	NA	NA	NA	NA	NA
Dividends	0.40	0.30	0.30	0.30	0.30	0.26	0.24	0.20	0.20	0.18
Payout Ratio	29%	32%	32%	31%	30%	6%	61%	26%	15%	29%

Cal. Yrs.	2003	2002	2001	2000	1999	1998	1997	1996	1995	1994
Prices - High	18.46	22.34	21.29	27.87	25.31	18.25	12.87	11.25	11.62	11.18
- Low	10.88	12.53	9.00	14.43	13.75	10.25	8.25	7.62	7.93	8.37
P/E Ratio - High	14	24	23	29	25	4	33	15	9	18
- Low	8	13	10	15	14	2	21	10	6	13

Income Statement Analysis (Million $)

	2004	2003	2002	2001	2000	1999	1998	1997	1996	1995
Revs.	8,934	8,445	9,363	10,105	9,766	9,347	9,189	8,645	7,881	7,545
Oper. Inc.	1,246	1,148	1,025	1,148	1,169	984	1,006	938	897	1,067
Depr.	28.3	276	277	272	272	286	313	290	286	268
Int. Exp.	62.0	30.0	34.0	58.0	78.0	69.0	69.0	75.4	77.0	65.4
Pretax Inc.	1,166	843	968	828	905	2,428	457	675	1,185	744
Eff. Tax Rate	38.5%	40.5%	39.8%	40.0%	41.0%	12.8%	40.0%	35.7%	18.8%	39.8%
Net Inc.	717	496	519	428	461	2,054	217	434	962	448
S&P Core Earnings	540	492	352	406	NA	NA	NA	NA	NA	NA

Balance Sheet & Other Fin. Data (Million $)

	2004	2003	2002	2001	2000	1999	1998	1997	1996	1995
Cash	3,129	2,262	1,375	563	817	1,222	1,098	313	1,646	243
Curr. Assets	4,433	3,606	2,682	2,068	2,285	2,318	2,031	1,545	2,800	2,548
Total Assets	7,873	7,246	4,719	4,088	4,126	4,550	4,301	4,120	5,267	4,570
Curr. Liab.	1,392	1,259	1,319	1,000	1,236	1,248	1,093	907	717	798
LT Debt	648	547	250	400	400	550	650	650	650	650
Common Equity	5,266	4,860	2,744	2,317	2,147	2,233	2,044	1,923	3,201	2,761
Total Cap.	6,048	5,532	3,171	2,860	2,666	2,894	2,797	2,810	4,148	3,717
Cap. Exp.	293	306	337	446	375	347	405	409	374	320
Cash Flow	1,000	772	796	700	733	2,340	530	724	1,248	716
Curr. Ratio	3.2	2.9	2.0	2.1	1.8	1.9	1.9	1.7	3.9	3.2
% LT Debt of Cap.	10.7	9.9	7.9	14.0	15.0	19.0	23.2	23.1	15.7	17.5
% Net Inc.of Revs.	8.0	5.9	5.5	4.2	4.7	22.0	2.4	5.0	12.2	5.9
% Ret. on Assets	9.5	8.0	11.8	10.4	10.7	46.4	5.2	9.2	19.6	10.3
% Ret. on Equity	14.2	13.0	20.5	19.2	21.4	96.0	10.9	16.9	32.3	17.2

Data as orig reptd.; bef. results of disc opers/spec. items. Per share data adj. for stk. divs.; EPS diluted. E-Estimated. NA-Not Available. NM-Not Meaningful. NR-Not Ranked. UR-Under Review.

Office: Three Limited Parkway, Columbus, OH 43216.
Telephone: 614-415-7000.
Website: http://www.limited.com
Chrmn & CEO: L.H. Wexner.
Vice Chrmn & COO: L.A. Schlesinger.

EVP & CFO: V.A. Hailey.
Dirs: E. M. Freedman, E. G. Gee, V. A. Hailey, J. L. Heskett, D. James, D. T. Kollat, L. A. Schlesinger, D. B. Shackelford, A. R. Tessler, L. H. Wexner, A. S. Wexner, R. Zimmerman.

Founded: in 1967.
Domicile: Delaware.
Employees: 111,100.
S&P Analyst: Marie Driscoll, CFA /CB/BK

Lincoln National Corp.

Recommendation: **BUY** ★★★★☆ SELL SELL HOLD BUY BUY

12-Month Target Price: $52.00
(as of May 05, 2004)

LNC has an approximate 0.07% weighting in the **S&P 500**

Sector: Financials
Sub-Industry: Life & Health Insurance
Peer Group: Life Insurance/Annuities - Larger

Summary: LNC offers annuities, life insurance, mutual funds, asset management and related advisory services to affluent individuals.

Quantitative Evaluations

S&P Earnings & Dividend Rank: B+

| D | C | B- | B | B+ | A- | A | A+ |

S&P Fair Value Rank: 1+

| 1 | 2 | 3 | 4 | 5 |
Lowest ——— Highest

Fair Value Calc.: $38.40 (Overvalued)

S&P Investability Quotient Percentile

98%

LNC scored higher than 98% of all companies for which an S&P Report is available.

Volatility: Average

| Low | Average | High |

Technical Evaluation: Neutral
Since 11/04, the technical indicators for LNC have been Neutral.

Relative Strength Rank: Moderate

41
1 Lowest ——— Highest 99

| Price as of 11/12/04: | $46.11 | 2004E S&P Core EPS: | $3.84 |

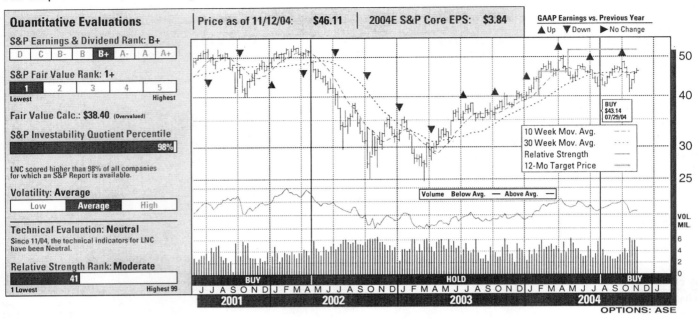

GAAP Earnings vs. Previous Year
▲ Up ▼ Down ► No Change

BUY $43.14 07/29/04

10 Week Mov. Avg.
30 Week Mov. Avg.
Relative Strength
12-Mo Target Price

Volume Below Avg. — Above Avg.

BUY   HOLD   BUY
J J A S O N D J F M A M J J A S O N D J F M A M J J A S O N D J F M A M J J A S O N D J
2001   2002   2003   2004

VOL. MIL.
OPTIONS: ASE

Analyst commentary prepared by Gregory Simcik, CFA /PMW/JWP

Highlights August 10, 2004

- We expect double-digit growth in operating earnings for the retirement segment in 2004, on higher expense assessments and net investment income, what we see as the attractiveness of guaranteed minimum benefits to consumers, and containment of benefits and operating expenses. We estimate low double-digit gains for operating earnings in the life segment, on modest growth in operating revenues and a decline in benefits and operating expenses.

- We expect operating earnings of the smaller investment management segment to climb nearly 33% in 2004, on higher fees and significant economies of scale. We see operating earnings of the equally small U.K. segment remaining subdued, primarily due to higher expenses.

- We forecast that total operating EPS will grow 18% in 2004, to $3.88, excluding $0.06 in one-time benefits related to a mortgage interest credit. Our operating estimate excludes $0.07 in net charges related to realized losses and restructuring, partly offset by a gain on business sale. We estimate that operating EPS will advance 11% in 2005, to $4.32, on 2.8% fewer shares. Our Standard and Poor's Core EPS estimates for 2004 and 2005 are $3.84 and $4.28, respectively, reflecting estimated pension expense.

Investment Rationale/Risk August 10, 2004

- We recommend accumulating the shares, which we expect to provide a total return that significantly exceeds our projected total return for the S&P 500. However, we think that the stock offers above-average risk, due to uncertainties associated with new guaranteed minimum benefits and sensitivity to equity markets.

- Risks to our recommendation and target price include dynamic hedging for guaranteed minimum benefits, sensitivity of operating results and reserves to volatility in the equity markets, difficulties in obtaining reinsurance for some products, currency risk with respect to the British pound, and changes in tax laws that potentially lessen the competitiveness of some products versus other investment vehicles.

- Our 12-month target price of $52 is based on a trailing P/E multiple of 12.9X our 12-month forward operating EPS estimate of $4.06, a discount to the peer group average historical multiple of 13.7X, to account for recent market volatility.

Key Stock Statistics

S&P Core EPS 2005E	4.28	52-week Range	$50.38-37.35
S&P Oper. EPS 2004E	3.88	12 Month P/E	11.3
P/E on S&P Oper. EPS 2004E	11.9	Beta	1.21
S&P Oper. EPS 2005E	4.32	Shareholders	10,058
Yield (%)	3.2%	Market Cap (B)	$ 8.1
Dividend Rate/Share	1.46	Shares Outstanding (M)	174.6

Value of $10,000 invested five years ago: **$ 11,270**

Dividend Data Dividends have been paid since 1920

Amount ($)	Date Decl.	Ex-Div. Date	Stock of Record	Payment Date
0.350	Mar. 11	Apr. 06	Apr. 09	May. 01 '04
0.350	May. 13	Jul. 07	Jul. 09	Aug. 01 '04
0.350	Sep. 09	Oct. 06	Oct. 08	Nov. 01 '04
0.365	Nov. 11	Jan. 06	Jan. 10	Feb. 01 '05

Revenues/Earnings Data Fiscal year ending December 31

Revenues (Million $)

	2004	2003	2002	2001	2000	1999
1Q	1,259	1,099	1,126	1,699	1,669	1,675
2Q	1,359	1,213	1,145	1,599	1,693	1,678
3Q	1,406	1,269	1,141	1,590	1,716	1,642
4Q	—	1,327	1,189	1,504	1,774	1,808
Yr.	—	5,284	4,635	6,381	6,852	6,804

Earnings Per Share ($)

	2004	2003	2002	2001	2000	1999
1Q	0.86	0.23	0.49	0.85	0.87	0.71
2Q	1.04	0.80	0.31	0.80	0.84	0.73
3Q	1.12	0.74	-0.68	0.61	0.71	0.66
4Q	E1.00	1.08	0.35	0.88	0.76	0.18
Yr.	E3.88	2.85	0.49	3.13	3.19	2.30

Next earnings report expected: early-February Source: S&P, Company Reports
EPS Estimates based on S&P Operating Earnings; historical GAAP earnings are as reported.

Lincoln National Corporation

Recommendation: **BUY** ★ ★ ★ ★ ☆   12-Month Target Price: **$52.00** (as of May 05, 2004)

Business Summary August 10, 2004

Lincoln National is a holding company with subsidiaries that operate multiple insurance and investment management businesses. According to the April 2003 editions of the Fortune 500 Largest U.S. Corporations and Fortune 500 by Industry Rankings, LNC is the 44th largest U.S. corporation, based on assets, and the eighth largest U.S. stock company in the Fortune 500 Life/Health Industry Ranking.

Operations are divided into four business segments: retirement (44% of income before federal income taxes and cumulative effect of accounting changes in 2003), life insurance (35%), investment management (3.3%), and Lincoln UK (6.2%). Primary operating subsidiaries include The Lincoln National Life Insurance Company, First Penn-Pacific Life Insurance Company, Lincoln Life & Annuity Company of New York, Delaware Management Holdings, Inc., Lincoln National (UK) plc, Lincoln Financial Advisors (LFA), a retailing distribution unit, and Lincoln Financial Distributors (LFD), a wholesaling distribution unit. Other operations, which includes results from LFA and LFD, corporate investment income, interest expense, some overhead expenses, and amortization of the gain on the sale of the reinsurance business, accounted for 11% of income before federal income taxes and the cumulative effect of accounting changes in 2003.

The retirement segment provides fixed and variable annuities to the individual annuities and employer-sponsored markets. The life insurance segment targets the affluent market, and underwrites and sells universal life, variable universal life, interest-sensitive whole life, corporate-owned life insurance (COLI), term-life insurance, and linked products such as universal life linked with long-term care benefits.

The Investment management segment offers retail and institutional mutual funds, separate and managed accounts, 529 college savings plans, and retirement plans and services, including 401(k) plans and administration services. Lincoln UK is licensed to do business throughout the U.K., and focuses primarily on retaining its existing customers and managing expenses for a closed block of business in the U.K., including accepting new deposits from and offering new products to existing policyholders. Offerings consist principally of unit-linked life and pension products, similar to U.S. variable life and annuity products.

In December 2001, Swiss Re acquired the company's reinsurance operations for $2.0 billion. LNC retained the capital supporting the operations, and the transaction freed up about $100 million in net retained capital. The sale included a series of indemnity reinsurance transactions, as well as the sale of certain stock companies and the recognition of a gain with respect to the reinsurance agreements that is being amortized into earnings over a period of 15 years. Following the transaction, the company paid $295 million to Swiss Re to settle disputed matters and to release LNC from further underwriting risk associated with the reinsurance business sold.

In December 2003, the company said it had received inquiries from regulators concerning the trading practices and procedures of its variable annuity and mutual fund operations. LNC added that it was not aware of any matters that might result in liabilities stemming from the probes.

Company Financials Fiscal Year ending December 31

Per Share Data ($)

(Year Ended December 31)	2003	2002	2001	2000	1999	1998	1997	1996	1995	1994
Tangible Bk. Val.	18.74	15.62	14.10	11.06	5.59	10.17	19.35	15.97	16.23	13.67
Oper. Earnings	NA	2.56	3.56	3.27	2.32	2.61	-0.25	2.08	1.48	1.88
Earnings	2.85	0.49	3.13	3.19	2.30	2.51	0.11	2.46	2.31	1.69
S&P Core Earnings	4.36	1.16	3.10	NA	NA	NA	NA	NA	NA	NA
Dividends	1.34	1.28	1.22	1.16	1.10	1.30	0.98	0.92	0.86	0.82
Payout Ratio	47%	NM	39%	36%	48%	52%	NM	37%	37%	49%
Prices - High	41.32	53.65	52.75	56.37	57.50	49.43	39.06	28.50	26.87	22.18
- Low	24.73	25.11	38.00	22.62	36.00	33.50	24.50	20.37	17.31	17.31
P/E Ratio - High	14	NM	17	18	25	20	NM	12	12	13
- Low	9	NM	12	7	16	13	NM	8	7	10

Income Statement Analysis (Million $)

	2003	2002	2001	2000	1999	1998	1997	1996	1995	1994
Life Ins. In Force	307,800	874	651,900	637,100	516,600	400,800	249,800	258,300	228,692	199,666
Prem. Inc.: Life	1,694	1,730	2,907	3,064	2,721	2,260	1,588	1,408	NA	NA
Prem. Inc.: A & H	3.98	20.3	341	410	698	635	573	793	NA	NA
Net Invest. Inc.	2,639	2,608	2,680	2,747	2,808	2,681	2,251	2,366	2,286	2,011
Total Revs.	5,284	4,645	6,362	6,852	6,798	6,087	4,898	6,721	6,633	6,984
Pretax Inc.	1,048	1.62	764	836	570	697	34.0	712	627	376
Net Oper. Inc.	NA	474	689	639	457	NA	257	434	307	390
Net Inc.	767	91.6	606	621	460	510	21.0	514	482	350
S&P Core Earnings	782	215	600	NA	NA	NA	NA	NA	NA	NA

Balance Sheet & Other Fin. Data (Million $)

	2003	2002	2001	2000	1999	1998	1997	1996	1995	1994
Cash & Equiv.	2,234	2,227	3,659	2,474	2,429	2,433	3,795	1,715	2,036	1,471
Premiums Due	352	213	400	297	260	775	621	651	538	565
Invest. Assets: Bonds	32,769	32,767	28,346	27,450	27,689	30,233	24,066	27,906	25,834	21,644
Invest. Assets: Stocks	3,319	337	471	550	604	543	660	993	1,165	1,039
Invest. Assets: Loans	6,119	6,151	6,475	6,624	6,628	6,233	4,051	4,031	3,790	3,406
Invest. Assets: Total	42,778	40,000	36,113	35,369	35,578	37,929	25,212	34,045	31,936	26,971
Deferred Policy Costs	3,192	2,971	2,885	3,071	2,800	1,964	1,624	1,892	1,437	2,444
Total Assets	106,745	93,133	98,001	99,844	103,096	99,836	77,175	71,713	63,258	49,330
Debt	1,459	1,512	1,336	1,457	1,457	712	808	626	659	420
Common Equity	5,811	5,296	5,263	4,953	4,264	5,388	4,983	4,467	4,375	2,730
% Return On Revs.	14.5	2.0	9.5	9.1	6.8	28.6	0.7	7.6	7.3	5.0
% Ret. on Assets	0.1	0.1	0.6	0.6	0.5	0.6	0.0	0.8	0.9	0.7
% Ret. on Equity	13.8	1.7	11.9	13.5	0.4	9.8	0.4	11.6	13.3	10.3
% Invest. Yield	7.1	6.9	7.5	7.7	7.6	7.9	7.5	7.2	7.3	7.1

Data as orig reptd.; bef. results of disc opers/spec. items. Per share data adj. for stk. divs. Bold denotes primary EPS (FASB 128)-prior periods restated. E-Estimated. NA-Not Available. NM-Not Meaningful. NR-Not Ranked. Hist. EPS data incl. real. inv. gains; oper. EPS est. excl. them.

Office: 1500 Market Street, Philadelphia, PA 19102.
Telephone: 215-448-1400.
Email: investorrelations@lnc.com
Website: http://www.lfg.com
Chrmn & CEO: J.A. Boscia.
EVP & CFO: R.C. Vaughan.

SVP & Chief Acctg Officer: C.J. Trumble.
SVP & General Counsel: D.L. Schoff.
Dirs: W. J. Avery, J. P. Barrett, T. D. Bell, J. A. Boscia, J. K. Britell, J. G. Drosdick, E. G. Johnson, M. L. Lachman, M. F. Mee, R. J. Ponder, J. S. Ruckelshaus, G. F. Tilton.

Founded: in 1905.
Domicile: Indiana.
Employees: 5,644.
S&P Analyst: Gregory Simcik, CFA /PMW/JWP

Linear Technology Corp.

Recommendation: **BUY** ★★★★★
NEU SEL HOLD BUY BUY

12-Month Target Price: $50.00
(as of October 06, 2004)

LLTC has an approximate 0.11% weighting in the **S&P 500**

Sector: Information Technology
Sub-Industry: Semiconductors
Peer Group: Semiconductors - Analog

Summary: This company manufactures high-performance linear integrated circuits.

Quantitative Evaluations

S&P Earnings & Dividend Rank: A

| D | C | B- | B | B+ | A- | **A** | A+ |

S&P Fair Value Rank: 4+

| 1 | 2 | 3 | **4** | 5 |
| Lowest | | | | Highest |

Fair Value Calc.: $38.80 (Fairly Valued)

S&P Investability Quotient Percentile

98%

LLTC scored higher than 98% of all companies for which an S&P Report is available.

Volatility: Average

| Low | **Average** | High |

Technical Evaluation: Bullish
Since 10/04, the technical indicators for LLTC have been Bullish.

Relative Strength Rank: Moderate

40

| 1 Lowest | | Highest 99 |

Price as of 11/12/04: **$38.05** | **2005E S&P Core EPS:** **$1.10**

GAAP Earnings vs. Previous Year ▲ Up ▼ Down ▶ No Change

10 Week Mov. Avg.
30 Week Mov. Avg.
Relative Strength
12-Mo Target Price

VOL. MIL.

BUY

J J A S O N D | J F M A M J J A S O N D | J F M A M J J A S O N D | J F M A M J J A S O N D | J
2001 | **2002** | **2003** | **2004**

OPTIONS: ASE, CBOE, P, Ph

Analyst commentary prepared by Amrit Tewary/CB/GG

Highlights October 14, 2004

- We forecast sales to advance 29% in FY 05 (Jun.) and 18% in FY 06, reflecting a cyclical expansion that we project for the semiconductor industry. FY 05 first quarter revenue grew 6% sequentially; company guidance was for 5% to 7% growth in what historically has been LLTC's slowest sales season of the year.

- Demand has been strong for small, powerful analog chips to manage power and signals in portable electronic products such as wireless phones that include PDAs and cameras. We forecast healthy demand for analog chips for a broader range of applications in communications, industrial and high-end consumer digital markets.

- The net margin is among the best in the industry, at 41% for the September quarter. Cash has risen to 92% of shareholders' equity, which we believe indicates financial flexibility. We believe LLTC will use cash to buy back shares and pay dividends. For FY 05, we estimate EPS of $1.35 and, after projected stock option expense, S&P Core EPS of $1.10. For FY 06, we estimate EPS of $1.60 and S&P Core EPS of $1.35.

Investment Rationale/Risk October 14, 2004

- We would buy shares of LLTC. We expect the company to outperform most chip peers during the current semiconductor upcycle, given its strong proprietary product portfolio, wide margins, diversified end markets, and balance sheet strength. Also, we think LLTC shares are attractively valued at current levels, based on our P/E and price-to-sales analyses.

- Risks to our opinion and target price include semiconductor industry cyclicality, competition, the risks of wafer fab ownership, and reliance on stock-based compensation that we view as moderate for a chipmaker but above that of most companies.

- Our 12-month target price of $50 for these high beta shares is based on our price-to-sales and P/E analyses. Our target price applies a P/E of 36X, above peers but below historical norms, to our forward 12-month EPS estimate. Also, our target price assumes a price to sales multiple of 15X, well above peers but below historical averages, applied to our FY 05 sales per share estimate. We think LLTC shares merit a premium valuation to most peers, given the company's above-average margins and below-average cyclicality for a chipmaker.

Key Stock Statistics

S&P Core EPS 2006E	1.35	52-week Range	$45.09-34.01
S&P Oper. EPS 2005E	1.35	12 Month P/E	33.7
P/E on S&P Oper. EPS 2005E	28.2	Beta	2.02
S&P Oper. EPS 2006E	1.60	Shareholders	1,682
Yield (%)	0.8%	Market Cap (B)	$ 11.7
Dividend Rate/Share	0.32	Shares Outstanding (M)	307.0

Value of $10,000 invested five years ago: **$ 10,522**

Dividend Data Dividends have been paid since 1992

Amount ($)	Date Decl.	Ex-Div. Date	Stock of Record	Payment Date
0.080	Jan. 13	Jan. 21	Jan. 23	Feb. 11 '04
0.080	Apr. 13	Apr. 21	Apr. 23	May. 12 '04
0.080	Jul. 21	Jul. 28	Jul. 30	Aug. 18 '04
0.080	Oct. 12	Oct. 20	Oct. 22	Nov. 10 '04

Revenues/Earnings Data Fiscal year ending June 30

Revenues (Million $)

	2005	2004	2003	2002	2001	2000
1Q	253.0	174.1	142.0	120.1	232.1	147.5
2Q	—	186.0	145.0	121.3	258.4	162.3
3Q	—	209.1	153.8	130.2	282.0	185.1
4Q	—	238.1	165.8	140.8	200.0	211.0
Yr.	—	807.3	606.6	512.3	972.6	705.9

Earnings Per Share ($)

	2005	2004	2003	2002	2001	2000
1Q	0.33	0.22	0.17	0.14	0.31	0.18
2Q	E0.32	0.23	0.18	0.14	0.34	0.20
3Q	E0.34	0.27	0.19	0.16	0.38	0.23
4Q	E0.36	0.31	0.21	0.17	0.26	0.27
Yr.	E1.35	1.02	0.74	0.60	1.29	0.88

Next earnings report expected: mid-January Source: S&P, Company Reports
EPS Estimates based on S&P Operating Earnings; historical GAAP earnings are as reported.

STANDARD &POOR'S

Linear Technology Corporation

Recommendation: **BUY** ★ ★ ★ ★ ★   12-Month Target Price: **$50.00** (as of October 06, 2004)

Business Summary October 14, 2004

Linear Technology Corp. has grown rapidly since incorporation in 1981. Annual revenues reached $100 million after 10 years of operations, and approached $1 billion in the boom year of FY 01 (Jun.). LLTC designs, makes and markets a broad line of high-performance standard linear integrated circuits (ICs) that address a wide range of real-world signal processing applications. Real-world phenomena, such as temperature, pressure, sound, images, speed, acceleration, position and rotation, are specifically analog in nature, consisting of continuously varying information. According to LLTC, advantages offered by operating in the linear, as opposed to the digital, IC market, include smaller capital requirements, greater price stability and market diversity, and less Asian competition.

LLTC's products are used in a wide variety of applications, including wireless and wireline telecommunications, networking, satellite systems, notebook and desk-top PCs, computer peripherals, video/multimedia, industrial instrumentation, medical devices, and high-end consumer products such as digital cameras and MP3 players. The company has expanded its customer base throughout its history. LLTC initially served primarily an industrial customer base, with a high percentage of revenues from the military market. Since the late 1980s, new products led to growth in the PC and hand-held device markets, and communication and networking markets contributed to growth significantly in recent years. The company sells its products to more than 15,000 original equipment manufacturers.

The company's product line includes operational and high-speed amplifiers, volt-

age regulators, voltage references, data converters, interface circuits, and other linear circuits, including buffers, battery monitors, comparators, drivers and filters.

LLTC targets the high-performance segments of the linear circuit market, which are characterized by higher precision, high power or micropower, higher speed, more subsystem integration on a single chip, and many other special features. A high degree of proprietary design content contributes to relatively stable pricing for the company's chips.

The company has fabrication and manufacturing facilities for six-inch wafers in Milpitas, CA, and Camas, WA. In FY 02, LLTC closed its oldest wafer fab, in Milpitas, contributing to a 16% overall workforce reduction as part of cost containment efforts during an industry downturn. However, the number of circuit design engineers increased 16%. The company performs test and assembly operations in Asia, and operates design facilities across the U.S. and in Singapore.

During FY 04 (FY 03), export sales, which were primarily to Europe and Asia, represented about 71% (68%) of net sales. LLTC sells both through a direct sales force and through distributors such as Arrow Electronics, which handled 15% of net sales in FY 04.

The company had no long-term debt over the past decade, and has maintained profitability, despite the cyclicality of sales in the semiconductor industry.

Company Financials Fiscal Year ending June 30

Per Share Data ($)

(Year Ended June 30)	2004	2003	2002	2001	2000	1999	1998	1997	1996	1995
Tangible Bk. Val.	5.87	5.80	5.63	5.59	4.20	2.95	2.46	1.94	1.48	1.05
Cash Flow	1.17	0.88	0.74	1.39	0.95	0.68	0.63	0.47	0.46	0.30
Earnings	1.02	0.74	0.60	1.29	0.88	0.61	0.57	0.43	0.43	0.28
S&P Core Earnings	0.79	0.50	0.40	1.10	NA	NA	NA	NA	NA	NA
Dividends	0.28	0.21	0.17	0.13	0.08	0.08	0.06	0.05	0.04	0.03
Payout Ratio	27%	28%	28%	10%	9%	12%	11%	12%	9%	12%
Prices - High	45.09	44.80	47.50	65.12	74.75	41.59	22.62	18.75	12.56	11.40
- Low	34.01	24.76	18.92	29.45	35.06	20.87	9.78	10.12	5.43	5.75
P/E Ratio - High	44	61	79	50	85	68	40	44	29	41
- Low	33	33	32	23	40	34	17	24	13	21

Income Statement Analysis (Million $)

	2004	2003	2002	2001	2000	1999	1998	1997	1996	1995
Revs.	807	607	512	973	706	507	485	379	378	265
Oper. Inc.	485	340	271	582	399	280	268	201	201	129
Depr.	48.7	45.9	46.3	35.8	25.0	22.0	20.1	12.4	10.2	8.56
Int. Exp.	Nil	Nil	Nil	Nil	Nil	Nil	Nil	Nil	Nil	Nil
Pretax Inc.	462	333	278	611	417	286	271	205	204	128
Eff. Tax Rate	29.0%	29.0%	29.0%	30.0%	31.0%	32.0%	33.3%	34.3%	34.2%	34.0%
Net Inc.	328	237	198	427	288	194	181	134	134	84.6
S&P Core Earnings	253	161	132	366	NA	NA	NA	NA	NA	NA

Balance Sheet & Other Fin. Data (Million $)

	2004	2003	2002	2001	2000	1999	1998	1997	1996	1995
Cash	204	136	212	321	230	787	638	443	322	250
Curr. Assets	1,832	1,776	1,728	1,728	1,310	905	768	559	419	317
Total Assets	2,088	2,057	1,988	2,017	1,507	1,047	893	680	530	368
Curr. Liab.	203	162	169	202	169	125	123	89.0	86.3	56.0
LT Debt	Nil	Nil	Nil	Nil	Nil	Nil	Nil	Nil	Nil	Nil
Common Equity	1,811	1,815	1,781	1,782	1,322	907	756	589	440	309
Total Cap.	1,811	1,815	1,819	1,815	1,339	922	770	591	443	312
Cap. Exp.	20.7	6.61	17.9	128	80.3	39.1	24.4	21.9	70.0	22.0
Cash Flow	377	282	244	463	313	216	201	147	144	93.2
Curr. Ratio	9.0	11.0	10.2	8.5	7.8	7.2	6.2	6.3	4.9	5.7
% LT Debt of Cap.	Nil	Nil	Nil	Nil	Nil	Nil	Nil	Nil	Nil	Nil
% Net Inc.of Revs.	40.7	39.0	38.6	43.9	40.8	38.3	37.3	35.4	35.4	31.9
% Ret. on Assets	15.8	11.7	9.9	24.3	22.5	20.0	23.0	22.2	29.8	26.6
% Ret. on Equity	18.1	13.2	11.1	27.5	25.8	23.3	26.4	26.1	35.7	31.8

Data as orig reptd.; bef. results of disc opers/spec. items. Per share data adj. for stk. divs.; EPS diluted. E-Estimated. NA-Not Available. NM-Not Meaningful. NR-Not Ranked. UR-Under Review.

Office: 1630 McCarthy Boulevard, Milpitas, CA 95035-7417.
Telephone: 408-432-1900.
Website: http://www.linear-tech.com
Chrmn & CEO: R.H. Swanson, Jr.
Pres: D.B. Bell.

COO & VP: L. Maier.
VP, CFO & Investor Contact: P. Coghlan 408-432-1900.
Secy: A.F. Scheiderman.
Dirs: D. S. Lee, L. T. McCarthy, R. M. Moley, R. H. Swanson, Jr., T. S. Volpe.

Founded: in 1981.
Domicile: Delaware.
Employees: 3,050.
S&P Analyst: Amrit Tewary/CB/GG

Liz Claiborne

Recommendation: **BUY** ★★★★☆   12-Month Target Price: **$45.00**
SELL | SELL | HOLD | BUY | BUY   (as of October 28, 2004)

LIZ has an approximate 0.04% weighting in the **S&P 500**

Sector: Consumer Discretionary
Sub-Industry: Apparel, Accessories & Luxury Goods
Peer Group: Designer Mens/Womens Apparel

Summary: LIZ designs and markets women's and men's apparel that is made by independent suppliers and sold through department and specialty stores worldwide.

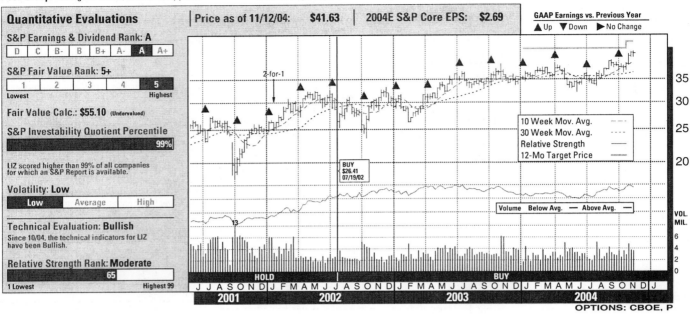

Quantitative Evaluations

S&P Earnings & Dividend Rank: A

| D | C | B- | B | B+ | A- | **A** | A+ |

S&P Fair Value Rank: 5+

| 1 | 2 | 3 | 4 | **5** |
| Lowest | | | | Highest |

Fair Value Calc.: $55.10 (Undervalued)

S&P Investability Quotient Percentile
99%

LIZ scored higher than 99% of all companies for which an S&P Report is available.

Volatility: Low

| **Low** | Average | High |

Technical Evaluation: Bullish
Since 10/04, the technical indicators for LIZ have been Bullish.

Relative Strength Rank: Moderate
65
1 Lowest   Highest 99

Price as of 11/12/04: **$41.63**   2004E S&P Core EPS: **$2.69**

GAAP Earnings vs. Previous Year
▲ Up ▼ Down ▶ No Change

10 Week Mov. Avg.
30 Week Mov. Avg.
Relative Strength
12-Mo Target Price

BUY $26.41 07/19/02

Volume Below Avg. — Above Avg.

VOL. MIL.

HOLD   BUY

J J A S O N D | J F M A M J J A S O N D | J F M A M J J A S O N D | J F M A M J J A S O N D J
2001   2002   2003   2004

OPTIONS: CBOE, P

Analyst commentary prepared by Marie Driscoll, CFA /PMW/BK

Highlights November 02, 2004

- A strong third quarter performance across LIZ's portfolio of bridge, better and contemporary apparel brands, non-apparel brands, and specialty retail drove a 7% consolidated sales increase, despite continued sales declines at the core Liz Claiborne brand. We project 8% sales growth for 2004, as we see a strong finish to the year, For 2005, we expect 7% growth. We see signs of improvement in the department store channel, in our view boding well for wholesale business. We look for double-digit growth at Ellen Tracy, Juicy Couture, and Mexx. We expect specialty retail, via Mexx, Sigrid Olsen, and Lucky Brands, to grow in the mid-teens, with new stores and an estimated mid-single-digit same-store sales gain. We anticipate high single-digit growth in the non-apparel/accessories business. For the longer term, we think that new management and design teams at Mexx Europe have created a multi-brand platform for international growth opportunities.

- We look for operating margins to widen by about 20 basis points in each of 2004 and 2005 driven by improved sourcing, fewer markdowns, a growing proportion of high-margin Mexx, and enhanced wholesale and retail inventory turns. We see the SG&A expense ratio rising, reflecting retail penetration.

- We expect $30 million interest expense for 2004, followed by a drop to $28 million in 2005. After taxes estimated at 35.2%, we project a 12% gain in 2004 EPS, to $2.85. For 2005, we estimate EPS of $3.15.

Investment Rationale/Risk November 02, 2004

- What we view as favorable valuation and a solid growth outlook are the basis of our accumulate recommendation. We view LIZ's broad diversification across brands, sales channels, and demographics, and its consistently strong financial results, as deserving of multiple expansion. We believe the company will gain market share in the next few years, as it assimilates recent acquisitions and extends the lines of many of its 36 brands. We view LIZ's International opportunities as significant.

- Risks to our recommendation and target price include changes in consumer sentiment and spending trends, continued access to sourcing, and geopolitical risk.

- We regard the stock as attractive, based on its historical P/E multiple range and the peer average P/E multiple. Our discounted cash flow analysis, which assumes five-year double-digit growth in free cash flow, tapering off to single digits, and a weighted average cost of capital of 11.3%, yields intrinsic value of $45. Our 12-month target price of $45 is based on a forward P/E multiple of about 14X applied to our 2005 EPS estimate, in line with the stock's historical P/E multiple.

Key Stock Statistics

S&P Core EPS 2005E	2.99	52-week Range	$42.23-32.09
S&P Oper. EPS 2004E	2.85	12 Month P/E	15.1
P/E on S&P Oper. EPS 2004E	14.6	Beta	1.15
S&P Oper. EPS 2005E	3.15	Shareholders	6,358
Yield (%)	0.5%	Market Cap (B)	$ 4.5
Dividend Rate/Share	0.23	Shares Outstanding (M)	108.5

Value of $10,000 invested five years ago: **$ 21,926**

Dividend Data Dividends have been paid since 1984

Amount ($)	Date Decl.	Ex-Div. Date	Stock of Record	Payment Date
0.056	Jan. 22	Feb. 19	Feb. 23	Mar. 15 '04
0.056	May. 20	May. 27	Jun. 01	Jun. 15 '04
0.056	Jul. 21	Aug. 23	Aug. 25	Sep. 15 '04
0.056	Oct. 05	Nov. 22	Nov. 25	Dec. 15 '04

Revenues/Earnings Data Fiscal year ending December 31

Revenues (Million $)

	2004	2003	2002	2001	2000	1999
1Q	1,103	1,076	892.9	826.6	809.5	700.8
2Q	1,026	959.4	789.5	727.0	661.7	607.7
3Q	1,307	1,174	1,041	1,008	879.0	821.0
4Q	—	1,032	993.9	886.5	754.0	677.1
Yr.	—	4,241	3,718	3,449	3,104	2,807

Earnings Per Share ($)

	2004	2003	2002	2001	2000	1999
1Q	0.62	0.59	0.48	0.44	0.42	0.35
2Q	0.46	0.41	0.36	0.31	0.29	0.25
3Q	1.03	0.89	0.78	0.69	0.63	0.54
4Q	E0.75	0.66	0.54	0.39	0.38	0.43
Yr.	E2.85	2.55	2.16	1.83	1.72	1.56

Next earnings report expected: late-February Source: S&P, Company Reports
EPS Estimates based on S&P Operating Earnings; historical GAAP earnings are as reported.

Liz Claiborne, Inc.

Recommendation: **BUY** ★ ★ ★ ★ ☆   12-Month Target Price: **$45.00** (as of October 28, 2004)

Business Summary November 02, 2004

Liz Claiborne designs and markets an extensive range of high-quality women's fashion apparel and accessories. It also sells a men's and children's apparel line, home fashion, and cosmetics, personal care and fragrances. The company believes it is one of the largest U.S. suppliers of women's branded apparel and accessories.

LIZ employs a multi-brand portfolio strategy, diversified across consumer groups, target markets, and distribution channels. Wholesale apparel and wholesale non-apparel accounted respectively for 67% and 13% of 2003 net sales, and for 65% and 12% of 2003 operating profits. Department and specialty stores brands include Dana Buchman, Ellen Tracy, Juicy Couture, and Sigrid Olsen labels at bridge prices; Liz Claiborne, Claiborne, Elisabeth and Realities at better prices; and Emma James in the upper moderate zone. Moderately priced lines available in national department stores include First Issue, Crazy Horse, and Villager. In addition, LIZ is a licensee for DKNY Jeans, DKNY Activewear, and Kenneth Cole of New York. The Liz Claiborne name is also licensed for a number of products, including women's shoes, home furnishings, optics, outerwear, sunglasses, watches, men's tailored clothing, and accessories. Licensing accounted for 0.7% of 2003 net sales and 4.5% of operating profits.

Products are manufactured in the U.S. and abroad. About 69% of 2003 total sales were made to the 100 largest customers, with Federated Department Stores, The May Department Stores Co., and Dillard Department Stores accounting for 12%, 8% and 7% of 2003 sales. LIZ products are available at more than 30,000 retail locations worldwide.

Products are also sold in 124 specialty retail stores and 196 outlet stores in the U.S., and 111 specialty retail stores, 67 outlets, and 553 concession stores outside the U.S. (as of March 2004). In 2003, all U.S.-based Liz Claiborne specialty retail stores were closed, and LIZ launched U.S. Mexx and Sigrid Olsen specialty retail store formats. Retail accounted for 20% of 2003 net sales and 19% of operating profits.

The 2004 capital budget is $125 million, reflecting planned new product launches and new store openings, as well as technology upgrades. In 2003, capital and in-store spending was $107 million. In addition, LIZ spent $222 million for acquisitions, which included additional payments of $46 million related to the Lucky Brands and Mexx Canada acquisitions.

In December 2003, the company acquired Enyce Holding LLC, a privately held designer, marketer and wholesaler of streetwear fashion apparel (2003 sales estimated at $95 million), for about $122 million. In April 2003, LIZ acquired Travis Jeans, Inc., the owner of Juicy Couture, a premium brand of sophisticated basics for women, men and children, for $53 million. In September 2002, Ellen Tracy, Inc., was acquired for about $180 million in stock and assumption of debt. In 2001, LIZ acquired Mexx Group B.V., a privately held fashion apparel and accessories company based in the Netherlands; in July 2002, it further consolidated control of the Mexx brand by acquiring Mexx Canada, a third-party distributor of Mexx products, with both wholesale and retail operations.

Company Financials Fiscal Year ending December 31

Per Share Data ($)

(Year Ended December 31)	2003	2002	2001	2000	1999	1998	1997	1996	1995	1994
Tangible Bk. Val.	6.73	5.43	5.71	5.45	5.95	7.67	6.97	7.19	6.71	6.39
Cash Flow	3.51	3.06	2.79	2.43	2.11	1.71	1.64	1.37	1.10	0.75
Earnings	2.55	2.16	1.83	1.72	1.56	1.29	1.32	1.07	0.85	0.53
S&P Core Earnings	2.39	2.00	1.68	NA	NA	NA	NA	NA	NA	NA
Dividends	0.23	0.23	0.23	0.23	0.23	0.23	0.23	0.23	0.23	0.23
Payout Ratio	9%	10%	12%	13%	14%	18%	17%	21%	27%	42%
Prices - High	38.90	33.25	27.47	24.15	20.34	27.43	28.96	22.56	15.00	13.31
- Low	26.23	23.55	18.00	15.46	15.43	12.50	19.06	13.12	7.18	7.68
P/E Ratio - High	15	15	15	14	13	21	22	21	18	25
- Low	10	11	10	9	10	10	14	12	9	15

Income Statement Analysis (Million $)

	2003	2002	2001	2000	1999	1998	1997	1996	1995	1994
Revs.	4,241	3,718	3,449	3,104	2,807	2,535	2,413	2,218	2,082	2,163
Oper. Inc.	575	493	780	402	368	340	323	278	229	186
Depr.	105	96.4	101	77.0	67.8	55.8	46.0	42.9	39.0	35.0
Int. Exp.	30.5	25.1	28.1	21.9	Nil	Nil	Nil	Nil	NA	NA
Pretax Inc.	438	362	300	288	302	267	293	249	203	131
Eff. Tax Rate	36.2%	36.2%	36.0%	36.0%	36.2%	36.5%	37.0%	37.5%	37.5%	37.0%
Net Inc.	280	231	192	185	192	169	185	156	127	83.0
S&P Core Earnings	259	213	176	NA	NA	NA	NA	NA	NA	NA

Balance Sheet & Other Fin. Data (Million $)

	2003	2002	2001	2000	1999	1998	1997	1996	1995	1994
Cash	344	276	161	54.4	37.9	230	138	529	438	330
Curr. Assets	1,348	1,203	1,106	911	859	1,075	1,057	1,142	1,065	1,023
Total Assets	2,607	2,296	1,951	1,512	1,412	1,393	1,305	1,383	1,329	1,290
Curr. Liab.	527	591	447	358	352	363	328	326	307	303
LT Debt	440	378	Nil	269	116	Nil	Nil	1.00	1.10	1.20
Common Equity	1,600	1,286	1,056	834	902	981	922	1,020	988	983
Total Cap.	2,094	1,705	1,093	1,139	1,044	999	932	1,030	997	986
Cap. Exp.	96.7	80.0	82.2	66.7	75.1	88.5	34.0	23.3	34.4	70.6
Cash Flow	385	328	294	262	260	225	231	199	166	118
Curr. Ratio	2.6	2.0	2.5	2.5	2.4	3.0	3.2	3.5	3.5	3.4
% LT Debt of Cap.	21.0	22.2	Nil	23.6	11.1	Nil	Nil	0.1	0.1	0.1
% Net Inc.of Revs.	6.6	6.2	5.6	5.9	6.9	6.7	7.7	7.1	6.1	3.8
% Ret. on Assets	11.5	10.9	11.1	12.6	13.7	12.6	13.7	11.5	9.8	6.6
% Ret. on Equity	19.3	19.7	20.3	21.3	20.4	17.8	19.0	15.5	12.9	8.5

Data as orig reptd.; bef. results of disc opers/spec. items. Per share data adj. for stk. divs. Bold denotes primary EPS - prior periods restated. E-Estimated. NA-Not Available. NM-Not Meaningful. NR-Not Ranked. UR-Under Review.

Office: 1441 Broadway, New York, NY 10018.
Telephone: 212-354-4900.
Email: investor_relations@liz.com
Website: http://www.lizclaiborne.com
Chrmn & CEO: P.R. Charron.

SVP & CFO: M. Scarpa.
VP, Treas & Investor Contact: R.J. Vill 212-295-7515.
Dirs: B. W. Aronson, P. R. Charron, R. J. Fernandez, M. Haben, N. J. Karch, K. P. Kopelman, K. Koplovitz, A. C. Martinez, O. R. Sockwell, H. Socol, P. E. Tierney, Jr.

Founded: in 1976.
Domicile: Delaware.
Employees: 13,000.
S&P Analyst: Marie Driscoll, CFA /PMW/BK

Lockheed Martin

Recommendation: **SELL** ★★☆☆☆
SELL | SELL | HOLD | BUY | BUY

12-Month Target Price: **$50.00**
(as of November 10, 2004)

LMT has an approximate 0.24% weighting in the **S&P 500**

Sector: Industrials
Sub-Industry: Aerospace & Defense
Peer Group: Aircraft Manufacturers

Summary: LMT is the world's largest military weapons manufacturer.

Quantitative Evaluations

S&P Earnings & Dividend Rank: B-
D | C | **B-** | B | B+ | A- | A | A+

S&P Fair Value Rank: 2+
1 | **2** | 3 | 4 | 5
Lowest | | | | Highest

Fair Value Calc.: $52.70 (Slightly Overvalued)

S&P Investability Quotient Percentile
54%

LMT scored higher than 54% of all companies
for which an S&P Report is available.

Volatility: Low
Low | Average | High

Technical Evaluation: Bullish
Since 11/04, the technical indicators for LMT
have been Bullish.

Relative Strength Rank: Moderate
64
1 Lowest | Highest 99

| Price as of 11/12/04: | **$58.56** | 2004E S&P Core EPS: | **$1.20** |

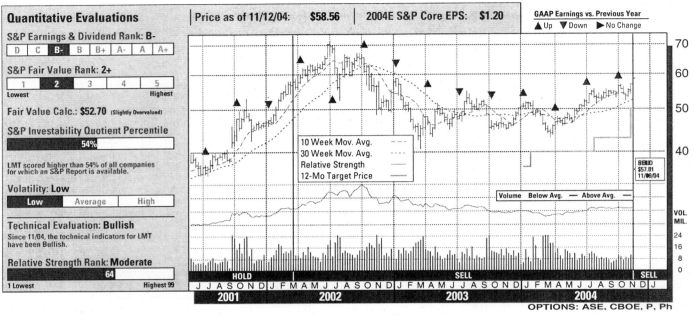

GAAP Earnings vs. Previous Year
▲ Up ▼ Down ► No Change

10 Week Mov. Avg. — — —
30 Week Mov. Avg. ....
Relative Strength
12-Mo Target Price

Volume Below Avg. ..... — Above Avg. —

BUILD
$57.81
11/08/04

HOLD | SELL | SELL
J J A S O N D | J F M A M J J A S O N D | J F M A M J J A S O N D | J F M A M J J A S O N D | J
2001 | 2002 | 2003 | 2004

OPTIONS: ASE, CBOE, P, Ph

Analyst commentary prepared by Robert E. Friedman, CPA /CB/JWP

Highlights 16-NOV-04

- We see revenues rising about 5% in 2005, primarily driven by a modest increase in military electronics sales. EBIT (earnings before interest and taxes) margins should rise fractionally, to at least 8.5%, on the increased electronics sales and ongoing production efficiencies. Following expected declines in pension expense, we estimate that reported and S&P Core EPS will advance about 20% and 40%, to $3.25 and $1.70, respectively. In projecting 2005 profitability performance, we are forecasting what we view as tepid debt-adjusted ROE of 12%.
- Looking at the long-term growth prospects of LMT's primary demand driver, the health of the U.S. military budget, we think sluggish growth in federal tax receipts, as well as political pressure to balance budgets, bolster social entitlement programs and fund larger homeland security and overseas peacekeeping initiatives, will likely prevent the company's sub-markets (the procurement and R&D sectors of the U.S. defense budget) from expanding at a sustainable average annual rate greater than 4%.
- In examining LMT's long-term profitability prospects, we believe that the Pentagon's desire for increasingly hi-tech systems could boost the rate of product obsolescence, which, in turn, could keep many of LMT's weapons systems from migrating toward more profitable fixed-price contract arrangements. Thus, we predict that LMT will likely post what we view as mediocre long-term 6% to 7.5% average annual free cash earnings growth and 12% to 15% ROE.

Investment Rationale/Risk 16-NOV-04

- We have an avoid opinion on LMT shares, as the stock is trading at a premium to our revised discounted cash flow (DCF)-based 12-month target price of $50 a share.
- Risks to our recommendation and target price primarily include any unexpected improvements to the structural growth prospects of LMT's military end markets, and/or structural improvements to the underlying economics of the military weapons business.
- Our revised free cash flow model, which values LMT by adding the discounted sum of annual free cash flow rising at an estimated 6% to 7.5% CAGR over the next 10 years, and matching 3% GDP growth thereafter, calculates LMT worth about $50 a share. We calculated our free cash CAGR estimate by multiplying our 12% to 15% long-term average ROE estimates by our projected 50% long-term earnings retention rate. Our relative valuation model, which compares a company's earnings yield (EPS divided by current stock price) with 10-year AAA-rated corporate bond yields, supports our contention that LMT is overvalued. Based on our projected 2005 S&P Core EPS of $1.70, the stock has an earnings yield of about 3.0%, versus a 4.7% yield for 10-year AAA corporate bonds.

Key Stock Statistics

S&P Core EPS 2005E	**1.70**	52-week Range	**$58.56-43.10**	
S&P Oper. EPS 2004E	**2.70**	12 Month P/E	**21.0**	
P/E on S&P Oper. EPS 2004E	**21.7**	Beta	**-0.11**	
S&P Oper. EPS 2005E	**3.25**	Shareholders	**45,425**	
Yield (%)	**1.7%**	Market Cap (B)	**$ 25.8**	
Dividend Rate/Share	**1.00**	Shares Outstanding (M)	**442.7**	

Value of $10,000 invested five years ago: **$ 33,143**

Dividend Data Dividends have been paid since 1995

Amount ($)	Date Decl.	Ex-Div. Date	Stock of Record	Payment Date
0.220	Jan. 22	Feb. 26	Mar. 01	Mar. 31 '04
0.220	Apr. 22	May. 27	Jun. 01	Jun. 30 '04
0.220	Aug. 05	Aug. 30	Sep. 01	Sep. 30 '04
0.250	Sep. 23	Nov. 29	Dec. 01	Dec. 30 '04

Revenues/Earnings Data Fiscal year ending December 31

Revenues (Million $)

	2004	2003	2002	2001	2000	1999
1Q	8,347	7,059	5,966	4,747	5,562	6,188
2Q	8,776	7,709	6,290	5,688	6,212	6,203
3Q	8,438	8,078	6,542	6,221	5,960	6,157
4Q	—	8,978	7,780	7,334	7,600	6,982
Yr.	—	31,824	26,578	23,990	25,329	25,530

Earnings Per Share ($)

	2004	2003	2002	2001	2000	1999
1Q	0.65	0.55	0.50	0.30	0.14	0.70
2Q	0.66	0.54	0.78	0.33	0.11	-0.11
3Q	0.69	0.48	0.66	-0.12	-1.74	0.57
4Q	E0.70	0.77	-0.76	-0.34	0.44	0.76
Yr.	E2.70	2.34	1.18	0.18	-1.05	1.92

Next earnings report expected: late-January Source: S&P, Company Reports
EPS Estimates based on S&P Operating Earnings; historical GAAP earnings are as reported.

Lockheed Martin Corporation

Recommendation: **SELL** ★★ ✩✩✩   12-Month Target Price: **$50.00** (as of November 10, 2004)

Business Summary 16-NOV-04

Lockheed Martin, the world's largest military weapons maker, conducts business through five operating segments.

LMT's Aeronautics segment (32% of gross revenues; 28% of operating profits; 6.8% profit margins in 2003) primarily makes fighter and military transport planes. Principal production programs consist of the C-130J military transport and the F-16 fighter. The segment's primary development programs include the F-35 Joint Strike fighter and the F-22 fighter. Boeing is the unit's primary competitor.

The Electronic Systems segment (28%; 35%; 9.5%) primarily makes land-, sea- and air-based missiles. Other offerings include various electronic surveillance and reconnaissance systems. ES's largest competitors include Raytheon's missile & electronics division and Europe's EADS.

LMT's Space Systems segment (19%; 16%; 6.7%) mostly makes satellites and payload-carrying rockets. The unit's primary competitors include Boeing, Northrop Grumman, EADS and Orbital Sciences. Based on the latest statistics provided by Space News, we believe the $43 billion-revenue space industry (primarily payload-carrying rocket and satellite manufacturing) is fairly oligopolistic; although there are more than 50 global space equipment makers, the five largest space equipment makers (Boeing, LMT, Raytheon, Northrop Grumman and EADS) account for more than 60% of annual space industry sales.

The Integrated Systems & Solutions segment (11%; 12%; 8.5%) mainly provides networking systems that coordinate the U.S. military's various communications functions. IS&S's primary competitors include Boeing and Northrop Grumman.

LMT's Information & Technology Services segment (10%; 9%; 7.1%) primarily provides various management, engineering and information technology services

to the U.S. government. We believe the $60 billion U.S. government IT market is fragmented; I&TS's main competitors include Northrop Grumman and General Dynamics.

In general, demand for military weapons systems is driven by growth in the U.S. defense budget, which accounts for about 40% of the global military weapons market (based on statistics provided by the Teal Group, an independent aerospace and defense research firm). In turn, growth in defense spending is driven by long-term military strategies, geopolitical climates, as well as political considerations. From FY 93 (Oct.) through FY 03, the procurement and R&D sectors of the U.S. defense budget grew at 8.6% and 2.9% average annual rates, respectively (based on U.S. Department of Defense statistics).

We believe that about 50% of LMT's year-end 2003 backlog of $77 billion consists of cost-plus contracts. Cost-plus contracts typically generate operating profit margins between 5% and 9%. In contrast, fixed price contracts typically generate EBIT (earnings before interest and taxes) margins of 10% to 15%.

Looking at LMT's historical financial performance, from 1993 through 2003, reported EPS grew at a 2.2% CAGR; per-share free cash flow expanded at a 1.8% CAGR; per-share equity growth (a proxy for growth in intrinsic value) grew at a 2.5% CAGR. In addition, debt-adjusted ROE averaged 7.1%. We believe LMT's quality of earnings is mediocre. Based on Standard & Poor's Core Earnings methodology, S&P Core EPS variance averaged -163%, primarily due to the reversal of non-operating pension income generated by LMT's overfunded pension plan.

Company Financials Fiscal Year ending December 31

Per Share Data ($)

(Year Ended December 31)	2003	2002	2001	2000	1999	1998	1997	1996	1995	1994
Tangible Bk. Val.	NM	NM	NM	NM	NM	NM	NM	NM	2.03	0.72
Cash Flow	3.69	2.40	2.08	1.36	3.30	5.27	5.37	6.73	4.24	5.17
Earnings	2.34	1.18	0.18	-1.05	1.92	2.63	3.04	3.40	1.64	2.66
S&P Core Earnings	2.20	-0.78	-2.29	NA	NA	NA	NA	NA	NA	NA
Dividends	0.58	0.44	0.44	0.44	0.88	0.82	0.80	0.78	0.35	NA
Payout Ratio	25%	37%	NM	NM	46%	31%	26%	23%	21%	NA
Prices - High	58.95	71.52	52.98	37.58	46.00	58.93	56.71	48.31	39.75	NA
- Low	40.64	45.85	31.00	16.50	16.37	41.00	39.12	36.50	25.00	NA
P/E Ratio - High	25	61	NM	NM	24	22	19	14	24	NA
- Low	17	39	NM	NM	9	16	13	11	15	NA

Income Statement Analysis (Million $)

	2003	2002	2001	2000	1999	1998	1997	1996	1995	1994
Revs.	31,824	26,578	23,990	25,329	25,530	26,266	28,069	26,875	22,853	22,906
Oper. Inc.	2,585	2,507	2,366	2,582	2,194	3,357	3,349	3,478	2,893	2,716
Depr.	609	558	823	968	529	1,005	1,052	1,197	921	937
Int. Exp.	487	581	700	919	809	861	842	700	288	304
Pretax Inc.	1,532	577	188	286	1,200	1,661	1,937	2,033	1,089	1,675
Eff. Tax Rate	31.3%	7.63%	58.0%	NM	38.6%	39.7%	32.9%	33.7%	37.4%	37.0%
Net Inc.	1,053	533	79.0	-424	737	1,001	1,300	1,347	682	1,055
S&P Core Earnings	994	-353	-989	NA	NA	NA	NA	NA	NA	NA

Balance Sheet & Other Fin. Data (Million $)

	2003	2002	2001	2000	1999	1998	1997	1996	1995	1994
Cash	1,010	2,738	912	1,505	455	285	Nil	Nil	653	639
Curr. Assets	9,401	10,626	10,778	11,259	10,696	10,611	10,105	9,940	8,177	8,143
Total Assets	26,175	25,758	27,654	30,349	30,012	28,744	28,361	29,257	17,648	18,049
Curr. Liab.	8,893	9,821	9,689	10,175	8,812	10,267	9,189	8,704	5,291	5,635
LT Debt	6,072	6,217	7,422	9,065	11,427	8,957	10,528	10,188	3,010	3,594
Common Equity	6,756	5,865	6,443	7,160	6,361	6,137	5,176	5,856	5,433	5,086
Total Cap.	12,828	12,082	14,857	16,961	17,788	15,094	15,704	16,044	9,433	9,680
Cap. Exp.	687	662	619	500	669	697	750	737	531	509
Cash Flow	1,662	1,091	902	544	1,266	2,006	2,299	2,544	1,603	1,932
Curr. Ratio	1.1	1.1	1.1	1.1	1.2	1.0	1.1	1.1	1.5	1.4
% LT Debt of Cap.	47.3	51.5	50.0	53.4	64.2	59.3	67.0	63.5	31.9	37.1
% Net Inc.of Revs.	3.3	2.0	0.3	NM	2.9	3.8	4.6	5.0	3.0	4.6
% Ret. on Assets	4.0	2.0	0.3	NM	2.5	3.5	4.5	5.8	3.8	6.0
% Ret. on Equity	16.7	8.7	1.2	NM	11.8	17.7	22.6	22.8	11.8	21.4

Data as orig reptd.; bef. results of disc opers/spec. items. Per share data adj. for stk. divs.; EPS diluted. E-Estimated. NA-Not Available. NM-Not Meaningful. NR-Not Ranked. UR-Under Review.

Office: 6801 Rockledge Drive, Bethesda, MD 20817.
Telephone: 301-897-6000.
Website: http://www.lockheedmartin.com
Chrmn: V. D. Coffman.
Pres, COO & CEO: R. J. Stevens.
EVP & CFO: C. E. Kubasik.

EVP: M. F. Camardo.
Dirs: E. C. Aldridge, Jr., N. D. Archibald, N. R. Augustine, M. C. Bennett, V. D. Coffman, G. S. King, D. H. McCorkindale, E. F. Murphy, J. W. Ralston, F. Savage, A. Stevens, R. J. Stevens, J. R. Ukropina, D. C. Yearley.

Founded: in 1909.
Domicile: Maryland.
Employees: 130,000.
S&P Analyst: Robert E. Friedman, CPA /CB/JWP

STANDARD &POOR'S

Loews Corp.

Recommendation: **HOLD** ★★★☆☆
SELL | SELL | HOLD | BUY | BUY

12-Month Target Price: **$65.00**
(as of July 29, 2004)

LTR has an approximate 0.11% weighting in the **S&P 500**

Sector: Financials
Sub-Industry: Multi-line Insurance
Peer Group: Insurers - Multi-Line - Larger

Summary: This conglomerate includes holdings in property casualty insurance, tobacco, offshore drilling, hotels, and natural gas pipelines.

Quantitative Evaluations

S&P Earnings & Dividend Rank: B-

| D | C | B- | B | B+ | A- | A | A+ |

S&P Fair Value Rank: NR

| 1 | 2 | 3 | 4 | 5 |
| Lowest | | | | Highest |

Fair Value Calc.: NA

S&P Investability Quotient Percentile

83%

LTR scored higher than 83% of all companies for which an S&P Report is available.

Volatility: Average

| Low | **Average** | High |

Technical Evaluation: Bullish

Since 10/04, the technical indicators for LTR have been Bullish.

Relative Strength Rank: Strong

76

1 Lowest | Highest 99

Price as of 11/12/04: $65.44 | **2004E S&P Core EPS: $5.47**

GAAP Earnings vs. Previous Year
▲ Up ▼ Down ► No Change

10 Week Mov. Avg.
30 Week Mov. Avg.
Relative Strength
12-Mo Target Price

OPTIONS: ASE, CBOE

Analyst commentary prepared by Gregory Simcik, CFA /CB/GG

Highlights August 30, 2004

- We project that operating earnings for the CNA Financial subsidiary will exceed $650 million in 2004, compared to a loss of $1.5 billion in 2003, on an improved combined ratio and substantially better reserve development.

- We expect operating earnings at the Lorillard subsidiary to decline over 10% in 2004, on promotional spending in a competitive cigarette market as well as a higher proportion of Lorillard earnings attributed to Carolina Group shares. We see operating losses for Diamond Offshore narrowing to $1 million, from $27 million in 2003.

- We forecast operating EPS of $5.75 in 2004, compared to an operating loss of $6.04 per share in 2003. Our 2004 estimate excludes $0.06 in charges for the early redemption of debt. We expect operating EPS to rise 5.6% in 2005, to $6.27. Our 2004 and 2005 Standard & Poor's Core Earnings per share estimates are $5.47 and $6.20, respectively, adjusted for projected stock option and pension expense.

Investment Rationale/Risk August 30, 2004

- Based on our target price, we believe LTR could offer investors a return that exceeds our expected return on the S&P 500 Index. However, due to the company's tobacco and environmental exposures, we believe LTR also presents above-average investor risk, and therefore we would not add to positions.

- Risks to our recommendation and target price include legal and regulatory risks associated with tobacco sales; increased price promotions in the cigarette market; higher state cigarette taxes; declines in the U.S. smoking population; energy market volatility; catastrophic, asbestos and environmental risk for CNA; and significant stock holdings, voting influence and management control by members of the Tisch family.

- Our 12-month target price of $65 is based on a sum-of-the-parts valuation, whereby we utilize multiples of 11.5X, 7.5X,10X and 10X for the CNA, CG, Texas Gas and Loews Hotels subsidiaries, respectively, applied to our 12-month forward operating earnings estimates. We then include a value for DO based on our S&P 12-month target price of $28, adjust the combined value for net corporate debt, and apply a 15% discount to account for Tisch family control.

Key Stock Statistics

S&P Core EPS 2005E	6.20	52-week Range	$65.78-41.76
S&P Oper. EPS 2004E	5.18	12 Month P/E	13.0
P/E on S&P Oper. EPS 2004E	12.6	Beta	0.65
S&P Oper. EPS 2005E	5.90	Shareholders	1,900
Yield (%)	0.9%	Market Cap (B)	$ 12.1
Dividend Rate/Share	0.60	Shares Outstanding (M)	185.5

Value of $10,000 invested five years ago: **$ 19,868**

Dividend Data Dividends have been paid since 1967

Amount ($)	Date Decl.	Ex-Div. Date	Stock of Record	Payment Date
0.150	Nov. 19	Nov. 26	Dec. 01	Dec. 15 '03
0.150	Feb. 17	Feb. 26	Mar. 01	Mar. 15 '04
0.150	May. 11	May. 27	Jun. 01	Jun. 14 '04
0.150	Aug. 17	Aug. 30	Sep. 01	Sep. 13 '04

Revenues/Earnings Data Fiscal year ending December 31

Revenues (Million $)

	2004	2003	2002	2001	2000	1999
1Q	3,491	3,949	4,792	5,104	4,674	5,559
2Q	3,915	4,250	4,652	4,319	5,332	5,649
3Q	3,785	3,940	4,079	4,841	5,776	5,431
4Q	—	4,336	3,972	5,154	5,556	4,859
Yr.	—	16,461	17,495	19,417	21,338	21,465

Earnings Per Share ($)

	2004	2003	2002	2001	2000	1999
1Q	0.05	0.87	1.23	2.67	0.91	0.91
2Q	1.98	1.02	0.84	-7.18	2.58	1.17
3Q	1.21	-7.60	1.05	0.85	3.45	1.26
4Q	E1.48	1.79	1.21	0.98	2.55	-0.99
Yr.	E5.18	-3.91	4.32	-2.75	9.44	2.40

Next earnings report expected: mid-February Source: S&P, Company Reports
EPS Estimates based on S&P Operating Earnings; historical GAAP earnings are as reported.

STANDARD &POOR'S

Loews Corporation

Stock Report
November 13, 2004
NYSE Symbol: **LTR**

Recommendation: **HOLD** ★ ★ ★ ☆ ☆   12-Month Target Price: **$65.00** (as of July 29, 2004)

Business Summary August 31, 2004

Loews Corp. is a holding company with interests in property casualty insurance (CNA Financial Corp., 91% stake), cigarettes (Lorillard Inc.), hotels (Loews Hotels Holding Corp.), offshore oil and gas drilling (Diamond Offshore Drilling, Inc., 54% stake), interstate natural gas pipelines (Texas Gas Transmission, LLC), and watches and clocks (Bulova Corp., 97% stake). LTR also has a 49% indirect stake in an oil tank shipping company (Hellespont Shipping Corp.).

CNA Financial Corp. (CNA; 71% of consolidated total revenue in 2003) is an insurance holding company whose subsidiaries consist primarily of property and casualty insurance companies. Lorillard, Inc., (CG; 20%) is a leading U.S. producer of tobacco products with its principal products marketed under the brand names Newport, Kent, True, Maverick, and Old Gold. The Loews Hotels division (1.7%) owns and/or operates 20 hotels in the U.S. and Canada. Diamond Offshore's (DO; 4.2%) business primarily consists of operating 45 offshore drilling rigs that are chartered on a contract basis for fixed terms by energy exploration companies. Texas Gas (0.9%) owns and operates a 5,800-mile natural gas pipeline system that originates in the Louisiana Gulf Coast and East Texas and runs north and east of the region. Bulova (1.0%) distributes and sells watches and clocks.

In November 2003, LTR purchased $750 million of convertible preferred stock from CNA and sold 18 million shares of CG tracking stock in a public offering. The preferred stock converted into 32.3 million shares of CNA common stock during April 2004 and raised LTR's stake in CNA to 91%. At March 31, 2004, outstanding CG tracking stock represented a 33% economic interest in the Carolina Group, whose principal assets and liabilities include the company's ownership interest in Lorillard, $2 billion of notional, intergroup debt owed by Carolina Group to Loews Group, and any and all liabilities, costs and expenses arising out of or related to tobacco-related businesses. The Loews Group consists of all LTR's assets and liabilities other than the 33% economic interest represented by the CG tracking stock and includes as an asset the notional intergroup debt of the Carolina Group.

In April 2004, 49%-owned Hellespont Shipping Corp. agreed to sell its four ultra-large crude oil tankers to Eurovav Luxembourg SA. In April 2004, CNA completed the sale of its individual life insurance business for approximately $700 million. In December 2003, CNA completed the sale of the majority of its group benefits business for approximately $530 million. In October 2003, CNA entered into an agreement to sell the renewal rights for most of the treaty business of CNA Re to Folksamerica. In May 2003, LTR acquired Texas Gas for $795 million in cash and the assumption of $250 million in debt.

Company Financials Fiscal Year ending December 31

Per Share Data ($)

(Year Ended December 31)	2003	2002	2001	2000	1999	1998	1997	1996	1995	1994
Tangible Bk. Val.	NM	59.64	48.70	54.83	45.73	42.71	38.76	35.52	32.75	22.81
Oper. Earnings	NA	NA	-6.81	5.71	3.03	1.98	4.15	NA	NA	2.18
Earnings	-3.91	4.49	-2.75	9.44	2.40	2.03	3.45	5.96	7.49	1.11
S&P Core Earnings	-5.99	7.89	-7.42	NA	NA	NA	NA	NA	NA	NA
Dividends	0.60	0.60	0.58	0.50	0.50	0.50	0.50	0.50	0.50	0.25
Relative Payout	NM	13%	NM	5%	21%	25%	14%	8%	7%	22%
Prices - High	49.48	62.30	72.50	104.93	52.25	54.12	57.81	47.93	39.93	25.68
- Low	38.25	37.50	41.05	38.25	29.25	39.00	42.75	36.25	21.65	21.12
P/E Ratio - High	NM	14	NM	11	22	27	17	8	5	23
- Low	NM	8	NM	4	12	19	12	6	3	19

Income Statement Analysis (Million $)

	2003	2002	2001	2000	1999	1998	1997	1996	1995	1994
Life Ins. In Force	388,968	437,751	497,732	534,781	469,990	394,394	311,598	237,009	166,047	127,433
Prem. Inc.: Life A & H	2,275	3,382	4,351	4,549	4,502	4,391	3,431	3,347	3,007	2,616
Prem. Inc.: Cas./Prop.	6,935	6,828	5,010	6,923	8,775	8,979	NA	10,127	8,724	6,837
Net Invest. Inc.	1,732	1,867	2,145	2,388	2,175	2,558	2,442	2,476	2,212	1,671
Total Revs.	3,288	17,495	19,417	21,338	21,465	21,208	20,139	20,442	18,677	13,515
Pretax Inc.	-751	1,647	-813	3,206	945	1,078	1,593	2,408	2,839	266
Net Oper. Inc.	NA	1,099	-1,328	1,134	658	452	954	14,491	NA	NA
Net Inc.	-468	983	-536	1,877	521	465	794	1,384	1,766	268
S&P Core Earnings	-1,112	1,594	-1,447	NA	NA	NA	NA	NA	NA	NA

Balance Sheet & Other Fin. Data (Million $)

	2003	2002	2001	2000	1999	1998	1997	1996	1995	1994
Cash & Equiv.	1.90	185	181	195	184	287	498	306	242	161
Premiums Due	20,468	16,601	19,453	15,302	13,529	13,071	NA	NA	NA	NA
Invest. Assets: Bonds	28,781	27,434	31,191	27,244	27,924	31,409	30,723	29,478	30,468	20,852
Invest. Assets: Stocks	888	1,121	1,646	2,683	4,024	2,381	1,163	1,136	1,214	1,438
Invest. Assets: Loans	NA	NA	NA	NA	NA	NA	NA	NA	309	244
Invest. Assets: Total	1,630	40,137	41,159	40,396	40,633	42,705	41,618	39,917	39,631	31,076
Deferred Policy Costs	2,533	2,551	2,424	2,418	2,436	2,422	2,142	1,854	1,493	1,025
Total Assets	2,725	70,520	75,251	70,877	69,464	70,906	69,577	67,683	65,058	50,336
Debt	2,032	5,652	5,920	6,040	5,706	5,967	5,906	4,371	4,248	2,144
Common Equity	-729	11,235	9,649	11,191	9,978	10,200	9,664	8,731	8,239	5,405
Comb. Loss-Exp. Ratio	146.6	110.3	158.6	113.6	120.9	114.2	108.2	108.4	107.0	110.0
% Return On Revs.	14.2	5.6	NM	8.8	2.4	2.2	4.5	6.8	9.5	2.0
% Ret. on Equity	NM	8.1	NM	4.9	5.2	4.7	8.6	16.3	25.9	4.6
% Invest. Yield	4.2	4.6	5.2	5.9	5.2	6.1	5.9	6.2	5.5	5.7

Data as orig reptd.; bef. results of disc opers/spec. items. Per share data adj. for stk. divs.; EPS diluted. E-Estimated. NA-Not Available. NM-Not Meaningful. NR-Not Ranked. Oper. EPS est. excl. real. inv. gains/losses; historical EPS data incl. them.

Office: 667 Madison Avenue, New York, NY 10021-8087.
Telephone: 212-521-2000.
Website: http://www.loews.com
Chrmn: P.R. Tisch.
Pres & CEO: J.S. Tisch.

SVP & CFO: P.W. Keegan.
SVP, Secy & General Counsel: G.W. Garson.
Dirs: J. L. Bower, J. Brademas, C. M. Diker, P. J. Fribourg, W. L. Harris, P. A. Laskawy, E. J. Noha, G. R. Scott, A. H. Tisch, P. R. Tisch, J. S. Tisch, J. M. Tisch, F. Wilpon.

Founded: in 1954.
Domicile: Delaware.
Employees: 22,700.
S&P Analyst: Gregory Simcik, CFA /CB/GG

Louisiana-Pacific

Recommendation: **HOLD** ★★★☆☆
SELL | SELL | HOLD | BUY | BUY

12-Month Target Price: **$26.00**
(as of April 28, 2004)

LPX has an approximate 0.02% weighting in the **S&P 500**

Sector: Materials
Sub-Industry: Forest Products
Peer Group: Forest Products - Larger

Summary: This major forest products company produces oriented strand board, plywood, lumber and other building products.

Quantitative Evaluations

S&P Earnings & Dividend Rank: B-

D | C | **B-** | B | B+ | A- | A | A+

S&P Fair Value Rank: 1-

1 | 2 | 3 | 4 | 5
Lowest | | | | Highest

Fair Value Calc.: $19.20 (Overvalued)

S&P Investability Quotient Percentile

94%

LPX scored higher than 94% of all companies for which an S&P Report is available.

Volatility: Average

Low | **Average** | High

Technical Evaluation: Bearish
Since 10/04, the technical indicators for LPX have been Bearish.

Relative Strength Rank: Moderate

33

1 Lowest | | Highest 99

Price as of 11/12/04: $25.15   **2004E S&P Core EPS:** $4.51

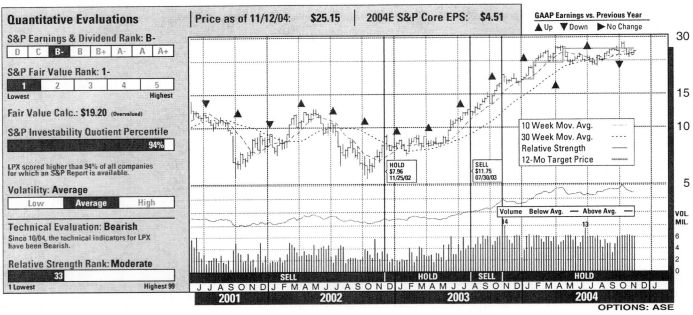

GAAP Earnings vs. Previous Year
▲ Up   ▼ Down   ▶ No Change

10 Week Mov. Avg.
30 Week Mov. Avg.
Relative Strength
12-Mo Target Price

HOLD $7.96 11/25/02
SELL $11.75 07/30/03

Volume   Below Avg. —   Above Avg. —

VOL. MIL.

SELL | HOLD | SELL | HOLD
J J A S O N D | J F M A M J J A S O N D | J F M A M J J A S O N D | J F M A M J J A S O N D | J
2001 | **2002** | **2003** | **2004**

OPTIONS: ASE

Analyst commentary prepared by Bryon J. Korutz/CB/BK

Highlights 15-NOV-04

- We expect sales to increase 17% in 2004, based on our projection of continued strength in wood products prices. For 2005, we see revenues dropping 12%, on an expected drop in volumes and prices.
- While OSB prices have dropped from early second quarter highs, we think prices are likely to improve in the near term. However, looking to the latter portion of 2004, we expect the supply of OSB and other wood products to outpace demand as the stronger home building season concludes, which should then put downward pressure on prices.
- For 2005, we expect a projected 7% drop in housing starts to put additional pressure on prices. In addition, we expect the industry to expand its capacity through the restart of previously closed OSB mills, as well as the addition of new mills. We think this planned expansion will lead to an imbalance between supply and demand, which, coupled with our forecast of a slowdown in housing starts, should cause prices, especially for OSB, to weaken in 2005.

Investment Rationale/Risk 15-NOV-04

- With the shares trading near our 12-month target price of $26, and with OSB prices expected to remain above last year's levels in the near term, we would hold LPX stock. We view favorably the company's actions in selling underperforming units and land, generating over $750 million from the asset sales. As a result of this program, the company had a cash and restricted cash balance at September 30, 2004, of $910 million. We expect that LPX will use proceeds to reduce debt and to fund cost reduction programs and capacity expansion projects.
- Risks to our recommendation and target price include a sooner and greater than anticipated decline in housing starts and OSB prices.
- Applying a peak historical price to sales ratio of 0.69X to our 2004 revenue estimate leads to a value for the shares of $17. By applying a forward peer P/E multiple of 20.7X to our 2005 EPS estimate of $1.35, we value the shares at $28. Blending these metrics leads to our 12-month target price of $26.

Key Stock Statistics

S&P Core EPS 2005E	**1.37**	52-week Range	**$28.31-16.54**
S&P Oper. EPS 2004E	**4.55**	12 Month P/E	**4.8**
P/E on S&P Oper. EPS 2004E	**5.5**	Beta	**1.83**
S&P Oper. EPS 2005E	**1.35**	Shareholders	**12,805**
Yield (%)	**1.6%**	Market Cap (B)	**$ 2.7**
Dividend Rate/Share	**0.40**	Shares Outstanding (M)	**109.3**

Value of $10,000 invested five years ago: **$ 22,997**

Dividend Data Dividends have been paid since 2004

Amount ($)	Date Decl.	Ex-Div. Date	Stock of Record	Payment Date
0.050	Feb. 02	Feb. 10	Feb. 12	Mar. 01 '04
0.075	May. 03	May. 13	May. 17	Jun. 01 '04
0.075	Aug. 02	Aug. 13	Aug. 17	Sep. 01 '04
0.100	Nov. 08	Nov. 12	Nov. 16	Dec. 01 '04

Revenues/Earnings Data Fiscal year ending December 31

Revenues (Million $)

	2004	2003	2002	2001	2000	1999
1Q	695.3	413.1	596.7	558.5	829.7	594.4
2Q	825.3	478.5	448.9	649.8	831.5	777.4
3Q	740.5	674.8	502.0	635.5	702.7	797.4
4Q	—	733.8	431.6	515.9	568.9	712.6
Yr.	—	2,300	1,943	2,360	2,933	2,879

Earnings Per Share ($)

	2004	2003	2002	2001	2000	1999
1Q	1.03	0.02	-0.03	-0.86	0.55	0.26
2Q	1.72	0.09	0.07	-0.09	0.20	0.79
3Q	0.96	1.03	0.18	-0.02	-0.39	0.65
4Q	E0.40	1.54	-0.44	-0.68	-0.50	0.34
Yr.	E4.55	2.67	-0.21	-1.64	-0.13	2.04

Next earnings report expected: early-February Source: S&P, Company Reports
EPS Estimates based on S&P Operating Earnings; historical GAAP earnings are as reported.

Louisiana-Pacific Corporation

Recommendation: **HOLD** ★ ★ ★ ☆ ☆   12-Month Target Price: **$26.00** (as of April 28, 2004)

Business Summary 15-NOV-04

Louisiana-Pacific, which holds about 23% of the U.S. market and 15% of the North American market, is one of North America's leading oriented strand board (OSB) producers. LPX also manufactures composite wood products, plastic building products, and engineered wood products.

The company has completed a major divestiture program aimed at selling underperforming and non-core assets. In May 2002, directors approved a plan to sell LPX's lumber, plywood and industrial panels units, and its 935,000 acres of timberlands, to focus on OSB, engineered wood products, composite wood products, and plastic building products. The sales were completed within the projected 12 to 18 months. Total proceeds generated exceeded $750 million, above the company's projection of $600 million to $700 million.

LPX is one of the largest North American producers of OSB, operating 14 plants with a combined annual capacity of 5.8 billion sq. ft. at the end of 2003 (56% of 2003 sales). The company's strategy for its OSB business is to increase investment in existing facilities in order to reduce costs and focus on the efficiency at its plants, improve net realizations relative to weighted-average OSB regional pricing, realize growth through new product introductions, expand capacity, and increase investment at existing facilities to reduce costs and improve efficiency.

The company also operates a composite wood segment (18%), which produces exterior siding and various cladding products for use in the residential and

commercial markets. Its composite wood products are classified into three categories. SmartSide siding (five plants, with 880 million sq. ft. of capacity, including specialty OSB plants) is an OSB-based siding, trim and fascia product line. LPX also produces hardboard siding and accessory products (two plants, with 505 million sq. ft. of capacity). The specialty OSB business includes a line of products focused on OSB substrates using overlay technologies for wood, such as concrete forms and project panels. Hardboard products include a number of lap and panel products.

LPX's plastic building products segment (9%) includes vinyl siding products and accessories, composite decking products and extruded plastic decorative moldings. At December 31, 2003, the company had two vinyl siding plants, with 3.2 million sq. ft. of annual production capacity, one plastic moldings plant, with 290 million lineal ft. of capacity, and two wood composite decking plants, with 28 million lineal ft. of capacity.

Through its engineered wood products business, the company manufactures and distributes engineered wood products (13%). LPX's engineered wood products include I-joists and laminated veneer lumber (LVL). At December 31, 2003, the company had annual production capacity of 10.6 million cubic ft. of LVL capacity at three plants, and 106 million lineal ft. of I-joist capacity at two plants.

Company Financials Fiscal Year ending December 31

Per Share Data ($)

(Year Ended December 31)	2003	2002	2001	2000	1999	1998	1997	1996	1995	1994
Tangible Bk. Val.	9.46	6.73	7.49	9.29	9.65	10.84	11.09	12.70	15.12	16.33
Cash Flow	3.93	1.06	-0.01	1.64	3.51	1.73	0.76	-0.08	1.41	4.94
Earnings	2.67	-0.21	-1.64	-0.13	2.04	0.02	-0.94	-1.87	-0.48	3.15
S&P Core Earnings	1.89	-0.63	-1.82	NA	NA	NA	NA	NA	NA	NA
Dividends	Nil	Nil	0.24	0.56	0.56	0.56	0.56	0.56	0.55	0.49
Payout Ratio	Nil	Nil	NM	NM	27%	NM	NM	NM	NM	15%
Prices - High	19.25	12.55	13.95	15.81	24.87	24.18	25.87	28.12	30.50	48.00
- Low	7.10	5.35	5.46	7.06	11.37	16.37	17.00	19.62	20.87	25.75
P/E Ratio - High	7	NM	NM	NM	12	NM	NM	NM	NM	15
- Low	3	NM	NM	NM	6	NM	NM	NM	NM	8

Income Statement Analysis (Million $)

	2003	2002	2001	2000	1999	1998	1997	1996	1995	1994
Revs.	2,300	1,943	2,360	2,933	2,879	2,297	2,403	2,486	2,843	3,040
Oper. Inc.	602	142	280	284	533	260	95.4	223	472	756
Depr.	135	132	170	184	156	185	184	192	203	197
Int. Exp.	88.5	95.8	95.6	81.0	47.9	37.5	30.9	21.3	16.2	14.5
Pretax Inc.	517	-18.1	-289	-25.3	357	14.0	-150	-327	-94.8	560
Eff. Tax Rate	45.1%	NM	NM	NM	39.1%	112.9%	NM	NM	NM	37.5%
Net Inc.	284	-21.5	-172	-13.8	217	2.00	-102	-201	-51.7	347
S&P Core Earnings	202	-63.8	-189	NA	NA	NA	NA	NA	NA	NA

Balance Sheet & Other Fin. Data (Million $)

	2003	2002	2001	2000	1999	1998	1997	1996	1995	1994
Cash	926	137	61.6	38.1	116	127	31.9	27.8	75.4	316
Curr. Assets	1,325	491	493	654	739	612	597	579	619	694
Total Assets	3,204	2,773	3,017	3,375	3,488	2,519	2,578	2,589	2,805	2,716
Curr. Liab.	290	273	310	378	541	367	319	345	449	345
LT Debt	1,021	1,070	1,152	1,184	1,015	460	572	459	201	210
Common Equity	1,410	1,132	1,081	2,590	1,360	1,223	1,286	1,428	1,656	1,849
Total Cap.	2,838	2,418	2,469	4,108	2,375	1,886	2,037	2,050	2,065	2,329
Cap. Exp.	83.6	44.3	69.2	188	88.3	77.8	205	266	413	352
Cash Flow	419	110	-1.40	171	373	187	82.1	-9.00	151	544
Curr. Ratio	4.6	1.8	1.6	1.7	1.4	1.7	1.9	1.7	1.4	2.0
% LT Debt of Cap.	36.0	44.3	46.7	28.8	42.7	24.4	28.1	22.4	9.8	9.0
% Net Inc.of Revs.	12.3	NM	NM	NM	7.5	0.1	NM	NM	NM	11.4
% Ret. on Assets	9.5	NM	NM	NM	7.2	0.1	NM	NM	NM	13.3
% Ret. on Equity	22.3	NM	NM	NM	16.8	0.2	NM	NM	NM	20.1

Data as orig reptd.; bef. results of disc opers/spec. items. Per share data adj. for stk. divs.; EPS diluted. E-Estimated. NA-Not Available. NM-Not Meaningful. NR-Not Ranked. UR-Under Review.

Office: 805 S.W. Broadway, Portland, OR 97205-3303.
Telephone: 503-821-5100.
Website: http://www.lpcorp.com
Chrmn & CEO: M. A. Suwyn.
EVP & CFO: C. M. Stevens.

EVP: R. W. Frost.
EVP: J. B. Kastelic.
Investor Contact: Becky Barkley (503-821-5100).
Dirs: E. G. Cook, A. W. Dunham, D. K. Frierson, P. W. Hansen, B. Lauderback, D. E. McCoy, L. C. Simpson, M. A. Suwyn, C. D. Watson.

Founded: in 1972.
Domicile: Delaware.
Employees: 7,100.
S&P Analyst: Bryon J. Korutz/CB/BK

Lowe's Companies

Recommendation: **BUY** ★★★★☆

12-Month Target Price: **$65.00**
(as of November 15, 2004)

LOW has an approximate 0.41% weighting in the **S&P 500**

Sector: Consumer Discretionary
Sub-Industry: Home Improvement Retail
Peer Group: Retail (Building Supplies)

Summary: This company retails building materials and supplies, lumber, hardware and appliances through more than 950 stores in 45 states.

Quantitative Evaluations

S&P Earnings & Dividend Rank: A+

| D | C | B- | B | B+ | A- | A | **A+** |

S&P Fair Value Rank: 4+

| 1 | 2 | 3 | **4** | 5 |
| Lowest | | | | Highest |

Fair Value Calc.: $63.20 (Slightly Undervalued)

S&P Investability Quotient Percentile

99%

LOW scored higher than 99% of all companies for which an S&P Report is available.

Volatility: Average

| Low | **Average** | High |

Technical Evaluation: Bullish
Since 9/04, the technical indicators for LOW have been Bullish.

Relative Strength Rank: Moderate

57

| 1 Lowest | | Highest 99 |

| Price as of 11/16/04: | **$58.08** | 2005E S&P Core EPS: | **$2.77** |

GAAP Earnings vs. Previous Year
▲ Up ▼ Down ► No Change

10 Week Mov. Avg.
30 Week Mov. Avg.
Relative Strength
12-Mo Target Price

Volume ▬ Below Avg. — Above Avg.

OPTIONS: ASE, CBOE, P, Ph

Analyst commentary prepared by Michael Souers/CB/BK

Highlights 17-NOV-04

- We forecast that sales will grow in the mid-teens in FY 06 (Jan.), with an estimated 140 to 160 net store openings, reflecting about 14% growth in total square footage. Same-store sales are expected to rise in the mid-single digits, on gains in traffic and average ticket, driven by improved merchandise assortments and healthy D-I-Y activity, bolstered by a solid housing market and favorable economic conditions.
- We think lower sourcing costs and inventory shrinkage, and firmer prices in lumber and building materials, will largely be offset by higher distribution and payroll-related expenses. With economies of scale from continued sales growth only partly offset by increased performance bonuses and advertising costs, we see operating margins widening by 20 to 30 basis points.
- We project lower interest expense, taxes at an effective rate of 38.5%, and a slightly lower share count, reflecting stock repurchases. Our FY 06 EPS estimate of $3.36 is 17% above our FY 05 forecast of $2.87. Our FY 05 EPS estimate excludes a charge of $0.16 from an accounting change.

Investment Rationale/Risk 17-NOV-04

- Based on our three-year EPS growth projection of 17%, and on the stock's P/E to growth ratio of 1.0X on our FY 05 EPS estimate, below the S&P 500, we believe the stock has appeal. We think improved economic conditions, including a recovering job market, will lead to strong consumer spending in 2005. In addition, we believe home improvement retailers will see solid gains, as consumers continue to focus on their homes. We see LOW's push into major U.S. metropolitan areas, where rival Home Depot (HD: buy; $43) has long dominated, helping to maintain revenue growth. Our recommendation is buy.
- Risks to our recommendation and target price include a potential slowdown in the economy; a sharp rise in interest rates, which could hurt home improvement related spending; and failure to execute LOW's metro market expansion strategy.
- At 17X our FY 06 estimate, LOW's shares trade in line with the S&P 500 and key peer HD. However, we believe LOW should carry a premium due to its above-average growth rate. Our 12-month target price of $65 is derived from our DCF (discounted cash flow) analysis, which assumes a weighted average cost of capital of 9.7% and a terminal growth rate of 3%.

Key Stock Statistics

S&P Core EPS 2006E	3.26	52-week Range	$60.54-45.90
S&P Oper. EPS 2005E	2.87	12 Month P/E	22.3
P/E on S&P Oper. EPS 2005E	21.0	Beta	1.12
S&P Oper. EPS 2006E	3.36	Shareholders	26,553
Yield (%)	0.3%	Market Cap (B)	$ 44.8
Dividend Rate/Share	0.16	Shares Outstanding (M)	771.8

Value of $10,000 invested five years ago: **$ 21,073**

Dividend Data Dividends have been paid since 1961

Amount ($)	Date Decl.	Ex-Div. Date	Stock of Record	Payment Date
0.001	Apr. 05	Apr. 14	Apr. 15	Apr. 30 '04
0.030	Apr. 02	Apr. 14	Apr. 16	Apr. 30 '04
0.040	May. 28	Jul. 14	Jul. 16	Jul. 30 '04
0.040	Sep. 13	Oct. 13	Oct. 15	Oct. 29 '04

Revenues/Earnings Data Fiscal year ending January 31

Revenues (Million $)

	2005	2004	2003	2002	2001	2000
1Q	8,681	7,118	6,471	5,276	4,467	3,772
2Q	10,169	8,666	7,488	6,127	5,264	4,435
3Q	9,064	7,802	6,415	5,454	4,504	3,909
4Q	—	7,252	6,118	5,253	4,544	3,789
Yr.	—	30,838	26,491	22,111	18,779	15,906

Earnings Per Share ($)

	2005	2004	2003	2002	2001	2000
1Q	0.57	0.53	0.44	0.29	0.25	0.17
2Q	0.89	0.75	0.59	0.42	0.36	0.30
3Q	0.66	0.55	0.43	0.32	0.27	0.22
4Q	E0.60	0.50	0.40	0.28	0.18	0.20
Yr.	E2.87	2.32	1.85	1.30	1.05	0.88

Next earnings report expected: late-February Source: S&P, Company Reports
EPS Estimates based on S&P Operating Earnings; historical GAAP earnings are as reported.

Lowe's Companies, Inc.

Recommendation: **BUY** ★ ★ ★ ★ ☆   12-Month Target Price: **$65.00** (as of November 15, 2004)

Business Summary 17-NOV-04

Lowe's Companies is the world's second largest home improvement retailer, after Atlanta-based Home Depot. Using a superstore format, the company's warehouse style stores focus on both do-it-yourself (D-I-Y) and professional customers. Retail customers are primarily D-I-Y homeowners and others buying for personal and family use. Commercial business customers include repair and remodeling contractors, electricians, landscapers, painters, plumbers, and commercial and residential building maintenance professionals.

Capitalizing on a growing number of U.S. households (now more than 100 million), and on historically high rates of home ownership, LOW has grown from a chain of 15 stores in FY 62 (Jan.) to 952 stores in 45 states, representing 108.8 million sq. ft. of selling space, at January 31, 2004. The company planned to open 140 new stores in FY 05, increasing square footage by 14%.

Since 1989, the company has been transforming its store base from a chain of small stores into a chain of destination home improvement warehouses. LOW has two prototypes: a 116,000 sq. ft. store for large markets and a 94,000 sq. ft. store used primarily to serve smaller markets. The prototypes feature an additional 31,000 sq. ft. and 26,000 sq. ft., respectively, for a lawn and garden center. A typical store stocks more than 40,000 items, with hundreds more available through the company's special order system.

LOW is focusing much of its future expansion on metropolitan markets with populations of 500,000 or more. Stores in these larger markets accounted for 46% of the total expansion in FY 04, and were to comprise a similar percentage of growth in FY 05.

In 1999, the company acquired Eagle Hardware and Garden, a 41-store chain of home improvement and garden centers in the western U.S. The acquisition spurred LOW's West Coast expansion, and provided a stepping stone into 10 new states, particularly in key metropolitan markets. In the FY 04 fourth quarter, to focus on its retail and commercial business, the company sold 26 commodity-focused locations operating under The Contractor Yard name.

Lowe's superstores combine the merchandise and services offerings of a: home fashions and interior design center; a lawn and garden center; an appliance dealer; an outdoor equipment dealer; a grill and patio furniture store; a hardware store; an air conditioning, heating, plumbing and electrical supply center; and a building materials supplier. LOW offers two proprietary credit cards, one for each customer category.

Contributions to sales by product line in FY 04 were as follows: fashion plumbing and electrical (12%); appliances (11%); lumber/plywood (9%); outdoor fashion (7%); millwork (7%); paint (7%); nursery (6%); flooring, (6%); tools (6%); rough plumbing and electrical (6%); hardware (6%); building materials (5%); outdoor power equipment (4%); cabinets/furniture (4%); walls & windows (3%); home organization (2%); and other (1%).

Company Financials Fiscal Year ending January 31

Per Share Data ($)

(Year Ended January 31)	2004	2003	2002	2001	2000	1999	1998	1997	1996	1995
Tangible Bk. Val.	13.10	10.62	8.60	7.18	6.15	4.45	3.71	3.20	2.58	2.23
Cash Flow	3.36	2.65	1.96	1.59	1.32	1.07	0.86	0.73	0.59	0.54
Earnings	2.32	1.85	1.30	1.05	0.88	0.68	0.51	0.43	0.35	0.36
S&P Core Earnings	2.25	1.73	1.22	1.01	NA	NA	NA	NA	NA	NA
Dividends	0.11	0.09	0.07	0.07	0.06	0.06	0.06	0.05	0.05	0.04
Payout Ratio	5%	5%	0%	7%	7%	9%	11%	12%	13%	12%

Cal. Yrs.	2003	2002	2001	2000	1999	1998	1997	1996	1995	1994
Prices - High	60.42	49.99	48.88	33.62	33.21	26.09	12.28	10.87	9.71	10.34
- Low	33.37	32.50	21.87	17.12	21.50	10.79	7.90	7.15	6.50	6.64
P/E Ratio - High	26	27	38	32	38	38	24	25	28	29
- Low	14	18	17	16	25	16	15	16	18	18

Income Statement Analysis (Million $)

	2004	2003	2002	2001	2000	1999	1998	1997	1996	1995
Revs.	30,838	26,491	22,111	18,779	15,906	12,245	10,137	8,600	7,075	6,111
Oper. Inc.	3,959	3,186	2,332	1,811	1,511	1,105	865	701	540	481
Depr.	781	645	534	409	337	272	241	198	150	110
Int. Exp.	180	203	199	146	123	95.0	73.3	65.1	54.7	44.8
Pretax Inc.	2,998	2,359	1,624	1,283	1,065	758	559	454	352	344
Eff. Tax Rate	37.9%	37.6%	37.0%	36.9%	36.8%	36.4%	36.0%	35.6%	35.1%	34.9%
Net Inc.	1,862	1,471	1,023	810	673	482	357	292	226	224
S&P Core Earnings	1,801	1,386	968	773	NA	NA	NA	NA	NA	NA

Balance Sheet & Other Fin. Data (Million $)

	2004	2003	2002	2001	2000	1999	1998	1997	1996	1995
Cash	1,624	1,126	799	456	491	223	195	70.0	171	268
Curr. Assets	6,687	5,568	4,920	4,175	3,710	2,586	2,110	1,851	1,604	1,557
Total Assets	19,042	16,109	13,736	11,376	9,012	6,345	5,219	4,435	3,556	3,106
Curr. Liab.	4,368	3,578	3,017	2,929	2,386	1,765	1,449	1,349	950	946
LT Debt	3,678	3,736	3,734	2,698	1,727	1,283	1,046	767	866	681
Common Equity	10,309	8,302	6,675	5,494	4,695	3,136	2,601	2,217	1,657	1,420
Total Cap.	14,644	12,516	10,713	8,443	6,622	4,579	3,771	3,086	2,607	2,150
Cap. Exp.	2,444	2,362	2,199	2,332	1,472	928	773	677	520	414
Cash Flow	2,643	2,116	1,557	1,219	1,010	754	598	490	376	333
Curr. Ratio	1.5	1.6	1.6	1.4	1.6	1.5	1.5	1.4	1.7	1.6
% LT Debt of Cap.	25.1	29.8	34.9	32.0	26.1	28.0	27.7	24.9	33.3	31.7
% Net Inc.of Revs.	6.0	5.6	4.6	4.3	4.2	3.9	3.5	3.4	3.2	3.7
% Ret. on Assets	10.6	9.9	8.2	7.9	8.4	8.3	7.4	7.3	6.8	8.2
% Ret. on Equity	20.0	19.6	16.8	15.9	16.2	16.8	14.8	15.1	14.7	18.9

Data as orig reptd.; bef. results of disc opers/spec. items. Per share data adj. for stk. divs.; EPS diluted. E-Estimated. NA-Not Available. NM-Not Meaningful. NR-Not Ranked. UR-Under Review.

Office: 1000 Lowes Blvd, Mooresville, NC 28117.
Telephone: 704-758-1000.
Website: http://www.lowes.com
Chrmn & CEO: R. L. Tillman.
Pres: R. A. Niblock.

EVP: L. D. Stone.
EVP: D. C. Pond.
Dirs: L. L. Berry, P. C. Browning, P. Fulton, D. E. Hudson, R. A. Ingram, R. K. Lochridge, C. Malone, R. A. Niblock, S. F. Page, O. T. Sloan, Jr., R. L. Tillman.

Founded: in 1952.
Domicile: North Carolina.
Employees: 147,000.
S&P Analyst: Michael Souers/CB/BK

LSI Logic

Recommendation: **HOLD** ★ ★ ★ ☆
SELL · SELL · HOLD · BUY · BUY

12-Month Target Price: **$5.50**
(as of September 14, 2004)

LSI has an approximate 0.02% weighting in the **S&P 500**

Sector: Information Technology
Sub-Industry: Semiconductors
Peer Group: Semiconductors - Logic - Larger Cos.

Summary: LSI is a leading supplier of complex, high-performance semiconductors and storage systems. It plans to spin off its storage operations through an IPO in 2004.

Quantitative Evaluations

S&P Earnings & Dividend Rank: C

| D | C | B- | B | B+ | A- | A | A+ |

S&P Fair Value Rank: 2-

| 1 | 2 | 3 | 4 | 5 |
| Lowest | | | | Highest |

Fair Value Calc.: $4.30 (Slightly Overvalued)

S&P Investability Quotient Percentile

27%

LSI scored lower than 73% of all companies for which an S&P Report is available.

Volatility: High

| Low | Average | High |

Technical Evaluation: Neutral

Since 11/04, the technical indicators for LSI have been Neutral.

Relative Strength Rank: Moderate

34

| 1 Lowest | | Highest 99 |

Price as of 11/12/04: $4.88 | **2004E S&P Core EPS:** $-1.81

GAAP Earnings vs. Previous Year
▲ Up ▼ Down ▶ No Change

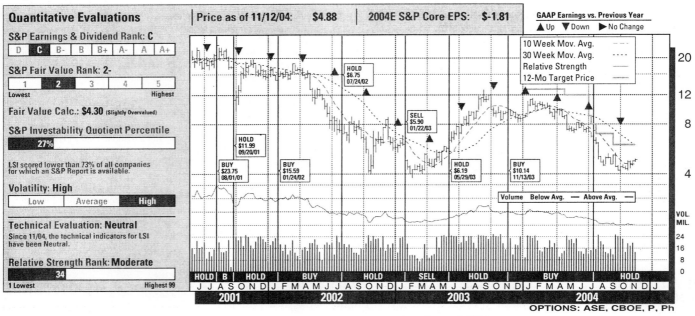

10 Week Mov. Avg.
30 Week Mov. Avg.
Relative Strength
12-Mo Target Price

Volume Below Avg. — Above Avg.

OPTIONS: ASE, CBOE, P, Ph

Analyst commentary prepared by Amrit Tewary/MF/BK

Highlights November 02, 2004

- After a projected decline of 2.4% in 2004, we expect sales to be flattish in 2005. We see orders and sales restricted by sluggish end market demand and an inventory correction in the distribution channel.

- In July, the company filed with the SEC indicating plans to spin off its storage systems operations via an IPO as soon as practical. We expect the initial sale of 20% of the unit, to be known as Engenio Information Technologies, Inc., with a planned NYSE ticker symbol of NGE, to be accomplished by the end of 2004. Storage systems accounted for 25% of 2004 third quarter sales, and have been important in the sales mix, as end markets for communications chips are lagging in the recovery. Following the planned IPO, LSI expects to own 80% of Engenio. It intends to distribute its remaining Engenio shares to LSI shareholders via a special dividend by the summer of 2005.

- Excluding goodwill amortization, acquisition, restructuring and other charges totaling $0.78 a share, the 2003 pro forma loss was $0.04 a share. We estimate pro forma EPS of $0.03 for 2004, with an increase to $0.26 seen for 2005. On a Standard & Poor's Core Earnings basis, we estimate a loss per share of $1.81 for 2004, and a loss of $0.43 for 2005.

Key Stock Statistics

S&P Core EPS 2005E	-0.43	52-week Range	$11.50-4.01
S&P Oper. EPS 2004E	0.03	12 Month P/E	NM
P/E on S&P Oper. EPS 2004E	NM	Beta	2.49
S&P Oper. EPS 2005E	0.26	Shareholders	3,842
Yield (%)	Nil	Market Cap (B)	$ 1.9
Dividend Rate/Share	Nil	Shares Outstanding (M)	384.9

Value of $10,000 invested five years ago: **$ 1,651**

Dividend Data

No cash dividends have been paid.

Investment Rationale/Risk November 02, 2004

- We would hold the shares. We believe the stock's price to sales ratio, which is below historical norms, fairly reflects our concerns about weakening demand trends and excess inventory in the distribution channel. We think the company will continue to be affected by weak order trends through the end of 2004, as it will likely take customers at least a few more months to reduce inventory.

- Risks to our opinion and target price include semiconductor industry cyclicality, execution risk for the storage unit IPO, wafer fabrication plant ownership, and competition heightened by new generations of programmable logic chips that substitute for some application-specific integrated circuits (ASIC) chips. We also view stock option expense as high compared to peers.

- Our 12-month target price of $5.50 is based on our historical price to sales model, in which we apply a price to sales ratio of 1.3X, below the stock's three-year average historical ratio of 2.0X, to our 2005 sales per share estimate. We believe the shares will continue trading below historical norms over the next 12 months, given the above-average near-term risks we see. Our target price also implies the application of a P/E of 22X, slightly below the average multiple for chip stocks in our coverage universe, to our 2005 pro forma EPS estimate.

Revenues/Earnings Data Fiscal year ending December 31

Revenues (Million $)

	2004	2003	2002	2001	2000	1999
1Q	452.4	372.8	412.5	517.2	615.2	456.8
2Q	447.9	407.2	437.8	465.2	644.3	501.0
3Q	380.2	450.2	487.0	396.7	727.6	540.0
4Q	—	462.9	479.7	405.8	750.6	584.9
Yr.	—	1,693	1,817	1,785	2,738	2,089

Earnings Per Share ($)

	2004	2003	2002	2001	2000	1999
1Q	0.02	-0.33	-0.47	-0.10	0.25	0.02
2Q	0.02	-0.43	-0.17	-0.91	0.21	0.03
3Q	-0.73	-0.08	-0.07	-1.09	0.06	0.17
4Q	E-0.04	0.02	-0.08	-0.68	0.18	0.29
Yr.	E0.03	-0.82	-0.79	-2.84	0.70	0.52

Next earnings report expected: late-January Source: S&P, Company Reports
EPS Estimates based on S&P Operating Earnings; historical GAAP earnings are as reported.

LSI Logic Corporation

Recommendation: **HOLD** ★ ★ ★ ☆ ☆   12-Month Target Price: **$5.50** (as of September 14, 2004)

Business Summary November 02, 2004

LSI Logic is best known as a leading supplier of application-specific and standard integrated circuits, although since 1998 it has diversified into storage components. Principal markets served include storage components (36% of 2003 revenues), storage systems (25%), consumer (20%), and communications (19%). Customers are generally electronic OEMs. LSI focuses on larger companies that make products in high volume.

The company operates in two main segments: semiconductors, which accounted for 75% of revenues in 2003, down from 82% of revenues in 2002 and 88% in 2001; and storage systems (25%, 18%, 12%). Semiconductors posted a loss from operations in 2003 and 2002, while storage systems showed income.

In November 2003, LSI announced plans to spin off its storage systems operations via an IPO. In a July 2004 SEC filing, the company indicated plans to sell 12.5 million Class A common shares of its storage unit, known as Engenio Information Technologies Inc., for $8 to $10 a share. After the planned offering, LSI expects to own all 50 million Class B common shares of Engenio, representing about 80% of the subsidiary's outstanding stock. The company intends to distribute the remaining Engenio shares to LSI shareholders by the summer of 2005 in a tax-free distribution, subject to favorable rulings on the tax status of the distribution.

The company emphasizes complex system-on-a-chip products that employ its CoreWare design methodology. Using sophisticated electronic design automation tools, customers add product features to pre-wired cores of industry-standard architecture protocols and algorithms that are electronically stitched together on a single chip. CoreWare methodology is based on application-specific integrated circuit (ASIC) technology: semiconductors designed to satisfy particular customer requirements. LSI is a large player in the global ASIC market, competing with companies such as IBM, Agere Systems, Philips Electronics, Texas Instruments, and Broadcom.

LSI's RapidChip technology aims to shorten customer design and delivery times by using pre-fabricated and proven silicon platforms upon which customers add their intellectual property.

The company has operations worldwide. Sales in the U.S. accounted for 51% of the total in 2003, with 40% coming from Asia, including Japan, and 8% from Europe. Most of LSI's wafers are manufactured at a company facility in Gresham, OR, and a facility in Tsukuba, Japan. The Tsukuba plant was sold in November 2003 to ROHM Co. Ltd., which now acts as a foundry provider to LSI. Taiwan Semiconductor has been a wafer foundry partner since April 2001.

LSI's semiconductors are used in a wide variety of applications, including digital video and audio, DVD recorders, wireless communications infrastructure, digital set-top boxes, high-speed metropolitan and wide area networks, optical networking, wireless local area networks, home networking, residential broadband gateways, and digital subscriber lines. The company supplies chips for Sony's Playstation II video game console. In 2003, Sony accounted for 13% of total revenues; IBM provided 15%.

Company Financials Fiscal Year ending December 31

Per Share Data ($)

(Year Ended December 31)	2003	2002	2001	2000	1999	1998	1997	1996	1995	1994
Tangible Bk. Val.	2.39	2.80	3.15	5.96	5.21	4.17	5.58	5.09	4.71	2.36
Cash Flow	-0.12	0.15	-1.32	1.81	1.62	0.41	1.14	1.13	1.46	0.97
Earnings	-0.82	-0.79	-2.84	0.70	0.52	-0.47	0.56	0.56	0.93	0.50
S&P Core Earnings	-1.33	-1.36	-3.47	NA	NA	NA	NA	NA	NA	NA
Dividends	Nil	Nil	Nil	Nil	Nil	Nil	Nil	Nil	Nil	Nil
Payout Ratio	Nil	Nil	Nil	Nil	Nil	Nil	Nil	Nil	Nil	Nil
Prices - High	12.90	18.60	26.10	90.37	35.68	14.68	23.43	19.81	31.25	11.34
- Low	3.78	3.97	9.70	16.30	8.06	5.25	9.31	8.50	9.12	3.87
P/E Ratio - High	NM	NM	NM	NM	69	NM	42	35	34	23
- Low	NM	NM	NM	NM	16	NM	17	15	10	8

Income Statement Analysis (Million $)

	2003	2002	2001	2000	1999	1998	1997	1996	1995	1994
Revs.	1,693	1,817	1,785	2,738	2,089	1,491	1,290	1,239	1,268	902
Oper. Inc.	171	155	-157	815	568	198	362	340	454	261
Depr.	263	349	533	404	367	248	166	147	136	104
Int. Exp.	30.7	52.0	44.6	41.6	40.0	8.48	1.50	13.6	16.3	18.5
Pretax Inc.	-284	-291	-1,030	380	224	-124	224	205	335	156
Eff. Tax Rate	NM	NM	NM	37.6%	29.0%	NM	28.0%	28.0%	28.0%	28.0%
Net Inc.	-309	-292	-992	237	159	-132	161	144	238	109
S&P Core Earnings	-505	-507	-1,214	NA	NA	NA	NA	NA	NA	NA

Balance Sheet & Other Fin. Data (Million $)

	2003	2002	2001	2000	1999	1998	1997	1996	1995	1994
Cash	270	449	757	236	251	200	105	717	686	429
Curr. Assets	1,390	1,626	1,769	2,072	1,288	820	870	1,051	1,137	731
Total Assets	3,448	4,143	4,626	4,197	3,207	2,800	2,127	1,953	1,850	1,270
Curr. Liab.	391	398	510	627	475	593	438	345	396	308
LT Debt	866	1,241	1,336	846	672	556	67.3	281	222	263
Common Equity	2,042	2,300	2,480	2,498	1,856	1,510	1,566	1,316	1,216	545
Total Cap.	2,916	3,665	3,995	3,481	2,610	2,207	1,689	1,607	1,453	937
Cap. Exp.	78.2	39.0	224	277	205	329	513	362	233	166
Cash Flow	-45.8	57.0	-459	641	526	116	327	294	374	212
Curr. Ratio	3.6	4.1	3.5	3.3	2.7	1.4	2.0	3.1	2.9	2.4
% LT Debt of Cap.	29.7	33.8	33.4	24.3	25.7	25.2	4.0	17.5	15.3	28.0
% Net Inc.of Revs.	NM	NM	NM	8.6	7.6	NM	12.5	11.9	18.8	12.1
% Ret. on Assets	NM	NM	NM	6.4	5.3	NM	7.9	7.7	15.3	9.7
% Ret. on Equity	NM	NM	NM	10.9	9.4	NM	11.2	11.6	27.0	24.7

Data as orig reptd.; bef. results of disc opers/spec. items. Per share data adj. for stk. divs.; EPS diluted. E-Estimated. NA-Not Available. NM-Not Meaningful. NR-Not Ranked. UR-Under Review.

Office: 1621 Barber Lane, Milpitas, CA 95035.
Telephone: 408-433-8000.
Email: investorrelations@lsil.com
Website: http://www.lsilogic.com
Chrmn & CEO: W.J. Corrigan.

EVP & CFO: B. Look.
VP, Secy, General Counsel & Investor Contact: D. Pursel 408-433-8000.
Dirs: T. Z. Chu, W. J. Corrigan, M. R. Currie, J. H. Keyes, R. D. Norby, M. J. O'Rourke, G. Reyes, L. W. Sonsini.

Founded: in 1980.
Domicile: Delaware.
Employees: 4,722.
S&P Analyst: Amrit Tewary/MF/BK

Lucent Technologies

Recommendation: **HOLD** ★ ★ ★ ☆ ☆
SELL SELL HOLD BUY BUY

12-Month Target Price: $4.00
(as of January 22, 2004)

LU has an approximate 0.15% weighting in the **S&P 500**

Sector: Information Technology
Sub-Industry: Communications Equipment
Peer Group: Core Network Systems

Summary: This former division of AT&T is one of the world's leading developers and manufacturers of telecommunications equipment, software and products.

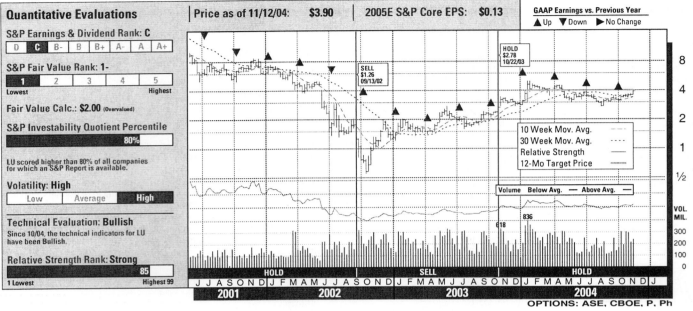

Quantitative Evaluations

S&P Earnings & Dividend Rank: C

| D | C | B- | B | B+ | A- | A | A+ |

S&P Fair Value Rank: 1-

| 1 | 2 | 3 | 4 | 5 |
| Lowest | | | | Highest |

Fair Value Calc.: $2.00 (Overvalued)

S&P Investability Quotient Percentile

80%

LU scored higher than 80% of all companies for which an S&P Report is available.

Volatility: High

| Low | Average | **High** |

Technical Evaluation: Bullish
Since 10/04, the technical indicators for LU have been Bullish.

Relative Strength Rank: Strong

85
1 Lowest   Highest 99

Price as of 11/12/04: $3.90   **2005E S&P Core EPS:** $0.13

GAAP Earnings vs. Previous Year
▲ Up   ▼ Down   ▶ No Change

10 Week Mov. Avg.
30 Week Mov. Avg.
Relative Strength
12-Mo Target Price

Volume Below Avg. — Above Avg.

OPTIONS: ASE, CBOE, P, Ph

Analyst commentary prepared by Kenneth M. Leon/PMW/BK

Highlights October 25, 2004

- Following a 13% sales increase in FY 04 (Sep.), we forecast 7% sales growth in FY 05. We think the mobility and worldwide services segments should continue to show double-digit growth, while the Integrated Network Services (INS) segment, which includes voice switching, broadband and optical equipment, may be flat in FY 05.

- We see signs of recovery in the overall telecom market, with pockets of opportunity in areas such as services, metro optical, voice over IP, broadband access, and high-speed wireless data. We estimate gross margins for FY 05 of 40% to 42%, reflecting a more favorable product sales mix, and efforts to reduce cost of sales. We expect operating expenses to level off, after showing improvements with lower R&D expenses and SG&A streamlined from prior restructurings.

- We estimate operating EPS of $0.18 for FY 05 and $0.20 for FY 06. On a Standard & Poor's Core Earnings basis, we look for $0.13 in FY 05 and $0.16 in FY 06, reflecting the projected impact, compared to estimated GAAP EPS, of stock option expense and pension cost adjustments.

Key Stock Statistics

S&P Core EPS 2006E	0.16	52-week Range	$5.00-2.70
S&P Oper. EPS 2005E	0.18	12 Month P/E	15.6
P/E on S&P Oper. EPS 2005E	21.7	Beta	NA
S&P Oper. EPS 2006E	0.20	Shareholders	1,476,691
Yield (%)	Nil	Market Cap (B)	$ 16.8
Dividend Rate/Share	Nil	Shares Outstanding (M)	4309.5

Value of $10,000 invested five years ago: **NA**

Dividend Data

Cash dividends were omitted in 2001.

Investment Rationale/Risk October 25, 2004

- We would hold the shares, trading below peers at 1.9X our FY 05 sales per share estimate. In our opinion, the company is beginning to improve its financial and operating metrics. We believe LU is benefiting from strong demand for wireless equipment using CDMA technology, but we think the company may continue to lag its competitors with those carriers that are deploying GSM and UMTS wireless systems. We forecast that LU's total sales will grow only in the upper single digits, well below peer levels, in FY 05 and FY 06.

- Risks to our recommendation and target price include slower improvement in telecom equipment markets than we anticipate, the potential loss of one of five customers that accounted for 22% of FY 03 total revenues, and the ability to deliver competitive products in the broadband and wireless markets, especially third generation wireless systems.

- Applying an enterprise value of 9.7X to our FY 05 EBITDA estimate, slightly below the peer average, and a ratio of 2.2X our FY 05 sales estimate, we arrive at our 12-month target price of $4.

Revenues/Earnings Data Fiscal year ending September 30

Revenues (Million $)

	2004	2003	2002	2001	2000	1999
1Q	2,259	2,075	3,579	4,346	8,065	9,204
2Q	2,194	2,403	3,516	5,907	8,355	8,220
3Q	2,190	1,965	2,949	5,886	8,713	9,315
4Q	2,402	2,027	2,277	5,155	8,680	10,575
Yr.	9,045	8,470	12,321	21,294	33,813	38,303

Earnings Per Share ($)

	2004	2003	2002	2001	2000	1999
1Q	0.07	-0.11	-0.14	-0.47	0.34	0.52
2Q	0.02	-0.14	-0.19	-1.00	0.19	0.16
3Q	0.08	-0.07	-2.34	-0.55	Nil	0.24
4Q	0.07	0.02	-0.84	-2.16	-0.01	0.30
Yr.	0.25	-0.29	-3.51	-4.18	0.51	1.10

Next earnings report expected: late-January   Source: S&P, Company Reports
EPS Estimates based on S&P Operating Earnings; historical GAAP earnings are as reported.

STANDARD &POOR'S

Lucent Technologies Inc.

Stock Report
November 13, 2004
NYSE Symbol: **LU**

Recommendation: **HOLD** ★ ★ ★ ☆ ☆   12-Month Target Price: **$4.00** (as of January 22, 2004)

Business Summary October 25, 2004

Lucent Technologies, formerly a unit of AT&T, is one of the world's leading manufacturers of telecommunications systems, software and products. The company is organized into two primary operating segments. Integrated Network Solutions (INS) focuses on wireline service providers, while the mobility segment focuses on wireless service providers.

The INS segment (33% of FY 04 (Sep.) total sales) focuses on providing end-to-end solutions for wireline service providers. Product offerings include circuit switching, packet switching, access, and optical networking products. LU believes that, over time, voice traffic will migrate from existing circuit switched infrastructure to a packet infrastructure driven by new packet based end-user devices.

The mobility segment (44%) focuses on global, wireless service providers with end-to-end solutions and products that support their needs for radio access, core networks, and network management systems. About 61% of FY 04 segment revenues were related to U.S. customers. LU's primary wireless focus is on two technologies: Code Division Multiple Access (CDMA) and Universal Mobile Tele-communication System (UMTS). Products include base stations, core network equipment, network management products and applications and service delivery products.

The services and other segment (23%) plans, consults and integrates support services as well as network engineering, provisioning, installation and warranty support. Even with weak markets, LU believes that services offer near-term

revenue potential, with an approximate $30 billion spent annually on services performed by third parties. Service gross margins, which are narrower than total company gross margins, rose to 25% in FY 04, from 19% in the FY 03, due to service mix changes between maintenance and professional services.

At the end of September 2003, LU completed its prior restructuring actions, and the company saw signs of stability in the overall telecom market. In October 2000, it spun off its enterprise network as Avaya. In December 2000, LU sold its non-core power systems business to Tyco International Ltd., for $2.5 billion in cash. In April 2001, it completed an IPO of its microelectronics products division as Agere Systems. In November 2001, it sold a significant portion of its optical fiber business to Furukawa Electric Co. In February 2002, the company sold its billing and customer care business to CSG Systems International.

In January 2004, the company announced a series of agreements with China Unicom and China Telecom, with total contract values exceeding $350 million. The agreements covered the entire range of LU's next generation network offerings and services. In July 2004, Verizon Wireless awarded the company an agreement worth at least $5 billion to supply a national, next-generation voice and data network. With this agreement, LU will continue as Verizon Wireless's primary next-generation network infrastructure supplier. LU will deploy a wireless broadband network using Qualcomm's CDMA2000 1xEV-DO technology. This will enable Verizon Wireless to offer voice, data, and video services in the future.

Company Financials Fiscal Year ending September 30

Per Share Data ($)

(Year Ended September 30)	2004	2003	2002	2001	2000	1999	1998	1997	1996	1995
Tangible Bk. Val.	NA	NM	NM	2.80	4.80	4.42	2.10	1.32	1.06	0.83
Cash Flow	NA	0.03	-3.07	-3.43	1.20	1.67	0.86	0.77	0.49	0.25
Earnings	0.25	-0.29	-3.51	-4.18	0.51	1.10	0.36	0.21	0.10	-0.34
S&P Core Earnings	NA	-0.50	-4.86	-3.87	NA	NA	NA	NA	NA	NA
Dividends	Nil	Nil	Nil	0.06	0.08	0.08	0.08	0.08	0.02	NA
Payout Ratio	Nil	Nil	Nil	NM	16%	7%	22%	35%	21%	NA
Prices - High	5.00	3.45	7.50	21.12	77.50	84.18	56.93	22.68	13.28	NA
- Low	2.70	1.24	0.55	5.00	12.18	47.00	18.35	11.18	6.75	NA
P/E Ratio - High	20	NM	NM	NM	NM	77	NM	NM	NM	NA
- Low	11	NM	NM	NM	NM	43	50	NM	NM	NA

Income Statement Analysis (Million $)

	2004	2003	2002	2001	2000	1999	1998	1997	1996	1995
Revs.	NA	8,470	12,321	21,294	33,813	38,303	30,147	26,360	15,859	21,413
Oper. Inc.	NA	633	-3,257	-6,336	6,308	7,494	3,795	3,081	1,424	493
Depr.	NA	978	1,470	2,536	2,318	1,806	1,334	1,450	937	1,493
Int. Exp.	NA	353	382	518	348	406	318	305	230	302
Pretax Inc.	NA	-1,003	-7,057	-19,823	3,003	5,443	2,330	1,502	388	-1,138
Eff. Tax Rate	NA	NM	NM	NM	44.0%	36.5%	57.3%	61.7%	36.9%	NM
Net Inc.	NA	-770	-11,826	-14,170	1,681	3,458	970	541	224	-867
S&P Core Earnings	NA	-1,980	-16,627	-13,160	NA	NA	NA	NA	NA	NA

Balance Sheet & Other Fin. Data (Million $)

	2004	2003	2002	2001	2000	1999	1998	1997	1996	1995
Cash	NA	4,507	2,894	2,390	1,467	1,816	685	1,350	2,241	3,843
Curr. Assets	NA	7,833	9,155	16,103	21,490	21,931	14,078	12,501	12,784	12,074
Total Assets	NA	15,765	17,791	33,664	48,792	38,775	26,720	23,811	22,626	21,117
Curr. Liab.	NA	5,015	6,326	10,169	10,877	11,778	10,428	10,738	10,713	11,563
LT Debt	NA	5,591	4,986	3,274	3,076	4,162	2,409	1,665	1,634	123
Common Equity	NA	-4,239	-4,734	11,023	26,172	13,584	5,534	3,387	3,387	2,329
Total Cap.	NA	2,220	1,932	16,283	30,514	17,746	7,943	5,052	4,320	2,452
Cap. Exp.	NA	291	449	1,390	2,701	2,215	1,626	1,635	939	1,277
Cash Flow	NA	105	-10,523	-11,662	3,999	5,264	2,304	1,991	1,161	626
Curr. Ratio	NA	1.6	1.4	1.6	2.0	1.9	1.4	1.2	1.2	1.8
% LT Debt of Cap.	NA	251.8	258.1	20.1	10.1	23.5	30.3	33.0	37.8	5.0
% Net Inc.of Revs.	NA	NM	NM	NM	5.0	9.0	3.2	2.1	1.4	NM
% Ret. on Assets	NA	NM	NM	NM	4.0	10.2	3.8	2.3	1.1	NA
% Ret. on Equity	NA	NM	NM	NM	8.4	32.5	21.7	17.8	10.9	NA

Data as orig. reptd. Yrs. ended Dec. pr. to 1996 (nine mos.); bef. results of disc. opers. and/or spec. items. Per share data adj. for stk. divs.; EPS diluted (primary prior to 1998). E-Estimated. NA-Not Available. NM-Not Meaningful. NR-Not Ranked.

Office: 600 Mountain Avenue, Murray Hill, NJ 07974.
Telephone: 908-582-8500.
Website: http://www.lucent.com
Chrmn, Pres & CEO: P.F. Russo.
EVP & CFO: F.A. D'Amelio.

SVP, Secy & General Counsel: R.J. Rawson.
Investor Contact: W. Zajack 973-509-0970.
Dirs: R. Denham, D. Goldin, E. E. Hagenlocker, C. A. Hills, K. J. Krapek, R. C. Levin, P. Russo, H. B. Schacht, F. A. Thomas, R. A. Williams, J. A. Young.

Founded: in 1995.
Domicile: Delaware.
Employees: 34,500.
S&P Analyst: Kenneth M. Leon/PMW/BK

Manor Care

Recommendation: **BUY** ★★★★☆ 12-Month Target Price: **$35.00**
(as of October 22, 2004)

HCR has an approximate 0.03% weighting in the **S&P 500**

Sector: Health Care
Sub-Industry: Health Care Facilities
Peer Group: Long-Term Care-- Larger

Summary: This provider of long-term health care services was formed through the 1998 merger of Health Care and Retirement Corp. and Manor Care Inc.

Quantitative Evaluations

S&P Earnings & Dividend Rank: NR

| D | C | B- | B | B+ | A- | A | A+ |

S&P Fair Value Rank: 3+

| 1 | 2 | **3** | 4 | 5 |
| Lowest | | | | Highest |

Fair Value Calc.: $33.20 (Slightly Overvalued)

S&P Investability Quotient Percentile

93%

HCR scored higher than 93% of all companies for which an S&P Report is available.

Volatility: Average

| Low | **Average** | High |

Technical Evaluation: Bullish

Since 10/04, the technical indicators for HCR have been Bullish.

Relative Strength Rank: Moderate

70

| 1 Lowest | | Highest 99 |

Price as of 11/12/04: $34.39 | **2004E S&P Core EPS:** $1.69

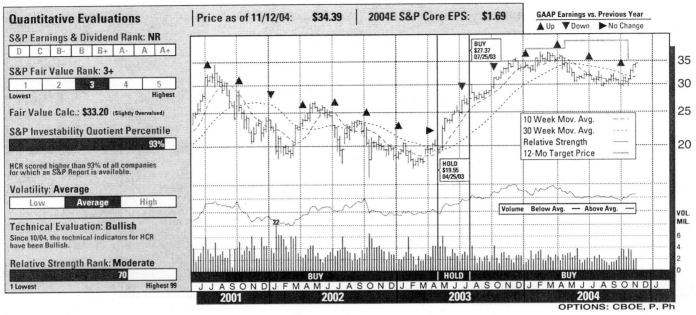

GAAP Earnings vs. Previous Year
▲ Up ▼ Down ► No Change

- 10 Week Mov. Avg.
- 30 Week Mov. Avg.
- Relative Strength
- 12-Mo Target Price

Volume Below Avg. — Above Avg.

OPTIONS: CBOE, P, Ph

Analyst commentary prepared by Cameron Lavey/CB/SB

Highlights October 29, 2004

- We look for revenues to grow 7% in 2004, to $3.2 billion, primarily on an increase in Medicare rates that was effective in October 2003. We also expect revenues to benefit from anticipated private pay per-diem price increases of 5%, a 3% rise in Medicaid rates, and additional contributions from the hospice and outpatient rehabilitation businesses, for which we see 5% higher occupancy rates over the course of 2004. We forecast revenue growth of 6% in 2005, as higher reimbursement rates offset a smaller number of facilities.

- We anticipate that well controlled labor costs, increased occupancy, and an improving payor mix will drive modest EBITDA margin expansion. We also expect lower interest expense, due to debt repurchases, and a 50 basis point reduction in the effective tax rate to help boost earnings.

- We estimate 2004 EPS at $1.85, up 41% from the level of 2003. We look for an additional gain of 14% in 2005, to $2.10.

Investment Rationale/Risk October 29, 2004

- We recommend accumulating the shares. We see high occupancy and increased Medicare exposure providing leverage on Medicare rate increases throughout 2004 and into 2005. We expect HCR to build on its success in leveraging its skilled nursing capabilities to provide Alzheimer's care, a premium service. We are encouraged by the company's active asset management (closing underperforming facilities and expanding in growth markets), build-up of higher value services, and what we view as healthy free cash flow, with gradual debt reduction likely. With a current dividend yield of about 1.8%, we view the shares as attractive.

- Risks to our opinion and target price include the possibility that Medicaid rate increases for long-term care will not return to historical levels for the foreseeable future, in light of continued budget pressures in some states; and potential changes in future Medicare and Medicaid rates.

- Our 12-month target price of $35 is derived by applying a P/E multiple of about 17X to our 2005 EPS estimate, in line with projected three-year growth, and is supported by our discounted cash flow valuation, which assumes a weighted average cost of capital of 8.3%.

Key Stock Statistics

S&P Oper. EPS 2004E	**1.85**	52-week Range	**$37.25-29.20**
P/E on S&P Oper. EPS 2004E	**18.6**	12 Month P/E	**19.4**
S&P Oper. EPS 2005E	**2.10**	Beta	**0.80**
Yield (%)	**1.6%**	Shareholders	**30,000**
Dividend Rate/Share	**0.56**	Market Cap (B)	**$ 3.0**
Shares Outstanding (M)	**86.4**		

Value of $10,000 invested five years ago: **$ 22,148**

Dividend Data Dividends have been paid since 2003

Amount ($)	Date Decl.	Ex-Div. Date	Stock of Record	Payment Date
0.140	Jan. 30	Feb. 11	Feb. 13	Feb. 27 '04
0.140	May. 03	May. 05	May. 07	May. 21 '04
0.140	Jul. 23	Aug. 05	Aug. 09	Aug. 23 '04
0.140	Oct. 22	Nov. 04	Nov. 08	Nov. 22 '04

Revenues/Earnings Data Fiscal year ending December 31

Revenues (Million $)

	2004	2003	2002	2001	2000	1999
1Q	797.3	730.5	716.0	638.2	545.7	531.9
2Q	799.1	750.6	728.4	663.3	581.3	530.5
3Q	806.8	761.3	732.9	687.6	604.5	536.7
4Q	—	787.1	728.1	704.9	624.9	536.3
Yr.	—	3,029	2,905	2,694	2,381	2,135

Earnings Per Share ($)

	2004	2003	2002	2001	2000	1999
1Q	0.46	0.33	0.33	0.24	-0.01	0.37
2Q	0.45	0.21	0.38	0.29	-0.03	0.30
3Q	0.45	0.35	0.38	0.30	0.20	0.31
4Q	E0.49	0.42	0.24	-0.18	0.22	-1.59
Yr.	E1.85	1.31	1.33	0.66	0.38	-0.51

Next earnings report expected: late-January Source: S&P, Company Reports
EPS Estimates based on S&P Operating Earnings; historical GAAP earnings are as reported.

Manor Care, Inc.

Recommendation: **BUY** ★ ★ ★ ☆   12-Month Target Price: **$35.00** (as of October 22, 2004)

Business Summary November 01, 2004

Manor Care, formed via the September 1998 merger of Health Care and Retirement and the original Manor Care Inc., provides a range of health care services, including skilled nursing care, assisted living, subacute medical and rehabilitation care, rehabilitation therapy, home health care, hospice care, and management services for subacute care and rehabilitation therapy.

The most significant portion of the company's business is related to skilled nursing care and assisted living. At September 30, 2004, it operated 282 skilled nursing facilities and 66 assisted living facilities. Certain centers have medical specialty units that provide subacute medical and rehabilitation care, and/or Alzheimer's care programs. Some assisted living facilities operate under the brand names Arden Courts and Springhouse. Arden Courts facilities specifically focus on providing care to persons suffering from early to middle-stage Alzheimer's disease and related memory impairment, while Springhouse facilities serve the general assisted living population of frail elderly. These facilities provide housing, personalized support and health care services in a non-institutional setting designed to address the needs of the elderly or Alzheimer's afflicted.

The home health care business specializes in all levels of home health, hospice care, and rehabilitation therapy from 94 offices, as of September 30, 2004, located in 24 states.

HCR provides rehabilitation therapy in its long-term care centers, other skilled nursing centers, hospitals, and 88 outpatient therapy clinics serving states in the Midwest and Mid-Atlantic, as well as Texas and Florida. The company provides program management services for subacute care and acute rehabilitation programs in hospitals and skilled nursing centers.

Capital spending in 2003 totaled $101.2 million, including $22.1 million to construct new facilities and expand existing facilities. In April 2002, the company sold its Mesquite, TX, acute care hospital, with 172 licensed beds, to Health Management Associates (HMA). It received $80 million in cash, and also purchased a 20% interest in the HMA entity that owns the hospital and one other in the same area, for $32 million. HCR has long-term management contracts with physician practices in the Midwest that specialize in vision care and refractive eye surgery. The company also owns a 97% interest in a medical transcription business that converts medical dictation into electronically formatted patient records.

In January 2004, HCR sold four skilled nursing facilities. In the second quarter of 2004, it elected to not renew the leases of three nursing centers and three assisted living centers, and sold one nursing center. In the third quarter of 2004, HCR opened one new nursing center and acquired one rehabilitation clinic and one hospice operation.

In 2003, revenues in the skilled nursing, assisted living and rehabilitation operations were generated from Medicaid (33%), Medicare (32%), and private pay and other (35%) sources.

In 2003, the company repurchased 6,940,647 of its shares for $145.1 million. In the first nine months of 2004, the company repurchased 3,363,000 shares for $108.2 million..

Company Financials Fiscal Year ending December 31

Per Share Data ($)

(Year Ended December 31)	2003	2002	2001	2000	1999	1998	1997	1996	1995	1994
Tangible Bk. Val.	9.87	9.68	9.28	8.87	8.72	10.35	6.78	NA	NA	NA
Cash Flow	2.72	2.58	1.90	1.55	0.57	0.67	2.32	NA	NA	NA
Earnings	1.31	1.33	0.66	0.38	-0.51	-0.42	1.40	NA	NA	NA
S&P Core Earnings	1.22	1.03	0.72	NA	NA	NA	NA	NA	NA	NA
Dividends	0.25	Nil	Nil	Nil	Nil	Nil	NA	NA	NA	NA
Payout Ratio	19%	Nil	Nil	Nil	Nil	Nil	NA	NA	NA	NA
Prices - High	35.83	27.01	34.50	21.18	33.50	35.00	NA	NA	NA	NA
- Low	17.19	16.20	17.31	6.43	12.75	23.50	NA	NA	NA	NA
P/E Ratio - High	27	20	52	56	NM	NM	NA	NA	NA	NA
- Low	13	12	26	17	NM	NM	NA	NA	NA	NA

Income Statement Analysis (Million $)

	2003	2002	2001	2000	1999	1998	1997	1996	1995	1994
Revs.	3,029	2,905	2,694	2,381	2,135	2,209	892	NA	NA	NA
Oper. Inc.	348	372	307	260	362	397	151	NA	NA	NA
Depr.	129	125	128	121	116	119	37.7	NA	NA	NA
Int. Exp.	41.9	37.7	50.8	60.7	54.0	46.6	17.2	NA	NA	NA
Pretax Inc.	190	213	130	61.7	-102	-24.1	101	NA	NA	NA
Eff. Tax Rate	37.5%	38.0%	47.3%	34.8%	NM	NM	30.7%	NA	NA	NA
Net Inc.	119	132	68.5	39.1	-55.2	-46.2	70.1	NA	NA	NA
S&P Core Earnings	111	101	74.0	NA	NA	NA	NA	NA	NA	NA

Balance Sheet & Other Fin. Data (Million $)

	2003	2002	2001	2000	1999	1998	1997	1996	1995	1994
Cash	86.3	30.6	26.7	24.9	12.0	33.7	7.46	NA	NA	NA
Curr. Assets	585	511	590	505	431	418	171	NA	NA	NA
Total Assets	2,397	2,307	2,424	2,358	2,281	2,715	936	NA	NA	NA
Curr. Liab.	388	642	391	473	409	504	121	NA	NA	NA
LT Debt	659	373	716	644	688	693	NA	NA	NA	NA
Common Equity	975	1,016	1,047	1,013	980	1,557	434	NA	NA	NA
Total Cap.	1,771	1,468	1,865	1,766	1,795	2,496	NA	NA	NA	NA
Cap. Exp.	101	92.5	89.4	117	166	296	NA	NA	NA	NA
Cash Flow	248	257	197	160	60.8	73.1	108	NA	NA	NA
Curr. Ratio	1.5	0.8	1.5	1.1	1.1	0.8	1.4	NA	NA	NA
% LT Debt of Cap.	37.2	25.4	38.4	36.5	38.3	27.8	NA	NA	NA	NA
% Net Inc.of Revs.	3.9	4.5	2.5	1.6	NM	NM	7.9	NA	NA	NA
% Ret. on Assets	5.0	5.6	2.9	1.7	NM	NM	8.1	NA	NA	NA
% Ret. on Equity	12.0	12.8	6.7	3.9	NM	NM	17.0	NA	NA	NA

Data as orig reptd.; bef. results of disc opers/spec. items. Per share data adj. for stk. divs.; EPS diluted. E-Estimated. NA-Not Available. NM-Not Meaningful. NR-Not Ranked. UR-Under Review.

Office: 333 N Summit St, Toledo, OH 43604-2617.
Telephone: 419-252-5500.
Email: info@hcr-manorcare.com
Website: http://www.hcr-manorcare.com
Chrmn, Pres & CEO: P.A. Ormond.
COO & EVP: M.K. Weikel.
EVP & CFO: G.G. Meyers.

VP & Chief Acctg Officer: S.C. Moler.
VP, Secy & General Counsel: R.J. Bixler.
VP & Investor Contact: W. Chenevert 419-252-5500.
Dirs: V. W. Colbert, J. F. Damico, J. H. Lemieux, W. H. Longfield, F. V. Malek, P. A. Ormond, J. T. Schwieters, R. G. Siefers, M. K. Weikel, G. R. Wilensky, T. L. Young.

Founded: in 1991.
Domicile: Delaware.
Employees: 61,000.
S&P Analyst: Cameron Lavey/CB/SB

Marathon Oil

Recommendation: HOLD ★ ★ ★ ☆ ☆
SELL SELL HOLD BUY BUY

12-Month Target Price: **$41.00**
(as of November 08, 2004)

MRO has an approximate 0.12% weighting in the **S&P 500**

Sector: Energy
Sub-Industry: Integrated Oil & Gas
Peer Group: Major Integrated Oil & Gas

Summary: MRO (formerly USX-Marathon Group, a part of USX Corp.) engages in worldwide exploration and production, and domestic refining, marketing and transportation.

Quantitative Evaluations

S&P Earnings & Dividend Rank: B+

D	C	B-	B	B+	A-	A	A+

S&P Fair Value Rank: 3-

1	2	3	4	5
Lowest				Highest

Fair Value Calc: $36.80 (Slightly Overvalued)

S&P Investability Quotient Percentile

98%

MRO scored higher than 98% of all companies for which an S&P Report is available.

Volatility: Average

Low	Average	High

Technical Evaluation: Bearish

Since 10/04, the technical indicators for MRO have been Bearish.

Relative Strength Rank: Weak

28

1 Lowest — Highest 99

Price as of 11/12/04: **$38.21** | 2004E S&P Core EPS: **$3.22**

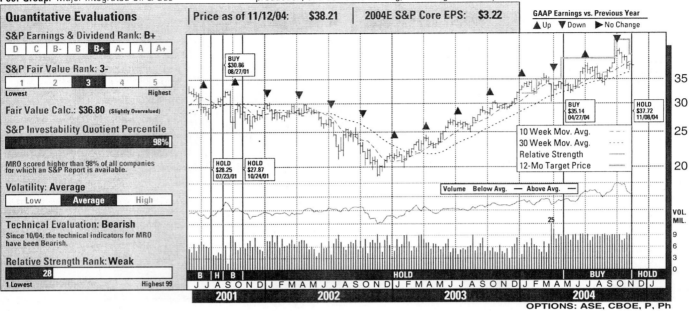

GAAP Earnings vs. Previous Year
▲ Up ▼ Down ► No Change

OPTIONS: ASE, CBOE, P, Ph

Analyst commentary prepared by T. Vital/DC/JWP

Highlights November 09, 2004

- Third quarter operating earnings dropped 22%, to $222 million, or $0.64, before special items. Results were $0.26 below our estimate, reflecting narrowed wholesale marketing margins for non-gasoline and non-distillate refined products, lower upstream volumes and higher derivative-related charges ($0.21 per share aftertax), and greater-than-expected operating costs.

- MRO's upstream production growth has been below average; we estimate that only 76% of production was replaced in 2003. As a result, the company has been realigning its upstream portfolio; about $1.2 billion in assets were sold in 2003. Hydrocarbon production dropped 13% in the third quarter, and MRO cut its 2004 target by 25,000 boe/d, to 335,000 boe/d, reflecting divestitures, field declines and weather-related downtime. We expect a 10% decline in 2004, before rising about 2% in 2005, and an average 3% per annum rise in 2006-08 on contributions from new core areas (West Africa, Russia and Norway). To fund upstream growth, 2004 capital spending is projected at $2.26 billion (60% E&P, 25% R&M), up from 2003's $2.18 billion.

- Strong prices boosted EBITDA before exploration expense (EBITDAX) by 16% in 2003, and we look for increases of 15% in 2004 and 2% in 2005. We expect that refining & marketing margins will experience pressure from high crude costs, but see wide sour crude price discounts aiding MRO refining & marketing results (about 60% of joint venture MAP's crude feedstocks are sour, about 60% from North American sources).

Investment Rationale/Risk November 09, 2004

- In March, MRO agreed to acquire from Ashland Inc. the 38% interest in the MAP refining joint venture that it did not already own, for $2.93 billion (to be funded through cash and equity). Closing is expected by the end of the 2005 first quarter, subject to regulatory approvals. We view the planned deal positively, as it would give the company full control of what we view as a high quality refining complex, providing a balance to upstream business risk.

- Risks to our recommendation and target price include negative trends in upstream production, changes in the market conditions affecting the oil and gas industry, and changes in operating conditions. We believe that MRO's integrated gas strategy is a strategic shift for the company and that it offers significant growth potential, but that its long-term, capital intensive projects create risk.

- Based on a blend of discounted cash flow and peer valuations, our 12-month target price is $41, representing 13X our 2005 EPS estimate of $3.14, a premium to peers. While we are encouraged by gains in MRO's global gas business and exploration success, its upstream growth has lagged its peers, and we would hold the shares.

Key Stock Statistics

S&P Core EPS 2005E	3.14	52-week Range	$42.60-28.82
S&P Oper. EPS 2004E	3.26	12 Month P/E	9.4
P/E on S&P Oper. EPS 2004E	11.7	Beta	0.54
S&P Oper. EPS 2005E	3.14	Shareholders	61,404
Yield (%)	2.9%	Market Cap (B)	$ 13.2
Dividend Rate/Share	1.12	Shares Outstanding (M)	346.1

Value of $10,000 invested five years ago: **$ 16,634**

Dividend Data Dividends have been paid since 1991

Amount ($)	Date Decl.	Ex-Div. Date	Stock of Record	Payment Date
0.250	Jan. 26	Feb. 13	Feb. 18	Mar. 10 '04
0.250	Apr. 28	May. 17	May. 19	Jun. 10 '04
0.250	Jul. 28	Aug. 16	Aug. 18	Sep. 10 '04
0.280	Oct. 27	Nov. 15	Nov. 17	Dec. 10 '04

Revenues/Earnings Data Fiscal year ending December 31

Revenues (Million $)

	2004	2003	2002	2001	2000	1999
1Q	10,693	10,033	6,419	8,722	7,855	4,851
2Q	12,592	9,643	8,078	9,168	8,710	5,481
3Q	12,249	10,253	8,437	8,330	9,228	6,490
4Q	—	11,101	8,530	6,846	8,631	7,505
Yr.	—	41,234	31,720	33,066	34,487	24,327

Earnings Per Share ($)

	2004	2003	2002	2001	2000	1999
1Q	0.83	0.98	0.22	1.62	0.81	0.38
2Q	1.01	0.80	0.54	1.88	1.18	0.43
3Q	0.64	0.90	0.23	0.62	0.38	0.74
4Q	E0.79	0.64	0.62	-2.90	-1.67	0.55
Yr.	E3.26	3.26	1.72	4.26	1.39	2.11

Next earnings report expected: late-January Source: S&P, Company Reports
EPS Estimates based on S&P Operating Earnings; historical GAAP earnings are as reported.

STANDARD &POOR'S

Marathon Oil Corporation

Stock Report
November 13, 2004
NYSE Symbol: **MRO**

Recommendation: HOLD ★ ★ ★ ☆   12-Month Target Price: **$41.00** (as of November 08, 2004)

Business Summary November 09, 2004

In January 2002, MRO (formerly USX-Marathon Group, a part of USX Corp.) began trading as a stand-alone company after USX-Marathon shareholders voted to separate USX's steel and energy businesses via a tax-free spinoff. In March 2004, MRO agreed to acquire from Ashland Inc. (ASH) the 38% interest in their Marathon Ashland Petroleum LLC (MAP) refining joint venture, for about $2.93 billion, as well as ASH's maleic anhydride operations, and 61 Valvoline Instant Oil Change centers for an additional $94 million; closing is expected by the end of the 2005 first quarter, subject to regulatory approvals.

MRO is engaged in oil and gas exploration and production (E&P; 12% of 2003 revenues, $1,514 million of 2003 operating income); refining, marketing and transportation (RM&T; 33%, $819 million); and integrated gas (5.4%, loss of $3 million) in the U.S. (93% of 2003 revenues), Canada (4%), the U.K. (2%), and Equatorial Guinea and elsewhere (1%).

The company replaced 124% of its 2003 barrel of oil equivalent (boe) production, excluding dispositions, at a finding and development (F&D) cost of $8.78 per boe. Excluding acquisitions and dispositions, the reserve replacement rate was 76% in 2003. In 2004, MRO expected to replace about 180% of production at a F&D cost under $5 per boe. In 2003, net liquid hydrocarbon production declined to 194,000 barrels per day (b/d, 55% from U.S. operations), from 207,000 b/d (57%) in 2002. Net natural gas production from continuing operations was 1,096 million cubic feet per day (MMcf per day, 67%) in 2003, versus 1,126 MMcf per day (66%) in 2002. At year-end 2002, net proved reserves declined to 1.042 billion barrels (Bbl; 70% developed, 55% liquids), versus 1.283 million Bbl (74%, 56%) in 2002, reflecting

the disposition of the Yates field. Worldwide production costs rose to $5.03 per boe in 2003, from $4.22 in 2002.

In 2003, MRO acquired Khanty Mansiyak Oil Corp. (KMOC) for $285 million, and sold its interest in CLAM Petroleum B.V., interests in several pipeline companies, and Yates field and gathering systems in West Texas.

In 1998, the company and ASH combined their RM&T operations into a joint venture, Marathon Ashland Petroleum LLC (MAP), owned 62% by MRO. In 2003, MAP owned and operated seven refineries (25% of throughput capacity at Garyville, LA; 24% Catlettsburg, KY; 21% Robinson, IL; 8% Detroit, MI; 8% Canton, OH; 7% Texas City, TX; and 7% St. Paul Park, MN), with throughput capacity of 935,000 b/d of crude oil. In 2003, refined product sales averaged 1.357 MMBbl per day (57% gasoline, 27% distillates, 7% feedstocks and special products, 5% asphalt, 2% propane, and 2% heavy fuel oil). MAP also operates a system of crude oil and refined product pipelines and terminals. It supplies about 3,900 Marathon and Ashland branded retail outlets. Retail sales of gasoline and convenience store merchandise are also made through a wholly owned MAP subsidiary, Speedway SuperAmerica LLC (SSA). The subsidiary had 1,775 retail outlets in nine states at the end of 2003.

In January 2004, MRO formed its integrated gas segment, which includes the company's Alaska LNG operations, Equatorial Guinea, methanol operations, and natural gas marketing and transportation activities, together with expenses related to integrated gas.

Company Financials Fiscal Year ending December 31

Per Share Data ($)

(Year Ended December 31)	2003	2002	2001	2000	1999	1998	1997	1996	1995	1994
Tangible Bk. Val.	18.39	15.13	15.97	15.53	15.40	14.00	12.52	11.62	10.01	11.01
Cash Flow	7.05	5.60	8.24	5.38	5.17	4.27	3.89	4.74	2.56	3.61
Earnings	3.26	1.72	4.26	1.39	2.11	1.05	1.58	2.33	-0.31	1.10
S&P Core Earnings	3.26	1.37	4.41	NA	NA	NA	NA	NA	NA	NA
Dividends	0.96	0.92	0.92	0.88	0.84	0.84	0.76	0.70	0.68	0.68
Payout Ratio	29%	53%	75%	63%	40%	80%	48%	30%	NM	62%
Prices - High	33.61	30.30	33.73	30.37	33.87	40.50	38.87	25.50	21.50	19.12
- Low	19.85	18.82	24.95	20.68	19.62	25.00	23.75	17.25	15.75	15.62
P/E Ratio - High	10	18	28	22	16	39	25	11	NM	17
- Low	6	11	20	15	9	24	15	7	NM	14

Income Statement Analysis (Million $)

	2003	2002	2001	2000	1999	1998	1997	1996	1995	1994
Revs.	40,963	31,464	33,019	34,487	24,212	21,726	15,668	16,332	13,871	10,215
Oper. Inc.	2,988	2,253	4,215	3,521	1,997	1,530	1,510	1,927	1,581	1,305
Depr. Depl. & Amort.	1,175	1,201	1,236	1,245	950	941	664	693	817	721
Int. Exp.	238	288	196	260	290	311	285	308	357	384
Pretax Inc.	1,898	1,098	2,781	1,412	1,425	701	672	991	-190	476
Eff. Tax Rate	30.8%	35.4%	27.3%	34.1%	22.7%	20.3%	32.1%	32.3%	NM	32.6%
Net Inc.	1,012	536	1,318	432	654	310	456	671	-83.0	321
S&P Core Earnings	1,014	428	1,367	NA	NA	NA	NA	NA	NA	NA

Balance Sheet & Other Fin. Data (Million $)

	2003	2002	2001	2000	1999	1998	1997	1996	1995	1994
Cash	1,396	488	657	340	111	137	36.0	32.0	77.0	28.0
Curr. Assets	6,040	4,479	4,411	4,985	4,102	2,976	2,018	2,046	1,888	1,737
Total Assets	19,482	17,812	16,129	15,232	15,705	14,544	10,565	10,151	10,109	10,951
Curr. Liab.	4,207	3,659	3,468	4,012	3,149	2,610	2,262	2,142	2,025	1,712
LT Debt	4,085	4,410	3,432	4,196	3,504	3,640	2,476	2,642	3,367	3,983
Common Equity	6,075	5,082	4,940	4,845	4,800	4,312	3,618	3,340	2,872	3,163
Total Cap.	12,171	12,908	11,632	12,235	11,552	10,992	7,596	7,342	7,493	8,676
Cap. Exp.	1,892	1,574	1,639	1,669	1,378	1,270	1,038	751	642	753
Cash Flow	2,187	1,737	2,546	1,677	1,604	1,251	1,120	1,364	734	1,036
Curr. Ratio	1.4	1.2	1.3	1.2	1.3	1.1	0.9	1.0	0.9	1.0
% LT Debt of Cap.	33.6	34.2	29.5	34.3	30.3	33.1	32.6	36.0	44.9	45.9
% Ret. on Assets	5.4	3.2	7.9	2.8	4.3	2.5	4.4	6.6	NM	2.9
% Ret. on Equity	18.1	10.7	22.4	9.0	14.4	7.8	13.1	21.6	NM	10.2

Data as orig. reptd.; bef. results of disc. opers. and/or spec. items. Per share data adj. for stk. divs. Revs. in quarterly table incl. oth. inc. EPS diuted. E-Estimated. NA-Not Available. NM-Not Meaningful. NR-Not Ranked.

Office: 5555 San Felipe Road, Houston, TX 77056-2723.
Telephone: 713-629-6600.
Website: http://www.marathon.com
Chrmn: T.J. Usher.
Pres & CEO: C.P. Cazalot, Jr.
SVP & CFO: J. Clark.

VP & Treas: P.C. Reinbolt.
VP, Secy & General Counsel: W.F. Schwind, Jr.
VP & Investor Contact: K.L. Matheny 713-296-4114.
Dirs: C. F. Bolden, Jr., C. P. Cazalot, Jr., D. A. Daberko, W. L. Davis, S. Jackson, P. Lader, C. R. Lee, D. H. Reilley, S. E. Schofield, T. J. Usher, D. C. Yearley.

Founded: in 1901.
Domicile: Delaware.
Employees: 27,007.
S&P Analyst: T. Vital/DC/JWP

Marriott International

Recommendation: **HOLD** ★★★☆☆

12-Month Target Price: **$51.00**
(as of July 01, 2004)

MAR has an approximate 0.12% weighting in the **S&P 500**

Sector: Consumer Discretionary
Sub-Industry: Hotels, Resorts & Cruise Lines
Peer Group: Hotel Companies - Larger

Summary: MAR's lodging brands include more than 2,000 hotels, most of which are managed by the company or are operated by others through franchise relationships.

Quantitative Evaluations

S&P Earnings & Dividend Rank: B+

| D | C | B- | B | B+ | A- | A | A+ |

S&P Fair Value Rank: 2+

| 1 | 2 | 3 | 4 | 5 |
| Lowest | | | | Highest |

Fair Value Calc.: $54.30 (Slightly Overvalued)

S&P Investability Quotient Percentile

95%

MAR scored higher than 95% of all companies for which an S&P Report is available.

Volatility: Low

| Low | Average | High |

Technical Evaluation: Bullish
Since 9/04, the technical indicators for MAR have been Bullish.

Relative Strength Rank: Strong

74

1 Lowest   Highest 99

Price as of 11/12/04: $57.61 | **2004E S&P Core EPS:** $2.24

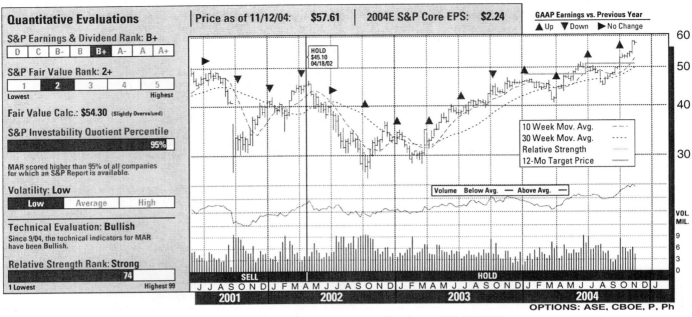

GAAP Earnings vs. Previous Year
▲ Up ▼ Down ► No Change

10 Week Mov. Avg.
30 Week Mov. Avg.
Relative Strength
12-Mo Target Price

Volume   Below Avg. — Above Avg.

OPTIONS: ASE, CBOE, P, Ph

Analyst commentary prepared by Tom Graves, CFA /PMW/BK

Highlights September 13, 2004

- We look for 2005 total revenue to increase 9%, to $10.8 billion, from the $10.0 billion that we project for 2004. We see growth drivers including higher revenue per available room at comparable hotels, and the presence of additional hotels in the Marriott lodging system.

- We estimate that MAR's lodging-related operating profit (including the company's timeshare business) will increase to $733 million in 2005, up 18% from the $623 million that we project for 2004. We estimate that the synthetic fuel business will lead to an EPS benefit of $0.40 in 2005, versus an anticipated contribution of $0.41 in 2004, with these benefits coming primarily from tax credits. We look for overall net income in 2005 to total $646 million ($2.75 a share), up from a projected $585 million ($2.42) in 2004.

- In April 2004, MAR announced a 13% rise in its dividend. The company closed its distribution services business in 2002, and completed the sale of its senior living business in the first quarter of 2003; these businesses were treated as discontinued operations in 2002 and 2003.

Investment Rationale/Risk September 13, 2004

- Our hold opinion on the stock reflects our view that the shares will get support from prospects for improvement in lodging industry fundamentals, including greater demand likely for business travel in 2005 and the latter part of 2004. In addition, we expect the company to repurchase some stock in the year ahead. In April 2004, directors boosted the stock buyback authorization by 20 million shares. As of mid-2004, MAR had authorization to acquire 24.7 million shares. However, we see earnings quality reduced by contributions related to synthetic fuel investments, and, to a lesser degree, by unexpensed stock option expense.

- Risks to our recommendation and target price include the possibility that terrorism fears will heighten, leading to lower than anticipated demand for hotel rooms.

- Our 12-month target price of $51 reflects our view that expectations of a further lodging industry upturn will help the shares to retain some of their P/E multiple premium (currently about 13%, based on projected 2005 EPS) to the level of the S&P 500.

Key Stock Statistics

S&P Core EPS 2005E	2.57	52-week Range	$58.18-40.64
S&P Oper. EPS 2004E	2.43	12 Month P/E	24.2
P/E on S&P Oper. EPS 2004E	23.7	Beta	1.08
S&P Oper. EPS 2005E	2.80	Shareholders	47,202
Yield (%)	0.6%	Market Cap (B)	$ 12.9
Dividend Rate/Share	0.34	Shares Outstanding (M)	223.6

Value of $10,000 invested five years ago: **$ 18,132**

Dividend Data Dividends have been paid since 1998

Amount ($)	Date Decl.	Ex-Div. Date	Stock of Record	Payment Date
0.075	Feb. 05	Mar. 30	Apr. 01	Apr. 28 '04
0.085	Apr. 30	Jun. 22	Jun. 24	Jun. 26 '04
0.085	Aug. 05	Sep. 07	Sep. 09	Oct. 18 '04
0.085	Nov. 04	Dec. 14	Dec. 16	Jan. 10 '05

Revenues/Earnings Data Fiscal year ending December 31

Revenues (Million $)

	2004	2003	2002	2001	2000	1999
1Q	2,252	2,023	1,808	2,461	2,167	1,895
2Q	2,402	2,016	2,034	2,450	2,391	2,042
3Q	2,304	2,109	1,924	2,373	2,303	1,995
4Q	—	2,866	2,675	2,868	3,156	2,807
Yr.	—	9,014	8,441	10,152	10,017	8,739

Earnings Per Share ($)

	2004	2003	2002	2001	2000	1999
1Q	0.47	0.36	0.32	0.47	0.37	0.38
2Q	0.67	0.51	0.50	0.50	0.50	0.42
3Q	0.55	0.38	0.45	0.39	0.43	0.36
4Q	E0.74	0.69	0.47	-0.48	0.59	0.44
Yr.	E2.43	1.94	1.74	0.92	1.89	1.51

Next earnings report expected: early-February Source: S&P, Company Reports
EPS Estimates based on S&P Operating Earnings; historical GAAP earnings are as reported.

Marriott International, Inc.

Recommendation: **HOLD** ★ ★ ★ ☆ ☆   12-Month Target Price: **$51.00** (as of July 01, 2004)

Business Summary September 13, 2004

As of January 2, 2004, Marriott International lodging and timeshare businesses included 2,718 properties, with 490,564 rooms or suites. This included 947 properties (249,503 rooms or suites) that MAR operated under long-term management or lease agreements, and six owned hotels (1,413). With its management agreements, the company typically earns a base fee, and may receive an incentive management fee that is based on hotel profits. MAR's lodging systems also included 1,765 franchised properties, with 239,648 rooms, that were operated by other parties. With franchise properties, the company generally received an initial application fee and continuing royalty fees.

By brand (including franchises), the lodging business, as of January 2, 2004, included 472 Marriott Hotels & Resorts, Marriott Conference Centers of JW Marriott Hotels & Resorts properties; 56 Ritz Carlton hotels; 126 Renaissance hotels; 192 Ramada International hotels; 616 Courtyard hotels; 524 Fairfield Inn properties; 110 SpringHill Suites properties; 449 Residence Inn hotels; 111 Town-Place Suites properties; 49 timeshare properties; and 13 Marriott Executive Apartments or other properties. In 2003, MAR's full-service lodging segment, which includes the Marriott, Ritz-Carlton, Renaissance and Ramada International businesses, accounted for 65% of total revenues.

The company's international presence, as of January 2, 2004, included 311 properties (49,982 rooms or suites) in Europe, 88 properties (30,177) in Asia, 39 (11,128) in the Middle East or Africa, 35 (8,733) in Canada, 10 (3,184) in Mexico, and 11 (2,679) in Australia.

The Marriott Vacation Club International timeshare business develops, sells and operates vacation timesharing resorts under four brands. At the end of 2003, there were 256,000 owners, up from 223,000 a year earlier. Of MAR's 49 timeshare properties at January 2,2004, 36 were in the continental U.S.

In October 2001, MAR acquired four coal-based synthetic fuel production facilities, for $46 million. The facilities produce significant losses, but these were outweighed in 2002 by tax credits related to synthetic fuel production. In June 2003, the company sold about a 50% interest in the synthetic fuel business. As of November 2003, MAR began accounting for results related to this business through the equity method.

The company's senior living business has been treated as a discontinued operation; the business was sold in the first quarter of 2003. As of January 3, 2003, MAR exited its distribution services business. Operating results of this business had been treated as discontinued operations. The after-tax cost to exit the business was $40 million.

In 2003, MAR repurchased 10.5 million common shares, at a total cost of $380 million. Through late April 2004, the company had purchased about 7.4 million additional shares, and was authorized to buy about 25 million more.

Company Financials Fiscal Year ending December 31

Per Share Data ($)

(Year Ended December 31)	2003	2002	2001	2000	1999	1998	1997	1996	1995	1994
Tangible Bk. Val.	10.33	9.13	7.11	5.61	4.26	3.36	NA	NA	NA	NA
Cash Flow	2.60	2.45	1.78	2.65	2.08	1.94	1.65	1.30	1.08	NA
Earnings	1.94	1.74	0.92	1.89	1.51	1.46	1.19	0.99	0.83	0.62
S&P Core Earnings	1.35	1.53	0.70	NA	NA	NA	NA	NA	NA	NA
Dividends	0.30	0.28	0.26	0.24	0.21	0.15	NA	NA	NA	NA
Payout Ratio	15%	16%	28%	12%	13%	10%	NA	NA	NA	NA
Prices - High	47.20	46.45	50.50	43.50	44.50	37.93	NA	NA	NA	NA
- Low	28.55	26.25	27.30	26.12	29.00	19.37	NA	NA	NA	NA
P/E Ratio - High	24	27	55	23	28	26	NA	NA	NA	NA
- Low	15	15	30	14	18	13	NA	NA	NA	NA

Income Statement Analysis (Million $)

	2003	2002	2001	2000	1999	1998	1997	1996	1995	1994
Revs.	9,014	8,441	10,152	10,017	8,739	7,968	9,046	7,267	6,255	5,746
Oper. Inc.	537	622	779	997	828	766	647	525	399	NA
Depr.	160	187	222	195	162	140	126	89.0	67.0	NA
Int. Exp.	110	86.0	109	100	61.0	30.0	22.0	37.0	9.00	7.00
Pretax Inc.	488	471	370	757	637	632	531	436	362	276
Eff. Tax Rate	NM	6.79%	36.2%	36.7%	37.2%	382.0%	39.0%	37.8%	39.2%	40.9%
Net Inc.	476	439	236	479	400	390	324	271	220	163
S&P Core Earnings	330	381	180	NA	NA	NA	NA	NA	NA	NA

Balance Sheet & Other Fin. Data (Million $)

	2003	2002	2001	2000	1999	1998	1997	1996	1995	1994
Cash	229	198	817	334	489	390	289	426	NA	NA
Curr. Assets	1,235	1,744	2,130	1,415	1,600	1,332	1,367	1,530	NA	NA
Total Assets	8,177	8,296	9,107	8,237	7,324	6,233	5,557	5,608	NA	NA
Curr. Liab.	1,770	2,207	1,802	1,917	1,743	1,412	1,639	1,748	NA	NA
LT Debt	1,391	1,553	2,815	2,016	1,676	1,267	112	413	NA	NA
Common Equity	4,050	3,679	3,478	3,267	2,908	2,570	2,586	2,549	NA	NA
Total Cap.	5,441	5,232	6,293	5,283	4,584	3,837	2,698	2,962	NA	NA
Cap. Exp.	210	292	560	1,095	929	937	NA	NA	NA	NA
Cash Flow	636	626	458	674	562	530	450	360	287	NA
Curr. Ratio	0.7	0.8	1.2	0.7	0.9	0.9	0.8	0.9	NA	NA
% LT Debt of Cap.	25.6	29.7	44.7	38.2	36.6	33.0	4.2	13.9	NA	NA
% Net Inc.of Revs.	5.3	5.2	2.3	4.8	4.6	4.9	3.6	3.7	3.5	2.8
% Ret. on Assets	5.8	5.0	2.7	6.2	5.9	6.8	6.6	NA	NA	NA
% Ret. on Equity	12.3	12.1	7.0	15.5	14.6	15.1	16.1	NA	NA	NA

Revenues for 1998 reflect a change in acctg. for various managed properties. Data pro forma prior to 3/27/98. Other data as orig. reptd. Data bef. results of disc. opers. and/or spec. items. Per share data adj. for stk. divs. as of ex-div. date. Bold denotes primary EPS. E-Estimated. NA-Not Available. NM-Not Meaningful. NR-Not Ranked.

Office: 10400 Fernwood Road, Bethesda, MD 20817.
Telephone: 301-380-3000.
Website: http://www.marriott.com
Chrmn & CEO: J.W. Marriott, Jr.
Pres & COO: W.J. Shaw.
EVP & CFO: A.M. Sorenson.

EVP & General Counsel: J. Ryan.
SVP & Treas: C.B. Handlon.
SVP & Investor Contact: L.E. Paugh .
Dirs: R. S. Braddock, A. M. Fudge, G. M. Grosvenor, L. W. Kellner, D. L. Lee, J. W. Marriott III, J. W. Marriott, Jr., F. D. McKenzie, G. Munoz, H. J. Pearce, R. W. Sant, W. J. Shaw, L. M. Small.

Founded: in 1971.
Domicile: Delaware.
Employees: 128,000.
S&P Analyst: Tom Graves, CFA /PMW/BK

Marshall & Ilsley Corp.

Recommendation: **HOLD** ★★★☆☆
SELL · STR · HOLD · BUY · STR BUY

12-Month Target Price: $42.00
(as of July 14, 2004)

MI has an approximate 0.09% weighting in the **S&P 500**

Sector: Financials
Sub-Industry: Regional Banks
Peer Group: Midwest/West Super Regional Banks

Summary: This bank holding company operates more than 200 offices in Wisconsin, in addition to offices in Arizona, Nevada, Minnesota, Missouri and Florida.

Quantitative Evaluations

S&P Earnings & Dividend Rank: A
| D | C | B- | B | B+ | A- | **A** | A+ |

S&P Fair Value Rank: 3+
| 1 | 2 | **3** | 4 | 5 |
Lowest — Highest

Fair Value Calc.: $41.00 (Slightly Overvalued)

S&P Investability Quotient Percentile
98%

MI scored higher than 98% of all companies for which an S&P Report is available.

Volatility: Low
| **Low** | Average | High |

Technical Evaluation: Bullish
Since 8/04, the technical indicators for MI have been Bullish.

Relative Strength Rank: Moderate
59
1 Lowest — Highest 99

| Price as of 11/12/04: | **$43.49** | 2004E S&P Core EPS: | **$2.49** |

GAAP Earnings vs. Previous Year
▲ Up ▼ Down ► No Change

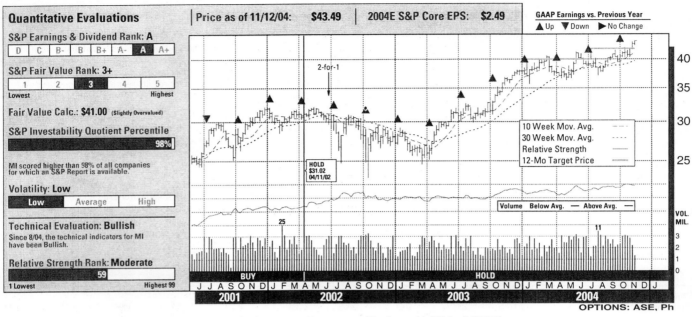

- 10 Week Mov. Avg.
- 30 Week Mov. Avg.
- Relative Strength
- 12-Mo Target Price

Volume Below Avg. — Above Avg.

OPTIONS: ASE, Ph

Analyst commentary prepared by James M. O'Brien/MF/JWP

Highlights November 08, 2004

- We expect the bank's net interest margin to compress for the remainder of 2004, in the wake of the Federal Reserve's recent actions on interest rates and MI's reliance on wholesale borrowings.

- Based on what we see as improved asset quality and healthier economic conditions, we believe that MI is likely to allow its loan loss reserve to move toward normalized historical levels in 2004. Our model calls for total provisions of about $51 million, down from $64 million in 2003. We think the company has made progress in improving the efficiency of its data processing subsidiary, Metavante, and our model assumes a modest additional improvement in 2004, together with increasing revenue contributions, especially from an anticipated pickup in loan growth that we believe can support our EPS estimates.

- All told, we see 2004 operating EPS advancing about 13%, to $2.69, from $2.38 in 2003 (which included $0.01 of Metavante's acquisition-related transition expenses), driven mainly by credit quality improvement as well as expense control and increased commercial loan demand. Our 2005 estimate is $3.00.

Investment Rationale/Risk November 08, 2004

- We would hold the shares on a total return basis. Using a long-term growth assumption of 10%, a discount rate of 8.3% to 8.4%, and a terminal P/E multiple of 13X to 15X projected EPS, we estimate intrinsic value of $41 to $42. Based on our view of the company's strong asset quality, solid capitalization, improving operating efficiency, and above-peer average profitability, we believe the stock deserves to trade in line with its mid-cap bank peers. We think that in an improving economy with increasing capital spending levels, the stock should trade about in line with its intrinsic value range.

- Risks to our recommendation and target price include potentially higher operating costs, the impact of a more sluggish economy than expected, and general interest rate risk.

- Our 12-month target price of $42 assumes a P/E of 14X our 2005 operating estimate, a slight discount to its peer group, as we think the growth rate could slow to a normalized 10% long term rate.

Key Stock Statistics

S&P Oper. EPS 2004E	2.69	52-week Range	$43.49-35.67
P/E on S&P Oper. EPS 2004E	16.2	12 Month P/E	16.6
S&P Oper. EPS 2005E	3.00	Beta	0.74
Yield (%)	1.9%	Shareholders	19,708
Dividend Rate/Share	0.84	Market Cap (B)	$ 9.7
Shares Outstanding (M)	222.8		

Value of $10,000 invested five years ago: **$ 13,804**

Dividend Data Dividends have been paid since 1938

Amount ($)	Date Decl.	Ex-Div. Date	Stock of Record	Payment Date
0.180	Feb. 19	Feb. 26	Mar. 01	Mar. 12 '04
0.210	Apr. 27	May. 26	May. 28	Jun. 11 '04
0.210	Aug. 19	Aug. 27	Aug. 31	Sep. 10 '04
0.210	Oct. 21	Nov. 26	Nov. 30	Dec. 10 '04

Revenues/Earnings Data Fiscal year ending December 31

Revenues (Million $)
	2004	2003	2002	2001	2000	1999
1Q	702.5	548.7	639.4	699.4	644.9	548.0
2Q	728.0	682.2	654.3	559.3	679.6	573.2
3Q	—	696.3	665.3	678.9	641.0	602.7
4Q	—	818.5	—	—	—	616.5
Yr.	—	2,746	2,650	2,712	2,676	2,342

Earnings Per Share ($)
	2004	2003	2002	2001	2000	1999
1Q	0.65	0.56	0.53	0.40	0.42	0.38
2Q	0.67	0.59	0.54	0.28	0.42	0.39
3Q	0.69	0.61	0.54	0.38	0.24	0.41
4Q	E0.68	0.62	0.55	0.49	0.39	0.41
Yr.	E2.69	2.38	2.16	1.54	1.45	1.57

Next earnings report expected: mid-January Source: S&P, Company Reports
EPS Estimates based on S&P Operating Earnings; historical GAAP earnings are as reported.

Recommendation: **HOLD** ★ ★ ★ ☆ ☆   12-Month Target Price: **$42.00** (as of July 14, 2004)

Business Summary November 08, 2004

Marshall & Ilsley Corp. has a diversified revenue mix, and the largest retail banking presence in Wisconsin, with 199 locations. In addition, it has retail offices in Arizona, Nevada, Missouri, Minnesota and Florida. The bank, with assets of $34.4 billion at December 31, 2003, also provides trust and investment management, equipment leasing, mortgage banking, financial planning, investments and insurance services.

Metavante Corp. (formerly M&I Data Services) supplies financial and data processing services and software to financial institutional customers across the U.S. and overseas. Data processing accounted for 29% of operating net revenues in each of 2003 and 2002.

Despite its interests in data processing and the diversification benefits this provides, MI remains a commercial bank, and derives a large portion of its total income from net interest income. Net interest income (the difference between the interest a bank receives on loans and other investments and the interest it pays on funds it borrows) is principally affected by the bank's ability to efficiently balance assets and liabilities in varying interest rate environments.

At December 31, 2003, the bulk of earning assets were financing loans and leases. Loans and leases were distributed as follows: commercial (30% of total loans and leases), real estate (63%), and personal (8%). Total average loans rose 16% in 2003, to $24.4 billion. The net interest margin (FTE basis) narrowed to 3.65%, from 3.96% in 2002.

In the 2001 third quarter, MI acquired Minnesota-based National City Bancorporation, with $1.2 billion in assets, in exchange for stock. Also in the quarter, MI acquired 12 branches in Arizona, with $538 million in assets and $455 million in deposits.

In March 2002, the company acquired Minnesota-based Richfield State Agency, with assets of $736 million and deposits of $548 million. Also in March, MI acquired Century Bancshares, based in Minnesota, with assets of $326 million and deposits of $280 million. Following these acquisitions, the bank operated 12 offices in Minnesota. In October 2002, MI acquired Mississippi Valley Bancshares, with assets of $2.1 billion and deposits of $1.7 billion, for $486 million in cash and common stock.

In May 2002, Metavante acquired Beneplan, Inc. a provider of third-party administration services for retirement benefit plans. In July, it acquired Paytrust, a bill management company. In August, it acquired Spectrum EBP, LLC, a privately-held company that exchanges online bills and payments.

Company Financials Fiscal Year ending December 31

Per Share Data ($)

(Year Ended December 31)	2003	2002	2001	2000	1999	1998	1997	1996	1995	1994
Tangible Bk. Val.	9.96	8.61	9.00	9.06	8.12	8.67	7.43	6.39	6.31	5.20
Earnings	2.38	2.16	1.54	1.45	1.57	1.31	1.21	1.04	0.98	0.48
S&P Core Earnings	2.28	2.07	1.49	NA	NA	NA	NA	NA	NA	NA
Dividends	0.70	0.55	0.57	0.52	0.47	0.43	0.39	0.36	0.33	0.30
Payout Ratio	29%	25%	37%	36%	30%	33%	32%	35%	33%	62%
Prices - High	38.46	32.12	32.12	31.12	36.37	31.12	31.12	17.81	13.25	12.00
- Low	24.60	23.11	23.53	19.12	27.18	19.68	16.18	12.18	9.00	8.87
P/E Ratio - High	16	15	21	22	23	24	26	17	14	25
- Low	10	11	15	13	17	15	13	12	9	19

Income Statement Analysis (Million $)

	2003	2002	2001	2000	1999	1998	1997	1996	1995	1994
Net Int. Inc.	1,057	1,006	843	673	705	676	564	506	491	491
Tax Equiv. Adj.	NA	32.2	31.2	31.0	28.7	26.2	22.8	13.9	9.57	9.58
Non Int. Inc.	1,194	1,089	1,020	978	850	726	596	488	420	367
Loan Loss Prov.	63.0	74.4	54.1	30.4	25.4	27.1	17.3	15.2	16.2	24.9
Exp./Op. Revs.	64.5%	61.9%	68.1%	65.4%	64.2%	67.1%	66.9%	67.5%	65.1%	76.0%
Pretax Inc.	758	719	501	470	528	465	370	313	300	168
Eff. Tax Rate	28.3%	33.2%	32.6%	32.5%	32.9%	35.2%	33.8%	35.1%	35.5%	43.7%
Net Inc.	544	480	338	317	355	301	245	203	193	94.4
% Net Int. Marg.	3.65	3.96	3.67	2.81	3.58	3.69	4.00	4.14	4.30	4.40
S&P Core Earnings	519	453	319	NA	NA	NA	NA	NA	NA	NA

Balance Sheet & Other Fin. Data (Million $)

	2003	2002	2001	2000	1999	1998	1997	1996	1995	1994
Money Mkt. Assets	163	250	947	163	175	146	81.0	85.4	134	254
Inv. Securities	5,607	5,209	4,464	5,848	5,575	5,192	4,969	3,839	2,909	2,295
Com'l Loans	14,254	6,586	10,815	9,649	4,754	4,078	3,865	3,249	3,211	2,933
Other Loans	10,896	17,011	8,480	7,938	11,580	9,918	8,776	6,053	5,658	5,859
Total Assets	34,373	32,875	27,254	26,078	24,370	21,566	19,477	14,763	13,343	12,613
Demand Deposits	4,715	4,462	3,559	3,130	2,831	2,929	2,723	2,471	2,363	2,199
Time Deposits	17,555	15,932	12,934	16,119	13,604	12,991	11,633	8,481	7,918	7,300
LT Debt	2,735	2,284	1,560	921	665	794	791	336	423	654
Common Equity	3,329	3,037	2,536	3,200	2,117	2,282	1,919	1,261	1,223	1,026
% Ret. on Assets	1.6	1.6	1.3	1.3	1.5	1.5	1.4	1.5	1.5	0.9
% Ret. on Equity	17.1	17.4	13.8	10.6	13.8	14.0	15.1	15.9	17.0	NA
% Loan Loss Resv.	1.4	1.4	1.4	1.3	1.4	1.6	1.6	1.7	1.8	1.8
% Loans/Deposits	113.1	117.2	117.0	91.4	99.4	88.0	87.4	85.0	86.3	92.6
% Equity to Assets	9.5	9.2	9.0	11.9	11.0	10.2	9.3	9.4	8.7	8.1

Data as orig reptd.; bef. results of disc opers/spec. items. Per share data adj. for stk. divs.; EPS diluted. E-Estimated. NA-Not Available. NM-Not Meaningful. NR-Not Ranked. UR-Under Review.

Office: 770 North Water Street, Milwaukee, WI 53202.
Telephone: 414-765-7801.
Website: http://www.micorp.com
Chrmn: J.B. Wigdale.
Pres & CEO: D.J. Kuester.
SVP & CFO: J.M. Presley.
SVP & Treas: D.H. Wilson.

SVP, Secy & General Counsel: R.J. Erickson.
Dirs: R. A. Abdoo, D. L. Andreas, A. N. Baur, J. F. Chait, B. E. Jacobs, D. R. Johnson, T. D. Kellner, D. J. Kuester, K. C. Lyall, J. A. Mellowes, E. L. Meyer, R. J. O'Toole, S. W. Orr, Jr., P. M. Platten III, R. A. Schaefer, J. S. Shiely, J. A. Urdan, D. S. Waller, G. E. Wardeberg, J. B. Wigdale.

Founded: in 1959.
Domicile: Wisconsin.
Employees: 12,244.
S&P Analyst: James M. O'Brien/MF/JWP

Marsh & McLennan

Recommendation: **HOLD** ★★★ ☆ ☆
SELL | SELL | HOLD | BUY | BUY

12-Month Target Price: $32.00
(as of October 26, 2004)

MMC has an approximate 0.13% weighting in the **S&P 500**

Sector: Financials
Sub-Industry: Insurance Brokers
Peer Group: Insurance Brokers & Related Services

Summary: This global professional services firm provides risk and insurance services, investment management, and consulting services through its operating companies.

Quantitative Evaluations

S&P Earnings & Dividend Rank: A

| D | C | B- | B | B+ | A- | **A** | A+ |

S&P Fair Value Rank: 4+

| 1 | 2 | 3 | **4** | 5 |
| Lowest | | | | Highest |

Fair Value Calc.: $27.60 (Fairly Valued)

S&P Investability Quotient Percentile

98%

MMC scored higher than 98% of all companies for which an S&P Report is available.

Volatility: High

| Low | Average | **High** |

Technical Evaluation: Bearish
Since 10/04, the technical indicators for MMC have been Bearish.

Relative Strength Rank: Weak

| 1 Lowest | | Highest 99 |

Price as of 11/12/04: $27.68 | **2004E S&P Core EPS:** $2.15

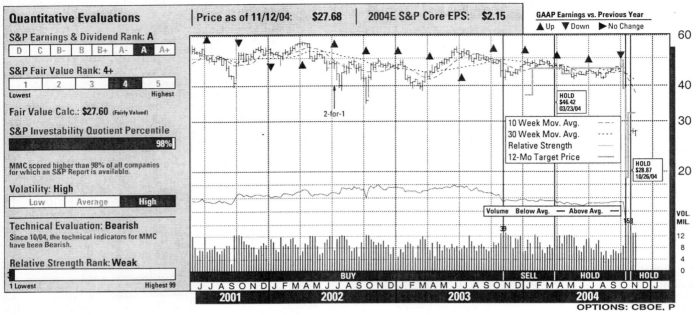

GAAP Earnings vs. Previous Year
▲ Up ▼ Down ► No Change

- 10 Week Mov. Avg.
- 30 Week Mov. Avg.
- Relative Strength
- 12-Mo Target Price

HOLD $46.42 03/23/04
HOLD $28.87 10/26/04

Volume Below Avg. — Above Avg.

BUY | SELL | HOLD | HOLD
J J A S O N D J F M A M J J A S O N D J F M A M J J A S O N D J F M A M J J A S O N D J
2001 | 2002 | 2003 | 2004

OPTIONS: CBOE, P

Analyst commentary prepared by Gregory Simcik, CFA /CB/BK

Highlights October 26, 2004

- We anticipate that revenues in 2004 will increase in the mid-single digits, on moderate organic revenue growth for risk and insurance services and consulting, currency effects from a weaker U.S. dollar in 2004, and contributions from acquisitions, offset by lower investment management revenues. We believe revenue gains at the risk and insurance services segment will be tempered by the elimination of brokering contingent commissions in the fourth quarter.

- With continuing declines in assets under management, reports of renegotiated fee structures, and the lingering impact of the recent $110 million regulatory settlement, we think margins at Putnam are likely to tighten in 2004.

- We project 2004 operating EPS of $2.88, up 2.5% from 2003. Our estimate excludes $0.12 in gains related to World Trade Center insurance settlements and $0.23 in losses related to regulatory settlements at Putnam. We estimate that operating EPS will decline nearly 10% in 2005, to $2.60, assuming $0.01 accretion from the Kroll acquisition, no brokering contingent commissions, and a 5% loss in remaining brokering revenue due primarily to client defections. Our 2005 estimate includes no provision for possible penalties associated with the New York Attorney General's civil suit against MMC.

Investment Rationale/Risk October 26, 2004

- Despite recent pro-active measures by the company to address concerns raised with allegations of bid-rigging and conflicts of interest, we believe MMC continues to face a number of regulatory, legal and operational challenges, including a civil lawsuit by the New York Attorney General and the recent elimination of high-margin contingent commissions. We also believe some of MMC's blue-chip clients could decide to sever relationships with the company given the allegations against it. Given these uncertainties, we believe MMC remains high risk and do not recommend investors add to current positions.

- Risks to our recommendation and target price include additional adverse effects from regulatory and legal investigations at the Marsh, Putnam and Mercer divisions, less than expected integration benefits, cost savings and growth at the newly acquired Kroll operations, a newly appointed CEO from outside the industry, and a softening property and casualty underwriting cycle.

- Our 12-month target price of $32 is based on a trailing P/E multiple of roughly 12X applied to our 2005 operating EPS estimate. We assume a multiple at a significant discount to MMC's long-term EPS growth rate of 14% to account for the high legal and operational risks that we believe the company faces from the bid-rigging allegations.

Key Stock Statistics

S&P Core EPS 2005E	2.16	52-week Range	$49.69-22.75
S&P Oper. EPS 2004E	2.88	12 Month P/E	12.1
P/E on S&P Oper. EPS 2004E	9.6	Beta	1.05
S&P Oper. EPS 2005E	2.60	Shareholders	11,363
Yield (%)	4.9%	Market Cap (B)	$ 14.4
Dividend Rate/Share	1.36	Shares Outstanding (M)	520.6

Value of $10,000 invested five years ago: **$ 7,583**

Dividend Data Dividends have been paid since 1923

Amount ($)	Date Decl.	Ex-Div. Date	Stock of Record	Payment Date
0.310	Nov. 20	Dec. 31	Jan. 05	Feb. 13 '04
0.310	Mar. 18	Apr. 06	Apr. 08	May. 14 '04
0.340	May. 20	Jul. 02	Jul. 07	Aug. 13 '04
0.340	Sep. 14	Oct. 13	Oct. 15	Nov. 15 '04

Revenues/Earnings Data Fiscal year ending December 31

Revenues (Million $)

	2004	2003	2002	2001	2000	1999
1Q	3,210	2,852	2,635	2,594	2,665	2,351
2Q	3,036	2,865	2,612	2,505	2,481	2,245
3Q	2,969	2,837	2,553	2,371	2,535	2,227
4Q	—	3,034	2,640	2,473	2,476	2,334
Yr.	—	11,588	10,440	9,943	10,157	9,157

Earnings Per Share ($)

	2004	2003	2002	2001	2000	1999
1Q	0.83	0.81	0.73	0.64	0.59	0.52
2Q	0.73	0.66	0.60	0.51	0.48	0.32
3Q	0.04	0.65	0.55	0.29	0.49	0.41
4Q	E0.48	0.69	0.57	0.26	0.49	0.08
Yr.	E2.88	2.81	2.45	1.70	2.05	1.31

Next earnings report expected: late-January Source: S&P, Company Reports
EPS Estimates based on S&P Operating Earnings; historical GAAP earnings are as reported.

Marsh & McLennan Companies, Inc.

Recommendation: **HOLD** ★ ★ ★ ☆ ☆   12-Month Target Price: **$32.00** (as of October 26, 2004)

Business Summary October 27, 2004

MMC operates three main businesses: risk and insurance services, investment management, and consulting. Although MMC has a strong global presence, it derives most of its revenues from the U.S. In 2003, MMC derived 63% of revenues from activities in the U.S., 15% from the U.K., 11% from Continental Europe, and 11% from other areas.

Risk and insurance services (59% of revenues and 67% of operating profits in 2003) include risk management and insurance brokering, intermediary reinsurance services for insurance and reinsurance organizations, and insurance program management. Services are conducted through three principal operating subsidiaries: Marsh, Guy Carpenter & Co., and MMC Capital. Marsh Inc. solidified its current position as the world's largest insurance broker following its $1.8 billion acquisition of rival insurance broker Johnson & Higgins in 1997 and its $2.2 billion acquisition of U.K.-based Sedgwick Group plc. in late 1998. Guy Carpenter & Co., Inc. provides reinsurance services worldwide. MMC Capital, Inc. develops and invests in insurance-related private equity investments on a global basis.

Investment management activities (17% of revenues and 19% of operating profits) are primarily carried out by Putnam Investments. The Boston-based Putnam organization is one of the largest U.S. investment management concerns, offering an array of fixed-income and equity products. At September 30, 2004, assets under management (AUM) amounted to $209 billion, a further decline from $240 billion at December 31, 2003, $251 billion at year-end 2002, and $315 billion at year-end 2001. At December 31, 2003, mutual funds accounted for 68% of AUM (65% in 2002), with institutional accounts representing the remaining 32% (35%).

Consulting services (24% of revenues and 14% of operating profits) are carried out by Mercer Inc., one of the world's largest consulting concerns. It provides consulting services in the areas of human resources, strategy, operations, marketing, organizational change, and economic and identity issues.

In April 2004, Putnam entered into the final settlements of charges by the SEC and the Massachusetts Secretary of the Commonwealth related to alleged short-term trading of Putnam mutual funds by employees in their personal accounts. Under the settlements, Putnam agreed, without admitting or denying the charges, to pay at least $110 million in fines, penalties, disgorgement and restitution, and to implement a number of remedial actions. In October 2004, Marsh was named as a defendant in a civil suit filed by the New York Attorney General on behalf of the state, as well as policyholders and shareholders, alleging the company was engaged in bid-rigging of insurance quotes obtained for its clients.

In July 2004, MMC completed its acquisition of Kroll Inc. for $1.9 billion in cash. MMC believes Kroll is the world's leading independent risk consulting company, providing a broad range of investigative, intelligence, financial, security and technology services. Management announced that Kroll will become part of Marsh Inc., which will be renamed Marsh Kroll, and that the transaction is expected to be accretive to earnings in 2005.

Company Financials Fiscal Year ending December 31

Per Share Data ($)

(Year Ended December 31)	2003	2002	2001	2000	1999	1998	1997	1996	1995	1994
Tangible Bk. Val.	NM	NM	NM	9.47	NM	NM	1.53	3.10	2.14	1.73
Cash Flow	3.52	3.10	2.61	2.94	2.07	1.98	1.19	1.38	1.23	1.14
Earnings	2.81	2.45	1.70	2.05	1.31	1.49	0.80	1.06	0.92	0.86
S&P Core Earnings	2.29	1.60	0.91	NA	NA	NA	NA	NA	NA	NA
Dividends	1.18	1.09	1.03	0.95	0.85	0.73	0.55	0.55	0.50	0.47
Payout Ratio	42%	44%	61%	46%	65%	49%	69%	52%	54%	54%
Prices - High	54.97	57.30	59.03	67.84	48.37	32.15	26.66	19.14	15.02	14.79
- Low	38.27	34.61	39.50	35.25	28.56	21.68	17.10	14.04	12.68	11.87
P/E Ratio - High	19	23	35	33	37	22	33	18	16	17
- Low	14	14	23	17	22	15	21	13	14	14

Income Statement Analysis (Million $)

	2003	2002	2001	2000	1999	1998	1997	1996	1995	1994
Revs.	11,588	10,440	9,943	10,157	9,157	7,190	6,009	4,149	3,770	3,435
Oper. Inc.	2,887	2,633	2,283	2,179	1,859	1,671	944	855	830	791
Depr.	391	359	520	488	400	251	199	140	135	121
Int. Exp.	185	160	196	247	233	140	106	61.6	62.8	50.6
Pretax Inc.	2,335	2,133	1,590	1,955	1,247	1,305	662	668	650	632
Eff. Tax Rate	33.0%	35.0%	37.7%	38.5%	41.8%	39.0%	39.7%	31.3%	38.0%	39.5%
Net Inc.	1,540	1,365	974	1,181	726	796	399	459	403	382
S&P Core Earnings	1,254	890	525	NA	NA	NA	NA	NA	NA	NA

Balance Sheet & Other Fin. Data (Million $)

	2003	2002	2001	2000	1999	1998	1997	1996	1995	1994
Cash	665	546	537	240	428	610	424	300	328	295
Curr. Assets	3,901	3,664	3,792	3,639	3,283	3,245	2,569	1,749	1,679	1,446
Total Assets	15,053	13,855	13,293	13,769	13,021	11,871	7,914	4,545	4,330	3,831
Curr. Liab.	4,089	3,863	3,938	4,119	4,318	5,002	2,379	1,556	1,570	1,392
LT Debt	2,910	2,891	2,334	2,347	2,357	1,590	1,240	458	411	409
Common Equity	5,451	5,018	5,173	5,228	4,170	3,659	3,199	1,889	1,666	1,461
Total Cap.	8,361	7,909	7,507	7,575	6,527	5,249	4,439	2,347	2,077	1,870
Cap. Exp.	436	423	433	472	358	297	202	157	137	149
Cash Flow	1,931	1,724	1,494	1,669	1,126	1,047	599	599	538	503
Curr. Ratio	1.0	0.9	1.0	0.9	0.8	0.6	1.1	1.1	1.1	1.0
% LT Debt of Cap.	34.8	36.6	31.1	31.0	36.1	30.3	27.9	19.6	19.8	21.9
% Net Inc.of Revs.	13.3	13.1	9.8	11.6	7.9	11.1	6.6	11.1	10.7	11.1
% Ret. on Assets	10.7	10.1	7.2	8.8	5.8	8.0	6.4	10.4	9.9	10.4
% Ret. on Equity	29.4	26.8	18.7	25.1	18.5	23.2	15.7	25.9	25.8	27.0

Data as orig reptd.; bef. results of disc opers/spec. items. Per share data adj. for stk. divs.; EPS diluted. E-Estimated. NA-Not Available. NM-Not Meaningful. NR-Not Ranked. UR-Under Review.

Office: 1166 Avenue of the Americas, New York, NY 10036-2774.
Telephone: 212-345-5000.
Email: shareowner-svcs@email.bankofny.com
Website: http://www.mmc.com
Pres & CEO: M.G. Cherkasky.
Vice Chrmn: M. Calbiallavetta.
SVP & CFO: S.S. Wijnberg.

SVP & General Counsel: W.L. Rosoff.
VP & Chief Acctg Officer: R.J. Rapport.
Investor Contact: B. Perlmutter 212-345-5000.
Dirs: L. W. Bernard, M. Cabiallavetta, Z. W. Carter, M. G. Cherkasky, P. Coster, C. A. Davis, R. F. Erburu, O. Fanjul, R. Groves, S. R. Hardis, G. S. King, D. A. Olsen, M. O. Schapiro, A. S. Simmons, A. J. Smith, C., L. of Monkton.

Founded: in 1923.
Domicile: Delaware.
Employees: 60,400.
S&P Analyst: Gregory Simcik, CFA /CB/BK

Masco Corp.

Recommendation: BUY ★★★★☆   12-Month Target Price: **$41.00**
(as of October 04, 2004)

MAS has an approximate 0.14% weighting in the **S&P 500**

Sector: Industrials
Sub-Industry: Building Products
Peer Group: Building Materials - Residential

Summary: MAS is one of the world's leading makers of faucets, cabinets, coatings and other consumer brand-name home improvement and building products.

Quantitative Evaluations

S&P Earnings & Dividend Rank: A-

| D | C | B- | B | B+ | A- | A | A+ |

S&P Fair Value Rank: 3+

| 1 | 2 | 3 | 4 | 5 |
| Lowest | | | | Highest |

Fair Value Calc.: $35.60 (Slightly Overvalued)

S&P Investability Quotient Percentile

99%

MAS scored higher than 99% of all companies for which an S&P Report is available.

Volatility: Low

| Low | Average | High |

Technical Evaluation: Bullish
Since 8/04, the technical indicators for MAS have been Bullish.

Relative Strength Rank: Moderate

67

| 1 Lowest | | Highest 99 |

| Price as of 11/15/04: | **$36.49** | 2004E S&P Core EPS: | **$2.16** |

GAAP Earnings vs. Previous Year
▲ Up ▼ Down ► No Change

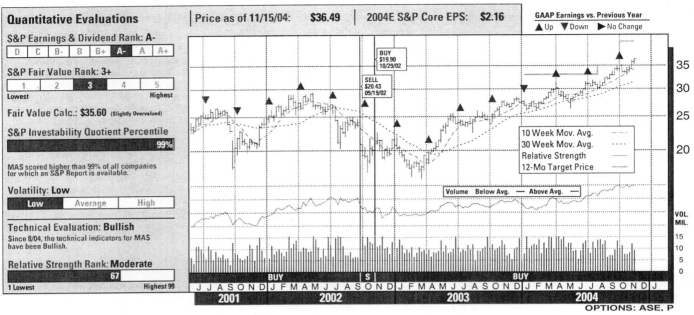

10 Week Mov. Avg.
30 Week Mov. Avg.
Relative Strength
12-Mo Target Price

Volume Below Avg. — Above Avg.

OPTIONS: ASE, P

Analyst commentary prepared by Michael W. Jaffe/CB/BK

Highlights 16-NOV-04

- We forecast a 7% sales gain in 2005, driven largely by professional demand. With our expectation that interest rates, though somewhat higher, will remain accommodative, we believe Masco's opportunities will stay strong through 2005. We see solid sales gains across many of Masco's segments, driven by market share gains, new product introductions and modest price increases. We also see stronger European sales, which we expect to be aided by Masco's efforts to expand foreign sales to more rapidly growing retail customers.
- We expect slightly wider net margins in 2005, on relatively healthy demand for Masco's products plus the likely ongoing benefits of its focus on holding down costs.
- Our 2004 forecast excludes $0.04 a share of first half gains related to the adjustment of a litigation accrual. EPS in 2003 before one-time items was $1.75.

Investment Rationale/Risk 16-NOV-04

- We believe that new home and home improvement markets will stay solid for the next couple of years, and that MAS's strong brand names and greater home center presence will enable it to gain market share and record earnings gains in that period. Based on these views and valuation considerations, we have a buy recommendation on the stock.
- Risks to our recommendation and target price include a more dramatic upturn in interest rates than we expect in the coming year, and the likely resultant impact that it would have on home and remodeling markets.
- Recently trading at almost 14X our 2005 EPS forecast, MAS was at a 13% discount to the S&P 500 and at the low end of its range for the past decade. We believe that MAS's business has cyclical qualities, but think its very strong positions in many of the markets it serves should allow it to trade at a market multiple. Based on our 2005 S&P Core Earnings estimate, which is only $0.05 a share below our operating forecast, we also think that the quality of earnings is high. All told, our 12-month target price is $41, or nearly 16X our 2005 EPS forecast.

Key Stock Statistics

S&P Core EPS 2005E	2.55	52-week Range	$36.51-25.88
S&P Oper. EPS 2004E	2.30	12 Month P/E	18.9
P/E on S&P Oper. EPS 2004E	15.9	Beta	0.71
S&P Oper. EPS 2005E	2.60	Shareholders	6,500
Yield (%)	2.0%	Market Cap (B)	$ 16.3
Dividend Rate/Share	0.72	Shares Outstanding (M)	448.0

Value of $10,000 invested five years ago: **$ 13,995**

Dividend Data Dividends have been paid since 1944

Amount ($)	Date Decl.	Ex-Div. Date	Stock of Record	Payment Date
0.160	Dec. 10	Jan. 07	Jan. 09	Feb. 09 '04
0.160	Mar. 18	Apr. 06	Apr. 09	May. 10 '04
0.160	Jun. 25	Jul. 07	Jul. 09	Aug. 09 '04
0.180	Sep. 13	Oct. 06	Oct. 08	Nov. 08 '04

Revenues/Earnings Data Fiscal year ending December 31

Revenues (Million $)

	2004	2003	2002	2001	2000	1999
1Q	2,806	2,498	2,100	1,911	1,746	1,391
2Q	3,061	2,788	2,314	2,085	1,871	1,567
3Q	3,173	2,918	2,518	2,247	1,893	1,704
4Q	—	2,862	2,487	2,115	1,733	1,645
Yr.	—	10,936	9,419	8,358	7,243	6,307

Earnings Per Share ($)

	2004	2003	2002	2001	2000	1999
1Q	0.52	0.32	0.31	0.25	0.39	0.36
2Q	0.65	0.46	0.43	0.30	0.41	0.41
3Q	0.64	0.53	0.24	-0.39	0.41	0.15
4Q	E0.53	0.19	0.37	0.26	0.10	0.40
Yr.	E2.30	1.51	1.33	0.42	1.31	1.28

Next earnings report expected: mid-February Source: S&P, Company Reports
EPS Estimates based on S&P Operating Earnings; historical GAAP earnings are as reported.

Masco Corporation

Recommendation: **BUY** ★★★★☆   12-Month Target Price: **$41.00** (as of October 04, 2004)

Business Summary 16-NOV-04

Masco is one of the largest U.S. makers of brand name consumer products for the home improvement and new construction markets; it derives most of its revenues from the sale of faucets, kitchen and bath cabinets, plumbing supplies and architectural coatings. Operations are focused on North America (80% of 2003 sales) and Europe (most of the other 20%). Home Depot accounted for 22% of 2003 sales.

The plumbing products division (24% of 2003 sales) is a major global faucet maker. MAS revolutionized faucets in 1954 with the Delta, and also offers the Peerless, Damixa and Mariani brands and private label faucets. The division also offers other bath products, including plumbing fittings and valves, bathtubs and shower enclosures, and spa items; brand names include Alsons, Aqua Glass, and Mixet. It also makes cabinets and related products (28%), including cabinetry for kitchen, bath, storage, home office and home entertainment applications, featuring the Kraftmaid, Merillat, and Hot Spring brands. MAS believes it is the largest U.S. maker of kitchen and bath cabinetry.

MAS sells decorative architectural items (14%), including paints and stains, and decorative bath and shower accessories; supplies and installs insulation products, and other building products such as fireplaces, cabinetry, gutters, shelving and windows (22%); and sells other specialty products (12%), such as windows and patio doors, electric staple guns, radiators, and lock sets used mostly in the hospitality area.

In 2002, MAS acquired more than 10 companies for a total of $1.2 billion in cash, stock, and assumed debt. The acquired units had combined annual sales of about $1 billion; the largest was Service Partners, LLC, which distributes and installs insulation and other building products. In 2003, the company bought PowerShot

Tool Co. (January 2003), a maker of fastening products, and several relatively small installation service companies.

Acquisitions made over the past several years have enabled Masco to build large positions in the markets it serves. In coming years, MAS plans fewer acquisitions and intends to focus more on internal growth, with an increased emphasis on cash flow and return on invested capital.

MAS raised net proceeds of $598 million from a May 2002 public offering of 22 million common shares. It also repurchased 37 million shares in 2003, at an average price of $22, and another 27 million shares in the first nine months of 2004, including 3 million in the third quarter.

In 2004's first quarter, MAS determined that several European businesses (total sales of over $350 million in 2003) were not core to its long-term growth strategy, and slated them for disposal. It expects to complete the disposals by early 2005, for net proceeds exceeding $300 million; two of these businesses, Germany-based Jung Pumpen and Spain-based Alvic Group, were sold in 2004's third quarter for a total of $191 million. MAS recognized a net gain of $0.21 a share in the quarter from the disposition of the two units, and also recognized a pretax charge of $31 million related to weaker than expected demand at certain other units that it planned to sell (all included in discontinued operations). A $118 million after-tax ($0.24 a share) goodwill impairment charge recorded in 2003's fourth quarter was mostly related to the disposal program. In 2003's third quarter, MAS sold its Baldwin Hardware and Weiser Lock businesses (total annual sales of $250 million) to Black & Decker. The units mostly distribute architectural hardware and lock-sets. Also in the quarter, MAS sold its Marvel Group unit. Total proceeds from the sales amounted to $289 million, mostly in cash.

Company Financials Fiscal Year ending December 31

Per Share Data ($)

(Year Ended December 31)	2003	2002	2001	2000	1999	1998	1997	1996	1995	1994
Tangible Bk. Val.	1.36	1.31	1.30	2.78	3.14	4.99	4.53	4.29	4.09	4.44
Cash Flow	2.00	1.85	1.02	1.84	1.68	1.78	1.48	1.23	0.91	0.99
Earnings	1.51	1.33	0.42	1.31	1.28	1.39	1.18	0.92	0.63	0.61
S&P Core Earnings	1.67	1.52	1.12	NA	NA	NA	NA	NA	NA	NA
Dividends	0.58	0.55	0.53	0.49	0.45	0.43	0.40	0.38	0.36	0.34
Payout Ratio	38%	41%	125%	37%	35%	31%	34%	41%	57%	56%
Prices - High	28.44	29.43	26.93	27.00	33.68	33.00	26.90	18.43	15.75	19.93
- Low	16.59	17.25	17.76	14.50	22.50	20.75	16.87	13.25	11.25	10.62
P/E Ratio - High	19	22	64	21	26	24	23	20	25	33
- Low	11	13	42	11	18	15	14	14	18	17

Income Statement Analysis (Million $)

	2003	2002	2001	2000	1999	1998	1997	1996	1995	1994
Revs.	10,936	9,419	8,358	7,243	6,307	4,345	3,760	3,237	2,927	4,468
Oper. Inc.	1,738	1,683	1,309	1,295	1,093	817	703	580	492	630
Depr.	244	220	269	238	182	136	116	100	90.0	121
Int. Exp.	262	237	239	191	120	85.3	79.8	74.7	73.8	105
Pretax Inc.	1,216	1,031	301	893	904	755	631	503	352	323
Eff. Tax Rate	38.1%	33.8%	34.0%	33.8%	37.0%	37.0%	39.4%	41.3%	NM	40.0%
Net Inc.	740	682	199	592	570	476	382	295	200	194
S&P Core Earnings	816	779	528	NA	NA	NA	NA	NA	NA	NA

Balance Sheet & Other Fin. Data (Million $)

	2003	2002	2001	2000	1999	1998	1997	1996	1995	1994
Cash	795	1,067	312	169	231	542	441	474	60.5	71.0
Curr. Assets	3,804	3,950	2,627	2,308	2,110	1,863	1,627	1,431	965	1,891
Total Assets	12,149	12,050	9,183	7,744	6,635	5,167	4,334	3,702	3,779	4,390
Curr. Liab.	2,099	1,932	1,237	1,078	846	847	620	518	446	601
LT Debt	3,848	4,316	3,628	3,018	2,431	1,391	1,322	1,236	1,577	1,593
Common Equity	5,456	5,294	4,120	3,426	3,137	2,729	2,229	1,840	1,655	2,113
Total Cap.	9,304	9,610	7,747	6,444	5,788	4,321	3,714	3,183	3,332	3,705
Cap. Exp.	271	285	274	388	351	189	167	138	165	191
Cash Flow	984	902	468	830	751	612	498	395	290	314
Curr. Ratio	1.8	2.0	2.1	2.1	2.5	2.2	2.6	2.8	2.2	3.1
% LT Debt of Cap.	41.4	44.9	46.8	46.8	42.0	32.2	35.6	38.8	47.3	43.0
% Net Inc.of Revs.	6.8	7.2	2.4	8.2	9.0	11.0	10.2	9.1	6.8	4.3
% Ret. on Assets	6.1	6.5	2.3	8.2	9.3	10.0	9.5	7.9	5.0	4.5
% Ret. on Equity	13.8	14.7	5.3	18.0	19.3	19.2	18.8	16.9	10.6	9.3

Data as orig reptd.; bef. results of disc opers/spec. items. Per share data adj. for stk. divs.; EPS diluted. E-Estimated. NA-Not Available. NM-Not Meaningful. NR-Not Ranked. UR-Under Review.

Office: 21001 Van Born Road, Taylor, MI 48180.
Telephone: 313-274-7400.
Website: http://www.masco.com
Chrmn & CEO: R. A. Manoogian.
Pres & COO: A. Barry.

VP & CFO: T. Wadhams.
SVP & General Counsel: J. R. Leekley.
Investor Contact: Samuel Cypert.
Dirs: T. G. Denomme, P. A. Dow, A. F. Earley, Jr., V. G. Istock, D. L. Johnston, J. M. Losh, W. B. Lyon, R. A. Manoogian, M. Van Lokeren.

Founded: in 1929.
Domicile: Delaware.
Employees: 61,000.
S&P Analyst: Michael W. Jaffe/CB/BK

Recommendation: **HOLD** ★★★★★
SELL SELL HOLD BUY BUY

12-Month Target Price: **$18.00**
(as of October 18, 2004)

MAT has an approximate 0.07% weighting in the **S&P 500**

Sector: Consumer Discretionary
Sub-Industry: Leisure Products
Peer Group: Toy-related Companies

Summary: This large toy company's brands and products include Barbie dolls, Fisher-Price toys, and Hot Wheels.

Quantitative Evaluations

S&P Earnings & Dividend Rank: B+

| D | C | B- | B | B+ | A- | A | A+ |

S&P Fair Value Rank: 5+

| 1 | 2 | 3 | 4 | 5 |
Lowest | | | | Highest

Fair Value Calc.: $21.50 (Slightly Undervalued)

S&P Investability Quotient Percentile

97%

MAT scored higher than 97% of all companies for which an S&P Report is available.

Volatility: Low

| Low | Average | High |

Technical Evaluation: Neutral
Since 10/04, the technical indicators for MAT have been Neutral.

Relative Strength Rank: Moderate

56

1 Lowest | Highest 99

| Price as of 11/12/04: | **$18.64** | 2004E S&P Core EPS: | **$1.15** |

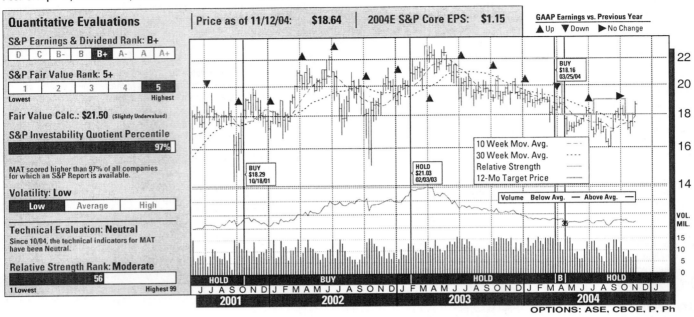

GAAP Earnings vs. Previous Year
▲ Up ▼ Down ▶ No Change

- 10 Week Mov. Avg.
- 30 Week Mov. Avg.
- Relative Strength
- 12-Mo Target Price

Volume Below Avg. — Above Avg.

OPTIONS: ASE, CBOE, P, Ph

Analyst commentary prepared by Amy Glynn/PMW/JWP

Highlights October 25, 2004

- We project a fractional sales increase for 2004, aided by currency benefits, as we expect pressures in the U.S. market and a challenging toy retailing environment to continue to restrict the top line. We think MAT is committed to revitalizing its fashion doll business, but we continue to believe that the impact of this strategy will not be evident until 2005. We see revenue growth in 2005 trending up from our 2004 forecast, but still see an increase only in the low single digits, in line with our estimate for the toy industry as a whole.

Investment Rationale/Risk October 25, 2004

- We view MAT's biggest challenge, and a potential catalyst for the stock, as the need to reinvigorate the top line by stemming declines of Barbie products, both in the U.S. and internationally. The company has indicated that early response to new products was positive, but until we see further evidence of consumer demand for the products, we think the shares should trade at a discount to the S&P 500. In addition, we see near-term concerns about the strength of the holiday season restricting the shares. Positive factors, in our opinion, include MAT's strong portfolio of leading consumer brands, its focus on the faster growing electronic learning aid space, and strong cash flow that has enabled it to reduce debt, increase the dividend, and increase share buybacks. We view the shares as fairly valued.

- Risks to our recommendation and target price include an uncertain toy retailing environment and the possibility of continued store closings, an inability to reinvigorate the top line, continued cost pressures, and a possible weak holiday season due to lack of demand for MAT products.

- At about 14X our 2005 EPS estimate, the stock trades at a premium to that of close peer Hasbro (HAS: hold, $17), but at a discount to the S&P 500. Our 12-month target price of $18 applies a P/E multiple of 14X to our 2005 EPS estimate, representing what we view as a justified discount to the S&P 500.

Key Stock Statistics

S&P Core EPS 2005E	**1.21**	52-week Range	**$20.50-15.94**
S&P Oper. EPS 2004E	**1.17**	12 Month P/E	**15.9**
P/E on S&P Oper. EPS 2004E	**15.9**	Beta	**0.01**
S&P Oper. EPS 2005E	**1.25**	Shareholders	**44,000**
Yield (%)	**2.1%**	Market Cap (B)	**$ 7.7**
Dividend Rate/Share	**0.40**	Shares Outstanding (M)	**415.0**

Value of $10,000 invested five years ago: **$ 14,205**

Dividend Data Dividends have been paid since 1990

Amount ($)	Date Decl.	Ex-Div. Date	Stock of Record	Payment Date
0.400	Nov. 21	Dec. 04	Dec. 08	Dec. 23 '03

Revenues/Earnings Data Fiscal year ending December 31

Revenues (Million $)

	2004	2003	2002	2001	2000	1999
1Q	780.9	745.3	742.0	732.0	693.3	879.0
2Q	804.0	769.0	804.4	854.3	817.8	1,040
3Q	1,667	1,705	1,669	1,613	1,584	1,825
4Q	—	1,741	1,669	1,605	1,575	1,771
Yr.	—	4,960	4,885	4,804	4,670	5,515

Earnings Per Share ($)

	2004	2003	2002	2001	2000	1999
1Q	0.02	0.07	-0.01	-0.05	-0.10	-0.01
2Q	0.06	0.05	0.04	-0.01	0.01	-0.50
3Q	0.61	0.61	0.57	0.46	0.24	0.32
4Q	E0.48	0.49	0.42	0.32	0.25	-0.04
Yr.	E1.17	1.22	1.03	0.71	0.40	-0.21

Next earnings report expected: early-February Source: S&P, Company Reports
EPS Estimates based on S&P Operating Earnings; historical GAAP earnings are as reported.

Mattel, Inc.

Recommendation: HOLD ★ ★ ★ ☆ ☆   12-Month Target Price: **$18.00** (as of October 18, 2004)

Business Summary October 25, 2004

Mattel is a major toy company, with brands that include Barbie and Fisher-Price. In 2003, MAT completed a financial realignment plan, first announced in the 2000 third quarter, that was designed to improve gross profits, SG&A expenses, operating income, and cash flows. The plan generated cumulative pretax cost savings of about $221 million, exceeding the initial target of $200 million. Cost savings of $55 million, $87 million and $79 million were realized in 2001, 2002 and 2003, respectively. The company incurred total pretax charges of $250 million since the plan's inception, including $26.3 million in 2003. In February 2003, as part of its financial realignment, MAT announced the consolidation of its US Girls and US Boys-Entertainment segments into one segment, renamed Mattel Brands US.

In 2003, net sales were about $5.0 billion, up from $4.9 billion in 2002. The company's portfolio of brands and products is grouped into three categories: Mattel Brands (61% of 2003 gross sales; 61% in 2002), Fisher-Price Brands (33%, 32%) and American Girl Brands (6%, 7%). Mattel Brands include Barbie, Polly Pocket!, ello, Hot Wheels, Matchbox and Tyco R/C vehicles and playsets, and Nickelodeon, Harry Potter, He-Man and Masters of the Universe, Batman and Justice League, among others. Fisher-Price includes Fisher-Price, Power Wheels, Sesame Street, Little People, Disney preschool and plush, Winnie the Pooh, Rescue Heroes, Barney, See 'N Say, Dora the Explorer, PowerTouch and View-Master. American Girl Brands are sold directly to consumers, and its children's publications are sold to certain retailers. Brand names include American Girl Today, the American Girls Collection, and Bitty Baby.

MAT operates in the U.S. and internationally. Revenues from the international segment provided 40% of consolidated gross sales in 2003. In the international segment, the geographic breakdown was as follows: Europe 62% of 2003 sales; Latin America 21%; Canada 9%; and Asia Pacific 8%.

The company's principal manufacturing facilities are located in countries such as China, Indonesia, Italy, Malaysia and Thailand. MAT also uses independent contractors to manufacture products. In the U.S., products are sold directly to large retailers, including discount and free-standing toy stores, chain stores, department stores and, to a limited extent, wholesalers. Internationally, products are sold to retailers and wholesalers, and through agents and distributors in countries in which the company has no direct presence. In 2003, the three largest customers, Wal-Mart ($1.0 billion), Toys "R" Us ($0.8 billion), and Target ($0.4 billion), accounted for 47% of consolidated net sales.

In November 2003, directors approved a $250 million increase in the share buyback program, bringing total authorized purchases to $500 million. In 2003, MAT repurchased about $244 million of stock. For 2004, one of the company's financial objectives was to maintain its 2003 year-end debt-to-capital ratio of about 25%, in an effort to achieve a long-term debt rating of A.

Company Financials Fiscal Year ending December 31

Per Share Data ($)

(Year Ended December 31)	2003	2002	2001	2000	1999	1998	1997	1996	1995	1994
Tangible Bk. Val.	3.49	2.92	1.46	0.59	1.36	1.64	4.06	3.84	3.09	2.25
Cash Flow	1.63	1.47	1.31	1.00	0.73	1.78	1.59	1.89	1.75	1.34
Earnings	1.22	1.03	0.71	0.40	-0.21	1.10	0.94	1.36	1.26	0.90
S&P Core Earnings	1.14	1.00	0.66	NA	NA	NA	NA	NA	NA	NA
Dividends	0.40	0.05	0.05	0.27	0.34	0.30	0.27	0.24	0.24	0.19
Payout Ratio	33%	5%	7%	67%	NM	27%	29%	18%	19%	21%
Prices - High	23.20	22.36	19.92	15.12	30.31	46.56	42.25	32.50	24.90	18.88
- Low	18.57	15.05	13.52	8.93	11.68	21.25	23.37	21.62	15.76	13.24
P/E Ratio - High	19	22	28	38	NM	42	45	24	20	21
- Low	15	15	19	22	NM	19	25	16	13	15

Income Statement Analysis (Million $)

	2003	2002	2001	2000	1999	1998	1997	1996	1995	1994
Revs.	4,960	4,885	4,804	4,670	5,515	4,782	4,835	3,786	3,639	3,205
Oper. Inc.	974	934	881	652	671	841	1,014	796	735	673
Depr.	184	192	263	256	390	215	190	149	133	124
Int. Exp.	80.6	114	155	153	152	111	90.1	75.5	74.0	55.4
Pretax Inc.	741	621	430	225	-111	465	425	546	533	394
Eff. Tax Rate	27.4%	26.8%	27.7%	24.5%	NM	28.6%	31.8%	30.8%	32.8%	35.0%
Net Inc.	538	455	311	170	-82.4	332	290	378	358	256
S&P Core Earnings	502	439	288	NA	NA	NA	NA	NA	NA	NA

Balance Sheet & Other Fin. Data (Million $)

	2003	2002	2001	2000	1999	1998	1997	1996	1995	1994
Cash	1,153	1,267	617	232	275	212	695	501	483	260
Curr. Assets	2,395	2,389	2,093	1,751	2,420	2,058	2,462	1,771	1,691	1,544
Total Assets	4,511	4,460	4,541	4,313	5,127	4,262	3,804	2,894	2,696	2,459
Curr. Liab.	1,468	1,649	1,597	1,502	1,818	1,317	1,173	960	848	916
LT Debt	589	640	1,021	1,242	1,184	984	664	364	464	360
Common Equity	2,216	1,979	1,738	1,403	1,963	1,819	1,726	1,448	1,275	1,052
Total Cap.	2,805	2,619	2,759	2,645	3,147	2,804	2,486	1,812	1,739	1,446
Cap. Exp.	101	167	101	162	212	783	223	209	207	163
Cash Flow	721	647	573	427	304	539	469	527	491	375
Curr. Ratio	1.6	1.4	1.3	1.2	1.3	1.6	2.1	1.8	2.0	1.7
% LT Debt of Cap.	21.0	24.4	37.0	47.0	37.6	35.1	26.7	20.1	26.7	24.9
% Net Inc.of Revs.	10.8	9.3	6.5	3.6	NM	6.9	6.0	10.0	9.8	8.0
% Ret. on Assets	12.0	10.1	7.0	3.8	NM	8.2	8.7	13.5	13.9	11.3
% Ret. on Equity	25.6	24.5	19.8	10.1	NM	17.8	17.1	27.7	30.3	26.8

Data as orig reptd.; bef. results of disc opers/spec. items. Per share data adj. for stk. divs.; EPS diluted. E-Estimated. NA-Not Available. NM-Not Meaningful. NR-Not Ranked. UR-Under Review.

Office: 333 Continental Boulevard, El Segundo, CA 90245-5012.
Telephone: 310-252-2000.
Website: http://www.mattel.com
Chrmn & CEO: R.A. Eckert.
SVP & Treas: W. Stavro.
SVP, Secy & General Counsel: R. Normile.

VP & Investor Contact: D. Douglas 310-252-2703.
CFO: K.M. Farr.
Dirs: E. P. Beard, H. Brown, M. J. Dolan, R. A. Eckert, T. M. Friedman, R. M. Loeb, A. L. Rich, C. A. Sinclair, G. C. Sullivan, J. L. Vogelstein, K. B. White.

Founded: in 1945.
Domicile: Delaware.
Employees: 25,000.
S&P Analyst: Amy Glynn/PMW/JWP

Maxim Integrated Products

Recommendation: **BUY** ★★★★★   **12-Month Target Price: $60.00**
(as of November 01, 2004)

MXIM has an approximate 0.13% weighting in the **S&P 500**

Sector: Information Technology
Sub-Industry: Semiconductors
Peer Group: Semiconductors - Analog

Summary: MXIM designs, develops and manufactures linear and mixed-signal integrated circuits used mainly in signal processing applications.

Quantitative Evaluations

S&P Earnings & Dividend Rank: B+

| D | C | B- | B | B+ | A- | A | A+ |

S&P Fair Value Rank: 5

| 1 | 2 | 3 | 4 | 5 |
| Lowest | | | | Highest |

Fair Value Calc.: $52.60 (Undervalued)

S&P Investability Quotient Percentile
95%

MXIM scored higher than 95% of all companies for which an S&P Report is available.

Volatility: Average

| Low | Average | High |

Technical Evaluation: Bullish
Since 10/04, the technical indicators for MXIM have been Bullish.

Relative Strength Rank: Weak
19
1 Lowest   Highest 99

Price as of 11/12/04: $42.51   **2005E S&P Core EPS:** $1.30

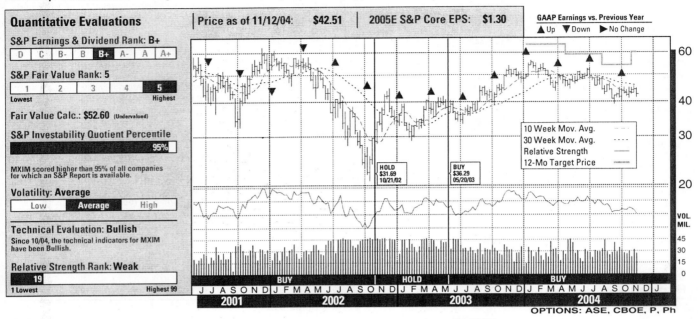

GAAP Earnings vs. Previous Year
▲ Up   ▼ Down   ► No Change

10 Week Mov. Avg.
30 Week Mov. Avg.
Relative Strength
12-Mo Target Price

HOLD $31.69 10/21/02
BUY $36.29 05/20/03

BUY   HOLD   BUY

J J A S O N D J F M A M J J A S O N D J F M A M J J A S O N D J F M A M J J A S O N D J
2001   2002   2003   2004

OPTIONS: ASE, CBOE, P, Ph

Analyst commentary prepared by Amrit Tewary/PMW/BK

Highlights November 03, 2004

- We forecast that revenues will advance about 27% in FY 05 (Jun.) and 18% in FY 06, reflecting our expectations that MXIM will outperform most peers during the remainder of the current cyclical expansion for the semiconductor industry. Operations acquired from Dallas Semiconductor in April 2001 added complementary product lines and helped MXIM enter new markets, although many Dallas operations have narrower margins than historical core business lines.

- We expect gross margins to widen to 73% by FY 06, from 70% in FY 04, due to improved manufacturing efficiencies. We expect R&D expenses and SG&A spending to increase less rapidly than revenues over the next few years, leading to significant operating profit margin expansion.

- MXIM has been buying back shares, and pays a larger dividend than most semiconductor companies. We project EPS of $1.77 for FY 05 and $2.14 for FY 06. Our S&P Core EPS estimates are $1.30 for FY 05 and $1.67 for FY 06, reflecting projected stock option expense.

Investment Rationale/Risk November 03, 2004

- We would buy the shares. We expect the company to outperform most chip peers during the current semiconductor up cycle, based on our view of its strong proprietary product portfolio, wide margins, diverse end markets and customers, and balance sheet strength. At about 25X our FY 05 EPS estimate of $1.77, well below historical norms, we view the shares as attractively priced. In addition, the shares appear undervalued, based on our historical price to sales ratio analysis.

- Risks to our opinion and target price include semiconductor industry cyclicality, increased competition, an inability to manage wafer fab operations effectively, and reliance on stock-based compensation that we view as moderately high compared to peer chipmakers.

- We see above-average price appreciation potential to our 12-month target price of $60. Our target price is based on our historical P/E multiple model, and is derived by applying a P/E multiple of 34X, above most peers but below the stock's average historical multiple, to our FY 05 EPS estimate. We think the shares merit a premium valuation to most chipmakers, in light of what we view as the company's highly profitable business model and below-average cyclicality for a chipmaker.

Key Stock Statistics

S&P Core EPS 2006E	1.67	52-week Range	$56.25-39.14
S&P Oper. EPS 2005E	1.77	12 Month P/E	31.0
P/E on S&P Oper. EPS 2005E	24.0	Beta	2.33
S&P Oper. EPS 2006E	2.14	Shareholders	1,538
Yield (%)	0.9%	Market Cap (B)	$ 13.8
Dividend Rate/Share	0.40	Shares Outstanding (M)	325.2

Value of $10,000 invested five years ago: **$ 10,580**

Dividend Data Dividends have been paid since 2002

Amount ($)	Date Decl.	Ex-Div. Date	Stock of Record	Payment Date
0.080	Feb. 05	Feb. 11	Feb. 16	Mar. 01 '04
0.080	Apr. 27	May. 05	May. 07	May. 28 '04
0.080	Aug. 06	Aug. 12	Aug. 16	Aug. 31 '04
0.100	Nov. 01	Nov. 10	Nov. 15	Nov. 30 '04

Revenues/Earnings Data Fiscal year ending June 30

Revenues (Million $)

	2005	2004	2003	2002	2001	2000
1Q	435.1	310.2	285.9	239.4	422.3	180.1
2Q	—	338.1	286.1	247.1	438.3	201.7
3Q	—	370.0	286.2	258.5	306.8	226.5
4Q	—	421.0	295.0	280.1	318.1	256.6
Yr.	—	1,439	1,153	1,025	1,577	864.9

Earnings Per Share ($)

	2005	2004	2003	2002	2001	2000
1Q	0.42	0.25	0.22	0.17	0.33	0.18
2Q	E0.43	0.28	0.23	0.18	0.34	0.20
3Q	E0.45	0.31	0.23	0.19	0.33	0.23
4Q	E0.47	0.36	0.24	0.20	-0.05	0.27
Yr.	E1.77	1.20	0.91	0.73	0.93	0.88

Next earnings report expected: early-February Source: S&P, Company Reports
EPS Estimates based on S&P Operating Earnings; historical GAAP earnings are as reported.

Maxim Integrated Products, Inc.

Recommendation: **BUY** ★ ★ ★ ★ ★   12-Month Target Price: **$60.00** (as of November 01, 2004)

Business Summary November 03, 2004

Maxim Integrated Products designs, develops, makes and markets a broad range of linear and mixed-signal integrated circuits known as analog circuits. Linear semiconductors handle continuously variable analog signals representing real-world phenomena (such as temperature, pressure, sound or speed). In contrast, digital semiconductors handle digital signals representing the zeroes and ones of binary arithmetic (the signal is either on or off, rather than continuous). Mixed-signal devices combine linear and digital functions. Compared to the digital integrated circuit market, the analog market is characterized by longer product life cycles, less foreign competition, lower capital requirements, and more stable growth rates that are less influenced by economic cycles.

In April 2001, the company expanded substantially by acquiring Dallas Semiconductor Corp. via an exchange of stock. The Dallas operations were similar to those of MXIM, and added complementary product lines in mixed-signal and digital chips. As of April 2001, Dallas was selling 390 proprietary products to 15,000 customers worldwide.

MXIM serves a broad range of electronics end markets. Segments include automotive, communications, consumer, data processing, industrial control, instrumentation, and medical. Products include data converters, interface circuits, delay lines, microcontrollers, microprocessor supervisors, operational amplifiers, power supplies, multiplexers, switches, battery chargers, battery management circuits, RF circuits, fiber optic transceivers, sensors and voltage references.

Applications for the company's products include global positioning systems, broadband networks, cable systems, PBX, video and wireless communications, flow control, robotics, automatic test equipment, data recorders, measuring instruments, bar code readers, disk drives, hand-held computers/PDAs, mainframes, servers, personal computers, point of sale terminals, and blood glucose meters.

A high degree of proprietary design content contributes to stable pricing conditions for the company's chips. The R&D budget was $306 million in FY 04 (Jun.), $272 million in FY 03, and $276 million in FY 02, which, despite an industry slowdown, was nearly equal to the $280 million spent in FY 01.

MXIM operates wafer fabrication facilities in San Jose, CA, Beaverton, OR, Dallas, TX, and San Antonio, TX, and uses outside silicon foundries for a small portion of production. During FY 04, the company continued a conversion to 8-inch wafer production capability at its Dallas and San Jose fabs. In October 2003, MXIM said it had purchased an 8-inch wafer plant in San Antonio, TX, from Philips, for $40 million in cash; production at the facility began in the fourth quarter of FY 04. The company operates test facilities in Cavite, the Philippines, and in Thailand.

International sales accounted for 70% of total revenue in FY 04, 67% in FY 03, 66% in FY 02, and 57% in FY 01. Like a number of analog chip makers, the company has a broad customer base of OEMs.

Company Financials Fiscal Year ending June 30

Per Share Data ($)

(Year Ended June 30)	2004	2003	2002	2001	2000	1999	1998	1997	1996	1995
Tangible Bk. Val.	6.51	6.38	5.44	6.36	3.95	3.24	2.42	3.66	1.32	0.76
Cash Flow	1.37	1.08	0.89	1.18	0.95	0.70	0.64	1.06	0.48	0.19
Earnings	1.20	0.91	0.73	0.93	0.88	0.65	0.59	0.47	0.43	0.15
S&P Core Earnings	0.82	0.50	0.24	0.57	NA	NA	NA	NA	NA	NA
Dividends	0.32	0.08	Nil	Nil	Nil	Nil	Nil	Nil	Nil	Nil
Payout Ratio	27%	9%	Nil	Nil	Nil	Nil	Nil	Nil	Nil	Nil
Prices - High	56.25	53.95	61.36	70.12	90.12	48.31	22.75	19.09	10.93	10.46
- Low	39.14	28.96	20.75	32.20	45.62	19.93	11.15	10.53	5.15	3.53
P/E Ratio - High	47	59	84	75	NM	55	39	41	25	71
- Low	33	32	28	35	52	23	19	22	12	24

Income Statement Analysis (Million $)

	2004	2003	2002	2001	2000	1999	1998	1997	1996	1995
Revs.	1,439	1,153	1,025	1,577	865	607	560	434	422	251
Oper. Inc.	668	507	402	699	405	294	270	216	199	69.0
Depr.	61.9	60.3	56.3	90.9	19.7	17.6	15.1	17.0	12.9	11.6
Int. Exp.	Nil	Nil	Nil	Nil	Nil	Nil	Nil	0.06	0.04	0.03
Pretax Inc.	626	462	387	505	425	297	270	208	190	60.0
Eff. Tax Rate	33.0%	33.0%	33.0%	33.7%	34.0%	34.0%	34.0%	34.0%	35.2%	35.0%
Net Inc.	420	310	259	335	281	196	178	137	123	39.0
S&P Core Earnings	285	170	84.7	205	NA	NA	NA	NA	NA	NA

Balance Sheet & Other Fin. Data (Million $)

	2004	2003	2002	2001	2000	1999	1998	1997	1996	1995
Cash	148	211	174	93.8	53.1	34.1	16.7	18.6	129	55.0
Curr. Assets	1,578	1,565	1,236	1,699	931	729	508	377	265	162
Total Assets	2,549	2,368	2,011	2,431	1,350	1,022	769	556	418	256
Curr. Liab.	319	216	229	325	208	121	130	85.2	88.4	66.0
LT Debt	Nil	Nil	Nil	Nil	Nil	Nil	Nil	Nil	Nil	Nil
Common Equity	2,112	2,070	1,741	2,101	1,118	879	631	466	325	179
Total Cap.	2,227	2,148	1,778	2,101	1,137	897	635	468	325	184
Cap. Exp.	232	84.1	90.4	337	176	54.3	109	44.2	75.1	35.5
Cash Flow	482	370	315	426	300	214	193	154	136	50.6
Curr. Ratio	5.0	7.2	5.4	5.2	4.5	6.0	3.9	4.4	3.0	2.5
% LT Debt of Cap.	Nil	Nil	Nil	Nil	Nil	Nil	Nil	Nil	Nil	NM
% Net Inc.of Revs.	29.2	26.8	25.3	21.2	32.4	32.3	31.8	31.6	29.1	16.0
% Ret. on Assets	17.1	14.1	11.7	14.8	23.7	21.9	26.9	28.1	36.6	17.9
% Ret. on Equity	20.1	16.2	13.5	17.5	28.1	26.0	32.5	34.6	48.9	25.2

Data as orig reptd.; bef. results of disc opers/spec. items. Per share data adj. for stk. divs. Bold denotes primary EPS - prior periods restated. E-Estimated. NA-Not Available. NM-Not Meaningful. NR-Not Ranked. UR-Under Review.

Office: 120 San Gabriel Drive, Sunnyvale, CA 94086.
Telephone: 408-737-7600.
Email: info@maxim-ic.com
Website: http://www.maxim-ic.com

Chrmn, Pres & CEO: J.F. Gifford.
VP, CFO & Investor Contact: C.W. Jasper 408-737-7600.
Dirs: J. R. Bergman, J. F. Gifford, B. K. Hagopian, A. R. Wazzan.
Founded: in 1983.

Domicile: Delaware.
Employees: 7,599.
S&P Analyst: Amrit Tewary/PMW/BK

The **McGraw·Hill** Companies

May Department Stores

Recommendation: **HOLD** ★★★☆☆
SELL SELL HOLD BUY BUY

12-Month Target Price: $28.00
(as of August 10, 2004)

MAY has an approximate 0.08% weighting in the **S&P 500**

Sector: Consumer Discretionary
Sub-Industry: Department Stores
Peer Group: Department Store Cos. - Larger

Summary: MAY, one of the largest U.S. retailers, operates about 500 department stores and nearly 700 bridal and formalwear stores.

Quantitative Evaluations

S&P Earnings & Dividend Rank: B+

| D | C | B- | B | **B+** | A- | A | A+ |

S&P Fair Value Rank: 5

| 1 | 2 | 3 | 4 | **5** |
Lowest | | | | Highest

Fair Value Calc.: $33.60 (Slightly Undervalued)

S&P Investability Quotient Percentile

91%

MAY scored higher than 91% of all companies for which an S&P Report is available.

Volatility: Average

| Low | **Average** | High |

Technical Evaluation: Bullish
Since 11/04, the technical indicators for MAY have been Bullish.

Relative Strength Rank: Strong

75

1 Lowest   Highest 99

Price as of 11/12/04: **$28.65** **2005E S&P Core EPS:** **$2.03**

GAAP Earnings vs. Previous Year
▲ Up ▼ Down ▶ No Change

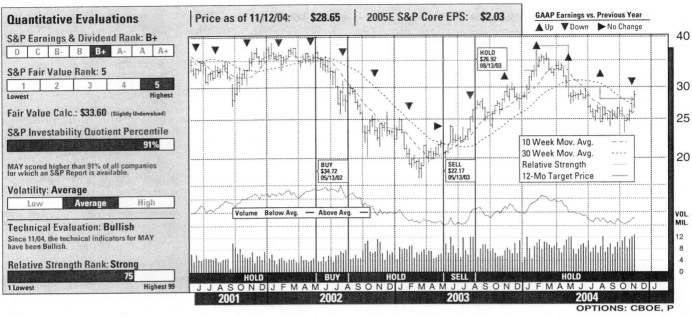

Analyst commentary prepared by Jason N. Asaeda/MF/BK

Highlights November 05, 2004

- Sales momentum has weakened since the start of FY 05 (Jan.), implying to us a slow turnaround in MAY's business. As a result, we look for same-store sales to be flat to down modestly, despite relatively easy comparisons. However, with an estimated $1.4 billion revenue contribution from the recently acquired up-scale Marshall Field's department store chain, we look for net revenues to increase 11% in FY 05, to nearly $14.7 billion. MAY also plans to open up to nine department stores and 52 bridal and formalwear stores, and to continue its divestiture of 34 department stores, announced in FY 04. As of July 31, 2004, the company had closed 19 stores, recording $350 million of an estimated $380 million in related asset impairment and other charges. MAY plans to have 24 stores closed by the end of FY 05.

- EBIT (earnings before interest and taxes) margins should widen, aided by the benefits of well controlled inventories, improved expense leverage, and cost savings from store divestitures and FY 03 division combinations. Reflecting the partial funding of MAY's $3.2 billion acquisition of Marshall Field's with $2.2 billion in notes, we look for a moderate increase in interest expense.

- We see FY 05 operating EPS of $2.16, and Standard & Poor's Core Earnings per share of $2.03, with the difference due to non-recurring items and estimated stock option expense.

Investment Rationale/Risk November 05, 2004

- We recommend holding the shares. We view favorably MAY's recent addition of Marshall Field's to its stable of department stores, as it has established the company's presence in the upper Midwest. The acquisition is also consistent with MAY's plan to reposition some of its moderate chains into more upscale retailers. In addition, the acquisition is likely to deliver cost synergies, helping sustain the company's margin expansion over the intermediate term. However, we see some integration risk, as both Marshall Field's and MAY are attempting turnarounds, and we have been disappointed by recent weakness in sales momentum. That said, we still believe that the company's turnaround initiatives are starting to pay off, and we look for measurable results in FY 06.

- Risks to our recommendation and target price include a possible decline in consumer spending due to economic and geopolitical uncertainties, or poor merchandise assortments. Also, with MAY facing more difficult historical sales comparisons over the next six months, we see modest potential for sales and/or earnings shortfalls.

- Our 12-month target price of $28 blends the stock's one-year historical forward P/E of 12X applied to our FY 06 operating EPS estimate of $2.47, and 0.5X our estimate of FY 06 sales.

Key Stock Statistics

S&P Core EPS 2006E	2.39	52-week Range	$36.48-23.04
S&P Oper. EPS 2005E	2.15	12 Month P/E	14.3
P/E on S&P Oper. EPS 2005E	13.3	Beta	0.78
S&P Oper. EPS 2006E	2.47	Shareholders	38,000
Yield (%)	3.4%	Market Cap (B)	$ 8.3
Dividend Rate/Share	0.97	Shares Outstanding (M)	291.4

Value of $10,000 invested five years ago: **$ 9,823**

Dividend Data Dividends have been paid since 1911

Amount ($)	Date Decl.	Ex-Div. Date	Stock of Record	Payment Date
0.240	Nov. 14	Nov. 26	Dec. 01	Dec. 15 '03
0.243	Feb. 12	Feb. 26	Mar. 01	Mar. 15 '04
0.243	Mar. 19	May. 27	Jun. 01	Jun. 15 '04
0.243	Aug. 20	Aug. 30	Sep. 01	Sep. 15 '04

Revenues/Earnings Data Fiscal year ending January 31

Revenues (Million $)

	2005	2004	2003	2002	2001	2000
1Q	2,963	2,873	3,096	3,153	3,050	3,053
2Q	2,956	300.0	3,030	3,173	3,131	3,713
3Q	3,483	2,976	2,992	3,202	3,328	3,173
4Q	—	4,494	4,373	4,647	5,004	4,789
Yr.	—	13,343	13,491	14,175	15,511	14,224

Earnings Per Share ($)

	2005	2004	2003	2002	2001	2000
1Q	0.24	0.23	0.23	0.34	0.35	0.34
2Q	0.33	-0.39	0.22	0.35	0.41	0.43
3Q	0.02	0.15	0.05	0.17	0.27	0.38
4Q	**E1.45**	1.38	1.26	1.36	1.59	1.45
Yr.	E2.15	1.41	1.76	2.22	2.62	2.60

Next earnings report expected: mid-February Source: S&P, Company Reports
EPS Estimates based on S&P Operating Earnings; historical GAAP earnings are as reported.

The May Department Stores Company

Recommendation: **HOLD** ★★★☆☆   12-Month Target Price: **$28.00** (as of August 10, 2004)

Business Summary November 05, 2004

May Department Stores is one of the largest U.S. department store companies. At November 2, 2004, the company operated 500 department stores, 229 David's Bridal stores, 458 After Hours Formalwear stores, and 11 Priscilla of Boston stores, in 46 states, the District of Columbia, and Puerto Rico.

MAY operates its department stores under 12 names: Lord & Taylor, Famous-Barr, Filene's, Foley's, Hecht's, Kaufmann's, L.S. Ayres, Meier & Frank, Robinsons-May, Strawbridge's, The Jones Store, and Marshall Field's. In FY 04 (Jan.), the company focused on delivering greater value through improvements in product and assortments; growing higher price-point categories; enhancing its selection of non-apparel gifts; and, repositioning Lord & Taylor to increase its distinctiveness.

MAY opened 10 department stores in FY 04, adding 1.7 million sq. ft. of retail space. The company planned to open nine department stores in FY 05: six to be built as anchors in traditional malls, and the remaining three in off-mall retail settings.

The Bridal Group includes David's Bridal, a bridal-related apparel retailer; After Hours Formalwear, a tuxedo rental and sales retailer; and Priscilla of Boston, an upscale bridal gown retailer. In FY 04, the Bridal Group expanded its national presence by opening 30 David's Bridal stores and 10 After Hours stores, and by acquiring 225 tuxedo stores, including 125 Gingiss Formalwear and Gary's Tux Shop stores; 64 Desmonds Formalwear stores; and, 25 Modern Tuxedo stores. It planned to open 52 new stores in FY 05.

The capital budget for 2002 through 2006 was projected at $4.1 billion, including about $1.6 billion for new stores totaling 12 million sq. ft., $1.2 billion to expand and remodel existing stores, and $370 million related to systems and operations.

In FY 03, the company completed a combination of its Pittsburgh-based Kaufmann's division with its Filene's division, headquartered in Boston. MAY also combined Portland-based Meier & Frank with Robinson-May, based in Los Angeles. The divisional combinations were expected to yield annual pretax savings of about $65 million. In FY 04, the company announced plans to divest 34 underperforming department stores, consisting of 32 Lord & Taylor stores, one Famous-Barr store, and one Jones Store location. Nine stores were closed in FY 04. When completed, the divestitures were expected to produce annual savings of about $50 million.

In July 2004, MAY acquired the Marshall Field's department store group, including 62 stores, three distribution centers, and $600 million of credit card receivables, and nine Mervyn's store locations from Target Corp., for $3.24 billion in cash. The company expects to realize pretax cost synergies of $85 million in FY 06, $140 million in FY 07, and $180 million annually thereafter.

In February 2004, directors approved a special repurchase of up to $500 million of company common stock. This program was indefinitely suspended in July in connection with the Marshall Field's acquisition. Prior to the suspension, MAY had repurchased $18 million of common stock.

Company Financials Fiscal Year ending January 31

Per Share Data ($)

(Year Ended January 31)	2004	2003	2002	2001	2000	1999	1998	1997	1996	1995
Tangible Bk. Val.	8.72	8.37	7.77	8.51	9.50	8.57	8.82	8.09	10.47	9.48
Cash Flow	3.43	3.51	4.39	4.58	4.28	3.46	3.14	3.00	2.71	3.04
Earnings	1.41	1.76	2.22	2.62	2.60	2.30	2.07	1.88	1.82	2.04
S&P Core Earnings	1.46	1.64	2.09	2.47	NA	NA	NA	NA	NA	NA
Dividends	0.95	0.95	0.93	0.89	0.89	0.84	0.80	0.77	0.74	0.67
Payout Ratio	67%	54%	42%	34%	34%	36%	39%	41%	41%	33%

Cal. Yrs.	2003	2002	2001	2000	1999	1998	1997	1996	1995	1994
Prices - High	30.82	38.86	41.25	33.93	45.37	47.25	38.08	34.83	30.25	30.08
- Low	17.81	20.10	27.00	19.18	29.18	33.16	29.08	26.66	21.91	21.50
P/E Ratio - High	22	18	18	13	17	20	18	19	17	15
- Low	13	9	12	7	11	14	14	14	12	11

Income Statement Analysis (Million $)

	2004	2003	2002	2001	2000	1999	1998	1997	1996	1995
Revs.	13,343	13,491	14,175	15,511	13,866	13,413	12,685	12,000	10,952	12,223
Oper. Inc.	1,835	1,813	2,052	2,858	2,279	2,112	1,990	1,882	1,743	1,914
Depr.	556	557	559	511	469	439	412	373	333	374
Int. Exp.	318	345	349	345	287	278	299	277	283	257
Pretax Inc.	639	820	1,144	1,402	1,523	1,395	1,279	1,232	1,160	1,296
Eff. Tax Rate	32.1%	33.9%	38.3%	38.8%	39.1%	39.1%	39.1%	39.2%	39.7%	39.7%
Net Inc.	434	542	706	858	927	849	779	749	700	782
S&P Core Earnings	434	542	484	642	791	NA	NA	NA	NA	NA

Balance Sheet & Other Fin. Data (Million $)

	2004	2003	2002	2001	2000	1999	1998	1997	1996	1995
Cash	564	55.0	52.0	156	41.0	112	199	102	159	55.0
Curr. Assets	5,143	4,722	4,925	5,270	5,115	4,987	4,878	5,035	5,097	4,910
Total Assets	12,097	11,936	11,920	11,574	10,935	10,533	9,930	10,059	10,122	9,472
Curr. Liab.	2,685	2,666	2,538	2,214	2,415	2,059	1,866	1,923	1,602	1,895
LT Debt	3,797	4,035	Nil	4,534	3,560	3,825	3,512	3,849	3,333	2,815
Common Equity	4,191	4,035	3,841	3,855	4,077	3,836	3,489	3,650	4,585	4,135
Total Cap.	8,996	9,045	4,823	9,274	8,492	8,470	8,107	8,247	8,664	7,388
Cap. Exp.	600	798	797	598	703	630	496	632	801	937
Cash Flow	990	1,081	1,265	1,369	1,396	1,270	1,173	1,122	1,014	1,137
Curr. Ratio	1.9	1.8	1.9	2.4	2.1	2.4	2.6	2.6	3.2	2.6
% LT Debt of Cap.	42.2	44.6	Nil	48.9	41.9	45.2	43.3	46.7	38.5	38.9
% Net Inc.of Revs.	3.3	4.0	5.0	5.5	6.7	6.3	6.1	6.2	6.4	6.4
% Ret. on Assets	3.6	4.5	6.0	7.6	8.6	8.3	7.8	7.5	7.2	8.6
% Ret. on Equity	10.6	13.3	18.3	21.6	23.4	22.7	22.4	18.1	15.6	19.6

Data as orig reptd.; bef. results of disc opers/spec. items. Per share data adj. for stk. divs.; EPS diluted. E-Estimated. NA-Not Available. NM-Not Meaningful. NR-Not Ranked. UR-Under Review.

Office: 611 Olive Street, St. Louis, MO 63101.
Telephone: 314-342-6300.
Website: http://www.maycompany.com
Chrmn & CEO: E.S. Kahn.
Pres: J.L. Dunham.
Vice Chrmn: W.P. McNamara.

EVP & CFO: T.D. Fingleton.
SVP & Treas: J.R. Kniffen.
Investor Contact: S. Bateman 314-342-6250.
Dirs: J. L. Dunham, M. J. Evans, E. S. Kahn, H. L. Kaplan, J. M. Kilts, R. E. Palmer, M. R. Quinlan, J. M. Roche, W. P. Stiritz, E. E. Whitacre, Jr., R. D. Wolfe.

Founded: in 1877.
Domicile: Delaware.
Employees: 110,000.
S&P Analyst: Jason N. Asaeda/MF/BK

Maytag Corp.

Recommendation: **HOLD** ★★★☆☆
SELL · SELL · HOLD · BUY · BUY

12-Month Target Price: **$20.00**
(as of November 09, 2004)

MYG has an approximate 0.01% weighting in the **S&P 500**

Sector: Consumer Discretionary
Sub-Industry: Household Appliances
Peer Group: Household Appliances

Summary: MYG produces appliances under the Maytag, Magic Chef, Admiral and Jenn-Air names, and floor care products under the Hoover name. The Dixie-Narco division makes vending equipment.

Quantitative Evaluations

S&P Earnings & Dividend Rank: B+

| D | C | B- | B | B+ | A- | A | A+ |

S&P Fair Value Rank: 4

| 1 | 2 | 3 | 4 | 5 |
| Lowest | | | | Highest |

Fair Value Calc.: $18.30 (Slightly Overvalued)

S&P Investability Quotient Percentile

64%

MYG scored higher than 64% of all companies for which an S&P Report is available.

Volatility: Average

| Low | Average | High |

Technical Evaluation: Bearish
Since 7/04, the technical indicators for MYG have been Bearish.

Relative Strength Rank: Moderate

59

| 1 Lowest | | Highest 99 |

Price as of 11/12/04: $20   **2004E S&P Core EPS:** $-0.35

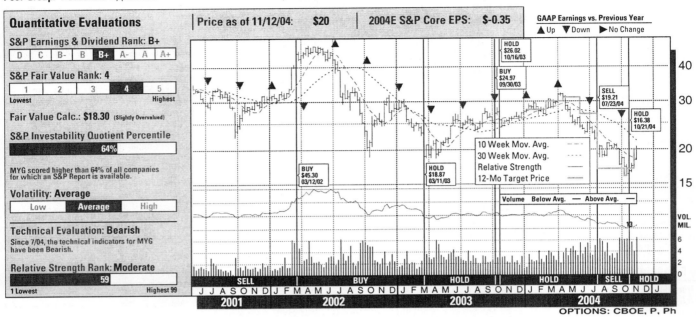

GAAP Earnings vs. Previous Year
▲ Up   ▼ Down   ► No Change

10 Week Mov. Avg.
30 Week Mov. Avg.
Relative Strength
12-Mo Target Price

Volume   Below Avg. — Above Avg.

OPTIONS: CBOE, P, Ph

Analyst commentary prepared by Amy Glynn, CFA /DC/JWP

Highlights November 15, 2004

- We see growth in the low to mid-single digits in U.S. industry shipments of major appliances in 2004. We expect demand for appliance products to be boosted by an improved economy, continued low, yet rising, interest rates, and recent housing market strength, in light of our belief that new homeowners may take a year or more to remodel their new homes. However, due to MYG-specific issues, such as continued weakness in the floor care segment and lost market share, we project revenues to be approximately flat in 2004. In 2005, we expect revenues to increase in the low single digits, aided, in part, by new product introductions in floor care. In November, MYG announced price increases in the range of 5% to 8%, effective January 2005, which will also help to boost the top line, in our view.

- We look for margins to narrow significantly in 2004, due to continued weakness in the company's floor care segment, higher raw material costs, and competitive pricing. We think that MYG is on track to reduce its annual costs through its "One Company" initiative, and see margins widening in 2005.

- For 2004, we project operating EPS of $0.98, before restructuring costs, goodwill impairment, and legal costs. We estimate operating EPS of $1.60 in 2005. On an S&P Core EPS basis, we project a loss of $0.35 for 2004, with profits seen at $1.22 in 2005.

Investment Rationale/Risk November 15, 2004

- We have a hold recomendation on the shares, based largely on valuation, as we think MYG's current challenges are reflected in the stock price. Furthermore, looking into 2005, we see significant opportunities for improvement, including easier comparisons, stemming declines in the floorcare business and MYG's plan to eliminate $150 million in annual costs. We think the shares are fairly valued at this level, trading at about 12.3X our 2005 EPS estimate. We think the stock's significant discount to the S&P 500 is justified due to near-term risks that we see.

- Risks to our opinion and target price include management execution, particularly with regard to MYG's "One Company" restructuring initiative, futher declines in business conditions, an unanticipated increase in competition, continued market share erosion and/or continued increases in raw material costs.

- Our 12-month target price of $20 is based on our historical P/E multiple model, and applies a target P/E multiple of 12.5X, below MYG's historical average, to our 2005 operating EPS estimate of $1.60.

Key Stock Statistics

S&P Core EPS 2005E	1.22	52-week Range	$32.21-15.30
S&P Oper. EPS 2004E	0.98	12 Month P/E	54.1
P/E on S&P Oper. EPS 2004E	20.4	Beta	1.60
S&P Oper. EPS 2005E	1.60	Shareholders	19,562
Yield (%)	3.6%	Market Cap (B)	$1.6
Dividend Rate/Share	0.72	Shares Outstanding (M)	79.2

Value of $10,000 invested five years ago: **$ 4,972**

Dividend Data Dividends have been paid since 1946

Amount ($)	Date Decl.	Ex-Div. Date	Stock of Record	Payment Date
0.180	Feb. 12	Feb. 26	Mar. 01	Mar. 15 '04
0.180	May. 13	May. 27	Jun. 01	Jun. 15 '04
0.180	Aug. 12	Aug. 30	Sep. 01	Sep. 15 '04
0.180	Nov. 11	Nov. 29	Dec. 01	Dec. 15 '04

Revenues/Earnings Data Fiscal year ending December 31

Revenues (Million $)

	2004	2003	2002	2001	2000	1999
1Q	1,219	1,136	1,178	1,009	1,095	1,106
2Q	1,152	1,163	1,193	1,010	1,104	1,085
3Q	1,186	1,221	1,168	1,171	1,056	1,069
4Q	—	1,272	1,127	1,134	991.3	1,063
Yr.	—	4,792	4,666	4,324	4,248	4,324

Earnings Per Share ($)

	2004	2003	2002	2001	2000	1999
1Q	0.49	0.44	0.75	0.99	0.89	0.95
2Q	-0.52	0.32	0.87	0.35	0.92	0.97
3Q	0.09	0.45	0.78	-0.48	0.74	0.92
4Q	E0.18	0.24	0.05	0.31	-0.12	0.82
Yr.	E0.98	1.46	2.44	2.13	2.44	3.66

Next earnings report expected: late-January Source: S&P, Company Reports
EPS Estimates based on S&P Operating Earnings; historical GAAP earnings are as reported.

Maytag Corporation

Recommendation: **HOLD** ★ ★ ★ ☆ ☆   12-Month Target Price: **$20.00** (as of November 09, 2004)

Business Summary November 15, 2004

Maytag produces home and commercial appliances. Its products are sold to customers throughout North America, and in international markets. The company was incorporated in Delaware in 1925.

The home appliances segment (95% of sales in 2003) manufactures laundry products, dishwashers, refrigerators, cooking appliances and floor care products. These products are sold mainly to major national retailers and independent retail dealers in North America and targeted international markets. Products are sold primarily under the Maytag, Amana, Hoover, Jenn-Air, and Magic Chef brand names.

Included in the home appliances segment is Maytag International, Inc., the company's international marketing subsidiary that administers the sale of home appliances and licensing of certain home appliance brands in markets outside of the U.S. MYG has also increased the company's emphasis on its in-home service business, Maytag Services, which repairs Maytag brand appliances as well as other brands.

The commercial appliances segment (5% of sales in 2003) makes commercial cooking equipment under the Jade brand name and vending equipment under the Dixie-Narco brand name. Dixie-Narco produces soft-drink vending equipment and money changers, sold to all major bottlers. In 1999, MYG bought Jade Range, a maker of heavy duty ranges and refrigeration units and residential ranges and outdoor grills, for $19 million in cash and stock. In the 2001 fourth quarter, the company sold G. S. Blodgett, a maker of commercial ovens, fryers and char-broilers for the foodservice industry.

Sales to Sears, Roebuck and Co. accounted for 15%, 13% and 12% of consolidated net sales in 2003, 2002 and 2001, respectively.

In May 2000, Home Depot began selling Maytag and Jenn-Air brand major appliances in selected markets.

In August 2001, MYG acquired Amana Appliances from Goodman Global Holding Co. for $325 million. In the first quarter of 2004, the company sold a former cooking appliance manufacturing facility in Indianapolis, Indiana.

In September 2004, the company completed the closing of its refrigeration plant in Galesburg, IL. As a result of this restructuring, which began in 2002, MYG recorded respective pretax charges of $48.4 million and $67.1 million in 2003 and 2002. In the first nine months of 2004, charges were $36.4 million. Total pretax restructuring charges are expected to be $160 million to $170 million, with the majority of remaining expenses expected to be incurred in the balance of 2004. The closure of the facility has resulted in a workforce reduction of approximately 1,420 positions through the end of the third quarter of 2004.

In the second quarter of 2004, the company announced a comprehensive restructuring plan to consolidate the Hoover Floor Care, Maytag Appliances, and Corporate Headquarters organizations. MYG anticipates that the restructuring plan will result in a workforce reduction of approximately 1,100 positions by the end of 2004. MYG expects this restructuring to result in annual cost savings of $150 million.

Company Financials Fiscal Year ending December 31

Per Share Data ($)

(Year Ended December 31)	2003	2002	2001	2000	1999	1998	1997	1996	1995	1994
Tangible Bk. Val.	NM	NM	NM	NM	NM	0.23	1.57	1.85	2.33	3.14
Cash Flow	3.56	4.52	4.16	4.38	5.77	4.63	3.27	2.45	0.91	2.53
Earnings	1.46	2.44	2.13	2.44	3.66	3.05	1.87	1.36	-0.14	1.42
S&P Core Earnings	1.82	1.89	1.44	NA	NA	NA	NA	NA	NA	NA
Dividends	0.72	0.72	0.72	0.72	0.72	0.70	0.64	0.56	0.52	0.50
Payout Ratio	49%	30%	34%	30%	20%	23%	34%	41%	NM	35%
Prices - High	30.70	47.94	37.40	47.75	74.81	64.50	37.56	22.87	21.50	20.12
- Low	17.90	18.84	22.25	25.00	31.25	35.37	19.75	17.50	14.50	14.00
P/E Ratio - High	21	20	18	20	20	21	20	17	NM	14
- Low	12	8	10	10	9	12	11	13	NM	10

Income Statement Analysis (Million $)

	2003	2002	2001	2000	1999	1998	1997	1996	1995	1994
Revs.	4,792	4,666	4,324	4,248	4,324	4,069	3,408	3,002	3,040	3,373
Oper. Inc.	470	590	458	628	723	671	496	420	400	442
Depr.	166	164	159	160	147	149	138	111	112	119
Int. Exp.	52.8	62.4	64.8	64.1	59.3	62.8	59.0	43.0	52.1	74.6
Pretax Inc.	173	296	212	332	531	471	301	228	-60.0	241
Eff. Tax Rate	33.8%	34.0%	14.2%	34.7%	36.8%	37.4%	36.5%	39.0%	1.25%	37.4%
Net Inc.	114	191	168	201	329	287	183	138	-15.0	151
S&P Core Earnings	144	148	114	NA	NA	NA	NA	NA	NA	NA

Balance Sheet & Other Fin. Data (Million $)

	2003	2002	2001	2000	1999	1998	1997	1996	1995	1994
Cash	6.76	8.11	109	27.2	28.8	28.6	28.0	28.0	141	110
Curr. Assets	1,304	1,324	1,370	1,077	1,022	969	935	905	910	1,130
Total Assets	3,024	3,104	3,156	2,669	2,636	2,588	2,514	2,330	2,125	2,504
Curr. Liab.	984	1,164	1,074	972	853	791	567	570	367	534
LT Debt	875	739	932	651	538	447	550	488	537	663
Common Equity	65.8	42.1	23.5	21.7	427	508	616	574	637	732
Total Cap.	941	781	1,081	860	1,158	1,149	1,364	1,160	1,188	1,433
Cap. Exp.	199	230	146	163	147	161	230	211	148	79.0
Cash Flow	280	355	327	361	476	435	321	249	97.0	270
Curr. Ratio	1.3	1.1	1.3	1.1	1.2	1.2	1.6	1.6	2.5	2.1
% LT Debt of Cap.	93.0	94.6	Nil	75.7	46.4	38.8	40.3	42.1	45.2	46.3
% Net Inc.of Revs.	2.4	4.1	3.9	4.7	7.6	7.0	5.4	4.6	NM	4.5
% Ret. on Assets	3.7	6.1	5.8	7.6	12.6	11.2	7.6	6.2	NM	6.1
% Ret. on Equity	211.9	582.8	NM	89.5	70.3	51.0	30.8	22.8	NM	22.9

Data as orig reptd.; bef. results of disc opers/spec. items. Per share data adj. for stk. divs.; EPS diluted. E-Estimated. NA-Not Available. NM-Not Meaningful. NR-Not Ranked. UR-Under Review.

Office: 403 West Fourth Street North, Newton, IA 50208.
Telephone: 641-792-7000.
Email: investor.relations@maytag.com
Website: http://www.maytag.com
Chrmn & CEO: R. F. Hake.
EVP & CFO: G. C. Moore.

SVP & General Counsel: R. K. Scholten.
SVP: M. W. Krivoruchka.
Dirs: B. R. Allen, H. L. Clark, Jr., L. Crown, R. F. Hake, W. R. Hicks, W. T. Kerr, J. A. McCaslin, B. G. Rethore, W. A. Reynolds, N. E. Stearns, Jr., F. G. Steingraber.

Founded: in 1893.
Domicile: Delaware.
Employees: 20,640.
S&P Analyst: Amy Glynn, CFA /DC/JWP

Recommendation: **SELL** ★ ★ ★ ★ ★
SELL SELL HOLD BUY BUY

12-Month Target Price: **$59.00**
(as of November 02, 2004)

MBI has an approximate 0.08% weighting in the **S&P 500**

Sector: Financials
Sub-Industry: Property & Casualty Insurance
Peer Group: Financial Guaranty/ Surety

Summary: MBIA is a leading provider of financial guarantee insurance and related services to public finance clients and financial institutions around the world.

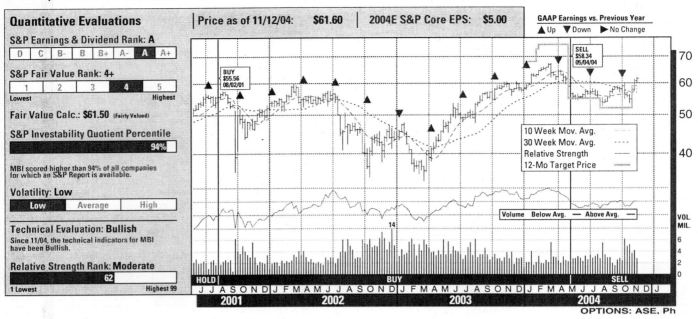

Quantitative Evaluations

S&P Earnings & Dividend Rank: A

| D | C | B- | B | B+ | A- | A | A+ |

S&P Fair Value Rank: 4+

| 1 | 2 | 3 | 4 | 5 |
| Lowest | | | | Highest |

Fair Value Calc.: $61.50 (Fairly Valued)

S&P Investability Quotient Percentile
94%

MBI scored higher than 94% of all companies for which an S&P Report is available.

Volatility: Low

| Low | Average | High |

Technical Evaluation: Bullish
Since 11/04, the technical indicators for MBI have been Bullish.

Relative Strength Rank: Moderate
62
1 Lowest   Highest 99

Price as of 11/12/04: $61.60   **2004E S&P Core EPS: $5.00**

GAAP Earnings vs. Previous Year
▲ Up   ▼ Down   ► No Change

BUY $55.56 08/02/01

SELL $58.34 05/04/04

10 Week Mov. Avg.
30 Week Mov. Avg.
Relative Strength
12-Mo Target Price

Volume   Below Avg. — Above Avg.

HOLD   BUY   SELL
J J A S O N D J F M A M J J A S O N D J F M A M J J A S O N D J F M A M J J A S O N D J
2001   2002   2003   2004

OPTIONS: ASE, Ph

Analyst commentary prepared by Catherine A. Seifert/MF/BK

Highlights August 25, 2004

- We see earned premiums increasing 15% to 20% in 2004, reflecting the strong (37%) rate of net written premium growth in 2003 (amid healthy production in the U.S. and in overseas municipal and structured finance operations). This should be partly offset by a sharp drop in premiums earned due to refundings (caused by an acceleration in the recognition of premiums as bonds are refunded amid dropping interest rates). However, our near term outlook is tempered by disappointing first half 2004 new business production. Adjusted direct premiums (ADP) declined 11%, year to year, in the first half of 2004, driven in part by a 64% drop in worldwide public finance ADP in the first quarter. This was due mainly to tighter credit spreads, which decreased insured penetration and increased competition.

- We are also concerned that as macro credit trends improve, the demand for structured finance credit enhancement products may decline. Both of these trends could hurt operating EPS growth.

- We see operating EPS of $5.20 in 2004 (versus $4.80 reported in 2003) and $5.80 in 2005.

Investment Rationale/Risk August 25, 2004

- We continue to recommend investors avoid the shares. MBI reported disappointing first quarter 2004 results, and although second quarter operating earnings of $1.34 a share (versus $1.21 a year earlier) actually beat our $1.25 a share estimate, we remain concerned about the company's ability to continue to produce this rate of profit growth in light of the previously mentioned downturn in business production . Moreover, rising interest rates, coupled with improving credit trends, could reduce demand for the company's credit enhancement products.

- Risks to our opinion and target price include a greater than expected pickup in production and a sharp rise in demand for credit enhancement products.

- We believe that what we see as MBI's lackluster near-term growth prospects will keep the shares under pressure. Our 12-month target price of $52 assumes that the shares' forward P/E multiple contracts to one that is slightly discounted to the peer group average and is at the low end of MBI's historical range.

Key Stock Statistics

S&P Oper. EPS 2004E	5.25	52-week Range	$67.34-52.55
P/E on S&P Oper. EPS 2004E	11.7	12 Month P/E	11.3
S&P Oper. EPS 2005E	5.75	Beta	0.90
Yield (%)	1.6%	Shareholders	798
Dividend Rate/Share	0.96	Market Cap (B)	$ 8.7
Shares Outstanding (M)	140.7		

Value of $10,000 invested five years ago: **$ 18,913**

Dividend Data Dividends have been paid since 1987

Amount ($)	Date Decl.	Ex-Div. Date	Stock of Record	Payment Date
0.200	Dec. 08	Dec. 17	Dec. 19	Jan. 15 '04
0.240	Mar. 11	Mar. 24	Mar. 26	Apr. 15 '04
0.240	Jun. 14	Jun. 23	Jun. 25	Jul. 15 '04
0.240	Sep. 10	Sep. 22	Sep. 24	Oct. 15 '04

Revenues/Earnings Data Fiscal year ending December 31

Revenues (Million $)

	2004	2003	2002	2001	2000	1999
1Q	327.5	280.9	252.3	229.0	254.4	236.8
2Q	340.4	310.7	258.4	206.6	262.5	235.4
3Q	476.0	313.0	282.5	246.5	266.2	215.1
4Q	—	325.8	357.6	256.1	274.3	216.1
Yr.	—	1,230	1,151	1,134	1,057	853.8

Earnings Per Share ($)

	2004	2003	2002	2001	2000	1999
1Q	1.42	1.54	1.08	0.87	0.89	0.06
2Q	1.47	1.51	0.97	0.96	0.87	0.37
3Q	1.29	1.31	1.11	1.03	0.88	0.85
4Q	—	1.25	0.84	1.05	0.92	0.85
Yr.	—	5.61	3.98	3.91	3.55	2.13

Next earnings report expected: early-February Source: S&P, Company Reports
EPS Estimates based on S&P Operating Earnings; historical GAAP earnings are as reported.

MBIA Inc.

Recommendation:  **SELL** ★ ★ ☆ ☆ ☆   12-Month Target Price: **$59.00** (as of November 02, 2004)

Business Summary August 25, 2004

MBIA Inc. (MBI), a dominant force in the municipal bond insurance market, has leveraged that strength and expanded into the structured finance market and into selected international markets. It is also engaged in asset management operations. At December 31, 2003, assets under management totaled $37.5 billion, up from $34.9 billion a year earlier. In early 2004, MBI announced plans to sell one of its asset management companies, 1838 Investment Advisors, LLC, which had year-end assets under management of $3.6 billion. The sale is expected to result in a small gain for MBI.

MBI offers insurance for new issues of municipal bonds, and for bonds traded in the secondary market, including bonds held in unit investment trusts and mutual funds. The economic value of municipal bond insurance to the governmental unit or agency offering bonds is a saving in interest costs reflecting the difference in yield on an insured bond from that on the same bond if uninsured. The company's guarantee also increases market acceptance for complex financings, and for municipal bonds of issuers that are not well known.

At December 31, 2003, the net par value of the company's insured debt obligations was $541.0 billion, of which general obligation municipal bonds accounted for 23%, utility bonds 11%, special revenue bonds 8%, health care bonds 6%, transportation bonds 5%, other U.S. municipal bonds 9%, non-U.S. municipal obliga-

tions 4%, U.S. structured finance obligations (asset/mortgage backed) 21%, and international structured finance 13%. Of the $541.0 billion of insured debt obligations at December 31, 2003, 17% had been issued outside the U.S., 11% had been issued by California, 7% by New York, 4% by Florida, and about 3% each by Texas, New Jersey, Pennsylvania, Illinois and Massachusetts.

MBI in recent years has expanded its presence in the structured finance (or asset-backed) markets to help offset slower growth in the more mature domestic public finance markets. However, in 2003, global public finance adjusted direct premiums (which equal upfront premiums and the estimated present value of current and future installment premiums) rose 58%, while global structured finance adjusted direct premiums (ADP) rose a more modest 7.0%. Total ADP growth in 2003 was 35%.

The company is the successor to the Municipal Bond Insurance Association, a voluntary association formed in 1974 by five multi-line insurance companies to insure municipal bonds. The association was reorganized in 1986, with four of the original five members participating. MBI's principal business in insuring municipal bonds unconditionally and irrevocably guarantees payment of principal and interest when due on insured municipal bonds.

Company Financials Fiscal Year ending December 31

Per Share Data ($)

(Year Ended December 31)	2003	2002	2001	2000	1999	1998	1997	1996	1995	1994
Tangible Bk. Val.	42.87	37.32	31.56	27.86	23.01	24.59	21.81	18.27	16.88	12.76
Oper. Earnings	NA	4.27	3.88	3.41	3.15	3.05	2.71	2.41	2.09	2.01
Earnings	5.61	3.98	3.91	3.55	2.13	2.88	2.81	2.48	2.14	2.06
S&P Core Earnings	5.25	3.91	3.81	NA	NA	NA	NA	NA	NA	NA
Dividends	0.80	0.68	0.60	0.55	0.53	0.52	0.51	0.48	0.44	0.38
Payout Ratio	14%	17%	15%	15%	25%	18%	18%	20%	20%	18%
Prices - High	60.72	60.11	57.49	50.79	47.91	53.95	44.91	34.87	25.83	21.75
- Low	34.14	34.93	36.00	24.20	30.08	30.70	30.29	23.33	18.45	15.75
P/E Ratio - High	11	15	15	14	23	19	16	14	12	11
- Low	6	9	9	7	14	11	11	9	9	8

Income Statement Analysis (Million $)

	2003	2002	2001	2000	1999	1998	1997	1996	1995	1994
Premium Inc.	733	589	524	446	443	425	297	252	215	218
Net Invest. Inc.	447	442	413	394	359	332	281	248	220	194
Oth. Revs.	590	120	197	217	605	156	75.1	46.0	27.0	27.4
Total Revs.	1,770	1,151	1,134	1,057	964	912	654	546	462	440
Pretax Inc.	1,149	793	791	715	388	565	480	408	345	329
Net Oper. Inc.	NA	NA	NA	NA	NA	NA	364	313	265	254
Net Inc.	814	587	583	529	321	433	374	322	271	260
S&P Core Earnings	761	577	568	NA	NA	NA	NA	NA	NA	NA

Balance Sheet & Other Fin. Data (Million $)

	2003	2002	2001	2000	1999	1998	1997	1996	1995	1994
Cash & Equiv.	452	298	297	246	229	148	23.2	112	110	76.4
Premiums Due	536	522	507	NA	NA	NA	13.4	0.98	6.10	0.90
Invest. Assets: Bonds	17,391	16,195	14,087	11,737	10,274	9,562	4,867	4,150	3,653	3,052
Invest. Assets: Stocks	Nil	Nil	Nil	Nil	Nil	Nil	Nil	Nil	Nil	Nil
Invest. Assets: Loans	Nil	Nil	Nil	Nil	Nil	Nil	Nil	205	212	139
Invest. Assets: Total	27,707	17,095	14,516	12,233	10,694	10,080	8,470	7,648	6,607	4,867
Deferred Policy Costs	320	302	278	274	252	230	154	148	140	133
Total Assets	30,268	18,852	16,200	13,894	12,264	11,797	9,811	8,562	7,267	5,456
Debt	8,870	1,033	805	795	689	689	474	374	374	299
Common Equity	6,259	5,493	4,783	4,223	3,513	3,792	3,048	2,480	2,234	1,705
Prop. & Cas. Loss Ratio	9.2	9.4	9.3	6.2	12.3	8.0	6.3	6.1	4.9	3.7
Prop. & Cas. Expense Ratio	12.8	16.8	13.4	22.1	23.6	16.8	26.2	28.3	29.3	28.8
Prop. & Cas. Combined Ratio	22.0	26.2	22.7	28.3	35.9	24.8	32.5	34.4	34.2	32.5
% Return On Revs.	46.0	51.0	51.4	50.0	33.2	47.5	57.2	59.1	58.7	59.2
% Ret. on Equity	13.8	11.4	13.0	13.7	8.8	12.7	13.5	13.7	13.8	15.8

Data as orig reptd.; bef. results of disc opers/spec. items. Per share data adj. for stk. divs.; EPS diluted. E-Estimated. NA-Not Available. NM-Not Meaningful. NR-Not Ranked. Hist. EPS data incl. real. inv. gains/losses; EPS estimates excl. them.

Office: 113 King Street, Armonk, NY 10504-1610.
Telephone: 914-273-4545.
Website: http://www.mbia.com
Chrmn: J.W. Brown.
CEO: G.C. Dunton.
VP & CFO: N. Ferreri.

VP & Secy: R.D. Wertheim.
Investor Contact: K.T. Brown 914-765-3648.
Dirs: J. W. Brown, E. Chaplin, D. C. Clapp, G. C. Dunton, C. L. Gaudiani, F. S. Johnson, D. P. Kearney, J. A. Lebenthal, L. H. Meyer, D. J. Perry, J. A. Rolls.

Founded: in 1973.
Domicile: Connecticut.
Employees: 701.
S&P Analyst: Catherine A. Seifert/MF/BK

MBNA Corp.

Recommendation: **BUY** ★★★★   12-Month Target Price: **$32.00**
(as of May 17, 2004)

KRB has an approximate 0.31% weighting in the **S&P 500**

Sector: Financials
Sub-Industry: Consumer Finance
Peer Group: Consumer Finance - Credit Cards

Summary: MBNA, one of the largest U.S. lenders through bank credit cards and a leading issuer of affinity cards, also provides retail deposit and financial transaction processing services.

Quantitative Evaluations

S&P Earnings & Dividend Rank: A+

| D | C | B- | B | B+ | A- | A | **A+** |

S&P Fair Value Rank: 5

| 1 | 2 | 3 | 4 | **5** |
| Lowest | | | | Highest |

Fair Value Calc.: $36.80 (Undervalued)

S&P Investability Quotient Percentile

99%

KRB scored higher than 99% of all companies for which an S&P Report is available.

Volatility: Average

| Low | **Average** | High |

Technical Evaluation: Bullish
Since 10/04, the technical indicators for KRB have been Bullish.

Relative Strength Rank: Moderate

61

| 1 Lowest | | Highest 99 |

| Price as of 11/12/04: | **$27** | 2004E S&P Core EPS: | **$2.01** |

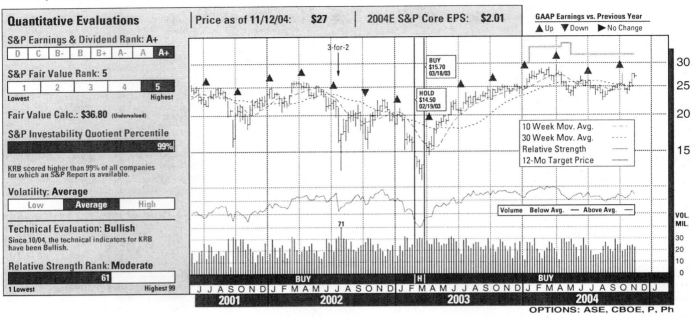

GAAP Earnings vs. Previous Year
▲ Up ▼ Down ► No Change

- 10 Week Mov. Avg.
- 30 Week Mov. Avg.
- Relative Strength
- 12-Mo Target Price

Volume Below Avg. — Above Avg.

OPTIONS: ASE, CBOE, P, Ph

Analyst commentary prepared by Evan M. Momios, CFA /MF/GG

Highlights August 18, 2004

- We believe MBNA's well established affinity-based marketing strategy, combined with an improving outlook for consumer spending and a sharp reduction in cash-out mortgage refinance volume, will support stronger loan growth in 2004 and 2005. We look for MBNA to report managed loan growth of 11% in 2004 and 12% in 2005.

- We think MBNA's history of stable credit quality will continue with gradually improving loss rates through 2004, in a strong economy with declining unemployment. In 2004's second quarter, net charge-offs were 4.95% of average managed loans, down from 4.99% in the first quarter and 5.35% in the 2003 second quarter. In our model, we assume net charge-off rates of 4.85% in 2004 and 4.80% in 2005.

- We see EPS of $2.07 in 2004, up 16% from $1.79 in 2003, followed by a 16% rise to $2.40 in 2005. Our 2004 and 2005 Standard & Poor's Core Earnings per share estimates are $2.01 and $2.35, respectively, primarily reflecting our projections of stock option expense.

Investment Rationale/Risk August 18, 2004

- We believe KRB shares are trading at discounts to peer and historical average levels due to investor concerns about the potential impact of increasing interest rates on the company's profitability. What KRB's current valuation does not reflect are the company's better than peer-average credit quality and its ability to generate above peer-average volume, in our view.

- Risks to our recommendation and target price include a significant deterioration of consumer sentiment that could have a negative impact on consumer spending and challenge volume growth; a decline in the demand for asset backed securities that could increase funding risk; and a more sizable increase than we expect in short-term interest rates, which could put additional pressure on the company's margin.

- Our 12-month target of $32 equates to 13.3X our 2005 EPS estimate, compared to 14.5X on average for peers currently, and versus 12.5X and 14.5X forward 12-month EPS on average for KRB during the past three and five years, respectively.

Key Stock Statistics

S&P Core EPS 2005E	**2.35**	52-week Range	**$29.68-22.35**
S&P Oper. EPS 2004E	**2.07**	12 Month P/E	**13.5**
P/E on S&P Oper. EPS 2004E	**13.0**	Beta	**1.22**
S&P Oper. EPS 2005E	**2.40**	Shareholders	**2,789**
Yield (%)	**1.8%**	Market Cap (B)	**$ 34.5**
Dividend Rate/Share	**0.48**	Shares Outstanding (M)	**1277.7**

Value of $10,000 invested five years ago: **$ 15,172**

Dividend Data Dividends have been paid since 1991

Amount ($)	Date Decl.	Ex-Div. Date	Stock of Record	Payment Date
0.120	Jan. 22	Mar. 11	Mar. 15	Apr. 01 '04
0.120	Apr. 22	Jun. 10	Jun. 14	Jul. 01 '04
0.120	Jul. 22	Sep. 13	Sep. 15	Oct. 01 '04
0.120	Oct. 21	Dec. 13	Dec. 15	Jan. 01 '05

Revenues/Earnings Data Fiscal year ending December 31

Revenues (Million $)

	2004	2003	2002	2001	2000	1999
1Q	2,976	2,732	2,512	2,288	1,778	1,445
2Q	2,968	2,812	2,529	2,433	1,861	1,615
3Q	—	3,002	2,556	2,672	2,035	1,663
4Q	—	3,139	2,834	2,751	2,195	1,747
Yr.	—	11,684	10,431	10,145	7,869	6,470

Earnings Per Share ($)

	2004	2003	2002	2001	2000	1999
1Q	0.40	0.33	0.28	0.23	0.19	0.15
2Q	0.51	0.42	0.35	0.29	0.23	0.18
3Q	0.56	0.51	0.30	0.36	0.29	0.23
4Q	E0.60	0.54	0.41	0.40	0.32	0.25
Yr.	E2.07	1.79	1.34	1.28	1.02	0.81

Next earnings report expected: late-January Source: S&P, Company Reports
EPS Estimates based on S&P Operating Earnings; historical GAAP earnings are as reported.

MBNA Corporation

Recommendation: **BUY** ★ ★ ★ ★ ★   12-Month Target Price: **$32.00** (as of May 17, 2004)

Business Summary August 18, 2004

MBNA is the world's largest independent credit card lender, as well as the leading issuer of affinity credit cards. Affinity credit cards are marketed to members of associations and customers of financial institutions. In addition to credit card lending, the company makes other types of consumer loans and offers insurance and deposit products. With its motto of "Getting the right customers and keeping them," KRB has rapidly increased both the number of card accounts and receivable balances in recent years. At the end of 2003, managed loans totaled $118.4 billion, up 10% from the level a year earlier. In 2003, the company added 10.7 million new accounts, and acquired the endorsement of 384 new groups.

MBNA offers standard, gold and Platinum Plus personal and business credit cards under either the MasterCard or Visa brand name and customizes them for thousands of endorsed affinity programs and for programs under its own brand name. In addition, the company offers customers even more customized, high-end credit card products such as the Quantum card. MBNA's card programs offer a variety of benefits and features based on the type of endorsing organization and need of the customer. These benefits and features include competitive interest rates, group-specific enhancements, rewards, or compensation to the endorsing organization based on the cardholder's usage. The company also offers business card products in the U.S. through MBNA Delaware and in the U.K. through MBNA Europe.

The company's other consumer loan products include unsecured lines of credit accessed by check, unsecured installment loans, and secured loans to individuals including home equity loans and airplane loans. It also offers money market deposit accounts and certificates of deposit. Insurance products include credit insurance offered to credit card customers, as well as automobile insurance and life insurance.

To attract new customers and gain new endorsements, KRB conducts extensive marketing campaigns. It uses a combination of direct mail, telemarketing, person-to-person and Internet marketing to market its credit cards. It has an in-house advertising agency, and telemarketing facilities in around the country.

As a lender, credit quality is of the utmost importance to the company. Decisions to extend credit are made using technology such as credit scoring models, as well as the insight of the credit analyst. Delinquency rates on the managed loan portfolio were 4.39% at the end of 2003, versus 4.88% in 2002 and 5.09% in 2001. Accounts are deemed delinquent if the minimum payment is not received by the date specified on the statement. Net credit losses are accounts that are 180 days overdue and written off, and are generally considered uncollectible. Net credit losses amounted to 5.08% of the managed loan portfolio in 2003, versus 4.99% in 2002 and 4.74% in 2001.

Company Financials Fiscal Year ending December 31

Per Share Data ($)

(Year Ended December 31)	2003	2002	2001	2000	1999	1998	1997	1996	1995	1994
Tangible Bk. Val.	6.20	4.63	4.08	3.03	2.16	1.53	1.42	1.32	1.07	0.77
Earnings	1.79	1.34	1.28	1.02	0.81	0.65	0.51	0.39	0.30	0.23
S&P Core Earnings	1.76	1.28	1.21	NA	NA	NA	NA	NA	NA	NA
Dividends	0.36	0.27	0.24	0.21	0.18	0.16	0.14	0.13	0.11	0.09
Payout Ratio	20%	20%	19%	21%	22%	25%	28%	32%	36%	41%
Prices - High	25.50	26.30	26.37	26.75	22.16	17.25	13.59	8.64	5.74	3.60
- Low	11.96	12.95	15.62	13.00	13.87	9.00	7.96	4.47	2.94	2.53
P/E Ratio - High	14	20	21	26	27	27	27	22	19	15
- Low	7	10	12	13	17	14	16	11	10	11

Income Statement Analysis (Million $)

	2003	2002	2001	2000	1999	1998	1997	1996	1995	1994
Net Int. Inc.	2,350	2,075	1,391	1,084	934	742	692	640	544	532
Tax Equiv. Adj.	0.76	1.07	1.68	2.37	1.93	1.86	1.89	1.79	1.79	1.65
Non Int. Inc.	7,825	6,753	6,940	5,093	4,208	3,229	2,813	1,896	1,425	1,014
Loan Loss Prov.	1,393	1,340	1,141	409	409	310	260	178	138	108
Exp./Op. Revs.	50.5%	53.3%	53.7%	59.1%	59.9%	60.6%	63.4%	62.0%	63.3%	64.4%
Pretax Inc.	3,659	2,785	2,715	2,120	1,655	1,254	1,022	731	585	441
Eff. Tax Rate	36.1%	36.6%	37.6%	38.1%	38.1%	38.1%	39.1%	35.1%	39.6%	39.6%
Net Inc.	2,338	1,766	1,694	1,313	1,024	776	623	474	353	267
% Net Int. Marg.	5.37	5.54	8.42	4.76	4.63	4.42	4.86	5.52	5.74	7.61
S&P Core Earnings	2,270	1,666	1,588	NA	NA	NA	NA	NA	NA	NA

Balance Sheet & Other Fin. Data (Million $)

	2003	2002	2001	2000	1999	1998	1997	1996	1995	1994
Money Mkt. Assets	4,865	5,348	3,031	700	2,014	1,526	2,086	877	574	268
Inv. Securities	4,716	4,141	3,547	3,050	3,046	1,880	2,509	2,318	2,096	2,002
Com'l Loans	Nil	Nil	Nil	Nil	Nil	Nil	Nil	Nil	Nil	Nil
Other Loans	33,624	28,727	24,634	19,955	17,664	13,468	11,162	10,129	8,135	5,707
Total Assets	59,113	52,857	45,448	38,678	30,859	25,806	21,306	17,035	13,229	9,672
Demand Deposits	10,210	8,481	7,220	5,815	568	498	312	234	170	101
Time Deposits	21,626	22,135	19,874	18,529	18,147	14,909	9,123	9,918	8,439	6,531
LT Debt	12,146	9,538	6,867	5,736	5,709	5,939	5,479	3,950	2,658	1,564
Common Equity	11,113	9,101	7,799	6,627	4,199	2,391	1,970	1,704	1,265	920
% Ret. on Assets	4.2	3.6	4.0	3.8	3.6	3.3	3.2	3.1	3.1	3.2
% Ret. on Equity	23.0	20.7	23.3	24.0	30.7	34.9	33.0	32.0	35.5	32.7
% Loan Loss Resv.	3.6	3.9	3.4	1.9	2.0	1.6	1.4	1.2	2.2	1.8
% Loans/Deposits	105.6	93.8	90.9	82.0	94.4	87.4	64.0	74.3	94.5	86.0
% Equity to Assets	18.1	17.2	17.1	15.6	11.6	9.3	9.6	9.8	9.6	9.7

Data as orig reptd.; bef. results of disc opers/spec. items. Per share data adj. for stk. divs. Bold denotes primary EPS - prior periods restated. E-Estimated. NA-Not Available. NM-Not Meaningful. NR-Not Ranked. UR-Under Review.

Office: 1100 North King Street, Wilmington, DE 19884-0131.
Telephone: 800-362-6255.
Website: http://www.mbna.com
Chrmn: R.D. Lerner.
Pres & CEO: B.L. Hammonds.
Vice Chrmn: R.K. Struthers.

Vice Chrmn: L.L. Weaver.
CFO: K.A. Vecchione.
Investor Contact: E.H. Murphy 302-432-0202.
Dirs: J. H. Berick, M. M. Boies, B. R. Civiletti, B. L. Hammonds, W. L. Jews, R. D. Lerner, S. L. Markowitz, W. B. Milstead, T. G. Murdough, Jr., L. S. Unger.

Founded: in 1990.
Domicile: Maryland.
Employees: 26,500.
S&P Analyst: Evan M. Momios, CFA /MF/GG

McCormick & Co.

Recommendation: **BUY** ★★★★☆
SELL | SELL | HOLD | BUY | BUY

12-Month Target Price: **$38.00**
(as of September 29, 2004)

MKC has an approximate 0.05% weighting in the **S&P 500**

Sector: Consumer Staples
Sub-Industry: Packaged Foods & Meats
Peer Group: Mid-sized Food Manufacturers

Summary: This company primarily produces spices, seasonings and flavorings for the retail food, foodservice and industrial markets. Trademarks include McCormick and Schilling.

Quantitative Evaluations

S&P Earnings & Dividend Rank: A

D	C	B-	B	B+	A-	A	A+

S&P Fair Value Rank: 2+

1	2	3	4	5
Lowest				Highest

Fair Value Calc.: $35.00 (Slightly Overvalued)

S&P Investability Quotient Percentile
99%

MKC scored higher than 99% of all companies for which an S&P Report is available.

Volatility: Low

Low	Average	High

Technical Evaluation: Bullish
Since 11/04, the technical indicators for MKC have been Bullish.

Relative Strength Rank: Moderate
61
1 Lowest — Highest 99

Price as of 11/12/04: $37.33   **2004E S&P Core EPS:** $1.50

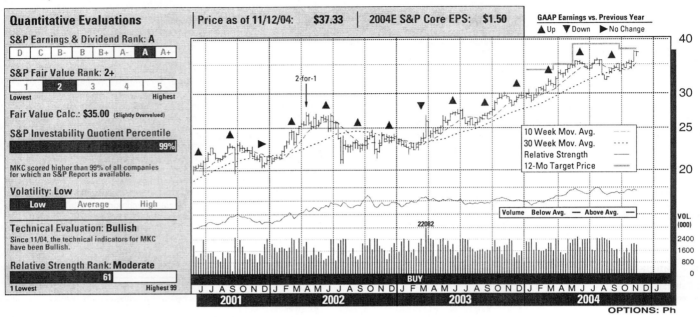

GAAP Earnings vs. Previous Year
▲ Up ▼ Down ▶ No Change

10 Week Mov. Avg.
30 Week Mov. Avg.
Relative Strength
12-Mo Target Price

Volume Below Avg. — Above Avg.

VOL. (000)
2400
1600
800
0

2-for-1

22082

BUY

J J A S O N D J F M A M J J A S O N D J F M A M J J A S O N D J F M A M J J A S O N D J
2001   2002   2003   2004

OPTIONS: Ph

Analyst commentary prepared by Richard Joy/CB/GG

Highlights August 05, 2004

- We project net sales growth of 11% to 12% in FY 04 (Nov.), reflecting core volume growth of 3% to 4%, price and mix improvements of 2% to 3% and contributions from the June 2003 acquisition of Zatarains. We expect sales growth of more than 15% for the consumer business and 8% to 9% growth for the industrial segment. We believe foreign currency translation should be a net positive factor, reflecting strength in the euro. Advertising spending will likely be in line with prior year levels due to spending behind new products. Operating profit margins are expected to widen, aided by modest price increases, a mix shift toward value-added products, and supply chain improvements. We expect total company operating profits to advance 13% to 14% in FY 04, with strong gains for both the consumer and industrial segments.

- Following lower interest expense and a modest reduction in shares outstanding, we see FY 04 EPS rising 12%, to $1.57, from EPS of $1.40 in FY 03. For FY 05, we expect a further 11% rise, to $1.74. For the longer term, we expect EPS growth of 10% to 12%.

- Our FY 04 and FY 05 Standard & Poor's Core Earnings per share estimates, reflecting projected stock option expense of $0.08 per share and a modest pension adjustment, are $1.50 and $1.67, respectively.

Key Stock Statistics

S&P Core EPS 2005E	1.67	52-week Range	$37.68-27.96
S&P Oper. EPS 2004E	1.56	12 Month P/E	24.9
P/E on S&P Oper. EPS 2004E	23.9	Beta	0.02
S&P Oper. EPS 2005E	1.75	Shareholders	10,600
Yield (%)	1.5%	Market Cap (B)	$ 4.6
Dividend Rate/Share	0.56	Shares Outstanding (M)	136.7

Value of $10,000 invested five years ago: $ 24,599

Dividend Data Dividends have been paid since 1925

Amount ($)	Date Decl.	Ex-Div. Date	Stock of Record	Payment Date
0.140	Nov. 25	Dec. 29	Dec. 31	Jan. 21 '04
0.140	Mar. 24	Apr. 01	Apr. 05	Apr. 16 '04
0.140	Jun. 22	Jun. 30	Jul. 02	Jul. 16 '04
0.140	Sep. 28	Oct. 06	Oct. 08	Oct. 22 '04

Investment Rationale/Risk August 05, 2004

- Our accumulate recommendation on the shares reflects our expectation for annual 10% to 12% EPS growth and solid gains for the company's businesses. The shares were recently trading at 19.6X our FY 05 EPS estimate of $1.74, a premium to the average P/E multiple for packaged food peers and the multiple for the S&P 500 Index. We believe this premium is warranted, given our growth outlook for the company. MKC's financial strength continues to improve, and free cash flow generation is rising. Internal volume trends remain solid, in our opinion, with volume gains exceeding category growth for several core product lines. We think long-term growth prospects are attractive, reflecting the company's dominant and expanding U.S. spice market share (over 45%), as well as its leading share of the European consumer market (over 20%).

- Risks to our recommendation and target price relate to competitive pressures in MKC's businesses, consumer acceptance of new product introductions, commodity cost inflation, and the company's ability to achieve sales and earnings growth forecasts.

- Our analysis of discounted free cash flow, using a weighted average cost of capital of 8.5%, suggest an intrinsic value for the shares in the low $40s. We have a 12-month target price of $39, which is derived from our analysis of discounted cash flows and comparable peer multiples.

Revenues/Earnings Data Fiscal year ending November 30

Revenues (Million $)

	2004	2003	2002	2001	2000	1999
1Q	572.4	485.4	518.9	533.5	462.4	441.5
2Q	596.2	527.9	552.6	567.1	485.7	468.2
3Q	613.5	557.6	545.0	570.7	495.9	476.8
4Q	—	698.7	703.4	701.0	679.5	620.4
Yr.	—	2,270	2,320	2,372	2,124	2,007

Earnings Per Share ($)

	2004	2003	2002	2001	2000	1999
1Q	0.27	0.23	0.24	0.19	0.18	0.13
2Q	0.30	0.27	0.24	0.19	0.18	0.04
3Q	0.33	0.28	0.25	0.25	0.23	0.18
4Q	E0.66	0.61	0.54	0.42	0.42	0.38
Yr.	E1.56	1.40	1.26	1.05	0.99	0.72

Next earnings report expected: late-January Source: S&P, Company Reports
EPS Estimates based on S&P Operating Earnings; historical GAAP earnings are as reported.

McCormick & Company, Incorporated

Recommendation: **BUY** ★★★★☆   12-Month Target Price: **$38.00** (as of September 29, 2004)

Business Summary August 06, 2004

Founded by Willoughby M. McCormick in 1889, McCormick & Co. is the world's largest spice company, with operations in the manufacture, marketing and distribution of spices, seasonings, flavorings and other specialty food products. The company markets its products to retail food, foodservice, and industrial markets under the McCormick and Schilling names.

McCormick operates in two business segments: consumer and industrial. The company had also previously owned a packaging business, which was sold during the third quarter of 2003. The consumer segment, which accounted for 51% of sales and 67% of operating profits in FY 03 (Nov.), sells spices, herbs, extracts, proprietary seasoning blends, sauces and marinades to the consumer food market. The industrial segment (49%, 33%) sells spices, herbs, extracts, proprietary seasonings, condiments, coatings and compound flavors to food processors, restaurant chains, distributors, warehouse clubs, and institutional operations.

Many spices and herbs purchased by the company are imported into the U.S. from the country of origin, although significant quantities of some materials, such as paprika, dehydrated vegetables, onion and garlic, and food ingredients other than spices and herbs, originate in the U.S. McCormick is a direct importer of certain raw materials, mainly black pepper, vanilla beans, cinnamon, herbs and seeds. The raw materials most important to the company are onion, garlic, and capsicums (paprika and chili peppers), which are produced in the U.S.; black pepper, most of which originates in India, Indonesia, Malaysia and Brazil; and

vanilla beans, a large portion of which the company sources from the Malagasy Republic and Indonesia.

Margin improvement for all business segments is a key element of the company's growth strategy. Gross profit margins (adjusted for the divestiture of the packaging segment) continued to rise in FY 03, reaching 39.6%, versus 39.1% in FY 02. This improvement reflects increasing sales of higher-margin, value-added products; reduced costs from customer and product segmentation; lower-cost procurement of materials and services on a global basis; use of trading exchanges in areas such as logistics; and improved expense containment.

In August 2000, the company completed the acquisition of the Ducros spice business from Eridania Beghin-Say, for FFr. 2.75 billion (approximately $379 million) in cash. In April 2003, MKC announced that it settled all purchase price adjustment claims arising from the Ducros, and received a $55 million payment from Cereol S.A. With annual sales of approximately $250 million, Ducros is the leading maker of consumer spices and herbs in Europe. In the European consumer spice market, Ducros and McCormick have a combined market share of more than 20%.

In June 2003, the company completed the acquisition of Zatarain's, the leading New Orleans-style food brand in the U.S., from Citigroup Venture Capital and other investors for $180 million in cash.

Company Financials Fiscal Year ending November 30

Per Share Data ($)

(Year Ended November 30)	2003	2002	2001	2000	1999	1998	1997	1996	1995	1994
Tangible Bk. Val.	0.28	0.62	NM	NM	1.70	1.57	1.59	1.82	2.08	1.81
Cash Flow	1.85	1.73	1.57	1.43	1.12	1.07	0.97	0.67	0.99	0.73
Earnings	1.40	1.26	1.05	0.99	0.72	0.71	0.65	0.27	0.60	0.38
S&P Core Earnings	1.28	1.12	0.90	NA	NA	NA	NA	NA	NA	NA
Dividends	0.46	0.37	0.40	0.38	0.34	0.32	0.30	0.28	0.26	0.24
Payout Ratio	33%	29%	38%	38%	48%	45%	47%	104%	43%	64%
Prices - High	30.21	27.25	23.27	18.87	17.31	18.21	14.18	12.68	13.31	12.37
- Low	21.71	20.70	17.00	11.87	13.31	13.53	11.31	9.43	9.06	8.87
P/E Ratio - High	22	22	22	19	24	26	22	47	22	33
- Low	16	16	16	12	19	19	18	35	15	24

Income Statement Analysis (Million $)

	2003	2002	2001	2000	1999	1998	1997	1996	1995	1994
Revs.	2,270	2,320	2,372	2,124	2,007	1,881	1,801	1,733	1,859	1,695
Oper. Inc.	366	353	324	287	252	240	217	215	264	256
Depr.	65.3	66.8	73.0	61.3	57.4	54.8	49.3	63.8	63.4	56.8
Int. Exp.	38.6	43.6	52.9	39.7	32.4	36.9	36.3	33.8	55.3	38.7
Pretax Inc.	286	257	212	204	163	159	150	67.3	151	95.0
Eff. Tax Rate	29.1%	28.9%	29.7%	32.6%	36.8%	34.6%	35.1%	35.4%	35.5%	35.6%
Net Inc.	199	180	147	138	103	104	97.4	43.5	97.5	61.2
S&P Core Earnings	182	158	126	NA	NA	NA	NA	NA	NA	NA

Balance Sheet & Other Fin. Data (Million $)

	2003	2002	2001	2000	1999	1998	1997	1996	1995	1994
Cash	25.1	47.3	31.3	23.9	12.0	17.7	13.5	22.4	12.5	15.6
Curr. Assets	762	725	636	620	491	504	507	534	671	658
Total Assets	2,148	1,931	1,772	1,660	1,189	1,259	1,256	1,327	1,614	1,569
Curr. Liab.	713	673	714	1,027	471	518	498	499	647	601
LT Debt	449	454	454	160	241	250	276	291	349	374
Common Equity	755	592	463	359	382	468	393	450	519	490
Total Cap.	1,226	1,046	943	523	628	643	671	746	894	883
Cap. Exp.	91.6	111	112	53.6	49.3	54.8	43.9	74.7	82.1	87.7
Cash Flow	265	247	220	199	161	159	147	107	161	118
Curr. Ratio	1.1	1.1	0.9	0.6	1.0	1.0	1.0	1.1	1.0	1.1
% LT Debt of Cap.	36.6	43.4	48.2	30.6	38.5	38.9	41.1	39.0	39.0	42.4
% Net Inc.of Revs.	8.8	7.8	6.2	6.5	5.1	5.5	5.4	2.5	5.2	3.6
% Ret. on Assets	9.8	9.7	8.5	9.7	8.4	8.3	7.5	3.0	6.1	4.2
% Ret. on Equity	29.6	34.1	35.7	37.1	26.8	24.1	23.1	9.0	19.3	12.8

Data as orig reptd.; bef. results of disc opers/spec. items. Per share data adj. for stk. divs.; EPS diluted. E-Estimated. NA-Not Available. NM-Not Meaningful. NR-Not Ranked. UR-Under Review.

Office: 18 Loveton Circle, Sparks, MD 21152-6000.
Telephone: 410-771-7301.
Website: http://www.mccormick.com
Chrmn, Pres, CEO & COO: R.J. Lawless.
EVP & CFO: F.A. Contino.
SVP, Secy & General Counsel: R.W. Skelton.

VP & Treas: P. Beard.
Investor Contact: J.L. Brooks 410-771-7244.
Dirs: B. H. Beracha, J. T. Brady, F. A. Contino, R. G. Davey, E. S. Dunn, Jr., J. M. Fitzpatrick, F. A. Hrabowski III, R. J. Lawless, M. M. Preston, W. E. Stevens, K. D. Weatherholtz.

Founded: in 1889.
Domicile: Maryland.
Employees: 8,000.
S&P Analyst: Richard Joy/CB/GG

McDonald's Corp.

Recommendation: **BUY** ★★★★☆
SELL SELL HOLD BUY BUY

12-Month Target Price: **$33.00**
(as of October 19, 2004)

MCD has an approximate 0.35% weighting in the **S&P 500**

Sector: Consumer Discretionary
Sub-Industry: Restaurants
Peer Group: Fast-food - Larger

Summary: MCD is the largest fast-food restaurant company in the world. At June 30, 2004, about 53% of its 31,244 restaurants were outside the U.S.

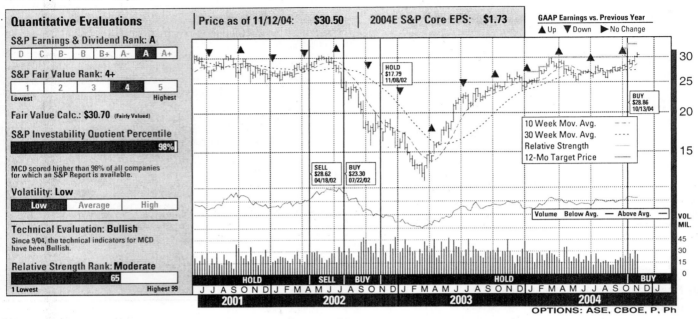

Quantitative Evaluations

S&P Earnings & Dividend Rank: A

| D | C | B- | B | B+ | A- | A | A+ |

S&P Fair Value Rank: 4+

| 1 | 2 | 3 | 4 | 5 |
| Lowest | | | | Highest |

Fair Value Calc.: $30.70 (Fairly Valued)

S&P Investability Quotient Percentile
98%

MCD scored higher than 98% of all companies for which an S&P Report is available.

Volatility: Low

| Low | Average | High |

Technical Evaluation: Bullish
Since 9/04, the technical indicators for MCD have been Bullish.

Relative Strength Rank: Moderate
65
1 Lowest   Highest 99

Price as of 11/12/04: **$30.50**   2004E S&P Core EPS: **$1.73**

GAAP Earnings vs. Previous Year
▲ Up ▼ Down ► No Change

HOLD $17.79 11/08/02

SELL $28.62 04/18/02   BUY $23.30 07/22/02

BUY $28.86 10/13/04

10 Week Mov. Avg.
30 Week Mov. Avg.
Relative Strength
12-Mo Target Price

Volume Below Avg. ▬ Above Avg. ▬ VOL. MIL.

HOLD | SELL | BUY | HOLD | BUY
J J A S O N D J F M A M J J A S O N D J F M A M J J A S O N D J F M A M J J A S O N D J
2001 2002 2003 2004

OPTIONS: ASE, CBOE, P, Ph

Analyst commentary prepared by Dennis P. Milton/PMW/JWP

Highlights October 20, 2004

■ MCD believes it can increase operating income 6% to 7% annually by increasing store count about 2%, boosting same-store sales 1% to 3%, and improving operating margins. We believe that strong competition in the fast food industry is likely to limit margin improvement over the longer term, but we think that the company can achieve its growth goal by using what we see as its superior product development capability to help increase the average check.

■ We expect strong revenue and earnings growth in 2004, as we see the company benefiting from a shift in its strategic plan, initiated in 2003, from extensive expansion and price discounting to a more intense focus on existing operations and menu upgrades. We expect systemwide sales and revenues to increase about 10%, driven by strong same-store sales growth in the U.S., and by positive translation effects from a weaker dollar. Operating margins should widen, due to reduced price discounting, well controlled corporate spending, and a lower effective tax rate, partially offset by higher food costs.

■ We project 2004 EPS of $1.91, up 34% from 2003's $1.43, excluding one-time items. After deducting $0.18 for projected stock option expense, we see 2004 Standard & Poor's Core Earnings of $1.73 a share. Our 2005 EPS estimate is $1.95.

Investment Rationale/Risk October 20, 2004

■ We would accumulate the shares. At 15X our 2004 EPS estimate, the shares trade in line with industry peers. We view this as an attractive valuation. We believe management is properly addressing operating shortcomings that we think hindered the company in recent years. In addition, although we believe MCD has only limited expansion prospects and faces strong competition from growing fast food and fast casual chains, we expect the company to produce strong sales results over the next few years as it shifts its menu focus to more upscale fare, enabling it to significantly increase the average check.

■ Risks to our opinion and target price include the potential for higher food costs, especially for beef; customer acceptance of MCD's new menu offerings; and exchange rate risk, in light of the company's substantial international business.

■ Our 12-month target price of $33 is based on a forward P/E multiple of 17X, a slight premium to industry peers, applied to our 2005 EPS estimate of $1.95. This is in line with our estimate of intrinsic value, based on our discounted cash flow model.

Key Stock Statistics

S&P Core EPS 2005E	1.77	52-week Range	$31.00-23.01
S&P Oper. EPS 2004E	1.91	12 Month P/E	19.3
P/E on S&P Oper. EPS 2004E	16.0	Beta	0.78
S&P Oper. EPS 2005E	1.97	Shareholders	953,000
Yield (%)	1.8%	Market Cap (B)	$ 38.3
Dividend Rate/Share	0.55	Shares Outstanding (M)	1257.2

Value of $10,000 invested five years ago: **$ 6,749**

Dividend Data Dividends have been paid since 1976

Amount ($)	Date Decl.	Ex-Div. Date	Stock of Record	Payment Date
0.400	Sep. 24	Nov. 12	Nov. 14	Dec. 01 '03
0.550	Sep. 14	Nov. 10	Nov. 15	Dec. 01 '04

Revenues/Earnings Data Fiscal year ending December 31

Revenues (Million $)

	2004	2003	2002	2001	2000	1999
1Q	4,400	3,800	3,597	3,512	3,344	3,035
2Q	4,729	4,281	3,862	3,708	3,561	3,407
3Q	4,926	4,505	4,047	3,879	3,749	3,444
4Q	—	4,555	3,899	3,772	3,590	3,373
Yr.	—	17,141	15,406	14,870	14,243	13,259

Earnings Per Share ($)

	2004	2003	2002	2001	2000	1999
1Q	0.40	0.29	0.28	0.29	0.33	0.29
2Q	0.47	0.37	0.39	0.34	0.39	0.37
3Q	0.61	0.43	0.38	0.42	0.41	0.39
4Q	E0.43	0.10	-0.27	0.21	0.34	0.35
Yr.	E1.91	1.18	0.77	1.25	1.46	1.39

Next earnings report expected: late-January Source: S&P, Company Reports
EPS Estimates based on S&P Operating Earnings; historical GAAP earnings are as reported.

STANDARD &POOR'S

McDonald's Corporation

Stock Report
November 13, 2004
NYSE Symbol: **MCD**

Recommendation: **BUY** ★ ★ ★ ☆   12-Month Target Price: **$33.00** (as of October 19, 2004)

Business Summary October 20, 2004

With one of the world's most widely known brand names, McDonald's serves about 47 million customers daily. The company operates and licenses more than 31,000 restaurants (30,000 McDonald's) in about 120 countries. At September 30, 2004, there were 13,647 McDonald's restaurants in the U.S., and 16,680 elsewhere.

McDonald's restaurants offer a substantially uniform menu, including hamburgers, french fries, chicken, fish, specialty sandwiches, beverages, and desserts. Most units also serve breakfast. To capture additional meal occasions, the company operates and franchises more than 1,000 restaurants under its Partner Brands concepts: Boston Market and Chipotle Mexican Grill. MCD also has a minority interest in a U.K.-based quick service food concept, Pret A Manger.

All restaurants are operated by MCD, franchisees, or affiliates under joint venture agreements. At September 30, 2004, there were 18,191 franchised restaurants (62% of 2003 systemwide sales), 9,095 company-owned restaurants (28%), and 4,072 affiliated restaurants (10%).

Systemwide sales totaled $45.9 billion in 2003, up 11% (5% in constant currencies) from $41.5 billion in 2002. Systemwide sales by geographic area in 2003 were: U.S., 48% (49% in 2002); Europe, 27% (25%); Asia/Pacific/Middle East/Africa, 16% (16%); Latin America, 3% (3%); Canada, 4% (4%), and Partner Brands 3% (3%). International business contributed 44% of operating income in 2003 (before corporate expenses, currency effect and one-time charges).

In 2003, comparable-store sales rose in the U.S. and Latin America, but declined elsewhere. After five consecutive quarters of declining same-store sales in the U.S., the company has posted a rebound since April 2003. It attributed this to a new corporate strategy that focuses on product development and investment in existing properties, rather than on expansion and price discounting. Sales were hurt by weak economic conditions in key European markets such as Germany and France, and by fears of BSE (Mad Cow disease) in Japan. However, systemwide sales and earnings benefited from positive translation effects due to a significantly weaker U.S. dollar.

MCD's stated operating priorities include fixing operating inadequacies in existing restaurants; taking a more integrated and focused approach to growth, with emphasis on increasing sales, margins and returns in existing restaurants; and ensuring the correct operating structure and resources, aligned behind focusing priorities that create benefits for its customers and restaurants. The company believes that by focusing on these areas, it can achieve annual operating earnings growth of 6% to 7%.

In 2004, the company planned to open about 500 traditional restaurants and 250 satellite restaurants, and expected to close about 200 traditional and 150 satellite units. Capital spending was projected at $1.5 billion to $1.6 billion. MCD expects to spend about $1.3 billion on dividends and share repurchases in 2004.

MCD does not currently expense stock option grants. Had they been expensed, EPS would have been reduced by $0.17 and $0.20 in 2003 and 2002, respectively.

Company Financials Fiscal Year ending December 31

Per Share Data ($)

(Year Ended December 31)	2003	2002	2001	2000	1999	1998	1997	1996	1995	1994
Tangible Bk. Val.	8.18	6.88	6.30	5.86	6.20	6.26	5.86	5.49	4.99	4.30
Cash Flow	2.08	1.59	2.08	2.20	2.07	1.73	1.71	1.64	1.52	1.29
Earnings	1.18	0.77	1.25	1.46	1.39	1.10	1.15	1.10	0.99	0.84
S&P Core Earnings	0.96	0.51	1.01	NA	NA	NA	NA	NA	NA	NA
Dividends	0.80	0.24	0.23	0.21	0.20	0.18	0.16	0.15	0.13	0.12
Payout Ratio	68%	31%	18%	15%	14%	16%	14%	13%	13%	14%
Prices - High	27.01	30.72	35.06	43.62	49.56	39.75	27.43	27.12	24.00	15.75
- Low	12.12	15.17	24.75	26.37	35.93	22.31	21.06	20.50	14.31	12.78
P/E Ratio - High	23	40	28	30	36	36	24	25	24	19
- Low	10	20	20	18	26	20	18	19	15	15

Income Statement Analysis (Million $)

	2003	2002	2001	2000	1999	1998	1997	1996	1995	1994
Revs.	17,141	15,406	14,870	14,243	13,259	12,421	11,409	10,687	9,795	8,321
Oper. Inc.	3,980	3,164	3,983	4,144	4,171	3,903	3,488	3,331	3,204	2,801
Depr.	1,148	1,051	1,086	1,011	956	881	794	743	709	629
Int. Exp.	388	360	452	430	396	414	363	365	363	326
Pretax Inc.	2,346	1,662	2,330	2,882	2,884	2,307	2,408	2,251	2,169	1,887
Eff. Tax Rate	35.7%	40.3%	29.8%	31.4%	32.5%	32.8%	31.8%	30.2%	34.2%	35.1%
Net Inc.	1,508	992	1,637	1,977	1,948	1,550	1,643	1,573	1,427	1,224
S&P Core Earnings	1,226	667	1,328	NA	NA	NA	NA	NA	NA	NA

Balance Sheet & Other Fin. Data (Million $)

	2003	2002	2001	2000	1999	1998	1997	1996	1995	1994
Cash	493	330	418	422	420	299	341	330	335	180
Curr. Assets	1,885	1,715	1,819	1,662	1,572	1,309	1,142	1,103	956	741
Total Assets	25,525	23,971	22,535	21,684	20,983	19,784	18,242	17,386	15,415	13,592
Curr. Liab.	2,486	2,422	2,248	2,361	3,274	2,497	2,985	2,135	1,795	2,451
LT Debt	9,343	9,704	8,556	7,844	5,632	6,189	4,834	4,803	4,258	2,935
Common Equity	11,982	10,281	9,488	9,204	9,639	9,464	8,851	8,360	7,503	6,446
Total Cap.	22,340	20,988	19,156	18,133	16,445	17,228	15,178	15,251	12,784	10,930
Cap. Exp.	1,307	2,004	1,906	1,945	1,868	1,879	2,111	2,375	2,064	1,539
Cash Flow	2,656	2,043	2,723	2,988	2,904	2,431	2,412	2,288	2,136	1,806
Curr. Ratio	0.8	0.7	0.8	0.7	0.5	0.5	0.4	0.5	0.5	0.3
% LT Debt of Cap.	41.8	46.2	44.7	43.3	34.2	35.9	31.8	31.5	33.3	26.9
% Net Inc.of Revs.	8.8	6.4	11.0	13.9	14.7	12.5	14.4	14.8	14.6	14.7
% Ret. on Assets	6.1	4.3	7.4	9.3	9.6	8.2	9.2	9.6	9.9	9.6
% Ret. on Equity	13.5	10.0	17.5	21.0	20.4	16.9	18.8	19.5	20.5	19.3

Data as orig reptd.; bef. results of disc opers/spec. items. Per share data adj. for stk. divs.; EPS diluted. E-Estimated. NA-Not Available. NM-Not Meaningful. NR-Not Ranked. UR-Under Review.

Office: McDonald's Plaza, Oak Brook, IL 60523.
Telephone: 630-623-3000.
Website: http://www.mcdonalds.com
Chrmn: A.J. McKenna.
Pres & CEO: C. Bell.
Sr EVP & CFO: M. Paull.

SVP, Secy & General Counsel: G. Santona.
Investor Contact: L. Ivinjack-Ciota 630-623-7428.
Dirs: H. Adams, Jr., C. H. Bell, E. A. Brennan, J. R. Cantalupo, R. A. Eckert, E. Hernandez, Jr., J. P. Jackson, D. G. Lubin, W. E. Massey, A. J. McKenna, C. D. McMillan, J. W. Rogers, Jr., T. L. Savage, R. W. Stone, R. N. Thurston, F. L. Turner.

Founded: in 1948.
Domicile: Delaware.
Employees: 418,000.
S&P Analyst: Dennis P. Milton/PMW/JWP

McGraw-Hill Companies

Recommendation: **NOT RANKED**   12-Month Target Price: **NA**

MHP has an approximate 0.15% weighting in the **S&P 500**

Sector: Consumer Discretionary
Sub-Industry: Publishing
Peer Group: Publishing - Large

Summary: The McGraw-Hill Companies is a leading information services organization serving worldwide markets in education, business, industry, other professions and government.

Quantitative Evaluations

S&P Earnings & Dividend Rank: NR

D	C	B-	B	B+	A-	A	A+

S&P Fair Value Rank: NR

1	2	3	4	5
Lowest				Highest

Fair Value Calc.: NA

S&P Investability Quotient Percentile
This company does not meet the inclusion criteria required for calculating an IQ value.

Volatility: Low

Low	Average	High

Technical Evaluation: Bullish
Since 9/04, the technical indicators for MHP have been Bullish.

Relative Strength Rank: Moderate

65
1 Lowest   Highest 99

Price as of 11/12/04:	**$87.15**	2004E S&P Core EPS:	**NA**

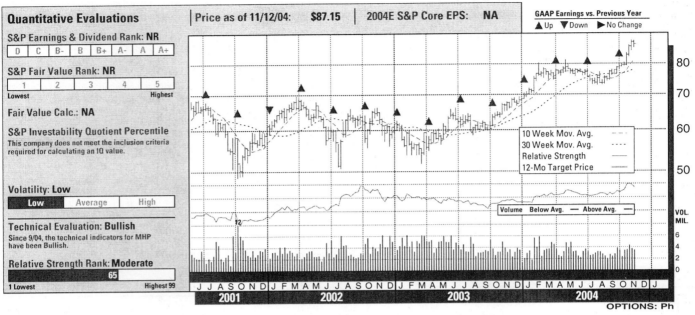

GAAP Earnings vs. Previous Year
▲ Up   ▼ Down   ► No Change

- 10 Week Mov. Avg.
- 30 Week Mov. Avg.
- Relative Strength
- 12-Mo Target Price

Volume ▢ Below Avg. — Above Avg.

Analyst commentary prepared by William H. Donald/CB/GG

Highlights August 20, 2004

- In July 2004, the company said that while it expects as much as a 5% decline in the grade school education market in 2004, it expects to outperform the market. MHP expects flat to modest growth in its Education segment overall. The company noted that for the fiscal year 2005, which began on July 1 for most states, general funding for grade school education is budgeted to grow at 4.9%, or 5.1% when total state funding is factored in. That compares with a 3% increase in fiscal 2004. MHP expects Financial Services to generate double digit revenue growth, and it expects Information and Media Services to show strong single digit to low double digit revenue growth.

- MHP expects Financial Services to maintain margins in 2004, and expects Information and Media Services to show improved margins, while operating margins in Education may decline slightly.

- Even with anticipated softness in the grade school marketplace, MHP expects income from continuing operations to increase in the high single digits in 2004, excluding the $0.30 net benefit from the 2003 sale of its equity interest in Rock-McGraw Inc. With a sharp rebound expected in the education market, MHP expects a return to double digit EPS growth in 2005.

Investment Rationale/Risk August 20, 2004

- Earnings estimates for McGraw-Hill from other analysts recently averaged about $3.61 a share for 2004 and $4.07 for 2005. Based on these estimates, MHP shares were trading at a P/E ratio of 21X projected 2004 EPS and 18X the estimate for 2005, versus averages for a select group of peers of 22X and 19X, respectively.

- MHP noted in its most recent 10Q report filed with the SEC that among the risks facing its business are prospective changes in the regulatory environment in the U.S. and abroad related to credit rating agencies that could affect Standard & Poor's. The company noted that risks also include the potential impact of economic and capital market activity on Standard & Poor's; the strengths of the U.S. and global economies; the strength of U.S. and international advertising markets; MHP's level of success in textbook adoptions in its educational publishing business; future levels of federal, state or local funding for educational materials; currency and foreign exchange fluctuations; and possible fluctuations in paper, printing and distribution costs.

- Standard & Poor's is a division of MHP, and provides no EPS estimates, target price, or stock opinion for the company.

Key Stock Statistics

Yield (%)	1.4%	52-week Range	$88.69-65.87
Dividend Rate/Share	1.20	12 Month P/E	23.1
Shares Outstanding (M)	189.9	Beta	0.54
Market Cap (B)	$ 16.5	Shareholders	5,089

Value of $10,000 invested five years ago: **$ 16,270**

Dividend Data Dividends have been paid since 1937

Amount ($)	Date Decl.	Ex-Div. Date	Stock of Record	Payment Date
0.300	Jan. 28	Feb. 23	Feb. 25	Mar. 10 '04
0.300	Apr. 28	May. 24	May. 26	Jun. 10 '04
0.300	Jul. 28	Aug. 24	Aug. 26	Sep. 10 '04
0.300	Oct. 28	Nov. 23	Nov. 26	Dec. 10 '04

Revenues/Earnings Data Fiscal year ending December 31

Revenues (Million $)

	2004	2003	2002	2001	2000	1999
1Q	911.6	830.8	846.6	846.4	784.2	716.5
2Q	1,230	1,172	1,191	1,149	1,016	922.7
3Q	1,696	1,603	1,577	1,535	1,394	1,318
4Q	—	1,222	1,172	1,115	1,086	1,034
Yr.	—	4,828	4,788	4,646	4,281	3,992

Earnings Per Share ($)

	2004	2003	2002	2001	2000	1999
1Q	0.39	0.21	0.15	0.10	0.22	0.12
2Q	0.86	0.74	0.70	0.61	0.55	0.45
3Q	1.69	1.51	1.42	1.22	1.10	0.96
4Q	—	1.12	0.69	-0.01	0.54	0.61
Yr.	—	3.58	2.96	1.92	2.41	2.14

Next earnings report expected: late-January Source: S&P, Company Reports
EPS Estimates based on S&P Operating Earnings; historical GAAP earnings are as reported.

The McGraw-Hill Companies, Inc.

Recommendation: **NOT RANKED**   12-Month Target Price: **NA**

Business Summary August 20, 2004

The McGraw-Hill Companies, Inc. is a leading provider of information products and services to business, professional and educational markets worldwide. The company believes that through acquisitions, new product and service development and a strong commitment to customer service, many of its business units have grown to be leaders in their respective fields. Well known brands include BusinessWeek, Standard & Poor's, Platts, F.W. Dodge, and Sweet's. Operations are conducted through over 300 offices in 33 countries worldwide.

McGraw-Hill Education (47% of revenues and 29% of profits in 2003) includes testing, grade school, college, vocational and professional publishing. Mc-Graw-Hill's publishing operations span the globe. This segment also contains the MH School division (elementary and secondary school textbooks and materials). In September 2000, MHP acquired Tribune Education, a leading publisher of supplementary education materials, for $635 million. In May 2001, MHP acquired Frank Schaffer Publications, a publisher of supplementary education materials. The Higher Education, Professional Publishing and International Group serves a global market. Higher education markets include college, university and post-graduate fields. Professional markets include engineering, science, medicine, health care, computer technology, business, government, training, and

general reference publishing. The company believes that a number of global trends point to healthy demand for professional books over the long term, including favorable demographics, growth in the number of college-educated adults, and strong worldwide growth in professional services.

The financial services segment (37% and 61%) consists of Standard & Poor's Credit Market Services, the world's leading provider of credit analysis and information, and Standard & Poor's Investment Services, which includes Advisor Services, Institutional Market Services, and Portfolio Services. Standard & Poor's Comstock was sold in February 2003.

The information and media services segment (16% and 10%) includes Business-Week magazine; the Construction Information Group, including F.W. Dodge and Sweet's; Aviation Week; the Healthcare Information Group; Platts energy market information; and a number of trade magazines, newsletters, directories, and video and online products. This segment also includes four ABC-affiliated TV stations in Denver (KMGH-TV); Indianapolis (WRTV); San Diego (KGTV); and Bakersfield, CA (KERO-TV).

Company Financials Fiscal Year ending December 31

Per Share Data ($)

(Year Ended December 31)	2003	2002	2001	2000	1999	1998	1997	1996	1995	1994
Tangible Bk. Val.	4.49	1.88	0.18	0.33	2.24	1.48	0.64	0.28	0.39	-0.30
Cash Flow	5.68	3.42	4.07	4.25	3.70	3.22	2.93	3.67	1.67	1.54
Earnings	3.58	2.96	1.92	2.41	2.14	1.71	1.46	2.48	1.14	1.03
S&P Core Earnings	2.87	2.30	1.19	NA	NA	NA	NA	NA	NA	NA
Dividends	1.08	1.02	0.98	0.94	0.86	0.78	0.72	0.66	0.60	0.58
Payout Ratio	30%	34%	51%	39%	40%	46%	49%	27%	53%	57%
Prices - High	70.00	69.70	70.87	67.68	63.12	51.65	37.68	24.62	21.90	19.31
- Low	51.74	50.71	48.70	41.87	47.12	34.25	22.43	18.62	15.90	15.62
P/E Ratio - High	20	24	37	28	29	30	26	10	19	19
- Low	14	17	25	17	22	20	15	8	14	15

Income Statement Analysis (Million $)

	2003	2002	2001	2000	1999	1998	1997	1996	1995	1994
Revs.	4,828	4,788	4,646	4,281	3,992	3,729	3,534	3,075	2,935	2,761
Oper. Inc.	1,369	1,037	1,044	1,128	984	851	779	662	509	477
Depr.	403	89.6	421	362	308	299	294	239	106	102
Int. Exp.	7.10	22.5	55.1	52.8	42.0	48.0	52.5	47.7	58.8	51.7
Pretax Inc.	1,130	905	615	767	698	560	471	815	386	345
Eff. Tax Rate	39.1%	36.3%	38.7%	38.5%	39.0%	39.0%	38.3%	39.2%	41.2%	41.2%
Net Inc.	688	577	377	472	426	342	291	496	227	203
S&P Core Earnings	552	446	233	NA	NA	NA	NA	NA	NA	NA

Balance Sheet & Other Fin. Data (Million $)

	2003	2002	2001	2000	1999	1998	1997	1996	1995	1994
Cash	696	58.2	53.5	3.17	6.49	10.5	4.77	3.43	10.3	8.00
Curr. Assets	2,256	1,674	1,813	1,802	1,554	1,429	1,464	1,350	1,240	1,124
Total Assets	5,394	5,032	5,161	4,931	4,089	3,788	3,724	3,642	3,104	3,009
Curr. Liab.	1,994	1,775	1,876	1,781	1,525	1,291	1,206	1,219	1,046	1,008
LT Debt	0.39	459	834	818	355	452	607	557	557	658
Common Equity	2,557	2,202	1,884	1,761	1,691	1,565	1,435	1,361	1,035	913
Total Cap.	2,758	2,861	2,908	2,742	2,182	2,147	2,153	2,068	1,733	1,700
Cap. Exp.	115	70.0	117	97.7	154	179	78.7	63.3	58.8	77.1
Cash Flow	1,091	666	798	834	734	641	584	734	334	305
Curr. Ratio	1.1	0.9	1.0	1.0	1.0	1.1	1.2	1.1	1.2	1.1
% LT Debt of Cap.	0.0	16.0	28.7	29.8	16.3	21.1	28.2	26.9	32.2	38.7
% Net Inc.of Revs.	14.2	12.0	8.1	11.0	10.7	9.2	8.2	16.1	7.7	7.4
% Ret. on Assets	13.2	11.3	7.5	10.4	10.8	9.1	7.9	14.8	7.4	6.7
% Ret. on Equity	29.1	28.2	20.5	27.7	26.3	22.7	20.8	41.4	23.3	23.3

Data as orig reptd.; bef. results of disc opers/spec. items. Per share data adj. for stk. divs.; EPS diluted. E-Estimated. NA-Not Available. NM-Not Meaningful. NR-Not Ranked. UR-Under Review.

Office: 1221 Avenue of the Americas, New York, NY 10020-1095.
Telephone: 212-512-2000.
Email: investor_relations@mcgraw-hill.com
Website: http://www.mcgraw-hill.com
Chrmn, Pres & CEO: H. McGraw III.
EVP & CFO: R.J. Bahash.
EVP & General Counsel: K.M. Vittor.

SVP & Treas: J. Weisenseel.
SVP & Secy: S.L. Bennett.
SVP & Investor Contact: D.S. Rubin 212-512-2000.
Dirs: P. Aspe, W. F. Bischoff, D. N. Daft, L. K. Lorimer, R. P. McGraw, H. W. McGraw III, H. W. McGraw, Jr., H. Ochoa-Brillembourg, J. H. Ross, E. B. Rust, Jr., K. L. Schmoke, S. Taurel.

Founded: in 1899.
Domicile: New York.
Employees: 16,068.
S&P Analyst: William H. Donald/CB/GG

The **McGraw·Hill** Companies

McKesson Corp.

Recommendation: **HOLD** ★★★★ ★
SELL · SELL · HOLD · BUY · BUY

12-Month Target Price: $27.00
(as of October 22, 2004)

MCK has an approximate 0.08% weighting in the **S&P 500**

Sector: Health Care
Sub-Industry: Health Care Distributors
Peer Group: Pharmaceuticals & Health Products

Summary: MCK (formerly McKesson HBOC) provides pharmaceutical supply management and information technologies to a broad range of healthcare customers.

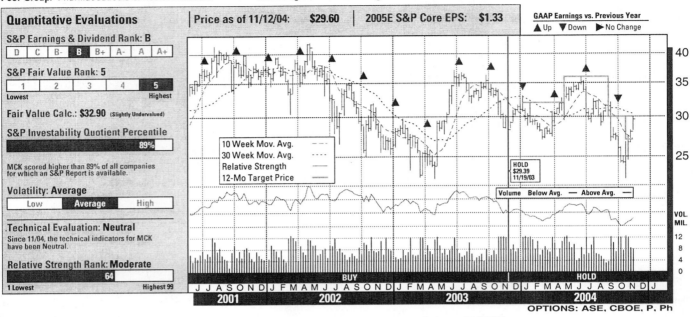

Quantitative Evaluations

S&P Earnings & Dividend Rank: B

| D | C | B- | **B** | B+ | A- | A | A+ |

S&P Fair Value Rank: 5

| 1 | 2 | 3 | 4 | **5** |
| Lowest | | | | Highest |

Fair Value Calc.: $32.90 (Slightly Undervalued)

S&P Investability Quotient Percentile
89%

MCK scored higher than 89% of all companies for which an S&P Report is available.

Volatility: Average

| Low | **Average** | High |

Technical Evaluation: Neutral
Since 11/04, the technical indicators for MCK have been Neutral.

Relative Strength Rank: Moderate
64
1 Lowest · Highest 99

Price as of 11/12/04: $29.60 | **2005E S&P Core EPS:** $1.33

GAAP Earnings vs. Previous Year
▲ Up ▼ Down ► No Change

10 Week Mov. Avg.
30 Week Mov. Avg.
Relative Strength
12-Mo Target Price

HOLD
$29.39
11/19/03

Volume Below Avg. — Above Avg.

VOL.
MIL.

BUY · HOLD

J J A S O N D | J F M A M J J A S O N D | J F M A M J J A S O N D | J F M A M J J A S O N D | J
2001 · 2002 · 2003 · 2004

OPTIONS: ASE, CBOE, P, Ph

Analyst commentary prepared by Phillip M. Seligman/PMW/BK

Highlights November 02, 2004

- We expect FY 05 (Mar.) operating revenue growth of 14%, reflecting our projection of a 15% increase for the core Pharmaceutical Solutions (P/S) segment. We reduced our sales growth estimate following MCK's warning that, with fewer than anticipated price increases in the first half, it expects third quarter EPS of $0.20 to $0.25, versus our earlier estimate of $0.50. The company expects price increases in the second half, but we see no indications that this will happen. In addition, we look for P/S operating margins to continue to narrow sharply, due to competition, demands by large customers, and changing dynamics in drugmaker-distributor relations.

Investment Rationale/Risk November 02, 2004

- We view MCK as more realistic in its reduced 2005 EPS guidance of $2.00 to $2.20 (down from $2.20 to $2.35), but we believe it may still be optimistic, in light of a challenging environment that we see. With only about 20% of dollar volumes now tied to fee-for-service, and many large drug makers still resistant to this business model, we think the company will remain highly dependent on the level and timing of price increases. We think drugmakers will slowly but eventually move to fee-for-service; we have low visibility regarding segment performance over the next few quarters. Despite this negative factor, we see demand for drug distribution and for MCK's Provider Technologies (P/T) services increasing, and, view the company's longer-term prospects favorably. However, we do not expect the stock to show any strength until P/S margin trends improve and P/T sales accelerate.

- Risks to our recommendation and target price include continued competitive pricing by MCK, additional account losses at M/S, increased competition and/or reduced hospital spending for I/S, and a potential negative outcome from a shareholder lawsuit related to the HBOC merger.

- In light of what we view as an expanding HBOC class-action litigation overhang, we have reduced our forward P/E multiple to 13X, below the level of the S&P 500. Applying this multiple to our calendar 2005 EPS estimate of $2.06 leads to our 12-month target price of $27.

Key Stock Statistics

S&P Core EPS 2006E	1.56	52-week Range	$35.90-22.61
S&P Oper. EPS 2005E	2.00	12 Month P/E	15.0
P/E on S&P Oper. EPS 2005E	14.8	Beta	0.29
S&P Oper. EPS 2006E	2.20	Shareholders	12,049
Yield (%)	0.8%	Market Cap (B)	$ 8.7
Dividend Rate/Share	0.24	Shares Outstanding (M)	293.9

Value of $10,000 invested five years ago: **$ 14,494**

Dividend Data Dividends have been paid since 1995

Amount ($)	Date Decl.	Ex-Div. Date	Stock of Record	Payment Date
0.060	Jan. 28	Feb. 26	Mar. 01	Apr. 01 '04
0.060	May. 26	Jun. 07	Jun. 09	Jul. 01 '04
0.060	Jul. 28	Aug. 30	Sep. 01	Oct. 01 '04
0.060	Oct. 28	Nov. 29	Dec. 01	Jan. 03 '05

Revenues/Earnings Data Fiscal year ending March 31

Revenues (Million $)

	2005	2004	2003	2002	2001	2000
1Q	19,187	16,524	13,623	11,654	9,729	8,697
2Q	19,934	16,810	13,690	12,159	9,874	9,050
3Q	—	18,232	14,921	13,197	11,029	9,891
4Q	—	17,940	14,886	12,991	11,409	9,305
Yr.	—	69,506	57,121	50,006	42,010	36,734

Earnings Per Share ($)

	2005	2004	2003	2002	2001	2000
1Q	0.55	0.53	0.39	0.36	0.22	0.25
2Q	0.29	0.53	0.43	0.27	0.22	0.21
3Q	E0.45	0.41	0.46	0.37	0.03	0.56
4Q	E0.71	0.73	0.62	0.42	-0.62	-0.31
Yr.	E2.00	2.19	1.90	1.43	-0.15	0.66

Next earnings report expected: late-January Source: S&P, Company Reports
EPS Estimates based on S&P Operating Earnings; historical GAAP earnings are as reported.

McKesson Corporation

Recommendation: **HOLD** ★ ★ ★ ☆ ☆   12-Month Target Price: **$27.00** (as of October 22, 2004)

Business Summary November 02, 2004

McKesson Corp. (formerly McKesson HBOC) is a leading distributor of medical products and supplies and healthcare information technology products and services. MCK aims to become the world leader in healthcare supply and comprehensive pharmaceutical management across the entire supply chain, from manufacturer to patient.

Pharmaceutical Solutions, which accounted for 94.6% of FY 04 (Mar.) operating revenues, primarily distributes ethical and proprietary drugs, medical-surgical supplies and health and beauty care products in North America. The business focuses on three primary customer segments: retail chains (pharmacies, food stores and mass merchandisers); retail independent pharmacies; and institutional providers in all 50 states and Canada. These customer categories accounted respectively for a 42%, 25% and 33% of the group's FY 03 revenues.

Medical-Surgical Solutions (3.6%) provides medical-surgical supplies, equipment, logistics and related services to the continuum of healthcare providers: hospitals, physicians' offices, long-term care and home care. It also makes and markets automated pharmacy systems to hospitals and retail pharmacies. Key products include the ROBOT-Rx robotic pharmacy dispensing and utilization tracking system; AcuDose-Rx unit-based cabinets that automate storage, dispensing and

tracking of drugs in patient areas; and AcuScan-Rx, which records, automates and streamlines drug administration and medication information requirements through bar code scanning.

Provider Technologies (1.8%) provides patient care, clinical, financial, managed care and strategic management software solutions to the healthcare industry. Products and services are sold to integrated delivery networks, hospitals, physicians' offices, home health providers, pharmacies, reference labs, and HMOs. IS products are designed to help automate individual hospital departments; provide care management services and medical call center management, data analysis and sharing and computer telephony and Internet links; document patient information for physicians and other clinicians; provide enterprise services such as UNIX support; and practice management applications.

MCK, together with AmeriSource Health, Cardinal Health, Fisher Scientific International, and Owens & Minor, formed an Internet-based company to provide commercially neutral product information focused on streamlining the process of identifying, buying and distributing pharmaceuticals, medical and surgical supplies, devices, and other lab products and services.

Company Financials Fiscal Year ending March 31

Per Share Data ($)

(Year Ended March 31)	2004	2003	2002	2001	2000	1999	1998	1997	1996	1995
Tangible Bk. Val.	12.66	10.57	9.81	8.55	8.40	5.89	7.11	5.74	9.38	9.01
Cash Flow	2.94	2.65	2.20	0.72	1.37	0.98	2.39	0.86	2.22	-1.46
Earnings	2.19	1.90	1.43	-0.15	0.66	0.31	1.59	0.06	1.45	-2.25
S&P Core Earnings	1.29	1.24	0.87	-0.39	NA	NA	NA	NA	NA	NA
Dividends	0.24	0.24	0.24	0.24	0.30	0.50	0.50	0.50	0.50	0.76
Payout Ratio	11%	13%	17%	NM	46%	161%	31%	NM	34%	NM

Cal. Yrs.	2003	2002	2001	2000	1999	1998	1997	1996	1995	1994
Prices - High	37.14	42.09	41.50	37.00	89.75	96.25	56.87	28.50	26.62	54.62
- Low	22.61	24.99	23.40	16.00	18.56	47.87	25.87	19.50	15.93	15.06
P/E Ratio - High	17	22	29	NM	NM	NM	36	NM	18	NM
- Low	10	13	16	NM	NM	NM	16	NM	11	NM

Income Statement Analysis (Million $)

	2004	2003	2002	2001	2000	1999	1998	1997	1996	1995
Revs.	69,506	57,121	50,006	42,010	36,734	30,382	20,857	12,887	13,716	13,171
Oper. Inc.	1,216	1,134	923	454	359	531	449	165	345	305
Depr.	232	204	208	246	201	199	86.0	72.0	71.3	69.8
Int. Exp.	120	121	119	118	120	124	103	56.0	46.7	46.0
Pretax Inc.	911	855	601	9.60	307	202	254	36.4	227	-71.0
Eff. Tax Rate	29.1%	34.3%	30.4%	NM	39.7%	57.9%	39.0%	86.0%	39.0%	NM
Net Inc.	647	562	419	-42.7	185	85.0	155	5.00	135	-193
S&P Core Earnings	380	364	255	-113	NA	NA	NA	NA	NA	NA

Balance Sheet & Other Fin. Data (Million $)

	2004	2003	2002	2001	2000	1999	1998	1997	1996	1995
Cash	718	534	563	446	606	269	36.0	230	477	693
Curr. Assets	13,004	11,254	10,699	9,164	7,966	6,500	4,106	3,761	2,665	2,699
Total Assets	16,240	14,353	13,324	11,530	10,373	9,082	5,608	5,173	3,504	3,479
Curr. Liab.	9,456	7,974	7,588	6,550	5,122	4,800	2,578	2,637	1,723	1,738
LT Debt	1,210	1,487	1,485	1,232	1,440	1,142	1,194	825	443	459
Common Equity	5,165	4,529	3,940	3,493	4,213	2,882	1,523	1,261	1,065	1,014
Total Cap.	6,375	6,016	5,425	4,724	5,653	4,024	2,796	1,541	1,564	1,532
Cap. Exp.	115	116	132	159	145	251	130	76.9	77.3	82.0
Cash Flow	879	766	626	203	386	284	241	77.0	207	-127
Curr. Ratio	1.4	1.4	1.4	1.4	1.6	1.4	1.6	1.4	1.5	1.6
% LT Debt of Cap.	19.0	24.7	27.4	26.1	25.5	28.4	42.7	53.5	28.3	29.9
% Net Inc.of Revs.	0.9	1.0	0.8	NM	0.5	0.3	0.7	Nil	1.0	NM
% Ret. on Assets	4.2	4.1	3.4	NM	1.9	1.2	2.9	0.1	3.9	NM
% Ret. on Equity	13.3	13.3	11.3	NM	4.8	3.9	10.7	0.4	13.0	NM

Data as orig. reptd.; pr. to 1995 for predecessor co. (Old McKesson); bef. results of disc. opers. and/or spec. items. Per share data adj. for stk. divs. as of ex-div. date. Bold denotes primary EPS. E-Estimated. NA-Not Available. NM-Not Meaningful. NR-Not Ranked.

Office: One Post Street, San Francisco, CA 94104-5296.
Telephone: 415-983-8300.
Email: investors@mckesson.com
Website: http://www.mckesson.com
Chrmn, Pres & CEO: J.H. Hammergren.
EVP & CTO: C. Smith.

EVP, Secy & General Counsel: I.D. Meyerson.
SVP, CFO & Investor Contact: J. Campbell 800-826-9360.
Dirs: W. A. Budd, J. H. Hammergren, A. F. Irby III, M. C. Jacobs, M. L. Knowles, D. M. Lawrence, R. W. Matshullat, J. V. Napier, J. E. Shaw, R. F. Syron.

Founded: in 1994.
Domicile: Delaware.
Employees: 24,600.
S&P Analyst: Phillip M. Seligman/PMW/BK

MeadWestvaco Corp.

Recommendation: HOLD ★★★☆☆
SELL SELL HOLD BUY BUY

12-Month Target Price: **$35.00**
(as of November 15, 2004)

MWV has an approximate 0.06% weighting in the **S&P 500**

Sector: Materials
Sub-Industry: Paper Products
Peer Group: Paper Products - Larger

Summary: This major producer of packaging and coated and specialty papers was formed through the January 2002 merger of Mead Corp. and Westvaco Corp.

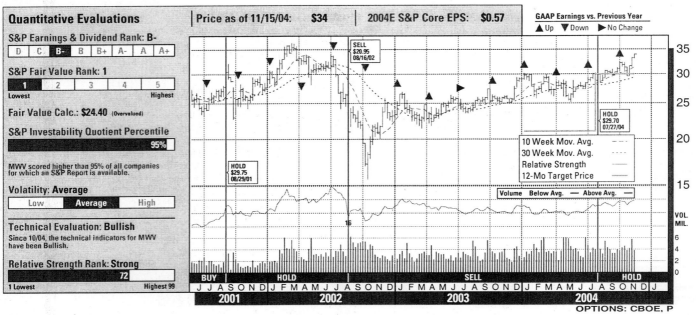

Quantitative Evaluations

S&P Earnings & Dividend Rank: B-
D | C | **B-** | B | B+ | A- | A | A+

S&P Fair Value Rank: 1
1 | 2 | 3 | 4 | 5
Lowest | | | | Highest

Fair Value Calc.: $24.40 (Overvalued)

S&P Investability Quotient Percentile
95%
MWV scored higher than 95% of all companies for which an S&P Report is available.

Volatility: Average
Low | **Average** | High

Technical Evaluation: Bullish
Since 10/04, the technical indicators for MWV have been Bullish.

Relative Strength Rank: Strong
72
1 Lowest | Highest 99

Price as of 11/15/04: **$34** | 2004E S&P Core EPS: **$0.57**

GAAP Earnings vs. Previous Year
▲ Up ▼ Down ► No Change

SELL $20.95 08/16/02
HOLD $29.75 08/29/01
HOLD $29.70 07/27/04

10 Week Mov. Avg. — — —
30 Week Mov. Avg. ·······
Relative Strength ——
12-Mo Target Price ——

Volume Below Avg. — Above Avg. ▬

VOL. MIL.
6 4 2 0

BUY | HOLD | SELL | HOLD
J J A S O N D | J F M A M J J A S O N D | J F M A M J J A S O N D | J F M A M J J A S O N D | J
2001 | 2002 | 2003 | 2004

OPTIONS: CBOE, P

Analyst commentary prepared by Bryon J. Korutz/PMW/JWP

Highlights 16-NOV-04

- After a rise of 7.5% that we project for 2004, we expect revenues to grow 4.5% in 2005, on firming paper and packaging fundamentals.
- S&P expects real GDP to grow about 4.5% and 3.5% in 2004 and 2005, respectively. With demand for packaging material and paper products typically tracking the economy, we think this will likely support improved volumes and price increases. In addition, we expect GDP growth to support better pricing and demand in the consumer and office products segment. We believe demand and prices for coated papers will improve, based on our projection of increased 9.3% increase advertising spending in 2005. However, we remain concerned about global overcapacity in coated papers. We see wider margins in 2004, on higher prices and improved manufacturing efficiencies, partly offset by higher energy and wood costs.
- We project 2004 S&P Core EPS of $0.57, with the difference from our operating estimate of $0.88 mainly due to projected pension expense.

Investment Rationale/Risk 16-NOV-04

- We expect a strengthening of the economy to boost the need for consumer packaging, and believe this will aid packaging prices. We also see the consumer and office products segment aided by a stronger economy. We see coated paper prices increasing, but we believe a global oversupply of coated papers could restrict a rise in prices. With the shares near our 12-month target price of $35, we would not add to positions.
- Risks to our recommendation and target price include a weaker than expected recovery in coated papers, and an unexpected downturn in the economy.
- Our DCF model, which assumes a weighted average cost of capital of 8.1% and an average growth rate of 10% over the next 10 years and 3.5% thereafter, values the shares at $35. By applying a peak P/E multiple of 11X to our 2006 EPS estimate of $3.05, we arrive at a value of $34. Our 12-month target price of $35 is a weighted average of our valuation metrics.

Key Stock Statistics

S&P Core EPS 2005E	**1.83**	52-week Range	**$33.96-24.92**
S&P Oper. EPS 2004E	**0.88**	12 Month P/E	**35.4**
P/E on S&P Oper. EPS 2004E	**38.5**	Beta	**1.01**
S&P Oper. EPS 2005E	**2.15**	Shareholders	**36,740**
Yield (%)	**2.7%**	Market Cap (B)	**$ 6.9**
Dividend Rate/Share	**0.92**	Shares Outstanding (M)	**202.7**

Value of $10,000 invested five years ago: **$ 13,041**

Dividend Data Dividends have been paid since 1892

Amount ($)	Date Decl.	Ex-Div. Date	Stock of Record	Payment Date
0.230	Jan. 27	Feb. 04	Feb. 06	Mar. 01 '04
0.230	Apr. 27	May. 05	May. 07	Jun. 01 '04
0.230	Jun. 22	Aug. 04	Aug. 06	Sep. 01 '04
0.230	Oct. 26	Nov. 03	Nov. 05	Dec. 01 '04

Revenues/Earnings Data Fiscal year ending December 31

Revenues (Million $)

	2004	2003	2002	2001	2000	1999
1Q	1,833	1,694	1,461	971.1	799.6	650.7
2Q	2,095	1,915	2,012	966.9	904.7	679.5
3Q	2,148	1,999	2,023	995.1	928.0	700.2
4Q	—	1,945	1,893	1,002	1,031	771.5
Yr.	—	7,553	7,242	3,935	3,663	2,802

Earnings Per Share ($)

	2004	2003	2002	2001	2000	1999
1Q	-0.01	-0.36	-0.37	0.33	0.50	0.25
2Q	0.24	-0.04	-0.04	0.18	0.70	0.27
3Q	0.52	0.14	0.09	0.28	0.53	0.35
4Q	E0.34	0.25	0.21	0.08	0.80	0.24
Yr.	E0.88	-0.01	-0.01	0.87	2.53	1.11

Next earnings report expected: late-January Source: S&P, Company Reports
EPS Estimates based on S&P Operating Earnings; historical GAAP earnings are as reported.

MeadWestvaco Corporation

Recommendation: **HOLD** ★ ★ ★ ☆ ☆   12-Month Target Price: **$35.00** (as of November 15, 2004)

Business Summary 16-NOV-04

MeadWestvaco Corp. was created through the January 2002 merger of Mead Corp. (MEA) and Westvaco Corp. (W). MWV conducts its operations through four business segments: packaging, papers, consumer and office products and specialty chemicals.

The packaging segment (53% of 2003 revenues) produces coated and uncoated, bleached and unbleached paperboard, linerboard and saturating kraft paperboard and consumer packaging for the beverage, cosmetics, food, health care, pharmaceutical, tobacco and media markets. The company operates 16 paperboard machines at six mills in the U.S. and Brazil. MWV has about 1.7 million short tons of bleached board capacity, 1.0 million short tons of coated natural kraft capacity, 0.5 million short tons of linerboard capacity, 0.4 million short tons of saturating kraft capacity, 0.09 million short tons of corrugating medium and 0.2 million short tons of unbleached paperboard capacity.

The paper segment (28%) produces, markets and distributes coated printing papers, carbonless copy papers and industrial specialty papers. The company has 2.1 million short tons of annual production capacity of coated papers, 0.3 million tons of carbonless papers capacity, 0.1 million short tons of uncoated free sheet capacity, and 0.06 million tons of specialty papers capacity, and operates 10 paper mills. Its coated papers are used to produce books, magazines, annual reports and catalogs. The segment also manufactures digital papers for commer-

cial and desktop printing, labels for food and beverages, envelopes, and carbonless paper for business forms.

The consumer and office products segment (14%) makes, markets and distributes school and office products, time management products, and envelopes. Products are distributed through the retail and commercial channels. The segment's consumer brands include Mead, AT-A-GLANCE, Cambridge, Five Star, Hilroy and Columbian. MWV operates eight plants and distribution centers and 13 envelope plants and print centers.

The specialty chemicals segment (5%) produces, markets and distributes specialty chemicals, derived from sawdust and other by-products of the pulp and papermaking process. These chemicals include activated carbon, printing ink resins, emulsifiers used in asphalt paving, and dyestuffs. The company also owns over 2.3 million acres of forest lands.

In 2003, MWV acquired AMCAL, Inc., for $12 million, and purchased essentially all of the assets of Day Runner, Inc., for $43 million. In January 2002, The Mead Corp. and Westvaco Corp. merged to form MeadWestvaco Corp., with 0.97 of a MWV share exchanged for each W share; and one MWV share, plus a special payment of $1.20, exchanged for each MEA share. At December 31, 2003, MWV completed the merger synergy program.

Company Financials Fiscal Year ending December 31

Per Share Data ($)

(Year Ended December 31)	2003	2002	2001	2000	1999	1998	1997	1996	1995	1994
Tangible Bk. Val.	19.89	20.44	17.34	23.17	21.65	22.39	22.35	21.69	20.49	18.48
Cash Flow	3.60	3.49	4.29	5.63	3.90	4.06	4.25	4.45	5.08	3.21
Earnings	-0.01	-0.01	0.87	2.53	1.11	1.30	1.58	2.09	2.80	1.03
S&P Core Earnings	-0.94	-1.37	-1.01	NA	NA	NA	NA	NA	NA	NA
Dividends	0.92	0.92	0.88	0.88	0.88	0.88	0.88	0.88	0.77	0.73
Payout Ratio	NM	NM	101%	35%	79%	68%	55%	42%	28%	71%
Prices - High	29.83	36.50	32.10	34.75	33.50	34.12	37.50	33.12	31.87	26.50
- Low	21.37	15.57	22.68	24.06	20.81	21.00	25.00	25.37	24.08	19.75
P/E Ratio - High	NM	NM	37	14	30	26	23	16	11	26
- Low	NM	NM	26	10	19	16	16	12	9	19

Income Statement Analysis (Million $)

	2003	2002	2001	2000	1999	1998	1997	1996	1995	1994
Revs.	7,553	7,242	3,935	3,663	2,802	2,886	2,982	3,045	3,272	2,607
Oper. Inc.	855	859	677	869	601	577	580	637	771	485
Depr.	724	674	347	314	280	281	269	240	230	219
Int. Exp.	291	309	208	192	124	110	93.3	105	108	115
Pretax Inc.	-29.0	-15.0	119	404	148	204	247	336	470	162
Eff. Tax Rate	NM	NM	25.6%	36.9%	24.9%	35.4%	34.0%	36.9%	39.8%	36.0%
Net Inc.	-2.00	-3.00	88.2	255	111	132	163	212	283	104
S&P Core Earnings	-188	-264	NA	NA	NA	NA	NA	NA	NA	NA

Balance Sheet & Other Fin. Data (Million $)

	2003	2002	2001	2000	1999	1998	1997	1996	1995	1994
Cash	225	372	81.2	255	109	105	175	115	152	75.0
Curr. Assets	2,426	2,431	1,016	1,064	738	739	805	716	787	631
Total Assets	12,487	12,921	6,787	6,570	4,897	5,009	4,899	4,437	4,253	3,983
Curr. Liab.	1,501	1,620	701	567	425	467	406	419	429	362
LT Debt	Nil	4,233	2,660	2,687	1,502	1,526	1,513	1,153	1,147	1,234
Common Equity	4,768	4,831	2,341	2,333	2,171	2,246	2,279	2,210	2,081	1,862
Total Cap.	6,446	10,821	6,009	5,927	4,472	4,541	4,494	4,018	3,824	3,621
Cap. Exp.	393	377	290	214	229	423	621	522	290	215
Cash Flow	722	671	436	569	392	413	432	453	514	323
Curr. Ratio	1.6	1.5	1.4	1.9	1.7	1.6	2.0	1.7	1.8	1.7
% LT Debt of Cap.	Nil	39.1	44.3	45.3	33.6	33.6	33.7	28.7	30.0	34.1
% Net Inc.of Revs.	NM	NM	2.2	7.0	4.0	4.6	5.5	7.0	8.7	4.0
% Ret. on Assets	NM	NM	1.3	4.4	2.2	2.7	3.5	4.9	6.9	2.6
% Ret. on Equity	NM	NM	3.8	11.3	5.0	5.8	7.3	9.9	14.4	5.6

Data as orig. reptd.; bef. results of disc. opers. and/or spec. items. Per share data adj. for stk. divs.; EPS diluted. Data prior to 2002 for Westvaco Corp. alone. E-Estimated. NA-Not Available. NM-Not Meaningful. NR-Not Ranked.

Office: 1 High Ridge Park, Stamford, CT 06905-1330.
Telephone: 203-461-7400.
Website: http://www.meadwestvaco.com
Chrmn & CEO: J. A. Luke, Jr.
Pres: J. A. Buzzard.
SVP & CFO: E. M. Rajkowski.

Secy, SVP & General Counsel: W. L. Willkie II.
Investor Contact: Mark F. Pomerleau (203-461-7616).
Dirs: J. G. Breen, M. E. Campbell, T. W. Cole, Jr., D. E. Collins, W. E. Hoglund, J. G. Kaiser, R. B. Kelson, J. A. Krol, S. J. Kropf, D. S. Luke, J. A. Luke, Jr., R. C. McCormack, L. J. Styslinger, Jr., J. L. Warner, J. L. Wilson, R. A. Zimmerman.

Founded: in 1846.
Domicile: Delaware.
Employees: 30,700.
S&P Analyst: Bryon J. Korutz/PMW/JWP

Medco Health Solutions

Recommendation: **HOLD** ★★★☆☆
SELL · SELL · HOLD · BUY · BUY
(as of November 12, 2004)

12-Month Target Price: $42.00

MHS has an approximate 0.10% weighting in the **S&P 500**

Sector: Health Care
Sub-Industry: Health Care Services

Summary: MHS, spun off from Merck & Co. in August 2003, is the largest U.S. pharmacy benefit manager (PBM) in terms of revenues and script count.

Quantitative Evaluations

S&P Earnings & Dividend Rank: NR

D	C	B-	B	B+	A-	A	A+

S&P Fair Value Rank: NR

1	2	3	4	5
Lowest				Highest

Fair Value Calc.: NA

S&P Investability Quotient Percentile

95%

MHS scored higher than 95% of all companies for which an S&P Report is available.

Volatility: Average

Low	Average	High

Technical Evaluation: NA

Relative Strength Rank: Strong

90

1 Lowest	Highest 99

Price as of 11/12/04:	**$39.02**	2004E S&P Core EPS:	**$1.40**

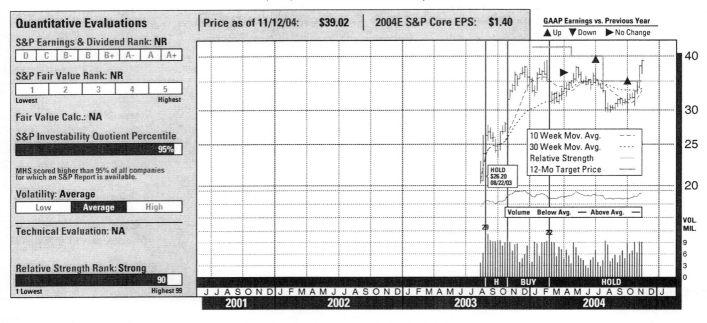

GAAP Earnings vs. Previous Year
▲ Up ▼ Down ▶ No Change

10 Week Mov. Avg.
30 Week Mov. Avg.
Relative Strength
12-Mo Target Price

HOLD $26.20 08/22/03

Volume Below Avg. — Above Avg.

H | BUY | HOLD

J J A S O N D | J F M A M J J A S O N D | J F M A M J J A S O N D | J F M A M J J A S O N D | J F M A M J J A S O N D | J
2001 | 2002 | 2003 | 2004

Analyst commentary prepared by Phillip M. Seligman/CB/JWP

Highlights 15-NOV-04

- We look for 2005 net revenue to rise about 4%, to $36.8 billion, from our 2004 estimate of $35.4 billion. We see improved account retention rates, new business, price increases on branded drugs, and increased script volumes enabled by the recent passage of the Medicare bill.
- We see EBITDA per adjusted prescription, which measures a PBM's profitability, continuing to rise in excess of 20%, on a favorable mix shift toward generic drugs, mail order penetration, and productivity enhancements. Another factor we believe has been aiding profits has been the rise in prescription orders processed through MHS's web site.
- We project 2005 EPS of $2.00, up from our 2004 estimate of $1.75. Both figures reflect the impact of amortization charges, which should cut 2005 EPS by $0.39, the same as we expect for 2004. Our projections for 2004 and 2005 Standard & Poor's Core Earnings per share are $1.40 and $1.60, respectively, mainly reflecting projected stock option expense and modest adjustments due to pension and post-retirement plans.

Investment Rationale/Risk 15-NOV-04

- We view MHS as a leading participant in the expanding PBM industry. While there has been increased scrutiny of the industry benefit managers, MHS's settlement with 20 states is now behind it. Also, while PBMs have received negative press, in our view reflecting a lack of transparency, we believe MHS's services and reputation for efficiency outweigh any concerns to potential customers, and note that it has been garnering new business. We think MHS's ability to attract and retain customers has improved, as it appears that the company will garner enough new business to more than compensate for accounts that it had lost.
- Risks to our recommendation and target price include increased competition, increased regulatory oversight and/or more stringent government regulations, continued margin pressures due to client demands for lower prices, and the potential loss of key client contracts.
- Given our view of good fundamentals, we think MHS's forward P/E merits a rise to the level we project for the S&P 500. Our 12-month target price of $42 equals 17.4X our 2005 cash EPS estimate of $2.40, which we use due to MHS's sharply higher amortization charges than peers.

Key Stock Statistics

S&P Core EPS 2005E	1.60	52-week Range	$39.20-29.40
S&P Oper. EPS 2004E	1.75	12 Month P/E	22.9
P/E on S&P Oper. EPS 2004E	22.3	Beta	NA
S&P Oper. EPS 2005E	2.00	Shareholders	140,597
Yield (%)	Nil	Market Cap (B)	$ 10.6
Dividend Rate/Share	Nil	Shares Outstanding (M)	272.5

Value of $10,000 invested five years ago: **NA**

Dividend Data

No cash dividends have been paid.

Revenues/Earnings Data Fiscal year ending December 31

Revenues (Million $)

	2004	2003	2002	2001	2000	1999
1Q	8,906	8,334	—	—	—	—
2Q	8,836	8,405	—	—	—	—
3Q	8,697	8,524	—	—	—	—
4Q	—	9,002	—	—	—	—
Yr.	—	34,265	32,959	29,071	22,266	—

Earnings Per Share ($)

	2004	2003	2002	2001	2000	1999
1Q	0.38	0.38	—	—	—	—
2Q	0.46	0.39	—	—	—	—
3Q	0.43	0.37	—	—	—	—
4Q	E0.46	0.43	—	—	—	—
Yr.	E1.75	1.57	1.18	0.95	0.80	—

Next earnings report expected: mid-February Source: S&P, Company Reports
EPS Estimates based on S&P Operating Earnings; historical GAAP earnings are as reported.

STANDARD &POOR'S

Medco Health Solutions, Inc.

Stock Report
November 15, 2004
NYSE Symbol: **MHS**

Recommendation: **HOLD** ★ ★ ★ ☆ ☆   12-Month Target Price: **$42.00** (as of November 12, 2004)

Business Summary 15-NOV-04

Medco Health Solutions was spun off to Merck & Co. (MRK) shareholders in a tax-free transaction on August 19, 2003. The company is one of the largest U.S. pharmacy benefit managers (PBMs). It provides programs and services to clients and members of pharmacy benefit plans, and to physicians and pharmacies that they use. Clients include managed care organizations; third-party benefit plan administrators; employers; government agencies; and union-sponsored benefit plans.

The company seeks to reduce the rate of increase of client drug expenditures (drug trend), and to save members money. It also continues to expand its home drug delivery business, reducing drug costs. In 2003, its network of mail-order pharmacies filled about 78 million prescriptions. MHS seeks to contain costs for clients and their members by encouraging the prescription of drugs on a plan's approved list of drugs (formulary) and the use of generics. It estimates that its service, technology, and cost containment initiatives let it limit average drug trend for plans that include both retail and home delivery to 10.2% in 2003, 12.9% in 2002, and 14.0% in 2001, versus a U.S. average of 13.4% in 2003, 15.3% in 2002, and 17.3% in 2000, as reported by the Centers for Medicare & Medicaid Services.

In 2003, MHS processed about 532 million prescriptions. Revenues and net income are derived from rebates and discounts on prescription drugs from pharmaceutical manufacturers, competitive discounts from retail pharmacies, negotiating favorable client pricing, including rebate sharing terms, shifting dispensing volumes from retail to home delivery, and the provision of services in a cost-efficient manner.

An SEC filing lists several risks for the company. With $1.5 billion in debt following its spinoff, a substantial portion of operating cash flow is expected to be dedicated to debt payments, reducing funds available for working capital, capital spending, acquisitions, and other purposes. There are pending lawsuits by plaintiffs alleging that MHS breached fiduciary obligations under ERISA. In June 2003, the U.S. Attorney's office for the Eastern District of Pennsylvania filed a notice of intervention with respect to two whistleblower complaints, filed in 2000, alleging improper pharmacy practices. MHS believes that an adverse determination in one of these suits could lead to significant damages.

Gross rebates recorded as received from MRK totaled $301.1 million through the separation date of August 19, 2003, $443.9 million in 2002, and $439.4 million in 2001. Under a five-year managed care agreement entered into with MRK effective July 2002, MRK provides MHS with rebates based in part on whether MRK products are included in formularies that MHS offers clients, and on whether MRK products achieve specified market share targets under plans for which MHS provides PBM services. If MHS fails to achieve the targets, it may have to pay substantial liquidated damages. Compliance with obligations under the agreement may affect its competitive position.

UnitedHealth Group accounted for 18% of 2003 net revenues. The 10 largest clients accounted for 46%.

Company Financials Fiscal Year ending December 31

Per Share Data ($)

(Year Ended December 31)	2003	2002	2001	2000	1999	1998	1997	1996	1995	1994
Tangible Bk. Val.	NM	NM	1.70	1.31	NA	NA	NA	NA	NA	NA
Cash Flow	2.62	2.13	2.15	1.87	NA	NA	NA	NA	NA	NA
Earnings	1.57	1.18	0.95	0.80	NA	NA	NA	NA	NA	NA
S&P Core Earnings	1.03	NA	NA	NA	NA	NA	NA	NA	NA	NA
Dividends	Nil	NA	NA	NA	NA	NA	NA	NA	NA	NA
Payout Ratio	Nil	NA	NA	NA	NA	NA	NA	NA	NA	NA
Prices - High	38.00	NA	NA	NA	NA	NA	NA	NA	NA	NA
- Low	20.20	NA	NA	NA	NA	NA	NA	NA	NA	NA
P/E Ratio - High	24	NA	NA	NA	NA	NA	NA	NA	NA	NA
- Low	13	NA	NA	NA	NA	NA	NA	NA	NA	NA

Income Statement Analysis (Million $)

	2003	2002	2001	2000	1999	1998	1997	1996	1995	1994
Revs.	34,265	32,959	29,071	22,266	NA	NA	NA	NA	NA	NA
Oper. Inc.	1,025	886	837	731	NA	NA	NA	NA	NA	NA
Depr.	283	257	323	289	NA	NA	NA	NA	NA	NA
Int. Exp.	Nil	73.5	Nil	Nil	NA	NA	NA	NA	NA	NA
Pretax Inc.	729	547	518	448	NA	NA	NA	NA	NA	NA
Eff. Tax Rate	41.6%	41.7%	50.5%	51.6%	NA	NA	NA	NA	NA	NA
Net Inc.	426	319	257	217	NA	NA	NA	NA	NA	NA
S&P Core Earnings	279	NA	NA	NA	NA	NA	NA	NA	NA	NA

Balance Sheet & Other Fin. Data (Million $)

	2003	2002	2001	2000	1999	1998	1997	1996	1995	1994
Cash	639	203	16.3	NA	NA	NA	NA	NA	NA	NA
Curr. Assets	3,760	3,044	2,534	NA	NA	NA	NA	NA	NA	NA
Total Assets	10,263	9,714	9,252	8,915	NA	NA	NA	NA	NA	NA
Curr. Liab.	2,605	2,370	1,809	NA	NA	NA	NA	NA	NA	NA
LT Debt	1,346	1,385	Nil	Nil	NA	NA	NA	NA	NA	NA
Common Equity	5,080	4,738	6,268	6,358	NA	NA	NA	NA	NA	NA
Total Cap.	7,604	7,305	7,423	7,502	NA	NA	NA	NA	NA	NA
Cap. Exp.	125	NA	322	251	NA	NA	NA	NA	NA	NA
Cash Flow	709	576	580	506	NA	NA	NA	NA	NA	NA
Curr. Ratio	1.4	1.3	1.4	NA	NA	NA	NA	NA	NA	NA
% LT Debt of Cap.	17.7	19.0	Nil	Nil	NA	NA	NA	NA	NA	NA
% Net Inc.of Revs.	1.2	1.0	0.9	1.0	NA	NA	NA	NA	NA	NA
% Ret. on Assets	4.2	NA	2.8	NA	NA	NA	NA	NA	NA	NA
% Ret. on Equity	7.3	NA	4.1	NA	NA	NA	NA	NA	NA	NA

Data as orig reptd.; bef. results of disc opers/spec. items. Per share data adj. for stk. divs.; EPS diluted. Pro forma data in 2002, balance sheet & book value as of Mar. 29, 2003. E-Estimated. NA-Not Available. NM-Not Meaningful. NR-Not Ranked.

Office: 100 Parsons Pond Drive, Franklin Lakes, NJ 07417.
Telephone: 201-269-3400.
Website: http://www.medcohealth.com
Chrmn, Pres & CEO: D. B. Snow, Jr.
EVP & COO: K. O. Klepper.
SVP & CFO: J. A. Reed.

Secy, SVP & General Counsel: D. S. Machlowitz.
SVP: J. P. Driscoll.
Investor Contact: Susan DeWitt (201-269-6187).
Dirs: H. W. Barker, Jr., J. L. Cassis, M. Goldstein, L. S. Lewin, E. H. Shortliffe, D. B. Snow, Jr., B. L. Strom, B. J. Wilson.

Founded: in 1983.
Domicile: Delaware.
Employees: 13,650.
S&P Analyst: Phillip M. Seligman/CB/JWP

MedImmune

Recommendation: **HOLD** ★★★☆☆
SELL | SELL | HOLD | BUY | BUY

12-Month Target Price: **$27.00**
(as of October 21, 2004)

MEDI has an approximate 0.06% weighting in the **S&P 500**

Sector: Health Care
Sub-Industry: Biotechnology
Peer Group: Biotech Therapeutics - Larger Capitalization

Summary: This biotech concern develops, manufactures and markets therapeutics and vaccines to treat and prevent certain infectious diseases and cancer.

Quantitative Evaluations

S&P Earnings & Dividend Rank: C

| D | **C** | B- | B | B+ | A- | A | A+ |

S&P Fair Value Rank: 1

| **1** | 2 | 3 | 4 | 5 |
| Lowest | | | | Highest |

Fair Value Calc.: $17.50 (Overvalued)

S&P Investability Quotient Percentile

89%

MEDI scored higher than 89% of all companies for which an S&P Report is available.

Volatility: Average

| Low | **Average** | High |

Technical Evaluation: Bullish
Since 10/04, the technical indicators for MEDI have been Bullish.

Relative Strength Rank: Moderate

61

| 1 Lowest | | Highest 99 |

| Price as of 11/12/04: | **$27.18** | 2004E S&P Core EPS: | **$-0.03** |

GAAP Earnings vs. Previous Year
▲ Up ▼ Down ▶ No Change

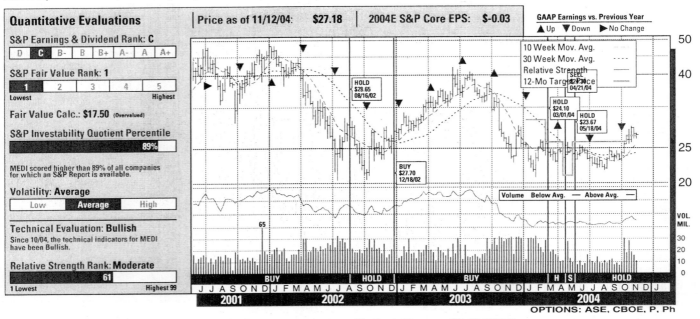

10 Week Mov. Avg.
30 Week Mov. Avg.
Relative Strength
12-Mo Target Price

Volume Below Avg. ─── Above Avg.

OPTIONS: ASE, CBOE, P, Ph

Analyst commentary prepared by Frank DiLorenzo, CFA /PMW/SRB

Highlights November 01, 2004

■ MEDI's third quarter pro forma loss of $0.22 a share (versus a loss of $0.06 in the 2003 period) was $0.01 wider than our estimate. Synagis sales of $61 million were $6 million above our forecast. Ethyol sales came in at $21 million for the quarter, $1 million below our view. The growth rate for Synagis sales has been moderating, while Ethyol sales have flattened out.

■ With MEDI providing up to 3 million doses of FluMist for the 2004/2005 flu season, we assume that the company could supply this many doses for 2005/2006. In a best case scenario, we think MEDI could supply 4 million to 5 million doses for the 2005/2006 flu season, which would result in some upside to our EPS estimate. The company is developing CAIV-T, a liquid formulated intranasal flu vaccine that could be stored in a refrigerator. We continue to forecast potential approval of CAIV-T for the 2007/2008 flu season as a best case scenario. FluMist is approved for ages 5 to 49, and MEDI is developing CAIV-T in an attempt to expand this experimental vaccine's approved usage to a wider age range, including the 6 months to 5 years group, as well as the elderly.

■ We project 2004 total revenues of $1.14 billion, and see $1.27 billion for 2005. Of this amount, we forecast Synagis sales at $936 million for 2004 and $1.05 billion for 2005. We estimate 2004 EPS of $0.26, and see an increase to $0.55 for 2005.

Key Stock Statistics

S&P Oper. EPS 2004E	0.26	52-week Range	$28.94-20.77
P/E on S&P Oper. EPS 2004E	NM	12 Month P/E	NM
S&P Oper. EPS 2005E	0.55	Beta	1.09
Yield (%)	Nil	Shareholders	1,975
Dividend Rate/Share	Nil	Market Cap (B)	$ 6.8
Shares Outstanding (M)	248.7		

Value of $10,000 invested five years ago: **$ 7,763**

Dividend Data

No cash dividends have been paid.

Investment Rationale/Risk November 01, 2004

■ We would hold the shares, based on valuation. We think that prospects for FluMist have improved at least through 2005, due to the inability of Chiron to supply its Fluvirin flu vaccine for the 2004/2005 flu season. However, relative to a number of other prominent biotech issues, we do not view the shares as undervalued, and we do not consider the company's prospects to be as strong as those of some peers. MEDI is developing Numax, a second-generation version of Synagis, but we believe the drug may offer only incremental sales gains, if it is approved. We continue to view CAIV-T as the company's best mid-term pipeline prospect.

■ Risks to our recommendation and target price include disappointing sales of Synagis, delayed or unsuccessful development of CAIV-T, potential increased competition in the flu vaccine market, and decreased FluMist supply in 2005 from the level of 2004.

■ Based on our 2005 EPS estimate, the stock's P/E multiple to growth (PEG) ratio of 2.0X is sharply above the S&P biotech peer average of 1.2X. Based on our net present value analysis (we assume over $1.3 billion in Synagis sales by 2008, and a 50% probability of CAIV-T approval by 2007, with peak sales of $500 million by 2014), our 12-month target price is $27.

Revenues/Earnings Data Fiscal year ending December 31

Revenues (Million $)

	2004	2003	2002	2001	2000	1999
1Q	489.0	435.9	329.6	245.2	198.3	128.7
2Q	93.68	117.8	63.72	33.37	29.50	10.24
3Q	92.58	99.4	72.63	47.41	57.36	48.91
4Q	—	407.8	381.8	292.7	238.2	173.7
Yr.	—	1,054	786.0	618.7	540.5	383.4

Earnings Per Share ($)

	2004	2003	2002	2001	2000	1999
1Q	0.44	0.43	-4.54	0.36	0.27	0.15
2Q	-0.40	0.05	-0.12	-0.04	-0.04	-0.06
3Q	-0.26	-0.07	-0.14	-0.09	0.03	0.03
4Q	E0.15	0.30	0.33	0.45	0.36	0.16
Yr.	E0.26	0.72	-4.40	0.68	0.66	0.44

Next earnings report expected: late-January Source: S&P, Company Reports
EPS Estimates based on S&P Operating Earnings; historical GAAP earnings are as reported.

MedImmune, Inc.

Recommendation: **HOLD** ★ ★ ★ ☆ ☆   12-Month Target Price: **$27.00** (as of October 21, 2004)

Business Summary November 01, 2004

MedImmune, the sixth largest U.S. biotech company in terms of revenues, is developing and commercializing treatments for infectious diseases, autoimmune disorders, and cancer. In January 2002, it acquired Aviron by exchanging 1.075 MEDI shares for each Aviron share. The impetus for the deal was Aviron's FluMist, an influenza vaccine that was approved by the FDA in June 2003.

Synagis, an injectable humanized monoclonal antibody, is effective in neutralizing respiratory syncytial virus (RSV) infection. RSV, typically seen in the fall, winter and early spring, is the most common cause of lower respiratory infections in pediatric patients. More than 125,000 infants are hospitalized with severe RSV disease in the U.S. annually, with about 325,000 infants (primarily premature babies) in the U.S. and a similar number outside the U.S. at risk of acquiring severe RSV yearly. Synagis is the only drug with FDA clearance to treat RSV. MEDI recorded Synagis sales of $849 million in 2003, up from $672 million in 2002.

The company co-markets Synagis with Abbott Labs in the U.S. Overseas, Abbott has exclusive marketing rights to the drug, which it buys from MEDI. European sales began in 1999. Japanese approval was granted in January 2002. In September 2003, Synagis was granted FDA approval to treat pediatric congenital heart disease. The company estimates that about 32,000 children are born with this condition in the U.S. each year. Numax, a next generation antibody to prevent RSV, is in Phase I/II testing.

FluMist is a vaccine delivered as a nasal spray to prevent influenza in adults and children. It is based on cold-adapted influenza technology that weakens live influenza strains until the vaccine is safe for humans. The vaccine is a frozen product that must be stored in a proper environment. In June 2003, the FDA approved FluMist for the prevention of flu in healthy individuals ages 5 to 49. FluMist was launched in time for the 2003/2004 flu season. Henry Schein will be the U.S. distributor for FluMist for the 2004/2005 flu season.

In April 2004, MEDI regained full FluMist rights from partner Wyeth, in exchange for milestones and royalties to Wyeth. MEDI is also developing CAIV-T, a liquid formulation of FluMist that would provide more convenient refrigerator storage. Trials of CAIV-T are being conducted with a goal of showing efficacy in children under 5 and adults over 49, as well as the 5 to 49 age group FluMist is approved for.

The company also markets CytoGam, an intravenous immune globulin product enriched in antibodies against cytomegalovirus (CMV) and used to prevent CMV disease associated with organ transplants; and Ethyol, a drug to alleviate side effects associated with chemotherapy. In October 2001, MEDI re-acquired U.S. marketing rights to Ethyol from Alza (a division of Johnson & Johnson). It markets Ethyol with its own oncology sales force of about 60 people.

MEDI is testing Vitaxin, a monoclonal antibody, in separate Phase II trials for the treatment of metastatic melanoma and prostate cancer. In May 2004, partner GlaxoSmithKline initiated a Phase III trial of a vaccine for human papillomaviruses, which can lead to genital warts and cervical cancer.

Company Financials Fiscal Year ending December 31

Per Share Data ($)

(Year Ended December 31)	2003	2002	2001	2000	1999	1998	1997	1996	1995	1994
Tangible Bk. Val.	6.57	6.16	4.87	3.99	2.63	1.28	0.28	0.56	0.41	0.39
Cash Flow	0.87	-4.25	0.72	0.69	0.46	0.31	-0.25	-0.22	-0.22	-0.20
Earnings	0.72	-4.40	0.68	0.66	0.44	0.30	-0.27	-0.24	-0.24	-0.21
S&P Core Earnings	0.38	-4.73	0.31	NA	NA	NA	NA	NA	NA	NA
Dividends	Nil	Nil	Nil	Nil	Nil	Nil	Nil	Nil	Nil	Nil
Payout Ratio	Nil	Nil	Nil	Nil	Nil	Nil	Nil	Nil	Nil	Nil
Prices - High	42.09	48.35	54.56	86.12	58.60	16.89	7.25	3.35	3.58	2.20
- Low	22.79	20.37	27.62	42.00	14.33	6.47	1.89	1.89	0.58	0.56
P/E Ratio - High	58	NM	80	NM	NM	56	NM	NM	NM	NM
- Low	32	NM	41	NM	NM	21	NM	NM	NM	NM

Income Statement Analysis (Million $)

	2003	2002	2001	2000	1999	1998	1997	1996	1995	1994
Revs.	1,054	848	619	540	383	201	81.0	41.1	27.4	18.9
Oper. Inc.	279	140	202	188	81.8	9.65	-34.7	-31.1	-22.5	-18.5
Depr.	37.7	36.8	9.12	7.32	5.00	3.46	2.75	1.80	1.55	1.49
Int. Exp.	10.3	9.11	0.59	0.47	3.18	4.04	3.48	2.26	0.25	0.26
Pretax Inc.	291	-1,050	228	209	86.3	8.81	-36.9	-29.5	-22.7	-18.8
Eff. Tax Rate	37.1%	NM	34.8%	30.8%	NM	NM	NM	NM	NM	NM
Net Inc.	183	-1,098	149	145	93.4	56.2	-36.9	-29.5	-22.7	-18.8
S&P Core Earnings	96.0	-1,180	69.1	NA	NA	NA	NA	NA	NA	NA

Balance Sheet & Other Fin. Data (Million $)

	2003	2002	2001	2000	1999	1998	1997	1996	1995	1994
Cash	788	1,423	788	526	270	135	30.0	115	38.0	22.5
Curr. Assets	1,103	743	594	688	402	216	100	133	49.0	32.3
Total Assets	2,795	2,188	1,219	1,007	648	353	170	164	57.3	44.7
Curr. Liab.	391	267	165	151	99	58.0	43.7	20.0	11.0	7.80
LT Debt	703	242	8.79	9.60	10.4	83.2	85.3	70.9	1.98	2.09
Common Equity	1,699	1,677	1,044	844	537	210	40.5	72.9	43.8	34.2
Total Cap.	2,402	1,920	1,053	853	547	293	126	144	45.8	36.3
Cap. Exp.	113	80.9	18.3	8.29	12.2	10.1	36.7	22.7	1.12	1.35
Cash Flow	221	-1,061	158	152	98.4	59.7	-34.1	-27.7	-21.1	-17.3
Curr. Ratio	2.8	2.8	3.6	4.5	4.1	3.7	2.3	6.7	4.4	4.1
% LT Debt of Cap.	29.3	12.6	0.8	1.1	1.9	28.4	67.7	49.3	4.3	5.8
% Net Inc.of Revs.	17.4	NM	24.1	26.8	24.4	28.0	NM	NM	NM	NM
% Ret. on Assets	7.4	NM	13.4	17.5	17.7	21.5	NM	NM	NM	NM
% Ret. on Equity	10.9	NM	15.8	21.0	23.8	44.9	NM	NM	NM	NM

Data as orig reptd.; bef. results of disc opers/spec. items. Per share data adj. for stk. divs.; EPS diluted. E-Estimated. NA-Not Available. NM-Not Meaningful. NR-Not Ranked. UR-Under Review.

Office: 35 West Watkins Mill Road, Gaithersburg, MD 20878.
Telephone: 301-417-0770.
Email: ir@medimmune.com
Website: http://www.medimmune.com
Chrmn: W.T. Hockmeyer.
Pres & COO: M.D. Booth.

Vice Chrmn & CEO: D.M. Mott.
SVP & CFO: L.S. Zoth.
Investor Contact: W. Roberts 301-527-4358.
Dirs: D. Baltimore, M. J. Barrett, M. D. Booth, J. H. Cavanaugh, B. H. Franklin, W. T. Hockmeyer, G. S. Macklin, D. M. Mott, E. Wyatt.

Founded: in 1987.
Domicile: Delaware.
Employees: 1,650.
S&P Analyst: Frank DiLorenzo, CFA /PMW/SRB

Medtronic, Inc.

Recommendation: **HOLD** ★★★☆☆
SELL SELL HOLD BUY BUY

12-Month Target Price: **$54.00**
(as of May 25, 2004)

MDT has an approximate 0.58% weighting in the **S&P 500**

Sector: Health Care
Sub-Industry: Health Care Equipment
Peer Group: Large Multi-Line Medical Device Manufacturers

Summary: MDT is a global medical device manufacturer with leadership positions in the pacemaker, defibrillator, orthopedic, diabetes management, and other medical markets.

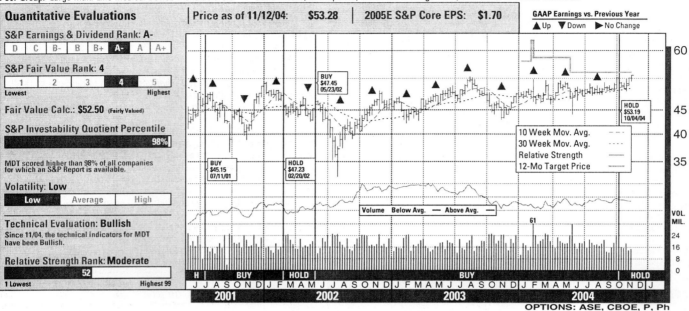

Quantitative Evaluations

Price as of 11/12/04: $53.28   **2005E S&P Core EPS:** $1.70

S&P Earnings & Dividend Rank: A-

| D | C | B- | B | B+ | **A-** | A | A+ |

S&P Fair Value Rank: 4

| 1 | 2 | 3 | **4** | 5 |
| Lowest | | | | Highest |

Fair Value Calc.: $52.50 (Fairly Valued)

S&P Investability Quotient Percentile 98%

MDT scored higher than 98% of all companies for which an S&P Report is available.

Volatility: Low

| **Low** | Average | High |

Technical Evaluation: Bullish
Since 11/04, the technical indicators for MDT have been Bullish.

Relative Strength Rank: Moderate 52
1 Lowest — Highest 99

Analyst commentary prepared by Robert M. Gold/MF

Highlights October 04, 2004

- We project FY 05 (Apr.) sales of $10.2 billion, driven by expected strong performance for defibrillators, spinal surgery, diabetes management, and neurology devices. In the pacemaker segment, we think flattening worldwide sales primarily reflect a mature market and ongoing usage of ICDs in some of the traditional pacemaker patient population, with new-generation devices incorporating both defibrillation and pacing technologies. Currency could provide a material boost to reported revenues, but hedging activities are likely to mute the bottom-line impact. Looking to FY 06, we anticipate that revenues will move toward $11 billion.

- We see gross margins widening, aided by new product launches that should favorably affect the sales mix, improved manufacturing efficiencies, and the positive impact of recent foreign exchange fluctuations. We expect R&D and SG&A costs to consume 9.8% and 31.5% of sales, respectively. We see EPS comparisons in FY 05 benefiting from a lower effective tax rate stemming from increased overseas manufacturing. We estimate free cash flow currently at an annualized $2 billion.

- We see FY 05 operating EPS of $1.85, up from $1.63 in FY 04. After adjusting for projected stock option expense, our FY 05 Standard & Poor's Core Earnings estimate is $1.70 a share. We believe the divergence between estimated S&P Core and operating EPS is modest relative to that of the company's medical device peers. Looking to FY 06, we expect EPS to advance 19%, to $2.20.

Key Stock Statistics

S&P Oper. EPS 2005E	1.85	52-week Range	$53.61-43.96
P/E on S&P Oper. EPS 2005E	28.8	12 Month P/E	32.1
S&P Oper. EPS 2006E	2.20	Beta	0.29
Yield (%)	0.6%	Shareholders	51,500
Dividend Rate/Share	0.34	Market Cap (B)	$ 64.5
Shares Outstanding (M)	1210.3		

Value of $10,000 invested five years ago: **$ 14,236**

Dividend Data Dividends have been paid since 1977

Amount ($)	Date Decl.	Ex-Div. Date	Stock of Record	Payment Date
0.073	Feb. 27	Mar. 31	Apr. 02	Apr. 30 '04
0.084	Jun. 24	Jun. 30	Jul. 02	Jul. 30 '04
0.084	Aug. 26	Sep. 29	Oct. 01	Oct. 29 '04
0.084	Oct. 21	Jan. 05	Jan. 07	Jan. 28 '05

Investment Rationale/Risk October 04, 2004

- In our view, the shares represent a core long term holding in the medical device subsector. We believe recent favorable Medicare reimbursement decisions and increased usage in the traditional pacemaker market will drive sustained growth within the implantable cardioverter defibrillator (ICD) growth in excess of 20% in the next three years, including an estimated 23% growth rate in 2004 and 2005. We see pacemaker sales, however, remaining soft. We think MDT can generate annual sales growth in the double digits in the coming five years, through sales of ICDs, spinal devices, diabetes management, and neurological devices. In the vascular segment, we believe the company's success in developing a drug-coated coronary stent is critical, and we expect MDT to compete in this area by mid-2006, assuming favorable data from ongoing clinical studies.

- Risks to our opinion and target price include the loss of market share in key product categories, unfavorable patent litigation, and adverse Medicare reimbursement rate adjustments.

- The shares, trading recently at 25.5X our calendar 2005 EPS estimate of $2.10, have reached parity with the company's large-cap cardiology device peers and our 12-month target price, and we therefore recently downgraded the stock to hold. Our 12-month target price of $54 assumes a calendar 2005 P/E multiple of about 25X and a forward P/E to growth ratio of 1.7X, in line with peers.

Revenues/Earnings Data Fiscal year ending April 30

Revenues (Million $)

	2005	2004	2003	2002	2001	2000
1Q	2,346	2,064	1,714	1,456	1,310	1,105
2Q	—	2,164	1,891	1,571	1,361	1,161
3Q	—	2,194	1,913	1,592	1,362	1,259
4Q	—	2,665	2,148	1,792	1,518	1,432
Yr.	—	9,087	7,665	6,411	5,552	5,015

Earnings Per Share ($)

	2005	2004	2003	2002	2001	2000
1Q	0.43	0.37	0.31	0.25	0.24	0.21
2Q	E0.45	0.39	0.25	0.05	0.26	0.23
3Q	E0.46	0.38	0.35	0.26	0.25	0.22
4Q	E0.51	0.47	0.40	0.25	0.29	0.26
Yr.	E1.85	1.60	1.30	0.80	0.85	0.90

Next earnings report expected: mid-November Source: S&P, Company Reports
EPS Estimates based on S&P Operating Earnings; historical GAAP earnings are as reported.

Medtronic, Inc.

Recommendation: **HOLD** ★ ★ ★ ☆ ☆   12-Month Target Price: **$54.00** (as of May 25, 2004)

Business Summary October 04, 2004

Formed in 1949, Medtronic has leading positions in many medical device categories, including cardiac rhythm management, neurological/spinal, vascular and cardiac surgery markets.

Cardiac rhythm management products (47% of FY 04 revenues) include implantable pacemakers to treat bradycardia (slow or irregular heartbeats). Bradycardia systems include pacemakers, leads and accessories. Some models are noninvasively programmed by a physician to adjust sensing, electrical pulse intensity, duration, rate and other factors, as well as pacers that can sense in both upper and lower heart chambers and produce appropriate impulses.

Implantable cardioverter defibrillators (ICDs) treat tachyarrhythmia (abnormally fast heart beats) by monitoring the heart; when very rapid heart rhythm is detected, they send electrical impulses or an electrical shock to restore normal rhythm. Cardiac resynchronization therapy (CRT) devices synchronize contractions of multiple heart chambers. In mid-2002, the FDA approved MDT's InSynch ICD, which offers CRT for heart failure, as well as advanced defibrillation capabilities for patients also at risk for potentially lethal tachyarrythmias that may lead to sudden cardiac arrest. In March 2003, the FDA approved the Insynch Marquis system, which combines the cardiac resynchronization of InSynch devices with state-of-the-art defibrillation therapies of the Marquis ICD platform. The company also sells external defibrillators.

Neurological and diabetes products (19%) include implantable neurostimulation systems, external and implantable drug administration devices, continuous glucose monitoring systems, hydrocephalic shunts and drainage devices, surgical instruments and diagnostic equipment.

Spinal, ear, nose and throat, and surgical navigation technologies (19%) products, which are used in surgical procedures of the head and spine, include thoracolumbar, cervical and interbody spinal devices, surgical navigation tools and surgical products. In July 2002, the FDA approved MDT's InFuse Bone Graft, a product containing a recombinant human bone morphogenetic protein that induces bone growth after spinal fusions.

Vascular products (9%) include coronary and peripheral stents and related delivery systems, stent grafts for minimally invasive abdominal aortic aneurysm repair, distal embolic protection systems, and a line of catheters, guidewires and accessories. The company is conducting clinical trials on a coronary stent coated with the experimental drug ABT-578, and hopes to gain FDA approval by late 2005.

Cardiac surgery products (6%) include positioning and stabilizing systems for beating heart surgery, perfusion systems, products for the repair and replacement of heart valves, and surgical accessories.

Company Financials Fiscal Year ending April 30

Per Share Data ($)

(Year Ended April 30)	2004	2003	2002	2001	2000	1999	1998	1997	1996	1995
Tangible Bk. Val.	3.18	2.21	1.10	3.53	2.61	1.99	1.68	1.34	1.41	1.45
Cash Flow	1.96	1.64	1.07	1.10	1.10	0.58	0.63	0.68	0.59	0.43
Earnings	1.60	1.30	0.80	0.85	0.90	0.40	0.48	0.56	0.47	0.32
S&P Core Earnings	1.46	1.10	0.76	0.91	NA	NA	NA	NA	NA	NA
Dividends	0.25	0.25	0.20	0.12	0.15	0.12	0.11	0.10	0.08	0.05
Payout Ratio	16%	19%	25%	14%	16%	30%	23%	17%	17%	16%

Cal. Yrs.	2003	2002	2001	2000	1999	1998	1997	1996	1995	1994
Prices - High	52.92	50.69	60.81	62.00	44.62	38.37	26.37	17.46	15.00	6.98
- Low	42.90	32.50	36.64	32.75	29.93	22.71	14.40	11.12	6.54	4.32
P/E Ratio - High	33	39	72	61	50	97	55	31	32	22
- Low	27	25	43	32	33	58	30	20	14	14

Income Statement Analysis (Million $)

	2004	2003	2002	2001	2000	1999	1998	1997	1996	1995
Revs.	9,087	7,665	6,411	5,552	5,015	4,134	2,605	2,438	2,169	1,742
Oper. Inc.	3,583	3,062	2,479	2,176	1,871	1,535	1,017	901	759	543
Depr.	443	408	330	297	243	213	138	117	112	107
Int. Exp.	56.5	7.20	Nil	74.0	13.0	28.8	8.16	9.38	7.96	9.00
Pretax Inc.	2,797	2,341	1,524	1,549	1,630	822	702	809	668	442
Eff. Tax Rate	29.9%	31.7%	35.4%	32.5%	32.6%	43.0%	34.8%	34.5%	34.4%	33.5%
Net Inc.	1,959	1,600	984	1,046	1,099	468	457	530	438	294
S&P Core Earnings	1,790	1,347	936	1,121	NA	NA	NA	NA	NA	NA

Balance Sheet & Other Fin. Data (Million $)

	2004	2003	2002	2001	2000	1999	1998	1997	1996	1995
Cash	1,594	1,470	411	1,030	448	376	383	251	461	324
Curr. Assets	5,313	4,606	3,488	3,757	3,013	2,395	1,552	1,238	1,343	1,104
Total Assets	14,111	12,321	10,905	7,039	5,669	4,870	2,775	2,409	2,503	1,947
Curr. Liab.	4,241	1,813	3,985	1,359	992	990	572	519	525	456
LT Debt	1.10	1,980	9.50	13.0	14.0	17.6	16.2	13.9	15.3	14.2
Common Equity	9,077	7,906	6,431	5,510	4,491	3,655	2,044	1,746	1,789	1,335
Total Cap.	9,486	10,191	6,674	5,523	4,520	3,703	2,074	1,762	1,850	1,385
Cap. Exp.	425	380	386	440	342	226	148	171	164	96.9
Cash Flow	2,402	2,008	1,314	1,343	1,342	681	595	647	549	401
Curr. Ratio	1.3	2.5	0.9	2.8	3.0	2.4	2.7	2.4	2.6	2.4
% LT Debt of Cap.	0.0	19.4	0.1	0.2	0.3	0.5	0.8	0.7	1.0	1.0
% Net Inc.of Revs.	21.6	20.9	15.3	18.8	21.9	11.3	17.6	21.7	20.1	16.9
% Ret. on Assets	14.8	13.8	11.0	16.5	20.6	11.0	17.6	21.3	19.7	16.5
% Ret. on Equity	23.1	22.3	16.5	20.9	26.6	14.8	24.1	29.5	28.0	24.7

Data as orig reptd.; bef. results of disc opers/spec. items. Per share data adj. for stk. divs. Bold denotes primary EPS - prior periods restated. E-Estimated. NA-Not Available. NM-Not Meaningful. NR-Not Ranked. UR-Under Review.

Office: 710 Medtronic Parkway, Minneapolis, MN 55432-5604.
Telephone: 763-514-4000.
Website: http://www.medtronic.com
Chrmn & CEO: A.D. Collins, Jr.
Pres & COO: W.A. Hawkins.
SVP & CFO: R.L. Ryan.

SVP, Secy & General Counsel: R.E. Lund.
VP & Treas: G. Ellis.
Investor Contact: T. Burns 763-505-2692.
Dirs: R. H. Anderson, M. R. Bonsignore, W. R. Brody, A. D. Collins, Jr., A. M. Gotto, Jr., S. A. Jackson, D. M. O'Leary, R. C. Pozen, J. Rosso, J. W. Schuler, G. M. Sprenger.

Founded: in 1957.
Domicile: Minnesota.
Employees: 30,900.
S&P Analyst: Robert M. Gold/MF

The McGraw·Hill Companies

Mellon Financial

Recommendation: **BUY ★★★★☆**   12-Month Target Price: **$33.00**
(as of October 19, 2004)

MEL has an approximate 0.12% weighting in the **S&P 500**

Sector: Financials
Sub-Industry: Asset Management & Custody Banks
Peer Group: East Super Regional Banks

Summary: This Pittsburgh-based bank holding company (formerly Mellon Bank) provides a full range of banking, investment and trust products to individuals, businesses and institutions.

Quantitative Evaluations

| Price as of 11/12/04: | $30.20 | 2004E S&P Core EPS: | $1.79 |

S&P Earnings & Dividend Rank: A-

| D | C | B- | B | B+ | A- | A | A+ |

S&P Fair Value Rank: 1+

| 1 | 2 | 3 | 4 | 5 |
| Lowest | | | | Highest |

Fair Value Calc.: $23.50 (Overvalued)

S&P Investability Quotient Percentile

96%

MEL scored higher than 96% of all companies for which an S&P Report is available.

Volatility: Average

| Low | Average | High |

Technical Evaluation: Bullish
Since 11/04, the technical indicators for MEL have been Bullish.

Relative Strength Rank: Moderate

58

1 Lowest   Highest 99

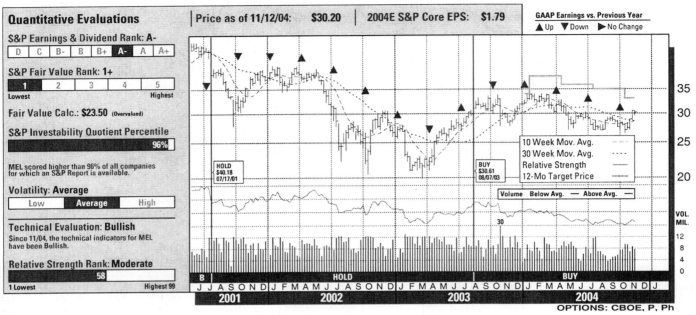

GAAP Earnings vs. Previous Year
▲ Up ▼ Down ► No Change

- 10 Week Mov. Avg.
- 30 Week Mov. Avg.
- Relative Strength
- 12-Mo Target Price

Volume   Below Avg. —   Above Avg. ■

HOLD $40.18 07/17/01

BUY $30.61 08/07/03

OPTIONS: CBOE, P, Ph

Analyst commentary prepared by Evan M. Momios, CFA /CB/BK

Highlights September 02, 2004

- We expect new business wins, equity market stability and strong economic conditions to boost revenue in 2004 from what we view as depressed 2003 levels. Based on 2004 first half results, we see MEL remaining focused on expense controls, and on track to achieve targeted operating expense savings. Our model assumes that operating leverage will remain positive for the rest of 2004.

- Net interest income, which comprises about 11% of total revenues, should remain relatively stable for the rest of the year, in the absence of a significant rise in interest rates. We see the primary risk to earnings in the company's ability to successfully execute its 2004 cost reduction plans to raise the profitability of its Human Resources business. However, MEL has thus far in 2004 reported cost savings that have exceeded our expectations and have increased our comfort level.

- We see 2004 EPS of $1.93, supported by share repurchases, increasing to $2.11 in 2005, implying annual EPS growth of approximately 9%, below our long-term annual EPS growth projection of 12%. Our 2005 estimate reflects our expectations of continued economic growth and equity market stability, outweighing higher staff-related expenses.

Investment Rationale/Risk September 02, 2004

- We have an accumulate recommendation on the stock based on its valuation discount versus peers, combined with the company's leverage to improving capital market conditions that we expect and its continued focus on expenses that we think will lead to stronger EPS growth than the Street anticipates.

- Risks to our recommendation and target price include a significant decline in U.S. equity markets that would have a direct impact on the company's EPS, as well as legislative, legal and regulatory risks.

- The stock has traded at 14X to 16X our 2004 EPS estimate of $1.93 during the past 12 months, versus 17X on average during the past two years, and 17X on average for its peer group. Our 12-month target price of $35 values the shares at 16.5X our 2005 EPS estimate, which we think is an appropriate discount to the historical average, in light of the uncertainty that we see for MEL's market sensitive businesses.

Key Stock Statistics

S&P Core EPS 2005E	1.98	52-week Range	$34.13-26.47
S&P Oper. EPS 2004E	1.90	12 Month P/E	16.4
P/E on S&P Oper. EPS 2004E	15.9	Beta	0.94
S&P Oper. EPS 2005E	2.00	Shareholders	22,351
Yield (%)	2.4%	Market Cap (B)	$ 12.8
Dividend Rate/Share	0.72	Shares Outstanding (M)	423.5

Value of $10,000 invested five years ago: **$ 8,988**

Dividend Data Dividends have been paid since 1895

Amount ($)	Date Decl.	Ex-Div. Date	Stock of Record	Payment Date
0.160	Jan. 20	Jan. 28	Jan. 30	Feb. 13 '04
0.180	Apr. 20	Apr. 28	Apr. 30	May. 14 '04
0.180	Jul. 21	Jul. 28	Jul. 30	Aug. 13 '04
0.180	Oct. 20	Oct. 27	Oct. 29	Nov. 15 '04

Revenues/Earnings Data Fiscal year ending December 31

Revenues (Million $)

	2004	2003	2002	2001	2000	1999
1Q	1,265	1,104	1,212	1,544	1,494	1,583
2Q	1,169	1,134	1,198	985.0	1,477	1,467
3Q	—	1,143	1,152	1,108	1,486	1,436
4Q	—	1,193	1,077	—	1,522	1,441
Yr.	—	4,550	4,737	4,055	5,979	5,986

Earnings Per Share ($)

	2004	2003	2002	2001	2000	1999
1Q	0.57	0.38	0.47	0.41	0.50	0.53
2Q	0.42	0.40	0.24	0.21	0.50	0.45
3Q	0.43	0.36	0.43	0.38	0.51	0.45
4Q	E0.48	0.43	0.38	-0.09	0.52	0.47
Yr.	E1.90	1.57	1.52	0.91	2.03	1.90

Next earnings report expected: mid-January Source: S&P, Company Reports
EPS Estimates based on S&P Operating Earnings; historical GAAP earnings are as reported.

Recommendation: **BUY** ★ ★ ★ ★ ☆   12-Month Target Price: **$33.00** (as of October 19, 2004)

Business Summary September 03, 2004

Founded in 1869 as T. Mellon and Sons' Bank, Mellon Financial (formerly Mellon Bank) operates through several well known entities, including Dreyfus Corp. and Founders Asset Management, two leading mutual fund companies; and Mellon Investor Services, which provides securities transfer services.

Operations are divided into six business sectors. Institutional Asset Management consists of Mellon Institutional Asset Management, with a number of institutional investment management subsidiaries, offering more than 100 equity, fixed income, and liquidity management products; and Mellon Global Investments, which distributes investment products internationally. Sector results are driven by end of period levels of managed assets and by the asset mix.

Mutual Funds consists of the activities of The Dreyfus Corporation (MEL's largest asset manager and leading provider of mutual funds), Founders Asset Management, and U.K.-based Newton Investment Management. Mutual Funds currently offers more than 200 investment products to individual investors and institutions domestically and internationally. Operating results are driven by average asset levels and the mix of assets managed.

Private Wealth Management provides investment management, wealth management, and private banking services to high net worth individuals, and includes the activities of Mellon United National Bank in Florida. Private Wealth Management operating results are driven by the level of assets under management and custody, the mix of assets, and the level of activity in client accounts.

Asset Servicing provides institutional trust and custody, foreign exchange, securities lending, transition management, and back office outsourcing for investment managers. Results of joint ventures are also included in this sector. Operating results are driven by factors that include interest rates, exchange rates, currency volatility, market value of assets under custody or administration, the level of transaction activity, and the type of services provided.

In 2003, the company reorganized its Human Resources business sector, and renamed it Human Resources and Investors Solutions. The sector provides consulting, outsourcing and administrative services to design, build and operate human resources and shareholder services solutions targeted at institutional clients and large corporations.

Treasury Services includes cash management, corporate banking, insurance premium financing, commercial real estate lending, corporate finance and derivative products, securities underwriting and trading, and the activities of Mellon 1st Business Bank in California.

Company Financials Fiscal Year ending December 31

Per Share Data ($)

(Year Ended December 31)	2003	2002	2001	2000	1999	1998	1997	1996	1995	1994
Tangible Bk. Val.	3.30	2.82	3.66	4.34	3.74	4.21	4.40	2.79	3.53	3.87
Earnings	1.57	1.52	0.91	2.03	1.90	1.63	1.44	1.29	1.13	0.60
S&P Core Earnings	1.38	1.09	0.52	NA	NA	NA	NA	NA	NA	NA
Dividends	0.57	0.49	0.82	0.86	0.78	0.71	0.65	0.59	0.50	0.39
Payout Ratio	36%	32%	90%	42%	41%	43%	45%	46%	44%	65%
Prices - High	33.83	40.80	51.62	51.93	40.18	40.18	32.40	18.68	14.12	10.09
- Low	19.89	20.42	27.75	26.81	31.00	22.50	17.25	12.06	7.65	7.50
P/E Ratio - High	22	27	57	26	21	25	23	14	13	17
- Low	13	13	30	13	16	14	12	9	7	12

Income Statement Analysis (Million $)

	2003	2002	2001	2000	1999	1998	1997	1996	1995	1994
Net Int. Inc.	569	610	574	1,328	1,430	1,491	1,467	1,478	1,548	1,508
Tax Equiv. Adj.	17.0	12.0	8.00	10.0	NA	8.00	NA	10.0	10.0	13.0
Non Int. Inc.	3,571	3,622	2,658	3,072	3,100	2,921	2,418	2,019	1,670	1,652
Loan Loss Prov.	7.00	172	-4.00	45.0	45.0	60.0	148	155	105	70.0
Exp./Op. Revs.	77.1%	73.7%	79.2%	64.8%	67.3%	68.2%	66.1%	62.6%	62.8%	74.8%
Pretax Inc.	988	993	675	1,582	1,563	1,340	1,169	1,151	1,092	711
Eff. Tax Rate	31.5%	32.8%	35.4%	36.3%	36.7%	35.1%	34.0%	36.3%	36.7%	39.1%
Net Inc.	677	667	436	1,007	989	870	771	733	691	433
% Net Int. Marg.	2.64	2.74	2.48	3.64	3.70	3.96	4.24	4.26	4.62	4.71
S&P Core Earnings	594	476	248	NA	NA	NA	NA	NA	NA	NA

Balance Sheet & Other Fin. Data (Million $)

	2003	2002	2001	2000	1999	1998	1997	1996	1995	1994
Money Mkt. Assets	3,694	4,791	5,683	4,193	1,502	945	1,083	1,076	922	883
Inv. Securities	11,253	11,742	9,709	8,932	6,356	7,021	4,849	6,486	5,432	5,125
Com'l Loans	NA	NA	NA	15,353	17,127	13,614	12,392	11,618	11,799	10,830
Other Loans	NA	NA	NA	11,016	13,121	18,479	16,750	15,775	15,891	15,903
Total Assets	33,983	36,231	34,360	50,364	47,946	50,777	44,892	42,596	40,646	38,644
Demand Deposits	6,054	11,074	9,537	10,545	9,588	9,976	7,975	8,692	6,458	5,979
Time Deposits	14,789	11,583	11,178	26,345	23,833	24,407	23,330	22,682	22,803	21,591
LT Debt	5,266	5,541	5,036	4,512	3,529	4,294	2,573	2,518	1,443	1,568
Common Equity	3,702	3,395	3,482	4,152	4,016	4,521	3,652	3,456	3,575	3,672
% Ret. on Assets	1.9	1.9	1.3	2.0	2.0	1.8	1.8	1.8	1.7	1.1
% Ret. on Equity	19.1	19.4	11.4	24.7	23.2	21.1	21.1	18.4	17.9	9.5
% Loan Loss Resv.	-1.4	1.5	1.5	1.5	1.3	1.5	1.6	1.9	1.7	2.3
% Loans/Deposits	35.8	37.2	41.2	71.5	90.5	93.3	93.1	87.3	94.6	97.0
% Equity to Assets	10.1	9.6	11.1	8.3	8.6	8.5	8.1	9.0	9.2	9.9

Data as orig reptd.; bef. results of disc opers/spec. items. Per share data adj. for stk. divs.; EPS diluted. E-Estimated. NA-Not Available. NM-Not Meaningful. NR-Not Ranked. UR-Under Review.

Office: One Mellon Center, Pittsburgh, PA 15258-0001.
Telephone: 412-234-5000.
Website: http://www.mellon.com
Chrmn & CEO: M.G. McGuinn.
Vice Chrmn: J.D. Aramanda.
Vice Chrmn: J.L. Leininger.
Vice Chrmn: A.P. Woods.

Vice Chrmn: S.E. Canter.
Investor Contact: S. Lackey 412-234-5601.
Dirs: C. R. Brown, R. E. Bruch, J. L Cohon, J. W. Connolly, S. G. Elliott, I. J. Gumberg, E. J. McAniff, M. G. McGuinn, R. Mehrabian, S. P. Mellon, M. A. Nordenberg, J. F. Orr III, D. S. Shapira, W. E. Strickland, Jr., J. Surma, Jr., W. W. von Schack.

Founded: in 1869.
Domicile: Pennsylvania.
Employees: 20,900.
S&P Analyst: Evan M. Momios, CFA /CB/BK

The **McGraw·Hill** Companies

Merck & Co.

Recommendation: **SELL** ★★☆☆☆   12-Month Target Price: **$23.00**
(as of November 09, 2004)

MRK has an approximate 0.53% weighting in the **S&P 500**

Sector: Health Care
Sub-Industry: Pharmaceuticals
Peer Group: Ethical Pharmaceuticals - Major

Summary: MRK is one of the world's largest prescription pharmaceuticals concerns. The Medco pharmaceutical benefits management unit was spun off to shareholders in August 2003.

Quantitative Evaluations

S&P Earnings & Dividend Rank: A+

| D | C | B- | B | B+ | A- | A | **A+** |

S&P Fair Value Rank: 4

| 1 | 2 | 3 | **4** | 5 |
| Lowest | | | | Highest |

Fair Value Calc.: $28.20 (Slightly Undervalued)

S&P Investability Quotient Percentile

93%

MRK scored higher than 93% of all companies for which an S&P Report is available.

Volatility: Average

| Low | **Average** | High |

Technical Evaluation: Bearish
Since 9/04, the technical indicators for MRK have been Bearish.

Relative Strength Rank: Weak

| 1 Lowest | | Highest 99 |

Price as of 11/12/04: $26.45 | **2004E S&P Core EPS:** $2.31

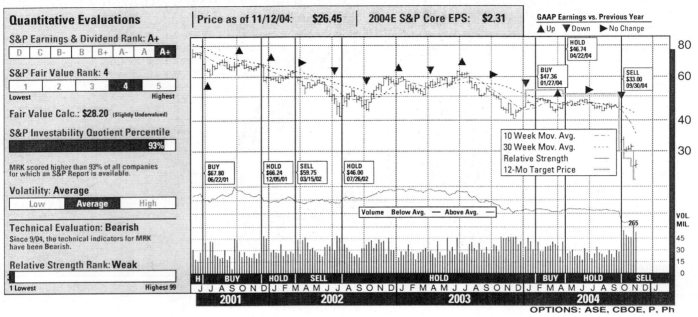

GAAP Earnings vs. Previous Year
▲ Up   ▼ Down   ► No Change

10 Week Mov. Avg.
30 Week Mov. Avg.
Relative Strength
12-Mo Target Price

Volume   Below Avg. — Above Avg. —

OPTIONS: ASE, CBOE, P, Ph

Analyst commentary prepared by H. B. Saftlas/MF/BK

Highlights November 11, 2004

- On September 30, 2004, MRK announced it was voluntarily withdrawing its Vioxx arthritis medication from the global market following new clinical trial results linking the drug with increased cardiovascular risks. We believe the Vioxx setback also casts considerable uncertainty with respect to the future of Arcoxia, Merck's second-generation COX-2 inhibitor. While the latter drug is now being widely sold abroad, the FDA is now requiring additional safety testing before it considers approving it. We expect total company sales to advance modestly to $5.1 billion in 2004, but decline about 6%-7% in 2005, reflecting the absence of Vioxx and likely continued slippage in Zocor.

- Inventory writedowns and other costs associated with the Vioxx recall resulted in a charge of $0.25 a share in the third quarter of 2004, and an additional charge of $0.25-$0.30 is expected in the fourth quarter. Despite ongoing cost streamlining measures, we expect gross margins to contract in 2005, largely reflecting the absence of Vioxx.

- We estimate EPS of $2.50 in 2005, versus the $2.60 seen for 2004, including Vioxx-related charges. After adjusting for projected option and pension expense, we forecast Standard & Poor's Core EPS of $2.21 in 2005, versus $2.31 in 2004.

Investment Rationale/Risk November 11, 2004

- We continue to recommend investors avoid the shares, largely due to ongoing fallout from Vioxx. Besides the impact of the Vioxx loss on future earnings, we believe MRK faces potentially large Vioxx-related legal liabilities. The Justice Dept. has begun a criminal investigation related to MRK's handling of Vioxx, while the SEC also launched an inquiry that we believe focuses on the adequacy of past Vioxx disclosure risks. We believe MRK's total legal liability costs may exceed $10 billion. Separately, we remain concerned over what we view as MRK's relatively lean pipeline for a company its size. We also note that the U.S. patent on Zocor (MRK's largest-selling drug) expires in July 2006.

- Risks to our recommendation and target price include the potential for earlier than expected approval of Arcoxia, delays in generic competition to Zocor, better than expected news flow related to MRK's pipeline, and positive developments in Vioxx litigation.

- With negative news flow related to Vioxx, we believe the shares should trade at a steep discount to peer drug stocks. We have a 12-month target price of $23, which applies a multiple of 9.2X to our 2005 EPS estimate, and assumes continuation of the $1.52 annual dividend (currently yielding close to 6%).

Key Stock Statistics

S&P Core EPS 2005E	2.21	52-week Range	$49.33-25.60
S&P Oper. EPS 2004E	2.60	12 Month P/E	9.7
P/E on S&P Oper. EPS 2004E	10.2	Beta	0.32
S&P Oper. EPS 2005E	2.50	Shareholders	233,000
Yield (%)	5.7%	Market Cap (B)	$ 58.7
Dividend Rate/Share	1.52	Shares Outstanding (M)	2217.6

Value of $10,000 invested five years ago: **$ 3,876**

Dividend Data Dividends have been paid since 1935

Amount ($)	Date Decl.	Ex-Div. Date	Stock of Record	Payment Date
0.370	Nov. 25	Dec. 03	Dec. 05	Jan. 02 '04
0.370	Feb. 24	Mar. 03	Mar. 05	Apr. 01 '04
0.370	May. 25	Jun. 02	Jun. 04	Jul. 01 '04
0.380	Jul. 27	Sep. 01	Sep. 03	Oct. 01 '04

Revenues/Earnings Data Fiscal year ending December 31

Revenues (Million $)

	2004	2003	2002	2001	2000	1999
1Q	5,631	5,571	12,169	11,345	8,851	7,537
2Q	6,022	5,525	12,810	11,893	9,477	8,018
3Q	5,538	5,762	12,893	11,920	10,568	8,196
4Q	—	5,627	13,918	12,558	11,467	8,963
Yr.	—	22,486	51,790	47,716	40,363	32,714

Earnings Per Share ($)

	2004	2003	2002	2001	2000	1999
1Q	0.73	0.68	0.71	0.71	0.62	0.54
2Q	0.79	0.79	0.77	0.78	0.73	0.61
3Q	0.60	0.83	0.83	0.84	0.78	0.64
4Q	E0.40	0.62	0.83	0.81	0.75	0.66
Yr.	E2.60	2.92	3.14	3.14	2.90	2.45

Next earnings report expected: late-January Source: S&P, Company Reports
EPS Estimates based on S&P Operating Earnings; historical GAAP earnings are as reported.

Merck & Co., Inc.

Recommendation: **SELL** ★★☆☆☆   12-Month Target Price: **$23.00** (as of November 09, 2004)

Business Summary November 11, 2004

Merck & Co. is one of the world's largest pharmaceutical companies, manufacturing and marketing a wide range of prescription drugs in many therapeutic classes in the U.S. and abroad. Foreign business is important, with subsidiaries outside of the U.S. accounting for 40% of total pharmaceutical and vaccine sales in 2003. MRK was originally founded in 1887 as a U.S. branch of E. Merck of Germany. It grew significantly in subsequent years through aggressive new drug development and acquisitions.

In August 2003, the company spun off its Medco Health Solutions pharmaceutical benefits management unit to MRK shareholders in a tax-free transaction. Shareholders received 0.1206 of a Medco share for each MRK share. Medco Health Solutions (NYSE: MHS; formerly Merck-Medco) provides mail-order drug and related services to 65 million people.

In September 2004, Merck announced it was removing its Vioxx COX-2 inhibitor arthritis medication from the market due an increased risk of cardiovascular events. As a result, Vioxx sales are not expected going forward. Vioxx sales were $2.5 billion in 2003. The company's second generation COX-2 drug, Arcoxia, is presently being sold in international markets. In October 2004, the FDA issued an "approvable letter" for Arcoxia, but added that additional safety tests would be required before the drug could be reconsidered for the U.S. market.

MRK's largest selling drug is Zocor (2003 sales of $5.0 billion), the world's second largest selling cholesterol lowering drug. Through a joint venture with Schering-Plough, the company also markets Zetia, a new type of cholesterol-lowering medicine that is especially effective in patients who do not respond to conventional statin therapy. Zetia had 2003 sales of $164 million. In July 2004, Merck/

Schering launched Vytorin, a combination of Zocor and Zetia for cholesterol reduction.

Other principal products include Cozaar/Hyzaar ($2.5 billion), a treatment for high blood pressure and congestive heart failure; Fosamax ($2.7 billion), a drug for osteoporosis (a bone-thinning disease that affects postmenopausal women); and Singulair ($2.0 billion), a treatment for asthma and seasonal allergic rhinitis.

As of September 2004, Zocor accounted for about 21% of the U.S. prescription statin cholesterol-lowering drug market, and Fosamax accounted for about 72% of the bisphosphonate osteoporosis market, based on data from IMS Health. Other key prescription pharmaceuticals include Vasotec/Vaseretic antihypertensives; Primaxin, an intravenous antibiotic; Crixivan, a protease inhibitor AIDS drug; and Proscar, a treatment for enlarged prostates. MRK is also a leading maker of vaccines.

The historical success of the company's drugs has enabled it to support a $3.2 billion R&D program (equal to 14% of sales in 2003), which MRK hopes will lead to an ongoing stream of blockbuster drugs in coming years. Key products in clinical trials include drugs for heart disease, diabetes, obesity, Alzheimer's disease, and infections, as well as several antiviral vaccines.

OTC medications such as Pepcid AC are offered through a venture with Johnson & Johnson. Merial, a leading animal health products company, is owned jointly by MRK and Rhone-Poulenc SA. Through a venture with Astra AB of Sweden, MRK books sales of Prilosec and other Astra drugs.

Company Financials Fiscal Year ending December 31

Per Share Data ($)

(Year Ended December 31)	2003	2002	2001	2000	1999	1998	1997	1996	1995	1994
Tangible Bk. Val.	6.13	4.88	3.77	3.23	2.43	1.91	2.45	2.17	2.00	1.58
Cash Flow	3.51	3.79	3.77	3.44	3.02	2.67	2.29	1.90	1.62	1.46
Earnings	2.92	3.14	3.14	2.90	2.45	2.15	1.87	1.60	1.35	1.19
S&P Core Earnings	2.71	2.81	2.87	NA	NA	NA	NA	NA	NA	NA
Dividends	1.46	1.42	1.38	1.26	1.10	0.95	0.87	0.74	0.64	0.58
Payout Ratio	50%	45%	44%	43%	45%	44%	47%	46%	47%	49%
Prices - High	63.50	64.50	95.25	96.68	87.37	80.87	54.09	42.12	33.62	19.75
- Low	40.57	38.50	56.80	52.00	60.93	50.68	39.00	28.25	18.18	14.06
P/E Ratio - High	22	21	30	33	36	38	29	26	25	17
- Low	14	12	18	18	25	24	21	18	13	12

Income Statement Analysis (Million $)

	2003	2002	2001	2000	1999	1998	1997	1996	1995	1994
Revs.	22,486	51,790	47,716	40,363	32,714	26,898	23,637	19,829	16,681	14,970
Oper. Inc.	9,912	11,361	11,192	10,686	9,056	7,655	6,701	5,912	5,262	5,075
Depr.	1,314	1,488	1,464	1,277	1,145	1,279	1,034	731	667	670
Int. Exp.	351	391	465	484	317	206	130	139	99	124
Pretax Inc.	9,220	10,214	10,693	10,133	8,842	8,295	6,594	5,685	4,889	4,509
Eff. Tax Rate	26.7%	30.0%	29.2%	29.6%	30.9%	34.8%	28.0%	29.2%	30.0%	31.5%
Net Inc.	6,590	7,150	7,282	6,822	5,891	5,248	4,614	3,881	3,335	2,997
S&P Core Earnings	6,089	6,395	6,649	NA	NA	NA	NA	NA	NA	NA

Balance Sheet & Other Fin. Data (Million $)

	2003	2002	2001	2000	1999	1998	1997	1996	1995	1994
Cash	1,201	2,243	2,144	2,537	2,022	2,606	1,125	2,181	3,349	2,270
Curr. Assets	11,527	14,834	12,962	13,353	11,259	10,229	8,213	7,727	8,618	6,922
Total Assets	40,588	47,561	44,007	39,910	35,633	31,853	25,812	24,293	23,832	21,857
Curr. Liab.	9,570	12,375	11,544	9,710	8,759	6,069	5,569	4,829	5,690	5,449
LT Debt	5,096	4,879	4,799	3,601	3,144	3,221	1,347	1,156	1,373	1,146
Common Equity	15,576	18,200	16,050	14,832	13,242	12,802	12,613	11,971	11,736	11,139
Total Cap.	24,588	28,008	25,686	23,454	52,175	21,491	16,645	15,437	13,109	14,735
Cap. Exp.	1,916	2,370	2,725	2,728	2,561	1,973	1,449	1,197	1,006	1,009
Cash Flow	7,904	8,638	8,746	8,099	7,035	6,527	5,648	4,612	4,002	3,667
Curr. Ratio	1.2	1.2	1.1	1.4	1.3	1.7	1.5	1.6	1.5	1.3
% LT Debt of Cap.	20.7	17.4	18.7	15.4	6.0	15.0	8.1	7.5	10.5	7.8
% Net Inc.of Revs.	29.3	13.8	15.3	16.9	18.0	19.5	19.5	19.6	20.0	20.0
% Ret. on Assets	15.0	15.6	17.3	18.1	17.4	18.2	18.4	16.1	14.6	14.4
% Ret. on Equity	39.0	41.7	47.2	48.6	20.1	41.3	37.5	33.1	29.2	28.4

Data as orig reptd.; bef. results of disc opers/spec. items. Per share data adj. for stk. divs.; EPS diluted. E-Estimated. NA-Not Available. NM-Not Meaningful. NR-Not Ranked. UR-Under Review.

Office: One Merck Drive, Whitehouse Station, NJ 08889-0100.
Telephone: 908-423-1000.
Website: http://www.merck.com
Chrmn, Pres & CEO: R.V. Gilmartin.
EVP & CFO: J.C. Lewent.
SVP & General Counsel: K.C. Frazier.

VP & Treas: C. Dorsa.
VP & Secy: C.A. Colbert.
Dirs: L. A. Bossidy, W. G. Bowen, J. B. Cole, W. M. Daley, R. V. Gilmartin, W. B. Harrison, Jr., W. N. Kelley, H. G. Miller, T. E. Shenk, S. O. Thier, W. P. Weeks, P. C. Wendell.

Founded: in 1891.
Domicile: New Jersey.
Employees: 63,200.
S&P Analyst: H. B. Saftlas/MF/BK

Mercury Interactive

Recommendation: **SELL** ★ ★ ★ ★ ★
SELL | SELL | HOLD | BUY | BUY

12-Month Target Price: **$33.00**
(as of October 21, 2004)

MERQ has an approximate 0.04% weighting in the **S&P 500**

Sector: Information Technology
Sub-Industry: Application Software
Peer Group: Security Software

Summary: MERQ develops, markets and supports a family of automated testing and monitoring solutions for business-critical enterprise and web applications.

Quantitative Evaluations

S&P Earnings & Dividend Rank: B

| D | C | B- | **B** | B+ | A- | A | A+ |

S&P Fair Value Rank: 5

| 1 | 2 | 3 | 4 | **5** |
| Lowest | | | | Highest |

Fair Value Calc.: $51.30 (Slightly Undervalued)

S&P Investability Quotient Percentile

67%

MERQ scored higher than 67% of all companies for which an S&P Report is available.

Volatility: Average

| Low | **Average** | High |

Technical Evaluation: Bullish

Since 10/04, the technical indicators for MERQ have been Bullish.

Relative Strength Rank: Strong

78

1 Lowest   Highest 99

Price as of 11/12/04: $44.06 | **2004E S&P Core EPS:** $-0.50

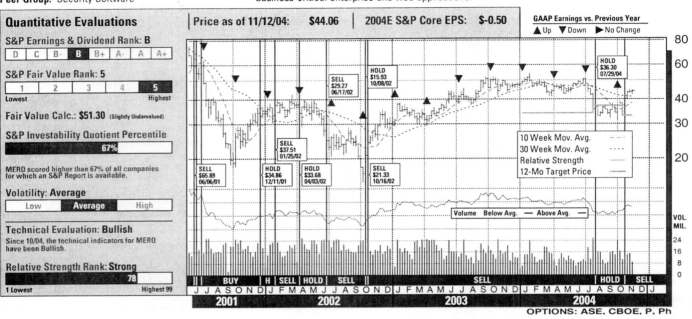

Analyst commentary prepared by Mark S. Basham/PMW/JWP

Highlights October 22, 2004

- We expect 2004 revenues to increase 32%. With growth in foreign markets expected to remain particularly strong, we estimate that about 15% of the projected growth will be due to positive currency effects. We attribute about 30% of the expected gains to acquisitions completed subsequent to the start of 2003. For 2005, we project that revenues will advance 10%, reflecting an expected slowing of the company's organic growth rate, and the anniversary of its most significant recent acquisitions.

- We look for gross margins to narrow by about two percentage points, as costs (in dollars) rise. We think that MERQ's spending on R&D will increase faster than revenues in each of 2004 and 2005, while selling and marketing spending growth will decelerate dramatically in response to the slowing of revenue growth. Our operating margin projections for each year are at the low end of the company's target range of 17% to 20%.

- We estimate 2004 operating EPS of $0.93, excluding stock-based compensation and acquisition-related charges, with 2005 EPS growing 24%, to $1.15. We believe that earnings quality remains questionable. Applying alternate fair value recognition policies, net stock-based compensation was $1.53 a share in 2003; we estimate such compensation at about $1.43 for 2004 and $1.50 for 2005, implying that Standard & Poor's Core Earnings would be negative.

Key Stock Statistics

S&P Core EPS 2005E	-0.35	52-week Range	$54.25-31.05
S&P Oper. EPS 2004E	0.93	12 Month P/E	66.8
P/E on S&P Oper. EPS 2004E	47.4	Beta	NA
S&P Oper. EPS 2005E	1.15	Shareholders	354
Yield (%)	Nil	Market Cap (B)	$ 4.1
Dividend Rate/Share	Nil	Shares Outstanding (M)	93.1

Value of $10,000 invested five years ago: **$ 9,446**

Dividend Data

No cash dividends have been paid.

Investment Rationale/Risk October 22, 2004

- We recently downgraded the shares to avoid, from hold, after a sharp rise in the share price to well above our 12-month target price. We believe the company's repurchase during the third quarter of 9.7 million shares fueled the rise in the stock. The purchase offset the expected dilutive effect of contingently convertible debt on EPS, when new accounting rules go into effect for periods ending after December 15, 2004. The new rules will be applied retroactively to such periods. Nevertheless, we do not see justification for a higher valuation than that implied by our target price, based on our longer-term revenue, profit, and cash flow projections.

- Risks to our recommendation and target price include faster corporate IT spending growth in 2005 than that contemplated by our view of some moderation from 2004 growth rates. The company had about $1.1 billion in cash and investments at September 30, 2004; use of this cash to make acquisitions, as MERQ has done in the past, could accelerate growth in revenue, earnings and cash flow above our expectations.

- Our 12-month target price is $33. Our discounted cash flow analysis suggests intrinsic value in the low $30 area. At our target price, the shares would have a P/E to projected growth (PEG) ratio of 2.4X, assuming a 12% longer-term growth rate. We view this premium as fair relative to the historical average of the Application Software peer group.

Revenues/Earnings Data Fiscal year ending December 31

Revenues (Million $)

	2004	2003	2002	2001	2000	1999
1Q	156.8	110.4	90.50	90.70	60.40	37.60
2Q	159.1	118.1	94.00	96.00	69.60	42.50
3Q	165.4	126.1	97.85	84.00	79.50	47.50
4Q	—	152.0	117.8	90.30	97.50	60.10
Yr.	—	506.5	400.1	361.0	307.0	187.7

Earnings Per Share ($)

	2004	2003	2002	2001	2000	1999
1Q	0.19	0.20	0.17	0.18	0.11	0.07
2Q	0.12	0.19	0.20	0.10	0.14	0.09
3Q	0.21	-0.08	0.15	-0.09	0.18	0.15
4Q	—	0.14	0.21	-0.01	0.28	0.15
Yr.	E0.93	0.45	0.74	0.20	0.70	0.39

Next earnings report expected: late-January Source: S&P, Company Reports
EPS Estimates based on S&P Operating Earnings; historical GAAP earnings are as reported.

Mercury Interactive Corporation

Recommendation: **SELL** ★ ★ ☆ ☆ ☆   12-Month Target Price: **$33.00** (as of October 21, 2004)

Business Summary October 22, 2004

Mercury Interactive Corp. develops, markets and supports Business Technology Optimization (BTO) solutions that it believes enable companies to test and deploy information technology-based processes and align them with key business objectives. Its Application Delivery, Application Management and IT governance products and services are designed to enable corporate development organizations, system integrators, and independent software developers to optimize the quality of information technology (IT) services and reduce spending on IT infrastructure. In 2003, the company organized its integrated software, services and best practices solutions into Optimization Centers to address each of its product lines.

Application Delivery products and services are intended to help organizations optimize the quality and performance of custom and pre-packaged software applications before they go into production. Quality Optimization Center products include Test Director, a single application that integrates the testing process from planning to defect tracking, and QuickTest Professional and WinRunner, for automated testing of software based on a variety of industry standard platforms. The Performance Optimization Center products include LoadRunner TestCenter, LoadRunner, LoadRunner and Deep Diagnostics for J2EE (Java 2 Enterprise Edition) and ProTune, for centralized large scale and enterprise application and infrastructure testing by emulating thousands of users and transactions. Variations of ProTune and Deep Diagnostics are also offered as managed services.

Application Management products and services are designed to assist customers in ensuring that software performs at the levels expected and meets required business goals. Performance Optimization Center products include Topaz Diagnostics, Topaz for Service Level Management, Topaz Business Availability and the Mercury Application Management Foundation (formerly Topaz Platform). Topaz products, as well as a component of the Foundation, are also offered as managed services.

IT Governance offerings are designed to manage the priorities, processes and people required to operate an Information Technology organization as a business, and align IT strategies and executions with overall business goals and regulations. The IT Governance Center product line offers support for quality programs such as Six-Sigma, CMMI, ITIL, ISO-9000 and COBIT. Workflow, security, execution and reporting services are integrated across the product line.

The company markets products through a direct sales and service organization that focuses on major accounts, and indirectly through alliance partners such as Accenture and IBM. MERQ maintains 68 sales and support offices worldwide. International sales accounted for 36%, 34% and 35% of total revenues in 2003, 2002 and 2001, respectively.

In August 2003, MERQ acquired privately held Kintana, a provider of IT governance software and services. Total consideration, including cash, stock, options assumed, and direct merger costs was $267 million. In May 2003, the company acquired Performant, a provider of J2EE diagnostics software, for total consideration of $23 million.

Company Financials Fiscal Year ending December 31

Per Share Data ($)

(Year Ended December 31)	2003	2002	2001	2000	1999	1998	1997	1996	1995	1994
Tangible Bk. Val.	3.26	3.85	2.75	3.57	2.56	1.99	1.69	1.54	1.47	0.77
Cash Flow	0.72	0.94	0.36	0.81	0.46	0.33	0.15	0.12	-0.06	0.12
Earnings	0.45	0.74	0.20	0.70	0.39	0.28	0.10	0.07	-0.10	0.10
S&P Core Earnings	-1.06	-0.45	-1.18	NA	NA	NA	NA	NA	NA	NA
Dividends	Nil	Nil	Nil	Nil	Nil	Nil	Nil	Nil	Nil	Nil
Payout Ratio	Nil	Nil	Nil	Nil	Nil	Nil	Nil	Nil	Nil	Nil
Prices - High	52.43	42.48	100.43	162.50	55.12	15.81	7.03	6.00	7.25	5.43
- Low	29.24	15.15	18.00	40.12	10.50	5.28	2.37	2.37	2.93	1.75
P/E Ratio - High	NM	57	NM	NM	NM	56	NM	86	NM	57
- Low	NM	20	NM	NM	NM	19	NM	34	NM	18

Income Statement Analysis (Million $)

	2003	2002	2001	2000	1999	1998	1997	1996	1995	1994
Revs.	506	400	361	307	188	121	76.7	54.6	39.5	23.5
Oper. Inc.	106	84.4	72.7	73.0	44.0	26.8	10.3	6.08	-4.30	5.76
Depr.	25.3	17.1	15.0	9.62	6.06	4.14	3.74	3.26	2.16	1.17
Int. Exp.	19.6	23.4	25.6	12.8	Nil	Nil	Nil	Nil	Nil	0.01
Pretax Inc.	57.7	82.4	30.3	80.9	42.0	27.3	9.63	5.78	-4.28	5.94
Eff. Tax Rate	28.0%	20.9%	41.2%	20.0%	21.1%	20.0%	30.4%	20.0%	NM	15.0%
Net Inc.	41.5	65.2	17.8	64.7	33.1	21.8	6.71	4.63	-5.25	5.05
S&P Core Earnings	-92.0	-38.4	-106	NA	NA	NA	NA	NA	NA	NA

Balance Sheet & Other Fin. Data (Million $)

	2003	2002	2001	2000	1999	1998	1997	1996	1995	1994
Cash	549	355	248	226	113	96.1	57.2	71.0	77.8	33.3
Curr. Assets	913	667	525	726	235	154	119	96.5	95.7	44.1
Total Assets	1,971	1,076	928	976	297	204	143	117	113	49.6
Curr. Liab.	390	290	196	173	97.7	58.0	30.4	18.5	20.2	10.4
LT Debt	811	317	377	500	Nil	Nil	Nil	Nil	Nil	Nil
Common Equity	700	445	354	303	200	146	113	99	92.6	39.2
Total Cap.	1,512	762	732	803	200	146	113	99	92.6	39.2
Cap. Exp.	17.1	8.16	22.1	45.6	23.9	14.9	11.8	4.60	6.96	3.20
Cash Flow	66.9	82.3	32.8	74.3	39.2	25.9	10.4	7.89	3.09	6.22
Curr. Ratio	2.3	2.3	2.7	4.2	2.4	2.6	3.9	5.2	4.7	4.2
% LT Debt of Cap.	53.7	41.6	51.6	62.3	Nil	Nil	Nil	Nil	Nil	Nil
% Net Inc.of Revs.	8.2	16.3	4.9	21.1	17.7	18.0	8.7	8.5	NM	21.5
% Ret. on Assets	2.7	6.5	1.9	10.2	13.2	12.6	5.1	4.0	NM	10.9
% Ret. on Equity	7.2	16.3	5.4	25.7	19.2	16.9	6.3	4.8	NM	13.8

Data as orig reptd.; bef. results of disc opers/spec. items. Per share data adj. for stk. divs. Bold denotes primary EPS - prior periods restated. E-Estimated. NA-Not Available. NM-Not Meaningful. NR-Not Ranked. UR-Under Review.

Office: 1325 Borregas Avenue, Sunnyvale, CA 94089.
Telephone: 408-822-5200.
Website: http://www.mercury.com
Chrmn, Pres & CEO: A. Landan.
EVP & CFO: D.P. Smith.

VP, Secy & General Counsel: S.J. Skaer.
Investor Contact: M. Levine 408-822-5464.
Dirs: B. Boston, I. Kohavi, A. Landan, C. Ostler, Y. Shamir, G. Yaron, A. Zingale.

Founded: in 1989.
Domicile: Delaware.
Employees: 2,322.
S&P Analyst: Mark S. Basham/PMW/JWP

Meredith Corp.

Recommendation: **BUY** ★★★★☆
SELL | SELL | HOLD | BUY | BUY

12-Month Target Price: **$60.00**
(as of September 02, 2004)

MDP has an approximate 0.02% weighting in the **S&P 500**

Sector: Consumer Discretionary
Sub-Industry: Publishing
Peer Group: Publishing - Large

Summary: MDP derives the bulk of its earnings from publishing magazines (primarily Better Homes and Gardens and Ladies' Home Journal) and ownership of 12 TV stations.

Quantitative Evaluations

S&P Earnings & Dividend Rank: A-

D	C	B-	B	B+	A-	A	A+

S&P Fair Value Rank: 3

1	2	3	4	5
Lowest				Highest

Fair Value Calc.: $51.80 (Fairly Valued)

S&P Investability Quotient Percentile
98%

MDP scored higher than 98% of all companies for which an S&P Report is available.

Volatility: Low

Low	Average	High

Technical Evaluation: Neutral
Since 11/04, the technical indicators for MDP have been Neutral.

Relative Strength Rank: Moderate
40
1 Lowest — Highest 99

Price as of 11/12/04: $52.38   **2005E S&P Core EPS:** $2.08

GAAP Earnings vs. Previous Year
▲ Up   ▼ Down   ► No Change

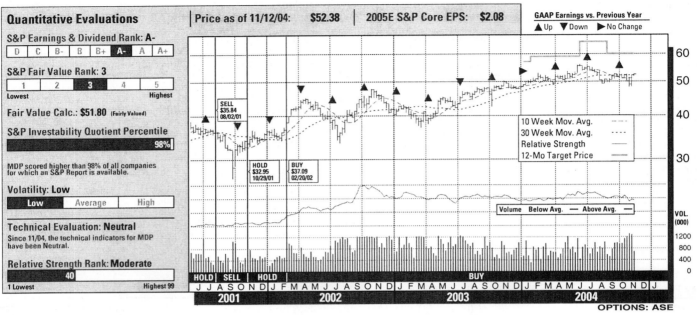

SELL $35.84 08/02/01
HOLD $32.95 10/29/01
BUY $37.09 02/20/02

10 Week Mov. Avg.
30 Week Mov. Avg.
Relative Strength
12-Mo Target Price

Volume   Below Avg. —   Above Avg. —

VOL. (000)
1200
800
400
0

HOLD | SELL | HOLD | BUY
J J A S O N D | J F M A M J J A S O N D | J F M A M J J A S O N D | J F M A M J J A S O N D | J F M A M J J A S O N D | J
2001 | 2002 | 2003 | 2004

OPTIONS: ASE

Analyst commentary prepared by William H. Donald/PMW/BK

Highlights September 07, 2004

- We expect total revenues in FY 05 (Jun.) to increase 9.4%, to $1.27 billion. We project that an advertising uptrend will continue through FY 05 for magazines and broadcasting. We also expect the company's magazines to gain advertising market share. For FY 06, we see a 13% advance in revenues, aided by further strengthening in advertising demand and pricing, particularly for magazines.

- Although we see profits under some pressure through FY 05, due to rising healthcare, pension, postal and programming expenses, profits should benefit from revenue gains and substantial savings resulting from recent downsizings and ongoing efficiency measures. We see operating income advancing 19.5% in FY 05, after a 14.5% gain in FY 04. We expect EBITDA margins to widen to 22.1%, from 20.5%. Looking ahead to FY 06, we see operating earnings advancing 22%, aided in part by expected revenue gains and operating efficiencies already in place.

- Aided by lower net interest expense, and after taxes expected to be unchanged at 38.7%, we expect FY 05 net income to grow 24%, to $137.8 million ($2.65 a share), from FY 04's $110.7 million ($2.14). For FY 06, we project a 19% advance in net income and a 17% gain in EPS, to $3.10, on more shares outstanding. We see S&P Core EPS of $1.80 for FY 05.

Key Stock Statistics

S&P Oper. EPS 2005E	2.70	52-week Range	$55.94-47.54
P/E on S&P Oper. EPS 2005E	19.4	12 Month P/E	23.1
S&P Oper. EPS 2006E	3.15	Beta	0.38
Yield (%)	0.9%	Shareholders	1,600
Dividend Rate/Share	0.48	Market Cap (B)	$ 2.1
Shares Outstanding (M)	50.0		

Value of $10,000 invested five years ago: **$ 15,526**

Dividend Data   Dividends have been paid since 1930

Amount ($)	Date Decl.	Ex-Div. Date	Stock of Record	Payment Date
0.120	Feb. 02	Feb. 25	Feb. 27	Mar. 15 '04
q.12	May. 12	May. 26	May. 28	Jun. 15 '04
0.120	Aug. 11	Aug. 27	Aug. 31	Sep. 15 '04
0.120	Nov. 08	Nov. 26	Nov. 30	Dec. 15 '04

Investment Rationale/Risk September 07, 2004

- We recommend accumulating the shares. The stock has historically traded at what we view as high P/E multiples, and toward the high end of its peer group range. Based on cash flow and earnings growth comparisons with peers, we think a premium valuation is warranted. We expect the company to continue to expand in growing markets. We see favorable demographic trends, and think MDP should continue to benefit, in terms of business growth and asset values, from its position as the largest publisher of shelter magazines and as a major group broadcaster. The company continues to outperform the magazine industry in circulation and advertising gains. We expect EPS growth to average in the mid- to high teens over the next five years.

- Risks to our recommendation and target price include a rapid rise in inflation, which affects paper costs; and an economic slowdown that would have a negative impact on advertising demand for MDP's print and broadcast properties.

- Based on discounted cash flow analysis (asssuming 15-year growth of 5% and a weighted average cost of capital of 9.9%) and expected stable relative P/E multiple comparisons, our 12-month target price is $60.

Revenues/Earnings Data   Fiscal year ending June 30

Revenues (Million $)

	2005	2004	2003	2002	2001	2000
1Q	288.9	272.7	250.1	236.6	250.2	260.4
2Q	—	280.4	251.7	228.0	260.9	266.1
3Q	—	299.6	278.2	256.2	272.3	286.9
4Q	—	309.1	300.1	267.2	269.8	283.7
Yr.	—	1,162	1,080	987.8	1,053	1,097

Earnings Per Share ($)

	2005	2004	2003	2002	2001	2000
1Q	0.50	0.37	0.32	0.17	0.32	0.34
2Q	E0.55	0.38	0.38	0.17	0.47	0.48
3Q	E0.75	0.67	0.50	0.35	0.37	0.47
4Q	E0.90	0.76	0.58	1.10	0.23	0.06
Yr.	E2.70	2.14	1.78	1.79	1.39	1.35

Next earnings report expected: late-January Source: S&P, Company Reports
EPS Estimates based on S&P Operating Earnings; historical GAAP earnings are as reported.

Meredith Corporation

Recommendation: **BUY** ★★★★☆   12-Month Target Price: **$60.00** (as of September 02, 2004)

Business Summary September 07, 2004

Meredith Corp. is a diversified media and marketing company with a long tradition of service to the home and family market. Operations primarily consist of magazine and book publishing, television broadcasting, and interactive and integrated marketing.

The company publishes 17 subscription-based magazines, including Better Homes and Gardens, Ladies' Home Journal, Successful Farming, WOOD, Country Home, Traditional Home, MORE, and Midwest Living. In addition, it produces about 170 special-interest publications. MDP also publishes about 300 home and family service books that are sold primarily through retail distribution outlets. In December 2002, the company acquired American Baby Group, a publisher with titles geared toward mothers-to-be and young mothers. American Baby's magazines include American Baby, First Year of Life, Childbirth, Healthy Kids en Espanol, Primeros 12 Meses, and Espera. American Baby produces television shows; owns six consumer sampling programs; provides custom publishing; and owns the American Baby Family Research Center and two Web sites. The company expected the acquisition to attract younger readers (particularly young families), and to help tap the fast growing U.S. Hispanic market.

Retail brand licensing efforts began in 1994, when MDP granted a license to Wal-Mart Stores to operate Better Homes and Gardens Garden Centers in its U.S. stores. In addition, GMAC Home Services, Inc. is licensed to use the Better Homes and Gardens trademark in connection with residential real estate marketing. Multicom Publishing is licensed to develop and publish CD-ROM titles based

on MDP's editorial products. Reader's Digest Association is licensed to market MDP-trademarked products. Global Vacation Group Inc. is also a licensee for vacation packages to selected destinations. The company also has marketing relationships with Sears, Home Depot, Carnival Cruise Lines, and DaimlerChrysler.

The company owns 11 network-affiliated TV stations, including WGNX-TV (CBS-Atlanta); KPHO (CBS), Phoenix, AZ; WNEM (CBS), Bay City-Saginaw-Flint, MI; KCTV (CBS), Kansas City, MO; WSMV (NBC), Nashville, TN; KVVU (FOX), Las Vegas, NV; KPTV-12 (UPN) and KPDX (FOX), Portland, OR; WHNS (FOX), Greenville, SC-Asheville, NC; KFXO (FOX), Bend, OR; and WFSB (CBS), Hartford-New Haven, CT.

MDP's consumer database contains more than 60 million names, making it one of the largest domestic databases among media companies. The database enables magazine and TV advertisers to precisely target marketing campaigns. In addition, the company has an extensive Internet presence, including 24 Web sites, and multi-year alliance agreements with leading Internet providers America Online and Microsoft Network.

In the FY 02 (Jun.) fourth quarter, the company recorded a noncash gain of $0.74 a share from the exchange of TV stations in Orlando and Ocala, FL, for a station in Portland, OR, as well as charges totaling $0.09 for noncash writeoffs. The second quarter included an unusual gain of $0.02.

Company Financials Fiscal Year ending June 30

Per Share Data ($)

(Year Ended June 30)	2004	2003	2002	2001	2000	1999	1998	1997	1996	1995
Tangible Bk. Val.	NM	NM	NM	NM	NM	NM	NM	1.01	NM	NM
Cash Flow	2.82	2.40	3.64	2.39	3.01	3.20	2.64	1.95	1.75	1.38
Earnings	2.14	1.78	1.79	1.39	1.35	1.67	1.46	1.22	0.97	0.72
S&P Core Earnings	2.01	1.64	0.92	0.92	NA	NA	NA	NA	NA	NA
Dividends	0.43	0.37	0.35	0.33	0.16	0.29	0.27	0.24	0.21	0.18
Payout Ratio	20%	22%	20%	24%	12%	17%	18%	20%	22%	25%
Prices - High	55.94	50.32	47.75	38.97	41.06	42.00	48.50	36.93	26.87	21.25
- Low	48.24	47.09	33.42	26.50	22.37	30.62	26.68	22.12	19.56	11.31
P/E Ratio - High	26	28	27	28	30	25	33	30	28	30
- Low	23	26	19	19	17	18	18	18	20	16

Income Statement Analysis (Million $)

	2004	2003	2002	2001	2000	1999	1998	1997	1996	1995
Revs.	1,162	1,080	988	1,053	1,097	1,036	1,010	855	867	885
Oper. Inc.	238	209	212	204	249	254	217	155	142	112
Depr.	35.2	31.4	93.8	51.6	87.6	82.6	64.5	40.4	44.1	36.4
Int. Exp.	22.7	27.8	33.2	32.9	34.9	22.0	14.7	1.30	5.50	15.1
Pretax Inc.	181	149	149	116	128	152	139	118	100	77.1
Eff. Tax Rate	38.7%	38.7%	38.7%	38.7%	44.3%	41.1%	42.6%	42.9%	45.4%	48.3%
Net Inc.	111	91.1	91.4	71.3	71.0	89.7	79.9	67.6	54.7	39.8
S&P Core Earnings	104	83.5	46.8	47.6	NA	NA	NA	NA	NA	NA

Balance Sheet & Other Fin. Data (Million $)

	2004	2003	2002	2001	2000	1999	1998	1997	1996	1995
Cash	58.7	22.3	28.2	36.3	22.9	11.0	4.95	125	13.8	17.0
Curr. Assets	314	268	272	291	289	256	247	337	211	262
Total Assets	1,466	1,437	1,460	1,438	1,440	1,423	1,067	761	734	882
Curr. Liab.	371	297	307	371	359	344	347	278	280	288
LT Debt	225	375	385	400	455	485	175	Nil	35.0	166
Common Equity	589	501	508	448	423	413	378	327	262	241
Total Cap.	912	948	985	907	926	932	372	350	322	462
Cap. Exp.	24.5	26.6	23.4	56.0	39.4	25.7	46.2	23.3	29.9	24.7
Cash Flow	146	123	185	123	159	172	144	108	99	76.3
Curr. Ratio	0.8	0.9	0.9	0.8	0.8	0.7	0.7	1.2	0.8	0.9
% LT Debt of Cap.	24.7	39.6	39.1	44.1	49.1	52.0	47.0	Nil	10.9	36.0
% Net Inc.of Revs.	9.5	8.4	9.3	6.8	6.5	8.7	7.9	7.9	6.3	4.5
% Ret. on Assets	7.6	6.3	6.3	5.0	5.0	7.2	8.7	9.0	7.4	4.6
% Ret. on Equity	20.4	18.1	19.1	16.4	17.0	22.7	22.7	23.0	21.7	16.0

Data as orig reptd.; bef. results of disc opers/spec. items. Per share data adj. for stk. divs. Bold denotes basic EPS (FASB 128)-prior periods restated. E-Estimated. NA-Not Available. NM-Not Meaningful. NR-Not Ranked. UR-Under Review.

Office: 1716 Locust Street, Des Moines, IA 50309-3023.
Telephone: 515-284-3000.
Website: http://www.meredith.com
Chrmn & CEO: W.T. Kerr.
Pres & COO: S.M. Lacy.
VP & CFO: S.V. Radia.

VP, Secy & General Counsel: J.S. Zieser.
Investor Contact: J. McCoy .
Dirs: H. M. Baum, M. S. Coleman, F. B. Henry, J. W. Johnson, W. T. Kerr, S. M. Lacy, R. E. Lee, D. J. Londoner, P. A. Marineau, M. Meredith Frazier, C. D. Peebler, N. L. Reding.

Founded: in 1902.
Domicile: Iowa.
Employees: 2,696.
S&P Analyst: William H. Donald/PMW/BK

Merrill Lynch

Recommendation: BUY ★★★★★ (SELL SELL HOLD BUY BUY) | **12-Month Target Price: $60.00** (as of July 13, 2004)

MER has an approximate 0.48% weighting in the **S&P 500**

Sector: Financials
Sub-Industry: Investment Banking & Brokerage
Peer Group: Investment Banking/Brokerage - Major

Summary: Merrill Lynch is one of the world's largest and most diversified securities brokerage concerns.

Quantitative Evaluations

S&P Earnings & Dividend Rank: A-

| D | C | B- | B | B+ | **A-** | A | A+ |

S&P Fair Value Rank: 2

| 1 | **2** | 3 | 4 | 5 |
| Lowest | | | | Highest |

Fair Value Calc.: $50.10 (Slightly Overvalued)

S&P Investability Quotient Percentile

91%

MER scored higher than 91% of all companies for which an S&P Report is available.

Volatility: Low

| **Low** | Average | High |

Technical Evaluation: Bullish

Since 10/04, the technical indicators for MER have been Bullish.

Relative Strength Rank: Moderate

66

| 1 Lowest | | Highest 99 |

Price as of 11/12/04: $56.95 | **2004E S&P Core EPS:** $4.17

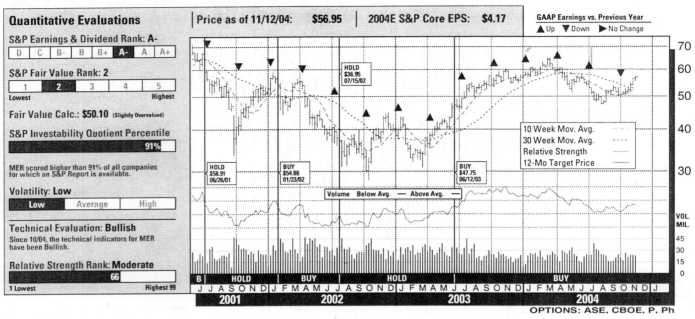

GAAP Earnings vs. Previous Year
▲ Up ▼ Down ► No Change

- 10 Week Mov. Avg.
- 30 Week Mov. Avg.
- Relative Strength
- 12-Mo Target Price

HOLD $36.95 07/15/02
HOLD $58.91 06/26/01
BUY $54.88 01/23/02
BUY $47.75 06/12/03

Volume Below Avg. — Above Avg.

OPTIONS: ASE, CBOE, P, Ph

Analyst commentary prepared by Robert Hansen, CFA /MF/JWP

Highlights November 03, 2004

- We think Merrill Lynch is benefiting from a growing economy, generally improving investor confidence, and relatively low interest rates. Although revenue suffered in the third quarter from sequential declines in brokerage, proprietary trading, and investment banking, results benefited from reduced compensation expenses, a lower tax rate, and aggressive stock buybacks. At the end of September 2004, total client assets were 7% higher than a year earlier, at nearly $1.5 trillion, while assets under management were up 1%, to $478 billion.

- Despite quarterly volatility in MER's various businesses, particularly in its sales and trading operations, we expect fundamentals to improve in 2005. We think MER's commission revenues are more stable than most expect given the mix of both retail and institutional clients. We expect Merrill to expand the number of financial advisers in its Global Private Client Group and expect total headcount to grow modestly in 2004 and 2005, after declining nearly 6% in 2003.

- We think that a positively sloped yield curve, higher corporate profits and anticipated improving investor sentiment will be positive drivers for Merrill's key businesses. We see EPS rising to $4.30 in 2004 and $4.70 in 2005, on higher revenue and prudent expense growth. We expect MER's acquisition of the energy trading operations of Entergy-Koch, which closed in the fourth quarter of 2004, to be accretive to EPS in 2005.

Investment Rationale/Risk November 03, 2004

- We find the shares attractive on a total return basis, given our view of Merrill's improving business momentum, broad business diversification, and prudent expense growth. We think the company's common share repurchase program, which was increased by $2 billion in July, will also help support the valuation. However, our enthusiasm is tempered by inconsistent client inflows and potential market share losses in its brokerage business.

- Risks to our recommendation and target price include stock and bond market volatility, various regulatory issues, and increased price competition, notably from discount brokers. We also note that trading revenues can be highly volatile in any given quarter.

- The stock recently traded at a P/E of nearly 12X our 2005 EPS estimate, which is a discount to the S&P 500 Index, the company's peer group, and Merrill's historical average over the past decade. Our 12-month target price is $60, which is 13X our 2005 EPS estimate. Having declined 8% thus far in 2004, versus a 4% gain for peers, we view the valuation as attractive and recommend accumulating the shares.

Key Stock Statistics

S&P Core EPS 2005E	4.37	52-week Range	$64.89-47.35
S&P Oper. EPS 2004E	4.30	12 Month P/E	11.3
P/E on S&P Oper. EPS 2004E	13.2	Beta	1.57
S&P Oper. EPS 2005E	4.70	Shareholders	19,720
Yield (%)	1.1%	Market Cap (B)	$ 53.5
Dividend Rate/Share	0.64	Shares Outstanding (M)	939.5

Value of $10,000 invested five years ago: **$ 15,294**

Dividend Data Dividends have been paid since 1961

Amount ($)	Date Decl.	Ex-Div. Date	Stock of Record	Payment Date
0.160	Jan. 26	Feb. 04	Feb. 06	Feb. 27 '04
0.160	Apr. 23	May. 05	May. 07	May. 26 '04
0.160	Jul. 26	Aug. 04	Aug. 06	Aug. 25 '04
0.160	Oct. 25	Nov. 03	Nov. 05	Nov. 24 '04

Revenues/Earnings Data Fiscal year ending December 31

Revenues (Million $)

	2004	2003	2002	2001	2000	1999
1Q	7,987	6,923	7,563	11,934	11,306	8,657
2Q	7,376	7,292	7,352	10,320	11,050	8,630
3Q	6,848	6,857	6,860	8,929	10,853	8,412
4Q	—	6,673	6,478	7,574	11,663	9,270
Yr.	—	27,745	28,253	38,757	44,872	34,879

Earnings Per Share ($)

	2004	2003	2002	2001	2000	1999
1Q	1.22	0.72	0.67	0.92	1.24	0.72
2Q	1.06	1.05	0.66	0.56	1.01	0.79
3Q	1.00	1.04	0.73	0.44	0.94	0.67
4Q	E1.10	1.23	0.56	-1.51	0.93	0.90
Yr.	E4.30	4.05	2.63	0.57	4.11	3.08

Next earnings report expected: late-January Source: S&P, Company Reports
EPS Estimates based on S&P Operating Earnings; historical GAAP earnings are as reported.

Merrill Lynch & Co., Inc.

Recommendation: **BUY** ★ ★ ★ ★   12-Month Target Price: **$60.00** (as of July 13, 2004)

Business Summary November 03, 2004

Merrill Lynch is one of the world's largest financial management and advisory companies. It consistently ranks among the largest debt and equity underwriters and mergers and acquisitions advisers on a global basis. MER has three operating segments: Global Markets and Investment Banking (GMI); the Global Private Client Group (GPC); and Merrill Lynch Investment Managers (MLIM). In 2003, GMI accounted for 50% of total net revenues, GPC for 44%, and MLIM for 7%.

GMI serves corporations, financial institutions and governments with comprehensive investment banking and strategic advisory services, including debt and equity trading, underwriting and origination, and mergers and acquisitions. As an investment banker, MER helps corporations and governments raise capital through debt and equity offerings. In its M&A advisory business, it advises corporations on such matters as takeovers, acquisitions, and corporate defenses. Business activity in this segment is supported by a worldwide staff of equity analysts, salespeople and traders. MER has equity trading activities around the globe. The company is investing in areas that it believes complement its existing capabilities and offer opportunities for future growth.

For individual investors, GPC provides service through a segmented offering that meets clients' needs at different levels. Private Wealth Advisors and their teams specialize in sophisticated solutions to meet the needs of MER's most affluent clients, Wealth Management Advisors provide personalized advice and guidance to high-net-worth individuals, while MER's Financial Advisory Center serves more than a million clients who have more basic financial needs. At the end of 2003, MER had about 13,500 private client advisers in about 640 offices with $1.3 trillion in total assets in private client accounts.

MLIM is one of the world's largest investment managers, with $500 billion of assets under management at year-end 2003, compared with $462 billion at the end of 2002. About 70% of MLIM's global assets under management were above benchmark or median for the 1-, 3- and 5- year periods ended December 2003. MLIM serves a globally diversified client base of mutual fund investors, high-net-worth individuals, pension funds, corporations, governments and other institutions.

In late 2001, in response to weak market and business conditions and industry overcapacity, MER launched a restructuring program to "right-size" the company. It recorded a $1.7 billion after-tax charge in the 2001 fourth quarter, in connection with the elimination of about 9,000 positions, real estate rationalization, and technology asset writedowns.

In December 2002, MER and other leading investment banks entered into a $1.4 billion agreement to settle allegations that their research was tainted with conflicts of interest and misled investors; MER's share was $200 million. The banks also agreed to make organizational changes to reduce conflicts of interest in their research departments and to help support independent research and investor education initiatives for a limited period of time.

Company Financials Fiscal Year ending December 31

Per Share Data ($)

(Year Ended December 31)	2003	2002	2001	2000	1999	1998	1997	1996	1995	1994
Tangible Bk. Val.	23.69	20.76	18.38	16.67	10.67	6.08	3.66	9.47	7.87	6.92
Cash Flow	4.05	2.63	0.57	4.11	3.09	1.50	3.00	2.64	NA	NA
Earnings	4.05	2.63	0.57	4.11	3.08	1.50	2.42	2.05	1.36	1.19
S&P Core Earnings	3.79	1.80	-0.51	NA	NA	NA	NA	NA	NA	NA
Dividends	0.64	0.64	0.64	0.60	0.53	0.46	0.38	0.29	0.25	0.22
Payout Ratio	16%	24%	112%	15%	17%	31%	16%	14%	19%	19%
Prices - High	60.47	59.32	80.00	74.62	51.25	54.56	39.09	21.28	16.18	11.40
- Low	30.75	28.21	33.50	36.31	31.00	17.87	19.62	12.34	8.65	8.06
P/E Ratio - High	15	23	NM	18	17	36	16	10	12	10
- Low	8	11	NM	9	10	12	8	6	6	7

Income Statement Analysis (Million $)

	2003	2002	2001	2000	1999	1998	1997	1996	1995	1994
Commissions	4,396	4,657	5,266	6,977	6,334	5,779	4,667	3,786	3,126	2,871
Int. Inc.	11,678	13,178	20,143	21,196	15,097	19,314	17,087	12,899	12,221	9,578
Total Revs.	27,745	28,253	38,757	44,872	34,879	35,853	31,731	25,011	21,513	18,233
Int. Exp.	7,782	9,836	17,072	18,280	13,205	18,306	16,109	11,895	11,248	8,609
Pretax Inc.	5,458	3,566	1,182	5,522	3,883	1,972	3,003	2,566	1,811	1,730
Eff. Tax Rate	26.9%	29.5%	51.5%	31.5%	32.6%	36.2%	36.5%	36.9%	38.5%	41.2%
Net Inc.	3,988	2,513	573	3,784	2,618	1,259	1,906	1,619	1,114	1,017
S&P Core Earnings	3,689	1,694	-441	NA	NA	NA	NA	NA	NA	NA

Balance Sheet & Other Fin. Data (Million $)

	2003	2002	2001	2000	1999	1998	1997	1996	1995	1994
Total Assets	494,518	447,928	419,419	407,200	328,071	299,804	292,819	213,016	176,857	163,749
Cash Items	25,321	17,586	93,357	78,548	26,852	23,725	17,416	9,003	8,503	7,265
Receivables	105,182	100,462	86,039	103,482	77,336	135,422	114,315	116,222	95,865	91,917
Secs. Owned	134,309	100,216	92,883	91,514	106,734	107,845	106,778	75,524	60,103	52,739
Sec. Borrowed	107,219	93,018	87,186	103,883	99,741	81,417	122,725	102,002	86,363	78,304
Due Brokers & Cust.	47,968	45,110	40,636	34,276	34,119	28,871	20,631	15,000	17,757	16,247
Other Liabs.	109,720	95,804	79,654	72,765	71,880	117,432	98,044	62,855	49,256	48,517
Capitalization:										
Debt	85,969	59,070	79,267	72,937	56,190	78,869	43,090	26,721	17,757	14,863
Equity	27,226	22,450	19,583	17,879	12,377	9,707	7,904	6,273	5,522	5,199
Total	113,620	81,945	99,275	91,241	68,992	85,576	52,055	33,940	23,481	20,681
% Return On Revs.	17.1	10.7	1.7	10.0	9.2	3.5	6.0	6.5	5.2	5.6
% Ret. on Assets	0.8	0.6	0.1	1.1	0.8	0.4	0.8	0.8	0.7	0.6
% Ret. on Equity	15.9	11.8	2.9	24.6	23.4	13.9	26.3	26.8	20.8	18.6

Data as orig reptd.; bef. results of disc opers/spec. items. Per share data adj. for stk. divs.; EPS diluted. E-Estimated. NA-Not Available. NM-Not Meaningful. NR-Not Ranked. UR-Under Review.

Office: 4 World Financial Center, New York, NY 10080.
Telephone: 212-449-1000.
Website: http://www.ml.com
Chrmn, Pres & CEO: E.S. O'Neal.
Vice Chrmn: H. McMahon.
Vice Chrmn: J.B. Quigley.

Vice Chrmn & SVP: S.R. Chapin.
EVP & CFO: A.L. Fakahany.
Investor Contact: T. Madon 866-607-1234.
Dirs: W. H. Clark, J. K. Conway, A. Cribiore, J. D. Finnegan, H. Neuburger, D. K. Newbigging, E. S. O'Neal, A. L. Peters, J. W. Prueher.

Founded: in 1820.
Domicile: Delaware.
Employees: 48,100.
S&P Analyst: Robert Hansen, CFA /MF/JWP

MetLife Inc.

Recommendation: **HOLD** ★★★☆☆
12-Month Target Price: **$43.00**
(as of October 07, 2004)

MET has an approximate 0.26% weighting in the **S&P 500**

Sector: Financials
Sub-Industry: Life & Health Insurance
Peer Group: Life/Health Insurers

Summary: MET became a leading publicly traded U.S. life insurer after its demutualization and April 2000 IPO.

Quantitative Evaluations

S&P Earnings & Dividend Rank: NR

D	C	B-	B	B+	A-	A	A+

S&P Fair Value Rank: 5

1	2	3	4	5
Lowest				Highest

Fair Value Calc.: $48.70 (Undervalued)

S&P Investability Quotient Percentile

96%

MET scored higher than 96% of all companies for which an S&P Report is available.

Volatility: Average

Low	Average	High

Technical Evaluation: Bullish
Since 11/04, the technical indicators for MET have been Bullish.

Relative Strength Rank: Moderate

43

1 Lowest	Highest 99

Price as of 11/12/04: $38.40 | **2004E S&P Core EPS:** $3.08

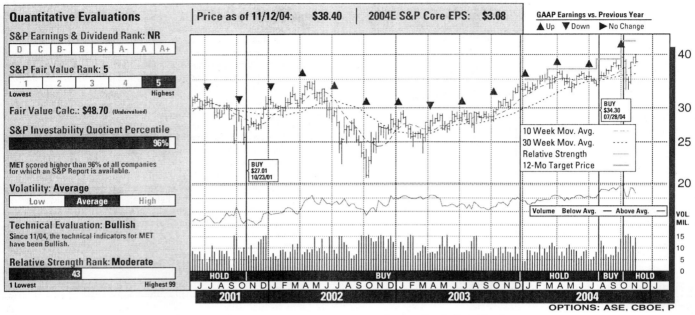

GAAP Earnings vs. Previous Year ▲ Up ▼ Down ▶ No Change

10 Week Mov. Avg.
30 Week Mov. Avg.
Relative Strength
12-Mo Target Price

Volume Below Avg. — Above Avg.

OPTIONS: ASE, CBOE, P

Analyst commentary prepared by Gregory Simcik, CFA /MF/GG

Highlights October 08, 2004

- We believe earnings growth for the institutional segment could exceed 20% in 2004, bolstered by easy comparisons with weak results in 2003. We think profits will increase at a single digit rate in the individual segment, aided by an expansion of the MetLife Financial Services distribution channel.

- We predict continued rapid growth in the international segment, which could account for 7.6% of total operating profits in 2004, up from 6.7% in 2003. We are also forecasting a 20%-plus rise in earnings for the auto and home segment, on 3.1% premium growth and improved underwriting margins. We estimate earnings will grow at a low double digit rate for the reinsurance segment and could nearly double for the smaller asset management segment.

- We expect consolidated operating EPS to rise 16% in 2004, to $3.27, and to rise 10% in 2005, to $3.60. Our 2004 and 2005 Standard & Poor's Core Earnings per share estimates are $3.08 and $3.59, respectively, reflecting projected stock option and pension expenses.

Investment Rationale/Risk October 08, 2004

- We believe MET offers investors a potential return comparable to that of the S&P 500 Index, and therefore have a hold recommendation on the shares. We believe higher interest rates should benefit investment spreads at MET, although probably not until 2005 at the earliest. We also believe growth in operating EPS could benefit from share repurchases, as MET has reiterated its goal to buy back at least $500 million in company stock during 2004.

- Risks to our recommendation and target price include the possibility that policies for some large group insurance buyers may not be renewed in a competitive environment. Additional risks include, in our view, exposure to asbestos-related liability claims, international operations in emerging markets, and catastrophic risks for homeowner and automobile lines.

- We base our 12-month target price of $43 on a trailing P/E multiple of 12X our 2005 operating EPS estimate, a slight premium to the historical multiple of 11.5X.

Key Stock Statistics

S&P Core EPS 2005E	3.59	52-week Range	$40.36-30.07
S&P Oper. EPS 2004E	3.45	12 Month P/E	9.6
P/E on S&P Oper. EPS 2004E	11.1	Beta	NA
S&P Oper. EPS 2005E	3.65	Shareholders	39,368
Yield (%)	1.2%	Market Cap (B)	$ 28.6
Dividend Rate/Share	0.46	Shares Outstanding (M)	744.3

Value of $10,000 invested five years ago: **NA**

Dividend Data Dividends have been paid since 2000

Amount ($)	Date Decl.	Ex-Div. Date	Stock of Record	Payment Date
0.230	Oct. 21	Nov. 05	Nov. 07	Dec. 15 '03
0.460	Sep. 28	Nov. 03	Nov. 05	Dec. 13 '04

Revenues/Earnings Data Fiscal year ending December 31

Revenues (Million $)

	2004	2003	2002	2001	2000	1999
1Q	9,503	8,364	7,973	7,971	—	—
2Q	9,579	8,862	8,244	7,811	8,111	—
3Q	10,048	8,816	8,120	7,970	7,744	—
4Q	—	9,747	8,810	8,399	8,426	—
Yr.	—	35,790	33,147	31,928	31,947	19,244

Earnings Per Share ($)

	2004	2003	2002	2001	2000	1999
1Q	0.87	0.38	0.41	0.37	—	—
2Q	1.12	0.78	0.50	0.41	0.44	—
3Q	0.93	0.74	0.43	0.21	0.31	—
4Q	E0.81	0.68	0.24	-0.41	0.74	—
Yr.	E3.45	2.57	1.58	0.62	1.49	1.21

Next earnings report expected: mid-February Source: S&P, Company Reports
EPS Estimates based on S&P Operating Earnings; historical GAAP earnings are as reported.

Recommendation: **HOLD** ★ ★ ★ ☆ ☆   12-Month Target Price: **$43.00** (as of October 07, 2004)

Business Summary October 08, 2004

MetLife (MET) is one of the largest insurance and financial services companies in the U.S. At the end of 2003, MET serviced approximately 13 million households and provided benefits to approximately 37 million employees and family members through their plan sponsors, including 88 of the FORTUNE 100 largest companies. MET also has international operations serving approximately 8 million customers in 10 countries at December 31, 2003. Formerly a mutual insurance company, MetLife demutualized and issued a publicly traded stock in 2000.

MET is organized into six business segments: institutional, individual, auto and home, international, reinsurance, and asset management. The institutional segment accounted for 40% of consolidated revenues in 2003 (39% in 2002), the individual segment accounted for 35% (38%), the auto and home segment accounted for 8.6% (9.0%), the international segment accounted for 7.1% (6.4%), the reinsurance segment accounted for 9.0% (7.5%), and the asset management segment accounted for 0.6% (0.7%).

The institutional segment offers group insurance and retirement and savings products, including life, non-medical health, long-term care, and dental insurance, as well as annuities, guaranteed interest contracts (GICs), and full service defined contribution programs for small and mid-sized companies. The individual segment offers traditional, universal, and variable life insurance, variable and fixed annuities, and products cross-sold from other segments. According to the Life Insurance Marketing and Research Association, MET was the second largest issuer of

individual variable life insurance, the fifth largest issuer of all individual life insurance products, and the fourth largest annuity writer in the U.S. for sales through September 30, 2003.

The auto and home segment offers insurance through employer-sponsored programs and a variety of retail distribution channels. Auto and homeowner's insurance represented 74% and 24%, respectively, of net premiums for the segment in 2003. The international segment offers a variety of insurance and retirement and savings products in Latin America and the Asia/Pacific region. The reinsurance segment includes the global business of Reinsurance Group of America (RGA), where MET held an approximate 52% stake at December 31, 2003. The asset management segment, State Street Research, includes a retail and institutional investment manager and a real estate investment advisor. At December 31, 2003, State Street Research had $47.5 billion of assets under management.

In August 2004, MET announced a definitive agreement to sell SSRM Holdings Inc, the holding company for State Street Research & Management Company and SSR Realty Advisors Inc., to BlackRock, Inc. for $375 million in cash and BlackRock stock, with the potential for additional contingent cash consideration. Management expected the deal could close in early 2005, subject to regulatory and fund shareholder approvals, and would not have a material impact on MET's 2005 operating earnings.

Company Financials Fiscal Year ending December 31

Per Share Data ($)

(Year Ended December 31)	2003	2002	2001	2000	1999	1998	1997	1996	1995	1994
Tangible Bk. Val.	27.94	24.83	22.43	21.53	NA	NA	NA	NA	NA	NA
Oper. Earnings	NA	NA	NA	NA	NA	NA	NA	NA	NA	NA
Earnings	2.57	1.58	0.62	1.49	1.21	NA	NA	NA	NA	NA
S&P Core Earnings	2.87	2.06	0.91	NA	NA	NA	NA	NA	NA	NA
Dividends	0.23	0.21	0.20	0.20	NA	NA	NA	NA	NA	NA
Payout Ratio	9%	13%	32%	13%	NA	NA	NA	NA	NA	NA
Prices - High	34.14	34.85	36.62	36.50	NA	NA	NA	NA	NA	NA
- Low	23.51	20.60	24.70	14.25	NA	NA	NA	NA	NA	NA
P/E Ratio - High	13	22	59	24	NA	NA	NA	NA	NA	NA
- Low	9	13	40	10	NA	NA	NA	NA	NA	NA

Income Statement Analysis (Million $)

	2003	2002	2001	2000	1999	1998	1997	1996	1995	1994
Life Ins. In Force	3,875,110	2,679,870	2,419,341	2,572,261	NA	NA	NA	NA	NA	NA
Prem. Inc.: Life	14,065	13,070	11,611	11,224	NA	NA	NA	NA	NA	NA
Prem. Inc.: A & H	3,537	3,052	2,744	2,377	NA	NA	NA	NA	NA	NA
Net Invest. Inc.	11,636	11,329	11,923	11,768	7,639	NA	NA	NA	NA	NA
Total Revs.	36,147	33,147	31,928	31,947	19,244	NA	NA	NA	NA	NA
Pretax Inc.	2,630	1,671	739	1,416	1,357	NA	NA	NA	NA	NA
Net Oper. Inc.	NA	NA	NA	NA	NA	NA	NA	NA	NA	NA
Net Inc.	1,943	1,155	473	953	918	NA	NA	NA	NA	NA
S&P Core Earnings	2,144	1,512	697	NA	NA	NA	NA	NA	NA	NA

Balance Sheet & Other Fin. Data (Million $)

	2003	2002	2001	2000	1999	1998	1997	1996	1995	1994
Cash & Equiv.	5,919	4,411	9,535	5,484	4,097	NA	NA	NA	NA	NA
Premiums Due	7,047	7,669	6,437	8,343	6,552	NA	NA	NA	NA	NA
Invest. Assets: Bonds	167,752	140,553	115,398	112,979	75,252	NA	NA	NA	NA	NA
Invest. Assets: Stocks	1,598	1,348	3,063	2,193	2,006	NA	NA	NA	NA	NA
Invest. Assets: Loans	34,998	33,666	31,893	30,109	16,805	NA	NA	NA	NA	NA
Invest. Assets: Total	218,099	188,335	162,222	156,527	105,187	NA	NA	NA	NA	NA
Deferred Policy Costs	12,943	11,727	11,167	10,618	4,416	NA	NA	NA	NA	NA
Total Assets	326,841	277,385	256,898	255,018	226,791	NA	NA	NA	NA	NA
Debt	5,703	5,690	4,884	3,516	3,350	NA	NA	NA	NA	NA
Common Equity	21,149	17,385	16,062	16,389	13,873	NA	NA	NA	NA	NA
% Return On Revs.	5.4	3.5	1.5	3.0	4.8	NA	NA	NA	NA	NA
% Ret. on Assets	0.6	0.4	0.2	0.4	NA	NA	NA	NA	NA	NA
% Ret. on Equity	10.1	6.9	2.9	6.3	NA	NA	NA	NA	NA	NA
% Invest. Yield	5.7	6.5	7.5	8.0	NA	NA	NA	NA	NA	NA

Data as orig reptd.; bef. results of disc opers/spec. items. Per share data adj. for stk. divs.; EPS diluted. E-Estimated. NA-Not Available. NM-Not Meaningful. NR-Not Ranked.Oper. EPS est. excl. real. inv. gains/losses; historical EPS data incl. them.

Office: 1 Madison Ave, New York, NY 10010-3681.
Telephone: 212-578-2211.
Website: http://www.metlife.com
Chrmn & CEO: R.H. Benmosche.
Pres & COO: C.R. Henrikson.
Vice Chrmn: S.G. Nagler.
EVP & CFO: W.J. Wheeler.

EVP & General Counsel: J.L. Libscomb.
Investor Contact: K. Helmintoller 212-578-5140.
Dirs: C. H. Barnette, R. H. Benmosche, B. A. Dole, Jr., C. W. Grise, J. R. Houghton, H. P. Kamen, H. L. Kaplan, J. M. Keane, C. R. Kinney, C. M. Leighton, S. M. Mathews, S. G. Nagler, J. J. Phelan, Jr., H. B. Price, K. J. Sicchitano, W. C. Steere, Jr.

Founded: in 1999.
Domicile: Delaware.
Employees: 49,000.
S&P Analyst: Gregory Simcik, CFA /MF/GG

MGIC Investment

Recommendation: **HOLD** ★★★☆☆
SELL SELL Hold BUY BUY

12-Month Target Price: $70.00
(as of October 14, 2004)

MTG has an approximate 0.06% weighting in the **S&P 500**

Sector: Financials
Sub-Industry: Thrifts & Mortgage Finance
Peer Group: Mortgage/Title Insurers

Summary: Through its Mortgage Guaranty Insurance Corp. unit, this holding company is a leading U.S. provider of private mortgage insurance (PMI) coverage.

Quantitative Evaluations

S&P Earnings & Dividend Rank: A

| D | C | B- | B | B+ | A- | A | A+ |

S&P Fair Value Rank: 5

| 1 | 2 | 3 | 4 | 5 |
| Lowest | | | | Highest |

Fair Value Calc.: $79.30 (Undervalued)

S&P Investability Quotient Percentile

98%

MTG scored higher than 98% of all companies for which an S&P Report is available.

Volatility: Average

| Low | Average | High |

Technical Evaluation: Bearish
Since 10/04, the technical indicators for MTG have been Bearish.

Relative Strength Rank: Moderate

38

| 1 Lowest | Highest 99 |

| Price as of 11/12/04: | **$67** | 2004E S&P Core EPS: | **$5.51** |

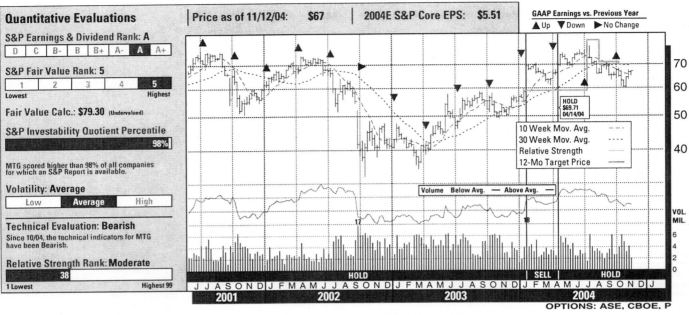

GAAP Earnings vs. Previous Year
▲ Up ▼ Down ▶ No Change

HOLD
$69.71
04/14/04

10 Week Mov. Avg.
30 Week Mov. Avg.
Relative Strength
12-Mo Target Price

Volume Below Avg. — Above Avg. —

HOLD | SELL | HOLD
2001 | 2002 | 2003 | 2004

OPTIONS: ASE, CBOE, P

Analyst commentary prepared by Erik J. Eisenstein/CB/JWP

Highlights October 19, 2004

- On a year-over-year basis, we expect a 1% decline in premiums earned in 2005, reflecting the effect of recent heavy refinancing activity. However, we expect the pace of refinancing to tail off in coming periods, reflecting the prior exhaustion of candidates coupled with higher fixed mortgage rates anticipated in the coming year. Heading into 2005, we expect this to be a net positive factor for MTG, despite reduced new insurance writing, reflecting increased persistence of in-force policies. As a result, we expect sequential increases in premiums earned to begin in the first quarter, and continue throughout 2005. With a reduction in contract underwriting revenue, due to an anticipated less vibrant mortgage origination market and lower realized gains, we see a 2% drop in revenue in 2004.

- We expect a 5% decline in losses and loss expenses in 2005, reflecting improved loss trends, based on our view of a stronger overall economy and labor market. After a projected 20% decrease in underwriting expenses, on a forecast reduction in new policy volume, we see total expenses down 9%.

- With our expectation of less income from joint ventures, we forecast that 2005 EPS will climb 8%, to $6.10, from $5.66 projected for 2004.

Key Stock Statistics

S&P Core EPS 2005E	6.03	52-week Range	$78.95-49.98
S&P Oper. EPS 2004E	5.66	12 Month P/E	12.6
P/E on S&P Oper. EPS 2004E	11.8	Beta	0.97
S&P Oper. EPS 2005E	6.10	Shareholders	164,000
Yield (%)	0.4%	Market Cap (B)	$ 6.6
Dividend Rate/Share	0.30	Shares Outstanding (M)	98.5

Value of $10,000 invested five years ago: **$ 11,578**

Dividend Data Dividends have been paid since 1991

Amount ($)	Date Decl.	Ex-Div. Date	Stock of Record	Payment Date
0.038	Jan. 29	Feb. 09	Feb. 11	Mar. 01 '04
0.038	May. 13	May. 20	May. 24	Jun. 09 '04
0.075	Jul. 29	Aug. 10	Aug. 12	Sep. 01 '04
0.075	Oct. 28	Nov. 08	Nov. 10	Dec. 01 '04

Investment Rationale/Risk October 19, 2004

- We project MTG's annual EPS growth rate in the five years beyond 2005 at 11.5%, reflecting a combination of positive and negative influences. On the plus side, we believe policies written during recent periods of record low mortgage rates will prove unusually persistent over that five-year period. On the downside, we remain concerned about increased competition from other financial institutions, including captive reinsurance subsidiaries of mortgage lenders. In addition, we see MTG with a larger subprime mortgage insurance business than its industry peers, giving rise, in our view, to a more volatile and cyclical earnings profile.

- Risks to our opinion and target price include competitive risks, as well as the risk that loss trends will not improve as rapidly as we project. Risks also include a significant decline in fixed mortgage rates, which could result in a further drop in persistency of in-force policies.

- Our 12-month target price of $70 is derived by applying a P/E multiple of 11.5X to our 2005 EPS estimate of $6.10, about in line with the stock's historical average. The multiple also indicates a P/E to growth (PEG) ratio of 1.0X, a bit below other financial institutions, which tend to trade at a 1.1 PEG ratio.

Revenues/Earnings Data Fiscal year ending December 31

Revenues (Million $)

	2004	2003	2002	2001	2000	1999
1Q	415.4	422.9	375.6	320.5	261.2	246.7
2Q	403.1	459.6	383.8	339.5	274.2	249.9
3Q	391.0	445.6	390.8	339.8	282.7	250.4
4Q	—	401.6	415.6	358.0	292.3	249.8
Yr.	—	1,685	1,566	1,358	1,110	996.8

Earnings Per Share ($)

	2004	2003	2002	2001	2000	1999
1Q	1.31	1.42	1.58	1.46	1.19	0.91
2Q	1.56	1.46	1.61	1.49	1.27	1.02
3Q	1.36	1.06	1.47	1.47	1.36	1.11
4Q	E1.43	1.05	1.37	1.50	1.23	1.25
Yr.	E5.66	4.99	6.04	5.93	5.05	4.30

Next earnings report expected: mid-January Source: S&P, Company Reports
EPS Estimates based on S&P Operating Earnings; historical GAAP earnings are as reported.

MGIC Investment Corporation

Recommendation: **HOLD** ★ ★ ★ ☆ ☆   12-Month Target Price: **$70.00** (as of October 14, 2004)

Business Summary October 19, 2004

By providing mortgage insurance on low down payment home loans, MGIC Investment seeks to make the dream of home ownership a reality for many Americans. Private mortgage insurance (PMI) lets home buyers purchase homes with down payments of under 20% by reducing default risk borne by lenders. In addition, by improving the credit quality of the underlying loans, mortgage insurance facilitates the sale of mortgage loans in the secondary market, principally to Freddie Mac and Fannie Mae. MTG has been the leading provider of mortgage insurance in terms of new insurance written since 1995.

Primary insurance may be written on a flow basis, in which loans are insured in individual, loan-by-loan transactions, or on a bulk basis, in which a portfolio of loans is insured in a single bulk transaction. MTG's writings of bulk insurance are in part sensitive to the volume of securitization involving non-conforming loans (loans that do not conform to the underwriting standards of Freddie Mac and Fannie Mae). New primary insurance written in bulk transactions increased to 27% of new primary insurance written in 2003, from 24% in 2002.

The company believes its competitive strengths lie in its risk management, productivity and financial strength and stability. MTG also competes by offering its customers a wide range of products and services designed to enhance profitability, including contract underwriting, eMagic.com and Defender. eMagic.com is a neutral website that provides access to all products and services necessary to assemble a home mortgage. Defender is an interactive voice and web response system that lenders can employ to help retain customers.

Effective March 31, 2003, MTG decided that it would not participate in certain risk sharing arrangements with mortgage lenders through captive mortgage reinsurance transactions. The captive mortgage insurance programs of larger lenders were not consistent with the company's position. As a result, the company experienced a reduction in business from such lenders in 2003 from the level of 2002.

The percentage of primary insured loans in default was 5.57% at December 31, 2003, up from 4.45% a year earlier and 3.46% at the end of 2001. The deterioration reflected the maturation of MTG's book of business and a higher volume of bulk business, together with a soft economy.

MTG owns about 46% of Credit-Based Asset Servicing and Securitization LLC and Litton Loan Servicing LP (collectively, C-BASS). C-BASS principally acquires and resolves delinquent single-family residential mortgage loans. MTG also owns 41.5% of Sherman Financial Group. Sherman purchases, services and securitizes delinquent consumer assets, such as credit card loans and Chapter 13 bankruptcy debt. Both C-BASS and Sherman are joint ventures with Radian Group.

In October 2002, directors authorized the repurchase of up to 5 million company common shares. In May 2003, directors authorized the purchase of an additional 5 million shares.

Company Financials Fiscal Year ending December 31

Per Share Data ($)

(Year Ended December 31)	2003	2002	2001	2000	1999	1998	1997	1996	1995	1994
Tangible Bk. Val.	38.58	33.87	28.47	23.07	16.79	15.05	13.07	11.59	9.57	7.17
Oper. Earnings	NA	NA	NA	NA	NA	3.29	2.73	NA	NA	NA
Earnings	4.99	6.04	5.93	5.05	4.30	3.39	2.75	2.17	1.75	1.35
S&P Core Earnings	4.72	5.71	5.53	NA	NA	NA	NA	NA	NA	NA
Dividends	0.11	0.10	0.10	0.10	0.10	0.10	0.10	0.08	0.08	0.08
Payout Ratio	2%	2%	2%	2%	2%	3%	4%	4%	5%	6%
Prices - High	58.77	74.40	77.31	71.50	62.75	74.50	66.93	38.87	31.00	17.12
- Low	35.30	33.60	50.56	31.93	30.12	24.25	34.93	25.25	16.37	12.50
P/E Ratio - High	12	12	13	14	15	22	24	18	18	13
- Low	7	6	9	6	7	7	13	12	9	9

Income Statement Analysis (Million $)

	2003	2002	2001	2000	1999	1998	1997	1996	1995	1994
Premium Inc.	1,366	1,182	1,042	890	793	763	709	617	507	404
Net Invest. Inc.	203	208	204	179	153	143	124	105	87.5	75.2
Oth. Revs.	117	176	111	41.7	51.1	65.4	35.0	23.2	23.8	23.0
Total Revs.	1,685	1,566	1,358	1,110	997	972	869	746	618	502
Pretax Inc.	640	898	932	789	681	555	465	365	291	217
Net Oper. Inc.	NA	NA	NA	NA	NA	NA	NA	NA	NA	NA
Net Inc.	494	629	639	542	470	385	324	258	208	160
S&P Core Earnings	468	595	597	NA	NA	NA	NA	NA	NA	NA

Balance Sheet & Other Fin. Data (Million $)

	2003	2002	2001	2000	1999	1998	1997	1996	1995	1994
Cash & Equiv.	83.2	69.5	85.4	57.0	49.0	46.1	40.4	37.2	38.9	27.8
Premiums Due	140	127	35.3	41.8	Nil	Nil	Nil	Nil	Nil	NA
Invest. Assets: Bonds	5,059	4,613	3,889	3,299	2,667	2,603	2,301	2,032	1,683	1,289
Invest. Assets: Stocks	8.28	10.8	20.7	22.0	Nil	4.63	116	4.04	3.84	3.60
Invest. Assets: Loans	Nil	Nil	Nil	Nil	Nil	Nil	Nil	Nil	Nil	Nil
Invest. Assets: Total	5,513	5,069	4,231	3,472	2,790	2,780	2,417	2,036	1,687	1,293
Deferred Policy Costs	32.6	31.9	32.1	25.8	22.4	24.1	27.0	32.0	38.0	42.9
Total Assets	5,917	5,300	4,567	3,858	3,104	3,051	2,618	2,222	1,875	1,476
Debt	315	677	472	397	425	442	238	35.4	35.8	36.1
Common Equity	4,859	4,128	3,020	2,465	1,776	1,641	1,487	1,366	1,121	838
Prop. & Cas. Loss Ratio	56.1	30.9	15.4	10.3	12.3	27.7	34.2	38.0	37.5	37.9
Prop. & Cas. Expense Ratio	14.1	14.8	16.5	16.4	19.7	19.6	18.4	21.6	24.6	28.1
Prop. & Cas. Combined Ratio	70.2	45.7	31.9	26.7	32.0	47.3	52.6	59.6	62.1	66.0
% Return On Revs.	29.3	40.2	47.1	48.8	47.2	39.7	37.3	34.6	41.1	31.9
% Ret. on Equity	11.0	16.2	23.3	25.6	27.5	24.7	22.7	20.7	21.2	20.6

Data as orig reptd.; bef. results of disc opers/spec. items. Per share data adj. for stk. divs.; EPS diluted. E-Estimated. NA-Not Available. NM-Not Meaningful. NR-Not Ranked. UR-Under Review.

Office: 250 East Kilbourn Avenue, Milwaukee, WI 53202.
Telephone: 414-347-6480.
Website: http://www.mgic.com
Pres & CEO: C.S. Culver.
EVP & CFO: J.M. Lauer.

SVP, Secy & General Counsel: J.H. Lane.
Investor Contact: M.J. Zimmerman 414-347-6596.
Dirs: J. A. Abbott, M. K. Bush, K. E. Case, C. S. Culver, D. S. Engelman, T. M. Hagerty, K. M. Jastrow II, D. P. Kearney, M. E. Lehman, W. A. McIntosh, L. M. Muma.

Founded: in 1984.
Domicile: Wisconsin.
Employees: 1,300.
S&P Analyst: Erik J. Eisenstein/CB/JWP

Micron Technology

Recommendation: HOLD ★ ★ ★ ☆ ☆
SELL | SELL | HOLD | BUY | BUY

12-Month Target Price: **$13.00**
(as of September 30, 2004)

MU has an approximate 0.07% weighting in the **S&P 500**

Sector: Information Technology
Sub-Industry: Semiconductors
Peer Group: Semiconductors - Memory

Summary: MU is a leading manufacturer of semiconductor memories and other semiconductor components.

Quantitative Evaluations

S&P Earnings & Dividend Rank: C

| D | C | B- | B | B+ | A- | A | A+ |

S&P Fair Value Rank: 5

| 1 | 2 | 3 | 4 | 5 |
| Lowest | | | | Highest |

Fair Value Calc.: $14.10 (Slightly Undervalued)

S&P Investability Quotient Percentile

93%

MU scored higher than 93% of all companies for which an S&P Report is available.

Volatility: High

| Low | Average | High |

Technical Evaluation: Bearish
Since 10/04, the technical indicators for MU have been Bearish.

Relative Strength Rank: Weak

25

| 1 Lowest | | Highest 99 |

| Price as of 11/12/04: | $12.01 | 2005E S&P Core EPS: | $0.16 |

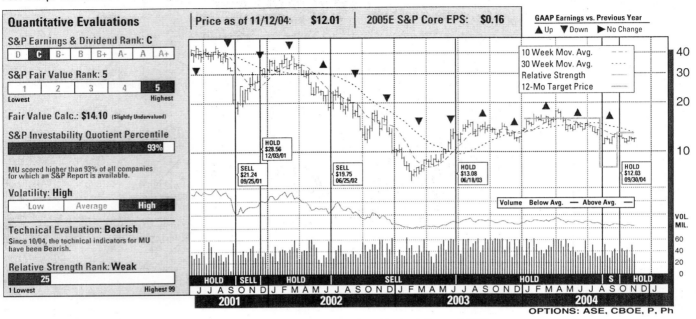

GAAP Earnings vs. Previous Year
▲ Up ▼ Down ► No Change

10 Week Mov. Avg.
30 Week Mov. Avg.
Relative Strength
12-Mo Target Price

HOLD $28.56 12/03/01
SELL $21.24 09/25/01
SELL $19.75 06/25/02
HOLD $13.08 06/18/03
HOLD $12.03 09/30/04

Volume   Below Avg. — Above Avg.

HOLD | SELL | HOLD | SELL | HOLD | S | HOLD
J J A S O N D | J F M A M J J A S O N D | J F M A M J J A S O N D | J F M A M J J A S O N D | J F M A M J J A S O N D | J
2001 | 2002 | 2003 | 2004

OPTIONS: ASE, CBOE, P, Ph

Analyst commentary prepared by Amrit Tewary/MF/BK

Highlights October 01, 2004

- We project that sales will rise about 15% in FY 05 (Aug.) from FY 04 levels. We expect strong unit volume growth to more than offset pricing pressures, especially for DRAM chips.

- On June 16, 2004, the company's Japanese subsidiary and Japanese DRAM maker Elpida Memory filed a petition against South Korea-based competitor Hynix Semiconductor seeking duties on Hynix imports into Japan. The petition parallels similar actions in Europe and the U.S. In September 2003, Intel made an equity investment of $450 million in MU, to support development of DDR2 memory products. We view this as an aid to MU's competitiveness.

- We estimate FY 05 EPS of $0.66, versus $0.24 posted in FY 04. After adjusting for projected stock option expense of $0.50 per share, we see 2005 Standard & Poor's Core Earnings of $0.16 per share.

Investment Rationale/Risk October 01, 2004

- We would hold MU shares. We expect November quarter sales results to benefit from healthy unit volume gains and stable pricing trends for DRAM chips. Also, we are encouraged by the relatively low levels of inventory within the company's distribution channel. However, we would be watchful for a potential imbalance in supply and demand during FY 05 (Aug.), as MU ramps 300 mm production. We believe an oversupply scenario could lead to severe pricing pressure.

- Risks to our opinion and target price include fluctuations in end-market demand; semiconductor industry cyclicality; competition; risks of financing, maintaining and managing wafer fabrication plants; and above-average share price volatility.

- Our 12-month target price of $13 is based on our price-to-sales model, and is derived by applying a multiple of 1.8X (below the historical norm) to our projected FY 05 sales per share. Our target price also implies a below historical-norm P/E of 20X our FY 05 EPS estimate. We believe a discount multiple is warranted, given some near-term macro concerns and the relatively large divergence between operating EPS and S&P Core EPS.

Key Stock Statistics

S&P Oper. EPS 2005E	0.66	52-week Range	$18.25-10.89
P/E on S&P Oper. EPS 2005E	18.2	12 Month P/E	50.0
S&P Oper. EPS 2006E	0.58	Beta	2.37
Yield (%)	Nil	Shareholders	3,944
Dividend Rate/Share	Nil	Market Cap (B)	$7.4
Shares Outstanding (M)	612.4		

Value of $10,000 invested five years ago: **$3,090**

Dividend Data

The most recent cash dividend was a payment of $0.05 a share in May 1996.

Revenues/Earnings Data Fiscal year ending August 31

Revenues (Million $)

	2004	2003	2002	2001	2000	1999
1Q	1,107	685.1	423.9	1,572	1,584	793.6
2Q	991.0	785.0	645.9	1,066	1,393	1,026
3Q	1,117	732.7	771.2	818.3	1,789	863.8
4Q	1,189	888.5	748.0	480.3	2,570	1,081
Yr.	4,404	3,091	2,589	3,936	7,336	3,764

Earnings Per Share ($)

	2004	2003	2002	2001	2000	1999
1Q	Nil	-0.52	-0.44	0.59	0.59	-0.10
2Q	-0.04	-1.02	-0.05	-0.01	0.29	0.04
3Q	0.13	-0.36	-0.04	-0.50	0.47	-0.05
4Q	0.14	-0.20	-0.97	-0.96	1.21	-0.04
Yr.	0.24	-2.11	-1.51	-0.88	2.56	-0.13

Next earnings report expected: late-December Source: S&P, Company Reports
EPS Estimates based on S&P Operating Earnings; historical GAAP earnings are as reported.

Micron Technology, Inc.

Recommendation: **HOLD** ★ ★ ★ ☆ ☆   12-Month Target Price: **$13.00** (as of September 30, 2004)

Business Summary October 01, 2004

Micron Technology is one of the largest global suppliers of dynamic random access memory (DRAM) chips, the most widely used semiconductor memory component in personal computers (PCs). The company's fortunes are linked to PC markets, and to the rise and fall of prices of commodity memory chips. DRAM sales accounted for 96% of total sales in FY 03 (Aug.).

About 82% of FY 03 total sales were to the computing market. Dell Computer and Hewlett-Packard together accounted for 28% of FY 03 sales.

The company's primary product in FY 03 was the 256 megabit double data rate synchronous DRAM (DDR SDRAM), which is available in various configurations, speeds, and package types. DDR SDRAM accounted for 60% of sales in FY 03, up from 21% in FY 02. The overall primary product in FY 02 was the 128 megabit SDRAM. Commercial volumes of next-generation 512 megabit and 1 gigabit DDR SDRAM began shipping in FY 03.

SDRAM operates faster than DRAM, partly because of a clock that synchronizes inputs. DDR SDRAM supports data transfers on both edges of each clock cycle, creating superior data throughput.

From 1993 to 1995, favorable industry dynamics led to strong growth in revenues and earnings at MU. However, prospects for strong profits led many competitors, primarily from Korea and Japan, to add significant productive capacity for DRAMs. Although the need for memory continued to grow with the PC industry, DRAM supply soon outstripped demand. As a result, prices for commodity DRAM products plummeted from FY 96 through FY 99. Although FY 00 saw some price stabilization, pricing softened again from FY 01 to FY 03. The company's average selling prices fell 17% in FY 03, while total megabits of semiconductor memory sold advanced 44%, contributing to a 19% increase in revenue.

In light of the commodity nature of DRAMs, diligent cost control is an essential ingredient for success in the industry. MU believes it is one of the most cost-efficient producers in the memory industry. As of December 2003, a transition of all manufacturing to advanced 0.11 micron line-width technology was about 60% completed. According to the company, the capability to move to leading-edge production technology helps it improve manufacturing efficiency by shrinking die sizes, thereby maximizing the number of units produced on a given silicon wafer.

The company operates manufacturing facilities in the U.S., Italy, Japan, Singapore and Scotland. In February 2003, in response to weak market conditions, MU announced a series of cost reduction initiatives, including a 10% reduction in workforce.

MU makes non-DRAM semiconductor products, including flash memory components (1% of total sales in FY 03) and complementary metal-oxide semiconductor (CMOS) image sensors (less than 1%). Static random access memory (SRAM) chips accounted for 2% of FY 02 sales, but further development of SRAM was suspended in March 2003.

Company Financials Fiscal Year ending August 31

Per Share Data ($)

(Year Ended August 31)	2004	2003	2002	2001	2000	1999	1998	1997	1996	1995
Tangible Bk. Val.	8.73	7.68	9.93	11.59	11.34	7.00	6.31	6.82	5.99	4.60
Cash Flow	2.13	-0.10	0.45	1.00	4.13	1.49	0.88	1.84	2.23	2.44
Earnings	0.24	-2.11	-1.51	-0.88	2.56	-0.13	-0.55	0.77	1.38	1.98
S&P Core Earnings	-0.09	-2.60	-2.14	-1.06	NA	NA	NA	NA	NA	NA
Dividends	Nil	Nil	Nil	Nil	Nil	Nil	Nil	Nil	0.08	0.08
Payout Ratio	Nil	Nil	Nil	Nil	Nil	Nil	Nil	Nil	5%	4%
Prices - High	18.25	15.66	39.50	49.61	97.50	42.50	27.81	30.03	22.00	47.37
- Low	10.89	6.60	9.50	16.39	28.00	17.12	10.03	11.00	8.31	10.62
P/E Ratio - High	76	NM	NM	NM	38	NM	NM	39	16	24
- Low	45	NM	NM	NM	11	NM	NM	14	6	5

Income Statement Analysis (Million $)

	2004	2003	2002	2001	2000	1999	1998	1997	1996	1995
Revs.	4.40	3,091	2,589	3,936	7,336	3,764	3,012	3,516	3,654	2,953
Oper. Inc.	1.44	133	152	138	3,288	796	113	864	1,338	1,496
Depr.	1.22	1,210	1,177	1,114	994	843	607	462	364	199
Int. Exp.	0.04	36.5	17.1	16.7	104	130	49.4	39.9	16.1	12.2
Pretax Inc.	0.23	-1,200	-999	-960	2,317	-91.5	-335	619	951	1,351
Eff. Tax Rate	32.2%	NM	NM	NM	34.4%	NM	NM	43.2%	37.6%	37.5%
Net Inc.	0.16	-1,273	-907	-521	1,504	-68.9	-234	332	594	844
S&P Core Earnings	-62.2	-1,578	-1,288	-626	NA	NA	NA	NA	NA	NA

Balance Sheet & Other Fin. Data (Million $)

	2004	2003	2002	2001	2000	1999	1998	1997	1996	1995
Cash	0.49	922	398	469	702	295	559	988	286	128
Curr. Assets	2.64	2,037	2,119	3,138	4,904	2,830	1,499	1,972	964	1,274
Total Assets	7.76	7,158	7,555	8,363	9,632	6,965	4,688	4,851	3,752	2,775
Curr. Liab.	0.97	993	753	687	1,648	922	740	750	665	605
LT Debt	1.03	997	361	445	934	1,528	758	762	315	129
Common Equity	5.61	5,038	6,367	7,135	6,432	3,964	2,693	2,883	2,502	1,896
Total Cap.	6.68	6,035	6,727	7,599	7,899	5,969	3,735	3,885	3,028	2,075
Cap. Exp.	1.08	822	760	1,489	1,188	804	707	517	1,426	730
Cash Flow	1.37	-63.3	270	593	2,499	774	373	794	957	1,043
Curr. Ratio	2.7	2.1	2.8	4.6	3.0	3.1	2.0	2.6	1.5	2.1
% LT Debt of Cap.	15.4	16.5	5.4	5.9	11.8	25.6	20.3	19.6	10.4	6.2
% Net Inc.of Revs.	3.6	NM	NM	NM	20.5	NM	NM	9.2	16.2	28.5
% Ret. on Assets	2.1	NM	NM	NM	18.1	NM	NM	7.7	16.4	39.2
% Ret. on Equity	3.0	NM	NM	NM	28.9	NM	NM	12.3	27.0	57.3

Data as orig reptd.; bef. results of disc opers/spec. items. Per share data adj. for stk. divs.; EPS diluted. E-Estimated. NA-Not Available. NM-Not Meaningful. NR-Not Ranked. UR-Under Review.

Office: 8000 South Federal Way, Boise, ID 83716.
Telephone: 208-368-4000.
Email: invrel@micron.com
Website: http://www.micron.com
Chrmn, Pres & CEO: S.R. Appleton.

VP & CFO: W.G. Stover, Jr.
VP, Secy & General Counsel: R.W. Lewis.
VP & Investor Contact: K.A. Bedard 208-368-4400.
Dirs: S. R. Appleton, J. W. Bagley, R. Foster, R. A. Lothrop, T. T. Nicholson, G. C. Smith, W. P. Weber.

Founded: in 1978.
Domicile: Delaware.
Employees: 17,900.
S&P Analyst: Amrit Tewary/MF/BK

The McGraw·Hill Companies

Microsoft Corp.

Recommendation: **BUY** ★★★★ 12-Month Target Price: **$33.00**
SELL | ... | ... | BUY | BUY
(as of November 16, 2004)

MSFT has an approximate 2.70% weighting in the **S&P 500**

Sector: Information Technology
Sub-Industry: Systems Software
Peer Group: Systems Software - Larger

Summary: Microsoft, the world's largest software company, develops PC software, including the Windows operating system and Office application suite.

Quantitative Evaluations

S&P Earnings & Dividend Rank: B+

| D | C | B- | B | B+ | A- | A | A+ |

S&P Fair Value Rank: 4

| 1 | 2 | 3 | 4 | 5 |
| Lowest | | | | Highest |

Fair Value Calc.: $29.90 (Slightly Undervalued)

S&P Investability Quotient Percentile

100%

MSFT scored higher than 100% of all companies for which an S&P Report is available.

Volatility: Low

| Low | Average | High |

Technical Evaluation: Neutral
Since 11/04, the technical indicators for MSFT have been Neutral.

Relative Strength Rank: Weak

| 18 |
| 1 Lowest | Highest 99 |

Price as of 11/16/04: **$27.12**   **2005E S&P Core EPS:** **$1.10**

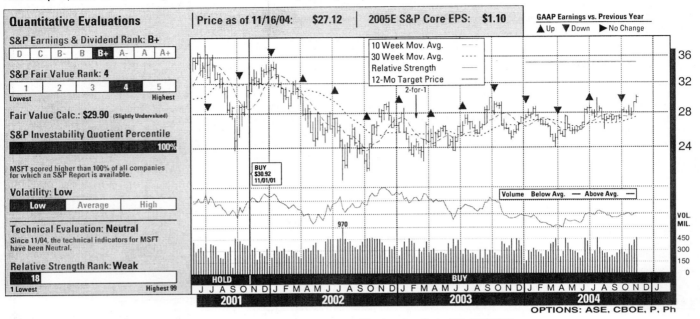

GAAP Earnings vs. Previous Year
▲ Up ▼ Down ▶ No Change

- 10 Week Mov. Avg.
- 30 Week Mov. Avg.
- Relative Strength
- 12-Mo Target Price

2-for-1

BUY
$30.92
11/01/01

970

Volume Below Avg. — Above Avg. —

VOL.
MIL.
450
300
150
0

HOLD   BUY
J J A S O N D | J F M A M J J A S O N D | J F M A M J J A S O N D | J F M A M J J A S O N D | J
2001   2002   2003   2004

OPTIONS: ASE, CBOE, P, Ph

Analyst commentary prepared by Jonathan Rudy, CFA /PMW/GG

Highlights October 26, 2004

- We expect revenues to increase about 7% in FY 05 (Jun.), driven in part by strong demand for MSFT's Server products. We believe that demand for Windows and Office XP will slow in FY 05.

- In FY 05, MSFT looks for 8% to 10% growth in worldwide PC unit shipments; this should continue to help results. We believe that relatively new products, such as Xbox, SQL Server, MSN, and the highly anticipated Longhorn platform in 2006, will boost revenues over the longer term. We view positively the company's recently announced $30 billion stock buyback program, $32 billion special dividend, and doubling of its regular dividend.

- We see operating margins widening in FY 05, primarily due to tighter cost controls, but due to the company's special dividend, we anticipate that investment income will decline sharply. We project FY 05 operating EPS of $1.25, followed by $1.40 in FY 06. Our FY 05 S&P Core EPS estimate of $1.10 reflects estimated equity compensation expense.

Investment Rationale/Risk October 26, 2004

- We would buy the shares, reflecting what we see as MSFT's strong balance sheet, market leadership, and discount to our estimate of intrinsic value, based on discounted cash flow analysis. We expect PC sales to remain strong in FY 05, driven by improving corporate demand. The company has continued to diversify its revenue stream into new areas, resulting in solid growth and profitability, while many competitors were severely affected by the technology downturn. We believe that MSFT's notable cash and short-term investment balance of over $64 billion, with no debt, provided the flexibility for the company's significant announcement of a planned stock buyback, special dividend, and a doubling of its regular dividend.

- Risks to our opinion and target price include a highly competitive software industry, and a rapidly changing technology landscape, such as a more rapid adoption of the Linux operating system than we currently anticipate.

- The stock is trading at a discount to our 12-month target price of $35, which is based on our discounted cash flow valuation model, assuming a discount rate of 13% to 14%.

Key Stock Statistics

S&P Oper. EPS 2005E	1.25	52-week Range	$30.20-24.01
P/E on S&P Oper. EPS 2005E	24.0	12 Month P/E	36.6
S&P Oper. EPS 2006E	1.40	Beta	1.65
Yield (%)	1.2%	Shareholders	141,975
Dividend Rate/Share	0.32	Market Cap (B)	$294.8
Shares Outstanding (M)	10871.6		

Value of $10,000 invested five years ago: **$ 6,799**

Dividend Data Dividends have been paid since 2003

Amount ($)	Date Decl.	Ex-Div. Date	Stock of Record	Payment Date
0.080	Jul. 20	Aug. 23	Aug. 25	Sep. 14 '04
0.080	Sep. 15	Nov. 15	Nov. 17	Dec. 02 '04
3.0 Spcl.	Jul. 20		Nov. 17	Dec. 02 '04

Revenues/Earnings Data Fiscal year ending June 30

Revenues (Million $)

	2005	2004	2003	2002	2001	2000
1Q	9,189	8,215	7,746	6,126	5,800	5,384
2Q	—	10,153	8,541	7,741	6,585	6,112
3Q	—	9,175	7,835	7,245	6,456	5,656
4Q	—	9,292	8,065	7,253	6,577	5,804
Yr.	—	36,835	32,187	28,365	25,296	22,956

Earnings Per Share ($)

	2005	2004	2003	2002	2001	2000
1Q	0.23	0.24	0.25	0.12	0.23	0.20
2Q	E0.33	0.14	0.24	0.21	0.24	0.22
3Q	E0.30	0.12	0.26	0.25	0.22	0.21
4Q	E0.30	0.25	0.18	0.14	0.01	0.22
Yr.	E1.25	0.75	0.92	0.71	0.69	0.85

Next earnings report expected: late-January Source: S&P, Company Reports
EPS Estimates based on S&P Operating Earnings; historical GAAP earnings are as reported.

Microsoft Corporation

Recommendation: **BUY** ★ ★ ★ ★ ★   12-Month Target Price: **$33.00** (as of November 16, 2004)

Business Summary October 26, 2004

Microsoft, the dominant player in the PC software market, rose to prominence on the popularity of its operating systems software. The company now leads the business applications software market, and has set its sights on becoming the leading provider of software and services for the Internet.

The company is best known for its operating systems software programs, which run about 90% of PCs currently in use. Its original DOS operating system gave way to Windows, a graphical user interface program run in conjunction with DOS, which made using a PC easier. MSFT's Client business segment includes Windows XP, Windows 2000, and other standard Windows operating systems. Windows XP, the latest version of the flagship PC operating system, was introduced in October 2001. The next generation of the Windows operating system, code-named Longhorn, is currently under development. MSFT is targeting broad availability of this operating system in calendar 2006.

MSFT's Server and Tools segment consists of server software licenses and client access licenses for Windows Server, SQL Server, Exchange Server, and other servers. Windows 2003 Server is the latest release of an operating system for servers, to help build and deploy distributed applications for networked PCs.

The Information Worker segment is responsible for developing and delivering technologies that focus on improving productivity for information workers in corporations. Office suite, which includes the popular Word (word processing), Excel (spreadsheet), PowerPoint (graphics), Access (database management) and Outlook (messaging and collaboration) software programs, dominates the application software market just as Windows dominates operating systems. MSFT Office System, the latest version, was introduced in October 2003.

The Business Solutions segment includes the businesses of Great Plains, bCentral and Navision. The segment develops and markets a wide range of business applications designed to help small and mid-market businesses become more connected with customers, employees, partners, and suppliers.

The MSN segment includes MSN Subscriptions and MSN Network Services. MSN Subscription services include MSN Internet access, which provides dial-up Internet access, and other premium services. MSN Network Services, which provides services on the Internet, including MSN Search, Messenger, and Hotmail. Partners include ESPN, Expedia and MSNBC.

The Mobile and Embedded Devices segment consists of Windows Mobile software, Windows Embedded device operating systems, MapPoint, and Windows Automotive. Windows Mobile software powers Pocket PC, Pocket PC Phone Edition, and Smartphone products.

The Home and Entertainment segment includes the Xbox video game system, PC games, the Home Products Division, and TV platform products.

In November 2001, the company agreed to settle a U.S. Department of Justice antitrust suit against MSFT. In November 2002, the federal judge who was overseeing the case largely approved the settlement, which had been opposed by nine of the 18 states that were a party to the suit. On June 30, 2004, the U.S. Court of Appeals for the District of Columbia Circuit unanimously affirmed the settlement and the final judgment.

Company Financials Fiscal Year ending June 30

Per Share Data ($)

(Year Ended June 30)	2004	2003	2002	2001	2000	1999	1998	1997	1996	1995
Tangible Bk. Val.	6.55	5.34	4.71	4.39	3.92	2.69	1.59	1.02	0.72	0.57
Cash Flow	0.86	1.05	0.80	0.83	0.92	0.80	0.51	0.38	0.26	0.17
Earnings	0.75	0.92	0.71	0.69	0.85	0.71	0.42	0.33	0.21	0.15
S&P Core Earnings	0.83	0.76	0.65	0.58	NA	NA	NA	NA	NA	NA
Dividends	0.16	0.32	Nil	Nil	Nil	Nil	Nil	Nil	Nil	Nil
Payout Ratio	21%	35%	Nil	Nil	Nil	Nil	Nil	Nil	Nil	Nil
Prices - High	30.20	30.00	35.31	38.07	59.31	59.96	36.00	18.84	10.76	6.82
- Low	27.05	22.55	20.70	21.43	20.12	34.00	15.54	10.09	4.99	3.64
P/E Ratio - High	40	33	50	55	70	84	86	57	50	47
- Low	36	25	29	31	24	48	37	31	23	25

Income Statement Analysis (Million $)

	2004	2003	2002	2001	2000	1999	1998	1997	1996	1995
Revs.	36,835	32,187	28,365	25,296	22,956	19,747	14,484	11,358	8,671	5,937
Oper. Inc.	10,220	14,656	12,994	13,256	11,685	10,938	7,964	5,687	3,558	2,307
Depr.	1,186	1,439	1,084	1,536	748	1,010	1,024	557	480	269
Int. Exp.	Nil	Nil	Nil	Nil	Nil	Nil	Nil	Nil	Nil	Nil
Pretax Inc.	12,196	14,726	11,513	11,525	14,275	11,891	7,117	5,314	3,379	2,167
Eff. Tax Rate	33.0%	32.1%	32.0%	33.0%	34.0%	34.5%	36.9%	35.0%	35.0%	32.9%
Net Inc.	8,168	9,993	7,829	7,721	9,421	7,785	4,490	3,439	2,195	1,453
S&P Core Earnings	9,042	8,339	7,051	6,518	NA	NA	NA	NA	NA	NA

Balance Sheet & Other Fin. Data (Million $)

	2004	2003	2002	2001	2000	1999	1998	1997	1996	1995
Cash	60,592	49,048	38,652	31,600	23,798	17,236	13,927	8,966	6,940	4,750
Curr. Assets	70,566	58,973	48,576	39,637	30,308	20,233	15,889	10,373	7,839	5,620
Total Assets	92,389	79,571	67,646	59,257	52,150	37,156	22,357	14,387	10,093	7,210
Curr. Liab.	14,969	13,974	12,744	11,132	9,755	8,718	5,730	3,610	2,425	1,347
LT Debt	Nil	Nil	Nil	Nil	Nil	Nil	Nil	Nil	Nil	Nil
Common Equity	74,825	61,020	52,180	47,289	41,368	27,458	15,647	9,797	6,908	5,333
Total Cap.	74,825	62,751	52,578	48,125	41,368	28,438	16,627	10,777	7,033	5,458
Cap. Exp.	1,109	891	770	1,103	879	583	656	499	494	495
Cash Flow	9,354	11,432	8,913	9,257	10,156	8,767	5,486	3,996	2,675	1,722
Curr. Ratio	4.7	4.2	3.8	3.6	3.1	2.3	2.8	2.9	3.2	4.2
% LT Debt of Cap.	Nil	Nil	Nil	Nil	Nil	Nil	Nil	Nil	Nil	Nil
% Net Inc.of Revs.	22.2	31.0	27.6	30.5	41.0	39.4	31.0	30.3	25.3	24.5
% Ret. on Assets	9.4	13.6	12.4	13.9	20.8	26.2	24.4	28.2	25.4	23.1
% Ret. on Equity	11.7	17.7	15.7	17.4	27.3	36.0	35.1	41.2	35.9	29.7

Data as orig reptd.; bef. results of disc opers/spec. items. Per share data adj. for stk. divs. Bold denotes primary EPS - prior periods restated. E-Estimated. NA-Not Available. NM-Not Meaningful. NR-Not Ranked. UR-Under Review.

Office: 1 Microsoft Way, Redmond, WA 98052-8300.
Telephone: 425-882-8080.
Email: msft@microsoft.com
Website: http://www.microsoft.com
Chrmn: W.H. Gates.
CEO: S.A. Ballmer.

SVP & CFO: J.G. Connors.
SVP, Secy & General Counsel: B. Smith.
Investor Contact: K. Srinivasan 425-706-3703.
Dirs: S. A. Ballmer, J. I. Cash, Jr., W. H. Gates III, R. V. Gilmartin, A. M. Korologos, D. F. Marquardt, C. H. Noski, H. Panke, J. A. Shirley.

Founded: in 1975.
Domicile: Washington.
Employees: 57,000.
S&P Analyst: Jonathan Rudy, CFA /PMW/GG

Millipore Corp.

Recommendation: **HOLD** ★ ★ ★ ☆ ☆

12-Month Target Price: **$52.00**
(as of October 20, 2004)

MIL has an approximate 0.02% weighting in the **S&P 500**

Sector: Health Care
Sub-Industry: Health Care Supplies
Peer Group: Disposable Medical Products

Summary: MIL provides technologies, tools and services for the development and production of new therapeutic drugs.

Quantitative Evaluations

S&P Earnings & Dividend Rank: B

| D | C | B- | **B** | B+ | A- | A | A+ |

S&P Fair Value Rank: 4-

| 1 | 2 | 3 | **4** | 5 |
| Lowest | | | | Highest |

Fair Value Calc.: $48.00 (Fairly Valued)

S&P Investability Quotient Percentile

97%

MIL scored higher than 97% of all companies for which an S&P Report is available.

Volatility: Average

| Low | **Average** | High |

Technical Evaluation: Bearish
Since 9/04, the technical indicators for MIL have been Bearish.

Relative Strength Rank: Weak

25
1 Lowest   Highest 99

Price as of 11/12/04: **$47.63** | **2004E S&P Core EPS:** **$1.78**

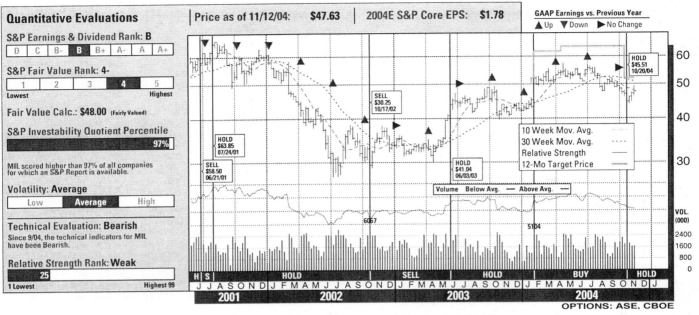

GAAP Earnings vs. Previous Year
▲ Up ▼ Down ► No Change

OPTIONS: ASE, CBOE

Analyst commentary prepared by Jeffrey Loo, CFA /CB/BK

Highlights October 25, 2004

- We have revised our 2004 and 2005 forecasts following our view of a disappointing third quarter in which sales grew 5% (only 1% growth after excluding the benefits of foreign exchange). We now see 2004 sales, inclusive of foreign exchange benefits, growing 9.6%, to about $876 million, revised from our original forecast of 12% growth to $894 million. In 2005, we see sales increasing 5.2%, to $921 million, reflecting a smaller expected benefit from foreign exchange.

- We see continued weakness over the next several quarters in European markets, notably France and Germany, where the reorganization of some pharmaceutical companies is disrupting purchases, and in Asia/Pacific markets, particularly Japan, where universities are slow to adapt to the change in funding to Independent Administrative Agency Status. Further, additional government changes have forced the reallocation of some funds away from research supplies. We see operating margins improving 70 basis points in 2005 due to a slight improvement in gross margins to 54.1% and from effective control of SG&A costs.

- Assuming effective tax rates of 23% and 22% in 2004 and 2005, respectively, our 2004 EPS estimate is $2.18, with $2.40 seen for 2005. We estimate 2004 Standard & Poor's Core Earnings of $1.78 a share.

Key Stock Statistics

S&P Oper. EPS 2004E	**2.18**	52-week Range	**$57.20-40.52**
P/E on S&P Oper. EPS 2004E	**21.8**	12 Month P/E	**20.9**
S&P Oper. EPS 2005E	**2.40**	Beta	**0.91**
Yield (%)	**Nil**	Shareholders	**2,484**
Dividend Rate/Share	**Nil**	Market Cap (B)	**$ 2.4**
Shares Outstanding (M)	**49.7**		

Value of $10,000 invested five years ago: **NA**

Dividend Data

No cash dividends have been paid since January 2002.

Investment Rationale/Risk October 25, 2004

- We recently downgraded our opinion on MIL shares to hold from accumulate based on our view of a challenging environment in several key overseas markets such as France, Germany and Japan. The European and Asia/Pacific markets account for about 54% of MIL's sales. However, we still see a robust North American market, with strong sales growth across product lines, despite a small 3% increase in the NIH budget expected in 2005. We see improved R&D spending on drug development and discovery, and continue to believe that MIL will benefit from an increasing industrywide drug pipeline and greater manufacturing capacity. We believe that there are about 2,000 biologic compounds in development or approved, including about 500 antibodies. We expect the production of new antibody products to aid MIL in the latter half of 2005 and into 2006. We also believe the capital market environment for small life science and biotech companies and startups remains strong, potentially leading to new sales for MIL.

- Risks to our recommendation and target price include a slowing of pharmaceutical R&D spending, prolonged slow adaptation to funding changes in Japan, and a potential reduction in government funding of research facilities.

- Based on our discounted cash flow and P/E to growth (PEG) ratio analyses, using a PEG ratio of 1.5X, in line with peers, our 12-month target price is $52.

Revenues/Earnings Data Fiscal year ending December 31

Revenues (Million $)

	2004	2003	2002	2001	2000	1999
1Q	222.5	187.4	166.6	162.5	224.8	180.4
2Q	224.7	196.4	176.1	167.9	238.9	187.5
3Q	210.7	200.1	175.6	157.7	239.4	188.6
4Q	—	215.8	185.9	168.8	250.6	214.7
Yr.	—	799.6	704.3	656.9	953.8	771.2

Earnings Per Share ($)

	2004	2003	2002	2001	2000	1999
1Q	0.55	0.44	0.40	0.15	0.56	0.25
2Q	0.57	0.46	0.46	0.43	0.67	0.32
3Q	0.50	0.50	0.39	0.33	0.61	0.37
4Q	E0.52	0.66	0.41	0.41	0.69	0.47
Yr.	E2.18	2.06	1.67	1.32	2.53	1.42

Next earnings report expected: late-January Source: S&P, Company Reports
EPS Estimates based on S&P Operating Earnings; historical GAAP earnings are as reported.

Millipore Corporation

Recommendation: **HOLD** ★ ★ ★ ☆ ☆   12-Month Target Price: **$52.00** (as of October 20, 2004)

Business Summary October 26, 2004

Millipore Corp. provides tools and services for the development and production of therapeutic drugs. MIL, which spun off its microelectronics unit in August 2001, focuses on solutions for drug manufacturing and other production processes, and on research and development tools for the life science industry. Operating revenues were up 14% in 2003, to $800 million.

The company directs its marketing efforts to three business segments: biotechnology (34% of 2003 sales), life science research (14%), and other bioscience (52%). MIL's offerings include consumable products, capital equipment, and services sold mainly to pharmaceutical, biotechnology, and life science research companies. Consumables and services accounted for 82% of 2003 sales, with the remaining 18% from hardware. The company sells more than 5,000 products (not including spare parts), including laboratory sample prep and screening kits, membrane filters tailored to different lab and production requirements, pumps, chromatography systems and columns, and water purification systems for laboratories and manufacturing. Manufacturing operations are conducted at sites located in the U.S., Europe, Japan and Brazil.

In 2003, revenues by geographic region were as follows: the Americas 44%, Europe 37%, and Asia/Pacific (the majority derived from Japan) 19%. Competitors include Amersham Biosciences, Apogent Technologies, Pall Corp., Qiagen, and United States Filter Corp.

MIL sells its products through a global sales network. In the U.S., the company primarily uses a direct sales force and web site sales. Outside the U.S., MIL has subsidiaries and branches in more than 30 countries, and also employs independent distributors.

The company concentrates its in-house R&D on the development of new products. It has augmented its product offerings and research capabilities through acquisitions and alliances.

MIL has said that its operations could be affected by an increasing number of biologic therapeutics being developed and approved over time, since its products are used in research laboratories, drug development programs, and drug manufacturing. According to the company, the drug industry is developing about 2,000 biologic compounds, including about 500 antibodies. Another factor affecting MIL's operations is industrywide biomanufacturing capacity, which it expects to continue to expand.

In August 2001, the company completed an IPO of 18% of a new microelectronics company, Mykrolis Corp. The IPO generated proceeds of $119 million. In February 2002, MIL distributed its remaining 82% stake in Mykrolis to its shareholders.

In January 2004, MIL entered into an alliance with HyClone Laboratories (a subsidiary of Fisher Scientific) to provide disposable bioprocessing products to the drug manufacturing industry.

Company Financials Fiscal Year ending December 31

Per Share Data ($)

(Year Ended December 31)	2003	2002	2001	2000	1999	1998	1997	1996	1995	1994
Tangible Bk. Val.	8.72	5.16	7.60	5.25	2.36	1.37	1.64	3.67	4.95	4.67
Cash Flow	2.88	2.39	1.96	3.51	2.40	1.23	0.04	1.70	2.51	1.59
Earnings	2.06	1.67	1.32	2.53	1.42	0.22	-0.89	1.00	1.90	1.09
S&P Core Earnings	1.67	1.41	1.08	NA	NA	NA	NA	NA	NA	NA
Dividends	Nil	Nil	0.44	0.44	0.44	0.42	0.49	0.35	0.32	0.30
Payout Ratio	Nil	Nil	33%	17%	31%	191%	NM	35%	17%	27%
Prices - High	49.37	60.95	66.85	77.37	42.12	38.43	52.00	47.12	41.50	28.50
- Low	29.90	27.25	42.65	36.25	23.43	17.25	33.50	33.62	22.87	19.18
P/E Ratio - High	24	36	51	31	30	NM	NM	47	22	26
- Low	15	16	32	14	17	NM	NM	34	12	18

Income Statement Analysis (Million $)

	2003	2002	2001	2000	1999	1998	1997	1996	1995	1994
Revs.	800	704	657	954	771	699	759	619	594	497
Oper. Inc.	166	160	150	216	149	89.2	41.8	92.0	147	118
Depr.	40.5	35.0	30.7	46.1	44.3	44.4	40.7	30.6	27.5	27.6
Int. Exp.	16.5	19.0	25.3	26.9	30.2	29.5	30.5	11.5	10.6	7.90
Pretax Inc.	112	104	78.4	154	82.4	8.54	-18.1	57.0	110	76.9
Eff. Tax Rate	10.1%	22.0%	19.0%	22.4%	21.9%	NA	NM	23.5%	22.5%	22.5%
Net Inc.	101	80.8	63.5	119	64.3	9.86	-38.8	43.6	85.4	59.6
S&P Core Earnings	82.0	68.5	51.8	NA	NA	NA	NA	NA	NA	NA

Balance Sheet & Other Fin. Data (Million $)

	2003	2002	2001	2000	1999	1998	1997	1996	1995	1994
Cash	147	101	62.5	58.4	51.1	36.0	2.24	46.9	23.8	30.2
Curr. Assets	516	390	312	465	359	305	352	312	262	259
Total Assets	951	786	916	875	793	762	766	683	531	528
Curr. Liab.	222	134	134	235	270	299	305	216	173	158
LT Debt	216	334	320	300	313	299	287	224	105	100
Common Equity	461	288	394	305	177	137	149	218	226	221
Total Cap.	677	622	759	605	490	436	436	442	332	322
Cap. Exp.	71.9	79.3	72.3	52.2	31.3	59.8	41.1	30.4	30.0	21.0
Cash Flow	141	116	94.2	165	109	54.3	1.88	74.2	113	87.2
Curr. Ratio	2.3	2.9	2.3	2.0	1.3	1.0	1.2	1.4	1.5	1.6
% LT Debt of Cap.	31.9	53.7	42.1	49.6	63.9	68.6	65.8	50.7	31.7	31.2
% Net Inc.of Revs.	12.6	11.5	9.7	12.5	8.3	1.4	NM	7.1	14.4	12.0
% Ret. on Assets	11.5	9.3	7.3	14.3	8.3	1.3	NM	7.2	16.0	10.8
% Ret. on Equity	26.9	23.7	18.2	49.4	41.4	6.9	NM	19.7	38.1	19.8

Data as orig. reptd.; bef. results of disc. opers. and/or spec. items. Per share data adj. for stk. divs.; EPS diluted (primary prior to 1998). E-Estimated. NA-Not Available. NM-Not Meaningful. NR-Not Ranked. Operating and net operating profit margins in 1997 and 1996 include pretax acquisition-related charges of $114 million and $68 million, respectively.

Office: 290 Concord Road, Billerica, MA 01821.
Telephone: 978-715-4321 .
Website: http://www.millipore.com
Chrmn, Pres & CEO: F.J. Lunger.
VP & CFO: K.B. Allen.

VP & General Counsel: J. Rudin.
Treas & Investor Contact: G.E. Helliwell .
Dirs: D. Bellus, R. C. Bishop, M. D. Booth, M. A. Hendricks, M. Hoffman, R. J. Lane, F. J. Lunger, J. F. Reno, E. M. Scolnick, K. E. Welke.

Founded: in 1954.
Domicile: Massachusetts.
Employees: 4,300.
S&P Analyst: Jeffrey Loo, CFA /CB/BK

Molex Inc.

Recommendation: **BUY** ★★★★☆   12-Month Target Price: **$34.00**
SELL SELL HOLD BUY BUY   (as of May 26, 2004)

MOLX has an approximate 0.05% weighting in the **S&P 500**

Sector: Information Technology
Sub-Industry: Electronic Manufacturing Services
Peer Group: Electronic Components - Larger Sales

Summary: Molex makes electrical and electronic devices primarily for OEMs in the computer, telecommunications, home appliance and home entertainment industries.

Quantitative Evaluations

S&P Earnings & Dividend Rank: A-

| D | C | B- | B | B+ | A- | A | A+ |

S&P Fair Value Rank: 5

| 1 | 2 | 3 | 4 | 5 |
| Lowest | | | | Highest |

Fair Value Calc.: $36.60 (Undervalued)

S&P Investability Quotient Percentile

95%

MOLX scored higher than 95% of all companies for which an S&P Report is available.

Volatility: Average

| Low | Average | High |

Technical Evaluation: Bullish

Since 11/04, the technical indicators for MOLX have been Bullish.

Relative Strength Rank: Moderate

42

| 1 Lowest | | Highest 99 |

| Price as of 11/12/04: | $30.53 | 2005E S&P Core EPS: | $1.26 |

GAAP Earnings vs. Previous Year
▲ Up ▼ Down ► No Change

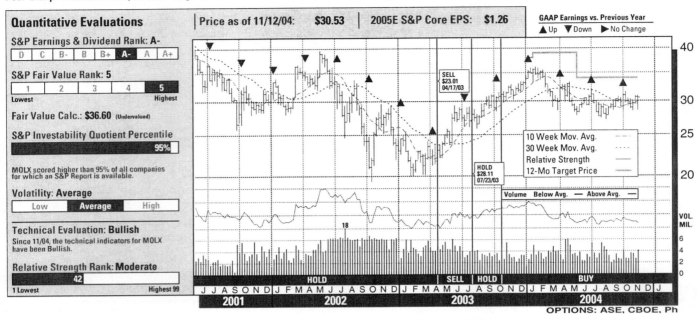

- 10 Week Mov. Avg.
- 30 Week Mov. Avg.
- Relative Strength
- 12-Mo Target Price

Volume Below Avg. — Above Avg. —

Analyst commentary prepared by Stewart Scharf/DC/BK

OPTIONS: ASE, CBOE, Ph

Highlights October 26, 2004

- We expect total revenues to advance close to 20% in FY 05 (Jun.), after approximately a 3% positive currency effect and 3% from acquisitions, reflecting strength in the telecom, mobile and data markets. We expect customer inventory levels to decline in the OEM and distribution channels, and see strong demand for new electronics products in the Far East, and a rebound in the Americas and Europe.

- We think gross margins will widen by 200 basis points, to 37%, in FY 05, as increased volume and pricing and an improving product mix offset higher, but moderating, copper and gold costs, as well as rising oil prices. We look for EBITDA margins to expand to 22%, from 20.4% in FY 04, as MOLX transfers production to the Far East South. We believe that restructuring efforts will save an estimated $20 million a year, reducing SG&A expenses by 200 basis points, to under 24% of sales.

- We think net profit margins (8.7% recently) may approach MOLX's 10% goal during FY 05. After a slightly higher projected tax rate of 27%, we see FY 05 EPS of $1.30, rising 15%, to $1.50 in FY 06. Earnings quality is sound, in our opinion, as our S&P Core Earnings estimate for 2005 is close to our operating EPS projection.

Investment Rationale/Risk October 26, 2004

- We continue to believe that investors should accumulate the shares of MOLX, based on our free cash model as well as our expectations of further profit leverage, as the company remains virtually debt free, in contrast with its leveraged peers. We expect MOLX to use excess cash for potential acquisitions, additional share buybacks and cash dividends (a 50% dividend hike was effected in late September 2004).

- Risks to our recommendation and target price include a smaller positive impact from foreign exchange, a slowdown in economic growth, less robust demand in the Far East, greater-than-expected price erosion due to further significant increases in raw material costs, and additional capacity in China and Japan.

- The stock is trading at 22X our FY 05 EPS estimate, a premium to the projected peer P/E and our forward multiple for the S&P 500. However, based on our discounted cash flow model, assuming a 4% perpetuity growth rate and a 7.8% weighted average cost of capital, the stock is selling at a 16% discount to its intrinsic value. In addition, the stock's average historical P/Es are above peers' P/Es. With what we see as an attractive, versus peers, P/E-to-EPS growth (PEG) ratio of 0.7X for FY 05, we maintain our 12-month target price at $34, a blend of these metrics.

Key Stock Statistics

S&P Oper. EPS 2005E	1.30	52-week Range	$36.10-27.07
P/E on S&P Oper. EPS 2005E	23.5	12 Month P/E	29.4
S&P Oper. EPS 2006E	1.50	Beta	1.73
Yield (%)	0.5%	Shareholders	2,851
Dividend Rate/Share	0.15	Market Cap (B)	$3.1
Shares Outstanding (M)	189.1		

Value of $10,000 invested five years ago: **$9,746**

Dividend Data Dividends have been paid since 1976

Amount ($)	Date Decl.	Ex-Div. Date	Stock of Record	Payment Date
0.025	Dec. 16	Dec. 26	Dec. 30	Jan. 26 '04
0.025	Mar. 16	Mar. 29	Mar. 31	Apr. 26 '04
0.025	Jun. 15	Jun. 28	Jun. 30	Jul. 26 '04
0.038	Aug. 02	Sep. 28	Sep. 30	Oct. 25 '04

Revenues/Earnings Data Fiscal year ending June 30

Revenues (Million $)

	2005	2004	2003	2002	2001	2000
1Q	640.2	496.8	469.3	430.4	625.9	492.0
2Q	—	549.0	454.6	416.5	629.3	543.0
3Q	—	569.1	443.2	408.3	599.8	567.6
4Q	—	631.8	476.1	456.3	510.5	614.6
Yr.	—	2,247	1,843	1,712	2,366	2,217

Earnings Per Share ($)

	2005	2004	2003	2002	2001	2000
1Q	0.29	0.17	0.15	0.13	0.33	0.23
2Q	E0.30	0.21	0.15	0.02	0.34	0.27
3Q	E0.33	0.24	0.13	0.10	0.31	0.29
4Q	E0.38	0.30	0.01	0.14	0.05	0.33
Yr.	E1.30	0.92	0.44	0.39	1.03	1.12

Next earnings report expected: mid-January Source: S&P, Company Reports
EPS Estimates based on S&P Operating Earnings; historical GAAP earnings are as reported.

Molex Incorporated

Recommendation: **BUY** ★★★★☆ 12-Month Target Price: **$34.00** (as of May 26, 2004)

Business Summary October 26, 2004

Molex is the world's second largest connector maker, operating 55 plants in 19 countries, and offering more than 100,000 products. The worldwide market for electronic connectors, cables and backplanes is estimated at about $28 billion, with MOLX holding an approximate 8% share.

MOLX's products include electrical and electronic devices such as terminals, connectors, cable assemblies, interconnection systems, fiber-optic interconnection systems, backplanes and mechanical and electronic switches. In FY 04 (Jun.), these products were sold to the following industries: computers (29%), telecommunications (20%), consumer products (21%), automotive (17%), industrial (9%), and other (4%).

The company's products are used in everything from computer equipment, data networking equipment, home entertainment products and wireless telecommunications products to household appliances, electronic medical equipment, and automotive equipment such as anti-lock braking systems.

MOLX sells primarily to OEMs, subcontractors and suppliers, through direct sales engineers and industrial distributors (U.S. and Canada), and through distributors, its own sales organizations and manufacturers' representative organizations (internationally). Customers include Cisco, Dell, Hewlett Packard, IBM, Motorola, Nokia, Ford, Sony, Samsung and Siemens.

Revenues outside the U.S. accounted for 70% of the FY 04 total, with 50% generated in Asia (22% in the Far East North and 28% in the Far East South), 17% in Europe and 3% in the non-U.S. Americas.

At September 30, 2004, order backlog was $314 million, up 51% from a year earlier. New orders rose 21%, to $622 million. Backlog of unfilled orders stood at $333 million ($324 million excluding positive foreign exchange) at FY 04 year-end,

up 79% from $186 million at the end of FY 03. Bookings in the FY 04 fourth quarter increased 45%, year to year, and 12% sequentially, to $680 million. Included in new orders were $20 million from a recent acquisition and an estimated $25 million due to customers advancing orders in anticipation of an announced price hike. MOLX includes a purchase order and scheduled delivery date in reported backlog only items. However, industry practice is moving toward indication orders, whereby customers initially provide a forecast, as opposed to a purchase order, and the order is not included in the backlog until the customer requests shipment.

In the first quarter of FY 05, MOLX repurchased 875,000 common shares for nearly $22 million under a $100 million share repurchase authorization. In FY 04, the company bought back 2,740,000 of its common shares for over $70 million under a $100 million repurchase program. In FY 03, the company repurchased 3,352,500 common shares for $75 million. MOLX projects capital spending of at least $190 million for FY 04.

In the fourth quarter of FY 03, MOLX incurred a pretax restructuring charge of $40.1 million ($0.15 a share, after tax) related to the active fiber optic operations for the telecom infrastructure market. In the second quarter of FY 02, MOLX incurred a $34 million pretax charge ($0.10 a share, after tax), for a reduction in staff of 800 to 900 employees, the lower current value of investments in other companies, and asset writedowns.

In the FY 04 second quarter, MOLX recorded a $5.0 million pretax gain on a stock sale and a $5.4 million positive equity adjustment resulting from an IPO completed by a company 20% owned by MOLX.

Company Financials Fiscal Year ending June 30

Per Share Data ($)

(Year Ended June 30)	2004	2003	2002	2001	2000	1999	1998	1997	1996	1995
Tangible Bk. Val.	10.05	9.10	8.64	8.25	7.83	6.94	6.47	6.30	5.74	5.62
Cash Flow	2.10	1.62	1.53	2.13	2.11	1.77	1.67	1.56	1.35	1.17
Earnings	0.92	0.44	0.39	1.03	1.12	0.91	0.92	0.85	0.74	0.63
S&P Core Earnings	0.85	0.39	0.39	1.01	NA	NA	NA	NA	NA	NA
Dividends	0.10	0.10	0.10	0.10	0.07	0.04	0.05	0.03	0.03	0.01
Payout Ratio	11%	23%	26%	10%	6%	4%	5%	4%	4%	2%
Prices - High	36.10	35.12	39.61	48.00	63.75	45.60	31.20	30.70	20.32	18.96
- Low	27.07	19.98	19.43	25.76	34.18	20.40	18.40	17.28	13.95	12.69
P/E Ratio - High	39	80	NM	47	57	50	34	36	27	30
- Low	29	45	50	25	31	22	20	20	19	20

Income Statement Analysis (Million $)

	2004	2003	2002	2001	2000	1999	1998	1997	1996	1995
Revs.	2,247	1,843	1,711	2,366	2,217	1,712	1,623	1,540	1,383	1,198
Oper. Inc.	450	-120	324	498	512	395	413	391	336	312
Depr.	228	229	224	218	196	169	149	139	120	105
Int. Exp.	Nil	Nil	Nil	Nil	Nil	Nil	Nil	Nil	NM	NM
Pretax Inc.	240	110	93.2	291	324	230	275	262	229	214
Eff. Tax Rate	26.5%	22.5%	17.9%	30.0%	31.1%	22.7%	33.7%	36.4%	36.4%	42.1%
Net Inc.	176	84.9	76.5	204	222	178	182	167	146	124
S&P Core Earnings	164	76.1	76.7	200	NA	NA	NA	NA	NA	NA

Balance Sheet & Other Fin. Data (Million $)

	2004	2003	2002	2001	2000	1999	1998	1997	1996	1995
Cash	339	350	313	208	241	183	205	326	283	313
Curr. Assets	1,169	962	915	892	1,023	881	868	874	735	773
Total Assets	2,572	2,335	2,254	2,214	2,247	1,902	1,640	1,637	1,461	1,441
Curr. Liab.	428	356	360	374	475	342	333	342	275	278
LT Debt	14.0	16.9	17.8	25.5	21.6	20.1	5.60	7.40	7.45	8.10
Common Equity	2,066	1,897	1,828	1,766	1,706	1,501	1,262	1,236	1,131	1,107
Total Cap.	2,081	1,914	1,846	1,793	1,734	1,526	1,274	1,258	1,152	1,128
Cap. Exp.	190	171	172	376	337	229	227	209	222	187
Cash Flow	404	314	300	422	419	347	331	305	265	229
Curr. Ratio	2.7	2.7	2.5	2.4	2.2	2.6	2.6	2.6	2.7	2.8
% LT Debt of Cap.	0.7	0.9	1.0	1.4	1.2	1.3	0.4	0.6	0.7	0.7
% Net Inc.of Revs.	7.8	4.6	4.5	8.6	10.0	10.4	11.2	10.8	10.6	10.4
% Ret. on Assets	7.2	3.7	3.4	9.1	10.7	10.1	11.1	10.8	10.1	9.6
% Ret. on Equity	8.9	4.6	4.3	11.7	13.9	12.9	14.6	14.1	13.0	12.4

Data as orig reptd.; bef. results of disc opers/spec. items. Per share data adj. for stk. divs.; EPS diluted. E-Estimated. NA-Not Available. NM-Not Meaningful. NR-Not Ranked. UR-Under Review.

Office: 2222 Wellington Court, Lisle, IL 60532.
Telephone: 630-969-4550.
Website: http://www.molex.com
Co-Chrmn: F.A. Krehbiel.
Co-Chrmn: J.H. Krehbiel.
Pres & COO: M.P. Slark.

Vice Chrmn & CEO: J.J. King.
VP, CFO & Treas: D.S. Bullock.
Investor Contact: N. Lefort 630-527-4344.
Dirs: M. J. Birck, D. K. Carnahan, M. L. Collins, E. D. Jannotta, J. J. King, F. A. Krehbiel, F. L. Krehbiel, J. H. Krehbiel, Jr., J. W. Laymon, D. G. Lubin, M. Naitoh, R. J. Potter, M. P. Slark.

Founded: in 1938.
Domicile: Delaware.
Employees: 21,225.
S&P Analyst: Stewart Scharf/DC/BK

Monsanto Co.

Recommendation: **SELL** ★★☆☆☆
SELL SELL HOLD BUY BUY

12-Month Target Price: **$35.00**
(as of October 06, 2004)

MON has an approximate 0.11% weighting in the **S&P 500**

Sector: Materials
Sub-Industry: Fertilizers & Agricultural Chemicals
Peer Group: Major Fertilizers & Agricultural Chemicals

Summary: Monsanto helps growers, grain processors and commercial customers control unwanted vegetation cost-effectively and in an environmentally sound way.

Quantitative Evaluations

S&P Earnings & Dividend Rank: NR

D	C	B-	B	B+	A-	A	A+

S&P Fair Value Rank: 2

1	2	3	4	5
Lowest				Highest

Fair Value Calc.: $37.40 (Overvalued)

S&P Investability Quotient Percentile

31%

MON scored lower than 69% of all companies for which an S&P Report is available.

Volatility: Average

Low	Average	High

Technical Evaluation: Bullish
Since 10/04, the technical indicators for MON have been Bullish.

Relative Strength Rank: Strong

87
1 Lowest   Highest 99

Price as of 11/12/04:	**$44.61**

2005E S&P Core EPS:	**$1.75**

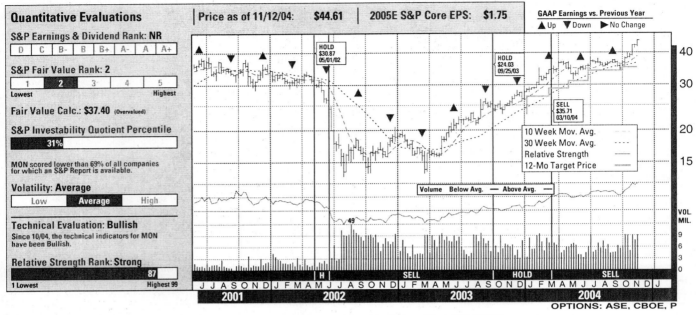

GAAP Earnings vs. Previous Year
▲ Up   ▼ Down   ► No Change

HOLD $30.87 05/01/02
HOLD $24.03 09/25/03
SELL $35.71 03/10/04

10 Week Mov. Avg.
30 Week Mov. Avg.
Relative Strength
12-Mo Target Price

Volume   Below Avg. — Above Avg.

VOL. MIL.

OPTIONS: ASE, CBOE, P

Analyst commentary prepared by Andrew West, CFA /DC/GG

Highlights October 08, 2004

- We expect FY 05 (Aug.) net sales to increase about 4%, to $5.7 billion, on higher pricing for genetically modified seeds and seed traits in the U.S., increased sales of these products to global markets, and a shift in MON's product mix and strategic focus to the seeds and genomics business, from herbicides. We expect higher herbicides volumes at lower prices, with Roundup off patent, allowing sales to rise at a slower rate.

- In chemicals, we think MON is pursuing a high volume, low cost producer strategy, and see increasing competition from other glyphosate-based herbicides pressuring product margins. In MON's growing and increasingly important seeds and genomics business, we expect widening margins on higher prices and market penetration. We believe these trends, combined with reduced overhead expense and significantly lower restructuring charges, will allow for operating margins, after depreciation, of almost 15%.

- We estimate that FY 05 operating EPS (excluding special expenses) will rise to $1.90 from $1.61 in FY 04, and project that Standard & Poor's Core Earnings will be 7% below FY 05 operating EPS, with the difference due to estimated pension and stock option expenses.

Investment Rationale/Risk October 08, 2004

- We believe the shares are somewhat overvalued and we would avoid them, considering MON's business risks and our moderate long-term growth expectations. MON is moving away from dependence on its herbicide business, where we expect greater competition and narrowing margins on patent expiry. We expect MON's biotechnology-driven seeds and traits business to drive MON's long-term growth, and see market share gains in global soybean, corn and cotton markets. We look for FY 05 free cash flow of about $675 million, growing about 3% annually through 2009, compared to about 6% annualized earnings growth in that period.

- Risks to our opinion and target price include the possibility of better than anticipated margin and market share growth, weaker than expected competition, lower than anticipated legal and regulatory exposures, and favorable changes in planting volumes or exchange rates.

- Our DCF model, assuming a 9% cost of capital and 3% terminal growth, calculates a value of $33. Our relative valuation model, which correlates historical peer group valuations with profitability and leverage, targets a forward price to sales multiple of 1.8X, and a price of $38. Blending our valuation approaches, our 12-month target price is $35.

Key Stock Statistics

S&P Oper. EPS 2005E	1.90	52-week Range	**$44.74-25.30**
P/E on S&P Oper. EPS 2005E	23.5	12 Month P/E	45.1
S&P Oper. EPS 2006E	2.05	Beta	**NA**
Yield (%)	1.3%	Shareholders	54,617
Dividend Rate/Share	0.58	Market Cap (B)	$ 11.9
Shares Outstanding (M)	267.0		

Value of $10,000 invested five years ago: **NA**

Dividend Data Dividends have been paid since 2001

Amount ($)	Date Decl.	Ex-Div. Date	Stock of Record	Payment Date
0.130	Dec. 03	Jan. 07	Jan. 09	Jan. 30 '04
0.130	Mar. 02	Apr. 06	Apr. 09	Apr. 30 '04
0.145	May. 04	Jul. 07	Jul. 09	Jul. 30 '04
0.145	Jul. 20	Oct. 06	Oct. 08	Oct. 29 '04

Revenues/Earnings Data Fiscal year ending August 31

Revenues (Million $)

	2004	2003	2002	2001	2000	1999
1Q	1,028	858.0	1,221	1,306	—	—
2Q	1,492	1,301	1,553	2,011	—	—
3Q	1,679	1,470	679.0	936.0	1,003	—
4Q	1,258	1,307	1,220	1,209	1,159	—
Yr.	5,457	4,936	4,673	5,462	5,493	5,248

Earnings Per Share ($)

	2004	2003	2002	2001	2000	1999
1Q	-0.29	-0.07	0.33	0.21	—	—
2Q	0.58	0.43	0.56	1.48	—	—
3Q	0.85	0.67	-0.63	-0.17	-0.25	—
4Q	-0.14	-0.72	0.23	-0.40	-0.20	—
Yr.	1.01	0.31	0.49	1.13	0.68	1.03

Next earnings report expected: early-January Source: S&P, Company Reports
EPS Estimates based on S&P Operating Earnings; historical GAAP earnings are as reported.

Monsanto Company

Recommendation: **SELL** ★ ★ ☆ ☆ ☆   12-Month Target Price: **$35.00** (as of October 06, 2004)

Business Summary October 08, 2004

Monsanto Co., a major producer of herbicides, seeds and other agricultural products, markets Roundup, the world's best selling herbicide. In 1970, the company discovered glyphosate, the main ingredient in Roundup. MON began marketing it under the Roundup brand in 1976. Roundup herbicides are used for agricultural, industrial and residential weed control, and are sold in more than 80 countries. In July 2003, the company changed its fiscal year end to August 31, from December 31.

MON operates in two segments: agricultural productivity, and seeds and genomics. The agricultural productivity segment (58% of sales and 55% of earnings before interest and taxes in the year ended August 31, 2004) consists of the company's crop protection products (Roundup herbicide and other glyphosate products), and its animal agriculture, Roundup lawn and garden products, and environmental technologies businesses. The seeds and genomics segment (42% of sales and 45% of earnings before interest and taxes) consists of the global seeds and related traits businesses, and technology platforms based on plant genomics, which increases the speed and power of genetic research. MON focuses on four key crops: corn, soybeans and other oilseeds, cotton and wheat.

In the year ended August 31, 2004, Roundup and other glyphosate-based herbicides accounted for 36% of total sales. Patents protecting Roundup herbicides expired in several countries in 1991, and patent protection for the active ingredient in Roundup herbicides expired in the U.S. in 2000. The Roundup herbicide had been the key to the company's growth strategy. Historically, MON selectively

reduced prices to encourage increased usage. The company sees primary drivers for Roundup growth in the future from Roundup use in conjunction with conservation tillage systems, and growth in Roundup Ready crops that tolerate the Roundup herbicide. Conservation tillage systems help farmers to reduce soil erosion by replacing plowing with the judicious use of herbicides to control weeds.

The crop protection business focuses on the herbicide market. In addition to Roundup, the business includes glyphosate sold to other major herbicide manufacturers, as well as selective herbicides that control specific weeds in corn, wheat and rice. MON's animal agriculture business focuses on improving animal productivity in the dairy and swine industries. The company produces the largest selling U.S. brand of recombinant bovine growth hormone, which increases milk production in dairy cows.

Prior to September 1, 1997, MON's predecessor company (today known as Pharmacia) operated an agricultural products business (the Ag business), a pharmaceuticals and nutrition business, and a chemical products business. On September 1, 1997, Pharmacia spun off the chemical products business to create a new company, Solutia. On September 1, 2000, Pharmacia spun off the Ag business to create the current company, Monsanto, in an IPO of more than 38 million shares, for net proceeds of $763 million. Pharmacia retained an 85% interest in MON following the offering. In August 2002, Pharmacia spun off its stake in MON via a dividend to Pharmacia shareholders.

Company Financials Fiscal Year ending August 31

Per Share Data ($)

(Year Ended August 31)	2004	2003	2002	2001	2000	1999	1998	1997	1996	1995
Tangible Bk. Val.	15.41	14.51	14.48	15.67	14.47	NM	NA	NA	NA	NA
Cash Flow	2.74	1.13	2.24	3.22	2.79	3.18	NA	NA	NA	NA
Earnings	1.01	0.31	0.49	1.13	0.68	1.03	NA	NA	NA	NA
S&P Core Earnings	1.35	1.22	0.01	1.05	NA	NA	NA	NA	NA	NA
Dividends	0.54	0.49	0.48	0.45	Nil	NA	NA	NA	NA	NA
Payout Ratio	53%	158%	98%	40%	Nil	NA	NA	NA	NA	NA
Prices - High	44.74	28.90	33.99	38.80	27.37	NA	NA	NA	NA	NA
- Low	28.07	13.55	13.20	26.87	19.75	NA	NA	NA	NA	NA
P/E Ratio - High	44	93	69	34	40	NA	NA	NA	NA	NA
- Low	28	44	27	24	29	NA	NA	NA	NA	NA

Income Statement Analysis (Million $)

	2004	2003	2002	2001	2000	1999	1998	1997	1996	1995
Revs.	5,457	3,373	4,673	5,462	5,493	5,248	NA	NA	NA	NA
Oper. Inc.	1,254	768	882	1,335	1,216	1,179	NA	NA	NA	NA
Depr.	452	302	460	554	546	547	NA	NA	NA	NA
Int. Exp.	91.0	57.0	59.0	99	214	269	NA	NA	NA	NA
Pretax Inc.	402	-38.0	202	463	334	263	NA	NA	NA	NA
Eff. Tax Rate	32.6%	NM	36.1%	35.9%	47.6%	43.0%	NA	NA	NA	NA
Net Inc.	271	-11.0	129	297	175	150	NA	NA	NA	NA
S&P Core Earnings	362	317	5.45	277	NA	NA	NA	NA	NA	NA

Balance Sheet & Other Fin. Data (Million $)

	2004	2003	2002	2001	2000	1999	1998	1997	1996	1995
Cash	1,037	511	428	307	131	26.0	NA	NA	NA	NA
Curr. Assets	4,931	4,962	4,424	4,797	4,973	4,027	NA	NA	NA	NA
Total Assets	9,164	9,461	8,890	11,429	11,726	11,101	NA	NA	NA	NA
Curr. Liab.	1,894	1,944	1,810	2,377	2,757	1,704	NA	NA	NA	NA
LT Debt	1,075	1,258	851	893	962	4,278	NA	NA	NA	NA
Common Equity	5,258	5,156	5,180	7,483	7,341	4,645	NA	NA	NA	NA
Total Cap.	6,333	6,414	6,031	8,376	8,303	8,923	NA	NA	NA	NA
Cap. Exp.	210	114	224	382	582	632	NA	NA	NA	NA
Cash Flow	723	291	589	851	721	697	NA	NA	NA	NA
Curr. Ratio	2.6	2.6	2.4	2.0	1.8	2.4	NA	NA	NA	NA
% LT Debt of Cap.	17.0	19.6	14.1	10.7	11.6	47.9	NA	NA	NA	NA
% Net Inc.of Revs.	5.0	NM	2.8	5.4	3.2	2.9	NA	NA	NA	NA
% Ret. on Assets	2.9	NM	1.3	2.6	1.5	1.4	NA	NA	NA	NA
% Ret. on Equity	5.2	NM	2.0	4.0	2.9	3.4	NA	NA	NA	NA

Data as orig reptd.; bef. results of disc opers/spec. items. Per share data adj. for stk. divs.; EPS diluted. E-Estimated. NA-Not Available. NM-Not Meaningful. NR-Not Ranked. UR-Under Review.

Office: 800 North Lindbergh Boulevard, St. Louis, MO 63167.
Telephone: 314-694-1000.
Email: info@monsanto.com
Website: http://www.monsanto.com
Chrmn, Pres & CEO: H. Grant.
EVP & CFO: T.K. Crews.

EVP, Secy & General Counsel: C.W. Burson.
VP & Treas: R.A. Paley.
Investor Contact: S. Foster 314-694-8148.
Dirs: F. V. AtLee III, J. Bachmann, H. Grant, G. S. King, S. R. Long, C. S. McMillan, W. U. Parfet, G. H. Poste, R. J. Stevens.

Founded: in 2000.
Domicile: Delaware.
Employees: 12,600.
S&P Analyst: Andrew West, CFA /DC/GG

Monster Worldwide

Recommendation: **SELL** ★☆☆☆☆
SELL SELL HOLD BUY BUY

12-Month Target Price: **$18.00**
(as of October 20, 2004)

MNST has an approximate 0.03% weighting in the **S&P 500**

Sector: Industrials
Sub-Industry: Employment Services
Peer Group: Staffing & Personnel Services over $1B Sales

Summary: Monster Worldwide is the online employment and recruitment leader, and is a leading recruitment services and advertising and marketing services agency.

Quantitative Evaluations

S&P Earnings & Dividend Rank: B-

| D | C | B- | B | B+ | A- | A | A+ |

S&P Fair Value Rank: 1-

| 1 | 2 | 3 | 4 | 5 |
| Lowest | | | | Highest |

Fair Value Calc.: $23.80 (Overvalued)

S&P Investability Quotient Percentile

22%

MNST scored lower than 78% of all companies for which an S&P Report is available.

Volatility: High

| Low | Average | High |

Technical Evaluation: Bullish
Since 9/04, the technical indicators for MNST have been Bullish.

Relative Strength Rank: Strong

82

| 1 Lowest | | Highest 99 |

| Price as of 11/12/04: | **$28.51** | 2004E S&P Core EPS: | **$0.30** |

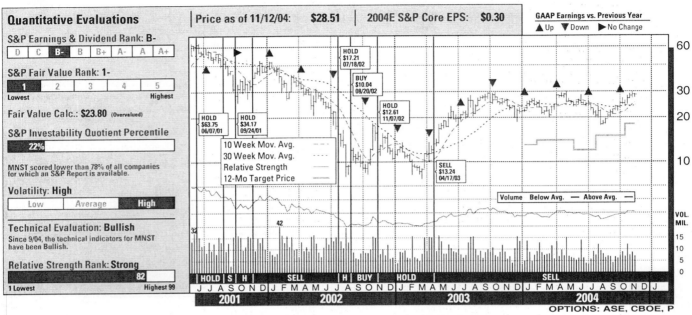

GAAP Earnings vs. Previous Year
▲ Up ▼ Down ► No Change

10 Week Mov. Avg. ---
30 Week Mov. Avg. ······
Relative Strength ——
12-Mo Target Price

Volume   Below Avg.   —— Above Avg.

OPTIONS: ASE, CBOE, P

Analyst commentary prepared by Mark S. Basham/PMW/JWP

Highlights 15-NOV-04

- We estimate that 2004 revenues will increase 25%, to $850 million, from $680 million in 2003. We see revenues from recent acquisitions accounting for $65 million of the increase, including $32 million from jobpilot, an online recruitment website operator in Europe that was acquired in April 2004, and $21 million from Tickle Inc., a provider of online career assessments that was acquired in May. We see organic growth driven by strong gains in online recruiting industrywide, partly offset by market share losses to top rivals HotJobs and CareerBuilder. In 2005, we project more modest industry growth, with ongoing share losses for MNST, resulting in revenue growth of 9% to 11%.
- We think margins will widen in 2004 and 2005, reflecting expected additional workforce cuts in the recruitment advertising segment. In the flagship Monster division, we think additional margin improvement will be difficult, after substantial cost cutting in 2002 and 2003, and in light of substantial new hirings. We project that marketing and promotional spending will be flat in 2005 with 2004's estimate $150 million to $155 million.
- We estimate 2004 EPS at $0.60, up from $0.40 in 2003, before reorganizational and other expenses. Reflecting estimated stock option expense, we see 2004 S&P Core EPS of $0.30. For 2005, we see earnings growth of 17%, to $0.70 ($0.40).

Investment Rationale/Risk 15-NOV-04

- We believe the current share price reflects extremely high job growth expectations that we think may be unrealistic, given S&P's expectations for moderate economic growth. We think that investors may be disappointed if robust job gains at levels that are typically seen as the economy expands after a recession are not sustained in this recovery. We believe a number of established and startup competitors are gaining market share, albeit in a growing market, as we view barriers to entry as relatively low.
- Risks to our recommendation and target price include the possibility that MNST's shift in marketing strategy away from deals for content and traffic with web portals AOL and MSN will not result in a loss of market share and, ultimately, its leading position in online recruiting, as we expect.
- Based on our discounted cash flow analysis, which assumes a weighted average cost of capital of 11% and a terminal growth rate of 3%, our 12-month target price is $18. We expect free cash flow of $70 million to $75 million in 2005, after negative free cash flow of $40 million in 2004, due in part to ongoing outlays for accrued business reorganization and separation costs.

Key Stock Statistics

S&P Core EPS 2005E	0.40	52-week Range	$29.94-17.60
S&P Oper. EPS 2004E	0.55	12 Month P/E	53.8
P/E on S&P Oper. EPS 2004E	51.8	Beta	NA
S&P Oper. EPS 2005E	0.70	Shareholders	1,774
Yield (%)	Nil	Market Cap (B)	$ 3.3
Dividend Rate/Share	Nil	Shares Outstanding (M)	119.1

Value of $10,000 invested five years ago: **NA**

Dividend Data

No cash dividends have been paid.

Revenues/Earnings Data Fiscal year ending December 31

Revenues (Million $)

	2004	2003	2002	2001	2000	1999
1Q	187.7	168.5	290.8	362.8	271.4	169.0
2Q	209.4	166.7	291.0	383.6	316.1	186.1
3Q	227.1	173.7	284.0	361.2	352.3	206.4
4Q	—	170.8	248.8	326.1	351.9	204.3
Yr.	—	679.6	1,115	1,448	1,292	765.8

Earnings Per Share ($)

	2004	2003	2002	2001	2000	1999
1Q	0.11	-1.04	0.06	0.05	0.08	-0.03
2Q	0.14	0.08	-0.68	0.17	0.08	0.04
3Q	0.17	0.11	0.12	0.23	0.23	-0.07
4Q	E0.19	0.11	-0.46	0.16	0.14	-0.03
Yr.	E0.55	0.06	-0.96	0.61	0.53	-0.09

Next earnings report expected: mid-February Source: S&P, Company Reports
EPS Estimates based on S&P Operating Earnings; historical GAAP earnings are as reported.

STANDARD &POOR'S

Monster Worldwide Inc.

Recommendation: **SELL** ★ ☆ ☆ ☆ ☆   12-Month Target Price: **$18.00** (as of October 20, 2004)

Business Summary 15-NOV-04

Monster Worldwide is a leading online recruitment and career leader through the Monster.com portal. It is also the world's largest Yellow Pages advertising agency, and provides recruitment advertising and related services. MNST's clients include more than 90 companies in the Fortune 100, and more than 490 in the Fortune 500. Formerly known as TMP Worldwide, the company adopted its current name and its stock began trading under the symbol MNST on May 1, 2003.

Monster.com is the leading global recruitment, hiring and career property on the web. Among the most visited locations on the Internet, Monster.com had more than 42 million registered users and 33.4 million resumes in its database as of December 2003, according to company statistics. In addition, the web site had over 1 million job postings. The website connects companies with qualified job seekers, offering innovative technology and services that provide greater control over the recruiting process. The Monster.com global network consists of local language and content sites in 22 countries, including the U.S., the U.K., Australia, Canada, Luxembourg, the Netherlands, Belgium, New Zealand, France, Singapore, Hong Kong, Germany, Spain, Ireland and India.

Monster.com offers various ancillary services. HMonster is a channel devoted to healthcare job postings. MonsterTRAK and Fastweb connect college students and alumni to college career centers and to college and scholarship sources. Monster Government Solutions develops and markets recruitment portals and related tools for governments.

The company's Yellow Pages division, also referred to as directional marketing services, develops marketing programs for national accounts, clients that sell products or services in multiple markets. The number of services that MNST offers has grown over the past 30 years from yellow pages ads to include a variety of services that connect businesses with consumers. Included in this division is Monstermoving.com, the leading online relocation information and services website.

Recruitment advertising, also referred to as the Advertising and Communications division, creates and places job ads in the classified sections of newspapers. This division has expanded to other services that help employers communicate with current and prospective employees.

In recent years, MNST grew aggressively via acquisitions; it made 55, using the purchase method of accounting, from 2000 to 2002. It also made a number of deals using pooling-of-interests accounting during that time. The result of this strategy was dismantled on March 31, 2003, when MNST spun off its staffing and executive search units into a newly formed, separate company, Hudson Highland Group, Inc. In a tax-free distribution, shareholders received one Hudson Highland common share for every 13 1/3 MNST common shares held. The company has since made several acquisitions, most notably jobpilot GmbH in April 2004, in exchange for 1 million MNST common shares and $61 million in cash.

Company Financials Fiscal Year ending December 31

Per Share Data ($)

(Year Ended December 31)	2003	2002	2001	2000	1999	1998	1997	1996	1995	1994
Tangible Bk. Val.	0.18	2.02	2.61	5.16	0.18	NM	NM	NM	NA	NA
Cash Flow	0.31	-0.46	1.28	1.11	0.35	0.43	0.48	-0.93	NA	NA
Earnings	0.06	-0.96	0.61	0.53	-0.09	0.07	0.19	-1.36	NA	NA
S&P Core Earnings	-0.08	-1.48	0.10	NA	NA	NA	NA	NA	NA	NA
Dividends	Nil	Nil	Nil	Nil	Nil	Nil	Nil	Nil	NA	NA
Payout Ratio	Nil	Nil	Nil	Nil	Nil	Nil	Nil	Nil	NA	NA
Prices - High	29.65	48.13	68.73	94.68	80.50	21.31	14.37	7.12	NA	NA
- Low	7.63	7.93	25.21	45.00	18.50	7.75	6.43	6.25	NA	NA
P/E Ratio - High	NM	NM	NM	NM	NM	NM	76	NM	NA	NA
- Low	NM	NM	NM	NM	NM	NM	34	NM	NA	NA

Income Statement Analysis (Million $)

	2003	2002	2001	2000	1999	1998	1997	1996	1995	1994
Revs.	680	1,115	1,448	1,292	766	407	237	163	NA	NA
Oper. Inc.	101	112	262	222	109	69.4	41.3	26.7	NA	NA
Depr.	28.0	55.5	76.0	62.6	35.0	22.2	14.0	8.89	NA	NA
Int. Exp.	Nil	4.90	10.6	9.49	17.0	13.7	11.0	14.6	NA	NA
Pretax Inc.	23.6	-130	125	114	-1.50	12.7	18.3	-48.5	NA	NA
Eff. Tax Rate	69.0%	NM	46.1%	50.5%	NM	66.6%	46.7%	NM	NA	NA
Net Inc.	7.32	-107	69.0	56.9	-7.40	4.25	9.62	-52.2	NA	NA
S&P Core Earnings	-8.07	-165	11.4	NA	NA	NA	NA	NA	NA	NA

Balance Sheet & Other Fin. Data (Million $)

	2003	2002	2001	2000	1999	1998	1997	1996	1995	1994
Cash	142	192	341	572	57.0	28.9	5.94	0.90	NA	NA
Curr. Assets	567	809	1,006	1,248	557	343	288	213	NA	NA
Total Assets	1,122	1,631	2,206	1,992	945	608	495	332	NA	NA
Curr. Liab.	640	799	930	853	565	360	282	225	NA	NA
LT Debt	2.09	3.92	9.13	28.0	71.0	118	116	71.0	NA	NA
Common Equity	468	813	1,229	1,058	281	123	96.9	31.3	NA	NA
Total Cap.	470	817	1,238	1,086	352	241	213	107	NA	NA
Cap. Exp.	21.6	46.7	73.6	78.9	NA	21.7	18.3	6.90	NA	NA
Cash Flow	35.4	-51.0	145	119	27.6	26.4	23.5	-43.6	NA	NA
Curr. Ratio	0.9	1.0	1.1	1.5	1.0	1.0	1.0	0.9	NA	NA
% LT Debt of Cap.	0.4	0.5	0.7	2.6	NA	48.9	54.4	66.1	NA	NA
% Net Inc.of Revs.	1.1	NM	4.8	4.4	NM	1.0	4.1	NM	NA	NA
% Ret. on Assets	0.5	NM	3.2	3.7	NM	0.8	2.3	NM	NA	NA
% Ret. on Equity	1.1	NM	6.0	8.2	NM	3.9	14.8	NM	NA	NA

Data as orig reptd.; bef. results of disc opers/spec. items. Per share data adj. for stk. divs. Bold denotes primary EPS - prior periods restated. E-Estimated. NA-Not Available. NM-Not Meaningful. NR-Not Ranked. UR-Under Review.

Office: 622 Third Avenue , New York, NY 10017-6707.
Telephone: 212-351-7000.
Email: corporate.communications@monsterworldwide.com
Website: http://www.monsterworldwide.com
Chrmn & CEO: A. J. McKelvey.
COO: W. M. Pastore.

SVP & CFO: M. Sileck.
EVP: P. M. Camara.
Investor Contact: Robert P. Jones (212-351-7032).
Dirs: G. R. Eisele, J. Gaulding, M. Kaufman, R. J. Kramer, A. J. McKelvey, D. A. Stein, J. Swann.

Founded: in 1967.
Domicile: Delaware.
Employees: 4,300.
S&P Analyst: Mark S. Basham/PMW/JWP

Moody's Corp.

Stock Report
November 13, 2004
NYSE Symbol: **MCO**

Recommendation: **BUY** ★★★★☆
SELL SELL HOLD BUY BUY

12-Month Target Price: **$85.00**
(as of October 27, 2004)

MCO has an approximate 0.11% weighting in the **S&P 500**

Sector: Financials
Sub-Industry: Specialized Finance
Peer Group: Financial Cos. - Misc.

Summary: MCO is a leading global credit rating, research and risk analysis concern.

Quantitative Evaluations

S&P Earnings & Dividend Rank: B

| D | C | B- | B | B | B+ | A- | A | A+ |

S&P Fair Value Rank: 1

| 1 | 2 | 3 | 4 | 5 |
Lowest | | | | Highest

Fair Value Calc.: $61.80 (Overvalued)

S&P Investability Quotient Percentile

97%

MCO scored higher than 97% of all companies for which an S&P Report is available.

Volatility: Low

| Low | Average | High |

Technical Evaluation: Bullish
Since 8/04, the technical indicators for MCO have been Bullish.

Relative Strength Rank: Strong

71

1 Lowest | Highest 99

Price as of 11/12/04: $80.30 | **2004E S&P Core EPS:** $2.50

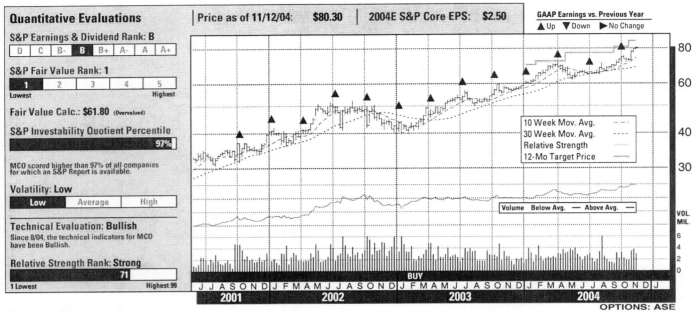

GAAP Earnings vs. Previous Year
▲ Up ▼ Down ▶ No Change

- - - 10 Week Mov. Avg.
········ 30 Week Mov. Avg.
Relative Strength
12-Mo Target Price

Volume Below Avg. — Above Avg.

BUY

J J A S O N D | J F M A M J J A S O N D | J F M A M J J A S O N D | J F M A M J J A S O N D | J
2001 | 2002 | 2003 | 2004

OPTIONS: ASE

Analyst commentary prepared by William H. Donald/DC/BK

Highlights September 15, 2004

- We expect revenues to rise about 16%, to $1.45 billion, in 2004, which should mark the fourth consecutive year of strong double digit growth. We are looking for gains in every business segment as well as a beneficial impact from foreign exchange translations. We believe global structured finance and corporate finance revenues will rise moderately. We project continued strong growth in the research business, and in the Moody's KMV business. For 2005, we expect total revenues to rise roughly 9.6%, to $1.59 billion.

- Aided by the increased revenues that we expect, we estimate EBITDA margins in 2004 will rise slightly, to 53.6% from 53.2% in 2003, despite the impact of investment spending and changes in the business mix. We project operating earnings will grow 15%, after a 23% advance in 2003. For 2005, we look for a 70 basis point margin improvement, to 54.3%, and an 11% rise in operating profits.

- After other items, including expected higher borrowing costs, and taxes at an estimated effective rate of 44.2%, versus 44.6% in 2003, we project a 13% increase in 2004 net income, to $412.3 million, from 2003's $363.9 million. We anticipate a 15% gain in operating EPS in 2004, to $2.75, from 2003's $2.39, which excludes about $0.04 in option expense and a $0.05 insurance recovery gain. We project operating EPS of $3.10 for 2005.

Investment Rationale/Risk September 15, 2004

- We regard the stock as attractive, based on our view of MCO's strong balance sheet, consistently wide operating margins, and heightened global growth opportunities. MCO is the only pure play publicly held credit rating concern. Based on these factors, we believe the stock warrants a premium P/E multiple relative to the S&P 500 and to other service companies.

- Risks to our recommendation and target price include the fact that the SEC is studying the credit rating industry to determine if there are anti-competitive practices, conflicts of interest, or disclosure, or other issues. We do not think that the SEC's action will have a major impact on MCO's business model. However, we think that changes in the competitive structure of the ratings industry would have an impact on market share and pricing over the longer term. Risks also include changes in the volume of debt securities issued in domestic and/or global capital markets, changes in interest rates and other volatility in the financial markets

- The stock is trading at a 16% discount to our intrinsic value estimate of $81, calculated by using our discounted cash flow model, which assumes 10-year average free cash flow growth of 13%, and a weighted average cost of capital of 10.5%. Our 12-month target price is also $81, based on a blend of our DCF model and relative P/E valuation.

Key Stock Statistics

S&P Oper. EPS 2004E	2.75	52-week Range	$80.92-55.60
P/E on S&P Oper. EPS 2004E	29.2	12 Month P/E	31.4
S&P Oper. EPS 2005E	3.10	Beta	NA
Yield (%)	0.4%	Shareholders	4,781
Dividend Rate/Share	0.30	Market Cap (B)	$ 11.9
Shares Outstanding (M)	147.9		

Value of $10,000 invested five years ago: **NA**

Dividend Data Dividends have been paid since 1934

Amount ($)	Date Decl.	Ex-Div. Date	Stock of Record	Payment Date
0.075	Dec. 09	Feb. 18	Feb. 20	Mar. 10 '04
0.075	Apr. 27	May. 18	May. 20	Jun. 10 '04
0.075	Jul. 28	Aug. 18	Aug. 20	Sep. 10 '04
0.075	Oct. 27	Nov. 17	Nov. 20	Dec. 10 '04

Revenues/Earnings Data Fiscal year ending December 31

Revenues (Million $)

	2004	2003	2002	2001	2000	1999
1Q	331.2	278.2	231.6	180.2	—	491.0
2Q	357.6	312.7	271.5	205.2	—	497.0
3Q	357.9	305.0	248.3	190.4	152.5	474.0
4Q	—	350.7	271.9	220.9	161.1	510.0
Yr.	—	1,247	1,023	796.7	602.3	1,972

Earnings Per Share ($)

	2004	2003	2002	2001	2000	1999
1Q	0.68	0.61	0.46	0.30	—	0.36
2Q	0.68	0.66	0.49	0.34	—	0.40
3Q	0.63	0.56	0.43	0.31	0.25	0.41
4Q	E0.66	0.56	0.45	0.37	0.25	0.39
Yr.	E2.75	2.39	1.83	1.32	0.97	1.56

Next earnings report expected: early-February Source: S&P, Company Reports
EPS Estimates based on S&P Operating Earnings; historical GAAP earnings are as reported.

Moody's Corporation

Recommendation: **BUY** ★ ★ ★ ★ ☆   12-Month Target Price: **$85.00** (as of October 27, 2004)

Business Summary September 24, 2004

Moody's Investors Service, the major operating subsidiary of Moody's Corp., is a global credit rating, research and risk analysis concern. It publishes rating opinions on a broad range of credit obligations issued in U.S. and international markets, including various corporate and governmental obligations, structured finance securities, and commercial paper programs. It also publishes investor-oriented credit research, including in-depth research on major issuers, industry studies, special comments and credit opinion handbooks, and provides risk management services. In April 2002, MCO acquired KMV Corp. (renamed Moody's KMV), a leading provider of quantitative services that help financial institutions and corporations manage credit-sensitive assets. Moody's KMV (MKMV) serves more than 1,500 clients in 60 countries.

Founded in 1900, Moody's employs more than 700 analysts based in 19 countries. It provides ratings and information on governmental and commercial entities in more than 100 countries.

Credit ratings help investors assess credit risks associated with fixed-income securities. They also create efficiencies in fixed-income markets by providing reliable, credible and independent assessments of credit risk. For issuers, company services increase market liquidity and may reduce transaction costs.

Ratings fees paid by issuers account for about 90% of total revenues. A substantial portion of revenues is thus dependent on the volume of debt securities issued in the global capital markets. MCO is therefore affected by the performance of, and the prospects for, major world economies, and by fiscal and monetary policies pursued by their governments. However, annual fee arrangements with frequent debt issuers, and annual fees from commercial paper and medium-term note programs, bank and insurance company financial strength ratings, mutual fund ratings, and other areas are less dependent on, or independent of, the volume of debt securities issued in the global capital markets.

Moody's Risk Management Services develops and distributes credit risk assessment software used by banks and other financial institutions in their portfolio management, commercial lending and other activities. It also provides modeling tools, analytics, credit education materials, seminars, computer-based lending simulations and more.

Moody's Investors Service and the Dun & Bradstreet operating company were separated into stand-alone entities on September 30, 2000. Each holder of "old" Dun & Bradstreet Corp. (D&B) received one share of "new" D&B for every two shares of old D&B held as of September 20, 2000. Old D&B changed its name to Moody's Corp. (NYSE: MCO), and new D&B assumed the name Dun & Bradstreet Corp. (NYSE: DNB). A holder of two Dun & Bradstreet shares at the record date received one share of new D&B and two MCO shares.

Company Financials Fiscal Year ending December 31

Per Share Data ($)

(Year Ended December 31)	2003	2002	2001	2000	1999	1998	1997	1996	1995	1994
Tangible Bk. Val.	NM	NM	NM	NM	NM	NM	NM	NM	NM	NM
Cash Flow	2.60	1.99	1.43	1.07	2.42	2.26	2.03	0.15	4.68	5.61
Earnings	2.39	1.83	1.32	0.97	1.56	1.44	1.27	-0.69	1.89	3.70
S&P Core Earnings	2.23	1.70	1.27	NA	NA	NA	NA	NA	NA	NA
Dividends	0.18	0.14	0.23	0.56	0.74	0.81	0.88	1.82	2.63	2.56
Payout Ratio	8%	7%	17%	57%	47%	56%	69%	NM	139%	69%
Prices - High	60.85	52.40	41.10	36.18	40.00	36.68	31.25	69.00	65.50	64.00
- Low	39.50	35.80	25.56	22.62	23.37	21.75	23.12	19.25	48.50	51.87
P/E Ratio - High	25	29	31	37	26	25	36	NM	35	17
- Low	17	20	19	23	15	15	18	NM	26	14

Income Statement Analysis (Million $)

	2003	2002	2001	2000	1999	1998	1997	1996	1995	1994
Revs.	1,247	1,023	797	602	1,972	1,935	1,811	1,783	5,415	4,896
Oper. Inc.	696	563	416	305	621	591	536	198	876	1,249
Depr.	32.6	25.0	17.0	16.6	141	142	132	141	475	324
Int. Exp.	21.8	21.0	16.5	3.60	5.00	12.0	53.0	37.0	53.0	39.0
Pretax Inc.	656	517	382	284	457	400	332	-14.0	444	879
Eff. Tax Rate	44.6%	44.1%	44.4%	44.2%	39.1%	38.5%	34.0%	NM	27.7%	28.4%
Net Inc.	364	289	212	159	256	246	219	-116	321	630
S&P Core Earnings	340	269	203	NA	NA	NA	NA	NA	NA	NA

Balance Sheet & Other Fin. Data (Million $)

	2003	2002	2001	2000	1999	1998	1997	1996	1995	1994
Cash	269	40.0	163	119	113	91.0	82.0	128	439	362
Curr. Assets	569	272	371	278	785	764	806	760	2,299	1,981
Total Assets	941	631	505	398	1,786	1,789	2,225	2,294	5,516	5,464
Curr. Liab.	432	462	359	253	1,415	1,353	1,497	2,008	2,834	2,187
LT Debt	300	300	300	300	Nil	Nil	Nil	Nil	Nil	Nil
Common Equity	-32.1	-327	-304	-283	-417	-371	-490	-455	1,183	1,319
Total Cap.	268	-27.0	-4.10	17.5	-115	-70.0	-188	-455	1,351	1,528
Cap. Exp.	17.9	18.0	14.8	12.3	44.1	55.0	51.0	58.0	286	273
Cash Flow	397	314	229	175	397	388	351	25.0	796	953
Curr. Ratio	1.3	0.6	1.0	1.1	0.6	0.6	0.5	0.4	0.8	0.9
% LT Debt of Cap.	112.0	NM	NM	NM	Nil	Nil	Nil	Nil	Nil	Nil
% Net Inc.of Revs.	29.2	28.2	26.6	26.3	13.0	12.7	12.1	NM	6.0	12.9
% Ret. on Assets	46.3	50.9	47.0	47.1	14.3	NA	10.2	NM	5.9	11.9
% Ret. on Equity	NM	NM	NM	NM	NM	NM	NM	NM	25.7	51.9

Data as orig reptd.; bef. results of disc opers/spec. items. Per share data adj. for stk. divs. Certain data for 1997 and 1996 restated. Bold denotes primary EPS -prior periods restated. E-Estimated. NA-Not Available. NM-Not Meaningful. NR-Not Ranked.

Office: 99 Church Street, New York, NY 10007.
Telephone: 212-553-0300.
Website: http://www.moodys.com
Chrmn, Pres & CEO: J. Rutherfurd, Jr.
COO & EVP: R.W. McDaniel.
SVP & CFO: J. Dering.

SVP & General Counsel: J.J. Goggins.
VP & Treas: R. Roy.
VP & Investor Contact: M.D. Courtian 212-553-7194.
Dirs: B. L. Anderson, M. J. Evans, R. R. Glauber, E. Kwist, C. Mack, R. W. McDaniel, Jr., H. A. McKinnell, Jr., J. Rutherfurd, Jr., J. K. Wulff.

Founded: in 1998.
Domicile: Delaware.
Employees: 2,300.
S&P Analyst: William H. Donald/DC/BK

Morgan Stanley

Recommendation: **BUY ★★★★**☆   12-Month Target Price: **$55.00**
(as of June 22, 2004)

MWD has an approximate 0.53% weighting in the **S&P 500**

Sector: Financials
Sub-Industry: Investment Banking & Brokerage
Peer Group: Investment Banking/Brokerage - Major

Summary: Morgan Stanley is among the largest securities firms in the U.S., with operations in the brokerage, underwriting and credit card businesses.

Quantitative Evaluations

S&P Earnings & Dividend Rank: A-

| D | C | B- | B | B+ | A- | A | A+ |

S&P Fair Value Rank: 1

| 1 | 2 | 3 | 4 | 5 |
Lowest | | | | Highest

Fair Value Calc.: $41.50 (Overvalued)

S&P Investability Quotient Percentile
91%

MWD scored higher than 91% of all companies for which an S&P Report is available.

Volatility: Average

| Low | Average | High |

Technical Evaluation: Neutral
Since 10/04, the technical indicators for MWD have been Neutral.

Relative Strength Rank: Moderate
53
1 Lowest   Highest 99

| Price as of 11/12/04: | **$53.13** | 2004E S&P Core EPS: | **$4.40** |

GAAP Earnings vs. Previous Year
▲ Up ▼ Down ► No Change

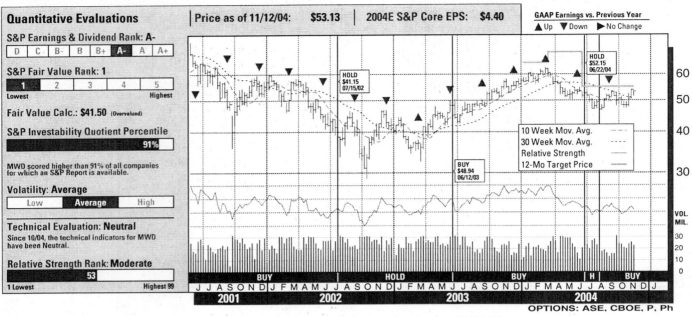

Legend:
- 10 Week Mov. Avg.
- 30 Week Mov. Avg.
- Relative Strength
- 12-Mo Target Price

Chart annotations: HOLD $41.15 07/15/02; HOLD $52.15 06/22/04; BUY $48.94 06/12/03

BUY | HOLD | BUY | H | BUY
J J A S O N D J F M A M J J A S O N D J F M A M J J A S O N D J F M A M J J A S O N D J
2001   2002   2003   2004

OPTIONS: ASE, CBOE, P, Ph

Analyst commentary prepared by Robert Hansen, CFA /CB/BK

Highlights September 23, 2004

- We think Morgan Stanley is benefiting from improved equity markets, a relatively steep yield curve, interest rate volatility, and tight credit spreads. However, FY 04 (Nov.) third quarter EPS of $0.76, versus $1.15 a year earlier, was significantly below our $1.10 estimate, largely due to increased legal costs and a sequential decline in principal transactions as the company bet wrong on the direction of interest rates. Although trading revenue can be volatile, we have less confidence in the company's risk management policies given the magnitude of the sequential revenue decline.

- We expect growth in sales and trading, investment banking, and commission and asset management revenue in FY 05. However, we see MWD losing market share in its brokerage, credit card and asset management segments. We see the Discover Credit Services segment negatively affecting results and expect MWD to dispose of the business in FY 05.

- We see continued prudent expense growth, particularly in compensation costs, which should also help profitability. We forecast EPS of $3.85 in FY 04 and $4.25 in FY 05.

Investment Rationale/Risk September 23, 2004

- We think the company's investment banking business, its largest segment, is well positioned, but believe the company's brokerage, credit card and asset management businesses lack competitive advantage. We see industry fundamentals improving, and we think the shares of MWD should trade near the peer group multiple.

- Risks to our recommendation and target price include stock and bond market volatility, potentially higher interest rates, increased competition, and regulatory issues. Trading revenue can also be highly volatile in a given quarter.

- At about 12X our FY 05 EPS estimate, the shares were recently at a notable discount to the peer group, the overall market, and the company's 10-year historical average of nearly 15X. Our 12-month target price is $55, which is 13X our FY 05 EPS estimate, near the peer average. We view the recent valuation as attractive, and would accumulate the shares.

Key Stock Statistics

S&P Core EPS 2005E	4.60	52-week Range	$62.83-46.54
S&P Oper. EPS 2004E	3.85	12 Month P/E	13.6
P/E on S&P Oper. EPS 2004E	13.8	Beta	2.06
S&P Oper. EPS 2005E	4.25	Shareholders	130,000
Yield (%)	1.9%	Market Cap (B)	$ 58.2
Dividend Rate/Share	1.00	Shares Outstanding (M)	1094.6

Value of $10,000 invested five years ago: **$ 10,108**

Dividend Data Dividends have been paid since 1993

Amount ($)	Date Decl.	Ex-Div. Date	Stock of Record	Payment Date
0.250	Dec. 18	Jan. 07	Jan. 09	Jan. 30 '04
0.250	Mar. 19	Apr. 06	Apr. 09	Apr. 30 '04
0.250	Jun. 14	Jul. 07	Jul. 09	Jul. 30 '04
0.250	Sep. 23	Oct. 06	Oct. 08	Oct. 29 '04

Revenues/Earnings Data Fiscal year ending November 30

Revenues (Million $)

	2004	2003	2002	2001	2000	1999
1Q	9,992	8,502	8,540	12,644	11,614	8,405
2Q	9,802	8,418	8,149	12,569	11,692	8,529
3Q	9,854	8,929	8,156	10,296	11,711	8,370
4Q	—	9,092	7,570	8,218	10,444	8,624
Yr.	—	34,933	32,415	43,727	45,413	33,928

Earnings Per Share ($)

	2004	2003	2002	2001	2000	1999
1Q	1.11	0.82	0.76	0.94	1.34	0.88
2Q	1.10	0.55	0.72	0.82	1.26	0.98
3Q	0.78	1.15	0.55	0.65	1.09	0.83
4Q	E0.88	0.92	0.67	0.78	1.06	1.42
Yr.	E3.85	3.45	2.69	3.19	4.73	4.10

Next earnings report expected: mid-December Source: S&P, Company Reports
EPS Estimates based on S&P Operating Earnings; historical GAAP earnings are as reported.

Morgan Stanley

Recommendation: **BUY** ★ ★ ★ ☆   12-Month Target Price: **$55.00** (as of June 22, 2004)

Business Summary September 23, 2004

Morgan Stanley is a global financial services company that maintains strong market positions in each of its four business segments: Institutional Securities, Individual Investor Group, Investment Management and Credit Services.

The company's Institutional Securities business (54% of FY 03 (Nov.) net revenues) provides worldwide financial advisory and capital raising services to a diverse group of domestic and international institutional clients. The business activities of this unit include investment banking, institutional sales and trading and principal investing activities, as well as aircraft leasing through Ansett Worldwide Aviation Services. As an investment banker, MWD helps raise capital for corporate clients through equity and debt offerings, and advises corporate clients on matters such as takeover defenses, acquisitions and restructurings. In its sales and trading operations, the company advises major buy side institutions on developments affecting their securities holdings, receiving either a commission or positive spread when the client places a buy or sell order.

The Individual Investor Group (19%) provides financial advice to individual clients, focusing on affluent and high net worth investors. MWD had about 11,000 financial advisers in nearly 450 branches at the end of FY 03. MWD had client assets of $565 billion at the end of FY 03, up from $517 billion at the end of FY 02.

The Investment Management business (12%) is one of the largest in the world. At the end of FY 03, it had $462 billion in assets under management or supervision, up

from $420 billion at the end of FY 02. The company's asset management group offers a wide range of domestic and international equity, bond and multi-class funds for both individual and institutional investors. MWD's portfolio managers are located in the U.S., Europe, Japan, Singapore and India.

Credit Services (16%) include the Discover Card and the Morgan Stanley Card as well as affinity cards. The business had about 46.1 million general purpose credit card accounts at the end of FY 03. MWD conducts substantial portions of its credit services business in the U.S. through Discover Bank, a wholly owned indirect subsidiary. Discover Bank is a state bank chartered under the laws of the State of Delaware, and has its deposits insured by the FDIC, pays FDIC assessments, and is subject to comprehensive regulation and periodic examination by the Delaware bank commissioner and by the FDIC.

In April 2003, MWD and nine other financial services firms reached a final settlement with the SEC, the New York State Attorney General's Office, the NYSE, and NASDAQ regarding allegations of conflicts of interest in investment research. MWD agreed to pay $125 million as part of the $1.4 billion settlement. MWD also agreed to make organizational changes to reduce conflicts of interest in its research departments. Since 2001, MWD has been named as a defendant in a number of civil actions, which it continues to defend itself against.

Company Financials Fiscal Year ending November 30

Per Share Data ($)

(Year Ended November 30)	2003	2002	2001	2000	1999	1998	1997	1996	1995	1994
Tangible Bk. Val.	21.52	19.43	17.36	16.91	14.79	11.88	10.99	8.69	6.91	5.84
Earnings	3.45	2.69	3.19	4.73	4.10	2.76	2.13	1.40	1.22	1.09
S&P Core Earnings	3.48	2.38	2.84	NA	NA	NA	NA	NA	NA	NA
Dividends	0.92	0.92	0.92	0.80	0.48	0.40	0.28	0.22	0.16	0.13
Payout Ratio	27%	34%	29%	17%	12%	14%	13%	16%	13%	11%
Prices - High	58.78	60.02	90.49	110.00	71.43	48.75	29.75	17.25	14.56	10.78
- Low	32.46	28.80	35.75	58.62	35.40	18.25	16.37	11.25	8.37	7.87
P/E Ratio - High	17	22	28	23	17	18	14	12	12	10
- Low	9	11	11	12	9	7	8	8	7	7

Income Statement Analysis (Million $)

	2003	2002	2001	2000	1999	1998	1997	1996	1995	1994
Net Int. Inc.	2,935	3,896	3,348	3,058	2,365	2,922	2,777	2,021	1,804	1,459
Non Int. Inc.	19,189	16,549	19,600	24,179	20,110	14,656	13,549	5,441	4,615	4,095
Loan Loss Prov.	1,267	1,336	1,052	810	529	1,173	1,493	1,232	744	548
Non Int. Exp.	16,636	15,725	17,264	18,746	14,281	15,530	12,052	5,917	4,280	3,791
Exp./Op. Revs.	76.3%	76.9%	75.2%	65.9%	63.2%	66.6%	NA	62.8%	66.7%	81.6%
Pretax Inc.	5,334	4,633	5,684	8,526	7,728	5,385	4,274	1,545	1,396	1,215
Eff. Tax Rate	29.0%	35.5%	36.5%	36.0%	38.0%	37.0%	39.5%	38.4%	38.7%	39.0%
Net Inc.	3,787	2,988	3,610	5,456	4,791	3,393	2,586	951	856	741
% Net Int. Marg.	5.40	5.50	5.57	6.08	8.47	9.00	8.45	8.16	8.47	9.05
S&P Core Earnings	3,830	2,658	3,203	NA	NA	NA	NA	NA	NA	NA

Balance Sheet & Other Fin. Data (Million $)

	2003	2002	2001	2000	1999	1998	1997	1996	1995	1994
Money Mkt. Assets	78,205	76,910	54,618	50,992	70,366	90,101	6,890	4,044	3,391	2,828
Inv. Securities	228,904	185,588	164,011	130,818	112,042	41,689	35,801	4,477	5,421	5,215
Tot. Loans	20,384	24,322	20,955	21,870	20,229	22,388	24,499	23,177	21,557	15,608
Total Assets	602,843	529,499	482,628	426,794	366,967	317,590	302,287	42,414	38,208	31,859
Demand Deposits	1,264	1,441	1,741	1,589	1,458	1,355	1,210	1,716	1,552	1,166
Time Deposits	11,575	12,316	10,535	10,341	8,939	6,842	7,783	5,497	4,639	4,043
LT Debt	68,410	43,985	40,851	36,830	28,604	27,435	18,627	8,144	6,732	5,293
Common Equity	24,933	21,951	20,437	18,796	16,344	13,445	14,079	5,165	4,834	4,108
% Ret. on Assets	0.7	0.6	0.8	1.4	1.4	NA	1.5	2.4	2.4	2.5
% Ret. on Equity	16.2	14.1	18.2	30.3	30.3	25.2	26.2	19.0	19.2	19.5
% Loan Loss Resv.	4.9	3.8	4.0	3.6	3.7	NA	NA	3.5	3.3	3.5
% Loans/Deposits	158.8	176.8	170.7	183.3	229.2	272.8	294.2	322.4	348.2	300.0
% Loans/Assets	3.9	4.5	4.7	5.4	6.2	7.5	13.8	53.6	53.9	49.0
% Equity to Assets	4.1	4.2	4.3	4.5	4.4	4.3	5.6	12.4	12.8	12.9

Data as orig. reptd.; for Dean Witter, Discover & Co. (yrs. ended Dec.) prior to 1997; bef. results of disc. opers. and/or spec. items. Per share data adj. for stk. divs.; EPS diluted. E-Estimated. NA-Not Available. NM-Not Meaningful. NR-Not Ranked.

Office: 1585 Broadway, New York, NY 10036.	EVP, Secy & General Counsel: D.G. Kempf, Jr.	Founded: in 1981.
Telephone: 212-761-4000.	CFO: D.H. Sidwell.	Domicile: Delaware.
Website: http://www.morganstanley.com	Chief Acctg Officer: J. Pace.	Employees: 51,196.
Chrmn & CEO: P.J. Purcell.	Dirs: S. H. Davies, J. E. Jacob, C. R. Kidder, C. F. Knight, J. W.	S&P Analyst: Robert Hansen, CFA /CB/BK
Pres: S.F. Newhouse.	Madigan, M. Marsh, M. Miles, P. J. Purcell, L. D. Tyson, K. Zumwinkel.	

Motorola

Recommendation: **BUY** ★★★★★   12-Month Target Price: **$22.00**
(as of July 20, 2004)

MOT has an approximate 0.39% weighting in the **S&P 500**

Sector: Information Technology
Sub-Industry: Communications Equipment
Peer Group: Wireless Equipment

Summary: This leading supplier of cellular telephone systems, semiconductors, two-way radios and paging equipment also offers information systems and other electronics products.

| Quantitative Evaluations | Price as of 11/12/04: $18.10 | 2004E S&P Core EPS: $0.53 |

S&P Earnings & Dividend Rank: B+
D | C | B- | B | **B+** | A- | A | A+

S&P Fair Value Rank: 2-
1 (Lowest) | **2** | 3 | 4 | 5 (Highest)

Fair Value Calc.: $15.00 (Overvalued)

S&P Investability Quotient Percentile
92%

MOT scored higher than 92% of all companies for which an S&P Report is available.

Volatility: Average
Low | **Average** | High

Technical Evaluation: Bearish
Since 11/04, the technical indicators for MOT have been Bearish.

Relative Strength Rank: Moderate
53
1 Lowest | Highest 99

Analyst commentary prepared by K. Leon/MF/JWP

Highlights October 22, 2004

- We expect 15% sales growth in 2005, based on our view of strong handset and wireless infrastructure markets. MOT's third quarter handset sales advanced 34% versus weaker sales in the prior year's same period, and average selling prices continue to trend higher, aided by a favorable product shift toward color display and integrated camera-ready phones. We believe better execution in the U.S. handset market, particularly CDMA handset shipments, may be material to MOT's performance. In the past, the company was late to market with new handsets, but we believe MOT is beginning to realize high volume shipments of new handsets introduced earlier in 2004.

- For 2005, we expect all major business segments to post double-digit sales growth, with the handset business leading with an 18% advance. We see 2005 gross margins staying at about 35%. We expect operating expenses to decrease as a percentage of sales, aided by cost control programs, despite higher research and development costs.

- Our EPS estimates (excluding special items) are $0.85 for 2004 and $1.00 for 2005. Our Standard & Poor's Core EPS estimates are $0.53 for 2004 and $0.88 in 2005, reflecting the estimated impact of stock option expense and pension cost adjustments.

Investment Rationale/Risk October 22, 2004

- We think the shares, priced below peers at 1X our 2004 sales estimate, are benefiting from stronger global demand for wireless products, and from the company's momentum in handsets and other key businesses. Despite a lower price for the IPO of FreeScale Semiconductor (FSL: $16), MOT's semiconductor unit, we believe the planned spinoff of the remaining FSL shares by the end of 2004 will be positive for shareholder value. With what we view as a growing portfolio of competitive handset products, we expect the company to gain market share in the fourth quarter and 2005 with a strong global market for handsets and wireless infrastructure.

- Risks to our recommendation and target price include a failure to successfully introduce and ship new products and technologies, a slower pace of recovery in the wireless infrastructure market including third generation upgrades, and the financial condition of the company's largest customers in the automotive, broadband, specialized mobile, and wireless infrastructure markets.

- Applying an assumed price to sales ratio of 1.4X to our 2005 sales estimates and using sum-of-the part analysis, we arrive at our 12-month target price of $22. The Personal Communications (handset) segment represents 58% of our enterprise value; no other segment accounts for over 13%.

Key Stock Statistics

S&P Core EPS 2005E	0.88	52-week Range	$20.89-12.39
S&P Oper. EPS 2004E	0.85	12 Month P/E	31.2
P/E on S&P Oper. EPS 2004E	21.3	Beta	1.37
S&P Oper. EPS 2005E	1.00	Shareholders	96,856
Yield (%)	0.9%	Market Cap (B)	$ 42.8
Dividend Rate/Share	0.16	Shares Outstanding (M)	2365.1

Value of $10,000 invested five years ago: **NA**

Dividend Data Dividends have been paid since 1942

Amount ($)	Date Decl.	Ex-Div. Date	Stock of Record	Payment Date
0.040	May. 04	Jun. 14	Jun. 15	Jul. 15 '04
0.040	Jul. 28	Sep. 13	Sep. 15	Oct. 15 '04
Stk.	—	Dec. 03	Nov. 26	Dec. 02 '04
0.040	Nov. 09	Dec. 13	Dec. 15	Jan. 14 '05

Revenues/Earnings Data Fiscal year ending December 31

Revenues (Million $)

	2004	2003	2002	2001	2000	1999
1Q	8,561	6,043	6,021	7,752	8,768	7,232
2Q	8,700	6,163	6,741	7,522	9,255	7,513
3Q	8,624	6,829	6,371	7,406	9,493	7,688
4Q	—	8,023	7,546	7,324	10,064	8,498
Yr.	—	27,058	26,679	30,004	37,580	30,931

Earnings Per Share ($)

	2004	2003	2002	2001	2000	1999
1Q	0.25	0.07	-0.20	-0.24	0.20	0.09
2Q	-0.09	0.05	-1.02	-0.35	0.09	0.11
3Q	0.20	0.05	0.05	-0.64	0.23	0.05
4Q	E0.26	0.20	0.08	-0.55	0.06	0.19
Yr.	E0.85	0.38	-1.09	-1.78	0.58	0.44

Next earnings report expected: late-January Source: S&P, Company Reports
EPS Estimates based on S&P Operating Earnings; historical GAAP earnings are as reported.

Motorola, Inc.

Recommendation: **BUY** ★★★★★   12-Month Target Price: **$22.00** (as of July 20, 2004)

Business Summary October 22, 2004

As the number of worldwide users of cellular telephones has climbed, Motorola has become a leading supplier to the expanding wireless industry. Although the company manufactures various electronic products, it is best known for its wireless products.

The Personal Communications segment (45% of 2004 third quarter sales) primarily manufactures personal two-way radios and wireless handsets in all three major digital standards: GSM, TDMA and CDMA. Nextel Communications accounted for 18% of total segment sales in 2003; China represented 9%. The segment is launching new handsets with color displays, integrated cameras, short messaging and web-based capability. In 2003, 75% of PCS handsets were manufactured in Asia, with 20% undertaken by third parties. MOT expected the outsourcing percentage to increase to 30% in 2004.

The Global Telecom Solutions unit (15%) makes wireless infrastructure communications systems. The segment's wireless infrastructure product portfolio includes radio base stations, base site controllers, associated software and services, and third-party switching for CDMA, GSM, iDEN and UMTS technologies. The company continues to build on its industry-leading position in push-to-talk over cellular (PoC) technology. During the 2004 second quarter, MOT announced a strategic relationship with France Telecom.

The Commercial, Government and Industrial Solutions segment (13%) manufactures analog and digital two-way radio voice and data products and privately operated systems for a wide range of governmental and industrial customers worldwide. MOT expects segment performance to continue to benefit from the need for safety and security solutions worldwide and the demand for larger, more complex systems. The 10 largest customers worldwide accounted for 16% of total segment sales in 2003.

The Broadband Communications segment (7%) manufactures digital systems and set-top terminals for broadband cable and satellite television networks; high speed data products, including cable modems and cable modem termination systems (CMTS), as well as Internet Protocol (IP)-based telephony products; and hybrid fiber/coaxial network transmission systems. Comcast accounted for 40% of total segment sales in 2003.

The Semiconductor Products segment (12%) manufactures a broad line of semiconductor devices for customers servicing the wireless, networking and automotive markets, and for standard products. Products manufactured by the segment and supplied to other Motorola affiliates, primarily the handset business, accounted for 23% of 2003 total segment sales.

The Integrated Electronics System Sector segment (8%) makes various products, including automotive and computer systems. In 2003, 63% of total segment sales were from four customers that included 18% to MOT, and 45% from the three largest U.S. automobile manufacturers.

In March 2004, the company and Nextel signed an agreement to extend their supply arrangements, allowing MOT to remain Nextel's preferred provider of iDEN infrastructure and handset equipment. The company owns 7% of Nextel's common shares.

Company Financials Fiscal Year ending December 31

Per Share Data ($)

(Year Ended December 31)	2003	2002	2001	2000	1999	1998	1997	1996	1995	1994
Tangible Bk. Val.	5.43	4.85	6.07	8.50	8.89	6.78	7.40	6.63	6.23	5.13
Cash Flow	1.09	-0.17	-0.63	1.70	1.60	0.69	1.91	1.89	2.03	1.74
Earnings	0.38	-1.09	-1.78	0.58	0.44	-0.54	0.65	0.63	0.98	0.88
S&P Core Earnings	0.08	-0.93	-2.23	NA	NA	NA	NA	NA	NA	NA
Dividends	0.16	0.16	0.16	0.16	0.16	0.16	0.16	0.15	0.13	0.09
Payout Ratio	42%	NM	NM	28%	37%	NM	25%	24%	14%	10%
Prices - High	14.40	17.12	25.12	61.54	49.83	21.95	30.16	22.83	27.50	20.37
- Low	7.58	7.30	10.50	15.81	20.85	12.79	18.00	14.70	17.16	14.04
P/E Ratio - High	38	NM	NM	NM	NM	NM	47	36	28	23
- Low	20	NM	NM	NM	NM	NM	28	23	18	16

Income Statement Analysis (Million $)

	2003	2002	2001	2000	1999	1998	1997	1996	1995	1994
Revs.	27,058	26,679	30,004	37,580	30,931	29,398	29,794	27,973	27,037	22,245
Oper. Inc.	2,694	2,059	-2,595	4,544	3,279	3,019	4,276	4,268	4,850	4,119
Depr.	1,667	2,108	2,552	2,522	2,182	2,197	2,329	2,308	1,919	1,525
Int. Exp.	295	668	645	494	305	301	216	249	213	207
Pretax Inc.	1,293	-3,446	-5,511	2,231	1,168	-1,374	1,816	1,775	2,782	2,437
Eff. Tax Rate	30.9%	NM	NM	40.9%	30.1%	NM	35.0%	35.0%	37.0%	36.0%
Net Inc.	893	-2,485	-3,937	1,318	817	-962	1,180	1,154	1,781	1,560
S&P Core Earnings	164	-2,084	-4,893	NA	NA	NA	NA	NA	NA	NA

Balance Sheet & Other Fin. Data (Million $)

	2003	2002	2001	2000	1999	1998	1997	1996	1995	1994
Cash	7,877	6,507	6,082	3,301	3,345	1,453	1,445	1,811	1,075	1,059
Curr. Assets	17,907	17,134	17,149	19,885	16,503	13,531	13,236	11,319	10,510	8,925
Total Assets	32,098	31,152	33,398	42,343	37,327	28,728	27,278	24,076	22,801	17,536
Curr. Liab.	9,433	9,810	9,698	16,257	12,416	11,440	9,055	7,995	7,793	5,917
LT Debt	7,161	7,674	8,857	4,778	3,573	2,633	2,144	1,931	1,949	1,127
Common Equity	12,689	11,239	13,691	18,612	16,344	12,222	13,272	11,795	11,048	9,096
Total Cap.	19,850	18,913	22,548	24,894	23,398	16,043	17,038	14,834	13,965	10,732
Cap. Exp.	655	607	1,321	4,131	2,684	3,221	2,874	2,973	4,225	3,320
Cash Flow	2,560	-377	-1,385	3,840	2,999	1,235	3,509	3,462	3,700	3,085
Curr. Ratio	1.9	1.7	1.8	1.2	1.3	1.2	1.5	1.4	1.4	1.5
% LT Debt of Cap.	36.1	40.6	39.3	19.2	15.3	16.4	12.6	13.0	14.0	10.5
% Net Inc.of Revs.	3.3	NM	NM	3.5	2.6	NM	4.0	4.1	6.6	7.0
% Ret. on Assets	2.8	NM	NM	3.2	2.5	NM	4.6	4.9	8.8	9.8
% Ret. on Equity	7.5	NM	NM	7.1	5.7	NM	9.4	10.1	14.4	19.7

Data as orig reptd.; bef. results of disc opers/spec. items. Per share data adj. for stk. divs.; EPS diluted. E-Estimated. NA-Not Available. NM-Not Meaningful. NR-Not Ranked. UR-Under Review.

Office: 1303 East Algonquin Road, Schaumburg, IL 60196.
Telephone: 800-262-8509.
Email: investors@motorola.com
Website: http://www.motorola.com
Chrmn & CEO: E.J. Zander.
Pres & COO: M.S. Zafirovski.

EVP & CFO: D. Devonshire.
EVP, Secy & General Counsel: A.P. Lawson.
SVP & Investor Contact: E. Gams 847-576-6873.
Dirs: H. L. Fuller, J. C. Lewent, W. E. Massey, N. Negroponte, I. Nooyi, J. E. Pepper, Jr., S. C. Scott III, R. Sommer, D. A. Warner III, J. A. White, M. S. Zafirovski, E. J. Zander.

Founded: in 1928.
Domicile: Delaware.
Employees: 88,000.
S&P Analyst: K. Leon/MF/JWP

M&T Bank

Recommendation: **SELL** ★★☆☆☆
SELL · SELL · HOLD · BUY · BUY

12-Month Target Price: **$94.00**
(as of October 18, 2004)

MTB has an approximate 0.11% weighting in the **S&P 500**

Sector: Financials
Sub-Industry: Regional Banks
Peer Group: Northeast Larger Regional Banks

Summary: This New York bank holding company is the parent of Manufacturers and Traders Trust Co. (M&T Bank).

Quantitative Evaluations

| Price as of 11/12/04: | $106.30 | 2004E S&P Core EPS: | $5.88 |

S&P Earnings & Dividend Rank: A+

| D | C | B- | B | B+ | A- | A | **A+** |

S&P Fair Value Rank: 2+

| 1 | **2** | 3 | 4 | 5 |
| Lowest | | | | Highest |

Fair Value Calc.: $96.40 (Slightly Overvalued)

S&P Investability Quotient Percentile

98%

MTB scored higher than 98% of all companies for which an S&P Report is available.

Volatility: Low

| **Low** | Average | High |

Technical Evaluation: Bullish
Since 9/04, the technical indicators for MTB have been Bullish.

Relative Strength Rank: Moderate

| | 65 | |
| 1 Lowest | | Highest 99 |

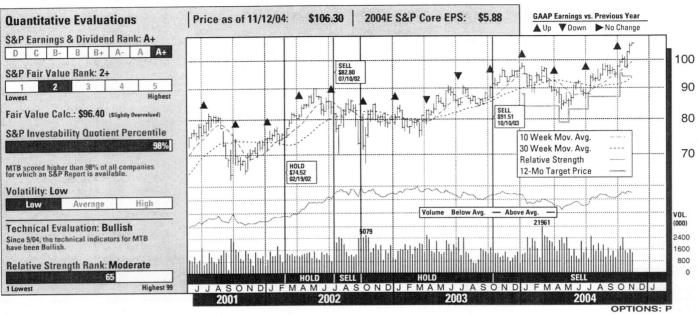

GAAP Earnings vs. Previous Year
▲ Up ▼ Down ▶ No Change

SELL $82.80 07/10/02
SELL $91.51 10/10/03
HOLD $74.52 02/19/02

10 Week Mov. Avg.
30 Week Mov. Avg.
Relative Strength
12-Mo Target Price

Volume Below Avg. — Above Avg.

$079
21961

VOL. (000)
2400
1600
800
0

HOLD | SELL | HOLD | SELL
J J A S O N D|J F M A M J J A S O N D|J F M A M J J A S O N D|J F M A M J J A S O N D|J
2001   2002   2003   2004

OPTIONS: P

Analyst commentary prepared by Erik J. Eisenstein/PMW/JWP

Highlights October 18, 2004

- We expect loan growth to accelerate in 2005 from the 2% rise, year to year, in the 2004 third quarter. As a result, we see 6% average earning asset growth in the coming year. Based on our projection of a narrower net interest margin in 2005, we see a 5% gain in net interest income. We forecast 15% lower loan loss provisions, based on our expectations of improvement in already above-average asset quality.

- We see higher trust income and a rise in deposit service charges outweighing a projected drop in mortgage banking revenue. As a result, we project a 6% advance in noninterest income. We forecast operating efficiency of 57.7%, somewhat better than the 58.3% seen for 2004. We anticipate a 12% gain in 2005 EPS, to $6.70, from $5.96 that we project for 2004.

- Our 2004 and 2005 estimates reflect the impact of MTB's decision to begin expensing the fair value of stock options in 2003. Accordingly, we view earnings quality as high relative to regional banking peers and the S&P 500. This view is reflected in our respective 2004 and 2005 S&P Core EPS estimates of $5.88 and $6.64.

Key Stock Statistics

S&P Core EPS 2005E	6.64	52-week Range	$106.65-82.90
S&P Oper. EPS 2004E	5.96	12 Month P/E	18.5
P/E on S&P Oper. EPS 2004E	17.8	Beta	0.36
S&P Oper. EPS 2005E	6.70	Shareholders	11,587
Yield (%)	1.5%	Market Cap (B)	$ 12.3
Dividend Rate/Share	1.60	Shares Outstanding (M)	116.1

Value of $10,000 invested five years ago: **$ 23,065**

Dividend Data Dividends have been paid since 1979

Amount ($)	Date Decl.	Ex-Div. Date	Stock of Record	Payment Date
0.400	Feb. 18	Feb. 25	Feb. 27	Mar. 31 '04
0.400	Apr. 21	May. 27	Jun. 01	Jun. 30 '04
0.400	Jul. 28	Aug. 31	Sep. 02	Sep. 30 '04
0.400	Oct. 27	Nov. 29	Dec. 01	Dec. 31 '04

Investment Rationale/Risk October 18, 2004

- We would avoid the shares, based on valuation. We see the April 2003 acquisition of Allfirst and resulting expansion into what we view as faster growing markets in Virginia and Maryland enhancing growth opportunities. We project the bank's EPS growth rate in the five years beyond 2005 at 10%, somewhat above peers.

- Risks to our recommendation and target price include the possibility that loan growth will accelerate more than we anticipate, leading to stronger fundamental results; and the possibility that MTB or a comparable regional bank will be acquired at a valuation higher than our target price.

- Our 12-month target price of $94 is derived by applying a P/E multiple to growth (PEG) ratio of 1.40X to our 2005 EPS estimate and five-year EPS growth forecast. In our view, MTB's earnings profile should be more consistent than that of its regional banking peers, due to what we see as lower relative interest rate and asset quality risk. We believe that a premium PEG ratio to the PEG of 1.30X for comparable regional banks is justified, based on our view of high relative earnings quality and consistency. Nevertheless, with the stock above our target price, we would avoid the shares.

Revenues/Earnings Data Fiscal year ending December 31

Revenues (Million $)

	2004	2003	2002	2001	2000	1999
1Q	774.3	568.4	585.4	664.7	470.9	429.3
2Q	792.9	809.3	582.6	662.3	480.8	426.1
3Q	828.0	795.7	589.6	646.4	498.4	445.6
4Q	—	784.2	596.4	623.5	647.4	460.0
Yr.	—	2,958	2,354	2,579	2,097	1,761

Earnings Per Share ($)

	2004	2003	2002	2001	2000	1999
1Q	1.30	1.23	1.25	0.85	0.86	0.83
2Q	1.53	1.10	1.26	0.94	0.91	0.80
3Q	1.56	1.28	1.23	0.98	0.94	0.83
4Q	E1.56	1.35	1.33	1.05	0.76	0.82
Yr.	E5.96	4.95	5.07	3.82	3.44	3.28

Next earnings report expected: mid-January Source: S&P, Company Reports
EPS Estimates based on S&P Operating Earnings; historical GAAP earnings are as reported.

M&T Bank Corporation

Recommendation:  SELL ★ ★ ★ ★ ★   12-Month Target Price: **$94.00** (as of October 18, 2004)

Business Summary October 18, 2004

M&T Bank Corp., headquartered in Buffalo, NY, operates primarily through its Manufacturers and Traders Trust Co. (M&T Bank) subsidiary, offering a wide range of commercial banking, trust and investment services.

In April 2003, the company acquired Baltimore-based Allfirst Financial, with 269 branches. The addition of Allfirst expanded MTB's consumer-oriented franchise to Washington, DC, Maryland, and Virginia. In 2003, as a result of the acquisition, assets, deposits and noninterest income grew 49%, 50% and 54%, respectively. At September 30, 2004, MTB was one of the 20 largest publicly traded U.S. bank holding companies in terms of asset size.

At September 30, 2004, M&T Bank conducted its retail banking operations through more than 650 branches, in New York, Pennsylvania, Maryland, Delaware, Virginia, West Virginia, and Washington, DC. Wholly owned M&T Mortgage Corp., a residential mortgage banking corporation, has offices in 16 states across the U.S.

Like a typical commercial bank, MTB derives the vast majority of its revenues from net interest income, the difference between the interest a bank receives on loans and other investments and the interest it pays on the funds it borrows. In 2003, net interest income accounted for 66% of total revenues, versus 71% in 2002. The principal factors that affect net interest income are the levels of earning assets, and management's ability to efficiently balance assets and liabilities in the context of a given interest rate environment. At December 31, 2003, the bulk of the bank's earning assets consisted of financing loans.

The loan and lease portfolio grew to $36.0 billion at the end of 2003, from $25.9 billion a year earlier, largely due to the Allfirst acquisition. Commercial real estate mortgage loans accounted for 33% of total loans (37% a year earlier), followed by consumer loans 31% (28%), commercial, financial and agricultural loans 25% (21%), residential real estate loans 7% (11%) and real estate construction loans 4% (4%).

The bank's loan quality improved somewhat in 2003. At December 31, 2003, nonperforming loans were equal to 0.67% of total loans outstanding, down from 0.84% a year earlier. Net chargeoffs in 2003 were $97 million (0.28% of average loans), down from $108 million (0.42%) in 2002. The provision for loan losses rose to $131 million, from $122 million. As a result, the allowance for loan losses increased to $614 million at December 31, 2003 (1.72% of outstanding loans), from $436 million (1.70%) a year earlier.

In February 2004, directors authorized the repurchase of 5 million common shares (4% of the shares outstanding). In the 2004 third quarter, MTB purchased 1,435,800 shares at an average cost of $94.20 each.

Company Financials Fiscal Year ending December 31

Per Share Data ($)

(Year Ended December 31)	2003	2002	2001	2000	1999	1998	1997	1996	1995	1994
Tangible Bk. Val.	21.43	20.23	17.84	16.10	14.88	13.72	15.59	13.55	12.53	10.30
Earnings	4.95	5.07	3.82	3.44	3.28	2.62	2.53	2.13	1.88	1.64
S&P Core Earnings	4.95	4.60	3.40	NA	NA	NA	NA	NA	NA	NA
Dividends	1.20	1.05	1.00	0.62	0.45	0.38	0.32	0.28	0.25	0.22
Payout Ratio	24%	21%	26%	18%	14%	15%	13%	13%	13%	13%
Prices - High	98.98	90.05	82.11	68.42	58.25	58.20	46.80	28.96	21.80	16.50
- Low	74.71	67.70	59.80	35.70	40.60	40.00	28.10	20.90	13.60	13.45
P/E Ratio - High	20	18	21	20	18	22	19	14	12	10
- Low	15	13	16	10	12	15	11	10	7	8

Income Statement Analysis (Million $)

	2003	2002	2001	2000	1999	1998	1997	1996	1995	1994
Net Int. Inc.	1,599	1,248	1,158	854	759	664	557	531	486	468
Tax Equiv. Adj.	16.3	14.0	17.5	10.5	7.71	7.19	5.84	4.50	4.60	4.00
Non Int. Inc.	831	513	476	325	282	269	161	170	150	124
Loan Loss Prov.	131	122	104	NA	44.5	43.2	46.0	43.0	40.0	61.0
Exp./Op. Revs.	59.6%	51.9%	57.4%	61.6%	59.4%	60.2%	58.7%	57.9%	58.5%	56.5%
Pretax Inc.	851	716	584	446	418	326	282	249	221	194
Eff. Tax Rate	32.5%	32.3%	35.2%	35.9%	36.5%	36.1%	37.5%	39.3%	40.8%	39.7%
Net Inc.	574	485	378	286	266	208	176	151	131	117
% Net Int. Marg.	4.09	4.36	4.23	4.02	4.02	3.97	4.38	4.45	4.43	4.89
S&P Core Earnings	574	440	336	NA	NA	NA	NA	NA	NA	NA

Balance Sheet & Other Fin. Data (Million $)

	2003	2002	2001	2000	1999	1998	1997	1996	1995	1994
Money Mkt. Assets	250	380	84.4	57.8	1,286	403	111	210	136	87.0
Inv. Securities	7,259	3,955	3,024	3,310	1,901	2,786	1,725	1,572	1,769	1,791
Com'l Loans	20,869	14,522	14,071	13,399	6,141	3,657	2,542	2,364	2,014	1,680
Other Loans	15,169	11,415	11,117	9,571	11,431	12,348	9,224	8,756	7,860	6,767
Total Assets	49,826	33,175	31,450	28,949	22,409	20,584	14,003	12,944	11,956	10,529
Demand Deposits	10,150	5,101	4,634	4,218	2,844	2,576	1,458	1,352	1,184	1,087
Time Deposits	20,756	16,564	16,946	16,014	12,530	12,161	9,705	9,161	8,286	7,156
LT Debt	5,535	4,497	3,462	3,415	1,744	1,568	428	178	193	96.2
Common Equity	5,717	3,182	2,939	38.0	44.5	1,602	1,018	906	806	681
% Ret. on Assets	1.4	1.5	1.3	1.1	1.2	1.2	1.3	1.2	1.2	1.2
% Ret. on Equity	12.9	15.8	13.4	12.7	15.6	15.9	18.3	17.3	17.1	16.6
% Loan Loss Resv.	1.7	1.7	1.7	1.6	-2.0	1.9	2.4	2.5	2.8	3.0
% Loans/Deposits	108.0	119.7	116.7	112.4	115.4	107.2	105.4	99.4	100.9	99.7
% Equity to Assets	10.8	9.5	9.3	8.8	7.9	7.6	7.1	6.9	6.6	6.8

Data as orig reptd.; bef. results of disc opers/spec. items. Per share data adj. for stk. divs.; EPS diluted. E-Estimated. NA-Not Available. NM-Not Meaningful. NR-Not Ranked. UR-Under Review.

Office: One M&T Plaza, Buffalo, NY 14203-2399.
Telephone: 716-842-5445.
Email: ir@mandtbank.com
Website: http://www.mandtbank.com
Chrmn, Pres & CEO: R.G. Wilmers.
EVP & CFO: M.P. Pinto.
EVP & Treas: A.C. Kugler.

Investor Contact: M.S. Piemonte 716-842-5445.
Dirs: W. F. Allyn, B. D. Baird, R. J. Bennett, C. A. Bontempo, R. T. Brady, E. Brumback, M. D. Buckley, P. J. Callan, R. C. Carballada, T. J. Cunningham III, D. Devorris, R. E. Garman, J. V. Glynn, D. C. Hathaway, D. R. Hawbaker, P. W. Hodgson, G. Kennedy, R. G. King, R. B. Newman II, J. G. Pereira, M. Pinto, R. E. Sadler, Jr., E. J. Sheehy, S. G. Sheetz, H. L. Washington, R. G. Wilmers.

Founded: in 1969.
Domicile: New York.
Employees: 14,000.
S&P Analyst: Erik J. Eisenstein/PMW/JWP

Mylan Laboratories

Recommendation: **HOLD** ★★★☆☆
SELL · SELL · HOLD · BUY · BUY

12-Month Target Price: $18.00
(as of July 26, 2004)

MYL has an approximate 0.04% weighting in the **S&P 500**

Sector: Health Care
Sub-Industry: Pharmaceuticals
Peer Group: Generic Drugs

Summary: This leading manufacturer of generic pharmaceuticals produces a broad range of generic drugs in varying strengths, and also sells several proprietary drugs.

Quantitative Evaluations

S&P Earnings & Dividend Rank: A-

D	C	B-	B	B+	**A-**	A	A+

S&P Fair Value Rank: 4

1	2	3	**4**	5
Lowest				Highest

Fair Value Calc.: $16.80 (Slightly Overvalued)

S&P Investability Quotient Percentile

89%

MYL scored higher than 89% of all companies for which an S&P Report is available.

Volatility: Average

Low	**Average**	High

Technical Evaluation: Bearish
Since 10/04, the technical indicators for MYL have been Bearish.

Relative Strength Rank: Weak

21
1 Lowest — Highest 99

Price as of 11/12/04: **$17.24**   **2005E S&P Core EPS:** **$0.72**

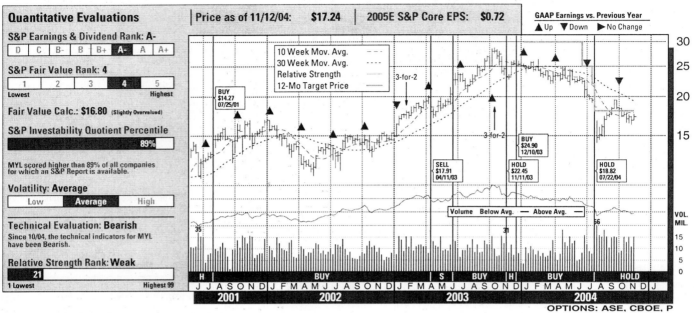

GAAP Earnings vs. Previous Year
▲ Up ▼ Down ► No Change

OPTIONS: ASE, CBOE, P

Analyst commentary prepared by Herman B. Saftlas/DC/BK

Highlights November 10, 2004

- We expect revenues in FY 05 (Mar.) to decline about 7%-8%, from FY 04's $1.38 billion, assuming Mylan continues as an independent entity (MYL has agreed to merge with King Pharmaceuticals (KG: $11; hold), but we believe the future of that deal remains in doubt). We think generic sales have come under pressure from intensified competitive pricing pressures throughout the industry, exacerbated by a larger presence of inexpensive authorized generics in the marketplace. Authorized generics are typically generics made by branded companies and sold through licensed distributors. Recent results have been adversely affected by new competition in generic versions of Prilosec, Sinemet and Macrobid. Although Mylan expects to introduce its much delayed generic version of Johnson & Johnson's (J&J) Duragesic pain patch in January 2005, we believe recent citizen petition filings by J&J may further delay that launch.

- We look for gross margins to contract under increased competitive pricing pressures, while net margins will probably suffer from higher SG&A spending, reduced other income and a higher tax rate.

- We project FY 05 operating EPS of $0.80, down from FY 04's $1.21. Boosted by greater contributions from new products, we estimate EPS will rebound to $1.00 in FY 06. After estimated option expense, we project Standard & Poor's Core EPS at $0.72 in FY 05, and $0.92 in FY 06.

Key Stock Statistics

S&P Core EPS 2006E	0.92	52-week Range	$26.35-14.24
S&P Oper. EPS 2005E	0.80	12 Month P/E	16.3
P/E on S&P Oper. EPS 2005E	21.6	Beta	0.32
S&P Oper. EPS 2006E	1.00	Shareholders	167,100
Yield (%)	0.7%	Market Cap (B)	$ 4.6
Dividend Rate/Share	0.12	Shares Outstanding (M)	269.1

Value of $10,000 invested five years ago: **$ 19,063**

Dividend Data Dividends have been paid since 1983

Amount ($)	Date Decl.	Ex-Div. Date	Stock of Record	Payment Date
0.030	Dec. 16	Dec. 29	Dec. 31	Jan. 15 '04
0.030	Mar. 22	Mar. 29	Mar. 31	Apr. 15 '04
0.030	Jun. 17	Jun. 28	Jun. 30	Jul. 15 '04
0.030	Sep. 20	Sep. 28	Sep. 30	Oct. 15 '04

Investment Rationale/Risk November 10, 2004

- In late October 2004, Mylan said it was re-evaluating its planned acquisition of King Pharmaceuticals following the latter's disclosure that a high rate of product returns may require it to restate earnings. In July 2004, MYL announced plans to acquire King for about $4 billion in MYL stock (terms called for each share of KG share to be exchanged for 0.9 MYL share). Investor Carl Icahn, holder of about 9.8% of MYL's shares, is attempting to block the acquisition. While King would bring a 1,200 cardiovascular drug salesforce that MYL could use to support the planned launch of its new branded nebivolol hypertension drug, we believe KG also brings widening generic competition to Levoxyl, patent risk to Altace, and an ongoing SEC investigation. Although we believe the deal would be initially dilutive, we think King could prove accretive if nebivolol turns out to be a major success.

- Risks to our recommendation and target price include risks that are common to all generic firms such as intense competitive pricing, the need for FDA approval for new products, and the need to successfully mount legal challenges to branded patents. Failure to successfully commercialize nebivolol is another risk for MYL.

- We have a 12-month target price of $18, which assumes a P/E multiple of

Revenues/Earnings Data Fiscal year ending March 31

Revenues (Million $)

	2005	2004	2003	2002	2001	2000
1Q	339.0	331.4	275.5	237.9	167.3	177.1
2Q	307.0	360.1	319.5	286.3	207.6	194.5
3Q	—	349.8	320.5	297.2	223.2	203.9
4Q	—	333.4	353.7	282.6	248.7	214.7
Yr.	—	1,375	1,269	1,104	846.7	790.1

Earnings Per Share ($)

	2005	2004	2003	2002	2001	2000
1Q	0.30	0.31	0.22	0.18	-0.26	0.11
2Q	0.18	0.33	0.24	0.22	0.12	0.12
3Q	E0.18	0.31	0.25	0.27	0.13	0.14
4Q	E0.20	0.27	0.27	0.24	0.15	0.15
Yr.	E0.80	1.21	0.97	0.91	0.13	0.52

Next earnings report expected: late-January Source: S&P, Company Reports
EPS Estimates based on S&P Operating Earnings; historical GAAP earnings are as reported.

Mylan Laboratories Inc.

Recommendation: **HOLD** ★ ★ ★ ☆ ☆   12-Month Target Price: **$18.00** (as of July 26, 2004)

Business Summary November 10, 2004

Mylan Laboratories is a leading manufacturer of generic pharmaceutical products in finished tablet, capsule and powder dosage forms, for resale by others. It began operations in 1961 as a privately owned company founded by Milan Puskar and an associate in White Sulphur Springs, WV. Generic drugs are typically sold at prices significantly below those of comparable branded products.

The company produces more than 115 generic drugs in more than 285 sizes and/or dosage strengths. The total includes nine generics that are available in extended release formulations. MYL also markets about 56 generic drugs under distribution agreements with other concerns. Generic drugs accounted for 80% of FY 04 (Mar.) revenues, with branded proprietary products providing the balance.

Generic drugs are the chemical equivalents of branded drugs, and are marketed after patent expirations on the primary products. Generic revenues increased 8.3% in FY 04, lifted by the inclusion of sales from generic Prilosec. Key therapeutic categories include antihypertensives (primarily nifedipine), antianxiety agents, analgesics, antianginals, antibiotics, antidepressants, and drugs that fight diabetes and diarrhea. MYL also offers an antigout drug, an antihistamine, anti-inflammatories, antipsychotics, anxiolytics, a bronchial dilator, diuretics and hypnotic agents. UDL Laboratories supplies unit dose generic drugs for the institutional and long-term care markets.

Through its Bertek Pharmaceuticals unit, the company markets several proprietary products. These include Annesteem, a generic version of Roche's Accutane acne treatment; Maxzide, a diuretic used to treat hypertension; Nitrek, a nitroglycerin transdermal patch; Clorpres, an antihypertensive agent; Acticin, a topical scabicidal agent; Sulfamylon, a topical antimicrobial cream used to treat patients with second and third degree burns; Zagam, a treatment for bronchitis; Digitek, a treatment for heart failure; Phenytek for seizures; and several wound care products. Through a venture with Penederm, Bertek co-promotes Mentax topical antifungal and Avita topical retinoic acid product.

Eldepryl, a treatment for Parkinson's disease, is marketed by Somerset Pharmaceuticals, jointly owned by the company and Watson Pharmaceuticals. Eldepryl is sold by Novartis under an agreement with Somerset. Somerset is also working on a selegiline patch treatment for depression.

R&D spending amounted to $100.8 million in FY 04 (equal to 7.3% of sales). MYL has 41 Abbreviated New Drug Applications (ANDAs) under review at the FDA, with branded sales of about $29 billion. Key proprietary branded pipeline products include nebivolol, a beta blocker antihypertensive; Apomorphine for Parkinson's disease; and other treatments for pain and fungal infections.

Company Financials Fiscal Year ending March 31

Per Share Data ($)

(Year Ended March 31)	2004	2003	2002	2001	2000	1999	1998	1997	1996	1995
Tangible Bk. Val.	5.30	4.39	3.97	2.97	3.00	2.49	2.24	1.90	1.98	1.69
Cash Flow	1.37	1.11	1.07	0.28	0.65	0.50	0.44	0.29	0.43	0.50
Earnings	1.21	0.97	0.91	0.13	0.52	0.43	0.36	0.23	0.38	0.45
S&P Core Earnings	1.05	0.89	0.84	0.40	NA	NA	NA	NA	NA	NA
Dividends	0.08	0.08	0.07	0.07	0.07	0.07	0.07	0.07	0.08	0.10
Payout Ratio	7%	18%	8%	55%	14%	17%	20%	31%	20%	22%

Cal. Yrs.	2003	2002	2001	2000	1999	1998	1997	1996	1995	1994
Prices - High	28.75	16.56	16.94	14.33	14.22	15.97	11.24	10.38	10.88	8.85
- Low	15.55	11.15	8.95	7.11	7.58	7.58	5.11	6.22	7.33	4.62
P/E Ratio - High	24	17	19	NM	27	37	31	45	28	20
- Low	13	12	12	NM	14	18	14	27	19	10

Income Statement Analysis (Million $)

	2004	2003	2002	2001	2000	1999	1998	1997	1996	1995
Revs.	1,375	1,269	1,104	847	790	721	555	440	393	396
Oper. Inc.	504	452	441	209	259	224	146	75.3	114	151
Depr.	44.3	40.6	46.1	42.4	35.7	26.9	21.7	17.3	13.5	12.7
Int. Exp.	Nil	Nil	Nil	Nil	Nil	Nil	Nil	Nil	NA	NA
Pretax Inc.	513	427	408	58.0	243	192	148	87.2	142	171
Eff. Tax Rate	34.7%	36.1%	36.3%	36.0%	36.5%	40.0%	32.1%	27.6%	27.8%	29.5%
Net Inc.	335	272	260	37.1	154	115	101	63.1	102	121
S&P Core Earnings	286	247	241	113	NA	NA	NA	NA	NA	NA

Balance Sheet & Other Fin. Data (Million $)

	2004	2003	2002	2001	2000	1999	1998	1997	1996	1995
Cash	687	687	617	285	303	260	104	140	189	180
Curr. Assets	1,318	1,228	1,062	879	687	583	430	379	379	331
Total Assets	1,875	1,745	1,617	1,466	1,341	1,207	848	778	778	546
Curr. Liab.	174	266	175	291	87.8	96.4	71.3	78.7	48.6	56.4
LT Debt	19.1	19.9	21.9	23.3	30.6	26.8	26.2	22.8	7.90	Nil
Common Equity	2,600	1,446	1,607	1,133	1,204	1,060	744	660	616	483
Total Cap.	2,642	1,479	1,646	1,175	1,253	1,110	776	689	633	483
Cap. Exp.	118	32.6	20.6	24.7	28.8	16.7	28.9	26.9	31.4	17.5
Cash Flow	379	313	306	79.5	190	142	122	80.5	116	134
Curr. Ratio	7.6	4.6	6.1	3.0	7.8	6.0	6.0	4.8	7.8	5.9
% LT Debt of Cap.	0.7	1.3	1.3	2.0	2.4	2.4	3.4	3.3	1.2	Nil
% Net Inc.of Revs.	24.3	21.5	23.6	4.4	19.5	16.0	18.1	14.4	26.0	30.5
% Ret. on Assets	18.5	16.2	16.9	2.6	12.1	11.2	12.4	8.6	16.5	25.4
% Ret. on Equity	14.1	19.1	17.7	3.2	13.6	12.8	14.4	9.9	18.6	28.0

Data as orig reptd.; bef. results of disc opers/spec. items. Per share data adj. for stk. divs.; EPS diluted. E-Estimated. NA-Not Available. NM-Not Meaningful. NR-Not Ranked. UR-Under Review.

Office: 1500 Corporate Drive, Canonsburg, PA 15317.
Telephone: 724-514-1800.
Email: investor_relations@mylan.com
Website: http://www.mylan.com
Chrmn: M. Puskar.
Pres & COO: L.J. DeBone.
Vice Chrmn & CEO: R.J. Coury.

SVP, Secy & General Counsel: R.L. Foster.
CFO: E.J. Borkowski.
Investor Contact: K. King 724-514-1800.
Dirs: W. Cameron, R. J. Coury, L. S. DeLynn, J. C. Gaisford, D. J. Leech, J. C. Maroon, M. Puskar, P. A. Sunseri, C. B. Todd, R. L. Vanderveen, S. A. Williams.

Founded: in 1970.
Domicile: Pennsylvania.
Employees: 2,800.
S&P Analyst: Herman B. Saftlas/DC/BK

Nabors Industries

Recommendation: **BUY** ★★★★★
SELL | BED | HOLD | BUY | BUY

12-Month Target Price: **$60.00**
(as of October 26, 2004)

NBR has an approximate 0.07% weighting in the **S&P 500**

Sector: Energy
Sub-Industry: Oil & Gas Drilling
Peer Group: Oil & Gas - Land Drilling

Summary: NBR is the world's largest oil and gas land drilling contractor.

Quantitative Evaluations

S&P Earnings & Dividend Rank: B

| D | C | B- | B | B+ | A- | A | A+ |

S&P Fair Value Rank: 4-

| 1 | 2 | 3 | 4 | 5 |
Lowest — Highest

Fair Value Calc.: $49.40 (Fairly Valued)

S&P Investability Quotient Percentile
93%

NBR scored higher than 93% of all companies for which an S&P Report is available.

Volatility: Average

| Low | Average | High |

Technical Evaluation: Neutral
Since 11/04, the technical indicators for NBR have been Neutral.

Relative Strength Rank: Moderate
52
1 Lowest — Highest 99

| Price as of 11/12/04: | **$49.44** | 2004E S&P Core EPS: | **$1.73** |

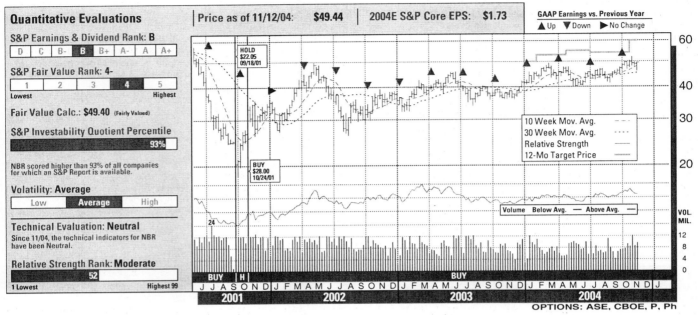

GAAP Earnings vs. Previous Year
▲ Up ▼ Down ► No Change

HOLD $22.05 09/18/01
BUY $28.00 10/24/01

10 Week Mov. Avg.
30 Week Mov. Avg.
Relative Strength
12-Mo Target Price

Volume Below Avg. — Above Avg.

VOL. MIL.

BUY | H | BUY
J J A S O N D | J F M A M J J A S O N D | J F M A M J J A S O N D | J F M A M J J A S O N D | J
2001 | 2002 | 2003 | 2004

OPTIONS: ASE, CBOE, P, Ph

Analyst commentary prepared by Stewart Glickman/MF/TV

Highlights November 02, 2004

- Third quarter EPS of $0.48 were $0.02 below our expectations. Revenues improved 10% sequentially in U.S. land drilling, and improved nicely in Canada after seasonal weakness in the second quarter in Canada. Alaska remained difficult. We estimate that U.S. land day-margins for NBR's fleet improved from second quarter levels, and expect further gains to occur in 2005.

- We continue to expect improvement both in utilization and in dayrates for NBR's fleet in 2004, although more so on dayrates, and we look for total U.S. land drilling activity to continue to strengthen, with gains both in dayrates and in rig count. We think that the company has enough excess capacity to take advantage of further improvements in the U.S. land drilling market.

- Offshore, we expect relatively slower growth from the Gulf of Mexico, while internationally, we see a modest improvement as this market has generally lagged any changes in the U.S. market. For 2004, we expect EPS of $1.82, rising to $2.55 in 2005. On an S&P Core Earnings basis, we see EPS of $1.73 and $2.47 in the respective years.

Investment Rationale/Risk November 02, 2004

- We recommend buying the stock, based in part on improving fundamentals that we foresee for land drilling. Through late October, the shares were up 20% year to date, versus a 28.0% gain in the S&P Oil & Gas Drilling Index. In addition, the stock was trading at an enterprise value of 11.2X our 2005 EBITDA estimate, versus an average of 9.9X for our peer group of land drillers, and at 11X our 2005 operating cash flow estimate, about in line with peers. We think NBR should trade at a modest premium, based in part on its leadership position in the industry and greater available equipment than peers.

- Risks to our recommendation and target price include lower than expected land drilling activity; reduced oil and natural gas prices; reduced dayrates for land drilling work; and operating margin pressure due to rising cost inflation.

- We continue to believe that land drilling activity has yet to reach its peak, and see NBR, the world's largest land driller, as poised to benefit. Our 12-month target price of $60 is based on the shares trading at an enterprise value of 12.5X our 2005 EBITDA estimate, accounting for the upside potential we see for dayrates, and blending with our projected 13.5X multiple of 2005 operating cash flows.

Key Stock Statistics

S&P Core EPS 2005E	2.47	52-week Range	$52.04-35.76
S&P Oper. EPS 2004E	1.82	12 Month P/E	29.8
P/E on S&P Oper. EPS 2004E	27.2	Beta	1.01
S&P Oper. EPS 2005E	2.55	Shareholders	2,241
Yield (%)	Nil	Market Cap (B)	$ 7.4
Dividend Rate/Share	Nil	Shares Outstanding (M)	149.5

Value of $10,000 invested five years ago: **$ 18,269**

Dividend Data

Class A dividends were paid from 1973 until omission in July 1982.

Revenues/Earnings Data Fiscal year ending December 31

Revenues (Million $)

	2004	2003	2002	2001	2000	1999
1Q	607.7	455.7	381.7	546.6	289.7	153.0
2Q	546.6	433.4	367.3	613.5	301.5	129.9
3Q	585.6	476.0	362.2	621.1	369.1	142.4
4Q	—	524.6	379.9	428.9	412.2	216.9
Yr.	—	1,880	1,466	2,225	1,409	642.3

Earnings Per Share ($)

	2004	2003	2002	2001	2000	1999
1Q	0.48	0.31	0.28	0.51	0.12	0.12
2Q	0.30	0.19	0.17	0.63	0.16	0.03
3Q	0.48	0.33	0.18	0.68	0.25	0.04
4Q	E0.57	0.42	0.18	0.35	0.35	0.06
Yr.	E1.82	1.25	0.81	2.18	0.89	0.23

Next earnings report expected: late-January Source: S&P, Company Reports
EPS Estimates based on S&P Operating Earnings; historical GAAP earnings are as reported.

STANDARD &POOR'S

Nabors Industries Ltd.

Recommendation: **BUY** ★ ★ ★ ★ ★   12-Month Target Price: **$60.00** (as of October 26, 2004)

Business Summary November 02, 2004

As the world's largest land drilling contractor, Nabors Industries Ltd. (formerly Nabors Industries, Inc.) owns a fleet of about 575 land drilling rigs. Formed as a Bermuda-exempt company in December 2001, but operating continuously in the drilling sector since the early 1900s, the company conducts oil, gas and geothermal land drilling operations in the lower 48 U.S. states, Alaska and Canada, and internationally, mainly in South and Central America, the Middle East and Africa. NBR also owns more than 750 land workover and well servicing rigs in the U.S. Southwest and West, and approximately 200 well servicing and workover rigs in Canada. It also markets 45 platform, 16 jackup and three barge rigs in the Gulf of Mexico and international markets; these rigs provide well servicing, workover and drilling services. The company also owns nine rigs through a joint venture in Saudi Arabia (a 50% interest in the venture's 17 rigs).

NBR's rigs include land-based rigs and offshore platform, jack-up and barge rigs. Rigs are classified by their depth capabilities and by whether their power systems are mechanical or electrical; the latter type convert diesel power to electricity to power the rig, which the company believes reduces drilling time and improves operating efficiency. These rigs, known as SCR rigs, are generally preferred by NBR's customers, and typically yield higher utilization and dayrates than similarly sized mechanical rigs. As of March 2004, the company had 401 land drilling rigs based in the U.S., of which 102 were stacked in inventory. NBR also had 81 rigs in Canada, with the remaining 93 rigs in international markets. Of the roughly 280 rigs in the U.S. that were part of the active fleet, 150 were of the SCR variety.

Substantially all of NBR's rigs were contracted in 2003 with daywork contracts, which provide for a basic rate per day when drilling (the dayrate) and for lower rates when the rig is moving, or when drilling operations are interrupted by

equipment breakdowns or adverse weather conditions. Well servicing and workover services are provided for existing wells where some form of artificial lift is required to bring oil to the surface.

The contract drilling segment (88% of 2003 revenues, and 96% of segment operating income) provides drilling, workover, well servicing and related services in the U.S. (including the Lower 48, Alaska, and offshore), Canada, and internationally. At the end of 2003, 58% of contract drilling revenues and 51% of total assets served customers in the U.S..

To supplement its primary business, NBR offers ancillary wellsite services, such as oilfield management, engineering, transportation, construction, maintenance, and well logging. As of March 2004, NBR had a fleet of 31 marine transportation and support vessels, primarily in the Gulf of Mexico, providing transport for supplies and crews for offshore rigs. A land transportation and hauling fleet consists of 240 rig and oilfield equipment hauling tractor-trailers, more than 300 fluid hauling trucks, about 800 fluid storage tanks, eight salt water disposal wells, and other equipment used in domestic drilling and well servicing. The six operating divisions that provide these products and services are not defined as reportable segments, but generated 11% of revenues in 2003.

NBR has grown from a land drilling business centered on Canada and Alaska to an international business with operations on land and offshore. In 1999, it acquired Bayard Drilling Technologies and Pool Energy Services. The company enhanced its core business in Canada, as well as its footing in instrumentation systems, with its 2001 acquisition of Command Drilling Corp., and its 2002 acquisitions of Enserco Energy Service Co. and Ryan Energy Technologies Inc.

Company Financials Fiscal Year ending December 31

Per Share Data ($)

(Year Ended December 31)	2003	2002	2001	2000	1999	1998	1997	1996	1995	1994
Tangible Bk. Val.	14.69	12.77	11.77	11.01	9.51	8.61	7.23	5.26	4.38	3.91
Cash Flow	2.72	2.11	3.19	1.89	1.06	1.87	1.60	1.25	0.93	0.28
Earnings	1.25	0.81	2.18	0.89	0.23	1.16	1.12	0.76	0.58	0.01
S&P Core Earnings	1.11	0.56	2.09	NA	NA	NA	NA	NA	NA	NA
Dividends	Nil	Nil	Nil	Nil	Nil	Nil	Nil	Nil	Nil	Nil
Payout Ratio	Nil	Nil	Nil	Nil	Nil	Nil	Nil	Nil	Nil	Nil
Prices - High	45.85	49.98	63.12	60.47	31.25	31.56	46.81	21.50	11.37	7.87
- Low	32.20	26.14	18.00	28.12	10.75	11.75	14.75	10.25	6.12	5.75
P/E Ratio - High	37	62	29	68	NM	27	42	28	20	NM
- Low	26	32	8	32	NM	10	13	13	11	NM

Income Statement Analysis (Million $)

	2003	2002	2001	2000	1999	1998	1997	1996	1995	1994
Revs.	1,880	1,466	2,121	1,327	639	968	1,029	720	573	423
Oper. Inc.	438	351	0.69	377	155	267	223	123	89.6	55.7
Depr. Depl. & Amort.	235	195	190	152	100	84.9	66.4	46.1	31.0	19.6
Int. Exp.	70.7	67.1	60.7	35.4	30.4	15.5	16.5	11.9	7.61	7.20
Pretax Inc.	175	141	542	227	45.6	200	182	81.6	58.6	4.20
Eff. Tax Rate	NM	13.7%	35.9%	40.2%	39.3%	37.5%	37.1%	13.6%	12.8%	84.7%
Net Inc.	192	121	348	135	27.7	125	115	70.6	51.1	0.70
S&P Core Earnings	172	83.7	332	NA	NA	NA	NA	NA	NA	NA

Balance Sheet & Other Fin. Data (Million $)

	2003	2002	2001	2000	1999	1998	1997	1996	1995	1994
Cash	1,532	1,331	919	551	112	47.3	3.92	104	15.2	45.1
Curr. Assets	1,516	1,370	1,031	1,018	461	266	306	329	183	160
Total Assets	5,603	5,064	4,152	3,137	2,398	1,450	1,234	871	584	419
Curr. Liab.	598	751	330	279	265	244	235	156	151	76.1
LT Debt	1,986	1,615	1,568	855	483	217	230	230	51.5	57.5
Common Equity	2,490	2,158	1,858	1,806	1,470	867	728	458	369	277
Total Cap.	4,849	4,175	3,711	2,759	2,046	1,157	986	706	424	335
Cap. Exp.	353	317	701	301	82.1	276	268	146	109	37.4
Cash Flow	427	317	538	288	128	210	181	117	82.1	20.3
Curr. Ratio	2.5	1.8	3.1	3.6	1.7	1.1	1.3	2.1	1.2	2.1
% LT Debt of Cap.	41.0	38.7	42.2	31.0	23.6	18.8	23.3	32.6	12.1	17.2
% Ret. on Assets	3.6	2.6	9.5	4.9	1.4	9.3	10.9	9.7	10.2	0.2
% Ret. on Equity	8.3	6.0	19.0	8.3	2.4	15.7	19.4	17.1	15.8	0.2

Data as orig reptd.; bef. results of disc opers/spec. items. Per share data adj. for stk. divs.; EPS diluted. E-Estimated. NA-Not Available. NM-Not Meaningful. NR-Not Ranked. UR-Under Review.

Office: International Trading Centre , Warren, St. Michael 77067, Barbados .
Telephone: 246-421-9471.
Website: http://www.nabors.com
Chrmn & CEO: E.M. Isenberg.
Pres & COO: A.G. Petrello.

VP & CFO: B.P. Koch.
VP & Secy: D. McLachlin.
Investor Contact: D.A. Smith 281-775-8038.
Dirs: E. M. Isenberg, J. L. Payne, A. G. Petrello, H. W. Schmidt, M. M. Sheinfeld, J. Wexler, M. J. Whitman.

Founded: in 1968.
Domicile: Bermuda.
Employees: 17,417.
S&P Analyst: Stewart Glickman/MF/TV

The McGraw·Hill Companies

National City

Recommendation: **BUY** ★★★★☆   SELL SELL HOLD BUY BUY

12-Month Target Price: $44.00
(as of September 13, 2004)

NCC has an approximate 0.23% weighting in the **S&P 500**

Sector: Financials
Sub-Industry: Regional Banks
Peer Group: Midwest/West Major Regional Banks

Summary: NCC, the third largest Ohio bank holding company, also has banking offices in Michigan, Kentucky, Indiana, Illinois, Missouri, and Pennsylvania.

Price as of 11/17/04:	$38.26	2004E S&P Core EPS:	$3.42

Quantitative Evaluations

S&P Earnings & Dividend Rank: A

D	C	B-	B	B+	A-	**A**	A+

S&P Fair Value Rank: 4-

1	2	3	**4**	5
Lowest				Highest

Fair Value Calc.: $40.40 (Slightly Undervalued)

S&P Investability Quotient Percentile

100%

NCC scored higher than 100% of all companies for which an S&P Report is available.

Volatility: Low

Low	Average	High

Technical Evaluation: Bullish
Since 10/04, the technical indicators for NCC have been Bullish.

Relative Strength Rank: Moderate

30

1 Lowest   Highest 99

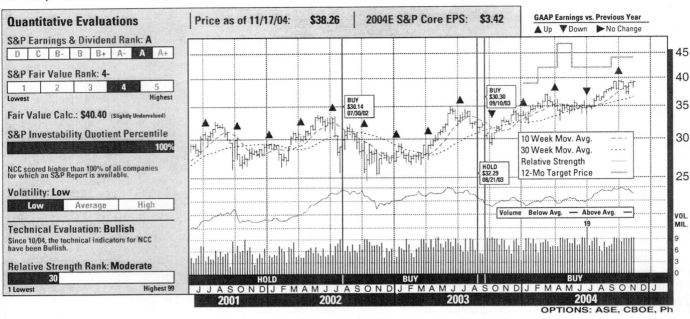

GAAP Earnings vs. Previous Year
▲ Up ▼ Down ► No Change

BUY $30.14 07/30/02
BUY $30.30 09/10/03
HOLD $32.29 08/21/03

10 Week Mov. Avg.
30 Week Mov. Avg.
Relative Strength
12-Mo Target Price

Volume Below Avg. — Above Avg.

VOL. MIL.

HOLD | BUY | BUY
J A S O N D | J F M A M J J A S O N D | J F M A M J J A S O N D | J F M A M J J A S O N D | J
2001 | 2002 | 2003 | 2004

OPTIONS: ASE, CBOE, Ph

Analyst commentary prepared by Evan M. Momios, CFA /CB/BK

Highlights 17-NOV-04

- The STARS recommendation for National City Corporation (NCC) has recently been changed to 4 from 5. The Highlights section of this Stock Report will be updated accordingly.

Investment Rationale/Risk 17-NOV-04

- The Investment Rationale/Risk section of this Stock Report will be updated shortly. For the latest news story on National City Corporation (NCC) from MarketScope, see below.

11/17/04 12:18 pm EST... S&P DOWNGRADES SHARES OF NATIONAL CITY CORP. TO BUY FROM STRONG BUY (NCC 38.52****): Shares of NCC have risen about 15% so far this year, significantly outperforming peers and the S&P 500. We think '05 results will be supported by operating efficiencies and improved credit quality. Trading at about 11.5X our '05 operating EPS estimate of $3.35, vs. about 12.5X on average for large capitalization peers, NCC shares remain undervalued, in our opinion, and should continue to be above-average performers. We are keeping our 12-month target price of $44, but based on the stock's potential total return, we believe the shares merit a buy recommendation. /E. Momios-CFA

Key Stock Statistics

S&P Core EPS 2005E	3.34	52-week Range	$39.66-32.01
S&P Oper. EPS 2004E	3.45	12 Month P/E	10.3
P/E on S&P Oper. EPS 2004E	11.4	Beta	0.36
S&P Oper. EPS 2005E	3.35	Shareholders	61,370
Yield (%)	3.7%	Market Cap (B)	$ 25.9
Dividend Rate/Share	1.40	Shares Outstanding (M)	677.5

Value of $10,000 invested five years ago: **$ 15,967**

Dividend Data Dividends have been paid since 1936

Amount ($)	Date Decl.	Ex-Div. Date	Stock of Record	Payment Date
0.320	Jan. 02	Jan. 08	Jan. 12	Feb. 01 '04
0.320	Apr. 01	Apr. 07	Apr. 12	May. 01 '04
0.350	Jul. 01	Jul. 08	Jul. 12	Aug. 01 '04
0.350	Oct. 01	Oct. 06	Oct. 11	Nov. 01 '04

Revenues/Earnings Data Fiscal year ending December 31

Revenues (Million $)

	2004	2003	2002	2001	2000	1999
1Q	2,462	2,622	2,248	2,346	2,158	2,051
2Q	2,261	2,534	2,209	2,325	2,321	2,065
3Q	—	2,037	2,064	2,233	2,270	2,014
4Q	—	2,400	2,207	2,189	2,344	2,163
Yr.	—	9,594	8,728	9,093	9,051	8,293

Earnings Per Share ($)

	2004	2003	2002	2001	2000	1999
1Q	1.16	1.05	0.73	0.55	0.53	0.54
2Q	0.83	0.94	0.63	0.57	0.56	0.56
3Q	0.86	0.56	0.61	0.58	0.54	0.57
4Q	E0.60	0.88	0.62	0.57	0.50	0.55
Yr.	E3.45	3.43	2.59	2.27	2.13	2.22

Next earnings report expected: mid-January Source: S&P, Company Reports
EPS Estimates based on S&P Operating Earnings; historical GAAP earnings are as reported.

National City Corporation

Recommendation: **BUY** ★★★★☆   12-Month Target Price: **$44.00** (as of September 13, 2004)

Business Summary October 19, 2004

National City Corp., one of the 10 largest U.S. banking holding companies, operates commercial banks with more than 1,100 offices, located mainly in Ohio, Kentucky, Illinois, Indiana, Michigan, Missouri and Pennsylvania.

The company operates in five major business lines. Consumer and small business financial services provides banking services such as deposit gathering and direct lending, dealer finance, education finance and lending-related insurance services. Consumer lending includes home equity, automobile, marine and recreational vehicle installment loans, student loans, and credit card and other unsecured personal and business lines of credit.

Wholesale banking provides credit-related and treasury management products, as well as capital markets and institutional services to corporations. Products include lines of credit, term loans, leases, investment real estate lending, asset-based lending, structured finance, syndicated lending, equity capital, treasury management, and international payment and clearing services.

National Consumer Finance originates residential mortgage and home equity loans, and also sells and services mortgage loans for third-party investors. The asset management business includes institutional asset management and personal wealth management.

National Processing (84% owned) includes Merchant Card Services, which authorizes, processes and performs financial settlement and reporting of credit card transactions, and payment services.

In 2003, average earning assets, from which interest income is derived, amounted to $106.8 billion, and consisted mainly of loans (92%) and investment securities (7%). Average sources of funds included interest-bearing deposits (43%), short-term borrowings (11%), long-term debt (21%), noninterest-bearing demand deposits (15%), shareholders' equity (8%), and other (2%).

At December 31, 2003, loans of $79.3 billion were divided: commercial 27%, residential real estate 35%, commercial real estate 12%, home equity 14%, credit card and other unsecured 3%, and other consumer 9%.

At the end of 2003, nonperforming assets, consisting primarily of nonaccrual and other real estate owned, totaled $657 million (0.83% of loans and related assets), down from $817 million (1.17%) a year earlier. The allowance for loan losses, which is set aside for possible loan defaults, was $1.13 billion (1.42% of loans), up from $1.10 billion (1.52%) a year earlier.

In April 2004, NCC acquired St. Louis, MO-based Allegiant Bancorp, for $492 million. In July 2004, the company acquired Cincinnati, OH-based Provident Financial Group for about $2.1 billion.

Company Financials Fiscal Year ending December 31

Per Share Data ($)

(Year Ended December 31)	2003	2002	2001	2000	1999	1998	1997	1996	1995	1994
Tangible Bk. Val.	13.47	11.70	12.15	11.06	9.44	10.69	10.14	9.93	9.40	8.18
Earnings	3.43	2.59	2.27	2.13	2.22	1.61	1.83	1.65	1.52	1.35
S&P Core Earnings	3.30	2.31	1.95	NA	NA	NA	NA	NA	NA	NA
Dividends	1.25	1.20	1.16	1.14	1.06	0.94	0.84	0.73	0.65	0.59
Payout Ratio	36%	46%	51%	54%	48%	58%	46%	45%	43%	44%
Prices - High	34.97	33.75	32.70	29.75	37.81	38.75	33.78	23.62	16.87	14.50
- Low	26.53	24.60	23.69	16.00	22.12	28.46	21.25	15.31	12.62	11.87
P/E Ratio - High	10	13	14	14	17	24	18	14	11	11
- Low	8	9	10	8	10	18	12	9	8	9

Income Statement Analysis (Million $)

	2003	2002	2001	2000	1999	1998	1997	1996	1995	1994
Net Int. Inc.	4,368	4,005	3,439	2,958	3,000	2,912	1,943	1,943	1,321	1,237
Tax Equiv. Adj.	NA	30.4	33.3	33.7	36.9	40.3	19.4	20.9	21.2	29.5
Non Int. Inc.	3,549	2,731	2,533	2,427	2,242	1,695	899	1,165	893	853
Loan Loss Prov.	638	682	605	287	250	201	140	146	97.5	79.4
Exp./Op. Revs.	51.6%	55.4%	56.0%	59.1%	56.9%	73.3%	71.0%	66.6%	65.8%	66.2%
Pretax Inc.	3,237	2,406	2,167	1,972	2,149	1,647	1,169	1,058	670	618
Eff. Tax Rate	34.6%	33.8%	35.9%	34.0%	34.6%	35.0%	31.0%	30.4%	30.5%	30.5%
Net Inc.	2,117	1,594	1,388	1,302	1,405	1,071	807	737	465	429
% Net Int. Marg.	4.11	4.34	4.71	3.85	3.99	4.11	4.25	4.44	4.44	4.65
S&P Core Earnings	2,038	1,429	1,201	NA	NA	NA	NA	NA	NA	NA

Balance Sheet & Other Fin. Data (Million $)

	2003	2002	2001	2000	1999	1998	1997	1996	1995	1994
Money Mkt. Assets	162	136	171	81.0	556	930	600	342	748	681
Inv. Securities	7,859	10,217	10,463	10,673	15,135	15,701	8,865	8,690	4,950	4,395
Com'l Loans	50,446	34,107	34,033	52,247	29,415	22,243	14,095	12,261	10,291	8,884
Other Loans	60,115	38,028	34,007	13,357	30,789	35,768	25,476	22,718	15,931	14,151
Total Assets	113,933	118,258	105,817	88,535	87,121	88,246	54,684	50,856	36,199	32,114
Demand Deposits	43,435	39,179	34,324	28,763	27,744	29,523	16,822	16,599	5,564	5,332
Time Deposits	20,495	25,940	28,806	26,494	22,322	28,724	20,039	19,401	19,637	19,140
LT Debt	23,666	22,730	17,316	18,145	15,038	9,009	4,810	2,994	1,215	744
Common Equity	9,329	8,308	7,381	6,740	5,698	6,977	4,281	4,432	2,735	2,414
% Ret. on Assets	1.8	1.4	1.4	1.5	1.6	1.5	1.5	1.5	1.4	1.4
% Ret. on Equity	24.2	20.3	19.7	20.9	22.2	18.7	18.5	17.7	18.1	17.1
% Loan Loss Resv.	1.2	1.1	1.2	1.3	1.5	1.7	1.8	2.0	1.9	2.0
% Loans/Deposits	148.0	141.7	130.0	125.3	114.9	106.3	103.5	102.0	104.0	94.1
% Equity to Assets	7.5	7.0	7.3	7.1	7.2	8.2	8.3	8.6	8.0	7.8

Data as orig reptd.; bef. results of disc opers/spec. items. Per share data adj. for stk. divs.; EPS diluted. E-Estimated. NA-Not Available. NM-Not Meaningful. NR-Not Ranked. UR-Under Review.

Office: 1900 East Ninth Street, Cleveland, OH 44114-3484.
Telephone: 216-222-2000.
Email: investor.relation@nationalcity.com
Website: http://www.nationalcity.com
Chrmn & CEO: D.A. Daberko.
Vice Chrmn: W.E. MacDonald III.
EVP & CFO: J.D. Kelly.

EVP, Secy & General Counsel: D.L. Zoeller.
SVP & Treas: T.A. Richlovsky.
Investor Contact: B. Figgie 216-222-9849.
Dirs: J. E. Barfield, J. S. Broadhurst, J. W. Brown, D. E. Collins, C. M. Connor, D. A. Daberko, D. E. Evans, J. T. Gorman, B. P. Healy, S. C. Lindner, P. A. Ormond, R. A. Paul, G. L. Shaheen, J. F. Tatar, J. S. Thorton, M. Weiss.

Founded: in 1845.
Domicile: Delaware.
Employees: 33,331.
S&P Analyst: Evan M. Momios, CFA /CB/BK

National Semiconductor

Recommendation: **HOLD** ★ ★ ★ ☆ ☆
SELL SELL HOLD BUY BUY

12-Month Target Price: $17.00
(as of November 02, 2004)

NSM has an approximate 0.05% weighting in the **S&P 500**

Sector: Information Technology
Sub-Industry: Semiconductors
Peer Group: Semiconductors - Analog

Summary: NSM is a leading manufacturer of a broad line of semiconductors, including analog, digital and mixed-signal integrated circuits.

Quantitative Evaluations

S&P Earnings & Dividend Rank: B-

| D | C | B- | B | B+ | A- | A | A+ |

S&P Fair Value Rank: 2+

| 1 | 2 | 3 | 4 | 5 |
| Lowest | | | | Highest |

Fair Value Calc.: $15.20 (Slightly Overvalued)

S&P Investability Quotient Percentile
80%

NSM scored higher than 80% of all companies for which an S&P Report is available.

Volatility: Average

| Low | Average | High |

Technical Evaluation: Neutral
Since 11/04, the technical indicators for NSM have been Neutral.

Relative Strength Rank: Moderate
48
1 Lowest   Highest 99

| Price as of 11/12/04: | $16.70 | 2005E S&P Core EPS: | $0.35 |

GAAP Earnings vs. Previous Year
▲ Up ▼ Down ► No Change

10 Week Mov. Avg.
30 Week Mov. Avg.
Relative Strength
12-Mo Target Price

Volume Below Avg. — Above Avg.

2-for-1

HOLD $16.11 10/26/04

HOLD   BUY   SELL   HOLD

J J A S O N D J F M A M J J A S O N D J F M A M J J A S O N D J F M A M J J A S O N D J
2001   2002   2003   2004

OPTIONS: ASE, CBOE, P, Ph

Analyst commentary prepared by Amrit Tewary/MF/BK

Highlights November 04, 2004

- Following a robust gain of 19% in FY 04 (May), we see sales declining 1.4% in FY 05. We believe chip customers have sharply slowed their order rates to adjust for weaker than expected end-market demand and a buildup of excess inventory. We expect most customer inventory adjustments to be completed over the next several months.

- NSM's gross margins widened to a record 55.0% in the FY 05 first quarter. We see gross margins narrowing to 49.5% in the second quarter, but recovering sequentially later in FY 05, due to continued emphasis on higher-margin analog products. We expect R&D costs and SG&A expenses to decrease from year-ago levels.

- We estimate EPS of $0.82 for FY 05. We forecast FY 05 S&P Core EPS of $0.35, including an estimated $0.46 of stock option expense.

Investment Rationale/Risk November 04, 2004

- We would hold the shares. We expect the semiconductor upcycle to continue through 2005, albeit at a slower pace. We believe the current inventory correction in the company's distribution channel will likely continue in the very short term. However, we expect most customer inventory adjustments to be completed over the next few months, leading to improved order bookings for NSM during the second half of FY 05. We believe the shares are fairly valued at current levels, based on our P/E multiple and price to sales ratio analyses.

- Risks to our recommendation and target price include the possibility that the current semiconductor industry upcycle will be shorter and less robust than we forecast; and a significant and prolonged deterioration in demand.

- Our 12-month target price of $17 is based on our historical price to sales ratio and P/E multiple models, which value the stock at a discount to historical norms. We believe a discount is warranted by what we expect to be declining sales in FY 05. Our target price applies a P/E multiple of 21X to our FY 05 EPS estimate, and a price to sales ratio of 3.3X to our FY 05 sales per share estimate.

Key Stock Statistics

S&P Core EPS 2006E	0.41	52-week Range	$24.35-11.85
S&P Oper. EPS 2005E	0.82	12 Month P/E	17.2
P/E on S&P Oper. EPS 2005E	20.4	Beta	1.99
S&P Oper. EPS 2006E	0.88	Shareholders	7,415
Yield (%)	Nil	Market Cap (B)	$ 6.0
Dividend Rate/Share	Nil	Shares Outstanding (M)	358.1

Value of $10,000 invested five years ago: **$ 9,742**

Dividend Data Dividends have been paid since 2005

Amount ($)	Date Decl.	Ex-Div. Date	Stock of Record	Payment Date
2-for-1	Apr. 19	May. 14	Apr. 29	May. 13 '04

Revenues/Earnings Data Fiscal year ending May 31

Revenues (Million $)

	2005	2004	2003	2002	2001	2000
1Q	548.0	424.8	420.6	339.3	640.8	481.1
2Q	—	473.5	422.3	366.5	595.0	513.9
3Q	—	513.6	404.3	369.5	475.6	548.9
4Q	—	571.2	425.3	419.5	401.2	595.3
Yr.	—	1,983	1,673	1,495	2,113	2,140

Earnings Per Share ($)

	2005	2004	2003	2002	2001	2000
1Q	0.31	0.08	0.01	-0.15	0.37	0.13
2Q	E0.14	0.17	0.02	-0.13	0.28	0.27
3Q	E0.17	0.24	-0.10	-0.11	0.11	0.84
4Q	E0.21	0.24	-0.01	0.05	-0.13	0.39
Yr.	E0.82	0.74	-0.09	-0.34	0.65	1.64

Next earnings report expected: early-December Source: S&P, Company Reports
EPS Estimates based on S&P Operating Earnings; historical GAAP earnings are as reported.

National Semiconductor Corporation

Recommendation: **HOLD** ★ ★ ★ ☆ ☆   12-Month Target Price: **$17.00** (as of November 02, 2004)

Business Summary November 05, 2004

National Semiconductor's CEO, Brian Halla, who joined the company in 1996, has led an effort to form a "new" NSM. The company's expertise has been primarily in analog intensive, digital and mixed-signal complex integrated circuits. In 1996, NSM spun off its logic, memory and discrete products (considered commodity-type components) as a separate company, Fairchild Semiconductor. The company now focuses on high-end analog chips.

CEO Halla has often said that information is analog, a key NSM strength. Analog and mixed-signal products process analog information, and convert analog to digital and vice versa. Analog devices, controlling continuously variable functions (such as light, color, sound and power), are used in automotive, telecommunications and industrial applications. About 84% of sales come from the Analog Group. In FY 04 (May), analog sales increased 23%, reflecting increased demand (unit shipments advanced 22%), led by sales of power management, audio, data conversion, and application-specific wireless products. Power management demand was largely driven by growth in wireless handsets.

The company markets its products globally to OEMs and original design manufacturers through a direct sales force. In addition, it markets products through distributors in its four business regions. Leading distributors include Arrow (which accounted for 10% of NSM's FY 04 sales) and Avnet (11%).

Wafer fabrication is concentrated in two facilities in the U.S. and one in Scotland.

Nearly all product assembly and final test operations are performed in several facilities in Asia.

In March 2003, NSM announced plans to sell its Information Appliances Group division. It completed the sale in August 2003, to Advanced Micro Devices (AMD). Products included the Geode Information Appliance-on-a-chip.

In August 2002, the company acquired DigitalQuake, Inc., a California-based development stage enterprise engaged in the development of flat panel display products. In April 2002, NSM acquired the Finnish company Fincitec Oy and a related Estonia-based company. These companies developed low-voltage, low-power application specific integrated circuits for battery powered devices.

In June 2001, NSM acquired Wireless Solutions Sweden AB, a developer of wireless solutions ranging from telemetry to mobile phones to wireless networking, including Bluetooth. The acquisition was accounted for using the purchase method, with a purchase price of $27.7 million for all Wireless Solutions common stock.

The company foresees continuing cash outlays for plant and equipment in FY 05, with its primary focus on extending its analog capacity and capabilities at its existing sites. NSM projected FY 05 capital expenditures at about the level of FY 04.

Company Financials Fiscal Year ending May 31

Per Share Data ($)

(Year Ended May 31)	2004	2003	2002	2001	2000	1999	1998	1997	1996	1995
Tangible Bk. Val.	4.21	4.17	4.46	4.70	4.63	2.67	5.62	6.03	5.76	5.16
Cash Flow	1.27	0.54	0.31	1.30	2.33	-1.81	0.59	0.91	1.56	1.75
Earnings	0.74	-0.09	-0.34	0.65	1.64	-3.02	-0.30	0.10	0.68	1.01
S&P Core Earnings	0.27	-0.59	-0.84	0.29	NA	NA	NA	NA	NA	NA
Dividends	Nil	Nil	Nil	Nil	Nil	Nil	Nil	Nil	Nil	Nil
Payout Ratio	Nil	Nil	Nil	Nil	Nil	Nil	Nil	Nil	Nil	Nil

Cal. Yrs.	2003	2002	2001	2000	1999	1998	1997	1996	1995	1994
Prices - High	22.62	18.65	17.55	42.96	25.93	14.12	21.43	13.81	16.81	12.50
- Low	6.27	4.97	9.85	8.56	4.43	3.71	10.81	6.50	8.25	7.18
P/E Ratio - High	31	NM	NM	66	16	NM	NM	NM	25	12
- Low	8	NM	NM	13	3	NM	NM	NM	12	7

Income Statement Analysis (Million $)

	2004	2003	2002	2001	2000	1999	1998	1997	1996	1995
Revs.	1,983	1,673	1,495	2,113	2,140	1,957	2,537	2,507	2,623	2,379
Oper. Inc.	582	248	81.9	517	550	20.2	342	357	447	495
Depr.	210	229	230	243	264	406	292	231	233	185
Int. Exp.	Nil	Nil	3.90	5.00	17.9	17.9	26.3	13.8	16.0	6.70
Pretax Inc.	334	-23.3	-123	307	643	-1,085	-100	57.3	247	329
Eff. Tax Rate	14.7%	NM	NM	19.4%	2.32%	NM	NM	52.0%	25.0%	19.7%
Net Inc.	285	-33.3	-122	246	628	-1,010	-99	27.5	185	264
S&P Core Earnings	104	-215	-298	108	NA	NA	NA	NA	NA	NA

Balance Sheet & Other Fin. Data (Million $)

	2004	2003	2002	2001	2000	1999	1998	1997	1996	1995
Cash	643	802	681	818	850	419	461	890	504	467
Curr. Assets	1,246	1,281	1,073	1,275	1,468	989	1,308	1,553	1,256	1,178
Total Assets	2,280	2,245	2,289	2,362	2,382	2,044	3,101	2,914	2,658	2,236
Curr. Liab.	461	367	404	472	628	665	794	791	677	686
LT Debt	Nil	19.9	20.4	26.0	48.6	416	391	324	351	82.5
Common Equity	1,681	1,706	1,781	1,768	1,643	701	1,859	1,749	1,557	1,234
Total Cap.	1,681	1,726	1,802	1,794	1,692	1,317	2,254	2,082	1,940	1,509
Cap. Exp.	215	171	138	228	170	303	622	593	628	479
Cash Flow	495	195	109	489	891	-604	194	259	412	438
Curr. Ratio	2.7	3.5	2.7	2.7	2.3	1.5	1.6	2.0	1.9	1.7
% LT Debt of Cap.	Nil	1.2	1.1	1.4	2.9	31.6	17.3	15.6	18.1	5.5
% Net Inc.of Revs.	14.4	NM	NM	11.6	29.3	NM	NM	1.1	7.1	11.1
% Ret. on Assets	12.6	NM	NM	10.3	28.4	NM	NM	1.0	7.6	13.3
% Ret. on Equity	16.8	NM	NM	14.4	49.3	NM	NM	1.7	12.8	23.4

Data as orig reptd.; bef. results of disc opers/spec. items. Per share data adj. for stk. divs.; EPS diluted. E-Estimated. NA-Not Available. NM-Not Meaningful. NR-Not Ranked. UR-Under Review.

Office: 2900 Semiconductor Dr, Santa Clara, CA 95052.
Telephone: 408-721-5000.
Email: invest.group@nsc.com
Website: http://www.national.com
Chrmn, Pres & CEO: B.L. Halla.

COO & EVP: D. Macleod.
SVP & CFO: L. Chew.
Secy: J.M. Clark, III.
Dirs: S. R. Appleton, G. P. Arnold, R. J. Danzig, R. J. Frankenberg, B. L. Halla, E. F. Kvamme, M. A. Maidique, E. R. McCracken.

Founded: in 1959.
Domicile: Delaware.
Employees: 9,700.
S&P Analyst: Amrit Tewary/MF/BK

Navistar International

Recommendation: **HOLD** ★ ★ ★ ★ ★
SELL · SELL · HOLD · BUY · BUY

12-Month Target Price: **$38.00**
(as of May 20, 2004)

NAV has an approximate 0.02% weighting in the **S&P 500**

Sector: Industrials
Sub-Industry: Construction & Farm Machinery & Heavy Trucks
Peer Group: Truck Manufacturers

Summary: NAV is a global maker of trucks, buses, and diesel engines.

Quantitative Evaluations

S&P Earnings & Dividend Rank: C

| D | C | B- | B | B+ | A- | A | A+ |

S&P Fair Value Rank: 1-

| 1 | 2 | 3 | 4 | 5 |

Lowest — Highest

Fair Value Calc.: $30.50 (Overvalued)

S&P Investability Quotient Percentile
This company does not meet the inclusion criteria required for calculating an IQ value.

Volatility: Average

| Low | Average | High |

Technical Evaluation: Neutral
Since 11/04, the technical indicators for NAV have been Neutral.

Relative Strength Rank: Moderate

69

1 Lowest — Highest 99

Price as of 11/12/04: $39.48 | **2004E S&P Core EPS:** $2.50

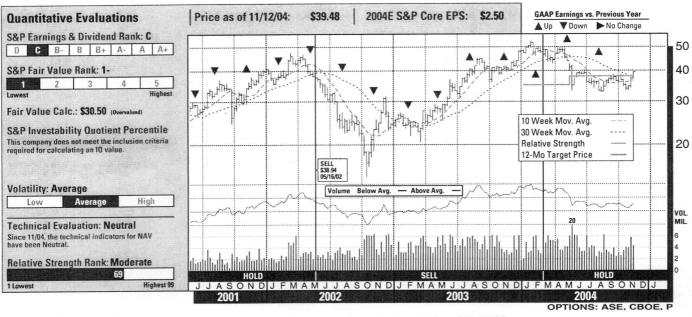

GAAP Earnings vs. Previous Year
▲ Up ▼ Down ► No Change

- 10 Week Mov. Avg.
- 30 Week Mov. Avg.
- Relative Strength
- 12-Mo Target Price

SELL $38.94 05/16/02

Volume Below Avg. — Above Avg. —

HOLD | SELL | HOLD

J J A S O N D J F M A M J J A S O N D J F M A M J J A S O N D J F M A M J J A S O N D J
2001 · 2002 · 2003 · 2004

OPTIONS: ASE, CBOE, P

Analyst commentary prepared by Anthony M. Fiore, CFA /JP/GG

Highlights August 31, 2004

- We think that a continued cyclical upturn in the truck manufacturing industry should lead to top line growth of about 10% in FY 05 (Oct.) for NAV. We anticipate that the replacement cycle, currently under way, will continue and should lead to higher unit volumes in FY 05. Furthermore, we believe there is a possibility of some additional demand being generated from fleet owners looking to purchase in advance of more stringent emission standards that are expected in 2007, although this may be more of a factor for NAV in FY 06.

- We expect a modest expansion of net margins in FY 05, based on our outlook for greater volumes as well as benefits from non-operational items, including decreased pension expense, Medicare benefit, and lower tax rate assumptions. So far in FY 04, operating leverage has been negatively affected by items such as higher steel prices and increased production costs related to emission standards. We see these factors abating over the next two to four quarters. For the longer term, we believe that earnings will continue to exhibit large swings due to the extreme cyclicality of the industry in which the company operates.

- Our Standard & Poor's Core Earnings estimates for FY 04 and FY 05 are $0.45 and $0.44 a share below our respective operating EPS forecasts. Most of the difference reflects projected stock option expense and pension cost adjustments.

Investment Rationale/Risk August 31, 2004

- Based on our belief that operating leverage at the company has been limited and also due to valuation considerations, we would not currently recommend adding to positions.

- Risks to our recommendation and target price include an unexpected downturn in the truck manufacturing market, continued raw material cost escalation, and further component shortages from suppliers.

- Our 12-month target price of $38 combines two separate valuation metrics. First, our discounted cash flow model, which assumes a 6.5% average annual free cash flow growth rate over the next 10 years, 3.5% growth in perpetuity, and a 9% weighted average cost of capital, indicates intrinsic value of about $34 a share. Second, in terms of price to earnings, the shares were recently trading at 9X our FY 05 EPS estimate. Applying a target P/E multiple of about 10X our FY 05 EPS estimate (14X our FY 04 EPS estimate) suggests a value of $40 a share. As in prior industry cycles, we expect the stock to trade at lower multiples during peak or near-peak EPS years.

Key Stock Statistics

S&P Core EPS 2005E	3.56	52-week Range	$52.95-32.72
S&P Oper. EPS 2004E	2.95	12 Month P/E	16.9
P/E on S&P Oper. EPS 2004E	13.4	Beta	1.70
S&P Oper. EPS 2005E	4.00	Shareholders	19,300
Yield (%)	Nil	Market Cap (B)	$ 2.8
Dividend Rate/Share	Nil	Shares Outstanding (M)	69.8

Value of $10,000 invested five years ago: **$ 9,784**

Dividend Data

Dividends on the common shares were omitted in 1981.

Revenues/Earnings Data Fiscal year ending October 31

Revenues (Million $)

	2004	2003	2002	2001	2000	1999
1Q	1,859	1,578	1,465	1,507	2,166	1,924
2Q	2,331	1,864	1,672	1,794	2,388	2,287
3Q	2,360	1,894	1,591	1,586	1,924	1,878
4Q	—	2,004	2,056	1,835	1,973	2,558
Yr.	—	7,340	6,784	6,722	8,451	8,647

Earnings Per Share ($)

	2004	2003	2002	2001	2000	1999
1Q	-0.34	-1.47	-0.88	-0.58	1.10	0.91
2Q	0.54	-0.18	-0.04	0.05	1.60	1.42
3Q	0.73	0.26	-0.26	0.03	1.58	3.86
4Q	E1.75	1.00	-6.67	0.11	-1.77	2.04
Yr.	E2.95	-0.21	-7.88	-0.39	2.58	8.20

Next earnings report expected: early-December Source: S&P, Company Reports
EPS Estimates based on S&P Operating Earnings; historical GAAP earnings are as reported.

The McGraw·Hill Companies

Navistar International Corporation

Recommendation: **HOLD** ★ ★ ★ ☆ ☆   12-Month Target Price: **$38.00** (as of May 20, 2004)

Business Summary August 31, 2004

Navistar International was created from the former International Harvester (IH). After shedding its construction and farm equipment businesses in the mid-1980s, the company's remaining truck and engine business was renamed Navistar. NAV operates in three principal industry segments: trucks, engines, and financial services.

The truck-making segment accounted for 72% of FY 03 (Oct.) revenues. The segment primarily makes a full line of diesel powered trucks and school buses for Class 5 through Class 8 truck markets in the U.S., Canada and Mexico. In general, these volatile and competitive end markets tend to move in response to cycles in the overall economy, and are particularly sensitive to fluctuations in the industrial sector. Since the last peak of 465,500 trucks in 1999, total industry shipments of Class 5 through Class 8 trucks in the U.S. and Canada declined in each subsequent year. At the end of FY 02, total industry deliveries were approximately 288,300 (NAV's market share was 33.9%), down from 312,700 (31.2%) in FY 01. For Mexico, industry retail deliveries in FY 02 totaled 21,900 (33.9%), versus 28,600 (31.2%). Competitors in the Class 5 through Class 8 markets include PACCAR, Ford, GM, DaimlerChrysler (including Freightliner, Sterling, and Western Star) and Volvo Global (including Volvo Trucks and Mack Trucks). Margins for this segment over the last six years averaged about 0.5%.

The company also makes diesel engines (24% of FY 03 revenues) for sale to

third-party truck manufacturers, as well as for use in its own trucks and school buses. Under a 10-year agreement that began in 2003, NAV supplies 7.3L diesel engines to Ford for use in Ford's diesel powered super duty trucks and vans. As of the end of FY 02, sales to Ford accounted for about 76% of total engine segment revenue. Primary competitors in the diesel engine manufacturing industry include Cummins, Caterpillar, and DaimlerChrysler's Detroit Diesel unit. Over the last six years, segment margins averaged about 15%.

NAV's manufacturing operations are capital intensive. In FY 03, FY 02 and FY 01, capital expenditures were equal to 2.9%, 3.7%, and 5.1% of revenues, respectively. For FY 04, management anticipated capital spending of about $200 million.

The company also has a small but profitable financing unit (4%) that provides financing and insurance to NAV's dealers and retail customers. Over the last six years, margins averaged about 33%.

For FY 03, NAV reported that its pension plan was underfunded by about $994 million. The company estimated that its total combined cash contribution would be about $450 million to $490 million for 2003 through 2005. To meet its 2003 requirement, in November 2002, the company sold $175 million of common stock to the pension plan.

Company Financials Fiscal Year ending October 31

Per Share Data ($)

(Year Ended October 31)	2003	2002	2001	2000	1999	1998	1997	1996	1995	1994
Tangible Bk. Val.	4.45	4.08	14.33	17.05	16.03	8.61	7.83	4.86	4.15	3.16
Cash Flow	2.60	-4.25	3.26	5.82	10.81	6.39	3.26	2.24	3.29	1.94
Earnings	-0.21	-7.88	-0.39	2.58	8.20	4.16	1.65	0.49	1.83	0.99
S&P Core Earnings	1.34	-10.38	-4.10	NA	NA	NA	NA	NA	NA	NA
Dividends	Nil	Nil	Nil	Nil	Nil	Nil	Nil	Nil	Nil	Nil
Payout Ratio	Nil	Nil	Nil	Nil	Nil	Nil	Nil	Nil	Nil	Nil
Prices - High	48.71	47.38	41.20	48.00	56.25	35.87	29.50	12.12	17.50	26.62
- Low	20.52	14.77	21.78	18.25	27.12	17.00	9.00	8.37	9.00	12.25
P/E Ratio - High	NM	NM	NM	19	7	9	18	25	10	27
- Low	NM	NM	NM	7	3	4	5	17	5	12

Income Statement Analysis (Million $)

	2003	2002	2001	2000	1999	1998	1997	1996	1995	1994
Revs.	7,320	6,764	6,722	8,451	8,582	7,830	6,321	5,705	6,292	5,305
Oper. Inc.	247	135	357	942	835	619	386	240	380	289
Depr.	191	220	217	199	174	159	120	101	81.0	72.0
Int. Exp.	272	154	161	146	135	105	74.0	83.0	87.0	91.0
Pretax Inc.	-45.0	-769	-47.0	224	591	410	242	105	262	158
Eff. Tax Rate	NM	NM	NM	29.0%	7.95%	27.1%	38.0%	38.1%	37.4%	35.4%
Net Inc.	-14.0	-476	-23.0	159	544	299	150	65.0	164	102
S&P Core Earnings	91.3	-626	-245	NA	NA	NA	NA	NA	NA	NA

Balance Sheet & Other Fin. Data (Million $)

	2003	2002	2001	2000	1999	1998	1997	1996	1995	1994
Cash	1,042	736	1,085	501	576	440	609	881	485	557
Curr. Assets	2,210	2,608	2,736	2,467	2,842	NA	NA	NA	NA	NA
Total Assets	6,900	6,943	7,067	6,945	6,928	6,178	5,516	5,326	5,566	5,056
Curr. Liab.	2,204	2,399	2,273	2,409	2,502	NA	NA	NA	NA	1,810
LT Debt	2,396	2,398	2,468	2,148	2,075	2,122	1,316	1,420	1,279	696
Common Equity	306	247	1,123	1,310	1,287	765	776	672	626	544
Total Cap.	2,706	2,649	3,595	3,462	3,366	3,891	2,336	2,092	1,905	1,513
Cap. Exp.	206	242	326	553	427	305	172	117	139	92.0
Cash Flow	177	-256	194	358	718	447	241	166	245	145
Curr. Ratio	1.0	1.1	1.2	1.0	1.1	NA	NA	NA	NA	NA
% LT Debt of Cap.	88.5	90.5	68.7	62.0	61.6	73.4	56.3	67.9	67.1	46.0
% Net Inc.of Revs.	NM	NM	NM	1.9	6.3	3.8	2.4	11.4	2.6	1.9
% Ret. on Assets	NM	NM	NM	2.3	8.3	5.1	2.8	1.2	3.1	2.0
% Ret. on Equity	NM	NM	NM	12.2	53.0	37.4	16.7	10.0	27.4	14.0

Data as orig reptd.; bef. results of disc opers/spec. items. Per share data adj. for stk. divs.; EPS diluted. E-Estimated. NA-Not Available. NM-Not Meaningful. NR-Not Ranked. UR-Under Review.

Office: 4201 Winfield Road , Warrenville, IL 60555.
Telephone: 630-753-5000.
Website: http://www.navistar.com
Chrmn, Pres & CEO: D.C. Ustian.
Vice Chrmn & CFO: R.C. Lannert.
SVP & General Counsel: S.K. Covey.

Treas: T. Endsley.
Secy: R.J. Perna.
Investor Contact: M. Oberle 630-753-2406.
Dirs: Y. M. Belton, E. Clariond, J. D. Correnti, A. J. Griffin, M. N. Hammes, J. R. Horne, J. H. Keyes, R. C. Lannert, D. McAllister, S. Morcott, W. F. Patient, D. C. Ustian.

Founded: in 1902.
Domicile: Delaware.
Employees: 14,200.
S&P Analyst: Anthony M. Fiore, CFA /JP/GG

Recommendation: **HOLD** ★★★ ☆☆   12-Month Target Price: **$53.00**
SELL SELL HOLD BUY BUY   (as of October 28, 2004)

NCR has an approximate 0.05% weighting in the **S&P 500**

Sector: Information Technology
Sub-Industry: Computer Hardware
Peer Group: Computer Hardware - Large System Vendors

Summary: NCR, spun off from AT&T in 1996, designs, develops, markets and services information technology products, services, systems and solutions worldwide.

Quantitative Evaluations

S&P Earnings & Dividend Rank: NR

D	C	B-	B	B+	A-	A	A+

S&P Fair Value Rank: 4

1	2	3	4	5
Lowest				Highest

Fair Value Calc.: $59.50 (Slightly Undervalued)

S&P Investability Quotient Percentile
This company does not meet the inclusion criteria required for calculating an IQ value.

Volatility: Average

Low	Average	High

Technical Evaluation: Bullish
Since 9/04, the technical indicators for NCR have been Bullish.

Relative Strength Rank: Strong

	79	
1 Lowest		Highest 99

Price as of 11/12/04: $57.39   **2004E S&P Core EPS: $-0.10**

GAAP Earnings vs. Previous Year
▲ Up ▼ Down ► No Change

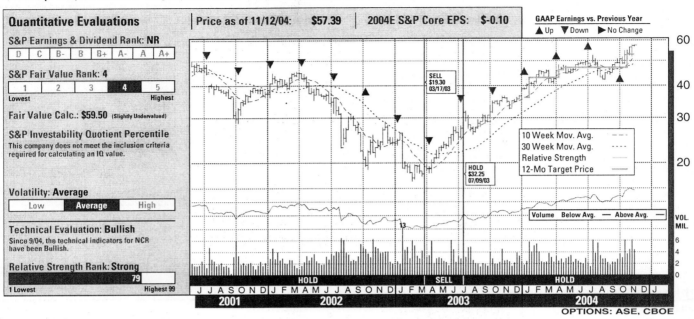

Analyst commentary prepared by Megan Graham-Hackett/PMW/BK

Highlights November 03, 2004

- We forecast a 5% increase in revenues in 2005, following an estimated 4% rise in 2004. We expect Data Warehousing solutions and Financial Self Service to continue to lead overall revenue growth for the company, and see Retail Store Automation's contributions as positive, depending on the pace of investments by retailers and synergies with a recent acquisition. We expect Financial Self Services revenues to continue to benefit from ATM upgrades by banks in the U.S. and in Europe and Asia. Customer Services has been reorganized to some degree, and we think that revenue pressures should be mitigated if NCR's management continues to execute well. However, we do not expect the impact of currency translations to be as favorable to 2005 revenue growth as it was in 2004.

- We project 2005 gross margins of 27.4%, somewhat higher than the 26.9% we expect for 2004, reflecting cost containment efforts by NCR. We project an effective tax rate of 25% for 2005.

- Our 2004 EPS estimate is $1.54; this includes real estate gains. Our 2004 S&P Core Earnings forecast is a loss of $0.10 a share, reflecting our estimate of stock option expense and pension costs. Our 2005 EPS estimate is $2.17.

Investment Rationale/Risk November 03, 2004

- We recommend holding existing positions. We view favorably what we see as NCR's strides in expense controls, but we believe that the revenue outlook remains modest, despite the benefits of currency fluctuations.

- Risks to our opinion and target price include multiple contraction as favorable currency translations could diminish; and a possible slowdown in the tech spending recovery, adversely affecting results.

- The stock's recent P/E multiple (based on our 2005 operating EPS estimate) was above peer levels, but the shares were trading below the level of peers on the basis of price to sales. Our 12-month target price of $53 is based on our discounted cash flow analysis, which assumes a weighted average cost of capital of 11.2%, and our price to sales ratio analysis. We believe the shares should trade at a price to sales ratio of about 0.8X our 2004 revenue estimate, based on the stock's historical trading average, and in line with peers.

Key Stock Statistics

S&P Core EPS 2005E	-0.11	52-week Range	$57.53-32.40
S&P Oper. EPS 2004E	1.54	12 Month P/E	22.8
P/E on S&P Oper. EPS 2004E	37.3	Beta	1.65
S&P Oper. EPS 2005E	2.17	Shareholders	400,000
Yield (%)	Nil	Market Cap (B)	$ 5.3
Dividend Rate/Share	Nil	Shares Outstanding (M)	93.2

Value of $10,000 invested five years ago: **$ 16,487**

Dividend Data

No cash dividends have been paid.

Revenues/Earnings Data Fiscal year ending December 31

Revenues (Million $)

	2004	2003	2002	2001	2000	1999
1Q	1,290	1,234	1,247	1,376	1,255	1,333
2Q	1,452	1,366	1,380	1,499	1,448	1,572
3Q	1,454	1,355	1,377	1,442	1,464	1,530
4Q	—	1,643	1,581	1,600	1,792	1,761
Yr.	—	5,598	5,585	5,917	5,959	6,196

Earnings Per Share ($)

	2004	2003	2002	2001	2000	1999
1Q	-0.05	-0.28	0.04	1.22	-0.05	0.03
2Q	1.27	-0.14	0.25	0.35	0.39	0.45
3Q	0.46	0.19	0.42	-0.07	0.55	0.53
4Q	E0.75	0.84	0.57	0.72	0.90	2.44
Yr.	E1.54	0.61	1.27	2.22	1.82	3.35

Next earnings report expected: late-January Source: S&P, Company Reports
EPS Estimates based on S&P Operating Earnings; historical GAAP earnings are as reported.

NCR Corporation

Recommendation: **HOLD** ★ ★ ★ ☆ ☆   12-Month Target Price: **$53.00** (as of October 28, 2004)

Business Summary November 03, 2004

NCR Corp. was spun off from AT&T as part of a restructuring announced in 1995; it had been acquired by AT&T in 1990, for $7.5 billion. In the next five years, NCR lost $3.9 billion, reflecting lost customers, uncontrolled costs, and a difficult relationship with AT&T. However, in 2000, NCR completed a five-year transition from selling commodity hardware (which generated losses) to providing solutions (including software and services) for customers.

The largest of NCR's segments is Customer Services (31% of total company revenues in 2003, including those for Data Warehousing). In 1998, NCR repositioned itself as a solutions supplier, rather than a hardware vendor.

The company is still probably best known as a leading supplier of Automated Teller Machines (ATMs). NCR's ATMs are included in the Financial Self Service segment (19.5%). The company anticipates growth from markets outside the U.S., and has aligned its sales strategy to better capitalize on such growth. NCR continues to believe that the Asia-Pacific region offers strong growth potential. The company also anticipates greater acceptance of ATMs with increased functionality, including automated cash acceptance, check cashing, bill payment, etc.

Retail Store Automation solutions (13.5%) include point-of-sale terminals, barcode scanners, kiosks, applications software and other related computer products.

For the longer term, Data Warehousing solutions (20.5%) is expected by the company to be one of the fastest growing areas in technology-related spending. NCR sees results in this area benefiting from growth in e-commerce. According to the company, data warehousing capabilities enable users to gain insight into consumer purchasing behavior and preferences, which in turn can be used to drive operational efficiency and profitability, as well as serve to enhance customer relationship management strategies. The company's Teradata technology is well recognized as a highly scalable platform, critical for data warehousing.

Systemedia solutions (8.4%) include business consumables such as paper and imaging supplies for printers. Payment and Imaging solutions (2.6%) consist of hardware, software and consulting and support services that enable item-based transactions to be digitally captured and processed.

NCR estimates that if it had recognized stock-based compensation expense in 2003, its pro forma earnings per share would have been $0.07, versus EPS of $0.61 that the company reported.

Company Financials Fiscal Year ending December 31

Per Share Data ($)

(Year Ended December 31)	2003	2002	2001	2000	1999	1998	1997	1996	1995	1994
Tangible Bk. Val.	18.69	12.61	20.81	12.91	17.05	13.78	13.14	13.82	11.98	NA
Cash Flow	3.89	4.56	6.47	5.50	6.91	4.76	3.82	2.73	-19.11	NA
Earnings	0.61	1.27	2.22	1.82	3.35	1.20	0.07	-1.07	-22.57	NA
S&P Core Earnings	0.58	-1.60	-1.07	NA	NA	NA	NA	NA	NA	NA
Dividends	Nil	Nil	Nil	Nil	Nil	Nil	Nil	Nil	NA	NA
Payout Ratio	Nil	Nil	Nil	Nil	Nil	Nil	Nil	Nil	NA	NA
Prices - High	39.47	45.49	50.00	53.68	55.75	41.87	41.37	40.75	NA	NA
- Low	16.92	18.80	28.59	32.37	26.68	23.50	25.87	30.87	NA	NA
P/E Ratio - High	65	36	23	29	17	35	NM	NM	NA	NA
- Low	28	15	13	18	8	20	NM	NM	NA	NA

Income Statement Analysis (Million $)

	2003	2002	2001	2000	1999	1998	1997	1996	1995	1994
Revs.	5,598	5,585	5,917	5,959	6,196	6,505	6,589	6,963	8,162	8,461
Oper. Inc.	445	517	609	566	436	516	364	515	-2,021	313
Depr.	315	328	423	361	358	364	383	385	350	415
Int. Exp.	26.0	19.0	18.0	13.0	12.0	13.0	15.0	56.0	90.0	44.0
Pretax Inc.	72.0	131	124	275	235	212	27.0	110	-2,416	-16.0
Eff. Tax Rate	19.4%	2.29%	NM	35.3%	NM	42.5%	74.1%	NM	NM	NM
Net Inc.	58.0	128	221	178	337	122	7.00	-109	-2,280	-203
S&P Core Earnings	55.0	-159	-106	NA	NA	NA	NA	NA	NA	NA

Balance Sheet & Other Fin. Data (Million $)

	2003	2002	2001	2000	1999	1998	1997	1996	1995	1994
Cash	689	526	336	357	763	514	1,129	1,203	NA	NA
Curr. Assets	2,422	2,186	1,963	2,234	2,541	2,632	3,271	3,318	NA	NA
Total Assets	5,480	4,672	4,855	5,106	4,895	4,892	5,293	5,280	NA	NA
Curr. Liab.	1,579	1,417	1,518	1,836	1,662	1,700	1,964	1,967	NA	NA
LT Debt	307	306	10.0	11.0	40.0	33.0	35.0	48.0	89.0	NA
Common Equity	1,875	1,325	2,027	1,758	1,596	1,447	1,353	1,396	1,210	NA
Total Cap.	2,204	1,651	2,059	1,796	1,685	1,524	1,652	1,733	NA	NA
Cap. Exp.	63.0	81.0	141	216	187	224	162	216	326	371
Cash Flow	373	456	644	539	695	486	390	276	-1,930	212
Curr. Ratio	1.5	1.5	1.3	1.2	1.5	1.5	1.7	1.7	NA	NA
% LT Debt of Cap.	13.9	18.5	0.5	0.6	2.4	2.2	2.1	2.8	NA	NA
% Net Inc.of Revs.	1.0	2.3	3.7	3.0	5.4	1.9	0.1	NM	NM	NM
% Ret. on Assets	1.1	2.7	4.4	3.6	6.9	2.4	0.1	NM	NA	NA
% Ret. on Equity	3.6	7.6	11.7	10.6	22.1	8.7	0.5	NM	NA	NA

Data as orig. reptd.; bef. results of disc. opers. and/or spec. items. Balance sheet data and book value for 1995 are pro forma as of Sep. 30, 1996. Per share data adj. for stk. divs.; EPS diluted (primary prior to 1998). E-Estimated. NA-Not Available. NM-Not Meaningful. NR-Not Ranked.

Office: 1700 S Patterson Blvd, Dayton, OH 45479.
Telephone: 937-445-5000.
Email: investor.relations@ncr.com
Website: http://www.ncr.com
Pres & CEO: M. Hurd.

SVP & CFO: P. Bocian.
SVP, Secy & General Counsel: J. Hoak.
Investor Contact: G. Swearingen 937-445-4700.
Dirs: E. P. Boykin, M. Frissora, M. V. Hurd, L. F. Levinson, V. L. Lund, L. Nyberg, C. K. Prahalad, J. M. Ringler, W. S. Stavropoulos.

Founded: in 1884.
Domicile: Maryland.
Employees: 29,000.
S&P Analyst: Megan Graham-Hackett/PMW/BK

Network Appliance

Recommendation: **SELL** ★ ★ ★ ★ ★
SELL SELL HOLD BUY BUY

12-Month Target Price: $21.00
(as of November 17, 2004)

NTAP has an approximate 0.10% weighting in the **S&P 500**

Sector: Information Technology
Sub-Industry: Computer Storage & Peripherals
Peer Group: Computer Peripherals - Storage (Large)

Summary: This company manufactures and supports high-performance network data storage devices that provide file service for data-intensive network environments.

Quantitative Evaluations

S&P Earnings & Dividend Rank: B

D	C	B-	B	B+	A-	A	A+

S&P Fair Value Rank: 3-

1	2	3	4	5
Lowest		3		Highest

Fair Value Calc.: $24.40 (Overvalued)

S&P Investability Quotient Percentile

90%

NTAP scored higher than 90% of all companies for which an S&P Report is available.

Volatility: High

Low	Average	High

Technical Evaluation: Bullish

Since 8/04, the technical indicators for NTAP have been Bullish.

Relative Strength Rank: Strong

96

1 Lowest — Highest 99

Price as of 11/17/04: $29.57 | **2005E S&P Core EPS:** $0.39

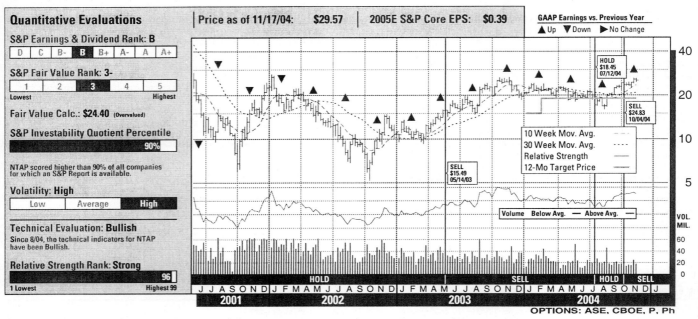

GAAP Earnings vs. Previous Year
▲ Up ▼ Down ► No Change

10 Week Mov. Avg.
30 Week Mov. Avg.
Relative Strength
12-Mo Target Price

Volume Below Avg. — Above Avg.

HOLD $18.45 07/12/04
SELL $24.83 10/04/04
SELL $15.49 05/14/03

HOLD .... SELL .... HOLD SELL
J J A S O N D J F M A M J J A S O N D J F M A M J J A S O N D J F M A M J J A S O N D J
2001 — 2002 — 2003 — 2004

OPTIONS: ASE, CBOE, P, Ph

Analyst commentary prepared by Richard N. Stice, CFA /MF/BK

Highlights October 04, 2004

- We expect revenues to advance about 33% in FY 05 (Apr.), following a 31% increase in FY 04. This reflects our view that information technology (IT) spending will improve over the next 12 months, particularly for products related to data storage, and that NTAP will continue to experience strength overseas. Moreover, we believe market share gains are likely.

- We see gross margins narrowing modestly, due to a shift in the business mix as NTAP's services revenue expands as a percentage of the total, as well as intensifying pricing pressures. We believe interest income will increase as a result of a higher interest rate environment and our expectation of continuing free cash flow generation.

- We project FY 05 EPS of $0.59, up 48% from FY 04's $0.40 (excluding a favorable tax benefit). Our FY 05 Standard & Poor's Core Earnings per share estimate is $0.38, with the difference attributable to projected stock option expense.

Investment Rationale/Risk October 04, 2004

- Our avoid recommendation is based on our view that the recent rise in the share price is not supported by current company or industry fundamentals. Moreover, we believe NTAP continues to face formidable competitive challenges, which are likely to negatively impact margins going forward. We are also concerned with the company's earnings quality, as we are projecting a 36% difference between FY 05 GAAP and S&P Core EPS.

- Risks to our recommendation and target price include demand rising at a faster rate than expected, abating pricing pressures and a contraction of the sales cycle.

- The shares trade at a premium to our relative P/E to growth measure, as well as to our intrinsic value calculation based on discounted cash flow analysis. Our assumptions include a weighted average cost of capital of 13.1%, a peak growth rate of 23% in year five, and an expected terminal growth rate of 3%. Combining the two metrics results in our 12-month target price of $19.

Key Stock Statistics

S&P Core EPS 2006E	0.53	52-week Range	$26.28-15.92
S&P Oper. EPS 2005E	0.62	12 Month P/E	61.6
P/E on S&P Oper. EPS 2005E	40.8	Beta	NA
S&P Oper. EPS 2006E	0.72	Shareholders	1,217
Yield (%)	Nil	Market Cap (B)	$ 10.6
Dividend Rate/Share	Nil	Shares Outstanding (M)	357.7

Value of $10,000 invested five years ago: **$ 11,014**

Dividend Data

No cash dividends have been paid.

Revenues/Earnings Data Fiscal year ending April 30

Revenues (Million $)

	2005	2004	2003	2002	2001	2000
1Q	358.4	260.5	206.8	200.4	231.2	103.3
2Q	375.2	275.6	215.2	194.7	260.8	124.7
3Q	—	297.3	228.5	198.3	288.4	151.3
4Q	—	337.0	241.6	204.9	225.8	200.0
Yr.	—	1,170	892.1	798.4	1,006	579.3

Earnings Per Share ($)

	2005	2004	2003	2002	2001	2000
1Q	0.13	0.08	0.05	Nil	0.01	0.04
2Q	0.15	0.13	0.05	-0.03	0.10	0.05
3Q	E0.16	0.11	0.06	0.02	0.09	0.06
4Q	E0.17	0.10	0.07	0.02	Nil	0.07
Yr.	E0.62	0.42	0.22	0.01	0.21	0.21

Next earnings report expected: mid-February Source: S&P, Company Reports
EPS Estimates based on S&P Operating Earnings; historical GAAP earnings are as reported.

Network Appliance, Inc.

Recommendation: **SELL** ★★☆☆☆   12-Month Target Price: **$21.00** (as of November 17, 2004)

Business Summary October 04, 2004

NTAP focuses on "simplifying the complex." This philosophy drives the entire company, from product design and system operation through support processes. NTAP believes this results in significant customer advantages, including reducing the total cost of ownership, and improving information availability and application performance.

The company provides enterprise network storage and data management solutions. These offerings provide consolidated storage, improved data center operations, economical business continuance, and efficient remote data access. NTAP's goal is to provide products that set the standard for simplicity and ease of operation, with what it believes to be one of the lowest total costs of ownership and highest returns on investment in the industry.

Products include filer storage, NearStore systems and NetCache appliances, as well as data management and content delivery software. Configured appliances range in price from $4,000 to over $1,000,000.

NTAP's filers are scalable, highly available, unified networked storage systems for data storage and simplifying data management. They are specifically designed for network-centric IT system architectures, and support both network-attached storage (NAS) and storage-attached networks (SAN) on a single platform.

NearStore products are designed for improving data backup and recovery architectures and archiving infrequently accessed files. The product complements and

significantly improves existing tape backup processes by inserting economical and simple to use disk-based storage between application storage and tape libraries, resulting in a highly efficient two stage backup configuration. NearStore can also be used as a mirror target within a data center, or for replicating data from distributed offices or branches to a central location.

The NetCache product line is a scalable suite of appliances, designed to solve complex web content delivery problems faced by enterprises and service providers. These appliances are deployed across the entire network, from the primary data center to remote points of presence and local offices worldwide.

The company believes Data ONTAP software offers a unique set of features to ensure mission critical availability levels, while lowering the total cost of ownership and the complexity typically associated with enterprise storage management.

NTAP's diversified customer base spans a number of large vertical markets including the energy, federal government, financial services, life sciences and telecommunications sectors. International customers accounted for 47% of revenues in FY 04 (Apr.), up from 42% in FY 03.

In February 2004, the company completed the acquisition of privately held Spinnaker Networks, a provider of networked storage products, for about $306 million in stock.

Company Financials Fiscal Year ending April 30

Per Share Data ($)

(Year Ended April 30)	2004	2003	2002	2001	2000	1999	1998	1997	1996	1995
Tangible Bk. Val.	2.91	2.75	2.39	2.21	1.54	1.02	0.64	0.41	0.15	NA
Cash Flow	0.56	0.38	0.14	0.33	0.26	0.14	0.18	0.02	0.03	-0.05
Earnings	0.42	0.22	0.01	0.21	0.21	0.12	0.07	Nil	0.03	-0.10
S&P Core Earnings	0.16	-0.28	-0.77	-0.52	NA	NA	NA	NA	NA	NA
Dividends	Nil	Nil	Nil	Nil	Nil	Nil	Nil	Nil	Nil	Nil
Payout Ratio	Nil	Nil	Nil	Nil	Nil	Nil	Nil	Nil	Nil	Nil

Cal. Yrs.	2003	2002	2001	2000	1999	1998	1997	1996	1995	1994
Prices - High	26.69	27.95	74.98	152.75	45.93	12.00	4.50	3.23	2.60	NA
- Low	9.26	5.18	6.00	33.87	9.53	3.25	1.32	1.25	0.84	NA
P/E Ratio - High	64	NM	NM	NM	NM	NM	62	98	NM	NA
- Low	22	NM	NM	NM	NM	NM	18	54	NM	NA

Income Statement Analysis (Million $)

	2004	2003	2002	2001	2000	1999	1998	1997	1996	1995
Revs.	1,170	892	798	1,006	579	289	166	93.3	46.6	14.8
Oper. Inc.	218	146	62.8	179	121	63.3	38.2	20.7	7.25	-4.52
Depr.	53.1	57.4	44.4	42.3	15.7	8.15	5.55	2.78	1.25	0.39
Int. Exp.	Nil	Nil	Nil	Nil	Nil	0.78	0.21	0.09	0.07	0.01
Pretax Inc.	170	97.8	2.53	133	114	57.0	33.5	4.04	6.60	-4.76
Eff. Tax Rate	10.8%	21.8%	NM	43.7%	35.5%	37.5%	37.5%	93.8%	Nil	Nil
Net Inc.	152	76.5	3.03	74.9	73.8	35.6	21.0	0.25	6.60	-4.76
S&P Core Earnings	59.5	-98.0	-256	-167	NA	NA	NA	NA	NA	NA

Balance Sheet & Other Fin. Data (Million $)

	2004	2003	2002	2001	2000	1999	1998	1997	1996	1995
Cash	241	284	211	466	279	221	37.3	21.5	24.6	1.79
Curr. Assets	1,089	853	679	636	533	315	99	56.6	40.4	8.74
Total Assets	1,877	1,319	1,109	1,036	592	346	116	68.9	45.4	10.6
Curr. Liab.	344	265	216	219	113	50.5	29.3	14.7	6.12	4.97
LT Debt	4.86	3.10	3.73	0.15	0.05	0.09	Nil	Nil	Nil	Nil
Common Equity	1,416	987	858	804	479	296	86.3	54.0	39.0	-7.26
Total Cap.	1,421	990	862	805	479	296	86.3	54.0	37.0	-7.30
Cap. Exp.	48.6	61.3	284	83.7	40.8	15.5	7.97	7.12	NA	NA
Cash Flow	205	134	47.4	117	89.5	43.8	26.5	3.03	7.85	-4.38
Curr. Ratio	3.2	3.2	3.2	2.9	4.7	6.2	3.4	3.9	6.6	1.8
% LT Debt of Cap.	0.3	0.3	0.4	0.0	0.0	0.0	Nil	Nil	Nil	Nil
% Net Inc.of Revs.	13.0	8.6	0.4	7.4	12.7	12.3	12.6	0.3	14.2	NA
% Ret. on Assets	9.5	6.3	0.3	9.2	15.7	15.4	22.7	0.4	23.5	NA
% Ret. on Equity	12.7	8.3	0.4	11.7	19.1	18.6	29.9	0.5	41.6	NA

Data as orig reptd.; bef. results of disc opers/spec. items. Per share data adj. for stk. divs.; EPS diluted. E-Estimated. NA-Not Available. NM-Not Meaningful. NR-Not Ranked. UR-Under Review.

Office: 495 East Java Drive, Sunnyvale, CA 94089.
Telephone: 408-822-6000.
Email: investor_relations@netapp.com
Website: http://www.netapp.com
Chrmn: D.T. Valentine.
Pres: T.F. Mendoza.

CEO: D.J. Warmenhoven.
SVP & CFO: S.J. Gomo.
Investor Contact: J. Baumann 408-822-3974.
Dirs: S. Ahuja, C. A. Bartz, M. R. Hallman, M. Leslie, N. G. Moore, S. Semmoto, G. T. Shaheen, D. T. Valentine, R. T. Wall, D. J. Warmenhoven.

Founded: in 1992.
Domicile: Delaware.
Employees: 2,844.
S&P Analyst: Richard N. Stice, CFA /MF/BK

Newell Rubbermaid

Recommendation: HOLD ★ ★ ★ ★ ★
SELL SELL HOLD BUY BUY

12-Month Target Price: **$23.00**
(as of October 29, 2004)

NWL has an approximate 0.06% weighting in the **S&P 500**

Sector: Consumer Discretionary
Sub-Industry: Housewares & Specialties
Peer Group: Houseware Products

Summary: This high-volume, brand-name consumer products concern has grown through acquisitions. Major product lines include housewares, home furnishings, office products and hardware.

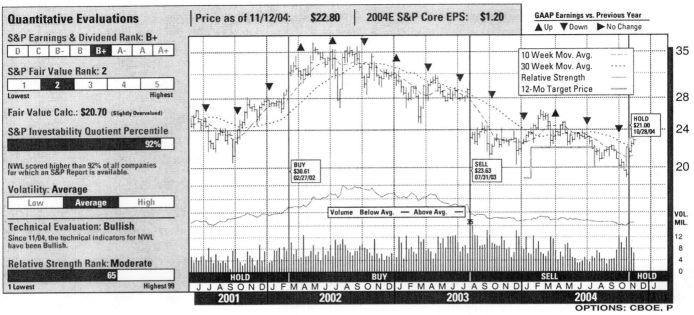

Quantitative Evaluations

S&P Earnings & Dividend Rank: B+

D | C | B- | B | **B+** | A- | A | A+

S&P Fair Value Rank: 2

1 | **2** | 3 | 4 | 5
Lowest | | | | Highest

Fair Value Calc.: $20.70 (Slightly Overvalued)

S&P Investability Quotient Percentile

92%

NWL scored higher than 92% of all companies for which an S&P Report is available.

Volatility: Average

Low | **Average** | High

Technical Evaluation: Bullish
Since 11/04, the technical indicators for NWL have been Bullish.

Relative Strength Rank: Moderate

65

1 Lowest | Highest 99

Price as of 11/12/04: **$22.80** | 2004E S&P Core EPS: **$1.20**

GAAP Earnings vs. Previous Year
▲ Up ▼ Down ► No Change

- 10 Week Mov. Avg.
- 30 Week Mov. Avg.
- Relative Strength
- 12-Mo Target Price

BUY $30.61 02/27/02

SELL $23.63 07/31/03

HOLD $21.00 10/28/04

Volume Below Avg. — Above Avg.

HOLD | BUY | SELL | HOLD
J J A S O N D|J F M A M J J A S O N D|J F M A M J J A S O N D|J F M A M J J A S O N D|J
2001 | **2002** | **2003** | **2004**

VOL. MIL.
35 / 28 / 24 / 20
12 / 8 / 4 / 0

OPTIONS: CBOE, P

Analyst commentary prepared by Howard Choe/PMW/BK

Highlights November 01, 2004

- We see net sales decreasing about 3% in 2004, reflecting the divestiture of some less profitable businesses and negative pricing, offset by favorable foreign exchange translations. We expect a decline in the cleaning and organization segment, largely due to NWL's planned exit of low margin product lines, as well as pricing pressures. We expect a slight increase in home fashions and in tools and hardware sales, due to positive trends in tool sales and favorable currency translations. Office products should also rise modestly, on improved sales in the commercial sector. For 2005, we expect sales to rise 2%.

- We expect operating margins to narrow slightly in 2004 from the level of 2003, as we do not expect the elimination of lower margin businesses and streamlining initiatives to fully offset the impact of higher marketing expenses tied to driving sales growth. We expect margin expansion of about 100 basis points in 2005, driven by greater leverage and cost controls.

- We estimate that 2004 operating EPS will decline 8%, to $1.37, from $1.49 in 2003 (excluding charges). We see $1.50 for 2005. We estimate S&P Core EPS of $1.20 for 2004 and $1.33 for 2005, reflecting estimated stock option and pension expenses.

Investment Rationale/Risk November 01, 2004

- We recently upgraded the shares to hold, from avoid, based on our view of improving sales and profit trends. The rate of decline has slowed for both measures, and we believe operating and net income will turn up in the fourth quarter, for the first time in more than a year. We believe sales will benefit from new product introductions, and the trimming of low margin products and effective cost controls should help improve profitability. In light of intense competition in many segments, we believe that the company needs to develop and market products that offer differentiation and benefits for consumers.

- Risks to our recommendation and target price include a slowdown in cost savings associated with the company's reorganization, weaker than expected demand for new products, and currency fluctuations.

- With the shares trading recently at a slight premium to peers, at a forward P/E multiple of 14X, we view them as fairly valued. Our 12-month target price of $23 is derived by applying a forward P/E multiple of 15X, a modest premium to peers, to our 2005 EPS estimate. In light of an improved sales and profit outlook, we expect the shares to perform in line with the S&P 500.

Key Stock Statistics

S&P Core EPS 2005E	**1.33**	52-week Range	**$26.41-19.05**
S&P Oper. EPS 2004E	**1.37**	12 Month P/E	**NM**
P/E on S&P Oper. EPS 2004E	**16.6**	Beta	**0.46**
S&P Oper. EPS 2005E	**1.50**	Shareholders	**22,632**
Yield (%)	**3.7%**	Market Cap (B)	**$ 6.3**
Dividend Rate/Share	**0.84**	Shares Outstanding (M)	**274.9**

Value of $10,000 invested five years ago: **$ 7,522**

Dividend Data Dividends have been paid since 1946

Amount ($)	Date Decl.	Ex-Div. Date	Stock of Record	Payment Date
0.210	Feb. 12	Feb. 19	Feb. 23	Mar. 12 '04
0.210	May. 13	May. 26	May. 28	Jun. 16 '04
0.210	Aug. 05	Aug. 12	Aug. 16	Sep. 03 '04
0.210	Nov. 04	Nov. 12	Nov. 16	Dec. 03 '04

Revenues/Earnings Data Fiscal year ending December 31

Revenues (Million $)

	2004	2003	2002	2001	2000	1999
1Q	1,541	1,736	1,597	1,611	1,551	1,516
2Q	1,736	1,976	1,895	1,725	1,712	1,597
3Q	1,672	1,945	1,948	1,768	1,687	1,610
4Q	—	2,093	2,014	1,806	1,762	1,690
Yr.	—	7,750	7,454	6,609	6,935	6,413

Earnings Per Share ($)

	2004	2003	2002	2001	2000	1999
1Q	0.12	0.06	0.19	0.14	0.28	-0.29
2Q	0.21	0.27	0.33	0.27	0.48	0.11
3Q	-0.86	0.27	0.29	0.31	0.46	0.26
4Q	E0.44	-0.77	0.36	0.27	0.35	0.25
Yr.	E1.37	-0.17	1.16	0.99	1.57	0.34

Next earnings report expected: late-January Source: S&P, Company Reports
EPS Estimates based on S&P Operating Earnings; historical GAAP earnings are as reported.

Newell Rubbermaid Inc.

Recommendation: **HOLD** ★ ★ ★ ☆ ☆   12-Month Target Price: **$23.00** (as of October 29, 2004)

Business Summary November 01, 2004

Newell Rubbermaid is a global manufacturer and marketer of name-brand consumer products distributed through volume purchasers, including discount stores and warehouse clubs, home centers, hardware stores, office superstores and contract stationers. The company's basic strategy is to merchandise a multi-product offering of everyday consumer products, backed by excellent customer service and new product development, to achieve maximum results for its shareholders.

Products are sold through five business segments: cleaning and organization (26% of 2003 sales, versus 26% in 2002), office products (22%, 23%), home fashions (16%, 19%), tools and hardware (16%, 19%) and other (21%, 22%). About 29% of 2003 sales were made outside the U.S. (27% in 2002).

NWL's cleaning and organization business is made up of Rubbermaid Home Products, Rubbermaid Food and Beverage, Rubbermaid Commercial Products, and Rubbermaid Europe and Canada. These divisions collectively design, manufacture and distribute indoor and outdoor organization, home storage, food storage and cleaning products.

The company's office products business consists of Sanford North America, Sanford Europe, Sanford Latin America, and Sanford Asia Pacific. These divisions make and sell pencils, pens, inks and other art supplies. Sanford North America also makes and sell markers, overhead projector pens, and highlighters.

NWL's home fashion business is conducted by Levolor/Kirsch, Home Decor Europe, and Swish UK. This group primarily designs, manufactures and distributes products including drapery hardware, blinds, shades, shelving and storage products.

The tools and hardware business is conducted by Irwin, Lenox, BernzOmatic, Shur-line and Amerock. This group makes, sources and sells hand tools, power tool accessories, propane torches, manual paint applicator products, cabinet hardware, and window and door hardware.

NWL's other business is comprised of Calphalon cookware and bakeware, Cookware Europe, Little Tikes, Graco, and Goody. Calphalon primarily makes and sells cookware and bakeware. Cookware Europe primarily make and sell glass products. The Little Tikes and Graco businesses makes and sells toys, high chairs, car seats, strollers and outdoor activity play equipment. Goody makes and sells hair care accessories.

In February 2004, the company sold its Panex cookware division, Frames Europe businesses in France, Spain and the U.K., and its Bulldog European tool business. In March 2004, NWL sold its Burnes Picture Frame, Anchor Glassware, and Mirro Cookware businesses to a privately held firm, for $310 million.

Company Financials Fiscal Year ending December 31

Per Share Data ($)

(Year Ended December 31)	2003	2002	2001	2000	1999	1998	1997	1996	1995	1994
Tangible Bk. Val.	NM	NM	0.44	0.97	2.38	1.57	2.20	3.58	2.60	2.79
Cash Flow	0.84	2.21	2.22	2.57	1.30	3.14	2.82	2.35	2.05	1.70
Earnings	-0.17	1.16	0.99	1.57	0.34	2.38	1.82	1.62	1.41	1.24
S&P Core Earnings	0.39	0.86	0.71	NA	NA	NA	NA	NA	NA	NA
Dividends	0.84	0.84	0.84	0.84	0.80	0.72	0.64	0.56	0.46	0.39
Payout Ratio	NM	72%	85%	54%	235%	30%	35%	35%	33%	31%
Prices - High	32.00	36.70	29.50	31.87	52.00	55.18	43.81	33.75	27.25	23.87
- Low	20.27	26.11	20.50	18.25	25.25	35.68	30.12	25.00	20.25	18.81
P/E Ratio - High	NM	32	30	20	NM	23	24	21	19	19
- Low	NM	23	21	12	NM	15	17	15	14	15

Income Statement Analysis (Million $)

	2003	2002	2001	2000	1999	1998	1997	1996	1995	1994
Revs.	7,750	7,454	6,909	6,935	6,413	3,720	3,234	2,873	2,498	2,075
Oper. Inc.	993	1,033	966	1,173	862	736	702	602	521	415
Depr.	278	281	329	293	272	148	162	116	102	72.5
Int. Exp.	140	111	137	130	100	60.4	73.6	57.0	49.8	30.0
Pretax Inc.	20.1	495	443	685	231	685	482	425	371	329
Eff. Tax Rate	NM	31.7%	34.2%	38.5%	58.7%	42.1%	39.5%	39.6%	40.0%	40.6%
Net Inc.	-46.6	312	265	422	95.4	396	290	256	222	196
S&P Core Earnings	108	232	190	NA	NA	NA	NA	NA	NA	NA

Balance Sheet & Other Fin. Data (Million $)

	2003	2002	2001	2000	1999	1998	1997	1996	1995	1994
Cash	144	55.1	6.80	31.7	102	57.5	36.1	4.36	58.8	14.9
Curr. Assets	3,000	3,080	2,851	2,897	2,739	1,591	1,382	1,108	1,133	918
Total Assets	7,481	7,389	7,266	7,262	6,724	4,328	3,944	3,005	2,931	2,488
Curr. Liab.	2,022	2,614	2,534	1,551	1,630	821	664	637	680	784
LT Debt	2,869	2,357	1,865	2,815	1,956	1,366	784	672	762	409
Common Equity	2,016	2,064	2,433	2,449	2,697	1,912	1,714	1,492	1,300	1,125
Total Cap.	4,887	4,426	4,373	5,358	4,738	3,300	3,096	2,211	2,093	1,552
Cap. Exp.	300	252	250	317	200	148	98.4	94.2	82.6	66.0
Cash Flow	232	592	593	714	367	544	452	373	324	268
Curr. Ratio	1.5	1.2	1.1	1.9	1.7	1.9	2.1	1.7	1.7	1.2
% LT Debt of Cap.	58.7	53.2	42.7	52.5	41.3	41.3	25.4	30.4	36.4	26.4
% Net Inc.of Revs.	NM	4.2	3.8	6.1	1.5	10.6	9.0	8.9	8.9	9.4
% Ret. on Assets	NM	4.3	3.6	6.0	1.5	9.5	8.4	8.6	8.2	8.8
% Ret. on Equity	NM	13.9	10.8	16.4	3.4	21.7	18.1	18.4	18.4	18.6

Data as orig reptd.; bef. results of disc opers/spec. items. Per share data adj. for stk. divs.; EPS diluted. E-Estimated. NA-Not Available. NM-Not Meaningful. NR-Not Ranked. UR-Under Review.

Office: 10B Glenlake Parkway NE, Atlanta, GA 30328-3473.
Telephone: 770-670-2232.
Email: investor.relations@newellco.com
Website: http://www.newellrubbermaid.com
Chrmn: W.D. Marohn.
Pres & CEO: J. Galli, Jr.
COO: J.J. Roberts.

COO: R.S. Parker.
VP & CFO: J.P. Robinson.
VP & Investor Contact: J.J. Herron 770-407-3994.
Dirs: T. E. Clarke, S. S. Cowen, A. F. Doody, J. Galli, Jr., W. D. Marohn, E. C. Millett, C. A. Montgomery, A. P. Newell, W. P. Sovey, G. R. Sullivan, R. G. Viault.

Founded: in 1903.
Domicile: Delaware.
Employees: 40,000.
S&P Analyst: Howard Choe/PMW/BK

Newmont Mining

Recommendation: **HOLD** ★★★☆☆
SELL SELL HOLD BUY BUY

12-Month Target Price: **$46.00**
(as of June 28, 2004)

NEM has an approximate 0.20% weighting in the **S&P 500**

Sector: Materials
Sub-Industry: Gold
Peer Group: Gold - Major Producers

Summary: Following its acquisition of Normandy Mining and Franco-Nevada, this company is the world's largest gold producer.

Quantitative Evaluations

S&P Earnings & Dividend Rank: B-

| D | C | B- | B | B+ | A- | A | A+ |

S&P Fair Value Rank: 1-

| 1 | 2 | 3 | 4 | 5 |
| Lowest | | | | Highest |

Fair Value Calc.: $38.70 (Overvalued)

S&P Investability Quotient Percentile

85%

NEM scored higher than 85% of all companies for which an S&P Report is available.

Volatility: Average

| Low | Average | High |

Technical Evaluation: Bullish
Since 8/04, the technical indicators for NEM have been Bullish.

Relative Strength Rank: Strong

76

| 1 Lowest | Highest 99 |

| Price as of 11/12/04: | **$49.65** | 2004E S&P Core EPS: | **$1.05** |

GAAP Earnings vs. Previous Year
▲ Up ▼ Down ► No Change

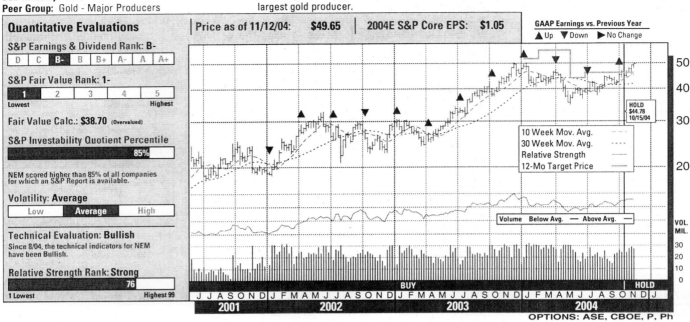

10 Week Mov. Avg.
30 Week Mov. Avg.
Relative Strength
12-Mo Target Price

HOLD
$44.78
10/15/04

Volume Below Avg. — Above Avg.

VOL. MIL.

OPTIONS: ASE, CBOE, P, Ph

Analyst commentary prepared by Leo J. Larkin/CB/BK

Highlights October 18, 2004

- Based on our forecast of higher gold and copper prices in 2004, we project a 30% to 35% sales gain, after a 21% increase in 2003. We see this growth as solely due to higher metals prices. We project 2004 average gold prices of at least $400 an oz., versus $363 in 2003. NEM projects 2004 equity gold production of 7.0 million to 7.2 million oz., versus 2003's 7.4 million oz. NEM projects total cash costs of $220 to $230 an oz., versus 2003's $203. The increase reflects the expected impact of a rise in the Australian dollar, mining of lower ore grades, and increased costs for royalties and taxes. We therefore see operating profit rising less rapidly than sales. With continued high levels of royalty income and another decline in interest expense expected, we see 2004 EPS rising, excluding unusual gains in 2003. Assuming flat gold production and a higher average gold price, we look for an increase in EPS in 2005.

- For the longer term, we see sales and EPS aided by a projected rise in the price of gold and continued strong profit contributions from base metals.

- According to data compiled by the World Bureau of Metal Statistics, global gold production this year through July declined to 1,281 metric tons, versus 1,375 metric tons of production in the same period in 2003.

Investment Rationale/Risk October 18, 2004

- On October 15, 2004, we downgraded NEM to hold, from accumulate, based on valuation. With gold prices seen in a trading range, and with the stock at 25X our 2005 EPS estimate, we believe NEM will just track the market. Accordingly, we would not add to positions. We recommend holding NEM as a way to benefit from a bull market in gold. We believe that gold is in a bull market for several reasons: we expect the gap between consumption and production to widen as production worldwide likely declines, despite higher prices; we see erratic financial market returns making gold and gold shares more attractive as alternative investments; and we believe that inflation will trend higher in 2005. With its production having greater exposure to the gold price than other major North American producers, we think NEM is well positioned to benefit from a rising gold price.

- The main risk to our recommendation and target price is that the bull market in gold ends and a drop in gold prices leads to lower EPS. Besides lower EPS, a lower gold price would reduce the level of reserves, which would likely result in a lower valuation for the stock. Finally, lower EPS would make it difficult for NEM to develop new mines without resorting to dilutive financing.

- Recently selling at 25X our 2005 EPS estimate, versus a P/E of 18X for the S&P 500, NEM appears expensive. However, we believe that a rising gold price should support the P/E on 2005's estimate. On that basis, we have a 12 month target price of $46.

Key Stock Statistics

S&P Core EPS 2005E	**1.75**	52-week Range	**$50.28-34.70**
S&P Oper. EPS 2004E	**1.10**	12 Month P/E	**48.7**
P/E on S&P Oper. EPS 2004E	**45.1**	Beta	**-0.09**
S&P Oper. EPS 2005E	**1.80**	Shareholders	**19,500**
Yield (%)	**0.8%**	Market Cap (B)	**$ 20.3**
Dividend Rate/Share	**0.40**	Shares Outstanding (M)	**443.9**

Value of $10,000 invested five years ago: **$ 24,523**

Dividend Data Dividends have been paid since 1934

Amount ($)	Date Decl.	Ex-Div. Date	Stock of Record	Payment Date
0.050	Feb. 04	Mar. 01	Mar. 03	Mar. 24 '04
0.075	Apr. 28	May. 28	Jun. 02	Jun. 23 '04
0.075	Jul. 28	Sep. 01	Sep. 03	Sep. 22 '04
0.100	Oct. 27	Nov. 29	Dec. 01	Dec. 21 '04

Revenues/Earnings Data Fiscal year ending December 31

Revenues (Million $)

	2004	2003	2002	2001	2000	1999
1Q	1,135	748.5	491.6	424.1	—	327.1
2Q	1,009	747.2	632.4	362.4	—	315.8
3Q	1,163	897.0	712.1	424.4	—	327.9
4Q	—	821.4	786.1	445.2	476.8	428.1
Yr.	—	3,214	2,622	1,656	1,809	1,399

Earnings Per Share ($)

	2004	2003	2002	2001	2000	1999
1Q	0.30	0.38	-0.06	-0.20	—	0.06
2Q	0.08	0.22	0.17	-0.17	—	0.04
3Q	0.29	0.28	0.05	0.11	—	-0.23
4Q	E0.40	0.36	0.19	0.10	0.12	0.28
Yr.	E1.10	1.23	0.39	-0.16	-0.06	0.15

Next earnings report expected: early-February Source: S&P, Company Reports
EPS Estimates based on S&P Operating Earnings; historical GAAP earnings are as reported.

Newmont Mining Corporation

Recommendation: **HOLD** ★ ★ ★ ☆ ☆   12-Month Target Price: **$46.00** (as of June 28, 2004)

Business Summary October 18, 2004

Following the completion of a three-way merger with Normandy Mining and Franco-Nevada in March 2002, Newmont Mining Corp. became the world's largest gold company. NEM issued 197 million common shares to accomplish the merger, doubling the number of shares outstanding.

The company expects annual gold production of 7.0 million oz. to 7.5 million oz. through 2006, with an increase thereafter. NEM projects future cash costs of $210 to $230 an oz., reflecting increased Australian and Canadian dollar rate assumptions, and anticipated higher energy-related costs. Excluding the impact of currency movements and higher energy-related costs, the company anticipates that total cash costs will trend down over time, as production from older, more mature mines is replaced by production from newer, low-cost operations.

As a general policy, NEM engages in only limited hedging of its production, because it anticipates higher gold prices over the long term, and seeks to provide shareholders with greater leverage to the price of gold. With the acquisition of Normandy, the company acquired gold hedges totaling about 4.9 million oz. At December 30, 2003, NEM had completely eliminated the hedge books of the Australian properties.

Production at North American operations totaled 2,902,600 oz. in 2003, versus 3,224,000 oz. in 2002.

Production in South America totaled 1,626,400 oz. in 2003, versus 1,426,300 oz. in 2002.

Production in Australia totaled 1,889,200 oz. in 2003, versus 1,684,600 oz. in 2002.

Gold production at Batu Hujua in Indonesia totaled 328,000 oz. in 2003, versus 278,000 equity oz. in 2002. Equity copper production totaled 343.4 million lbs., versus 362.3 million lbs. in 2002.

Equity gold production totaled 7.38 million oz. in 2003, versus 7.63 million oz. in 2002. NEM's average realized price per oz. was $366 in 2003, versus $313 in 2002. Cash costs per oz. were $203 in 2003, versus $189 in 2002. Total production cost per oz. was $266 in 2003, versus $250 in 2002.

In 2003, 39% (42% in 2002) of NEM's equity production came from North America, 22% (19%) from South America, 26% (22%) from Australia and 13% (13%) from other overseas locations.

Gold reserves totaled 91.3 million oz. at the end of 2003, versus 86.9 million oz. at the end of 2002, using a gold price of $325 per oz. for 2003 and $300 per oz. for 2002. Copper reserves totaled 7.6 billion lbs. at 2002 year end, versus 6.0 billion lbs. at the end of 2001.

EPS in the 2003 fourth quarter increased to $0.33 (excluding unusual gains of $0.03), on a 2.8% sales gain, from $0.19 in the 2002 period. The sharp rise was due mostly to an increase in the average price of gold to $394 an oz., from $325 an oz. in the 2002 period. EPS also benefited from higher copper prices and lower interest expense.

Company Financials Fiscal Year ending December 31

Per Share Data ($)

(Year Ended December 31)	2003	2002	2001	2000	1999	1998	1997	1996	1995	1994
Tangible Bk. Val.	8.39	2.77	7.49	8.11	8.66	8.62	10.17	10.30	7.89	4.48
Cash Flow	2.60	1.75	1.38	1.40	1.58	-0.45	2.14	2.11	2.40	1.76
Earnings	1.23	0.39	-0.16	-0.06	0.15	-2.27	0.44	0.86	1.17	0.70
S&P Core Earnings	1.05	0.25	-0.26	NA	NA	NA	NA	NA	NA	NA
Dividends	0.17	0.12	0.12	0.12	0.12	0.12	0.39	0.48	0.48	0.48
Payout Ratio	14%	31%	NM	NM	80%	NM	89%	56%	41%	69%
Prices - High	50.28	32.75	25.23	28.37	30.06	34.87	47.50	60.75	46.25	48.07
- Low	24.08	18.52	14.00	12.75	16.37	13.25	26.56	43.87	33.12	33.87
P/E Ratio - High	41	84	NM	NM	NM	NM	NM	71	40	69
- Low	20	47	NM	NM	NM	NM	NM	51	28	48

Income Statement Analysis (Million $)

	2003	2002	2001	2000	1999	1998	1997	1996	1995	1994
Revs.	3,214	2,658	1,656	1,809	1,399	1,454	1,573	768	639	597
Oper. Inc.	1,184	852	435	568	457	500	582	172	162	160
Depr.	564	506	300	359	240	289	266	125	107	91.0
Int. Exp.	88.6	130	86.4	94.6	62.6	78.8	77.1	49.4	36.0	10.0
Pretax Inc.	544	268	-10.2	10.1	112	-471	132	74.6	142	54.0
Eff. Tax Rate	38.0%	7.43%	NM	NM	12.9%	NM	48.2%	NM	8.35%	NM
Net Inc.	510	150	-23.3	-82.3	24.8	-360	68.4	85.1	113	76.0
S&P Core Earnings	435	96.7	-52.8	NA	NA	NA	NA	NA	NA	NA

Balance Sheet & Other Fin. Data (Million $)

	2003	2002	2001	2000	1999	1998	1997	1996	1995	1994
Cash	1,459	402	149	158	55.3	79.1	146	198	71.0	174
Curr. Assets	2,360	1,113	709	612	534	513	641	456	290	370
Total Assets	11,050	10,155	4,062	3,917	3,383	3,187	3,614	2,081	1,774	1,657
Curr. Liab.	834	693	486	399	274	212	395	224	194	153
LT Debt	887	1,701	1,190	1,129	1,014	1,201	1,179	585	604	594
Common Equity	7,747	5,722	1,469	1,389	1,452	1,440	1,591	1,025	743	386
Total Cap.	9,614	8,434	2,955	2,925	2,627	2,733	2,938	1,716	1,429	1,347
Cap. Exp.	501	300	402	421	221	216	415	231	309	402
Cash Flow	1,075	652	269	270	264	-71.4	334	210	208	151
Curr. Ratio	2.8	1.6	1.5	1.5	1.9	2.4	1.6	2.0	1.5	2.4
% LT Debt of Cap.	9.2	20.2	40.3	38.6	38.6	43.9	40.1	34.1	42.3	44.1
% Net Inc.of Revs.	15.9	5.7	NM	NM	1.8	NM	4.3	11.1	17.7	12.7
% Ret. on Assets	4.8	2.1	NM	NM	0.7	NM	2.4	4.4	6.6	5.3
% Ret. on Equity	7.6	4.0	NM	NM	1.7	NM	5.2	9.6	18.0	20.9

Data as orig reptd.; bef. results of disc opers/spec. items. Per share data adj. for stk. divs.; EPS diluted. E-Estimated. NA-Not Available. NM-Not Meaningful. NR-Not Ranked. UR-Under Review.

Office: 1700 Lincoln Street, Denver, CO 80203-4500.
Telephone: 303-863-7414.
Website: http://www.newmont.com
Chrmn & CEO: W.W. Murdy.
Pres: P. Lassonde.
SVP & CFO: B.D. Hansen.

VP & Treas: T.P. Mahoney.
VP, Secy & General Counsel: B.D. Banks.
Investor Contact: R. Ball .
Dirs: G. A. Barton, V. A. Calarco, M. S. Hamson, L. I. Higdon, Jr., P. Lassonde, R. J. Miller, W. W. Murdy, R. A. Plumbridge, J. B. Prescott, M. K. Reilly, D. C. Roth, S. Schulich, J. V. Taranik.

Auditor: PricewaterhouseCoopers.
Founded: in 1916.
Domicile: Delaware.
Employees: 13,400.
S&P Analyst: Leo J. Larkin/CB/BK

The **McGraw·Hill** Companies

New York Times

Recommendation: **HOLD** ★ ★ ★ ☆ ☆
SELL · SELL · HOLD · BUY · BUY

12-Month Target Price: **$46.00**
(as of September 20, 2004)

NYT has an approximate 0.06% weighting in the **S&P 500**

Sector: Consumer Discretionary
Sub-Industry: Publishing
Peer Group: Newspaper Cos. - Large

Summary: This diversified communications company publishes newspapers, operates radio and television stations, and has equity holdings in newsprint and paper mills.

Quantitative Evaluations

S&P Earnings & Dividend Rank: A-

| D | C | B- | B | B+ | A- | A | A+ |

S&P Fair Value Rank: 1

| **1** | 2 | 3 | 4 | 5 |
| Lowest | | | | Highest |

Fair Value Calc.: $27.30 (Overvalued)

S&P Investability Quotient Percentile

89%

NYT scored higher than 89% of all companies for which an S&P Report is available.

Volatility: Low

| **Low** | Average | High |

Technical Evaluation: Bullish

Since 11/04, the technical indicators for NYT have been Bullish.

Relative Strength Rank: Moderate

41

| 1 Lowest | | Highest 99 |

Price as of 11/12/04: **$41.52** | **2004E S&P Core EPS:** **$1.79**

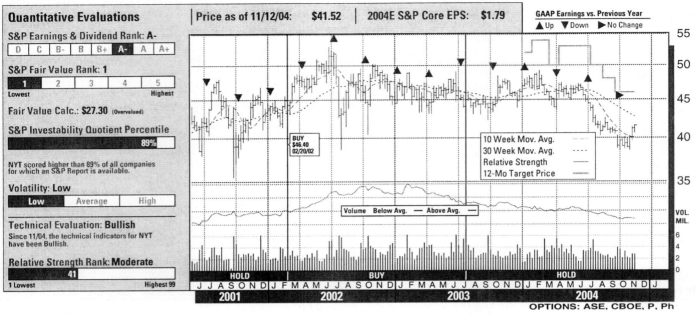

GAAP Earnings vs. Previous Year
▲ Up ▼ Down ► No Change

BUY
$46.40
02/20/02

10 Week Mov. Avg.
30 Week Mov. Avg.
Relative Strength
12-Mo Target Price

Volume ☐ Below Avg. — Above Avg. ☐

HOLD | BUY | HOLD
J J A S O N D | J F M A M J J A S O N D | J F M A M J J A S O N D | J F M A M J J A S O N D | J
2001 | 2002 | 2003 | 2004

OPTIONS: ASE, CBOE, P, Ph

Analyst commentary prepared by William H. Donald/CB/JWP

Highlights July 16, 2004

- We see revenues growing 4.1% in 2004, to about $3.36 billion, from $3.23 billion in 2003. We look for newspaper advertising revenues to rise 3.2%, largely in the second half; we see circulation revenues up slightly, while other print revenues increase 14%. We anticipate a 14% advance in broadcasting, boosted by political advertising, and a 19% rise in digital revenues.

- We project that operating margins will widen slightly, to 16.8%, from 16.7% in 2003, despite pressures from rising newsprint and employee benefit costs. Operating earnings should rise 5%.

- After non-operating items, including an expected 4% rise in interest expense, and taxes estimated at 39.3%, versus 39.6%, we expect 2004 net income to increase 2.2%, to $309.2 million, from 2003's $302.7 million. With fewer shares outstanding, we expect EPS to increase about 3%, to $2.06, from 2003's $1.98. We project a 13% advance in 2005 EPS, to $2.31.

Investment Rationale/Risk July 16, 2004

- We view the shares as fairly valued and would hold existing positions. Although the stock usually trades at a modest discount to peers, NYT's recent P/E multiple of 21X our 2004 EPS estimate was in line with the peer average.

- Risks to our recommendation and target price include the health of the New York City economy, which can be significantly affected by the state of the financial markets and the financial services industries, as well as the level of tourism.

- Although our 12-month target price of $50 provides moderate upside potential, we would not add to positions considering the tentativeness of the current advertising recovery. Our target price assumes that NYT will be trading at a 22X multiple of our $2.31 EPS estimate for 2005. Based on our EPS estimates for peers, our target price for NYT assumes its multiple will be more closely aligned with the historical peer relationship.

Key Stock Statistics

S&P Oper. EPS 2004E	1.97	52-week Range	$49.23-38.47
P/E on S&P Oper. EPS 2004E	21.1	12 Month P/E	21.4
S&P Oper. EPS 2005E	2.30	Beta	0.69
Yield (%)	1.5%	Shareholders	10,700
Dividend Rate/Share	0.62	Market Cap (B)	$ 6.0
Shares Outstanding (M)	145.1		

Value of $10,000 invested five years ago: **$ 11,080**

Dividend Data Dividends have been paid since 1958

Amount ($)	Date Decl.	Ex-Div. Date	Stock of Record	Payment Date
0.145	Nov. 20	Nov. 26	Dec. 01	Dec. 19 '03
0.145	Feb. 19	Feb. 26	Mar. 01	Mar. 19 '04
0.155	Apr. 13	May. 27	Jun. 01	Jun. 18 '04
0.155	Jun. 17	Aug. 30	Sep. 01	Sep. 17 '04

Revenues/Earnings Data Fiscal year ending December 31

Revenues (Million $)

	2004	2003	2002	2001	2000	1999
1Q	801.9	783.7	737.1	778.1	843.2	739.1
2Q	823.9	801.9	772.2	760.3	885.6	779.4
3Q	773.8	759.3	729.5	696.9	787.0	729.7
4Q	—	882.3	840.2	780.6	951.5	882.5
Yr.	—	3,227	3,079	3,016	3,489	3,131

Earnings Per Share ($)

	2004	2003	2002	2001	2000	1999
1Q	0.38	0.45	0.35	0.36	0.47	0.34
2Q	0.50	0.47	0.51	0.15	0.59	0.47
3Q	0.33	0.33	0.38	0.28	0.44	0.34
4Q	E0.76	0.73	0.69	0.49	0.83	0.59
Yr.	E1.97	1.98	1.94	1.26	2.32	1.73

Next earnings report expected: late-January Source: S&P, Company Reports
EPS Estimates based on S&P Operating Earnings; historical GAAP earnings are as reported.

The New York Times Company

Recommendation: HOLD ★ ★ ★ ☆ ☆   12-Month Target Price: **$46.00** (as of September 20, 2004)

Business Summary July 16, 2004

The New York Times Co. has diversified interests in newspapers, broadcasting, information services, and forest products.

The Newspaper Group includes The New York Times; The New England Newspaper Group, which includes The Boston Globe and the Worcester Telegram & Gazette; the International Herald Tribune; 15 regional newspapers; newspaper wholesalers; and information services. The New York Times is circulated in all 50 states, U.S. territories, and worldwide. Its average circulation in the 12 months through September 2003 was 1,132,000 copies daily; Sunday circulation was 1,682,100. The Boston Globe, New England's largest newspaper, had circulation of 446,400 daily and 695,500 Sunday. Circulation for the Worcester Telegram & Gazette was 102,600 daily and 120,700 Sunday. Regional newspaper circulation was 620,816 daily and 669,700 Sunday.

The Broadcasting Group, based in Memphis, includes eight network-affiliated TV stations (WNEP-TV, serving the Wilkes-Barre/Scranton area of Pennsylvania; WQAD-TV, serving the Quad-Cities area of Illinois and Iowa; KFSM-TV in Fort Smith, AR; WHNT-TV in Huntsville, AL; KFOR-TV in Oklahoma City, OK; WHO-TV in Des Moines, IA; WREG-TV in Memphis, TN; and WTKR-TV, serving the Norfolk, VA, area); and two radio stations (WQXR-FM and WQEW-AM in NYC). The company also operates news, photo and graphics services; manages news and feature syndicates; has several electronic publishing and new media activities;

owns a video production company; and has minority interests in a Canadian newsprint mill and in a supercalendered paper mill in Maine.

The company's Internet sites are consolidated under a separate division, New York Times Digital. The sites, which total more than 40, include NYTimes.com, Boston.com, NYToday.com, WineToday.com, and Abuzz.

The company has a 17% ownership interest in New England Sport Ventures, LLC (NESV), which owns the Boston Red Sox baseball club, including Fenway Park and about 80% of New England Sports Network, a regional cable television sports network. The company also owns 50% of DTC, a digital cable channel co-owned with Discovery Communications, Inc.

On April 2, 2001, the company sold four golf magazines and related interests for $435 million, thereby ending its magazine interests. The sale netted $241.3 million, or $1.49 a share. In April 1999, NYT and Scholastic Inc. jointly launched a bi-weekly teen magazine called The New York Times Upfront, sold in classroom sets or through home delivery.

In 2003, newspaper publishing accounted for 93% of revenues and 91% of operating profits; television broadcasting for 4% and 6%, respectively; and New York Times Digital (NYTD) provided 3% of revenues and 3% of profits. Losses from joint ventures amounted to $8.2 million.

Company Financials Fiscal Year ending December 31

Per Share Data ($)

(Year Ended December 31)	2003	2002	2001	2000	1999	1998	1997	1996	1995	1994
Tangible Bk. Val.	NM	NM	NM	NM	0.83	1.12	1.77	0.90	1.05	0.84
Cash Flow	2.95	2.93	2.48	3.65	2.83	2.46	2.21	1.20	1.37	1.77
Earnings	1.98	1.94	1.26	2.32	1.73	1.49	1.33	0.43	0.70	1.03
S&P Core Earnings	1.77	1.35	0.72	NA	NA	NA	NA	NA	NA	NA
Dividends	0.57	0.53	0.49	0.45	0.41	0.37	0.32	0.29	0.28	0.28
Payout Ratio	29%	27%	39%	19%	24%	25%	24%	66%	40%	27%
Prices - High	49.06	53.00	47.98	49.87	49.93	40.68	33.25	19.93	15.43	14.75
- Low	43.29	38.60	35.48	32.62	26.50	20.50	18.18	12.87	10.06	10.62
P/E Ratio - High	25	27	38	21	29	27	25	46	22	14
- Low	22	20	28	14	15	14	14	30	14	10

Income Statement Analysis (Million $)

	2003	2002	2001	2000	1999	1998	1997	1996	1995	1994
Revs.	3,227	3,079	3,016	3,489	3,131	2,937	2,866	2,615	2,409	2,358
Oper. Inc.	687	698	568	864	769	703	629	448	368	365
Depr.	148	153	194	228	197	188	174	148	139	154
Int. Exp.	44.8	48.7	51.4	64.1	52.5	46.9	45.0	50.3	49.0	34.9
Pretax Inc.	500	491	340	673	538	506	437	198	229	383
Eff. Tax Rate	39.6%	39.0%	40.5%	40.9%	42.4%	43.3%	40.0%	57.3%	40.6%	45.3%
Net Inc.	303	300	202	398	310	287	262	84.5	136	213
S&P Core Earnings	268	208	116	NA	NA	NA	NA	NA	NA	NA

Balance Sheet & Other Fin. Data (Million $)

	2003	2002	2001	2000	1999	1998	1997	1996	1995	1994
Cash	39.4	37.0	52.0	69.0	63.9	36.0	107	39.1	91.4	41.4
Curr. Assets	603	563	560	611	615	522	616	479	463	412
Total Assets	3,805	3,634	3,439	3,607	3,496	3,465	3,639	3,540	3,377	3,138
Curr. Liab.	760	736	861	877	674	628	697	654	517	451
LT Debt	726	729	599	637	598	598	545	637	638	523
Common Equity	1,392	1,362	1,150	1,281	1,449	1,531	1,728	1,623	1,612	1,544
Total Cap.	2,350	2,164	1,813	2,024	2,188	2,295	2,460	2,450	2,419	2,245
Cap. Exp.	121	161	90.4	85.3	73.4	82.6	153	211	201	186
Cash Flow	450	453	396	626	508	475	436	232	275	368
Curr. Ratio	0.8	0.8	0.7	0.7	0.9	0.8	0.9	0.7	0.9	0.9
% LT Debt of Cap.	30.9	33.7	33.0	31.5	27.3	26.1	22.2	26.0	26.4	23.3
% Net Inc.of Revs.	9.4	9.7	6.7	11.4	9.9	9.8	9.2	3.2	5.6	9.0
% Ret. on Assets	8.1	8.5	5.7	11.2	8.9	8.1	7.3	2.4	4.2	6.7
% Ret. on Equity	22.7	23.9	16.6	29.1	20.8	17.6	15.6	5.2	8.6	13.6

Data as orig reptd.; bef. results of disc opers/spec. items. Per share data adj. for stk. divs.; EPS diluted. E-Estimated. NA-Not Available. NM-Not Meaningful. NR-Not Ranked. UR-Under Review.

Office: 229 W. 43rd St., New York, NY 10036.
Telephone: 212-556-1234.
Website: http://www.nytco.com
: D. Thurm.
Chrmn: A.O. Sulzberger, Jr.
Pres & CEO: R.T. Lewis.

Vice Chrmn & SVP: M. Golden.
SVP & CFO: L.P. Forman.
VP & Investor Contact: C.J. Mathis 212-556-1981.
Dirs: J. F. Akers, B. C. Barnes, R. E. Cesan, J. H. Dryfoos, M. Golden, W. E. Kennard, R. T. Lewis, D. E. Liddle, E. R. Marram, H. B. Schacht, D. M. Stewart, C. J. Sulzberger, A. P. Sulzberger Jr.

Founded: in 1896.
Domicile: New York.
Employees: 12,400.
S&P Analyst: William H. Donald/CB/JWP

NEXTEL Communications

Recommendation: **BUY** ★★★★★ 12-Month Target Price: **$30.00**
SELL | SELL | HOLD | BUY | BUY
(as of October 22, 2004)

NXTL has an approximate 0.28% weighting in the **S&P 500**

Sector: Telecommunication Services
Sub-Industry: Wireless Telecommunication Services
Peer Group: National (Domestic)

Summary: NXTL is the leading provider of specialized mobile radio communications services.

Quantitative Evaluations

S&P Earnings & Dividend Rank: B-

| D | C | **B-** | B | B+ | A- | A | A+ |

S&P Fair Value Rank: 3-

| 1 | 2 | **3** | 4 | 5 |
Lowest | | | | Highest

Fair Value Calc.: $26.30 (Slightly Overvalued)

S&P Investability Quotient Percentile

53%

NXTL scored higher than 53% of all companies
for which an S&P Report is available.

Volatility: Average

| Low | **Average** | High |

Technical Evaluation: Bullish
Since 10/04, the technical indicators for NXTL
have been Bullish.

Relative Strength Rank: Moderate

70

1 Lowest   Highest 99

Price as of 11/12/04: **$27.39**   **2004E S&P Core EPS:** **$2.93**

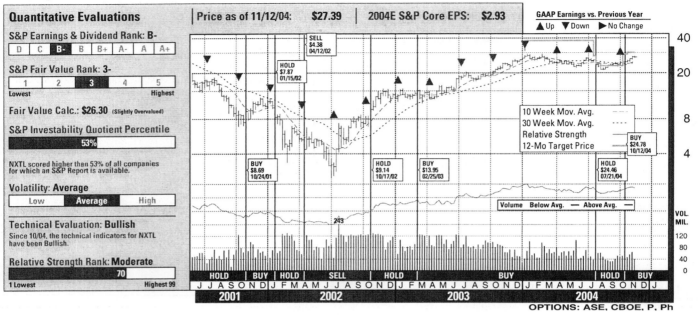

GAAP Earnings vs. Previous Year
▲ Up ▼ Down ▶ No Change

10 Week Mov. Avg.
30 Week Mov. Avg.
Relative Strength
12-Mo Target Price

Volume Below Avg. — Above Avg. —

OPTIONS: ASE, CBOE, P, Ph

Analyst commentary prepared by Kenneth M. Leon/MF/GG

Highlights October 26, 2004

- Following 21% service revenue growth in 2004, we expect service revenues to increase 18% in 2005, paced by 3.1 million net annual new U.S. customers, $65 monthly revenue per user and monthly customer churn of 1.5%, below the 2.5% industry average. We believe Direct Connect's continuing strong growth among high-value individual purchasers and the Nationwide Direct Connect program boost NXTL's operating performance above peers.

- We see EBITDA service margins of 43% to 45% in 2005, on economies of scale and a continued reduction in billing expenses from outsourcing. Our EBITDA service margin estimates take into account NXTL's expanding prepaid service through Boost Mobile and increased development costs of 3G field trials and marketing efforts. Boost Mobile had 800,000 subscribers at the end of the September quarter, representing 5.2% of NXTL's 15.3 million subscriber base, but nearly 26% of total net subscriber additions in the 2004 third quarter. Increased handset subsidies have slowed EBITDA margin improvement.

- Before special items, operating EPS in 2003 was $1.39. With the company guiding to a 38% tax rate beginning in the 2004 third quarter, we estimate 2004 operating EPS of $1.85, and see $1.80 for 2005. We estimate 2004 Standard & Poor's Core Earnings of $2.93 a share, which excludes the tax rate effect on a GAAP basis, and see $1.55 for 2005; we project stock option expense as a moderately negative factor for earnings quality in both years.

Key Stock Statistics

S&P Core EPS 2005E	1.55	52-week Range	$29.37-21.18
S&P Oper. EPS 2004E	1.85	12 Month P/E	10.0
P/E on S&P Oper. EPS 2004E	14.8	Beta	2.12
S&P Oper. EPS 2005E	1.80	Shareholders	4,100
Yield (%)	Nil	Market Cap (B)	$ 29.6
Dividend Rate/Share	Nil	Shares Outstanding (M)	1111.3

Value of $10,000 invested five years ago: **$ 6,027**

Dividend Data

No cash dividends have been paid.

Investment Rationale/Risk October 26, 2004

- While the shares have lagged the S&P 500 Index and are down 10.5% year to date, we believe the current valuation at 14X our 2005 earnings estimate reflects higher capital outlays for licensed spectrum and 3G network upgrades. However, we expect NXTL to generate positive free cash flow in 2004 through 2006, with EBITDA growing annually at 20%, above peers.

- Risks to our recommendation and target price include increased competition from Verizon Wireless and other leading wireless carriers in the business and government markets, where NXTL has the largest market share; regulatory delays on new radio spectrum to be awarded to the company by the FCC; higher cash payments for the new spectrum, which may be well in excess of our $3 billion estimate; and delays in upgrading to a third generation network.

- With the planned acquisition of AT&T Wireless (AWE: hold, $15) by Cingular Wireless, NXTL will become the largest pure play in the wireless sub-industry. In our opinion, management has a strong track record in meeting its strategic and financial objectives. Our 12-month target price of $30 is based on a blend of forward P/E multiple (using 16.7X our 2005 earnings estimate) and enterprise value (6.6X our 2005 EBITDA estimate) analyses. With the stock priced below peers on a P/E basis, we would buy NXTL.

Revenues/Earnings Data Fiscal year ending December 31

Revenues (Million $)

	2004	2003	2002	2001	2000	1999
1Q	3,103	2,371	1,957	1,742	1,079	663.8
2Q	3,289	2,556	2,154	1,881	1,260	793.1
3Q	3.40	2,887	2,279	1,992	1,416	889.0
4Q	—	3,006	2,331	2,074	1,646	980.0
Yr.	—	10,820	8,721	7,689	5,714	3,326

Earnings Per Share ($)

	2004	2003	2002	2001	2000	1999
1Q	0.51	0.20	-0.82	-0.56	-0.45	-0.83
2Q	1.12	0.27	0.37	-0.56	-0.38	-0.52
3Q	0.52	0.32	0.55	-0.87	-0.31	-0.55
4Q	E0.41	0.56	1.38	-2.25	-0.08	-0.43
Yr.	E1.85	1.36	1.78	-4.27	-1.21	-2.29

Next earnings report expected: mid-February Source: S&P, Company Reports
EPS Estimates based on S&P Operating Earnings; historical GAAP earnings are as reported.

Please read the Required Disclosures and Reg. AC certification on the last page of this report.

The McGraw·Hill Companies

NEXTEL Communications, Inc.

Recommendation: **BUY** ★ ★ ★ ★ ★   12-Month Target Price: **$30.00** (as of October 22, 2004)

Business Summary October 26, 2004

Nextel, the fifth largest U.S. wireless phone carrier, ended 2003 with 12.3 million subscribers, an increase of nearly 2.3 million from the level a year earlier. The company believes it has made major inroads into the blue-collar business market, due to its distinctive two-way radio service, Direct Connect, which provides instant communication at the push of a button (with no dialing, ringing, or reply delays), and new product offerings. NXTL has completed the full deployment of Nationwide Direct Connect, and is introducing an innovative voice coding technology that it expects to double its cellular capacity and enhance voice quality.

NXTL's wireless services are targeted at small and mid-sized businesses such as construction and manufacturing, and at government employees. In December 2002, the company announced the signing of a $200 million contract to provide nationwide Enhanced Specialized Mobile Radio services to all U.S. federal agencies, as well as to state and local agencies with federal funding, and it planned to offer unique interoperability advantages for emergency preparedness and response. NXTL has a number of important strategic and commercial relationships with Motorola, which is a significant shareholder. Motorola, as the company's sole supplier, provides the iDEN infrastructure equipment and substantially all the handsets used throughout the market. Motorola provides handset service and repair, transmitter and receiver site rent, and training.

In addition to its directly owned domestic wireless business, the company has a 32% ownership interest in publicly traded Nextel Partners, an affiliate that provides service in small and medium-sized U.S. markets. In November 2002, the

Nextel International (NII) subsidiary, which offers wireless services in Brazil, Mexico, Argentina and Peru, emerged from bankruptcy. NXTL recorded a $1.2 billion gain in 2002 as a result of deconsolidating NII Holdings.

Capital spending totaled $1.8 billion in 2003, and NXTL forecasts 2004 expenditures of about $2.2 billion. As part of its 2004 capital spending, the company expects to spend $900 million for the core-iDEN network, $350 million for IT and other network projects, $600 million for 2,200 new cell sites and land costs for future cell sites, and $350 million for development work on new applications. Some of the new features cover WiDEN, a next generation network platform that can increase data speeds of the current iDEN network up to 4X by boosting the capacity of existing radio channels, and the new 6:1 vocoder software upgrade.

In February 2004, NXTL announced that it would test a wireless broadband service in the Raleigh-Durham, NC, market, using Flarion Technologies FLASH-OFDM technology. The trial will provide wireless broadband access on laptop and desktop computers, pocket PCs, and similar devices. The company said it had seen impressive results with the technology in extensive laboratory testing. Under real world conditions, NXTL has been running market trials with service price plans in the Raleigh-Durham, NC market. For broadband wireless services, we expect NXTL to make a decision on whether it will use the Flarion technology or Qualcomm's (QCOM: buy, $41) CDMA 1xEV-DO in the first quarter of 2005.

Company Financials Fiscal Year ending December 31

Per Share Data ($)

(Year Ended December 31)	2003	2002	2001	2000	1999	1998	1997	1996	1995	1994
Tangible Bk. Val.	NM	NM	NM	NM	NM	NM	NM	NM	NM	-0.49
Cash Flow	2.91	3.07	-1.73	0.46	-0.72	-1.50	-2.09	-0.35	-0.33	0.01
Earnings	1.36	1.78	-4.27	-1.21	-2.29	-2.99	-3.21	-1.25	-1.16	-0.76
S&P Core Earnings	0.89	0.21	-4.46	NA	NA	NA	NA	NA	NA	NA
Dividends	Nil	Nil	Nil	Nil	Nil	Nil	Nil	Nil	Nil	Nil
Payout Ratio	Nil	Nil	Nil	Nil	Nil	Nil	Nil	Nil	Nil	Nil
Prices - High	28.17	14.67	38.62	82.93	58.69	17.06	16.00	12.00	10.87	23.37
- Low	10.89	2.50	6.87	22.62	12.50	7.68	6.06	6.37	4.68	6.62
P/E Ratio - High	21	8	NM	NM	NM	NM	NM	NM	NM	NM
- Low	8	1	NM	NM	NM	NM	NM	NM	NM	NM

Income Statement Analysis (Million $)

	2003	2002	2001	2000	1999	1998	1997	1996	1995	1994
Revs.	10,820	8,721	7,689	5,714	3,326	1,847	739	333	225	194
Oper. Inc.	4,216	3,166	-1,800	1,264	535	-220	-411	245	-173	-44.2
Depr.	1,694	1,595	1,746	1,265	1,004	832	526	401	236	195
Int. Exp.	844	1,048	1,403	1,245	878	656	407	227	115	NA
Pretax Inc.	1,650	1,777	-2,959	-678	-1,298	-1,054	-1,309	-863	-532	-291
Eff. Tax Rate	6.85%	22.0%	NM	NM	NM	NM	NM	NM	NM	NM
Net Inc.	1,537	1,386	-3,094	-711	-1,270	-1,519	-1,568	-556	-331	-193
S&P Core Earnings	948	134	-3,471	NA	NA	NA	NA	NA	NA	NA

Balance Sheet & Other Fin. Data (Million $)

	2003	2002	2001	2000	1999	1998	1997	1996	1995	1994
Cash	806	1,846	2,565	2,609	4,701	321	433	140	409	474
Curr. Assets	3,688	4,650	5,723	6,458	6,620	1,053	840	309	505	504
Total Assets	20,510	21,484	22,064	22,686	18,410	11,573	9,228	6,472	5,513	2,889
Curr. Liab.	2,817	2,756	4,577	2,722	2,831	1,182	769	376	365	NA
LT Debt	9,725	12,279	14,720	14,629	10,312	7,710	5,038	2,783	1,653	1,163
Common Equity	5,836	2,710	-865	1,745	2,283	-61.0	1,912	2,508	2,645	1,269
Total Cap.	17,527	17,759	16,921	19,450	15,499	10,379	8,430	6,097	5,138	2,432
Cap. Exp.	1,716	1,863	3,418	3,518	1,947	2,082	1,597	435	271	NA
Cash Flow	3,173	2,962	-1,348	345	-458	-836	-1,052	-155	-95.0	2.10
Curr. Ratio	1.3	1.7	1.3	2.4	2.3	0.9	1.1	0.8	1.4	NA
% LT Debt of Cap.	55.5	69.1	87.0	75.2	66.5	74.3	59.8	45.6	32.2	47.8
% Net Inc.of Revs.	14.2	15.9	NM	NM	NM	NM	NM	NM	NM	NM
% Ret. on Assets	7.3	6.4	NM	NM	NM	NM	NM	NM	NM	NM
% Ret. on Equity	34.6	148.2	NM	NM	NM	NM	NM	NM	NM	NM

Data as orig. reptd.; bef. results of disc. opers. and/or spec. items. Per share data adj. for stk. divs.; EPS diluted. E-Estimated. NA-Not Available. NM-Not Meaningful. NR-Not Ranked.

Office: 2001 Edmund Halley Drive, Reston, VA 20191.
Telephone: 703-433-4000.
Website: http://www.nextel.com
Chrmn: W.E. Conway.
Pres & CEO: T.M. Donahue.

Vice Chrmn: M. O'Brien.
COO & EVP: T.N. Kelly.
EVP & CFO: P.N. Saleh.
Dirs: K. J. Bane, J. T. Bryan, W. E. Conway, Jr., T. M. Donahue, F. M. Drendel, J. Hill, W. E. Kennard, M. E. O'Brien, D. M. Weibling.

Founded: in 1987.
Domicile: Delaware.
Employees: 17,000.
S&P Analyst: Kenneth M. Leon/MF/GG

Nicor Inc.

Recommendation: **HOLD** ★★★☆☆
SELL | SELL | HOLD | BUY | BUY

12-Month Target Price: $39.00
(as of October 08, 2004)

GAS has an approximate 0.02% weighting in the **S&P 500**

Sector: Utilities
Sub-Industry: Gas Utilities
Peer Group: Diversified - Larger

Summary: This holding company's Nicor Gas subsidiary is one of the largest U.S. natural gas distributors.

Quantitative Evaluations

S&P Earnings & Dividend Rank: B+

| D | C | B- | B | B+ | A- | A | A+ |

S&P Fair Value Rank: 2

| 1 | 2 | 3 | 4 | 5 |
| Lowest | | | | Highest |

Fair Value Calc.: $35.20 (Slightly Overvalued)

S&P Investability Quotient Percentile

86%

GAS scored higher than 86% of all companies for which an S&P Report is available.

Volatility: Low

| Low | Average | High |

Technical Evaluation: Bullish
Since 8/04, the technical indicators for GAS have been Bullish.

Relative Strength Rank: Moderate

51

1 Lowest   Highest 99

Price as of 11/12/04: $38.49   **2004E S&P Core EPS:** $2.00

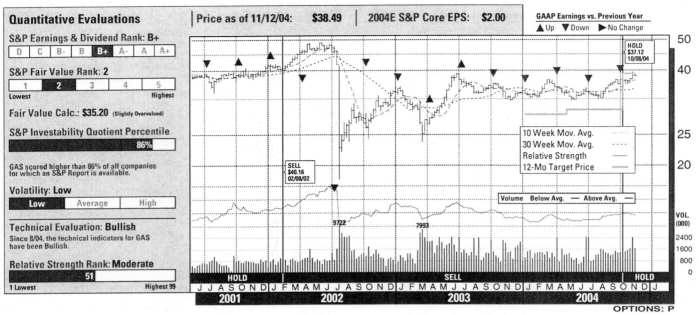

GAAP Earnings vs. Previous Year
▲ Up   ▼ Down   ► No Change

Legend:
- 10 Week Mov. Avg.
- 30 Week Mov. Avg.
- Relative Strength
- 12-Mo Target Price

Volume   Below Avg. — Above Avg.

HOLD $37.12 10/08/04

SELL $40.16 02/08/02

Analyst commentary prepared by Yogeesh Wagle /PMW/JWP

Highlights October 11, 2004

- Our 2004 EPS estimate excludes the potential impact of a regulatory review of GAS's historical performance-based rate (PBR) plan and related insurance recoveries. We expect the PBR review to be completed in 2004 or 2005. Our 2004 EPS estimate includes $0.07 of first half asset sale gains, as such gains have been a recurring phenomenon in recent periods.

- We look for 2004 operating EPS to increase nearly 7%, with increasing contributions from Tropical Shipping, higher asset sale gains, and new fixed bill retail energy products (in Other Energy Ventures) outweighing higher utility operating and maintenance costs and the impact of warmer than normal winter weather. In the absence of regulatory rate relief for rising utility costs, we see limited EPS growth prospects through 2006. However, lower legal expense and improving shipping results should, in our opinion, have a positive impact on EPS over the next few years. In 2005, we look for about 2% EPS growth, with lower legal fees and increasing contributions from Tropical Shipping and Other Energy Ventures, outweighing lower asset sale gains and a higher income tax rate.

- Reported 2003 EPS includes $0.39 in one-time gains. Our 2004 operating and Standard & Poor's Core Earnings estimates exclude a first quarter litigation charge of $0.52 a share. Our 2004 S&P Core EPS estimate of $2.00 primarily reflects the exclusion of pension income and asset sale gains.

Key Stock Statistics

S&P Core EPS 2005E	2.14	52-week Range	$39.65-32.03
S&P Oper. EPS 2004E	2.05	12 Month P/E	27.3
P/E on S&P Oper. EPS 2004E	18.8	Beta	0.39
S&P Oper. EPS 2005E	2.20	Shareholders	25,000
Yield (%)	4.8%	Market Cap (B)	$ 1.7
Dividend Rate/Share	1.86	Shares Outstanding (M)	44.1

Value of $10,000 invested five years ago: **$ 12,839**

Dividend Data Dividends have been paid since 1954

Amount ($)	Date Decl.	Ex-Div. Date	Stock of Record	Payment Date
0.465	Nov. 20	Dec. 29	Dec. 31	Feb. 01 '04
0.465	Mar. 18	Mar. 29	Mar. 31	May. 01 '04
0.465	Apr. 19	Jun. 28	Jun. 30	Aug. 01 '04
0.465	Jul. 15	Sep. 28	Sep. 30	Nov. 01 '04

Investment Rationale/Risk October 11, 2004

- We recently upgraded the shares to hold, from sell. The shares trade in line with peers, based on our 2005 EPS estimates. However, the stock's price to trailing operating cash flow multiple is at a discount to peers. The company is considering filing for regulatory rate relief, but we believe a filing is unlikely until outstanding regulatory issues are resolved. We view the dividend as secure, but with the payout ratio over 80%, versus a peer average of about 66%, we see limited future growth. On the positive side, we think that GAS's unregulated Chicago hub operations should see better results, on greater demand for natural gas. Although the tropical shipping business has likely seen disruptions from recent hurricanes, we expect post-hurricane rebuilding to boost cargo container volume.

- Risks to our recommendation and target price include a potentially unfavorable resolution of the regulatory PBR review, a denial of regulatory rate relief for higher utility costs, lower than expected insurance recoveries for litigation expense, and slower than expected growth in unregulated operations.

- We believe the shares would be fairly valued at a P/E multiple of 16X projected 2005 EPS, a slight premium to peers. Assuming appreciation in line with our longer-term EPS growth forecast of 3%, our 12-month target price is $39.

Revenues/Earnings Data Fiscal year ending December 31

Revenues (Million $)

	2004	2003	2002	2001	2000	1999
1Q	1,116	1,171	588.0	1,474	659.3	576.4
2Q	429.5	452.8	352.2	373.0	348.4	271.8
3Q	299.9	294.8	252.4	244.4	301.0	227.3
4Q	—	743.9	704.7	453.0	989.4	539.0
Yr.	—	2,663	1,897	2,544	2,298	1,615

Earnings Per Share ($)

	2004	2003	2002	2001	2000	1999
1Q	0.44	1.14	0.82	0.85	0.83	0.82
2Q	0.36	0.54	0.50	0.59	0.66	0.56
3Q	-0.26	0.01	0.67	0.73	-1.37	0.42
4Q	E0.91	0.79	0.89	1.01	0.85	0.83
Yr.	E2.05	2.48	2.88	3.17	1.00	2.62

Next earnings report expected: early-February Source: S&P, Company Reports
EPS Estimates based on S&P Operating Earnings; historical GAAP earnings are as reported.

Nicor Inc.

Recommendation: **HOLD** ★ ★ ★ ☆ ☆   12-Month Target Price: **$39.00** (as of October 08, 2004)

Business Summary October 11, 2004

Nicor seeks earnings growth through investment in unregulated operations, including its Tropical Shipping and Other Energy Ventures divisions. However, the company's main operating segment remains its regulated gas utility operations.

As of the end of 2003, Nicor Gas (84.5% of 2003 segment operating profit) served 2.08 million customers in a service territory that encompasses most of the northern third of Illinois, excluding Chicago. In 2003, Nicor Gas delivered 494.2 billion cubic feet (Bcf) of natural gas, of which 47% went to residential customers, 27% to commercial customers, and 26% to industrial customers. This contrasts with 519.1 Bcf delivered in 2002 and 475.2 Bcf delivered in 2001. The company has an extensive storage and transmission system that provides flexibility. The system is directly connected to eight interstate pipelines, and includes seven owned underground gas storage facilities, with about 140 Bcf of top storage capacity.

From 2000 through 2002, regulators provided Nicor with a performance-based rate (PBR) plan that allowed the utility to earn a profit on savings generated for customers by procuring natural gas at lower than prevailing market prices. Accounting for the PBR plan was brought into question in 2002, leading GAS to restate prior financial statements and not record PBR income for 2002. As of mid-2004, regulators were evaluating testimony alleging that GAS should refund up to $190 million to customers.

Nicor Gas is also engaged in non-traditional natural gas storage and transportation activities through its Chicago Hub, which serves marketers, other distributors, and electric power facilities. Though within regulated operations, contributions from the Chicago Hub (net income $7.3 million in 2003, $15.4 million in 2002 and $13 million in 2001) can lead to the utility earning higher than regulated allowed rates of return.

GAS's Tropical Shipping unit (11.5% of EBIT) is one of the largest containerized cargo carriers in the Caribbean, with a fleet of 10 owned and five chartered vessels, with total container container capacity of about 5,100 TEUs, serving 25 ports. Total volumes shipped in 2003 were 177,100 TEUs, up from 175,100 TEUs in 2002 and 145,700 TEUs in 2001.

The company's Other Energy Ventures (4.0%) include Nicor Services and Solutions, Nicor Enerchange, the Horizon Pipeline, and Nicor Energy. Nicor's Services and Solutions businesses offer service contracts covering the maintenance or repair of gas piping and major appliances and provide utility-bill management and natural gas price protection plans. Nicor Enerchange engages in wholesale natural gas marketing and trading in the Midwest, and administers the Chicago Hub. GAS is also a 50% joint venture owner of the 74-mile Illinois Horizon natural gas pipeline.

In the 2002 third quarter, GAS wrote down to zero its 50% joint venture interest in Nicor Energy, a competitive retail energy marketer. Accounting irregularities were discovered at Nicor Energy in 2002, leading to a restatement of results since 2000, and prompting a regulatory review. In March 2003, Nicor Energy finished assigning all customers to qualified energy providers as part of its exit from the retail energy business.

Company Financials Fiscal Year ending December 31

Per Share Data ($)

(Year Ended December 31)	2003	2002	2001	2000	1999	1998	1997	1996	1995	1994
Tangible Bk. Val.	17.15	16.55	16.39	15.56	16.76	15.97	15.43	14.75	13.59	13.25
Cash Flow	5.73	6.00	6.46	4.12	5.58	5.25	5.29	4.92	4.17	4.03
Earnings	2.48	2.88	3.17	1.00	2.62	2.42	2.61	2.42	1.96	2.07
S&P Core Earnings	2.45	2.30	1.99	NA	NA	NA	NA	NA	NA	NA
Dividends	1.86	1.84	1.76	1.66	1.54	1.46	1.40	1.32	1.28	1.26
Payout Ratio	75%	64%	56%	166%	59%	60%	54%	55%	65%	60%
Prices - High	39.30	49.00	42.37	43.87	42.93	44.43	42.93	37.12	28.50	29.25
- Low	23.70	18.09	34.00	29.37	31.18	37.12	30.00	25.37	21.75	21.87
P/E Ratio - High	16	17	13	44	16	18	16	15	15	14
- Low	10	6	11	29	12	15	11	10	11	11

Income Statement Analysis (Million $)

	2003	2002	2001	2000	1999	1998	1997	1996	1995	1994
Revs.	2,663	1,897	2,544	2,298	1,615	1,465	1,993	1,851	1,480	1,609
Oper. Inc.	189	227	244	507	352	345	361	358	302	297
Depr.	144	138	149	144	140	137	131	125	112	103
Int. Exp.	37.3	38.5	44.9	48.6	45.1	46.6	49.1	47.8	42.7	40.3
Pretax Inc.	169	186	217	61.1	190	178	197	189	154	161
Eff. Tax Rate	35.2%	31.0%	33.8%	23.6%	34.6%	34.4%	35.0%	35.8%	35.3%	31.8%
Net Inc.	110	128	144	46.7	124	116	128	121	100	110
S&P Core Earnings	108	102	90.4	NA	NA	NA	NA	NA	NA	NA

Balance Sheet & Other Fin. Data (Million $)

	2003	2002	2001	2000	1999	1998	1997	1996	1995	1994
Cash	50.3	75.2	10.7	55.8	42.5	13.0	5.20	33.2	26.4	42.3
Curr. Assets	916	708	518	915	508	465	535	573	390	418
Total Assets	3,797	2,899	2,575	2,885	2,452	2,365	2,395	2,439	2,259	2,210
Curr. Liab.	1,069	1,099	826	1,312	746	579	622	700	626	600
LT Debt	497	396	446	347	436	557	550	518	469	459
Common Equity	755	728	728	708	788	759	744	730	688	683
Total Cap.	1,813	1,514	1,514	1,548	1,173	1,539	1,606	1,516	1,397	1,375
Cap. Exp.	181	193	186	158	154	136	113	120	157	172
Cash Flow	253	266	292	191	264	253	259	246	212	212
Curr. Ratio	0.8	0.6	0.6	0.7	0.7	0.8	0.9	1.3	0.6	0.7
% LT Debt of Cap.	27.4	26.1	28.8	29.6	28.3	34.7	36.3	34.2	33.6	33.4
% Net Inc.of Revs.	4.1	6.7	5.6	2.0	7.7	7.9	6.4	6.5	6.7	6.8
% Ret. on Assets	3.3	4.7	5.3	1.8	5.1	4.9	5.3	5.2	4.5	5.1
% Ret. on Equity	14.8	12.3	20.0	6.2	16.0	15.4	17.3	17.1	14.5	16.1

Data as orig reptd.; bef. results of disc opers/spec. items. Per share data adj. for stk. divs. Bold denotes primary EPS - prior periods restated. E-Estimated. NA-Not Available. NM-Not Meaningful. NR-Not Ranked. UR-Under Review.

Office: 1844 Ferry Road, Naperville, IL 60563-9600.
Telephone: 630-305-9500.
Website: http://www.nicorinc.com
Chrmn & CEO: T.L. Fisher.
Pres: R.M. Strobel.
EVP & CFO: R.L. Hawley.

VP & Treas: G.M. Behrens.
VP, Secy & General Counsel: P.C. Gracey.
Investor Contact: M. Knox 630-305-9500.
Dirs: R. M. Beavers, Jr., B. P. Bickner, J. H. Birdsall III, T. A. Donahoe, T. L. Fisher, J. E. Jones, D. J. Keller, W. A. Osborn, J. Rau, J. F. Riordan, R. M. Strobel, P. A. Wier.

Founded: in 1953.
Domicile: Illinois.
Employees: 3,500.
S&P Analyst: Yogeesh Wagle /PMW/JWP

NIKE, Inc.

Recommendation: **BUY** ★★★★☆
SELL SELL HOLD BUY BUY

12-Month Target Price: **$89.00**
(as of March 19, 2004)

NKE has an approximate 0.21% weighting in the **S&P 500**

Sector: Consumer Discretionary
Sub-Industry: Footwear
Peer Group: Footwear - Athletic

Summary: NIKE is the world's leading designer and marketer of high-quality athletic footwear, athletic apparel and accessories.

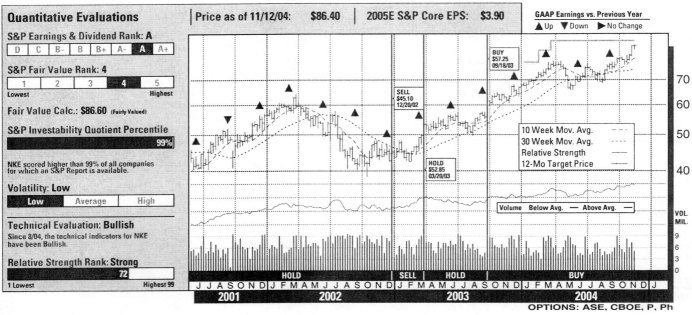

	Price as of 11/12/04: **$86.40**	2005E S&P Core EPS: **$3.90**

Quantitative Evaluations

S&P Earnings & Dividend Rank: A
D · C · B- · B · B+ · A- · **A** · A+

S&P Fair Value Rank: 4
1 · 2 · 3 · **4** · 5
Lowest — Highest

Fair Value Calc.: $86.60 (Fairly Valued)

S&P Investability Quotient Percentile
99%

NKE scored higher than 99% of all companies for which an S&P Report is available.

Volatility: Low
Low · Average · High

Technical Evaluation: Bullish
Since 8/04, the technical indicators for NKE have been Bullish.

Relative Strength Rank: Strong
72
1 Lowest — Highest 99

GAAP Earnings vs. Previous Year
▲ Up ▼ Down ▶ No Change

10 Week Mov. Avg.
30 Week Mov. Avg.
Relative Strength
12-Mo Target Price

Volume Below Avg. — Above Avg.

OPTIONS: ASE, CBOE, P, Ph

Analyst commentary prepared by Yogeesh Wagle/PMW/JWP

Highlights September 23, 2004

- We expect sales growth in the high single digits in FY 05 (May), driven by contributions from the Converse acquisition and by improved sales at Nike Golf, as well as international growth, mainly in the European and Asia-Pacific regions. U.S. apparel sales should post mid-single-digit gains. U.S. footwear sales are likely to be up slightly, on improved sales of marquee products, continued popularity of retro/classics, and firmer pricing.

- We expect operating margins to widen, on a sales mix shift to higher margin products, favorable currency effects, improved sourcing, and supply chain upgrades, partly offset by increased advertising expenditures.

- After expected lower interest expense, and taxes at an estimated rate of 34.8%, we project that FY 05 EPS will increase 18%, to $4.15, from $3.51 in FY 04. For FY 06, we see mid-single-digit revenue growth, mainly on mid-teens gains in international footwear and apparel, combined with greater operating efficiency, resulting in EPS of $4.62.

Investment Rationale/Risk September 23, 2004

- We recommend accumulating the shares. At 19X our FY 05 EPS estimate, the shares are near the level of the S&P 500, but below their historical average. We see upside potential, reflecting greater demand for performance products in the U.S. and increased penetration in higher growth Asia-Pacific markets. In addition, we think the shares should command a premium to peers, given our view of the company's proven ability to market technologically advanced athletic shoes at premium prices, and what we see as its market leader status. We think the Converse acquisition will enable NKE to leverage its distribution and marketing strength to build on Converse's iconic brand name.

- Risks to our recommendation and target price include a possible slowdown in the ongoing economic expansion in the U.S., and a drop in consumer sentiment precipitated by potential terrorist acts. International risks include possible political unrest, economic weakness, supply disruptions, and unfavorable currency fluctuations.

- Our 12-month target price of $89 is equal to about 21X our FY 05 EPS estimate, in line with the stock's five-year historical average P/E multiple.

Key Stock Statistics

S&P Core EPS 2006E	4.46	52-week Range	$86.52-60.69
S&P Oper. EPS 2005E	4.15	12 Month P/E	23.1
P/E on S&P Oper. EPS 2005E	20.8	Beta	0.73
S&P Oper. EPS 2006E	4.62	Shareholders	19,069
Yield (%)	0.9%	Market Cap (B)	$ 16.0
Dividend Rate/Share	0.80	Shares Outstanding (M)	262.5

Value of $10,000 invested five years ago: **$ 18,979**

Dividend Data Dividends have been paid since 1984

Amount ($)	Date Decl.	Ex-Div. Date	Stock of Record	Payment Date
0.200	Nov. 24	Dec. 11	Dec. 15	Jan. 05 '04
0.200	Feb. 17	Mar. 11	Mar. 15	Apr. 05 '04
0.200	May. 10	Jun. 10	Jun. 14	Jul. 05 '04
0.200	Aug. 09	Sep. 09	Sep. 13	Oct. 04 '04

Revenues/Earnings Data Fiscal year ending May 31

Revenues (Million $)

	2005	2004	2003	2002	2001	2000
1Q	3,562	3,025	2,796	2,614	2,637	2,501
2Q	—	2,837	2,515	2,337	2,199	2,060
3Q	—	2,904	2,401	2,260	2,170	2,162
4Q	—	3,487	2,985	2,682	2,483	2,273
Yr.	—	12,253	10,697	9,893	9,489	8,995

Earnings Per Share ($)

	2005	2004	2003	2002	2001	2000
1Q	1.21	0.98	0.81	0.75	0.77	0.70
2Q	E0.80	0.66	0.57	0.48	0.44	0.38
3Q	E0.82	0.74	0.47	0.46	0.35	0.52
4Q	E1.30	1.13	0.92	0.77	0.60	0.46
Yr.	E4.15	3.51	2.77	2.46	2.16	2.07

Next earnings report expected: mid-December Source: S&P, Company Reports
EPS Estimates based on S&P Operating Earnings; historical GAAP earnings are as reported.

NIKE, Inc.

Recommendation: **BUY** ★★★★☆   12-Month Target Price: **$89.00** (as of March 19, 2004)

Business Summary September 23, 2004

NIKE designs, develops and markets worldwide high quality footwear, apparel, equipment and accessory products. The company's athletic footwear products are designed for specific sports, casual and leisure purposes. As the world's largest supplier of athletic footwear, NKE puts considerable emphasis on high-quality construction and innovative design. Basketball, cross-training, running, children's shoes, and women's shoes are currently the top selling categories, and are expected to remain the top sellers for the near term. NKE also markets shoes for tennis, golf, soccer, baseball, football, bicycling and volleyball, wrestling, cheerleading, aquatic activities, auto racing, and other athletic and recreational uses.

NKE has a significant non-footwear business, and markets sports apparel, athletic bags and accessory items to complement its athletic footwear line. These items are sold through the same distribution channels. In addition, the company sells sports equipment under the NIKE brand including sport balls, timepieces, eyewear, skates, bats, gloves and other equipment designed for specific sporting activities. NKE has agreements with licensees to produce and sell Nike-branded swimwear, cycling apparel, maternity exercise wear, school supplies, timepieces and electronic media devices.

Through wholly owned Cole Haan Holdings Inc., the company sells a line of dress and casual footwear and accessories for men, women and children under the Cole Haan, g Series and Bragano brand name. Wholly owned subsidiary, Bauer

NIKE Hockey Inc., makes and markets ice skates, skate blades, in-line roller skates, protective gear, hockey sticks, and hockey jerseys and accessories under the Bauer and Nike brand names.

In April 2002, NKE acquired Hurley International, a provider of action sports apparel for surfing, skateboarding and snowboarding and youth lifestyle apparel under the Hurley brand name.

In September 2003, the company acquired Converse, Inc., for $305 million, plus the assumption of certain liabilities. Converse, which had revenues of $205 million in 2002, is a widely recognized designer, distributor and marketer of apparel and footwear under the Converse, Chuck Taylor, All Star, One Star, and Jack Purcell brand names.

Virtually all products are manufactured by independent contractors. Products are sold to about 28,000 retail accounts in the U.S. and, through independent distributors, licensees and subsidiaries, in about 120 countries worldwide. NKE estimates that its products are sold in more than 23,000 retail accounts outside the U.S. Sales outside the U.S. accounted for 53% of the total in FY 04 (May), up from 51% in FY 03. Most footwear is produced outside the U.S.; apparel is produced both in the U.S. and abroad. The company also operates about 165 retail outlets in the U.S. and 165 outside the U.S., consisting of Niketowns, Nike stores, Nike factory stores, employee-only stores, and Cole Haan stores.

Company Financials Fiscal Year ending May 31

Per Share Data ($)

(Year Ended May 31)	2004	2003	2002	2001	2000	1999	1998	1997	1996	1995
Tangible Bk. Val.	16.27	14.44	12.78	11.53	10.11	10.28	9.81	9.28	6.81	5.14
Cash Flow	4.44	3.66	7.01	2.88	2.75	2.25	1.98	3.15	2.22	1.60
Earnings	3.51	2.77	2.46	2.16	2.07	1.57	1.35	2.68	1.89	1.36
S&P Core Earnings	3.35	2.62	2.32	2.05	NA	NA	NA	NA	NA	NA
Dividends	0.52	0.52	0.48	0.48	0.48	0.48	0.44	0.35	0.35	0.23
Payout Ratio	15%	19%	20%	22%	23%	31%	33%	13%	19%	17%

Cal. Yrs.	2003	2002	2001	2000	1999	1998	1997	1996	1995	1994
Prices - High	68.54	64.28	60.06	57.00	66.93	52.68	76.37	64.00	35.18	19.12
- Low	42.38	38.53	35.50	25.81	38.75	31.00	37.75	31.75	17.18	11.56
P/E Ratio - High	20	26	24	26	32	34	57	24	19	14
- Low	12	16	14	12	19	20	28	12	9	9

Income Statement Analysis (Million $)

	2004	2003	2002	2001	2000	1999	1998	1997	1996	1995
Revs.	12,253	10,697	9,893	9,489	8,995	8,777	9,553	9,187	6,471	4,761
Oper. Inc.	1,802	1,485	1,291	1,212	1,150	1,054	1,049	1,518	1,073	757
Depr.	252	239	224	197	188	198	185	138	97.2	71.1
Int. Exp.	25.0	42.9	47.6	58.7	45.0	44.0	60.0	52.3	39.5	24.5
Pretax Inc.	1,450	1,123	2,035	921	919	745	653	1,295	899	650
Eff. Tax Rate	34.8%	34.1%	17.2%	36.0%	37.0%	39.5%	38.7%	38.5%	38.5%	38.5%
Net Inc.	946	740	1,686	590	579	451	400	796	553	400
S&P Core Earnings	897	698	632	559	NA	NA	NA	NA	NA	NA

Balance Sheet & Other Fin. Data (Million $)

	2004	2003	2002	2001	2000	1999	1998	1997	1996	1995
Cash	828	634	576	304	254	198	109	445	262	216
Curr. Assets	5,512	4,680	4,158	3,625	3,596	3,265	3,533	3,831	2,727	2,046
Total Assets	7,892	6,714	6,443	5,820	5,857	5,248	5,397	5,361	3,952	3,143
Curr. Liab.	2,009	2,015	1,836	1,787	2,140	1,447	1,704	1,867	1,467	1,108
LT Debt	682	552	626	436	470	386	379	296	9.58	10.6
Common Equity	4,782	3,991	3,839	3,495	3,136	3,335	3,262	3,156	2,431	1,965
Total Cap.	5,464	4,543	4,465	3,931	3,607	3,721	3,641	3,452	2,443	1,993
Cap. Exp.	214	186	283	318	420	384	506	466	216	154
Cash Flow	1,198	979	1,909	787	767	645	585	934	650	471
Curr. Ratio	2.7	2.3	2.3	2.0	1.7	2.3	2.1	2.0	1.9	1.9
% LT Debt of Cap.	12.5	12.1	14.0	11.1	13.0	10.4	10.4	8.6	0.4	0.5
% Net Inc.of Revs.	7.7	6.9	17.0	6.2	6.4	5.1	4.2	8.7	8.5	8.4
% Ret. on Assets	12.9	11.3	27.5	10.1	10.4	8.5	7.4	17.1	15.6	14.5
% Ret. on Equity	21.6	18.9	46.0	17.8	17.9	13.7	12.5	28.5	25.2	21.6

Data as orig reptd.; bef. results of disc opers/spec. items. Per share data adj. for stk. divs.; EPS diluted. E-Estimated. NA-Not Available. NM-Not Meaningful. NR-Not Ranked. UR-Under Review.

Office: One Bowerman Drive, Beaverton, OR 97005-6453.
Telephone: 503-641-6453.
Website: http://www.nikebiz.com
Chrmn, Pres & CEO: P.H. Knight.
VP & CFO: D.W. Blair.

VP & Secy: L.D. Stewart.
Investor Contact: P.M. Catlett 800-640-8007.
Dirs: T. E. Clarke, J. K. Conway, R. D. DeNunzio, A. B. Graf, Jr., D. J. Hayes, D. G. Houser, J. P. Jackson, P. H. Knight, O. C. Smith, J. R. Thompson, Jr.

Founded: in 1964.
Domicile: Oregon.
Employees: 24,667.
S&P Analyst: Yogeesh Wagle/PMW/JWP

NiSource Inc.

Recommendation: **HOLD** ★ ★ ★ ☆ ☆
SELL · SELL · HOLD · BUY · BUY

12-Month Target Price: **$22.00**
(as of April 30, 2004)

NI has an approximate 0.05% weighting in the **S&P 500**

Sector: Utilities
Sub-Industry: Gas Utilities
Peer Group: Diversified - Larger

Summary: NI, the third largest U.S. gas distribution utility and the fourth largest gas pipeline company, also provides electric utility services.

Quantitative Evaluations

S&P Earnings & Dividend Rank: B+

| D | C | B- | B | **B+** | A- | A | A+ |

S&P Fair Value Rank: 3

| 1 | 2 | **3** | 4 | 5 |
| Lowest | | | | Highest |

Fair Value Calc.: $20.70 (Slightly Overvalued)

S&P Investability Quotient Percentile

68%

NI scored higher than 68% of all companies for which an S&P Report is available.

Volatility: Low

| **Low** | Average | High |

Technical Evaluation: Neutral
Since 10/04, the technical indicators for NI have been Neutral.

Relative Strength Rank: Moderate

38
1 Lowest | Highest 99

| Price as of 11/12/04: | **$21.48** | 2004E S&P Core EPS: | **$1.50** |

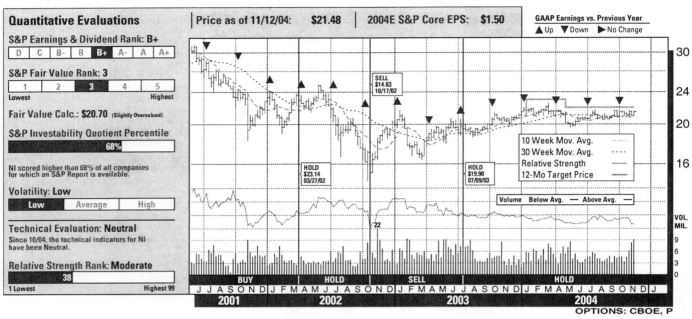

GAAP Earnings vs. Previous Year
▲ Up ▼ Down ▶ No Change

- 10 Week Mov. Avg.
- 30 Week Mov. Avg.
- Relative Strength
- 12-Mo Target Price

Volume Below Avg. ▪ Above Avg. ▫

VOL.
MIL.

SELL $14.83 10/17/02

HOLD $23.14 03/27/02

HOLD $19.90 07/09/03

BUY · HOLD · SELL · HOLD
2001 · 2002 · 2003 · 2004

OPTIONS: CBOE, P

Analyst commentary prepared by Craig K. Shere, CFA /CB/GG

Highlights August 19, 2004

- We expect 2004 gross revenues to decline by less than 5%, as the effects of milder winter weather (reducing demand for natural gas utility services) and lower interruptible gas supply sales outweigh higher electric sales and natural gas prices. We expect continued historically high natural gas prices to restrict industrial demand for NI's gas distribution services.

- We expect margins to widen, as lower labor costs and increased summer power capacity utilization outweigh the impact of lower winter natural gas demand. NI expects 2004 pretax pension expense to decrease by $20 million to $30 million. We see interest expense down over 10%, due to a reduction in debt associated with asset sales, a mandatory conversion of certain debt to equity in 2003, and reduced interest costs due to 2003 debt refinancings. In 2005, we look for flat EPS, as the absence of one-time 2004 legal, insurance and property tax adjustments and lower electric contributions offset higher weather driven natural gas results.

- Reported 2003 EPS included a third quarter asset sale gain of $0.04. Our Standard & Poor's Core Earnings estimate is $0.15 below our operating EPS forecast, due to negative adjustments to pension expense accounting and the full expensing of employee stock options.

Investment Rationale/Risk August 19, 2004

- Excluding changes in working capital, NiSource's average quarterly free cash flow after capital expenditures and dividends has been a negative $6.5 million over the 14 quarters since the beginning of 2001. With industrial natural gas demand down, we see few growth drivers for NI in coming years. At the same time, we believe it will be difficult to keep expenses down, given rising pension, insurance and health care costs. Longer term, we believe NiSource can produce about 3% average annual EPS growth, below the utility peer group average.

- Risks to our recommendation and target price include declines in Midwest power margins for Whiting Clean Energy, unusually mild winter and summer weather, weak economic growth, higher interest rates, high natural gas prices and their effect on consumption patterns, and delays in the proposed Millennium Pipeline Project.

- Based on our view of below-average EPS growth prospects, we believe NiSource should trade at a discount to peer valuations. We believe NI would be fairly valued at a 2005 P/E multiple of 12.9X (versus a regulated utility group average of over 13.8X). From this fair value, we look for appreciation in line with long-term EPS growth. Our 12-month target price is $22.

Key Stock Statistics

S&P Core EPS 2005E	1.56	52-week Range	$22.53-19.65
S&P Oper. EPS 2004E	1.60	12 Month P/E	13.3
P/E on S&P Oper. EPS 2004E	13.4	Beta	0.55
S&P Oper. EPS 2005E	1.65	Shareholders	42,034
Yield (%)	4.3%	Market Cap (B)	$ 5.7
Dividend Rate/Share	0.92	Shares Outstanding (M)	263.5

Value of $10,000 invested five years ago: **$ 12,934**

Dividend Data Dividends have been paid since 1987

Amount ($)	Date Decl.	Ex-Div. Date	Stock of Record	Payment Date
0.230	Jan. 05	Jan. 28	Jan. 30	Feb. 20 '04
0.230	Mar. 24	Apr. 28	Apr. 30	May. 20 '04
0.230	May. 11	Jul. 28	Jul. 30	Aug. 20 '04
0.230	Aug. 24	Oct. 27	Oct. 29	Nov. 19 '04

Revenues/Earnings Data Fiscal year ending December 31

Revenues (Million $)

	2004	2003	2002	2001	2000	1999
1Q	2,473	2,525	2,208	3,798	1,106	891.5
2Q	1,245	1,141	1,376	1,875	1,003	680.8
3Q	979.8	898.3	1,067	1,756	1,179	688.0
4Q	—	1,683	1,841	2,029	2,742	885.0
Yr.	—	6,247	6,492	9,459	6,031	3,145

Earnings Per Share ($)

	2004	2003	2002	2001	2000	1999
1Q	0.82	0.87	1.17	0.85	0.62	0.62
2Q	0.13	0.15	0.11	-0.06	0.17	0.18
3Q	0.08	0.09	0.12	-0.10	0.38	0.22
4Q	E0.57	0.53	0.59	0.32	Nil	0.25
Yr.	E1.60	1.63	2.00	1.01	1.08	1.27

Next earnings report expected: early-February Source: S&P, Company Reports
EPS Estimates based on S&P Operating Earnings; historical GAAP earnings are as reported.

NiSource Inc.

Recommendation: **HOLD** ★★★☆☆   12-Month Target Price: **$22.00** (as of April 30, 2004)

Business Summary August 20, 2004

NiSource is the third largest U.S. natural gas distributor (measured by customers served), the fourth largest owner of U.S. natural gas interstate pipelines (by route miles), and one of the largest owners of underground natural gas storage. It also provides electric utility services in northern Indiana. The company's operating divisions include Gas Distribution (45.2% of 2003 year-end segment assets), Gas Transmission and Storage (21.6%), Electric operations (22.8%) and Other operations (10.4%). Excluding losses from Other operations and corporate expense, segment operating income in 2003 was derived 43.2% from Gas Distribution, 34.0% from Gas Transmission and Storage, and 22.8% from Electric.

Gas Distribution operations provide gas utility service to nearly 3.3 million customers, in nine states. The division owns and operates 55,469 miles of pipeline, 30,429 acres of underground storage, and eight storage wells. In 2003, total sales and transportation volumes were 878.9 MDTH, down from 924.2 MDTH in 2002.

Gas Transmission and Storage operates 16,021 miles of interstate natural gas pipelines and 841,992 acres of underground storage. In 2003, total throughput was 1,238.9 MDTH, down from 1,314.3 MDTH in 2002. The division is working to develop the proposed Millennium Pipeline to access additional Canadian gas supply. Phase 1 of the Millennium project, a 186-mile section in New York state, is expected to be in service by November 2006.

Electric operations are conducted by NI's Northern Indiana subsidiary. At the end of 2003, Northern Indiana generated and distributed electricity for 437,375 electric utility customers. The utility operates three coal-fired plants (2,574 MW), five gas-fired plants (306 MW), and two hydroelectric plants (10 MW). In 2003, the utility generated 77.2% of its electric requirements, and purchased 22.8% .

Other operations include the Whiting Clean Energy project, a 525-MW gas-fired cogeneration plant, and various real estate holdings. After being placed into service in 2002, Whiting was unable to deliver originally projected levels of steam. Whiting lost about $30 million after taxes in 2003; as of March 2004, management expected similar results in 2004. The segment also owns NI's corporate headquarters and other Indiana residential and development property held for sale.

In March 2004, NI attributed a stabilization of its credit rating (which had been on negative credit watch) in 2003 to a 20% dividend cut announced July 2003, the sale of non-core assets, and the sale of common equity. During 2003, the company raised $586.5 million in cash from the sale of assets, and $344.1 million from the remarketing of convertible debt instruments in February 2003 (this also involved the issuance of 13.1 million common shares).

In January and August 2003, the company sold its exploration and production operations, for $425 million and the assumption of $213 million in liabilities for forward sales contracts. In October, NI sold its Primary Energy electric assets, for $325.4 million in cash and assumed debt.

Company Financials Fiscal Year ending December 31

Per Share Data ($)

(Year Ended December 31)	2003	2002	2001	2000	1999	1998	1997	1996	1995	1994
Tangible Bk. Val.	0.70	NM	NM	NM	9.88	9.20	9.59	9.17	8.96	8.64
Cash Flow	3.53	4.70	4.07	3.84	NA	NA	NA	NA	NA	NA
Earnings	1.63	2.00	1.01	1.08	1.27	1.59	1.53	1.44	1.36	1.24
S&P Core Earnings	1.67	1.43	0.32	NA	NA	NA	NA	NA	NA	NA
Dividends	1.10	1.16	1.16	1.08	1.02	0.96	0.90	0.84	0.78	0.72
Payout Ratio	67%	58%	115%	100%	80%	60%	59%	58%	57%	58%
Prices - High	21.97	24.99	32.55	31.50	30.93	33.75	24.93	20.12	19.25	16.50
- Low	16.39	14.51	18.25	12.75	16.37	24.65	19.00	17.62	14.62	13.06
P/E Ratio - High	13	12	32	29	24	21	16	14	14	13
- Low	10	7	18	12	13	16	12	12	11	11

Income Statement Analysis (Million $)

	2003	2002	2001	2000	1999	1998	1997	1996	1995	1994
Revs.	6,247	6,492	9,459	6,031	3,145	2,933	2,587	1,822	1,722	1,676
Oper. Inc.	1,116	1,203	1,009	568	773	678	660	612	594	553
Depr.	497	574	642	374	311	256	250	215	201	194
Int. Exp.	469	533	605	325	184	129	121	107	100	93.8
Pretax Inc.	662	680	416	298	NA	NA	NA	NA	NA	NA
Eff. Tax Rate	35.4%	34.4%	44.1%	43.7%	33.5%	34.2%	35.5%	38.6%	36.1%	33.2%
Net Inc.	426	426	212	147	160	194	191	177	175	164
S&P Core Earnings	437	305	67.9	NA	NA	NA	NA	NA	NA	NA

Balance Sheet & Other Fin. Data (Million $)

	2003	2002	2001	2000	1999	1998	1997	1996	1995	1994
Cash	27.3	56.2	128	193	NA	NA	NA	NA	NA	NA
Curr. Assets	2,063	1,869	2,567	4,918	NA	NA	NA	NA	NA	NA
Total Assets	16,624	16,897	17,374	19,697	NA	NA	NA	NA	NA	NA
Curr. Liab.	2,609	4,177	4,729	6,893	NA	NA	NA	NA	NA	NA
LT Debt	6,075	5,448	6,214	6,148	NA	NA	NA	NA	NA	NA
Common Equity	4,416	4,175	3,469	3,415	NA	NA	NA	NA	NA	NA
Total Cap.	10,490	11,581	11,515	11,483	4,903	3,725	2,370	142	3,191	3,174
Cap. Exp.	575	622	668	366	NA	NA	NA	NA	NA	NA
Cash Flow	923	1,000	854	521	NA	NA	NA	NA	NA	NA
Curr. Ratio	0.8	0.4	0.5	0.7	NA	NA	NA	NA	NA	NA
% LT Debt of Cap.	57.9	47.0	54.0	53.5	NA	NA	NA	NA	NA	NA
% Net Inc.of Revs.	6.8	6.6	2.2	2.4	NA	NA	NA	NA	NA	NA
% Ret. on Assets	2.5	2.5	1.1	1.1	NA	NA	NA	NA	NA	NA
% Ret. on Equity	9.9	11.1	6.2	6.2	NA	NA	NA	NA	NA	NA

Data as orig reptd.; bef. results of disc opers/spec. items. Per share data adj. for stk. divs.; EPS diluted. E-Estimated. NA-Not Available. NM-Not Meaningful. NR-Not Ranked. UR-Under Review.

Office: 801 East 86th Avenue, Merrillville, IN 46410-6272.
Telephone: 877-647-5990.
Email: questions@nisource.com
Website: http://www.nisource.com
Chrmn, Pres & CEO: G.L. Neale.
Vice Chrmn: S.P. Adik.

COO & EVP: S.W. Miller.
EVP & CFO: M.W. O'Donnell.
EVP & General Counsel: P.V. Fazio, Jr.
VP & Investor Contact: D.E. Senchak 219-647-6085.
Dirs: S. P. Adik, S. C. Beering, A. J. Decio, D. E. Foster, G. L. Neale, I. M. Rolland, J. W. Thompson, R. J. Welsh, C. Y. Woo, R. A. Young.

Founded: in 1912.
Domicile: Delaware.
Employees: 8,614.
S&P Analyst: Craig K. Shere, CFA /CB/GG

Noble Corp.

Recommendation: **HOLD** ★ ★ ★ ★
SELL | SELL | HOLD | BUY | BUY

12-Month Target Price: $49.00
(as of October 22, 2004)

NE has an approximate 0.06% weighting in the **S&P 500**

Sector: Energy
Sub-Industry: Oil & Gas Drilling
Peer Group: Oil & Gas - Offshore Drilling

Summary: NE principally provides contract drilling services for the oil and gas industry worldwide.

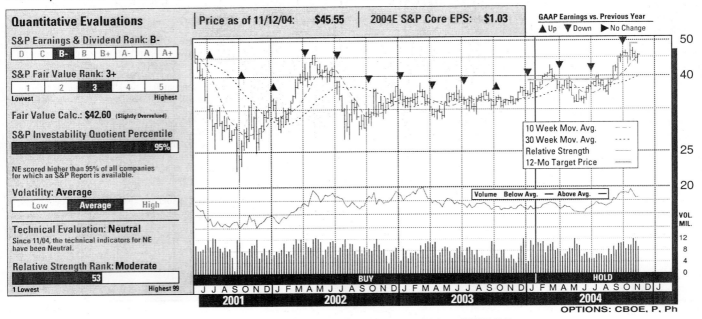

Quantitative Evaluations	**Price as of 11/12/04:**	**$45.55**	**2004E S&P Core EPS:**	**$1.03**

GAAP Earnings vs. Previous Year ▲ Up ▼ Down ► No Change

S&P Earnings & Dividend Rank: B-
D | C | B- | B | B+ | A- | A | A+

S&P Fair Value Rank: 3+
1 | 2 | **3** | 4 | 5
Lowest | | | | Highest

Fair Value Calc.: $42.60 (Slightly Overvalued)

S&P Investability Quotient Percentile 95%

NE scored higher than 95% of all companies for which an S&P Report is available.

Volatility: Average
Low | Average | High

Technical Evaluation: Neutral
Since 11/04, the technical indicators for NE have been Neutral.

Relative Strength Rank: Moderate
53
1 Lowest | Highest 99

Legend:
10 Week Mov. Avg.
30 Week Mov. Avg.
Relative Strength
12-Mo Target Price

Volume   Below Avg. — Above Avg.

BUY | HOLD

J J A S O N D | J F M A M J J A S O N D | J F M A M J J A S O N D | J F M A M J J A S O N D | J
2001 | 2002 | 2003 | 2004

VOL. MIL.
12
8
4
0

OPTIONS: CBOE, P, Ph

Analyst commentary prepared by Stewart Glickman/PMW/JWP

Highlights October 26, 2004

- Third quarter results declined from those of 2003, due in part to reduced utilization and dayrates in the North Sea, as well as a charge of $0.04 a share due to the impact of Hurricane Ivan in the Gulf of Mexico. The North Sea was weaker, year to year, but we think that fundamentals in the region have been strengthening recently, with the exception of Norway, where an ongoing strike has adversely affected rig demand. Results in West Africa were also stronger than in recent quarters, while the Middle East region remained very active.

- The average dayrate for NE's drilling rigs in international markets rose 1% sequentially, but declined 2.8% domestically. Lower domestic dayrates were offset by significantly higher utilization, which rose to 89% in the third quarter, from 79% in the second quarter. At the end of the third quarter, net debt was about 15% of total capitalization, about equal to the historical average, but below recent levels.

- We see the strongest ongoing improvement in international markets, led by the Middle East, West Africa, and the North Sea (excluding Norway). We expect overall operating margins to be flat to down slightly through the end of 2004, before widening in 2005. We see 2004 EPS of $1.08, followed by $2.02 in 2005. We project Standard & Poor's Core Earnings of $0.93 a share for 2004 and $1.89 for 2005.

Key Stock Statistics

S&P Core EPS 2005E	1.89	52-week Range	$48.00-33.29
S&P Oper. EPS 2004E	1.08	12 Month P/E	49.0
P/E on S&P Oper. EPS 2004E	42.2	Beta	0.97
S&P Oper. EPS 2005E	2.02	Shareholders	1,564
Yield (%)	Nil	Market Cap (B)	$ 6.2
Dividend Rate/Share	Nil	Shares Outstanding (M)	135.4

Value of $10,000 invested five years ago: **$ 16,948**

Dividend Data

No dividends have been paid on the common stock. Debt agreements currently prohibit payments. A stockholder rights plan was adopted in 1995.

Investment Rationale/Risk October 26, 2004

- We recommend holding the shares, which we view as fairly valued. The stock is trading at an enterprise value of 12.7X our 2005 EBITDA estimate, in line with the peer group average of 12.4X. On a price to operating cash flow basis, the share are trading at a 14.1X multiple, slightly above the 13.5X peer group average. We think a slight premium is warranted, in light of NE's relatively higher historical returns on capital employed (ROCE), as well as we what we view as a strong position in the Middle East, a region with what we regard as favorable drilling growth prospects.

- Risks to our recommendation and target price include a possible return to soft market conditions in the North Sea and West Africa; significant reductions in exploration and production spending by major oil producers and national oil companies; and lower oil and natural gas prices.

- We view favorably what we see as NE's solid returns on capital employed (ROCE), which we estimate at 7.1% for 2003, the highest among the company's peers. We expect high single-digit ROCE for 2005, above the peer average, and see this warranting a slight premium to peer valuations. Blending our projections for enterprise value to EBITDA, price to net equity, and price to operating cash flow metrics, our 12-month target price is $49.

Revenues/Earnings Data Fiscal year ending December 31

Revenues (Million $)

	2004	2003	2002	2001	2000	1999
1Q	245.4	245.0	235.5	222.4	184.8	180.1
2Q	253.0	247.9	247.4	246.7	230.7	175.5
3Q	265.6	254.7	234.7	272.8	225.9	176.8
4Q	—	239.8	251.1	260.5	241.2	173.5
Yr.	—	987.4	986.4	1,002	882.6	705.9

Earnings Per Share ($)

	2004	2003	2002	2001	2000	1999
1Q	0.21	0.30	0.39	0.40	0.19	0.20
2Q	0.26	0.33	0.43	0.50	0.32	0.21
3Q	0.23	0.40	0.37	0.58	0.33	0.19
4Q	E0.39	0.23	0.39	0.48	0.38	0.12
Yr.	E1.08	1.25	1.57	1.97	1.22	0.72

Next earnings report expected: late-January Source: S&P, Company Reports
EPS Estimates based on S&P Operating Earnings; historical GAAP earnings are as reported.

Noble Corporation

Recommendation: **HOLD** ★ ★ ★ ☆ ☆   12-Month Target Price: **$49.00** (as of October 22, 2004)

Business Summary October 26, 2004

In April 2002, Noble Drilling Corp. shareholders approved a corporate restructuring that effectively changed the company's place of incorporation from Delaware to the Cayman Islands. The restructuring was completed April 30, 2002, upon the merger of an indirect subsidiary of Noble Corp., a newly formed Cayman Islands company, with and into Noble Drilling. Noble Corp. (NE) became the parent holding company of Noble Drilling and the other companies in the Noble corporate group.

The company believes that the level of drilling activity and the number of announced discoveries in water depths greater than 5,000 ft. have increased significantly in recent years. Accordingly, NE has focused on increasing the number of rigs in its fleet capable of deepwater offshore drilling. It intends to expand international and offshore deepwater drilling capabilities through acquisitions, rig upgrades and modifications, and via redeployment of assets. A key to the company's deepwater strategy is the Noble EVA-4000 semisubmersible conversion program. The EVA-4000 is a proprietary design through which NE has converted submersible drilling rigs into ultra-deepwater semisubmersibles. The company believes the EVA-4000 program completes the conversion at a lower cost and more rapidly than new construction.

NE provides contract drilling services in offshore markets worldwide. The company has a fleet of 57 offshore drilling rigs, with options to purchase two additional jackup rigs in 2004. Currently owned rigs include floating deepwater units (including 13 semisubmersibles and three dynamically positioned drillships, seven of which are designed to operate in depths greater than 5,000 ft.), 37 independent leg, cantilever jackup rigs (including 26 premium units that operate in depths of 300 ft. or more, four that operate in depths of 360 ft. or more, and 11 that operate in water depths of 250 ft.), and three submersibles. Of these drilling units, nine can operate in harsh environments. Contract drilling operations (67% of 2003 contract drilling revenues originated outside the U.S.) accounted for 91% of total revenues in 2003; labor and turnkey contract drilling for 3%; and engineering, consulting and other for 6%.

At the end of 2003, over 65% of the company's fleet was deployed in international markets, including the North Sea, Brazil, West Africa, the Middle East, India and Venezuela.

In 2003, average utilization for NE's international fleet fell to 84%, from 95% in 2002, while U.S. utilization declined to 81%, from 84%. Dayrates for the international fleet dropped to $56,735, from $61,708, while for the U.S. fleet, dayrates increased to $70,457, from $58,802.

NE has continued to expand its technological applications for the drilling industry. In 2001, the company acquired for $6.56 million Maurer Engineering Inc., which was renamed Maurer Technology Inc., and was integrated into the Noble Engineering & Development Ltd. unit.

Company Financials Fiscal Year ending December 31

Per Share Data ($)

(Year Ended December 31)	2003	2002	2001	2000	1999	1998	1997	1996	1995	1994
Tangible Bk. Val.	16.31	14.90	13.44	11.80	10.60	10.00	8.77	7.01	4.48	4.53
Cash Flow	2.36	2.51	2.85	2.04	1.39	1.77	2.56	1.19	0.34	0.62
Earnings	1.25	1.57	1.97	1.22	0.72	1.23	1.98	0.66	-0.08	0.11
S&P Core Earnings	1.11	1.43	1.83	NA	NA	NA	NA	NA	NA	NA
Dividends	Nil	Nil	Nil	Nil	Nil	Nil	Nil	Nil	Nil	Nil
Payout Ratio	Nil	Nil	Nil	Nil	Nil	Nil	Nil	Nil	Nil	Nil
Prices - High	38.40	45.95	54.00	53.50	32.87	34.68	38.18	22.00	9.12	9.12
- Low	30.46	27.00	20.80	27.25	12.00	10.75	15.50	8.00	5.00	5.25
P/E Ratio - High	31	29	27	44	46	28	19	33	NM	83
- Low	24	17	11	22	17	9	8	12	NM	48

Income Statement Analysis (Million $)

	2003	2002	2001	2000	1999	1998	1997	1996	1995	1994
Revs.	987	986	1,002	883	706	788	713	514	328	352
Oper. Inc.	366	400	503	379	245	301	261	128	47.7	66.5
Depr. Depl. & Amort.	148	125	119	111	89.0	72.0	77.9	52.2	36.5	39.5
Int. Exp.	40.3	42.6	47.8	54.6	33.1	5.20	12.9	18.8	12.2	12.4
Pretax Inc.	187	243	350	226	124	231	380	102	4.87	27.0
Eff. Tax Rate	11.0%	13.9%	24.6%	26.8%	24.3%	29.8%	30.5%	22.2%	67.2%	21.0%
Net Inc.	166	210	264	166	95.3	162	264	79.3	1.59	21.5
S&P Core Earnings	148	190	245	NA	NA	NA	NA	NA	NA	NA

Balance Sheet & Other Fin. Data (Million $)

	2003	2002	2001	2000	1999	1998	1997	1996	1995	1994
Cash	139	274	288	177	137	217	66.4	174	64.5	145
Curr. Assets	422	466	494	379	291	438	265	388	188	240
Total Assets	3,190	3,066	2,751	2,596	2,432	2,179	1,506	1,367	741	740
Curr. Liab.	244	281	208	205	233	350	153	152	86.4	82.3
LT Debt	542	590	550	650	731	461	138	240	130	127
Common Equity	2,178	1,989	1,778	1,577	1,398	1,310	1,149	925	519	352
Total Cap.	2,927	2,779	2,526	2,372	2,197	1,828	1,351	1,216	654	655
Cap. Exp.	307	268	134	125	422	541	391	217	91.2	56.0
Cash Flow	315	335	382	276	184	234	342	132	30.9	48.3
Curr. Ratio	1.7	1.7	2.4	1.8	1.2	1.3	1.7	2.6	2.2	2.9
% LT Debt of Cap.	18.5	21.2	21.8	27.4	33.3	25.2	10.2	19.7	19.9	19.3
% Ret. on Assets	5.3	7.2	9.9	6.6	4.1	8.8	18.4	7.5	0.2	2.8
% Ret. on Equity	8.0	11.1	15.7	11.1	7.0	13.2	25.5	10.9	NM	2.3

Data as orig reptd.; bef. results of disc opers/spec. items. Per share data adj. for stk. divs. Bold denotes primary EPS - prior periods restated. E-Estimated. NA-Not Available. NM-Not Meaningful. NR-Not Ranked. UR-Under Review.

Office: 13135 South Dairy Ashford, Sugar Land, TX 77478.
Telephone: 281-276-6100.
Website: http://www.noblecorp.com
Chrmn & CEO: J.C. Day.
SVP & CFO: M.A. Jackson.

SVP & Secy: J.J. Robertson.
VP & Investor Contact: J.T. Rynd 281-276-6100.
Dirs: M. A. Cawley, L. J. Chazen, L. R. Corbett, J. C. Day, M. E. Leland, J. E. Little, M. P. Ricciardello, W. A. Sears.
Auditor: PricewaterhouseCoopers.

Founded: in 1939.
Domicile: Cayman Islands.
Employees: 3,364.
S&P Analyst: Stewart Glickman/PMW/JWP

STANDARD &POOR'S

Nordstrom, Inc.

Recommendation: **HOLD** ★★★★ **12-Month Target Price: $47.00**
SELL SELL HOLD BUY BUY
(as of November 04, 2004)

JWN has an approximate 0.06% weighting in the **S&P 500**

Sector: Consumer Discretionary
Sub-Industry: Department Stores
Peer Group: Department Store Cos. - Larger

Summary: This Seattle-based specialty retailer of apparel and accessories, widely known for its emphasis on service, operates about 150 stores in 27 states.

Quantitative Evaluations

S&P Earnings & Dividend Rank: B+

| D | C | B- | B | B+ | A- | A | A+ |

S&P Fair Value Rank: 4-

| 1 | 2 | 3 | 4 | 5 |
| Lowest | | | | Highest |

Fair Value Calc.: $45.80 (Fairly Valued)

S&P Investability Quotient Percentile

97%

JWN scored higher than 97% of all companies for which an S&P Report is available.

Volatility: Average

| Low | Average | High |

Technical Evaluation: Bullish

Since 10/04, the technical indicators for JWN have been Bullish.

Relative Strength Rank: Strong

77

1 Lowest | Highest 99

| Price as of 11/12/04: | $45.72 | 2005E S&P Core EPS: | $2.48 |

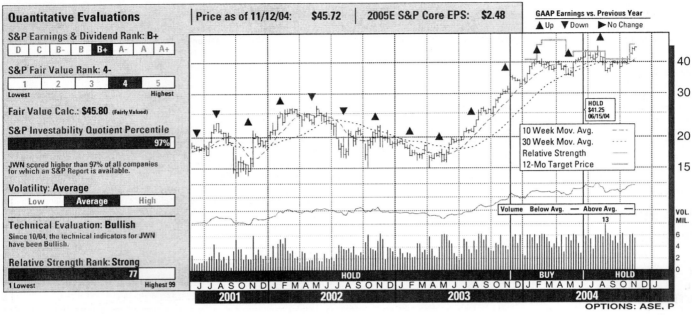

GAAP Earnings vs. Previous Year
▲ Up ▼ Down ► No Change

HOLD $41.25 06/15/04

10 Week Mov. Avg.
30 Week Mov. Avg.
Relative Strength
12-Mo Target Price

Volume Below Avg. ▬ Above Avg.

VOL. MIL.

HOLD | BUY | HOLD

J J A S O N D J F M A M J J A S O N D J F M A M J J A S O N D J F M A M J J A S O N D J
2001 | 2002 | 2003 | 2004

OPTIONS: ASE, P

Analyst commentary prepared by Jason N. Asaeda/MF/GG

Highlights August 25, 2004

- We see net sales rising about 6.5% in FY 05 (Jan.), to $6.9 billion, with about $6.6 billion of retail sales and $300 million of Internet sales. Retail sales are expected to reflect a mid single-digit same-store sales increase and the opening of two full-line stores. We see sales likely to be driven by the inclusion of more color, fashion and newness in apparel assortments, better merchandise flow to stores, and superior customer service levels.

- Earnings before interest and taxes (EBIT) margins should widen, on supply chain initiatives, greater sales leverage, and productivity gains from technology investments, partly offset by incremental new store expenses and higher incentive compensation costs. Factoring lower interest expense and service charge income from the credit card operation (which JWN does not consider to be a profit center), we look for pretax margins to increase 240 basis points, to 8.5%.

- After modest share dilution, we expect FY 05 operating EPS of $2.48, and Standard & Poor's Core Earnings per share of $2.40; the difference mainly reflects estimated option expense.

Investment Rationale/Risk August 25, 2004

- We would hold the shares, based on valuation. In our view, JWN has made considerable headway with a turnaround since early FY 04, mainly due to investment in a perpetual inventory management system that the company says has enabled it to better serve customers, measure each store's potential, and maintain and reinforce collaboration among stores and merchants. We think this bodes well for potentially sustainable sales and earnings growth in coming years, as JWN more accurately forecasts trends and plans inventory and expenses.

- Risks to our recommendation and target price include a possible decline in consumer spending due to geopolitical and economic uncertainties. Investors should also note that in the early stages of a period of rising interest rates, retail stocks have tended to underperform.

- We calculate intrinsic value of $40, using our DCF model, which assumes a cost of capital of 13% and a terminal growth rate of 5%. Our 12-month target price of $41 reflects the stock's two-year historical forward P/E of 15X our $2.80 FY 06 operating EPS estimate, and our DCF analysis.

Key Stock Statistics

S&P Core EPS 2006E	2.80	52-week Range	$46.30-29.76
S&P Oper. EPS 2005E	2.55	12 Month P/E	19.8
P/E on S&P Oper. EPS 2005E	17.9	Beta	1.56
S&P Oper. EPS 2006E	2.95	Shareholders	75,717
Yield (%)	1.1%	Market Cap (B)	$ 6.5
Dividend Rate/Share	0.52	Shares Outstanding (M)	141.4

Value of $10,000 invested five years ago: **$ 21,008**

Dividend Data Dividends have been paid since 1971

Amount ($)	Date Decl.	Ex-Div. Date	Stock of Record	Payment Date
0.110	Nov. 18	Nov. 25	Nov. 28	Dec. 15 '03
0.110	Feb. 18	Feb. 25	Feb. 27	Mar. 15 '04
0.110	May. 18	May. 26	May. 28	Jun. 15 '04
0.130	Aug. 19	Aug. 27	Aug. 31	Sep. 15 '04

Revenues/Earnings Data Fiscal year ending January 31

Revenues (Million $)

	2005	2004	2003	2002	2001	2000
1Q	1,535	1,344	1,246	1,218	1,146	1,039
2Q	1,953	1,795	1,656	1,546	1,449	1,443
3Q	—	1,421	1,323	1,239	1,254	1,110
4Q	—	1,933	1,751	1,632	1,656	1,532
Yr.	—	6,492	5,975	5,634	5,529	5,124

Earnings Per Share ($)

	2005	2004	2003	2002	2001	2000
1Q	0.48	0.20	-0.08	0.18	0.25	0.22
2Q	0.75	0.48	0.27	0.29	0.35	0.51
3Q	E0.45	0.33	0.14	0.08	-0.03	0.25
4Q	E0.87	0.74	0.44	0.38	0.20	0.50
Yr.	E2.55	1.76	0.76	0.92	0.78	1.46

Next earnings report expected: late-November Source: S&P, Company Reports
EPS Estimates based on S&P Operating Earnings; historical GAAP earnings are as reported.

Nordstrom, Inc.

Recommendation: **HOLD** ★ ★ ★ ☆ ☆   12-Month Target Price: **$47.00** (as of November 04, 2004)

Business Summary August 25, 2004

Nordstrom was founded in 1901 by John W. Nordstrom with his profits from the Gold Rush of 1897. The company began with a single small shoe store in Seattle, WA. As of May 2004, it was operating 93 Nordstrom fashion specialty stores from Alaska to Virginia, selling full lines of medium to upscale apparel, shoes and accessories for women, men and children. JWN was also operating 49 Nordstrom Rack clearance and off-price stores, five Faconnable boutiques, a freestanding shoe store in Hawaii, and one clearance store under the name Last Chance. In addition, the company was operating 31 international Faconnable boutiques, mostly in Europe, and has a direct sales division.

The ambience for full-line stores is upscale, with an emphasis on customer service. The stores feature a wide selection of style, size and color in each merchandise category. Nordstrom Rack stores purchase merchandise directly from manufacturers, and also serve as outlets for clearance merchandise from the company's full-line stores.

Faconnable, which was acquired in 2000 for $169 million, is a wholesaler and retailer of men's and women's apparel and accessories. The Nordstrom.com subsidiary includes the company's Internet and catalog businesses. In May 2002, JWN acquired the minority stake in Nordstrom.com owned by Benchmark Capital Partners and Madron Investment Group, for $70 million.

Merchandise category sales in FY 04 (Jan.) were: 36% women's apparel; 20% shoes; 19% women's accessories; 17% men's apparel and furnishings; 4% chil-dren's apparel and accessories; and 4% other. Sales per sq. ft. increased to $327 in FY 04 from $319 in FY 03.

JWN's operations are seasonal. The second quarter, which includes the company's Anniversary Sales, accounts for about 28% of annual net sales. The fourth quarter, which includes the holiday season, accounts for about 30% of annual net sales.

The company has expanded its use of information systems to provide greater flexibility in merchandising and responding to customer needs. Detailed sales information is available in all full-line stores. JWN began implementation of a perpetual inventory system in 2002, and is replacing its point of sale system; it expects this to be substantially completed by the fall of 2004.

JWN opened four full-line stores and two Rack stores in FY 04, increasing its retail square footage by 4%, to about 19.1 million sq. ft. The company plans to spend $725 million to $775 million over the next three years on capital projects, including $240 million to $250 million in FY 04. In comparison to the previous three years, JWN plans to open fewer stores, slow spending on information systems, and increase spending on improvement of existing facilities.

In 1995, directors authorized $1.1 billion of share buybacks. The company had purchased 39 million shares, for a total of $1 billion, as of January 31, 2004. Purchase authority of $82 million remained.

Company Financials Fiscal Year ending January 31

Per Share Data ($)

(Year Ended January 31)	2004	2003	2002	2001	2000	1999	1998	1997	1996	1995
Tangible Bk. Val.	10.79	9.09	8.75	8.12	8.98	9.26	9.67	9.25	8.77	8.17
Cash Flow	3.57	2.49	2.55	2.33	2.88	2.63	2.23	1.88	1.83	1.91
Earnings	1.76	0.76	0.92	0.78	1.46	1.41	1.20	0.91	1.01	1.24
S&P Core Earnings	1.67	0.62	0.80	0.83	NA	NA	NA	NA	NA	NA
Dividends	0.41	0.38	0.35	0.32	0.35	0.30	0.27	0.25	0.25	0.19
Payout Ratio	23%	50%	38%	41%	24%	21%	22%	27%	25%	16%

Cal. Yrs.	2003	2002	2001	2000	1999	1998	1997	1996	1995	1994
Prices - High	35.50	26.87	22.97	34.50	44.81	40.37	34.09	26.75	22.62	24.87
- Low	15.00	15.60	13.80	14.12	21.68	21.42	16.93	17.12	17.50	15.50
P/E Ratio - High	20	35	25	44	31	29	28	29	22	20
- Low	9	20	15	18	15	15	14	19	17	13

Income Statement Analysis (Million $)

	2004	2003	2002	2001	2000	1999	1998	1997	1996	1995
Revs.	6,492	5,975	5,634	5,529	5,124	5,028	4,852	4,453	4,114	3,987
Oper. Inc.	585	424	363	335	467	458	393	310	321	475
Depr.	251	234	218	203	194	180	160	156	134	111
Int. Exp.	91.0	86.2	73.5	63.0	54.0	49.0	35.5	45.6	46.7	39.1
Pretax Inc.	398	196	204	167	332	338	307	244	272	336
Eff. Tax Rate	39.0%	47.1%	39.0%	38.9%	38.9%	38.8%	39.4%	39.3%	39.4%	39.5%
Net Inc.	243	104	125	102	203	207	186	148	165	203
S&P Core Earnings	229	83.9	107	109	NA	NA	NA	NA	NA	NA

Balance Sheet & Other Fin. Data (Million $)

	2004	2003	2002	2001	2000	1999	1998	1997	1996	1995
Cash	476	208	331	25.0	27.0	241	24.8	28.3	24.5	32.5
Curr. Assets	2,455	2,073	2,055	1,813	1,565	1,680	1,595	1,532	1,613	1,398
Total Assets	4,466	4,096	4,049	3,608	3,062	3,115	2,865	2,703	2,733	2,397
Curr. Liab.	1,050	870	948	951	867	769	943	787	832	690
LT Debt	1,605	1,342	1,351	1,100	747	805	320	329	366	298
Common Equity	1,634	1,372	1,314	1,229	1,185	1,317	1,475	1,473	1,423	1,344
Total Cap.	3,239	2,714	2,666	2,329	1,932	2,122	1,775	1,915	1,789	1,642
Cap. Exp.	258	328	390	321	305	291	260	204	253	232
Cash Flow	494	338	342	305	397	387	346	304	299	314
Curr. Ratio	2.3	2.4	2.2	1.9	1.8	2.2	1.7	1.9	1.9	2.0
% LT Debt of Cap.	49.5	49.4	50.7	47.2	38.7	37.9	17.8	17.2	20.5	18.1
% Net Inc.of Revs.	3.7	1.7	2.2	1.8	4.0	4.1	3.8	3.3	4.0	5.1
% Ret. on Assets	5.7	2.5	3.3	3.1	6.6	6.9	6.7	5.4	6.4	8.9
% Ret. on Equity	16.2	7.7	9.8	8.5	16.3	14.8	12.6	10.2	11.9	16.2

Data as orig reptd.; bef. results of disc opers/spec. items. Per share data adj. for stk. divs.; EPS diluted (primary prior to 1998). E-Estimated. NA-Not Available. NM-Not Meaningful. NR-Not Ranked. UR-Under Review.

Office: 1617 Sixth Avenue, Seattle, WA 98101-1707.
Telephone: 206-628-2111.
Email: invrelations@nordstrom.com
Website: http://www.nordstrom.com
Chrmn: B.A. Nordstrom.
Pres: B.W. Nordstrom.

EVP & CFO: M.G. Koppel.
VP & Secy: D.L. Mackie.
Investor Contact: S. Allen 206-303-3200.
Dirs: D. W. Gittinger, E. Hernandez, Jr., J. P. Jackson, J. A. McMillan, B. A. Nordstrom, J. N. Nordstrom, A. E. Osborne, Jr., W. D. Ruckel-shaus, A. A. Winter.

Founded: in 1901.
Domicile: Washington.
Employees: 46,000.
S&P Analyst: Jason N. Asaeda/MF/GG

Norfolk Southern

Recommendation: **HOLD** ★★★☆   12-Month Target Price: **$32.00**
(as of October 20, 2004)

NSC has an approximate 0.12% weighting in the **S&P 500**

Sector: Industrials
Sub-Industry: Railroads
Peer Group: Railroads (U.S.) - Major

Summary: This railroad operates 21,500 route miles serving 22 Eastern states and Canada, and owns a 58% stake in Conrail.

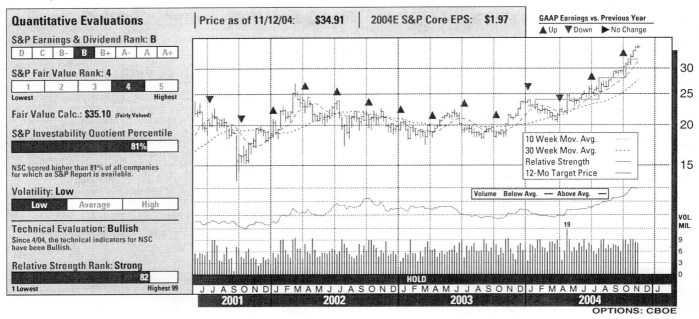

Quantitative Evaluations	Price as of 11/12/04: **$34.91**	2004E S&P Core EPS: **$1.97**

S&P Earnings & Dividend Rank: B

| D | C | B- | **B** | B+ | A- | A | A+ |

S&P Fair Value Rank: 4

| 1 | 2 | 3 | **4** | 5 |
| Lowest | | | | Highest |

Fair Value Calc.: $35.10 (Fairly Valued)

S&P Investability Quotient Percentile
81%

NSC scored higher than 81% of all companies for which an S&P Report is available.

Volatility: Low

| **Low** | Average | High |

Technical Evaluation: Bullish
Since 4/04, the technical indicators for NSC have been Bullish.

Relative Strength Rank: Strong
82
1 Lowest   Highest 99

GAAP Earnings vs. Previous Year
▲ Up ▼ Down ► No Change

10 Week Mov. Avg.
30 Week Mov. Avg.
Relative Strength
12-Mo Target Price

Volume Below Avg. — Above Avg. ▬

HOLD

J J A S O N D | J F M A M J J A S O N D | J F M A M J J A S O N D | J F M A M J J A S O N D | J
2001   2002   2003   2004

OPTIONS: CBOE

Analyst commentary prepared by Andrew West, CFA /PMW

Highlights October 21, 2004

- We project revenue increases of 12% in 2004 and 5% in 2005. We see an anticipated growing economy boosting general merchandise shipments, and expect the company to benefit from some improvement in price levels. We expect intermodal revenue to lead the growth in 2004, with an advance of about 20%, reflecting recent new service offerings that we think will help convert highway shipping to rail. We see coal revenues up 14%, boosted by price increases, export volumes, and utility inventory building. We believe that what we view as NSC's superior system speed and service may help boost market share.

- We expect margins to reach 22% in 2004, above the five-year average of 16%, benefiting from improved rail service and asset utilization, and only moderate increases in compensation and fuel expenses. We expect interest expense to decrease, as NSC continues to cut debt.

- We forecast 2004 operating EPS of $2.20, followed by an increase of 11% in 2005, to $2.45. We project 2004 Standard & Poor's Core EPS of $1.97, after estimated option and pension expenses. We expect two charges recorded in 2003 to lead to a reduction of certain costs reported in 2004, reducing our estimate of earnings quality.

Investment Rationale/Risk October 21, 2004

- We believe the shares are fairly valued, based on our longer-term growth outlook for NSC. Over the next six years, we expect annual revenue growth to average about 5%. We anticipate widening operating profit margins, stabilizing at about 20% for the longer term, generating 15% annualized earnings growth, and an increasing dividend over the next six years. We project 2004 free cash flow exceeding $1.3 billion, followed by a slight decline over the ensuing five years, on an expected rise in capital expenditure requirements.

- Risks to our opinion and target price include unfavorable fuel prices, weaker than expected economic and freight demand growth, legal and regulatory risks, declining railroad system fluidity, weather, and rising interest rates.

- Our discounted cash flow model, which assumes an 8% cost of capital and 3% terminal growth, estimates intrinsic value of $28. Our relative valuation model, which relates historical peer group valuations to profitability and leverage, targets a forward price to sales multiple of 1.9X, or $37. Blending our models, we arrive at our 12-month target price of $32.

Key Stock Statistics

S&P Core EPS 2005E	2.26	52-week Range	$35.59-20.38
S&P Oper. EPS 2004E	2.20	12 Month P/E	19.5
P/E on S&P Oper. EPS 2004E	15.9	Beta	0.52
S&P Oper. EPS 2005E	2.45	Shareholders	52,091
Yield (%)	1.1%	Market Cap (B)	$ 13.8
Dividend Rate/Share	0.40	Shares Outstanding (M)	396.0

Value of $10,000 invested five years ago: **$ 16,468**

Dividend Data Dividends have been paid since 1901

Amount ($)	Date Decl.	Ex-Div. Date	Stock of Record	Payment Date
0.080	Apr. 26	May. 05	May. 07	Jun. 10 '04
0.100	Jul. 27	Aug. 04	Aug. 06	Sep. 10 '04
0.100	Jul. 27	Aug. 04	Aug. 06	Sep. 10 '04
0.100	Oct. 25	Nov. 03	Nov. 05	Dec. 10 '04

Revenues/Earnings Data Fiscal year ending December 31

Revenues (Million $)

	2004	2003	2002	2001	2000	1999
1Q	1,693	1,561	1,498	1,540	1,508	1,030
2Q	1,813	1,633	1,593	1,592	1,592	1,194
3Q	1,857	1,598	1,598	1,508	1,535	1,500
4Q	—	1,676	1,581	1,530	1,524	1,471
Yr.	—	6,468	6,270	6,170	6,159	5,195

Earnings Per Share ($)

	2004	2003	2002	2001	2000	1999
1Q	0.40	0.54	0.22	0.16	-0.12	0.30
2Q	0.54	0.35	0.31	0.28	0.30	0.20
3Q	0.72	0.35	0.32	0.20	0.26	0.05
4Q	E0.66	0.13	0.33	0.30	0.01	0.08
Yr.	E2.20	1.05	1.18	0.94	0.45	0.63

Next earnings report expected: late-January Source: S&P, Company Reports
EPS Estimates based on S&P Operating Earnings; historical GAAP earnings are as reported.

Recommendation: **HOLD** ★ ★ ★ ☆ ☆   12-Month Target Price: **$32.00** (as of October 20, 2004)

Business Summary October 21, 2004

Norfolk Southern provides rail transportation service in the eastern U.S, with an extensive intermodal network and a significant automotive business. NSC owns 58% of Conrail's shares, with CSX holding the remainder, and holds 50% voting rights. NSC and CSX operate certain separate portions of Conrail's rail routes and assets. NSC's non-rail activities includes real estate, natural resources, and telecommunications.

In June 2003, NSC and CSX filed a joint petition with the Surface Transportation Board (STB) seeking to establish direct ownership and control of the Conrail subsidiaries currently operated by CSX and NSC. Under the proposed transaction, CSX would directly own the New York Central Line, and NSC would directly own the Pennsylvania Line. Completion of the transaction was subject both to STB approval and to an IRS ruling qualifying it as a non-taxable disposition.

As of December 31, 2003, NSC's rail network encompassed 21,500 miles in 22 states and Ontario, Canada. Most of the Conrail lines acquired were located in the Northeast and Midwest. In addition, NSC and CSX Transportation share Conrail lines in New York/New Jersey, the Monongahela coal fields of Pennsylvania, and Detroit. Access to Conrail's Pennsylvania line increased the size of NSC's service system by nearly 50%, and provided access to major ports in the Northeast.

Technically, the company leases routes from Conrail Inc. NSC makes lease and rent payments to Conrail for use of that company's assets. For income statement

purposes, NSC records a charge ($419 million in 2003) that is net of equity income from Conrail.

Total revenue ton miles rose 2.2% in 2003, to 183 billion, while revenue per ton mile rose 0.9%, to $.0353. As of December 31, 2003, the average age of NSC's 2,572 unit locomotive fleet was 15.3 years, and that of its 75,485 unit freight car fleet was 26.6 years.

Coal, coke, and iron ore has been the largest commodity group in terms of revenues (23% of rail operating revenues in each 2003 and 2002). The company handled a total of 172 million tons of coal, coke, and iron ore in 2003.

NSC's intermodal traffic accounted for 19% of 2003 and 2002 revenues, with about 45% representing international shipments. Shipments for truckload carriers grew in response to driver shortages and trucking capacity constraints.

General merchandise freight consists of automotive (14% and 15% of rail operating revenues in 2003 and 2002, respectively), chemicals (12%, 12%), metals and construction (11%, 11%), paper, clay and forest products (10%, 10%), and agriculture, consumer products, and government (11%, 10%).

Non-transportation activities include telecommunications; acquisition and leasing of coal, oil, gas and timberlands; commercial real estate; and leasing or sale of rail property and equipment.

Company Financials Fiscal Year ending December 31

Per Share Data ($)

(Year Ended December 31)	2003	2002	2001	2000	1999	1998	1997	1996	1995	1994
Tangible Bk. Val.	17.83	16.71	15.78	15.17	15.53	15.61	14.44	13.27	12.48	11.73
Cash Flow	2.40	2.50	2.27	1.80	1.91	2.83	2.98	3.15	2.87	2.62
Earnings	1.05	1.18	0.94	0.45	0.63	1.65	1.84	2.03	1.81	1.63
S&P Core Earnings	0.95	0.70	0.41	NA	NA	NA	NA	NA	NA	NA
Dividends	0.30	0.26	0.24	0.80	0.80	0.80	0.80	0.75	0.69	0.64
Payout Ratio	29%	22%	26%	178%	127%	48%	43%	37%	38%	39%
Prices - High	24.62	26.98	24.11	22.75	36.43	41.75	38.12	32.20	27.20	24.91
- Low	17.35	17.20	13.41	11.93	19.62	27.43	28.20	25.45	20.16	19.50
P/E Ratio - High	23	23	26	51	58	25	21	16	15	15
- Low	17	15	14	27	31	17	15	13	11	12

Income Statement Analysis (Million $)

	2003	2002	2001	2000	1999	1998	1997	1996	1995	1994
Revs.	6,468	6,270	6,170	6,159	5,195	4,221	4,223	4,770	4,668	4,642
Oper. Inc.	1,592	1,158	1,521	1,150	1,207	1,502	1,645	1,626	1,500	1,519
Depr.	528	515	514	517	489	450	432	429	414	404
Int. Exp.	497	518	553	551	561	516	385	159	152	139
Pretax Inc.	586	706	553	250	351	845	998	1,197	1,115	1,049
Eff. Tax Rate	29.9%	34.8%	34.5%	31.2%	31.9%	25.4%	30.0%	35.6%	36.1%	36.3%
Net Inc.	411	460	362	172	239	630	699	770	713	668
S&P Core Earnings	365	270	155	NA	NA	NA	NA	NA	NA	NA

Balance Sheet & Other Fin. Data (Million $)

	2003	2002	2001	2000	1999	1998	1997	1996	1995	1994
Cash	284	184	204	Nil	37.0	5.00	34.0	403	329	307
Curr. Assets	1,425	1,299	1,047	849	1,371	913	1,103	1,457	1,343	1,338
Total Assets	20,596	19,956	19,418	18,976	19,250	18,180	17,350	11,416	10,905	10,588
Curr. Liab.	1,801	1,853	2,386	1,887	1,924	1,117	1,093	1,190	1,206	1,132
LT Debt	6,800	7,006	7,027	7,339	7,556	7,483	7,398	1,800	1,553	1,548
Common Equity	6,976	6,500	6,090	5,824	5,932	5,921	5,445	4,978	4,829	4,685
Total Cap.	17,008	16,561	15,943	15,958	16,225	15,998	15,372	6,827	8,733	8,494
Cap. Exp.	720	689	746	731	912	956	875	688	659	713
Cash Flow	939	975	876	689	728	1,080	1,131	1,199	1,127	1,072
Curr. Ratio	0.8	0.7	0.4	0.4	0.7	0.8	1.0	1.2	1.1	1.2
% LT Debt of Cap.	40.0	42.3	44.1	46.0	46.6	46.8	48.1	26.4	17.8	18.2
% Net Inc.of Revs.	6.4	7.3	5.9	2.8	4.6	14.9	16.6	16.1	15.3	14.4
% Ret. on Assets	2.0	2.3	1.9	0.9	1.3	3.5	4.9	6.9	6.7	6.5
% Ret. on Equity	6.1	7.3	6.1	2.9	4.0	11.1	13.4	15.7	15.0	14.6

Data as orig reptd.; bef. results of disc opers/spec. items. Per share data adj. for stk. divs.; EPS diluted. E-Estimated. NA-Not Available. NM-Not Meaningful. NR-Not Ranked. UR-Under Review.

Office: Three Commercial Place, Norfolk, VA 23510-2191.
Telephone: 757-629-2680.
Website: http://www.nscorp.com
Chrmn & CEO: D.R. Goode.
Pres: C.W. Moorman.
Vice Chrmn: L.I. Prillaman.

Vice Chrmn & COO: S.C. Tobias.
Vice Chrmn & CFO: H.C. Wolf.
Investor Contact: L. McGruder 757-629-2861.
Dirs: G. L. Baliles, G. R. Carter, A. D. Correll, D. R. Goode, L. Hilliard, B. M. Joyce, S. F. Leer, J. M. O'Brien, H. W. Pote, J. P. Reason.

Founded: in 1980.
Domicile: Virginia.
Employees: 28,753.
S&P Analyst: Andrew West, CFA /PMW

Northern Trust Corp.

Recommendation: **BUY** ★★★★☆
SELL | SELL | HOLD | BUY | BUY

12-Month Target Price: **$47.00**
(as of October 29, 2004)

NTRS has an approximate 0.09% weighting in the **S&P 500**

Sector: Financials
Sub-Industry: Asset Management & Custody Banks
Peer Group: Financial Services - Diversified

Summary: Chicago-based Northern Trust is a leading provider of fiduciary, asset management and private banking services.

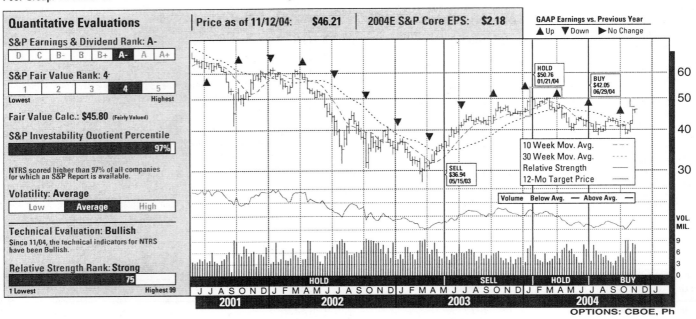

Quantitative Evaluations

S&P Earnings & Dividend Rank: A-
D | C | B- | B | B+ | **A-** | A | A+

S&P Fair Value Rank: 4
1 | 2 | 3 | **4** | 5
Lowest | | | | Highest

Fair Value Calc.: $45.80 (Fairly Valued)

S&P Investability Quotient Percentile
97%

NTRS scored higher than 97% of all companies for which an S&P Report is available.

Volatility: Average
Low | **Average** | High

Technical Evaluation: Bullish
Since 11/04, the technical indicators for NTRS have been Bullish.

Relative Strength Rank: Strong
75
1 Lowest | Highest 99

Price as of 11/12/04: $46.21 | **2004E S&P Core EPS:** $2.18

GAAP Earnings vs. Previous Year
▲ Up   ▼ Down   ► No Change

Analyst commentary prepared by Evan Momios, CFA /MF/JWP

Highlights November 01, 2004

- Better than expected investment asset growth, stronger equity market performance than in recent years, new business wins, and expense control continued to support operating results in the first nine months of 2004. We believe benign equity market conditions in the quarters ahead and new business wins will continue to support revenue growth primarily from higher trust fees. Rising interest rates are likely to boost revenue in 2005, in our view. We estimate net interest income to account for about 26% of total revenue in 2004 and 2005, compared to approximately 28% in 2003.

- We see expenses remaining under control. In our view, the company's credit quality is strong enough to justify our expectation for limited loan loss provision requirements in the remainder of 2004 and into 2005, assuming that economic growth sustains its current pace.

- Overall, excluding third-quarter 2004 litigation charges, we see operating EPS advancing to $2.32 in 2004, and to $2.55 in 2005, from $1.89 in 2003, reflecting the benefits of a strong economy and what we expect to be better equity market conditions than in recent years. Our S&P Core EPS estimates are $2.18 and $2.51 for 2004 and 2005, respectively, reflecting stock option and pension related adjustments.

Investment Rationale/Risk November 01, 2004

- We believe NTRS shares merit an accumulate recommendation on a total return basis, based on the stock's low valuation compared to historical levels and our view of the company's improving operating outlook versus recent years. We believe the company's leading position in the affluent market, and its focus in ultra wealthy clients, will result in above peer average revenue growth in a stable or modestly rising equity market.

- Risks to our recommendation and target price include a significant decline in economic activity, a serious geopolitical event that could impact equity markets, legal and regulatory risks.

- The shares were recently trading at about 18X our 2004 operating EPS estimate, compared to 21X and 25X 12-month forward EPS, on average, during the past three and five years, respectively. Our 12-month target price of $47 is equal to approximately 18.5X our 2005 EPS estimate, and assumes modest P/E multiple expansion from current levels. Although our outlook for asset managers and custody banks remains positive, our enthusiasm is moderated by a number of macro-economic and geopolitical uncertainties that could result in mixed equity market performance in the intermediate future, and consequently could increase the stock's volatility and restrain the company's revenue growth.

Key Stock Statistics

S&P Core EPS 2005E	2.51	52-week Range	**$51.35-38.40**
S&P Oper. EPS 2004E	2.32	12 Month P/E	20.6
P/E on S&P Oper. EPS 2004E	19.9	Beta	1.13
S&P Oper. EPS 2005E	2.55	Shareholders	3,288
Yield (%)	1.6%	Market Cap (B)	$ 10.1
Dividend Rate/Share	0.76	Shares Outstanding (M)	219.2

Value of $10,000 invested five years ago: **$ 9,780**

Dividend Data Dividends have been paid since 1896

Amount ($)	Date Decl.	Ex-Div. Date	Stock of Record	Payment Date
0.190	Nov. 18	Dec. 08	Dec. 10	Jan. 02 '04
0.190	Feb. 17	Mar. 08	Mar. 10	Apr. 01 '04
0.190	Apr. 20	Jun. 08	Jun. 10	Jul. 01 '04
0.190	Jul. 19	Sep. 08	Sep. 10	Oct. 01 '04

Revenues/Earnings Data Fiscal year ending December 31

Revenues (Million $)

	2004	2003	2002	2001	2000	1999
1Q	680.9	630.2	714.2	882.9	798.2	656.3
2Q	695.9	671.3	719.3	560.7	892.8	672.3
3Q	686.7	645.9	678.6	785.9	923.2	710.7
4Q	—	650.5	663.0	728.7	933.9	774.4
Yr.	—	2,598	2,775	3,262	3,548	2,804

Earnings Per Share ($)

	2004	2003	2002	2001	2000	1999
1Q	0.57	0.43	0.56	0.55	0.49	0.41
2Q	0.59	0.36	0.56	0.57	0.53	0.43
3Q	0.52	0.51	0.43	0.55	0.53	0.45
4Q	E0.58	0.58	0.43	0.45	0.54	0.46
Yr.	E2.32	1.89	1.97	2.11	2.08	1.74

Next earnings report expected: late-January Source: S&P, Company Reports
EPS Estimates based on S&P Operating Earnings; historical GAAP earnings are as reported.

Northern Trust Corporation

Recommendation: **BUY** ★★★★☆   12-Month Target Price: **$47.00** (as of October 29, 2004)

Business Summary November 01, 2004

Northern Trust, founded in 1889, is a Chicago-based bank holding company and a leading provider of a broad array of financial services, including personal fiduciary, asset management, personal and private banking and master trust/custody, global custody and treasury management services. At December 31, 2003, the company's assets totaled $41 billion, and administered trust assets were $2.2 trillion, including $479 billion of assets under management. NTRS's strategy is to focus on expanding its two principal business units: corporate and institutional services, and personal financial services.

The Personal Financial Services (PFS) unit provides personal trust and investment management services, estate administration, banking (including private banking) and residential real estate mortgage lending. PFS focuses on small/mid-size businesses, executives, retirees and high net worth individuals. PFS is one of the largest U.S. bank managers of personal trust assets, with $104 billion in assets under management and $195 billion in assets under administration at the end of 2003. The company currently has 83 PFS offices in 16 states, more than 250 portfolio managers, and more than 250 trust, custody, and estate administrators.

The Corporate and Institutional Services unit is a leading provider of master trust, master custody and related services to retirement plans, institutional clients and international clients. Master trust and custody includes worldwide custody, settle-

ment and reporting; cash management; and performance analysis services. Trust and custody relationships often include investment management, securities lending, transition management and commission recapture services. This unit also offers a full range of commercial banking services, mainly to domestic corporations and global financial institutions.

Through Northern Trust Global Investments (NTGI), the company provides a broad range of investment management and related services and products to clients that include institutional and individual separately managed accounts, bank common and collective funds, registered investment companies, collective investment schemes and unregistered private investment funds.

In June 2003, NTRS sold its Northern Trust Retirement Consulting (NTRC) unit, and recognized a pretax loss of $20.2 million. NTRC provided retirement related services to 200 companies and about 1 million individuals. In January 2003, the company acquired Deutsche Bank's global passive equity, enhanced equity, and passive fixed income businesses, for a total payment of about $117 million. In April 2003, NTRS acquired Atlanta-based private wealth manager Legacy South, for total consideration of $11.5 million, to be paid over a 16-month period. At the end of 2002, Legacy South had $300 million in assets under management.

Company Financials Fiscal Year ending December 31

Per Share Data ($)

(Year Ended December 31)	2003	2002	2001	2000	1999	1998	1997	1996	1995	1994
Tangible Bk. Val.	13.88	13.04	11.97	10.54	9.25	7.54	6.62	5.93	5.28	5.13
Earnings	1.89	1.97	2.11	2.08	1.74	1.52	1.33	1.10	0.94	0.79
S&P Core Earnings	1.63	1.64	1.82	NA	NA	NA	NA	NA	NA	NA
Dividends	0.70	0.68	0.64	0.56	0.48	0.42	0.38	0.32	0.27	0.23
Payout Ratio	37%	35%	30%	27%	28%	28%	28%	29%	29%	29%
Prices - High	48.75	62.67	82.25	92.12	54.62	44.93	35.75	18.87	14.00	10.81
- Low	27.64	30.41	41.40	46.75	40.15	27.87	17.00	12.31	7.93	8.06
P/E Ratio - High	26	32	39	44	31	30	27	17	15	14
- Low	15	15	20	22	23	18	13	11	8	10

Income Statement Analysis (Million $)

	2003	2002	2001	2000	1999	1998	1997	1996	1995	1994
Net Int. Inc.	548	602	595	569	519	477	438	388	358	338
Tax Equiv. Adj.	52.4	48.7	52.6	53.3	38.6	35.9	32.7	33.6	37.6	33.4
Non Int. Inc.	1,542	1,537	1,580	1,537	1,235	1,070	934	778	677	630
Loan Loss Prov.	2.50	37.5	66.5	24.0	12.5	9.00	9.00	12.0	6.00	6.00
Exp./Op. Revs.	68.1%	67.2%	61.8%	62.6%	62.8%	63.0%	65.0%	64.0%	66.1%	69.9%
Pretax Inc.	631	669	732	730	617	543	472	387	321	262
Eff. Tax Rate	32.9%	33.2%	33.4%	33.6%	34.3%	34.8%	34.4%	33.2%	31.4%	30.3%
Net Inc.	423	447	488	485	405	354	309	259	220	182
% Net Int. Marg.	1.73	1.93	2.02	2.02	2.05	2.08	2.18	2.25	2.30	2.36
S&P Core Earnings	365	369	418	NA	NA	NA	NA	NA	NA	NA

Balance Sheet & Other Fin. Data (Million $)

	2003	2002	2001	2000	1999	1998	1997	1996	1995	1994
Money Mkt. Assets	9,565	9,332	10,546	5,865	3,439	1,174	5,275	3,197	1,784	2,642
Inv. Securities	9,471	6,594	6,331	7,270	6,244	5,848	4,198	4,815	5,760	5,053
Com'l Loans	4,702	5,137	5,767	5,708	5,485	4,615	4,082	3,818	3,708	3,107
Other Loans	13,111	12,927	12,213	12,437	9,890	9,032	8,506	7,119	6,198	5,484
Total Assets	41,450	39,478	39,665	36,022	28,708	27,870	25,315	21,608	19,934	18,562
Demand Deposits	5,767	6,602	7,110	5,375	4,945	3,928	3,961	3,887	3,313	2,830
Time Deposits	20,503	19,460	17,909	17,453	16,426	14,275	12,399	9,909	9,175	8,904
LT Debt	1,341	1,284	1,485	1,356	1,427	1,426	1,225	733	352	792
Common Equity	3,055	2,880	2,653	2,342	2,055	1,820	1,619	1,424	1,282	1,111
% Ret. on Assets	1.0	1.1	1.3	1.5	1.4	1.3	1.3	1.2	1.1	1.0
% Ret. on Equity	14.2	16.1	19.4	21.8	20.7	20.3	20.0	18.8	17.7	16.7
% Loan Loss Resv.	0.8	0.9	0.9	0.9	1.0	1.1	1.2	1.4	1.5	1.7
% Loans/Deposits	67.8	69.3	71.9	79.5	71.9	75.0	76.9	79.3	79.3	73.2
% Equity to Assets	7.3	7.0	6.6	6.8	6.8	6.5	6.5	6.5	6.2	5.9

Data as orig reptd.; bef. results of disc opers/spec. items. Per share data adj. for stk. divs. Bold denotes primary EPS - prior periods restated. E-Estimated. NA-Not Available. NM-Not Meaningful. NR-Not Ranked. UR-Under Review.

Office: 50 South LaSalle Street, Chicago, IL 60675.
Telephone: 312-630-6000.
Website: http://www.northerntrust.com
Chrmn, Pres & CEO: W.A. Osborn.
Vice Chrmn: P.R. Pero.
EVP & CFO: S.L. Fradkin.

EVP & General Counsel: K.R. Welsh.
Investor Contact: B.J. Fleming 312-444-7811.
Dirs: D. L. Burnham, D. E. Cross, S. Crown, R. S. Hamada, R. A. Helman, D. C. Jain, D. C. Jain, A. L. Kelly, R. C. McCormack, E. J. Mooney, W. A. Osborn, J. W. Rowe, H. B. Smith, W. D. Smithburg.

Founded: in 1889.
Domicile: Delaware.
Employees: 8,056.
S&P Analyst: Evan Momios, CFA /MF/JWP

North Fork Bancorporation

Recommendation: **HOLD** ★ ★ ★ ☆   12-Month Target Price: **$29.00**
(as of October 27, 2004)

NFB has an approximate 0.13% weighting in the **S&P 500**

Sector: Financials
Sub-Industry: Regional Banks
Peer Group: Northeast Larger Regional Banks

Summary: This Long Island-based mutli-bank holding company, with about $55 billion in assets, serves the New York metropolitan area.

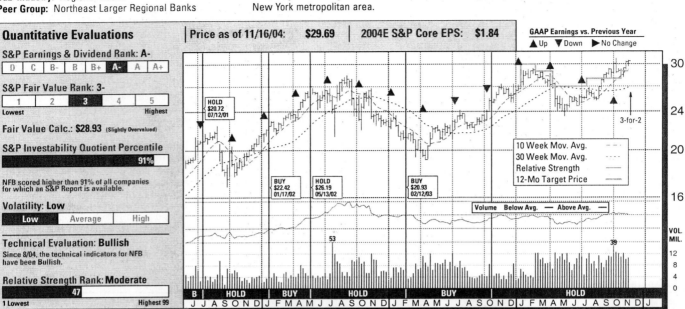

Quantitative Evaluations

S&P Earnings & Dividend Rank: A-

| D | C | B- | B | B+ | A- | A | A+ |

S&P Fair Value Rank: 3-

| 1 | 2 | 3 | 4 | 5 |
| Lowest | | | | Highest |

Fair Value Calc.: $28.93 (Slightly Overvalued)

S&P Investability Quotient Percentile
91%

NFB scored higher than 91% of all companies for which an S&P Report is available.

Volatility: Low

| Low | Average | High |

Technical Evaluation: Bullish
Since 8/04, the technical indicators for NFB have been Bullish.

Relative Strength Rank: Moderate
47
1 Lowest   Highest 99

Price as of 11/16/04: **$29.69**   2004E S&P Core EPS: **$1.84**

GAAP Earnings vs. Previous Year
▲ Up   ▼ Down   ► No Change

Analyst commentary prepared by Erik J. Eisenstein/CB/BK

Highlights October 29, 2004

- We expect a 79% advance in average earning assets in 2005, reflecting the full-year effect of the May 2004 acquisition of The Trust Company of New Jersey, and the October 2004 acquisition of GreenPoint Financial (GPT). We also think NFB's net interest margin will contract significantly as a result of the GreenPoint acquisition and despite the expected benefit of growth in noninterest bearing deposits. We therefore see a 69% advance in net interest income . We forecast a 47% rise in loan loss provisions, below expected loan growth on anticipated economic growth.

- Our forecast calls for noninterest income to more than double, with the full-year benefit of GreenPoint Mortgage and, to a lesser extent, fees on an anticipated larger deposit base. We expect operating expenses to rise about 83% in the coming year.

- With a higher projected share count, we forecast a 21% increase in 2005 EPS, to $3.40, from $2.80 projected for 2004. Our 2004 and 2005 Standard & Poor's Core Earnings projections are $2.76 and $3.34, respectively, reflecting our view of above-average earnings quality relative to other regional banks.

Investment Rationale/Risk October 29, 2004

- Prior to the acquisition of GPT, we saw NFB as a fundamentally strong regional bank with superior operating and lending margins. We take a mixed view of the recent GPT acquisition. Based on our view of a relatively low price offered for GPT, and potential cost savings, we view the deal as likely to be accretive to 2005 EPS. However, including GPT's thrift and mortgage banking operations, we see NFB as having somewhat tighter lending and operating margins and being more exposed to interest rate risk.

- Risks to our opinion and target price include interest rate risk and integration risk associated with the acquisition of GPT.

- Our 12-month target price of $44 is derived by applying a P/E multiple in line with peers to our 2005 EPS estimate. The in-line valuation reflects our view of roughly offsetting positive and negative valuation factors. We see earnings quality and the 3.1% dividend yield as above average, relative to peers. On the other hand, we also see EPS growth as more volatile than that of other regional banks beyond 2005. In addition, we see potential execution risk associated with a major acquisition, despite our view of NFB as an adept acquirer.

Key Stock Statistics

S&P Core EPS 2005E	2.23	52-week Range	$30.81-23.45
S&P Oper. EPS 2004E	1.87	12 Month P/E	16.3
P/E on S&P Oper. EPS 2004E	16.3	Beta	0.20
S&P Oper. EPS 2005E	2.27	Shareholders	8,745
Yield (%)	3.0%	Market Cap (B)	$ 13.9
Dividend Rate/Share	0.88	Shares Outstanding (M)	467.8

Value of $10,000 invested five years ago: **$ 25,088**

Dividend Data Dividends have been paid since 1994

Amount ($)	Date Decl.	Ex-Div. Date	Stock of Record	Payment Date
0.300	Mar. 23	Apr. 28	Apr. 30	May. 17 '04
0.300	Jun. 22	Jul. 28	Jul. 30	Aug. 16 '04
0.330	Sep. 28	Oct. 27	Oct. 29	Nov. 15 '04
3-for-2	Sep. 28	Nov. 16	Oct. 29	Nov. 15 '04

Revenues/Earnings Data Fiscal year ending December 31

Revenues (Million $)

	2004	2003	2002	2001	2000	1999
1Q	309.4	330.8	314.5	305.5	273.2	210.9
2Q	338.6	329.8	322.9	296.7	313.4	224.1
3Q	379.4	297.8	336.8	306.3	302.3	223.7
4Q	—	307.6	339.4	310.3	303.4	232.1
Yr.	—	1,266	1,313	1,219	1,175	890.8

Earnings Per Share ($)

	2004	2003	2002	2001	2000	1999
1Q	0.45	0.45	0.41	0.33	0.27	0.25
2Q	0.45	0.41	0.43	0.33	0.33	0.28
3Q	0.47	0.42	0.44	0.35	0.28	0.27
4Q	E0.49	0.45	0.45	0.37	0.30	0.28
Yr.	E1.87	1.73	1.72	1.37	0.93	1.08

Next earnings report expected: mid-January Source: S&P, Company Reports
EPS Estimates based on S&P Operating Earnings; historical GAAP earnings are as reported.

North Fork Bancorporation, Inc.

Recommendation: **HOLD** ★ ★ ★ ☆ ☆   12-Month Target Price: **$29.00** (as of October 27, 2004)

Business Summary November 01, 2004

North Fork Bancorporation attained a 2003 return on equity of 27%, return on assets of 1.9%, and core operating efficiency ratio (noninterest expenses divided by net revenue) of 34%. In addition to its banking business, the company, through subsidiaries, offers related financial services, such as asset management, brokerage, and sales of alternative investment products. In 2003, NFB opened nine branches. It planned to open additional branches in 2004.

In May, 2004, the company acquired The Trust Company of New Jersey (TCNJ), with $4.2 billion in assets and 93 branches in the northern part of New Jersey, via an exchange of stock valued at $726 million.

In October 2004, NFB acquired GreenPoint Financial (GPT), which owns Green-Point Mortgage and GreenPoint Bank, with 90 branches in the New York metropolitan area, via an exchange of stock valued at $6.3 billion. Following the acquisition, the company had $55 billion in assets and operated 350 branches throughout the New York metropolitan area, New Jersey and Connecticut. Also in October, NFB agreed to sell GreenPoint Credit LLC, the manufactured housing finance business it acquired as part of the GPT acquisition, to Green Tree Servicing LLC. The transaction is expected to close in the fourth quarter, subject to receipt of certain necessary consents to transfer servicing to Green Tree.

In November 2001, the company acquired Commercial Bank of New York, with 10 Manhattan branches and $900 million in deposits. In February 2000, it acquired JSB Financial and Reliance Bancorp, in exchange for about $570 million and $352

million in stock, respectively. JSB, with $1.7 billion in assets, operated 13 retail branches in the New York City area and Long Island. Reliance, with $2.4 billion in assets, operated 29 retail branches in the New York City area and on Long Island.

The vast majority of revenue is derived from interest on loans. Total loans, which increased 8.6% in 2003, to $12.3 billion, were divided as follows: multi-family mortgage 29% (32% in 2002), commercial mortgage 23% (19%), residential mortgage 20% (22%), commercial 17% (16%), consumer loans, 9% (9%), and construction and land loans 2% (2%).

Deposits are the major (and most cost effective) source of funds for lending operations. Totaling $15.1 billion at the end of 2003, deposits (by type) were divided: 27% demand; 25% savings; 30% NOW and money market; 12% time; and 6% certificates of deposits, $100,000 and over.

In the 2003 third quarter, NFB completed a balance sheet repositioning that included a reduction of $2.5 billion in mortgage-backed securities, through a combination of sales and portfolio cash flows. In connection with the plan, the company restructured $1 billion of long-term borrowings, resulting in a charge of $12 million in the second quarter.

In January 2003, directors authorized the repurchase of 5 million company common shares. In June 2003, directors authorized an increase in the number of shares then available for purchase to 8 million, from 4 million.

Company Financials Fiscal Year ending December 31

Per Share Data ($)

(Year Ended December 31)	2003	2002	2001	2000	1999	1998	1997	1996	1995	1994
Tangible Bk. Val.	4.61	4.58	4.13	3.59	2.80	3.53	3.96	2.57	2.53	2.24
Earnings	1.73	1.72	1.37	0.93	1.08	0.79	0.80	0.43	0.47	0.28
S&P Core Earnings	1.69	1.66	1.33	NA	NA	NA	NA	NA	NA	NA
Dividends	0.72	0.65	0.54	0.48	0.48	0.32	0.25	0.17	0.12	0.06
Payout Ratio	42%	38%	40%	52%	45%	40%	31%	39%	26%	20%
Prices - High	27.34	28.49	22.48	16.66	17.83	18.36	15.00	8.05	5.61	3.75
- Low	19.10	20.81	14.87	9.62	11.41	9.41	7.50	5.02	3.00	2.77
P/E Ratio - High	16	17	16	18	17	23	19	19	12	13
- Low	11	12	11	10	11	12	9	12	6	10

Income Statement Analysis (Million $)

	2003	2002	2001	2000	1999	1998	1997	1996	1995	1994
Net Int. Inc.	816	842	687	592	449	425	278	231	141	133
Tax Equiv. Adj.	NA	22.2	19.4	14.5	8.75	5.51	7.40	3.82	1.97	1.86
Non Int. Inc.	140	120	100	99	59.4	54.9	35.4	29.2	20.9	19.0
Loan Loss Prov.	26.3	25.0	17.8	17.0	6.00	15.5	6.00	6.80	9.00	3.28
Exp./Op. Revs.	36.2%	31.7%	33.7%	42.7%	34.3%	47.5%	39.1%	32.9%	42.0%	60.3%
Pretax Inc.	599	636	506	376	339	243	191	112	90.7	46.6
Eff. Tax Rate	33.9%	34.4%	34.5%	37.6%	35.0%	30.9%	37.6%	44.4%	42.5%	36.3%
Net Inc.	396	417	331	235	220	168	119	62.4	52.2	29.7
% Net Int. Marg.	4.24	4.93	4.83	4.39	4.16	4.48	4.69	4.50	5.18	4.83
S&P Core Earnings	386	403	322	NA	NA	NA	NA	NA	NA	NA

Balance Sheet & Other Fin. Data (Million $)

	2003	2002	2001	2000	1999	1998	1997	1996	1995	1994
Money Mkt. Assets	531	27.6	351	310	63.8	17.0	11.8	2.30	1.35	0.75
Inv. Securities	7,319	8,864	5,754	4,558	4,823	4,552	2,779	2,158	1,157	773
Com'l Loans	4,960	3,971	1,767	2,539	1,959	1,624	743	982	246	241
Other Loans	7,385	7,399	8,633	6,871	4,671	4,107	3,281	2,136	1,739	1,583
Total Assets	20,962	21,413	17,232	14,841	12,108	10,680	6,829	5,751	3,303	2,718
Demand Deposits	8,600	6,765	2,703	2,025	2,438	1,263	906	735	452	331
Time Deposits	6,517	6,428	8,601	7,144	4,107	2,214	1,385	3,391	2,083	2,012
LT Debt	1,486	1,918	1,794	795	199	199	36.0	35.0	35.0	75.0
Common Equity	1,478	1,514	1,437	1,214	619	831	602	458	310	255
% Ret. on Assets	1.9	2.2	2.1	1.6	1.9	1.9	1.9	1.1	1.8	1.0
% Ret. on Equity	26.5	28.3	25.0	21.2	30.4	23.4	22.5	14.5	18.5	12.1
% Loan Loss Resv.	1.0	1.0	1.0	1.0	1.0	1.3	1.5	1.7	2.6	2.8
% Loans/Deposits	81.7	86.2	92.0	102.5	101.1	88.9	79.8	69.8	75.6	77.1
% Equity to Assets	7.1	7.6	8.3	7.8	6.4	8.2	8.4	7.8	9.7	8.3

Data as orig reptd.; bef. results of disc opers/spec. items. Per share data adj. for stk. divs.; EPS diluted. E-Estimated. NA-Not Available. NM-Not Meaningful. NR-Not Ranked. UR-Under Review.

Office: 275 Broad Hollow Road, Melville, NY 11747.
Telephone: 631-844-1004.
Website: http://www.northforkbank.com
Chrmn, Pres & CEO: J.A. Kanas.

Vice Chrmn: J. Bohlsen.
EVP, CFO & Investor Contact: D.M. Healy 631-844-1258.
Dirs: J. Bohlsen, A. C. Dickerson, L. A. Gerard, D. M. Healy, J. A. Kanas, R. A. Nielson, J. F. Reeve, G. H. Rowsom, K. R. Schmeller.

Founded: in 1980.
Domicile: Delaware.
Employees: 2,979.
S&P Analyst: Erik J. Eisenstein/CB/BK

Northrop Grumman

Recommendation: **SELL** ★☆☆☆☆
SELL SELL HOLD BUY BUY

12-Month Target Price: **$40.00**
(as of July 29, 2004)

NOC has an approximate 0.18% weighting in the **S&P 500**

Sector: Industrials
Sub-Industry: Aerospace & Defense
Peer Group: Aircraft Manufacturers

Summary: Based on revenues, NOC is the world's third-largest defense contractor.

Quantitative Evaluations

S&P Earnings & Dividend Rank: B+

| D | C | B- | B | B+ | A- | A | A+ |

S&P Fair Value Rank: 5+

| 1 | 2 | 3 | 4 | 5 |
| Lowest | | | | Highest |

Fair Value Calc.: $81.20 (Undervalued)

S&P Investability Quotient Percentile

66%

NOC scored higher than 66% of all companies for which an S&P Report is available.

Volatility: Low

| Low | Average | High |

Technical Evaluation: Neutral
Since 11/04, the technical indicators for NOC have been Neutral.

Relative Strength Rank: Moderate

55

| 1 Lowest | | Highest 99 |

| Price as of 11/12/04: | **$55.14** | 2004E S&P Core EPS: | **$1.94** |

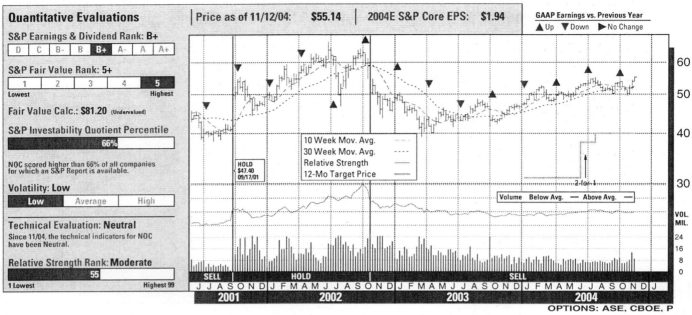

GAAP Earnings vs. Previous Year
▲ Up ▼ Down ► No Change

10 Week Mov. Avg.
30 Week Mov. Avg.
Relative Strength
12-Mo Target Price

HOLD
$47.40
09/17/01

2-for-1

Volume   Below Avg. — Above Avg.

VOL.
MIL.
24
16
8
0

SELL   HOLD   SELL
J J A S O N D J F M A M J J A S O N D J F M A M J J A S O N D J F M A M J J A S O N D J
2001   2002   2003   2004

OPTIONS: ASE, CBOE, P

Analyst commentary prepared by Robert E. Friedman, CPA /MF/JWP

Highlights August 27, 2004

- We see greater Pentagon demand for NOC's ships, surveillance aircraft, radar and computer systems driving a 10% rise in 2004 revenues. However, we expect 2004 EBIT margins to remain at somewhat over 7%, as we see much of near-term sales being generated under 5%-plus margin cost-plus development contracts. Nevertheless, we see a spike in near-term sales and the absence of restructuring charges driving a 35% increase in 2004 EPS, to $2.91.

- We are not as optimistic about the company's longer-term financial prospects. Looking at demand drivers, we believe sluggish growth in tax receipts, as well as political pressures to balance budgets, bolster huge federal entitlement programs, and fund homeland security and overseas peacekeeping initiatives, will likely prevent the procurement and R&D sectors of the U.S. military budget from expanding at a long-term annual rate greater than 4%.

- With regard to NOC's longer-term profitability prospects, we believe that the Pentagon's desire for increasingly hi-tech systems could boost the rate of product obsolescence. This could prevent many of the company's weapons systems from migrating toward more profitable fixed-price contract arrangements. We therefore project that NOC will post operating profit margins of 7% to 9% for the longer term, with a 5% to 7% free cash EPS compound annual growth rate (CAGR) and 10% to 13% average ROE.

Investment Rationale/Risk August 27, 2004

- We are maintaining our sell opinion on the shares. We think that the stock continues to trade at a material premium to our intrinsic value-based target price of $40.

- Risks to our recommendation and target price include potential unexpected improvements in the structural growth and economics of the global defense industry.

- Our revised cash flow model (which values the stock by adding the sum of future free cash flow growing at a 5% to 7% CAGR over the next 10 years, and at 3.0% thereafter) indicates that the stock is worth about $40 a share, which is our 12-month target price.

Key Stock Statistics

S&P Oper. EPS 2004E	2.91	52-week Range	$55.25-45.07
P/E on S&P Oper. EPS 2004E	18.9	12 Month P/E	19.4
S&P Oper. EPS 2005E	3.25	Beta	-0.21
Yield (%)	1.7%	Shareholders	39,500
Dividend Rate/Share	0.92	Market Cap (B)	$ 19.6
Shares Outstanding (M)	358.5		

Value of $10,000 invested five years ago: **$ 21,625**

Dividend Data Dividends have been paid since 1951

Amount ($)	Date Decl.	Ex-Div. Date	Stock of Record	Payment Date
0.400	Feb. 17	Feb. 26	Mar. 01	Mar. 13 '04
0.460	May. 12	May. 20	May. 24	Jun. 05 '04
2-for-1	May. 12	Jun. 22	May. 28	Jun. 21 '04
0.230	Aug. 17	Aug. 26	Aug. 30	Sep. 11 '04

Revenues/Earnings Data Fiscal year ending December 31

Revenues (Million $)

	2004	2003	2002	2001	2000	1999
1Q	7,105	5,866	3,931	1,986	2,080	2,099
2Q	7,374	6,627	4,231	3,663	1,856	2,274
3Q	7,408	6,619	4,214	3,605	1,731	2,122
4Q	—	7,094	4,830	4,304	2,229	2,506
Yr.	—	26,206	17,206	13,558	7,618	8,995

Earnings Per Share ($)

	2004	2003	2002	2001	2000	1999
1Q	0.63	0.46	0.64	0.71	1.24	0.75
2Q	0.79	0.55	0.77	0.64	1.25	0.82
3Q	0.80	0.60	0.59	0.42	1.06	0.92
4Q	E0.74	0.56	0.86	0.64	0.99	0.98
Yr.	E2.91	2.16	2.86	2.40	4.41	3.47

Next earnings report expected: early-February Source: S&P, Company Reports
EPS Estimates based on S&P Operating Earnings; historical GAAP earnings are as reported.

Recommendation: **SELL** ★☆☆☆☆   12-Month Target Price: **$40.00** (as of July 29, 2004)

Business Summary August 27, 2004

Northrop Grumman, a leading defense contractor, conducts business through six segments.

Electronic Sensors & Systems (22% of 2003 revenues; 29% of operating profits; 9.8% profit margins) is a leading maker of airborne radar and other hi-tech military electronics. Major competitors include Raytheon, Britain's BAE Systems, and France's Thales.

Ships (20%; 15%; 5.4%) primarily makes conventional battleships and nuclear-powered aircraft carriers. General Dynamics is the segment's primary competitor.

Information Technology (18%; 14%; 5.9%) develops and operates computer systems, primarily for various U.S. government agencies, including the Pentagon. Primary competitors include defense contractors Lockheed Martin and General Dynamics, as well as civilian IT providers.

Mission Systems (15%; 13%; 6.3%) primarily puts together complex information systems used by the the U.S. military. MS's primary competitors include Boeing, Raytheon and France-based Thales.

Integrated Systems (14%; 19%; 10%) designs and puts together highly sophisticated electronic battlefield surveillance and communications systems. Primary competitors include Boeing and Lockheed Martin.

Space Technology (11%; 10%; 6.8%) mostly makes electronic components and systems for military satellites, rockets and missiles. Primary competitors include Lockheed Martin and Boeing.

From 1996 through 2003, revenues more than tripled, reflecting an aggressive acquisition program. During this period, per share net operating earnings showed a seven-year compound annual growth rate (CAGR) of 0.1%. Per share retained earnings growth (a proxy for intrinsic value growth) declined at a 4.2% CAGR during this period. Primary profitability performance ratios, such as operating profit margins, net profit margins and debt-adjusted return on equity, stood at seven-year average levels of 7.2%, 4.4% and 8.3%, respectively.

Based on Standard & Poor's Core Earnings methodology, quality of earnings is mediocre. Over the past seven years, the reported earnings to S&P Core variance was 101%, primarily due to the reversal of non-operating gains from NOC's pension plans.

The company estimates that 60% to 70% of backlog consists of cost-plus contracts. NOC estimates that these cost-plus contracts have operating profit margins of about 5%. Under cost-plus contracts, the U.S. government reimburses defense contractors for the costs incurred in building weapons systems, and remits any additional rewards-based fees.

Demand for NOC's offerings is primarily driven by growth in the procurement and research and development sectors of the U.S. defense budget, which accounts for about 40% of global military weapons spending. The market for military weapons systems is mature. Based on U.S. Department of Defense statistics, from FY 93 (Oct.) through FY 03, the procurement and R&D sectors of the total U.S. defense budget grew at 1.5% and 1.8% average annual rates, respectively.

Company Financials Fiscal Year ending December 31

Per Share Data ($)

(Year Ended December 31)	2003	2002	2001	2000	1999	1998	1997	1996	1995	1994
Tangible Bk. Val.	NM	NM	NM	NM	NM	NM	NM	NM	NM	-4.58
Cash Flow	4.05	5.29	6.31	7.08	6.23	4.25	6.16	5.57	5.41	3.10
Earnings	2.16	2.86	2.40	4.41	3.47	1.40	2.99	2.17	2.56	0.36
S&P Core Earnings	2.42	-0.95	-2.85	NA	NA	NA	NA	NA	NA	NA
Dividends	0.80	0.80	0.80	0.80	0.80	0.80	0.80	0.80	0.80	0.80
Payout Ratio	37%	28%	33%	18%	23%	57%	27%	37%	31%	NM
Prices - High	50.55	67.50	55.28	46.93	37.96	69.50	63.93	42.12	32.12	23.68
- Low	41.50	43.60	38.20	21.31	23.50	29.65	35.68	28.87	19.87	17.25
P/E Ratio - High	23	24	23	11	11	50	21	19	13	66
- Low	19	15	16	5	7	21	12	13	8	48

Income Statement Analysis (Million $)

	2003	2002	2001	2000	1999	1998	1997	1996	1995	1994
Revs.	26,206	17,206	13,558	7,618	8,995	8,902	9,153	8,071	6,818	6,711
Oper. Inc.	1,538	1,391	1,649	1,479	1,358	1,149	1,298	1,025	819	750
Depr.	682	525	645	381	389	393	418	367	283	269
Int. Exp.	497	422	373	175	224	233	257	270	137	109
Pretax Inc.	1,131	1,009	699	975	762	312	651	384	409	65.0
Eff. Tax Rate	28.6%	30.9%	38.9%	35.9%	36.6%	37.8%	37.5%	39.1%	38.4%	46.2%
Net Inc.	808	697	427	625	483	194	407	234	252	35.0
S&P Core Earnings	892	-223	-487	NA	NA	NA	NA	NA	NA	NA

Balance Sheet & Other Fin. Data (Million $)

	2003	2002	2001	2000	1999	1998	1997	1996	1995	1994
Cash	342	1,412	464	319	142	44.0	63.0	44.0	18.0	17.0
Curr. Assets	5,745	15,835	4,589	2,526	2,793	3,033	2,936	2,597	2,072	2,431
Total Assets	33,009	42,266	20,886	9,622	9,285	9,536	9,677	9,422	5,455	6,047
Curr. Liab.	6,361	11,373	5,132	2,688	2,464	2,367	2,715	2,600	1,715	1,964
LT Debt	5,410	9,398	5,033	1,605	2,000	2,562	2,500	2,950	1,163	1,633
Common Equity	15,785	14,322	7,391	3,919	3,257	2,850	2,623	2,128	1,459	1,290
Total Cap.	22,067	24,209	13,443	5,800	5,321	5,412	5,198	5,139	2,653	2,939
Cap. Exp.	635	538	393	274	201	211	238	194	133	134
Cash Flow	1,490	1,222	1,072	1,006	872	587	825	601	535	304
Curr. Ratio	0.9	1.4	0.9	0.9	1.1	1.3	1.1	1.0	1.2	1.2
% LT Debt of Cap.	24.5	38.8	37.4	27.7	37.6	47.3	48.1	57.4	43.8	55.6
% Net Inc.of Revs.	3.1	4.1	3.1	8.2	5.4	2.2	4.4	2.9	3.7	0.5
% Ret. on Assets	2.1	2.2	2.8	6.6	5.1	2.0	4.3	3.1	4.4	0.8
% Ret. on Equity	5.4	6.4	7.6	17.4	15.8	7.1	17.1	13.0	18.3	2.7

Data as orig reptd.; bef. results of disc opers/spec. items. Per share data adj. for stk. divs.; EPS diluted. E-Estimated. NA-Not Available. NM-Not Meaningful. NR-Not Ranked. UR-Under Review.

Office: 1840 Century Park East, Los Angeles, CA 90067-2199.
Telephone: 310-553-6262.
Email: investor_relations@mail.northgrum.com
Website: http://www.northropgrumman.com
Chrmn, Pres & CEO: R.D. Sugar.
VP & CFO: C.H. Noski.
VP & Treas: J.L. Sanford.

VP & Secy: J.H. Mullan.
VP & General Counsel: W.B. Terry.
VP & Investor Contact: G. Kent 310-553-6262.
Dirs: J. T. Chain, Jr., L. W. Coleman, J. M. Cook, V. Fazio, P. Frost, C. R. Larson, C. H. Noski, J. H. Nussbaum, P. A. Odeen, A. L. Peters, K. W. Sharer, J. B. Slaughter, R. D. Sugar.

Founded: in 1939.
Domicile: Delaware.
Employees: 122,600.
S&P Analyst: Robert E. Friedman, CPA /MF/JWP

Novell, Inc.

Recommendation: **HOLD** ★★★☆☆
SELL · SELL · HOLD · BUY · BUY

12-Month Target Price: **$8.00**
(as of August 12, 2004)

NOVL has an approximate 0.03% weighting in the **S&P 500**

Sector: Information Technology
Sub-Industry: Systems Software
Peer Group: Systems Software - Larger

Summary: NOVL is a leading vendor of directory-enabled networking software, with its NetWare product line and related offerings.

Quantitative Evaluations

S&P Earnings & Dividend Rank: C

| D | **C** | B- | B | B+ | A- | A | A+ |

S&P Fair Value Rank: 1

| **1** | 2 | 3 | 4 | 5 |
| Lowest | | | | Highest |

Fair Value Calc.: $5.40 (Overvalued)

S&P Investability Quotient Percentile

41%

NOVL scored lower than 59% of all companies for which an S&P Report is available.

Volatility: High

| Low | Average | **High** |

Technical Evaluation: Neutral
Since 10/04, the technical indicators for NOVL have been Neutral.

Relative Strength Rank: Moderate

39

| 1 Lowest | | Highest 99 |

Price as of 11/12/04: $7.15 | **2004E S&P Core EPS: $-0.17**

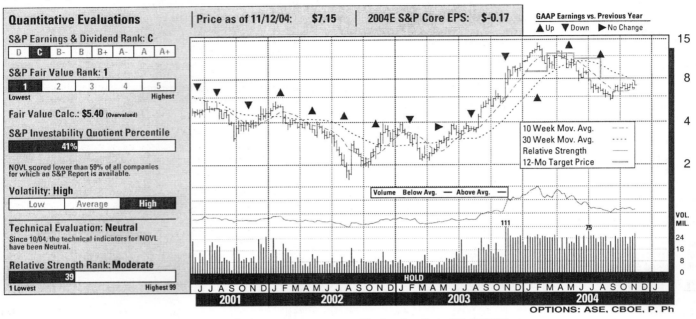

GAAP Earnings vs. Previous Year
▲ Up ▼ Down ► No Change

- - - 10 Week Mov. Avg.
· · · 30 Week Mov. Avg.
—— Relative Strength
—— 12-Mo Target Price

Volume Below Avg. — Above Avg. —

HOLD

2001 2002 2003 2004

OPTIONS: ASE, CBOE, P, Ph

Analyst commentary prepared by Jonathan Rudy, CFA /MF/JWP

Highlights August 27, 2004

- We expect revenues to increase approximately 6% in FY 04 (Oct.), following a 2% decline in FY 03, driven mainly by recent acquisitions, such as that of SUSE Linux. We see 5% revenue growth in FY 05.

- Revenue growth has historically benefited from the company's new product introductions, but sales of the company's core NetWare product line have continued to fall below our expectations. However, we expect new products focused mainly on the company's Linux offerings, due to its acquisitions of SUSE Linux and Ximian, to drive future revenue growth.

- We expect operating margins to widen, benefiting from recent cost-cutting initiatives. We project operating EPS of $0.16 in FY 04, up from operating EPS of $0.02 (excluding one-time charges) in FY 03. We see EPS of $0.22 in FY 05. Our Standard & Poor's Core Earnings estimate of a loss of $0.17 a share for FY 04 includes the potential impact of stock option expense.

Investment Rationale/Risk August 27, 2004

- Despite the discount to our target price, we would not add to positions of these high beta shares due to what we consider the company's poor execution in recent years. NOVL has undergone numerous strategy changes over the past couple of years, culminating in multiple restructuring charges and acquisitions. However, the company has a strong balance sheet, in our view, with over $1.50 per share in net cash and investments. The shares trade at a discount to peer levels with an enterprise value to sales of 1.6X.

- Risks to our opinion and target price include a rapidly changing technology landscape and the fact that NOVL competes directly with Microsoft in multiple product lines. We also believe that NOVL is highly dependent on an overall improvement in corporate IT spending.

- Based primarily on a blend of relative enterprise value to sales and P/E to growth metrics, our 12-month target price is $8 a share.

Key Stock Statistics

S&P Oper. EPS 2004E	0.16	52-week Range	$14.24-5.62
P/E on S&P Oper. EPS 2004E	44.7	12 Month P/E	NM
S&P Oper. EPS 2005E	0.22	Beta	NA
Yield (%)	Nil	Shareholders	9,080
Dividend Rate/Share	Nil	Market Cap (B)	$ 2.7
Shares Outstanding (M)	375.9		

Value of $10,000 invested five years ago: **$ 3,387**

Dividend Data

No cash dividends have been paid.

Revenues/Earnings Data Fiscal year ending October 31

Revenues (Million $)

	2004	2003	2002	2001	2000	1999
1Q	267.1	260.0	277.9	245.0	316.0	285.8
2Q	293.6	276.0	273.9	240.8	302.4	315.6
3Q	304.6	282.8	282.3	246.7	270.0	326.8
4Q	—	286.8	300.3	307.6	273.3	344.6
Yr.	—	1,106	1,134	1,040	1,162	1,273

Earnings Per Share ($)

	2004	2003	2002	2001	2000	1999
1Q	0.03	-0.03	0.03	0.01	0.13	0.09
2Q	-0.04	-0.08	-0.08	-0.48	0.09	0.11
3Q	0.06	-0.03	0.03	-0.06	0.03	0.14
4Q	E0.07	-0.29	-0.25	-0.26	-0.11	0.21
Yr.	E0.16	-0.44	-0.28	-0.79	0.15	0.55

Next earnings report expected: late-November Source: S&P, Company Reports
EPS Estimates based on S&P Operating Earnings; historical GAAP earnings are as reported.

Novell, Inc.

Recommendation: **HOLD** ★ ★ ★ ☆ ☆   12-Month Target Price: **$8.00** (as of August 12, 2004)

Business Summary August 27, 2004

Novell provides e-business solutions and Net services software designed to secure and power the networked world (the Internet, intranets, and extranets; wired to wireless; corporate and public) across leading operating systems. The company's network solutions provide essential network management, messaging, and groupware capabilities, integrated through the company's directory services. In FY 03 (Oct.), NOVL organized its operations into four segments based on geographic areas and Celerant Management Consulting. The three geographic areas are the Americas, EMEA, and Asia Pacific.

The Americas region accounted for 48% of net sales in FY 03, down from 53% in FY 02. EMEA comprised 31% of net sales in FY 03, up from 28% in FY 02, and Asia Pacific accounted for 8%, up from 7% in FY 02. Celerant comprised 13% of net sales in FY 03, up from 11% in FY 02.

NOVL's management also reviews revenue by solution category. These solution categories are: Identity management and Web services, Cross-platform services, Worldwide services, and Celerant Management Consulting.

The identity management and Web services category provides solutions that help customers with their identity management and security issues. Products include Secure-Login/Single Sign-On, DirXML, iChain, exteNd, and BorderManager. Products in this category are branded as Nsure and exteNd.

NOVL's cross-platform services category provides solutions that offer an effective and open approach to networking and collaboration services, including file, print, messaging, scheduling, workspace, etc., while using a cross-platform approach.

Products include NetWare, GroupWise, ZENworks, and Novell iFolder. These products are branded as Nterprise.

Worldwide services includes comprehensive worldwide information technology consulting, education, and support services that apply business solutions to customers' business situations, providing the business knowledge and technical expertise to help customers implement identity management, Web services, and cross-platform services. Services in this category are branded as Ngage.

Celerant Management Consulting provides operational strategy and implementation consulting services to a wide range of customers across various sectors.

In July 2002, NOVL acquired Silverstream Software, for about $212 million in cash. Silverstream's products are designed to unify and repurpose existing applications and information by harnessing the value of customers' prior technology investments and helping them deliver Web-based applications that are reliable, scalable and secure.

In August 2003, NOVL acquired Ximian, Inc., a privately-held company and provider of desktop and server solutions that enable enterprise Linux adoption. Terms were not disclosed. In January 2004, NOVL acquired SUSE Linux AG, a privately-held company and distributor of commercial Linux for enterprise servers, for about $210 million in cash. These acquisitions expand NOVL's ability to support Linux solutions, providing the company with Linux desktop, groupware, and management technologies.

Company Financials Fiscal Year ending October 31

Per Share Data ($)

(Year Ended October 31)	2003	2002	2001	2000	1999	1998	1997	1996	1995	1994
Tangible Bk. Val.	1.89	2.31	2.98	3.80	4.57	4.42	4.46	4.67	5.22	4.08
Cash Flow	-0.27	-0.09	-0.53	0.39	0.75	0.50	0.04	0.65	1.15	0.80
Earnings	-0.44	-0.28	-0.79	0.15	0.55	0.29	-0.22	0.35	0.90	0.56
S&P Core Earnings	-0.45	-0.47	-1.27	NA	NA	NA	NA	NA	NA	NA
Dividends	Nil	Nil	Nil	Nil	Nil	Nil	Nil	Nil	Nil	Nil
Payout Ratio	Nil	Nil	Nil	Nil	Nil	Nil	Nil	Nil	Nil	Nil
Prices - High	10.77	5.64	9.12	44.56	41.18	19.00	13.00	15.62	23.25	26.25
- Low	2.14	1.57	2.96	4.87	16.06	6.81	6.28	8.75	13.75	13.75
P/E Ratio - High	NM	NM	NM	NM	75	66	NM	45	26	47
- Low	NM	NM	NM	33	29	23	NM	25	15	25

Income Statement Analysis (Million $)

	2003	2002	2001	2000	1999	1998	1997	1996	1995	1994
Revs.	1,105	1,134	1,040	1,162	1,273	1,084	1,007	1,375	2,041	1,998
Oper. Inc.	52.3	103	46.1	98.2	293	175	-53.6	232	546	547
Depr.	61.1	68.8	86.7	81.9	70.2	76.2	91.1	105	94.2	86.4
Int. Exp.	Nil	Nil	Nil	Nil	Nil	Nil	Nil	Nil	NA	NA
Pretax Inc.	-55.0	-92.2	-277	70.7	244	142	-151	180	509	297
Eff. Tax Rate	NM	NM	NM	30.0%	21.8%	28.0%	NM	30.0%	33.5%	30.5%
Net Inc.	-162	-103	-262	49.5	191	102	-78.3	126	338	207
S&P Core Earnings	-167	-172	-384	NA	NA	NA	NA	NA	NA	NA

Balance Sheet & Other Fin. Data (Million $)

	2003	2002	2001	2000	1999	1998	1997	1996	1995	1994
Cash	752	636	705	698	895	1,007	1,033	1,025	1,321	862
Curr. Assets	1,031	920	1,027	1,007	1,336	1,436	1,470	1,591	1,925	1,453
Total Assets	1,568	1,665	1,904	1,712	1,942	1,924	1,911	2,049	2,417	1,963
Curr. Liab.	626	592	611	455	440	415	322	365	461	463
LT Debt	Nil	Nil	Nil	Nil	Nil	Nil	Nil	Nil	Nil	Nil
Common Equity	934	1,066	1,271	1,245	1,492	1,493	1,565	1,616	1,938	1,487
Total Cap.	941	1,074	1,293	1,257	1,503	1,509	1,589	1,685	1,956	1,501
Cap. Exp.	39.5	27.6	33.3	57.8	69.2	57.4	64.8	101	84.5	73.5
Cash Flow	-101	-34.3	-175	131	261	178	12.8	231	432	293
Curr. Ratio	1.6	1.6	1.7	2.2	3.0	3.5	4.6	4.4	4.2	3.1
% LT Debt of Cap.	Nil	Nil	Nil	Nil	Nil	Nil	Nil	Nil	Nil	Nil
% Net Inc.of Revs.	NM	NM	NM	4.3	15.0	9.4	NM	9.2	16.6	10.3
% Ret. on Assets	NM	NM	NM	2.7	9.9	5.3	NM	5.7	15.4	11.6
% Ret. on Equity	NM	NM	NM	3.6	12.8	6.7	NM	7.1	19.8	14.8

Data as orig reptd.; bef. results of disc opers/spec. items. Per share data adj. for stk. divs. Bold denotes primary EPS - prior periods restated. E-Estimated. NA-Not Available. NM-Not Meaningful. NR-Not Ranked. UR-Under Review.

Office: 404 Wyman St Ste 500, Waltham, MA 02451-1212.
Telephone: 781-464-8000.
Website: http://www.novell.com
Chrmn, Pres & CEO: J.L. Messman.
Vice Chrmn: C. Stone.
SVP & CFO: J.S. Tibbetts, Jr.

SVP, Secy & General Counsel: J.A. LaSala, Jr.
Investor Contact: B. Smith 781-464-8052.
Dirs: A. Aiello, F. Corrado, R. Crandall, W. Mackie, C. Malone, J. L. Messman, R. L. Nolan, T. G. Plaskett, J. W. Poduska, Sr., J. D. Robinson III, K. B. White.

Founded: in 1983.
Domicile: Delaware.
Employees: 5,734.
S&P Analyst: Jonathan Rudy, CFA /MF/JWP

Novellus Systems

Recommendation: **HOLD** ★★★☆☆   SELL | SELL | HOLD | BUY | BUY

12-Month Target Price: $27.00
(as of October 14, 2004)

NVLS has an approximate 0.04% weighting in the **S&P 500**

Sector: Information Technology
Sub-Industry: Semiconductor Equipment
Peer Group: Semiconductor Equipment - Larger Front-end

Summary: NVLS manufactures, markets and services automated wafer fabrication systems for the deposition of thin films.

Quantitative Evaluations

S&P Earnings & Dividend Rank: B-

D | C | **B-** | B | B+ | A- | A | A+

S&P Fair Value Rank: 3+

1 | 2 | **3** | 4 | 5
Lowest | | | | Highest

Fair Value Calc.: $26.50 (Slightly Overvalued)

S&P Investability Quotient Percentile — 93%

NVLS scored higher than 93% of all companies for which an S&P Report is available.

Volatility: Average

Low | **Average** | High

Technical Evaluation: Neutral
Since 11/04, the technical indicators for NVLS have been Neutral.

Relative Strength Rank: Moderate — 44
1 Lowest | Highest 99

| Price as of 11/12/04: | $27.05 | 2004E S&P Core EPS: | $0.25 |

GAAP Earnings vs. Previous Year ▲ Up ▼ Down ► No Change

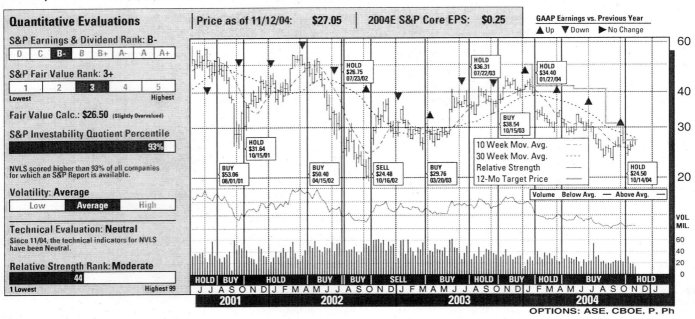

Analyst commentary prepared by Colin McArdle/CB/GG

OPTIONS: ASE, CBOE, P, Ph

Highlights October 15, 2004

- We expect 2004 sales to climb 45%, followed by 8% growth in 2005, as a semiconductor industry upturn accelerates and demand for copper-related deposition tools continues to grow. Third quarter sales and EPS were in line with our expectations, though forward guidance cited a slowdown in demand for semiconductor equipment.

- Current quarter revenue visibility appears impaired for many technology companies. NVLS has said it is experiencing weaker demand due to increasing inventories and questions about demand for chips. The company said it continued to receive production orders for its CMP equipment in the third quarter, and we believe NVLS has the technological know-how to transform this product line, acquired in 2002, into an offering competitive with that of CMP leader Applied Materials (AMAT: accumulate, $16).

- We believe the company's copper electroplating line remains dominant, despite emerging competition from AMAT, and we also see opportunity in the nascent low-k dielectrics market. We forecast 2004 EPS of $0.99, followed by an advance to $1.35 in 2005.

Investment Rationale/Risk October 15, 2004

- We expect overall spending on semiconductor capital equipment to grow 40% in 2004, followed by 10%-15% growth in 2005. We believe that what we view as NVLS's strong footing in deposition equipment for copper interconnects positions it well in the current semiconductor equipment market as inventory issues unwind. We suggest investors hold the shares, in view of strong third quarter results and our longer term optimism for the group as this chip cycle progresses.

- Risks to our recommendation and target price include increasing competition and the threat of pricing pressures, as well as technological obsolescence. NVLS also has some customer concentration issues.

- Capitalizing projected 2005 EPS of $1.35 at a peer group multiple of 20X, we arrive at our 12-month target price of $27. The company has nearly $6.50 a share in cash and equivalents, and no long term debt.

Key Stock Statistics

S&P Core EPS 2005E	1.22	52-week Range	$44.80-22.89
S&P Oper. EPS 2004E	0.99	12 Month P/E	31.4
P/E on S&P Oper. EPS 2004E	27.3	Beta	NA
S&P Oper. EPS 2005E	1.35	Shareholders	994
Yield (%)	Nil	Market Cap (B)	$ 3.8
Dividend Rate/Share	Nil	Shares Outstanding (M)	139.8

Value of $10,000 invested five years ago: **$ 9,177**

Dividend Data

Amount ($)	Date Decl.	Ex-Div. Date	Stock of Record	Payment Date
0.050	Oct. 21	Dec. 16	Dec. 20	Dec. 27 '04

Revenues/Earnings Data Fiscal year ending December 31

Revenues (Million $)

	2004	2003	2002	2001	2000	1999
1Q	262.9	238.4	169.7	458.7	198.7	115.2
2Q	338.2	239.1	222.2	376.9	335.0	130.9
3Q	415.9	221.1	230.5	303.7	250.1	154.9
4Q	—	226.5	217.6	200.0	389.9	191.7
Yr.	—	925.1	840.0	1,339	1,174	592.7

Earnings Per Share ($)

	2004	2003	2002	2001	2000	1999
1Q	0.11	0.08	0.03	0.55	0.19	0.08
2Q	0.25	0.05	0.08	0.40	0.57	0.10
3Q	0.45	-0.23	0.03	-0.10	0.29	0.18
4Q	E0.19	0.07	0.02	0.12	0.69	0.27
Yr.	E0.99	-0.03	0.15	0.97	1.75	0.64

Next earnings report expected: late-January Source: S&P, Company Reports
EPS Estimates based on S&P Operating Earnings; historical GAAP earnings are as reported.

Novellus Systems, Inc.

Recommendation: **HOLD** ★ ★ ★ ☆ ☆   12-Month Target Price: **$27.00** (as of October 14, 2004)

Business Summary October 15, 2004

Novellus is the second largest maker of deposition equipment used to deposit conductive and insulating layers on semiconductor wafers to form integrated circuits (ICs). In addition, through the 2001 acquisition of GaSonics International, the company entered the market for wafer surface preparation equipment. Through the December 2002 acquisition of SpeedFam-IPEC, NVLS entered the chemical mechanical planarization (CMP) equipment market. These two types of equipment are complementary to deposition equipment.

The company's product line of deposition equipment includes chemical vapor deposition (CVD), physical vapor deposition (PVD), and electroplating (ECD) equipment, all of which are used to form the layers of wiring and insulation, known as the interconnect, of ICs. High-density plasma CVD (HDP) and plasma-enhanced CVD (PECVD) systems employ a chemical plasma to deposit all of the insulating layers and some of the conductive layers on the surface of a wafer. PVD systems deposit conductive layers through a process known as sputtering. ECD systems deposit conductive layers of copper on wafers, through a process known as electrochemical deposition.

Although NVLS's original tool sets established it as a leader in CVD, the company has recently centered its product strategy around the emergence of the copper interconnect market. Copper has lower resistance and capacitance values than aluminum, the conductive metal generally used in ICs, offering increased speed and decreased chip size. The company's SABRE tool offers a complete solution for the deposition of copper interconnects and holds the leading market share in copper.

Surface preparation products, including photoresist strip and clean, are becoming increasingly important with the industry's migration to copper interconnects. Surface preparation systems remove photoresist and other potential contaminants from a wafer before proceeding with the next deposition step.

The company aims to increase its market share in the worldwide thin film deposition market, and to strengthen its position as a leading supplier of semiconductor processing equipment. NVLS's strategy is to provide customers with systems that achieve the highest levels of wafer throughput, yield (the percentage of functioning ICs to the total produced), and film quality. The company will continue to focus its marketing efforts on major semiconductor manufacturers. Sales to the 10 largest customers accounted for 76% of sales in 2003.

The semiconductor industry that NVLS serves is global in scope. Export sales accounted for 65% of 2003 revenue, up from 61% in 2002.

In December 2002, the company acquired chemical mechanical planarization (CMP) tool maker SpeedFam-IPEC, in exchange for about $290 million in stock and assumption of debt, strengthening its position in copper-related tools.

Company Financials Fiscal Year ending December 31

Per Share Data ($)

(Year Ended December 31)	2003	2002	2001	2000	1999	1998	1997	1996	1995	1994
Tangible Bk. Val.	12.42	12.69	13.04	11.49	6.47	3.63	2.98	3.83	2.85	2.21
Cash Flow	0.43	0.45	1.32	2.04	0.89	0.73	-0.78	1.06	0.88	0.49
Earnings	-0.03	0.15	0.97	1.75	0.64	0.50	-0.96	0.95	0.80	0.45
S&P Core Earnings	-0.44	-0.35	0.55	NA	NA	NA	NA	NA	NA	NA
Dividends	Nil	Nil	Nil	Nil	Nil	Nil	Nil	Nil	Nil	Nil
Payout Ratio	Nil	Nil	Nil	Nil	Nil	Nil	Nil	Nil	Nil	Nil
Prices - High	45.50	54.48	58.70	70.25	42.79	19.77	22.12	10.75	14.54	9.41
- Low	24.93	19.40	25.37	24.93	14.95	6.95	7.95	5.25	7.12	4.29
P/E Ratio - High	NM	NM	61	40	67	39	NM	11	18	21
- Low	NM	NM	26	14	23	14	NM	6	9	9

Income Statement Analysis (Million $)

	2003	2002	2001	2000	1999	1998	1997	1996	1995	1994
Revs.	925	840	1,339	1,174	593	519	534	462	374	225
Oper. Inc.	56.5	46.3	273	328	130	103	112	148	123	67.7
Depr.	69.6	44.3	51.9	40.1	29.8	23.8	18.3	11.3	7.65	3.97
Int. Exp.	0.91	1.02	1.15	2.33	1.70	4.87	2.74	0.47	0.23	0.29
Pretax Inc.	-15.3	22.9	209	342	114	80.0	-121	145	125	68.1
Eff. Tax Rate	NM	NM	31.0%	31.0%	33.0%	34.0%	NM	35.0%	34.0%	34.0%
Net Inc.	-5.03	22.9	144	236	76.6	52.8	-95.7	94.0	82.5	44.9
S&P Core Earnings	-67.2	-50.7	81.6	NA	NA	NA	NA	NA	NA	NA

Balance Sheet & Other Fin. Data (Million $)

	2003	2002	2001	2000	1999	1998	1997	1996	1995	1994
Cash	497	616	551	571	182	81.2	59.3	177	150	137
Curr. Assets	1,572	1,634	2,517	1,827	733	399	351	374	318	234
Total Assets	2,339	2,494	3,010	2,015	910	552	493	460	365	265
Curr. Liab.	221	382	1,138	505	140	111	127	86.1	92.0	50.8
LT Debt	Nil	Nil	Nil	Nil	Nil	Nil	65.0	65.0	Nil	Nil	Nil
Common Equity	2,072	2,056	1,872	1,511	770	375	301	374	273	214
Total Cap.	2,072	2,075	1,872	1,511	770	440	366	374	273	214
Cap. Exp.	31.1	26.8	80.0	68.5	28.8	36.1	36.2	35.2	19.3	6.90
Cash Flow	64.5	67.2	196	276	106	76.7	-77.4	105	90.2	48.9
Curr. Ratio	7.1	4.3	2.2	3.6	5.2	3.6	2.8	4.3	3.5	4.6
% LT Debt of Cap.	Nil	Nil	Nil	Nil	Nil	14.7	17.8	NM	NM	Nil
% Net Inc.of Revs.	NM	2.7	10.8	20.1	12.9	10.2	NM	20.4	22.1	20.0
% Ret. on Assets	NM	0.8	5.5	16.1	10.5	10.1	NM	22.8	26.0	21.7
% Ret. on Equity	NM	1.2	8.2	20.7	13.4	15.6	NM	29.1	33.9	26.9

Data as orig reptd.; bef. results of disc opers/spec. items. Per share data adj. for stk. divs.; EPS diluted. E-Estimated. NA-Not Available. NM-Not Meaningful. NR-Not Ranked. UR-Under Review.

Office: 4000 North First Street, San Jose, CA 95134-1568.
Telephone: 408-943-9700.
Email: info@novellus.com
Website: http://www.novellus.com
Chrmn & CEO: R.S. Hill.
Pres: S. Somekh.

VP & CFO: K. Royal.
VP, Treas & Secy: R.S. Yim.
VP & Investor Contact: M. Grech 408-943-9700.
Dirs: N. R. Bonke, Y. A. El-Mansy, R. S. Hill, J. D. Litster, Y. Nishi, G. G. Possley, A. D. Rhoads, W. R. Spivey, D. A. Whitaker.

Founded: in 1984.
Domicile: California.
Employees: 2,902.
S&P Analyst: Colin McArdle/CB/GG

Nucor Corp.

Recommendation: **HOLD** ★ ★ ★ ☆ ☆   12-Month Target Price: **$46.00**
(as of September 09, 2004)

NUE has an approximate 0.07% weighting in the **S&P 500**

Sector: Materials
Sub-Industry: Steel
Peer Group: Minimilll Steelmakers and Suppliers

Summary: NUE, the largest U.S. minimill, is currently gaining market share in flat roll sheet and strip steel.

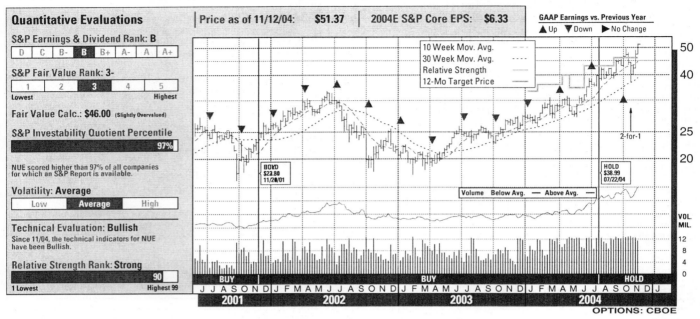

Price as of 11/12/04: **$51.37**	2004E S&P Core EPS: **$6.33**

Quantitative Evaluations

S&P Earnings & Dividend Rank: B

| D | C | B- | B | B+ | A- | A | A+ |

S&P Fair Value Rank: 3-

| 1 | 2 | 3 | 4 | 5 |
| Lowest | | | | Highest |

Fair Value Calc.: $46.00 (Slightly Overvalued)

S&P Investability Quotient Percentile   97%

NUE scored higher than 97% of all companies
for which an S&P Report is available.

Volatility: Average

| Low | Average | High |

Technical Evaluation: Bullish
Since 11/04, the technical indicators for NUE
have been Bullish.

Relative Strength Rank: Strong   90

1 Lowest   Highest 99

Analyst commentary prepared by Leo Larkin/PMW/GG

Highlights September 10, 2004

- We see 2004 sales advancing about 70%, after growth of 30.5% in 2003, mostly reflecting expected higher revenue per ton. We see the increase resulting from rising demand and from NUE's decision to impose a raw material surcharge. We see 2004 volume up 11%, based on our expectations of 4.4% real GDP growth in 2004, versus 3.1% in 2003. Excluding acquisitions, we believe volume rose 4% to 5% in 2003. Other positive factors that we anticipate for sales include a stabilization of non-residential construction markets, the likely absence of operational problems at the Decatur plant, and a small rise in the level of imports. Aided by much lower startup costs, expected higher operating rates, and the imposition of raw material surcharges, we expect EPS to post a sizable advance in 2004.

- We anticipate that sales growth in 2005 will trail 2004's robust gain, as increases in the volume of tons shipped are partly offset by an expected price decline. We believe rising U.S. steel production and a likely increase in imports will lead to lower prices in 2005. We also anticipate a contraction in margins, and a decline in EPS from 2004 levels.

- For the longer term, we see sales and EPS aided by industry consolidation and the introduction of new steelmaking technology.

Investment Rationale/Risk September 10, 2004

- We would hold the shares for potential capital gains and dividend income. In our view, EPS reached a cyclical trough in 2003. We see free cash flow growth accelerating, on a combination of rising net income and a decline in capital spending as a percentage of depreciation for the next several years. We think this will enable the company to accelerate dividend increases, make acquisitions, and invest in new steelmaking technology. From 1995 through 2004, NUE raised the dividend at a compound annual rate of 13%. However, in light of our belief that 2004 EPS could represent a peak or near peak in cycle EPS, we would not add to positions.

- Risks to our opinion and target price include the possibility of a 2005 EPS decline greater than we currently anticipate, due to unanticipated weakness in end markets.

- Following the company's upward revision of its third quarter EPS guidance in early September, we raised our 2004 EPS estimate to $12.75, from $10.45, based on the more positive outlook. We also adjusted our DCF model to account for greater free cash flow that we anticipate based on the increased EPS estimate. Based on our DCF analysis, our 12-month target price is $91.

Key Stock Statistics

S&P Core EPS 2005E	4.86	52-week Range	$51.59-25.26
S&P Oper. EPS 2004E	6.80	12 Month P/E	10.8
P/E on S&P Oper. EPS 2004E	7.6	Beta	1.39
S&P Oper. EPS 2005E	4.90	Shareholders	61,000
Yield (%)	1.0%	Market Cap (B)	$ 8.2
Dividend Rate/Share	0.52	Shares Outstanding (M)	159.1

Value of $10,000 invested five years ago: **$ 19,639**

Dividend Data Dividends have been paid since 1973

Amount ($)	Date Decl.	Ex-Div. Date	Stock of Record	Payment Date
0.210	Feb. 25	Mar. 29	Mar. 31	May. 11 '04
0.210	Jun. 02	Jun. 28	Jun. 30	Aug. 11 '04
0.260	Sep. 09	Sep. 28	Sep. 30	Nov. 11 '04
2-for-1 Stk.	Sep. 09	Oct. 18	Sep. 30	Oct. 15 '04

Revenues/Earnings Data Fiscal year ending December 31

Revenues (Million $)

	2004	2003	2002	2001	2000	1999
1Q	2,286	1,480	1,028	1,028	1,200	893.8
2Q	2,762	1,520	1,142	1,079	1,214	997.2
3Q	3,240	1,604	1,166	1,053	1,163	1,027
4Q	—	1,661	1,233	979.6	1,009	1,092
Yr.	—	6,266	4,802	4,139	4,586	4,009

Earnings Per Share ($)

	2004	2003	2002	2001	2000	1999
1Q	0.72	0.12	0.13	0.21	0.47	0.16
2Q	1.59	0.06	0.38	0.21	0.49	0.29
3Q	2.59	0.10	0.25	0.13	0.43	0.39
4Q	E1.90	0.13	0.28	0.17	0.52	0.56
Yr.	E6.80	0.40	1.03	0.73	1.90	1.40

Next earnings report expected: late-January Source: S&P, Company Reports
EPS Estimates based on S&P Operating Earnings; historical GAAP earnings are as reported.

Recommendation: **HOLD** ★ ★ ★ ☆ ☆   12-Month Target Price: **$46.00** (as of September 09, 2004)

Business Summary September 10, 2004

Nucor is the largest U.S. minimill steelmaker. The company's product offerings include hot-rolled steel (angles, rounds, channels, sheet, wide flange beams, pilings, billets, blooms, beam blanks, and plate), cold rolled steel, cold finished steel, steel joists and joist girders, steel deck, and steel fasteners.

The company manufactures the broadest range of products of any U.S. steel company, and is by far the most profitable. In contrast to the old line integrated steel companies, Nucor makes raw steel by melting scrap in electric arc furnaces, a far less capital intensive method than integrated steelmaking, which requires mining of raw materials for conversion into liquid steel via blast furnaces and coke ovens. Its sheet plants use the company's revolutionary thin slab casting process, which transforms molten steel into 2 inch thick slab.

Scrap and scrap substitutes comprise the major component of cost for Nucor's steelmaking. Their average cost was $137 per ton in 2003, versus $110 per ton in 2002 and $101 per ton in 2001.

Shipments to outside customers totaled 16,263,000 tons in 2003, versus 12,314,000 tons in 2002. Steel production totaled 17,441,000 tons in 2003, versus 13,622,000 tons in 2002. The increase in shipments and production reflected the acquisition of Trico Steel in July 2002 and Birmingham Steel in December 2002.

Nucor's principal competitors for traditional minimill construction market steel products include Bayou Steel, Chaparral Steel, and Gerdau Ameri Steel.

Competition in flat roll carbon sheet includes the old line integrated companies, and new minimill players such as BHP-North Star, Gallatin Steel, and Steel Dynamics.

In April 2003, the company said it had signed an agreement with Companhia Vale Do Rio Doce (CRVD) to build and operate an environmentally friendly pig iron project in northern Brazil. Nucor was to invest $10 million, in return for a 22% interest in the venture. The project will utilize two conventional mini-blast furnaces to produce 380,000 metric tons of pig iron a year, using iron ore supplied by CRVD. Nucor plans to purchase the plant's production. Production is scheduled to begin in late 2004.

In December 2003, Nucor said it was instituting a $20 per ton raw materials surcharge on all steel mill products, beginning with shipments on January 1, 2004. The company said the surcharge would be adjusted on the third Monday of every month, based on raw material cost changes from the previous month, and applied to shipments on the first day of the following month. Nucor said a rapid and unprecedented rise in raw material costs had outpaced the company's ability to react appropriately through normal price changes.

In September 2004, the company said it expected to report third quarter EPS of $4.40 to $4.60, versus earlier guidance of $3.20 to $3.40. NUE attributed the upward revision to wider margins.

Company Financials Fiscal Year ending December 31

Per Share Data ($)

(Year Ended December 31)	2003	2002	2001	2000	1999	1998	1997	1996	1995	1994
Tangible Bk. Val.	14.90	14.86	14.15	13.73	12.98	11.87	10.66	9.17	7.89	6.42
Cash Flow	2.72	3.00	2.59	3.49	2.87	2.94	2.91	2.46	2.58	2.21
Earnings	0.40	1.04	0.73	1.90	1.40	1.50	1.68	1.42	1.57	1.30
S&P Core Earnings	0.30	0.92	0.65	NA	NA	NA	NA	NA	NA	NA
Dividends	0.40	0.38	0.34	0.30	0.26	0.23	0.20	0.16	0.14	0.09
Payout Ratio	100%	37%	47%	16%	18%	15%	12%	11%	9%	7%
Prices - High	29.39	35.07	28.25	28.21	30.90	30.31	31.46	31.50	31.62	36.00
- Low	17.51	18.00	16.72	14.75	20.81	17.62	22.37	22.56	21.00	24.37
P/E Ratio - High	73	34	39	15	22	20	19	22	20	28
- Low	44	17	23	8	15	12	13	16	13	19

Income Statement Analysis (Million $)

	2003	2002	2001	2000	1999	1998	1997	1996	1995	1994
Revs.	6,266	4,802	4,139	4,586	4,009	4,151	4,184	3,647	3,462	2,976
Oper. Inc.	468	601	469	737	631	665	678	570	605	528
Depr.	364	307	289	259	257	253	218	182	174	158
Int. Exp.	24.6	22.9	22.0	24.1	20.5	10.0	9.28	8.11	9.28	14.6
Pretax Inc.	90.8	310	174	478	379	415	460	388	432	357
Eff. Tax Rate	4.51%	22.0%	35.0%	35.0%	35.5%	36.5%	36.0%	36.0%	36.5%	36.5%
Net Inc.	62.8	162	113	311	245	264	294	248	276	227
S&P Core Earnings	47.9	143	101	NA	NA	NA	NA	NA	NA	NA

Balance Sheet & Other Fin. Data (Million $)

	2003	2002	2001	2000	1999	1998	1997	1996	1995	1994
Cash	350	219	462	491	572	309	283	104	202	102
Curr. Assets	1,621	1,424	1,374	1,381	1,539	1,129	1,126	828	831	639
Total Assets	4,492	4,381	3,759	3,722	3,730	3,227	2,984	2,620	2,296	2,002
Curr. Liab.	630	592	484	558	531	487	524	466	477	382
LT Debt	904	879	460	460	390	215	168	153	107	173
Common Equity	2,342	2,323	2,201	2,131	2,262	2,073	1,876	1,609	1,382	1,123
Total Cap.	3,423	3,419	2,946	2,904	2,934	2,570	2,321	2,028	1,710	1,535
Cap. Exp.	215	244	261	415	375	503	307	537	263	185
Cash Flow	427	469	402	570	501	517	512	430	449	384
Curr. Ratio	2.6	2.4	2.8	2.5	2.9	2.3	2.1	1.8	1.7	1.7
% LT Debt of Cap.	26.4	25.7	15.6	15.9	13.3	8.4	7.2	7.5	6.3	11.3
% Net Inc.of Revs.	1.0	3.4	2.7	6.8	6.1	6.4	7.0	6.8	8.0	7.6
% Ret. on Assets	1.4	4.0	3.0	8.3	7.0	8.5	10.5	10.1	12.8	11.8
% Ret. on Equity	2.7	5.1	5.2	14.2	11.3	13.4	16.9	16.6	22.0	22.4

Data as orig reptd.; bef. results of disc opers/spec. items. Per share data adj. for stk. divs.; EPS diluted. E-Estimated. NA-Not Available. NM-Not Meaningful. NR-Not Ranked. UR-Under Review.

Office: 2100 Rexford Road, Charlotte, NC 28211.
Telephone: 704-366-7000.
Email: info@nucor.com
Website: http://www.nucor.com
Pres, Vice Chrmn & CEO: D.R. DiMicco.

EVP, CFO & Treas: T.S. Lisenby.
Secy: A.R. Eagle.
Dirs: P. C. Browning, C. C. Daley, Jr., D. R. DiMicco, H. B. Gantt, V. F. Haynes, J. D. Hlavacek, R. J. Milchovich, T. A. Waltermire.
Auditor: PricewaterhouseCoopers.

Founded: in 1940.
Domicile: Delaware.
Employees: 9,900.
S&P Analyst: Leo Larkin/PMW/GG

NVIDIA Corp.

Stock Report
November 13, 2004
NASDAQ Symbol: **NVDA**

Recommendation: **HOLD** ★★★☆☆
SELL · SELL · HOLD · BUY · BUY

12-Month Target Price: $19.00
(as of November 05, 2004)

NVDA has an approximate 0.03% weighting in the **S&P 500**

Sector: Information Technology
Sub-Industry: Semiconductors
Peer Group: Semiconductors - Graphics

Summary: NVDA develops and markets 3D graphics processors and related software for personal computers, workstations and digital entertainment platforms.

Quantitative Evaluations

S&P Earnings & Dividend Rank: B-

| D | C | B- | B | B+ | A- | A | A+ |

S&P Fair Value Rank: 4-

| 1 | 2 | 3 | 4 | 5 |
| Lowest | | | | Highest |

Fair Value Calc.: $17.80 (Fairly Valued)

S&P Investability Quotient Percentile

17%

NVDA scored lower than 83% of all companies for which an S&P Report is available.

Volatility: High

| Low | Average | High |

Technical Evaluation: Bullish
Since 11/04, the technical indicators for NVDA have been Bullish.

Relative Strength Rank: Strong

92
1 Lowest   Highest 99

Price as of 11/12/04: $18.10 | **2005E S&P Core EPS:** $0.06

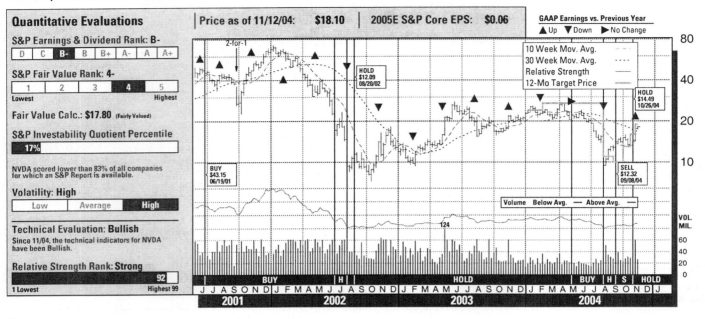

GAAP Earnings vs. Previous Year
▲ Up ▼ Down ▶ No Change

10 Week Mov. Avg.
30 Week Mov. Avg.
Relative Strength
12-Mo Target Price

Analyst commentary prepared by Amrit Tewary/MF/JWP

Highlights November 10, 2004

- We expect sales to grow 7.8% in FY 05 (Jan.) and another 10.8% in FY 06. We project a multi-year semiconductor industry expansion that should to boost the company's core markets in graphics processor units (GPUs) for PCs.

- In August 2003, rival ATI Technologies won a contract to design the GPU for Microsoft's next generation Xbox video game console; NVDA is the current GPU maker for Xbox. Despite this design loss, we do not expect revenues to be affected through FY 05, as the original Xbox finishes its run. Revenues from Xbox provide an estimated 15% to 20% of total sales.

- We expect the operating margin to narrow in FY 05, as we see higher R&D and SG&A expenses outweighing a wider gross margin. For FY 06, we see margins widening significantly on a more favorable product mix and operating cost controls. The company became debt free in the FY 04 third quarter, after redeeming its convertible debt. We estimate FY 05 EPS of $0.47, and forecast $0.83 for FY 06. Including an adjustment for estimated stock option expense, we project S&P Core Earnings per share of $0.06 for FY 04 and $0.40 for FY 06.

Investment Rationale/Risk November 10, 2004

- We would hold shares of NVDA, as we expect them to perform in line with chip peers over the next 12 months. We believe the company is gaining traction at customers with its newer, higher-end graphics chips. We expect strength in the higher end graphics processor segment to offset intensifying competitive pressure in the lower end and mainstream segments.

- Risks to our opinion and target price include the possibility that a sharp deterioration in the macroeconomic environment will lead to softer than anticipated PC end market demand in upcoming quarters, thus negatively impacting NVDA's graphics chip sales. Other risks include increased competition and potential strategic lapses by the company.

- Our 12-month target price of $19 is based on our P/E and price-to-sales analyses. Our target price is derived by applying a P/E multiple of 23X, below the stock's average historical multiple, to our FY 06 EPS estimate. Our target also applies a price-to-sales ratio of 1.5X, below historical norms, to our FY 06 sales per share estimate. We expect most chip stocks to trade at a discount to historical norms, given our view that the industry is entering the latter stage of the current upcycle.

Key Stock Statistics

S&P Core EPS 2006E	0.40	52-week Range	$27.35-9.30
S&P Oper. EPS 2005E	0.47	12 Month P/E	41.1
P/E on S&P Oper. EPS 2005E	38.5	Beta	NA
S&P Oper. EPS 2006E	0.83	Shareholders	436
Yield (%)	Nil	Market Cap (B)	$ 3.0
Dividend Rate/Share	Nil	Shares Outstanding (M)	166.5

Value of $10,000 invested five years ago: **$ 24,976**

Dividend Data

No cash dividends have been paid.

Revenues/Earnings Data Fiscal year ending January 31

Revenues (Million $)

	2005	2004	2003	2002	2001	2000
1Q	471.9	405.0	582.9	240.9	148.5	71.02
2Q	456.1	459.8	427.3	259.9	169.3	78.02
3Q	515.6	486.1	430.3	365.0	197.7	97.02
4Q	—	472.1	468.9	503.7	219.8	128.5
Yr.	—	1,823	1,909	1,369	735.3	374.5

Earnings Per Share ($)

	2005	2004	2003	2002	2001	2000
1Q	0.12	0.12	0.47	0.16	0.09	0.04
2Q	0.03	0.14	0.03	0.20	0.15	0.05
3Q	0.15	0.04	-0.32	0.24	0.18	0.09
4Q	E0.17	0.14	0.30	0.43	0.20	0.10
Yr.	E0.47	0.43	0.54	1.03	0.62	0.27

Next earnings report expected: mid-February Source: S&P, Company Reports
EPS Estimates based on S&P Operating Earnings; historical GAAP earnings are as reported.

The **McGraw·Hill** Companies

NVIDIA Corporation

Recommendation: HOLD ★ ★ ★ ★ ★   12-Month Target Price: **$19.00** (as of November 05, 2004)

Business Summary November 10, 2004

NVIDIA Corp. designs, develops and markets high-performance graphics processing units (GPUs), media and communications processors (MCPs), ultra-low power media processors (UMPs), and related software for PCs and digital entertainment platforms, ranging from professional workstations to video game consoles to handheld electronic devices. It aims to be the "most important visual computing company in the world."

Interactive 3D graphics displays are an integral part of many computing applications for workstations, consumer and commercial desktop and laptop PCs, personal digital assistants, cellular phones, and gaming consoles. NVDA's products are designed into products offered by nearly all leading PC OEMs.

The company believes that PC interactive 3D graphics capability represents one of the primary means by which users differentiate between systems. NVDA thinks that PC users can easily differentiate the quality of graphics, and prefer displays that provide a superior visual experience.

NVDA's products provide high levels of visual quality, realistic imagery and motion, and complex object and scene interaction. The company offers a "top to bottom" family of graphics processors, serving various 3D and 2D sub-markets in a full spectrum of price points. At the high end are the NVIDIA GeForce FX and GeForce4 GPUs (graphics processing units), which are designed to deliver high performance and cinematic quality graphics for interactive entertainment and digital image editing. The workstation market is addressed by the Quadro family of GPUs. The nForce family of MCPs offers a comprehensive set of multimedia

capabilities and works with Advanced Micro Devices microprocessors. Products for handheld PDAs and wireless phones are available in the GoForce family of UMPs.

In March 2000, the company agreed to develop and supply graphics chips for Microsoft's Xbox video game console. The XGPU and MCP products form a two-processor chipset that powers the Xbox system's graphics, audio and networking capabilities. In August 2003, rival ATI Technologies won the contract for the GPU for the next-generation Xbox.

In August 2003, NVDA acquired MediaQ Inc., for $70 million cash, in an effort to add expertise in graphics and multimedia technology for the wireless mobile device market.

Sales are concentrated among a few large customers at the head of a distribution channel that serves a broad base of end customers. In FY 04 (Jan.), Edom Technology, an Asian distributor, accounted for 21% of sales; Microsoft for 15%; Atlantic Semiconductor, a distributor, 12%; and sales to Micro-Star, a contract electronics manufacturer, 12%. Sales outside the Americas accounted for 75% of total sales in FY 04.

The company runs on a fabless model, relying on contract manufacturers that include Taiwan Semiconductor, IBM, and United Microelectronics for wafer fabrication.

Company Financials Fiscal Year ending January 31

Per Share Data ($)

(Year Ended January 31)	2004	2003	2002	2001	2000	1999	1998	1997	1996	1995
Tangible Bk. Val.	5.50	5.43	4.56	2.80	1.02	0.56	NM	NA	NA	NA
Cash Flow	0.91	0.88	1.29	0.72	0.42	0.07	-0.05	NA	NA	NA
Earnings	0.43	0.54	1.03	0.62	0.28	0.04	-0.07	NA	NA	NA
S&P Core Earnings	-0.01	-0.66	0.30	0.35	NA	NA	NA	NA	NA	NA
Dividends	Nil	Nil	Nil	Nil	Nil	Nil	NA	NA	NA	NA
Payout Ratio	Nil	Nil	Nil	Nil	Nil	Nil	NA	NA	NA	NA

Cal. Yrs.	2003	2002	2001	2000	1999	1998	1997	1996	1995	1994
Prices - High	27.75	72.66	70.25	44.00	11.87	NA	NA	NA	NA	NA
- Low	9.33	7.20	14.12	8.75	3.00	NA	NA	NA	NA	NA
P/E Ratio - High	65	NM	68	71	42	NA	NA	NA	NA	NA
- Low	22	NM	14	14	11	NA	NA	NA	NA	NA

Income Statement Analysis (Million $)

	2004	2003	2002	2001	2000	1999	1998	1997	1996	1995
Revs.	1,823	1,909	1,369	735	375	158	29.1	3.90	NA	NA
Oper. Inc.	172	202	299	144	67.6	8.52	-2.10	-2.20	NA	NA
Depr.	82.0	58.2	43.5	15.7	9.00	4.01	1.36	0.80	NA	NA
Int. Exp.	12.0	Nil	16.2	4.85	Nil	Nil	Nil	NA	NA	NA
Pretax Inc.	86.7	151	253	145	60.4	4.49	-3.60	-3.10	NA	NA
Eff. Tax Rate	14.1%	39.7%	30.0%	32.0%	32.2%	7.96%	Nil	Nil	NA	NA
Net Inc.	74.4	90.8	177	99	41.0	4.13	-3.60	-3.10	NA	NA
S&P Core Earnings	-1.44	-104	49.4	54.7	NA	NA	NA	NA	NA	NA

Balance Sheet & Other Fin. Data (Million $)

	2004	2003	2002	2001	2000	1999	1998	1997	1996	1995
Cash	604	1,028	798	699	61.6	50.3	6.60	NA	NA	NA
Curr. Assets	1,053	1,352	1,234	930	173	101	19.3	NA	NA	NA
Total Assets	1,399	1,617	1,503	1,017	203	113	25.0	NA	NA	NA
Curr. Liab.	334	379	433	309	76.2	47.1	3.20	NA	NA	NA
LT Debt	9.46	305	306	300	1.46	2.00	1.90	NA	NA	NA
Common Equity	1,051	933	764	407	127	64.2	6.90	NA	NA	NA
Total Cap.	1,061	1,238	1,070	707	129	66.2	8.80	NA	NA	NA
Cap. Exp.	128	63.1	97.0	36.3	11.6	7.90	0.16	NA	NA	NA
Cash Flow	156	149	220	114	50.0	8.14	-2.24	NA	NA	NA
Curr. Ratio	3.2	3.6	2.8	3.0	2.3	2.1	6.0	NA	NA	NA
% LT Debt of Cap.	0.9	24.6	28.6	42.4	1.1	3.0	21.5	NA	NA	NA
% Net Inc.of Revs.	4.1	4.8	12.9	13.4	10.9	2.6	NM	NA	NA	NA
% Ret. on Assets	4.9	5.8	14.0	16.1	25.9	5.8	NM	NA	NA	NA
% Ret. on Equity	7.5	10.7	30.2	36.9	42.9	11.3	NM	NA	NA	NA

Data as orig reptd.; bef. results of disc opers/spec. items. Per share data adj. for stk. divs. Bold denotes primary EPS - prior periods restated. E-Estimated. NA-Not Available. NM-Not Meaningful. NR-Not Ranked. UR-Under Review.

Office: 2701 San Tomas Expressway, Santa Clara, CA 95050.
Telephone: 408-486-2000.
Email: ir@nvidia.com
Website: http://www.nvidia.com
Pres & CEO: J. Huang.
VP & General Counsel: D.M. Shannon.

VP & Investor Contact: M. Hara 408-486-2000.
CFO: M.D. Burkett.
Secy: E.C. Jensen.
Dirs: S. Chu, T. Coxe, J. C. Gaither, J. Huang, H. C. Jones, W. J. Miller, A. B. Seawell, M. A. Stevens.

Founded: in 1993.
Domicile: Delaware.
Employees: 1,825.
S&P Analyst: Amrit Tewary/MF/JWP

Occidental Petroleum

Recommendation: **BUY** ★★★★☆
SELL SELL HOLD BUY BUY

12-Month Target Price: **$65.00**
(as of October 11, 2004)

OXY has an approximate 0.21% weighting in the **S&P 500**

Sector: Energy
Sub-Industry: Integrated Oil & Gas
Peer Group: Major Integrated Oil & Gas

Summary: Occidental Petroleum is a global oil and gas exploration and production company, with a chemicals division.

Quantitative Evaluations

S&P Earnings & Dividend Rank: B+

D	C	B-	B	B+	A-	A	A+

S&P Fair Value Rank: 2-

1	2	3	4	5
Lowest				Highest

Fair Value Calc.: $54.00 (Slightly Overvalued)

S&P Investability Quotient Percentile

91%

OXY scored higher than 91% of all companies for which an S&P Report is available.

Volatility: Low

Low	Average	High

Technical Evaluation: Bullish
Since 6/04, the technical indicators for OXY have been Bullish.

Relative Strength Rank: Moderate

57

1 Lowest	Highest 99

Price as of 11/12/04:	$57.91	2004E S&P Core EPS:	$6.24

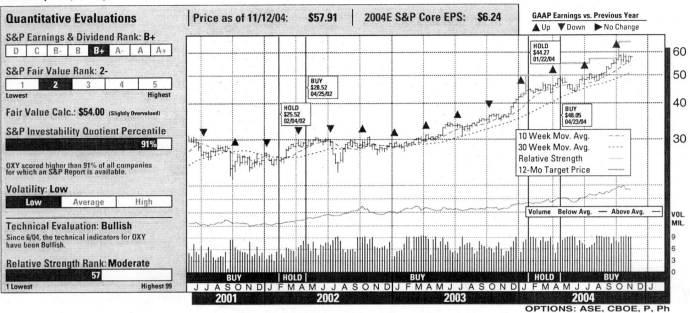

GAAP Earnings vs. Previous Year
▲ Up ▼ Down ► No Change

- 10 Week Mov. Avg.
- 30 Week Mov. Avg.
- Relative Strength
- 12-Mo Target Price

Volume Below Avg. — Above Avg.

OPTIONS: ASE, CBOE, P, Ph

Analyst commentary prepared by T. J. Vital/MF/PMW/GG

Highlights October 22, 2004

- Third quarter operating EPS exceeded our expectations by $0.20, on greater than expected natural gas price realizations, higher gas production from Oman, and wider chemical margins. Chemical results in the quarter were boosted by stronger chlorine pricing, and OxyChem implemented a $20 per ton increase in the second quarter, and announced an additional $20 per ton raise to be effective on October 1 to most accounts; other U.S. chlor-alkali producers announced similar increases. EBITDA climbed 31% in 2003, on improved demand and stronger pricing. We expect gains of 33% in 2004 and 12% in 2005.

- Hydrocarbon production rose 3.1% in the quarter, and we expect growth of over 3.5% in 2004 and nearly 2.5% in 2005. OXY expected fourth quarter volumes to remain near third quarter levels. In August, the company said it had been informed that Ecuador was considering terminating OXY's participation contract for Block 15, based on an assertion that the company had breached its agreement; OXY regards this as incorrect. Ecuadorian operations represent 8% of the company's production and 4% of its proved reserves.

- In April 2003, the company made three Permian Basin acquisitions (73 million bbl. of proved reserves), for about $235 million. As a result, OXY raised its production forecast by 10,000 b/d through 2006. It expected 575,000 b/d for 2004, 590,000 b/d for 2005, and 620,000 b/d for 2006. We view reserve replacement as strong, and calculate the organic rate at 131% for 2003.

Key Stock Statistics

S&P Core EPS 2005E	6.29	52-week Range	$59.42-35.60
S&P Oper. EPS 2004E	6.27	12 Month P/E	10.5
P/E on S&P Oper. EPS 2004E	9.2	Beta	0.55
S&P Oper. EPS 2005E	6.30	Shareholders	52,635
Yield (%)	1.9%	Market Cap (B)	$ 22.9
Dividend Rate/Share	1.10	Shares Outstanding (M)	394.7

Value of $10,000 invested five years ago: **$ 31,500**

Dividend Data Dividends have been paid since 1975

Amount ($)	Date Decl.	Ex-Div. Date	Stock of Record	Payment Date
0.260	Nov. 04	Dec. 08	Dec. 10	Jan. 15 '04
0.275	Feb. 12	Mar. 08	Mar. 10	Apr. 15 '04
0.275	Apr. 30	Jun. 08	Jun. 10	Jul. 15 '04
0.275	Jul. 15	Sep. 08	Sep. 10	Oct. 15 '04

Investment Rationale/Risk October 22, 2004

- We would accumulate the shares, recently yielding 1.9%, and with what we project as solid growth prospects at low finding and development, acquisition and reserve replacement costs relative to those of peers. In April, the U.S. eased sanctions against Libya. This enabled OXY, which wrote off 217 million bbl. of Libyan oil after its departure in 1986, to return to that country. With the majority of the company's reserves and production focused on oil and in maturing areas of the U.S., we expect OXY's upstream growth to be driven by Middle East projects. To fund upstream growth, OXY expects capital spending to increase 29%, to $1.8 billion (including $0.3 billion for the Dolphin Project) in 2004, with a further rise in 2005, on increased investments in the Dolphin Project, Libya, and possible acquisitions (such as in the Permian Basin).

- Risks to our recommendation and target price include geopolitical risk associated with upstream growth in certain international regions (such as the Middle East and Libya); and the impact of high feedstock and energy costs on its chemical operations.

- Using an average of our DCF analysis and market and peer multiple valuations, our 12-month target price is $65, equal to 10X our 2005 EPS estimate, a slight discount to peers.

Revenues/Earnings Data Fiscal year ending December 31

Revenues (Million $)

	2004	2003	2002	2001	2000	1999
1Q	2,580	2,371	1,523	4,475	2,574	1,344
2Q	2,769	2,266	1,867	3,845	3,195	1,647
3Q	3,067	2,319	1,963	3,285	3,863	2,113
4Q	—	2,370	1,985	2,380	3,943	2,506
Yr.	—	9,447	7,338	13,985	13,575	7,610

Earnings Per Share ($)

	2004	2003	2002	2001	2000	1999
1Q	1.23	1.03	0.33	1.37	0.74	-0.17
2Q	1.46	0.97	0.63	1.26	1.53	0.03
3Q	1.88	1.14	1.25	1.18	1.09	0.35
4Q	E1.72	0.97	0.84	-0.65	0.90	1.33
Yr.	E6.27	4.11	3.07	3.17	4.26	1.58

Next earnings report expected: late-January Source: S&P, Company Reports
EPS Estimates based on S&P Operating Earnings; historical GAAP earnings are as reported.

Occidental Petroleum Corporation

Recommendation: **BUY** ★ ★ ★ ★ ☆   12-Month Target Price: **$65.00** (as of October 11, 2004)

Business Summary October 22, 2004

Conducting business through subsidiaries, Occidental Petroleum is a global oil and gas exploration and production (65% of 2003 segment revenues; 94% of 2003 pretax operating profit) and chemical (35%; 6%) company.

The oil and gas segment explores for, develops, produces and markets crude oil and natural gas. The company has active oil and gas operations in the U.S. (principally in California, the Hugoton area in Kansas and Oklahoma, the Permian field in West Texas and New Mexico, and the Gulf of Mexico) and internationally (Colombia, Ecuador, Oman, Pakistan, Qatar, Russia, the U.A.E., and Yemen).

Since purchasing a 78% stake in the giant Elk Hills field in 1998, OXY has become the largest independent oil and gas producer in California. Total worldwide barrel of oil equivalent (BOE) production averaged 547,000 per day in 2003, up from 515,000 per day in 2002. Crude oil and liquids production rose to 419,000 barrels per day (b/d; 61% U.S.) in 2003, from 381,000 bpd in 2002. Natural gas production declined to 606 million cubic feet per day (MMcf/d; 88% U.S.) in 2003, from 627 MMcf/d in 2002. Excluding acquisitions, OXY replaced 184% of worldwide oil and gas production in 2003, at an average finding and development cost of $4.27 per BOE, compared to 140% in 2002, at an average cost of $4.65. Excluding acquisitions, the three-year (2001-2003) average reserve replacement was 156% at an average finding and development cost of $4.53 per BOE. Crude oil represented about 83% of 2003 proved reserves and 77% of 2003 production. Proved oil reserves at the end of 2003 totaled 1.97 billion bbl. (81% developed; 74% U.S.),

compared to 1.97 Bbbl. (78%, 74%) in 2002. Natural gas proven reserves totaled 2.049 trillion cubic feet (70% developed; 70% U.S.) in 2003, compared to 2.049 Tcf (85%; 89%) in 2002.

In April 2000, the company sold its 29.2% stock interest in Canadian Occidental Petroleum Ltd., for about $700 million. Funds were used in part for the purchase of Altura Energy Ltd. in the Permian Basin, for $3.6 billion, and the purchase of ARCO Long Beach Inc. (the owner of the Long Beach Unit's operating contractor, THUMS), for $68 million. During 2003, OXY made several complementary acquisitions in the Permian Basin, for about $317 million. In 2002, OXY acquired a 24.5% interest in Dolphin Energy Ltd. (the Dolphin Project for the development and production of natural gas from Qatar's North Field, with startup slated for 2006), for $310 million. It expects to invest about $1 billion for its 24.5% share in the Dolphin Project over the next three years. In 2003, Dolphin Energy signed two 25-year contracts to supply about 1 Bcf/d of natural gas to two entities in the U.A.E.; a third contract is being negotiated with the Emirate of Dubai.

The OxyChem subsidiary manufactures basic chemicals (principally chlorine and caustic soda), vinyls, petrochemicals and specialty products. OXYChem has enhanced its position in core markets by entering into alliances that offer cost savings. In 1998, the company became a partner in the Equistar Chemicals, L.P. alliance (with a 29.5% interest). In August 2002, OXY exchanged its Equistar interest for a 21% equity interest in Lyondell Chemical Co.

Company Financials Fiscal Year ending December 31

Per Share Data ($)

(Year Ended December 31)	2003	2002	2001	2000	1999	1998	1997	1996	1995	1994
Tangible Bk. Val.	20.49	16.71	15.06	12.90	9.57	8.97	8.46	11.57	10.37	9.88
Cash Flow	7.13	5.73	5.77	6.69	3.84	3.26	2.78	5.00	4.21	2.48
Earnings	4.11	3.07	3.17	4.26	1.58	0.88	0.39	1.86	1.31	-0.36
S&P Core Earnings	4.05	2.55	3.40	NA	NA	NA	NA	NA	NA	NA
Dividends	1.04	1.00	1.00	1.00	1.00	1.00	1.00	1.00	1.00	1.00
Payout Ratio	25%	33%	32%	23%	63%	114%	NM	54%	76%	NM
Prices - High	42.98	30.75	31.10	25.56	24.56	30.43	30.75	27.25	24.37	22.37
- Low	27.17	22.98	21.87	15.75	14.62	16.62	21.75	20.12	18.00	15.12
P/E Ratio - High	10	10	10	6	16	35	79	15	19	NM
- Low	7	7	7	4	9	19	56	11	14	NM

Income Statement Analysis (Million $)

	2003	2002	2001	2000	1999	1998	1997	1996	1995	1994
Revs.	9,326	7,338	13,985	13,574	7,610	6,596	8,016	10,557	10,423	9,236
Oper. Inc.	4,281	3,119	3,638	3,826	1,831	1,297	1,835	2,316	2,143	1,539
Depr. Depl. & Amort.	1,177	1,012	971	901	805	835	822	921	922	882
Int. Exp.	332	295	392	518	498	559	434	484	579	589
Pretax Inc.	2,884	1,662	1,892	3,196	1,257	688	528	1,152	913	109
Eff. Tax Rate	42.5%	25.4%	29.8%	45.1%	50.2%	52.8%	58.9%	39.4%	44.1%	131.2%
Net Inc.	1,595	1,163	1,186	1,569	568	325	217	698	511	-36.0
S&P Core Earnings	1,568	963	1,273	NA	NA	NA	NA	NA	NA	NA

Balance Sheet & Other Fin. Data (Million $)

	2003	2002	2001	2000	1999	1998	1997	1996	1995	1994
Cash	683	146	199	97.0	214	96.0	113	279	520	129
Curr. Assets	2,474	1,873	1,483	2,067	1,688	2,795	1,916	2,190	2,519	2,258
Total Assets	18,168	16,548	17,850	19,414	14,125	15,252	15,282	17,634	17,815	17,989
Curr. Liab.	2,526	2,235	1,890	2,740	1,967	2,931	1,870	2,470	2,657	2,201
LT Debt	3,993	4,452	4,528	5,658	4,854	5,367	4,925	4,511	4,819	6,114
Common Equity	7,929	6,318	5,634	4,774	3,523	3,120	2,304	3,809	3,305	3,132
Total Cap.	13,235	12,085	13,489	13,977	9,372	9,555	10,239	12,211	12,069	13,142
Cap. Exp.	1,601	1,236	1,401	952	601	1,074	1,549	1,185	979	1,103
Cash Flow	2,772	2,175	2,157	2,470	1,366	1,143	951	1,619	1,340	770
Curr. Ratio	1.0	0.8	0.8	0.8	0.9	1.0	1.0	0.9	1.0	1.0
% LT Debt of Cap.	30.2	36.8	33.6	40.5	51.8	56.2	48.1	36.9	40.0	46.5
% Ret. on Assets	9.2	6.8	6.4	9.4	3.9	2.1	1.3	3.9	2.9	NM
% Ret. on Equity	22.4	19.5	22.8	37.8	16.9	12.6	6.2	17.0	9.2	NM

Data as orig reptd.; bef. results of disc opers/spec. items. Per share data adj. for stk. divs.; EPS diluted. E-Estimated. NA-Not Available. NM-Not Meaningful. NR-Not Ranked. UR-Under Review.

Office: 10889 Wilshire Boulevard, Los Angeles, CA 90024-4201.
Telephone: 310-208-8800.
Email: investorrelations_newyork@oxy.com
Website: http://www.oxy.com
Chrmn & CEO: R.R. Irani.
Pres: D.R. Laurance.
Sr EVP & CFO: S.I. Chazen.

EVP, Secy & General Counsel: D.P. de Brier.
VP & Chief Acctg Officer: S.P. Dominick, Jr.
VP & Investor Contact: K.J. Huffman 212-603-8183.
Dirs: R. W. Burkle, J. S. Chalsty, E. P. Djerejian, R. C. Dreier, J. E. Feick, R. R. Irani, D. R. Laurance, I. W. Maloney, R. Segovia, A. D. Syriani, R. Tomich, W. L. Weisman.

Founded: in 1920.
Domicile: Delaware.
Employees: 7,133.
S&P Analyst: T. J. Vital/MF/PMW/GG

Recommendation: **HOLD** ★ ★ ★ ☆ ☆
SELL SELL HOLD BUY BUY

12-Month Target Price: **$33.00**
(as of August 12, 2004)

OMX has an approximate 0.03% weighting in the **S&P 500**

Sector: Consumer Discretionary
Sub-Industry: Specialty Stores
Peer Group: Office Products Retailers

Summary: This retail and business to business office products distributor operates about 900 superstores.

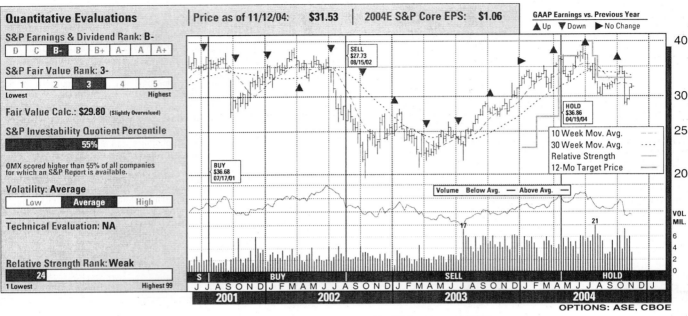

Quantitative Evaluations	
S&P Earnings & Dividend Rank: B-	

D C **B-** B B+ A- A A+

S&P Fair Value Rank: 3-

1 2 **3** 4 5
Lowest Highest

Fair Value Calc.: $29.80 (Slightly Overvalued)

S&P Investability Quotient Percentile
55%

OMX scored higher than 55% of all companies for which an S&P Report is available.

Volatility: Average

Low **Average** High

Technical Evaluation: NA

Relative Strength Rank: Weak
24
1 Lowest   Highest 99

Price as of 11/12/04: **$31.53** | 2004E S&P Core EPS: **$1.06**

Analyst commentary prepared by Michael Souers/JP/BK

Highlights November 08, 2004

- We expect revenues to increase on a comparable basis in the low- to mid-single digits in 2005 excluding the paper and building products business, which the company divested on October 29. We look for same-store sales growth in the low single digits in office supply retail operations, aided by ongoing store remodeling and customer service enhancement efforts. We think OMX's contract segment will produce mid-single digit revenue growth through additional account wins as well as greater business from existing accounts as it leverages cross-selling opportunities with retail.

- After an initial increase in operating expenses due to lower margins and continued losses from OfficeMax Direct, we expect operating margins to improve on continuing synergies resulting from recent acquisition activity and the leveraging of expenses over a higher revenue base.

- We anticipate sharply lower interest expense as OMX uses a large part of its cash proceeds from asset sales to pay down debt. We project a large reduction in the share count due to share buybacks and estimate 2005 EPS of $2.33.

Investment Rationale/Risk November 08, 2004

- We recommend holding the shares. The recently completed sale of its paper, forest products and timberland assets for approximately $3.7 billion leaves the company in a much better financial position, in our opinion. With the cash received from the sale of assets, OMX is planning on retiring between $2.2 and $2.3 billion in total debt and using between $800 million and $1 billion ($9 to $11 in cash per share) for either a special dividend or share repurchases. However, we believe it is unclear whether the company can effectively compete with behemoths Staples (SPLS: $30; accumulate) and Office Depot (ODP: $16; accumulate).

- Risks to our opinion and target price include a slowdown in economic growth; a sharp rise in interest rates that could dampen capital spending by businesses; and the negative effects of potential terrorist attacks on consumer spending.

- At about 13X our 2005 EPS estimate, OMX trades on a par with ODP but at a significant discount to SPLS. Our 12-month target price of $33 assumes that the company will continue to trade at the low end of comparable ranges with peers.

Key Stock Statistics

S&P Oper. EPS 2004E	1.40	52-week Range	$38.01-27.27
P/E on S&P Oper. EPS 2004E	22.5	12 Month P/E	16.9
S&P Oper. EPS 2005E	2.33	Beta	1.15
Yield (%)	1.9%	Shareholders	14,223
Dividend Rate/Share	0.60	Market Cap (B)	$ 2.8
Shares Outstanding (M)	88.0		

Value of $10,000 invested five years ago: **$ 9,195**

Dividend Data Dividends have been paid since 1935

Amount ($)	Date Decl.	Ex-Div. Date	Stock of Record	Payment Date
0.150	Dec. 12	Dec. 29	Jan. 01	Jan. 15 '04
0.150	Feb. 13	Mar. 30	Apr. 01	Apr. 15 '04
0.150	Apr. 16	Jun. 29	Jul. 01	Jul. 15 '04
0.150	Jul. 30	Sep. 29	Oct. 01	Oct. 15 '04

Revenues/Earnings Data Fiscal year ending December 31

Revenues (Million $)

	2004	2003	2002	2001	2000	1999
1Q	3,530	1,853	1,788	1,901	1,946	1,611
2Q	3,401	1,928	1,888	1,890	1,926	1,678
3Q	3,651	2,111	1,935	1,874	1,921	1,789
4Q	—	2,352	1,801	1,757	1,865	1,874
Yr.	—	8,245	7,412	7,422	7,807	6,953

Earnings Per Share ($)

	2004	2003	2002	2001	2000	1999
1Q	0.66	-0.38	-0.17	-0.68	0.60	0.22
2Q	0.52	-0.12	Nil	0.28	0.46	0.92
3Q	0.63	0.48	0.09	0.20	1.33	0.74
4Q	E0.24	0.05	0.05	-0.78	0.34	1.18
Yr.	E1.40	0.07	-0.03	-0.96	2.73	3.06

Next earnings report expected: late-January Source: S&P, Company Reports
EPS Estimates based on S&P Operating Earnings; historical GAAP earnings are as reported.

OfficeMax Incorporated

Recommendation: **HOLD** ★ ★ ★ ☆ ☆   12-Month Target Price: **$33.00** (as of August 12, 2004)

Business Summary November 08, 2004

OfficeMax (formerly Boise Cascade Corporation) is a business to business and retail office products distributor through direct sales, catalog, the Internet and about 900 superstores. Until late October 2004, it produced and distributed paper, packaging and wood products, and distributed office products and building materials. The company had recently focused on a long-term strategy of growth in its distribution businesses and had reduced the number of production facilities it operated, as well as its holdings of timberland.

In late October 2004, the company sold its paper, forest products, and timberland assets for about $3.7 billion to affiliates of Boise Cascade, LLC, a new company. In November 2004, it changed its name to OfficeMax Incorporated. Prior to these changes, Boise Office Solutions (49% of 2003 sales) distributed a broad line of products for office use. Most merchandise is purchased from outside manufacturers, with the exception of office papers, which are from the company's own operations. Products include office supplies, paper, technology products and office furniture. In December 2003, as part of its strategy of moving away from manufacturing, the former Boise Cascade acquired OfficeMax, Inc., a retailer of office products, for $1.3 billion. Following the purchase, Office Solutions was split into two segments: contract, which operates 80 distribution centers; and retail, with about 970 superstores.

Boise Building Solutions (33%) made lumber, structural panels (plywood and oriented strand board), particleboard, and engineered wood products. The segment's engineered lumber consisted of laminated veneer lumber, wood I-joists, and laminated beams. At December 31, 2003, BCC had 1,780 million sq. ft. of plywood and veneer production capacity, 440 million sq. ft. of oriented strand board (OSB) capacity, 200 million sq. ft. of particleboard capacity, 380 million

board feet of lumber capacity, 19 million cu. ft. of laminated veneer lumber capacity, and 150 million sq. ft. of Brazilian veneer capacity. Most production was sold to independent wholesalers and dealers, and through the company's 27 wholesale building distribution centers, which sell mostly to retail lumber dealers, home centers focusing on the do-it-yourself market, and industrial customers. The company's wood products are used primarily in housing, industrial construction, and manufactured products. About 21% of the lumber, panels, and engineered wood products sold by the company's distribution operations was produced internally. In April 2004, the company agreed to divest its OSB production capacity through the sale of Voyageur Panel Ltd., a Canada-based, 47%-owned joint venture that operated its OSB plant.

Boise Paper Solutions produced uncoated free sheet papers, including office, printing, forms, envelope and specialty papers. It also produces newsprint, containerboard, corrugated containers and market pulp. At the end of 2003, the company's five paper and containerboard mills had an annual production capacity of 2.9 million short tons. BCC also operated six paper distribution centers. The division accounted for 19% of 2003 sales, with uncoated papers accounting for 56% of segment revenues, followed by containerboard and corrugated products at 20%.

The former Boise Cascade owned or controlled 2.4 million acres of U.S. timberland. Its timberland resources supplied Boise Building Solutions and Boise Paper Solutions with about 47% of their combined fiber needs in 2003. During 2003, company saw mills processed 175 million cu. ft. of sawtimber (used to make lumber and veneers), and 239 million cu. ft. of pulpwood (used in paper making).

Company Financials Fiscal Year ending December 31

Per Share Data ($)

(Year Ended December 31)	2003	2002	2001	2000	1999	1998	1997	1996	1995	1994
Tangible Bk. Val.	9.55	14.72	18.07	21.81	18.10	14.93	17.47	21.88	25.77	18.76
Cash Flow	5.20	5.24	4.13	7.49	7.68	4.31	3.65	4.09	10.78	3.13
Earnings	0.07	-0.03	-0.96	2.73	3.06	-0.85	-1.19	-0.63	5.93	-3.08
S&P Core Earnings	0.39	-1.15	-1.84	NA	NA	NA	NA	NA	NA	NA
Dividends	0.60	0.60	0.60	0.60	0.60	0.60	0.60	0.60	0.60	0.60
Payout Ratio	NM	NM	NM	22%	20%	NM	NM	NM	10%	NM
Prices - High	32.89	38.81	38.00	43.93	47.18	40.37	45.56	47.25	47.50	30.50
- Low	20.72	19.61	26.99	21.75	28.75	22.25	27.75	27.37	26.25	19.00
P/E Ratio - High	NM	NM	NM	16	15	NM	NM	NM	8	NM
- Low	NM	NM	NM	8	9	NM	NM	NM	4	NM

Income Statement Analysis (Million $)

	2003	2002	2001	2000	1999	1998	1997	1996	1995	1994
Revs.	8,245	7,412	7,422	7,807	6,953	6,162	5,494	5,108	5,074	4,140
Oper. Inc.	483	459	515	656	704	495	365	367	873	350
Depr.	308	307	296	298	289	283	256	233	241	236
Int. Exp.	133	118	128	151	145	160	137	146	137	149
Pretax Inc.	19.3	1.00	-47.6	298	356	-15.0	-28.0	31.3	589	-65.0
Eff. Tax Rate	11.5%	NM	NM	39.0%	40.0%	NM	NM	38.2%	39.2%	NM
Net Inc.	17.1	11.3	-42.5	179	200	-25.7	-30.0	9.05	352	-63.0
S&P Core Earnings	22.6	-67.3	-106	NA	NA	NA	NA	NA	NA	NA

Balance Sheet & Other Fin. Data (Million $)

	2003	2002	2001	2000	1999	1998	1997	1996	1995	1994
Cash	125	65.2	56.7	62.8	66.9	74.4	64.0	261	52.0	29.5
Curr. Assets	2,501	1,296	1,245	1,577	1,531	1,368	1,354	1,355	1,313	918
Total Assets	7,376	4,947	4,934	5,267	5,138	4,967	4,970	4,711	4,656	4,294
Curr. Liab.	1,977	1,054	1,266	1,014	1,125	1,130	894	933	770	658
LT Debt	2,191	1,611	1,144	1,823	1,717	1,734	1,903	1,526	1,579	1,856
Common Equity	2,157	1,258	1,458	1,654	1,523	1,187	1,251	1,323	1,346	818
Total Cap.	4,598	3,176	3,203	3,973	3,774	3,535	3,852	3,538	3,295	3,358
Cap. Exp.	228	219	305	297	221	229	280	789	409	271
Cash Flow	312	305	238	460	472	241	190	197	593	119
Curr. Ratio	1.3	1.2	1.0	1.6	1.4	1.2	1.5	1.5	1.7	1.4
% LT Debt of Cap.	47.7	50.7	35.7	45.9	45.5	49.1	49.4	43.1	47.9	55.3
% Net Inc.of Revs.	0.2	0.2	NM	2.3	2.9	NM	NM	0.2	6.9	NM
% Ret. on Assets	0.3	0.2	NM	3.4	4.0	NM	NM	0.2	7.9	NM
% Ret. on Equity	0.2	0.8	NM	10.2	12.7	NM	NM	NM	27.8	NM

Data as orig reptd.; bef. results of disc opers/spec. items. Per share data adj. for stk. divs.; EPS diluted. E-Estimated. NA-Not Available. NM-Not Meaningful. NR-Not Ranked. UR-Under Review.

Office: 1111 W Jefferson St, Boise, ID 83728-0071.
Telephone: 208-384-6161.
Email: investor@bc.com
Website: http://www.bc.com
Chrmn & CEO: G.J. Harad.
SVP & CFO: T. Crumley.

SVP & General Counsel: J.W. Holleran.
VP & Treas: W.M. Rancourt.
VP & Investor Contact: V. Hannity 208-384-6390.
Dirs: W. F. Bryant, C. S. Farley, R. Gangwal, R. R. Goodmanson, E. E. Hagenlocker, G. J. Harad, G. G. Michael, A. W. Reynolds, J. E. Shaw, C. M. Ticknor, W. W. Woods, Jr., F. R. de Luzuriaga.

Founded: in 1931.
Domicile: Delaware.
Employees: 55,618.
S&P Analyst: Michael Souers/JP/BK

Office Depot

Recommendation: **BUY** ★ ★ ★ ★ ☆
SELL | SELL | HOLD | BUY | BUY

12-Month Target Price: $18.00
(as of October 20, 2004)

ODP has an approximate 0.05% weighting in the **S&P 500**

Sector: Consumer Discretionary
Sub-Industry: Specialty Stores
Peer Group: Office Products Retailers

Summary: Office Depot is a leading operator of office products superstores and mail order catalogs.

Quantitative Evaluations

S&P Earnings & Dividend Rank: B+

| D | C | B- | B | **B+** | A- | A | A+ |

S&P Fair Value Rank: 5

| 1 | 2 | 3 | 4 | **5** |
| Lowest | | | | Highest |

Fair Value Calc.: $20.00 (Slightly Undervalued)

S&P Investability Quotient Percentile
87%

ODP scored higher than 87% of all companies for which an S&P Report is available.

Volatility: Average

| Low | **Average** | High |

Technical Evaluation: Bullish
Since 10/04, the technical indicators for ODP have been Bullish.

Relative Strength Rank: Moderate
65
1 Lowest   Highest 99

Price as of 11/12/04: $17.05   **2004E S&P Core EPS:** $1.08

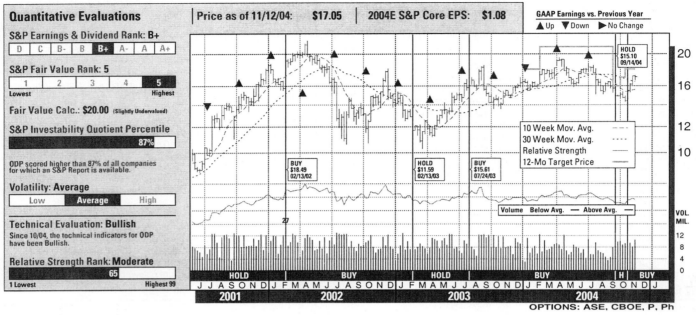

GAAP Earnings vs. Previous Year
▲ Up ▼ Down ► No Change

- 10 Week Mov. Avg.
- 30 Week Mov. Avg.
- Relative Strength
- 12-Mo Target Price

Volume Below Avg. — Above Avg.

OPTIONS: ASE, CBOE, P, Ph

Analyst commentary prepared by Michael Souers/JP/BK

Highlights October 26, 2004

- We expect sales to grow in the mid to high single digits in 2005 on ODP's expansion of retail and delivery operations in the Northeast, modest gains in the U.S. contract business and e-commerce, and continued international penetration, mainly in Europe. We see continued improvement in same-store sales at North American retail, on better sales of furniture and technology items, coupled with further gains from the new Ink Depots, merchandise upgrades, and heightened marketing efforts.

- We think improved sourcing and inventory management, along with cost savings from the consolidation of distribution facilities, should drive modest margin expansion. In addition, we believe that ODP's plans for stock buybacks of up to $500 million over the next two years will have a positive effect on EPS growth.

- After our projections for slightly lower interest expense, taxes of 32.0%, and a 2%-3% lower share count, reflecting ODP's plans for share repurchases, we estimate 2005 EPS of $1.26, a 12% increase from our 2004 EPS estimate of $1.13.

Investment Rationale/Risk October 26, 2004

- We recommend accumulating the shares based on valuation. Trading at 12X our 2005 EPS estimate, the shares are trading at a discount to the valuation of peers and the S&P 500. Although we remain concerned over the lack of progress in the Guilbert acquisition, ODP's North American Retail division is showing signs of improvement due to higher product margins and better cost control. In addition, we view the recent change in ODP's top management as a positive for the company. ODP's balance sheet provides considerable financial flexibility in our opinion, with nearly $4 in cash per share and our view of manageable debt levels.

- Risks to our opinion and target price include a slowdown in economic growth, a sharp rise in interest rates that could dampen capital spending by businesses, negative effects of potential terrorist attacks on consumer spending, and unfavorable currency fluctuations.

- At recent levels, ODP traded at a significant discount to its primary rival Staples (SPLS: accumulate, $28) in terms of P/E and P/E-to-growth multiples. Our 12-month target price of $18 is based on our DCF analysis, which assumes a weighted average cost of capital of 10.3% and a terminal growth rate of 3.5%.

Key Stock Statistics

S&P Core EPS 2005E	1.21	52-week Range	$19.50-13.87
S&P Oper. EPS 2004E	1.13	12 Month P/E	16.2
P/E on S&P Oper. EPS 2004E	15.1	Beta	1.27
S&P Oper. EPS 2005E	1.26	Shareholders	3,723
Yield (%)	Nil	Market Cap (B)	$ 5.3
Dividend Rate/Share	Nil	Shares Outstanding (M)	312.4

Value of $10,000 invested five years ago: **$ 14,218**

Dividend Data

No cash dividends have been paid.

Revenues/Earnings Data Fiscal year ending December 31

Revenues (Million $)

	2004	2003	2002	2001	2000	1999
1Q	3,605	3,056	3,022	3,018	3,066	2,623
2Q	3,162	2,816	2,622	2,554	2,633	2,343
3Q	3,328	3,236	2,871	2,782	2,823	2,579
4Q	—	3,251	2,842	2,800	3,048	2,719
Yr.	—	12,359	11,357	11,154	11,570	10,263

Earnings Per Share ($)

	2004	2003	2002	2001	2000	1999
1Q	0.37	0.33	0.32	0.19	0.32	0.25
2Q	0.25	0.19	0.18	0.14	0.18	0.19
3Q	E0.28	0.29	0.27	0.20	0.16	Nil
4Q	E0.23	0.15	0.21	0.13	-0.57	0.24
Yr.	E1.13	0.96	0.98	0.66	0.16	0.69

Next earnings report expected: mid-February Source: S&P, Company Reports
EPS Estimates based on S&P Operating Earnings; historical GAAP earnings are as reported.

Office Depot, Inc.

Recommendation: **BUY** ★ ★ ★ ★ ☆   12-Month Target Price: **$18.00** (as of October 20, 2004)

Business Summary October 26, 2004

Office Depot operates a chain of high-volume office products warehouse stores that sell brand name and private label office products primarily to small and medium-size businesses. At December 31, 2003, the company's North American retail division operated 900 superstores in 44 states, the District of Columbia, and Canada. The business services group sells to large and medium-size businesses through a dedicated sales force, catalogs (under the Viking and Office Depot names), call centers, and the Internet. The international division operated in 21 countries through 199 retail office supply stores, catalogs, and delivery operations. Sales by product group in 2003 were as follows: office products and machine supplies 56%; technology and related products 22%; and office furniture and other 22%.

After expanding its store base aggressively from 1995 to 2000, ODP adopted a more conservative strategy in 2001, scaling back new store openings and closing underperforming stores. In 2001, the company also began to reduce square footage of new stores from its typical 27,500 sq. ft., to match the needs of new markets and fill in existing markets. The 36 new stores opened in 2003 averaged about 14,000 sq. ft. each. Each store offers about 7,000 brand name office products, including general office supplies, business machines and computers, office furniture, and other business-related products. ODP also offers Office Depot products in grocery stores and other retail outlets.

In addition to large businesses, the company's business services group offers delivery and contract services to individuals, small and home office businesses,

and educational institutions and government agencies. ODP also offers specialized services designed to aid customers in improving efficiencies and reducing costs. The Viking business, acquired in 1998, sells a wide variety of office products to small and medium-size businesses through direct marketing catalogs and programs.

ODP's website provides the same assortment of products offered to catalog customers. In 1999, the company introduced its first international website, in the U.K. At the end of 2003, ODP operated 31 international websites, in countries that included Germany, the Netherlands, Italy, Australia, Japan, France and Austria. Worldwide e-commerce sales grew to $2.6 billion in 2003, from $2.1 billion in 2002.

In January 2003, the company sold its Australian operations, with no significant impact on net income. In April 2003, ODP expanded its presence in Spain, opening six new office supply superstores. Also in April, the company agreed to acquire the contract sales business of Guilbert, S.A., from Pinault Printemps Redout, for 815 million euros ($869 million), effectively doubling the size of ODP's European operations. The acquisition was completed in June 2003.

In March 2004, ODP agreed to acquire from Toys "R" Us, Inc., 124 former Kids "R" Us stores, for $197 million in cash, plus the assumption of lease payments and other obligations. The company expected to convert 50 to 60 of the stores into Office Depot locations, and to sell the remaining properties.

Company Financials Fiscal Year ending December 31

Per Share Data ($)

(Year Ended December 31)	2003	2002	2001	2000	1999	1998	1997	1996	1995	1994
Tangible Bk. Val.	5.77	6.61	5.28	4.66	5.06	4.86	7.23	4.09	3.45	2.30
Cash Flow	1.75	1.59	1.27	0.86	1.08	0.93	1.49	0.89	0.84	0.67
Earnings	0.96	0.98	0.66	0.16	0.69	0.61	0.65	0.54	0.57	0.46
S&P Core Earnings	0.91	0.92	0.58	NA	NA	NA	NA	NA	NA	NA
Dividends	Nil	Nil	Nil	Nil	Nil	Nil	Nil	Nil	Nil	Nil
Payout Ratio	Nil	Nil	Nil	Nil	Nil	Nil	Nil	Nil	Nil	Nil
Prices - High	18.50	21.96	18.70	14.87	26.00	24.83	16.00	17.08	21.41	18.00
- Low	10.28	10.60	7.12	5.87	9.00	10.58	8.41	8.58	12.66	12.58
P/E Ratio - High	19	22	28	93	38	41	25	32	38	39
- Low	11	11	11	37	13	17	13	16	22	27

Income Statement Analysis (Million $)

	2003	2002	2001	2000	1999	1998	1997	1996	1995	1994
Revs.	12,359	11,357	11,154	11,570	10,263	8,998	6,718	6,069	5,314	4,266
Oper. Inc.	719	707	562	433	615	659	405	322	309	243
Depr.	248	201	199	206	169	141	102	82.5	64.8	49.6
Int. Exp.	54.8	46.2	44.3	33.9	26.1	22.4	21.6	26.1	22.6	19.7
Pretax Inc.	445	479	314	92.5	414	389	263	213	222	179
Eff. Tax Rate	32.1%	35.0%	36.0%	46.6%	37.8%	40.0%	39.4%	39.3%	40.3%	41.3%
Net Inc.	302	311	201	49.3	258	233	160	129	132	105
S&P Core Earnings	286	292	178	NA	NA	NA	NA	NA	NA	NA

Balance Sheet & Other Fin. Data (Million $)

	2003	2002	2001	2000	1999	1998	1997	1996	1995	1994
Cash	791	877	563	151	219	705	200	51.4	62.0	32.0
Curr. Assets	3,577	3,210	2,806	2,699	2,631	2,780	2,021	1,822	1,731	1,274
Total Assets	6,145	4,766	4,332	4,196	4,276	4,113	2,981	2,740	2,531	1,904
Curr. Liab.	2,277	1,992	2,102	1,908	1,944	1,531	1,138	1,128	1,022	787
LT Debt	829	412	318	598	321	471	447	417	495	394
Common Equity	2,794	2,297	1,848	1,601	1,908	2,029	1,329	1,156	1,003	715
Total Cap.	3,868	2,774	2,230	2,200	2,229	2,500	1,777	1,573	1,497	1,109
Cap. Exp.	212	202	207	268	396	255	94.3	177	220	175
Cash Flow	550	512	400	255	426	374	262	212	197	155
Curr. Ratio	1.6	1.6	1.3	1.4	1.4	1.8	1.8	1.6	1.7	1.6
% LT Debt of Cap.	21.4	14.9	14.2	27.2	14.4	18.8	25.2	26.5	33.1	35.5
% Net Inc.of Revs.	2.4	2.7	1.8	0.4	2.5	2.6	2.4	2.1	2.5	2.5
% Ret. on Assets	5.5	6.8	4.7	1.2	6.2	6.6	5.6	4.9	6.0	6.7
% Ret. on Equity	11.9	15.0	11.7	2.8	13.1	13.9	12.9	12.0	15.4	16.1

Data as orig reptd.; bef. results of disc opers/spec. items. Per share data adj. for stk. divs. Bold denotes primary EPS - prior periods restated. E-Estimated. NA-Not Available. NM-Not Meaningful. NR-Not Ranked. UR-Under Review.

Office: 2200 Old Germantown Road, Delray Beach, FL 33445.
Telephone: 561-438-4800.
Email: investor.relations@officedepot.com
Website: http://www.officedepot.com
Chrmn & CEO: N.R. Austrian.
EVP & CFO: C. Brown.

EVP, Secy & General Counsel: D.C. Fannin.
VP & Investor Contact: E. Dunn 800-937-3600.
Dirs: L. A. Ault III, N. R. Austrian, C. R. Cohen, D. I. Fuente, B. Gaines, B. Gordon, W. S. Hedrick, J. L. Heskett, M. J. Myers, M. B. Nelson, F. P. Scruggs, Jr., P. J. Solomon.

Founded: in 1986.
Domicile: Delaware.
Employees: 46,000.
S&P Analyst: Michael Souers/JP/BK

Omnicom Group

Recommendation: **BUY** ★★★★☆
SELL SELL HOLD BUY BUY

12-Month Target Price: **$85.00**
(as of October 26, 2004)

OMC has an approximate 0.14% weighting in the **S&P 500**

Sector: Consumer Discretionary
Sub-Industry: Advertising
Peer Group: Advertising Agencies

Summary: OMC owns the DDB Worldwide, BBDO Worldwide and TBWA Worldwide advertising agency networks; it also owns more than 100 marketing and specialty services firms.

Quantitative Evaluations

S&P Earnings & Dividend Rank: A+

D	C	B-	B	B+	A-	A	A+

S&P Fair Value Rank: 4+

1	2	3	4	5
Lowest				Highest

Fair Value Calc.: $80.50 (Slightly Overvalued)

S&P Investability Quotient Percentile
86%

OMC scored higher than 86% of all companies for which an S&P Report is available.

Volatility: Average

Low	Average	High

Technical Evaluation: Bullish
Since 9/04, the technical indicators for OMC have been Bullish.

Relative Strength Rank: Strong
79

1 Lowest — Highest 99

Price as of 11/12/04:	$83.53	2004E S&P Core EPS:	$4.24

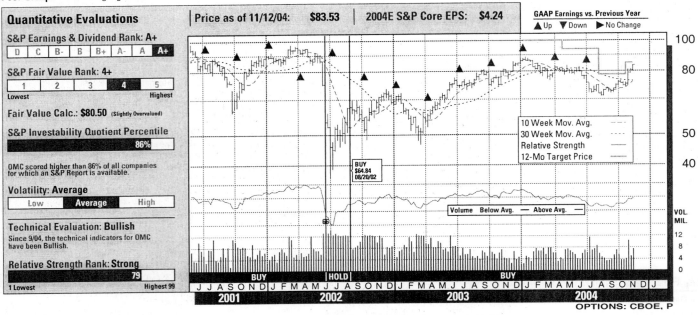

GAAP Earnings vs. Previous Year
▲ Up ▼ Down ► No Change

10 Week Mov. Avg. ┄┄
30 Week Mov. Avg. ┈┈
Relative Strength ──
12-Mo Target Price ┅┅

BUY $64.84 08/20/02

Volume Below Avg. — Above Avg.

BUY | HOLD | BUY

J J A S O N D J F M A M J J A S O N D J F M A M J J A S O N D J F M A M J J A S O N D J
2001   2002   2003   2004

OPTIONS: CBOE, P

VOL. MIL.
12
8
4
0

100
80
50
40

Analyst commentary prepared by William H. Donald/PMW/BK

Highlights August 16, 2004

■ We recently lowered our outlook for global advertising growth through 2005, in the wake of heightened terrorism concerns and mixed economic signals. We now look for OMC's 2004 revenues to increase 11%, to about $9.6 billion. We see a major part of revenue growth continuing to come from currency translation gains and acquisitions. For 2005, we project a 12% advance in revenues, to $10.7 billion, including 4% to 5% reflecting currency translation effects. We look for about 6% organic growth, and up to 2% from potential acquisitions.

■ We see operating margins under pressure, as a result of upfront costs associated with gaining new business, severance payments, changes in the revenue mix, and greater utilization of freelance labor. However, we expect these pressures to ease over the course of 2005. We see 2004 operating earnings advancing 13.5%, after a gain of 6% in 2003. We see 2004 operating margins unchanged at 13.5%. For 2005, we expect margin improvement, to 14.2%, and a 17% advance in operating earnings.

■ After non-operating items, including taxes, and minority interests, we anticipate an 8.7% advance in net operating earnings in 2004, to $734.4 million ($3.85 a share), from $675.9 million ($3.59) reported for 2003. For 2005, we project a 14% gain, to $4.40.

Key Stock Statistics

S&P Oper. EPS 2004E	3.85	52-week Range	$88.82-66.43
P/E on S&P Oper. EPS 2004E	21.7	12 Month P/E	21.2
S&P Oper. EPS 2005E	4.40	Beta	1.29
Yield (%)	1.1%	Shareholders	3,633
Dividend Rate/Share	0.90	Market Cap (B)	$15.6
Shares Outstanding (M)	186.3		

Value of $10,000 invested five years ago: **$ 10,528**

Dividend Data Dividends have been paid since 1986

Amount ($)	Date Decl.	Ex-Div. Date	Stock of Record	Payment Date
0.200	Dec. 16	Dec. 23	Dec. 26	Jan. 06 '04
0.225	Feb. 17	Mar. 03	Mar. 05	Apr. 02 '04
0.225	May. 25	Jun. 04	Jun. 08	Jul. 01 '04
0.225	Sep. 14	Sep. 22	Sep. 24	Oct. 07 '04

Investment Rationale/Risk August 16, 2004

■ We recently downgraded the shares to accumulate, from buy, to reflect our more cautious outlook for general global advertising through 2005. The stock's performance, like that of its peers, has been weak year to date versus the S&P 500. Through mid-August, the shares fell 23%. We think this was due largely to worries about potential earn-out obligations totaling nearly $500 million, related to acquired agencies; and to the pace of global business spending in the wake of heightened terrorism and mixed economic signals. However, we believe the company will outperform its peers in revenue growth, profitability, and rate of earnings growth over the next three years. The stock traded recently at 18X our 2004 EPS projection, and at 15X our 2005 estimate. We expect EPS growth to average in the high teens in the five years through 2008, versus mid-teens average growth that we expect for OMC's peer group.

■ Risks to our recommendation and target price include the company's future financial condition and results of operations, changes in general economic conditions in the U.S. and abroad, increased competition, and currency fluctuations.

■ Reflecting reductions in our EPS estimates, we recently lowered our 12-month target price to $78. Our discounted cash flow analysis assumes that the stock will trade at a forward P/E multiple of about 18X our 2005 EPS estimate, in line with the recent 2004 multiple.

Revenues/Earnings Data Fiscal year ending December 31

Revenues (Million $)

	2004	2003	2002	2001	2000	1999
1Q	2,231	1,937	1,732	1,601	1,379	1,147
2Q	2,408	2,150	1,917	1,747	1,520	1,270
3Q	2,319	2,029	1,768	1,571	1,453	1,211
4Q	—	2,506	2,119	1,970	1,802	1,502
Yr.	—	8,621	7,536	6,889	6,154	5,131

Earnings Per Share ($)

	2004	2003	2002	2001	2000	1999
1Q	0.72	0.69	0.68	0.54	0.78	0.37
2Q	1.10	1.02	1.00	0.81	0.70	0.59
3Q	E0.79	0.72	0.68	0.50	0.48	0.39
4Q	E1.26	1.17	1.08	0.87	0.78	0.66
Yr.	E3.85	3.59	3.44	2.70	2.73	2.01

Next earnings report expected: mid-February Source: S&P, Company Reports
EPS Estimates based on S&P Operating Earnings; historical GAAP earnings are as reported.

STANDARD &POOR'S

Omnicom Group Inc.

Recommendation: **BUY** ★★★★☆   12-Month Target Price: **$85.00** (as of October 26, 2004)

Business Summary August 16, 2004

Omnicom Group, a global advertising and marketing services company, is one of the world's largest corporate communications companies. The company's organic growth rate in the past eight years has exceeded that of its industry, leading to a rapid expansion in market share worldwide. At the end of 2003, OMC ranked first in worldwide gross income, up from third in 2001 and fourth in 1990.

OMC is comprised of more than 1,500 subsidiary agencies, operating in more than 100 countries. It operates as three independent global agency networks: the BBDO Worldwide Network, the DDB Worldwide Network, and the TBWA Worldwide Network. In addition, OMC's Diversified Agency Services group includes more than 100 marketing services and specialized advertising agency groups. The company's growth has been augmented significantly by acquisitions. OMC's companies provide an extensive range of marketing and corporate communications services, including advertising, media planning and buying, promotional marketing, sports and event marketing, direct marketing, crisis communications, custom publishing, database management, field marketing, digital and interactive marketing, public relations, marketing research, brand consultancy, directory and business-to-business advertising, health care communications, recruitment communications, and other specialty communications.

Non-advertising marketing and communications services accounted for 57% of revenues in 2003, up from 30% 13 years earlier. Customer relationship management (CRM) revenues accounted for 34%, public relations for 11%, and specialty communications 12%. Advertising and media services accounted for the remaining 43%. In 2003, OMC had more than 5,000 clients. The company's 10 largest and 200 largest clients accounted for 17.9% and 50.7% of consolidated revenue, respectively. The largest client accounted for about 5.0% of revenue, and no other single client accounted for over 2.5%. Each agency network has its own clients, and the networks compete with each other in the same markets.

The breadth, depth and diversity of OMC's business reduce its exposure to any single industry, or to an economic reversal in any world region. They also provides the company with significant opportunities to benefit from growth in non-advertising services, such as public relations, event marketing, etc. Such expenditures are growing faster than traditional advertising expenditures.

Operations cover the major regions of North America, the U.K., Europe, the Middle East, Africa, Latin America, the Far East, and Australia. In 2003, about 45% of commissions and fees came from international operations.

Company Financials Fiscal Year ending December 31

Per Share Data ($)

(Year Ended December 31)	2003	2002	2001	2000	1999	1998	1997	1996	1995	1994
Tangible Bk. Val.	NM	NM	NM	NM	NM	NM	NM	NM	-1.89	-1.51
Cash Flow	4.20	4.07	3.75	3.63	2.59	2.38	1.92	1.70	1.43	1.24
Earnings	3.59	3.44	2.70	2.73	2.01	1.68	1.37	1.15	0.95	0.79
S&P Core Earnings	3.37	3.12	2.47	NA	NA	NA	NA	NA	NA	NA
Dividends	0.80	0.80	0.78	0.70	0.60	0.50	0.45	0.38	0.33	0.31
Payout Ratio	22%	23%	29%	26%	30%	30%	33%	33%	35%	39%
Prices - High	87.60	97.35	98.20	100.93	107.50	58.50	42.37	26.06	18.75	13.43
- Low	46.50	36.50	59.10	68.12	55.93	37.00	22.25	17.75	12.46	10.93
P/E Ratio - High	24	28	36	37	53	35	31	23	20	17
- Low	13	11	22	25	28	22	16	16	13	14

Income Statement Analysis (Million $)

	2003	2002	2001	2000	1999	1998	1997	1996	1995	1994
Revs.	8,621	7,536	6,889	6,154	5,131	4,092	3,125	2,642	2,258	1,756
Oper. Inc.	1,289	1,224	1,179	1,065	821	693	506	412	343	267
Depr.	124	120	211	187	97.1	133	103	85.8	72.0	62.8
Int. Exp.	57.9	45.5	72.8	76.5	84.9	69.6	43.1	34.1	43.3	34.8
Pretax Inc.	1,137	1,087	908	923	689	545	411	326	243	200
Eff. Tax Rate	33.5%	34.5%	38.8%	40.0%	39.7%	39.6%	38.0%	38.0%	40.2%	37.2%
Net Inc.	676	643	503	499	363	285	222	176	140	108
S&P Core Earnings	631	584	456	NA	NA	NA	NA	NA	NA	NA

Balance Sheet & Other Fin. Data (Million $)

	2003	2002	2001	2000	1999	1998	1997	1996	1995	1994
Cash	1,529	667	472	517	576	648	556	523	335	257
Curr. Assets	7,286	5,637	5,234	5,367	4,712	3,981	2,988	2,425	2,106	1,602
Total Assets	14,499	11,820	10,617	9,891	9,018	6,910	4,966	4,056	3,528	2,852
Curr. Liab.	7,762	6,840	6,644	6,625	6,009	4,796	3,579	2,863	2,502	1,987
LT Debt	2,537	1,945	1,340	1,245	712	716	342	205	290	187
Common Equity	3,466	2,569	2,178	1,548	1,553	1,086	981	801	552	541
Total Cap.	6,394	4,687	3,677	2,970	2,708	1,893	1,273	1,068	903	770
Cap. Exp.	141	117	149	150	130	89.7	76.1	48.8	49.6	38.5
Cash Flow	800	763	714	685	460	418	325	262	212	171
Curr. Ratio	0.9	0.8	0.8	0.8	0.8	0.8	0.8	0.8	0.8	0.8
% LT Debt of Cap.	39.7	41.5	36.4	41.9	26.3	37.8	68.1	19.2	32.2	24.3
% Net Inc.of Revs.	7.8	8.5	7.3	8.1	7.1	7.0	7.1	6.7	6.2	6.2
% Ret. on Assets	5.1	5.7	4.9	5.3	4.5	4.8	4.9	4.7	4.3	4.0
% Ret. on Equity	22.4	27.1	27.0	32.2	27.9	27.6	23.3	26.1	27.5	22.1

Data as orig reptd.; bef. results of disc opers/spec. items. Per share data adj. for stk. divs. Bold denotes basic EPS (FASB 128)-prior periods restated. E-Estimated. NA-Not Available. NM-Not Meaningful. NR-Not Ranked. UR-Under Review.

Office: 437 Madison Avenue, New York, NY 10022-7001.
Telephone: 212-415-3600.
Email: IR@OmnicomGroup.com
Website: http://www.omnicomgroup.com
Chrmn: B. Crawford.
Pres & CEO: J.D. Wren.

Vice Chrmn: P. Mead.
EVP, CFO & Investor Contact: R.J. Weisenburger 212-415-3600.
SVP, Secy & General Counsel: M.J. O'Brien.
Dirs: R. C. Clark, L. S. Coleman, Jr., E. M. Cook, B. Crawford, S. S. Denison, M. A. Henning, J. R. Murphy, J. R. Purcell, L. J. Rice, G. L. Roubos, J. D. Wren.

Founded: in 1944.
Domicile: New York.
Employees: 58,500.
S&P Analyst: William H. Donald/PMW/BK

Oracle Corp.

Recommendation: **BUY** ★★★★ ☆   12-Month Target Price: **$15.00**
(as of April 19, 2004)

ORCL has an approximate 0.63% weighting in the **S&P 500**

Sector: Information Technology
Sub-Industry: Systems Software
Peer Group: Database

Summary: ORCL is the world's largest supplier of information management software.

Quantitative Evaluations

S&P Earnings & Dividend Rank: B

| D | C | B- | **B** | B+ | A- | A | A+ |

S&P Fair Value Rank: 5+

| 1 | 2 | 3 | 4 | **5** |
| Lowest | | | | Highest |

Fair Value Calc.: $14.70 (Slightly Undervalued)

S&P Investability Quotient Percentile

97%

ORCL scored higher than 97% of all companies for which an S&P Report is available.

Volatility: Average

| Low | **Average** | High |

Technical Evaluation: Bullish
Since 9/04, the technical indicators for ORCL have been Bullish.

Relative Strength Rank: Strong

81

| 1 Lowest | | Highest 99 |

Price as of 11/12/04: **$13.39** | **2005E S&P Core EPS:** **$0.48**

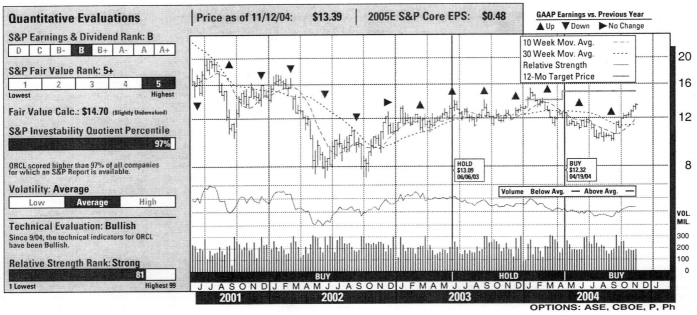

GAAP Earnings vs. Previous Year
▲ Up ▼ Down ► No Change

- 10 Week Mov. Avg.
- 30 Week Mov. Avg.
- Relative Strength
- 12-Mo Target Price

HOLD $13.09 06/06/03

BUY $12.32 04/19/04

Volume Below Avg. — Above Avg.

OPTIONS: ASE, CBOE, P, Ph

Analyst commentary prepared by Jonathan Rudy, CFA /MF/BK

Highlights November 03, 2004

- In November 2004, ORCL increased its cash tender offer for PeopleSoft (PSFT: hold, $23) to $24 per share (approximately $8.9 billion), from $21 a share ($7.7 billion). In May, ORCL reduced its offer to $21 a share, from an earlier offer of $26 a share ($9.4 billion). ORCL made an initial offer, valued at $5.1 billion, in June 2003. In September 2004, a federal judge ruled in favor of the company and against the Department of Justice, refusing to block the proposed merger on anti-trust grounds. However, the outcome of the proposed combination is still unclear, in our view, with two significant hurdles remaining: PSFT's poison pill and its lawsuit against ORCL seeking $1 billion in damages.

- On a stand-alone basis, we expect ORCL's revenues to increase about 7% in FY 05 (May). We see software license sales continuing to grow, with an anticipated 8% gain, following an 8% increase in FY 04. We expect operating margins to widen further, as management continues to target cost-cutting and productivity-enhancing measures. We project FY 05 operating EPS of $0.58 (excluding one-time items), up 16% from FY 04's $0.50 (excluding one-time items), and we see a rise to $0.65 in FY 06.

- Our FY 05 Standard & Poor's Core EPS projection of $0.48 reflects estimated stock option expense.

Investment Rationale/Risk November 03, 2004

- We recommend accumulating the shares, primarily due to what we view as ORCL's solid execution and attractive valuation. However, we see the ongoing legal battle over the potential acquisition of PSFT remaining a concern. We believe the company is highly profitable, with operating margins of about 40%, return on equity exceeding 35%, no debt, and strong cash flow from operations. The stock traded recently at 19X our calendar 2005 EPS estimate of $0.61, and at a P/E to growth (PEG) ratio of 1.3X, a discount to peer levels, despite ORCL's greater profitability.

- Risks to our recommendation and target price include a rapidly changing technology landscape, such as a rapid adoption of open source database technology; intense competition from IBM (IBM: accumulate, $86) and Microsoft (MSFT: buy, $28); and legal and regulatory risks associated with ORCL's tender offer for PSFT.

- Our 12-month target price of $15 is based on a blend of relative P/E multiple and P/E to growth ratio metrics, and our discounted cash flow analysis.

Key Stock Statistics

S&P Oper. EPS 2005E	0.58	52-week Range	$15.51-9.78
P/E on S&P Oper. EPS 2005E	23.1	12 Month P/E	25.8
S&P Oper. EPS 2006E	0.65	Beta	1.75
Yield (%)	Nil	Shareholders	26,514
Dividend Rate/Share	Nil	Market Cap (B)	$ 68.7
Shares Outstanding (M)	5128.5		

Value of $10,000 invested five years ago: **$ 8,976**

Dividend Data

No cash dividends have been paid.

Revenues/Earnings Data Fiscal year ending May 31

Revenues (Million $)

	2005	2004	2003	2002	2001	2000
1Q	2,215	2,072	2,028	2,265	2,262	1,985
2Q	—	2,498	2,309	2,380	2,660	2,322
3Q	—	2,509	2,307	2,254	2,674	2,449
4Q	—	3,076	2,832	2,774	3,264	3,374
Yr.	—	10,156	9,475	9,673	10,860	10,130

Earnings Per Share ($)

	2005	2004	2003	2002	2001	2000
1Q	0.10	0.08	0.06	0.09	0.09	0.04
2Q	E0.14	0.12	0.10	0.10	0.11	0.07
3Q	E0.14	0.12	0.11	0.09	0.10	0.13
4Q	E0.20	0.19	0.16	0.12	0.15	0.82
Yr.	E0.58	0.50	0.43	0.39	0.44	1.05

Next earnings report expected: mid-December Source: S&P, Company Reports
EPS Estimates based on S&P Operating Earnings; historical GAAP earnings are as reported.

Oracle Corporation

Recommendation: **BUY** ★★★★☆   12-Month Target Price: **$15.00** (as of April 19, 2004)

Business Summary November 03, 2004

Oracle Corp. is the world's largest provider of enterprise software. The company's software products fall into two broad categories: database technology software and business applications software.

Database technology software provides a platform for developing and deploying applications on the Internet and corporate intranets. The platform includes database management software, application server, collaboration software, and development tools that allow users to create, retrieve and modify the various types of data stored in a computer system. The Oracle relational database management system (DBMS) is a key component of the company's Internet platform, and enables storage, manipulation and retrieval of relational, object-relational, multi-dimensional and other types of data. In FY 04, ORCL released the latest version of its database technology software, Oracle10g. The Oracle Database 10g with Real Application Clusters acts as a single database in a cluster, and does not require the data to be separated on multiple computers. New software license revenues from database technology products accounted for 29%, and 28% of total revenues in FY 04, and FY 03, respectively.

The company also offers Oracle Application Server, an open-software platform for developing, deploying and managing distributed Internet software application programs. It provides the infrastructure necessary to run Internet-computing applications. In October 2000, ORCL introduced Oracle9i Application Server (Oracle9i AS), an open software platform, based on industry standards, that is intended to make it easier for developers to build Internet Web sites and applications.

Business applications software automates the performance of specific business data processing functions for customer relationship management, supply chain management, financial management, procurement, project management, and human resources management. Oracle E-Business Suite Release 11i is a fully integrated and Internet-enabled set of software applications that is designed to enable companies to manage the entire business cycle on a global basis and to solve end to end business problems. New software license revenues from applications software provided 6%, and 7% of total revenues in FY 04, and FY 03, respectively.

ORCL's software business is comprised of new software licenses and software license updates and product support. The software business contributed 79% of total revenue in FY 04 (May), up from 76% in FY 03. The services business, which is comprised of consulting, advanced product services, and education, accounted for 21% of total revenue in FY 04, versus 24% in FY 03.

On June 9, 2003, the company began an unsolicited cash tender offer of $16 a share, or about $5.1 billion, for PeopleSoft, Inc. (PSFT) common shares. On June 18, 2003, ORCL increased the offer to $19.50 a share ($6.2 billion). On February 4, 2004, it increased the offer to $9.4 billion ($26 a share). On May 14, 2004, it reduced the offer to $21 a share, or about $7.7 billion. On November 1, 2004, ORCL increased its offer to $24 a share, or approximately $8.9 billion.

Company Financials Fiscal Year ending May 31

Per Share Data ($)

(Year Ended May 31)	2004	2003	2002	2001	2000	1999	1998	1997	1996	1995
Tangible Bk. Val.	1.55	1.21	1.13	1.12	1.15	1.29	0.51	0.40	0.32	0.21
Cash Flow	0.55	0.49	0.45	0.50	1.10	0.43	0.19	0.18	0.14	0.10
Earnings	0.50	0.43	0.39	0.44	1.05	0.22	0.14	0.14	0.10	0.07
S&P Core Earnings	0.46	0.37	0.34	0.36	NA	NA	NA	NA	NA	NA
Dividends	Nil	Nil	Nil	Nil	Nil	Nil	Nil	Nil	Nil	Nil
Payout Ratio	Nil	Nil	Nil	Nil	Nil	Nil	Nil	Nil	Nil	Nil

Cal. Yrs.	2003	2002	2001	2000	1999	1998	1997	1996	1995	1994
Prices - High	14.03	17.50	35.00	46.46	28.34	7.47	7.02	5.66	3.61	2.29
- Low	10.64	7.25	10.16	21.50	5.25	2.95	3.48	2.92	1.97	1.29
P/E Ratio - High	28	41	90	NM	27	34	52	42	36	31
- Low	21	17	26	NM	5	14	26	22	20	17

Income Statement Analysis (Million $)

Revs.	18,773	9,475	9,673	10,860	10,130	8,827	7,144	5,684	4,223	2,967
Oper. Inc.	4,098	3,767	3,934	4,124	6,475	2,619	1,740	1,565	1,124	797
Depr.	234	327	363	347	314	320	329	265	220	148
Int. Exp.	21.0	16.0	20.0	24.0	18.9	21.4	16.7	6.81	6.60	7.00
Pretax Inc.	3,945	3,425	3,408	3,971	10,123	1,982	1,328	1,284	920	659
Eff. Tax Rate	32.0%	32.6%	34.7%	35.5%	37.8%	34.9%	38.7%	36.0%	34.3%	33.0%
Net Inc.	2,681	2,307	2,224	2,561	6,297	1,290	814	821	603	442
S&P Core Earnings	2,459	2,049	1,923	2,119	NA	NA	NA	NA	NA	NA

Balance Sheet & Other Fin. Data (Million $)

Cash	4,138	4,737	3,095	5,888	7,872	1,786	1,920	890	841	586
Curr. Assets	11,336	9,227	8,728	8,963	10,883	5,447	4,323	3,271	2,284	1,617
Total Assets	12,763	11,064	10,800	11,030	13,077	7,260	5,819	4,624	3,357	2,425
Curr. Liab.	4,272	4,158	3,960	3,917	5,862	3,046	2,484	1,922	1,455	1,055
LT Debt	163	175	298	301	301	304	304	300	0.90	81.7
Common Equity	7,995	6,320	6,117	6,278	6,461	7,391	2,958	2,370	1,870	1,211
Total Cap.	8,217	6,681	6,619	6,906	7,028	7,831	3,278	2,676	1,880	1,321
Cap. Exp.	189	291	278	313	263	347	328	391	308	262
Cash Flow	2,915	2,634	2,587	2,908	6,611	1,290	1,142	1,086	823	589
Curr. Ratio	2.7	2.2	2.2	2.3	1.9	1.8	1.7	1.7	1.6	1.5
% LT Debt of Cap.	2.0	2.6	4.5	4.4	4.3	3.9	9.3	11.2	0.1	6.2
% Net Inc.of Revs.	14.3	24.3	23.0	23.6	62.2	14.6	11.4	14.5	14.3	14.9
% Ret. on Assets	22.6	21.1	20.4	21.2	61.9	19.7	15.6	20.6	20.9	22.0
% Ret. on Equity	37.5	37.1	35.9	40.2	124.0	19.4	30.5	38.7	39.1	45.2

Data as orig reptd.; bef. results of disc opers/spec. items. Per share data adj. for stk. divs.; EPS diluted. E-Estimated. NA-Not Available. NM-Not Meaningful. NR-Not Ranked. UR-Under Review.

Office: 500 Oracle Parkway, Redwood Shores, CA 94065-1675.
Telephone: 650-506-7000.
Email: investor_us@oracle.com
Website: http://www.oracle.com
Chrmn & EVP: J.O. Henley.
Pres: S.A. Catz.
Pres: C.E. Phillips, Jr.

CEO: L.J. Ellison.
SVP, Secy & General Counsel: D. Cooperman.
Investor Contact: S. Mills 650-607-5176.
Dirs: J. Berg, H. R. Bingham, M. J. Boskin, S. A. Catz, L. J. Ellison, H. Garcia-Molina, J. Grundfest, J. O. Henley, J. F. Kemp, D. L. Lucas, C. Phillips.

Founded: in 1977.
Domicile: Delaware.
Employees: 41,658.
S&P Analyst: Jonathan Rudy, CFA /MF/BK

Recommendation: **BUY** ★★★★★   12-Month Target Price: **$84.00**
SELL SELL HOLD BUY BUY
(as of October 04, 2004)

PCAR has an approximate 0.12% weighting in the **S&P 500**

Sector: Industrials
Sub-Industry: Construction & Farm Machinery & Heavy Trucks
Peer Group: Truck Manufacturers

Summary: This heavy-duty truck manufacturer produces the well known Peterbilt and Kenworth brand heavy-duty highway trucks.

Quantitative Evaluations

S&P Earnings & Dividend Rank: B+

| D | C | B- | B | B+ | A- | A | A+ |

S&P Fair Value Rank: 3

| 1 | 2 | 3 | 4 | 5 |
| Lowest | | | | Highest |

Fair Value Calc.: $74.20 (Slightly Overvalued)

S&P Investability Quotient Percentile

100%

PCAR scored higher than 100% of all companies for which an S&P Report is available.

Volatility: Average

| Low | Average | High |

Technical Evaluation: Bullish

Since 11/04, the technical indicators for PCAR have been Bullish.

Relative Strength Rank: Strong

90

| 1 Lowest | Highest 99 |

Price as of 11/12/04: $78.83   2004E S&P Core EPS: $5.21

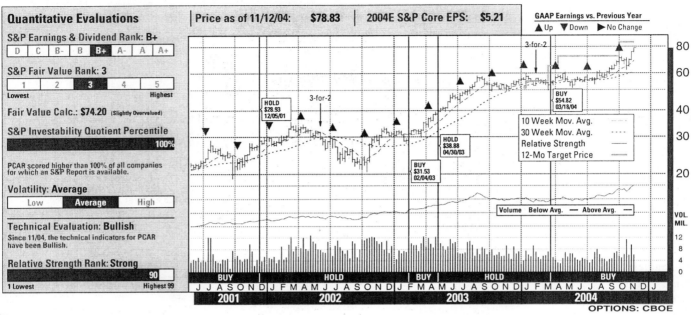

GAAP Earnings vs. Previous Year
▲ Up ▼ Down ► No Change

HOLD $28.93 12/05/01
3-for-2
HOLD $38.88 04/30/03
BUY $31.53 02/04/03
BUY $54.82 03/18/04
3-for-2

10 Week Mov. Avg.
30 Week Mov. Avg.
Relative Strength
12-Mo Target Price

Volume Below Avg. — Above Avg.

BUY | HOLD | BUY | HOLD | BUY
J J A S O N D | J F M A M J J A S O N D | J F M A M J J A S O N D | J F M A M J J A S O N D | J
2001 2002 2003 2004

OPTIONS: CBOE

Analyst commentary prepared by Anthony M. Fiore, CFA /PMW/BK

Highlights October 22, 2004

- We expect net sales and revenues to increase about 15% in 2005, following a projected advance of about 30% in 2004. We expect improved carrier profitability, coupled with an aging motor fleet, to drive strong replacement demand for heavy-duty trucks in 2005. In addition, we see sales in 2005 benefiting from projected expansion in Europe, combined with expected market share gains in the U.S. medium duty (Class 5-7) truck industry.

- We anticipate a further expansion of operating margins in 2005. We see higher truck volumes contributing to improvement in overall gross margins, and expect benefits from ongoing cost-control efforts to lead to a decline in selling, general and administrative expenses as a percentage of sales. For the longer term, we believe that earnings will continue to exhibit large swings, due to the highly cyclical nature of the global truck industry.

- We regard the quality of earnings as very high versus peers, with only a minimal difference between our Standard & Poor's Core EPS estimates and our operating EPS forecasts.

Investment Rationale/Risk October 22, 2004

- We believe PCAR is well positioned to benefit from continued strength in global truck demand, due to a cyclical upswing that we believe occurs on average every three to five years. We are maintaining our buy recommendation on the shares, based on our outlook for strong growth in revenues and earnings in 2005.

- Risks to our recommendation and target price include an unexpected downturn in the North American and/or European truck markets; potential for supply disruptions; and continued escalation of raw material costs.

- Our 12-month target price of $84 a share combines two valuation metrics. Our discounted cash flow model, which assumes a 9% to 10% average annual free cash flow growth rate over the next 10 years, 3.5% growth in perpetuity, and an 8.4% weighted average cost of capital, indicates intrinsic value of about $83. In terms of relative valuation, the shares traded recently at a P/E multiple of about 11X our 2005 EPS estimate. Applying a P/E multiple of 13X, in line with historical norms, to our 2005 estimate leads to a value of about $85. Blending these two methodologies leads to our target price.

Key Stock Statistics

S&P Core EPS 2005E	6.49	52-week Range	$78.85-49.61
S&P Oper. EPS 2004E	5.23	12 Month P/E	16.8
P/E on S&P Oper. EPS 2004E	15.1	Beta	0.99
S&P Oper. EPS 2005E	6.50	Shareholders	2,287
Yield (%)	1.0%	Market Cap (B)	$ 13.7
Dividend Rate/Share	0.80	Shares Outstanding (M)	173.6

Value of $10,000 invested five years ago: **$ 46,058**

Dividend Data Dividends have been paid since 1943

Amount ($)	Date Decl.	Ex-Div. Date	Stock of Record	Payment Date
0.150	Dec. 09	Feb. 13	Feb. 18	Mar. 05 '04
0.200	Apr. 27	May. 17	May. 19	Jun. 04 '04
0.200	Jul. 13	Aug. 16	Aug. 18	Sep. 07 '04
0.200	Sep. 21	Nov. 16	Nov. 18	Dec. 06 '04

Revenues/Earnings Data Fiscal year ending December 31

Revenues (Million $)

	2004	2003	2002	2001	2000	1999
1Q	2,501	1,803	1,502	1,528	2,331	2,154
2Q	2,787	1,895	1,802	1,523	2,023	2,271
3Q	2,775	1,940	1,996	1,501	1,647	2,175
4Q	—	2,083	1,919	1,536	1,544	2,327
Yr.	—	7,721	7,219	6,089	7,437	9,021

Earnings Per Share ($)

	2004	2003	2002	2001	2000	1999
1Q	1.03	0.63	0.27	0.26	0.88	0.68
2Q	1.34	0.71	0.42	0.23	0.76	0.79
3Q	1.41	0.75	0.74	0.23	0.54	0.81
4Q	E1.48	0.90	0.70	0.29	0.36	1.01
Yr.	E5.23	2.99	2.13	1.01	2.55	3.29

Next earnings report expected: early-February Source: S&P, Company Reports
EPS Estimates based on S&P Operating Earnings; historical GAAP earnings are as reported.

PACCAR Inc.

Recommendation: **BUY** ★★★★ 12-Month Target Price: **$84.00** (as of October 04, 2004)

Business Summary October 25, 2004

Originally incorporated in 1924 as the Pacific Car and Foundry Company, and tracing its roots back to the Seattle Car Manufacturing Company, PACCAR has grown into a multinational company with principal businesses that include the design, manufacture and distribution of high-quality light, medium and heavy-duty commercial trucks and related aftermarket parts.

The company's heavy-duty (class 8) diesel trucks are marketed under the Peterbilt, Kenworth, DAF and Foden names. In addition, through its Peterbilt and Kenworth divisions, PCAR competes in the North American medium duty (class 6/7) markets and the European light/medium (6 to 15 metric ton) commercial vehicle market with DAF cab-over-engine trucks.

PCAR operates in a highly cyclical industry. The North American heavy duty truck industry hit bottom in 1991, with 98,600 unit sales. Industry sales climbed through the 1990s, peaking at a record 263,000 units in 1999. However, North American industry sales dropped to approximately 165,000 units in 2002. The company's primary competition in this market includes Navistar, Freightliner (a subsidiary of DaimlerChrysler), and Mack Trucks (a division of Volvo trucks).

Because of high fixed manufacturing costs, size is significant in the truck making business. In general, the higher the production rate, the lower the per truck manufacturing costs. According to the company, lower per truck manufacturing costs, as well as brand name recognition, are big advantages in the very competitive heavy truck industry.

In an effort to mitigate sales and earnings cyclicality, PCAR focuses on truck design and assembly, leaving the production of major components to outside suppliers. It believes this strategy has served the company well when volatile demand for heavy trucks tails off during cyclical downturns.

In 2003, the company's truck production and related aftermarket parts distribution businesses accounted for 94% of revenues and 84% of operating income. Segment profit margins in 2003, 2002 and 2001, were 8.3%, 7.1% and 3.5%, respectively; in the boom years of 2000, 1999 and 1998, segment profit margins were 6.9%, 9.0% and 7.4%, respectively.

PCAR also manufactures industrial winches under the Braden, Carco and Gearmatic names. Sales of winches provided less than 1% of net sales in 2003, 2002 and 2001.

Like other big truck makers, the company aims to capitalize on a growing trend toward truck leasing and financing. The Finance Services segment accounted for 6.0% of 2003 revenues, but generated 16% of operating income; it posted 26%, 17% and 8% operating margins in 2003, 2002 and 2001, respectively. The rebound in margins in 2003 resulted from a decrease in loan loss provisions. In 2003, 2002 and 2001, provisions for loan losses were $29 million, $53 million and $87 million, respectively.

Company Financials Fiscal Year ending December 31

Per Share Data ($)

(Year Ended December 31)	2003	2002	2001	2000	1999	1998	1997	1996	1995	1994
Tangible Bk. Val.	16.56	13.68	12.68	12.68	11.55	10.04	8.53	7.76	7.15	6.57
Cash Flow	4.51	3.38	2.05	3.47	4.15	3.08	2.61	1.61	1.86	1.53
Earnings	2.99	2.13	1.01	2.55	3.29	2.36	1.96	1.15	1.44	1.17
S&P Core Earnings	2.97	2.00	0.84	NA	NA	NA	NA	NA	NA	NA
Dividends	1.04	0.65	0.53	0.53	1.07	0.93	0.92	0.56	0.89	0.67
Payout Ratio	35%	30%	53%	21%	32%	40%	47%	48%	62%	57%
Prices - High	58.38	35.32	30.79	24.11	28.00	29.66	26.44	16.25	12.13	13.72
- Low	27.84	20.46	19.00	16.11	17.55	16.44	13.47	9.27	8.72	8.88
P/E Ratio - High	20	17	31	9	9	13	13	14	8	12
- Low	9	10	19	6	5	7	7	8	6	8

Income Statement Analysis (Million $)

	2003	2002	2001	2000	1999	1998	1997	1996	1995	1994
Revs.	8,195	7,219	6,089	7,437	9,021	7,895	6,764	4,600	4,848	4,490
Oper. Inc.	1,313	1,012	672	1,122	1,243	931	790	516	575	471
Depr.	268	218	180	156	147	124	112	81.1	72.4	63.2
Int. Exp.	3.50	249	275	294	223	192	170	152	146	NA
Pretax Inc.	806	574	255	665	923	653	536	313	400	320
Eff. Tax Rate	34.6%	35.2%	32.0%	33.6%	36.8%	36.1%	35.5%	35.8%	36.8%	36.1%
Net Inc.	527	372	174	442	584	417	346	201	253	205
S&P Core Earnings	523	349	145	NA	NA	NA	NA	NA	NA	NA

Balance Sheet & Other Fin. Data (Million $)

	2003	2002	2001	2000	1999	1998	1997	1996	1995	1994
Cash	1,724	1,308	1,062	910	1,059	837	676	508	609	553
Curr. Assets	2,599	2,102	1,834	1,861	2,119	2,070	1,756	1,548	1,137	NA
Total Assets	9,940	8,703	7,914	8,271	7,933	6,795	5,600	5,299	4,391	3,928
Curr. Liab.	1,482	1,258	1,134	1,268	1,534	1,519	1,214	1,352	688	NA
LT Debt	1,557	1,552	1,547	1,655	1,475	1,311	1,334	1,145	1,160	631
Common Equity	3,246	2,601	2,253	2,249	2,111	1,764	1,498	1,358	1,251	1,175
Total Cap.	4,803	4,152	3,800	3,904	3,585	3,075	2,987	2,655	2,562	1,838
Cap. Exp.	111	78.8	83.9	143	256	193	133	123	94.0	81.0
Cash Flow	794	590	354	598	731	541	458	282	325	268
Curr. Ratio	1.8	1.7	1.6	1.5	1.4	1.4	1.4	1.1	1.7	NA
% LT Debt of Cap.	32.4	37.4	40.7	42.4	41.1	42.6	44.7	43.1	45.3	34.3
% Net Inc.of Revs.	6.4	5.2	2.9	5.9	6.5	5.3	5.1	4.4	5.3	4.6
% Ret. on Assets	5.6	4.5	2.1	5.5	7.9	6.7	6.4	4.1	6.1	5.7
% Ret. on Equity	18.0	15.3	7.7	20.3	30.1	25.6	24.2	15.4	20.9	17.9

Data as orig reptd.; bef. results of disc opers/spec. items. Per share data adj. for stk. divs. Bold denotes primary EPS - prior periods restated. E-Estimated. NA-Not Available. NM-Not Meaningful. NR-Not Ranked. UR-Under Review.

Office: 777 106th Avenue NE, Bellevue, WA 98004-5017.
Telephone: 425-468-7400.
Website: http://www.paccar.com
Chrmn & CEO: M.C. Pigott.
Pres: T.E. Plimpton.

Vice Chrmn: M.A. Tembreull.
VP & General Counsel: G.G. Morie.
Dirs: J. M. Fluke, Jr., G. Grinstein, D. K. Newbigging, M. C. Pigott, J. C. Pigott, W. G. Reed, Jr., H. C. Stonecipher, M. A. Tembreull, H. A. Wagner.

Founded: in 1905.
Domicile: Delaware.
Employees: 17,000.
S&P Analyst: Anthony M. Fiore, CFA /PMW/BK

Pactiv Corp.

Recommendation: **HOLD** ★★★☆☆
SELL SELL HOLD BUY BUY

12-Month Target Price: $25.00
(as of July 23, 2004)

PTV has an approximate 0.03% weighting in the **S&P 500**

Sector: Materials
Sub-Industry: Metal & Glass Containers
Peer Group: Metal, Glass & Plastic Containers and Packaging Products

Summary: Pactiv Corp., spun off by Tenneco in 1999, is a leading provider of advanced packaging solutions for consumer, institutional and industrial markets.

Quantitative Evaluations

S&P Earnings & Dividend Rank: NR

D	C	B-	B	B+	A-	A	A+

S&P Fair Value Rank: 3+

1	2	**3**	4	5
Lowest				Highest

Fair Value Calc.: $23.30 (Slightly Overvalued)

S&P Investability Quotient Percentile

64%

PTV scored higher than 64% of all companies for which an S&P Report is available.

Volatility: Low

Low	Average	High

Technical Evaluation: Bullish
Since 11/04, the technical indicators for PTV have been Bullish.

Relative Strength Rank: Moderate

60

1 Lowest		Highest 99

Price as of 11/12/04:	$25	2004E S&P Core EPS:	$0.25

GAAP Earnings vs. Previous Year
▲ Up ▼ Down ► No Change

HOLD $23.26 07/23/04

- - - 10 Week Mov. Avg.
...... 30 Week Mov. Avg.
—— Relative Strength
—— 12-Mo Target Price

Volume Below Avg. — Above Avg.

VOL. MIL.

BUY   HOLD

J J A S O N D | J F M A M J J A S O N D | J F M A M J J A S O N D | J F M A M J J A S O N D | J
2001   2002   2003   2004

OPTIONS: ASE, Ph

Analyst commentary prepared by Stewart Scharf/CB/MJ

Highlights October 29, 2004

- We expect organic sales to advance in the mid- to high single digits in 2005 (before 2% to 3% from positive foreign exchange and acquisitions), following 5% growth seen for 2004. We see these gains driven by our forecast of greater demand in North America for new Hefty consumer products, as well as for foodservice/food packaging, and protective and flexible products. We also expect market conditions to improve in Europe.
- We think gross margins (before D&A) will widen modestly in 2005, from our projection of 28% for 2004, as PTV's pricing initiatives will likely begin to kick in and offset the higher resin prices we see. We believe EBITDA margins should widen from our 18% forecast for 2004, as cost savings from plant consolidations will likely offset increased promotional spending. However, the amount of margin improvement during 2005 will depend on the direction of resin prices (the company estimates that a $0.01 drop in resin costs results in a $0.05 rise in EPS). We look for expected strong free cash flow generation to be earmarked mainly for share buybacks; FCF should expand from our $270 million projection for 2004 (adjusted for $36 million in cash for restructuring) as PTV improves working capital.
- We estimate 2004 EPS of $1.40 (before a $0.39 restructuring charge, but after $0.20 of pension income), rising 18%, to $1.65, in 2005. We view earnings quality as subpar, as our 2005 S&P Core EPS estimate is 34% below our operating EPS projection.

Key Stock Statistics

S&P Core EPS 2005E	1.09	52-week Range	$25.28-19.80
S&P Oper. EPS 2004E	1.40	12 Month P/E	22.5
P/E on S&P Oper. EPS 2004E	17.9	Beta	0.58
S&P Oper. EPS 2005E	1.65	Shareholders	43,051
Yield (%)	Nil	Market Cap (B)	$ 3.8
Dividend Rate/Share	Nil	Shares Outstanding (M)	150.3

Value of $10,000 invested five years ago: **$ 18,567**

Dividend Data

No cash dividends have been paid.

Investment Rationale/Risk October 29, 2004

- PTV recently projected 2004 EPS at the low end of its guided range. We continue to suggest that investors not add to their holdings in the shares. This assessment is based on our valuation models and volatile raw material prices, which may have an adverse impact on earnings into 2005.
- Risks to our recommendation and target price include a significant rise in resin prices that PTV is unable to recover via pricing actions, a softer global economic rebound, a negative effect from foreign currencies, and lower pension income.
- We expect interest coverage and leverage ratios to improve from recent levels of 6.3X and 2.1X, respectively, in line with peers. We see PTV's return on investment (ROI) staying near 12%, which is on par with the ROI of other consumer packaging companies. With the stock recently trading at 14X our 2005 EPS projection, modestly below peer levels, we view the stock as fairly valued. We have a 12-month target price of $25, applying a 15X P/E, near PTV's five-year historical forward multiple, and on par with our projected P/E for the S&P 500. Based on our DCF model, with 3% terminal growth and an 8.5% WACC, the shares are 8% below intrinsic value.

Revenues/Earnings Data Fiscal year ending December 31

Revenues (Million $)

	2004	2003	2002	2001	2000	1999
1Q	775.0	717.0	647.0	695.0	738.0	666.0
2Q	858.0	810.0	728.0	745.0	820.0	738.0
3Q	865.0	793.0	727.0	717.0	778.0	754.0
4Q	—	818.0	778.0	710.0	798.0	763.0
Yr.	—	3,138	2,880	2,812	3,134	2,921

Earnings Per Share ($)

	2004	2003	2002	2001	2000	1999
1Q	Nil	0.27	0.26	0.18	0.17	0.03
2Q	0.33	0.37	0.38	0.28	0.24	0.28
3Q	0.37	0.16	0.37	0.28	0.24	0.01
4Q	E0.35	0.41	0.37	0.29	0.05	-1.00
Yr.	E1.40	1.21	1.37	1.03	0.70	-0.67

Next earnings report expected: late-January Source: S&P, Company Reports
EPS Estimates based on S&P Operating Earnings; historical GAAP earnings are as reported.

Pactiv Corporation

Recommendation: **HOLD** ★★★☆☆   12-Month Target Price: **$25.00** (as of July 23, 2004)

Business Summary November 01, 2004

Pactiv Corp., a global supplier of specialty packaging and consumer products, seeks growth through internal programs, complemented by strategic acquisitions and new product introductions. Over 80% of sales come from products that hold the leading or second market share position. In 2003, Wal-Mart Stores accounted for over 11% of sales.

PTV operates three units: consumer products (Hefty), foodservice/food packaging, and protective and flexible packaging. Consumer products sales accounted for 28% of total sales in 2003 ($195 million in operating income); foodservice/food packaging 44% ($178 million); and protective and flexible packaging 28% ($58 million). The company operates 80 manufacturing facilities in 14 countries. Foreign sales account for about 23% of the total.

The company manufactures consumer products such as foam and molded fiber disposable tableware, and disposable aluminum cookware. It sells many products under recognized brand names, such as Hefty, Baggies, Hefty One-Zip, Kordite, and E-Z Foil. In 2003, new products included Hefty Hearty Meals plates and bowls, Zoo Pals slider bags for children, Sports Pals plates, and OneZip school bags.

PTV makes food packaging products for the food processing industry, including molded fiber egg cartons, foam meat trays, aluminum containers, and modified atmosphere packaging. The company expected case ready meat packaging sales to reach $150 million by the end of 2004. New products introduced in 2003 included new barrier trays for meat packaging, and containers for agricultural products.

The company also makes packaging for cushioning, surface protection and insulation in the automotive, electronic, durable goods, building and construction products industries.

Flexible packaging products provide solutions for consumer, medical, pharmaceutical, chemical, hygiene and industrial applications. Products include liners for disposable diapers, wrap-around sleeves for glass and plastic bottles, and disposable surgical kits.

PTV has projected 2004 after-tax pension income of $31 million ($0.19 a share), down from 2003's $39 million ($0.25). Assuming a 9% return on pension assets, the company will not be required to contribute to the plan for the next 10 years. PTV says that a 50-basis point change in the assumed rate of return on plan assets would result in an average change in pension income of $25 million a year between 2004 and 2013. An equal change in the discount rate would result in an average change of $10 million a year over that period.

In September 2004, PTV revised its 2004 EPS forecast to a range of $1.40 to $1.45 from its earlier projection of $1.50 to $1.56.

The company expects to incur $60 million of after-tax restructuring charges ($36 million in cash) in 2004, including $44 million recognized in the first quarter.

Through the first nine months of 2004, PTV repurchased 10.1 million of its shares at an average cost of $22.71 a share.

PTV projected 2004 capital spending of $110 million to $120 million, with depreciation and amortization of $175 million.

Company Financials Fiscal Year ending December 31

Per Share Data ($)

(Year Ended December 31)	2003	2002	2001	2000	1999	1998	1997	1996	1995	1994
Tangible Bk. Val.	0.77	1.79	4.91	3.79	2.19	NA	NA	NA	NA	NA
Cash Flow	2.24	2.35	2.14	1.84	0.43	1.43	NA	NA	NA	NA
Earnings	1.21	1.37	1.03	0.70	-0.67	0.39	NA	NA	NA	NA
S&P Core Earnings	1.00	-0.23	-0.57	NA	NA	NA	NA	NA	NA	NA
Dividends	Nil	Nil	Nil	Nil	Nil	NA	NA	NA	NA	NA
Payout Ratio	Nil	Nil	Nil	Nil	Nil	NA	NA	NA	NA	NA
Prices - High	24.03	24.47	18.10	13.31	14.50	NA	NA	NA	NA	NA
- Low	17.55	15.35	11.26	7.50	9.31	NA	NA	NA	NA	NA
P/E Ratio - High	20	18	18	19	NM	NA	NA	NA	NA	NA
- Low	15	11	11	11	NM	NA	NA	NA	NA	NA

Income Statement Analysis (Million $)

	2003	2002	2001	2000	1999	1998	1997	1996	1995	1994
Revs.	3,138	2,880	2,812	3,134	2,921	2,791	NA	NA	NA	NA
Oper. Inc.	630	617	574	570	498	466	NA	NA	NA	NA
Depr.	163	158	177	185	184	175	NA	NA	NA	NA
Int. Exp.	96.0	96.0	107	134	146	164	NA	NA	NA	NA
Pretax Inc.	314	367	284	207	-159	124	NA	NA	NA	NA
Eff. Tax Rate	37.6%	39.8%	41.5%	44.0%	NM	46.0%	NA	NA	NA	NA
Net Inc.	195	220	165	113	-112	66.0	NA	NA	NA	NA
S&P Core Earnings	160	-36.0	-91.1	NA	NA	NA	NA	NA	NA	NA

Balance Sheet & Other Fin. Data (Million $)

	2003	2002	2001	2000	1999	1998	1997	1996	1995	1994
Cash	140	127	41.0	26.0	12.0	18.0	NA	NA	NA	NA
Curr. Assets	982	904	740	900	866	1,031	NA	NA	NA	NA
Total Assets	3,706	3,412	4,060	4,341	4,588	4,749	NA	NA	NA	NA
Curr. Liab.	474	501	459	512	920	1,703	NA	NA	NA	NA
LT Debt	1,336	1,224	1,211	1,560	1,741	1,186	NA	NA	NA	NA
Common Equity	1,061	897	1,689	1,539	1,350	1,286	NA	NA	NA	NA
Total Cap.	2,617	2,282	3,502	3,595	3,432	2,848	NA	NA	NA	NA
Cap. Exp.	112	126	145	135	1,129	NA	NA	NA	NA	NA
Cash Flow	358	378	342	298	72.0	241	NA	NA	NA	NA
Curr. Ratio	2.1	1.8	1.6	1.8	0.9	0.6	NA	NA	NA	NA
% LT Debt of Cap.	51.1	53.6	34.6	43.4	50.7	41.6	NA	NA	NA	NA
% Net Inc.of Revs.	6.2	7.6	5.9	3.6	NM	2.4	NA	NA	NA	NA
% Ret. on Assets	5.5	5.9	4.0	2.5	NM	NA	NA	NA	NA	NA
% Ret. on Equity	19.9	17.0	10.2	7.8	NM	NA	NA	NA	NA	NA

Data as orig reptd.; bef. results of disc opers/spec. items. Data for 1998 pro forma. Per share data adj. for stk. divs.; EPS diluted. E-Estimated. NA-Not Available. NM-Not Meaningful. NR-Not Ranked.

Office: 1900 West Field Court, Lake Forest, IL 60045-4828.
Telephone: 847-482-2000.
Email: investorrelations@pactiv.com
Website: http://www.pactiv.com
Chrmn, Pres & CEO: R.L. Wambold.

SVP & CFO: A.A. Campbell.
VP & General Counsel: J.V. Faulkner, Jr.
VP & Investor Contact: C. Hanneman 847-482-2429.
Dirs: L. D. Brady, K. D. Brooksher, R. J. Darnall, M. R. Henderson, R. B. Porter, R. L. Wambold, N. Wesley.

Founded: in 1965.
Domicile: Delaware.
Employees: 16,000.
S&P Analyst: Stewart Scharf/CB/MJ

Recommendation: **HOLD** ★★★☆ | 12-Month Target Price: **$27.00**
(as of March 05, 2004)

PLL has an approximate 0.03% weighting in the **S&P 500**

Sector: Industrials
Sub-Industry: Industrial Machinery
Peer Group: Control and/or Filter Products-- Specialized

Summary: PLL is a leading producer of filters for the healthcare and aircraft industries.

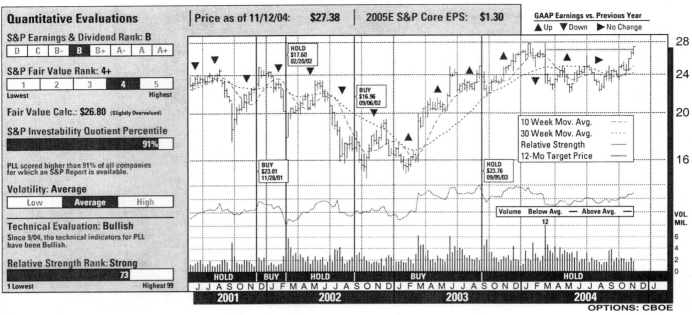

Quantitative Evaluations

S&P Earnings & Dividend Rank: B

| D | C | B- | B | B+ | A- | A | A+ |

S&P Fair Value Rank: 4+

| 1 | 2 | 3 | 4 | 5 |
| Lowest | | | | Highest |

Fair Value Calc.: $26.80 (Slightly Overvalued)

S&P Investability Quotient Percentile

91%

PLL scored higher than 91% of all companies for which an S&P Report is available.

Volatility: Average

| Low | Average | High |

Technical Evaluation: Bullish
Since 9/04, the technical indicators for PLL have been Bullish.

Relative Strength Rank: Strong

73

1 Lowest — Highest 99

Price as of 11/12/04: $27.38 | **2005E S&P Core EPS: $1.30**

GAAP Earnings vs. Previous Year
▲ Up ▼ Down ▶ No Change

- 10 Week Mov. Avg.
- 30 Week Mov. Avg.
- Relative Strength
- 12-Mo Target Price

Volume Below Avg. — Above Avg.

OPTIONS: CBOE

Analyst commentary prepared by Stewart Scharf/PMW/BK

Highlights September 08, 2004

- We expect FY 05 (Jul.) sales growth (after positive foreign exchange) in the mid-single digits, as strength in general industrial and a recovery in biopharmaceutical and medical sales outweigh low-single-digit growth projected for the aerospace segment. We project at least 10% growth for microelectronics, but think that sales may soften sequentially, due to a slowdown in the semiconductor sector. We believe that the majority of the sales growth will come from the Western Hemisphere.

- Gross margins should widen slightly in FY 05 from FY 04's 49%, on a more favorable product mix. We see FY 05 EBITDA margins widening from 18% of sales in FY 04, as $10 million in projected cost savings from PLL's CoRe cost-reduction program, which includes plant rationalizations and the realignment of divisions, outweigh higher consulting, pension and insurance costs.

- After taxes at an effective rate projected at 24%, we estimate FY 05 EPS of $1.45, with a gain to $1.60 seen for FY 06. Our FY 05 Standard & Poor's Core Earnings projection, mainly reflecting estimated stock option expense, is $1.30.

Investment Rationale/Risk September 08, 2004

- With FY 04 fourth quarter EPS below our estimate, uncertain microelectronics markets, and based on our valuation models, we would not add to positions.

- Risks to our recommendation and target price include continued weakness in the biopharmaceutical division, a severe downturn in the semiconductor market, slower growth in Asia, a softer global economy, and less robust capital spending for water projects.

- At 16X our FY 05 EPS estimate, the stock trades on par with the P/E multiple of the S&P 500 (adjusted for fiscal year), but somewhat below the level of PLL's closest peers. With the shares at a modest premium to intrinsic value, based on our DCF model, which assumes a terminal growth rate of 3% and a weighted average cost of capital of 9%, and with a P/E multiple to EPS growth ratio (PEG) of 1.1X, slightly below peer levels, we view the stock as fairly valued. Applying a forward P/E multiple on a par with that of peers, our 12-month target price is $27.

Key Stock Statistics

S&P Oper. EPS 2005E	1.45	52-week Range	$28.04-22.00
P/E on S&P Oper. EPS 2005E	18.9	12 Month P/E	22.8
S&P Oper. EPS 2006E	1.60	Beta	1.04
Yield (%)	1.3%	Shareholders	4,605
Dividend Rate/Share	0.36	Market Cap (B)	$ 3.4
Shares Outstanding (M)	124.0		

Value of $10,000 invested five years ago: **$ 13,796**

Dividend Data Dividends have been paid since 1974

Amount ($)	Date Decl.	Ex-Div. Date	Stock of Record	Payment Date
0.090	Jan. 22	Feb. 04	Feb. 06	Feb. 20 '04
0.090	Apr. 14	Apr. 28	Apr. 30	May. 14 '04
0.090	Jul. 20	Aug. 02	Aug. 04	Aug. 19 '04
0.090	Oct. 14	Oct. 26	Oct. 28	Nov. 12 '04

Revenues/Earnings Data Fiscal year ending July 31

Revenues (Million $)

	2004	2003	2002	2001	2000	1999
1Q	374.3	332.2	274.1	278.1	267.1	249.8
2Q	428.1	388.5	285.4	304.7	294.7	278.3
3Q	463.9	421.5	302.4	321.1	318.1	299.9
4Q	504.5	471.4	428.9	331.5	344.2	319.1
Yr.	1,771	1,614	1,291	1,235	1,224	1,147

Earnings Per Share ($)

	2004	2003	2002	2001	2000	1999
1Q	0.19	-0.19	0.16	0.21	0.20	0.11
2Q	0.20	0.25	0.15	0.24	0.27	0.13
3Q	0.37	0.33	0.21	0.30	0.34	-0.23
4Q	0.44	0.44	0.07	0.21	0.37	0.40
Yr.	1.20	0.83	0.59	0.95	1.18	0.41

Next earnings report expected: early-December Source: S&P, Company Reports
EPS Estimates based on S&P Operating Earnings; historical GAAP earnings are as reported.

Pall Corporation

Recommendation: **HOLD** ★ ★ ★ ☆ ☆   12-Month Target Price: **$27.00** (as of March 05, 2004)

Business Summary September 08, 2004

Pall Corp. is a global producer of filters for healthcare, aerospace and industrial markets, serving customers in the life sciences and industrial markets. The company divides these markets into five segments: Medical and BioPharmaceuticals (life sciences), and General Industrial, Aerospace and Microelectronics (industrial business). Disposable replacement products account for 75% of annual sales. In September 2004, PLL said that, as part of cost-saving initiatives, it would combine its operations into three integrated businesses: Life Sciences, comprising Medical and BioPharmaceuticals; Aeropower, comprising Aerospace and General Industrial's Machinery & Equipment business; and Pall Process Technologies, comprising Food & Beverage, Fuels & Chemicals, Power Generation, Municipal Water and Microelectronics.

In September 2004, PLL said that the Michigan Department of Environmental Quality (MEDQ) had given it one year to demonstrate that its proposed clean-up method for its Unit E aquifer could be an approved remedy. The MEDQ has identified an alternative methodology if the company is unable to resolve the issues. PLL noted that costs for an alternative remedy could be significant, and are not reflected in its FY 04 (Jul.) balance sheet.

The life sciences segment contributed 41% of total revenues ($149 million in operating profit) in FY 04. The biopharmaceutical division makes filter products used in production and development of drugs, and food and beverage filters that help produce yeast- and bacteria-free water. The rapidly growing blood division offers hospitals and blood centers blood filters that reduce leukocyte (white cells) and other bloodborne viral contaminants, such as bacteria. Biopharmaceutical sales accounted for 52% of the segment's total sales in FY 04 ($85 million in operating profit), while medical products (blood and cardiovascular filtration)

accounted for 48% ($64 million profits). PLL estimates the market potential for medical filters at $4.3 billion. In March 2004, the FDA granted clearance to the company to market its enhanced Bacteria Detection System.

The industrial segment (59% of total revenues; $160 million in operating profit) makes filters and separation products for three markets. The aerospace division (17% of segment revenues; $44 million profits) includes both commercial and military markets. The general industrial division (64%; $78 million profits) produces filters for the aluminum, paper, automobile, oil, gas, chemical, petrochemical and power industries. The microelectronics (19%; $38 million profits) unit makes products for the semiconductor, data storage and photographic film industries.

In FY 04, revenues from the Western Hemisphere accounted for 38% of the total, Europe 41%, and Asia 21%.

In FY 04, pretax restructuring and other charges included nearly $21 million ($0.11 a share, after taxes) to increase environmental reserves. In addition, $4.8 million ($0.03, after tax) was recorded to restructure operations in Europe and Japan. The charges were partly offset by a $7.6 million gain ($0.04, after tax) on the sale of investment in Oiltools in the fourth quarter, and a $5.6 million ($0.03, after tax) first quarter adjustment to decrease a pension liability.

In September 2004, PLL projected FY 05 capital spending at $70 million, with depreciation and amortization of $90 million, dividends of $45 million, share repurchases of $100 million, free cash flow of $160 million (after dividend payments and capital expenditures), and EPS of $1.38 to $1.52. At the end of FY 04, net debt was equal to 24% of capitalization.

Company Financials Fiscal Year ending July 31

Per Share Data ($)

(Year Ended July 31)	2004	2003	2002	2001	2000	1999	1998	1997	1996	1995
Tangible Bk. Val.	6.21	5.16	NM	6.29	5.41	5.09	5.32	5.84	5.73	5.13
Cash Flow	1.90	1.51	1.19	1.53	1.68	1.01	1.33	1.03	1.61	1.40
Earnings	1.20	0.83	0.59	0.95	1.18	0.41	0.75	0.53	1.21	1.04
S&P Core Earnings	1.16	0.70	0.42	0.83	NA	NA	NA	NA	NA	NA
Dividends	0.27	0.36	0.52	0.68	0.50	0.64	0.60	0.54	0.47	0.41
Payout Ratio	23%	43%	88%	71%	42%	156%	81%	102%	39%	39%
Prices - High	28.04	27.00	24.48	26.25	25.00	26.18	26.62	26.12	29.37	27.87
- Low	22.00	15.01	14.68	17.50	17.12	15.75	19.37	19.50	19.62	18.37
P/E Ratio - High	23	33	41	28	21	64	36	49	24	27
- Low	18	18	25	18	15	38	26	37	16	18

Income Statement Analysis (Million $)

	2004	2003	2002	2001	2000	1999	1998	1997	1996	1995
Revs.	1,771	1,614	1,291	1,235	1,224	1,147	1,087	1,062	960	823
Oper. Inc.	320	299	215	256	274	160	216	182	248	212
Depr.	88.9	83.9	74.0	71.5	63.4	74.8	73.1	62.8	46.8	41.7
Int. Exp.	20.5	24.4	14.3	16.6	14.1	18.4	7.87	2.84	12.0	10.9
Pretax Inc.	198	143	100	150	188	58.9	135	86.1	198	167
Eff. Tax Rate	23.4%	27.9%	26.7%	21.5%	22.2%	12.6%	30.6%	21.8%	30.0%	29.0%
Net Inc.	152	103	73.2	118	147	51.5	93.6	67.3	139	119
S&P Core Earnings	148	87.4	52.1	102	NA	NA	NA	NA	NA	NA

Balance Sheet & Other Fin. Data (Million $)

	2004	2003	2002	2001	2000	1999	1998	1997	1996	1995
Cash	199	127	105	54.9	81.0	86.7	12.1	18.0	106	111
Curr. Assets	1,070	938	916	779	753	744	602	607	581	525
Total Assets	2,140	2,017	2,027	1,549	1,507	1,488	1,347	1,266	1,185	1,075
Curr. Liab.	419	421	438	314	438	558	394	301	330	288
LT Debt	489	490	620	359	224	117	112	62.1	46.7	68.8
Common Equity	1,054	935	820	770	761	731	766	825	732	652
Total Cap.	1,559	1,439	1,478	1,149	1,006	869	899	915	815	754
Cap. Exp.	61.3	62.2	69.9	77.8	66.5	71.2	85.1	88.6	82.2	66.5
Cash Flow	241	187	147	190	210	126	167	130	185	161
Curr. Ratio	2.6	2.2	2.1	2.5	1.7	1.3	1.5	2.0	1.8	1.8
% LT Debt of Cap.	31.3	34.0	41.9	31.2	22.3	13.4	12.4	6.8	5.7	9.1
% Net Inc.of Revs.	8.6	6.4	5.7	9.6	12.0	4.5	8.6	6.3	14.4	14.5
% Ret. on Assets	7.3	5.1	NA	7.7	9.8	3.6	7.2	5.5	12.3	11.7
% Ret. on Equity	15.2	11.8	NA	15.4	19.7	6.9	11.8	8.6	20.0	19.2

Data as orig reptd.; bef. results of disc opers/spec. items. Per share data adj. for stk. divs. Bold denotes primary EPS - prior periods restated. E-Estimated. NA-Not Available. NM-Not Meaningful. NR-Not Ranked. UR-Under Review.

Office: 2200 Northern Boulevard, East Hills, NY 11548.
Telephone: 516-484-5400.
Email: invrel@pall.com
Website: http://www.pall.com
Chrmn & CEO: E. Krasnoff.
Pres & CFO: M. Wilson.

COO: D. Stevens.
Investor Contact: D. Foster 516-801-9246.
Dirs: A. Appel, D. J. Carroll, Jr., J. H. Haskell, Jr., U. Haynes, Jr., E. Krasnoff, E. W. Martin, Jr., K. L. Plourde, H. Shelley, E. L. Snyder, E. Travaglianti, J. D. Watson, M. Wilson.

Founded: in 1946.
Domicile: New York.
Employees: 10,300.
S&P Analyst: Stewart Scharf/PMW/BK

Parametric Technology

Recommendation: **HOLD** ★ ★ ★ ☆ ☆
SELL SELL HOLD BUY BUY

12-Month Target Price: $5.50
(as of September 21, 2004)

PMTC has an approximate 0.01% weighting in the **S&P 500**

Sector: Information Technology
Sub-Industry: Application Software
Peer Group: Computer Aided Designing

Summary: PMTC, a leader in mechanical design automation, is attempting to shift its focus to collaborative product development software solutions.

Quantitative Evaluations

S&P Earnings & Dividend Rank: C

D	C	B-	B	B+	A-	A	A+

S&P Fair Value Rank: 5

1	2	3	4	5
Lowest				Highest

Fair Value Calc.: $6.30 (Slightly Undervalued)

S&P Investability Quotient Percentile

37%

PMTC scored lower than 63% of all companies for which an S&P Report is available.

Volatility: High

Low	Average	High

Technical Evaluation: Bullish
Since 11/04, the technical indicators for PMTC have been Bullish.

Relative Strength Rank: Moderate

61

1 Lowest   Highest 99

Price as of 11/12/04:   **$5.53** | **2005E S&P Core EPS:**   **$0.04**

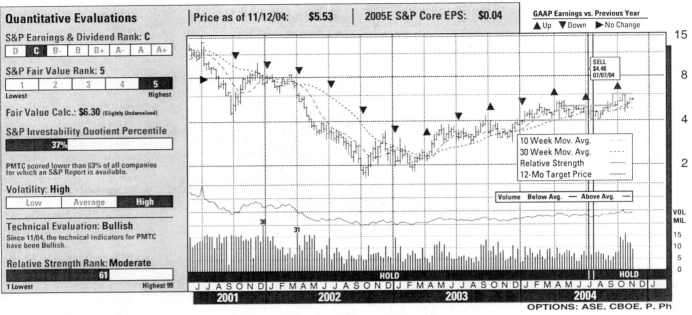

GAAP Earnings vs. Previous Year
▲ Up ▼ Down ► No Change

SELL $4.48 07/07/04

10 Week Mov. Avg.
30 Week Mov. Avg.
Relative Strength
12-Mo Target Price

Volume   Below Avg. — Above Avg.

HOLD   HOLD

J J A S O N D J F M A M J J A S O N D J F M A M J J A S O N D J F M A M J J A S O N D J
2001   2002   2003   2004

OPTIONS: ASE, CBOE, P, Ph

Analyst commentary prepared by Jonathan Rudy, CFA /MF/GG

Highlights October 21, 2004

- We project that revenues will increase about 4% in FY 05 (Sep.), rebounding from a 2% decline in FY 04. We believe results for The Windchill product line, PMTC's solution for product lifecycle management (PLM), have been disappointing, but there has been some recent sequential improvement.

- Sales of the company's flagship product for mechanical design automation, Pro/ENGINEER, continue to be weak. We think this is primarily due to the protracted slowdown in the manufacturing sector. However, we believe that PMTC is beginning to improve operationally, following multiple restructurings.

- With improved cost controls, we anticipate that the company will continue to improve its profitability in FY 05, with projected operating EPS of $0.28 for the year (excluding amortization and one-time charges), up from $0.25 in FY 04 on an operating basis. Our FY 05 Standard & Poor's Core Earnings estimate is $0.04 a share, reflecting estimated stock option expense.

Investment Rationale/Risk October 21, 2004

- We have a hold recommendation on the shares, primarily due to what we view as better than expected recent execution, and the shares trading at a discount to peers with an enterprise value at 2.1X sales. However, overall results have been disappointing over the past two years, in our view. PMTC has undergone restructurings in seven out of the past nine quarters, leading us to believe that its quality of earnings is weaker than those of its peers. Nevertheless, we view the balance sheet as strong, with nearly $1.10 a share in cash and investments, and no debt. We would hold existing positions.

- Risks to our opinion and target price include a rapidly changing technology landscape, pricing pressures due to intense competition in the enterprise software sector, and a weaker salesforce execution than we anticipate.

- Our 12-month target price of $5.50 is based on relative P/E multiple to growth ratio and enterprise value to sales metrics.

Key Stock Statistics

S&P Oper. EPS 2005E	0.28	52-week Range	$6.07-2.84
P/E on S&P Oper. EPS 2005E	19.8	12 Month P/E	42.5
Yield (%)	Nil	Beta	NA
Dividend Rate/Share	Nil	Shareholders	5,771
Shares Outstanding (M)	269.1	Market Cap (B)	$1.5

Value of $10,000 invested five years ago: **$ 2,763**

Dividend Data

No cash dividends have been paid.

Revenues/Earnings Data Fiscal year ending September 30

Revenues (Million $)

	2004	2003	2002	2001	2000	1999
1Q	156.8	172.0	195.4	234.9	239.0	250.1
2Q	164.7	171.0	179.9	245.1	227.1	263.3
3Q	168.4	165.2	178.1	229.1	227.3	264.1
4Q	170.1	163.7	188.6	225.4	235.0	250.0
Yr.	660.0	671.9	742.0	934.6	928.4	1,058

Earnings Per Share ($)

	2004	2003	2002	2001	2000	1999
1Q	-0.10	-0.04	-0.02	0.05	0.04	0.11
2Q	0.01	-0.06	-0.07	0.03	-0.02	0.04
3Q	0.06	-0.13	-0.10	-0.01	-0.01	0.13
4Q	0.15	-0.14	-0.16	-0.10	0.03	0.17
Yr.	0.13	-0.37	-0.36	-0.03	-0.01	0.43

Next earnings report expected: late-January Source: S&P, Company Reports
EPS Estimates based on S&P Operating Earnings; historical GAAP earnings are as reported.

Recommendation: HOLD ★ ★ ★ ☆ ☆   12-Month Target Price: **$5.50** (as of September 21, 2004)

Business Summary October 21, 2004

Parametric Technology has been going through a product transition in recent years. As a result, the company is now organized into two business units, Design Solutions, which includes mechanical computer-aided design (MCAD) products, and Collaboration and Control Solutions, which includes the Windchill product line.

Historically, the company's core business has been developing mechanical CAD/ CAM/CAE solutions through its Pro/ENGINEER design software. PMTC is now attempting to leverage its strength in mechanical design software to succeed in shifting its focus to product lifecycle management (PLM) software solutions.

PLM solutions include software and services that use the Internet to assist in the collaborative efforts in developing, building and managing products throughout their entire lifecycle. PLM combines many smaller, formerly isolated markets that address various phases of the product life cycle, including product data management, component and supplier management, visualization and digital mockup, computer-aided design, manufacturing and engineering, enterprise application integration, program and project management, manufacturing planning and maintenance, repair and overhaul.

PMTC believes demand for its PLM solutions will be driven by a need on the part of manufacturers to deliver more custom-tailored goods faster and at lower prices, while relying more heavily on geographically dispersed and dynamic supply chains.

The company's enterprise PLM solution is a Web-based product called Windchill. The Windchill enterprise suite enables manufacturers to leverage the Internet in their product development and delivery process from customer driven engineer-to-order through development, manufacturing and retirement. Windchill Link solutions use a series of point solutions that employ the Web-based Windchill architecture; each is designed to address business-critical manufacturing functions.

PMTC's Design Solutions segment encompasses a broad range of engineering disciplines essential to the development of virtually all manufactured products, ranging from consumer products to jet aircraft. These software tools, which include the company's core Pro/ENGINEER software, are designed to enable end-users to reduce their time-to-market and manufacturing costs for their products and to improve product quality by easily evaluating multiple design alternatives and sharing data. During the 2003 first quarter, PMTC released Pro ENGINEER Wildfire, the latest release of the company's Pro/ENGINEER design solution.

Collaboration and Control (Windchill) based solutions revenue accounted for 26% of total revenue in FY 03, up from 24% in FY 02. Design Solutions accounted for 74% of total revenue in FY 03, down from 76% in FY 02. Sales to customers outside North America were 63% of the total in FY 03, up from 58% in FY 02.

Company Financials Fiscal Year ending September 30

Per Share Data ($)

(Year Ended September 30)	2004	2003	2002	2001	2000	1999	1998	1997	1996	1995
Tangible Bk. Val.	NA	0.54	0.90	1.18	1.47	1.31	1.22	2.52	2.01	1.48
Cash Flow	NA	-0.21	-0.08	0.26	0.27	0.65	0.49	0.91	0.58	0.34
Earnings	0.13	-0.37	-0.36	-0.03	-0.01	0.43	0.38	0.82	0.52	0.30
S&P Core Earnings	NA	-0.56	-0.77	-0.34	NA	NA	NA	NA	NA	NA
Dividends	Nil	Nil	Nil	Nil	Nil	Nil	Nil	Nil	Nil	Nil
Payout Ratio	Nil	Nil	Nil	Nil	Nil	Nil	Nil	Nil	Nil	Nil
Prices - High	6.07	4.35	8.44	17.00	32.87	35.93	36.31	32.12	28.37	18.12
- Low	3.85	1.80	1.64	3.97	7.37	11.68	8.50	18.75	12.93	8.00
P/E Ratio - High	47	NM	NM	NM	NM	84	96	39	55	60
- Low	30	NM	NM	NM	NM	27	22	23	25	27

Income Statement Analysis (Million $)

	2004	2003	2002	2001	2000	1999	1998	1997	1996	1995
Revs.	NA	672	742	935	928	1,058	1,018	809	600	394
Oper. Inc.	NA	-7.09	25.3	117	92.1	294	344	349	222	128
Depr.	NA	41.6	72.6	76.4	78.8	62.3	29.9	22.4	16.8	9.50
Int. Exp.	NA	Nil	Nil	Nil	0.37	0.62	13.3	Nil	Nil	NM
Pretax Inc.	NA	-82.4	-74.3	-10.9	-5.07	181	204	337	216	128
Eff. Tax Rate	NA	NM	NM	NM	NM	34.2%	48.2%	35.0%	36.2%	39.4%
Net Inc.	NA	-98.3	-93.6	-8.21	-3.98	119	106	219	138	77.4
S&P Core Earnings	NA	-147	-201	-90.5	NA	NA	NA	NA	NA	NA

Balance Sheet & Other Fin. Data (Million $)

	2004	2003	2002	2001	2000	1999	1998	1997	1996	1995
Cash	NA	205	179	217	326	240	206	154	434	308
Curr. Assets	NA	416	501	516	628	705	594	691	562	400
Total Assets	NA	578	675	798	925	1,017	833	832	659	454
Curr. Liab.	NA	298	316	360	362	457	420	187	146	82.0
LT Debt	NA	Nil	Nil	Nil	Nil	Nil	Nil	Nil	Nil	NM
Common Equity	NA	195	290	400	529	521	327	645	512	371
Total Cap.	NA	197	290	400	529	521	359	645	512	371
Cap. Exp.	NA	20.8	29.7	61.4	37.0	35.2	36.2	28.0	29.7	12.9
Cash Flow	NA	-56.6	-21.0	68.2	74.8	182	136	242	155	86.9
Curr. Ratio	NA	1.4	1.6	1.4	1.7	1.5	1.4	3.7	3.8	4.9
% LT Debt of Cap.	NA	Nil	Nil	Nil	Nil	Nil	Nil	Nil	NM	NM
% Net Inc.of Revs.	NA	NM	NM	NM	NM	11.3	10.4	27.1	23.0	19.6
% Ret. on Assets	NA	NM	NM	NM	NM	13.1	12.7	29.4	24.8	20.4
% Ret. on Equity	NA	NM	NM	NM	NM	27.9	21.7	37.9	31.2	24.9

Data as orig reptd.; bef. results of disc opers/spec. items. Per share data adj. for stk. divs. Bold denotes primary EPS - prior periods restated. E-Estimated. NA-Not Available. NM-Not Meaningful. NR-Not Ranked. UR-Under Review.

Office: 140 Kendrick Street , Needham , MA 02494.
Telephone: 781-370-5000.
Website: http://www.ptc.com
Pres & CEO: C.R. Harrison.
EVP & CFO: N. Moses.

SVP & General Counsel: A.C. vonStaats.
Investor Contact: M. Mendola 781-370-6151.
Dirs: R. N. Goldman, D. K. Grierson, C. R. Harrison, O. B. Marx III, M. E. Porter, N. G. Posternak.

Founded: in 1985.
Domicile: Massachusetts.
Employees: 3,500.
S&P Analyst: Jonathan Rudy, CFA /MF/GG

Parker Hannifin

Recommendation: **HOLD** ★★★ ★ ★
SELL SELL HOLD BUY BUY

12-Month Target Price: **$66.00**
(as of October 07, 2004)

PH has an approximate 0.08% weighting in the **S&P 500**

Sector: Industrials
Sub-Industry: Industrial Machinery
Peer Group: Pumps/Fluid/Filter Equip. (Manufacturing)

Summary: PH is a global maker of industrial pumps, valves and hydraulics. Its products are used in everything from jet engines to trucks and autos and utility turbines.

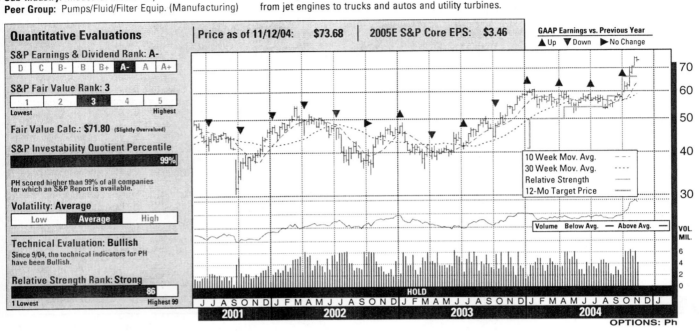

| Price as of 11/12/04: | $73.68 | 2005E S&P Core EPS: | $3.46 |

Quantitative Evaluations

S&P Earnings & Dividend Rank: A-
| D | C | B- | B | B+ | A- | A | A+ |

S&P Fair Value Rank: 3
| 1 | 2 | 3 | 4 | 5 |
Lowest — Highest

Fair Value Calc.: $71.80 (Slightly Overvalued)

S&P Investability Quotient Percentile
99%

PH scored higher than 99% of all companies for which an S&P Report is available.

Volatility: Average
| Low | Average | High |

Technical Evaluation: Bullish
Since 9/04, the technical indicators for PH have been Bullish.

Relative Strength Rank: Strong
86
1 Lowest — Highest 99

GAAP Earnings vs. Previous Year
▲ Up ▼ Down ► No Change

10 Week Mov. Avg.
30 Week Mov. Avg.
Relative Strength
12-Mo Target Price

Volume Below Avg. — Above Avg. —
VOL. MIL.

HOLD

J J A S O N D J F M A M J J A S O N D J F M A M J J A S O N D J F M A M J J A S O N D J
2001   2002   2003   2004

OPTIONS: Ph

Analyst commentary prepared by Robert E. Friedman, CPA /PMW/JWP

Highlights October 11, 2004

- We project 5% revenue growth in FY 05 (Jun.), driven primarily by automotive and machine tool demand for PH's industrial components (70% of revenues) and by rebounding commercial aviation demand for various aircraft equipment and components (15%). We believe the company will be able to maintain EBIT (earnings before interest and taxes) margins of about 10%, driven by the modest increase in volume sales that we project, and by operating efficiencies from ongoing cost containment programs.

- Aided by restrained growth in non-operating expenses, we expect FY 05 EPS to advance about 20%, to $3.52. On a Standard & Poor's Core Earnings basis, we project that EPS will be up about 15%, to $3.46. On the profitability side of the equation, we believe PH will generate FY 05 debt-adjusted return on equity (ROE) of 15%.

- We are relatively optimistic about the company's longer-term prospects. A combination of what we see as solid end market growth prospects and PH's history, in our view, of respectable cost containment measures should enable the company to generate a free cash earnings per share compound annual growth rate (CAGR) of 10%, with average ROE of about 15%.

Investment Rationale/Risk October 11, 2004

- With the shares are trading at a modest discount to our 12-month target price of $66, we would not add to positions.

- Risks to our recommendation and target price include unexpected structural deterioration in PH's primary long-term demand drivers, or in its business economics.

- Our free cash flow model (which values the stock by adding the discounted sum of projected cash earnings growing at a 10% CAGR over the next 10 years, and at 3.0% thereafter) indicates that the stock is worth about $66 a share, which is our 12-month target price. Our relative valuation model, which compares a company's earnings yield with 10-year AAA-rated bond yields, supports our opinion that the stock is trading at a modest discount. Based on our FY 05 S&P Core EPS estimate of $3.46, the stock is generating an earnings yield of 5.7%, versus 10-year AAA bond yields of about 4.7%.

Key Stock Statistics

S&P Oper. EPS 2005E	3.52	52-week Range	$75.45-51.65
P/E on S&P Oper. EPS 2005E	20.9	12 Month P/E	20.8
Yield (%)	1.0%	Beta	1.09
Dividend Rate/Share	0.76	Shareholders	4,955
Shares Outstanding (M)	119.5	Market Cap (B)	$ 8.8

Value of $10,000 invested five years ago: **$ 17,896**

Dividend Data Dividends have been paid since 1949

Amount ($)	Date Decl.	Ex-Div. Date	Stock of Record	Payment Date
0.190	Jan. 29	Feb. 17	Feb. 19	Mar. 05 '04
0.190	Apr. 22	May. 18	May. 20	Jun. 04 '04
0.190	Jul. 23	Aug. 18	Aug. 20	Sep. 03 '04
0.190	Oct. 27	Nov. 16	Nov. 18	Dec. 03 '04

Revenues/Earnings Data Fiscal year ending June 30

Revenues (Million $)
	2005	2004	2003	2002	2001	2000
1Q	1,947	1,587	1,586	1,476	1,477	1,242
2Q	—	1,621	1,517	1,437	1,460	1,239
3Q	—	1,906	1,647	1,578	1,534	1,394
4Q	—	1,993	1,661	1,658	1,485	1,480
Yr.	—	7,107	6,411	6,149	5,980	5,355

Earnings Per Share ($)
	2005	2004	2003	2002	2001	2000
1Q	1.11	0.48	0.52	0.52	1.09	0.67
2Q	E0.75	0.47	0.32	0.25	0.68	0.68
3Q	E0.94	0.90	0.42	0.45	0.80	0.97
4Q	E1.03	1.05	0.42	-0.10	0.42	0.99
Yr.	E3.52	2.91	1.68	1.12	2.99	3.31

Next earnings report expected: mid-January Source: S&P, Company Reports
EPS Estimates based on S&P Operating Earnings; historical GAAP earnings are as reported.

Parker Hannifin Corporation

Recommendation: **HOLD** ★★★ ☆☆   12-Month Target Price: **$66.00** (as of October 07, 2004)

Business Summary October 11, 2004

With about $7 billion in annual revenues, Parker Hannifin is one of the world's largest makers of components that control the flow of industrial fluids. It is also a major global maker of components that move and/or control the operation of a variety of machinery and equipment. PH's offerings include a wide range of valves, pumps, hydraulics, filters and related products. The company's components are used in everything from jet engines to medical devices, farm tractors, and utility turbines.

Primary customers include makers and users of civilian and military aircraft, agricultural machinery, trucks and autos, power generators, and construction machinery. In FY 04 (Jun.) no single customer accounted for over 4% of total sales. Principal competitors include Honeywell International, Eaton Corp., and U.K.-based Invensys plc.

U.S. markets account for most of the company's revenues. In FY 04, North American sales accounted for nearly 70% of total revenues; international markets accounted for the balance.

PH's Industrial segment (69% of FY 04 revenues; 52% of operating profits; and 6% profit margins) makes valves, pumps, seals, and hydraulic components for a broad range of industries. The company's industrial components are sold to manufacturers (as part of original equipment) and to end users (as replacement parts). Replacement part sales are generally more profitable than original equipment sales. PH's industrial components are designed for both standard and custom specifications. Custom-made components are typically more profitable than standard components.

Demand for the company's industrial components is primarily driven by strength of global capital spending levels. Based on U.S. Census Bureau statistics, from 1993 through 2003, non-defense, non-aerospace capital spending rose at a 3.7% average annual rate.

The more profitable Aerospace segment (17%; 32%; 14%) primarily makes hydraulic, pneumatic and fuel equipment used in civilian and military airframes and jet engines. It also makes aircraft wheels and brakes for small planes and military aircraft. PH sells aircraft components to aircraft manufacturers as new equipment, and to end-users (such as airlines) as replacement parts. As with industrial components, aircraft-related replacement parts sales are generally more profitable than are original equipment sales.

Demand for PH's aircraft components is driven primarily by growth in the global passenger jetliner fleet of planes seating more than 100 passengers. Based on statistics provided by independent research firm Avitas, Inc., and global airline trade group International Air Transport Association (IATA), from 1993 through 2003, this fleet grew at a 3.0% average annual rate.

PH's Climate & Industrial Controls unit (10%; 13%; 10%) makes refrigeration and air conditioning systems. The Other unit (3%; 2%; 6%) makes pre-fab industrial buildings.

From FY 97 through FY 04, net operating EPS, free cash flow per share, and net worth per share grew at 2.4%, 13% and 8.0% compound annual growth rates, respectively. Return on equity (ROE) averaged 14% during this period.

Company Financials Fiscal Year ending June 30

Per Share Data ($)

(Year Ended June 30)	2004	2003	2002	2001	2000	1999	1998	1997	1996	1995
Tangible Bk. Val.	14.08	11.45	12.27	13.43	14.94	12.62	11.68	11.32	9.57	9.75
Cash Flow	5.01	3.85	3.55	5.29	5.17	4.68	4.52	3.98	3.43	3.06
Earnings	2.91	1.68	1.12	2.99	3.31	2.83	2.88	2.46	2.15	1.97
S&P Core Earnings	3.00	0.91	0.56	1.78	NA	NA	NA	NA	NA	NA
Dividends	0.76	0.74	0.72	0.70	0.51	0.64	0.60	0.51	0.48	0.45
Payout Ratio	26%	44%	64%	23%	15%	23%	21%	21%	22%	23%
Prices - High	75.45	59.80	54.88	50.10	54.00	51.43	52.62	51.25	29.41	27.66
- Low	51.73	35.82	34.52	30.40	31.00	29.50	26.56	24.91	21.25	18.38
P/E Ratio - High	26	36	49	17	16	18	18	21	14	14
- Low	18	21	31	10	9	10	9	10	10	9

Income Statement Analysis (Million $)

	2004	2003	2002	2001	2000	1999	1998	1997	1996	1995
Revs.	7,107	6,411	6,149	5,980	5,355	4,959	4,633	4,091	3,586	3,214
Oper. Inc.	817	639	628	836	829	741	733	633	546	502
Depr.	253	259	282	265	206	202	183	170	141	120
Int. Exp.	73.4	81.6	82.0	90.4	59.2	63.7	52.8	46.7	36.7	31.0
Pretax Inc.	494	297	218	534	562	478	504	425	374	348
Eff. Tax Rate	30.0%	34.0%	40.3%	35.5%	34.5%	35.0%	35.9%	35.5%	36.0%	37.4%
Net Inc.	346	196	130	344	368	311	323	274	240	218
S&P Core Earnings	357	107	65.0	204	NA	NA	NA	NA	NA	NA

Balance Sheet & Other Fin. Data (Million $)

	2004	2003	2002	2001	2000	1999	1998	1997	1996	1995
Cash	184	246	46.0	23.7	68.5	33.3	30.5	69.0	64.0	63.8
Curr. Assets	2,537	2,397	2,236	2,196	2,153	1,775	1,780	1,500	1,402	1,246
Total Assets	6,257	5,986	5,733	5,338	4,646	3,706	3,525	2,999	2,886	2,302
Curr. Liab.	1,260	1,424	1,360	1,413	1,186	755	989	716	767	653
LT Debt	954	966	1,089	857	702	725	513	433	440	237
Common Equity	2,982	2,521	2,584	2,529	2,309	1,854	1,683	1,547	1,384	1,192
Total Cap.	4,015	3,508	3,750	3,518	3,089	2,610	2,226	2,006	1,849	1,452
Cap. Exp.	142	158	207	345	230	230	237	189	202	152
Cash Flow	599	455	412	609	575	513	506	444	381	338
Curr. Ratio	2.0	1.7	1.6	1.6	1.8	2.3	1.8	2.1	1.8	1.9
% LT Debt of Cap.	23.8	27.5	29.0	24.4	22.7	27.8	23.0	21.6	23.8	16.3
% Net Inc.of Revs.	4.9	3.1	2.1	5.8	6.9	6.3	7.0	6.7	6.7	6.8
% Ret. on Assets	5.6	3.3	2.3	6.9	8.8	8.6	9.9	9.3	9.2	10.3
% Ret. on Equity	12.6	7.7	5.1	14.2	17.7	17.6	20.0	18.7	18.6	20.2

Data as orig reptd.; bef. results of disc opers/spec. items. Per share data adj. for stk. divs. Bold denotes primary EPS - prior periods restated. E-Estimated. NA-Not Available. NM-Not Meaningful. NR-Not Ranked. UR-Under Review.

Office: 6035 Parkland Boulevard, Cleveland, OH 44124-4141.
Telephone: 216-896-3000.
Website: http://www.parker.com
Chrmn: D.E. Collins.
Pres & CEO: D.E. Washkewicz.
VP & CFO: T.K. Pistell.

VP & Treas: P. Huggins.
VP, Secy & General Counsel: T.A. Piraino, Jr.
Investor Contact: C. Groudle 216-896-3000.
Dirs: J. G. Breen, D. E. Collins, W. E. Kassling, R. J. Kohlhepp, P. W. Likins, G. Mazzaupi, K. Mueller, C. Oborun, H. R. Ortino, A. L. Rayfield, W. R. Schmitt, D. L. Starnes, N. W. Vande Steeg, D. E. Washkewicz.

Founded: in 1924.
Domicile: Ohio.
Employees: 48,447.
S&P Analyst: Robert E. Friedman, CPA /PMW/JWP

Paychex, Inc.

Recommendation: **HOLD** ★★★★★
SELL | SELL | HOLD | BUY | BUY

12-Month Target Price: **$35.00**
(as of September 16, 2003)

PAYX has an approximate 0.12% weighting in the **S&P 500**

Sector: Information Technology
Sub-Industry: Data Processing & Outsourced Services
Peer Group: Billing & Payroll Services

Summary: PAYX provides computerized payroll accounting services to small and medium-size concerns throughout the U.S.

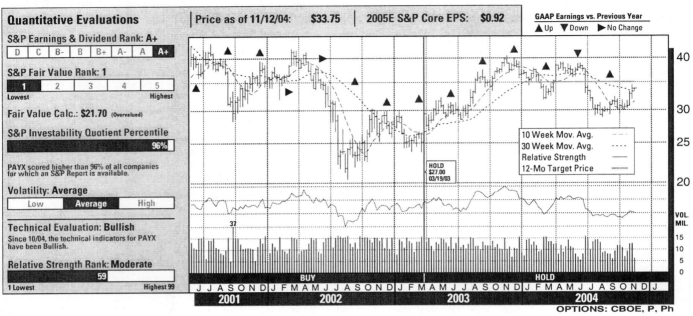

Quantitative Evaluations

S&P Earnings & Dividend Rank: A+
D | C | B- | B | B+ | A- | A | **A+**

S&P Fair Value Rank: 1
1 | 2 | 3 | 4 | 5
Lowest | | | | Highest

Fair Value Calc.: $21.70 (Overvalued)

S&P Investability Quotient Percentile
96%

PAYX scored higher than 96% of all companies for which an S&P Report is available.

Volatility: Average
Low | **Average** | High

Technical Evaluation: Bullish
Since 10/04, the technical indicators for PAYX have been Bullish.

Relative Strength Rank: Moderate
59
1 Lowest | Highest 99

Price as of 11/12/04: **$33.75** | 2005E S&P Core EPS: **$0.92**

GAAP Earnings vs. Previous Year
▲ Up ▼ Down ► No Change

10 Week Mov. Avg.
30 Week Mov. Avg.
Relative Strength
12-Mo Target Price

HOLD $27.00 03/19/03

BUY | HOLD

J J A S O N D J F M A M J J A S O N D J F M A M J J A S O N D J F M A M J J A S O N D J
2001 | 2002 | 2003 | 2004

OPTIONS: CBOE, P, Ph

Analyst commentary prepared by Stephanie S. Crane/PMW/JWP

Highlights September 24, 2004

- We look for revenues to increase 11% in FY 05 (May), after a 17% advance posted in FY 04. We see growth in the payroll and benefits segments partly offset by lower interest earned on funds held for clients. We expect revenues to be aided by PAYX's recent acquisitions of Advantage Payroll Services and InterPay, Inc.

- We project FY 05 growth in the core payroll client base in the low double digits, including further penetration of add-on services, such as Taxpay and direct deposit. The company has also said it is making a more aggressive move into the human resources and benefits area. The human resources business provides higher revenues per employee and wider margins than traditional payroll outsourcing.

- We see operating margins widening slightly in FY 05, to 36%, from 33% in FY 04. We expect EPS to grow about 19%, to $0.95. Our FY 05 Standard & Poor's Core Earnings projection $0.92 reflects estimated stock option expense.

Investment Rationale/Risk September 24, 2004

- We have a hold recommendation on the shares. We see the company benefiting from solid execution and strong profitability levels, wider than those of peers, due to strong cost controls, and a move into higher margin areas such as paying taxes for customers, direct deposit, check signing, and employee benefit administrative services.

- Risks to our recommendation and target price stem from volatility in the small to medium sized business environment; and the impact of competition on pricing and margins.

- We see the shares as fairly valued at current levels. Our 12-month target price of $35 is derived from a peer-based P/E to growth ratio of 1.12X, as well as our discounted cash flow analysis. The latter assumes a discount rate of 11.2% and a perpetual growth rate of 4%.

Key Stock Statistics

S&P Oper. EPS 2005E	0.95	52-week Range	$40.00-28.83
P/E on S&P Oper. EPS 2005E	35.5	12 Month P/E	41.2
Yield (%)	1.5%	Beta	0.64
Dividend Rate/Share	0.52	Shareholders	19,201
Shares Outstanding (M)	378.2	Market Cap (B)	$ 12.8

Value of $10,000 invested five years ago: **$ 13,044**

Dividend Data Dividends have been paid since 1988

Amount ($)	Date Decl.	Ex-Div. Date	Stock of Record	Payment Date
0.120	Jan. 09	Jan. 29	Feb. 02	Feb. 16 '04
0.120	Apr. 08	Apr. 29	May. 03	May. 17 '04
0.120	Jul. 08	Jul. 29	Aug. 02	Aug. 16 '04
0.130	Oct. 06	Oct. 28	Nov. 01	Nov. 15 '04

Revenues/Earnings Data Fiscal year ending May 31

Revenues (Million $)

	2005	2004	2003	2002	2001	2000
1Q	345.0	309.3	252.7	234.8	203.9	166.4
2Q	—	312.1	268.8	233.0	208.1	172.4
3Q	—	342.6	287.8	242.8	229.3	192.2
4Q	—	330.4	289.8	244.3	228.6	197.2
Yr.	—	1,294	1,099	954.9	869.9	728.1

Earnings Per Share ($)

	2005	2004	2003	2002	2001	2000
1Q	0.23	0.21	0.20	0.19	0.16	0.11
2Q	E0.23	0.21	0.20	0.18	0.16	0.12
3Q	E0.25	0.21	0.19	0.18	0.18	0.13
4Q	E0.25	0.16	0.19	0.18	0.18	0.14
Yr.	E0.95	0.80	0.78	0.73	0.68	0.51

Next earnings report expected: mid-December Source: S&P, Company Reports
EPS Estimates based on S&P Operating Earnings; historical GAAP earnings are as reported.

Paychex, Inc.

Recommendation: **HOLD** ★ ★ ★ ☆ ☆   12-Month Target Price: **$35.00** (as of September 16, 2003)

Business Summary September 24, 2004

In FY 04 (May), Paychex, which provides payroll processing, human resources and benefits services for small to medium-size businesses, recorded its 14th consecutive year of record revenues and net income. A streak of 10 consecutive years of net income growth exceeding 30% ended in FY 02, as growth slowed to 8%, followed gains of 7% in FY 03 and 3% in FY 04, in a difficult economic environment.

PAYX, founded in 1971, began by serving the payroll accounting services of businesses with fewer than 200 employees. It currently has more than 100 locations, serves more than 490,000 clients throughout the U.S., and ranks as the second largest U.S. payroll accounting services company. PAYX operates primarily in the U.S., and its addressable market consists of 6 million small to mid-sized companies. About 99% of these have fewer than 100 employees, and represent the company's primary customers.

The company's payroll segment prepares payroll checks, earnings statements, internal accounting records and all federal, state and local payroll tax returns, and provides collection and remittance of payroll obligations. PAYX's tax filing and payment services, including Taxpay, used by 87% of clients, provide automatic tax filing and payment, preparation and submission of tax returns, plus deposit of funds with tax authorities. Employee Payment Services (used by 60% of clients) provides a variety of ways for businesses to pay employees, including the traditional paper check, direct bank deposit, a debit and purchase card option, and a special type of check called Readychex.

PAYX's ability to continually expand its client base and increase the use of ancillary services has led to consistent growth for this segment. Client retention rates are typically about 80%, as many customers go out of business, reflecting the failure rate for small companies in general.

The Human Resources/Professional Employer Organization (HRS/PEO) segment provides employee benefits, management and human resources services. The Paychex Administrative Services (PAS) product offers businesses a bundled package that includes payroll, employer compliance, human resource and employee benefit administration and employee risk management. As of May 31, 2004, the PAS and PEO products combined served more than 157,000 client employees.

PAYX offers 401(k) plan recordkeeping services, group benefits' and workers' compensation insurance services, section 125 Plans, and management services directly to clients. The company's outsourcing services provide regulatory compliance, healthcare benefits, 401(k) administration, and other services.

In September 2002, the company acquired Advantage Payroll Services Inc. for $314 million in cash, including the redemption of preferred stock and the repayment of debt. In April 2003, PAYX acquired InterPay Inc., for $182 million in cash.

Company Financials Fiscal Year ending May 31

Per Share Data ($)

(Year Ended May 31)	2004	2003	2002	2001	2000	1999	1998	1997	1996	1995
Tangible Bk. Val.	1.88	1.55	2.43	2.00	1.50	1.18	0.90	0.69	0.55	0.41
Cash Flow	1.02	0.89	0.80	0.75	0.57	0.43	0.33	0.25	0.19	0.15
Earnings	0.80	0.78	0.73	0.68	0.51	0.37	0.28	0.20	0.15	0.11
S&P Core Earnings	0.80	0.72	0.66	0.65	NA	NA	NA	NA	NA	NA
Dividends	0.44	0.33	0.33	0.22	0.18	0.12	0.08	0.07	0.06	0.03
Payout Ratio	55%	56%	45%	32%	35%	32%	29%	35%	39%	25%

Cal. Yrs.	2003	2002	2001	2000	1999	1998	1997	1996	1995	1994
Prices - High	40.54	42.15	51.00	61.25	29.91	24.47	15.33	12.56	6.56	3.57
- Low	23.76	20.39	28.27	24.16	15.70	13.37	7.55	6.02	3.39	2.50
P/E Ratio - High	51	54	70	90	59	66	55	63	43	31
- Low	30	26	39	36	31	36	27	30	22	22

Income Statement Analysis (Million $)

	2004	2003	2002	2001	2000	1999	1998	1997	1996	1995
Revs.	1,294	1,099	955	870	728	597	494	400	325	267
Oper. Inc.	516	444	393	700	283	210	153	112	81.4	62.1
Depr.	82.8	43.4	29.5	26.4	23.9	22.1	18.8	15.3	13.9	11.0
Int. Exp.	Nil	Nil	Nil	Nil	Nil	Nil	Nil	Nil	Nil	0.20
Pretax Inc.	450	432	395	364	275	200	144	104	72.7	54.4
Eff. Tax Rate	32.6%	32.0%	30.5%	30.0%	31.0%	30.5%	29.1%	27.5%	28.0%	28.2%
Net Inc.	303	293	275	255	190	139	102	75.2	52.3	39.0
S&P Core Earnings	304	272	252	243	NA	NA	NA	NA	NA	NA

Balance Sheet & Other Fin. Data (Million $)

	2004	2003	2002	2001	2000	1999	1998	1997	1996	1995
Cash	219	79.9	61.9	45.8	47.1	343	251	183	117	83.7
Curr. Assets	3,280	3,033	2,815	2,791	2,363	1,793	1,479	1,141	165	124
Total Assets	3,950	3,691	2,953	2,907	2,456	1,873	1,550	1,201	220	168
Curr. Liab.	2,722	2,588	2,023	2,144	1,887	1,432	1,216	946	28.1	26.7
LT Debt	Nil	Nil	Nil	Nil	Nil	Nil	Nil	Nil	Nil	0.50
Common Equity	1,235	1,077	924	745	563	436	330	252	191	140
Total Cap.	1,249	1,084	924	745	563	436	330	252	191	141
Cap. Exp.	50.6	60.2	54.4	45.3	32.9	22.1	28.2	18.0	17.0	12.3
Cash Flow	386	337	304	281	214	161	121	90.5	66.3	50.1
Curr. Ratio	1.2	1.2	1.4	1.3	1.3	1.3	1.2	1.2	5.9	4.7
% LT Debt of Cap.	Nil	Nil	Nil	Nil	Nil	Nil	Nil	Nil	Nil	0.4
% Net Inc.of Revs.	23.4	26.7	28.7	29.3	26.1	23.3	20.7	18.8	16.1	14.7
% Ret. on Assets	7.9	8.8	9.4	9.5	8.8	8.1	7.4	7.4	26.9	26.2
% Ret. on Equity	26.2	29.3	32.6	38.7	38.0	36.3	35.2	34.0	31.7	31.5

Data as orig reptd.; bef. results of disc opers/spec. items. Per share data adj. for stk. divs. Bold denotes primary EPS - prior periods restated. E-Estimated. NA-Not Available. NM-Not Meaningful. NR-Not Ranked. UR-Under Review.

Office: 911 Panorama Trail South, Rochester, NY 14625-2396.
Telephone: 585-385-6666.
Website: http://www.paychex.com
Chrmn: B.T. Golisano.
Pres & CEO: J.J. Judge.

SVP, CFO & Secy: J.M. Morphy.
Investor Contact: J. Shuler 585-383-3406.
Dirs: G. T. Clark, D. J. Flaschen, B. T. Golisano, P. Horsley, G. M. Inman, J. R. Sebo, J. M. Tucci.

Founded: in 1979.
Domicile: Delaware.
Employees: 9,400.
S&P Analyst: Stephanie S. Crane/PMW/JWP

Penney (J.C.)

Recommendation: **HOLD** ★ ★ ★ ☆ ☆   12-Month Target Price: **$42.00**

SELL | SELL | HOLD | BUY | BUY

(as of November 16, 2004)

JCP has an approximate 0.11% weighting in the **S&P 500**

Sector: Consumer Discretionary
Sub-Industry: Department Stores
Peer Group: Department Store Cos. - Larger

Summary: JCP is one of the largest U.S. retailers through its department stores and catalog operations.

Quantitative Evaluations

S&P Earnings & Dividend Rank: B-

D | C | **B-** | B | B+ | A- | A | A+

S&P Fair Value Rank: 2-

1 | **2** | 3 | 4 | 5
Lowest | | | | Highest

Fair Value Calc.: $35.20 (Slightly Overvalued)

S&P Investability Quotient Percentile

90%

JCP scored higher than 90% of all companies
for which an S&P Report is available.

Volatility: Average

Low | **Average** | High

Technical Evaluation: Neutral
Since 11/04, the technical indicators for JCP
have been Neutral.

Relative Strength Rank: Moderate

65

1 Lowest | Highest 99

| Price as of 11/16/04: | **$39.98** | 2005E S&P Core EPS: | **$1.91** |

GAAP Earnings vs. Previous Year
▲ Up   ▼ Down   ► No Change

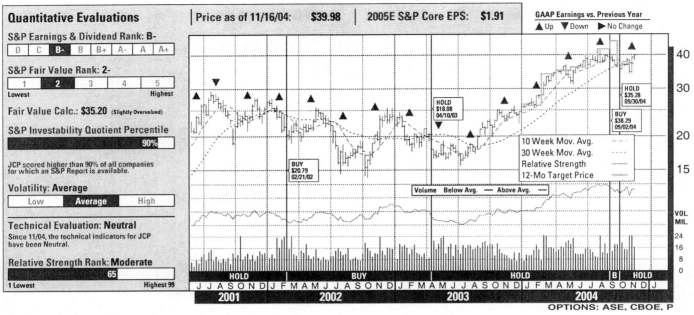

Analyst commentary prepared by Jason N. Asaeda/DC/TV

Highlights November 05, 2004

- From a projected $18.8 billion in FY 05 (Jan.), we expect sales to rise about 4% in FY 06, to $19.5 billion, with $16.6 billion from retail stores and $2.9 billion from catalog/Internet channels. At retail, we look for same-store sales to increase in the mid-single digits, and think JCP could gain market share with the addition of several new stores, mainly in off-mall locations. Based, in part, on recent store visits, we think JCP is doing a good job of driving store traffic with easier-to-shop store layouts, faster-turning fashion apparel, and home offerings that better emphasize design, quality, and value. We also see an improvement in sales being driven by the company's ability to reach a broad audience via its multi-channel sales strategy.

- We look for earnings before interest and taxes (EBIT) margins to widen, on the benefits of centralized merchandising and marketing initiatives, an improved store environment, and savings from a $200 million cost reduction plan.

- We estimate FY 05 operating EPS of $2.10 and Standard & Poor's Core EPS of $1.91, and FY 06 operating EPS of $2.70 and S&P Core EPS of $2.59. The differences reflect projected stock option and pension expenses.

Investment Rationale/Risk November 05, 2004

- We continue to view JCP's assortments, value proposition and multi-channel sales strategy favorably, and believe these factors will likely work in the company's favor this upcoming holiday shopping season. We also think JCP will benefit in FY 06 from the branding and fashion experience of Myron Ullman III, most recently Directeur General at LVMH Moet Hennessey Louis Vuitton, chosen by directors to succeed Allen Questrom as chairman and CEO, effective December 1. That said, we are seeing competing moderate chains stepping up their merchandising and marketing initiatives to match JCP's success, and are concerned that the company's fundamentals could weaken post-holiday as the chains regain their footing in the marketplace.

- Risks to our recommendation and target price include a decline in sales due to poor merchandise planning, unforeseen shifts in fashion trends, adverse weather conditions, and heightened competition.

- We derive our 12-month target price of $37 by blending a peer-average forward P/E multiple of 14X to our FY 06 operating EPS estimate of $2.70 for JCP, and a value of $37 derived by our DCF analysis. Our DCF model assumes a cost of capital of 8% and a terminal growth rate of 4%.

Key Stock Statistics

S&P Core EPS 2006E	2.59	52-week Range	$41.50-22.29
S&P Oper. EPS 2005E	2.32	12 Month P/E	NM
P/E on S&P Oper. EPS 2005E	17.2	Beta	0.91
S&P Oper. EPS 2006E	2.80	Shareholders	46,524
Yield (%)	1.3%	Market Cap (B)	$ 11.5
Dividend Rate/Share	0.50	Shares Outstanding (M)	288.2

Value of $10,000 invested five years ago: **$ 19,512**

Dividend Data Dividends have been paid since 1922

Amount ($)	Date Decl.	Ex-Div. Date	Stock of Record	Payment Date
0.125	Dec. 10	Jan. 07	Jan. 09	Feb. 01 '04
0.125	Mar. 19	Apr. 06	Apr. 09	May. 01 '04
0.125	May. 14	Jul. 07	Jul. 09	Aug. 01 '04
0.125	Sep. 17	Oct. 06	Oct. 08	Nov. 01 '04

Revenues/Earnings Data Fiscal year ending January 31

Revenues (Million $)

	2005	2004	2003	2002	2001	2000
1Q	4,033	7,493	7,728	7,522	7,528	7,569
2Q	3,857	7,313	7,198	7,211	7,207	7,309
3Q	4,461	7,985	7,872	7,729	7,538	7,978
4Q	—	6,098	9,549	9,542	9,573	9,834
Yr.	—	17,786	32,347	32,004	31,846	32,510

Earnings Per Share ($)

	2005	2004	2003	2002	2001	2000
1Q	0.38	0.05	0.29	0.13	-0.63	0.61
2Q	0.23	-0.03	-0.05	-0.23	-0.10	0.12
3Q	0.50	0.31	0.30	0.09	-0.30	0.51
4Q	E1.11	0.83	0.68	0.32	-1.26	-0.08
Yr.	E2.32	1.21	1.25	0.32	-2.29	1.16

Next earnings report expected: late-February Source: S&P, Company Reports
EPS Estimates based on S&P Operating Earnings; historical GAAP earnings are as reported.

J.C. Penney Company, Inc.

Recommendation: **HOLD** ★ ★ ★ ☆ ☆   12-Month Target Price: **$42.00** (as of November 16, 2004)

Business Summary November 05, 2004

J.C. Penney Co.'s main business is the operation of its eponymous department store chain, with 1,018 JCPenney stores throughout the U.S. and Puerto Rico, and 60 Renner department stores in Brazil, as of September 29, 2004. The company formerly operated 2,735 Eckerd stores, one of the largest U.S. drug store chains in the U.S.

Over the past decade, JCP has shed its image as a mass merchandiser, transforming itself into a moderate-priced department store chain. Since 2001, it has focused on a five-year turnaround strategy to improve its stores to competitive levels of profitability. Key components of the strategy are to provide competitive, fashionable merchandise assortments; offer a compelling and appealing marketing program; present vibrant and energized store environments; have and maintain a competitive expense structure; and attract and retain an experienced and professional workforce.

In FY 04 (Jan.), JCP developed a new store distribution center network as part of efforts to centralize merchandising, marketing and operating processes. The network, comprised of 13 store support centers (SSCs), facilitates the movement of merchandise from suppliers to stores, to improve in-stock positions, and to reduce costs, time and handling from the distribution process.

Also in FY 04, the company closed 36 department stores, including its six Mexican stores, and opened six new and relocated stores. Total new square footage declined about 2.4 million sq. ft., to 105 million sq. ft.

The direct-to-customer business includes catalogs and the Internet. Since January 2000, JCP has eliminated about 40% of the catalog's infrastructure, including fulfillment centers, telemarketing centers, and outlet stores. The company views the Internet channel, jcpenney.com, as an attractive shopping venue for an expanding base of customers.

In January 2003, the company announced a new cost reduction program, expected to result in annualized cost savings exceeding $200 million when fully implemented. JCP expects to achieve initial savings in FY 05 from: the closing of a catalog telemarketing center; the transfer of management responsibility to the company for six SSCs outsourced to third parties; restructuring efforts in department store operations, catalog, and related corporate support functions; and further refinement of marketing expenditures.

In the FY 04 fourth quarter, JCP announced plans to sell Eckerd. Eckerd's net assets were classified as held for sale, and results of its operations and its financial position reported as discontinued operations. In April 2004, the company signed definitive sales agreements with The Jean Coutu Group Inc. and CVS Corp. for a total of $4.525 billion in cash. The sale was completed in July 2004. JCP has committed $3.5 billion in net sales proceeds and another $1.1 billion in existing cash for debt reduction and share buybacks.

Company Financials Fiscal Year ending January 31

Per Share Data ($)

(Year Ended January 31)	2004	2003	2002	2001	2000	1999	1998	1997	1996	1995
Tangible Bk. Val.	18.54	12.04	11.46	NM	14.28	15.04	15.50	15.73	23.58	23.27
Cash Flow	2.68	3.45	3.00	0.36	3.87	4.40	4.46	4.13	5.15	5.65
Earnings	1.21	1.25	0.32	-2.29	1.16	2.19	2.10	2.29	3.48	4.29
S&P Core Earnings	1.24	0.66	0.15	-2.47	NA	NA	NA	NA	NA	NA
Dividends	0.50	0.50	0.50	0.50	2.19	2.18	2.14	2.08	1.92	1.68
Payout Ratio	41%	40%	156%	NM	188%	100%	102%	91%	55%	38%

Cal. Yrs.	2003	2002	2001	2000	1999	1998	1997	1996	1995	1994
Prices - High	26.42	27.75	29.50	22.50	54.43	78.75	68.25	57.00	50.00	59.00
- Low	15.57	14.07	10.50	8.62	17.68	42.62	44.87	44.00	39.87	41.00
P/E Ratio - High	22	22	92	NM	47	36	32	25	14	14
- Low	13	11	33	NM	15	19	21	19	11	10

Income Statement Analysis (Million $)

	2004	2003	2002	2001	2000	1999	1998	1997	1996	1995
Revs.	17,786	32,347	32,004	31,846	32,510	30,678	30,546	22,653	20,562	21,706
Oper. Inc.	1,184	1,681	1,473	873	1,681	2,253	1,687	1,075	1,200	2,292
Depr.	394	667	717	695	710	637	584	381	341	323
Int. Exp.	261	388	386	427	673	663	648	414	383	320
Pretax Inc.	546	584	203	-886	531	955	925	909	1,341	1,699
Eff. Tax Rate	33.3%	36.5%	43.8%	NM	36.7%	37.8%	38.8%	37.8%	37.5%	37.8%
Net Inc.	364	371	114	-568	336	594	566	565	838	1,057
S&P Core Earnings	345	171	41.0	-650	NA	NA	NA	NA	NA	NA

Balance Sheet & Other Fin. Data (Million $)

	2004	2003	2002	2001	2000	1999	1998	1997	1996	1995
Cash	2,994	2,474	2,840	944	1,233	96.0	287	131	173	261
Curr. Assets	6,513	8,353	8,677	7,257	8,472	11,125	11,484	11,712	9,409	9,468
Total Assets	18,300	17,867	18,048	19,742	20,888	23,638	23,493	22,088	17,102	16,202
Curr. Liab.	3,754	4,159	4,499	4,235	4,465	5,970	6,137	7,966	4,020	4,481
LT Debt	5,114	4,940	5,179	5,448	5,844	7,143	6,986	4,565	4,080	3,335
Common Equity	5,121	6,037	5,766	5,860	6,782	6,694	6,831	5,526	5,509	5,292
Total Cap.	11,756	12,701	12,539	12,843	14,087	15,829	15,668	11,879	11,152	9,989
Cap. Exp.	373	658	631	648	631	744	824	704	717	550
Cash Flow	733	1,011	802	94.0	1,010	1,193	1,110	946	1,179	1,340
Curr. Ratio	1.7	2.0	1.9	1.7	1.9	1.9	1.9	1.5	2.3	2.1
% LT Debt of Cap.	43.5	38.9	41.3	42.4	41.5	45.1	44.6	38.4	36.6	33.4
% Net Inc.of Revs.	2.0	1.1	0.4	NM	1.0	1.9	1.9	2.5	4.1	4.9
% Ret. on Assets	2.0	2.1	0.1	NM	1.5	2.5	2.5	2.9	4.8	6.9
% Ret. on Equity	6.1	5.8	1.9	NM	4.5	8.2	8.6	9.5	14.8	19.9

Data as orig reptd.; bef. results of disc opers/spec. items. Per share data adj. for stk. divs.; EPS diliuted. E-Estimated. NA-Not Available. NM-Not Meaningful. NR-Not Ranked. UR-Under Review.

Office: 6501 Legacy Drive, Plano, TX 75024-3698.
Telephone: 972-431-1000.
Website: http://www.jcpenney.net
Chrmn & CEO: A. Questrom.
EVP & CFO: R.B. Cavanaugh.

EVP, Secy & General Counsel: C.R. Lotter.
Investor Contact: E. Akresh 972-431-1000.
Dirs: C. C. Barrett, A. Burns, M. Clark, T. J. Engibous, K. B. Foster, V. E. Jordan, Jr., B. Osborne, J. C. Pfeiffer, A. Questrom, A. W. Richards, L. H. Roberts, C. S. Sanford, Jr., R. G. Turner.

Founded: in 1902.
Domicile: Delaware.
Employees: 147,000.
S&P Analyst: Jason N. Asaeda/DC/TV

PeopleSoft, Inc.

Recommendation: HOLD ★ ★ ★ ★ ★   **12-Month Target Price:** **$24.00**
(as of November 01, 2004)

PSFT has an approximate 0.08% weighting in the **S&P 500**

Sector: Information Technology
Sub-Industry: Application Software
Peer Group: Enterprise Applications - Larger

Summary: Oracle Corp. has offered to acquire this enterprise software developer for $24 a share.

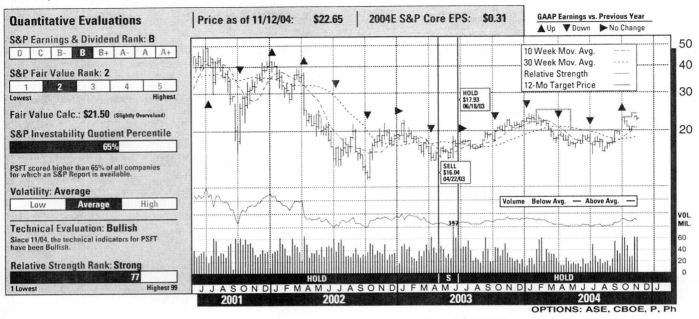

Quantitative Evaluations	Price as of 11/12/04: $22.65	2004E S&P Core EPS: $0.31

S&P Earnings & Dividend Rank: B
D C B- **B** B+ A- A A+

S&P Fair Value Rank: 2
1 **2** 3 4 5
Lowest   Highest

Fair Value Calc.: $21.50 (Slightly Overvalued)

S&P Investability Quotient Percentile
65%
PSFT scored higher than 65% of all companies for which an S&P Report is available.

Volatility: Average
Low **Average** High

Technical Evaluation: Bullish
Since 11/04, the technical indicators for PSFT have been Bullish.

Relative Strength Rank: Strong
77
1 Lowest   Highest 99

GAAP Earnings vs. Previous Year
▲ Up ▼ Down ► No Change

10 Week Mov. Avg.
30 Week Mov. Avg.
Relative Strength
12-Mo Target Price

HOLD $17.93 06/18/03
SELL $16.04 04/22/03
Volume Below Avg. — Above Avg.

HOLD | S | HOLD
J J A S O N D | J F M A M J J A S O N D | J F M A M J J A S O N D | J F M A M J J A S O N D | J
2001   2002   2003   2004

OPTIONS: ASE, CBOE, P, Ph

Analyst commentary prepared by Jonathan Rudy, CFA /CB/JWP

Highlights November 03, 2004

- On November 1, 2004, Oracle Corp. (ORCL: buy, $12) increased its cash tender offer for PSFT to $24 a share (valuing the company at approximately $8.9 billion), from $21 a share. Earlier, in May 2004, ORCL had lowered its offer to $21 a share, from $26 a share. On September 9, 2004, a federal judge ruled that an ORCL/PSFT combination would not violate antitrust laws. This decision overturned a previous ruling by the Department of Justice that the acquisition of PSFT by ORCL would violate antitrust laws.

- On a stand-alone basis, we expect PSFT's revenues to advance about 22% in 2004, and approximately 19% in 2005, following a 16% increase in 2003, with results seen primarily benefiting from the 2003 acquisition of JDEC. We project 2004 operating EPS of $0.68 (excluding one-time items), and see $0.77 in 2005.

- Our 2004 Standard & Poor's Core Earnings estimate of $0.31 a share reflects the projected impact of stock option expense.

Investment Rationale/Risk November 03, 2004

- We believe it is increasingly likely that ORCL will be able to acquire PSFT, with PSFT recently terminating the contract of its president/CEO, who was in open opposition to the offer, and with ORCL winning an appeal of the DOJ's antitrust decision. ORCL's cash offer of $24 per share values the stock at an enterprise value of 2.6X sales, 3.2X our 2004 revenue estimate, and 31X our 2005 EPS estimate, a fair value, in our opinion, in light of PSFT's declining license revenue.

- Risks to our opinion and target price include a rapidly changing technology landscape, customer losses due to ORCL's hostile tender offer for PSFT, integration risk from the acquisition of J.D. Edwards, and intense competition in the software industry.

- Our 12-month target price is $24, based primarily on ORCL's cash tender offer, in addition to relative enterprise value to sales and P/E to growth metrics.

Key Stock Statistics

S&P Oper. EPS 2004E	0.68	52-week Range	$24.04-15.39
P/E on S&P Oper. EPS 2004E	33.3	12 Month P/E	NM
S&P Oper. EPS 2005E	0.77	Beta	NA
Yield (%)	Nil	Shareholders	2,800
Dividend Rate/Share	Nil	Market Cap (B)	$ 8.3
Shares Outstanding (M)	366.9		

Value of $10,000 invested five years ago: **$ 14,653**

Dividend Data

No cash dividends have been paid.

Revenues/Earnings Data Fiscal year ending December 31

Revenues (Million $)

	2004	2003	2002	2001	2000	1999
1Q	643.1	460.3	483.3	503.1	375.4	305.4
2Q	647.3	497.4	482.2	532.6	420.1	312.2
3Q	698.8	624.1	471.2	509.4	443.1	303.1
4Q	—	685.2	512.3	528.2	497.8	372.3
Yr.	—	2,267	1,949	2,073	1,736	1,429

Earnings Per Share ($)

	2004	2003	2002	2001	2000	1999
1Q	0.07	0.12	0.14	0.11	0.06	-0.73
2Q	0.03	0.11	0.11	0.15	0.05	0.01
3Q	0.06	-0.02	0.14	0.16	0.23	0.02
4Q	E0.20	0.05	0.18	0.18	0.14	-0.02
Yr.	E0.68	0.25	0.57	0.59	0.48	-0.67

Next earnings report expected: late-January Source: S&P, Company Reports
EPS Estimates based on S&P Operating Earnings; historical GAAP earnings are as reported.

PeopleSoft, Inc.

Recommendation: **HOLD** ★ ★ ★ ☆ ☆   12-Month Target Price: **$24.00** (as of November 01, 2004)

Business Summary November 03, 2004

PeopleSoft designs, markets and supports a family of enterprise application software products for use throughout large and medium sized organizations worldwide. The company provides enterprise application software for customer relationship management, human capital management, financial management, and supply chain management, along with a range of industry-specific products. Within each application suite, PSFT offers embedded analytics and portal applications. In addition, the company offers a suite of products for application integration and analytic capability, including portal applications.

PSFT's first product was a human resource management system, shipped starting in December 1988. Since then, the company has expanded its product offerings significantly. Until recently, PSFT focused on enterprise resource planning, or ERP, software. This back-office software provides a foundation for business processes for customers, suppliers, and employees, such as general ledger, payables, billing, payroll, and enterprise planning.

The company's human resources management software helps organizations manage employee positions and compensation; recruit, hire, and train employees; promote, allocate, and retire personnel; and comply with local and international regulatory requirements. Other software products include applications for financial management, student administration, treasury management, enterprise performance management, project management, sales and logistics, materials management, supply chain planning, and procurement.

In August 2003, the company completed its acquisition of J.D. Edwards for cash

and stock totaling about $1.8 billion. As a result of this acquisition, PSFT offers three product families that address specific customer needs across a range of company sizes and industries: PeopleSoft Enterprise (formerly PeopleSoft 8), PeopleSoft EnterpriseOne (formerly J.D. Edwards 5), and PeopleSoft World (formerly J.D. Edwards World Software).

In June 2001, PSFT began shipping a solution called PeopleSoft Customer Relationship Management (CRM), which was built from the Vantive products. PeopleSoft CRM is a suite of customer relationship management products that help companies to sell, support, analyze and service customers through many channels of interaction including the Internet, telephone call center, facsimile, email, or directly through sales and service representatives.

PeopleSoft Supply Chain Management helps organizations in three main categories: Supplier Relationship Management, Customer Fulfillment Management, and Supply Chain Planning.

The company began shipping its first pure Internet application suite, PeopleSoft 8, now PeopleSoft Enterprise, in September 2000, marking PSFT's largest technological advance in enterprise software in more than a decade. PeopleSoft 8 includes newly developed, pure Internet collaborative applications that enable organizations to create a real-time, collaborative network of customers, employees and suppliers.

Company Financials Fiscal Year ending December 31

Per Share Data ($)

(Year Ended December 31)	2003	2002	2001	2000	1999	1998	1997	1996	1995	1994
Tangible Bk. Val.	4.11	6.08	5.23	3.79	2.70	2.84	1.87	1.18	0.80	0.50
Cash Flow	0.76	0.89	0.91	0.76	-0.30	0.78	0.59	0.26	0.18	0.11
Earnings	0.25	0.57	0.59	0.48	-0.67	0.55	0.44	0.15	0.14	0.07
S&P Core Earnings	-0.23	0.01	0.19	NA	NA	NA	NA	NA	NA	NA
Dividends	Nil	Nil	Nil	Nil	Nil	Nil	Nil	Nil	Nil	Nil
Payout Ratio	Nil	Nil	Nil	Nil	Nil	Nil	Nil	Nil	Nil	Nil
Prices - High	23.05	42.65	53.87	50.00	26.37	57.43	39.50	26.12	11.75	4.93
- Low	14.40	11.75	15.78	12.00	11.50	16.50	15.31	8.56	3.75	1.62
P/E Ratio - High	92	75	91	NM	NM	NM	90	NM	87	71
- Low	58	21	27	NM	NM	NM	35	NM	28	23

Income Statement Analysis (Million $)

	2003	2002	2001	2000	1999	1998	1997	1996	1995	1994
Revs.	2,267	1,949	2,073	1,736	1,429	1,314	816	450	228	113
Oper. Inc.	339	364	355	188	-141	294	205	112	56.2	29.0
Depr.	176	101	103	84.2	97.3	58.2	38.9	26.7	11.3	7.30
Int. Exp.	Nil	Nil	Nil	4.01	4.11	Nil	Nil	Nil	Nil	Nil
Pretax Inc.	139	283	290	237	-166	242	176	61.7	48.9	23.9
Eff. Tax Rate	37.9%	35.5%	33.9%	38.6%	NM	40.7%	38.5%	41.9%	40.0%	39.0%
Net Inc.	85.0	183	192	146	-178	143	108	35.9	29.4	14.6
S&P Core Earnings	-77.5	3.61	61.9	NA	NA	NA	NA	NA	NA	NA

Balance Sheet & Other Fin. Data (Million $)

	2003	2002	2001	2000	1999	1998	1997	1996	1995	1994
Cash	439	319	434	647	414	480	268	197	126	88.0
Curr. Assets	2,011	2,351	2,133	1,616	1,359	1,164	726	397	244	149
Total Assets	4,225	2,849	2,548	1,985	1,688	1,441	898	540	314	172
Curr. Liab.	589	776	839	770	752	668	481	287	156	78.0
LT Debt	Nil	Nil	Nil	68.0	69.0	89.4	Nil	Nil	Nil	Nil
Common Equity	2,859	1,956	1,592	1,024	765	664	417	253	157	93.3
Total Cap.	2,859	1,956	1,592	1,092	834	754	417	253	157	93.3
Cap. Exp.	250	93.3	92.0	102	57.2	100	55.4	57.1	53.2	18.2
Cash Flow	261	284	295	230	-80.5	201	147	62.6	40.6	21.8
Curr. Ratio	3.4	3.0	2.5	2.1	1.8	1.7	1.5	1.4	1.6	1.9
% LT Debt of Cap.	Nil	Nil	Nil	6.2	8.3	11.9	Nil	Nil	Nil	Nil
% Net Inc.of Revs.	3.8	9.4	9.2	8.4	NM	10.9	13.3	8.0	12.9	12.9
% Ret. on Assets	2.4	6.7	8.5	7.9	NM	12.2	15.1	8.3	12.1	3.5
% Ret. on Equity	3.5	10.3	14.6	16.3	NM	26.5	32.3	17.3	21.1	17.6

Data as orig reptd.; bef. results of disc opers/spec. items. Per share data adj. for stk. divs.; EPS diluted. E-Estimated. NA-Not Available. NM-Not Meaningful. NR-Not Ranked. UR-Under Review.

Office: 4460 Hacienda Drive, Pleasanton, CA 94588-2761.
Telephone: 925-225-3000.
Email: investor_relations@peoplesoft.com
Website: http://www.peoplesoft.com
Chrmn & CEO: D.A. Duffield.
Pres & EVP: P. Wilmington.

Pres, SVP & CFO: K.T. Parker.
Vice Chrmn: A. Bhusri.
SVP, Secy & General Counsel: A.S. Jordan.
Investor Contact: B. Okunski.
Dirs: A. G. Battle, A. Bhursi, D. A. Duffield, F. J. Fanzilli, Jr., S. Goldby, M. J. Maples, C. J. Yansouni.

Founded: in 1986.
Domicile: Delaware.
Employees: 12,163.
S&P Analyst: Jonathan Rudy, CFA /CB/JWP

Peoples Energy

Recommendation: **HOLD** ★ ★ ★ ☆ ☆
SELL | SELL | HOLD | BUY | BUY

12-Month Target Price: **$44.00**
(as of October 29, 2004)

PGL has an approximate 0.02% weighting in the **S&P 500**

Sector: Utilities
Sub-Industry: Gas Utilities
Peer Group: Diversified - Larger

Summary: This diversified energy company focuses on gas distribution, power generation, oil and gas production, asset-based gas wholesaling, and retail energy services.

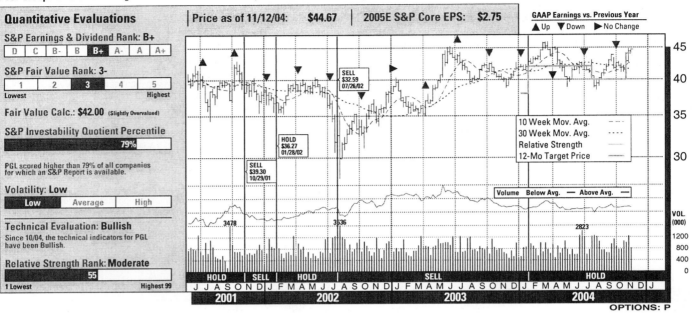

Quantitative Evaluations

S&P Earnings & Dividend Rank: B+

| D | C | B- | B | B+ | A- | A | A+ |

S&P Fair Value Rank: 3-

| 1 | 2 | 3 | 4 | 5 |
| Lowest | | | | Highest |

Fair Value Calc.: $42.00 (Slightly Overvalued)

S&P Investability Quotient Percentile

79%

PGL scored higher than 79% of all companies for which an S&P Report is available.

Volatility: Low

| Low | Average | High |

Technical Evaluation: Bullish
Since 10/04, the technical indicators for PGL have been Bullish.

Relative Strength Rank: Moderate

55

1 Lowest — Highest 99

Price as of 11/12/04: $44.67 **2005E S&P Core EPS:** $2.75

GAAP Earnings vs. Previous Year
▲ Up ▼ Down ► No Change

Chart legend:
- 10 Week Mov. Avg.
- 30 Week Mov. Avg.
- Relative Strength
- 12-Mo Target Price

Volume Below Avg. — Above Avg. —

VOL. (000)
1200
800
400
0

Chart annotations: SELL $32.59 07/26/02; HOLD $36.27 01/28/02; SELL $39.30 10/29/01; 3478; 3536; 2823

HOLD	SELL	HOLD	SELL	HOLD
J J A S O N D	J F M A M J J A S O N D	J F M A M J J A S O N D	J F M A M J J A S O N D	J
2001	2002	2003	2004	

OPTIONS: P

Analyst commentary prepared by Craig K. Shere, CFA /PMW/JWP

Highlights July 30, 2004

- Our FY 04 (Sep.) operating EPS estimate excludes expected fourth quarter asset sale gains (which PGL estimates at about $0.10) and severance charges. Our longer-term EPS estimates assume that Aquila, a distressed buyer of power from PGL's 50%-owned Elwood plant in Chicago, will continue to make payments on its long-term supply contract (which is at above market prices).

- We expect FY 04 operating EPS to drop over 10%, as higher pension expense, the impact of warmer weather, lower midstream earnings (due to reduced natural gas price volatility), production shortfalls, and over 5% more shares outstanding outweigh one-time tax benefits. In the third quarter, an expensive dry hole, delayed production from new wells, and the shut-in of capacity due to the temporary loss of pipeline transportation boosted costs and reduced production volumes. For FY 05, we see 9% EPS growth, as normal winter weather, lower production costs, higher production volumes, flat pension expense, savings from the FY 04 severance program, and growth in unregulated operations outweigh about 6% greater interest expense and a higher effective tax rate.

- Our FY 04 Standard & Poor's Core EPS projection is $0.14 below our operating EPS estimate, primarily due to pension accounting adjustments, the inclusion of severance expense, and estimated stock option expense.

Key Stock Statistics

S&P Oper. EPS 2005E	2.80	52-week Range	$46.03-38.50
P/E on S&P Oper. EPS 2005E	16.0	12 Month P/E	19.5
S&P Oper. EPS 2006E	2.90	Beta	-0.05
Yield (%)	4.8%	Shareholders	20,892
Dividend Rate/Share	2.16	Market Cap (B)	$ 1.7
Shares Outstanding (M)	37.6		

Value of $10,000 invested five years ago: **$ 14,993**

Dividend Data Dividends have been paid since 1937

Amount ($)	Date Decl.	Ex-Div. Date	Stock of Record	Payment Date
0.530	Dec. 05	Dec. 18	Dec. 22	Jan. 15 '04
0.540	Feb. 04	Mar. 18	Mar. 22	Apr. 15 '04
0.540	Jun. 02	Jun. 18	Jun. 22	Jul. 15 '04
0.540	Aug. 04	Sep. 20	Sep. 22	Oct. 15 '04

Investment Rationale/Risk July 30, 2004

- We are increasingly confident that PGL will return to earnings growth in FY 05 and beyond, based on our expectations of continued strength in unregulated operations and more normal winter weather in anticipated for 2004-05 (after a warmer than normal 2003-04). Despite higher commodity prices, we see PGL continuing to find accretive acquisitions for its oil and gas production operations. The company has a history of annual dividend increases, but with its FY 05 payout ratio at about 77%, we expect only modest increases over the next couple years.

- Risks to our recommendation and target price include the potential default of one of Elwood's wholesale power purchasers, a prolonged decline in natural gas prices, inability to find accretive acquisitions, higher interest rates, and warmer than usual winter weather.

- The stock's price to book ratio is about in line with peers, but its P/E multiple and price to trailing operating cash flow multiples are at premiums. Based on our expectations of above-average EPS growth, already reflected in our FY 05 EPS estimate, we believe the stock should trade at a P/E multiple on projected 2005 EPS in line with the 13.6X utility average (as of late July). We look for appreciation in line with our longer-term EPS growth rate projection of 6%. Our 12-month target price is $40. Total investor returns are augmented by a dividend yield of over 5%.

Revenues/Earnings Data Fiscal year ending September 30

Revenues (Million $)

	2004	2003	2002	2001	2000	1999
1Q	604.9	549.1	377.6	717.0	412.5	313.5
2Q	927.0	903.8	522.8	1,074	525.2	500.8
3Q	401.1	398.1	347.1	318.5	261.3	218.7
4Q	332.2	287.3	235.0	160.9	219.1	171.1
Yr.	2,265	2,138	1,483	2,270	1,418	1,194

Earnings Per Share ($)

	2004	2003	2002	2001	2000	1999
1Q	0.85	0.87	0.87	1.03	0.83	0.66
2Q	1.46	1.77	1.55	1.76	1.62	1.86
3Q	0.15	0.22	0.04	0.33	0.31	0.20
4Q	-0.16	0.04	0.05	0.38	-0.32	-0.11
Yr.	2.29	2.87	2.51	2.74	2.44	2.61

Next earnings report expected: late-January Source: S&P, Company Reports
EPS Estimates based on S&P Operating Earnings; historical GAAP earnings are as reported.

Peoples Energy Corporation

Recommendation: **HOLD** ★ ★ ★ ☆ ☆   12-Month Target Price: **$44.00** (as of October 29, 2004)

Business Summary July 30, 2004

Peoples Energy is seeking to expand its unregulated business activities. The company's unregulated businesses (including power generation, midstream natural gas services, oil and gas production and retail energy services) accounted for 30.4% of FY 03 (Sep.) operating segment profit before allocation of corporate overhead, up from 23.1% in FY 02. The company targets 10% to 15% long-term earnings growth from these diversified businesses.

PGL's regulated gas utilities (Peoples Gas and North Shore Gas) purchase, store, distribute, sell and transport natural gas through a 6,000-mile distribution system that serves the Chicago and 54 communities in northeastern Illinois. At the end of FY 03, Peoples Gas served about 825,000 customers in Chicago, while North Shore Gas served 150,000 customers in suburban communities.

The Power Generation segment develops, constructs, owns and operates natural gas-fired power plants. PGL and Dominion Energy are equal investors in Elwood Energy, which owns a 1,400 megawatt peaking facility near Chicago. PGL is also a 27% owner in the Southeast Chicago Project, a 350 MW Chicago peaking facility. PGL is evaluating the potential construction of a 280 MW peaking plant in New Mexico, a 1,150 MW baseload plant in Oregon, and potential projects in Texas.

Both Elwood and the Southeast Chicago Project have sold their capacity through long-term contracts. Aquila, one of the three companies contracting for Elwood power, was downgraded to junk credit status in the 2002 fourth quarter.

Midstream Services provides wholesale natural gas services to utilities, marketers, pipelines and electric generators in the Midwest. Through Peoples Gas and Peoples Energy Resources, the segment operates a natural gas hub and a natural gas liquids peaking facility, and has several contractual relationships for pipeline transportation and storage. In December 2003, the company said it was expanding this division's wholesale marketing and asset management activities.

The Retail Energy Services segment provides competitive retail natural gas and electricity supply as a part of the deregulation of Illinois energy markets. The unit is one of the largest nonutility retail energy marketers in northern Illinois. In the FY 03 third quarter, PGL became the natural gas provider for the State of Illinois, increasing the unit's total natural gas volumes by 5%.

Through its Oil and Gas Production operations, PGL engages in low to moderate risk drilling opportunities (primarily for natural gas), and acquires proved reserves with upside potential (realized through drilling, production enhancements and reservoir optimization). During FY 03, the unit's total production increased over 33%, to 25,798 MMcfe. It also has an equity investment in EnerVest, which develops and manages oil and gas producing properties.

Company Financials Fiscal Year ending September 30

Per Share Data ($)

(Year Ended September 30)	2004	2003	2002	2001	2000	1999	1998	1997	1996	1995
Tangible Bk. Val.	NA	23.11	22.74	22.76	22.02	21.66	20.94	20.43	19.48	18.38
Earnings	2.29	2.87	2.51	2.74	2.44	2.61	2.25	2.81	2.96	1.78
S&P Core Earnings	NA	2.55	1.08	1.97	NA	NA	NA	NA	NA	NA
Dividends	2.15	2.11	2.07	2.03	1.99	1.95	1.91	1.87	1.83	1.80
Payout Ratio	94%	74%	82%	74%	82%	75%	85%	67%	62%	101%
Prices - High	46.03	45.25	40.45	44.62	46.93	40.25	40.12	39.87	37.37	32.00
- Low	38.50	34.93	27.80	34.35	26.18	31.75	32.12	31.25	29.62	24.25
P/E Ratio - High	20	16	16	16	19	15	18	14	13	18
- Low	17	12	11	13	11	12	14	11	10	14

Income Statement Analysis (Million $)

	2004	2003	2002	2001	2000	1999	1998	1997	1996	1995
Revs.	NA	2,138	1,483	2,270	1,418	1,194	1,138	1,274	1,199	1,033
Depr.	NA	112	99	95.0	101	83.5	77.2	74.1	70.6	66.4
Maint.	NA	NA	NA	NA	NA	NA	44.0	47.6	45.6	41.7
Fxd. Chgs. Cov.	NA	3.95	3.21	2.46	3.10	4.40	6.71	8.32	7.34	4.79
Constr. Credits	NA	NA	NA	NA	1.12	1.96	Nil	Nil	Nil	Nil
Eff. Tax Rate	NA	36.3%	34.2%	34.6%	33.4%	36.2%	64.8%	31.3%	32.7%	29.7%
Net Inc.	NA	104	89.1	97.1	86.4	92.6	79.4	98.4	103	62.2
S&P Core Earnings	NA	92.5	38.7	69.7	NA	NA	NA	NA	NA	NA

Balance Sheet & Other Fin. Data (Million $)

	2004	2003	2002	2001	2000	1999	1998	1997	1996	1995
Gross Prop.	NA	2,962	2,972	2,890	2,682	2,462	2,254	2,134	2,046	2,088
Cap. Exp.	NA	187	201	266	248	229	116	89.4	85.6	95.9
Net Prop.	NA	1,838	1,952	1,940	1,810	1,650	1,490	1,419	1,391	1,373
Capitalization:										
LT Debt	NA	744	554	644	420	522	517	527	527	622
% LT Debt	NA	46.7	40.7	44.4	35.1	40.4	41.0	42.4	43.6	49.2
Pfd.	NA	Nil	Nil	Nil	Nil	Nil	Nil	Nil	Nil	Nil
% Pfd.	NA	Nil	Nil	Nil	Nil	Nil	Nil	Nil	Nil	Nil
Common	NA	848	806	806	777	769	741	716	681	642
% Common	NA	53.3	59.3	55.6	64.9	59.6	58.9	57.7	56.4	50.7
Total Cap.	NA	2,028	1,767	1,814	1,570	1,621	1,561	1,527	1,474	1,510
% Oper. Ratio	NA	93.8	91.6	95.1	91.8	91.3	86.2	89.7	88.9	89.8
% Earn. on Net Prop.	NA	10.6	8.8	24.0	9.2	9.9	7.8	9.4	9.6	7.7
% Return On Revs.	NA	4.9	6.0	4.3	6.1	7.8	7.0	7.7	8.6	6.0
% Return On Invest. Capital	NA	8.1	8.2	10.0	8.7	8.3	17.0	6.6	9.8	17.1
% Return On Com. Equity	NA	12.6	11.1	12.3	11.2	12.3	10.9	14.1	15.6	9.6

Data as orig reptd.; bef. results of disc opers/spec. items. Per share data adj. for stk. divs.; EPS diluted. E-Estimated. NA-Not Available. NM-Not Meaningful. NR-Not Ranked. UR-Under Review.

Office: 130 East Randolph Street, Chicago, IL 60601-6207.
Telephone: 312-240-4000.
Email: corporatecommunications@pecorp.com
Website: http://www.peoplesenergy.com
Chrmn, Pres & CEO: T.M. Patrick.
SVP & CFO: T.A. Nardi.

Secy: P.H. Kauffman.
Investor Contact: M.A. Wall 312-240-7534.
Dirs: J. R. Boris, W. J. Brodsky, P. S. Cafferty, J. Higgins, D. C. Jain, M. E. Lavin, H. J. Livingston, Jr., L. H. McKeever, T. M. Patrick, R. P. Toft, A. R. Velasquez.

Founded: in 1855.
Domicile: Illinois.
Employees: 2,396.
S&P Analyst: Craig K. Shere, CFA /PMW/JWP

Recommendation: **BUY** ★★★★★
[SELL | SELL | HOLD | BUY | BUY]

12-Month Target Price: **$62.00**
(as of April 13, 2004)

PEP has an approximate 0.80% weighting in the **S&P 500**

Sector: Consumer Staples
Sub-Industry: Soft Drinks
Peer Group: Soft Drinks

Summary: PEP is a major international producer of branded beverage and snack food products.

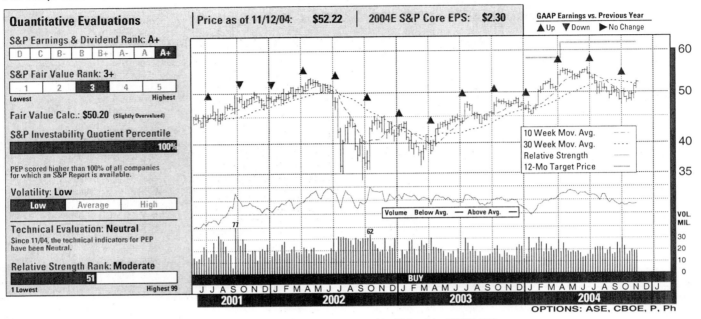

Quantitative Evaluations

| Price as of 11/12/04: | **$52.22** | 2004E S&P Core EPS: | **$2.30** |

GAAP Earnings vs. Previous Year
▲ Up ▼ Down ► No Change

S&P Earnings & Dividend Rank: A+

| D | C | B- | B | B+ | A- | A | **A+** |

S&P Fair Value Rank: 3+

| 1 | 2 | **3** | 4 | 5 |
| Lowest | | | | Highest |

Fair Value Calc.: $50.20 (Slightly Overvalued)

S&P Investability Quotient Percentile

100%

PEP scored higher than 100% of all companies for which an S&P Report is available.

Volatility: Low

| **Low** | Average | High |

Technical Evaluation: Neutral
Since 11/04, the technical indicators for PEP have been Neutral.

Relative Strength Rank: Moderate

| 51 |
| 1 Lowest | Highest 99 |

10 Week Mov. Avg.
30 Week Mov. Avg.
Relative Strength
12-Mo Target Price

Volume — Below Avg. — Above Avg.

VOL. MIL.

BUY
J J A S O N D J F M A M J J A S O N D J F M A M J J A S O N D J F M A M J J A S O N D J
2001 **2002** **2003** **2004**

OPTIONS: ASE, CBOE, P, Ph

Analyst commentary prepared by Richard Joy/PMW/JWP

Highlights July 26, 2004

- We expect net sales to advance about 7% in 2004, reflecting contributions from new products, a favorable pricing environment, and modest foreign exchange benefits. We expect segment operating income to advance 10% to 11%, reflecting favorable pricing and product mix benefits, improved operating efficiency, and productivity gains. By segment, we see operating profits for North American beverages rising in the high single digits, and expect profits for Frito Lay North America to increase 7% to 8%. For the PepsiCo International segment, we believe operating profits will climb 21% to 23%, while we believe the Quaker Foods business will see profits decline 2% to 3%.

- After higher bottler equity income, a modest reduction in net interest expense, fewer shares outstanding, and the inclusion of $0.16 a share of estimated option expense, we estimate operating EPS of $2.31 for 2004, a 13% gain from 2003 operating EPS of $2.05. For 2005, we project a 12% rise, to $2.58. We expect operating free cash flow to exceed $3.5 billion in 2004.

- Our respective 2004 and 2005 Standard & Poor's Core EPS projections, reflecting pension cost adjustment of $0.01 in each year, are $2.30 and $2.57.

Investment Rationale/Risk July 26, 2004

- We recommend buying the shares on a total return basis, based on our view of solid profit growth and growing free cash flows. Based on the company's leading positions in several fast growing food and beverage categories, we believe PEP is poised to deliver 11% to 12% annual EPS growth for the longer term. At a recent P/E multiple of 22X our 2004 EPS estimate, the shares are valued at a discount to comparable global consumer products companies, but at a premium to the S&P 500. We view this premium as warranted, in light of what we see as PEP's promising longer-term prospects stemming from its large market positions in the growing worldwide packaged beverage and snack industries.

- Risks to our recommendation and target price include unfavorable weather conditions in the company's markets, inability to meet volume and revenue growth targets, increased popularity of low carbohydrate diets, and consumer acceptance of new product introductions.

- Our 12-month target price of $62 is derived from our analysis of peers and historical multiples, and our discounted free cash flow model, which assumes a weighted average cost of capital of 9%, 15-year average operating profit growth of 7.5% and a terminal growth rate of 3.5%.

Key Stock Statistics

S&P Core EPS 2005E	2.57	52-week Range	**$55.71-45.30**
S&P Oper. EPS 2004E	2.31	12 Month P/E	21.9
P/E on S&P Oper. EPS 2004E	22.6	Beta	0.41
S&P Oper. EPS 2005E	2.60	Shareholders	214,000
Yield (%)	1.8%	Market Cap (B)	$ 88.0
Dividend Rate/Share	0.92	Shares Outstanding (M)	1684.5

Value of $10,000 invested five years ago: **$ 16,236**

Dividend Data Dividends have been paid since 1952

Amount ($)	Date Decl.	Ex-Div. Date	Stock of Record	Payment Date
0.160	Nov. 21	Dec. 10	Dec. 12	Jan. 02 '04
0.160	Jan. 29	Mar. 10	Mar. 12	Mar. 31 '04
0.230	May. 05	Jun. 09	Jun. 11	Jun. 30 '04
0.230	Jul. 23	Sep. 08	Sep. 10	Sep. 30 '04

Revenues/Earnings Data Fiscal year ending December 31

Revenues (Million $)

	2004	2003	2002	2001	2000	1999
1Q	6,131	5,530	5,101	5,330	4,191	5,114
2Q	7,070	6,538	6,178	6,713	4,928	4,982
3Q	7,257	6,830	6,376	6,906	4,909	4,591
4Q	—	8,073	7,457	7,986	6,410	5,680
Yr.	—	26,971	25,112	26,935	20,438	20,367

Earnings Per Share ($)

	2004	2003	2002	2001	2000	1999
1Q	0.46	0.45	0.36	0.32	0.29	0.22
2Q	0.61	0.58	0.49	0.44	0.38	0.49
3Q	0.79	0.62	0.54	0.34	0.40	0.32
4Q	E0.59	0.52	0.46	0.37	0.41	0.33
Yr.	E2.31	2.05	1.85	1.47	1.48	1.37

Next earnings report expected: early-February Source: S&P, Company Reports
EPS Estimates based on S&P Operating Earnings; historical GAAP earnings are as reported.

PepsiCo, Inc.

Recommendation: **BUY** ★ ★ ★ ★ ★   12-Month Target Price: **$62.00** (as of April 13, 2004)

Business Summary July 26, 2004

Originally incorporated in 1919, PepsiCo is a leader in the global snack and beverage industry. The company manufactures, markets and sells a variety of salty, convenient, sweet and grain-based snacks, carbonated and non-carbonated beverages, and foods. PepsiCo is organized into four business segments: Frito-Lay North America (FLNA), PepsiCo Beverages North America (PBNA), PepsiCo International (PI) and Quaker Foods North America (QFNA).

FLNA (34% of 2003 sales, 41% of operating profits) produces the best-selling line of snack foods in the U.S., including Fritos brand corn chips, Lay's and Ruffles potato chips, Doritos and Tostitos tortilla chips, Cheetos cheese-flavored snacks, Rold Gold pretzels, Sunchips multigrain snacks, Grandma's cookies, Quaker Fruit and Oatmeal bars, Cracker Jack candy-coated popcorn and Quaker rice cakes. FLNA branded products are sold to independent distributors and retailers. Products are transported from Frito-Lay's manufacturing plants to major distribution centers, principally by company-owned trucks.

PBNA (29%, 31%) manufactures or uses contract manufacturers, markets and sells beverage concentrates, fountain syrups and finished goods, under the brands Pepsi, Mountain Dew, Sierra Mist, Mug, SoBe, Gatorade, Tropicana Pure Premium, Dole, Tropicana Season's Best, Tropicana Twister and Propel. PBNA also manufactures, markets and sells ready-to-drink tea and coffee products

through joint ventures with Lipton and Starbucks. In additions, it markets the Aquafina water brand and licenses it to its bottlers. Pepsi-Cola bottlers are licensed by PepsiCo to manufacture, sell and distribute, within defined territories, beverages and syrups bearing the Pepsi-Cola beverage trademarks.

PI (32%, 20%) manufactures through consolidated businesses, as well as through noncontrolled affiliates, a number of leading salty and sweet snack brands including Sabritas, Gamesa and Alegro in Mexico, Walkers in the United Kingdom, and Smith's in Australia. PI also manufactures, markets and sells beverage concentrates, fountain syrups and finished goods under the brands Pepsi, 7UP, Mirinda, Mountain Dew, Gatorade and Tropicana outside North America. These brands are sold to franchise bottlers, independent distributors and retailers. However, in certain markets, PI operates its own bottling plants and distribution facilities. International division products are available in approximately 200 countries.

QFNA (5%, 8%) manufactures, markets and sells Cap'n Crunch and Life ready-to-eat cereals, Quaker hot cereals, Rice-A-Roni and Near East flavored rice products, Pasta Roni pasta products, Aunt Jemima mixes and syrups and Quaker grits.

Company Financials Fiscal Year ending December 31

Per Share Data ($)

(Year Ended December 31)	2003	2002	2001	2000	1999	1998	1997	1996	1995	1994
Tangible Bk. Val.	3.82	2.37	1.90	1.91	1.48	NM	0.72	NM	NM	-0.63
Cash Flow	2.75	2.47	2.07	2.13	2.06	2.12	1.65	1.79	2.08	2.09
Earnings	2.05	1.85	1.47	1.48	1.37	1.31	0.95	0.72	1.00	1.11
S&P Core Earnings	2.03	1.54	1.20	NA	NA	NA	NA	NA	NA	NA
Dividends	0.63	0.59	0.58	0.56	0.53	0.51	0.49	0.45	0.39	0.35
Payout Ratio	31%	32%	39%	38%	39%	39%	52%	62%	39%	32%
Prices - High	48.88	53.50	50.46	49.93	42.56	44.81	41.31	35.87	29.37	20.56
- Low	36.24	34.00	40.25	29.68	30.12	27.56	28.25	27.25	16.93	14.62
P/E Ratio - High	24	29	34	34	31	34	43	50	29	19
- Low	18	18	27	20	22	21	30	38	17	13

Income Statement Analysis (Million $)

	2003	2002	2001	2000	1999	1998	1997	1996	1995	1994
Revs.	26,971	25,112	26,935	20,438	20,367	22,348	20,917	31,645	30,421	28,472
Oper. Inc.	6,208	6,066	5,490	4,185	3,915	4,106	4,058	5,087	5,247	4,778
Depr.	1,221	1,112	1,082	960	1,032	1,234	1,106	1,719	1,740	1,577
Int. Exp.	163	178	219	221	363	395	478	600	682	645
Pretax Inc.	4,992	4,868	4,029	3,210	3,656	2,263	2,309	2,047	2,432	2,664
Eff. Tax Rate	28.5%	31.9%	33.9%	32.0%	43.9%	11.9%	35.4%	43.9%	34.0%	33.0%
Net Inc.	3,568	3,313	2,662	2,183	2,050	1,993	1,491	1,149	1,606	1,784
S&P Core Earnings	3,543	2,749	2,164	NA	NA	NA	NA	NA	NA	NA

Balance Sheet & Other Fin. Data (Million $)

	2003	2002	2001	2000	1999	1998	1997	1996	1995	1994
Cash	820	1,638	683	864	964	311	2,883	786	1,498	1,488
Curr. Assets	6,930	6,413	5,853	4,604	4,173	4,362	6,251	5,139	5,546	5,072
Total Assets	25,327	23,474	21,695	18,339	17,551	22,660	20,101	24,512	25,432	24,792
Curr. Liab.	6,415	6,052	4,998	3,935	3,788	7,914	4,257	5,139	5,230	5,270
LT Debt	1,702	2,187	2,651	2,346	2,812	4,028	4,946	8,439	8,509	8,841
Common Equity	11,896	9,250	8,648	7,249	6,881	6,401	6,939	6,623	7,313	6,856
Total Cap.	14,837	13,196	12,821	10,956	10,902	12,432	13,582	16,840	17,707	17,669
Cap. Exp.	1,345	1,437	1,324	1,067	1,118	1,405	1,506	2,287	2,104	2,253
Cash Flow	4,786	4,421	3,744	3,143	3,082	3,227	2,597	2,868	3,346	3,361
Curr. Ratio	1.1	1.1	1.2	1.2	1.1	0.6	1.5	1.0	1.0	1.0
% LT Debt of Cap.	11.5	16.6	20.7	21.4	25.8	32.4	36.4	50.1	48.1	50.0
% Net Inc.of Revs.	13.2	13.2	9.9	10.7	10.1	8.9	7.1	3.6	5.3	6.3
% Ret. on Assets	14.6	14.7	12.5	12.2	10.2	9.3	7.1	4.6	6.4	7.4
% Ret. on Equity	33.3	37.0	32.8	30.9	30.9	29.9	22.0	16.5	22.7	27.2

Data as orig reptd.; bef. results of disc opers/spec. items. Per share data adj. for stk. divs. Bold denotes diluted EPS (FASB 128)-prior periods restated. E-Estimated. NA-Not Available. NM-Not Meaningful. NR-Not Ranked.

Office: 700 Anderson Hill Road, Purchase, NY 10577.
Telephone: 914-253-2000.
Website: http://www.pepsico.com
Chrmn & CEO: S.S. Reinemund.
Pres & CFO: I.K. Nooyi.
SVP & Treas: L.L. Nowell III.

SVP, Secy & General Counsel: D.R. Andrews.
VP & Investor Contact: K. Luke 914-253-3691.
Dirs: J. F. Akers, R. E. Allen, R. L. Hunt, A. C. Martinez, I. K. Nooyi, F. D. Raines, S. S. Reinemund, S. P. Rockefeller, J. J. Schiro, F. A. Thomas, C. M. Trudell, S. D. Trujillo, D. Vasella.

Founded: in 1916.
Domicile: North Carolina.
Employees: 143,000.
S&P Analyst: Richard Joy/PMW/JWP

Pepsi Bottling Group

Recommendation: **HOLD** ★ ★ ★ ☆ ☆
SELL SELL HOLD BUY BUY

12-Month Target Price: $30.00
(as of September 28, 2004)

PBG has an approximate 0.07% weighting in the **S&P 500**

Sector: Consumer Staples
Sub-Industry: Soft Drinks
Peer Group: Soft Drink Bottlers

Summary: This company is the world's largest manufacturer, seller and distributor of carbonated and non-carbonated Pepsi-Cola beverages.

Quantitative Evaluations

S&P Earnings & Dividend Rank: NR

D	C	B-	B	B+	A-	A	A+

S&P Fair Value Rank: 2+

1	2	3	4	5
Lowest				Highest

Fair Value Calc.: $24.90 (Overvalued)

S&P Investability Quotient Percentile

71%

PBG scored higher than 71% of all companies for which an S&P Report is available.

Volatility: Low

Low	Average	High

Technical Evaluation: Neutral
Since 10/04, the technical indicators for PBG have been Neutral.

Relative Strength Rank: Moderate

47

1 Lowest	Highest 99

Price as of 11/12/04: $29   2004E S&P Core EPS: $1.54

GAAP Earnings vs. Previous Year
▲ Up ▼ Down ▶ No Change

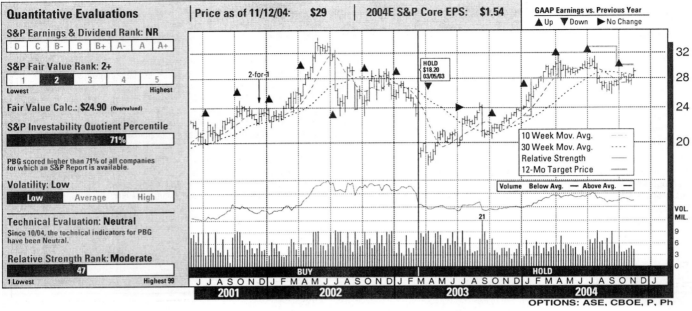

- 10 Week Mov. Avg.
- 30 Week Mov. Avg.
- Relative Strength
- 12-Mo Target Price

Volume Below Avg. — Above Avg. —

OPTIONS: ASE, CBOE, P, Ph

Analyst commentary prepared by Richard Joy/MF/BK

Highlights October 11, 2004

- We expect PBG's net revenues to rise 4% to 5% in 2005, reflecting up to 2% comparable worldwide volume growth, up to a 3% increase in net revenues per case, and a modest foreign currency translation benefit. While volume comparisons should benefit from strong bottled water growth and the addition of new beverage products, we think carbonated soft drink trends will remain sluggish. We expect net revenues per case to benefit from new products and higher pricing, as well as channel and package mix improvements.

- We expect EBITDA to rise more than 7% in 2005, to $1.72 billion. Following repurchases that we expect to reduce shares by up to 3%, we think EPS will climb 10% in 2005, to $1.90, from anticipated EPS of $1.73 in 2004. Longer-term, we project 8% to 10% annual EPS growth.

- Our 2004 and 2005 Standard & Poor's Core Earnings per share projections, reflecting estimated stock option expense of $0.15 per share and per share pension plan cost adjustments of $0.04 and $0.02, respectively, are $1.54 and $1.73, respectively.

Investment Rationale/Risk October 11, 2004

- Our hold recommendation on the shares primarily reflects our concerns about rising commodity costs, sluggish carbonated soft drink volume trends and competitive pressures in Mexico. Despite these concerns, we believe PBG should post a free cash flow growth in excess of 10% in 2005, along with widening margins and improving returns on capital. With the stock recently at 15X our 2005 EPS estimate, a discount to the P/E multiple for the S&P 500 Index and at a modest premium to peers, we view PBG as a worthwhile holding.

- Risks to our recommendation and target price include a rise in competitive pressures for PBG's business in Mexico, an inability to meet volume and revenue growth targets, and unfavorable weather conditions in the company's markets.

- We have a 12-month target price of $30, which is derived from our analysis of comparable peer multiples and discounted free cash flows. Our DCF assumptions include a weighted average cost of capital of 9% and an expected terminal growth rate of 3%.

Key Stock Statistics

S&P Core EPS 2005E	1.73	52-week Range	$31.40-22.01
S&P Oper. EPS 2004E	1.73	12 Month P/E	17.1
P/E on S&P Oper. EPS 2004E	16.8	Beta	0.65
S&P Oper. EPS 2005E	1.90	Shareholders	55,540
Yield (%)	0.7%	Market Cap (B)	$ 7.3
Dividend Rate/Share	0.20	Shares Outstanding (M)	250.1

Value of $10,000 invested five years ago: **$ 34,566**

Dividend Data Dividends have been paid since 1999

Amount ($)	Date Decl.	Ex-Div. Date	Stock of Record	Payment Date
0.010	Nov. 21	Dec. 10	Dec. 12	Jan. 02 '04
0.010	Mar. 04	Mar. 10	Mar. 12	Mar. 31 '04
0.050	Mar. 25	Jun. 09	Jun. 11	Jun. 30 '04
0.050	Aug. 10	Sep. 08	Sep. 10	Sep. 30 '04

Revenues/Earnings Data Fiscal year ending December 31

Revenues (Million $)

	2004	2003	2002	2001	2000	1999
1Q	2,067	1,874	1,772	1,647	1,545	1,452
2Q	2,675	2,532	2,209	2,060	1,913	1,831
3Q	2,934	2,810	2,455	2,274	2,125	2,036
4Q	—	3,049	2,780	2,462	2,399	2,186
Yr.	—	10,265	9,216	8,443	7,982	7,505

Earnings Per Share ($)

	2004	2003	2002	2001	2000	1999
1Q	0.19	0.14	0.19	0.09	0.06	-0.01
2Q	0.53	0.47	0.47	0.39	0.29	0.07
3Q	0.73	0.67	0.61	0.51	0.41	0.30
4Q	E0.30	0.26	0.20	0.05	0.01	-0.09
Yr.	E1.73	1.52	1.46	1.03	0.77	0.46

Next earnings report expected: late-January Source: S&P, Company Reports
EPS Estimates based on S&P Operating Earnings; historical GAAP earnings are as reported.

The Pepsi Bottling Group, Inc.

Recommendation: **HOLD** ★ ★ ★ ☆ ☆   12-Month Target Price: **$30.00** (as of September 28, 2004)

Business Summary October 11, 2004

The Pepsi Bottling Group is the world's largest manufacturer, seller and distributor of carbonated and non-carbonated Pepsi-Cola beverages. The company has exclusive rights to manufacture, sell and distribute Pepsi-Cola beverages in all or a portion of 41 states, the District of Columbia, eight Canadian provinces, Spain, Greece, Turkey, Mexico and Russia. The company was separated from PepsiCo via a March 1999 IPO. As of February 20, 2004, PepsiCo's ownership represented 46% of the voting power of all classes of PBG's voting stock.

The company's brands include some of the most well recognized trademarks in the world, and include Pepsi-Cola, Diet Pepsi, Mountain Dew, Lipton Brisk, Lipton's Iced Tea, 7UP outside the U.S., Pepsi Max, Pepsi One, Slice, Sierra Mist, Mug, Aquafina, Starbucks Frappaccino and Miranda, which are bottled under licenses from PepsiCo or PepsiCo joint ventures.

According to the company, the market shares for carbonated soft drinks sold under trademarks owned by PepsiCo in its territories range from 15.4% to approximately 38.8%. PBG's market share for carbonated soft drinks sold under PepsiCo trademarks for each country where it operates is as follows: Canada 40.9%; Russia 24.7%; Turkey 21.5%; Spain 12.8%; and Greece 11.3%. In addition, market share for PBG's territories and the territories of other bottlers in Mexico is 14.5% for carbonated soft drinks sold under trademarks owned by PepsiCo and carbonated water sold under the Garci Crespo trademark.

PBG has established an extensive production and distribution system to deliver products directly to stores without using wholesalers or middlemen. As of December 27, 2003, the company operated 98 soft drink production facilities worldwide, as well as 514 distribution facilities. PBG also owns or leases and operates approximately 40,900 vehicles, and owns more than 1.8 million soft drink dispensing and vending machines.

The company's strategy includes a major push into the cold drink, or vending machine, distribution channel, which yields higher profits per unit than other channels of distribution. PBG expects a substantial part of new capital investment to go for continuing its push toward expanding vending machine distribution. Another key part of the company's strategy entails acquisitions and international markets. PBG has been designated an anchor bottler by PepsiCo, providing it with the ability to make acquisitions of additional smaller Pepsi bottlers in territories in Pepsi's U.S. bottling system that account for about 12.6% of total system volume, without getting specific prior approval from PepsiCo.

In November 2002, PBG completed the acquisition of Mexican bottler Pepsi-Gemex S.A. de C.V., for $1.1 billion. Headquartered in Mexico City, Pepsi-Gemex is the second largest bottler of Pepsi-Cola beverages outside of the United States, and owns Mexico's largest purified water company, Electropura.

Company Financials Fiscal Year ending December 31

Per Share Data ($)

(Year Ended December 31)	2003	2002	2001	2000	1999	1998	1997	1996	1995	1994
Tangible Bk. Val.	NM	NM	NM	NM	NM	NM	NA	NA	NA	NA
Cash Flow	3.57	3.00	2.77	2.23	2.43	2.96	NA	NA	NA	NA
Earnings	1.52	1.46	1.03	0.77	0.46	-0.39	NA	NA	NA	NA
S&P Core Earnings	1.42	1.18	0.78	NA	NA	NA	NA	NA	NA	NA
Dividends	0.04	0.04	0.04	0.04	0.02	NA	NA	NA	NA	NA
Payout Ratio	3%	3%	4%	5%	4%	NA	NA	NA	NA	NA
Prices - High	27.62	34.80	25.00	21.25	12.62	NA	NA	NA	NA	NA
- Low	17.00	21.65	15.81	8.12	7.75	NA	NA	NA	NA	NA
P/E Ratio - High	18	24	24	28	27	NA	NA	NA	NA	NA
- Low	11	15	15	11	17	NA	NA	NA	NA	NA

Income Statement Analysis (Million $)

	2003	2002	2001	2000	1999	1998	1997	1996	1995	1994
Revs.	10,265	9,216	8,443	7,982	7,505	7,041	NA	NA	NA	NA
Oper. Inc.	1,524	1,349	1,190	1,025	901	749	NA	NA	NA	NA
Depr.	568	451	514	435	505	472	NA	NA	NA	NA
Int. Exp.	239	191	194	192	202	221	NA	NA	NA	NA
Pretax Inc.	710	700	482	397	209	-192	NA	NA	NA	NA
Eff. Tax Rate	33.5%	31.6%	28.2%	34.0%	33.5%	NM	NA	NA	NA	NA
Net Inc.	422	428	305	229	118	-146	NA	NA	NA	NA
S&P Core Earnings	394	347	229	NA	NA	NA	NA	NA	NA	NA

Balance Sheet & Other Fin. Data (Million $)

	2003	2002	2001	2000	1999	1998	1997	1996	1995	1994
Cash	1,235	222	277	318	190	36.0	NA	NA	NA	NA
Curr. Assets	3,039	1,737	1,548	1,584	1,493	1,318	NA	NA	NA	NA
Total Assets	11,544	10,027	7,857	7,736	7,619	7,322	NA	NA	NA	NA
Curr. Liab.	2,478	1,248	1,081	967	947	1,025	NA	NA	NA	NA
LT Debt	4,493	4,523	3,285	3,271	3,268	3,361	NA	NA	NA	NA
Common Equity	1,881	1,824	1,601	1,646	1,563	-238	NA	NA	NA	NA
Total Cap.	8,191	7,960	6,226	6,295	6,287	4,325	NA	NA	NA	NA
Cap. Exp.	644	623	593	515	560	507	NA	NA	NA	NA
Cash Flow	990	879	819	664	623	326	NA	NA	NA	NA
Curr. Ratio	1.2	1.4	1.4	1.6	1.6	1.3	NA	NA	NA	NA
% LT Debt of Cap.	54.9	56.8	52.8	52.0	51.9	77.7	NA	NA	NA	NA
% Net Inc.of Revs.	4.1	4.6	3.6	2.9	1.6	NM	NA	NA	NA	NA
% Ret. on Assets	3.9	4.8	3.9	3.0	1.6	NM	NA	NA	NA	NA
% Ret. on Equity	22.8	25.0	18.8	14.3	17.8	NM	NA	NA	NA	NA

Data as orig reptd.; bef. results of disc opers/spec. items. Per share data adj. for stk. divs.; EPS diluted. E-Estimated. NA-Not Available. NM-Not Meaningful. NR-Not Ranked. UR-Under Review.

Office: One Pepsi Way, Somers, NY 10589-2204.
Telephone: 914-767-6000.
Email: shareholder.relations@pepsi.com
Website: http://www.pbg.com
Chrmn & CEO: J.T. Cahill.

SVP & CFO: A.H. Drewes.
SVP, Secy & General Counsel: P.C. McGuire.
Investor Contact: M.W. Settino 914-767-7216.
Dirs: L. G. Alvarado, B. H. Beracha, J. T. Cahill, I. D. Hall, T. E. Kean, S. Kronick, B. J. McGarvie, M. D. Moore, C. G. Small, C. E. Weatherup.

Founded: in 1999.
Domicile: Delaware.
Employees: 66,000.
S&P Analyst: Richard Joy/MF/BK

PerkinElmer, Inc.

Recommendation: **HOLD** ★★★☆☆
SELL | SELL | HOLD | BUY | BUY

12-Month Target Price: $20.00
(as of September 10, 2004)

PKI has an approximate 0.03% weighting in the **S&P 500**

Sector: Health Care
Sub-Industry: Health Care Equipment
Peer Group: Life Science Research Products

Summary: This diversified technology company (formerly EG&G Inc.) provides advanced scientific and technical products and services worldwide.

Quantitative Evaluations

S&P Earnings & Dividend Rank: B

D | C | B- | **B** | B+ | A- | A | A+

S&P Fair Value Rank: 4-

1 | 2 | 3 | **4** | 5
Lowest | | | | Highest

Fair Value Calc.: $21.40 (Slightly Overvalued)

S&P Investability Quotient Percentile

59%

PKI scored higher than 59% of all companies for which an S&P Report is available.

Volatility: Average

Low | **Average** | High

Technical Evaluation: Bullish
Since 10/04, the technical indicators for PKI have been Bullish.

Relative Strength Rank: Strong

90
1 Lowest | Highest 99

Price as of 11/12/04: $22.14 | **2004E S&P Core EPS:** $0.68

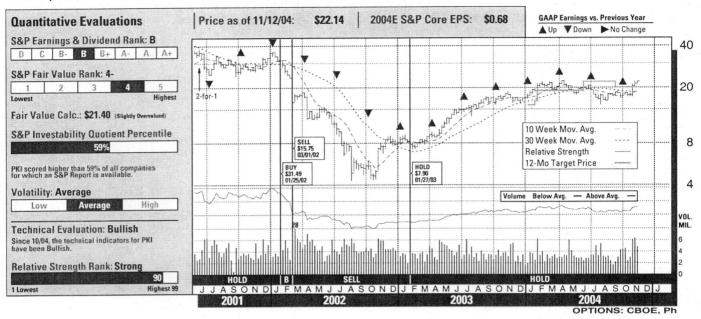

GAAP Earnings vs. Previous Year
▲ Up ▼ Down ► No Change

10 Week Mov. Avg.
30 Week Mov. Avg.
Relative Strength
12-Mo Target Price

Volume Below Avg. — Above Avg. —

OPTIONS: CBOE, Ph

Analyst commentary prepared by Bryon J. Korutz/CB/GG

Highlights September 10, 2004

- We expect 2004 revenues to increase 5.0%, followed by an anticipated gain of 6.0% in 2005. We expect new products to aid the company's prospects, and see the potential for significant growth in Asia, especially in China, over the longer term, although we see the possibility of a near-term slowdown in China. We expect demand to firm in the bio-pharmaceutical area, and also expect continued volume growth in biomedical imaging. We believe aerospace markets have bottomed, but remain cautious regarding the pace of the recovery.

- We see wider EBITDA margins, on lower SG&A expenses, due to staff cuts and plant closings, as PKI integrates its life sciences and analytical units. We project annualized cost savings totaling $45 million by the end of 2004, due to the Life and Analytical Sciences unit consolidation in 2002. We think a new financing arrangement should ease some liquidity concerns, as the company focuses on improving productivity, cash flow and working capital.

- We see 2004 Standard & Poor's Core Earnings of $0.68 a share, reflecting $0.14 of projected stock option expense and $0.01 of pension costs.

Investment Rationale/Risk September 10, 2004

- We expect the shares to be average performers over the next 12 months. We would not add to existing positions, due to our concerns about the company's exposure to China, even though this is currently small.

- Risks to our recommendation and target price include slower than anticipated recovery in the aerospace market, and a possible greater than expected slowing of the Chinese economy.

- Our first valuation metric, which applies a forward peer P/E multiple of 20X to our 2005 EPS estimate of $1.05, indicates that the stock is worth $21 a share. Our discounted cash flow model, which values PKI by adding the sum of future free cash flows growing at estimated initial average annual rates of 7% to 14% over a 10-year forecast period and at 3.5% thereafter, and uses a WACC of 8.8%, indicates an intrinsic value of $18. Our 12-month target price of $20 is based on a weighted average of these valuation metrics.

Key Stock Statistics

S&P Core EPS 2005E	0.90	52-week Range	$22.59-15.05
S&P Oper. EPS 2004E	0.88	12 Month P/E	33.5
P/E on S&P Oper. EPS 2004E	25.2	Beta	1.99
S&P Oper. EPS 2005E	1.05	Shareholders	8,568
Yield (%)	1.3%	Market Cap (B)	$ 2.8
Dividend Rate/Share	0.28	Shares Outstanding (M)	128.1

Value of $10,000 invested five years ago: **$ 11,864**

Dividend Data Dividends have been paid since 1965

Amount ($)	Date Decl.	Ex-Div. Date	Stock of Record	Payment Date
0.070	Jan. 29	Apr. 21	Apr. 23	May. 14 '04
0.070	Jun. 02	Jul. 21	Jul. 23	Aug. 13 '04
0.070	Aug. 04	Oct. 20	Oct. 22	Nov. 12 '04
0.070	Nov. 03	Jan. 19	Jan. 21	Feb. 11 '05

Revenues/Earnings Data Fiscal year ending December 31

Revenues (Million $)

	2004	2003	2002	2001	2000	1999
1Q	393.4	358.4	346.3	334.9	243.0	357.5
2Q	412.6	377.1	383.1	331.8	398.7	304.3
3Q	403.4	367.1	366.0	302.1	431.9	388.4
4Q	—	432.6	409.6	361.2	462.4	427.2
Yr.	—	1,535	1,505	1,330	1,695	1,363

Earnings Per Share ($)

	2004	2003	2002	2001	2000	1999
1Q	0.10	0.03	-0.23	0.13	0.09	0.15
2Q	0.16	0.08	0.03	0.30	0.30	-0.03
3Q	0.19	0.11	0.08	0.21	0.02	-0.07
4Q	E0.31	0.21	0.01	-0.49	0.41	0.30
Yr.	E0.88	0.43	-0.03	-0.01	1.32	0.30

Next earnings report expected: late-January Source: S&P, Company Reports
EPS Estimates based on S&P Operating Earnings; historical GAAP earnings are as reported.

PerkinElmer, Inc.

Recommendation: **HOLD** ★ ★ ★ ☆ ☆   12-Month Target Price: **$20.00** (as of September 10, 2004)

Business Summary September 10, 2004

PerkinElmer is a global technology company with operations in more than 125 countries. It provides products and systems to telecom, medical, pharmaceutical, chemical, semiconductor, aerospace and photographic markets. PKI projected that it would achieve 2004 pretax cost savings of $5 million to $20 million, related to the October 2002 combination of its Life Sciences and Analytical Instruments businesses, forming the Life and Analytical Sciences unit. The company's other operating segments are Optoelectronics and Fluid Sciences. International sales accounted for 53% of the 2003 total.

The Life and Analytical Sciences business unit accounted for 65% of total sales in 2003, and $94.7 million of operating profit. Life and Analytical Sciences provides drug discovery, genetic screening and environmental and chemical analysis tools, including instruments, reagents, consumables and services. Its instruments are used for scientific research and clinical applications. For drug discovery, PKI offers a wide range of instrumentation, software and consumables, including reagents, based on its core expertise in fluorescent, chemiluminescent and radioactive labeling, and the detection of nucleic acids and proteins. For genetic screening laboratories, it provides software, reagents and analysis tools to test for various inherited disorders. For chemical analysis, the company offers analytical tools employing technologies such as molecular and atomic spectroscopy, high-pressure liquid chromatography, gas chromatography and thermal analysis.

The Optoelectronics unit (23%; $42.2 million) makes products that include digital imaging, sensor and specialty lighting components to customers in biomedical, consumer products and other specialty end markets. PKI supplies amorphous silicon digital X-ray detectors, a technology for medical imaging and radiation therapy. The company's specialty lighting technologies include xenon flashtubes, ceramic xenon light sources, and laser pump sources.

The Fluid Sciences unit (12%; $17.9 million) makes fluid control and containments systems for turbine engines and semiconductor fabrication facilities. In the aerospace market, PKI provides sealing and pneumatic systems for large commercial transport aircraft, military, business and regional jets. In the semiconductor equipment market, the company provides components, sub-assembly integration and processing services to many of the world's leading semiconductor equipment manufacturers.

In 2003, PKI incurred a $2.0 million restructuring charge in the Life and Analytical Sciences business, and a $0.3 million restructuring charge in the Optoelectronics business; mainly for headcount reductions. The charges were related to efforts to improve performance and take advantage of synergies created through the integration of the Life Sciences and Analytical Instruments businesses.

Company Financials Fiscal Year ending December 31

Per Share Data ($)

(Year Ended December 31)	2003	2002	2001	2000	1999	1998	1997	1996	1995	1994
Tangible Bk. Val.	NM	NM	NM	NM	NM	0.92	2.75	2.75	2.56	2.89
Cash Flow	1.06	0.58	0.77	1.62	1.01	1.66	0.82	1.01	0.91	0.04
Earnings	0.43	-0.03	-0.01	1.32	0.30	1.11	0.34	0.58	0.53	-0.29
S&P Core Earnings	0.25	-0.34	-0.68	NA	NA	NA	NA	NA	NA	NA
Dividends	0.28	0.28	0.28	0.28	0.28	0.28	0.28	0.28	0.28	0.28
Payout Ratio	65%	NM	NM	21%	92%	25%	84%	49%	53%	NM
Prices - High	18.71	36.30	52.31	60.50	22.50	16.87	12.31	12.56	12.25	9.50
- Low	7.22	4.28	21.27	19.00	12.75	9.43	9.00	8.12	6.50	6.87
P/E Ratio - High	44	NM	NM	46	74	15	37	22	23	NM
- Low	17	NM	NM	14	42	9	27	14	12	NM

Income Statement Analysis (Million $)

	2003	2002	2001	2000	1999	1998	1997	1996	1995	1994
Revs.	1,535	1,505	1,330	1,695	1,363	1,408	1,461	1,427	1,420	1,333
Oper. Inc.	211	131	196	263	177	144	132	129	122	97.0
Depr.	80.2	76.6	80.5	79.1	66.1	50.4	44.6	40.9	39.4	36.8
Int. Exp.	Nil	Nil	Nil	Nil	28.3	11.4	12.5	13.4	8.50	5.40
Pretax Inc.	80.9	-8.55	34.2	144	44.9	156	54.0	80.4	86.1	-17.0
Eff. Tax Rate	32.0%	NM	NM	40.4%	36.8%	34.6%	43.3%	32.2%	36.9%	NM
Net Inc.	55.0	-4.13	-0.62	86.1	28.4	102	30.6	54.5	54.3	-32.1
S&P Core Earnings	31.2	-43.1	-71.3	NA	NA	NA	NA	NA	NA	NA

Balance Sheet & Other Fin. Data (Million $)

	2003	2002	2001	2000	1999	1998	1997	1996	1995	1994
Cash	202	317	138	126	127	95.6	57.9	47.8	76.0	75.7
Curr. Assets	766	991	997	893	815	565	488	455	469	481
Total Assets	2,608	2,836	2,919	2,260	1,715	1,185	832	823	804	793
Curr. Liab.	452	698	708	718	852	524	286	260	250	282
LT Debt	544	614	598	583	115	130	114	115	115	0.80
Common Equity	1,349	1,252	1,364	728	551	400	328	365	367	445
Total Cap.	1,893	1,866	1,962	1,312	666	530	443	480	482	446
Cap. Exp.	16.6	37.8	88.7	70.6	41.1	NA	48.7	80.5	61.8	37.3
Cash Flow	135	72.4	79.9	165	94.5	152	75.3	95.4	93.7	5.00
Curr. Ratio	1.7	1.4	1.4	1.2	1.0	1.1	1.7	1.8	1.9	1.7
% LT Debt of Cap.	28.7	32.9	30.5	44.5	17.3	24.5	25.9	24.0	23.9	0.2
% Net Inc.of Revs.	3.6	NM	NM	5.1	2.1	7.2	2.1	3.8	3.8	NM
% Ret. on Assets	2.0	NM	NM	4.3	2.0	10.1	3.7	6.7	6.8	NM
% Ret. on Equity	4.2	NM	NM	13.5	6.0	28.0	8.8	14.9	13.4	NM

Data as orig reptd.; bef. results of disc opers/spec. items. Per share data adj. for stk. divs.; EPS diluted. E-Estimated. NA-Not Available. NM-Not Meaningful. NR-Not Ranked. UR-Under Review.

Office: 45 William Street, Wellesley, MA 02481-4008.
Telephone: 781-237-5100.
Website: http://www.perkinelmer.com
Chrmn, Pres & CEO: G.L. Summe.
SVP & CFO: R.F. Friel.

SVP, Clerk & General Counsel: T.L. Carlson.
VP, Chief Acctg Officer & Treas: J.D. Capello.
Investor Contact: D. Sutherby 781-431-4306.
Dirs: T. J. Erickson, N. A. Lopardo, A. P. Michas, J. C. Mullen, V. L. Sato, G. Schmergel, K. J. Sicchitano, G. L. Summe, G. R. Tod.

Founded: in 1947.
Domicile: Massachusetts.
Employees: 10,000.
S&P Analyst: Bryon J. Korutz/CB/GG

Pfizer Inc.

Recommendation: **HOLD** ★ ★ ★ ☆ ☆
SELL · SELL · HOLD · BUY · BUY

12-Month Target Price: **$32.00**
(as of October 20, 2004)

PFE has an approximate 1.88% weighting in the **S&P 500**

Sector: Health Care
Sub-Industry: Pharmaceuticals
Peer Group: Ethical Pharmaceuticals - Major

Summary: PFE, the world's largest drug company, with about 11% of the global market, acquired Pharmacia in April 2003, in exchange for 1.8 billion PFE shares.

Quantitative Evaluations

S&P Earnings & Dividend Rank: A

| D | C | B- | B | B+ | A- | **A** | A+ |

S&P Fair Value Rank: 5+

| 1 | 2 | 3 | 4 | **5** |
| Lowest | | | | Highest |

Fair Value Calc.: $45.10 (Undervalued)

S&P Investability Quotient Percentile
100%

PFE scored higher than 100% of all companies for which an S&P Report is available.

Volatility: Low

| **Low** | Average | High |

Technical Evaluation: Bearish
Since 9/04, the technical indicators for PFE have been Bearish.

Relative Strength Rank: Weak

| **11** |
| 1 Lowest | Highest 99 |

Price as of 11/12/04: **$27.45**   **2004E S&P Core EPS:** **$2.03**

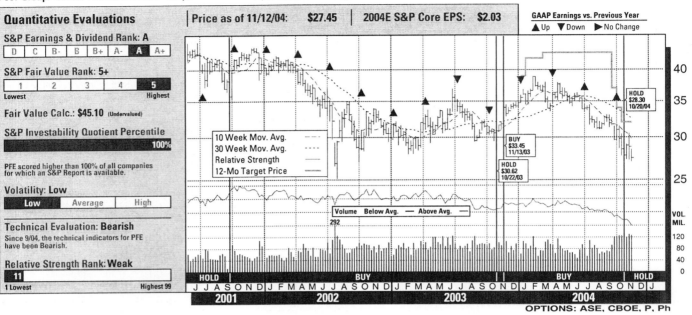

GAAP Earnings vs. Previous Year
▲ Up ▼ Down ► No Change

- 10 Week Mov. Avg. ---
- 30 Week Mov. Avg. ····
- Relative Strength
- 12-Mo Target Price

HOLD $28.30 10/20/04
BUY $33.45 11/13/03
HOLD $30.62 10/22/03

Volume Below Avg. — Above Avg.
292

VOL. MIL.

HOLD | BUY | BUY | HOLD
J J A S O N D J F M A M J J A S O N D J F M A M J J A S O N D J F M A M J J A S O N D J
2001   2002   2003   2004

OPTIONS: ASE, CBOE, P, Ph

Analyst commentary prepared by H. B. Saftlas/CB/GG

Highlights October 22, 2004

- We expect total revenues to grow about 5%-6% in 2005, to over $55 billion. Key growth drivers should be Lipitor, the dominant product in the expanding cholesterol reduction market; Celebrex and Bextra, COX-2 inhibitor treatments for arthritis and pain; and Norvasc, a leading drug for hypertension and congestive heart failure. Sales of Celebrex and Bextra will probably benefit from the recent removal of Merck's (MRK: avoid, $31) Vioxx COX-2 from the market because of elevated risks of heart attack and stroke (Celebrex has not been associated with those risks). New products such as Lyrica anti-convulsant and Caduet heart drug should also bolster volume. However, we project lower sales for Viagra, Accupril, Diflucan, Neurontin and Zithromax, with declines in the last four products stemming from generic competition.

- Gross margins should hold steady at about 86%, in our opinion. As a percentage of total sales, both SG&A costs and R&D expenses should be lower than in 2004, helped by merger-related cost savings and synergies estimated at $4.0 billion in 2005, up from an indicated $3.5 billion in 2004.

- We project 2005 operating EPS of $2.36, up from an indicated $2.13 in 2004. After projected stock option expense and pension adjustments, we estimate Standard & Poor's Core EPS of $2.26 for 2005, and $2.03 for 2004.

Key Stock Statistics

S&P Core EPS 2005E	2.26	52-week Range	$38.89-27.02
S&P Oper. EPS 2004E	2.13	12 Month P/E	22.9
P/E on S&P Oper. EPS 2004E	12.9	Beta	0.41
S&P Oper. EPS 2005E	2.36	Shareholders	288,819
Yield (%)	2.5%	Market Cap (B)	$206.7
Dividend Rate/Share	0.68	Shares Outstanding (M)	7531.0

Value of $10,000 invested five years ago: **$ 8,878**

Dividend Data Dividends have been paid since 1901

Amount ($)	Date Decl.	Ex-Div. Date	Stock of Record	Payment Date
0.170	Dec. 15	Feb. 11	Feb. 13	Mar. 05 '04
0.170	Apr. 22	May. 12	May. 14	Jun. 04 '04
0.170	Jun. 24	Aug. 11	Aug. 13	Sep. 03 '04
0.170	Oct. 28	Nov. 09	Nov. 12	Dec. 03 '04

Investment Rationale/Risk October 22, 2004

- We recently downgraded our opinion on the shares to hold from accumulate, reflecting our belief that forward valuation expansion could be more restrained amid the protracted slide in pharmaceutical sector valuations and slowing trends in Pfizer's top-line growth. Pfizer recently cautioned investors that it expects a substantial impact from the loss of patent exclusivity of several key products such as Diflucan, Neurontin, Accupril and Zithromax in 2005. While ongoing merger synergies should buoy earnings, we believe sales growth over the next few years may be challenged by patent expirations, new competition in the cholesterol market, and uncertainties in the R&D pipeline. Recently priced at less than 12X our 2005 EPS estimate, the shares are valued sharply below the S&P 500.

- Risks to our recommendation and target price include failure to successfully develop pipeline drugs, possible passage by Congress of a drug reimportation program, and adverse patent litigation outcomes.

- Our 12-month target price of $32 is derived by applying a P/E of 13.5X to our $2.36 EPS estimate for 2005. At that level, the stock would have a 2005 P/E-to-growth ratio of 1.3X, in line with peer pharmaceutical companies. Our target price is also close to our calculation of intrinsic value, derived from our DCF model, which assumes decelerating cash flow growth over 10 years and a weighted average cost of capital of 8.0%.

Revenues/Earnings Data Fiscal year ending December 31

Revenues (Million $)

	2004	2003	2002	2001	2000	1999
1Q	12,487	8,525	7,747	7,645	4,315	3,927
2Q	12,274	9,993	7,296	7,686	7,041	3,779
3Q	12,831	12,504	7,996	7,898	7,205	3,992
4Q	—	14,167	9,333	9,030	8,105	4,506
Yr.	—	45,188	32,373	32,259	29,574	16,204

Earnings Per Share ($)

	2004	2003	2002	2001	2000	1999
1Q	0.30	0.40	0.37	0.30	0.31	0.21
2Q	0.38	-0.49	0.30	0.29	0.18	0.18
3Q	0.43	0.29	0.37	0.33	0.22	0.18
4Q	E0.61	0.08	0.43	0.30	0.23	0.25
Yr.	E2.13	0.22	1.47	1.22	0.59	0.82

Next earnings report expected: late-January Source: S&P, Company Reports
EPS Estimates based on S&P Operating Earnings; historical GAAP earnings are as reported.

The **McGraw·Hill** Companies

Pfizer Inc.

Recommendation: **HOLD** ★ ★ ★ ☆ ☆   12-Month Target Price: **$32.00** (as of October 20, 2004)

Business Summary October 25, 2004

Pfizer traces its roots back to 1849, when it was founded by Charles Pfizer and Charles Erhart as a chemical products company. Following its acquisitions of Warner-Lambert Co. in June 2000 and Pharmacia Corp. in April 2003, PFE now ranks as the world's largest prescription pharmaceuticals company, accounting for about 11% of the global market. In March 2003, the company sold its confectionery and shaving products businesses, for $5.1 billion.

The company's drug portfolio is unmatched in terms of breadth and depth throughout the global pharmaceutical market. The diverse line spans medicines to treat major conditions such as cancer, epilepsy, depression and high blood pressure. About 14 PFE drugs are the leaders in their respective therapeutic markets, eight are among the world's top selling products, and 10 generate sales exceeding $1 billion a year. The company's broad range of drugs reduces its dependence on any single product. Foreign sales accounted for 41% of total revenues in 2003.

Principal cardiovasculars include Lipitor, the world's largest selling cholesterol-lowering agent, as well as the biggest drug in any therapeutic category in 2003 (sales of $9.2 billion in 2003), and antihypertensives such as Norvasc ($4.3 billion), Accupril ($706 million) and Cardura ($594 million). Infectious disease drugs consist of Zithromax broad-spectrum antibiotic ($2.0 billion) and Diflucan antifungal agent ($1.2 billion); key central nervous system medicines are Zoloft antidepressant ($3.1 billion) and Neurontin anti-convulsant ($2.7 billion).

Other drugs sold include Celebrex and Bextra COX-2 inhibitors for arthritis and pain (combined sales of $2.6 billion), Viagra for male erectile dysfunction ($1.9 billion), Zyrtec antihistamine ($1.3 billion), Xalatan for glaucoma ($623 million), Detrol and LA/Detrol treatments for incontinence ($544 million), anticancer agents ($713 million), and Genotropin growth hormone ($481 million).

The animal health division ($1.6 billion in sales) offers one of the largest selling and broadest product lines in its field. Principal products include feed additives, vaccines, antibiotics, antihelmintics, and other veterinary products. Consumer products ($3 billion in sales) include a broad line of OTC products, including well known brands such as Ben-Gay and Desitin ointments; Sudafed and Benadryl cough and cold medications; Motrin pain reliever; Nicorette nicotine chewing gum and transdermal patch; and Listerine mouthwash.

R&D spending totaled $7.1 billion in 2003, equal to 15.8% of total revenues. The R&D pipeline includes more than 130 new molecular entities, as well as another 95 projects representing new uses for existing medicines. Compounds under development include new treatments for atherosclerosis, diabetes, osteoporosis, breast cancer, neuropathic pain, epilepsy, anxiety disorders, Parkinson's disease, and many other conditions. PFE believes it is seen as a partner of choice for potentially lucrative product licensing deals with other pharmaceutical companies and smaller biotechnology concerns.

Company Financials Fiscal Year ending December 31

Per Share Data ($)

(Year Ended December 31)	2003	2002	2001	2000	1999	1998	1997	1996	1995	1994
Tangible Bk. Val.	0.85	3.04	2.64	2.26	2.11	2.06	2.03	1.43	1.11	1.15
Cash Flow	0.78	1.64	1.39	0.74	0.96	0.63	0.69	0.61	0.51	0.43
Earnings	0.22	1.47	1.22	0.59	0.82	0.49	0.57	0.50	0.41	0.35
S&P Core Earnings	0.29	1.35	1.09	NA	NA	NA	NA	NA	NA	NA
Dividends	0.60	0.52	0.44	0.36	0.31	0.25	0.23	0.20	0.17	0.16
Payout Ratio	273%	35%	36%	61%	37%	51%	40%	40%	42%	45%
Prices - High	36.92	42.46	46.75	49.25	50.04	42.97	26.66	15.20	11.14	6.61
- Low	27.90	25.13	34.00	30.00	31.54	23.68	13.43	10.04	6.20	4.42
P/E Ratio - High	NM	29	38	83	61	87	47	31	27	19
- Low	NM	17	28	51	38	48	24	20	15	13

Income Statement Analysis (Million $)

	2003	2002	2001	2000	1999	1998	1997	1996	1995	1994
Revs.	45,188	32,373	32,259	29,574	16,204	13,544	12,504	11,306	10,021	8,281
Oper. Inc.	17,061	13,436	12,147	9,758	5,091	4,092	3,780	3,444	2,527	2,248
Depr.	4,078	1,036	1,068	968	542	534	502	430	374	289
Int. Exp.	270	251	49.0	386	223	136	147	170	205	142
Pretax Inc.	3,263	11,796	10,329	5,781	4,448	2,594	3,088	2,804	2,299	1,862
Eff. Tax Rate	49.7%	22.1%	24.8%	35.4%	28.0%	24.7%	28.0%	31.0%	32.1%	30.0%
Net Inc.	1,639	9,181	7,752	3,718	3,199	1,950	2,213	1,929	1,554	1,298
S&P Core Earnings	2,147	8,441	6,862	NA	NA	NA	NA	NA	NA	NA

Balance Sheet & Other Fin. Data (Million $)

	2003	2002	2001	2000	1999	1998	1997	1996	1995	1994
Cash	1,520	1,878	1,036	1,099	739	1,552	877	1,637	1,512	2,019
Curr. Assets	29,741	24,781	18,450	17,187	11,191	9,931	6,820	6,468	6,152	5,788
Total Assets	116,775	46,356	39,153	33,510	20,574	18,302	15,336	14,667	12,729	11,099
Curr. Liab.	23,657	18,555	13,640	11,981	9,185	7,192	5,305	5,640	5,187	4,826
LT Debt	5,755	3,140	2,609	1,123	525	527	729	687	833	604
Common Equity	65,158	19,950	18,293	16,076	8,887	8,810	7,933	6,954	5,507	4,324
Total Cap.	84,370	23,454	21,354	17,579	9,713	9,534	8,818	7,944	6,553	5,179
Cap. Exp.	2,641	1,758	2,203	2,191	1,561	1,198	943	774	696	672
Cash Flow	5,717	10,217	8,820	4,686	3,741	2,484	2,715	2,359	1,928	1,588
Curr. Ratio	1.3	1.3	1.4	1.4	1.2	1.4	1.3	1.1	1.2	1.2
% LT Debt of Cap.	6.8	13.4	12.2	6.4	5.4	5.5	8.3	8.6	12.7	11.7
% Net Inc.of Revs.	3.6	28.4	24.0	12.6	19.7	14.4	17.7	17.1	15.5	15.7
% Ret. on Assets	2.0	21.5	21.3	11.5	16.5	11.6	14.8	14.1	13.0	12.8
% Ret. on Equity	3.9	48.0	45.1	24.8	36.2	23.3	29.7	31.0	31.6	32.0

Data as orig reptd.; bef. results of disc opers/spec. items. Per share data adj. for stk. divs.; EPS diluted. E-Estimated. NA-Not Available. NM-Not Meaningful. NR-Not Ranked. UR-Under Review.

Office: 235 East 42nd Street, New York, NY 10017-5755.
Telephone: 212-573-2323.
Website: http://www.pfizer.com
Chrmn & CEO: H.A. McKinnell.
EVP & CFO: D.L. Shedlarz.
SVP & General Counsel: J.B. Kindler.

VP & Secy: M.M. Foran.
Investor Contact: J.R. Gardner .
Dirs: M. S. Brown, M. A. Burns, R. N. Burt, W. D. Cornwell, W. H. Gray III, C. J. Horner, W. R. Howell, S. O. Ikenberry, G. A. Lorch, H. A. McKinnell, D. G. Mead, F. D. Raines, R. J. Simmons, W. C. Steere, Jr., J. Valles.

Founded: in 1849.
Domicile: Delaware.
Employees: 122,000.
S&P Analyst: H. B. Saftlas/CB/GG

Recommendation: **SELL** ★★☆☆☆
SELL | SELL | HOLD | BUY | BUY

12-Month Target Price: **$30.00**
(as of October 29, 2004)

PCG has an approximate 0.12% weighting in the **S&P 500**

Sector: Utilities
Sub-Industry: Electric Utilities
Peer Group: Electric & Gas- Larger

Summary: This energy holding company is the parent of Pacific Gas and Electric Co., which recently emerged from bankruptcy reorganization.

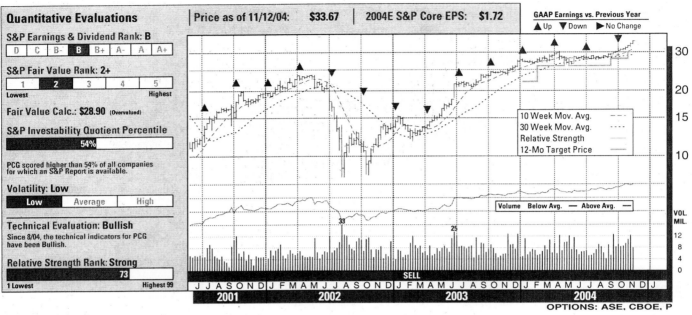

Quantitative Evaluations

S&P Earnings & Dividend Rank: B

D | C | B- | **B** | B+ | A- | A | A+

S&P Fair Value Rank: 2+

1 | **2** | 3 | 4 | 5
Lowest | | | | Highest

Fair Value Calc.: $28.90 (Overvalued)

S&P Investability Quotient Percentile

54%

PCG scored higher than 54% of all companies for which an S&P Report is available.

Volatility: Low

Low | Average | High

Technical Evaluation: Bullish
Since 8/04, the technical indicators for PCG have been Bullish.

Relative Strength Rank: Strong

73

1 Lowest | Highest 99

Price as of 11/12/04: **$33.67**

2004E S&P Core EPS: **$1.72**

GAAP Earnings vs. Previous Year
▲ Up ▼ Down ▶ No Change

10 Week Mov. Avg.
30 Week Mov. Avg.
Relative Strength
12-Mo Target Price

Volume Below Avg. — Above Avg.

VOL. MIL.

SELL

J J A S O N D | J F M A M J J A S O N D | J F M A M J J A S O N D | J F M A M J J A S O N D | J
2001 | 2002 | 2003 | 2004

OPTIONS: ASE, CBOE, P

Analyst commentary prepared by Justin McCann/PMW/JWP

Highlights September 15, 2004

- After an anticipated 9% advance in 2004 from 2003 operating EPS of $1.93 (which included $0.45 that had been reported as a non-operating recovery of previously written-off power costs), we expect a 4% to 5% increase in 2005. With the bankruptcy court having approved (on May 3, 2004) the reorganization plan of National Energy & Gas Transmission (formerly PG&E National Energy Group), PCG's equity interest in its former subsidiary was eliminated.

- With its April 2004 emergence from bankruptcy, Pacific Gas and Electric regained its investment grade credit rating, paid $8.4 billion in allowed creditor claims, and deposited $1.8 billion in escrow for disputed claims. The payments were made using proceeds from a $6.7 billion bond offering, $2.4 billion in cash, $800 million from term loans, and $300 million from a credit facility.

- On May 27, 2004, the California Public Utilities Commission (CPUC) adopted the proposals of the December 2003 settlement agreement, and approved rate revenue increases of $236 million for electric distribution, $52 million for gas distribution, and $38 million for electric generation.

Key Stock Statistics

S&P Core EPS 2005E	1.93	52-week Range	$33.82-23.43
S&P Oper. EPS 2004E	2.10	12 Month P/E	3.9
P/E on S&P Oper. EPS 2004E	16.0	Beta	0.37
S&P Oper. EPS 2005E	2.20	Shareholders	110,740
Yield (%)	Nil	Market Cap (B)	$ 13.6
Dividend Rate/Share	Nil	Shares Outstanding (M)	403.1

Value of $10,000 invested five years ago: **$ 14,562**

Dividend Data

No cash dividends have been paid since January 2001.

Investment Rationale/Risk September 15, 2004

- We think that the emergence of Pacific Gas and Electric from bankruptcy, the restoration of its investment grade credit rating, and the elimination of PCG's equity interest in its former National Energy Group subsidiary have restored greatly needed stability to both the utility and the holding company, but we would still avoid the shares. In the absence of a dividend, we believe the stock is overvalued at an approximate peer P/E multiple of 13.5X our 2004 EPS estimate.

- Risks to our opinion and target price include significantly better than expected earnings performance, and a major increase in the average P/E multiple of the group as a whole.

- With the dividend not expected to be restored before the second half of 2005, and based on our expectations of gradually rising interest rates and a modest contraction in the peer P/E multiple, we believe the shares should trade at about a 5% discount to the approximate peer P/E multiple of 13.4X based on our 2005 EPS estimates. Our 12-month target price of $28 is equal to a P/E multiple of 12.7X applied to our 2005 EPS estimate of $2.20.

Revenues/Earnings Data Fiscal year ending December 31

Revenues (Million $)

	2004	2003	2002	2001	2000	1999
1Q	2,722	2,065	2,935	6,675	5,008	5,257
2Q	2,749	2,729	2,938	5,013	5,638	4,820
3Q	2,623	3,103	3,654	6,301	7,504	6,380
4Q	—	2,538	2,968	4,978	8,082	4,795
Yr.	—	10,435	12,495	22,959	26,232	20,820

Earnings Per Share ($)

	2004	2003	2002	2001	2000	1999
1Q	7.21	-0.21	1.71	-2.62	0.77	0.37
2Q	0.88	0.81	0.75	2.07	0.68	0.46
3Q	0.53	1.24	1.17	2.12	0.67	0.50
4Q	E0.46	0.09	-3.72	1.42	-11.28	-1.49
Yr.	E2.10	1.96	-0.15	2.99	-9.18	0.04

Next earnings report expected: NA Source: S&P, Company Reports
EPS Estimates based on S&P Operating Earnings; historical GAAP earnings are as reported.

PG&E Corporation

Recommendation: **SELL** ★ ★ ☆ ☆ ☆   12-Month Target Price: **$30.00** (as of October 29, 2004)

Business Summary September 15, 2004

PG&E Corp. was formed as the holding company for Pacific Gas and Electric Co. (PG&E) and its operating subsidiaries on January 1, 1997.

On April 12, 2004, PG&E, one of the largest investor-owned U.S. gas and electric utilities, emerged from Chapter 11 bankruptcy protection under the terms of a December 2003 settlement agreement with the California Public Utility Commission (CPUC). The utility had filed for bankruptcy protection in April 2001, as it was unable to recover about $9 billion of debt it had incurred due to a rate freeze that prevented it from passing through the surging costs of its wholesale power purchases. Although PG&E would no longer be subject to the oversight of the bankruptcy court, the court would retain jurisdiction to hear and determine disputes related to the settlement agreement with the CPUC and the reorganization plan.

In September 2001, PG&E had filed a plan of reorganization that proposed splitting the parent company and its utility into stand-alone companies, with the power generation operations and the electric and natural gas transmission businesses being transferred to newly created units of the parent company. However, in June 2003, the company announced a proposed settlement agreement with the staff of the CPUC. Under the proposed settlement, PG&E would remain an integrated utility subject to the CPUC, and could establish a $2.2 billion after-tax regulatory asset that would be recovered in rates over nine years, beginning January 1, 2004. The CPUC and bankruptcy court approved the settlement in December 2003.

In 2003, PG&E provided electricity (72.7% of revenues) to about 4.9 million customers, and gas (27.3%) to about 3.9 million customers, in northern and central California.

As of December 31, 2003, PG&E owned and operated 118 generating facilities with a net operating capacity of 6,420 MW. The utility's Diablo Canyon nuclear facility consists of two units, each capable of generating 1,087 MW of power per day. The hydroelectric system consists of 110 generating units at 68 powerhouses, including a pumped storage facility, with a total generating capacity of 3,896 MW. The utility also owns six fossil fuel-fired power plants with a collective generating capacity of 350 MW.

PCG formed the PG&E National Energy Group (NEG) in 1999 to integrate the power generation, gas transmission and energy trading and services businesses. In November 2002, NEG defaulted on the repayment of $431 million of a credit facility. NEG ceased payments on its obligations, and entered into discussions with lenders regarding a restructuring of its commitments. In July 2003, NEG filed for Chapter 11 bankruptcy protection. In October 2003, the unit was renamed National Energy Gas & Transmission, Inc. (NEGT). On May 3, 2004, the bankruptcy court approved NEGT's plan of reorganization, which eliminated PCG's equity interest.

In 1996, California passed legislation that restructured the state's power market. The bill included a non-bypassable competitive transition charge for recovery of stranded costs, and a 10% rate reduction (implemented in January 1998) for residential and small commercial customers.

Company Financials Fiscal Year ending December 31

Per Share Data ($)

(Year Ended December 31)	2003	2002	2001	2000	1999	1998	1997	1996	1995	1994
Tangible Bk. Val.	10.11	8.92	11.87	8.74	19.13	21.06	21.28	20.60	19.68	20.06
Earnings	1.96	-0.15	2.99	-9.18	0.04	1.88	1.75	1.75	2.99	2.21
S&P Core Earnings	2.05	-1.08	1.59	NA	NA	NA	NA	NA	NA	NA
Dividends	Nil	Nil	Nil	1.20	1.20	1.20	1.20	1.77	1.96	1.96
Payout Ratio	Nil	Nil	Nil	NM	NM	64%	69%	101%	66%	89%
Prices - High	27.98	23.75	20.93	31.81	34.00	35.06	30.93	28.37	30.62	35.00
- Low	11.69	8.00	6.50	17.00	20.25	29.06	20.87	19.50	24.25	21.37
P/E Ratio - High	14	NM	7	NM	NM	19	18	16	10	16
- Low	6	NM	2	NM	NM	15	12	11	8	10

Income Statement Analysis (Million $)

	2003	2002	2001	2000	1999	1998	1997	1996	1995	1994
Revs.	10,435	12,495	22,959	26,232	20,820	19,942	15,400	9,610	9,622	10,447
Depr.	1,222	1,309	1,068	3,659	1,780	1,609	1,889	1,222	1,360	1,397
Maint.	NA	NA	NA	NA	NA	NA	NA	NA	477	457
Fxd. Chgs. Cov.	2.23	2.94	2.48	3.01	2.99	2.65	2.90	2.90	3.80	3.15
Constr. Credits	NA	NA	NA	NA	Nil	Nil	Nil	Nil	31.0	32.0
Eff. Tax Rate	36.7%	NM	35.8%	NM	95.0%	44.2%	43.4%	42.4%	40.1%	45.4%
Net Inc.	791	-57.0	1,090	-3,324	13.0	719	716	755	1,339	1,007
S&P Core Earnings	830	-404	580	NA	NA	NA	NA	NA	NA	NA

Balance Sheet & Other Fin. Data (Million $)

	2003	2002	2001	2000	1999	1998	1997	1996	1995	1994
Gross Prop.	29,222	31,179	33,012	28,469	28,067	29,844	20,472	33,310	32,227	31,668
Cap. Exp.	1,698	3,032	2,665	1,758	1,584	1,619	1,822	1,230	932	1,107
Net Prop.	18,107	16,928	19,167	16,591	16,776	17,633	20,472	19,008	18,918	19,399
Capitalization:										
LT Debt	9,924	11,590	9,527	5,516	9,484	10,523	7,659	7,821	8,049	8,675
% LT Debt	70.2	76.2	68.8	63.5	57.9	56.6	35.7	46.0	46.0	47.5
Pfd.	Nil	Nil	Nil	Nil	Nil	Nil	539	840	840	870
% Pfd.	Nil	Nil	Nil	Nil	Nil	Nil	2.71	4.90	4.80	4.80
Common	4,215	3,613	4,322	3,172	6,886	8,066	8,897	8,363	8,599	8,635
% Common	29.8	23.8	31.2	36.5	42.1	43.4	41.5	49.1	49.2	47.7
Total Cap.	15,122	16,786	15,668	10,536	19,748	22,733	21,424	21,345	21,814	22,475
% Oper. Ratio	80.4	67.2	90.3	84.1	90.9	92.8	92.3	86.0	80.6	84.4
% Earn. on Net Prop.	14.6	31.2	15.0	34.7	5.1	5.0	8.8	7.1	10.5	8.4
% Return On Revs.	7.6	NM	4.7	NM	0.1	3.6	4.6	7.9	13.9	9.6
% Return On Invest. Capital	13.9	22.8	16.7	29.1	9.7	6.4	9.0	6.5	6.0	7.7
% Return On Com. Equity	20.2	NM	29.1	NM	0.2	8.5	8.3	8.5	14.7	11.1

Data as orig reptd.; bef. results of disc opers/spec. items. Per share data adj. for stk. divs.; EPS diluted. E-Estimated. NA-Not Available. NM-Not Meaningful. NR-Not Ranked. UR-Under Review.

Office: One Market , San Francisco, CA 94105.
Telephone: 415-267-7000.
Email: invrel@pg-corp.com
Website: http://www.pgecorp.com
Chrmn, Pres & CEO: R.D. Glynn, Jr.
SVP & CFO: P.A. Darbee.

SVP & General Counsel: B.R. Worthington.
VP & Treas: L.T. Barnes, Jr.
VP & Investor Contact: G. Togneri 415-267-7080.
Dirs: D. R. Andrews, L. S. Biller, D. A. Coulter, C. L. Cox, W. S. Davila, R. D. Glynn, Jr., D. M. Lawrence, M. S. Metz, C. E. Reichardt, B. L. Williams.

Founded: in 1995.
Domicile: California.
Employees: 20,600.
S&P Analyst: Justin McCann/PMW/JWP

Phelps Dodge

Recommendation: **SELL** ★ ★ ☆ ☆ ☆   12-Month Target Price: **$60.00**
(as of April 28, 2004)

PD has an approximate 0.08% weighting in the **S&P 500**

Sector: Materials
Sub-Industry: Diversified Metals & Mining
Peer Group: Copper Mining

Summary: PD, the world's second largest copper producer, is also a world leader in the production of molybdenum and among the leading producers of magnet wire and carbon black.

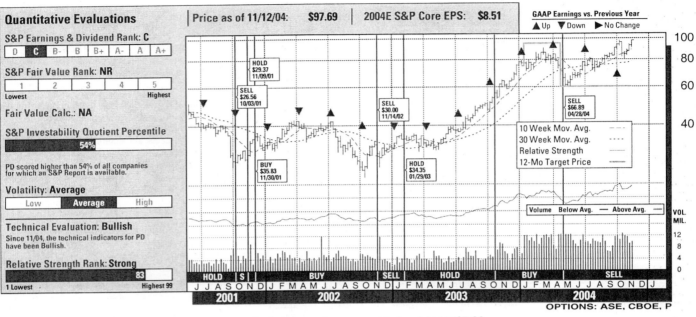

Quantitative Evaluations	Price as of 11/12/04: $97.69	2004E S&P Core EPS: $8.51

S&P Earnings & Dividend Rank: C

| D | C | B- | B | B+ | A- | A | A+ |

S&P Fair Value Rank: NR

| 1 | 2 | 3 | 4 | 5 |
| Lowest | | | | Highest |

Fair Value Calc.: NA

S&P Investability Quotient Percentile

54%

PD scored higher than 54% of all companies for which an S&P Report is available.

Volatility: Average

| Low | Average | High |

Technical Evaluation: Bullish
Since 11/04, the technical indicators for PD have been Bullish.

Relative Strength Rank: Strong

83

| 1 Lowest | Highest 99 |

Analyst commentary prepared by Leo J. Larkin/CB/GG

Highlights August 30, 2004

- Following a rise of 11% in 2003, we look for sales to climb 45% to 50% in 2004, based on our expectations of higher copper prices, another strong gain for specialty chemicals, and a rebound in wire and copper. We look for an average copper price of $1.20 a lb. in 2004, versus 2003's average price of $0.81. Our copper price projection rests on our expectations of flat to lower world output, coupled with rising demand. We expect PD's 2004 copper production to total 2.35 billion lbs., up from 2003 output of 2.10 billion lbs., as the company restarts some currently idle capacity. Aided by vigorous company-wide cost cutting, a higher operating rate projected for the mining segment, and another solid contribution expected from non-copper units, we see operating income rising. Benefiting further from anticipated lower interest expense, we expect PD to post sizable earnings in 2004.

- Assuming a lower average copper price than in 2004, we look for a decline in sales and EPS in 2005.

- According to data compiled by the World Bureau of Metal Statistics, there was a deficit in copper totaling 509,000 metric tons in 2004's first four months, versus a deficit of 81,000 metric tons a year earlier.

Investment Rationale/Risk August 30, 2004

- We recommend avoiding the shares, based on our belief that 2004 could represent peak or near peak of cycle EPS. Following release of second quarter 2004 results, we increased our 2004 EPS estimate to $8.85, from $8.35, on greater than expected strength in the copper price. However, we are keeping our estimate of $8.05 for 2005, as we believe that the price of copper may trail 2004's projected average of $1.20 a lb. Our expectations of a possible decline in the average price of copper in 2005 are based on the assumption that growth from China will slow from 2004 levels. In addition, supply will likely increase, as we think that producers may respond to higher prices by restarting idle capacity. Although copper may remain in a deficit in 2005, the deficit could narrow from 2004 levels, putting downward pressure on prices.

- The main risk to our recommendation and target price is that copper market conditions prove to be stronger than expected and that peak of cycle EPS occurs in 2005 or 2006 instead of 2004.

- Based on our expectation that the stock will trade at a P/E on 2005's projected EPS similar to that seen at the last cycle peak in 1995, our 12-month target price is $60.

Key Stock Statistics

S&P Core EPS 2005E	7.76	52-week Range	$97.94-58.50
S&P Oper. EPS 2004E	10.10	12 Month P/E	12.6
P/E on S&P Oper. EPS 2004E	9.7	Beta	1.42
S&P Oper. EPS 2005E	8.05	Shareholders	18,502
Yield (%)	1.0%	Market Cap (B)	$ 9.3
Dividend Rate/Share	1.00	Shares Outstanding (M)	95.5

Value of $10,000 invested five years ago: **$ 18,264**

Dividend Data Dividends have been paid since 2004

Amount ($)	Date Decl.	Ex-Div. Date	Stock of Record	Payment Date
0.250	Jun. 02	Aug. 11	Aug. 13	Sep. 03 '04
0.250	Oct. 07	Nov. 09	Nov. 12	Dec. 03 '04

Revenues/Earnings Data Fiscal year ending December 31

Revenues (Million $)

	2004	2003	2002	2001	2000	1999
1Q	1,597	978.0	918.5	1,101	1,120	663.1
2Q	1,651	962.2	966.8	1,064	1,113	691.1
3Q	1,847	1,031	941.2	937.0	1,193	742.7
4Q	—	1,171	895.5	901.2	1,099	1,018
Yr.	—	4,143	3,722	4,002	4,525	3,114

Earnings Per Share ($)

	2004	2003	2002	2001	2000	1999
1Q	1.90	-0.30	-0.03	0.21	0.25	0.01
2Q	2.30	-0.21	-0.46	-1.41	-0.48	-0.99
3Q	2.95	-0.04	-0.34	-1.28	0.50	0.27
4Q	E2.95	0.70	-2.58	-1.00	0.10	-2.91
Yr.	E10.10	0.06	-3.54	-3.47	0.37	-4.13

Next earnings report expected: late-January Source: S&P, Company Reports
EPS Estimates based on S&P Operating Earnings; historical GAAP earnings are as reported.

Phelps Dodge Corporation

Recommendation: **SELL** ★ ★ ☆ ☆ ☆   12-Month Target Price: **$60.00** (as of April 28, 2004)

Business Summary August 31, 2004

Phelps Dodge, the world's second largest copper producer, is the world's largest producer of continuous-cast copper rod and molybdenum, and also produces wire and cable and specialty chemicals.

PD posted EPS of $0.70 in the 2003 fourth quarter, versus a loss of $2.58 in the 2002 period. Results in the 2003 quarter benefited from higher copper production, an increase in the average price of copper to $0.93 a lb., from $0.70, much lower charges, and a 14-fold gain in operating profits in the non-copper units. Results in 2002 included an after-tax charge of $2.12 a share for asset impairments, a litigation settlement and insurance settlements; results in the 2003 quarter included charges of $0.20 a share for environmental claims and other charges.

In 1999, the company acquired Cyprus Amax Minerals. Excluding acquired cash of $785 million, the purchase price was $749 million in cash, plus 20.6 million common shares. Following the merger, PD became the world's second largest copper producer.

The mining segment accounted for 68% of 2003 revenues (67% in 2002), and had an operating profit of $265.2 million, versus an operating loss of $65.0 million in 2002. The industrial segment, which consists of carbon black and wire and cable operations, accounted for 32% of 2003 revenues, and had operating profit of $68.5 million, versus $30.6 million.

The mining unit produces copper from mines in the U.S., Chile and Peru. Copper production for PD's own account was 1,059,300 metric tons in 2003, versus 1,028,800 metric tons in 2002.

The average price of copper (based on the London Metal Exchange) was $0.81 per lb. in 2003, versus $0.71 per lb. in 2002 and $0.72 in 2001. The company's chief competitors in copper are Freeport McMoran Copper & Gold, Chile's state-owned Corporacion Nacional del Cobre de Chile (Codelco), Grupo Mexico, and Southern Peru Copper.

According to the World Bureau of Metals Statistics, there was a deficit of 196,000 metric tons in 2003, versus a surplus of 345,000 metric tons in 2002 and a surplus of 1,004,000 metric tons in 2001.

Industrial operations include PD Wire & Cable Group, the world's leading producer of insulated magnet wire for use in motors, generators and transformers; and Columbian Chemicals Co., one of the world's largest producers of carbon black.

Commercially recoverable copper reserves totaled 21.1 million metric tons at the end of 2003, versus 21 million metric tons at the end of 2002 and 23.0 million metric tons at the end of 2001.

In June 2002, the company sold 10 million common shares and 2 million convertible preferred shares. Net proceeds totaling about $592 million were used for debt reduction. Following the sale, shares outstanding totaled about 88.7 million, up from 78.7 million at the end of 2001.

Company Financials Fiscal Year ending December 31

Per Share Data ($)

(Year Ended December 31)	2003	2002	2001	2000	1999	1998	1997	1996	1995	1994
Tangible Bk. Val.	29.03	31.63	34.40	37.24	39.01	40.22	39.23	39.92	36.58	28.87
Cash Flow	2.40	1.44	2.45	6.24	1.19	8.20	11.18	10.79	13.86	6.56
Earnings	0.06	-3.54	-3.47	0.37	-4.13	3.26	6.63	6.97	10.65	3.81
S&P Core Earnings	-0.05	-3.77	-5.60	NA	NA	NA	NA	NA	NA	NA
Dividends	Nil	Nil	0.75	2.00	2.00	2.00	2.00	1.95	1.80	1.69
Payout Ratio	Nil	Nil	NM	NM	NM	62%	30%	28%	17%	44%
Prices - High	79.42	42.51	55.68	73.00	70.62	71.75	89.62	77.62	70.50	65.00
- Low	30.11	22.90	25.74	36.06	41.87	43.87	59.87	54.62	51.87	47.62
P/E Ratio - High	NM	NM	NM	NM	NM	22	14	11	7	17
- Low	NM	NM	NM	NM	NM	13	9	8	5	13

Income Statement Analysis (Million $)

	2003	2002	2001	2000	1999	1998	1997	1996	1995	1994
Revs.	4,143	3,722	4,002	4,525	3,114	3,063	3,914	3,786	4,185	3,289
Oper. Inc.	658	437	389	753	468	525	940	973	1,297	753
Depr.	423	410	465	464	329	293	284	250	223	195
Int. Exp.	145	187	226	213	120	94.0	62.0	68.0	65.0	57.3
Pretax Inc.	74.1	-394	-263	55.0	-422	333	594	698	1,076	384
Eff. Tax Rate	65.2%	NM	NM	34.5%	NM	40.2%	30.3%	31.6%	30.0%	27.3%
Net Inc.	18.1	-289	-273	29.0	-255	191	409	462	747	271
S&P Core Earnings	-5.29	-316	-440	NA	NA	NA	NA	NA	NA	NA

Balance Sheet & Other Fin. Data (Million $)

	2003	2002	2001	2000	1999	1998	1997	1996	1995	1994
Cash	684	350	387	250	234	222	158	471	609	287
Curr. Assets	1,790	1,428	1,504	1,508	1,693	980	1,051	1,422	1,555	1,208
Total Assets	7,273	7,029	7,619	7,831	8,229	5,037	4,965	4,816	4,646	4,134
Curr. Liab.	1,015	784	1,014	1,418	1,418	651	701	686	605	650
LT Debt	Nil	1,948	2,522	1,963	2,172	836	857	555	613	622
Common Equity	3,062	2,812	2,707	3,106	3,278	2,588	2,511	2,756	2,678	2,188
Total Cap.	3,544	5,193	5,730	5,600	5,932	4,026	3,806	3,821	3,722	3,119
Cap. Exp.	151	130	263	397	201	318	662	513	408	376
Cash Flow	427	121	192	493	74.0	484	693	712	970	466
Curr. Ratio	1.8	1.8	1.5	1.1	1.2	1.5	1.5	2.1	2.6	1.9
% LT Debt of Cap.	Nil	37.5	44.0	35.1	36.6	20.8	22.5	14.5	16.5	20.0
% Net Inc.of Revs.	0.4	NM	NM	0.6	NM	6.2	10.4	12.2	17.8	8.2
% Ret. on Assets	0.3	NM	NM	0.4	NM	3.8	8.4	9.8	17.0	6.9
% Ret. on Equity	0.2	NM	NM	0.9	NM	7.5	15.5	17.0	30.7	12.9

Data as orig reptd.; bef. results of disc opers/spec. items. Per share data adj. for stk. divs.; EPS diluted. E-Estimated. NA-Not Available. NM-Not Meaningful. NR-Not Ranked. UR-Under Review.

Office: 1 N Central Ave, Phoenix, AZ 85004-4464.
Telephone: 602-366-8100.
Website: http://www.phelpsdodge.com
Chrmn & CEO: J.S. Whisler.
Pres & COO: T.R. Snider.
SVP & CFO: R.G. Peru.

SVP & General Counsel: S.D. Colton.
VP & Investor Contact: S.K. Rideout 602-366-7856.
Dirs: R. N. Burt, A. W. Durham, W. A. Franke, R. D. Johnson, M. L. Knowles, R. D. Krebs, J. C. Madonna, G. R. Parker, W. J. Post, J. E. Thompson, J. S. Whisler.

Founded: in 1885.
Domicile: New York.
Employees: 13,000.
S&P Analyst: Leo J. Larkin/CB/GG

Pinnacle West Capital

Recommendation: **HOLD** ★★★☆☆
SELL SELL HOLD BUY BUY

12-Month Target Price: $42.00
(as of October 25, 2004)

PNW has an approximate 0.04% weighting in the **S&P 500**

Sector: Utilities
Sub-Industry: Electric Utilities
Peer Group: Electric Cos. (Domestic) - Midsized

Summary: This utility holding company is the parent of Arizona Public Service, Arizona's largest electric utility.

Quantitative Evaluations

S&P Earnings & Dividend Rank: A

D	C	B-	B	B+	A-	A	A+

S&P Fair Value Rank: 3

1	2	3	4	5
Lowest				Highest

Fair Value Calc.: $43.80 (Slightly Overvalued)

S&P Investability Quotient Percentile
81%

PNW scored higher than 81% of all companies for which an S&P Report is available.

Volatility: Low

Low	Average	High

Technical Evaluation: Bullish
Since 8/04, the technical indicators for PNW have been Bullish.

Relative Strength Rank: Moderate
61
1 Lowest   Highest 99

Price as of 11/12/04:	**$45.14**	2004E S&P Core EPS:	**$2.19**

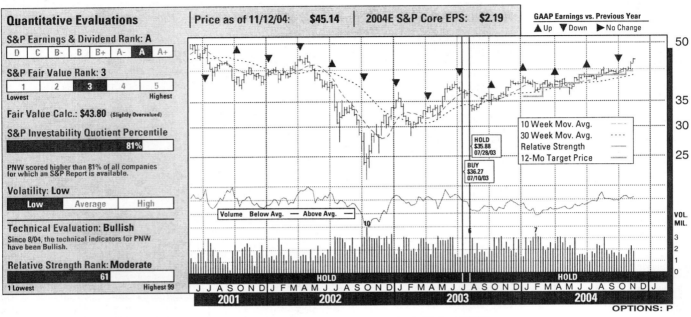

GAAP Earnings vs. Previous Year
▲ Up   ▼ Down   ► No Change

HOLD $35.88 07/28/03
BUY $36.27 07/10/03

- 10 Week Mov. Avg.
- 30 Week Mov. Avg.
- Relative Strength
- 12-Mo Target Price

Volume Below Avg. — Above Avg.

HOLD   HOLD
J J A S O N D J F M A M J J A S O N D J F M A M J J A S O N D J F M A M J J A S O N D J
  2001   2002   2003   2004

OPTIONS: P

Analyst commentary prepared by Justin McCann/CB/GG

Highlights September 15, 2004

- Following an anticipated 9% increase in 2004 from 2003's EPS from continuing operations of $2.44 (before $0.19 in tax credits related to prior years), we expect EPS to increase more than 20% in 2005. We expect earnings from marketing and trading to be negligible, but we see EPS continuing to benefit from strong customer growth and accelerating asset sales from the SunCor real estate unit.

- In August 2004, Arizona Public Service (APS) reached a rate settlement agreement with the staff of the Arizona Corporation Commission (ACC) and other concerned parties. The agreement included a rate increase of $75.5 million (4.21%); this was less than half of the $175 million (9.8%) rate increase requested by APS in June 2003, but well above the $142 million rate decrease previously recommended by the ACC staff. PNW expects the ACC to make a ruling on the agreement by the end of 2004.

- The settlement agreement also approved the transfer to APS of power plants currently owned by PNW's non-regulated Pinnacle West Energy. The transfer (which would have to be approved by federal regulators) would increase the APS rate base by $700 million, after a disallowance of $148 million that is expected to result in an after-tax write-off of $88 million. The agreement did not include the utility's requested recovery of a prior $234 million writeoff.

Investment Rationale/Risk September 15, 2004

- After having slightly underperformed the S&P Electric Utility Index in 2003 and 2004 to date, we expect the stock to trade at a P/E multiple on our 2005 EPS estimate that more closely approximates the company's peers, and to remain relatively flat over the next 12 months. However, with the federal tax rate on dividends having been reduced from the earned rate to 15%, we think the shares should be supported by the consistency of PNW's dividend growth, which has been at a higher rate than its peers.

- Risks to our investment recommendation and target price include a worse than expected commission decision on APS's rate case settlement agreement, and a significant decline in the average P/E multiple of the group as a whole.

- Although the dividend payout ratio of 71% of our EPS estimate for 2004 is slightly above the industry average, we expect PNW to continue to increase its annual dividend by $0.10 a share. However, until there has been a final ACC ruling on the pending rate case, we believe the shares are fairly valued at the lower end of an approximate peer P/E multiple range of 13X to 13.5X our 2005 EPS estimates. Our 12-month target price is $41.

Key Stock Statistics

S&P Core EPS 2005E	2.91	52-week Range	$45.34-36.30
S&P Oper. EPS 2004E	2.50	12 Month P/E	16.0
P/E on S&P Oper. EPS 2004E	18.1	Beta	0.24
S&P Oper. EPS 2005E	3.15	Shareholders	36,876
Yield (%)	4.2%	Market Cap (B)	$ 4.1
Dividend Rate/Share	1.90	Shares Outstanding (M)	91.6

Value of $10,000 invested five years ago: **$ 15,095**

Dividend Data Dividends have been paid since 1993

Amount ($)	Date Decl.	Ex-Div. Date	Stock of Record	Payment Date
0.450	Jan. 21	Jan. 29	Feb. 02	Mar. 01 '04
0.450	Mar. 17	Apr. 29	May. 03	Jun. 01 '04
0.450	Jul. 16	Jul. 29	Aug. 02	Sep. 01 '04
0.475	Oct. 20	Oct. 28	Nov. 01	Dec. 01 '04

Revenues/Earnings Data Fiscal year ending December 31

Revenues (Million $)

	2004	2003	2002	2001	2000	1999
1Q	574.4	552.6	380.2	938.8	488.1	438.5
2Q	722.7	683.3	496.8	1,294	756.5	544.1
3Q	886.8	847.7	719.4	1,574	1,607	894.3
4Q	—	734.2	416.6	744.7	838.1	546.4
Yr.	—	2,818	2,637	4,551	3,690	2,423

Earnings Per Share ($)

	2004	2003	2002	2001	2000	1999
1Q	0.33	0.22	0.63	0.73	0.64	0.36
2Q	0.78	0.60	0.89	0.79	1.06	0.81
3Q	1.14	1.20	1.19	1.91	1.37	0.28
4Q	E0.45	0.50	-0.17	0.42	0.50	0.53
Yr.	E2.50	2.52	2.53	3.85	3.56	1.97

Next earnings report expected: late-January Source: S&P, Company Reports
EPS Estimates based on S&P Operating Earnings; historical GAAP earnings are as reported.

Pinnacle West Capital Corporation

Recommendation: **HOLD** ★ ★ ★ ★ ★   12-Month Target Price: **$42.00** (as of October 25, 2004)

Business Summary September 15, 2004

Pinnacle West Capital is the holding company for Arizona Public Service (APS), which, with more than 931,500 customers, is Arizona's largest electric utility. APS provides service to the entire state, with the exception of Tucson and about 50% of the Phoenix area.

In 2003, the regulated electricity segment accounted for 70.2% of PNW's consolidated revenues (76.3% in 2002, 75.5% in 2001); the marketing and trading segment, 13.9% (12.4%, 19.2%); the real estate segment, 12.8% (9.0%, 5.0%); and other, 3.1% (2.3%, 0.3%).

Residential customers accounted for 48.4% of PNW's regulated electric sales in 2003 (45.0% in 2002, 35.7% in 2001); business customers, 47.5% (46.1%, 37.2%); and wholesale and other, 4.1% (8.9%, 27.1%).

Consolidated fuel sources in 2003 were: purchased power and net interchange 54.4% (49.9% in 2002, 45.6% in 2001); coal, 20.1% (23.8%, 27.3%); nuclear, 14.7% (17.7%, 18.3%); and other, 10.8% (8.6%, 8.8%).

APS has a 29.1% owned or leased interest in the Palo Verde Nuclear Generating Station's Units 1 and 3, and a 17.0% interest in Unit 2; It has a 100% interest in Units 1, 2 and 3, and a 15% interest in Units 4 and 5 of the coal-fueled Four Corners Steam Generating Station; and a 14.0% in Units 1, 2 and 3 of the coal-fueled Navajo Steam Generating Station (NGS).

In September 1999, the Arizona Corporation Commission (ACC) approved an APS settlement agreement that initiated a series of rate reductions, totaling 7.5%, from October 1, 1999 (but retroactive to July 1, 1999), through July 1, 2003. The agreement called for a regulatory disallowance of $234 million pretax (recorded as a net reduction of regulatory assets), but gave APS an opportunity to recover $350 million of stranded costs (net present value was calculated by APS at $533 million) through a competitive transition charge valid through December 31, 2004. The agreement also permitted APS to defer for later recovery prudent and reasonable costs of compliance with the provisions of the agreement, system benefits costs in excess of the levels included in the new rates, and costs associated with various service obligations (including the "provider of last resort" service) through adjustment clauses that would commence on July 1, 2004.

Capital spending for Arizona Public Service was about $429 million in 2003. The utility projected capital expenditures of $426 million for 2004, $562 million for 2005, and $655 million for 2006.

PNW's non-utility subsidiaries include Pinnacle West Energy, which conducts unregulated power generation operations; APS Energy Services, which provides commodity energy and energy related products; SunCor, which owns, develops and sells real estate property in Arizona, New Mexico, and Utah; and El Dorado, an investment firm.

Company Financials Fiscal Year ending December 31

Per Share Data ($)

(Year Ended December 31)	2003	2002	2001	2000	1999	1998	1997	1996	1995	1994
Tangible Bk. Val.	29.81	28.23	29.46	28.09	26.00	25.50	23.90	22.51	21.50	20.32
Earnings	2.52	2.53	3.85	3.56	1.97	2.85	2.76	2.41	2.28	2.30
S&P Core Earnings	2.43	1.65	3.00	NA	NA	NA	NA	NA	NA	NA
Dividends	1.73	1.63	1.53	1.43	1.32	1.23	1.13	1.03	0.93	0.83
Payout Ratio	68%	64%	40%	40%	67%	43%	41%	43%	41%	36%
Prices - High	40.48	46.68	50.70	52.68	43.37	49.25	42.75	32.25	28.87	22.87
- Low	28.34	21.70	37.65	25.68	30.18	39.37	27.62	26.25	19.62	16.00
P/E Ratio - High	16	18	13	15	22	17	15	13	13	10
- Low	11	9	10	7	15	14	10	11	9	7

Income Statement Analysis (Million $)

	2003	2002	2001	2000	1999	1998	1997	1996	1995	1994
Revs.	2,818	2,637	4,551	3,690	2,423	2,131	1,995	1,818	1,670	1,685
Depr.	438	425	428	394	386	380	368	300	244	237
Maint.	NA	NA	NA	NA	NA	NA	NA	NA	NA	NA
Fxd. Chgs. Cov.	2.43	2.64	3.80	3.95	3.61	3.17	2.93	2.80	1.81	2.18
Constr. Credits	14.2	NA	NA	NA	11.7	18.6	16.2	14.7	14.1	9.38
Eff. Tax Rate	31.4%	39.1%	39.5%	42.5%	38.4%	40.4%	38.9%	37.8%	39.1%	38.0%
Net Inc.	231	215	327	302	270	243	236	211	200	201
S&P Core Earnings	223	140	255	NA	NA	NA	NA	NA	NA	NA

Balance Sheet & Other Fin. Data (Million $)

	2003	2002	2001	2000	1999	1998	1997	1996	1995	1994
Gross Prop.	10,470	16,316	9,285	8,383	7,805	7,876	7,730	7,145	6,947	6,827
Cap. Exp.	693	896	1,041	659	343	319	308	259	296	255
Net Prop.	7,310	12,842	5,907	5,133	4,779	5,062	5,043	4,655	4,647	4,624
Capitalization:										
LT Debt	2,898	2,882	2,673	1,955	2,206	2,144	2,244	2,372	2,511	2,589
% LT Debt	50.6	51.8	51.7	45.1	50.0	49.8	50.5	52.0	53.9	55.9
Pfd.	Nil	Nil	Nil	Nil	Nil	Nil	171	219	269	269
% Pfd.	Nil	Nil	Nil	Nil	Nil	Nil	3.80	4.80	5.80	5.80
Common	2,830	2,686	2,499	2,383	2,206	2,163	2,027	1,970	1,881	1,776
% Common	49.4	48.2	48.3	54.9	50.0	50.2	45.6	43.2	40.3	38.3
Total Cap.	7,057	6,777	6,237	5,481	5,599	5,678	5,856	5,995	6,086	6,052
% Oper. Ratio	86.6	81.7	89.9	87.7	83.1	75.7	74.0	77.1	74.0	75.6
% Earn. on Net Prop.	6.8	4.2	24.6	13.6	12.2	11.2	11.0	11.7	9.4	8.9
% Return On Revs.	8.2	8.2	7.2	8.2	11.1	11.4	11.8	11.6	12.0	11.9
% Return On Invest. Capital	6.2	7.7	7.9	8.2	7.5	13.9	7.0	6.8	7.2	7.7
% Return On Com. Equity	8.4	8.3	13.4	13.2	12.3	11.6	11.8	11.0	10.9	11.7

Data as orig reptd.; bef. results of disc opers/spec. items. Per share data adj. for stk. divs.; EPS diluted. E-Estimated. NA-Not Available. NM-Not Meaningful. NR-Not Ranked. UR-Under Review.

Office: 400 North 5th Street, Phoenix, AZ 85004-3902.
Telephone: 602-250-1000.
Website: http://www.pinnaclewest.com
Chrmn & CEO: W.J. Post.
Pres & COO: J.E. Davis.
EVP & CFO: D. Brandt.
VP & Treas: B.M. Gomez.

VP, Secy & General Counsel: N.C. Loftin.
Investor Contact: R.L. Hickman 602-250-5668.
Investor Contact: L. Malagon 602-250-5671.
Dirs: E. N. Basha, J. E. Davis, M. L. Gallagher, P. Grant, R. A. Herberger, Jr., M. O. Hesse, W. S. Jamieson, Jr., H. S. Lopez, K. L. Munro, B. J. Nordstrom, W. J. Post, W. L. Stewart.

Founded: in 1920.
Domicile: Arizona.
Employees: 7,200.
S&P Analyst: Justin McCann/CB/GG

Pitney Bowes

Recommendation: **BUY** ★★★★☆
SELL | SELL | HOLD | BUY | BUY
(as of April 13, 2004)

12-Month Target Price: **$48.00**

PBI has an approximate 0.09% weighting in the **S&P 500**

Sector: Industrials
Sub-Industry: Office Services & Supplies
Peer Group: Office Equipment - Hardware

Summary: PBI, the world's largest manufacturer of mailing systems, also provides production and document management equipment, facilities management services and lease financing.

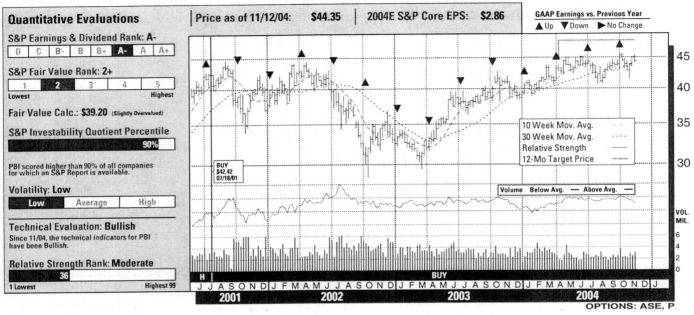

Quantitative Evaluations

S&P Earnings & Dividend Rank: A-
D | C | B- | B | B+ | **A-** | A | A+

S&P Fair Value Rank: 2+
1 | **2** | 3 | 4 | 5
Lowest | | | | Highest

Fair Value Calc.: $39.20 (Slightly Overvalued)

S&P Investability Quotient Percentile
90%
PBI scored higher than 90% of all companies for which an S&P Report is available.

Volatility: Low
Low | Average | High

Technical Evaluation: Bullish
Since 11/04, the technical indicators for PBI have been Bullish.

Relative Strength Rank: Moderate
36
1 Lowest | Highest 99

Price as of 11/12/04: **$44.35** | 2004E S&P Core EPS: **$2.86**

GAAP Earnings vs. Previous Year
▲ Up ▼ Down ▶ No Change

10 Week Mov. Avg.
30 Week Mov. Avg.
Relative Strength
12-Mo Target Price

BUY $42.42 07/18/01

Volume   Below Avg. — Above Avg.

OPTIONS: ASE, P

Analyst commentary prepared by Stephanie S. Crane/MF/JWP

Highlights November 05, 2004

- Following third quarter results, we continue to believe that small business demand for mailing systems has escalated, as evidenced by demand for PBI's low- to mid-range meters, with early signs of a moderate pickup in enterprise spending as demand for high-end production mailing equipment expands.

- We look for revenue in 2004 to grow 6%, with a 7% increase seen in 2005. We expect growth to come from a continued economic recovery, migration to digital meters (now two thirds of PBI's U.S. meter base), strengthening international markets, and acquisition activity. We also expect to see incremental growth from Secap and PSI, recent acquisitions that are now fully integrated and expanded.

- We see margins widening from 55% in 2003 to 56% in 2004, as a result of a more favorable product mix and cost cutting efforts. We think ongoing stock repurchases (5.4 million in 2003) may provide an additional boost to EPS. We forecast 2004 EPS of $2.51, up about 4% from 2003's $2.42 (before charges). For 2005, we expect EPS of $2.85.

Investment Rationale/Risk November 05, 2004

- We find the shares attractive based on our view of PBI's large recurring revenue stream (77% of revenue in 2003), a leadership position within its market, and a better than average dividend yield of 3%. In addition, we see a strengthening economy, synergies from recent acquisitions, and new product introductions focusing on digital technology leading to steady revenue growth and widening margins in coming periods.

- Risks to our recommendation and target price come from increased competition in the document management outsourcing market, which would have an impact on pricing within Pitney Bowes Management Services division. This division contributes over 25% of revenues.

- At recent levels, the shares traded at a discount to their historical average, the S&P 500, and our intrinsic value calculation. Our discounted cash flow assumptions include a weighted average cost of capital of 8% and an expected terminal growth rate of 3%. Our 12-month target price is $48. We would accumulate the shares on a total return basis.

Key Stock Statistics

S&P Oper. EPS 2004E	2.51	52-week Range	$45.73-38.22
P/E on S&P Oper. EPS 2004E	17.7	12 Month P/E	19.1
S&P Oper. EPS 2005E	2.85	Beta	0.44
Yield (%)	2.8%	Shareholders	27,011
Dividend Rate/Share	1.22	Market Cap (B)	$ 10.2
Shares Outstanding (M)	230.6		

Value of $10,000 invested five years ago: **NA**

Dividend Data Dividends have been paid since 1934

Amount ($)	Date Decl.	Ex-Div. Date	Stock of Record	Payment Date
0.305	Feb. 04	Feb. 18	Feb. 20	Mar. 12 '04
0.305	Apr. 12	May. 19	May. 21	Jun. 12 '04
0.305	Jul. 12	Aug. 18	Aug. 20	Sep. 12 '04
0.305	Nov. 08	Nov. 17	Nov. 19	Dec. 12 '04

Revenues/Earnings Data Fiscal year ending December 31

Revenues (Million $)

	2004	2003	2002	2001	2000	1999
1Q	1,172	1,091	1,050	966.3	945.0	1,082
2Q	1,206	1,134	1,081	1,021	998.0	1,105
3Q	1,218	1,137	1,114	1,044	960.0	1,090
4Q	—	1,215	1,165	1,091	978.0	1,188
Yr.	—	4,577	4,410	4,122	3,881	4,432

Earnings Per Share ($)

	2004	2003	2002	2001	2000	1999
1Q	0.54	0.48	0.53	0.42	0.50	0.52
2Q	0.58	0.50	0.59	0.76	0.56	0.58
3Q	0.58	0.50	0.61	0.49	0.63	0.69
4Q	E0.67	0.61	0.08	0.41	0.55	0.66
Yr.	E2.51	2.10	1.81	2.08	2.18	2.42

Next earnings report expected: early-February Source: S&P, Company Reports
EPS Estimates based on S&P Operating Earnings; historical GAAP earnings are as reported.

Pitney Bowes Inc.

Recommendation: **BUY** ★ ★ ★ ★ ☆   12-Month Target Price: **$48.00** (as of April 13, 2004)

Business Summary November 05, 2004

Pitney Bowes had its beginnings in the early 1920s, when it introduced its first postage meter devices. Over the years, the company has built up this business to provide customers with a complete line of mail room solutions. PBI now offers a complete line of digital and networked solutions, leveraging its mailing expertise to offer office equipment and value-added services and solutions that are designed to allow businesses to be more efficient and reduce costs. The company also provides lease financing and other financial services to customers and other businesses.

The Global Mailing segment, which accounted for 69% of 2003 revenue (68% in 2002), encompasses the rental of postage meters and the sale, rental and financing of mailing equipment, including mail finishing and software based mail creation equipment. Products include postage meters, mailing machines, letter and parcel scales, mail openers, mailroom furniture, presort machines, and postal payment solutions.

The Enterprise Solutions segment (28% of revenues in both 2003 and 2002) comprises two divisions: Pitney Bowes Management Services (PBMS) and Document Messaging Technologies (DMT). PBMS is a major provider of on- and off-site services that let customers manage the creation, processing, storage, retrieval, distribution and tracking of documents and messages in both paper and digital form. The unit focuses on facilities management contracts for advanced mailing, secure mail services, reprographic, document management and other

high value services. The DMT business involves the servicing and financing of high-speed software-enabled production mail systems, sorting equipment, incoming mail systems, electronic statement, billing and payment solutions, and mailing software.

The Capital Services division (3%, 4%) consists of external financing for non-Pitney Bowes products, including the strategic financing of third party equipment. Asset and fee-based income is generated by financing or arranging transactions of critical large ticket customer assets. In January 2003, PBI said it would stop active pursuit of long-term Capital Services financing transactions, including long-term financing of postal and related equipment. The company plans to continue to provide lease financing for its products through its internal financing operations. In the past, PBI directly financed or arranged financing for commercial and non-commercial aircraft, real estate, locomotives, railcars, and office equipment.

In August 2002, PBI acquired PSI, the largest U.S. presort company, for about $127 million in cash and $39 million in assumption of debt. PSI prepares, sorts and aggregates mail to earn postal discounts and expedite delivery for customers.

In October 2003, PBI acquired DDD for $49.5 million, of which $24.8 million was in cash. DDD provides fulfillment services, secure mail processing, logistics support and record and information management.

Company Financials Fiscal Year ending December 31

Per Share Data ($)

(Year Ended December 31)	2003	2002	2001	2000	1999	1998	1997	1996	1995	1994
Tangible Bk. Val.	NM	0.10	1.05	4.34	5.28	5.26	5.96	6.86	6.20	5.03
Cash Flow	3.32	2.98	3.44	3.55	4.05	3.31	2.21	2.48	2.23	1.96
Earnings	2.10	1.81	2.08	2.18	2.42	2.03	1.80	1.56	1.34	1.10
S&P Core Earnings	1.87	1.34	0.81	NA	NA	NA	NA	NA	NA	NA
Dividends	1.20	1.18	1.16	1.14	1.02	0.90	0.80	0.69	0.60	0.52
Payout Ratio	57%	65%	56%	52%	42%	44%	44%	44%	45%	47%
Prices - High	42.75	44.41	44.70	54.12	73.31	66.37	45.75	30.68	24.12	23.18
- Low	29.45	28.55	32.00	24.00	40.87	42.21	26.81	20.93	15.00	14.62
P/E Ratio - High	20	25	21	25	30	33	25	20	18	21
- Low	14	16	15	11	17	21	15	13	11	13

Income Statement Analysis (Million $)

	2003	2002	2001	2000	1999	1998	1997	1996	1995	1994
Revs.	4,577	4,410	4,122	3,881	4,433	4,221	4,100	3,859	3,555	3,271
Oper. Inc.	1,291	1,276	1,046	1,316	1,526	1,375	1,303	1,160	1,109	999
Depr.	289	264	317	321	412	361	300	278	272	268
Int. Exp.	168	185	193	201	184	169	209	204	226	194
Pretax Inc.	721	619	766	803	985	864	803	684	619	567
Eff. Tax Rate	31.4%	29.3%	32.9%	29.9%	33.1%	34.3%	34.3%	31.4%	34.1%	38.5%
Net Inc.	495	438	514	563	659	568	526	469	408	348
S&P Core Earnings	440	324	199	NA	NA	NA	NA	NA	NA	NA

Balance Sheet & Other Fin. Data (Million $)

	2003	2002	2001	2000	1999	1998	1997	1996	1995	1994
Cash	294	315	232	198	254	129	139	137	88.6	76.0
Curr. Assets	2,513	2,553	2,557	2,627	3,343	2,509	2,464	2,222	2,101	2,084
Total Assets	8,891	8,732	8,318	7,901	8,223	7,661	7,893	8,156	7,845	7,400
Curr. Liab.	2,647	3,350	3,083	2,882	2,873	2,722	3,373	3,305	3,502	3,978
LT Debt	3,151	2,317	2,419	2,192	2,308	2,023	1,068	1,300	1,063	802
Common Equity	1,086	852	890	1,283	1,624	1,734	1,870	2,237	2,069	1,742
Total Cap.	5,898	4,706	4,584	4,704	5,015	4,680	4,146	4,260	3,947	3,001
Cap. Exp.	286	225	256	269	305	298	244	272	338	346
Cash Flow	784	702	832	884	1,071	929	646	747	679	616
Curr. Ratio	0.9	0.8	0.8	0.9	1.2	0.9	0.7	0.7	0.6	0.5
% LT Debt of Cap.	53.4	49.2	52.8	46.6	46.0	43.2	25.8	30.5	26.9	26.7
% Net Inc.of Revs.	10.8	9.9	12.5	14.5	14.9	13.5	12.8	12.2	11.5	10.7
% Ret. on Assets	5.6	5.1	6.3	7.0	8.3	7.3	6.6	5.9	5.3	5.0
% Ret. on Equity	51.1	50.3	47.3	38.7	40.3	31.5	25.6	21.8	21.4	19.7

Data as orig reptd.; bef. results of disc opers/spec. items. Per share data adj. for stk. divs.; EPS diluted. E-Estimated. NA-Not Available. NM-Not Meaningful. NR-Not Ranked. UR-Under Review.

Office: 1 Elmcroft Rd, Stamford, CT 06926-0700.
Telephone: 203-351-6858.
Email: investorrelations@pb.com
Website: http://www.pitneybowes.com
Chrmn & CEO: M.J. Critelli.
Pres & COO: M.D. Martin.

EVP & CFO: B.P. Nolop.
SVP & General Counsel: M.C. Mayes.
Investor Contact: C.F. McBride 203-351-6349.
Dirs: L. G. Alvarado, C. G. Campbell, M. J. Critelli, J. P. Einhorn, E. Green, H. L. Henkel, J. H. Keyes, J. S. McFarlane, E. R. Menasce, M. I. Roth, D. L. Shedlarz, R. E. Weissmann.

Founded: in 1920.
Domicile: Delaware.
Employees: 32,474.
S&P Analyst: Stephanie S. Crane/MF/JWP

Plum Creek Timber

Recommendation: **SELL** ★★ ☆ ☆ ☆
SELL SELL HOLD BUY BUY

12-Month Target Price: **$25.00**
(as of January 22, 2004)

PCL has an approximate 0.06% weighting in the **S&P 500**

Sector: Financials
Sub-Industry: Real Estate Investment Trusts
Peer Group: REITs - Specialty

Summary: Following its October 2001 acquisition of The Timber Co., this REIT now owns and manages more than 8.0 million acres of timberlands in 20 states.

Quantitative Evaluations

S&P Earnings & Dividend Rank: NR

D	C	B-	B	B+	A-	A	A+

S&P Fair Value Rank: 2

1	2	3	4	5
Lowest				Highest

Fair Value Calc.: $35.10 (Slightly Overvalued)

S&P Investability Quotient Percentile

41%

PCL scored lower than 59% of all companies for which an S&P Report is available.

Volatility: Low

Low	Average	High

Technical Evaluation: Bullish
Since 8/04, the technical indicators for PCL have been Bullish.

Relative Strength Rank: Strong

77

1 Lowest		Highest 99

Price as of 11/12/04: $38.81 | **2004E S&P Core EPS:** $1.47

GAAP Earnings vs. Previous Year
▲ Up ▼ Down ► No Change

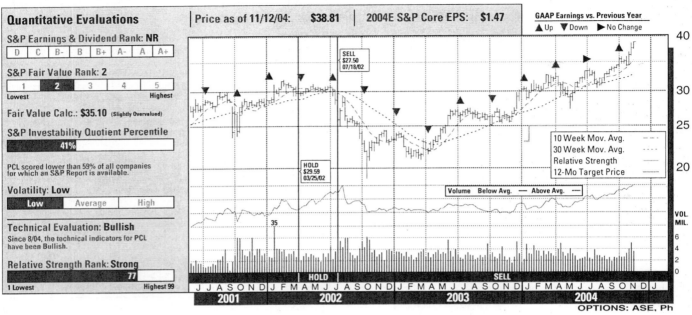

10 Week Mov. Avg.
30 Week Mov. Avg.
Relative Strength
12-Mo Target Price

Volume Below Avg. — Above Avg.

OPTIONS: ASE, Ph

Analyst commentary prepared by Bryon J. Korutz/MF/BK

Highlights November 04, 2004

- We expect revenues of this timber REIT to increase 18% in 2004, followed by a drop of 2.3% seen for 2005. Standard & Poor's projects that real GDP will grow 4.5% in 2004. Overall, we see this anticipated increase supporting improved demand and prices for pulpwood, as a firming U.S. economy will likely lead to greater demand for certain grades of paper.

- We see continued recovery in pulpwood prices, based on our expectation that the U.S. economy will continue to strengthen. We believe that average wood products prices in 2004 will exceed those reached in 2003, based on our projection of a 4.4% increase in housing starts. With sawlog prices typically mirroring lumber prices, we look for sawlog prices to remain steady for the balance of 2004. Sequentially, harvest volumes in the north should equal those reached in the third quarter, but drop in the south. Looking to 2005, we expect sawlog and wood products prices to decline, based on our expectations of a 7.0% drop in housing starts in 2005.

- We estimate operating EPS of $1.47 a share in 2004, declining to $1.30 in 2005.

Investment Rationale/Risk November 04, 2004

- Reflecting our expectations of weakening sawlog prices in 2005, and with the shares above our 12-month target price of $25, we would avoid the stock. However, on the positive side, we see pulpwood demand and prices rising, as demand for paper increases in step with what we view as a strengthening U.S. economy and expected firming sales in its real estate segment.

- Risks to our recommendation and target price include lesser declines in log demand and prices than we expect.

- Our first valuation metric, which applies a peer forward P/E multiple of 13.8X to our 2005 EPS estimate of $1.30, indicates a potential value of $18 a share. Our dividend discount model indicates that the stock has an intrinsic value of about $27 a share. Blending our valuation metrics, our 12-month target price is $25.

Key Stock Statistics

S&P Core EPS 2005E	1.30	52-week Range	$38.81-25.42
S&P Oper. EPS 2004E	1.47	12 Month P/E	20.8
P/E on S&P Oper. EPS 2004E	26.4	Beta	0.53
S&P Oper. EPS 2005E	1.30	Shareholders	28,221
Yield (%)	3.7%	Market Cap (B)	$ 7.1
Dividend Rate/Share	1.44	Shares Outstanding (M)	183.6

Value of $10,000 invested five years ago: **$ 20,673**

Dividend Data Dividends have been paid since 1989

Amount ($)	Date Decl.	Ex-Div. Date	Stock of Record	Payment Date
0.350	Oct. 28	Nov. 10	Nov. 13	Nov. 26 '03
0.350	Feb. 02	Feb. 11	Feb. 13	Feb. 27 '04
0.360	Jul. 27	Aug. 13	Aug. 17	Aug. 31 '04
0.360	Nov. 02	Nov. 10	Nov. 15	Nov. 30 '04

Revenues/Earnings Data Fiscal year ending December 31

Revenues (Million $)

	2004	2003	2002	2001	2000	1999
1Q	497.0	273.0	275.0	117.0	58.95	178.2
2Q	341.0	318.0	271.0	100.0	53.15	184.3
3Q	363.0	290.0	310.0	141.0	41.54	52.00
4Q	—	315.0	281.0	240.0	55.42	46.05
Yr.	—	1,196	1,137	598.0	209.1	460.6

Earnings Per Share ($)

	2004	2003	2002	2001	2000	1999
1Q	0.84	0.18	0.30	0.32	1.16	0.20
2Q	0.31	0.31	0.29	0.24	0.30	0.33
3Q	0.42	0.25	0.38	0.42	0.14	0.73
4Q	E0.29	0.30	0.29	1.25	0.30	0.38
Yr.	E1.47	1.04	1.26	2.58	1.91	1.72

Next earnings report expected: late-January Source: S&P, Company Reports
EPS Estimates based on S&P Operating Earnings; historical GAAP earnings are as reported.

Plum Creek Timber Company, Inc.

Recommendation: **SELL** ★ ★ ☆ ☆ ☆   12-Month Target Price: **$25.00** (as of January 22, 2004)

Business Summary November 04, 2004

Plum Creek Timber Co., a real estate investment trust (REIT), is the second largest U.S. private timberland owner. PCL owns about 8.1 million acres of timberlands, in 21 states. In addition, the trust operates four wood products manufacturing facilities. PCL attempts to maximize the value of its timberlands through intensive silviculture management techniques. It diversifies its timber holdings through the acquisition of timberlands.

The trust conducts operations through five business segments: Northern resources and Southern resources (accounting together for 58% of 2003 revenues), manufacturing (31%), real estate (10%), and natural resources (1%).

The Northern resources segment encompasses 3.7 million acres of timberlands, in Idaho, Maine, Michigan, Montana, New Hampshire, Oregon, Pennsylvania, Washington, West Virginia, western Virginia, and Wisconsin. The segment has an estimated 132 million tons of standing timber. Harvested logs are sold primarily to U.S. mills, and for export to Canada, with a small portion going to Pacific Rim countries.

The Southern resources segment consists of 4.1 million acres of timberlands (including 350,000 acres of leased land), located in Alabama, Arkansas, Florida, Georgia, Louisiana, Mississippi, North and South Carolina, Oklahoma, Texas, and eastern Virginia. The segment has an estimated 165 million tons of standing

timber. Harvested logs are sold to third party mills that produce forest products, including lumber, plywood, oriented strand board, and pulp and paper products.

The real estate segment is involved in selling higher and better use lands. PCL estimates that, out of its 8.1 million acres, about 1.35 million acres are of higher and better use timberlands, which it expects to sell over the next 15 years for conservation, residential, and recreational purposes. It also estimates that it has 1.4 million acres of non-strategic timberlands.

The trust's manufacturing operations include four lumber mills, two plywood plants, two medium density fiberboard (MDF) facilities, and two lumber remanufacturing facilities. The facilities convert logs into lumber, plywood, and other wood products, and convert sawdust and wood shavings into MDF. PCL's plywood products focus on the specialty plywood products market, which includes boat, recreational vehicle, and fiberglass-reinforced panel manufacturing.

In the 2004 first quarter, PCL agreed to sell its working interest in its natural resources joint venture to its partner, Geomet, for $27 million, with contingent additional sales proceeds of up to $3 million payable in 2008. The transaction closed in the 2004 second quarter. PCL retained its royalty interest in the project and the sales agreement provided for contingent sales proceeds of up to $3 million payable in 2008.

Company Financials Fiscal Year ending December 31

Per Share Data ($)

(Year Ended December 31)	2003	2002	2001	2000	1999	1998	1997	1996	1995	1994
Tangible Bk. Val.	11.57	12.04	12.21	7.46	7.70	8.78	10.14	10.58	5.76	5.49
Cash Flow	1.63	1.82	3.00	2.47	3.10	3.12	3.93	6.74	4.07	3.69
Earnings	1.04	1.26	2.58	1.91	1.72	0.90	1.72	4.71	2.17	2.36
S&P Core Earnings	1.04	1.24	2.57	NA	NA	NA	NA	NA	NA	NA
Dividends	1.40	1.49	2.85	2.28	2.28	2.26	2.16	2.00	1.90	1.62
Payout Ratio	135%	118%	110%	119%	133%	NM	126%	42%	88%	69%
Prices - High	30.75	31.98	30.00	29.81	32.12	34.87	36.00	27.75	26.75	32.50
- Low	20.88	18.92	23.30	21.50	23.12	23.43	25.75	22.87	19.87	19.62
P/E Ratio - High	30	25	12	16	19	39	21	6	12	14
- Low	20	15	9	11	13	26	15	5	9	8

Income Statement Analysis (Million $)

	2003	2002	2001	2000	1999	1998	1997	1996	1995	1994
Revs.	1,196	1,137	598	209	461	699	726	634	585	579
Oper. Inc.	410	443	305	166	206	210	244	222	213	218
Depr.	107	105	55.0	38.9	59.7	69.3	70.2	56.9	54.1	54.1
Int. Exp.	117	103	54.0	46.8	63.5	60.6	60.4	50.1	46.8	47.4
Pretax Inc.	186	235	196	132	100	76.0	112	225	111	113
Eff. Tax Rate	NM	0.85%	NM	NM	NM	0.68%	0.07%	0.60%	0.50%	0.80%
Net Inc.	192	233	338	132	113	75.4	112	224	111	95.9
S&P Core Earnings	193	229	336	NA	NA	NA	NA	NA	NA	NA

Balance Sheet & Other Fin. Data (Million $)

	2003	2002	2001	2000	1999	1998	1997	1996	1995	1994
Cash	260	246	193	181	115	114	135	124	87.6	60.9
Curr. Assets	405	378	306	195	133	210	232	222	174	149
Total Assets	4,387	4,289	4,122	1,250	1,251	1,438	1,301	1,356	826	823
Curr. Liab.	168	155	149	180	74.2	80.9	74.0	69.0	62.4	55.8
LT Debt	2,031	1,839	1,667	560	643	943	745	763	517	531
Common Equity	2,119	2,222	2,247	507	533	405	470	490	234	223
Total Cap.	4,187	4,105	3,952	1,066	1,176	1,348	1,215	1,253	751	754
Cap. Exp.	246	231	59.0	21.7	25.6	54.9	28.3	19.3	30.7	26.0
Cash Flow	299	338	393	171	173	145	182	281	165	150
Curr. Ratio	2.4	2.4	2.1	1.1	1.8	2.6	3.1	3.2	2.8	2.7
% LT Debt of Cap.	48.5	44.8	42.2	52.5	54.7	69.9	61.3	60.9	68.8	70.4
% Net Inc.of Revs.	16.1	20.5	56.5	63.1	24.6	10.8	15.4	35.3	19.0	16.6
% Ret. on Assets	4.4	5.5	11.8	10.5	8.4	5.5	8.5	20.7	13.4	11.7
% Ret. on Equity	8.8	10.4	28.3	25.4	24.2	17.2	23.2	61.7	48.5	46.2

Data as orig reptd.; bef. results of disc opers/spec. items. Per share data adj. for stk. divs. Bold denotes primary EPS - prior periods restated. E-Estimated. NA-Not Available. NM-Not Meaningful. NR-Not Ranked. UR-Under Review.

Office: 999 3rd Ave Ste 4300, Seattle, WA 98104-4096.
Telephone: 206-467-3600.
Email: info@plumcreek.com
Website: http://www.plumcreek.com
Chrmn: D.D. Leland.
Pres & CEO: R.R. Holley.

EVP & CFO: W.R. Brown.
SVP, Secy & General Counsel: J.A. Kraft.
VP & Treas: D.W. Lambert.
Investor Contact: J. Hobbs 800-858-5347.
Dirs: I. B. Davidson, R. R. Holley, R. Josephs, D. D. Leland, J. G. McDonald, H. R. Moghadam, J. H. Scully, S. C. Tobias, C. B. Webb.

Founded: in 1989.
Domicile: Delaware.
Employees: 2,040.
S&P Analyst: Bryon J. Korutz/MF/BK

PMC-Sierra, Inc.

Recommendation: **SELL** ★★☆☆☆
SELL SELL HOLD BUY BUY

12-Month Target Price: **$7.00**
(as of September 21, 2004)

PMCS has an approximate 0.02% weighting in the **S&P 500**

Sector: Information Technology
Sub-Industry: Semiconductors
Peer Group: Semiconductors Communications IC

Summary: PMC-Sierra designs, develops, markets and supports high-performance semiconductor networking solutions for advanced communications markets.

Quantitative Evaluations

S&P Earnings & Dividend Rank: C

| D | C | B- | B | B+ | A- | A | A+ |

S&P Fair Value Rank: 1-

| 1 | 2 | 3 | 4 | 5 |
| Lowest | | | | Highest |

Fair Value Calc.: $6.30 (Overvalued)

S&P Investability Quotient Percentile
66%

PMCS scored higher than 66% of all companies for which an S&P Report is available.

Volatility: High

| Low | Average | High |

Technical Evaluation: Bullish
Since 11/04, the technical indicators for PMCS have been Bullish.

Relative Strength Rank: Strong
78
1 Lowest   Highest 99

| Price as of 11/12/04: | $11.23 | 2004E S&P Core EPS: | $-0.35 |

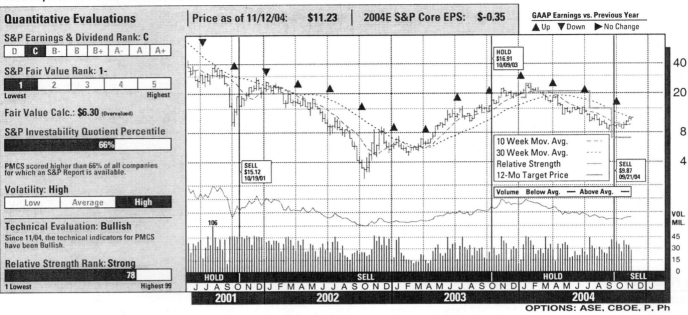

GAAP Earnings vs. Previous Year
▲ Up   ▼ Down   ▶ No Change

HOLD $16.91 10/09/03

10 Week Mov. Avg.
30 Week Mov. Avg.
Relative Strength
12-Mo Target Price

Volume Below Avg. — Above Avg. —

SELL $15.12 10/19/01

SELL $9.87 09/21/04

106

VOL. MIL.
45
30
15
0

HOLD   SELL   HOLD   SELL

J J A S O N D J F M A M J J A S O N D J F M A M J J A S O N D J F M A M J J A S O N D J
2001   2002   2003   2004

OPTIONS: ASE, CBOE, P, Ph

Analyst commentary prepared by Zaineb Bokhari/MF/JWP

Highlights November 08, 2004

- Results for the third quarter of 2004 were negatively impacted by an abrupt slowdown in asymmetric DSL line deployments in China and excess supply chain inventory of semiconductor components in general. We expect these market conditions to persist over the next several months, and look for revenues to decline sequentially in the December quarter. We expect revenues to increase 19% in 2004, as strong revenue growth in the first half of the year offsets weaker growth expected for the second half. We look for revenue growth of 1.3% in 2005, due to difficult year to year comparisons, particularly in the first half of the year.

- We expect gross margins to widen to 70% in 2004, from 65% in 2003, supported by the high volume of sales in the first half of 2004. We expect gross margins to narrow modestly in 2005, but we look for an improvement throughout the year as sales volumes recover from the expected lows in the December 2004 quarter. We see operating margins widening in 2005 from 2004 as the company maintains tight control over discretionary spending in the weaker sales environment.

- We estimate 2004 pro forma EPS, excluding goodwill, acquisition expenses and other items, of $0.18, rising to $0.22 in 2005. Our Standard and Poor's Core EPS estimates are for losses of $0.35 in 2004 and $0.33 in 2005, reflecting option-related expense.

Investment Rationale/Risk November 08, 2004

- We continue to recommend that investors avoid these very volatile shares. We view the company as exposed to demand for communications equipment, which has been very volatile, and note that we have low visibility into results in coming periods. Visibility is further impacted due to the company's volatile "turns business" which represents orders placed and shipped in the same quarter. In addition, we think the company lacks economies of scale that would enable it to capture the manufacturing efficiency of a traditional semiconductor supplier.

- Risks to our opinion and target price include stronger than expected demand for communications equipment.

- PMCS's earnings recovery has been choppy, although we believe there is a possibility of a rapid pickup once demand returns. Our 12-month target price of $7 is based on a P/E multiple of 32X applied to our 2005 EPS estimate. This reflects a P/E to growth ratio of 1.3X, based on our longer-term projection of 25% annual growth.

Key Stock Statistics

S&P Core EPS 2005E	-0.33	52-week Range	$24.91-8.22
S&P Oper. EPS 2004E	0.18	12 Month P/E	44.9
P/E on S&P Oper. EPS 2004E	62.4	Beta	NA
S&P Oper. EPS 2005E	0.22	Shareholders	1,423
Yield (%)	Nil	Market Cap (B)	$ 2.0
Dividend Rate/Share	Nil	Shares Outstanding (M)	178.2

Value of $10,000 invested five years ago: **$ 2,359**

Dividend Data

No cash dividends have been paid.

Revenues/Earnings Data Fiscal year ending December 31

Revenues (Million $)

	2004	2003	2002	2001	2000	1999
1Q	78.66	55.39	51.44	119.9	114.2	50.14
2Q	85.70	60.38	54.51	94.13	150.2	59.29
3Q	71.17	63.10	59.58	61.56	198.1	71.60
4Q	—	70.62	52.56	47.16	231.7	80.60
Yr.	—	249.5	218.1	322.7	694.7	262.5

Earnings Per Share ($)

	2004	2003	2002	2001	2000	1999
1Q	0.09	-0.07	-0.08	-0.38	0.16	0.09
2Q	0.08	-0.05	-0.07	-1.39	0.22	0.27
3Q	0.03	0.02	-0.05	-0.20	-0.31	0.13
4Q	E Nil	0.05	-0.18	-1.82	0.24	0.15
Yr.	E0.18	-0.05	-0.38	-3.80	0.41	0.59

Next earnings report expected: late-January Source: S&P, Company Reports
EPS Estimates based on S&P Operating Earnings; historical GAAP earnings are as reported.

PMC-Sierra, Inc.

Recommendation: **SELL** ★ ★ ☆ ☆ ☆   12-Month Target Price: **$7.00** (as of September 21, 2004)

Business Summary November 08, 2004

PMC-Sierra designs, develops, markets and supports high-performance semiconductor networking solutions for broadband communications. The company's chips are used in high-speed transmission and networking systems that are being used to restructure the global telecommunications and data communications infrastructure. PMCS offers more than 120 integrated circuit components, used in equipment for the Access, Metro, Enterprise/Storage and Consumer segments of the Internet infrastructure. Less than 10% of revenue comes from Storage or Consumer, and the company aims to expand in these areas. Chip offerings include transceivers, framers and mappers, packet cell and cell processors, traffic managers and switch fabrics, serializers/deserializers, and microprocessors. PMCS also provides related technical service and support to equipment manufacturers.

The primary growth drivers for PMCS's business are the emergence of the Internet, the upgrade of corporate data networks, and remote access. The common element of these drivers is high bandwidth demand for data. Legacy telecommunications networks were designed for voice processing, but new network deployments are being optimized for data transfer and packet processing. Increased data traffic has led to emphasis on network infrastructure systems designed to handle large amounts of information without sacrificing speed of data transfer. Excess capacity in communication service provider infrastructures contributed to revenue declines since the boom year of 2002.

The communications chip markets are global: 52% of 2003 sales came from

outside the U.S., up from 5% in 2002 and 42% in 2001. The customer base includes Nortel, Alcatel, Samsung and Lucent. In 2003, Cisco Systems and Hewlett-Packard each accounted for over 10% of sales.

As a fabless semiconductor supplier, PMCS outsources production to independent foundries and chip assemblers; this lets the company focus on design efforts. Foundry partners include Chartered Semiconductor, Taiwan Semiconductor, and IBM. PMCS avoids the overhead associated with owning and maintaining a fabrication plant, allowing consistently wide gross margins (typically above 70% in boom times, and near 58% at the 2001 industry cycle bottom) compared to those of most vertically integrated chip companies. The company's chips have highly complex design content, and sell in relatively low volumes; this also contributes to wide gross margins.

The company's executive offices and much of its operations are located in Santa Clara, CA, and Burnaby, BC. PMCS has design centers across the U.S. and Canada. In 2003, 36% of orders were handled by distributors.

PMCS has pursued a large number of acquisitions to add technological expertise and let the company address larger market segments. Eight acquisitions in 2000 helped boost headcount substantially, from 660 at the end of 1999 to 1,726 at the end of 2000. Restructuring prompted by an industry downturn brought headcount down to 1,099 at the end of 2002, and to 930 at 2003 year end.

Company Financials Fiscal Year ending December 31

Per Share Data ($)

(Year Ended December 31)	2003	2002	2001	2000	1999	1998	1997	1996	1995	1994
Tangible Bk. Val.	1.25	1.14	1.59	3.24	1.61	0.85	0.69	0.34	0.63	0.23
Cash Flow	0.12	-0.13	-3.22	0.82	0.74	0.09	0.33	-0.31	0.29	-0.02
Earnings	-0.05	-0.38	-3.80	0.41	0.59	-0.02	0.26	-0.41	0.21	-0.10
S&P Core Earnings	-0.43	-0.94	-3.35	NA	NA	NA	NA	NA	NA	NA
Dividends	Nil	Nil	Nil	Nil	Nil	Nil	Nil	Nil	Nil	Nil
Payout Ratio	Nil	Nil	Nil	Nil	Nil	Nil	Nil	Nil	Nil	Nil
Prices - High	22.81	26.80	111.75	255.50	80.56	16.40	8.78	6.18	7.18	2.03
- Low	4.64	2.70	9.37	60.00	15.67	5.71	3.46	1.96	1.90	0.84
P/E Ratio - High	NM	NM	NM	NM	NM	NM	33	NM	34	NM
- Low	NM	NM	NM	NM	NM	NM	13	NM	9	NM

Income Statement Analysis (Million $)

	2003	2002	2001	2000	1999	1998	1997	1996	1995	1994
Revs.	249	218	323	695	262	162	127	188	189	109
Oper. Inc.	23.5	-33.0	-93.1	251	119	74.7	56.7	36.5	36.4	4.00
Depr.	28.4	42.4	98.0	74.2	21.2	14.2	9.20	10.9	8.89	6.66
Int. Exp.	Nil	Nil	Nil	Nil	Nil	0.96	1.90	1.28	0.89	0.44
Pretax Inc.	-15.8	-83.9	-657	178	132	20.0	50.0	-38.4	34.7	-7.07
Eff. Tax Rate	NM	NM	NM	57.6%	31.6%	NM	31.5%	NM	30.9%	NM
Net Inc.	-7.99	-65.0	-639	75.3	90.0	-2.88	34.3	-48.1	24.0	-8.58
S&P Core Earnings	-74.5	-159	-563	NA	NA	NA	NA	NA	NA	NA

Balance Sheet & Other Fin. Data (Million $)

	2003	2002	2001	2000	1999	1998	1997	1996	1995	1994
Cash	290	75.8	152	256	84.1	33.9	69.2	42.1	45.9	15.9
Curr. Assets	464	476	494	571	254	123	93.5	68.3	110	56.7
Total Assets	553	729	855	1,126	342	197	149	130	185	92.0
Curr. Liab.	147	247	280	230	89.1	54.9	34.9	47.9	77.2	32.9
LT Debt	175	275	275	0.56	1.08	5.22	9.10	18.4	8.98	6.23
Common Equity	226	199	272	851	236	126	90.6	48.4	81.0	34.6
Total Cap.	401	476	576	896	246	134	115	79.3	108	58.9
Cap. Exp.	11.7	3.14	27.8	104	30.7	21.5	8.20	4.00	10.9	6.60
Cash Flow	20.4	-22.6	-541	149	111	11.3	43.5	-37.2	32.9	-1.90
Curr. Ratio	3.2	1.9	1.8	2.5	2.9	2.2	2.7	1.4	1.4	1.7
% LT Debt of Cap.	43.6	57.7	47.8	0.1	0.4	3.9	7.9	23.2	8.3	10.6
% Net Inc.of Revs.	NM	NM	NM	10.8	34.3	NM	27.0	NM	12.7	NM
% Ret. on Assets	NM	NM	NM	9.9	32.9	NM	24.6	NM	17.3	NM
% Ret. on Equity	NM	NM	NM	14.0	49.1	NM	49.4	NM	41.5	NM

Data as orig reptd.; bef. results of disc opers/spec. items. Per share data adj. for stk. divs. Bold denotes primary EPS - prior periods restated. E-Estimated. NA-Not Available. NM-Not Meaningful. NR-Not Ranked. UR-Under Review.

Office: 3975 Freedom Cir, Santa Clara, CA 95054.
Telephone: 408-239-8000.
Email: investor_relations@pmc-sierra.com
Website: http://www.pmc-sierra.com
Chrmn: A. Balkanski.
Pres & CEO: R.L. Bailey.

Vice Chrmn: J. Diller.
COO: G. Aasen.
VP & CFO: A. Krock.
Investor Contact: D. Climie 408-988-8276.
Dirs: R. Bailey, A. Balkanski, R. Belluzzo, J. V. Diller, W. Kurtz, F. J. Marshall, L. O. Wilks.

Founded: in 1983.
Domicile: Delaware.
Employees: 930.
S&P Analyst: Zaineb Bokhari/MF/JWP

The McGraw·Hill Companies

STANDARD &POOR'S

PNC Financial Services

Recommendation: **HOLD** ★★★☆☆
SELL · SELL · HOLD · BUY · BUY

12-Month Target Price: **$57.00**
(as of January 21, 2004)

PNC has an approximate 0.14% weighting in the **S&P 500**

Sector: Financials
Sub-Industry: Regional Banks
Peer Group: Northeast Larger Regional Banks

Summary: This bank holding company (formerly PNC Bank Corp.) conducts regional banking, wholesale banking and asset management businesses.

Quantitative Evaluations

S&P Earnings & Dividend Rank: B+

| D | C | B- | B | B+ | A- | A | A+ |

S&P Fair Value Rank: 2

| 1 | 2 | 3 | 4 | 5 |
Lowest   Highest

Fair Value Calc.: $49.70 (Slightly Overvalued)

S&P Investability Quotient Percentile

93%

PNC scored higher than 93% of all companies for which an S&P Report is available.

Volatility: Low

| Low | Average | High |

Technical Evaluation: Neutral
Since 11/04, the technical indicators for PNC have been Neutral.

Relative Strength Rank: Moderate

| 52 |
1 Lowest   Highest 99

Price as of 11/12/04: $55.70 | **2004E S&P Core EPS:** $4.10

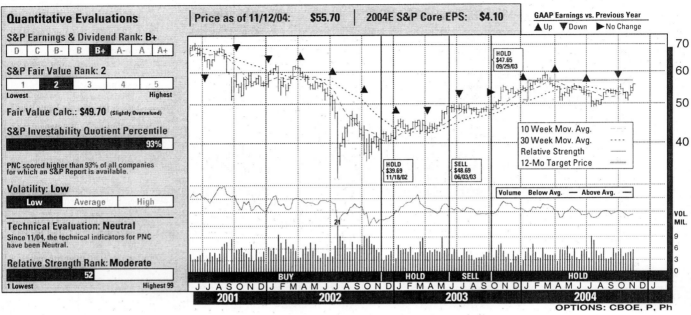

GAAP Earnings vs. Previous Year
▲ Up ▼ Down ► No Change

HOLD $47.65 09/29/03
HOLD $39.69 11/18/02
SELL $48.69 06/03/03

10 Week Mov. Avg.
30 Week Mov. Avg.
Relative Strength
12-Mo Target Price

Volume Below Avg. — Above Avg. —

VOL. MIL.
9 6 3 0

BUY | HOLD | SELL | HOLD
J J A S O N D J F M A M J J A S O N D J F M A M J J A S O N D J F M A M J J A S O N D J
2001   2002   2003   2004

OPTIONS: CBOE, P, Ph

Analyst commentary prepared by James M. O'Brien /CB/BK

Highlights 15-NOV-04

- We believe 2004 third quarter results were mostly driven by an improvement in credit quality and balance sheet growth. For the rest of 2004 and into 2005, we expect growth in fee income, which accounts for two-thirds of total revenue, and tighter expense controls to be the main drivers of results.
- We think asset quality has stabilized, with solid improvement demonstrated thus far in 2004. We believe expense control remains one of management's challenges. Our model assumes that expense growth will trail fee income growth in the quarters ahead.
- Overall, we expect 2004 operating EPS to increase to $4.06, from $3.65 in 2003. Our 2004 EPS estimate reflects our growth expectations of 10% a year for the longer term, and is based primarily on our assumptions of a stronger economy and slightly rising interest rates in coming periods. Our 2005 EPS estimate is $4.50.

Investment Rationale/Risk 15-NOV-04

- We believe that regulatory risk has lessened, and do not see regulatory concerns as likely to be the primary determinants of the stock's performance in coming quarters, following the lifting of the company's formal written agreement with federal regulators in September 2003. However, we think the uncertainty revolving around the pending Riggs National Corp. acquisition could distract senior management and create short-term investor uncertainty. In our view, investors eventually will focus on PNC's fundamental outlook, which we view as remaining neutral. We think that fee income growth and improved credit quality will be the main drivers in 2005, partly offset by relatively weak loan volumes in most of the bank's business units.
- Risks to our recommendation and target price include acquisition integration risk, and general interest rate and economic risk.
- The stock traded recently at 12X our 2005 EPS estimate, versus an average multiple of 12X for the past two years, and 14X for the past three years. Our 12-month target price of $57 reflects a peer P/E multiple of 13X our 2005 EPS estimate of $4.50.

Key Stock Statistics

S&P Oper. EPS 2004E	4.06	52-week Range	$59.79-48.90
P/E on S&P Oper. EPS 2004E	13.7	12 Month P/E	13.2
S&P Oper. EPS 2005E	4.50	Beta	0.62
Yield (%)	3.6%	Shareholders	50,034
Dividend Rate/Share	2.00	Market Cap (B)	$ 15.7
Shares Outstanding (M)	282.4		

Value of $10,000 invested five years ago: **$ 11,045**

Dividend Data Dividends have been paid since 1865

Amount ($)	Date Decl.	Ex-Div. Date	Stock of Record	Payment Date
0.500	Jan. 06	Jan. 12	Jan. 14	Jan. 24 '04
0.500	Apr. 06	Apr. 12	Apr. 14	Apr. 24 '04
0.500	Jul. 06	Jul. 12	Jul. 14	Jul. 24 '04
0.500	Oct. 07	Oct. 13	Oct. 15	Oct. 24 '04

Revenues/Earnings Data Fiscal year ending December 31

Revenues (Million $)

	2004	2003	2002	2001	2000	1999
1Q	1,577	1,487	1,648	1,873	1,889	2,021
2Q	1,395	1,468	1,674	1,799	1,908	1,868
3Q	—	1,493	1,540	1,691	1,901	1,863
4Q	—	1,521	1,507	1,317	1,925	1,914
Yr.	—	5,969	6,369	6,680	7,623	7,666

Earnings Per Share ($)

	2004	2003	2002	2001	2000	1999
1Q	1.15	0.92	1.11	0.89	1.01	1.05
2Q	1.07	0.65	1.12	1.00	1.01	1.03
3Q	0.91	1.00	1.00	0.84	1.01	1.06
4Q	E0.93	1.08	0.97	-1.52	1.06	1.01
Yr.	E4.06	3.65	4.20	1.26	4.09	4.15

Next earnings report expected: late-January Source: S&P, Company Reports
EPS Estimates based on S&P Operating Earnings; historical GAAP earnings are as reported.

The PNC Financial Services Group, Inc.

Recommendation: **HOLD** ★ ★ ★ ☆ ☆   12-Month Target Price: **$57.00** (as of January 21, 2004)

Business Summary 15-NOV-04

PNC Financial Services Group (formerly PNC Bank Corp.) is a bank holding company that operates regional banking, corporate banking, real estate finance, asset-based lending, wealth management, asset management and global fund services. Its primary market area includes Pennsylvania, New Jersey, Delaware, Ohio and Kentucky.

Operations are currently divided into seven lines of business. Regional community banking provides credit, deposit, branch-based brokerage and electronic banking products and services to retail customers, as well as deposit, credit, treasury management and capital markets products to small businesses. Corporate banking provides credit, equipment leasing, capital markets and treasury management products and services mainly to mid-size corporations and government entities. PNC Real Estate Finance provides credit, capital markets, treasury management, commercial mortgage loan servicing and other products to developers, owners and investors in commercial real estate. PNC Business Credit provides asset-based lending, capital markets and treasury management products and services to middle market customers nationally. PNC Advisors offers customized investment products and services, including full-service brokerage, to affluent customers. BlackRock, which is 69%-owned, manages assets for institutions and individuals through a variety of fixed income, liquidity, equity and alternative

investment products, including the proprietary BlackRock family of funds. PFPC, the largest full-service mutual fund transfer agent, provides a range of fund services to the investment management industry.

In 2003, average earning assets, from which interest income is derived, amounted to $55.2 billion, and consisted mainly of loans (63%) and investment securities (28%). Average sources of funds included interest-bearing deposits (51%), noninterest-bearing deposits (17%), other borrowings (14%), shareholders' equity (10%) and other (7%).

At December 31, 2003, nonperforming assets, mainly non-accrual loans and foreclosed assets, totaled $328 million (0.92% of loans and related assets), versus $418 million (1.13%) a year earlier. The allowance for loan losses, which is set aside for possible loan defaults, was $632 million (1.85% of loans), versus $673 million (1.90%) a year earlier. Net chargeoffs (loans written off as uncollectible) were $211 million (0.61% of average loans) in 2003, versus $211 million (0.60%). In January 2004, PNC acquired United National Bancorp, a bank holding company with over $3 billion in assets. United Trust, a subsidiary provides commercial and retail banking services through 45 branches in New Jersey and seven branches in Pennsylavania.

Company Financials Fiscal Year ending December 31

Per Share Data ($)

(Year Ended December 31)	2003	2002	2001	2000	1999	1998	1997	1996	1995	1994
Tangible Bk. Val.	14.22	14.78	12.19	13.37	12.07	11.49	12.47	13.08	13.21	15.80
Earnings	3.65	4.20	1.26	4.09	4.15	3.60	3.28	2.90	1.19	2.57
S&P Core Earnings	3.53	3.83	0.92	NA	NA	NA	NA	NA	NA	NA
Dividends	1.94	1.92	1.92	1.83	1.68	1.58	1.50	1.42	1.40	1.31
Payout Ratio	53%	46%	152%	45%	40%	44%	46%	49%	118%	51%
Prices - High	55.55	62.80	75.81	75.00	62.00	66.75	58.75	39.75	32.37	31.62
- Low	41.63	32.70	51.14	36.00	43.00	38.75	36.50	27.50	21.12	20.00
P/E Ratio - High	15	15	60	18	15	19	18	14	27	12
- Low	11	8	41	9	10	11	11	9	18	8

Income Statement Analysis (Million $)

	2003	2002	2001	2000	1999	1998	1997	1996	1995	1994
Net Int. Inc.	1,996	2,197	2,262	2,164	2,433	2,573	2,495	2,444	2,142	1,936
Tax Equiv. Adj.	NA	NA	NA	18.0	22.0	49.0	99	35.0	46.6	33.5
Non Int. Inc.	3,141	3,108	2,412	2,871	2,723	2,503	1,759	1,373	1,240	931
Loan Loss Prov.	177	309	903	136	163	225	70.0	Nil	6.00	60.1
Exp./Op. Revs.	67.7%	60.8%	71.4%	60.8%	60.3%	63.6%	61.5%	60.0%	72.0%	61.0%
Pretax Inc.	1,600	1,858	564	1,848	1,891	1,710	1,618	1,527	627	902
Eff. Tax Rate	33.7%	33.4%	33.2%	34.3%	33.2%	34.8%	35.0%	35.0%	34.9%	32.4%
Net Inc.	1,029	1,200	377	1,214	1,264	1,115	1,052	992	408	610
% Net Int. Marg.	3.64	3.99	3.84	3.64	3.68	3.85	3.94	3.83	3.15	3.40
S&P Core Earnings	993	1,093	270	NA	NA	NA	NA	NA	NA	NA

Balance Sheet & Other Fin. Data (Million $)

	2003	2002	2001	2000	1999	1998	1997	1996	1995	1994
Money Mkt. Assets	50.0	3,658	1,335	1,151	1,148	1,014	1,526	774	1,611	809
Inv. Securities	16,409	17,421	15,243	7,053	8,759	8,088	8,522	11,917	15,839	20,921
Com'l Loans	15,987	22,335	23,134	28,635	24,198	25,182	19,989	18,062	16,812	12,445
Other Loans	18,093	13,115	14,840	21,966	26,572	32,468	34,668	33,736	32,244	23,689
Total Assets	68,168	66,377	69,568	69,844	75,413	77,207	75,120	73,260	73,404	64,145
Demand Deposits	11,505	9,538	10,124	8,490	8,441	9,943	10,158	10,937	10,707	6,992
Time Deposits	33,736	35,444	37,180	39,174	38,227	37,553	37,491	34,739	36,192	28,019
LT Debt	7,667	9,112	8,922	7,266	9,395	10,994	11,523	11,744	10,398	11,754
Common Equity	6,735	6,943	5,822	6,649	5,939	6,036	5,377	5,862	5,767	4,375
% Ret. on Assets	1.5	1.8	0.5	1.7	1.7	1.5	1.4	1.4	0.5	1.0
% Ret. on Equity	15.0	18.7	5.9	19.0	20.8	19.2	18.4	17.0	7.1	14.1
% Loan Loss Resv.	1.8	1.8	1.5	1.3	1.2	1.3	1.8	2.3	2.6	2.8
% Loans/Deposits	78.4	82.4	89.1	109.6	119.7	121.4	111.8	113.4	105.2	102.5
% Equity to Assets	10.2	9.4	8.9	9.0	7.8	7.5	7.6	7.9	7.6	7.1

Data as orig reptd.; bef. results of disc opers/spec. items. Per share data adj. for stk. divs.; EPS diluted. E-Estimated. NA-Not Available. NM-Not Meaningful. NR-Not Ranked. UR-Under Review.

Office: 249 Fifth Avenue, Pittsburgh, PA 15222-2707.
Telephone: 412-762-2000.
Email: corporate.communiations@pncbank.com
Website: http://www.pnc.com
Chrmn & CEO: J. E. Rohr.
CFO & Vice Chrmn: W. S. Demchak.

Vice Chrmn: W. C. Mutterperl.
Dirs: P. W. Chellgren, R. N. Clay, J. G. Cooper, G. A. Davidson, Jr., R. Kelson, B. C. Lindsay, A. Massaro, T. H. O'Brien, J. G. Pepper, J. E. Rohr, L. K. Steffes, D. F. Strigl, S. G. Thieke, T. J. Usher, M. A. Washington, H. H. Wehmeier.

Founded: in 1922.
Domicile: Pennsylvania.
Employees: 23,200.
S&P Analyst: James M. O'Brien /CB/BK

Power-One, Inc.

Recommendation: **HOLD** ★★★☆☆ | SELL SELL HOLD BUY BUY

12-Month Target Price: **$9.00**
(as of September 23, 2004)

PWER has an approximate 0.01% weighting in the **S&P 500**

Sector: Industrials
Sub-Industry: Electrical Components & Equipment
Peer Group: Power Supply - Larger

Summary: PWER manufactures power conversion products designed primarily for communications infrastructure applications.

Quantitative Evaluations

S&P Earnings & Dividend Rank: NR

| D | C | B- | B | B+ | A- | A | A+ |

S&P Fair Value Rank: 1

| 1 | 2 | 3 | 4 | 5 |
Lowest — Highest

Fair Value Calc.: $5.20 (Overvalued)

S&P Investability Quotient Percentile

66%

PWER scored higher than 66% of all companies for which an S&P Report is available.

Volatility: High

| Low | Average | **High** |

Technical Evaluation: Bullish
Since 11/04, the technical indicators for PWER have been Bullish.

Relative Strength Rank: Strong

88
1 Lowest — Highest 99

| Price as of 11/12/04: | **$8.52** | 2004E S&P Core EPS: | **$-0.39** |

GAAP Earnings vs. Previous Year
▲ Up ▼ Down ▶ No Change

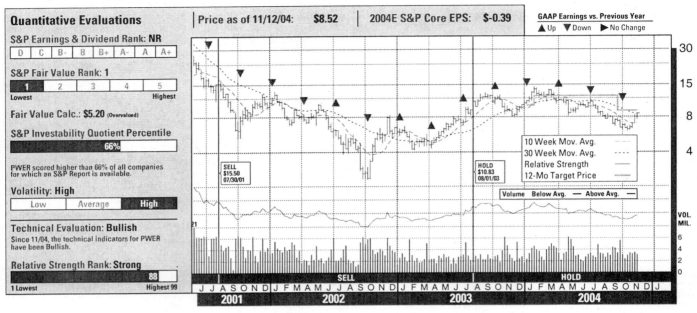

- 10 Week Mov. Avg.
- 30 Week Mov. Avg.
- Relative Strength
- 12-Mo Target Price

Volume Below Avg. — Above Avg.

SELL $15.50 07/30/01
HOLD $10.83 08/01/03

SELL — HOLD
J J A S O N D J F M A M J J A S O N D J F M A M J J A S O N D J F M A M J J A S O N D J
2001 2002 2003 2004

Analyst commentary prepared by Bryon J. Korutz/MF/BK

Highlights November 12, 2004

- We see sales gains of about 7.7% in 2004 and 10% in 2005. We see sales boosted by the introduction of new products, and by improved demand related to an expected increase in capital spending at wireless companies. We project that demand for PWER's AC/DC and DC/DC power supplies will firm, but see weakness in DC power systems.

- In light of ongoing aggressive cost cuts, and based on our expectations that sales conditions will likely grow slightly more favorable as 2004 progresses, we expect the company to post a small profit in the fourth quarter. Looking to 2005, we see gross margins widening to 40%, from 37% expected in 2004. We think that PWER's cash and investment balance of about $86.5 million at the end of the 2004 third quarter, combined with what we view as a low level of debt, should enable the company to be one of the surviving industry suppliers.

- We forecast a loss of $0.39 a share for 2004 under Standard & Poor's Core Earnings methodology, with the difference from our operating estimate of a loss of $0.12 reflecting projected option expense.

Investment Rationale/Risk November 12, 2004

- We would not add to positions in the shares, despite what appears to be a favorable valuation, reflecting our concerns about the stock's volatility and the pace of recovery in the company's end markets.

- Risks to our recommendation and target price include slower recovery of end markets and weakness in the acceptance of new products.

- Our discounted cash flow model, which assumes a weighted average cost of capital of 14.9% over the next five years and 10.9% thereafter, a compound average annual free cash flow growth rate of 5.4% over the next 15 years, and 3% growth in perpetuity, values the stock at $9 a share. A historical price to sales ratio of 2.67X applied to our 2005 revenue estimate gives value of $10 a share. Our 12-month target price of $9 is a blend of our two valuation metrics.

Key Stock Statistics

S&P Core EPS 2005E	-0.12	52-week Range	$14.38-6.00
S&P Oper. EPS 2004E	-0.12	12 Month P/E	NM
P/E on S&P Oper. EPS 2004E	NM	Beta	NA
S&P Oper. EPS 2005E	0.10	Shareholders	344
Yield (%)	Nil	Market Cap (B)	$0.715
Dividend Rate/Share	Nil	Shares Outstanding (M)	83.9

Value of $10,000 invested five years ago: **$ 12,244**

Dividend Data

No cash dividends have been paid.

Revenues/Earnings Data Fiscal year ending December 31

Revenues (Million $)

	2004	2003	2002	2001	2000	1999
1Q	68.65	56.32	48.40	169.9	77.01	34.83
2Q	72.51	69.33	56.19	92.90	113.8	46.57
3Q	67.24	63.66	60.04	53.10	150.4	61.24
4Q	—	67.02	66.03	47.88	169.7	62.76
Yr.	—	256.3	230.7	363.7	511.0	205.4

Earnings Per Share ($)

	2004	2003	2002	2001	2000	1999
1Q	-0.03	-0.04	-0.09	0.20	-0.02	-0.07
2Q	-0.05	-0.01	-0.13	-1.02	0.14	0.04
3Q	-0.06	-0.04	-2.45	-0.55	0.20	0.08
4Q	E-0.05	-0.12	0.06	-1.00	0.23	0.10
Yr.	E-0.12	-0.22	-2.62	-2.36	0.56	0.18

Next earnings report expected: late-January Source: S&P, Company Reports
EPS Estimates based on S&P Operating Earnings; historical GAAP earnings are as reported.

Power-One, Inc.

Recommendation: **HOLD** ★ ★ ★ ☆ ☆   12-Month Target Price: **$9.00** (as of September 23, 2004)

Business Summary November 12, 2004

A maker of power conversion products, Power-One develops products primarily for the communications infrastructure market. Growth in its primary market had been fueled by the proliferation of Internet usage and the convergence of voice, data and video applications. However, several years of exceptionally strong growth in infrastructure markets came to an abrupt halt in late 2000. With hundreds of different products, PWER believes it is one of only a few companies that can power virtually every segment of a communications infrastructure network. In 2003, 63% of revenues (56% in 2002) came from sales outside North America (mainly Europe).

PWER has four primary divisions: Compact Advanced Power Solutions (CAPS), Energy Solutions (ES), Silicon Power Systems (SPS), and di/dt. CAPS consists of the original Power-One AC/DC business and the high-density board-mounted DC/DC businesses obtained through the acquisitions of IPD in 1999 and Melcher in 1998. ES represents a combination of PWER's HC Power and Powec acquisitions in 2000. SPS is a new division that is engaged in developing next-generation silicon-based DC/DC technology. SPS's maXyz product line, introduced in 2003, was developed specifically for the Intermediate Bus Architecture market. In 2004, it introduced its Z-Series product line, a new digital power management architecture. In February 2003, the company acquired di/dt Inc., a designer and manufacturer of high-density DC/DC converters used primarily in the communications and networking environments, for $12.4 million.

Products made by the company include AC/DC power supplies that power communications and networking equipment, as well as industrial, automatic/semiconductor test, transportation, medical and other electronic equipment; DC/DC converters to control power on communications printed circuit boards; and DC power systems used by communications and Internet service providers. PWER designs its products mostly for higher-end communications infrastructure markets, rather than for use in PCs, mobile phones, or other consumer products.

AC/DC power supplies convert alternating current from a primary power source, such as a wall outlet, into a precisely controlled direct current. Nearly all electronic devices that plug into AC wall outlets require some type of AC/DC power supply. DC/DC converters modify an existing DC voltage level to other DC levels to meet the power needs of various subsystems and components within electronic equipment. DC power systems power and back up large communications infrastructure equipment.

In 2003, 62% of sales were to communications infrastructure equipment markets, 16% to industrial markets, 8% to transportation, and 14% to other areas. Cisco Systems accounted for 15% of 2003 sales, down from 16% in 2002, and was the only customer to account for over 10% of sales in either year.

Company Financials Fiscal Year ending December 31

Per Share Data ($)

(Year Ended December 31)	2003	2002	2001	2000	1999	1998	1997	1996	1995	1994
Tangible Bk. Val.	2.62	2.85	4.06	6.00	2.60	1.12	1.67	NA	NA	NA
Cash Flow	-0.03	-2.36	-1.90	0.87	0.64	0.28	0.36	0.32	NA	NA
Earnings	-0.22	-2.62	-2.36	0.56	0.18	0.11	0.19	NA	NA	NA
S&P Core Earnings	-0.45	-2.08	-2.32	NA	NA	NA	NA	NA	NA	NA
Dividends	Nil	Nil	Nil	Nil	Nil	Nil	Nil	NA	NA	NA
Payout Ratio	Nil	Nil	Nil	Nil	Nil	Nil	Nil	NA	NA	NA
Prices - High	12.80	13.25	52.50	89.81	15.75	5.83	6.62	NA	NA	NA
- Low	4.15	2.33	5.32	10.66	2.06	1.75	4.54	NA	NA	NA
P/E Ratio - High	NM	NM	NM	NM	89	53	35	NA	NA	NA
- Low	NM	NM	NM	NM	12	16	24	NA	NA	NA

Income Statement Analysis (Million $)

	2003	2002	2001	2000	1999	1998	1997	1996	1995	1994
Revs.	256	231	364	511	205	103	91.6	74.2	NA	NA
Oper. Inc.	3.89	-82.2	-88.8	94.8	32.8	17.1	20.9	14.2	NA	NA
Depr.	16.0	20.9	36.1	24.2	14.3	8.96	6.25	6.22	NA	NA
Int. Exp.	1.04	1.13	2.50	6.45	Nil	0.81	3.18	4.22	NA	NA
Pretax Inc.	-19.2	-223	-187	66.4	16.5	8.06	11.8	3.79	NA	NA
Eff. Tax Rate	NM	NM	NM	33.9%	39.1%	28.9%	30.1%	10.4%	NA	NA
Net Inc.	-18.2	-211	-186	43.9	10.0	5.73	8.23	3.40	NA	NA
S&P Core Earnings	-36.9	-167	-183	NA	NA	NA	NA	NA	NA	NA

Balance Sheet & Other Fin. Data (Million $)

	2003	2002	2001	2000	1999	1998	1997	1996	1995	1994
Cash	100	107	79.7	137	63.6	10.8	32.0	1.68	NA	NA
Curr. Assets	227	222	271	503	166	66.4	71.8	32.6	NA	NA
Total Assets	350	361	520	782	283	154	113	72.7	NA	NA
Curr. Liab.	72.6	72.0	54.8	126	44.5	34.2	10.5	23.0	NA	NA
LT Debt	Nil	8.91	7.60	9.41	3.96	7.64	Nil	26.3	NA	NA
Common Equity	281	287	458	634	232	108	100	1.13	NA	NA
Total Cap.	282	296	472	655	238	119	102	43.7	NA	NA
Cap. Exp.	7.32	7.01	30.5	52.2	27.1	11.6	5.20	NA	NA	NA
Cash Flow	-2.15	-190	-150	68.1	24.4	14.7	13.0	9.61	NA	NA
Curr. Ratio	3.1	3.1	4.9	4.0	3.7	1.9	6.9	1.4	NA	NA
% LT Debt of Cap.	Nil	3.0	1.6	1.4	1.7	6.4	Nil	60.1	NA	NA
% Net Inc.of Revs.	NM	NM	NM	8.6	4.9	5.6	9.0	4.6	NA	NA
% Ret. on Assets	NM	NM	NM	8.1	4.6	4.3	8.9	NA	NA	NA
% Ret. on Equity	NM	NM	NM	10.1	5.9	5.5	13.3	NA	NA	NA

Data as orig reptd.; bef. results of disc opers/spec. items. Per share data adj. for stk. divs. Bold denotes primary EPS - prior periods restated. E-Estimated. NA-Not Available. NM-Not Meaningful. NR-Not Ranked. UR-Under Review.

Office: 740 Calle Plano, Camarillo, CA 93012-8583.
Telephone: 805-987-8741.
Website: http://www.power-one.com
Chrmn & CEO: S.J. Goldman.
Pres & COO: W.T. Yeates.

SVP, CFO, Chief Acctg Officer & Treas: E.K. Schnopp.
Secy & General Counsel: R.H. Holliday.
Investor Contact: M. Goeller .
Dirs: K. R. Bishop, H. Brandli, S. J. Goldman, J. E. Jacoby, M. Mel-liar-Smith, J. Walters.

Founded: in 1973.
Domicile: Delaware.
Employees: 2,371.
S&P Analyst: Bryon J. Korutz/MF/BK

PPG Industries

Recommendation: **HOLD** ★★★☆☆
SELL · SELL · HOLD · BUY · BUY

12-Month Target Price: **$65.00**
(as of January 07, 2004)

PPG has an approximate 0.10% weighting in the **S&P 500**

Sector: Materials
Sub-Industry: Diversified Chemicals
Peer Group: Major Diversified Companies

Summary: PPG is a leading manufacturer of coatings and resins, flat and fiber glass, and industrial and specialty chemicals.

Quantitative Evaluations

S&P Earnings & Dividend Rank: B

| D | C | B- | **B** | B+ | A- | A | A+ |

S&P Fair Value Rank: 2-

| 1 | **2** | 3 | 4 | 5 |
| Lowest | | | | Highest |

Fair Value Calc.: $58.90 (Slightly Overvalued)

S&P Investability Quotient Percentile

95%

PPG scored higher than 95% of all companies for which an S&P Report is available.

Volatility: Low

| **Low** | Average | High |

Technical Evaluation: Bullish

Since 10/04, the technical indicators for PPG have been Bullish.

Relative Strength Rank: Moderate

69

1 Lowest · Highest 99

Price as of 11/12/04: $66.99 | **2004E S&P Core EPS:** $4.02

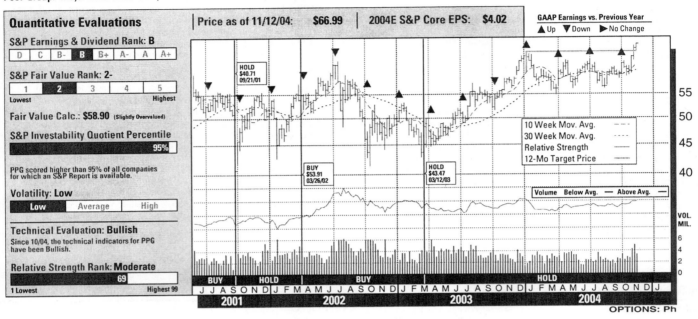

GAAP Earnings vs. Previous Year
▲ Up ▼ Down ► No Change

HOLD $40.71 09/21/01

BUY $53.91 03/26/02

HOLD $43.47 03/12/03

10 Week Mov. Avg. — — —
30 Week Mov. Avg. ·······
Relative Strength ————
12-Mo Target Price ———

Volume Below Avg. — Above Avg.

VOL. MIL.
6
4
2
0

55
50
45
40

BUY | HOLD | BUY | HOLD
J J A S O N D J F M A M J J A S O N D J F M A M J J A S O N D J F M A M J J A S O N D J
2001 | 2002 | 2003 | 2004

OPTIONS: Ph

Analyst commentary prepared by Richard O'Reilly, CFA /CB/BK

Highlights August 12, 2004

- We expect sales and earnings of this diversified company to continue to advance for the rest of 2004 and 2005. We see the chemicals unit bolstered by a rebound in chlor-alkali prices in the second half of 2004, despite margin pressures due to higher energy costs. We look for auto products to benefit from projected modestly higher new vehicle sales in 2004; flat glass should be helped by better trends in commercial construction. Industrial and packaging coatings should continue to benefit from a stronger industrial sector, while architectural coatings should grow together with its key home center customer.

- PPG is restructuring its fiberglass business, which has been hurt by a downturn in electronics demand and lower prices. While the optical products business continued to post good growth in early 2004, we think gains will begin to slow, as 2003 included the European introduction of a new generation of lenses.

- The tax rate for 2004 is projected at 24%, down from 35% for 2003. We believe post-retirement benefit costs will likely decline in 2004 by about $0.09 a share, after a $0.55 increase in 2003. We see quarterly charges of $0.03 a share continuing into 2005, related to PPG's asbestos settlement obligation. Our 2004 Standard & Poor's Core Earnings estimate is $4.02 a share.

Investment Rationale/Risk August 12, 2004

- We would hold the shares, based on EPS growth that we see for the rest of 2004 and 2005, assuming increasing industrial activity. The stock is trading at a P/E multiple, based on our 2004 EPS estimate, in line with that of the S&P 500. We view PPG as a well run company with an attractive strategy of investing globally in several growth businesses to help provide greater earnings consistency, while remaining a low-cost producer in its glass and commodity chemicals operations.

- Risks to our recommendation and target price include slower than expected industrial activity, and greater industry capacity in key product lines.

- Dividends have been increased for 33 consecutive years, and the yield is well above that of the S&P 500. Our 12-month target price of $65 assumes the the stock's P/E multiple based on projected 2005 EPS will remain in line with that of the S&P 500.

Key Stock Statistics

S&P Core EPS 2005E	4.42	52-week Range	$67.00-54.81
S&P Oper. EPS 2004E	3.90	12 Month P/E	18.6
P/E on S&P Oper. EPS 2004E	17.2	Beta	0.82
S&P Oper. EPS 2005E	4.30	Shareholders	28,337
Yield (%)	2.7%	Market Cap (B)	$ 11.5
Dividend Rate/Share	1.80	Shares Outstanding (M)	171.9

Value of $10,000 invested five years ago: **$ 12,821**

Dividend Data Dividends have been paid since 1899

Amount ($)	Date Decl.	Ex-Div. Date	Stock of Record	Payment Date
0.440	Jan. 15	Feb. 12	Feb. 17	Mar. 12 '04
0.450	Apr. 15	May. 06	May. 10	Jun. 11 '04
0.450	Jul. 15	Aug. 06	Aug. 10	Sep. 10 '04
0.450	Oct. 22	Nov. 08	Nov. 10	Dec. 10 '04

Revenues/Earnings Data Fiscal year ending December 31

Revenues (Million $)

	2004	2003	2002	2001	2000	1999
1Q	2,264	2,071	1,875	2,099	2,087	1,803
2Q	2,429	2,304	2,134	2,164	2,210	1,947
3Q	2,409	2,206	2,068	1,999	2,078	1,954
4Q	—	2,175	1,990	1,907	1,992	2,053
Yr.	—	8,756	8,067	8,169	8,367	7,757

Earnings Per Share ($)

	2004	2003	2002	2001	2000	1999
1Q	0.67	0.49	0.25	0.33	0.79	0.70
2Q	1.06	0.89	-2.03	0.92	1.17	1.05
3Q	1.12	0.83	0.87	0.55	0.86	0.56
4Q	E1.00	0.71	0.55	0.49	0.75	0.92
Yr.	E3.90	2.92	-0.36	2.29	3.57	3.23

Next earnings report expected: mid-January Source: S&P, Company Reports
EPS Estimates based on S&P Operating Earnings; historical GAAP earnings are as reported.

Recommendation: **HOLD** ★ ★ ★ ☆ ☆   12-Month Target Price: **$65.00** (as of January 07, 2004)

Business Summary August 12, 2004

PPG is one of the world's leading producers of original and refinish automotive and industrial coatings (used in appliance, industrial equipment and packaging markets) and is a major North American supplier of architectural coatings (Pittsburgh, Olympic, Porter and Lucite brands). From early 1997 through 2000, it made 18 coatings acquisitions, primarily automotive and industrial, in the Americas and Europe, with combined annual sales of $1.6 billion. The company is a global supplier of aircraft coatings and sealants. PPG also produces metal pretreatments, adhesives and sealants for the automotive industry, and sealants for architectural insulating glass.

The company is also one of the world's largest producers of flat glass and fabricated glass. Major markets include original and replacement glass for automobiles, commercial and residential construction, aircraft transparencies, furniture and various industrial uses. These businesses aim for cash generation and earnings growth. PPG is the world's second largest producer of continuous strand and chopped strand fiberglass, including plastic reinforcement yarns and electronic and specialty materials, for transportation, construction, electronics, recreational and industrial uses. It also provides claims processing services to insurance companies and the automotive after-market through LYNX Services.

PPG is the world's third largest producer of chlorine and caustic soda (used in a wide variety of industrial applications), vinyl chloride monomer (for use in polyvinyl chloride resins) and chlorinated solvents. These commodity chemicals are highly cyclical; volumes declined in 2003. The company's ECU (electrochemical unit) prices in 2003 averaged about 45% higher than 2002's reduced level. Specialty chemicals include silica compounds, Transitions photochromic lenses, optical resins, and fine chemicals (phosgene derivatives and pharmaceutical intermediates). The newest version of Transitions lenses, called Next Generations, was introduced in early 2002, helping sales for the business to grow by over 20% in each of 2002 and 2003.

The company aims to achieve faster and more consistent earnings growth by improving its mix of businesses through internal growth and acquisitions. It has focused resources on its higher growth businesses, consisting of coatings and specialty chemicals. PPG made 23 acquisitions, for $2 billion, from early 1997 through 2000. In May 2002, the company agreed to settle all current and future personal injury claims against it and 50%-owned Pittsburgh Corning for asbestos products. In 2002, PPG recorded a related after-tax charge of $495 million, reflecting the current value of cash contributions over a 21-year period, plus 1.4 million common shares.

Sales and operating profits by product group in 2003 were: coatings (55% and 70%), glass (25% and 7%) and chemicals (20% and 23%). International operations contributed 36% of sales and 35% of operating profits.

Company Financials Fiscal Year ending December 31

Per Share Data ($)

(Year Ended December 31)	2003	2002	2001	2000	1999	1998	1997	1996	1995	1994
Tangible Bk. Val.	7.36	3.49	9.10	8.57	8.30	13.09	14.10	13.49	13.21	12.35
Cash Flow	5.23	1.99	4.93	6.20	12.99	6.69	6.04	5.89	5.41	3.93
Earnings	2.92	-0.36	2.29	3.57	3.23	4.48	3.94	3.96	3.80	2.43
S&P Core Earnings	3.48	1.76	1.17	NA	NA	NA	NA	NA	NA	NA
Dividends	1.73	1.70	1.68	1.60	1.52	1.42	1.33	1.26	1.18	1.12
Payout Ratio	59%	NM	73%	45%	47%	32%	34%	32%	31%	46%
Prices - High	64.42	62.86	59.75	65.06	70.75	76.62	67.50	62.25	47.87	42.12
- Low	42.61	41.39	38.99	36.00	47.93	49.12	48.62	42.87	34.87	33.75
P/E Ratio - High	22	NM	26	18	22	17	17	16	13	17
- Low	15	NM	17	10	15	11	12	11	9	14

Income Statement Analysis (Million $)

	2003	2002	2001	2000	1999	1998	1997	1996	1995	1994
Revs.	8,756	8,067	8,169	8,629	7,757	7,510	7,379	7,218	7,058	6,331
Oper. Inc.	1,367	1,309	1,371	1,649	1,528	1,659	1,689	1,658	1,511	1,329
Depr.	394	398	447	447	419	383	373	364	352	318
Int. Exp.	107	128	169	161	133	110	105	108	94.0	91.0
Pretax Inc.	843	-28.0	666	1,017	973	1,294	1,175	1,240	1,248	856
Eff. Tax Rate	34.8%	NM	37.1%	36.3%	38.7%	36.0%	37.0%	37.9%	38.5%	38.0%
Net Inc.	500	-60.0	387	620	568	801	714	744	768	515
S&P Core Earnings	597	300	197	NA	NA	NA	NA	NA	NA	NA

Balance Sheet & Other Fin. Data (Million $)

	2003	2002	2001	2000	1999	1998	1997	1996	1995	1994
Cash	499	117	108	111	158	128	129	70.0	106	62.0
Curr. Assets	3,537	2,945	2,703	3,093	3,062	2,660	2,584	2,296	2,276	2,168
Total Assets	8,424	7,863	8,452	9,125	8,914	7,387	6,868	6,441	6,194	5,894
Curr. Liab.	2,139	1,920	1,955	2,543	2,384	1,912	1,662	1,796	1,629	1,425
LT Debt	1,339	1,699	1,699	1,810	1,836	1,081	1,257	834	736	773
Common Equity	2,911	2,150	3,080	3,097	3,106	2,880	2,509	2,483	2,569	2,557
Total Cap.	4,475	4,044	5,453	5,578	5,560	4,488	4,254	3,393	3,660	3,703
Cap. Exp.	217	238	291	561	490	487	466	476	448	NA
Cash Flow	894	338	834	1,067	987	1,184	1,087	1,108	1,120	832
Curr. Ratio	1.7	1.5	1.4	1.2	1.3	1.4	1.6	1.3	1.4	1.5
% LT Debt of Cap.	29.9	42.0	31.2	32.4	33.0	24.0	29.5	24.6	20.1	20.9
% Net Inc.of Revs.	5.7	NM	4.7	7.2	7.3	10.7	9.7	10.3	10.9	8.1
% Ret. on Assets	6.1	NM	4.4	6.9	7.0	11.2	10.7	11.8	12.7	9.1
% Ret. on Equity	19.8	NM	12.5	20.0	19.0	29.7	28.6	29.4	30.0	20.8

Data as orig reptd.; bef. results of disc opers/spec. items. Per share data adj. for stk. divs.; EPS diluted. E-Estimated. NA-Not Available. NM-Not Meaningful. NR-Not Ranked. UR-Under Review.

Office: 1 Ppg Pl, Pittsburgh, PA 15272.
Telephone: 412-434-3131.
Website: http://www.ppg.com
Chrmn & CEO: R.W. LeBoeuf.
Pres & COO: C.E. Bunch.
SVP & CFO: W.H. Hernandez.

SVP & General Counsel: J.C. Diggs.
VP & Investor Contact: D.B. Atkinson .
Dirs: J. G. Berges, C. E. Bunch, E. B. Davis, Jr., V. F. Haynes, M. J. Hooper, A. J. Krowe, R. W. LeBoeuf, R. Mehrabian, R. Ripp, T. J. Usher, D. R. Whitwam.

Founded: in 1883.
Domicile: Pennsylvania.
Employees: 32,900.
S&P Analyst: Richard O'Reilly, CFA /CB/BK

Recommendation: **HOLD** ★★★☆☆
SELL · SELL · HOLD · BUY · BUY

12-Month Target Price: **$51.00**
(as of October 20, 2004)

PPL has an approximate 0.09% weighting in the **S&P 500**

Sector: Utilities
Sub-Industry: Electric Utilities
Peer Group: Electric Cos. (Domestic) - Large

Summary: This Pennsylvania-based holding company for PPL Utilities also has holdings in the U.K., Europe, and Latin America.

Quantitative Evaluations

S&P Earnings & Dividend Rank: B

| D | C | B- | **B** | B+ | A- | A | A+ |

S&P Fair Value Rank: 2-

| 1 | **2** | 3 | 4 | 5 |
| Lowest | | | | Highest |

Fair Value Calc.: $44.50 (Overvalued)

S&P Investability Quotient Percentile

82%

PPL scored higher than 82% of all companies for which an S&P Report is available.

Volatility: Low

| **Low** | Average | High |

Technical Evaluation: Bullish
Since 9/04, the technical indicators for PPL have been Bullish.

Relative Strength Rank: Strong

72

| 1 Lowest | | Highest 99 |

Price as of 11/12/04: $53.73 | **2004E S&P Core EPS:** $3.07

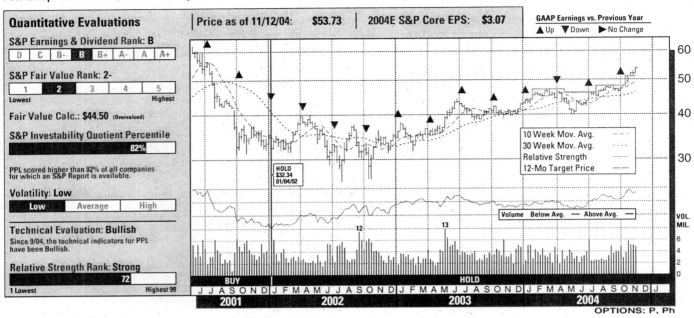

GAAP Earnings vs. Previous Year
▲ Up ▼ Down ► No Change

- - - 10 Week Mov. Avg.
······ 30 Week Mov. Avg.
Relative Strength
12-Mo Target Price

Volume Below Avg. — Above Avg.

HOLD $32.34 01/04/02

BUY | HOLD

J J A S O N D | J F M A M J J A S O N D | J F M A M J J A S O N D | J F M A M J J A S O N D | J F M A M J J A S O N D | J
2001 | **2002** | **2003** | **2004**

OPTIONS: P, Ph

Analyst commentary prepared by Justin McCann/CB/JWP

Highlights August 27, 2004

- After an anticipated flat performance in 2004 (compared with 2003's EPS from ongoing operations of $3.71), we expect operating EPS in 2005 to increase nearly 7%. We expect results in 2004 to be restricted by the higher operating expenses projected for the regulated utility and the dilutive impact of the May 2004 conversion of equity participating securities into 10 million common shares. However, we see this being largely offset by an expected increase in earnings from the power supply business and an anticipated reduction in interest costs.

- PPL has filed for a $164 million increase (8%) in its Pennsylvania electric distribution rates. The state commission is expected to issue a decision by the end of 2004, with rates expected to go into effect on January 1, 2005. The company has also filed for a rate increase for its U.K. utility operations. We expect a ruling by December, with U.K. rates expected to go into effect on April 1, 2005.

- PPL reported operating earnings of $0.72 a share for the second quarter of 2004. This excluded net credits of $0.09 in unusual items, including a non-cash credit of $0.13 for the transfer of PPL's interest in the Brazilian electric utility CEMAR.

Investment Rationale/Risk August 27, 2004

- After outperformance in 2003 and year to date in 2004, we expect the stock to perform more in line with the company's electric utility peers over the next 12 months. We believe PPL can realize annual EPS growth of 3% to 5% over the next few years, but we expect the performance of the shares over the coming year to be restricted by the uncertainties related to the pending rate cases in Pennsylvania and the U.K.

- Risks to our recommendation and target price include potential unfavorable rate case rulings, significantly lower results from the unregulated operations, and a major shift in the average P/E multiple of the peer group as a whole.

- The stock's dividend yield (recently about 3.5%) is below the peer average, but the payout ratio (44% of our EPS estimate for 2004) is also below that of peers. We see this providing increased financial flexibility. In light of PPL's exposure to the wholesale power market, we expect the shares to continue to trade at about a 9% discount to the approximate 13.3X peer P/E multiple on our EPS estimate for 2005. Our 12-month target price is $48.

Key Stock Statistics

S&P Core EPS 2005E	3.50	52-week Range	$53.77-39.67
S&P Oper. EPS 2004E	3.70	12 Month P/E	12.2
P/E on S&P Oper. EPS 2004E	14.5	Beta	0.57
S&P Oper. EPS 2005E	4.00	Shareholders	83,783
Yield (%)	3.1%	Market Cap (B)	$ 10.2
Dividend Rate/Share	1.64	Shares Outstanding (M)	188.9

Value of $10,000 invested five years ago: **$ 23,412**

Dividend Data Dividends have been paid since 1946

Amount ($)	Date Decl.	Ex-Div. Date	Stock of Record	Payment Date
0.385	Nov. 21	Dec. 08	Dec. 10	Jan. 01 '04
0.410	Feb. 27	Mar. 08	Mar. 10	Apr. 01 '04
0.410	May. 28	Jun. 08	Jun. 10	Jul. 01 '04
0.410	Aug. 27	Sep. 08	Sep. 10	Oct. 01 '04

Revenues/Earnings Data Fiscal year ending December 31

Revenues (Million $)

	2004	2003	2002	2001	2000	1999
1Q	1,520	1,487	1,351	1,566	1,413	1,067
2Q	1,362	1,338	1,288	1,409	1,297	1,004
3Q	1,465	1,456	1,476	1,438	1,458	1,386
4Q	—	1,296	1,314	1,312	1,505	1,133
Yr.	—	5,587	5,429	5,725	5,683	4,590

Earnings Per Share ($)

	2004	2003	2002	2001	2000	1999
1Q	0.99	1.06	1.00	1.52	0.99	0.76
2Q	0.82	0.67	-0.18	0.80	0.64	0.40
3Q	1.03	0.97	0.80	1.04	0.94	1.07
4Q	E0.91	1.44	0.71	-2.19	0.79	0.93
Yr.	E3.70	4.15	2.35	1.15	3.36	3.14

Next earnings report expected: late-January Source: S&P, Company Reports
EPS Estimates based on S&P Operating Earnings; historical GAAP earnings are as reported.

Please read the Required Disclosures and Reg. AC certification on the last page of this report.

The McGraw·Hill Companies

PPL Corporation

Recommendation: **HOLD** ★ ★ ★ ☆ ☆   12-Month Target Price: **$51.00** (as of October 20, 2004)

Business Summary August 29, 2004

PPL Corp. (formerly PP&L Resources) is a holding company formed in 1995 by Pennsylvania Power & Light (now operating as PPL Electric Utilities), its main subsidiary, which supplies electricity to 1.3 million customers in a 10,000 square mile area in 29 counties of central-eastern Pennsylvania. PPL Gas Utilities distributes natural gas to 105,000 customers in Pennsylvania and a few hundred in Maryland.

Operating revenues by business segment in 2003 were as follows: utility 66.4% (67.7% in 2002, 59.8% in 2001); wholesale energy marketing 21.7% (18.3%, 19.5%); energy related businesses 8.9% (10.3%, 13.0%); unregulated retail electric and gas 2.7% (3.4%, 7.0%); and net energy trading margins 0.2% (0.3%, 0.7%).

Wholly owned PPL Energy Supply was formed in 2000 as the holding company for the company's competitive energy businesses. Its major operating facilities are PPL Generation, PPL Global, and PPL EnergyPlus.

PPL Generation owns and operates, through subsidiaries, power plants in Pennsylvania, Montana, Maine, Connecticut, Arizona, Illinois, and New York. At December 31, 2003, it had 11,527 MW of generating capacity, with about 74% provided by the Pennsylvania plants. The Pennsylvania plants are operated in conjunction with PJM Interconnection, LLC, which operates the electric transmission network and electric energy market in the Mid-Atlantic region.

In September 2002, PPL Global acquired the remaining 49% interest in Western Power Distribution in the U.K., for $236 million and the assumption of $2.1 billion in non-recourse debt. PPL Global has a 95.4% interest in the Chilean electric distribution company, Empressa Emel S. A. It also had an 89.6% interest in the Brazilian electric utility, Cia Energetica do Maranhao (CEMAR). Following a bankruptcy filing by CEMAR, Brazilian regulators assumed full control of the utility in August 2002. In April 2004, PPL transfered its entire interest in CEMAR to a Brazilian firm. PPL also has holdings in Bolivia, El Salvador, Spain and Peru.

PPL EnergyPlus markets the power produced by PPL Generation (as well as purchased power, natural gas, and oil) to wholesale and retail markets in the U.S. It also purchases and sells energy forward and futures contracts as well as other commodity-based financial instruments in accordance with PPL's risk management policies.

In 1998, the Pennsylvania Public Utility Commission issued an order allowing Pennsylvania Power & Light to recover (over 11 years beginning January 1, 1999) $2.97 billion in stranded costs, with authorization to issue transition bonds that would securitize up to $2.85 billion of its stranded costs.

In August 2001, PPL sold $800 million of bonds through the securitization of its electricity transmission and distribution business. Proceeds were used for generation projects. The process involved the separation of regulated units from PPL Corp. and its non-regulated units, and bids for a power supply contract from 2002 through the end of 2009. PPL Energy Plus was the successful bidder for the contract.

Company Financials Fiscal Year ending December 31

Per Share Data ($)

(Year Ended December 31)	2003	2002	2001	2000	1999	1998	1997	1996	1995	1994
Tangible Bk. Val.	11.06	11.74	13.96	13.30	11.20	11.87	16.77	16.73	16.13	15.06
Earnings	4.15	2.35	1.15	3.36	3.14	2.29	1.80	2.05	2.05	1.41
S&P Core Earnings	3.90	1.58	1.80	NA	NA	NA	NA	NA	NA	NA
Dividends	1.54	1.35	1.06	1.06	1.00	1.34	1.67	1.67	1.67	1.67
Payout Ratio	37%	57%	92%	32%	32%	59%	93%	81%	81%	118%
Prices - High	44.33	39.95	62.36	46.12	32.00	28.93	24.25	26.00	26.50	27.25
- Low	31.65	26.00	30.99	18.37	20.37	20.87	19.00	21.62	17.87	18.62
P/E Ratio - High	11	17	54	14	10	13	13	13	13	19
- Low	8	11	27	5	6	9	11	11	9	13

Income Statement Analysis (Million $)

	2003	2002	2001	2000	1999	1998	1997	1996	1995	1994
Revs.	5,587	5,429	5,725	5,683	4,590	3,786	3,049	2,910	2,752	2,725
Depr.	380	367	254	261	257	338	374	363	302	289
Maint.	NA	314	269	261	215	182	184	191	186	180
Fxd. Chgs. Cov.	2.72	2.49	3.08	2.95	3.20	3.45	3.25	3.77	3.20	2.99
Constr. Credits	NA	NA	NA	NA	NA	Nil	NA	NA	12.1	13.1
Eff. Tax Rate	18.5%	29.5%	54.4%	36.3%	26.1%	39.3%	42.7%	45.4%	42.8%	42.4%
Net Inc.	748	425	221	513	478	379	296	329	350	244
S&P Core Earnings	674	240	262	NA	NA	NA	NA	NA	NA	NA

Balance Sheet & Other Fin. Data (Million $)

	2003	2002	2001	2000	1999	1998	1997	1996	1995	1994
Gross Prop.	17,775	16,406	12,477	11,418	10,717	10,489	10,336	10,242	10,235	9,998
Cap. Exp.	771	648	565	460	318	304	310	360	403	505
Net Prop.	10,446	9,566	6,135	5,948	5,644	4,363	6,766	6,905	7,122	7,127
Capitalization:										
LT Debt	8,145	6,562	5,906	4,717	4,103	3,092	2,698	2,968	2,967	3,092
% LT Debt	71.1	74.0	75.3	69.1	71.8	60.3	47.0	48.0	50.0	54.4
Pfd.	51.0	82.0	82.0	97.0	Nil	347	347	466	466	466
% Pfd.	0.45	0.92	1.05	1.42	Nil	6.70	6.10	7.50	7.90	7.80
Common	3,259	2,224	1,857	2,012	1,613	1,790	2,809	2,745	2,497	2,454
% Common	28.5	25.1	23.7	29.5	28.2	34.9	49.0	44.4	42.1	40.8
Total Cap.	13,710	11,274	9,332	6,880	7,328	5,317	8,075	8,075	8,356	8,290
% Oper. Ratio	78.9	76.8	81.1	84.0	84.8	79.8	82.1	80.9	79.1	81.6
% Earn. on Net Prop.	13.4	17.5	14.2	28.6	22.3	10.3	8.0	8.0	8.1	7.1
% Return On Revs.	13.4	7.8	3.9	9.0	10.4	10.0	9.7	11.3	12.7	9.0
% Return On Invest. Capital	10.0	12.6	12.4	14.3	11.3	13.1	9.4	6.5	6.8	6.6
% Return On Com. Equity	26.2	17.5	8.7	28.3	28.1	16.5	10.7	12.3	12.8	8.7

Data as orig reptd.; bef. results of disc opers/spec. items. Per share data adj. for stk. divs.; EPS diluted. E-Estimated. NA-Not Available. NM-Not Meaningful. NR-Not Ranked. UR-Under Review.

Office: 2 N 9th St, Allentown, PA 18101-1179.
Telephone: 610-774-5151.
Email: invrel@pplweb.com
Website: http://www.pplweb.com
Chrmn, Pres & CEO: W.F. Hecht.
EVP & CFO: J.R. Biggar.

SVP, Secy & General Counsel: R.J. Grey.
VP & Treas: J.E. Abel.
Investor Contact: T.J. Paukovits 610-774-4124.
Dirs: F. M. Bernthal, J. R. Biggar, J. W. Conway, E. A. Deaver, L. K. Goeser, W. F. Hecht, S. Heydt, W. K. Smith, S. M. Stalnecker.

Founded: in 1920.
Domicile: Pennsylvania.
Employees: 12,256.
S&P Analyst: Justin McCann/CB/JWP

Praxair

Recommendation: **HOLD** ★ ★ ★ ☆ ☆
SELL SELL HOLD BUY BUY

12-Month Target Price: **$46.00**
(as of October 08, 2004)

PX has an approximate 0.13% weighting in the **S&P 500**

Sector: Materials
Sub-Industry: Industrial Gases
Peer Group: Industrial Gases

Summary: PX is the largest producer of industrial gases in North and South America, and one of the largest worldwide. It also provides ceramic and metallic coatings.

Quantitative Evaluations

S&P Earnings & Dividend Rank: A

| D | C | B- | B | B+ | A- | **A** | A+ |

S&P Fair Value Rank: 3

| 1 | 2 | **3** | 4 | 5 |
| Lowest | | | | Highest |

Fair Value Calc.: $41.30 (Slightly Overvalued)

S&P Investability Quotient Percentile

99%

PX scored higher than 99% of all companies for which an S&P Report is available.

Volatility: Low

| **Low** | Average | High |

Technical Evaluation: Bullish

Since 8/04, the technical indicators for PX have been Bullish.

Relative Strength Rank: Moderate

60

| 1 Lowest | Highest 99 |

Price as of 11/12/04: **$44.47** | **2004E S&P Core EPS:** **$1.95**

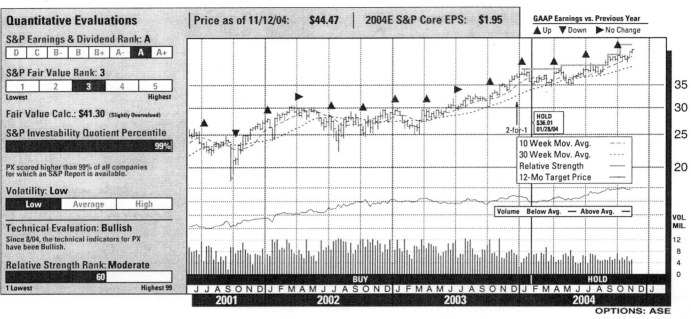

GAAP Earnings vs. Previous Year
▲ Up ▼ Down ► No Change

HOLD $36.01 01/28/04

2-for-1

10 Week Mov. Avg.
30 Week Mov. Avg.
Relative Strength
12-Mo Target Price

Volume ■ Below Avg. — Above Avg.

VOL. MIL.

BUY | HOLD

J J A S O N D J F M A M J J A S O N D J F M A M J J A S O N D J F M A M J J A S O N D J
2001 | 2002 | 2003 | 2004

OPTIONS: ASE

Analyst commentary prepared by Richard O'Reilly, CFA /CB/GG

Highlights September 10, 2004

- We project that 2004 sales will grow 13% to 15%, aided by favorable currency exchange rates, with continued good gains into 2005. We expect U.S. gases volumes to show high single digit growth, versus 2003's sluggish 1% trend, assuming a continuing uptick in industrial activity and gains in key end markets such as health care and petroleum refining.

- We see selling price increases likely to remain modest, before contractual pass-through of any changes in natural gas prices. We also expect Europe and Asia to post continued good sales gains. Surface Technologies should see a continued pickup in coatings services, while we think the aviation repair business is starting to see signs of a recovery.

- Despite high U.S. power costs and projected higher pension and medical expenses of about $20 million, we see operating profit margins recovering in 2004 to about 17%, from 2003's reduced 16.4%. Interest expense will likely be flat to modestly higher, and we project the effective tax rate at 25%, versus 2003's 22.6%. With a debt to capital ratio of 47% at June 30, 2004, we expect PX to ramp up share buybacks.

Investment Rationale/Risk September 10, 2004

- We have a hold opinion on the shares. The stock's P/E multiple, based on our 2005 EPS estimate, is at what we view as an appropriate premium to that of the S&P 500, versus a discount in the the past two years. The company is concentrating on several less capital intensive, faster growing global markets. We believe that a continuing pickup in the U.S. industrial economy should translate into stronger U.S. volume growth.

- Risks to our recommendation and target price include unexpected slowdowns in industrial activity and higher-than-expected power costs.

- Our 12-month target price of $43 is based on our 2005 EPS forecast of $2.30 and a discount cash flow model assuming 10.4% weighted average cost of capital and average annual growth in free cash flow of 8% over the next 10 years. We see the stock's S&P Earnings and Dividend Ranking of A (the dividend has been raised for 11 consecutive years) adding to the investment appeal of the shares, and we would hold existing positions.

Key Stock Statistics

S&P Core EPS 2005E	2.20	52-week Range	$44.58-33.50
S&P Oper. EPS 2004E	2.08	12 Month P/E	21.9
P/E on S&P Oper. EPS 2004E	21.4	Beta	0.98
S&P Oper. EPS 2005E	2.35	Shareholders	24,770
Yield (%)	1.3%	Market Cap (B)	$ 14.4
Dividend Rate/Share	0.60	Shares Outstanding (M)	324.7

Value of $10,000 invested five years ago: **$ 19,826**

Dividend Data Dividends have been paid since 1992

Amount ($)	Date Decl.	Ex-Div. Date	Stock of Record	Payment Date
0.150	Jan. 27	Mar. 03	Mar. 05	Mar. 15 '04
0.150	Apr. 28	Jun. 03	Jun. 07	Jun. 15 '04
0.150	Jul. 27	Sep. 02	Sep. 07	Sep. 15 '04
0.150	Oct. 26	Dec. 03	Dec. 07	Dec. 15 '04

Revenues/Earnings Data Fiscal year ending December 31

Revenues (Million $)

	2004	2003	2002	2001	2000	1999
1Q	1,531	1,337	1,232	1,335	1,230	1,118
2Q	1,603	1,401	1,307	1,314	1,265	1,149
3Q	1,674	1,414	1,292	1,271	1,275	1,169
4Q	—	1,461	1,297	1,238	1,273	1,203
Yr.	—	5,613	5,128	5,158	5,043	4,639

Earnings Per Share ($)

	2004	2003	2002	2001	2000	1999
1Q	0.49	0.40	0.39	0.39	0.36	0.34
2Q	0.53	0.46	0.46	0.39	0.38	0.34
3Q	0.53	0.46	0.40	0.19	0.38	0.35
4Q	E0.53	0.47	0.43	0.36	0.02	0.35
Yr.	E2.08	1.77	1.66	1.32	1.13	1.36

Next earnings report expected: late-January Source: S&P, Company Reports
EPS Estimates based on S&P Operating Earnings; historical GAAP earnings are as reported.

Praxair, Inc.

Recommendation: **HOLD** ★ ★ ★ ☆ ☆   12-Month Target Price: **$46.00** (as of October 08, 2004)

Business Summary September 10, 2004

Since its 1992 spinoff from Union Carbide Corp., PX, the largest producer of industrial gases in North and South America, has expanded its operations to 40 countries. Foreign sales accounted for 50% of the total in 2003, with Brazil alone providing 10%. The purchase from CBI Industries of that company's Liquid Carbonic business in 1996 made PX the world's largest supplier of carbon dioxide. The acquisition added significantly to exposure to non-cyclical food and beverage markets. The company is also concentrating on several less capital intensive, faster growing global markets, such as health care and electronics, in addition to core industrial gases. In June 2004, PX acquired Home Care Supply, Inc., the largest private U.S. home respiratory and medical equipment provider, for $245 million. With annual sales of $170 million, the acquisition doubled PX's U.S. home care business. PX reduced its capital spending in recent years, but has projected 2004 spending of $700 million.

PX conducts its industrial gases business through four operating segments: North America (62% of sales and 59% of profits in 2003), South America (12%, 19%), Europe (12%, 12%) and Asia (7%, 7%). The industrial gases business involves the production, distribution and sale of atmospheric gases (oxygen, nitrogen, argon and rare gases), carbon dioxide, hydrogen, helium, acetylene, and specialty gases. Atmospheric gases are produced through air separation processes, primarily cryogenic, while other gases are produced by various methods. PX also

produces specialty products for use in the electronics industry. The business also includes the construction and sale of equipment to produce industrial gases. The company has developed noncryogenic air separation processes that open new markets consisting of small users, and that help to optimize production capacity by lowering production costs. Major customers include aerospace, beverage, chemicals, electronics, food processing, health care, glass, metal fabrication, petroleum, primary metals, and pulp/paper concerns. Consumption of industrial gases has historically increased at 1.5X to 2X the rate of local industrial production growth in countries in which PX does business.

Industrial gases are supplied to customers through three basic methods: on-site/pipeline (24% of total 2003 sales), merchant (31%) and packaged (32%). At the end of 2003, the company had 262 cryogenic air separation plants worldwide (170 in North America), 85 carbon dioxide plants (51), and 30 hydrogen plants (24). S.A. White Martins (Brazil, 99.2% owned) is the largest producer of industrial gases in South America.

The Surface Technologies business (7%, 3%) applies metallic and ceramic coatings and powders to parts and equipment provided by customers, provides aircraft engine and airframe component overhaul services, and manufactures electric arc, plasma and oxygen fuel spray equipment.

Company Financials Fiscal Year ending December 31

Per Share Data ($)

(Year Ended December 31)	2003	2002	2001	2000	1999	1998	1997	1996	1995	1994
Tangible Bk. Val.	6.00	4.03	7.58	3.97	3.70	3.36	2.89	2.39	3.37	2.72
Cash Flow	3.33	3.12	2.84	2.59	2.73	2.73	2.62	2.22	2.80	1.70
Earnings	1.77	1.66	1.32	1.13	1.36	1.30	1.27	0.89	0.91	0.73
S&P Core Earnings	1.67	1.38	1.05	NA	NA	NA	NA	NA	NA	NA
Dividends	0.46	0.38	0.34	0.31	0.28	0.25	0.22	0.19	0.16	0.14
Payout Ratio	26%	23%	26%	28%	21%	19%	17%	21%	18%	19%
Prices - High	38.26	30.55	27.96	27.46	29.06	26.93	29.00	25.06	17.06	12.31
- Low	25.01	22.27	18.25	15.15	16.00	15.34	19.62	15.75	9.87	8.12
P/E Ratio - High	22	18	21	24	21	21	23	28	19	17
- Low	14	13	14	13	12	12	16	18	11	11

Income Statement Analysis (Million $)

	2003	2002	2001	2000	1999	1998	1997	1996	1995	1994
Revs.	5,613	5,128	5,158	5,043	4,639	4,833	4,735	4,449	3,146	2,711
Oper. Inc.	1,444	1,358	1,333	1,220	1,199	1,310	1,230	1,125	812	737
Depr.	517	483	499	471	445	467	444	420	279	273
Int. Exp.	151	206	224	224	204	260	216	220	125	112
Pretax Inc.	735	726	585	493	638	607	633	350	434	346
Eff. Tax Rate	23.7%	21.8%	23.1%	20.9%	23.8%	20.9%	23.9%	31.4%	28.2%	23.7%
Net Inc.	585	548	432	363	441	425	416	282	262	203
S&P Core Earnings	552	454	343	NA	NA	NA	NA	NA	NA	NA

Balance Sheet & Other Fin. Data (Million $)

	2003	2002	2001	2000	1999	1998	1997	1996	1995	1994
Cash	50.0	39.0	39.0	31.0	76.0	34.0	43.0	63.0	15.0	63.0
Curr. Assets	1,449	1,286	1,276	1,361	1,335	1,394	1,497	1,666	930	840
Total Assets	8,305	7,401	7,715	7,762	7,722	8,096	7,810	7,538	4,134	3,520
Curr. Liab.	1,117	1,100	1,194	1,439	1,725	1,289	1,366	2,550	1,029	889
LT Debt	2,661	2,510	2,725	2,641	2,111	2,895	2,874	1,703	933	893
Common Equity	3,088	2,340	2,477	2,357	2,290	2,332	2,122	2,122	1,121	839
Total Cap.	5,944	5,014	5,363	5,156	4,835	5,789	5,592	4,195	2,462	2,286
Cap. Exp.	983	498	595	704	653	781	902	893	600	326
Cash Flow	1,102	1,031	931	834	886	892	860	696	758	476
Curr. Ratio	1.3	1.2	1.1	0.9	0.8	1.1	1.1	0.7	0.9	0.9
% LT Debt of Cap.	44.8	50.1	50.8	51.2	43.7	50.0	51.4	40.6	37.9	39.1
% Net Inc.of Revs.	10.4	10.7	8.4	7.2	9.5	8.8	8.8	6.3	8.4	7.5
% Ret. on Assets	7.4	7.3	5.6	4.7	5.6	5.3	5.4	4.9	6.9	5.9
% Ret. on Equity	21.6	22.8	17.9	15.6	19.1	19.1	20.6	18.5	26.8	27.2

Data as orig reptd.; bef. results of disc opers/spec. items. Per share data adj. for stk. divs.; EPS diluted. E-Estimated. NA-Not Available. NM-Not Meaningful. NR-Not Ranked. UR-Under Review.

Office: 39 Old Ridgebury Road, Danbury, CT 06810-5113.
Telephone: 203-837-2000.
Website: http://www.praxair.com
Chrmn, Pres & CEO: D.H. Reilley.
SVP & CFO: J.S. Sawyer.
VP & Treas: M.J. Allan.

VP, Secy & General Counsel: D.H. Chaifetz.
Investor Contact: E.T. Hirsch 203-837-2354.
Dirs: A. Achaval, C. W. Gargalli, I. D. Hall, R. L. Kuehn, Jr., R. W. LeBoeuf, B. F. Payton, G. J. Ratcliffe, Jr., D. H. Reilley, W. T. Smith, H. M. Watson, Jr.

Founded: in 1988.
Domicile: Delaware.
Employees: 25,438.
S&P Analyst: Richard O'Reilly, CFA /CB/GG

Principal Financial Group

Recommendation: **HOLD** ★★★☆☆
SELL SELL HOLD BUY BUY

12-Month Target Price: $37.00
(as of November 02, 2004)

PFG has an approximate 0.11% weighting in the **S&P 500**

Sector: Financials
Sub-Industry: Other Diversified Financial Services
Peer Group: Financial & Investment Services

Summary: PFG offers businesses, individuals and other clients various financial products and services, including insurance and retirement and investment services.

Quantitative Evaluations

S&P Earnings & Dividend Rank: NR

| D | C | B- | B | B+ | A- | A | A+ |

S&P Fair Value Rank: 3+

| 1 | 2 | **3** | 4 | 5 |
Lowest ——— Highest

Fair Value Calc.: $36.80 (Slightly Overvalued)

S&P Investability Quotient Percentile
82%

PFG scored higher than 82% of all companies for which an S&P Report is available.

Volatility: Low

| **Low** | Average | High |

Technical Evaluation: Bullish
Since 10/04, the technical indicators for PFG have been Bullish.

Relative Strength Rank: Moderate
63
1 Lowest ——— Highest 99

| Price as of 11/12/04: | **$38.74** | 2004E S&P Core EPS: | **$2.17** |

GAAP Earnings vs. Previous Year
▲ Up ▼ Down ► No Change

10 Week Mov. Avg.
30 Week Mov. Avg.
Relative Strength
12-Mo Target Price

HOLD $28.86 08/21/02

Volume Below Avg. — Above Avg.

Analyst commentary prepared by Gregory Simcik, CFA /PMW/GG

Highlights August 25, 2004

- We expect operating earnings to increase 13% in 2004 for the USAMA segment, on higher fees and other revenue, and flat operating expenses, despite additional overhead expenses allocated to the segment from the former mortgage banking segment during the 2004 second half.

- We estimate high-single-digit operating earnings growth for the IAMA segment, aided by recent acquisitions, but offset somewhat by the recent disposition of the Argentine subsidiary. We believe operating earnings for the life and health segment will grow only in the mid-single digits in 2004, as PFG pursues new strategies to spur growth in the segment, including new products and refined product distribution.

- We expect total operating EPS from continuing operations to increase 13% in 2004, to $2.31, on 2.8% fewer shares. We project total operating EPS growth of 15% for 2005, to $2.66, on 1.9% fewer shares. Our respective Standard & Poor's Core Earnings projections are $2.17 and $2.63 a share, reflecting estimated stock option and pension expenses.

Investment Rationale/Risk August 25, 2004

- We believe PFG could reinvest proceeds from the sale of the mortgage banking business in higher growth businesses and/or buy back more stock under its share repurchase authorization. However, we also see the shares offering above-average risk in a period of uncertainty for equity markets. At their current level, we view the shares as offering a return comparable to our expected return for the S&P 500, and would hold existing positions.

- Risks to our recommendation and target price include volatility in results due to large case sales for asset accumulation operations, sensitivity of operations to fluctuations in the equity markets, purchase price and integration risks associated with potential acquisitions, and currency risks.

- We base our 12-month target price of $36 on a sum-of-the-parts valuation that includes the sales price for the mortgage banking segment, and multiples of 15X, 14.5X and 11X applied to our 12-month forward unleveraged operating earnings estimates for the USAMA, IAMA, and life and health segments, respectively, with the combined value adjusted for corporate debt. Our multiple for USAMA is in line with the average for publicly traded peers. Our multiples for IAMA and life and health are at modest discounts to peers, due to additional international risks for IAMA and slower growth for life and health.

Key Stock Statistics

S&P Core EPS 2005E	2.63	52-week Range	$39.68-31.16
S&P Oper. EPS 2004E	2.31	12 Month P/E	15.1
P/E on S&P Oper. EPS 2004E	16.8	Beta	NA
S&P Oper. EPS 2005E	2.66	Shareholders	585,801
Yield (%)	1.4%	Market Cap (B)	$ 11.9
Dividend Rate/Share	0.55	Shares Outstanding (M)	307.0

Value of $10,000 invested five years ago: **NA**

Dividend Data Dividends have been paid since 2002

Amount ($)	Date Decl.	Ex-Div. Date	Stock of Record	Payment Date
0.450	Oct. 24	Nov. 05	Nov. 07	Dec. 08 '03
0.550	Oct. 22	Nov. 09	Nov. 12	Dec. 17 '04

Revenues/Earnings Data Fiscal year ending December 31

Revenues (Million $)

	2004	2003	2002	2001	2000	1999
1Q	2,257	2,297	2,228	—	—	—
2Q	1,980	2,412	2,336	—	—	—
3Q	2,089	2,266	1,996	2,457	—	—
4Q	—	2,479	2,424	—	—	—
Yr.	—	9,404	9,223	8,818	8,885	—

Earnings Per Share ($)

	2004	2003	2002	2001	2000	1999
1Q	0.62	0.47	0.68	—	—	—
2Q	0.40	0.62	0.33	—	—	—
3Q	0.62	0.68	0.12	0.32	—	—
4Q	E0.61	0.60	0.64	—	—	—
Yr.	E2.31	2.23	1.77	1.02	1.74	—

Next earnings report expected: early-February Source: S&P, Company Reports
EPS Estimates based on S&P Operating Earnings; historical GAAP earnings are as reported.

Principal Financial Group, Inc.

Recommendation: **HOLD** ★ ★ ★ ☆ ☆   12-Month Target Price: **$37.00** (as of November 02, 2004)

Business Summary August 25, 2004

The Principal Financial Group is a leading provider of retirement savings, investment and insurance products and services, with about 15 million customers and $144.9 billion in assets under management at December 31, 2003. According to surveys conducted by CFO magazine, PFG serviced more 401(k) plans in the U.S. in 2002 than any other CFO, mutual fund, or insurance company. According to the Spectrem Group, it held the leading market share in 2002, based on number of plans in the 401(k) market for businesses with fewer than 500 employees. According to the Investment Company Institute, the company ranked in the top quartile of U.S. mutual fund managers in terms of total mutual fund assets under management at November 30, 2003.

PFG's businesses are organized into four operating segments. The U.S. Asset Management and Accumulation segment (USAMA), which accounted for 39% of 2003 operating revenue (41% in 2002), provides retirement savings and related investment products and services, and asset management operations, with a concentration on small and medium-sized businesses. Segment account values totaled $91.7 billion at December 31, 2003.

The International Asset Management and Accumulation segment (IAMA), consists of Principal International and offers retirement products and services, annuities, mutual funds and life insurance through subsidiaries in Chile, Mexico, Hong Kong and India, with joint ventures in Brazil, Japan and Malaysia. IAMA accounted for 4.3% of operating revenues in 2003 (3.9%). Assets under management totaled $7.5 billion at December 31, 2003.

The life and health insurance segment, which accounted for 42% of operating revenues in 2003 (43%), offers individual and group life and disability insurance, as well as group health, dental and vision insurance. The recently divested mortgage banking segment accounted for 15% of operating revenues in 2003 (13%). The corporate and other segment accounted for 0.1% of operating revenues in 2003 (-0.2%) and includes, among other things, intersegment eliminations and the company's financing activities.

In June 2004, PFG acquired an interest in a coal-based synthetic fuel production facility, for total consideration of $37 million. Fuel produced through 2007 qualifies for tax credits, and the company has agreed to make additional payments to the seller based on its pro rata allocation of tax credits.

In May 2004, the company formed a joint venture with Punjab National Bank and Vijaya Bank to sell mutual funds and related financial services in India; PFG will own 65% of the venture. In January 2004, the company purchased Dao Heng Fund Management in Hong Kong, an additional 45% stake in Post Advisory Group, and the Molloy Companies, which offer consultative, administrative and claims services for insured and self-funded health plans. In June 2003, PFG agreed to purchase the remaining 50% stake in IDBI-Principal Asset Management Company, for about $20.3 million. In February 2003, it purchased AFORE Tepeyac S.A. de C.V. in Mexico, for about $53.5 million.

In July 2004, PFG sold its Argentine subsidiary, and completed the sale of its entire mortgage banking group to Citigroup, for estimated net proceeds of $630 million, subject to post-closing adjustments.

Company Financials Fiscal Year ending December 31

Per Share Data ($)

(Year Ended December 31)	2003	2002	2001	2000	1999	1998	1997	1996	1995	1994
Tangible Bk. Val.	22.12	19.32	10.59	14.89	NA	NA	NA	NA	NA	NA
Oper. Earnings	NA	2.46	1.96	NA	NA	NA	NA	NA	NA	NA
Earnings	2.23	1.77	1.02	1.74	NA	NA	NA	NA	NA	NA
S&P Core Earnings	2.38	1.85	1.69	NA	NA	NA	NA	NA	NA	NA
Dividends	0.45	0.25	Nil	NA	NA	NA	NA	NA	NA	NA
Payout Ratio	20%	14%	Nil	NA	NA	NA	NA	NA	NA	NA
Prices - High	34.67	31.50	24.75	NA	NA	NA	NA	NA	NA	NA
- Low	25.21	22.00	18.50	NA	NA	NA	NA	NA	NA	NA
P/E Ratio - High	16	18	24	NA	NA	NA	NA	NA	NA	NA
- Low	11	12	18	NA	NA	NA	NA	NA	NA	NA

Income Statement Analysis (Million $)

	2003	2002	2001	2000	1999	1998	1997	1996	1995	1994
Life Ins. In Force	136,530	137,794	62,309	60,389	NA	NA	NA	NA	NA	NA
Prem. Inc.: Life	1,500	1,824	2,089	1,792	NA	NA	NA	NA	NA	NA
Prem. Inc.: A & H	2,135	2,058	2,033	2,205	NA	NA	NA	NA	NA	NA
Net Invest. Inc.	3,420	3,305	3,395	3,172	NA	NA	NA	NA	NA	NA
Total Revs.	9,404	8,823	8,818	8,885	NA	NA	NA	NA	NA	NA
Pretax Inc.	954	666	449	872	NA	NA	NA	NA	NA	NA
Net Oper. Inc.	NA	864	711	NA	NA	NA	NA	NA	NA	NA
Net Inc.	728	620	370	627	NA	NA	NA	NA	NA	NA
S&P Core Earnings	778	647	608	NA	NA	NA	NA	NA	NA	NA

Balance Sheet & Other Fin. Data (Million $)

	2003	2002	2001	2000	1999	1998	1997	1996	1995	1994
Cash & Equiv.	2,344	1,685	1,218	940	NA	NA	NA	NA	NA	NA
Premiums Due	720	460	531	572	NA	NA	NA	NA	NA	NA
Invest. Assets: Bonds	37,553	34,287	30,030	29,328	NA	NA	NA	NA	NA	NA
Invest. Assets: Stocks	713	379	834	579	NA	NA	NA	NA	NA	NA
Invest. Assets: Loans	14,312	11,900	11,898	12,359	NA	NA	NA	NA	NA	NA
Invest. Assets: Total	55,578	48,996	44,773	44,403	NA	NA	NA	NA	NA	NA
Deferred Policy Costs	1,572	1,414	1,373	1,338	NA	NA	NA	NA	NA	NA
Total Assets	107,754	89,861	88,351	86,838	NA	NA	NA	NA	NA	NA
Debt	2,767	1,333	1,378	1,391	NA	NA	NA	NA	NA	NA
Common Equity	7,400	13,314	6,820	6,624	NA	NA	NA	NA	NA	NA
% Return On Revs.	7.7	7.0	4.2	7.1	NA	NA	NA	NA	NA	NA
% Ret. on Assets	0.7	0.7	0.4	NA	NA	NA	NA	NA	NA	NA
% Ret. on Equity	10.4	4.6	5.7	NA	NA	NA	NA	NA	NA	NA
% Invest. Yield	6.5	7.0	7.8	NA	NA	NA	NA	NA	NA	NA

Data as orig reptd.; bef. results of disc opers/spec. items. Per share data adj. for stk. divs.; EPS diluted. E-Estimated. NA-Not Available. NM-Not Meaningful. NR-Not Ranked. UR-Under Review.

Office: 711 High Street, Des Moines, IA 50392.
Telephone: 515-247-5111.
Website: http://www.principal.com
Chrmn, Pres & CEO: J.B. Griswell.
EVP & CFO: M.S. Gersie.

EVP & General Counsel: K.E. Shaff.
VP & Investor Contact: J. Effrein 800-986-3343 Opt. 4.
Dirs: B. J. Bernard, J. Carter-Miller, G. E. Costley, D. J. Drury, D. Gelatt, S. L. Helton, C. S. Johnson, W. T. Kerr, R. L. Keyser, V. H. Loewenstein, A. Mathrani, F. F. Pena, E. E. Tallett.

Founded: in 1998.
Domicile: Delaware.
Employees: 14,976.
S&P Analyst: Gregory Simcik, CFA /PMW/GG

Procter & Gamble

Recommendation: **BUY** ★★★★★   12-Month Target Price: **$65.00**
(as of April 30, 2004)

PG has an approximate 1.26% weighting in the **S&P 500**

Sector: Consumer Staples
Sub-Industry: Household Products
Peer Group: Household Products

Summary: This leading consumer products company markets household and personal care products in more than 140 countries.

Quantitative Evaluations

S&P Earnings & Dividend Rank: A

| D | C | B- | B | B+ | A- | A | A+ |

S&P Fair Value Rank: 3+

| 1 | 2 | 3 | 4 | 5 |
| Lowest | | | | Highest |

Fair Value Calc.: $50.70 (Slightly Overvalued)

S&P Investability Quotient Percentile

100%

PG scored higher than 100% of all companies for which an S&P Report is available.

Volatility: Low

| Low | Average | High |

Technical Evaluation: Bearish
Since 10/04, the technical indicators for PG have been Bearish.

Relative Strength Rank: Moderate

38

| 1 Lowest | Highest 99 |

| Price as of 11/12/04: | $54.60 | 2005E S&P Core EPS: | $2.35 |

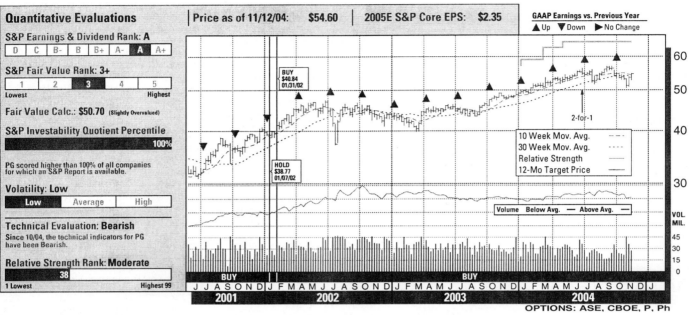

GAAP Earnings vs. Previous Year
▲ Up ▼ Down ► No Change

BUY $40.84 01/31/02
HOLD $38.77 01/07/02
2-for-1

10 Week Mov. Avg.
30 Week Mov. Avg.
Relative Strength
12-Mo Target Price

Volume Below Avg. — Above Avg.

OPTIONS: ASE, CBOE, P, Ph

Analyst commentary prepared by Howard Choe/PMW/GG

Highlights August 19, 2004

- We expect sales to increase about 6% in FY 05 (Jun.), driven largely by higher volume growth. We believe currency translation will have a neutral effect. We see the bulk of volume growth as likely to come from sales of PG's leading brands, and from new product introductions. We expect volume growth to be led by the beauty and healthcare segments.

- We expect raw material costs to moderate in FY 05, and see better cost controls leading to wider gross margins. We also see operating margins widening, due to marketing, research and administrative costs that are similar to the level of FY 04 as a percentage of sales.

- We estimate that FY 05 EPS will advance 12%, to $2.59, from $2.32 in FY 04. We project FY 05 Standard & Poor's Core Earnings of $2.35 a share, with the difference from our operating estimate primarily reflecting projected stock option expense.

Investment Rationale/Risk August 19, 2004

- We are maintaining our buy opinion on the shares, reflecting our view of PG's solid fundamentals and outlook. We expect the company to continue to benefit from its focus on its larger brands, an improved product mix, and cost savings resulting from restructuring initiatives. PG has also been successful, in our view, in offering consumers an attractive price/value proposition, as well as innovative new products.

- Risks to our recommendation and target price include unfavorable currency translation, increased competition, greater promotional spending, and low consumer acceptance of new products.

- The shares are trading in line with the level of PG's large-cap peers, at about 22X our calendar 2004 EPS estimate. Our 12-month target price of $65 was derived from a combination of our relative valuation and discounted cash flow analyses. Based on what we see as the company's higher level of execution and consistency in earnings and cash flow growth, we believe the stock should trade at a premium to peers.

Key Stock Statistics

S&P Oper. EPS 2005E	2.60	52-week Range	$56.95-47.50
P/E on S&P Oper. EPS 2005E	21.0	12 Month P/E	22.6
Yield (%)	1.8%	Beta	-0.15
Dividend Rate/Share	1.00	Shareholders	1,426,000
Shares Outstanding (M)	2536.7	Market Cap (B)	$138.5

Value of $10,000 invested five years ago: **NA**

Dividend Data Dividends have been paid since 1891

Amount ($)	Date Decl.	Ex-Div. Date	Stock of Record	Payment Date
0.500	Mar. 09	Apr. 21	Apr. 23	May. 14 '04
2-for-1	Mar. 09	Jun. 21	May. 21	Jun. 18 '04
0.250	Jul. 13	Jul. 21	Jul. 23	Aug. 16 '04
0.250	Oct. 12	Oct. 20	Oct. 22	Nov. 15 '04

Revenues/Earnings Data Fiscal year ending June 30

Revenues (Million $)

	2005	2004	2003	2002	2001	2000
1Q	13,744	12,195	10,796	9,766	9,969	9,919
2Q	—	13,221	11,005	10,403	10,182	10,588
3Q	—	13,029	10,656	9,900	9,511	9,783
4Q	—	12,962	10,920	10,169	9,582	9,661
Yr.	—	51,407	43,377	40,238	39,244	39,951

Earnings Per Share ($)

	2005	2004	2003	2002	2001	2000
1Q	0.73	0.63	0.52	0.40	0.41	0.40
2Q	E0.72	0.65	0.53	0.32	0.42	0.39
3Q	E0.60	0.55	0.46	0.37	0.32	0.26
4Q	E0.55	0.50	0.34	0.32	-0.12	0.18
Yr.	E2.60	2.32	1.84	1.54	1.04	1.24

Next earnings report expected: late-January Source: S&P, Company Reports
EPS Estimates based on S&P Operating Earnings; historical GAAP earnings are as reported.

The Procter & Gamble Company

Recommendation: **BUY** ★ ★ ★ ★ ★   12-Month Target Price: **$65.00** (as of April 30, 2004)

Business Summary August 19, 2004

Procter & Gamble's goal is to create the most successful global brands in every category everywhere that it competes. With brands like Crest toothpaste, Pampers disposable diapers, and Tide detergent in its family of products, the company believes that it has assembled a portfolio of premier consumer brands in a variety of categories, selling about 300 products to more than 5 billion consumers in 140 countries.

PG believes it has made substantial progress over the past two years in strengthening its businesses. The company focuses on six drivers to success: consumer focus, strategic choices, operational excellence and financial discipline, organizational structure, and brand-building capability.

In June 1999, the company embarked on a sweeping restructuring program that was to be completed by 2005. However, due to faster than expected implementation, the program was largely completed in calendar 2003. The program resulted in cumulative after-tax charges of $3.79 billion, lower than the original estimate of $4.4 billion, and led to separation packages provided to 21,600 employees worldwide as of June 30, 2003. PG's long-term sales growth rate target is 4% to 6%. It projects net operating earnings growth rate in double digits. Part of the anticipated earnings growth is seen resulting from annual after-tax savings of about $1.65 billion by 2004.

In 1999, PG reorganized itself into five Global Business Units (GBUs), aiming to leverage its size by developing products and strategies globally. The company believes this has increase innovation, and has let products be introduced more quickly than in the past. The GBUs are supported by seven Market Development Organizations, which act as sales agents for all PG products in each local region.

The fabric and home care division, which sells cleaning detergents such as Tide, Cascade and Downy, contributed 29% of sales in FY 03 (Jun.). The baby and family care division, which sells bathroom tissue and paper towels with brands such as Bounty and Charmin, accounted for 23% of sales. Beauty care, which sells personal care products under brands such as Cover Girl, Pantene and Secret, accounted for 28% of sales. Food and beverage, selling brands such as Pringles and Folgers, accounted for 7% of sales. Healthcare, selling brands such as Crest, Vicks and Pepto-Bismol, accounted for 13% of sales.

In FY 03, North America accounted for 54% of total sales, Europe, Middle East and Africa for 29%; Asia 11%; and Latin America 6%.

In September 2003, PG acquired a controlling interest in Wella AG, a beauty care company, for about $7 billion (including the assumption of debt). The acquisition was financed via a combination of cash and debt. Wella, which sells products in more than 150 countries, focuses on professional and retail hair care, cosmetics and fragrances. In FY 02, PG spun off its Jif peanut butter and Crisco shortening businesses. Also in FY 02, the company acquired the Clairol hair care business from Bristol-Myers Squibb Co., for $4.95 billion in cash.

Company Financials Fiscal Year ending June 30

Per Share Data ($)

(Year Ended June 30)	2004	2003	2002	2001	2000	1999	1998	1997	1996	1995
Tangible Bk. Val.	NM	0.43	NM	0.78	0.68	1.31	1.28	3.00	2.02	1.49
Cash Flow	3.18	2.41	2.11	1.85	2.01	2.00	1.80	1.77	1.57	1.38
Earnings	2.32	1.84	1.54	1.04	1.24	1.30	1.28	1.22	1.07	0.93
S&P Core Earnings	2.17	1.58	1.28	0.81	NA	NA	NA	NA	NA	NA
Dividends	0.93	0.82	0.76	0.70	0.64	0.57	0.51	0.45	0.40	0.35
Payout Ratio	40%	45%	49%	68%	52%	44%	39%	37%	37%	38%
Prices - High	56.95	49.96	47.37	40.86	59.18	57.81	47.40	41.68	27.75	22.37
- Low	48.88	39.78	37.04	27.98	26.37	41.00	32.56	25.90	19.84	15.15
P/E Ratio - High	25	27	31	39	48	45	37	34	26	24
- Low	21	22	24	27	21	32	25	21	19	16

Income Statement Analysis (Million $)

	2004	2003	2002	2001	2000	1999	1998	1997	1996	1995
Revs.	51,407	43,377	40,238	39,244	39,951	38,125	37,154	35,764	35,284	33,434
Oper. Inc.	19,827	9,556	8,371	7,007	8,145	8,401	7,653	6,975	6,173	5,432
Depr.	1,733	1,703	1,693	2,271	2,191	2,148	1,598	1,487	1,358	1,253
Int. Exp.	629	561	603	794	722	650	548	457	484	488
Pretax Inc.	9,350	7,530	6,383	4,616	5,536	5,838	5,708	5,249	4,669	4,000
Eff. Tax Rate	30.7%	31.1%	31.8%	36.7%	36.0%	35.5%	33.8%	34.9%	34.7%	33.9%
Net Inc.	6,481	5,186	4,352	2,922	3,542	3,763	3,780	3,415	3,046	2,645
S&P Core Earnings	5,922	4,313	3,486	2,165	NA	NA	NA	NA	NA	NA

Balance Sheet & Other Fin. Data (Million $)

	2004	2003	2002	2001	2000	1999	1998	1997	1996	1995
Cash	5,469	5,912	3,427	2,306	1,415	2,294	1,549	2,350	2,520	2,178
Curr. Assets	17,115	15,220	12,166	10,889	10,146	11,358	10,577	10,786	10,807	10,842
Total Assets	57,048	43,706	40,776	34,387	34,366	32,113	30,966	27,544	27,730	28,125
Curr. Liab.	22,147	12,358	12,704	9,846	10,141	10,761	9,250	7,798	7,825	8,648
LT Debt	12,554	11,475	11,201	9,792	8,916	6,231	5,765	4,143	4,670	5,161
Common Equity	15,752	14,606	12,072	10,309	10,550	10,277	10,415	10,187	9,836	8,676
Total Cap.	32,093	29,057	25,984	22,696	21,828	18,651	16,608	14,889	17,030	16,281
Cap. Exp.	2,024	1,482	1,679	2,486	3,018	2,828	2,559	2,129	2,179	2,146
Cash Flow	8,083	6,764	5,921	5,193	5,733	5,802	5,274	4,798	4,301	3,796
Curr. Ratio	0.8	1.2	1.0	1.1	1.0	1.1	1.1	1.4	1.4	1.3
% LT Debt of Cap.	39.1	39.5	43.1	43.1	40.8	33.4	34.7	27.8	27.4	31.7
% Net Inc.of Revs.	12.6	12.0	10.8	7.4	8.9	9.9	10.2	9.5	8.6	7.9
% Ret. on Assets	12.9	12.3	11.6	8.5	10.7	11.9	12.9	12.4	10.9	9.9
% Ret. on Equity	41.8	37.9	37.8	28.0	34.0	35.3	35.7	33.1	31.8	32.7

Data as orig reptd.; bef. results of disc opers/spec. items. Per share data adj. for stk. divs. Bold denotes primary EPS - prior periods restated. E-Estimated. NA-Not Available. NM-Not Meaningful. NR-Not Ranked. UR-Under Review.

Office: One Procter & Gamble Plaza, Cincinnati, OH 45202.
Telephone: 513-983-1100.
Website: http://www.pg.com
Chrmn, Pres & CEO: A.G. Lafley.
Vice Chrmn: B.L. Byrnes.
Vice Chrmn: S. Arnold.
Vice Chrmn: R.K. Clark.

Vice Chrmn: R. McDonald.
Treas & Investor Contact: J.P. Goodwin 800-742-6253.
Dirs: N. R. Augustine, B. L. Byrnes, R. K. Clark, S. Cook, D. De Sole, J. T. Gorman, A. G. Lafley, C. R. Lee, L. M. Martin, W. J. McNerney, Jr., J. A. Rodgers, J. F. Smith, Jr., R. Snyderman, R. D. Storey, M. v. Whitman, E. Zedillo.

Founded: in 1837.
Domicile: Ohio.
Employees: 110,000.
S&P Analyst: Howard Choe/PMW/GG

Progressive Corp.

Recommendation: **HOLD** ★★★☆☆
SELL SELL HOLD BUY BUY

12-Month Target Price: **$103.00**
(as of November 04, 2004)

PGR has an approximate 0.18% weighting in the **S&P 500**

Sector: Financials
Sub-Industry: Property & Casualty Insurance
Peer Group: Commercial/Personal Insurers - National

Summary: This leading underwriter of nonstandard auto and other specialty personal lines coverages has expanded its product line and evolved into a full-service auto insurer.

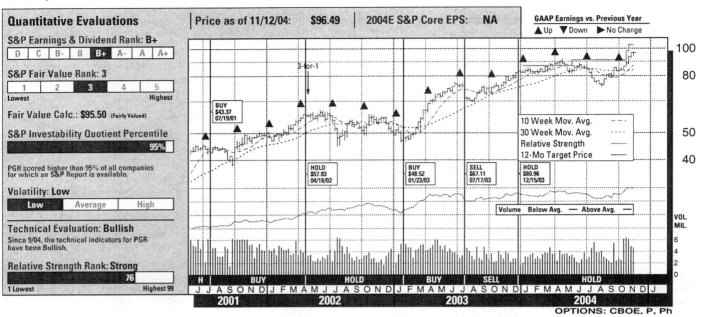

Quantitative Evaluations

S&P Earnings & Dividend Rank: B+
D | C | B- | B | **B+** | A- | A | A+

S&P Fair Value Rank: 3
1 | 2 | **3** | 4 | 5
Lowest | | | | Highest

Fair Value Calc.: $95.50 (Fairly Valued)

S&P Investability Quotient Percentile
95%

PGR scored higher than 95% of all companies for which an S&P Report is available.

Volatility: Low
Low | Average | High

Technical Evaluation: Bullish
Since 9/04, the technical indicators for PGR have been Bullish.

Relative Strength Rank: Strong
76
1 Lowest | Highest 99

Price as of 11/12/04: $96.49 | **2004E S&P Core EPS:** NA

Price as of 11/12/04: **$96.49**

GAAP Earnings vs. Previous Year
▲ Up ▼ Down ► No Change

3-for-1

BUY $43.37 07/19/01
HOLD $57.83 04/18/02
BUY $48.52 01/23/03
SELL $67.11 07/17/03
HOLD $80.96 12/15/03

10 Week Mov. Avg.
30 Week Mov. Avg.
Relative Strength
12-Mo Target Price

Volume Below Avg. — Above Avg.

VOL. MIL.

H | BUY | HOLD | BUY | SELL | HOLD
J J A S O N D J F M A M J J A S O N D J F M A M J J A S O N D J F M A M J J A S O N D J
2001 | 2002 | 2003 | 2004

OPTIONS: CBOE, P, Ph

Analyst commentary prepared by Catherine A. Seifert/MF/JWP

Highlights November 12, 2004

- We believe earned premium growth in 2005 will likely continue to slow to around 12%, from an expected 12% to 15% in 2004. Although this rate of growth remains above that of many of PGR's peers, it is below the company's previous rates of growth. This reflects, in our view, a combination of PGR's shifting business model to one of a standard lines carrier, and to the company's less aggressive pricing strategy. In the first nine months of 2004, net written premiums rose 9%, year over year. Earned premiums were up 12% during the same period.

- Underwriting margins in recent periods have benefited from favorable claim trends, particularly in the personal auto line, where claim frequency trends have been very favorable, in our view. Despite an industrywide surge in catastrophe losses, PGR's underwriting results improved in the first nine months of 2004. This was evidenced by a lower combined loss and expense ratio of 86.3%, versus 87.9% in the 2003 interim.

- Our operating EPS estimates of $6.95 for 2004 and $6.60 for 2005 (versus $5.65 in 2003) assume that double digit earned premium growth will be partly offset by an erosion in underwriting margins amid an uptick in some competitive pressures and a slight deterioration in the unusually favorable claim trends.

Investment Rationale/Risk November 12, 2004

- While we acknowledge PGR's above average rate of premium growth and its historically superior (to peers) underwriting results, we remain concerned about the sustainability of both of these trends. At current levels, the shares trade at a premium to peers, both on a forward price/earnings and a price/book basis. Consequently, we see no reason to add to holdings.

- Risks to our recommendation and target price include a possible sharp rise in loss costs and increased price competition in PGR's core personal auto line. Also, the New York Attorney General (AG) has alleged that certain insurance brokers have have acted improperly in the use of incentive commissions paid in the placement of certain commercial lines insurance policies. Certain commercial lines insurers have also been investigated as part of this probe. We think PGR shares could come under pressure if the AG discovers some wrongdoing on the part of personal lines carriers and the way they market their products.

- Our 12-month target price of $103 assumes that PGR shares continue to trade at a premium to peers, both on a forward price/book basis and on a forward P/E basis. PGR's lack of meaningful exposure to the record industry catastrophe losses, year to date, and thus far to the Spitzer investigation, will likely buoy the shares' near term valuation, in our opinion.

Key Stock Statistics

S&P Oper. EPS 2004E	**6.95**	52-week Range	**$97.29-73.10**
P/E on S&P Oper. EPS 2004E	**13.9**	12 Month P/E	**13.3**
S&P Oper. EPS 2005E	**6.60**	Beta	**0.79**
Yield (%)	**0.1%**	Shareholders	**4,101**
Dividend Rate/Share	**0.12**	Market Cap (B)	**$ 19.3**
Shares Outstanding (M)	**200.1**		

Value of $10,000 invested five years ago: **$ 30,817**

Dividend Data Dividends have been paid since 1965

Amount ($)	Date Decl.	Ex-Div. Date	Stock of Record	Payment Date
0.025	Apr. 16	Jun. 09	Jun. 11	Jun. 30 '04
0.030	Aug. 20	Sep. 08	Sep. 10	Sep. 30 '04
0.030	Aug. 20	Sep. 16	Sep. 20	Sep. 30 '04
0.030	Oct. 15	Dec. 08	Dec. 10	Dec. 31 '04

Revenues/Earnings Data Fiscal year ending December 31

Revenues (Million $)

	2004	2003	2002	2001	2000	1999
1Q	3,280	2,720	2,069	1,774	1,602	1,410
2Q	3,367	2,921	2,259	1,863	1,653	1,525
3Q	3,387	3,081	2,419	1,860	1,752	1,585
4Q	—	3,170	—	1,988	—	1,605
Yr.	—	11,892	9,294	7,488	6,771	6,124

Earnings Per Share ($)

	2004	2003	2002	2001	2000	1999
1Q	2.09	1.32	0.78	0.39	-0.21	0.47
2Q	1.76	1.29	0.71	0.46	-0.06	0.50
3Q	1.77	1.45	0.80	0.43	0.26	0.33
4Q	—	1.63	0.69	0.56	0.21	0.02
Yr.	—	5.69	2.99	1.83	0.21	1.32

Next earnings report expected: late-January Source: S&P, Company Reports
EPS Estimates based on S&P Operating Earnings; historical GAAP earnings are as reported.

The Progressive Corporation

Recommendation: **HOLD** ★ ★ ★ ☆ ☆   12-Month Target Price: **$103.00** (as of November 04, 2004)

Business Summary November 12, 2004

The Progressive Corp. is a regional auto insurer that has expanded from a specialty writer of nonstandard coverage into a full-service auto insurer. Until 1999, the company had been aggressively pricing its policies and accepting narrower profit margins. Consequently, PGR's written premium growth had been much greater than that of the overall property-casualty insurance industry. Beginning in late 1999 and continuing into 2000, the company refocused its efforts on its underwriting results, and began to raise its premium rates, which slowed its rate of growth. During 2001-2003, PGR began to ramp up its growth rate again. During 2003, net written premiums grew 26%, reflecting a 24% rise in personal lines business written through agents, a 29% increase in direct written personal lines premiums, and a 35% surge in commercial auto written premiums, partly offset by a 39% drop in other written premiums. Personal lines business accounted for 88% of all net written premiums in 2003. Policies in force rose 19% in 2003, to 8.2 million at year end, from 6.9 million a year earlier. Underwriting results (as measured by the combined loss/expense ratio) improved during 2003. PGR's combined ratio equaled 87.3% in 2003, versus 92.4% in 2002. These ratios consisted of a loss ratio of 67.4% in 2003 (versus 70.9% in 2002); and an expense ratio of 19.9% in 2003 (versus 21.5% in 2002).

PGR's core business (93% of 2003's $10.5 billion in personal lines net premiums written) consists of underwriting private passenger automobile insurance. Based on 2002 year end industry net written premium data (latest available), the com-

pany was the third largest private U.S. passenger auto insurer. PGR's other lines of business include recreational vehicle, motorcycle and small commercial vehicle insurance, collateral protection, directors' and officers' liability insurance, and fidelity coverage for financial institutions.

Historically, the bulk of the company's core business consisted of nonstandard insurance programs, which provide coverage for accounts rejected or canceled by other companies. However, as part of a strategy to expand its share of the personal automobile insurance market, PGR is underwriting standard and preferred risk automobile insurance coverage.

PGR distributes its core personal lines products through an array of channels, including independent agents and strategic alliance agency relationships (69% of personal lines net premiums written in 2003). Distribution through direct channels, including a toll free telephone line and the Internet, accounted for 31% of net written premiums in 2003.

The company is licensed to sell its policies throughout the U.S. In 2003, Florida accounted for 11% of direct premiums written, Texas 9%, New York 7%, Ohio 6%, California 6%, Georgia 5%, Pennsylvania 5%, and all other states the remaining 51%.

Company Financials Fiscal Year ending December 31

Per Share Data ($)

(Year Ended December 31)	2003	2002	2001	2000	1999	1998	1997	1996	1995	1994
Tangible Bk. Val.	23.38	17.28	14.76	13.01	12.55	11.76	9.85	7.82	6.44	4.98
Oper. Earnings	NA	3.22	2.16	0.25	1.19	2.00	1.49	1.36	0.95	0.92
Earnings	5.69	2.99	1.83	0.21	1.32	2.04	1.77	1.38	1.09	1.20
S&P Core Earnings	5.61	3.15	2.09	NA	NA	NA	NA	NA	NA	NA
Dividends	0.10	0.10	0.09	0.09	0.09	0.08	0.08	0.08	0.07	0.07
Payout Ratio	2%	3%	5%	44%	7%	4%	5%	6%	7%	6%
Prices - High	84.68	60.49	50.60	37.00	58.08	57.33	40.29	24.08	16.50	13.50
- Low	46.25	44.75	27.37	15.00	22.83	31.33	20.50	13.45	11.58	9.25
P/E Ratio - High	15	20	28	NM	44	28	23	17	15	11
- Low	8	15	15	NM	17	15	12	10	11	8

Income Statement Analysis (Million $)

	2003	2002	2001	2000	1999	1998	1997	1996	1995	1994
Premium Inc.	11,341	8,884	7,162	6,348	5,684	4,948	4,190	3,199	2,727	2,191
Net Invest. Inc.	465	455	414	385	341	295	275	226	199	159
Oth. Revs.	54.5	34.3	24.7	37.4	99	49.6	144	53.0	85.6	66.0
Total Revs.	11,861	9,373	7,600	6,771	6,124	5,292	4,608	3,478	3,012	2,415
Pretax Inc.	1,860	981	588	31.8	412	661	579	442	346	380
Net Oper. Inc.	NA	718	486	55.4	267	449	336	309	NA	NA
Net Inc.	1,255	667	411	46.1	295	457	400	314	251	274
S&P Core Earnings	1,234	702	469	NA	NA	NA	NA	NA	NA	NA

Balance Sheet & Other Fin. Data (Million $)

	2003	2002	2001	2000	1999	1998	1997	1996	1995	1994
Cash & Equiv.	110	94.8	86.4	73.1	68.2	71.7	23.3	62.0	56.0	56.8
Premiums Due	2,351	1,959	1,497	1,567	1,761	1,456	1,161	821	650	542
Invest. Assets: Bonds	9,133	7,713	5,949	4,784	4,533	4,219	4,301	3,568	3,076	2,704
Invest. Assets: Stocks	2,751	2,004	2,050	2,012	1,666	1,013	970	882	692	476
Invest. Assets: Loans	Nil	Nil	Nil	Nil	Nil	Nil	Nil	Nil	Nil	Nil
Invest. Assets: Total	12,532	10,284	8,226	6,983	6,428	5,674	5,270	4,450	3,768	3,180
Deferred Policy Costs	412	364	317	310	343	299	260	200	182	162
Total Assets	16,282	13,564	11,122	10,052	9,705	8,463	7,560	6,184	5,353	4,675
Debt	1,490	1,489	1,096	749	1,049	777	776	776	676	676
Common Equity	5,060	3,768	3,251	2,870	2,753	2,557	2,136	1,677	1,392	1,066
Prop. & Cas. Loss Ratio	67.4	70.9	73.6	83.2	75.0	68.5	71.1	70.2	71.6	NA
Prop. & Cas. Expense Ratio	18.8	20.4	21.0	21.0	22.1	22.4	20.7	19.8	21.4	NA
Prop. & Cas. Combined Ratio	86.2	91.3	94.7	104.2	97.1	90.9	91.8	90.0	93.0	NA
% Return On Revs.	10.6	7.1	5.4	0.7	4.8	8.6	278.2	9.0	8.3	11.3
% Ret. on Equity	28.4	19.3	13.4	1.6	11.1	19.5	21.0	20.5	19.7	NA

Data as orig reptd.; bef. results of disc opers/spec. items. Per share data adj. for stk. divs.; EPS diluted. E-Estimated. NA-Not Available. NM-Not Meaningful. NR-Not Ranked. EPS ests. excl. real. inv. gains/losses; historical EPS data include them.

Office: 6300 Wilson Mills Road, Mayfield Village, OH 44143.
Telephone: 440-461-5000.
Website: http://www.progressive.com
Chrmn: P.B. Lewis.
Pres & CEO: G.M. Renwick.
VP & CFO: W.T. Forrester.

VP, Chief Acctg Officer & Investor Contact: J.W. Basch 440-446-2851.
VP & Treas: T.A. King.
Dirs: M. N. Allen, B. C. Ames, C. Davis, S. Hardis, B. Healy, J. D. Kelly, P. Laskawy, P. Lewis, N. Matthews, G. M. Renwick, D. B. Shackelford, B. T. Sheares.

Founded: in 1965.
Domicile: Ohio.
Employees: 25,834.
S&P Analyst: Catherine A. Seifert/MF/JWP

Progress Energy

Recommendation: **HOLD** ★ ★ ★ ☆ ☆
SELL | SELL | HOLD | BUY | BUY

12-Month Target Price: $43.00
(as of November 04, 2004)

PGN has an approximate 0.10% weighting in the **S&P 500**

Sector: Utilities
Sub-Industry: Electric Utilities
Peer Group: Electric Cos. (Domestic) - Large

Summary: This holding company was renamed after the acquisition of St. Petersburg-based Florida Progress Corp. by Raleigh-based CP&L Energy.

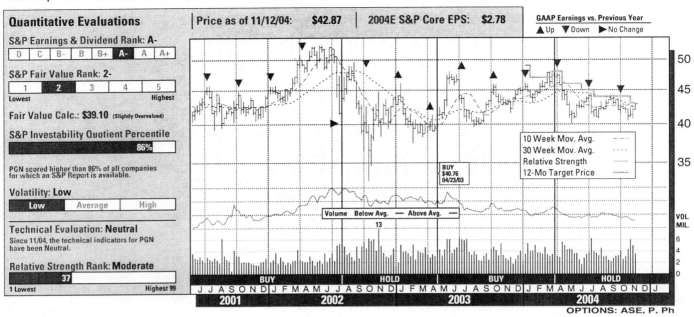

Quantitative Evaluations	Price as of 11/12/04: **$42.87**	2004E S&P Core EPS: **$2.78**

S&P Earnings & Dividend Rank: A-

D | C | B- | B | B+ | **A-** | A | A+

S&P Fair Value Rank: 2-

1 | **2** | 3 | 4 | 5
Lowest — Highest

Fair Value Calc.: $39.10 (Slightly Overvalued)

S&P Investability Quotient Percentile
86%

PGN scored higher than 86% of all companies for which an S&P Report is available.

Volatility: Low

Low | Average | High

Technical Evaluation: Neutral
Since 11/04, the technical indicators for PGN have been Neutral.

Relative Strength Rank: Moderate
37
1 Lowest — Highest 99

GAAP Earnings vs. Previous Year
▲ Up ▼ Down ► No Change

10 Week Mov. Avg.
30 Week Mov. Avg.
Relative Strength
12-Mo Target Price

BUY $40.76 04/23/03

Volume Below Avg. — Above Avg. —

VOL. MIL.

BUY | HOLD | BUY | HOLD
J J A S O N D | J F M A M J J A S O N D | J F M A M J J A S O N D | J F M A M J J A S O N D | J
2001 | **2002** | **2003** | **2004**

OPTIONS: ASE, P, Ph

Analyst commentary prepared by Justin McCann/PMW/JWP

Highlights September 28, 2004

- Following an anticipated 14% decline in 2004 from 2003's EPS from ongoing operations of $3.56, we expect EPS to rebound nearly 20% in 2005. Operating results in 2004 are expected to be hurt about $0.55 due to the loss of synthetic fuel related tax credits. Since these credits are tied to projected tax liabilities (which are expected to be significantly reduced due to the impact of recent hurricanes), we expect a significant reduction in production and earnings from synfuel operations.

- Aided by continued customer growth, we estimate a 2% to 3% increase in earnings from the regulated utilities. However, we believe this will be partly offset by a decrease in regulated wholesale sales, higher fixed costs in the unregulated generation business, and increased benefit-related costs.

- We do not expect any new major equity issuances over the next several years, and believe a foundation has been set for EPS growth in 2005 and 2006. PGN hopes to accelerate the reduction of its debt. We believe that it will attempt to sell its Progress Rail Services subsidiary earlier than its original target date of the end of 2006.

Investment Rationale/Risk September 28, 2004

- In light of expected total return, including the stock's above-average dividend yield, we would hold existing positions. We believe the stock is fairly valued at a discount of over 8% to the average peer P/E multiple of 13.2X our 2005 estimates, due to the potential for an unfavorable IRS review of PGN's synthetic fuel tax credits, as well as the relatively modest earnings performance expected for 2005.

- Risks to our recommendation and target price include a sharp decline in the average P/E multiple of the group as a whole, as well as potential for significant tax liabilities if synthetic fuel-related tax credits are not approved by the IRS. A pending IRS field audit recommendation is due by the final quarter of 2004, and is expected to be unfavorable; PGN could then appeal the recommendation in a process that could take up to two years.

- Based on our expectations of rising interest rates and a modest contraction in the average peer group P/E multiple, we expect the shares to trade at about 12X our 2005 EPS estimate of $3.65. Our 12-month target price is $44.

Key Stock Statistics

S&P Core EPS 2005E	**3.37**	52-week Range	**$47.95-40.09**
S&P Oper. EPS 2004E	**3.00**	12 Month P/E	**15.5**
P/E on S&P Oper. EPS 2004E	**14.3**	Beta	**0.16**
S&P Oper. EPS 2005E	**3.55**	Shareholders	**70,118**
Yield (%)	**5.4%**	Market Cap (B)	**$ 10.6**
Dividend Rate/Share	**2.30**	Shares Outstanding (M)	**246.8**

Value of $10,000 invested five years ago: **$ 15,883**

Dividend Data Dividends have been paid since 1937

Amount ($)	Date Decl.	Ex-Div. Date	Stock of Record	Payment Date
0.575	Dec. 10	Jan. 08	Jan. 12	Feb. 02 '04
0.575	Mar. 17	Apr. 07	Apr. 12	May. 01 '04
0.575	May. 12	Jul. 08	Jul. 12	Aug. 02 '04
0.575	Sep. 17	Oct. 06	Oct. 11	Nov. 01 '04

Revenues/Earnings Data Fiscal year ending December 31

Revenues (Million $)

	2004	2003	2002	2001	2000	1999
1Q	2,234	2,187	1,787	1,908	877.1	762.9
2Q	2,430	2,050	1,959	2,316	892.3	762.8
3Q	2,775	2,458	2,277	2,331	1,084	1,025
4Q	—	2,048	1,922	1,907	1,265	806.1
Yr.	—	8,743	7,945	8,461	4,119	3,358

Earnings Per Share ($)

	2004	2003	2002	2001	2000	1999
1Q	0.45	0.89	0.58	0.77	0.56	0.63
2Q	0.63	0.65	0.56	0.56	0.70	0.43
3Q	1.24	1.40	0.72	1.77	1.93	0.97
4Q	E0.52	0.47	0.66	-0.42	-0.07	0.51
Yr.	E3.00	3.40	2.53	2.64	3.03	2.55

Next earnings report expected: late-January Source: S&P, Company Reports
EPS Estimates based on S&P Operating Earnings; historical GAAP earnings are as reported.

Progress Energy, Inc.

Recommendation: **HOLD** ★ ★ ★ ☆ ☆   12-Month Target Price: **$43.00** (as of November 04, 2004)

Business Summary September 28, 2004

Progress Energy changed its name from CP&L Energy in December 2000.

On November 30, 2000, the company acquired Florida Progress Corp. (FPC), for about $5.4 billion in cash (65%) and stock (35%), plus the assumption of $2.7 billion of FPC debt. FPC was the holding company for Florida Power (now operating as Progress Energy Florida), which provides electricity to about 1.5 million customers in central, northern and Gulf Coast Florida.

CP&L Energy was formed in June 2000, as the holding company for Carolina Power & Light Co. (now operating as Progress Energy Carolinas), a utility providing electricity to 1.3 million customers in eastern and western North Carolina and central South Carolina, and, after the 1999 acquisition of North Carolina Natural Gas (in exchange for about $354 million in stock), natural gas to 178,000 customers in eastern and southern North Carolina. On September 30, 2003, PGN completed the sale of North Carolina Natural Gas, for $425 million in cash.

Utility operations accounted for 77% of PGN's consolidated revenues in 2003 (83% in 2002), nonregulated, diversified businesses for 23% (17%).

Carolina Power & Light received authorization from the North Carolina Utility Commission (in December 1998) and the South Carolina Public Service Commission (January 1999) to accelerate the amortization of its nuclear generating

assets, effective from January 1, 2000, through 2004. Annual amortization has ranged from $106 million to $150 million, for a total of $750 million.

In 2003, the company realigned its nonregulated businesses into the following segments: Competitive Commercial Operations, which is engaged in nonregulated electric generation operations and in marketing activities primarily in the southeastern United States; Fuels, which is mainly engaged in natural gas production in Texas and Louisiana, as well as coal mining and related services, and the production of synthetic fuels and related services, both of which are located in Kentucky, West Virginia, and Virginia; and Rail Services, which is engaged in rail and railcar-related services in 23 states, Mexico and Canada.

Through its Fuels business segment, PGN produces and sells coal-based solid synthetic fuel, which can qualify for tax credits if certain requirements are satisfied (such as there being a significant difference in the chemical composition of the end product from the feedstock used). These tax credits are subject to review by the IRS and, if not approved, there could be a significant tax liability owed that could have a major impact on earnings and cash flows.

The company also has other nonregulated businesses, including telecommunications primarily in the eastern U.S., and energy services, which do not meet the requirements for separate segment reporting.

Company Financials Fiscal Year ending December 31

Per Share Data ($)

(Year Ended December 31)	2003	2002	2001	2000	1999	1998	1997	1996	1995	1994
Tangible Bk. Val.	13.78	12.43	10.58	7.48	19.43	19.20	18.18	17.16	16.36	15.95
Earnings	3.40	2.53	2.64	3.03	2.55	2.75	2.66	2.66	2.48	2.03
S&P Core Earnings	3.44	2.04	2.59	NA	NA	NA	NA	NA	NA	NA
Dividends	2.24	2.18	2.12	2.06	2.00	1.94	1.88	1.82	1.76	1.70
Payout Ratio	66%	86%	80%	68%	78%	71%	71%	68%	71%	84%
Prices - High	48.00	52.70	49.25	49.37	47.87	49.62	42.68	38.75	34.62	30.00
- Low	37.45	32.84	38.78	28.25	29.25	39.18	32.75	33.75	26.12	22.50
P/E Ratio - High	14	21	19	16	19	18	16	15	14	15
- Low	11	13	15	9	11	14	12	13	11	11

Income Statement Analysis (Million $)

	2003	2002	2001	2000	1999	1998	1997	1996	1995	1994
Revs.	8,743	7,945	8,461	4,119	3,358	3,130	3,024	2,996	3,007	2,877
Depr.	1,040	820	1,090	740	496	487	482	387	364	398
Maint.	NA	NA	NA	NA	NA	NA	NA	NA	197	207
Fxd. Chgs. Cov.	2.16	1.64	1.75	2.60	4.23	4.50	4.25	4.13	3.67	3.44
Constr. Credits	7.00	8.13	18.0	20.7	11.5	6.82	4.92	6.42	8.50	9.50
Eff. Tax Rate	NM	NM	NM	29.8%	40.3%	39.2%	37.6%	40.8%	39.2%	35.0%
Net Inc.	811	552	542	478	382	399	388	391	373	313
S&P Core Earnings	819	445	532	NA	NA	NA	NA	NA	NA	NA

Balance Sheet & Other Fin. Data (Million $)

	2003	2002	2001	2000	1999	1998	1997	1996	1995	1994
Gross Prop.	25,172	23,021	22,541	21,028	12,233	10,797	10,475	10,197	9,822	9,546
Cap. Exp.	1,018	2,109	1,216	950	765	527	450	457	344	301
Net Prop.	17,056	12,541	12,445	11,677	7,257	6,300	6,294	6,400	6,329	6,349
Capitalization:										
LT Debt	10,027	9,840	9,577	5,983	3,029	2,614	2,416	2,526	2,610	2,531
% LT Debt	57.4	59.6	61.5	52.4	46.6	46.5	45.6	47.1	49.0	48.1
Pfd.	Nil	Nil	Nil	Nil	59.4	59.4	59.4	144	144	144
% Pfd.	Nil	Nil	Nil	Nil	0.91	1.06	1.10	2.70	2.70	2.70
Common	7,444	6,677	6,004	5,424	3,413	2,949	2,819	2,690	2,575	2,586
% Common	42.6	40.4	38.5	47.6	52.5	52.4	53.2	50.2	48.3	49.2
Total Cap.	18,398	17,656	17,241	13,476	8,337	7,514	7,239	7,420	7,288	7,141
% Oper. Ratio	66.8	85.4	83.5	87.1	82.4	79.3	80.6	82.8	82.3	84.7
% Earn. on Net Prop.	8.2	8.3	10.3	7.6	12.1	10.2	8.9	8.1	8.4	7.0
% Return On Revs.	9.3	6.9	6.4	11.6	11.4	12.8	12.8	13.1	12.4	10.9
% Return On Invest. Capital	8.2	7.2	9.2	7.1	7.3	7.8	7.7	7.8	8.0	7.1
% Return On Com. Equity	11.5	8.7	9.4	10.8	11.9	13.7	13.9	14.5	14.1	11.6

Data as orig reptd.; bef. results of disc opers/spec. items. Per share data adj. for stk. divs. Bold denotes primary EPS - prior periods restated. E-Estimated. NA-Not Available. NM-Not Meaningful. NR-Not Ranked. UR-Under Review.

Office: 410 S Wilmington St, Raleigh, NC 27601-1849.
Telephone: 919-546-6111.
Email: shareholder.relations@progress-energy.com
Website: http://www.progress-energy.com
Chrmn, Pres, CEO & COO: R.B. McGehee.
EVP & CFO: G.S. Chatas.
SVP, Secy & General Counsel: J.R. McArthur.

VP & Treas: T.R. Sullivan.
Secy & General Counsel: W.D. Johnson.
Investor Contact: B. Drennan 919-546-7474.
Dirs: E. B. Borden, J. E. Bostic, Jr., D. L. Burner, C. W. Coker, R. L. Daugherty, W. D. Frederick, Jr., W. O. McCoy, R. B. McGehee, E. M. McKee, J. H. Mullin III, R. A. Nunis, P. S. Rummell, C. A. Saladrigas, J. G. Wittner.

Founded: in 1926.
Domicile: North Carolina.
Employees: 15,300.
S&P Analyst: Justin McCann/PMW/JWP

Recommendation: **BUY** ★★★★ ☆   **12-Month Target Price: $42.00**
(SELL SELL HOLD BUY BUY)   (as of October 29, 2004)

PLD has an approximate 0.07% weighting in the **S&P 500**

Sector: Financials
Sub-Industry: Real Estate Investment Trusts
Peer Group: REITs - Specialty

Summary: This REIT (formerly ProLogis Trust) is the largest publicly held, U.S.-based owner and operator of distribution facilities, with operations in North America, Europe and Japan.

Quantitative Evaluations

S&P Earnings & Dividend Rank: B+

| D | C | B- | B | B+ | A- | A | A+ |

S&P Fair Value Rank: NR

| 1 | 2 | 3 | 4 | 5 |
| Lowest | | | | Highest |

Fair Value Calc.: NA

S&P Investability Quotient Percentile

95%

PLD scored higher than 95% of all companies for which an S&P Report is available.

Volatility: Average

| Low | **Average** | High |

Technical Evaluation: Bullish
Since 6/04, the technical indicators for PLD have been Bullish.

Relative Strength Rank: Strong

76

| 1 Lowest | | Highest 99 |

| **Price as of 11/12/04:** | **$40.39** | **2004E S&P Core EPS:** | **$1.11** |

GAAP Earnings vs. Previous Year
▲ Up   ▼ Down   ► No Change

SELL $29.43 10/23/03
BUY $34.04 07/30/04
HOLD $27.29 07/28/03

10 Week Mov. Avg.
30 Week Mov. Avg.
Relative Strength
12-Mo Target Price

Volume   Below Avg.   — Above Avg. —

22   48

VOL. MIL.
6
4
2
0

HOLD	SELL	HOLD	BUY
J J A S O N D	J F M A M J J A S O N D	J F M A M J J A S O N D	J F M A M J J A S O N D	J
2001	2002	2003	2004

Analyst commentary prepared by Robert McMillan/CB/JWP

Highlights November 02, 2004

- Demand for distribution and warehouse space in North America has been lukewarm during most of 2004, but we think it should improve in 2005 on stronger economic growth around the world. Demand in Europe and Asia should continue to be robust in 2005.

- After an 8.8% advance in 2003, we look for rental income to rise almost 20% in 2004 and 15% in 2005, driven principally by the acquisition of Keystone Properties and strength in the Asian and European operations; this should offset sluggish growth in the North American portfolio, which has been constrained by sluggish rent growth. Average same-store occupancy rose by 0.76% during the third quarter of 2004; same-store net operating income rose by 0.67%. Even though we look for an increase in leasing activity, we doubt the trust will be able to meaningfully raise rental rates on new and expiring leases until some time in 2005. We think continuing acquisition activity, combined with the disposition of underperforming assets, will help PLD increase revenues and earnings.

- We project operating EPS of $1.13 in 2004 and $1.25 in 2005; we see FFO of $2.42 and $2.65 in 2004 and 2005.

Key Stock Statistics

S&P Core EPS 2005E	**1.24**	52-week Range	**$40.39-27.62**
S&P Oper. EPS 2004E	**1.13**	12 Month P/E	**22.3**
P/E on S&P Oper. EPS 2004E	**35.7**	Beta	**0.21**
S&P Oper. EPS 2005E	**1.25**	Shareholders	**9,600**
Yield (%)	**3.6%**	Market Cap (B)	**$ 7.3**
Dividend Rate/Share	**1.46**	Shares Outstanding (M)	**181.8**

Value of $10,000 invested five years ago: **$ 26,320**

Dividend Data Dividends have been paid since 1994

Amount ($)	Date Decl.	Ex-Div. Date	Stock of Record	Payment Date
0.365	Feb. 02	Feb. 11	Feb. 13	Feb. 27 '04
q.365	May. 03	May. 12	May. 14	May. 28 '04
0.365	Aug. 02	Aug. 13	Aug. 17	Aug. 31 '04
0.365	Nov. 01	Nov. 12	Nov. 16	Nov. 30 '04

Investment Rationale/Risk November 02, 2004

- We think the shares have attractive appreciation potential over the next 12 months on a total return basis. Their 3.8% dividend yield adds to their attractiveness.

- Risks to our recommendation and target price include slower than expected growth in demand for industrial space and consequently revenues, higher than expected expenses, and rising interest rates.

- Our 12-month target price is $42 a share, assuming that PLD delivers FFO of $2.52 over the next four quarters, and that the shares trade at about 16.5X our trailing 12-month FFO projection. This is higher than the historical multiple of about 11X, but in line with current levels, and we think it can be sustained by what we view as PLD's improving operating prospects, as well as investor enthusiasm for REITs and their relatively high dividends. We expect dividends, currently providing a 3.8% yield, to continue to rise in tandem with growth, to meet the 90% payout ratio required of REITs.

Revenues/Earnings Data Fiscal year ending December 31

Revenues (Million $)

	2004	2003	2002	2001	2000	1999
1Q	150.9	159.9	172.3	162.2	163.0	93.77
2Q	150.1	169.4	174.5	163.5	153.4	137.2
3Q	148.8	116.8	134.9	150.8	163.7	173.9
4Q	—	213.1	193.3	76.94	163.9	153.9
Yr.	—	734.1	675.0	552.3	643.5	567.2

Earnings Per Share ($)

	2004	2003	2002	2001	2000	1999
1Q	0.19	0.21	0.31	0.25	0.28	0.02
2Q	0.39	0.26	0.31	0.26	0.12	0.08
3Q	0.42	-0.04	0.14	0.28	0.29	0.44
4Q	E0.26	0.72	0.44	-0.27	0.27	0.22
Yr.	E1.13	1.16	1.20	0.52	0.96	0.81

Next earnings report expected: early-February Source: S&P, Company Reports
EPS Estimates based on S&P Operating Earnings; historical GAAP earnings are as reported.

STANDARD &POOR'S

ProLogis

Recommendation: **BUY** ★★★★☆   12-Month Target Price: **$42.00** (as of October 29, 2004)

Business Summary November 03, 2004

ProLogis (formerly ProLogis Trust, and prior to that Security Capital Industrial Trust) is a real estate investment trust (REIT) that owns and operates industrial distribution and temperature-controlled distribution facilities in North America, Europe and Japan. The trust's investment strategy focuses on generic industrial distribution facilities in markets with attractive long-term growth prospects in which PLD can achieve a strong market position by acquiring and developing flexible facilities for warehousing and light manufacturing uses.

PLD's business is organized into two main operating segments -- property operations and CDFS (corporate distribution facilities services). The property operations segment (79% of 2003 operating income) is involved in long-term ownership, management and leasing of industrial distribution facilities, usually adaptable for both distribution and light manufacturing or assembly uses. The trust earns income from rents and reimbursement of property operating expenses from unaffiliated customers, and management fees from entities in which it has an ownership interest. As of December 31, 2003, the trust owned, managed, or had under development 1,737 distribution centers containing 230.4 million sq. ft. of space in North America, Europe and Japan.

ProLogis develops distribution properties in the CDFS business segment (21% of 2003 operating income), with the intent to contribute the property to a property fund or to sell the property to a third party. Also in the CDFS business segment, ProLogis acquires properties with the intent to contribute them to a property fund, generally after rehabilitation and/or repositioning activities have been completed. These properties, along with their operations, are included in the property operations segment after they are completed or acquired through the date they are contributed or sold. The gains and losses realized from the contributions or sales of these properties are included in the CDFS business segment's income because they were developed or acquired in that segment. At December 31, 2003, there were 119 CDFS business segment operating properties aggregating 20.4 million square feet at a total investment of $928.3 million that were included in the property operations segment's investments on an interim basis.

PLD has sought to develop a customer base diverse in terms of industry concentration and geography. At December 31, 2003, the company had 3,785 customers, with the largest customer accounting for 2.4% of annual base rent. The top 25 customers accounted for 22% of base rent. The company leases its operating properties to customers under agreements that are generally classified as operating leases

At December 31, 2003, the stabilized industrial distribution facility portfolio of 205.8 million sq. ft. was 90.2% leased and 89.6% occupied, versus 91.2% leased and 89.5% occupied a year earlier. Rental rates in 2003 for both new and renewed leases for previously leased space (42.8 million square feet) for all properties including those owned by the property funds decreased by 4.8%, as compared to rental rate growth of 2.0% in 2002 and 14.6% in 2001 on similar transactions.

Company Financials Fiscal Year ending December 31

Per Share Data ($)

(Year Ended December 31)	2003	2002	2001	2000	1999	1998	1997	1996	1995	1994
Tangible Bk. Val.	14.35	13.96	12.94	13.53	13.86	12.83	13.13	12.41	12.30	12.04
Earnings	1.16	1.20	0.52	0.96	0.81	0.51	0.04	0.63	0.61	0.57
S&P Core Earnings	1.14	1.17	0.49	NA	NA	NA	NA	NA	NA	NA
Dividends	1.44	1.42	1.42	1.38	1.34	1.30	1.24	1.07	1.01	0.94	0.85
Payout Ratio	124%	118%	NM	140%	160%	267%	245%	160%	153%	149%
Prices - High	32.62	26.00	23.30	24.68	22.18	26.50	25.50	22.50	17.75	18.25
- Low	23.63	20.96	19.35	17.56	16.75	19.75	18.87	16.50	14.50	11.50
P/E Ratio - High	28	22	45	26	27	52	NM	36	29	32
- Low	20	17	37	18	20	39	NM	26	24	20

Income Statement Analysis (Million $)

	2003	2002	2001	2000	1999	1998	1997	1996	1995	1994
Rental Income	Nil	449	466	480	492	345	285	227	154	70.6
Mortgage Income	Nil	Nil	Nil	Nil	Nil	Nil	18.0	6.46	4.62	1.09
Total Income	734	675	574	644	567	368	302	233	159	71.7
General Exp.	210	91.0	83.0	78.0	76.7	58.1	51.7	112	75.5	36.1
Interest Exp.	155	153	164	172	172	104	52.7	38.8	32.0	7.57
Prov. for Losses	Nil	Nil	Nil	Nil	Nil	Nil	Nil	Nil	Nil	Nil
Depr.	165	153	143	151	152	101	76.6	59.9	39.8	18.2
Net Inc.	251	249	128	214	182	111	39.7	79.4	48.7	25.1
S&P Core Earnings	208	210	86.8	NA	NA	NA	NA	NA	NA	NA

Balance Sheet & Other Fin. Data (Million $)

	2003	2002	2001	2000	1999	1998	1997	1996	1995	1994
Cash	1,009	111	28.0	57.9	69.3	63.1	25.0	4.77	22.2	21.3
Total Assets	6,369	5,924	5,604	5,946	5,848	4,331	3,034	2,462	1,834	1,195
Real Estate Invest.	5,854	5,396	4,588	4,689	4,975	3,658	3,006	2,509	1,828	1,176
Loss Reserve	Nil	Nil	Nil	Nil	Nil	Nil	Nil	Nil	Nil	Nil
Net Invest.	5,007	4,683	4,013	4,213	4,608	3,403	2,835	2,400	1,771	1,155
ST Debt	Nil	222	49.3	69.7	43.5	42.9	20.0	56.9	93.0	167
Capitalization:										
Debt	2,991	2,510	2,529	2,555	2,413	1,796	857	652	458	138
Equity	2,586	2,486	2,276	2,236	2,243	1,583	1,542	1,163	1,001	778
Total	6,089	5,439	5,251	5,574	5,428	4,104	2,379	2,264	1,653	981
% Earn & Depr/Assets	6.8	7.0	4.7	6.2	6.6	5.7	4.2	6.5	5.8	4.8
Price Times Book Value:										
Hi	2.3	1.9	1.8	1.8	1.6	4.0	1.9	1.8	1.4	1.5
Low	1.6	1.5	1.5	1.3	1.2	3.0	1.4	1.3	1.2	1.0

Data as orig reptd.; bef. results of disc opers/spec. items. Per share data adj. for stk. divs.; EPS diluted. E-Estimated. NA-Not Available. NM-Not Meaningful. NR-Not Ranked. UR-Under Review.

Office: 14100 East 35th Place, Aurora, CO 80011-1631.
Telephone: 303-375-9292.
Email: info@prologis.com
Website: http://www.prologis.com
Chrmn & CEO: K.D. Brooksher.
Vice Chrmn: I.F. Lyons III.

CFO: W.C. Rakowich.
Secy & General Counsel: E.S. Nekritz.
Investor Contact: R.L. Kennedy 303-576-2690.
Trustees: K. D. Brooksher, S. L. Feinberg, G. L. Fotiades, D. P. Jacobs, N. Kroes, I. F. Lyons III, W. C. Rakowich, J. H. Schwartz, K. N. Stensby, D. M. Steuert, J. A. Teixeira, W. D. Zollars.

Founded: in 1991.
Domicile: Maryland.
Employees: 725.
S&P Analyst: Robert McMillan/CB/JWP

Providian Financial

Recommendation: **HOLD** ★ ★ ★ ☆ ☆
SELL | SELL | HOLD | BUY | BUY

12-Month Target Price: $16.00
(as of October 21, 2004)

PVN has an approximate 0.04% weighting in the **S&P 500**

Sector: Financials
Sub-Industry: Consumer Finance
Peer Group: Consumer Finance - Credit Cards

Summary: This consumer lender offers a range of lending products, including credit cards, as well as fee-based products and services.

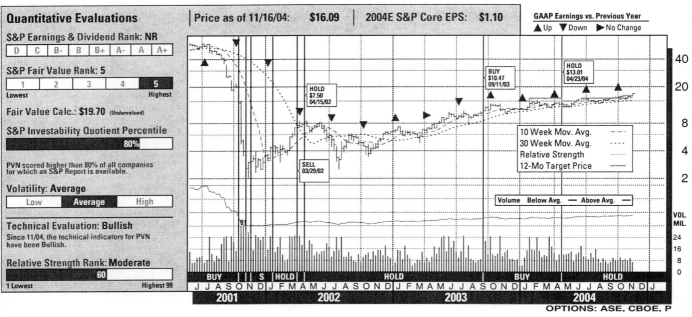

Quantitative Evaluations

S&P Earnings & Dividend Rank: NR

| D | C | B- | B | B+ | A- | A | A+ |

S&P Fair Value Rank: 5

| 1 | 2 | 3 | 4 | 5 |
| Lowest | | | | Highest |

Fair Value Calc.: $19.70 (Undervalued)

S&P Investability Quotient Percentile
80%

PVN scored higher than 80% of all companies for which an S&P Report is available.

Volatility: Average

| Low | Average | High |

Technical Evaluation: Bullish
Since 11/04, the technical indicators for PVN have been Bullish.

Relative Strength Rank: Moderate
60
1 Lowest — Highest 99

Price as of 11/16/04: **$16.09** | 2004E S&P Core EPS: **$1.10**

GAAP Earnings vs. Previous Year
▲ Up ▼ Down ▶ No Change

- 10 Week Mov. Avg.
- 30 Week Mov. Avg.
- Relative Strength
- 12-Mo Target Price

Volume Below Avg. — Above Avg.

HOLD $7.50 04/15/02
SELL 03/29/02
BUY $10.47 09/11/03
HOLD $13.01 04/23/04

BUY | S | HOLD | HOLD | BUY | HOLD
J J A S O N D | J F M A M J J A S O N D | J F M A M J J A S O N D | J F M A M J J A S O N D | J F M A M J J A S O N D J
2001 | 2002 | 2003 | 2004

OPTIONS: ASE, CBOE, P

Analyst commentary prepared by Evan M. Momios, CFA /CB/BK

Highlights 17-NOV-04

- Results for the first nine months of 2004 reinforced our opinion that PVN has made significant progress in a turnaround plan designed to upgrade the credit quality of its customer base, boost profitability and capital strength, and increase revenues. Managed loans fell 14% in 2003, as PVN sold higher risk portions of its portfolio. We look for managed loans to grow 6% in 2004, and in the 6% to 7% range in 2005, as we think the company is likely to remain focused on growing loans while preserving credit quality. Our model assumes that margins will stabilize at current levels in the remainder of 2004 and narrow modestly over the longer term as PVN's loan portfolio mix tilts toward lower credit risk and lower yielding credits.

- We expect credit quality improvement to continue to support EPS growth, but we see its contribution declining progressively in the quarters ahead. We believe noninterest expenses are likely to rise from third quarter 2004 levels as new product introductions and account growth require higher marketing expenses, offsetting modest operating efficiency improvements.

- Overall, we look for 2004 EPS to increase to $1.15, from $0.67 in 2003, and we see $1.35 for 2005. Our 2004 and 2005 S&P Core Earnings per share estimates are $1.10 and $1.30, respectively, reflecting the projected impact of employee stock options.

Investment Rationale/Risk 17-NOV-04

- We advise investors to hold but not add to positions, based on our view that the stock's current valuation fully reflects the company's progress in improving its risk profile and its growth prospects. We believe PVN has made significant progress in improving the credit quality of its receivables portfolio, but we think investors are likely to focus on volume growth, which we see remaining modest for the near term.

- Risks to our recommendation and target price include a possible deterioration of consumer confidence that could affect consumer spending, a rise in unemployment that could threaten credit quality, and a serious geopolitical event that could shock the U.S. economy.

- As of mid-November, the shares were trading at about 12X our 2005 EPS estimate, versus 11X to 12X on average for larger peers with what we consider better credit quality and more diversified business models. We think this reflects the company's progress on the credit quality front. Our 12-month target price of $16 equates to approximately 12X our 2005 EPS estimate and reflects our view that the shares are fully valued at current levels and that the stock's valuation multiple is sustainable.

Key Stock Statistics

S&P Core EPS 2005E	1.30	52-week Range	$16.85-9.97
S&P Oper. EPS 2004E	1.15	12 Month P/E	14.5
P/E on S&P Oper. EPS 2004E	14.7	Beta	1.68
S&P Oper. EPS 2005E	1.35	Shareholders	8,151
Yield (%)	Nil	Market Cap (B)	$ 4.7
Dividend Rate/Share	Nil	Shares Outstanding (M)	292.7

Value of $10,000 invested five years ago: **$ 4,064**

Dividend Data

Quarterly cash dividends were suspended in late 2001. The most recent dividend payment was $0.03 a share in September 2001.

Revenues/Earnings Data Fiscal year ending December 31

Revenues (Million $)

	2004	2003	2002	2001	2000	1999
1Q	645.1	769.7	1,646	1,585	1,355	768.9
2Q	671.4	685.0	914.4	1,586	1,477	944.4
3Q	705.5	681.3	853.6	1,502	1,441	1,090
4Q	—	645.4	659.1	857.2	1,674	1,233
Yr.	—	2,781	4,073	5,530	5,948	4,037

Earnings Per Share ($)

	2004	2003	2002	2001	2000	1999
1Q	0.35	0.02	0.02	0.80	0.60	0.39
2Q	0.24	0.13	0.31	0.82	0.21	0.43
3Q	0.34	0.29	0.15	0.20	0.68	0.52
4Q	E0.22	0.23	0.04	-1.39	0.73	0.55
Yr.	E1.15	0.67	0.52	0.49	2.23	1.89

Next earnings report expected: mid-January Source: S&P, Company Reports
EPS Estimates based on S&P Operating Earnings; historical GAAP earnings are as reported.

Providian Financial Corporation

Recommendation: **HOLD** ★ ★ ★ ☆ ☆   12-Month Target Price: **$16.00** (as of October 21, 2004)

Business Summary 17-NOV-04

Providian Financial primarily provides consumer loans through Visa and Master-Card credit cards. The company was a wholly owned subsidiary of Providian Corp. until its June 1997 spinoff. At December 31, 2003, managed loans totaled $16.9 billion, down from $19.6 billion a year earlier. Total accounts at December 31, 2003, amounted to 10.5 million, down from 12.0 million a year earlier.

During 2003, PVN's credit measures strengthened. Total 30-day or more delinquencies amounted to 9.29% of managed loans on December 31, 2003, versus 11.11% at the end of 2002. Net credit losses represent the principal amount of losses from customers who have not paid their existing loan balances, less any recoveries in the current period. In 2003, net credit losses amounted to 15.82% of average managed loans, down from 16.29% in 2002.

Since June 2002, PVN has been focusing on what it believes is a more balanced marketing strategy designed to generate a balanced mix of new business originated across the broad middle to prime market segments to achieve more stable earnings and lower, less volatile credit loss rates. The company uses credit, income, demographic, and psychographic criteria developed by its marketing department to define its primary target market, which it calls Mainstream America. Credit card products are marketed through direct mail and telemarketing channels as well as television and the Internet. In 2003, PVN launched a number of new strategic partnership programs that offer co-branded and affinity cards to targeted audiences.

In October 2001, the company launched a strategic action plan designed to mitigate sources of underperformance, focus its business on markets posting strong risk-adjusted returns, and manage for solid capital, reserves and liquidity. In 2002 and 2003, PVN completed several actions designed to further its goals under the October 2001 strategic plan, and its goal of establishing and maintaining a strong capital position for regulatory purposes. These actions included the sale of the company's interests in the Providian Master Trust in February 2002, generating cash proceeds of $2.8 billion; the sale of its international operations in April and May 2002; the sale of certain higher risk receivables in June 2002; and the completion of various securitization transactions.

In February 2004, PVN launched its New Providian strategy and a new brand identity and logo: Providian-Providing More. The main focus of the strategy is to reinforce customer loyalty and the responsible use of credit. The Providian Real Information program gives customers free access to their credit scores, and information on managing their credit. The Real Rewards program rewards customers with gift certificates or points for on-time payments over a period of time, for making purchases, and for carrying a balance. The company expected to introduce a number of proprietary products based on these themes in 2004.

Company Financials Fiscal Year ending December 31

Per Share Data ($)

(Year Ended December 31)	2003	2002	2001	2000	1999	1998	1997	1996	1995	1994
Tangible Bk. Val.	8.01	7.39	6.70	7.11	4.73	2.86	2.09	1.49	NA	NA
Earnings	0.67	0.52	0.49	2.23	1.89	1.02	0.67	0.54	NA	NA
S&P Core Earnings	0.59	0.51	0.25	NA	NA	NA	NA	NA	NA	NA
Dividends	Nil	Nil	0.09	0.13	0.10	0.08	0.03	NA	NA	NA
Payout Ratio	Nil	Nil	18%	6%	5%	7%	5%	NA	NA	NA
Prices - High	13.14	8.49	64.06	67.00	69.00	37.84	15.60	NA	NA	NA
- Low	4.87	2.50	2.00	29.06	34.75	14.18	9.70	NA	NA	NA
P/E Ratio - High	20	16	NM	30	37	37	23	NA	NA	NA
- Low	7	5	NM	13	18	14	15	NA	NA	NA

Income Statement Analysis (Million $)

	2003	2002	2001	2000	1999	1998	1997	1996	1995	1994
Net Int. Inc.	473	919	1,653	1,825	1,175	595	399	408	NA	NA
Tax Equiv. Adj.	NA	NA	NA	NA	NA	NA	NA	NA	NA	NA
Non Int. Inc.	1,675	2,381	2,942	3,248	2,412	1,266	635	412	NA	NA
Loan Loss Prov.	622	1,292	2,014	1,515	1,099	546	149	127	NA	NA
Exp./Op. Revs.	55.9%	54.8%	51.1%	48.7%	74.4%	44.3%	55.5%	52.7%	NA	NA
Pretax Inc.	324	200	234	1,086	917	491	311	262	NA	NA
Eff. Tax Rate	39.5%	24.5%	39.5%	40.0%	40.0%	39.6%	38.5%	37.9%	NA	NA
Net Inc.	196	151	141	652	550	296	191	162	NA	NA
% Net Int. Marg.	9.74	11.5	9.14	11.1	12.2	11.4	NA	NA	NA	NA
S&P Core Earnings	173	144	70.3	NA	NA	NA	NA	NA	NA	NA

Balance Sheet & Other Fin. Data (Million $)

	2003	2002	2001	2000	1999	1998	1997	1996	1995	1994
Money Mkt. Assets	3,235	3,601	1,611	307	1,298	298	115	172	NA	NA
Inv. Securities	1,886	1,857	1,324	2,572	581	434	173	7.17	NA	NA
Com'l Loans	Nil	NA	Nil	Nil	Nil	Nil	Nil	Nil	NA	NA
Other Loans	6,281	6,908	12,970	13,770	11,610	5,741	2,961	2,950	NA	NA
Total Assets	14,275	16,710	19,938	18,055	14,341	7,231	4,449	4,381	NA	NA
Demand Deposits	63.0	56.7	71.2	79.8	63.9	48.2	32.1	28.3	NA	NA
Time Deposits	10,038	12,652	15,247	13,034	10,474	4,624	3,181	3,362	NA	NA
LT Debt	1,164	982	1,064	1,135	1,118	560	82.0	165	NA	NA
Common Equity	2,325	2,139	1,908	2,032	1,099	803	595	420	NA	NA
% Ret. on Assets	1.3	0.8	0.7	4.0	5.1	5.1	4.4	NA	NA	NA
% Ret. on Equity	8.8	7.5	7.2	38.7	51.5	42.4	35.5	NA	NA	NA
% Loan Loss Resv.	10.0	14.7	14.9	10.5	8.9	7.9	4.9	3.1	NA	NA
% Loans/Deposits	62.2	54.4	84.7	105.0	109.8	122.9	NA	120.9	NA	NA
% Equity to Assets	14.4	11.0	10.4	10.4	9.9	12.0	12.3	NA	NA	NA

Data as orig reptd.; bef. results of disc opers/spec. items. Per share data adj. for stk. divs.; EPS diluted. E-Estimated. NA-Not Available. NM-Not Meaningful. NR-Not Ranked. UR-Under Review.

Office: 201 Mission Street, San Francisco, CA 94105.
Telephone: 415-543-0404.
Website: http://www.providian.com
Chrmn, Pres & CEO: J. Saunders.
CFO & Vice Chrmn: A. Vuoto.
Secy, General Counsel & Vice Chrmn: E. Richey.

Vice Chrmn: C. Chen.
Investor Contact: Jack Carsky (415-278-4977).
Dirs: J. L. Douglas, R. D. Field, J. D. Grissom, R. J. Higgins, J. P. Holdcroft, F. W. McFarlan, R. M. Owades, F. Ruiz de Luzuriaga, J. Saunders, J. A. Truelove.

Founded: in 1981.
Domicile: Delaware.
Employees: 4,525.
S&P Analyst: Evan M. Momios, CFA /CB/BK

Prudential Financial

Recommendation: **HOLD** ★ ★ ★ ☆ ☆
SELL | SELL | HOLD | BUY | BUY

12-Month Target Price: $51.00
(as of October 22, 2004)

PRU has an approximate 0.23% weighting in the **S&P 500**

Sector: Financials
Sub-Industry: Life & Health Insurance
Peer Group: Life Insurance/Annuities - Larger

Summary: Through its subsidiaries, Prudential provides a wide range of insurance, investment management and other financial products and services to customers in the U.S. and overseas.

Quantitative Evaluations

S&P Earnings & Dividend Rank: NR

D	C	B-	B	B+	A-	A	A+

S&P Fair Value Rank: 3+

1	2	3	4	5
Lowest				Highest

Fair Value Calc.: $47.50 (Fairly Valued)

S&P Investability Quotient Percentile

96%

PRU scored higher than 96% of all companies for which an S&P Report is available.

Volatility: Low

Low	Average	High

Technical Evaluation: Bullish
Since 11/04, the technical indicators for PRU have been Bullish.

Relative Strength Rank: Moderate

43

1 Lowest | Highest 99

Price as of 11/12/04: **$48** | **2004E S&P Core EPS:** **$2.77**

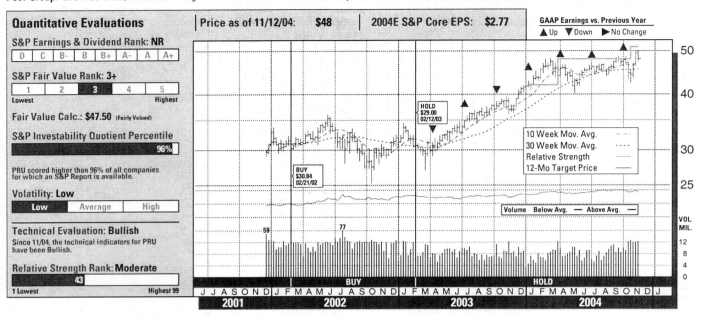

GAAP Earnings vs. Previous Year
▲ Up ▼ Down ▶ No Change

BUY $30.84 02/21/02
HOLD $29.00 02/12/03

10 Week Mov. Avg.
30 Week Mov. Avg.
Relative Strength
12-Mo Target Price

Volume Below Avg. — Above Avg.

Analyst commentary prepared by Gregory Simcik, CFA /PMW/BK

Highlights October 26, 2004

- We expect solid growth for the financial services businesses in 2004, due to continuing strong organic growth in the company's international operations and contributions from the recent American Skandia, Cigna and Hyundai acquisitions.

- We remain somewhat skeptical regarding PRU's goal of 12% return on equity (ROE) by the end of 2005, especially since its average historical ROE has been in the mid-single digits.

- We forecast that operating EPS from continuing operations will advance 29% in 2004, to $3.28, on 5.9% fewer shares. We estimate that operating EPS will grow over 30% in 2005, to $4.25. Our respective S&P Core EPS projections are $2.77 and $3.72, reflecting estimated stock option and pension expenses.

Investment Rationale/Risk October 26, 2004

- We would hold existing positions. While the shares trade at a discount to our 12-month target price, we think that the potential upside is offset by risks that we see, including an investigation by the New York State Attorney General of relationships and practices among group life underwriters and insurance brokers.

- Risks to our recommendation and target price include currency risk, reserving risks for new guaranteed minimum benefits, the pricing and availability of reinsurance for some products, integration risks from acquisitions, regulatory risks, legal and operational risks associated with the New York Attorney General's investigations, and continuing labor unionization efforts for agents.

- Our 12-month target price of $51 is based on a trailing P/E multiple of 12X applied to our 2005 operating EPS estimate, in line with PRU's stated ROE goal.

Key Stock Statistics

S&P Core EPS 2005E	3.72	52-week Range	$50.00-36.35
S&P Oper. EPS 2004E	3.43	12 Month P/E	13.0
P/E on S&P Oper. EPS 2004E	14.0	Beta	NA
S&P Oper. EPS 2005E	4.25	Shareholders	3,366,793
Yield (%)	1.3%	Market Cap (B)	$ 24.5
Dividend Rate/Share	0.63	Shares Outstanding (M)	511.0

Value of $10,000 invested five years ago: **NA**

Dividend Data Dividends have been paid since 2002

Amount ($)	Date Decl.	Ex-Div. Date	Stock of Record	Payment Date
0.500	Nov. 11	Nov. 21	Nov. 25	Dec. 18 '03
0.625	Nov. 09	Nov. 19	Nov. 23	Dec. 20 '04

Revenues/Earnings Data Fiscal year ending December 31

Revenues (Million $)

	2004	2003	2002	2001	2000	1999
1Q	4,755	6,785	6,684	6,747	—	—
2Q	6,884	7,304	6,637	7,168	—	—
3Q	7,327	6,693	6,679	6,356	—	—
4Q	—	7,125	6,675	6,906	—	—
Yr.	—	27,907	26,675	27,177	26,514	—

Earnings Per Share ($)

	2004	2003	2002	2001	2000	1999
1Q	0.72	0.42	0.47	—	—	—
2Q	0.98	0.21	0.20	—	—	—
3Q	1.09	0.48	0.68	—	—	—
4Q	E0.80	0.95	Nil	—	—	—
Yr.	E3.43	2.06	1.36	0.07	0.82	—

Next earnings report expected: mid-February Source: S&P, Company Reports
EPS Estimates based on S&P Operating Earnings; historical GAAP earnings are as reported.

Prudential Financial, Inc.

Recommendation: **HOLD** ★ ★ ★ ☆ ☆   12-Month Target Price: **$51.00** (as of October 22, 2004)

Business Summary October 26, 2004

Prudential is one of the largest U.S. financial services companies, and also serves individual and institutional customers in more than 30 other countries. In December 2001, the company completed its demutualization, its IPO of 126.5 million common shares, and a private placement of 2 million Class B shares. The common stock reflects the performance of the financial services businesses, while the Class B stock reflects the performance of PRU's closed block of business; there is no legal separation of the two businesses. On the date of demutualization, PRU also co-issued 13.8 million equity security units with Prudential Capital Financial Trust I, and issued $1.75 billion in notes associated with the closed block business.

The closed block business represents a number of insurance products no longer offered, including certain participating insurance and annuity policies. At December 31, 2003, PRU began to put in place reinsurance contracts necessary to transfer a portion of the risks associated with the closed block business.

The financial services business conducts its operation through three divisions as well as the corporate and other segment: insurance, investments, and international insurance and investments. The insurance division accounted for 37% of 2003 operating revenues from continuing operations, the investments division 27%, the international insurance and investments division 33%, and corporate and other 2.7%.

The insurance division consists of two segments. The individual life and annuities unit distributes variable, universal and term life insurance, fixed and variable annuities, and other non-participating life insurance protection products to the

U.S. retail market. The group insurance unit distributes group life, disability and related insurance products through employee and member benefit plans. Individual life and annuities accounted for 46% of the division's operating revenues in 2003, and group insurance 54%.

The investment division provides investment management, financial advisory, retirement, and other asset management products and services to retail and institutional clients. Retirement accounted for 46% of the division's operating revenues in 2003, financial advisory activities 26%, investment management 25%, and other asset management 2.0%.

The international insurance and investments division primarily distributes individual life insurance products in Japan, Korea, and other Asian, Latin American and European countries. PRU also provides private banking, asset management and financial advisory services to retail and institutional clients outside the U.S. Insurance accounted for 94% of the division's operating revenues in 2003, and investments for 6%.

In May 2003, the company acquired American Skandia, for $1.2 billion. In July 2003, PRU completed a combination of retail securities brokerage operations with Wachovia in a 38%-owned joint venture. In the 2003 fourth quarter, the company sold its property and casualty business in a several transactions. In February 2004, PRU purchased an 80% stake in Hyundai Investment and Securities Co., with the remaining interest possibly to be acquired in three to six years. In April 2004, the company acquired Cigna's retirement business, for $2.1 billion in cash.

Company Financials Fiscal Year ending December 31

Per Share Data ($)

(Year Ended December 31)	2003	2002	2001	2000	1999	1998	1997	1996	1995	1994
Tangible Bk. Val.	39.65	37.89	34.90	NA	NA	NA	NA	NA	NA	NA
Oper. Earnings	NA	NA	NA	NA	NA	NA	NA	NA	NA	NA
Earnings	2.06	1.36	0.07	0.82	NA	NA	NA	NA	NA	NA
S&P Core Earnings	1.91	1.56	NA	NA	NA	NA	NA	NA	NA	NA
Dividends	0.50	0.40	Nil	NA	NA	NA	NA	NA	NA	NA
Payout Ratio	24%	29%	Nil	NA	NA	NA	NA	NA	NA	NA
Prices - High	42.21	36.00	33.74	NA	NA	NA	NA	NA	NA	NA
- Low	27.03	25.25	27.50	NA	NA	NA	NA	NA	NA	NA
P/E Ratio - High	20	26	NM	NA	NA	NA	NA	NA	NA	NA
- Low	13	19	NM	NA	NA	NA	NA	NA	NA	NA

Income Statement Analysis (Million $)

	2003	2002	2001	2000	1999	1998	1997	1996	1995	1994
Life Ins. In Force	1,928,650	1,800,788	1,768,038	NA	NA	NA	NA	NA	NA	NA
Prem. Inc.: Life	10,972	10,897	10,078	NA	NA	NA	NA	NA	NA	NA
Prem. Inc.: A & H	806	586	515	NA	NA	NA	NA	NA	NA	NA
Net Invest. Inc.	8,681	8,832	9,151	9,467	NA	NA	NA	NA	NA	NA
Total Revs.	27,907	26,675	27,177	26,514	NA	NA	NA	NA	NA	NA
Pretax Inc.	1,958	64.0	-227	525	NA	NA	NA	NA	NA	NA
Net Oper. Inc.	NA	NA	NA	NA	NA	NA	NA	NA	NA	NA
Net Inc.	1,308	256	-170	304	NA	NA	NA	NA	NA	NA
S&P Core Earnings	1,047	895	-403	NA	NA	NA	NA	NA	NA	NA

Balance Sheet & Other Fin. Data (Million $)

	2003	2002	2001	2000	1999	1998	1997	1996	1995	1994
Cash & Equiv.	9,746	11,688	20,364	19,994	NA	NA	NA	NA	NA	NA
Premiums Due	Nil	Nil	Nil	NA	NA	NA	NA	NA	NA	NA
Invest. Assets: Bonds	132,011	128,075	110,316	NA	NA	NA	NA	NA	NA	NA
Invest. Assets: Stocks	6,703	2,807	2,272	NA	NA	NA	NA	NA	NA	NA
Invest. Assets: Loans	27,621	22,094	28,299	NA	NA	NA	NA	NA	NA	NA
Invest. Assets: Total	181,041	183,094	165,834	169,251	NA	NA	NA	NA	NA	NA
Deferred Policy Costs	7,826	7,031	6,868	6,751	NA	NA	NA	NA	NA	NA
Total Assets	321,274	292,746	293,030	298,414	NA	NA	NA	NA	NA	NA
Debt	5,610	4,757	5,304	14,812	NA	NA	NA	NA	NA	NA
Common Equity	21,292	21,330	20,453	20,692	NA	NA	NA	NA	NA	NA
% Return On Revs.	4.7	1.0	NM	1.1	NA	NA	NA	NA	NA	NA
% Ret. on Assets	0.4	0.1	NM	NA	NA	NA	NA	NA	NA	NA
% Ret. on Equity	6.1	1.2	NM	NA	NA	NA	NA	NA	NA	NA
% Invest. Yield	4.8	5.1	5.8	NA	NA	NA	NA	NA	NA	NA

Data as orig reptd.; bef. results of disc opers/spec. items. Per share data adj. for stk. divs.; EPS diluted. E-Estimated. NA-Not Available. NM-Not Meaningful. NR-Not Ranked. UR-Under Review.

Office: 751 Broad Street, Newark, NJ 07102.
Telephone: 973-802-6000.
Email: investor.relations@prudential.com
Website: http://www.prudentialfinancial.com
Chrmn, Pres & CEO: A.F. Ryan.
Vice Chrmn: V.L. Banta.
Vice Chrmn: M.B. Grier.

Vice Chrmn: J.R. Strangfeld, Jr.
Vice Chrmn: R.A. Lawson.
Dirs: F. E. Agnew, F. K. Becker, G. Caperton, G. F. Casellas, J. G. Cullen, W. H. Gray III, J. F. Hanson, G. H. Hiner, C. J. Horner, K. J. Krapek, A. F. Ryan, I. F. Schmertz, R. M. Thomson, J. A. Unruh, S. C. Van Ness.

Founded: in 1875.
Domicile: New Jersey.
Employees: 39,422.
S&P Analyst: Gregory Simcik, CFA /PMW/BK

Public Service Enterprise Group

Recommendation: **HOLD** ★★★☆☆   12-Month Target Price: **$42.00**
(as of August 02, 2004)

PEG has an approximate 0.10% weighting in the **S&P 500**

Sector: Utilities
Sub-Industry: Multi-Utilities & Unregulated Power

Summary: This holding company owns Public Service Electric and Gas (PSE&G), with a service area that encompasses 70% of New Jersey, and also invests in energy-related businesses.

Quantitative Evaluations

S&P Earnings & Dividend Rank: B+

D	C	B-	B	B+	A-	A	A+

S&P Fair Value Rank: 2-

1	2	3	4	5
Lowest				Highest

Fair Value Calc.: $39.20 (Overvalued)

S&P Investability Quotient Percentile

70%

PEG scored higher than 70% of all companies for which an S&P Report is available.

Volatility: Low

Low	Average	High

Technical Evaluation: Bullish
Since 10/04, the technical indicators for PEG have been Bullish.

Relative Strength Rank: Moderate

61

1 Lowest	Highest 99

Price as of 11/12/04:	$45.08	2004E S&P Core EPS:	$3.40

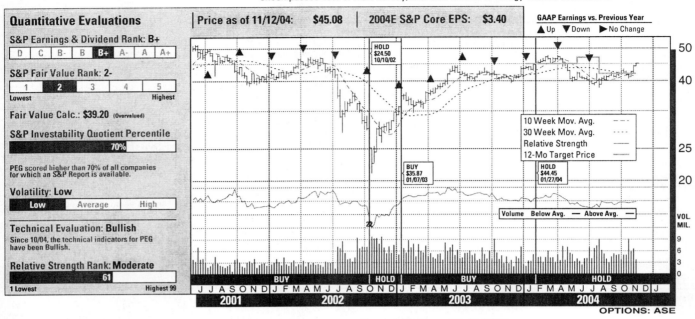

GAAP Earnings vs. Previous Year
▲ Up ▼ Down ► No Change

- 10 Week Mov. Avg.
- 30 Week Mov. Avg.
- Relative Strength
- 12-Mo Target Price

Volume Below Avg. — Above Avg.

OPTIONS: ASE

Analyst commentary prepared by Craig K. Shere, CFA /PMW/BK

Highlights August 11, 2004

- PEG's Power division began providing a portion of the PSE&G New Jersey utility's power needs directly, as part of a competitively won contract, in June 2004. As a result, reported revenues and cost of goods sold should fall in the 2004 second half, due to intercompany eliminations. Our 2004 operating EPS estimate excludes about $0.05 of non-cash gains from nuclear retirement funds net of first quarter charges for one-time debt refinancing and lease termination expenses.

- We look for 2004 and 2005 EPS to be negatively affected by increased operating and maintenance expense related to nuclear and coal plants. EPS in 2005 and 2006 should be negatively affected by a November 2005 conversion of debt for equity. We look for about a 12% decline in 2004 operating EPS (excluding nuclear decommissioning fund income), as a transmission bottleneck in March combined with rising natural gas prices and plant outages to increase second quarter purchased power expenses. We expect the transmission constraint to continue into mid-2005, but look for increased plant availability and lower natural gas prices to mitigate this effect.

- Our 2004 and 2005 Standard & Poor's Core EPS projections exceed our operating EPS estimates, due to the inclusion of income from PEG's nuclear decommissioning fund and positive accounting adjustments for pension and other post-retirement benefit expenses.

Key Stock Statistics

S&P Core EPS 2005E	3.74	52-week Range	$47.72-38.10
S&P Oper. EPS 2004E	3.20	12 Month P/E	14.3
P/E on S&P Oper. EPS 2004E	14.1	Beta	0.25
S&P Oper. EPS 2005E	3.35	Shareholders	110,373
Yield (%)	4.9%	Market Cap (B)	$ 10.7
Dividend Rate/Share	2.20	Shares Outstanding (M)	237.2

Value of $10,000 invested five years ago: **$ 14,938**

Dividend Data Dividends have been paid since 1907

Amount ($)	Date Decl.	Ex-Div. Date	Stock of Record	Payment Date
0.540	Nov. 18	Dec. 04	Dec. 08	Dec. 31 '03
0.550	Jan. 20	Mar. 04	Mar. 08	Mar. 31 '04
0.550	Apr. 20	Jun. 04	Jun. 08	Jun. 30 '04
0.550	Jul. 22	Sep. 07	Sep. 09	Sep. 30 '04

Investment Rationale/Risk August 11, 2004

- We believe the stock is trading near fair value, and would hold existing positions. The stock's price to book and price to trailing operating cash flow multiples are in line with those of multi-utility peers. In light of a significant lowering of EPS guidance in the second quarter of 2004, we believe PEG's discounted 2005 P/E multiple versus that of multi-utility peers is appropriate. Despite a projected 2005 dividend payout ratio over 60% (above the peer average), we believe PEG will continue modest annual growth in its annual dividend, following an initial $0.01 quarterly rise in 2004.

- Risks to our recommendation and target price include the failure to complete plants under construction on time and on budget, the ability to continue hedging over 75% of electric generating capacity, potential defaults of leveraged lease counterparties, tax rulings affecting leveraged leases, potentially rising interest rates, timely completion of plant maintenance, milder than normal weather, and narrower wholesale power margins.

- In light of earnings volatility seen in the 2004 first half, we believe the stock is fairly valued at a P/E ratio of about 11.5X estimated 2005 EPS, versus a diversified multi-utility peer P/E multiple of 12.5X. PEG's stated long-term EPS growth target is 4% to 6%. We look for the shares to appreciate in line with the long-term EPS growth rate. Our 12-month target price is $42.

Revenues/Earnings Data Fiscal year ending December 31

Revenues (Million $)

	2004	2003	2002	2001	2000	1999
1Q	3,221	3,364	1,914	2,814	1,924	1,795
2Q	2,290	2,419	1,469	2,171	1,521	1,436
3Q	—	2,805	2,328	2,401	1,525	1,606
4Q	—	—	2,679	2,429	1,981	1,660
Yr.	—	11,116	8,390	9,815	6,848	6,497

Earnings Per Share ($)

	2004	2003	2002	2001	2000	1999
1Q	1.14	1.42	0.87	1.22	1.25	0.85
2Q	0.50	0.66	-1.10	0.67	0.66	0.83
3Q	E0.95	0.93	1.00	0.82	0.66	1.01
4Q	E0.52	0.69	1.19	0.95	0.98	0.61
Yr.	E3.20	3.72	1.99	3.67	3.55	3.29

Next earnings report expected: NA Source: S&P, Company Reports
EPS Estimates based on S&P Operating Earnings; historical GAAP earnings are as reported.

STANDARD &POOR'S

Public Service Enterprise Group Incorporated

Stock Report
November 13, 2004
NYSE Symbol: **PEG**

Recommendation: **HOLD** ★ ★ ★ ☆ ☆   12-Month Target Price: **$42.00** (as of August 02, 2004)

Business Summary August 11, 2004

Public Service Enterprise Group seeks to minimize earnings and cash flow volatility by entering into long-term contracts for most of its competitive wholesale power generation, and by reducing its exposure to international operations over time. At the end of 2003, the company's New Jersey utility operations served 2.03 million electric customers and 1.67 million natural gas customers. PEG has three primary operating unit: Public Service Electric and Gas Co. - PSE&G (46% of assets at the end of 2003), Power (27%), and Energy Holdings (27%).

As a part of New Jersey utility deregulation, PSE&G transferred its power generating and gas supply operations to PEG's unregulated Power division in 2000 and 2002, respectively. In July 2003, the utility's electric distribution operations received a $159.5 million regulatory rate increase. PSE&G makes money from the delivery of electricity and gas, with the cost of the commodities passed through to ratepayers.

Based on the proximity of its plants to PSE&G's customer base, Power has been able to win competitive bids for a significant portion of the utility's electricity supply obligations. Power seeks to lock in pricing for at least 75% of anticipated electric output over an 18- to 24-month period. At the end of 2003, Power had 13,751 MW of generation, but projects under construction were expected to increase capacity to 16,000 MW. In 2003, 87% of the division's generation was produced by its baseload nuclear and coal-fired plants (representing nearly 50% of total generating capacity).

Power's generating fleet is concentrated in the Pennsylvania, New Jersey, and Maryland Interconnection (known as PJM), but the division acquired plants in Connecticut in 2002, and has been constructing facilities in New York and the Mid-West in 2003 and 2004. In addition to its electric business, Power provides PSE&G with all of the utility's gas commodity supply needs under a contract running through 2007.

At the end of 2003, PSEG Energy Holdings assets were comprised 40% of leveraged leases, 23% international power plants, 20% international electric distribution facilities, 6% U.S. power plants, and 11% other and passive investments. PSEG Global manages generation and distribution operations, and PSEG Resources manages leveraged leases. In 2003, Global refocused its strategy from accelerated growth investment to enhancing the value of existing holdings and divesting non-core holdings. At the end of 2003, 34% of Resources' lessees were below investment grade; 80% were related to U.S. and foreign energy projects. In February 2004, PEG said it expected a gradual decline in Resources' earnings, due to the maturation of its portfolio and the absence of significant new investments.

PEG has materially reduced capital spending as part of a plan to reduce debt and increase free cash flow. In 2004 and 2005, it expected capital expenditures of $1.22 billion and $770 million, respectively, versus capital spending that declined from $2.03 billion to $1.35 billion between 2001 and 2003.

Company Financials Fiscal Year ending December 31

Per Share Data ($)

(Year Ended December 31)	2003	2002	2001	2000	1999	1998	1997	1996	1995	1994
Tangible Bk. Val.	20.84	14.78	16.93	19.21	18.50	21.86	21.72	21.60	21.57	20.93
Earnings	3.72	1.99	3.67	3.55	3.29	2.79	2.41	2.42	2.71	2.78
S&P Core Earnings	4.03	3.06	3.16	NA	NA	NA	NA	NA	NA	NA
Dividends	2.16	2.16	2.16	2.16	2.16	2.16	2.16	2.16	2.16	2.16
Payout Ratio	58%	109%	59%	61%	66%	77%	90%	89%	80%	78%
Prices - High	44.50	47.25	51.55	50.00	42.62	42.75	31.81	32.12	30.62	32.00
- Low	32.09	20.00	36.87	25.68	32.00	30.31	22.87	25.12	26.00	23.87
P/E Ratio - High	12	24	14	14	13	15	13	13	11	12
- Low	9	10	10	7	10	11	9	10	10	9

Income Statement Analysis (Million $)

	2003	2002	2001	2000	1999	1998	1997	1996	1995	1994
Revs.	11,116	8,390	9,815	6,848	6,497	5,931	6,370	6,041	6,164	5,916
Depr.	527	571	522	362	536	669	630	607	674	630
Maint.	NA	NA	NA	NA	NA	NA	281	318	313	308
Fxd. Chgs. Cov.	2.43	2.38	2.46	2.88	3.20	2.87	2.69	2.97	3.07	2.97
Constr. Credits	NA	NA	NA	NA	NA	13.0	20.0	18.0	42.5	46.6
Eff. Tax Rate	35.3%	37.3%	NM	39.1%	43.8%	39.5%	37.0%	33.1%	34.8%	30.6%
Net Inc.	852	416	763	764	723	644	560	612	662	679
S&P Core Earnings	925	638	656	NA	NA	NA	NA	NA	NA	NA

Balance Sheet & Other Fin. Data (Million $)

	2003	2002	2001	2000	1999	1998	1997	1996	1995	1994
Gross Prop.	17,406	16,562	14,886	11,968	11,156	18,386	17,982	16,400	16,628	16,245
Cap. Exp.	1,351	1,814	2,053	959	582	535	542	586	827	999
Net Prop.	12,422	11,449	10,064	7,702	7,078	11,026	11,217	11,179	11,187	11,098
Capitalization:										
LT Debt	13,025	12,391	11,061	6,505	5,783	4,813	4,925	4,622	5,243	5,234
% LT Debt	70.2	75.7	72.8	60.2	59.1	43.3	45.5	44.2	46.1	46.6
Pfd.	Nil	Nil	Nil	Nil	Nil	1,208	683	681	685	685
% Pfd.	Nil	Nil	Nil	Nil	Nil	10.9	6.30	6.50	6.00	6.10
Common	5,529	3,987	4,137	4,294	3,996	5,098	5,211	5,213	5,445	5,311
% Common	29.8	24.3	27.2	39.8	40.9	45.8	48.2	49.8	47.9	47.9
Total Cap.	22,750	19,302	18,403	13,906	12,707	14,825	14,556	14,128	14,860	14,548
% Oper. Ratio	86.5	78.8	76.9	79.6	80.4	80.0	82.5	82.5	81.0	80.0
% Earn. on Net Prop.	17.3	14.3	21.3	18.9	20.4	10.7	9.9	5.5	10.4	10.6
% Return On Revs.	7.7	5.0	7.8	11.2	11.1	10.9	8.8	10.2	10.7	11.5
% Return On Invest. Capital	8.1	9.3	9.6	10.8	9.5	8.1	10.1	7.5	10.4	8.2
% Return On Com. Equity	18.1	10.2	18.8	18.4	15.9	12.5	10.7	11.5	12.3	13.0

Data as orig reptd.; bef. results of disc opers/spec. items. Per share data adj. for stk. divs. Bold denotes primary EPS - prior periods restated. E-Estimated. NA-Not Available. NM-Not Meaningful. NR-Not Ranked. UR-Under Review.

Office: 80 Park Plaza, Newark, NJ 07102-4109.
Telephone: 973-430-7000.
Email: stkserv@pseg.com
Website: http://www.pseg.com
Chrmn, Pres & CEO: E.J. Ferland.
EVP & CFO: T.M. O'Flynn.

SVP & General Counsel: R.E. Selover.
Treas: M.A. Plawner.
Investor Contact: P. Rosengren 973-430-5911.
Dirs: C. Dorsa, E. H. Drew, E. J. Ferland, A. R. Gamper, Jr., C. K. Harper, W. V. Hickey, S. A. Jackson, T. A. Renyi, R. J. Swift.

Founded: in 1985.
Domicile: New Jersey.
Employees: 9,613.
S&P Analyst: Craig K. Shere, CFA /PMW/BK

Pulte Homes

Recommendation: **HOLD** ★ ★ ★ ☆ ☆
SELL | SELL | HOLD | BUY | BUY

12-Month Target Price: **$59.00**
(as of October 26, 2004)

PHM has an approximate 0.07% weighting in the **S&P 500**

Sector: Consumer Discretionary
Sub-Industry: Homebuilding
Peer Group: Homebuilders - National

Summary: This builder of a wide range of single-family homes and condominiums in 27 states is the leading U.S. developer of active adult communities, and has a mortgage banking unit.

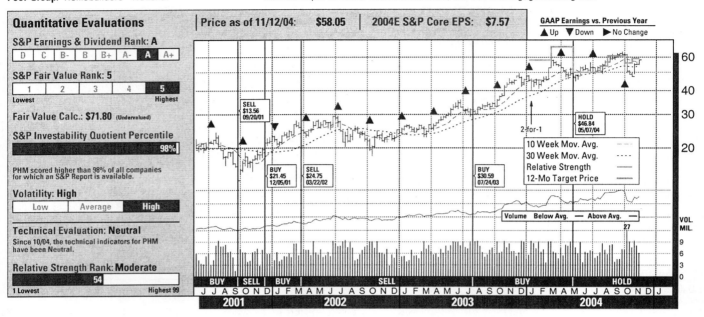

Quantitative Evaluations

S&P Earnings & Dividend Rank: A

D	C	B-	B	B+	A-	A	A+

S&P Fair Value Rank: 5

1	2	3	4	5
Lowest				Highest

Fair Value Calc.: $71.80 (Undervalued)

S&P Investability Quotient Percentile

98%

PHM scored higher than 98% of all companies for which an S&P Report is available.

Volatility: High

Low	Average	High

Technical Evaluation: Neutral
Since 10/04, the technical indicators for PHM have been Neutral.

Relative Strength Rank: Moderate

54

1 Lowest | Highest 99

Price as of 11/12/04: $58.05 | **2004E S&P Core EPS:** $7.57

GAAP Earnings vs. Previous Year
▲ Up ▼ Down ► No Change

Chart legend:
- 10 Week Mov. Avg.
- 30 Week Mov. Avg.
- Relative Strength
- 12-Mo Target Price

Volume Below Avg. — Above Avg.

Analyst commentary prepared by Michael W. Jaffe/CB/BK

Highlights November 01, 2004

- We see PHM's revenues rising about 12% in 2005, driven by a larger number of active neighborhoods, as we see PHM continuing its active program of new community openings. We also see 2005 being lifted by closings on the company's large order backlog. However, in light of our outlook for higher, but still accommodative, mortgage rates, we think PHM will lose some of its pricing power in 2005, and see relatively flat average prices for homes sold in that year.

- We expect comparatively even net margins in 2005. We see margins aided by the likely benefits of better overhead leverage, and our projection of ongoing efforts by Pulte to improve operating efficiencies and construction practices. We see these factors being offset by the somewhat more competitive conditions that we anticipate in housing markets in the coming year, community startup costs, and a likely ongoing shift in PHM's mortgage originations toward less profitable adjustable rate issues.

- Our 2004 and 2005 Standard & Poor's Core Earnings forecasts each fall only $0.03 a share below our operating EPS estimate, with the difference related to projected option costs in excess of those that we expect PHM to record (about $0.07 a share in each year).

Investment Rationale/Risk November 01, 2004

- We expect housing markets to remain in pretty good shape over the coming year, based on our outlook for higher, but still accommodative, mortgage rates, and some ongoing economic growth. We also have a positive view of PHM's position as the largest U.S. builder of homes for buyers over 50 years of age, as we believe that mature buyers are least affected by mortgage rates, as many are able to pay cash for homes. However, after factoring in the maturity of the current housing cycle, our interest rate outlook and valuation considerations, we would not add to positions in the shares.

- The primary risk to our recommendation and target price is a sharper than expected upturn in mortgage rates.

- The shares recently traded at a little over 6X our 2005 EPS forecast, which was slightly below peers and in the lower half of Pulte's historical valuation. We expect PHM shares to be supported over the coming year by the still solid operating performance that we forecast, but think their upside will be limited by investor concerns about housing market prospects. Our 12-month target price is $59, or about 7X our 2005 EPS estimate. We would hold the shares, but believe that the potential level of appreciation is too modest to warrant additional purchases.

Key Stock Statistics

S&P Core EPS 2005E	8.47	52-week Range	$64.07-40.00
S&P Oper. EPS 2004E	7.60	12 Month P/E	8.9
P/E on S&P Oper. EPS 2004E	7.6	Beta	0.97
S&P Oper. EPS 2005E	8.50	Shareholders	1,527
Yield (%)	0.3%	Market Cap (B)	$ 7.4
Dividend Rate/Share	0.20	Shares Outstanding (M)	127.6

Value of $10,000 invested five years ago: **$ 50,059**

Dividend Data Dividends have been paid since 1977

Amount ($)	Date Decl.	Ex-Div. Date	Stock of Record	Payment Date
2-for-1	Dec. 11	Jan. 05	Dec. 23	Jan. 02 '04
0.050	Feb. 11	Mar. 12	Mar. 16	Apr. 01 '04
0.050	May. 13	Jun. 15	Jun. 17	Jul. 01 '04
0.050	Sep. 15	Sep. 23	Sep. 27	Oct. 01 '04

Revenues/Earnings Data Fiscal year ending December 31

Revenues (Million $)

	2004	2003	2002	2001	2000	1999
1Q	2,039	1,553	1,379	839.8	775.8	682.5
2Q	2,519	1,958	1,686	1,058	982.6	834.1
3Q	2,967	2,400	1,860	1,482	1,054	937.1
4Q	—	3,138	2,548	2,002	1,347	1,241
Yr.	—	9,049	7,472	5,382	4,159	3,730

Earnings Per Share ($)

	2004	2003	2002	2001	2000	1999
1Q	1.02	0.70	0.56	0.46	0.29	0.27
2Q	1.45	0.98	0.73	0.70	0.58	0.43
3Q	1.99	1.28	0.92	0.77	0.73	0.54
4Q	E3.14	1.94	1.39	0.99	1.01	0.80
Yr.	E7.60	4.91	3.60	3.01	2.59	2.04

Next earnings report expected: late-January Source: S&P, Company Reports
EPS Estimates based on S&P Operating Earnings; historical GAAP earnings are as reported.

Pulte Homes, Inc.

Recommendation: **HOLD** ★ ★ ★ ★ ★   12-Month Target Price: **$59.00** (as of October 26, 2004)

Business Summary November 02, 2004

Pulte Homes has more than quadrupled its home sales since 1990. Its total of 39,813 units sold in 2003 consisted of 32,693 domestic unit sales, plus international and sales made through affiliates. The company operates in 27 states and 45 markets throughout the U.S., and also has operations in Mexico, Puerto Rico, and Argentina (foreign sales accounted for 3% of revenues in 2003). PHM targets buyers in nearly all home categories, but has recently concentrated its expansion efforts on affordable housing and on mature buyers (age 50 and over). In line with the latter strategy, in July 2001, it acquired Del Webb Corp., the leading U.S. builder of active adult communities ($1.9 billion in FY 01 revenues on 7,038 home closings), for a total of $1.9 billion in stock, cash, and assumption of debt.

The company focuses on building single-family detached homes, which account for about 80% to 85% of unit volume. PHM's average price for U.S. homes sold in 2003 was $259,000, with about 75% of closings ranging in price from $100,000 to $350,000.

Orders in 2004's third quarter increased 19%, year to year, to $3.0 billion (up 11% in units, to 10,109 homes). Order backlog at September 30, 2004, totaled $6.4 billion (20,400 units), up 38% (23% in units) from the year-earlier level.

PHM normally designs its homes; with construction then performed by subcontractors under supervision of the company's on-site superintendents.

With mature age brackets expected to be the fastest growing segment of the U.S. population in coming years, the company has concentrated on attaining a leading position in active adult/retirement markets.

To assist its home sales effort, PHM offers mortgage banking and title insurance services through Pulte Mortgage and other units.

The company also has operations in Mexico, Puerto Rico, and Argentina. PHM's initial foreign offerings focused on affordable and social interest housing, but with its late 2000 entry into Argentina, it developed a fully amenitized project for higher-income individuals in the suburbs of Buenos Aires. As of early 2004, the company was evaluating long-term strategies for its international operations.

In October 2001, PHM reached a settlement with the FDIC related to the company's discontinued First Heights Bank operations. Pulte agreed to pay the FDIC $41.5 million, with the FDIC retaining all amounts previously withheld from First Heights. The suit centered on tax benefits and other matters involved in First Heights' 1988 acquisition of five failed and insolvent Texas thrifts. Separately, in August 2001, the United States Court of Federal Claims ruled that the U.S. had breached a contract related to PHM's acquisition of the First Heights businesses; in September 2003, the U.S. Court of Federal Claims issued a final judgment awarding PHM $48.7 million in non-taxable damages in the case, with appeals filed by the government and PHM the following month.

Company Financials Fiscal Year ending December 31

Per Share Data ($)

(Year Ended December 31)	2003	2002	2001	2000	1999	1998	1997	1996	1995	1994
Tangible Bk. Val.	24.26	18.82	15.27	15.01	12.63	10.68	9.55	8.91	7.04	6.47
Cash Flow	5.23	3.84	3.33	2.76	2.19	1.21	0.66	0.70	0.51	0.68
Earnings	4.91	3.60	3.01	2.59	2.04	1.15	0.57	0.63	0.45	0.56
S&P Core Earnings	4.89	3.53	2.86	NA	NA	NA	NA	NA	NA	NA
Dividends	0.08	0.08	0.08	0.08	0.08	0.07	0.06	0.06	0.06	0.06
Payout Ratio	2%	2%	3%	3%	4%	6%	11%	10%	13%	11%
Prices - High	49.41	29.87	25.12	22.50	15.62	18.09	10.62	8.65	8.65	9.65
- Low	22.72	18.10	13.05	7.62	8.37	9.96	6.81	6.00	5.03	4.53
P/E Ratio - High	10	8	8	9	8	16	19	14	19	17
- Low	5	5	4	3	4	9	12	10	11	8

Income Statement Analysis (Million $)

	2003	2002	2001	2000	1999	1998	1997	1996	1995	1994
Revs.	9,049	7,472	5,382	4,159	3,730	2,867	2,524	2,384	2,029	1,756
Oper. Inc.	997	746	601	429	350	222	135	145	144	203
Depr.	40.2	29.8	32.9	14.2	13.5	5.04	7.81	6.75	6.30	13.2
Int. Exp.	Nil	Nil	81.6	65.1	56.8	51.1	26.6	53.3	73.0	96.6
Pretax Inc.	996	729	492	355	286	166	81.0	102	82.0	104
Eff. Tax Rate	38.0%	39.0%	38.5%	38.5%	37.8%	39.0%	38.5%	38.3%	40.5%	39.8%
Net Inc.	617	445	302	218	178	101	49.8	63.2	48.8	62.4
S&P Core Earnings	615	436	288	NA	NA	NA	NA	NA	NA	NA

Balance Sheet & Other Fin. Data (Million $)

	2003	2002	2001	2000	1999	1998	1997	1996	1995	1994
Cash	404	613	72.1	184	51.7	125	245	190	292	160
Curr. Assets	NA	NA	NA	NA	NA	NA	NA	NA	NA	NA
Total Assets	8,063	6,888	5,714	2,886	2,597	2,350	2,151	1,985	2,048	1,941
Curr. Liab.	NA	NA	NA	NA	NA	NA	NA	NA	NA	NA
LT Debt	1,962	1,913	1,738	678	526	570	584	436	589	563
Common Equity	3,448	2,760	2,277	1,248	1,093	921	813	829	761	711
Total Cap.	5,418	4,674	4,015	1,926	1,619	1,492	1,397	1,265	1,350	1,274
Cap. Exp.	39.1	NA	NA	NA	NA	NA	Nil	Nil	Nil	Nil
Cash Flow	657	474	335	233	192	106	57.6	70.0	55.2	75.6
Curr. Ratio	NA	NA	NA	NA	NA	NA	NA	NA	NA	NA
% LT Debt of Cap.	36.2	40.9	43.3	35.2	32.5	38.2	41.8	34.5	43.6	44.2
% Net Inc.of Revs.	6.8	6.0	5.6	5.3	4.8	3.5	2.0	2.7	2.4	3.6
% Ret. on Assets	8.3	7.1	7.0	8.1	7.2	4.5	2.4	3.2	2.4	2.2
% Ret. on Equity	19.9	17.7	17.2	18.7	17.7	11.7	6.1	8.0	6.6	9.9

Data as orig reptd.; bef. results of disc opers/spec. items. Per share data adj. for stk. divs.; EPS diluted (primary prior to 1998). E-Estimated. NA-Not Available. NM-Not Meaningful. NR-Not Ranked. UR-Under Review.

Office: 100 Bloomfield Hills Pkwy Ste 300, Bloomfield Hills, MI 48304-2950.
Telephone: 248-647-2750.
Website: http://www.pulte.com
Chrmn: W.J. Pulte.
Pres & CEO: R.J. Dugas, Jr.
COO & EVP: S.C. Petruska.

EVP & CFO: R.A. Cregg.
SVP, Secy & General Counsel: J.R. Stoller.
VP & Investor Contact: J.P. Zeumer 248-433-4597.
Dirs: D. K. Anderson, D. J. Dugas, Jr., D. J. Kelly-Ennis, D. N. McCammon, P. J. O'Meara, W. J. Pulte, B. W. Reznicek, M. E. Rossi, A. E. Schwartz, F. J. Sehn, J. J. Shea, W. B. Smith.

Founded: in 1969.
Domicile: Michigan.
Employees: 10,800.
S&P Analyst: Michael W. Jaffe/CB/BK

The **McGraw·Hill** Companies

STANDARD &POOR'S

QLogic Corp.

Recommendation: **BUY** ★★★★☆
SELL | SELL | HOLD | BUY | BUY

12-Month Target Price: **$35.00**
(as of October 05, 2004)

QLGC has an approximate 0.03% weighting in the **S&P 500**

Sector: Information Technology
Sub-Industry: Computer Storage & Peripherals

Summary: QLGC designs and supplies semiconductor and board-level I/O (input/output) and enclosure management products.

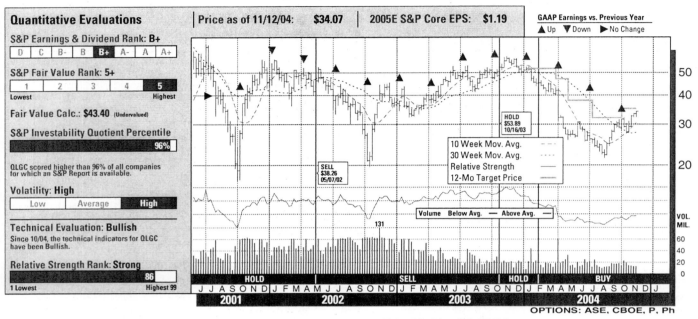

| Quantitative Evaluations | Price as of 11/12/04: | $34.07 | 2005E S&P Core EPS: | $1.19 |

S&P Earnings & Dividend Rank: B+
D | C | B- | B | **B+** | A- | A | A+

S&P Fair Value Rank: 5+
1 | 2 | 3 | 4 | **5**
Lowest — Highest

Fair Value Calc.: $43.40 (Undervalued)

S&P Investability Quotient Percentile — 96%

QLGC scored higher than 96% of all companies for which an S&P Report is available.

Volatility: High
Low | Average | **High**

Technical Evaluation: Bullish
Since 10/04, the technical indicators for QLGC have been Bullish.

Relative Strength Rank: Strong — 86
1 Lowest — Highest 99

GAAP Earnings vs. Previous Year
▲ Up ▼ Down ▶ No Change

SELL $38.26 05/07/02
HOLD $53.89 10/16/03

10 Week Mov. Avg.
30 Week Mov. Avg.
Relative Strength
12-Mo Target Price

Volume Below Avg. — Above Avg.

131

VOL. MIL.

HOLD | SELL | HOLD | BUY
J J A S O N D|J F M A M J J A S O N D|J F M A M J J A S O N D|J F M A M J J A S O N D|J
2001 | 2002 | 2003 | 2004

OPTIONS: ASE, CBOE, P, Ph

Analyst commentary prepared by Richard N. Stice, CFA /CB/GG

Highlights October 15, 2004

- We expect revenues to increase about 10% in FY 06 (Mar.), following an estimated 5% gain in FY 05. This reflects our expectations of an improving economic climate, gains in market share, and a rise in information technology spending, particularly for data storage products.

- We think that gross margins should remain in the upper 60% area, boosted by manufacturing efficiencies and a more favorable business mix. However, we believe these factors are likely to be outweighed by more aggressive pricing as the industry turns its focus toward the small and medium-sized business market. We expect EPS to be aided by continuing share repurchases. QLGC recently implemented a $100 million stock repurchase program.

- We see FY 06 operating EPS of $1.70, up 6% from FY 05's anticipated $1.60 (excluding $0.04 of special charges). Our FY 05 and FY 06 Standard & Poor's Core Earnings per share estimates are $1.19 and $1.23, respectively, reflecting projected stock option expense.

Investment Rationale/Risk October 15, 2004

- We recommend accumulating the shares. According to recent industry figures, QLGC is the largest provider of Fibre Channel host bus adapters, which are components used in networked storage environments. We view positively the company's execution and capital structure. Gross margins in the latest quarter widened by 140 basis points, year to year. We expect the company to continue to generate free cash flow, and see the balance sheet as strong, with a current ratio in excess of 14 and no long term debt.

- Risks to our recommendation and target price include a potential slowing of demand in the storage networking sector, loss of market share, and a greater than expected decline in average selling prices.

- Our 12-month target price of $35 is based on an intrinsic value calculation utilizing our discounted cash flow analysis. Our assumptions include a weighted average cost of capital of 12.2% and an expected terminal growth rate of 4%.

Key Stock Statistics

S&P Core EPS 2006E	1.23	52-week Range	$57.59-21.44
S&P Oper. EPS 2005E	1.60	12 Month P/E	23.7
P/E on S&P Oper. EPS 2005E	21.3	Beta	NA
S&P Oper. EPS 2006E	1.70	Shareholders	632
Yield (%)	Nil	Market Cap (B)	$ 3.2
Dividend Rate/Share	Nil	Shares Outstanding (M)	92.5

Value of $10,000 invested five years ago: **$ 5,673**

Dividend Data

No cash dividends have been paid.

Revenues/Earnings Data Fiscal year ending March 31

Revenues (Million $)

	2005	2004	2003	2002	2001	2000
1Q	129.8	126.2	98.96	89.90	76.77	43.19
2Q	134.6	132.3	107.1	80.88	85.97	47.49
3Q	—	137.1	114.2	83.63	95.13	52.34
4Q	—	128.3	120.6	92.26	99.7	60.13
Yr.	—	523.9	440.8	344.2	357.5	203.1

Earnings Per Share ($)

	2005	2004	2003	2002	2001	2000
1Q	0.34	0.33	0.24	0.20	0.20	0.15
2Q	0.38	0.35	0.24	0.17	-0.01	0.18
3Q	E0.41	0.36	0.29	0.18	0.26	0.20
4Q	E0.43	0.34	0.31	0.20	0.27	0.17
Yr.	E1.60	1.39	1.09	0.74	0.72	0.70

Next earnings report expected: mid-January Source: S&P, Company Reports
EPS Estimates based on S&P Operating Earnings; historical GAAP earnings are as reported.

Recommendation: **BUY** ★★★★☆   12-Month Target Price: **$35.00** (as of October 05, 2004)

Business Summary October 15, 2004

QLogic Corp. designs and develops storage networking infrastructure components sold to OEMs, distributors, resellers, and system integrators. QLGC produces the controller chips, management enclosure chips, host bus adapters (HBAs), fabric switches, and management software that provide the connectivity infrastructure for storage networks of every size. The company serves customers with solutions based on various SAN technologies, including Small Computer Systems Interface (SCSI), Internet SCSI (iSCSI), and Fibre Channel.

In late 2003, the University of California, Berkeley, published an updated report measuring the amount of digital information generated in the world each year. The report concluded that the world was generating over 1.6 million terabytes (1 terabyte equals about 1 million books) of magnetically recorded information a year. The study added that the volume of information was doubling every year.

During the past few years, iSCSI has emerged as a new SAN technology, allowing SCSI commands to be transported over standard Ethernet infrastructure. This technology provides an entry point for small and medium-sized businesses to incorporate the benefits of SANs. By using an Ethernet infrastructure that already exists in nearly every business environment, small and medium-sized businesses can implement SANs without training new people on the deployment or management of the network.

The company's technology is found primarily in server, workstation, storage subsystem, and hard disk drive solutions targeted at storage intensive enterprise applications such as data warehousing, data mining, and online transaction processing; media rich environments such as film and video, broadcast, medical imaging and computer-aided design; and server clustering, high speed backup, and data replication.

QLGC markets and distributes its products through OEM manufacturer partners, system integrators, resellers and a direct sales organization. It also uses a network of independent manufacturers' representatives and regional and international distributors.

International revenues accounted for 56% of net revenues in FY 04 (Mar.), up from 54% in FY 03. Sun Microsystems and Fujitsu each accounted for over 10% of FY 04 sales. The five largest customers accounted for 56% of FY 04 revenues, down from 60% in FY 03. QLGC works closely with independent hardware and software vendors, as well as with developers and integrators who create, test and evaluate complementary storage networking products. Key alliance partners include Cisco Systems, Microsoft, and Computer Associates.

The company continues to invest heavily in research and development, and to expand its capabilities to address emerging technologies in a rapidly evolving storage networking industry. In FY 04, QLGC's R&D spending totaled $87.8 million, up from $81.3 million in FY 03.

Company Financials Fiscal Year ending March 31

Per Share Data ($)

(Year Ended March 31)	2004	2003	2002	2001	2000	1999	1998	1997	1996	1995
Tangible Bk. Val.	9.22	8.00	6.65	5.67	3.27	2.13	3.41	0.52	0.37	0.35
Cash Flow	1.54	1.24	0.88	0.84	0.76	0.39	0.49	0.18	0.07	0.10
Earnings	1.39	1.09	0.74	0.72	0.70	0.35	0.21	0.12	0.02	0.04
S&P Core Earnings	1.03	0.70	0.44	0.32	NA	NA	NA	NA	NA	NA
Dividends	Nil	Nil	Nil	Nil	Nil	Nil	Nil	Nil	Nil	Nil
Payout Ratio	Nil	Nil	Nil	Nil	Nil	Nil	Nil	Nil	Nil	Nil

Cal. Yrs.	2003	2002	2001	2000	1999	1998	1997	1996	1995	1994
Prices - High	58.72	57.10	99.12	203.25	83.75	16.82	5.67	3.54	1.17	1.28
- Low	32.13	19.66	17.21	39.68	11.62	3.00	2.31	0.81	0.51	0.40
P/E Ratio - High	42	52	NM	NM	NM	49	27	30	78	29
- Low	23	18	NM	NM	NM	9	11	7	34	9

Income Statement Analysis (Million $)

	2004	2003	2002	2001	2000	1999	1998	1997	1996	1995
Revs.	524	441	344	358	203	117	81.4	68.9	53.8	57.7
Oper. Inc.	214	157	99	132	78.8	36.7	20.9	12.4	3.64	5.80
Depr.	14.8	14.7	13.0	10.8	4.80	3.37	2.43	3.02	2.45	2.40
Int. Exp.	Nil	Nil	Nil	Nil	0.02	0.08	0.11	0.13	0.15	0.10
Pretax Inc.	216	159	106	117	81.7	38.9	21.8	9.83	1.20	3.33
Eff. Tax Rate	38.0%	35.0%	33.0%	41.2%	34.0%	34.0%	38.6%	40.5%	44.6%	40.9%
Net Inc.	134	103	70.7	68.8	54.0	25.7	13.4	5.85	0.67	1.97
S&P Core Earnings	99	67.0	42.1	30.5	NA	NA	NA	NA	NA	NA

Balance Sheet & Other Fin. Data (Million $)

	2004	2003	2002	2001	2000	1999	1998	1997	1996	1995
Cash	157	138	76.1	128	64.1	43.2	64.1	19.1	8.41	1.15
Curr. Assets	854	748	587	490	177	131	108	31.1	23.0	17.3
Total Assets	929	817	670	571	267	173	136	37.0	28.5	24.6
Curr. Liab.	60.8	66.7	51.0	47.8	24.2	20.2	17.6	11.3	9.67	6.80
LT Debt	Nil	Nil	Nil	Nil	Nil	Nil	0.14	0.35	0.58	0.85
Common Equity	868	751	619	524	243	153	118	24.4	16.3	15.6
Total Cap.	868	751	619	524	243	153	118	24.7	16.9	16.5
Cap. Exp.	22.3	15.7	14.5	16.7	40.0	6.77	3.92	3.90	1.20	NA
Cash Flow	149	118	83.7	79.6	58.8	29.1	15.8	8.87	3.12	4.37
Curr. Ratio	14.0	11.2	11.5	10.3	7.3	6.5	6.2	2.7	2.4	2.5
% LT Debt of Cap.	Nil	Nil	Nil	Nil	Nil	Nil	0.1	1.4	3.4	5.2
% Net Inc.of Revs.	25.5	23.5	20.5	19.2	26.6	21.9	16.5	8.5	1.2	3.4
% Ret. on Assets	15.3	13.9	11.4	14.2	24.5	16.6	15.5	17.9	2.5	8.3
% Ret. on Equity	16.5	15.1	12.4	15.6	27.3	19.0	18.8	28.8	4.2	13.4

Data as orig reptd.; bef. results of disc opers/spec. items. Per share data adj. for stk. divs.; EPS diluted. E-Estimated. NA-Not Available. NM-Not Meaningful. NR-Not Ranked. UR-Under Review.

Office: 26650 Aliso Viejo Pkwy, Aliso Viejo, CA 92656-2674.
Telephone: 949-389-6000.
Website: http://www.qlogic.com
Chrmn, Pres & CEO: H.K. Desai.

VP, CFO & Investor Contact: T. Massetti 949-389-7533.
Secy: M.R. Manning.
Dirs: L. R. Carter, H. K. Desai, J. R. Fiebiger, B. S. Iyer, C. L. Miltner, G. D. Wells.

Founded: in 1992.
Domicile: Delaware.
Employees: 819.
S&P Analyst: Richard N. Stice, CFA /CB/GG

QUALCOMM Inc.

Recommendation: **BUY** ★★★★ 12-Month Target Price: **$45.00**
(as of August 17, 2004)

QCOM has an approximate 0.59% weighting in the **S&P 500**

Sector: Information Technology
Sub-Industry: Communications Equipment
Peer Group: Wireless Equipment

Summary: QCOM focuses on developing products and services based on its CDMA digital wireless technology.

Quantitative Evaluations

S&P Earnings & Dividend Rank: B

| D | C | B- | B | B+ | A- | A | A+ |

S&P Fair Value Rank: 3-

| 1 | 2 | 3 | 4 | 5 |
| Lowest | | 3 | | Highest |

Fair Value Calc.: $37.10 (Slightly Overvalued)

S&P Investability Quotient Percentile

89%

QCOM scored higher than 89% of all companies for which an S&P Report is available.

Volatility: Average

| Low | Average | High |

Technical Evaluation: Neutral

Since 11/04, the technical indicators for QCOM have been Neutral.

Relative Strength Rank: Moderate

40

| 1 Lowest | | Highest 99 |

Price as of 11/12/04: $40.20 | **2005E S&P Core EPS:** $1.05

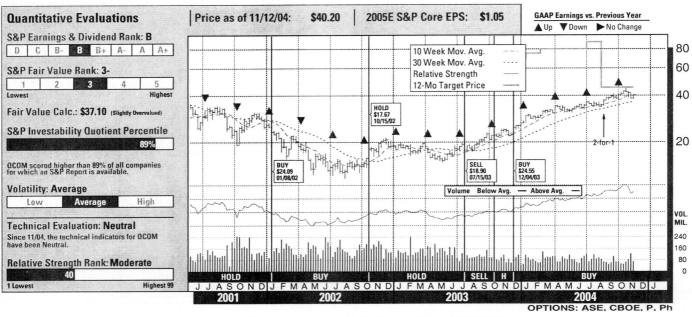

GAAP Earnings vs. Previous Year
▲ Up ▼ Down ► No Change

- 10 Week Mov. Avg.
- 30 Week Mov. Avg.
- Relative Strength
- 12-Mo Target Price

HOLD $17.67 10/15/02
BUY $24.09 01/08/02
SELL $18.90 07/15/03
BUY $24.55 12/04/03
2-for-1

Volume Below Avg. — Above Avg.

VOL. MIL.
240
160
80
0

HOLD	BUY	HOLD	SELL	H	BUY
J J A S O N D	J F M A M J J A S O N D	J F M A M J J A S O N D	J F M A M J J A S O N D	J F M A M J J A S O N D J
2001	2002	2003	2004

OPTIONS: ASE, CBOE, P, Ph

Analyst commentary prepared by Kenneth M. Leon/PMW/JWP

Highlights November 09, 2004

- We expect total revenues to climb 26% in FY 05 (Sep.), followed by a 20% advance in FY 06, driven by growing global demand for code division multiple access (CDMA) integrated chipsets and gains for license royalties. In early November, QCOM said first quarter chipset shipments should be 38 million to 39 million units, flat sequentially, due to capacity constraints. In regard to license fee revenues, the company estimated calendar 2005 CDMA handset shipments of 218 million to 228 million, up from 168 million to 172 million forecast for 2004. We reduced our forecast from 180 million to 175 million CDMA handset shipments in calendar 2004.

- With CDMA handset sales in 2005 expected to reach 220 million to 230 million units, based on our forecast, and with the average selling price per unit seen flat to up 3%, we estimate FY 05 revenue growth of 22% to 25% for the very profitable licensing business. We expect FY 05 and FY 06 gross margins of 67% to 69%, versus 69% in FY 04, as we have increased our forecast for sales and marketing and R&D expenses.

- Excluding QSI, the unprofitable investment segment under GAAP reporting, we project FY 05 operating EPS of $1.20, up from FY 04's $1.09; our FY 06 estimate is $1.50. Our FY 05 and FY 06 S&P Core EPS projections are $1.05 and $1.35, respectively, after estimated stock option expense and other adjustments.

Key Stock Statistics

S&P Core EPS 2006E	1.35	52-week Range	$44.41-21.80
S&P Oper. EPS 2005E	1.20	12 Month P/E	39.0
P/E on S&P Oper. EPS 2005E	33.5	Beta	1.76
S&P Oper. EPS 2006E	1.50	Shareholders	10,519
Yield (%)	0.7%	Market Cap (B)	$ 65.4
Dividend Rate/Share	0.28	Shares Outstanding (M)	1627.8

Value of $10,000 invested five years ago: **$ 10,512**

Dividend Data Dividends have been paid since 2003

Amount ($)	Date Decl.	Ex-Div. Date	Stock of Record	Payment Date
0.100	Mar. 02	May. 26	May. 28	Jun. 25 '04
2-for-1	Jul. 13	Aug. 16	Jul. 23	Aug. 13 '04
0.070	Jul. 13	Aug. 25	Aug. 27	Sep. 24 '04
0.070	Nov. 10	Dec. 06	Dec. 08	Jan. 05 '05

Investment Rationale/Risk November 09, 2004

- After declining from a recent 52-week high, we think the shares have further upside potential. The stock is priced near peer levels on the basis of FY 05 P/E multiple, but we see QCOM growing faster, as we anticipate a strong handset replacement market in Europe and the U.S., and rising demand for CDMA handsets in China, India, Japan, and South Korea. We view the company as having a very attractive financial model, with wide gross margins, no long term debt, and $7.6 billion in cash at the end of the FY 04 fourth quarter.

- Risks to our opinion and target price include the possibility that developed countries will not keep up with the high replacement rate expected for more advanced CDMA handsets using either 1X-EV-DO or WCDMA technologies; slower than expected wireless subscriber growth in emerging countries such as China and India; accounting issues related to license royalties; and the company's dependence on a limited number of third-party manufacturers to provide subassemblies and parts for its CDMA chipsets as it tries to meet growing demand.

- Applying a P/E multiple of 34X to our FY 05 EPS estimate, a premium to peers that we think is warranted by what we view as above-average growth potential, we arrive at our 12-month target price of $45.

Revenues/Earnings Data Fiscal year ending September 30

Revenues (Million $)

	2004	2003	2002	2001	2000	1999
1Q	1,242	857.5	698.6	684.0	1,120	941.2
2Q	1,216	1,043	696.1	713.3	727.7	932.4
3Q	1,341	921.6	770.9	640.0	713.5	1,004
4Q	1,118	908.8	873.9	650.8	635.0	1,060
Yr.	4,880	3,971	3,040	2,680	3,197	3,937

Earnings Per Share ($)

	2004	2003	2002	2001	2000	1999
1Q	0.21	0.15	0.09	-0.24	0.12	0.04
2Q	0.27	0.07	0.03	0.09	0.13	-0.04
3Q	0.29	0.12	-0.01	-0.18	0.10	0.04
4Q	0.23	0.18	0.12	-0.03	0.09	0.09
Yr.	1.03	0.51	0.22	-0.36	0.43	0.15

Next earnings report expected: late-January Source: S&P, Company Reports
EPS Estimates based on S&P Operating Earnings; historical GAAP earnings are as reported.

QUALCOMM Incorporated

Recommendation: **BUY** ★ ★ ★ ★ ★   12-Month Target Price: **$45.00** (as of August 17, 2004)

Business Summary November 09, 2004

QUALCOMM develops, makes and markets digital wireless telecommunications products and services based on its code division multiple access (CDMA) technology. The company reports results in four operating segments: CDMA technology (QCT), technology licensing (QTL), wireless and Internet (QWI), and strategic initiatives (QSI).

The QCT segment, which accounted for 59% of total sales in FY 04 (Sep.), provides integrated circuits and system software solutions to many of the world's leading wireless handset and infrastructure manufacturers. The company uses a fabless business model, employing several independent semiconductor foundries to manufacture all of its semiconductor products. In FY 04, QCOM announced a convergence platform using three chipsets that address all major third generation interfaces and include popular digital electronics features for wireless devices.

QCT's current competitors include major semiconductor companies such as Texas Instruments, STMicroelectronics, Freescale, VIA Telecom, NEC, Infineon and Philips, as well as major telecommunications equipment companies such as Motorola, Nokia, Ericsson, Samsung and Matsushita, which design their own integrated circuits and software for certain products.

The digital wireless standard known as CDMA offers superior performance to that of other digital technologies, allowing a greater number of calls within the allocated frequency. QCOM holds a number of patents related to CDMA, and derives royalties from licensing its technology to wireless manufacturers. Royalties are paid when manufacturers earn revenue from the sale of CDMA-based equipment. The technology licensing business (QTL) accounted for 25% of FY 04 revenues.

The company's third-generation CDMA2000 1X technology was commercially deployed in South Korea in October 2000. In North America, most CDMA-based operators had commercially deployed CDMA2000 1X at the end of FY 03. As of October 2004, 10 wireless phone operators had commercially deployed CDMA 1xEV-DO technology, in South Korea, the U.S., Japan, Brazil, Guatamala, Romania, and the Czech Republic. The European Community and certain carriers in Japan have focused on another third generation wireless mode, known as WCDMA, based on QCOM's CDMA technology. TD-SDCDMA, a third CDMA mode, is the least developed, but is supported by the Chinese government.

The QWI segment accounted for 16% of FY 04 sales. It provides satellite-based two-way data messaging and position reporting equipment to transportation companies. QWI shipped 43,400 OmniTRACs units in FY 04, bringing the total to 520,000 units shipped. QWI also includes the BREW product and service for software developers and interface device suppliers.

In November 2004, the company announced plans to begin commercial operations in 2006 for the delivery of low-cost multimedia content to multiple subscribers. MediaFLO USA will offer a nationwide FLO technology-based network as a shared resource for U.S. wireless operators and their customers. The new network plans to use 700 MHz spectrum. QCOM expects to invest $800 million over five years to build and operate MediaFLO. Starting with the FY 05 first quarter, the business unit will be reported in the QSI segment.

Revenue from customers in South Korea, the U.S. and Japan accounted respectively for 43%, 21% and 18% of total consolidated revenues in FY 04 (45%, 23% and 15% in FY 03). The increase in revenues from customers in Japan was primarily attributed to higher royalties from licensees in Japan using CDMA2000 and WCDMA.

Company Financials Fiscal Year ending September 30

Per Share Data ($)

(Year Ended September 30)	2004	2003	2002	2001	2000	1999	1998	1997	1996	1995
Tangible Bk. Val.	5.69	4.54	2.77	2.82	3.14	2.22	0.83	0.92	0.78	0.76
Cash Flow	1.13	0.62	0.47	-0.14	0.57	0.28	0.21	0.16	0.07	0.07
Earnings	1.03	0.51	0.22	-0.36	0.43	0.15	0.09	0.08	0.02	0.03
S&P Core Earnings	0.83	0.74	0.34	-0.68	NA	NA	NA	NA	NA	NA
Dividends	0.19	0.12	Nil	Nil	Nil	Nil	Nil	Nil	Nil	Nil
Payout Ratio	18%	24%	Nil	Nil	Nil	Nil	Nil	Nil	Nil	Nil
Prices - High	44.41	27.42	26.67	44.68	100.00	92.51	4.21	4.49	3.40	3.42
- Low	26.66	14.79	11.60	19.15	25.75	3.26	2.35	2.44	1.89	1.28
P/E Ratio - High	43	54	NM	NM	NM	NM	46	57	NM	NM
- Low	26	29	NM	NM	NM	21	26	31	NM	NM

Income Statement Analysis (Million $)

	2004	2003	2002	2001	2000	1999	1998	1997	1996	1995
Revs.	4,880	3,971	3,040	2,680	3,197	3,937	3,348	2,096	814	387
Oper. Inc.	2,266	1,684	1,068	877	1,105	564	385	191	49.4	51.5
Depr.	163	180	394	320	244	158	142	93.6	56.8	30.9
Int. Exp.	Nil	30.7	25.7	10.2	4.92	54.0	8.06	11.0	3.40	2.10
Pretax Inc.	2,313	1,285	461	-426	1,197	320	197	111	26.6	39.9
Eff. Tax Rate	25.4%	35.6%	22.0%	NM	44.0%	33.1%	20.4%	14.8%	21.1%	24.3%
Net Inc.	1,725	827	360	-531	670	201	109	91.9	21.0	30.2
S&P Core Earnings	1,395	610	274	-512	NA	NA	NA	NA	NA	NA

Balance Sheet & Other Fin. Data (Million $)

	2004	2003	2002	2001	2000	1999	1998	1997	1996	1995
Cash	7,635	4,561	2,581	2,581	2,521	660	176	249	346	567
Curr. Assets	7,227	5,949	3,941	3,055	2,730	2,978	1,537	1,550	751	705
Total Assets	10,820	8,822	6,510	5,747	6,063	4,535	2,567	2,275	1,185	941
Curr. Liab.	894	808	675	521	472	876	882	567	326	105
LT Debt	Nil	123	0.23	Nil	Nil	660	664	667	10.9	33.5
Common Equity	9,664	7,599	5,265	4,890	5,516	2,872	958	1,024	845	800
Total Cap.	9,664	7,722	5,271	4,896	5,563	3,584	1,661	1,691	856	833
Cap. Exp.	332	231	114	114	163	180	322	163	217	100
Cash Flow	1,888	1,007	754	-211	914	359	250	186	77.8	61.1
Curr. Ratio	8.1	7.4	5.8	5.9	5.8	3.4	1.7	2.7	2.3	6.7
% LT Debt of Cap.	Nil	1.6	0.0	Nil	Nil	18.4	39.9	39.4	1.3	4.0
% Net Inc.of Revs.	35.3	20.8	11.8	NM	21.0	5.1	3.2	4.4	2.6	7.8
% Ret. on Assets	17.6	10.8	5.9	NM	12.6	5.7	4.5	5.3	2.6	4.6
% Ret. on Equity	20.0	12.7	7.1	NM	16.0	10.5	11.0	9.8	2.6	6.1

Data as orig reptd.; bef. results of disc opers/spec. items. Per share data adj. for stk. divs.; EPS diluted. E-Estimated. NA-Not Available. NM-Not Meaningful. NR-Not Ranked. UR-Under Review.

Office: 5775 Morehouse Drive, San Diego, CA 92121-1714.
Telephone: 858-587-1121.
Email: ir@qualcomm.com
Website: http://www.qualcomm.com
Chrmn & CEO: I.M. Jacobs.
Pres & COO: A.S. Thornley.

EVP & CFO: W.E. Keitel.
SVP & General Counsel: L. Lupin.
VP & Investor Contact: B. Davidson 858-658-4813.
Dirs: R. C. Atkinson, A. A. Coffman, R. V. Dittamore, D. L. Dougan, I. M. Jacobs, R. E. Kahn, D. A. Nelles, P. M. Sacerdote, B. Scowcroft, M. I. Stern, R. J. Sulpizio.

Founded: in 1985.
Domicile: Delaware.
Employees: 7,600.
S&P Analyst: Kenneth M. Leon/PMW/JWP

Quest Diagnostics

Recommendation: **HOLD** ★ ★ ★ ☆ ☆
SELL | SELL | HOLD | BUY | BUY

12-Month Target Price: **$93.00**
(as of November 15, 2004)

DGX has an approximate 0.09% weighting in the **S&P 500**

Sector: Health Care
Sub-Industry: Health Care Services
Peer Group: Diagnostic Test Services

Summary: This company provides diagnostic testing, information and services to physicians, hospitals, managed care organizations, employers and government agencies.

Quantitative Evaluations	**Price as of 11/16/04:** $92.05 **2004E S&P Core EPS:** $4.41

S&P Earnings & Dividend Rank: NR

| D | C | B- | B | B+ | A- | A | A+ |

S&P Fair Value Rank: 3+

| 1 | 2 | **3** | 4 | 5 |
| Lowest | | | | Highest |

Fair Value Calc.: $88.00 (Slightly Overvalued)

S&P Investability Quotient Percentile
91%

DGX scored higher than 91% of all companies for which an S&P Report is available.

Volatility: Low

| **Low** | Average | High |

Technical Evaluation: Bullish
Since 10/04, the technical indicators for DGX have been Bullish.

Relative Strength Rank: Moderate
61
1 Lowest   Highest 99

GAAP Earnings vs. Previous Year
▲ Up   ▼ Down   ▶ No Change

Analyst commentary prepared by Jeffrey Loo, CFA /CB/BK

Highlights 17-NOV-04

- We see 2004 sales growing about 8%, to $5.1 billion, reflecting a full year contribution from Unilab, 2% to 3% organic requisition growth, and an increase of 3% to 4% in average revenue per requisition due to a greater proportion of gene-based and esoteric tests along with a greater number of tests ordered per requisition. We see continued increases in patient recognition that diagnostic tests are beneficial for the early detection and possible prevention of disease. We see these trends continuing in 2005, resulting in 5% sales growth, to about $5.35 billion.

- We see operating margins improving 80 basis points, to 17.6%, on improving gross margins and increased operational efficiency from Six Sigma initiatives and further implementation of DGX's eMaxx'r' clinical connectivity Internet portal, which we believe helps lower bad debt expense through more orderly and timely collection of physician and patient information, such as insurance coverage. Bad debt expense of 4.6% in the third quarter reflected DGX's continued focus on this area. We see bad debt levels in the low 4% area in the future. About 30% of tests are now ordered through eMaxx'r', and we expect a gradual increase over the next several quarters as DGX rolls out its connectivity systems to more physicians.

- Our 2004 and 2005 EPS estimates are $4.89 and $5.44, respectively, and are based on higher sales and increased margins from improved operational efficiency. Our 2004 S&P Core Earnings estimate is $4.41 a share.

Investment Rationale/Risk 17-NOV-04

- We believe DGX's fundamentals are solid, and that it will benefit from an aging population, more esoteric testing, and a continuing shift from capitated to fee-for-service. However, we think DGX continues to face pricing pressure from third-party payers, including a five-year Medicare price freeze that began January 1, 2004, which we see pressuring revenue per requisition growth. DGX's Medicare mix increased after the Unilab acquisition. We also believe DGX will face increased competition from regional laboratories, particularly for higher margin esoteric tests. A handful of new labs recently received venture funding and have been active in their expansion plans. Also, DGX was able to expand revenue and earnings in recent years through acquisitions. In our view, however, a paucity of acquisition candidates of size (i.e., over $100 million in revenue) will limit this source of growth. Absent significant job creation, we believe lab utilization will be adversely affected.

- Risks to our recommendation and target price include further pricing pressure from third-party payers resulting in a decline in revenue per requisition; continued slow job creation weighing on utilization and possibly lowering the number of tests ordered; and increased competition from other labs.

- Our 12-month target price of $93 is based on a blend of our DCF analysis, utilizing a WACC of 9.3% and a terminal growth rate of 3%, and relative value analysis. This target price represents a P/E of 17X our estimated 2005 EPS, in line with peers and the S&P 500.

Key Stock Statistics

S&P Oper. EPS 2004E	**4.89**	52-week Range	**$92.05-68.85**
P/E on S&P Oper. EPS 2004E	**18.8**	12 Month P/E	**20.1**
S&P Oper. EPS 2005E	**5.44**	Beta	**0.41**
Yield (%)	**0.7%**	Shareholders	**5,900**
Dividend Rate/Share	**0.60**	Market Cap (B)	**$ 9.3**
Shares Outstanding (M)	**101.2**		

Value of $10,000 invested five years ago: **$ 61,818**

Dividend Data Dividends have been paid since 2004

Amount ($)	Date Decl.	Ex-Div. Date	Stock of Record	Payment Date
0.150	Oct. 21	Jan. 06	Jan. 08	Jan. 23 '04
0.150	Feb. 19	Apr. 05	Apr. 07	Apr. 21 '04
0.150	May. 04	Jul. 02	Jul. 07	Jul. 21 '04
0.150	Jul. 22	Oct. 06	Oct. 08	Oct. 22 '04

Revenues/Earnings Data Fiscal year ending December 31

Revenues (Million $)

	2004	2003	2002	2001	2000	1999
1Q	1,256	1,093	946.8	882.5	857.5	381.8
2Q	1,298	1,220	1,069	931.6	877.1	394.0
3Q	1,290	1,221	1,059	903.2	850.2	614.8
4Q	—	1,204	1,034	910.4	836.4	814.5
Yr.	—	4,738	4,108	3,628	3,421	2,205

Earnings Per Share ($)

	2004	2003	2002	2001	2000	1999
1Q	1.10	0.86	0.67	0.37	0.20	0.12
2Q	1.20	1.12	0.87	0.48	0.32	0.21
3Q	1.26	1.12	0.87	0.51	0.30	-0.10
4Q	E1.25	1.02	0.82	0.52	0.30	-0.17
Yr.	E4.89	4.12	3.23	1.88	1.11	-0.02

Next earnings report expected: late-January Source: S&P, Company Reports
EPS Estimates based on S&P Operating Earnings; historical GAAP earnings are as reported.

Quest Diagnostics Incorporated

Recommendation: **HOLD** ★ ★ ★ ☆ ☆   12-Month Target Price: **$93.00** (as of November 15, 2004)

Business Summary 17-NOV-04

Quest Diagnostics is the largest independent U.S. clinical lab provider. The company offers a broad range of clinical laboratory testing services used by physicians in the detection, diagnosis, evaluation, monitoring and treatment of diseases and other medical conditions. Tests range from routine (such as blood cholesterol tests) to highly complex esoteric (such as gene-based testing and molecular diagnostics testing). DGX also provides clinical trial testing for the development of new drugs and clinical lab testing in Mexico and Puerto Rico.

The company processes more than 130 million requisitions (order forms completed by physicians indicating tests to be performed) annually. Customers include physician practices, managed care organizations, hospitals, governmental institutions, employers, and other independent clinical laboratories.

At the end of 2003, DGX had a network of 30 principal laboratories in major metropolitan areas throughout the U.S., 155 smaller "rapid response" (STAT) laboratories, and approximately 1,925 patient service centers in the U.S., along with facilities in Mexico City, San Juan, PR, and near London, England. The company also operates two esoteric testing laboratories and research and development facilities at its Nichols Institute unit (one in San Juan Capistrano, CA, and one in Chantilly, VA). In 2003, DGX launched its eMaxx'r' Internet portal to physicians nationwide, which enables doctors to order diagnostic tests and review laboratory results online, as well as check patients' insurance eligibility in real time and view clinical information from many sources.

DGX's laboratory testing business consists of routine, esoteric and clinical trial testing. Routine testing generated 80% of net revenues in 2003 (83% in 2002), esoteric testing 16% (13% in 2002), and clinical trials under 3% (less than 3% in 2002). The balance of revenues came from foreign operations.

Routine tests measure important health parameters such as the function of the kidney, heart, liver, thyroid and other organs. Commonly ordered tests include blood cholesterol level tests; complete blood cell counts; pap smears; HIV-related tests; urinalyses; pregnancy tests; and alcohol and other substance-abuse tests.

Esoteric tests are performed less frequently than routine tests, and/or require more sophisticated equipment and materials, professional hands-on attention, and more highly skilled personnel. As a result, they are generally priced substantially higher than routine tests. Esoteric tests are generally in the fields of endocrinology and metabolism, genetics, hematology, immunology, microbiology, oncology, serology, special chemistry, and toxicology.

In February 2003, DGX acquired Unilab Corp., substantially increasing its presence in California. In connection with the acquisition and as part of its settlement with the Federal Trade Commission, DGX sold certain assets to LabCorp for $4.5 million, including the assignment of four agreements with independent physician associations and leases for 46 patient service centers.

Company Financials Fiscal Year ending December 31

Per Share Data ($)

(Year Ended December 31)	2003	2002	2001	2000	1999	1998	1997	1996	1995	1994
Tangible Bk. Val.	NM	NM	NM	NM	NM	1.20	0.45	NA	0.48	NA
Cash Flow	5.58	4.63	3.40	2.54	1.28	1.58	0.90	NA	1.19	NA
Earnings	4.12	3.23	1.88	1.11	-0.02	0.45	-0.39	NA	-0.39	NA
S&P Core Earnings	3.60	2.83	1.65	NA	NA	NA	NA	NA	NA	NA
Dividends	Nil	Nil	Nil	Nil	Nil	Nil	Nil	Nil	NA	NA
Payout Ratio	Nil	Nil	Nil	Nil	Nil	Nil	Nil	Nil	NA	NA
Prices - High	74.99	96.14	75.75	73.12	16.46	11.53	10.43	7.87	NA	NA
- Low	47.36	49.09	36.60	14.56	8.87	7.25	7.12	6.62	NA	NA
P/E Ratio - High	18	30	40	66	NM	26	NM	NA	NA	NA
- Low	11	15	19	13	NM	16	NM	NA	NA	NA

Income Statement Analysis (Million $)

	2003	2002	2001	2000	1999	1998	1997	1996	1995	1994
Revs.	4,738	4,108	3,628	3,421	2,205	1,459	1,529	1,616	1,629	NA
Oper. Inc.	950	724	559	452	243	163	151	166	183	NA
Depr.	154	131	148	134	90.8	68.8	76.4	99	90.9	NA
Int. Exp.	59.8	53.7	70.5	120	69.8	44.0	46.0	74.9	50.7	NA
Pretax Inc.	755	557	343	210	19.8	53.9	-19.1	-676	-15.7	NA
Eff. Tax Rate	39.9%	39.5%	43.4%	45.7%	NM	50.1%	NM	NM	NM	NA
Net Inc.	437	322	184	105	-1.27	26.9	-22.3	-626	-22.5	NA
S&P Core Earnings	377	279	162	NA	NA	NA	NA	NA	NA	NA

Balance Sheet & Other Fin. Data (Million $)

	2003	2002	2001	2000	1999	1998	1997	1996	1995	1994
Cash	155	96.8	122	171	27.3	203	162	42.0	40.0	NA
Curr. Assets	996	824	877	981	873	578	572	511	700	NA
Total Assets	4,301	3,324	2,931	2,865	2,878	1,360	1,401	1,395	1,612	NA
Curr. Liab.	724	636	659	955	701	309	295	249	394	NA
LT Debt	1,029	797	820	761	1,171	413	482	515	515	NA
Common Equity	2,397	1,769	1,336	1,031	862	567	541	538	604	NA
Total Cap.	3,426	2,565	2,156	1,793	2,046	2,034	1,024	1,054	1,119	NA
Cap. Exp.	175	155	149	116	76.0	39.6	30.8	70.4	93.1	NA
Cash Flow	591	454	332	239	89.6	95.7	54.1	-527	68.4	NA
Curr. Ratio	1.4	1.3	1.3	1.0	1.2	1.9	1.9	2.1	1.8	NA
% LT Debt of Cap.	30.0	31.0	38.0	42.4	57.6	42.1	47.1	48.9	46.0	NA
% Net Inc.of Revs.	9.2	7.8	5.1	3.1	NM	1.8	NM	NM	NM	NA
% Ret. on Assets	11.5	10.3	6.3	3.7	NM	1.9	NM	NM	NA	NA
% Ret. on Equity	20.9	20.8	15.5	11.1	NM	4.9	NM	NM	NA	NA

Data as orig. reptd.; bef. results of disc. opers. and/or spec. items. Per share data adj. for stk. divs.; EPS diluted. Balance Sheet Data and Book Value for 1995 are pro forma as of Sep. 30, 1996. E-Estimated. NA-Not Available. NM-Not Meaningful. NR-Not Ranked.

Office: One Malcolm Avenue, Teterboro, NJ 07608.
Telephone: 201-393-5000.
Email: investor@questdiagnostics.com
Website: http://www.questdiagnostics.com
Chrmn: K. W. Freeman.
Pres, COO & CEO: S. N. Mohapatra.

SVP & CFO: R. A. Hagemann.
SVP & General Counsel: M. E. Prevoznik.
Investor Contact: Laure Park (201-393-5030).
Dirs: J. C. Baldwin, W. F. Buehler, J. F. Flaherty III, K. W. Freeman, W. R. Grant, R. Haggerty, S. Mohapatra, D. C. Stanzione, G. R. Wilensky, J. B. Ziegler.

Founded: in 1967.
Domicile: Delaware.
Employees: 37,200.
S&P Analyst: Jeffrey Loo, CFA /CB/BK

STANDARD &POOR'S

Qwest Communications

Recommendation: HOLD ★★★★★
SELL SELL HOLD BUY BUY

12-Month Target Price: **$4.00**
(as of October 13, 2003)

Q has an approximate 0.06% weighting in the **S&P 500**

Sector: Telecommunication Services
Sub-Industry: Integrated Telecommunication Services
Peer Group: Regional Bell Operating Companies (RBOC's)

Summary: This company is a facilities-based provider of multimedia communications, including local phone service in 14 states.

Quantitative Evaluations

S&P Earnings & Dividend Rank: C

| D | C | B- | B | B+ | A- | A | A+ |

S&P Fair Value Rank: NR

| 1 | 2 | 3 | 4 | 5 |
| Lowest | | | | Highest |

Fair Value Calc.: NA

S&P Investability Quotient Percentile

20%

Q scored lower than 80% of all companies for which an S&P Report is available.

Volatility: High

| Low | Average | High |

Technical Evaluation: Bullish
Since 9/04, the technical indicators for Q have been Bullish.

Relative Strength Rank: Strong

88

1 Lowest   Highest 99

Price as of 11/12/04: **$3.90**   **2004E S&P Core EPS:** **$-0.93**

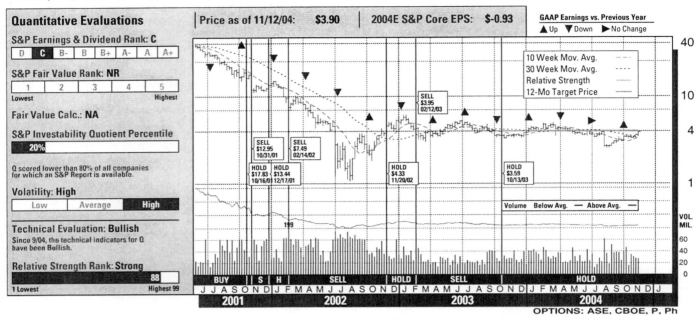

GAAP Earnings vs. Previous Year
▲ Up ▼ Down ► No Change

- 10 Week Mov. Avg.
- 30 Week Mov. Avg.
- Relative Strength
- 12-Mo Target Price

Volume Below Avg. — Above Avg.

OPTIONS: ASE, CBOE, P, Ph

Analyst commentary prepared by Todd Rosenbluth/CB/BK

Highlights November 09, 2004

- We see 2004 revenues declining about 3%, due to a decrease in local service revenues stemming from access line losses and sluggish data revenues. However, we believe customer retention will improve in 2005, as the company further bundles long-distance and wireless services, helping to keep revenues relatively stable. We project that revenues will fall fractionally in 2005.

- We expect EBITDA margins to expand slightly, to 26% in 2005, from an expected 25% in 2004, a level still below peers, as higher selling expenses due to the launch of new lower margin services are outweighed by workforce reductions and lower wireless service costs. We expect depreciation charges to decrease, and think interest expense, although still viewed as high, will be down slightly, as bank facilities have been refinanced and debt maturities extended.

- We see an operating loss of $0.64 a share for 2004; the inclusion of projected stock option expenses and pension adjustments leads to our 2004 Standard & Poor's Core Earnings projection of a loss of $0.93. We see an operating loss of $0.38 for 2005. Results in 2003 exclude charges of $0.15 a share for a termination agreement and $0.09 for asset impairment, and income of $1.38 from discontinued operations. Third quarter 2004 results include a $0.14 litigation reserve charge.

Investment Rationale/Risk November 09, 2004

- We believe customer retention will improve in 2005, with additional long-distance penetration in Q's core states and implementation of a nationwide wireless resale offering from Sprint PCS. However, we see the shares restricted by the company's relatively weak margins and high debt load. Third quarter results were below our expectations, with revenue and EBITDA reduced by access line losses and pricing pressures.

- Risks to our opinion and target price include Q's history of accounting probes, relatively high long-term debt relative to EBITDA, access line losses, multiple litigation issues, and weak demand for telecom services.

- Despite operational challenges and a history of accounting probes, we are using a slightly higher enterprise value to estimated EBITDA multiple for the stock than for Bell peers to arrive at our 12-month target price of $4. We believe this is warranted by the improving outlook we see in 2005. We think the shares have less support than peers, which all offer a dividend yield of over 3%. We would not add to positions in these volatile shares.

Key Stock Statistics

S&P Oper. EPS 2004E	-0.64	52-week Range	$5.00-2.56
P/E on S&P Oper. EPS 2004E	NM	12 Month P/E	NM
S&P Oper. EPS 2005E	-0.38	Beta	NA
Yield (%)	Nil	Shareholders	408,000
Dividend Rate/Share	Nil	Market Cap (B)	$ 7.1
Shares Outstanding (M)	1815.9		

Value of $10,000 invested five years ago: **$ 1,688**

Dividend Data

A dividend of $0.05 a share was paid in June 2001.

Revenues/Earnings Data Fiscal year ending December 31

Revenues (Million $)

	2004	2003	2002	2001	2000	1999
1Q	3,481	3,624	3,985	5,051	3,377	1,581
2Q	3,442	3,596	3,915	5,222	3,450	1,597
3Q	3,449	3,570	3,776	4,766	4,765	1,018
4Q	—	3,498	3,709	4,656	5,018	1,157
Yr.	—	14,288	15,385	19,695	16,610	3,928

Earnings Per Share ($)

	2004	2003	2002	2001	2000	1999
1Q	-0.17	-0.07	-0.59	0.01	0.45	0.01
2Q	-0.07	-0.07	-10.48	-1.99	-0.14	0.03
3Q	-0.31	-0.39	-0.07	-0.09	-0.15	Nil
4Q	E-0.14	-0.22	-0.62	-0.32	-0.07	0.56
Yr.	E-0.64	-0.76	-10.48	-2.38	-0.06	0.60

Next earnings report expected: late-February Source: S&P, Company Reports
EPS Estimates based on S&P Operating Earnings; historical GAAP earnings are as reported.

Recommendation: **HOLD** ★ ★ ★ ☆ ☆   12-Month Target Price: **$4.00** (as of October 13, 2003)

Business Summary November 09, 2004

Following the June 2000 acquisition of Baby Bell U.S. WEST, Inc. (USW), Qwest Communications International (Q) provides local and long-distance telecommunications services, wireless, data and video services in 14 states: Arizona, Colorado, Idaho, Iowa, Minnesota, Montana, Nebraska, New Mexico, North Dakota, Oregon, South Dakota, Utah, Washington and Wyoming. The company also provides secure broadband data, voice and video communications outside its local service area, as well as globally.

Q offers wireline voice services (96% of 2003 revenues) that include basic local exchange telephone services for roughly 15.7 million access lines for consumers and business and interLATA long-distance voice services in all states of its local territory. By the end of the third quarter of 2004, 4.4 million access lines had Q for long distance. The company also provides intraLATA long-distance services to customers nationwide, including its 27 local service areas, and provides interLATA long-distance services to customers outside local service areas. In addition, Q provides other voice services, such as public telephone service and collocation services that host another provider's telecom equipment in Q's facilities.

The company also offers a broad range of products and professional services to enable customers to transport voice, data, and video telecommunications at speeds starting at 14.4 kilobits per second. Q's services include ATM, frame relay, private lines, and DSL services, and allow, for example, business customers to transfer files to one another, as well as letting consumers access email and Internet services. Data and Internet services accounted for 27% of 2003 revenues. Q began to offer VoIP service in Minnesota in December 2003, with deployments in other markets planned for 2004.

Q operates its wireless segment (4% of revenues) in selected markets in its local service area, including Denver, Seattle, Portland and Phoenix. In August 2003, it entered into a five-year reseller agreement with national carrier Sprint PCS. Services began being offered under the Qwest name beginning in March 2004; Q retained control of all marketing, customer services, pricing and promotional offerings.

Through Qwest Dex, the company was the largest telephone directory publisher in the local service area. In August 2002, Q agreed to sell Qwest Dex for $7.05 billion to two private equity groups. The first stage of the transaction, valued at $2.75 billion, closed in the 2002 fourth quarter; the second stage, valued at $4.30 billion, closed in September 2003. In July 2004, Q agreed to sell its licenses and related wireless network to Verizon Wireless for $418 million. The deal, subject to regulatory approval, is expected to close in early 2005.

In October 2003, Q completed the initial stage of a one-year internal review of its accounting practices, filing its 2002 10-K financial report. It restated initially reported revenues by $945 million for 2000, and $1.5 billion for 2001. This included the results of improperly accounting for transfers of optical capacity for cash, contemporaneous transfers of optical capacity, directory publishing, and wireless promotions. In October 2004, Q settled the matter with the SEC and agreed to pay a $250 million fine.

Company Financials Fiscal Year ending December 31

Per Share Data ($)

(Year Ended December 31)	2003	2002	2001	2000	1999	1998	1997	1996	1995	1994
Tangible Bk. Val.	NM	NM	1.28	5.37	4.95	0.82	0.93	1.35	NA	NA
Cash Flow	1.07	-10.48	0.83	2.56	1.13	-1.15	0.09	0.03	-0.05	-0.02
Earnings	-0.76	-9.84	-2.38	-0.06	0.60	-1.51	0.04	-0.02	-0.08	-0.02
S&P Core Earnings	-0.81	-7.38	-1.39	NA	NA	NA	NA	NA	NA	NA
Dividends	Nil	Nil	0.05	Nil	Nil	Nil	Nil	NA	NA	NA
Payout Ratio	Nil	Nil	NM	Nil	Nil	Nil	Nil	NA	NA	NA
Prices - High	6.15	15.19	48.18	66.00	52.37	25.65	17.21	NA	NA	NA
- Low	3.01	1.07	11.08	32.12	25.03	11.00	5.50	NA	NA	NA
P/E Ratio - High	NM	NM	NM	NM	87	NM	NM	NA	NA	NA
- Low	NM	NM	NM	NM	42	NM	NM	NA	NA	NA

Income Statement Analysis (Million $)

	2003	2002	2001	2000	1999	1998	1997	1996	1995	1994
Revs.	14,288	15,385	19,695	16,610	3,928	2,243	697	231	125	71.0
Depr.	3,167	3,847	5,335	3,342	404	202	20.3	16.2	10.0	2.40
Maint.	NA	NA	NA	NA	NA	NA	NA	NA	NA	NA
Constr. Credits	NA	NA	NA	NA	NA	NA	NA	NA	NA	NA
Eff. Tax Rate	NM	NM	NM	NM	21.4%	NM	38.4%	NM	NM	NM
Net Inc.	-1,313	-17,625	-3,958	-81.0	459	-844	14.5	-6.97	-25.1	-6.90
S&P Core Earnings	-1,382	-12,411	-2,327	NA	NA	NA	NA	NA	NA	NA

Balance Sheet & Other Fin. Data (Million $)

	2003	2002	2001	2000	1999	1998	1997	1996	1995	1994
Gross Prop.	45,094	44,580	55,099	48,318	4,469	2,811	657	NA	NA	NA
Net Prop.	18,149	18,995	29,977	25,583	4,109	2,655	615	NA	NA	NA
Cap. Exp.	2,088	2,764	8,543	6,597	1,900	1,413	346	NA	NA	NA
Total Cap.	14,744	16,924	56,852	58,493	9,425	6,545	1,012	NA	NA	NA
Fxd. Chgs. Cov.	0.2	0.1	1.3	2.4	4.9	NM	2.2	NA	NA	NA
Capitalization:										
LT Debt	15,639	19,754	20,197	15,421	2,368	2,307	631	NA	NA	NA
Pfd.	Nil	Nil	Nil	Nil	Nil	Nil	Nil	NA	NA	NA
Common	-1,016	-2,830	36,655	41,304	7,001	4,238	382	NA	NA	NA
% Return On Revs.	NM	NM	NM	NM	11.7	NM	2.1	NA	NA	NA
% Return On Invest. Capital	5.1	12.4	NM	7.6	8.0	2.9	NA	NA	NA	NA
% Return On Com. Equity	NM	NM	NM	NM	8.2	NA	NA	NA	NA	NA
% Earn. on Net Prop.	17.5	17.1	26.4	32.9	22.4	18.0	NA	NA	NA	NA
% LT Debt of Cap.	106.9	116.7	35.5	27.2	25.3	35.2	62.3	NA	NA	NA
Capital. % Pfd.	Nil	Nil	Nil	Nil	Nil	Nil	Nil	NA	NA	NA
Capital. % Common	-6.9	-16.7	64.5	72.8	74.7	64.8	37.7	NA	NA	NA

Data as orig reptd.; bef. results of disc opers/spec. items. Per share data adj. for stk. divs.; EPS diluted. E-Estimated. NA-Not Available. NM-Not Meaningful. NR-Not Ranked. UR-Under Review.

Office: 1801 California Street, Denver, CO 80202-2658.
Telephone: 303-992-1400.
Email: investor.relations@qwest.com
Website: http://www.qwest.com
Chrmn & CEO: R.C. Notebaert.

Vice Chrmn & CFO: O.G. Shaffer.
EVP, Secy & General Counsel: R.N. Baer.
Dirs: L. G. Alvarado, P. F. Anschutz, C. L. Biggs, K. D. Brooksher, T. J. Donohue, J. L. Haines, C. Y. Harvey, P. S. Hellman, V. Khosla, R. C. Notebaert, F. Popoff, C. D. Slater.

Founded: in 1983.
Domicile: Delaware.
Employees: 47,000.
S&P Analyst: Todd Rosenbluth/CB/BK

RadioShack Corp.

Recommendation: **HOLD** ★★★★ ☆
SELL SELL HOLD BUY BUY

12-Month Target Price: **$32.00**
(as of October 04, 2004)

RSH has an approximate 0.05% weighting in the **S&P 500**

Sector: Consumer Discretionary
Sub-Industry: Computer & Electronics Retail
Peer Group: Retailers/Resellers

Summary: This consumer electronics retailer operates the RadioShack chain, which has more than 7,000 stores (including dealers/franchises).

Quantitative Evaluations

S&P Earnings & Dividend Rank: B+

| D | C | B- | B | B+ | A- | A | A+ |

S&P Fair Value Rank: 5+

| 1 | 2 | 3 | 4 | 5 |
| Lowest | | | | Highest |

Fair Value Calc.: $40.50 (Undervalued)

S&P Investability Quotient Percentile — 97%

RSH scored higher than 97% of all companies for which an S&P Report is available.

Volatility: Average

| Low | Average | High |

Technical Evaluation: Bullish
Since 9/04, the technical indicators for RSH have been Bullish.

Relative Strength Rank: Strong — 75

| 1 Lowest | | Highest 99 |

| Price as of 11/12/04: | **$32.46** | 2004E S&P Core EPS: | **$1.81** |

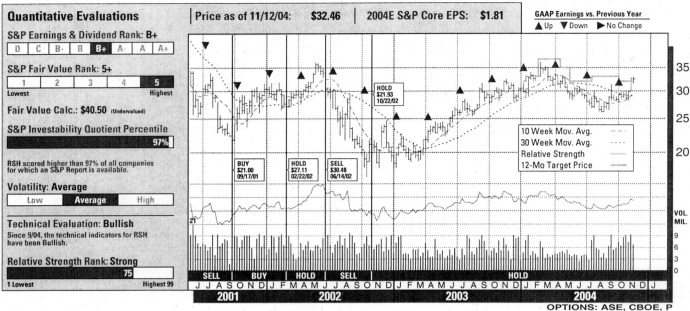

GAAP Earnings vs. Previous Year
▲ Up ▼ Down ▶ No Change

HOLD $21.93 10/22/02

BUY $21.00 09/17/01

HOLD $27.11 02/22/02

SELL $30.48 06/14/02

10 Week Mov. Avg.
30 Week Mov. Avg.
Relative Strength
12-Mo Target Price

SELL | BUY | HOLD | SELL | HOLD

J J A S O N D | J F M A M J J A S O N D | J F M A M J J A S O N D | J F M A M J J A S O N D | J
2001 | 2002 | 2003 | 2004

VOL. MIL.
9 6 3 0

OPTIONS: ASE, CBOE, P

Analyst commentary prepared by Amy Glynn, CFA /MF/BK

Highlights October 28, 2004

▪ We look for 2004 revenues to increase approximately 3%. We expect strong growth in the wireless communications department to drive overall sales growth for the company. In addition, we believe that the parts, batteries and accessories area will contribute a larger portion of revenues throughout all of the company's departments. However, we expect top-line growth to be restricted by lackluster expansion in several non-wireless categories. Looking into 2005, we estimate revenue growth of about 6%, toward the low end of updated October company guidance. Included in our growth forecast are expected revenues from RSH's entry into SAM's CLUB via the acquisition of certain assets from Wireless Retail, Inc.

▪ We think that margins will widen due to improved efficiencies generated from supply chain management initiatives and a shift in the sales mix toward higher margin products.

▪ We estimate 2004 operating EPS of $2.09, up from $1.77 in 2003. We project 2004 Standard & Poor's Core Earnings of $1.81, after $0.28 of projected stock option expense. We look for 2005 operating EPS of $2.40, representing about 15% earnings growth, below the company's forecast of 19% to 21% growth. Our 2005 Standard & Poor's Core EPS estimate is $2.11.

Investment Rationale/Risk October 28, 2004

▪ In September, RSH announced a new three-year growth plan, expected to start in 2005, which includes an accelerated rollout of the latest store format, international expansion, and strategic alliances with retailers and manufacturers. With our view of limited opportunities to grow square footage, but strong free cash flow, we think RSH's decision to re-evaluate its business and explore new sources of growth makes sense. However, we are concerned with execution, as RSH has a multi-pronged strategy, and is partly reliant on areas outside of the core retail business. In addition, we have little detail about how much capital will be invested in each of the growth areas. At 12X our 2005 EPS estimate, the shares are at a discount to peers on a P/E basis. However, we believe a discount P/E multiple is warranted, partly due to our view of limited store expansion opportunities versus peers, and partly due to the very early stage of the growth plan and the execution risk that we perceive.

▪ Risks to our opinion and target price include adverse changes in national and regional U.S. economic conditions; increased competition among consumer electronics retailers; an unexpected loss of business from a major supplier; a reduction in the growth rate of the wireless industry; and management execution risk.

▪ Our 12-month target price of $32 is based on our historical P/E model and is derived by applying a below-peer P/E multiple of 13.3X to our 2005 estimate.

Key Stock Statistics

S&P Core EPS 2005E	2.11	52-week Range	$36.24-26.04
S&P Oper. EPS 2004E	2.09	12 Month P/E	16.1
P/E on S&P Oper. EPS 2004E	15.5	Beta	1.23
S&P Oper. EPS 2005E	2.40	Shareholders	29,083
Yield (%)	0.8%	Market Cap (B)	$ 5.1
Dividend Rate/Share	0.25	Shares Outstanding (M)	158.5

Value of $10,000 invested five years ago: **$ 5,209**

Dividend Data Dividends have been paid since 1987

Amount ($)	Date Decl.	Ex-Div. Date	Stock of Record	Payment Date
0.250	Oct. 17	Dec. 04	Dec. 08	Dec. 26 '03
0.250	Sep. 24	Nov. 29	Dec. 01	Dec. 20 '04

Revenues/Earnings Data Fiscal year ending December 31

Revenues (Million $)

	2004	2003	2002	2001	2000	1999
1Q	1,093	1,070	1,034	1,140	1,047	890.2
2Q	1,054	1,025	998.1	1,040	1,023	886.7
3Q	1,102	1,064	1,047	1,081	1,140	960.3
4Q	—	1,490	1,498	1,516	1,584	1,389
Yr.	—	4,649	4,577	4,776	4,795	4,126

Earnings Per Share ($)

	2004	2003	2002	2001	2000	1999
1Q	0.41	0.33	0.31	0.23	0.35	0.27
2Q	0.42	0.34	0.28	0.21	0.38	0.30
3Q	0.43	0.34	0.25	0.23	0.39	0.29
4Q	E0.82	0.77	0.63	0.18	0.74	0.58
Yr.	E2.09	1.77	1.45	0.85	1.84	1.43

Next earnings report expected: mid-February Source: S&P, Company Reports
EPS Estimates based on S&P Operating Earnings; historical GAAP earnings are as reported.

RadioShack Corporation

Recommendation: **HOLD** ★★★☆☆   12-Month Target Price: **$32.00** (as of October 04, 2004)

Business Summary October 28, 2004

The company changed its name to RadioShack Corp. (from Tandy Corp.) in May 2000, reflecting its operation of the large RadioShack consumer electronics retail chain. At December 31, 2003, the RadioShack chain included 5,121 company-operated stores located throughout the U.S., as well as in Puerto Rico and the U.S. Virgin Islands. As of year-end 2003, the company also had a network of 1,921 dealer/franchise stores, including 55 located outside the U.S. These stores largely provide products to smaller communities.

Sales at comparable company-owned stores in the RadioShack chain advanced 2% in 2003, following a 1% decline in 2002, a 1% rise in 2001 and an 11% gain in 2000. Overall, company-owned stores average about 2,450 sq. ft., and are located in major malls and strip centers, as well as individual storefronts. Each store carries an assortment of electronic parts, batteries and accessories; wireless and conventional phones; audio/video equipment; direct-to-home (DTH) satellite systems; PCs; and specialized products such as home air cleaners and unique toys. RSH also provides access to third-party services, such as cellular and PCS phone and DTH satellite activation, long-distance telephone service, prepaid wireless airtime, and extended service plans.

RSH has formed strategic alliances with various suppliers of products and services. The company has a sales incentive agreement with Echostar Satellite Corp. (DISH Network) to acquire subscribers for the multi-channel audio/video programming direct broadcast satellite services of DISH Network in the U.S. Through its telecommunications relationship with Sprint Communications Co. and Sprint PCS, RSH customers have access to wireless PCS telephones and service, prepaid

calling cards and long-distance telephone service, as well as residential telephones and related telephony products. In addition, the company has an alliance with Verizon Wireless related to cellular phone service. Hewlett-Packard Co. is the sole supplier of PCs sold through RadioShack retail outlets.

In 2003, RSH repurchased 9.9 million of its common shares for $251 million. In 2002, the company bought back about 10.8 million common shares for $275 million. In March 2004, RSH indicated that it planned to spend $200 million to $250 million on stock purchases in 2004. EPS in 2002 included a net benefit of about $0.03 a share from unusual items, consisting of a charge related to the settlement of a lawsuit, an impairment charge, and a favorable litigation settlement. In 2001, results included a net negative impact of about $0.66 a share from unusual items, including a writedown of non-strategic inventory, a charge related to the closing of underperforming stores prior to their lease expiration, a loss related to an asset sale, an impairment charge related to a writeoff of goodwill, restructuring costs, and a loss on an Internet-related investment. In 1998, RSH sold its unprofitable Computer City retail business to CompUSA Inc.

In October 2004, RSH announced that it began operating wireless kiosks in 542 SAM'S CLUB locations, a division of Wal-Mart Stores. RSH's entry resulted from RSH's acquisition of certain assets from Wireless Retail, Inc., which had been operating SAM's CLUB's wireless business. In 2003, wireless sales at SAM'S CLUB exceeded $150 million. RSH expects accelerated sales and accretive earnings from the SAM'S CLUB distribution channel in 2006.

Company Financials Fiscal Year ending December 31

Per Share Data ($)

(Year Ended December 31)	2003	2002	2001	2000	1999	1998	1997	1996	1995	1994
Tangible Bk. Val.	4.73	4.24	4.04	4.46	3.70	3.84	4.69	5.11	6.03	5.82
Cash Flow	2.31	1.97	1.41	2.38	1.87	0.73	1.24	0.07	1.15	0.90
Earnings	1.77	1.45	0.85	1.84	1.43	0.27	0.82	-0.41	0.78	0.73
S&P Core Earnings	1.49	1.18	1.06	NA	NA	NA	NA	NA	NA	NA
Dividends	0.25	0.22	0.22	0.22	0.15	0.20	0.20	0.20	0.18	0.16
Payout Ratio	14%	15%	25%	12%	10%	74%	25%	NM	24%	22%
Prices - High	32.48	36.21	56.50	72.93	79.50	31.93	23.00	14.78	16.09	12.65
- Low	18.74	16.99	20.10	35.06	20.59	15.18	10.15	8.53	9.12	7.68
P/E Ratio - High	18	25	66	40	56	NM	28	NM	21	17
- Low	11	12	24	19	14	NM	12	NM	12	11

Income Statement Analysis (Million $)

	2003	2002	2001	2000	1999	1998	1997	1996	1995	1994
Revs.	4,649	4,577	4,776	4,795	4,126	4,788	5,372	6,286	5,839	4,991
Oper. Inc.	576	510	583	736	597	424	434	261	428	440
Depr.	92.0	94.7	108	107	90.2	99	97.2	109	92.0	84.8
Int. Exp.	35.7	43.4	50.8	53.9	37.2	45.4	46.1	36.0	33.7	30.0
Pretax Inc.	473	425	292	594	481	100	304	-146	343	360
Eff. Tax Rate	36.9%	38.0%	42.8%	38.0%	38.0%	38.5%	38.5%	NM	38.3%	37.6%
Net Inc.	299	263	167	368	298	61.3	187	-91.6	212	224
S&P Core Earnings	252	211	200	NA	NA	NA	NA	NA	NA	NA

Balance Sheet & Other Fin. Data (Million $)

	2003	2002	2001	2000	1999	1998	1997	1996	1995	1994
Cash	635	447	401	131	165	64.5	106	122	143	206
Curr. Assets	1,667	1,707	1,714	1,818	1,403	1,299	1,716	1,940	2,048	2,556
Total Assets	2,244	1,707	2,245	2,577	2,142	1,994	2,318	2,583	2,722	3,244
Curr. Liab.	858	829	826	1,232	925	880	976	1,194	960	1,206
LT Debt	541	591	565	303	319	235	236	104	141	153
Common Equity	769	729	714	812	758	748	959	1,165	1,501	1,370
Total Cap.	1,311	1,320	1,344	1,284	1,150	1,083	1,295	1,369	1,742	2,004
Cap. Exp.	190	107	139	120	102	132	118	175	227	181
Cash Flow	391	354	270	470	383	155	278	17.0	304	270
Curr. Ratio	1.9	2.1	2.1	1.5	1.5	1.5	1.8	1.6	2.1	2.1
% LT Debt of Cap.	41.3	44.8	42.1	23.6	27.8	21.7	18.2	7.6	8.1	7.7
% Net Inc.of Revs.	6.4	5.8	3.5	7.7	7.2	1.3	3.5	NM	3.7	4.5
% Ret. on Assets	13.4	13.3	6.9	15.6	14.4	2.8	7.6	NM	7.1	7.3
% Ret. on Equity	39.9	35.9	21.2	46.2	38.8	6.5	17.0	NM	12.3	13.6

Data as orig reptd.; bef. results of disc opers/spec. items. Per share data adj. for stk. divs.; EPS diluted. E-Estimated. NA-Not Available. NM-Not Meaningful. NR-Not Ranked. UR-Under Review.

Office: 100 Throckmorton St, Ste 1800, Fort Worth, TX 76102.
Telephone: 817-415-3700.
Email: investor.relations@radioshack.com
Website: http://www.radioshackcorporation.com
Chrmn & CEO: L.H. Roberts.
Pres & COO: D.J. Edmondson.
SVP & CFO: D. Johnson.

SVP, Secy & General Counsel: M.C. Hill.
Investor Contact: J. Grant 817-415-7833.
Dirs: F. J. Belatti, R. E. Elmquist, R. S. Falcone, D. R. Feehan, R. J. Hernandez, L. V. Jackson, R. J. Kamerschen, H. E. Lockhart, J. L. Messman, W. G. Morton, Jr., T. G. Plaskett, L. H. Roberts, E. D. Woodbury.

Founded: in 1899.
Domicile: Delaware.
Employees: 39,500.
S&P Analyst: Amy Glynn, CFA /MF/BK

Raytheon Co.

Recommendation: **HOLD** ★ ★ ★ ★ ★
SELL | SELL | HOLD | BUY | BUY

12-Month Target Price: $36.00
(as of August 05, 2004)

RTN has an approximate 0.16% weighting in the **S&P 500**

Sector: Industrials
Sub-Industry: Aerospace & Defense
Peer Group: Electronics/Defense

Summary: Raytheon, the second largest U.S. military contractor, specializes in making high-tech missiles and electronics.

Quantitative Evaluations

Price as of 11/12/04:	**$38.79**	2004E S&P Core EPS:	**$1.38**

S&P Earnings & Dividend Rank: B-

D | C | **B-** | B | B+ | A- | A | A+

S&P Fair Value Rank: 4-

1 (Lowest) | 2 | 3 | **4** | 5 (Highest)

Fair Value Calc.: $37.80 (Slightly Overvalued)

S&P Investability Quotient Percentile

73%

RTN scored higher than 73% of all companies for which an S&P Report is available.

Volatility: Low

Low | Average | High

Technical Evaluation: Bullish

Since 10/04, the technical indicators for RTN have been Bullish.

Relative Strength Rank: Moderate

63

1 Lowest | Highest 99

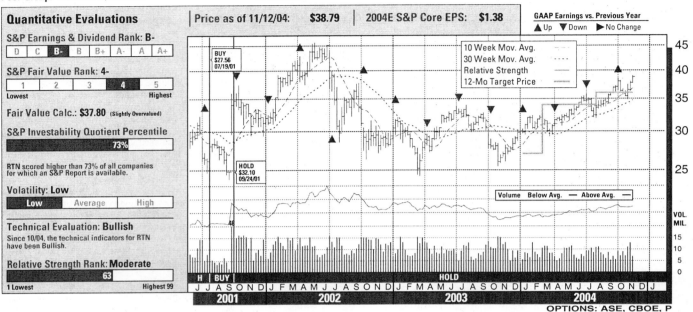

GAAP Earnings vs. Previous Year
▲ Up ▼ Down ► No Change

10 Week Mov. Avg.
30 Week Mov. Avg.
Relative Strength
12-Mo Target Price

BUY $27.56 07/19/01
HOLD $32.10 09/24/01

Volume Below Avg. — Above Avg.

H | BUY | HOLD
J J A S O N D | J F M A M J J A S O N D | J F M A M J J A S O N D | J F M A M J J A S O N D | J
2001 | **2002** | **2003** | **2004**

OPTIONS: ASE, CBOE, P

Analyst commentary prepared by Robert E. Friedman, CPA /MF

Highlights August 13, 2004

■ We believe increased Pentagon demand for RTN's missiles and military electronics (75% of revenues), will lead to a 10% advance in 2004 revenues. We believe near-term top-line results will also be augmented by a rebound in sales of RTN's business and regional airline jets, due to recovering North American and European economies.

■ However, we think that ongoing production inefficiencies should continue to put downward pressure on operating profits, resulting in a slip in earnings before interest and taxes (EBIT) margins from 10% to 9% levels. However, an anticipated 15% decline in interest expense (from early debt retirement) should allow RTN to post a 12% rise in 2004 EPS, to $1.44 (Our 2004 EPS estimate excludes a $0.51 lawsuit settlement charge and $0.06 early debt retirement charge). On a S&P Core Earnings basis, we are also forecasting a 12% EPS increase, to $1.38. In estimating near-term profitability performance, we predict RTN will generate ROE in the low 6% area.

■ Looking at RTN's long-term prospects, we believe accelerating demand primarily for the company's radar, communications and guidance equipment will drive revenue growth. However, intensifying competition should keep a lid on pricing power, thereby preventing RTN from boosting free cash earnings greater than a 7% compound annual growth rate (CAGR), and from posting ROE of more than 13%.

Investment Rationale/Risk August 13, 2004

■ We are maintaining our hold opinion on RTN shares, as the stock is trading near our DCF-based 12-month target price.

■ Risks to our recommendation and target price primarily include any unexpected structural deterioration of RTN's U.S. military end-markets and/or structural deterioration of RTN's underlying business economics.

■ Our free cash flow models (which value RTN by adding the sum of free cash earnings growing at a projected 5% to 7% CAGR over the next 10 years, and 3.0% thereafter) calculate the stock to be worth about $36 a share. Another intrinsic value model (which incorporates several variables, including our projections of 10% to 13% average ROE, a 7% long-term risk-free bond rate, and RTN's net asset value of $25 a share) also indicates a value of about $36 a share, which is our 12-month target price.

Key Stock Statistics

S&P Oper. EPS 2004E	**0.87**	52-week Range	**$38.98-26.90**
P/E on S&P Oper. EPS 2004E	**44.6**	12 Month P/E	**48.5**
S&P Oper. EPS 2005E	**1.65**	Beta	**0.09**
Yield (%)	**2.1%**	Shareholders	**17,689**
Dividend Rate/Share	**0.80**	Market Cap (B)	**$ 17.5**
Shares Outstanding (M)	**451.1**		

Value of $10,000 invested five years ago: **$ 15,156**

Dividend Data Dividends have been paid since 1964

Amount ($)	Date Decl.	Ex-Div. Date	Stock of Record	Payment Date
0.200	Dec. 17	Dec. 30	Jan. 02	Jan. 30 '04
0.200	Mar. 24	Apr. 01	Apr. 05	May. 03 '04
0.200	Jun. 23	Jul. 02	Jul. 07	Aug. 04 '04
0.200	Sep. 23	Sep. 30	Oct. 04	Nov. 01 '04

Revenues/Earnings Data Fiscal year ending December 31

Revenues (Million $)

	2004	2003	2002	2001	2000	1999
1Q	4,676	4,201	3,911	3,968	4,231	5,025
2Q	4,929	4,429	4,095	4,307	4,124	5,210
3Q	4,936	4,378	4,092	3,961	4,160	4,776
4Q	—	5,101	4,662	4,631	4,380	4,830
Yr.	—	18,109	16,760	16,867	16,895	19,841

Earnings Per Share ($)

	2004	2003	2002	2001	2000	1999
1Q	0.24	0.27	0.37	0.28	0.24	0.76
2Q	-0.22	0.45	0.54	0.33	0.28	0.84
3Q	0.41	0.05	0.56	-0.73	0.39	-0.48
4Q	E0.45	0.52	0.38	0.15	0.55	0.21
Yr.	E0.87	1.29	1.85	0.01	1.46	1.34

Next earnings report expected: late-January Source: S&P, Company Reports
EPS Estimates based on S&P Operating Earnings; historical GAAP earnings are as reported.

STANDARD &POOR'S

Raytheon Company

Recommendation: **HOLD** ★ ★ ★ ☆ ☆   12-Month Target Price: **$36.00** (as of August 05, 2004)

Business Summary August 13, 2004

This $20 billion-revenue military weapons maker conducts business through three general operating segments:

RTN's military weapons segment (76% of revenues, 95% of operating income and 10% operating profit margins in 2003) primarily makes highly sophisticated electronics systems and missiles. The unit is the world's largest maker of military electronics and missiles. Major competitors include Lockheed Martin, Northrop Grumman, Boeing, Britain's BAE Systems, and Europe's MBDA. About 55% of military weapons backlog consists of more profitable fixed price contracts (10%-15% profit margins), and about 45% consists less profitable cost-plus contracts (5%-10% profit margins).

RTN's primary missile and military electronics markets are volatile and slow-growing. Based on statistics provided by the Aerospace Industries Association, an aerospace and defense industry trade organization, from 1993 through 2003, the $13 billion-revenue U.S. missile market grew at 10-year average annual rate of 3.0%. According to the AIA, the $30-billion defense-related search and navigation instrument market, a proxy for the military electronics market, grew at a 10-year average annual rate of 2.9%.

In general, demand for military weapons systems is driven by growth in the U.S. defense budget, which accounts for about 40% of total global military weapons sales. In turn, growth in defense spending is driven by long-term military strategic planning, geopolitical climates and political considerations. Based on Pentagon statistics, from FY 93 through FY 03, the procurement and R&D sectors of the U.S. defense budget grew at 8.6% and 2.9% average annual rates, respectively.

The Raytheon Aircraft Company segment (11%; 0%; NM) makes small, pis-

ton-powered aircraft; turboprop-powered aircraft for commuter airlines; a line of corporate jets; and military training aircraft. Over the last several years, RAC has been plagued by new product delays and cost overruns.

Based on revenues, RAC is the world's fifth-largest corporate jet maker. Canada-based Bombardier, General Dynamics' Gulfstream division, Textron's Cessna division and France's Dassault are the world's first-, second-, third- and fourth-largest corporate jet makers. The $9 billion global corporate jet market is oligopolistic; based on statistics provided by independent aviation research firm Teal Group, the five largest corporate jet makers account for 99% of global corporate jet sales.

Demand for RTN's business jets is primarily driven by the health of corporate budgets and fractional (or time-share) market. Based on statistics provided by trade group General Aviation Manufacturers Association, from 1994 through 2003, the U.S. small plane (corporate jet and piston) market (in unit sales) grew at a 9% average annual rate.

RTN's Other segment (3%; -2%; NM) primarily provides services to the aircraft fractional ownership industry.

Looking at RTN's historical financial performance, from 1993 through 2003, reported net operating EPS declined at a compound average growth rate (CAGR) of 6.6%; per-share equity growth (a proxy for growth in intrinsic value) grew at a 4.3% CAGR. In addition, ROE averaged 8.9%. Based on Standard & Poor's Core Earnings methodology, 10-year average S&P Core EPS variance stood at -18%, primarily due to reversals of non-operating pension income generated by RTN's historically overfunded pension plan.

Company Financials Fiscal Year ending December 31

Per Share Data ($)

(Year Ended December 31)	2003	2002	2001	2000	1999	1998	1997	1996	1995	1994
Tangible Bk. Val.	NM	NM	NM	NM	NM	NM	NM	6.44	7.26	12.92
Cash Flow	2.22	2.74	2.03	3.50	3.46	4.75	4.07	4.77	4.77	3.29
Earnings	1.29	1.85	0.01	1.46	1.34	2.53	2.18	3.21	3.25	2.25
S&P Core Earnings	1.11	-0.25	-2.68	NA	NA	NA	NA	NA	NA	NA
Dividends	0.80	0.80	0.80	0.80	0.80	0.80	0.80	0.79	0.75	0.73
Payout Ratio	62%	43%	NM	55%	60%	32%	37%	25%	23%	32%
Prices - High	33.97	45.70	37.44	35.81	76.56	60.75	60.50	56.12	47.25	34.43
- Low	24.31	26.30	23.95	17.50	22.18	40.68	41.75	43.37	31.43	30.25
P/E Ratio - High	26	25	NM	25	57	24	28	17	15	15
- Low	19	14	NM	12	17	16	19	14	10	13

Income Statement Analysis (Million $)

	2003	2002	2001	2000	1999	1998	1997	1996	1995	1994
Revs.	18,109	16,760	16,867	16,895	19,841	19,530	13,673	12,331	11,716	10,013
Oper. Inc.	1,709	2,118	1,488	2,319	2,251	2,797	2,036	1,602	1,584	1,353
Depr.	393	364	729	694	724	761	457	369	371	275
Int. Exp.	537	497	660	736	713	739	397	256	197	49.0
Pretax Inc.	762	1,074	117	877	828	1,467	790	1,083	1,192	900
Eff. Tax Rate	29.8%	29.7%	95.7%	43.2%	44.8%	41.1%	33.3%	29.8%	33.5%	33.7%
Net Inc.	535	755	5.00	498	457	864	527	761	792	597
S&P Core Earnings	460	-105	-970	NA	NA	NA	NA	NA	NA	NA

Balance Sheet & Other Fin. Data (Million $)

	2003	2002	2001	2000	1999	1998	1997	1996	1995	1994
Cash	661	544	1,214	871	230	421	296	139	210	202
Curr. Assets	6,585	7,190	8,362	8,013	8,931	8,637	9,233	5,604	5,275	4,985
Total Assets	23,668	23,946	26,636	26,777	28,110	27,939	28,598	11,126	9,841	7,395
Curr. Liab.	3,849	5,107	5,753	4,865	7,886	6,680	11,886	4,692	3,690	3,283
LT Debt	7,376	7,138	6,875	9,054	7,298	8,163	4,406	1,500	1,488	24.5
Common Equity	9,162	8,870	11,290	10,823	10,959	10,856	10,425	4,598	4,292	3,928
Total Cap.	16,538	16,008	18,743	20,650	18,810	19,580	15,617	6,098	5,780	3,953
Cap. Exp.	428	458	486	431	532	509	459	406	329	267
Cash Flow	928	1,119	734	1,192	1,181	1,625	984	1,130	1,163	872
Curr. Ratio	1.7	1.4	1.5	1.6	1.1	1.3	0.8	1.2	1.4	1.5
% LT Debt of Cap.	44.6	44.6	36.7	43.8	38.8	41.7	28.2	24.6	25.8	0.6
% Net Inc.of Revs.	3.0	4.5	0.0	2.9	2.3	4.4	3.9	6.2	6.8	6.0
% Ret. on Assets	2.2	3.0	0.0	1.8	1.6	3.1	2.7	7.3	9.2	8.5
% Ret. on Equity	5.9	7.5	0.0	4.6	4.2	8.1	7.0	17.2	19.3	15.2

Data as orig. reptd.; bef. results of disc. opers. and/or spec. items. Per share data adj. for stk. divs. as of ex-div. date. Bold denotes diluted EPS (FASB 128). E-Estimated. NA-Not Available. NM-Not Meaningful. NR-Not Ranked. Historical/forecasted EPS based on ongoing operations.

Office: 870 Winter St, Waltham, MA 02451.
Telephone: 781-522-3000.
Email: invest@raytheon.com
Website: http://www.raytheon.com
Chrmn, Pres & CEO: W.H. Swanson.
SVP & CFO: E.S. Pliner.

SVP & General Counsel: J.B. Stephens.
VP & Treas: R.A. Goglia.
VP & Investor Contact: T.C. Oliver 781-860-2304.
Dirs: B. M. Barrett, F. Colloredo-Mansfeld, J. M. Deutch, T. E. Everhart, F. M. Poses, W. B. Rudman, M. C. Ruettgers, R. L. Skates, W. R. Spivey, L. G. Stuntz, W. H. Swanson, J. H. Tilelli, Jr.

Founded: in 1928.
Domicile: Delaware.
Employees: 77,700.
S&P Analyst: Robert E. Friedman, CPA /MF

Reebok International

Recommendation: **BUY** ★★★★ ☆   12-Month Target Price: **$42.00**
SELL | SELL | HOLD | BUY | BUY   (as of October 21, 2004)

RBK has an approximate 0.02% weighting in the **S&P 500**

Sector: Consumer Discretionary
Sub-Industry: Footwear
Peer Group: Footwear - Athletic

Summary: RBK is a leading producer of athletic footwear and apparel sold in the U.S. and overseas.

Quantitative Evaluations

S&P Earnings & Dividend Rank: B

D	C	B-	**B**	B+	A-	A	A+

S&P Fair Value Rank: 4

1	2	3	**4**	5
Lowest				Highest

Fair Value Calc.: $41.30 (Slightly Undervalued)

S&P Investability Quotient Percentile

99%

RBK scored higher than 99% of all companies for which an S&P Report is available.

Volatility: Average

Low	**Average**	High

Technical Evaluation: Bullish

Since 10/04, the technical indicators for RBK have been Bullish.

Relative Strength Rank: Moderate

68

1 Lowest	Highest 99

Price as of 11/12/04: **$39.06** | 2004E S&P Core EPS: **$2.74**

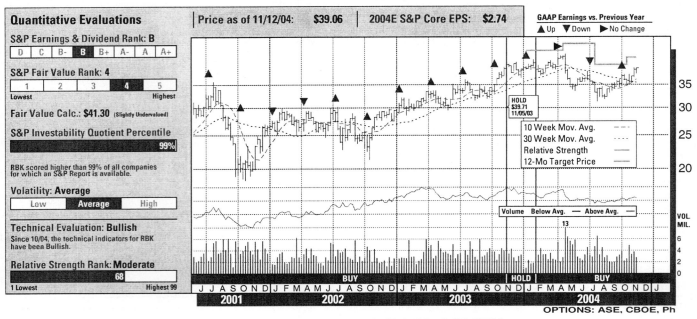

GAAP Earnings vs. Previous Year
▲ Up   ▼ Down   ▶ No Change

HOLD
$39.71
11/05/03

10 Week Mov. Avg.
30 Week Mov. Avg.
Relative Strength
12-Mo Target Price

Volume   Below Avg. — Above Avg.

VOL. MIL.

OPTIONS: ASE, CBOE, Ph

Analyst commentary prepared by Marie Driscoll, CFA /CB/GG

Highlights October 25, 2004

- We see 2005 revenues rising 6% to 8%, aided by solid growth in apparel sales as double-digit gains in sports licensed products outweigh declines in branded products. We also expect continued expansion in international markets and the 2004 acquisition of The Hockey Company to contribute to top-line growth. U.S. footwear sales will likely rise about 2% to 3%, driven by increased sales of performance shoes and Rbk products.

- We expect slight gross margin expansion, as we see firmer pricing in performance footwear and gains from improved sourcing outweighing pricing pressures in branded apparel. We think increased marketing expenditures in support of new products will only partly offset greater expense leverage; we see operating margins widening by 40 to 50 basis points.

- With lower interest expense, reflecting refinanced debt, we project 2005 EPS of $3.35, an increase of 14% from our 2004 EPS estimate of $2.95. Our 2004 EPS estimate excludes $0.11 in charges related to the early redemption of debt. Based on our estimates for 2004 and 2005 Standard & Poor's Core Earnings, we believe that RBK's earnings quality is relatively high, reflecting about a 5% impact from potential stock option expensing.

Key Stock Statistics

S&P Core EPS 2005E	3.15	52-week Range	$42.95-31.25
S&P Oper. EPS 2004E	2.95	12 Month P/E	14.1
P/E on S&P Oper. EPS 2004E	13.2	Beta	0.43
S&P Oper. EPS 2005E	3.35	Shareholders	6,006
Yield (%)	0.8%	Market Cap (B)	$ 2.3
Dividend Rate/Share	0.30	Shares Outstanding (M)	58.1

Value of $10,000 invested five years ago: **$ 42,971**

Dividend Data Dividends have been paid since 2003

Amount ($)	Date Decl.	Ex-Div. Date	Stock of Record	Payment Date
0.150	Feb. 10	Mar. 03	Mar. 05	Mar. 19 '04
0.150	Jul. 27	Aug. 17	Aug. 19	Sep. 03 '04

Investment Rationale/Risk October 25, 2004

- In 2004, we think RBK will face tougher competition domestically as a major customer, Foot Locker, mends ties with rival Nike. In addition, branded apparel sales have been in a downtrend. On the plus side, we think RBK stands to benefit from resurgent consumer spending and firmer pricing domestically, and from continued growth in Asia and Eastern Europe. In our view, the company's Rbk products have been well received by younger consumers, a key demographic in footwear. We believe The Hockey Company purchase provides RBK with a competitive entry in the ice hockey sporting goods and apparel market.

- Risks to our recommendation and target price include a potential slowdown in the U.S. economy or a drop in consumer sentiment. International risks include possible political unrest, economic weakness, supply disruptions, and unfavorable currency fluctuations.

- We think the shares are attractive at 10.8X our 2005 EPS estimate, about a 30% discount to peer Nike (NKE: accumulate, $81) and the S&P 500. On a P/E multiple to growth basis, the shares also appear slightly undervalued versus the S&P 500 and NKE. Our 12-month target price of $42 is equal to 12.5X our 2005 EPS estimate, reflecting a discount to the stock's historical P/E average, based on our view of weakness in branded apparel.

Revenues/Earnings Data Fiscal year ending December 31

Revenues (Million $)

	2004	2003	2002	2001	2000	1999
1Q	831.9	798.3	736.0	769.9	769.8	785.8
2Q	813.6	802.6	717.4	711.0	685.1	697.4
3Q	1,165	1,041	911.6	847.3	787.8	793.9
4Q	—	843.6	762.8	664.6	622.5	622.8
Yr.	—	3,485	3,128	2,993	2,865	2,900

Earnings Per Share ($)

	2004	2003	2002	2001	2000	1999
1Q	0.63	0.63	0.58	0.68	0.56	0.32
2Q	0.35	0.41	0.39	0.24	0.19	0.08
3Q	1.36	0.96	0.81	0.66	0.56	0.06
4Q	E0.60	0.44	0.27	0.09	0.11	-0.26
Yr.	E2.95	2.43	2.04	1.66	1.40	0.20

Next earnings report expected: late-January Source: S&P, Company Reports
EPS Estimates based on S&P Operating Earnings; historical GAAP earnings are as reported.

 STANDARD &POOR'S

STANDARD &POOR'S

Recommendation: BUY ★★★★☆   12-Month Target Price: **$42.00** (as of October 21, 2004)

Business Summary October 28, 2004

Reebok International is the third largest global designer and marketer of sports and fitness and casual footwear, apparel and accessories. In addition to its eponymous Reebok brand, the company's sells products under several other brands, including Rockport, which it owns, and the Greg Norman Collection, Ralph Lauren, and Polo Footwear, for which it is a licensee. RBK believes the development of multiple brands sold through multiple channels will enable it reach a broader range of consumers and will offer a hedge against market trend risks.

Domestic sales of footwear and apparel under the Reebok brand accounted for 45% of 2003's total sales. Product categories include lifestyle footwear and apparel that capitalize on the "retro" look under the Reebok Classic brand, footwear and apparel for children, sold under the Reebok and Weebok brand names, and performance products, marketed to athletic consumers, designed for basketball, running, walking, fitness, soccer, tennis and other sports. The performance category also includes RBK's sports licensing agreements: a December 2000 alliance with the National Football League to manufacture, market and sell NFL licensed merchandise, and an agreement with the NBA, signed in 2001, covering apparel, footwear, and certain accessories.

The Rbk product line, introduced in 2002, features street-inspired footwear, apparel and accessories designed to appeal to young, fashion-oriented consumers. The company has developed footwear collections featuring hip-hop artists Jay-Z and 50 Cent, which are marketed through a strategy that emphasizes the connection between sports, music, fashion and entertainment.

Reebok products are distributed primarily through specialty athletic retailers, sporting goods stores, department stores, and through company stores. International operations concentrated mainly in Europe, the Far East and Latin America, contributed 38% of 2003's total sales.

The Rockport Company designs, produces and distributes specially designed comfort footwear for men and women under the Rockport brand, and apparel via a licensee. Products include casual, dress, outdoor performance, golf and fitness walking shoes. Rockport products are sold predominantly through selected higher-end national and local shoe store chains, department stores, independent shoe stores, and outfitters, and through independently owned Rockport retail shops. The Ralph Lauren footwear business offers a broad range of footwear products sold under the Polo Sport brand name. Extended offerings include the RLX line of high performance athletic footwear, and the Lauren collection for women.

The Greg Norman division produces a collection of apparel, footwear and accessories under the Greg Norman name and logo, including golf apparel, men's casual sportswear such as leather jackets and sweaters, activewear, and swimwear; mostly at upper-end price points.

Effective June 30, 2004, RBK acquired Montreal-based The Hockey Company Inc., a designer, manufacturer and marketer of hockey apparel and equipment, for $204 million in cash, plus the assumption of $125 million of debt.

Company Financials Fiscal Year ending December 31

Per Share Data ($)

(Year Ended December 31)	2003	2002	2001	2000	1999	1998	1997	1996	1995	1994
Tangible Bk. Val.	16.22	13.57	10.90	9.45	8.17	8.05	7.83	5.58	11.11	12.24
Cash Flow	3.24	2.72	2.13	2.21	1.06	1.26	3.13	2.61	2.56	3.40
Earnings	2.43	2.04	1.66	1.40	0.20	0.42	2.32	2.00	2.07	3.02
S&P Core Earnings	2.32	1.92	1.43	NA	NA	NA	NA	NA	NA	NA
Dividends	0.15	Nil	Nil	Nil	Nil	Nil	Nil	0.23	0.30	0.30
Payout Ratio	6%	Nil	Nil	Nil	Nil	Nil	Nil	11%	14%	10%
Prices - High	40.70	30.25	35.75	28.33	22.75	33.18	52.87	45.25	39.62	40.25
- Low	28.52	21.25	18.50	6.93	7.81	12.56	27.62	25.37	24.12	28.37
P/E Ratio - High	17	15	22	20	NM	79	23	23	19	13
- Low	12	10	11	5	NM	30	12	13	12	9

Income Statement Analysis (Million $)

	2003	2002	2001	2000	1999	1998	1997	1996	1995	1994
Revs.	3,485	3,128	2,993	2,865	2,900	3,225	3,644	3,478	3,481	3,280
Oper. Inc.	288	247	221	204	187	189	323	308	402	453
Depr.	35.6	32.0	36.6	46.2	48.6	48.0	47.4	42.9	38.6	32.2
Int. Exp.	25.6	23.8	17.6	22.1	49.7	60.7	64.4	42.2	25.7	16.5
Pretax Inc.	234	195	156	136	28.0	37.0	158	238	276	417
Eff. Tax Rate	30.8%	31.0%	31.0%	36.1%	36.0%	32.2%	7.90%	35.4%	36.3%	36.9%
Net Inc.	157	132	103	80.9	11.0	23.9	135	139	165	254
S&P Core Earnings	147	120	84.7	NA	NA	NA	NA	NA	NA	NA

Balance Sheet & Other Fin. Data (Million $)

	2003	2002	2001	2000	1999	1998	1997	1996	1995	1994
Cash	694	642	413	269	282	180	210	232	80.4	84.0
Curr. Assets	1,727	1,614	1,295	1,225	1,243	1,362	1,465	1,463	1,343	1,337
Total Assets	1,990	1,861	1,543	1,463	1,564	1,740	1,756	1,756	1,656	1,649
Curr. Liab.	566	580	449	488	624	612	577	517	432	506
LT Debt	353	353	351	345	370	554	63.9	854	254	132
Common Equity	1,034	885	720	608	529	524	507	381	895	991
Total Cap.	1,387	1,238	1,071	953	899	1,111	1,178	1,269	1,185	1,144
Cap. Exp.	44.5	27.6	27.4	29.2	51.2	53.6	23.9	30.0	63.6	61.8
Cash Flow	193	164	139	127	59.7	71.9	183	182	203	287
Curr. Ratio	3.1	2.8	2.9	2.5	2.0	2.2	2.5	2.8	3.1	2.6
% LT Debt of Cap.	25.5	28.5	32.8	36.2	41.2	49.9	54.2	67.3	21.5	11.5
% Net Inc.of Revs.	4.5	4.2	3.4	2.8	0.4	0.7	3.7	4.0	4.8	7.8
% Ret. on Assets	8.2	7.7	6.8	5.3	0.7	1.4	7.6	8.1	10.0	17.0
% Ret. on Equity	16.4	16.4	15.5	14.2	2.1	4.6	30.4	21.8	17.5	28.1

Data as orig reptd.; bef. results of disc opers/spec. items. Per share data adj. for stk. divs.; EPS diluted. E-Estimated. NA-Not Available. NM-Not Meaningful. NR-Not Ranked. UR-Under Review.

Office: 1895 J W Foster Blvd, Canton , MA 02021.
Telephone: 781-401-5000.
Website: http://www.reebok.com
Chrmn & CEO: P.B. Fireman.
EVP & CFO: K.I. Watchmaker.

SVP & General Counsel: D.A. Pace.
Investor Contact: N. Kerman 781-401-7152.
Dirs: N. Axelrod, P. R. Duncan, P. B. Fireman, R. G. Lesser, G. Nunes, D. L. Patrick, D. E. Puhy, T. M. Ryan, B. E. Tatelman.

Founded: in 1979.
Domicile: Massachusetts.
Employees: 7,760.
S&P Analyst: Marie Driscoll, CFA /CB/GG

Regions Financial

Recommendation: **HOLD** ★★★☆   12-Month Target Price: **$35.00**
(as of October 15, 2004)

RF has an approximate 0.15% weighting in the **S&P 500**

Sector: Financials
Sub-Industry: Regional Banks
Peer Group: Southeast Major Regional Banks

Summary: With the 2004 acquisition of Union Planters, this major southeastern bank holding company now has total assets of about $84 billion and operates some 1,400 offices in 15 states.

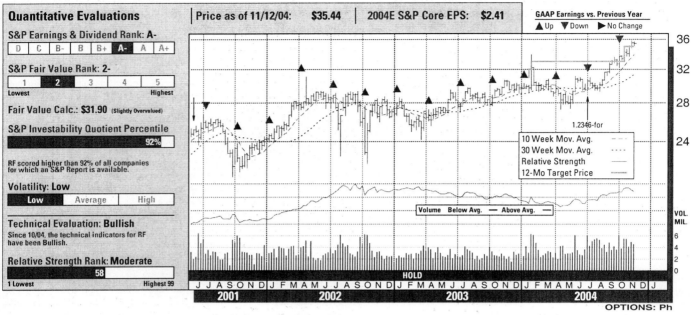

Quantitative Evaluations

S&P Earnings & Dividend Rank: A-
| D | C | B- | B | B+ | A- | A | A+ |

S&P Fair Value Rank: 2-
| 1 | 2 | 3 | 4 | 5 |
Lowest — Highest

Fair Value Calc.: $31.90 (Slightly Overvalued)

S&P Investability Quotient Percentile — 92%

RF scored higher than 92% of all companies for which an S&P Report is available.

Volatility: Low
| Low | Average | High |

Technical Evaluation: Bullish
Since 10/04, the technical indicators for RF have been Bullish.

Relative Strength Rank: Moderate — 58
1 Lowest — Highest 99

Price as of 11/12/04: $35.44   **2004E S&P Core EPS:** $2.41

GAAP Earnings vs. Previous Year — ▲ Up ▼ Down ► No Change

Chart legend:
- 10 Week Mov. Avg.
- 30 Week Mov. Avg.
- Relative Strength
- 12-Mo Target Price

1.2346-for

Volume Below Avg. — Above Avg.

HOLD

J J A S O N D | J F M A M J J A S O N D | J F M A M J J A S O N D | J F M A M J J A S O N D | J
2001 | 2002 | 2003 | 2004

VOL. MIL.

OPTIONS: Ph

Analyst commentary prepared by James M. O'Brien/CB/BK

Highlights 12-NOV-04

- We expect mortgage banking revenue to moderate for the remainder of 2004 with the recent bottoming in interest rates. We see revenue growth at Morgan Keegan coming under pressure from higher long-term interest rates, which was the case in the second and third quarters.

- Assuming that economic conditions remain strong, we expect commercial loan growth to improve moderately, late in 2004. We see the net interest margin remaining stable for most of the year, and expect it to widen later in 2004, reflecting the recent increase in short-term interest rates. We believe credit quality has stabilized and see it as likely to improve further. We expect operating expense growth to remain under control. Union Planters, a Memphis-based bank holding company, was acquired in the second quarter of 2004.

- We estimate 2004 EPS of $2.41 for the combined entity, and project 2005 EPS of $2.63, as we think the merged company can operate a more efficient mortgage business.

Investment Rationale/Risk 12-NOV-04

- We expect earnings growth to slow in coming quarters, but we think that the stock's dividend yield will help somewhat to support the shares. We believe the company remains well positioned in most target markets, and view it as having a healthy presence in the faster growing areas of the Southeast. We believe this should further support the shares, helping to minimize downside risk.

- Risks to our recommendation and target price include heightened credit costs at legacy Union Planters, a subdued rebound in C&I loan growth, general interest rate risk, and merger integration risk.

- Assuming a growth rate of 6.5% (declining to a constant rate of 4.5% in five years), and a dividend payout ratio of 40% (growing to a constant ratio of 45% in five years), our dividend discount model estimates intrinsic value at $34 to $35 a share for various discount rates. Based on our expectations of slowing earnings growth, we believe the stock will perform in line with the S&P 500 in the coming year. Our 12-month target price of $35 is based on a P/E multiple of about 13X our 2005 EPS estimate, in line with peer P/E multiples.

Key Stock Statistics

S&P Oper. EPS 2004E	2.41	52-week Range	$35.84-27.26
P/E on S&P Oper. EPS 2004E	14.7	12 Month P/E	15.4
S&P Oper. EPS 2005E	2.63	Beta	0.45
Yield (%)	3.7%	Shareholders	49,740
Dividend Rate/Share	1.33	Market Cap (B)	$ 16.4
Shares Outstanding (M)	462.1		

Value of $10,000 invested five years ago: **$ 17,361**

Dividend Data Dividends have been paid since 1968

Amount ($)	Date Decl.	Ex-Div. Date	Stock of Record	Payment Date
.0816 Spl.	Jan. 26	Mar. 16	Mar. 18	Apr. 01 '04
0.330	Jan. 22	Mar. 16	Mar. 18	Apr. 01 '04
0.412	Apr. 22	Jun. 15	Jun. 17	Jul. 01 '04
0.333	Oct. 21	Oct. 28	Nov. 01	Nov. 15 '04

Revenues/Earnings Data Fiscal year ending December 31

Revenues (Million $)

	2004	2003	2002	2001	2000	1999
1Q	901.2	917.6	920.2	956.0	947.0	809.6
2Q	885.0	940.1	929.4	1,063	930.2	819.9
3Q	—	888.6	967.4	1,014	971.4	865.3
4Q	—	871.6	978.9	1,004	986.8	876.0
Yr.	—	3,618	3,796	4,038	3,835	3,392

Earnings Per Share ($)

	2004	2003	2002	2001	2000	1999
1Q	0.61	0.58	0.53	0.46	0.53	0.46
2Q	0.58	0.59	0.54	0.40	0.46	0.49
3Q	0.55	0.59	0.57	0.48	0.47	0.48
4Q	E0.63	0.59	0.57	0.49	0.47	0.48
Yr.	E2.41	2.35	2.20	1.81	1.93	1.90

Next earnings report expected: mid-January Source: S&P, Company Reports
EPS Estimates based on S&P Operating Earnings; historical GAAP earnings are as reported.

Regions Financial Corporation

Recommendation: **HOLD** ★ ★ ★ ☆ ☆   12-Month Target Price: **$35.00** (as of October 15, 2004)

Business Summary 12-NOV-04

Regions Financial Corp., a Birmingham, AL-based bank holding company, operates primarily in the southeastern U.S., with operations consisting of banking, brokerage and investment services, mortgage banking, insurance brokerage, credit life insurance, commercial accounts receivable factoring and specialty financing. At December 31, 2003, Regions Bank, through which banking operations are conducted, had 681 full service banking offices in Alabama, Arkansas, Florida, Georgia, Louisiana, North Carolina, South Carolina, Tennessee and Texas. Since beginning operations in 1971, a substantial portion of the company's growth has come from acquisitions. Through the end of 2003, RF had completed 102 acquisitions, representing $28.2 billion in assets.

Bank-related operations include Morgan Keegan (acquired in 2001), a regional full-service brokerage and investment bank. Morgan Keegan, which operates 142 offices, offers products and services including securities brokerage, asset management, financial planning, mutual funds, securities underwriting, sales and trading, and investment banking. The company also operates Regions Mortgage (RMI) and EquiFirst Corp., which are involved in mortgage banking. RMI's primary business is the origination and servicing of mortgage loans for long-term investors. EquiFirst typically originates mortgage loans that are sold to third-party investors with servicing released.

In 2003, average earnings assets, from which interest income is derived, totaled

$44.2 billion and consisted of loans (71%), investment securities (21%) and other (8%). Average sources of funds, used in the lending business, included interest-bearing deposits (55%), noninterest-bearing deposits (11%), short-term borrowings (11%), long-term debt (11%), shareholders' equity (9%), and other (3%).

Total loans of $32.1 billion at the end of 2003 were divided as follows: real estate mortgage 40%, commercial 30%, consumer 19% and real estate construction 11%.

Nonperforming assets (primarily loans where interest and principal payments are not being received as per original terms) at December 31, 2003, amounted to $338.6 million (1.05% of loans and other real estate), versus $356.9 million (1.15%) a year earlier. The allowance for loan losses, which is set aside for possible loan defaults, was $437.2 million (1.41% of net loans), up from $419.2 million (1.41%). Net chargeoffs, or the amount of loans actually written off as uncollectible, totaled $104.6 million (0.33% of average loans) in 2003, versus $111.8 million (0.36%) in 2002.

During 2002, the company expanded into the Dallas, TX, market through the acquisition of Brookhollow Bancshares ($167 million in assets); and into the Houston, TX, market by buying Independence Bank, National Association ($112 million). In the second quarter of 2004, RF acquired Union Planters, a $31.9 billion bank holding company headquartered in Memphis, TN.

Company Financials Fiscal Year ending December 31

Per Share Data ($)

(Year Ended December 31)	2003	2002	2001	2000	1999	1998	1997	1996	1995	1994
Tangible Bk. Val.	16.25	15.29	10.58	11.00	9.75	9.72	9.56	8.75	9.07	8.21
Earnings	2.35	2.20	1.81	1.93	1.90	1.52	1.74	1.50	1.52	1.38
S&P Core Earnings	2.32	2.11	1.63	NA	NA	NA	NA	NA	NA	NA
Dividends	1.00	0.94	0.91	0.87	0.79	0.72	0.62	0.57	0.53	0.49
Payout Ratio	43%	43%	50%	45%	42%	47%	36%	38%	35%	35%
Prices - High	30.69	31.10	26.72	22.67	33.71	36.95	36.44	21.86	18.22	14.88
- Low	24.16	21.95	20.84	14.83	18.78	23.38	20.80	16.40	12.55	12.04
P/E Ratio - High	13	14	15	12	18	24	21	15	12	11
- Low	10	10	11	8	10	15	12	11	8	9

Income Statement Analysis (Million $)

	2003	2002	2001	2000	1999	1998	1997	1996	1995	1994
Net Int. Inc.	1,475	1,498	1,425	1,389	1,426	1,325	829	700	497	436
Tax Equiv. Adj.	NA	NA	NA	NA	NA	NA	NA	13.3	10.5	10.6
Non Int. Inc.	1,373	1,207	950	641	537	468	258	221	160	143
Loan Loss Prov.	122	128	165	127	114	60.5	41.8	29.0	20.7	19.0
Exp./Op. Revs.	64.6%	65.1%	64.2%	55.2%	54.2%	61.6%	55.2%	59.3%	56.7%	58.2%
Pretax Inc.	912	869	718	742	785	635	445	338	258	217
Eff. Tax Rate	28.5%	28.7%	29.1%	28.9%	33.1%	33.6%	32.7%	32.1%	33.2%	32.8%
Net Inc.	652	620	509	528	525	422	300	230	173	146
% Net Int. Marg.	3.49	3.73	3.66	3.55	3.94	4.25	4.20	4.27	4.10	4.26
S&P Core Earnings	647	592	458	NA	NA	NA	NA	NA	NA	NA

Balance Sheet & Other Fin. Data (Million $)

	2003	2002	2001	2000	1999	1998	1997	1996	1995	1994
Money Mkt. Assets	1,491	1,424	1,502	112	90.3	427	127	54.0	76.4	70.6
Inv. Securities	9,088	8,995	7,847	8,994	10,913	7,969	4,451	3,901	3,025	2,609
Com'l Loans	9,914	10,842	9,912	9,070	8,230	7,144	3,856	2,830	1,992	1,871
Other Loans	22,501	20,144	21,225	22,402	19,992	17,286	12,572	10,505	7,665	7,277
Total Assets	48,598	47,939	45,383	43,688	42,714	36,832	23,034	18,930	13,709	12,839
Demand Deposits	5,718	5,148	5,085	4,513	4,420	4,577	2,368	1,909	1,535	1,450
Time Deposits	27,015	27,779	26,463	27,510	25,569	23,773	15,383	13,139	9,361	8,643
LT Debt	5,712	5,386	4,748	4,478	1,751	571	400	447	553	519
Common Equity	4,452	4,178	4,036	3,458	3,065	3,000	1,913	1,599	1,125	1,014
% Ret. on Assets	1.4	1.3	1.1	1.2	1.3	1.4	1.4	1.3	1.3	1.3
% Ret. on Equity	15.1	15.1	13.6	16.2	17.3	17.2	17.1	15.2	15.8	16.0
% Loan Loss Resv.	1.4	1.3	1.3	1.2	1.2	1.3	1.2	1.3	1.4	1.3
% Loans/Deposits	102.1	98.7	100.7	98.7	95.7	85.9	91.5	85.9	87.8	90.4
% Equity to Assets	8.9	8.8	8.4	7.5	7.6	8.2	8.4	8.5	8.1	8.1

Data as orig reptd.; bef. results of disc opers/spec. items. Per share data adj. for stk. divs.; EPS diluted. E-Estimated. NA-Not Available. NM-Not Meaningful. NR-Not Ranked. UR-Under Review.

Office: 417 North 20th Street, Birmingham, AL 35203-0247.
Telephone: 205-944-1300.
Email: askus@regionsbank.com
Website: http://www.regions.com
Chrmn, Pres & CEO: C. E. Jones, Jr.
COO & Vice Chrmn: R. D. Horsley.
EVP & CFO: D. B. Jordon.

EVP: W. E. Askew.
Investor Contact: Jenifer M. Goforth (205-326-7090).
Dirs: J. B. Boone, Jr., J. S. French, M. H. Greene, R. D. Horsley, C. E. Jones, Jr., S. W. Matlock, A. B. Morgan, Jr., M. Portera, J. W. Rothenstreich, W. W. Stewart, L. J. Styslinger III, J. H. Watson, C. K. Wilson, Jr., H. W. Witt.

Founded: in 1970.
Domicile: Delaware.
Employees: 16,180.
S&P Analyst: James M. O'Brien/CB/BK

Reynolds American

Recommendation: **BUY** ★★★★☆   12-Month Target Price: **$74.00**
(as of September 28, 2004)

RAI has an approximate 0.10% weighting in the **S&P 500**

Sector: Consumer Staples
Sub-Industry: Tobacco
Peer Group: Tobacco/Cigarettes

Summary: RAI, the second largest U.S. cigarette manufacturer, was formed via the mid-2004 merger of R.J. Reynolds and Brown & Williamson.

Quantitative Evaluations

S&P Earnings & Dividend Rank: NR

| D | C | B- | B | B+ | A- | A | A+ |

S&P Fair Value Rank: 2-

| 1 | **2** | 3 | 4 | 5 |
| Lowest | | | | Highest |

Fair Value Calc.: $61.90 (Overvalued)

S&P Investability Quotient Percentile

74%

RAI scored higher than 74% of all companies for which an S&P Report is available.

Volatility: Average

| Low | **Average** | High |

Technical Evaluation: Neutral

Since 11/04, the technical indicators for RAI have been Neutral.

Relative Strength Rank: Moderate

52

1 Lowest   Highest 99

| Price as of 11/12/04: | $72.92 | 2004E S&P Core EPS: | $6.43 |

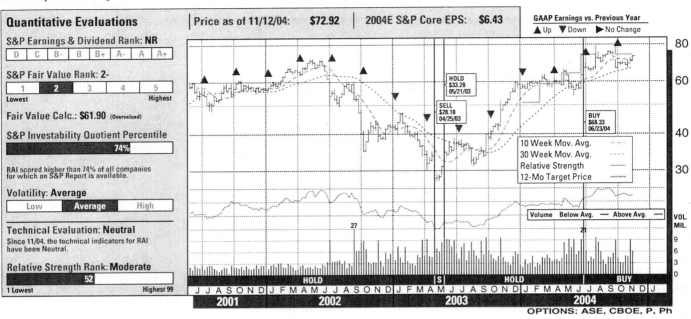

GAAP Earnings vs. Previous Year
▲ Up   ▼ Down   ▶ No Change

HOLD $33.28 05/21/03
SELL $28.18 04/25/03
BUY $68.33 06/23/04

10 Week Mov. Avg.
30 Week Mov. Avg.
Relative Strength
12-Mo Target Price

Volume Below Avg. — Above Avg.

VOL. MIL.

OPTIONS: ASE, CBOE, P, Ph

Analyst commentary prepared by Anishka Clarke/CB/BK

Highlights November 03, 2004

- Reflecting the mid-2004 merger of RJRT and Brown & Williamson, we see double-digit sales growth in 2005, following a similar increase in 2004. We anticipate about 1% internal growth, as we anticipate continued share gains for focus brands Camel, Salem and Pall Mall. We see competitive pressure in the menthol category limiting growth for the Kool brand. Overall, we expect competition from deep discount brands and an increased marketing focus from rival premium brands to limit internal sales growth. Also, we believe the reduction in marketing for certain brands, including Doral and Winston, will hinder long-term sales growth.

- We anticipate faster realization of cost synergies from the merger, and see a likely improvement in gross margins. Cost savings at the SG&A level are likely to continue in 2005. We look for savings from changes to sales programs, increased outsourcing, and facility consolidation to boost operating margins.

- We expect higher interest expense in 2005, and an effective tax rate of about 36%. We look for 2005 EPS of $7.40, up 8% from our 2004 EPS projection of $6.86, which excludes legal settlement costs but includes favorable tax treatments for 2004.

Investment Rationale/Risk November 03, 2004

- We are maintaining our accumulate opinion on the shares, which we view as undervalued on a total return basis. We attribute current share price pressure to the ongoing $280 billion Department of Justice trial. Still, we believe $600 million in anticipated synergies can be achieved within two years, with the majority of benefits coming in 2005 and beyond. We also continue to see significant cost savings aiding margin expansion in the longer term. However, despite a larger brand portfolio, we remain cautious about revenue growth potential, as a new combined brand strategy is not clear. We do not regard high growth sales as likely.

- Risks to our recommendation and target price include a near-term negative impact on trading multiples due to ongoing litigation.

- Assuming a longer-term growth rate of 1% and a cost of capital of 10.5%, our DCF analysis calculates intrinsic value of $74 a share. With ongoing trials expected to put pressure on trading multiples, we apply a forward P/E multiple of 10X, in line with the historical average, to our 2005 EPS estimate of $7.40 to arrive at our 12-month target price of $74.

Key Stock Statistics

S&P Core EPS 2005E	7.37	52-week Range	$76.19-50.27
S&P Oper. EPS 2004E	6.86	12 Month P/E	28.1
P/E on S&P Oper. EPS 2004E	10.6	Beta	0.17
S&P Oper. EPS 2005E	7.40	Shareholders	26,000
Yield (%)	5.2%	Market Cap (B)	$ 10.8
Dividend Rate/Share	3.80	Shares Outstanding (M)	148.0

Value of $10,000 invested five years ago: **$ 50,477**

Dividend Data   Dividends have been paid since 1999

Amount ($)	Date Decl.	Ex-Div. Date	Stock of Record	Payment Date
0.950	Dec. 09	Dec. 17	Dec. 19	Jan. 02 '04
0.950	Feb. 04	Mar. 08	Mar. 10	Apr. 01 '04
0.950	May. 05	May. 08	Jun. 10	Jul. 01 '04
0.950	Aug. 18	Sep. 08	Sep. 10	Oct. 01 '04

Revenues/Earnings Data   Fiscal year ending December 31

Revenues (Million $)

	2004	2003	2002	2001	2000	1999
1Q	1,218	1,218	1,515	1,950	1,922	—
2Q	1,352	1,431	1,705	2,269	2,085	1,907
3Q	1,866	1,384	1,585	2,273	2,119	1,991
4Q	—	1,234	1,406	2,093	2,041	1,976
Yr.	—	5,267	6,211	8,585	8,167	7,567

Earnings Per Share ($)

	2004	2003	2002	2001	2000	1999
1Q	1.43	0.84	1.79	0.98	0.77	—
2Q	1.76	0.83	2.29	1.26	1.07	-0.36
3Q	2.28	-41.31	1.56	1.31	1.16	0.88
4Q	E1.61	-4.53	-1.16	0.93	0.45	1.00
Yr.	E6.86	-44.08	4.64	4.48	3.46	1.80

Next earnings report expected: late-January Source: S&P, Company Reports
EPS Estimates based on S&P Operating Earnings; historical GAAP earnings are as reported.

Please read the Required Disclosures and Reg. AC certification on the last page of this report.

The McGraw·Hill Companies

Reynolds American, Inc.

Recommendation: **BUY** ★ ★ ★ ☆   12-Month Target Price: **$74.00** (as of September 28, 2004)

Business Summary November 04, 2004

On July 30, 2004, R.J. Reynolds Tobacco Co. (RJRT) merged with Brown & Williamson (B&W), the U.S. operations of British American Tobacco (BTI), to form a new publicly traded company, Reynolds American, Inc. Shareholders of RJRT received a 58% interest in the new entity, and shareholders of B&W received 42%. Combining RJRT and B&W, the second and third largest players, RAI is the second largest U.S. cigarette manufacturer, with a combined market share of over 32%.

RAI is the parent company of RJRT, Santa Fe Natural Tobacco, which RJRT acquired in 2002, and Lane Limited, which was purchased from BTI for $400 million as part of the merger.

During 2003, RJRT implemented a significant restructuring plan, targeting cost savings of $1 billion by the end of 2005 through a significant workforce reduction, asset divestitures and associated exit activities. It also announced a shift in marketing strategy to improve profitability, directing most of its spending to its Camel and Salem brands, which together accounted for 48% of RJRT's volume at the end of 2003. Total volume in 2003 was 83.5 billion units, which represented a 22.5% share of the market. The company's other brands include Winston, Doral, Vantage, More and Now. In 2003, it began distributing Eclipse, a cigarette that primarily heats rather than burns tobacco, in an effort to reduce second-hand smoke. The product is offered in selected retail chain outlets.

The operations of B&W also underwent restructuring in 2003, including productivity improvements and major cost savings efforts across the company. In 2003, B&W had sales of 38.8 billion units and had market share of 9.8% at year end. Principal brands include Kool, Pall Mall, Capri, Misty and GPC.

Through its subsidiaries, RAI is now a defendant in a number of product-liability lawsuits related to cigarettes. The lawsuits charge that lung cancer and other diseases, as well as addiction, have resulted from the use of, or exposure to, RAI's tobacco products. At December 31, 2003, there were 1,592 active cases pending against RJRT.

In November 1998, the major U.S. cigarette manufacturers, including RJRT and B&W, entered into what was termed a Master Settlement Agreement (MSA) with attorneys general representing the remaining 46 states that had not previously settled their Medicaid cost recovery claims against the industry. Under terms of the agreement, tobacco companies were to pay the states over $8 billion annually at least through 2025. In addition, cigarette manufacturers agreed to fund anti-smoking campaigns, establish a national public health foundation intended to reduce smoking among youths, and accept a number of marketing restrictions. RJRT's cash payments under the MSA and other existing settlement agreements totaled $1.8 billion in 2003, down from $2.5 billion in 2002.

Company Financials Fiscal Year ending December 31

Per Share Data ($)

(Year Ended December 31)	2003	2002	2001	2000	1999	1998	1997	1996	1995	1994
Tangible Bk. Val.	NM	NM	NM	NM	NM	NM	NA	NA	NA	NA
Cash Flow	-41.62	6.69	9.44	8.21	6.21	NA	NA	NA	NA	NA
Earnings	-44.08	4.64	4.48	3.46	1.80	-2.75	NA	NA	NA	NA
S&P Core Earnings	18.87	21.58	20.00	NA	NA	NA	NA	NA	NA	NA
Dividends	3.80	3.73	3.30	3.10	0.78	NA	NA	NA	NA	NA
Payout Ratio	NM	80%	74%	90%	43%	NA	NA	NA	NA	NA
Prices - High	60.14	71.90	62.70	50.25	34.00	NA	NA	NA	NA	NA
- Low	27.52	34.83	44.18	15.75	16.00	NA	NA	NA	NA	NA
P/E Ratio - High	NM	15	14	15	19	NA	NA	NA	NA	NA
- Low	NM	8	10	5	9	NA	NA	NA	NA	NA

Income Statement Analysis (Million $)

	2003	2002	2001	2000	1999	1998	1997	1996	1995	1994
Revs.	5,267	6,211	8,585	8,167	7,567	5,716	NA	NA	NA	NA
Oper. Inc.	873	1,200	1,409	1,399	1,368	NA	NA	NA	NA	NA
Depr.	151	184	491	485	482	NA	NA	NA	NA	NA
Int. Exp.	111	147	150	168	268	176	NA	NA	NA	NA
Pretax Inc.	-3,918	683	892	748	510	-340	NA	NA	NA	NA
Eff. Tax Rate	NM	38.8%	50.2%	52.9%	61.8%	NM	NA	NA	NA	NA
Net Inc.	-3,689	418	444	352	195	-299	NA	NA	NA	NA
S&P Core Earnings	1,615	1,947	1,980	NA	NA	NA	NA	NA	NA	NA

Balance Sheet & Other Fin. Data (Million $)

	2003	2002	2001	2000	1999	1998	1997	1996	1995	1994
Cash	1,523	1,584	2,020	2,543	1,177	3,036	NA	NA	NA	NA
Curr. Assets	3,331	3,992	3,856	3,871	2,468	4,138	NA	NA	NA	NA
Total Assets	9,677	14,651	15,050	15,554	14,377	16,301	NA	NA	NA	NA
Curr. Liab.	2,865	3,427	2,792	2,776	3,068	3,885	NA	NA	NA	NA
LT Debt	1,671	1,755	1,631	1,674	1,653	2,065	NA	NA	NA	NA
Common Equity	3,057	6,716	8,026	8,436	7,064	7,555	NA	NA	NA	NA
Total Cap.	5,534	9,707	11,383	11,966	10,347	11,073	NA	NA	NA	NA
Cap. Exp.	70.0	111	74.0	60.0	55.0	NA	NA	NA	NA	NA
Cash Flow	-3,538	602	935	837	677	NA	NA	NA	NA	NA
Curr. Ratio	1.2	1.2	1.4	1.4	0.8	1.1	NA	NA	NA	NA
% LT Debt of Cap.	30.2	18.1	14.3	14.0	16.0	18.6	NA	NA	NA	NA
% Net Inc.of Revs.	NM	6.7	5.2	4.3	2.6	NM	NA	NA	NA	NA
% Ret. on Assets	NM	2.8	2.9	2.4	1.2	NM	NA	NA	NA	NA
% Ret. on Equity	NM	5.7	5.4	4.5	2.3	NM	NA	NA	NA	NA

Data as orig reptd. for R.J. Reynolds; bef. results of disc opers/spec. items. Per share data adj. for stk. divs.; EPS diluted. E-Estimated. NA-Not Available. NM-Not Meaningful. NR-Not Ranked. UR-Under Review.

Office: 401 North Main Street, Winston-Salem, NC 27102-2866.
Telephone: 336-741-5500.
Email: talktorjrt@rjrt.com
Website: http://www.rjrholdings.com
Chrmn, Pres & CEO: A.J. Schindler.
EVP & CFO: D.M. Neal.

EVP & General Counsel: C.A. Blixt.
SVP & Chief Acctg Officer: T.R. Adams.
SVP & Treas: D.A. Fawley.
Dirs: M. K. Bush, J. T. Chain, Jr., A. D. Frazier, Jr., E. V. Goings, D. Ilitch, N. Mensah, R. S. Miller, Jr., A. J. Schindler, J. P. Viviano, T. C. Wajnert.

Founded: in 1875.
Domicile: Delaware.
Employees: 7,000.
S&P Analyst: Anishka Clarke/CB/BK

Source: S&P, Company Reports

Robert Half International

Recommendation: HOLD ★ ★ ★ ☆ ☆
SELL SELL HOLD BUY BUY

12-Month Target Price: $30.00
(as of April 23, 2004)

RHI has an approximate 0.04% weighting in the **S&P 500**

Sector: Industrials
Sub-Industry: Employment Services
Peer Group: Staffing & Personnel Services over $1B Sales

Summary: RHI is the world's largest specialized provider of temporary and permanent personnel in the fields of accounting and finance.

Quantitative Evaluations

S&P Earnings & Dividend Rank: B

| D | C | B- | **B** | B+ | A- | A | A+ |

S&P Fair Value Rank: 1-

| **1** | 2 | 3 | 4 | 5 |
| Lowest | | | | Highest |

Fair Value Calc.: $23.80 (Overvalued)

S&P Investability Quotient Percentile

94%

RHI scored higher than 94% of all companies for which an S&P Report is available.

Volatility: Average

| Low | **Average** | High |

Technical Evaluation: Bullish

Since 11/04, the technical indicators for RHI have been Bullish.

Relative Strength Rank: Moderate

48

| 1 Lowest | Highest 99 |

Price as of 11/12/04: $27.78   **2004E S&P Core EPS:** $0.65

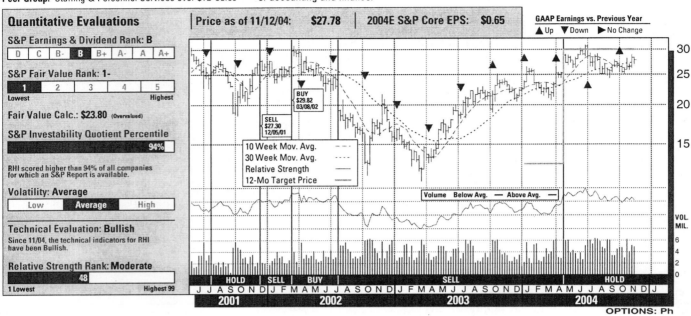

GAAP Earnings vs. Previous Year
▲ Up ▼ Down ► No Change

10 Week Mov. Avg.
30 Week Mov. Avg.
Relative Strength
12-Mo Target Price

Volume   Below Avg. — Above Avg. —

OPTIONS: Ph

Analyst commentary prepared by Michael W. Jaffe/CB/BK

Highlights October 25, 2004

- We expect revenues to grow about 12% in 2005. The recession of 2001 caused many businesses to cut staff or put hiring plans on hold, but RHI's business started to show signs of a solid recovery in early 2004. We see that trend continuing through at least 2005, based on our outlook for ongoing economic gains. We also expect RHI to benefit from demand related to a heightened focus on internal accounting controls and other corporate governance require- ments, in light of some corporate scandals over the past few years. We see flat revenues from Protiviti, as we think a likely reduction in revenues related to Sarbanes Oxley (as a good number of companies will be in compliance with the Act) will be offset by expected ongoing growth in Protiviti's client base for other services.

- Operating margins should widen in 2005, on the better demand trends that we see and the expected operating leverage generated by the forecasted in- creased in revenue. However, Protiviti, which has been profitable since the first quarter of 2004, will likely see relatively similar profits in 2005, as we see its performance limited by the likely loss of some of its Sarbanes Oxley business; Protiviti accounted for $0.11 of EPS in the first nine months of 2004.

- We see Standard & Poor's Core Earnings falling $0.12 a share below our operating income forecasts in both 2004 and 2005, with the difference reflecting projected option expense.

Investment Rationale/Risk October 25, 2004

- RHI's performance started to revive in early 2004, as temporary worker markets finally picked up, and we believe the greater need for internal accounting controls in U.S. corporations also began to assist its performance. Although the U.S. labor market went into somewhat of a lull in the middle of 2004, we expect a better economy to revive the hiring picture again in coming periods. We believe that situation would make RHI a good holding, but we would not add to positions based on valuation considerations.

- Risks to our recommendation and target price include an unexpected downturn in the U.S. economy and a resultant return to soft labor markets.

- The shares recently traded at about 25X our 2005 EPS forecast, which was substantially above the multiple sported by the S&P 500. However, we believe that lofty multiple will be supported by the ongoing labor market rebound that we forecast, and its likely positive effect on RHI over the next few years. Based on that outlook, we have a 12-month target price of $30, or almost 29X our 2005 EPS estimate (a little less than twice the multiple of the S&P 500), for this volatile stock.

Key Stock Statistics

S&P Core EPS 2005E	0.93	52-week Range	$30.98-20.45
S&P Oper. EPS 2004E	0.77	12 Month P/E	50.5
P/E on S&P Oper. EPS 2004E	36.1	Beta	1.23
S&P Oper. EPS 2005E	1.05	Shareholders	1,900
Yield (%)	0.9%	Market Cap (B)	$ 4.8
Dividend Rate/Share	0.24	Shares Outstanding (M)	172.3

Value of $10,000 invested five years ago: **$ 18,973**

Dividend Data Dividends have been paid since 2004

Amount ($)	Date Decl.	Ex-Div. Date	Stock of Record	Payment Date
0.060	Apr. 22	May. 21	May. 25	Jun. 15 '04
0.060	Jul. 28	Aug. 23	Aug. 25	Sep. 15 '04
0.060	Oct. 28	Nov. 22	Nov. 24	Dec. 15 '04

Revenues/Earnings Data Fiscal year ending December 31

Revenues (Million $)

	2004	2003	2002	2001	2000	1999
1Q	572.3	473.2	468.5	719.3	632.9	485.0
2Q	641.2	483.0	473.1	648.4	671.0	497.1
3Q	708.0	501.1	484.8	574.7	689.6	529.5
4Q	—	517.7	478.6	510.5	705.9	569.8
Yr.	—	1,975	1,905	2,453	2,699	2,081

Earnings Per Share ($)

	2004	2003	2002	2001	2000	1999
1Q	0.09	-0.02	0.05	0.26	0.24	0.19
2Q	0.18	Nil	0.02	0.21	0.25	0.18
3Q	0.24	0.03	-0.02	0.13	0.26	0.19
4Q	E0.25	0.03	-0.04	0.07	0.26	0.21
Yr.	E0.77	0.04	0.01	0.67	1.00	0.77

Next earnings report expected: late-January Source: S&P, Company Reports
EPS Estimates based on S&P Operating Earnings; historical GAAP earnings are as reported.

STANDARD &POOR'S

Robert Half International Inc.

Stock Report
November 13, 2004
NYSE Symbol: **RHI**

Recommendation: HOLD ★ ★ ★ ☆ ☆   12-Month Target Price: **$30.00** (as of April 23, 2004)

Business Summary October 25, 2004

Robert Half International is the world's largest specialized staffing service in the fields of accounting and finance. In May 2002, RHI expanded its offerings to include risk consulting and internal audit services through its Protiviti unit. In 2003, the company derived 88% of its revenue base from activities in temporary and consultant staffing, 5% from permanent placement staffing, and the remaining 7% from risk consulting and internal audit services. Foreign operations accounted for 18% of RHI's revenues in 2003. At the end of 2003, the company's staffing businesses had more than 325 offices, in 43 states, the District of Columbia, and 10 foreign nations, while Protiviti had 30 offices in 20 states and six foreign nations. It placed about 175,000 employees on temporary assignments in 2003.

RHI's Accountemps temporary services division offers customers an economical means of dealing with uneven or peak work loads for accounting, tax and finance personnel. The temporary workers are employees of Accountemps, and are paid by Accountemps only when working on customer assignments. The customer pays a fixed rate for hours worked. If the client converts the temporary hire to a permanent worker, it typically pays a one-time fee for the conversion.

RHI offers permanent placement services through Robert Half Finance & Accounting, which specializes in accounting, financial, tax and banking personnel. Fees for successful permanent placements are paid only by the employer and are usually a percentage of the new employee's annual salary.

Since the early 1990s, the company has expanded into additional specialty fields. In 1991, OfficeTeam was formed to provide skilled temporary administrative and office personnel. In 1992, RHI acquired Robert Half Legal (formerly The Affiliates), which places temporary and regular employees in paralegal, legal administrative and other legal support positions. In 1994, Robert Half Technology (formerly RHI Consulting) was created to concentrate on the placement of temporary and contract information technology professionals. In 1997, the company established Robert Half Management Resources (formerly RHI Management Resources) to provide senior level project professionals specializing in the accounting and finance fields. The Creative Group, which started up in 1999, provides project staffing in the advertising, marketing and web design fields. In 2003, Accountemps provided 42% of revenues, OfficeTeam 25%, other placement businesses 26%, and Protiviti 7%.

Prior to 1986, the company was primarily a franchiser of Accountemps and Robert Half Finance & Accounting offices. Since 1986, RHI has acquired all franchised locations (the last was purchased in July 2003).

In May 2002, RHI hired 765 professionals, including more than 50 partners, who had been part of Arthur Andersen LLP's U.S. internal audit and business risk consulting practices. Robert Half hired these individuals to staff its newly formed Protiviti unit, which specializes in internal auditing, and in business and technology risk consulting.

The company repurchased 6.9 million shares in 2002, for a total of $132 million, and another 1.6 million shares on the open market in 2003, for $24.6 million.

Company Financials Fiscal Year ending December 31

Per Share Data ($)

(Year Ended December 31)	2003	2002	2001	2000	1999	1998	1997	1996	1995	1994
Tangible Bk. Val.	3.65	3.41	3.69	3.13	2.27	1.89	1.32	0.75	0.42	0.14
Cash Flow	0.42	0.42	1.07	1.30	0.98	0.82	0.59	0.40	0.27	0.20
Earnings	0.04	0.01	0.67	1.00	0.77	0.70	0.50	0.33	0.23	0.15
S&P Core Earnings	-0.11	-0.17	0.51	NA	NA	NA	NA	NA	NA	NA
Dividends	Nil	Nil	Nil	Nil	Nil	Nil	Nil	Nil	Nil	Nil
Payout Ratio	Nil	Nil	Nil	Nil	Nil	Nil	Nil	Nil	Nil	Nil
Prices - High	25.18	30.90	30.90	38.62	24.18	30.12	21.53	13.83	7.43	4.45
- Low	11.44	11.94	18.50	12.34	10.21	14.50	11.12	6.50	3.27	2.12
P/E Ratio - High	NM	NM	46	39	32	43	43	41	33	29
- Low	NM	NM	28	12	13	21	22	19	14	14

Income Statement Analysis (Million $)

	2003	2002	2001	2000	1999	1998	1997	1996	1995	1994
Revs.	1,975	1,905	2,453	2,699	2,081	1,793	1,303	899	629	446
Oper. Inc.	75.0	71.2	261	348	268	240	172	113	77.0	54.0
Depr.	65.9	72.3	73.1	56.6	39.1	24.6	17.7	11.9	8.30	7.30
Int. Exp.	Nil	Nil	Nil	Nil	Nil	Nil	Nil	0.71	0.77	1.57
Pretax Inc.	11.7	3.50	196	302	235	221	159	104	69.1	45.2
Eff. Tax Rate	45.5%	38.0%	38.3%	38.3%	39.7%	40.5%	41.0%	41.1%	41.7%	42.2%
Net Inc.	6.39	2.17	121	186	141	132	93.7	61.1	40.3	26.1
S&P Core Earnings	-18.4	-30.2	91.1	NA	NA	NA	NA	NA	NA	NA

Balance Sheet & Other Fin. Data (Million $)

	2003	2002	2001	2000	1999	1998	1997	1996	1995	1994
Cash	377	317	347	239	151	166	131	80.2	41.3	2.60
Curr. Assets	699	643	686	672	491	430	334	218	134	67.7
Total Assets	980	936	994	971	777	704	561	416	301	228
Curr. Liab.	189	184	177	237	176	153	122	86.6	55.9	29.6
LT Debt	2.34	2.40	2.48	2.54	2.60	3.40	4.53	5.07	1.50	3.10
Common Equity	789	745	806	719	576	522	419	308	228	177
Total Cap.	791	747	808	721	601	551	439	329	245	198
Cap. Exp.	36.5	48.3	84.7	74.0	52.6	67.2	32.0	18.0	8.42	4.77
Cash Flow	72.3	74.5	194	243	181	156	111	73.0	48.6	33.4
Curr. Ratio	3.7	3.5	3.9	2.8	2.8	2.8	2.7	2.5	2.4	2.3
% LT Debt of Cap.	0.3	0.3	0.3	0.4	0.4	0.6	1.1	1.6	0.6	1.6
% Net Inc.of Revs.	0.3	0.1	4.9	6.9	6.8	7.3	7.2	6.8	6.4	5.9
% Ret. on Assets	0.7	0.2	12.3	21.3	19.1	20.8	19.2	17.1	15.2	11.8
% Ret. on Equity	0.8	0.3	15.9	28.7	25.7	28.0	25.8	22.8	19.9	16.5

Data as orig reptd.; bef. results of disc opers/spec. items. Per share data adj. for stk. divs.; EPS diluted. E-Estimated. NA-Not Available. NM-Not Meaningful. NR-Not Ranked. UR-Under Review.

Office: 2884 Sand Hill Rd Ste 200, Menlo Park, CA 94025-7072.
Telephone: 650-234-6000.
Website: http://www.rhii.com
Chrmn & CEO: H.M. Messmer, Jr.
Pres, Vice Chrmn & CFO: M.K. Waddell.

COO: P.F. Gentzkow.
VP & Treas: M. Buckley.
VP, Secy & General Counsel: S. Karel.
Dirs: A. S. Berwick, Jr., F. P. Furth, E. W. Gibbons, H. M. Messmer, Jr., T. J. Ryan, J. S. Schaub, M. K. Waddell.

Founded: in 1967.
Domicile: Delaware.
Employees: 182,300.
S&P Analyst: Michael W. Jaffe/CB/BK

Rockwell Automation

Recommendation: **HOLD** ★ ★ ★ ☆ ☆
SELL | SELL | HOLD | BUY | BUY

12-Month Target Price: $45.00
(as of November 04, 2004)

ROK has an approximate 0.08% weighting in the **S&P 500**

Sector: Industrials
Sub-Industry: Electrical Components & Equipment
Peer Group: Electronic Components

Summary: This former aerospace and defense contractor (formerly Rockwell International) now primarily manufactures automated industrial equipment and power generators.

Quantitative Evaluations

S&P Earnings & Dividend Rank: B+

| D | C | B- | B | B+ | A- | A | A+ |

S&P Fair Value Rank: 1

| 1 | 2 | 3 | 4 | 5 |
| Lowest | | | | Highest |

Fair Value Calc.: $32.70 (Overvalued)

S&P Investability Quotient Percentile
98%

ROK scored higher than 98% of all companies for which an S&P Report is available.

Volatility: Average

| Low | **Average** | High |

Technical Evaluation: Bullish
Since 10/04, the technical indicators for ROK have been Bullish.

Relative Strength Rank: Strong
86
1 Lowest   Highest 99

Price as of 11/12/04: $45.81 | **2005E S&P Core EPS:** $2.02

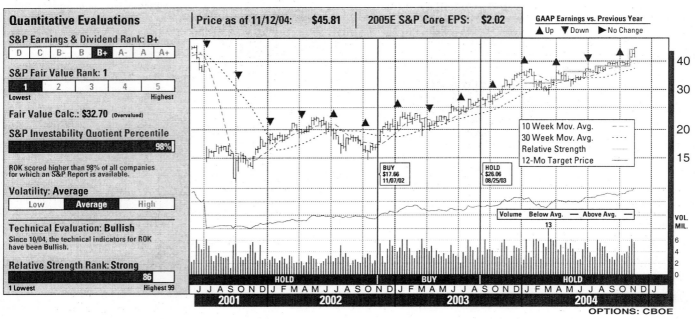

GAAP Earnings vs. Previous Year — ▲ Up ▼ Down ▶ No Change

10 Week Mov. Avg.
30 Week Mov. Avg.
Relative Strength
12-Mo Target Price

BUY $17.66 11/07/02
HOLD $26.06 08/25/03

Volume — Below Avg. — Above Avg.

OPTIONS: CBOE

Analyst commentary prepared by John F. Hingher, CFA /PMW/BK

Highlights November 09, 2004

- We think that continued positive readings in the monthly Purchasing Managers' Index suggest a sustainable uptrend for industrial equipment spending following a burst of pent-up demand early in 2004. For FY 05 (Sep.), we see a combination of modest organic growth (led by customer capital investment); rising, but still favorable, interest rates; and a weak U.S. dollar leading to average sales growth of 7%.

- Aided by the higher expected sales, we project wider margins in FY 05, reflecting benefits of cost rationalization actions. We expect the company to be able to offset higher raw material costs in the power systems business with productivity improvements and price increases.

- We expect earnings from continued operation to grow 29% in FY 05, to $418 million, up from FY 04's $324 million, excluding one-time items. For the longer term, we think ROK's lean operating structure and what we see as its strong balance sheet position it well to take advantage of the current upturn in business investment spending. Our FY 05 EPS estimate is $2.20, with S&P Core EPS of $2.02 seen.

Investment Rationale/Risk November 09, 2004

- We are maintaining our hold opinion on the shares, as we believe that our expectations of improving capital spending, what we see as management's proven ability to deliver solid cash flow, and a 1.6% dividend yield are fairly reflected in the current price.

- Risks to our recommendation and target price include delays in customer capital spending, higher raw material costs, and delayed benefits from facilities rationalization actions.

- Our discounted cash flow model, which assumes a weighted average cost of capital of 10%, free cash flow growth of 9% to 10% a year for the next 10 years, and 3.5% perpetual growth, indicates that the shares are somewhat undervalued. In terms of relative valuation, the shares traded recently at 20X our forward 12-month EPS estimate of $2.20, above their historical average multiple, and at a slight premium to a peer average P/E multiple of 19X. Blending these methodologies leads to our 12-month target price of $45.

Key Stock Statistics

S&P Oper. EPS 2005E	2.20	52-week Range	$45.98-28.45
P/E on S&P Oper. EPS 2005E	20.8	12 Month P/E	21.1
Yield (%)	1.4%	Beta	0.93
Dividend Rate/Share	0.66	Shareholders	39,021
Shares Outstanding (M)	184.3	Market Cap (B)	$ 8.4

Value of $10,000 invested five years ago: **NA**

Dividend Data Dividends have been paid since 1948

Amount ($)	Date Decl.	Ex-Div. Date	Stock of Record	Payment Date
0.165	Feb. 04	Feb. 12	Feb. 17	Mar. 08 '04
0.165	Apr. 16	May. 13	May. 17	Jun. 07 '04
0.165	Jun. 02	Aug. 12	Aug. 16	Sep. 07 '04
0.165	Nov. 03	Nov. 10	Nov. 15	Dec. 06 '04

Revenues/Earnings Data Fiscal year ending September 30

Revenues (Million $)

	2004	2003	2002	2001	2000	1999
1Q	1,016	984.0	939.0	1,107	1,660	1,608
2Q	1,113	1,029	958.0	1,171	1,784	1,701
3Q	1,164	1,033	995.0	1,027	1,820	1,808
4Q	1,206	1,058	1,017	974.0	1,887	1,926
Yr.	4,411	4,104	3,909	4,279	7,151	7,043

Earnings Per Share ($)

	2004	2003	2002	2001	2000	1999
1Q	0.30	0.22	0.16	0.38	0.81	0.70
2Q	0.41	0.26	0.31	0.38	0.85	0.74
3Q	0.66	0.67	0.47	-0.15	0.90	0.77
4Q	0.51	0.33	0.26	0.07	0.78	0.80
Yr.	1.85	1.49	1.20	0.68	3.35	3.01

Next earnings report expected: late-January Source: S&P, Company Reports
EPS Estimates based on S&P Operating Earnings; historical GAAP earnings are as reported.

Rockwell Automation, Inc.

Recommendation: **HOLD** ★ ★ ★ ★ ★   12-Month Target Price: **$45.00** (as of November 04, 2004)

Business Summary November 09, 2004

In the early 1990s, Rockwell Automation (formerly Rockwell International) operated a broad range of manufacturing businesses: military electronics, semiconductor equipment, telecom gear, truck parts and automated equipment. Following a series of divestitures that included the June 2001 spinoff of Rockwell Collins, the company now focuses primarily on automation products and platforms. Its three main operating segments are Control Systems, Power Systems, and FirstPoint Contact (formerly Electronic Commerce).

The Control Systems (CS) segment (80% of FY 03 revenues and 88% of operating profits; 12% profit margins) supplies industrial automation products, systems, software and services focused on helping customers improve control and improve manufacturing processes. CS is divided into three units: the Components and Packaged Applications Group (CPAG); the Automation Control and Information Group (ACIG); and Global Manufacturing Solutions (GMS).

CPAG (40% of CS sales) produces industrial components, power control and motor management products. ACIG (40%) products include programmable logic controllers (PLCs), which are used to automate the control and monitoring of industrial plants and processes. GMS (20%) provides multi-vendor automation and information systems and solutions designed to help customers improve their manufacturing operations. These products are marketed primarily under the Rockwell Automation, Allen-Bradley, and Rockwell Software brand names. Major markets served include consumer products, food and beverage, transportation, metals,

mining, pulp and paper, petroleum, specialty chemicals, pharmaceuticals, electric power, water treatment, electronic assembly, and semiconductor fabrication. Competitors include Emerson Electric, GE, Schneider Electric, and Siemens. Over the past five years, segment margins averaged 14.5%.

The Power Systems segment (17%, 12%; 8%) makes power transmission components, gear reducers, speed drives, shaft mounted reducers, conveyor pulleys, shaft couplings, clutches, motor brakes, mounted bearings and motors. Products are marketed mainly under the Dodge and Reliance Electric brand names. Major markets served include mining, aggregate, food/beverage, forestry, petrochemicals, metals, unit handling, air handling and environmental. Competitors include ABB Ltd., Baldor Electric Co., Emerson, GE, Regal-Beloit Corp., and Siemens. Over the past five years, margins for this segment averaged 6.7%.

The FirstPoint Contact segment (3%, 0%; 0.9%) makes products that include automatic call distributors, computer telephony integration software, information collection, reporting, queuing and management systems, call center systems and consulting services. Major markets served include service, transportation, energy, health care, retail, telecommunications and financial. Competitors include Apropos Technology, Inc., Aspect Communications Corp., Avaya, Inc., Cisco Systems, and Nortel Networks. Over the past five years, segment margins averaged about 1%.

Company Financials Fiscal Year ending September 30

Per Share Data ($)

(Year Ended September 30)	2004	2003	2002	2001	2000	1999	1998	1997	1996	1995
Tangible Bk. Val.	NA	2.41	2.61	2.23	6.90	6.56	10.05	14.67	11.17	8.08
Cash Flow	NA	2.53	2.29	5.39	4.80	4.74	0.99	5.00	5.03	6.05
Earnings	1.85	1.49	1.20	0.68	3.35	3.01	-0.55	2.97	2.55	3.42
S&P Core Earnings	NA	1.16	0.75	-0.06	NA	NA	NA	NA	NA	NA
Dividends	0.66	0.66	0.66	0.93	1.02	1.02	1.02	1.16	1.16	1.08
Payout Ratio	36%	44%	55%	137%	30%	34%	NM	42%	45%	32%
Prices - High	45.98	36.10	22.79	49.45	54.50	64.93	61.62	70.62	64.62	48.00
- Low	28.45	18.75	14.71	11.78	27.68	39.93	32.12	44.37	47.50	35.00
P/E Ratio - High	25	24	19	73	16	22	NM	26	25	14
- Low	15	13	12	17	8	13	NM	16	19	10

Income Statement Analysis (Million $)

	2004	2003	2002	2001	2000	1999	1998	1997	1996	1995
Revs.	NA	4,104	3,909	4,279	7,151	7,043	6,752	7,762	10,373	12,981
Oper. Inc.	NA	543	488	1,079	1,223	1,203	1,001	1,367	1,544	1,849
Depr.	NA	198	206	872	276	337	306	484	542	571
Int. Exp.	NA	52.0	66.0	83.0	73.0	84.0	58.0	27.0	32.0	170
Pretax Inc.	NA	299	233	168	943	890	25.0	923	896	1,226
Eff. Tax Rate	NA	5.69%	3.00%	25.6%	32.6%	34.6%	536.0%	36.5%	38.1%	39.4%
Net Inc.	NA	282	226	125	636	582	-109	586	555	742
S&P Core Earnings	NA	220	142	-12.0	NA	NA	NA	NA	NA	NA

Balance Sheet & Other Fin. Data (Million $)

	2004	2003	2002	2001	2000	1999	1998	1997	1996	1995
Cash	NA	226	289	121	190	356	103	283	715	665
Curr. Assets	NA	1,736	1,775	1,697	3,206	3,582	4,096	3,684	5,358	5,805
Total Assets	NA	3,986	4,024	4,074	6,390	6,704	7,170	7,971	10,065	12,505
Curr. Liab.	NA	820	966	867	1,820	2,108	1,983	1,970	4,281	4,111
LT Debt	NA	764	767	922	924	911	908	156	161	1,776
Common Equity	NA	1,587	1,609	1,600	2,669	2,637	3,245	4,811	4,256	3,781
Total Cap.	NA	2,388	2,534	2,693	3,593	3,548	4,153	4,967	4,417	5,558
Cap. Exp.	NA	109	104	157	315	377	408	683	866	685
Cash Flow	NA	480	432	997	912	919	197	1,070	1,097	1,313
Curr. Ratio	NA	2.1	1.8	2.0	1.8	1.7	2.1	1.9	1.3	1.4
% LT Debt of Cap.	NA	32.0	30.3	34.2	25.7	25.7	21.9	3.2	3.6	31.9
% Net Inc.of Revs.	NA	6.9	5.8	2.9	8.9	8.3	NM	7.5	5.4	5.7
% Ret. on Assets	NA	7.1	5.6	2.7	9.8	8.4	NM	6.5	5.8	6.6
% Ret. on Equity	NA	17.6	14.1	5.9	24.4	19.8	NM	12.9	13.8	20.7

Data as orig. reptd.; bef. results of disc. opers. and/or spec. items. Per share data adj. for stk. divs.; EPS diluted. E-Estimated. NA-Not Available. NM-Not Meaningful. NR-Not Ranked.

Office: 777 East Wisconsin Avenue, Milwaukee, WI 53202.
Telephone: 414-212-5200.
Website: http://www.rockwellautomation.com
Chrmn & CEO: D.H. Davis, Jr.
SVP & CFO: M.A. Bless.

SVP, Secy & General Counsel: D.M. Hagerman.
Investor Contact: N.J. Franz 414-212-5211.
Dirs: B. C. Alewine, J. M. Cook, D. H. Davis, Jr., W. H. Gray III, V. Istock, W. T. McCormick, Jr., B. M. Rockwell, D. Speer, J. F. Toot, Jr., K. F. Yontz.

Founded: in 1928.
Domicile: Delaware.
Employees: 21,500.
S&P Analyst: John F. Hingher, CFA /PMW/BK

Rockwell Collins

Recommendation: **HOLD** ★ ★ ★ ★ ★   12-Month Target Price: **$37.00**
(as of October 12, 2004)

COL has an approximate 0.06% weighting in the **S&P 500**

Sector: Industrials
Sub-Industry: Aerospace & Defense
Peer Group: Aerospace/Defense Instrumentation

Summary: COL is one of the world's largest makers of commercial and military cockpit controls.

Quantitative Evaluations

S&P Earnings & Dividend Rank: NR

D	C	B-	B	B+	A-	A	A+

S&P Fair Value Rank: 4

1	2	3	4	5
Lowest				Highest

Fair Value Calc.: $39.10 (Fairly Valued)

S&P Investability Quotient Percentile

95%

COL scored higher than 95% of all companies for which an S&P Report is available.

Volatility: Average

Low	Average	High

Technical Evaluation: Bullish

Since 11/04, the technical indicators for COL have been Bullish.

Relative Strength Rank: Strong

74

1 Lowest	Highest 99

Price as of 11/12/04:	**$39.77**	2005E S&P Core EPS:	**$1.54**

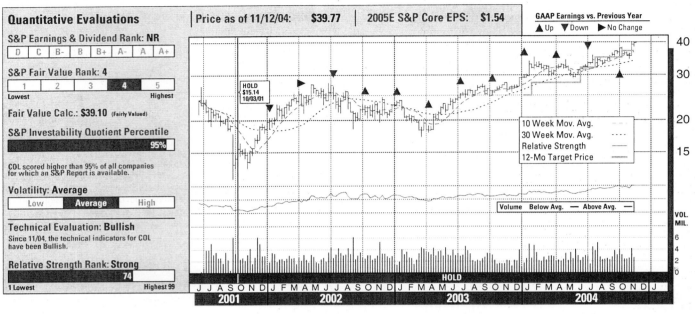

GAAP Earnings vs. Previous Year
▲ Up ▼ Down ▶ No Change

HOLD $15.14 10/03/01

- - - 10 Week Mov. Avg.
······ 30 Week Mov. Avg.
—— Relative Strength
▨▨ 12-Mo Target Price

Volume Below Avg. —— Above Avg.

Analyst commentary prepared by Robert E. Friedman, CPA /DC/BK

Highlights October 13, 2004

- We are estimating that COL will post about a 10% hike in FY 05 (Sep.) revenues, driven by an expected 12%+ advance in higher-margin government/military aircraft-related component sales (54% of revenues), and an 8% rise in commercial aerospace-related component sales (46%).

- Consequently, we project that the volume sales hikes will allow operating profit margins (earnings before interest and taxes, or EBIT) to expand to about 16%, primarily driven by the greater proportion of higher-margin military electronics sales. As a result, we are forecasting that COL will post a FY 05 reported EPS increase of about 16%, to $1.94, and an S&P Core EPS advance of 19%, to $1.54. In addition, we estimate that COL will be able to generate return on equity (ROE) exceeding 20%.

- Looking at the company's long-term prospects, we believe COL can post cash earnings growth of 7.5% to 10% annually, with 15% to 20% ROE. However, we see mature commercial aircraft markets as well as the substantial bargaining power of the company's largest airline customers limiting the magnitude of future potential earnings growth and returns.

Investment Rationale/Risk October 13, 2004

- We are maintaining our hold opinion on COL, as the stock is trading near our revised DCF-based 12-month target price of $37 a share.

- Risks to our recommendation and target price include any unexpected structural deterioration in COL's primary commercial and military endmarkets, and/or structural deterioration in COL's underlying business economics.

- Our free cash flow model, which values COL basically by adding the sum of cash earnings with projected 10-year compound annual growth rates (CAGR) of 7.5% to 10%, and at 3.0% thereafter, values COL at about $37, which is our 12-month target price. We calculated our CAGR assumptions by multiplying our sustainable 15% to 20% average ROE estimates by one minus our projected 50% earnings retention rate. Our relative valuation model, which compares a company's earnings yield with 10-year AAA-rated bond yields, supports our opinion that the stock is trading near our fair value appraisals. Based on our FY 05 S&P Core EPS estimate of $1.54, the stock is generating an earnings yield of 4.3%, near 10-year AAA bond yields of about 4.7%.

Key Stock Statistics

S&P Oper. EPS 2005E	**1.94**	52-week Range	**$39.89-25.72**
P/E on S&P Oper. EPS 2005E	**20.5**	12 Month P/E	**23.8**
Yield (%)	**1.2%**	Beta	**NA**
Dividend Rate/Share	**0.48**	Shareholders	**35,508**
Shares Outstanding (M)	**177.0**	Market Cap (B)	**$ 7.0**

Value of $10,000 invested five years ago: **NA**

Dividend Data Dividends have been paid since 2001

Amount ($)	Date Decl.	Ex-Div. Date	Stock of Record	Payment Date
0.090	Feb. 11	Feb. 19	Feb. 23	Mar. 15 '04
0.090	May. 03	May. 13	May. 17	Jun. 07 '04
0.120	Jun. 30	Aug. 10	Aug. 12	Sep. 07 '04
0.120	Nov. 02	Nov. 10	Nov. 15	Dec. 06 '04

Revenues/Earnings Data Fiscal year ending September 30

Revenues (Million $)

	2004	2003	2002	2001	2000	1999
1Q	628.0	561.0	563.0	587.0	563.0	—
2Q	719.0	618.0	608.0	690.0	618.0	—
3Q	744.0	620.0	623.0	727.0	627.0	—
4Q	839.0	743.0	698.0	816.0	702.0	—
Yr.	2,930	2,542	2,492	2,820	2,510	—

Earnings Per Share ($)

	2004	2003	2002	2001	2000	1999
1Q	0.38	0.27	0.26	0.30	—	—
2Q	0.39	0.33	0.31	0.31	—	—
3Q	0.42	0.43	0.33	0.36	—	—
4Q	0.48	0.40	0.38	-0.26	—	—
Yr.	1.67	1.43	1.28	0.72	1.35	—

Next earnings report expected: late-January Source: S&P, Company Reports
EPS Estimates based on S&P Operating Earnings; historical GAAP earnings are as reported.

Rockwell Collins, Inc.

Recommendation: **HOLD** ★★★ ☆☆   12-Month Target Price: **$37.00** (as of October 12, 2004)

Business Summary October 13, 2004

Rockwell Collins is a major global cockpit controls maker. It conducts its business through two operating segments: Commercial Systems and Government Systems.

Commercial Systems, which accounted for 50% of revenues and 35% of operating profits in FY 03 (Sep.), and had 11% operating profit margins, primarily makes cockpit control equipment and inflight entertainment systems. CS also provides a range of repair and overhaul services.

The segment sells to the large-passenger jet market (manufacturers and big airlines) and the small-passenger jet market (regional and business jet makers and regional airlines). Primary large-jet manufacturing customers include Boeing and Airbus. Principal small-jet makers include Canada's Bombardier, Brazil's Embraer, the General Dynamics Gulfstream unit, and Textron's Cessna division. The commercial aviation electronics equipment market totals $4.5 billion.

The cockpit controls business is concentrated: Honeywell, COL, and France's Thales account for substantially all industry sales. The inflight entertainment industry operates as a duopoly, with the company and Japan's Matsushita each controlling about 50% of the market.

Demand for commercial aviation electronics (avionics) is primarily driven by airline profitability and air traffic growth. Based on Air Transport Association statistics, from 1993 through 2002, the U.S. airline industry generated operating earnings as high as $5.4 billion, and losses as much as $11.3 billion. Based on the latest statistics provided by independent aviation research firm Avitas, Inc., from 1991 through 2001, passenger air traffic grew at a 2.2% annual rate. From 1994 through 2003, demand for commercial aircraft cockpit controls grew at a 2.0% average annual rate, based on statistics provided by the Aerospace Industries Association (AIA).

Government Systems (45%; 53%; 17%) primarily makes communication radios and cockpit displays installed in military jets. The segment also makes navigation equipment embedded in guided missiles. Major customers include defense industry giants Lockheed Martin, Raytheon, and Northrop Grumman. COL's served military market stands at about $6 billion. The company competes primarily with Raytheon.

Demand for military cockpit controls is driven by growth in the procurement and research & development segments of the U.S. military budget (40% of global military spending). In turn, growth in procurement and R&D budgets is driven by the U.S. military's anticipated long-term needs, the current geopolitical environment, and U.S. government budget allocations.

Based on U.S. Defense Department statistics, in the last 10 years (government FY 94 (Oct.) through FY 03), procurement and R&D budgets grew at 1.8% and 3.0% average annual rates, respectively. From 1994 through 2003, defense-related cockpit controls equipment grew at a 4.1% average annual rate, based on statistics provided by the AIA.

Fixed price contracts (which typically generate profit margins of 10% to 15%), versus cost-plus contracts (which typically generate profit margins of 5% to 9%), accounted for 90% of 2003 total sales.

Company Financials Fiscal Year ending September 30

Per Share Data ($)

(Year Ended September 30)	2004	2003	2002	2001	2000	1999	1998	1997	1996	1995
Tangible Bk. Val.	NA	2.21	2.93	4.48	NA	NA	NA	NA	NA	NA
Cash Flow	NA	2.02	1.85	1.47	1.87	NA	NA	NA	NA	NA
Earnings	1.67	1.43	1.28	0.72	1.35	NA	NA	NA	NA	NA
S&P Core Earnings	NA	0.82	0.46	NA	NA	NA	NA	NA	NA	NA
Dividends	0.39	0.36	0.36	Nil	NA	NA	NA	NA	NA	NA
Payout Ratio	23%	25%	28%	Nil	NA	NA	NA	NA	NA	NA
Prices - High	39.89	30.10	28.00	27.12	NA	NA	NA	NA	NA	NA
- Low	29.16	17.20	18.50	11.80	NA	NA	NA	NA	NA	NA
P/E Ratio - High	24	21	22	38	NA	NA	NA	NA	NA	NA
- Low	17	12	14	16	NA	NA	NA	NA	NA	NA

Income Statement Analysis (Million $)

	2004	2003	2002	2001	2000	1999	1998	1997	1996	1995
Revs.	NA	2,542	2,492	2,820	2,510	NA	NA	NA	NA	NA
Oper. Inc.	NA	440	427	492	492	NA	NA	NA	NA	NA
Depr.	NA	105	105	131	99	NA	NA	NA	NA	NA
Int. Exp.	NA	3.00	6.00	3.00	20.0	NA	NA	NA	NA	NA
Pretax Inc.	NA	368	341	224	381	NA	NA	NA	NA	NA
Eff. Tax Rate	NA	29.9%	30.8%	37.9%	32.5%	NA	NA	NA	NA	NA
Net Inc.	NA	258	236	139	257	NA	NA	NA	NA	NA
S&P Core Earnings	NA	148	86.8	59.1	NA	NA	NA	NA	NA	NA

Balance Sheet & Other Fin. Data (Million $)

	2004	2003	2002	2001	2000	1999	1998	1997	1996	1995
Cash	NA	66.0	49.0	60.0	20.0	NA	NA	NA	NA	NA
Curr. Assets	NA	1,427	1,438	1,639	1,531	NA	NA	NA	NA	NA
Total Assets	NA	2,591	2,560	2,628	2,628	NA	NA	NA	NA	NA
Curr. Liab.	NA	901	1,043	1,135	1,073	NA	NA	NA	NA	NA
LT Debt	NA	Nil	Nil	Nil	Nil	NA	NA	NA	NA	NA
Common Equity	NA	833	987	1,110	1,086	NA	NA	NA	NA	NA
Total Cap.	NA	833	987	1,110	1,086	NA	NA	NA	NA	NA
Cap. Exp.	NA	72.0	62.0	110	NA	NA	NA	NA	NA	NA
Cash Flow	NA	363	341	270	356	NA	NA	NA	NA	NA
Curr. Ratio	NA	1.6	1.4	1.4	1.4	NA	NA	NA	NA	NA
% LT Debt of Cap.	NA	Nil	Nil	Nil	Nil	NA	NA	NA	NA	NA
% Net Inc.of Revs.	NA	10.1	9.5	4.9	10.2	NA	NA	NA	NA	NA
% Ret. on Assets	NA	10.0	9.1	5.9	NA	NA	NA	NA	NA	NA
% Ret. on Equity	NA	28.4	22.5	13.8	NA	NA	NA	NA	NA	NA

Data as orig reptd.; bef. results of disc opers/spec. items. Per share data adj. for stk. divs. Bold denotes primary EPS -prior periods restated. Pro forma data in 2000, bal. sh. as of Mar. 31, 2001. E-Estimated. NA-Not Available. NM-Not Meaningful. NR-Not Ranked.

Office: 400 Collins Road NE, Cedar Rapids, IA 52498.
Telephone: 319-295-6835.
Email: investorrelations@rockwellcollins.com
Website: http://www.rockwellcollins.com
Chrmn, Pres & CEO: C.M. Jones.

COO & EVP: R.M. Chiusano.
SVP & CFO: L.A. Erickson.
SVP, Secy & General Counsel: G.R. Chadick.
VP & Treas: P.E. Allen.
Investor Contact: D. Brehm 319-295-7575.

Dirs: D. R. Beall, A. J. Carbone, M. P. Carns, C. A. Davis, R. J. Ferris, C. L. Shavers, J. F. Toot, Jr.
Employees: 14,300.
S&P Analyst: Robert E. Friedman, CPA /DC/BK

Rohm & Haas

Recommendation: **HOLD** ★★★☆
SELL · SELL · HOLD · BUY · BUY

12-Month Target Price: $44.00
(as of December 18, 2003)

ROH has an approximate 0.09% weighting in the **S&P 500**

Sector: Materials
Sub-Industry: Specialty Chemicals
Peer Group: Specialty Chemicals (Larger)

Summary: One of the world's largest producers of specialty chemicals and plastics, ROH also supplies salt products.

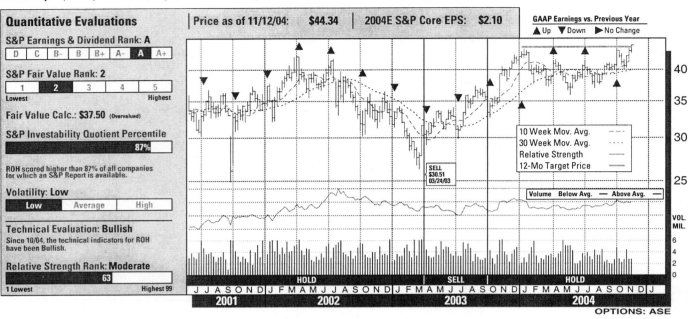

Quantitative Evaluations

S&P Earnings & Dividend Rank: A
D | C | B- | B | B+ | A- | **A** | A+

S&P Fair Value Rank: 2
1 | **2** | 3 | 4 | 5
Lowest — Highest

Fair Value Calc.: $37.50 (Overvalued)

S&P Investability Quotient Percentile
87%
ROH scored higher than 87% of all companies for which an S&P Report is available.

Volatility: Low
Low | Average | High

Technical Evaluation: Bullish
Since 10/04, the technical indicators for ROH have been Bullish.

Relative Strength Rank: Moderate
63
1 Lowest — Highest 99

Price as of 11/12/04: $44.34 | **2004E S&P Core EPS:** $2.10

GAAP Earnings vs. Previous Year
▲ Up ▼ Down ► No Change

10 Week Mov. Avg.
30 Week Mov. Avg.
Relative Strength
12-Mo Target Price

SELL $30.51 03/24/03

Volume Below Avg. — Above Avg.

HOLD | SELL | HOLD
J J A S O N D | J F M A M J J A S O N D | J F M A M J J A S O N D | J F M A M J J A S O N D | J
2001 | 2002 | 2003 | 2004

OPTIONS: ASE

Analyst commentary prepared by Richard O'Reilly, CFA /CB/GG

Highlights September 13, 2004

- We expect sales to grow about 12% in 2004, aided by favorable currency rates and price increases announced in response to a rapid rise in raw material costs. We see volume growth in the mid- to high single digit range, versus 2003's 2.5% rate, for most chemicals-related segments.

- We see 2004 salt sales likely to be similar to those of 2003, which included strong demand for ice control salt, due to severe weather in early 2003. ROH did not make any acquisitions in 2003, and reduced debt by about $378 million. Interest expense should edge up from 2003's level, due to reduced capitalized interest expense, despite further debt reduction during the year.

- We believe hikes in selling prices will offset about 50% of a projected $250 million increase (with the majority in the second half) in raw material costs for 2004. We expect the adhesives business to begin to recover in 2004, as a result of restructuring actions of the past two years. We project an effective tax rate of about 30%, down from 2003's 32.3%. In 2004, we expect pension expense to be $0.09 a share higher than last year, and stock option expense modestly lower.

Investment Rationale/Risk September 13, 2004

- We have a hold opinion on the stock. We view the company's fundamentals as somewhat favorable, although the gap between raw material costs and selling prices has widened during 2004, due to a rapid rise in raw material costs. We expect to see improved volume growth in both 2004 and 2005, after relatively flat volumes for most of 2003. Based on our 2005 EPS estimate, the shares were recently trading at a P/E multiple modestly above that of the S&P 500 and specialty chemicals peers.

- Risks to our recommendation and target price include ROH's inability to offset unexpected increases in raw material costs and successfully introduce new products.

- Our 12-month target price is $44, based on a historical trailing 12-month P/E multiple applied to our 2005 EPS estimate. The dividend, increased in 2004 for the 27th consecutive year, provides an above-market average yield that we expect to continue to advance over the longer term.

Key Stock Statistics

S&P Core EPS 2005E	2.31	52-week Range	$44.34-35.90
S&P Oper. EPS 2004E	2.15	12 Month P/E	20.8
P/E on S&P Oper. EPS 2004E	20.6	Beta	1.01
S&P Oper. EPS 2005E	2.40	Shareholders	9,037
Yield (%)	2.3%	Market Cap (B)	$ 10.0
Dividend Rate/Share	1.00	Shares Outstanding (M)	224.8

Value of $10,000 invested five years ago: **$ 12,851**

Dividend Data Dividends have been paid since 1927

Amount ($)	Date Decl.	Ex-Div. Date	Stock of Record	Payment Date
0.220	Feb. 02	Feb. 11	Feb. 13	Mar. 01 '04
0.250	May. 03	May. 12	May. 14	Jun. 01 '04
0.250	Jul. 26	Aug. 11	Aug. 13	Sep. 01 '04
0.250	Sep. 24	Nov. 03	Nov. 05	Dec. 01 '04

Revenues/Earnings Data Fiscal year ending December 31

Revenues (Million $)

	2004	2003	2002	2001	2000	1999
1Q	1,832	1,613	1,381	1,572	1,765	940.0
2Q	1,801	1,570	1,457	1,408	1,771	1,144
3Q	1,803	1,591	1,454	1,346	1,693	1,577
4Q	—	1,647	1,435	1,340	1,650	1,678
Yr.	—	6,421	5,727	5,666	6,879	5,339

Earnings Per Share ($)

	2004	2003	2002	2001	2000	1999
1Q	0.51	0.37	0.38	0.22	0.56	0.64
2Q	0.52	-0.02	0.42	-0.94	0.35	-0.06
3Q	0.61	0.45	0.35	0.24	0.38	0.26
4Q	E0.51	0.49	0.16	0.17	0.32	0.41
Yr.	E2.15	1.30	0.98	-0.31	1.61	1.27

Next earnings report expected: early-February Source: S&P, Company Reports
EPS Estimates based on S&P Operating Earnings; historical GAAP earnings are as reported.

Rohm and Haas Company

Recommendation: **HOLD** ★ ★ ★ ☆ ☆    12-Month Target Price: **$44.00** (as of December 18, 2003)

Business Summary September 14, 2004

Rohm & Haas is one of the world's largest specialty chemical companies, with annual sales of about $6.5 billion. As a result of the 1999 purchase of Morton International Inc., the company is now a leading global maker of chemicals used in coatings, adhesives, sealants, plastics, and electronic materials. ROH is the world's largest producer of acrylic acid, used in many of its products.

International operations accounted for 53% of sales in 2003.

Coatings (30% of sales and 31% of income in 2003) include polymers and resins (including opaque polymers, emulsions, rheology modifiers, binders, thickeners, dispersants) for paints, coatings, inks, paper, textile, nonwoven materials, construction products and leather finishes. The segment also includes liquid and powder coatings for automobiles, appliances, furniture and equipment. In September 2002, the company acquired the powder coatings business of Ferro Corp., for $60 million. The purchase boosted annual sales of ROH's powder coatings business to $300 million. Adhesives and sealants (9%, 2%) consist of materials for use in pressure sensitive tapes and labels, laminated food packaging, graphic arts, and industrial products.

Performance chemicals (19%, 12%) include plastic additives (global supplier of impact modifiers, processing aids, thermal stabilizers and lubricants); consumer and industrial specialties (biocides, water-soluble polymers, dispersants, an-

timicrobials, and scale inhibitors for industrial, household cleaning and personal care products); and process chemicals (ion exchange and fluid process chemicals for water treatment and food and chemical processing, and inorganic chemicals (sodium borohydride)). The monomer segment (16%, 19%) produces methyl methacrylate, acrylic acid and specialty monomer.

The electronic materials segment (15%, 23%) provides technology for use in telecommunications, consumer electronics and household appliances. Microelectronics (about 57% of segment sales) provides an extensive assortment of critical chemicals needed to reproduce complicated circuitry designs on integrated circuits. Rodel provides high-tech pads and slurries used to make ultra smooth and uniform layers on integrated circuits. The printed wiring board business provides essential chemistry for use in the manufacture of high-density printed circuits and circuit boards, and the electronic and industrial finishing business provides coatings processes for interconnection, corrosion resistant, and decorative applications.

Salt (11%, 13%) includes Morton, the leading consumer salt brand in the U.S., and the Windsor brand in Canada; it also sells products for animal consumption, water conditioning, highway and residential ice control, and food and industrial processing.

Company Financials Fiscal Year ending December 31

Per Share Data ($)

(Year Ended December 31)	2003	2002	2001	2000	1999	1998	1997	1996	1995	1994
Tangible Bk. Val.	0.13	NM	NM	NM	NM	8.77	8.51	7.84	7.58	6.70
Cash Flow	3.44	3.04	2.24	4.39	5.87	4.04	3.67	3.19	2.60	2.40
Earnings	1.30	0.98	-0.31	1.61	1.27	2.52	2.13	1.82	1.41	1.26
S&P Core Earnings	0.90	0.23	-0.91	NA	NA	NA	NA	NA	NA	NA
Dividends	0.86	0.82	0.80	0.78	0.74	0.69	0.63	0.57	0.52	0.48
Payout Ratio	66%	84%	NM	48%	58%	27%	30%	32%	37%	38%
Prices - High	43.05	42.60	38.70	49.43	49.25	38.87	33.75	27.50	21.62	22.83
- Low	26.26	30.19	24.90	24.37	28.12	26.00	23.54	18.29	16.50	17.75
P/E Ratio - High	33	43	NM	31	39	15	16	15	15	18
- Low	20	31	NM	15	22	10	11	10	12	14

Income Statement Analysis (Million $)

	2003	2002	2001	2000	1999	1998	1997	1996	1995	1994
Revs.	6,421	5,727	5,666	6,879	5,339	3,720	3,999	3,986	3,884	3,545
Oper. Inc.	1,264	1,066	973	1,395	1,220	898	896	839	765	717
Depr.	478	457	562	613	902	276	279	262	242	231
Int. Exp.	126	132	182	241	159	34.0	39.0	54.0	57.0	60.0
Pretax Inc.	415	320	-64.0	576	465	690	616	530	441	407
Eff. Tax Rate	30.6%	31.9%	NM	39.4%	46.2%	34.1%	32.6%	31.5%	33.8%	35.1%
Net Inc.	288	218	-70.0	354	249	453	410	363	292	264
S&P Core Earnings	200	50.9	-202	NA	NA	NA	NA	NA	NA	NA

Balance Sheet & Other Fin. Data (Million $)

	2003	2002	2001	2000	1999	1998	1997	1996	1995	1994
Cash	196	295	92.0	92.0	57.0	16.0	40.0	11.0	43.0	127
Curr. Assets	2,527	2,543	2,421	2,781	2,497	1,287	1,397	1,456	1,421	1,440
Total Assets	9,445	9,706	10,350	11,267	11,256	3,648	3,900	3,933	3,916	3,861
Curr. Liab.	1,797	1,621	1,624	2,194	2,510	875	850	886	828	932
LT Debt	2,468	2,872	2,720	3,225	3,122	409	509	562	606	629
Common Equity	3,357	3,333	3,815	3,693	3,475	1,488	1,671	1,597	1,648	1,486
Total Cap.	6,775	7,402	7,831	8,228	7,847	2,157	2,510	2,501	2,550	2,402
Cap. Exp.	339	407	401	391	323	229	254	334	417	339
Cash Flow	766	675	492	967	1,149	723	682	625	527	488
Curr. Ratio	1.4	1.6	1.5	1.3	1.0	1.5	1.6	1.6	1.7	1.5
% LT Debt of Cap.	36.4	38.8	34.7	39.2	39.8	19.0	20.2	22.5	23.8	26.2
% Net Inc.of Revs.	4.5	3.8	NM	5.1	4.7	12.2	10.3	9.1	7.5	7.4
% Ret. on Assets	3.0	2.2	NM	3.1	3.3	12.0	10.5	9.2	7.5	7.1
% Ret. on Equity	8.9	5.9	NM	9.8	10.0	28.3	24.7	21.9	18.2	18.4

Data as orig reptd.; bef. results of disc opers/spec. items. Per share data adj. for stk. divs.; EPS diluted. E-Estimated. NA-Not Available. NM-Not Meaningful. NR-Not Ranked. UR-Under Review.

Office: 100 Independence Mall West, Philadelphia, PA 19106.
Telephone: 215-592-3000.
Website: http://www.rohmhaas.com
Chrmn & CEO: R.L. Gupta.
Pres & COO: J.M. Fitzpatrick.
VP & CFO: J.M. Croisetiere.

VP, Secy & General Counsel: R.A. Lonergan.
Investor Contact: G.S. O'Brien 215-592-2928.
Dirs: W. J. Avery, J. M. Fitzpatrick, E. G. Graves, Sr., R. L. Gupta, D. W. Haas, T. W. Haas, J. A. Henderson, R. L. Keyser, J. P. Montoya, S. O. Moose, G. S. Omenn, G. L. Rogers, R. H. Schmitz, M. C. Whittington.

Founded: in 1909.
Domicile: Delaware.
Employees: 17,245.
S&P Analyst: Richard O'Reilly, CFA /CB/GG

Rowan Companies

Recommendation: **BUY** ★★★★☆
SELL SELL HOLD BUY BUY

12-Month Target Price: $29.00
(as of July 15, 2004)

RDC has an approximate 0.02% weighting in the **S&P 500**

Sector: Energy
Sub-Industry: Oil & Gas Drilling
Peer Group: Oil & Gas - Offshore Drilling

Summary: RDC performs contract oil and natural gas drilling, provides contract aviation services, and builds heavy equipment and offshore drilling rigs.

Quantitative Evaluations

S&P Earnings & Dividend Rank: B-

| D | C | B- | B | B+ | A- | A | A+ |

S&P Fair Value Rank: 1-

| 1 | 2 | 3 | 4 | 5 |
| Lowest | | | | Highest |

Fair Value Calc.: $19.70 (Overvalued)

S&P Investability Quotient Percentile

75%

RDC scored higher than 75% of all companies for which an S&P Report is available.

Volatility: Average

| Low | Average | High |

Technical Evaluation: Neutral
Since 11/04, the technical indicators for RDC have been Neutral.

Relative Strength Rank: Weak

23

| 1 Lowest | Highest 99 |

| Price as of 11/12/04: | $24.67 | 2004E S&P Core EPS: | $0.13 |

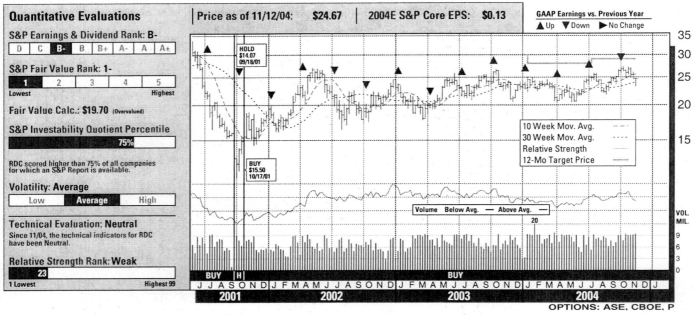

GAAP Earnings vs. Previous Year
▲ Up ▼ Down ► No Change

- 10 Week Mov. Avg.
- 30 Week Mov. Avg.
- Relative Strength
- 12-Mo Target Price

Volume Below Avg. — Above Avg. —

OPTIONS: ASE, CBOE, P

Analyst commentary prepared by Stewart Glickman/DC/BK

Highlights October 18, 2004

- Third quarter EPS fell slightly shy of our expectations, but Gulf of Mexico (GOM) utilization improved sequentially to 97%, from 88%. GOM dayrates were 19% higher year to year, and 10% higher sequentially. Looking to the rest of 2004 and to 2005, we expect the number of rigs mobilizing away from the Gulf of Mexico to other regions in the world to dwindle, as the tightening jackup supply situation is yielding improved dayrates, and expected drilling activity in the GOM for 2005 should be robust. RDC has typically commanded a higher average dayrate than the industry, due to a larger number of premium jackups. We see this trend continuing.

- All told, we estimate return on capital employed of 1.4% for 2004, with an increase to 4.7% for 2005. In October, the company said that all 24 of its offshore rigs had been under contract since June, and the company's land rigs had been 100% utilized for 21 consecutive months.

- For 2004, we estimate EPS before one-time impairment charges of $0.23, followed by a gain to $0.82 in 2005. On a Standard & Poor's Core Earnings basis, we project EPS of $0.13 and $0.71 in the respective years.

Investment Rationale/Risk October 18, 2004

- We recommend accumulating the stock. Through mid October, the shares were up 12% in 2004, versus an increase of 29% for the S&P Oil & Gas Drilling Index. The shares traded recently at an enterprise value of 11.4X our 2005 EBITDA estimate, below the peer average of 11.9X. However, we note that the shares have historically traded at a premium to peer levels. We look for EBITDA to rise nearly 60% in 2004, and to increase nearly another 80% in 2005. The shares are trading in line with peers on a price to operating cash flow basis, and at a slight premium on a price to net equity basis.

- Risks to our recommendation and target price include lower than expected dayrates and utilization; reduced drilling activity in the GOM; and delays in rig redeployments that might lead to lost operating days.

- Our 12-month target price of $29 is based on a blend of enterprise value to estimated 2005 EBITDA, price to operating cash flow and price to net equity valuations. We assume that the shares should trade an an enterprise value of 12.5X projected 2005 EBITDA, in line with the stock's historical average.

Key Stock Statistics

S&P Core EPS 2005E	0.71	52-week Range	$27.26-20.44
S&P Oper. EPS 2004E	0.23	12 Month P/E	NM
P/E on S&P Oper. EPS 2004E	NM	Beta	1.36
S&P Oper. EPS 2005E	0.82	Shareholders	2,000
Yield (%)	Nil	Market Cap (B)	$ 2.6
Dividend Rate/Share	Nil	Shares Outstanding (M)	106.8

Value of $10,000 invested five years ago: **$ 17,345**

Dividend Data

No cash dividends have been paid.

Revenues/Earnings Data Fiscal year ending December 31

Revenues (Million $)

	2004	2003	2002	2001	2000	1999
1Q	170.5	131.3	137.8	193.5	127.7	100.0
2Q	190.9	158.1	148.5	210.4	143.2	119.2
3Q	234.6	193.9	184.2	191.3	190.8	119.9
4Q	—	195.8	146.8	135.8	184.2	121.4
Yr.	—	679.1	617.3	731.1	646.0	460.6

Earnings Per Share ($)

	2004	2003	2002	2001	2000	1999
1Q	-0.11	-0.18	0.92	0.33	0.07	-0.12
2Q	-0.02	-0.07	-0.09	0.36	0.12	-0.03
3Q	0.09	0.12	0.11	0.22	0.27	0.01
4Q	E0.21	0.05	-0.03	-0.10	0.29	0.03
Yr.	E0.23	-0.08	0.90	0.80	0.74	-0.12

Next earnings report expected: mid-January Source: S&P, Company Reports
EPS Estimates based on S&P Operating Earnings; historical GAAP earnings are as reported.

Rowan Companies, Inc.

Recommendation: **BUY** ★ ★ ★ ☆   12-Month Target Price: **$29.00** (as of July 15, 2004)

Business Summary October 18, 2004

Rowan Companies, a major provider of international and domestic contract drilling and aviation services, also operates a mini-steel mill, a manufacturing facility that produces heavy equipment, and a marine construction division.

At the end of 2003, RDC owned a fleet of 42 drilling rigs, including 24 offshore rigs (23 jackups and one semisubmersible capable of drilling in water depths up to 1,200 ft.) and 18 land drilling rigs. Drilling operations (62% of 2003 revenues) are conducted primarily in the Gulf of Mexico, the North Sea, offshore eastern Canada, and in Texas and Louisiana.

The company's jackup rigs perform both exploratory and development drilling, and, in certain areas, well workover operations. Its larger, deepwater jackups can drill to depths of 20,000 ft. to 30,000 ft. in maximum water depths of 250 ft. to 490 ft. At March 31, 2004, RDC's offshore fleet included 16 cantilever jack-up rigs, with three harsh environment Gorilla Class rigs, three enhanced Super Gorilla class rigs, seven conventional jackup rigs (including five rigs with skid base capability), and one semisubmersible rig. The company operates two of the cantilever jackup rigs under operating leases expiring in 2008. The Gorilla Class rigs (Gorillas II, III and IV) are heavier-duty rigs intended to drill up to 30,000 ft. in water depths up to 328 ft. in extreme hostile environments (winds up to 100 miles per hour and seas up to 90 ft.). During 1998, RDC launched the first of three Super Gorilla Class rigs, Rowan Gorilla V, an enhanced Gorilla Class rig; it completed the Rowan Gorilla VI

in 2000 and the Super Gorilla VII in 2001. The Super Gorilla VIII was completed in the 2003 third quarter. In 2001, RDC began development of the Tarzan class jackup rig, specifically designed for deeper drilling (more than 15,000 ft.) in water depths less than 250 ft. in the Gulf of Mexico.

RDC's worldwide rig utilization rate increased to 89% in 2003, from 87% in 2002; average dayrates increased over 20%. Land rig utilization was 74% in 2003, with an average day rate of $10,700 (67%, $10,000).

The manufacturing division (20%) operates a mini-steel mill that recycles scrap and produces steel plate; a manufacturing facility that produces heavy equipment such as front-end loaders; and a marine group that has designed and/or built about 33% of all mobile offshore jackup drilling rigs, including all 23 operated by the company.

Era Aviation (18%) provides contract and charter helicopter and fixed wing aviation services in Alaska, Louisiana, Texas, and the western U.S. Its fleet consists of 92 helicopters and 19 fixed-wing aircraft.

Capital expenditures in 2003 totaled $250 million, up slightly from $240 million in 2002. For 2004, RDC projected capital spending of $130 million to $150 million.

Company Financials Fiscal Year ending December 31

Per Share Data ($)

(Year Ended December 31)	2003	2002	2001	2000	1999	1998	1997	1996	1995	1994
Tangible Bk. Val.	11.95	12.09	11.84	11.17	8.69	8.77	7.53	5.80	5.06	5.25
Cash Flow	0.84	1.72	1.52	1.36	0.54	2.00	2.28	1.25	0.37	-0.33
Earnings	-0.08	0.90	0.80	0.74	-0.12	1.43	1.76	0.70	-0.22	-0.27
S&P Core Earnings	-0.05	-0.31	0.65	NA	NA	NA	NA	NA	NA	NA
Dividends	Nil	Nil	Nil	Nil	Nil	Nil	Nil	Nil	Nil	Nil
Payout Ratio	Nil	Nil	Nil	Nil	Nil	Nil	Nil	Nil	Nil	Nil
Prices - High	26.72	27.03	33.89	34.25	21.68	32.50	43.93	24.50	10.00	9.25
- Low	17.70	16.04	11.10	19.06	8.50	9.00	16.75	8.87	5.37	5.75
P/E Ratio - High	NM	30	42	46	NM	23	25	35	NM	NM
- Low	NM	18	14	26	NM	6	10	13	NM	NM

Income Statement Analysis (Million $)

	2003	2002	2001	2000	1999	1998	1997	1996	1995	1994
Revs.	679	617	731	646	461	706	695	571	471	438
Oper. Inc.	89.0	65.1	193	170	45.1	232	230	127	48.3	49.4
Depr. Depl. & Amort.	86.9	78.1	68.5	58.9	54.7	49.7	47.1	47.9	50.6	50.8
Int. Exp.	15.9	15.9	13.1	12.1	11.5	1.24	16.2	27.5	27.7	27.5
Pretax Inc.	-12.0	133	120	111	-14.5	194	173	60.5	-17.7	-22.5
Eff. Tax Rate	NM	35.0%	35.9%	36.7%	NM	35.7%	9.73%	NM	NM	NM
Net Inc.	-7.77	86.3	77.0	70.2	-9.67	124	156	61.3	-18.4	-23.0
S&P Core Earnings	-4.74	-30.2	62.8	NA	NA	NA	NA	NA	NA	NA

Balance Sheet & Other Fin. Data (Million $)

	2003	2002	2001	2000	1999	1998	1997	1996	1995	1994
Cash	58.2	179	237	193	87.1	149	108	97.2	90.0	111
Curr. Assets	444	470	507	483	325	366	412	317	273	254
Total Assets	2,191	2,055	1,939	1,678	1,356	1,249	1,122	899	802	805
Curr. Liab.	150	116	201	104	202	79.6	81.5	85.3	73.0	58.0
LT Debt	569	513	438	372	297	310	256	267	248	249
Common Equity	1,137	1,132	1,108	1,053	724	730	653	496	429	442
Total Cap.	1,924	1,811	1,674	1,516	1,099	1,116	984	765	681	695
Cap. Exp.	250	243	305	216	205	248	181	118	33.9	33.0
Cash Flow	79.1	164	145	129	45.0	174	204	109	32.1	27.8
Curr. Ratio	3.0	4.1	2.5	4.6	1.6	4.6	5.1	3.7	3.8	4.4
% LT Debt of Cap.	29.6	28.3	26.2	24.5	27.0	27.8	26.0	34.9	36.4	35.7
% Ret. on Assets	NM	4.3	4.3	4.6	NM	10.5	15.5	7.2	NM	NM
% Ret. on Equity	NM	7.7	7.1	7.9	NM	18.0	27.2	13.3	NM	NM

Data as orig reptd.; bef. results of disc opers/spec. items. Per share data adj. for stk. divs. Bold denotes primary EPS - prior periods restated. E-Estimated. NA-Not Available. NM-Not Meaningful. NR-Not Ranked. UR-Under Review.

Office: 2800 Post Oak Boulevard, Houston, TX 77056-6127.
Telephone: 713-621-7800.
Email: ir@rowancompanies.com
Website: http://www.rowancompanies.com
Chrmn, Pres & CEO: D.F. McNease.
Vice Chrmn & Chief Admin: R.G. Croyle.

SVP & Treas: E.E. Thiele.
VP & Investor Contact: W.C. Provine 713-960-7575.
Secy: M.H. Hay.
Dirs: H. O. Boswell, R. G. Croyle, W. T. Fox III, G. Hearne, F. R. Lausen, H. E. Lentz, D. F. McNease, L. Moynihan, C. R. Palmer, P. D. Peacock.

Founded: in 1923.
Domicile: Delaware.
Employees: 5,395.
S&P Analyst: Stewart Glickman/DC/BK

Ryder System

Recommendation: HOLD ★ ★ ★ ☆ ☆   12-Month Target Price: **$51.00**
(as of October 25, 2004)

R has an approximate 0.03% weighting in the **S&P 500**

Sector: Industrials
Sub-Industry: Air Freight & Logistics
Peer Group: Logistics Providers

Summary: R provides truck leasing and rental, logistics, and supply chain management solutions worldwide.

Quantitative Evaluations

S&P Earnings & Dividend Rank: B

| D | C | B- | **B** | B+ | A- | A | A+ |

S&P Fair Value Rank: NR

| 1 | 2 | 3 | 4 | 5 |
| Lowest | | | | Highest |

Fair Value Calc.: NA

S&P Investability Quotient Percentile

84%

R scored higher than 84% of all companies for which an S&P Report is available.

Volatility: Average

| Low | **Average** | High |

Technical Evaluation: Bullish

Since 6/04, the technical indicators for R have been Bullish.

Relative Strength Rank: Strong

83

1 Lowest   Highest 99

Price as of 11/12/04: **$53.67** | 2004E S&P Core EPS: **$1.98**

GAAP Earnings vs. Previous Year
▲ Up ▼ Down ▶ No Change

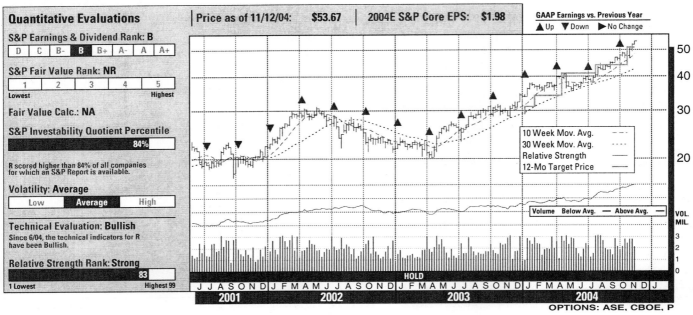

- 10 Week Mov. Avg.
- 30 Week Mov. Avg.
- Relative Strength
- 12-Mo Target Price

Volume Below Avg. — Above Avg. —

HOLD

| J J A S O N D | J F M A M J J A S O N D | J F M A M J J A S O N D | J F M A M J J A S O N D | J |
| 2001 | 2002 | 2003 | 2004 |

OPTIONS: ASE, CBOE, P

Analyst commentary prepared by Andrew West, CFA /DC/JWP

Highlights October 28, 2004

- We forecast revenue growth of 6% in 2004, and 5% in 2005. We anticipate both internal and acquisition-led growth in R's largest segment, fleet management solutions; little growth in contract carriage; and flat to weaker revenues at supply chain solutions. We expect leasing demand to improve, supported by the general economic expansion and tight trucking capacity.

- We look for operating margins to widen, primarily due to larger revenue contributions relative to fixed costs on higher rates and asset utilization. We see less room for cutting overhead expenses in 2004, although we expect pension costs to decline. We expect 2004 capital expenditures of over $1.2 billion to help renew the company's fleet, reduce lease expense, and lead to increased depreciation charges and higher debt levels.

- We forecast that 2004 EPS will climb 47%, to $3.11, from $2.12 in 2003, and rise 5% in 2005, to $3.25. We project 2004 Standard & Poor's Core EPS of $1.98, reflecting estimated option and pension expenses, restructuring reversals, and gains on asset sales, indicating our significant concerns regarding earnings quality.

Investment Rationale/Risk October 28, 2004

- After a number of restructurings in the past decade, we believe R has passed the peak of its cost-cutting phase, and expect the company to focus more on a strategy of profitable revenue growth, supported by increased capital spending and acquisitions. We forecast 15% annual earnings growth and 17% free cash flow growth over the next six years, with 2004 and 2005 growing more rapidly from a low base, supported by the economic recovery.

- Risks to our opinion and target price include lower than expected increases in economic growth, leasing demand, and lease rates; changes in accounting assumptions; and rising interest rates, which could unfavorably affect R in light of its financial leverage.

- Our discounted cash flow model assumes an 8% cost of capital and 3.5% terminal growth, and targets intrinsic value at $55. Our relative value model, which relates historical peer group valuations to profitability and leverage, estimates a forward price to sales multiple of 0.6X ($48). Blending these models, we arrive at our 12-month target price of $51.

Key Stock Statistics

S&P Core EPS 2005E	2.95	52-week Range	$53.70-28.14
S&P Oper. EPS 2004E	3.11	12 Month P/E	18.3
P/E on S&P Oper. EPS 2004E	17.3	Beta	0.83
S&P Oper. EPS 2005E	3.25	Shareholders	12,565
Yield (%)	1.1%	Market Cap (B)	$ 3.5
Dividend Rate/Share	0.60	Shares Outstanding (M)	64.3

Value of $10,000 invested five years ago: **$ 26,795**

Dividend Data Dividends have been paid since 1976

Amount ($)	Date Decl.	Ex-Div. Date	Stock of Record	Payment Date
0.150	Feb. 12	Feb. 19	Feb. 23	Mar. 19 '04
0.150	May. 07	May. 18	May. 20	Jun. 18 '04
0.150	Jul. 16	Aug. 18	Aug. 20	Sep. 17 '04
0.150	Oct. 08	Nov. 17	Nov. 19	Dec. 17 '04

Revenues/Earnings Data Fiscal year ending December 31

Revenues (Million $)

	2004	2003	2002	2001	2000	1999
1Q	1,212	1,194	1,150	1,282	1,309	1,154
2Q	1,269	1,197	1,209	1,294	1,332	1,215
3Q	1,306	1,194	1,212	1,243	1,339	1,262
4Q	—	1,217	1,205	1,188	1,357	1,322
Yr.	—	4,802	4,776	5,006	5,337	4,952

Earnings Per Share ($)

	2004	2003	2002	2001	2000	1999
1Q	0.53	0.33	0.27	0.07	0.33	0.15
2Q	0.97	0.55	0.47	0.33	0.50	0.29
3Q	0.83	0.63	0.54	-0.09	0.20	0.51
4Q	E0.80	0.61	0.52	Nil	0.46	0.10
Yr.	E3.11	2.12	1.80	0.31	1.49	1.06

Next earnings report expected: early-February Source: S&P, Company Reports
EPS Estimates based on S&P Operating Earnings; historical GAAP earnings are as reported.

Ryder System, Inc.

Recommendation: **HOLD** ★ ★ ★ ☆ ☆   12-Month Target Price: **$51.00** (as of October 25, 2004)

Business Summary October 28, 2004

Ryder System has undertaken a series of corporate restructurings and asset divestitures. During the 1990s, it sold assets accounting for over 50% of revenues. A reorganizational plan was implemented in January 2000 that was designed to make the company's earnings less cyclical and seasonal and its business less capital intensive, and to allow for better client service. Business operations are currently full-service leasing, short-term truck rental, truck maintenance services, logistics services, and dedicated contract carriage.

Fleet management solutions (FMS; 63% of 2003 revenues and 72% of pretax profits) provides full service truck leasing to more than 13,300 customers worldwide, ranging from large national enterprises to small companies, with a fleet of 135,000 vehicles as of December 31, 2003. Under a full service lease, the company provides customers with vehicles, maintenance, supplies and related equipment necessary for operation, while customers furnish and supervise their own drivers, and dispatch and exercise control over the vehicles.

FMS also services customer vehicles under maintenance contracts, and provides short-term truck rental to commercial customers to supplement their fleets during peak periods. A range of vehicles, from heavy-duty tractors and trailers to light-duty trucks, is available for commercial short-term rental. FMS also provides additional services, including fleet management, freight management, and insurance programs. In 2003, segment pretax profits declined, with increased pension expenses outweighing improved rental results.

Supply chain solutions (SCS; 27%, 15%) provides global integrated logistics support of entire customer supply chains, from inbound raw materials supply through finished goods distribution, management of carriers, and inventory deployment and overall supply chain design and management. Services include combinations of logistics systems and information technology design, the provision of vehicles and equipment (including maintenance and drivers), warehouse and transportation management, vehicle dispatch, and just-in-time delivery.

The dedicated contract carriage segment (DCC; 10%, 12%) combines the equipment, maintenance and administrative services of a full-service lease with additional services, including driver hiring and training, routing and scheduling, fleet sizing, and other technical support.

The company's FMS segment has historically disposed of revenue earning equipment at prices in excess of book value. Net gains on vehicle sales accounted for 12% of net profits in 2003 (15% in 2002).

Effective December 31, 2003, R acquired General Car and Truck Leasing System, a commercial truck leasing and rental company, for $105 million, subject to adjustments. The company expected the acquisition, which included 4,200 vehicles and 700 customers, to add about $75 million to revenues. Effective March 1, 2004, R acquired the fleet and contract maintenance agreement assets of Ruan Leasing Co. for $145 million, subject to adjustments. The acquisition is expected by R to add about $125 million in annualized revenues.

In May 2004, the company sold its corporate headquarters for $39 million in cash, resulting in a $14 million gain in the second quarter.

Company Financials Fiscal Year ending December 31

Per Share Data ($)

(Year Ended December 31)	2003	2002	2001	2000	1999	1998	1997	1996	1995	1994
Tangible Bk. Val.	18.09	14.97	17.51	17.43	16.87	11.51	11.17	11.01	12.30	10.91
Cash Flow	11.90	10.65	9.30	11.20	10.12	11.12	10.29	9.20	11.48	10.39
Earnings	2.12	1.80	0.31	1.49	1.06	2.16	2.05	-0.39	1.96	1.95
S&P Core Earnings	2.26	0.84	-0.76	NA	NA	NA	NA	NA	NA	NA
Dividends	0.60	0.60	0.60	0.60	0.60	0.60	0.60	0.60	0.60	0.60
Payout Ratio	28%	33%	194%	40%	57%	28%	29%	NM	31%	31%
Prices - High	34.65	31.09	23.19	25.12	28.75	40.56	37.12	31.12	26.12	28.00
- Low	20.00	21.05	16.06	14.81	18.81	19.43	27.12	22.62	21.00	19.87
P/E Ratio - High	16	17	75	17	27	19	18	NM	13	14
- Low	9	12	52	10	18	9	13	NM	11	10

Income Statement Analysis (Million $)

	2003	2002	2001	2000	1999	1998	1997	1996	1995	1994
Revs.	4,802	4,776	5,006	5,337	4,952	5,189	4,894	5,519	5,167	4,686
Oper. Inc.	905	854	798	906	997	1,115	1,097	943	1,210	1,074
Depr.	625	552	545	580	623	665	654	779	756	666
Int. Exp.	96.2	91.7	119	154	184	199	189	207	191	145
Pretax Inc.	212	176	30.7	141	117	258	264	-17.6	264	261
Eff. Tax Rate	36.2%	36.0%	39.2%	37.0%	37.9%	38.4%	39.4%	NM	41.2%	41.1%
Net Inc.	136	113	18.7	89.0	72.9	159	160	-31.3	155	154
S&P Core Earnings	145	53.1	-46.3	NA	NA	NA	NA	NA	NA	NA

Balance Sheet & Other Fin. Data (Million $)

	2003	2002	2001	2000	1999	1998	1997	1996	1995	1994
Cash	141	104	118	122	113	138	78.0	191	93.0	76.0
Curr. Assets	1,107	1,024	982	928	1,209	1,110	1,092	1,148	884	759
Total Assets	5,279	4,767	4,924	5,475	5,770	5,709	5,509	5,645	5,894	5,014
Curr. Liab.	1,074	862	1,014	1,302	1,450	1,363	1,090	1,155	1,120	1,093
LT Debt	1,449	1,389	1,392	1,604	1,819	2,100	2,268	2,237	2,411	1,795
Common Equity	1,344	1,108	1,231	1,253	1,205	1,095	1,061	1,106	1,240	1,129
Total Cap.	3,688	3,431	3,625	3,874	4,035	4,003	4,054	4,029	4,299	3,494
Cap. Exp.	725	600	657	1,289	1,734	1,369	1,042	1,303	2,152	1,769
Cash Flow	760	665	564	669	696	824	813	748	911	819
Curr. Ratio	1.0	1.2	1.0	0.7	0.8	0.8	1.0	1.0	0.8	0.7
% LT Debt of Cap.	39.3	40.5	38.4	41.4	45.1	52.5	55.9	55.6	56.1	51.4
% Net Inc.of Revs.	2.8	2.4	0.4	1.7	1.5	3.1	3.3	NM	3.0	3.3
% Ret. on Assets	2.7	2.3	0.4	1.6	1.3	2.8	2.9	NM	2.8	3.3
% Ret. on Equity	11.1	9.6	1.5	7.2	1.1	14.7	14.8	NM	13.1	14.4

Data as orig reptd.; bef. results of disc opers/spec. items. Per share data adj. for stk. divs.; EPS diluted. E-Estimated. NA-Not Available. NM-Not Meaningful. NR-Not Ranked. UR-Under Review.

Office: 3600 N.W. 82nd Avenue, Doral, FL 33166.
Telephone: 305-593-3726.
Email: ryderforinvestor@ryder.com
Website: http://www.ryder.com
Chrmn, Pres & CEO: G.T. Swienton.

EVP & CFO: T. Leinbach.
EVP, Secy & General Counsel: V.A. O'Meara.
Investor Contact: B. Brunn 305-500-4053.
Dirs: J. M. Berra, J. L. Dionne, D. I. Fuente, L. M. Martin, D. Mudd, E. A. Renna, A. J. Smith, G. T. Swienton, H. E. Tookes II, C. A. Varney.

Founded: in 1955.
Domicile: Florida.
Employees: 26,700.
S&P Analyst: Andrew West, CFA /DC/JWP

Sabre Holdings

Recommendation: **HOLD** ★ ★ ★ ☆ ☆   **12-Month Target Price: $25.00**
(as of October 28, 2004)

TSG has an approximate 0.03% weighting in the **S&P 500**

Sector: Information Technology
Sub-Industry: Data Processing & Outsourced Services
Peer Group: Data Processors - Misc.

Summary: TSG, spun off from AMR (the parent of American Airlines) in March 2000, offers a variety of travel-related services.

Quantitative Evaluations

S&P Earnings & Dividend Rank: NR

| D | C | B- | B | B+ | A- | A | A+ |

S&P Fair Value Rank: 5+

| 1 | 2 | 3 | 4 | **5** |
| Lowest | | | | Highest |

Fair Value Calc.: $24.20 (Slightly Undervalued)

S&P Investability Quotient Percentile

92%

TSG scored higher than 92% of all companies for which an S&P Report is available.

Volatility: Average

| Low | **Average** | High |

Technical Evaluation: Bearish
Since 10/04, the technical indicators for TSG have been Bearish.

Relative Strength Rank: Weak

17
| 1 Lowest | Highest 99 |

Price as of 11/12/04: $22.58   **2004E S&P Core EPS: $0.98**

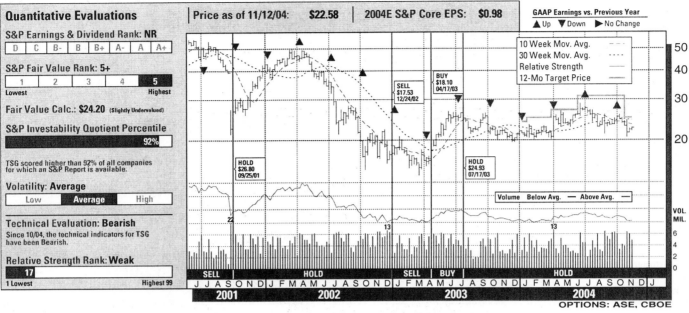

GAAP Earnings vs. Previous Year
▲ Up ▼ Down ► No Change

- - - 10 Week Mov. Avg.
······ 30 Week Mov. Avg.
Relative Strength
12-Mo Target Price

Analyst commentary prepared by Scott H. Kessler/MF/BK

OPTIONS: ASE, CBOE

Highlights October 29, 2004

- After basically flat revenues in 2003, reflecting reduced airline industry capacity, sluggish global economies, geopolitical concerns, and perceived inconveniences due to increased airport security measures, we expect adjusted revenues to advance 9% in 2004 and 8% in 2005, largely due to a projected rebound in demand for travel services. We believe continuing penetration of online, corporate and international markets will contribute to revenue growth and margin expansion, paced by Travelocity.

- In the 2003 fourth quarter, TSG took actions intended to improve profitability. It began to integrate the GetThere segment into other business units, and furloughed what we estimate were about 500 employees. We expect margins to benefit from these actions, and from a more favorable revenue mix, despite increased marketing spending associated with Travelocity (which launched a new television, radio and print advertising campaign in January 2004).

- We see EPS benefiting from a $100 million stock repurchase authorization announced in October 2004. The company previously announced a $100 million buyback program in October 2003. The discrepancies between our estimates for annual per-share operating earnings and Standard & Poor's Core Earnings large reflect stock option expenses.

Investment Rationale/Risk October 29, 2004

- We think the issues that discouraged travel through mid-2003, such as SARS and the Iraq war, have largely dissipated. We believe improving consumer sentiment and spending will contribute to growth in 2004 and 2005 revenues and profits. However, we believe the air travel industry still faces substantial challenges, particularly due to pricing pressures and excess capacity based largely on the lack of a sizable and sustained rebound in corporate demand. TSG, in our view, also faces notable competition from InterActiveCorp, Orbitz (whose acquisition by Cendant we expect to be completed by December 2004, pending necessary approvals), priceline.com, and the like, and from airline and hotel company websites.

- Risks to our recommendation and target price include geopolitical unrest or activity that negatively impacts demand for travel offerings, and actions that make a competitor considerably better positioned strategically.

- Based on relative analysis (where recently, TSG's P/E was below and its P/E-to-growth rate was in line with those of peers) and our discounted cash flow model (whose assumptions include a weighted average cost of capital of 14.6% and average free cash flow growth through 2008 of 18%), our 12-month target price is $25.

Key Stock Statistics

S&P Core EPS 2005E	1.08	52-week Range	$28.85-19.58
S&P Oper. EPS 2004E	1.41	12 Month P/E	20.2
P/E on S&P Oper. EPS 2004E	16.0	Beta	1.54
S&P Oper. EPS 2005E	1.58	Shareholders	12,011
Yield (%)	1.3%	Market Cap (B)	$ 3.1
Dividend Rate/Share	0.30	Shares Outstanding (M)	135.5

Value of $10,000 invested five years ago: **$ 5,862**

Dividend Data Dividends have been paid since 2003

Amount ($)	Date Decl.	Ex-Div. Date	Stock of Record	Payment Date
0.075	Jan. 20	Jan. 28	Jan. 30	Feb. 17 '04
0.075	Apr. 20	Apr. 28	Apr. 30	May. 14 '04
0.075	Jul. 20	Jul. 28	Jul. 30	Aug. 16 '04
0.075	Oct. 26	Nov. 03	Nov. 05	Nov. 15 '04

Revenues/Earnings Data Fiscal year ending December 31

Revenues (Million $)

	2004	2003	2002	2001	2000	1999
1Q	539.8	543.8	549.4	573.4	644.9	638.1
2Q	550.9	507.2	536.8	582.0	661.8	639.0
3Q	544.4	526.8	517.4	524.8	667.0	617.0
4Q	—	467.4	453.0	422.8	643.4	540.5
Yr.	—	2,045	2,056	2,103	2,617	2,435

Earnings Per Share ($)

	2004	2003	2002	2001	2000	1999
1Q	0.31	0.45	0.64	Nil	0.48	0.71
2Q	0.42	0.05	0.47	0.04	0.46	0.48
3Q	0.49	0.18	0.40	0.13	0.34	0.61
4Q	E0.20	-0.10	0.01	-0.52	-0.23	0.74
Yr.	E1.41	0.58	1.50	-0.35	1.11	2.54

Next earnings report expected: late-January Source: S&P, Company Reports
EPS Estimates based on S&P Operating Earnings; historical GAAP earnings are as reported.

Sabre Holdings Corp.

Recommendation: **HOLD** ★ ★ ★ ☆ ☆   12-Month Target Price: **$25.00** (as of October 28, 2004)

Business Summary October 29, 2004

Sabre Holdings is a worldwide leader (based on revenues) in travel-related commerce, marketing travel offerings, and providing distribution and technology solutions for the travel industry. It serves travel agents, individual travelers, companies managing business travelers, and travel suppliers through the Sabre Travel Network, Travelocity, and Sabre Airline Solutions business segments.

The Sabre global distribution system (often referred to as a GDS) and other similar systems are a principal means of air travel distribution in the U.S. and in many international regions. Through the Sabre GDS, travel agencies, corporate travel departments, and individual consumers can access information about and can book reservations for airline trips, hotel stays, car rentals, cruises, and tour packages.

The Sabre Travel Network, which markets the Sabre GDS, accounts for a majority of TSG's revenues (71% and 75% in 2003 and 2002, respectively, including inter-segment revenues). As of December 2003, travel agencies with about 53,000 locations in more than 113 countries subscribed to the Sabre system. Subscribers could make reservations with 430 airlines, 41 car rental companies, 220 tour operators, 9 cruise lines, 35 railroads, and 249 hotel companies covering 60,600 hotels worldwide.

In April 2002, the company acquired the 30% interest that it did not already own in Travelocity (18%, 15%), a leading provider (based on gross bookings and reve-

nues) of consumer-focused services for both leisure and unmanaged business travelers. Travelocity is the exclusive provider of travel booking services for America Online, and for some of Yahoo's North American websites. It acts as an agency by receiving fees from travel providers for sales of their offerings. More recently, it began a merchant business by purchasing wholesale inventory from air carriers, hotels, and car rental companies, and selling them independently or as part of packages. Travelocity also garners revenues from advertising on its websites.

The Sabre Airline Solutions segment (11%, 10%) provides airline software systems and consulting services. The segment's suite of software products help airlines and other travel providers increase their revenues, streamline their operations, improve workflow and raise productivity. The company provided custom and off-the-shelf software solutions to more than 200 airlines as of December 2003.

During the 2003 fourth quarter, TSG integrated its GetThere business unit (which accounted for about 2% of revenues in each of 2002 and 2001) into its three other operating businesses. GetThere's corporate travel businesses was moved to Sabre Travel Network, its supplier website went to Sabre Airline Solutions, and its technology and development infrastructure was moved to Travelocity. GetThere is no longer a separate business. TSG acquired GetThere in October 2000, for $757 million.

Company Financials Fiscal Year ending December 31

Per Share Data ($)

(Year Ended December 31)	2003	2002	2001	2000	1999	1998	1997	1996	1995	1994
Tangible Bk. Val.	5.60	5.51	2.83	NM	9.72	7.35	5.79	4.36	3.08	NA
Cash Flow	1.55	2.32	2.95	3.77	4.52	3.68	2.94	2.69	2.55	NA
Earnings	0.58	1.50	-0.35	1.11	2.54	1.78	1.53	1.44	1.20	NA
S&P Core Earnings	0.15	1.18	-0.75	NA	NA	NA	NA	NA	NA	NA
Dividends	0.21	Nil	Nil	5.20	Nil	Nil	Nil	Nil	Nil	NA
Payout Ratio	36%	Nil	Nil	NM	Nil	Nil	Nil	Nil	Nil	NA
Prices - High	27.50	49.98	54.98	53.50	72.00	44.87	37.00	33.37	NA	NA
- Low	14.00	14.85	21.22	22.31	38.25	23.00	23.25	25.62	NA	NA
P/E Ratio - High	47	33	NM	48	28	25	24	23	NA	NA
- Low	24	10	NM	20	15	13	15	18	NA	NA

Income Statement Analysis (Million $)

	2003	2002	2001	2000	1999	1998	1997	1996	1995	1994
Revs.	2,045	2,056	2,103	2,617	2,435	2,306	1,784	1,622	1,463	NA
Oper. Inc.	302	434	429	596	631	598	493	492	456	NA
Depr.	136	117	438	346	258	248	185	165	171	NA
Int. Exp.	24.1	23.4	41.2	31.7	9.99	19.5	21.7	27.4	Nil	NA
Pretax Inc.	127	339	11.5	236	528	371	324	306	252	NA
Eff. Tax Rate	34.7%	36.8%	NM	52.1%	37.1%	37.6%	38.3%	39.0%	39.0%	NA
Net Inc.	83.3	214	-47.0	144	332	232	200	187	154	NA
S&P Core Earnings	22.3	169	-100	NA	NA	NA	NA	NA	NA	NA

Balance Sheet & Other Fin. Data (Million $)

	2003	2002	2001	2000	1999	1998	1997	1996	1995	1994
Cash	923	912	667	145	6.63	8.01	11.3	443	NA	NA
Curr. Assets	1,368	1,312	1,092	693	976	944	874	695	501	NA
Total Assets	2,956	2,757	2,376	2,650	1,951	1,927	1,524	1,287	1,100	NA
Curr. Liab.	503	500	564	1,266	525	401	317	290	172	NA
LT Debt	588	436	400	149	Nil	318	318	318	387	NA
Common Equity	1,680	1,642	1,042	791	1,262	954	757	570	393	NA
Total Cap.	2,279	2,101	1,662	1,227	1,262	1,285	1,087	931	780	NA
Cap. Exp.	71.5	62.6	158	190	168	320	218	186	165	NA
Cash Flow	219	331	391	490	590	480	385	352	325	NA
Curr. Ratio	2.7	2.6	1.9	0.5	1.9	2.4	2.8	2.4	2.9	NA
% LT Debt of Cap.	25.8	20.7	24.1	12.1	Nil	24.7	29.3	34.2	49.6	NA
% Net Inc.of Revs.	4.1	10.4	NM	5.5	13.6	10.1	11.2	11.5	10.5	NA
% Ret. on Assets	2.9	8.3	NM	6.3	17.1	13.4	14.2	18.5	NA	NA
% Ret. on Equity	5.0	16.0	NM	14.0	30.0	27.1	30.1	NM	NA	NA

Data as orig. reptd.; bef. results of disc. opers. and/or spec. items. Per share data adj. for stk. divs.; EPS diluted (primary prior to 1998). Data for 1996 are pro forma. E-Estimated. NA-Not Available. NM-Not Meaningful. NR-Not Ranked.

Office: 3150 Sabre Drive, Southlake, TX 76092-2103.
Telephone: 682-605-1000.
Email: contact.us@sabre.com
Website: http://www.sabre-holdings.com
Chrmn: P.C. Ely, Jr.
Pres & CEO: S. Gilland.

EVP & CFO: J.M. Jackson.
EVP & General Counsel: D. Schwarte.
SVP & Treas: J. Murphy.
VP & Investor Contact: K. Fugate 866-722-7347.
Dirs: R. S. Caldwell, P. C. Ely, Jr., M. S. Gilliland, R. G. Lindner, G. W. Marschel, Jr., B. L. Martin, P. B. Strobel, M. A. Taylor, R. L. Thomas.

Founded: in 1996.
Domicile: Delaware.
Employees: 6,200.
S&P Analyst: Scott H. Kessler/MF/BK

SAFECO Corp.

Recommendation: **HOLD** ★★★☆☆
SELL SELL HOLD BUY BUY
12-Month Target Price: **$50.00**
(as of April 20, 2004)

SAFC has an approximate 0.05% weighting in the **S&P 500**

Sector: Financials
Sub-Industry: Property & Casualty Insurance
Peer Group: Commercial/Personal Insurers - National

Summary: SAFC has sold its life insurance and investments unit to better focus on its property-casualty insurance operations.

Quantitative Evaluations

S&P Earnings & Dividend Rank: B-

| D | C | B- | B | B+ | A- | A | A+ |

S&P Fair Value Rank: 2

| 1 | 2 | 3 | 4 | 5 |
| Lowest | | | | Highest |

Fair Value Calc.: $40.60 (Overvalued)

S&P Investability Quotient Percentile

98%

SAFC scored higher than 98% of all companies for which an S&P Report is available.

Volatility: Low

| Low | Average | High |

Technical Evaluation: Neutral

Since 11/04, the technical indicators for SAFC have been Neutral.

Relative Strength Rank: Moderate

50

| 1 Lowest | | Highest 99 |

| Price as of 11/12/04: | $47.89 | 2004E S&P Core EPS: | $3.25 |

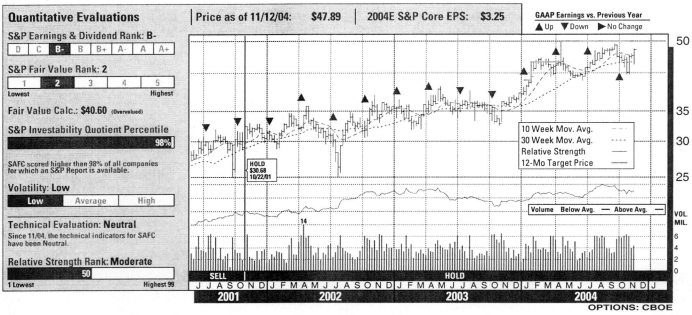

GAAP Earnings vs. Previous Year
▲ Up ▼ Down ▶ No Change

10 Week Mov. Avg.
30 Week Mov. Avg.
Relative Strength
12-Mo Target Price

HOLD $30.68 10/22/01

Volume   Below Avg. — Above Avg. —

OPTIONS: CBOE

Analyst commentary prepared by Catherine A. Seifert/PMW/BK

Highlights October 21, 2004

- We expect 2004 to be a transition year for the company, as it restructures its property-casualty operations and sells its life and investment division. SAFC sold its life and investments business on August 2, 2004, for proceeds $1.51 billion, of which $623 million was used to repurchase 13.2 million common shares, and $735.2 million was used to repurchase debt. The company reported third quarter operating EPS (from continuing operations) of $0.39, versus an operating loss of $0.06 in the 2003 period. Results include the after-tax impact of catastrophe claims of $0.96, versus $0.10. In the first nine months of 2004, net earned premiums increased 13%, exceeding our assumption of 10% to 12% growth in earned premiums, on favorable premium pricing and policy retention trends, partly offset by the disruptive effects of the restructuring.

- We anticipate that SAFC will succeed in its attempt to reduce its operating expenses. The combined loss/expense ratio of 92.4% for the first nine months of 2004 was an improvement from the ratio of 102.7% in the 2003 period, despite higher catastrophe claims.

- A rebound in operating EPS that we anticipate, to $4.25 for 2004 and $4.50 for 2005, is skewed by a number of after-tax charges incurred in 2003, including a third quarter workers' compensation reserve boost of $133.3 million and a fourth quarter restructuring charge of $8 million. Our estimate of 2004 operating EPS does not take into account the impact of the sale.

Key Stock Statistics

S&P Oper. EPS 2004E	4.25	52-week Range	$49.41-35.85
P/E on S&P Oper. EPS 2004E	11.3	12 Month P/E	12.1
S&P Oper. EPS 2005E	4.50	Beta	0.24
Yield (%)	1.8%	Shareholders	64,500
Dividend Rate/Share	0.88	Market Cap (B)	$ 6.1
Shares Outstanding (M)	126.8		

Value of $10,000 invested five years ago: **$ 18,026**

Dividend Data Dividends have been paid since 1933

Amount ($)	Date Decl.	Ex-Div. Date	Stock of Record	Payment Date
0.185	Feb. 04	Apr. 06	Apr. 09	Apr. 26 '04
0.185	May. 05	Jul. 07	Jul. 09	Jul. 26 '04
0.220	Aug. 02	Oct. 06	Oct. 08	Oct. 25 '04
0.220	Nov. 03	Jan. 12	Jan. 14	Jan. 24 '05

Investment Rationale/Risk October 21, 2004

- The shares of this property-casualty insurer fell, together with those of peers, after New York State Attorney General Elliot Spitzer filed suit against insurance broker Marsh & McLennan (MMC: sell, $25) on October 14, 2004, alleging, among other things, that MMC engaged in bid rigging in the placement of certain insurance accounts. A number of insurers (but not SAFC) were mentioned in the investigation. As a result, we think that the entire sector has come under intense selling pressure. Although third quarter results indicated, in our view, that the company is making headway in improving the profitability of its underlying book of business, our enthusiasm is tempered by the risk to investor sentiment that we see associated with the investigation.

- Risks to our opinion and target price include a deterioration in claim trends, a sharp increase in premium price competition, SAFC's inability to successfully implement its restructuring, and a broadening of the investigation into certain insurance industry practices .

- Our 12-month target price of $50 assumes that the shares will trade at a forward P/E multiple of 11X applied to our 2005 operating EPS estimate of $4.50. This represents a modest premium to the peer group average.

Revenues/Earnings Data Fiscal year ending December 31

Revenues (Million $)

	2004	2003	2002	2001	2000	1999
1Q	1,498	1,763	1,713	1,733	1,762	1,666
2Q	1,556	1,872	1,798	1,716	1,768	1,666
3Q	1,567	1,781	1,795	1,708	1,809	1,762
4Q	—	1,943	1,760	1,706	1,780	1,677
Yr.	—	7,358	7,065	6,863	7,118	6,866

Earnings Per Share ($)

	2004	2003	2002	2001	2000	1999
1Q	1.33	0.65	0.50	-6.89	0.23	0.87
2Q	1.78	0.81	0.82	-0.11	0.23	0.54
3Q	0.04	-0.21	0.59	-1.22	0.36	0.12
4Q	—	1.19	0.42	0.06	0.08	0.34
Yr.	—	2.44	2.33	-8.18	0.90	1.90

Next earnings report expected: late-January Source: S&P, Company Reports
EPS Estimates based on S&P Operating Earnings; historical GAAP earnings are as reported.

SAFECO Corporation

Recommendation: **HOLD** ★ ★ ★ ☆ ☆   12-Month Target Price: **$50.00** (as of April 20, 2004)

Business Summary October 21, 2004

Seattle-based insurer SAFECO has faced a difficult property-casualty market with mixed success in recent years. By early 2001, a full-scale management shake-up occurred, and a new CEO and president was appointed. The company also underwrites life and health insurance. To better focus on its core property-casualty operations, in late 2003, SAFC put its life and investment operations up for sale. In early 2004, an investor group led by White Mountains Insurance Group, Ltd., and Berkshire Hathaway Inc. agreed to acquire SAFC's life and investment units, for about $1.35 billion. Mellon Financial Corp. agreed to acquire Safeco Trust Company for an undisclosed amount. Revenues (before realized investment losses) totaled $7.5 billion in 2003, with property-casualty premiums accounting for 66%, life insurance and investment revenues for 12%, and net investment income for 22%.

Property-casualty insurance is the company's principal line of business. SAFC was the 18th largest U.S. property-casualty insurance company, based on 2002 direct written premiums (latest available data). Earned premiums exceeded $4.9 billion in 2003, up 8.9% from earned premiums of over $4.5 billion in 2002. Through about 7,300 independent agents and brokers, most major lines of personal and commercial p-c coverage are offered in nearly all states, although much of SAFC's business is concentrated in the Pacific Northwest. In 2003, business

written in California accounted for 17% of earned premiums; Washington accounted for 12%, Texas 10%, and Oregon 6%.

Safeco Personal Insurance (66% of 2003 earned premiums) primarily underwrites personal auto insurance and homeowners coverage. It was the 14th largest U.S. writer of auto insurance and the 10th largest writer of homeowners' insurance, based on 2002 (latest available) direct written premiums. The division also offers an array of umbrella, earthquake, dwelling fire, inland marine, recreational vehicle, motorcycle and boat insurance coverage for individuals.

Safeco Business Insurance (30% of 2003 earned premiums) offers a line of commercial insurance products designed for small to medium sized businesses (defined as customers who pay $100,00 or less in annual written premiums). Principal products offered by the segment include commercial multi-peril, workers' compensation, property, general liability, and commercial auto. The Surety and Other segment (4% of earned premiums in 2003) provides surety bonds for construction, performance, and legal matters that include appeals, probate and bankruptcies. SAFC was the fifth largest U.S. writer of surety bonds, based on 2002 (latest available) direct written premiums. The other line of business primarily consist of businesses that are being exited or run off.

Company Financials Fiscal Year ending December 31

Per Share Data ($)

(Year Ended December 31)	2003	2002	2001	2000	1999	1998	1997	1996	1995	1994
Tangible Bk. Val.	34.92	30.69	27.70	26.48	22.80	31.01	29.28	32.58	31.61	22.48
Oper. Earnings	NA	NA	NA	0.19	1.32	2.07	3.02	3.02	2.84	2.29
Earnings	2.44	2.33	-8.18	0.90	1.90	2.51	3.31	3.48	3.17	2.50
S&P Core Earnings	2.80	1.77	-1.43	NA	NA	NA	NA	NA	NA	NA
Dividends	0.74	0.74	0.93	1.48	1.44	1.34	1.22	1.11	1.02	0.94
Relative Payout	30%	32%	NM	164%	76%	53%	37%	32%	32%	38%
Prices - High	39.79	38.00	32.95	35.87	46.75	56.00	55.37	42.25	39.25	29.87
- Low	32.50	24.99	21.50	18.00	21.81	38.25	36.50	30.87	25.12	23.37
P/E Ratio - High	16	16	NM	40	25	22	17	12	12	12
- Low	13	11	NM	20	11	15	11	9	8	9

Income Statement Analysis (Million $)

	2003	2002	2001	2000	1999	1998	1997	1996	1995	1994
Life Ins. In Force	667,378	67,001	57,511	55,262	48,175	45,206	NA	NA	NA	NA
Prem. Inc.: Life A & H	868	778	637	503	361	353	290	266	262	277
Prem. Inc.: Cas./Prop.	4,902	4,521	4,473	4,563	4,383	4,208	2,817	2,275	2,162	2,053
Net Invest. Inc.	1,680	1,672	1,649	1,627	1,585	1,519	1,245	1,117	1,075	992
Total Revs.	7,358	7,065	6,863	7,118	31.0	6,547	4,709	3,965	3,723	3,537
Pretax Inc.	441	418	-1,458	114	287	418	573	578	514	390
Net Oper. Inc.	NA	27.8	-1,062	69.0	221	335	366	380	357	288
Net Inc.	339	301	-1,045	115	252	352	430	439	399	314
S&P Core Earnings	388	229	-184	NA	NA	NA	NA	NA	NA	NA

Balance Sheet & Other Fin. Data (Million $)

	2003	2002	2001	2000	1999	1998	1997	1996	1995	1994
Cash & Equiv.	550	3,482	593	529	440	398	728	296	300	293
Premiums Due	1,640	1,626	973	1,063	1,058	978	954	467	445	419
Invest. Assets: Bonds	26,207	24,278	21,444	20,830	19,564	20,576	19,987	14,530	11,997	9,611
Invest. Assets: Stocks	1,279	1,083	1,597	1,816	2,005	2,037	1,880	1,299	1,119	855
Invest. Assets: Loans	936	926	924	823	861	630	584	506	472	472
Invest. Assets: Total	28,807	26,771	24,875	23,811	22,931	24,160	22,451	16,889	16,132	13,467
Deferred Policy Costs	639	626	627	605	599	521	545	396	356	389
Total Assets	35,845	34,656	30,093	31,512	30,573	30,892	29,468	19,918	18,768	15,902
Debt	1,966	1,968	1,592	1,617	3,159	3,458	2,360	1,233	1,068	983
Common Equity	5,023	4,432	3,635	4,695	4,295	5,576	5,462	4,115	3,983	2,829
Comb. Loss-Exp. Ratio	100.1	105.3	118.7	111.4	108.4	102.6	98.7	98.3	99.7	103.8
% Return On Revs.	4.6	4.3	NM	1.6	3.8	5.4	9.1	11.1	10.7	8.9
% Ret. on Equity	7.2	7.5	NM	2.6	5.1	12.6	0.0	9.4	11.7	11.2
% Invest. Yield	6.0	5.1	6.8	7.0	6.7	12.6	6.5	6.7	7.4	7.6

Data as orig reptd.; bef. results of disc opers/spec. items. Per share data adj. for stk. divs.; EPS diluted. E-Estimated. NA-Not Available. NM-Not Meaningful. NR-Not Ranked. EPS ests. excl. inv. gains/losses; historical EPS include them.

Office: Safeco Plaza, Seattle, WA 98185.
Telephone: 206-545-5000.
Website: http://www.safeco.com
Chrmn, Pres & CEO: M.S. McGavick.
SVP, CFO & Secy: C.B. Mead.
SVP & General Counsel: J.W. Ruddy.

VP & Chief Acctg Officer: M.S. Hebert.
Investor Contact: N. Fuller 206-545-3399.
Dirs: J. W. Brown, P. J. Campbell, R. S. Cline, J. Green III, G. T. Hutton, W. W. Krippaehne, Jr., M. S. McGavick, W. G. Reed, Jr., N. B. Rice, J. M. Runstad.

Founded: in 1929.
Domicile: Washington.
Employees: 11,200.
S&P Analyst: Catherine A. Seifert/PMW/BK

The **McGraw·Hill** Companies

Safeway Inc.

Recommendation: **BUY** ★ ★ ★ ★ 12-Month Target Price: **$20.00**
SELL SELL HOLD BUY BUY (as of October 20, 2004)

SWY has an approximate 0.08% weighting in the **S&P 500**

Sector: Consumer Staples
Sub-Industry: Food Retail
Peer Group: Food Chain Cos. - Large

Summary: This major food retailer operates about 1,800 stores in the U.S. and Canada.

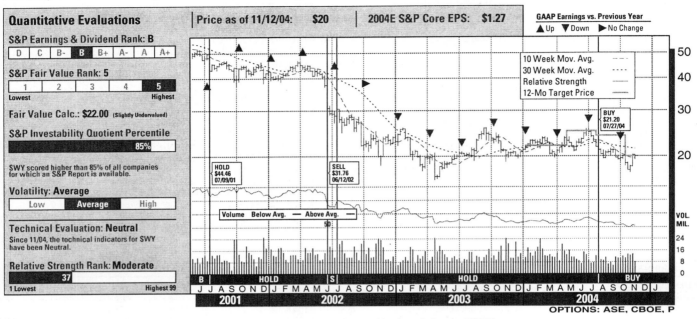

Quantitative Evaluations

S&P Earnings & Dividend Rank: B

| D | C | B- | **B** | B+ | A- | A | A+ |

S&P Fair Value Rank: 5

| 1 | 2 | 3 | 4 | **5** |
Lowest | | | | Highest

Fair Value Calc.: $22.00 (Slightly Undervalued)

S&P Investability Quotient Percentile
85%

SWY scored higher than 85% of all companies for which an S&P Report is available.

Volatility: Average

| Low | **Average** | High |

Technical Evaluation: Neutral
Since 11/04, the technical indicators for SWY have been Neutral.

Relative Strength Rank: Moderate
37
1 Lowest | Highest 99

Price as of 11/12/04: $20 **2004E S&P Core EPS:** $1.27

GAAP Earnings vs. Previous Year
▲ Up   ▼ Down   ▶ No Change

- 10 Week Mov. Avg.
- 30 Week Mov. Avg.
- Relative Strength
- 12-Mo Target Price

HOLD $44.46 07/09/01
SELL $31.76 06/12/02
BUY $21.20 07/27/04

Volume   Below Avg.   Above Avg.

VOL. MIL.

B | HOLD | S | HOLD | BUY
J J A S O N D J F M A M J J A S O N D J F M A M J J A S O N D J F M A M J J A S O N D J
2001 | 2002 | 2003 | 2004

OPTIONS: ASE, CBOE, P

Analyst commentary prepared by Joseph Agnese/DC/BK

Highlights October 21, 2004

- We expect sales to increase 1% to 3% in 2005, reflecting low single-digit gains for same-store sales, and about 2% more sq. ft. of selling space as the company has plans for 245 store remodelings. We believe SWY should benefit from improving consumer confidence due to a recovering economy, despite significant challenges from increased competition.

- We believe the company is focusing on defending its market share. We therefore expect high levels of promotional spending and reduced product prices to pressure gross margins. In addition, we see a shift in product mix toward lower margin fuel sales contributing to gross margin erosion. Overall, we look for operating margins to widen as a significant restructuring in labor contracts coupled with improved shrink controls and efficiency gains due to centralized marketing and procurement functions should help the company leverage any rise in sales.

- Interest expense should be lower, in our opinion, reflecting the company's focus on reducing debt levels. In all, we project 2005 operating EPS of $1.70, up significantly from our 2004 operating EPS estimate of $1.30, including our estimate of a $0.57 impact following a labor union strike in Southern California during the first quarter.

Key Stock Statistics

S&P Core EPS 2005E	1.69	52-week Range	$25.64-17.26
S&P Oper. EPS 2004E	1.30	12 Month P/E	NM
P/E on S&P Oper. EPS 2004E	15.4	Beta	0.50
S&P Oper. EPS 2005E	1.70	Shareholders	13,700
Yield (%)	Nil	Market Cap (B)	$ 8.9
Dividend Rate/Share	Nil	Shares Outstanding (M)	447.5

Value of $10,000 invested five years ago: **$ 5,050**

Dividend Data

No cash dividends have been paid.

Investment Rationale/Risk October 21, 2004

- We recommend accumulating the stock. We view the shares, trading below historical levels, as undervalued, given our expectation for an improving sales environment in 2005 and better sales leverage due to the restructuring of labor contracts.

- Risks to our recommendation and target price include a more intense competitive environment than anticipated, disruptions caused by labor disputes, and a slowdown in the economy.

- With the stock recently trading at 10.7X our 2005 EPS estimate of $1.70, below its historical average P/E multiple of 11.7X, we believe the shares are attractively valued. The company has been trying to recover market share due a labor union strike in Southern California in early 2004, and the shares were down 14.3% in 2004 through mid October, versus a decrease of 7.9% for the S&P Food Retail Index and a 0.1% rise for the S&P 500. Assuming that the economy continues to improve steadily, and that employee costs are better controlled, we project five-year annual EPS growth of 7% to 9%. Based on our historical forward 12-month P/E analysis, our 12-month target price is $20, equal to 11.8X our 2005 EPS estimate of $1.70.

Revenues/Earnings Data Fiscal year ending December 31

Revenues (Million $)

	2004	2003	2002	2001	2000	1999
1Q	7,639	8,043	7,367	7,666	7,086	6,113
2Q	8,361	8,248	7,514	7,986	7,418	6,337
3Q	8,297	8,277	7,508	7,962	7,457	6,475
4Q	—	10,985	10,011	10,686	10,015	9,935
Yr.	—	35,553	32,399	34,301	31,977	28,860

Earnings Per Share ($)

	2004	2003	2002	2001	2000	1999
1Q	0.10	0.36	0.66	0.55	0.48	0.40
2Q	0.35	0.36	0.62	0.59	0.55	0.46
3Q	0.35	0.45	0.60	0.60	0.53	0.44
4Q	E0.51	-1.57	-0.77	0.70	0.58	0.59
Yr.	E1.30	-0.38	1.20	2.44	2.13	1.88

Next earnings report expected: mid-February Source: S&P, Company Reports
EPS Estimates based on S&P Operating Earnings; historical GAAP earnings are as reported.

Safeway Inc.

Recommendation: BUY ★ ★ ★ ☆   12-Month Target Price: **$20.00** (as of October 20, 2004)

Business Summary October 21, 2004

Safeway is one of the largest U.S. food and drug retailers, operating 1,817 stores, located principally in California, Oregon, Washington, Alaska, Colorado, Arizona, Texas, and the Mid-Atlantic region. To support its store network, SWY has a network of distribution, manufacturing and food processing facilities. The company seeks to provide value to customers by maintaining high store standards and a wide selection of high quality produce and meat at competitive prices.

The company focuses on differentiating itself with quality perishables and meat. In an effort to develop a reputation for having the best produce in the market, and the most tender meat, SWY is introducing a higher standard of merchandising, revisiting product quality and selection and enhancing the in-store environment. The company has developed a line of about 1,369 corporate brand products since 1993, under the Safeway Select banner. SWY manufactures about 24% of its private label merchandise in company-owned plants. SWY's plant operations include milk, bread baking, ice cream, cheese and meat packaging, soft drink bottling, fruit and vegetable processing, other food processing, and pet food plants. In addition, SWY has 17 distribution/warehousing centers that collectively provide the majority of all products to Safeway stores.

SWY continues to expand by opening new stores. During 2003, the company

invested $934 million ($1.5 billion in 2002), excluding acquisitions, to open 40 (75) new stores, of which 22 (51) were new locations and 18 (24) were replacements, and completed 75 (203) remodels. SWY closed 31 stores in 2003, and 40 in 2002. At the end of 2003, the company projected capital spending for 2004, excluding acquisitions, at $1.2 billion to $1.4 billion, based on plans to open about 45 new or replacement stores, and to remodel 160 to 165 existing locations. SWY is putting a growing emphasis on opening larger store formats, to accommodate a variety of wider-margin specialty departments, such as deli counters and bakeries. Although current stores average 45,000 sq. ft., a typical new store averages 55,000 sq. ft. However, smaller stores are expected to continue to be an important part of the company's network in smaller communities.

Acquisitions over the past few years have helped make the company one of the largest U.S. food and drug retailers, with sales exceeding $32 billion in 2002. In February 2001, SWY acquired Genuardi's, for about $530 million in cash. Genuardi's operated 39 stores in the greater Philadelphia, PA, area, including New Jersey and Delaware. The company also holds a 49% interest in Casa Ley, S.A. de C.V., a chain of 99 food and general merchandise stores in western Mexico. In 1999, SWY acquired Carr-Gottstein Foods and Randall's.

Company Financials Fiscal Year ending December 31

Per Share Data ($)

(Year Ended December 31)	2003	2002	2001	2000	1999	1998	1997	1996	1995	1994
Tangible Bk. Val.	2.79	1.77	1.67	1.35	NM	NM	0.68	1.98	1.10	0.74
Cash Flow	1.57	2.91	4.29	3.77	3.24	2.63	2.38	1.68	1.36	1.18
Earnings	-0.38	1.20	2.44	2.13	1.88	1.59	1.25	0.97	0.68	0.51
S&P Core Earnings	1.21	2.42	2.19	NA	NA	NA	NA	NA	NA	NA
Dividends	Nil	Nil	Nil	Nil	Nil	Nil	Nil	Nil	Nil	Nil
Payout Ratio	Nil	Nil	Nil	Nil	Nil	Nil	Nil	Nil	Nil	Nil
Prices - High	25.83	46.90	61.37	62.68	62.43	61.37	31.71	22.68	12.87	7.96
- Low	16.20	18.45	37.44	30.75	29.31	30.50	21.06	11.21	7.65	4.81
P/E Ratio - High	NM	39	25	29	33	39	25	24	19	16
- Low	NM	15	15	14	16	19	17	12	11	10

Income Statement Analysis (Million $)

	2003	2002	2001	2000	1999	1998	1997	1996	1995	1994
Revs.	35,553	32,399	34,301	31,977	28,860	24,484	22,484	17,269	16,398	15,627
Oper. Inc.	2,167	3,190	3,535	3,119	2,698	2,134	1,841	1,231	1,058	938
Depr.	864	813	946	838	700	533	561	339	330	326
Int. Exp.	442	369	447	457	362	244	247	183	205	225
Pretax Inc.	141	1,320	2,095	1,867	1,674	1,397	1,076	768	557	424
Eff. Tax Rate	NM	56.9%	40.1%	41.5%	42.0%	42.2%	42.3%	40.0%	41.0%	41.0%
Net Inc.	-170	569	1,254	1,092	971	807	622	461	328	250
S&P Core Earnings	538	1,140	1,122	NA	NA	NA	NA	NA	NA	NA

Balance Sheet & Other Fin. Data (Million $)

	2003	2002	2001	2000	1999	1998	1997	1996	1995	1994
Cash	175	73.7	68.5	91.7	106	46.0	77.0	79.7	74.8	61.0
Curr. Assets	3,508	4,259	3,312	3,224	3,052	2,320	2,030	1,654	1,515	1,438
Total Assets	15,097	16,047	17,463	15,965	14,900	11,390	8,494	5,545	5,194	5,022
Curr. Liab.	3,464	3,936	3,883	3,780	3,583	2,894	2,539	2,030	1,939	1,824
LT Debt	7,072	7,522	6,712	5,822	6,357	4,651	3,041	1,729	1,950	2,024
Common Equity	3,644	3,628	5,890	5,390	4,086	3,082	2,149	1,187	796	644
Total Cap.	11,139	11,727	13,100	11,721	10,822	7,950	5,487	2,915	2,855	2,819
Cap. Exp.	936	1,371	1,793	1,573	1,334	1,075	758	542	451	340
Cash Flow	694	1,381	2,200	1,930	1,671	1,340	1,183	800	658	577
Curr. Ratio	1.0	1.1	0.9	0.9	0.9	0.8	0.8	0.8	0.8	0.8
% LT Debt of Cap.	63.5	64.1	51.2	49.7	58.7	58.5	55.4	59.3	68.3	71.8
% Net Inc.of Revs.	NM	1.8	3.7	3.4	3.4	3.3	2.8	2.7	2.0	1.6
% Ret. on Assets	NM	3.4	7.5	7.1	7.4	8.1	8.9	8.6	6.5	4.9
% Ret. on Equity	NM	11.9	22.2	23.0	27.1	30.9	37.3	46.5	45.7	48.2

Data as orig reptd.; bef. results of disc opers/spec. items. Per share data adj. for stk. divs. Bold denotes primary EPS - prior periods restated. E-Estimated. NA-Not Available. NM-Not Meaningful. NR-Not Ranked. UR-Under Review.

Office: 5918 Stoneridge Mall Road, Pleasanton, CA 94588-3229.
Telephone: 925-467-3000.
Website: http://www.safeway.com
Chrmn, Pres & CEO: S.A. Burd.
SVP, CFO & Chief Acctg Officer: D.F. Bond.

SVP & General Counsel: R.A. Gordon.
SVP & Investor Contact: M.C. Plaisance 925-467-3000.
Dirs: S. A. Burd, J. H. Greene, Jr., P. Hazen, H. L. Lopez, R. I. MacDonnell, P. A. Magowan, G. R. Roberts, R. A. Stirn, W. Y. Tauscher.

Founded: in 1915.
Domicile: Delaware.
Employees: 208,000.
S&P Analyst: Joseph Agnese/DC/BK

St. Jude Medical

Stock Report
November 13, 2004
NYSE Symbol: **STJ**

Recommendation: **HOLD** ★★★☆☆
SELL SELL HOLD BUY BUY

12-Month Target Price: **$80.00**
(as of September 29, 2004)

STJ has an approximate 0.12% weighting in the **S&P 500**

Sector: Health Care
Sub-Industry: Health Care Equipment
Peer Group: Large Multi-Line Medical Device Manufacturers

Summary: The leading maker of mechanical heart valves, this company also produces pacemakers, defibrillators and other cardiac devices.

Quantitative Evaluations

S&P Earnings & Dividend Rank: B

| D | C | B- | **B** | B+ | A- | A | A+ |

S&P Fair Value Rank: 1+

| **1** | 2 | 3 | 4 | 5 |
| Lowest | | | | Highest |

Fair Value Calc.: $57.10 (Overvalued)

S&P Investability Quotient Percentile
96%

STJ scored higher than 96% of all companies for which an S&P Report is available.

Volatility: Average

| Low | **Average** | High |

Technical Evaluation: Bullish
Since 9/04, the technical indicators for STJ have been Bullish.

Relative Strength Rank: Moderate
54

| 1 Lowest | | Highest 99 |

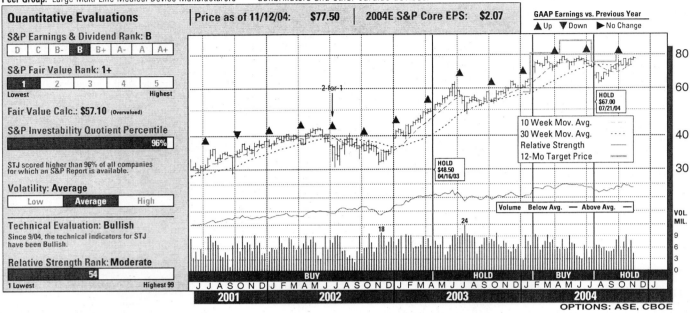

Price as of 11/12/04: **$77.50** | 2004E S&P Core EPS: **$2.07**

GAAP Earnings vs. Previous Year
▲ Up ▼ Down ▶ No Change

10 Week Mov. Avg.
30 Week Mov. Avg.
Relative Strength
12-Mo Target Price

Volume Below Avg. — Above Avg.

OPTIONS: ASE, CBOE

Analyst commentary prepared by Robert M. Gold/CB/JWP

Highlights October 22, 2004

- In our opinion, St. Jude is poised to capture additional share in the U.S. implantable cardioverter defibrillator (ICD) market in coming quarters, reflecting the launch of its cardiac resynchronization therapy (CRT) devices. Largely driven by CRT, but aided by relatively easy year-ago comparisons, we expect that ICD sales in the second half of 2004 will rise 60%, to $330 million. In other areas such as cardiac pacing, vascular sealing and cardiac surgery, however, we are concerned about a more competitive landscape.

- We look for 14% revenue growth in 2004, to $2.2 billion, with currency adding 3% to reported growth. Our estimate includes $575 million of ICD sales, pacemaker sales of $900 million, $150 million of EP catheter sales, $175 million of vascular sealing revenues, $280 million of cardiac surgery sales, and $95 million of other product sales. We model gross margins for 2004 at 71.2% of sales, with SG&A expenses consuming an estimated 33.5% to 34.0%, and R&D outlays representing 12.5% of revenues. We estimate the effective tax rate at 26.5%. Looking into 2005, we believe revenues will approach $2.6 billion.

Investment Rationale/Risk October 22, 2004

- Given the prospect of reduced currency tailwinds, rising competitive pressures across business categories, and the stock's high valuation relative to the S&P 500, we maintain our hold opinion. From our perspective, the company's CRT launch should help St. Jude compete for large hospital contracts over the coming year, as a broader product offering should appeal to hospital administrators seeking to limit the number of product vendors to which they are exposed. However, we think STJ will remain at a disadvantage to some of its competitors with far broader product lines and the ability to provide bundled product offerings, and we have some concerns regarding the potential for some ICD price erosion in coming quarters. We think the company will be able to gain significant EPS leverage from a rising number of ICD implantations among the Medicare population in 2005 and 2006.

- Risks to our recommendation and target price include failure to successfully commercialize new products in a timely manner, adverse changes to Medicare and private pay reimbursement rates, and negative patent litigation outcomes.

- Our 12-month target price is $80; at that level, STJ would command a 2005 P/E to projected three-year EPS growth ratio of 1.5X, in line with cardiovascular peers. Based on our perception of increasing competition in key product categories and uncertainties in the vascular sealing and pacing markets, we think a 2005 P/E of 29X is reasonable, given our three-year projected EPS growth rate of 20%.

Key Stock Statistics

S&P Oper. EPS 2004E	2.30	52-week Range	$79.03-58.38
P/E on S&P Oper. EPS 2004E	33.7	12 Month P/E	39.7
S&P Oper. EPS 2005E	2.80	Beta	0.11
Yield (%)	Nil	Shareholders	3,234
Dividend Rate/Share	Nil	Market Cap (B)	$ 13.7
Shares Outstanding (M)	177.0		

Value of $10,000 invested five years ago: **$ 55,445**

Dividend Data

Amount ($)	Date Decl.	Ex-Div. Date	Stock of Record	Payment Date
2-for-1	—	Nov. 23	Nov. 01	Nov. 22 '04

Revenues/Earnings Data Fiscal year ending December 31

Revenues (Million $)

	2004	2003	2002	2001	2000	1999
1Q	548.4	441.4	371.2	326.1	295.5	266.7
2Q	556.6	495.1	404.4	336.1	300.9	290.7
3Q	578.3	477.4	404.9	337.0	287.0	275.8
4Q	—	518.6	409.5	348.2	295.4	281.3
Yr.	—	1,933	1,590	1,347	1,179	1,115

Earnings Per Share ($)

	2004	2003	2002	2001	2000	1999
1Q	0.52	0.43	0.34	0.27	0.10	-0.07
2Q	0.53	0.43	0.38	0.25	0.20	0.21
3Q	0.49	0.46	0.39	0.18	0.22	-0.22
4Q	E0.64	0.51	0.40	0.28	0.24	0.21
Yr.	E2.30	1.83	1.51	0.96	0.76	0.15

Next earnings report expected: late-January Source: S&P, Company Reports
EPS Estimates based on S&P Operating Earnings; historical GAAP earnings are as reported.

St. Jude Medical, Inc.

Recommendation: **HOLD** ★★★☆☆   12-Month Target Price: **$80.00** (as of September 29, 2004)

Business Summary October 22, 2004

St. Jude Medical, originally formed to produce mechanical heart valves, has expanded into several medical device industry areas, including cardiac rhythm management (CRM), cardiology and vascular access, and cardiac surgery. Sales outside the U.S. accounted for 42% of revenues in 2003.

Cardiac rhythm management products (71% of 2003 sales) include pacemakers and related systems used to treat patients with hearts that beat too slowly (bradycardia). Current pacemakers, including the Identity ADx, Integrity ADx, Verity ADx, Affinity, Entity and Regency lines, offer STJ technological features such as the AF Suppression Pacing Algorithm (designed to suppress atrial fibrillation) and the beat-by-beat Autocapture pacing System that lets the pacemaker monitor every paced beat to verify that the heart has been stimulated, deliver a back-up pulse in the event of non-stimulation, continuously measure threshold, and adjust energy output to match changing patient needs. The Identity family of pacemakers, launched in February 2002, expanded the feature set to include a suite of arrhythmia diagnostics, including dial-channel stored electrograms. Outside the U.S., STJ also sells the Genesis System, a device-based ventricular resynchronization system designed to treat congestive heart failure and suppress atrial fibrillation.

Implantable cardioverter defibrillators (ICDs) are used to treat patients with hearts that beat too fast (tachycardia), monitoring the heartbeat and delivering higher energy electrical impulses to end ventricular tachycardia and ventricular fibrillation. ICD products include the Atlas (approved by the FDA in December 2001),

Photon and Contour lines. Outside the U.S., STJ also sells the Profile ICDs. The company hopes to gain FDA approval in 2004 to sell its Epic HF ICD, Atlas+ HF ICD, Aescula 1055K left-heart lead, and QuickSite left-heart lead.

The Cardiology and Vascular Access (15%) division makes specialized disposable cardiovascular devices such as percutaneous (through the skin) catheter introducers, diagnostic guidewires, vascular closure devices, angiography catheters, electrophysiology catheters, and bipolar temporary pacing catheters.

The Cardiac Surgery unit (14%) consists of the heart valve group and the Anastomotic Technology group. Heart valve replacements or repair products may be needed when a natural heart valve has deteriorated due to congenital defects or disease. STJ offers both mechanical and tissue replacement heart valves. Its mechanical valve has been implanted in more than 1.4 million patients. The company also markets the Toronto SPV stentless tissue valve, the world's leading stentless tissue valve; and the SJM Biocor tissue valves. The division has also developed a suture-free device, the Symmetry Bypass System Aortic Connector, which lets cardiac surgeons attach vein grafts to the aorta during coronary bypass artery graft procedures without sutures.

R&D spending in 2003 totaled $241.1 million, or 12.5% of sales, up from $200.3 million (12.6%) in 2002. For 2004, management anticipates that R&D spending will consume 12.5% to 13.0% of sales.

Company Financials Fiscal Year ending December 31

Per Share Data ($)

(Year Ended December 31)	2003	2002	2001	2000	1999	1998	1997	1996	1995	1994
Tangible Bk. Val.	6.03	6.53	4.55	2.99	2.04	2.88	3.49	2.93	2.76	3.96
Cash Flow	2.24	1.92	1.47	1.29	0.65	1.15	0.66	0.84	1.19	0.62
Earnings	1.83	1.51	0.96	0.76	0.15	0.75	0.30	0.56	0.91	0.56
S&P Core Earnings	1.63	1.26	0.76	NA	NA	NA	NA	NA	NA	NA
Dividends	Nil	Nil	Nil	Nil	Nil	Nil	Nil	Nil	Nil	0.10
Payout Ratio	Nil	Nil	Nil	Nil	Nil	Nil	Nil	Nil	Nil	18%
Prices - High	64.00	43.12	39.03	31.25	20.37	19.84	21.46	23.00	21.62	13.66
- Low	38.76	30.52	22.22	11.81	11.46	9.59	13.50	14.81	11.83	8.25
P/E Ratio - High	35	29	41	41	NM	26	73	41	24	24
- Low	21	20	23	16	NM	13	46	26	13	15

Income Statement Analysis (Million $)

	2003	2002	2001	2000	1999	1998	1997	1996	1995	1994
Revs.	1,933	1,590	1,347	1,179	1,115	1,016	994	809	724	360
Oper. Inc.	533	445	347	326	300	263	212	260	234	148
Depr.	76.7	74.9	90.3	92.3	85.7	68.9	66.1	44.9	40.3	8.31
Int. Exp.	Nil	Nil	Nil	Nil	Nil	23.7	14.4	3.54	12.9	3.71
Pretax Inc.	459	373	228	177	67.0	186	88.2	142	188	106
Eff. Tax Rate	26.0%	26.0%	24.3%	27.2%	63.8%	30.5%	38.0%	35.0%	30.9%	25.5%
Net Inc.	339	276	173	129	24.2	129	54.7	92.2	129	79.0
S&P Core Earnings	301	231	136	NA	NA	NA	NA	NA	NA	NA

Balance Sheet & Other Fin. Data (Million $)

	2003	2002	2001	2000	1999	1998	1997	1996	1995	1994
Cash	461	402	148	108	88.9	88.0	28.5	185	166	137
Curr. Assets	1,492	1,114	798	705	690	682	743	665	520	434
Total Assets	2,556	1,951	1,629	1,533	1,554	1,385	1,459	1,301	1,016	920
Curr. Liab.	510	375	322	297	283	203	252	293	193	113
LT Debt	352	Nil	123	295	477	375	220	172	120	255
Common Equity	1,604	1,577	1,184	941	794	806	987	836	703	552
Total Cap.	2,046	1,577	1,307	1,235	1,272	1,181	1,207	1,008	823	807
Cap. Exp.	49.6	62.2	63.1	39.7	69.4	74.2	94.0	95.0	43.0	18.8
Cash Flow	416	351	263	221	110	198	121	137	169	88.0
Curr. Ratio	2.9	3.0	2.5	2.4	2.4	3.4	3.0	2.3	2.7	3.9
% LT Debt of Cap.	17.2	Nil	9.4	23.8	37.6	31.7	18.2	17.1	14.6	31.6
% Net Inc.of Revs.	17.6	17.4	12.8	11.0	2.2	12.7	5.5	11.4	17.8	22.0
% Ret. on Assets	15.1	15.4	10.9	8.4	1.6	9.1	4.0	7.9	13.3	10.9
% Ret. on Equity	21.3	20.0	16.2	14.9	3.0	14.4	6.0	11.8	20.6	15.3

Data as orig reptd.; bef. results of disc opers/spec. items. Per share data adj. for stk. divs.; EPS diluted. E-Estimated. NA-Not Available. NM-Not Meaningful. NR-Not Ranked. UR-Under Review.

Office: One Lillehei Plaza, St. Paul, MN 55117.
Telephone: 651-483-2000.
Website: http://www.sjm.com
Chrmn, Pres & CEO: D.J. Starks.
EVP, CFO & Treas: J.C. Heinmiller.

VP, Secy, General Counsel & Investor Contact: K.T. O'Malley
651-483-2000.
Dirs: R. Devenuti, S. M. Essig, T. H. Garrett III, M. A. Rocca, D. J. Starks, D. A. Thompson, S. Widensohler, W. Yarno, F. Yin.
Auditor: Ernst & Young.

Founded: in 1976.
Domicile: Minnesota.
Employees: 7,391.
S&P Analyst: Robert M. Gold/CB/JWP

St. Paul Travelers

Recommendation: **SELL** ★ ★ ☆ ☆ ☆
(SELL SELL HOLD BUY BUY)

12-Month Target Price: **$30.00**
(as of August 05, 2004)

STA has an approximate 0.22% weighting in the **S&P 500**

Sector: Financials
Sub-Industry: Property & Casualty Insurance
Peer Group: Commercial/Personal Insurers - National

Summary: Formed via the 2004 merger of Travelers Property Casualty Corp. and Saint Paul Cos., STA is a leading provider of commercial property-liability and homeowners and auto insurance.

Quantitative Evaluations

S&P Earnings & Dividend Rank: NR

D	C	B-	B	B+	A-	A	A+

S&P Fair Value Rank: 2-

1	2	3	4	5
Lowest				Highest

Fair Value Calc.: $32.20 (Slightly Overvalued)

S&P Investability Quotient Percentile

79%

STA scored higher than 79% of all companies for which an S&P Report is available.

Volatility: Average

Low	Average	High

Technical Evaluation: Bullish
Since 11/04, the technical indicators for STA have been Bullish.

Relative Strength Rank: Moderate

64

1 Lowest	Highest 99

Price as of 11/12/04:	$36.54	2004E S&P Core EPS:	$2.85

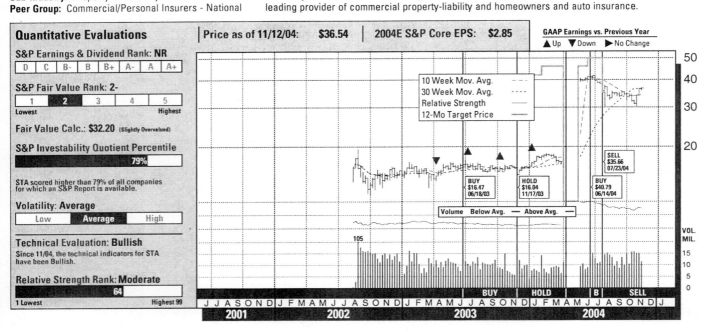

GAAP Earnings vs. Previous Year
▲ Up ▼ Down ► No Change

Analyst commentary prepared by Catherine A. Seifert/CB/JWP

Highlights August 13, 2004

- We expect earned premium growth for the combined companies in the mid- to high single digit range in 2004, on strong written premium growth for personal lines, partially offset by more moderate written premium growth in the commercial and specialty lines.

- Total revenue growth will not likely be as robust, in our view, reflecting only a low single digit rise in net investment income, due to the relatively low interest rate environment. We expect that underwriting results in 2004 will improve from 2003's levels, assuming the low levels of catastrophe losses experienced in the first half of 2004 do not increase significantly for the second half of the year.

- We expect operating earnings per share (defined as net income before realized investment gains or losses) to reach $3.15 in 2004. Our estimate includes $1.54 and $0.04 in after-tax reserve adjustment and restructuring charges, respectively, associated with the St. Paul merger. We forecast operating EPS of $5.25 in 2005, up 11% from 2004's level, excluding the merger-related charges.

Investment Rationale/Risk August 13, 2004

- We recently downgraded the shares to avoid from accumulate after STA announced a $1.6 billion pretax charge to boost surety and construction reserves and to account for certain uncollectible reinsurance agreements associated with the historical St. Paul businesses. We believe the need to shore up St. Paul reserves in the context of a "merger of equals" reduces management credibility at a time of increased uncertainty due to the merger, and advise investors to avoid the shares on the added risk.

- Risks to our recommendation and target price include better than expected asbestos and environmental claims and reserves development, higher than expected revenue and cost synergies associated with the merger, lower than anticipated levels of catastrophe losses, and a lessening of price competition for a number of property and casualty lines.

- Our $30 target price assumes a 12-month forward price/tangible book multiple of 1.3X, a modest discount to the peer group average. We choose a lower multiple to account for the additional merger-related risks.

Key Stock Statistics

S&P Oper. EPS 2004E	2.30	52-week Range	$41.75-14.82
P/E on S&P Oper. EPS 2004E	15.9	12 Month P/E	NM
S&P Oper. EPS 2005E	4.80	Beta	NA
Yield (%)	2.4%	Shareholders	16,848
Dividend Rate/Share	0.88	Market Cap (B)	$ 24.4
Shares Outstanding (M)	668.8		

Value of $10,000 invested five years ago: **NA**

Dividend Data Dividends have been paid since 2003

Amount ($)	Date Decl.	Ex-Div. Date	Stock of Record	Payment Date
0.080	Jan. 22	Feb. 02	Feb. 04	Feb. 27 '04
0.220	Apr. 29	Jun. 08	Jun. 10	Jun. 30 '04
0.220	Jul. 28	Sep. 08	Sep. 10	Sep. 30 '04
0.220	Oct. 27	Dec. 08	Dec. 10	Dec. 31 '04

Revenues/Earnings Data Fiscal year ending December 31

Revenues (Million $)

	2004	2003	2002	2001	2000	1999
1Q	4,128	3,603	3,233	3,058	—	—
2Q	6,181	3,749	3,320	2,983	—	—
3Q	6,261	3,746	3,564	3,012	—	—
4Q	—	4,042	4,153	3,178	—	—
Yr.	—	15,139	14,270	12,231	—	—

Earnings Per Share ($)

	2004	2003	2002	2001	2000	1999
1Q	1.34	0.34	0.43	—	—	—
2Q	—	0.44	0.33	—	—	—
3Q	—	0.42	0.33	—	—	—
4Q	—	0.49	-0.79	—	—	—
Yr.	—	1.68	0.23	1.06	—	—

Next earnings report expected: late-January Source: S&P, Company Reports
EPS Estimates based on S&P Operating Earnings; historical GAAP earnings are as reported.

Please read the Required Disclosures and Reg. AC certification on the last page of this report.

The **McGraw·Hill** Companies

STANDARD
&POOR'S

The St. Paul Travelers Companies, Inc.

Stock Report
November 13, 2004
NYSE Symbol: **STA**

Recommendation: **SELL** ★ ★ ☆ ☆ ☆   12-Month Target Price: **$30.00** (as of August 05, 2004)

Business Summary August 15, 2004

The St. Paul Travelers Companies Inc. was formed on April 1, 2004, as a result of the acquisition of Travelers Property Casualty Corp. by The Saint Paul Companies. Under terms of the transaction, each Travelers common share was exchanged for 0.4334 of a share of common stock of The Saint Paul Companies (now known as The St. Paul Travelers Companies, Inc.). For accounting purposes, the transaction was structured as a reverse acquisition, with Travelers treated as the acquirer. The company will also continue to hold the 79% ownership interest in John Nuveen & Co. that was held by Saint Paul. On a pro forma basis, the new entity is believed to be the second largest commercial lines insurer in the United States. The $20.6 billion in estimated 2003 pro forma net written premiums for the combined entity were divided as follows: middle market commercial lines 24%, small commercial lines 15%, national commercial accounts 5%, construction 6%, surety 5%, financial and professional services 4%, other specialty commercial lines 17%, and personal lines 24%.

Founded in Saint Paul, MN, in 1853, The St. Paul Companies is the 14th largest property-casualty insurer in the U.S. Operating revenues (which exclude realized investment gains and/ or losses) totaled just under $8.8 billion in 2003 (down from nearly $9.2 billion in 2002), and were divided: earned premiums 80%, net invest-ment income 13%, asset management fees 5%, and other 2%. Net written premi-ums totaled $7.5 billion in 2003, up 5.6% from $7.1 billion in 2002. During 2003, commercial lines accounted for 30% of net written premiums, general commercial

lines 33%, surety and construction 16%, international and Lloyds 18%, and runoff operations (primary health care and reinsurance) 3%. The combined loss and expense ratio in 2003 improved to 102.5%, from 109.6% in 2002 (both presented on a statutory basis.)

Headquartered in Hartford, CT, Travelers Property Casualty Corp. is the fifth largest property-casualty insurer in the U.S. The company is also the third largest commercial lines insurer and the eighth largest personal lines insurer. Operating revenues totaled $15.1 billion in 2003 (up from $14.1 billion in 2002), and were divided: earned premiums 83%, net investment income 12%, fee income 4%, and other 1%. Net written premiums totaled $13.2 billion in 2003, up nearly 11% from $11.9 billion in 2002. During 2003, commercial lines accounted for 62% of net written premiums, while personal lines accounted for the remaining 38%. The combined loss and expense ratio equaled 96.9% in 2003, an improvement over the 117.4% reported for 2002. The commercial lines segment reported a combined ratio of 98.4% (versus 128.9% in 2002), while the personal lines segment reported a combined ratio of 94.4% (versus 99.4%).

John Nuveen & Co., 79%-owned at the end of 2003, underwrites and trades municipal bonds and tax-exempt unit investment trusts and markets tax-exempt open-end and closed-end funds. Assets under management rose 20% during 2003, to $95.4 billion.

Company Financials Fiscal Year ending December 31

Per Share Data ($)

(Year Ended December 31)	2003	2002	2001	2000	1999	1998	1997	1996	1995	1994
Tangible Bk. Val.	9.52	10.29	6.66	NA	NA	NA	NA	NA	NA	NA
Oper. Earnings	NA	NA	NA	NA	NA	NA	NA	NA	NA	NA
Earnings	1.68	0.23	1.06	NA	NA	NA	NA	NA	NA	NA
S&P Core Earnings	3.71	0.14	NA	NA	NA	NA	NA	NA	NA	NA
Dividends	0.28	Nil	NA	NA	NA	NA	NA	NA	NA	NA
Payout Ratio	17%	Nil	NA	NA	NA	NA	NA	NA	NA	NA
Prices - High	17.42	19.50	NA	NA	NA	NA	NA	NA	NA	NA
- Low	12.98	12.09	NA	NA	NA	NA	NA	NA	NA	NA
P/E Ratio - High	10	85	NA	NA	NA	NA	NA	NA	NA	NA
- Low	8	53	NA	NA	NA	NA	NA	NA	NA	NA

Income Statement Analysis (Million $)

	2003	2002	2001	2000	1999	1998	1997	1996	1995	1994
Premium Inc.	12,545	11,155	9,411	NA	NA	NA	NA	NA	NA	NA
Net Invest. Inc.	1,869	1,881	2,034	NA	NA	NA	NA	NA	NA	NA
Oth. Revs.	725	1,234	786	NA	NA	NA	NA	NA	NA	NA
Total Revs.	15,139	14,270	12,231	NA	NA	NA	NA	NA	NA	NA
Pretax Inc.	2,229	-260	1,389	NA	NA	NA	NA	NA	NA	NA
Net Oper. Inc.	NA	NA	NA	NA	NA	NA	NA	NA	NA	NA
Net Inc.	1,696	216	1,062	NA	NA	NA	NA	NA	NA	NA
S&P Core Earnings	1,615	41.1	NA	NA	NA	NA	NA	NA	NA	NA

Balance Sheet & Other Fin. Data (Million $)

	2003	2002	2001	2000	1999	1998	1997	1996	1995	1994
Cash & Equiv.	714	432	NA	NA	NA	NA	NA	NA	NA	NA
Premiums Due	4,090	3,861	NA	NA	NA	NA	NA	NA	NA	NA
Invest. Assets: Bonds	33,046	30,003	NA	NA	NA	NA	NA	NA	NA	NA
Invest. Assets: Stocks	733	852	NA	NA	NA	NA	NA	NA	NA	NA
Invest. Assets: Loans	211	258	32,843	NA	NA	NA	NA	NA	NA	NA
Invest. Assets: Total	38,652	38,425	NA	NA	NA	NA	NA	NA	NA	NA
Deferred Policy Costs	925	873	NA	NA	NA	NA	NA	NA	NA	NA
Total Assets	64,872	64,138	57,599	NA	NA	NA	NA	NA	NA	NA
Debt	2,675	2,744	3,755	NA	NA	NA	NA	NA	NA	NA
Common Equity	11,987	10,137	9,729	NA	NA	NA	NA	NA	NA	NA
Prop. & Cas. Loss Ratio	NA	NA	80.7	NA	NA	NA	NA	NA	NA	NA
Prop. & Cas. Expense Ratio	NA	NA	27.3	NA	NA	NA	NA	NA	NA	NA
Prop. & Cas. Combined Ratio	96.9	117.4	108.0	NA	NA	NA	NA	NA	NA	NA
% Return On Revs.	11.2	1.6	8.7	NA	NA	NA	NA	NA	NA	NA
% Ret. on Equity	15.3	NA	NA	NA	NA	NA	NA	NA	NA	NA

Data as orig reptd.; bef. results of disc opers/spec. items. Data for Travelers prior to April 2004. Balance sheet & per share data pro forma in 2001. Per share data adj. for stk. divs.; EPS diluted (primary prior to 1998). E-Estimated.
NA-Not Available. NM-Not Meaningful. NR-Not Ranked.

Office: 385 Washington Street, Saint Paul, MN 55102.
Telephone: 651-310-7911.
Website: http://www.stpaultravelers.com
Chrmn: R.I. Lipp.
Pres & CEO: J.S. Fishman.
EVP & Chief Admin: A. Bessette.
EVP & Investor Contact: M. Olivo 860-277-8330.

SVP & Secy: B.A. Backberg.
Dirs: H. P. Berkowitz, K. J. Bialkin, C. H. Byrd, J. H. Dasburg, L. B. Disharoon, J. M. Dolan, K. M. Duberstein, J. S. Fishman, L. G. Graev, M. D. Hartzband, T. R. Hodgson, W. H. Kling, J. A. Lawrence, R. I. Lipp, B. J. McGarvie, G. D. Nelson, C. Otis, Jr., J. M. Peek, N. A. Roseman, C. W. Scharf, G. M. Sprenger, F. J. Tasco, L. J. Thomsen.

Founded: in 1853.
Domicile: Minnesota.
Employees: 9,300.
S&P Analyst: Catherine A. Seifert/CB/JWP

Sanmina-SCI Corp.

Recommendation: **BUY** ★★★★★   12-Month Target Price: **$11.00**
SELL SELL HOLD BUY BUY   (as of October 08, 2004)

SANM has an approximate 0.04% weighting in the **S&P 500**

Sector: Information Technology
Sub-Industry: Electronic Manufacturing Services
Peer Group: Circuit Boards/Microelectronics - Larger Sales

Summary: SANM (formerly Sanmina Corp.), a provider of customized integrated manufacturing services to OEMs in the electronics industry, acquired SCI Systems in December 2001.

Quantitative Evaluations

S&P Earnings & Dividend Rank: C

| D | C | B- | B | B+ | A- | A | A+ |

S&P Fair Value Rank: 5

| 1 | 2 | 3 | 4 | 5 |
| Lowest | | | | Highest |

Fair Value Calc.: $11.20 (Undervalued)

S&P Investability Quotient Percentile

59%

SANM scored higher than 59% of all companies for which an S&P Report is available.

Volatility: High

| Low | Average | **High** |

Technical Evaluation: Bullish
Since 10/04, the technical indicators for SANM have been Bullish.

Relative Strength Rank: Strong

90

1 Lowest   Highest 99

Price as of 11/12/04: **$9**   2005E S&P Core EPS: **$0.33**

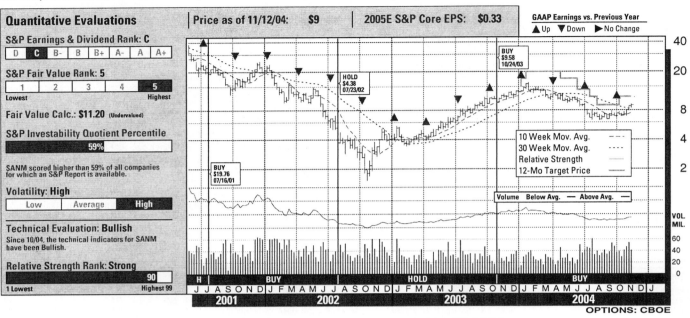

GAAP Earnings vs. Previous Year
▲ Up ▼ Down ► No Change

BUY $9.58 10/24/03

HOLD $4.38 07/23/02

BUY $19.76 07/16/01

- - - 10 Week Mov. Avg.
····· 30 Week Mov. Avg.
Relative Strength
12-Mo Target Price

Volume Below Avg. — Above Avg.

VOL. MIL.

H | BUY | HOLD | BUY
J J A S O N D | J F M A M J J A S O N D | J F M A M J J A S O N D | J F M A M J J A S O N D | J
2001 | **2002** | **2003** | **2004**

OPTIONS: CBOE

Analyst commentary prepared by Richard N. Stice, CFA /MF/BK

Highlights November 01, 2004

- We expect revenues to increase about 13% in FY 05 (Sep.), following an advance of 18% in FY 04. We see growth being driven by improving end market demand in SANM's primary vertical markets, and by the ramping up of several new customer wins. We expect other areas of growth to include original design manufacturing, where we see the company expanding revenues by 30%-50% in FY 05.

- We see gross margins as likely to widen, aided by higher volumes, a more favorable business mix, rising capacity utilization, and the benefits of cost reduction efforts. We see interest expense continuing to decline as a result of the company's recent moves to lower its debt profile.

- We forecast FY 05 operating EPS of $0.46, up 92% from FY 04's $0.24 (excluding $0.25 of special charges). Our Standard & Poor's Core Earnings estimate FY 05 is $0.33, reflecting projected stock option expense.

Investment Rationale/Risk November 01, 2004

- We recommend buying these high beta shares. Our recommendation is based in part on our positive view of the electronics manufacturing services (EMS) industry. Over the past few years, we believe SANM has enhanced its industry presence, diversified its product and service offerings, and produced a number of synergies. In addition, with the company's restructuring plans expected to be largely completed by 2005, and end market demand picking up, in our estimation, near-term results may be stronger than previously anticipated.

- Risks to our recommendation and target price include a possible loss of market share, further restructuring of business operations beyond those currently stated, and an inability to expand the design manufacturing business.

- Our 12-month target price of $11 combines discounted cash flow (DCF) analysis with a relative price to sales measure. Our DCF model assumes a weighted average cost of capital of 10.4% and an expected terminal growth rate of 3%.

Key Stock Statistics

S&P Oper. EPS 2005E	**0.46**	52-week Range	**$15.51-6.30**
P/E on S&P Oper. EPS 2005E	**19.6**	12 Month P/E	**NM**
S&P Oper. EPS 2006E	**0.64**	Beta	**NA**
Yield (%)	**Nil**	Shareholders	**2,731**
Dividend Rate/Share	**Nil**	Market Cap (B)	**$ 4.7**
Shares Outstanding (M)	**521.1**		

Value of $10,000 invested five years ago: **$ 3,705**

Dividend Data

No cash dividends have been paid. A bank credit agreement currently prohibits the payment of cash dividends.

Revenues/Earnings Data Fiscal year ending September 30

Revenues (Million $)

	2004	2003	2002	2001	2000	1999
1Q	2,970	2,537	1,130	1,390	763.7	275.5
2Q	2,862	2,444	2,411	1,191	875.2	281.1
3Q	3,070	2,649	2,618	776.6	1,001	309.5
4Q	3,301	2,732	2,602	600.7	1,272	348.6
Yr.	12,204	10,361	8,762	4,054	3,912	1,215

Earnings Per Share ($)

	2004	2003	2002	2001	2000	1999
1Q	0.03	-0.01	-0.12	0.34	0.15	Nil
2Q	-0.09	-0.06	-0.08	0.19	0.17	0.12
3Q	0.02	-0.02	-0.01	0.09	0.01	0.13
4Q	0.01	-0.17	-5.10	-0.52	0.30	0.14
Yr.	-0.02	-0.27	-5.60	0.12	0.64	0.38

Next earnings report expected: late-January Source: S&P, Company Reports
EPS Estimates based on S&P Operating Earnings; historical GAAP earnings are as reported.

Sanmina-SCI Corporation

Recommendation: **BUY** ★ ★ ★ ★ ★   12-Month Target Price: **$11.00** (as of October 08, 2004)

Business Summary November 01, 2004

Sanmina-SCI Corp. operates in the electronic manufacturing services (EMS) industry.

The company offers its OEM customers end-to-end services that span the entire product life cycle, from product design and engineering to after market service and support. Products manufactured by SANM for OEMs include wireless and wireline communications switches, personal computers, high-end computers and servers, medical imaging systems and digital satellite set-top boxes. Products are made in more than 20 countries, on five continents. The company seeks to locate facilities either near customers in major electronics industry centers, or in low-cost locations.

SANM has also begun to offer product designs that the customer can either brand or integrate into their own system solution. In this model, it takes on the role of the original design manufacturer (ODM). For ODM products, the company retains intellectual property rights and earns royalty or licensing fees, in addition to manufacturing revenue associated with building and shipping the product.

The company targets markets that it believes offer significant growth opportunities, and for which OEMs sell complex products that are subject to rapid technological change. SANM's approach to its target markets is two-fold. It intends to strengthen its significant presence in the communications and computing mar-

kets, while also focusing on other under penetrated sectors, such as the automotive, defense, industrial and semiconductor capital equipment segments.

Historically, SANM has had substantial recurring sales from existing customers. SANM typically enters into supply agreements with its major OEM customers that range from three to five years. Many of these agreements have have been entered into in connection with divestiture transactions, in which the company acquires plants, equipment and inventory from the OEM. In these situations, the customer typically agrees to purchase its requirements for particular products and geographic areas from SANM. However, these contracts generally do not obligate the customer to purchase minimum quantities of products.

Revenues are concentrated among a handful of customers. In FY 03 (Sep.), sales to the 10 largest customers accounted for 68.5% of net sales, up from 65.8% in FY 02. The two largest customers in FY 03, IBM and Hewlett-Packard, accounted for 28.8% and 9.6% of net sales, respectively. FY 03 international sales provided 70% of the total, up from 56% in FY 02.

In January 2003, SANM reached an agreement with IBM to provide a range of additional manufacturing services in North America and Europe. The company's revenues over the three-year term of the agreement were expected to exceed $3.6 billion.

Company Financials Fiscal Year ending September 30

Per Share Data ($)

(Year Ended September 30)	2004	2003	2002	2001	2000	1999	1998	1997	1996	1995
Tangible Bk. Val.	NA	2.23	2.50	4.85	4.54	2.47	1.70	1.08	0.71	0.45
Cash Flow	NA	0.17	-5.08	0.67	1.14	0.58	0.47	0.37	0.26	0.13
Earnings	-0.02	-0.27	-5.60	0.12	0.64	0.38	0.36	0.17	0.20	0.13
S&P Core Earnings	NA	-0.37	-2.11	-0.01	NA	NA	NA	NA	NA	NA
Dividends	Nil	Nil	Nil	Nil	Nil	Nil	Nil	Nil	Nil	Nil
Payout Ratio	Nil	Nil	Nil	Nil	Nil	Nil	Nil	Nil	Nil	Nil
Prices - High	15.51	12.81	23.80	54.75	60.50	27.31	15.62	11.34	7.09	3.57
- Low	6.30	3.43	1.52	11.64	21.06	12.37	4.90	4.75	2.53	1.60
P/E Ratio - High	NM	NM	NM	NM	95	72	44	41	35	28
- Low	NM	NM	NM	NM	33	33	14	17	13	13

Income Statement Analysis (Million $)

	2004	2003	2002	2001	2000	1999	1998	1997	1996	1995
Revs.	NA	10,361	8,762	4,054	3,912	1,215	723	405	265	168
Oper. Inc.	NA	357	331	456	545	220	139	81.5	53.4	31.7
Depr.	NA	223	250	181	157	48.8	27.3	12.9	8.10	4.68
Int. Exp.	NA	130	98.0	55.2	Nil	Nil	0.69	5.10	5.16	0.73
Pretax Inc.	NA	-198	-2,814	82.8	330	148	107	67.1	45.3	28.0
Eff. Tax Rate	NA	NM	NM	51.1%	40.3%	36.6%	36.5%	39.0%	38.0%	39.2%
Net Inc.	NA	-137	-2,697	40.4	197	93.7	68.2	40.9	28.1	17.0
S&P Core Earnings	NA	-193	-1,018	-1.97	NA	NA	NA	NA	NA	NA

Balance Sheet & Other Fin. Data (Million $)

	2004	2003	2002	2001	2000	1999	1998	1997	1996	1995
Cash	NA	1,083	1,065	568	993	136	153	122	115	107
Curr. Assets	NA	4,169	4,159	2,583	2,585	885	342	234	185	163
Total Assets	NA	7,450	7,518	3,640	3,639	1,202	468	303	231	188
Curr. Liab.	NA	2,036	2,054	492	712	217	115	60.3	40.0	34.0
LT Debt	NA	1,926	1,975	1,219	1,144	355	5.77	86.3	86.3	86.3
Common Equity	NA	3,323	3,415	1,841	1,701	626	344	156	104	67.1
Total Cap.	NA	5,339	5,407	3,121	2,907	982	350	242	190	154
Cap. Exp.	NA	70.7	93.0	188	199	65.3	29.0	30.2	21.8	9.93
Cash Flow	NA	85.4	-2,447	221	355	142	95.4	53.8	36.2	17.7
Curr. Ratio	NA	2.0	2.0	5.2	3.6	4.1	3.0	3.9	4.6	4.8
% LT Debt of Cap.	NA	36.1	36.5	39.1	39.3	36.2	1.6	35.6	45.4	56.0
% Net Inc.of Revs.	NA	NM	NM	1.0	5.0	7.7	9.4	10.1	10.6	10.1
% Ret. on Assets	NA	NM	NM	1.1	7.0	10.1	17.7	15.3	13.4	13.5
% Ret. on Equity	NA	NM	NM	2.2	15.4	16.9	27.3	31.5	32.9	29.9

Data as orig reptd.; bef. results of disc opers/spec. items. Per share data adj. for stk. divs.; EPS diluted. E-Estimated. NA-Not Available. NM-Not Meaningful. NR-Not Ranked. UR-Under Review.

Office: 2700 North First Street, San Jose, CA 95134.
Telephone: 408-964-3500.
Email: info@sanmina-sci.com
Website: http://www.sanmina-sci.com
Chrmn & CEO: J. Sola.

Pres & COO: R.W. Furr.
EVP & CFO: D.L. White.
Investor Contact: P. Bombino 408-964-3610.
Dirs: J. Bolger, N. R. Bonke, R. Furr, M. M. Rosati, A. E. Sapp, Jr., W. Shortridge, P. J. Simone, J. Sola, B. Vonderschmitt, J. M. Ward.

Founded: in 1989.
Domicile: Delaware.
Employees: 45,008.
S&P Analyst: Richard N. Stice, CFA /MF/BK

Sara Lee

Recommendation: **HOLD** ★ ★ ★ ☆ ☆
SELL | SELL | HOLD | BUY | BUY

12-Month Target Price: $23.00
(as of August 05, 2004)

SLE has an approximate 0.17% weighting in the **S&P 500**

Sector: Consumer Staples
Sub-Industry: Packaged Foods & Meats
Peer Group: Very Large Food Manufacturers

Summary: SLE is a diversified producer of branded food products (meats, fresh and frozen baked goods and coffee products), as well as personal apparel and household care products.

Quantitative Evaluations

S&P Earnings & Dividend Rank: A-

| D | C | B- | B | B+ | A- | A | A+ |

S&P Fair Value Rank: 5

| 1 | 2 | 3 | 4 | 5 |
| Lowest | | | | Highest |

Fair Value Calc.: $25.40 (Slightly Undervalued)

S&P Investability Quotient Percentile

97%

SLE scored higher than 97% of all companies for which an S&P Report is available.

Volatility: Low

| Low | Average | High |

Technical Evaluation: Bullish

Since 10/04, the technical indicators for SLE have been Bullish.

Relative Strength Rank: Moderate

| | 62 | |
| 1 Lowest | | Highest 99 |

| Price as of 11/12/04: | **$24.32** | 2005E S&P Core EPS: | **$1.60** |

GAAP Earnings vs. Previous Year
▲ Up ▼ Down ► No Change

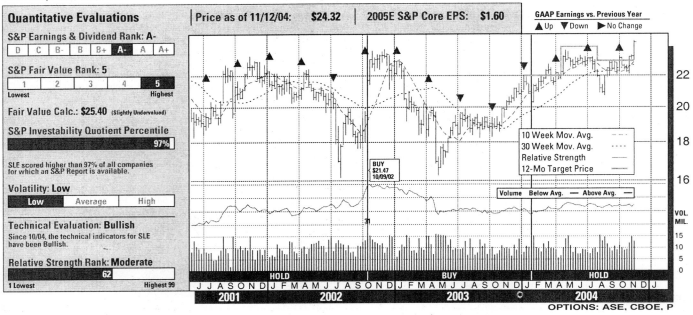

10 Week Mov. Avg. ---
30 Week Mov. Avg. ....
Relative Strength
12-Mo Target Price

Volume Below Avg. — Above Avg.

BUY
$21.47
10/09/02

HOLD | BUY | HOLD
J J A S O N D | J F M A M J J A S O N D | J F M A M J J A S O N D | J F M A M J J A S O N D J
2001 | 2002 | 2003 | 2004

OPTIONS: ASE, CBOE, P

Analyst commentary prepared by Richard Joy/MF

Highlights August 13, 2004

- We believe net sales in FY 05 (Jun.) will advance 2% to 3%, as modest volume growth, higher prices and a foreign currency benefit outweigh the divestiture of Italian hosiery operations. We anticipate continued commodity inflation, representing an incremental $260 million over FY 04, will continue to be a drag on earnings. By business segment, we expect operating profits for the meats and beverage divisions to decline in FY 05, while profits for the bakery segment should rise at a mid- to high-single digit rate. For the household products segment, we expect profits to grow at a mid-single digits rate, while profits in the apparel division are likely to be even with the prior year. Marketing spending will likely rise substantially, as the company spends on new product introductions, such as the launch of its Senseo coffee machine in the U.S., and works to build market share for its strategic brands. We expect total operating profits to rise 4% to 5% in FY 05.

- Following a higher interest expense, an increase in the effective tax rate to 20% from 17.5%, and a reduction in shares outstanding, we expect FY 05 EPS of $1.65, up 4% from FY 04 EPS of $1.59. For FY 06 we expect a further 6% rise to $1.75. For the longer term, we expect annual EPS growth of 7% to 8%.

- Our FY 05 and FY 06 Standard & Poor's Core Earnings per share projections, reflecting estimated stock option expense of $0.05 per share and a modest pension adjustment, are $1.60 and $1.70, respectively.

Key Stock Statistics

S&P Core EPS 2006E	1.70	52-week Range	$24.43-20.13
S&P Oper. EPS 2005E	1.66	12 Month P/E	14.0
P/E on S&P Oper. EPS 2005E	14.7	Beta	0.37
S&P Oper. EPS 2006E	1.75	Shareholders	90,300
Yield (%)	3.2%	Market Cap (B)	$ 19.1
Dividend Rate/Share	0.79	Shares Outstanding (M)	784.8

Value of $10,000 invested five years ago: **$ 10,118**

Dividend Data Dividends have been paid since 1946

Amount ($)	Date Decl.	Ex-Div. Date	Stock of Record	Payment Date
0.188	Jan. 29	Feb. 26	Mar. 01	Apr. 01 '04
0.188	Apr. 29	May. 27	Jun. 01	Jul. 01 '04
0.188	Jun. 24	Aug. 30	Sep. 01	Oct. 01 '04
0.198	Oct. 29	Nov. 29	Dec. 01	Jan. 03 '05

Investment Rationale/Risk August 13, 2004

- We have a hold recommendation on the shares, reflecting our expectations for mixed operating results for the company's businesses. Results in recent quarters have been affected by weakness in the intimates and underwear segment and higher commodity costs, which we believe will continue in FY 05. We see strong operating cash flow and an annual contingency payment related to the European tobacco divestiture likely to finance a dividend hike, continued debt reduction, and higher share repurchases, while increasing focus on core brands should begin to lead to profit margin improvement and lower capital requirements. We like SLE's long-term prospects, and view the shares as worth holding at a recent level of about 12.4X our calendar 2005 EPS estimate of $1.70, a discount to the P/E multiples of comparable food industry peers and the S&P 500 Index.

- Risks to our recommendation and target price relate to competitive pressures in SLE's businesses, commodity cost inflation, consumer acceptance of new products and the company's ability to achieve sales and earnings growth forecasts.

- Our analysis of discounted cash flows, using a weighted average cost of capital of 9%, suggests an intrinsic value for the shares in the low- to mid-$20s. We have a 12-month target price of $23, derived from an analysis of peer multiples and our discounted free cash flow model.

Revenues/Earnings Data Fiscal year ending June 30

Revenues (Million $)

	2005	2004	2003	2002	2001	2000
1Q	4,861	4,666	4,534	4,518	4,455	4,239
2Q	—	5,017	4,776	4,990	4,757	4,634
3Q	—	4,745	4,350	4,200	4,308	4,175
4Q	—	5,138	4,631	4,495	4,227	4,463
Yr.	—	19,566	18,291	17,628	17,747	17,511

Earnings Per Share ($)

	2005	2004	2003	2002	2001	2000
1Q	0.44	0.29	0.38	0.30	0.27	0.26
2Q	E0.39	0.39	0.42	0.20	0.17	0.40
3Q	E0.37	0.47	0.33	0.31	0.28	0.27
4Q	E0.46	0.44	0.37	0.43	1.15	0.33
Yr.	E1.66	1.59	1.50	1.23	1.87	1.27

Next earnings report expected: late-January Source: S&P, Company Reports
EPS Estimates based on S&P Operating Earnings; historical GAAP earnings are as reported.

Please read the Required Disclosures and Reg. AC certification on the last page of this report.

The **McGraw·Hill** Companies

Sara Lee Corporation

Recommendation: **HOLD** ★ ★ ★ ☆ ☆   12-Month Target Price: **$23.00** (as of August 05, 2004)

Business Summary August 13, 2004

Sara Lee, best known for its familiar baked goods, also boasts many other branded food and non-food products, ranging from Ball Park franks to the Wonderbra. The company aims to build leadership brands in three highly focused global businesses: food and beverages, intimates and underwear, and household products. SLE has operations in 55 countries, and markets branded products in nearly 200 nations.

In recent years, SLE has worked to reshape and refocus itself around three core businesses. The company divested several businesses, including its PYA/Monarch foodservice operation (December 2000) and its Coach leather goods unit (April 2001). It regarded these businesses as valuable companies that did not fit its narrower business focus. SLE has been using proceeds from the divestitures to repurchase stock, retire debt, and fund acquisitions. The company tripled the size of its bakery business with the August 2001 acquisition of The Earthgrains Co., one of the largest U.S. fresh bread companies, for about $2.9 billion.

The Sara Lee food and beverage business (53% of FY 03 (Jun.) total sales; 44% of operating profits) consists of packaged meats and baked goods. The company's pork, poultry and beef products are sold to supermarkets, warehouse clubs, and

other customers in the U.S., Europe and Mexico. Brands include Ball Park, Best's, Kahn's, and Hillshire Farm. Sara Lee bakery produces a wide variety of fresh and frozen baked and specialty items. Core products are bread, specialty breads, refrigerated dough, bagels, frozen and fresh pies, pound cakes, cheesecakes, danishes, and specialty desserts, marketed worldwide through multiple channels of distribution. The Sara Lee beverage segment includes the Douwe Egberts, Chock Full O'Nuts, MJB, and Hills Bros. coffee brands, and Pickwick tea brands.

Intimates and underwear (35%, 38%) products include such personal products as hosiery (Hanes, L'eggs, Sheer Energy, Underalls, Dim, Pretty Polly) and underwear and intimate apparel (Bali, Dim, Hanes, Playtex). The household products segment (12%, 18%) includes brands such as Kiwi shoe care and Sanex skin care products.

The company's established financial goals include real annual EPS growth of 8% to 10% over time, a total debt to capital ratio below 40%, and after-tax return on invested capital in excess of 20%. SLE repurchased common stock valued at $305 million in FY 03, $138 million in FY 02, and $643 million in FY 01.

Company Financials Fiscal Year ending June 30

Per Share Data ($)

(Year Ended June 30)	2004	2003	2002	2001	2000	1999	1998	1997	1996	1995
Tangible Bk. Val.	NM	NM	NM	NM	NM	NM	NM	0.35	0.46	NM
Cash Flow	2.53	2.44	1.94	2.80	1.92	1.83	0.08	1.72	1.57	1.37
Earnings	1.59	1.50	1.23	1.87	1.27	1.26	-0.57	0.99	0.92	0.81
S&P Core Earnings	1.67	1.30	1.00	0.92	NA	NA	NA	NA	NA	NA
Dividends	0.60	0.61	0.59	0.57	0.54	0.49	0.45	0.41	0.37	0.34
Payout Ratio	38%	41%	48%	30%	43%	39%	NM	40%	40%	41%
Prices - High	24.43	23.13	23.84	24.75	25.31	28.75	31.81	28.87	20.25	16.87
- Low	20.17	16.25	16.15	18.26	13.37	21.06	22.15	18.25	14.93	12.12
P/E Ratio - High	15	15	19	13	20	23	NM	28	22	21
- Low	13	11	13	10	11	17	NM	18	16	15

Income Statement Analysis (Million $)

	2004	2003	2002	2001	2000	1999	1998	1997	1996	1995
Revs.	19,566	18,291	17,628	17,747	17,511	20,012	20,011	19,734	18,624	17,719
Oper. Inc.	2,386	2,345	2,138	2,191	2,345	2,304	2,391	2,323	2,185	2,010
Depr.	734	674	582	599	602	553	618	680	634	606
Int. Exp.	271	276	304	270	252	237	224	202	228	243
Pretax Inc.	1,542	1,484	1,185	1,851	1,567	1,671	-443	1,484	1,378	1,219
Eff. Tax Rate	17.5%	17.7%	14.8%	13.4%	26.1%	28.7%	NM	32.0%	33.6%	34.0%
Net Inc.	1,272	1,221	1,010	1,603	1,158	1,191	-523	1,009	916	804
S&P Core Earnings	1,336	1,047	806	768	NA	NA	NA	NA	NA	NA

Balance Sheet & Other Fin. Data (Million $)

	2004	2003	2002	2001	2000	1999	1998	1997	1996	1995
Cash	638	942	298	548	314	279	273	272	243	202
Curr. Assets	5,746	5,953	4,986	5,083	5,974	4,987	5,220	5,391	5,081	4,928
Total Assets	14,883	15,084	13,753	10,167	11,611	10,521	10,989	12,953	12,602	12,431
Curr. Liab.	5,423	5,199	5,463	4,958	6,759	5,953	5,733	5,016	4,642	4,844
LT Debt	4,171	5,157	4,326	2,640	2,248	1,892	2,270	1,933	1,842	1,817
Common Equity	2,948	1,870	1,534	899	1,007	1,034	1,561	4,280	4,320	3,939
Total Cap.	7,194	7,806	7,252	4,646	4,271	3,866	4,718	7,394	7,356	6,882
Cap. Exp.	530	746	669	532	647	535	474	547	542	480
Cash Flow	2,006	1,895	1,592	2,191	1,748	1,732	71.0	1,663	1,523	1,372
Curr. Ratio	1.1	1.1	0.9	1.0	0.9	0.8	0.9	1.1	1.1	1.0
% LT Debt of Cap.	58.0	66.1	59.7	56.8	52.6	48.9	48.1	26.1	25.1	26.4
% Net Inc.of Revs.	6.5	6.7	5.7	9.0	6.6	6.0	NM	5.1	5.0	4.5
% Ret. on Assets	8.4	8.5	8.4	14.7	10.6	11.1	NM	7.9	7.1	6.7
% Ret. on Equity	52.8	71.7	83.0	167.1	112.3	90.9	NM	22.9	21.6	21.2

Data as orig reptd.; bef. results of disc opers/spec. items. Per share data adj. for stk. divs. Bold denotes primary EPS - prior periods restated. E-Estimated. NA-Not Available. NM-Not Meaningful. NR-Not Ranked. UR-Under Review.

Office: 3 First National Plz, Chicago, IL 60602-4226.
Telephone: 312-726-2600.
Website: http://www.saralee.com
Chrmn, Pres & CEO: C.S. McMillan.
Pres & COO: B. Barnes.
EVP & CFO: L.M. de Kool.

EVP, Secy & General Counsel: R.A. Palmore.
SVP & Chief Acctg Officer: W. Szypulski.
SVP, Treas & Investor Contact: D. Ferguson 312-726-2600.
Dirs: B. C. Barnes, J. T. Battenberg, III, C. W. Coker, J. S. Crown, W. D. Davis, V. E. Jordan, Jr., L. T. Koellner, J. D. Manley, C. S. McMillan, I. Prosser, R. L. Ridgway, R. L. Thomas, C. J. van Lede.

Founded: in 1941.
Domicile: Maryland.
Employees: 150,400.
S&P Analyst: Richard Joy/MF

SBC Communications

Recommendation: **SELL** ★★ ☆ ☆ ☆
SELL SELL HOLD BUY BUY
(as of October 04, 2004)

12-Month Target Price: **$23.00**

SBC has an approximate 0.80% weighting in the **S&P 500**

Sector: Telecommunication Services
Sub-Industry: Integrated Telecommunication Services
Peer Group: Regional Bell Operating Companies (RBOC's)

Summary: SBC is the second largest U.S. provider of local telephone and wireless service, through its 60%-owned Cingular joint venture with BellSouth.

Quantitative Evaluations

S&P Earnings & Dividend Rank: B+

D	C	B-	B	B+	A-	A	A+

S&P Fair Value Rank: 2

1	2	3	4	5
Lowest				Highest

Fair Value Calc.: $23.80 (Slightly Overvalued)

S&P Investability Quotient Percentile

71%

SBC scored higher than 71% of all companies for which an S&P Report is available.

Volatility: Low

Low	Average	High

Technical Evaluation: Neutral
Since 11/04, the technical indicators for SBC have been Neutral.

Relative Strength Rank: Moderate

45

1 Lowest   Highest 99

Price as of 11/12/04: $26.67   **2004E S&P Core EPS:** $1.15

GAAP Earnings vs. Previous Year
▲ Up ▼ Down ► No Change

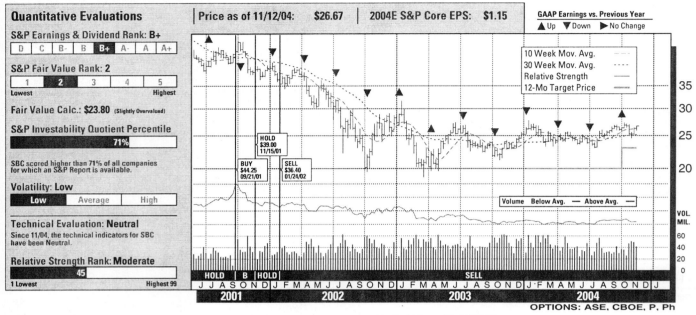

Analyst commentary prepared by Todd Rosenbluth/CB/BK

OPTIONS: ASE, CBOE, P, Ph

Highlights October 22, 2004

- Including revenues from Cingular, we look for combined 2004 revenue for SBC to be up 2%, with declines in local voice revenues stemming from line losses and wireless substitution outweighed by growth in long distance and DSL services, trends we see continuing in 2005. We see Cingular's organic growth providing modest top-line benefits. However, we expect the planned acquisition of AT&T Wireless (AWE: hold, $15), subject to regulatory approvals, to boost revenues significantly in 2005.

- While we believe that SBC's EBITDA margins will be helped moderately as wholesale access rates increase in a number of SBC's territories, margins should remain under pressure, in our view, into 2005. We see margin contraction resulting from SBC's high labor related costs, the buildout of new services, such as satellite, and the company's aggressive bundling efforts. In 2005, we expect that the planned integration of AWE will cause SBC's margins to contract further. We see EBITDA margins narrowing to 33% in 2004 and 30% in 2005, from 34% in 2003.

- We see 2004 operating EPS of $1.46, with Standard & Poor's Core Earnings of $1.15; the difference reflects projected pension adjustments. In 2005, we see operating EPS of $0.94, hurt by expected AWE integration, amortization and financing charges.

Investment Rationale/Risk October 22, 2004

- SBC's third quarter results were ahead of our expectations, in part reflecting non-operating benefits, but we remain concerned that margins will be pressured. We see challenges to SBC's wireless unit following the planned AWE deal closing, particularly related to the company's branding efforts, customer base, and pricing strategy. We believe investors should avoid SBC shares, given our concern that future growth will be offset by access line losses and necessary aggressive customer retention plans. We see risks related to SBC's management succession plans. In addition, we do not look for SBC to generate sufficient earnings to support the dividend in 2005, causing shareholders' equity to decline.

- Risks to our recommendation and target price include a positive change in federal regulations for the telecom segment, consolidation in either the wireline or wireless arena that would eliminate a competitor, and a sustainable recovery in demand for telecom services.

- Our discounted cash flow valuation, assuming a WACC of 8.3%, modest projected declines in cash flow through 2008, and 0% to 2% cash flow growth thereafter, indicates the stock is overvalued. In light of SBC's P/E and enterprise value/EBITDA multiples being above peer levels, anticipated declining operating cash flow, and below-peer margins, our blended 12-month target price is $23.

Key Stock Statistics

S&P Core EPS 2005E	0.68	52-week Range	$27.73-22.83
S&P Oper. EPS 2004E	1.46	12 Month P/E	14.4
P/E on S&P Oper. EPS 2004E	18.3	Beta	0.74
S&P Oper. EPS 2005E	0.94	Shareholders	960,050
Yield (%)	4.7%	Market Cap (B)	$ 88.4
Dividend Rate/Share	1.25	Shares Outstanding (M)	3315.4

Value of $10,000 invested five years ago: **$ 6,221**

Dividend Data Dividends have been paid since 1984

Amount ($)	Date Decl.	Ex-Div. Date	Stock of Record	Payment Date
0.313	Dec. 12	Jan. 07	Jan. 10	Feb. 02 '04
0.313	Mar. 26	Apr. 06	Apr. 10	May. 03 '04
0.313	Jun. 25	Jul. 07	Jul. 10	Aug. 02 '04
0.313	Sep. 24	Oct. 06	Oct. 08	Nov. 01 '04

Revenues/Earnings Data Fiscal year ending December 31

Revenues (Million $)

	2004	2003	2002	2001	2000	1999
1Q	10,128	10,333	10,522	11,190	12,582	7,317
2Q	10,314	10,204	10,843	11,477	13,211	7,395
3Q	10,292	10,239	10,556	11,338	13,454	12,534
4Q	—	10,067	11,217	11,903	12,239	12,896
Yr.	—	40,843	43,138	45,908	51,476	49,489

Earnings Per Share ($)

	2004	2003	2002	2001	2000	1999
1Q	0.59	0.74	0.48	0.54	0.53	0.56
2Q	0.35	0.42	0.53	0.61	0.54	0.59
3Q	0.38	0.37	0.51	0.61	0.88	0.33
4Q	E0.36	0.28	0.71	0.37	0.38	0.50
Yr.	E1.46	1.80	2.23	2.14	2.32	1.90

Next earnings report expected: late-January Source: S&P, Company Reports
EPS Estimates based on S&P Operating Earnings; historical GAAP earnings are as reported.

STANDARD &POOR'S

SBC Communications Inc.

Recommendation: **SELL** ★ ★ ☆ ☆ ☆   12-Month Target Price: **$23.00** (as of October 04, 2004)

Business Summary October 25, 2004

SBC Communications is the second largest U.S. local telephone service provider, with 52.9 million phone lines in 13 states as of September 2004 (down from 55.3 million in September 2003); and the second largest wireless carrier, through its 60%-owned Cingular Wireless joint venture with BellSouth (BLS). The company has grown through mergers with fellow Bell companies Pacific Telesis (a $16.5 billion acquisition in 1997) and Ameritech ($62 billion, 1999). SBC seeks to expand through its wireless, data and long-distance businesses.

The wireline segment, which accounted for 73% of normalized operating revenues (including Cingular) in 2003, consists of local, network access and long-distance services, and messaging and Internet services. SBC finished 2003 with more than 7 million UNE-P wholesale lines. The FCC approved SBC's application to provide interLATA long-distance service for calls originating in Kansas, Oklahoma, Arkansas, Missouri and California by the end of 2002. The company received access to long-distance markets in Michigan in September 2003, and in Illinois, Indiana, Ohio and Wisconsin in October 2003. As of September 2004, SBC served 19.8 million long-distance lines, up from 11.5 million at September 2003.

In October 2001, due to a weakening U.S. economy and an uncertain regulatory environment, SBC initially scaled back its broadband deployment. During 2003, SBC's partnership with Yahoo! helped increase its broadband penetration. As of September 2004, SBC had 4.7 million DSL customers.

Cingular Wireless (18% of normalized operating revenues in 2003) began opera-

tions in October 2000, through the merger of wireless operations of SBC and BLS. The joint venture launched a nationwide advertising campaign in January 2001, to reinforce brand awareness for the newly created brand. Cingular's net subscriber base increased nearly 10% in the one-year period ended September 2004, bringing it to 25.7 million. Cingular has completely deployed 2.5G GPRS-based services in its GSM markets. In early 2003, Cingular restructured its marketing and sales organizations, and began addressing pricing strategies intended to strengthen its competitive position. In February 2004, Cingular agreed to buy AT&T Wireless (AWE), one of its competitors, for $41 billion in cash. The planned deal, which awaits regulatory and shareholder approval, is expected to close in late 2004 and be dilutive until 2007.

In June 2004, SBC also sold a large portion of its stake in Danish telecom TDC A/S, raising $2.1 billion for debt reduction. In the 2004 third quarter, SBC sold its 50% stake in directory operations in Illinois and part of Indiana to co-owner R.H. Donnelly for $1.5 billion in cash, to help finance its pending wireless acquisition. In September, Standard & Poor's Credit Market Services downgraded SBC's long-term rating to A, from A+ and has kept a negative watch outlook.

In 2003, SBC changed the accounting for its directory business to the amortization method, in which revenues and direct expenses are recognized ratably over the life of the directory.

Company Financials Fiscal Year ending December 31

Per Share Data ($)

(Year Ended December 31)	2003	2002	2001	2000	1999	1998	1997	1996	1995	1994
Tangible Bk. Val.	11.09	9.51	8.62	7.38	5.87	4.95	3.60	3.59	2.89	4.69
Cash Flow	4.16	4.79	2.25	5.16	4.37	4.66	3.47	3.58	3.33	3.06
Earnings	1.80	2.23	2.14	2.32	1.90	2.05	0.80	1.73	1.55	1.37
S&P Core Earnings	1.50	1.21	1.39	NA	NA	NA	NA	NA	NA	NA
Dividends	1.37	1.07	1.02	1.01	0.97	0.94	0.89	0.85	0.82	0.78
Payout Ratio	76%	48%	48%	43%	51%	46%	111%	49%	53%	57%
Prices - High	31.65	40.99	53.06	59.00	59.93	54.87	38.06	30.12	29.25	22.18
- Low	18.85	19.57	36.50	34.81	44.06	35.00	24.62	23.00	19.81	18.37
P/E Ratio - High	18	18	25	25	32	27	48	17	19	16
- Low	10	9	17	15	23	17	31	13	13	13

Income Statement Analysis (Million $)

	2003	2002	2001	2000	1999	1998	1997	1996	1995	1994
Revs.	40,843	43,138	45,908	51,476	49,489	28,777	24,856	13,898	12,670	11,619
Depr.	7,870	8,578	9,077	9,748	8,553	5,177	4,922	2,240	2,170	2,038
Maint.	NA	NA	NA	NA	NA	NA	NA	NA	NA	NA
Constr. Credits	NA	NA	NA	NA	NA	NA	NA	NA	11.2	NA
Eff. Tax Rate	32.9%	28.5%	36.1%	38.2%	39.4%	36.2%	36.9%	35.7%	32.3%	32.3%
Net Inc.	5,971	7,473	7,260	7,967	6,573	4,068	1,474	2,101	1,889	1,649
S&P Core Earnings	5,000	4,048	4,717	NA	NA	NA	NA	NA	NA	NA

Balance Sheet & Other Fin. Data (Million $)

	2003	2002	2001	2000	1999	1998	1997	1996	1995	1994
Gross Prop.	133,923	131,755	127,524	119,753	116,332	73,466	65,286	31,595	29,256	29,256
Net Prop.	52,128	48,490	49,827	47,195	46,571	29,920	27,339	14,007	12,988	17,317
Cap. Exp.	5,219	6,808	11,189	13,124	10,304	5,927	5,766	3,027	2,336	2,350
Total Cap.	69,607	62,705	58,476	54,079	49,351	27,888	24,967	12,340	11,928	16,893
Fxd. Chgs. Cov.	8.1	7.1	7.1	8.0	7.5	7.1	3.2	7.4	4.6	4.4
Capitalization:										
LT Debt	16,060	18,536	17,133	16,492	17,415	12,612	12,019	5,505	5,672	5,848
Pfd.	Nil	Nil	Nil	Nil	Nil	Nil	1,000	Nil	Nil	Nil
Common	38,248	33,199	32,491	30,463	26,726	12,927	9,892	6,835	6,256	8,356
% Return On Revs.	14.6	17.3	15.8	15.5	13.3	14.1	5.9	15.2	14.9	14.2
% Return On Invest. Capital	10.9	14.6	15.9	18.3	17.3	26.7	12.0	28.5	15.9	13.0
% Return On Com. Equity	16.7	22.6	23.1	27.9	26.6	35.4	15.1	32.1	25.9	20.7
% Earn. on Net Prop.	28.5	35.0	63.6	43.7	44.4	24.1	8.6	15.6	20.0	11.6
% LT Debt of Cap.	29.6	35.8	34.5	35.1	39.5	49.4	52.4	44.7	47.6	41.2
Capital. % Pfd.	Nil	Nil	Nil	Nil	Nil	Nil	4.4	Nil	Nil	Nil
Capital. % Common	70.4	64.2	65.5	64.9	60.5	50.6	43.2	55.4	52.4	58.8

Data as orig reptd.; bef. results of disc opers/spec. items. Per share data adj. for stk. divs.; EPS diluted. E-Estimated. NA-Not Available. NM-Not Meaningful. NR-Not Ranked. UR-Under Review.

Office: 175 East Houston, San Antonio, TX 78205-2255.
Telephone: 210-821-4105.
Website: http://www.sbc.com
Chrmn & CEO: E.E. Whitacre, Jr.
Pres: W.M. Daley.
CFO: R.L. Stephenson.
General Counsel: J.D. Ellis.

Investor Contact: D. Cessac 210-351-2058.
Dirs: G. F. Amelio, C. C. Barksdale, J. E. Barnes, A. A. Busch III, W. P. Clark, M. K. Eby, Jr., H. E. Gallegos, J. T. Hay, J. A. Henderson, B. R. Inman, C. F. Knight, L. M. Martin, J. B. McCoy, M. S. Metz, T. Rembe, S. D. Ritchey, J. M. Roche, C. Slim Helu, L. D. Tyson, P. P. Upton, E. E. Whitacre, Jr.

Founded: in 1983.
Domicile: Delaware.
Employees: 168,950.
S&P Analyst: Todd Rosenbluth/CB/BK

Recommendation: **HOLD** ★★★☆☆
SELL SELL HOLD BUY BUY

12-Month Target Price: **$20.00**
(as of October 21, 2004)

SGP has an approximate 0.25% weighting in the **S&P 500**

Sector: Health Care
Sub-Industry: Pharmaceuticals
Peer Group: Ethical Pharmaceuticals - Major

Summary: SGP is a leading producer of prescription and OTC pharmaceuticals and has important interests in sun care, animal health and foot care products.

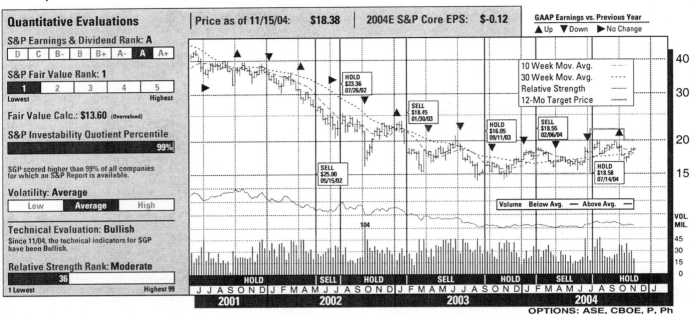

Quantitative Evaluations

S&P Earnings & Dividend Rank: A

| D | C | B- | B | B+ | A- | **A** | A+ |

S&P Fair Value Rank: 1

| **1** | 2 | 3 | 4 | 5 |
| Lowest | | | | Highest |

Fair Value Calc.: $13.60 (Overvalued)

S&P Investability Quotient Percentile
99%
SGP scored higher than 99% of all companies for which an S&P Report is available.

Volatility: Average

| Low | **Average** | High |

Technical Evaluation: Bullish
Since 11/04, the technical indicators for SGP have been Bullish.

Relative Strength Rank: Moderate
| 36 | |
| 1 Lowest | Highest 99 |

Price as of 11/15/04: $18.38

2004E S&P Core EPS: $-0.12

GAAP Earnings vs. Previous Year
▲ Up ▼ Down ▶ No Change

10 Week Mov. Avg.
30 Week Mov. Avg.
Relative Strength
12-Mo Target Price

HOLD $23.36 07/26/02
SELL $18.45 01/30/03
HOLD $16.05 09/11/03
SELL $18.55 02/06/04
SELL $25.00 05/15/02
HOLD $18.58 07/14/04

Volume Below Avg. — Above Avg.

104

VOL. MIL.

HOLD | SELL | HOLD | SELL | HOLD | SELL | HOLD
J J A S O N D | J F M A M J J A S O N D | J F M A M J J A S O N D | J F M A M J J A S O N D | J
2001 | 2002 | 2003 | 2004

OPTIONS: ASE, CBOE, P, Ph

Analyst commentary prepared by H. B. Saftlas/MF/BK

Highlights 16-NOV-04

- We project total revenues will advance about 7% in 2005. Growth should reflect strength in sales of Remicade for rheumatoid arthritis, Nasonex nasal steroid for asthma, and Temodar anticancer agent. We also see stablization in the Claritin/Clarinex and Intron A franchises, while sales of PEG Intron/Rebetol for hepatitis C should benefit from recent approval for marketing in Japan. Greater sales of new drugs such Noxafil antifungal and Asmanex anti-asthma should also augment volume. In addition, we expect modest growth in sales of animal health and consumer products.

- Although we see further modest attrition in gross margins, overall profitability should benefit from ongoing cost-cutting measures, which should result in reduced SG&A and R&D spending as a percentage of total revenues. We also forecast a significant increase in equity income from SGP's joint venture with Merck, reflecting projected sharply higher sales of the venture's Zetia and Vytorin cholesterol-lowering drugs.

- After factoring in payment accruals and dilution associated with a recent $1.25 billion offering of convertible preferred, we project operating EPS of $0.17 for 2005, versus a projected $0.05 a share loss for 2004. Adjusting for projected stock option and pension expenses, we estimate S&P Core EPS of $0.10 in 2005, versus an expected loss of $0.12 in 2004.

Investment Rationale/Risk 16-NOV-04

- We reiterate our hold recommendation on the shares. We believe that investors have discounted likely losses for the next few quarters, and will now focus on anticipated positive news. In our opinion, the key drivers for future growth will be Zetia and Vytorin cholesterol-lowering agents, which are marketed through a joint venture with Merck. Approved in July 2004, Vytorin (a Zetia/Zocor combination) is the first and only cholesterol therapy that both inhibits cholesterol production in the liver and blocks cholesterol absorption in the intestine. Competitively priced, and supported by strong clinicals and marketing muscle, Vytorin has the potential to capture over 15% of the $20 billion cholesterol drug market, in our view. We also see some stabilizing trends in SGP's established Intron A and Claritin franchises, while we think its R&D pipeline is beginning to show signs of life. We also believe SGP has made significant progress in resolving its consent decree issues.

- Risks to our recommendation and target price include failure by Vytorin to live up to expectations, other pipeline disappointments, and possible worsening of SGP's legal and regulatory problems.

- Our 12-month target price of $20 is based on our discounted cash flow model, which assumes steady free cash flow growth over 10 years and a 7.1% weighted average cost of capital.

Key Stock Statistics

S&P Core EPS 2005E	0.10	52-week Range	$20.10-14.88
S&P Oper. EPS 2004E	-0.05	12 Month P/E	NM
P/E on S&P Oper. EPS 2004E	NM	Beta	0.24
S&P Oper. EPS 2005E	0.17	Shareholders	46,000
Yield (%)	1.2%	Market Cap (B)	$ 27.1
Dividend Rate/Share	0.22	Shares Outstanding (M)	1472.8

Value of $10,000 invested five years ago: **$ 3,686**

Dividend Data Dividends have been paid since 1952

Amount ($)	Date Decl.	Ex-Div. Date	Stock of Record	Payment Date
0.055	Jan. 27	Feb. 04	Feb. 06	Feb. 26 '04
q.055	Apr. 27	May. 05	May. 07	May. 28 '04
0.055	Jun. 21	Aug. 04	Aug. 06	Aug. 31 '04
0.055	Sep. 28	Nov. 03	Nov. 05	Nov. 30 '04

Revenues/Earnings Data Fiscal year ending December 31

Revenues (Million $)

	2004	2003	2002	2001	2000	1999
1Q	1,963	2,082	2,556	2,319	2,389	2,186
2Q	2,147	2,338	2,833	2,630	2,626	2,451
3Q	1,978	1,998	2,421	2,382	2,383	2,236
4Q	—	1,948	2,370	2,471	2,418	2,303
Yr.	—	8,334	10,180	9,802	9,815	9,176

Earnings Per Share ($)

	2004	2003	2002	2001	2000	1999
1Q	-0.05	0.12	0.41	0.38	0.42	0.36
2Q	-0.04	0.12	0.43	0.43	0.43	0.37
3Q	0.01	-0.18	0.29	0.41	0.40	0.35
4Q	E-0.01	-0.12	0.21	0.10	0.39	0.34
Yr.	E-0.05	-0.06	1.34	1.32	1.64	1.42

Next earnings report expected: late-January Source: S&P, Company Reports
EPS Estimates based on S&P Operating Earnings; historical GAAP earnings are as reported.

Schering-Plough Corporation

Recommendation: **HOLD** ★ ★ ★ ☆ ☆   12-Month Target Price: **$20.00** (as of October 21, 2004)

Business Summary 16-NOV-04

Schering-Plough is a leading maker of niche-oriented prescription pharmaceuticals. It also has interests in animal health products, over-the-counter (OTC) medications, and consumer products. The company traces its history to Ernst Schering, a Berlin chemist who founded the company in 1864. International operations accounted for 57% of sales in 2003. In mid-April 2003, Fred Hassan (formerly chairman and CEO of Pharmacia Corp.) was elected chairman and CEO of SGP.

Anti-infective and anticancer products (37% of 2003 sales) are SGP's largest product category, with Intron A the principal drug in this segment. With sales of about $1.9 billion, the company's Intron A is the largest selling interferon. While it is used to treat a wide variety of cancers and viral infections, the bulk of Intron A sales now comprise a formulation of PEG-Intron A used in combination with Valeant Pharmaceuticals' (formerly ICN Pharmaceuticals) ribavirin to treat hepatitis C. Other anti-infective/anticancer drugs include Eulexin for prostate cancer, Cedax antibiotic, Temodar anticancer, Netromycin antibiotic, and Ethyol cytoprotective agent.

Prescription respiratory/allergy drugs are the company's second largest product category (24%). SGP's leading product in this category is Clarinex nonsedating antihistamine (sales of $498 million in 2003). Prior to the expiration of patents on the older prescription version of Claritin, the company launched its improved Clarinex antihistamine. SGP also shifted its Rx Claritin products to OTC formulations, which are included in the Consumer Health Care division. Other prescription allergy/respiratory drugs include Nasonex ($301 million), Proventil ($125 million), Vancenase and Vanceril.

Cardiovasculars (6%) consist of Imdur, an oral nitrate; Nitro-Dur, a nitroglycerin patch; K-Dur, a potassium supplement; and Integrilin, a platelet inhibiting agent. Zetia, a novel lipid-lowering agent, is sold through a joint venture with Merck & Co. SGP booked equity income from this venture of $54 million in 2003, comprised of $113 million of operating profits, plus a $20 million milestone payment, less $79 million for R&D costs. In July 2004, the FDA approved Vytorin, a combination of Zetia with Merck's Zocor statin cholesterol agent. Vytorin is also marketed through SGP's joint venture with Merck.

Dermatologicals (6%) include steroids such as Diprolene and Elocon; and Lotrisone, a topical antifungal and anti-inflammatory cream. Other drugs (7%) include Prandin for diabetes and Remicade anti-inflammatory. SGP is also a leading maker of animal health products (8%).

Consumer health care products (12%) largely comprise OTC Claritin, which had sales of $415 million in 2003. Other products in this division include medications such as Afrin nasal spray, Chlor-Trimeton allergy tablets, Coricidin and Drixoral cold remedies, Gyne-Lotrimin for vaginal yeast infections, foot care items sold under the Dr. Scholl's and other names, and Coppertone and other sun care products.

R&D expenses totaled $1.5 billion in 2003, equal to 17.6% of net sales. Key R&D projects include Noxafil, an antifungal; a combination of Claritin with Merck's Singulair asthma drug; Asmanex, an anti-asthma drug; and PEG-Intron for leukemia and melanoma.

Company Financials Fiscal Year ending December 31

Per Share Data ($)

(Year Ended December 31)	2003	2002	2001	2000	1999	1998	1997	1996	1995	1994
Tangible Bk. Val.	4.57	4.07	4.41	3.75	3.11	2.33	1.59	1.41	1.11	0.95
Cash Flow	0.22	1.28	1.54	1.84	1.60	0.44	1.11	0.94	0.82	0.71
Earnings	-0.06	1.34	1.32	1.64	1.42	1.18	0.98	0.83	0.71	0.60
S&P Core Earnings	0.16	1.17	1.41	NA	NA	NA	NA	NA	NA	NA
Dividends	0.57	0.67	0.62	0.55	0.49	0.43	0.55	0.32	0.29	0.25
Payout Ratio	NM	50%	47%	33%	34%	36%	56%	39%	41%	41%
Prices - High	23.75	36.25	57.25	60.00	60.81	57.75	32.00	18.28	15.18	9.48
- Low	14.16	16.10	32.35	30.50	40.25	30.34	15.87	12.62	8.87	6.81
P/E Ratio - High	NM	27	43	37	43	49	33	22	21	16
- Low	NM	12	25	19	28	26	16	15	12	11

Income Statement Analysis (Million $)

	2003	2002	2001	2000	1999	1998	1997	1996	1995	1994
Revs.	8,334	10,180	9,802	9,815	9,176	8,077	6,778	5,656	5,104	4,657
Oper. Inc.	975	2,941	3,248	3,394	3,015	2,566	2,159	1,820	1,609	1,407
Depr.	417	372	320	299	264	238	200	173	157	158
Int. Exp.	81.0	Nil	Nil	44.0	29.0	19.0	40.0	56.0	69.0	68.0
Pretax Inc.	-46.0	2,563	2,523	3,188	2,795	2,326	1,913	1,606	1,395	1,213
Eff. Tax Rate	NM	23.0%	23.0%	24.0%	24.5%	24.5%	24.5%	24.6%	24.5%	24.0%
Net Inc.	-92.0	1,974	1,943	2,423	2,110	1,756	1,444	1,213	1,053	922
S&P Core Earnings	247	1,717	2,070	NA	NA	NA	NA	NA	NA	NA

Balance Sheet & Other Fin. Data (Million $)

	2003	2002	2001	2000	1999	1998	1997	1996	1995	1994
Cash	4,218	3,521	2,716	2,397	1,876	1,259	714	536	322	161
Curr. Assets	9,147	8,272	6,519	5,720	4,909	3,958	2,920	2,365	1,956	1,739
Total Assets	15,102	14,136	12,174	10,805	9,375	7,840	6,507	5,398	4,665	4,326
Curr. Liab.	4,609	4,729	3,917	3,645	3,209	3,032	2,891	2,599	2,362	2,029
LT Debt	2,410	Nil	Nil	Nil	Nil	4.00	46.0	47.0	87.0	186
Common Equity	7,337	8,142	7,125	6,119	5,165	4,002	2,821	2,060	1,623	1,574
Total Cap.	9,981	8,500	7,427	6,333	5,449	4,297	3,145	2,374	1,965	2,006
Cap. Exp.	701	770	759	763	543	389	405	325	294	272
Cash Flow	325	2,346	2,263	2,722	2,374	1,994	1,644	1,386	1,210	1,080
Curr. Ratio	2.0	1.7	1.7	1.6	1.5	1.3	1.0	0.9	0.8	0.9
% LT Debt of Cap.	24.1	Nil	Nil	Nil	Nil	0.1	1.4	2.0	4.4	9.3
% Net Inc.of Revs.	NM	19.4	19.8	24.7	23.0	21.7	21.3	21.5	20.6	19.8
% Ret. on Assets	NM	15.0	16.9	24.0	24.5	24.5	24.3	24.1	23.4	21.8
% Ret. on Equity	NM	25.9	29.3	42.9	46.0	51.5	59.2	65.9	65.9	59.6

Data as orig reptd.; bef. results of disc opers/spec. items. Per share data adj. for stk. divs.; EPS diluted. E-Estimated. NA-Not Available. NM-Not Meaningful. NR-Not Ranked. UR-Under Review.

Office: 2000 Galloping Hill Road, Kenilworth, NJ 07033.
Telephone: 908-298-4000.
Website: http://www.schering-plough.com
Chrmn & CEO: F. Hassan.
EVP & CFO: R. J. Bertolini.

EVP & General Counsel: T. J. Sabatino, Jr.
EVP: C. S. Cox.
Dirs: H. W. Becherer, F. Hassan, D. H. Komansky, P. Leder, E. R. McGrath, D. L. Miller, C. E. Mundy, Jr., R. d. Osborne, P. F. Russo, K. C. Turner, A. Weinbach, R. F. van Oordt.

Founded: in 1970.
Domicile: New Jersey.
Employees: 30,500.
S&P Analyst: H. B. Saftlas/MF/BK

Schlumberger Ltd.

Recommendation: **HOLD** ★ ★ ★ ☆ ☆
SELL · SELL · HOLD · BUY · BUY
(as of October 22, 2004)

12-Month Target Price: $68.00

SLB has an approximate 0.35% weighting in the **S&P 500**

Sector: Energy
Sub-Industry: Oil & Gas Equipment & Services
Peer Group: Oil & Gas - Services & Equipment - Large

Summary: This company supplies services and technology to the petroleum, utility, semiconductor, smart card, network and Internet solutions industries.

Quantitative Evaluations

S&P Earnings & Dividend Rank: B-

| D | C | B- | B | B+ | A- | A | A+ |

S&P Fair Value Rank: 1

| 1 | 2 | 3 | 4 | 5 |
| Lowest | | | | Highest |

Fair Value Calc.: $46.70 (Overvalued)

S&P Investability Quotient Percentile

94%

SLB scored higher than 94% of all companies for which an S&P Report is available.

Volatility: Average

| Low | Average | High |

Technical Evaluation: Bearish

Since 10/04, the technical indicators for SLB have been Bearish.

Relative Strength Rank: Moderate

40

1 Lowest — Highest 99

Price as of 11/12/04: $65.65 | **2004E S&P Core EPS:** $1.75

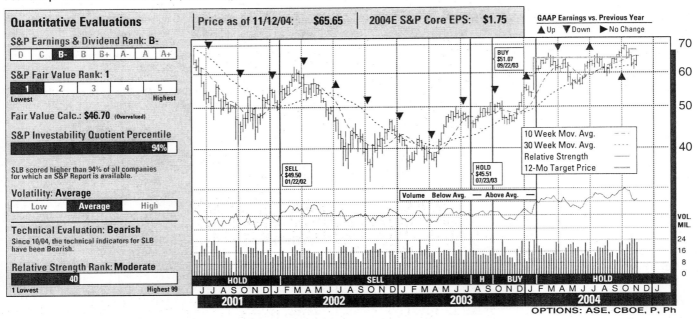

GAAP Earnings vs. Previous Year
▲ Up ▼ Down ▶ No Change

BUY $51.07 09/22/03
SELL $49.50 01/22/02
HOLD $45.51 07/23/03

10 Week Mov. Avg.
30 Week Mov. Avg.
Relative Strength
12-Mo Target Price

Volume Below Avg. — Above Avg.

HOLD | SELL | H | BUY | HOLD
J J A S O N D J F M A M J J A S O N D J F M A M J J A S O N D J F M A M J J A S O N D J
2001 · 2002 · 2003 · 2004

OPTIONS: ASE, CBOE, P, Ph

Analyst commentary prepared by Stewart Glickman/CB/GG

Highlights October 27, 2004

- Third quarter EPS of $0.52 (before certain charges) was $0.01 below our expectations. Oilfield services revenues grew 16%, year over year, led by double-digit gains in drilling and measurements, well servicing, well completions, wireline, and integrated project management businesses. Geographically, the strongest activity was registered in India, Russia, Mexico and the U.S. (land). For all of 2004, we look for oilfield revenues to increase about 17%. We also expect operating margins to average about 17% for the year.

- SLB sold a majority of its SchlumbergerSema businesses in January 2004, for total consideration of about $1.8 billion. At September 30, the company's long-term debt stood at $3.7 billion, representing a debt to capital ratio of about 39%, down significantly from the $6.1 billion at December 31, 2003 (51%).

- With about 75% of revenues from outside North America, we expect 2004 to be a strong year for international operations, reflecting our expectations of strong capital spending by state-owned oil companies. For 2004, we see EPS from continuing operations of $2.08 ($1.75 on an S&P Core Earnings basis). For 2005, we see EPS of $2.52 ($2.19). The divergence between projected operating and Core earnings is due in nearly equal proportions to adjustments for projected stock option expensing and pension gains.

Investment Rationale/Risk October 27, 2004

- We recommend holding the stock. Through late October, the shares were up about 21% in 2004, versus a 31% gain for the S&P Oil & Gas Equipment and Services Index. The shares were trading at an enterprise value of 12.5X our 2005 EBITDA estimate, above the peer multiple of 11.6X, and at a modest premium on a price to net equity basis as well. On a price to cash flow basis, however, the shares are trading at a 13.3X multiple, below the 16.3X peer group average.

- Risks to our recommendation and target price include a decline in oil and gas exploration and production activity; reduced demand for integrated systems in oilfield services; and political risk in emerging markets.

- Applying an enterprise value multiple of 13X to our 2005 EBITDA estimate, in line with the slight premium to its peer group at which the stock has traded over the past three years, and blending this with our price to operating cash flow and price to net equity valuations, our 12-month target price is $68.

Key Stock Statistics

S&P Core EPS 2005E	2.19	52-week Range	$69.89-45.95
S&P Oper. EPS 2004E	2.08	12 Month P/E	36.7
P/E on S&P Oper. EPS 2004E	31.6	Beta	1.03
S&P Oper. EPS 2005E	2.52	Shareholders	24,770
Yield (%)	1.1%	Market Cap (B)	$ 38.7
Dividend Rate/Share	0.75	Shares Outstanding (M)	588.7

Value of $10,000 invested five years ago: **$ 13,263**

Dividend Data Dividends have been paid since 1957

Amount ($)	Date Decl.	Ex-Div. Date	Stock of Record	Payment Date
0.188	Jan. 22	Feb. 23	Feb. 25	Apr. 08 '04
0.188	Apr. 22	May. 28	Jun. 02	Jul. 03 '04
0.188	Jul. 22	Aug. 30	Sep. 01	Oct. 08 '04
0.188	Oct. 21	Dec. 20	Dec. 22	Jan. 07 '05

Revenues/Earnings Data Fiscal year ending December 31

Revenues (Million $)

	2004	2003	2002	2001	2000	1999
1Q	3,041	3,263	3,257	2,910	2,214	2,474
2Q	2,881	3,485	3,337	3,635	2,422	2,232
3Q	2,966	3,474	3,446	3,624	2,537	2,311
4Q	—	3,671	3,434	3,577	2,862	2,258
Yr.	—	14,059	13,474	13,746	10,035	8,752

Earnings Per Share ($)

	2004	2003	2002	2001	2000	1999
1Q	0.22	0.26	0.30	0.41	0.24	0.16
2Q	0.43	0.24	0.34	-0.16	0.27	0.23
3Q	0.50	-0.09	0.30	0.34	0.35	0.25
4Q	E0.58	0.40	-4.92	0.32	0.41	0.11
Yr.	E2.08	0.81	-4.18	0.91	1.27	0.58

Next earnings report expected: late-January Source: S&P, Company Reports
EPS Estimates based on S&P Operating Earnings; historical GAAP earnings are as reported.

Schlumberger Limited

Recommendation: **HOLD** ★★★☆☆   12-Month Target Price: **$68.00** (as of October 22, 2004)

Business Summary October 28, 2004

As a global oilfield and information services company with major activity in the energy industry, Schlumberger operates in four primary business segments: Oilfield Services (64% of 2003 revenues; 69% in 2002), SchlumbergerSema (19%, 22%), WesternGECO (9%, 11%), and Other.

Oilfield Services provides exploration and production services, solutions and technology to the petroleum industry. It is managed geographically via 27 GeoMarkets grouped into four geographic areas (North America, South America, Europe/CIS/Africa, and the Middle East/Asia). GeoMarkets bring together geographically focused teams to meet local needs and provide customized solutions. New technology development is provided by 13 Service Groups, to introduce solutions in delivery of products and services within GeoMarkets. Oilfield services are organized into seven technology segments: wireline services, providing information technology to evaluate the reservoir, plan and monitor wells, and evaluate and monitor production; drilling & measurements, including directional drilling, measurement while drilling and logging while drilling services; well services, constructing mostly oil and gas wells; well completions & productivity; integrated project management; and Schlumberger Information Solutions.

In 2001, SLB shifted its strategic focus toward providing totally integrated systems to the oilfield services sector with the purchase of Bull CP8 (for $313 million) and Sema plc (for $5.19 billion). As a result of these acquisitions, the SchlumbergerSema business segment was created, combining Sema, Bull CP8, and certain businesses of Schlumberger Test & Transactions and Resource Management

Services (including CellNet and Convergent). After selling most of the SchlumbergerSema businesses in January 2004, SLB retained Sema's strategic activities for the oil & gas industry, and operations that provide connectivity with the upstream oil & gas business.

WesternGECO provides worldwide comprehensive reservoir imaging, monitoring and development services, with seismic crews and data processing centers, as well as a large multiclient seismic library. Services include 3D and time-lapse (4D) seismic surveys, and multi-component surveys for delineating prospects and reservoir management. The segment is owned 70% by Schlumberger and 30% by Baker Hughes.

The company also offers a wide ranging portfolio of hardware and software products through Schlumberger Volume Products. SLB has more than 20 years of expertise in the smart card industry, and has sold more than 2.5 billion smart cards to date. Product expertise includes cards, payphones, point of sale terminals, mass transit terminals, meters and trading systems.

In July 2003, SLB divested its NPTest semiconductor testing business, which provided advanced test and diagnostic systems to the semiconductor industry, for proceeds of $220 million in cash. In August 2003, the company sold its Verification Systems businesses via a proceed-free management buyout, and in October 2003, SLB divested its parking solutions business for $84 million in cash.

Company Financials Fiscal Year ending December 31

Per Share Data ($)

(Year Ended December 31)	2003	2002	2001	2000	1999	1998	1997	1996	1995	1994
Tangible Bk. Val.	3.74	1.40	2.27	11.73	11.29	12.48	11.10	8.91	7.48	6.98
Cash Flow	27.59	-1.51	4.17	3.45	2.39	3.83	4.41	3.55	3.04	2.70
Earnings	0.81	-4.18	0.91	1.27	0.58	1.81	2.52	1.74	1.34	1.10
S&P Core Earnings	0.67	-1.79	0.12	NA	NA	NA	NA	NA	NA	NA
Dividends	0.75	0.75	0.75	0.75	0.75	0.75	1.13	0.75	0.71	0.60
Payout Ratio	93%	NM	82%	59%	129%	41%	45%	43%	53%	54%
Prices - High	56.24	62.43	82.81	88.87	70.68	86.43	94.43	54.12	35.25	31.50
- Low	35.62	33.40	40.84	53.50	45.43	40.06	49.00	32.68	25.06	25.00
P/E Ratio - High	69	NM	91	70	NM	48	37	31	26	29
- Low	44	NM	45	42	NM	22	19	19	19	23

Income Statement Analysis (Million $)

	2003	2002	2001	2000	1999	1998	1997	1996	1995	1994
Revs.	13,893	13,474	13,746	9,611	8,395	11,816	10,648	8,956	7,622	6,697
Oper. Inc.	16,779	-456	3,165	2,084	1,327	2,428	2,622	1,895	1,581	1,373
Depr. Depl. & Amort.	15,709	1,545	1,896	1,271	1,021	1,137	973	885	820	776
Int. Exp.	334	368	385	276	193	150	87.0	0.72	82.0	63.0
Pretax Inc.	568	-2,230	1,126	959	470	1,323	1,669	675	770	617
Eff. Tax Rate	36.9%	NM	51.1%	23.8%	29.9%	23.4%	22.3%	NM	16.8%	13.2%
Net Inc.	473	-2,418	522	733	329	1,014	1,296	851	649	536
S&P Core Earnings	393	-1,034	67.7	NA	NA	NA	NA	NA	NA	NA

Balance Sheet & Other Fin. Data (Million $)

	2003	2002	2001	2000	1999	1998	1997	1996	1995	1994
Cash	234	168	178	3,040	4,390	3,957	1,761	1,359	1,121	1,232
Curr. Assets	10,369	7,185	7,705	7,493	8,606	8,805	6,071	5,043	4,024	3,824
Total Assets	20,041	19,435	22,326	17,173	15,081	16,078	12,097	10,325	8,910	8,322
Curr. Liab.	6,795	6,451	6,218	3,991	3,474	3,919	3,630	3,474	2,765	2,787
LT Debt	6,097	6,029	6,216	3,573	3,183	3,285	1,069	637	613	394
Common Equity	11,763	5,606	8,378	8,295	7,721	8,119	6,695	5,626	4,964	4,583
Total Cap.	18,258	12,188	15,231	12,474	10,904	11,404	7,764	6,263	5,577	4,977
Cap. Exp.	1,025	1,366	2,053	1,323	792	1,887	1,496	1,158	939	783
Cash Flow	16,181	-872	2,418	2,003	1,350	2,151	2,269	1,736	1,469	1,312
Curr. Ratio	1.5	1.1	1.2	1.9	2.5	2.2	1.7	1.4	1.5	1.4
% LT Debt of Cap.	33.4	49.5	40.8	28.6	29.2	28.8	13.8	10.1	11.0	7.9
% Ret. on Assets	2.4	NM	2.6	4.5	2.1	7.2	11.6	8.8	7.5	6.6
% Ret. on Equity	4.1	NM	6.3	9.1	4.2	13.7	21.0	16.0	13.6	12.0

Data as orig reptd.; bef. results of disc opers/spec. items. Per share data adj. for stk. divs.; EPS diluted. E-Estimated. NA-Not Available. NM-Not Meaningful. NR-Not Ranked. UR-Under Review.

Office: 153 East 53rd Street, New York, NY 10022-4624.
Telephone: 212-350-9400.
Email: irsupport@slb.com
Website: http://www.slb.com
Chrmn & CEO: A. Gould.
EVP & CFO: J. Perraud.

VP & Investor Contact: D. Pferdehirt 212-350-9432.
Chief Acctg Officer: F. Sorgie.
Treas: M. Soublin.
Dirs: J. Deutch, J. S. Gorelick, A. Gould, T. Isaac, A. Lajous, A. Levy-Lang, D. Primat, N. Seydoux, L. G. Stuntz, S. Ullring.

Founded: in 1956.
Domicile: Netherlands Antilles.
Employees: 77,000.
S&P Analyst: Stewart Glickman/CB/GG

Schwab (Charles)

Recommendation: **SELL** ★ ★ ☆ ☆ ☆
SELL SELL HOLD BUY BUY

12-Month Target Price: **$9.00**
(as of November 12, 2004)

SCH has an approximate 0.13% weighting in the **S&P 500**

Sector: Financials
Sub-Industry: Investment Banking & Brokerage
Peer Group: Discount/Online Brokers

Summary: This company's Charles Schwab & Co. subsidiary is among the largest brokerage firms in the U.S., serving primarily retail clients.

Quantitative Evaluations

S&P Earnings & Dividend Rank: A-

| D | C | B- | B | B+ | A- | A | A+ |

S&P Fair Value Rank: 3

| 1 | 2 | 3 | 4 | 5 |
| Lowest | | | | Highest |

Fair Value Calc.: $10.10 (Slightly Overvalued)

S&P Investability Quotient Percentile

78%

SCH scored higher than 78% of all companies for which an S&P Report is available.

Volatility: Average

| Low | Average | High |

Technical Evaluation: Bullish

Since 11/04, the technical indicators for SCH have been Bullish.

Relative Strength Rank: Strong

83

| 1 Lowest | Highest 99 |

Price as of 11/16/04: **$10.45** **2004E S&P Core EPS:** **$0.28**

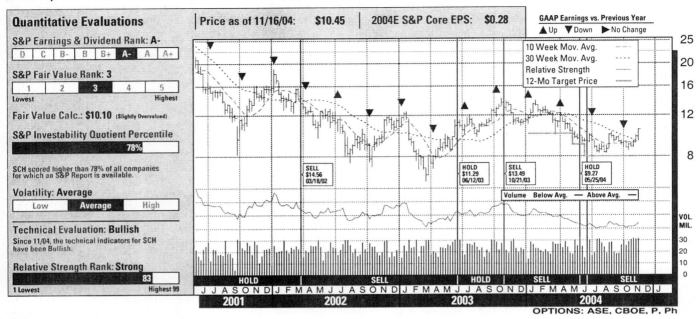

GAAP Earnings vs. Previous Year
▲ Up ▼ Down ► No Change

10 Week Mov. Avg.
30 Week Mov. Avg.
Relative Strength
12-Mo Target Price

SELL $14.56 03/18/02
HOLD $11.29 06/12/03
SELL $13.49 10/21/03
HOLD $9.27 05/25/04

Volume Below Avg. — Above Avg. —

HOLD | SELL | HOLD | SELL | SELL
J J A S O N D J F M A M J J A S O N D J F M A M J J A S O N D J F M A M J J A S O N D J
2001 | 2002 | 2003 | 2004

OPTIONS: ASE, CBOE, P, Ph

Analyst commentary prepared by Robert Hansen, CFA /MF/BK

Highlights 17-NOV-04

- We think that Schwab is losing its competitive differentiation as a discount broker as it moves toward becoming a full-service brokerage. We think reductions in commissions and fees for its largest and most active investors that started in mid-June will restrict revenue growth. Despite lower commission rates, we expect SCH to lose market share in 2005, since its commission rates remain higher than those of online competitors. We think the company is losing customer loyalty as it focuses on retaining its most profitable customers.
- Trading volumes declined significantly in both the second and third quarters, after surging in the first quarter. We attribute this to seasonality, Nasdaq declines, and interest rate concerns. We think that SCH's investing services options have been viewed as overly complex and expensive by customers. We expect the company to sell its U.S. Trust asset management division, and to incur a large loss, as we see deteriorating performance. We see a loss on SCH's sale of its capital markets group (a strategic business, in our view), which closed in the fourth quarter.
- We forecast EPS of $0.37 for 2004 and $0.45 for 2005, aided by continued net client inflows, growth in asset-based revenue, and cost reductions. After projected stock option expense, our Standard & Poor's Core EPS estimates are $0.28 for 2004 and $0.39 for 2005.

Investment Rationale/Risk 17-NOV-04

- We think that the shares are trading at a premium to peers, due to the company's brand recognition, established client base, and recurring asset-based fees. However, we think the premium will narrow, as we expect increased price competition and market share losses. In addition, we project a lower valuation for the shares, based on recent management changes and our view of the company's unsuccessful acquisition strategy. We view SCH's corporate governance policies negatively in our valuation of the shares and would prefer that the company split the roles of chairman and CEO.
- Risks to our recommendation and target price include higher trading volumes, reduced competition, lower interest rates, and equity market gains.
- Despite price weakness thus far in 2004, the shares still trade at about 23X our 2005 EPS estimate, a significant premium to asset management and brokerage peers that we follow. Our 12-month target price of $9 is equal to 20X our 2005 EPS estimate. We have a sell recommendation on the shares, given their premium valuation and our view of increased price competition.

Key Stock Statistics

S&P Core EPS 2005E	0.39	52-week Range	$13.92-8.25
S&P Oper. EPS 2004E	0.37	12 Month P/E	37.3
P/E on S&P Oper. EPS 2004E	28.2	Beta	1.96
S&P Oper. EPS 2005E	0.45	Shareholders	12,400
Yield (%)	0.8%	Market Cap (B)	$ 14.1
Dividend Rate/Share	0.08	Shares Outstanding (M)	1347.0

Value of $10,000 invested five years ago: **$ 3,895**

Dividend Data Dividends have been paid since 1989

Amount ($)	Date Decl.	Ex-Div. Date	Stock of Record	Payment Date
0.014	Jan. 20	Feb. 03	Feb. 05	Feb. 19 '04
0.020	Apr. 20	May. 03	May. 05	May. 19 '04
0.020	Jul. 19	Aug. 03	Aug. 05	Aug. 19 '04
0.020	Oct. 27	Nov. 03	Nov. 05	Nov. 19 '04

Revenues/Earnings Data Fiscal year ending December 31

Revenues (Million $)

	2004	2003	2002	2001	2000	1999
1Q	1,190	900.0	1,059	1,200	1,726	951.6
2Q	1,112	1,018	1,049	1,071	1,405	982.1
3Q	1,000	1,051	1,031	1,023	1,323	883.7
4Q	—	1,118	996.0	1,059	1,335	1,127
Yr.	—	4,087	4,135	4,353	5,788	3,945

Earnings Per Share ($)

	2004	2003	2002	2001	2000	1999
1Q	0.12	0.05	0.06	0.07	0.22	0.11
2Q	0.08	0.09	0.07	-0.01	0.09	0.12
3Q	0.03	0.09	Nil	0.01	0.10	0.10
4Q	E0.09	0.11	-0.06	-0.01	0.10	0.13
Yr.	E0.37	0.35	0.07	0.06	0.51	0.47

Next earnings report expected: late-January Source: S&P, Company Reports
EPS Estimates based on S&P Operating Earnings; historical GAAP earnings are as reported.

The Charles Schwab Corporation

Recommendation: **SELL** ★ ★ ☆ ☆ ☆   12-Month Target Price: **$9.00** (as of November 12, 2004)

Business Summary 17-NOV-04

The Charles Schwab Corp. is a financial holding company that is engaged, through subsidiaries, in securities brokerage and related financial services. The company provides its services through four segments, including Individual Investor, Institutional Investor, Capital Markets, and U.S. Trust. Other subsidiaries include Charles Schwab Investment Management (CSIM), the investment adviser for Schwab's proprietary mutual funds; Schwab Capital Markets L.P., a market maker in Nasdaq and other securities providing trade execution services primarily to broker-dealers and institutional clients; and CyberTrader, Inc., an electronic trading technology and brokerage concern that provides services to highly active, online traders.

Through the Individual Investor segment (57% of 2003 operating revenue), the company provides retail brokerage and banking services. Through various types of brokerage accounts, Schwab offers the purchase and sale of securities, including Nasdaq, exchange-listed and other equity securities, options, mutual funds, unit investment trusts, variable annuities and fixed income investments. Schwab also offers certain clients initial and secondary public stock offerings, debt underwritings, and access to futures and commodities trading. In addition, the company provides clients with access to a variety of life insurance and annuity products through third-party insurance companies. The company, through subsidiaries, serves 7.5 million active client accounts, and held client assets of $966.7 billion at December 31, 2003.

Through its Institutional Investor segment (20%), SCH provides custodial, trade execution and support services to investment advisers, serves company 401(k) plan sponsors and third-party administrators, and supports company stock option plans. In April 2004, SCH said that its Institutional segment had surpassed $300 billion in custodied assets on behalf of about 5,000 adviser firms and their 1.2 million accounts. SCH launched Schwab Advisor Network in May 2002, which refers affluent investors to carefully selected local investment advisers.

The Capital Markets segment (7%) provides trade execution services in Nasdaq, exchange-listed and other securities primarily to broker-dealers, including Schwab, and institutional clients. In January 2004, SCH acquired SoundView Technology Group, a research-driven securities firm focused on technology companies, for about $340 million in cash.

U.S. Trust Corp. (15%) is a wealth management concern that, through subsidiaries, provided fiduciary services and private banking services through 37 client offices at the end of 2003. In October 2003, U.S. Trust acquired the Private Asset Management group of State Street Corp., which had $12 billion in assets under management, for about $365 million in cash.

According to the company's 2004 proxy statement, directors and executive officers as a group (22 persons) owned 21% of the company's stock, including 19% by chairman C.R. Schwab.

Company Financials Fiscal Year ending December 31

Per Share Data ($)

(Year Ended December 31)	2003	2002	2001	2000	1999	1998	1997	1996	1995	1994
Tangible Bk. Val.	2.56	0.55	2.58	2.69	1.81	1.15	0.91	0.67	0.47	0.38
Cash Flow	0.35	0.30	0.30	0.70	0.59	0.39	0.32	0.27	NA	NA
Earnings	0.35	0.07	0.06	0.51	0.47	0.28	0.22	0.19	0.14	0.11
S&P Core Earnings	0.27	-0.02	-0.09	NA	NA	NA	NA	NA	NA	NA
Dividends	0.05	0.04	0.04	0.04	0.04	0.04	0.03	0.03	0.02	0.01
Payout Ratio	14%	63%	73%	8%	8%	13%	13%	14%	13%	12%
Prices - High	14.20	19.00	33.00	44.75	51.66	22.83	9.83	4.87	4.29	1.82
- Low	6.25	7.22	8.13	22.45	16.95	6.16	4.50	2.66	1.63	1.17
P/E Ratio - High	41	NM	NM	88	NM	81	45	25	30	16
- Low	18	NM	NM	44	NM	22	20	14	11	10

Income Statement Analysis (Million $)

	2003	2002	2001	2000	1999	1998	1997	1996	1995	1994
Commissions	1,207	1,206	1,355	2,294	1,863	1,309	1,174	954	751	546
Int. Inc.	970	1,186	1,857	2,589	1,471	1,127	900	681	568	363
Total Revs.	4,328	4,480	5,281	7,139	4,713	3,388	2,300	1,851	1,420	1,065
Int. Exp.	241	345	928	1,352	768	652	546	426	357	198
Pretax Inc.	710	168	135	1,231	971	577	447	394	277	224
Eff. Tax Rate	33.5%	42.3%	42.2%	41.7%	39.4%	39.6%	39.6%	40.7%	37.7%	39.7%
Net Inc.	472	97.0	78.0	718	589	348	270	234	173	135
S&P Core Earnings	357	-31.5	-131	NA	NA	NA	NA	NA	NA	NA

Balance Sheet & Other Fin. Data (Million $)

	2003	2002	2001	2000	1999	1998	1997	1996	1995	1994
Total Assets	45,866	39,705	40,464	38,154	29,299	22,264	16,482	13,779	10,552	7,918
Cash Items	2,832	3,114	4,407	3,302	10,547	11,399	7,571	7,869	5,856	4,587
Receivables	9,137	7,067	10,066	16,680	17,543	9,980	8,019	5,244	4,088	3,010
Secs. Owned	4,023	1,716	1,700	1,603	340	242	283	128	114	Nil
Sec. Borrowed	Nil	Nil	Nil	Nil	Nil	Nil	Nil	Nil	Nil	Nil
Due Brokers & Cust.	2,661	1,476	27,822	26,785	25,171	19,867	14,498	12,280	9,346	7,084
Other Liabs.	1,330	1,302	1,327	1,277	931	618	478	361	327	195
Capitalization:										
Debt	772	642	730	770	407	351	361	284	246	171
Equity	4,461	4,011	4,163	4,230	2,274	1,429	1,145	855	633	467
Total	5,233	4,653	4,893	5,000	2,681	1,780	1,506	1,139	879	638
% Return On Revs.	15.1	3.0	2.0	14.8	20.7	10.3	16.2	12.7	12.2	12.7
% Ret. on Assets	1.1	0.2	0.2	2.0	2.3	1.8	1.8	2.0	1.9	1.8
% Ret. on Equity	11.1	2.4	1.9	21.1	31.8	27.5	27.0	31.5	31.4	32.0

Data as orig reptd.; bef. results of disc opers/spec. items. Per share data adj. for stk. divs.; EPS diluted. E-Estimated. NA-Not Available. NM-Not Meaningful. NR-Not Ranked. UR-Under Review.

Office: 120 Kearny Street, San Francisco, CA 94108.
Telephone: 415-627-7000.
Email: investor.relations@schwab.com
Website: http://www.schwab.com
Chrmn & CEO: C. R. Schwab.
EVP & CFO: C. V. Dodds.

Vice Chrmn: D. G. Lepore.
EVP: W. L. Atwell.
Investor Contact: Richard G. Fowler (415-636-2787).
Dirs: N. H. Bechtle, C. P. Butcher, D. G. Fisher, A. M. Frank, F. C. Herringer, S. T. McLin, D. S. Pottruck, C. R. Schwab, G. P. Shultz, P. A. Sneed, R. O. Walther, R. N. Wilson, D. B. Yoffie.

Auditor: Deloitte & Touche.
Founded: in 1971.
Domicile: Delaware.
Employees: 16,700.
S&P Analyst: Robert Hansen, CFA /MF/BK

Scientific-Atlanta

Recommendation: **BUY** ★ ★ ★ ☆   12-Month Target Price: **$32.00**
(as of September 28, 2004)

SFA has an approximate 0.04% weighting in the **S&P 500**

Sector: Information Technology
Sub-Industry: Communications Equipment
Peer Group: Cable and Broadcast Equipment

Summary: SFA manufactures broadband communications systems and satellite-based video, voice and data communications networks.

Quantitative Evaluations

S&P Earnings & Dividend Rank: A-

| D | C | B- | B | B+ | A- | A | A+ |

S&P Fair Value Rank: 4-

| 1 | 2 | 3 | 4 | 5 |
| Lowest | | | | Highest |

Fair Value Calc.: $29.50 (Slightly Overvalued)

S&P Investability Quotient Percentile

94%

SFA scored higher than 94% of all companies for which an S&P Report is available.

Volatility: Average

| Low | Average | High |

Technical Evaluation: Bullish
Since 11/04, the technical indicators for SFA have been Bullish.

Relative Strength Rank: Moderate

66

1 Lowest   Highest 99

Price as of 11/12/04: **$30.12**   **2005E S&P Core EPS:** **$1.10**

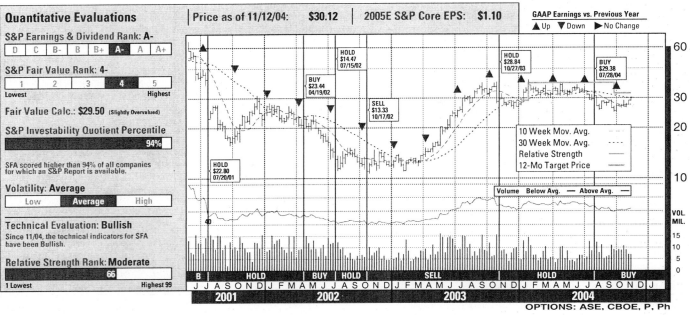

GAAP Earnings vs. Previous Year
▲ Up   ▼ Down   ▶ No Change

- 10 Week Mov. Avg.
- 30 Week Mov. Avg.
- Relative Strength
- 12-Mo Target Price

Volume Below Avg. —   Above Avg. —

OPTIONS: ASE, CBOE, P, Ph

Analyst commentary prepared by A. Bensinger/CB/MWJ

Highlights September 29, 2004

- We expect sales, following an 18% increase in FY 04 (Jun.), to advance 19% in FY 05, reflecting our outlook for improved spending by the company's cable operator customers, particularly in digital video recording (DVR) set-top boxes. Overall digital set-top sales have benefited from substantial new orders from Cablevision, which ended its supplier relationship with Sony at the end of 2002. We see transmission product sales up slightly, on higher expected demand from international customers.

- We see FY 05 set-top box volume at 4.7 million units, including more than two million DVR boxes. We project that gross margins will remain steady at about 37%, as higher sales volume and material cost reductions from engineering re-design will likely offset lower set-top box selling prices that we forecast. Despite our view of incremental hiring, we see SG&A and R&D expenses decreasing slightly as a percentage of sales.

- With higher interest income expected on an improved cash position, we see operating EPS of $1.62 for FY 05, versus the $1.30 posted for FY 04. On a Standard & Poor's Core Earnings basis, we estimate EPS of $1.10 for FY 05, largely reflecting projected stock option expense.

Investment Rationale/Risk September 29, 2004

- We view the company's business model and balance sheet as attractive, with net margins of 12%, more than double the peer average, more than $8 a share in cash, and a debt to equity ratio well below peer levels. We see SFA benefiting from an upgrade cycle to digital recording video set-top boxes. Based on our relative and intrinsic analyses, we think the stock is undervalued, and would accumulate the shares.

- Risks to our recommendation and target price include increased customer acceptance of plug and play cable compatibility, delays in the deployment of digital video recording set tops, lower consumer spending, and the loss of a major customer.

- Applying a blend of average group forward P/E multiple, price to sales, and book value ratios, we have a 12-month target price of $32. Our target is further supported, in our view, by our discounted cash flow analysis, which indicates a fair value slightly under $32. Our DCF model assumes a weighted average cost of capital of 11.7% and growth in average annual free cash flow of 14% over the next five years.

Key Stock Statistics

S&P Oper. EPS 2005E	**1.64**	52-week Range	**$38.59-24.61**
P/E on S&P Oper. EPS 2005E	**18.4**	12 Month P/E	**20.2**
Yield (%)	**0.1%**	Beta	**2.26**
Dividend Rate/Share	**0.04**	Shareholders	**5,272**
Shares Outstanding (M)	**153.3**	Market Cap (B)	**$ 4.6**

Value of $10,000 invested five years ago: **$ 9,377**

Dividend Data Dividends have been paid since 1976

Amount ($)	Date Decl.	Ex-Div. Date	Stock of Record	Payment Date
0.010	Feb. 12	Feb. 25	Feb. 27	Mar. 15 '04
0.010	May. 13	May. 26	May. 28	Jun. 15 '04
0.010	Aug. 11	Aug. 25	Aug. 27	Sep. 14 '04
0.010	Nov. 08	Nov. 17	Nov. 19	Dec. 08 '04

Revenues/Earnings Data Fiscal year ending June 30

Revenues (Million $)

	2005	2004	2003	2002	2001	2000
1Q	452.7	395.6	311.6	410.1	597.2	349.3
2Q	—	416.6	352.0	418.2	631.4	372.7
3Q	—	437.0	382.6	452.7	663.7	440.7
4Q	—	458.8	404.2	390.1	619.6	552.6
Yr.	—	1,708	1,450	1,671	2,512	1,715

Earnings Per Share ($)

	2005	2004	2003	2002	2001	2000
1Q	0.36	0.28	0.07	0.23	0.67	0.16
2Q	E0.39	0.33	0.10	0.25	0.42	0.20
3Q	E0.42	0.35	0.18	0.28	0.46	0.23
4Q	E0.47	0.45	0.31	-0.10	0.44	0.35
Yr.	E1.64	1.41	0.65	0.66	1.99	0.94

Next earnings report expected: late-January Source: S&P, Company Reports
EPS Estimates based on S&P Operating Earnings; historical GAAP earnings are as reported.

STANDARD &POOR'S

Scientific-Atlanta, Inc.

Recommendation: **BUY** ★ ★ ★ ★ ☆   12-Month Target Price: **$32.00** (as of September 28, 2004)

Business Summary September 29, 2004

Scientific-Atlanta produces a wide variety of broadband products for the cable television industry, including satellite communications equipment that transports programming from its source to geographically distributed headends, optical communications products that transport information within metropolitan areas to individual neighborhoods, and radio frequency (RF) electronics products that provide connectivity within the neighborhoods to each consumer's home.

The company's primary product is the Explorer digital set-top box, which is designed to enable subscribers to access new services such as e-mail over television, video-on-demand, Web browsing, Internet Protocol (IP) services, digital video recording, and electronic commerce. The company shipped 3.2 million Explorer set-tops in FY 03 (Jun.), down from 3.4 million units in FY 02.

During FY 03, SFA introduced the Explorer 8000 set-top, which adds digital video recording capabilities that allow the cable subscriber to pause, rewind, fast forward, record, and replay live analog and digital TV programs using a built-in hard drive. The company also introduced the Explorer 3250 high definition (HD) set-top to improve upon previous generations of HD set-tops by offering enhanced installation features, nearly 30% faster processing speed, increased memory, additional audio options and stretch and zoom capabilities for HD Televisions.

The company's transmission products enable operators to transmit video and data over the same network, with a reverse path for customers to communicate back to the operator. Sales of optoelectronic products accounted for 9% of total sales

in FY 03, versus 11% in FY 02. RF distribution products constituted 6% of total sales in FY 03, down from 7% in FY 02.

The company's software subsidiary, PowerTV, Inc., develops operating software products for the advanced digital interactive cable television markets.

International sales increased to 22% of the total in FY 03, from 20% in FY 02. The largest customers included Time Warner (24% of total sales in FY 03), Cablevision Systems (19%), Comcast Corporation (11%), Cox Communications (6%), and Charter Communications (5%). In June 2002, major customer Adelphia (5%) filed for Chapter 11 bankruptcy.

In August 2002, SFA announced a worldwide restructuring of operations, to align costs with reduced sales levels. The restructuring, which included a 6% workforce reduction (400 positions), was substantially completed by December 2002. In the second half of FY 03, the company reduced its workforce by another 150 positions.

In April 2000, ViaSat Inc. acquired the company's satellite network business (4% of FY 00 total sales). SFA retained the satellite television networks business, now known as the Media Networks business. In January 2002, the company acquired BarcoNet, NV, a Belgium-based provider of multimedia distribution solutions for broadband cable and broadcast applications.

Company Financials Fiscal Year ending June 30

Per Share Data ($)

(Year Ended June 30)	2004	2003	2002	2001	2000	1999	1998	1997	1996	1995
Tangible Bk. Val.	9.98	8.00	7.61	8.70	7.58	4.72	3.94	3.35	2.97	3.04
Cash Flow	1.89	1.12	1.04	2.39	1.25	0.94	0.81	0.67	0.29	0.61
Earnings	1.41	0.65	0.66	1.99	0.94	0.65	0.51	0.39	0.05	0.42
S&P Core Earnings	1.17	0.34	0.26	1.18	NA	NA	NA	NA	NA	NA
Dividends	0.04	0.04	0.04	0.04	0.02	0.03	0.03	0.03	0.03	0.03
Payout Ratio	3%	6%	6%	2%	2%	5%	6%	8%	67%	7%
Prices - High	38.59	37.45	28.18	65.80	94.00	33.25	13.96	12.46	10.18	12.43
- Low	24.61	10.99	10.10	15.75	24.40	11.06	5.87	7.12	6.00	5.68
P/E Ratio - High	27	58	43	33	NM	51	27	32	NM	30
- Low	17	17	15	8	26	17	11	18	NM	14

Income Statement Analysis (Million $)

	2004	2003	2002	2001	2000	1999	1998	1997	1996	1995
Revs.	1,708	1,450	1,671	2,512	1,715	1,243	1,181	1,168	1,048	1,147
Oper. Inc.	361	236	225	473	253	122	102	127	74.0	120
Depr.	75.1	71.4	59.9	66.3	50.7	46.1	48.3	43.2	36.6	29.8
Int. Exp.	0.78	0.87	0.87	0.41	0.56	0.64	0.48	0.48	0.67	0.78
Pretax Inc.	308	152	158	510	223	146	115	89.2	10.6	93.4
Eff. Tax Rate	29.3%	34.0%	34.1%	34.6%	30.0%	30.0%	30.0%	32.0%	32.0%	32.0%
Net Inc.	218	100	104	334	156	102	80.8	60.6	7.20	63.5
S&P Core Earnings	181	51.5	41.2	198	NA	NA	NA	NA	NA	NA

Balance Sheet & Other Fin. Data (Million $)

	2004	2003	2002	2001	2000	1999	1998	1997	1996	1995
Cash	442	360	563	563	844	319	175	107	21.0	80.0
Curr. Assets	1,708	1,324	1,549	1,549	1,151	831	716	597	563	615
Total Assets	2,270	1,919	2,003	2,003	1,779	1,062	940	824	763	785
Curr. Liab.	306	274	394	394	380	268	259	250	262	276
LT Debt	7.70	8.57	8.60	Nil	0.10	0.37	1.00	1.81	0.40	0.77
Common Equity	2,165	2,023	1,348	1,509	1,215	738	632	533	464	474
Total Cap.	2,173	2,031	1,356	1,509	1,329	739	633	534	464	475
Cap. Exp.	30.7	24.4	105	105	82.8	51.4	40.6	53.1	60.8	64.8
Cash Flow	293	172	164	400	207	148	129	104	43.8	93.3
Curr. Ratio	5.6	4.8	3.9	3.9	3.0	3.1	2.8	2.4	2.1	2.2
% LT Debt of Cap.	0.4	0.4	0.6	Nil	0.0	0.1	0.2	0.3	0.1	0.2
% Net Inc.of Revs.	12.8	6.9	6.2	13.3	9.0	8.2	6.8	5.2	0.7	5.6
% Ret. on Assets	10.4	5.2	5.3	17.6	11.0	10.2	9.2	7.6	1.0	8.9
% Ret. on Equity	10.4	5.2	7.1	24.5	16.0	14.9	13.9	12.2	1.6	14.0

Data as orig reptd.; bef. results of disc opers/spec. items. Per share data adj. for stk. divs.; EPS diluted. E-Estimated. NA-Not Available. NM-Not Meaningful. NR-Not Ranked. UR-Under Review.

Office: 5030 Sugarloaf Parkway, Lawrenceville, GA 30044-2869.
Telephone: 770-236-5000.
Email: investor@sciatl.com
Website: http://www.scientificatlanta.com
Chrmn, Pres & CEO: J.F. McDonald.

SVP, CFO & Treas: J.W. Eidson.
SVP, Secy & General Counsel: M. Veysey.
Dirs: M. H. Antonini, J. I. Cash, Jr., D. W. Dorman, W. E. Kassling, M. B. Mangum, J. F. McDonald, T. F. McGuirk, D. J. McLaughlin, J. V. Napier, S. Nunn.

Founded: in 1951.
Domicile: Georgia.
Employees: 7,538.
S&P Analyst: A. Bensinger/CB/MWJ

The **McGraw-Hill** Companies

Sealed Air

Recommendation: HOLD ★★★☆☆
SELL | SELL | HOLD | BUY | BUY

12-Month Target Price: **$51.00**
(as of October 27, 2004)

SEE has an approximate 0.04% weighting in the **S&P 500**

Sector: Materials
Sub-Industry: Paper Packaging
Peer Group: Packaging - Consumer Products

Summary: This company is a leading global manufacturer of a wide range of food and protective packaging materials and systems.

Quantitative Evaluations

S&P Earnings & Dividend Rank: NR

D	C	B-	B	B+	A-	A	A+

S&P Fair Value Rank: 2

1	2	3	4	5
Lowest				Highest

Fair Value Calc.: $48.60 (Slightly Overvalued)

S&P Investability Quotient Percentile

24%

SEE scored lower than 76% of all companies for which an S&P Report is available.

Volatility: Average

Low	Average	High

Technical Evaluation: Bullish
Since 11/04, the technical indicators for SEE have been Bullish.

Relative Strength Rank: Moderate

70

1 Lowest		Highest 99

Price as of 11/12/04: $52.83 | **2004E S&P Core EPS:** $2.64

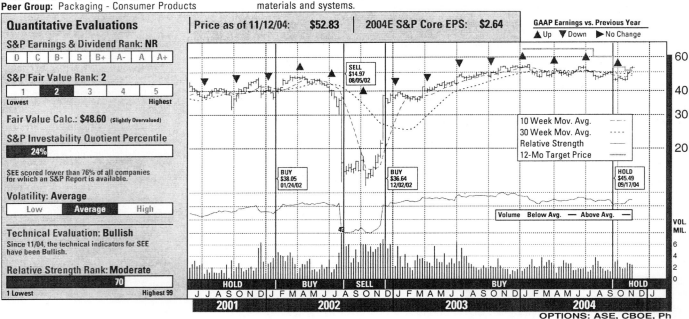

GAAP Earnings vs. Previous Year
▲ Up ▼ Down ► No Change

SELL $14.97 08/05/02
BUY $38.05 01/24/02
BUY $36.64 12/02/02
HOLD $45.49 09/17/04

10 Week Mov. Avg.
30 Week Mov. Avg.
Relative Strength
12-Mo Target Price

Volume Below Avg. — Above Avg. —

HOLD | BUY | SELL | BUY | HOLD
J J A S O N D | J F M A M J J A S O N D | J F M A M J J A S O N D | J F M A M J J A S O N D | J F M A M J J A S O N D | J
2001 | 2002 | 2003 | 2004

OPTIONS: ASE, CBOE, Ph

Analyst commentary prepared by Stewart Scharf/CB/JWP

Highlights October 29, 2004

- We anticipate net sales growth in the high single digits in 2005, following our forecast of 5% growth in 2004 (before 3% positive foreign exchange), primarily on increased demand for new protective/specialty packaging products. We expect food packaging sales to remain weak on a U.S. ban on Canadian beef, and restrictions on U.S. beef imports from various countries (mainly Japan, Korea and Mexico) as a result of the Mad Cow disease scare in late 2003. Japan recently announced that it plans to resume U.S. imports of beef from cattle 20 months of age or less by early 2005.

- Following our projection of narrower gross margins in 2004, as higher raw material costs and product mix shifts in food packaging outweigh price hikes and margin expansion on the protective materials side, we expect operating (EBITDA) margins to expand during 2005 from 19% recently, on a larger proportion of wider margin products, such as case-ready meat and vertical pouch packaging, and improved operating efficiencies. We see restructuring efforts leading to annualized cost savings of $15 million to $20 million, with some savings achieved during 2005.

- We project 2004 EPS of $2.65 (before dilution of $0.09 due to an accounting change for convertible debt, and charges of about $0.18 to $0.20 for debt redemption and $0.07 to $0.10 for restructuring). We see EPS of $3.15 for 2005. Our Standard & Poor's Core EPS estimates virtually match our operating projections.

Investment Rationale/Risk October 29, 2004

- We anticipate that free cash flow (FCF) will exceed $300 million in 2005, and expect SEE to use excess cash for further debt paydowns, share buybacks and niche acquisitions. However, with rising petrochemical prices and uncertain markets, and based on our valuations, we view the stock as fairly valued.

- Risks to our recommendation and target price include a slower than expected economic rebound, further significant increases in resin prices, additional delays in resolving import restrictions on U.S. beef, the possibility of another Mad Cow disease scare, negative foreign exchange effects, and failure of Congress to pass an asbestos trust fund.

- The stock is trading at under 16X our 2005 EPS estimate, well below its historical average P/E multiple of 23X, but on par with our projected multiple for the S&P 500 Index and at a premium to peers. Our discounted cash flow (DCF) analysis indicates that the stock is at a modest discount to intrinsic value, assuming a perpetual growth rate of 3.5% and a weighted average cost of capital (WACC) of 8.25%. Our 12-month target price is $51, based on average peer historical forward P/E multiples.

Key Stock Statistics

S&P Core EPS 2005E	3.14	52-week Range	$54.90-44.06
S&P Oper. EPS 2004E	2.65	12 Month P/E	21.3
P/E on S&P Oper. EPS 2004E	19.9	Beta	1.64
S&P Oper. EPS 2005E	3.15	Shareholders	8,997
Yield (%)	Nil	Market Cap (B)	$ 4.4
Dividend Rate/Share	Nil	Shares Outstanding (M)	83.6

Value of $10,000 invested five years ago: **$ 9,788**

Dividend Data

Dividends, initiated in 1975, were discontinued in 1989.

Revenues/Earnings Data Fiscal year ending December 31

Revenues (Million $)

	2004	2003	2002	2001	2000	1999
1Q	913.1	822.9	746.1	758.3	741.5	678.9
2Q	923.7	865.6	786.3	761.6	756.8	695.1
3Q	944.2	908.7	825.8	766.2	773.3	714.8
4Q	—	934.8	846.1	781.4	796.1	750.8
Yr.	—	3,532	3,204	3,067	3,068	2,840

Earnings Per Share ($)

	2004	2003	2002	2001	2000	1999
1Q	0.64	0.52	0.56	0.25	0.45	0.34
2Q	0.66	0.56	0.61	0.30	0.44	0.40
3Q	0.69	0.41	0.62	0.37	0.46	0.43
4Q	E0.66	0.50	-6.13	0.30	0.56	0.50
Yr.	E2.65	2.00	-4.30	1.22	1.93	1.68

Next earnings report expected: late-January Source: S&P, Company Reports
EPS Estimates based on S&P Operating Earnings; historical GAAP earnings are as reported.

Sealed Air Corporation

Recommendation: **HOLD** ★ ★ ★ ☆ ☆   12-Month Target Price: **$51.00** (as of October 27, 2004)

Business Summary November 01, 2004

Sealed Air Corp., with a broader global presence following its merger with the Cryovac packaging business of W.R. Grace in 1998, is a leading protective and specialty packaging company. It expects an increasing proportion of sales to come from outside the U.S. Foreign operations accounted for 45% of sales in 2003, with Europe accounting for 26% of total sales. At September 30, 2004, Europe accounted for nearly 30% of sales.

The company operates in two business segments: food packaging products (62% of 2003 net sales; 63% of operating profits), and protective and specialty packaging products (38%; 37%). Surface protection and other cushioning products include air cellular packaging materials, and plastic sheets containing encapsulated air bubbles that protect products from damage through shock or vibration during shipment, under the Bubble Wrap and Air Cap brand names. SEE's engineered products consist of its Instapak foam-in-place packaging systems, which provide protection packaging for various products, including computer, electronic and communications equipment, and void-fill packaging of office supplies, books and other small products. The company also makes Jiffy protective mailers and other durable mailers and bags.

Food packaging products primarily consists of flexible materials and related systems marketed mainly under the Cryovac trademark for a broad range of perishable food applications. Cryovac products include shrink bags, shrink films and laminated films. The segment also manufactures polystyrene foam trays that are used by supermarkets and food processors to protect and display fresh meat, poultry and produce. In addition, it sells rigid packaging and absorbent pads used for food packaging, including its Dri-Loc pads. About 9% of U.S. beef is exported.

In October 2004, the company reiterated its revised 2004 EPS guidance of $2.60 to $2.70, which it had reduced in September from $2.80 to $2.90. SEE repurchased $27 million of its common stock in the 2004 third quarter, following $34 million in the second quarter, bringing the total number of shares repurchased year to date to over 1.7 million, for $86 million. The company lowered its projected 2004 capital expenditures to $100 million, from a range of $125 million to $150 million.

In the 2003 fourth quarter, SEE repurchased at a premium nearly $123 million of senior notes due July 2008, and $50 million of senior notes due May 2009, resulting in a loss on debt repurchase of $33.6 million ($0.22 a share). Prior to the July 2003 redemption of the company's 25,789,399 Series A convertible preferred shares for $51 each, plus accrued dividends, each preferred share was eligible for conversion into 0.885 of a common share. The redemption was financed by the July 2003 private placement of $1.3 billion of senior notes. The recapitalization was expected to eliminate 24 million common shares, on an if-converted basis, with a net reduction of 17 million shares, assuming that 6 million shares from the debt offering were converted into common stock if the stock exceeds $70 a share. During 2003, SEE incurred a net charge of $24.7 million ($0.26 a share) on the redemption and repurchase of convertible preferred stock. EPS in 2003 were $2.45, before net charges of $0.45.

In the 2002 fourth quarter, the company incurred a charge exceeding $841 million to settle asbestos-related and fraudulent transfer claims related to its 1998 acquisition of the Cryovac packaging unit of W.R. Grace, which was operating under bankruptcy protection. A loss of $6.13 a share in the 2002 fourth quarter reflected asbestos settlement and restructuring charges totaling $6.81 a share.

Company Financials Fiscal Year ending December 31

Per Share Data ($)

(Year Ended December 31)	2003	2002	2001	2000	1999	1998	1997	1996	1995	1994
Tangible Bk. Val.	NM	NM	NM	NM	NM	NM	5.69	NA	NA	NA
Cash Flow	3.91	-2.34	3.84	4.33	3.41	2.44	2.38	NA	NA	NA
Earnings	2.00	-4.30	1.22	1.93	1.68	0.12	1.17	NA	NA	NA
S&P Core Earnings	2.03	2.58	1.25	NA	NA	NA	NA	NA	NA	NA
Dividends	Nil	Nil	Nil	Nil	Nil	Nil	NA	NA	NA	NA
Payout Ratio	Nil	Nil	Nil	Nil	Nil	Nil	NA	NA	NA	NA
Prices - High	54.47	48.39	47.10	61.87	68.43	68.00	NA	NA	NA	NA
- Low	35.00	12.70	28.80	26.37	44.50	27.37	NA	NA	NA	NA
P/E Ratio - High	27	NM	39	32	41	NM	NA	NA	NA	NA
- Low	17	NM	24	14	26	NM	NA	NA	NA	NA

Income Statement Analysis (Million $)

	2003	2002	2001	2000	1999	1998	1997	1996	1995	1994
Revs.	3,532	3,204	3,067	3,068	2,840	2,507	1,480	NA	NA	NA
Oper. Inc.	693	1,766	641	687	648	524	155	NA	NA	NA
Depr.	154	166	221	220	147	178	93.0	NA	NA	NA
Int. Exp.	134	65.3	76.4	64.5	58.1	53.6	19.0	NA	NA	NA
Pretax Inc.	377	-392	297	413	396	199	143	NA	NA	NA
Eff. Tax Rate	36.2%	NM	47.3%	45.5%	46.6%	63.3%	38.5%	NA	NA	NA
Net Inc.	240	-309	157	225	211	73.0	88.0	NA	NA	NA
S&P Core Earnings	189	227	111	NA	NA	NA	NA	NA	NA	NA

Balance Sheet & Other Fin. Data (Million $)

	2003	2002	2001	2000	1999	1998	1997	1996	1995	1994
Cash	365	127	13.8	11.2	13.7	45.0	48.0	NA	NA	NA
Curr. Assets	1,428	1,056	776	877	803	845	2,176	NA	NA	NA
Total Assets	4,704	4,261	3,908	4,048	3,855	4,040	3,773	NA	NA	NA
Curr. Liab.	1,190	1,153	627	675	582	535	1,358	NA	NA	NA
LT Debt	2,260	868	788	944	665	997	48.5	NA	NA	NA
Common Equity	1,124	813	850	753	551	437	468	NA	NA	NA
Total Cap.	3,418	3,039	3,215	3,301	3,193	3,425	322	NA	NA	NA
Cap. Exp.	124	91.6	146	114	75.1	82.4	24.3	NA	NA	NA
Cash Flow	366	-197	322	381	287	179	181	NA	NA	NA
Curr. Ratio	1.2	0.9	1.2	1.3	1.4	1.6	1.6	NA	NA	NA
% LT Debt of Cap.	66.1	28.6	24.5	28.6	20.8	29.1	15.1	NA	NA	NA
% Net Inc.of Revs.	6.8	NM	5.1	7.3	7.4	2.9	5.9	NA	NA	NA
% Ret. on Assets	5.4	NM	3.9	5.7	5.3	1.9	2.0	NA	NA	NA
% Ret. on Equity	21.9	NM	12.7	24.7	28.3	0.2	16.0	NA	NA	NA

Data as orig reptd.; bef. results of disc opers/spec. items. Per share data adj. for stk. divs.; EPS diluted. Certain 1998 data pro forma. E-Estimated. NA-Not Available. NM-Not Meaningful. NR-Not Ranked.

Office: Park 80 East, Saddle Brook, NJ 07663-5291.
Telephone: 201-791-7600.
Website: http://www.sealedair.com
Pres & CEO: W.V. Hickey.
SVP & CFO: D. Kelsey.

VP, Secy & General Counsel: H.K. White.
Treas: T.S. Christie.
Investor Contact: P.H. Cook 201-791-7600.
Dirs: H. Brown, M. Chu, L. R. Codey, T. D. Dunphy, C. F. Farrell, Jr., W. V. Hickey, K. P. Manning, W. J. Marino.

Founded: in 1996.
Domicile: Delaware.
Employees: 17,600.
S&P Analyst: Stewart Scharf/CB/JWP

The McGraw·Hill Companies

Sears, Roebuck

Recommendation: HOLD ★ ★ ★ ☆ ☆
SELL SELL HOLD BUY BUY

12-Month Target Price: $50.00
(as of November 17, 2004)

S has an approximate 0.10% weighting in the **S&P 500**

Sector: Consumer Discretionary
Sub-Industry: Department Stores
Peer Group: Department Store Cos. - Larger

Summary: This multi-line retailer provides a wide array of merchandise and services in the U.S. and Canada.

Quantitative Evaluations

S&P Earnings & Dividend Rank: B+

| D | C | B- | B | B+ | A- | A | A+ |

S&P Fair Value Rank: 2+

| 1 | 2 | 3 | 4 | 5 |
| Lowest | | | | Highest |

Fair Value Calc.: $41.90 (Overvalued)

S&P Investability Quotient Percentile

67%

S scored higher than 67% of all companies for which an S&P Report is available.

Volatility: High

| Low | Average | High |

Technical Evaluation: Bullish
Since 11/04, the technical indicators for S have been Bullish.

Relative Strength Rank: Strong

97
1 Lowest   Highest 99

Price as of 11/17/04: $52.99 | **2004E S&P Core EPS:** $0.90

GAAP Earnings vs. Previous Year
▲ Up ▼ Down ► No Change

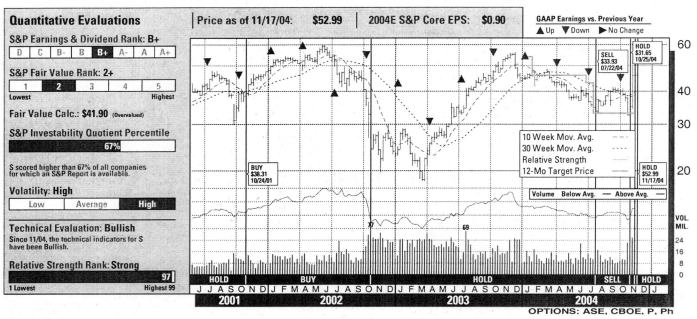

10 Week Mov. Avg.
30 Week Mov. Avg.
Relative Strength
12-Mo Target Price

Volume   Below Avg. — Above Avg. —

OPTIONS: ASE, CBOE, P, Ph

Analyst commentary prepared by Jason N. Asaeda/MF/BK

Highlights 17-NOV-04

- The STARS recommendation for Sears, Roebuck and Co. (S) has recently been changed to 3 from 1. The Highlights section of this Stock Report will be updated accordingly.

Investment Rationale/Risk 17-NOV-04

- The Investment Rationale/Risk section of this Stock Report will be updated shortly. For the latest news story on Sears, Roebuck and Co. (S) from Market-Scope, see below.

11/17/04 12:55 pm EST... UPDATE - S&P MAINTAINS HOLD OPINION ON SHARES OF SEARS, ROEBUCK (S 55.69***): We share S's view that merger agreed to today with Kmart (118.62, NR), pending approvals, would have product, cost, and competitive synergies. We think these are achievable but see integration and execution risks, given divergent cultures and customer mix. S believes cash option at $50 offers attractive premium to historical mid-$30's share price. Based on a.m. call, we conclude S's dividend will likely end after merger. Nonetheless, our opinion remains hold, since some metrics, including price/sales and real estate valuations, suggest a competing bid is not out of the question. /J.Asaeda

Key Stock Statistics

S&P Core EPS 2005E	1.31	52-week Range	$56.06-31.21
S&P Oper. EPS 2004E	1.70	12 Month P/E	5.5
P/E on S&P Oper. EPS 2004E	27.1	Beta	0.61
S&P Oper. EPS 2005E	1.90	Shareholders	149,591
Yield (%)	1.7%	Market Cap (B)	$ 11.2
Dividend Rate/Share	0.92	Shares Outstanding (M)	212.0

Value of $10,000 invested five years ago: **$ 17,792**

Dividend Data Dividends have been paid since 1935

Amount ($)	Date Decl.	Ex-Div. Date	Stock of Record	Payment Date
0.230	Feb. 04	Feb. 25	Feb. 27	Apr. 01 '04
0.230	May. 13	May. 26	May. 28	Jul. 01 '04
0.230	Aug. 11	Aug. 27	Aug. 31	Oct. 01 '04
0.230	Oct. 13	Nov. 26	Nov. 30	Jan. 03 '05

Revenues/Earnings Data Fiscal year ending December 31

Revenues (Million $)

	2004	2003	2002	2001	2000	1999
1Q	7,794	8,880	9,037	8,857	8,973	9,037
2Q	8,781	10,196	10,142	10,226	10,076	9,992
3Q	8,295	9,794	9,669	9,753	9,627	9,538
4Q	—	12,254	12,518	12,242	12,374	12,504
Yr.	—	41,124	41,366	41,078	40,937	41,071

Earnings Per Share ($)

	2004	2003	2002	2001	2000	1999
1Q	-0.09	0.60	0.98	0.53	0.65	0.38
2Q	0.24	1.04	0.71	-0.60	1.11	0.86
3Q	-0.29	0.52	0.59	0.80	0.81	0.62
4Q	E1.59	10.84	2.67	1.52	1.32	1.98
Yr.	E1.70	11.86	4.94	2.24	3.88	3.81

Next earnings report expected: late-January Source: S&P, Company Reports
EPS Estimates based on S&P Operating Earnings; historical GAAP earnings are as reported.

Sears, Roebuck and Co.

Recommendation: **HOLD** ★ ★ ★ ☆ ☆   12-Month Target Price: **$50.00** (as of November 17, 2004)

Business Summary November 12, 2004

Sears, Roebuck and Co. is a leading retailer of appliances and home and automotive products and related services. Since 2002, the company has focused on repositioning its core business of full-line stores. S has said that changes included centralized cashiers, better presentation standards, narrowed apparel assortments, the introduction of several proprietary brands, and improved customer service. The company has also expanded its assortment of key hardlines, and exited certain non-core, low profit businesses. In addition, in June 2002, S acquired Lands' End, Inc., a leading direct merchant of apparel, home products and soft luggage, for $1.8 billion.

In 2003, the company became a more focused retailer, selling its credit and financial products business, which included U.S. credit card operations and related credit protection and insurance products. In November 2003, S sold substantially all assets and liabilities of its credit business to Citibank (USA) N.A. (an affiliate of Citigroup, Inc.), for $31.8 billion. Under a long-term marketing and servicing alliance, Citibank N.A. is expected to provide credit and customer services benefits to Sears Card and Sears Gold MasterCard holders, and to support the company's zero-percent financing program. S expects to receive annual performance payments from Citibank N.A., based on the level of new account and credit sales generation, and on other activities.

With the sale of its credit business, S's financial reporting was changed in 2004 to reflect two operating segments: Domestic and International. The Domestic segment comprised the former Retail and Related Services segment, including revenues earned from the Citibank N.A. relationship; and the former Corporate and

Other segment. The International segment represents the results of operations of Sears Canada.

At the end of 2003, the former Retail and Related Services segment consisted of about 871 full-line Sears department stores and 1,105 specialty stores, including Sears Hardware and Orchard Supply Hardware stores, independently owned hardline dealer stores (located in small communities), and The Great Outdoors home decorating and remodeling stores.

The Retail segment's Direct to Consumer business included Lands' End online, catalog and retail operations. Lands' End offers traditionally styled casual clothing for men, women and children. Direct to Consumer also included direct marketing of goods and services memberships, merchandise through specialty catalogs, and impulse and continuity merchandise.

The Retail segment's Product Repair Services business provides service contracts, product installation, and repair services for all major brands of home products through a national network of about 10,000 service technicians. It also sells and services residential cooling and heating systems.

S's former Corporate and Other segment includes home improvement services, mainly siding and windows through Sears Home Improvement Services.

The company conducts retail, credit and corporate operations in Canada through Sears Canada Inc., a consolidated, 54%-owned subsidiary.

Company Financials Fiscal Year ending December 31

Per Share Data ($)

(Year Ended December 31)	2003	2002	2001	2000	1999	1998	1997	1996	1995	1994
Tangible Bk. Val.	20.61	16.12	19.12	20.33	18.53	15.80	15.00	12.63	10.40	26.18
Cash Flow	15.06	7.66	4.52	6.49	6.04	4.74	4.96	4.87	3.93	NM
Earnings	11.86	4.94	2.24	3.88	3.81	2.74	2.99	3.12	2.53	3.16
S&P Core Earnings	1.74	3.40	1.47	NA	NA	NA	NA	NA	NA	NA
Dividends	0.92	0.92	0.92	0.92	0.92	0.92	0.92	0.92	1.26	1.60
Payout Ratio	8%	19%	41%	24%	24%	34%	31%	29%	50%	51%
Prices - High	56.06	59.90	48.93	43.50	53.18	65.00	65.25	53.87	61.25	55.12
- Low	18.25	19.71	29.90	25.25	26.68	39.06	38.75	38.25	29.37	42.12
P/E Ratio - High	5	12	22	11	14	24	22	17	24	17
- Low	2	4	13	7	7	14	13	12	12	13

Income Statement Analysis (Million $)

	2003	2002	2001	2000	1999	1998	1997	1996	1995	1994
Revs.	41,124	41,366	41,078	40,937	41,071	41,322	41,296	38,236	34,925	54,559
Oper. Inc.	4,035	4,210	4,408	4,587	4,570	4,460	4,664	4,145	3,707	3,818
Depr.	909	875	751	901	848	830	786	697	578	649
Int. Exp.	1,025	1,143	1,415	1,248	1,268	1,428	1,409	1,370	1,377	1,340
Pretax Inc.	5,449	2,453	1,223	2,223	2,419	1,838	2,138	2.05	1,728	1,712
Eff. Tax Rate	36.8%	35.0%	38.2%	37.4%	37.4%	41.6%	42.7%	39.6%	40.7%	20.9%
Net Inc.	3,397	1,584	735	1,343	1,453	1,027	1,188	1,271	1,025	1,244
S&P Core Earnings	500	1,089	484	NA	NA	NA	NA	NA	NA	NA

Balance Sheet & Other Fin. Data (Million $)

	2003	2002	2001	2000	1999	1998	1997	1996	1995	1994
Cash	9,057	1,962	1,064	842	729	495	358	660	606	1,421
Curr. Assets	18,196	39,983	36,105	28,794	28,667	29,271	30,682	28,447	26,441	NA
Total Assets	27,723	50,409	44,317	36,899	36,954	37,675	38,700	36,167	33,130	91,896
Curr. Liab.	13,759	18,597	15,584	15,796	13,701	14,109	15,790	14,950	14,607	NA
LT Debt	4,218	21,304	18,921	11,020	12,884	13,631	13,071	12,170	10,044	9,713
Common Equity	6,401	6,753	6,119	6,769	6,839	6,066	5,862	4,945	4,060	9,240
Total Cap.	10,619	28,057	25,040	17,789	19,723	19,697	18,933	17,115	14,429	22,448
Cap. Exp.	925	1,035	1,126	1,084	1,033	1,212	1,328	1,189	1,183	1,120
Cash Flow	4,306	2,459	1,486	2,244	2,301	1,857	1,974	1,943	1,550	NM
Curr. Ratio	1.3	2.1	2.3	1.8	2.1	2.1	1.9	1.9	1.8	NA
% LT Debt of Cap.	39.7	75.9	75.6	61.9	65.3	69.2	69.0	71.1	28.1	43.3
% Net Inc.of Revs.	8.3	3.8	1.8	3.3	3.5	2.5	2.9	3.3	2.9	2.3
% Ret. on Assets	8.7	3.3	1.8	3.6	3.9	2.8	3.2	3.7	2.9	1.4
% Ret. on Equity	51.6	24.6	11.4	19.7	22.5	31.1	22.0	27.7	14.6	12.5

Data as orig reptd.; bef. results of disc opers/spec. items. Per share data adj. for stk. divs. Bold denotes primary EPS - prior periods restated. E-Estimated. NA-Not Available. NM-Not Meaningful. NR-Not Ranked. UR-Under Review.

Office: 3333 Beverly Road, Hoffman Estates, IL 60179.
Telephone: 847-286-2500.
Email: invrel@sears.com
Website: http://www.sears.com
Chrmn, Pres & CEO: A.J. Lacy.

SVP & CFO: G.R. Richter.
SVP & General Counsel: A.L. Zopp.
Investor Contact: S.A. Bohaboy 847-286-7419.
Dirs: H. Adams, Jr., B. C. Barnes, W. L. Bax, D. J. Carty, W. J. Farrell, M. A. Miles, H. B. Price, D. A. Terrell, R. Yzaguirre.

Founded: in 1886.
Domicile: New York.
Employees: 249,000.
S&P Analyst: Jason N. Asaeda/MF/BK

Sempra Energy

Recommendation: **HOLD** ★ ★ ★ ☆ ☆   SELL | SELL | HOLD | BUY | BUY

12-Month Target Price: $38.00
(as of August 05, 2004)

SRE has an approximate 0.08% weighting in the **S&P 500**

Sector: Utilities
Sub-Industry: Multi-Utilities & Unregulated Power

Summary: This gas and electric utility is also engaged in unregulated power, liquefied natural gas, and international energy projects.

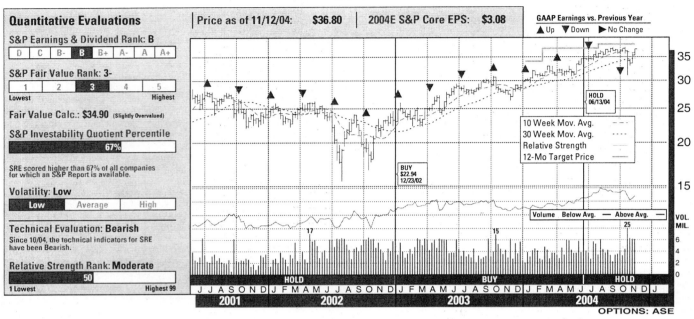

Quantitative Evaluations

S&P Earnings & Dividend Rank: B

D | C | B- | **B** | B+ | A- | A | A+

S&P Fair Value Rank: 3-

1 | 2 | **3** | 4 | 5
Lowest   Highest

Fair Value Calc.: $34.90 (Slightly Overvalued)

S&P Investability Quotient Percentile

67%

SRE scored higher than 67% of all companies for which an S&P Report is available.

Volatility: Low

Low | Average | High

Technical Evaluation: Bearish
Since 10/04, the technical indicators for SRE have been Bearish.

Relative Strength Rank: Moderate

50

1 Lowest   Highest 99

Price as of 11/12/04: $36.80   **2004E S&P Core EPS:** $3.08

Analyst commentary prepared by Craig K. Shere, CFA /CB/BK

Highlights August 16, 2004

- We see 2004 revenues growing about 18%, driven by higher pass-through utility expenses, a 70% increase in megawatts sold to California under CDWR contracts, full-year contributions from three power plants (2,125 MW) completed in 2003, a $25 million pipeline rate increase and growing volumes on the Bajanorte pipeline, partly offset by much lower authorizations of utility performance-based ratemaking awards and the absence of nuclear plant incentive performance awards.

- We believe margins will narrow, as the effects of increased pass-through utility expenses offset greater contributions from wider margin CDWR contracts. We expect other income to grow, due to economic growth in service territories for unconsolidated South American utility operations. Taking into account over 9% additional outstanding shares, we look for operating EPS to grow about 4%.

- Reported 2003 EPS includes $0.10 of gains for one-time tax benefits and regulatory settlements net of asset impairments and other charges.

Investment Rationale/Risk August 16, 2004

- In early June 2004, SRE outlined a targeted 2008 EPS range that represents almost 5% annual compound growth from our 2004 operating EPS estimate. Due to SRE's exposure to more volatile wholesale power and energy trading operations, we believe SRE should trade at a discounted P/E multiple versus its more regulated multi-utility peers.

- Risks to our recommendation and target price include SRE's failure to complete its planned LNG projects, declining wholesale power margins, potential losses from energy and metals trading, higher interest rates and a weaker economy.

- We believe SRE is fairly valued at its current 2005 P/E multiple of 11.5X, vs. about 12.7X for multi-utility peers. The stock trades at slight premiums to peers based on price-to-book and price to trailing operating cash flow multiples. We look for the shares to appreciate in line with our view of 5% long-term EPS growth potential. Our 12-month target price is $38.

Key Stock Statistics

S&P Core EPS 2005E	3.13	52-week Range	$37.27-26.36
S&P Oper. EPS 2004E	3.20	12 Month P/E	10.6
P/E on S&P Oper. EPS 2004E	11.5	Beta	0.16
S&P Oper. EPS 2005E	3.25	Shareholders	60,000
Yield (%)	2.7%	Market Cap (B)	$ 8.6
Dividend Rate/Share	1.00	Shares Outstanding (M)	233.4

Value of $10,000 invested five years ago: **$ 21,737**

Dividend Data Dividends have been paid since 1998

Amount ($)	Date Decl.	Ex-Div. Date	Stock of Record	Payment Date
0.250	Dec. 03	Dec. 19	Dec. 23	Jan. 15 '04
0.250	Feb. 23	Mar. 18	Mar. 22	Apr. 15 '04
0.250	Jun. 08	Jun. 21	Jun. 23	Jul. 15 '04
0.250	Sep. 14	Sep. 27	Sep. 29	Oct. 15 '04

Revenues/Earnings Data Fiscal year ending December 31

Revenues (Million $)

	2004	2003	2002	2001	2000	1999
1Q	2,360	1,923	1,460	3,242	1,460	1,191
2Q	1,996	1,840	1,488	1,900	1,530	1,517
3Q	2,165	2,058	1,384	1,510	1,832	1,254
4Q	—	2,066	1,688	1,377	2,321	1,473
Yr.	—	7,887	6,020	8,029	7,143	5,435

Earnings Per Share ($)

	2004	2003	2002	2001	2000	1999
1Q	0.96	0.56	0.71	0.88	0.49	0.42
2Q	0.55	0.56	0.70	0.66	0.55	0.35
3Q	0.98	1.00	0.73	0.46	0.55	0.45
4Q	E0.75	1.11	0.65	0.52	0.47	0.44
Yr.	E3.20	3.24	2.79	2.52	2.06	1.66

Next earnings report expected: late-February Source: S&P, Company Reports
EPS Estimates based on S&P Operating Earnings; historical GAAP earnings are as reported.

Sempra Energy

Recommendation: **HOLD** ★ ★ ★ ☆ ☆   12-Month Target Price: **$38.00** (as of August 05, 2004)

Business Summary August 17, 2004

Sempra Energy operates in the regulated Utilities and unregulated Global Enterprises segments. The Utilities segment (contributing almost 60% of 2003 recurring segment income) includes Southern California Gas Company (SoCalGas) and San Diego Gas & Electric (SDG&E). Global Enterprises (over 40%) includes risk management and infrastructure units.

At the end of 2003, SRE's Utilities segment served 6.2 million natural gas customers and 1.3 million electric customers primarily in Southern California and also in portions of central California. In addition to its local distribution service, the segment owns over 3,000 miles of transmission and storage pipeline. During 2003, the FERC approved an approximate $25 million pretax transmission rate increase. However, SDG&E's nuclear incentive-pricing ratemaking (contributing $53 million after-tax in 2003) expired at the end of 2003.

During 2003, SRE's California Utilities earned $72.8 million pretax from Performance Based Ratemaking (PBR) awards. PBR awards are earned when the utilities save costs for ratepayers, but awards do not become income until officially granted by the utility commission. At the end of 2003, $53.6 million in pretax awards had yet to be officially granted. By mid-2004, SRE expects a regulatory decision regarding its proposals to meet future electricity demand (including the transfer of a $600 million power plant to SDG&E from Global Enterprise's Energy Resources division).

Global Enterprise's risk management divisions include Sempra Energy Trading (SET) and Solutions (SES). Global Enterprise's largest 2003 earnings contributor was SET, which derived its net trading margin from gas (26%), oil--crude & products (24%), metals (18%), power (13%) and other (19%). At 2003 year end, 83.4% of the value of SET's contracts settled in cash within 24 months. SES procures electricity and natural gas for commercial and industrial customers. In February 2004, SRE noted that increasing competition was having a negative effect on Solutions' margins.

Global Enterprise's infrastructure divisions include Sempra Energy Resources (SER) and International (SEI). SER is a competitive wholesale power producer. In March 2004, SER agreed to acquire a 50% interest in a $430 million acquisition of six active Texas power plants (975 MW net) and four inactive plants (930 MW net). The acquisition was facilitated by Sempra Energy Partners, formed in 2003 to pursue asset acquisitions in the distressed energy market. During 2003, SER finished constructing three new power plants (2,125 MW net). A significant portion of SER earnings come from a long term power supply contract (expiring in 2011) with California.

SEI operates and develops distribution utilities and transmission systems in Mexico and South America. SEI is pursuing claims against the Argentine government for changes to natural gas tariffs. Through Sempra Energy LNG Corp., SEI is also pursuing development of two liquefied natural gas (LNG) terminals in Louisiana (costing $700 million) and Baja California, Mexico ($300 million for SRE's 50% interest). The company plans to begin construction in 2004 and bring the LNG facilities into operation in 2007.

Company Financials Fiscal Year ending December 31

Per Share Data ($)

(Year Ended December 31)	2003	2002	2001	2000	1999	1998	1997	1996	1995	1994
Tangible Bk. Val.	17.14	13.78	13.17	12.27	12.60	12.14	12.56	12.21	11.70	11.18
Cash Flow	6.12	5.68	5.35	NA	NA	NA	NA	NA	NA	NA
Earnings	3.24	2.79	2.52	2.06	1.66	1.24	1.82	1.77	1.67	NA
S&P Core Earnings	3.29	2.16	1.76	NA	NA	NA	NA	NA	NA	NA
Dividends	1.00	1.00	1.00	1.00	1.56	1.56	1.27	1.24	1.22	NA
Payout Ratio	31%	36%	40%	49%	94%	126%	70%	NA	NA	NA
Prices - High	30.90	26.25	28.61	24.87	26.00	29.31	NA	NA	NA	NA
- Low	22.25	15.50	17.31	16.18	17.12	23.75	NA	NA	NA	NA
P/E Ratio - High	10	9	11	12	16	24	NA	NA	NA	NA
- Low	7	6	7	8	10	19	NA	NA	NA	NA

Income Statement Analysis (Million $)

	2003	2002	2001	2000	1999	1998	1997	1996	1995	1994
Revs.	7,887	6,020	8,029	7,037	5,360	5,481	5,069	4,496	4,166	NA
Oper. Inc.	939	987	993	NA	1,617	1,536	1,503	1,508	NA	NA
Depr.	615	596	579	563	879	929	604	586	521	NA
Int. Exp.	327	323	352	301	229	207	107	103	117	132
Pretax Inc.	742	721	731	NA	NA	NA	NA	NA	NA	NA
Eff. Tax Rate	6.33%	20.2%	29.1%	38.6%	31.2%	31.9%	41.1%	41.3%	39.7%	NA
Net Inc.	695	575	518	429	394	294	432	427	401	359
S&P Core Earnings	708	445	362	NA	NA	NA	NA	NA	NA	NA

Balance Sheet & Other Fin. Data (Million $)

	2003	2002	2001	2000	1999	1998	1997	1996	1995	1994
Cash	432	455	605	NA	NA	NA	NA	NA	NA	NA
Curr. Assets	7,886	7,010	4,808	NA	NA	NA	NA	NA	NA	NA
Total Assets	22,009	17,757	15,156	NA	NA	NA	NA	NA	NA	NA
Curr. Liab.	8,348	7,247	5,524	NA	NA	NA	NA	NA	NA	NA
LT Debt	4,199	4,487	3,840	NA	NA	NA	NA	NA	NA	NA
Common Equity	3,890	2,825	2,692	NA	NA	NA	NA	NA	NA	NA
Total Cap.	8,807	8,202	7,474	7,093	6,813	6,489	7,309	6,859	NA	NA
Cap. Exp.	1,049	1,214	1,068	NA	NA	NA	NA	NA	NA	NA
Cash Flow	1,310	1,171	1,097	NA	NA	NA	NA	NA	NA	NA
Curr. Ratio	0.9	1.0	0.9	NA	NA	NA	NA	NA	NA	NA
% LT Debt of Cap.	47.7	54.7	51.4	NA	NA	NA	NA	NA	NA	NA
% Net Inc.of Revs.	8.8	9.6	6.5	NA	NA	NA	NA	NA	NA	NA
% Ret. on Assets	3.3	3.5	3.4	NA	NA	NA	NA	NA	NA	NA
% Ret. on Equity	20.7	20.8	20.0	NA	NA	NA	NA	NA	NA	NA

Data as orig reptd.; bef. results of disc opers/spec. items. Per share data adj. for stk. divs.; EPS diluted. E-Estimated. NA-Not Available. NM-Not Meaningful. NR-Not Ranked. UR-Under Review.

Office: 101 Ash Street, San Diego, CA 92101-3017.
Telephone: 619-696-2000.
Email: investor@sempra.com
Website: http://www.sempra.com
Chrmn & CEO: S.L. Baum.
Pres & COO: D.E. Felsinger.
EVP & CFO: N.E. Schmale.

EVP & General Counsel: M.J. Chaudhri.
VP & Investor Contact: D.V. Arriola 619-696-2901.
Dirs: S. L. Baum, H. H. Bertea, J. G. Brocksmith, Jr., H. L. Carter, R. A. Collato, D. E. Felsinger, D. K. Fletcher, W. D. Godbold, Jr., W. D. Jones, R. G. Newman, W. G. Ouchi, W. C. Rusnack, W. P. Rutledge, N. E. Schmale.

Founded: in 1998.
Domicile: California.
Employees: 13,000.
S&P Analyst: Craig K. Shere, CFA /CB/BK

Sherwin-Williams

Recommendation: **BUY** ★★★★☆   12-Month Target Price: **$46.00**
SELL | SELL | HOLD | BUY | BUY   (as of October 25, 2004)

SHW has an approximate 0.06% weighting in the **S&P 500**

Sector: Consumer Discretionary
Sub-Industry: Home Improvement Retail
Peer Group: Retail (Building Supplies)

Summary: SHW, the largest U.S. producer of paints, is also a major seller of wallcoverings and related products.

Quantitative Evaluations

S&P Earnings & Dividend Rank: A

| D | C | B- | B | B+ | A- | A | A+ |

S&P Fair Value Rank: 2+

| 1 | 2 | 3 | 4 | 5 |
Lowest | | | | Highest

Fair Value Calc.: $40.90 (Slightly Overvalued)

S&P Investability Quotient Percentile

99%

SHW scored higher than 99% of all companies for which an S&P Report is available.

Volatility: Low

| Low | Average | High |

Technical Evaluation: Bullish
Since 10/04, the technical indicators for SHW have been Bullish.

Relative Strength Rank: Moderate

66

1 Lowest | Highest 99

| Price as of 11/12/04: | **$45.44** | 2004E S&P Core EPS: | **$2.60** |

GAAP Earnings vs. Previous Year
▲ Up   ▼ Down   ► No Change

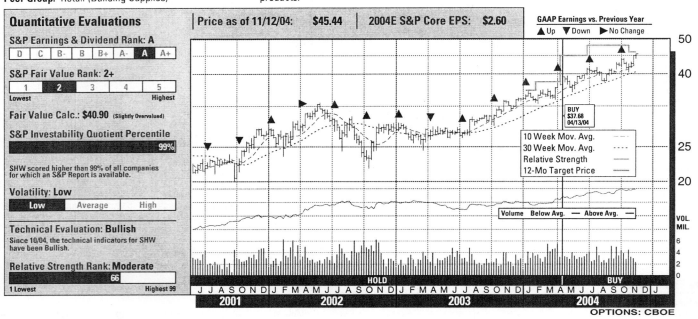

BUY
$37.68
04/13/04

10 Week Mov. Avg.
30 Week Mov. Avg.
Relative Strength
12-Mo Target Price

Volume Below Avg. — Above Avg.

VOL. MIL.

HOLD | BUY

J J A S O N D J F M A M J J A S O N D J F M A M J J A S O N D J F M A M J J A S O N D J
2001 | 2002 | 2003 | 2004

OPTIONS: CBOE

Analyst commentary prepared by Michael Souers/JP/BK

Highlights October 29, 2004

- We expect mid- to high single digit sales growth in 2005. Paint store segment sales gains will likely be driven by new store additions and low single digit same-store sales increases, which should benefit from greater do-it-yourself (DIY) activity and architectural paint sales to commercial customers. We believe consumer paints will also benefit from robust DIY activity and new product introductions, while automotive finishes sales will likely gain on greater international penetration. We look for international coatings revenues to grow on improving economic conditions in South American markets.

- We expect margins to remain relatively flat as rising raw material costs and continuing investments in new stores and in the Asia-Pacific market will likely offset the benefits of leveraging expenses over a greater sales base and improved manufacturing efficiencies.

- After slightly lower interest expense, taxes at 35.0%, and 1%-2% fewer shares, reflecting SHW's active buyback program, we estimate 2005 EPS of $3.00, representing a 13% increase from our 2004 EPS estimate of $2.65. We regard earnings quality as good, with Standard & Poor's Core Earnings adjustments reducing our 2005 and 2004 EPS estimates by less than 5%.

Investment Rationale/Risk October 29, 2004

- We recommend accumulating the shares. In our opinion, favorable economic indicators such as continued strength in building materials retail sales and existing home sales, albeit at a slower pace compared to 2004, should continue to support DIY activity in 2005. Furthermore, we anticipate improved business spending to boost growth in industrial maintenance and product finish applications. The company's Asia-Pacific investments should, in our opinion, provide long-term growth in markets with fast-growing economies for industrial coating and finishes and architectural paint sales to commercial customers. Lastly, SHW continues to expand its paint store base at a healthy clip, in our opinion. The company plans to add 32 stores in the fourth quarter of 2004, bringing total new stores for 2004, excluding acquisitions, to 65.

- Risks to our opinion and target price include a significant slowdown in economic growth; a sharp rise in interest rates, which could dampen home-related spending; the negative effects of potential terrorist attacks on consumer spending; and a negative ruling on SHW's pending lead pigment litigation case in Rhode Island.

- At 14X our 2005 EPS estimate, SHW shares recently traded below their historical average P/E and below the P/E multiple of the S&P 500. Our 12-month target price of $46 is equal to about 15X our 2005 estimate, on par with the stock's historical P/E.

Key Stock Statistics

S&P Core EPS 2005E	2.95	52-week Range	$45.44-31.50
S&P Oper. EPS 2004E	2.65	12 Month P/E	17.3
P/E on S&P Oper. EPS 2004E	17.1	Beta	0.69
S&P Oper. EPS 2005E	3.00	Shareholders	11,398
Yield (%)	1.5%	Market Cap (B)	$ 6.4
Dividend Rate/Share	0.68	Shares Outstanding (M)	141.3

Value of $10,000 invested five years ago: **$ 22,617**

Dividend Data Dividends have been paid since 1979

Amount ($)	Date Decl.	Ex-Div. Date	Stock of Record	Payment Date
0.170	Feb. 04	Feb. 19	Feb. 23	Mar. 15 '04
0.170	Apr. 28	May. 26	May. 28	Jun. 11 '04
0.170	Jul. 21	Aug. 18	Aug. 20	Sep. 03 '04
0.170	Oct. 20	Nov. 09	Nov. 12	Nov. 26 '04

Revenues/Earnings Data Fiscal year ending December 31

Revenues (Million $)

	2004	2003	2002	2001	2000	1999
1Q	1,320	1,148	1,149	1,158	1,222	1,128
2Q	1,618	1,472	1,453	1,408	1,429	1,384
3Q	1,677	1,503	1,426	1,367	1,412	1,345
4Q	—	1,285	1,156	1,133	1,149	1,146
Yr.	—	5,408	5,185	5,067	5,212	5,004

Earnings Per Share ($)

	2004	2003	2002	2001	2000	1999
1Q	0.35	0.21	0.23	0.23	0.25	0.17
2Q	0.87	0.75	0.70	0.58	0.71	0.63
3Q	0.92	0.82	0.74	0.58	0.66	0.66
4Q	E0.51	0.48	0.38	0.29	-1.55	0.34
Yr.	E2.65	2.26	2.04	1.68	0.10	1.80

Next earnings report expected: early-February Source: S&P, Company Reports
EPS Estimates based on S&P Operating Earnings; historical GAAP earnings are as reported.

STANDARD &POOR'S

The Sherwin-Williams Company

Recommendation: **BUY** ★ ★ ★ ☆   12-Month Target Price: **$46.00** (as of October 25, 2004)

Business Summary October 29, 2004

With several acquisitions in recent years, Sherwin-Williams continues its quest to become "America's Paint Company." Already the largest producer and distributor of paints and varnishes in the U.S. and the third largest worldwide, the company had about 2,688 paint stores in 48 states, Puerto Rico, the Virgin Islands, Mexico and Canada as of 2003 year-end. In 2002, U.S. manufacturers shipped an estimated 1,463 million gallons of paint and allied products valued at about $17.2 billion. SHW aims to expand its business through acquisitions in the fragmented paint industry. Its largest acquisitions to date were Pratt & Lambert United, Inc. (1996), enhancing access to the independent dealer and mass merchandising distribution channels in the U.S.; and Thompson Minwax Holding Corp. (1997), providing leading brands in the stain and varnish category.

The company has been selling paint for 130 years, and believes it has consistently been on the leading edge of technology in the paint industry. With the constant introduction of new products, SHW continues to meet technological challenges. A streak of 23 consecutive years of earnings growth (excluding one-time expenses) ended in 2001.

SHW has five business segments: Paint Stores (65% of revenues in 2003), Consumer (22%), Automotive Finishes (8%), International Coatings (5%), and Administrative (nil). The paint stores sell paint, wallcoverings, floor coverings, window treatments, industrial maintenance products and finishes, and assorted tools. Products are marketed to the DIY, professional painting, industrial maintenance and home building markets, and to manufacturers of products that require a factory finish. The paint store segment opened 51 stores in 2003, down from 70 new stores in 2002. Brands include Sherwin-Williams labeled architectural coatings, industrial finishes, Dutch Boy, Pratt & Lambert, Martin-Senour, Dupli-Color, Krylon, Thompson's and Minwax, as well as private label brands.

The consumer segment makes architectural paints, stains, varnishes, industrial maintenance products, wood finishing products, paint applicators, corrosion inhibitors, and paint related products. About 46% of segment sales are through the paint stores segment, with the balance to third party customers such as independent dealers, mass merchandisers, and home improvement centers. Automotive finishes develops, makes and distributes various motor vehicle finish, refinish, and touch-up products, primarily throughout North and South America, the Caribbean, and Italy. Sherwin-Williams branded automotive finish and refinish products are sold through 128 company-operated branches in the U.S., and in Canada (16), Jamaica (14) and Chile (21). The international coatings segment manufactures and licenses architectural paints, stains, varnishes, industrial maintenance products, product finishes, wood finishing products and paint-related products worldwide. A majority of segment sales come from South America, including 34 company-operated paint stores in Chile, 23 in Brazil, and one in Uruguay. The administrative segment primarily relates to corporate headquarters.

Company Financials Fiscal Year ending December 31

Per Share Data ($)

(Year Ended December 31)	2003	2002	2001	2000	1999	1998	1997	1996	1995	1994
Tangible Bk. Val.	2.95	4.05	3.69	3.18	2.32	1.76	0.86	2.19	3.19	5.58
Cash Flow	3.13	2.86	2.39	0.77	2.42	2.17	2.48	1.08	0.77	1.50
Earnings	2.26	2.04	1.68	0.10	1.80	1.57	1.50	1.33	1.17	1.07
S&P Core Earnings	2.14	1.81	1.62	NA	NA	NA	NA	NA	NA	NA
Dividends	0.62	0.60	0.58	0.54	0.48	0.45	0.50	0.35	0.32	0.28
Payout Ratio	27%	29%	35%	NM	27%	29%	33%	26%	27%	25%
Prices - High	34.77	33.24	28.23	27.62	32.87	37.87	33.37	28.87	20.75	17.87
- Low	24.42	21.75	19.73	17.12	18.75	19.43	24.12	19.50	16.00	14.75
P/E Ratio - High	15	16	17	NM	18	24	22	22	18	17
- Low	11	11	12	NM	10	12	16	15	14	14

Income Statement Analysis (Million $)

	2003	2002	2001	2000	1999	1998	1997	1996	1995	1994
Revs.	5,408	5,185	5,066	5,212	5,004	4,934	4,881	4,133	3,274	3,100
Oper. Inc.	690	670	599	676	680	629	613	495	384	383
Depr.	117	116	109	109	105	97.8	90.2	76.0	63.0	73.7
Int. Exp.	38.7	40.5	54.6	62.0	61.2	72.0	80.8	25.0	3.00	3.20
Pretax Inc.	523	497	424	143	490	440	427	375	318	299
Eff. Tax Rate	36.5%	37.5%	38.0%	88.8%	38.0%	38.0%	39.0%	38.9%	37.0%	37.5%
Net Inc.	332	311	263	16.0	304	273	261	229	201	187
S&P Core Earnings	316	276	254	NA	NA	NA	NA	NA	NA	NA

Balance Sheet & Other Fin. Data (Million $)

	2003	2002	2001	2000	1999	1998	1997	1996	1995	1994
Cash	303	164	119	2.90	18.6	19.1	3.53	1.90	269	251
Curr. Assets	1,715	1,506	1,507	1,552	1,597	1,547	1,532	1,416	1,239	1,189
Total Assets	3,683	3,432	3,628	3,751	4,052	4,065	4,036	2,995	2,141	1,962
Curr. Liab.	1,154	1,083	1,141	1,115	1,190	1,112	1,116	1,051	619	597
LT Debt	503	507	504	624	624	730	844	143	24.0	20.0
Common Equity	1,174	1,300	1,319	1,472	1,699	1,716	1,592	1,401	1,212	1,053
Total Cap.	1,962	1,849	1,991	2,095	2,323	2,446	2,436	1,544	1,236	1,074
Cap. Exp.	117	127	82.6	133	134	146	164	123	108	78.7
Cash Flow	449	426	372	125	409	371	351	305	264	260
Curr. Ratio	1.5	1.4	1.3	1.4	1.3	1.4	1.4	1.4	2.0	2.0
% LT Debt of Cap.	25.6	27.4	25.3	29.8	26.9	29.9	34.6	9.3	1.9	1.9
% Net Inc.of Revs.	6.1	6.0	5.2	0.3	6.1	5.5	5.3	5.5	6.1	6.0
% Ret. on Assets	9.3	8.8	7.1	0.4	7.5	6.7	7.4	8.9	9.8	9.8
% Ret. on Equity	26.8	23.7	18.9	1.0	17.8	16.5	17.4	17.5	17.7	18.3

Data as orig reptd.; bef. results of disc opers/spec. items. Per share data adj. for stk. divs. Bold denotes primary EPS - prior periods restated. E-Estimated. NA-Not Available. NM-Not Meaningful. NR-Not Ranked. UR-Under Review.

Office: 101 Prospect Avenue N.W., Cleveland, OH 44115-1075.
Telephone: 216-566-2000.
Website: http://www.sherwin.com
Chrmn & CEO: C.M. Connor.
Pres & COO: J.M. Scaminace.
SVP, CFO & Treas: S. Hennessy.

SVP & Investor Contact: C.G. Ivy .
VP, Secy & General Counsel: L.E. Stellato.
Dirs: J. C. Boland, J. G. Breen, D. E. Collins, C. M. Connor, D. E. Evans, S. J. Kropf, R. W. Mahoney, G. E. McCullough, A. M. Mixon III, C. E. Moll, J. G. Morikis, J. M. Scaminace, R. K. Smucker, L. E. Stellato.

Founded: in 1866.
Domicile: Ohio.
Employees: 25,777.
S&P Analyst: Michael Souers/JP/BK

The McGraw·Hill Companies

STANDARD
&POOR'S

Siebel Systems

Recommendation: **HOLD** ★★★☆☆
SELL · SELL · HOLD · BUY · BUY

12-Month Target Price: **$10.00**
(as of October 04, 2004)

SEBL has an approximate 0.04% weighting in the **S&P 500**

Sector: Information Technology
Sub-Industry: Application Software
Peer Group: Marketing/Customer Service Software

Summary: Siebel is the leading provider of sales, marketing and customer service information software systems.

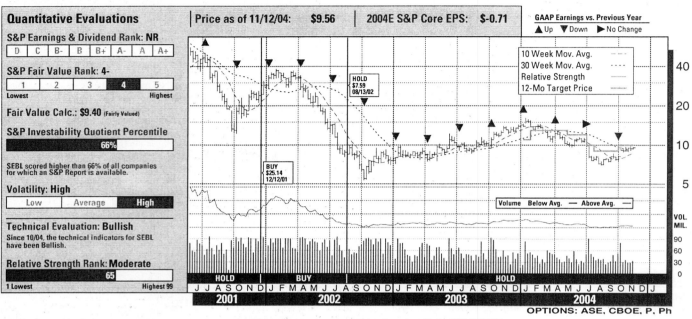

Quantitative Evaluations	Price as of 11/12/04: $9.56	2004E S&P Core EPS: $-0.71

S&P Earnings & Dividend Rank: NR

D C B- B B+ A- A A+

S&P Fair Value Rank: 4-

1 2 3 **4** 5
Lowest   Highest

Fair Value Calc.: $9.40 (Fairly Valued)

S&P Investability Quotient Percentile
66%

SEBL scored higher than 66% of all companies for which an S&P Report is available.

Volatility: High

Low Average **High**

Technical Evaluation: Bullish
Since 10/04, the technical indicators for SEBL have been Bullish.

Relative Strength Rank: Moderate
65
1 Lowest   Highest 99

Analyst commentary prepared by Jonathan Rudy, CFA /DC/GG

Highlights October 26, 2004

- We expect revenues to decrease about 3% in 2004, following a 17% drop in 2003. However, we see revenues increasing 3% in 2005. We believe SEBL has been negatively affected by a difficult information technology (IT) spending environment. Nevertheless, the company has been able to maintain its market leadership in the Customer Relationship Management (CRM) market. The 2004 launch of Siebel 7.7 (the company's latest version of its e-business Application Suite) includes new industry-specific products that should contribute to growth over the longer term, in our opinion.

- We look for a 1% drop in license revenues and a 4% decline in maintenance and consulting revenues in 2004. However, we anticipate license revenues rebounding in 2005 with a 6% increase. We see maintenance and consulting revenues rising 2% in 2005. We expect operating margins to widen as recent cost controls should lower operating expense levels.

- We believe that SEBL will benefit from lower expense levels due to a recent restructuring. We estimate operating EPS of $0.21 for 2004 and $0.27 for 2005.

Investment Rationale/Risk October 26, 2004

- We have a hold opinion on the shares, as we believe attractive relative valuation levels are offset by company-specific challenges. We believe SEBL is particularly vulnerable to the impact of option expensing. Our Standard & Poor's 2004 Core Earnings estimate of a loss of $0.71 reflects projected stock option expense that is significantly greater than peer levels. However, SEBL remains the clear market share leader in the area of sales, marketing and customer service software, in our opinion. With the stock trading at a discount to peer levels, at an enterprise value to sales of 2.1X, and with the balance sheet showing over $2.1 billion in cash and short-term investments and little debt, we would hold existing positions.

- Risks to our recommendation and target price include a rapidly changing technology landscape; intense competition in the software industry, resulting in continuous pricing pressure; and a potential slowdown in global information technology spending.

- Our 12-month target price of $10 is based on relative enterprise value to sales and P/E to growth valuation metrics.

Key Stock Statistics

S&P Oper. EPS 2004E	0.21	52-week Range	$16.19-6.97
P/E on S&P Oper. EPS 2004E	45.5	12 Month P/E	NM
S&P Oper. EPS 2005E	0.27	Beta	NA
Yield (%)	Nil	Shareholders	1,740
Dividend Rate/Share	Nil	Market Cap (B)	$ 4.9
Shares Outstanding (M)	508.2		

Value of $10,000 invested five years ago: **$ 2,925**

Dividend Data

No cash dividends have been paid.

Revenues/Earnings Data Fiscal year ending December 31

Revenues (Million $)

	2004	2003	2002	2001	2000	1999
1Q	329.3	332.8	477.9	588.7	319.7	134.1
2Q	301.1	333.3	405.6	549.7	397.5	164.4
3Q	321.4	317.1	357.2	428.5	496.5	195.3
4Q	—	366.7	394.7	481.4	581.6	268.0
Yr.	—	1,354	1,635	2,048	1,795	790.9

Earnings Per Share ($)

	2004	2003	2002	2001	2000	1999
1Q	0.06	0.01	0.12	0.15	-0.10	0.05
2Q	0.02	0.02	0.06	0.15	0.04	0.06
3Q	-0.12	0.04	-0.19	0.07	0.13	0.07
4Q	E0.08	0.08	-0.08	0.13	0.15	0.10
Yr.	E0.21	-0.01	-0.08	0.49	0.24	0.27

Next earnings report expected: late-January Source: S&P, Company Reports
EPS Estimates based on S&P Operating Earnings; historical GAAP earnings are as reported.

Siebel Systems, Inc.

Recommendation: **HOLD** ★ ★ ★ ☆ ☆   12-Month Target Price: **$10.00** (as of October 04, 2004)

Business Summary October 26, 2004

Siebel Systems is the leading provider of e-business applications software, which helps organizations manage customer, partner and employee relationships.

SEBL's customer relationship management applications enable organizations to sell to, market to, and service their customers across multiple channels, including the Web, call centers, field, resellers, retail, and dealer networks.

The company's partner relationship management applications seamlessly unite the organization's partners, resellers and customers in one global information system to facilitate greater collaboration and increased revenues, productivity, and customer satisfaction.

Siebel 7.5, the latest version of SEBL's e-business software, is a comprehensive suite of Web-based e-business software applications, providing organizations with a single view of the customer across multiple distribution channels. It provides support for sales, marketing and customer services organizations, and seamlessly unites the organization's partners, resellers and customers into a single global information system. Siebel 7.7 is scheduled for release in 2004.

Siebel Sales, the company's core application product, enables teams of sales and marketing professionals to manage sales information throughout the entire sales cycle. Siebel Service enables teams of customer service, sales and marketing professionals to ensure complete customer satisfaction by using closed-loop, service request management capabilities.

Siebel Call Center provides both Sales and Service functionality that enables call center agents to provide both sales and customer service assistance.

Siebel Marketing and Analytics lets marketing professionals, sales and service managers and business analysts monitor overall company performance and the effectiveness of company programs and activities. It extracts information from other Siebel products into a customer data mart, designed for fast data analysis.

Siebel Employee Relationship Management (ERM) is a set of applications that supports organizational learning, organizational performance and employee service.

Making data available from one application to another, as well as connecting multiple applications to create coordinated processes, is known as integration. SEBL's Universal Application Network (UAN) is a design and set of technical standards for data and process integration that is supported by leading integration consultants and makers of integration servers, the software environment that shares data.

The company also provides implementation consulting and other technical services to license customers, in connection with alliance partners.

International license revenues in 2003 totaled $240 million, equal to 50% of software license revenues, down from $291 million (42%) in 2002. Total international revenues in 2003 were $567 million, 42% of total revenues, down from $619 million (38%) in 2002.

Company Financials Fiscal Year ending December 31

Per Share Data ($)

(Year Ended December 31)	2003	2002	2001	2000	1999	1998	1997	1996	1995	1994
Tangible Bk. Val.	3.81	3.84	3.74	2.89	1.70	0.81	0.40	0.30	0.08	NA
Cash Flow	0.31	0.25	0.72	0.33	0.32	0.14	0.01	0.02	0.00	NA
Earnings	-0.01	-0.08	0.49	0.24	0.27	0.11	-0.01	0.02	0.00	NA
S&P Core Earnings	-0.93	-2.27	-1.02	NA	NA	NA	NA	NA	NA	NA
Dividends	Nil	Nil	Nil	Nil	Nil	Nil	Nil	Nil	NA	NA
Payout Ratio	Nil	Nil	Nil	Nil	Nil	Nil	Nil	Nil	NA	NA
Prices - High	14.56	38.38	84.50	119.87	46.00	9.25	6.17	3.78	NA	NA
- Low	8.58	5.33	12.24	32.75	7.87	3.78	1.65	1.06	NA	NA
P/E Ratio - High	NM	NM	NM	NM	NM	86	NM	NM	NA	NA
- Low	NM	NM	NM	NM	NM	35	NM	NM	NA	NA

Income Statement Analysis (Million $)

	2003	2002	2001	2000	1999	1998	1997	1996	1995	1994
Revs.	1,354	1,635	2,048	1,795	791	392	119	39.2	8.00	0.10
Oper. Inc.	233	265	836	410	205	93.8	33.8	7.91	0.51	-1.70
Depr.	157	154	120	51.4	22.3	13.5	3.89	1.20	0.14	0.10
Int. Exp.	14.9	20.0	Nil	Nil	6.06	Nil	0.00	0.01	Nil	Nil
Pretax Inc.	-5.31	-55.8	404	384	197	73.1	10.0	8.11	0.53	-1.77
Eff. Tax Rate	NM	NM	37.0%	42.3%	38.0%	41.4%	124.2%	38.0%	40.0%	Nil
Net Inc.	-3.40	-35.7	255	222	122	42.9	-2.43	5.03	0.32	-1.77
S&P Core Earnings	-462	-1,083	-467	NA	NA	NA	NA	NA	NA	NA

Balance Sheet & Other Fin. Data (Million $)

	2003	2002	2001	2000	1999	1998	1997	1996	1995	1994
Cash	584	668	799	751	608	80.0	31.3	72.4	11.4	NA
Curr. Assets	2,397	2,588	2,190	1,843	1,129	382	135	90.6	15.2	NA
Total Assets	2,851	3,033	2,745	2,162	1,227	442	149	100	16.1	NA
Curr. Liab.	688	648	609	582	251	151	36.6	18.1	6.10	NA
LT Debt	113	412	300	300	300	Nil	Nil	Nil	Nil	NA
Common Equity	2,050	1,957	1,836	1,280	675	291	113	81.2	9.92	NA
Total Cap.	2,163	2,369	2,136	1,580	976	291	113	81.4	9.93	NA
Cap. Exp.	15.0	70.8	251	162	42.8	39.2	6.68	7.34	0.87	NA
Cash Flow	154	118	374	175	144	56.3	1.46	6.22	0.46	NA
Curr. Ratio	3.5	4.0	3.6	3.2	4.5	2.5	3.7	5.0	2.5	NA
% LT Debt of Cap.	5.2	17.4	14.0	19.0	30.7	Nil	Nil	Nil	Nil	NA
% Net Inc.of Revs.	NM	NM	12.4	12.4	15.4	11.0	NM	12.8	4.0	NA
% Ret. on Assets	NM	NM	10.4	12.9	14.6	14.5	NM	8.7	NA	NA
% Ret. on Equity	NM	NM	16.3	12.8	25.3	21.3	NM	11.0	NA	NA

Data as orig reptd.; bef. results of disc opers/spec. items. Per share data adj. for stk. divs. Bold denotes primary EPS - prior periods restated. E-Estimated. NA-Not Available. NM-Not Meaningful. NR-Not Ranked. UR-Under Review.

Office: 2207 Bridgepointe Parkway , San Mateo, CA 94404.
Telephone: 650-295-5000 .
Website: http://www.siebel.com
Chrmn: T.M. Siebel.
Vice Chrmn & VP: P.A. House.
CEO: J.M. Lawrie.

SVP & CFO: K.A. Goldman.
SVP & CTO: E.Y. Abbo.
SVP & Investor Contact: M.D. Hanson 650-295-5000.
Dirs: J. C. Gaither, P. A. House, J. M. Lawrie, M. F. Racicot, E. E. Schmidt, C. R. Schwab, G. T. Shaheen, T. M. Siebel, A. M. Spence, J. W. White.

Founded: in 1993.
Domicile: Delaware.
Employees: 4,972.
S&P Analyst: Jonathan Rudy, CFA /DC/GG

Sigma-Aldrich Corp.

Recommendation: HOLD ★ ★ ★ ☆   12-Month Target Price: **$63.00**
(as of April 26, 2004)

SIAL has an approximate 0.04% weighting in the **S&P 500**

Sector: Materials
Sub-Industry: Specialty Chemicals
Peer Group: Specialty Chemicals (Larger)

Summary: This company makes and sells a wide range of biochemicals, organic chemicals and chromatography products.

Quantitative Evaluations

S&P Earnings & Dividend Rank: A+

| D | C | B- | B | B+ | A- | A | **A+** |

S&P Fair Value Rank: 1

| **1** | 2 | 3 | 4 | 5 |
| Lowest | | | | Highest |

Fair Value Calc.: $43.60 (Overvalued)

S&P Investability Quotient Percentile

99%

SIAL scored higher than 99% of all companies for which an S&P Report is available.

Volatility: Low

| **Low** | Average | High |

Technical Evaluation: Bullish

Since 11/04, the technical indicators for SIAL have been Bullish.

Relative Strength Rank: Moderate

44

1 Lowest   Highest 99

| Price as of 11/15/04: | **$58.57** | 2004E S&P Core EPS: | **$3.20** |

GAAP Earnings vs. Previous Year
▲ Up   ▼ Down   ▶ No Change

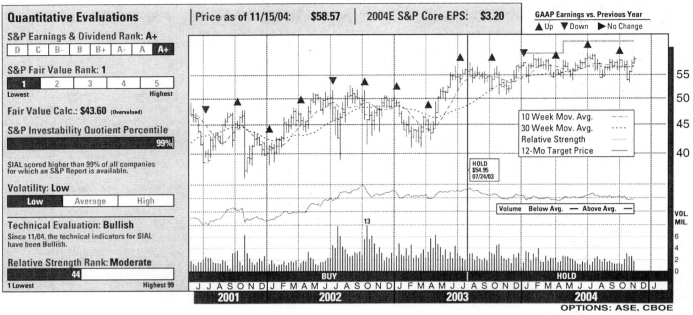

- 10 Week Mov. Avg.
- 30 Week Mov. Avg.
- Relative Strength
- 12-Mo Target Price

HOLD $54.95 07/24/03

Volume   Below Avg. — Above Avg.

HOLD

BUY

J J A S O N D J F M A M J J A S O N D J F M A M J J A S O N D J F M A M J J A S O N D J
2001   2002   2003   2004

OPTIONS: ASE, CBOE

Analyst commentary prepared by Richard O'Reilly, CFA /CB/JWP

Highlights 16-NOV-04

- We project that sales in 2005 will grow about 7%, close to the 7%-8% rate expected for 2004, but with a smaller contribution from favorable currency exchange. We expect volumes to show growth in 2005 after a flat comparison expected for 2004 (on top of a nearly 3% decline in 2003), on new products and marketing initiatives, and assuming a pickup in pharmaceutical markets. We expect fine chemicals sales to rebound, driven by record order levels.
- We see price increases continuing at the recent 2.3% annual rate, but below those of the past several years due to greater competitive pressures. Two acquisitions made during the 2004 second quarter should add about 1% to annual sales growth. We expect pretax margins for 2005 to be similar to 2004's 22.5%, aided by additional process improvements. We project an effective tax rate of 26% for 2004, down from 30.2% in 2003, due to a one-time tax benefit; we expect the tax rate to be about 31% in 2005.
- EPS comparisons should benefit from additional modest share repurchases; SIAL, which resumed buying back stock in the latter half of 2002, has acquired 35% of its shares since November 1999. We project 2004 Standard & Poor's Core Earnings per share of $3.20, reflecting projected option expense of about $0.15.

Investment Rationale/Risk 16-NOV-04

- We have a hold recommendation on the shares, which were little changed year to date through mid-November. We believe SIAL will achieve 2004 EPS growth greater than its 10% goal, before a one-time tax benefit, and can maintain return on equity of over 20%, but we see this driven largely by favorable currency exchange. We expect sales volumes to be flat for the full year, with some rebound in 2005, boosted by new marketing initiatives and an expanded sales force.
- Risks to our recommendation and target price include unexpected weakness in key markets such as pharmaceutical and academia, greater price competition, adverse currency exchange movements, and an inability to successfully introduce new products.
- The shares traded recently at a P/E multiple, based on our 2004 forecast of operating EPS of $3.15 (excluding tax benefits), modestly higher than that of the S&P 500. Assuming a similar premium multiple based on our 2005 EPS forecast, our 12-month target price is $63. We see the stock's Standard & Poor's Earnings and Dividend Ranking of A+ (the dividend has been raised each year since 1975) adding to its investment appeal.

Key Stock Statistics

S&P Core EPS 2005E	**3.20**	52-week Range	**$59.96-51.16**
S&P Oper. EPS 2004E	**3.35**	12 Month P/E	**18.3**
P/E on S&P Oper. EPS 2004E	**17.5**	Beta	**0.16**
S&P Oper. EPS 2005E	**3.35**	Shareholders	**1,036**
Yield (%)	**1.2%**	Market Cap (B)	**$ 4.0**
Dividend Rate/Share	**0.68**	Shares Outstanding (M)	**69.1**

Value of $10,000 invested five years ago: **$ 20,758**

Dividend Data   Dividends have been paid since 1970

Amount ($)	Date Decl.	Ex-Div. Date	Stock of Record	Payment Date
0.170	Feb. 10	Feb. 26	Mar. 01	Mar. 15 '04
0.170	May. 04	May. 27	Jun. 01	Jun. 15 '04
0.170	Aug. 10	Aug. 30	Sep. 01	Sep. 15 '04
0.170	Nov. 09	Nov. 29	Dec. 01	Dec. 15 '04

Revenues/Earnings Data   Fiscal year ending December 31

Revenues (Million $)

	2004	2003	2002	2001	2000	1999
1Q	368.1	334.7	301.6	305.6	290.1	333.0
2Q	348.6	327.1	304.3	293.7	273.8	318.4
3Q	340.6	314.2	304.8	287.7	269.8	323.9
4Q	—	322.2	296.3	292.3	262.6	252.1
Yr.	—	1,298	1,207	1,179	1,096	1,038

Earnings Per Share ($)

	2004	2003	2002	2001	2000	1999
1Q	0.89	0.72	0.54	0.48	0.53	0.44
2Q	0.85	0.67	-0.30	0.49	2.52	0.44
3Q	0.81	0.66	0.63	0.45	0.35	0.44
4Q	E0.80	0.67	0.92	0.45	0.40	0.39
Yr.	E3.35	2.68	1.78	1.87	3.83	1.71

Next earnings report expected: mid-February Source: S&P, Company Reports
EPS Estimates based on S&P Operating Earnings; historical GAAP earnings are as reported.

Sigma-Aldrich Corporation

Recommendation: **HOLD** ★ ★ ★ ☆ ☆   12-Month Target Price: **$63.00** (as of April 26, 2004)

Business Summary 16-NOV-04

Sigma-Aldrich, well known for its extensive catalog business, is one of the world's largest providers of research chemicals, reagents, chromatography products, and related products. In July 2003, the company said that all activities related to discontinuing its diagnostics business had been completed; all told, SIAL sold product lines representing about 70% of diagnostics sales in 2001 (sales of $65 million, and a loss of $0.16 a share). It recorded a related one-time charge of $0.85 a share from discontinued operations in the 2002 second quarter. In May 2000, the company sold its B-Line Systems metals business (reported as discontinued operations in 1999) for $430 million. SIAL intends to boost annual sales growth for its continuing chemical business to 10% through continued global expansion by entering new countries; increasing distribution of its catalogs; and acquisitions, joint ventures and partnerships, especially in life sciences products.

Foreign sales accounted for 57% of the total in 2003.

SIAL distributes more than 85,000 chemical products, under the Sigma, Aldrich, Fluka and Supelco brands names, for use primarily in research and development, in diagnosis of disease, and as specialty chemicals for manufacturing. About 75% of sales are to customers in the life sciences, with the remaining 25% used in high technology applications. Customer sectors include pharmaceutical (40% of sales), academia (30%), chemical industry (20%), and hospitals and commercial laboratories (10%). The company itself produces about 40,000 products, accounting for 55% of 2003 net sales of chemical products. Remaining products are purchased from outside sources.

The Scientific Research unit (59% of sales in 2003) supplies biochemicals, organic and inorganic compounds, reagents, and related equipment for use in university, governmental, non-profit agency, and pharmaceutical industry research. The Biotechnology unit (23%) supplies products used in biotechnology, genomic and proteomics research and chromatography. Sigma-Genosys (acquired in 1998) is a major maker of custom synthetic DNA products, synthetic peptides and genes to the life science product categories. SIAL believe it is the leading supplier of products used in cell signaling and neuroscience. The Fine Chemicals unit (18%) is a medium-sized supplier of bulk quantities of organic, inorganic and biochemicals to pharmaceutical, biotechnology and industrial customers.

Through the end of 2002, the company had sold product lines accounting for about 70% of the $65 million of 2001 sales of the discontinued diagnostics business. Efforts to sell other product lines and inventories were concluded by the end of the 2003 first quarter. The business reported an after-tax loss of $3.7 million ($0.05 a share) in 2002, with net income of $1.1 million ($0.02) in the first quarter of 2003.

SIAL also offers about 80,000 esoteric chemicals (less than 1% of total sales) as a special service to customers that screen them for potential applications.

Company Financials Fiscal Year ending December 31

Per Share Data ($)

(Year Ended December 31)	2003	2002	2001	2000	1999	1998	1997	1996	1995	1994
Tangible Bk. Val.	12.83	10.90	6.75	7.34	11.58	10.96	10.56	9.42	8.27	7.02
Cash Flow	3.65	3.45	2.82	2.47	2.13	2.25	2.08	1.93	1.73	1.48
Earnings	2.68	1.78	1.87	1.66	1.47	1.64	1.62	1.48	1.32	1.10
S&P Core Earnings	2.55	2.10	1.76	NA	NA	NA	NA	NA	NA	NA
Dividends	0.50	0.35	0.33	0.32	0.29	0.28	0.26	0.23	0.19	0.17
Payout Ratio	19%	19%	18%	19%	20%	17%	16%	16%	14%	15%
Prices - High	57.91	52.80	51.49	40.87	35.25	42.75	41.12	32.06	25.87	27.62
- Low	40.94	38.16	36.25	20.18	24.50	25.75	26.87	23.75	16.25	15.00
P/E Ratio - High	22	30	28	25	24	26	25	22	20	25
- Low	15	21	19	12	17	16	17	16	12	14

Income Statement Analysis (Million $)

	2003	2002	2001	2000	1999	1998	1997	1996	1995	1994
Revs.	1,298	1,207	1,179	1,096	1,038	1,194	1,127	1,035	960	851
Oper. Inc.	353	323	291	284	275	305	302	277	247	210
Depr.	69.3	66.3	71.4	67.6	66.9	61.8	48.1	45.2	40.9	36.7
Int. Exp.	10.1	13.8	18.2	10.2	Nil	0.92	0.73	1.82	1.65	2.91
Pretax Inc.	273	272	202	203	204	243	253	230	204	170
Eff. Tax Rate	30.2%	31.4%	30.2%	31.5%	27.1%	31.4%	34.3%	35.6%	35.5%	35.2%
Net Inc.	190	187	141	139	149	166	166	148	132	110
S&P Core Earnings	180	155	133	NA	NA	NA	NA	NA	NA	NA

Balance Sheet & Other Fin. Data (Million $)

	2003	2002	2001	2000	1999	1998	1997	1996	1995	1994
Cash	128	52.4	37.6	31.1	43.8	24.3	46.2	104	84.0	9.70
Curr. Assets	815	695	727	714	775	773	707	667	610	502
Total Assets	1,548	1,390	1,440	1,348	1,432	1,433	1,244	1,100	985	852
Curr. Liab.	257	266	398	335	106	142	119	110	108	105
LT Debt	176	177	178	101	0.20	0.41	0.55	3.79	13.8	14.5
Common Equity	999	882	810	859	1,259	1,216	1,073	942	825	700
Total Cap.	1,176	1,059	987	960	1,260	1,217	1,061	946	839	714
Cap. Exp.	57.7	60.7	110	69.2	91.8	130	109	93.8	60.2	72.0
Cash Flow	260	253	212	207	216	228	214	193	173	147
Curr. Ratio	3.2	2.6	1.8	2.1	7.3	5.4	5.9	6.0	5.6	4.8
% LT Debt of Cap.	15.0	16.7	18.0	10.5	0.0	0.0	0.0	0.4	1.6	2.0
% Net Inc.of Revs.	14.7	15.5	11.9	12.7	14.3	13.9	14.7	14.3	13.7	13.0
% Ret. on Assets	12.7	13.2	10.1	10.0	10.4	12.4	14.2	14.2	14.3	13.7
% Ret. on Equity	20.2	22.1	16.9	13.1	12.0	14.5	16.4	16.7	17.3	17.1

Data as orig reptd.; bef. results of disc opers/spec. items. Per share data adj. for stk. divs.; EPS diluted. E-Estimated. NA-Not Available. NM-Not Meaningful. NR-Not Ranked. UR-Under Review.

Office: 3050 Spruce Street, St. Louis, MO 63103.
Telephone: 314-771-5765.
Website: http://www.sigma-aldrich.com
Chrmn & CEO: D. R. Harvey.
Pres & COO: J. Nagarkatti.

Secy & CFO: M. R. Hogan.
Investor Contact: Kirk A. Richter (314-286-8004).
Dirs: N. V. Fedoroff, D. R. Harvey, W. L. McCollum, W. C. O'Neil, Jr., J. P. Reinhard, J. W. Sandweiss, D. D. Spatz, B. A. Toan.

Founded: in 1951.
Domicile: Delaware.
Employees: 5,920.
S&P Analyst: Richard O'Reilly, CFA /CB/JWP

Simon Property Group

Recommendation: **BUY** ★★★★ 12-Month Target Price: **$69.00**
SELL SELL HOLD BUY BUY
(as of October 28, 2004)

SPG has an approximate 0.12% weighting in the **S&P 500**

Sector: Financials
Sub-Industry: Real Estate Investment Trusts
Peer Group: REITs - Regional Malls

Summary: Simon Property Group is the largest U.S. REIT that focuses on regional malls and community shopping centers.

Quantitative Evaluations

S&P Earnings & Dividend Rank: B+

| D | C | B- | B | B+ | A- | A | A+ |

S&P Fair Value Rank: NR

| 1 | 2 | 3 | 4 | 5 |
| Lowest | | | | Highest |

Fair Value Calc.: NA

S&P Investability Quotient Percentile

89%

SPG scored higher than 89% of all companies for which an S&P Report is available.

Volatility: Average

| Low | Average | High |

Technical Evaluation: Bullish
Since 10/04, the technical indicators for SPG have been Bullish.

Relative Strength Rank: Strong

74

1 Lowest   Highest 99

Price as of 11/12/04: **$61.71**   **2004E S&P Core EPS:** **$1.48**

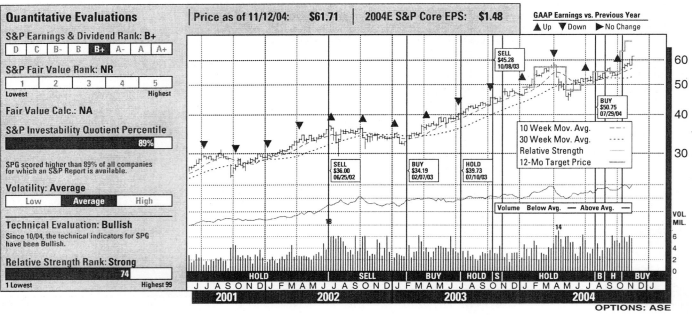

GAAP Earnings vs. Previous Year
▲ Up ▼ Down ▶ No Change

10 Week Mov. Avg.
30 Week Mov. Avg.
Relative Strength
12-Mo Target Price

Volume Below Avg. — Above Avg.

Analyst commentary prepared by R. McMillan/PMW/BK

Highlights October 29, 2004

■ We expect the trust to continue to benefit from what we view as a successful strategy of operating large and strategically located regional malls and shopping centers in major metropolitan markets. We see the recent acquisition of Chelsea Property Group (CPG), with its focus on upscale outlet malls, enhancing SPG's overall portfolio.

■ After growing 8.9% in 2003, we look for total revenues to advance about 9% in 2004 and nearly 28% in 2005, due to higher rents and tenant reimbursements, as well as the CPG acquisition. Comparable sales per sq. ft. in SPG's regional mall portfolio rose to $421 in the 2004 third quarter, from $398 in the 2003 period, while occupancy dipped slightly, to 91.8%, from 91.9%; average rent per sq. ft. rose 3.8%, year to year. Looking ahead, we believe that an improving economy and healthy retail sales bode well for the trust's results. We anticipate strong demand for space, enabling SPG to continue to achieve double-digit rent increases when expired leases are renewed. Rising tenant sales, a portion of which the trust collects as percentage rent, should also bolster revenues.

■ We see EPS of $1.48 for 2004 and $1.60 for 2005, with respective FFO per share of $4.35 and $4.85.

Investment Rationale/Risk October 29, 2004

■ We would buy the shares for their total return potential. The shares offer a dividend yield of about 4.5%.

■ Risks to our recommendation and target price include slower than expected growth in consumer spending and rental income growth, higher than normal retailer bankruptcies, and the impact of rising interest rates.

■ Our 12-month target price of $69 assumes that SPG will deliver FFO of $4.72 a share over the next four quarters (ending September 2005), and that the shares will trade at about 14.5X our trailing 12-month FFO projection. Although this is higher than the historical multiple of about 9X, we think the multiple will continue to widen as long as SPG demonstrates that its acquisition of CPG is proceeding well and that its operating trends are improving. We expect the dividend, to continue to rise in tandem with growth, to meet the 90% REIT payout requirement.

Key Stock Statistics

S&P Core EPS 2005E	1.60	52-week Range	$61.73-44.39
S&P Oper. EPS 2004E	1.48	12 Month P/E	34.1
P/E on S&P Oper. EPS 2004E	41.7	Beta	-0.02
S&P Oper. EPS 2005E	1.60	Shareholders	2,239
Yield (%)	4.2%	Market Cap (B)	$ 13.6
Dividend Rate/Share	2.60	Shares Outstanding (M)	221.1

Value of $10,000 invested five years ago: **$ 35,707**

Dividend Data Dividends have been paid since 1994

Amount ($)	Date Decl.	Ex-Div. Date	Stock of Record	Payment Date
0.650	May. 06	May. 13	May. 17	May. 28 '04
0.650	Jul. 28	Aug. 13	Aug. 17	Aug. 31 '04
0.410	Oct. 04	Oct. 15	Oct. 13	Nov. 30 '04
0.240	Oct. 27	Nov. 15	Nov. 17	Nov. 30 '04

Revenues/Earnings Data Fiscal year ending December 31

Revenues (Million $)

	2004	2003	2002	2001	2000	1999
1Q	584.3	547.8	494.9	487.2	477.9	446.1
2Q	601.6	566.3	517.5	488.3	487.7	454.0
3Q	623.5	566.6	550.8	500.6	493.9	466.9
4Q	—	659.9	622.6	569.2	561.3	528.0
Yr.	—	2,314	2,186	2,045	2,013	1,895

Earnings Per Share ($)

	2004	2003	2002	2001	2000	1999
1Q	0.24	0.29	0.17	0.19	0.21	0.21
2Q	0.34	0.33	0.91	0.21	0.24	0.22
3Q	0.36	0.27	0.33	0.21	0.24	0.25
4Q	E0.54	0.64	0.52	0.25	0.44	0.32
Yr.	E1.48	1.53	1.93	0.87	1.13	1.00

Next earnings report expected: early-February Source: S&P, Company Reports
EPS Estimates based on S&P Operating Earnings; historical GAAP earnings are as reported.

STANDARD &POOR'S

Simon Property Group, Inc.

Stock Report
November 13, 2004
NYSE Symbol: **SPG**

Recommendation: **BUY** ★★★★★   12-Month Target Price: **$69.00** (as of October 28, 2004)

Business Summary October 29, 2004

Simon Property Group is a REIT that owns, develops, manages, leases and acquires primarily regional malls and community shopping centers. At December 31, 2003, it owned 246 income-producing properties in North America, consisting of 175 regional malls, 67 community shopping centers, and four office and mixed-use properties in 37 states and Canada. The trust also owned nine retail real estate properties in Canada and Europe, and held four parcels of land for future development. SPG wholly owns 156 properties, controls 14 in which it has a joint venture interest, and holds the remaining 76 through unconsolidated joint venture interests. The trust is the managing or co-managing general partner or member of 235 of its properties. In 2003, regional malls, community centers, and the remaining portfolio accounted respectively for 91.3%, 5.6% and 3.1% of total annualized base rent.

Regional malls generally contain two or more anchors and a wide variety of smaller stores located in enclosed malls connecting the anchors. Additional stores, frequently called freestanding stores, are usually located along the perimeter of the parking area. SPG's 175 regional malls range in size from about 200,000 sq. ft. to 2.9 million sq. ft. of gross leasable area (GLA), with all but four regional malls exceeding 400,000 sq. ft. As of the end of 2003, its regional malls contained in the aggregate more than 18,500 occupied stores, including more than 700 anchors, mostly national retailers.

Community shopping centers are generally unenclosed, and are smaller than regional malls. SPG's 67 community shopping centers generally range in size from about 50,000 sq. ft. to 950,000 sq. ft. of GLA. Community shopping centers are generally of three types. The trust owns power centers that are designed to serve a larger trade area and contain at least two anchors, and usually as many as five to seven, that are usually national retailers among the leaders in their markets, and occupy more than 70% of the GLA in the center. It also owns traditional community centers that focus primarily on value-oriented and convenience goods and services. These centers are usually anchored by a supermarket, discount retailer, or drugstore and are designed to service a neighborhood area. In addition, SPG owns open air centers adjacent to its regional malls, designed to take advantage of the drawing power of the mall as lifestyle centers that are typically open air centers, and containing at least 50,000 sq. ft. of GLA of specialty retail regional mall type tenants, as well as restaurants.

In June 2004, the trust agreed to pay a total of $3.5 billion ($66 a share) in cash and preferred and common stock, and to assume $1.3 billion of debt and preferred equity, to acquire Chelsea Property Group, a REIT that specializes in operating premium outlet shopping centers. The acquisition was completed in October 2004. In 2003, SPG invested $1.1 billion in new properties, either through acquisitions or by increasing its ownership stakes. It also sold 13 non-core properties, consisting of seven regional malls, five community centers, and one mixed-use property.

Company Financials Fiscal Year ending December 31

Per Share Data ($)

(Year Ended December 31)	2003	2002	2001	2000	1999	1998	1997	1996	1995	1994
Tangible Bk. Val.	14.66	13.87	13.00	14.29	15.36	15.70	11.11	10.45	2.28	1.18
Earnings	1.53	1.93	0.87	1.13	1.00	1.01	1.08	1.02	1.08	0.71
S&P Core Earnings	1.55	2.07	0.97	NA	NA	NA	NA	NA	NA	NA
Dividends	2.40	2.18	2.08	2.02	2.02	2.02	2.01	2.12	1.95	1.90
Payout Ratio	157%	113%	NM	179%	202%	200%	186%	208%	178%	268%
Prices - High	48.59	36.95	30.97	27.12	30.93	34.87	34.37	31.00	26.00	23.70
- Low	31.70	28.80	23.75	21.50	20.43	25.81	27.87	21.12	22.50	19.10
P/E Ratio - High	32	19	36	24	31	34	32	30	24	39
- Low	21	15	27	19	20	26	26	21	21	32

Income Statement Analysis (Million $)

	2003	2002	2001	2000	1999	1998	1997	1996	1995	1994
Rental Income	1,423	1,386	1,320	1,284	1,207	900	680	469	331	429
Mortgage Income	Nil	Nil	Nil	Nil	Nil	Nil	Nil	Nil	Nil	Nil
Total Income	2,314	2,186	2,045	2,013	1,895	1,405	1,054	748	554	474
General Exp.	611	788	712	674	655	495	228	409	303	259
Interest Exp.	615	603	622	667	580	420	288	208	150	150
Prov. for Losses	Nil	8.97	8.41	9.64	8.50	6.60	Nil	3.46	2.90	4.24
Depr.	498	423	453	420	382	268	201	136	92.7	75.9
Net Inc.	339	1,109	201	242	210	160	137	88.8	62.6	42.3
S&P Core Earnings	288	371	169	NA	NA	NA	NA	NA	NA	NA

Balance Sheet & Other Fin. Data (Million $)

	2003	2002	2001	2000	1999	1998	1997	1996	1995	1994
Cash	536	397	255	214	155	130	787	70.4	63.0	105
Total Assets	15,685	14,905	13,794	13,911	14,199	13,277	7,663	5,896	2,556	2,277
Real Estate Invest.	14,972	14,250	13,187	13,038	12,794	11,850	6,867	5,301	2,162	1,900
Loss Reserve	Nil	20.5	24.7	20.1	14.6	14.5	Nil	Nil	Nil	Nil
Net Invest.	12,415	12,027	11,311	11,558	11,697	11,127	6,406	5,022	2,009	1,829
ST Debt	1,481	940	665	1,164	1,162	1,030	390	49.8	Nil	7.10
Capitalization:										
Debt	8,786	8,606	8,176	7,904	9,109	7,973	5,078	3,632	1,981	1,931
Equity	2,971	2,653	2,327	2,515	3,246	3,409	2,465	1,012	233	57.3
Total	13,241	12,074	11,381	10,958	12,355	11,382	6,939	4,937	2,214	1,988
% Earn & Depr/Assets	5.5	10.7	4.7	4.7	4.3	4.1	5.0	5.3	6.4	6.0
Price Times Book Value:										
Hi	3.3	2.7	2.4	1.9	2.0	2.2	3.1	3.0	11.4	2.4
Low	2.2	2.1	1.8	1.5	1.3	1.6	2.5	2.0	9.9	1.9

Data as orig reptd.; bef. results of disc opers/spec. items. Per share data adj. for stk. divs.; EPS diluted. E-Estimated. NA-Not Available. NM-Not Meaningful. NR-Not Ranked. UR-Under Review.

Office: 115 West Washington Street, Indianapolis, IN 46204.
Telephone: 317-636-1600.
Website: http://www.simon.com
Chrmn: M. Simon.
Chrmn: H. Simon.
Pres & COO: R.S. Sokolov.

CEO: D. Simon.
EVP & CFO: S.E. Sterrett.
VP & Investor Contact: S.J. Doran 800-461-3439.
Trustees: B. Bayh, M. E. Bergstein, L. W. Bynoe, M. D. DeBartolo York, K. N. Horn, G. W. Miller, F. W. Petri, M. Simon, H. Simon, D. Simon, J. A. Smith, Jr., R. S. Sokolov, P. J. Ward, P. S. van den Berg.

Auditor: Ernst & Young, Indianapolis, IN.
Founded: in 1993.
Domicile: Delaware.
Employees: 4,040.
S&P Analyst: R. McMillan/PMW/BK

Recommendation: **HOLD** ★ ★ ★ ☆ ☆
SELL · SELL · HOLD · BUY · BUY

12-Month Target Price: $50.00
(as of November 03, 2004)

SLM has an approximate 0.20% weighting in the **S&P 500**

Sector: Financials
Sub-Industry: Consumer Finance
Peer Group: Student Loans

Summary: This company (formerly USA Education) is the leading U.S. provider of post-secondary educational financial services.

Quantitative Evaluations

Price as of 11/12/04: $50.61 **2004E S&P Core EPS:** $3.45

S&P Earnings & Dividend Rank: A-

| D | C | B- | B | B+ | A- | A | A+ |

S&P Fair Value Rank: 1+

| 1 | 2 | 3 | 4 | 5 |
| Lowest | | | | Highest |

Fair Value Calc.: $40.30 (Overvalued)

S&P Investability Quotient Percentile
93%

SLM scored higher than 93% of all companies for which an S&P Report is available.

Volatility: Average

| Low | Average | High |

Technical Evaluation: Bullish
Since 10/04, the technical indicators for SLM have been Bullish.

Relative Strength Rank: Strong
87
1 Lowest   Highest 99

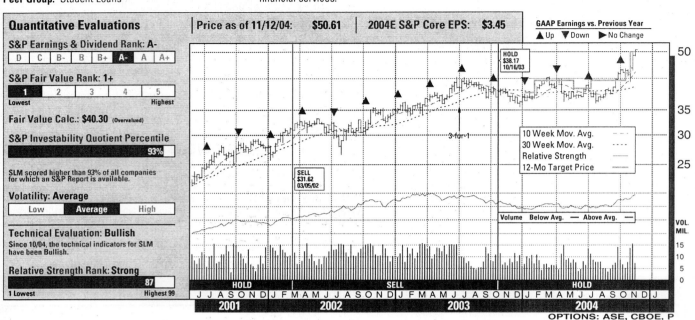

GAAP Earnings vs. Previous Year
▲ Up ▼ Down ► No Change

- 10 Week Mov. Avg.
- 30 Week Mov. Avg.
- Relative Strength
- 12-Mo Target Price

Volume Below Avg. — Above Avg.

OPTIONS: ASE, CBOE, P

Analyst commentary prepared by Erik J. Eisenstein/MF/BK

Highlights November 05, 2004

- We project average on-balance-sheet student loan growth of about 16% in 2005. With forecasted 18% off-balance-sheet loan growth, we see 17% overall average managed loan growth. We forecast a narrower net interest spread, on higher borrowing costs. As a result, we expect a 6% decline in net interest income, despite the anticipated gain in on-balance-sheet assets. We see loan loss provisions up about 21%. We project weaker derivative results, in the absence of a $386 million positive derivative market value adjustment in the 2004 second quarter. Nevertheless, we see other revenue rising about 2%, on expected higher gains on student loan securitizations, as well as servicing and securitization revenue.

- With growth of 16% expected for noninterest expenses, we see EPS down 12% in 2005, to $3.15, from $3.56 projected for 2004, reflecting our view of difficult comparisons. However, with SLM continuing to enjoy strong student loan originations as it winds down its government sponsored activities, we forecast five-year EPS growth beyond 2005 of about 14%.

- Our S&P Core EPS projections for 2004 and 2005 are $3.45 and $2.98, respectively, reflecting estimated stock-based compensation expense.

Investment Rationale/Risk November 05, 2004

- In light of our view that higher tuition costs will likely continue to fuel demand for student loans, and that the company should be able to boost its origination market share through its preferred lending channel initiatives, we see SLM's growth prospects far exceeding those of most financial institutions. However, our fundamental view is tempered by the possibility that growth could be threatened by competitive pressures, inasmuch as we view the student debt market as commodity-like. Also, given our view of heavy regulation of the industry, we see an element of long-term political risk. However, as a result of the recent elections, we think SLM is more likely to achieve a favorable resolution of the Higher Education Act reauthorization process in 2005.

- Risks to our recommendation and target price include political risk, as well as competitive threats to SLM's market share.

- Our 12-month target price of $50 is derived by applying a P/E multiple of 16X to our 2005 EPS estimate, about the historical average, reflecting our view of about average historical political risk, and a bit above our projected five-year EPS growth rate. We would hold the shares on a total return basis.

Key Stock Statistics

S&P Core EPS 2005E	2.98	52-week Range	$50.61-35.60
S&P Oper. EPS 2004E	3.56	12 Month P/E	15.0
P/E on S&P Oper. EPS 2004E	14.2	Beta	-0.05
S&P Oper. EPS 2005E	3.15	Shareholders	531
Yield (%)	1.5%	Market Cap (B)	$ 22.1
Dividend Rate/Share	0.76	Shares Outstanding (M)	436.0

Value of $10,000 invested five years ago: **$ 32,957**

Dividend Data Dividends have been paid since 1983

Amount ($)	Date Decl.	Ex-Div. Date	Stock of Record	Payment Date
0.170	Jan. 29	Mar. 03	Mar. 05	Mar. 19 '04
0.190	May. 14	Jun. 02	Jun. 04	Jun. 18 '04
0.190	Jul. 30	Sep. 01	Sep. 03	Sep. 17 '04
0.190	Oct. 29	Dec. 01	Dec. 03	Dec. 17 '04

Revenues/Earnings Data Fiscal year ending December 31

Revenues (Million $)

	2004	2003	2002	2001	2000	1999
1Q	915.1	1,109	1,158	929.1	995.3	722.0
2Q	1,509	1,047	702.2	1,191	932.4	769.9
3Q	1,047	1,013	404.0	411.6	1,105	820.7
4Q	—	955.9	968.1	983.4	1,134	946.8
Yr.	—	4,160	3,232	3,515	4,166	3,259

Earnings Per Share ($)

	2004	2003	2002	2001	2000	1999
1Q	0.64	0.88	0.88	0.05	0.31	0.23
2Q	1.36	0.80	0.26	0.56	0.24	0.25
3Q	0.80	0.76	-0.14	-0.42	0.18	0.25
4Q	E0.76	0.57	0.64	0.56	0.19	0.29
Yr.	E3.56	3.01	1.64	0.76	0.92	1.02

Next earnings report expected: mid-January Source: S&P, Company Reports
EPS Estimates based on S&P Operating Earnings; historical GAAP earnings are as reported.

SLM Corporation

Recommendation: **HOLD** ★ ★ ★ ☆ ☆   12-Month Target Price: **$50.00** (as of November 03, 2004)

Business Summary November 05, 2004

SLM Corp. (formerly USA Education, Inc.) is the largest U.S. private source of funding, delivery and servicing support for higher education loans, primarily through its participation in the Federal Family Education Loan Program (FFELP). The company's primary business is to originate and hold student loans.

The company was chartered by an Act of Congress in 1972, but in 1997, it was rechartered as a private sector corporation, with new management assuming control following an extended proxy battle. The reorganization led SLM to reassess its bank-oriented loan purchase strategy. As a result, it changed the focus of its marketing efforts to the college campus, specifically financial aid offices. Pursuant to its reorganization as a private company, SLM has substantially completed the wind down of its government sponsored activities. As of October 2004, it expected to complete the transition by the end of the 2005 first quarter.

In 1998, SLM began to originate a small amount of FFELP loans. In order to accelerate loan origination efforts, the company completed two strategic acquisitions: Nellie Mae in 1999, and Student Loan Funding Resources in 2000.

Through dedicated lender relationships and direct origination, the company intended to build its preferred channel, loans originated and serviced on the SLM's servicing platform that are committed for sale to or owned from inception by the company. The company believes loans acquired or originated in this fashion are more profitable, as they are acquired at a lower average cost and have a longer average life and lower servicing costs. Loan volume disbursed from SLM's preferred channel increased 23% in 2003, to $15.2 billion.

Insurance is provided on FFELP loans by certain state or non-profit guarantee

agencies, which are reinsured by the federal government. Most FFELP loans originated after October 1, 1993, are 98% reinsured, resulting in 2% risk sharing for the holders of these loans.

In addition to federal loan programs, which have statutory limits on annual and total borrowings, SLM offers private credit loan programs to bridge the gap between the cost of education and a student's aid package and self-financing resources. Private loan originations were $3.3 billion in 2003, up 39% from the level of 2002.

In July 2000, the company acquired USA Group's guarantee servicing, student loan servicing and secondary market operations. In January 2002, to expand and diversify its in-house expertise in the area of student loan delinquency, default prevention, and collection services, SLM acquired two collection companies.

In October 2004, SLM acquired Southwest Student Services Corp., the ninth largest U.S. holder of federal student loans, with a $4.8 billion portfolio. In September, the company acquired a majority interest in Arrow Financial Services, an accounts receivable management company. SLM expected the acquisition to extend its reach in the debt recovery industry. In November 2003, the company acquired Academic Management Services Corp., a student loan originator and tuition plan provider. In April, SLM acquired Pioneer Mortgage, a Michigan-based mortgage banking company. In December 2002, the company purchased First Trust Financial, a mortgage banking company with operations in New England.

At June 30, 2004, the company had authorization remaining to enter into share repurchase and equity forward contracts for 21 million common shares.

Company Financials Fiscal Year ending December 31

Per Share Data ($)

(Year Ended December 31)	2003	2002	2001	2000	1999	1998	1997	1996	1995	1994
Tangible Bk. Val.	4.55	3.08	3.59	2.54	1.43	1.33	1.30	1.48	1.43	1.63
Earnings	3.01	1.64	0.76	0.92	1.02	0.98	0.93	0.71	0.51	0.48
S&P Core Earnings	2.75	1.40	0.53	NA	NA	NA	NA	NA	NA	NA
Dividends	0.59	0.28	0.24	0.22	0.20	0.19	0.17	0.16	0.14	0.14
Payout Ratio	20%	17%	32%	24%	20%	19%	19%	23%	28%	28%
Prices - High	42.91	35.65	29.33	22.75	17.97	17.12	15.72	9.35	6.75	4.75
- Low	33.73	25.66	18.62	9.27	13.16	9.16	8.47	6.02	3.13	2.97
P/E Ratio - High	14	22	39	25	18	17	17	13	13	10
- Low	11	16	25	10	13	9	9	9	6	6

Income Statement Analysis (Million $)

	2003	2002	2001	2000	1999	1998	1997	1996	1995	1994
Interest On: Mtges.	2,197	2,124	2,625	2,977	2,569	2,293	2,711	2,900	2,974	2,351
Interest On: Invest.	151	87.9	373	501	240	295	573	543	719	500
Int. Exp.	1,022	1,203	2,124	2,837	2,115	1,925	2,526	2,577	3,021	2,142
Guaranty Fees	Nil	Nil	Nil	Nil	Nil	Nil	Nil	Nil	Nil	Nil
Loan Loss Prov.	147	117	66.0	32.1	34.4	Nil	Nil	Nil	Nil	17.0
Admin. Exp.	808	690	708	586	359	361	269	199	161	130
Pretax Inc.	2,183	1,223	617	712	752	750	765	608	512	579
Eff. Tax Rate	35.7%	35.3%	36.2%	33.1%	31.9%	31.7%	31.8%	30.2%	27.6%	28.8%
Net Inc.	1,404	792	384	465	501	501	511	424	371	412
S&P Core Earnings	1,276	664	261	NA	NA	NA	NA	NA	NA	NA

Balance Sheet & Other Fin. Data (Million $)

	2003	2002	2001	2000	1999	1998	1997	1996	1995	1994
Mtges.	51,078	43,541	42,037	38,635	34,852	29,825	32,765	38,016	39,514	38,951
Invest.	5,268	4,231	5,072	5,206	5,185	3,990	5,076	7,436	7,614	10,435
Cash & Equiv.	1,652	758	715	734	590	116	54.0	271	1,253	2,262
Total Assets	64,611	53,175	52,874	48,792	44,025	37,210	39,909	47,630	50,002	52,961
ST Debt	18,735	25,619	31,065	30,464	37,491	26,588	23,176	22,517	17,447	16,016
LT Debt	23,211	22,242	17,285	14,911	4,496	8,811	14,541	22,606	30,083	34,319
Equity	3,564	1,833	1,507	1,250	676	654	675	834	867	1,257
% Ret. on Assets	2.4	1.5	0.8	1.0	1.2	1.3	1.2	0.9	0.7	0.8
% Ret. on Equity	25.8	47.4	27.8	48.2	75.1	75.5	67.7	49.9	35.0	35.5
Equity/Assets Ratio	10.9	3.1	2.7	2.1	1.6	1.7	1.7	1.7	2.1	2.7
Price Times Book Value:										
Hi	9.4	11.6	8.2	8.9	12.6	12.9	12.1	6.3	4.7	2.9
Low	7.4	8.3	5.2	3.6	9.2	6.9	6.5	4.1	2.2	1.8

Data as orig reptd.; bef. results of disc opers/spec. items. Per share data adj. for stk. divs.; EPS diluted. E-Estimated. NA-Not Available. NM-Not Meaningful. NR-Not Ranked. UR-Under Review.

Office: 11600 Sallie Mae Drive, Reston, VA 20193.
Telephone: 703-810-3000.
Website: http://www.salliemae.com
Chrmn: E.A. Fox.
Pres & COO: T.J. Fitzpatrick.
Vice Chrmn & CEO: A.L. Lord.

EVP & General Counsel: M.M. Keler.
SVP & Investor Contact: K. deLaski 703-810-3000.
Dirs: C. L. Daley, W. M. Diefenderfer III, T. J. Fitzpatrick, E. A. Fox, D. S. Gilleland, E. A. Goode, A. T. Grant, R. F. Hunt, B. J. Lambert III, A. L. Lord, B. A. Munitz, A. A. Porter, Jr., W. Schoellkopf, S. L. Shapiro, B. L. Williams.

Founded: in 1972.
Domicile: Delaware.
Employees: 7,500.
S&P Analyst: Erik J. Eisenstein/MF/BK

Snap-on Inc.

Recommendation: HOLD ★ ★ ★ ★   12-Month Target Price: **$30.00**
(as of September 29, 2004)

SNA has an approximate 0.02% weighting in the **S&P 500**

Sector: Consumer Discretionary
Sub-Industry: Household Appliances
Peer Group: Hardware & Tools

Summary: This company is the largest manufacturer and distributor of hand tools, storage units and diagnostic equipment for professional mechanics and industry.

Quantitative Evaluations

S&P Earnings & Dividend Rank: B

| D | C | B- | **B** | B+ | A- | A | A+ |

S&P Fair Value Rank: 1

| **1** | 2 | 3 | 4 | 5 |
| Lowest | | | | Highest |

Fair Value Calc.: $25.00 (Overvalued)

S&P Investability Quotient Percentile

85%

SNA scored higher than 85% of all companies for which an S&P Report is available.

Volatility: Low

| **Low** | Average | High |

Technical Evaluation: Neutral

Since 11/04, the technical indicators for SNA have been Neutral.

Relative Strength Rank: Moderate

32

| 1 Lowest | Highest 99 |

Price as of 11/12/04: $30.50 | **2004E S&P Core EPS:** $1.55

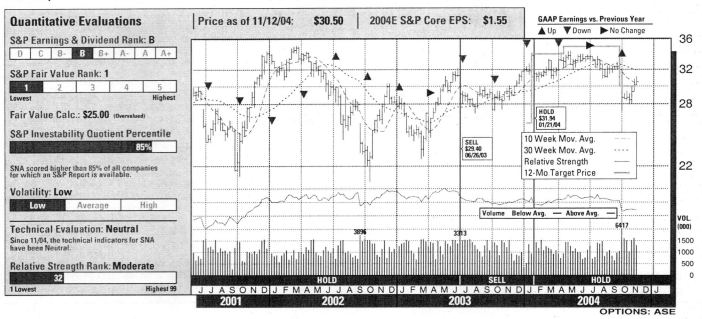

GAAP Earnings vs. Previous Year
▲ Up ▼ Down ▶ No Change

HOLD $31.94 01/21/04

SELL $29.40 06/26/03

10 Week Mov. Avg.
30 Week Mov. Avg.
Relative Strength
12-Mo Target Price

Volume Below Avg. — Above Avg.

3896 3313 6417

VOL. (000)

OPTIONS: ASE

Analyst commentary prepared by Amy Glynn, CFA /CB/MGH

Highlights November 04, 2004

- We project total revenue growth in the mid- to high single digits for 2004, on increased contributions from the dealer group as well as from the commercial and industrial group. We think the addition of new dealers will help the dealer group post sales gains during the year. In addition, we expect sales comparisons in the commercial and industrial group to benefit from an improvement in the economy. We forecast total sales growth in the mid-single digits for 2005, aided by pricing and new product introductions.

- We see operating margins narrowing in 2004, in light of SNA's recent comment that benefits from U.S. hand tool plant consolidations have not yet reached expectations. We expect to see the impact of this consolidation in the first half of 2005. In addition, steel prices continue to pressure margins, as price adjustments taken in July were not enough to offset the dramatic rise in steel costs. We think SNA will raise prices again in late 2004/early 2005 to offset higher steel prices.

- We estimate 2004 operating EPS of $1.67 per share. Our projection is before an estimated $0.26 of continuous improvement costs. For 2005, we see operating EPS of $1.88, on mid-single digit revenue growth and benefits from the U.S. plant consolidations.

Investment Rationale/Risk November 04, 2004

- With two recent downward earnings revisions, we think SNA will struggle in the next couple of quarters with weak demand and rising steel prices. In our view, SNA also needs to demonstrate that its restructuring initiatives will have a noticeable impact on its bottom line, which we don't foresee until 2005. However, SNA's 3.4% dividend yield and ongoing share repurchase program should provide some support for the stock price, in our opinion, and we think the shares merit holding. Longer term, SNA should also benefit from stronger demand and its move toward a more efficient cost structure.

- Risks to our opinion and target price include an unexpected weakening in SNA's major markets, insufficient market acceptance of new products, increased competition, and adverse changes in currency exchange rates or raw material prices.

- Our 12-month target price of $30 is based on our historical P/E model, which applies a target P/E of 16X to our 2005 operating EPS estimate. In recent years, the shares have traded in a P/E multiple range of 12X to 22X current year operating EPS, with an average multiple of about 17X. Given the current challenges, we think a discount to SNA's historical average is warranted.

Key Stock Statistics

S&P Core EPS 2005E	1.76	52-week Range	$34.41-27.15
S&P Oper. EPS 2004E	1.67	12 Month P/E	23.6
P/E on S&P Oper. EPS 2004E	18.3	Beta	1.07
S&P Oper. EPS 2005E	1.88	Shareholders	10,280
Yield (%)	3.3%	Market Cap (B)	$ 1.8
Dividend Rate/Share	1.00	Shares Outstanding (M)	57.5

Value of $10,000 invested five years ago: **$ 11,946**

Dividend Data Dividends have been paid since 1939

Amount ($)	Date Decl.	Ex-Div. Date	Stock of Record	Payment Date
0.250	Jan. 23	Feb. 13	Feb. 18	Mar. 10 '04
0.250	Apr. 23	May. 18	May. 20	Jun. 10 '04
0.250	Jun. 25	Aug. 18	Aug. 20	Sep. 10 '04
0.250	Oct. 22	Nov. 17	Nov. 19	Dec. 10 '04

Revenues/Earnings Data Fiscal year ending December 31

Revenues (Million $)

	2004	2003	2002	2001	2000	1999
1Q	616.3	543.1	510.0	527.4	544.4	452.6
2Q	612.1	565.2	547.2	525.6	563.2	473.1
3Q	550.9	525.6	502.4	508.1	511.8	453.2
4Q	—	599.3	549.5	534.6	556.3	566.7
Yr.	—	2,233	2,109	2,096	2,176	1,946

Earnings Per Share ($)

	2004	2003	2002	2001	2000	1999
1Q	0.22	0.37	0.37	0.51	0.60	0.55
2Q	0.38	0.38	0.50	0.15	0.78	0.42
3Q	0.39	0.30	0.33	0.01	0.48	0.72
4Q	E0.42	0.30	0.56	-0.30	0.24	0.47
Yr.	E1.67	1.35	1.76	0.37	2.10	2.16

Next earnings report expected: early-February Source: S&P, Company Reports
EPS Estimates based on S&P Operating Earnings; historical GAAP earnings are as reported.

Snap-on Incorporated

Recommendation: **HOLD** ★ ★ ★ ☆ ☆   12-Month Target Price: **$30.00** (as of September 29, 2004)

Business Summary November 08, 2004

Snap-on (formerly Snap-on Tools) manufactures and markets tool, diagnostic and equipment solutions for professional tool and equipment users. Its customers include automotive technicians, vehicle service centers, manufacturers, industrial tool and equipment users, and those involved in commercial applications such as construction, electrical and agriculture.

In 1996, as part of an effort to become a complete solutions provider to the transportation and industrial service markets worldwide, SNA acquired John Bean Co., a producer of wheel and brake service equipment. In 1997, it bought a 50% interest in Thomson Corp.'s Mitchell Repair Information business, a provider of vehicle repair information for service establishments. Also in 1997, the company acquired Computer Aided Service, Inc., a developer of repair shop management and point of sale systems and diagnostics equipment; and purchased Hofman Werkstatt-Technik, a European leader in under-car equipment technology. In 1998, SNA acquired Hein-Werner Corp., a leading worldwide maker and marketer of automotive collision repair equipment. In 1999, it purchased Sandvik Saw and Tools (renamed Bahco). Bahco produces and supplies professional hand tools. The company also purchased three other businesses in 1999, as well as the remaining 40% interest in Mitchell Repair.

The company makes hand tools (wrenches, screwdrivers, sockets, pliers and similar items), power tools (pneumatic impact wrenches, ratchets, power drills, sanders and polishers), tool storage units (tool chests and roll cabinets), and electronic tools and shop equipment (automotive diagnostic equipment, wheel balancing and aligning equipment, battery chargers and other items). Acquisitions have expanded its product lines, especially in electronic diagnostics and emissions test and repair equipment, and opened new distribution channels.

In 2002, SNA reorganized into three reportable business segments: the Snap-on dealer group (47% of 2003 sales); the commercial and industrial group (45%); and the diagnostics and information group (8%). The Snap-on dealer group serves the worldwide franchised dealer van channel. The commercial and industrial group provides tools and equipment products to a broad range of industrial and commercial customers worldwide through direct, distributor, and other non-franchised channels. The diagnostics and information group provides diagnostic equipment, vehicle service information, business management systems, equipment repair services, and other solutions for customers in the worldwide vehicle service and repair marketplace.

The company manages mobile van sales for automotive technicians who are served by a worldwide network of dealers, the majority of which are franchised. Industrial products are sold by company salespeople. Dealers operate out of walk-in vans that carry an inventory of products. Snap-on Diagnostics uses a company salesforce to sell equipment, diagnostics and software to repair shops and OEMs.

Company Financials Fiscal Year ending December 31

Per Share Data ($)

(Year Ended December 31)	2003	2002	2001	2000	1999	1998	1997	1996	1995	1994
Tangible Bk. Val.	8.29	6.27	6.01	6.53	6.69	9.60	12.74	12.30	11.07	11.08
Cash Flow	2.38	2.65	1.54	3.23	3.10	0.68	3.06	2.68	2.35	2.00
Earnings	1.35	1.76	0.37	2.10	2.16	-0.08	2.44	2.16	1.84	1.53
S&P Core Earnings	1.31	0.92	0.09	NA	NA	NA	NA	NA	NA	NA
Dividends	1.00	0.97	0.96	0.94	0.90	0.86	0.82	0.76	0.72	0.72
Payout Ratio	74%	55%	NM	45%	42%	NM	34%	35%	39%	47%
Prices - High	32.38	35.15	34.40	32.43	37.81	46.43	46.31	38.25	31.50	29.58
- Low	22.60	20.71	21.15	20.87	26.43	25.50	34.25	27.33	20.66	19.33
P/E Ratio - High	24	20	93	15	18	NM	19	18	17	19
- Low	17	12	57	10	12	NM	14	13	11	13

Income Statement Analysis (Million $)

	2003	2002	2001	2000	1999	1998	1997	1996	1995	1994
Revs.	2,233	2,109	2,096	2,176	1,946	1,773	1,672	1,485	1,292	1,254
Oper. Inc.	167	217	168	270	228	102	232	188	157	188
Depr.	60.3	51.7	68.0	66.2	55.4	45.0	38.4	31.9	31.5	30.1
Int. Exp.	24.4	28.7	35.5	40.7	27.4	21.3	17.7	12.6	13.3	10.8
Pretax Inc.	117	161	47.6	193	198	10.8	239	209	180	154
Eff. Tax Rate	32.6%	36.0%	54.8%	36.1%	35.7%	NM	37.0%	37.3%	37.0%	36.0%
Net Inc.	78.7	103	21.5	123	127	-4.78	150	131	113	98.0
S&P Core Earnings	76.6	53.9	5.49	NA	NA	NA	NA	NA	NA	NA

Balance Sheet & Other Fin. Data (Million $)

	2003	2002	2001	2000	1999	1998	1997	1996	1995	1994
Cash	96.1	18.4	6.70	6.10	17.6	15.0	25.7	15.4	16.2	9.00
Curr. Assets	1,132	1,051	1,139	1,186	1,206	1,080	1,022	1,017	947	873
Total Assets	2,139	1,994	1,974	2,050	2,150	1,675	1,641	1,521	1,361	1,235
Curr. Liab.	567	552	549	538	453	458	353	341	336	238
LT Debt	303	304	446	473	247	247	151	150	144	109
Common Equity	1,011	830	869	844	825	762	892	828	751	766
Total Cap.	1,348	1,168	1,339	1,342	1,099	1,018	1,055	985	899	882
Cap. Exp.	29.4	45.8	53.6	57.6	35.4	46.8	55.4	52.3	31.6	41.8
Cash Flow	139	155	89.5	189	183	40.2	189	163	145	128
Curr. Ratio	2.0	1.9	2.1	2.2	2.7	2.4	2.9	3.0	2.8	3.7
% LT Debt of Cap.	22.5	26.0	33.3	35.3	22.4	24.2	14.3	15.2	16.0	12.4
% Net Inc.of Revs.	3.5	4.9	1.0	5.7	6.5	NM	9.0	8.9	8.7	7.8
% Ret. on Assets	3.8	5.2	1.1	5.9	6.7	NM	9.5	9.1	8.7	8.0
% Ret. on Equity	8.5	12.9	2.4	14.7	16.0	NM	17.5	16.7	14.9	13.3

Data as orig reptd.; bef. results of disc opers/spec. items. Per share data adj. for stk. divs.; EPS diluted. E-Estimated. NA-Not Available. NM-Not Meaningful. NR-Not Ranked. UR-Under Review.

Office: 10801 Corporate Drive, Pleasant Prairie, WI 53158.
Telephone: 262-656-5200.
Website: http://www.snapon.com
Chrmn, Pres & CEO: D.F. Elliott.
SVP & CFO: M.M. Ellen.
VP & Treas: B.A. Metzger.

VP, Secy & General Counsel: S.F. Marrinan.
VP & Investor Contact: W.H. Pfund 262-656-6488.
Dirs: B. S. Chelberg, R. J. Decyk, D. F. Elliott, J. F. Fiedler, A. L. Kelly, W. D. Lehman, J. D. Michaels, L. Nyberg, F. S. Ptak, E. H. Rensi, R. F. Teerlink.

Founded: in 1920.
Domicile: Delaware.
Employees: 12,400.
S&P Analyst: Amy Glynn, CFA /CB/MGH

Solectron Corp.

Recommendation: HOLD ★ ★ ★ ☆ ☆
SELL SELL HOLD BUY BUY

12-Month Target Price: **$6.00**
(as of September 29, 2004)

SLR has an approximate 0.05% weighting in the **S&P 500**

Sector: Information Technology
Sub-Industry: Electronic Manufacturing Services
Peer Group: Circuit Boards/Microelectronics - Larger Sales

Summary: SLR is a major provider of electronic manufacturing services to OEMs in the computer, telecom, datacom, consumer and other industries.

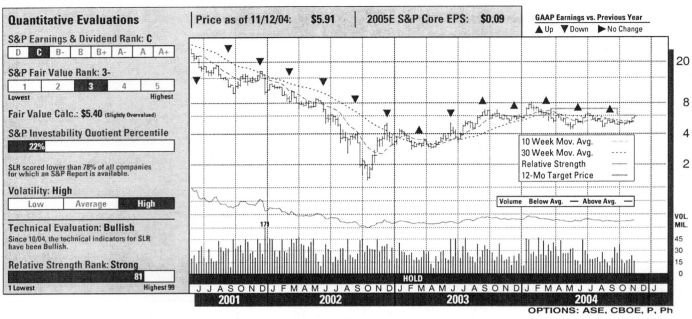

Quantitative Evaluations	Price as of 11/12/04: $5.91	2005E S&P Core EPS: $0.09

S&P Earnings & Dividend Rank: C
D | **C** | B- | B | B+ | A- | A | A+

S&P Fair Value Rank: 3-
1 | 2 | **3** | 4 | 5
Lowest ... Highest

Fair Value Calc.: $5.40 (Slightly Overvalued)

S&P Investability Quotient Percentile
22%
SLR scored lower than 78% of all companies for which an S&P Report is available.

Volatility: High
Low | Average | **High**

Technical Evaluation: Bullish
Since 10/04, the technical indicators for SLR have been Bullish.

Relative Strength Rank: Strong
81
1 Lowest ... Highest 99

GAAP Earnings vs. Previous Year
▲ Up ▼ Down ► No Change

10 Week Mov. Avg.
30 Week Mov. Avg.
Relative Strength
12-Mo Target Price

Volume Below Avg. — Above Avg.

VOL. MIL.
45
30
15
0

HOLD

J J A S O N D | J F M A M J J A S O N D | J F M A M J J A S O N D | J F M A M J J A S O N D | J
2001 | 2002 | 2003 | 2004

OPTIONS: ASE, CBOE, P, Ph

Analyst commentary prepared by Richard N. Stice, CFA /CB/DRJ

Highlights September 29, 2004

- We expect revenues to increase about 9% in FY 05 (Aug.), following an 18% rise in FY 04. The projected growth reflects new program wins and what we view as strengthening end markets. For the longer term, we believe industry fundamentals are robust, and see demand being driven by expansion of the relatively low penetration rate of outsourcing into electronics manufacturing, and by the potential benefits that the outsourcing model provides to OEMs.

- We see gross margins widening on rising volumes, a shift of production to lower cost regions, and a more favorable business mix. We expect interest expense to continue to decline, as the company recently repurchased about $950 million of convertible notes.

- We forecast FY 05 operating EPS of $0.23, versus breakeven results in FY 04 (excluding $0.29 of special charges). We see Standard & Poor's Core Earnings per share of $0.09 in FY 05, which reflects projected stock option expense.

Investment Rationale/Risk September 29, 2004

- We would hold existing positions. Although SLR was slow to respond to the economic downturn that began in 2001, we believe the company's restructuring benefits are paying off, with operating expenses declining notably over the past several quarters. In addition, SLR returned to operating profitability in the FY 04 third quarter. However, we remain concerned about what we view as the company's relatively narrow gross margins, high debt load, and lack of consistent free cash flow generation.

- Risks to our recommendation and target price include a prolonged slowdown in the communications and networking markets, additional restructuring requirements beyond those currently projected, and the inability to sell excess or obsolete inventory to third parties.

- Our 12-month target price of $6 is based on a combination of relative price to sales and discounted cash flow analyses. Our DCF assumptions include a weighted average cost of capital of 10.3% and an expected terminal growth rate of 3%.

Key Stock Statistics

S&P Oper. EPS 2005E	0.23	52-week Range	$8.20-4.39
P/E on S&P Oper. EPS 2005E	25.7	12 Month P/E	NM
S&P Oper. EPS 2006E	0.31	Beta	NA
Yield (%)	Nil	Shareholders	8,130
Dividend Rate/Share	Nil	Market Cap (B)	$ 5.7
Shares Outstanding (M)	961.7		

Value of $10,000 invested five years ago: **$ 1,384**

Dividend Data

No cash dividends have been paid.

Revenues/Earnings Data Fiscal year ending August 31

Revenues (Million $)

	2004	2003	2002	2001	2000	1999
1Q	2,697	3,137	3,152	5,696	2,502	1,946
2Q	2,887	2,818	2,975	5,419	2,860	1,908
3Q	3,040	2,816	3,033	3,983	3,592	2,152
4Q	3,014	2,814	3,117	3,595	4,736	2,386
Yr.	11,638	11,014	12,276	18,692	14,138	8,391

Earnings Per Share ($)

	2004	2003	2002	2001	2000	1999
1Q	-0.06	-0.09	-0.08	0.29	0.18	0.13
2Q	-0.11	-0.13	-0.19	0.18	0.16	0.13
3Q	-0.08	-3.74	-0.35	-0.28	0.20	0.15
4Q	-0.05	-0.21	-3.21	-0.38	0.27	0.17
Yr.	-0.29	-3.75	-3.98	-0.19	0.80	0.57

Next earnings report expected: mid-December Source: S&P, Company Reports
EPS Estimates based on S&P Operating Earnings; historical GAAP earnings are as reported.

Solectron Corporation

Recommendation: **HOLD** ★ ★ ★ ☆ ☆   12-Month Target Price: **$6.00** (as of September 29, 2004)

Business Summary October 01, 2004

Solectron Corp. seeks to offer customers significant competitive advantages by outsourcing their electronics supply chain service needs. Elements of its strategy include capitalizing on industry growth trends, concentrating on core and emerging markets, developing and maintaining cost competitiveness, establishing long-term strategic relationships, and having diverse geographic operations.

SLR provides electronics supply chain services to OEMs in several segments of the electronics industry. Products related to the company's business include networking equipment such as routers and switches, telecom equipment, note-books, desktops, cellular phones, home game consoles, and X-ray equipment. SLR offers a comprehensive range of services that consist of collaborative design support, supply chain design and sourcing, product testing, full product manufac-turing, and product repair and warranty service.

According to the company, benefits that electronic manufacturing service (EMS) providers offer to OEMs include reduced time to market, lower total costs, better asset utilization, and access to leading manufacturing and service technologies. In addition, the company believes that employing an EMS company lets OEMs allocate resources toward core competencies, including R&D and marketing efforts.

SLR has shifted its manufacturing capacity to lower-cost locations over the past few years: to Mexico, Eastern Europe, and particularly Asia. This reflects its belief that OEMs will be driven by the cost advantages associated with these locations, among other factors, in coming years. At the end of FY 03 (Aug.), the company had about 70% of its manufacturing capacity, in terms of headcount and equip-ment, and 50% in terms of square footage, located in these regions.

In FY 03, Hewlett-Packard (HP) and Nortel Networks each accounted for 12% of net sales, while Cisco Systems provided 11%. The 10 largest customers contrib-uted a total of 61% of net sales, down from 68% in FY 02 and 72% in FY 01. Sales outside the U.S. accounted for 64% of the total, down from 66% in FY 02.

In the FY 03 second quarter, the company reached a manufacturing and supply agreement to assemble printed circuit boards and memory modules for HP's mid- and high-end enterprise servers, as well as for other products. In connection with the agreement, SLR paid $5 million to acquire certain operating assets. At anticipated production levels, the contract would generate about $1.4 billion in sales for the company over five years.

During FY 03, SLR recorded restructuring and impairment costs of $469.6 million related to continuing operations. This included employee severance and benefit charges related to the elimination of 9,500 full-time positions; about 57% of the positions were in the Americas region, 31% in Europe, and 12% in Asia/Pacific. Facilities and equipment subject to restructuring were located primarily in the Americas and Europe.

Company Financials Fiscal Year ending August 31

Per Share Data ($)

(Year Ended August 31)	2004	2003	2002	2001	2000	1999	1998	1997	1996	1995
Tangible Bk. Val.	2.32	1.48	3.16	4.81	6.28	5.16	5.02	2.00	1.67	1.36
Cash Flow	-0.03	-3.43	-3.50	0.64	1.21	0.91	1.28	0.57	0.48	0.40
Earnings	-0.29	-3.75	-3.98	-0.19	0.80	0.57	0.41	0.34	0.27	0.23
S&P Core Earnings	-0.34	-2.57	-1.93	-0.15	NA	NA	NA	NA	NA	NA
Dividends	Nil	Nil	Nil	Nil	Nil	Nil	Nil	Nil	Nil	Nil
Payout Ratio	Nil	Nil	Nil	Nil	Nil	Nil	Nil	Nil	Nil	Nil
Prices - High	8.20	6.89	12.42	41.95	52.62	49.00	23.37	11.84	7.51	5.64
- Low	4.39	2.80	1.39	9.65	24.54	18.64	8.85	5.89	3.62	2.76
P/E Ratio - High	NM	NM	NM	NM	66	87	57	35	27	25
- Low	NM	NM	NM	NM	31	33	21	17	13	12

Income Statement Analysis (Million $)

	2004	2003	2002	2001	2000	1999	1998	1997	1996	1995
Revs.	11,638	11,014	12,276	18,692	14,138	8,391	5,288	3,694	2,817	2,066
Oper. Inc.	-366	145	204	985	994	622	423	345	260	185
Depr.	227	264	377	536	251	183	124	105	84.8	61.4
Int. Exp.	144	210	244	176	71.6	36.5	24.8	26.6	15.7	9.50
Pretax Inc.	-252	-2,524	-3,578	-158	740	432	299	238	173	120
Eff. Tax Rate	NM	NM	NM	NM	32.3%	32.0%	33.5%	33.7%	34.0%	34.0%
Net Inc.	-252	-3,105	-3,110	-124	501	294	199	158	114	79.5
S&P Core Earnings	-297	-2,129	-1,506	-96.9	NA	NA	NA	NA	NA	NA

Balance Sheet & Other Fin. Data (Million $)

	2004	2003	2002	2001	2000	1999	1998	1997	1996	1995
Cash	1,430	1,519	1,918	2,482	1,476	1,326	225	225	229	149
Curr. Assets	4,666	4,954	6,660	8,704	8,628	3,994	1,888	1,476	1,145	726
Total Assets	5,817	6,530	11,014	12,930	10,376	4,835	2,411	1,852	1,452	941
Curr. Liab.	2,159	3,235	3,005	2,689	3,217	1,113	841	544	358	371
LT Debt	1,221	1,818	3,184	5,028	3,320	923	386	386	387	30.0
Common Equity	2,379	1,422	4,773	5,151	3,802	2,793	1,181	919	701	538
Total Cap.	3,600	3,240	7,957	10,178	7,122	3,716	1,567	1,305	1,087	568
Cap. Exp.	150	137	242	537	506	426	244	188	115	114
Cash Flow	-24.9	-2,841	-2,733	413	752	477	323	263	199	141
Curr. Ratio	2.2	1.5	2.2	3.2	2.7	3.6	2.2	2.7	3.2	2.0
% LT Debt of Cap.	33.9	56.1	40.0	49.4	46.6	24.8	24.6	29.6	35.6	5.3
% Net Inc.of Revs.	NM	NM	NM	NM	3.5	3.5	3.8	4.3	4.1	3.9
% Ret. on Assets	NM	NM	NM	NM	6.3	8.1	9.3	9.6	9.5	9.4
% Ret. on Equity	NM	NM	NM	NM	14.4	14.8	18.9	19.5	18.4	18.4

Data as orig reptd.; bef. results of disc opers/spec. items. Per share data adj. for stk. divs.; EPS diluted. E-Estimated. NA-Not Available. NM-Not Meaningful. NR-Not Ranked. UR-Under Review.

Office: 777 Gibraltar Drive, Milpitas, CA 95035.
Telephone: 408-957-8500.
Website: http://www.solectron.com
Pres & CEO: M. Cannon.

EVP & CFO: K. Patel.
VP, Treas & Investor Contact: P. Hayes .
Dirs: M. Cannon, R. A. D'Amore, H. Fridrich, W. R. Graber, W. Hasler, P. Low, C. W. Scott, O. Yamada, C. Yansouni.

Founded: in 1977.
Domicile: Delaware.
Employees: 57,000.
S&P Analyst: Richard N. Stice, CFA /CB/DRJ

Southern Co.

Recommendation: HOLD ★★★☆☆
SELL | SELL | HOLD | BUY | BUY

12-Month Target Price: **$31.00**
(as of October 21, 2004)

SO has an approximate 0.22% weighting in the **S&P 500**

Sector: Utilities
Sub-Industry: Electric Utilities
Peer Group: Electric Cos. (Domestic) - Very Large

Summary: This Atlanta-based energy holding company is one of the largest U.S. electricity producers.

Quantitative Evaluations

S&P Earnings & Dividend Rank: A-

| D | C | B- | B | B+ | A- | A | A+ |

S&P Fair Value Rank: 3-

| 1 | 2 | 3 | 4 | 5 |
Lowest — Highest

Fair Value Calc.: $32.10 (Slightly Overvalued)

S&P Investability Quotient Percentile
88%

SO scored higher than 88% of all companies for which an S&P Report is available.

Volatility: Low

| Low | Average | High |

Technical Evaluation: Bullish
Since 7/04, the technical indicators for SO have been Bullish.

Relative Strength Rank: Moderate
65
1 Lowest — Highest 99

| Price as of 11/12/04: | $33.16 | 2004E S&P Core EPS: | $1.75 |

GAAP Earnings vs. Previous Year
▲ Up ▼ Down ► No Change

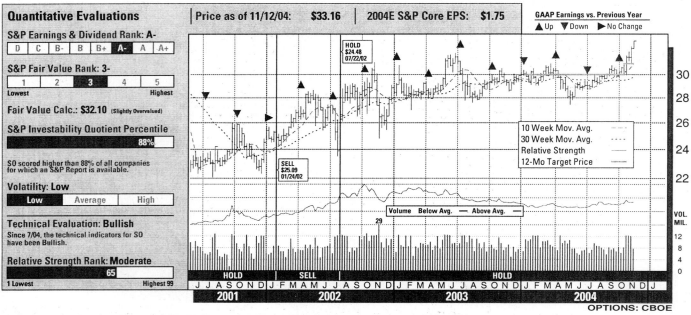

10 Week Mov. Avg.
30 Week Mov. Avg.
Relative Strength
12-Mo Target Price

Volume   Below Avg. — Above Avg.

VOL. MIL.

HOLD   SELL   HOLD
J J A S O N D | J F M A M J J A S O N D | J F M A M J J A S O N D | J F M A M J J A S O N D | J
2001   2002   2003   2004

OPTIONS: CBOE

Analyst commentary prepared by Justin McCann/PMW/BK

Highlights September 22, 2004

- After an expected 1% increase in 2004 from 2003 operating EPS of $1.97 (which excludes a one-time charge of $0.05 and an $0.11 settlement gain), we project that EPS will be up about 4% in 2005. We see anticipated earnings growth for the regulated utilities in 2004 partly offset by an earnings decline at the unregulated competitive generation business after a very strong performance in 2003.

- SO reported second quarter operating EPS of $0.48, versus $0.49 in the 2003 quarter. Earnings benefited from customer growth of 1.8% and more favorable weather, but this was outweighed by higher fuel and purchased power costs and the shifting of certain operation and maintenance expenses from the first quarter.

- With long-term contracts seen reducing risk, we expect the competitive generation business to increase its income to over $300 million by 2007, from $224 million in 2003. We see the utilities recording annual customer growth of about 1.5% and demand growth of about 2%, and expect SO to post average annual EPS growth exceeding 5% for the longer term.

Investment Rationale/Risk September 22, 2004

- We expect the stock to continue to trade at an approximate 10% premium to the average peer P/E multiple of 13.3X to 13.5X based on our 2005 EPS estimates. We view this premium as justified by the relative predictability of SO's earnings and dividend stream (with an S&P Earnings/Dividend ranking of A-) and its A credit rating a couple of notches above the industry average. We view the shares as fairly valued.

- Risks to our recommendation and target price include the potential failure of a counterparty to a purchase power agreement to fulfill its contract, and a significant decline in the average P/E multiple of the group as a whole.

- With the payout ratio (72% of our operating EPS estimate for 2004) within a targeted range of 70% to 75%, we expect annual dividends to continue to grow 2% to 2.5%, or nearly half our projection of average annual EPS growth of 5% over the longer term. Based on our view that the shares will continue to trade at a premium to peers, but that the P/E multiple will remain relatively flat, our 12-month target price is $30.

Key Stock Statistics

S&P Core EPS 2005E	1.84	52-week Range	$33.16-27.44
S&P Oper. EPS 2004E	2.01	12 Month P/E	16.9
P/E on S&P Oper. EPS 2004E	16.5	Beta	-0.48
S&P Oper. EPS 2005E	2.05	Shareholders	134,068
Yield (%)	4.3%	Market Cap (B)	$ 24.5
Dividend Rate/Share	1.43	Shares Outstanding (M)	738.2

Value of $10,000 invested five years ago: **NA**

Dividend Data Dividends have been paid since 1948

Amount ($)	Date Decl.	Ex-Div. Date	Stock of Record	Payment Date
0.350	Apr. 19	Apr. 29	May. 03	Jun. 05 '04
0.358	Jul. 19	Jul. 29	Aug. 02	Sep. 04 '04
0.358	Jul. 19	Jul. 29	Aug. 02	Sep. 04 '04
0.358	Oct. 18	Oct. 28	Nov. 01	Dec. 06 '04

Revenues/Earnings Data Fiscal year ending December 31

Revenues (Million $)

	2004	2003	2002	2001	2000	1999
1Q	2,755	2,553	2,214	2,270	2,052	2,442
2Q	3,009	2,859	2,631	2,561	2,522	2,791
3Q	3,441	3,319	3,248	3,165	3,198	3,737
4Q	—	2,564	2,457	2,200	2,294	2,616
Yr.	—	11,251	10,549	10,200	10,066	11,585

Earnings Per Share ($)

	2004	2003	2002	2001	2000	1999
1Q	0.45	0.41	0.32	0.26	0.38	0.32
2Q	0.47	0.59	0.46	0.40	0.52	0.45
3Q	0.87	0.84	0.83	0.79	0.95	0.90
4Q	E0.21	0.17	0.23	0.16	0.16	0.19
Yr.	E2.01	2.02	1.85	1.61	1.52	1.86

Next earnings report expected: late-January Source: S&P, Company Reports
EPS Estimates based on S&P Operating Earnings; historical GAAP earnings are as reported.

Recommendation: **HOLD** ★ ★ ★ ☆ ☆   12-Month Target Price: **$31.00** (as of October 21, 2004)

Business Summary September 22, 2004

The Southern Company is one of the largest producers of electricity in the U.S.

With more than 38,000 megawatts of generating capacity, this Atlanta-based utility holding company serves more than 4.1 million customers in the Southeast through five integrated subsidiaries: Alabama Power, Georgia Power, Gulf Power, Mississippi Power, and Savannah Electric & Power. The Southern Power subsidiary serves both the utility subsidiaries and the wholesale power market.

SO's electric revenues accounted for 90.9% of consolidated revenues in 2003 (93.8% in 2002, 94.7% in 2001). Electric revenues by customer class in 2003 were: residential 34.8% (35.9% in 2002, 33.8% in 2001); commercial 30.0% (30.4%, 30.8%); industrial 21.0% (21.0%, 22.3%); wholesale 13.3% (11.8%, 12.2%), and other 0.9% (0.9%, 0.9%).

Sources of fuel for the Southern system in 2003 were: coal 71% (69% in 2002, 72% in 2001%); nuclear 16% (16%, 16%); hydroelectric 4% (3%, 3%) and gas 9% (12%, 9%).

In January 2001, SO announced the formation of a new subsidiary, Southern Power Company (SPC), to own, manage and finance wholesale generating assets in the Southeast. Energy from SPC's assets was to be marketed to wholesale customers through the Southern Company Generation and Energy Marketing subsidiary. SPC had 4,800 megawatts of generating capacity at December 31, 2003.

The company operates, through subsidiaries, 34 hydroelectric generating stations,

32 fossil fuel generating stations, three nuclear generating stations, and 10 combined cycle/cogeneration stations. SO has projected its construction additions or acquisitions of property at $2.16 billion for 2004, $2.25 billion for 2005, and $2.58 billion for 2005.

SO is also the parent company for a system service company that provides, at cost, specialized service to the parent and its subsidiaries; Southern Telecom, which provides wholesale fiber optic solutions to telecommunication providers in the Southeast; Southern Communications Services (Southern LINC), which provides digital, wireless communications services to SO's five utility subsidiaries, as well as to the general public within the Southeast; and Southern Nuclear, which provides services to SO's nuclear power plants.

In June 2002, the company formed Southern Company GAS, a wholly owned unit that began operation in August 2002 as a retail gas marketer in Georgia. In July 2002, the unit acquired for about $60 million from The New Power Company (out of bankruptcy) 210,000 Georgia retail gas customers.

In April 2001, SO completed the spinoff of its remaining interest in Mirant Corp. (NYSE: MIR). In October 2000, it had completed an IPO of 19.7% of its Southern Energy subsidiary (renamed Mirant in January 2001), a global independent power producer with energy marketing and risk management businesses. Gross proceeds to SO from the IPO were $1.47 billion.

Company Financials Fiscal Year ending December 31

Per Share Data ($)

(Year Ended December 31)	2003	2002	2001	2000	1999	1998	1997	1996	1995	1994
Tangible Bk. Val.	12.92	11.56	10.87	15.12	6.14	8.77	10.52	12.49	11.99	12.46
Earnings	2.02	1.85	1.61	1.52	1.86	1.40	1.42	1.68	1.66	1.52
S&P Core Earnings	1.85	1.35	1.12	NA	NA	NA	NA	NA	NA	NA
Dividends	1.39	1.35	1.34	1.34	1.34	1.34	1.30	1.26	1.22	1.18
Payout Ratio	69%	74%	83%	88%	72%	96%	92%	75%	73%	78%
Prices - High	32.00	31.14	35.72	35.00	29.62	31.56	26.25	25.87	25.00	22.06
- Low	27.00	23.22	20.89	20.37	22.06	23.93	19.87	21.12	19.37	17.00
P/E Ratio - High	16	17	22	23	16	23	18	15	15	15
- Low	13	13	13	13	12	17	14	13	12	11

Income Statement Analysis (Million $)

	2003	2002	2001	2000	1999	1998	1997	1996	1995	1994
Revs.	11,251	10,549	10,155	10,066	11,585	11,403	12,611	10,358	9,180	8,297
Depr.	1,027	1,047	1,173	1,171	1,307	1,539	1,246	996	904	821
Maint.	937	961	909	852	945	887	763	782	683	660
Fxd. Chgs. Cov.	4.21	3.80	3.25	2.87	2.71	2.63	2.68	3.77	3.31	3.28
Constr. Credits	25.0	22.0	NA	NA	NA	NA	20.0	23.0	25.0	29.0
Eff. Tax Rate	29.3%	28.6%	33.3%	37.2%	33.2%	38.8%	42.7%	39.9%	39.2%	38.9%
Net Inc.	1,474	1,318	1,119	994	1,276	977	972	1,127	1,103	989
S&P Core Earnings	1,351	964	776	NA	NA	NA	NA	NA	NA	NA

Balance Sheet & Other Fin. Data (Million $)

	2003	2002	2001	2000	1999	1998	1997	1996	1995	1994
Gross Prop.	43,722	41,764	38,104	35,972	38,620	37,363	34,044	34,190	33,093	30,694
Cap. Exp.	2,002	2,717	2,617	2,225	2,560	2,005	1,859	1,229	1,401	1,536
Net Prop.	29,418	26,315	23,084	21,622	24,544	24,124	22,110	23,269	23,026	21,117
Capitalization:										
LT Debt	10,587	8,956	10,941	10,457	14,443	13,020	10,274	7,935	8,306	7,593
% LT Debt	52.3	50.7	57.8	49.4	60.8	57.1	46.3	42.7	44.9	44.1
Pfd.	Nil	Nil	Nil	Nil	Nil	Nil	2,237	1,402	1,432	1,432
% Pfd.	Nil	Nil	Nil	Nil	Nil	Nil	10.0	7.60	7.70	8.30
Common	9,648	8,710	7,984	10,690	9,296	9,797	9,647	9,216	8,772	8,186
% Common	47.7	49.3	42.2	50.6	39.2	42.9	43.5	49.7	47.4	47.6
Total Cap.	25,809	22,937	24,147	26,436	29,662	24,790	27,997	24,454	24,877	23,063
% Oper. Ratio	79.7	80.5	81.9	82.0	81.7	82.6	84.6	82.1	79.5	79.3
% Earn. on Net Prop.	10.0	10.1	10.7	11.4	8.5	7.3	8.6	8.0	8.5	8.3
% Return On Revs.	13.1	12.5	11.0	9.9	11.0	8.6	7.7	10.9	12.0	11.9
% Return On Invest. Capital	8.9	8.5	7.4	7.3	9.6	13.8	10.4	7.9	7.9	7.6
% Return On Com. Equity	16.1	15.8	12.0	10.0	13.4	10.0	10.3	12.5	13.0	12.5

Data as orig reptd.; bef. results of disc opers/spec. items. Per share data adj. for stk. divs.; EPS diluted. E-Estimated. NA-Not Available. NM-Not Meaningful. NR-Not Ranked. UR-Under Review.

Office: 270 Peachtree Street, N.W., Atlanta, GA 30303.
Telephone: 404-506-5000.
Email: investors@southerncompany.com
Website: http://www.southernco.com
Chrmn & CEO: D. Ratcliffe.
EVP, CFO & Treas: T.A. Fanning.

EVP & General Counsel: G.E. Holland Jr.
Investor Contact: G. Kundert 404-506-5135.
Investor Contact: J. Stewart 404-506-0747.
Dirs: D. P. Amos, D. J. Bern, F. S. Blake, T. F. Chapman, B. S. Gordon, D. M. James, Z. T. Pate, J. N. Purcell, D. M. Ratcliffe, G. J. St. Pe.

Founded: in 1945.
Domicile: Delaware.
Employees: 25,762.
S&P Analyst: Justin McCann/PMW/BK

Southwest Airlines

Recommendation: BUY ★★★★ ☆
SELL SELL HOLD BUY BUY

12-Month Target Price: **$20.00**
(as of November 11, 2004)

LUV has an approximate 0.11% weighting in the **S&P 500**

Sector: Industrials
Sub-Industry: Airlines
Peer Group: Airlines (U.S.) - Major

Summary: LUV, the sixth largest U.S. airline, offers discounted fares, primarily for short-haul, point-to-point flights.

Quantitative Evaluations

Price as of 11/12/04:	**$16**	2004E S&P Core EPS:	**$0.39**

S&P Earnings & Dividend Rank: A

D	C	B-	B	B+	A-	**A**	A+

S&P Fair Value Rank: 2+

1	**2**	3	4	5
Lowest				Highest

Fair Value Calc.: $14.60 (Slightly Overvalued)

S&P Investability Quotient Percentile

92%

LUV scored higher than 92% of all companies for which an S&P Report is available.

Volatility: Average

Low	**Average**	High

Technical Evaluation: Bullish
Since 10/04, the technical indicators for LUV have been Bullish.

Relative Strength Rank: Moderate

67

1 Lowest	Highest 99

GAAP Earnings vs. Previous Year
▲ Up ▼ Down ► No Change

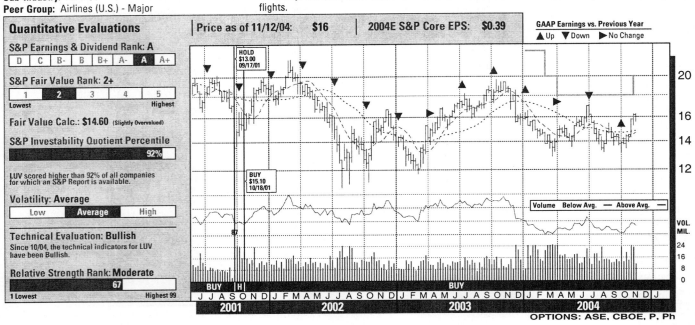

Analyst commentary prepared by Jim Corridore/DC/JWP

OPTIONS: ASE, CBOE, P, Ph

Highlights November 15, 2004

- We look for 2005 revenues to grow about 12%, reflecting our expectations that LUV will add about 10% to capacity and that modestly improving industry demand should lead to slightly higher load factors and average airfares. We are seeing some signs of a modest rise in travel demand in peak seasonal periods. However, revenue, booking and pricing trends have not been strong in non-peak periods. We think LUV plans to increase the number of flights it has out of Chicago Midway, which we believe is an attempt to take advantage of the bankruptcy of ATA Holdings, parent of ATA Airlines, the tenth largest airline in the U.S. LUV is also likely to add at least one new city in 2005, in our view.

- We see margins as likely to widen, with increased revenue yields and cost savings from closing some reservation centers outweighing higher expected labor, fuel and maintenance costs, as well as increased promotion and other costs to add Philadelphia as a new market. Although the company is 80% hedged on oil prices in 2005 at a price of $25 a barrel, LUV is exposed to rising oil prices on the remaining 20% of its fuel requirements.

- We estimate 2005 EPS of $0.65, up 44% from the $0.45 we are forecasting for 2004. On a Standard & Poor's Core Earnings basis, we project 2005 EPS of $0.59. LUV has no defined benefit pension plan, but tends to use stock options to compensate employees more liberally than other airlines. We see stock option expense deducting about $0.06 from EPS in 2005.

Investment Rationale/Risk November 15, 2004

- We have a buy recommendation on LUV, reflecting our belief that it is the financially strongest, and operationally best positioned U.S. airline, as well as our expectations of increased investor interest in the sector if industry conditions improve. The company has posted 31 consecutive years of profitable operations, and we see the quality of those earnings as very high, since LUV has no pension issues. In our view, the company has ample cash, and its debt to total capitalization is significantly below peer levels. We think these measures warrant a premium valuation to the S&P 500. We believe the stock should also benefit from LUV's strong oil hedge position, somewhat insulating the shares from current high oil prices.

- Risks to our recommendation and target price include the possibility that one or more of the other low cost carriers enters into a market share war with LUV. In addition, although the company is the best hedged among U.S. airlines, in our view, continued high oil prices could drive investor sentiment away from airline stocks, even with LUV's strong hedge position relative to the rest of the industry.

- We think the stock will see some P/E multiple expansion over the next 12 months. Our 12-month target price of $20 is equal to about 31X our 2005 EPS estimate of $0.65, in the middle of LUV's five-year historical P/E range. We expect the shares to remain volatile due to difficult industry conditions and fluctuating oil prices.

Key Stock Statistics

S&P Core EPS 2005E	0.59	52-week Range	**$18.70-12.88**
S&P Oper. EPS 2004E	0.45	12 Month P/E	40.0
P/E on S&P Oper. EPS 2004E	35.6	Beta	0.85
S&P Oper. EPS 2005E	0.65	Shareholders	12,114
Yield (%)	0.1%	Market Cap (B)	$ 12.5
Dividend Rate/Share	0.02	Shares Outstanding (M)	779.6

Value of $10,000 invested five years ago: **$ 14,143**

Dividend Data Dividends have been paid since 1976

Amount ($)	Date Decl.	Ex-Div. Date	Stock of Record	Payment Date
0.005	Nov. 21	Dec. 03	Dec. 05	Jan. 06 '04
0.005	Jan. 15	Mar. 02	Mar. 04	Mar. 25 '04
0.005	May. 19	Jun. 08	Jun. 10	Jun. 30 '04
0.005	Jul. 15	Aug. 31	Sep. 02	Sep. 23 '04

Revenues/Earnings Data Fiscal year ending December 31

Revenues (Million $)

	2004	2003	2002	2001	2000	1999
1Q	1,484	1,351	1,257	1,429	1,243	1,076
2Q	1,716	1,515	1,473	1,554	1,461	1,220
3Q	1,674	1,553	1,391	1,335	1,479	1,235
4Q	—	1,517	1,401	1,238	1,467	1,204
Yr.	—	5,937	5,522	5,555	5,650	4,736

Earnings Per Share ($)

	2004	2003	2002	2001	2000	1999
1Q	0.03	0.03	0.03	0.15	0.12	0.12
2Q	0.14	0.30	0.13	0.22	0.24	0.19
3Q	0.15	0.13	0.09	0.19	0.23	0.16
4Q	E0.13	0.08	0.05	0.08	0.19	0.12
Yr.	E0.45	0.54	0.30	0.63	0.79	0.59

Next earnings report expected: late-January Source: S&P, Company Reports
EPS Estimates based on S&P Operating Earnings; historical GAAP earnings are as reported.

Southwest Airlines Co.

Recommendation: **BUY** ★★★★☆   12-Month Target Price: **$20.00** (as of November 11, 2004)

Business Summary November 15, 2004

Southwest Airlines was the sixth largest U.S. airline in 2003, based on revenue passenger miles. At December 31, 2003, it served 59 airports in 58 cities in 30 states. LUV specializes in low fare, point-to-point, short-haul, high-frequency service. Since 1993, it has concentrated its expansion program on markets in the East. Although 80% of its work force belongs to unions, the company believes that it has generally enjoyed harmonious labor relations. LUV began service to Philadelphia in May 2004.

The company primarily offers short-haul flights that require no connections through a hub. The average flight length in 2003 was 558 miles, with an average duration of about 1.5 hours; about 79% of customers fly nonstop. By eschewing the hub-and-spoke structure favored by other major airlines, avoiding interlining, feeder services and congested airports, LUV has been able to keep aircraft turnaround times low. In addition, by serving mainly short-haul markets, the company believes it holds down food costs, as well as ground service that keeps aircraft out of service and requires leasing more airport gate space. In 2003, the average aircraft turnaround time was about 25 minutes.

LUV's strategy to control costs includes flying only one aircraft type, simplifying scheduling, maintenance and pilot training. At the end of 2003, the company operated 388 Boeing 737s; the average age of the fleet was 9.6 years. In June 2000, LUV placed the largest order in its history, for 94 Boeing 737-700s, with a list price of $4.5 billion, to be delivered between 2002 and 2007. After the September

11 terrorist attacks, the company deferred delivery of 19 aircraft to help stabilize cash flow. For 2004, it had firm orders to take delivery of 47 aircraft.

The company has one of the industry's lowest cost structures; it spent $0.0760 per seat-mile in 2003, up from $0.0741 in 2002. Savings are realized by offering only unrestricted coach seats, with no assigned seating, reducing ticketing costs. In addition, LUV books over 85% of customers electronically. Since 1996, it has let passengers book flights through its Web site; about 54% of 2003 passenger revenues were obtained this way. Despite its low costs, the company delivers consistently high levels of service, and ranks high in on-time performance, baggage handling, and customer satisfaction as tracked by the Department of Transportation.

About 80% of employees are covered by collective bargaining agreements. LUV is negotiating with its flight attendants union. In May 2002, the company gave pilots a pay raise and contract extension to September 2006, although the current contract was not amendable until 2004.

In 2003, the company announced that it would add blended winglets to its fleet of 737-700 aircraft, retrofitting these planes through 2005. The addition of the wing enhancements should extend the range of the planes, save fuel, lower engine maintenance costs, and reduce takeoff noise. In November 2003, LUV announced the consolidation of nine reservation centers into six, effective February 28, 2004.

Company Financials Fiscal Year ending December 31

Per Share Data ($)

(Year Ended December 31)	2003	2002	2001	2000	1999	1998	1997	1996	1995	1994
Tangible Bk. Val.	6.40	5.69	5.23	4.57	3.79	3.21	2.69	2.24	1.95	1.71
Cash Flow	1.00	0.74	1.03	1.14	0.90	0.83	0.67	0.51	0.45	0.45
Earnings	0.54	0.30	0.63	0.79	0.59	0.55	0.41	0.27	0.24	0.24
S&P Core Earnings	0.48	0.23	0.61	NA	NA	NA	NA	NA	NA	NA
Dividends	0.02	0.02	0.01	0.01	0.01	0.01	0.01	0.01	0.01	0.01
Payout Ratio	3%	6%	2%	1%	2%	2%	2%	3%	3%	3%
Prices - High	19.69	22.00	23.32	23.32	15.72	10.55	7.77	6.56	5.90	7.70
- Low	11.72	10.90	11.25	10.00	9.58	6.80	4.19	4.07	3.23	3.06
P/E Ratio - High	36	73	37	30	26	19	19	24	24	32
- Low	22	36	18	13	16	12	10	15	13	13

Income Statement Analysis (Million $)

	2003	2002	2001	2000	1999	1998	1997	1996	1995	1994
Revs.	5,937	5,522	5,555	5,650	4,736	4,164	3,817	3,406	2,873	2,592
Oper. Inc.	867	774	949	1,302	1,030	909	720	534	470	470
Depr.	384	356	318	281	249	225	196	183	157	153
Int. Exp.	58.0	89.3	49.3	42.3	22.9	30.7	43.7	59.3	58.8	53.4
Pretax Inc.	708	393	828	1,017	774	705	517	341	305	300
Eff. Tax Rate	37.6%	38.6%	38.2%	38.5%	38.7%	38.5%	38.5%	39.3%	40.2%	40.1%
Net Inc.	442	241	511	625	474	433	318	207	183	179
S&P Core Earnings	385	188	486	NA	NA	NA	NA	NA	NA	NA

Balance Sheet & Other Fin. Data (Million $)

	2003	2002	2001	2000	1999	1998	1997	1996	1995	1994
Cash	1,865	1,815	2,280	523	419	379	623	582	317	175
Curr. Assets	2,313	2,232	2,520	832	631	574	806	751	473	315
Total Assets	9,878	8,954	8,997	6,670	5,652	4,716	4,246	3,723	3,256	2,823
Curr. Liab.	172	1,434	2,239	1,298	960	851	869	765	611	522
LT Debt	1,332	1,553	1,327	761	872	623	628	650	661	583
Common Equity	5,052	4,422	4,014	3,451	2,836	2,398	2,009	1,648	1,427	1,239
Total Cap.	7,804	7,202	6,399	5,065	4,400	3,570	3,076	2,749	2,370	2,055
Cap. Exp.	1,238	603	998	1,135	1,168	947	689	677	729	789
Cash Flow	826	597	829	907	723	659	513	391	339	333
Curr. Ratio	13.4	1.6	1.1	0.6	0.7	0.7	0.9	1.0	0.8	0.6
% LT Debt of Cap.	17.1	21.6	20.7	15.0	19.8	17.5	20.4	24.5	27.9	28.4
% Net Inc.of Revs.	7.4	4.4	9.2	11.1	10.0	10.4	8.3	6.1	6.4	6.9
% Ret. on Assets	4.7	2.7	6.5	10.1	9.2	9.7	8.0	5.9	6.0	6.6
% Ret. on Equity	9.3	5.7	13.7	19.9	18.1	19.7	17.4	13.5	13.7	15.6

Data as orig reptd.; bef. results of disc opers/spec. items. Per share data adj. for stk. divs.; EPS diluted. E-Estimated. NA-Not Available. NM-Not Meaningful. NR-Not Ranked. UR-Under Review.

Office: P.O. Box 36611, Dallas, TX 75235-1611.
Telephone: 214-792-4000.
Website: http://www.southwest.com
Chrmn: H. D. Kelleher.
Vice Chrmn & CEO: G. C. Kelly.
Pres, Secy & COO: C. C. Barrett.

VP & CFO: L. Wright.
Investor Contact: Tammy Romo (214-792-4415).
Dirs: C. C. Barrett, L. Caldera, C. W. Crockett, W. H. Cunningham, W. P. Hobby, T. C. Johnson, H. D. Kelleher, G. Kelly, R. W. King, N. Loeffler, J. T. Montford, J. M. Morris.

Founded: in 1967.
Domicile: Texas.
Employees: 32,847.
S&P Analyst: Jim Corridore/DC/JWP

Sovereign Bancorp

Recommendation: **BUY** ★★★★☆   12-Month Target Price: **$24.00**
(as of July 21, 2004)

SOV has an approximate 0.07% weighting in the **S&P 500**

Sector: Financials
Sub-Industry: Thrifts & Mortgage Finance
Peer Group: Major Savings & Loan Companies

Summary: This $56 billion bank holding company has branches in Pennsylvania, New Jersey, Connecticut, New Hampshire, Rhode Island, Massachusetts, and New York.

Quantitative Evaluations

S&P Earnings & Dividend Rank: B+

D	C	B-	B	B+	A-	A	A+

S&P Fair Value Rank: 3-

1	2	3	4	5
Lowest				Highest

Fair Value Calc.: $21.50 (Slightly Overvalued)

S&P Investability Quotient Percentile

97%

SOV scored higher than 97% of all companies for which an S&P Report is available.

Volatility: Low

Low	Average	High

Technical Evaluation: Neutral
Since 11/04, the technical indicators for SOV have been Neutral.

Relative Strength Rank: Moderate

45

1 Lowest   Highest 99

	Price as of 11/12/04:	**$22.45**	2004E S&P Core EPS:	**$1.35**

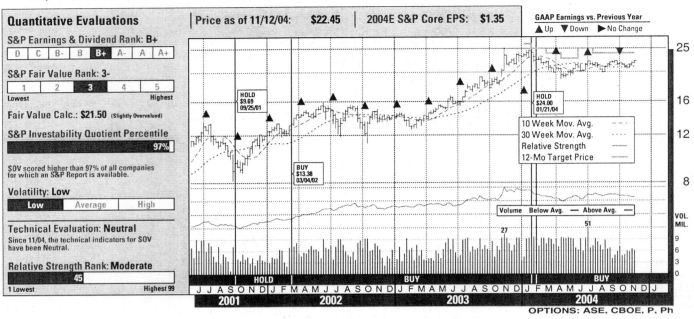

GAAP Earnings vs. Previous Year
▲ Up   ▼ Down   ▶ No Change

- 10 Week Mov. Avg.
- 30 Week Mov. Avg.
- Relative Strength
- 12-Mo Target Price

OPTIONS: ASE, CBOE, P, Ph

Analyst commentary prepared by Erik J. Eisenstein/CB/BK

Highlights November 03, 2004

- We see average earning assets growing 26% in 2005, on projected improvement in commercial credit demand, the full-year effect of the July 2004 acquisition of Seacoast Financial Services Corp., and the expected acquisition of Waypoint Financial early in the coming year, subject to required approvals. We see the net interest margin benefiting from higher short-term interest rates, and estimate that net interest income will increase 32%. We expect a 37% reduction in loan loss provisions, reflecting projected economic improvement.

- We see noninterest income up 15%, despite lower projected mortgage banking income and gains on securities sales, on higher consumer and commercial banking fees. General and administrative expenses should rise 22%, a bit slower than asset growth, due to expected improved operating efficiency and reduced mortgage originations.

- We estimate 2005 EPS of $1.94, up 15% from $1.69 seen in 2004, excluding acquisition-related charges and a 2004 third quarter charge of $0.13 for early extinguishment of debt.

Investment Rationale/Risk November 03, 2004

- We would accumulate the shares. We view SOV as likely to fundamentally outperform regional banking peers in coming years. We see above-average growth potential in the company's retail and commercial banking businesses, as well as its New England franchise, which we think will be bolstered by the acquisitions of First Essex and Seacoast Financial. We also have confidence in the company's ability to effectively integrate recent and planned acquisitions, informed by its track record. We project annual EPS growth of 10% for the five years beyond 2005, above the peer rate of 9%.

- Risks to our recommendation and target price include interest rate risk, in particular the risk that the short-term interest rate increases we anticipate will not fully materialize, resulting in a narrower than expected net interest margin. Risks also include execution risk associated with integrating recent and planned acquisitions.

- Our 12-month target price of $24 is derived by applying a P/E to growth (PEG) ratio of 1.25X, in line with peer levels, to our 2005 EPS and five-year EPS growth estimates.

Key Stock Statistics

S&P Core EPS 2005E	1.90	52-week Range	$24.75-19.31	
S&P Oper. EPS 2004E	1.69	12 Month P/E	16.5	
P/E on S&P Oper. EPS 2004E	13.3	Beta	0.91	
S&P Oper. EPS 2005E	1.94	Shareholders	18,359	
Yield (%)	0.5%	Market Cap (B)	$ 7.7	
Dividend Rate/Share	0.12	Shares Outstanding (M)	343.3	

Value of $10,000 invested five years ago: **$ 28,093**

Dividend Data Dividends have been paid since 1987

Amount ($)	Date Decl.	Ex-Div. Date	Stock of Record	Payment Date
0.025	Dec. 18	Jan. 29	Feb. 02	Feb. 17 '04
0.030	Mar. 24	Apr. 29	May. 03	May. 17 '04
0.030	Jun. 24	Jul. 29	Aug. 02	Aug. 16 '04
0.030	Sep. 23	Oct. 28	Nov. 01	Nov. 15 '04

Revenues/Earnings Data Fiscal year ending December 31

Revenues (Million $)

	2004	2003	2002	2001	2000	1999
1Q	627.6	621.5	602.4	687.9	493.1	400.3
2Q	639.7	621.5	622.1	681.8	545.9	410.7
3Q	714.1	601.8	634.5	665.5	649.3	450.9
4Q	—	607.2	633.1	613.3	690.0	475.7
Yr.	—	2,452	2,492	2,649	2,378	1,738

Earnings Per Share ($)

	2004	2003	2002	2001	2000	1999
1Q	0.33	0.27	0.25	0.05	0.12	0.28
2Q	0.42	0.37	0.32	0.12	-0.22	0.30
3Q	0.24	0.37	0.33	0.03	-0.07	0.31
4Q	E0.45	0.38	0.33	0.30	-0.01	0.14
Yr.	E1.69	1.38	1.23	0.48	-0.18	1.01

Next earnings report expected: late-January Source: S&P, Company Reports
EPS Estimates based on S&P Operating Earnings; historical GAAP earnings are as reported.

Sovereign Bancorp Inc.

Recommendation: **BUY** ★★★★☆ 12-Month Target Price: **$24.00** (as of July 21, 2004)

Business Summary November 04, 2004

Sovereign Bancorp, once a small thrift, has grown into a large banking franchise, largely via acquisitions. From 1990 through October 2004, SOV had acquired 24 financial institutions, branch networks and/or related businesses. Of these acquisitions, 16, with assets totaling $26 million, were completed since 1995. As of September 2004, the company had $56 billion in assets, and about 535 banking offices, in Connecticut, Massachusetts, New Hampshire, New Jersey, New York, Pennsylvania, and Rhode Island. Pro forma of pending acquisitions (subject to necessary approvals), SOV was one of the 20 largest banking institutions in the U.S.

In May 2004, SOV said it believed excess capital generation, improving credit quality, and an asset sensitive asset/liability profile would drive double-digit earnings growth though 2007. The company expected this growth to be aided by continued operating and tax efficiency, and by manageable levels of growth for loans, deposits and fee revenue. SOV's EPS goals of $1.90 to $2.00 for 2005, $2.10 to at least $2.20 for 2006, and at least $2.40 for 2007, imply 10% to 15% annual growth in earnings.

At December 31, 2003, total loans of $26.1 billion were 19% residential real estate loans, 42% commercial loans, and 38% consumer loans (mostly home equity and auto loans).

At December 31, 2003, deposits totaling $27.3 billion consisted of 16% demand accounts, 22% NOW accounts, 4% customer repurchase agreements, 11% savings accounts, 25% money markets, and 22% CDs.

The allowance for loan losses at December 31, 2003, was $327.9 million (equal to 148.7% of total nonperforming assets), up from $298.8 million (116.2%) a year earlier. Net chargeoffs in 2003 totaled $132.8 million (0.55% of average total loans), compared to $127.3 million (0.58%) in 2002. Nonperforming assets totaled $220.4 million (0.51% of total assets) at December 31, 2003, versus $257.1 million (0.65%).

In July 2004, the company acquired Massachusetts-based Seacoast Financial Services Corp. (FESX), the operator of CompassBank and Nantucket Bank, with $5.3 billion in assets, in exchange for stock valued at $1.1 billion.

In February 2004, SOV acquired Massachusetts-based First Essex Bancorp (FESX), with $1.7 billion in assets, and 20 offices in Massachusetts and New Hampshire, for $418 million in cash and common stock.

In March 2004, the company agreed to acquire Waypoint Financial Corp. (WYPT), with $5.3 billion in assets, and 65 banking offices, in Pennsylvania and Maryland. The transaction, valued at $980 million in cash and common stock, is expected to be completed in early 2005, subject to shareholder and regulatory approval.

In May 2003, directors authorized the repurchase of up to 5 million company common shares. After repurchasing 100,000 shares under this program, in October 2004, directors authorized the repurchase of an additional 15.5 million outstanding shares.

Company Financials Fiscal Year ending December 31

Per Share Data ($)

(Year Ended December 31)	2003	2002	2001	2000	1999	1998	1997	1996	1995	1994
Tangible Bk. Val.	6.62	5.27	3.40	2.14	6.03	4.74	5.02	3.75	2.93	3.31
Earnings	1.38	1.23	0.48	-0.18	1.01	0.85	0.63	0.60	0.69	0.63
S&P Core Earnings	1.38	1.21	0.40	NA	NA	NA	NA	NA	NA	NA
Dividends	0.10	0.10	0.10	0.10	0.10	0.07	0.07	0.06	0.06	0.06
Payout Ratio	7%	8%	21%	NM	9%	9%	11%	10%	9%	9%
Prices - High	25.20	15.90	13.50	9.96	26.25	22.75	18.43	9.63	7.20	7.63
- Low	12.60	11.20	7.15	6.25	7.00	8.75	8.94	6.36	4.86	4.86
P/E Ratio - High	18	13	28	NM	26	27	29	16	10	12
- Low	9	9	15	NM	7	10	14	11	7	8

Income Statement Analysis (Million $)

	2003	2002	2001	2000	1999	1998	1997	1996	1995	1994
Net Int. Inc.	1,206	1,160	1,054	855	615	494	341	217	174	155
Loan Loss Prov.	162	147	97.1	56.5	30.0	28.0	37.2	2.50	1.00	4.10
Non Int. Inc.	456	381	411	230	130	106	38.5	26.7	25.8	14.6
Non Int. Exp.	968	979	1,175	1,013	446	360	212	158	113	91.0
Pretax Inc.	598	467	209	-106	269	211	130	83.0	85.9	74.9
Eff. Tax Rate	25.6%	26.7%	12.7%	NM	33.3%	35.4%	40.3%	38.0%	34.4%	38.0%
Net Inc.	402	342	123	-41.0	179	136	77.6	51.5	56.4	46.4
% Net Int. Marg.	3.42	3.61	3.57	3.19	2.86	2.56	2.68	2.59	2.54	2.96
S&P Core Earnings	401	336	101	NA	NA	NA	NA	NA	NA	NA

Balance Sheet & Other Fin. Data (Million $)

	2003	2002	2001	2000	1999	1998	1997	1996	1995	1994
Total Assets	43,505	39,524	35,475	33,458	26,607	21,914	14,336	9,433	8,078	6,564
Loans	25,821	22,829	20,135	21,656	14,094	11,152	9,833	9,096	7,712	4,359
Deposits	27,344	26,785	23,298	24,499	11,720	12,323	7,890	5,052	5,039	4,027
Capitalization:										
Debt	12,124	6,240	6,869	5,367	316	4,108	858	1,092	1,018	440
Equity	3,260	2,764	2,202	1,949	1,821	1,204	682	376	327	304
Total	15,587	9,205	2,202	7,315	2,138	5,312	1,733	1,568	1,445	744
% Ret. on Assets	1.0	0.9	0.4	NM	19.2	82.7	12.6	5.5	16.9	0.8
% Ret. on Equity	13.3	13.8	5.9	NM	11.9	13.8	13.5	12.9	NA	16.5
% Loan Loss Resv.	1.3	1.3	1.3	1.2	-0.9	1.2	0.9	0.4	0.5	0.8
% Risk Based Capital	12.1	7.5	10.7	10.3	14.9	10.3	12.2	15.1	12.6	12.7
Price Times Book Value:										
Hi	3.8	3.0	2.9	4.6	4.4	4.8	4.4	2.0	1.7	2.3
Low	1.9	2.1	1.8	2.9	1.2	1.9	2.1	1.3	1.1	1.5

Data as orig reptd.; bef. results of disc opers/spec. items. Per share data adj. for stk. divs.; EPS diluted. E-Estimated. NA-Not Available. NM-Not Meaningful. NR-Not Ranked. UR-Under Review.

Office: 1500 Market St, Philadelphia, PA 19102-2100.
Telephone: 215-557-4630.
Email: investor@sovereignbank.com
Website: http://www.sovereignbank.com
Chrmn, Pres & CEO: J.S. Sidhu.

EVP & CFO: J.D. Hogan.
SVP & Chief Acctg Officer: L.E. McAlee, Jr.
SVP & Investor Contact: T. Barnhart 610-208-8681.
Dirs: K. G. Champagne, P. M. Ehlerman, R. V. Gilbane, B. Hard, A. C. Hove, Jr., D. K. Rothermel, J. S. Sidhu, C. C. Troilo, Sr.

Founded: in 1984.
Domicile: Pennsylvania.
Employees: 8,106.
S&P Analyst: Erik J. Eisenstein/CB/BK

STANDARD
&POOR'S

Sprint Corp.

Recommendation: **HOLD** ★★★☆☆
SELL SELL HOLD BUY BUY

12-Month Target Price: **$21.00**
(as of October 15, 2004)

FON has an approximate 0.29% weighting in the **S&P 500**

Sector: Telecommunication Services
Sub-Industry: Integrated Telecommunication Services
Peer Group: Telecommunications (Long Distance)

Summary: Sprint, which offers local, long-distance and wireless services, recombined its tracking stocks in April 2004.

Quantitative Evaluations

S&P Earnings & Dividend Rank: B+

| D | C | B- | B | B+ | A- | A | A+ |

S&P Fair Value Rank: 1-

| 1 | 2 | 3 | 4 | 5 |
| Lowest | | | | Highest |

Fair Value Calc.: $16.30 (Overvalued)

S&P Investability Quotient Percentile

89%

FON scored higher than 89% of all companies for which an S&P Report is available.

Volatility: Average

| Low | Average | High |

Technical Evaluation: Bullish
Since 7/04, the technical indicators for FON have been Bullish.

Relative Strength Rank: Strong

76

| 1 Lowest | | Highest 99 |

Price as of 11/12/04: **$22.35**   **2004E S&P Core EPS:** **$0.62**

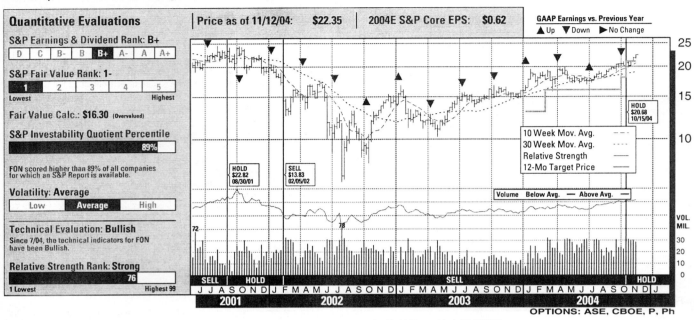

GAAP Earnings vs. Previous Year ▲ Up ▼ Down ▶ No Change

HOLD $22.82 08/30/01

SELL $13.83 02/05/02

HOLD $20.68 10/15/04

10 Week Mov. Avg.
30 Week Mov. Avg.
Relative Strength
12-Mo Target Price

Volume Below Avg. — Above Avg.

VOL. MIL.

SELL | HOLD | SELL | HOLD

J J A S O N D | J F M A M J J A S O N D | J F M A M J J A S O N D | J F M A M J J A S O N D | J
2001   2002   2003   2004

OPTIONS: ASE, CBOE, P, Ph

Analyst commentary prepared by Todd Rosenbluth/PMW/BK

Highlights October 20, 2004

- Combining Sprint PCS with Sprint's traditional wireline operations, we see FON's revenues up about 3% in 2004. We expect wireless operations to grow 14%, aided by higher penetration of the company's Vision data offering and a pickup in wholesale subscribers. For 2005, we project revenue growth of 2%, with wireless data growth outweighing wireline pressures that we see due to wireless substitution and increased competition from the Bells and from long-distance and cable carriers.

- We expect total 2005 EBITDA margins to widen to 30%, from 29% that we project for 2004, as increased wireless minutes of use and workforce reductions outweigh expected higher advertising expenses. Depreciation charges should decline significantly, as capital spending is cut from earlier levels and a long-distance network writedown occurs. We also see lower interest expense.

- We see 2004 operating EPS of $0.92 for the combined FON, and project $1.24 for 2005. Our 2004 Standard & Poor's Core EPS projection is $0.62, reflecting estimated stock option expense and pension adjustments. We see 2005 S&P Core Earnings of $0.88.

Investment Rationale/Risk October 20, 2004

- Following third quarter results, we still see challenges in long-distance and local operations from pricing pressure and substitution, but we believe results will continue to be aided by modest revenue per household growth in local operations and by wireless gains. We believe Sprint's revenues and net subscriber count will benefit from pending merger activity among national wireless carriers, and from wholesale relationships. We think that the company's business mix will continue to shift away from weak long-distance operations, and toward what we see as higher growth wireless activity.

- Risks to our opinion and target price include regulatory changes that affect either wireless or local wireline operations, weaker demand for telecom services, and decreased wholesale wireless traffic.

- The shares trade above the level of wireline peers on a P/E multiple basis. However, we believe the premium is justified, in light of what we see as FON's stronger earnings growth prospects. Our 12-month target price of $21 assumes that the shares will trade at a slight discount to Baby Bell peers on a forward enterprise value/EBITDA basis. The shares also offer a dividend yield of about 2.5%. We would hold existing positions.

Key Stock Statistics

S&P Core EPS 2005E	0.88	52-week Range	$22.35-14.72
S&P Oper. EPS 2004E	0.92	12 Month P/E	NM
P/E on S&P Oper. EPS 2004E	24.3	Beta	1.33
S&P Oper. EPS 2005E	1.24	Shareholders	62,000
Yield (%)	2.2%	Market Cap (B)	$ 32.5
Dividend Rate/Share	0.50	Shares Outstanding (M)	1452.6

Value of $10,000 invested five years ago: **$ 3,377**

Dividend Data Dividends have been paid since 1939

Amount ($)	Date Decl.	Ex-Div. Date	Stock of Record	Payment Date
0.125	Feb. 11	Mar. 08	Mar. 10	Mar. 31 '04
0.125	Apr. 20	Jun. 07	Jun. 09	Jun. 30 '04
0.125	Aug. 10	Sep. 07	Sep. 09	Sep. 30 '04
0.125	Oct. 11	Dec. 07	Dec. 09	Dec. 30 '04

Revenues/Earnings Data Fiscal year ending December 31

Revenues (Million $)

	2004	2003	2002	2001	2000	1999
1Q	67.07	3,581	4,029	4,358	4,404	4,172
2Q	6,869	3,530	3,965	4,310	4,446	4,244
3Q	6,922	3,538	3,805	4,244	4,444	4,341
4Q	—	3,536	3,659	4,012	4,394	4,407
Yr.	—	14,185	15,182	16,924	17,688	17,160

Earnings Per Share ($)

	2004	2003	2002	2001	2000	1999
1Q	0.15	0.31	0.32	0.36	0.50	0.47
2Q	0.16	0.10	0.12	0.33	0.41	0.44
3Q	-1.32	-0.48	0.54	0.18	0.43	0.41
4Q	E0.32	0.40	0.28	-1.02	0.11	0.49
Yr.	E0.92	0.33	1.18	-0.16	1.45	1.97

Next earnings report expected: early-February Source: S&P, Company Reports
EPS Estimates based on S&P Operating Earnings; historical GAAP earnings are as reported.

STANDARD
&POOR'S

Sprint Corporation

Stock Report
November 13, 2004
NYSE Symbol: **FON**

Recommendation: **HOLD** ★ ★ ★ ☆ ☆   12-Month Target Price: **$21.00** (as of October 15, 2004)

Business Summary October 20, 2004

On April 23, 2004, Sprint Corp. recombined its tracking stocks into a single class of stock. Each PCS share was converted into 0.50 of an FON share. The company's Sprint PCS wireless business contributed 47% of 2003 revenues, while the wireline segment was split between the Local Telephone (23% of 2003 revenue) and Global Markets (30%) divisions.

As of September 2004, the PCS Group provided nationwide service to 23.2 million subscribers (up from 20.3 million at the end of 2003) by providing its own digital network, expanding its wholesale business with Virgin Mobile, affiliating with other companies mainly in and around smaller cities, roaming on other providers' analog cellular networks using multi-mode handsets, and roaming on other providers' digital networks that use code division multiple access (CDMA) technology. Direct customers comprised of 75% of Sprint's customer base, with the remaining customers split between affiliate and wholesale providers. In August 2003, Sprint and Qwest Communications signed a wholesale agreement for PCS to serve as the exclusive third-party provider of wireless services for Qwest, including the PCS Vision offering of advanced wireless data services. Qwest will continue to provide sales and service support to all its wireless customers, including the promotion and sale of handsets, price plans and data services and customer service.

The Local Telephone division (LTD) is the largest independent U.S. incumbent local exchange carrier (ILEC). LTD consists mainly of regulated local phone

companies serving about 7.7 million access lines as of September 2004 in 18 states, including Florida, Ohio and Texas. In addition to traditional ILEC customer services, the unit earns revenue from access charges paid by other carriers for access to FON's local network and consumer long-distance services in the LTD service territory. As of September 2003, Sprint was also offering DSL service to 432,000 customers.

Beginning in 2000, FON combined its long-distance operation, Sprint ION, broadband fixed wireless services, and certain other ventures into the Global Markets division (GMD). The GMD unit is the third largest traditional U.S. long-distance carrier in terms of revenues (after AT&T and MCI) and in 2004 has been competing with aggressive Baby Bells for market share. To increase its business and data revenues, GMD is expanding its ability to provide web and applications hosting, consulting services, and collocation services.

In January 2003, the company sold its Directory Publishing business to R.H. Donnelley, for $2.23 billion. In the 2003 second quarter, Sprint decided to wind down its Web-hosting business, and recorded a $348 million pretax charge. A pretax charge of $1.22 billion in the 2003 third quarter was related to a revaluation of the fair value of Sprint's fixed wireless spectrum. In the third quarter of 2004, FON took a $3.5 billion ($1.53 a share) charge for the impairment of its long distance network.

Company Financials Fiscal Year ending December 31

Per Share Data ($)

(Year Ended December 31)	2003	2002	2001	2000	1999	1998	1997	1996	1995	1994
Tangible Bk. Val.	14.40	11.45	11.41	13.95	10.42	10.45	10.52	9.91	6.65	5.48
Cash Flow	3.12	4.14	2.60	4.00	-4.35	7.19	3.07	3.27	3.45	3.39
Earnings	0.33	1.18	-0.16	1.45	1.97	1.78	1.09	1.40	1.36	1.27
S&P Core Earnings	1.12	1.26	-0.12	NA	NA	NA	NA	NA	NA	NA
Dividends	0.50	0.50	0.50	0.50	0.50	0.50	0.50	0.50	0.50	0.50
Payout Ratio	152%	42%	NM	34%	25%	28%	46%	36%	37%	40%
Prices - High	16.76	20.47	29.31	67.81	75.93	42.65	30.31	22.75	20.56	20.06
- Low	10.22	6.65	18.50	19.62	36.87	27.62	19.18	16.93	12.93	13.06
P/E Ratio - High	51	17	NM	47	39	24	28	16	15	16
- Low	31	6	NM	14	19	16	18	12	9	10

Income Statement Analysis (Million $)

	2003	2002	2001	2000	1999	1998	1997	1996	1995	1994
Revs.	14,185	15,182	16,924	17,688	17,016	17,135	14,874	14,045	12,765	12,662
Oper. Inc.	4,376	4,488	4,238	5,101	-5,059	3,075	4,178	3,858	3,388	3,266
Depr.	2,519	2,645	2,449	2,267	2,129	2,705	1,726	1,591	1,466	1,478
Int. Exp.	236	295	57.0	76.0	182	895	280	301	318	407
Pretax Inc.	434	1,453	-129	2,170	-2,797	698	1,583	1,912	1,480	1,404
Eff. Tax Rate	32.3%	28.0%	NM	40.5%	37.9%	56.2%	39.8%	37.7%	36.1%	35.5%
Net Inc.	294	1,046	-146	1,292	-1,736	457	953	1,191	946	884
S&P Core Earnings	1,030	1,132	-112	NA	NA	NA	NA	NA	NA	NA

Balance Sheet & Other Fin. Data (Million $)

	2003	2002	2001	2000	1999	1998	1997	1996	1995	1994
Cash	1,635	641	134	122	104	605	102	1,151	124	123
Curr. Assets	4,378	3,327	3,485	4,512	4,282	4,388	3,773	4,353	3,619	2,189
Total Assets	21,862	23,043	24,164	23,649	21,803	33,231	18,185	16,953	15,196	14,936
Curr. Liab.	2,359	4,320	6,298	5,004	4,301	4,551	3,077	3,314	5,142	3,055
LT Debt	2,627	2,736	3,258	3,482	4,531	11,942	3,755	2,981	3,253	4,605
Common Equity	13,372	11,814	11,704	12,343	10,514	12,202	9,025	8,520	4,643	4,525
Total Cap.	17,632	16,385	16,514	17,101	15,980	26,221	13,809	12,360	8,772	10,426
Cap. Exp.	1,674	2,181	5,295	4,105	3,534	42,311	2,863	2,434	1,857	2,016
Cash Flow	2,821	3,698	2,310	3,566	-3,858	3,156	2,678	2,781	2,412	2,359
Curr. Ratio	1.9	0.8	0.6	0.9	1.0	1.0	1.2	1.3	0.7	0.7
% LT Debt of Cap.	14.9	16.7	19.7	20.4	28.4	45.5	27.1	24.1	37.1	44.2
% Net Inc.of Revs.	2.1	6.9	NM	7.3	10.2	2.6	6.4	8.5	7.4	7.0
% Ret. on Assets	1.3	4.4	NM	5.7	8.5	1.8	5.4	7.4	6.4	6.0
% Ret. on Equity	2.3	8.8	NM	11.2	17.7	4.2	10.8	18.1	20.6	20.7

Data as orig reptd.; bef. results of disc opers/spec. items. Does not reflect 4/04 combination. Per share data adj. for stk. divs.; EPS diluted. E-Estimated. NA-Not Available. NM-Not Meaningful. NR-Not Ranked. UR-Under Review.

Office: 6299 Sprint Parkway, Overland Park, KS 66251.
Telephone: 816-501-6827.
Email: investorrelation.sprintcom@mail.sprint.com
Website: http://www.sprint.com
Chrmn & CEO: G.D. Forsee.
Pres & COO: L. Lauer.
EVP & CFO: R.J. Dellinger.

EVP & General Counsel: T.A. Gerke.
SVP & Treas: G.M. Betts.
VP & Investor Contact: K. Fawkes 816-501-6827.
Dirs: D. Ausley, G. M. Bethune, E. L. Draper, Jr., G. D. Forsee, D. A. Henretta, I. O. Hockaday, Jr., L. K. Lorimer, C. E. Rice, L. W. Smith, G. Storch, W. H. Swanson.

Founded: in 1925.
Domicile: Kansas.
Employees: 41,200.
S&P Analyst: Todd Rosenbluth/PMW/BK

Stanley Works

Recommendation: **HOLD** ★ ★ ★ ☆
SELL · SELL · HOLD · BUY · BUY

12-Month Target Price: **$47.00**
(as of May 10, 2004)

SWK has an approximate 0.04% weighting in the **S&P 500**

Sector: Consumer Discretionary
Sub-Industry: Household Appliances
Peer Group: Hardware & Tools

Summary: This company is a worldwide producer of tools, hardware and specialty hardware for home improvement, consumer, industrial and professional use.

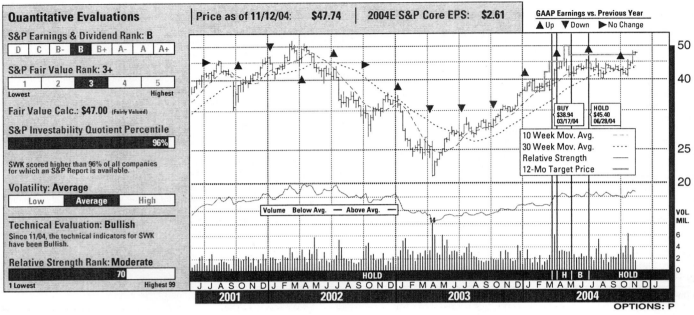

Quantitative Evaluations

S&P Earnings & Dividend Rank: B
| D | C | B- | **B** | B+ | A- | A | A+ |

S&P Fair Value Rank: 3+
| 1 | 2 | **3** | 4 | 5 |
Lowest — Highest

Fair Value Calc.: $47.00 (Fairly Valued)

S&P Investability Quotient Percentile
96%

SWK scored higher than 96% of all companies for which an S&P Report is available.

Volatility: Average
| Low | **Average** | High |

Technical Evaluation: Bullish
Since 11/04, the technical indicators for SWK have been Bullish.

Relative Strength Rank: Moderate
70
1 Lowest — Highest 99

Price as of 11/12/04: $47.74   **2004E S&P Core EPS:** $2.61

GAAP Earnings vs. Previous Year
▲ Up ▼ Down ▶ No Change

10 Week Mov. Avg.
30 Week Mov. Avg.
Relative Strength
12-Mo Target Price

Analyst commentary prepared by Amy Glynn, CFA /PMW/JWP

Highlights November 04, 2004

- We project that 2004 revenues from continuing operations will increase about 18% from the $2.7 billion posted in 2003, aided by acquisitions and strong organic sales growth. We look for organic revenue growth in the mid-single digits in 2005, aided by some price increases. We think that SWK will pursue additional acquisitions in 2005.

- Despite cost inflation, we expect operating margins to widen in 2004, due to benefits from restructuring initiatives. We forecast further gains in 2005, although we see the level of improvement moderating somewhat.

- We see 2004 operating EPS of $2.88. Our 2004 S&P Core EPS estimate is $2.61, reflecting our projections of $0.11 for stock option expense and $0.16 for pension costs. We look for 2005 operating EPS of $3.15 and S&P Core EPS of $2.85. SWK expects 2004 free cash flow to be at the upper end of its earlier projection of $250 million to $300 million. Over the near term, we believe the company will use free cash flow to make accretive acquisitions, pay dividends, and continue to reduce debt. For the longer term, SWK expects to continue to grow via acquisitions, by entering related markets through brand name and distribution leverage, and by pursuing global expansion opportunities.

Investment Rationale/Risk November 04, 2004

- We are encouraged by strong demand from home center and mass merchant customers, strength in the company's security solutions and industrial tools businesses, better pricing, and improved execution. We believe revenue growth over the next few years will be boosted by the recent repositioning of SWK's product portfolio toward higher growth businesses. We also think the company is taking the necessary steps to improve its cost structure. However, we would hold the shares, primarily based on valuation.

- Risks to our opinion and target price include an unexpected weakening in the company's major markets, acquisition integration risk, increased competition, adverse changes in currency exchange rates or raw material prices, and the inability of the company to meet expectations for sales growth and profitability.

- Our 12-month target price of $47 is based on our historical P/E multiple model, and applies a P/E multiple of 15X to our 2005 operating EPS estimate of $3.15. The shares provide an indicated dividend yield of about 2.5%.

Key Stock Statistics

S&P Core EPS 2005E	2.85	52-week Range	$48.35-32.09
S&P Oper. EPS 2004E	2.88	12 Month P/E	12.8
P/E on S&P Oper. EPS 2004E	16.6	Beta	0.89
S&P Oper. EPS 2005E	3.15	Shareholders	14,053
Yield (%)	2.3%	Market Cap (B)	$ 3.9
Dividend Rate/Share	1.12	Shares Outstanding (M)	81.9

Value of $10,000 invested five years ago: **$ 20,124**

Dividend Data Dividends have been paid since 1877

Amount ($)	Date Decl.	Ex-Div. Date	Stock of Record	Payment Date
0.260	Jan. 23	Mar. 04	Mar. 08	Mar. 30 '04
0.260	Apr. 23	Jun. 02	Jun. 04	Jun. 29 '04
0.280	Jul. 22	Sep. 01	Sep. 03	Sep. 28 '04
0.280	Oct. 14	Nov. 24	Nov. 29	Dec. 21 '04

Revenues/Earnings Data Fiscal year ending December 31

Revenues (Million $)
	2004	2003	2002	2001	2000	1999
1Q	778.6	632.2	616.7	626.2	695.0	683.7
2Q	794.7	652.6	649.1	676.5	702.8	685.5
3Q	791.2	665.6	665.5	676.1	684.4	692.0
4Q	—	727.7	661.7	645.6	666.0	691.0
Yr.	—	2,678	2,594	2,624	2,749	2,752

Earnings Per Share ($)
	2004	2003	2002	2001	2000	1999
1Q	0.70	0.22	0.56	0.54	0.54	0.34
2Q	0.73	0.11	0.72	0.58	0.58	0.28
3Q	0.76	0.46	0.62	0.62	0.56	0.56
4Q	E0.70	0.38	0.20	0.07	0.54	0.49
Yr.	E2.88	1.14	2.10	1.81	2.22	1.67

Next earnings report expected: late-January Source: S&P, Company Reports
EPS Estimates based on S&P Operating Earnings; historical GAAP earnings are as reported.

The Stanley Works

Recommendation: **HOLD** ★ ★ ★ ☆ ☆   12-Month Target Price: **$47.00** (as of May 10, 2004)

Business Summary November 04, 2004

The Stanley Works, founded in 1843 and incorporated in 1852, is a worldwide producer of tools and door products for professional, industrial and consumer use. In 2003, the company had net sales of $2.7 billion from continuing operations, and employed about 13,500 people worldwide.

In 1997, the company's then CEO, John Trani, outlined a new strategy. He emphasized that, in light of the fragmented nature of the hard goods industry, he believed that SWK's greatest asset, its well recognized and respected brand name, was not being fully utilized, and said he would triple the advertising budget. The company would also invest much more in developing new products and product extensions to help make SWK a one-stop shop for its customers, such as the domestic big box (e.g., Home Depot) retail channel.

Foreign operations, largely in Europe, accounted for 31% of sales in 2003.

In 2003 and 2002, 16% and 21% of sales, respectively, were to one customer. In 2001, 18% of sales were to Home Depot, up from 17% in 2000.

The Tools segment (74% of 2003 sales) produces tools for carpenters and mechanics, pneumatic and hydraulic tools, and tool sets. Carpenters' tools include measuring instruments, planes, hammers, knives and blades, garden tools, screwdrivers, saws, chisels, boring tools, masonry, tile and drywall tools, as well as electronic stud sensors, levels, alignment tools and elevation measuring systems. Mechanics' tools include hand tools such as wrenches, sockets, electronic diagnostic tools, tool boxes and high-density industrial storage and retrieval systems. SWK's pneumatic tools include fastening tools and fasteners and pneumatic air tools. Hydraulic tools include hand-held tools as well as mounted

demolition hammers and compactors designed to work on skid steer loaders, mini-excavators, backhoes and large excavators.

As of 2003, the Doors segment (26%) made commercial and residential doors, both automatic and manual, as well as closet doors and systems, home decor and door and consumer hardware. Products included residential insulated steel, reinforced fiberglass and wood entrance door systems, vinyl patio doors, mirrored closet doors and closet organizing systems, automatic doors and related door hardware products. The residential doors unit was divested in March 2004.

In October 2004, SWK announced plans to divest its Home Decor business, with about $150 million in annual sales. Subject to necessary approvals, the transaction was expected to close in the 2004 fourth quarter.

In 2002, the company acquired Best Lock Corp., a global provider of security access control systems, for $316 million. SWK acquired three small businesses in 2003, at a total cost of $23.4 million, and five small businesses at a total cost of $42.7 million in 2002.

In April 2003, SWK announced restructuring plans to improve the profitability of certain businesses. The restructuring, completed in 2003, included a workforce reduction of more than 1,000, the exit from the Mac Tools retail channel, and the impairment of certain fixed assets and inventories related to the future consolidation of two distribution facilities. In 2001, the company undertook restructuring activities that resulted in the closure of 13 facilities and an employment reduction of 2,200.

Company Financials Fiscal Year ending December 31

Per Share Data ($)

(Year Ended December 31)	2003	2002	2001	2000	1999	1998	1997	1996	1995	1994
Tangible Bk. Val.	2.65	5.05	7.05	6.59	6.18	5.33	5.67	7.68	6.79	6.52
Cash Flow	2.16	2.90	2.76	3.17	2.62	2.41	0.34	1.93	1.58	2.10
Earnings	1.14	2.10	1.81	2.22	1.67	1.53	-0.47	1.09	0.67	1.40
S&P Core Earnings	1.12	1.43	1.30	NA	NA	NA	NA	NA	NA	NA
Dividends	1.03	0.99	0.94	0.90	0.87	0.83	0.77	0.73	0.71	0.69
Payout Ratio	90%	47%	52%	41%	52%	54%	NM	67%	107%	49%
Prices - High	37.87	52.00	46.97	31.87	35.00	57.25	47.37	32.81	26.68	22.43
- Low	20.84	27.31	28.06	18.43	22.00	23.50	28.00	23.62	17.81	17.43
P/E Ratio - High	33	25	26	14	21	37	NM	30	40	16
- Low	18	13	16	8	13	15	NM	22	27	12

Income Statement Analysis (Million $)

	2003	2002	2001	2000	1999	1998	1997	1996	1995	1994
Revs.	2,678	2,593	2,624	2,749	2,752	2,729	2,670	2,671	2,624	2,511
Oper. Inc.	342	360	412	424	321	331	331	342	324	330
Depr.	86.5	71.2	82.9	83.3	86.0	79.7	72.4	74.7	81.2	63.3
Int. Exp.	34.2	28.5	18.9	34.6	33.0	31.0	24.7	28.0	35.6	33.6
Pretax Inc.	133	273	237	294	231	215	174	174	113	202
Eff. Tax Rate	27.3%	32.1%	33.1%	33.8%	35.1%	36.0%	NM	44.4%	47.6%	37.9%
Net Inc.	96.7	185	158	194	150	138	-41.9	96.9	59.1	125
S&P Core Earnings	94.7	127	113	NA	NA	NA	NA	NA	NA	NA

Balance Sheet & Other Fin. Data (Million $)

	2003	2002	2001	2000	1999	1998	1997	1996	1995	1994
Cash	204	122	115	93.6	88.0	110	152	84.0	75.4	69.3
Curr. Assets	1,201	1,190	1,141	1,094	1,091	1,086	1,005	911	915	889
Total Assets	2,424	2,418	2,056	1,885	1,891	1,933	1,759	1,660	1,670	1,701
Curr. Liab.	754	681	826	707	693	702	623	382	388	422
LT Debt	535	564	197	249	290	345	284	343	391	387
Common Equity	1,032	1,165	844	933	737	669	608	780	735	744
Total Cap.	1,567	1,729	1,041	1,181	1,027	1,014	892	1,123	1,142	1,146
Cap. Exp.	31.4	37.2	55.7	59.8	78.0	56.9	73.3	78.7	66.5	66.0
Cash Flow	183	256	241	278	236	218	30.5	172	140	189
Curr. Ratio	1.6	1.7	1.4	1.5	1.6	1.5	1.6	2.4	2.4	2.1
% LT Debt of Cap.	34.1	32.6	18.9	21.1	28.2	34.0	31.8	30.6	34.2	33.8
% Net Inc.of Revs.	3.6	7.1	6.0	7.1	5.5	5.0	NM	3.7	2.3	5.0
% Ret. on Assets	4.0	8.3	8.0	10.3	7.8	7.5	NM	5.9	3.5	7.7
% Ret. on Equity	8.8	16.9	20.0	20.8	20.8	21.6	NM	12.8	8.0	17.6

Data as orig reptd.; bef. results of disc opers/spec. items. Per share data adj. for stk. divs.; EPS diluted. E-Estimated. NA-Not Available. NM-Not Meaningful. NR-Not Ranked. UR-Under Review.

Office: 1000 Stanley Drive, New Britain, CT 06053.
Telephone: 860-225-5111.
Website: http://www.stanleyworks.com
Chrmn & CEO: J.F. Lundgren.
EVP & CFO: J. Loree.

VP, Secy & General Counsel: B.H. Beatt.
Investor Contact: G. Gould 860-827-3833.
Dirs: J. G. Breen, S. B. Brown, V. W. Colbert, E. A. Kampouris, E. S. Kraus, J. Lundgren, J. D. Opie, K. D. Wriston.

Founded: in 1843.
Domicile: Connecticut.
Employees: 13,500.
S&P Analyst: Amy Glynn, CFA /PMW/JWP

Staples, Inc.

Recommendation: **BUY** ★★★★☆
SELL · SELL · HOLD · BUY · BUY

12-Month Target Price: **$35.00**
(as of August 17, 2004)

SPLS has an approximate 0.14% weighting in the **S&P 500**

Sector: Consumer Discretionary
Sub-Industry: Specialty Stores
Peer Group: Office Products Retailers

Summary: This leading operator of office products superstores has more than 1,500 units in the U.S. and internationally.

Quantitative Evaluations

S&P Earnings & Dividend Rank: B+

| D | C | B- | B | B+ | A- | A | A+ |

S&P Fair Value Rank: 3-

| 1 | 2 | 3 | 4 | 5 |
| Lowest | | | | Highest |

Fair Value Calc.: $30.80 (Fairly Valued)

S&P Investability Quotient Percentile 98%

SPLS scored higher than 98% of all companies for which an S&P Report is available.

Volatility: Average

| Low | Average | High |

Technical Evaluation: Bullish
Since 10/04, the technical indicators for SPLS have been Bullish.

Relative Strength Rank: Moderate 49
1 Lowest   Highest 99

| Price as of 11/12/04: | **$30.50** | 2005E S&P Core EPS: | **$1.18** |

GAAP Earnings vs. Previous Year
▲ Up ▼ Down ▶ No Change

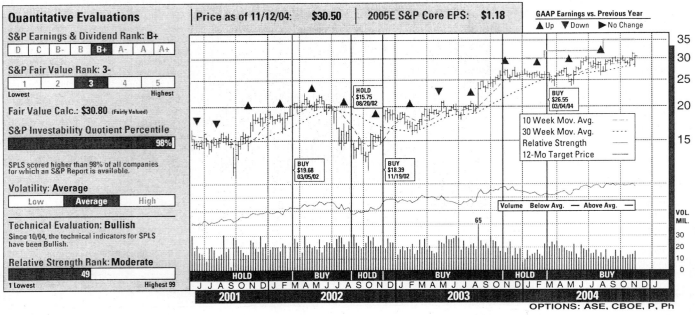

10 Week Mov. Avg.
30 Week Mov. Avg.
Relative Strength
12-Mo Target Price

Volume Below Avg. — Above Avg.

OPTIONS: ASE, CBOE, P, Ph

Analyst commentary prepared by Yogeesh Wagle/PMW/BK

Highlights September 23, 2004

- We project 8% to 10% sales growth in FY 05 (Jan.), aided by account growth at the delivery business division, continued international penetration, and store additions in North America and Europe. We see same-store sales gains of 2% to 4%, on modest increases in customer traffic and average ticket, fueled by the company's remodeling and marketing initiatives. Internet sales should continue to see robust growth.

- We think gross margins should widen, as benefits from a growing private label business, supply chain initiatives, lower sourcing costs, and modest leverage from occupancy costs outweigh greater penetration of lower margin national accounts. Despite expected higher advertising and payroll related expenses, partly offset by continued efficiency improvements and positive operating leverage, we see operating margins widening moderately.

- We project slightly lower interest expense, taxes at an effective rate of 37.0%, and lower share count. We estimate FY 05 EPS of $1.40, up 26% from FY 04's $1.11 (before one-time charges). For FY 06, we see 7% to 9% revenue growth, driven mainly by international expansion, a widening of 50 to 60 basis points in margins, and fewer shares outstanding, resulting in EPS of $1.64.

Investment Rationale/Risk September 23, 2004

- We would accumulate the shares. We believe greater business spending, particularly by small to medium size businesses, and an improving job market bode well for SPLS. We think Europe will continue to offer growth opportunities in retail and in the delivery business, as the company builds on its 2002 acquisition of Guilbert's mail order business. At 18X our FY 06 EPS estimate, the shares trade near the level of the S&P 500, but above those of key peer Office Depot (ODP: hold, $18). Our DCF model, which assumes an 11% average cost of capital and a 4% perpetual growth rate, indicates intrinsic value of $33 to $35.

- Risks to our recommendation and target price include a slowdown in economic growth, slower than expected capital spending and hiring by businesses, and higher interest rates. International risks include economic and political instability and unfavorable currency movements.

- Our 12-month target price of $35 is equal to 21X our FY 06 EPS estimate. This is a premium to the valuation of primary peer ODP, which we believe is justified by what we view as SPLS's leadership position in the key North American retail market.

Key Stock Statistics

S&P Oper. EPS 2005E	**1.40**	52-week Range	**$31.52-23.69**
P/E on S&P Oper. EPS 2005E	**21.8**	12 Month P/E	**24.4**
S&P Oper. EPS 2006E	**1.64**	Beta	**0.95**
Yield (%)	**0.7%**	Shareholders	**7,677**
Dividend Rate/Share	**0.20**	Market Cap (B)	**$ 15.2**
Shares Outstanding (M)	**497.6**		

Value of $10,000 invested five years ago: **$ 17,581**

Dividend Data Dividends have been paid since 2004

Amount ($)	Date Decl.	Ex-Div. Date	Stock of Record	Payment Date
0.200	Mar. 04	Apr. 22	Apr. 26	May. 17 '04

Revenues/Earnings Data Fiscal year ending January 31

Revenues (Million $)

	2005	2004	2003	2002	2001	2000
1Q	3,452	3,147	2,745	2,667	2,556	2,072
2Q	3,089	2,869	2,426	2,314	2,201	1,840
3Q	—	3,485	3,090	2,834	2,802	2,394
4Q	—	3,681	3,335	2,929	3,115	2,588
Yr.	—	13,181	11,596	10,744	10,674	8,842

Earnings Per Share ($)

	2005	2004	2003	2002	2001	2000
1Q	0.25	0.05	0.20	0.09	0.10	0.11
2Q	0.24	0.18	0.13	0.09	0.10	0.11
3Q	E0.40	0.33	0.27	0.20	0.19	0.20
4Q	E0.50	0.42	0.35	0.20	-0.23	0.26
Yr.	E1.40	0.99	0.94	0.63	0.15	0.67

Next earnings report expected: mid-November Source: S&P, Company Reports
EPS Estimates based on S&P Operating Earnings; historical GAAP earnings are as reported.

Staples, Inc.

Recommendation: **BUY** ★ ★ ★ ☆   12-Month Target Price: **$35.00** (as of August 17, 2004)

Business Summary September 23, 2004

Staples is a leading office supplies distributor, with global retail, catalog, e-commerce, and contract stationer operations. In 2001, the company launched its Back to Brighton strategy to drive profitable sales growth, boost profit margins, and increase asset productivity. Under this strategy, which focuses on the needs of small business customers, SPLS introduced a new store format, Dover, with a more efficient, smaller layout, lower sightlines, and signage hanging from the ceiling to improve navigability. It planned to open new stores in this format, and to convert older stores to it. Other initiatives included enhancing customer service, adding more Staples brand products, improving the supply chain to achieve better in-stock positions, and reducing sourcing costs. In 2003, the company launched a new marketing campaign touting its promise to make buying office products easy.

At January 31, 2004, SPLS operated 1,559 high-volume office superstores, mostly in North America (1,358 stores), but also in five European countries: the U.K. (93), Germany (53), the Netherlands (40), Portugal (14) and Belgium (1). The company operated 343 new or remodeled stores with its Dover format at the end of FY 04 (Jan.). In FY 05, it planned to add 95 new stores in North America, and to remodel 50 existing stores in the Dover format; it also planned to open 20 new stores in Europe.

Stores operate under the names Staples--The Office Superstore and Staples Express. A prototype superstore has about 20,000 sq. ft. of sales area, carries about 8,000 stock items, and is generally located in a suburban area. Express

stores range from 6,000 sq. ft. to 10,000 sq. ft. in size, stock about 6,000 items, and are located in downtown business areas. In FY 04, total sales by segment were: North American Retail 59%; North American Delivery 28%; and Europe 13%. Sales by product line were: office supplies and services 42%; business machines and telecommunications services 30%; computers and related products 21%; and office furniture 7%.

Delivery operations comprise the catalog business, Staples Direct and Quill Corporation; the contract stationer businesses; and the Internet e-commerce business, Staples.com. Quill, acquired in May 1998, is a direct mail catalog business serving medium-sized businesses. In July 2002, the company acquired Medical Arts Press, a provider of specialized printed products and supplies to medical offices, for $383 million in cash, and merged it into Quill.

In October 2002, SPLS acquired Guilbert's European mail order business, for about $788 million, gaining access to four new countries: Belgium, France, Spain and Italy, and strengthening its competitive position in Great Britain. The company believed that the acquired business, renamed Staples European Catalogue, provided a platform for continued penetration of Europe's growing mail-order market.

Contract stationer operations, Staples National Advantage and Staples Business Advantage, serve medium- to large-size businesses that seek more services than those provided by the traditional retail and mail order businesses.

Company Financials Fiscal Year ending January 31

Per Share Data ($)

(Year Ended January 31)	2004	2003	2002	2001	2000	1999	1998	1997	1996	1995
Tangible Bk. Val.	4.51	2.61	3.94	3.29	2.98	3.27	2.19	1.86	1.49	0.86
Cash Flow	1.55	1.51	1.10	0.63	1.01	1.03	0.52	0.43	0.32	0.22
Earnings	0.99	0.94	0.63	0.15	0.67	0.41	0.34	0.28	0.20	0.13
S&P Core Earnings	0.91	0.87	0.48	0.31	NA	NA	NA	NA	NA	NA
Dividends	Nil	Nil	Nil	Nil	Nil	Nil	Nil	Nil	Nil	Nil
Payout Ratio	Nil	Nil	Nil	Nil	Nil	Nil	Nil	Nil	Nil	Nil
Cal. Yrs.	2003	2002	2001	2000	1999	1998	1997	1996	1995	1994
Prices - High	27.87	22.45	19.45	28.75	35.93	30.79	13.38	10.05	8.62	4.88
- Low	15.73	11.68	11.02	10.25	16.43	10.58	7.61	5.59	4.24	2.89
P/E Ratio - High	28	24	31	NM	54	75	39	35	41	39
- Low	16	12	17	NM	25	26	22	20	20	23

Income Statement Analysis (Million $)

	2004	2003	2002	2001	2000	1999	1998	1997	1996	1995
Revs.	13,181	11,596	10,744	10,674	8,937	7,123	5,181	3,968	3,068	2,000
Oper. Inc.	1,081	950	768	719	708	514	355	260	191	110
Depr.	283	267	249	231	174	99	83.4	56.0	43.6	28.7
Int. Exp.	20.2	20.6	27.2	45.2	17.1	17.4	23.1	20.1	19.9	8.39
Pretax Inc.	778	662	431	244	516	306	213	173	120	63.9
Eff. Tax Rate	37.0%	32.6%	38.5%	75.5%	39.0%	39.5%	38.5%	38.5%	38.5%	37.5%
Net Inc.	490	446	265	59.7	315	185	131	106	73.7	39.9
S&P Core Earnings	450	413	221	147	NA	NA	NA	NA	NA	NA

Balance Sheet & Other Fin. Data (Million $)

	2004	2003	2002	2001	2000	1999	1998	1997	1996	1995
Cash	457	596	395	264	110	358	355	106	111	71.0
Curr. Assets	3,479	2,717	2,403	2,356	2,192	2,064	1,666	1,151	926	640
Total Assets	6,503	5,721	4,093	3,989	3,814	3,179	2,455	1,788	1,403	1,008
Curr. Liab.	2,123	2,175	1,596	1,711	1,455	1,265	941	603	422	350
LT Debt	567	732	350	441	501	205	509	391	344	249
Common Equity	3,663	2,659	2,054	1,764	1,829	1,657	967	762	611	385
Total Cap.	4,230	3,441	2,411	2,205	2,330	1,862	1,476	1,153	955	634
Cap. Exp.	278	265	340	450	355	322	183	200	116	64.7
Cash Flow	773	713	514	291	489	285	214	162	117	68.6
Curr. Ratio	1.6	1.2	1.5	1.4	1.5	1.6	1.8	1.9	2.2	1.8
% LT Debt of Cap.	13.4	21.3	14.5	20.0	21.5	11.0	34.5	33.9	36.0	39.3
% Net Inc.of Revs.	3.7	3.8	2.5	0.6	3.5	2.6	2.5	2.7	2.4	2.0
% Ret. on Assets	8.0	9.1	6.6	1.5	9.0	6.6	6.2	6.7	6.1	4.7
% Ret. on Equity	15.5	18.9	13.9	3.3	18.1	14.1	15.1	15.5	14.8	11.1

Data as orig reptd.; bef. results of disc opers/spec. items. Per share data adj. for stk. divs.; EPS diluted. E-Estimated. NA-Not Available. NM-Not Meaningful. NR-Not Ranked. UR-Under Review.

Office: 500 Staples Drive , Framingham , MA 01702.
Telephone: 508-253-5000.
Email: investor@staples.com
Website: http://www.staples.com
Chrmn: T.G. Stemberg.
Pres & CEO: R.L. Sargent.

Vice Chrmn: B.L. Anderson.
Vice Chrmn: J.S. Vassalluzzo.
COO: M.A. Miles, Jr.
Dirs: B. L. Anderson, B. C. Barnes, A. M. Blank, M. E. Burton, G. L. Crittenden, R. J. Currie, G. J. Mitchell, J. L. Moody, R. T. Moriarty, R. C. Nakasone, R. L. Sargent, T. G. Stemberg, M. Trust, P. F. Walsh.

Founded: in 1985.
Domicile: Delaware.
Employees: 60,633.
S&P Analyst: Yogeesh Wagle/PMW/BK

The **McGraw·Hill** Companies

Starbucks Corp.

Recommendation: **HOLD** ★★★☆☆
SELL · HOLD · BUY

12-Month Target Price: **$55.00**
(as of November 12, 2004)

SBUX has an approximate 0.20% weighting in the **S&P 500**

Sector: Consumer Discretionary
Sub-Industry: Restaurants
Peer Group: Fast-food - Larger

Summary: SBUX purchases and roasts high-quality whole bean coffees, which it sells, together with fresh, rich-brewed coffees, primarily through approximately 8,600 retail stores.

Quantitative Evaluations

S&P Earnings & Dividend Rank: B+

D	C	B-	B	B+	A-	A	A+

S&P Fair Value Rank: 2-

1	2	3	4	5
Lowest				Highest

Fair Value Calc.: $51.70 (Slightly Overvalued)

S&P Investability Quotient Percentile

96%

SBUX scored higher than 96% of all companies for which an S&P Report is available.

Volatility: Low

Low	Average	High

Technical Evaluation: Bullish

Since 10/04, the technical indicators for SBUX have been Bullish.

Relative Strength Rank: Strong

82

1 Lowest		Highest 99

Price as of 11/15/04: $55.16 | **2005E S&P Core EPS: $1.04**

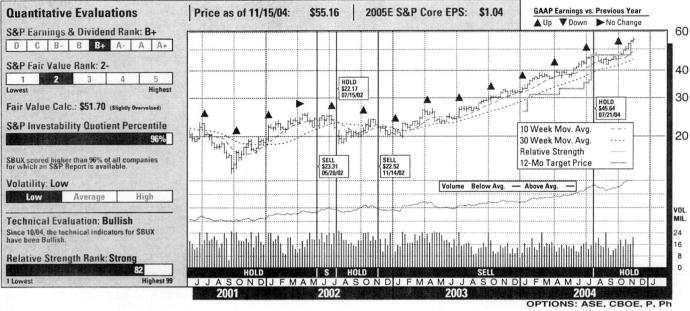

GAAP Earnings vs. Previous Year
▲ Up ▼ Down ► No Change

Analyst commentary prepared by Dennis Milton/PMW/BK

OPTIONS: ASE, CBOE, P, Ph

Highlights 15-NOV-04

- SBUX recently raised its long-term global target to 30,000 retail locations, from 25,000. The company plans to add at least 1,500 units annually for the next several years, as it expands operations worldwide. It targets annual revenue growth of 20%, with EPS gains of 20% to 25%, over the next three years. In FY 05 (Sep.), SBUX expects to open about 1,075 new stores in the U.S., and another 425 internationally.

- We expect retail revenues to increase about 18% in FY 05, due to expansion and average unit growth of about 6%, partly offset by one fewer week in the fiscal year (FY 04 had 53 weeks). We see specialty revenues growing about 15%, primarily due to increased royalty revenues and a further significant increase in licensee stores. We believe margins will widen slightly, benefiting from leverage of a larger sales base over fixed costs, partly offset by higher food, labor and maintenance costs. and by expenses related to expansion.

- We anticipate FY 05 EPS of $1.15, up 21% from $0.95 in FY 04. Our FY 05 S&P Core EPS forecast, including estimated stock option expense of $0.11, is $1.04.

Investment Rationale/Risk 15-NOV-04

- At 53X our FY 05 S&P Core EPS estimate of $1.04, the shares are trading at a significant premium to industry peers and the S&P 500. In our opinion, this premium is justified. We believe the company's growth prospects are excellent. We expect expansion to fuel revenue growth at a compound annual rate of 20% over the next several years. Based on what we view as SBUX's demonstrated ability to expand while still achieving impressive same-store sales growth and, more recently, significant operating margin expansion, we view the shares as fairly valued.

- Risks to our opinion and target price include a potentially negative impact on customer traffic from planned price increases, a lack of customer acceptance of the company's food initiatives, and the possibility that aggressive expansion in the U.S. will increase cannibalization rates.

- Our 12-month target price of $55 applies a P/E multiple of 46X, in the middle of the historical range, to our calendar 2005 EPS estimate of $1.20. We believe investors will continue to reward what we view as the company's strong sales execution, despite a significant valuation premium to peers. Investors should be aware that SBUX's use of stock option grants may dilute future earnings.

Key Stock Statistics

S&P Oper. EPS 2005E	**1.15**	52-week Range	**$56.55-30.00**
P/E on S&P Oper. EPS 2005E	**48.1**	12 Month P/E	**58.1**
Yield (%)	**Nil**	Beta	**0.46**
Dividend Rate/Share	**Nil**	Shareholders	**12,137**
Shares Outstanding (M)	**397.5**	Market Cap (B)	**$ 21.9**

Value of $10,000 invested five years ago: **$ 39,150**

Dividend Data

No cash dividends have been paid.

Revenues/Earnings Data Fiscal year ending September 30

Revenues (Million $)

	2004	2003	2002	2001	2000	1999
1Q	1,281	1,004	805.3	667.4	527.0	405.6
2Q	1,241	954.2	783.2	629.3	504.7	375.8
3Q	1,319	1,037	835.2	662.8	555.5	423.8
4Q	1,453	1,081	865.2	689.5	582.0	474.8
Yr.	5,294	4,076	3,289	2,649	2,169	1,680

Earnings Per Share ($)

	2004	2003	2002	2001	2000	1999
1Q	0.27	0.20	0.17	0.13	0.09	0.07
2Q	0.19	0.13	0.08	0.08	0.06	0.05
3Q	0.24	0.17	0.14	0.12	0.09	0.07
4Q	0.25	0.17	0.15	0.14	0.01	0.09
Yr.	0.95	0.67	0.54	0.46	0.25	0.27

Next earnings report expected: late-January Source: S&P, Company Reports
EPS Estimates based on S&P Operating Earnings; historical GAAP earnings are as reported.

STANDARD &POOR'S

Starbucks Corporation

Stock Report
November 16, 2004
NASDAQ Symbol: **SBUX**

Recommendation: **HOLD** ★ ★ ★ ☆ ☆   12-Month Target Price: **$55.00** (as of November 12, 2004)

Business Summary 15-NOV-04

Starbucks Corp.'s rapid growth in retail outlets throughout the U.S. has made its name synonymous with specialty coffee. A caffeine-fueled expansion has brought the number of Starbucks retail stores to 8,569 at October 3, 2004, from 165 stores at the end of FY 92 (Sep.). Company revenues grew 30% in FY 04, to nearly $5.3 billion, and have posted a compound annual growth rate of about 26% over the past five years.

The company's objective is to rapidly expand its retail operations, grow its specialty operations, and selectively pursue new product introduction and the development of new channels of distribution.

Retail stores accounted for 84% of FY 04 net sales (down from 85% in FY 03). Stores are typically clustered in high-traffic, high-visibility locations in each market. They are located in office buildings, downtown and suburban retail centers, and kiosks placed in building lobbies, airport terminals and supermarkets. In FY 03 (latest available), the retail store sales mix by product type was 78% beverages, 12% food items, 5% whole bean coffees, and 5% coffee-related hardware items.

SBUX seeks to expand its retail business by increasing its share in existing markets and opening stores in new markets in which it sees an opportunity to become the leading specialty coffee retailer. It opened a net total of 599 company-owned stores in FY 04, and plans to open about 650 in FY 05. At October, 2004, SBUX operated 4,293 stores in the U.S., and 887 stores in Canada, the U.K., Australia, Singapore and Thailand.

Specialty operations, which accounted for 16% of total revenues in FY 04 (15% in FY 03), aims to develop the Starbucks brand outside the company-owned retail store environment through a number of channels. SBUX has licensing agreements (39% of specialty revenues in FY 03) (latest available) with prominent retailers in North America, Central America, Europe, the Middle East, Africa and Asia. As of October 3, 2004, there were 3,354 licensed retail stores worldwide. The company has more than 12,800 foodservice accounts (27%), through which it sells whole bean and ground coffee to various coffee distributors, hotels, airlines and restaurants. SBUX also has a licensing agreement (25%) with Kraft, Inc., which markets and distributes the company's whole bean and ground coffees to more than 19,000 grocery and warehouse club accounts. Several other initiatives, including the company's e-commerce site and product development partnerships with Pepsi-Cola and Dreyer's Ice Cream, account for the remainder (9%) of specialty sales.

In the FY 03 fourth quarter, SBUX acquired Seattle Coffee Co., which includes Seattle's Best Coffee and Torrefazione Italia coffee brands, for $72 million.

The company bought back 2.2 million common shares in the first nine months of FY 04, for about $82.2 million. At July 27, 2004, authorization remained to purchase about 12.4 million shares.

SBUX does not currently expense stock options. Had they been expensed in FY 03 (latest available), FY 02 and FY 01, EPS would have been reduced by $0.09, $0.10 and $0.11, respectively.

Company Financials Fiscal Year ending September 30

Per Share Data ($)

(Year Ended September 30)	2004	2003	2002	2001	2000	1999	1998	1997	1996	1995
Tangible Bk. Val.	NA	5.04	4.40	3.56	3.00	2.58	2.22	1.68	1.46	1.10
Cash Flow	NA	1.31	1.10	0.91	0.95	0.55	0.41	0.35	0.27	0.18
Earnings	0.95	0.67	0.54	0.46	0.25	0.27	0.19	0.18	0.14	0.09
S&P Core Earnings	NA	0.58	0.46	0.36	NA	NA	NA	NA	NA	NA
Dividends	Nil	Nil	Nil	Nil	Nil	Nil	Nil	Nil	Nil	Nil
Payout Ratio	Nil	Nil	Nil	Nil	Nil	Nil	Nil	Nil	Nil	Nil
Prices - High	56.55	33.43	25.70	25.65	25.40	20.50	14.98	11.18	10.06	5.87
- Low	32.90	19.62	18.44	13.46	11.56	9.93	7.18	6.53	3.62	2.78
P/E Ratio - High	60	50	48	56	NM	76	80	64	75	64
- Low	35	29	34	29	NM	37	38	37	27	30

Income Statement Analysis (Million $)

	2004	2003	2002	2001	2000	1999	1998	1997	1996	1995
Revs.	NA	4,076	3,289	2,649	2,169	1,680	1,309	967	697	465
Oper. Inc.	NA	646	504	430	334	264	199	146	96.4	70.0
Depr.	NA	259	221	177	272	108	80.9	58.2	39.4	24.8
Int. Exp.	NA	Nil	Nil	Nil	Nil	1.36	1.38	7.27	8.70	3.77
Pretax Inc.	NA	436	341	289	161	164	116	93.3	68.5	43.1
Eff. Tax Rate	NA	38.5%	37.0%	37.3%	41.1%	38.0%	41.2%	38.5%	38.5%	39.4%
Net Inc.	NA	268	215	181	94.6	102	68.4	57.4	42.1	26.1
S&P Core Earnings	NA	231	181	143	NA	NA	NA	NA	NA	NA

Balance Sheet & Other Fin. Data (Million $)

	2004	2003	2002	2001	2000	1999	1998	1997	1996	1995
Cash	NA	201	175	113	70.8	0.07	102	70.1	229	62.4
Curr. Assets	NA	924	848	594	460	387	337	317	340	205
Total Assets	NA	2,730	2,293	1,851	1,493	1,253	993	851	727	468
Curr. Liab.	NA	609	537	445	313	252	179	139	101	71.0
LT Debt	NA	4.35	5.08	5.79	6.48	7.02	Nil	167	167	81.4
Common Equity	NA	2,082	1,727	1,376	1,148	961	794	532	452	312
Total Cap.	NA	2,087	1,754	1,406	1,180	1,001	813	708	626	397
Cap. Exp.	NA	357	375	384	316	262	202	170	102	129
Cash Flow	NA	528	436	358	367	209	149	116	81.5	50.9
Curr. Ratio	NA	1.5	1.6	1.3	1.5	1.5	1.9	2.3	3.4	2.9
% LT Debt of Cap.	NA	0.2	0.3	0.4	0.5	0.7	Nil	23.6	26.6	20.5
% Net Inc.of Revs.	NA	6.6	6.5	6.8	4.4	6.1	5.2	5.9	6.0	5.6
% Ret. on Assets	NA	10.9	10.4	10.8	6.9	9.1	7.4	7.3	7.1	11.2
% Ret. on Equity	NA	14.1	13.9	14.4	9.0	11.6	10.3	11.7	11.0	12.4

Data as orig reptd.; bef. results of disc opers/spec. items. Per share data adj. for stk. divs.; EPS diluted. E-Estimated. NA-Not Available. NM-Not Meaningful. NR-Not Ranked. UR-Under Review.

Office: 2401 Utah Avenue South, Seattle, WA 98134.
Telephone: 206-447-1575.
Email: investorrelations@starbucks.com
Website: http://www.starbucks.com
Chrmn: H. Schultz.
Pres & CEO: O. C. Smith.

EVP & CFO: M. Casey.
Secy, EVP & General Counsel: P. E. Boggs.
Investor Contact: Tracy Moran (206-442-7806).
Dirs: B. Bass, H. P. Behar, B. Bradley, C. J. Foley, O. Lee, G. B. Maffei, A. I. Prentice, H. Schultz, J. G. Shennan, Jr., O. C. Smith, M. E. Ullman III, C. E. Weatherup.

Founded: in 1985.
Domicile: Washington.
Employees: 74,000.
S&P Analyst: Dennis Milton/PMW/BK

Starwood Hotels & Resorts

Recommendation: **HOLD** ★★★☆☆
SELL · SELL · HOLD · BUY · BUY

12-Month Target Price: $50.00
(as of October 22, 2004)

HOT has an approximate 0.10% weighting in the **S&P 500**

Sector: Consumer Discretionary
Sub-Industry: Hotels, Resorts & Cruise Lines
Peer Group: Hotel Companies - Larger

Summary: HOT is one of the world's largest lodging companies, with more than 700 hotels, including the Sheraton, Westin, St. Regis, W, and Four Points by Sheraton brands.

Quantitative Evaluations

S&P Earnings & Dividend Rank: NR

| D | C | B- | B | B+ | A- | A | A+ |

S&P Fair Value Rank: 1-

| 1 | 2 | 3 | 4 | 5 |
| Lowest | | | | Highest |

Fair Value Calc.: $37.80 (Overvalued)

S&P Investability Quotient Percentile

70%

HOT scored higher than 70% of all companies for which an S&P Report is available.

Volatility: Average

| Low | Average | High |

Technical Evaluation: Bullish
Since 9/04, the technical indicators for HOT have been Bullish.

Relative Strength Rank: Strong

71

1 Lowest — Highest 99

Price as of 11/12/04: $50.94   **2004E S&P Core EPS:** $1.21

GAAP Earnings vs. Previous Year
▲ Up   ▼ Down   ▶ No Change

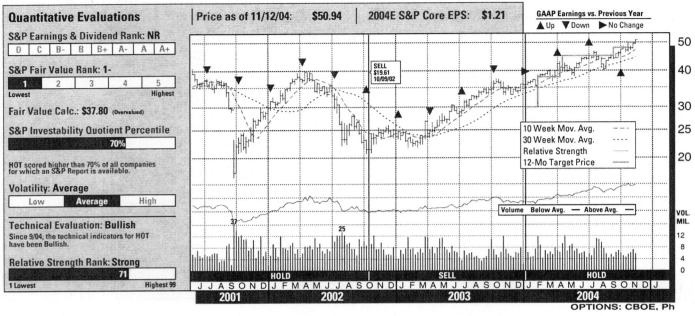

10 Week Mov. Avg.
30 Week Mov. Avg.
Relative Strength
12-Mo Target Price

Volume   Below Avg. — Above Avg.

VOL. MIL.

HOLD · SELL · HOLD

J J A S O N D J F M A M J J A S O N D J F M A M J J A S O N D J F M A M J J A S O N D J
2001   2002   2003   2004

OPTIONS: CBOE, Ph

Analyst commentary prepared by Tom Graves, CFA /PMW/BK

Highlights September 14, 2004

- For the company as currently constituted, we look for 2005 revenues from continuing operations to increase about 7%, to $5.6 billion, from $5.3 billion projected for 2004, including increases in revenue per available room at comparable-owned hotels, and higher revenue related to management and franchising operations. Our projection includes revenue from properties that might be divested, but excludes revenue from any properties that HOT might add from the Le Meridien hotel business, of which the company has acquired some senior debt.

- Before special items, we estimate 2005 net income of $426 million ($2.00 a share), up 37% from the $311 million ($1.46) that we project for 2004. Our 2004 EPS estimate excludes a $0.06 net benefit from special items. In 2003, the net effect of special items on earnings from continuing operations was about $0.35 a share, primarily due to impairment charges. For each of 2004 and 2005, we expect an effective tax rate below 25%, largely due to tax exempt income of a subsidiary trust. In 2003, HOT had an effective rate, before special items, of about 4%.

Investment Rationale/Risk September 14, 2004

- Our hold opinion on the stock is based on our view that the share price fairly reflects favorable prospects for a further hotel industry upturn, as well as an opportunity for HOT to benefit from a prospective acquisition of equity, properties, or management agreements related to the Le Meridien business, and the company's projected cash generation.

- Risks to our recommendation and target price include the possibility that terrorism fears could heighten, leading to lower than expected demand for hotel rooms.

- Based on our 2005 EPS estimates, the stock is trading at a sharp P/E multiple premium (recently about 43%) to the S&P 500. The company's recent level of unexpensed stock options also raises our concerns about earnings quality. We expect these factors to limit the stock's upside in the coming year. Our 12-month target price is $48. At this price, we believe the shares would still trade at a P/E multiple premium to the S&P 500. The stock has an indicated dividend yield of about 1.9%.

Key Stock Statistics

S&P Core EPS 2005E	1.61	52-week Range	$50.94-33.07
S&P Oper. EPS 2004E	1.50	12 Month P/E	28.3
P/E on S&P Oper. EPS 2004E	34.0	Beta	1.10
S&P Oper. EPS 2005E	1.90	Shareholders	20,000
Yield (%)	1.6%	Market Cap (B)	$ 10.6
Dividend Rate/Share	0.84	Shares Outstanding (M)	207.3

Value of $10,000 invested five years ago: **$ 24,008**

Dividend Data Dividends have been paid since 1995

Amount ($)	Date Decl.	Ex-Div. Date	Stock of Record	Payment Date
0.840	Dec. 19	Dec. 29	Dec. 31	Jan. 21 '04

Revenues/Earnings Data Fiscal year ending December 31

Revenues (Million $)

	2004	2003	2002	2001	2000	1999
1Q	1,227	1,073	1,096	1,014	1,008	851.0
2Q	1,363	1,220	1,232	1,110	1,151	968.0
3Q	1,336	1,140	1,157	965.0	1,114	956.0
4Q	—	1,197	1,174	878.0	1,105	1,087
Yr.	—	4,630	4,659	3,967	4,345	3,862

Earnings Per Share ($)

	2004	2003	2002	2001	2000	1999
1Q	0.16	-0.58	0.16	0.30	0.26	-4.86
2Q	0.56	0.42	0.37	0.55	0.56	0.73
3Q	0.49	0.23	0.26	0.14	0.50	0.23
4Q	E0.44	0.42	0.42	-0.28	0.64	0.51
Yr.	E1.50	0.51	1.20	0.73	1.96	-3.41

Next earnings report expected: early-February Source: S&P, Company Reports
EPS Estimates based on S&P Operating Earnings; historical GAAP earnings are as reported.

Please read the Required Disclosures and Reg. AC certification on the last page of this report.

The **McGraw·Hill** Companies

Recommendation: **HOLD** ★ ★ ★ ☆ ☆   12-Month Target Price: **$50.00** (as of October 22, 2004)

Business Summary September 14, 2004

Starwood Hotels is one of the world's largest hotel companies, with operations in about 80 countries. At December 31, 2003, the company's business included 738 properties, with about 229,000 rooms, in 82 countries, In addition, HOT operates some vacation ownership resorts.

HOT's hotel brands include St. Regis (luxury full-service hotels and resorts), The Luxury Collection (luxury full-service hotels and resorts), Westin (luxury and upscale full-service hotels and resorts), Sheraton (full-service hotels and resorts), W (boutique full-service urban hotels), and Four Points (moderately priced full-service hotels). At December 31, 2003, the company's hotel business included 394 Sheratons (135,000 rooms), 121 Westins (52,000 rooms), 49 properties (8,000 rooms) in the St. Regis or Luxury Collection groups, 138 Four Points (25,000 rooms), and 18 hotels (5,000 rooms) in the W chain. Of HOT's 738 affiliated properties, the company wholly owned, majority owned, or leased 140 properties (50,000 rooms), and managed 286 properties (98,000 rooms), including entities in which HOT had a minority equity interest; there were also 312 hotels (81,000) for which the company received franchise fees.

At the end of 2003, the company had 18 vacation ownership resorts in the U.S. and the Bahamas, including six that were actively selling vacation ownership interests, four under construction, two expected to start construction shortly, and six that had sold all existing inventory. In 2003, HOT made capital expenditures of about $140 million related to the vacation ownership business.

In December 2003, Lehman Brothers Holdings Inc. and Starwood announced the acquisition at a discount of all of the outstanding senior debt (about $1.3 billion) of Le Meridien Hotels and Resorts Ltd. Subsequently, HOT said it had funded its $200 million share of the acquisition through a high yield junior participation in the debt. As of late 2003, the Le Meridien portfolio included more than 120 upscale hotels and resorts with significant concentration in major European cities and resort destinations. In January 2004, the company said it had acquired Bliss, with operations that included spas and product sales, from LVMH Moet Hennessy Louis Vuitton. HOT said Bliss had 2003 revenues of $40 million.

Excluding special items, HOT had 2003 net income of $176 million ($0.86 a share). This excludes such items as impairment charges related to a portfolio of 18 U.S. non-core hotels that were held for sale, and a favorable settlement of tax matters.

In 2003, the company received about $1.1 billion of proceeds from various asset sales, including the sale of the Hotel Principe di Savoia in Milan, Italy; four hotels and an interest in some undeveloped land in Costa Smeralda, Italy; and 16 U.S. hotels that HOT considered to be non-core.

In December 1999, HOT sold most of its gaming assets, including Caesars World, Inc., for about $3 billion, to Park Place Entertainment Corp. The sale excluded the Desert Inn property, which was sold in June 2000 for $270 million. Proceeds were used primarily for debt reduction.

HOT common shares are attached and trade together with Class B shares that are related to a company subsidiary that is a real estate investment trust. HOT says that the trust is not subject to federal income tax on its taxable income at corporate rates provided that it distributes annually all of its taxable income to its shareholders and complies with certain other requirements.

Company Financials Fiscal Year ending December 31

Per Share Data ($)

(Year Ended December 31)	2003	2002	2001	2000	1999	1998	1997	1996	1995	1994
Tangible Bk. Val.	4.55	3.57	2.35	2.50	2.16	1.43	NA	NA	NA	NA
Cash Flow	2.58	2.28	3.29	4.30	-0.86	3.73	NA	NA	NA	NA
Earnings	0.51	1.20	0.73	1.96	-3.41	0.67	NA	NA	NA	NA
S&P Core Earnings	0.12	0.77	0.52	NA	NA	NA	NA	NA	NA	NA
Dividends	0.84	0.84	0.80	0.69	0.60	2.04	NA	NA	NA	NA
Payout Ratio	165%	70%	110%	35%	NM	NM	NA	NA	NA	NA
Prices - High	37.60	39.94	40.89	37.50	37.75	57.87	61.50	36.91	20.08	13.50
- Low	21.68	19.00	17.10	19.75	19.50	18.75	33.50	19.66	10.00	6.00
P/E Ratio - High	74	33	56	19	NM	86	NA	NA	NA	NA
- Low	43	16	23	10	NM	28	NA	NA	NA	NA

Income Statement Analysis (Million $)

	2003	2002	2001	2000	1999	1998	1997	1996	1995	1994
Revs.	4,630	4,659	3,967	4,345	3,862	4,710	NA	NA	NA	NA
Oper. Inc.	1,698	1,856	1,191	1,509	1,329	1,361	NA	NA	NA	NA
Depr.	429	222	526	481	476	556	NA	NA	NA	NA
Int. Exp.	287	338	369	439	516	639	NA	NA	NA	NA
Pretax Inc.	-5.00	252	200	610	533	43.0	NA	NA	NA	NA
Eff. Tax Rate	NM	1.59%	23.0%	33.0%	NM	NM	NA	NA	NA	NA
Net Inc.	105	246	151	401	-638	141	NA	NA	NA	NA
S&P Core Earnings	27.6	157	107	NA	NA	NA	NA	NA	NA	NA

Balance Sheet & Other Fin. Data (Million $)

	2003	2002	2001	2000	1999	1998	1997	1996	1995	1994
Cash	508	216	157	189	436	290	NA	NA	NA	NA
Curr. Assets	1,245	950	897	1,048	1,176	1,077	NA	NA	NA	NA
Total Assets	11,894	12,259	12,461	12,660	12,923	16,101	NA	NA	NA	NA
Curr. Liab.	1,644	2,199	1,587	1,805	2,303	2,074	NA	NA	NA	NA
LT Debt	4,393	4,449	5,269	5,074	4,779	8,111	NA	NA	NA	NA
Common Equity	4,326	6,357	3,756	3,851	3,690	4,202	NA	NA	NA	NA
Total Cap.	9,676	11,882	10,380	10,417	10,167	13,580	NA	NA	NA	NA
Cap. Exp.	307	82.0	477	544	521	832	NA	NA	NA	NA
Cash Flow	534	468	677	882	-162	697	NA	NA	NA	NA
Curr. Ratio	0.8	0.4	0.6	0.6	0.5	0.5	NA	NA	NA	NA
% LT Debt of Cap.	45.4	37.4	50.8	48.7	47.0	59.7	NA	NA	NA	NA
% Net Inc.of Revs.	NM	5.3	3.8	9.2	NM	3.0	NA	NA	NA	NA
% Ret. on Assets	NM	2.0	1.2	3.1	NM	NA	NA	NA	NA	NA
% Ret. on Equity	NM	3.9	4.0	10.6	NM	NA	NA	NA	NA	NA

Data as orig reptd.; bef. results of disc opers/spec. items. Per share data adj. for stk. divs. Bold denotes primary EPS - prior periods restated. E-Estimated. NA-Not Available. NM-Not Meaningful. NR-Not Ranked. UR-Under Review.

Office: 1111 Westchester Avenue, White Plains, NY 10604.
Telephone: 914-640-8100.
Website: http://www.starwoodhotels.com
Chrmn: B.S. Sternlicht.
Pres: S.M. Hankin.
Pres: T.W. Darnall.

CEO: S.J. Heyer.
COO: R.F. Cotter.
Investor Contact: P.S. Styles .
Dirs: C. Barshefsky, J. Chapus, B. W. Duncan, E. Hippeau, G. J. Mitchell, S. R. Quazzo, T. O. Ryder, B. S. Sternlicht, D. W. Yih, K. C. Youngblood.

Founded: in 1969.
Domicile: Maryland.
Employees: 110,000.
S&P Analyst: Tom Graves, CFA /PMW/BK

State Street Corp.

Recommendation: **HOLD** ★★★☆☆
SELL | SELL | HOLD | BUY | BUY

12-Month Target Price: **$46.00**
(as of October 12, 2004)

STT has an approximate 0.14% weighting in the **S&P 500**

Sector: Financials
Sub-Industry: Asset Management & Custody Banks
Peer Group: Investment Management Cos. - Larger

Summary: This bank holding company, with $9.4 trillion in assets under custody and $1.1 trillion in assets under management, is a leading servicer of financial assets worldwide.

Quantitative Evaluations

S&P Earnings & Dividend Rank: A

| D | C | B- | B | B+ | A- | A | A+ |

S&P Fair Value Rank: 4

| 1 | 2 | 3 | 4 | 5 |
| Lowest | | | | Highest |

Fair Value Calc.: $47.10 (Slightly Undervalued)

S&P Investability Quotient Percentile
94%

STT scored higher than 94% of all companies for which an S&P Report is available.

Volatility: Average

| Low | Average | High |

Technical Evaluation: Bullish
Since 11/04, the technical indicators for STT have been Bullish.

Relative Strength Rank: Moderate
45
1 Lowest — Highest 99

Price as of 11/12/04: $45.76 | **2004E S&P Core EPS:** $2.39

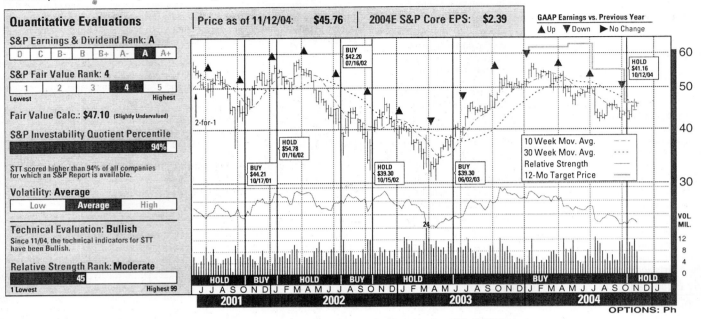

GAAP Earnings vs. Previous Year
▲ Up ▼ Down ► No Change

Analyst commentary prepared by Evan Momios, CFA /CB/BK

Highlights October 13, 2004

- We continue to believe that long-term macro trends remain intact, including outsourcing of custody services, growth of worldwide pension systems, development of more complex investment vehicles, consolidation among financial processing providers, and increasing pressure on public retirement systems. We think strong expected economic conditions, combined with expected equity market stability and what we view as STT's success in gaining new assets from existing and new clients in recent quarters, bode well for long-term revenue growth prospects.

- In the short term, however, our outlook is less optimistic following third quarter 2004 results that in our view demonstrated that the company needs to better align its operating expenses with its market sensitive revenue model. We believe the company's announced cost cutting initiatives could help in that direction and support results in the longer term. The challenge, in our view, will be to ensure that cost cutting does not put revenue growth opportunities at risk.

- Following disappointing third quarter 2004 results, we reduced our 2004 operating EPS estimate by $0.21, to $2.48 and our 2005 operating EPS estimate by $0.34, to $2.70.

Investment Rationale/Risk October 13, 2004

- We recently downgraded our recommendation on the shares to hold, from accumulate, following an earnings disappointment for the second consecutive quarter. We believe the newly appointed CEO is facing a challenging task in reducing the company's expenses while at the same time pursuing revenue growth opportunities.

- Risks to our recommendation and target price include a severe flattening or inversion of the Treasury yield curve; failure to implement announced cost cutting initiatives; legal and regulatory risks; and a serious geopolitical event that could impact global capital markets.

- Our 12-month target price of $46 is equal to about 17X our 2005 EPS estimate. We see this as reasonable based on our view of the company's subdued short-term operating outlook, the company's need to strengthen expense controls, its success in winning new clients, and the stock's historical valuation range. Based on our 2005 EPS estimate, a five-year projected EPS growth rate of 10%, and terminal P/E multiples of 16X to 18X, we estimate the stock's intrinsic value in the $43 to $49 range for various discount rates.

Key Stock Statistics

S&P Core EPS 2005E	2.62	52-week Range	$56.90-39.91
S&P Oper. EPS 2004E	2.48	12 Month P/E	14.6
P/E on S&P Oper. EPS 2004E	18.5	Beta	1.19
S&P Oper. EPS 2005E	2.70	Shareholders	5,454
Yield (%)	1.4%	Market Cap (B)	$15.3
Dividend Rate/Share	0.64	Shares Outstanding (M)	333.4

Value of $10,000 invested five years ago: **$13,158**

Dividend Data Dividends have been paid since 1910

Amount ($)	Date Decl.	Ex-Div. Date	Stock of Record	Payment Date
0.150	Dec. 18	Dec. 30	Jan. 02	Jan. 15 '04
0.150	Mar. 18	Mar. 30	Apr. 01	Apr. 15 '04
0.160	Jun. 17	Jun. 29	Jul. 01	Jul. 15 '04
0.160	Sep. 16	Sep. 29	Oct. 01	Oct. 15 '04

Revenues/Earnings Data Fiscal year ending December 31

Revenues (Million $)

	2004	2003	2002	2001	2000	1999
1Q	1,219	1,213	981.0	1,491	1,431	1,116
2Q	1,469	1,282	1,003	1,463	1,424	1,185
3Q	1,424	1,287	956.0	1,413	1,494	1,197
4Q	—	1,673	1,456	1,270	1,339	1,476
Yr.	—	5,463	4,396	5,637	5,027	4,974

Earnings Per Share ($)

	2004	2003	2002	2001	2000	1999
1Q	0.63	0.29	0.54	0.37	0.46	0.37
2Q	0.65	-0.07	0.54	0.50	0.45	0.38
3Q	0.52	0.60	0.56	0.51	0.46	0.39
4Q	E0.58	1.33	1.46	0.52	0.45	0.76
Yr.	E2.48	2.15	3.10	1.90	1.82	1.89

Next earnings report expected: mid-January Source: S&P, Company Reports
EPS Estimates based on S&P Operating Earnings; historical GAAP earnings are as reported.

State Street Corporation

Recommendation: **HOLD** ★★★☆☆   12-Month Target Price: **$46.00** (as of October 12, 2004)

Business Summary October 13, 2004

Best known as a leading provider of services in the post-trade phase of the investment process, which includes custody, accounting, fund administration and performance, State Street Corp. is one of the largest U.S. providers of trust services, with $9.4 trillion of assets under custody and $1.1 trillion of assets under management at the end of 2003.

Operations are conducted in two business lines: investment servicing (85% of operating revenues in 2003) and investment management (15%). Investment servicing includes accounting, custody, daily pricing, operations outsourcing for investment managers, securities lending, foreign exchange, trustee and record-keeping, deposit and short-term investment facilities, lease financing, and performance, risk and compliance analytics. The company also provides shareholder services, which include mutual fund and collective fund shareholder accounting, through 50%-owned affiliates Boston Financial Data Services and International Financial Data Services. Investment management provides a range of services for managing financial assets, including investment management, investment research and trading services primarily for institutional investors worldwide. These services include active and passive U.S. and non-U.S. equity and fixed income strategies, and other related services such as securities lending. In December 2002, STT sold its corporate trust business and recorded a gain of $495 million.

In 2003, average earning assets, from which interest income is derived, amounted to $73.57 billion, and consisted mainly of loans (8%), investment securities (42%), interest-bearing deposits with other banks (31%), and federal funds sold, securities purchased under resale agreements and trading account assets (20%). Average sources of funds included U.S. interest-bearing deposits (7%), foreign deposits (36%), noninterest-bearing demand deposits (9%), short-term borrowings (33%), long-term debt (2%), shareholders' equity (6%), and other (7%).

The company had no non-accrual loans at either December 31, 2003, or December 31, 2002. The allowance for loan losses, set aside for possible loan defaults, was $61 million (1.21% of loans) at the end of 2003, unchanged (1.46%) from the level a year earlier. There were no chargeoffs in 2003, versus less than $1 million of net chargeoffs in 2002.

In January 2003, STT completed the primary closing of its acquisition of a substantial part of the global securities services business of Deutsche Bank, for about $1.1 billion. In July 2003, it closed the acquisitions of Deutsche Bank's business units in Italy and Austria. In the period ending on the one-year anniversary of the primary closing, the company was to make additional payments of up to an estimated 360 million euros, based on performance. At December 31, 2003, GSS accounted for about 22% of total custody assets. In October 2003, STT sold its Private Asset Management business. It recognized a related net gain of $0.56 a share in the 2003 fourth quarter.

Company Financials Fiscal Year ending December 31

Per Share Data ($)

(Year Ended December 31)	2003	2002	2001	2000	1999	1998	1997	1996	1995	1994
Tangible Bk. Val.	11.66	12.92	11.87	10.13	8.31	7.19	6.20	5.47	4.82	4.03
Earnings	2.15	3.10	1.90	1.82	1.89	1.33	1.16	0.90	0.74	0.68
S&P Core Earnings	1.41	2.01	1.83	NA	NA	NA	NA	NA	NA	NA
Dividends	0.56	0.48	0.41	0.35	0.29	0.25	0.22	0.19	0.17	0.15
Payout Ratio	26%	15%	21%	19%	15%	19%	19%	21%	22%	22%
Prices - High	53.63	58.36	63.93	68.40	47.62	37.15	31.84	17.12	11.56	10.78
- Low	30.37	32.11	36.25	31.21	27.75	23.93	15.65	10.43	7.00	6.90
P/E Ratio - High	25	19	34	38	25	28	27	19	16	16
- Low	14	10	19	17	15	18	13	12	9	10

Income Statement Analysis (Million $)

	2003	2002	2001	2000	1999	1998	1997	1996	1995	1994
Net Int. Inc.	810	979	1,025	894	781	745	641	551	429	367
Tax Equiv. Adj.	51.0	61.0	67.0	65.0	40.0	40.0	44.0	37.0	34.9	23.8
Non Int. Inc.	368	571	2,782	2,665	2,255	1,997	1,673	1,292	1,107	982
Loan Loss Prov.	Nil	4.00	10.0	9.00	80.0	17.0	16.0	8.00	8.00	11.6
Exp./Op. Revs.	83.0%	74.2%	75.0%	74.3%	76.9%	75.4%	73.5%	74.4%	74.7%	74.0%
Pretax Inc.	1,112	1,555	930	906	968	657	564	447	367	320
Eff. Tax Rate	35.1%	34.7%	32.5%	34.3%	36.1%	33.6%	32.6%	34.5%	32.6%	35.2%
Net Inc.	722	1,015	628	595	619	436	380	293	247	207
% Net Int. Marg.	1.17	1.42	1.66	1.66	1.66	1.90	2.18	2.23	2.01	NA
S&P Core Earnings	473	658	604	NA	NA	NA	NA	NA	NA	NA

Balance Sheet & Other Fin. Data (Million $)

	2003	2002	2001	2000	1999	1998	1997	1996	1995	1994
Money Mkt. Assets	31,694	46,342	37,991	44,083	35,616	26,399	16,450	16,952	12,233	7,615
Inv. Securities	38,215	28,071	20,781	13,740	14,703	9,737	10,375	9,387	6,360	8,414
Com'l Loans	2,768	2,052	3,289	3,476	2,326	4,721	3,919	3,701	3,144	2,522
Other Loans	2,253	2,122	2,052	1,797	1,967	1,588	1,643	1,012	842	711
Total Assets	87,534	85,794	69,896	69,298	60,896	47,082	37,975	36,524	25,785	21,730
Demand Deposits	7,893	7,279	9,390	10,009	8,943	8,386	7,785	6,395	5,082	4,212
Time Deposits	39,623	38,189	29,169	27,928	25,202	19,153	17,093	13,124	11,565	9,691
LT Debt	2,222	1,270	1,217	1,219	921	922	774	511	175	128
Common Equity	5,747	4,787	3,845	3,262	2,652	2,311	1,995	1,775	1,588	1,231
% Ret. on Assets	0.8	1.3	0.9	0.9	1.1	1.0	1.1	1.1	1.0	1.0
% Ret. on Equity	13.7	23.5	17.7	20.1	24.9	20.3	20.2	17.5	16.9	17.8
% Loan Loss Resv.	1.2	1.5	1.1	1.1	1.1	1.3	1.5	1.6	1.6	1.8
% Loans/Deposits	10.6	9.2	13.9	13.9	12.6	22.9	22.4	24.2	23.9	23.3
% Equity to Assets	6.1	5.5	5.1	4.5	4.6	5.1	5.4	5.9	6.1	5.7

Data as orig reptd.; bef. results of disc opers/spec. items. Per share data adj. for stk. divs.; EPS diluted. E-Estimated. NA-Not Available. NM-Not Meaningful. NR-Not Ranked. UR-Under Review.

Office: 225 Franklin Street, Boston, MA 02110-2875.
Telephone: 617-786-3000.
Email: ir@statestreet.com
Website: http://www.statestreet.com
Chrmn & CEO: R.E. Logue.
Vice Chrmn: J.R. Towers.
EVP & CFO: E.J. Resch.

EVP & Treas: S.M. Gavell.
EVP, Secy & General Counsel: C. Cutrell.
SVP & Investor Contact: S.K. MacDonald 617-786-3000.
Dirs: T. E. Albright, K. F. Burnes, T. S. Casner, N. F. Darehshori, A. L. Goldstein, D. P. Gruber, L. A. Hill, C. R. Lamantia, R. E. Logue, A. Poe, R. P. Sergel, R. L. Skates, G. L. Summe, J. R. Towers, D. C. Walsh, R. E. Weissman.

Founded: in 1832.
Domicile: Massachusetts.
Employees: 19,850.
S&P Analyst: Evan Momios, CFA /CB/BK

Stryker Corp.

Recommendation: **BUY** ★★★★☆
SELL | SELL | HOLD | BUY | BUY

12-Month Target Price: **$53.00**
(as of October 15, 2004)

SYK has an approximate 0.16% weighting in the **S&P 500**

Sector: Health Care
Sub-Industry: Health Care Equipment
Peer Group: Orthopedic Products

Summary: SYK makes specialty surgical and medical products such as orthopedic implants, endoscopic items and hospital beds, and operates a chain of physical therapy clinics.

Quantitative Evaluations

S&P Earnings & Dividend Rank: B+

| D | C | B- | B | B+ | A- | A | A+ |

S&P Fair Value Rank: 3

| 1 | 2 | 3 | 4 | 5 |
Lowest — Highest

Fair Value Calc.: $43.10 (Slightly Overvalued)

S&P Investability Quotient Percentile

98%

SYK scored higher than 98% of all companies for which an S&P Report is available.

Volatility: Average

| Low | Average | High |

Technical Evaluation: Bearish
Since 10/04, the technical indicators for SYK have been Bearish.

Relative Strength Rank: Weak

21
1 Lowest — Highest 99

| Price as of 11/12/04: | $44.48 | 2004E S&P Core EPS: | $1.37 |

GAAP Earnings vs. Previous Year
▲ Up ▼ Down ► No Change

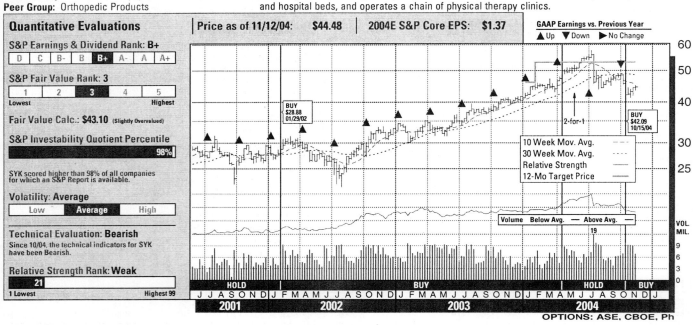

- 10 Week Mov. Avg.
- 30 Week Mov. Avg.
- Relative Strength
- 12-Mo Target Price

Volume Below Avg. — Above Avg.

BUY $28.88 01/29/02

2-for-1

BUY $42.09 10/15/04

HOLD | BUY | HOLD | BUY
J J A S O N D J F M A M J J A S O N D J F M A M J J A S O N D J F M A M J J A S O N D J
2001 | 2002 | 2003 | 2004

OPTIONS: ASE, CBOE, Ph

Analyst commentary prepared by Robert M. Gold/DC/BK

Highlights October 20, 2004

- We see 2005 revenues approximating $4.9 billion, up from an estimated $4.3 billion in 2004. In terms of foreign currency impact, we are not modeling any material upside from currency in 2005, following an estimated $105 million benefit in 2004. By category, we see reconstructive joint implant sales (knees, hips and extremities) growing about 15%, to $3.0 billion, versus the $2.6 billion we look for in 2004; medical/surgical revenues (arthroscopy, endoscopy, surgical instrument, hospital beds and stretchers) of $1.6 billion from an estimated $1.5 billion; and physical therapy revenues reaching $270 million from an estimated $250 million.

- In our opinion, foreign currency will continue to boost reported revenue growth, and, to a lesser extent, earnings growth into the 2004 fourth quarter. We expect that currency's will boost reported fourth quarter sales by up to $10 million, based on current exchange rates. However, we do not think that currency will have a meaningful impact on results during 2005. We look for a 2004 gross margin of 65%. We project that SG&A costs will consume 39% of sales, while R&D expenditures equal about 5% of sales. We see the effective tax rate for 2004 at 30.0%.

- Our 2004 operating EPS forecast is $1.43, with 2005 EPS seen advancing to $1.70. Our respective Standard & Poor's Core EPS projections are $1.37 and $1.63, reflecting estimated stock option expense. We believe the divergence between operating and Core EPS is modest relative to the company's peers.

Key Stock Statistics

S&P Core EPS 2005E	1.63	52-week Range	$57.66-39.26
S&P Oper. EPS 2004E	1.43	12 Month P/E	42.0
P/E on S&P Oper. EPS 2004E	31.1	Beta	0.51
S&P Oper. EPS 2005E	1.70	Shareholders	3,195
Yield (%)	0.2%	Market Cap (B)	$ 17.9
Dividend Rate/Share	0.07	Shares Outstanding (M)	402.0

Value of $10,000 invested five years ago: **$ 27,043**

Dividend Data Dividends have been paid since 1992

Amount ($)	Date Decl.	Ex-Div. Date	Stock of Record	Payment Date
q.07	—	Dec. 29	Dec. 31	Jan. 30 '04
0.140	Dec. 02	Dec. 29	Dec. 31	Jan. 30 '04
2-for-1	Apr. 20	May. 17	May. 03	May. 14 '04

Investment Rationale/Risk October 20, 2004

- Following a recent decline, we would accumulate the stock, and believe it now offers both solid long term fundamentals and a reasonable valuation. We also view the company's balance sheet as strong; as of September 30, 2004, the company had retired all $1.5 billion of debt incurred in the 1998 acquisition of Howmedica Inc. Long term debt was down to $3.9 million, from $18.8 million at the end of 2003. We believe that SYK will pursue strategic acquisitions using available borrowing capacity and free cash flow. For 2004, we estimate free cash flow will exceed $400 million. Based on our bullish view of the global orthopedics industry, and Stryker's strong position in it, we think SYK is an attractive investment in the group.

- Risks to our opinion and target price include possible unfavorable patent litigation outcomes, adverse Medicare reimbursement rate adjustments, and a significant loss of orthopedic device market share in the U.S. and/or Europe.

- With the shares recently trading nearly 30% below their 52-week high, we believe their valuation has become more attractive and we therefore upgraded SYK to accumulate from hold. Following the decline, the shares were priced at 24X our 2005 EPS estimate, a modest discount to our orthopedics universe and below the stock's average multiple over the past three years. Our 12-month target price of $53 is equal to about 31X our 2005 EPS forecast, representing a 2005 P/E to projected three-year growth ratio of 1.7X, in line with peers.

Revenues/Earnings Data Fiscal year ending December 31

Revenues (Million $)

	2004	2003	2002	2001	2000	1999
1Q	1,035	846.9	702.9	634.2	562.1	522.4
2Q	1,043	891.7	733.9	639.0	566.5	523.3
3Q	1,029	885.4	745.6	619.3	548.4	498.9
4Q	—	1,001	829.2	709.8	612.4	599.1
Yr.	—	3,625	3,012	2,602	2,289	2,104

Earnings Per Share ($)

	2004	2003	2002	2001	2000	1999
1Q	0.33	0.26	0.20	0.16	0.13	-0.05
2Q	0.37	0.27	0.21	0.16	0.13	-0.01
3Q	0.04	0.27	0.18	0.15	0.13	Nil
4Q	E0.40	0.33	0.26	0.20	0.17	0.11
Yr.	E1.43	1.11	0.85	0.67	0.55	0.05

Next earnings report expected: late-January Source: S&P, Company Reports
EPS Estimates based on S&P Operating Earnings; historical GAAP earnings are as reported.

STANDARD &POOR'S

Stryker Corporation

Stock Report
November 13, 2004
NYSE Symbol: SYK

Recommendation: **BUY** ★ ★ ★ ★ ☆   12-Month Target Price: **$53.00** (as of October 15, 2004)

Business Summary October 20, 2004

Stryker Corp. traces its origins to a business founded in 1941 by Dr. Homer H. Stryker, a leading orthopedic surgeon and the inventor of several orthopedic products. The company has significant exposure to the artificial hip, prosthetic knee, and trauma product areas. International sales accounted for 36% of the total in 2003.

Orthopedic implants (58% of 2003 sales) consist of products such as hip, knee, shoulder and spinal implants, associated implant instrumentation, trauma-related products, and bone cement. Artificial joints are made of cobalt chromium, titanium alloys, ceramics, or ultra-high molecular weight polyethylene, and are implanted in patients whose natural joints have been damaged by arthritis, osteoporosis, other diseases, or injury. SYK also sells trauma-related products, used primarily in the fixation of fractures resulting from sudden injury, and including internal fixation devices such as nails, plates and screws, and external fixation devices such as pins, wires and connection bars. The division also sells Simplex bone cement, a material used to secure cemented implants to bone, and the OP-1 Bone Growth Device. Composed of recombinant human osteogenic protein-1 and a bioresorbable collagen matrix, the product induces the formation of new bone when implanted into existing bone, and is approved to treat long bone fractures in patients in whom use of autograft treatments has failed or is not a feasible option. Stryker continues to develop OP-1 for spinal indications, including spinal stenosis.

The medical and surgical equipment unit (36%) operates through four units. Stryker Instruments sells powered surgical drills, saws, fixation and reaming equipment, as well as other instruments used for drilling, burring, rasping or cutting bone, wiring or pinning bone fractures, and preparing hip or knee surfaces for the placement of artificial hip or knee joints. Stryker Endoscopy offers medical video cameras, light sources, arthroscopes, laparascopes, powered surgical instruments, and disposable suction/irrigation devices. Stryker Medical offers 30 types of specialty stretchers customized for acute care and specialty surgical facilities. Stryker Leibinger makes plate and screw systems for craniomaxillofacial surgery to repair small bones in the hands, face and head, and sells a proprietary bone substitute material, BoneSource.

Through a network of 374 outpatient centers in 25 states and the District of Columbia, the Physiotherapy Associates (6%) division provides physical, occupational and speech therapy services to patients recovering from orthopedic or neurological illness and injury. During 2003, Physiotherapy and Stryker received a subpoena concerning a Department of Justice investigation into the unit's billing coding practices. Revenues from billings to U.S. federal health care programs approximated 14% of division sales in 2003 and 2002.

During 2003, spending on research and development totaled $180.2 million (5.0% of sales), up from $141.4 million (4.7%) in 2002. New product launches in 2003 included the Trident Ceramic Acetabular System, Simplex P with Tobramycin Bone Cement, and the CORE platform of micro powered surgical instruments in the U.S. and the System 5 heavy-duty, battery-powered surgical instruments in Europe.

Company Financials Fiscal Year ending December 31

Per Share Data ($)

(Year Ended December 31)	2003	2002	2001	2000	1999	1998	1997	1996	1995	1994
Tangible Bk. Val.	2.98	1.42	0.65	0.04	NM	NM	1.48	1.25	1.12	0.88
Cash Flow	1.71	1.30	1.09	0.97	0.46	0.20	0.40	0.36	0.30	0.24
Earnings	1.11	0.85	0.67	0.55	0.05	0.10	0.32	0.27	0.23	0.19
S&P Core Earnings	1.07	0.80	0.63	NA	NA	NA	NA	NA	NA	NA
Dividends	0.07	0.06	0.05	0.03	0.03	0.03	0.03	0.03	0.01	0.01
Payout Ratio	6%	7%	7%	5%	60%	27%	9%	9%	5%	5%
Prices - High	42.68	33.73	31.60	28.87	18.31	13.93	11.32	8.03	7.31	4.68
- Low	29.82	21.92	21.65	12.21	11.10	7.75	6.06	4.96	4.51	2.96
P/E Ratio - High	38	40	47	52	NM	NM	35	30	32	25
- Low	27	26	32	22	NM	NM	19	18	20	16

Income Statement Analysis (Million $)

	2003	2002	2001	2000	1999	1998	1997	1996	1995	1994
Revs.	3,625	3,012	2,602	2,289	2,104	1,103	980	910	872	682
Oper. Inc.	901	751	645	600	329	226	217	169	186	141
Depr.	230	186	172	169	163	37.6	33.3	34.7	28.7	20.9
Int. Exp.	22.6	40.3	67.9	96.6	123	12.2	4.12	4.35	6.32	3.68
Pretax Inc.	653	507	406	335	29.8	60.0	196	160	163	128
Eff. Tax Rate	30.5%	31.8%	33.0%	34.0%	34.9%	34.0%	35.7%	38.4%	41.0%	39.8%
Net Inc.	454	346	272	221	19.4	39.6	125	104	87.0	72.4
S&P Core Earnings	436	324	257	NA	NA	NA	NA	NA	NA	NA

Balance Sheet & Other Fin. Data (Million $)

	2003	2002	2001	2000	1999	1998	1997	1996	1995	1994
Cash	65.9	37.8	50.1	54.0	80.0	142	351	368	265	202
Curr. Assets	1,398	1,151	993	997	1,110	1,312	757	754	624	541
Total Assets	3,159	2,816	2,424	2,431	2,581	2,886	985	994	855	768
Curr. Liab.	851	708	533	617	670	699	303	252	174	179
LT Debt	18.8	491	721	877	1,181	1,488	4.45	90.0	97.0	95.3
Common Equity	2,155	1,498	1,056	855	672	643	657	530	454	358
Total Cap.	2,174	1,989	1,777	1,731	1,853	2,148	653	706	656	556
Cap. Exp.	145	139	162	80.7	76.2	51.2	35.2	26.7	36.2	29.2
Cash Flow	683	532	444	390	182	77.2	159	139	116	93.3
Curr. Ratio	1.6	1.6	1.9	1.6	1.7	1.9	2.5	3.0	3.6	3.0
% LT Debt of Cap.	0.9	24.7	40.6	50.6	63.8	69.3	0.7	12.7	14.8	17.1
% Net Inc.of Revs.	12.5	11.5	10.4	9.7	0.9	3.6	12.8	11.5	10.0	10.6
% Ret. on Assets	15.2	13.2	11.2	8.8	0.7	2.0	12.7	11.3	10.7	11.9
% Ret. on Equity	24.8	27.1	28.4	29.0	2.9	6.1	20.5	21.2	21.4	22.4

Data as orig reptd.; bef. results of disc opers/spec. items. Per share data adj. for stk. divs.; EPS diluted. E-Estimated. NA-Not Available. NM-Not Meaningful. NR-Not Ranked. UR-Under Review.

Office: 2725 Fairfield Rd, Portage, MI 49002-1752.
Telephone: 269-385-2600.
Website: http://www.strykercorp.com
Chrmn, Pres & CEO: J.W. Brown.
Pres & COO: S.P. MacMillan.

VP, CFO, Secy & Investor Contact: D.H. Bergy 269-385-2600.
General Counsel: C.E. Hall.
Dirs: J. W. Brown, H. E. Cox, Jr., D. M. Engelman, J. H. Grossman, J. S. Lillard, W. U. Parfet, R. E. Stryker.

Founded: in 1946.
Domicile: Michigan.
Employees: 14,762.
S&P Analyst: Robert M. Gold/DC/BK

SunGard Data Systems

Recommendation: **HOLD** ★ ★ ★ ☆ ☆
SELL · SELL · HOLD · BUY · BUY

12-Month Target Price: $29.00
(as of October 04, 2004)

SDS has an approximate 0.07% weighting in the **S&P 500**

Sector: Information Technology
Sub-Industry: Data Processing & Outsourced Services
Peer Group: Financial Services Processors & Services

Summary: This large specialized provider of proprietary investment support systems also offers outsourcing and hosting for online and other business applications.

Quantitative Evaluations

S&P Earnings & Dividend Rank: B+

D	C	B-	B	B+	A-	A	A+

S&P Fair Value Rank: 5

1	2	3	4	5
Lowest				Highest

Fair Value Calc.: $36.40 (Undervalued)

S&P Investability Quotient Percentile

94%

SDS scored higher than 94% of all companies for which an S&P Report is available.

Volatility: Average

Low	Average	High

Technical Evaluation: Bullish
Since 10/04, the technical indicators for SDS have been Bullish.

Relative Strength Rank: Moderate
55
1 Lowest   Highest 99

Price as of 11/12/04: $26.63 | **2004E S&P Core EPS: $1.15**

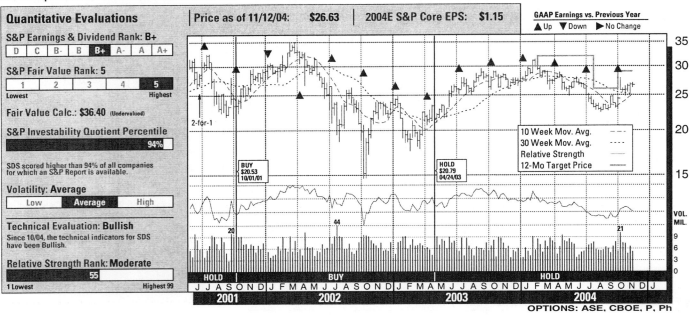

GAAP Earnings vs. Previous Year
▲ Up ▼ Down ► No Change

10 Week Mov. Avg.
30 Week Mov. Avg.
Relative Strength
12-Mo Target Price

BUY $20.53 10/01/01
HOLD $20.79 04/24/03

2-for-1

OPTIONS: ASE, CBOE, P, Ph

Analyst commentary prepared by Stephanie S. Crane/MF/GG

Highlights October 22, 2004

- Reflecting our view of still somewhat restrained corporate technology spending, we project EPS growth of 10% in 2004. However, we project annual EPS growth of 14% to 16% over the next three years. SDS is a leader in investment support systems and software (52% of 2004 second quarter sales), and we believe it will continue to leverage its position to win new contracts. SDS has also been benefiting from demand for its availability services (33%), as corporations continue to outsource computer operations.

- Over the past couple of years, SDS acquired the disaster recovery assets of Comdisco and U.K.-based Guardian iT (a large European supplier of business continuity solutions), for $1.1 billion in cash and stock. In October 2004, SDS announced the proposed spinoff of its Availability Services business, in part, we believe, to enable both of the company's primary operating units to better pursue and execute on opportunities. Pending necessary regulatory and IRS approvals, we expect the spinoff to be completed by March 2005. Shareholder approval is not required.

- As a result of acquisitions, SDS has also established a Higher Education and Public Sector Systems segment (15%) to diversify its revenues and enable cross-selling. In September, the company sold its electronics communications network, Brut, to NASDAQ, for which it garnered an after-tax gain of $47 million, or $0.16 per share.

Key Stock Statistics

S&P Oper. EPS 2004E	1.40	52-week Range	$31.65-22.40
P/E on S&P Oper. EPS 2004E	19.0	12 Month P/E	17.3
S&P Oper. EPS 2005E	1.59	Beta	0.90
Yield (%)	Nil	Shareholders	7,850
Dividend Rate/Share	Nil	Market Cap (B)	$7.7
Shares Outstanding (M)	288.4		

Value of $10,000 invested five years ago: **$ 22,663**

Dividend Data

No cash dividends have been paid.

Investment Rationale/Risk October 22, 2004

- Despite an improving economy, we think financial services companies remain somewhat hesitant to make new investments in technology. However, they appear to be committing some of their budgets to the company's straight-through processing offerings, which should provide returns on investment and productivity benefits. We believe existing customers are also spending a greater percentage of their resources on the company's software and services. In our view, the planned spinoff of the Availability Services company through a tax-free distribution to shareholders would promote better business focus and a more attractive company valuation.

- Risks to our opinion and target price include customers potentially delaying IT spending due to required Sarbanes-Oxley compliance, companies increasingly fulfilling continuity services internally rather than relying on an outside vendor, newer acquisitions not adding as much value as we expected, and the spinoff of Availability Services being delayed or cancelled.

- The stock's recent P/E of 17 was comparable to that of the S&P 500, but its P/E-to-growth (PEG) ratio of 1.1 was well below the index's. Based on comparisons with the S&P 500 Data Processing Services Sub-Industry (where SDS had P/E and PEG ratios less than those of its peers), our 12-month target price is $29. We believe the company's pending spinoff of its Availability Services business would contribute to shareholder value.

Revenues/Earnings Data Fiscal year ending December 31

Revenues (Million $)

	2004	2003	2002	2001	2000	1999
1Q	840.6	674.5	594.2	440.8	384.7	319.6
2Q	898.7	734.0	623.3	462.2	401.1	333.4
3Q	899.3	742.4	644.2	463.3	413.2	351.7
4Q	—	804.3	682.5	562.4	461.7	388.3
Yr.	—	2,955	2,593	1,929	1,661	1,445

Earnings Per Share ($)

	2004	2003	2002	2001	2000	1999
1Q	0.29	0.26	0.24	0.20	0.15	-0.08
2Q	0.35	0.31	0.28	0.22	0.20	0.15
3Q	0.52	0.31	0.27	0.22	0.21	0.14
4Q	E0.41	0.38	0.33	0.23	0.24	0.18
Yr.	E1.40	1.27	1.12	0.86	0.78	0.39

Next earnings report expected: mid-February Source: S&P, Company Reports
EPS Estimates based on S&P Operating Earnings; historical GAAP earnings are as reported.

SunGard Data Systems Inc.

Recommendation: **HOLD** ★ ★ ★ ☆ ☆   12-Month Target Price: **$29.00** (as of October 04, 2004)

Business Summary October 22, 2004

SunGard Data Systems provides software and processing solutions, primarily for financial services, and also offers information availability solutions. The company's strategy entails upgrading and enhancing its offerings, acquiring complementary businesses, providing straight-through processing, building strong customer relationships, maintaining financial strength, and promoting an entrepreneurial culture.

Investment Support Systems (which accounted for 54% of revenues in both 2003 and 2002) offers order routing, trading support, execution and clearing, position keeping and tracking, regulatory and tax compliance and reporting, and investment accounting and record keeping (brokerage and trading systems); manages and services the portfolios of high net worth individuals (wealth management systems); automates risk management and trading operations (treasury and risk management systems); tracks investment activities, values portfolios, performs complex accounting calculations and general ledger postings, and generates reports (investment management systems); and addresses accounting activities associated with defined contribution retirement plans such as 401(k) plans (benefit, insurance and investor accounting systems).

Through Availability Services (which contributed 40% of 2003 revenues and 41% in 2002), SDS enables customers to ensure the continuity of their business information. High-availability solutions include a combination of a dedicated network, servers and storage per customer. Traditional business continuity operations

allow clients to restore processing operations several hours to two days after an interruption. SDS also provides offerings that allow customers to relocate important business processes, and range from generic office space to dedicated trading rooms

Higher Education and Public Sector Systems (6%, 5%) provides specialized enterprise resource planning (ERP) and administrative solutions to institutions of higher learning, school districts, and other non-profit organizations, as well as to government entities. Offerings are related to accounting; personnel; fundraising; grant and project management; student administration and reporting for educational and non-profit organizations; and accounting, personnel, utility billing, land management, public safety, and justice administration for government entities.

Through nine acquisitions in 2003, SDS bolstered its offerings in trust tax and compliance products and services (Trust Tax Services of America), registered brokerage (Andover Brokerage), financial management and public safety and justice solutions for government agencies and utilities (H.T.E.), software for the energy industry (Caminus), risk management solutions (Reech Capital), technology and services for managed account and separately managed account strategies (London Pacific Advisory Services), global insurance industry and government sector software and services (Sherwood International), investment management and portfolio accounting solutions (Forbatec), and credit risk solutions for Basel II compliance (Whitelight Systems). In 2002, SDS completed nine acquisitions.

Company Financials Fiscal Year ending December 31

Per Share Data ($)

(Year Ended December 31)	2003	2002	2001	2000	1999	1998	1997	1996	1995	1994
Tangible Bk. Val.	3.26	3.05	4.18	4.29	3.89	2.25	1.57	1.20	1.52	1.40
Cash Flow	2.33	1.82	1.25	1.11	0.58	1.05	0.96	0.61	0.65	0.51
Earnings	1.27	1.12	0.86	0.79	0.39	0.55	0.43	0.20	0.31	0.28
S&P Core Earnings	1.01	0.94	0.76	NA	NA	NA	NA	NA	NA	NA
Dividends	Nil	Nil	Nil	Nil	Nil	Nil	Nil	Nil	Nil	Nil
Payout Ratio	Nil	Nil	Nil	Nil	Nil	Nil	Nil	Nil	Nil	Nil
Prices - High	29.60	35.10	32.49	27.50	20.96	20.00	15.71	11.87	8.12	5.12
- Low	17.50	14.70	20.00	11.50	8.43	10.84	9.25	6.87	4.43	3.93
P/E Ratio - High	23	31	38	35	54	36	36	59	26	18
- Low	14	13	23	15	22	20	21	34	14	14

Income Statement Analysis (Million $)

	2003	2002	2001	2000	1999	1998	1997	1996	1995	1994
Revs.	2,955	2,593	1,929	1,661	1,445	1,160	862	670	533	437
Oper. Inc.	932	828	582	495	397	322	242	182	139	106
Depr.	311	203	109	88.7	76.8	108	94.8	70.9	54.7	35.9
Int. Exp.	11.7	13.1	3.64	2.24	2.32	1.74	2.58	Nil	Nil	0.67
Pretax Inc.	615	543	410	357	190	208	134	63.6	85.1	72.5
Eff. Tax Rate	39.8%	40.1%	40.1%	40.3%	61.6%	42.9%	42.0%	45.1%	42.8%	40.6%
Net Inc.	370	326	246	213	73.2	119	77.5	34.9	48.7	43.1
S&P Core Earnings	297	271	217	NA	NA	NA	NA	NA	NA	NA

Balance Sheet & Other Fin. Data (Million $)

	2003	2002	2001	2000	1999	1998	1997	1996	1995	1994
Cash	479	440	396	256	287	258	64.9	46.1	115	103
Curr. Assets	1,363	1,135	1,118	912	787	584	310	237	281	222
Total Assets	4,000	3,282	2,898	1,845	1,565	1,075	786	679	580	486
Curr. Liab.	1,047	871	749	395	348	312	225	210	148	113
LT Debt	187	188	355	7.94	5.52	2.82	2.80	4.40	3.24	4.90
Common Equity	2,766	2,222	1,794	1,442	1,211	761	559	465	422	359
Total Cap.	2,953	2,410	2,149	1,450	1,216	764	562	469	432	372
Cap. Exp.	182	121	102	99	95.8	63.6	54.4	11.7	4.71	34.3
Cash Flow	682	529	355	302	150	227	172	106	103	79.0
Curr. Ratio	1.3	1.3	1.5	2.3	2.3	1.9	1.4	1.1	1.9	2.0
% LT Debt of Cap.	6.3	7.8	16.5	0.5	0.5	0.4	0.5	0.9	0.8	1.3
% Net Inc.of Revs.	12.5	12.6	12.8	12.8	5.1	10.3	9.0	5.2	9.1	9.9
% Ret. on Assets	10.2	10.5	10.4	12.5	5.3	12.8	10.6	5.5	9.1	9.5
% Ret. on Equity	14.8	16.2	15.2	16.1	7.1	18.0	15.2	7.9	12.5	12.8

Data as orig reptd.; bef. results of disc opers/spec. items. Per share data adj. for stk. divs.; EPS diluted. E-Estimated. NA-Not Available. NM-Not Meaningful. NR-Not Ranked. UR-Under Review.

Office: 680 East Swedesford Road, Wayne, PA 19087.
Telephone: 610-341-8700.
Website: http://www.sungard.com
Chrmn: J.L. Mann.
Pres & CEO: C. Conde.
SVP, CFO & Treas: M.J. Ruane.

SVP & General Counsel: L.A. Gross.
Investor Contact: M. Hopkins 610-341-4357.
Dirs: G. S. Bentley, M. C. Brooks, C. Conde, R. De Oliveira, H. C. Duques, A. A. Eisenstat, B. Goldstein, J. Haugen, R. E. King, J. L. Mann, M. I. Ruddock.

Founded: in 1982.
Domicile: Delaware.
Employees: 10,000.
S&P Analyst: Stephanie S. Crane/MF/GG

Recommendation: **SELL** ★★☆☆☆
SELL SELL HOLD BUY BUY

12-Month Target Price: **$70.00**
(as of July 22, 2004)

SUN has an approximate 0.05% weighting in the **S&P 500**

Sector: Energy
Sub-Industry: Oil & Gas Refining, Marketing & Transportation
Peer Group: Refining and/or Marketing

Summary: SUN is primarily a petroleum refiner and marketer, with interests in logistics and cokemaking.

Quantitative Evaluations

S&P Earnings & Dividend Rank: B+

| D | C | B- | B | B+ | A- | A | A+ |

S&P Fair Value Rank: 3+

| 1 | 2 | 3 | 4 | 5 |
Lowest — Highest

Fair Value Calc.: $75.00 (Fairly Valued)

S&P Investability Quotient Percentile
98%

SUN scored higher than 98% of all companies for which an S&P Report is available.

Volatility: Average

| Low | Average | High |

Technical Evaluation: Bullish
Since 9/04, the technical indicators for SUN have been Bullish.

Relative Strength Rank: Moderate
66
1 Lowest — Highest 99

Price as of 11/12/04: $76.36   **2004E S&P Core EPS:** $7.10

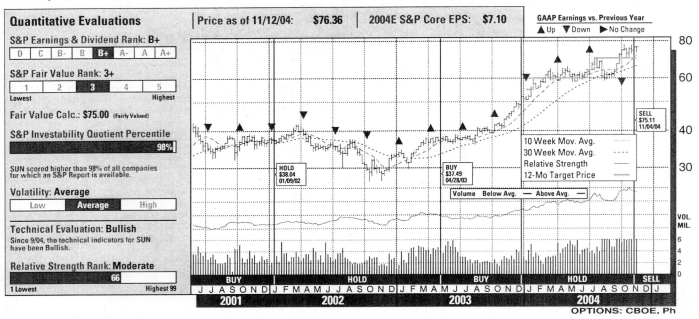

GAAP Earnings vs. Previous Year
▲ Up ▼ Down ▶ No Change

10 Week Mov. Avg.
30 Week Mov. Avg.
Relative Strength
12-Mo Target Price

Volume Below Avg. — Above Avg.

BUY / HOLD / BUY / HOLD / SELL
2001 2002 2003 2004

OPTIONS: CBOE, Ph

Analyst commentary prepared by T. Vital/CB/BK

Highlights November 05, 2004

- Third quarter operating earnings declined 3.2%, to $120 million, or $1.60 per share, $0.04 below our estimate, reflecting increased planned maintenance in the Northeast Refining Complex and higher than expected operating expenses, partially offset by higher than expected chemical pricing. SUN's January 2004 purchase of the Eagle Point refinery contributed $30 million to third quarter earnings. Operating results excluded a $34 million after-tax loss from the early extinguishment of debt, and an $18 million after-tax gain from an income tax settlement.

- Planned 2004 capital spending has been boosted to $750 million ($175 million for the clean fuels program, which should total $400 million to $500 million by 2006), from $425 million ($23 million) in 2003. Stock buybacks remain a significant part of SUN's overall strategy, with 3.7 million shares repurchased for $236 million during the first nine months of 2004; about $550 million of authorizations remain outstanding.

- EBITDA nearly tripled in 2003, and we expect a 41% hike in 2004 on strong demand and higher throughputs, but we expect a 26% drop in 2005 on reduced demand stemming from projected slower economic growth.

Investment Rationale/Risk November 05, 2004

- As a diversified refiner focused on light/sweet crude feedstocks, we expect SUN to continue to benefit from a recovery in the chemical sector, but we see downside risk to its U.S. refining margins from projected slower economic growth and a build in U.S. refined product inventories. However, SUN has increased its financial flexibility through debt refinancing and reduction, which should help it weather changes in the industrial climate. In September 2004, SUN issued $250 million of 10-year, 4 7/8% notes, and repurchased $352 million of various higher interest rate (6 3/4% to 9 3/8%) debt issues; SUN projects annual pretax interest savings of about $15 million. As of September 30, 2004, net debt to capital dropped to 38%, from 42% at 2003 year end.

- Risks to our recommendation and target price include the company's diversification into petrochemicals, lubricants, logistics and coke, which could offset earnings volatility from its refining and marketing operations.

- Based on a blend of discounted cash flow analysis and multiples valuations, our 12-month target price is $70, which represents 12X our 2005 EPS estimate, a premium to peers reflecting SUN's diversified business base. We would avoid SUN shares, as they are trading above this level.

Key Stock Statistics

S&P Core EPS 2005E	5.69	52-week Range	$78.03-44.74
S&P Oper. EPS 2004E	7.35	12 Month P/E	12.5
P/E on S&P Oper. EPS 2004E	10.4	Beta	0.37
S&P Oper. EPS 2005E	5.88	Shareholders	250,000
Yield (%)	1.6%	Market Cap (B)	$ 5.6
Dividend Rate/Share	1.20	Shares Outstanding (M)	73.1

Value of $10,000 invested five years ago: **$ 36,681**

Dividend Data Dividends have been paid since 1904

Amount ($)	Date Decl.	Ex-Div. Date	Stock of Record	Payment Date
0.275	Jan. 08	Feb. 06	Feb. 10	Mar. 10 '04
0.275	Apr. 01	May. 06	May. 10	Jun. 10 '04
0.300	Jul. 01	Aug. 06	Aug. 10	Sep. 10 '04
0.300	Oct. 07	Nov. 08	Nov. 10	Dec. 10 '04

Revenues/Earnings Data Fiscal year ending December 31

Revenues (Million $)

	2004	2003	2002	2001	2000	1999
1Q	5,245	4,570	2,931	3,627	3,187	1,933
2Q	6,276	4,189	3,556	3,916	3,634	2,373
3Q	6,558	4,594	3,812	3,588	3,702	2,651
4Q	—	4,576	4,085	2,932	3,738	3,111
Yr.	—	17,929	14,384	14,063	14,300	10,068

Earnings Per Share ($)

	2004	2003	2002	2001	2000	1999
1Q	1.17	1.12	-1.40	1.24	0.75	0.21
2Q	3.07	1.04	0.12	2.35	2.44	0.28
3Q	1.39	1.40	-0.13	0.99	-0.29	0.15
4Q	E1.46	0.47	0.79	0.05	1.80	0.42
Yr.	E7.35	4.03	-0.62	4.85	4.70	1.07

Next earnings report expected: late-January Source: S&P, Company Reports
EPS Estimates based on S&P Operating Earnings; historical GAAP earnings are as reported.

Sunoco, Inc.

Recommendation: **SELL** ★ ★ ☆ ☆ ☆   12-Month Target Price: **$70.00** (as of July 22, 2004)

Business Summary November 05, 2004

As the eighth largest U.S. refiner, based on refining capacity, Sunoco or its predecessors have been active in the petroleum industry since 1886. Sunoco, Inc. (SUN), the holding company, is a non-operating holding company. The company operates in five business segments: Refining and Supply (40% of 2003 sales; 56% of 2003 pretax income), Retail Marketing (42%; 19%), Chemicals (9%; 11%), Logistics (7%; 5%) and Coke (2%; 9%).

The Refining and Supply business manufactures petroleum products, commodity petrochemicals, and lubricants. As of December 31, 2003, SUN owned and operated four refineries, located in Marcus Hook and Philadelphia, PA (505,000 barrels per day, b/d), Toledo, OH (140,000 b/d), and Tulsa, OK (85,000 b/d). In January 2004, SUN purchased the Eagle Point (150,000 b/d) refinery from El Paso Corp. for $235 million, including an estimated $124 million for crude oil and refined product inventory. Virtually all of the crude oil processed at the company's refineries is light sweet crude, acquired through third parties from West Africa (63% of 2003 purchases), the U.S. (22%), Canada (7%), the North Sea (5%), and elsewhere. Product sales rose 2.6%, to 842,900 b/d, in 2003 (gasoline 30%, middle distillates 43%, residual fuels 14%, petrochemicals 2%, lubricants 3%, and other).

SUN estimates that clean fuels spending to comply with Tier II gasoline and diesel specifications will range between $400 million and $500 million by 2006.

Retail Marketing consists of the retail sale of gasoline and middle distillates, as well as the operation of convenience stores in 25 states, primarily on the East

Coast and in the Midwest. At December 31, 2003, SUN had 4,528 retail gasoline outlets (45% company-owned or leased, and 55% distributor outlets). In April 2004, the company purchased some 385 retail gasoline sites under the Mobil brand from ConocoPhillips for about $187 million, plus inventory. Branded fuel sales rose 6.1%, to 316,800 b/d, in 2003, reflecting wider retail margins and contributions from the 193 Speedway retail sites purchased from Marathon Ashland Petroleum LLC in June 2003.

During 2003, petrochemicals production declined 0.4%, to 5,718 million lbs. (phenol and related products 46%, polypropylene 27%, propylene 14%, plasticizers 10%, and other 3%). In March 2003, SUN secured a long-term supply of propylene and acquired a 400 million lb/y polypropylene facility from Equistar Chemicals L.P for $198 million. In January 2004, SUN sold its plasticizer business to BASF for about $90 million.

Logistics operations are conducted primarily through Sunoco Logistics Partners L.P., a master limited partnership that is 75.3% owned by SUN. Activities include the operation of crude oil and refined product pipelines and terminals, and marketing activities in the U.S.

The Coke business makes high-quality, blast furnace coke at its Indiana Harbor facility in East Chicago, IN, and its Jewell facility in Vansant, VA, and produces metallurgical coal production from mines in Virginia primarily for use at the Jewell cokemaking facility. Coke sales declined 6.2%, to 2.024 million tons, in 2003.

Company Financials Fiscal Year ending December 31

Per Share Data ($)

(Year Ended December 31)	2003	2002	2001	2000	1999	1998	1997	1996	1995	1994
Tangible Bk. Val.	20.47	18.10	21.75	20.06	16.73	16.82	10.41	9.45	12.82	17.07
Cash Flow	8.71	3.70	8.77	8.10	4.10	5.44	4.93	-0.80	5.99	4.26
Earnings	4.03	-0.62	4.85	4.70	1.07	2.95	2.70	-4.43	2.24	0.91
S&P Core Earnings	4.26	-1.40	3.75	NA	NA	NA	NA	NA	NA	NA
Dividends	1.03	1.00	1.00	1.00	1.00	1.00	1.00	1.00	1.40	1.80
Payout Ratio	25%	NM	21%	21%	93%	34%	37%	NM	63%	198%
Prices - High	52.60	42.25	42.73	34.56	39.43	44.31	46.37	32.62	32.87	35.25
- Low	29.67	27.02	29.12	21.93	22.87	29.50	24.00	21.87	24.75	25.12
P/E Ratio - High	13	NM	9	7	37	15	17	NM	15	39
- Low	7	NM	6	5	21	10	9	NM	11	28

Income Statement Analysis (Million $)

	2003	2002	2001	2000	1999	1998	1997	1996	1995	1994
Revs.	17,866	14,299	14,063	14,062	9,889	8,413	10,464	11,233	8,370	7,702
Oper. Inc.	934	313	954	948	331	605	680	225	575	562
Depr. Depl. & Amort.	363	329	321	298	276	257	259	267	341	359
Int. Exp.	111	108	103	78.0	82.0	71.0	71.0	79.0	105	97.0
Pretax Inc.	495	-73.0	587	596	150	389	385	-408	319	155
Eff. Tax Rate	37.0%	NM	32.2%	31.0%	35.3%	28.0%	31.7%	NM	28.8%	14.8%
Net Inc.	312	-47.0	398	411	97.0	280	263	-281	227	97.0
S&P Core Earnings	330	-106	307	NA	NA	NA	NA	NA	NA	NA

Balance Sheet & Other Fin. Data (Million $)

	2003	2002	2001	2000	1999	1998	1997	1996	1995	1994
Cash	431	390	42.0	239	87.0	38.0	33.0	67.0	14.0	117
Curr. Assets	2,068	1,898	1,510	1,683	1,456	1,180	1,248	1,535	1,460	1,508
Total Assets	6,922	6,441	5,932	5,426	5,196	4,849	4,667	5,025	5,184	6,465
Curr. Liab.	2,170	1,776	1,778	1,646	1,766	1,384	1,464	1,817	1,530	1,915
LT Debt	1,350	1,453	1,142	933	878	823	824	835	888	1,073
Common Equity	1,556	1,394	1,642	1,702	4,782	1,514	739	690	949	1,863
Total Cap.	3,940	3,816	3,335	2,885	5,897	2,512	2,359	2,273	2,709	3,606
Cap. Exp.	425	385	331	465	374	457	380	408	545	848
Cash Flow	675	282	719	709	373	517	478	-59.0	545	456
Curr. Ratio	1.0	1.1	0.8	1.0	0.8	0.9	0.9	0.8	1.0	0.8
% LT Debt of Cap.	34.3	38.1	34.2	32.3	14.9	32.8	34.9	36.8	32.8	29.8
% Ret. on Assets	4.7	NM	7.0	7.7	1.9	5.9	5.4	NM	3.9	1.6
% Ret. on Equity	21.2	NM	23.8	25.6	2.0	23.1	30.7	NM	14.5	5.0

Data as orig reptd.; bef. results of disc opers/spec. items. Per share data adj. for stk. divs.; EPS diluted. E-Estimated. NA-Not Available. NM-Not Meaningful. NR-Not Ranked. UR-Under Review.

Office: 1801 Market Street, Philadelphia, PA 19103-1699.
Telephone: 215-977-3000.
Email: sunocoonline@sunocoinc.com
Website: http://www.sunocoinc.com
Chrmn, Pres & CEO: J.G. Drosdick.
SVP & CFO: T.W. Hofmann.

SVP & Chief Admin: C.K. Valutas.
SVP & General Counsel: M.S. Kuritzkes.
VP & Investor Contact: T.P. Delaney 215-977-6106.
Dirs: R. J. Darnall, J. G. Dorsdick, U. F. Fairbairn, T. P. Gerrity, R. Greco, J. G. Kaiser, R. D. Kennedy, R. Lenny, N. S. Matthews, R. A. Pew, G. J. Ratcliffe, J. G. Rowe, J. K. Wulff.

Founded: in 1886.
Domicile: Pennsylvania.
Employees: 14,900.
S&P Analyst: T. Vital/CB/BK

Sun Microsystems

Recommendation: **HOLD** ★ ★ ★ ☆ ☆
SELL | SELL | HOLD | BUY | BUY

12-Month Target Price: $6.00
(as of January 15, 2004)

SUNW has an approximate 0.15% weighting in the **S&P 500**

Sector: Information Technology
Sub-Industry: Computer Hardware
Peer Group: Computer Hardware - Large System Vendors

Summary: SUNW makes high-performance workstations for engineering, scientific and technical markets, and also sells servers and operating system software.

Quantitative Evaluations

S&P Earnings & Dividend Rank: C

| D | **C** | B- | B | B+ | A- | A | A+ |

S&P Fair Value Rank: 1-

| **1** | 2 | 3 | 4 | 5 |
| Lowest | | | | Highest |

Fair Value Calc.: $2.70 (Overvalued)

S&P Investability Quotient Percentile

26%

SUNW scored lower than 74% of all companies for which an S&P Report is available.

Volatility: High

| Low | Average | **High** |

Technical Evaluation: Bullish
Since 9/04, the technical indicators for SUNW have been Bullish.

Relative Strength Rank: Strong

| | | **87** |
| 1 Lowest | | Highest 99 |

| **Price as of 11/12/04:** | **$4.86** | **2005E S&P Core EPS:** | **$-0.17** |

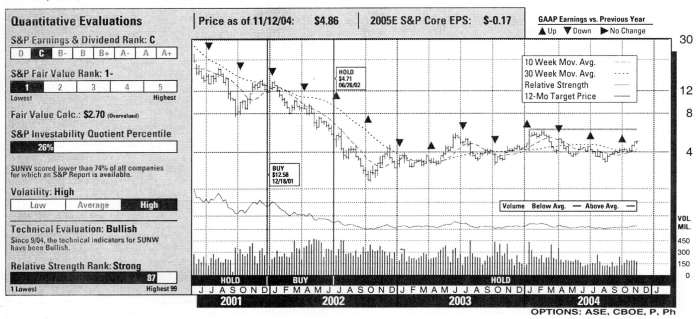

GAAP Earnings vs. Previous Year
▲ Up ▼ Down ▶ No Change

- 10 Week Mov. Avg.
- 30 Week Mov. Avg.
- Relative Strength
- 12-Mo Target Price

Volume Below Avg. — Above Avg. —

OPTIONS: ASE, CBOE, P, Ph

Analyst commentary prepared by M. Graham-Hackett/CB/BK

Highlights October 18, 2004

- We project a 6% decline in revenues in FY 05 (Jun.), following a 2.2% decrease in FY 04. In our opinion, FY 04 revenues reflected a gradual recovery in IT spending overall, but continued competitive pricing pressures in the server market, as well as a negative impact from a mix shift, reflecting Sun's new lower-end product offerings. For FY 05, we believe the current trend of a gradual IT spending recovery should continue, but see product mix and pricing pressure continuing to weigh on revenues.

- We expect stiff pricing competition and the impact of Sun's increased low-end sales mix to negatively affect gross margin in FY 05. Nevertheless, we expect cost reduction efforts to more than offset these effects and see gross margins widening to 41.4% in FY 05, from 40.4% in FY 04. Sun's efforts to reduce expenses have recently shown benefits to the company's bottom line, and we expect these efforts to continue as the company tries to build better operating leverage into its business.

- We expect earnings per share of $0.01 for FY 05, versus a loss of $0.23 a share in FY 04. Our FY 05 S&P Core Earnings projection is for a loss of $0.17 a share, reflecting projected stock option expense.

Investment Rationale/Risk October 18, 2004

- We would hold the shares. We believe the company faces competitive threats from Windows and Linux operating systems. However, we think that Sun's recent entry into the Linux-based server market may offset these pressures. From a macro perspective, while we do not see technology spending likely to return to the heady rates of 1999 and 2000, we do expect modest growth to resume in this market over the next several years.

- Risks to our opinion and target price include the possibility that as tech spending recovers, the company may face a user migration away from UNIX systems, which account for the majority of Sun's sales; and a possible general deterioration in technology spending.

- Sun has more than $7 billion in cash and investments (both long and short term), including approximately $2 billion received from Microsoft Corp., related to the resolution of patent disputes and a technology collaboration deal. Our 12-month target price of $6 is based on our price to sales and DCF analyses. Our target price assumes that the stock will trade at 1.7X our calendar 2005 revenue per share estimate; we base this on our review of the stock's historical average, and on the range of its peers.

Key Stock Statistics

S&P Oper. EPS 2005E	0.01	52-week Range	$5.93-3.29
P/E on S&P Oper. EPS 2005E	NM	12 Month P/E	NM
Yield (%)	Nil	Beta	NA
Dividend Rate/Share	Nil	Shareholders	23,400
Shares Outstanding (M)	3363.1	Market Cap (B)	$ 16.3

Value of $10,000 invested five years ago: **$ 1,746**

Dividend Data

No cash dividends have been paid.

Revenues/Earnings Data Fiscal year ending June 30

Revenues (Million $)

	2005	2004	2003	2002	2001	2000
1Q	2,628	2,536	2,747	2,861	5,045	3,145
2Q	—	2,888	2,915	3,108	5,115	3,554
3Q	—	2,651	2,790	3,107	4,095	4,005
4Q	—	3,110	2,982	3,420	3,995	5,017
Yr.	—	11,185	11,434	12,496	18,250	15,721

Earnings Per Share ($)

	2005	2004	2003	2002	2001	2000
1Q	-0.05	-0.09	-0.04	-0.06	0.15	0.08
2Q	E Nil	-0.04	-0.72	-0.13	0.12	0.11
3Q	E Nil	-0.23	Nil	-0.01	0.04	0.15
4Q	E0.01	0.23	-0.32	0.02	-0.03	0.21
Yr.	E0.01	-0.12	-1.07	-0.18	0.29	0.55

Next earnings report expected: mid-January Source: S&P, Company Reports
EPS Estimates based on S&P Operating Earnings; historical GAAP earnings are as reported.

Sun Microsystems, Inc.

Recommendation: **HOLD** ★ ★ ★ ☆ ☆   12-Month Target Price: **$6.00** (as of January 15, 2004)

Business Summary October 19, 2004

Sun Microsystems, founded in 1982, invented the workstation. The company continues to rely on its concept that the network is the computer. Sun is a leading supplier of networked computing products, including workstations, servers and storage products, that primarily use the company's own Scaleable Processor Architecture (SPARC) microprocessors and its Solaris software. Computer systems accounted for 52% of net revenues in FY 04 (Jun.), network storage products more than 13%, support services 27%, and professional services nearly 8%.

A workstation is a type of computer used for engineering applications (CAD/CAM), desktop publishing, software development, and other applications that need a moderate amount of computing power and high-quality graphics capabilities. In terms of computing power, workstations fall between PCs and minicomputers. UNIX has been the most common operating system for workstations, but Microsoft's Windows NT has posed a formidable challenge. Sun's workstations range from low cost UltraSPARC-based workstations to high end, multi-processor color graphics systems. Systems include the Sun Blade line and the Sun Fire V880z.

The company's servers can be used for file sharing, letting users access data distributed across multiple storage devices and networks, or as compute resources, to distribute compute-intensive applications across multiple processors, ranging from the low-end workgroup severs to data center servers. Sun's data center servers, including the Sun Fire E25K, are used for server consolidations as well as data mining and warehousing. Sun's midrange enterprise servers such as the Sun Fire E6900 and E4900, and E2900, are based on the UltraSPARC IV microprocessor and feature dual-threaded capability. The company's entry-level

line include the Sun Fire V480 and Sun Fire V880. Sun introduced its first x86 entry level server, the V60, in FY 03, and introduced its Sun Fire V20Z AMD Opteron-based server in FY 04.

The company has steadily invested in advancing its presence in storage. In the mid-range, Sun's storage line includes the StorEdge A5200 Array and T3 Array, as well as the StorEdge 6320, 6120 and 3910. In the high end, Sun's storage systems include the StorEdge 9980 and 9970, which combine Hitachi Data Systems' high-end storage products with Sun's own resource management and file management software under an OEM deal signed in FY 02.

In FY 02, the company introduced Solaris 9, its popular Unix operating system. Solaris 9's features include identity management and enhanced security and manageability. Sun's latest version of Solaris, Solaris 10, features "self-healing," or predictive capabilities to improve the performance and reliability of a system.

Sun is also known for inventing Java object-oriented programming language. Java has attracted significant interest in the software development industry because of its portability; software created in Java can run on any type of system. As a result, it is a popular tool for designing software for distribution over the Internet.

Sales to General Electric Co. and its subsidiaries in the aggregate accounted for approximately 14%, 11% and 12%, respectively, of Sun's FY 04, FY 03 and FY 02 total net revenues.

The company estimates that its FY 04 loss of $0.12 a share would have been a $0.37 loss if stock option expense had been included.

Company Financials Fiscal Year ending June 30

Per Share Data ($)

(Year Ended June 30)	2004	2003	2002	2001	2000	1999	1998	1997	1996	1995
Tangible Bk. Val.	1.77	1.88	2.32	2.63	2.23	1.55	1.17	0.93	0.76	0.67
Cash Flow	0.10	-0.79	0.12	0.65	0.78	0.51	0.38	0.36	0.24	0.19
Earnings	-0.12	-1.07	-0.18	0.29	0.55	0.32	0.24	0.25	0.15	0.11
S&P Core Earnings	-0.67	-0.81	-0.38	0.14	NA	NA	NA	NA	NA	NA
Dividends	Nil	Nil	Nil	Nil	Nil	Nil	Nil	Nil	Nil	Nil
Payout Ratio	Nil	Nil	Nil	Nil	Nil	Nil	Nil	Nil	Nil	Nil
Prices - High	5.93	5.64	14.41	35.12	64.65	41.50	11.04	6.66	4.39	2.49
- Low	3.29	3.02	2.34	7.52	25.12	10.89	4.70	3.23	2.25	0.93
P/E Ratio - High	NM	NM	NM	NM	NM	NM	46	27	29	22
- Low	NM	NM	NM	26	46	34	19	13	15	8

Income Statement Analysis (Million $)

	2004	2003	2002	2001	2000	1999	1998	1997	1996	1995
Revs.	11,185	11,434	12,496	18,250	15,721	11,726	9,791	8,598	7,095	5,902
Oper. Inc.	3.00	694	239	2,540	5,574	2,269	1,746	1,391	1,017	741
Depr.	730	918	970	1,229	776	627	440	342	284	241
Int. Exp.	37.0	43.0	58.0	100	84.0	0.68	1.57	7.46	9.11	17.8
Pretax Inc.	437	-2,653	-1,048	1,584	2,771	1,606	1,176	1,121	709	523
Eff. Tax Rate	NM	NM	NM	38.1%	33.1%	35.8%	35.1%	32.0%	32.8%	31.9%
Net Inc.	-388	-3,429	-587	981	1,854	1,031	763	762	476	356
S&P Core Earnings	-2,166	-2,581	-1,253	471	NA	NA	NA	NA	NA	NA

Balance Sheet & Other Fin. Data (Million $)

	2004	2003	2002	2001	2000	1999	1998	1997	1996	1995
Cash	3,601	3,062	2,885	1,472	1,849	1,089	822	660	990	1,228
Curr. Assets	7,303	6,779	7,777	7,934	6,877	6,116	4,148	3,728	3,034	2,934
Total Assets	14,503	12,985	16,522	18,181	14,152	8,420	5,711	4,697	3,801	3,545
Curr. Liab.	5,113	4,129	5,057	5,146	4,759	3,227	2,123	1,849	1,489	1,331
LT Debt	1,175	1,531	1,449	1,705	1,720	Nil	74.6	106	60.2	91.0
Common Equity	6,438	6,491	10,085	10,586	7,309	4,812	3,514	2,742	2,251	2,123
Total Cap.	7,613	8,022	11,534	13,035	9,393	4,812	3,588	2,848	2,312	2,214
Cap. Exp.	8,469	373	559	1,292	982	739	830	554	296	242
Cash Flow	342	-2,511	383	2,210	2,630	1,658	1,203	1,104	760	596
Curr. Ratio	1.4	1.6	1.5	1.5	1.4	1.9	2.0	2.0	2.0	2.2
% LT Debt of Cap.	15.4	19.1	12.6	13.1	18.3	Nil	2.1	3.9	2.6	4.1
% Net Inc.of Revs.	NM	NM	NM	5.4	11.8	8.8	7.8	8.9	6.7	6.0
% Ret. on Assets	NM	NM	NM	6.1	16.4	14.6	14.7	17.9	13.0	11.0
% Ret. on Equity	NM	NM	NM	11.0	30.5	24.8	24.4	30.5	21.8	18.9

Data as orig reptd.; bef. results of disc opers/spec. items. Per share data adj. for stk. divs.; EPS diluted. E-Estimated. NA-Not Available. NM-Not Meaningful. NR-Not Ranked. UR-Under Review.

Office: 4150 Network Circle, Santa Clara, CA 95054.
Telephone: 650-960-1300.
Email: investor-relations@sun.com
Website: http://www.sun.com
Chrmn & CEO: S.G. McNealy.
Pres & COO: J.I. Schwartz.

EVP & CFO: S.T. McGowan.
EVP & CTO: G.M. Papadopoulos.
SVP, Secy & General Counsel: M.A. Dillon.
Investor Contact: J. DeCoster 415-294-4482.
Dirs: J. L. Barksdale, S. Bennett, L. J. Doerr, R. J. Fisher, M. Lehman, S. G. McNealy, M. K. Oshman, N. O. Seligman, L. Turner.

Founded: in 1982.
Domicile: Delaware.
Employees: 32,600.
S&P Analyst: M. Graham-Hackett/CB/BK

The McGraw-Hill Companies

SunTrust Banks

Recommendation: **HOLD** ★★★☆☆
SELL SELL HOLD BUY BUY

12-Month Target Price: **$75.00**
(as of January 12, 2004)

STI has an approximate 0.24% weighting in the **S&P 500**

Sector: Financials
Sub-Industry: Regional Banks
Peer Group: Southeast Major Regional Banks

Summary: This bank holding company operates through subsidiaries in Florida, Georgia, Maryland, Tennessee, Virginia, and the District of Columbia.

Quantitative Evaluations

S&P Earnings & Dividend Rank: A+

D	C	B-	B	B+	A-	A	A+

S&P Fair Value Rank: 2

1	2	3	4	5
Lowest				Highest

Fair Value Calc.: $68.00 (Slightly Overvalued)

S&P Investability Quotient Percentile

98%

STI scored higher than 98% of all companies for which an S&P Report is available.

Volatility: Low

Low	Average	High

Technical Evaluation: Bullish
Since 10/04, the technical indicators for STI have been Bullish.

Relative Strength Rank: Moderate

57

1 Lowest   Highest 99

Price as of 11/12/04:	**$73.10**	2004E S&P Core EPS:	**$5.01**

GAAP Earnings vs. Previous Year
▲ Up   ▼ Down   ► No Change

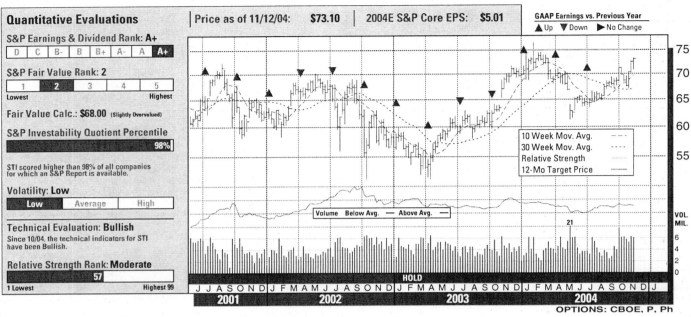

10 Week Mov. Avg.
30 Week Mov. Avg.
Relative Strength
12-Mo Target Price

Volume   Below Avg. — Above Avg.

HOLD

J J A S O N D | J F M A M J J A S O N D | J F M A M J J A S O N D | J F M A M J J A S O N D | J
2001 | **2002** | **2003** | **2004**

OPTIONS: CBOE, P, Ph

VOL. MIL.

Analyst commentary prepared by James M. O'Brien /CB/BK

Highlights August 20, 2004

■ In May 2004, SunTrust agreed to acquire National Commerce Financial (NCF: $32) for about $7 billion in cash and stock. The deal is expected to close in the 2004 fourth quarter, subject to necessary approvals.

■ On a standalone basis, we believe STI's loan growth is likely to accelerate in 2004, to 6%, although growth in corporate lending should continue to remain below long-term historical trends until possibly late in the year. Based on our expectations for a small increase in short-term interest rates over the balance of 2004, and the current shape of the Treasury yield curve, we believe the net interest margin is likely to remain flat. We believe relevant asset quality metrics could improve further in a stronger economy. We forecast high single digit growth for noninterest income, reflecting momentum in non-mortgage related lines. Expense control measures put in place in early 2002, as well as a series of system enhancements, still have not been fully realized, in our opinion.

■ All told, we see EPS rising to $5.19 in 2004, from $4.73 in 2003. Our 2005 EPS estimate is $5.58, which was reduced from $5.65 after the acquisition announcement, to reflect potential dilution from the planned deal.

Investment Rationale/Risk August 20, 2004

■ Despite our view that the company's earnings track record is more stable and consistent than peers, and STI's significant stake in Coca-Cola (which provides sizable dividends), we think the shares deserve a P/E multiple in line with peers.

■ Risks to our recommendation and target price include acquisition integration risk, potentially weaker than expected corporate lending, and general interest rate risk.

■ Assuming long-term growth of 9% (declining to a constant rate of 4.5% in five years), a dividend payout ratio of 40% (increasing to a constant 45% in five years), and a discount rate of 8.2%, our dividend discount model estimates an intrinsic value of $68. Our 12-month target price of $75 is based on an in-line peer median P/E multiple of about 13X our 2005 EPS estimate. WE would hold, but not add to, positions.

Key Stock Statistics

S&P Oper. EPS 2004E	5.19	52-week Range	$76.65-61.27
P/E on S&P Oper. EPS 2004E	14.1	12 Month P/E	14.8
S&P Oper. EPS 2005E	5.58	Beta	0.42
Yield (%)	2.7%	Shareholders	68,000
Dividend Rate/Share	2.00	Market Cap (B)	$ 26.2
Shares Outstanding (M)	358.2		

Value of $10,000 invested five years ago: **$ 11,077**

Dividend Data Dividends have been paid since 1985

Amount ($)	Date Decl.	Ex-Div. Date	Stock of Record	Payment Date
0.500	Feb. 10	Feb. 26	Mar. 01	Mar. 15 '04
0.500	Apr. 20	May. 26	May. 31	Jun. 15 '04
0.500	Aug. 10	Aug. 30	Sep. 01	Sep. 15 '04
0.500	Nov. 10	Nov. 29	Dec. 01	Dec. 15 '04

Revenues/Earnings Data Fiscal year ending December 31

Revenues (Million $)

	2004	2003	2002	2001	2000	1999
1Q	1,769	1,766	1,913	2,270	2,048	1,887
2Q	1,811	1,771	1,918	2,156	2,116	1,922
3Q	—	1,752	1,852	2,060	2,211	1,953
4Q	—	1,783	1,845	1,949	2,244	1,858
Yr.	—	7,072	7,527	8,435	8,619	7,620

Earnings Per Share ($)

	2004	2003	2002	2001	2000	1999
1Q	1.26	1.17	1.06	1.14	1.04	0.87
2Q	1.29	1.17	1.20	1.25	1.05	0.91
3Q	E1.30	1.18	1.21	1.15	1.10	1.00
4Q	E1.34	1.21	1.20	1.16	1.11	0.71
Yr.	E5.19	4.73	4.66	4.70	4.30	3.50

Next earnings report expected: NA Source: S&P, Company Reports
EPS Estimates based on S&P Operating Earnings; historical GAAP earnings are as reported.

SunTrust Banks, Inc.

Recommendation: **HOLD** ★ ★ ★ ☆ ☆   12-Month Target Price: **$75.00** (as of January 12, 2004)

Business Summary August 20, 2004

With more than $125 billion in assets, SunTrust is an Atlanta-based bank holding company that operates 1,201 branches located in Florida, Georgia, Maryland, Tennessee, Virginia and the District of Columbia. Primary businesses include traditional deposit, credit and trust and investment services. The company also provides mortgage banking, credit-related insurance, asset management, brokerage and capital market services. At year end 2003, it had trust assets of $159.0 billion, and a mortgage servicing portfolio of $69.0 billion.

Principal operating units include retail, which offers loans, deposits and other fee-based services for consumer and private banking clients; commercial, which provides lending, treasury management, financial risk management products and corporate card services; corporate and investment banking, which offers corporate banking, treasury management, international banking and leasing to firms with over $250 million in annual revenues; private client services, which provides asset management products and professional services to individual and institutional clients; and mortgage, which originates mortgage loans through retail, broker and correspondent channels.

Loans totaled $80.7 billion at the end of 2003 and were divided: commercial 38%; real estate construction 6%; residential mortgages 30%; other real estate 12%; and consumer loans 15%.

Average earning assets amounted to $109.3 billion in 2003, and consisted mainly of loans (70%) and investment securities (20%). Average sources of funds, which the

bank uses to fund its lending business, included time deposits (8%), NOW/money market accounts (32%), savings deposits (6%), other interest-bearing deposits (3%), short-term borrowings (11%), long-term debt (12%), shareholders' equity (7%), noninterest-bearing deposits (17%), and other (6%).

At year-end 2003, nonperforming assets, which include mainly non-accrual and restructured loans and other real estate owned, were $378.1 million (0.47% of loans and other real estate owned), down from $542.0 million (0.74%) a year earlier. The provision for loan losses, which is held in anticipation of actual losses, was $941.9 million (1.17% of loans) at the end of 2003, versus $930.1 million (1.27%) at the end of 2002. Net chargeoffs, or the amount of loans actually written off as uncollectible, were $311.1 million in 2003 (0.41% of average loans), versus $422.3 million (0.59%) in 2002.

The company owned Coca-Cola Co. common shares, with a market value of about $2.5 billion at year end 2003.

In June 2003, STI completed the acquisition of Lighthouse Financial Services, Inc. based in Hilton Head, South Carolina. STI acquired approximately $637 million in assets, $567 million in loans, and $421 million in deposits. In addition, STI paid $131 million in a combination of cash and STI stock. In July 2003, the bank completed the acquisition of Sun America Mortgage, one the top mortgage lenders in Metro Atlanta.

Company Financials Fiscal Year ending December 31

Per Share Data ($)

(Year Ended December 31)	2003	2002	2001	2000	1999	1998	1997	1996	1995	1994
Tangible Bk. Val.	29.73	25.46	26.67	25.07	22.13	22.99	23.38	20.88	17.66	13.90
Earnings	4.73	4.66	4.70	4.30	3.50	3.04	3.13	2.76	2.47	2.19
S&P Core Earnings	4.80	4.38	4.50	NA	NA	NA	NA	NA	NA	NA
Dividends	1.80	1.72	1.60	1.48	1.38	1.00	0.93	0.83	0.74	0.66
Payout Ratio	38%	37%	34%	34%	39%	33%	30%	30%	29%	30%
Prices - High	71.73	70.20	72.35	68.06	79.81	87.75	75.25	52.50	35.43	25.68
- Low	51.44	51.48	57.29	41.62	60.43	54.00	44.12	32.00	23.62	21.75
P/E Ratio - High	15	15	15	16	23	26	24	19	14	12
- Low	11	11	12	10	17	16	14	12	10	10

Income Statement Analysis (Million $)

	2003	2002	2001	2000	1999	1998	1997	1996	1995	1994
Net Int. Inc.	3,320	3,244	3,253	3,108	3,145	2,929	1,894	1,784	1,676	1,620
Tax Equiv. Adj.	45.0	39.5	40.8	40.4	42.5	46.4	36.6	40.1	49.6	55.7
Non Int. Inc.	2,179	2,187	2,003	1,767	1,769	1,708	933	804	720	703
Loan Loss Prov.	314	470	275	134	170	215	117	116	112	138
Exp./Op. Revs.	68.4%	61.5%	59.2%	58.0%	59.3%	62.8%	59.6%	61.5%	59.5%	58.9%
Pretax Inc.	1,909	1,823	2,020	1,920	1,696	1,498	1,026	903	826	782
Eff. Tax Rate	30.2%	27.0%	32.2%	32.6%	33.7%	35.2%	35.0%	31.7%	31.5%	33.1%
Net Inc.	1,332	1,332	1,369	1,294	1,124	971	667	617	565	523
% Net Int. Marg.	3.08	3.41	NA	3.55	3.88	3.97	4.11	4.40	4.50	4.60
S&P Core Earnings	1,351	1,253	1,310	NA	NA	NA	NA	NA	NA	NA

Balance Sheet & Other Fin. Data (Million $)

	2003	2002	2001	2000	1999	1998	1997	1996	1995	1994
Money Mkt. Assets	3,243	2,820	3,025	2,223	1,869	2,027	1,180	1,815	1,425	1,095
Inv. Securities	25,607	23,445	19,656	18,810	18,317	17,559	11,729	10,551	9,677	9,319
Com'l Loans	30,682	28,694	28,946	30,781	26,933	24,590	14,387	11,966	10,560	9,552
Other Loans	50,050	44,474	40,013	41,459	39,069	40,496	25,749	23,428	20,741	18,996
Total Assets	125,393	117,323	104,741	103,496	95,390	93,170	57,983	52,468	46,471	42,709
Demand Deposits	24,185	21,250	19,200	15,064	14,201	14,066	8,928	8,900	7,821	7,654
Time Deposits	57,004	58,456	48,337	54,469	45,900	44,968	29,270	27,990	25,362	24,565
LT Debt	15,314	11,880	12,661	8,945	6,017	5,808	3,172	1,565	1,002	930
Common Equity	9,731	16,030	15,064	14,536	13,691	8,179	5,199	4,880	4,270	3,453
% Ret. on Assets	1.1	1.2	1.3	1.3	1.2	1.3	1.2	1.2	1.3	1.3
% Ret. on Equity	14.4	8.6	9.3	9.2	8.0	14.5	13.2	13.5	14.6	14.8
% Loan Loss Resv.	1.1	1.1	1.2	1.2	1.3	1.5	1.9	2.0	2.2	2.3
% Loans/Deposits	106.3	101.5	108.5	106.4	112.4	110.3	137.1	96.0	94.3	88.6
% Equity to Assets	7.6	14.0	14.2	14.2	14.8	8.9	9.1	9.3	8.7	8.5

Data as orig reptd.; bef. results of disc opers/spec. items. Per share data adj. for stk. divs.; EPS diluted. E-Estimated. NA-Not Available. NM-Not Meaningful. NR-Not Ranked. UR-Under Review.

Office: 303 Peachtree St NE, Atlanta, GA 30308-3201.
Telephone: 404-588-7711.
Website: http://www.suntrust.com
Chrmn, Pres & CEO: L.P. Humann.
Vice Chrmn: J.W. Spiegel.
Vice Chrmn: J.W. Clay, Jr.
Vice Chrmn: J.M. Wells III.

Vice Chrmn: T.J. Hoepner.
Treas & Investor Contact: G. Peacock, Jr. 404-658-4879
Dirs: R. M. Beall, R. M. Beall II, J. H. Brown, A. D. Correll, J. C. Crowe, J. C. Crowe, D. N. Daft, P. C. Frist, D. H. Hughes, L. P. Humann, M. D. Ivester, J. H. Lanier, G. G. Minor III, L. L. Prince, F. S. Royal, K. H. Williams.

Founded: in 1891.
Domicile: Georgia.
Employees: 27,578.
S&P Analyst: James M. O'Brien /CB/BK

Supervalu Inc.

Recommendation: **HOLD** ★★★☆☆
SELL | SELL | HOLD | BUY | BUY

12-Month Target Price: $30.00
(as of February 17, 2004)

SVU has an approximate 0.04% weighting in the **S&P 500**

Sector: Consumer Staples
Sub-Industry: Food Retail

Summary: SVU, one of the largest U.S. food wholesalers, is also the 11th largest supermarket retailer.

Quantitative Evaluations

S&P Earnings & Dividend Rank: A-

| D | C | B- | B | B+ | A- | A | A+ |

S&P Fair Value Rank: 5

| 1 | 2 | 3 | 4 | **5** |
| Lowest | | | | Highest |

Fair Value Calc.: $37.60 (Slightly Undervalued)

S&P Investability Quotient Percentile

93%

SVU scored higher than 93% of all companies for which an S&P Report is available.

Volatility: Average

| Low | **Average** | High |

Technical Evaluation: Bullish
Since 10/04, the technical indicators for SVU have been Bullish.

Relative Strength Rank: Strong

78

1 Lowest | Highest 99

Price as of 11/12/04: $32.17 | **2005E S&P Core EPS: $2.03**

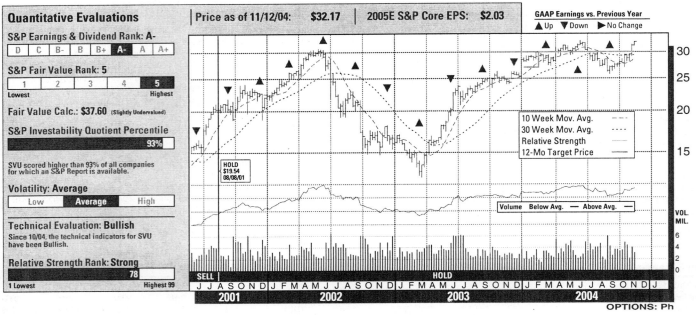

Analyst commentary prepared by Joseph Agnese/PMW/BK

Highlights October 18, 2004

- We see FY 06 (Feb.) revenues growing about 4%, on same-store sales gains in the low single digits and the addition of 125 to 150 new extreme value combination stores. We expect conversions of extreme value stores into combination stores to continue, as major remodelings are completed on regional banner stores. Despite intense competition, we see retail sales growing in the mid-single digits, spurred by an improving economy and modest inflation. However, we believe sales could be restricted as customers continue to trade down to lower priced goods. We think food distribution sales should decline in the low single digits, as we expect customer attrition to be only partly offset by new business wins.

- We expect gross margins to benefit from a shift in the business mix, due to growth of wider margin retail stores. Despite our projection of significantly higher employee benefit costs, we see operating margins widening, on increased sales of wider margin general merchandise products. In addition, we expect improved distribution efficiencies, as the company operates facilities at greater capacities.

- After expected lower interest expense, due to a reduction in debt levels, we look for FY 06 operating EPS of $2.55, up 7.1% from our estimate of $2.38 for FY 05.

Investment Rationale/Risk October 18, 2004

- We expect comparable-store sales to increase in FY 06, driven by ongoing economic improvement and by expansion of combination dollar/general merchandise stores under the Save-A-Lot banner, despite the effects of intense competition in the retail food industry. We believe the company will post modest earnings growth as it focuses on expanding its extreme value combination store format, despite an intense competitive environment. In our opinion, customer counts should remain steady, due to SVU's value focus.

- Risks to our opinion and target price include deterioration in the economic environment, and increased retail or food distribution competition.

- The shares traded recently at 12X our calendar 2004 EPS estimate of $2.40, below the peer group average of 13X. We believe the stock is fairly valued at a P/E multiple to growth ratio of 1.5X, based on our five-year estimated EPS growth rate of 8%. Applying a P/E multiple of 12X to our 12-month forward EPS estimate of $2.46, in line with the historical average, we arrive at our 12-month target price of $30. We would hold existing positions. The shares also offer a 2.1% dividend yield.

Key Stock Statistics

S&P Oper. EPS 2005E	2.38	52-week Range	$32.49-24.03
P/E on S&P Oper. EPS 2005E	13.5	12 Month P/E	11.8
S&P Oper. EPS 2006E	2.55	Beta	0.52
Yield (%)	1.9%	Shareholders	6,782
Dividend Rate/Share	0.61	Market Cap (B)	$ 4.3
Shares Outstanding (M)	134.3		

Value of $10,000 invested five years ago: **$ 17,127**

Dividend Data Dividends have been paid since 1936

Amount ($)	Date Decl.	Ex-Div. Date	Stock of Record	Payment Date
0.145	Feb. 11	Feb. 26	Mar. 01	Mar. 15 '04
0.145	Apr. 07	May. 27	Jun. 01	Jun. 15 '04
0.152	Aug. 11	Aug. 30	Sep. 01	Sep. 15 '04
0.152	Oct. 06	Nov. 29	Dec. 01	Dec. 15 '04

Revenues/Earnings Data Fiscal year ending February 28

Revenues (Million $)

	2005	2004	2003	2002	2001	2000
1Q	5,912	5,836	5,654	6,932	6,953	5,290
2Q	4,487	4,591	4,340	4,715	5,334	4,146
3Q	—	4,739	4,553	4,610	5,420	5,362
4Q	—	5,044	4,613	4,651	5,487	5,542
Yr.	—	20,210	19,160	20,909	23,194	20,339

Earnings Per Share ($)

	2005	2004	2003	2002	2001	2000
1Q	1.09	0.55	0.57	0.45	0.53	0.55
2Q	0.57	0.46	0.44	0.39	0.43	0.37
3Q	E0.57	0.36	0.43	0.44	0.36	0.42
4Q	E0.65	0.70	0.48	0.26	-0.70	0.52
Yr.	E2.38	2.07	1.91	1.53	0.62	1.87

Next earnings report expected: late-December Source: S&P, Company Reports
EPS Estimates based on S&P Operating Earnings; historical GAAP earnings are as reported.

Recommendation: **HOLD** ★ ★ ★ ★ ★   12-Month Target Price: **$30.00** (as of February 17, 2004)

Business Summary October 18, 2004

Supervalu, organized in 1925 as the successor to two wholesale grocery concerns established in the 1870s, has grown into the largest U.S. food distributor to supermarkets, and the 11th largest food retailer. Retail operations are conducted through extreme value stores, regional price superstores, and regional supermarkets.

Extreme value food stores are operated primarily under the Sav-A-Lot banner, and typically average 15,000 sq. ft. The stores stock about 1,250 high volume items, usually focusing on a single size for each product sold, with the majority consisting of privately created or controlled branded products that emphasize quality and characteristics comparable to those of national brands. At the end of FY 04 (Feb.), the company operated 1,225 extreme value stores, in 37 states; 821 of the stores were licensed. SVU purchased 53 dollar store general merchandise stores in its acquisition of Deal$-Nothing Over a Dollar in May 2002. During FY 04, the company converted or opened 166 combination extreme value stores, offering both food and dollar-priced general merchandise.

Price supercenters carry more than 45,000 items, and range from 45,000 sq. ft. to 100,000 sq. ft., averaging about 64,000 sq. ft. The stores emphasize value and selection, while offering convenient one-stop shopping. Most of the company's price superstores offer traditional dry grocery departments along with perishable departments and pharmacies. The stores operate principally under the Cub Foods, Shop 'n Save, Shoppers Food Warehouse and Biggs' banners. At the end of FY 04, SVU operated 199 price superstores and franchised another 29 stores.

Supermarkets generally carry about 32,000 items, range in size from 30,000 sq. ft. to 65,000 sq. ft., and average 50,000 sq. ft. SVU operated 59 stores under the Scott's, Hornbachers' and Farm Fresh banners as of the end of FY 04.

In FY 04, distribution sales accounted for nearly 48% of total revenues. With margins of only 2.3%, the segment is less profitable than the retail food segment. The company offers and supplies customers with a variety and selection of food and non-food products, including groceries, meats, dairy products, frozen foods, deli, bakery, fresh fruits and vegetables, health and beauty aids, general merchandise, seasonal items, and tobacco products. In addition to its own corporate retail stores and licensed Sav-A-Lot stores, SVU was affiliated with 3,130 retail food stores as the primary supplier to about 2,470 stores, and as a secondary supplier to 660 stores. Distribution customers are located in 48 states, and range from small convenience stores to 200,000 sq. ft. supercenters. In September 2003, the company exchanged its New England operations for the former Fleming Midwest operations that were then owned by C&S Wholesale Grocers, Inc.

Company Financials Fiscal Year ending February 28

Per Share Data ($)

(Year Ended February 28)	2004	2003	2002	2001	2000	1999	1998	1997	1996	1995
Tangible Bk. Val.	4.84	3.24	2.54	1.43	1.40	6.10	5.81	6.04	5.27	4.79
Cash Flow	4.34	4.14	4.08	3.20	4.03	3.48	3.66	3.04	2.83	1.70
Earnings	2.07	1.91	1.53	0.62	1.87	1.57	1.82	1.30	1.22	0.30
S&P Core Earnings	2.03	1.61	1.24	0.39	NA	NA	NA	NA	NA	NA
Dividends	0.57	0.56	0.55	0.54	0.54	0.53	0.52	0.50	0.49	0.57
Payout Ratio	27%	29%	36%	87%	29%	33%	28%	38%	40%	188%
Cal. Yrs.	2003	2002	2001	2000	1999	1998	1997	1996	1995	1994
Prices - High	28.84	30.81	24.10	22.87	28.87	28.93	21.12	16.50	16.43	20.06
- Low	12.60	14.75	12.60	11.75	16.81	20.18	14.06	13.56	11.25	11.00
P/E Ratio - High	14	16	16	37	15	18	12	13	13	66
- Low	6	8	8	19	9	13	8	10	9	36

Income Statement Analysis (Million $)

	2004	2003	2002	2001	2000	1999	1998	1997	1996	1995
Revs.	20,210	19,160	20,909	23,194	20,339	17,421	17,201	16,552	16,486	16,564
Oper. Inc.	919	870	904	860	800	652	636	613	585	553
Depr.	302	297	341	344	277	234	230	232	219	199
Int. Exp.	166	182	194	213	154	124	134	137	140	138
Pretax Inc.	455	408	344	154	448	316	385	281	268	16.0
Eff. Tax Rate	38.4%	37.0%	40.1%	46.8%	45.8%	39.6%	40.0%	37.6%	37.7%	NM
Net Inc.	280	257	206	82.0	243	191	231	175	166	43.0
S&P Core Earnings	276	217	166	51.2	NA	NA	NA	NA	NA	NA

Balance Sheet & Other Fin. Data (Million $)

	2004	2003	2002	2001	2000	1999	1998	1997	1996	1995
Cash	292	29.2	12.0	11.0	11.0	8.00	6.00	6.54	5.00	4.84
Curr. Assets	2,037	1,647	1,604	2,092	2,178	1,583	1,612	1,601	1,554	1,646
Total Assets	6,153	5,896	5,825	6,407	6,495	4,266	4,093	4,283	4,283	4,305
Curr. Liab.	1,872	1,525	1,701	2,341	2,510	1,522	1,457	1,369	1,327	1,447
LT Debt	1,634	2,020	1,875	2,008	1,954	1,246	1,261	1,420	1,446	1,460
Common Equity	2,210	2,009	1,918	1,793	1,821	1,300	1,196	1,301	1,210	1,187
Total Cap.	3,986	4,146	3,873	3,831	3,778	2,606	2,499	2,765	2,699	2,653
Cap. Exp.	328	383	293	398	408	240	231	245	236	298
Cash Flow	582	554	547	426	520	425	461	407	385	242
Curr. Ratio	1.1	1.1	0.9	0.9	0.9	1.0	1.1	1.2	1.2	1.1
% LT Debt of Cap.	41.0	48.7	48.4	52.4	51.7	47.8	50.5	51.4	53.6	55.0
% Net Inc.of Revs.	1.4	1.3	1.0	0.4	1.2	1.1	1.3	1.1	1.0	0.3
% Ret. on Assets	4.6	4.4	3.4	1.3	4.5	4.6	5.5	4.2	3.9	1.1
% Ret. on Equity	13.3	13.2	11.1	4.5	15.6	15.3	18.5	14.0	13.8	3.6

Data as orig reptd.; bef. results of disc opers/spec. items. Per share data adj. for stk. divs.; EPS diluted. E-Estimated. NA-Not Available. NM-Not Meaningful. NR-Not Ranked. UR-Under Review.

Office: 11840 Valley View Road, Eden Prairie, MN 55344.
Telephone: 952-828-4000.
Website: http://www.supervalu.com
Chrmn, Pres & CEO: J. Noddle.
EVP & CFO: P.K. Knous.
SVP & Treas: S.M. Smith.

VP & Investor Contact: Y. Scharton .
Secy & General Counsel: J.P. Breedlove.
Dirs: I. Cohen, R. Daly, L. A. Del Santo, S. E. Engel, E. C. Gage, G. L. Keith, Jr., R. L. Knowlton, C. M. Lillis, J. Noddle, H. Perlmutter, M. Peterson, S. S. Rogers.

Founded: in 1871.
Domicile: Delaware.
Employees: 55,200.
S&P Analyst: Joseph Agnese/PMW/BK

Symantec Corp.

Recommendation: **BUY** ★★★★☆
SELL · SELL · HOLD · BUY · BUY

12-Month Target Price: **$65.00**
(as of October 25, 2004)

SYMC has an approximate 0.17% weighting in the **S&P 500**

Sector: Information Technology
Sub-Industry: Systems Software
Peer Group: Security Software

Summary: SYMC provides content security solutions, including antivirus software.

Quantitative Evaluations

S&P Earnings & Dividend Rank: B

| D | C | B- | **B** | B+ | A- | A | A+ |

S&P Fair Value Rank: 2-

| 1 | **2** | 3 | 4 | 5 |
| Lowest | | | | Highest |

Fair Value Calc.: $55.70 (Slightly Overvalued)

S&P Investability Quotient Percentile **95%**

SYMC scored higher than 95% of all companies for which an S&P Report is available.

Volatility: Average

| Low | **Average** | High |

Technical Evaluation: Bullish
Since 7/04, the technical indicators for SYMC have been Bullish.

Relative Strength Rank: Strong

81
1 Lowest   Highest 99

| Price as of 11/12/04: | **$60.97** | 2005E S&P Core EPS: | **$1.27** |

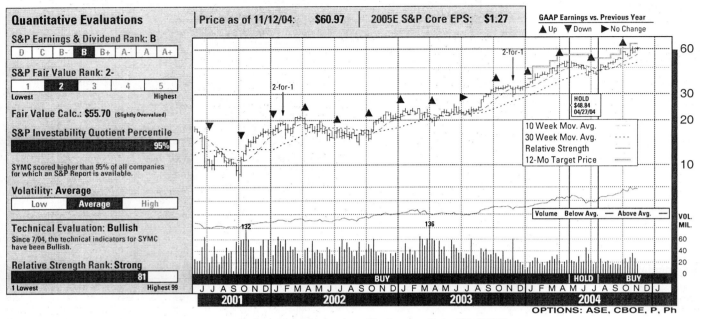

GAAP Earnings vs. Previous Year
▲ Up   ▼ Down   ▶ No Change

- 10 Week Mov. Avg.
- 30 Week Mov. Avg.
- Relative Strength
- 12-Mo Target Price

Volume   Below Avg. ▮   Above Avg. ▮

HOLD $48.84 04/27/04

BUY | HOLD | BUY

2001 2002 2003 2004

OPTIONS: ASE, CBOE, P, Ph

Analyst commentary prepared by Jonathan Rudy, CFA /MF/BK

Highlights October 27, 2004

- We see revenues increasing by about 33% in FY 05 (Mar.), driven by continued strength in SYMC's consumer antivirus business. We expect results to benefit from recent acquisitions as well as from the company's push into the enterprise market, adding to its traditional focus on the retail market.

- We expect the enterprise business to continue to grow, helped by agreements with IBM and Intel, as well as by other partnerships. On the retail side, despite intense competitive pressures, SYMC has managed to increase its revenues and add to its leading market share in recent quarters. The company has several new products in the pipeline; we look for this to further boost revenues.

- We estimate operating margins will widen in FY 05. Despite more shares outstanding, we forecast FY 05 EPS of $1.65 (excluding one-time items and goodwill amortization). Our FY 05 Standard & Poor's Core Earnings estimate of $1.27 a share reflects the potential impact of stock option expense.

Investment Rationale/Risk October 27, 2004

- We have an accumulate opinion on the shares, reflecting our belief that SYMC has strong company execution, as well as a more reasonable valuation level following a recent selloff in the share price. We believe that SYMC can grow earnings annually at about 15%-18% over the next couple of years, including recent acquisitions. The shares trade at a discount to the Internet Security peer group, based on their P/E to projected growth ratio of about 1.6X.

- Risks to our recommendation and target price include a rapidly changing technology landscape, intense competition in the Internet security software industry, and a potential slowdown in corporate information technology (IT) spending.

- Using a blend of relative valuations, based on enterprise value to projected sales, P/E to expected growth, and our discounted cash flow model, which assumes a weighted average cost of capital of about 12% and a perpetual growth rate of 3%, we arrive at our 12-month target price of $65.

Key Stock Statistics

S&P Oper. EPS 2005E	**1.65**	52-week Range	**$62.45-28.55**
P/E on S&P Oper. EPS 2005E	**37.0**	12 Month P/E	**44.8**
S&P Oper. EPS 2006E	**1.85**	Beta	**1.64**
Yield (%)	**Nil**	Shareholders	**773**
Dividend Rate/Share	**Nil**	Market Cap (B)	**$ 19.2**
Shares Outstanding (M)	**315.1**		

Value of $10,000 invested five years ago: **$ 48,657**

Dividend Data

Amount ($)	Date Decl.	Ex-Div. Date	Stock of Record	Payment Date
2-for-1	Oct. 22	Nov. 20	Nov. 05	Nov. 19 '03
2-for-1 Stk.	Oct. 20	Dec. 01	Nov. 11	Nov. 30 '04

Revenues/Earnings Data Fiscal year ending March 31

Revenues (Million $)

	2005	2004	2003	2002	2001	2000
1Q	556.6	391.1	316.0	228.0	191.4	175.1
2Q	618.3	428.7	325.2	242.4	192.3	182.5
3Q	—	493.9	375.6	290.3	219.3	200.8
4Q	—	556.4	390.0	310.8	250.6	187.2
Yr.	—	1,870	1,407	1,071	853.5	745.7

Earnings Per Share ($)

	2005	2004	2003	2002	2001	2000
1Q	0.33	0.18	0.18	-0.07	0.15	0.10
2Q	0.38	0.25	0.17	-0.04	0.15	0.11
3Q	E0.43	0.32	0.22	Nil	0.05	0.35
4Q	E0.45	0.33	0.21	0.02	-0.09	0.12
Yr.	E1.65	1.07	0.77	-0.10	0.24	0.68

Next earnings report expected: late-January Source: S&P, Company Reports
EPS Estimates based on S&P Operating Earnings; historical GAAP earnings are as reported.

Symantec Corporation

Recommendation: **BUY** ★★★★☆   12-Month Target Price: **$65.00** (as of October 25, 2004)

Business Summary October 27, 2004

Symantec, a world leader in Internet security technology, provides a broad range of content and network security solutions to individuals and enterprises. The company is a leading provider of virus protection, firewall, virtual private network, vulnerability management, intrusion detection, remote management technologies, and security services to consumers and enterprises worldwide.

The company is organized into five operating segments: Consumer Products, Enterprise Security, Enterprise Administration, Services, and Other.

The Consumer Products segment accounted for 47% of net revenues in FY 04 (Mar.), up from 41% in FY 03. The segment's charter is to ensure that consumers and their information are secure and protected in a connected world. Primary product lines include Norton AntiVirus software for protection against, and detection and elimination of, computer viruses, and Norton Internet Security, a fully integrated suite that provides total Internet protection for the home computer. Other products include Norton SystemWorks, Norton Utilities, and Norton CleanSweep.

The Enterprise Security and Administration segments accounted for 39% and 12% of total net revenues in FY 04, respectively, versus 42% and 15% in FY 03. The objective of the Enterprise Security segment is to provide a broad range of security solutions for SYMC's enterprise customers. The segment focuses on two areas: content and network security. The Enterprise Administration segment offers products that enable companies to be more effective and efficient within

their Information Technology (IT) departments. Products include pcAnywhere and Ghost Corporate Edition.

The Services division provides fee-based technical support and consulting services to enterprise customers to assist them with the planning, design and implementation of enterprise security solutions in the anti-virus and Internet content filtering technologies.

The Other business segment is comprised of sunset products, products nearing the end of their life cycle, and operations from the web access management product line, which was divested in August 2001.

International revenues accounted for 52% of the total in FY 04, versus 49% in FY 03.

As of March 31, 2004, SYMC had acquired 33 companies since its 1989 IPO. In December 2000, the company acquired AXENT Technologies in a stock transaction valued at about $975 million.

In June 2004, SYMC acquired Brightmail, Inc., a developer of e-mail services and software for application service providers, Internet service providers, portals and enterprises. The purchase price was estimated at $370 million in cash when the acquisition was first announced in May.

Company Financials Fiscal Year ending March 31

Per Share Data ($)

(Year Ended March 31)	2004	2003	2002	2001	2000	1999	1998	1997	1996	1995
Tangible Bk. Val.	3.93	5.77	2.52	1.94	2.22	1.19	1.39	0.98	0.84	0.69
Cash Flow	1.24	2.02	0.04	0.35	0.86	0.31	0.46	0.02	-0.10	0.28
Earnings	1.07	0.77	-0.10	0.24	0.68	0.21	0.36	0.12	-0.19	0.19
S&P Core Earnings	0.84	0.53	-0.37	0.06	NA	NA	NA	NA	NA	NA
Dividends	Nil	Nil	Nil	Nil	Nil	Nil	Nil	Nil	Nil	Nil
Payout Ratio	Nil	Nil	Nil	Nil	Nil	Nil	Nil	Nil	Nil	Nil

Cal. Yrs.	2003	2002	2001	2000	1999	1998	1997	1996	1995	1994
Prices - High	35.00	23.09	18.37	20.40	17.32	8.15	6.93	5.78	8.31	4.90
- Low	18.18	13.60	7.80	6.84	3.12	2.17	3.00	2.18	4.03	2.46
P/E Ratio - High	33	30	78	NM	25	38	20	49	NM	25
- Low	17	18	33	NM	5	10	8	19	NM	13

Income Statement Analysis (Million $)

	2004	2003	2002	2001	2000	1999	1998	1997	1996	1995
Revs.	1,870	1,407	1,071	854	746	593	578	472	445	335
Oper. Inc.	607	453	70.3	291	191	90.0	126	57.6	-0.95	60.0
Depr.	74.9	95.7	38.8	32.0	42.9	24.0	25.2	22.7	19.7	13.3
Int. Exp.	21.2	21.2	9.17	Nil	0.02	1.80	1.22	1.40	1.49	2.40
Pretax Inc.	542	364	45.5	141	257	83.2	112	30.3	-44.3	38.3
Eff. Tax Rate	31.6%	31.7%	NM	54.6%	33.9%	39.6%	24.1%	14.2%	NM	25.7%
Net Inc.	371	248	-28.2	63.9	170	50.2	85.1	26.0	-39.7	28.5
S&P Core Earnings	282	157	-106	14.8	NA	NA	NA	NA	NA	NA

Balance Sheet & Other Fin. Data (Million $)

	2004	2003	2002	2001	2000	1999	1998	1997	1996	1995
Cash	2,410	1,706	1,375	557	432	193	226	160	129	105
Curr. Assets	2,842	1,988	1,563	782	546	316	329	238	237	180
Total Assets	4,456	3,266	2,503	1,792	846	563	476	342	298	221
Curr. Liab.	1,287	895	579	413	227	217	153	109	102	84.5
LT Debt	600	607	3.63	2.36	1.55	1.50	6.00	15.0	15.5	25.4
Common Equity	2,426	1,764	1,320	1,377	619	345	318	218	180	111
Total Cap.	3,071	2,371	1,324	1,379	620	347	323	233	196	137
Cap. Exp.	111	192	141	61.2	28.5	25.1	26.3	27.1	35.8	17.7
Cash Flow	445	344	10.6	95.9	213	74.2	110	48.8	-20.0	41.8
Curr. Ratio	2.2	2.2	2.7	1.9	2.4	1.5	2.1	2.2	2.3	2.1
% LT Debt of Cap.	19.5	25.6	0.3	0.2	0.3	2.1	1.8	6.4	7.9	18.6
% Net Inc.of Revs.	19.8	17.7	NM	7.5	22.8	8.5	14.7	5.5	NM	8.5
% Ret. on Assets	9.6	8.6	NM	4.8	24.1	9.7	20.8	8.2	NM	13.9
% Ret. on Equity	17.7	16.1	NM	6.4	35.3	15.2	31.8	13.0	NM	32.5

Data as orig reptd.; bef. results of disc opers/spec. items. Per share data adj. for stk. divs.; EPS diluted. E-Estimated. NA-Not Available. NM-Not Meaningful. NR-Not Ranked. UR-Under Review.

Office: 20330 Stevens Creek Boulevard, Cupertino, CA 95014-2132.
Telephone: 408-517-8000.
Email: investor-relations@symantec.com
Website: http://www.symantec.com
Chrmn & CEO: J.W. Thompson.
Pres & COO: J.G. Schwarz.

SVP & CFO: G. Myers.
SVP, Secy & General Counsel: A. Courvillle.
VP & CTO: R.A. Clyde.
Investor Contact: H. Corcos 408-517-8324.
Dirs: T. Amochaev, W. Coleman III, F. Lion, D. Mahoney, R. S. Miller, G. Reyes, D. Schulman, J. W. Thompson.

Founded: in 1983.
Domicile: Delaware.
Employees: 5,300.
S&P Analyst: Jonathan Rudy, CFA /MF/BK

Symbol Technologies

Recommendation: **SELL** ★ ★ ☆ ☆ ☆
SELL | SELL | HOLD | BUY | BUY

12-Month Target Price: **$12.00**
(as of July 27, 2004)

SBL has an approximate 0.03% weighting in the **S&P 500**

Sector: Information Technology
Sub-Industry: Electronic Equipment Manufacturers
Peer Group: Scanners/Bar Codes

Summary: SBL develops, makes and sells portable bar-code scanning equipment that uses laser technology to read data encoded in bar-code symbols.

Quantitative Evaluations

S&P Earnings & Dividend Rank: B-

| D | C | B- | B | B+ | A- | A | A+ |

S&P Fair Value Rank: 2-

| 1 | 2 | 3 | 4 | 5 |
Lowest — Highest

Fair Value Calc.: $13.70 (Slightly Overvalued)

S&P Investability Quotient Percentile

81%

SBL scored higher than 81% of all companies for which an S&P Report is available.

Volatility: High

| Low | Average | **High** |

Technical Evaluation: Bullish
Since 10/04, the technical indicators for SBL have been Bullish.

Relative Strength Rank: Strong

78

1 Lowest — Highest 99

Price as of 11/12/04: **$15.24**   **2004E S&P Core EPS:** **$0.34**

GAAP Earnings vs. Previous Year
▲ Up ▼ Down ▶ No Change

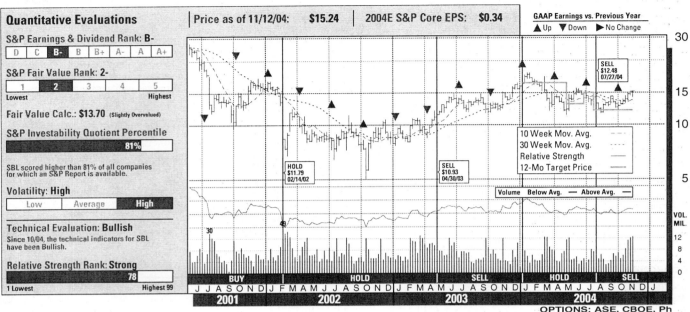

10 Week Mov. Avg.
30 Week Mov. Avg.
Relative Strength
12-Mo Target Price

Volume Below Avg. — Above Avg. —

OPTIONS: ASE, CBOE, Ph

Analyst commentary prepared by Stephanie S. Crane/MF/MGH

Highlights November 08, 2004

- We expect revenues in 2004 to increase 13%, following the 9% growth witnessed in 2003. We expect increases in IT spending related to warehouse and shipping logistics, route accounting and wireless mobility to drive product revenues, specifically as we see the company focusing new product launches in these areas. We expect revenue from product sales to grow 17%, paced by new products in wireless handhelds, but expect services to decline 2.5%, as SBL focuses on building its Global Services program.

- We see gross margins for 2004 at 46%, widening from 44% in 2003, on higher volumes and cost efficiencies. We expect R&D spending to remain at 9% to 10% of sales, due to strong emphasis on new product development, and project SG&A expenses at 26% of sales. Operating margins are expected to widen to 8% in 2004, from 0.5% in 2003, on operating efficiencies.

- We estimate 2004 operating EPS of $0.44, up from 2003's $0.23. This factors in an expected $0.05 dilutive impact from the planned acquisition of Matrics. We see 2004 Standard & Poor's Core Earnings per share of $0.34, reflecting projected stock option expense.

Investment Rationale/Risk November 08, 2004

- We recommend avoiding the shares. Our recommendation is based on several factors. The acquisition of Matrics, a provider of radio frequency identification (RFID) systems, for $230 million, planned for closing at the end of the year, could dilute 2004 earnings per share by as much as $0.05, with dilution extending through 2005. We also expect Symbol's growth to continue sluggish in the near term as the company works to rebuild its service business.

- Risks to our recommendation and target price include less aggressive competition than expected, as well as a slower shift to alternate technologies.

- The price to sales ratio, at 1.6X, is at the low end of the 10-year historical average. Combining this metric with our intrinsic value calculation using discounted cash flow analysis, we arrive at our 12-month target price of $12.

Key Stock Statistics

S&P Oper. EPS 2004E	0.44	52-week Range	$19.37-11.30
P/E on S&P Oper. EPS 2004E	34.6	12 Month P/E	49.2
Yield (%)	0.1%	Beta	2.08
Dividend Rate/Share	0.02	Shareholders	1,702
Shares Outstanding (M)	239.3	Market Cap (B)	$ 3.6

Value of $10,000 invested five years ago: **$ 8,346**

Dividend Data Dividends have been paid since 1997

Amount ($)	Date Decl.	Ex-Div. Date	Stock of Record	Payment Date
0.010	Feb. 10	Mar. 17	Mar. 19	Apr. 09 '04
0.010	Jul. 26	Sep. 15	Sep. 17	Oct. 08 '04

Revenues/Earnings Data Fiscal year ending December 31

Revenues (Million $)

	2004	2003	2002	2001	2000	1999
1Q	419.6	386.4	317.6	450.2	320.0	259.7
2Q	432.8	373.8	329.1	340.2	341.4	274.1
3Q	442.7	377.1	382.0	331.2	373.3	293.0
4Q	—	393.0	372.9	331.1	414.8	312.5
Yr.	—	1,530	1,402	1,453	1,450	1,139

Earnings Per Share ($)

	2004	2003	2002	2001	2000	1999
1Q	0.03	-0.13	0.02	0.12	0.15	0.12
2Q	0.12	0.03	-0.11	-0.27	0.17	0.14
3Q	0.09	0.05	0.14	-0.16	0.19	0.15
4Q	E0.10	0.07	-0.30	0.06	-0.84	0.16
Yr.	E0.44	0.01	-0.25	-0.24	-0.33	0.54

Next earnings report expected: mid-March Source: S&P, Company Reports
EPS Estimates based on S&P Operating Earnings; historical GAAP earnings are as reported.

Symbol Technologies, Inc.

Recommendation: **SELL** ★ ★ ☆ ☆ ☆   12-Month Target Price: **$12.00** (as of July 27, 2004)

Business Summary November 08, 2004

Symbol Technologies has grown from a manufacturer of bar-code scanning products to become a global provider of wireless networking and information systems that allow access to information over local area networks (LANs), wide area networks (WANs), and the Internet. The company makes scanner integrated mobile and wireless information management systems that consist of mobile computing devices, wireless local area networks (WLAN), bar code readers, network appliances, peripherals, software, and programming tools.

The company's bar-code reading devices are designed to capture and decode one- and two-dimensional bar code symbols and store, process and transmit information. SBL's mobile computing devices are microprocessor-based, light-weight and battery-operated hand-held computers. Information may be captured by a bar-code reader, or may be manually entered via a keyboard, touch screen, or pen computer display/entry device, and transmitted instantly by a host computer across a WLAN, or in some cases via a modem. SBL's wireless communication solutions connect its mobile computing devices to wireless WANs and LANs. Based on spread spectrum RF technology, the company's WLAN products provide real-time wireless data communication at data rates of up to 11 Mbps, and in combination with its telephony products, can provide wireless voice and data over TCP/IP data networks.

Products are sold through a direct sales force, OEMs, value-added resellers, and sales representatives and distributors. As part of its restructuring, management has implemented an aggressive program to monitor and approve its partners both on a financial and a technological basis, approving over 5,000 partners so far within a two tiered distribution system. This system was introduced in the Americas in the second quarter of 2003 and is expected in Asia by 2004.

SBL's global services organization provides a full range of professional and customer support services, from project planning and network design, through integration and installation, to ongoing service and support. Management's strategy for the service segment focuses on leveraging the repair business into more advanced solutions that can be linked to sales of their extensive product line. To boost margins in this segment, SBL has moved to lower cost regions such as El Paso, TX, and the Czech Republic. In Europe, it is focusing on reducing shared costs by centralizing key administrative functions.

In October 2003, the company completed a restatement of its financial documents, providing unaudited data for 1998 through 2003. The restatements pointed to misrepresentation of sales with an emphasis on timing irregularities, improper accounting for accounts receivables, inventory impairment, engineering expenses, accruals, reserves and pre-payments, restructuring, acquisitions, and stock options. For the five-year period, revenue was reduced by $223 million to a cumulative $6.12 billion, from a previously reported $6.34 billion, while gross margin was reduced by $101 million, to a cumulative $2.15 billion, from $2.25 billion.

Company Financials Fiscal Year ending December 31

Per Share Data ($)

(Year Ended December 31)	2003	2002	2001	2000	1999	1998	1997	1996	1995	1994
Tangible Bk. Val.	2.53	2.38	3.35	3.64	2.56	2.09	1.71	1.45	1.32	1.62
Cash Flow	0.30	0.05	-0.01	0.06	0.86	0.70	0.56	0.44	0.39	0.27
Earnings	0.01	-0.25	-0.24	-0.33	0.54	0.44	0.34	0.24	0.23	0.18
S&P Core Earnings	0.15	-0.15	-0.35	NA	NA	NA	NA	NA	NA	NA
Dividends	0.02	0.02	0.02	0.01	0.01	0.01	0.01	Nil	Nil	Nil
Payout Ratio	NM	NM	NM	NM	2%	2%	2%	Nil	Nil	Nil
Prices - High	17.70	17.50	37.33	46.02	28.88	19.07	8.87	6.51	5.34	4.52
- Low	8.01	4.98	9.50	17.08	11.55	7.24	5.62	4.19	3.21	2.05
P/E Ratio - High	NM	NM	NM	NM	53	43	26	27	24	26
- Low	NM	NM	NM	NM	21	16	17	17	14	12

Income Statement Analysis (Million $)

	2003	2002	2001	2000	1999	1998	1997	1996	1995	1994
Revs.	1,530	1,402	1,453	1,449	1,139	978	774	657	555	465
Oper. Inc.	149	139	-8.90	171	243	200	158	136	113	81.3
Depr.	68.8	69.3	53.5	82.1	66.2	55.2	45.3	39.5	34.3	18.0
Int. Exp.	10.6	16.8	20.7	16.4	8.14	5.82	5.50	4.89	4.56	5.31
Pretax Inc.	3.90	-82.6	-80.4	-79.6	171	139	110	81.1	75.0	58.3
Eff. Tax Rate	15.5%	NM	NM	NM	32.0%	33.0%	36.0%	38.0%	38.0%	40.0%
Net Inc.	3.29	-57.8	-54.7	-69.0	116	93.0	70.2	50.3	46.5	35.0
S&P Core Earnings	38.0	-33.7	-80.3	NA	NA	NA	NA	NA	NA	NA

Balance Sheet & Other Fin. Data (Million $)

	2003	2002	2001	2000	1999	1998	1997	1996	1995	1994
Cash	150	76.1	81.0	63.4	30.1	16.3	60.0	34.3	63.7	31.4
Curr. Assets	734	690	1,000	1,078	584	480	400	352	317	266
Total Assets	1,647	1,572	1,893	2,093	1,048	838	679	614	544	474
Curr. Liab.	536	474	340	458	233	184	158	131	107	74.3
LT Debt	99	136	310	308	100	64.6	40.3	50.5	60.8	59.9
Common Equity	921	888	1,181	1,202	640	531	454	400	353	316
Total Cap.	1,020	1,023	1,491	1,598	740	596	494	450	414	386
Cap. Exp.	60.6	34.7	98.5	79.7	70.0	89.3	42.7	34.7	36.6	24.8
Cash Flow	72.1	11.6	-1.20	13.1	183	148	116	89.8	80.8	53.0
Curr. Ratio	1.4	1.5	2.9	2.4	2.5	2.6	2.5	2.7	3.0	3.6
% LT Debt of Cap.	9.7	13.3	20.8	19.3	13.5	10.8	8.2	11.2	14.7	15.5
% Net Inc.of Revs.	0.2	NM	NM	NM	10.2	9.5	9.1	7.7	8.4	7.5
% Ret. on Assets	0.2	NM	NM	NM	12.3	12.3	10.9	8.7	9.2	7.6
% Ret. on Equity	0.4	NM	NM	NM	19.9	18.9	16.5	13.4	13.9	11.8

Data as orig reptd.; bef. results of disc opers/spec. items. Per share data adj. for stk. divs.; EPS diluted. E-Estimated. NA-Not Available. NM-Not Meaningful. NR-Not Ranked. UR-Under Review.

Office: 1 Symbol Plz, Holtsville, NY 11742-1300.
Telephone: 631-738-2400.
Email: info@symbol.com
Website: http://www.symbol.com
Chrmn: S. Iannuzzi.
Pres, CEO & COO: W. Nuti.

SVP & CFO: M. Greenquist.
SVP, Secy & General Counsel: P.M. Lieb.
VP & Chief Acctg Officer: J.M. Conboy.
Investor Contact: N. Tully 631-738-5050.
Dirs: R. Chrenc, S. Iannuzzi, E. Kozel, W. R. Nuti, G. Samenuk, M. A. Yellin.

Founded: in 1973.
Domicile: Delaware.
Employees: 5,300.
S&P Analyst: Stephanie S. Crane/MF/MGH

Synovus Financial

Recommendation: HOLD ★★★☆☆
SELL | SELL | HOLD | BUY | BUY

12-Month Target Price: **$29.00**
(as of October 15, 2003)

SNV has an approximate 0.08% weighting in the **S&P 500**

Sector: Financials
Sub-Industry: Regional Banks
Peer Group: Southeast Major Regional Banks

Summary: SNV owns about 40 community banks in Georgia and four other southern states, and has an 81% interest in one of the world's largest bankcard processing companies.

Quantitative Evaluations

S&P Earnings & Dividend Rank: A+

| D | C | B- | B | B+ | A- | A | **A+** |

S&P Fair Value Rank: 3-

| 1 | 2 | **3** | 4 | 5 |
| Lowest | | | | Highest |

Fair Value Calc.: $26.60 (Slightly Overvalued)

S&P Investability Quotient Percentile

96%

SNV scored higher than 96% of all companies for which an S&P Report is available.

Volatility: Low

| **Low** | Average | High |

Technical Evaluation: Bullish
Since 9/04, the technical indicators for SNV have been Bullish.

Relative Strength Rank: Moderate

| 54 |
| 1 Lowest | Highest 99 |

Price as of 11/12/04: **$27.88**   **2004E S&P Core EPS:** **$1.40**

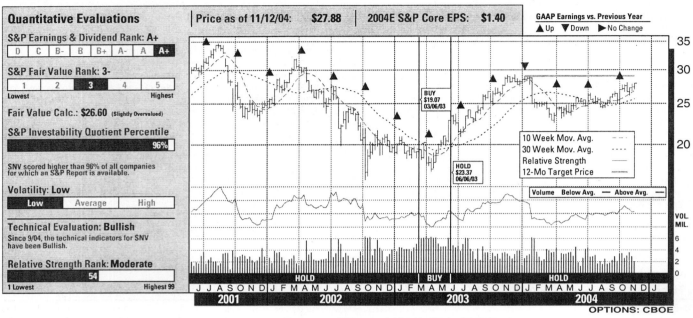

GAAP Earnings vs. Previous Year
▲ Up   ▼ Down   ▶ No Change

BUY $19.07 03/06/03

HOLD $23.37 06/06/03

10 Week Mov. Avg.
30 Week Mov. Avg.
Relative Strength
12-Mo Target Price

Volume Below Avg. — Above Avg.

VOL. MIL.
6 4 2 0

HOLD | BUY | HOLD
J J A S O N D | J F M A M J J A S O N D | J F M A M J J A S O N D | J F M A M J J A S O N D | J
2001 | 2002 | 2003 | 2004

OPTIONS: CBOE

Analyst commentary prepared by James M. O'Brien/PMW/BK

Highlights November 11, 2004

- We see an earnings gain of about 11% in 2005, driven by expected loan growth in the high single to low double digits, slightly above the average for our regional bank universe; a small widening of the net interest margin, based on the assumption of slowly rising short-term interest rates; and fee income growth of about 6%, based on management's guidance for a pickup in activity at bankcard data subsidiary Total System Services.

- We see the loan portfolio continuing to benefit from a dynamic service territory that consists of states in the Southeast with economic growth rates well above the national average. Credit quality strengthened again in the third quarter; we attribute this to sound underwriting, and expect further improvement in the fourth quarter. We expect the efficiency ratio to trend modestly lower.

- We see 2004 EPS of $1.40, up from 2003's $1.28, and expect an increase to $1.55 in 2005, assuming higher interest rates. This is within the company's guidance of a gain of 8% to 10%.

Investment Rationale/Risk November 11, 2004

- At recent levels, the stock was trading at about 18X our 2005 EPS estimate, well above the P/E multiples of regional bank peers, but below its three- and five-year multiples of 20X and 21X. We view the premium valuation as warranted and sustainable, based on what we see as SNV's above-average growth prospects beyond 2004. However, we do not expect the shares to outperform the S&P 500 over the next 12 months, in light of our expectations of 2005 EPS growth below our view of the company's longer-term potential.

- Risks to our recommendation and target price include general interest rate and economic risks, and a slowdown in the capital markets.

- Based on our 2005 EPS estimate of $1.55, and assuming a 50% payout ratio, cost of equity of 9.0% to 8.6%, and a growth rate of 12%, declining to 6% in five years and to 4.5% five years later, our dividend discount model calculates intrinsic value of $25 to $27 a share a year from now. Blending this with our relative valuation model, our 12-month target price is $29.

Key Stock Statistics

S&P Oper. EPS 2004E	1.40	52-week Range	$29.25-22.50
P/E on S&P Oper. EPS 2004E	19.9	12 Month P/E	20.4
S&P Oper. EPS 2005E	1.55	Beta	0.74
Yield (%)	2.5%	Shareholders	29,827
Dividend Rate/Share	0.69	Market Cap (B)	$ 8.6
Shares Outstanding (M)	309.4		

Value of $10,000 invested five years ago: **$ 14,492**

Dividend Data Dividends have been paid since 1930

Amount ($)	Date Decl.	Ex-Div. Date	Stock of Record	Payment Date
0.165	Nov. 20	Dec. 17	Dec. 19	Jan. 02 '04
0.173	Feb. 26	Mar. 17	Mar. 19	Apr. 01 '04
0.173	May. 19	Jun. 16	Jun. 18	Jul. 01 '04
0.173	Aug. 19	Sep. 15	Sep. 17	Oct. 01 '04

Revenues/Earnings Data Fiscal year ending December 31

Revenues (Million $)

	2004	2003	2002	2001	2000	1999
1Q	646.8	585.0	547.4	516.6	450.9	371.7
2Q	648.6	612.0	558.1	550.8	474.6	398.4
3Q	—	613.4	580.7	513.8	487.9	412.6
4Q	—	620.3	603.7	487.5	518.0	445.1
Yr.	—	2,431	2,290	2,069	1,931	1,628

Earnings Per Share ($)

	2004	2003	2002	2001	2000	1999
1Q	0.34	0.30	0.28	0.25	0.22	0.18
2Q	0.34	0.32	0.29	0.26	0.22	0.19
3Q	0.35	0.33	0.31	0.27	0.23	0.21
4Q	E0.38	0.34	0.35	0.29	0.26	0.22
Yr.	E1.40	1.28	1.21	1.05	0.92	0.80

Next earnings report expected: late-January Source: S&P, Company Reports
EPS Estimates based on S&P Operating Earnings; historical GAAP earnings are as reported.

Synovus Financial Corp.

Recommendation: **HOLD** ★ ★ ★ ☆ ☆   12-Month Target Price: **$29.00** (as of October 15, 2003)

Business Summary November 12, 2004

Synovus Financial (the name was created by combining the words synergy, which means interaction of separate components such that the result is greater than the sum of its parts, and novus, which means of superior quality and different from others in the same category) operates with a decentralized, community-focused management structure that it believes enables it to offer tailored financial services to customers. The company has 40 bank subsidiaries, in Georgia, Florida, Alabama, South Carolina, and Tennessee.

Operations are divided into two segments: financial services and transaction processing services. Financial services provides commercial banking, retail banking, trust services, mortgage banking, securities brokerage and insurance services. Transaction processing includes consumer credit, debit, commercial, retail and stored value card processing and related services, as well as debt collection and bankruptcy management services and the provision of software solutions for commercial card management programs. SNV holds an 81% interest in Total System Services, Inc., one of the world's largest bankcard data processing concerns.

In 2003, average earning assets, from which interest income is derived, amounted to $18.1 billion, and consisted mainly of loans (87%) and investment securities (13%). Sources of funds used in the lending business included interest-bearing deposits (62%), noninterest-bearing deposits (12%), borrowings (13%), shareholders' equity (11%), and other (3%).

At December 31, 2003, nonperforming assets, consisting primarily of nonaccrual loans and other real estate owned, totaled $95.9 million (0.58% of loans and related assets), versus $93.3 million (0.64%) a year earlier. The allowance for loan losses, which is set aside for possible loan defaults, was $266.1 million (1.37% of loans), versus $199.8 million (1.38%) a year earlier. Net chargeoffs, or the amount of loans actually written off as uncollectible, were $56.1 million (0.36% of average loans) in 2003, versus $44.2 million (0.33%) in 2002.

SNV holds an 81% interest in Total System Services (TSYS), one of the world's largest credit, debit, commercial, stored value, chip and retail card processing companies. TSYS provides card production, statement preparation, electronic commerce services, portfolio management services, account acquisition, credit evaluation, risk management, and customer service throughout the U.S., Canada, Mexico, Honduras, the Caribbean, and Europe, representing more than 231 million cardholder accounts.

In November 2003, the company announced plans to charter a new bank in the Jacksonville, FL, market. Subject to approval by federal and state banking regulators, SNV anticipated that the bank would open in the spring of 2004. In February 2004, the company acquired People Florida Banking Corp., the parent of Peoples Bank, which had about $255.6 million in assets and operated four offices, including its headquarters in Palm Harbor, FL.

Company Financials Fiscal Year ending December 31

Per Share Data ($)

(Year Ended December 31)	2003	2002	2001	2000	1999	1998	1997	1996	1995	1994
Tangible Bk. Val.	6.50	6.40	5.75	4.98	4.35	3.96	3.43	3.00	2.66	2.22
Earnings	1.28	1.21	1.05	0.92	0.80	0.70	0.62	0.53	0.44	0.38
S&P Core Earnings	1.23	1.17	0.97	NA	NA	NA	NA	NA	NA	NA
Dividends	0.66	0.59	0.51	0.44	0.34	0.28	0.24	0.20	0.16	0.13
Payout Ratio	52%	49%	49%	48%	43%	40%	39%	37%	36%	35%
Prices - High	29.25	31.93	34.74	27.37	25.12	25.91	22.41	14.83	8.96	5.88
- Low	17.24	16.48	22.75	14.00	17.25	17.25	13.11	7.77	5.25	4.92
P/E Ratio - High	23	26	33	30	31	37	36	28	20	15
- Low	13	14	22	15	22	25	21	15	12	13

Income Statement Analysis (Million $)

	2003	2002	2001	2000	1999	1998	1997	1996	1995	1994
Net Int. Inc.	763	718	630	562	513	441	412	375	342	260
Tax Equiv. Adj.	7.39	7.26	7.25	6.00	5.30	4.54	4.42	4.60	5.10	5.00
Non Int. Inc.	1,592	1,009	936	833	739	561	489	426	340	264
Loan Loss Prov.	71.8	65.3	51.7	44.3	34.0	26.7	32.3	31.8	25.8	22.1
Exp./Op. Revs.	50.7%	62.1%	64.0%	66.2%	68.4%	67.0%	66.7%	66.7%	69.5%	69.4%
Pretax Inc.	638	588	510	428	363	302	268	219	179	134
Eff. Tax Rate	34.9%	33.8%	35.0%	34.8%	34.2%	34.6%	34.9%	36.3%	36.2%	35.7%
Net Inc.	389	365	312	263	225	187	165	140	115	86.4
% Net Int. Marg.	NA	4.65	4.65	4.70	5.07	5.22	5.26	5.19	5.15	5.11
S&P Core Earnings	375	351	286	NA	NA	NA	NA	NA	NA	NA

Balance Sheet & Other Fin. Data (Million $)

	2003	2002	2001	2000	1999	1998	1997	1996	1995	1994
Money Mkt. Assets	177	97.8	27.6	380	94.0	54.1	93.3	38.2	125	33.5
Inv. Securities	2,529	2,238	2,088	2,078	1,994	1,818	1,655	1,639	1,487	1,147
Com'l Loans	13,686	11,791	9,809	8,495	6,789	5,225	4,411	4,002	3,670	1,589
Other Loans	2,779	2,673	2,609	2,257	2,289	2,195	2,204	2,073	1,857	2,741
Total Assets	21,633	19,036	16,658	14,908	12,547	10,498	9,260	8,612	7,928	6,115
Demand Deposits	2,834	2,303	1,985	1,727	1,625	1,362	2,385	2,212	2,074	809
Time Deposits	13,108	11,625	10,162	9,435	7,815	7,180	5,323	4,991	4,654	4,219
LT Debt	1,576	1,336	1,053	841	319	127	126	97.0	107	120
Common Equity	2,245	2,041	1,695	1,417	1,227	1,071	904	784	694	580
% Ret. on Assets	1.9	2.0	2.0	1.9	1.9	1.9	1.8	1.7	1.5	1.5
% Ret. on Equity	18.1	19.6	20.0	19.9	19.3	19.0	19.6	19.1	18.0	17.5
% Loan Loss Resv.	1.4	1.4	1.3	1.4	1.4	1.5	1.6	1.6	1.5	1.5
% Loans/Deposits	104.1	105.6	105.5	96.3	97.1	86.8	85.8	82.9	81.9	86.1
% Equity to Assets	10.5	10.5	9.9	9.6	10.0	10.0	9.4	8.9	8.4	8.6

Data as orig reptd.; bef. results of disc opers/spec. items. Per share data adj. for stk. divs. Bold denotes primary EPS - prior periods restated. E-Estimated. NA-Not Available. NM-Not Meaningful. NR-Not Ranked. UR-Under Review.

Office: One Arsenal Place, 901 Front Avenue, Columbus, GA 31901.
Telephone: 706-649-5220.
Website: http://www.synovus.com
Chrmn: J.D. Yancey.
Pres & COO: R.E. Anthony.
Vice Chrmn: W.M. Deriso, Jr.
Vice Chrmn: F.L. Green III.

Vice Chrmn: E.R. James.
Investor Contact: P.A. Reynolds 706-649-5220.
Dirs: D. P. Amos, R. E. Anthony, J. E. Beverly, J. H. Blanchard, R. Y. Bradley, F. W. Brumley, E. W. Camp, C. E. Floyd, G. W. Garrard, Jr., T. M. Goodrich, V. N. Hansford, J. P. Illges III, A. W. Jones III, M. H. Lampton, J. Moulton, H. L. Page, J. N. Purcell, M. T. Stith, W. B. Turner, Jr., J. D. Yancey.

Founded: in 1888.
Domicile: Georgia.
Employees: 10,909.
S&P Analyst: James M. O'Brien/PMW/BK

Sysco Corp.

Recommendation: **BUY** ★★★★★   12-Month Target Price: **$39.00**
SELL | SELL | HOLD | BUY | BUY   (as of November 01, 2004)

SYY has an approximate 0.20% weighting in the **S&P 500**

Sector: Consumer Staples
Sub-Industry: Food Distributors
Peer Group: Food & Health Distributors

Summary: SYY is the largest U.S. marketer and distributor of foodservice products, serving about 420,000 customers.

Quantitative Evaluations

S&P Earnings & Dividend Rank: A+

| D | C | B- | B | B+ | A- | A | A+ |

S&P Fair Value Rank: 2+

| 1 | 2 | 3 | 4 | 5 |
Lowest | | | | Highest

Fair Value Calc.: $31.10 (Slightly Overvalued)

S&P Investability Quotient Percentile   **100%**

SYY scored higher than 100% of all companies
for which an S&P Report is available.

Volatility: Low

| Low | Average | High |

Technical Evaluation: Bullish
Since 11/04, the technical indicators for SYY
have been Bullish.

Relative Strength Rank: Moderate   **68**
1 Lowest   Highest 99

| Price as of 11/12/04: | **$35.25** | 2005E S&P Core EPS: | **$1.51** |

GAAP Earnings vs. Previous Year
▲ Up ▼ Down ► No Change

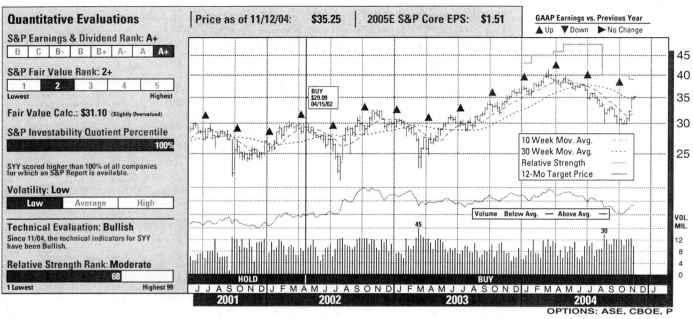

BUY
$29.09
04/15/02

10 Week Mov. Avg.
30 Week Mov. Avg.
Relative Strength
12-Mo Target Price

Volume Below Avg. — Above Avg.

VOL. MIL.

HOLD   BUY
J J A S O N D J F M A M J J A S O N D J F M A M J J A S O N D J F M A M J J A S O N D J
2001   2002   2003   2004

OPTIONS: ASE, CBOE, P

Analyst commentary prepared by Anishka Clarke/PMW/GG

Highlights August 23, 2004

- We expect sales to increase about 10% in FY 05 (Jun.), somewhat slower than in FY 04, despite food cost inflation in the high single digits. We think that a recent slowdown in restaurant sales, driven by a softening U.S. economy, could persist for the near term. We also see a change in client focus toward multi-unit and marketing associate served business limiting revenue growth in the near term. We expect inflation to moderate by early 2005.

- We see some gross margin expansion, despite higher food price inflation, as the proportion of marketing associate-served sales, which offer wider margins than those provided by SYY's traditional business, rises. In addition, gross margins should benefit from an increase in the sales of private label products, which currently account for about 57% of marketing associate-served business, and for 49% of all traditional broadline sales, excluding Canadian operations.

- Despite increased costs associated with the startup of SYY''s first redistribution center in February 2005, we see operating margins benefiting from improved productivity, due in part to a companywide information systems implementation and improved compensation programs. With further share repurchases expected, we look for FY 05 EPS to grow 15%, to $1.58.

Investment Rationale/Risk August 23, 2004

- We are maintaining our buy opinion on the stock, based on valuation and our growth expectations. Our growth outlook is based on what we see as favorable industry trends, including increased dining out and efficiency gains from industry consolidation. We see significant cross-selling opportunities, as current customers receive, on average, only 35% of their products through the company. We are also encouraged by SYY's strong focus on attaining and building customer relationships that will improve operating metrics. For the longer term, we believe the planned redistribution centers will provide significant cost savings opportunities in handling and distribution.

- Risks to our recommendation and target price include SYY's ability to continue to grow in double digits in light of its significant size and reach, and a recent slowdown in restaurant sales.

- Our DCF analysis, assuming a weighted average cost of capital of 8.5% and a 3% terminal growth rate, suggests intrinsic value of $44. Applying a forward peer P/E multiple of 21X to our $1.69 calendar 2005 EPS estimate suggests a value of $36. Combining our two models, we arrive at our 12-month target price of $40.

Key Stock Statistics

S&P Oper. EPS 2005E	1.50	52-week Range	$41.27-29.48
P/E on S&P Oper. EPS 2005E	23.5	12 Month P/E	25.2
S&P Oper. EPS 2006E	1.77	Beta	0.42
Yield (%)	1.7%	Shareholders	15,293
Dividend Rate/Share	0.60	Market Cap (B)	$ 22.6
Shares Outstanding (M)	639.8		

Value of $10,000 invested five years ago: **$ 19,023**

Dividend Data Dividends have been paid since 1970

Amount ($)	Date Decl.	Ex-Div. Date	Stock of Record	Payment Date
0.130	Feb. 13	Mar. 31	Apr. 02	Apr. 23 '04
0.130	May. 14	Jun. 30	Jul. 02	Jul. 23 '04
0.130	Sep. 03	Sep. 29	Oct. 01	Oct. 22 '04
0.150	Nov. 12	Jan. 05	Jan. 07	Jan. 28 '05

Revenues/Earnings Data Fiscal year ending June 30

Revenues (Million $)

	2005	2004	2003	2002	2001	2000
1Q	7.53	7,134	6,424	5,829	5,360	4,657
2Q	—	7,037	6,349	5,591	5,291	4,652
3Q	—	7,026	6,395	5,620	5,345	4,723
4Q	—	8,139	6,972	6,311	5,789	5,272
Yr.	—	29,335	26,140	23,351	21,785	19,303

Earnings Per Share ($)

	2005	2004	2003	2002	2001	2000
1Q	0.35	0.32	0.28	0.24	0.21	0.15
2Q	E0.37	0.34	0.28	0.24	0.21	0.16
3Q	E0.34	0.30	0.26	0.23	0.21	0.15
4Q	E0.45	0.43	0.37	0.31	0.26	0.21
Yr.	E1.50	1.37	1.18	1.01	0.88	0.68

Next earnings report expected: late-January Source: S&P, Company Reports
EPS Estimates based on S&P Operating Earnings; historical GAAP earnings are as reported.

Sysco Corporation

Recommendation: **BUY** ★ ★ ★ ★ ★   12-Month Target Price: **$39.00** (as of November 01, 2004)

Business Summary August 23, 2004

Sysco is the largest marketer and distributor of foodservice products in North America. The company recently held an 11.7% share of the foodservice industry in the U.S. and Canada. As of June 2003, SYY operated a fleet of about 8,570 delivery vehicles, from 145 distribution facilities and self-serve centers throughout the continental U.S., Alaska, and parts of Canada, providing products and services to about 420,000 restaurants, hotels, schools, hospitals, retirement homes, and other foodservice operations: nearly anywhere a meal is prepared away from home.

The company was formed in 1970, when shareholders of nine companies exchanged their stock for SYY common stock. Since its formation, the company has grown significantly, with sales increasing from $115 million to over $26 billion, via internal expansion and acquisitions. Through the end of FY 03 (Jun.), the company had made 73 acquisitions since inception.

SYY operates in both the traditional and chain restaurant segments of the food service industry. Traditional food service customers include restaurants, hospitals, schools, hotels and industrial caterers. Chain restaurant customers (supported by SYGMA Network operations) include regional pizza and national hamburger, chicken and steak chain operations. FY 03 and FY 02 sales were derived as follows: restaurants (63%), hospitals and nursing homes (10%), schools and colleges (6%), hotels and motels (6%), and other (15%). Wendy's International, Inc., accounted for 5% of FY 03 total sales, and for 45% of SYGMA segment sales.

Sales growth of 11.9% in FY 03 reflected 6.7% real sales growth, 5.2% growth from acquisitions, and no food inflation. The company's long-term goal is to attain real sales growth in the upper single digits; minimum growth in EPS of 500 basis points above the real sales growth rate; 37% return on equity; and long term debt equal to 35% to 40% of capitalization. SYY seeks to expand its traditional business by focusing on its marketing associate-served sales to independent customers. These customers generally provide wider margins than do larger traditional customers. The company has been increasing distribution to independent customers, which accounted for 56% of broadline food service sales in FY 03, up from 55% in FY 02. SYY is also emphasizing the sale of Sysco-branded products, which typically carry wider margins than other branded products. During FY 03, Sysco brand products accounted for 49% of total broadline sales, up from 48% in FY 02. The company also hopes to benefit from the growing home meal replacement industry with its SYGMA Network subsidiary (11.2% of total sales), which specializes in customized service to chain restaurants.

Company Financials Fiscal Year ending June 30

Per Share Data ($)

(Year Ended June 30)	2004	2003	2002	2001	2000	1999	1998	1997	1996	1995
Tangible Bk. Val.	2.11	1.68	1.85	2.07	1.90	1.71	1.57	1.68	1.70	1.57
Cash Flow	1.80	1.59	1.47	1.27	1.02	0.84	0.74	0.66	0.58	0.52
Earnings	1.37	1.18	1.01	0.88	0.68	0.54	0.48	0.43	0.38	0.35
S&P Core Earnings	1.31	1.08	0.92	0.82	NA	NA	NA	NA	NA	NA
Dividends	0.61	0.40	0.32	0.26	0.18	0.20	0.17	0.14	0.12	0.10
Payout Ratio	45%	34%	32%	30%	26%	36%	35%	33%	32%	29%
Prices - High	41.27	37.57	32.58	30.12	30.43	20.56	14.34	11.81	9.06	8.12
- Low	29.48	22.90	21.25	21.75	13.06	12.46	9.96	7.31	6.90	6.21
P/E Ratio - High	30	32	32	34	45	38	30	28	24	24
- Low	22	19	21	25	19	23	21	17	18	18

Income Statement Analysis (Million $)

	2004	2003	2002	2001	2000	1999	1998	1997	1996	1995
Revs.	29,335	26,140	23,351	21,784	19,303	17,423	15,328	14,455	13,395	12,118
Oper. Inc.	1,816	1,597	1,439	1,286	1,030	873	772	703	639	586
Depr.	284	273	278	248	220	206	181	160	145	131
Int. Exp.	69.9	72.2	62.9	71.0	71.0	73.0	58.0	47.0	44.0	38.6
Pretax Inc.	1,475	1,260	1,101	967	738	594	533	496	454	418
Eff. Tax Rate	38.5%	38.3%	38.3%	38.3%	38.5%	39.1%	39.0%	39.0%	39.0%	39.7%
Net Inc.	907	778	680	597	454	362	325	303	277	252
S&P Core Earnings	868	710	618	559	NA	NA	NA	NA	NA	NA

Balance Sheet & Other Fin. Data (Million $)

	2004	2003	2002	2001	2000	1999	1998	1997	1996	1995
Cash	200	421	230	136	159	149	110	118	108	134
Curr. Assets	3,851	3,630	3,185	2,985	2,733	2,409	2,180	1,964	1,922	1,787
Total Assets	7,848	6,937	5,990	5,469	4,814	4,097	3,780	3,437	3,325	3,095
Curr. Liab.	3,127	2,701	2,239	2,090	1,783	1,428	1,324	1,114	1,038	945
LT Debt	1,231	1,249	1,176	961	1,024	998	867	686	582	542
Common Equity	7,585	2,198	2,133	2,148	1,762	1,427	1,357	1,400	1,475	1,404
Total Cap.	9,503	3,945	3,750	3,379	3,032	2,669	2,456	2,323	2,288	2,151
Cap. Exp.	530	436	416	341	266	287	259	211	236	202
Cash Flow	1,191	1,051	958	845	674	567	506	463	422	383
Curr. Ratio	1.2	1.3	1.4	1.4	1.5	1.7	1.6	1.8	1.9	1.9
% LT Debt of Cap.	13.0	31.7	31.4	28.4	33.8	37.4	35.3	29.6	25.4	25.2
% Net Inc.of Revs.	3.1	3.0	2.9	2.7	2.4	2.1	2.1	2.1	2.1	2.1
% Ret. on Assets	12.3	12.0	12.0	11.6	10.2	9.2	9.0	9.0	8.6	8.5
% Ret. on Equity	13.1	35.9	32.1	30.5	28.5	26.0	23.6	21.1	19.2	19.1

Data as orig reptd.; bef. results of disc opers/spec. items. Per share data adj. for stk. divs.; EPS diluted. E-Estimated. NA-Not Available. NM-Not Meaningful. NR-Not Ranked. UR-Under Review.

Office: 1390 Enclave Parkway, Houston, TX 77077-2099.
Telephone: 281-584-1390.
Website: http://www.sysco.com
Chrmn & CEO: R.J. Schneiders.
Pres & COO: T.E. Lankford.
SVP & Treas: D.D. Sanders.

VP & General Counsel: M.C. Nichols.
Investor Contact: T.R. Spigelmyer 281-584-1390.
Dirs: C. G. Campbell, J. M. Cassaday, J. B. Craven, J. Golden, J. A. Hafner, T. E. Lankford, R. G. Merrill, R. J. Schnieders, P. S. Sewell, J. K. Stubblefield, Jr., R. G. Tilghman, J. M. Ward.

Founded: in 1969.
Domicile: Delaware.
Employees: 47,800.
S&P Analyst: Anishka Clarke/PMW/GG

Target Corp.

Recommendation: HOLD ★★★☆☆   12-Month Target Price: **$50.00**
(as of October 11, 2004)

TGT has an approximate 0.43% weighting in the **S&P 500**

Sector: Consumer Discretionary
Sub-Industry: General Merchandise Stores
Peer Group: General Merchandise

Summary: TGT operates over 1,146 Target and 125 SuperTarget discount stores across the U.S.

Quantitative Evaluations

S&P Earnings & Dividend Rank: A+

D	C	B-	B	B+	A-	A	A+

S&P Fair Value Rank: 4

1	2	3	4	5
Lowest				Highest

Fair Value Calc.: $51.80 (Fairly Valued)

S&P Investability Quotient Percentile
This company does not meet the inclusion criteria required for calculating an IQ value.

Volatility: Low

Low	Average	High

Technical Evaluation: Bullish
Since 9/04, the technical indicators for TGT have been Bullish.

Relative Strength Rank: Strong

	74	
1 Lowest		Highest 99

Price as of 11/12/04: $52.02   **2005E S&P Core EPS: $2.12**

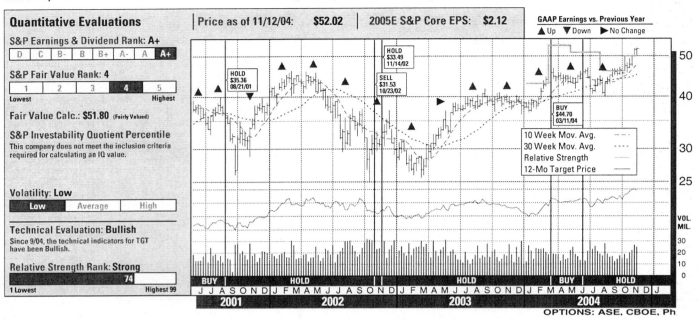

GAAP Earnings vs. Previous Year — ▲ Up ▼ Down ▶ No Change

10 Week Mov. Avg. — — —
30 Week Mov. Avg. ·······
Relative Strength
12-Mo Target Price

OPTIONS: ASE, CBOE, Ph

Analyst commentary prepared by Jason N. Asaeda/CB/BK

Highlights October 14, 2004

- We see revenues down 2% in FY 05 (Jan.), to $47.3 billion, in the likely absence of department store revenues in the second half. In late July, TGT completed the sale of the Marshall Field's business to The May Department Stores Co. (MAY: hold, $24) for $3.24 billion in cash. The company also announced plans to sell its Mervyn's business to an investment consortium for $1.65 billion in cash.

- For Target discount stores, we look for sales to rise 11%, to $46 billion, on a 4%-6% same-store sales increase and the addition of 8%-10% retail square footage. Improved in-stock levels and an increased focus on food and consumables -- particularly at the newer "Greatland" format stores -- should drive shopping frequency. We look for fashion-focused, well-edited apparel selections and marketing efforts that convey a stronger value message to also provide a sales lift.

- EBIT (earnings before interest and taxes) margins should widen, on improved sales leverage and better sourcing and inventory management, partly offset by expected increases in employee-related benefits, and the likely absence of the $27 million LIFO credit recorded in FY 04. We estimate FY 05 operating EPS of $2.23, and Standard & Poor's Core Earnings of $2.12, with the difference due to projected stock option and pension costs.

Investment Rationale/Risk October 14, 2004

- We would hold the shares, based on valuation. In our view, TGT's sale of its department store divisions will likely enhance shareholder value, as the company plans to use proceeds to reduce debt, repurchase shares, and invest in its core namesake business. Combined with our expectation of 10%-11% annual sales growth for TGT's namesake discount store division, and effective inventory and cost controls, we look for sustained margin expansion over the next few years. We also expect sales and earnings visibility to improve, as the company will operate as a pure play discounter. However, with the shares recently trading at a premium to the S&P 500 Index, we see favorable TGT prospects as fully reflected in its valuation.

- Risks to our recommendation and target price include lower-than-anticipated sales growth due to cutbacks in consumer discretionary spending. TGT also faces growing competition from Wal-Mart Stores, Inc. (WMT: accumulate, $52), as well as moderate department stores Sears, Roebuck & Co. (S: avoid, $38) and J.C. Penney Co., Inc. (JCP: hold, $37), which are expanding off-mall.

- Our 12-month target price of $50 blends a forward P/E of 21X applied to our FY 06 operating EPS estimate of $2.60, and a price-to-sales ratio of 0.7X applied to our FY 06 sales estimate, the five-year historical averages.

Key Stock Statistics

S&P Core EPS 2006E	2.50	52-week Range	$52.25-36.19
S&P Oper. EPS 2005E	2.24	12 Month P/E	14.7
P/E on S&P Oper. EPS 2005E	23.2	Beta	1.02
S&P Oper. EPS 2006E	2.60	Shareholders	17,582
Yield (%)	0.6%	Market Cap (B)	$ 47.0
Dividend Rate/Share	0.32	Shares Outstanding (M)	903.3

Value of $10,000 invested five years ago: **$ 16,397**

Dividend Data Dividends have been paid since 1965

Amount ($)	Date Decl.	Ex-Div. Date	Stock of Record	Payment Date
0.070	Jan. 15	Feb. 18	Feb. 20	Mar. 10 '04
0.070	Mar. 11	May. 18	May. 20	Jun. 10 '04
0.080	Jun. 09	Aug. 18	Aug. 20	Sep. 10 '04
0.080	Sep. 09	Nov. 17	Nov. 20	Dec. 10 '04

Revenues/Earnings Data Fiscal year ending January 31

Revenues (Million $)

	2005	2004	2003	2002	2001	2000
1Q	11,587	10,322	9,594	8,345	7,746	7,214
2Q	10,556	10,984	10,068	8,952	8,251	7,752
3Q	10,909	11,286	10,194	9,354	8,582	8,009
4Q	—	15,571	14,061	13,237	12,324	10,390
Yr.	—	48,163	43,917	39,888	36,903	33,702

Earnings Per Share ($)

	2005	2004	2003	2002	2001	2000
1Q	0.48	0.38	0.38	0.28	0.26	0.21
2Q	0.40	0.39	0.38	0.30	0.28	0.25
3Q	—	0.33	0.30	0.20	0.24	0.26
4Q	E0.94	0.91	0.75	0.73	0.61	0.56
Yr.	E2.24	2.01	1.81	1.51	1.38	1.27

Next earnings report expected: mid-February Source: S&P, Company Reports
EPS Estimates based on S&P Operating Earnings; historical GAAP earnings are as reported.

Target Corporation

Recommendation: **HOLD** ★ ★ ★ ☆ ☆   12-Month Target Price: **$50.00** (as of October 11, 2004)

Business Summary October 15, 2004

Target Corp.'s main business is the operation of its eponymous upscale discount store chain, with 1,272 locations (including 126 SuperTarget stores) as of July 31, 2004. The company's discontinued operations are comprised of Mervyn's, a mid-market promotional department store chain, and Marshall Field's, a traditional department store chain.

In July 2004, TGT completed the sale of its entire Marshall Field's business unit, including three distribution centers and about $600 million of credit card receivables, as well as nine Mervyn's store locations to The May Department Stores Co. for $3.2 billion in cash. Prior to the sale, the company had attempted to increase merchandise excitement and newness at Marshall Field's through exclusive design partnerships, the development of proprietary brands, and increased emphasis on holidays and special events. Marshall Field's contributed 5.4% of total FY 04 (Jan.) revenues.

Also in July, TGT reached definitive agreements to sell its Mervyn's business unit to an investment consortium for $1.65 billion in cash. In FY 05, the company has attempted to strengthen Mervyn's competitive position by upgrading its merchandise assortment, expanding the number of national brands, and adding new brands. TGT expects the deal, subject to closing conditions, to occur in the FY 05 third quarter. Mervyn's accounted for 7.4% of total FY 04 revenues.

At its Target business unit, TGT strives to appeal to sophisticated style and quality standards of customers by infusing its assortment with fashion newness, trusted brands, and exclusive designer names such as Isaac Mizrahi. Under the "Expect More. Pay Less." brand promise, the company also believes it satisfies customer demand for value by matching Wal-Mart's prices on identical and similar items in local markets, and by pricing its differentiated products at deep discounts. In FY 04 (Jan.), TGT opened 101 new discount stores and SuperTarget locations; SuperTarget stores combine food and general merchandise under one roof. Target contributed 85.9% of total FY 04 revenues.

To support sales and earnings growth, TGT offers credit to qualified customers in each of its business segments. In FY 04, credit card operations contributed 2.9% ($1.4 billion) of total revenues. The company, which has operated proprietary credit card programs for many years, began a national rollout of the Target Visa credit card in 2001. By the end of FY 04, TGT had reached nearly $5.9 billion in total average credit card receivables, with Target Visa contributing about $3.9 billion.

Capital spending in FY 04 was about $3.0 billion, mostly for the addition of new Target units. In FY 05, TGT plans to invest $3.2-$3.4 billion, mostly in new square footage for Target stores (8%-10%, of which 30% would be SuperTargets), and in distribution and systems infrastructure.

Company Financials Fiscal Year ending January 31

Per Share Data ($)

(Year Ended January 31)	2004	2003	2002	2001	2000	1999	1998	1997	1996	1995
Tangible Bk. Val.	12.14	10.38	8.68	7.27	6.43	5.71	4.78	4.05	3.64	3.54
Cash Flow	3.45	3.14	2.70	2.41	2.19	1.87	1.61	1.29	1.05	1.09
Earnings	2.01	1.81	1.51	1.38	1.27	1.02	0.85	0.52	0.34	0.48
S&P Core Earnings	1.95	1.70	1.42	1.37	NA	NA	NA	NA	NA	NA
Dividends	0.26	0.24	0.21	0.20	0.20	0.18	0.17	0.15	0.15	0.14
Payout Ratio	13%	13%	14%	14%	16%	18%	19%	30%	43%	29%

Cal. Yrs.	2003	2002	2001	2000	1999	1998	1997	1996	1995	1994
Prices - High	41.80	46.15	41.74	39.18	38.50	27.12	18.50	10.15	6.70	7.23
- Low	25.60	24.90	26.00	21.62	25.03	15.71	8.96	5.76	5.27	5.40
P/E Ratio - High	21	25	28	28	30	27	22	20	20	15
- Low	13	14	17	16	20	15	11	11	16	11

Income Statement Analysis (Million $)

	2004	2003	2002	2001	2000	1999	1998	1997	1996	1995
Revs.	48,163	43,917	39,888	36,903	33,702	30,951	27,757	25,371	23,516	21,311
Oper. Inc.	4,839	4,476	3,759	3,418	3,183	2,734	2,435	2,009	1,537	1,671
Depr.	1,320	1,212	1,079	940	854	780	693	650	594	531
Int. Exp.	559	588	464	425	393	398	416	442	442	439
Pretax Inc.	2,960	2,676	2,216	2,053	1,936	1,556	1,326	783	501	714
Eff. Tax Rate	37.8%	38.2%	38.0%	38.4%	38.8%	38.2%	39.5%	39.5%	38.0%	39.2%
Net Inc.	1,841	1,654	1,374	1,264	1,185	962	802	474	311	434
S&P Core Earnings	1,791	1,553	1,289	1,247	NA	NA	NA	NA	NA	NA

Balance Sheet & Other Fin. Data (Million $)

	2004	2003	2002	2001	2000	1999	1998	1997	1996	1995
Cash	716	758	499	356	220	255	211	201	175	147
Curr. Assets	12,928	11,935	9,648	7,304	6,483	6,005	5,561	5,440	4,955	4,959
Total Assets	31,392	28,603	24,154	19,490	17,143	15,666	14,191	13,389	12,570	11,697
Curr. Liab.	8,314	7,523	7,054	6,301	5,850	5,057	4,556	4,111	3,523	3,390
LT Debt	10,217	10,186	8,088	5,634	4,521	4,452	4,425	4,808	4,959	4,488
Common Equity	11,065	9,443	7,860	6,519	5,862	5,043	4,180	3,519	3,146	3,043
Total Cap.	21,282	21,080	15,948	12,153	10,383	10,585	9,635	9,278	9,047	7,725
Cap. Exp.	3,004	3,221	3,163	2,528	1,918	1,657	1,354	1,301	1,505	1,095
Cash Flow	3,161	2,866	2,453	2,204	2,039	1,742	1,495	1,124	905	946
Curr. Ratio	1.6	1.6	1.4	1.2	1.1	1.2	1.2	1.3	1.4	1.5
% LT Debt of Cap.	48.0	48.3	50.7	46.4	43.5	42.1	45.9	51.8	54.9	58.1
% Net Inc.of Revs.	3.8	3.8	3.4	3.4	3.5	3.1	2.9	1.9	1.4	2.0
% Ret. on Assets	6.1	6.3	6.3	6.9	7.2	6.4	6.0	3.7	2.6	3.9
% Ret. on Equity	18.0	19.1	19.1	20.4	21.7	20.8	20.8	14.2	9.5	14.3

Data as orig reptd.; bef. results of disc opers/spec. items. Per share data adj. for stk. divs.; EPS diluted. E-Estimated. NA-Not Available. NM-Not Meaningful. NR-Not Ranked. UR-Under Review.

Office: 1000 Nicollet Mall, Minneapolis, MN 55403.
Telephone: 612-304-6073.
Website: http://www.target.com
Chrmn & CEO: R.J. Ulrich.
Vice Chrmn: G.L. Storch.
EVP & CFO: D.A. Scovanner.

EVP, Secy & General Counsel: J.T. Hale.
Investor Contact: S. Kahn 612-370-6735.
Dirs: R. Austin, C. Darden, R. A. Enrico, W. W. George, E. Hoffman, M. J. Hooper, J. A. Johnson, R. M. Kovacevich, A. M. Mulcahy, S. W. Sanger, W. R. Staley, G. W. Tamke, S. D. Trujillo, R. J. Ulrich.

Founded: in 1902.
Domicile: Minnesota.
Employees: 328,000.
S&P Analyst: Jason N. Asaeda/CB/BK

TECO Energy

Recommendation: **SELL** ★ ★ ☆ ☆ ☆
SELL SELL HOLD BUY BUY

12-Month Target Price: $13.00
(as of October 25, 2004)

TE has an approximate 0.03% weighting in the **S&P 500**

Sector: Utilities
Sub-Industry: Electric Utilities
Peer Group: Electric & Gas - Mid-sized & Smaller

Summary: TE owns Tampa Electric Co., which serves the Tampa Bay region in west central Florida, and has significant diversified operations related to its core business.

Quantitative Evaluations

Price as of 11/12/04: $15.15 | **2004E S&P Core EPS:** $0.75

S&P Earnings & Dividend Rank: B+

| D | C | B- | B | B+ | A- | A | A+ |

S&P Fair Value Rank: 3-

| 1 | 2 | 3 | 4 | 5 |
| Lowest | | | | Highest |

Fair Value Calc.: $14.00 (Slightly Overvalued)

S&P Investability Quotient Percentile

| 61% |

TE scored higher than 61% of all companies for which an S&P Report is available.

Volatility: Low

| Low | Average | High |

Technical Evaluation: Bullish
Since 8/04, the technical indicators for TE have been Bullish.

Relative Strength Rank: Strong

| | 74 | |
| 1 Lowest | | Highest 99 |

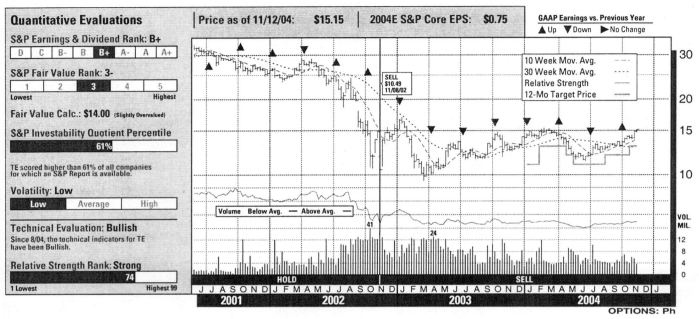

GAAP Earnings vs. Previous Year
▲ Up ▼ Down ▶ No Change

10 Week Mov. Avg.
30 Week Mov. Avg.
Relative Strength
12-Mo Target Price

SELL $10.49 11/08/02

Volume Below Avg. — Above Avg. —

HOLD | SELL

J J A S O N D | J F M A M J J A S O N D | J F M A M J J A S O N D | J F M A M J J A S O N D | J
2001 | 2002 | 2003 | 2004

VOL. MIL.

OPTIONS: Ph

Analyst commentary prepared by Justin McCann/CB/GG

Highlights August 23, 2004

- Excluding one-time net charges that include write-offs of power project investments, we expect TE to return to profitability in 2004, after a restated loss from continuing operations of $0.08 a share in 2003. We believe 2003 operating results, excluding special charges and goodwill impairments, were hurt by a combination of depressed power prices and costs related to the power plant development program at Teco Wholesale Generation.

- With the company's February 2004 decision to exit the state-of-the-art Union and Gila River power projects, which resulted in a 2003 after-tax impairment charge of $762 million ($4.24 a share), we expect TE to focus on its core Florida utility operations. We expect 2004 sales growth of about 2.5% at Tampa Electric, and 4% to 5% customer growth and higher per customer usage at Peoples Gas.

- Results in the first half of 2004 were hurt by the impact of mild weather, but we expect full-year results to benefit from a return to normal weather for Tampa Electric, and an improved economy for the coal and transportation businesses.

Investment Rationale/Risk August 23, 2004

- We expect the stock, which underperformed the S&P Electric Utilities Index in 2003 and the first half of 2004, to continue to underperform over the near term. We think that TE's liquidity position has improved, but we still see cause for concern. Excluding $49.5 million in restricted cash, consolidated cash and equivalents totaled $85.6 million at June 30, 2004; $537.5 million was available under a bank credit facility.

- Risks to our recommendation and target price include a significant increase in the average P/E multiple of the Electric Utility group as a whole, and much better than expected improvement in earnings of TE's non-regulated operations.

- Directors cut the dividend 46% with the May 2003 payment, but the payout ratio still exceeds 85% of our 2004 EPS estimate, well above the industry average. We believe the shares should trade at a modest discount to the peer P/E multiple of about 13.3X, based on our 2005 EPS estimates, and we have a 12-month target price of $12.

Key Stock Statistics

S&P Core EPS 2005E	0.92	52-week Range		$15.38-11.30
S&P Oper. EPS 2004E	0.78	12 Month P/E		NM
P/E on S&P Oper. EPS 2004E	19.4	Beta		0.29
S&P Oper. EPS 2005E	0.95	Shareholders		22,097
Yield (%)	5.0%	Market Cap (B)		$ 3.0
Dividend Rate/Share	0.76	Shares Outstanding (M)		198.8

Value of $10,000 invested five years ago: **$ 9,265**

Dividend Data Dividends have been paid since 1900

Amount ($)	Date Decl.	Ex-Div. Date	Stock of Record	Payment Date
0.190	Jan. 27	Feb. 03	Feb. 05	Feb. 15 '04
0.190	Apr. 28	May. 04	May. 06	May. 15 '04
0.190	Jul. 28	Aug. 03	Aug. 05	Aug. 15 '04
0.190	Oct. 22	Oct. 28	Nov. 01	Nov. 15 '04

Revenues/Earnings Data Fiscal year ending December 31

Revenues (Million $)

	2004	2003	2002	2001	2000	1999
1Q	642.3	651.8	606.6	671.1	524.5	446.4
2Q	713.0	695.3	677.7	641.9	559.5	491.7
3Q	742.3	759.1	731.0	677.8	614.7	555.9
4Q	—	633.8	660.5	657.8	596.0	490.0
Yr.	—	2,740	2,676	2,649	2,295	1,983

Earnings Per Share ($)

	2004	2003	2002	2001	2000	1999
1Q	0.15	-0.12	0.50	0.53	0.42	0.37
2Q	-0.44	0.03	0.56	0.52	0.46	0.39
3Q	0.27	0.03	0.72	0.71	0.65	0.32
4Q	E0.17	-0.02	0.20	0.47	0.44	0.33
Yr.	E0.78	-0.08	1.95	2.24	1.97	1.53

Next earnings report expected: early-February Source: S&P, Company Reports
EPS Estimates based on S&P Operating Earnings; historical GAAP earnings are as reported.

Recommendation: **SELL** ★ ★ ☆ ☆ ☆   12-Month Target Price: **$13.00** (as of October 25, 2004)

Business Summary August 24, 2004

With its Tampa Electric subsidiary serving the growing electricity demands of Tampa, FL, and its adjacent communities, TECO Energy (TE) has diversified into such non-regulated businesses as coal operations, transportation, energy production, and real estate.

Contributions by business segment in 2003 were as follows: Tampa Electric (54.5% of revenues, $98.9 million in net income); TECO Coal (10.2%, $77.1 million); Peoples Gas System (14.0%, $24.5 million); TECO Transport (8.9%, $15.3 million); other unregulated businesses (9.1%, a loss of $4.4 million); and TECO Wholesale Generation (3.3%, a loss of $147.6 million).

Tampa Electric serves more than 612,000 customers in west central Florida, including Hillsborough, Polk, Pasco and Pinellas counties. The customer mix in 2003 (based on revenues) was as follows: residential 48.4% (47.6% in 2001); commercial 29.0% (29.0%); industrial 9.7% (10.0%); and other (including bulk power for resale) 12.9% (13.4%). The company has five active electric generating plants and four combustion turbine units, with a total net generating capacity of 3,256 megawatts. Fuel sources for Tampa Electric in 2003 were: coal, 78%; natural gas, 21%, and oil, 1%.

In 1997, TE acquired Lykes Energy Inc., the parent of Peoples Gas System (PGS), Florida's largest natural gas distributor, via an exchange of stock valued at about $300 million. PGS has retail operations in all of the state's major metropolitan communities, and serves more than 281,000 customers. In February 2000, PGS formed a joint venture, US Propane, L.P., with the propane operations of Atmos Energy, AGL Resources, and Piedmont Natural Gas. In August 2000, each partner contributed its propane operations to the venture, which was to focus on the Southeast.

Unregulated businesses include TECO Coal, with properties in Kentucky, Virginia and Tennessee; TECO Transport, which consists of four subsidiaries that transport, store and transfer coal and other bulk commodities to Tampa Electric (38% in 2003, 43% in 2002, 45% in 2001) and third parties (62%, 57%, 55%); and TECO Wholesale Generation (TGW) (formerly Teco Power Services), which has subsidiaries that have interests in independent power projects in Florida, Virginia, Hawaii, Arkansas, Mississippi, Texas, Arizona and Guatemala.

Other unregulated operations include TECO Solutions, which offers various energy products and services, such as TECO Gas Services and TECO Propane Ventures, LLC; TECO Properties; and TECO Investments. TE also has an approximate 19% interest in EEGSA, which distributes electricity to more than 717,000 customers in Guatemala.

In July 2003, TE announced that the proceeds from the April 2003 sale of a 49% interest in its synfuel facilities were being held in escrow pending a review by the IRS of test procedures used to qualify for synthetic-fuel tax credits. In November 2003, the company said that the IRS had ruled the procedures were in compliance with requirements, and the proceeds held in escrow had been recovered.

Company Financials Fiscal Year ending December 31

Per Share Data ($)

(Year Ended December 31)	2003	2002	2001	2000	1999	1998	1997	1996	1995	1994
Tangible Bk. Val.	8.55	13.75	12.94	11.93	11.19	11.42	11.04	10.73	10.00	9.33
Earnings	-0.08	1.95	2.24	1.97	1.53	1.52	1.61	1.71	1.60	1.32
S&P Core Earnings	0.24	1.75	2.04	NA	NA	NA	NA	NA	NA	NA
Dividends	0.93	1.41	1.37	1.33	1.29	1.23	1.17	1.10	1.05	0.99
Payout Ratio	NM	72%	61%	68%	84%	81%	72%	65%	66%	76%
Prices - High	17.00	29.05	32.97	33.18	28.00	30.62	28.18	27.00	25.75	22.62
- Low	9.47	10.02	24.75	17.25	18.37	24.75	22.75	23.00	20.00	18.12
P/E Ratio - High	NM	15	15	17	18	20	18	16	16	17
- Low	NM	5	11	9	12	16	14	13	12	14

Income Statement Analysis (Million $)

	2003	2002	2001	2000	1999	1998	1997	1996	1995	1994
Revs.	2,740	2,676	2,649	2,295	1,983	1,958	1,862	1,473	1,392	1,351
Depr.	326	303	298	268	232	228	225	185	175	174
Maint.	152	162	151	140	125	129	114	92.2	101	101
Fxd. Chgs. Cov.	2.30	2.43	2.51	2.59	3.30	3.95	3.88	3.69	3.44	3.47
Constr. Credits	27.4	9.60	2.60	0.70	0.50	Nil	0.20	22.9	19.3	5.70
Eff. Tax Rate	NM	NM	NM	6.87%	30.2%	28.8%	30.9%	26.1%	23.8%	22.6%
Net Inc.	-14.7	298	304	251	201	200	211	201	186	153
S&P Core Earnings	44.4	267	277	NA	NA	NA	NA	NA	NA	NA

Balance Sheet & Other Fin. Data (Million $)

	2003	2002	2001	2000	1999	1998	1997	1996	1995	1994
Gross Prop.	8,040	8,215	7,544	6,560	8,501	5,601	5,360	4,722	4,491	4,096
Cap. Exp.	591	1,065	966	688	426	296	213	268	433	309
Net Prop.	5,679	5,464	4,838	3,970	6,064	3,308	3,237	2,957	2,874	2,620
Capitalization:										
LT Debt	4,393	3,973	2,043	1,575	1,208	1,280	1,080	996	995	1,024
% LT Debt	73.0	43.2	50.9	51.1	46.0	45.9	42.8	43.7	44.9	47.3
Pfd.	Nil	Nil	Nil	Nil	Nil	Nil	Nil	20.0	55.0	55.0
% Pfd.	Nil	Nil	Nil	Nil	Nil	Nil	Nil	0.90	2.50	2.50
Common	1,622	5,223	1,972	1,507	1,418	1,508	1,445	1,262	1,167	1,084
% Common	27.0	56.8	49.1	48.9	54.0	54.1	57.2	55.4	52.6	50.1
Total Cap.	6,537	9,719	4,545	3,564	3,284	3,334	3,048	2,761	2,675	2,620
% Oper. Ratio	83.7	84.0	83.7	82.8	83.0	82.6	82.9	81.5	81.4	83.4
% Earn. on Net Prop.	0.3	7.6	9.6	10.9	7.3	12.1	13.3	9.3	9.4	8.8
% Return On Revs.	NM	11.1	11.5	10.9	10.1	10.2	11.4	13.6	13.4	11.3
% Return On Invest. Capital	9.6	6.4	11.9	12.4	9.7	11.3	10.9	10.6	10.2	8.9
% Return On Com. Equity	NM	6.5	17.5	17.2	13.7	13.6	15.6	16.5	16.5	14.5

Data as orig reptd.; bef. results of disc opers/spec. items. Per share data adj. for stk. divs.; EPS diluted. E-Estimated. NA-Not Available. NM-Not Meaningful. NR-Not Ranked. UR-Under Review.

Office: 702 North Franklin Street, Tampa, FL 33602.
Telephone: 813-228-4111.
Website: http://www.tecoenergy.com
Chrmn & CEO: S. Hudson.
Pres & COO: J.B. Ramil.
EVP & CFO: G.L. Gillette.

SVP & General Counsel: S.M. McDevitt.
Investor Contact: M.M. Kane 813-228-1772.
Dirs: C. D. Ausley, S. L. Baldwin, R. D. Fagan, J. L. Ferman, Jr., L. Guinot, Jr., I. D. Hall, S. Hudson, T. L. Rankin, W. D. Rockford, W. P. Sovey, J. T. Touchton, J. A. Urquhart, J. O. Welch, Jr.

Founded: in 1899.
Domicile: Florida.
Employees: 5,753.
S&P Analyst: Justin McCann/CB/GG

Tektronix

Recommendation: **HOLD** ★★★☆☆
SELL   SELL   HOLD   BUY   BUY

12-Month Target Price: $36.00
(as of June 30, 2004)

TEK has an approximate 0.03% weighting in the **S&P 500**

Sector: Information Technology
Sub-Industry: Electronic Equipment Manufacturers
Peer Group: Measuring Instruments

Summary: This test, measurement and monitoring company provides measurement solutions to the semiconductor, computer, telecommunications and other industries.

Quantitative Evaluations

S&P Earnings & Dividend Rank: B-

| D | C | B- | B | B+ | A- | A | A+ |

S&P Fair Value Rank: 2+

| 1 | 2 | 3 | 4 | 5 |
| Lowest | | | | Highest |

Fair Value Calc.: $29.90 (Slightly Overvalued)

S&P Investability Quotient Percentile

96%

TEK scored higher than 96% of all companies for which an S&P Report is available.

Volatility: Average

| Low | Average | High |

Technical Evaluation: Neutral
Since 10/04, the technical indicators for TEK have been Neutral.

Relative Strength Rank: Moderate

63

| 1 Lowest | | Highest 99 |

| Price as of 11/12/04: | **$33.09** | 2005E S&P Core EPS: | **$1.19** |

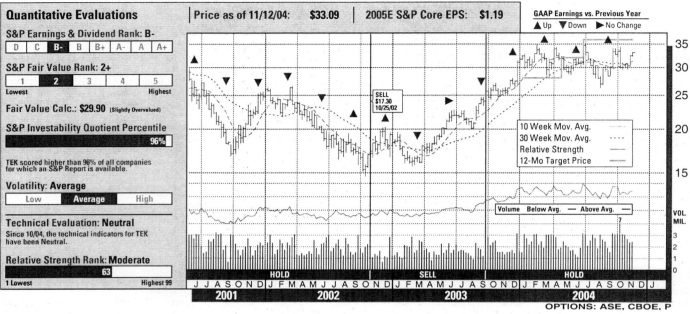

GAAP Earnings vs. Previous Year
▲ Up ▼ Down ► No Change

- 10 Week Mov. Avg.
- 30 Week Mov. Avg.
- Relative Strength
- 12-Mo Target Price

Volume Below Avg. — Above Avg.

OPTIONS: ASE, CBOE, P

Analyst commentary prepared by Bryon J. Korutz/CB/BK

Highlights 15-NOV-04

- We expect sales to advance 14% in FY 05 (May). Overall, we expect to see gradual improvement in sales, as global economies start to recover from their recent downturn.
- In addition, we anticipate that greater demand for new logic analyzers, oscilloscopes, and other test products will boost sales. We project that most sales growth will come from European and Asian markets, particularly from China. We believe that the recent opening of the company's Shanghai manufacturing facility will increase TEK's access to Asian markets. We think the company has taken effective action to improve its sales force, in an effort to more effectively sell its products. We expect gross margins to widen, benefiting from increased sales and an improved cost structure. We view TEK's acquisition of Inet Technologies as positive, as it should position TEK to deliver all network and monitoring and protocol testing needs to its communication customers.
- We project FY 05 operating EPS of $1.45, and see FY 04 Standard & Poor's Core Earnings of $1.19 a share; the difference mainly reflects projected stock option expense.

Investment Rationale/Risk 15-NOV-04

- Based on our belief that end markets have reached a cyclical bottom and have started to improve, and with the shares trading near our 12-month target price of $36, we would hold existing positions.
- Risks to our recommendation and target price include a slowdown in the Chinese economy and slower than anticipated acceptance of new products.
- Applying a forward peer P/E multiple of 22X to our FY 05 EPS estimate of $1.45, we value the stock at $32 a share. Our discounted cash flow model, which assumes a weighted average cost of capital of 9.6%, compound average free cash flow growth of 13.6% over 15 years (versus 14.6% over the past 10 years), and 4% thereafter, values the shares at $37. Our blended valuation model, which represents a weighted average of our valuation metrics, results in our 12-month target price of $36.

Key Stock Statistics

S&P Oper. EPS 2005E	**1.45**	52-week Range	**$35.00-25.10**
P/E on S&P Oper. EPS 2005E	**22.8**	12 Month P/E	**19.9**
Yield (%)	**0.7%**	Beta	**1.30**
Dividend Rate/Share	**0.24**	Shareholders	**2,882**
Shares Outstanding (M)	**91.7**	Market Cap (B)	**$ 3.0**

Value of $10,000 invested five years ago: **$ 20,818**

Dividend Data Dividends have been paid since 2003

Amount ($)	Date Decl.	Ex-Div. Date	Stock of Record	Payment Date
0.040	Dec. 22	Jan. 07	Jan. 09	Jan. 26 '04
0.040	Mar. 22	Apr. 06	Apr. 09	Apr. 26 '04
0.040	Jun. 24	Jul. 07	Jul. 09	Jul. 26 '04
0.060	Sep. 23	Oct. 06	Oct. 08	Oct. 25 '04

Revenues/Earnings Data Fiscal year ending May 31

Revenues (Million $)

	2005	2004	2003	2002	2001	2000
1Q	250.5	201.4	198.5	216.6	278.2	436.1
2Q	—	217.9	203.6	214.6	325.1	261.3
3Q	—	243.5	186.7	203.6	326.9	277.0
4Q	—	257.8	202.3	208.5	305.1	301.5
Yr.	—	920.6	791.0	843.3	1,235	1,121

Earnings Per Share ($)

	2005	2004	2003	2002	2001	2000
1Q	0.43	0.13	0.24	0.08	0.28	-0.09
2Q	E0.49	0.42	0.10	0.09	0.38	0.16
3Q	E0.32	0.50	0.01	0.11	0.43	-0.18
4Q	E0.35	0.31	0.05	0.05	0.37	0.32
Yr.	E1.45	1.37	0.40	0.33	1.46	0.13

Next earnings report expected: mid-December   Source: S&P, Company Reports
EPS Estimates based on S&P Operating Earnings; historical GAAP earnings are as reported.

STANDARD &POOR'S

Tektronix, Inc.

Recommendation: **HOLD** ★★★☆☆   12-Month Target Price: **$36.00** (as of June 30, 2004)

Business Summary 15-NOV-04

Tektronix has completed a transition from a portfolio company to a business that focuses solely on test, measurement and monitoring. The company has been emphasizing growing markets, expansion in key geographic areas, innovative products, strategic alliances and acquisitions, and cost controls. TEK conducts operations on a geographic regional basis in the Americas, Europe, the Middle East, Africa and the Pacific, including Japan.

Test and measurement products include a broad range of instruments designed to allow an engineer to measure, test or calibrate electrical and optical circuits, mechanical motion, sound or radio waves. The oscilloscope is TEK's primary measurement product. Oscilloscopes measure an electrical event and display the measurement on the screen of a cathode ray tube. Logic Analyzers are debugging tools used to capture, display and analyze streams of digital data that occur simultaneously over many channels. TEK also produces video test products, which include waveform monitors, MPEG test products, and video signal genera- tors. Finally, the company also produces network monitoring and protocol testing products, as well as signal source and radio frequency test products.

The company's customers are electronic and computer equipment component manufacturers and service providers, semiconductor manufacturers, communica- tions and networking companies, private industrial firms, governmental organiza- tions, public utilities, educational institutions, radio stations, television stations, and networks.

TEK maintains its own direct sales and field maintenance organization. Sales to end customers are made through TEK's direct sales organization and local subsidiaries or independent distributors.

The company devotes a significant portion of its resources to design and develop new and enhanced products that can be manufactured cost effectively and sold at competitive prices and to meet their customers' needs. These activities include: research on basic devices and techniques, the design and development of products, components and specialized equipment and the development of processes needed for production. The vast majority of Tektronix research and development is devoted to enhancing and developing its own products.

In September 2004, TEK acquired Inet, a global provider of communications software solutions that enable network operators to more strategically and profit- ably operate their businesses. Tektronix acquired all of Inet s outstanding com- mon stock for $12.50 per share, consisting of $6.25 per share in cash and $6.25 per share in Tektronix common stock. Prior to the close of the transaction on September 30, 2004, Inet had 39.6 million shares of common stock outstanding.

TEK's main competitor is Agilent Technologies (formerly the measurement busi- ness of Hewlett-Packard).

Company Financials Fiscal Year ending May 31

Per Share Data ($)

(Year Ended May 31)	2004	2003	2002	2001	2000	1999	1998	1997	1996	1995
Tangible Bk. Val.	9.39	8.32	9.48	10.41	10.28	6.63	7.18	7.70	6.89	6.39
Cash Flow	1.72	0.79	0.77	1.92	0.59	0.25	1.44	1.77	1.47	1.31
Earnings	1.37	0.40	0.33	1.46	0.13	-0.54	0.80	1.15	1.00	0.88
S&P Core Earnings	0.65	-0.25	-0.23	0.83	NA	NA	NA	NA	NA	NA
Dividends	Nil	Nil	Nil	0.18	0.24	0.24	0.23	0.20	0.20	0.20
Payout Ratio	Nil	Nil	Nil	12%	185%	NM	29%	17%	20%	23%
Cal. Yrs.	**2003**	**2002**	**2001**	**2000**	**1999**	**1998**	**1997**	**1996**	**1995**	**1994**
Prices - High	32.25	26.60	40.50	43.65	20.00	24.09	23.20	17.41	20.62	13.50
- Low	15.65	14.64	16.75	17.18	8.78	6.84	16.08	9.91	10.45	7.87
P/E Ratio - High	24	76	NM	30	NM	NM	29	15	21	15
- Low	11	42	NM	12	NM	NM	20	9	10	9

Income Statement Analysis (Million $)

	2004	2003	2002	2001	2000	1999	1998	1997	1996	1995
Revs.	921	791	843	1,235	1,121	1,861	2,086	1,940	1,769	1,940
Oper. Inc.	144	90.5	104	220	115	100	219	223	185	152
Depr.	29.8	33.5	41.0	44.8	44.1	74.8	65.9	59.6	47.0	40.7
Int. Exp.	2.21	6.87	10.0	13.0	15.8	15.7	10.1	12.1	14.0	10.1
Pretax Inc.	167	33.3	47.0	220	19.6	-75.2	123	169	142	110
Eff. Tax Rate	29.3%	NM	35.0%	36.4%	35.0%	NM	33.0%	32.0%	30.0%	25.9%
Net Inc.	118	35.1	30.5	140	12.7	-51.2	82.3	115	100	81.2
S&P Core Earnings	55.5	-21.9	-22.0	79.5	NA	NA	NA	NA	NA	NA

Balance Sheet & Other Fin. Data (Million $)

	2004	2003	2002	2001	2000	1999	1998	1997	1996	1995
Cash	149	190	263	292	684	39.7	121	143	37.0	32.0
Curr. Assets	545	588	747	936	1,112	720	749	752	754	651
Total Assets	1,331	1,391	1,384	1,542	1,535	1,359	1,377	1,317	1,328	1,210
Curr. Liab.	249	237	273	336	330	497	350	304	365	381
LT Debt	0.50	55.0	57.0	128	150	151	151	152	202	105
Common Equity	871	779	927	1,013	978	622	785	771	675	603
Total Cap.	871	834	984	1,141	1,128	772	936	923	877	708
Cap. Exp.	18.6	17.2	16.4	31.5	42.3	108	155	112	107	102
Cash Flow	148	68.7	71.5	185	56.9	23.6	148	174	147	122
Curr. Ratio	2.2	2.5	2.7	2.8	3.4	1.4	2.1	2.5	2.1	1.7
% LT Debt of Cap.	0.1	6.6	5.8	11.2	13.3	19.5	19.2	16.5	23.0	14.8
% Net Inc.of Revs.	12.8	4.4	3.6	11.3	1.1	NM	3.9	5.9	5.6	5.5
% Ret. on Assets	8.7	2.5	2.1	9.2	0.9	NM	6.1	8.7	7.8	7.4
% Ret. on Equity	14.3	4.1	3.1	14.1	1.6	NM	10.6	15.9	15.6	15.2

Data as orig reptd.; bef. results of disc opers/spec. items. Per share data adj. for stk. divs.; EPS diluted. E-Estimated. NA-Not Available. NM-Not Meaningful. NR-Not Ranked. UR-Under Review.

Office: 14200 S.W. Karl Braun Drive, Beaverton, OR 97077.
Telephone: 503-627-7111.
Email: investor-relations@tektronix.com
Website: http://www.tek.com
Chrmn, Pres & CEO: R. H. Wills.

SVP & CFO: C. Slade.
SVP: D. E. Coreson.
VP: R. D. McBee.
Dirs: P. L. Alker, A. G. Ames, G. B. Cameron, D. N. Campbell, F. C. Gill, M. A. McPeak, R. H. Wills, C. J. Yansouni.

Founded: in 1946.
Domicile: Oregon.
Employees: 3,834.
S&P Analyst: Bryon J. Korutz/CB/BK

Tellabs, Inc.

Recommendation: HOLD ★ ★ ★ ★   12-Month Target Price: **$9.00**
(as of October 26, 2004)

TLAB has an approximate 0.03% weighting in the **S&P 500**

Sector: Information Technology
Sub-Industry: Communications Equipment
Peer Group: Core Network Systems

Summary: This company manufactures voice and data equipment used in public and private communications networks worldwide.

Quantitative Evaluations

S&P Earnings & Dividend Rank: B

| D | C | B- | B | B+ | A- | A | A+ |

S&P Fair Value Rank: 5

| 1 | 2 | 3 | 4 | 5 |
| Lowest | | | | Highest |

Fair Value Calc.: $9.20 (Slightly Undervalued)

S&P Investability Quotient Percentile
98%

TLAB scored higher than 98% of all companies for which an S&P Report is available.

Volatility: High

| Low | Average | High |

Technical Evaluation: Bearish
Since 10/04, the technical indicators for TLAB have been Bearish.

Relative Strength Rank: Weak
17
1 Lowest   Highest 99

| Price as of 11/12/04: | $8.40 | 2004E S&P Core EPS: | $0.23 |

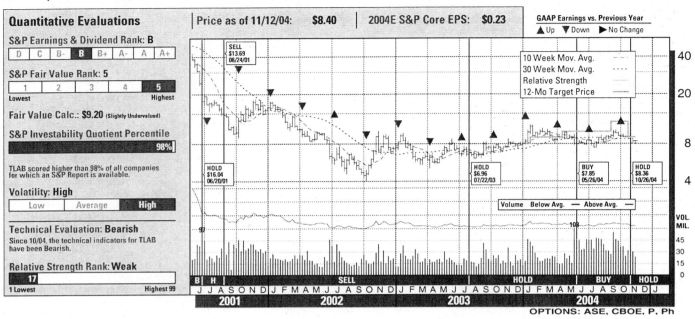

GAAP Earnings vs. Previous Year
▲ Up   ▼ Down   ▶ No Change

10 Week Mov. Avg.
30 Week Mov. Avg.
Relative Strength
12-Mo Target Price

Volume   Below Avg. — Above Avg. —

Analyst commentary prepared by K. Leon/CB/BK

OPTIONS: ASE, CBOE, P, Ph

Highlights October 27, 2004

- Following an 18% sales increase in 2004, we forecast 9% sales growth in 2005, as we expect the company to experience a slowdown in demand for its broadband and transport equipment. In May 2004, TLAB agreed to acquire Advanced Fibre Communications (AFCI; hold, $16), a leader in broadband access, for about $1.9 billion in cash and stock. In September 2004, the terms were amended to a deal valued at $1.5 billion as a result of AFCI's weaker operating quarter results and outlook. The transaction is expected to close in early December 2004, subject to necessary approvals. Based on the amended terms of the deal, TLAB sees the acquisition as accretive to pretax income in 2005, excluding special items.

- As a stand-alone company, we expect TLAB's gross margins to narrow to 52% to 53% in 2005, from 59% in the 2004 second quarter, due to an unfavorable product mix change and slower demand for higher margin transport products. We see total operating expenses rising 3% in 2005, based on expectations of more prudent research and development spending and more focused sales and marketing costs.

- All told, we see 2004 EPS of $0.36, followed by $0.37 in 2005. Our Standard & Poor's Core Earnings per share estimates are $0.23 for 2004 and $0.22 for 2005, reflecting projected stock option expense and other one-time adjustments.

Key Stock Statistics

S&P Core EPS 2005E	0.22	52-week Range	$11.37-7.30
S&P Oper. EPS 2004E	0.36	12 Month P/E	40.0
P/E on S&P Oper. EPS 2004E	23.3	Beta	NA
S&P Oper. EPS 2005E	0.37	Shareholders	6,700
Yield (%)	Nil	Market Cap (B)	$ 3.5
Dividend Rate/Share	Nil	Shares Outstanding (M)	416.2

Value of $10,000 invested five years ago: **$ 1,217**

Dividend Data

No cash dividends have been paid.

Investment Rationale/Risk October 27, 2004

- We view the shares as fairly valued versus peers and the S&P 500. We believe the company may be challenged to realize double-digit sales growth in 2005, as we estimate slower demand from wireless and wireline customers. However, strong cost controls should enable TLAB to realize improved profitability.

- Risks to our recommendation and target price include failure to complete and successfully integrate the proposed AFCI acquisition over the next six months; lower than expected market penetration for the company's new broadband products; weaker demand for its core transport products; and a drop in customer satisfaction, as 37% of total sales in 2003 were realized from the largest U.S. wireline carriers.

- Applying the stock's P/E multiple of 24X on our 2004 estimate to our 2005 EPS estimate and an enterprise value of 10.8X to our 2005 EBITDA estimate, we arrive at our 12-month target price of $9. Based on TLAB's $1.3 billion of cash equivalents and its debt-free balance sheet, and with the stock trading at an enterprise value of 3X our 2005 sales projection, near peer levels, we would hold the shares.

Revenues/Earnings Data Fiscal year ending December 31

Revenues (Million $)

	2004	2003	2002	2001	2000	1999
1Q	263.8	222.5	371.5	772.1	631.3	469.6
2Q	304.3	234.1	344.6	509.4	785.5	540.4
3Q	284.3	244.5	288.1	448.2	812.1	594.5
4Q	—	279.3	312.8	470.0	1,159	714.9
Yr.	—	980.4	1,317	2,200	3,387	2,320

Earnings Per Share ($)

	2004	2003	2002	2001	2000	1999
1Q	0.03	-0.10	0.01	0.29	0.29	0.26
2Q	0.12	-0.27	-0.35	-0.43	0.38	0.32
3Q	0.11	-0.16	-0.22	-0.12	0.45	0.35
4Q	E0.10	-0.06	-0.21	-0.20	0.71	0.46
Yr.	E0.36	-0.58	-0.76	-0.44	1.82	1.36

Next earnings report expected: late-January Source: S&P, Company Reports
EPS Estimates based on S&P Operating Earnings; historical GAAP earnings are as reported.

Tellabs, Inc.

Recommendation: **HOLD** ★ ★ ★ ☆ ☆   12-Month Target Price: **$9.00** (as of October 26, 2004)

Business Summary October 27, 2004

Tellabs designs, manufactures, markets and services optical networking, next-generation switching and broadband access solutions. The company's voice and data transport and network access systems are used by telephone companies, long-distance carriers, alternate service providers, wireless service providers, cable operators, government agencies, utilities and businesses.

The company's transport systems (47% of sales in the 2004 third quarter) are designed to help service providers lower costs, generate more revenues, and efficiently manage bandwidth as the end-user demand for communication services grows. Product offerings include the Tellabs 5000 (formerly TITAN) series of digital-cross connect systems, the new Tellabs 6400 (formerly Ocular OSX) product line, the Tellabs 6500 Transport Switch (formerly TITAN 6500 Multiservice Transport Switch), and the Tellabs 7100 (formerly TITAN 6100) series of optical transport systems.

TLAB's managed access solutions (26%) provide seamless integration of circuit-switched voice and data, IP-data and voice-over-Internet protocol (VoIP) services, and access capacity expansion through digital subscriber line (DSL) technology. Products include the Tellabs 8100 (formerly MartisDXX) for international markets and Tellabs 6300 (formerly FOCUS) series of managed access and transport systems, the Tellabs 7200 (formerly FOCUS 6200) Optical Transport System for international markets, and the Tellabs 2300 (formerly CABLESPAN) telephony distribution systems that support cable television providers and alternate access carriers.

The company's data and voice quality products (10%) consist primarily of the Tellabs 3000 (formerly VERITY) family of broadband and narrowband echo cancellers, and Tellabs Voice-Quality Enhancement (VQE) solutions that enable wireless and wireline providers to improve voice quality in long-distance, wireless, and private networks.

The remaining portion of sales in the 2004 third quarter came from services revenues (17%). Services provides customers on a worldwide basis with network deployment services, traffic management services and other support services for technical assistance, system maintenance, systems performance improvement and skills enhancement.

Sales to customers in the U.S. accounted for 61% of the total in 2003, with 39% from international customers. The largest single group of customers was the Incumbent Local Exchange Carriers (ILECs), which include BellSouth, Verizon, SBC, and Qwest Communications. Sales to ILECs accounted for 37% of total net sales in 2003. Verizon (including Verizon Wireless) was the company's largest customer, at 21%.

In May 2004, TLAB agreed to acquire Advanced Fibre Communications (AFCI), for about $1.9 billion in cash and stock (1.55 TLAB common shares and $7 in cash for each AFCI share). In August 2004, the deal was amended to about $1.5 billion ($12 in cash and 0.504 of a share of TLAB for each AFCI share). Subject to necessary approvals, the transaction is expected to close in early December 2004.

Company Financials Fiscal Year ending December 31

Per Share Data ($)

(Year Ended December 31)	2003	2002	2001	2000	1999	1998	1997	1996	1995	1994
Tangible Bk. Val.	3.76	4.45	5.55	6.26	4.85	3.40	2.40	1.47	1.09	0.71
Cash Flow	-0.32	-0.41	-0.06	2.09	1.56	1.18	0.83	0.41	0.38	0.25
Earnings	-0.58	-0.76	-0.44	1.82	1.36	1.03	0.71	0.32	0.32	0.20
S&P Core Earnings	-0.71	-1.03	-0.68	NA	NA	NA	NA	NA	NA	NA
Dividends	Nil	Nil	Nil	Nil	Nil	Nil	Nil	Nil	Nil	Nil
Payout Ratio	Nil	Nil	Nil	Nil	Nil	Nil	Nil	Nil	Nil	Nil
Prices - High	9.73	17.47	67.12	76.93	77.25	46.56	32.50	23.37	13.18	7.00
- Low	5.07	4.00	8.98	37.62	32.37	15.68	16.00	7.62	5.87	2.73
P/E Ratio - High	NM	NM	NM	42	57	45	46	73	42	35
- Low	NM	NM	NM	21	24	15	23	24	19	14

Income Statement Analysis (Million $)

	2003	2002	2001	2000	1999	1998	1997	1996	1995	1994
Revs.	980	1,317	2,200	3,387	2,319	1,660	1,204	869	635	494
Oper. Inc.	-77.1	-12.7	70.9	1,117	832	593	410	276	180	119
Depr.	110	143	158	116	84.6	56.1	46.9	32.6	24.0	19.5
Int. Exp.	0.70	0.90	0.51	0.63	0.58	0.29	0.41	1.17	0.12	1.77
Pretax Inc.	-245	-328	-245	1,109	816	590	400	175	163	97.8
Eff. Tax Rate	NM	NM	NM	31.5%	31.5%	32.5%	34.0%	32.6%	28.9%	26.0%
Net Inc.	-242	-313	-182	760	559	398	264	118	116	72.4
S&P Core Earnings	-295	-427	-277	NA	NA	NA	NA	NA	NA	NA

Balance Sheet & Other Fin. Data (Million $)

	2003	2002	2001	2000	1999	1998	1997	1996	1995	1994
Cash	246	1,019	1,102	1,022	966	643	109	90.4	162	74.7
Curr. Assets	1,499	1,534	1,945	2,322	1,786	1,253	863	475	366	221
Total Assets	2,608	2,623	2,866	3,073	2,353	1,628	1,183	744	552	390
Curr. Liab.	208	257	320	412	274	218	226	132	99	82.0
LT Debt	Nil	Nil	3.39	2.85	2.85	2.85	2.90	2.85	2.85	2.85
Common Equity	2,219	2,290	2,466	2,628	2,048	1,377	933	591	433	293
Total Cap.	2,319	2,290	2,490	2,637	2,058	1,391	936	601	447	297
Cap. Exp.	9.50	34.1	208	208	99	75.9	84.7	64.8	35.0	23.0
Cash Flow	-131	-171	-24.5	876	644	454	311	151	139	91.9
Curr. Ratio	7.2	6.0	6.1	5.6	6.5	5.7	3.8	5.6	3.7	2.7
% LT Debt of Cap.	Nil	Nil	0.1	0.1	0.1	0.2	0.0	0.5	1.0	1.0
% Net Inc.of Revs.	NM	NM	NM	22.4	24.1	24.0	21.9	13.6	18.3	14.6
% Ret. on Assets	NM	NM	NM	28.0	28.0	28.3	27.4	18.2	24.5	20.1
% Ret. on Equity	NM	NM	NM	32.5	32.5	34.5	34.6	23.0	32.0	29.0

Data as orig reptd.; bef. results of disc opers/spec. items. Per share data adj. for stk. divs.; EPS diluted. E-Estimated. NA-Not Available. NM-Not Meaningful. NR-Not Ranked. UR-Under Review.

Office: 1415 W Diehl Rd, Naperville, IL 60563-2349.
Telephone: 630-378-8800.
Website: http://www.tellabs.com
Chrmn: M.J. Birck.
Pres & CEO: K.A. Prabhu.

EVP & CFO: T.J. Wiggins.
SVP, Secy & General Counsel: J. Sheehan.
Investor Contact: J. Springer 630-798-3603.
Dirs: M. J. Birck, B. Hedfors, M. Hobson, F. A. Krehbiel, M. E. Lavin, S. P. Marshall, K. A. Prabhu, W. F. Souders, J. H. Suwinski.

Founded: in 1974.
Domicile: Delaware.
Employees: 3,515.
S&P Analyst: K. Leon/CB/BK

Temple-Inland

Recommendation: **HOLD** ★ ★ ★ ★ ★
SELL SELL HOLD BUY BUY

12-Month Target Price: $68.00
(as of July 27, 2004)

TIN has an approximate 0.03% weighting in the **S&P 500**

Sector: Materials
Sub-Industry: Paper Packaging
Peer Group: Containers and Packaging (Paper)

Summary: This major producer of corrugated containers and containerboard also makes building products, and has financial services operations as well.

Quantitative Evaluations

S&P Earnings & Dividend Rank: B

| D | C | B- | **B** | B+ | A- | A | A+ |

S&P Fair Value Rank: 4-

| 1 | 2 | 3 | **4** | 5 |
| Lowest | | | | Highest |

Fair Value Calc.: $63.20 (Fairly Valued)

S&P Investability Quotient Percentile

97%

TIN scored higher than 97% of all companies for which an S&P Report is available.

Volatility: Low

| **Low** | Average | High |

Technical Evaluation: Bearish

Since 10/04, the technical indicators for TIN have been Bearish.

Relative Strength Rank: Weak

21

| 1 Lowest | | Highest 99 |

| Price as of 11/12/04: | **$62.18** | 2004E S&P Core EPS: | **$3.20** |

GAAP Earnings vs. Previous Year
▲ Up ▼ Down ▶ No Change

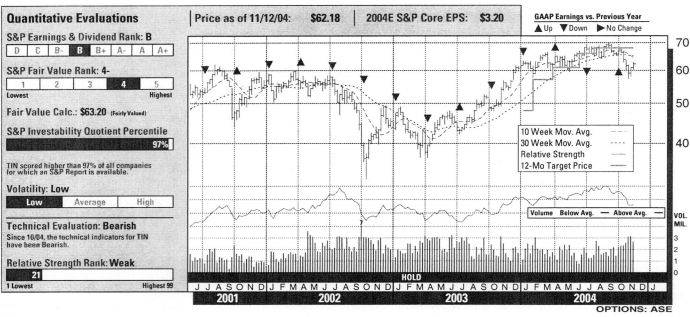

10 Week Mov. Avg.
30 Week Mov. Avg.
Relative Strength
12-Mo Target Price

Volume Below Avg. — Above Avg. —

VOL. MIL.

HOLD

J J A S O N D | J F M A M J J A S O N D | J F M A M J J A S O N D | J F M A M J J A S O N D | J
2001 | **2002** | **2003** | **2004**

OPTIONS: ASE

Analyst commentary prepared by Bryon J. Korutz/CB/JWP

Highlights 15-NOV-04

■ After a rise of 2.0% seen for 2004, we expect revenue to grow 4.0% in 2005. S&P projects real GDP growth of 4.5% for 2004. We see this supporting improved demand and price increases for TIN's corrugated containers and containerboard, as we expect a firming economy to stimulate the manufacturing sector and boost movement of goods.

■ Corrugated box demand and pricing have firmed, and we see demand remaining steady into 2005. We also expect a third containerboard price increase in early 2005 and see a resultant price hike in boxes to be phased in. In the forest products segment, we see average wood products prices in 2005 below levels reached in 2004, based on our projection of a 7.0% drop in housing starts. Overall, we see higher packaging wood products prices, cost reductions, and facility consolidations boosting margins to 8.9% in 2004, from 4.0% in 2003.

■ Based on S&P Core Earnings methodology, we see TIN earning $3.20 a share in 2004 and $4.03 and 2005. The difference from our operating earnings estimates is related mainly to projected stock option expense, partly offset by projected net pension gains.

Investment Rationale/Risk 15-NOV-04

■ We view as positive TIN's sale of its third party mortgage servicing portfolio. We see this divestiture reducing the volatility of the financial services segment. Based on our expectations of a firming in the packaging segment, partly offset by our view of a weakening outlook for wood products prices in late 2004 and in 2005, we would not add to positions.

■ Risks to our recommendation and target price include a weaker than expected recovery in paper packaging prices and demand.

■ Our relative valuation, calculated by applying an average forward peer P/E multiple of about 15.7X to our 2005 EPS estimate of $4.05, indicates that the stock is worth about $64. Our DCF model, which assumes a weighted average cost of capital of 7.7%, compound average annual free cash flow growth of 6.0% over the 15-year forecast period, and 3.0% growth in perpetuity, values the stock at $71. Our 12-month target price of $68 is a blend of our two metrics.

Key Stock Statistics

S&P Core EPS 2005E	**4.03**	52-week Range	**$70.02-53.66**
S&P Oper. EPS 2004E	**3.22**	12 Month P/E	**50.6**
P/E on S&P Oper. EPS 2004E	**19.3**	Beta	**1.17**
S&P Oper. EPS 2005E	**4.05**	Shareholders	**5,425**
Yield (%)	**2.3%**	Market Cap (B)	**$ 3.5**
Dividend Rate/Share	**1.44**	Shares Outstanding (M)	**55.7**

Value of $10,000 invested five years ago: **$ 11,533**

Dividend Data Dividends have been paid since 1984

Amount ($)	Date Decl.	Ex-Div. Date	Stock of Record	Payment Date
q.36	May. 07	May. 27	Jun. 01	Jun. 15 '04
0.360	Aug. 06	Aug. 30	Sep. 01	Sep. 15 '04
1.0 Spcl.	Nov. 08	Nov. 29	Dec. 01	Dec. 15 '04
0.360	Nov. 05	Nov. 29	Dec. 01	Dec. 15 '04

Revenues/Earnings Data Fiscal year ending December 31

Revenues (Million $)

	2004	2003	2002	2001	2000	1999
1Q	1,148	1,135	1,020	1,053	1,066	850.0
2Q	1,218	1,182	1,190	1,062	1,096	904.0
3Q	1,194	1,170	1,157	1,057	1,081	955.0
4Q	—	1,166	1,151	1,000	1,043	973.0
Yr.	—	4,653	4,518	4,172	4,286	3,682

Earnings Per Share ($)

	2004	2003	2002	2001	2000	1999
1Q	0.24	-0.32	0.30	0.24	1.04	0.46
2Q	0.98	2.86	0.31	0.58	1.20	0.87
3Q	0.71	-0.06	0.28	0.90	0.87	1.07
4Q	E0.85	-0.70	0.36	0.54	0.72	1.03
Yr.	E3.22	1.78	1.25	2.26	3.83	3.43

Next earnings report expected: early-February Source: S&P, Company Reports
EPS Estimates based on S&P Operating Earnings; historical GAAP earnings are as reported.

Recommendation:  HOLD ★ ★ ★ ☆ ☆   12-Month Target Price: **$68.00** (as of July 27, 2004)

Business Summary 15-NOV-04

Temple-Inland has diverse operations in the areas of forest products and financial services. In forest products, it makes both corrugated packaging products and building materials. In April 2002, the company acquired Gaylord Container Corp. for $847 million, mostly for the acquisition of Gaylord's notes.

The corrugated packaging segment (58% of 2003 sales) makes containerboard. The company converted 82% of its containerboard into corrugated packaging and point-of-purchase displays in 2003, and offered the rest on the open market. TIN's boxes range from commodity brown boxes to intricate die cut containers that can be printed with multi-color graphics. The segment's corrugated boxes are sold to customers in the food, paper, glass containers, chemical, appliance and plastics industries. The segment also produces litho-laminated corrugated packaging, high graphics folding cartons, and multi-wall corrugated board. At December 31, 2003, the company operated five linerboard mills and one medium mill, with total annual capacity of 3.3 million tons, and 79 converting and other facilities. TIN also owns an interest in a gypsum facing paper joint venture.

The forest products segment (17%) produces wood products, including lumber, particleboard, medium density fiberboard, gypsum wallboard and fiberboard. TIN's building products are used primarily in home construction, remodeling, and repair and cabinet and furniture production. At December 31, 2003, the company operated five lumber mills with annual production capacity of 1,034 million board feet,

one fiberboard mill with 460 million square feet of capacity, five particleboard mills with 860 million square feet of capacity, four gypsum wallboard mills with 2,000 million square feet of capacity, and four medium density fiberboard mills with 540 million square feet of capacity.

At the end of 2003, the company managed 2.0 million acres of owned and leased timberlands in Texas, Louisiana, Georgia and Alabama. In 2003, the timberlands supplied 57% of TIN's saw timber needs and 43% of its pine pulpwood needs. As part of an ongoing effort to enhance return on investment, the company determined that 1.8 million acres were strategic and would not be sold. It identified 110,000 acres as non-strategic, and 160,000 acres were identified as higher and better use land. Since completing the study, TIN has sold 78,000 acres of non-strategic land. In 2003, it sold about 2,436 acres of higher and better use land, for $12 million.

The financial services segment (25%) includes a savings bank, mortgage banking operations, a real estate development unit, and an insurance brokerage. Guaranty Bank conducts business through banking centers in Texas and California. Commercial and residential lending activities are conducted in 123 offices, in 28 states and the District of Columbia. The company is also involved in the development of 55 residential subdivisions, in Texas, California, Colorado, Florida, Georgia, Missouri, Tennessee and Utah.

Company Financials Fiscal Year ending December 31

Per Share Data ($)

(Year Ended December 31)	2003	2002	2001	2000	1999	1998	1997	1996	1995	1994
Tangible Bk. Val.	29.33	28.84	34.90	37.41	35.69	35.93	36.30	36.34	35.48	31.83
Cash Flow	6.80	6.25	6.67	8.24	7.43	6.12	5.68	6.97	8.88	6.07
Earnings	1.78	1.25	2.26	3.83	3.43	1.21	0.90	2.39	5.01	2.35
S&P Core Earnings	1.83	0.20	0.95	NA	NA	NA	NA	NA	NA	NA
Dividends	1.70	1.28	1.28	1.28	1.28	1.28	1.28	1.24	1.14	1.02
Payout Ratio	96%	102%	57%	33%	37%	106%	142%	52%	23%	43%
Prices - High	62.86	59.99	62.15	67.68	77.50	67.25	69.43	55.37	55.75	56.75
- Low	36.86	32.69	40.35	34.62	53.62	42.68	49.62	39.75	41.50	43.00
P/E Ratio - High	35	48	27	18	23	56	77	23	11	24
- Low	21	26	18	9	16	35	55	17	8	18

Income Statement Analysis (Million $)

	2003	2002	2001	2000	1999	1998	1997	1996	1995	1994
Revs.	4,653	4,518	4,172	4,286	3,682	3,740	3,625	3,460	3,460	2,938
Oper. Inc.	316	511	491	654	610	546	467	515	716	545
Depr.	270	260	216	225	225	275	268	254	216	208
Int. Exp.	135	133	98.0	104	95.0	106	110	113	95.4	176
Pretax Inc.	-97.0	107	177	320	306	124	95.0	156	431	193
Eff. Tax Rate	NM	39.3%	37.3%	39.1%	37.6%	46.0%	46.3%	14.8%	34.8%	32.1%
Net Inc.	97.0	65.0	111	195	191	67.0	51.0	133	281	131
S&P Core Earnings	99	10.8	46.0	NA	NA	NA	NA	NA	NA	NA

Balance Sheet & Other Fin. Data (Million $)

	2003	2002	2001	2000	1999	1998	1997	1996	1995	1994
Cash	399	455	590	322	284	244	188	228	358	315
Curr. Assets	NA	NA	NA	NA	NA	NA	NA	NA	NM	NA
Total Assets	21,143	21,760	18,687	18,142	16,186	15,990	14,364	12,947	12,764	12,251
Curr. Liab.	NA	NA	NA	NA	NA	NA	NA	NA	NM	NA
LT Debt	2,155	6,124	1,859	1,897	1,691	2,018	1,605	1,791	1,734	1,531
Common Equity	1,968	1,949	1,896	1,833	1,927	1,998	2,045	2,015	1,975	1,783
Total Cap.	4,130	8,309	4,059	4,002	3,814	4,258	3,873	3,871	3,926	3,477
Cap. Exp.	159	125	210	257	204	214	251	290	420	483
Cash Flow	367	325	327	420	416	342	319	387	497	339
Curr. Ratio	NA	NA	NA	NA	NA	NA	NA	NA	NM	NA
% LT Debt of Cap.	52.2	73.7	45.8	47.4	44.3	47.4	41.4	42.8	44.2	44.0
% Net Inc.of Revs.	NM	1.4	2.7	4.5	5.2	1.8	1.4	3.9	8.1	4.5
% Ret. on Assets	NM	0.3	0.6	1.1	1.2	0.4	0.4	1.1	2.2	1.1
% Ret. on Equity	NM	3.4	6.0	10.4	9.7	3.3	2.5	6.7	15.0	7.5

Data as orig reptd.; bef. results of disc opers/spec. items. Per share data adj. for stk. divs.; EPS diluted. E-Estimated. NA-Not Available. NM-Not Meaningful. NR-Not Ranked. UR-Under Review.

Office: 1300 MoPac Expressway South, Austin, TX 78746.
Telephone: 512-434-5800.
Email: investorrelations@templeinland.com
Website: http://www.temple-inland.com
Chrmn & CEO: K. M. Jastrow II.
EVP: H. C. Maxwell.
EVP: D. E. Stahl.

CFO: R. D. Levy.
Investor Contact: Chris L. Nines (512-434-5587).
Dirs: P. M. Anderson, A. M. Beschloss, D. M. Carlton, R. Cizik, E. L. Draper, Jr., A. M. Frank, J. T. Hackett, J. M. Heller, B. R. Inman, K. M. Jastrow II, J. A. Johnson, W. A. Reed, H. A. Sklenar, L. E. Temple, A. Temple III.

Founded: in 1983.
Domicile: Delaware.
Employees: 18,000.
S&P Analyst: Bryon J. Korutz/CB/JWP

Tenet Healthcare

Recommendation: **SELL** ★★☆☆☆
SELL · ·HOLD· · BUY

12-Month Target Price: $9.00
(as of October 15, 2004)

THC has an approximate 0.05% weighting in the **S&P 500**

Sector: Health Care
Sub-Industry: Health Care Facilities
Peer Group: Hospital Management

Summary: Tenet Healthcare, the second largest U.S. for-profit hospital manager, with acute care facilities in 14 states, also operates other health care facilities and related businesses.

Quantitative Evaluations

S&P Earnings & Dividend Rank: C

| D | C | B- | B | B+ | A- | A | A+ |

S&P Fair Value Rank: 1

| 1 | 2 | 3 | 4 | 5 |
| Lowest | | | | Highest |

Fair Value Calc.: $5.50 (Overvalued)

S&P Investability Quotient Percentile

21%

THC scored lower than 79% of all companies for which an S&P Report is available.

Volatility: High

| Low | Average | High |

Technical Evaluation: Neutral
Since 11/04, the technical indicators for THC have been Neutral.

Relative Strength Rank: Moderate

41

| 1 Lowest | | Highest 99 |

Price as of 11/12/04: **$10.99** **2004E S&P Core EPS:** **$-0.52**

GAAP Earnings vs. Previous Year
▲ Up ▼ Down ► No Change

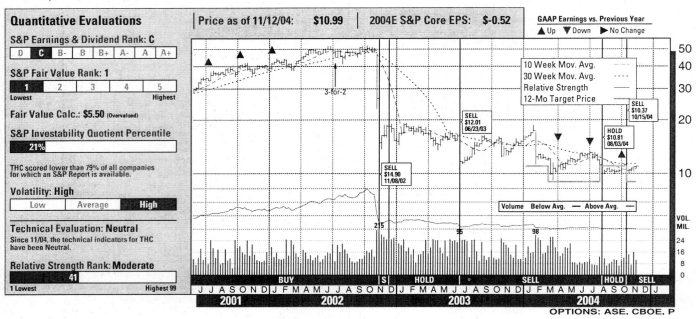

Analyst commentary prepared by Cameron Lavey/CB/JWP

OPTIONS: ASE, CBOE, P

Highlights November 04, 2004

■ For the company as currently constituted, we look for 2005 revenue to increase 2.0%, to $10.4 billion, reflecting higher Medicare reimbursement rates, partially offset by lower managed care pricing and flat inpatient and outpatient volume growth. We believe that deteriorating negotiating leverage with managed care will continue to be a significant challenge for THC for the rest of 2004 and the first half of 2005.

■ Although first quarter volumes rose sequentially, volumes declined in the second and third quarters, suggesting possible market share erosion. Our 2004 EPS forecast reflects this concern, as well as our expectations of rising supply costs and higher bad debt expense. We see the company making progress in controlling labor costs over the course of the year.

■ We estimate an operating loss of $0.17 in 2004, which excludes numerous charges, including litigation and restructuring charges. We anticipate a return to profitability in 2005, with EPS of $0.15. After removing gains from asset sales, and including restructuring charges and litigation settlements, we estimate 2004 S&P Core Earnings at a loss of $0.52.

Investment Rationale/Risk November 04, 2004

■ We believe that industry conditions, including increases in self-pay revenues and higher labor and supply costs, remain challenging. In addition, we think that THC faces additional company-specific risks. Specifically, we are concerned about THC's inconsistent volume growth, increased bad debt expense, and ongoing litigation exposure. We also think that hospital divestitures are slightly behind schedule.

■ Risks to our opinion and target price include the possibility that THC sells the targeted hospitals on more favorable terms than we anticipate. Additional risks include an increase in patient volumes, better expense control, and lower levels of bad debt.

■ Given the negative free cash flow and EPS, we use a sum-of-the-parts model to arrive at our 12-month target price of $9. Our model incorporates slightly lower asset values, based on recent data from THC's hospital divestitures. We would avoid the shares.

Key Stock Statistics

S&P Oper. EPS 2004E	-0.17	52-week Range	$18.73-9.15
P/E on S&P Oper. EPS 2004E	NM	12 Month P/E	NM
S&P Oper. EPS 2005E	0.15	Beta	-0.19
Yield (%)	Nil	Shareholders	9,600
Dividend Rate/Share	Nil	Market Cap (B)	$ 5.1
Shares Outstanding (M)	466.7		

Value of $10,000 invested five years ago: **$ 8,011**

Dividend Data

Dividends, initiated in 1973, were omitted beginning in 1993. A special dividend of $0.01 a share was paid in March 2000.

Revenues/Earnings Data Fiscal year ending December 31

Revenues (Million $)

	2004	2003	2002	2001	2000	1999
1Q	2,669	3,417	—	3,297	2,893	2,873
2Q	2,570	3,346	—	3,394	2,915	2,780
3Q	2,440	3,268	—	3,484	3,036	2,850
4Q	—	3,181	—	3,738	3,209	2,911
Yr.	—	13,212	8,743	13,913	12,053	11,414

Earnings Per Share ($)

	2004	2003	2002	2001	2000	1999
1Q	-0.04	0.03	—	0.45	0.32	0.27
2Q	-0.45	-0.28	—	0.38	0.36	0.29
3Q	-0.11	-0.50	—	0.57	0.40	0.08
4Q	E-0.03	-2.34	—	0.64	0.31	0.08
Yr.	E-0.17	-3.01	0.93	2.04	1.39	0.72

Next earnings report expected: mid-March Source: S&P, Company Reports
EPS Estimates based on S&P Operating Earnings; historical GAAP earnings are as reported.

The McGraw·Hill Companies

Tenet Healthcare Corporation

Recommendation: **SELL** ★ ★ ☆ ☆ ☆   12-Month Target Price: **$9.00** (as of October 15, 2004)

Business Summary November 04, 2004

Tenet Healthcare ranks as the second largest U.S. for-profit hospital manager. At September 30, 2004, it owned or operated 70 U.S. general hospitals in continuing operations, with 18,090 licensed beds in 14 states. The largest concentrations of hospital beds were in California, Florida and Texas. The company's hospitals offer acute care services. Several hospitals also offer open-heart surgery, neonatal intensive care, neurosciences, orthopedic services, and oncology services.

THC also owns and operates a small number of rehabilitation hospitals, specialty hospitals, and long-term care facilities, a psychiatric facility, and medical office buildings located on or near the general hospital properties.

Hospital net patient revenues in 2003 were derived from Medicare (26%), managed care (49%), Medicaid (9%), and indemnity/other sources (16%).

On a same-facility basis (under company management for at least one year), admissions rose 1.7% in 2003, to 946,640, from 930,655 in 2002; net inpatient revenue per patient day declined 5.1%, to $1,708 ($1,799). The average length of stay declined slightly to 5.3 days, from 5.4, while the number of outpatient visits decreased by 0.1%, to 8,427,096 (8,433,526).

In March 2003, THC announced its intentions to divest or consolidate 14 general hospitals that no longer fit its core operating strategy of building competitive networks of hospitals in major markets. As of September 2004, it had sold all 14 of these hospitals. THC completed construction in June 2004 on a 118-bed general

hospital and medical complex in Frisco, TX, and a 90-bed hospital in Bartlett, TN, with an opening that occurred in July 2004.

In January 2004, the company said it intended to divest an additional 27 hospitals, including 19 in California and eight in Louisiana, Massachusetts, Missouri and Texas. A recent study of the capital expenditures required to comply with California's seismic regulations for hospitals prompted the divestiture plans in that state. THC said it intended to focus its financial and management resources on its remaining core group of 69 U.S. hospitals, including the two recently constructed hospitals. As of September 30, 2004, THC had sold seven of the 27 target hospitals and entered into agreements to sell an additional 13 by the end of 2004. The company expects proceeds, including tax benefits, of about $600 million from the sale of the 27 hospitals.

In January 2003, THC was sued by the U.S. Justice Department for allegedly submitting false claims to Medicare. In October 2003, the Justice Department served THC with a subpoena related to its investigation of Medicare outlier payments to hospitals. In September 2003, the U.S. Senate launched an investigation into the company's corporate governance practices with respect to federal health care programs. In October 2004, additional investigations were announced into THC's medical directorship arrangements and physician relocation agreements. As of October 2004, no settlement had been reached with respect to the ongoing lawsuits and investigations.

Company Financials Fiscal Year ending December 31

Per Share Data ($)

(Year Ended December 31)	2003	2002	2001	2000	1999	1998	1997	1996	1995	1994
Tangible Bk. Val.	4.85	4.40	4.40	3.45	1.57	1.01	0.31	0.17	0.05	6.62
Cash Flow	-2.00	1.54	3.24	2.51	1.85	1.71	1.79	0.81	2.29	1.47
Earnings	-3.01	0.93	2.04	1.39	0.72	0.53	0.81	-0.16	1.27	0.73
S&P Core Earnings	0.27	1.54	1.24	NA	NA	NA	NA	NA	NA	NA
Dividends	Nil	Nil	Nil	Nil	0.01	Nil	Nil	Nil	Nil	Nil
Payout Ratio	Nil	Nil	Nil	Nil	1%	Nil	Nil	Nil	Nil	Nil
Prices - High	19.25	52.50	41.85	30.50	18.12	27.29	23.25	15.83	13.83	13.00
- Low	11.32	13.70	24.66	11.29	10.25	15.83	14.25	12.08	8.91	8.33
P/E Ratio - High	NM	56	21	22	25	52	29	NM	11	18
- Low	NM	15	12	8	14	30	18	NM	7	11

Income Statement Analysis (Million $)

	2003	2002	2001	2000	1999	1998	1997	1996	1995	1994
Revs.	13,212	8,743	13,913	12,053	11,414	10,880	9,895	8,691	5,559	3,318
Oper. Inc.	1,072	1,676	2,797	2,244	1,935	1,858	1,809	1,597	1,099	623
Depr.	471	302	604	554	533	556	460	443	321	195
Int. Exp.	296	147	327	456	479	485	464	417	312	138
Pretax Inc.	-1,829	777	1,799	1,156	639	481	669	-21.0	746	338
Eff. Tax Rate	NM	38.5%	40.9%	40.1%	43.5%	46.8%	40.2%	NM	NM	39.9%
Net Inc.	-1,404	459	1,025	678	340	249	378	-73.0	-73.0	194
S&P Core Earnings	123	760	NA	NA	NA	NA	NA	NA	NA	NA

Balance Sheet & Other Fin. Data (Million $)

	2003	2002	2001	2000	1999	1998	1997	1996	1995	1994
Cash	619	210	38.0	62.0	135	29.0	155	151	201	294
Curr. Assets	4,248	3,792	3,394	3,226	3,594	3,962	2,890	2,391	1,545	1,624
Total Assets	12,298	13,780	13,814	12,995	13,161	13,771	12,833	11,705	8,332	7,918
Curr. Liab.	2,394	2,381	2,584	2,166	1,912	2,022	1,767	1,869	1,134	1,356
LT Debt	4,039	3,872	3,919	4,202	5,668	6,391	5,829	5,022	3,191	3,273
Common Equity	4,361	5,723	5,619	5,079	4,066	3,870	3,558	3,224	2,636	1,986
Total Cap.	8,404	10,121	10,227	9,835	10,225	10,701	9,810	8,678	6,221	5,560
Cap. Exp.	753	490	889	601	619	592	534	406	370	264
Cash Flow	-933	761	1,629	1,232	873	805	838	370	719	389
Curr. Ratio	1.8	1.6	1.3	1.5	1.9	2.0	1.6	1.3	1.4	1.2
% LT Debt of Cap.	48.1	38.3	38.3	42.7	55.4	59.7	59.4	57.9	51.3	58.9
% Net Inc.of Revs.	NM	5.2	7.4	5.6	3.0	2.3	3.8	NM	7.2	5.9
% Ret. on Assets	NM	NM	7.6	5.2	2.5	1.9	3.1	NM	4.9	3.4
% Ret. on Equity	NM	NM	19.2	14.8	8.6	6.7	11.1	NM	17.3	11.8

Data as orig reptd.; bef. results of disc opers/spec. items. Per share data adj. for stk. divs.; EPS diluted (primary prior to 1998). Prior to 2002 (7 mos.), fiscal yr. ended May 31 of the fol. cal. yr. E-Estimated. NA-Not Available. NM-Not Meaningful. NR-Not Ranked.

Office: 3820 State Street, Santa Barbara, CA 93105-5106.
Telephone: 805-563-7000.
Email: feedback@tenethealth.com
Website: http://www.tenethealth.com
Chrmn & CEO: J.C. Barbakow.
Pres: T. Fetter.
Vice Chrmn: B.P. Schochet.

COO: R.J. Jennings.
CFO: S.D. Farber.
Investor Contact: T. Rice 805-563-7188.
Dirs: L. Biondi, S. Cloud, Jr., T. Fetter, V. B. Honeycutt, J. Kane, E. Kangas, J. R. Kerrey, F. D. Loop, M. Lozano, R. C. Nakasone, J. A. Unruh.

Auditor: KPMG.
Founded: in 1967.
Domicile: Nevada.
Employees: 109,759.
S&P Analyst: Cameron Lavey/CB/JWP

Teradyne, Inc.

Recommendation: **HOLD** ★★★☆☆
SELL · SELL · HOLD · BUY · BUY

12-Month Target Price: **$18.00**
(as of November 02, 2004)

TER has an approximate 0.03% weighting in the **S&P 500**

Sector: Information Technology
Sub-Industry: Semiconductor Equipment
Peer Group: Semiconductor Equipment - Back-end

Summary: This maker of automatic test equipment (ATE), used primarily by the semiconductor and telecommunications industries, also makes backplane connectors.

Quantitative Evaluations

Price as of 11/12/04:	$16.79	2004E S&P Core EPS:	$0.30

S&P Earnings & Dividend Rank: C

D	**C**	B-	B	B+	A-	A	A+

S&P Fair Value Rank: 1-

1	2	3	4	5
Lowest				Highest

Fair Value Calc.: $9.90 (Overvalued)

S&P Investability Quotient Percentile
82%

TER scored higher than 82% of all companies for which an S&P Report is available.

Volatility: High

Low	Average	**High**

Technical Evaluation: Bullish
Since 10/04, the technical indicators for TER have been Bullish.

Relative Strength Rank: Moderate
68
1 Lowest   Highest 99

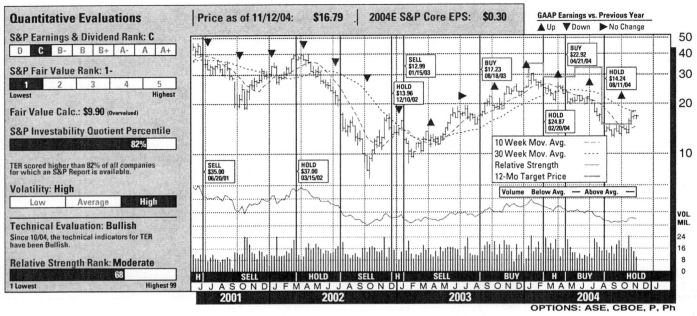

GAAP Earnings vs. Previous Year
▲ Up ▼ Down ► No Change

10 Week Mov. Avg.
30 Week Mov. Avg.
Relative Strength
12-Mo Target Price

Volume Below Avg. — Above Avg.

OPTIONS: ASE, CBOE, P, Ph

Analyst commentary prepared by Colin McArdle/MF/MWJ

Highlights November 05, 2004

- We expect sales to decline more than 10% in 2005, as orders appeared to be slowing in the second half of 2004, in line with with a period when chip demand was slowing and inventories were rising. During the last two years, the company reduced its break-even quarterly sales rate to $340 million, in order to ensure profitability even in a downturn.

- In the 2004 third quarter, TER recorded its third quarterly profit in a row, on an operating basis, after more than two years of losses. In its semiconductor test segment, orders were particularly strong for the Catalyst (wireless orders) and J750 (microcontroller, automotive, image sensors, embedded flash) systems. Circuit board assembly test orders rose in the quarter, and the large connections systems segment, excluding a business exited in the fourth quarter of 2004, saw a 5% decline.

- We project operating EPS of $0.81 in 2004 and $0.65 in 2005, with Standard & Poor's Core Earnings of $0.30 and $0.15 in the respective years.

Investment Rationale/Risk November 05, 2004

- We recommend holding the stock, based on our view of a continuing measured recovery in the semiconductor industry that is sensitive to economic vagaries and slowing end demand for semiconductors. We note that the stock's beta is high. We believe that the period of underinvestment from 2001 to 2003 was reversed in the first half of 2004, with orders up strongly for test equipment makers. We see the current slowdown persisting through the next few quarters as higher inventories are digested.

- Risks to our recommendation and target price include competition from larger semiconductor testing companies, as well as a global decrease in demand for chips.

- Applying a P/E multiple of 28X our 2005 EPS estimate of $0.65, our 12-month target price is $18. This is in line with TER's growth rate and with peers.

Key Stock Statistics

S&P Core EPS 2005E	0.15	52-week Range	$30.70-12.53
S&P Oper. EPS 2004E	0.81	12 Month P/E	22.1
P/E on S&P Oper. EPS 2004E	20.7	Beta	NA
S&P Oper. EPS 2005E	0.65	Shareholders	4,724
Yield (%)	Nil	Market Cap (B)	$ 3.3
Dividend Rate/Share	Nil	Shares Outstanding (M)	194.1

Value of $10,000 invested five years ago: **$ 3,964**

Dividend Data

No cash dividends have been paid.

Revenues/Earnings Data Fiscal year ending December 31

Revenues (Million $)

	2004	2003	2002	2001	2000	1999
1Q	430.6	334.6	248.0	605.2	615.4	344.4
2Q	526.5	331.5	309.9	365.8	747.5	400.9
3Q	457.8	329.2	330.7	249.4	859.5	497.0
4Q	—	357.6	333.6	220.2	821.6	548.5
Yr.	—	1,353	1,222	1,441	3,044	1,791

Earnings Per Share ($)

	2004	2003	2002	2001	2000	1999
1Q	0.20	-0.41	-0.42	0.30	0.52	0.10
2Q	0.39	-0.28	-0.28	-0.23	0.71	0.20
3Q	0.21	-0.28	-0.91	-0.59	0.90	0.35
4Q	E0.02	-0.06	-2.31	-0.63	0.74	0.42
Yr.	E0.81	-1.03	-3.93	-1.15	2.86	1.07

Next earnings report expected: mid-January Source: S&P, Company Reports
EPS Estimates based on S&P Operating Earnings; historical GAAP earnings are as reported.

Teradyne, Inc.

Recommendation: **HOLD** ★ ★ ★ ☆ ☆   12-Month Target Price: **$18.00** (as of November 02, 2004)

Business Summary November 05, 2004

Founded in 1960, Teradyne is now the world's largest manufacturer of automatic test equipment (ATE) for the electronics industry. Its products include systems to test semiconductors (55% of 2003 revenues), connection systems (26%), assembly test systems (11%), and other test systems (8%). As a result of a severe industry downturn, TER reduced its workforce by about 4,200 employees over the past two years, and has taken other steps to restructure the business, including eliminating product lines, reducing the number of operating facilities, and outsourcing certain manufacturing.

As electronic systems have become more complex, the need for products to test the systems has grown dramatically in recent years. Semiconductor and electronics makers use the company's systems to measure product performance, improve quality, reduce time to market, enhance manufacturing, minimize labor costs, and improve production yields. TER's test systems are all computer controlled, and programming and operating software is supplied both as an integral part of the product and as a separately priced enhancement.

The company's semiconductor test systems are used by chipmakers and subcontractors in the design and testing of many types of chips, including logic, memory, mixed signal, and system-on-a-chip integrated circuits. Test system prices can reach $3 million.

In the memory test market, where reducing cost is particularly crucial, TER's Probe-One system delivers one of the shortest test times per wafer, and one of the lowest test costs. The company pioneered the system-on-a-chip test market in

1996, with the Catalyst test system; the Catalyst Tiger, introduced in 2000, extended Catalyst's capabilities to very high device operating speeds. In digital logic test, TER's J750 and J750k test systems provide 64 channels of test capability on a single circuit board, significantly reducing tester size. In April 2002, TER introduced the FLEX, its next generation high throughput SoC test system, combining parallel test capability and the ability to test different device types.

The company's backplane connection systems are used principally by the computer, telecommunications and military/aerospace industries. A backplane is a panel that supports the circuit boards in an electronic assembly, and carries the wiring that connects the boards to each other and to other system elements.

TER expanded its printed circuit board (PCB) test and inspection business via the October 2001 acquisition of Genrad for about $264 million (including the assumption of debt). TER believed the purchase of Genrad, a leading maker of ATE and software for PCB tests, strengthened its product line, added to its presence in Europe and Asia, and let it compete more effectively in the PCB market.

The three largest customers accounted for 21% of 2003 sales, versus 23% in 2002. The semiconductor and electronics business is global in scope; 63% of 2003 sales were to customers outside the U.S., versus 54% the year before.

The company has spent $929 million (16% of sales) on research and development over the past three years.

Company Financials Fiscal Year ending December 31

Per Share Data ($)

(Year Ended December 31)	2003	2002	2001	2000	1999	1998	1997	1996	1995	1994
Tangible Bk. Val.	4.33	4.97	8.69	9.89	6.77	6.13	5.63	5.11	4.60	3.39
Cash Flow	-0.22	-3.06	-0.36	3.42	1.56	1.04	1.08	0.85	1.20	0.69
Earnings	-1.03	-3.93	-1.15	2.86	1.07	0.59	0.74	0.55	0.95	0.48
S&P Core Earnings	-1.44	-4.25	-1.65	NA	NA	NA	NA	NA	NA	NA
Dividends	Nil	Nil	Nil	Nil	Nil	Nil	Nil	Nil	Nil	Nil
Payout Ratio	Nil	Nil	Nil	Nil	Nil	Nil	Nil	Nil	Nil	Nil
Prices - High	26.31	40.20	47.21	115.43	66.00	24.21	29.59	13.87	21.43	8.56
- Low	8.75	7.10	18.43	23.00	20.62	7.50	11.81	5.56	8.03	5.09
P/E Ratio - High	NM	NM	NM	40	62	41	40	25	23	18
- Low	NM	NM	NM	8	19	13	16	10	8	11

Income Statement Analysis (Million $)

	2003	2002	2001	2000	1999	1998	1997	1996	1995	1994
Revs.	1,353	1,222	1,441	3,044	1,791	1,489	1,266	1,172	1,191	677
Oper. Inc.	47.3	-192	-1.54	813	345	210	234	174	288	130
Depr.	152	160	139	102	86.4	76.3	59.2	50.9	43.1	31.5
Int. Exp.	20.9	21.8	4.09	1.84	1.66	1.57	2.25	2.43	3.00	1.71
Pretax Inc.	-186	-561	-326	740	274	146	193	140	250	103
Eff. Tax Rate	NM	NM	NM	30.0%	30.0%	30.0%	34.0%	33.0%	36.3%	31.0%
Net Inc.	-194	-718	-202	518	192	102	128	93.5	159	70.9
S&P Core Earnings	-270	-777	-290	NA	NA	NA	NA	NA	NA	NA

Balance Sheet & Other Fin. Data (Million $)

	2003	2002	2001	2000	1999	1998	1997	1996	1995	1994
Cash	586	541	586	464	387	298	74.7	250	182	203
Curr. Assets	769	809	1,207	1,378	908	759	727	617	740	447
Total Assets	1,785	1,895	2,542	2,356	1,568	1,313	1,252	1,097	1,024	656
Curr. Liab.	281	279	296	619	392	256	278	225	230	139
LT Debt	408	451	452	8.35	8.95	13.2	13.1	15.6	18.7	8.80
Common Equity	950	1,028	1,764	1,707	1,153	1,026	937	842	760	493
Total Cap.	1,357	1,479	2,216	1,737	1,176	1,057	974	872	794	517
Cap. Exp.	30.8	46.4	198	235	120	119	106	59.4	79.2	29.6
Cash Flow	-41.5	-559	-63.5	620	278	178	187	144	202	102
Curr. Ratio	2.7	2.9	4.1	2.2	2.3	3.0	2.6	2.7	3.2	3.2
% LT Debt of Cap.	30.0	30.5	20.4	0.5	0.8	1.2	1.4	1.8	2.4	1.7
% Net Inc.of Revs.	NM	NM	NM	17.0	10.7	6.9	10.1	8.0	13.4	10.5
% Ret. on Assets	NM	NM	NM	26.4	13.3	8.0	10.9	8.8	17.9	11.7
% Ret. on Equity	NM	NM	NM	36.2	17.6	10.4	14.3	11.7	23.9	15.4

Data as orig reptd.; bef. results of disc opers/spec. items. Per share data adj. for stk. divs.; EPS diluted. E-Estimated. NA-Not Available. NM-Not Meaningful. NR-Not Ranked. UR-Under Review.

Office: 321 Harrison Avenue, Boston, MA 02118.
Telephone: 617-482-2700.
Email: investorrelations@teradyne.com
Website: http://www.teradyne.com
Chrmn: G. Chamillard.
Pres & CEO: M.A. Bradley.

VP & CFO: G.R. Beecher.
VP & General Counsel: E. Casal.
Investor Contact: T.B. Newman, Jr. 617-422-2425
Dirs: J. W. Bagley, M. Bradley, A. Carnesale, G. W. Chamillard, J. P. Mulroney, V. M. O'Reilly, R. A. Vallee, P. S. Wolpert.

Founded: in 1960.
Domicile: Massachusetts.
Employees: 6,100.
S&P Analyst: Colin McArdle/MF/MWJ

Texas Instruments

Recommendation: **HOLD** ★ ★ ★ ☆ ☆
SELL SELL HOLD BUY BUY

12-Month Target Price: $25.00
(as of October 18, 2004)

TXN has an approximate 0.39% weighting in the **S&P 500**

Sector: Information Technology
Sub-Industry: Semiconductors
Peer Group: Semiconductors - Analog

Summary: One of the world's largest manufacturers of semiconductors, this company also produces sensors, controls and educational products.

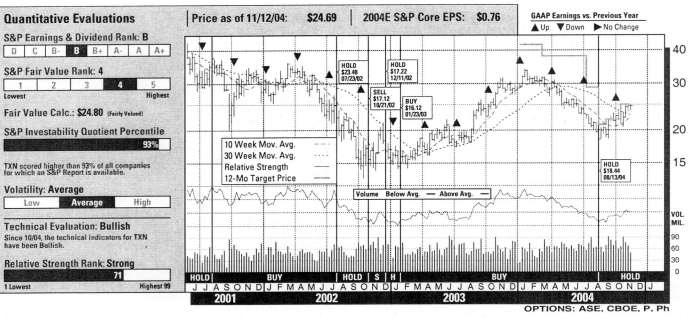

Quantitative Evaluations

S&P Earnings & Dividend Rank: B

| D | C | B- | **B** | B+ | A- | A | A+ |

S&P Fair Value Rank: 4

| 1 | 2 | 3 | **4** | 5 |
| Lowest | | | | Highest |

Fair Value Calc.: $24.80 (Fairly Valued)

S&P Investability Quotient Percentile
93%

TXN scored higher than 93% of all companies for which an S&P Report is available.

Volatility: Average

| Low | **Average** | High |

Technical Evaluation: Bullish
Since 10/04, the technical indicators for TXN have been Bullish.

Relative Strength Rank: Strong
71
| 1 Lowest | | Highest 99 |

Price as of 11/12/04: **$24.69**   **2004E S&P Core EPS:** **$0.76**

Analyst commentary prepared by Amrit Tewary/PMW/BK

Highlights October 20, 2004

- We estimate that revenues will advance 27% in 2004 and rise about 1% in 2005, reflecting our expectations of robust worldwide semiconductor industry sales growth in 2004, followed by a moderation in 2005, during what we expect to be the last year of the current upcycle. The company recently announced a new profit-sharing plan for employees that we believe should control bonus costs better than in the past. We project that gross margins will widen to 45% in 2004 and 46% in 2005, from 40% in 2003.

- EPS amounted to $0.46 in 2003 (before gains on sales of Micron Technology shares of $0.13 in the third quarter and $0.09 in the fourth quarter). We project that EPS will increase to $1.04 in 2004 and $1.11 in 2005.

- We believe stock option expense is about in line with peer levels. We estimate 2004 Standard & Poor's Core Earnings of $0.76 a share, and see $0.84 for 2005.

Investment Rationale/Risk October 20, 2004

- We would hold existing positions. Although the shares are down significantly thus far in 2004, we think current valuation multiples are warranted, in light of what we see as elevated near-term risks. We believe chip order rates will continue to be sluggish for the near term, as some distributor and OEM customers will likely require several more quarters to clear out excess channel inventory. We also believe that macroeconomic concerns will continue to affect demand for the near term. We therefore think that the seasonal upswing in the upcoming holiday season will not be as strong as we previously anticipated.

- Risks to our recommendation and target price include fluctuations in demand for semiconductors, competition in chip design and price, and the challenges of operating wafer plants.

- Our 12-month target price of $25 applies a target P/E multiple of 23X, below historical norms, to our 2005 EPS estimate. Our target price values TXN at a discount to its average historical price to sales ratio in recent years. We think a discount is warranted in light of what we regard as above-average near-term risk.

Key Stock Statistics

S&P Core EPS 2005E	0.84	52-week Range	$33.98-18.06
S&P Oper. EPS 2004E	1.04	12 Month P/E	23.3
P/E on S&P Oper. EPS 2004E	23.7	Beta	1.76
S&P Oper. EPS 2005E	1.11	Shareholders	28,058
Yield (%)	0.4%	Market Cap (B)	$ 42.7
Dividend Rate/Share	0.10	Shares Outstanding (M)	1727.9

Value of $10,000 invested five years ago: **$ 5,369**

Dividend Data Dividends have been paid since 1962

Amount ($)	Date Decl.	Ex-Div. Date	Stock of Record	Payment Date
0.021	Jan. 15	Jan. 28	Jan. 30	Feb. 09 '04
0.021	Apr. 14	Apr. 28	Apr. 30	May. 17 '04
0.021	Jul. 15	Jul. 28	Jul. 30	Aug. 16 '04
0.025	Sep. 16	Oct. 28	Nov. 01	Nov. 22 '04

Revenues/Earnings Data Fiscal year ending December 31

Revenues (Million $)

	2004	2003	2002	2001	2000	1999
1Q	2,936	2,192	1,827	2,528	2,653	2,039
2Q	3,241	2,339	2,162	2,037	2,843	2,346
3Q	3,250	2,533	2,248	1,849	3,160	2,385
4Q	—	2,770	2,146	1,786	3,033	2,554
Yr.	—	9,834	8,383	8,201	11,875	9,468

Earnings Per Share ($)

	2004	2003	2002	2001	2000	1999
1Q	0.21	0.07	-0.02	0.13	0.25	0.15
2Q	0.25	0.07	0.05	-0.11	0.75	0.20
3Q	0.32	0.25	0.11	-0.07	0.38	0.24
4Q	E0.27	0.28	-0.34	-0.07	0.37	0.26
Yr.	E1.04	0.68	-0.20	-0.12	1.73	0.84

Next earnings report expected: late-January Source: S&P, Company Reports
EPS Estimates based on S&P Operating Earnings; historical GAAP earnings are as reported.

Recommendation: **HOLD** ★ ★ ★ ☆ ☆   12-Month Target Price: **$25.00** (as of October 18, 2004)

Business Summary October 20, 2004

Texas Instruments is one of the world's 10 largest semiconductor companies, in terms of revenues. It has design, sales or manufacturing operations in more than 25 countries. The company has increasingly concentrated on digital signal processors (DSPs), and on analog and mixed-signal integrated circuits. Semiconductors grew from less than 60% of revenues in 1996 to 87% in the boom year of 2000, and accounted for 85% in 2003.

DSP and analog product lines are largely complementary. These chips work together to enable electronic devices to benefit from digitization of electronic signals. Analog technology converts real-world signals, such as sound, light and pressure, into the zeros and ones of the digital world. DSP chips then process signal information in real time. Analog chips also convert signals back to analog format.

The DSP market has recently been a fast growing area of the semiconductor industry, driven by strong demand for devices such as wireless phones, modems, and computer networking gear. Increased use of digital components in embedded systems in automobiles, appliances, and manufacturing equipment could also enhance market opportunities. DSPs accounted for 35% of semiconductor revenues in 2003, up from 30% in 2002; analog chips provided 40% (40%); and the remaining 25% (30%) came from other chip products such as standard logic, ASICs, RISC microprocessors, microcontrollers, and digital imaging devices.

The company's focused DSP strategy required a multi-year restructuring. In 1997,

TXN sold its defense electronics business to Raytheon Co. In 1998, it sold its struggling dynamic random access memory (DRAM) operations to Micron Technology (MU), taking some payment in stock; after selling some shares in prior years, it sold its remaining 57 million MU shares in the second half of 2003. In 2000, the company acquired Toccata Technology, a developer of digital-audio amplifier technology; Dot Wireless, a developer of CDMA third-generation wireless technology; Alantro Communications, a developer of wireless local area networking technology; and, most notably, Burr-Brown Corp., a high-end analog chip maker with expertise in data converters and amplifiers. In 2001, TXN acquired Graychip, a developer of digital converters used for high-speed signal processing applications. In 2003, the company acquired Radia Communications, a semiconductor company focused on systems for 802.11 wireless local area networking products.

In 2003, TXN had about 30,000 customers; Nokia accounted for 14% of total revenue. Over 80% of sales were made outside the U.S. Distributors handled 25% of 2003 sales.

In addition to semiconductors, the company has two other principal segments. The Sensors & Controls segment (10% of 2003 sales) sells electrical and electronic controls, sensors, and radio frequency identification systems to the commercial and industrial markets. The Educational & Productivity Solutions unit (5%) is a leading supplier of educational and graphing calculators.

Company Financials Fiscal Year ending December 31

Per Share Data ($)

(Year Ended December 31)	2003	2002	2001	2000	1999	1998	1997	1996	1995	1994
Tangible Bk. Val.	6.35	5.73	6.42	6.71	5.39	4.19	3.80	2.69	2.70	2.05
Cash Flow	1.57	0.78	0.94	2.49	1.47	0.97	0.89	0.56	1.19	0.89
Earnings	0.68	-0.20	-0.12	1.73	0.84	0.26	0.19	-0.03	0.70	0.45
S&P Core Earnings	0.40	-0.16	-0.34	NA	NA	NA	NA	NA	NA	NA
Dividends	0.09	0.09	0.09	0.09	0.09	0.09	0.09	0.09	0.08	0.06
Payout Ratio	12%	NM	NM	5%	10%	33%	45%	NM	11%	13%
Prices - High	31.67	35.94	54.68	99.78	55.75	22.60	17.81	8.54	10.46	5.59
- Low	13.90	13.10	20.10	35.00	21.50	10.06	7.76	5.06	4.29	3.81
P/E Ratio - High	47	NM	NM	58	66	89	94	NM	15	12
- Low	20	NM	NM	20	26	39	41	NM	6	8

Income Statement Analysis (Million $)

	2003	2002	2001	2000	1999	1998	1997	1996	1995	1994
Revs.	9,834	8,383	8,201	11,875	9,468	8,460	9,750	9,940	13,128	10,315
Oper. Inc.	2,493	1,977	1,246	3,715	2,751	1,543	1,724	878	2,350	1,748
Depr.	1,528	1,689	1,828	1,376	1,055	1,144	1,109	904	756	665
Int. Exp.	39.0	57.0	61.0	75.0	75.0	75.0	94.0	108	69.0	58.0
Pretax Inc.	1,250	-346	-426	4,578	2,019	617	713	-23.0	1,619	1,042
Eff. Tax Rate	4.16%	NM	NM	32.6%	30.4%	34.0%	57.6%	NM	32.8%	33.7%
Net Inc.	1,198	-344	-201	3,087	1,406	407	302	-46.0	1,088	691
S&P Core Earnings	701	-275	-587	NA	NA	NA	NA	NA	NA	NA

Balance Sheet & Other Fin. Data (Million $)

	2003	2002	2001	2000	1999	1998	1997	1996	1995	1994
Cash	1,818	949	431	745	662	540	1,015	978	1,553	1,290
Curr. Assets	7,709	6,126	5,775	8,115	6,055	4,846	6,103	4,454	5,518	4,017
Total Assets	15,510	14,679	15,779	17,720	15,028	11,250	10,849	9,360	9,215	6,989
Curr. Liab.	2,200	1,934	1,580	2,813	2,628	2,196	2,496	2,486	3,188	2,199
LT Debt	628	833	1,211	1,216	1,097	1,027	1,286	1,697	804	808
Common Equity	11,864	10,734	11,879	12,588	9,255	6,527	5,914	4,097	4,095	3,039
Total Cap.	12,551	11,696	13,421	14,273	11,346	7,935	7,200	5,794	4,899	3,847
Cap. Exp.	800	802	1,790	2,762	1,373	1,031	1,238	2,063	1,439	1,076
Cash Flow	2,726	1,345	1,627	4,463	2,461	1,551	1,411	858	1,844	1,356
Curr. Ratio	3.5	3.2	3.7	2.9	2.3	2.2	2.4	1.8	1.7	1.8
% LT Debt of Cap.	5.0	7.1	9.0	8.5	9.7	12.9	17.9	29.3	16.4	21.0
% Net Inc.of Revs.	12.2	NM	NM	26.0	14.8	4.8	3.1	NM	8.3	6.7
% Ret. on Assets	7.9	NM	NM	18.6	10.6	3.7	3.0	NM	13.4	10.5
% Ret. on Equity	10.6	NM	NM	27.9	17.6	6.5	6.0	NM	30.5	25.6

Data as orig reptd.; bef. results of disc opers/spec. items. Per share data adj. for stk. divs.; EPS diluted. E-Estimated. NA-Not Available. NM-Not Meaningful. NR-Not Ranked. UR-Under Review.

Office: 12500 TI Blvd, Dallas, TX 75243-0199.
Telephone: 972-995-3773.
Website: http://www.ti.com
Chrmn: T.J. Engibous.
Pres & CEO: R.K. Templeton.
SVP & CFO: K. March.

SVP, Secy & General Counsel: J.F. Hubach.
SVP & Investor Contact: T. West .
Dirs: J. R. Adams, D. L. Boren, D. A. Carp, C. S. Cox, T. J. Engibous, G. W. Fronterhouse, D. R. Goode, P. H. Patsley, W. R. Sanders, R. J. Simmons, R. K. Templeton, C. Whitman.

Founded: in 1938.
Domicile: Delaware.
Employees: 34,154.
S&P Analyst: Amrit Tewary/PMW/BK

The **McGraw·Hill** Companies

Textron Inc.

Recommendation: **HOLD** ★★★☆☆ | **12-Month Target Price: $61.00**
(as of November 03, 2004)

TXT has an approximate 0.09% weighting in the **S&P 500**

Sector: Industrials
Sub-Industry: Industrial Conglomerates
Peer Group: Aerospace/Transportation/Defense

Summary: This conglomerate primarily makes industrial bolts and screws, and industrial equipment and components, as well as Cessna business jets and Bell helicopters.

Quantitative Evaluations

S&P Earnings & Dividend Rank: B+

| D | C | B- | B | B+ | A- | A | A+ |

S&P Fair Value Rank: 2-

| 1 | 2 | 3 | 4 | 5 |
| Lowest | | | | Highest |

Fair Value Calc.: $64.10 (Slightly Overvalued)

S&P Investability Quotient Percentile

97%

TXT scored higher than 97% of all companies for which an S&P Report is available.

Volatility: Average

| Low | **Average** | High |

Technical Evaluation: Bullish

Since 10/04, the technical indicators for TXT have been Bullish.

Relative Strength Rank: Strong

73

| 1 Lowest | Highest 99 |

Price as of 11/12/04: $71.50 | **2004E S&P Core EPS: $1.34**

GAAP Earnings vs. Previous Year
▲ Up   ▼ Down   ▶ No Change

- 10 Week Mov. Avg.
- 30 Week Mov. Avg.
- Relative Strength
- 12-Mo Target Price

Volume Below Avg. — Above Avg. —

VOL. MIL.

HOLD

J J A S O N D | J F M A M J J A S O N D | J F M A M J J A S O N D | J F M A M J J A S O N D | J
2001 | 2002 | 2003 | 2004

OPTIONS: Ph

Analyst commentary prepared by Robert E. Friedman, CPA /CB/JWP

Highlights November 05, 2004

- We are forecasting a 5% rise in 2005 revenues, as we anticipate that modest global economic growth and capital spending will spur modest near-term demand for TXT's industrial components, consumer leisure products and business jets.

- We project that the modest hike in sales volume, the absence of large restructuring charges, well controlled SG&A expenses, and benefits from prior-year cost-cutting initiatives will allow EBIT (earnings before interest and taxes) margins to rise to 8.5%-plus levels. As a result, we expect 2005 EPS to climb about 45%, to $3.75, and Standard & Poor's Core EPS to advance about 80%, to $2.41. Regarding projected 2005 profitability performance, we are forecasting that TXT will post what we view as middling debt-adjusted ROE of about 8%.

- Looking at TXT's long-term financial prospects, we believe the mature and highly cyclical aircraft and automotive markets may prevent the company from generating outsized sustainable earnings growth and profitability returns. However, we believe free cash earnings could still expand at a 7% compound annual growth rate (CAGR), with return on equity (ROE) averaging about 15%, at best. Therefore, we think long-term book value (net equity) growth, a key measure of shareholder returns, could grow at a 5%-10% CAGR.

Investment Rationale/Risk November 05, 2004

- We are maintaining our hold opinion on TXT, as the shares are trading at a modest premium to our 12-month target price of $61 a share.

- Risks to our recommendation and target price primarily include any unexpected structural deterioration of TXT's primary end-markets, and/or structural deterioration of TXT's underlying business economics.

- Our free cash earnings models, which value TXT by basically adding the discounted sum of free cash earnings growing at a projected 10-year CAGR of 7%, suggest that the stock is worth about $61 a share. We calculate our estimated 10-year, 7% free cash earnings CAGR by multiplying our projected 15% ROE estimates by our projected 50% earnings retention ratio. Our relative valuation model, which compares a company's earnings yield (EPS divided by current stock price) with 10-year AAA-rated corporate bond yields, supports our tempered view of TXT shares. Based on our projected 2005 S&P Core EPS of $2.41, the stock is currently trading at an earnings yield of 4.0%, versus 10-year AAA corporate bond yields of 4.7%.

Key Stock Statistics

S&P Core EPS 2005E	2.41	52-week Range	$71.79-47.72
S&P Oper. EPS 2004E	2.60	12 Month P/E	30.9
P/E on S&P Oper. EPS 2004E	27.5	Beta	1.13
S&P Oper. EPS 2005E	3.75	Shareholders	19,000
Yield (%)	2.0%	Market Cap (B)	$ 9.9
Dividend Rate/Share	1.40	Shares Outstanding (M)	138.6

Value of $10,000 invested five years ago: **$ 11,233**

Dividend Data Dividends have been paid since 1942

Amount ($)	Date Decl.	Ex-Div. Date	Stock of Record	Payment Date
0.325	Feb. 25	Mar. 10	Mar. 12	Apr. 01 '04
0.325	Apr. 28	Jun. 09	Jun. 11	Jul. 01 '04
0.325	Jul. 28	Sep. 08	Sep. 10	Oct. 01 '04
0.350	Oct. 21	Dec. 08	Dec. 10	Jan. 03 '05

Revenues/Earnings Data Fiscal year ending December 31

Revenues (Million $)

	2004	2003	2002	2001	2000	1999
1Q	2,354	2,399	2,418	3,040	3,293	2,749
2Q	2,547	2,530	2,824	3,288	3,277	2,887
3Q	2,569	2,231	2,554	2,810	3,208	2,709
4Q	—	2,699	2,862	3,183	3,312	3,234
Yr.	—	9,859	10,658	12,321	13,090	11,579

Earnings Per Share ($)

	2004	2003	2002	2001	2000	1999
1Q	0.26	0.49	0.40	0.79	1.06	0.93
2Q	0.71	0.62	0.74	0.88	1.23	1.05
3Q	0.73	0.34	0.51	-2.34	1.08	0.95
4Q	E0.90	0.60	0.95	1.81	-1.53	1.12
Yr.	E2.60	2.05	2.60	1.16	1.90	4.05

Next earnings report expected: late-January Source: S&P, Company Reports
EPS Estimates based on S&P Operating Earnings; historical GAAP earnings are as reported.

Textron Inc.

Recommendation: **HOLD** ★ ★ ★ ☆ ☆   12-Month Target Price: **$61.00** (as of November 03, 2004)

Business Summary November 10, 2004

This $10 billion-revenue industrial and finance conglomerate conducts business through five operating segments:

TXT's Bell segment (24% of 2003 revenues; 31% of operating profits; 10% profit margins) is a major civil and military helicopter maker. Based on revenues, Bell is the world's third-largest helicopter maker; EADS's Eurocopter unit, AgustaWestland, United Technologies' Sikorsky unit and Boeing's helicopter operations are the world's first-, second-, fourth- and fifth-largest helicopter manufacturers, respectively. The $15 billion-revenue helicopter-manufacturing industry is oligopolistic: based on statistics provided by United Technologies, the five largest helicopter makers account for about 85% of industry revenues.

Demand for military helicopters is primarily driven by strategic military needs and growth in the U.S. Defense procurement budget. From 1993 through 2003, the U.S. defense procurement budget grew at a 1.5% average annual rate. Demand for commercial helicopters is primarily driven by the health of corporate budgets. Based on statistics provided by industry trade group Aerospace Industries Association, from 1994 through 2003, the U.S. commercial helicopter market (in unit sales) grew at a 10% average annual rate.

TXT's Cessna segment (23%; 26%; 8.7%) primarily makes the Cessna brand aircraft (Citation business jets and Cessna single-piston airplanes). Based on revenues, Cessna is the world's third-largest corporate jet maker. Canada's Bombardier, General Dynamics' Gulfstream division, France's Dassault and Raytheon's aircraft-making unit are the world's first-, second-, fourth- and fifth-largest corporate aircraft makers, respectively. The $9 billion global corporate jet market is oligopolistic; based on statistics provided by the independent aviation

research firm Teal Group, the five largest corporate jet makers account for 99% of global corporate jet sales.

Demand for small planes is primarily driven by the health of corporate budgets. Based on statistics provided by the General Aviation Manufacturers Association (GAMA, a small plane-making industry trade organization), from 1994 through 2003, the U.S. small plane (corporate jet and piston) market (in unit sales) grew at a 10% average annual rate.

The Industrial Products segment (29%; 19%; 4.9%) makes a variety of industrial and consumer products, primarily E-Z-GO golf carts; components, assemblies, telecom test equipment, professional lawn-mowing and turf maintenance equipment and trucks.

TXT's Fastening Systems segment (18%; 9%; 3.8%) makes industrial bolts, screws and other fasteners for the aircraft, auto and business equipment-making industries.

Textron Finance (5.8%; 16%; 21%), provides a wide range of commercial financing and lease financing arrangements. TF's largest competitor is GE Capital (GEC). CIT is another major TF competitor.

From 1993 through 2003, TXT's per-share net worth expanded at a CAGR of 5.6%; per-share free cash earnings contracted at a 7.1% CAGR; and ROE averaged 11%. Based on the Standard & Poor's Core EPS methodology, TXT's Standard & Poor's Core EPS variance averaged 22% over the last seven years, primarily due to non-operating gains generated by TXT's pension plans.

Company Financials Fiscal Year ending December 31

Per Share Data ($)

(Year Ended December 31)	2003	2002	2001	2000	1999	1998	1997	1996	1995	1994
Tangible Bk. Val.	16.18	12.92	12.40	11.60	10.56	5.54	9.10	9.42	10.52	7.76
Cash Flow	4.65	5.23	4.76	5.28	6.90	4.87	5.84	5.05	5.13	4.61
Earnings	2.05	2.60	1.16	1.90	4.05	2.68	3.29	2.80	2.76	2.40
S&P Core Earnings	1.18	0.27	-1.40	NA	NA	NA	NA	NA	NA	NA
Dividends	1.30	1.30	1.30	1.30	1.26	1.11	1.00	0.88	0.78	0.70
Payout Ratio	63%	50%	NM	68%	9%	41%	30%	31%	28%	29%
Prices - High	57.99	53.60	60.47	77.50	98.00	80.93	70.75	48.87	38.68	30.31
- Low	26.00	32.20	31.29	40.68	65.87	52.06	45.00	34.56	24.31	23.25
P/E Ratio - High	28	21	52	41	24	30	22	17	14	13
- Low	13	12	27	21	16	19	14	12	9	10

Income Statement Analysis (Million $)

	2003	2002	2001	2000	1999	1998	1997	1996	1995	1994
Revs.	9,859	10,658	12,321	13,090	11,579	9,683	10,544	9,274	9,973	9,681
Oper. Inc.	1,171	1,285	1,461	2,074	1,702	1,439	2,109	1,945	2,041	1,815
Depr.	356	368	514	494	440	361	435	387	415	398
Int. Exp.	283	330	459	492	260	315	726	731	813	665
Pretax Inc.	388	464	393	585	1,004	737	922	827	813	754
Eff. Tax Rate	27.6%	21.6%	57.8%	52.6%	37.9%	39.9%	39.5%	38.9%	39.5%	40.8%
Net Inc.	281	364	166	277	623	443	558	482	479	433
S&P Core Earnings	161	38.5	-202	NA	NA	NA	NA	NA	NA	NA

Balance Sheet & Other Fin. Data (Million $)

	2003	2002	2001	2000	1999	1998	1997	1996	1995	1994
Cash	843	307	260	289	209	53.0	87.0	47.0	99	49.0
Curr. Assets	3,592	3,887	4,017	3,914	3,735	4,355	NA	NA	NA	NA
Total Assets	15,090	15,505	16,052	16,370	16,393	13,721	18,610	18,235	23,172	20,925
Curr. Liab.	2,256	2,239	3,075	3,263	3,256	3,919	NA	NA	NA	NA
LT Debt	6,144	7,038	5,962	6,648	6,142	4,192	10,496	10,346	10,249	8,137
Common Equity	3,680	3,395	3,923	3,982	4,365	2,984	3,215	3,169	3,397	2,866
Total Cap.	10,224	10,842	10,253	10,957	10,826	7,511	14,207	14,012	13,661	11,019
Cap. Exp.	301	296	532	527	532	475	412	343	283	302
Cash Flow	637	732	680	771	1,062	803	992	869	893	830
Curr. Ratio	1.6	1.7	1.3	1.2	1.1	1.1	NA	NA	NA	NA
% LT Debt of Cap.	60.1	64.9	58.1	60.7	56.7	55.8	73.9	73.8	75.0	73.8
% Net Inc.of Revs.	2.9	3.4	1.3	2.1	5.4	4.6	5.3	2.0	4.8	4.5
% Ret. on Assets	1.8	2.3	1.0	1.7	4.1	2.7	3.0	2.7	2.2	2.2
% Ret. on Equity	7.9	9.9	4.2	6.6	16.9	14.3	17.4	14.7	15.3	15.6

Data as orig reptd.; bef. results of disc opers/spec. items. Per share data adj. for stk. divs.; EPS diluted. E-Estimated. NA-Not Available. NM-Not Meaningful. NR-Not Ranked. UR-Under Review.

Office: 40 Westminster Street, Providence, RI 02903-2525.
Telephone: 401-421-2800.
Website: http://www.textron.com
Chrmn, Pres & CEO: L.B. Campbell.
EVP & CFO: T.R. French.
EVP & Secy: J.D. Butler.

EVP & General Counsel: T. O'Donnell.
EVP & Investor Contact: M.L. Howell 401-457-2228.
Dirs: H. J. Arnelle, K. M. Bader, T. Beck, L. B. Campbell, R. K. Clark, R. S. Dickson, I. J. Evans, L. K. Fish, J. T. Ford, P. E. Gagne, J. D. Macomber, B. H. Rowe, S. F. Segnar, M. D. Walker, T. B. Wheeler, P. of Bayswater.

Founded: in 1928.
Domicile: Delaware.
Employees: 43,000.
S&P Analyst: Robert E. Friedman, CPA /CB/JWP

Thermo Electron

Recommendation: **HOLD** ★★★☆☆
SELL · SELL · HOLD · BUY · BUY

12-Month Target Price: **$31.00**
(as of October 28, 2004)

TMO has an approximate 0.04% weighting in the **S&P 500**

Sector: Health Care
Sub-Industry: Health Care Equipment
Peer Group: Life Science Research Products

Summary: This maker of analytical instruments, biomedical equipment, cogeneration systems and process equipment has sold minority interests in several publicly traded subsidiaries.

Quantitative Evaluations

S&P Earnings & Dividend Rank: B-

D	C	B-	B	B+	A-	A	A+

S&P Fair Value Rank: 5

1	2	3	4	5
Lowest				Highest

Fair Value Calc.: $32.70 (Slightly Undervalued)

S&P Investability Quotient Percentile

89%

TMO scored higher than 89% of all companies for which an S&P Report is available.

Volatility: Average

Low	Average	High

Technical Evaluation: Bullish
Since 11/04, the technical indicators for TMO have been Bullish.

Relative Strength Rank: Moderate

64

1 Lowest	Highest 99

Price as of 11/12/04: $29.96   **2004E S&P Core EPS:** $1.00

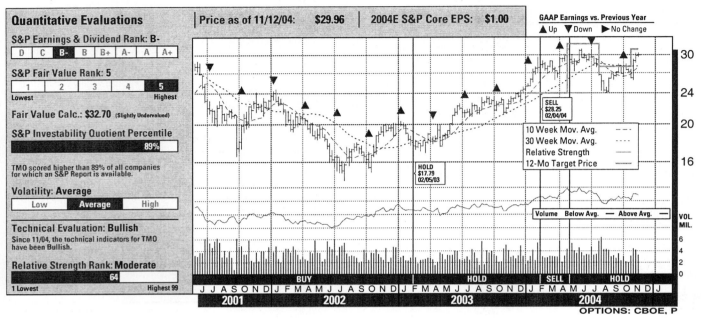

GAAP Earnings vs. Previous Year
▲ Up ▼ Down ► No Change

- 10 Week Mov. Avg. — —
- 30 Week Mov. Avg. ......
- Relative Strength ——
- 12-Mo Target Price ——

Volume Below Avg. — Above Avg.

VOL. MIL.

SELL $28.25 02/04/04

HOLD $17.79 02/05/03

BUY | HOLD | SELL | HOLD

J J A S O N D | J F M A M J J A S O N D | J F M A M J J A S O N D | J F M A M J J A S O N D | J
2001 · 2002 · 2003 · 2004

OPTIONS: CBOE, P

Analyst commentary prepared by Stewart Scharf/PMW/BK

Highlights November 01, 2004

- We expect organic revenues to grow in the high single digits in 2005, up from our projection of a 5% increase in 2004, reflecting strength in life and lab sciences, and a gradual pickup in measurement and control. We see positive foreign currencies and net acquisitions adding at least 10% to organic growth. We expect sequential improvement in the book-to-bill ratio (1.01X at September 30, 2004), as TMO focuses on new products and short lead times of one to two quarters.

- We see gross margins widening sequentially to near 50% in 2005, on a more favorable product mix. EBITDA margins should approach 16%, as we expect SG&A expenses (27% of revenues in the third quarter) to be well controlled, as the company focuses on core operations and achieves further productivity gains, with further strength likely in China and a recovery seen in Europe, especially in the U.K. and Germany.

- We see 2004 operating EPS of $1.25 (before $0.12 of amortization of acquisition-related intangible assets and a $0.02 restructuring charge); we expect EPS to reach $1.40 in 2005. We project S&P Core EPS of $1.00 for 2004, reflecting estimated stock option expense and amortization of assets; for 2005, we see S&P Core EPS of $1.30, as TMO begins to expense stock options.

Investment Rationale/Risk November 01, 2004

- Third quarter earnings exceeded our estimate, but we expect the stock to track to S&P 500, based on valuation. We view favorably TMO's agreement to sell its optical technologies unit, subject to necessary approvals, and to focus on its core instruments businesses.

- Risks to our recommendation and target price include a slower than expected economic recovery, especially in Europe; competitive pricing pressures; a slowdown in production in China; potential negative foreign currency impact; a decrease in the number of accretive acquisitions; and reduced demand for new mass spectrometry systems.

- The stock is trading at 20X our 2005 EPS estimate, a modest premium to the level of TMO's closest peers. Our DCF model indicates that the shares are at a modest premium to intrinsic value, assuming a 3.5% growth rate in perpetuity and a weighted average cost of capital of 8%. Applying a forward P/E multiple close to the stock's average historical highs, we arrive at our 12-month target price of $31.

Key Stock Statistics

S&P Core EPS 2005E	1.30	52-week Range	$31.40-22.70
S&P Oper. EPS 2004E	1.25	12 Month P/E	16.6
P/E on S&P Oper. EPS 2004E	24.0	Beta	1.15
S&P Oper. EPS 2005E	1.40	Shareholders	10,430
Yield (%)	Nil	Market Cap (B)	$ 4.8
Dividend Rate/Share	Nil	Shares Outstanding (M)	159.9

Value of $10,000 invested five years ago: **NA**

Dividend Data

No cash dividends have been paid.

Revenues/Earnings Data Fiscal year ending December 31

Revenues (Million $)

	2004	2003	2002	2001	2000	1999
1Q	582.0	500.2	491.3	573.1	598.9	1,010
2Q	525.3	516.4	509.1	542.5	609.5	1,092
3Q	542.3	497.1	517.2	512.9	581.0	1,077
4Q	—	583.4	568.8	559.7	577.0	659.0
Yr.	—	2,097	2,086	2,188	2,281	2,471

Earnings Per Share ($)

	2004	2003	2002	2001	2000	1999
1Q	0.26	0.19	0.34	0.12	0.09	0.17
2Q	0.30	0.32	0.23	0.05	0.15	-1.49
3Q	0.26	0.24	0.23	0.14	0.07	0.22
4Q	E0.38	0.30	0.25	-0.04	0.10	0.13
Yr.	E1.25	1.04	1.12	0.27	0.36	-0.11

Next earnings report expected: early-February   Source: S&P, Company Reports
EPS Estimates based on S&P Operating Earnings; historical GAAP earnings are as reported.

Recommendation: **HOLD** ★ ★ ★ ★ ★   12-Month Target Price: **$31.00** (as of October 28, 2004)

Business Summary November 01, 2004

Thermo Electron Corp. develops and manufactures technology-based instrument systems, components and solutions used to monitor, collect and analyze data.

In July 2004, the company sold its Spectra-Physics optical technologies unit to Newport Corp. (NEWP), for $200 million in cash, $50 million in NEWP common stock, and a $50 million note. TMO retained a small business in the optical segment that makes digital cameras used in its scientific instruments division. Spectra-Physics had $212 million in revenues in 2003, 10% of TMO's total. The company restated its historical financial statements to reflect the discontinued operation; it expected this to have a negative impact of $0.07 a share for 2004, net of an estimated $0.01 of interest income from divestiture proceeds. In the 2004 second quarter, TMO recorded an after-tax gain on the sale of $0.20 a share.

TMO's growth strategy focuses on improving productivity, internal growth by investing proceeds from sales of non-core businesses to pursue technological developments in high growth markets, and niche acquisitions. In January 2004, the company acquired French laboratory equipment provider Jouan SA (about $92 million in 2003 sales), for $137 million, plus assumption of nearly $9 million of debt. In September 2004, TMO acquired InnaPhase Corp., a supplier of laboratory information management systems with annual sales of $26 million, for $65 million. The company expected InnaPhase to add $0.02 to 2005 EPS. Through late October 2004, TMO had acquired four companies in 2004, with total sales of $185 million.

Under a reorganization plan, the company split into three independent entities: Life and Laboratory Sciences (62% of 2003 revenues; $211 million of adjusted operating income); recently discontinued Optical Technologies (10%; $0.7 million);

and Measurement and Control (29%; $57 million). Laboratory Sciences serves the biotechnology, laboratory and healthcare industries, through five divisions: bioscience technologies, analytical instruments, spectroscopy, informatics and services, and clinical diagnostics. The Optical Technologies segment makes products for the scientific instrument, biomedical and telecommunications industries. Measurement Control provides sensors, monitors and control systems to industrial markets through three divisions: process instruments, environmental instruments, and temperature control.

In July 2004, directors authorized the repurchase of $100 million of debt and equity through July 22, 2005. As of late 2004, the company's previous $100 million buyback plan was virtually complete. In 2003, TMO purchased 3 million shares, for $58 million. In November 2003, the company said it would begin expensing stock options in 2005. Option expense was $0.12 a share in 2003. In 2003, TMO spent $268 million to redeem debt securities, including its 4% convertible subordinated debentures ($197 million principal) due 2005. The conversion price was $35.77.

In 2003, the company reported diluted GAAP EPS from continuing operations of $1.04. Adjusted reported EPS was $1.09. TMO incurred pretax restructuring charges of $48.7 million, and pretax amortization of acquisition-related intangible assets of $9.9 million.

In June 2004, TMO appointed vice president of financial operations P.M. Wilver as CFO, effective October 1, 2004. Mr. Wilver succeeded T. Melas-Kyriazi, who left the company to pursue other interests.

Company Financials Fiscal Year ending December 31

Per Share Data ($)

(Year Ended December 31)	2003	2002	2001	2000	1999	1998	1997	1996	1995	1994
Tangible Bk. Val.	5.00	3.79	1.33	6.34	5.03	1.51	1.60	1.60	3.59	8.63
Cash Flow	1.35	1.35	0.81	0.94	0.63	1.90	2.13	2.13	1.79	1.50
Earnings	1.04	1.12	0.27	0.36	-0.11	1.04	1.41	1.35	1.11	0.93
S&P Core Earnings	0.79	0.50	0.02	NA	NA	NA	NA	NA	NA	NA
Dividends	Nil	Nil	Nil	Nil	Nil	Nil	Nil	Nil	Nil	Nil
Payout Ratio	Nil	Nil	Nil	Nil	Nil	Nil	Nil	Nil	Nil	Nil
Prices - High	25.40	24.60	30.62	31.24	20.25	44.25	44.50	44.37	34.66	21.27
- Low	16.89	14.33	16.55	14.00	12.50	13.56	28.37	29.75	19.50	16.00
P/E Ratio - High	24	22	NM	87	NM	43	32	33	31	23
- Low	16	13	NM	39	NM	13	20	22	18	17

Income Statement Analysis (Million $)

	2003	2002	2001	2000	1999	1998	1997	1996	1995	1994
Revs.	2,097	2,086	2,188	2,281	2,471	3,868	3,558	3,558	2,207	1,585
Oper. Inc.	292	264	265	296	362	538	543	543	332	242
Depr.	58.5	56.4	99	97.5	114	162	136	136	84.9	62.3
Int. Exp.	18.7	Nil	71.8	Nil	Nil	104	93.1	93.1	76.9	61.7
Pretax Inc.	219	288	70.7	185	37.5	392	488	488	299	204
Eff. Tax Rate	21.0%	32.3%	38.1%	60.7%	NM	43.6%	35.8%	35.8%	33.0%	34.0%
Net Inc.	173	195	49.6	62.0	-14.6	177	239	239	140	103
S&P Core Earnings	131	79.3	5.63	NA	NA	NA	NA	NA	NA	NA

Balance Sheet & Other Fin. Data (Million $)

	2003	2002	2001	2000	1999	1998	1997	1996	1995	1994
Cash	304	339	298	506	282	397	594	594	462	998
Curr. Assets	1,395	1,772	1,965	2,466	2,517	3,301	3,094	3,094	22,021	1,683
Total Assets	3,389	3,647	3,825	4,863	5,182	6,332	5,796	5,796	3,745	3,020
Curr. Liab.	685	1,104	1,142	729	1,066	1,138	1,092	1,092	715	537
LT Debt	230	451	728	1,528	1,566	2,026	1,743	1,550	1,116	1,050
Common Equity	2,383	2,033	1,908	2,534	2,014	2,248	1,998	1,998	1,299	990
Total Cap.	2,624	2,495	2,650	4,098	4,026	5,025	3,925	4,065	2,947	2,426
Cap. Exp.	46.1	51.2	84.8	74.0	87.2	148	112	125	63.0	60.0
Cash Flow	231	252	148	160	99	339	375	375	225	166
Curr. Ratio	2.0	1.6	1.7	3.4	2.4	2.9	2.8	2.8	2.8	3.1
% LT Debt of Cap.	8.7	18.1	27.4	37.3	38.9	40.3	44.4	38.1	37.9	43.3
% Net Inc.of Revs.	8.2	9.4	2.3	2.7	NM	4.6	6.7	6.7	6.3	6.5
% Ret. on Assets	4.9	5.2	1.1	1.2	NM	2.9	4.1	5.0	4.1	3.7
% Ret. on Equity	7.8	9.9	2.2	2.7	NM	8.3	12.0	14.5	12.0	10.9

Data as orig reptd.; bef. results of disc opers/spec. items. Per share data adj. for stk. divs.; EPS diluted. E-Estimated. NA-Not Available. NM-Not Meaningful. NR-Not Ranked. UR-Under Review.

Office: 81 Wyman Street, Waltham, MA 02254-9046.
Telephone: 781-622-1000.
Website: http://www.thermo.com
Chrmn: J. Manzi.
Pres & CEO: M.E. Dekkers.

VP & CFO: T. Melas-Kyriazi.
VP, Secy & General Counsel: S.H. Hoogasian.
VP & Investor Contact: J.T. Corcoran 781-622-1306.
Dirs: M. E. Dekkers, J. L. LaMattina, P. J. Manning, J. P. Manzi, R. A. McCabe, R. W. O'Leary, M. E. Porter, E. S. Ullian.

Founded: in 1956.
Domicile: Delaware.
Employees: 11,000.
S&P Analyst: Stewart Scharf/PMW/BK

Recommendation: **HOLD** ★★★★★
SELL SELL HOLD BUY BUY

12-Month Target Price: **$80.00**
(as of October 18, 2004)

MMM has an approximate 0.59% weighting in the **S&P 500**

Sector: Industrials
Sub-Industry: Industrial Conglomerates
Peer Group: Conglomerates - Domestic

Summary: This diversified technology company has operations in electronics, health care, industrial, consumer and office, telecommunications, safety and security and other markets.

Quantitative Evaluations

S&P Earnings & Dividend Rank: A-

| D | C | B- | B | B+ | A- | A | A+ |

S&P Fair Value Rank: 1

| 1 | 2 | 3 | 4 | 5 |
| Lowest | | | | Highest |

Fair Value Calc.: $57.00 (Overvalued)

S&P Investability Quotient Percentile
99%

MMM scored higher than 99% of all companies for which an S&P Report is available.

Volatility: Low

| Low | Average | High |

Technical Evaluation: Neutral
Since 11/04, the technical indicators for MMM have been Neutral.

Relative Strength Rank: Moderate
47
| 1 Lowest | Highest 99 |

Price as of 11/12/04: $82.68 **2004E S&P Core EPS:** $3.58

GAAP Earnings vs. Previous Year
▲ Up ▼ Down ► No Change

- 10 Week Mov. Avg.
- 30 Week Mov. Avg.
- Relative Strength
- 12-Mo Target Price

2-for-1

Volume Below Avg. — Above Avg.

VOL. MIL.
24 16 8 0

HOLD
J J A S O N D J F M A M J J A S O N D J F M A M J J A S O N D J F M A M J J A S O N D J
2001 **2002** **2003** **2004**

OPTIONS: ASE, CBOE, P, Ph

Analyst commentary prepared by Anthony M. Fiore, CFA /CB/JWP

Highlights October 19, 2004

- We see revenues increasing 5% to 8% in 2005, following a projected advance of about 11% in 2004. We expect top-line growth in 2005 to benefit from further penetration of the Asia-Pacific and Latin America regions, the development of adjacent market opportunities, an expanding pipeline of new products, and contributions from acquisitions. Moreover, we believe that sustained global economic growth should help boost sales of MMM's more cyclical Industrial and Electro and Communications businesses.

- We see a modest expansion of operating margins in 2005, due to expected benefits from Six Sigma, improving volumes, and an increasing percentage of higher margin Display and Graphics and Health Care sales. Operating margins (before one-time items), which averaged about 18% from 1994-2003, were 24% in the third quarter of 2004. Over the next few years, we believe that continued efforts to streamline this diverse company will enable MMM to maintain above average profitability.

- Our Standard & Poor's Core Earnings estimates for 2004 and 2005 are each $0.14 a share below our respective operating EPS forecasts, with the difference reflecting projected stock option expense and pension and post-retirement cost adjustments.

Investment Rationale/Risk October 19, 2004

- We have a hold recommendation on the shares. While we expect favorable end market conditions to continue over the next 12 months, we believe that our outlook is largely reflected in the price of the stock.

- Risks to our recommendation and target price include an unexpected downturn in the global economy; a greater than expected moderation of growth in the optical display business; execution risk associated with acquisitions and/or cost savings initiatives; and unanticipated litigation expenses related to product liability.

- Our discounted cash flow model, which assumes an 8% average annual free cash flow growth rate over the next 10 years, 3.5% growth in perpetuity, and an 8.6% weighted average cost of capital, indicates intrinsic value of about $79. In terms of relative valuation, the shares traded recently at a P/E multiple of about 18X our 2005 EPS estimate of $4.07. Applying a target P/E multiple of 20X, in line with historical norms, suggests a value of $81 a share. Blending these two valuation metrics leads to our 12-month target price of $80.

Key Stock Statistics

S&P Core EPS 2005E	3.93	52-week Range	$90.29-73.31
S&P Oper. EPS 2004E	3.72	12 Month P/E	22.9
P/E on S&P Oper. EPS 2004E	22.2	Beta	0.52
S&P Oper. EPS 2005E	4.07	Shareholders	125,636
Yield (%)	1.7%	Market Cap (B)	$ 64.4
Dividend Rate/Share	1.44	Shares Outstanding (M)	778.5

Value of $10,000 invested five years ago: **$ 18,872**

Dividend Data Dividends have been paid since 1916

Amount ($)	Date Decl.	Ex-Div. Date	Stock of Record	Payment Date
0.360	Feb. 10	Feb. 18	Feb. 20	Mar. 12 '04
0.360	May. 11	May. 19	May. 21	Jun. 12 '04
0.360	Aug. 09	Aug. 18	Aug. 20	Sep. 12 '04
0.360	Nov. 08	Nov. 17	Nov. 19	Dec. 12 '04

Revenues/Earnings Data Fiscal year ending December 31

Revenues (Million $)

	2004	2003	2002	2001	2000	1999
1Q	4,939	4,318	3,890	4,170	4,052	3,776
2Q	5,012	4,580	4,161	4,079	4,224	3,863
3Q	4,969	4,616	4,143	3,967	4,252	3,997
4Q	—	4,718	4,138	3,863	4,136	4,023
Yr.	—	18,232	16,332	16,079	16,724	15,659

Earnings Per Share ($)

	2004	2003	2002	2001	2000	1999
1Q	0.90	0.64	0.57	0.57	0.60	0.48
2Q	0.97	0.78	0.59	0.25	0.59	0.59
3Q	0.97	0.83	0.69	0.50	0.63	0.57
4Q	E0.88	0.77	0.65	0.48	0.50	0.55
Yr.	E3.72	3.02	2.50	1.79	2.32	2.17

Next earnings report expected: mid-January Source: S&P, Company Reports
EPS Estimates based on S&P Operating Earnings; historical GAAP earnings are as reported.

Please read the Required Disclosures and Reg. AC certification on the last page of this report.

The McGraw·Hill Companies

STANDARD &POOR'S

3M Company

Stock Report
November 13, 2004
NYSE Symbol: **MMM**

Recommendation: **HOLD** ★ ★ ★ ☆ ☆   12-Month Target Price: **$80.00** (as of October 18, 2004)

Business Summary October 19, 2004

In September 2002, MMM announced that it would strategically realign its organization for faster growth and closer focus on markets and customers. The realignment resulted in seven new reportable business segments, versus six used in 2002. The new reportable units are Health Care; Industrial; Consumer and Office; Display and Graphics; Electro and Communications; Safety, Security and Protection Services; and Transportation.

The Health Care segment (22% of 2003 revenue, and 26% of operating profit; 26% operating margin) serves markets worldwide including medical, surgical, pharmaceutical, dental, health information systems and other markets. Products provided include medical and pharmaceutical products, drug delivery systems, dental products, health information systems, and personal care and related products.

The Industrial segment (18%, 12%; 14%) serves a broad range of markets, from aerospace and plastics to metal working and packaging. Products include abrasives, engineered adhesives, industrial tape, packaging systems, superabrasives and microfinishing systems, surface conditioning products, Dyneon materials, performance materials, specialty materials and filtration products.

The Consumer and Office segment (14%, 12%; 18%) serves markets that include consumer, office, education and foodservice markets. Products include office supply products, stationery products, construction and home improvement products, protective material products, home care, and visual systems products.

The Display and Graphics segment (16%, 23%; 30%) serves markets that include electronic display, touch screen, commercial graphics and traffic control materials.

The Electro and Communications segment (10%, 6.5%; 14%) serves the electronic and telecommunications markets with products that speed the delivery of information and ideas, while also reducing costs. This segment also serves the electrical power markets. Products include electronic and interconnect solutions, microinterconnect systems, telecommunications products and electrical products.

The Safety, Security and Protection Services segment (11%, 11%; 23%) strives to increase the safety, security and productivity of workers, facilities and systems around the world. Products include occupational health and safety, commercial care, safety and security, industrial mineral, food services trade, consumer safety and light management, and corrosion protection products.

The Transportation segment (8.4%, 9.9%; 25%) serves automotive manufacturers, automotive body shops, the aerospace and marine industries, and other general transportation related industries.

In December 2002, the company acquired the precision lens business of Corning Inc., for about $850 million. The business, which makes lens systems for rear projection televisions, now operates under the name 3M Precision Optics, Inc., and is part of the Display and Graphics segment.

Company Financials Fiscal Year ending December 31

Per Share Data ($)

(Year Ended December 31)	2003	2002	2001	2000	1999	1998	1997	1996	1995	1994
Tangible Bk. Val.	6.62	4.91	6.23	7.17	7.06	7.39	7.32	7.54	8.21	8.02
Cash Flow	4.23	3.70	3.15	3.60	3.28	2.55	3.57	2.87	2.58	2.75
Earnings	3.02	2.50	1.79	2.32	2.17	1.49	2.53	1.82	1.56	1.57
S&P Core Earnings	2.91	1.71	0.94	NA	NA	NA	NA	NA	NA	NA
Dividends	1.32	1.24	1.20	1.16	1.12	1.10	1.06	0.96	0.94	0.88
Payout Ratio	44%	50%	67%	50%	52%	74%	42%	53%	60%	56%
Prices - High	85.40	65.77	63.50	61.46	51.68	48.93	52.75	42.93	34.93	28.56
- Low	59.73	50.00	42.93	39.09	34.65	32.81	40.00	30.62	25.37	23.18
P/E Ratio - High	28	26	35	26	24	33	21	24	22	18
- Low	20	20	24	17	16	22	16	17	16	15

Income Statement Analysis (Million $)

	2003	2002	2001	2000	1999	1998	1997	1996	1995	1994
Revs.	18,232	16,332	16,079	16,724	15,659	15,021	15,070	14,236	13,460	15,079
Oper. Inc.	4,770	4,000	3,274	3,898	3,828	3,398	3,545	3,374	3,159	3,254
Depr.	964	954	1,089	1,025	900	866	870	883	859	1,003
Int. Exp.	84.0	80.0	124	111	109	139	94.0	79.0	102	87.0
Pretax Inc.	3,657	3,005	2,186	2,974	2,880	1,952	3,440	2,479	2,168	2,154
Eff. Tax Rate	32.9%	32.1%	32.1%	34.5%	35.8%	35.1%	36.1%	35.7%	36.2%	35.8%
Net Inc.	2,403	1,974	1,430	1,857	1,763	1,213	2,121	1,516	1,306	1,322
S&P Core Earnings	2,319	1,356	750	NA	NA	NA	NA	NA	NA	NA

Balance Sheet & Other Fin. Data (Million $)

	2003	2002	2001	2000	1999	1998	1997	1996	1995	1994
Cash	1,836	618	616	302	387	448	230	744	772	491
Curr. Assets	7,720	6,059	6,296	6,379	6,066	6,318	6,168	6,486	6,395	6,928
Total Assets	17,600	15,329	14,606	14,522	13,896	14,153	13,238	13,364	14,183	13,496
Curr. Liab.	5,082	4,457	4,509	4,754	3,819	4,386	3,983	3,789	3,724	3,605
LT Debt	1,735	2,140	1,520	971	1,480	1,614	1,015	851	1,203	1,031
Common Equity	7,885	5,993	6,086	6,531	6,289	5,936	5,926	6,294	6,884	6,734
Total Cap.	9,620	8,133	7,606	7,502	7,769	8,133	7,391	7,135	8,087	8,321
Cap. Exp.	677	763	980	1,115	1,039	1,430	1,406	1,109	1,088	1,148
Cash Flow	3,367	2,928	2,519	2,882	2,663	2,079	2,991	2,399	2,165	2,325
Curr. Ratio	1.5	1.4	1.4	1.3	1.6	1.4	1.5	1.7	1.7	1.9
% LT Debt of Cap.	18.0	26.3	20.0	12.9	19.1	19.8	13.7	11.9	14.9	12.4
% Net Inc.of Revs.	13.2	12.1	8.9	11.1	11.3	8.1	14.1	10.6	9.7	8.8
% Ret. on Assets	14.6	13.2	9.8	13.1	12.6	8.9	15.9	11.0	9.6	10.4
% Ret. on Equity	34.6	32.7	22.7	29.0	28.8	20.5	34.7	23.0	19.2	20.2

Data as orig reptd.; bef. results of disc opers/spec. items. Per share data adj. for stk. divs.; EPS diluted. E-Estimated. NA-Not Available. NM-Not Meaningful. NR-Not Ranked. UR-Under Review.

Office: 3M Center, St. Paul, MN 55144-1000.
Telephone: 651-733-1110.
Email: innovation@mmm.com
Website: http://www.mmm.com
Chrmn & CEO: W.J. McNerney, Jr.
SVP & CFO: P.D. Campbell.
SVP & General Counsel: R.F. Ziegler.

Treas: W.J. Schmoll.
Secy: G. Larson.
Investor Contact: M. Ginter 651-733-8206.
Dirs: L. G. Alvarado, E. A. Brennan, V. D. Coffman, M. L. Eskew, E. M. Liddy, W. J. McNerney, Jr., R. S. Morrison, A. L. Peters, R. L. Ridgway, K. W. Sharer, L. W. Sullivan.

Founded: in 1902.
Domicile: Delaware.
Employees: 67,072.
S&P Analyst: Anthony M. Fiore, CFA /CB/JWP

Tiffany & Co.

Recommendation: **SELL** ★★☆☆☆
SELL | SELL | HOLD | BUY | BUY

12-Month Target Price: **$28.00**
(as of November 11, 2004)

TIF has an approximate 0.04% weighting in the **S&P 500**

Sector: Consumer Discretionary
Sub-Industry: Specialty Stores
Peer Group: Jewelry Retailers

Summary: Tiffany is a leading international retailer, designer, manufacturer and distributor of fine jewelry and gift items.

Quantitative Evaluations

S&P Earnings & Dividend Rank: A

| D | C | B- | B | B+ | A- | A | A+ |

S&P Fair Value Rank: 3

| 1 | 2 | 3 | 4 | 5 |
| Lowest | | | | Highest |

Fair Value Calc.: $32.30 (Slightly Undervalued)

S&P Investability Quotient Percentile

61%

TIF scored higher than 61% of all companies for which an S&P Report is available.

Volatility: Average

| Low | Average | High |

Technical Evaluation: Neutral

Since 11/04, the technical indicators for TIF have been Neutral.

Relative Strength Rank: Moderate

34

| 1 Lowest | | Highest 99 |

| Price as of 11/12/04: | $31.19 | 2005E S&P Core EPS: | $1.43 |

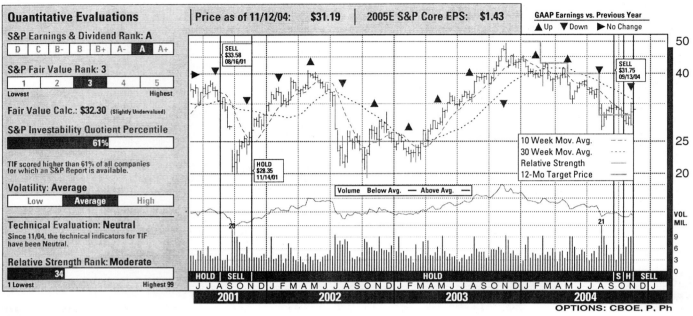

GAAP Earnings vs. Previous Year
▲ Up ▼ Down ▶ No Change

SELL $33.58 08/16/01

HOLD $28.35 11/14/01

SELL $31.75 09/13/04

10 Week Mov. Avg.
30 Week Mov. Avg.
Relative Strength
12-Mo Target Price

Volume Below Avg. — Above Avg.

HOLD | SELL | HOLD | S H | SELL

J J A S O N D | J F M A M J J A S O N D | J F M A M J J A S O N D | J F M A M J J A S O N D | J
2001 | **2002** | **2003** | **2004**

OPTIONS: CBOE, P, Ph

Analyst commentary prepared by Jason N. Asaeda/PMW/GG

Highlights 11-NOV-04

- The STARS recommendation for Tiffany & Co. (TIF) has recently been changed to 2 from 3. The Highlights section of this Stock Report will be updated accordingly.

Investment Rationale/Risk 11-NOV-04

- The Investment Rationale/Risk section of the Stock Report will be updated shortly.

Key Stock Statistics

S&P Core EPS 2006E	1.60	52-week Range	$45.81-27.00
S&P Oper. EPS 2005E	1.44	12 Month P/E	22.3
P/E on S&P Oper. EPS 2005E	21.7	Beta	2.23
S&P Oper. EPS 2006E	1.65	Shareholders	4,845
Yield (%)	0.8%	Market Cap (B)	$ 4.6
Dividend Rate/Share	0.24	Shares Outstanding (M)	146.1

Value of $10,000 invested five years ago: **$ 10,309**

Dividend Data Dividends have been paid since 1988

Amount ($)	Date Decl.	Ex-Div. Date	Stock of Record	Payment Date
0.050	Nov. 20	Dec. 17	Dec. 19	Jan. 12 '04
0.050	Feb. 19	Mar. 17	Mar. 19	Apr. 12 '04
0.060	May. 20	Jun. 17	Jun. 21	Jul. 12 '04
0.060	Aug. 19	Sep. 16	Sep. 20	Oct. 11 '04

Revenues/Earnings Data Fiscal year ending January 31

Revenues (Million $)

	2005	2004	2003	2002	2001	2000
1Q	457.0	395.8	347.1	336.4	345.1	272.3
2Q	476.6	442.5	374.4	371.3	374.4	307.1
3Q	461.1	430.1	366.0	333.1	372.1	322.7
4Q	—	731.6	619.0	565.8	576.4	559.8
Yr.	—	2,000	1,707	1,607	1,668	1,462

Earnings Per Share ($)

	2005	2004	2003	2002	2001	2000
1Q	0.27	0.24	0.22	0.20	0.20	0.11
2Q	0.25	0.28	0.22	0.24	0.26	0.15
3Q	0.14	0.19	0.24	0.16	0.24	0.15
4Q	E0.79	0.74	0.60	0.55	0.56	0.56
Yr.	E1.44	1.45	1.28	1.15	1.26	0.98

Next earnings report expected: late-February Source: S&P, Company Reports
EPS Estimates based on S&P Operating Earnings; historical GAAP earnings are as reported.

Tiffany & Co.

Recommendation: **SELL** ★ ★ ☆ ☆ ☆   12-Month Target Price: **$28.00** (as of November 11, 2004)

Business Summary October 14, 2004

Founded by Charles Lewis Tiffany in 1837, Tiffany & Co. has become an internationally known jeweler and specialty retailer. Jewelry purchases drive sales and earnings growth. The company also sells timepieces and clocks; sterling silver merchandise, including flatware, hollowware, trophies, key holders, picture frames and desk accessories; stainless steel flatware; crystal, glassware, china and other tableware; custom engraved stationery; writing instruments; fashion accessories; and fragrance products. TIF also sells other brands of timepieces and tableware in the U.S.

Products are sold via four distribution channels: U.S. retail, comprised of company-owned stores (47% of FY 04 (Jan.) net sales); international retail (39%), including direct marketing sales; U.S. direct marketing (10%); and specialty retail (4%), which reflects the results of Little Switzerland, Inc., a wholly owned specialty retailer of jewelry, watches, crystal, china and giftware in the Caribbean; and the company's investment in Temple St. Clair L.L.C., a privately held designer and wholesaler of fine jewelry in the U.S.

At the end of FY 04, TIF had company-operated stores and department store boutiques in 90 international locations. The U.S. retail business consisted of the New York flagship store and 50 branch stores. The New York store is undergoing a multi-year renovation to increase selling space and add floor space for customer service and special exhibitions. TIF plans to open three to five new U.S. branch stores a year.

Japan accounted for 24% of FY 04 net sales, down from 26% in FY 03, reflecting

lower unit volume in silver jewelry. The company has a commercial relationship with Mitsukoshi, a leading Japanese department store operator.

Direct marketing includes business-to-business, catalog and Internet sales. TIF distributes a selection of more than 2,400 products through tiffany.com.

In FY 04, 57% of jewelry merchandise, based on cost, was produced by the company. A substantial majority of non-jewelry merchandise is purchased from others.

Products containing one or more diamonds accounted for 40% of FY 04 net sales. TIF has historically purchased cut diamonds, but in FY 04, began to purchase rough diamonds from Aber Resources Ltd. and other sellers. The company also built a diamond sorting and processing facility in Belgium, and a diamond cutting/polishing facility in Canada. TIF has a 14.7% equity investment in Aber, which has a 40% stake in the Diavik Diamonds Project in Canada. The company is obligated to buy at least $50 million of diamonds annually from Aber over the next 10 years.

In May 2004, the company said it planned to open two stores in the fall of 2004, under the Iridesse trade name, focusing exclusively on pearls and pearl jewelry, with price points ranging from about $100 to $40,000. Four additional Iridesse stores are planned for 2005, with at least 20 stores to be opened within five years. Through Iridesse, TIF hopes to establish itself in the pearl jewelry market.

Company Financials Fiscal Year ending January 31

Per Share Data ($)

(Year Ended January 31)	2004	2003	2002	2001	2000	1999	1998	1997	1996	1995
Tangible Bk. Val.	10.01	8.34	7.15	6.34	5.23	3.72	3.18	2.74	2.07	1.71
Cash Flow	2.06	1.80	1.58	1.56	1.25	0.83	0.66	0.57	0.45	0.36
Earnings	1.45	1.28	1.15	1.26	0.98	0.63	0.51	0.42	0.30	0.23
S&P Core Earnings	1.37	1.16	1.09	1.20	NA	NA	NA	NA	NA	NA
Dividends	0.18	0.16	0.15	0.15	0.11	0.09	0.07	0.05	0.04	0.04
Payout Ratio	12%	13%	13%	12%	11%	14%	13%	11%	12%	15%

Cal. Yrs.	2003	2002	2001	2000	1999	1998	1997	1996	1995	1994
Prices - High	49.45	41.00	38.25	45.37	45.00	13.00	12.15	10.56	6.85	5.45
- Low	21.60	19.40	19.90	27.09	12.62	6.75	8.43	6.17	3.62	3.56
P/E Ratio - High	34	32	33	36	46	21	24	25	23	24
- Low	15	15	17	22	13	11	17	15	12	15

Income Statement Analysis (Million $)

	2004	2003	2002	2001	2000	1999	1998	1997	1996	1995
Revs.	2,000	1,707	1,607	1,668	1,462	1,169	1,018	922	803	683
Oper. Inc.	446	397	375	374	298	191	155	130	99	81.2
Depr.	90.4	78.0	64.6	46.7	41.5	29.7	22.1	20.8	18.8	16.5
Int. Exp.	14.9	15.1	19.8	16.2	15.0	9.33	8.04	9.50	12.3	12.9
Pretax Inc.	343	300	289	318	248	156	128	103	69.0	51.6
Eff. Tax Rate	37.1%	36.6%	40.0%	40.0%	41.3%	42.1%	43.0%	43.2%	43.2%	43.1%
Net Inc.	216	190	174	191	146	90.1	72.8	58.4	39.2	29.3
S&P Core Earnings	204	173	164	181	NA	NA	NA	NA	NA	NA

Balance Sheet & Other Fin. Data (Million $)

	2004	2003	2002	2001	2000	1999	1998	1997	1996	1995
Cash	276	156	174	196	217	189	107	117	82.0	44.3
Curr. Assets	1,348	1,070	954	1,005	892	816	631	569	502	402
Total Assets	2,391	1,924	1,630	1,568	1,344	1,057	827	739	654	551
Curr. Liab.	395	300	341	337	281	293	250	226	219	167
LT Debt	393	297	179	242	250	194	91.0	93.0	102	102
Common Equity	1,468	1,208	1,037	925	757	516	444	378	264	222
Total Cap.	1,884	1,505	1,216	1,168	1,007	711	535	471	366	326
Cap. Exp.	273	220	171	108	171	62.8	51.0	40.0	26.5	19.0
Cash Flow	306	268	238	237	187	120	94.9	79.0	58.0	45.8
Curr. Ratio	3.4	3.6	2.8	3.0	3.2	2.8	2.5	2.5	2.3	2.4
% LT Debt of Cap.	20.9	19.7	14.7	20.7	24.8	27.3	17.0	19.7	27.9	31.1
% Net Inc.of Revs.	10.8	11.1	10.8	11.4	10.0	7.7	7.2	6.3	4.9	4.3
% Ret. on Assets	10.0	10.7	10.9	13.1	12.1	9.6	9.3	8.4	6.5	5.6
% Ret. on Equity	16.1	16.9	17.7	22.7	22.9	18.8	17.7	18.2	16.2	14.3

Data as orig reptd.; bef. results of disc opers/spec. items. Per share data adj. for stk. divs.; EPS dluted. E-Estimated. NA-Not Available. NM-Not Meaningful. NR-Not Ranked. UR-Under Review.

Office: 727 Fifth Avenue, New York, NY 10022.
Telephone: 212-755-8000.
Website: http://www.tiffany.com
Chrmn & CEO: M.J. Kowalski.
Pres: J.E. Quinn.

EVP & CFO: J.N. Fernandez.
SVP, Secy & General Counsel: P.B. Dorsey.
Investor Contact: M.L. Aaron 212-230-5301.
Dirs: R. Bravo, W. R. Chaney, S. L. Hayes III, A. F. Kohnstamm, M. J.
Kowalski, C. K. Marquis, J. T. Presby, J. E. Quinn, W. A. Shutzer.

Founded: in 1837.
Domicile: Delaware.
Employees: 6,862.
S&P Analyst: Jason N. Asaeda/PMW/GG

Time Warner

Recommendation: BUY ★ ★ ★ ★
SELL | SELL | HOLD | BUY | BUY

12-Month Target Price: $19.00
(as of April 15, 2004)

TWX has an approximate 0.72% weighting in the **S&P 500**

Sector: Consumer Discretionary
Sub-Industry: Movies & Entertainment
Peer Group: Entertainment Content Providers - Larger

Summary: This leading media company (formerly AOL Time Warner) has operations in areas such as online access and content, cable systems/networks, publishing, filmed entertainment and music.

Quantitative Evaluations

S&P Earnings & Dividend Rank: C

| D | C | B- | B | B+ | A- | A | A+ |

S&P Fair Value Rank: 5

| 1 | 2 | 3 | 4 | 5 |
| Lowest | | | | Highest |

Fair Value Calc.: $22.40 (Undervalued)

S&P Investability Quotient Percentile

71%

TWX scored higher than 71% of all companies for which an S&P Report is available.

Volatility: Low

| Low | Average | High |

Technical Evaluation: Bullish

Since 11/04, the technical indicators for TWX have been Bullish.

Relative Strength Rank: Moderate

51

1 Lowest   Highest 99

| Price as of 11/15/04: | $17.38 | 2004E S&P Core EPS: | $0.52 |

GAAP Earnings vs. Previous Year
▲ Up ▼ Down ▶ No Change

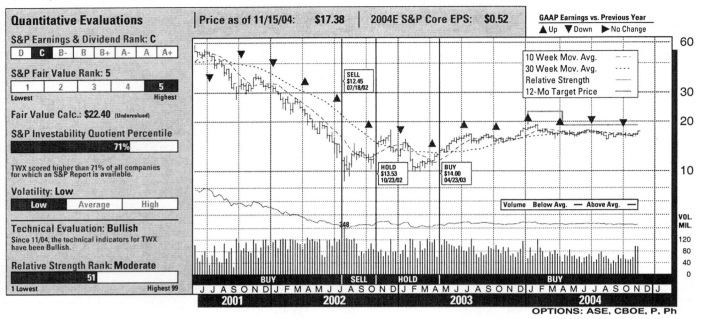

10 Week Mov. Avg.
30 Week Mov. Avg.
Relative Strength
12-Mo Target Price

Volume Below Avg. — Above Avg.

OPTIONS: ASE, CBOE, P, Ph

Analyst commentary prepared by Tuna N. Amobi, CFA, CPA /PMW/BK

Highlights 18-NOV-04

- We expect consolidated revenues to grow about 9% in 2004 (pro forma for the Music segment, which was discontinued in 2003) and 7% in 2005. We see strong growth in cable networks advertising and affiliate/distribution revenues, and further gains in cable system subscription revenues with increased penetration of broadband services, including high-speed Internet access, digital video, and, starting in 2005, digital phone (VoIP). Our 2004 outlook is tempered by difficult film studio comparisons, but we see continued gains from DVD sales and stronger contributions from TV production. At America Online, we anticipate that advertising revenues will benefit in 2005 from increased contributions from paid search, and from the recent acquisition of Ad.com.

- Margins should reflect advertising and subscription growth at the cable businesses (networks and systems), partly offset by higher programming costs and new-product marketing expenses. In addition, AOL's margins should improve, with further declines in variable network costs and an increase in higher-margin ad revenues. Comparisons should benefit from the sale of the unprofitable Time Life business in 2003. We estimate EBITDA of about $10.1 billion for 2004 and $11.0 billion for 2005.

- We forecast 2004 EPS of $0.67 (S&P Core EPS of $0.52, after estimated stock option and pension expenses), and $0.78 in 2005 ($0.62).

Investment Rationale/Risk 18-NOV-04

- Our recommendation is buy. After a transition year in 2003 that culminated in a restructuring of TWX's balance sheet and a simplification of its operating structure, we believe this leading media and entertainment conglomerate is better positioned for continued organic growth of its core businesses and possible strategic acquisitions. After a recently aborted bid for film studio Metro-Goldwyn-Mayer, the company has affirmed its intentions to explore a bid for Adelphia Communications. We believe the cable system business offers a platform for organic growth in free cash flow, as it rapidly deploys advanced services that complement its "triple-play" offering. We estimate that TWX will generate free cash flow of $4.3 billion in 2004 and $5.4 billion in 2005.

- Risks to our recommendation and target price include a pending investigation by the government of certain accounting disclosure practices, and what we expect to be continued rapid attrition of the core narrowband subscriber base at AOL. We also see risks from competitive pressures, film volatility, potential acquisition risk, and macroeconomic exposure.

- Our 12-month target price of $19 is based primarily on DCF analysis, and is equal to 18X estimated 2005 free cash flow per share, and enterprise value of 11X estimated 2005 EBITDA, both in line with peer levels.

Key Stock Statistics

S&P Core EPS 2005E	0.62	52-week Range	$19.30-15.28
S&P Oper. EPS 2004E	0.67	12 Month P/E	29.4
P/E on S&P Oper. EPS 2004E	26.0	Beta	2.16
S&P Oper. EPS 2005E	0.78	Shareholders	67,750
Yield (%)	Nil	Market Cap (B)	$76.5
Dividend Rate/Share	Nil	Shares Outstanding (M)	4580.4

Value of $10,000 invested five years ago: $ 2,339

Dividend Data

No cash dividends have been paid.

Revenues/Earnings Data Fiscal year ending December 31

Revenues (Million $)

	2004	2003	2002	2001	2000	1999
1Q	10,090	9,230	9,407	9,080	8,316	1,467
2Q	10,888	9,922	10,203	9,202	8,908	1,621
3Q	9,965	9,503	9,963	9,320	8,758	1,836
4Q	—	10,904	11,388	10,632	10,231	1,929
Yr.	—	39,565	40,961	38,234	36,213	6,886

Earnings Per Share ($)

	2004	2003	2002	2001	2000	1999
1Q	0.15	0.09	Nil	-0.31	0.20	0.07
2Q	0.19	0.23	0.09	-0.17	0.23	0.10
3Q	0.11	0.12	-0.01	-0.22	0.22	0.17
4Q	E0.18	0.24	-10.04	-0.41	0.14	0.13
Yr.	E0.67	0.68	-10.01	-1.11	0.79	0.48

Next earnings report expected: late-January Source: S&P, Company Reports
EPS Estimates based on S&P Operating Earnings; historical GAAP earnings are as reported.

Recommendation: **BUY** ★★★★☆   12-Month Target Price: **$19.00** (as of April 15, 2004)

Business Summary 18-NOV-04

In January 2001, online access and content company America Online (AOL) merged with cable systems and media concern Time Warner, forming AOL Time Warner (the company changed its name to Time Warner in October 2003), in a transaction valued at over $106 billion. Revenues consist of subscriptions (52% of 2003 revenues), advertising (15%), and content and other (33%).

AOL, the global leader in online services, had about 31.6 million subscribers worldwide at March 31, 2004. AOL's operations also include CompuServe, Netscape, Wal-Mart connect, AOL for Broadband, premium services such as MusicNet@AOL and AOL Call Alert, and messaging and Web properties such as AOL Instant Messenger, ICQ, Moviefone and MapQuest. In August 2004, America Online acquired online advertising company Advertising.com, for $445 million.

The 82%-owned Time Warner Cable segment is the second largest U.S. cable operator, serving about 10.9 million cable subscribers. With a substantially upgraded plant, it also offers high speed data and other interactive digital services, such as high-definition television, video-on-demand, personal video recorders, and telephony. Major clusters include New York City, Houston and Tampa.

Filmed Entertainment is mainly Warner Bros., a global unit with leading positions in feature films, TV, home video, animation, and product/brand licensing. It has hit film and TV shows that include Harry Potter, the Matrix, Friends, ER, and The West Wing. New Line Cinema is an independent film producer, with hits such as the Lord of the Rings trilogy. The Networks segment includes world news leader CNN; leading pay TV services HBO and Cinemax; leading cable networks TNT, TBS and Cartoon; Turner Classic Movies; and the WB broadcast network. In May 2003, TWX sold its 50% stake in Comedy Central to Viacom, for $1.2 billion in cash.

The Publishing segment, mainly Time Inc., owns 130 magazine titles worldwide, including Time, People, Time, Sports Illustrated, Fortune, Entertainment Weekly, and In Style, and 77 titles published by IPC Group Ltd. in the U.K. and Australia. In December 2003, TWX sold its Time Life Inc. direct marketing operations to a private venture group, for consideration based on meeting future performance targets.

The SEC and the Department of Justice are investigating certain accounting and disclosure practices at the company, mainly at America Online. In the 2004 third quarter, TWX established a reserve of $500 million in connection with the investigations. In addition, following its determination that AOL Europe should have been consolidated starting in March 2000, it plans to restate results for 2000 and 2001.

In March 2004, TWX sold its WMG recorded music and its Warner/Chappell music publishing operations to a private investor group, for $2.6 billion in cash, with an option to reacquire up to 19.9% within three years. Also in the 2004 first quarter, it sold its 85% stake in Turner sports (NBA and NHL teams). In October, the company sold its DVD/CD manufacturing business to Cinram international, Inc., for $1 billion in cash.

In December 2003, the company announced a merger of its Kansas City and Texas 50%-owned joint ventures with Comcast in cable systems that serve about 1.5 million subscribers. In March 2003, it restructured its TWE partnership, taking full control of Warner Bros., HBO, WB Network, Court TV, and Comedy Central, retaining a 79% interest in Time Warner Cable (TWC), and offering Comcast, its TWE partner, a 21% interest in TWC (with an option to reduce this stake by 4% recently granted to Comcast), $2.1 billion in cash, and $1.5 billion in stock.

Company Financials Fiscal Year ending December 31

Per Share Data ($)

(Year Ended December 31)	2003	2002	2001	2000	1999	1998	1997	1996	1995	1994
Tangible Bk. Val.	NM	NM	NM	2.51	2.44	1.17	0.12	0.03	0.08	0.07
Cash Flow	1.92	-8.62	0.97	0.61	0.61	0.42	0.11	-0.25	0.11	0.04
Earnings	0.68	-10.01	-1.11	0.79	0.48	0.30	0.05	-0.33	0.02	-0.03
S&P Core Earnings	0.41	-3.32	-1.08	NA	NA	NA	NA	NA	NA	NA
Dividends	Nil	Nil	Nil	Nil	Nil	Nil	Nil	Nil	Nil	Nil
Payout Ratio	Nil	Nil	Nil	Nil	Nil	Nil	Nil	Nil	Nil	Nil
Prices - High	18.32	32.92	58.51	83.37	83.37	95.81	40.00	5.69	4.43	2.89
- Low	9.90	8.70	27.40	32.75	32.75	32.50	5.15	1.98	1.39	0.76
P/E Ratio - High	27	NM	NM	NM	NM	NM	NM	NM	NM	NM
- Low	15	NM	NM	NM	NM	NM	NM	NM	NM	NM

Income Statement Analysis (Million $)

	2003	2002	2001	2000	1999	1998	1997	1996	1995	1994
Revs.	39,565	40,961	38,234	7,703	6,886	4,777	2,600	1,685	1,094	394
Oper. Inc.	11,502	11,593	9,906	2,271	1,776	851	341	101	249	103
Depr.	5,724	5,595	9,203	444	363	298	132	124	159	72.1
Int. Exp.	1,863	1,900	1,576	55.0	40.0	20.0	13.0	1.60	1.40	1.00
Pretax Inc.	4,731	-44,156	-4,465	1,884	2,014	1,096	92.0	-499	62.3	-18.5
Eff. Tax Rate	29.0%	NM	NM	38.9%	38.8%	30.5%	NM	NM	52.2%	NM
Net Inc.	3,146	-44,574	-4,921	1,152	1,232	762	92.0	-499	29.8	-33.6
S&P Core Earnings	1,979	-14,686	-4,771	NA	NA	NA	NA	NA	NA	NA

Balance Sheet & Other Fin. Data (Million $)

	2003	2002	2001	2000	1999	1998	1997	1996	1995	1994
Cash	3,040	1,730	719	2,610	2,490	887	631	125	129	64.1
Curr. Assets	12,268	11,155	10,274	4,671	4,428	1,979	930	323	271	133
Total Assets	121,783	115,450	208,559	10,827	10,673	5,348	2,214	847	959	406
Curr. Liab.	15,518	13,395	12,972	2,328	2,395	1,725	894	554	290	133
LT Debt	Nil	27,354	22,792	1,411	1,630	348	372	50.0	19.3	19.5
Common Equity	56,038	52,817	152,071	6,778	6,161	3,033	598	100	513	218
Total Cap.	62,939	96,042	189,714	8,189	7,791	3,381	970	205	668	273
Cap. Exp.	2,761	3,023	3,634	485	642	301	297	150	50.3	57.8
Cash Flow	8,870	-38,979	4,282	1,596	1,595	1,060	224	-375	189	38.4
Curr. Ratio	0.8	0.8	0.8	2.0	1.8	1.1	1.0	0.6	0.9	1.0
% LT Debt of Cap.	Nil	28.5	12.0	17.2	20.9	10.3	38.4	24.4	2.9	7.1
% Net Inc.of Revs.	8.0	NM	NM	15.0	17.9	16.0	3.5	NM	2.7	NM
% Ret. on Assets	2.7	NM	NM	10.9	15.3	18.5	6.0	NM	4.4	NM
% Ret. on Equity	5.8	NM	NM	17.6	26.6	37.8	25.3	NM	8.2	NM

Prior to 2000 (pro forma), years ended Jun. of the fol. cal. yr. Data as orig reptd.; bef. results of disc opers/spec. items. Per share data adj. for stk. divs.; EPS diluted (primary prior to 1998). E-Estimated. NA-Not Available. NM-Not Meaningful. NR-Not Ranked.

Office: 1 Time Warner Ctr, New York, NY 10019-8016.
Telephone: 212-484-8000.
Email: aoltwir@aoltw.com
Website: http://www.timewarner.com
Chrmn & CEO: R. D. Parsons.
EVP & CFO: W. H. Pace.

Secy, EVP & General Counsel: P. T. Cappuccio.
EVP: E. Adler.
Investor Contact: John K. Martin (212-484-6579).
Dirs: J. L. Barksdale, S. F. Bollenbach, S. M. Case, F. J. Caufield, R. C. Clark, M. Gilburne, C. A. Hills, R. Mark, M. A. Miles, K. J. Novack, R. D. Parsons, F. D. Raines, R. E. Turner, F. T. Vincent.

Founded: in 1985.
Domicile: Delaware.
Employees: 80,000.
S&P Analyst: Tuna N. Amobi, CFA, CPA /PMW/BK

TJX Companies

Recommendation: **HOLD** ★ ★ ★ ★ ★
SELL SELL HOLD BUY BUY

12-Month Target Price: $27.00
(as of November 16, 2004)

TJX has an approximate 0.11% weighting in the **S&P 500**

Sector: Consumer Discretionary
Sub-Industry: Apparel Retail
Peer Group: Off-Price Apparel Retailers

Summary: TJX operates seven chains of off-price apparel and home fashion specialty stores in the U.S., Canada, Ireland and the U.K.

Quantitative Evaluations

S&P Earnings & Dividend Rank: A

| D | C | B- | B | B+ | A- | A | A+ |

S&P Fair Value Rank: 4+

| 1 | 2 | 3 | 4 | 5 |
| Lowest | | | | Highest |

Fair Value Calc.: $25.30 (Slightly Undervalued)

S&P Investability Quotient Percentile

95%

TJX scored higher than 95% of all companies for which an S&P Report is available.

Volatility: Average

| Low | Average | High |

Technical Evaluation: Bullish

Since 10/04, the technical indicators for TJX have been Bullish.

Relative Strength Rank: Moderate

60

| 1 Lowest | Highest 99 |

Price as of 11/16/04: $24.52 | **2005E S&P Core EPS:** $1.29

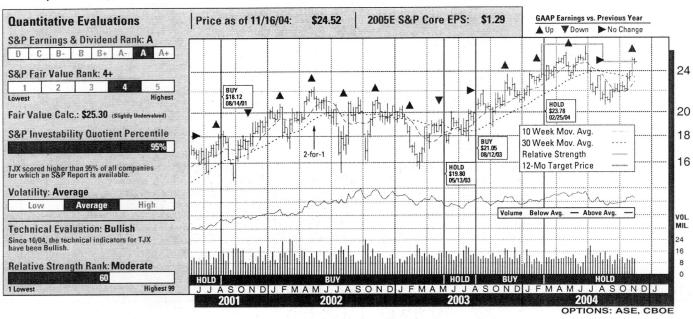

GAAP Earnings vs. Previous Year
▲ Up ▼ Down ▶ No Change

BUY $18.12 08/14/01
2-for-1
HOLD $19.80 05/13/03
BUY $21.05 08/12/03
HOLD $23.78 02/25/04

10 Week Mov. Avg.
30 Week Mov. Avg.
Relative Strength
12-Mo Target Price

Volume Below Avg. — Above Avg.

VOL. MIL.

HOLD | BUY | HOLD | BUY | HOLD
J J A S O N D J F M A M J J A S O N D J F M A M J J A S O N D J F M A M J J A S O N D J
2001 | 2002 | 2003 | 2004

OPTIONS: ASE, CBOE

Analyst commentary prepared by Marie Driscoll, CFA /MF/GG

Highlights August 23, 2004

- We project 10% to 11% total sales growth for FY 05 (Jan.), on expected contributions from new stores and a low single digit same-store sales increase. TJX expects to add about 200 stores in FY 05, expanding all concepts, including another 21 Canada-based Winners and HomeSense stores, and 30 more T.K. Maxx units in the U.K. and Ireland. We see recently acquired Bob's Stores adding about $450 million to sales. We expect currency exchange rates to aid international sales and profits translations, but to a lesser degree than in FY 04.

- We look for a modest narrowing of operating margins, as improved merchandise margins and inventory management is offset by merchandise misses at HomeGoods, and the company calibrates store level operations at Bob's Stores and A.J. Wright. We expect SG&A costs to rise slightly as a percentage of sales, on higher labor, freight and insurance costs.

- With $550 million of share buybacks likely, we see FY 05 EPS of $1.40, up 9% from FY 04's $1.28. Our FY 05 Standard & Poor's Core Earnings estimate of $1.29 a share reflects what we view as above-average earnings quality.

Investment Rationale/Risk August 23, 2004

- We recommend holding TJX shares. We expect TJX to benefit from increased demand for better apparel, but the maturity of the core MarMaxx division tempers our enthusiasm. We see ample operating cash flow to fund expansion, investments in infrastructure, and likely share buybacks. We expect international operations, A.J. Wright, HomeGoods and Bob's Stores to drive long-term growth.

- Risks to our recommendation and target price include consumer confidence, spending habits and buying preferences, merchandise availability, and geopolitical risk.

- Our 12-month target price of $25 incorporates historical, relative and intrinsic valuation methodologies. TJX recently traded at 13X our FY 06 EPS estimate, about a 10% discount to the S&P 500 and at about par with key peers. Based on our projected 15% long-term earnings growth rate, the stock's P/E multiple to growth ratio (based on our FY 05 EPS estimate) is roughly 1.0X, about a 20% discount to the level of the S&P 500 as well as its retail peer group.

Key Stock Statistics

S&P Core EPS 2006E	1.54	52-week Range	$26.82-20.64
S&P Oper. EPS 2005E	1.40	12 Month P/E	16.9
P/E on S&P Oper. EPS 2005E	17.8	Beta	0.86
S&P Oper. EPS 2006E	1.65	Shareholders	49,915
Yield (%)	0.7%	Market Cap (B)	$ 12.0
Dividend Rate/Share	0.18	Shares Outstanding (M)	488.8

Value of $10,000 invested five years ago: **$ 22,132**

Dividend Data Dividends have been paid since 1980

Amount ($)	Date Decl.	Ex-Div. Date	Stock of Record	Payment Date
0.035	Dec. 16	Feb. 10	Feb. 12	Mar. 04 '04
0.045	Apr. 07	May. 11	May. 13	Jun. 03 '04
0.045	Jun. 01	Aug. 10	Aug. 12	Sep. 02 '04
0.045	Sep. 09	Nov. 08	Nov. 11	Dec. 02 '04

Revenues/Earnings Data Fiscal year ending January 31

Revenues (Million $)

	2005	2004	2003	2002	2001	2000
1Q	3,353	2,789	2,666	2,271	2,108	1,952
2Q	3,414	3,046	2,765	2,488	2,258	2,099
3Q	3,817	3,387	3,045	2,742	2,461	2,257
4Q	—	4,106	3,505	3,209	2,751	2,527
Yr.	—	13,328	11,981	10,709	9,579	8,795

Earnings Per Share ($)

	2005	2004	2003	2002	2001	2000
1Q	0.33	0.22	0.27	0.22	0.22	0.20
2Q	0.24	0.24	0.24	0.20	0.20	0.18
3Q	0.41	0.36	0.28	0.27	0.28	0.25
4Q	E0.42	0.47	0.29	0.28	0.24	0.22
Yr.	E1.40	1.28	1.08	0.97	0.93	0.83

Next earnings report expected: late-February   Source: S&P, Company Reports
EPS Estimates based on S&P Operating Earnings; historical GAAP earnings are as reported.

The TJX Companies, Inc.

Recommendation: **HOLD** ★★★☆☆   12-Month Target Price: **$27.00** (as of November 16, 2004)

Business Summary August 23, 2004

With $13 billion in annual revenues, TJX is by far the largest U.S. off-price family apparel and home fashion retailer via its seven retail concepts. At January 31, 2004, The MarMaxx Group operated 745 T.J. Maxx stores in 47 states, and 673 Marshalls stores in 42 states and Puerto Rico. TJX also operates 160 Winners, a Canadian off-price family apparel chain; 182 HomeGoods, a U.S. off-price home goods chain; T.K. Maxx, a family off-price apparel chain with 147 stores in the U.K. and Ireland, and 25 HomeSense stores, a Canadian home goods chain; 31 Bob's Stores, acquired in December 2003, emphasize men's clothing along with casual family apparel and footwear. The 99 A.J. Wright stores offer apparel, home fashion and gifts for the moderate income shopper, while TJX's other retail concepts target the middle to upper-middle demographic.

TJX added 188 stores in FY 04 (Jan.), raising its store count 10%, to 2,031, excluding the 31 Bob's Stores. In FY 05, it plans to add 60 stores to The MarMaxx Group, 40 HomeGoods stores, 32 A.J. Wright locations, 25 T.K. Maxx stores in the U.K. and Ireland, 15 HomeSense units, eight new Winners locations, and two additional Bob's Stores.

TJX has retained the separate identities of the T.J. Maxx and Marshalls stores, while operating a common buying and merchandising organization and consolidated administrative functions, thus allowing TJX to operate with a lower cost structure. Although merchandise is similar at Marshalls and T.J. Maxx, Marshalls offers a full-line shoe department, a larger men's department, and costume jewelry, rather than fine jewelry. In FY 04, T.J. Maxx tested expanded jewelry and accessories departments, and plans to expand 282 more in FY 05. Marshalls intends to expand its footwear offering in 67 stores in FY 05.

TJX purchases much of its inventory opportunistically, with only a small percentage specifically manufactured to order. TJX buyers are in the market weekly, and by maintaining a liquid inventory position, buyers can buy close to need, enabling them to buy into current consumer demand while offering rapidly changing merchandise at everyday prices below department and specialty store regular prices. TJX acquires large quantities of merchandise at significant discounts from initial wholesale prices. Generally, purchases are for current selling seasons, with a limited quantity of packaway merchandise intended for a future selling season.

FY 04 capital spending totaled $409 million, versus $397 million in FY 03. The company plans $500 million in capital spending in FY 05, including $188 million for new stores, $221 million for store renovations and improvements, and $91 million for its office and distribution centers. TJX's planned rate of new store growth is 8% to 9% annually for the next several years.

In July 2002, TJX completed a $1.0 billion share repurchase program, and announced plans to buy back an additional $1.0 billion of stock. Through the first quarter of FY 05, TJX purchased 48.6 million of its shares, at a cost of $956 million.

Company Financials Fiscal Year ending January 31

Per Share Data ($)

(Year Ended January 31)	2004	2003	2002	2001	2000	1999	1998	1997	1996	1995
Tangible Bk. Val.	2.74	2.36	2.14	1.85	1.55	1.59	1.39	1.20	0.43	0.71
Cash Flow	1.75	1.46	1.34	1.23	1.08	0.85	0.60	0.47	0.24	0.26
Earnings	1.28	1.08	0.97	0.93	0.83	0.65	0.43	0.30	0.09	0.13
S&P Core Earnings	1.21	1.01	0.91	0.90	NA	NA	NA	NA	NA	NA
Dividends	0.13	0.12	0.11	0.07	0.07	0.06	0.07	0.04	0.07	0.07
Payout Ratio	10%	11%	11%	7%	8%	9%	15%	12%	76%	53%

Cal. Yrs.	2003	2002	2001	2000	1999	1998	1997	1996	1995	1994
Prices - High	23.70	22.45	20.30	15.75	18.50	15.00	9.64	6.03	2.39	3.67
- Low	15.54	15.30	13.56	6.96	8.25	7.75	4.78	2.12	1.39	1.78
P/E Ratio - High	19	21	21	17	22	23	22	20	26	29
- Low	12	14	14	7	10	12	11	7	15	14

Income Statement Analysis (Million $)

	2004	2003	2002	2001	2000	1999	1998	1997	1996	1995
Revs.	13,328	11,981	10,709	9,579	8,795	7,949	7,389	6,689	4,448	3,843
Oper. Inc.	1,334	1,171	1,104	1,064	1,022	842	652	530	274	244
Depr.	238	208	204	176	160	137	125	127	85.9	76.5
Int. Exp.	27.3	25.4	25.6	34.7	20.4	1.69	4.50	37.4	44.2	26.2
Pretax Inc.	1,068	938	874	865	854	704	522	366	109	142
Eff. Tax Rate	38.4%	38.3%	38.2%	37.8%	38.3%	38.5%	41.3%	41.6%	41.6%	41.7%
Net Inc.	658	578	540	538	527	433	307	214	63.6	83.0
S&P Core Earnings	619	546	506	519	NA	NA	NA	NA	NA	NA

Balance Sheet & Other Fin. Data (Million $)

	2004	2003	2002	2001	2000	1999	1998	1997	1996	1995
Cash	246	492	493	133	372	461	404	475	209	42.0
Curr. Assets	2,452	2,241	2,116	1,722	1,701	1,743	1,683	1,662	1,687	1,046
Total Assets	4,397	3,940	3,596	2,932	2,805	2,748	2,610	2,561	2,746	1,638
Curr. Liab.	1,691	1,566	1,315	1,229	1,366	1,307	1,218	1,182	1,278	758
LT Debt	692	694	702	319	319	220	221	244	691	239
Common Equity	1,552	1,409	1,341	1,219	1,119	1,221	1,091	977	482	498
Total Cap.	2,369	2,145	2,043	1,538	1,439	1,441	1,392	1,379	1,186	880
Cap. Exp.	409	397	449	257	239	208	192	119	112	128
Cash Flow	897	786	744	714	687	566	420	341	140	152
Curr. Ratio	1.5	1.4	1.6	1.4	1.2	1.3	1.4	1.4	1.3	1.4
% LT Debt of Cap.	29.2	32.3	34.4	20.8	22.2	15.3	15.8	17.7	58.2	27.2
% Net Inc.of Revs.	4.9	4.8	5.0	5.6	6.0	5.4	4.1	3.2	1.4	2.2
% Ret. on Assets	15.8	15.3	16.6	18.8	19.0	16.2	11.9	8.2	2.9	5.4
% Ret. on Equity	44.5	42.1	42.2	46.0	45.0	37.2	28.5	29.3	13.1	15.5

Data as orig reptd.; bef. results of disc opers/spec. items. Per share data adj. for stk. divs.; EPS diluted. E-Estimated. NA-Not Available. NM-Not Meaningful. NR-Not Ranked. UR-Under Review.

Office: 770 Cochituate Road, Framingham, MA 01701.
Telephone: 508-390-1000.
Website: http://www.tjx.com
Chrmn: B. Cammarata.
Pres & CEO: E.J. English.
Sr EVP & CFO: J. Naylor.

Sr EVP & Chief Admin: D. Campbell.
VP & Treas: M.B. Reynolds.
VP & Investor Contact: S. Lang 508-390-2323.
Dirs: D. Brandon, B. Cammarata, G. L. Crittenden, G. Deegan, E. J. English, D. F. Hightower, R. G. Lesser, J. F. O'Brien, R. F. Shapiro, W. B. Shire, F. H. Wiley.

Founded: in 1956.
Domicile: Delaware.
Employees: 105,000.
S&P Analyst: Marie Driscoll, CFA /MF/GG

The McGraw·Hill Companies

STANDARD
&POOR'S

Torchmark Corp.

Recommendation: HOLD ★★★☆☆ 12-Month Target Price: $56.00
(as of October 21, 2004)

TMK has an approximate 0.06% weighting in the **S&P 500**

Sector: Financials
Sub-Industry: Life & Health Insurance
Peer Group: Life/Health Insurers

Summary: This financial services company derives most of its earnings from life and health insurance operations.

Quantitative Evaluations

| Price as of 11/12/04: | $55.71 | 2004E S&P Core EPS: | $4.13 |

S&P Earnings & Dividend Rank: A

| D | C | B- | B | B+ | A- | A | A+ |

S&P Fair Value Rank: 5+

| 1 | 2 | 3 | 4 | 5 |
| Lowest | | | | Highest |

Fair Value Calc.: $61.10 (Slightly Undervalued)

S&P Investability Quotient Percentile

97%

TMK scored higher than 97% of all companies for which an S&P Report is available.

Volatility: Low

| Low | Average | High |

Technical Evaluation: Bullish
Since 10/04, the technical indicators for TMK have been Bullish.

Relative Strength Rank: Moderate

55

| 1 Lowest | Highest 99 |

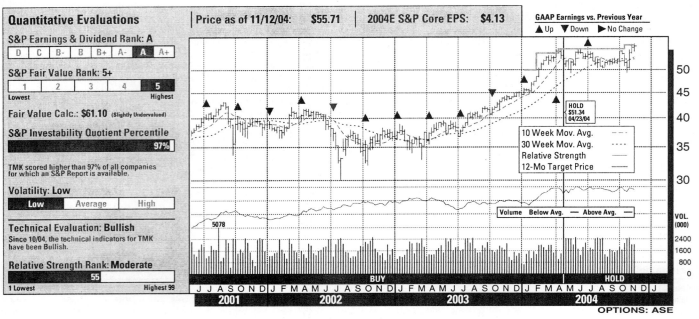

GAAP Earnings vs. Previous Year
▲ Up ▼ Down ► No Change

HOLD
$51.34
04/23/04

10 Week Mov. Avg.
30 Week Mov. Avg.
Relative Strength
12-Mo Target Price

Volume Below Avg. — Above Avg.

VOL.
(000)
2400
1600
800
0

BUY   HOLD

J J A S O N D | J F M A M J J A S O N D | J F M A M J J A S O N D | J F M A M J J A S O N D | J
2001   2002   2003   2004

OPTIONS: ASE

Analyst commentary prepared by Gregory Simcik, CFA /CB/JWP

Highlights October 25, 2004

- We expect premiums to rise 4.7% in 2004, with health insurance premium growth likely to lag life insurance premium growth on lower sales of Medicare supplemental health products.

- We expect the combined ratio for life insurance to remain essentially flat, with a moderate expansion for health insurance. We believe the Iraq war could continue to adversely affect claims in the company's military distribution channel and that a pending settlement regarding an unprofitable closed block of cancer supplemental insurance could reduce losses for this block of business beginning in 2005.

- We project a 9.8% rise in operating EPS in 2004, to $4.25, on 2.9% fewer shares due to share repurchases. Our estimate excludes $0.02 in realized investment gains and a $0.04 loss from non-recurring items. We expect operating EPS to grow 9.4% in 2005, to $4.65. Our 2004 and 2005 Standard & Poor's Core Earnings per share estimates are $4.13 and $4.56, respectively, reflecting projected stock option and pension expenses.

Investment Rationale/Risk October 25, 2004

- We believe TMK shares may modestly outperform our expected return for the S&P 500 Index going forward. However, we also believe TMK faces above average risk on a number of significant operating challenges. Therefore, we recommend investors hold, but not add to, current positions in the stock.

- Risks to our recommendation and target price include possible market trends in senior health care that promote alternatives to TMK's Medicare supplemental policies, continuing difficulties in recruiting new life insurance sales agents, continuing high claims for policies covering U.S. military personnel in Iraq and Afghanistan, as well as potential declines in demand for TMK's juvenile life and limited-benefit hospital-surgical policies, which are becoming significant contributors to premium growth for TMK.

- We arrived at our 12-month target price of $56 by applying the company's historical trailing P/E multiple of 12X to our 2005 operating EPS estimate.

Key Stock Statistics

S&P Core EPS 2005E	4.56	52-week Range	$56.33-43.59
S&P Oper. EPS 2004E	4.25	12 Month P/E	13.9
P/E on S&P Oper. EPS 2004E	13.1	Beta	0.44
S&P Oper. EPS 2005E	4.65	Shareholders	5,332
Yield (%)	0.8%	Market Cap (B)	$ 6.1
Dividend Rate/Share	0.44	Shares Outstanding (M)	109.7

Value of $10,000 invested five years ago: **$ 17,023**

Dividend Data Dividends have been paid since 1933

Amount ($)	Date Decl.	Ex-Div. Date	Stock of Record	Payment Date
0.110	Mar. 02	Mar. 31	Apr. 02	Apr. 30 '04
0.110	May. 03	Jun. 30	Jul. 02	Jul. 30 '04
0.110	Aug. 02	Oct. 04	Oct. 06	Nov. 01 '04
0.110	Oct. 28	Jan. 03	Jan. 05	Feb. 01 '05

Revenues/Earnings Data Fiscal year ending December 31

Revenues (Million $)

	2004	2003	2002	2001	2000	1999
1Q	772.5	718.4	689.7	674.8	619.0	567.5
2Q	764.0	734.3	633.5	689.0	615.1	507.2
3Q	—	730.4	715.8	686.7	640.5	565.8
4Q	—	747.5	699.0	656.6	641.2	586.4
Yr.	—	2,931	2,738	2,707	2,516	2,227

Earnings Per Share ($)

	2004	2003	2002	2001	2000	1999
1Q	1.05	0.85	0.80	0.79	0.68	0.61
2Q	1.04	0.95	0.52	0.78	0.65	0.26
3Q	E1.07	0.94	0.98	0.82	0.77	0.55
4Q	E1.09	0.98	0.89	0.67	0.73	0.56
Yr.	E4.25	3.73	3.18	3.11	2.82	1.93

Next earnings report expected: late-November Source: S&P, Company Reports
EPS Estimates based on S&P Operating Earnings; historical GAAP earnings are as reported.

Torchmark Corporation

Recommendation: **HOLD** ★ ★○★ ★ ★   12-Month Target Price: **$56.00** (as of October 21, 2004)

Business Summary October 25, 2004

Torchmark Corp.'s principal operating subsidiaries are Liberty National Life Insurance Co., Globe Life and Accident Insurance Co., United American Insurance Co., American Income Life Insurance Co., United Investors Life Insurance Co., and American Income Life Insurance Co. The subsidiaries are licensed to sell insurance in all 50 states, the District of Columbia, Puerto Rico, Guam, the Virgin Islands, New Zealand, and Canada. Distribution is through direct solicitation, independent agents, and exclusive agents.

TMK's subsidiaries offer a full line of nonparticipating ordinary individual life products and health insurance (primarily Medicare supplemental coverage). Fixed and variable annuities are also offered. In 2003, the life insurance underwriting margin of $326 million accounted for 65% of the total underwriting margin, versus 62% in 2002; the health insurance underwriting margin of $164 million accounted for 33% (35%); and the annuities underwriting margin of $11 million accounted 2.1% (2.8%). Total excess investment income rose 29% in 2003 to $321 million.

Annualized life and health insurance premiums in force at the end of 2003 totaled $2.5 billion, with Medicare supplemental sales accounting for 27%, direct response life insurance 16%, other health insurance 15%, and other life insurance policies 42%. Annuity reserves at the end of 2002 (latest available) were $2.2 billion (down from $3.0 billion at the end of 2001), with 29% fixed and 71% variable, versus 21% fixed and 79% variable in 2001. In its 2002 annual report, the company

noted that variable annuity deposits had declined following the termination in 2001 of a contract with a variable annuity distributor.

Annualized life insurance premium issued in 2003 totaled $382.3 million (up 14% from $334.0 million in 2002); 43% was distributed through the direct response channel, 14% through the exclusive agent channel, 28% through the American Income Agency channel, and 15% through United American, TMK's health insurance company, and other channels. Health insurance premiums issued in 2003 totaled $228.1 million (up 14% from $201.8 million in 2002). United American (UA) independent agents accounted for 46% of the volume, UA branch office sales for 31%, and direct response channels for 5.8%, American Income Agency sales for 5.8%, and exclusive agents for 5.1%.

In 1998, as part of a long-term plan to enhance shareholder value and narrow its focus, the company sold a 36% stake in Waddell & Reed (W&R), its mutual fund/asset management unit, in an IPO. TMK shareholders then received the remaining 64% of W&R through a tax-free spinoff completed in November 1998, with three W&R shares distributed for every 10 TMK shares held. The spinoff reduced the company's shareholders' equity by about $174 million.

In 2003, TMK repurchased about 6 million of its common shares, valued at $225 million.

Company Financials Fiscal Year ending December 31

Per Share Data ($)

(Year Ended December 31)	2003	2002	2001	2000	1999	1998	1997	1996	1995	1994
Tangible Bk. Val.	25.39	20.91	17.24	14.34	12.05	13.48	10.05	7.81	7.21	4.70
Oper. Earnings	3.87	3.51	3.12	2.85	2.45	2.29	NA	2.22	1.97	1.91
Earnings	3.73	3.18	3.11	2.82	1.93	1.81	2.56	2.24	1.90	1.86
S&P Core Earnings	3.68	3.39	2.73	NA	NA	NA	NA	NA	NA	NA
Dividends	0.38	0.36	0.36	0.36	0.36	0.58	0.59	0.58	0.57	0.56
Payout Ratio	10%	11%	12%	13%	19%	32%	23%	26%	30%	30%
Prices - High	45.75	42.17	43.25	41.18	38.00	49.81	42.81	26.06	22.62	24.75
- Low	33.00	30.02	32.56	18.75	24.56	31.81	25.00	20.12	17.12	16.18
P/E Ratio - High	12	13	14	15	20	28	17	12	12	13
- Low	9	9	10	7	13	18	10	9	9	9

Income Statement Analysis (Million $)

	2003	2002	2001	2000	1999	1998	1997	1996	1995	1994
Life Ins. In Force	126,737	118,660	113,055	108,319	101,846	96,339	91,870	86,948	80,391	74,835
Prem. Inc.: Life	1,246	1,221	1,144	1,082	1,018	960	910	855	772	602
Prem. Inc.: A & H	1,034	1,019	1,011	911	825	760	739	733	751	768
Net Invest. Inc.	557	519	492	472	447	460	434	405	382	330
Total Revs.	2,931	2,738	2,707	2,516	2,220	2,158	1,849	2,206	2,067	1,923
Pretax Inc.	655	580	597	553	393	410	516	495	428	387
Net Oper. Inc.	446	424	393	365	328	324	336	316	281	275
Net Inc.	430	383	391	362	259	256	338	319	272	269
S&P Core Earnings	424	408	343	NA	NA	NA	NA	NA	NA	NA

Balance Sheet & Other Fin. Data (Million $)

	2003	2002	2001	2000	1999	1998	1997	1996	1995	1994
Cash & Equiv.	155	140	129	154	127	104	126	110	95.2	70.0
Premiums Due	80.7	70.4	67.5	75.0	53.5	130	127	112	122	224
Invest. Assets: Bonds	8,103	7,194	6,526	5,950	5,680	5,768	5,860	5,328	5,210	4,505
Invest. Assets: Stocks	57.4	24.5	0.57	0.54	29.0	10.0	12.0	8.86	10.6	32.0
Invest. Assets: Loans	704	401	393	374	245	358	301	271	246	202
Invest. Assets: Total	8,795	7,784	7,154	6,471	6,399	6,413	6,538	5,940	5,779	5,236
Deferred Policy Costs	2,330	2,184	2,066	1,942	1,742	1,503	1,371	1,254	1,121	1,017
Total Assets	13,461	12,361	12,428	12,963	12,132	11,249	10,967	9,801	9,364	8,404
Debt	693	552	681	366	372	383	564	792	792	793
Common Equity	3,240	2,851	2,497	2,202	1,993	2,260	1,933	1,629	1,589	1,243
% Return On Revs.	14.7	14.0	14.4	14.4	11.7	11.9	18.3	14.4	13.2	14.0
% Ret. on Assets	3.3	3.1	3.1	2.9	2.2	2.3	3.3	3.3	3.1	3.4
% Ret. on Equity	14.1	14.3	16.6	17.2	12.2	12.2	19.0	19.8	19.2	20.2
% Invest. Yield	6.7	7.0	7.2	7.5	6.8	7.1	7.0	6.9	7.1	7.1

Data as orig reptd.; bef. results of disc opers/spec. items. Per share data adj. for stk. divs.; EPS diluted. E-Estimated. NA-Not Available. NM-Not Meaningful. NR-Not Ranked. Historical EPS data incl. realized investment gains; oper. EPS estimates excl. them.

Office: 2001 Third Avenue South, Birmingham, AL 35233.
Telephone: 205-325-4200.
Website: http://www.torchmarkcorp.com
Chrmn & CEO: C.B. Hudson.
EVP & CFO: G.L. Coleman.
EVP & General Counsel: L.M. Hutchison.

VP & Treas: M.J. Klyce.
VP & Secy: C.A. McCoy.
VP & Investor Contact: J.L. Lane 972-569-3627.
Dirs: C. E. Adair, D. L. Boren, J. M. Farley, L. T. Hagopian, C. B. Hudson, J. L. Lanier, Jr., M. S. McAndrew, H. T. McCormick, G. J. Records, R. K. Richey, L. C. Smith, P. J. Zucconi.

Founded: in 1900.
Domicile: Delaware.
Employees: 4,868.
S&P Analyst: Gregory Simcik, CFA /CB/JWP

Toys "R" Us

Recommendation: **HOLD** ★★★☆ 12-Month Target Price: **$20.00**
(as of October 27, 2004)

TOY has an approximate 0.04% weighting in the **S&P 500**

Sector: Consumer Discretionary
Sub-Industry: Specialty Stores
Peer Group: Toy Stores

Summary: This company is one of the world's largest toy retailers, and also operates retail stores dedicated to babies.

Analyst commentary prepared by Yogeesh Wagle/CB/JWP

Highlights October 28, 2004

- There have been numerous reports of TOY exploring the possibility of selling its toy business and focusing on the fast-growing Babies "R" Us unit. However, we think there is still a great deal of uncertainty related to the timing and structure of a possible transaction. Assuming no sale of the toy business, we look for FY 06 (Jan.) net sales to fall slightly from our projection of $11.6 billion in FY 05. We see a slight decline in U.S. toy store sales and the closings of freestanding Kids "R" Us and Imaginarium stores as likely to be partially offset by modest sales growth at the company's international toy, Babies "R" Us, and toysrus.com businesses.

- We expect operating margins to widen slightly, benefiting from the company's emphasis on carrying exclusive toy products, cost savings from restructuring efforts, some easing in promotional activity, and TOY's exit from unprofitable stores.

- After expected lower net interest expense, we estimate FY 06 EPS of $1.05, up 15% from our FY 05 estimate of $0.91. Our FY 05 EPS number excludes the impact of an accounting change and charges related to restructuring and store closings.

Investment Rationale/Risk October 28, 2004

- We think TOY is facing continued pressure on market share and margins from mass market giants such as Wal-Mart Stores (WMT: accumulate, $52) and Target Corp. (TGT: hold, $48). In addition, we have yet to see a viable long-term strategy from TOY to effectively compete with these retailers. On the positive side, the company's July closing and sale of 146 free-standing Kids "R" Us stores and its planned closing of 36 Imaginarium stores should enable TOY to increase its focus on the faster-growing Babies "R" Us and international divisions. We think TOY will likely also benefit from rising consumer spending and an easing promotional pricing environment in 2005. We think the company could gain some market share as other toy retailers reduce their store count.

- Risks to our recommendation and target price include the possibility of a slowdown in the ongoing economic expansion in the U.S. and a drop in consumer sentiment precipitated by terrorist acts. International risks include possible political unrest, economic weakness, supply disruptions and unfavorable currency fluctuations in markets abroad.

- At 16.5X our FY 06 EPS estimate, the shares trade at a premium to the S&P 500. Our 12-month target price of $20 is based on a P/E of 19X our FY 06 estimate, slightly above the stock's three-year historical average.

Key Stock Statistics

S&P Core EPS 2006E	0.87	52-week Range	$19.90-10.21
S&P Oper. EPS 2005E	0.91	12 Month P/E	27.2
P/E on S&P Oper. EPS 2005E	21.8	Beta	1.55
S&P Oper. EPS 2006E	1.05	Shareholders	31,820
Yield (%)	Nil	Market Cap (B)	$ 4.2
Dividend Rate/Share	Nil	Shares Outstanding (M)	214.1

Value of $10,000 invested five years ago: **$ 12,167**

Dividend Data

No cash dividends have been paid.

Revenues/Earnings Data Fiscal year ending January 31

Revenues (Million $)

	2005	2004	2003	2002	2001	2000
1Q	2,058	2,170	2,095	2,061	2,319	2,166
2Q	2,022	2,138	2,070	2,021	1,994	2,204
3Q	—	2,321	2,271	2,178	2,220	2,465
4Q	—	4,937	4,869	4,759	4,799	5,027
Yr.	—	11,566	11,305	11,019	11,332	11,862

Earnings Per Share ($)

	2005	2004	2003	2002	2001	2000
1Q	-0.13	-0.03	-0.02	-0.09	0.93	0.07
2Q	0.28	-0.05	-0.08	-0.15	0.01	0.05
3Q	E-0.15	-0.18	-0.13	-0.22	-0.32	0.06
4Q	E1.10	0.67	1.30	0.80	1.23	0.98
Yr.	E0.91	0.41	1.09	0.96	1.88	1.14

Next earnings report expected: mid-November Source: S&P, Company Reports
EPS Estimates based on S&P Operating Earnings; historical GAAP earnings are as reported.

Toys "R" Us, Inc.

Recommendation: **HOLD** ★ ★ ★ ☆ ☆   12-Month Target Price: **$20.00** (as of October 27, 2004)

Business Summary October 28, 2004

Through its 1,501 stores (as of January 31, 2004), TOY sells toys, clothing and other items for children. Its flagship Toys "R" Us chain included 685 company-operated stores in the U.S., including four Geoffrey stores. Sales from the U.S. toy stores totaled $6.47 billion in FY 04 (Jan.), down 4.1% from FY 03's $6.74 billion. TOY has been reformatting its U.S. toy stores, moving toward organizing merchandise based on some relatively new themes or concepts. It has also been increasing the number of combo stores, which include a greater amount of space for apparel. In addition, it expects a growing portion of sales to come from products that are exclusive to its U.S. toy stores. Including franchises, the company had 574 toy stores outside the U.S.

In August 2000, the company formed an alliance with Amazon.com, creating a co-branded Internet store for toys and video games. The new toy store debuted in 2000, and was followed by a co-branded baby products store in the first half of 2001. In FY 04, the Internet division had sales of $376 million, up from $340 million in FY 03. The division's operating loss, net of minority interest, narrowed to $18 million in FY 04, versus $37 million for the prior year.

In FY 01, TOY recorded a one-time gain of $0.93 a share related to an April 2000 IPO of equity of its Toys "R" Us business in Japan. Subsequent to the transaction, TOY's ownership percentage of the Japanese business declined to 48%, from 80%. Hence, various financial items (including sales) related to the Japan business are no longer being consolidated in TOY's financial statements.

As of January 31, 2004, TOY's Babies "R" Us business had 198 stores. FY 04 net sales from this business totaled $1.76 billion, up 10% from FY 03's $1.60 billion.

In May 2002, the company sold 14,950,000 common shares for $253 million, and 8,050,000 equity linked security units for $390 million. Each security note consists of a contract to purchase, for $50, a specified number of common shares in August 2005, and a senior note due 2007, with a principal amount of $50.

In 2003, TOY announced it would close all 146 of its free-standing Kids "R" Us stores and 36 free-standing Imaginarium stores. The company expected the closings to boost operating earnings by about $8 million in FY 05, and by about $20 million annually thereafter. In conjunction with the closings, TOY recorded costs and charges of $147 million in the fourth quarter of FY 04 and expected to record additional charges of approximately $25 million during FY 05. In March 2004, TOY announced it had entered into an agreement with Office Depot, Inc., in which Office Depot had agreed to acquire 124 of the former Kids "R" Us stores for $197 million in cash, plus the assumption of certain liabilities. In lieu of free-standing Kids "R" Us and Imaginarium stores, the company plans to offer these concepts within Toys "R" Us and Babies "R" Us formats.

Company Financials Fiscal Year ending January 31

Per Share Data ($)

(Year Ended January 31)	2004	2003	2002	2001	2000	1999	1998	1997	1996	1995
Tangible Bk. Val.	18.19	17.37	15.64	15.52	13.82	13.06	14.44	13.29	12.57	12.26
Cash Flow	2.05	2.61	1.82	3.23	2.27	0.46	2.58	2.28	1.16	2.41
Earnings	0.41	1.09	0.96	1.88	1.14	-0.50	1.70	1.54	0.53	1.85
S&P Core Earnings	0.25	0.91	0.06	0.84	NA	NA	NA	NA	NA	NA
Dividends	Nil	Nil	Nil	Nil	Nil	Nil	Nil	Nil	Nil	Nil
Payout Ratio	Nil	Nil	Nil	Nil	Nil	Nil	Nil	Nil	Nil	Nil

Cal. Yrs.	2003	2002	2001	2000	1999	1998	1997	1996	1995	1994
Prices - High	14.80	23.10	31.00	20.00	24.75	32.75	37.12	37.62	30.87	40.87
- Low	7.70	8.51	16.81	9.75	13.12	15.62	24.37	20.50	21.62	29.62
P/E Ratio - High	36	21	32	11	22	NM	22	24	58	22
- Low	19	8	18	5	12	NM	14	13	41	16

Income Statement Analysis (Million $)

	2004	2003	2002	2001	2000	1999	1998	1997	1996	1995
Revs.	11,566	11,305	11,019	11,332	11,862	11,170	11,038	9,932	9,427	8,746
Oper. Inc.	695	788	665	685	798	536	1,097	1,020	940	1,073
Depr.	348	317	308	290	278	255	253	206	192	161
Int. Exp.	142	119	117	127	91.0	102	85.0	102	109	90.9
Pretax Inc.	138	361	91.0	637	440	-106	772	673	265	844
Eff. Tax Rate	36.2%	36.6%	26.4%	36.6%	36.6%	NM	36.5%	36.5%	44.2%	37.0%
Net Inc.	88.0	229	67.0	404	279	-132	490	427	148	532

Balance Sheet & Other Fin. Data (Million $)

	2004	2003	2002	2001	2000	1999	1998	1997	1996	1995
Cash	2,003	1,083	283	275	584	410	214	761	203	370
Curr. Assets	4,684	3,560	2,631	2,907	2,873	2,597	2,904	3,160	2,419	2,531
Total Assets	10,218	9,397	8,076	8,003	8,353	7,899	7,963	8,023	6,738	6,571
Curr. Liab.	2,772	2,378	2,000	2,351	2,838	2,491	2,325	2,541	2,093	2,137
LT Debt	2,349	2,139	1,816	1,567	1,230	1,222	851	409	827	785
Common Equity	4,222	4,030	3,414	3,418	3,680	3,624	4,428	4,191	3,432	3,429
Total Cap.	7,118	6,727	5,678	5,457	5,272	5,179	5,498	5,322	4,487	4,434
Cap. Exp.	256	398	705	402	533	373	494	415	468	586
Cash Flow	436	546	375	694	557	123	743	633	340	693
Curr. Ratio	1.7	1.5	1.3	1.2	1.0	1.0	1.3	1.2	1.2	1.2
% LT Debt of Cap.	33.0	31.8	32.0	28.7	23.3	23.6	15.4	17.1	18.4	17.7
% Net Inc.of Revs.	0.8	2.0	0.6	3.6	2.4	NM	4.4	4.3	1.6	6.1
% Ret. on Assets	0.9	2.6	0.8	4.9	3.4	NM	6.1	5.8	2.2	8.5
% Ret. on Equity	2.1	6.2	2.0	11.4	7.6	NM	11.4	11.2	4.3	16.4

Data as orig reptd.; bef. results of disc opers/spec. items. Per share data adj. for stk. divs.; EPS diluted. E-Estimated. NA-Not Available. NM-Not Meaningful. NR-Not Ranked. UR-Under Review.

Office: 1 Geoffrey Way, Wayne, NJ 07470-2035.
Telephone: 973-617-3500.
Website: http://www.toysrus.com
Chrmn, Pres & CEO: J.H. Eyler, Jr.
Vice Chrmn: R.L. Markee.

EVP, Secy & General Counsel: C.K. Kay.
CFO: R.L. Arthur.
Dirs: R. Costin, J. Eyler, R. N. Farah, P. A. Georgescu, C. A. Hallman, C. Hill, N. Karch, N. S. Matthews, A. B. Newman, F. Noonan.

Founded: in 1927.
Domicile: Delaware.
Employees: 65,000.
S&P Analyst: Yogeesh Wagle/CB/JWP

The McGraw·Hill Companies

Transocean

Recommendation: HOLD ★★★☆☆
SELL SELL HOLD BUY BUY

12-Month Target Price: $39.00
(as of October 26, 2004)

RIG has an approximate 0.11% weighting in the **S&P 500**

Sector: Energy
Sub-Industry: Oil & Gas Drilling
Peer Group: Oil & Gas - Offshore Drilling

Summary: This offshore contract driller (formerly Transocean Sedco Forex), formed through the 1999 merger of Transocean Offshore and Sedco Forex, acquired R&B Falcon in 2001.

Quantitative Evaluations

S&P Earnings & Dividend Rank: B-

| D | C | B- | B | B+ | A- | A | A+ |

S&P Fair Value Rank: 1

| 1 | 2 | 3 | 4 | 5 |
| Lowest | | | | Highest |

Fair Value Calc.: $27.80 (Overvalued)

S&P Investability Quotient Percentile

62%

RIG scored higher than 62% of all companies for which an S&P Report is available.

Volatility: Average

| Low | Average | High |

Technical Evaluation: Neutral
Since 10/04, the technical indicators for RIG have been Neutral.

Relative Strength Rank: Strong

75

| 1 Lowest | Highest 99 |

Price as of 11/12/04: $37.07 | **2004E S&P Core EPS:** $0.38

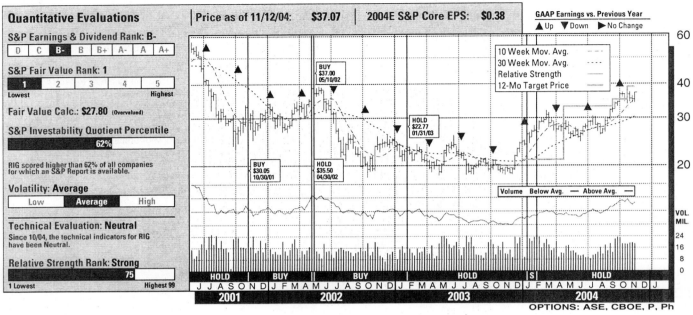

Analyst commentary prepared by Stewart Glickman/PMW/BK

Highlights September 22, 2004

- We believe that prospects for the company's high-specification semisubmersibles will continue to improve through 2004, as the deepwater rig market is expected to tighten. The North Sea market, which has been relatively weak, appears to be improving, although a strike in Norway that began in July, and which appears likely to continue into the fourth quarter resulted in lost revenues of about $7 million to $8 million in the third quarter. The West Africa jackup market appears to be improving. In the mid-water market, we do not anticipate a recovery until 2005, as we see that market as oversupplied. In the shallow Gulf of Mexico (GOM) jackup market, we expect gradual improvement in utilization and dayrates, and see stronger gains in the deepwater GOM.

- In September 2004, the company sold 17,940,000 TODCO Class A common shares at $15.75 each, including an underwriters' over-allotment option, reducing RIG's stake in TODCO to 47% (82% voting power). We expect proceeds of about $270 million to be used to help reduce debt; at June 30, 2004, long term debt stood at about $2.7 billion.

- For 2004, we see EPS of $0.49, followed by a gain to $1.07 in 2005. On an S&P Core Earnings basis, we expect EPS of $0.38 and $1.02, respectively.

Investment Rationale/Risk September 22, 2004

- Through mid-September, the shares were up 37% in 2004, versus a 16% gain in the S&P Oil & Gas Drilling index. The stock is trading at an enterprise value of 11.3X our 2005 EBITDA estimate, in line with the peer group average of 11.2X. In addition, the shares are trading at 12.6X our 2005 operating cash flow per share estimate, versus 12.0X for our peer group. We think recent stock price gains were due in part to an uptick in activity in deepwater markets.

- Risks to our recommendation and target price include lower than expected drilling activity in the North Sea and the Far East; a continued labor strike in Norway; lower oil and natural gas prices; and continued weakness in mid-water markets.

- We expect the deepwater market to tighten further toward the end of 2004, and see a turnaround in the mid-water market in 2005. As a result, we look for earnings to grow strongly in 2005. Our 12-month target price of $35 is based on our view that the stock will trade at an enterprise value of 11.5X our 2005 EBITDA estimate. We would maintain positions in the shares.

Key Stock Statistics

S&P Core EPS 2005E	1.02	52-week Range	$37.34-18.55
S&P Oper. EPS 2004E	0.49	12 Month P/E	51.5
P/E on S&P Oper. EPS 2004E	75.7	Beta	1.46
S&P Oper. EPS 2005E	1.07	Shareholders	17,564
Yield (%)	Nil	Market Cap (B)	$ 11.9
Dividend Rate/Share	Nil	Shares Outstanding (M)	320.8

Value of $10,000 invested five years ago: **$ 13,149**

Dividend Data

Dividends, paid since 1993, were discontinued in June 2002.

Revenues/Earnings Data Fiscal year ending December 31

Revenues (Million $)

	2004	2003	2002	2001	2000	1999
1Q	652.0	616.0	667.9	550.1	300.9	189.0
2Q	633.2	603.9	646.2	752.2	299.2	162.0
3Q	651.8	622.9	695.2	770.2	314.5	165.0
4Q	—	591.5	664.6	747.6	314.9	131.0
Yr.	—	2,434	2,674	2,820	1,230	648.0

Earnings Per Share ($)

	2004	2003	2002	2001	2000	1999
1Q	0.07	0.15	0.24	0.11	0.15	0.10
2Q	0.15	-0.14	0.25	0.26	0.17	0.25
3Q	0.48	0.03	0.79	0.30	0.22	0.29
4Q	E0.21	0.02	-8.71	0.19	-0.04	-0.11
Yr.	E0.49	0.06	-7.42	0.86	0.50	0.53

Next earnings report expected: early-February Source: S&P, Company Reports
EPS Estimates based on S&P Operating Earnings; historical GAAP earnings are as reported.

STANDARD &POOR'S

Transocean Inc.

Stock Report
November 13, 2004
NYSE Symbol: **RIG**

Recommendation: HOLD ★ ★ ★ ☆ ☆   12-Month Target Price: **$39.00** (as of October 26, 2004)

Business Summary September 22, 2004

Transocean (formerly Transocean Sedco Forex), the world's largest offshore drilling company, acquired R&B Falcon (FLC) on January 31, 2001, for about $9.6 billion. In May 2002, the company adopted its current name. Transocean Sedco Forex had been formed in December 1999, upon the merger of Transocean Offshore and Sedco Forex Holdings (the former offshore contract drilling unit of Schlumberger). As one of the pioneers in offshore drilling, RIG invented the first jackup rig, the first semisubmersible rig, and the first drillship. The company focuses mainly on deepwater drilling activity, where the deepwater sector is typically defined as that which begins in water depths of 4,500 ft., and extending to practical maximum depth, which is currently at about 10,000 ft. of water. The mid-water market typically covers water depths of 300 ft. to 4,500 ft., while the shallow water market covers water depths of up to 300 ft..

In July 2002, RIG announced plans to divest its Gulf of Mexico shallow and inland water business, which had been part of R&B Falcon. In December 2002, R&B Falcon changed its name to TODCO; in January 2004, the former shallow water and inland water business became known as the TODCO segment. In February 2004, RIG completed an IPO of 13.8 million TODCO Class A common shares, about 23% of the common shares outstanding. At March 1, 2004, RIG held the remaining 77% interest in TODCO (with 94% of the voting power). After a September 2004 public offering of 17,940,000 TODCO shares at $15.75 each, RIG's stake was reduced to 47% (82% voting power). The company plans eventually to dispose of its interest.

The company is engaged in both exploration and development drilling activity. At March 1, 2004, excluding TODCO, RIG owned or operated 96 mobile offshore drilling units, consisting of 32 high-specification semisubmersibles and drillships (floaters), 26 other floaters, 26 jackup rigs, and 12 other rigs. At February 27, 2004, the company's active fleet was geographically diversified, in the U.S. Gulf of Mexico (14 units), Canada (1), Brazil (10), the North Sea (17), the Mediterranean and Middle East (9), the Caspian Sea (1), Africa (18), India (10), and Asia and Australia (16). The TODCO fleet consists of 24 jackup rigs, 30 drilling barges, nine land rigs, three submersible drilling rigs, and four other drilling rigs.

RIG's operations are aggregated into two reportable segments; Transocean Drilling and TODCO. The Transocean Drilling segment ($2.2 billion in 2003 revenues, $423 million in operating income) consists of floaters, jackups and other rigs used to support offshore drilling activities and services. The TODCO segment ($228 million in revenues, $118 million operating loss) consists of RIG's interest in TODCO, which conducts jackup, drilling barge, land rig, submersible and other operations in the U.S. Gulf of Mexico and inland waters, Mexico, Trinidad, and Venezuela. Of total company-wide revenues of $2.4 billion in 2003, 31% was generated in operations in the U.S., 13% in Brazil; 9% in the U.K., and the remaining 47% in other countries. The company's largest clients include Petrobras (11.8% of total 2003 revenues), BP (11.1%) and Shell (10.7%).

In 2003, the average company-wide dayrate was $67,200 ($74,800 in 2002). Average utilization fell to 57% in 2003, from 59% in 2002.

In May 2002, directors voted to cease paying cash dividends (a final payment of $0.03 a share was made June 13, 2002), in an attempt to implement an optimal capital structure, and for more efficient allocation of cash flow.

Company Financials Fiscal Year ending December 31

Per Share Data ($)

(Year Ended December 31)	2003	2002	2001	2000	1999	1998	1997	1996	1995	1994
Tangible Bk. Val.	15.55	15.42	13.94	14.08	18.61	12.96	9.29	8.39	6.40	5.66
Cash Flow	1.65	-5.85	2.85	1.73	0.90	4.56	2.38	1.74	0.73	0.66
Earnings	0.06	-7.42	0.86	0.50	0.53	3.41	1.38	1.08	0.83	0.23
S&P Core Earnings	0.01	1.47	0.64	NA	NA	NA	NA	NA	NA	NA
Dividends	Nil	0.06	0.15	0.12	0.12	0.12	0.12	0.12	0.12	0.12
Payout Ratio	Nil	NM	17%	24%	23%	4%	9%	11%	15%	53%
Prices - High	25.90	39.30	57.69	65.50	36.50	59.93	60.50	35.68	24.62	10.75
- Low	18.40	18.10	23.05	29.25	19.62	23.00	26.12	20.56	8.87	7.81
P/E Ratio - High	NM	NM	67	NM	69	18	44	33	30	48
- Low	NM	NM	27	NM	37	7	19	19	11	35

Income Statement Analysis (Million $)

	2003	2002	2001	2000	1999	1998	1997	1996	1995	1994
Revs.	2,434	2,674	2,820	1,230	648	1,090	892	529	323	243
Oper. Inc.	759	1,114	1,159	375	181	577	320	154	79.0	45.4
Depr. Depl. & Amort.	508	500	625	259	132	117	103	46.6	27.0	24.5
Int. Exp.	202	212	224	3.02	10.3	23.9	22.9	7.22	2.52	2.00
Pretax Inc.	21.6	-2,489	361	144	48.8	487	207	122	75.1	20.2
Eff. Tax Rate	13.9%	NM	23.8%	25.4%	NM	29.5%	31.5%	35.9%	37.5%	37.2%
Net Inc.	18.4	-2,368	272	107	58.1	343	142	78.0	46.9	12.7
S&P Core Earnings	2.63	471	204	NA	NA	NA	NA	NA	NA	NA

Balance Sheet & Other Fin. Data (Million $)

	2003	2002	2001	2000	1999	1998	1997	1996	1995	1994
Cash	474	1,214	853	34.5	166	69.5	54.2	24.2	113	46.8
Curr. Assets	1,179	1,912	1,737	448	559	362	307	252	195	128
Total Assets	11,663	12,665	17,020	6,359	6,140	3,251	2,755	2,443	524	493
Curr. Liab.	511	1,504	1,144	495	529	192	185	231	62.0	48.5
LT Debt	3,612	3,630	4,539	1,430	1,188	814	728	392	30.0	30.0
Common Equity	7,193	7,141	10,989	4,004	3,910	1,979	1,621	1,628	364	321
Total Cap.	10,848	10,879	15,846	5,794	5,482	3,023	2,520	2,212	480	424
Cap. Exp.	496	141	506	575	537	573	406	213	18.9	59.2
Cash Flow	527	-1,868	897	367	190	460	245	125	41.5	37.2
Curr. Ratio	2.3	1.3	1.5	0.9	1.1	1.9	1.7	1.1	3.1	2.6
% LT Debt of Cap.	33.3	33.4	28.6	24.7	21.7	26.9	28.9	17.8	6.3	7.1
% Ret. on Assets	0.2	NM	2.3	1.7	1.5	11.4	5.5	5.3	9.2	2.6
% Ret. on Equity	0.3	NM	3.6	2.7	2.6	19.1	8.7	7.9	13.7	4.0

Data as orig reptd.; bef. results of disc opers/spec. items. Per share data adj. for stk. divs. Bold denotes primary EPS - prior periods restated. E-Estimated. NA-Not Available. NM-Not Meaningful. NR-Not Ranked. UR-Under Review.

Office: 4 Greenway Plaza, Houston, TX 77046.
Telephone: 713-232-7500.
Email: info@houston.deepwater.com
Website: http://www.deepwater.com
Chrmn: J.M. Talbert.
Pres & CEO: R.L. Long.
COO & EVP: J.P. Cahuzac.

SVP, CFO & Treas: G.L. Cauthen.
SVP, Secy & General Counsel: E.B. Brown.
Investor Contact: J.L. Chastain 713-232-7551.
Dirs: V. E. Grijalva, A. Lindenauer, R. Long, P. B. Loyd, Jr., M. B. McNamara, R. L. Monti, R. A. Pattarozzi, K. Siem, R. M. Sprague, I. C. Strachan, J. M. Talbert.

Founded: in 1953.
Domicile: Cayman Islands.
Employees: 10,100.
S&P Analyst: Stewart Glickman/PMW/BK

Tribune Co.

Recommendation: **BUY** ★★★★☆
SELL | SELL | HOLD | BUY | BUY

12-Month Target Price: $50.00
(as of October 28, 2004)

TRB has an approximate 0.13% weighting in the **S&P 500**

Sector: Consumer Discretionary
Sub-Industry: Publishing
Peer Group: Newspaper Cos. - Large

Summary: This leading media company has interests in radio and television broadcasting, newspaper publishing and the Internet.

Quantitative Evaluations

S&P Earnings & Dividend Rank: A-

| D | C | B- | B | B+ | **A-** | A | A+ |

S&P Fair Value Rank: 2-

| 1 | **2** | 3 | 4 | 5 |
| Lowest | | | | Highest |

Fair Value Calc.: $38.30 (Slightly Overvalued)

S&P Investability Quotient Percentile

83%

TRB scored higher than 83% of all companies for which an S&P Report is available.

Volatility: Low

| **Low** | Average | High |

Technical Evaluation: Neutral

Since 10/04, the technical indicators for TRB have been Neutral.

Relative Strength Rank: Moderate

43

| 1 Lowest | | Highest 99 |

Price as of 11/12/04: **$43.95** | 2004E S&P Core EPS: **$1.48**

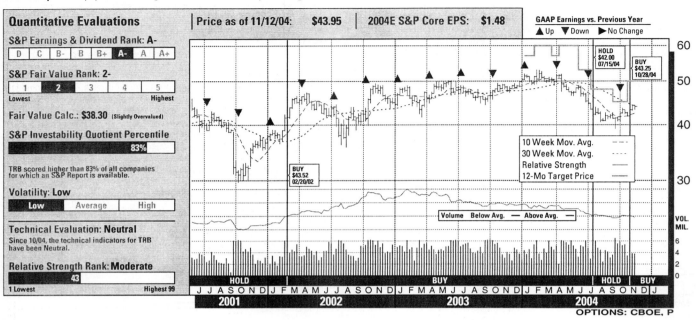

GAAP Earnings vs. Previous Year
▲ Up ▼ Down ► No Change

- 10 Week Mov. Avg.
- 30 Week Mov. Avg.
- Relative Strength
- 12-Mo Target Price

Volume Below Avg. — Above Avg.

OPTIONS: CBOE, P

Analyst commentary prepared by William H. Donald/CB/JWP

Highlights 15-NOV-04

- We look for total revenues to rise nearly 8% in 2005, to about $6.2 billion, including a 6.6% gain in newspaper advertising, and low double-digit gains for both TV and radio. The anticipated growth comes on top of 3% improvement in total revenues that we estimate for 2004. Although revenues benefited in 2004 from unusually strong political advertising, the year was also characterized by generally soft newspaper and radio advertising, and lower newspaper circulation income in the wake of circulation misstatements at Hoy, New York, and Newsday.

- In the absence of unusual items, we look for operating earnings to advance 22% and EBITDA margins to widen to 29.1% in 2005. Including about $17 million of downsizing costs, and our estimate of about $90 million ($0.28 a share, net) to settle advertiser claims with regard to misstated circulation at Newsday and Hoy, New York, we look for 2004 operating earnings to decline 5.5%. We see EBITDA margins narrowing to 26.3% in 2004, from 2003's 28.4%.

- For 2005, we project a 37% advance in net income, to nearly $832 million, with EPS of $2.45, assuming no additional unusual charges. We estimate 2004 net income of about $608 million ($1.75 a share). This is 32% below the $891 million ($2.61) reported for 2003, which included $241 million ($0.52) of unusual pretax gains.

Investment Rationale/Risk 15-NOV-04

- We expect the stock to rebound from its September low. We think the impact of circulation misstatements on revenues and profits could be less than anticipated, and we see signs of a strengthening advertising outlook. The stock's recent P/E multiple of 18X our 2005 EPS estimate of $2.45 is in line with peer levels, but we believe TRB will return to a premium P/E level in the months ahead. Thus, we have a buy recommendation on the shares.

- Risks to our opinion and target price include a slower than expected recovery in the Chicago, New York and Los Angeles economies, which can be significantly affected by the health of the financial markets and financial services industries, the entertainment industries and tourism; and the potential for additional negative fallout from the misstatements of circulation at TRB's publications.

- Our 12-month target price of $50 assumes that the stock will outpace the S&P 500, and beat the performance that we project for peers. Based on our DCF analysis, the shares are trading at a discount to intrinsic value, which we calculate at about $51. Our assumptions include a weighted average cost of capital of 9.4% and perpetuity cash flow growth of 4.5%.

Key Stock Statistics

S&P Core EPS 2005E	1.92	52-week Range	$53.00-39.20
S&P Oper. EPS 2004E	1.75	12 Month P/E	21.9
P/E on S&P Oper. EPS 2004E	25.1	Beta	0.62
S&P Oper. EPS 2005E	2.45	Shareholders	7,032
Yield (%)	1.1%	Market Cap (B)	$ 14.0
Dividend Rate/Share	0.48	Shares Outstanding (M)	318.3

Value of $10,000 invested five years ago: **$ 8,472**

Dividend Data Dividends have been paid since 1902

Amount ($)	Date Decl.	Ex-Div. Date	Stock of Record	Payment Date
0.120	Feb. 11	Feb. 24	Feb. 26	Mar. 11 '04
0.120	May. 12	May. 25	May. 27	Jun. 10 '04
0.120	Jul. 28	Aug. 24	Aug. 26	Sep. 09 '04
0.120	Oct. 20	Nov. 22	Nov. 24	Dec. 08 '04

Revenues/Earnings Data Fiscal year ending December 31

Revenues (Million $)

	2004	2003	2002	2001	2000	1999
1Q	1,332	1,290	1,234	1,293	782.5	719.9
2Q	1,496	1,450	1,381	1,367	1,335	836.9
3Q	1,414	1,386	1,340	1,276	1,359	836.7
4Q	—	1,470	1,430	1,318	1,502	828.0
Yr.	—	5,595	5,384	5,253	4,910	3,222

Earnings Per Share ($)

	2004	2003	2002	2001	2000	1999
1Q	0.35	0.41	0.18	0.20	0.26	1.31
2Q	0.29	0.67	0.33	0.21	0.46	3.39
3Q	0.37	0.53	0.71	-0.49	0.22	0.45
4Q	E0.74	1.00	0.57	0.32	0.11	0.48
Yr.	E1.75	2.61	1.80	0.28	0.99	5.62

Next earnings report expected: late-January Source: S&P, Company Reports
EPS Estimates based on S&P Operating Earnings; historical GAAP earnings are as reported.

Tribune Company

Recommendation:  BUY ★ ★ ★ ☆   12-Month Target Price: **$50.00** (as of October 28, 2004)

Business Summary 15-NOV-04

Tribune Co.'s operations include 14 daily newspapers; 26 television stations; and radio superstation WGN-AM, Chicago. The company is also one of the largest providers of interactive news and information services in the U.S., and the largest multimedia company in four of the five most populous states: California, New York, Illinois and Florida. Its media operations are located in 20 of the 30 most populous U.S. markets, and reach more than 80% of U.S. households. TRB believes that it is the only media organization with TV stations, newspapers and websites in the three leading U.S. markets: New York, Chicago, and Los Angeles.

Tribune Publishing, the third largest U.S. newspaper group in circulation, includes 11 market-leading newspapers: The Los Angeles Times, Chicago Tribune, Newsday (New York), The Baltimore Sun, Sun-Sentinel (Florida), The Orlando Sentinel, The Hartford Courant, The Morning Call (Pennsylvania), The (Stamford) Advocate, Greenwich Time, and Daily Press (VA). The company also publishes five Spanish-language dailies.

Tribune Broadcasting owns and operates 26 major market television stations, including national superstation WGN-TV, and reaches more than 80% of U.S. television households. Most of the stations are affiliated with The WB Network, in which the company owns a 22% interest. The TV stations are located in New York, Los Angeles, Chicago, Philadelphia, Boston, Dallas, Washington, DC, Atlanta, Houston, Seattle, Miami, Denver, Sacramento, St. Louis, Portland, San Diego, Indianapolis, Hartford, Grand Rapids, MI, New Orleans, Harrisburg, PA, and Al-

bany, NY. TRB also owns 31% of The TV Food Network; 9% of The Golf Channel; 50% of Central Florida News 13; 33% of Classified Ventures LLC; 50% of Career Holdings, Inc.; 20% of Digital City, Inc.; 23% of Image Builders Software Inc.; and 25% of Interealty Corp. Tribune Entertainment develops, produces and syndicates first-run television programming, and TRB also owns the Chicago Cubs baseball team.

TRB Interactive operates more than 50 leading interactive news and information sites in major markets across the U.S., including 18 of the 30 leading markets. It has a 16% equity interest in SoftKey International, a publisher and distributor of multimedia software, and other interests.

In June 2000, TRB acquired The Times Mirror Co. (TMC), a publisher of newspapers and magazines, for about $8 billion. In September 2000, as part of a plan to divest non-core assets, it sold Tribune Education to The McGraw-Hill Cos., for $680 million. It also sold TMC's Jeppesen Sanderson, Inc. (the world's leading provider of flight information services), to Boeing Co., for $1.5 billion. Times Mirror Magazines, the publisher of 20 titles, including Field & Stream, Popular Science, GOLF Magazine and Outdoor Life, was sold in December 2000, for $475 million. The company is in litigation with the IRS concerning a disputed $600 million tax liability dating back to 1998, when TMC disposed of two subsidiaries for $1.6 billion in what it termed a tax-free reorganization.

Company Financials Fiscal Year ending December 31

Per Share Data ($)

(Year Ended December 31)	2003	2002	2001	2000	1999	1998	1997	1996	1995	1994
Tangible Bk. Val.	NM	NM	NM	NM	NM	NM	NA	-0.81	0.27	NM
Cash Flow	3.26	2.43	1.82	2.27	6.44	2.21	2.02	2.02	1.54	1.35
Earnings	2.61	1.80	0.28	0.99	5.62	1.51	1.41	1.07	0.88	0.83
S&P Core Earnings	2.02	1.06	0.05	NA	NA	NA	NA	NA	NA	NA
Dividends	0.44	0.44	0.44	0.40	0.36	0.34	0.32	0.30	0.28	0.26
Payout Ratio	17%	24%	157%	40%	6%	23%	23%	28%	32%	31%
Prices - High	51.77	49.49	45.90	55.18	60.87	37.53	31.34	22.06	17.21	16.12
- Low	41.60	35.66	29.71	27.87	30.15	22.37	17.75	14.15	12.68	12.21
P/E Ratio - High	20	27	NM	56	11	25	22	21	20	19
- Low	16	20	NM	28	5	15	13	13	14	15

Income Statement Analysis (Million $)

	2003	2002	2001	2000	1999	1998	1997	1996	1995	1994
Revs.	5,595	5,384	5,253	4,910	3,222	2,981	2,720	2,406	2,245	2,155
Oper. Inc.	1,589	1,499	1,244	1,404	993	898	815	633	526	512
Depr.	228	223	442	371	222	196	173	143	121	115
Int. Exp.	198	213	255	241	113	88.5	86.5	47.8	21.8	20.6
Pretax Inc.	1,415	940	269	597	526	705	659	474	413	429
Eff. Tax Rate	37.0%	35.3%	58.7%	45.3%	NM	41.2%	40.3%	40.4%	40.5%	43.5%
Net Inc.	891	609	111	310	1,483	414	394	283	245	242
S&P Core Earnings	669	337	17.1	NA	NA	NA	NA	NA	NA	NA

Balance Sheet & Other Fin. Data (Million $)

	2003	2002	2001	2000	1999	1998	1997	1996	1995	1994
Cash	248	106	65.8	116	631	12.4	66.6	274	22.9	21.8
Curr. Assets	1,605	1,525	1,364	1,491	2,085	945	848	887	546	544
Total Assets	14,280	14,078	14,505	14,676	8,798	5,936	4,778	3,701	3,288	2,786
Curr. Liab.	1,264	1,154	1,533	1,449	861	828	706	673	557	530
LT Debt	2,350	3,227	3,685	4,007	2,694	1,616	1,521	980	757	411
Common Equity	6,941	5,806	5,294	5,513	3,189	2,063	1,522	1,227	1,056	1,262
Total Cap.	11,635	11,448	11,479	12,039	7,415	4,675	3,710	2,397	2,361	1,894
Cap. Exp.	194	187	266	302	135	140	104	93.3	118	92.0
Cash Flow	1,095	807	553	681	1,687	591	547	496	399	339
Curr. Ratio	1.3	1.3	0.9	1.0	2.4	1.1	1.2	1.3	1.0	1.0
% LT Debt of Cap.	20.2	28.2	32.1	33.3	36.3	34.6	41.0	40.9	32.1	21.7
% Net Inc.of Revs.	15.9	11.3	2.1	6.3	46.0	13.9	14.5	11.8	11.0	11.2
% Ret. on Assets	6.3	4.3	0.8	2.7	20.1	7.7	9.3	8.1	8.1	9.1
% Ret. on Equity	13.6	10.5	2.1	7.1	55.8	22.1	27.3	23.2	18.4	19.5

Data as orig reptd.; bef. results of disc opers/spec. items. Per share data adj. for stk. divs.; EPS diluted. E-Estimated. NA-Not Available. NM-Not Meaningful. NR-Not Ranked. UR-Under Review.

Office: 435 North Michigan Avenue, Chicago, IL 60611.
Telephone: 312-222-9100.
Website: http://www.tribune.com
Chrmn, Pres & CEO: D. FitzSimons.
Secy, General Counsel & SVP: C. H. Kenney.

SVP: D. C. Grenesko.
SVP: L. E. Lewin.
Investor Contact: Ruthellyn Musil (312-222-3787).
Dirs: J. Chandler, D. J. FitzSimons, J. Fuller, B. D. Holden, W. A. Osborn, W. Stinehart, Jr., D. S. Taft, K. C. Turner.

Founded: in 1847.
Domicile: Delaware.
Employees: 23,800.
S&P Analyst: William H. Donald/CB/JWP

T. Rowe Price Group

Recommendation: **BUY** ★★★★☆
SELL SELL HOLD BUY BUY

12-Month Target Price: **$60.00**
(as of September 14, 2004)

TROW has an approximate 0.07% weighting in the **S&P 500**

Sector: Financials
Sub-Industry: Asset Management & Custody Banks
Peer Group: Investment Management Cos. - Larger

Summary: This company (formerly T. Rowe Price Associates) operates one of the largest no-load mutual fund complexes in the U.S.

Quantitative Evaluations

S&P Earnings & Dividend Rank: A

D	C	B-	B	B+	A-	A	A+

S&P Fair Value Rank: 3-

1	2	3	4	5
Lowest				Highest

Fair Value Calc.: $57.00 (Slightly Overvalued)

S&P Investability Quotient Percentile

89%

TROW scored higher than 89% of all companies for which an S&P Report is available.

Volatility: Average

Low	Average	High

Technical Evaluation: Bullish

Since 10/04, the technical indicators for TROW have been Bullish.

Relative Strength Rank: Strong

86

1 Lowest — Highest 99

Price as of 11/12/04: $59.97   **2004E S&P Core EPS:** $2.12

GAAP Earnings vs. Previous Year
▲ Up   ▼ Down   ▶ No Change

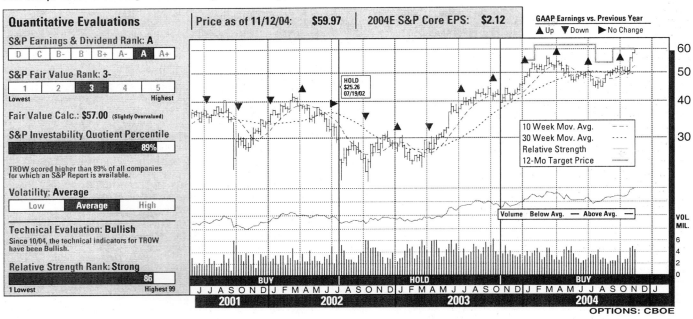

10 Week Mov. Avg.
30 Week Mov. Avg.
Relative Strength
12-Mo Target Price

HOLD
$25.26
07/19/02

Volume   Below Avg. — Above Avg.

VOL.
MIL.

BUY   HOLD   BUY
J J A S O N D J F M A M J J A S O N D J F M A M J J A S O N D J F M A M J J A S O N D J
2001   2002   2003   2004

OPTIONS: CBOE

Analyst commentary prepared by Robert Hansen, CFA /MF/JWP

Highlights October 29, 2004

- T. Rowe Price has experienced impressive revenue and earnings growth over the past year, due to, in our opinion, equity market appreciation and improved net client inflows. We think the company maintains a strong competitive advantage given its global franchise, multiple distribution channels, and broad line of no-load fund offerings. We see market share gains given our view of the company's superior fund performance, low expense ratios, and excellent client service.

- Third quarter results benefited from a 2.5% sequential rise in assets under management, to $212 billion, largely due to net inflows. Net inflows were $5.8 billion, versus $4.2 billion in the previous quarter. We believe that the company is seeing good growth in its mutual funds, separate accounts, and sub-advised relationships. We also see significant growth opportunities for TROW overseas, particularly, in Europe.

- We estimate EPS of $2.41 in 2004 and $2.80 in 2005, on widening operating margins and a higher level of assets under management. We forecast strong growth in management fees in 2005, aided by the continued shift that we see toward higher margin equity funds and away from bond and money market funds. We do not expect a material impact from ongoing regulatory inquiries.

Investment Rationale/Risk October 29, 2004

- We believe the shares should trade at a significant premium to peers based on our view of the company's impressive EPS growth, consistent net inflows, and high proportion of client assets in equity funds. We think a premium valuation is also justified given the company's low debt balances and diversified client base. We believe T. Rowe Price's broad line of no-load mutual funds makes it easy for investors to reallocate assets among funds--which is not the case at some smaller fund companies--contributing to increased client retention, in our opinion.

- Risks to our investment recommendation and target price include stock and bond market volatility, reduced investor confidence, and potentially increased competition.

- The shares, which recently traded at 19X our 2005 EPS estimate, have risen about 11% thus far in 2004. Our 12-month target price of $60 is equal to 21X our 2005 EPS estimate, a significant premium to peers, but comparable to their historical average. We would accumulate the shares on a total retirn basis, given that we expect TROW to gain market share, as we see the industry consolidating.

Key Stock Statistics

S&P Core EPS 2005E	**2.50**	52-week Range	**$60.13-40.00**
S&P Oper. EPS 2004E	**2.41**	12 Month P/E	**25.9**
P/E on S&P Oper. EPS 2004E	**24.9**	Beta	**1.57**
S&P Oper. EPS 2005E	**2.80**	Shareholders	**3,900**
Yield (%)	**1.3%**	Market Cap (B)	**$ 7.7**
Dividend Rate/Share	**0.76**	Shares Outstanding (M)	**128.1**

Value of $10,000 invested five years ago: **$ 17,907**

Dividend Data Dividends have been paid since 1986

Amount ($)	Date Decl.	Ex-Div. Date	Stock of Record	Payment Date
0.190	Dec. 11	Dec. 23	Dec. 26	Jan. 09 '04
0.190	Mar. 09	Mar. 19	Mar. 23	Apr. 06 '04
0.190	Jun. 03	Jun. 23	Jun. 25	Jul. 09 '04
0.190	Sep. 09	Sep. 23	Sep. 27	Oct. 08 '04

Revenues/Earnings Data Fiscal year ending December 31

Revenues (Million $)

	2004	2003	2002	2001	2000	1999
1Q	306.5	219.5	242.0	280.5	316.3	245.8
2Q	310.5	238.3	240.3	262.1	300.7	245.8
3Q	317.0	259.1	221.6	243.6	303.7	259.9
4Q	—	283.4	219.6	241.3	291.6	284.9
Yr.	—	996.5	925.8	1,028	1,212	1,036

Earnings Per Share ($)

	2004	2003	2002	2001	2000	1999
1Q	0.58	0.31	0.41	0.38	0.58	0.41
2Q	0.60	0.42	0.40	0.40	0.54	0.41
3Q	0.62	0.51	0.34	0.39	0.53	0.48
4Q	E0.61	0.53	0.37	0.35	0.43	0.55
Yr.	E2.41	1.77	1.52	1.52	2.08	1.85

Next earnings report expected: late-January Source: S&P, Company Reports
EPS Estimates based on S&P Operating Earnings; historical GAAP earnings are as reported.

The McGraw-Hill Companies

T. Rowe Price Group, Inc.

Recommendation: **BUY** ★★★★☆   12-Month Target Price: **$60.00** (as of September 14, 2004)

Business Summary October 29, 2004

T. Rowe Price Group (TROW) is the successor to an investment counseling business formed by the late T. Rowe Price in 1937. It is now the investment adviser to the T. Rowe Price family of no-load mutual funds, and is one of the largest publicly held U.S. mutual fund complexes. At the end of 2003, TROW had $190 billion in assets under management, up from $141 billion at the end of 2002. At the end of 2003, 71% of assets under management were invested in equity securities, and 29% were invested in bond and money market securities.

Mutual funds are pooled investments representing the savings of many individuals that are invested in stocks, bonds and other assets managed by a portfolio manager in the hope of either outperforming a market average or meeting a similar goal. No-load funds are sold without a sales commission. TROW also manages private accounts for individuals and institutions. Its assets under management are accumulated from a diversified client base that is accessed across several distribution methods. At the end of 2003, assets under management were sourced about 20%-30% from each of the following: individual U.S. investors, U.S. defined contribution retirement plans, third-party distributors, and institutional investors. TROW's international clients accounted for 4% of total assets under management at the end of 2003.

Revenues primarily come from fees for managing portfolios. Investment advisory

fees, which accounted for 78% of 2003 revenues, depend largely on the total value and composition of assets under management. Fluctuations in financial markets and in the composition of assets under management affect revenues and results of operations. Other revenues are obtained from billing the funds for transfer agent and record keeping functions, investment income and gains, and assorted services such as discount brokerage.

The company employs fundamental and quantitative security analyses in the performance of its investment advisory functions, and maintains substantial internal equity and fixed income investment research capabilities. It performs original industry and company research, using such sources as inspection of corporate activities, management interviews, company-published financial and other information, financial newspapers and magazines, corporate rating services, and field checks with suppliers and competitors in the same industry and particular business sector. TROW also uses research provided by brokerage firms in a supportive capacity and information received from private economists, political observers, commentators, government experts, and market and security analysts. Its stock selection process for some investment portfolios is based on quantitative analyses using computerized data modeling.

Company Financials Fiscal Year ending December 31

Per Share Data ($)

(Year Ended December 31)	2003	2002	2001	2000	1999	1998	1997	1996	1995	1994
Tangible Bk. Val.	5.31	3.82	3.35	2.42	6.35	5.05	4.09	2.96	2.34	1.83
Cash Flow	2.21	1.92	41.43	2.66	2.26	1.59	2.71	0.80	NA	NA
Earnings	1.77	1.52	1.52	2.08	1.85	1.34	1.12	0.80	0.63	0.50
S&P Core Earnings	1.55	1.33	1.30	NA	NA	NA	NA	NA	NA	NA
Dividends	0.70	0.65	0.61	0.54	0.40	0.34	0.28	0.23	0.17	0.14
Payout Ratio	40%	43%	40%	26%	22%	25%	25%	28%	28%	28%
Prices - High	47.59	42.69	43.93	49.93	43.25	42.87	36.87	22.81	14.18	9.56
- Low	38.37	21.25	23.44	30.06	25.87	20.87	18.25	10.65	6.75	6.15
P/E Ratio - High	27	28	29	24	23	32	33	29	23	19
- Low	22	14	15	14	14	16	16	13	11	12

Income Statement Analysis (Million $)

	2003	2002	2001	2000	1999	1998	1997	1996	1995	1994
Income Int.	3.91	3.06	32.8	59.1	37.5	28.5	22.0	17.0	12.8	NA
Income Other	995	923	995	1,153	999	858	733	569	427	NA
Total Income	999	926	1,027	1,212	1,036	886	755	586	439	382
General Exp.	585	552	603	690	589	540	461	381	281	NA
Interest Exp.	3.29	4.96	12.7	9.72	Nil	Nil	Nil	Nil	Nil	NA
Depr.	45.3	50.6	80.5	53.7	32.6	32.6	29.0	18.1	14.6	NA
Net Inc.	227	194	196	269	239	174	144	99	76.5	61.2
S&P Core Earnings	198	169	167	NA	NA	NA	NA	NA	NA	NA

Balance Sheet & Other Fin. Data (Million $)

	2003	2002	2001	2000	1999	1998	1997	1996	1995	1994
Cash	237	111	79.7	80.5	358	284	200	115	81.4	60.0
Receivables	121	96.8	104	131	122	101	86.8	73.2	55.8	46.7
Cost of Investments	273	216	154	250	279	220	193	169	150	NA
Total Assets	1,547	1,370	1,313	1,469	998	797	646	479	365	297
Loss Reserve	Nil	Nil	Nil	Nil	Nil	Nil	Nil	Nil	Nil	NA
ST Debt	Nil	Nil	NA	NA	NA	NA	NA	Nil	Nil	NA
Capitalization:										
Debt	Nil	Nil	104	312	17.7	Nil	Nil	Nil	Nil	13.4
Equity	1,329	1,189	1,078	991	770	614	487	346	274	216
Total	1,329	1,189	1,181	1,304	848	667	537	384	296	245
Price Times Bk. Val.: High	9.0	11.2	13.1	20.6	6.8	8.5	9.0	7.7	6.1	5.2
Price Times Bk. Val.: Low	7.2	5.6	7.0	12.4	4.1	4.1	4.5	3.6	2.9	3.4
Cash Flow	273	245	276	323	272	207	173	117	91.1	NA
% Exp./Op. Revs.	65.8	65.7	67.8	62.2	60.0	64.7	64.9	68.0	67.3	68.3
% Earn & Depr/Assets	18.7	18.3	19.9	26.2	30.3	28.6	30.8	27.6	27.5	NA

Data as orig reptd.; bef. results of disc opers/spec. items. Per share data adj. for stk. divs. Bold denotes primary EPS - prior periods restated. E-Estimated. NA-Not Available. NM-Not Meaningful. NR-Not Ranked. UR-Under Review.

Office: 100 East Pratt Street, Baltimore, MD 21202.
Telephone: 410-345-2000.
Email: info@troweprice.com
Website: http://www.troweprice.com
Chrmn & Pres: G.A. Roche.
Vice Chrmn & VP: M.D. Testa.
Vice Chrmn & VP: J.S. Riepe.

VP & CFO: K.V. Moreland.
VP & Treas: J.P. Croteau.
Investor Contact: S.E. Norwitz 410-345-2124.
Dirs: E. C. Bernard, J. T. Brady, D. W. Garrett, D. B. Hebb, Jr., H. H. Hopkins, J. A. Kennedy, C., J. H. Laporte, R. L. Menschel, W. T. Reynolds, J. S. Riepe, G. A. Roche, B. C. Rogers, A. Sommer, M. D. Testa, A. M. Whittemore.

Founded: in 1937.
Domicile: Maryland.
Employees: 3,783.
S&P Analyst: Robert Hansen, CFA /MF/JWP

TXU Corp.

Recommendation: **BUY** ★★★★ ☆
SELL SELL HOLD BUY BUY

12-Month Target Price: **$74.00**
(as of October 27, 2004)

TXU has an approximate 0.17% weighting in the **S&P 500**

Sector: Utilities
Sub-Industry: Electric Utilities
Peer Group: Electric & Gas- Larger

Summary: This Dallas-based energy holding company provides energy services to customers in Texas.

Quantitative Evaluations

S&P Earnings & Dividend Rank: B

| D | C | B- | **B** | B+ | A- | A | A+ |

S&P Fair Value Rank: 3+

| 1 | 2 | **3** | 4 | 5 |
| Lowest | | | | Highest |

Fair Value Calc.: $59.10 (Slightly Overvalued)

S&P Investability Quotient Percentile

74%

TXU scored higher than 74% of all companies for which an S&P Report is available.

Volatility: Average

| Low | **Average** | High |

Technical Evaluation: Bullish

Since 12/03, the technical indicators for TXU have been Bullish.

Relative Strength Rank: Strong

95

| 1 Lowest | Highest 99 |

Price as of 11/12/04: $64.28 | **2004E S&P Core EPS:** $2.60

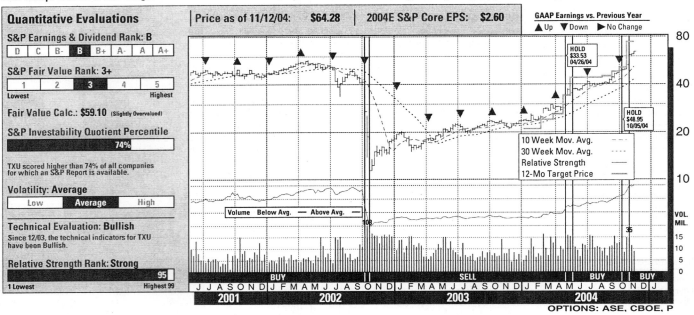

GAAP Earnings vs. Previous Year
▲ Up ▼ Down ▶ No Change

HOLD $33.53 04/26/04
HOLD $48.95 10/05/04

10 Week Mov. Avg.
30 Week Mov. Avg.
Relative Strength
12-Mo Target Price

Volume Below Avg. — Above Avg.

VOL. MIL.

BUY | SELL | BUY | BUY

J J A S O N D | J F M A M J J A S O N D | J F M A M J J A S O N D | J F M A M J J A S O N D | J
2001 | 2002 | 2003 | 2004

OPTIONS: ASE, CBOE, P

Analyst commentary prepared by Justin McCann/PMW/BK

Highlights November 01, 2004

- After anticipated 2004 EPS of $2.75, we expect a restructured TXU to more than double its EPS in 2005. We expect the company's aggressive share repurchase plan (including its highly dilutive convertible securities) to boost EPS by about $0.90, and its commission-approved 2004 fuel adjustment revenues to add about $0.82. We also expect to see EPS benefit by over $0.55 from a sharp decline in both SG&A and O&M expenses. Other factors expected to contribute to the sharp rise in 2005 EPS are reduced purchased power costs and wider margins at the electric delivery operations.

- Following restructuring-related asset sales announced in April and May, TXU estimated after-tax proceeds of about $1.9 billion from the July 30 sale of its Australian unit, about $410 million from the June 2 sale of TXU Fuel, and an additional $1.22 billion from the October 1 sale of TXU Gas. On September 29, the company said it had reached a mutual agreement not to pursue a planned energy trading joint venture with Credit Suisse First Boston.

- Approximately $3.5 billion in estimated net proceeds from asset sales enabled TXU to repurchase $1.84 billion of convertible preferred stock (reducing diluted shares by 9%) and to complete the repurchase of 20 million common share shares by September 28. Directors authorized the buyback of an additional 50 million shares, with completion expected by the end of November.

Key Stock Statistics

S&P Core EPS 2005E	5.54	52-week Range	$64.39-20.87
S&P Oper. EPS 2004E	2.75	12 Month P/E	NM
P/E on S&P Oper. EPS 2004E	23.4	Beta	-0.32
S&P Oper. EPS 2005E	5.65	Shareholders	64,226
Yield (%)	3.5%	Market Cap (B)	$ 18.7
Dividend Rate/Share	2.25	Shares Outstanding (M)	291.2

Value of $10,000 invested five years ago: **$ 20,110**

Dividend Data Dividends have been paid since 1946

Amount ($)	Date Decl.	Ex-Div. Date	Stock of Record	Payment Date
0.125	Feb. 20	Mar. 03	Mar. 05	Apr. 01 '04
0.125	May. 21	Jun. 02	Jun. 04	Jul. 01 '04
0.125	Aug. 20	Sep. 01	Sep. 03	Oct. 01 '04
0.563	Oct. 25	Dec. 01	Dec. 03	Jan. 03 '05

Investment Rationale/Risk November 01, 2004

- We recently upgraded the shares to buy, from hold. Based on a sharp increase in our earnings outlook for 2005 and our preliminary EPS estimate for 2006 ($6.50), we believe the shares are undervalued at a recent level of less than 11X our 2005 EPS. Despite a sharp advance year to date in 2004, we see significant upside potential over the next 12 months. In addition, with a 350% increase in the annual dividend (effective with the January payment), from $0.50 to $2.25, the yield has risen from less than 1% to well over 3.5%, making it competitive with (although at the lower end of the range) the yields of its lower growth industry peers.

- Risks to our recommendation and target price include lower than anticipated results from the power and energy operations, an inability to stem the loss of customers to other suppliers, and a reduction in the average P/E multiple of the group as a whole.

- Although we view TXU as having significant earnings growth potential over the next two years, well above the average rate in the low to mid-single digits for its electric utility peers, we expect the shares to trade at a discount to the industry average, due to the greater volatility and risks of the energy business. We expect the P/E multiple to widen, and to show about a 2% discount to the projected peer P/E multiple of about 13.4X applied to our 2005 EPS estimates. Our 12-month target price is $74.

Revenues/Earnings Data Fiscal year ending December 31

Revenues (Million $)

	2004	2003	2002	2001	2000	1999
1Q	2,992	2,760	2,453	8,375	4,776	4,468
2Q	2,296	2,617	2,505	6,127	4,592	3,729
3Q	2,743	3,104	2,918	6,603	5,834	4,435
4Q	—	2,527	2,158	6,822	6,807	4,486
Yr.	—	11,008	10,034	27,927	22,009	17,118

Earnings Per Share ($)

	2004	2003	2002	2001	2000	1999
1Q	0.56	0.34	1.02	0.76	0.71	0.65
2Q	-0.29	0.49	0.64	0.78	0.87	0.35
3Q	0.37	1.01	0.88	1.28	1.25	1.31
4Q	E0.36	0.20	-1.81	0.31	0.61	1.24
Yr.	E2.75	2.03	-0.55	3.12	3.43	3.53

Next earnings report expected: mid-February Source: S&P, Company Reports
EPS Estimates based on S&P Operating Earnings; historical GAAP earnings are as reported.

TXU Corp.

Recommendation: **BUY** ★ ★ ★ ★ ★   12-Month Target Price: **$74.00** (as of October 27, 2004)

Business Summary November 01, 2004

On October 1, 2004, TXU Corp., a Dallas-based energy holding company, completed the sale (announced in June 2004) of its TXU Gas Company subsidiary, for $1.905 billion in cash. The gas company is one of the largest U.S. gas distribution businesses, and the largest in Texas. It serves more than 1.4 million customers in the north central, eastern and western parts of Texas, through about 26,000 miles of distribution mains. It also has one of the largest U.S. pipelines, with about 6,162 miles of gathering and transmission pipelines in Texas, and underground storage reserves with 40 Bcf of capacity.

On July 30, 2004, the company completed the sale (announced in April 2004) of its TXU Australia subsidiary, for $3.72 billion. The unit distributes electricity to about 582,000 customers and natural gas to about 480,000 customers. Earlier, on June 2, 2004, TXU completed the sale (also announced in April) of TXU Fuel Co., the gas transportation business of TXU Energy (with 1,900 miles of intrastate pipeline), for $500 million.

In May 2004, TXU formed a limited partnership, Capgemini Energy L.P., in a 10-year contract with Capgemini, valued at over $3.5 billion. The company, which will hold less than a 3% interest in the partnership, was to transfer 2,700 employees to Capgemini Energy effective July 1, 2004. The partnership will provide customer service support to TXU. On the same day, TXU entered into a memorandum of understanding with Credit Suisse First Boston to work on an equally owned investment in an energy marketing and trading business. On September 29, 2004, the companies said they had mutually agreed not to pursue the joint venture.

In January 2002, TXU Electric Company (renamed TXU US Holdings Company) separated into new businesses. The restructuring resulted from 1999 legislation that deregulated the electric utility industry in Texas. The regulated transmission and distribution business was transferred to the newly formed Oncor Electric Delivery Company.

Unregulated operations were transferred to newly formed TXU Energy Company. The company's unregulated subsidiaries include TXU Generation, which owns or leases 20,400 megawatts of generating capacity; TXU Energy Trading, which trades electricity and gas; and TXU Energy Retail, which provides electricity and related services to more than 2.7 million retail customers.

In August 2000, TXU Communications contributed its telecommunications business to TXU Communications Ventures, a wholly owned subsidiary of Pinnacle One, in exchange for a 50% interest in Pinnacle One. On March 1, 2003, TXU consolidated the remaining interest and debt of Pinnacle One. In April 2004, the company sold TXU Communications Ventures, for $524 million and the purchaser's assumption of $3 million in debt.

Company Financials Fiscal Year ending December 31

Per Share Data ($)

(Year Ended December 31)	2003	2002	2001	2000	1999	1998	1997	1996	1995	1994
Tangible Bk. Val.	11.70	9.87	1.54	NM	2.96	4.92	21.96	26.64	25.10	28.74
Earnings	2.03	0.55	3.12	3.43	3.53	2.79	2.85	3.35	-0.61	2.40
S&P Core Earnings	2.03	0.54	2.55	NA	NA	NA	NA	NA	NA	NA
Dividends	0.50	1.93	2.40	2.40	2.30	2.20	2.13	2.02	2.81	3.08
Payout Ratio	25%	NM	77%	70%	65%	79%	75%	60%	NM	128%
Prices - High	23.96	57.05	50.00	45.25	47.18	48.06	42.00	43.75	41.25	43.12
- Low	15.00	10.10	34.81	25.93	32.75	38.37	31.50	38.50	30.12	29.62
P/E Ratio - High	12	NM	16	13	13	17	15	13	NM	18
- Low	7	NM	11	8	9	14	11	11	NM	12

Income Statement Analysis (Million $)

	2003	2002	2001	2000	1999	1998	1997	1996	1995	1994
Revs.	11,008	10,034	27,927	22,009	17,118	14,736	7,946	6,551	5,639	5,664
Depr.	949	949	1,418	1,214	1,271	1,147	667	621	564	550
Maint.	NA	NA	NA	NA	NA	NA	NA	344	290	305
Fxd. Chgs. Cov.	2.03	1.78	1.48	1.78	1.82	1.80	2.20	2.26	2.29	2.05
Constr. Credits	NA	NA	NA	11.0	10.0	9.00	8.90	11.0	15.0	22.0
Eff. Tax Rate	29.9%	34.9%	NM	26.9%	31.3%	41.5%	36.4%	31.4%	30.2%	32.9%
Net Inc.	737	175	831	916	985	740	660	754	-139	543
S&P Core Earnings	716	153	661	NA	NA	NA	NA	NA	NA	NA

Balance Sheet & Other Fin. Data (Million $)

	2003	2002	2001	2000	1999	1998	1997	1996	1995	1994
Gross Prop.	31,820	29,543	22,480	32,051	33,090	31,110	25,287	25,562	24,616	24,001
Cap. Exp.	956	996	1,626	1,382	1,632	1,173	446	434	434	444
Net Prop.	20,920	19,642	22,480	23,301	23,640	22,867	18,571	17,599	17,746	17,669
Capitalization:										
LT Debt	13,629	12,426	17,049	16,986	17,875	16,566	8,759	8,668	9,175	7,888
% LT Debt	54.1	72.3	52.2	69.4	68.2	66.8	52.1	54.9	57.2	50.4
Pfd.	Nil	Nil	Nil	Nil	Nil	Nil	1,200	1,084	1,134	1,258
% Pfd.	Nil	Nil	Nil	Nil	Nil	Nil	7.20	6.90	7.10	8.00
Common	11,566	4,766	15,612	7,476	8,334	8,246	6,843	6,033	5,732	6,490
% Common	45.9	27.7	47.8	30.6	31.8	33.2	40.7	38.2	35.7	41.5
Total Cap.	29,864	21,552	33,440	29,084	30,671	29,078	20,362	19,226	19,393	19,168
% Oper. Ratio	93.8	94.7	92.4	90.3	87.5	86.9	80.7	69.4	68.3	76.5
% Earn. on Net Prop.	14.2	12.9	8.9	10.6	11.2	11.9	10.5	11.3	10.1	7.5
% Return On Revs.	6.7	1.7	3.0	4.2	5.8	5.0	8.3	11.5	NM	9.6
% Return On Invest. Capital	6.2	6.4	7.2	8.4	8.5	8.9	9.6	10.4	NM	7.0
% Return On Com. Equity	6.5	2.5	5.2	11.4	11.9	9.8	10.3	12.8	NM	8.3

Data as orig reptd.; bef. results of disc opers/spec. items. Per share data adj. for stk. divs. Bold denotes diluted EPS (FASB 128)-prior periods restated. E-Estimated. NA-Not Available. NM-Not Meaningful. NR-Not Ranked. Due to different levels of shs. outstg., the reported EPS for the 1998 individual quarters do not add up to the full year EPS.

Office: 1601 Bryan St, Dallas, TX 75201-3411.
Telephone: 214-812-4600.
Email: investor@txu.com
Website: http://www.txu.com
Chrmn: E. Nye.
Pres & CEO: C.J. Wilder.
EVP & CFO: H.D. Farell.

EVP & Secy: P. Tinkham.
EVP & General Counsel: E. Peterson.
Investor Contact: T. Hogan 214-812-4641.
Dirs: D. C. Bonham, W. M. Griffin, K. Laday, J. E. Little, E. Nye, J. E. Oesterreicher, M. W. Ranger, H. H. Richardson, J. Wilder, E. G. de Planque.

Founded: in 1944.
Domicile: Texas.
Employees: 14,235.
S&P Analyst: Justin McCann/PMW/BK

Tyco International

Recommendation: HOLD ★ ★ ★ ★ ★
SELL | SELL | HOLD | BUY | BUY

12-Month Target Price: $33.00
(as of August 03, 2004)

TYC has an approximate 0.63% weighting in the **S&P 500**

Sector: Industrials
Sub-Industry: Industrial Conglomerates
Peer Group: Conglomerates - Domestic

Summary: This global diversified company provides products and services in the areas of fire and security, electronics, health care, engineered products, plastics and adhesives.

Quantitative Evaluations

S&P Earnings & Dividend Rank: B-

| D | C | B- | B | B+ | A- | A | A+ |

S&P Fair Value Rank: 3

| 1 | 2 | 3 | 4 | 5 |
| Lowest | | | | Highest |

Fair Value Calc.: $32.70 (Slightly Overvalued)

S&P Investability Quotient Percentile

59%

TYC scored higher than 59% of all companies for which an S&P Report is available.

Volatility: Average

| Low | Average | High |

Technical Evaluation: Bullish
Since 11/04, the technical indicators for TYC have been Bullish.

Relative Strength Rank: Strong

75

1 Lowest | Highest 99

Price as of 11/12/04: $34.47   **2004E S&P Core EPS:** $1.25

GAAP Earnings vs. Previous Year
▲ Up   ▼ Down   ► No Change

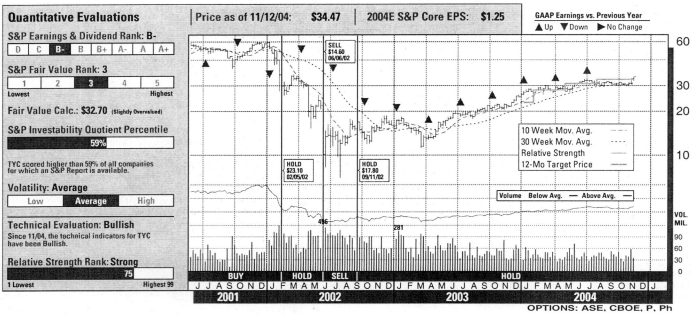

SELL $14.60 06/06/02

HOLD $23.10 02/05/02

HOLD $17.80 09/11/02

10 Week Mov. Avg.
30 Week Mov. Avg.
Relative Strength
12-Mo Target Price

Volume   Below Avg.   ─ Above Avg.

BUY | HOLD | SELL | HOLD

J J A S O N D J F M A M J J A S O N D J F M A M J J A S O N D J F M A M J J A S O N D J
2001 | 2002 | 2003 | 2004

OPTIONS: ASE, CBOE, P, Ph

Analyst commentary prepared by Michael W. Jaffe/CB/BK

Highlights August 27, 2004

- We expect sales to increase 7% in FY 05 (Sep.), on the likely benefits of the healthy economy we forecast. We see health care sales aided by demographic trends, and expect a solid revenue revival in electronics, where demand has picked up after a sizable downturn in recent years. We also expect engineered products and services revenues to be aided by better client markets. However, we see fire and security revenues restricted by soft (although, in our view, firming) commercial construction markets.

- We expect net margins to widen in FY 05, on our outlook for better organic sales, and improved operating efficiencies that we see emanating from TYC's initiatives.

- Our FY 04 operating estimate excludes $0.06 a share of charges in the first nine months of the year from restructuring and divestiture actions, plus the early retirement of a small amount of debt. Our Standard & Poor's Core Earnings estimates for FY 04 and FY 05 are $0.22 and $0.16 a share, respectively, below our operating earnings forecasts, with the differences reflecting projected options and pension plan costs in both years and the inclusion of charges in FY 04.

Investment Rationale/Risk August 27, 2004

- We think TYC operates solid businesses, and has greatly improved its financial footing through certain asset and debt sales in the past two years, and high levels of free cash flow in recent periods. Since his July 2002 appointment to replace Dennis Kozlowski, who was forced out of his leadership posts in mid-2002 by criminal charges, Edward Breen has overseen major changes in upper management, directors and business practices. Based on these factors, valuation metrics and other considerations, we would hold TYC.

- Risks to our recommendation and target price include a worse than expected global economy, and any other negative consequences related to actions of TYC's former leaders.

- The stock recently traded at a little over 17X our FY 05 EPS forecast, a 10% premium to the S&P 500's forward multiple. Tyco's business outlook now appears solid, in our view, but in light of major uncertainties, such as TYC's substantial level of goodwill ($26.1 billion at June 30, 2004) and shareholder lawsuits, we think it is near an appropriate valuation. Our 12-month target price is $33, or about 18X our FY 05 EPS estimate.

Key Stock Statistics

S&P Core EPS 2005E	1.69	52-week Range	$34.47-21.42
S&P Oper. EPS 2004E	1.61	12 Month P/E	33.1
P/E on S&P Oper. EPS 2004E	21.4	Beta	1.82
S&P Oper. EPS 2005E	1.85	Shareholders	34,700
Yield (%)	0.1%	Market Cap (B)	$ 69.1
Dividend Rate/Share	0.05	Shares Outstanding (M)	2005.5

Value of $10,000 invested five years ago: **$ 8,602**

Dividend Data Dividends have been paid since 1975

Amount ($)	Date Decl.	Ex-Div. Date	Stock of Record	Payment Date
0.013	Dec. 11	Dec. 30	Jan. 02	Feb. 02 '04
0.013	Jan. 23	Mar. 30	Apr. 01	May. 03 '04
0.013	May. 12	Jun. 29	Jul. 01	Aug. 02 '04
0.013	Aug. 06	Sep. 29	Oct. 01	Nov. 01 '04

Revenues/Earnings Data Fiscal year ending September 30

Revenues (Million $)

	2004	2003	2002	2001	2000	1999
1Q	9,701	8,927	8,579	8,029	6,639	5,214
2Q	10,041	8,989	8,611	8,810	7,070	5,239
3Q	10,451	9,413	9,104	8,680	7,418	5,820
4Q	—	9,473	9,350	8,517	7,805	6,225
Yr.	—	36,801	35,644	34,037	28,932	22,497

Earnings Per Share ($)

	2004	2003	2002	2001	2000	1999
1Q	0.34	0.28	0.47	0.57	0.46	-0.07
2Q	0.37	0.06	-1.03	0.63	0.50	0.07
3Q	0.43	0.27	-0.23	0.64	0.58	0.12
4Q	E0.41	-0.11	-0.75	0.70	1.12	0.46
Yr.	E1.61	0.52	-1.54	2.55	2.64	0.62

Next earnings report expected: NA Source: S&P, Company Reports
EPS Estimates based on S&P Operating Earnings; historical GAAP earnings are as reported.

Tyco International Ltd.

Recommendation: **HOLD** ★★★☆☆   12-Month Target Price: **$33.00** (as of August 03, 2004)

Business Summary August 27, 2004

Tyco International, a global conglomerate, underwent an executive upheaval in FY 02 (Sep.). In June 2002, Dennis Kozlowski resigned as chairman and CEO, just before being charged with evading over $1 million in New York sales taxes on art purchases. Allegations of misuse of company funds by Mr. Kozlowski and other executives followed, and in September 2002, the Manhattan District Attorney filed charges of financial fraud against Mr. Kozlowski, former CFO Mark Swartz and former counsel Mark Belnick (Mr. Belnick was acquitted of these charges in July 2004). On the same day, the SEC filed a civil fraud suit against the three, and TYC sued Mr. Kozlowski, alleging that he had misappropriated money and assets (it later filed against Messrs. Swartz and Belnick). TYC claimed that starting in 1996, Messrs. Kozlowski and Swartz were the main recipients of over $600 million of unauthorized bonuses, interest-free loans, and forgiveness of these loans.

TYC's subsequent forensic review of its prior accounting and governance practices (concluded in late 2002) did not uncover any systemic fraud, but found several incorrect accounting entries. It also decided that prior management had used aggressive accounting that, even when in accordance with generally accepted accounting principles, inflated earnings. In total, TYC recorded $6.8 billion of pretax charges (as restated) from continuing operations for the year ($3.06 a share, net), with the largest part for the $3.3 billion writedown of its global undersea network.

Operations consist of Fire and Security Services (31% of sales and 8% of operating profits in FY 03, before losses from Tyco Global Network; TGN); Electronics (28%, 30%); Health Care (23%, 50%); Engineered Products and Services (13%, 8%); and Plastics and Adhesives (5%, 4%). Tyco derived 46% of its revenues outside the U.S. in FY 03.

In Fire and Security, TYC is the world's largest fire protection concern, and the largest provider of security solutions to residential, business and governmental customers.

The Electronics division is the world's leading supplier of passive electronic components.

In Health Care, the company is a major provider of medical devices and disposable medical products.

The Engineered Products and Services segment ranks as the world's leading pipe and valve manufacturer.

Plastics and Adhesives mostly makes packaging products.

Tyco completed a review of its core businesses in FY 03's fourth quarter, and started a divestiture and restructuring program. Under the program, TYC planned to sell its TGN undersea fiber optic telecommunications system, as that market has been challenged by major overcapacity. Tyco also started a broader program to increase its focus on core operations, and would exit certain businesses that did not meet its criteria for strategic fit or financial returns. Combined FY 03 revenues of businesses being considered for divestiture totaled $2 billion. TYC recorded $174 million of pretax charges for restructuring and divestiture actions in the first nine months of FY 04. Through June 2004, it had also closed 142 facilities, cut its workforce by 5,300 and exited 17 businesses under the program.

In July 2002, TYC sold 100% of CIT Group for $4.6 billion.

Company Financials Fiscal Year ending September 30

Per Share Data ($)

(Year Ended September 30)	2003	2002	2001	2000	1999	1998	1997	1996	1995	1994
Tangible Bk. Val.	NM	NM	NM	0.42	0.10	NM	1.30	1.15	1.04	0.58
Cash Flow	1.25	-0.52	3.72	3.60	1.40	1.49	0.84	0.64	0.58	0.52
Earnings	0.52	-1.54	2.55	2.64	0.62	1.01	0.65	0.51	0.36	0.34
S&P Core Earnings	0.49	-1.20	2.05	NA	NA	NA	NA	NA	NA	NA
Dividends	0.05	0.05	0.05	0.05	0.05	0.05	0.05	0.05	0.05	0.06
Payout Ratio	10%	NM	2%	2%	8%	5%	8%	10%	14%	19%
Prices - High	27.18	58.81	63.21	59.18	53.87	39.09	22.75	14.00	8.90	6.90
- Low	11.20	6.98	39.24	32.00	22.50	20.12	12.93	8.09	5.81	5.35
P/E Ratio - High	52	NM	25	22	87	39	35	28	18	20
- Low	22	NM	15	12	36	20	20	16	11	16

Income Statement Analysis (Million $)

	2003	2002	2001	2000	1999	1998	1997	1996	1995	1994
Revs.	36,801	35,644	34,037	28,932	22,497	12,311	6,598	5,090	4,535	3,263
Oper. Inc.	5,568	6,509	8,865	7,393	4,977	2,490	899	666	618	312
Depr.	1,472	2,033	2,141	1,644	1,322	566	120	83.0	133	66.2
Int. Exp.	1,148	1,077	777	845	547	236	90.8	62.0	63.0	45.0
Pretax Inc.	1,803	-2,811	6,004	6,465	1,651	1,718	688	524	385	201
Eff. Tax Rate	42.4%	NM	21.4%	29.8%	37.6%	31.5%	39.1%	40.8%	43.7%	38.0%
Net Inc.	1,035	-3,070	4,671	4,520	1,031	1,177	419	310	217	125
S&P Core Earnings	994	-2,369	3,755	NA	NA	NA	NA	NA	NA	NA

Balance Sheet & Other Fin. Data (Million $)

	2003	2002	2001	2000	1999	1998	1997	1996	1995	1994
Cash	4,329	6,383	2,587	1,265	1,762	820	171	69.4	66.0	6.19
Curr. Assets	17,240	19,765	NA	12,816	11,163	5,743	2,447	1,696	1,452	1,048
Total Assets	63,545	66,414	111,287	40,404	32,362	16,527	5,888	3,954	3,381	2,416
Curr. Liab.	10,572	19,632	NA	11,679	9,179	5,048	1,735	1,292	1,085	811
LT Debt	18,251	16,487	38,503	9,462	9,109	4,652	919	512	506	413
Common Equity	26,369	24,791	31,737	17,033	12,333	6,137	3,052	1,938	1,635	1,079
Total Cap.	44,733	41,320	70,542	27,630	21,946	10,847	3,996	2,469	2,151	1,506
Cap. Exp.	1,170	1,709	1,798	1,704	1,633	781	199	123	119	73.0
Cash Flow	2,507	-1,037	6,812	6,165	2,353	1,743	539	393	350	191
Curr. Ratio	1.6	1.0	NA	1.1	1.2	1.1	1.4	1.3	1.3	1.3
% LT Debt of Cap.	40.8	39.9	54.6	34.2	41.5	42.9	23.0	20.7	23.5	27.4
% Net Inc.of Revs.	2.8	NM	13.7	15.6	4.6	9.6	6.4	6.1	4.8	3.8
% Ret. on Assets	1.6	NM	6.2	12.4	3.7	8.7	8.5	8.5	6.6	5.1
% Ret. on Equity	4.1	NM	19.2	30.7	9.3	24.6	16.8	17.4	14.4	12.5

Data as orig. reptd.; bef. results of disc. opers. and/or spec. items. Per share data adj. for stk. divs.; EPS diluted (primary prior to 1998). Yrs. ended Jun. 30 prior to 1998. E-Estimated. NA-Not Available. NM-Not Meaningful.

Office: 90 Pitts Bay Road, Pembroke HM 08, Bermuda.
Telephone: 441-292-8674.
Email: info@tyco.com
Website: http://www.tyco.com
Chrmn & CEO: E. Breen.
EVP & CFO: D.J. FitzPatrick.
EVP & General Counsel: W.B. Lytton.

SVP & Chief Acctg Officer: C.A. Davidson.
SVP & Treas: M. Hund-Mejean.
Investor Contact: E. Arditte 609-720-4621.
Dirs: D. C. Blair, E. D. Breen, G. W. Buckley, B. Duperreault, B. Gordon, J. A. Krol, H. C. McCall, M. J. McDonald, B. R. O'Neill, S. S. Wijnberg, J. B. York.

Auditor: PricewaterhouseCoopers.
Founded: in 1984.
Domicile: Bermuda.
Employees: 258,600.
S&P Analyst: Michael W. Jaffe/CB/BK

Union Pacific

Recommendation: **HOLD** ★★★☆☆
SELL · SELL · HOLD · BUY · BUY

12-Month Target Price: $61.00
(as of October 21, 2004)

UNP has an approximate 0.15% weighting in the **S&P 500**

Sector: Industrials
Sub-Industry: Railroads
Peer Group: Railroads (U.S.) - Major

Summary: UNP operates the largest U.S. railroad, with 33,000 miles of rail serving the western two-thirds of the country.

Quantitative Evaluations

S&P Earnings & Dividend Rank: B

| D | C | B- | **B** | B+ | A- | A | A+ |

S&P Fair Value Rank: 3-

| 1 | 2 | **3** | 4 | 5 |
| Lowest | | | | Highest |

Fair Value Calc.: $61.90 (Slightly Overvalued)

S&P Investability Quotient Percentile

72%

UNP scored higher than 72% of all companies for which an S&P Report is available.

Volatility: Low

| **Low** | Average | High |

Technical Evaluation: Bullish
Since 9/04, the technical indicators for UNP have been Bullish.

Relative Strength Rank: Moderate

61

| 1 Lowest | | Highest 99 |

| Price as of 11/12/04: | **$64.69** | 2004E S&P Core EPS: | **$2.26** |

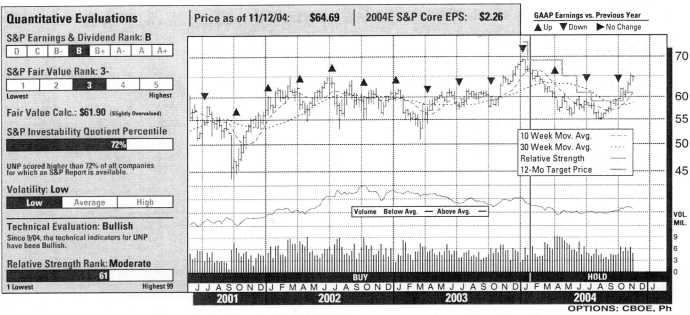

GAAP Earnings vs. Previous Year
▲ Up ▼ Down ► No Change

- 10 Week Mov. Avg.
- 30 Week Mov. Avg.
- Relative Strength
- 12-Mo Target Price

Volume Below Avg. — Above Avg. —

VOL. MIL.

BUY — HOLD

J J A S O N D | J F M A M J J A S O N D | J F M A M J J A S O N D | J F M A M J J A S O N D | J
2001 — 2002 — 2003 — 2004

OPTIONS: CBOE, Ph

Analyst commentary prepared by Andrew West, CFA /PMW/GG

Highlights October 22, 2004

- We forecast 2004 revenue growth of about 5%, reflecting a strengthening U.S. economy. We expect the industrial products, chemicals, and intermodal sectors to lead UNP's growth, with coal shipments up moderately, on increasing production and electric utility demand. We expect revenues in the automobile sector to remain relatively weak. For 2005, we project 5% revenue growth, with higher freight rates making a greater contribution.

- We see rail operating margins weakening in 2004, as system fluidity and efficiency has declined substantially in response to higher freight volumes, and fuel prices reach record highs. We forecast higher capital spending and personnel expenses targeted at removing bottlenecks and repairing customer service perceptions, and higher depreciation charges. Interest expense should decrease, on lower debt levels and rates. We expect gradually improving system fluidity to help margins improve in 2005.

- We estimate 2004 EPS of $2.70, down 34% from 2003's EPS from continuing operations of $4.07. We project a 59% increase in 2005, to $4.30. Our 2004 S&P Core EPS estimate is $2.26, reflecting estimated stock option and pension expenses.

Investment Rationale/Risk October 22, 2004

- We expect the stock to perform in line with the S&P 500 over the next 12 months. We view valuation as fair, based on our longer-term outlook, as we expect current operational difficulties to be gradually overcome. We see performance linked to a demonstration by UNP that it can improve efficiency and service levels. We project historically weak 2004 free cash flow of under $700 million, recovering to about $1.4 billion in six years ($1.6 billion for earnings).

- Risks to our opinion and target price include the possibility that system fluidity may be impaired longer or cost more to remedy than expected, sustained high fuel prices, severe weather, weaker than expected economic activity, and interest rate volatility.

- Our discounted cash flow model, which assumes a 7% cost of capital and a 3% terminal growth rate, sets value at $60. Our relative valuation model, correlating historical peer group valuations with profitability and leverage, suggests a forward price to sales multiple of 1.3X, and a price of $61. Combining our models leads to our 12-month target price of $61.

Key Stock Statistics

S&P Core EPS 2005E	3.96	52-week Range	$69.56-54.80
S&P Oper. EPS 2004E	2.70	12 Month P/E	21.0
P/E on S&P Oper. EPS 2004E	24.0	Beta	0.36
S&P Oper. EPS 2005E	4.30	Shareholders	32,364
Yield (%)	1.9%	Market Cap (B)	$ 16.8
Dividend Rate/Share	1.20	Shares Outstanding (M)	259.6

Value of $10,000 invested five years ago: **$ 13,566**

Dividend Data Dividends have been paid since 1900

Amount ($)	Date Decl.	Ex-Div. Date	Stock of Record	Payment Date
0.300	Feb. 26	Mar. 08	Mar. 10	Apr. 01 '04
0.300	May. 28	Jun. 07	Jun. 09	Jul. 01 '04
0.300	Jul. 29	Sep. 03	Sep. 08	Oct. 01 '04

Revenues/Earnings Data Fiscal year ending December 31

Revenues (Million $)

	2004	2003	2002	2001	2000	1999
1Q	2,893	2,736	2,967	2,943	2,913	2,740
2Q	3,029	2,894	3,154	2,998	2,979	2,773
3Q	3,076	2,956	3,199	3,026	3,070	2,893
4Q	—	2,965	3,171	3,006	2,952	2,867
Yr.	—	11,551	12,491	11,973	11,878	11,273

Earnings Per Share ($)

	2004	2003	2002	2001	2000	1999
1Q	0.63	0.60	0.86	0.72	0.74	0.52
2Q	0.60	1.10	1.15	0.95	0.96	0.77
3Q	0.77	1.21	1.63	1.04	1.00	0.86
4Q	E0.71	1.28	1.41	1.06	0.63	0.95
Yr.	E2.70	4.07	5.05	3.77	3.34	3.12

Next earnings report expected: late-January Source: S&P, Company Reports
EPS Estimates based on S&P Operating Earnings; historical GAAP earnings are as reported.

Union Pacific Corporation

Recommendation: **HOLD** ★ ★ ★ ☆ ☆   12-Month Target Price: **$61.00** (as of October 21, 2004)

Business Summary October 22, 2004

Following the 2003 sale of its Overnite trucking subsidiary, Union Pacific is focusing on operating the largest U.S. railroad. The Union Pacific rail system (accounting for 89% of revenues in 2003) spans more than 33,000 miles, linking Pacific Coast and Gulf Coast ports to midwest and eastern gateways. The railroad serves the western two-thirds of the U.S., and maintains coordinated schedules with other carriers for the handling of freight to and from the Atlantic Coast, the Pacific Coast, the Southeast, the Southwest, Canada and Mexico.

The company's core business strategy involves providing what it considers premium service for a premium price, a business mix that maximizes profitability, leveraging of volume across the system, increased productivity by working smarter, and maximizing asset utilization. UNP views service reliability and efficiency as linchpins of its strategy, and a key to its ability to take market share from the trucking industry.

UNP's energy transport operations (primarily coal) provided 22% of rail freight revenues and grew 3% in 2003, industrial products 20% and 7%, intermodal 19% and 4%, chemicals 14% and 1%, automotive 11% and 1%, and agricultural 14% and 5%.

Revenue carloads grew 1% in 2003, to 9.2 million; revenue ton-miles grew 3%, to 533 billion; and gross ton miles rose 3%, to a record 1.0 trillion. From 1999 to 2003, million gross ton miles per employee rose from 17.3 to 22.0.

The railroad completed the integration of the Southern Pacific's railroad assets in 2001; these assets were acquired in 1996, for $4.1 billion, significantly expanding operations. Between mid-1997 and late 1998, UNP experienced serious operating problems on its rail system. Part of the problem stemmed from difficulties in integrating the information systems of the Southern Pacific and Union Pacific railroads. In 1999, service returned to normal levels, but UNP incurred $45 million of charges due to the merger. In 2000 and 2001, the company incurred additional costs of $10 million and $89 million, respectively, to integrate Southern Pacific. In 1995, the company acquired Chicago and North Western.

Overnite Corp. (10.5% of 2002 revenues), a trucking company, was sold in an October 2003 IPO, raising net proceeds of about $610 million, and rendering it a discontinued operation in 2003.

Other operations include the development and expansion of the company's technology and telecommunication assets, and self-insurance.

Included in 2004 first quarter expenses was a charge related to an Arkansas Supreme Court decision upholding a $35.8 million jury verdict, including interest, against the railroad for a 1998 grade-crossing accident. In addition, UNP recorded a $38.6 million reduction in state tax liabilities.

In July 2004, UNP indicated that 2004 capital spending would be $2.25 billion, with increased acquisitions and the rental of locomotives. The company anticipated that train crews would increase to 18,500, from 16,685, to handle traffic growth and congestion.

Company Financials Fiscal Year ending December 31

Per Share Data ($)

(Year Ended December 31)	2003	2002	2001	2000	1999	1998	1997	1996	1995	1994
Tangible Bk. Val.	47.85	41.99	38.30	35.07	32.29	29.93	30.79	30.51	26.62	20.36
Cash Flow	7.92	9.19	7.87	7.34	6.91	1.78	5.97	6.86	6.15	9.55
Earnings	4.07	5.05	3.77	3.34	3.12	-2.57	1.74	3.36	3.01	4.66
S&P Core Earnings	3.76	3.83	2.82	NA	NA	NA	NA	NA	NA	NA
Dividends	0.99	0.83	0.80	0.80	0.80	1.03	1.72	1.72	1.72	1.66
Payout Ratio	24%	16%	21%	24%	26%	NM	99%	51%	57%	36%
Prices - High	69.50	65.15	60.70	52.81	67.87	63.75	72.98	74.50	70.12	67.12
- Low	50.90	52.99	43.75	34.25	39.00	37.31	56.25	48.25	45.62	43.75
P/E Ratio - High	17	13	16	16	22	NM	42	22	23	14
- Low	13	10	12	10	13	NM	32	14	15	9

Income Statement Analysis (Million $)

	2003	2002	2001	2000	1999	1998	1997	1996	1995	1994
Revs.	11,551	12,491	11,973	11,878	11,273	10,553	11,079	8,786	7,486	7,798
Oper. Inc.	3,200	3,530	2,072	2,043	2,887	1,446	2,296	2,295	1,983	2,501
Depr.	1,067	1,206	1,174	1,140	1,083	1,070	1,043	762	642	1,005
Int. Exp.	574	633	701	723	733	714	605	501	450	337
Pretax Inc.	1,637	2,016	1,533	1,310	1,202	-696	676	1,113	933	1,419
Eff. Tax Rate	35.5%	33.5%	37.0%	35.7%	34.9%	NM	36.1%	34.1%	33.7%	32.5%
Net Inc.	1,056	1,341	966	842	783	-633	432	733	619	958
S&P Core Earnings	972	1,003	708	NA	NA	NA	NA	NA	NA	NA

Balance Sheet & Other Fin. Data (Million $)

	2003	2002	2001	2000	1999	1998	1997	1996	1995	1994
Cash	527	369	113	105	175	176	90.0	191	230	121
Curr. Assets	2,089	2,152	1,542	1,285	1,314	1,502	1,415	1,334	1,679	1,822
Total Assets	33,460	32,764	31,551	30,499	29,888	29,374	28,764	27,914	19,446	15,942
Curr. Liab.	2,456	2,701	2,692	2,962	2,885	2,932	3,247	3,056	1,899	2,505
LT Debt	7,822	8,928	9,386	9,644	9,926	10,011	8,285	7,900	6,232	4,090
Common Equity	12,354	10,651	9,575	8,662	8,001	7,393	8,225	8,225	6,364	5,131
Total Cap.	29,345	28,057	26,843	25,449	24,642	23,712	22,762	22,064	16,310	12,077
Cap. Exp.	1,752	1,887	1,736	1,783	1,834	2,111	2,101	1,360	1,058	1,597
Cash Flow	2,123	2,547	2,140	1,982	1,866	437	1,475	1,495	1,261	1,963
Curr. Ratio	0.9	0.8	0.6	0.4	0.5	0.5	0.4	0.4	0.9	0.7
% LT Debt of Cap.	26.7	31.8	35.0	37.9	40.3	42.2	36.3	35.8	38.2	33.9
% Net Inc.of Revs.	9.1	10.7	8.1	7.1	6.9	NM	3.9	8.3	8.3	12.8
% Ret. on Assets	3.2	4.2	3.1	2.8	2.6	NM	1.5	3.1	3.7	6.2
% Ret. on Equity	9.2	13.3	10.6	10.1	10.2	NM	5.3	10.0	10.8	19.1

Data as orig reptd.; bef. results of disc opers/spec. items. Per share data adj. for stk. divs.; EPS diluted (primary prior to 1998). E-Estimated. NA-Not Available. NM-Not Meaningful. NR-Not Ranked. UR-Under Review.

Office: 1416 Dodge Street, Omaha, NE 68179.
Telephone: 402-271-5777.
Website: http://www.up.com
Chrmn, Pres & CEO: R.K. Davidson.
COO: I.J. Evans.
EVP & CFO: J. Young.

SVP, Secy & General Counsel: C.W. von Bernuth.
VP, Treas & Investor Contact: M.S. Jones 402-271-6111.
Dirs: P. F. Anschutz, R. K. Davidson, E. B. Davis, Jr., T. J. Donohue, A. W. Dunham, S. F. Eccles, I. Evans, E. T. Gerry, Jr., J. R. Hope, R. J. Mahoney, E. Z. Ponce de Leon, S. R. Rogel.

Founded: in 1862.
Domicile: Utah.
Employees: 46,400.
S&P Analyst: Andrew West, CFA /PMW/GG

Unisys Corp.

Recommendation: **SELL** ★ ☆ ☆ ☆ ☆
SELL | SELL | HOLD | BUY | BUY

12-Month Target Price: $10.00
(as of July 15, 2004)

UIS has an approximate 0.03% weighting in the **S&P 500**

Sector: Information Technology
Sub-Industry: IT Consulting & Other Services
Peer Group: Information Technology Services - Larger Cos.

Summary: Unisys is a leading worldwide supplier of information services and technology solutions to more than 60,000 customers in 100 countries.

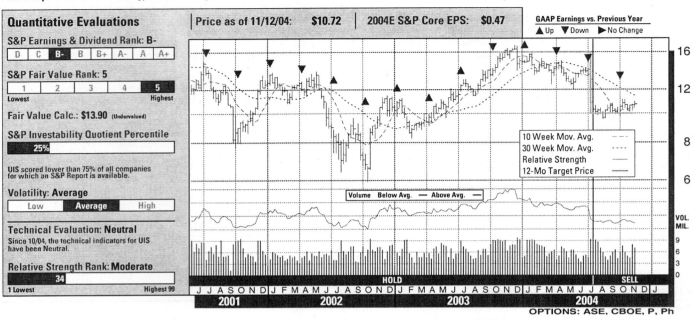

Quantitative Evaluations

S&P Earnings & Dividend Rank: B-

| D | C | B- | B | B+ | A- | A | A+ |

S&P Fair Value Rank: 5

| 1 | 2 | 3 | 4 | 5 |
| Lowest | | | | Highest |

Fair Value Calc.: $13.90 (Undervalued)

S&P Investability Quotient Percentile

| 25% |

UIS scored lower than 75% of all companies for which an S&P Report is available.

Volatility: Average

| Low | Average | High |

Technical Evaluation: Neutral
Since 10/04, the technical indicators for UIS have been Neutral.

Relative Strength Rank: Moderate

| 34 |
| 1 Lowest | Highest 99 |

Price as of 11/12/04: $10.72 | **2004E S&P Core EPS:** $0.47

GAAP Earnings vs. Previous Year
▲ Up ▼ Down ► No Change

- 10 Week Mov. Avg.
- 30 Week Mov. Avg.
- Relative Strength
- 12-Mo Target Price

Volume Below Avg. — Above Avg.

HOLD | SELL

J J A S O N D | J F M A M J J A S O N D | J F M A M J J A S O N D | J F M A M J J A S O N D | J
2001 | 2002 | 2003 | 2004

OPTIONS: ASE, CBOE, P, Ph

Analyst commentary prepared by Stephanie S. Crane /CB/GG

Highlights October 22, 2004

- We expect revenues to increase 1% in 2004, following a 5% rise in 2003, due to slower momentum in UIS's services business, with weakness persisting in the company's hardware segment. We see an eventual upturn in 2005 being driven by a likely pickup in IT spending, as corporations begin to allocate funds to new projects.

- In the third quarter of 2004, revenues and earnings at UIS declined versus 2003, falling short of expectations due to weakness in both the services and technology businesses, a departure from consistent growth exhibited in the past six quarters. The disappointment came from deferrals in enterprise server contracts in the second quarter that provided lower revenue than originally expected.

- We look for operating margins of 3.3%, narrowing from the 7% witnessed in 2003, on weaker revenues in the second half of 2004. We project SG&A expenses at 19% of revenues, reflecting the benefits of continued cost control efforts. We estimate 2004 EPS of $0.68, after accounting for $0.19 of pension expenses. Our 2005 EPS estimate is $1.07. Our Standard & Poor's Core Earnings estimate for 2004 is $0.47, based on projected stock option expense.

Investment Rationale/Risk October 22, 2004

- We recommend avoiding the shares. We believe the strong performance of the stock over the past year was due, in part, to the company's position in the IT services industry, which we believe is benefiting from a growing outsourcing trend. However, we think the company's hardware business, which accounted for 21% of 2003 revenues, is unlikely to improve significantly over the near term, as customers remain cautious in their spending.

- Risks to our recommendation and target price include less than expected competition in the outsourcing and IT services space, which could bolster pricing and relieve pressure on profit margins.

- Our 12-month target price of $10 is based on our relative P/E to growth (PEG) analysis, and on our intrinsic value estimate, using our discounted cash flow (DCF) analysis. Our DCF assumptions include a weighted average cost of capital of 10% and an expected terminal growth rate of 3%.

Key Stock Statistics

S&P Core EPS 2005E	0.77	52-week Range	$16.85-9.57
S&P Oper. EPS 2004E	0.68	12 Month P/E	19.1
P/E on S&P Oper. EPS 2004E	15.8	Beta	1.30
S&P Oper. EPS 2005E	1.07	Shareholders	26,300
Yield (%)	Nil	Market Cap (B)	$ 3.6
Dividend Rate/Share	Nil	Shares Outstanding (M)	335.9

Value of $10,000 invested five years ago: **$ 4,720**

Dividend Data

Common dividends, paid since 1895, were omitted in September 1990. Preferred dividends, suspended in February 1991, were reinstated in January 1993. In February 1994, UIS retired the dividend arrearage on its Series A preferred shares with an $80 million payment.

Revenues/Earnings Data Fiscal year ending December 31

Revenues (Million $)

	2004	2003	2002	2001	2000	1999
1Q	1,463	1,399	1,363	1,624	1,669	1,823
2Q	1,388	1,425	1,360	1,461	1,597	1,896
3Q	1,446	1,450	1,332	1,376	1,691	1,866
4Q	—	1,638	1,553	1,557	1,928	1,960
Yr.	—	5,911	5,607	6,018	6,885	7,545

Earnings Per Share ($)

	2004	2003	2002	2001	2000	1999
1Q	0.09	0.12	0.10	0.22	0.34	0.31
2Q	0.06	0.16	0.13	0.09	0.18	0.37
3Q	0.07	0.17	0.18	0.07	0.14	0.47
4Q	E0.34	0.33	0.27	-0.53	0.12	0.46
Yr.	E0.68	0.78	0.69	-0.16	0.77	1.63

Next earnings report expected: mid-January Source: S&P, Company Reports
EPS Estimates based on S&P Operating Earnings; historical GAAP earnings are as reported.

Unisys Corporation

Recommendation: **SELL** ★ ★ ☆ ☆ ☆   12-Month Target Price: **$10.00** (as of July 15, 2004)

Business Summary October 25, 2004

In recent years, UIS has been making a transition in its business model, in an effort to strengthen its capabilities as a services-led, technology-based solutions provider. As part of this transformation, the company has moved away from low margin, commodity-type products and services toward higher end, value added opportunities, such as business process outsourcing, managed infrastructure services, business consulting, enterprise security, and high end server technology. During this period, the IT services and technology industry has experienced a severe contraction in demand, resulting from a weak economic environment worldwide.

The company operates through two business units: services and technology.

The services segment provides end-to-end services and solutions designed to help clients improve their competitiveness and efficiency in the global marketplace. UIS's portfolio of offerings includes systems integration and consulting; outsourcing, which includes the management of a customer's internal information systems and specific business processes such as payment processing, mortgage administration, and cargo management; infrastructure services involving the design, management and support of customer desktops, servers, mobile and wireless systems, and networks; and enterprise-wide security solutions to protect systems, networks, applications and data. Services revenue provided 80% of total revenue in 2003, up from 76% in 2002, 74% in 2001 and 69% in 2000.

The technology group develops servers and related products designed to operate in transaction intensive, mission critical environments. Major offerings include enterprise class servers based on Cellular MultiProcessing architecture, such as the ClearPath Plus family of servers, which integrates proprietary and open platforms, and the ES7000 family of servers, which provide enterprise class attributes on Intel-based servers; operating system software and middleware to power high-end servers; and specialized technologies, including payment systems, chip testing, and peripheral support products. Revenues from the technology group accounted for 20% in 2003, down from 24% in 2002, 26% in 2001 and 31% in 2000.

The primary vertical markets served by the company worldwide include financial services, communications, transportation, commercial, and the public sector, including the U.S. federal government. Products and services are marketed primarily through a direct sales force.

UIS has a large international presence; export sales accounted for 53% of 2003 revenues, down from 55% in 2002 and 57% in 2001. At December 31, 2003, the company had 24 major facilities in the U.S., with aggregate floor space of about 5.1 million sq. ft., and 24 facilities outside the U.S., with 2.4 million sq. ft. of floor space. International facilities are located primarily in Australia, Brazil, France, Germany, the Netherlands, South Africa, Switzerland, and the U.K.

At December 31, 2003, the company owned about 28% of the voting common stock of Nihon Unisys, Ltd., a publicly traded Japanese company. Nihon is the exclusive supplier of UIS's hardware and software products in Japan.

Company Financials Fiscal Year ending December 31

Per Share Data ($)

(Year Ended December 31)	2003	2002	2001	2000	1999	1998	1997	1996	1995	1994
Tangible Bk. Val.	3.65	2.12	6.06	6.89	6.29	0.38	NM	NM	NM	NM
Cash Flow	1.81	1.16	0.79	1.63	2.51	2.04	1.39	0.91	-2.24	1.69
Earnings	0.78	0.69	-0.16	0.77	1.63	1.06	-5.30	-0.34	-4.37	-0.07
S&P Core Earnings	0.39	-0.56	-1.46	NA	NA	NA	NA	NA	NA	NA
Dividends	Nil	Nil	Nil	Nil	Nil	Nil	Nil	Nil	Nil	Nil
Payout Ratio	Nil	Nil	Nil	Nil	Nil	Nil	Nil	Nil	Nil	Nil
Prices - High	16.85	13.84	19.70	36.06	49.68	35.37	16.50	9.12	11.75	16.50
- Low	8.25	5.92	7.70	9.12	20.93	13.31	5.75	5.37	5.50	8.25
P/E Ratio - High	22	20	NM	47	30	33	NM	NM	NM	NM
- Low	11	9	NM	12	13	13	NM	NM	NM	NM

Income Statement Analysis (Million $)

	2003	2002	2001	2000	1999	1998	1997	1996	1995	1994
Revs.	5,911	5,607	6,018	6,885	7,545	7,208	6,636	6,371	6,202	7,400
Oper. Inc.	770	578	298	698	1,226	1,076	1,722	556	-454	791
Depr.	343	155	302	271	265	266	1,218	228	244	300
Int. Exp.	69.6	66.5	70.0	79.8	128	172	233	250	202	204
Pretax Inc.	381	333	-46.5	379	770	604	-759	93.7	-781	153
Eff. Tax Rate	32.0%	33.0%	NM	35.4%	32.1%	35.9%	NM	34.1%	NM	29.4%
Net Inc.	259	223	-49.9	245	523	387	-854	61.8	-627	108
S&P Core Earnings	132	-183	-463	NA	NA	NA	NA	NA	NA	NA

Balance Sheet & Other Fin. Data (Million $)

	2003	2002	2001	2000	1999	1998	1997	1996	1995	1994
Cash	636	302	326	378	464	605	803	1,035	1,120	885
Curr. Assets	2,258	1,946	2,204	2,587	2,846	2,817	2,887	3,133	3,219	3,142
Total Assets	5,475	4,981	5,769	5,718	5,890	5,578	5,591	6,967	7,113	7,324
Curr. Liab.	2,054	2,185	2,323	2,686	2,619	2,583	2,577	2,465	3,147	2,509
LT Debt	1,048	748	745	536	950	1,105	1,438	2,271	1,533	1,864
Common Equity	1,395	856	2,113	2,186	1,953	97.0	-214	187	290	1,034
Total Cap.	2,444	1,604	2,858	2,722	2,904	2,622	2,644	4,027	3,393	4,469
Cap. Exp.	251	196	199	198	220	207	302	162	195	226
Cash Flow	601	378	252	516	751	546	253	157	-383	288
Curr. Ratio	1.1	0.9	0.9	1.0	1.1	1.1	1.1	1.3	1.0	1.3
% LT Debt of Cap.	42.9	46.6	26.1	19.7	32.7	42.1	54.4	56.4	45.2	41.7
% Net Inc.of Revs.	4.4	4.0	NM	3.6	6.9	5.4	NM	0.1	NM	1.5
% Ret. on Assets	4.9	4.1	NM	4.2	9.1	6.9	NM	NM	NM	1.5
% Ret. on Equity	23.0	15.0	NM	11.8	47.6	NA	NM	NM	NM	NM

Data as orig reptd.; bef. results of disc opers/spec. items. Per share data adj. for stk. divs.; EPS diluted. E-Estimated. NA-Not Available. NM-Not Meaningful. NR-Not Ranked. UR-Under Review.

Office: Unisys Way, Blue Bell, PA 19424.
Telephone: 215-986-4011.
Website: http://www.unisys.com
Chrmn & CEO: L.A. Weinbach.
Pres & COO: J.W. McGrath.
Vice Chrmn: G.R. Gazerwitz.

SVP & CFO: J.B. Haugen.
SVP, Secy & General Counsel: N.S. Sundheim.
VP & Investor Contact: J.F. McHale 215-986-4011.
Dirs: J. P. Bolduc, J. J. Duderstadt, H. C. Duques, M. J. Espe, D. K. Fletcher, G. D. Fosler, R. J. Hogan, E. A. Huston, C. M. Jones, T. E. Martin, L. A. Weinbach.

Founded: in 1886.
Domicile: Delaware.
Employees: 37,300.
S&P Analyst: Stephanie S. Crane /CB/GG

UnitedHealth Group

Recommendation: **HOLD** ★★★☆☆
SELL SELL HOLD BUY BUY

12-Month Target Price: **$71.00**
(as of October 19, 2004)

UNH has an approximate 0.49% weighting in the **S&P 500**

Sector: Health Care
Sub-Industry: Managed Health Care
Peer Group: Managed Care - Large

Summary: This leading health care services company (formerly United HealthCare) provides health benefit services to more than 18.7 million individuals across the U.S.

Quantitative Evaluations

S&P Earnings & Dividend Rank: A

D	C	B-	B	B+	A-	A	A+

S&P Fair Value Rank: 4-

1	2	3	4	5
Lowest				Highest

Fair Value Calc.: $83.30 (Slightly Undervalued)

S&P Investability Quotient Percentile

99%

UNH scored higher than 99% of all companies for which an S&P Report is available.

Volatility: Average

Low	Average	High

Technical Evaluation: Bullish
Since 11/04, the technical indicators for UNH have been Bullish.

Relative Strength Rank: Strong

85

1 Lowest   Highest 99

Price as of 11/12/04: **$81.50**   2004E S&P Core EPS: **$3.70**

GAAP Earnings vs. Previous Year
▲ Up ▼ Down ▶ No Change

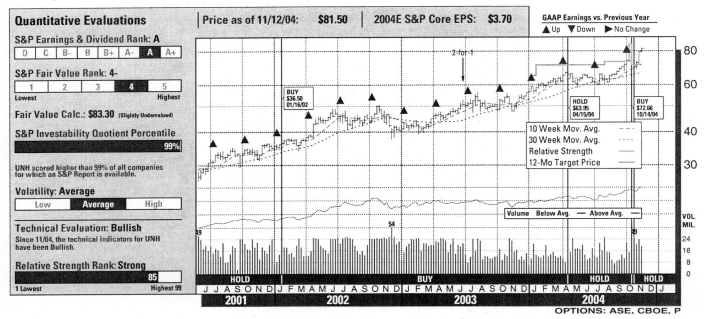

- 10 Week Mov. Avg.
- 30 Week Mov. Avg.
- Relative Strength
- 12-Mo Target Price

Volume Below Avg. —— Above Avg.

OPTIONS: ASE, CBOE, P

Analyst commentary prepared by Phillip M. Seligman/PMW/JWP

Highlights October 20, 2004

- We project 2005 revenue growth exceeding 20%, to over $44 billion, from our estimated 2004 revenues of about $37 billion. We see the advance driven by the July acquisition of Oxford Health Plans (OHP), an average 9% net premium increase, an increase in enrollment, and continued gains at most, if not all, non-health plan units.

- We expect medical cost trends to rise modestly from 2004's 8% to 8.5% levels, as the positive impact of effective care management and lower drug cost trends is increasingly offset by newer and costlier clinical care technologies. In addition, an increase in utilization trends, particularly in elective situations, is possible, in our view, assuming that the economic recovery is sustained. We expect the SG&A cost ratio to continue to decline, aided by specific, actionable operating cost reductions that the company identified to be in excess of $200 million, and $80 million to $100 million in savings from the OHP merger.

- Despite 54.7 million additional shares outstanding as a result of the OHP acquisition, we believe EPS should continue to grow at 20% or more annually at least for the next three to five years. For 2005, we see EPS of $4.75, up 21% from our 2004 EPS estimate of $3.92. Our 2004 and 2005 Standard & Poor's Core EPS projections, reflecting estimated stock option expense, are $3.70 and $4.50, respectively, about 5% below our corresponding operating EPS estimates.

Investment Rationale/Risk October 20, 2004

- We believe that UNH has shown strong, consistent performance, and continues to have a robust operating outlook. Nevertheless, we do not anticipate much price appreciation for the shares for the foreseeable future. A recent sectorwide plunge in shares of managed care organizations suggests to us that investors are concerned about a possible probe of the sector by New York Attorney General Spitzer, and about the outcome of the U.S. presidential election. We also think that recent news of the managed care sector's high profits, while its accounts face high premium rates, will put pressure on future premium rate hikes.

- Risks to our recommendation and target price include a potential government probe, election uncertainty, increased competition, higher than expected medical costs, lower than expected premium yields, and a weaker job market.

- We applied a forward P/E multiple of 15X, modestly above peer levels, to our 2005 EPS estimate of $4.75, to arrive at our 12-month target price of $71. With the shares trading near our target price, we would hold current positions.

Key Stock Statistics

S&P Core EPS 2005E	4.50	52-week Range	$82.20-48.83
S&P Oper. EPS 2004E	3.92	12 Month P/E	22.2
P/E on S&P Oper. EPS 2004E	20.8	Beta	0.22
S&P Oper. EPS 2005E	4.75	Shareholders	13,361
Yield (%)	0.0%	Market Cap (B)	$ 54.2
Dividend Rate/Share	0.03	Shares Outstanding (M)	664.7

Value of $10,000 invested five years ago: **$ 60,620**

Dividend Data Dividends have been paid since 1990

Amount ($)	Date Decl.	Ex-Div. Date	Stock of Record	Payment Date
a.03	Feb. 06	Mar. 30	Apr. 01	Apr. 16 '04

Revenues/Earnings Data Fiscal year ending December 31

Revenues (Million $)

	2004	2003	2002	2001	2000	1999
1Q	8,144	6,975	6,013	5,680	5,099	4,809
2Q	8,704	7,087	6,078	5,813	5,220	4,858
3Q	9,859	7,238	6,247	5,941	5,369	4,903
4Q	—	7,523	6,682	6,020	5,434	4,992
Yr.	—	28,823	25,020	23,454	21,122	19,562

Earnings Per Share ($)

	2004	2003	2002	2001	2000	1999
1Q	0.88	0.65	0.46	0.32	0.26	0.18
2Q	0.93	0.71	0.51	0.34	0.25	0.19
3Q	1.04	0.77	0.56	0.36	0.27	0.20
4Q	E1.07	0.83	0.60	0.38	0.32	0.23
Yr.	E3.92	2.96	2.13	1.40	1.09	0.80

Next earnings report expected: late-January Source: S&P, Company Reports
EPS Estimates based on S&P Operating Earnings; historical GAAP earnings are as reported.

UnitedHealth Group

Recommendation: **HOLD** ★ ★ ★ ☆ ☆   12-Month Target Price: **$71.00** (as of October 19, 2004)

Business Summary October 20, 2004

UnitedHealth Group, a U.S. leader in healthcare management, provides a broad range of healthcare products and services, including health maintenance organizations (HMOs), point of service (POS) plans, preferred provider organizations (PPOs), and managed fee for service programs. It also offers managed behavioral health services, utilization management, workers' compensation and disability management services, specialized provider networks, and third-party administration services.

The company's products and services use several core competencies, including medical information management, healthcare delivery management, health benefit administration, risk assessment and pricing, health benefit design, and provider contracting and risk sharing. These capabilities allow UNH to provide comprehensive managed care services such as health maintenance organization, insurance and self-funded healthcare coverage products, as well as unbundled healthcare management and cost containment products such as mental health and substance abuse services, utilization review services, specialized provider networks, and employee assistance programs.

UNH operates in six broad markets nationwide, assuming the financial risks of providing healthcare services. Plans charge members a fixed annual premium, while entering into contractual arrangements with independent health care providers to help manage medical and hospital use, quality and costs. At December

31, 2003, risk and fee-based health plan enrollment totaled 9,630,000, including commercial (8,295,000), Medicare (230,000) and Medicaid (1,105,000) members. Its Uniprise segment provides network-based health services, business-to-business transaction services, consumer connectivity, and technology support services to large employers and health plans in return for administrative fees; it generally assumes no responsibility for healthcare costs. At December 31, 2003, Uniprise enrollment totaled 9,060,000. UNH also provided Medicare supplement health insurance products to nearly 4.0 million AARP members at December 31, 2003.

The company also develops and markets specialty services to HMOs, PPOs, insurers, providers, Blue Cross/Blue Shield plans, third-party administrators, employers, labor unions and government agencies. These include care management and benefit administration; transplant networks; workers' compensation and disability management; demand management; geriatric care management; behavioral health; management of dental care benefits; medical stop loss insurance; and third-party administration.

Heath Care Services' UnitedHealthcare division and Uniprise, which together account for 96% of total revenues, serve 18.7 million members through more than 350,000 network physicians and about 3,500 network hospitals throughout the U.S.

UNH acquired Mid Atlantic Medical Services in the 2004 first quarter.

Company Financials Fiscal Year ending December 31

Per Share Data ($)

(Year Ended December 31)	2003	2002	2001	2000	1999	1998	1997	1996	1995	1994
Tangible Bk. Val.	2.47	1.58	1.76	1.23	1.50	2.07	2.95	2.28	2.08	3.60
Cash Flow	3.44	2.53	1.80	1.46	1.13	-0.01	0.76	0.62	0.54	0.50
Earnings	2.96	2.13	1.40	1.09	0.80	-0.28	0.57	0.44	0.39	0.41
S&P Core Earnings	2.74	1.98	1.24	NA	NA	NA	NA	NA	NA	NA
Dividends	0.02	0.02	0.02	0.01	0.01	0.01	0.01	0.01	0.01	0.01
Payout Ratio	1%	1%	1%	1%	1%	NM	1%	2%	2%	2%
Prices - High	58.67	50.50	36.40	31.71	17.50	18.48	15.03	17.25	16.40	13.84
- Low	39.20	33.92	25.25	11.59	9.84	7.39	10.60	7.50	8.53	9.31
P/E Ratio - High	20	24	26	29	22	NM	27	39	42	34
- Low	13	16	18	11	12	NM	19	17	22	23

Income Statement Analysis (Million $)

	2003	2002	2001	2000	1999	1998	1997	1996	1995	1994
Revs.	28,823	25,020	23,454	20,890	19,343	17,106	11,563	9,889	5,511	3,769
Oper. Inc.	3,234	2,441	1,831	1,215	957	619	657	544	549	570
Depr.	299	255	265	247	233	185	146	133	94.5	64.1
Int. Exp.	95.0	90.0	94.0	72.0	49.0	4.00	NM	0.59	0.77	2.16
Pretax Inc.	2,840	2,096	1,472	1,155	894	-46.0	742	581	460	468
Eff. Tax Rate	35.7%	35.5%	38.0%	36.3%	36.5%	NM	38.0%	38.7%	37.0%	38.0%
Net Inc.	1,825	1,352	913	736	568	-166	460	356	286	288
S&P Core Earnings	1,689	1,260	812	NA	NA	NA	NA	NA	NA	NA

Balance Sheet & Other Fin. Data (Million $)

	2003	2002	2001	2000	1999	1998	1997	1996	1995	1994
Cash	2,262	1,831	1,810	1,619	2,151	1,644	1,256	1,647	1,804	1,654
Curr. Assets	6,120	5,174	4,946	4,405	4,568	4,280	2,193	2,740	2,867	1,908
Total Assets	17,634	14,164	12,486	11,053	10,273	9,701	7,623	6,997	6,161	3,489
Curr. Liab.	8,768	8,379	7,491	6,570	5,892	5,342	2,570	2,643	2,434	664
LT Debt	1,750	950	900	650	400	249	19.0	31.0	39.0	24.3
Common Equity	5,128	4,428	3,891	3,688	3,863	4,038	4,534	3,823	3,188	2,795
Total Cap.	6,878	5,378	4,791	4,338	4,263	4,287	4,553	4,354	3,227	2,825
Cap. Exp.	352	419	425	245	196	210	187	165	109	79.6
Cash Flow	2,124	1,607	1,178	983	801	-9.00	577	460	380	352
Curr. Ratio	0.7	0.6	0.7	0.7	0.8	0.8	0.9	1.0	1.2	2.9
% LT Debt of Cap.	25.4	17.7	18.8	15.0	9.4	5.8	0.4	0.7	1.2	0.9
% Net Inc.of Revs.	6.3	43.4	32.9	37.5	2.9	NM	4.0	3.6	5.2	7.6
% Ret. on Assets	11.5	10.1	7.8	6.9	5.7	NM	6.3	5.4	5.9	11.2
% Ret. on Equity	38.2	32.5	24.1	19.5	14.4	NM	10.3	9.3	9.3	14.9

Data as orig reptd.; bef. results of disc opers/spec. items. Per share data adj. for stk. divs. Bold denotes primary EPS - prior periods restated. E-Estimated. NA-Not Available. NM-Not Meaningful. NR-Not Ranked. UR-Under Review.

Office: 9900 Bren Road East, Minnetonka, MN 55343.
Telephone: 952-936-1300.
Website: http://www.unitedhealthgroup.com
Chrmn & CEO: W.W. McGuire.
Pres & COO: S.J. Hemsley.
CFO: P.J. Erlandson.

Secy & General Counsel: D.J. Lubben.
Investor Contact: L. Destefano 952-936-7265.
Dirs: W. C. Ballard, Jr., R. T. Burke, S. Hemsley, J. A. Johnson, T. H. Kean, D. W. Leatherdale, W. W. McGuire, M. O. Mundinger, R. L. Ryan, D. E. Shalala, W. G. Spears, G. R. Wilensky.

Auditor: Deloitte & Touche.
Founded: in 1974.
Domicile: Minnesota.
Employees: 33,000.
S&P Analyst: Phillip M. Seligman/PMW/JWP

United Parcel Service

Recommendation: **BUY** ★★★★
SELL SELL HOLD BUY BUY

12-Month Target Price: **$96.00**
(as of September 27, 2004)

UPS has an approximate 0.86% weighting in the **S&P 500**

Sector: Industrials
Sub-Industry: Air Freight & Logistics
Peer Group: Air Freight & Couriers

Summary: UPS is the world's largest express delivery company, and has established itself as a facilitator of e-commerce.

Quantitative Evaluations

S&P Earnings & Dividend Rank: NR

D	C	B-	B	B+	A-	A	A+

S&P Fair Value Rank: 2

1	**2**	3	4	5
Lowest				Highest

Fair Value Calc.: $73.60 (Slightly Overvalued)

S&P Investability Quotient Percentile

100%

UPS scored higher than 100% of all companies for which an S&P Report is available.

Volatility: Low

Low	Average	High

Technical Evaluation: Bullish
Since 9/04, the technical indicators for UPS have been Bullish.

Relative Strength Rank: Strong

75

1 Lowest		Highest 99

Price as of 11/12/04:	**$84.55**	2004E S&P Core EPS:	**$2.67**

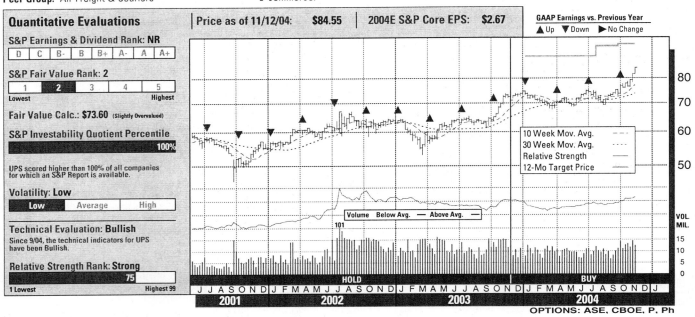

GAAP Earnings vs. Previous Year ▲ Up ▼ Down ► No Change

- 10 Week Mov. Avg.
- 30 Week Mov. Avg.
- Relative Strength
- 12-Mo Target Price

Volume Below Avg. ─ Above Avg. ─

HOLD | BUY

J J A S O N D | J F M A M J J A S O N D | J F M A M J J A S O N D | J F M A M J J A S O N D | J
2001 | 2002 | 2003 | 2004

VOL. MIL.

OPTIONS: ASE, CBOE, P, Ph

Analyst commentary prepared by Jim Corridore/DC/JWP

Highlights November 05, 2004

- We expect 2005 revenues to grow 8%-10%, on top of projected growth of about 10% in 2004. We look for 2005 revenues to be aided by recently enacted rate increases averaging 2.9% for Express, Ground and Deferred Delivery Services; these rate increases were at the high end of the 2.5%-3% increase we were projecting. We see international volumes and revenues rising about 20%, aided by strong export activity out of China. We expect the domestic ground package delivery business to benefit from increased demand and market share gains. We foresee improving demand for UPS's high-yield Next Day Air and domestic deferred delivery services.

- We expect operating margins to widen slightly, as increased fuel costs are offset by fuel surcharges on delivery services, lower compensation costs as a percentage of revenues, and lower purchased transportation costs. We look for the roll-out of the company's new package flow technology to aid margins. UPS estimates that the technology will help it cut costs by $400 million in 2005, and $600 million annually by 2007. We see UPS experiencing fixed cost leverage as a higher revenue base is leveraged over the existing infrastructure.

- We estimate 2004 EPS of $2.95, up 21% from 2003's $2.44 from operations. For 2005, we project EPS of $3.40, up 15% from our 2004 estimate. We forecast Standard & Poor's Core Earnings of $2.67 for 2004 and $3.00 in 2005, reflecting estimated pension and stock option expenses.

Investment Rationale/Risk November 05, 2004

- We think investors are likely to continue to rotate into cargo stocks as the U.S. economy continues to strengthen, and we look for the stock's P/E multiple to expand as UPS benefits from improving industry fundamentals. We think UPS may make other significant acquisitions, on top of the October 2004 announcement that it plans to acquire CNF Inc.'s Menlo Forwarding division. We believe the proposed Menlo purchase adds capabilities in the delivery of large, heavy packages.

- Risks to our recommendation and target price include a possible price war between UPS and FedEx, as well as the possibility that DHL will be successful in its efforts to build a strong U.S. ground business. In addition, UPS is in mediation with its pilots union concerning a new contract. Although we think a settlement will eventually be reached, there is a risk of an eventual strike, in our opinion, as well as a significant rise in labor costs.

- We think the stock can trade at a P/E multiple of 28X our 2005 EPS estimate of $3.40, resulting in our target price of $96. This P/E is toward the high end of the stock's historical range, and at a large premium to the S&P 500. However, we believe it is warranted by UPS's high returns on assets and invested capital, what we view as strong cash from operations, and its position as the world's largest package delivery company.

Key Stock Statistics

S&P Core EPS 2005E	3.00	52-week Range	$84.64-67.51
S&P Oper. EPS 2004E	2.95	12 Month P/E	29.0
P/E on S&P Oper. EPS 2004E	28.7	Beta	NA
S&P Oper. EPS 2005E	3.40	Shareholders	14,409
Yield (%)	1.3%	Market Cap (B)	$ 49.7
Dividend Rate/Share	1.12	Shares Outstanding (M)	1124.4

Value of $10,000 invested five years ago: **NA**

Dividend Data Dividends have been paid since 2000

Amount ($)	Date Decl.	Ex-Div. Date	Stock of Record	Payment Date
0.250	Nov. 13	Nov. 20	Nov. 24	Jan. 05 '04
0.280	Feb. 12	Feb. 19	Feb. 23	Mar. 09 '04
0.280	May. 06	May. 13	May. 17	Jun. 02 '04
0.280	Aug. 12	Aug. 19	Aug. 23	Sep. 08 '04

Revenues/Earnings Data Fiscal year ending December 31

Revenues (Million $)

	2004	2003	2002	2001	2000	1999
1Q	8,919	8,015	7,579	7,510	7,220	6,331
2Q	8,871	8,226	7,682	7,566	7,284	6,560
3Q	8,952	8,312	7,754	7,481	7,400	6,715
4Q	—	8,932	8,257	8,089	7,900	7,446
Yr.	—	33,485	31,272	30,646	29,771	27,052

Earnings Per Share ($)

	2004	2003	2002	2001	2000	1999
1Q	0.67	0.54	0.50	0.48	0.67	0.44
2Q	0.72	0.61	0.54	0.55	0.60	-0.77
3Q	0.78	0.65	0.51	0.50	0.60	0.52
4Q	E0.86	0.75	1.32	0.57	0.63	0.56
Yr.	E2.95	2.55	2.87	2.12	2.50	0.77

Next earnings report expected: late-January Source: S&P, Company Reports
EPS Estimates based on S&P Operating Earnings; historical GAAP earnings are as reported.

United Parcel Service, Inc.

Recommendation: **BUY** ★★★★★   12-Month Target Price: **$96.00** (as of September 27, 2004)

Business Summary November 05, 2004

United Parcel Service is the world's largest express and package delivery company. It is also a leading commerce facilitator, offering various logistics and financial services. The company, which had been privately held since its founding in 1907, made its initial public offering of Class B stock in November 1999.

The company seeks to position itself as the primary coordinator of the flow of goods, information and funds throughout the entire supply chain (the movement from the raw materials and parts stage through final consumption of the finished product). Within the U.S., UPS estimates that it carries goods having a value in excess of 6% of the U.S. gross domestic product, or 2% of the world GDP.

Domestic package delivery services accounted for 75% of revenues in 2003. About 78% of the 12.4 million daily domestic shipments handled by UPS in 2003 was moved by its ground delivery service, which is available to every address in the 48 contiguous states in the U.S. Domestic air delivery is provided throughout the U.S., including next day air, which is guaranteed by 10:00 a.m. to more than 74% of the U.S. population, and by noon to an additional 15% of the population.

UPS entered the international arena in 1975. In 2003, it handled 1.27 million international shipments per day. Its international package delivery service (17% of total revenues in 2003) is growing faster than its domestic business, and this trend is expected to continue over the next few years. In January 2001, the Department of Transportation granted the company the right to fly directly from the U.S. to China; it began direct service in April 2001. In April 2002, UPS opened a new intra-Asia hub in the Philippines, to enable future growth in Asia.

Non-package businesses, 8% of 2003 revenues, comprise a fast growing segment. The Supply Chain Solutions Group provides logistics and distribution services, international trade management, and transportation and freight using multi-modal transportation. UPS Capital provides asset-based lending, global trade finance and export/import lending. UPS Consulting provides supply chain design and re-engineering advice.

In 2003, the company announced plans for significant improvements in its package sorting and delivery systems. UPS expects to invest $600 million over the next several years to simplify and optimize package sorting and delivery. It sees this resulting in significantly improved efficiency, reliability and flexibility. Upon completion, estimated by 2007, the company expects to save about $600 million annually, through productivity improvements and driving about 100 million fewer miles a year.

At December 31, 2003, UPS had about 228,000 employees (64% of the total workforce) employed under a national master agreement with the International Brotherhood of Teamsters. In October 2002, the Teamsters ratified a new agreement that runs through July 31, 2008. At the end of 2003, the company owned, operated or chartered about 600 aircraft, and operated a ground fleet of more than 88,000 vehicles.

Company Financials Fiscal Year ending December 31

Per Share Data ($)

(Year Ended December 31)	2003	2002	2001	2000	1999	1998	1997	1996	1995	1994
Tangible Bk. Val.	12.03	11.09	9.14	8.58	10.31	13.10	5.42	NA	NA	NA
Cash Flow	3.91	4.20	3.41	3.50	1.77	5.15	1.77	1.87	NA	NA
Earnings	2.55	2.87	2.12	2.50	0.77	1.57	0.81	1.01	NA	NA
S&P Core Earnings	2.46	2.48	1.70	NA	NA	NA	NA	NA	NA	NA
Dividends	0.92	0.76	0.76	0.81	Nil	NA	NA	NA	NA	NA
Payout Ratio	36%	26%	36%	32%	Nil	NA	NA	NA	NA	NA
Prices - High	74.87	67.10	62.50	69.75	76.93	NA	NA	NA	NA	NA
- Low	53.00	54.25	46.15	49.50	50.00	NA	NA	NA	NA	NA
P/E Ratio - High	29	23	29	28	NM	NA	NA	NA	NA	NA
- Low	21	19	22	20	NM	NA	NA	NA	NA	NA

Income Statement Analysis (Million $)

	2003	2002	2001	2000	1999	1998	1997	1996	1995	1994
Revs.	33,485	31,272	30,646	29,771	27,052	24,788	22,458	22,368	21,045	19,576
Oper. Inc.	5,994	5,560	5,358	5,685	5,127	4,202	2,761	2,993	NA	NA
Depr.	1,549	1,464	1,396	1,173	1,139	1,112	1,063	964	NA	NA
Int. Exp.	121	173	184	205	228	227	187	95.0	77.0	29.0
Pretax Inc.	4,370	5,009	3,937	4,834	2,088	2,902	1,553	1,910	1,708	1,575
Eff. Tax Rate	33.7%	35.0%	38.4%	39.3%	57.7%	40.0%	41.5%	40.0%	38.9%	40.1%
Net Inc.	2,898	3,254	2,425	2,934	883	1,741	909	1,146	1,043	943
S&P Core Earnings	2,790	2,820	1,948	NA	NA	NA	NA	NA	NA	NA

Balance Sheet & Other Fin. Data (Million $)

	2003	2002	2001	2000	1999	1998	1997	1996	1995	1994
Cash	2,951	2,211	1,616	1,952	6,278	1,629	460	NA	NA	NA
Curr. Assets	9,853	8,738	7,597	7,124	11,138	5,425	4,477	NA	NA	NA
Total Assets	28,909	26,357	24,636	21,662	23,043	17,067	15,912	14,954	12,645	11,182
Curr. Liab.	5,518	5,555	4,629	4,501	4,198	3,717	3,398	NA	NA	NA
LT Debt	3,149	3,495	4,648	2,981	1,912	2,191	2,583	2,573	1,729	1,127
Common Equity	14,852	12,455	10,248	9,735	12,474	7,598	6,087	5,901	5,151	4,647
Total Cap.	18,001	15,950	14,896	12,716	14,386	9,789	8,676	8,474	6,880	NA
Cap. Exp.	1,947	1,658	2,372	2,147	1,476	1,645	1,984	2,333	NA	NA
Cash Flow	4,447	4,718	3,821	4,107	2,022	2,853	1,972	2,110	NA	NA
Curr. Ratio	1.8	1.6	1.6	1.6	2.7	1.5	1.3	NA	NA	NA
% LT Debt of Cap.	17.5	21.9	31.2	23.4	13.3	22.4	29.8	30.4	25.1	19.5
% Net Inc.of Revs.	8.7	10.4	7.9	9.9	3.3	7.0	4.0	5.1	5.0	4.8
% Ret. on Assets	10.5	12.8	10.5	13.1	4.4	10.6	5.9	8.3	8.8	NA
% Ret. on Equity	21.2	28.7	24.3	26.4	8.8	25.4	21.0	20.7	21.3	NA

Data as orig reptd.; bef. results of disc opers/spec. items. Per share data adj. for stk. divs. Bold denotes primary EPS - prior periods restated. E-Estimated. NA-Not Available. NM-Not Meaningful. NR-Not Ranked. UR-Under Review.

Office: 55 Glenlake Parkway N.E., Atlanta, GA 30328.
Telephone: 404-828-6000.
Website: http://www.ups.com
Chrmn & CEO: M. Eskew.
COO & SVP: J. Beystehner.
SVP, CFO & Treas: D.S. Davis.

SVP & Secy: A.E. Hill.
Investor Contact: K. Kuehn 404-828-6977.
Dirs: C. Darden, M. L. Eskew, J. P. Kelly, A. M. Livermore, G. E. MacDougal, V. A. Pelson, L. N. Soupata, R. M. Teeter, J. W. Thompson, C. B. Tome.

Founded: in 1907.
Domicile: Delaware.
Employees: 355,000.
S&P Analyst: Jim Corridore/DC/JWP

U.S. Bancorp

Recommendation: **BUY** ★★★★★   12-Month Target Price: **$35.00**
(as of September 08, 2004)

USB has an approximate 0.52% weighting in the **S&P 500**

Sector: Financials
Sub-Industry: Diversified Banks
Peer Group: Midwest/West Major Regionals

Summary: This bank holding company was formed through the February 2001 merger of Minneapolis-based U.S. Bancorp and Milwaukee-based Firstar Corp.

Quantitative Evaluations

Price as of 11/12/04:	$30.48	2004E S&P Core EPS:	$2.16

S&P Earnings & Dividend Rank: NR

| D | C | B- | B | B+ | A- | A | A+ |

S&P Fair Value Rank: 3+

| 1 | 2 | 3 | 4 | 5 |
| Lowest | | | | Highest |

Fair Value Calc.: $29.50 (Slightly Overvalued)

S&P Investability Quotient Percentile

97%

USB scored higher than 97% of all companies for which an S&P Report is available.

Volatility: Low

| Low | Average | High |

Technical Evaluation: Neutral
Since 11/04, the technical indicators for USB have been Neutral.

Relative Strength Rank: Moderate

56

| 1 Lowest | | Highest 99 |

GAAP Earnings vs. Previous Year
▲ Up ▼ Down ▶ No Change

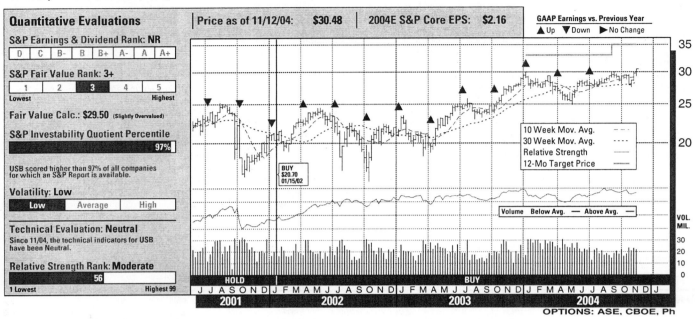

10 Week Mov. Avg.
30 Week Mov. Avg.
Relative Strength
12-Mo Target Price

Volume Below Avg. — Above Avg.

OPTIONS: ASE, CBOE, Ph

Analyst commentary prepared by Evan M. Momios, CFA /PMW/JWP

Highlights September 09, 2004

- We expect loan growth to continue in the low single digits through 2004, as we see growth in commercial lending beginning to accelerate, offsetting slower growth in home equity and mortgage lending. USB is one of the most profitable large cap banks in terms of returns on equity and on assets. We see this reflecting its focus on revenue growth and cost controls, and what we view as its attractive mix of high-margin businesses. More than 40% of revenues are derived from fee-based businesses, including payment processing and asset management.

- We believe earnings growth will accelerate in the second half of 2004, after a stronger first half than we expected, as nonperforming assets continue to decline, the net interest margin begins to expand, and commercial loan growth gradually increases. We expect share repurchases to remain elevated for the remainder of the year, as USB continues to generate excess cash.

- Overall, we see EPS increasing from $1.92 in 2003 to $2.20 in 2004 and $2.45 in 2005, aided by a healthy U.S. economy that we expect. Our respective 2004 and 2005 Standard & Poor's Core Earnings projections of $2.16 and $2.42 reflect estimated small pension plan adjustments.

Investment Rationale/Risk September 09, 2004

- We see USB as well positioned to benefit from an improving economy that we think will lead to accelerating growth in commercial lending, asset management, and payment processing revenues. We also think that the company's retail business will benefit from USB's ongoing expansion in western markets via new in-store branches. We view this as a cost-effective and shareholder friendly way to build revenues, in contrast to making a large acquisition.

- Risks to our recommendation and target price include a severe economic downturn in combination with higher short term interest rates that could result in an inverted yield curve, legal and regulatory risks, and a serious geopolitical event that could hurt U.S. equity markets.

- Our 12-month target price of $35 is supported by our discounted cash flow analysis, which assumes longer-term EPS growth of 11% annually. Our 12-month target price is equivalent to a P/E multiple of about 14X applied to our 2005 EPS estimate, versus a current level of about 13.5X our 2004 EPS estimate. Currently yielding 3.2%, we would buy the shares on a total return basis.

Key Stock Statistics

S&P Core EPS 2005E	2.42	52-week Range	$30.48-24.89
S&P Oper. EPS 2004E	2.20	12 Month P/E	14.9
P/E on S&P Oper. EPS 2004E	13.9	Beta	0.77
S&P Oper. EPS 2005E	2.45	Shareholders	74,340
Yield (%)	3.1%	Market Cap (B)	$ 57.3
Dividend Rate/Share	0.96	Shares Outstanding (M)	1879.3

Value of $10,000 invested five years ago: **NA**

Dividend Data Dividends have been paid since 1863

Amount ($)	Date Decl.	Ex-Div. Date	Stock of Record	Payment Date
0.240	Dec. 16	Dec. 29	Dec. 31	Jan. 15 '04
0.240	Mar. 17	Mar. 29	Mar. 31	Apr. 15 '04
0.240	Jun. 15	Jun. 28	Jun. 30	Jul. 15 '04
0.240	Sep. 15	Sep. 28	Sep. 30	Oct. 15 '04

Revenues/Earnings Data Fiscal year ending December 31

Revenues (Million $)

	2004	2003	2002	2001	2000	1999
1Q	3,576	3,697	3,690	4,420	1,661	1,581
2Q	3,478	3,801	3,813	4,154	1,732	1,597
3Q	—	3,489	3,978	4,026	1,781	1,616
4Q	—	3,584	3,492	3,843	1,824	1,630
Yr.	—	14,571	15,422	16,443	6,998	6,424

Earnings Per Share ($)

	2004	2003	2002	2001	2000	1999
1Q	0.52	0.46	0.41	0.21	0.31	0.29
2Q	0.54	0.48	0.43	0.29	0.32	0.29
3Q	E0.56	0.49	0.45	0.02	0.32	0.03
4Q	E0.58	0.50	0.44	0.36	0.37	0.27
Yr.	E2.20	1.92	1.73	0.88	1.32	0.87

Next earnings report expected: NA Source: S&P, Company Reports
EPS Estimates based on S&P Operating Earnings; historical GAAP earnings are as reported.

U.S. Bancorp

Recommendation: **BUY** ★★★★★   12-Month Target Price: **$35.00** (as of September 08, 2004)

Business Summary September 09, 2004

U.S. Bancorp, headquartered in Minneapolis, is the eighth largest U.S. bank holding company, with $189 billion in assets at December 31, 2003, and about 2,243 banking offices, in 24 states in the Midwest and West.

Operations are divided into four business segments. Consumer banking (41% of net revenues in 2003) offers products and services to the consumer market and small businesses through branch offices, ATMs, telephone customer service and telesales, online banking and direct mail. Payment services (19%) specializes in credit and debit card products, corporate and purchasing card services, and ATM and merchant processing. Private client, trust and asset management (11%) provides mutual fund processing services, trust, private banking and financial advisory services. Wholesale banking (21%) includes lending, depository, treasury management and other financial services to middle-market, large corporate, financial institution and public sector clients. Treasury and corporate support includes the company's investment portfolios, funding, capital management and asset securitization activities, and interest rate risk management.

In 2003, average earning assets, from which interest income is derived, consisted mainly of loans (76%) and investment securities (23%). Average sources of funds included interest-bearing deposits 45%, noninterest-bearing deposits 17%,

short-term borrowings 6%, long-term debt 17%, shareholders' equity 10%, and other 5%.

Nonperforming assets, which include mainly nonperforming loans and other real estate, totaled $1.1 billion (0.97% of loans and other real estate) at December 31, 2003, down from $1.4 billion (1.18%) a year earlier. The allowance for loan losses, which is set aside for possible loan defaults, was $2.37 billion (2.00% of loans) at the end of 2003, down from $2.42 billion (2.08%) a year earlier. Net chargeoffs, or the amount of loans written off as uncollectible, were $1.25 billion (1.06% of average loans) in 2003, versus $1.37 billion (1.20%) in 2002.

In December 2002, USB acquired the corporate trust business of State Street Corp. The transaction boosted assets under administration to $1.36 trillion, one of the highest levels in the corporate trust industry. At December 31, 2003, total assets under administration totalled $1.73 trillion.

In December 2003, the company completed the spinoff of Piper Jaffray Cos. As a result, USB restated historical financial results related to its former subsidiary as discontinued operations. In addition, it recorded a one-time, after-tax charge of $6.7 million in the 2003 fourth quarter.

Company Financials Fiscal Year ending December 31

Per Share Data ($)

(Year Ended December 31)	2003	2002	2001	2000	1999	1998	1997	1996	1995	1994
Tangible Bk. Val.	5.77	4.93	4.64	7.11	4.66	5.38	NA	NA	NA	NA
Earnings	1.92	1.73	0.88	1.32	0.87	0.65	0.78	0.64	0.58	0.55
S&P Core Earnings	1.89	1.59	0.66	NA	NA	NA	NA	NA	NA	NA
Dividends	0.86	0.78	0.75	0.65	0.40	Nil	NA	NA	NA	NA
Payout Ratio	45%	45%	85%	49%	46%	Nil	NA	NA	NA	NA
Prices - High	30.00	24.50	26.06	28.00	35.33	31.31	NA	NA	NA	NA
- Low	18.56	16.05	16.50	15.37	19.56	23.50	NA	NA	NA	NA
P/E Ratio - High	16	14	30	21	41	48	NA	NA	NA	NA
- Low	10	9	19	12	22	36	NA	NA	NA	NA

Income Statement Analysis (Million $)

	2003	2002	2001	2000	1999	1998	1997	1996	1995	1994
Net Int. Inc.	7,189	6,840	6,409	2,699	2,643	1,413	1,366	1,243	1,174	1,112
Tax Equiv. Adj.	28.2	36.6	55.9	45.1	54.3	43.3	40.6	39.1	38.5	39.6
Non Int. Inc.	5,068	5,569	5,030	1,505	1,388	859	770	643	559	NA
Loan Loss Prov.	1,254	1,349	2,529	222	187	114	124	97.0	67.1	NA
Exp./Op. Revs.	45.7%	83.7%	57.5%	55.0%	59.9%	65.7%	57.3%	61.6%	62.7%	NA
Pretax Inc.	5,651	5,103	2,634	1,927	1,413	638	785	624	575	NA
Eff. Tax Rate	34.4%	34.8%	35.2%	31.4%	38.0%	32.6%	34.0%	33.4%	33.7%	NA
Net Inc.	3,710	3,326	1,707	1,284	875	430	519	415	380	358
% Net Int. Marg.	4.49	4.61	4.45	NA	4.09	4.46	NA	NA	NA	NA
S&P Core Earnings	3,655	3,062	1,280	NA	NA	NA	NA	NA	NA	NA

Balance Sheet & Other Fin. Data (Million $)

	2003	2002	2001	2000	1999	1998	1997	1996	1995	1994
Money Mkt. Assets	NA	1,332	1,607	200	897	2.75	150	NA	NA	NA
Inv. Securities	43,334	28,488	26,608	13,866	13,114	6,432	7,196	NA	NA	NA
Com'l Loans	65,768	68,811	71,703	28,498	26,198	15,241	NA	NA	NA	NA
Other Loans	52,467	47,440	42,702	25,208	24,428	10,627	NA	NA	NA	NA
Total Assets	189,286	180,027	171,390	77,585	72,788	38,476	37,100	NA	NA	NA
Demand Deposits	32,470	35,106	31,212	10,980	10,300	10,498	6,181	NA	NA	NA
Time Deposits	86,582	80,428	74,007	45,298	41,586	18,353	21,658	NA	NA	NA
LT Debt	33,816	31,582	28,542	3,877	5,038	1,709	1,371	NA	NA	NA
Common Equity	19,242	18,101	16,461	6,528	6,309	3,530	3,185	NA	NA	NA
% Ret. on Assets	2.0	1.9	1.0	1.7	1.2	1.2	NA	NA	NA	NA
% Ret. on Equity	19.7	19.2	10.8	20.0	13.6	13.7	NA	NA	NA	NA
% Loan Loss Resv.	2.0	2.0	2.1	1.3	1.4	1.5	1.6	NA	NA	NA
% Loans/Deposits	100.5	100.6	111.4	95.4	98.8	89.7	NA	NA	NA	NA
% Equity to Assets	10.2	9.8	9.4	8.5	8.8	8.8	NA	NA	NA	NA

Results prior to 2001 for Firstar Corp.; Data as orig. reptd. (pro forma prior to Star Banc merger); bef. results of disc. opers. and/or spec. items. Per share data adj. for stk. divs. as of ex-div. date. Bold denotes primary EPS. E-Estimated. NA-Not Available. NM-Not Meaningful. NR-Not Ranked.

Office: 800 Nicollet Mall, Minneapolis, MN 55402-7000.
Telephone: 612-973-1111.
Website: http://www.usbank.com
Chrmn & CEO: J.A. Grundhofer.
Pres, Vice Chrmn & COO: R.K. Davis.
Vice Chrmn: A. Cecere.
Vice Chrmn: E. Grzedzinski.

Vice Chrmn: W.L. Chenevich.
Investor Contact: H.D. McCullough 612-303-0786.
Dirs: L. L. Ahlers, A. D. Collins, Jr., P. H. Coors, J. C. Dannemiller, V. B. Gluckman, J. F. Grundhofer, J. A. Grundhofer, D. W. Johnson, J. W. Johnson, J. W. Levin, D. B. O'Maley, O. M. Owens, T. E. Petry, R. G. Reiten, C. D. Schnuck, W. R. Staley, P. T. Stokes, J. J. Stollenwerk.

Founded: in 1929.
Domicile: Delaware.
Employees: 0.
S&P Analyst: Evan M. Momios, CFA /PMW/JWP

United States Steel

Recommendation: **HOLD** ★★★ ☆ ☆
SELL SELL HOLD BUY BUY

12-Month Target Price: $43.00
(as of November 02, 2004)

X has an approximate 0.05% weighting in the **S&P 500**

Sector: Materials
Sub-Industry: Steel
Peer Group: Integrated Steelmakers - Domestic

Summary: This company manufactures and sells a wide variety of steel sheet, plate, tubular and tin products, coke, and taconite pellets.

Quantitative Evaluations

S&P Earnings & Dividend Rank: B-

| D | C | B- | B | B+ | A- | A | A+ |

S&P Fair Value Rank: 2-

| 1 | 2 | 3 | 4 | 5 |
| Lowest | | | | Highest |

Fair Value Calc.: $35.70 (Overvalued)

S&P Investability Quotient Percentile

68%

X scored higher than 68% of all companies for which an S&P Report is available.

Volatility: High

| Low | Average | High |

Technical Evaluation: Bullish
Since 11/04, the technical indicators for X have been Bullish.

Relative Strength Rank: Strong

93

1 Lowest — Highest 99

Price as of 11/12/04: $45.59   **2004E S&P Core EPS:** $4.49

GAAP Earnings vs. Previous Year
▲ Up ▼ Down ► No Change

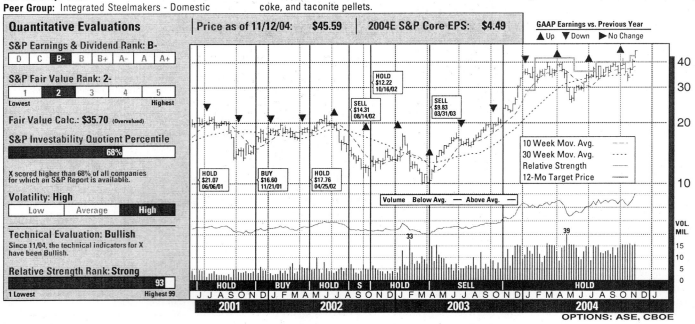

HOLD $12.22 10/16/02
SELL $14.31 08/14/02
SELL $9.83 03/31/03
HOLD $21.07 06/06/01
BUY $16.60 11/21/01
HOLD $17.76 04/25/02

10 Week Mov. Avg.
30 Week Mov. Avg.
Relative Strength
12-Mo Target Price

Volume Below Avg. — Above Avg.

VOL. MIL.

OPTIONS: ASE, CBOE

Analyst commentary prepared by Leo Larkin/MF/BK

Highlights November 04, 2004

- Based on S&P's forecast of 3.5% GDP growth in 2005, versus estimated GDP growth of 4.5% in 2004, we look for 2% sales growth in 2005, versus 50% projected for 2004. In our view, there should be a sharp deceleration in sales growth as a lower average price per ton offsets a forecasted volume gain of 7%. Sharply higher sales in 2004 have reflected higher prices, along with the inclusion of National and Sartid for the full year. Nothwithstanding our expectation for continued economic growth in the U.S. and Europe, we expect to see lower prices due to increased supply. At 2003 year-end, distributor and end user inventories of steel products were low; at the end of 2004, we believe that such inventories will be higher. We also see rising domestic production and increased imports adding to supply in 2005 and placing downward pressure on prices. As a result, we look for declines in operating margins and EPS in 2005.

- X's long-term sales and EPS should benefit from consolidation of the global steel industry and a gradual decline in costs for employee pension and health care.

- According to data compiled by the American Iron and Steel Institute, domestic steel shipments through the first eight months of 2004 rose 9.5%, year to year, while consumption (domestic shipments plus imports minus exports) increased 17%.

Investment Rationale/Risk November 04, 2004

- Following third quarter 2004 EPS, we raised our 12-month target price to $43 on a more positive earnings outlook. Third quarter margins were much better than we anticipated. On that basis, we increased our 2005 estimate to $5.35, from $4.25. We recommend holding X as a highly leveraged special situation turn-around. We believe X's merger with National should lower its costs and increase its future EPS. Adding to X's appeal, in our view, the global market is undergoing consolidation, and the industry appears to be gaining pricing power for the first time in over a decade. However, we wouldn't add to holdings given our belief that 2004 could represent peak cycle EPS.

- Risks to our opinion and target price include asbestos liabilities. In 2003, X incurred litigation expenses totaling $25 million to settle an asbestos-related lawsuit. X has been subject to about 34,000 asbestos claims over the past 12 years, but most have been dismissed or settled for immaterial amounts. While this most recent case could prove to be an aberration, we see it as a cause for concern.

- Recently selling at 7X our 2005 EPS estimate, versus a P/E of 9X for rival Nucor (NUE: hold, $47), X appears expensive given Nucor's superior EPS record and what we see as its much stronger balance sheet. However, we believe that given X's turnaround potential, the shares could sell at about 8X our 2005 estimate, which is at the lower end of their historical range. On that basis, our 12-month target price is $43.

Key Stock Statistics

S&P Core EPS 2005E	3.58	52-week Range	$45.69-22.50
S&P Oper. EPS 2004E	7.05	12 Month P/E	10.1
P/E on S&P Oper. EPS 2004E	6.5	Beta	1.89
S&P Oper. EPS 2005E	5.35	Shareholders	37,800
Yield (%)	0.4%	Market Cap (B)	$ 5.2
Dividend Rate/Share	0.20	Shares Outstanding (M)	113.7

Value of $10,000 invested five years ago: **$ 18,317**

Dividend Data Dividends have been paid since 1991

Amount ($)	Date Decl.	Ex-Div. Date	Stock of Record	Payment Date
0.050	Jan. 27	Feb. 13	Feb. 18	Mar. 10 '04
0.050	Apr. 27	May. 17	May. 19	Jun. 10 '04
0.050	Jul. 27	Aug. 16	Aug. 18	Sep. 10 '04
0.050	Oct. 26	Nov. 15	Nov. 17	Dec. 10 '04

Revenues/Earnings Data Fiscal year ending December 31

Revenues (Million $)

	2004	2003	2002	2001	2000	1999
1Q	2,963	1,898	1,434	1,564	1,582	1,211
2Q	3,466	2,362	1,807	1,737	1,629	1,304
3Q	3,729	2,508	1,914	1,660	1,462	1,334
4Q	—	2,681	1,899	1,414	1,417	1,462
Yr.	—	9,458	7,054	6,375	6,090	5,380

Earnings Per Share ($)

	2004	2003	2002	2001	2000	1999
1Q	0.36	-0.35	-0.93	-0.10	0.45	-0.13
2Q	1.62	-0.01	0.28	-0.34	0.62	0.59
3Q	2.72	-3.47	1.04	-0.26	0.19	-0.37
4Q	E2.35	-0.26	0.10	-1.95	-1.59	0.35
Yr.	E7.05	-4.09	0.62	-2.45	-0.33	0.48

Next earnings report expected: late-January Source: S&P, Company Reports
EPS Estimates based on S&P Operating Earnings; historical GAAP earnings are as reported.

United States Steel Corporation

Recommendation: **HOLD** ★ ★ ★ ☆ ☆   12-Month Target Price: **$43.00** (as of November 02, 2004)

Business Summary November 04, 2004

On December 31, 2001, USX Corp. announced the completion of the tax-free spinoff of its steel and steel-related businesses into a freestanding, publicly traded company known as United States Steel Corporation (X). On January 2, 2002, X began trading on the New York Stock Exchange as an independent company.

In 2003, domestic shipments totaled 14.4 million tons, versus 10.7 million tons in 2002. Revenue per ton was $426, versus $427 in 2002. In 2003, there was an operating loss per ton of $5, versus a per ton loss of $3 in 2002.

In 2003, domestic raw steel production totaled 14.9 million tons, versus 11.5 million tons in 2002. Domestic raw steel capacity utilization was 88.3% in 2003, versus 90.1% in 2002.

In November 2000, X acquired U.S. Steel Kosice s.r.o (USSK), a holding company for the steel and related assets of VSZ a.s., for a cash price of $69 million. Located in Kosice, Slovakia, VSZ's steel operations produce flat roll sheet and tin mill products for sale within a 375-mile radius of Kosice. USSK had shipments of 4.8 million tons in 2003, versus 3.9 million tons in 2002. Revenue per ton was $358, versus $276 in 2002. Per ton profit was $42 in 2003, versus $28 in 2002. USSK's production totaled 4.8 million tons in 2003, versus 4.4 million tons in 2002.

On May 20, 2003, X completed its acquisition of National Steel, for an aggregate purchase price of about $1.05 billion, consisting of about $850 million in cash, and the assumption of certain liabilities totaling about $200 million. As a result, its

U.S.-based operations have about 17 million tons of capacity. X estimated that the merged company would achieve annual cost savings of about $400 million by the end of 2004, via workforce reductions, operational synergies, and administrative cost reductions.

On September 12, 2003, a wholly owned subsidiary of X completed the acquisition of Serbian steelmaker Sartid a.d. (Sartid) and related subsidiaries for some $23 million. Sartid is an integrated steelmaker with some 2.4 million tons of capacity.

In the 2003 third quarter, X incurred a $618 million pretax charge ($3.89 a share) in connection with a planned workforce reduction. The charges consist of cash payments totaling $113 million, $408 million in pension and other post-retirement curtailment losses, and pension settlement losses of $97 million. The quarter also included a pretax asset impairment charge of $46 million from a non-monetary asset exchange.

On April 19, 2004, X redeemed $187 million principal amount of its 10 3/4% senior notes at a 10.75% premium, resulting in a reduction in the principal amount outstanding to $348 million. It also redeemed $72 million principal amount of its 9 3/4% senior notes at a 9.75% premium, resulting in a reduction of the principal amount outstanding to $378 million. The redemptions were funded out of $294 million in net proceeds from the sale of 8.0 million shares of X's common stock at $38.50 a share in March 2004.

Company Financials Fiscal Year ending December 31

Per Share Data ($)

(Year Ended December 31)	2003	2002	2001	2000	1999	1998	1997	1996	1995	1994
Tangible Bk. Val.	7.98	15.81	28.16	21.54	23.22	22.22	18.78	14.38	16.11	11.25
Cash Flow	-0.57	4.24	1.42	3.72	3.93	6.72	7.89	6.49	7.86	6.52
Earnings	-4.09	0.62	-2.45	-0.33	0.48	3.92	4.88	3.00	3.53	2.35
S&P Core Earnings	-1.06	-4.10	-8.47	NA	NA	NA	NA	NA	NA	NA
Dividends	0.20	0.20	0.55	1.00	1.00	1.00	1.00	1.00	1.00	1.00
Payout Ratio	NM	32%	NM	NM	NM	26%	20%	33%	28%	43%
Prices - High	37.05	22.00	22.00	32.93	34.25	43.06	40.75	37.87	39.12	45.62
- Low	9.61	10.66	13.00	12.68	21.75	20.43	25.37	24.12	29.12	30.25
P/E Ratio - High	NM	35	NM	NM	71	11	8	13	11	19
- Low	NM	17	NM	NM	45	5	5	8	8	13

Income Statement Analysis (Million $)

	2003	2002	2001	2000	1999	1998	1997	1996	1995	1994
Revs.	9,458	7,054	6,286	6,090	5,380	6,189	6,814	6,547	6,456	6,066
Oper. Inc.	316	478	-150	422	520	763	949	652	815	627
Depr.	363	350	344	360	304	283	303	292	318	314
Int. Exp.	148	136	153	115	75.0	53.0	98.0	128	142	160
Pretax Inc.	-860	13.0	-546	-1.00	76.0	537	686	367	453	248
Eff. Tax Rate	NM	NM	NM	NM	32.9%	32.2%	34.1%	25.1%	33.1%	19.0%
Net Inc.	-406	61.0	-218	-21.0	51.0	364	452	275	303	201
S&P Core Earnings	-109	-398	-755	NA	NA	NA	NA	NA	NA	NA

Balance Sheet & Other Fin. Data (Million $)

	2003	2002	2001	2000	1999	1998	1997	1996	1995	1994
Cash	316	243	147	219	22.0	9.00	18.0	23.0	52.0	20.0
Curr. Assets	3,107	2,440	2,073	2,717	1,981	1,275	1,531	1,428	1,444	1,780
Total Assets	7,838	7,977	8,337	8,711	7,525	6,693	6,694	6,580	6,521	6,480
Curr. Liab.	2,130	1,372	1,259	1,391	1,266	1,016	1,334	1,299	1,519	1,267
LT Debt	1,890	1,408	1,434	2,485	1,151	712	456	1,014	923	1,432
Common Equity	867	2,027	2,506	1,917	2,053	2,090	1,634	1,559	1,337	913
Total Cap.	2,989	3,658	4,672	5,070	3,555	2,805	2,486	2,644	2,331	2,441
Cap. Exp.	316	258	287	244	287	310	261	337	324	248
Cash Flow	-59.0	411	126	331	346	638	742	545	621	490
Curr. Ratio	1.5	1.8	1.6	2.0	1.6	1.3	1.1	1.1	1.0	1.4
% LT Debt of Cap.	63.2	38.5	30.7	49.0	32.4	25.4	18.3	38.4	39.6	58.7
% Net Inc.of Revs.	NM	0.9	NM	NM	0.9	5.9	6.6	4.2	4.7	3.3
% Ret. on Assets	NM	0.7	NM	NM	0.7	5.4	6.8	4.2	4.7	3.0
% Ret. on Equity	NM	2.7	NM	NM	2.0	18.4	31.7	17.5	12.4	22.8

Data as orig reptd.; bef. results of disc opers/spec. items. Per share data adj. for stk. divs.; EPS diluted. E-Estimated. NA-Not Available. NM-Not Meaningful. NR-Not Ranked. UR-Under Review.

Office: 600 Grant Street, Pittsburgh, PA 15219-2800.
Telephone: 412-433-1121.
Email: shareholderservices@uss.com
Website: http://www.ussteel.com
Chrmn: T.J. Usher.
Pres & CEO: J.P. Surma, Jr.

Vice Chrmn, Secy & General Counsel: D.D. Sandman.
EVP & CFO: G.R. Haggerty.
VP & Treas: L.T. Brockway.
Investor Contact: J.J. Quaid 412-433-1184.
Dirs: J. G. Cooper, R. J. Darnall, J. Drosdick, S. A. Jackson, C. R. Lee, F. Lucchino, D. D. Sandman, S. E. Schofield, T. Usher, D. C. Yearley.

Founded: in 2001.
Domicile: Delaware.
Employees: 47,000.
S&P Analyst: Leo Larkin/MF/BK

United Technologies

Recommendation: **HOLD** ★★★☆☆
SELL SELL HOLD BUY BUY

12-Month Target Price: **$100.00**
(as of September 27, 2004)

UTX has an approximate 0.45% weighting in the **S&P 500**

Sector: Industrials
Sub-Industry: Aerospace & Defense
Peer Group: Aerospace/Transportation/Defense

Summary: This company's business portfolio includes Pratt & Whitney jet engines, Sikorsky helicopters, Otis elevators and Carrier air conditioners.

Quantitative Evaluations

Price as of 11/12/04:	**$97.75**	2004E S&P Core EPS:	**$4.00**

S&P Earnings & Dividend Rank: A+

D	C	B-	B	B+	A-	A	**A+**

S&P Fair Value Rank: 3-

1	2	**3**	4	5
Lowest				Highest

Fair Value Calc.: $96.30 (Fairly Valued)

S&P Investability Quotient Percentile

99%

UTX scored higher than 99% of all companies for which an S&P Report is available.

Volatility: Low

Low	Average	High

Technical Evaluation: Bullish

Since 11/04, the technical indicators for UTX have been Bullish.

Relative Strength Rank: Moderate

53

1 Lowest	Highest 99

GAAP Earnings vs. Previous Year
▲ Up ▼ Down ► No Change

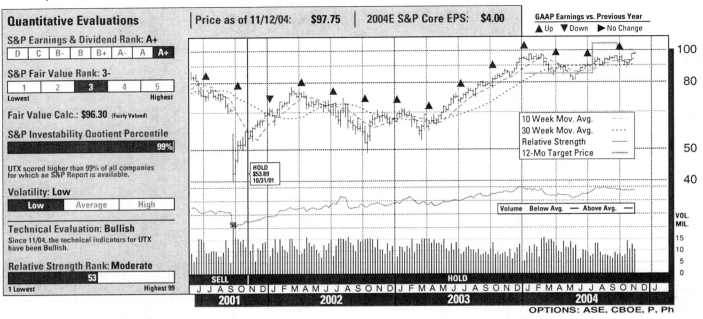

- 10 Week Mov. Avg.
- 30 Week Mov. Avg.
- Relative Strength
- 12-Mo Target Price

HOLD
$53.89
10/31/01

Volume Below Avg. — Above Avg. —

SELL   HOLD
J J A S O N D J F M A M J J A S O N D J F M A M J J A S O N D J F M A M J J A S O N D J
2001   2002   2003   2004

OPTIONS: ASE, CBOE, P, Ph

VOL.
MIL.
15
10
5
0

Analyst commentary prepared by Robert Friedman/MF/JWP

Highlights September 27, 2004

- We believe incremental sales from acquisitions, solid organic growth and a weak U.S. dollar will help propel a 7%+ increase in 2005 revenues. However, we think the ailing airline industry and sluggish Boeing and Airbus production rates will continue to restrict near-term demand for UTX's jet engines, aircraft components and overhaul services. In addition, we expect the potential for moderating residential and commercial building starts to hamper near-term demand for Carrier heating, ventilating and air conditioning (HVAC) systems.

- However, we think strong sales growth in the Otis Elevator segment and ongoing cost cutting will allow UTX to boost EBIT margins to the 14% level. In the absence of expected $500 million in 2004 restructuring charges, we project that in 2005, UTX should post a 10%+ operating EPS increase, to $6.22; a 30%+ S&P Core EPS increase, to $5.31; and ROE of 19%.

- Looking at UTX's long-term prospects, we believe the company's ongoing migration toward operating businesses that generate recurring earnings streams and solid returns on capital will allow it to produce a respectable debt-adjusted return on equity (ROE) of 17%. However, in our opinion, UTX's large capital base and mature end markets may prevent long-term free cash flow from expanding at a greater than 8.5% compound annual growth rate (CAGR).

Investment Rationale/Risk September 27, 2004

- We are maintaining our hold opinion on UTX, as the stock is trading only at a modest discount to our DCF-based 12-month target price of $100.

- Risks to our recommendation and target price include unexpected structural deterioration in the economics of UTX's aerospace and industrial businesses, which, in turn, could force UTX to post 10-year free cash EPS growth at lower rates than our 8.5% CAGR projection, and ROE lower than our 17% estimate.

- Our free cash flow model (which assumes free cash earnings growing at an 8.5% CAGR over the next 10 years, and 3% thereafter) leads to our 12-month target price of $100. We calculated our 10-year free cash flow CAGR of 8.5% by multiplying our 17% ROE estimate by our projected earnings retention ratio of 50%. We believe another valuation metric, which compares a company's earnings yield to 10-year AAA-rated bond yields, gives credence to our hold recommendation. Based on our 2004 S&P Core EPS estimate of $4.00, the stock is sporting an earnings yield of 4.4%, near 10-year AAA bond yields of about 4.7%.

Key Stock Statistics

S&P Core EPS 2005E	**5.31**	52-week Range	**$98.25-80.67**
S&P Oper. EPS 2004E	**5.60**	12 Month P/E	**18.1**
P/E on S&P Oper. EPS 2004E	**17.5**	Beta	**0.97**
S&P Oper. EPS 2005E	**6.22**	Shareholders	**26,000**
Yield (%)	**1.4%**	Market Cap (B)	**$ 50.0**
Dividend Rate/Share	**1.40**	Shares Outstanding (M)	**511.0**

Value of $10,000 invested five years ago: **$ 18,695**

Dividend Data Dividends have been paid since 1936

Amount ($)	Date Decl.	Ex-Div. Date	Stock of Record	Payment Date
0.350	Feb. 03	Feb. 18	Feb. 20	Mar. 10 '04
0.350	Apr. 14	May. 19	May. 21	Jun. 10 '04
0.350	Jun. 09	Aug. 18	Aug. 20	Sep. 10 '04
0.350	Oct. 13	Nov. 17	Nov. 19	Dec. 10 '04

Revenues/Earnings Data Fiscal year ending December 31

Revenues (Million $)

	2004	2003	2002	2001	2000	1999
1Q	8,646	6,702	6,374	6,671	6,390	5,442
2Q	9,622	7,790	7,324	7,332	6,961	6,041
3Q	9,339	7,954	7,299	6,920	6,465	6,127
4Q	—	8,588	7,215	6,974	6,767	6,517
Yr.	—	31,034	28,212	27,897	26,583	24,127

Earnings Per Share ($)

	2004	2003	2002	2001	2000	1999
1Q	1.14	1.00	0.92	0.86	0.74	0.57
2Q	1.66	1.26	1.23	1.16	1.00	0.83
3Q	1.43	1.27	1.21	1.12	0.98	0.16
4Q	E1.26	1.16	1.06	0.69	0.84	0.10
Yr.	E5.60	4.69	4.42	3.83	3.55	1.65

Next earnings report expected: mid-January Source: S&P, Company Reports
EPS Estimates based on S&P Operating Earnings; historical GAAP earnings are as reported.

STANDARD &POOR'S

United Technologies Corporation

Stock Report
November 13, 2004
NYSE Symbol: **UTX**

Recommendation: **HOLD** ★ ★ ★ ☆ ☆   12-Month Target Price: **$100.00** (as of September 27, 2004)

Business Summary September 27, 2004

This multi-industry holding company conducts business through five business segments.

Carrier (29% of revenues, 21% of operating profits, and 10% operating profit margins in 2003) is the world's largest maker of commercial and residential heating, ventilating and air-conditioning (HVAC) equipment. Carrier is expanding its presence in commercial refrigeration, currently dominated by Ingersoll-Rand's Thermo King unit.

Otis (25%, 32%, 17%) is the world's largest maker of elevators and escalators. The segment also generates recurring revenues from servicing Otis equipment; it has service contracts on substantially all Otis-made elevators and escalators. The division is greatly expanding its presence in Eastern Europe, Russia and China. Otis accounts for about 25% of the world's new elevator market. Otis's largest competitor, Swiss-based Schindler Elevator Co., commands about 15% of the market. Other competitors include Germany-based ThyssenKrupp, and Finland-based Kone Corp.

Pratt & Whitney (24%, 27%, 15%) is one of the world's "Big Three" jet engine makers (the others are GE and Rolls Royce). Pratt & Whitney, which generates about 30% of segment revenues from jet engine sales to Boeing and Airbus, also makes engines for military jet fighters and transports. Aircraft spare parts and overhaul service operations are an important source of high margin, recurring revenues. Demand for commercial jet engines and spare parts is primarily driven by growth in the world's airline fleet. Based on the latest data provided by independent research firm Avitas Inc. and global airline trade group International

Air Transport Association (IATA), from 1992 through 2002, the global airline fleet expanded at a 2.4% average annual rate.

The Flight Systems (FS) segment (18%, 19%, 14%) primarily makes Sikorsky helicopters, as well as aircraft fuel systems, propellers and power generators. Sikorsky's largest competitor is Textron's Bell Helicopter unit, the world's largest maker of commercial and military helicopters.

UTX's newest segment, U.K.-based Chubb (4%, 1%, 4.8%) is a major global security systems provider that UTX purchased for $1 billion in 2003. Chubb generates recurring revenue and earnings streams from long-term contracts on more than 900,000 security systems. With more than 20,000 security system providers worldwide, the $110 billion-revenue security services industry is fragmented. Primary competitors include Tyco International's ADT unit, U.K.-based Kidde PLC, and Sweden-based Securitas AB.

From 1996 through 2003, UTX shares far outperformed the S&P 500, rising at a seven-year CAGR of 18%, versus 6.0% for the Index. The outperformance reflected a seven-year net operating EPS CAGR of 15%, a free cash flow CAGR of 14%, and a debt-adjusted average ROE of 16%.

UTX has recorded several large restructuring charges and asset writedowns. In 2003, 2002, 2001 and 1999, the company incurred restructuring charges and asset writedowns totaling $199 million, $321 million, $348 million and $842 million, respectively.

Company Financials Fiscal Year ending December 31

Per Share Data ($)

(Year Ended December 31)	2003	2002	2001	2000	1999	1998	1997	1996	1995	1994
Tangible Bk. Val.	-4.63	2.92	3.32	1.90	1.60	5.84	6.75	7.62	7.03	6.17
Cash Flow	6.28	5.86	5.63	5.25	3.32	4.25	3.72	3.36	3.00	2.57
Earnings	4.69	4.42	3.83	3.55	1.65	2.52	2.10	1.73	1.43	1.10
S&P Core Earnings	4.31	2.63	2.27	NA	NA	NA	NA	NA	NA	NA
Dividends	1.14	0.98	0.90	0.83	0.76	0.70	0.62	0.55	0.51	0.48
Payout Ratio	24%	22%	23%	23%	46%	28%	29%	32%	36%	43%
Prices - High	96.75	77.75	87.50	79.75	75.96	56.25	44.46	35.25	24.43	18.00
- Low	53.51	48.83	40.10	46.50	51.62	33.50	32.56	22.62	15.56	13.75
P/E Ratio - High	21	18	23	22	46	22	21	20	17	16
- Low	11	11	10	13	31	13	15	13	11	13

Income Statement Analysis (Million $)

	2003	2002	2001	2000	1999	1998	1997	1996	1995	1994
Revs.	31,034	28,212	27,897	26,583	23,844	25,687	24,495	23,273	22,624	21,161
Oper. Inc.	4,644	4,384	4,138	3,999	2,361	2,993	2,598	2,395	2,254	2,108
Depr.	799	727	905	859	844	854	848	853	844	793
Int. Exp.	375	381	426	382	260	204	195	237	260	294
Pretax Inc.	3,470	3,276	2,807	2,758	1,257	1,963	1,764	1,560	1,344	1,076
Eff. Tax Rate	27.1%	27.1%	26.9%	30.9%	25.9%	31.7%	32.5%	33.5%	34.5%	35.7%
Net Inc.	2,361	2,236	1,938	1,808	841	1,255	1,072	906	750	585
S&P Core Earnings	2,147	1,298	1,113	NA	NA	NA	NA	NA	NA	NA

Balance Sheet & Other Fin. Data (Million $)

	2003	2002	2001	2000	1999	1998	1997	1996	1995	1994
Cash	1,623	2,080	1,558	748	957	550	755	1,127	900	386
Curr. Assets	12,364	11,751	11,263	10,662	10,627	9,355	9,248	9,611	8,952	8,228
Total Assets	34,648	29,090	26,969	25,364	24,366	18,375	16,719	16,745	15,958	15,624
Curr. Liab.	10,295	7,903	8,371	9,344	9,215	7,735	7,311	7,390	6,659	6,553
LT Debt	4,257	4,632	4,237	3,476	3,086	1,575	1,275	1,437	1,649	1,885
Common Equity	11,707	10,506	8,369	7,662	7,117	3,998	3,658	4,306	4,021	3,752
Total Cap.	16,673	16,445	13,899	12,514	11,664	6,994	6,362	6,810	7,031	6,572
Cap. Exp.	530	586	793	937	762	866	843	794	780	759
Cash Flow	3,160	2,963	2,843	2,667	1,685	2,109	1,888	1,753	1,567	1,356
Curr. Ratio	1.2	1.5	1.3	1.1	1.2	1.2	1.3	1.3	1.3	1.3
% LT Debt of Cap.	25.5	28.2	30.5	27.8	26.5	22.5	20.0	21.1	23.5	28.7
% Net Inc.of Revs.	7.6	7.9	6.9	6.8	3.5	4.9	4.4	3.9	3.3	2.8
% Ret. on Assets	7.4	8.0	7.4	7.3	4.0	7.2	6.4	5.5	4.7	3.8
% Ret. on Equity	23.9	23.0	24.2	24.5	14.6	32.8	27.7	21.6	18.6	15.5

Data as orig reptd.; bef. results of disc opers/spec. items. Per share data adj. for stk. divs.; EPS diluted. E-Estimated. NA-Not Available. NM-Not Meaningful. NR-Not Ranked. UR-Under Review.

Office: One Financial Plaza, Hartford, CT 06103.
Telephone: 860-728-7000.
Email: invrelations@corphq.utc.com
Website: www.utc.com
Chrmn, Pres & CEO: G.A. David.
VP & Treas: T.I. Rogan.

VP & Secy: D.A. Valentine.
General Counsel: W.H. Trachsel.
Investor Contact: P. Jackson 860-728-7912.
Dirs: B. Bernard, G. A. David, J. Garnier, J. S. Gorelick, C. R. Lee, R. D. McCormick, H. Mcgraw III, S. F. Page, F. P. Popoff, H. P. Swygert, A. Villeneuve, H. A. Wagner, S. I. Weill, C. T. Whitman.

Founded: in 1934.
Domicile: Delaware.
Employees: 203,300.
S&P Analyst: Robert Friedman/MF/JWP

Univision Communications

Recommendation: **BUY** ★★★★☆

SELL | SELL | HOLD | BUY | BUY

12-Month Target Price: $40.00
(as of August 06, 2004)

UVN has an approximate 0.09% weighting in the **S&P 500**

Sector: Consumer Discretionary
Sub-Industry: Broadcasting & Cable TV
Peer Group: Television Stations

Summary: UVN is the leading U.S. Spanish language media company.

Quantitative Evaluations

S&P Earnings & Dividend Rank: NR

D	C	B-	B	B+	A-	A	A+

S&P Fair Value Rank: 5

1	2	3	4	5
Lowest				Highest

Fair Value Calc.: $31.80 (Slightly Undervalued)

S&P Investability Quotient Percentile

95%

UVN scored higher than 95% of all companies for which an S&P Report is available.

Volatility: Average

Low	Average	High

Technical Evaluation: Neutral
Since 11/04, the technical indicators for UVN have been Neutral.

Relative Strength Rank: Weak

16

1 Lowest	Highest 99

Price as of 11/12/04: $29.93 | **2004E S&P Core EPS:** $0.59

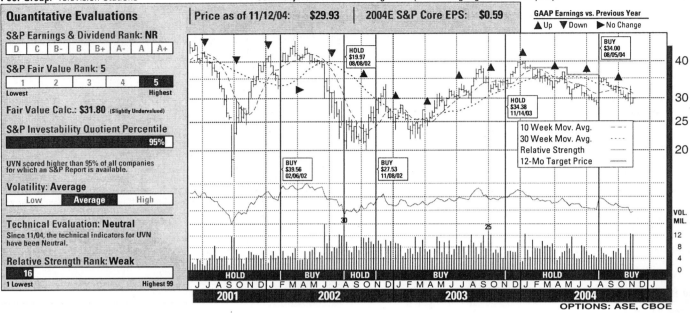

GAAP Earnings vs. Previous Year
▲ Up ▼ Down ▶ No Change

Analyst commentary prepared by Tuna N. Amobi, CFA, CPA /CB/GG

OPTIONS: ASE, CBOE

Highlights August 15, 2004

- We estimate consolidated revenue growth of about 18% in 2004 (on a pro forma basis assuming that the radio segment was acquired at the start of 2003), with 14% growth seen in 2005. We expect the key growth drivers to include UVN's continued strong ratings across its TV and radio channels, increasing benefits of the radio integration, and additional opportunities in the fast-growing Hispanic advertising market. Our outlook also reflects the 2004 first quarter adoption of FIN 46, which requires the consolidation of variable interest entities, namely the 50%-owned Mexico-based Disa records and the two Puerto Rico TV stations owned by Raycom Media; in line with management's guidance, this consolidation should not affect reported earnings.

- Continued improvements in operating leverage should generating meaningful margin expansion across the core businesses. We believe the new, fast growing Telefutura broadcast network is on track to generate positive operating cash flow in 2004. In addition, we see further cost savings from the continued integration of the radio acquisition (the former Hispanic Broadcasting). After radio start-up costs and higher TV programming expenses, we see pro forma EBITDA advancing 25% and 19% in 2004 and 2005, respectively, from about $480 million in 2003 (as adjusted for merger costs).

- With reduced interest expense reflecting a recent debt refinancing, we estimate EPS of $0.74 in 2004 ($0.61 S&P Core, after deducting employee stock options expense), and $0.90 in 2005 ($0.76 S&P Core).

Key Stock Statistics

S&P Core EPS 2005E	0.73	52-week Range	$40.05-28.38
S&P Oper. EPS 2004E	0.72	12 Month P/E	42.1
P/E on S&P Oper. EPS 2004E	41.6	Beta	1.56
S&P Oper. EPS 2005E	0.87	Shareholders	302
Yield (%)	Nil	Market Cap (B)	$ 7.7
Dividend Rate/Share	Nil	Shares Outstanding (M)	324.2

Value of $10,000 invested five years ago: **$ 6,734**

Dividend Data

No cash dividends have been paid.

Investment Rationale/Risk August 15, 2004

- We recommend accumulating the shares, based mainly on our view of UVN's position as the pre-eminent Spanish language media conglomerate in the fastest-growing segment of the broadcast industry. The company has been gaining an increasing share of the Hispanic TV audience, helping it to gradually narrow an audience-to-revenues gap compared with the major English-language broadcasters. Separately, we think management's recent estimate of nearly $13 million in annual synergies from last year's radio acquisition could prove conservative. In addition, like Telefutura, several recent radio start-ups are starting to turn the corner to profitability. In the longer term, the merging music and online businesses could prove a strong growth platform.

- Risks to our recommendation and target price include a concentration of UVN's business with two foreign-based TV programming suppliers; potential competitive pressures from NBC-affiliated Telemundo; concerns with new audience measurement initiatives; and advertising exposure to macroeconomic factors.

- After recovering 17% within two days after the early August release of better-than-expected second quarter results, the stock now trades at 1.6X P/E-to-growth, 30X free cash flow and 19X EV/EBITDA. While we view these as sizable premium multiples to broadcast peers, we see additional potential upside from management's somewhat cautious third quarter guidance (with strong ratings for "Copa America") and current demographic shifts. Our 12-month target price is $40, which we see as a warranted premium to peers.

Revenues/Earnings Data Fiscal year ending December 31

Revenues (Million $)

	2004	2003	2002	2001	2000	1999
1Q	352.9	261.7	214.4	194.9	181.5	138.0
2Q	495.3	320.2	322.8	237.5	231.1	172.4
3Q	477.4	321.1	269.8	221.7	212.0	177.3
4Q	—	408.1	284.2	233.8	238.9	205.3
Yr.	—	1,311	1,091	887.9	863.5	693.1

Earnings Per Share ($)

	2004	2003	2002	2001	2000	1999
1Q	0.09	0.05	0.03	0.03	0.09	0.04
2Q	0.24	0.16	0.09	0.12	0.14	0.09
3Q	0.21	0.16	0.08	0.04	0.13	0.10
4Q	E0.18	0.17	0.14	0.05	0.17	0.13
Yr.	E0.72	0.55	0.34	0.23	0.57	0.36

Next earnings report expected: mid-February Source: S&P, Company Reports
EPS Estimates based on S&P Operating Earnings; historical GAAP earnings are as reported.

Univision Communications Inc.

Recommendation: **BUY** ★★★☆   12-Month Target Price: **$40.00** (as of August 06, 2004)

Business Summary August 17, 2004

Univision Communications is the leading U.S. Spanish language media company. The company aims to benefit from rapid expansion of the Hispanic population and rising advertiser awareness of Hispanic buying power. In September 2003, UVN acquired Hispanic Broadcasting Corp. (HBC), the largest U.S. Spanish language radio broadcaster, with 66 radio stations in 17 of the 25 leading Hispanic markets. Each HBC common share was exchanged for 0.85 of a UVN Class A share.

UVN's principal business, television broadcasting, consists of the Univision, Galavision and TeleFutura TV networks, 56 owned and operated broadcast television stations (36 full power and 20 low power), which are largely affiliated with the Univision and TeleFutura networks, and a TV production business. The Univision network is the most popular U.S. Spanish language broadcast network, reaching more than 98% of all U.S. Hispanic households. Galavision is the leading U.S. Spanish general entertainment cable network, reaching about 5.7 million Hispanic households.

With assets received from the $1.1 billion cash acquisition of USA Broadcasting in December 2001, UVN in January 2002 launched its second network, TeleFutura, a general interest Spanish language broadcast network, to counter-program traditional lineups and draw new Spanish TV viewers. The deal gave UVN duopolies in seven of the eight leading Hispanic markets. TeleFutura's signal covers about 79% of all U.S. Hispanic households.

Formerly HBC, Univision Radio owns and/or operates 68 radio stations in 17 of the top 25 U.S. Hispanic markets and operates four stations in Puerto Rico. Its radio stations cover approximately 73% of all U.S. Hispanic radio listeners and have nearly 10 million listeners weekly.

The music segment consists of Univision Music Group, launched in April 2001 to record and publish the music of developing and established Latin artists. In April 2002, UVN acquired the Fonovisa Music Group, Televisa's Latin music company, with about 120 recording artists and a substantial record and music publishing catalog. UVN holds a 50% interest in Mexico-based Disa Records, the world's second largest Spanish language record label. Univision Online, Inc. operates an Internet portal, Univision.com, that provides Spanish language content for Hispanics in the U.S., Mexico and Latin America.

On December 23, 2003, the company entered into a 40-year lease for a three-story building with approximately 92,500 square feet for the relocation of its owned and/or operated television and radio stations and studio facilities in Puerto Rico. The company has an option that expires on December 31, 2004, to acquire the two television stations it operates in Puerto Rico for $190 million. If UVN exercises this option, it will be required to offer its two primary TV programming providers, Televisa (Mexico) and Venesion (Venezuela), the right to acquire 15% and 10% interests, respectively, in those stations for a pro rata portion of the purchase price.

Company Financials Fiscal Year ending December 31

Per Share Data ($)

(Year Ended December 31)	2003	2002	2001	2000	1999	1998	1997	1996	1995	1994
Tangible Bk. Val.	NM	NM	NM	0.77	NM	NM	NM	NM	-2.62	NA
Cash Flow	0.85	0.64	0.58	0.60	0.62	0.32	0.61	0.25	0.28	NA
Earnings	0.55	0.34	0.23	0.57	0.36	0.05	0.36	0.16	0.03	NA
S&P Core Earnings	0.43	0.20	0.09	NA	NA	NA	NA	NA	NA	NA
Dividends	Nil	Nil	Nil	Nil	Nil	Nil	Nil	Nil	Nil	NA
Payout Ratio	Nil	Nil	Nil	Nil	Nil	Nil	Nil	Nil	Nil	NA
Prices - High	39.95	47.00	52.25	62.68	51.59	21.00	17.84	10.06	NA	NA
- Low	21.83	16.40	16.30	24.00	17.06	10.53	7.93	5.75	NA	NA
P/E Ratio - High	73	NM	NM	NM	NM	NM	50	64	NA	NA
- Low	40	NM	NM	NM	NM	NM	22	37	NA	NA

Income Statement Analysis (Million $)

	2003	2002	2001	2000	1999	1998	1997	1996	1995	1994
Revs.	1,311	1,091	888	863	693	577	460	370	321	NA
Oper. Inc.	434	332	300	289	267	196	163	107	112	NA
Depr.	84.9	78.8	84.1	28.0	64.0	64.4	58.6	39.5	54.2	NA
Int. Exp.	75.2	91.1	56.0	31.5	27.5	37.5	41.8	41.7	42.2	NA
Pretax Inc.	261	148	118	225	175	50.3	63.7	24.3	12.0	NA
Eff. Tax Rate	40.4%	41.5%	53.5%	48.0%	52.3%	80.3%	NM	23.5%	40.0%	NA
Net Inc.	155	86.5	54.7	117	83.5	9.93	83.2	18.6	7.20	NA
S&P Core Earnings	122	49.8	20.3	NA	NA	NA	NA	NA	NA	NA

Balance Sheet & Other Fin. Data (Million $)

	2003	2002	2001	2000	1999	1998	1997	1996	1995	1994
Cash	76.7	35.7	381	54.5	22.6	13.0	10.7	11.6	14.4	NA
Curr. Assets	521	385	596	250	178	154	139	112	106	NA
Total Assets	7,643	3,402	3,164	1,448	974	938	968	884	882	NA
Curr. Liab.	289	223	270	363	142	153	144	120	142	NA
LT Debt	1,368	1,432	1,662	378	303	377	461	498	556	NA
Common Equity	5,103	1,558	813	695	514	395	346	262	223	NA
Total Cap.	7,265	3,106	2,850	1,079	826	781	819	760	779	NA
Cap. Exp.	56.3	92.3	130	64.7	39.0	41.0	35.2	12.6	16.1	NA
Cash Flow	240	165	139	144	147	73.8	141	58.1	61.4	NA
Curr. Ratio	1.8	1.7	2.2	0.7	1.3	1.0	1.0	0.9	0.7	NA
% LT Debt of Cap.	18.8	46.1	58.3	35.0	36.7	48.3	56.3	65.5	71.4	NA
% Net Inc.of Revs.	11.9	7.9	6.2	13.5	12.1	1.7	18.1	7.6	2.2	NA
% Ret. on Assets	2.8	2.6	2.4	9.7	8.7	1.0	9.0	2.1	NA	NA
% Ret. on Equity	4.7	7.3	7.2	19.3	18.3	2.5	27.2	7.6	NA	NA

Data as orig reptd.; bef. results of disc opers/spec. items. Per share data adj. for stk. divs.; EPS diluted. E-Estimated. NA-Not Available. NM-Not Meaningful. NR-Not Ranked. UR-Under Review.

Office: 1999 Avenue of the Stars, Los Angeles, CA 90067-4613.
Telephone: 310-556-7676.
Website: http://www.univision.com
Chrmn & CEO: A.J. Perenchio.
Vice Chrmn & Secy: R.V. Cahill.
COO: R. Rodriguez.

Sr EVP & Investor Contact: A. Hobson 310-556-7676.
EVP & CFO: G.W. Blank.
Dirs: F. Aguirre, E. Azcarraga Jean, G. A. Cisneros, A. De Angoitia, H. Gaba, A. F. Horn, A. J. Perenchio, J. G. Perenchio, A. Rivera, R. Rodriguez, M. T. Tichenor, Jr.

Founded: in 1992.
Domicile: Delaware.
Employees: 4,300.
S&P Analyst: Tuna N. Amobi, CFA, CPA /CB/GG

Unocal Corp.

Recommendation: **HOLD** ★★★☆☆

12-Month Target Price: **$44.00**
(as of October 28, 2004)

UCL has an approximate 0.11% weighting in the **S&P 500**

Sector: Energy
Sub-Industry: Oil & Gas Exploration & Production
Peer Group: Exploration & Production - Large

Summary: UCL is an international oil and gas exploration and production (E&P) company, with businesses in trade and marketing, pipelines and storage, and geothermal and power.

Quantitative Evaluations

S&P Earnings & Dividend Rank: B

| D | C | B- | **B** | B+ | A- | A | A+ |

S&P Fair Value Rank: 4-

| 1 | 2 | 3 | **4** | 5 |
Lowest — Highest

Fair Value Calc.: $45.40 (Slightly Undervalued)

S&P Investability Quotient Percentile
81%

UCL scored higher than 81% of all companies for which an S&P Report is available.

Volatility: Average

| Low | **Average** | High |

Technical Evaluation: Bullish
Since 11/04, the technical indicators for UCL have been Bullish.

Relative Strength Rank: Moderate
66
1 Lowest — Highest 99

| Price as of 11/12/04: | **$44.16** | 2004E S&P Core EPS: | **$3.56** |

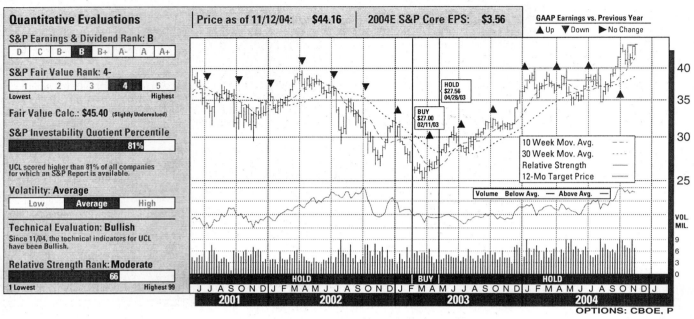

GAAP Earnings vs. Previous Year
▲ Up ▼ Down ► No Change

10 Week Mov. Avg.
30 Week Mov. Avg.
Relative Strength
12-Mo Target Price

Volume   Below Avg. — Above Avg. —

HOLD $27.56 04/28/03
BUY $27.00 02/11/03

OPTIONS: CBOE, P

Analyst commentary prepared by Charles LaPorta, CFA /PMW/GG

Highlights August 23, 2004

- Second quarter operating EPS of $0.86 exceeded our estimate by $0.06, reflecting higher than expected hydrocarbon price realizations, partly offset by production volumes that were below expectations. Second quarter hydrocarbon production declined 1.3% sequentially, and was below our expectations, reflecting the sale of oil and gas producing assets in North America in 2003, as well as lower volumes from production sharing contracts (PSCs) in Asia due to higher commodity prices.

- We expect third quarter production to average 403,600 b/d, about equal to that of the second quarter, and see full-year production averaging 406,000 b/d, reflecting lower volumes from PSCs, due to high commodity prices, continued North American production declines, and more conservative production expectations from the West Seno field in Indonesia.

- EBITDAX (earnings before interest, taxes, depreciation, amortization and exploration expense) climbed 31% in 2003, on higher prices, but we expect a decline of about 3% in 2004, on lower volumes, and a drop of over 10% in 2005, on projected lower prices. Removal of recognized pension losses makes our S&P Core Earnings projections higher than our operating estimates.

Investment Rationale/Risk August 23, 2004

- We remain concerned about UCL's North American production declines, as well as its ability to reduce unit operating costs and finding and development costs, particularly in North America. The organic reserve replacement ratio was 133% in 2003, versus 82% in 2002, but this upstream improvement boosted capital spending 3% in 2003, to $1.7 billion. Large development projects in Southeast Asia and the Caspian Sea are driving 2004 spending, but lower capital requirements in the Gulf of Mexico deepwater are expected to keep 2004 spending at 2003 levels.

- Risks to our recommendation and target price include events that would cause substantial and sustained declines in oil and gas prices; a persistent inability to replace reserves; and potential acts of terrorism on UCL's production facilities.

- Based on a blend of our DCF and market valuations, using our estimate of UCL's production growth and our oil and gas price projections, our 12-month target price is $40, equal to 13X our 2005 EPS estimate. We think this premium to peer levels is justified, based on what we view as a history of solid reserve replacement.

Key Stock Statistics

S&P Core EPS 2005E	3.39	52-week Range	$44.20-30.90
S&P Oper. EPS 2004E	4.30	12 Month P/E	10.6
P/E on S&P Oper. EPS 2004E	10.3	Beta	0.46
S&P Oper. EPS 2005E	4.50	Shareholders	20,485
Yield (%)	1.8%	Market Cap (B)	$ 11.6
Dividend Rate/Share	0.80	Shares Outstanding (M)	263.2

Value of $10,000 invested five years ago: **$ 15,386**

Dividend Data Dividends have been paid since 1916

Amount ($)	Date Decl.	Ex-Div. Date	Stock of Record	Payment Date
0.200	Dec. 05	Jan. 07	Jan. 09	Feb. 09 '04
0.200	Feb. 10	Apr. 07	Apr. 12	May. 12 '04
0.200	May. 24	Jul. 08	Jul. 12	Aug. 12 '04
0.200	Jul. 28	Oct. 07	Oct. 12	Nov. 12 '04

Revenues/Earnings Data Fiscal year ending December 31

Revenues (Million $)

	2004	2003	2002	2001	2000	1999
1Q	1,892	1,789	1,049	2,214	1,856	1,231
2Q	1,980	1,620	1,368	1,696	2,216	1,555
3Q	1,993	1,541	1,297	1,579	2,347	1,588
4Q	—	1,589	1,583	1,260	2,783	1,683
Yr.	—	6,539	5,297	6,752	9,202	6,057

Earnings Per Share ($)

	2004	2003	2002	2001	2000	1999
1Q	1.00	0.82	0.09	1.16	0.51	0.03
2Q	1.04	0.65	0.46	0.95	1.00	0.04
3Q	1.22	0.58	0.41	0.42	0.71	0.18
4Q	E1.17	0.65	0.38	-0.13	0.70	0.31
Yr.	E4.30	2.70	1.34	2.43	2.93	0.46

Next earnings report expected: early-February Source: S&P, Company Reports
EPS Estimates based on S&P Operating Earnings; historical GAAP earnings are as reported.

Please read the Required Disclosures and Reg. AC certification on the last page of this report.

The McGraw·Hill Companies

Unocal Corporation

Recommendation: **HOLD** ★★★☆☆   12-Month Target Price: **$44.00** (as of October 28, 2004)

Business Summary August 23, 2004

As one of the world's largest independent exploration, development and production companies, Unocal Corp. has principal operations in North America and Asia. Other activities include ownership in proprietary and common carrier pipelines, natural gas storage facilities, and the marketing and trading of hydrocarbon commodities. Reportable business segments include exploration and production (41% of 2003 sales; 2003 segment earnings of $1,020 million), trade (47%, loss of $2 million), midstream (9%, income of $71 million), geothermal and power (2%, income of $50 million), and other.

Proved reserves declined to 1.759 billion barrels oil equivalent (BOE) at the end of 2003, from 1.774 billion BOE a year earlier. UCL replaced 149% of its 2003 natural gas and crude oil production through discoveries and extensions, improved recovery and revisions. Finding, development and acquisition costs (FD&A) were about $7.05 per BOE in 2003, an improvement over the prior year's $11.97. Faced by rising production costs, the company planned to focus in 2004 on improving its per unit operating costs and F&D costs, especially in its North American operations.

Net proved liquid reserves at the end of 2003 totaled 675 million bbl. (MMBbls; 32% Far East, 21% U.S. Lower 48, 10% Alaska, 8% Canada, and 29% elsewhere), versus 681 MMBbls (29% Far East, 24% U.S. Lower 48, 11% Alaska, 8% Canada, and 28% elsewhere) in 2002. Net proved natural gas reserves totaled 6.505 trillion cubic feet (Tcf; 61% Far East, 21% U.S. Lower 48, 5% Canada, 3% Alaska, and 10% elsewhere), compared to 6.559 Tcf (58% Far East, 26% U.S. Lower 48, 5% Canada, 3% Alaska, and 8% elsewhere). The company's net liquids production averaged

about 160,000 bbl. per day (b/d; 37% Far East, 27% U.S. Lower 48, 13% Alaska, 11% Canada, and 12% elsewhere) in 2003, compared to 167,000 b/d (32% Far East, 31% U.S. Lower 48, 14% Alaska, 11% Canada, and 12% elsewhere) in 2002. Net natural gas production averaged 1.728 billion cubic feet (Bcf; 51% Far East, 36% U.S. Lower 48, 5% Canada, 3% Alaska, and 5% elsewhere) per day in 2003, compared to 1.826 Bcf (46% Far East, 39% U.S. Lower 48, 5% Canada, 4% Alaska, and 6% elsewhere) per day in 2002. Production costs averaged $4.01 per BOE in 2003, versus $3.70 in 2002.

The trade segment externally markets UCL's hydrocarbon production. Activities include transporting and selling the company's production.

The midstream segment is comprised of the company's pipelines and North America gas storage businesses. The pipelines business includes UCL's equity interests in certain petroleum pipeline companies (e.g., 23.44% in Colonial Pipeline Co., 27.75% in the Trans-Andean oil pipeline) and wholly owned pipeline systems throughout the U.S. Also included is wholly owned Unocal Pipeline Co., which owns a 1.36% participation interest in the TransAlaska Pipeline Systems (TAPS).

UCL produces geothermal energy. It has more than 35 years experience in geothermal resource exploration, reservoir delineation, and management. The company operates major geothermal fields producing steam for power generation projects in Indonesia and the Philippines; combined installed electrical generating capacity was 1,120 megawatts at the end of 2003.

Company Financials Fiscal Year ending December 31

Per Share Data ($)

(Year Ended December 31)	2003	2002	2001	2000	1999	1998	1997	1996	1995	1994
Tangible Bk. Val.	15.51	12.84	13.41	11.72	9.45	9.14	9.92	9.08	9.77	9.43
Cash Flow	6.79	5.65	6.09	6.62	3.71	3.93	6.23	5.43	5.05	4.27
Earnings	2.70	1.34	2.43	2.93	0.46	0.54	2.65	1.76	0.91	0.36
S&P Core Earnings	2.56	0.95	2.10	NA	NA	NA	NA	NA	NA	NA
Dividends	0.80	0.80	0.80	0.80	0.80	0.80	0.80	0.80	0.80	0.80
Payout Ratio	30%	60%	33%	27%	174%	148%	30%	45%	88%	NM
Prices - High	37.08	39.70	40.00	40.12	46.62	42.12	45.87	42.12	30.50	30.75
- Low	24.97	26.58	29.51	25.00	27.50	28.31	36.12	27.75	24.75	24.37
P/E Ratio - High	14	30	16	14	NM	78	17	24	34	85
- Low	9	20	12	9	NM	52	14	16	27	68

Income Statement Analysis (Million $)

	2003	2002	2001	2000	1999	1998	1997	1996	1995	1994
Revs.	6,539	5,224	6,664	8,914	5,842	5,003	5,781	5,101	8,425	6,904
Oper. Inc.	2,562	1,672	1,173	2,715	1,100	873	1,633	1,724	1,776	1,348
Depr. Depl. & Amort.	988	1,071	967	971	833	867	962	914	1,022	947
Int. Exp.	223	212	225	243	264	177	183	294	326	308
Pretax Inc.	1,241	616	1,092	1,236	250	305	771	758	463	294
Eff. Tax Rate	42.1%	45.4%	41.4%	40.2%	48.4%	57.4%	13.2%	39.8%	43.8%	57.8%
Net Inc.	710	330	599	723	113	130	669	456	260	124
S&P Core Earnings	671	235	510	NA	NA	NA	NA	NA	NA	NA

Balance Sheet & Other Fin. Data (Million $)

	2003	2002	2001	2000	1999	1998	1997	1996	1995	1994
Cash	404	168	190	235	332	238	338	217	94.0	148
Curr. Assets	1,991	1,375	1,295	1,802	1,631	1,388	1,501	3,228	1,576	1,528
Total Assets	11,798	10,760	10,425	10,010	8,967	7,952	7,530	9,123	9,891	9,337
Curr. Liab.	2,085	1,632	1,422	1,845	1,559	1,376	1,160	1,622	1,316	1,257
LT Debt	3,157	3,524	3,419	2,914	3,375	3,080	2,691	2,940	3,698	3,461
Common Equity	4,009	3,298	3,124	2,719	2,184	2,202	2,314	2,275	2,417	2,302
Total Cap.	7,909	7,690	7,619	6,643	6,221	5,414	5,142	6,085	6,837	6,919
Cap. Exp.	1,718	1,670	1,727	1,302	1,171	1,704	1,427	1,398	1,459	1,272
Cash Flow	1,698	1,401	1,566	1,694	946	997	1,631	1,352	1,246	1,035
Curr. Ratio	1.0	0.8	0.9	1.0	1.0	1.0	1.3	2.0	1.2	1.2
% LT Debt of Cap.	39.9	45.8	44.9	43.9	54.3	56.9	42.2	48.3	54.1	50.0
% Ret. on Assets	6.3	3.1	5.9	7.6	1.3	1.7	8.0	48.0	2.7	1.3
% Ret. on Equity	19.4	10.3	20.5	29.5	5.2	5.8	29.2	18.7	9.5	3.6

Data as orig. reptd.; bef. results of disc. opers. and/or spec. items. Per share data adj. for stk. divs.; EPS diluted. Revs.in quarterly table incl. oth. inc. E-Estimated. NA-Not Available. NM-Not Meaningful. NR-Not Ranked.

Office: 2141 Rosecrans Avenue, El Segundo, CA 90245.
Telephone: 310-726-7600.
Email: investor_relations@unocal.com
Website: http://www.unocal.com
Chrmn & CEO: C.R. Williamson.
Pres & COO: J.H. Bryant.
Vice Chrmn: J.W. Creighton.

EVP & CFO: T.G. Dallas.
SVP & General Counsel: S.H. Gillespie.
VP & Investor Contact: R.E. Wright 310-726-7665.
Dirs: C. Arnold, J. W. Creighton, Jr., J. W. Crownover, F. P. McClean, R. D. McCormick, D. B. Rice, K. W. Sharer, M. A. Suwyn, M. v. Whitman, C. R. Williamson.

Founded: in 1890.
Domicile: Delaware.
Employees: 6,700.
S&P Analyst: Charles LaPorta, CFA /PMW/GG

UnumProvident Corp.

Recommendation: HOLD ★★★☆ 　　12-Month Target Price: **$15.00**
SELL SELL HOLD BUY BUY 　　(as of August 04, 2004)

UNM has an approximate 0.04% weighting in the **S&P 500**

Sector: Financials
Sub-Industry: Life & Health Insurance
Peer Group: Health/Disability Insurers

Summary: This leading provider of individual and group disability coverage was formed through the June 1999 merger of Provident Cos. and UNUM Corp.

Quantitative Evaluations

S&P Earnings & Dividend Rank: B

| D | C | B- | **B** | B+ | A- | A | A+ |

S&P Fair Value Rank: 4-

| 1 | 2 | 3 | **4** | 5 |
| Lowest | | | | Highest |

Fair Value Calc.: $15.10 (Slightly Undervalued)

S&P Investability Quotient Percentile

86%

UNM scored higher than 86% of all companies for which an S&P Report is available.

Volatility: Average

| Low | Average | High |

Technical Evaluation: Bearish
Since 10/04, the technical indicators for UNM have been Bearish.

Relative Strength Rank: Weak

11

| 1 Lowest | | Highest 99 |

| Price as of 11/12/04: | **$13.45** | 2004E S&P Core EPS: | **$0.01** |

GAAP Earnings vs. Previous Year
▲ Up ▼ Down ► No Change

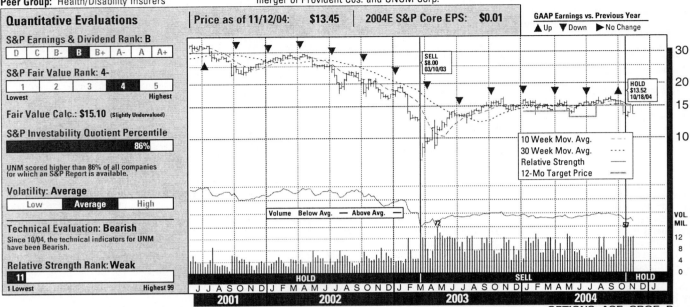

10 Week Mov. Avg.
30 Week Mov. Avg.
Relative Strength
12-Mo Target Price

SELL $8.00 03/10/03
HOLD $13.52 10/18/04

Volume Below Avg. — Above Avg.

OPTIONS: ASE, CBOE, P

Analyst commentary prepared by Gregory Simcik, CFA /CB/BK

Highlights October 20, 2004

- Excluding charges for reserve strengthening, we expect 2004 pretax operating earnings to increase 15% for the income protection segment. We forecast that pretax operating earnings will decline 11% for the life and accident segment, and see operating earnings growing in the high single digits for the Colonial segment.

- For the closed block individual income protection segment, we expect pretax operating earnings of $137 million in 2004, excluding charges for writeoffs. Comparisons should benefit from the absence of $70 million of amortization, due to the early 2004 writeoffs of all intangibles, including deferred acquisition costs.

- Excluding charges for reserve strengthening and writeoffs, we project that 2004 consolidated operating earnings will advance about 20%, to $521 million ($1.74 a share). We forecast consolidated operating EPS growth of 9% in 2005, to $1.89. Our Standard & Poor's Core Earnings per share estimates for 2004 and 2005 are $0.01 and $1.86, respectively, including projected charges for reserve strengthening, writeoffs, our forecast of stock option expense, and pension expense adjustments.

Investment Rationale/Risk October 20, 2004

- Following the recent pullback in the stock price, we recommend maintaining, but not adding to, current positions. Although we believe the recent job market stabilization could benefit claims trends in the income protection segment, we also believe UNM faces significant challenges, including industry-wide investigations of group underwriters by the New York Attorney General related to possible illegal insurance broker activity, increased examinations of UNM's claims handling practices by state insurance departments, and recent downgrades of UNM by some debt rating agencies that potentially create public relations problems and could adversely affect sales and client retention.

- Risks to our recommendation and target price include negative publicity and unfavorable findings with the New York Attorney General's investigations and state insurance department market conduct examinations; client retention problems due to price increases for income protection products; and possible additional writedowns, reserve strengthenings and/or dilutive issuances of new securities associated with the income protection segment.

- We base our 12-month target price of $15 on a sum-of-the-parts analysis that includes an enterprise value for each segment and adjusts for debt. We assign respective values of 9X, 11X, 13X and 8X our 12-month forward operating earning estimates for the income protection, life and accident, Colonial, and closed block individual income protection segments, including estimated amortization for the closed block segment.

Key Stock Statistics

S&P Core EPS 2005E	1.86	52-week Range	$16.85-11.41
S&P Oper. EPS 2004E	1.65	12 Month P/E	NM
P/E on S&P Oper. EPS 2004E	8.2	Beta	0.73
S&P Oper. EPS 2005E	1.80	Shareholders	19,628
Yield (%)	2.2%	Market Cap (B)	$ 4.0
Dividend Rate/Share	0.30	Shares Outstanding (M)	296.5

Value of $10,000 invested five years ago: **$ 4,911**

Dividend Data Dividends have been paid since 1925

Amount ($)	Date Decl.	Ex-Div. Date	Stock of Record	Payment Date
0.075	Jan. 12	Jan. 22	Jan. 26	Feb. 20 '04
0.075	Apr. 15	Apr. 22	Apr. 26	May. 21 '04
0.075	Jul. 13	Jul. 22	Jul. 26	Aug. 20 '04
0.075	Oct. 12	Oct. 21	Oct. 25	Nov. 19 '04

Revenues/Earnings Data Fiscal year ending December 31

Revenues (Million $)

	2004	2003	2002	2001	2000	1999
1Q	2,624	2,395	2,331	2,341	2,394	984.4
2Q	2,509	2,529	2,402	2,363	2,424	2,273
3Q	2,655	2,556	2,450	2,377	2,312	2,433
4Q	—	2,511	2,431	2,314	2,303	3,648
Yr.	—	9,992	9,613	9,395	9,432	9,330

Earnings Per Share ($)

	2004	2003	2002	2001	2000	1999
1Q	-1.93	-1.02	0.30	0.75	0.56	0.54
2Q	0.25	0.36	0.40	0.60	0.59	-0.08
3Q	0.55	0.36	0.45	0.52	0.57	-0.91
4Q	E0.42	-0.71	0.39	0.52	0.62	0.56
Yr.	E1.65	-0.96	1.68	2.39	2.33	-0.77

Next earnings report expected: early-February Source: S&P, Company Reports
EPS Estimates based on S&P Operating Earnings; historical GAAP earnings are as reported.

UnumProvident Corporation

Recommendation: **HOLD** ★ ★ ★ ☆ ☆   12-Month Target Price: **$15.00** (as of August 04, 2004)

Business Summary October 21, 2004

UnumProvident, based in Chattanooga, TN, believes it is the largest provider of group and individual income protection products in North America and the U.K. The company was formed via the 1999 merger of Provident Companies, Inc., an individual income protection insurance provider, and Unum Corp., a group income protection insurance provider.

Operations are organized into five segments: income protection, life and accident, colonial, other, and corporate. Income protection accounted for 69% of operating revenue in 2003 (69% in 2002), life and accident 21% (21%), Colonial 7.7% (7.5%), other 2.0% (2.4%), and corporate 0.3% (0.4%).

The income protection segment includes group income protection insurance, recently issued and closed block individual income protection insurance, long-term care insurance, and disability management services. The life and accident segment includes group life insurance, accidental death and dismemberment insurance, and brokerage voluntary life insurance, including universal life.

The Colonial segment includes a broad line of products sold mainly to employees through payroll deduction, including income protection, life, and cancer and critical illness products. The other segment includes products that are no longer actively marketed, including individual and corporate-owned life insurance, reinsurance pools and management operations, group pension, health insurance, and individual annuities. In 2004, UNM began separate reporting of results from the closed block individual income protection lines.

After lower claim resolution rates in the 2003 first quarter, UNM increased its group income protection claim reserves by $454 million pretax. In the 2003 fourth quarter, it boosted its group income protection reserves by another $440 million pretax. At December 31, 2003, consolidated reserves for future policy and contract benefits totaled $31.1 billion. In 2003, the company sold $1.15 billion in equity and equity-related securities in a move to restore balance sheet strength.

In 2002 and 2003, the company saw increased market conduct examinations by state insurance departments, focused on its disability claims handling policies and practices. As a result, a coordinated examination of UNM's disability claims handling policies and practices was organized by the states of Massachusetts, Maine and Tennessee in 2003. At December 31, 2003, 44 states and the District of Columbia were participating in this effort. In early 2004, the company said that the New York State Attorney General had indicated a review of disability claims handling and in October 2004, UNM announced that it was subpoenaed for information in the NY Attorney General's probe of insurance broker activity.

During 2003, UNM acquired the U.K. group income protection group from Sun Life Assurance Co. of Canada, with renewal rights for about $37.2 million. Effective January 1, 2004, the company took over management and administration duties for the U.K. portion of Swiss Life's group income protection claims portfolio, with Swiss Life reinsuring this portfolio with UNM. In 2003, the company agreed to sell its Canadian branch to RBC Insurance; the transaction closed in the second quarter of 2004. In January, 2004, UNM sold its Unum Japan Accident Insurance Co. to Hitachi Capital Corp.

Company Financials Fiscal Year ending December 31

Per Share Data ($)

(Year Ended December 31)	2003	2002	2001	2000	1999	1998	1997	1996	1995	1994
Tangible Bk. Val.	22.94	25.58	21.74	20.29	17.82	20.05	17.69	17.34	16.48	11.16
Oper. Earnings	NA	2.52	2.44	2.37	-1.00	2.14	1.77	1.52	1.36	1.60
Earnings	-0.96	1.68	2.39	2.33	-0.77	1.82	1.84	1.46	1.14	1.35
S&P Core Earnings	-0.54	2.35	2.30	NA	NA	NA	NA	NA	NA	NA
Dividends	0.37	0.59	0.59	0.59	0.35	0.40	0.38	0.36	0.36	0.52
Payout Ratio	NM	35%	25%	25%	NM	22%	21%	25%	32%	38%
Prices - High	19.54	29.70	33.75	31.93	56.87	42.43	39.06	25.75	16.93	15.93
- Low	5.91	16.30	22.25	11.93	26.00	26.12	23.18	14.25	10.25	10.75
P/E Ratio - High	NM	18	14	14	NM	23	21	18	15	12
- Low	NM	10	9	5	NM	14	13	10	9	8

Income Statement Analysis (Million $)

	2003	2002	2001	2000	1999	1998	1997	1996	1995	1994
Life Ins. In Force	787,199	712,826	642,988	583,848	567,215	158,317	138,341	102,665	98,953	81,860
Prem. Inc.: Life	1,800	1,683	1,554	1,448	1,452	503	1,287	646	647	NA
Prem. Inc.: A & H	5,816	5,770	5,524	5,608	5,391	1,845	NA	501	486	1,383
Net Invest. Inc.	2,158	2,086	2,003	2,060	2,060	1,374	1,355	1,090	1,221	1,239
Total Revs.	9,992	9,613	9,395	9,432	9,330	3,938	3,553	2,292	2,555	2,762
Pretax Inc.	-435	1,019	825	866	-166	403	380	226	176	201
Net Oper. Inc.	NA	614	593	NA	NA	368	NA	151	136	158
Net Inc.	-265	817	582	564	-183	254	247	146	116	135
S&P Core Earnings	-150	568	564	NA	NA	NA	NA	NA	NA	NA

Balance Sheet & Other Fin. Data (Million $)

	2003	2002	2001	2000	1999	1998	1997	1996	1995	1994
Cash & Equiv.	663	734	2,515	1,958	836	366	401	288	302	335
Premiums Due	6,243	5,986	6,224	6,047	765	98.4	73.9	72.3	75.5	63.0
Invest. Assets: Bonds	31,187	27,486	24,393	22,589	22,357	15,142	17,342	11,145	12,618	11,596
Invest. Assets: Stocks	39.1	27.9	10.9	24.5	38.0	2.10	10.0	4.90	5.30	7.00
Invest. Assets: Loans	3,353	3,344	3,510	3,679	3,595	2,107	1,984	1,749	1,679	2,864
Invest. Assets: Total	35,028	31,152	28,324	26,604	26,549	17,333	19,434	13,317	14,751	15,018
Deferred Policy Costs	3,052	2,982	2,675	2,424	2,391	465	363	422	272	638
Total Assets	49,718	45,260	42,443	40,364	38,448	23,088	23,178	14,993	16,301	17,150
Debt	2,789	1,914	2,304	1,915	1,467	900	725	200	200	203
Common Equity	7,271	9,398	5,940	5,576	4,983	3,409	3,123	1,582	1,496	1,013
% Return On Revs.	NM	8.5	6.2	6.0	NM	6.5	7.0	6.4	4.5	4.9
% Ret. on Assets	NM	1.9	1.4	1.4	NM	1.1	1.3	0.9	0.7	0.8
% Ret. on Equity	NM	9.1	10.1	10.7	NM	7.7	10.0	9.5	8.2	9.6
% Invest. Yield	6.5	7.0	7.3	7.8	NM	7.9	7.6	7.8	8.2	8.2

Data as orig reptd.; bef. results of disc opers/spec. items. Per share data adj. for stk. divs.; EPS diluted. E-Estimated. NA-Not Available. NM-Not Meaningful. NR-Not Ranked. Realized inv. gains/losses incl. in historical EPS; excl. from estimates.

Office: 1 Fountain Square, Chattanooga, TN 37402-1307.
Telephone: 423-755-1011.
Website: http://www.unumprovident.com
Pres & CEO: T.R. Watjen.
EVP, Chief Admin & General Counsel: F.D. Copeland.
SVP & CFO: R.C. Greving.

Secy: S.N. Roth.
Investor Contact: T.A. White 423-755-8996.
Dirs: W. L. Armstrong, E. M. Caulfield, J. S. Fossel, R. E. Goldsberry, T. A. Kinser, A. S. MacMillan, Jr., H. O. Maclellan, Jr., C. W. Pollard, L. R. Pugh, J. W. Rowe, W. J. Ryan, T. R. Watjen.

Founded: in 1887.
Domicile: Delaware.
Employees: 13,400.
S&P Analyst: Gregory Simcik, CFA /CB/BK

Recommendation: **BUY** ★★★★★ | 12-Month Target Price: **$44.00**
(as of October 21, 2004)

UST has an approximate 0.07% weighting in the **S&P 500**

Sector: Consumer Staples
Sub-Industry: Tobacco
Peer Group: Tobacco - Diversified

Summary: UST is a leading producer of moist smokeless tobacco products, marketed under such leading brand names as Copenhagen and Skoal. It also imports and produces wines.

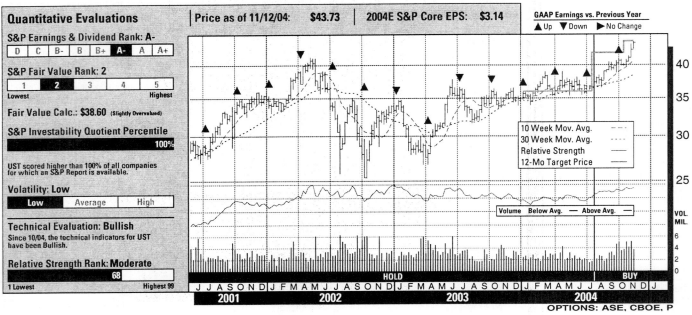

Quantitative Evaluations

S&P Earnings & Dividend Rank: A-
D | C | B- | B | B+ | **A-** | A | A+

S&P Fair Value Rank: 2
1 | **2** | 3 | 4 | 5
Lowest — Highest

Fair Value Calc.: $38.60 (Slightly Overvalued)

S&P Investability Quotient Percentile
100%
UST scored higher than 100% of all companies for which an S&P Report is available.

Volatility: Low
Low | Average | High

Technical Evaluation: Bullish
Since 10/04, the technical indicators for UST have been Bullish.

Relative Strength Rank: Moderate
68
1 Lowest — Highest 99

Price as of 11/12/04: $43.73 | **2004E S&P Core EPS:** $3.14

GAAP Earnings vs. Previous Year
▲ Up ▼ Down ► No Change

- 10 Week Mov. Avg.
- 30 Week Mov. Avg.
- Relative Strength
- 12-Mo Target Price

Volume | Below Avg. — Above Avg.

HOLD | BUY

J J A S O N D | J F M A M J J A S O N D | J F M A M J J A S O N D | J F M A M J J A S O N D | J
2001 | 2002 | 2003 | 2004

OPTIONS: ASE, CBOE, P

Analyst commentary prepared by Anishka Clarke/PMW/BK

Highlights October 28, 2004

- We expect net sales to advance 5% in 2005, following an estimated 4% rise in 2004. We believe continued strength in Red Seal, UST's price-value tobacco brand, and Skoal, one of its premium brands, will support volume growth in 2005. We also look for Husky, the sub-price value brand, new line extensions, and pouches to boost sales. Although Copenhagen products will likely see increased investment, we anticipate weak 2005 sales. Growth in wine sales should continue at a double-digit pace, in our view.

- We look for a slight improvement in gross margins, aided by volume growth and an effort to reduce promotional activity. We look for continued brand building activity, especially in the premium category, with modest growth from the incremental $24 million spent in 2004. SG&A expenses should rise at a controlled rate, in our view, and we project operating margins of about 51%. Interest expense should remain flat, reflecting stabilizing debt levels.

- With further share repurchases expected, we see 2005 EPS rising 7%, to $3.37, from our 2004 EPS estimate of $3.16, adjusted for favorable taxation. We project 2004 S&P Core EPS of $3.14, reflecting estimated stock option and pension-related items.

Investment Rationale/Risk October 28, 2004

- We are maintaining our buy opinion on the shares, based on valuation, and as trends continue to improve. Smokeless tobacco industry volumes have risen in the mid-single digits since the end of 2003. We attribute positive momentum to the successful sub-price value category and increased marketing initiatives that have led to a slowdown in the decline of the premium category. We believe UST will continue to benefit from overall industry trends, increased marketing investments, new products, and packaging innovations. For the longer term, we see a continued focus on premium products leading to margin expansion, despite lower growth potential. We look for products such as Husky and Red Seal to support volume growth in the near-term.

- Risks to our recommendation and target price include the company's exposure to the cigarette industry and its associated legal risks, which may continue to depress stock multiples.

- Using our two-stage discounted cash flow model, assuming a five-year annual sales growth rate of 5% and a weighted average cost of capital of 10.5%, we calculate intrinsic value of $45 a share. Our 12-month target price is $44, based on a blend of our intrinsic value estimate with a historical P/E multiple of 12X applied to our 2005 EPS estimate of $3.37.

Key Stock Statistics

S&P Core EPS 2005E	3.37	52-week Range	$43.91-33.93
S&P Oper. EPS 2004E	3.16	12 Month P/E	20.3
P/E on S&P Oper. EPS 2004E	13.8	Beta	0.43
S&P Oper. EPS 2005E	3.38	Shareholders	7,242
Yield (%)	4.8%	Market Cap (B)	$ 7.2
Dividend Rate/Share	2.08	Shares Outstanding (M)	165.2

Value of $10,000 invested five years ago: **$ 20,977**

Dividend Data Dividends have been paid since 1912

Amount ($)	Date Decl.	Ex-Div. Date	Stock of Record	Payment Date
0.520	Feb. 19	Mar. 11	Mar. 15	Mar. 31 '04
0.520	May. 04	Jun. 14	Jun. 15	Jun. 30 '04
0.520	Jul. 29	Sep. 10	Sep. 14	Sep. 30 '04
0.520	Oct. 28	Dec. 13	Dec. 15	Dec. 31 '04

Revenues/Earnings Data Fiscal year ending December 31

Revenues (Million $)

	2004	2003	2002	2001	2000	1999
1Q	433.3	420.0	375.2	383.0	368.3	350.1
2Q	464.6	438.9	432.3	422.2	392.0	378.1
3Q	462.0	437.6	451.3	417.8	389.9	383.4
4Q	—	446.2	424.0	447.4	397.4	400.8
Yr.	—	1,743	1,683	1,670	1,548	1,512

Earnings Per Share ($)

	2004	2003	2002	2001	2000	1999
1Q	0.73	0.66	0.61	0.66	0.62	0.60
2Q	0.92	0.77	0.80	0.74	0.69	0.70
3Q	0.80	0.74	0.77	0.75	0.69	0.69
4Q	E0.79	-0.27	-3.82	0.82	0.70	0.78
Yr.	E3.16	1.90	-1.61	2.97	2.70	2.68

Next earnings report expected: late-January Source: S&P, Company Reports
EPS Estimates based on S&P Operating Earnings; historical GAAP earnings are as reported.

STANDARD &POOR'S

UST Inc.

Recommendation: **BUY** ★ ★ ★ ★   12-Month Target Price: **$44.00** (as of October 21, 2004)

Business Summary October 28, 2004

UST, the leading U.S. producer of smokeless tobacco, has seen its profit growth restricted by intensified price competition. In recent years, the company's smokeless tobacco sales volumes (level with 2002 at 636.1 million cans), market share, and earnings have come under pressure from increasing competition from rivals that generally sell their smokeless tobacco products at substantially lower prices than UST's products. The company addressed these pressures in mid-1997, introducing a low-priced tobacco product, Red Seal, in areas in which price competition was fiercest. Since then, the company has introduced pouches, as well as successful line extensions in existing products.

Although UST still holds a substantial share (about 73%) of the highly profitable U.S. smokeless tobacco market, its share has declined from 86% in 1991. The company's moist smokeless tobacco products include Copenhagen and Skoal, the world's two best selling brands of moist smokeless tobacco. Moist brands also include Skoal Long Cut, Skoal Bandits, Copenhagen Long Cut, and Rooster. Other tobacco products carry the names Bruton, CC, and Red Seal. The company's tobacco products (86.4% of 2003 revenues) are sold throughout the U.S., principally to chain stores and tobacco and grocery wholesalers. In 1986, federal legislation was enacted regulating smokeless tobacco products by requiring health warning notices on smokeless tobacco packages and advertising and by prohibiting the advertising of smokeless tobacco products on electronic media. In recent years, other proposals have been made at federal, state and local levels for additional regulation of tobacco products, including a requirement for addi-

tional warning notices on cigar products, a significant increase in federal excise taxes, a ban or further restriction of all advertising and promotion, regulation of environmental tobacco smoke, and increased regulation of the manufacturing and marketing of tobacco products.

In addition to its smokeless tobacco offerings, UST is also a significant importer and producer of wines, and has other operations. A premium cigar business was divested in March 2004. Wines (11.2% of 2003 revenues) consist of premium varietal and blended wines dominated by Washington State-produced Chateau Ste. Michelle and Columbia Crest, and Villa Mt. Eden, a premium-quality California wine. Case volume for Columbia Crest and Chateau Ste. Michelle accounted for 77.9% of the company's premium wine case volume in 2003.

Other businesses (2.4% of 2003 revenues) include UST's international operation, which markets moist smokeless tobacco; and formerly included the manufacture and marketing of premium cigars (Don Tomas and Astral).

In March 2004, UST paid $200 million and transferred its cigar operations to Swedish Match North America, to dismiss, without prejudice, a case brought by that company. In January 2003, the Supreme Court declined to hear UST's appeal in the Conwood antitrust case, letting stand a $1.1 billion award against the company. UST paid $1.3 billion in 2003, from restricted deposits set aside in 2002 in satisfaction of the award.

Company Financials Fiscal Year ending December 31

Per Share Data ($)

(Year Ended December 31)	2003	2002	2001	2000	1999	1998	1997	1996	1995	1994
Tangible Bk. Val.	NM	NM	3.47	1.66	1.20	2.57	2.37	1.53	1.53	1.79
Cash Flow	2.15	-1.31	3.23	2.94	2.89	2.61	2.53	2.57	2.30	2.00
Earnings	1.90	-1.61	2.97	2.70	2.68	2.44	2.37	2.42	2.16	1.87
S&P Core Earnings	3.02	3.13	2.84	NA	NA	NA	NA	NA	NA	NA
Dividends	2.00	1.92	1.84	1.76	1.68	1.62	1.62	1.48	1.30	1.12
Payout Ratio	105%	NM	62%	65%	63%	66%	68%	61%	60%	60%
Prices - High	37.79	41.35	36.00	28.87	34.93	36.87	36.93	35.87	36.00	31.50
- Low	26.73	25.30	23.37	13.87	24.06	24.56	25.50	28.25	26.50	23.62
P/E Ratio - High	20	NM	12	11	13	15	16	15	17	17
- Low	14	NM	8	5	9	10	11	12	12	13

Income Statement Analysis (Million $)

	2003	2002	2001	2000	1999	1998	1997	1996	1995	1994
Revs.	1,743	1,683	1,670	1,548	1,512	1,423	1,402	1,397	1,325	1,198
Oper. Inc.	958	912	876	792	813	764	742	779	737	669
Depr.	41.6	49.7	43.2	39.6	37.0	31.7	30.5	28.3	29.1	28.2
Int. Exp.	76.9	46.1	66.2	47.4	13.5	4.42	8.40	7.29	4.80	4.62
Pretax Inc.	515	-444	799	718	763	734	704	745	705	641
Eff. Tax Rate	38.1%	NM	38.5%	38.5%	38.5%	38.0%	37.6%	37.7%	39.0%	39.5%
Net Inc.	319	-271	492	442	469	455	439	464	430	388
S&P Core Earnings	505	528	470	NA	NA	NA	NA	NA	NA	NA

Balance Sheet & Other Fin. Data (Million $)

	2003	2002	2001	2000	1999	1998	1997	1996	1995	1994
Cash	438	382	272	96.0	75.0	33.2	6.93	54.5	69.4	50.7
Curr. Assets	1,248	2,291	892	691	580	507	442	444	426	382
Total Assets	1,726	2,765	2,012	1,646	1,016	913	827	807	785	741
Curr. Liab.	521	1,462	222	170	261	197	167	307	281	161
LT Debt	1,140	1,140	863	869	411	100	100	100	100	125
Common Equity	-115	2,161	581	271	2,761	468	438	282	294	362
Total Cap.	1,029	3,301	1,627	1,326	3,172	568	538	382	394	492
Cap. Exp.	45.1	57.2	47.2	51.1	59.3	56.3	58.1	44.7	35.3	27.7
Cash Flow	360	-222	535	481	506	487	470	492	459	416
Curr. Ratio	2.4	1.6	4.0	4.1	2.2	2.6	2.7	1.4	1.5	2.4
% LT Debt of Cap.	110.8	34.5	53.0	65.5	13.0	17.6	18.6	26.2	25.4	25.4
% Net Inc.of Revs.	18.3	NM	29.4	28.6	31.0	32.0	31.3	33.2	32.4	32.4
% Ret. on Assets	14.2	NM	26.9	33.2	48.7	52.3	53.7	58.3	56.3	54.7
% Ret. on Equity	NM	NM	115.4	187.5	19.3	100.5	122.0	161.2	131.0	96.3

Data as orig reptd.; bef. results of disc opers/spec. items. Per share data adj. for stk. divs. Bold denotes primary EPS - prior periods restated. E-Estimated. NA-Not Available. NM-Not Meaningful. NR-Not Ranked. UR-Under Review.

Office: 100 West Putnam Ave, Greenwich, CT 06830.
Telephone: 203-661-1100.
Website: http://www.ustinc.com
Chrmn, Pres & CEO: V.A. Gierer, Jr.

EVP & General Counsel: R.H. Verheij.
SVP & CFO: R.T. D'Alessandro.
Dirs: J. Barr, J. P. Clancey, E. H. DeHority, Jr., P. Diaz Dennis, E. J. Eisenman, V. A. Gierer, Jr., J. E. Heid, P. J. Neff, R. J. Rossi.

Founded: in 1911.
Domicile: Delaware.
Employees: 5,212.
S&P Analyst: Anishka Clarke/PMW/BK

Valero Energy

Recommendation: **BUY** ★★★★☆
SELL | SELL | HOLD | BUY | BUY

12-Month Target Price: $47.00
(as of October 12, 2004)

VLO has an approximate 0.10% weighting in the **S&P 500**

Sector: Energy
Sub-Industry: Oil & Gas Refining, Marketing & Transportation
Peer Group: Refining and/or Marketing

Summary: Valero Energy is the third largest U.S. petroleum refiner, with total refining capacity of nearly 2 million barrels of oil per day.

Quantitative Evaluations

S&P Earnings & Dividend Rank: B

D	C	B-	**B**	B+	A-	A	A+

S&P Fair Value Rank: 5

1	2	3	4	**5**
Lowest				Highest

Fair Value Calc.: $47.20 (Slightly Undervalued)

S&P Investability Quotient Percentile

87%

VLO scored higher than 87% of all companies for which an S&P Report is available.

Volatility: Average

Low	**Average**	High

Technical Evaluation: Bullish

Since 9/04, the technical indicators for VLO have been Bullish.

Relative Strength Rank: Moderate

64

1 Lowest — Highest 99

Price as of 11/12/04:	**$42.26**	2004E S&P Core EPS:	**$6.18**

GAAP Earnings vs. Previous Year
▲ Up ▼ Down ► No Change

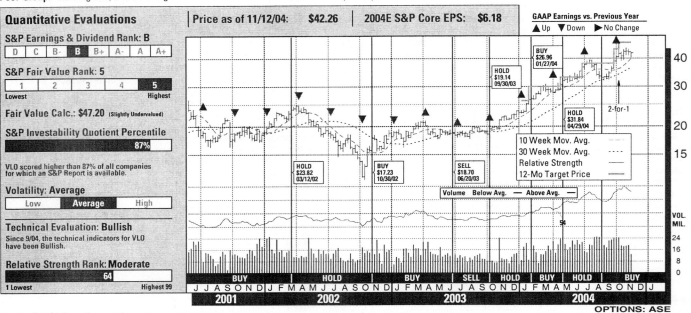

10 Week Mov. Avg.
30 Week Mov. Avg.
Relative Strength
12-Mo Target Price

Volume Below Avg. — Above Avg.

VOL.
MIL.
24
16
8
0

| BUY | HOLD | BUY | SELL | HOLD | BUY | HOLD | BUY |
J J A S O N D J F M A M J J A S O N D J F M A M J J A S O N D J F M A M J J A S O N D J
2001   2002   2003   2004

OPTIONS: ASE

Analyst commentary prepared by T. Vital/PMW/GG

Highlights October 13, 2004

- Wide sour crude discounts and high throughput volumes boosted second quarter operating earnings to $629.6 million ($2.28 a share, as adjusted, $0.28 above our estimate). Results benefited from contributions from the recently acquired Aruba and St. Charles refineries, which added about $80 million and $56 million, respectively, to operating income during the quarter. In July, VLO scheduled a two-for-one stock split for October, and announced a 6.7% dividend hike.

- With the phase-in of Tier II federal lower sulfur gasoline regulations in 2004, demand for sweet (lower sulfur) crude increased, and price discounts on sour crude feedstocks widened. Increased OPEC production of lower quality crudes has moved the global crude slate toward heavier blends, which are generally high in sulfur. We expect these trends to continue through 2005, we think that VLO's EPS will increase by about $1 for each dollar volume improvement in the heavy crude discount.

- Throughput volumes climbed 62% in the second quarter, reflecting recent acquisitions, and we expect 2004 volumes to grow 20%. EBITDA climbed 88% in 2003, and we expect an advance of 104% in 2004, on strong demand, before a drop of 15% in 2005, on projected lower pricing. The addition of a new 45,000 b/d coker unit at the Texas City refinery in December 2003 should add about $125 million to 2004 operating income.

Key Stock Statistics

S&P Core EPS 2005E	4.87	52-week Range	$44.48-21.25
S&P Oper. EPS 2004E	6.22	12 Month P/E	8.0
P/E on S&P Oper. EPS 2004E	6.8	Beta	0.83
S&P Oper. EPS 2005E	4.93	Shareholders	52,000
Yield (%)	0.8%	Market Cap (B)	$ 10.8
Dividend Rate/Share	0.32	Shares Outstanding (M)	256.6

Value of $10,000 invested five years ago: **$ 50,107**

Dividend Data Dividends have been paid since 1997

Amount ($)	Date Decl.	Ex-Div. Date	Stock of Record	Payment Date
0.150	Apr. 29	May. 17	May. 19	Jun. 16 '04
0.150	Jul. 15	Aug. 09	Aug. 11	Sep. 09 '04
2-for-1	Jul. 27	Oct. 08	Sep. 23	Oct. 07 '04
0.080	Oct. 21	Nov. 08	Nov. 10	Dec. 15 '04

Investment Rationale/Risk October 13, 2004

- We would accumulate the shares. VLO faces investment costs of $1.56 billion through 2007 ($750 million projected through 2004) to meet lower sulfur fuel U.S. federal Tier II mandates, but we view its ability to process low-cost heavy/sour crude feedstocks (about 70% of its 2004 crude purchases were sour) as a strategic advantage. Due to increased environmental costs, 2004 capital spending should rise to $1.7 billion ($375 million for Tier II, $235 million for regulatory, $270 million for turnarounds), from 2003's $1.11 billion ($380 million, $140 million, $140 million).

- Risks to our recommendation and target price include relatively high environmental spending through 2006, amid a leveraged balance sheet (net debt was 39% of capitalization at June 30, 2004) reflecting recent acquisitions; and potential adverse developments in MTBE litigation.

- Based on our price and margin projections, and blending our DCF and peer analyses, our 12-month target price is $47, equal to 9.5X our 2005 EPS estimate, a slight discount to peers, reflecting VLO's environmental spending needs. We think U.S. refining margins peaked in the 2004 second quarter, but with product markets tight, we think that U.S. refining margins have shifted toward higher highs and higher lows, and we expect heavy/sour crude price discounts to continue, aiding VLO's earnings and cash flow.

Revenues/Earnings Data Fiscal year ending December 31

Revenues (Million $)

	2004	2003	2002	2001	2000	1999
1Q	11,082	9,693	5,122	3,769	2,929	1,337
2Q	13,808	8,844	6,522	4,499	3,373	1,825
3Q	14,339	9,922	7,192	3,859	4,249	2,162
4Q	—	9,509	8,110	2,861	4,121	2,638
Yr.	—	37,969	26,976	14,988	14,671	7,961

Earnings Per Share ($)

	2004	2003	2002	2001	2000	1999
1Q	0.91	0.76	-0.18	1.06	0.27	-0.03
2Q	2.28	0.54	0.05	2.12	0.76	-0.20
3Q	1.57	0.75	0.14	0.79	1.01	0.20
4Q	E1.40	0.51	0.41	0.41	0.73	0.15
Yr.	E6.22	2.54	0.41	4.42	2.80	0.13

Next earnings report expected: late-January Source: S&P, Company Reports
EPS Estimates based on S&P Operating Earnings; historical GAAP earnings are as reported.

Please read the Required Disclosures and Reg. AC certification on the last page of this report.

The **McGraw·Hill** Companies

Valero Energy Corporation

Recommendation: **BUY** ★★★★☆   12-Month Target Price: **$47.00** (as of October 12, 2004)

Business Summary October 13, 2004

In 2001, Valero Energy (formerly Valero Refining and Marketing Co.) merged with Ultramar Diamond Shamrock (UDS), creating the third largest U.S. refiner, in terms of refining capacity. The company's business segments are refining (86% of 2003 operating revenue, 87% of operating income) and retail (14%, 13%). In 2003, VLO served customers in the U.S. (87% of 2003 revenues), Canada (11%), and other countries; no single customer accounted for over 10% of consolidated operating revenues. In March 2004, VLO acquired El Paso Corp.'s 315,000 b/d Aruba refinery and certain related businesses, for $465 million plus $162 million in working capital. In July 2003, the company purchased Orion Refining Corp.'s 215,000 b/d refinery in St. Charles Parish, LA, for $400 million, plus $149 million of hydrocarbon inventory.

The refining segment includes refining operations, wholesale marketing, product supply and distribution, and transportation operations. At December 31, 2003, the company owned and operated 14 refineries in the U.S. and Canada, with a combined throughput capacity of about 2.13 million barrels per day (b/d). The refining segment by region consisted of Gulf Coast (six refineries, 53% of throughput capacity), Mid-Continent (two, 15%), West Coast (three, 13%) and Northeast (two, 19%). According to the company, VLO has the most complex refining systems among the U.S. independent refiners, with a Nelson complexity rating of 11.6, versus a peer group average of 9.2. In 2003, about 49% of feedstock crudes were sour, 35% sweet, and 16% blendstocks and other feedstocks. About 70% of VLO's crude oil feedstock requirements are purchased through term contracts, with the remainder generally purchased on the spot market. Average

refinery yields for 2003 were composed of 54% gasoline and blendstocks, 28% distillates such as home heating oil, diesel fuel and jet fuel, and 18% asphalt, lubricants, petrochemicals, and other heavy products. Of the gasoline that VLO produces, about 30% is reformulated gasoline and CARB gasoline, which sells at a premium to conventional grades of gasoline. About 80% of the company's distillate slate is low-sulfur diesel, CARB diesel and jet fuel, which sell at a premium to high-sulfur heating oil.

VLO is one of the largest independent retailers of refined products in the central and southwest U.S. Its retail operations are segregated geographically into two groups: the U.S. System (sales of 129,000 b/d in 2003) and the Northeast System (79,000 b/d). In the U.S., VLO marketed refined products through about 1,150 company-operated sites in the U.S. (half owned/half leased) under a variety of brand names, including Corner Store, Ultramart, and Stop N Go. In VLO's California retail facilities, the company promoted its Valero brand, and in its Mid-Continent and Southwest retail facilities, its Diamond Shamrock brand was promoted. VLO's Northeast System involved retail operations in eastern Canada, where the company supplied refined products through about 475 retail stores, and distributed gasoline to about 575 dealers and independent jobbers.

At the end of 2003, the company held a 46% ownership stake in Valero L.P. (VLI), a master limited partnership that owns and operates crude oil and refined product pipelines and storage facilities primarily in Texas, New Mexico, Colorado, Oklahoma, California, and New Jersey.

Company Financials Fiscal Year ending December 31

Per Share Data ($)

(Year Ended December 31)	2003	2002	2001	2000	1999	1998	1997	1996	1995	1994
Tangible Bk. Val.	11.71	6.48	7.81	12.55	9.68	9.70	10.32	NA	NA	NA
Cash Flow	4.62	2.46	5.50	3.73	0.94	0.28	1.56	NA	NA	NA
Earnings	2.54	0.42	4.42	2.80	0.13	-0.42	1.02	0.26	NA	NA
S&P Core Earnings	2.49	0.27	4.29	NA	NA	NA	NA	NA	NA	NA
Dividends	0.21	0.20	0.17	0.16	0.16	0.11	0.08	NA	NA	NA
Payout Ratio	8%	48%	4%	6%	128%	NM	8%	NA	NA	NA
Prices - High	23.54	24.98	26.30	19.31	12.65	18.25	17.56	NA	NA	NA
- Low	16.10	11.57	15.75	9.25	8.34	8.81	13.46	NA	NA	NA
P/E Ratio - High	9	60	6	7	NM	NM	17	NA	NA	NA
- Low	6	28	4	3	NM	NM	13	NA	NA	NA

Income Statement Analysis (Million $)

	2003	2002	2001	2000	1999	1998	1997	1996	1995	1994
Revs.	37,969	26,976	14,988	14,671	7,961	5,539	5,756	2,758	NA	NA
Oper. Inc.	1,733	920	1,139	723	162	198	276	145	NA	NA
Depr. Depl. & Amort.	511	449	138	112	92.4	78.7	65.2	55.0	NA	NA
Int. Exp.	278	256	102	83.0	55.4	32.5	42.5	41.4	NA	NA
Pretax Inc.	989	164	895	528	20.2	-83.1	176	39.1	NA	NA
Eff. Tax Rate	36.9%	35.5%	37.0%	35.8%	29.2%	NM	36.3%	42.5%	NA	NA
Net Inc.	622	91.5	564	339	14.3	-47.3	112	22.5	NA	NA
S&P Core Earnings	604	60.0	547	NA	NA	NA	NA	NA	NA	NA

Balance Sheet & Other Fin. Data (Million $)

	2003	2002	2001	2000	1999	1998	1997	1996	1995	1994
Cash	369	409	346	14.6	60.1	11.2	9.94	NA	NA	NA
Curr. Assets	3,817	3,536	4,113	1,285	829	640	789	352	NA	NA
Total Assets	15,664	14,465	14,337	4,308	2,979	2,726	2,493	1,986	NA	NA
Curr. Liab.	3,064	3,007	4,730	1,039	719	498	597	301	NA	NA
LT Debt	4,245	4,867	2,805	1,042	785	822	430	353	NA	NA
Common Equity	5,535	4,308	4,203	1,527	1,085	1,085	1,159	1,076	NA	NA
Total Cap.	11,585	10,592	8,884	3,149	2,146	2,117	1,846	1,655	NA	NA
Cap. Exp.	976	628	394	195	101	166	69.2	NA	NA	NA
Cash Flow	1,128	541	701	451	107	31.4	172	66.2	NA	NA
Curr. Ratio	1.2	1.2	0.9	1.2	1.2	1.3	1.3	1.2	NA	NA
% LT Debt of Cap.	36.6	45.9	31.6	33.0	36.5	NM	62.8	21.3	NA	NA
% Ret. on Assets	4.1	0.6	6.0	9.3	0.5	NM	4.9	NA	NA	NA
% Ret. on Equity	12.5	2.2	19.7	26.0	1.3	NM	10.0	NA	NA	NA

Data as orig reptd.; bef. results of disc opers/spec. items. Per share data adj. for stk. divs.; EPS diluted. E-Estimated. NA-Not Available. NM-Not Meaningful. NR-Not Ranked. UR-Under Review.

Office: One Valero Place, San Antonio, TX 78212.	COO & EVP: W.R. Klesse.	Auditor: Ernst & Young.
Telephone: 210-370-2000.	EVP & CFO: M.S. Ciskowski.	Founded: in 1955.
Email: investorrelations@valero.com	EVP & Chief Admin: K.D. Booke.	Domicile: Delaware.
Website: http://www.valero.com	VP & Investor Contact: L. Bailey 210-370-2139.	Employees: 19,621.
Chrmn & CEO: W.E. Greehey.	Dirs: E. G. Biggs, W. E. Bradford, R. K. Calgaard, J. D. Choate, R. M.	S&P Analyst: T. Vital/PMW/GG
Pres: G.C. King.	Escobedo, W. E. Greehey, B. Marbut, S. K. Purcell.	

Veritas Software

Recommendation: **BUY** ★★★★★   12-Month Target Price: **$28.00**
SELL SELL HOLD BUY BUY
(as of October 07, 2004)

VRTS has an approximate 0.09% weighting in the **S&P 500**

Sector: Information Technology
Sub-Industry: Systems Software
Peer Group: Systems Software - Larger

Summary: VRTS is a leading supplier of enterprise data storage management solutions.

Quantitative Evaluations

S&P Earnings & Dividend Rank: B-

| D | C | B- | B | B+ | A- | A | A+ |

S&P Fair Value Rank: 4-

| 1 | 2 | 3 | 4 | 5 |
| Lowest | | | | Highest |

Fair Value Calc.: $23.10 (Slightly Undervalued)

S&P Investability Quotient Percentile

89%

VRTS scored higher than 89% of all companies for which an S&P Report is available.

Volatility: High

| Low | Average | High |

Technical Evaluation: Bullish
Since 10/04, the technical indicators for VRTS have been Bullish.

Relative Strength Rank: Moderate

67

| 1 Lowest | | Highest 99 |

Price as of 11/12/04: $21.96   **2004E S&P Core EPS:** $0.10

GAAP Earnings vs. Previous Year
▲ Up   ▼ Down   ▶ No Change

- - - 10 Week Mov. Avg.
..... 30 Week Mov. Avg.
—— Relative Strength
—— 12-Mo Target Price

BUY $20.34 10/07/04

Volume Below Avg. ▪ — Above Avg. —

HOLD   BUY

J J A S O N D | J F M A M J J A S O N D | J F M A M J J A S O N D | J F M A M J J A S O N D | J
   2001   2002   2003   2004

OPTIONS: ASE, CBOE, P, Ph

Analyst commentary prepared by Jonathan Rudy, CFA /MF/GG

Highlights October 28, 2004

- In June 2004, VRTS restated revenues for 2001 to 2003 after an internal probe found accounting problems with the way service revenue was recognized. The restatements reduced reported revenue by $3 million in 2001, $1 million in 2002, and $24 million in 2003. However, we believe that the long-term fundamentals in the storage industry remain solid and that VRTS continues to gain market share.

- We expect 2005 revenues to advance about 15%, as the company continues to gain share in the storage software market. We also see VRTS benefiting from the 2003 acquisitions of Jareva Technologies and Precise Software. We expect operating margins to narrow slightly in 2005, to about 26%. Despite an increase in the number of shares outstanding, and excluding amortization and one-time charges, we expect operating EPS to increase about 15% in 2004, to $0.92, from $0.80 in 2003. For 2005, we project an 11% increase in EPS to $1.02.

- Our 2004 Standard & Poor's Core Earnings estimate of $0.10 a share reflects the potential impact of projected stock option expense.

Investment Rationale/Risk October 28, 2004

- We have a buy recommendation on the shares, primarily due to our belief that recent data points indicate stronger enterprise software spending than we had previously anticipated, in addition to our view of the company's strong balance sheet and discount valuation to peers. VRTS has approximately $3.75 per share in net cash/investments. With VRTS trading at about 22X our 2005 operating EPS estimate of $1.02, and at a P/E to growth rate of 1.2X, a discount to peers, we believe the shares are attractively valued.

- Risks to our recommendation and target price include a rapidly changing technology landscape, a slowdown in global information technology spending, and intense competition in the enterprise software sector.

- Our 12-month target price of $28 is based primarily on our discounted cash flow analysis and relative P/E multiple to growth and enterprise value to sales metrics. The assumptions in our DCF model include approximately 20% annual growth in free cash flow over the next five years, a 15% discount rate, and a 3% perpetual growth rate.

Key Stock Statistics

S&P Oper. EPS 2004E	0.92	52-week Range	$40.68-16.30
P/E on S&P Oper. EPS 2004E	23.9	12 Month P/E	20.3
S&P Oper. EPS 2005E	1.02	Beta	NA
Yield (%)	Nil	Shareholders	217,000
Dividend Rate/Share	Nil	Market Cap (B)	$9.3
Shares Outstanding (M)	422.1		

Value of $10,000 invested five years ago: **$4,584**

Dividend Data

No cash dividends have been paid.

Revenues/Earnings Data Fiscal year ending December 31

Revenues (Million $)

	2004	2003	2002	2001	2000	1999
1Q	485.8	390.1	370.4	387.4	244.6	71.90
2Q	485.0	408.4	364.7	390.2	275.4	114.7
3Q	496.7	446.6	365.7	340.2	317.2	183.4
4Q	—	502.0	405.7	374.4	370.1	226.2
Yr.	—	1,747	1,507	1,492	1,207	596.1

Earnings Per Share ($)

	2004	2003	2002	2001	2000	1999
1Q	0.22	0.10	0.11	-0.40	-0.44	0.06
2Q	0.20	0.11	0.06	-0.32	-0.43	-0.59
3Q	0.22	0.17	0.09	-0.40	-0.37	-0.48
4Q	E0.27	0.43	-0.12	-0.51	-0.31	-0.44
Yr.	E0.92	0.81	0.14	-1.63	-1.55	-1.59

Next earnings report expected: late-January Source: S&P, Company Reports
EPS Estimates based on S&P Operating Earnings; historical GAAP earnings are as reported.

Please read the Required Disclosures and Reg. AC certification on the last page of this report.

Veritas Software Corporation

Recommendation: **BUY** ★★★★★   12-Month Target Price: **$28.00** (as of October 07, 2004)

Business Summary October 28, 2004

Veritas Software is a leading independent supplier of storage software products and services. Storage software includes storage management and data protection software as well as clustering, replication and storage area networking software. The company's products are designed to provide protection against data loss and file corruption, rapid recovery after disk or computer system failure, the ability to process large files efficiently, and the ability to manage and back up data distributed on large networks of systems without interrupting users.

VRTS emerged as the largest independent storage software provider following its 1999 acquisition of the Network and Storage Management Group (NSMG) of Seagate Software. Prior to this acquisition, the company focused primarily on sales of storage management software to the UNIX platform. The NSMG acquisition enabled VRTS to offer products targeted at the Windows NT market (the earlier edition of Windows 2000 and Windows XP).

Data protection products are designed to protect, back up, and restore data. Products include Veritas NetBackup, Veritas NetBackup Storage Migrator, and Veritas Global Data Manager, among others. File and volume management products improve the manageability and performance of business critical data. Products include Veritas Volume Manager, and Veritas File System. High availability, clustering and replication products make key businesses applications more available in complex computing environments. Products include Veritas Cluster Server, Veritas File Replicator and Veritas Storage Replicator. Application solutions are integrated solutions to help businesses optimize their storage management strate-

gies. Products include Veritas Foundation Suite, and Veritas Database editions for Oracle, Sybase and DB2.

The company has key OEM relationships with Dell, IBM, Hewlett-Packard, Sun Microsystems and Microsoft. VRTS has also integrated its solutions in a range of product suites optimized for specific applications including Oracle, Sybase, NFS, SAP and web-based environments.

In December 2000, VRTS, Seagate Technology, and a private investor group announced a transaction in which VRTS acquired all of its common stock held by Seagate Technology, certain other securities, and cash. In the transaction, the company issued to Seagate shareholders 109.3 million shares, in return for 128 million VRTS common shares. The main effect of the transaction for VRTS was to reduce the number of shares outstanding, therefore boosting EPS.

In January 2003, the company acquired Jareva Technologies, Inc., a privately held provider of automated server provisioning products, for about $62 million in cash. Jareva's software allows businesses to automatically deploy additional servers without manual intervention.

In June 2003, VRTS acquired Precise Software Solutions Ltd., a public company based in Israel, for about $609 million in cash and stock. Precise Software develops software that monitors and analyzes the performance of network infrastructure such as web and application servers, databases, and network storage equipment.

Company Financials Fiscal Year ending December 31

Per Share Data ($)

(Year Ended December 31)	2003	2002	2001	2000	1999	1998	1997	1996	1995	1994
Tangible Bk. Val.	3.98	3.92	3.24	1.66	0.43	0.79	0.50	0.30	0.23	0.15
Cash Flow	1.11	0.55	0.82	0.76	-1.51	0.25	0.12	0.06	0.12	0.12
Earnings	0.81	0.14	-1.63	-1.55	-1.59	0.22	0.10	0.06	0.01	0.02
S&P Core Earnings	0.11	-0.55	-2.32	NA	NA	NA	NA	NA	NA	NA
Dividends	Nil	Nil	Nil	Nil	Nil	Nil	Nil	Nil	Nil	Nil
Payout Ratio	Nil	Nil	Nil	Nil	Nil	Nil	Nil	Nil	Nil	Nil
Prices - High	39.40	49.89	108.75	174.00	98.58	14.44	7.98	5.55	2.58	0.80
- Low	15.55	10.29	17.30	72.41	12.88	5.27	2.24	1.65	0.52	0.27
P/E Ratio - High	49	NM	NM	NM	NM	65	78	96	36	37
- Low	19	NM	NM	NM	NM	24	22	28	7	12

Income Statement Analysis (Million $)

	2003	2002	2001	2000	1999	1998	1997	1996	1995	1994
Revs.	1,747	1,507	1,492	1,207	596	211	121	36.1	24.1	15.1
Oper. Inc.	-585	407	411	367	-336	61.8	31.8	13.7	8.61	3.12
Depr.	128	175	978	925	24.1	7.48	3.21	1.70	1.18	0.67
Int. Exp.	30.4	30.8	29.4	31.6	15.7	5.70	1.21	Nil	0.02	0.12
Pretax Inc.	392	128	-542	-526	-468	59.8	23.8	11.6	10.6	3.05
Eff. Tax Rate	9.76%	55.3%	NM	NM	NM	13.6%	4.25%	15.8%	7.21%	7.01%
Net Inc.	354	57.4	-651	-620	-503	51.6	22.7	9.77	9.87	2.84
S&P Core Earnings	48.9	-225	-926	NA	NA	NA	NA	NA	NA	NA

Balance Sheet & Other Fin. Data (Million $)

	2003	2002	2001	2000	1999	1998	1997	1996	1995	1994
Cash	823	764	538	887	148	139	75.6	5.27	2.35	8.69
Curr. Assets	2,844	2,546	2,062	1,383	862	277	225	42.3	32.1	21.6
Total Assets	5,348	4,200	3,799	4,083	4,233	349	242	47.8	35.0	23.2
Curr. Liab.	812	665	518	458	231	78.5	36.8	5.03	4.34	4.20
LT Debt	901	460	444	429	451	100	100	NA	NA	NA
Common Equity	3,544	2,884	2,723	2,983	3,393	170	104	41.8	30.1	18.8
Total Cap.	4,444	3,344	3,281	3,625	4,002	270	204	NA	NA	NA
Cap. Exp.	81.2	108	146	135	59.7	23.4	6.20	NA	5.50	NA
Cash Flow	482	232	327	305	-479	59.1	26.0	11.5	11.1	3.51
Curr. Ratio	3.5	3.8	4.0	3.0	3.7	3.5	6.1	8.4	7.4	5.1
% LT Debt of Cap.	20.3	13.8	13.5	11.8	11.3	37.1	48.9	NA	NA	NA
% Net Inc.of Revs.	20.2	3.8	NM	NM	NM	24.5	18.8	27.1	41.0	18.9
% Ret. on Assets	7.4	1.4	NM	NM	NM	17.5	15.7	23.6	33.9	NA
% Ret. on Equity	11.0	2.0	NM	NM	NM	37.7	31.2	27.2	40.4	NA

Data as orig reptd.; bef. results of disc opers/spec. items. Per share data adj. for stk. divs.; EPS diluted. E-Estimated. NA-Not Available. NM-Not Meaningful. NR-Not Ranked. UR-Under Review.

Office: 350 Ellis Street, Mountain View, CA 94043.
Telephone: 650-527-8000.
Email: IR@veritas.com
Website: http://www.veritas.com
Chrmn, Pres & CEO: G.L. Bloom.
Vice Chrmn: G.W. Squire.

EVP & CFO: E. Gillis.
SVP, Secy & General Counsel: J. Brigden.
Investor Contact: R. Budig 650-527-4047.
Dirs: G. L. Bloom, S. D. Brooks, M. Brown, K. J. Lauk, W. Pade, D. J. Roux, G. W. Squire, C. M. Ticknor, V. P. Unruh.

Founded: in 1982.
Domicile: Delaware.
Employees: 6,518.
S&P Analyst: Jonathan Rudy, CFA /MF/GG

Verizon Communications

Recommendation: **BUY** ★★★★★   **12-Month Target Price: $44.00**
SELL SELL HOLD BUY BUY   (as of August 12, 2004)

VZ has an approximate 1.06% weighting in the **S&P 500**

Sector: Telecommunication Services
Sub-Industry: Integrated Telecommunication Services
Peer Group: Regional Bell Operating Companies (RBOC's)

Summary: VZ, which offers wireline and wireless services, was created through the mid-2000 merger of Bell Atlantic Corp. and GTE Corp.

Quantitative Evaluations

S&P Earnings & Dividend Rank: B

| D | C | B- | **B** | B+ | A- | A | A+ |

S&P Fair Value Rank: 2

| 1 | **2** | 3 | 4 | 5 |
| Lowest | | | | Highest |

Fair Value Calc.: $37.70 (Slightly Overvalued)

S&P Investability Quotient Percentile
92%

VZ scored higher than 92% of all companies for which an S&P Report is available.

Volatility: Low

| **Low** | Average | High |

Technical Evaluation: Bullish
Since 11/04, the technical indicators for VZ have been Bullish.

Relative Strength Rank: Moderate
58
1 Lowest   Highest 99

Price as of 11/12/04: **$42.22** | **2004E S&P Core EPS:** **$1.89**

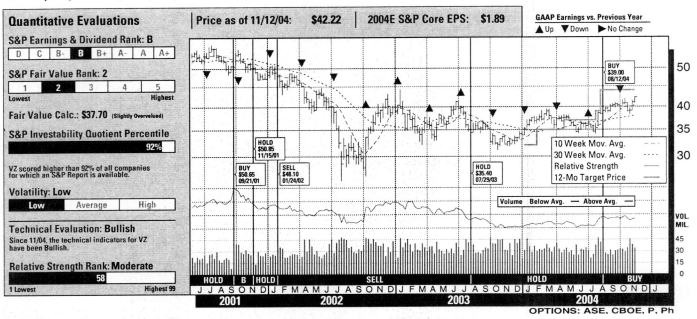

GAAP Earnings vs. Previous Year
▲ Up   ▼ Down   ► No Change

Analyst commentary prepared by Todd Rosenbluth/PMW/JWP

Highlights November 02, 2004

- We expect 2005 revenues to rise 3%, following a likely 5.5% increase in 2004, with strong customer growth in the wireless joint venture and long-distance and DSL penetration outweighing a decline in the domestic telecom unit's voice revenues stemming from fewer access lines. We expect access line erosion to persist, due to broadband and wireless substitution. We believe the wireless unit will continue to gain market share, even though two of its peers have merged. For 2005, we see wireless revenue growth of 7%, after an expected 23% advance in 2004, aided by data revenue gains and the net addition of subscribers.

- We see EBITDA margins widening to 41% in 2005, from a likely 40% in 2004, on staff reductions, increased wholesale access rates, and other costs controls. In the 2004 third quarter, despite higher pension costs, due to higher medical expenses and revised assumptions, margins widened, as wireless customer acquisition costs held steady despite strong growth.

- We see 2004 operating EPS of $2.51, and S&P Core EPS of $1.89, with the difference largely due to a pension cost adjustment. We see 2005 operating EPS of $2.65 and S&P Core EPS of $2.08. In the 2004 first half, the company recorded charges of $0.17 a share for severance and pension benefits related to recent workforce reductions.

Key Stock Statistics

S&P Core EPS 2005E	**2.08**	52-week Range	**$42.27-31.81**
S&P Oper. EPS 2004E	**2.51**	12 Month P/E	**35.2**
P/E on S&P Oper. EPS 2004E	**16.8**	Beta	**0.92**
S&P Oper. EPS 2005E	**2.65**	Shareholders	**1,335,000**
Yield (%)	**3.6%**	Market Cap (B)	**$116.9**
Dividend Rate/Share	**1.54**	Shares Outstanding (M)	**2769.0**

Value of $10,000 invested five years ago: **$ 7,850**

Dividend Data Dividends have been paid since 1984

Amount ($)	Date Decl.	Ex-Div. Date	Stock of Record	Payment Date
0.385	Dec. 04	Jan. 07	Jan. 09	Feb. 02 '04
0.385	Mar. 08	Apr. 06	Apr. 09	May. 03 '04
0.385	Jun. 03	Jul. 07	Jul. 09	Aug. 02 '04
0.385	Sep. 02	Oct. 06	Oct. 08	Nov. 01 '04

Investment Rationale/Risk November 02, 2004

- With most of the major U.S. wireless carriers having reported third quarter results, we believe VZ's wireless segment remains the clear industry leader, and we expect market share gains to continue into 2005. In addition, we believe the company is taking appropriate steps in focusing capital spending on growth initiatives such as wireless broadband and its fiber buildout. We see this helping to offset competition. We see cash flow as strong enough to support the dividend. Although we see wireline pressures, we believe VZ's overall growth prospects exceed those of the other RBOCs, and think that the shares deserve a premium valuation.

- Risks to our opinion and target price include pricing pressures in the wireline and wireless segments, customer migration, and earnings quality issues due to pension income.

- Based on our 2005 sales estimate, our sum-of-the-parts analysis values VZ at about $45 a share, reflecting our view of the telco's relatively stronger prospects. Our DCF analysis assumes an 8.2% weighted average cost of capital and cash flow growth ranging from -1% to 1% from 2004 to 2007, with 1% to 2% growth for the next 10 years. Our blended 12-month target price is $44. Combined with a dividend yield of about 4%, we would buy the shares for total return.

Revenues/Earnings Data Fiscal year ending December 31

Revenues (Million $)

	2004	2003	2002	2001	2000	1999
1Q	17,136	16,490	16,375	16,266	14,532	7,967
2Q	17,383	16,829	16,835	16,909	16,769	8,295
3Q	18,206	17,155	17,201	17,004	16,533	8,304
4Q	—	17,278	17,214	17,011	16,873	8,608
Yr.	—	67,752	67,625	67,190	64,707	33,174

Earnings Per Share ($)

	2004	2003	2002	2001	2000	1999
1Q	0.43	0.63	Nil	0.65	0.56	0.72
2Q	0.64	0.46	-0.78	-0.38	1.79	0.74
3Q	0.63	0.64	1.60	0.69	0.97	0.74
4Q	E0.65	-0.53	0.83	-0.75	0.62	0.46
Yr.	E2.51	1.27	1.67	0.22	3.95	2.66

Next earnings report expected: late-January   Source: S&P, Company Reports
EPS Estimates based on S&P Operating Earnings; historical GAAP earnings are as reported.

Verizon Communications Inc.

Recommendation: **BUY** ★★★★★   12-Month Target Price: **$44.00** (as of August 12, 2004)

Business Summary November 02, 2004

Verizon Communications was formed through the $60 billion merger of Bell Atlantic Corp. and GTE Corp. in June 2000. As of September 2004, VZ was the largest U.S. provider of both wireline and wireless communications, with 53.7 million access lines (down 4.4% from the level a year earlier) and 42.1 million wireless customers (up 17%). However, following a merger of two wireless carriers in October, Verizon Wireless has the second largest customer base.

The domestic telecom segment, which serves a territory consisting of 32 states and the District of Columbia, generated 58% of total operating revenues in 2003. The segment provides exchange telecommunications services among customers within a local access and transport area (LATA), including local private voice and data services, switched local residential and business services, and toll services within or outside a LATA. VZ finished the 2004 third quarter with 6.7 million resale and UNE-P lines (up nearly 1.3 million, year to year). As of September 2004, it had 17.3 million long-distance customers, and had received FCC approval to enter in-region long-distance markets in all of its local markets for 18 months. In 2003, the company began bundling its local and long-distance service with its DSL service offering. As of September 2004, about 53% of VZ's residential local service customers had also purchased DSL and/or long-distance from the company. In addition, VZ has begun rolling out advanced fiber based broadband services in nine states as part of its plan to equip one million homes and business with the technology in 2004.

In 2003, primarily as a result of a voluntary separation plan in the fourth quarter,

the Domestic Telecom unit's workforce was reduced by more than 22,500. The company recorded a charge of $1.04 a share in the fourth quarter, for severance and pension benefits. In the 2004 second quarter, the company recorded charges of $0.03 a share for asset writedowns and $0.01 for employee pension benefits.

Verizon Wireless, a joint venture of VZ (55%) and Vodafone (45%), combines the wireless operations of Bell Atlantic Mobile, GTE Wireless, AirTouch and Primeco. In December 2001, VZ acquired Price Communications Wireless for $1.7 billion, adding about 560,000 customers. In January 2003, the company withdrew a registration statement for an IPO of its wireless group. Vodafone has an option that began in July 2003 to put a portion of its 45% ownership back to Verizon Wireless. As of September, the unit had a 17.5% penetration rate and a 1.5% monthly churn rate, among the industry's best. In January 2004, Verizon Wireless began expanding its BroadbandAccess EV-DO network nationally, which had been tested in San Diego and Washington, DC, and announced plans to spend $1 billion on it over the next two years.

The International segment includes operations, investments and contracts in the Americas, Europe and Asia. At December 31, 2003, the company's International segment managed about 9 million access lines and provided wireless services to about 30 million customers. VZ's Information Services segment is the world's leader in print and online directory publishing, with nearly 1,900 directory titles. In addition to producing print Yellow Pages in 48 states and six countries, the segment also consists of an online directory called Superpages.com.

Company Financials Fiscal Year ending December 31

Per Share Data ($)

(Year Ended December 31)	2003	2002	2001	2000	1999	1998	1997	1996	1995	1994
Tangible Bk. Val.	NM	NM	NM	12.79	10.22	8.39	8.24	8.47	7.64	6.94
Cash Flow	6.14	6.56	5.22	8.43	6.59	5.62	5.29	4.92	5.14	NA
Earnings	1.27	1.67	0.22	3.95	2.66	1.87	1.57	1.98	2.13	1.60
S&P Core Earnings	1.76	1.91	0.58	NA	NA	NA	NA	NA	NA	NA
Dividends	1.54	1.54	1.54	1.54	1.54	1.54	1.49	1.43	1.40	1.37
Payout Ratio	122%	92%	NM	39%	58%	82%	95%	72%	66%	85%
Prices - High	44.31	51.09	57.40	66.00	69.50	61.18	45.87	37.43	34.43	29.81
- Low	31.10	26.01	43.80	39.06	50.62	40.43	28.37	27.56	24.18	24.18
P/E Ratio - High	35	31	NM	17	26	33	29	19	16	19
- Low	25	16	NM	10	19	22	18	14	11	15

Income Statement Analysis (Million $)

	2003	2002	2001	2000	1999	1998	1997	1996	1995	1994
Revs.	67,752	67,625	67,190	64,707	33,174	31,566	30,194	13,081	13,430	13,791
Depr.	13,617	13,423	13,657	12,261	6,221	5,870	5,864	2,595	2,627	2,652
Maint.	NA	NA	NA	NA	NA	NA	NA	NA	NA	NA
Constr. Credits	NA	NA	NA	NA	NA	NA	NA	NA	NA	NA
Eff. Tax Rate	19.7%	21.7%	64.2%	38.9%	37.8%	40.2%	38.4%	36.8%	38.2%	38.7%
Net Inc.	3,509	4,584	590	10,810	4,208	2,991	2,455	1,739	1,862	1,402
S&P Core Earnings	4,859	5,250	1,557	NA	NA	NA	NA	NA	NA	NA

Balance Sheet & Other Fin. Data (Million $)

	2003	2002	2001	2000	1999	1998	1997	1996	1995	1994
Gross Prop.	180,975	178,028	169,586	158,957	89,238	83,065	77,437	34,758	33,554	33,746
Net Prop.	75,316	74,496	74,419	69,504	39,299	36,816	35,039	15,916	15,921	16,938
Cap. Exp.	11,884	11,984	17,371	17,633	8,675	7,447	6,638	2,553	2,627	2,699
Total Cap.	96,281	122,120	116,888	115,923	39,091	33,678	29,522	14,881	14,597	18,228
Fxd. Chgs. Cov.	2.5	5.5	3.5	3.7	6.8	5.0	4.3	6.0	6.0	4.9
Capitalization:										
LT Debt	16,759	44,791	45,657	42,491	18,664	17,846	13,265	5,960	6,407	6,806
Pfd.	Nil	Nil	Nil	Nil	Nil	Nil	200	145	145	85.0
Common	33,466	33,720	32,539	36,342	15,880	13,026	12,789	7,423	6,685	6,081
% Return On Revs.	5.2	6.8	0.9	16.7	12.7	9.5	8.1	13.3	13.9	10.2
% Return On Invest. Capital	8.4	7.6	4.0	15.4	16.9	18.3	17.2	19.7	21.0	9.8
% Return On Com. Equity	10.6	13.5	1.8	33.5	29.1	23.2	24.3	24.7	29.2	19.6
% Earn. on Net Prop.	28.1	34.5	50.5	38.3	22.3	18.4	21.0	18.5	18.8	10.2
% LT Debt of Cap.	33.4	36.6	58.4	53.9	54.0	57.8	50.5	44.1	48.4	52.5
Capital. % Pfd.	Nil	Nil	Nil	Nil	Nil	Nil	0.8	1.1	1.1	0.6
Capital. % Common	66.6	42.9	41.6	46.1	46.0	42.2	48.7	54.9	50.5	46.9

Data as orig reptd.; bef. results of disc opers/spec. items. Per share data adj. for stk. divs.; EPS diluted. E-Estimated. NA-Not Available. NM-Not Meaningful. NR-Not Ranked. UR-Under Review.

Office: 1095 Avenue of the Americas, New York, NY 10036.
Telephone: 212-395-2121.
Website: http://www.verizon.com
Chrmn & CEO: I.G. Seidenberg.
Pres & Vice Chrmn: L.T. Babbio, Jr.
EVP & CFO: D.A. Toben.

EVP & General Counsel: W.P. Barr.
SVP & Treas: W.F. Heitmann.
SVP & Investor Contact: T.A. Bartlett 212-395-2121.
Dirs: J. R. Barker, R. L. Carrion, R. W. Lane, S. O. Moose, J. Neubauer, T. H. O'Brien, H. B. Price, I. G. Seidenberg, W. V. Shipley, J. R. Stafford, R. D. Storey.

Auditor: Ernst & Young.
Founded: in 1983.
Domicile: Delaware.
Employees: 229,500.
S&P Analyst: Todd Rosenbluth/PMW/JWP

V. F. Corp.

Recommendation: HOLD ★ ★ ★ ★ ★
SELL SELL HOLD BUY BUY

12-Month Target Price: **$56.00**
(as of November 17, 2004)

VFC has an approximate 0.05% weighting in the **S&P 500**

Sector: Consumer Discretionary
Sub-Industry: Apparel, Accessories & Luxury Goods
Peer Group: Designer Mens/Womens Apparel

Summary: This global apparel company produces jeans, decorated knitwear and sportswear, intimate apparel, children's playwear, and specialty apparel under several well known brand names.

Quantitative Evaluations

S&P Earnings & Dividend Rank: B+

| D | C | B- | B | B+ | A- | A | A+ |

S&P Fair Value Rank: 4-

| 1 | 2 | 3 | 4 | 5 |
| Lowest | | | | Highest |

Fair Value Calc.: $57.50 (Slightly Undervalued)

S&P Investability Quotient Percentile

98%

VFC scored higher than 98% of all companies for which an S&P Report is available.

Volatility: Low

| Low | Average | High |

Technical Evaluation: Bullish
Since 10/04, the technical indicators for VFC have been Bullish.

Relative Strength Rank: Moderate

62

| 1 Lowest | | Highest 99 |

| Price as of 11/17/04: | **$54.68** | 2004E S&P Core EPS: | **$3.85** |

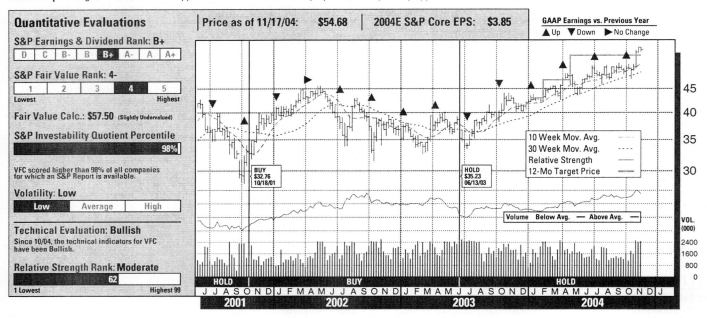

GAAP Earnings vs. Previous Year ▲ Up ▼ Down ► No Change

- 10 Week Mov. Avg.
- 30 Week Mov. Avg.
- Relative Strength
- 12-Mo Target Price

BUY $32.76 10/18/01
HOLD $35.23 06/13/03

Volume Below Avg. — Above Avg.

VOL. (000) 2400 1600 800 0

HOLD | BUY | HOLD
J J A S O N D J F M A M J J A S O N D J F M A M J J A S O N D J F M A M J J A S O N D J
2001 2002 2003 2004

Analyst commentary prepared by Marie Driscoll, CFA /DC/GG

Highlights August 02, 2004

- We expect 2004 sales to grow about 13%, on contributions from Nautica (acquired in August 2003) and Vans (acquired in June 2004), additional penetration of Lee and Wrangler brands in international markets, and continued gains for The North Face brand of outdoor products.

- We see slightly lower U.S. jeanswear sales, reflecting the impact of Levi Strauss's July 2003 entry into the mass market channel, and a shift in mix toward lower-priced products. We expect VFC's Wrangler brand to experience pricing and margin pressure.

- We look for operating margins to narrow slightly despite lower-cost sourcing, cost savings from restructuring, and VFC's exit from certain unprofitable businesses. We expect VF Corp. will increase marketing spending for Nautica and its outdoor and sportswear businesses. In addition, the company has allocated $45 million ($0.27 per share) of SG&A expenses to fuel future growth. After expected level interest expense and taxes estimated at 35%, we project 2004 EPS of $3.96, up 10% from 2003's $3.61. Our 2004 Standard and Poor's Core Earnings estimate is $3.71, reflecting estimated pension expense and projected option expense.

Investment Rationale/Risk August 02, 2004

- Our hold recommendation on the shares balances what we view as attractive valuation against what we regard as VFC's reliance on acquisitions for sales and earnings growth. With more than two-thirds of its businesses in mature and commodity-type deflationary categories and channels, we think it will be hard for the company to meet its goal of 6% annual revenue growth beyond 2004.

- Risks to our opinion and target price include fashion and inventory risk, and integration risk for recent acquisitions.

- Our 12-month target price of $53 is equal to a historical forward P/E multiple of 12.2X our 2005 EPS estimate of $4.38. Our DCF model yields intrinsic value of $51. The stock, recently yielding 2.2% and trading at 12X our 2004 EPS estimate, is at a 30% discount to the S&P 500 and a 15% discount to peer branded apparel companies.

Key Stock Statistics

S&P Core EPS 2005E	4.18	52-week Range	$55.29-40.16
S&P Oper. EPS 2004E	4.10	12 Month P/E	13.4
P/E on S&P Oper. EPS 2004E	13.3	Beta	0.61
S&P Oper. EPS 2005E	4.45	Shareholders	5,779
Yield (%)	2.0%	Market Cap (B)	$ 6.1
Dividend Rate/Share	1.08	Shares Outstanding (M)	111.1

Value of $10,000 invested five years ago: **$ 20,760**

Dividend Data Dividends have been paid since 1941

Amount ($)	Date Decl.	Ex-Div. Date	Stock of Record	Payment Date
0.260	Feb. 17	Mar. 05	Mar. 09	Mar. 19 '04
0.260	Apr. 27	Jun. 09	Jun. 11	Jun. 21 '04
0.260	Jul. 22	Sep. 08	Sep. 10	Sep. 20 '04
0.270	Oct. 21	Dec. 08	Dec. 10	Dec. 20 '04

Revenues/Earnings Data Fiscal year ending December 31

Revenues (Million $)

	2004	2003	2002	2001	2000	1999
1Q	1,433	1,250	1,212	1,423	1,355	1,358
2Q	1,270	1,135	1,160	1,323	1,330	1,365
3Q	1,793	1,435	1,400	1,477	1,600	1,465
4Q	—	1,387	1,311	1,295	1,463	1,364
Yr.	—	5,207	5,084	5,519	5,748	5,552

Earnings Per Share ($)

	2004	2003	2002	2001	2000	1999
1Q	0.93	0.83	0.67	0.67	0.68	0.69
2Q	0.80	0.68	0.79	0.60	0.69	0.64
3Q	1.38	1.14	1.15	0.90	0.86	0.85
4Q	E0.98	0.96	0.69	-1.03	0.08	0.81
Yr.	E4.10	3.61	3.24	1.19	2.27	2.99

Next earnings report expected: mid-February Source: S&P, Company Reports
EPS Estimates based on S&P Operating Earnings; historical GAAP earnings are as reported.

V. F. Corporation

Recommendation: **HOLD** ★ ★ ★ ☆ ☆   12-Month Target Price: **$56.00** (as of November 17, 2004)

Business Summary August 02, 2004

V.F. Corp. is the world's largest apparel manufacturer, and holds the leading position in several market categories, including jeanswear, intimate apparel, workwear and daypacks.

In the U.S., the company holds about 20% of the jeans market, with its Lee, Wrangler, Rustler, Riders, Brittania, Chic and Gitano brands. It also makes and markets Lee, Wrangler, Maverick, Old Axe, and H.I.S. jeanswear and related products in Europe, and markets Lee and Wrangler brands in Canada, Mexico, and South America.

VFC entered the sportswear market with the August 2003 acquisition of Nautica Enterprises, Inc. Nautica is principally a brand of men's sportswear sold in department and specialty stores as well as 115 Nautica outlet stores. The Nautica brand is licensed for several apparel categories not produced by the company and for nonapparel products that generate over $400 million in wholesale sales annually.

VFC's U.S. intimate apparel brands include Bestform, Curvation and Vassarette in the discount store channel, and Vanity Fair, Lily of France, Exquisite Form, and the licensed Tommy Hilfiger and Natori labels in the department, chain and specialty store channel. Products include bras, panties, daywear, shapewear and sleepwear. The company also has a private label lingerie business with various national chain, discount and specialty stores. In Europe, VFC sells women's intimate apparel under additional labels such as Lou, Bolero, Gemma, Intima Cherry, Belcor and Variance.

The outdoor apparel and equipment segment includes the North Face brand of outdoor apparel and equipment, and the JansSport and Eastpak brands of daypacks and backpacks. VFC's occupational apparel segment produces workwear, career and safety apparel sold under the Red Kap, Horace Small Apparel Company, PST and Bulwark brands.

The all other segment includes its activewear apparel businesses, which designs, makes and markets imprinted sports apparel under licenses granted by the four major American professional sports leagues and NASCAR, most major colleges and universities and other organizations, and 110 retail outlet stores that sell a broad selection of excess quantities of company products.

Capital spending totaled $86.6 million in 2003, versus $64.5 million and $78.3 million in 2002 and 2001, respectively, and generally related to maintenance spending for worldwide manufacturing and other facilities. VFC projected that 2004 capital expenditures would reach $90 million.

In the 2001 fourth quarter, the company began a strategic repositioning program designed to exit underperforming businesses and aggressively reduce its overall cost structure. It incurred charges of $26 million, $114 million and $117 million in 2002, 2001 and 2000, respectively. Moves included closing excess production capacity, and exiting underperforming businesses, including U.S. swimwear, specialty workwear, and private label knitwear. In May 2004, VFC sold its infants' and children's apparel businesses, with products sold under the Healthtex and Lee brands, and the licensed Nike name. The company expects the transaction to be about neutral to 2004 earnings.

Company Financials Fiscal Year ending December 31

Per Share Data ($)

(Year Ended December 31)	2003	2002	2001	2000	1999	1998	1997	1996	1995	1994
Tangible Bk. Val.	8.61	10.91	9.97	9.71	10.08	9.36	8.69	8.67	6.97	6.41
Cash Flow	4.64	4.35	0.00	3.73	5.71	4.39	3.87	3.57	2.51	3.33
Earnings	3.61	3.24	1.19	2.27	2.99	3.10	2.70	2.32	1.21	2.10
S&P Core Earnings	3.70	2.75	0.77	NA	NA	NA	NA	NA	NA	NA
Dividends	1.01	0.97	0.93	0.89	0.85	0.81	0.77	0.73	0.69	0.65
Payout Ratio	28%	30%	78%	39%	28%	26%	29%	31%	57%	31%
Prices - High	44.08	45.64	42.70	36.90	55.00	54.68	48.25	34.93	28.56	26.87
- Low	32.62	31.50	28.15	20.93	27.43	33.43	32.25	23.81	23.37	22.12
P/E Ratio - High	12	14	36	16	18	18	18	15	24	13
- Low	9	10	24	9	9	11	12	10	19	11

Income Statement Analysis (Million $)

	2003	2002	2001	2000	1999	1998	1997	1996	1995	1994
Revs.	5,207	5,084	5,519	5,748	5,552	5,479	5,222	5,137	5,062	4,972
Oper. Inc.	718	729	516	683	820	845	761	718	522	697
Depr.	104	107	169	173	335	161	156	161	168	159
Int. Exp.	61.4	71.3	93.4	88.7	71.4	62.0	50.0	62.8	77.0	80.3
Pretax Inc.	599	562	263	432	596	631	585	508	284	456
Eff. Tax Rate	33.5%	35.1%	47.6%	38.1%	38.5%	38.5%	40.0%	41.1%	44.6%	39.8%
Net Inc.	398	364	138	267	366	388	351	300	157	275
S&P Core Earnings	406	303	84.6	NA	NA	NA	NA	NA	NA	NA

Balance Sheet & Other Fin. Data (Million $)

	2003	2002	2001	2000	1999	1998	1997	1996	1995	1994
Cash	515	496	332	119	79.9	63.0	124	271	84.0	60.0
Curr. Assets	2,209	2,075	2,031	2,110	1,877	1,848	1,601	1,706	1,668	1,551
Total Assets	4,246	3,503	4,103	4,358	4,027	3,837	3,323	3,450	3,447	3,336
Curr. Liab.	872	875	814	1,006	1,113	1,033	766	766	868	912
LT Debt	956	602	904	905	518	522	516	519	614	517
Common Equity	1,951	1,658	2,113	2,192	2,164	2,046	1,841	1,974	1,772	1,734
Total Cap.	2,938	2,297	3,062	3,145	2,733	2,622	2,439	2,562	2,469	2,335
Cap. Exp.	86.6	64.5	81.6	125	150	189	154	139	155	133
Cash Flow	502	472	304	437	698	549	503	457	321	429
Curr. Ratio	2.5	2.4	2.5	2.1	1.7	1.8	2.1	2.2	1.9	1.7
% LT Debt of Cap.	32.6	26.2	29.5	28.8	18.9	19.9	21.1	20.3	24.9	22.1
% Net Inc.of Revs.	7.6	7.2	2.5	4.6	6.6	7.1	6.7	5.9	3.1	5.5
% Ret. on Assets	10.3	9.6	3.3	6.4	9.3	10.8	10.4	8.6	4.6	8.9
% Ret. on Equity	22.1	19.3	6.3	12.1	17.1	20.0	18.3	15.8	8.7	16.5

Data as orig reptd.; bef. results of disc opers/spec. items. Per share data adj. for stk. divs. Bold denotes primary EPS - prior periods restated. E-Estimated. NA-Not Available. NM-Not Meaningful. NR-Not Ranked. UR-Under Review.

Office: 105 Corporate Center Boulevard , Greensboro, NC 27408.
Telephone: 336-424-6000.
Email: irrequest@vfc.com
Website: http://www.vfc.com
Chrmn, Pres & CEO: M.J. McDonald.
VP & CFO: R.K. Shearer.

VP & Treas: F.C. Pickard, III.
VP, Secy & General Counsel: C.S. Cummings.
VP & Investor Contact: C. Knoebel 336-424-6189.
Dirs: E. E. Crutchfield, J. Ernesto de Bedout, U. F. Fairbairn, B. S. Feigin, G. Fellows, D. Hesse, R. J. Hurst, W. A. McCollough, M. J. McDonald, M. R. Sharp, R. G. Viault.

Founded: in 1899.
Domicile: Pennsylvania.
Employees: 52,300.
S&P Analyst: Marie Driscoll, CFA /DC/GG

Viacom Inc.

Recommendation: HOLD ★★★☆☆
SELL · SELL · HOLD · BUY · BUY

12-Month Target Price: $40.00
(as of July 13, 2004)

VIA.B has an approximate 0.57% weighting in the **S&P 500**

Sector: Consumer Discretionary
Sub-Industry: Movies & Entertainment
Peer Group: Entertainment Content Providers - Larger

Summary: Viacom includes cable networks, the CBS Corp. TV businesses, the Paramount movie business, Infinity Broadcasting Corp., and a majority equity interest in Blockbuster Inc.

Quantitative Evaluations

S&P Earnings & Dividend Rank: B-

| D | C | B- | B | B+ | A- | A | A+ |

S&P Fair Value Rank: 4

| 1 | 2 | 3 | 4 | 5 |
| Lowest | | | | Highest |

Fair Value Calc.: $36.70 (Fairly Valued)

S&P Investability Quotient Percentile

78%

VIA.B scored higher than 78% of all companies for which an S&P Report is available.

Volatility: NA

| Low | Average | High |

Technical Evaluation: NA

Relative Strength Rank: Moderate

45

| 1 Lowest | | Highest 99 |

Price as of 11/12/04: $36.05 | **2004E S&P Core EPS:** $1.47

GAAP Earnings vs. Previous Year
▲ Up ▼ Down ► No Change

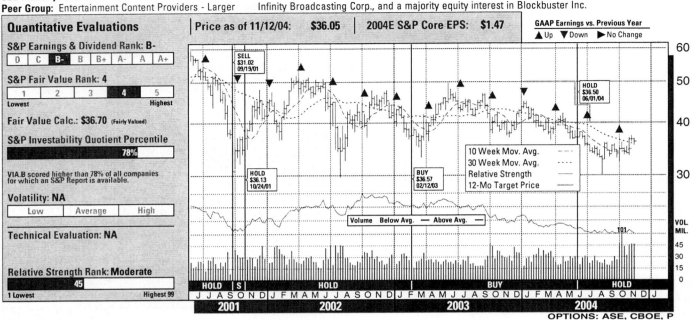

- 10 Week Mov. Avg.
- 30 Week Mov. Avg.
- Relative Strength
- 12-Mo Target Price

Volume Below Avg. — Above Avg.

VOL. MIL.

OPTIONS: ASE, CBOE, P

Analyst commentary prepared by Tuna N. Amobi, CFA, CPA /PMW/JWP

Highlights November 03, 2004

- Pro forma for Blockbuster, we estimate consolidated revenue growth of about 8% in each of 2004 and 2005, driven mainly by continued strong growth for MTV and other cable networks businesses. We also see continued strong ratings at CBS, meaningful ratings improvement at UPN, and relatively modest growth at the TV stations. We expect growth in the high single digits at the outdoor segment, as rates and occupancies continue to firm. However, we are less optimistic about Infinity Radio, which has lagged the radio industry. We think potential exists for strong growth of home entertainment revenues, but we remain cautious on the theatrical performance slate at Paramount.

- We anticipate continued margin expansion, reflecting high-margin advertising growth at cable networks and improved operating leverage at the outdoor segment (outweighing the impact of unprofitable outstanding transit contracts). In addition, radio margins should begin to reflect continuing cost control initiatives in 2005. Pro forma for Blockbuster, we estimate consolidated EBITDA growth of 13% and 9% in 2004 and 2005, to nearly $6.3 billion and $6.9 billion, respectively.

- Assuming a 10% to 11% decline in shares outstanding by the end of 2005, due to an estimated stock buyback of $5.5 billion to $6.0 billion through the end 2005 under a new $8 billion program, and with reduced interest expenses expected, we project EPS of $1.59 for 2004 (S&P Core EPS of $1.47, after estimated stock option and pension expenses), and see $1.85 for 2005 ($1.72).

Investment Rationale/Risk November 03, 2004

- We would hold the shares, which we see benefiting from a continued but gradual recovery in advertising spending. In our view, the recent divestiture of the Blockbuster (BBI: hold, $7) video retail chain enabled the company to shed a mature, declining business, and should allow management to increasingly focus on expanding into faster-growth businesses. Separately, we think that aggressive execution of a new stock buyback plan should offer some catalyst for the shares. Leverage ratios continue to support our view of significant balance sheet flexibility. We project free cash flow of about $2.9 billion and $3.2 billion in 2004 and 2005, respectively. We see longer-term growth platforms including international expansion in Asia and Europe, Internet distribution, video games, and Spanish-language audiences.

- Risks to our recommendation and target price include potential vulnerability to macroeconomic uncertainties due to a high exposure to advertising-dependent businesses; regulatory exposure; and film volatility.

- Our 12-month target price of $40 is based on discounted cash flow (DCF) analysis. We believe the stock's ratios of 10X for enterprise value to EBITDA and 18X for price to free cash flow, based on our 2005 estimates, are consistent with current multiples in the media and entertainment universe. Relative to the S&P 500, our target price implies a P/E premium of about 30%, based on our 2005 estimate.

Key Stock Statistics

S&P Core EPS 2005E	1.72	52-week Range	$45.05-30.09
S&P Oper. EPS 2004E	1.59	12 Month P/E	NM
P/E on S&P Oper. EPS 2004E	22.7	Beta	1.32
S&P Oper. EPS 2005E	1.85	Shareholders	65,684
Yield (%)	0.8%	Market Cap (B)	$ 57.8
Dividend Rate/Share	0.28	Shares Outstanding (M)	1734.9

Value of $10,000 invested five years ago: **$ 8,082**

Dividend Data Dividends have been paid since 2003

Amount ($)	Date Decl.	Ex-Div. Date	Stock of Record	Payment Date
0.060	Jan. 28	Feb. 25	Feb. 27	Apr. 01 '04
0.060	May. 19	May. 27	Jun. 01	Jul. 01 '04
0.060	Jul. 21	Aug. 27	Aug. 31	Oct. 01 '04
0.070	Oct. 28	Nov. 26	Nov. 30	Jan. 01 '05

Revenues/Earnings Data Fiscal year ending December 31

Revenues (Million $)

	2004	2003	2002	2001	2000	1999
1Q	6,772	6,051	5,672	5,752	3,026	2,951
2Q	6,842	6,418	5,850	5,717	4,851	3,003
3Q	5,485	6,600	6,307	5,714	5,811	3,332
4Q	—	7,516	6,778	6,040	6,356	3,572
Yr.	—	26,585	24,606	23,223	20,044	12,859

Earnings Per Share ($)

	2004	2003	2002	2001	2000	1999
1Q	0.41	0.26	0.21	Nil	0.10	0.08
2Q	0.43	0.37	0.31	0.01	-0.41	0.08
3Q	0.42	0.40	0.36	-0.11	0.02	0.16
4Q	E0.40	-0.22	0.36	-0.02	0.25	0.19
Yr.	E1.59	0.81	1.24	-0.13	-0.30	0.51

Next earnings report expected: early-February Source: S&P, Company Reports
EPS Estimates based on S&P Operating Earnings; historical GAAP earnings are as reported.

Please read the Required Disclosures and Reg. AC certification on the last page of this report.

The **McGraw·Hill** Companies

Viacom Inc.

Recommendation: **HOLD** ★ ★ ★ ☆ ☆   12-Month Target Price: **$40.00** (as of July 13, 2004)

Business Summary November 03, 2004

Viacom, a major entertainment and media company, reflects several acquisitions, including that of CBS Corp. in 2000. As of March 2004, National Amusement, Inc., controlled by Sumner Redstone, VIA's chairman and CEO, owned about 71% of VIA's voting Class A common stock.

Segment contributions to consolidated revenues in 2003 were as follows: Cable Networks 21%, Television 29%, Infinity Radio 8%, Outdoor 7%, Entertainment 15%, and Video 22%. Intercompany revenue eliminations, as a percentage of total revenues, were 2% for 2003. The company generated 18% of total revenues from international regions in 2003, with 58% of total international revenues of $4.0 billion generated in Europe and 23% in Canada.

In October 2004, VIA completed the spinoff of 81.5%-owned Blockbuster Inc. (BBI). Based on an exchange ratio of one VIA share for 5.15 BBI shares, VIA accepted about 28 million shares in exchange for 144 million of BBI Class A and Class B shares.

The Cable Networks business includes MTV: Music Television, Nickelodeon/Nick at Nite, VH1 Music First, TV Land, Comedy Central, the BET Cable Network, Spike TV, Country Music Television, and Showtime. The Television segment includes ownership of the CBS and UPN television broadcast networks, 39 TV stations, and VIA's TV production and syndication business.

The Radio segment includes the operation of about 186 Infinity radio stations. Revenues and EBITDA in 2003 totaled $2.1 billion and $1.0 billion, respectively. The Outdoor segment is comprised of various outdoor advertising displays in U.S. and international markets. The Entertainment segment includes Paramount Pictures,

which produces and distributes theatrical movies; Paramount Parks, which owns and operates five theme parks; movie theatre and music publishing operations; and a book publishing business (Simon and Schuster), which in prior years was reported as a distinct publishing segment.

In October 2004, the company announced a new $8 billion stock buyback program that replaced an existing $3 billion plan begun in 2002, and announced a 17% increase in the quarterly cash dividend. Also in October, VIA announced a deal to merge its FM radio station in San Francisco with Spanish Broadcasting, which would give the company a 10% equity interest in the Spanish radio broadcaster, with an option to raise the stake to 15%.

In June 2004, VIA named Tom Freston and Leslie Moonves, formerly CEOs of MTV Networks and CBS Entertainment, respectively, as its new co-COOs, replacing former COO Mel Karmazin. The company also announced a succession plan, with current chairman and CEO Redstone to relinquish his CEO role within three years, and either Mr. Freston or Mr. Moonves next in line for CEO.

In August 2004, the company agreed to pay $1.75 a share to merge 38%-owned SportsLine.com with its CBS Sports unit. In 2003, VIA acquired America Online's 50% stake (giving it full ownership) in the Comedy Central cable network, for about $1.2 billion in cash. In May 2002, it acquired KCAL-TV, for about $650 million in cash. In January 2001, VIA acquired BET Holdings II, Inc., which operates the BET Cable Network and BET Jazz: The Jazz Channel, for about $3 billion, including the net issuance of about 43 million Class B common shares.

Company Financials Fiscal Year ending December 31

Per Share Data ($)

(Year Ended December 31)	2003	2002	2001	2000	1999	1998	1997	1996	1995	1994
Tangible Bk. Val.	NM	NM	NM	NM	NM	NM	NM	NM	-7.11	-7.70
Cash Flow	1.38	1.78	1.66	1.52	1.71	0.95	1.78	1.27	1.30	0.61
Earnings	0.81	1.24	-0.13	-0.30	0.51	-0.10	0.45	0.15	0.21	0.13
S&P Core Earnings	1.20	1.04	-0.38	NA	NA	NA	NA	NA	NA	NA
Dividends	0.12	Nil	Nil	Nil	Nil	Nil	Nil	Nil	Nil	Nil
Payout Ratio	15%	Nil	Nil	Nil	Nil	Nil	Nil	Nil	Nil	Nil
Prices - High	49.75	51.89	59.50	75.87	60.43	37.12	21.12	23.81	27.12	22.50
- Low	33.11	29.75	28.25	44.31	35.37	20.25	12.62	14.87	20.12	10.87
P/E Ratio - High	61	42	NM	NM	NM	NM	47	NM	NM	NM
- Low	41	24	NM	NM	NM	NM	28	NM	NM	NM

Income Statement Analysis (Million $)

	2003	2002	2001	2000	1999	1998	1997	1996	1995	1994
Revs.	26,585	24,606	22,223	20,044	12,859	12,096	13,206	12,084	11,689	7,363
Oper. Inc.	5,957	5,542	4,667	4,243	2,162	1,529	1,696	2,181	2,314	824
Depr.	1,000	946	3,087	2,224	845	777	943	818	821	216
Int. Exp.	776	848	963	822	449	622	782	832	868	536
Pretax Inc.	2,861	3,695	656	436	783	96.0	1,060	468	632	395
Eff. Tax Rate	55.9%	39.2%	NM	NM	52.5%	145.0%	65.1%	63.2%	66.0%	70.8%
Net Inc.	1,435	2,207	-220	-364	372	-44.0	375	171	215	131
S&P Core Earnings	2,087	1,845	-656	NA	NA	NA	NA	NA	NA	NA

Balance Sheet & Other Fin. Data (Million $)

	2003	2002	2001	2000	1999	1998	1997	1996	1995	1994
Cash	851	631	727	935	681	267	292	209	464	598
Curr. Assets	7,736	7,167	7,206	7,832	5,198	5,065	5,714	5,718	5,199	5,255
Total Assets	89,849	89,754	90,810	82,646	24,486	23,613	28,289	28,834	29,026	28,274
Curr. Liab.	7,585	7,341	7,562	7,758	4,400	5,633	5,053	4,269	4,099	4,131
LT Debt	9,683	10,205	10,824	12,474	Nil	3,813	7,423	9,856	10,712	10,402
Common Equity	63,205	62,488	62,717	47,967	11,132	11,450	12,184	11,394	10,894	10,592
Total Cap.	73,812	74,337	75,884	67,481	12,379	15,863	19,607	22,450	22,806	22,194
Cap. Exp.	534	537	515	659	706	604	530	599	731	365
Cash Flow	2,435	3,152	2,867	1,860	1,216	676	1,318	929	976	271
Curr. Ratio	1.0	1.0	1.0	1.0	1.2	0.9	1.1	1.3	1.3	1.3
% LT Debt of Cap.	13.1	13.7	14.3	18.5	Nil	24.0	37.8	43.9	47.0	46.9
% Net Inc.of Revs.	5.4	9.0	NM	NM	2.9	NM	2.8	1.4	1.9	1.8
% Ret. on Assets	1.6	2.4	NM	NM	1.5	NM	1.3	0.6	0.8	0.6
% Ret. on Equity	2.3	3.5	NM	NM	3.3	NM	2.7	0.9	1.3	0.8

Data as orig reptd.; bef. results of disc opers/spec. items. Per share data adj. for stk. divs. Bold denotes primary EPS - prior periods restated. E-Estimated. NA-Not Available. NM-Not Meaningful. NR-Not Ranked. UR-Under Review.

Office: 1515 Broadway, New York, NY 10036.
Telephone: 212-258-6000.
Email: info@viacom.com
Website: http://www.viacom.com
Chrmn & CEO: S.M. Redstone.
Pres & COO: L. Moonves.
Pres & COO: T. Freston.

EVP & CFO: R.J. Bressler.
EVP, Secy & General Counsel: M.D. Fricklas.
SVP & Investor Contact: M.M. Shea 212-258-6515.
Dirs: G. S. Abrams, D. R. Andelman, J. A. Califano, Jr., W. S. Cohen, P. P. Dauman, A. C. Greenberg, J. Leschly, D. T. McLaughlin, S. Redstone, S. M. Redstone, F. V. Salerno, W. Schwartz, P. Stonesifer, R. D. Walter.

Founded: in 1986.
Domicile: Delaware.
Employees: 117,750.
S&P Analyst: Tuna N. Amobi, CFA, CPA /PMW/JWP

Visteon Corp.

Recommendation: **HOLD** ★★★☆☆
SELL | SELL | HOLD | BUY | BUY

12-Month Target Price: $7.50
(as of October 22, 2004)

VC has an approximate 0.01% weighting in the **S&P 500**

Sector: Consumer Discretionary
Sub-Industry: Auto Parts & Equipment
Peer Group: Automobile Original Equipment - Larger Cos.

Summary: Visteon is the world's second largest supplier of automotive systems, modules and components.

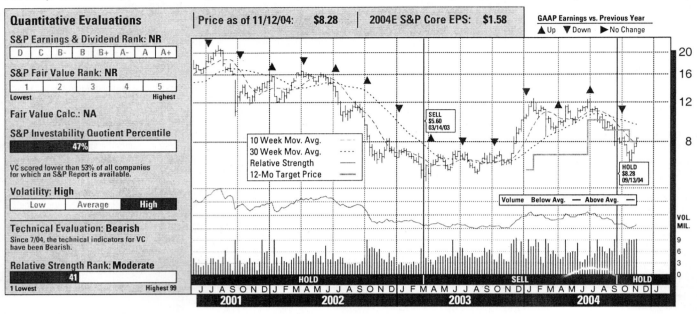

Quantitative Evaluations

S&P Earnings & Dividend Rank: NR

| D | C | B- | B | B+ | A- | A | A+ |

S&P Fair Value Rank: NR

| 1 | 2 | 3 | 4 | 5 |
| Lowest | | | | Highest |

Fair Value Calc.: NA

S&P Investability Quotient Percentile

47%

VC scored lower than 53% of all companies for which an S&P Report is available.

Volatility: High

| Low | Average | High |

Technical Evaluation: Bearish
Since 7/04, the technical indicators for VC have been Bearish.

Relative Strength Rank: Moderate
41
1 Lowest — Highest 99

Price as of 11/12/04: $8.28

2004E S&P Core EPS: $1.58

GAAP Earnings vs. Previous Year
▲ Up ▼ Down ► No Change

- 10 Week Mov. Avg.
- 30 Week Mov. Avg.
- Relative Strength
- 12-Mo Target Price

SELL $5.60 03/14/03

HOLD $8.28 09/13/04

Volume Below Avg. — Above Avg. —

HOLD | SELL | HOLD

J J A S O N D J F M A M J J A S O N D J F M A M J J A S O N D J F M A M J J A S O N D J
2001 | 2002 | 2003 | 2004

Analyst commentary prepared by Efraim Levy, CFA /PMW/GG

Highlights October 27, 2004

- We believe North American automotive light vehicle sales volume will total about 17.0 million units in 2005, following an expected 16.6 million units in 2004, up slightly from 2003 levels. VC's sales are heavily dependent on the volume of its former parent, Ford. In 2005, we expect revenues to rise 3% to 5%, reflecting 2% to 4% lower Ford sales, but 22% higher non-Ford sales. We believe the company will see contributions from its investments in new products. Increased volume, combined with cost reduction efforts, should help margins. However, we expect steel and other commodity costs to rise as contracts expire and are renewed at sharply higher prices.

- We see a significant portion of expected operational earnings improvement in 2005 stemming from employee movement from VC to Ford, with new and replacement employees receiving significantly lower wages. Cost-cutting actions should also contribute.

- Excluding special items, 2003 pro forma EPS was $2.12. Our 2004 EPS forecast excludes special and one-time charges. For the longer term, we expect non-Ford revenues to rise faster than sales to Ford, which accounted for 76% of 2003 revenues; in 2004 and 2005, we expect Ford's share to drop to about 70% and 67% of sales, respectively.

Investment Rationale/Risk October 27, 2004

- We would hold existing positions. We think the stock's lower price to sales ratio than that of most peers reflects its weaker margins and dependence on Ford for sales and earnings. Book value declined sharply from the level at September 30, 2003, as the company announced mostly non-cash charges for the fourth quarter aggregating $756 million after tax ($6.02 a share). In addition, net charges aggregated $9.35 a share in the first nine months of 2004, further reducing book value. The 2004 charges were mostly non-cash, and some of them may be restored in the future. Historically, the shares have traded at a discount to the S&P 500. Historical and projected differences in operating earnings from Standard & Poor's Core Earnings primarily reflect net pension credits, partly offset by option expense.

- Risks to our recommendation and target price include declines in automobile demand and production volume, especially for Ford vehicles; pricing pressures; and unfavorable raw material cost trends.

- We project negative cash flow for both 2004 and 2005. After cutting our 2005 EPS forecast to $0.06, we do not regard P/E multiple as a meaningful measure of valuation. Applying a price to sales ratio of 0.07X to our 2005 revenue per share estimate leads us to 12-month target price of $7.50. The price to sales ratio is in line with the cyclical stock's historical range.

Key Stock Statistics

S&P Core EPS 2005E	2.46	52-week Range	$12.50-6.31
S&P Oper. EPS 2004E	-0.76	12 Month P/E	NM
P/E on S&P Oper. EPS 2004E	NM	Beta	NA
S&P Oper. EPS 2005E	0.06	Shareholders	120,062
Yield (%)	2.9%	Market Cap (B)	$ 1.1
Dividend Rate/Share	0.24	Shares Outstanding (M)	129.5

Value of $10,000 invested five years ago: **NA**

Dividend Data Dividends have been paid since 2000

Amount ($)	Date Decl.	Ex-Div. Date	Stock of Record	Payment Date
0.060	Jan. 16	Jan. 28	Jan. 30	Mar. 01 '04
0.060	Apr. 13	Apr. 28	Apr. 30	Jun. 01 '04
0.060	Jul. 15	Jul. 28	Jul. 30	Sep. 01 '04
0.060	Oct. 18	Oct. 27	Oct. 29	Dec. 01 '04

Revenues/Earnings Data Fiscal year ending December 31

Revenues (Million $)

	2004	2003	2002	2001	2000	1999
1Q	4,972	4,704	4,469	4,723	5,225	—
2Q	4,870	4,613	5,039	4,905	5,309	—
3Q	4,154	3,884	4,344	3,722	4,404	—
4Q	—	4,459	4,543	4,493	4,529	—
Yr.	—	17,660	18,395	17,843	19,467	18,676

Earnings Per Share ($)

	2004	2003	2002	2001	2000	1999
1Q	0.23	-0.12	-0.57	0.24	1.13	—
2Q	0.24	-1.33	0.56	-0.31	1.25	—
3Q	-10.86	-1.34	-0.40	-0.74	0.37	—
4Q	E0.25	-6.87	-0.27	-0.11	-0.67	—
Yr.	E-0.76	-9.65	-0.68	-0.91	2.08	2.16

Next earnings report expected: late-January Source: S&P, Company Reports
EPS Estimates based on S&P Operating Earnings; historical GAAP earnings are as reported.

The McGraw·Hill Companies

Visteon Corporation

Recommendation: **HOLD** ★ ★ ★ ☆ ☆   12-Month Target Price: **$7.50** (as of October 22, 2004)

Business Summary October 27, 2004

In June 2000, Ford Motor spun off its Visteon Corp. subsidiary to shareholders. VC is the world's second largest supplier of automotive systems, modules and components to global vehicle manufacturers, trailing only Delphi Automotive Systems, the former GM automotive parts manufacturing subsidiary. In the spinoff, Ford shareholders received 0.130933 of a VC share for each Ford common or Class B share owned.

The company operates in three business segments, and is a leading Tier 1 supplier in two of them.

The comfort, communication & safety segment includes climate control systems and interior/exterior systems product groups. The climate control systems product group makes systems, modules and components for fluid transport, air handling, heat exchange and compressors. The interior/exterior systems product group produces systems, modules and components for cockpits, instrument panels, interior trim and seats, lighting and bumpers.

The dynamics and energy conversion segment consists of the energy transformation systems and chassis systems product groups. The energy systems product group makes systems, modules and components for energy management, distributed power generation, electrical conversions, and fuel storage and delivery products. The chassis systems product group produces systems, modules and components for axle and driveline, steering and chassis products.

The glass segment produces glass products for Ford and aftermarket customers, and float glass for commercial architecture.

In December 2000, VC wrote down the value of its glass segment by $200 million.

In 2003, Ford accounted for 76% of sales (80% in 2002). The company aimed to boost non-Ford business to 28% of sales in 2004.

In 2003, VC posted after-tax special charges $947 million, including $468 million for a deferred tax allowance.

In September 2004, the company said it expected to record non-cash pretax charges of $825 million to $900 million in the third quarter, related to its deferred tax assets.

VC aims to be the world's leading consumer-focused, technology-driven automotive systems company. Its strategy includes capitalizing on its core Ford business, improving operating performance, expanding non-Ford business, using e-commerce to cut costs and improve sales, exploiting in-house technology and systems engineering leadership, expanding aftermarket business, and streamlining and focusing the product portfolio.

Over the past decade, in terms of vehicles sold, North American truck sales have moved from about two-thirds of car sales to volume exceeding cars. The company believes its expertise and experience as Ford's largest supplier give it an edge in the growing truck market.

In the first nine months of 2004, net charges aggregated $9.35 a share, including third quarter charges of $872 million for increased valuation allowances against deferred tax asset, a $314 million reduction the net book value of the steering systems product group, and $25 million for early retirement and relocation programs to reduce the number of employees leased from Ford Motor.

Company Financials Fiscal Year ending December 31

Per Share Data ($)

(Year Ended December 31)	2003	2002	2001	2000	1999	1998	1997	1996	1995	1994
Tangible Bk. Val.	14.40	23.09	25.32	26.76	22.42	NA	NA	NA	NA	NA
Cash Flow	-4.28	4.19	4.18	7.28	7.17	NA	NA	NA	NA	NA
Earnings	-9.65	-0.68	-0.91	2.08	2.16	NA	NA	NA	NA	NA
S&P Core Earnings	-6.94	0.51	0.03	NA	NA	NA	NA	NA	NA	NA
Dividends	0.24	0.24	0.24	0.12	NA	NA	NA	NA	NA	NA
Payout Ratio	NM	NM	NM	6%	NA	NA	NA	NA	NA	NA
Prices - High	10.48	16.78	21.72	19.25	NA	NA	NA	NA	NA	NA
- Low	5.34	6.38	10.45	9.75	NA	NA	NA	NA	NA	NA
P/E Ratio - High	NM	NM	NM	9	NA	NA	NA	NA	NA	NA
- Low	NM	NM	NM	5	NA	NA	NA	NA	NA	NA

Income Statement Analysis (Million $)

	2003	2002	2001	2000	1999	1998	1997	1996	1995	1994
Revs.	17,660	18,395	17,843	19,467	18,676	NA	NA	NA	NA	NA
Oper. Inc.	295	546	549	1,337	1,190	NA	NA	NA	NA	NA
Depr.	674	627	666	676	651	NA	NA	NA	NA	NA
Int. Exp.	94.0	103	131	167	176	NA	NA	NA	NA	NA
Pretax Inc.	-1,150	-117	-169	439	445	NA	NA	NA	NA	NA
Eff. Tax Rate	NM	NM	NM	32.6%	33.5%	NA	NA	NA	NA	NA
Net Inc.	-1,213	-87.0	-118	270	281	NA	NA	NA	NA	NA
S&P Core Earnings	-873	63.4	5.05	NA	NA	NA	NA	NA	NA	NA

Balance Sheet & Other Fin. Data (Million $)

	2003	2002	2001	2000	1999	1998	1997	1996	1995	1994
Cash	956	1,278	1,181	1,477	700	NA	NA	NA	NA	NA
Curr. Assets	4,410	4,737	4,753	5,005	4,474	NA	NA	NA	NA	NA
Total Assets	10,964	11,170	11,078	11,325	10,886	NA	NA	NA	NA	NA
Curr. Liab.	3,572	3,466	3,435	3,804	3,749	NA	NA	NA	NA	NA
LT Debt	1,467	1,298	1,293	1,397	1,400	NA	NA	NA	NA	NA
Common Equity	1,858	5,956	3,291	3,505	2,915	NA	NA	NA	NA	NA
Total Cap.	3,325	7,257	4,597	4,920	4,614	NA	NA	NA	NA	NA
Cap. Exp.	879	723	752	793	NA	NA	NA	NA	NA	NA
Cash Flow	-539	540	548	946	932	NA	NA	NA	NA	NA
Curr. Ratio	1.2	1.4	1.4	1.3	1.2	NA	NA	NA	NA	NA
% LT Debt of Cap.	44.1	17.9	28.1	28.4	48.0	NA	NA	NA	NA	NA
% Net Inc.of Revs.	NM	NM	NM	1.4	1.5	NA	NA	NA	NA	NA
% Ret. on Assets	NM	NM	NM	2.3	NA	NA	NA	NA	NA	NA
% Ret. on Equity	NM	NM	NM	10.8	NA	NA	NA	NA	NA	NA

Data as orig reptd.; bef. results of disc opers/spec. items. Per share data adj. for stk. divs.; EPS diluted. E-Estimated. NA-Not Available. NM-Not Meaningful. NR-Not Ranked. UR-Under Review.

Office: 17000 Rotunda Drive, Dearborn, MI 48120.
Telephone: 800-847-8366.
Email: vcstock@visteon.com
Website: http://www.visteon.com
Chrmn & CEO: P.J. Pestillo.
Pres & COO: M.F. Johnston.
EVP & CFO: J.F. Palmer.

SVP, Secy & General Counsel: S.L. Fox.
VP & Chief Acctg Officer: G. Minor.
Investor Contact: D. Fiebig 313-755-3699.
Investor Contact: C.K. Collins 313-755-3357.
Dirs: M. C. Gottschalk, W. H. Gray III, S. Hamp, P. L. Higgins, R. H. Jenkins, M. F. Johnston, K. J. Krapek, P. J. Pestillo, C. L. Schaffer, T. Stallkamp, J. D. Thornton.

Founded: in 2000.
Domicile: Delaware.
Employees: 72,000.
S&P Analyst: Efraim Levy, CFA /PMW/GG

Vulcan Materials

Recommendation: **HOLD** ★★★☆☆
SELL SELL HOLD BUY BUY

12-Month Target Price: **$50.00**
(as of June 01, 2004)

VMC has an approximate 0.05% weighting in the **S&P 500**

Sector: Materials
Sub-Industry: Construction Materials
Peer Group: Construction (Cement & Aggregates)

Summary: VMC is the largest U.S. producer of construction aggregates, and a leading maker of a wide variety of industrial chemicals.

Quantitative Evaluations

S&P Earnings & Dividend Rank: A-

| D | C | B- | B | B+ | **A-** | A | A+ |

S&P Fair Value Rank: 3

| 1 | 2 | **3** | 4 | 5 |
| Lowest | | | | Highest |

Fair Value Calc.: $49.00 (Slightly Overvalued)

S&P Investability Quotient Percentile
98%

VMC scored higher than 98% of all companies for which an S&P Report is available.

Volatility: Low

| **Low** | Average | High |

Technical Evaluation: Bullish
Since 10/04, the technical indicators for VMC have been Bullish.

Relative Strength Rank: Moderate
47
1 Lowest ___ Highest 99

Price as of 11/12/04: **$50.50**   **2004E S&P Core EPS:** **$2.49**

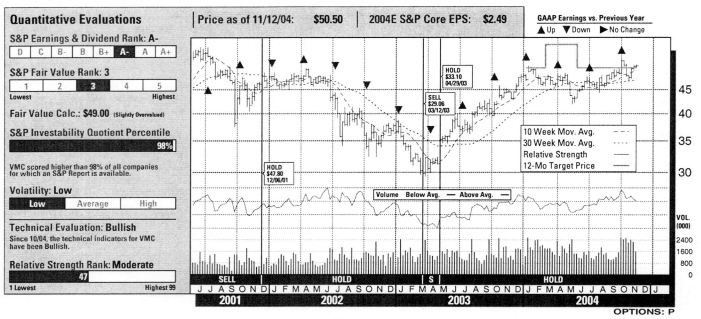

GAAP Earnings vs. Previous Year
▲ Up ▼ Down ► No Change

10 Week Mov. Avg. — — —
30 Week Mov. Avg. ·········
Relative Strength ____
12-Mo Target Price ____

HOLD $33.10 04/29/03
SELL $29.06 03/12/03
HOLD $47.80 12/06/01

Volume Below Avg. — Above Avg.

SELL HOLD S HOLD

VOL. (000)
2400
1600
800
0

J J A S O N D J F M A M J J A S O N D J F M A M J J A S O N D J F M A M J J A S O N D J
2001 2002 2003 2004

OPTIONS: P

Analyst commentary prepared by Leo J. Larkin/PMW/JWP

Highlights August 10, 2004

- We project a 2004 sales gain of 10% to 11%, after a 9.2% increase in 2003, based on S&P's forecast of 4.6% GDP growth for 2004, versus 2003's growth of 3.1%. We see both segments posting solid gains in pricing and volume. We expect increased industrial demand to boost chemical segment sales. A slower decline in private nonresidential construction spending and a projected increase in highway spending should aid construction aggregates. Reflecting an expected return to profitability in chemicals, and some abatement of raw material cost pressures for both units, we expect operating profits to advance. Benefiting further from reduced interest expense, we expect 2004 EPS to post a 19% gain.

- Based on S&P's forecast of 3.9% GDP growth in 2005 and our expectations of a sustained upturn in non-residential construction spending, we look for another increase in sales and EPS. For the longer term, we sales and EPS benefiting from continued consolidation of the construction materials industry.

- According to data compiled by the U.S. Census Bureau, total construction spending through May 2004 was up 8.9%, year to year.

Investment Rationale/Risk August 10, 2004

- At a recent yield of 2.3%, and trading at 18X our 2004 EPS estimate, we believe the shares are worth holding. In addition to compound EPS growth of 10.5% from 1994 through 2003, the company increased its dividends at a compound annual rate of 9.2%. With an upturn in construction in progress and what we view as a likely rebound in chemicals, we believe VMC can sustain its recent growth rate for EPS and dividends.

- Risks to our recommendation and target price include the possibility of weaker than expected end markets for the company's main products, potentially leading the stock's P/E multiple to contract.

- We look for another solid gain in EPS and dividends in 2005, but we do not foresee an expansion in the stock's P/E multiple. We expect the stock to trade at 18X our 2005 EPS estimate, toward the upper end of its historical range. Based on our projection of 2005 EPS of $2.85, our 12-month target price is $50.

Key Stock Statistics

S&P Oper. EPS 2004E	**2.60**	52-week Range	**$52.13-41.94**
P/E on S&P Oper. EPS 2004E	**19.4**	12 Month P/E	**20.1**
S&P Oper. EPS 2005E	**2.85**	Beta	**0.69**
Yield (%)	**2.1%**	Shareholders	**3,693**
Dividend Rate/Share	**1.04**	Market Cap (B)	**$ 5.2**
Shares Outstanding (M)	**102.4**		

Value of $10,000 invested five years ago: **$ 13,364**

Dividend Data Dividends have been paid since 1934

Amount ($)	Date Decl.	Ex-Div. Date	Stock of Record	Payment Date
0.260	Feb. 13	Feb. 25	Feb. 27	Mar. 10 '04
0.260	May. 14	May. 26	May. 28	Jun. 10 '04
0.260	Jul. 09	Aug. 24	Aug. 26	Sep. 10 '04
0.260	Oct. 08	Nov. 22	Nov. 24	Dec. 10 '04

Revenues/Earnings Data Fiscal year ending December 31

Revenues (Million $)

	2004	2003	2002	2001	2000	1999
1Q	617.5	566.7	587.1	569.1	515.0	482.2
2Q	816.3	766.8	681.4	825.3	665.1	611.5
3Q	891.2	829.9	785.8	843.1	681.2	656.4
4Q	—	728.7	676.0	728.1	631.0	605.6
Yr.	—	2,892	2,797	3,020	2,492	2,356

Earnings Per Share ($)

	2004	2003	2002	2001	2000	1999
1Q	0.14	0.01	0.11	0.06	0.23	0.26
2Q	0.85	0.65	0.64	0.78	0.75	0.61
3Q	0.96	0.91	0.75	0.90	0.84	0.84
4Q	E0.60	0.59	0.36	0.44	0.47	0.64
Yr.	E2.60	2.18	1.86	2.17	2.29	2.35

Next earnings report expected: early-February Source: S&P, Company Reports
EPS Estimates based on S&P Operating Earnings; historical GAAP earnings are as reported.

Vulcan Materials Company

Recommendation: HOLD ★ ★ ★ ☆ ☆   12-Month Target Price: **$50.00** (as of June 01, 2004)

Business Summary August 10, 2004

Vulcan Materials is the largest U.S. producer of construction aggregates, and is also a significant producer of industrial and specialty chemicals.

In 2003, construction materials accounted for 80% of net sales (78% in 2002), and posted earnings before interest and income taxes of $388.7 million ($383.2 million). Chemicals accounted for 20% (22%) of net sales, and incurred a $27.6 million loss, versus a $63.8 million loss before interest and income taxes in 2002.

The construction materials division produces and sells construction aggregates (72% of 2003 construction materials sales), asphaltic products and placement (14%), ready-mix concrete (10%), and other products (4%). Shipments of aggregates totaled 232.8 million tons, versus 217.3 million tons in 2002. Other products include asphalt mix, ready-mix concrete, trucking services, barge transportation, and paving construction.

Sales of aggregates by end use in 2003 were as follows: highways, streets and airports (25%), other public works (9%), government buildings (11%), residential buildings (26%), private nonresidential buildings (25%), agricultural, chemical and industrial (2%), and railroad ballast (2%).

In 2002, the company paid about $43.4 million for acquisitions, versus $139 million for acquisitions in 2001. In 2000, VMC acquired various assets of Tarmac America for $226.9 million in cash and related working capital. The acquisition added about

500 million tons of proven and probable aggregates reserves, and extended the company's presence into the eastern U.S.

At the end of 2003, VMC estimated that it had proven and probable aggregates reserves totaling 10.6 billion tons, sufficient to support an average life of 48 years at current operating rates.

The company's main competitors in the aggregates business are La Farge North America, Martin Marietta Materials, and Texas Industries.

The chemical unit produces chlorine, caustic soda, hydrochloric acid, sodium chlorite, potassium chemicals and chlorinated organic chemicals, which are sold principally to the chemical processing, polymer, refrigerant, foam-blowing, food and pharmaceutical, pulp and paper, and water management industries. In 2003, VMC divested its Performance Chemicals unit.

Sales of chemicals in 2003 by end use were as follows: process and intermediate chemicals (64%), industrial durables and nondurables (18%), and consumer nondurables (18%).

In its 2004 second quarter report, VMC reaffirmed its guidance for 2004 EPS of $2.45 to $2.65. It projected EPS of $0.90 to $1.00 for the third quarter.

Company Financials Fiscal Year ending December 31

Per Share Data ($)

(Year Ended December 31)	2003	2002	2001	2000	1999	1998	1997	1996	1995	1994
Tangible Bk. Val.	12.01	11.04	10.02	9.00	8.63	11.47	9.81	8.60	7.59	6.79
Cash Flow	4.87	4.47	4.89	4.43	4.37	3.86	3.21	2.85	2.56	1.86
Earnings	2.18	1.86	2.17	2.29	2.35	2.50	2.03	1.79	1.54	0.89
S&P Core Earnings	1.89	1.51	1.81	NA	NA	NA	NA	NA	NA	NA
Dividends	0.97	0.94	0.90	0.84	0.78	0.69	0.63	0.56	0.49	0.44
Payout Ratio	44%	51%	41%	37%	33%	28%	31%	31%	32%	49%
Prices - High	48.60	49.95	55.30	48.87	51.25	44.66	34.64	22.16	20.12	18.83
- Low	28.75	32.35	37.50	36.50	34.31	31.33	18.41	17.70	16.04	14.66
P/E Ratio - High	22	27	25	21	22	18	17	12	13	21
- Low	13	17	17	16	15	13	9	10	10	16

Income Statement Analysis (Million $)

	2003	2002	2001	2000	1999	1998	1997	1996	1995	1994
Revs.	2,892	2,797	3,020	2,492	2,356	1,776	1,679	1,569	1,461	1,253
Oper. Inc.	618	560	649	573	565	481	409	387	361	244
Depr.	277	268	278	232	207	138	121	113	111	107
Int. Exp.	54.1	55.0	61.3	48.1	48.6	7.23	6.91	8.64	11.4	10.7
Pretax Inc.	311	260	324	312	352	375	301	286	258	146
Eff. Tax Rate	28.3%	25.8%	31.3%	29.6%	31.8%	31.7%	30.4%	33.9%	35.7%	32.8%
Net Inc.	223	190	223	220	240	256	209	189	166	98.0
S&P Core Earnings	194	155	186	NA	NA	NA	NA	NA	NA	NA

Balance Sheet & Other Fin. Data (Million $)

	2003	2002	2001	2000	1999	1998	1997	1996	1995	1994
Cash	417	171	101	55.3	52.8	181	129	50.8	21.9	8.00
Curr. Assets	1,050	790	730	695	625	576	487	394	362	337
Total Assets	3,637	3,448	3,398	3,229	2,839	1,659	1,449	1,321	1,216	1,181
Curr. Liab.	543	298	344	572	387	211	208	195	177	211
LT Debt	339	858	906	685	699	76.5	81.9	85.5	90.0	97.0
Common Equity	1,803	1,697	1,604	1,471	1,324	1,154	1,025	884	797	732
Total Cap.	2,573	2,993	2,829	2,426	2,273	1,329	1,162	1,056	979	912
Cap. Exp.	194	249	287	340	315	203	161	152	109	100
Cash Flow	501	458	501	452	447	394	330	301	277	205
Curr. Ratio	1.9	2.7	2.1	1.2	1.6	2.7	2.3	2.0	2.1	1.6
% LT Debt of Cap.	13.2	28.7	32.0	28.3	30.7	5.8	7.0	8.1	9.2	10.7
% Net Inc.of Revs.	7.7	6.8	7.4	8.8	10.2	14.4	12.5	12.0	11.4	7.8
% Ret. on Assets	6.3	5.6	6.7	7.2	10.7	16.5	15.1	14.9	13.8	8.7
% Ret. on Equity	12.8	11.5	14.5	15.7	19.4	23.5	21.6	22.5	21.7	13.7

Data as orig reptd.; bef. results of disc opers/spec. items. Per share data adj. for stk. divs.; EPS diluted. E-Estimated. NA-Not Available. NM-Not Meaningful. NR-Not Ranked. UR-Under Review.

Office: 1200 Urban Center Drive, Birmingham, AL 35242-5014.
Telephone: 205-298-3000.
Email: ir@vmcmail.com
Website: http://www.vulcanmaterials.com
Chrmn & CEO: D.M. James.
SVP, CFO & Treas: M.E. Tomkins.

SVP, Secy & General Counsel: W.F. Denson III.
Investor Contact: M. Warren 205-298-3220.
Dirs: P. J. Carroll, Jr., L. D. DeSimone, P. W. Farmer, H. A. Franklin, D. M. James, A. M. Korologos, D. J. McGregor, J. V. Napier, D. B. Rice, O. R. Smith, V. Trosino.

Founded: in 1910.
Domicile: New Jersey.
Employees: 8,838.
S&P Analyst: Leo J. Larkin/PMW/JWP

Wachovia Corp.

Recommendation: **BUY** ★★★★★   12-Month Target Price: **$58.00**
SELL | SELL | HOLD | BUY | BUY
(as of October 07, 2004)

WB has an approximate 0.77% weighting in the **S&P 500**

Sector: Financials
Sub-Industry: Diversified Banks
Peer Group: Money Center Banks

Summary: This bank holding company, the fourth largest in the U.S., operates banking offices in 11 East Coast states and Washington, DC.

Quantitative Evaluations

S&P Earnings & Dividend Rank: A-

| D | C | B- | B | B+ | A- | A | A+ |

S&P Fair Value Rank: 3+

| 1 | 2 | 3 | 4 | 5 |
| Lowest | | | | Highest |

Fair Value Calc.: $50.60 (Slightly Overvalued)

S&P Investability Quotient Percentile

99%

WB scored higher than 99% of all companies
for which an S&P Report is available.

Volatility: Low

| Low | Average | High |

Technical Evaluation: Bullish
Since 10/04, the technical indicators for WB
have been Bullish.

Relative Strength Rank: Strong

74
1 Lowest — Highest 99

| Price as of 11/12/04: | $52.85 | 2004E S&P Core EPS: | $3.84 |

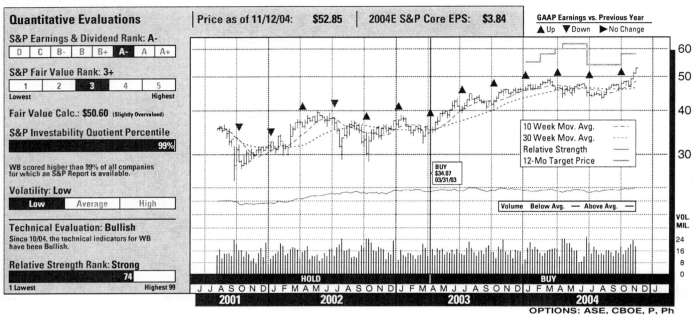

GAAP Earnings vs. Previous Year
▲ Up ▼ Down ► No Change

- 10 Week Mov. Avg.
- 30 Week Mov. Avg.
- Relative Strength
- 12-Mo Target Price

BUY
$34.07
03/31/03

Volume Below Avg. — Above Avg. —

VOL. MIL.
24
16
8
0

HOLD | BUY
J J A S O N D J F M A M J J A S O N D J F M A M J J A S O N D J F M A M J J A S O N D J
2001 2002 2003 2004

OPTIONS: ASE, CBOE, P, Ph

Analyst commentary prepared by Evan Momios, CFA /CB/BK

Highlights October 19, 2004

- We believe the planned acquisition of SouthTrust (SOTR: buy, $43), expected to close in the 2004 fourth quarter, subject to necessary approvals, will be beneficial for WB's operating results and shareholders. We believe the relative size of the two companies (SOTR has about one-eighth of WB's assets) and the successful integration of Wachovia/FirstUnion reduce integration risk.

- In our view, the proposed deal will further strengthen WB's middle market and retail loan portfolio, accelerate its ongoing expansion in the lucrative and high-growth Texas market, and generate excess capital that we think management is likely to use for stock repurchases. Although management has not projected any revenue synergies, we believe that revenue growth is likely to accelerate as the two organizations exchange with each other and adopt best sales practices. We also think that management's cost savings projection of 36% of SOTR's total expenses is reasonable, as it translates to what we view as a modest 3% of combined expenses.

- We see 2004 operating EPS (excluding merger charges) of $3.95, up from $3.40 in 2003. For 2005, we expect EPS to rise to $4.30, up 9% from our 2004 EPS estimate, slightly below our long-term growth projection of 10%.

Investment Rationale/Risk October 19, 2004

- We recommend buying the shares, based on the company's focus on expense control, credit quality, and productivity improvements, which we believe should allow for balanced above peer-average long-term growth in a variety of economic and interest rate scenarios. At about 12X our $3.95 operating EPS estimate for 2004, the shares are trading at a small discount to large-cap bank peers, despite our view of WB's above peer average long-term growth prospects.

- Risks to our recommendation and target price include a severe economic downturn in combination with higher short-term interest rates that could result in an inverted yield curve; legal and regulatory risks; and a serious geopolitical event affecting equity markets.

- Our 12-month target price of $58 equates to 13.5X our 2005 operating EPS estimate, and is at the lower end of our terminal value and discounted cash flow model valuations, which are based mainly on the assumption of a five-year EPS growth rate of about 10%, and on discount rates of 8.6% to 8.8%.

Key Stock Statistics

S&P Core EPS 2005E	4.22	52-week Range	$52.85-43.05
S&P Oper. EPS 2004E	3.95	12 Month P/E	14.4
P/E on S&P Oper. EPS 2004E	13.4	Beta	0.75
S&P Oper. EPS 2005E	4.30	Shareholders	170,205
Yield (%)	3.5%	Market Cap (B)	$ 84.8
Dividend Rate/Share	1.84	Shares Outstanding (M)	1603.6

Value of $10,000 invested five years ago: **NA**

Dividend Data Dividends have been paid since 1914

Amount ($)	Date Decl.	Ex-Div. Date	Stock of Record	Payment Date
0.400	Jan. 15	Feb. 25	Feb. 27	Mar. 15 '04
0.400	Apr. 20	May. 26	May. 28	Jun. 15 '04
0.400	Aug. 17	Aug. 27	Aug. 31	Sep. 15 '04
0.460	Oct. 18	Nov. 26	Nov. 30	Dec. 15 '04

Revenues/Earnings Data Fiscal year ending December 31

Revenues (Million $)

	2004	2003	2002	2001	2000	1999
1Q	6,756	5,776	5,930	5,599	6,155	5,522
2Q	6,618	5,841	6,004	5,450	5,426	5,330
3Q	6,893	6,315	5,802	4,976	6,648	5,252
4Q	—	6,542	5,855	6,371	6,017	5,980
Yr.	—	24,474	23,591	22,396	24,246	22,084

Earnings Per Share ($)

	2004	2003	2002	2001	2000	1999
1Q	0.94	0.76	0.66	0.59	0.85	0.73
2Q	0.95	0.77	0.62	0.64	-2.27	0.90
3Q	0.96	0.82	0.66	-0.31	0.86	0.84
4Q	E0.99	0.83	0.66	0.54	0.65	0.86
Yr.	E3.95	3.17	2.60	1.45	0.12	3.33

Next earnings report expected: mid-January Source: S&P, Company Reports
EPS Estimates based on S&P Operating Earnings; historical GAAP earnings are as reported.

Wachovia Corporation

Recommendation: **BUY** ★★★★★   12-Month Target Price: **$58.00** (as of October 07, 2004)

Business Summary October 19, 2004

With over $400 billion in assets, Wachovia Corp. is the fourth largest bank holding company in the U.S., and the largest East Coast bank with offices spanning from Connecticut to Florida. The company substantially increased its size through its September 2001 merger with First Union Corp.

The company operates through four main business segments: General Bank, Capital Management, Wealth Management, and Corporate and Investment Bank. General Bank (58% of net income in 2003) operates the largest domestic retail and commercial bank on the East Coast (2,600 offices) with operations in 11 states from Connecticut to Florida and in Washington, DC. Capital Management (11%) comprises retail brokerage services and investment management, and provides institutional trust and insurance services. Wealth Management (4%) consists of financial, trust, gift and tax planning; investment management; private banking; insurance and retirement planning; and other wealth products and advisory services. Corporate and Investment Bank (28%) offers a range of fixed income and equity products, cash management, and other services to large corporate and institutional clients.

In 2003, average earning assets, from which interest income is derived, amounted to $292.4 billion, and consisted mainly of loans and leases (54%) and investment securities (33%). Average sources of funds included savings and NOW accounts (15%), time deposits (11%), money market accounts (15%), foreign deposits (2%), noninterest-bearing demand deposits (12%), short-term borrowings (18%), long-term debt (10%), shareholders' equity (9%) and other (8%).

At December 31, 2003, nonperforming assets, consisting primarily of nonaccrual loans and foreclosed properties, were $1.15 billion (0.69% of loans and related assets), versus $1.74 billion (1.11%) a year earlier. The allowance for loan losses, set aside for possible loan defaults, was $2.50 billion (1.51% of loans), versus $2.80 billion (1.72%) a year earlier. Net chargeoffs, or the amount of loans actually written off as uncollectible, were $652 million (0.41% of average loans) in 2003, down from $1.12 billion (0.73%) in 2002.

In July 2003, Wachovia and Prudential Financial combined their retail brokerage operations (with Wachovia holding a 62% interest). The merger created the third largest brokerage firm in the U.S., with combined client assets of $603.1 billion, 11,500 registered representatives, and 3,300 brokerage locations in 49 states and Washington, DC, at December 31, 2003. Management expects the transaction to be accretive to EPS in 2004, excluding merger-related and restructuring expenses.

Company Financials Fiscal Year ending December 31

Per Share Data ($)

(Year Ended December 31)	2003	2002	2001	2000	1999	1998	1997	1996	1995	1994
Tangible Bk. Val.	15.27	14.48	11.50	11.92	11.22	12.36	14.71	12.46	13.14	11.52
Earnings	3.17	2.60	1.45	0.12	3.33	2.95	2.99	2.68	2.93	2.49
S&P Core Earnings	3.09	2.32	1.14	NA	NA	NA	NA	NA	NA	NA
Dividends	1.25	1.00	0.96	1.92	1.88	1.58	1.22	1.10	0.98	0.86
Payout Ratio	39%	38%	66%	NM	56%	54%	41%	41%	34%	35%
Prices - High	46.74	39.88	36.60	38.87	65.75	65.93	53.00	38.87	29.75	24.00
- Low	32.12	28.57	25.22	23.50	32.00	40.93	36.31	25.56	20.68	19.50
P/E Ratio - High	15	15	25	NM	20	22	18	15	10	10
- Low	10	11	17	NM	10	14	12	10	7	8

Income Statement Analysis (Million $)

	2003	2002	2001	2000	1999	1998	1997	1996	1995	1994
Net Int. Inc.	10,607	9,823	7,775	7,277	7,452	7,277	5,743	4,996	3,263	3,034
Tax Equiv. Adj.	256	218	159	117	118	117	Nil	84.0	82.3	92.7
Non Int. Inc.	9,309	7,836	7,003	5,682	6,995	6,198	3,362	2,322	1,429	1,166
Loan Loss Prov.	586	1,479	1,947	691	692	691	840	375	180	100
Exp./Op. Revs.	65.4%	65.3%	65.8%	89.6%	60.8%	67.5%	61.4%	63.1%	62.3%	62.4%
Pretax Inc.	6,080	4,667	2,293	703	4,831	3,965	2,710	2,310	1,559	1,415
Eff. Tax Rate	30.1%	23.3%	29.4%	80.4%	33.3%	27.1%	30.0%	35.1%	35.0%	34.6%
Net Inc.	4,247	3,579	1,619	138	3,223	2,891	1,896	1,499	1,013	925
% Net Int. Marg.	3.72	3.92	3.57	3.81	3.79	3.81	4.36	4.21	4.41	4.78
S&P Core Earnings	4,144	3,187	1,255	NA	NA	NA	NA	NA	NA	NA

Balance Sheet & Other Fin. Data (Million $)

	2003	2002	2001	2000	1999	1998	1997	1996	1995	1994
Money Mkt. Assets	61,747	45,827	46,180	36,109	27,542	12,675	13,907	11,274	5,971	3,523
Inv. Securities	100,445	75,804	58,467	49,246	53,035	53,988	23,590	16,683	15,171	11,482
Com'l Loans	107,466	109,097	61,258	87,447	80,619	79,689	28,111	23,639	21,289	17,521
Other Loans	58,105	54,000	102,543	36,313	54,947	59,720	72,148	72,219	45,513	37,181
Total Assets	401,032	341,839	330,452	254,170	253,024	237,363	157,274	157,274	96,740	77,314
Demand Deposits	48,683	44,640	43,464	30,315	31,375	35,614	21,753	18,632	11,788	10,524
Time Deposits	172,542	146,878	143,989	112,353	109,672	106,853	81,136	76,183	53,212	48,435
LT Debt	36,730	39,662	41,733	35,809	31,975	22,949	8,042	7,660	6,444	3,429
Common Equity	32,428	32,078	28,438	15,347	16,709	17,173	12,032	10,008	6,152	5,398
% Ret. on Assets	1.1	1.1	0.6	0.1	1.3	1.5	1.3	1.1	1.2	1.3
% Ret. on Equity	13.2	11.8	7.4	0.9	19.2	19.8	17.2	16.5	17.4	16.5
% Loan Loss Resv.	1.5	1.7	-1.8	1.4	1.3	1.3	1.3	1.4	1.5	1.8
% Loans/Deposits	74.8	85.2	87.4	86.7	96.1	97.7	94.2	101.1	101.0	91.6
% Equity to Assets	8.7	9.0	7.5	6.3	6.9	7.4	7.4	6.6	6.6	7.5

Data as orig reptd.; bef. results of disc opers/spec. items. Per share data adj. for stk. divs.; EPS diluted. Prior to 2001, data for First Union Corp. E-Estimated. NA-Not Available. NM-Not Meaningful. NR-Not Ranked.

Office: One Wachovia Center, Charlotte, NC 28288-0013.
Telephone: 704-374-6565.
Website: http://www.wachovia.com
Chrmn, Pres & CEO: G.K. Thompson.
CFO: R.P. Kelly.
Investor Contact: A. Lehman .

Dirs: J. D. Baker II, J. S. Balloun, R. J. Brown, P. C. Browning, J. T. Casteen III, W. H. Goodwin, Jr., R. A. Ingram, D. M. James, W. D. Malone, Jr., M. J. McDonald, J. Neubauer, L. U. Noland III, V. L. Richey, R. G. Shaw, L. L. Smith, K. Thompson, J. C. Whitaker, Jr., D. D. Young.

Founded: in 1879.
Domicile: North Carolina.
Employees: 86,670.
S&P Analyst: Evan Momios, CFA /CB/BK

Walgreen Co.

Recommendation: **BUY** ★ ★ ★ ★
SELL | SELL | HOLD | BUY | BUY

12-Month Target Price: **$43.00**
(as of January 12, 2004)

WAG has an approximate 0.36% weighting in the **S&P 500**

Sector: Consumer Staples
Sub-Industry: Drug Retail
Peer Group: Drug Stores

Summary: WAG, the largest U.S. retail drug chain in terms of revenues, operates more than 4,500 drug stores in 44 states and Puerto Rico.

Quantitative Evaluations

S&P Earnings & Dividend Rank: A+

| D | C | B- | B | B+ | A- | A | **A+** |

S&P Fair Value Rank: 4

| 1 | 2 | 3 | **4** | 5 |
| Lowest | | | | Highest |

Fair Value Calc.: $38.70 (Fairly Valued)

S&P Investability Quotient Percentile **100%**

WAG scored higher than 100% of all companies for which an S&P Report is available.

Volatility: Low

| **Low** | Average | High |

Technical Evaluation: Bullish
Since 11/04, the technical indicators for WAG have been Bullish.

Relative Strength Rank: Moderate

| | 63 | |
| 1 Lowest | | Highest 99 |

| Price as of 11/12/04: | **$39.24** | 2005E S&P Core EPS: | **NA** |

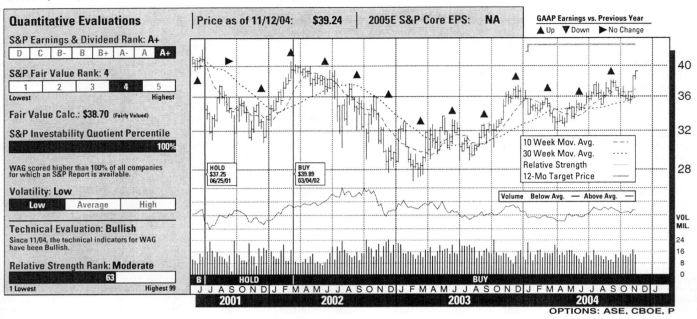

GAAP Earnings vs. Previous Year
▲ Up   ▼ Down   ► No Change

10 Week Mov. Avg.
30 Week Mov. Avg.
Relative Strength
12-Mo Target Price

Volume   Below Avg. —   Above Avg. —

HOLD $37.25 06/25/01
BUY $39.89 03/04/02

VOL. MIL.

OPTIONS: ASE, CBOE, P

Analyst commentary prepared by Joseph Agnese/PMW/JWP

Highlights September 28, 2004

- We see sales advancing 14% to 16% in FY 05 (Aug.), fueled by the expected opening of about 450 new stores, pharmacy same-store sales gains in the low to mid-teens, and front-end same-store sales growth in the mid-single digits. We see front-end growth benefiting from an improving economy that we expect to result in consumer preference for shopping based on convenience rather than on price. Prescription sales growth should continue to benefit from an aging population, new drug introductions, and moderate drug price inflation.

- We expect margins to benefit from improved leverage of new stores and increased sales of generic drugs, which carry lower prices but wider margins than branded counterparts. However, we think that margin gains may be largely offset by a shift in product mix toward lower margin pharmacy sales, as well as higher employee costs and an increased proportion of lower margin third party prescription sales.

- We look for FY 05 EPS to increase 15%, to $1.52, from $1.32 seen in FY 04, excluding one-time gains.

Investment Rationale/Risk September 28, 2004

- We recommend buying the shares. We see valuation benefiting from a more favorable economic and competitive environment in 2004. We see continued improvement in the U.S. economy leading to improved store traffic conditions, as consumers take advantage of WAG's convenient locations and product offerings.

- Risks to our recommendation and target price include a weaker than expected economy, and increased competition from peers and other formats.

- The stock traded recently at 24X our FY 05 EPS estimate, at about 1.5X our projected longer-term EPS growth rate of 16%, and at a premium to the shares of other drug chains we cover. We believe the above-average multiples are justified by what we see as WAG's long history of stable earnings growth, strong balance sheet, and leadership position in its industry. Our 12-month target price of $43 is equal to 28X our FY 05 EPS estimate of $1.52, in line with the stock's average historical P/E multiple.

Key Stock Statistics

S&P Oper. EPS 2005E	1.52	52-week Range	$39.29-32.00
P/E on S&P Oper. EPS 2005E	25.8	12 Month P/E	29.7
Yield (%)	0.5%	Beta	0.27
Dividend Rate/Share	0.21	Shareholders	104,128
Shares Outstanding (M)	1024.5	Market Cap (B)	$ 40.2

Value of $10,000 invested five years ago: **$ 15,358**

Dividend Data Dividends have been paid since 1933

Amount ($)	Date Decl.	Ex-Div. Date	Stock of Record	Payment Date
0.043	Jan. 14	Feb. 17	Feb. 19	Mar. 12 '04
0.043	Apr. 14	May. 19	May. 21	Jun. 12 '04
0.053	Jul. 14	Aug. 18	Aug. 20	Sep. 11 '04
0.053	Oct. 13	Nov. 10	Nov. 15	Dec. 11 '04

Revenues/Earnings Data Fiscal year ending August 31

Revenues (Million $)

	2004	2003	2002	2001	2000	1999
1Q	8,721	7,485	6,559	5,614	4,823	4,016
2Q	9,782	8,446	7,489	6,429	5,609	4,691
3Q	9,579	8,328	7,398	6,296	5,394	4,571
4Q	9,427	8,246	7,235	6,284	5,381	4,560
Yr.	37,508	32,505	28,681	24,623	21,207	17,839

Earnings Per Share ($)

	2004	2003	2002	2001	2000	1999
1Q	0.25	0.22	0.18	0.15	0.13	0.11
2Q	0.42	0.36	0.32	0.29	0.23	0.20
3Q	0.33	0.29	0.25	0.21	0.19	0.16
4Q	0.32	0.27	0.24	0.21	0.21	0.16
Yr.	1.32	1.14	0.99	0.86	0.76	0.62

Next earnings report expected: early-January Source: S&P, Company Reports
EPS Estimates based on S&P Operating Earnings; historical GAAP earnings are as reported.

Walgreen Co.

Recommendation: **BUY** ★★★★★   12-Month Target Price: **$43.00** (as of January 12, 2004)

Business Summary September 28, 2004

Walgreen has gained prescription market share in all but one of its 50 leading markets within the past five years. In FY 04 (Aug.), Chicago-based WAG, one of the largest U.S. retail drug store chain in terms of revenues and profitability, posted its 30th consecutive year of record sales and earnings. Sales increased 15% in FY 04, to $37.5 billion. Earnings before special items advanced 16%, to $1.36 billion.

In 1909, the company's founder, Charles Rudolph Walgreen Sr., purchased one of the busiest drug stores on Chicago's South Side, and transformed it by constructing an ice cream fountain that featured his own brand of ice cream. The ice cream fountain was the forerunner of the famous Walgreen's soda fountain, which became the main attraction for customers from the 1920s through the 1950s. People lined up to buy a product that WAG invented in the early 1920s: the milkshake.

WAG has long resisted the merger fever that has spread through the drug store industry. Instead, it stresses internal growth strategies: large-scale infiltration of new markets, and relocation of units to free-standing stores; and convenience, including 24-hour operations and drive-through pharmacy service.

As of August 31, 2004, the company operated 4,582 drug stores, in 44 states and Puerto Rico, up from 4,227 a year earlier. There were large concentrations of stores in Florida, Illinois and Texas. Internally, WAG is growing faster than any other drug store chain. It opened 436 net new stores (including closures and relocations) during FY 04. The company plans to open 450 units in FY 05, with a goal of 7,000 total stores by FY 10.

Pharmacy sales accounted for 63% of total sales in FY 04, up from 62% in FY 03. WAG, which was already a leading dispenser of prescriptions in the U.S., boosted pharmacy sales 18% in FY 04, versus a 17% gain in FY 03 (including a gain of 14% for comparable drugs, versus 13%).

The company's technological advances include satellite linkage to all stores and facilities, point-of-sale scanning and implementation of the strategic inventory management system (SIMS), uniting all elements of the purchasing, distribution and sales cycle. This is designed to reduce inventory, improve in-stock positions, and provide faster reaction to sales trends.

Healthcare Plus, WAG's pharmacy mail-order subsidiary, offers sales, marketing and operational support for third-party retail and mail-order prescriptions through two facilities. The company has also formed a pharmacy benefits manager, WHP Health Initiatives, targeting small to medium-size employers and HMOs.

Company Financials Fiscal Year ending August 31

Per Share Data ($)

(Year Ended August 31)	2004	2003	2002	2001	2000	1999	1998	1997	1996	1995
Tangible Bk. Val.	NA	7.02	6.08	5.11	4.19	3.47	2.86	2.40	2.08	1.82
Cash Flow	NA	1.47	1.29	1.12	0.99	0.82	0.72	0.60	0.52	0.46
Earnings	1.32	1.14	0.99	0.86	0.76	0.62	0.54	0.44	0.38	0.33
S&P Core Earnings	NA	1.07	0.93	0.80	NA	NA	NA	NA	NA	NA
Dividends	0.18	0.16	0.15	0.14	0.14	0.13	0.13	0.12	0.11	0.10
Payout Ratio	14%	14%	15%	16%	18%	21%	23%	27%	29%	30%
Prices - High	39.29	37.42	40.70	45.29	45.75	33.93	30.21	16.81	10.90	7.84
- Low	32.00	26.90	27.70	28.70	22.06	22.68	14.78	9.62	7.28	5.40
P/E Ratio - High	30	33	41	53	60	55	56	38	29	24
- Low	24	24	28	33	29	37	28	22	19	17

Income Statement Analysis (Million $)

	2004	2003	2002	2001	2000	1999	1998	1997	1996	1995
Revs.	NA	32,505	28,681	24,623	21,207	17,839	15,307	13,363	11,778	10,395
Oper. Inc.	NA	2,194	1,932	1,668	1,454	1,226	1,024	872	750	652
Depr.	NA	346	307	269	230	210	189	164	147	132
Int. Exp.	NA	Nil	Nil	3.10	0.40	0.40	1.00	2.00	2.00	2.00
Pretax Inc.	NA	1,889	1,637	1,423	1,263	1,027	877	712	607	524
Eff. Tax Rate	NA	37.8%	37.8%	37.8%	38.5%	39.2%	38.8%	38.8%	38.8%	38.7%
Net Inc.	NA	1,176	1,019	886	777	624	537	436	372	321
S&P Core Earnings	NA	1,104	955	820	NA	NA	NA	NA	NA	NA

Balance Sheet & Other Fin. Data (Million $)

	2004	2003	2002	2001	2000	1999	1998	1997	1996	1995
Cash	NA	1,017	450	16.9	12.8	142	144	73.0	9.00	22.0
Curr. Assets	NA	6,358	5,167	4,394	3,550	3,222	2,623	2,326	2,019	1,813
Total Assets	NA	11,406	9,879	8,834	7,104	5,907	4,902	4,207	3,634	3,253
Curr. Liab.	NA	3,421	2,955	3,012	2,304	1,924	1,580	1,439	1,182	1,078
LT Debt	NA	Nil	Nil	Nil	Nil	Nil	Nil	Nil	Nil	Nil
Common Equity	NA	7,196	6,230	5,207	4,234	3,484	2,849	2,373	3,634	1,793
Total Cap.	NA	7,424	6,407	5,344	4,336	3,559	2,938	2,486	3,779	1,935
Cap. Exp.	NA	795	934	1,237	1,119	696	641	485	365	310
Cash Flow	NA	1,522	1,327	1,155	1,007	834	726	600	519	453
Curr. Ratio	NA	1.9	1.7	1.5	1.5	1.7	1.7	1.6	1.7	1.7
% LT Debt of Cap.	NA	Nil	Nil	Nil	Nil	Nil	Nil	Nil	Nil	Nil
% Net Inc.of Revs.	NA	3.6	3.6	3.6	3.7	3.5	3.5	3.3	3.2	3.0
% Ret. on Assets	NA	11.0	10.9	11.1	11.9	11.5	11.8	11.1	10.8	10.4
% Ret. on Equity	NA	17.5	17.8	18.8	20.1	19.7	20.6	19.7	10.8	19.0

Data as orig reptd.; bef. results of disc opers/spec. items. Per share data adj. for stk. divs. Bold denotes primary EPS - prior periods restated. E-Estimated. NA-Not Available. NM-Not Meaningful. NR-Not Ranked. UR-Under Review.

Office: 200 Wilmot Road, Deerfield, IL 60015.
Telephone: 847-940-2500.
Email: investor.relations@walgreens.com
Website: http://www.walgreens.com
Chrmn & CEO: D.W. Bernauer.
Pres & COO: J.A. Rein.
SVP & CFO: W. Rudolphsen.

SVP & Treas: J.W. Gleeson.
SVP, Secy & General Counsel: J.A. Oettinger.
Investor Contact: R. Hans 847-940-2500.
Dirs: D. W. Bernauer, W. C. Foote, J. J. Howard, A. G. McNally, C. Reed, J. Rein, D. Y. Schwartz, J. B. Schwemm, C. R. Walgreen, III, M. M. von Ferstel.

Auditor: Deloitte & Touche.
Founded: in 1901.
Domicile: Illinois.
Employees: 154,000.
S&P Analyst: Joseph Agnese/PMW/JWP

Wal-Mart Stores

Recommendation: **BUY** ★★★★☆
SELL | SELL | HOLD | BUY | BUY
12-Month Target Price: **$62.00**
(as of August 11, 2004)

WMT has an approximate 2.19% weighting in the **S&P 500**

Sector: Consumer Staples
Sub-Industry: Hypermarkets & Super Centers
Peer Group: Retail - General Merchandise

Summary: WMT, the largest retailer in North America, operates a chain of discount department stores, wholesale clubs, and combination discount stores and supermarkets.

Quantitative Evaluations

| Price as of 11/12/04: | $56.85 | 2005E S&P Core EPS: | $2.40 |

GAAP Earnings vs. Previous Year
▲ Up ▼ Down ► No Change

S&P Earnings & Dividend Rank: A+

| D | C | B- | B | B+ | A- | A | A+ |

S&P Fair Value Rank: 3+

| 1 | 2 | 3 | 4 | 5 |
| Lowest | | 3 | | Highest |

Fair Value Calc.: $54.10 (Slightly Overvalued)

S&P Investability Quotient Percentile

100%

WMT scored higher than 100% of all companies for which an S&P Report is available.

Volatility: Low

| Low | Average | High |

Technical Evaluation: Bullish

Since 11/04, the technical indicators for WMT have been Bullish.

Relative Strength Rank: Moderate

57

| 1 Lowest | | Highest 99 |

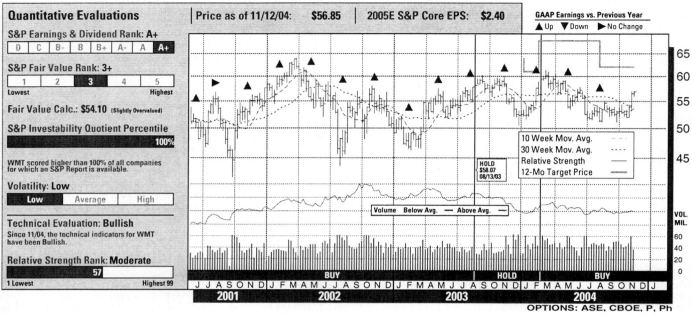

10 Week Mov. Avg.
30 Week Mov. Avg.
Relative Strength
12-Mo Target Price

HOLD $58.07 08/13/03

Volume — Below Avg. — Above Avg.

VOL. MIL.

BUY | HOLD | BUY
J J A S O N D | J F M A M J J A S O N D | J F M A M J J A S O N D | J F M A M J J A S O N D | J
2001 | 2002 | 2003 | 2004

OPTIONS: ASE, CBOE, P, Ph

Analyst commentary prepared by Joseph Agnese/MF/BK

Highlights August 18, 2004

- We expect FY 05 (Jan.) net sales to grow about 12%, to $287 billion, driven by a modest same-store sales increase and the addition of about 8% to square footage (50 million sq. ft. of new retail space), including 230 to 240 new U.S. supercenters (about 140 would be relocations or expansions of existing discount stores), and 130 to 140 international units. We see low price leadership in the U.S., continued expansion of the company's successful food business, additional refinements to apparel selections, and continued inroads into international markets as likely to be key sales drivers. We also believe renewed emphasis on small business customers and price leadership is boosting results at Sam's Club.

- We see EBIT (earnings before interest and taxes) margins benefiting from lower apparel markdowns, an improved product mix, and global sourcing efforts.

- Aided by modest share repurchases, we see both operating EPS and Standard & Poor's Core Earnings per share of $2.40 for FY 05.

Investment Rationale/Risk August 18, 2004

- We recommend accumulating the shares. We view WMT as remaining well positioned to increase its U.S. market share, due to continued low price leadership and an expanding merchandise assortment with improving quality. We concur with the company's view of a more favorable consumer spending outlook. We think easier same-store sales comparisons in the FY 05 first half should give WMT an opportunity to better leverage operating expenses. These factors bode well, in our opinion, for a return to more robust sales and earnings growth over the next few years.

- Risks to our recommendation and target price include greater competition, and economic pressures reflecting rising unemployment or lower consumer confidence.

- Based on our P/E multiple and DCF analyses (assuming a weighted average cost of capital of 9.0%), our 12-month target price is $62.

Key Stock Statistics

S&P Oper. EPS 2005E	2.40	52-week Range	$61.31-50.50
P/E on S&P Oper. EPS 2005E	23.7	12 Month P/E	25.7
S&P Oper. EPS 2006E	2.71	Beta	0.74
Yield (%)	0.9%	Shareholders	333,604
Dividend Rate/Share	0.52	Market Cap (B)	$241.2
Shares Outstanding (M)	4242.5		

Value of $10,000 invested five years ago: **$ 10,021**

Dividend Data Dividends have been paid since 1973

Amount ($)	Date Decl.	Ex-Div. Date	Stock of Record	Payment Date
0.130	Mar. 02	Mar. 17	Mar. 19	Apr. 05 '04
0.130	Mar. 02	May. 19	May. 21	Jun. 07 '04
0.130	Mar. 02	Aug. 18	Aug. 20	Sep. 07 '04
0.130	Mar. 02	Dec. 15	Dec. 17	Jan. 03 '05

Revenues/Earnings Data Fiscal year ending January 31

Revenues (Million $)

	2005	2004	2003	2002	2001	2000
1Q	65,443	57,224	54,960	48,052	42,985	34,717
2Q	70,466	63,232	59,694	52,799	46,112	38,470
3Q	—	63,035	58,797	52,738	45,676	40,432
4Q	—	75,190	71,073	64,210	56,556	51,394
Yr.	—	258,681	244,524	217,799	191,329	165,013

Earnings Per Share ($)

	2005	2004	2003	2002	2001	2000
1Q	0.50	0.41	0.37	0.31	0.30	0.25
2Q	0.62	0.52	0.46	0.36	0.36	0.28
3Q	E0.54	0.46	0.41	0.33	0.31	0.29
4Q	E0.75	0.63	0.57	0.49	0.45	0.43
Yr.	E2.40	2.03	1.81	1.50	1.40	1.25

Next earnings report expected: mid-November Source: S&P, Company Reports
EPS Estimates based on S&P Operating Earnings; historical GAAP earnings are as reported.

The McGraw·Hill Companies

Wal-Mart Stores, Inc.

Recommendation: **BUY** ★★★★☆   12-Month Target Price: **$62.00** (as of August 11, 2004)

Business Summary August 18, 2004

Wal-Mart, the largest retailer in North America, has set its sights on other parts of the world. As of January 31, 2004, the company operated 1,478 Wal-Mart Stores, 1,471 Supercenters, 538 Sam's Clubs, and 64 Neighborhood Markets in the U.S. Internationally, WMT operated 11 units in Argentina, 25 in Brazil, 235 in Canada, 34 in China, 92 in Germany, 15 in Korea, 623 in Mexico, 53 in Puerto Rico, and 267 in the U.K.

The company's operations are divided into three divisions: Wal-Mart, Sam's Club, and International. In FY 04 (Jan.), the Wal-Mart segment, comprised of discount stores, Supercenters and Neighborhood Markets, had sales of $174.2 billion, up 11% from the level of FY 03. Sam's Club sales totaled $34.5 billion, up 8.9%. In international markets, in which WMT operates a variety of formats, some via joint ventures, sales were up nearly 17%, to $47.6 billion.

In May 2003, WMT sold McLane Company, Inc., a wholly owned wholesale distributor, to Berkshire Hathaway, for about $1.5 billion. As a result of the sale, McLane, which contributed $15 billion in FY 03 net sales, was classified as a discontinued operation.

The average U.S. Wal-Mart discount store has about 98,000 sq. ft., and carries a wide variety of general merchandise. The average Supercenter is much larger, with about 187,000 sq. ft. Most Supercenters, which carry a broader assortment of groceries, developed from the relocation or expansion of WMT discount stores.

Nationally advertised merchandise accounts for a majority of sales at Wal-Mart Stores and Supercenters, but the company also markets limited lines of merchandise under store brands. WMT's Neighborhood Markets, which offer groceries, pharmaceuticals and general merchandise, have an average size of about 43,000 sq. ft.

Sam's Clubs are membership only operations in the U.S., Puerto Rico and Mexico, averaging about 127,000 sq. ft. Merchandise includes bulk displays of name brand hard goods, some soft goods and institutional size grocery items. Each Sam's Club also carries products such as sporting goods, toys and books; most clubs have fresh food departments.

During FY 04, WMT opened 41 new and relocated or expanded three discount stores; added 83 new and relocated or expanded from discount stores 130 supercenters; opened 15 new Neighborhood Markets; added 13 new and relocated or expanded 21 Sam's Clubs; and opened 91 and relocated or expanded 38 international locations. The company ended FY 04 with about 607 million sq. ft. of retail space.

The company aims to increase productivity, pass on cost reductions to customers via an everyday low pricing strategy, and provide a more complete assortment of merchandise in its stores. WMT achieved about $12 billion in price rollbacks in the Wal-Mart division in FY 04.

Company Financials Fiscal Year ending January 31

Per Share Data ($)

(Year Ended January 31)	2004	2003	2002	2001	2000	1999	1998	1997	1996	1995
Tangible Bk. Val.	7.83	6.78	5.95	4.99	3.69	4.75	4.13	3.75	3.22	2.77
Cash Flow	2.91	2.58	2.22	2.04	1.78	1.41	1.15	0.99	0.88	0.82
Earnings	2.03	1.81	1.50	1.40	1.25	0.99	0.78	0.67	0.59	0.59
S&P Core Earnings	2.03	1.79	1.47	1.39	NA	NA	NA	NA	NA	NA
Dividends	0.30	0.30	0.28	0.24	0.18	0.15	0.14	0.11	0.10	0.09
Payout Ratio	15%	17%	19%	17%	14%	16%	17%	16%	17%	15%

Cal. Yrs.	2003	2002	2001	2000	1999	1998	1997	1996	1995	1994
Prices - High	60.20	63.94	58.75	69.00	70.25	41.37	20.96	14.12	13.81	14.62
- Low	46.25	43.72	42.00	41.43	38.68	18.78	11.00	9.54	10.25	10.50
P/E Ratio - High	30	35	39	49	56	42	27	21	23	25
- Low	23	24	28	30	31	19	14	14	17	18

Income Statement Analysis (Million $)

	2004	2003	2002	2001	2000	1999	1998	1997	1996	1995
Revs.	256,329	246,525	217,799	191,329	165,013	137,634	117,958	104,859	93,627	82,494
Oper. Inc.	16,525	17,076	15,367	12,392	10,684	8,418	6,796	5,871	5,416	5,120
Depr.	3,852	3,432	3,290	2,868	2,375	1,872	1,634	1,463	1,304	1,070
Int. Exp.	996	543	1,326	1,374	1,022	797	784	889	938	776
Pretax Inc.	14,193	12,719	10,751	10,116	9,083	7,323	5,719	4,850	4,346	4,262
Eff. Tax Rate	36.1%	35.3%	36.2%	36.5%	36.8%	37.4%	37.0%	37.0%	36.8%	37.1%
Net Inc.	8,861	8,039	6,671	6,295	5,575	4,430	3,526	3,056	2,740	2,681
S&P Core Earnings	8,861	7,955	6,592	6,235	NA	NA	NA	NA	NA	NA

Balance Sheet & Other Fin. Data (Million $)

	2004	2003	2002	2001	2000	1999	1998	1997	1996	1995
Cash	5,199	2,758	2,161	2,054	1,856	1,879	1,447	883	83.0	45.0
Curr. Assets	34,421	30,483	28,246	26,555	24,356	21,132	19,352	17,993	17,331	15,338
Total Assets	104,912	94,685	83,451	78,130	70,349	49,996	45,384	39,604	37,541	32,819
Curr. Liab.	37,418	32,617	27,282	28,949	25,803	16,762	14,460	10,957	11,454	9,973
LT Debt	20,099	19,608	18,732	15,655	16,674	9,607	9,674	10,016	10,600	9,709
Common Equity	43,623	39,337	35,102	31,343	25,834	21,112	18,503	17,143	14,756	12,726
Total Cap.	65,206	60,307	56,169	49,181	44,546	33,234	30,115	28,647	26,087	22,846
Cap. Exp.	10,308	9,355	8,383	8,042	6,183	3,734	2,636	2,643	3,566	3,734
Cash Flow	12,713	11,471	9,961	9,163	7,950	6,302	5,160	4,519	4,044	3,751
Curr. Ratio	0.9	0.9	1.0	0.9	0.9	1.3	1.3	1.6	1.5	1.5
% LT Debt of Cap.	30.8	32.5	33.3	31.8	37.4	28.9	32.1	35.0	40.6	40.6
% Net Inc.of Revs.	3.5	3.3	3.1	3.3	3.4	3.2	3.0	2.9	2.9	3.3
% Ret. on Assets	8.9	9.0	8.3	8.5	9.3	9.3	8.3	7.9	7.8	9.1
% Ret. on Equity	21.3	21.6	20.1	22.0	23.8	22.4	19.8	19.2	19.9	19.9

Data as orig reptd.; bef. results of disc opers/spec. items. Per share data adj. for stk. divs. Bold denotes primary EPS - prior periods restated. E-Estimated. NA-Not Available. NM-Not Meaningful. NR-Not Ranked. UR-Under Review.

Office: 702 S.W. 8th Street, Bentonville, AR 72716.
Telephone: 479-273-4000.
Website: http://www.walmartstores.com
Chrmn: S.R. Walton.
Pres & CEO: H.L. Scott, Jr.
Vice Chrmn: T.M. Coughlin.

EVP, CFO & Investor Contact: T.M. Schoewe 479-273-4000.
EVP, Secy & General Counsel: T.D. Hyde.
Dirs: J. Breyer, M. M. Burns, T. M. Coughlin, S. C. Gault, D. Glass, R. A. Hernandez, D. G. Lepore, J. D. Opie, J. P. Reason, H. L. Scott, Jr., J. C. Shewmaker, J. H. Villarreal, S. R. Walton, J. T. Walton.

Founded: in 1945.
Domicile: Delaware.
Employees: 1,500,000.
S&P Analyst: Joseph Agnese/MF/BK

Washington Mutual

Recommendation: HOLD ★★★ ☆ ☆
SELL | SELL | HOLD | BUY | BUY

12-Month Target Price: $41.00
(as of October 21, 2004)

WM has an approximate 0.32% weighting in the **S&P 500**

Sector: Financials
Sub-Industry: Thrifts & Mortgage Finance
Peer Group: Major Savings & Loan Companies

Summary: WM is the largest U.S. savings institution, with about $289 billion in assets.

Quantitative Evaluations

S&P Earnings & Dividend Rank: A

| D | C | B- | B | B+ | A- | **A** | A+ |

S&P Fair Value Rank: 3+

| 1 | 2 | **3** | 4 | 5 |
| Lowest | | | | Highest |

Fair Value Calc.: $39.10 (Slightly Overvalued)

S&P Investability Quotient Percentile
89%

WM scored higher than 89% of all companies for which an S&P Report is available.

Volatility: Average

| Low | **Average** | High |

Technical Evaluation: Neutral
Since 11/04, the technical indicators for WM have been Neutral.

Relative Strength Rank: Moderate
39
1 Lowest — Highest 99

Price as of 11/12/04: **$40.06** **2004E S&P Core EPS:** **$2.80**

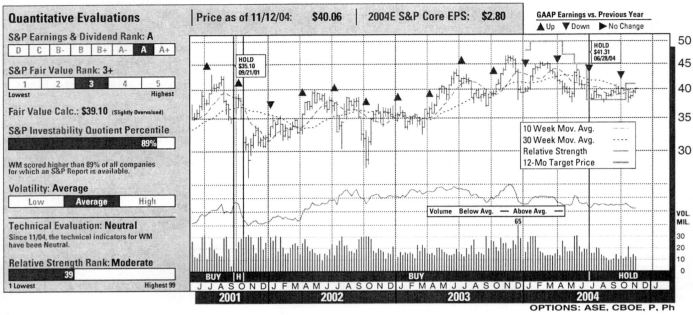

GAAP Earnings vs. Previous Year
▲ Up ▼ Down ▶ No Change

HOLD $35.10 09/21/01
HOLD $41.31 06/28/04

10 Week Mov. Avg.
30 Week Mov. Avg.
Relative Strength
12-Mo Target Price

Volume Below Avg. — Above Avg.
65

VOL. MIL.
50 45 40 35 30
30 20 10 0

BUY | H | BUY | HOLD
J J A S O N D | J F M A M J J A S O N D | J F M A M J J A S O N D | J F M A M J J A S O N D | J
2001 | 2002 | 2003 | 2004

OPTIONS: ASE, CBOE, P, Ph

Analyst commentary prepared by Erik J. Eisenstein/MF/JWP

Highlights October 29, 2004

- We expect average earning assets to grow 5% in 2005, muted by the full-year effect of heavy refinancing activity in 2004. We also expect earning assets to be hampered by reduced balances of loans held for sale, on a slower projected mortgage origination market. We project that the net interest margin will widen on a year-over-year basis, leading to an 8% increase in net interest income.

- We think credit quality will improve in 2005 as the economy continues to recover, leading to a 2% drop in loan loss provisions. We see noninterest income rising about 16%, helped in part by increased fees on a larger deposit base. We also expect higher mortgage rates to lead to improved mortgage servicing results in 2005, offsetting an expected decline in mortgage originations. We were encouraged by the sequential improvement in the operating efficiency ratio in the 2004 third quarter. In 2005, we forecast that operating expenses will be up only 2%, with expansion spending outweighing lower costs associated with reduced mortgage volume and efforts to cut expenses.

- Overall, we project that 2005 EPS will gain 33%, to $3.80, from $2.85 projected for 2004, benefitting from what we see as an easy comparison.

Investment Rationale/Risk October 29, 2004

- We recommend holding the shares on a total return basis. We have a positive view of WM's consumer bank. We see its retail store banking concept as innovative and a source of competitive advantage relative to other depository institutions. We believe expansion of this concept to new locations will stimulate earnings growth in coming years. We view WM's mortgage banking operations, which have expanded through acquisitions in recent years, less positively. Although these operations have generally bolstered results in prior periods, we believe they will expose the company to greater interest rate risk than it has faced in the past. Moreover, we continue to see execution risk associated with efforts to fully integrate these operations.

- Risks to our recommendation and target price include interest rate and execution risk.

- Our 12-month target price of $41 implies a P/E multiple of 10.8X, somewhat below the historical average, applied to our 2005 EPS estimate.

Key Stock Statistics

S&P Core EPS 2005E	3.78	52-week Range	$46.79-36.80
S&P Oper. EPS 2004E	2.85	12 Month P/E	11.7
P/E on S&P Oper. EPS 2004E	14.1	Beta	0.31
S&P Oper. EPS 2005E	3.80	Shareholders	51,293
Yield (%)	4.5%	Market Cap (B)	$ 35.0
Dividend Rate/Share	1.80	Shares Outstanding (M)	873.1

Value of $10,000 invested five years ago: **$ 19,586**

Dividend Data Dividends have been paid since 1986

Amount ($)	Date Decl.	Ex-Div. Date	Stock of Record	Payment Date
0.430	Apr. 19	Apr. 28	Apr. 30	May. 14 '04
0.440	Jul. 21	Jul. 28	Jul. 30	Aug. 13 '04
0.440	Jul. 21	Jul. 28	Jul. 30	Aug. 13 '04
0.450	Oct. 20	Oct. 27	Oct. 29	Nov. 15 '04

Revenues/Earnings Data Fiscal year ending December 31

Revenues (Million $)

	2004	2003	2002	2001	2000	1999
1Q	3,958	4,523	4,690	4,664	3,727	3,206
2Q	3,646	4,664	4,793	4,741	3,862	3,324
3Q	4,075	4,562	4,793	4,428	3,996	3,429
4Q	—	4,264	4,760	3,859	4,181	3,612
Yr.	—	18,013	19,037	17,692	15,767	13,571

Earnings Per Share ($)

	2004	2003	2002	2001	2000	1999
1Q	0.73	1.05	0.98	0.77	0.55	0.51
2Q	0.55	1.10	1.01	0.91	0.61	0.52
3Q	0.76	1.09	1.01	0.85	0.57	0.55
4Q	E0.81	0.91	1.03	0.62	0.63	0.53
Yr.	E2.85	4.12	4.05	3.15	2.36	2.11

Next earnings report expected: late-January Source: S&P, Company Reports
EPS Estimates based on S&P Operating Earnings; historical GAAP earnings are as reported.

Recommendation: **HOLD** ★ ★ ★ ☆ ☆   12-Month Target Price: **$41.00** (as of October 21, 2004)

Business Summary October 29, 2004

For the better part of a decade, Washington Mutual focused on building scale and leading national positions in retail banking, mortgage lending, and select commercial lending businesses through both internal growth and acquisitions. As a result, WM was the largest U.S. savings institution, with assets of $289 billion at September 30, 2004, and more than 2,300 offices at October 20, 2004. Now focused on leveraging the power of that franchise, the company's strategy is to maximize household growth and multiple product relationships, improve service levels, and drive operational efficiencies. WM is committed to identifying and eliminating $1 billion in annualized noninterest expense by the second quarter of 2005. In July 2004, the company announced plans to eliminate about 2,690 positions in its mortgage banking and commercial businesses.

WM is also focused on opening new retail banking locations. After opening 143 new locations in 2002 and acquiring an additional 123 as part of the Dime acquisition, WM opened 260 locations in 2003. In 2004, WM plans to open an additional 250 locations, including 50 in Florida, 50 in Illinois, 30 in Texas, and 35 in the New York/New Jersey area. The company plans to open 250 new locations annually thereafter.

At the end of 2003, home loans accounted for 57% of WM's loan portfolio (58% at year-end 2002), multifamily loans 12% (13%), home equity loans and other lines of credit 16% (11%), purchased specialty mortgage finance loans 7% (7%), and other 8% (10%).

Home loans basically consist of mortgages extended to homebuyers for the purchase of a one-four family house. Mortgages can also be issued to refinance existing debt. Home equity loans and lines of credit generally provide higher

margins than home loans and represent an opportunity to expand the non-home portfolio. Multifamily loans are mortgages extended to individuals or corporations to buy, construct, develop or refinance apartment buildings.

Savings products offered include checking accounts, certificates of deposit of various maturities and regular savings accounts. The company is attempting to build up its checking account base as a means to lower its cost of funds and generate fee income. In addition, checking accounts, which are viewed as constituting the primary customer relationship with the bank, can be used to cross-sell other products. Deposits in checking accounts comprised 63% of total deposits at year-end 2003 (59% at year-end 2002), savings accounts 7% (7%), money market deposit accounts 12% (13%), and time deposit accounts 18% (22%).

In January 2002, WM acquired Dime Bancorp, with $15 billion in deposits and 123 branches in the New York area.

In October 2002, the company acquired Homeside Lending, Inc., one of the 10 largest residential mortgage lenders in the U.S., for about $1.3 billion. In January 2004, WM sold its Washington Mutual Finance subsidiary, which offered installment and real estate-secured loans to consumers in small communities. In connection with the sale, WM recorded a $676 million pretax gain in the first quarter.

In July 2003, directors authorized the buyback of 100 million common shares. In the 2004 second quarter, WM purchased 266,484 shares, at an average price of $42.73 each.

Company Financials Fiscal Year ending December 31

Per Share Data ($)

(Year Ended December 31)	2003	2002	2001	2000	1999	1998	1997	1996	1995	1994
Tangible Bk. Val.	15.38	14.36	13.44	11.21	9.16	9.37	9.09	7.98	9.60	7.98
Earnings	4.12	4.05	3.15	2.36	2.11	1.71	0.83	0.38	1.19	1.13
S&P Core Earnings	4.05	3.94	3.03	NA	NA	NA	NA	NA	NA	NA
Dividends	1.40	1.06	0.90	0.76	0.65	0.55	0.47	0.40	0.34	0.31
Payout Ratio	34%	26%	29%	32%	31%	37%	57%	106%	29%	28%
Prices - High	46.85	39.98	42.99	37.29	30.50	34.44	32.27	20.38	13.11	11.11
- Low	32.40	27.80	26.52	14.41	16.45	17.83	18.77	11.61	7.38	7.00
P/E Ratio - High	11	10	14	16	14	20	39	54	11	10
- Low	8	7	8	6	8	10	23	31	6	6

Income Statement Analysis (Million $)

	2003	2002	2001	2000	1999	1998	1997	1996	1995	1994
Net Int. Inc.	7,629	8,341	6,876	4,311	4,452	4,292	2,656	1,191	578	571
Loan Loss Prov.	42.0	595	575	185	167	162	207	202	10.0	20.0
Non Int. Inc.	5,174	4,022	1,883	1,985	1,509	1,524	751	259	107	108
Non Int. Exp.	7,408	6,382	4,167	3,126	2,910	3,284	2,300	1,025	382	384
Pretax Inc.	6,029	6,154	4,311	2,984	2,884	2,369	901	223	292	275
Eff. Tax Rate	37.1%	36.7%	36.6%	36.4%	37.0%	37.2%	46.5%	42.8%	34.7%	37.3%
Net Inc.	3,793	3,896	2,732	1,899	1,817	1,487	482	114	191	172
% Net Int. Marg.	3.11	3.48	3.32	2.38	2.63	2.88	3.03	2.89	3.05	3.60
S&P Core Earnings	3,735	3,788	2,616	NA	NA	NA	NA	NA	NA	NA

Balance Sheet & Other Fin. Data (Million $)

	2003	2002	2001	2000	1999	1998	1997	1996	1995	1994
Total Assets	275,178	268,298	242,506	194,716	186,514	165,493	96,981	44,552	21,633	18,458
Loans	174,394	145,875	131,587	118,612	113,497	108,371	67,140	30,467	12,536	12,555
Deposits	153,181	155,516	107,182	79,574	81,130	85,492	50,986	24,080	10,597	9,778
Capitalization:										
Debt	22,123	22,198	23,883	29,951	28,313	45,198	23,791	7,918	3,936	3,817
Equity	19,742	20,134	14,063	10,166	9,053	9,344	5,191	2,398	1,592	1,305
Total	41,865	42,332	38,048	40,117	37,366	54,542	29,100	10,316	5,527	5,122
% Ret. on Assets	1.4	1.5	1.2	1.0	1.0	1.0	0.5	0.3	1.0	1.0
% Ret. on Equity	19.1	22.8	22.5	19.8	19.8	20.2	9.3	3.9	11.9	13.7
% Loan Loss Resv.	0.6	0.9	0.9	-0.8	0.9	1.0	1.0	1.2	1.1	1.0
% Risk Based Capital	10.8	11.4	10.9	11.4	11.2	12.1	NA	NA	11.5	14.9
Price Times Book Value:										
Hi	2.0	2.8	3.2	3.3	3.3	3.7	3.9	2.6	1.4	1.4
Low	2.1	1.9	2.0	1.3	1.8	1.9	2.3	1.5	0.8	0.9

Data as orig reptd.; bef. results of disc opers/spec. items. Per share data adj. for stk. divs. Bold denotes primary EPS - prior periods restated. E-Estimated. NA-Not Available. NM-Not Meaningful. NR-Not Ranked. UR-Under Review.

Office: 1201 3rd Ave, Seattle, WA 98101.
Telephone: 206-461-2000.
Website: http://www.wamu.com
Chrmn, Pres & CEO: K.K. Killinger.
Vice Chrmn: W.A. Longbrake.
Vice Chrmn: C.T. Tall.

EVP & CFO: T.W. Casey.
SVP & General Counsel: F.L. Chapman.
Investor Contact: J. DeGrande 206-461-3186.
Dirs: D. P. Beighle, A. V. Farrell, S. E. Frank, K. K. Killinger, P. D. Matthews, M. K. Murphy, M. Osmer-McQuade, M. E. Pugh, W. G. Reed, Jr., E. A. Sanders, W. D. Schulte, J. H. Stever, W. B. Wood, Jr.

Founded: in 1889.
Domicile: Washington.
Employees: 63,720.
S&P Analyst: Erik J. Eisenstein/MF/JWP

Recommendation: HOLD ★ ★ ★ ☆ ☆
SELL SELL HOLD BUY BUY

12-Month Target Price: **$30.00**
(as of October 28, 2004)

WMI has an approximate 0.16% weighting in the **S&P 500**

Sector: Industrials
Sub-Industry: Environmental Services
Peer Group: Solid Waste Management

Summary: WMI is the largest U.S. trash hauling/disposal concern.

Quantitative Evaluations

S&P Earnings & Dividend Rank: B

| D | C | B- | **B** | B+ | A- | A | A+ |

S&P Fair Value Rank: 3

| 1 | 2 | **3** | 4 | 5 |
| Lowest | | | | Highest |

Fair Value Calc.: $28.20 (Slightly Overvalued)

S&P Investability Quotient Percentile

76%

WMI scored higher than 76% of all companies for which an S&P Report is available.

Volatility: Average

| Low | **Average** | High |

Technical Evaluation: Bullish
Since 11/04, the technical indicators for WMI have been Bullish.

Relative Strength Rank: Moderate

59

| 1 Lowest | | Highest 99 |

Price as of 11/12/04: $29.71 | **2004E S&P Core EPS:** $1.25

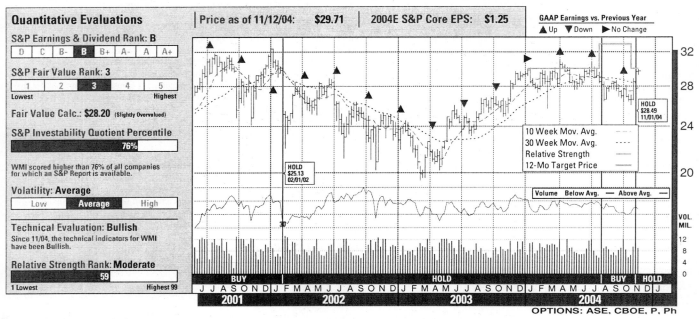

GAAP Earnings vs. Previous Year
▲ Up ▼ Down ▶ No Change

10 Week Mov. Avg.
30 Week Mov. Avg.
Relative Strength
12-Mo Target Price

Volume Below Avg. — Above Avg. —

HOLD $28.49 11/01/04
HOLD $25.13 02/01/02

BUY | HOLD | BUY | HOLD

J J A S O N D J F M A M J J A S O N D J F M A M J J A S O N D J F M A M J J A S O N D J
2001 | 2002 | 2003 | 2004

OPTIONS: ASE, CBOE, P, Ph

Analyst commentary prepared by Stewart Scharf/PMW/BK

Highlights November 01, 2004

- We expect internal revenue growth in the mid- to high single digits in 2005, following growth near 5% that we see for 2004, driven by improving volume as well as pricing initiatives; total revenue growth (including acquisitions and positive effects from commodity recycling prices) should be near 9% in 2005.

- We think 2005 gross margins (before depreciation and amortization) should widen by 100 basis points, to near 36%, on cost savings from routing initiatives, and from likely stabilizing fuel costs. We expect EBITDA margins to widen to near 26%, as WMI leverages its cost structure, leading to a projected $45 million in annualized cost savings, which should outweigh higher insurance costs. SG&A expenses should drop below 10% of revenues. We expect free cash flow generation of at least $950 million in 2004 to be used for additional share buybacks ($425 million to $500 million seen for 2004), as well as potential accretive acquisitions and dividends (a 6.5% hike in the 2005 first quarter).

- We estimate that the effective tax rate will drop to about 30% in 2004, and project 2004 EPS of $1.35, followed by $1.65 in 2005. We see S&P Core EPS of $1.25 for 2004 and $1.56 for 2005, reflecting estimated stock option expense.

Investment Rationale/Risk November 01, 2004

- We would not add to positions, based on uncertain market conditions, higher fuel and steel costs, and our valuation models which suggest that the shares are fairly valued. We expect a three-year, $1.2 billion annual stock purchase and dividend program. We expect WMI to maintain debt of about 60% of capitalization, below the level of its closest competitors.

- Risks to our recommendation and target price include a further significant rise in fuel costs, a slower economic rebound than we anticipate, and a potential inability to raise prices enough to meet return on invested capital (ROIC) goals, especially in the Midwest and South.

- We expect ROIC eventually to exceed WMI's 5.5% weighted average cost of capital by 500 basis points, and project total enterprise value to EBITDA above 9.0X for 2005, exceeding the peer average. The stock offers what we view as an attractive dividend yield of 2.6%, but the shares trade at 17X our 2005 EPS estimate, a premium to the multiple of the S&P 500 as well as that of peers. Our 12-month target price of $30 is based on the stock's average historical forward P/E multiple.

Key Stock Statistics

S&P Core EPS 2005E	1.56	52-week Range	$31.00-25.67
S&P Oper. EPS 2004E	1.35	12 Month P/E	19.6
P/E on S&P Oper. EPS 2004E	22.0	Beta	0.29
S&P Oper. EPS 2005E	1.65	Shareholders	19,555
Yield (%)	2.5%	Market Cap (B)	$ 17.2
Dividend Rate/Share	0.75	Shares Outstanding (M)	579.9

Value of $10,000 invested five years ago: **$ 16,764**

Dividend Data Dividends have been paid since 1998

Amount ($)	Date Decl.	Ex-Div. Date	Stock of Record	Payment Date
0.188	Jan. 30	Feb. 26	Mar. 01	Mar. 25 '04
0.188	May. 17	May. 27	Jun. 01	Jun. 25 '04
0.188	Aug. 17	Aug. 30	Sep. 01	Sep. 24 '04
0.188	Oct. 13	Nov. 29	Dec. 01	Dec. 23 '04

Revenues/Earnings Data Fiscal year ending December 31

Revenues (Million $)

	2004	2003	2002	2001	2000	1999
1Q	2,896	2,716	2,609	2,719	3,217	3,071
2Q	3,138	2,915	2,825	2,915	3,266	3,335
3Q	3,274	2,975	2,896	2,897	3,125	3,385
4Q	—	2,968	2,812	2,791	2,884	3,336
Yr.	—	11,574	11,142	11,322	12,492	13,127

Earnings Per Share ($)

	2004	2003	2002	2001	2000	1999
1Q	0.25	0.18	0.22	0.20	0.09	0.58
2Q	0.37	0.30	0.35	0.30	Nil	0.51
3Q	0.52	0.35	0.38	0.05	-0.31	-1.53
4Q	E0.33	0.39	0.39	0.25	0.06	-0.18
Yr.	E1.35	1.21	1.33	0.80	-0.16	-0.64

Next earnings report expected: mid-February Source: S&P, Company Reports
EPS Estimates based on S&P Operating Earnings; historical GAAP earnings are as reported.

STANDARD &POOR'S

Waste Management, Inc.

Stock Report
November 13, 2004
NYSE Symbol: **WMI**

Recommendation: **HOLD** ★ ★ ★ ☆ ☆   12-Month Target Price: **$30.00** (as of October 28, 2004)

Business Summary November 01, 2004

Waste Management, the largest U.S. waste disposal company, is completing a three-year turnaround plan that has refocused the company on its core North American operations in an effort to boost overall performance. WMI provides collection, transfer, recycling and resource recovery, as well as disposal services. It also owns U.S. waste-to-energy facilities. The waste industry tends to lag economic recoveries by six to nine months.

The company divested most of its non-solid waste operations in 2000, and continues to focus on improving customer service and operating efficiencies. To support its business strategy, WMI adopted a new organizational structure in March 2002. It moved to three field management layers, from four, and reduced the number of field layers with administrative and functional staff to two, from four. The new structure refocused more than 1,200 sites, 900 districts, and a number of divisions into 1,200 operating units that report to 82 market areas. In 2003, WMI acquired $561 million in annualized revenues, for $344 million. The company expects to spend $250 million on tuck-in acquisitions in 2004.

In 2003, the North American solid waste (NASW) business accounted for virtually all operating revenues. Revenues from NASW were 57% collection, 19% landfill, 6% waste-to-energy (Wheelabrator Technologies unit), 11% transfer, and 6.5% recycling and other. At the end of 2003, WMI owned or operated 284 solid waste and five hazardous waste landfills, with average remaining landfill life of 26 years (36 years when considering remaining permitted capacity, probable expansion capacity, and projected annual disposal volume.) The company also operated 366 transfer stations and 17 waste-to-energy facilities. At September 30, 2004, the internalization rate (waste disposed of at company-owned landfills) was 65%. WMI had 289 active landfills in 2003, handling over 117 million tons of disposal

volume, including 1.8 million tons of volume disposed of in hazardous waste landfills.

In January 2003, WMI formed a new recycling organization, Recycle America Alliance (RAA), intended to optimize the capacity and improve the earnings of its recycling line by combining assets and operations with other recycling processors.

In the 2004 third quarter, WMI recorded income of $0.12 a share from favorable tax audit settlements. In the 2003 fourth quarter, it recorded pretax income of $17 million ($0.04 a share, after tax) from a litigation settlement and a lower tax rate. In 2003, the company incurred $44 million of pretax restructuring charges, including a $20 million restructuring charge in the first quarter to cover a net workforce reduction of 700 employees and 270 contract workers, expected to result in $50 million of annualized cost savings, and $23 million in the second quarter, as the company cut an additional 600 employees and 200 contract workers. WMI planned to reduce its 15,000 commercial and residential routes by 10%, realizing a projected $180 million of annual expense savings. In 2003, the company exceeded its goal of reducing 750 routes for savings of about $18 million. In March 2002, it recorded a $37 million pretax restructuring charge for costs related to its new organizational structure; it recorded another $1 million of charges in the third quarter of 2002.

Following $240 million of share buybacks in the 2004 third quarter, WMI had purchased a total of 72 million shares (12% of its common shares outstanding) since the start of 2002. In 2003, it bought back 22 million shares, for $574 million.

Company Financials Fiscal Year ending December 31

Per Share Data ($)

(Year Ended December 31)	2003	2002	2001	2000	1999	1998	1997	1996	1995	1994
Tangible Bk. Val.	0.24	0.21	0.43	NM	NM	NM	4.51	4.57	4.32	0.90
Cash Flow	3.44	5.29	2.97	2.14	1.99	1.25	2.47	1.33	1.57	1.47
Earnings	1.21	1.33	0.80	-0.16	-0.64	-1.31	1.26	0.24	0.55	0.61
S&P Core Earnings	1.09	1.17	1.04	NA	NA	NA	NA	NA	NA	NA
Dividends	0.01	0.01	0.01	0.01	0.02	0.02	Nil	Nil	Nil	Nil
Payout Ratio	1%	1%	1%	NM	NM	NM	Nil	Nil	Nil	Nil
Prices - High	29.72	31.25	32.50	28.31	60.00	58.18	44.12	34.25	22.50	15.12
- Low	19.39	20.20	22.51	13.00	14.00	34.43	28.62	17.25	10.00	10.37
P/E Ratio - High	25	23	41	NM	NM	NM	35	NM	41	25
- Low	16	15	28	NM	NM	NM	23	NM	18	17

Income Statement Analysis (Million $)

	2003	2002	2001	2000	1999	1998	1997	1996	1995	1994
Revs.	11,574	11,142	11,322	12,492	13,127	12,703	2,614	1,313	457	176
Oper. Inc.	2,841	2,870	3,034	3,216	2,154	4,010	983	448	141	51.7
Depr.	1,265	2,444	1,371	1,429	1,614	1,499	303	153	56.4	18.8
Int. Exp.	439	462	541	748	770	681	104	45.5	41.3	11.4
Pretax Inc.	1,129	1,240	792	344	-139	-676	463	78.1	18.9	21.6
Eff. Tax Rate	35.8%	34.2%	35.9%	NM	NM	NM	41.0%	57.8%	60.4%	35.9%
Net Inc.	719	823	503	-97.0	-395	-767	273	32.9	30.3	13.8
S&P Core Earnings	643	725	653	NA	NA	NA	NA	NA	NA	NA

Balance Sheet & Other Fin. Data (Million $)

	2003	2002	2001	2000	1999	1998	1997	1996	1995	1994
Cash	135	264	730	94.0	181	88.7	51.2	23.5	13.2	6.60
Curr. Assets	2,588	2,700	3,124	2,457	6,221	3,881	655	340	120	37.0
Total Assets	20,656	19,631	19,490	18,565	22,681	22,715	6,623	2,831	908	323
Curr. Liab.	3,332	3,173	3,721	2,937	7,489	4,294	569	320	105	28.4
LT Debt	7,997	8,062	7,709	8,372	8,399	11,114	2,724	1,158	335	154
Common Equity	5,563	5,308	5,392	4,801	4,403	4,372	2,629	1,155	403	108
Total Cap.	15,473	13,389	14,241	14,067	13,540	16,069	5,674	2,322	738	278
Cap. Exp.	1,200	1,287	1,328	1,313	1,327	1,651	436	348	84.6	40.9
Cash Flow	1,984	3,267	1,874	1,332	1,219	732	577	186	86.6	32.1
Curr. Ratio	0.8	0.9	0.9	0.8	0.8	0.9	1.2	1.1	1.1	1.3
% LT Debt of Cap.	51.7	60.2	54.1	59.5	62.0	69.2	48.0	49.9	45.4	55.4
% Net Inc.of Revs.	6.2	7.4	4.4	NM	NM	NM	10.5	2.5	6.7	7.8
% Ret. on Assets	3.5	4.2	2.6	NM	NM	NM	4.1	1.4	3.6	4.3
% Ret. on Equity	13.2	15.4	9.9	NM	NM	NM	10.4	3.2	10.7	13.3

Data as orig reptd.; bef. results of disc opers/spec. items. Per share data adj. for stk. divs. Bold denotes primary EPS - prior periods restated. E-Estimated. NA-Not Available. NM-Not Meaningful. NR-Not Ranked. UR-Under Review.

Office: 1001 Fannin Street, Houston, TX 77002.
Telephone: 713-512-6200.
Website: http://www.wm.com
Chrmn: A.M. Myers.
Pres & COO: L. O'Donnell III.
CEO: D.P. Steiner.

SVP & CFO: R.G. Simpson.
SVP & General Counsel: R.L. Wittenbraker.
Investor Contact: G. Nikkel 713-265-1358.
Dirs: P. S. Cafferty, F. M. Clark, Jr., R. S. Miller, A. M. Myers, J. C. Pope, W. R. Reum, S. G. Rothmeier, D. P. Steiner, C. Vogt.

Founded: in 1894.
Domicile: Delaware.
Employees: 51,700.
S&P Analyst: Stewart Scharf/PMW/BK

Waters Corp.

Recommendation: **BUY** ★★★★★   **12-Month Target Price: $56.00**
(as of June 24, 2004)

WAT has an approximate 0.05% weighting in the **S&P 500**

Sector: Health Care
Sub-Industry: Health Care Equipment
Peer Group: Life Science Research Products

Summary: This company manufactures high performance liquid chromatography, thermal analysis and mass spectrometry products.

Quantitative Evaluations

S&P Earnings & Dividend Rank: B

| D | C | B- | **B** | B+ | A- | A | A+ |

S&P Fair Value Rank: 4+

| 1 | 2 | 3 | **4** | 5 |
| Lowest | | | | Highest |

Fair Value Calc.: $46.00 (Fairly Valued)

S&P Investability Quotient Percentile

97%

WAT scored higher than 97% of all companies for which an S&P Report is available.

Volatility: Average

| Low | **Average** | High |

Technical Evaluation: Neutral
Since 11/04, the technical indicators for WAT have been Neutral.

Relative Strength Rank: Moderate

57

| 1 Lowest | | Highest 99 |

Price as of 11/12/04: $45.63   **2004E S&P Core EPS:** $1.63

GAAP Earnings vs. Previous Year
▲ Up ▼ Down ▶ No Change

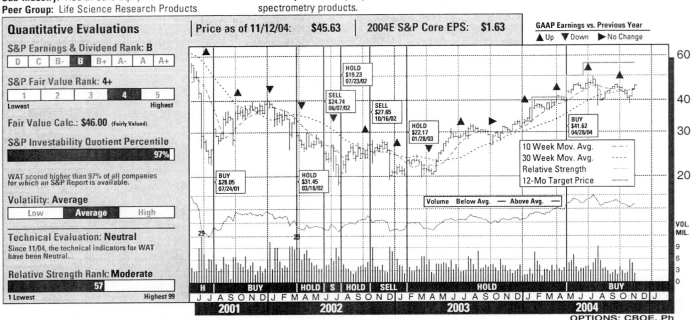

Analyst commentary prepared by Jeffrey Loo, CFA /CB/JWP

Highlights 15-NOV-04

- We see sales of $1.10 billion in 2004, increasing to $1.23 billion in 2005 on higher sales across all product lines. Shipments of WAT's new Acquity UPLC began in the third quarter, and we see sales doubling in the fourth quarter with continued strong sales into 2005. WAT will also begin shipping its new Q-Tof Premier Mass Spectrometry system and eLab notebook in the fourth quarter. We believe the new Q-Tof Premier will drive Mass Spectrometry sales and reverse the sluggish sales trend this unit has experienced over the past two years, primarily due to a patent litigation lawsuit that was finally settled in March 2004. The eLab notebook is part of its new informatics division, and we see sales in this unit reaching $50 million in 2005. We also see increased service contracts as its installed base grows, and we think sales at its Thermal Analysis unit should continue to post strong sales growth on high industrial demand.
- We expect foreign exchange to continue to aid results, but we believe these benefits will lessen in 2005. We see wider gross margins from new products, together with increasing sales in the new informatics segment, and expect operating margins to widen by 60 basis points through fixed cost leverage, partly offset by a transition of the sales force in Asia from a distributor network to direct sales.
- We see WAT's effective tax rate declining to 21% on increased manufacturing volume in Ireland. We estimate 2004 operating EPS of $1.79, and see 2005 EPS of $2.06. Our 2004 Standard & Poor's Core Earnings estimate is $1.63 a share.

Key Stock Statistics

S&P Oper. EPS 2004E	1.79	52-week Range	$49.80-29.86	
P/E on S&P Oper. EPS 2004E	25.5	12 Month P/E	26.7	
S&P Oper. EPS 2005E	2.06	Beta	0.84	
Yield (%)	Nil	Shareholders	286	
Dividend Rate/Share	Nil	Market Cap (B)	$ 5.4	
Shares Outstanding (M)	118.2			

Value of $10,000 invested five years ago: **$ 19,599**

Dividend Data

No cash dividends have been paid.

Investment Rationale/Risk 15-NOV-04

- We have a strong buy recommendation on the stock based on our view of continued strength in its pharmaceutical, biotechnology and industrial end markets. Geographically, we see continued strong demand in the U.S. and Asia along with improving conditions in Europe. We see its greatest growth potential in Asia, where we believe countries such as China, India and Korea will continue to build infrastructure in pharmaceutical and industrial markets. New products, such as the Acquity UPLC and the Q-Tof Premier MS system, should lead to improved growth and profitability, with sales accelerating in 2005. We see some adverse impact on HPLC sales, but we believe the higher priced Acquity UPLC, together with wider margin proprietary consumables, will drive sales and boost margins in 2005.
- Risks to our recommendation and target price include continued declining growth in government research budgets, continued sluggish sales of mass spectrometry systems, greater than expected cannibalization of HPLC sales due to the introduction of the Acquity UPLC, and a general slowdown of equipment sales.
- We believe the shares deserve a premium valuation over peers due to our view of WAT's stronger growth profile. Based on a blend of our DCF model, which assumes a weighted average cost of capital of 9.3%, and a terminal growth rate of 4%, and P/E to growth ratio analysis using a PEG ratio of 1.5X, our 12-month target price is $56.

Revenues/Earnings Data Fiscal year ending December 31

Revenues (Million $)

	2004	2003	2002	2001	2000	1999
1Q	255.1	221.0	200.3	201.0	180.2	160.4
2Q	260.5	231.8	217.2	206.8	197.4	172.3
3Q	264.8	230.4	216.1	202.7	191.9	171.1
4Q	—	275.1	256.4	248.7	225.5	200.7
Yr.	—	958.2	890.0	859.2	795.1	704.4

Earnings Per Share ($)

	2004	2003	2002	2001	2000	1999
1Q	0.33	0.26	0.27	0.28	0.23	0.17
2Q	0.49	0.33	0.28	0.29	0.28	0.21
3Q	0.42	0.29	0.29	0.28	0.27	0.21
4Q	E0.60	0.47	0.30	-0.01	0.37	0.32
Yr.	E1.79	1.34	1.12	0.84	1.14	0.92

Next earnings report expected: late-January Source: S&P, Company Reports
EPS Estimates based on S&P Operating Earnings; historical GAAP earnings are as reported.

Waters Corporation

Recommendation: **BUY** ★ ★ ★ ★ ★   12-Month Target Price: **$56.00** (as of June 24, 2004)

Business Summary 15-NOV-04

Waters Corp. operates in the analytical instrument industry, with manufacturing and distribution expertise in three complementary technologies: HPLC (high performance liquid chromatography) instruments, columns and other consumables, and related service; thermal analysis (TA) and rheology instruments; and mass spectrometry (MS) instruments that can be integrated with other analytical instruments.

The Waters division is the world's largest maker of HPLC instruments, chromatography columns, and related consumables. It has the largest market share in the U.S., Europe, and non-Japan Asia, and a leading position in Japan. HPLC is the largest product segment of the analytical instrument market. Instruments are used in many industries to detect, identify, monitor and measure chemical, physical and biological composition of materials, and to purify a range of compounds.

HPLC is the standard technique to identify and analyze constituent components of various chemicals and materials. Its unique performance capabilities let it separate and identify 80% of known chemicals and materials. HPLC is used to analyze substances in a variety of industries for R&D, quality control, and process engineering applications. Pharmaceutical and life science industries use HPLC primarily to identify new drugs.

The Micromass division is a leader in the manufacture and support of organic, inorganic, stable isotope, and ICP mass spectrometers typically coupled with HPLC, chemical electrophoresis, chemical electrophoresis chromatography, gas chromatography or elemental analysis systems. MS is an analytical technique used to identify unknown compounds, quantify known materials, and elucidate the structural and chemical properties of molecules by measuring the masses of individual molecules that have been converted into ions. These products serve diverse markets, including pharmaceutical and environmental industries.

The TA Instruments division makes and services thermal analysis and rheology instruments used for the physical characterization of polymers and related materials. Thermal analysis measures physical characteristics of materials as a function of temperature. Changes in temperature affect several characteristics of materials, such as their physical state, weight, dimension and mechanical and electrical properties, which may be measured using thermal analysis techniques. As a result, thermal analysis is widely used to develop, produce and characterize materials in industries such as plastics, chemicals and pharmaceuticals.

In January 2003, WAT acquired the rheology instruments and services business of Rheometric Scientific, Inc., for $17 million in cash, and the assumption of $6 million of liabilities. It integrated the business with its TA Instruments unit. In July 2003, the company purchased privately held Creon Lab Control, which provides scientific data management solutions that allow researchers to analyze and share data and collaborate electronically. In March 2004, WAT acquired privately held NuGenesis Technologies Corp. for about $43 million. NuGenesis and Creon Lab formed the company's new lab informatics market segment.

Company Financials Fiscal Year ending December 31

Per Share Data ($)

(Year Ended December 31)	2003	2002	2001	2000	1999	1998	1997	1996	1995	1994
Tangible Bk. Val.	2.67	NM	3.19	2.21	0.98	NM	NM	NM	NA	-0.25
Cash Flow	1.60	1.40	1.08	1.36	1.14	0.78	0.09	0.28	0.22	0.21
Earnings	1.34	1.12	0.84	1.14	0.92	0.57	-0.08	0.15	0.14	0.12
S&P Core Earnings	1.18	0.99	1.07	NA	NA	NA	NA	NA	NA	NA
Dividends	Nil	Nil	Nil	Nil	Nil	Nil	Nil	Nil	Nil	NA
Payout Ratio	Nil	Nil	Nil	Nil	Nil	Nil	Nil	Nil	Nil	NA
Prices - High	33.42	39.25	85.37	90.93	33.84	21.87	12.10	8.40	4.56	NA
- Low	19.79	17.86	22.33	21.96	18.12	9.12	5.78	4.18	3.31	NA
P/E Ratio - High	25	35	NM	80	37	39	NM	56	18	NA
- Low	15	16	NM	19	20	16	NM	28	13	NA

Income Statement Analysis (Million $)

	2003	2002	2001	2000	1999	1998	1997	1996	1995	1994
Revs.	958	890	859	795	704	619	465	391	333	307
Oper. Inc.	271	251	258	240	205	164	113	87.9	58.6	48.7
Depr.	33.8	37.2	34.0	29.4	28.9	27.2	20.0	16.7	7.71	11.3
Int. Exp.	2.37	2.48	1.26	Nil	8.95	18.3	13.7	14.7	30.3	19.9
Pretax Inc.	224	195	147	211	168	102	7.47	31.1	17.2	18.4
Eff. Tax Rate	23.6%	22.1%	22.3%	26.0%	27.0%	26.7%	211.0%	36.1%	18.1%	18.0%
Net Inc.	171	152	115	156	122	74.4	-8.29	19.9	14.1	15.1
S&P Core Earnings	150	134	147	NA	NA	NA	NA	NA	NA	NA

Balance Sheet & Other Fin. Data (Million $)

	2003	2002	2001	2000	1999	1998	1997	1996	1995	1994
Cash	357	313	227	75.5	3.80	5.50	3.11	0.60	3.20	22.8
Curr. Assets	715	636	523	344	247	252	213	144	127	149
Total Assets	1,131	1,011	887	692	584	578	552	366	300	321
Curr. Liab.	379	320	281	221	198	186	171	83.0	70.9	69.8
LT Debt	125	Nil	Nil	Nil	81.1	218	305	210	159	186
Common Equity	590	665	582	452	292	150	62.3	57.8	58.1	53.6
Total Cap.	715	665	582	452	373	377	376	275	223	246
Cap. Exp.	34.6	37.9	42.4	35.4	19.4	15.0	18.2	10.1	6.26	NA
Cash Flow	205	189	148	186	151	101	10.8	35.6	21.8	25.5
Curr. Ratio	1.9	2.0	1.9	1.6	1.3	1.4	1.2	1.7	1.9	2.1
% LT Debt of Cap.	17.5	Nil	Nil	Nil	21.7	57.8	81.1	76.4	71.1	75.7
% Net Inc.of Revs.	17.8	17.1	13.3	19.6	17.4	12.0	NM	5.1	4.2	4.9
% Ret. on Assets	15.9	16.0	14.5	24.4	21.1	13.2	NM	6.0	4.5	NA
% Ret. on Equity	27.2	24.3	22.2	42.0	55.3	69.1	NM	32.7	79.6	NA

Data as orig reptd.; bef. results of disc opers/spec. items. Per share data adj. for stk. divs.; EPS diluted. E-Estimated. NA-Not Available. NM-Not Meaningful. NR-Not Ranked. UR-Under Review.

Office: 34 Maple Street, Milford, MA 01757-3696.
Telephone: 508-478-2000.
Email: info@waters.com
Website: http://www.waters.com
Chrmn & CEO: D. A. Berthiaume.
EVP: J. R. Nelson.

EVP: A. G. Caputo.
SVP: B. K. Mazar.
Investor Contact: Gene Cassis (508-482-2349).
Dirs: J. Bekenstein, M. J. Berendt, D. A. Berthiaume, P. Caldwell, E. Conard, L. H. Glimcher, W. J. Miller, T. P. Salice.

Founded: in 1991.
Domicile: Delaware.
Employees: 3,900.
S&P Analyst: Jeffrey Loo, CFA /CB/JWP

Watson Pharmaceuticals

Recommendation: **HOLD** ★★★☆☆
SELL | SELL | HOLD | BUY | BUY

12-Month Target Price: **$31.00**
(as of June 29, 2004)

WPI has an approximate 0.03% weighting in the **S&P 500**

Sector: Health Care
Sub-Industry: Pharmaceuticals
Peer Group: Generic Drugs

Summary: WPI manufactures and markets proprietary and off-patent pharmaceutical products.

Quantitative Evaluations

S&P Earnings & Dividend Rank: B+

| D | C | B- | B | B+ | A- | A | A+ |

S&P Fair Value Rank: 5

| 1 | 2 | 3 | 4 | 5 |
| Lowest | | | | Highest |

Fair Value Calc.: $34.40 *(Undervalued)*

S&P Investability Quotient Percentile
82%

WPI scored higher than 82% of all companies
for which an S&P Report is available.

Volatility: Average

| Low | Average | High |

Technical Evaluation: Bullish
Since 11/04, the technical indicators for WPI
have been Bullish.

Relative Strength Rank: Moderate
38
1 Lowest — Highest 99

Price as of 11/15/04: $28.60 **2004E S&P Core EPS: $1.75**

GAAP Earnings vs. Previous Year
▲ Up ▼ Down ▶ No Change

- 10 Week Mov. Avg.
- 30 Week Mov. Avg.
- Relative Strength
- 12-Mo Target Price

Volume Below Avg. — Above Avg. —

HOLD $45.20 12/12/03
BUY $42.32 11/05/03

VOL. MIL.

J J A S O N D J F M A M J J A S O N D J F M A M J J A S O N D J F M A M J J A S O N D J
2001   2002   2003   2004

OPTIONS: ASE, CBOE, Ph

Analyst commentary prepared by Phillip M. Seligman/PMW/JWP

Highlights 17-NOV-04

- We forecast that 2005 revenues will be flat to up modestly from our 2004 estimate of $1.6 billion, much slower than growth of nearly 10% that we projected earlier. In our view, WPI should benefit from 17 generic products it planned to launch in 2004, and from its expected 2005 launches of eight to 10 generic products. However, our 2005 revenue estimate also assumes that the favorable impact of these sales will be tempered by a continued decline in sales of oral contraceptives (OCs), competitive pricing pressures on other generic drugs, a delay in the launch of Emsam antidepressant, and only a modest pickup in the sales of Oxytrol transdermal patch for urinary incontinence.

- We expect gross margins to widen slightly, mainly on more favorable branded and generic product mixes, partly offset by potential market share losses in OCs and competitive pricing pressures. We expect the SG&A cost ratio to decline, as WPI benefits from a recent streamlining of operations and the elimination of the contract sales force for Oxytrol. However, we believe R&D spending will increase modestly as a percentage of revenues, to support new product development.

- We look for 2005 EPS of $2.20, following our 2004 operating EPS estimate of $1.85. After projected stock option expense, we see 2004 S&P Core EPS of $1.75, followed by $1.98 for 2005.

Key Stock Statistics

S&P Core EPS 2005E	1.98	52-week Range	$50.12-24.50
S&P Oper. EPS 2004E	1.85	12 Month P/E	21.2
P/E on S&P Oper. EPS 2004E	15.6	Beta	0.31
S&P Oper. EPS 2005E	2.20	Shareholders	3,602
Yield (%)	Nil	Market Cap (B)	$ 3.1
Dividend Rate/Share	Nil	Shares Outstanding (M)	109.5

Value of $10,000 invested five years ago: **$ 7,601**

Dividend Data

No cash dividends have been paid.

Investment Rationale/Risk 17-NOV-04

- We are encouraged by WPI's focus on R&D. As of late October, it had more than 100 products in development, representing $60 billion in brand sales. This included 32 ANDAs on file with the FDA as of late October, 17 that it planned to file by the end of 2004, and at least 20 filings expected annually in coming years. However, we are concerned that plans to launch eight to 10 generics in 2005 will limit revenue growth into 2006. We are encouraged by WPI's plan to restructure its brand business and to install separate presidents for the brand and generics businesses. However, we think the departure of president and COO J. Papa and the likelihood of the new positions being unfilled until mid-2005 may impede the restructuring and normal operations, and put the company at a competitive disadvantage.

- Risks to our recommendation and target price include increased competition, business disruption during management's business strategy change and cost reduction initiative, and the loss of patent protection for Ferrlecit, an intravenous iron product.

- We think revenue growth will decelerate until 2005, after which we expect the number of new product launches per year to increase and the restructuring and management realignment to have been completed. Our 12-month target price of $31 is based on applying a forward P/E multiple of about 14X, a discount to peer levels, to our 2005 EPS estimate.

Revenues/Earnings Data Fiscal year ending December 31

Revenues (Million $)

	2004	2003	2002	2001	2000	1999
1Q	409.7	336.9	285.7	296.9	172.2	159.2
2Q	399.4	355.9	300.1	299.0	200.2	170.2
3Q	408.0	358.8	307.9	270.9	179.3	171.2
4Q	—	406.2	329.6	293.9	254.8	188.5
Yr.	—	1,458	1,223	1,161	811.5	689.2

Earnings Per Share ($)

	2004	2003	2002	2001	2000	1999
1Q	0.42	0.44	0.30	0.58	1.48	0.23
2Q	0.32	0.47	0.56	0.61	0.96	0.47
3Q	0.13	0.47	0.38	-0.55	-0.55	0.38
4Q	E0.49	0.48	0.40	0.43	-0.02	0.75
Yr.	E1.85	1.86	1.64	1.07	1.65	1.83

Next earnings report expected: early-February Source: S&P, Company Reports
EPS Estimates based on S&P Operating Earnings; historical GAAP earnings are as reported.

Watson Pharmaceuticals, Inc.

Recommendation: **HOLD** ★ ★ ★ ☆ ☆   12-Month Target Price: **$31.00** (as of June 29, 2004)

Business Summary 17-NOV-04

Watson Pharmaceuticals manufactures and sells branded and off-patent (generic) pharmaceuticals, and develops advanced drug delivery systems designed primarily to enhance the therapeutic benefits of pharmaceutical compounds. WPI targets difficult to produce niche off-patent pharmaceuticals, in an effort to minimize competition with traditional commodity-oriented generic drug companies. To reduce its dependence on the volatile generic market, the company is building up its branded drug business. WPI currently markets more than 30 branded pharmaceuticals, and more than 120 generic drug products.

Total revenues in 2003 were divided as follows: generic drugs 47%; and branded drugs 53%, divided into three groups: women's health products, general products and urology, and nephrology.

Key branded women's health brands are Levora, Trivora and Nor-QD oral contraceptives, and Alora estrogen replacement. WPI is currently the second largest producer of oral contraceptives, offering 17 products. This business has been strengthened by a supply agreement with Johnson & Johnson under which WPI sells branded generic versions of several popular J&J oral contraceptives.

The company also sells branded dermatologicals such as Monodox and Cleocin-T acne treatments, and Cordran and Cormax topical corticosteroids; and nephrology products that include INFeD and Ferrlecit iron replacements. Other important branded lines are Dilacor XR and Microzide antihypertensives, Norco and Maxidone analgesics, and Unithroid for hypothyroidism. In early 2003, the FDA ap-

proved WPI's new Oxytrol oxybutynin transdermal patch to treat urinary incontinence.

Currently marketed generic products include tranquilizers, anti-hypertensives, diuretics, anti-ulcers, anti-psychotics, anti-inflammatories, analgesics, hormone replacements, anti-spasmodics and anti-diarrheals. Many of the pharmaceuticals incorporate WPI's novel proprietary drug delivery systems, such as transmucosal, vaginal and transdermal systems that allow for defined rates of drug release.

The company sells its products primarily through distributors and chain drug stores, such as AmeriSourceBergen (17% of total sales in 2003), McKesson HBOC (15%), Cardinal Health (12%), and Walgreen (11%). Much of WPI's growth has stemmed from acquisitions and investments in pharmaceutical joint ventures. In July 2000, the company acquired Schein Pharmaceuticals, the maker of 100 generic and branded products, including Ferrlecit intravenous therapy for iron deficiency in hemodialysis patients. WPI also has a 50% interest in Somerset Pharmaceuticals, which makes the Eldepryl treatment for Parkinson's disease.

R&D spending totaled $102.1 million in 2003, equal to 7.0% of net revenues. The company has a number of abbreviated new drug applications (ANDAs) for off-patent products pending before the FDA, and several ethical drugs are under development. Principal new products under development include oral fentanyl for pain management and Ferrlecit for cancer.

Company Financials Fiscal Year ending December 31

Per Share Data ($)

(Year Ended December 31)	2003	2002	2001	2000	1999	1998	1997	1996	1995	1994
Tangible Bk. Val.	5.54	4.33	3.79	0.98	5.00	3.08	3.14	5.20	3.98	3.25
Cash Flow	2.78	2.45	2.01	2.34	2.28	1.66	1.17	1.06	0.72	0.61
Earnings	1.86	1.64	1.07	1.65	1.83	1.32	1.01	0.98	0.65	0.53
S&P Core Earnings	1.64	1.36	0.52	NA	NA	NA	NA	NA	NA	NA
Dividends	Nil	Nil	Nil	Nil	Nil	Nil	Nil	Nil	Nil	Nil
Payout Ratio	Nil	Nil	Nil	Nil	Nil	Nil	Nil	Nil	Nil	Nil
Prices - High	50.12	33.25	66.39	71.50	62.93	63.00	34.12	24.75	25.25	14.75
- Low	26.90	17.95	26.50	33.68	26.50	30.50	16.00	13.00	10.00	6.37
P/E Ratio - High	27	20	62	43	34	48	34	25	39	28
- Low	14	11	25	20	14	23	16	13	16	12

Income Statement Analysis (Million $)

	2003	2002	2001	2000	1999	1998	1997	1996	1995	1994
Revs.	1,458	1,223	1,161	812	689	556	338	194	153	87.1
Oper. Inc.	439	386	404	227	281	237	152	89.0	57.6	31.9
Depr.	100	86.6	101	71.4	44.0	31.3	14.6	6.25	5.24	3.01
Int. Exp.	25.8	22.1	27.8	24.3	11.1	7.06	NA	Nil	Nil	0.52
Pretax Inc.	318	279	199	355	273	199	145	109	72.8	30.0
Eff. Tax Rate	36.2%	37.0%	41.5%	52.0%	34.4%	39.3%	37.6%	32.8%	34.1%	37.7%
Net Inc.	203	176	116	171	179	121	90.2	73.3	47.9	18.7
S&P Core Earnings	178	146	56.3	NA	NA	NA	NA	NA	NA	NA

Balance Sheet & Other Fin. Data (Million $)

	2003	2002	2001	2000	1999	1998	1997	1996	1995	1994
Cash	574	273	329	238	116	72.7	82.8	211	122	56.5
Curr. Assets	1,323	921	890	831	435	293	247	280	198	87.1
Total Assets	3,283	2,663	2,528	2,580	1,439	1,070	755	420	322	130
Curr. Liab.	339	375	245	280	129	94.8	100	21.4	29.0	12.0
LT Debt	723	332	416	438	150	150	2.39	2.90	3.57	5.06
Common Equity	2,057	1,798	1,672	1,548	1,055	750	565	383	289	111
Total Cap.	2,924	2,282	2,274	2,242	1,292	955	604	398	293	118
Cap. Exp.	151	87.5	62.0	34.3	26.8	26.5	14.6	10.2	22.5	20.0
Cash Flow	303	262	218	242	223	152	105	79.5	53.1	21.7
Curr. Ratio	3.9	2.5	3.6	3.0	3.4	3.1	2.5	13.1	6.8	7.2
% LT Debt of Cap.	24.7	14.5	18.3	19.6	11.6	15.7	0.4	0.1	1.2	4.3
% Net Inc.of Revs.	13.9	14.4	10.0	21.0	26.0	21.7	26.7	37.8	31.3	21.5
% Ret. on Assets	6.8	6.8	4.6	8.4	13.9	13.2	15.4	19.8	16.4	15.9
% Ret. on Equity	10.5	10.1	7.2	13.1	19.3	18.4	19.0	21.8	18.7	18.5

Data as orig reptd.; bef. results of disc opers/spec. items. Per share data adj. for stk. divs.; EPS diluted. E-Estimated. NA-Not Available. NM-Not Meaningful. NR-Not Ranked. UR-Under Review.

Office: 311 Bonnie Circle, Corona, CA 92880-2882.
Telephone: 909-493-5300.
Website: http://www.watsonpharm.com
Chrmn & CEO: A. Y. Chao.
Pres & COO: J. Papa.

EVP & CFO: C. P. Slacik.
EVP: J. Nash.
Investor Contact: Patricia Eisenhaur (909-493-5600).
Dirs: A. Y. Chao, M. J. Fedida, M. J. Feldman, A. F. Hummel, C. M. Klema, J. Michelson, R. R. Taylor, A. L. Turner, F. G. Weiss.

Founded: in 1983.
Domicile: Nevada.
Employees: 3,983.
S&P Analyst: Phillip M. Seligman/PMW/JWP

WellPoint Health Networks

Recommendation: HOLD ★★★☆☆
SELL SELL HOLD BUY BUY

12-Month Target Price: $127.00
(as of November 09, 2004)

WLP has an approximate 0.17% weighting in the **S&P 500**

Sector: Health Care
Sub-Industry: Managed Health Care
Peer Group: Managed Care - Large

Summary: This managed care company, which serves 16 million medical and 47 million specialty members, has agreed to be acquired by Anthem, Inc.

Quantitative Evaluations

S&P Earnings & Dividend Rank: B+

| D | C | B- | B | B+ | A- | A | A+ |

S&P Fair Value Rank: 3-

| 1 | 2 | 3 | 4 | 5 |
| Lowest | | | | Highest |

Fair Value Calc.: $104.10 (Slightly Overvalued)

S&P Investability Quotient Percentile
98%

WLP scored higher than 98% of all companies for which an S&P Report is available.

Volatility: Average

| Low | Average | High |

Technical Evaluation: Neutral

Since 11/04, the technical indicators for WLP have been Neutral.

Relative Strength Rank: Strong

88
1 Lowest   Highest 99

| Price as of 11/12/04: | $117.64 | 2004E S&P Core EPS: | $6.96 |

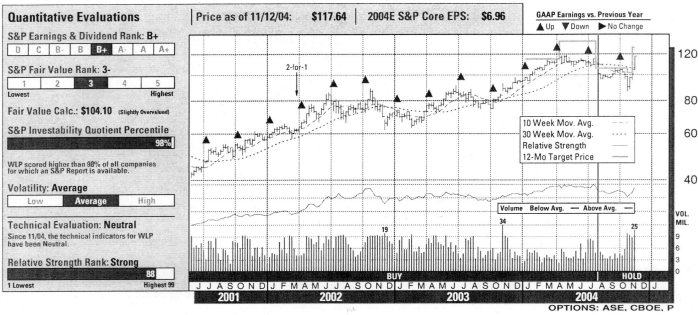

GAAP Earnings vs. Previous Year
▲ Up ▼ Down ► No Change

2-for-1

- - - 10 Week Mov. Avg.
..... 30 Week Mov. Avg.
—— Relative Strength
—— 12-Mo Target Price

Volume Below Avg. — Above Avg.

VOL. MIL.

BUY   HOLD

J J A S O N D | J F M A M J J A S O N D | J F M A M J J A S O N D | J F M A M J J A S O N D | J
2001   2002   2003   2004

OPTIONS: ASE, CBOE, P

Analyst commentary prepared by Phillip M. Seligman/PMW/JWP

Highlights November 02, 2004

▪ The company has agreed to be acquired by its slightly smaller Blues peer Anthem, Inc. (ATH: hold, $82), in a transaction that was originally expected to close in mid-2004, subject to necessary approvals. Until the closing, which we think will likely be delayed, we will continue to follow WLP in its current configuration. For 2005, we look for operating revenues to advance about 11%, to about $26.0 billion, from our 2004 estimate of $23.4 billion, with organic enrollment up at least 4%. The company notes that membership growth in its key geographic areas (California, Georgia and Texas) has been strong, and we see this trend sustainable through 2005.

▪ We expect the commercial medical loss ratio (MLR) to be flat, plus or minus up to 50 basis points, with our projected 2004 level. We see improving medical management practices and the pricing of products above medial cost increases sustaining this trend. We see the SG&A cost ratio continuing to decline, on increased penetration of IT utilization and the spreading of fixed SG&A costs over an expanding membership base.

▪ We project 2005 EPS of $8.50, excluding investment gains, versus our 2004 EPS estimate of $7.65. Our S&P EPS projections for 2004 and 2005, reflecting estimated stock option expense and modest pension adjustments, are 9.2% and 9.0% below our respective operating EPS estimates.

Key Stock Statistics

S&P Core EPS 2005E	7.73	52-week Range	$119.06-86.50
S&P Oper. EPS 2004E	7.65	12 Month P/E	15.8
P/E on S&P Oper. EPS 2004E	15.4	Beta	0.07
S&P Oper. EPS 2005E	8.50	Shareholders	1,251
Yield (%)	Nil	Market Cap (B)	$ 18.4
Dividend Rate/Share	Nil	Shares Outstanding (M)	156.4

Value of $10,000 invested five years ago: **$ 33,458**

Dividend Data

No cash dividends have been paid since 1996.

Investment Rationale/Risk November 02, 2004

▪ The company's premium yields have been above medical cost trends, but we see the spread contracting over time, on industrywide pricing pressures. We view WLP's performance as healthy, and, with good management execution, see it as sustainable. However, we think customers may see excess profits and increasingly balk at steep rate hikes. Meanwhile, we see risk in the California Insurance Commissioner's opposition to the proposed ATH merger, citing corporate governance issues. Three other states recently began to reconsider their approvals, but for other reasons. We expect the deal, if it occurs, to be postponed and restructured.

▪ Risks to our opinion and target price include increased competition, higher than expected medical costs, lower than expected premium yields, a weakened job market, and the possibility that the planned acquisition fails to occur. Risks also include an expansion of the insurance industry probe by New York State Attorney General Eliot Spitzer and other state attorneys general to the health insurance industry.

▪ In light of uncertainty surrounding insurance company probes and the planned ATH merger, we see greater volatility and a likelihood of valuation compression. Based on applying a forward P/E multiple of 12X, a modest premium to the level of the managed care industry, to our 2005 EPS estimate, our 12-month target price is $102.

Revenues/Earnings Data Fiscal year ending December 31

Revenues (Million $)

	2004	2003	2002	2001	2000	1999
1Q	5,646	4,841	3,943	2,615	2,145	1,771
2Q	5,780	4,940	4,299	3,145	2,289	1,857
3Q	5,848	5,049	4,515	3,245	2,353	1,892
4Q	—	5,530	4,581	3,422	2,442	1,966
Yr.	—	20,360	17,339	12,429	9,229	7,485

Earnings Per Share ($)

	2004	2003	2002	2001	2000	1999
1Q	1.85	1.29	0.97	0.74	0.61	0.52
2Q	1.86	1.49	1.10	0.76	0.65	0.52
3Q	1.97	1.63	1.38	0.82	0.69	0.56
4Q	E1.96	1.73	1.18	0.83	0.69	0.60
Yr.	E7.65	6.16	4.64	3.15	2.64	2.19

Next earnings report expected: late-January Source: S&P, Company Reports
EPS Estimates based on S&P Operating Earnings; historical GAAP earnings are as reported.

WellPoint Health Networks Inc.

Recommendation: **HOLD** ★ ★ ★ ☆ ☆   12-Month Target Price: **$127.00** (as of November 09, 2004)

Business Summary November 02, 2004

On October 26, 2003, the company agreed to be acquired by its slightly smaller Blues peer, Anthem, Inc., with the transaction expected to close in mid-2004, subject to necessary approvals.

WellPoint Health Networks, the former not-for-profit California Blue Cross health plan, has become one of the largest investor-owned U.S. managed care companies. Principal products are health maintenance organization (HMO), preferred provider organization (PPO), and Point-of-Service (POS) health plans. WLP also offers a range of specialty health care products, marketed as separate plans or incorporated into broader medical plans. At December 31, 2003, it had total medical membership of 15.0 million, versus 13.8 million a year earlier. By geographic markets, members were located in California (44.8%), Georgia (14.5%), Missouri (9.4%), Illinois (4.8%), Wisconsin (3.9%), Texas (3.3%), other states (12.6%), BlueCard Host Members (6.7%). Specialty services were provided to 44.7 million individuals.

HMO plans are marketed primarily in California under the Blue Cross banner, and outside California principally under the UNICARE name. WLP provides healthcare services through a network of about 31,000 primary care and specialist physicians, and about 427 hospitals in California. Outside of California, it provides services through a network of 92,700 primary care and specialist physicians, and 870 hospitals.

About 60% of California members are in WLP's PPO plan. WLP's PPO provider network includes about 48,000 physicians and 440 hospitals. PPO plans are similar to HMO plans, in that they provide for health care delivery at lower costs than

traditional health insurance, but members have an option to receive care from providers who are not part of the network, typically at substantial out-of-pocket costs.

Through its specialty care networks, WLP provides pharmacy (31.2 million members at December 31, 2003), dental (3.3 million), as well as life insurance (3.1 million) and products to individuals covered through disability insurance (603,409) and behavioral health (7.4 million).

The company also offers Medicare supplemental plans, which typically pay the difference between healthcare cost incurred and the amount paid by Medicare, while using the PPO and HMO provider networks.

In January 2002, WLP acquired RightCHOICE Managed Care Inc., serving 3.0 million medical members in the Midwest (primarily Missouri), for $1.3 billion (30% cash, 70% stock).

In April 2003, the company said it would drop its plans to acquire CareFirst BlueCross BlueShield, serving 3.1 million medical members primarily in Maryland, Delaware, and the District of Columbia, following the Maryland Insurance Commissioner's decision to disapprove CareFirst's conversion to for-profit status.

In September 2003, WLP acquired Cobalt Corp., a Blue Cross Blue Shield licensee, serving 675,000 medical members in Wisconsin, for $885 million (48% in cash and 52% in stock).

Company Financials Fiscal Year ending December 31

Per Share Data ($)

(Year Ended December 31)	2003	2002	2001	2000	1999	1998	1997	1996	1995	1994
Tangible Bk. Val.	14.13	10.52	8.14	8.45	7.14	6.60	3.76	2.39	7.77	6.42
Cash Flow	7.26	5.53	3.96	3.21	2.88	2.67	2.04	1.81	1.01	1.15
Earnings	6.16	4.64	3.15	2.64	2.19	2.27	1.64	1.52	0.91	1.07
S&P Core Earnings	5.81	4.17	2.87	NA	NA	NA	NA	NA	NA	NA
Dividends	Nil	Nil	Nil	Nil	Nil	Nil	Nil	5.00	Nil	Nil
Payout Ratio	Nil	Nil	Nil	Nil	Nil	Nil	Nil	NM	Nil	Nil
Prices - High	98.10	89.20	61.45	60.75	48.50	43.93	30.56	19.56	18.50	18.50
- Low	63.13	57.57	40.82	28.46	24.12	21.03	16.25	11.68	13.50	12.12
P/E Ratio - High	16	19	20	23	22	19	19	13	20	17
- Low	10	12	13	11	11	9	10	8	15	11

Income Statement Analysis (Million $)

	2003	2002	2001	2000	1999	1998	1997	1996	1995	1994
Revs.	20,360	17,339	12,429	9,229	7,485	6,478	5,826	4,170	3,107	2,792
Oper. Inc.	1,820	1,394	933	710	617	501	525	434	395	375
Depr.	174	115	110	75.4	68.8	55.0	57.1	37.7	22.0	15.2
Int. Exp.	50.6	60.4	49.9	24.0	20.2	26.9	36.7	36.6	Nil	Nil
Pretax Inc.	1,559	1,163	699	564	487	392	382	340	303	352
Eff. Tax Rate	40.0%	40.0%	40.6%	39.3%	39.0%	18.5%	40.5%	40.5%	40.6%	39.4%
Net Inc.	935	698	415	342	297	320	227	202	180	213
S&P Core Earnings	883	627	379	NA	NA	NA	NA	NA	NA	NA

Balance Sheet & Other Fin. Data (Million $)

	2003	2002	2001	2000	1999	1998	1997	1996	1995	1994
Cash	1,427	1,356	1,028	567	505	411	284	313	1,070	371
Curr. Assets	1,641	8,213	5,873	4,500	3,816	3,434	3,506	2,538	2,463	586
Total Assets	14,789	11,303	7,472	5,505	4,593	4,226	4,533	3,406	2,679	2,386
Curr. Liab.	7,081	5,752	4,066	3,073	2,527	2,183	2,344	1,545	840	875
LT Debt	1,238	1,012	838	401	348	300	388	625	Nil	Nil
Common Equity	6,115	4,512	2,673	2,220	1,885	1,315	1,223	870	1,670	1,419
Total Cap.	7,724	5,542	3,511	2,621	2,233	1,615	1,611	1,495	1,670	1,419
Cap. Exp.	153	102	92.9	46.9	39.0	78.0	58.4	43.3	25.2	22.1
Cash Flow	1,109	813	525	418	366	375	284	240	202	228
Curr. Ratio	0.2	1.4	1.4	1.5	1.5	1.6	1.5	1.6	2.9	0.7
% LT Debt of Cap.	16.0	18.3	23.9	15.3	15.6	18.6	24.1	41.8	Nil	Nil
% Net Inc.of Revs.	4.6	4.0	3.3	3.7	4.0	4.9	3.9	4.9	5.8	7.6
% Ret. on Assets	7.1	7.4	6.4	6.8	6.7	7.3	5.7	6.7	7.0	9.9
% Ret. on Equity	17.6	19.4	17.0	16.7	15.5	25.2	21.7	15.9	11.6	16.1

Data as orig reptd.; bef. results of disc opers/spec. items. Per share data adj. for stk. divs. Bold denotes primary EPS - prior periods restated. E-Estimated. NA-Not Available. NM-Not Meaningful. NR-Not Ranked. UR-Under Review.

Office: One Wellpoint Way, Thousand Oaks, CA 91362.
Telephone: 805-557-6655.
Website: http://www.wellpoint.com
Chrmn & CEO: L.D. Schaeffer.
EVP & CFO: D.A. Colby.

EVP, Secy & General Counsel: T.C. Geiser.
VP & Investor Contact: J. Cygul 805-557-6789.
Dirs: R. E. Birk, S. P. Burke, W. H. Bush, J. A. Hill, W. Y. Jobe, R. G. Peru, J. G. Pisano, E. A. Sanders, L. D. Schaeffer.

Founded: in 1992.
Domicile: Delaware.
Employees: 19,100.
S&P Analyst: Phillip M. Seligman/PMW/JWP

Wells Fargo

Recommendation: **HOLD** ★★★☆☆
SELL | SELL | HOLD | BUY | BUY

12-Month Target Price: **$65.00**
(as of September 30, 2004)

WFC has an approximate 0.96% weighting in the **S&P 500**

Sector: Financials
Sub-Industry: Diversified Banks
Peer Group: Midwest/West Major Regionals

Summary: This San Francisco-based bank holding company provides banking, insurance, investment, mortgage and consumer finance services throughout North America.

Quantitative Evaluations

S&P Earnings & Dividend Rank: A

D	C	B-	B	B+	A-	A	A+

S&P Fair Value Rank: 3

1	2	3	4	5
Lowest		3		Highest

Fair Value Calc.: $60.30 (Slightly Overvalued)

S&P Investability Quotient Percentile

97%

WFC scored higher than 97% of all companies for which an S&P Report is available.

Volatility: Low

Low	Average	High

Technical Evaluation: Bullish
Since 11/04, the technical indicators for WFC have been Bullish.

Relative Strength Rank: Moderate

54

1 Lowest | Highest 99

Price as of 11/12/04:	**$62.57**	2004E S&P Core EPS:	**$3.91**

GAAP Earnings vs. Previous Year
▲ Up ▼ Down ▶ No Change

- 10 Week Mov. Avg.
- 30 Week Mov. Avg.
- Relative Strength
- 12-Mo Target Price

Volume Below Avg. — Above Avg.

VOL. MIL.

J J A S O N D | J F M A M J J A S O N D | J F M A M J J A S O N D | J F M A M J J A S O N D | J
2001 | **2002** | **2003** | **2004**

HOLD

OPTIONS: ASE, CBOE, P, Ph

Analyst commentary prepared by Evan M. Momios, CFA /MF/BK

Highlights October 04, 2004

- We think that WFC's strong sales culture, diverse product mix, high credit quality standards, and exposure to attractive growth regions support its ability to achieve above-average revenue and earnings growth consistency for the longer term. However, we expect 2004 revenue growth below historical levels and below what we view as WFC's potential.

- We estimate 2004 total loan growth of 8%, after 18% growth in 2003, on significantly lower residential mortgage originations, partly offset by stronger commercial loans. We believe WFC's large mortgage servicing portfolio should offset some of the expected decline in mortgage origination fees and loan sale gains. We see the net interest margin widening to 4.90% by the fourth quarter, from 4.83% in the second quarter.

- We project EPS of $4.17 for 2004 and $4.55 for 2005. We forecast Standard & Poor's Core Earnings of $3.91 a share for 2004 and $4.30 for 2005, mainly due to estimated stock option expense.

Investment Rationale/Risk October 04, 2004

- As of the end of September, the shares were little changed in 2004, underperforming peers and the S&P 500. We believe the relative underperformance reflects lingering concerns about WFC's exposure to a slowing mortgage origination market and the possible impact of employee stock option expensing on EPS.

- Risks to our recommendation and target price include a severe economic downturn in combination with higher short-term interest rates that could result in an inverted yield curve; litigation and regulatory risks; and a serious geopolitical event that could affect equity markets.

- The stock's average P/E multiple was 16X and 14X in the past five years and three years, respectively. Our 12-month target price of $65 assumes that in a year, the stock will trade at a P/E multiple of about 14X our 2005 EPS estimate, similar to its current P/E on estimated 2004 EPS. We would hold the stock, which has a dividend yield of about 3.1%.

Key Stock Statistics

S&P Core EPS 2005E	4.30	52-week Range	$62.57-54.32
S&P Oper. EPS 2004E	4.10	12 Month P/E	15.6
P/E on S&P Oper. EPS 2004E	15.3	Beta	0.36
S&P Oper. EPS 2005E	4.55	Shareholders	96,634
Yield (%)	3.1%	Market Cap (B)	$105.9
Dividend Rate/Share	1.92	Shares Outstanding (M)	1691.9

Value of $10,000 invested five years ago: **$ 14,919**

Dividend Data Dividends have been paid since 1939

Amount ($)	Date Decl.	Ex-Div. Date	Stock of Record	Payment Date
0.450	Jan. 27	Feb. 04	Feb. 06	Mar. 01 '04
0.450	Apr. 27	May. 05	May. 07	Jun. 01 '04
0.480	Jul. 27	Aug. 04	Aug. 06	Sep. 01 '04
0.480	Oct. 25	Nov. 03	Nov. 05	Dec. 01 '04

Revenues/Earnings Data Fiscal year ending December 31

Revenues (Million $)

	2004	2003	2002	2001	2000	1999
1Q	7,955	7,561	6,982	7,295	6,421	5,215
2Q	8,269	7,637	7,005	5,361	6,678	5,310
3Q	8,305	8,170	7,044	7,099	6,925	5,450
4Q	—	8,257	7,443	7,137	7,545	5,820
Yr.	—	31,800	28,473	26,891	27,568	21,795

Earnings Per Share ($)

	2004	2003	2002	2001	2000	1999
1Q	1.03	0.88	0.80	0.67	0.61	0.53
2Q	1.00	0.90	0.82	-0.05	0.61	0.55
3Q	1.02	0.92	0.84	0.67	0.47	0.57
4Q	E1.05	0.95	0.86	0.69	0.65	0.58
Yr.	E4.10	3.65	3.32	1.97	2.33	2.23

Next earnings report expected: mid-January Source: S&P, Company Reports
EPS Estimates based on S&P Operating Earnings; historical GAAP earnings are as reported.

Wells Fargo & Company

Recommendation: **HOLD** ★ ★ ★ ☆ ☆   12-Month Target Price: **$65.00** (as of September 30, 2004)

Business Summary October 04, 2004

Tracing its roots to a business founded by Henry Wells and William Fargo in 1852, Wells Fargo is now the fifth largest U.S. bank holding company, with about $388 billion in assets. The company provides banking, insurance, investments, mortgage and consumer finance through about 5,900 financial services stores across North America. The company's strategy is focused on cross selling financial products to its client base. At the end of 2003, WFC estimated that each of its current customers had an average of more than four products. The company's goal is eight products per customer, which WFC sees as half of estimated potential demand.

Operations are divided into three lines of business. Community banking (70% of net income in 2003) offers diversified financial products and services to individual consumers and small businesses, as well as investment management and other services to retail customers and high net worth individuals, insurance and securities brokerage. Lending products include residential mortgages, lines of credit, equipment and transportation loans, and equity lines. Wholesale banking (23%) serves businesses with over $10 million in annual sales with commercial loans and lines of credit, asset-based lending, equipment leasing, international trade facilities, foreign exchange services, treasury management, investment management, institutional fixed income and equity sales. Wells Fargo financial (7%) consists of consumer finance and auto finance operations, including direct install-

ment loans to individuals and purchase of sales finance contracts from retail merchants.

In 2003, average earning assets, from which interest income is derived, amounted to $318.2 billion and mainly consisted of loans, including mortgages, and leases (86%) and investment securities (10%). Average sources of funds included interest-bearing deposits (43%), noninterest-bearing deposits (20%), short-term borrowings (8%), long-term debt (14%), shareholders' equity (8%) and other (7%).

At the end of 2003, nonperforming assets, consisting mainly of nonaccrual loans, foreclosed assets and other real estate owned, were $1.67 billion (0.43% of assets), down from $1.69 billion (0.48%) a year earlier. The allowance for loan losses, which is set aside for possible loan defaults, was $3.89 billion (1.54% of loans), versus $3.82 billion (1.98%) a year earlier. Net chargeoffs, or the amount of loans actually written off as uncollectible, were $1.72 billion (0.81% of average loans) in 2003, versus $1.68 billion (0.96%) in 2002.

Acquisitions in 2003 included certain assets of Syracuse, NY-based Telmark, LLC ($660 million in assets), Seattle, WA-based Pacific Northwest Bancorp ($3.3 billion), Grand Junction, CO-based Two Rivers Corp. ($74 million), and 14 smaller acquisitions of asset management, commercial real estate brokerage, bankruptcy and insurance brokerage businesses with total assets of $136 million.

Company Financials Fiscal Year ending December 31

Per Share Data ($)

(Year Ended December 31)	2003	2002	2001	2000	1999	1998	1997	1996	1995	1994
Tangible Bk. Val.	14.07	12.22	9.80	9.18	7.91	6.77	9.01	7.97	7.10	5.40
Earnings	3.65	3.32	1.97	2.33	2.23	1.17	1.75	1.54	1.38	1.23
S&P Core Earnings	3.56	3.13	1.68	NA	NA	NA	NA	NA	NA	NA
Dividends	1.50	1.10	1.00	0.90	0.79	0.70	0.61	0.53	0.45	0.38
Payout Ratio	41%	33%	51%	39%	35%	60%	35%	34%	33%	31%
Prices - High	59.18	53.44	54.81	56.37	49.93	43.87	39.50	23.43	17.37	14.12
- Low	43.27	43.30	38.25	31.37	32.18	27.50	21.37	15.25	11.31	10.50
P/E Ratio - High	16	16	28	24	22	37	23	15	13	12
- Low	12	13	19	13	14	24	12	10	8	9

Income Statement Analysis (Million $)

	2003	2002	2001	2000	1999	1998	1997	1996	1995	1994
Net Int. Inc.	16,007	14,855	12,460	10,865	9,355	8,990	4,033	3,701	3,269	2,804
Tax Equiv. Adj.	NA	NA	NA	65.0	64.0	59.0	44.5	32.2	34.0	29.0
Non Int. Inc.	12,323	9,348	7,227	9,565	6,653	6,427	2,924	2,612	1,901	1,718
Loan Loss Prov.	1,722	1,733	1,780	1,329	1,045	1,545	525	395	312	165
Exp./Op. Revs.	60.7%	52.2%	65.5%	57.7%	60.9%	68.4%	63.5%	64.5%	65.3%	68.0%
Pretax Inc.	9,477	8,854	5,479	6,549	5,948	3,293	2,050	1,782	1,423	1,181
Eff. Tax Rate	34.6%	35.5%	37.5%	38.5%	37.0%	40.8%	34.1%	35.2%	32.8%	32.2%
Net Inc.	6,202	5,710	3,423	4,026	3,747	1,950	1,351	1,154	956	800
% Net Int. Marg.	5.08	5.57	5.36	5.35	5.66	5.79	5.74	5.63	5.58	5.67
S&P Core Earnings	6,055	5,374	2,894	NA	NA	NA	NA	NA	NA	NA

Balance Sheet & Other Fin. Data (Million $)

	2003	2002	2001	2000	1999	1998	1997	1996	1995	1994
Money Mkt. Assets	2,745	3,174	2,530	1,598	1,554	1,517	1,501	2,701	777	765
Inv. Securities	32,953	27,947	40,308	38,655	38,518	31,997	18,731	16,959	16,004	14,837
Com'l Loans	48,729	47,292	47,547	60,541	46,538	41,830	12,878	12,125	11,234	9,155
Other Loans	204,344	149,342	124,952	10,583	72,926	66,164	31,757	29,029	36,455	29,695
Total Assets	387,798	349,259	307,569	272,426	218,102	202,475	88,540	80,175	72,134	59,316
Demand Deposits	74,387	74,094	65,362	55,096	42,916	43,732	16,253	14,296	11,624	9,283
Time Deposits	173,140	142,822	121,904	114,463	89,792	90,056	39,204	35,834	30,405	27,141
LT Debt	63,642	50,205	38,530	32,981	24,160	19,709	12,767	13,082	13,677	9,186
Common Equity	34,255	30,107	26,996	26,103	21,860	20,296	6,755	5,875	5,010	3,334
% Ret. on Assets	1.7	1.7	1.2	1.6	1.8	1.0	1.6	1.5	1.4	1.4
% Ret. on Equity	19.3	20.0	12.8	16.2	17.6	14.2	21.2	20.0	21.9	22.6
% Loan Loss Resv.	1.3	1.5	1.8	2.1	2.5	2.9	2.9	2.6	2.0	2.1
% Loans/Deposits	117.0	117.3	110.9	104.7	93.8	79.0	76.7	78.6	109.5	103.6
% Equity to Assets	8.7	8.7	9.2	9.7	10.0	10.2	7.4	7.5	6.3	6.2

Data as orig. reptd.; bef. results of disc opers. and/or spec. items. Data for 1997 and prior years based on Norwest Corp. before merger with Wells Fargo. Per share data adj. for stk. divs. as of ex-div. date. Bold denotes primary EPS. E-Estimated. NA-Not Available. NM-Not Meaningful. NR-Not Ranked.

Office: 420 Montgomery Street, San Francisco, CA 94163.
Telephone: 800-333-0343.
Website: http://www.wellsfargo.com
Chrmn, Pres & CEO: R.M. Kovacevich.
EVP & CFO: H.I. Atkins.
EVP & General Counsel: J.M. Strother.

Investor Contact: B. Strickland 415-396-0523.
Dirs: J. A. Blanchard III, S. E. Engel, E. Hernandez, Jr., R. L. Joss, R. C. King, R. M. Kovacevich, R. D. McCormick, C. H. Milligan, B. F. Montoya, P. J. Quigley, D. B. Rice, J. M. Runstad, S. W. Sanger, S. G. Swenson, M. W. Wright.

Founded: in 1929.
Domicile: Delaware.
Employees: 140,000.
S&P Analyst: Evan M. Momios, CFA /MF/BK

Wendy's International

Recommendation: **BUY** ★★★★☆
SELL | SEC | HOLD | BUY | BUY

12-Month Target Price: **$38.00**
(as of October 22, 2004)

WEN has an approximate 0.04% weighting in the **S&P 500**

Sector: Consumer Discretionary
Sub-Industry: Restaurants
Peer Group: Fast-food - Larger

Summary: Wendy's operates or franchises close to 6,600 Wendy's, about 2,600 Tim Hortons, and about 300 Baja Fresh restaurants, mainly in the U.S. and Canada.

Quantitative Evaluations

S&P Earnings & Dividend Rank: A-

| D | C | B- | B | B+ | A- | A | A+ |

S&P Fair Value Rank: 3

| 1 | 2 | **3** | 4 | 5 |
Lowest — Highest

Fair Value Calc.: $34.40 (Slightly Overvalued)

S&P Investability Quotient Percentile
97%

WEN scored higher than 97% of all companies for which an S&P Report is available.

Volatility: Average

| Low | **Average** | High |

Technical Evaluation: Neutral
Since 11/04, the technical indicators for WEN have been Neutral.

Relative Strength Rank: Moderate
50
1 Lowest — Highest 99

Price as of 11/12/04: $35.84   **2004E S&P Core EPS: $2.13**

GAAP Earnings vs. Previous Year
▲ Up ▼ Down ▶ No Change

10 Week Mov. Avg.
30 Week Mov. Avg.
Relative Strength
12-Mo Target Price

BUY $36.93 05/01/02

HOLD | BUY | HOLD | BUY
J J A S O N D J F M A M J J A S O N D J F M A M J J A S O N D J F M A M J J A S O N D J
2001 | 2002 | 2003 | 2004

OPTIONS: CBOE, P

Analyst commentary prepared by Dennis Milton/DC/GG

Highlights October 26, 2004

- We believe WEN has successfully captured market share in the fast food industry over the past few years by offering higher quality products and service than some of its larger fast food competitors. The company is pursuing an expansion strategy to extend the Wendy's chain to more than 8,000 units, the Tim Hortons chain to more than 3,800 units, and Baja Fresh to 600 to 700 units over the next five to seven years.

- We think WEN will be able to produce compound annual earnings growth of 9% to 10% over the next several years, primarily due to moderate expected same-store sales growth and more restaurants in operation. Despite strong industry competition, we also see some operating margin improvement from the leveraging of fixed costs over a larger sales base.

- In 2005, we expect EPS to grow 11%, to $2.50, from our 2004 EPS estimate of $2.25. Our projection is based on continued expansion, same store sales growth of about 3% at Wendy's and 5% at Tim Horton's, and improved operating margins. We look for most of the company's operating income growth to occur in the second half of the year, where comparisons are more favorable. Our 2005 Standard & Poor's Core earnings estimate, which includes $0.15 of projected expense for stock option grants, is $2.35.

Investment Rationale/Risk October 26, 2004

- We would accumulate the shares at their recent valuation of 14.5X our 2004 EPS estimate, a slight discount to peer levels. Despite recent weakness in Wendy's sales trends, we do not believe a discount is warranted, given our view of the company's superior growth prospects and solid operating history. We expect WEN to continue to gain market share well into the future, as a result of its expansion program, reductions in long-term expansion plans of rivals, and a continuing increase in U.S. disposable income, which we see aiding the company's results due to its high end positioning in the quick service restaurant (QSR) segment. We are especially impressed with the growth prospects of the Tim Hortons chain, which already accounts for more than 40% of the company's operating income and is rapidly expanding in the U.S.

- Risks to our opinion and target price include rising food costs, which could have a negative impact on margins, and the lack of customer acceptance of new product offerings.

- Our 12-month target price of $38 is based on a forward P/E multiple of 15X, in line with peers, and our 2005 EPS estimate of $2.50, and is supported by our estimate of intrinsic value, according to our discounted cash flow model.

Key Stock Statistics

S&P Core EPS 2005E	2.35	52-week Range	$42.75-31.74
S&P Oper. EPS 2004E	2.25	12 Month P/E	16.1
P/E on S&P Oper. EPS 2004E	15.9	Beta	0.30
S&P Oper. EPS 2005E	2.50	Shareholders	74,400
Yield (%)	1.3%	Market Cap (B)	$ 4.1
Dividend Rate/Share	0.48	Shares Outstanding (M)	114.0

Value of $10,000 invested five years ago: **$ 15,769**

Dividend Data Dividends have been paid since 1976

Amount ($)	Date Decl.	Ex-Div. Date	Stock of Record	Payment Date
0.120	Feb. 02	Feb. 10	Feb. 12	Feb. 27 '04
0.120	Apr. 26	Apr. 29	May. 03	May. 17 '04
0.120	Jul. 23	Jul. 29	Aug. 02	Aug. 16 '04
0.120	Oct. 21	Oct. 28	Nov. 01	Nov. 15 '04

Revenues/Earnings Data Fiscal year ending December 31

Revenues (Million $)

	2004	2003	2002	2001	2000	1999
1Q	834.8	694.0	612.4	555.5	519.8	476.5
2Q	908.9	786.0	684.0	609.6	569.9	528.5
3Q	914.0	806.5	722.1	610.4	577.6	540.7
4Q	—	862.4	711.7	615.7	572.3	533.8
Yr.	—	3,149	2,730	2,391	2,237	2,072

Earnings Per Share ($)

	2004	2003	2002	2001	2000	1999
1Q	0.45	0.38	0.39	0.33	0.30	0.25
2Q	0.62	0.53	0.54	0.47	0.43	0.39
3Q	0.60	0.58	0.52	0.44	0.41	0.39
4Q	E0.58	0.56	0.44	0.41	0.29	0.33
Yr.	E2.25	2.05	1.89	1.65	1.44	1.32

Next earnings report expected: late-January Source: S&P, Company Reports
EPS Estimates based on S&P Operating Earnings; historical GAAP earnings are as reported.

Wendy's International, Inc.

Recommendation: **BUY** ★★★★☆   12-Month Target Price: **$38.00** (as of October 22, 2004)

Business Summary October 26, 2004

Wendy's International is the world's third largest quick service restaurant (QSR) chain. It was founded in 1969 as Wendy's Old Fashioned Hamburgers by the late Dave Thomas, who was known as the company's spokesperson until his passing in 2002. In addition to Wendy's, the company also owns the Tim Hortons and Baja Fresh restaurant concepts.

Wendy's restaurants offer a relatively standard menu featuring hamburgers and filet of chicken breast sandwiches, which are prepared to order with the customer's choice of condiments. The company's share of the U.S. QSR hamburger market was 14% in 2003. At September 26, 2004, there were 5,854 Wendy's restaurants in the U.S., 373 in Canada, and 345 outside of North America. About 78% of the restaurants were operated by a system of more than 500 franchisees. Average net sales per domestic restaurant was $1.29 million in 2003, up slightly from $1.28 million in 2002.

Each Tim Hortons unit offers coffee, cappuccino, fresh baked goods, and, in some units, sandwiches and soups. It has 70% of the coffee and fresh baked goods market in Canada. At September 26, 2004, there were 2,399 Tim Hortons units in Canada and 233 units in the U.S. About 96% of the units were operated by franchisees. Average sales per Canadian unit were C$1.62 million in 2003, up 4.5% from C$1.56 million in 2002.

Baja Fresh offers a range of fast-casual fresh Mexican food. At September 26, 2004, there were 305 Baja Fresh units, predominantly in the western U.S. Average net sales volume was $1.37 million in 2003, down from $1.50 million in 2002.

Systemwide sales in 2003 were approximately $8.0 billion for Wendy's restaurants,

$2.1 billion for Tim Hortons, and $300 million for Baja Fresh. Retail sales accounted for 80% of total revenues, with franchise revenues accounting for the remainder.

WEN intends to increase its revenues through new unit development and by boosting same-store sales. In 2003, the company opened 321 Wendy's, 211 Tim Hortons, and 74 Baja Fresh restaurants. Comparable-store sales grew 0.9% at domestic Wendy's units, 4.8% at Tim Hortons Canada units, and 4.5% at Tim Hortons U.S. units, but fell 4.6% at Baja Fresh units. For 2004, WEN plans to open 550 to 600 new restaurants, focused primarily on the Wendy's North America and Hortons Canada markets. Capital spending is expected to total between $300 million and $350 million in 2004.

In 2002, the company invested a combined $22 million for minority positions in Cafe Express, a fast casual restaurant chain based in the southwestern U.S., and Pasta Pomodoro, a fast casual restaurant chain featuring fresh Italian food. In February 2004, the company increased its ownership of Cafe Express to a 70% majority position.

From 1998 to 2003, WEN repurchased 36.8 million common shares, for $885 million. At January 31, 2004, it had $366 million remaining under its existing buyback authorization.

The company does not currently expense stock options. Had stock options been expensed, EPS would have been reduced by $0.10, $0.09 and $0.06 in 2003, 2002 and 2001, respectively.

Company Financials Fiscal Year ending December 31

Per Share Data ($)

(Year Ended December 31)	2003	2002	2001	2000	1999	1998	1997	1996	1995	1994
Tangible Bk. Val.	12.15	9.84	9.40	9.48	8.60	9.37	9.78	8.89	7.47	6.37
Cash Flow	3.51	3.10	2.62	2.31	2.06	1.63	1.68	1.91	1.56	1.59
Earnings	2.05	1.89	1.65	1.44	1.32	0.95	0.97	1.20	0.90	0.93
S&P Core Earnings	1.94	1.74	1.54	NA	NA	NA	NA	NA	NA	NA
Dividends	0.24	0.24	0.24	0.24	0.24	0.24	0.24	0.24	0.24	0.24
Payout Ratio	12%	13%	15%	17%	18%	25%	25%	20%	27%	26%
Prices - High	41.55	41.60	30.50	27.12	31.68	25.18	27.93	23.00	22.75	18.50
- Low	23.97	26.15	20.00	14.00	19.68	18.12	19.62	16.75	14.37	13.25
P/E Ratio - High	20	22	18	19	24	27	29	19	25	20
- Low	12	14	12	10	15	19	20	14	16	14

Income Statement Analysis (Million $)

	2003	2002	2001	2000	1999	1998	1997	1996	1995	1994
Revs.	3,149	2,730	2,391	2,237	2,072	1,948	2,037	1,897	1,746	1,370
Oper. Inc.	586	531	453	424	389	346	335	356	306	199
Depr.	168	143	123	113	103	100	105	95.0	84.4	68.1
Int. Exp.	45.8	41.5	30.2	28.9	10.2	19.8	18.9	20.3	20.4	18.7
Pretax Inc.	378	346	307	271	269	208	219	255	165	149
Eff. Tax Rate	37.5%	36.8%	37.0%	37.5%	38.0%	40.6%	40.5%	38.8%	33.3%	35.0%
Net Inc.	236	219	194	170	167	123	131	156	110	97.2
S&P Core Earnings	221	200	181	NA	NA	NA	NA	NA	NA	NA

Balance Sheet & Other Fin. Data (Million $)

	2003	2002	2001	2000	1999	1998	1997	1996	1995	1994
Cash	171	172	111	170	211	161	234	224	214	135
Curr. Assets	463	331	266	319	350	314	382	337	321	203
Total Assets	3,164	2,667	2,076	1,958	1,884	1,838	1,942	1,781	1,509	1,086
Curr. Liab.	528	360	297	296	284	249	213	208	296	207
LT Debt	693	682	651	448	449	446	250	242	337	145
Common Equity	1,980	1,449	1,030	1,126	1,065	1,068	1,184	1,057	822	681
Total Cap.	2,805	2,239	1,763	1,647	1,584	1,575	1,715	1,562	1,207	866
Cap. Exp.	342	331	301	276	248	242	295	307	218	142
Cash Flow	404	362	317	283	270	224	236	251	191	165
Curr. Ratio	0.9	0.9	0.9	1.1	1.2	1.3	1.8	1.6	1.1	1.0
% LT Debt of Cap.	24.7	30.4	36.9	27.2	28.3	28.3	14.6	15.5	27.9	16.7
% Net Inc.of Revs.	7.5	8.0	8.1	7.6	8.0	6.3	6.4	8.2	6.3	7.1
% Ret. on Assets	8.0	9.2	9.6	8.8	9.0	6.5	7.0	9.5	8.1	9.3
% Ret. on Equity	13.8	17.7	18.0	15.5	15.6	11.0	11.7	16.6	14.4	15.1

Data as orig reptd.; bef. results of disc opers/spec. items. Per share data adj. for stk. divs.; EPS diluted. E-Estimated. NA-Not Available. NM-Not Meaningful. NR-Not Ranked. UR-Under Review.

Office: 4288 West Dublin-Granville Road, Dublin, OH 43017-0256.
Telephone: 614-764-3100.
Email: investor_relations@wendys.com
Website: http://www.wendys.com
Chrmn, Pres & CEO: J.T. Schuessler.
EVP & CFO: K.B. Anderson.

EVP & Treas: J.F. Catherwood.
EVP, Secy & General Counsel: L.M. McCorkle, Jr.
Investor Contact: M. Gordon 614-764-3019.
Dirs: K. B. Anderson, A. B. Crane, J. Hill, P. D. House, T. F. Keller, W. E. Kirwan, D. P. Lauer, J. R. Lewis, J. F. Millar, J. V. Pickett, J. T. Schuessler, J. R. Thompson.

Founded: in 1969.
Domicile: Ohio.
Employees: 53,000.
S&P Analyst: Dennis Milton/DC/GG

Weyerhaeuser Co.

Recommendation: **SELL** ★☆☆☆☆   **12-Month Target Price: $54.00**
SELL SELL HOLD BUY BUY   (as of May 11, 2004)

WY has an approximate 0.15% weighting in the **S&P 500**

Sector: Materials
Sub-Industry: Forest Products
Peer Group: Forest Products - Larger

Summary: One of the world's largest integrated forest products companies, WY grows timber; makes and sells forest products; and engages in real estate construction and development.

Quantitative Evaluations

| Price as of 11/12/04: | **$66.85** | 2004E S&P Core EPS: | **$4.84** |

S&P Earnings & Dividend Rank: B

| D | C | B- | **B** | B+ | A- | A | A+ |

S&P Fair Value Rank: 2-

| 1 | **2** | 3 | 4 | 5 |
| Lowest | | | | Highest |

Fair Value Calc.: $60.40 (Slightly Overvalued)

S&P Investability Quotient Percentile

95%

WY scored higher than 95% of all companies for which an S&P Report is available.

Volatility: Average

| Low | **Average** | High |

Technical Evaluation: Neutral
Since 11/04, the technical indicators for WY have been Neutral.

Relative Strength Rank: Moderate

55

| 1 Lowest | | Highest 99 |

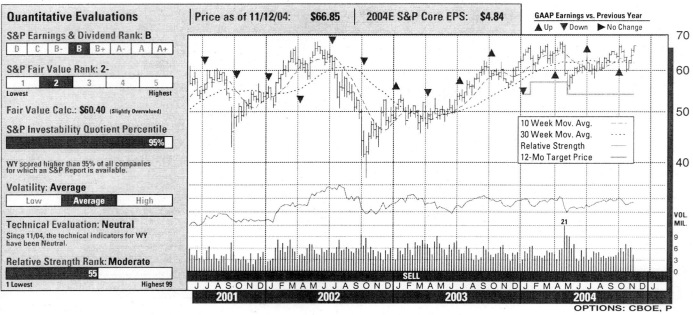

GAAP Earnings vs. Previous Year
▲ Up   ▼ Down   ► No Change

10 Week Mov. Avg.
30 Week Mov. Avg.
Relative Strength
12-Mo Target Price

VOL. MIL.

SELL

J J A S O N D J F M A M J J A S O N D J F M A M J J A S O N D J F M A M J J A S O N D J
2001   2002   2003   2004

OPTIONS: CBOE, P

Analyst commentary prepared by Bryon Korutz/CB/GG

Highlights October 26, 2004

- We expect revenues to increase 13% in 2004, with average wood product prices above those reached in 2003. However, we see wood product prices weakening over the balance of the year, based on a seasonal slowdown in housing starts. For 2005, we see a 7.0% drop in housing starts placing downward pressure on wood product prices, with average wood product prices below 2004 levels.

- With regard to WY's paper and packaging products, Standard & Poor's sees real GDP rising 4.3% in 2004, and we expect this to lead to improved demand and prices for paper and packaging, as demand for these products typically tracks the economic cycle. We see continued price improvement in 2005, based on our projected increase in business expenditures. All told, we project that margins will benefit from the higher prices and operating leverage related to the increased production. We estimate that operating margins will increase to 11.7% in 2004, from 6.2% the year before. We see operating margins dropping to 9.2% in 2005, on our forecasted decline in demand and prices for wood products.

- Our 2004 Standard & Poor's Core Earnings estimate is $4.84, reflecting, in part, the effect of projected option expense and pension costs.

Investment Rationale/Risk October 26, 2004

- Based on our expectations that wood product prices will come under pressure in the latter part of 2004 and into 2005, and with the shares above our 12-month target price of $54, we would avoid WY stock.

- Risks to our recommendation and target price include softer than expected declines in wood product prices and housing starts.

- Our DCF model, assuming a WACC of 8.2%, a compound annual growth rate of 5.2% over the next 15 years, and 3.0% growth in perpetuity, values the stock at $59. Applying a peer forward P/E multiple of 13X to our 2005 EPS estimate of $3.85 results in a value of $50. By taking a weighted average of our valuation metrics, we reach our 12-month target price of $54 a share.

Key Stock Statistics

S&P Core EPS 2005E	3.73	52-week Range	$68.05-55.06
S&P Oper. EPS 2004E	5.28	12 Month P/E	13.3
P/E on S&P Oper. EPS 2004E	12.7	Beta	1.05
S&P Oper. EPS 2005E	3.85	Shareholders	13,726
Yield (%)	2.4%	Market Cap (B)	$ 16.1
Dividend Rate/Share	1.60	Shares Outstanding (M)	241.2

Value of $10,000 invested five years ago: **$ 11,800**

Dividend Data Dividends have been paid since 1933

Amount ($)	Date Decl.	Ex-Div. Date	Stock of Record	Payment Date
0.400	Jan. 08	Jan. 28	Jan. 30	Mar. 01 '04
0.400	Apr. 13	Apr. 28	Apr. 30	Jun. 01 '04
0.400	Jul. 09	Jul. 28	Jul. 30	Aug. 30 '04
0.400	Oct. 07	Oct. 27	Oct. 29	Nov. 29 '04

Revenues/Earnings Data Fiscal year ending December 31

Revenues (Million $)

	2004	2003	2002	2001	2000	1999
1Q	5,037	4,614	3,991	3,553	3,925	2,665
2Q	5,893	4,930	4,922	3,842	4,189	3,044
3Q	5,849	5,184	4,890	3,752	3,824	3,120
4Q	—	5,145	4,718	3,398	4,042	3,433
Yr.	—	19,873	18,521	14,545	15,980	12,262

Earnings Per Share ($)

	2004	2003	2002	2001	2000	1999
1Q	0.54	-0.19	0.24	0.49	1.04	0.21
2Q	1.57	0.71	0.32	0.78	0.89	0.81
3Q	2.45	0.37	0.06	0.41	0.90	1.18
4Q	E1.37	0.41	0.57	-0.07	0.88	0.78
Yr.	E5.28	1.30	1.09	1.61	3.72	2.98

Next earnings report expected: late-January Source: S&P, Company Reports
EPS Estimates based on S&P Operating Earnings; historical GAAP earnings are as reported.

Please read the Required Disclosures and Reg. AC certification on the last page of this report.

The **McGraw·Hill** Companies

Weyerhaeuser Company

Recommendation: **SELL** ★★☆☆☆   12-Month Target Price: **$54.00** (as of May 11, 2004)

Business Summary October 26, 2004

Weyerhaeuser, one of the largest integrated forest products companies, is primarily engaged in growing and harvesting timber; the production, distribution and sale of wood and paper products; and real estate development.

Through its timberlands segment (7.0% of 2003 sales), WY operates 6.0 million acres of company-owned timberlands and leases 800,000 acres of timberlands in 10 states. Through Weyerhaeuser Canada, the company has long-term licenses on 29.9 million acres in five Canadian provinces, and owns 663,000 acres in British Columbia. Through wholly owned subsidiaries, WY also participates in timberland joint ventures worldwide.

The company's wood products businesses (42%) produce and sell softwood and hardwood lumber, plywood and veneer, composite panels, oriented strand board, and engineered lumber. Products are sold primarily through WY's 73 customer service centers. Building materials are sold to wholesalers, home improvement centers, manufactured housing companies, industrial manufacturers, and users. At December 31, 2003, the company's annual production capacity of softwood lumber was 7.7 billion board feet, 2.7 billion square feet of plywood and veneer, 1.1 billion square feet of composite panels, 4.4 billion square feet of OSB, and 0.4 billion board feet of hardwood lumber.

Products made by the pulp and paper unit (19%) include papergrade, absorbent, dissolving and specialty pulp grades. Paper products include coated and uncoated papers, which are used in the printing and publishing industries as well as

for office use. WY also produces bleached board, used in the production of liquid containers. The company's newsprint business is a joint venture with Nippon Paper Industries, which produces newsprint for U.S. and Japanese markets. At December 31, 2003, WY's annual production capacity for pulp was 2.8 million metric tons, 3.0 million tons of paper, 0.2 million tons of coated groundwood, 0.3 million tons of liquid packaging board, and 2.2 million tons of paper converting capacity.

The containerboard, packaging and recycling segment (22%) manufactures corrugating medium, linerboard and kraft paper. WY operates packaging plants that supply corrugated boxes to a range of industrial, agricultural and consumer products in the U.S. and Mexico. At December 31, 2003, annual production capacity for containerboard was 6.3 million tons, 106.0 million square feet of corrugated packaging, and 0.2 million tons of kraft bags. The company also operates a wastepaper collection system that collects and processes all major grades of recovered papers.

Through Weyerhaeuser Real Estate Company (10%), the company is involved in the development of single-family housing and residential lots, including the development of master-planned communities.

In March 2002, WY acquired Willamette Industries (WLL). The total value of the transaction was about $7.9 billion: $6.1 billion to acquire all WLL stock for $55.50 a share in cash, plus the assumption of $1.8 billion of debt.

Company Financials Fiscal Year ending December 31

Per Share Data ($)

(Year Ended December 31)	2003	2002	2001	2000	1999	1998	1997	1996	1995	1994
Tangible Bk. Val.	17.44	15.80	25.45	25.95	27.15	22.74	23.31	23.25	22.54	20.86
Cash Flow	7.23	6.63	5.94	7.52	6.07	4.55	4.85	5.45	6.96	5.46
Earnings	1.30	1.09	1.61	3.72	2.98	1.47	1.71	2.34	3.93	2.86
S&P Core Earnings	0.70	-0.75	NA	NA	NA	NA	NA	NA	NA	NA
Dividends	1.60	1.60	1.60	1.60	1.60	1.60	1.60	1.60	1.50	1.20
Payout Ratio	123%	147%	99%	43%	54%	109%	94%	68%	38%	42%
Prices - High	64.70	68.09	63.50	74.50	73.93	62.00	63.93	49.87	50.37	51.25
- Low	45.40	37.35	42.77	36.06	49.56	36.75	42.62	39.50	36.87	35.75
P/E Ratio - High	50	62	39	20	25	42	37	21	13	18
- Low	35	34	27	10	17	25	25	17	9	12

Income Statement Analysis (Million $)

	2003	2002	2001	2000	1999	1998	1997	1996	1995	1994
Revs.	19,873	18,521	14,545	15,980	12,262	10,766	11,210	11,114	11,788	10,398
Oper. Inc.	2,716	2,455	1,689	2,536	1,902	1,385	1,486	1,687	2,514	1,754
Depr.	1,318	1,225	876	859	640	616	628	617	621	534
Int. Exp.	796	771	344	351	277	273	297	405	411	391
Pretax Inc.	436	371	516	1,323	970	463	539	720	1,244	920
Eff. Tax Rate	33.9%	35.0%	31.4%	36.5%	36.5%	36.5%	36.5%	35.7%	35.8%	36.0%
Net Inc.	288	241	354	840	616	294	342	463	799	589
S&P Core Earnings	156	-168	2.35	NA	NA	NA	NA	NA	NA	NA

Balance Sheet & Other Fin. Data (Million $)

	2003	2002	2001	2000	1999	1998	1997	1996	1995	1994
Cash	202	122	204	123	1,643	35.0	122	33.0	34.0	112
Curr. Assets	4,021	3,888	3,061	3,288	4,543	2,170	2,294	2,225	2,235	NA
Total Assets	28,109	28,219	18,293	18,195	18,339	12,834	13,075	13,596	13,253	13,007
Curr. Liab.	2,525	2,994	1,863	2,704	2,934	1,499	1,384	1,483	1,603	NA
LT Debt	12,397	12,721	5,715	5,114	4,453	4,662	4,743	5,328	4,736	4,586
Common Equity	7,109	6,623	6,695	6,832	7,173	4,526	4,649	4,604	4,486	4,290
Total Cap.	23,800	23,400	14,787	14,323	13,611	10,592	10,931	11,369	10,529	9,965
Cap. Exp.	608	930	660	848	487	615	656	879	996	1,102
Cash Flow	1,606	1,466	1,230	1,699	1,256	910	970	1,080	1,420	1,123
Curr. Ratio	1.6	1.3	1.6	1.2	1.5	1.4	1.7	1.5	1.4	NA
% LT Debt of Cap.	52.1	54.4	38.6	35.7	32.7	44.0	43.4	40.5	45.0	46.0
% Net Inc.of Revs.	1.4	1.3	2.4	5.3	5.0	2.7	3.1	4.2	6.8	5.7
% Ret. on Assets	1.0	1.0	1.9	4.6	4.0	2.3	2.6	3.5	6.1	4.6
% Ret. on Equity	4.2	3.6	5.2	12.0	10.5	6.4	7.4	10.2	18.2	14.3

Data as orig. reptd.; bef. results of disc. opers. and/or spec. items. Per share data adj. for stk. divs.; EPS diluted. Ratios are affected by inclusion of non-forest products opers. E-Estimated. NA-Not Available. NM-Not Meaningful. NR-Not Ranked.

Office: 33663 Weyerhaeuser Way South, Federal Way, WA 98003.
Telephone: 253-924-2345.
Email: invrelations@weyerhaeuser.com
Website: http://www.weyerhaeuser.com
Chrmn, Pres & CEO: S.R. Rogel.
COO & EVP: R.E. Hanson.
EVP & CFO: R.J. Taggart.

VP & Chief Acctg Officer: S.J. Hillyard.
VP & Treas: J.W. Nitta.
VP & Investor Contact: K.F. McAuley 253-924-2058.
Dirs: R. F. Haskayne, R. J. Herbold, M. R. Ingram, J. I. Kieckhefer, A. G. Langbo, D. F. Mazankowski, N. W. Piasecki, S. R. Rogel, W. D. Ruckelshaus, R. H. Sinkfield, D. M. Steuert, J. N. Sullivan, C. R. Williamson.

Founded: in 1900.
Domicile: Washington.
Employees: 55,162.
S&P Analyst: Bryon Korutz/CB/GG

Whirlpool Corp.

Recommendation: HOLD ★ ★ ★ ☆ ☆
SELL SELL HOLD BUY BUY

12-Month Target Price: $59.00
(as of October 20, 2004)

WHR has an approximate 0.04% weighting in the **S&P 500**

Sector: Consumer Discretionary
Sub-Industry: Household Appliances
Peer Group: Household Appliances

Summary: WHR is the world's second largest manufacturer of home appliances. Sears, Roebuck is its largest customer.

Quantitative Evaluations

S&P Earnings & Dividend Rank: B

| D | C | B- | **B** | B+ | A- | A | A+ |

S&P Fair Value Rank: 4+

| 1 | 2 | 3 | **4** | 5 |
| Lowest | | | | Highest |

Fair Value Calc.: $62.70 (Slightly Overvalued)

S&P Investability Quotient Percentile

97%

WHR scored higher than 97% of all companies for which an S&P Report is available.

Volatility: Average

| Low | **Average** | High |

Technical Evaluation: Neutral
Since 11/04, the technical indicators for WHR have been Neutral.

Relative Strength Rank: Moderate

57

1 Lowest   Highest 99

| Price as of 11/12/04: | **$64.10** | 2004E S&P Core EPS: | **$5.51** |

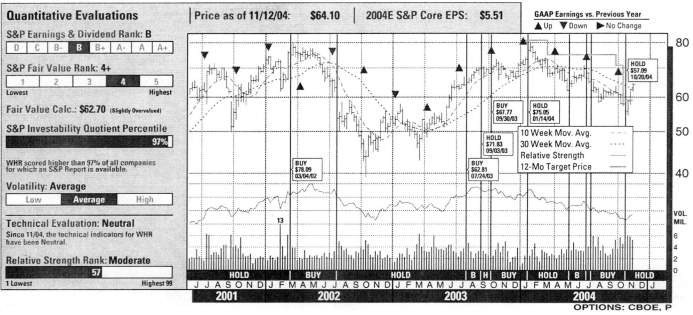

GAAP Earnings vs. Previous Year
▲ Up   ▼ Down   ▶ No Change

HOLD $57.09 10/20/04
BUY $67.77 09/30/03
HOLD $75.05 01/14/04
HOLD $71.83 09/03/03
BUY $78.09 03/04/02
BUY $62.81 07/24/03

10 Week Mov. Avg.
30 Week Mov. Avg.
Relative Strength
12-Mo Target Price

HOLD | BUY | HOLD | B|H| BUY | HOLD | B | BUY | HOLD
J J A S O N D|J F M A M J J A S O N D|J F M A M J J A S O N D|J F M A M J J A S O N D|J F M A M J J A S O N D|J
2001 **2002** **2003** **2004**

OPTIONS: CBOE, P

Analyst commentary prepared by Amy Glynn, CFA /PMW/BK

Highlights October 21, 2004

- We forecast 2004 sales growth in the mid-single digits, and project a similar sales gain for 2005. We expect relatively low interest rates, a sustained economic recovery, recent housing strength, and improved consumer confidence to help U.S. appliance industry shipments improve moderately into 2005. We see European comparisons continuing to benefit from strong demand for several new major appliance products. We expect Latin American sales to benefit from improved economic conditions in the region.

- We expect gross and operating margins to narrow in 2004, due to rising raw material pricing and logistics costs. WHR has been working on productivity initiatives to offset the increased costs, but we do not expect to see the full benefit of this until 2005, when we project that operating margins will widen. WHR has also been increasing prices an average of 10% across all regions and products lines, in a move to offset the higher costs.

- We project 2004 operating EPS of $5.89, slightly down from $5.91 posted in 2003. Our 2004 S&P Core EPS estimate is $5.51, after adjustments for projected stock option expense and pension-related items. We see 2005 operating EPS and Core EPS of $6.26 and $5.87, respectively.

Key Stock Statistics

S&P Core EPS 2005E	5.87	52-week Range	$80.00-54.53
S&P Oper. EPS 2004E	5.89	12 Month P/E	10.3
P/E on S&P Oper. EPS 2004E	10.9	Beta	0.97
S&P Oper. EPS 2005E	6.26	Shareholders	8,078
Yield (%)	2.7%	Market Cap (B)	$ 4.3
Dividend Rate/Share	1.72	Shares Outstanding (M)	66.4

Value of $10,000 invested five years ago: **$ 10,069**

Dividend Data Dividends have been paid since 1929

Amount ($)	Date Decl.	Ex-Div. Date	Stock of Record	Payment Date
0.430	Dec. 16	Feb. 25	Feb. 27	Mar. 15 '04
0.430	Apr. 20	May. 18	May. 20	Jun. 15 '04
0.430	Aug. 17	Aug. 25	Aug. 27	Sep. 15 '04
0.430	Oct. 19	Nov. 16	Nov. 18	Dec. 15 '04

Investment Rationale/Risk October 21, 2004

- We think global industry demand trends remain positive, and we see this boding well for WHR, which we view as a leader in the industry. However, we think concerns about rising raw material prices will restrict the shares for the next 12 months. We would hold the shares, which we see somewhat supported by a dividend yield of nearly 3%. We expect company moves such as price hikes, additional productivity efforts, and an accelerated rate of innovation/introduction of new products to help restore margins in 2005.

- Risks to our opinion and target price include unfavorable changes in business conditions and growth prospects in WHR's markets, increased competition, rising raw material prices, and management execution risk.

- Our 12-month target price of $59 is based on our historical P/E multiple model, and applies a target P/E multiple of 9.5X to our 2005 EPS estimate. We think concerns about rising raw material costs will limit near-term P/E multiple expansion. Our target P/E multiple is below the stock's five-year historical average.

Revenues/Earnings Data Fiscal year ending December 31

Revenues (Million $)

	2004	2003	2002	2001	2000	1999
1Q	3,007	2,716	2,574	2,517	2,590	2,486
2Q	3,264	2,988	2,737	2,585	2,586	2,617
3Q	3,318	3,113	2,759	2,594	2,570	2,719
4Q	—	3,359	2,947	2,647	2,579	2,689
Yr.	—	12,176	11,016	10,343	10,325	10,511

Earnings Per Share ($)

	2004	2003	2002	2001	2000	1999
1Q	1.43	1.32	1.21	0.49	1.52	0.36
2Q	1.53	1.35	0.91	1.10	1.66	1.30
3Q	1.50	1.48	1.46	-1.40	0.98	1.40
4Q	E1.43	1.76	0.20	0.31	1.00	1.51
Yr.	E5.89	5.91	3.78	0.50	5.20	4.56

Next earnings report expected: early-February Source: S&P, Company Reports
EPS Estimates based on S&P Operating Earnings; historical GAAP earnings are as reported.

Please read the Required Disclosures and Reg. AC certification on the last page of this report.

The McGraw·Hill Companies

STANDARD & POOR'S

Whirlpool Corporation

Stock Report
November 13, 2004
NYSE Symbol: **WHR**

Recommendation: **HOLD** ★ ★ ★ ☆ ☆   12-Month Target Price: **$59.00** (as of October 20, 2004)

Business Summary October 21, 2004

Whirlpool manufactures a full line of household appliances and other products for home and commercial use. Products are made in 13 countries, and marketed in more than 170. Growth in recent years has been aided by acquisitions, including the purchase of the appliance business of N.V. Philips Electronics of the Netherlands in the early 1990s. In Latin America and Asia, growth is being fueled by partnerships with existing local appliance companies.

Major product categories include home laundry appliances (32% of 2003 sales); home refrigerators and freezers (29%); home cooking appliances (16%); and other appliances (23%).

Sears, Roebuck and Co. accounted for 18% of WHR's 2003 sales.

The company's sales advanced 10.5% in 2003 on a 5.6% rise in product shipments. North America, Europe, Latin America, and Asia all posted higher net sales. For the year, global sales were increased when converted to U.S. dollars, due to currency fluctuations.

In 2003, 64% of total sales were made in North America. Major brands in the U.S. include Whirlpool, KitchenAid, Roper, Kenmore, Estate, and Crosley & Kirkland Signature. Major brands in Canada are Inglis, Admiral, Speed Queen, Roper, Whirlpool and KitchenAid. About 22% of total sales were made in Europe, where brand names include Polar, Bauknecht, Ignis, Laden, Whirlpool and KitchenAid.

Markets also include Latin America and Asia. About 11% of total sales were in

Latin America, where WHR distributes its major home appliances under the Whirlpool, Brastemp, Consul, and Eslabon de Lugo brand names. About 3% of sales were in Asia.

In 1999, WHR incurred charges totaling $60 million ($0.79 a share) related to Brazilian currency devaluation. WHR believed it had taken the steps needed to limit its exposure to Brazilian currency moves.

In December 2000, the company announced plans for a global restructuring that resulted in total pre-tax costs of $387 million, and is expected to result in annualized cost savings of more than $200 million when fully implemented. The plan calls for the elimination of about 7,500 positions worldwide, of which about 6,900 had been eliminated as of December 31, 2003.

In February 2004, WHR forecast 2004 EPS of $6.20 to $6.35. The company said 2003 fourth quarter U.S. industry unit shipments of major appliances increased 8.1%, year to year. It expected shipments in the U.S. to increase 2% in 2004. In addition, WHR projected that 2004 industry shipments would grow 3% in Europe, about 5% to 10% in Latin America, and about 5% to 10% in Asia.

Through December 31, 2003, the company had repurchased about 13.7 million common shares, for $749 million, under buyback authorizations aggregating $1 billion.

Company Financials Fiscal Year ending December 31

Per Share Data ($)

(Year Ended December 31)	2003	2002	2001	2000	1999	1998	1997	1996	1995	1994
Tangible Bk. Val.	15.23	5.82	11.10	13.97	14.29	14.01	11.25	14.08	12.61	13.38
Cash Flow	12.00	9.62	6.32	10.39	9.64	9.71	4.13	6.32	6.55	5.62
Earnings	5.91	3.78	0.50	5.20	4.56	4.06	-0.62	2.08	2.80	2.10
S&P Core Earnings	5.71	2.12	-1.91	NA	NA	NA	NA	NA	NA	NA
Dividends	1.36	1.36	1.02	1.36	1.36	1.36	1.36	1.36	1.36	1.22
Payout Ratio	23%	36%	NM	26%	30%	33%	NM	65%	49%	58%
Prices - High	73.35	79.80	74.20	68.31	78.25	75.25	69.50	61.37	60.87	73.50
- Low	42.80	39.23	45.87	31.50	40.93	43.68	45.25	44.25	49.25	44.62
P/E Ratio - High	12	21	NM	13	17	19	NM	30	22	35
- Low	7	10	NM	6	9	11	NM	21	18	21

Income Statement Analysis (Million $)

	2003	2002	2001	2000	1999	1998	1997	1996	1995	1994
Revs.	12,176	11,016	10,343	10,325	10,511	10,323	8,617	8,696	8,163	8,104
Oper. Inc.	1,219	1,207	1,147	1,178	1,261	1,126	710	754	775	904
Depr.	427	405	396	371	386	438	356	318	282	266
Int. Exp.	137	143	162	180	166	260	168	236	207	165
Pretax Inc.	652	468	89.0	580	510	565	-104	223	314	351
Eff. Tax Rate	35.0%	41.2%	48.3%	34.5%	38.6%	37.0%	NM	36.4%	31.8%	50.1%
Net Inc.	414	262	34.0	367	347	310	-46.0	156	209	158
S&P Core Earnings	401	147	-130	NA	NA	NA	NA	NA	NA	NA

Balance Sheet & Other Fin. Data (Million $)

	2003	2002	2001	2000	1999	1998	1997	1996	1995	1994
Cash	249	192	316	114	261	636	578	129	149	72.0
Curr. Assets	3,865	3,327	3,311	3,237	3,177	3,882	4,281	3,812	3,541	3,078
Total Assets	7,361	6,631	6,967	6,902	6,826	7,935	8,270	8,015	7,800	6,655
Curr. Liab.	3,589	3,505	3,082	3,303	2,892	3,267	3,676	4,022	3,829	2,988
LT Debt	1,134	1,092	1,295	795	714	1,087	1,074	955	983	885
Common Equity	1,301	796	2,126	1,684	1,867	2,001	1,771	1,926	1,877	1,723
Total Cap.	2,734	2,083	3,725	2,801	2,738	3,854	3,035	3,269	3,273	2,924
Cap. Exp.	423	430	378	375	437	523	378	336	483	418
Cash Flow	841	667	430	738	733	748	310	474	491	424
Curr. Ratio	1.1	0.9	1.1	1.0	1.1	1.2	1.2	1.0	0.9	1.0
% LT Debt of Cap.	41.5	52.4	34.8	28.4	26.1	28.2	35.4	29.3	30.0	30.3
% Net Inc.of Revs.	3.4	2.4	0.3	3.6	3.3	3.0	NM	NM	2.6	1.9
% Ret. on Assets	5.9	3.9	0.5	5.3	4.7	3.8	NM	2.0	2.9	2.5
% Ret. on Equity	40.6	22.8	1.5	20.7	17.9	16.4	NM	8.2	11.6	9.3

Data as orig reptd.; bef. results of disc opers/spec. items. Per share data adj. for stk. divs. Bold denotes primary EPS - prior periods restated. E-Estimated. NA-Not Available. NM-Not Meaningful. NR-Not Ranked. UR-Under Review.

Office: 2000 N M 63, Benton Harbor, MI 49022-2692.
Telephone: 269-923-5000.
Email: info@whirlpool.com
Website: http://www.whirlpool.com
Chrmn & CEO: D.R. Whitwam.
Pres & COO: J.M. Fettig.

EVP & CFO: R.S. Barrett.
Secy: R.T. Kenagy.
Investor Contact: T.C. Filstrup 269-923-3189.
Dirs: G. T. DiCamillo, J. M. Fettig, A. D. Gilmour, K. J. Hempel, M. F. Johnston, J. M. Kilts, A. G. Langbo, M. L. Marsh, P. G. Stern, J. D. Stoney, M. D. White, D. R. Whitwam.

Founded: in 1906.
Domicile: Delaware.
Employees: 68,407.
S&P Analyst: Amy Glynn, CFA /PMW/BK

Williams Companies

Recommendation: **HOLD** ★★★★★
SELL · SELL · HOLD · BUY · BUY

12-Month Target Price: **$15.00**
(as of November 04, 2004)

WMB has an approximate 0.07% weighting in the **S&P 500**

Sector: Energy
Sub-Industry: Oil & Gas Refining, Marketing & Transportation

Summary: WMB's core business segments are exploration and production, midstream gas and liquids, and gas pipeline.

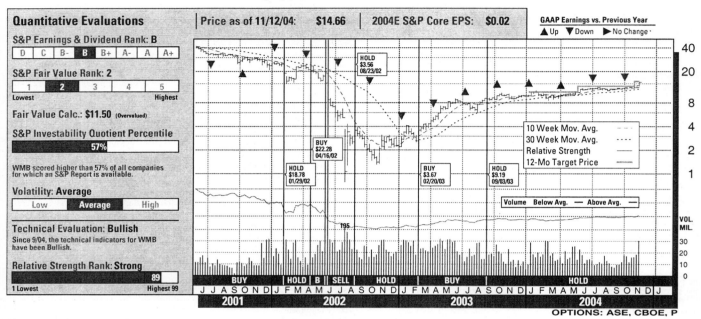

Quantitative Evaluations

S&P Earnings & Dividend Rank: B
| D | C | B- | **B** | B+ | A- | A | A+ |

S&P Fair Value Rank: 2
| 1 | **2** | 3 | 4 | 5 |
Lowest | | | | Highest

Fair Value Calc.: $11.50 (Overvalued)

S&P Investability Quotient Percentile
57%
WMB scored higher than 57% of all companies for which an S&P Report is available.

Volatility: Average
| Low | **Average** | High |

Technical Evaluation: Bullish
Since 9/04, the technical indicators for WMB have been Bullish.

Relative Strength Rank: Strong
89
1 Lowest   Highest 99

Price as of 11/12/04: **$14.66**   2004E S&P Core EPS: **$0.02**

GAAP Earnings vs. Previous Year
▲ Up ▼ Down ► No Change

10 Week Mov. Avg.
30 Week Mov. Avg.
Relative Strength
12-Mo Target Price

Volume Below Avg. — Above Avg.

HOLD $3.56 08/23/02
BUY $22.28 04/16/02
HOLD $18.78 01/29/02
BUY $3.67 02/20/03
HOLD $9.19 09/03/03

OPTIONS: ASE, CBOE, P

Analyst commentary prepared by Craig K. Shere, CFA /GG

Highlights August 18, 2004

- In August, the company projected 2004 segment profits (before corporate overhead, interest and taxes) of $1.1 billion to $1.4 billion, versus reported segment profits of $1.3 billion in 2003. Results in 2003 were aided by $151 million of asset sale gains, net of one-time charges, and contributions from Canadian midstream assets sold in the 2004 third quarter.

- Excluding discontinued Canadian operations, one-time gains and power operations (which WMB is scaling back), we look for a $5 million decrease in segment profit, as lower hedged natural gas prices, the full-year effects of divested production properties, and increasing pipeline unit costs outweigh contributions from new midstream deepwater projects. For 2005, we look for positive segment profit growth, driven by higher natural gas production and realized gas prices. We expect the company to file rate cases for price increases on its pipeline units by the end of 2006.

- Our 2004 operating EPS estimate excludes an estimated $0.09 in net one-time charges (including costs for early debt retirement and asset sale gains). Our 2004 Standard & Poor's Core EPS projection is $0.33 less than our operating EPS estimate, due to the inclusion of net-one time charges to operating businesses and exclusion of asset sale gains.

Investment Rationale/Risk August 18, 2004

- With core cash flows expected to rise, and capital spending declining, reflecting the completion of pipeline and midstream projects, we expect WMB to realize substantial free cash flow over the next few years. Despite improving cash flow, we do not anticipate a dividend increase prior to 2006, in light of the company's desire to pay down debt in an effort to regain an investment-grade credit rating.

- Risks to our recommendation and target price include changes in power margins and natural gas prices, divestitures of power trading contracts, changes in rates for WMB's FERC regulated pipelines, natural gas production growth rates, and changes in credit ratings.

- As a large pipeline company with other operations significantly hedged, we believe WMB should trade in line with the 1.7X average utility price to book multiple (versus a current P/B of 1.5X). We believe this higher multiple will be increasingly achievable as WMB continues to pay down debt with its growing levels of free cash flow after capital expenditures. Our 12-month target price is $13.

Key Stock Statistics

S&P Core EPS 2005E	0.64	52-week Range	$14.75-8.49
S&P Oper. EPS 2004E	0.45	12 Month P/E	NM
P/E on S&P Oper. EPS 2004E	32.6	Beta	1.67
S&P Oper. EPS 2005E	0.65	Shareholders	164,000
Yield (%)	0.3%	Market Cap (B)	$ 8.2
Dividend Rate/Share	0.04	Shares Outstanding (M)	556.5

Value of $10,000 invested five years ago: **NA**

Dividend Data Dividends have been paid since 1974

Amount ($)	Date Decl.	Ex-Div. Date	Stock of Record	Payment Date
0.010	Nov. 20	Dec. 10	Dec. 12	Dec. 29 '03
0.010	Jan. 23	Mar. 10	Mar. 12	Mar. 29 '04
0.010	May. 20	Jun. 09	Jun. 11	Jun. 28 '04
0.010	Jul. 16	Aug. 25	Aug. 27	Sep. 13 '04

Revenues/Earnings Data Fiscal year ending December 31

Revenues (Million $)

	2004	2003	2002	2001	2000	1999
1Q	3,114	4,833	1,622	3,096	2,428	1,944
2Q	3,049	3,657	1,057	2,815	2,859	1,993
3Q	3,373	4,795	1,266	2,805	2,882	2,207
4Q	—	3,549	1,703	2,319	3,229	2,449
Yr.	—	16,834	5,608	11,035	10,398	8,593

Earnings Per Share ($)

	2004	2003	2002	2001	2000	1999
1Q	0.01	-0.09	0.05	0.78	0.27	0.13
2Q	-0.03	0.17	-0.59	0.69	0.78	0.04
3Q	0.03	0.04	-0.35	0.44	0.27	0.06
4Q	E0.15	-0.16	-0.26	-0.20	0.57	0.13
Yr.	E0.45	-0.03	-1.14	1.67	1.95	0.36

Next earnings report expected: mid-February Source: S&P, Company Reports
EPS Estimates based on S&P Operating Earnings; historical GAAP earnings are as reported.

The Williams Companies, Inc.

Recommendation: **HOLD** ★★★☆☆   12-Month Target Price: **$15.00** (as of November 04, 2004)

Business Summary August 18, 2004

The Williams Companies has sought to strengthen its balance sheet in the wake of credit, accounting, regulatory and operating difficulties negatively affecting the energy merchant industry in 2002 and 2003. (The company's credit rating fell to junk status as of July 2002.) In 2003, WMB raised $2.73 billion in cash from the sale of businesses and investments, up from $2.57 billion in 2002 and $408 million in 2001. As of May 2004, the company projected capital spending of $725 million to $825 million for 2004 (down from $957 million in 2003 and $1.67 billion in 2002).

In May 2004, based on reduced capital spending and growing operating cash flow, WMB projected free cash flow after capital expenditures of $700 million to $1 billion through 2005 (excluding a $25 million cash use in the 2004 first quarter). Combined with asset sales of $856 to $956 million (including $356 million in the 2004 first quarter), excess cash on hand, changes in working capital, and expected conversion of $1.1 billion of debt into equity in the 2005 first quarter, the company believes it can cut debt by $4.7 to $5.4 billion in the two years through 2005 (including $711 million of 2004 first quarter debt reduction). If WMB is able to exit its power business, management hopes the company can regain an investment-grade credit rating by about 2006.

Operations include exploration and production (E&P), midstream gas and liquids, gas pipeline, and power. In 2003, excluding power, recurring segment profit was derived 26% from E&P, 26% from midstream, and 48% from pipeline. WMB views E&P as its primary growth segment. With 57% of proved natural gas and oil reserves undeveloped at the end of 2003, E&P believes it has up to 10 years of

low-risk, high-return drilling opportunities. In 2003, WMB drilled 900 gross wells (419 net), with nearly a 99% success rate.

The Midstream division provides natural gas gathering, processing and treating, and natural gas liquid fractionation, storage and marketing. WMB sold its Alaska refinery for $304 million in March 2004, and intends to sell additional Midstream assets before the end of 2004. Midstream's capital spending was expected to drop in 2004, due to the completion of new deepwater drilling and pipeline projects in 2003.

The Gas Pipeline division is the fifth largest owner (by miles) of U.S. interstate pipeline. WMB's nearly 15,000 miles of pipeline include the Transcontinental Gas Pipeline (Transco), Northwest Pipeline, and a 50% ownership interest in the Gulfstream pipeline. Major Transco and Northwest expansion projects were completed in 2003 and early 2004, adding capacity equal to nearly 10% of system deliveries in 2002. In May 2003, the company sold its Texas Gas Pipeline for about $1.05 billion.

In June 2002, the company announced plans to exit the power business. WMB expects the unit's remaining contractual commitments to produce positive free cash flows over time, but believes that its volatility and collateral demands are detrimental to the company's credit profile. In May 2004, WMB said that there had been few qualified bidders for the Power division.

Company Financials Fiscal Year ending December 31

Per Share Data ($)

(Year Ended December 31)	2003	2002	2001	2000	1999	1998	1997	1996	1995	1994
Tangible Bk. Val.	5.96	7.15	9.43	13.26	11.69	8.34	9.35	10.35	9.68	5.15
Cash Flow	1.27	0.53	3.17	3.80	2.04	1.82	2.49	2.35	2.19	1.00
Earnings	-0.03	-1.14	1.67	1.95	0.36	0.32	1.04	1.08	0.93	0.82
S&P Core Earnings	-0.26	-1.34	1.40	NA	NA	NA	NA	NA	NA	NA
Dividends	0.04	0.42	0.68	0.60	0.60	0.60	0.54	0.47	0.36	0.28
Payout Ratio	NM	NM	41%	31%	167%	171%	52%	43%	39%	34%
Prices - High	10.73	26.35	46.44	49.75	53.75	36.93	28.62	19.50	14.83	11.12
- Low	2.51	0.78	20.80	29.50	28.00	20.00	18.12	14.16	8.16	7.37
P/E Ratio - High	NM	NM	28	26	NM	NM	28	18	16	14
- Low	NM	NM	12	15	NM	NM	17	13	9	9

Income Statement Analysis (Million $)

	2003	2002	2001	2000	1999	1998	1997	1996	1995	1994
Revs.	16,834	5,608	11,035	10,398	8,593	7,658	4,410	3,531	2,856	1,751
Oper. Inc.	1,849	1,566	3,389	2,602	1,591	1,372	1,414	1,271	998	465
Depr.	671	775	798	832	742	646	500	411	369	150
Int. Exp.	1,241	1,325	747	1,010	668	515	405	360	278	146
Pretax Inc.	71.0	-617	1,533	1,415	316	247	543	545	401	247
Eff. Tax Rate	51.3%	NM	41.1%	39.1%	51.0%	44.6%	32.8%	33.6%	25.4%	33.1%
Net Inc.	15.2	-502	835	873	162	147	351	362	299	165
S&P Core Earnings	-144	-699	703	NA	NA	NA	NA	NA	NA	NA

Balance Sheet & Other Fin. Data (Million $)

	2003	2002	2001	2000	1999	1998	1997	1996	1995	1994
Cash	2,316	2,019	1,301	1,211	1,092	503	81.3	115	90.0	36.0
Curr. Assets	8,795	12,886	12,938	15,477	6,517	3,532	2,256	1,890	1,344	1,457
Total Assets	27,022	34,989	38,906	40,197	25,289	18,647	13,879	12,419	10,495	5,226
Curr. Liab.	6,270	11,309	13,495	16,804	5,772	4,439	3,027	2,199	2,050	1,474
LT Debt	Nil	11,896	10,621	10,532	9,746	6,366	4,565	4,377	2,874	1,308
Common Equity	4,102	4,778	6,044	5,892	5,585	4,155	3,430	3,260	3,014	1,406
Total Cap.	4,186	20,723	21,532	20,693	18,475	13,193	9,973	9,425	7,456	3,476
Cap. Exp.	957	1,824	1,922	4,904	3,513	1,708	1,162	819	828	326
Cash Flow	657	274	1,633	1,705	901	786	840	763	669	306
Curr. Ratio	1.4	1.1	1.0	0.9	1.1	0.8	0.7	0.9	0.7	1.0
% LT Debt of Cap.	Nil	57.4	49.3	50.9	52.8	48.3	45.8	46.4	38.5	37.6
% Net Inc.of Revs.	0.1	NM	7.6	8.4	1.9	1.9	7.9	10.3	46.1	9.4
% Ret. on Assets	0.0	NM	2.3	2.7	0.7	0.9	2.7	3.2	16.8	3.4
% Ret. on Equity	0.0	NM	14.0	15.2	3.3	3.7	10.2	11.2	13.5	11.0

Data as orig reptd.; bef. results of disc opers/spec. items. Per share data adj. for stk. divs.; EPS diluted. E-Estimated. NA-Not Available. NM-Not Meaningful. NR-Not Ranked. UR-Under Review.

Office: 1 Williams Ctr, Tulsa, OK 74172-0140.
Telephone: 918-573-2000.
Website: http://www.williams.com
Chrmn, Pres & CEO: S.J. Malcolm:
SVP & CFO: D. Chappel.
SVP & General Counsel: J.J. Bender.

Treas: T. Campbell.
Investor Contact: A. Oliver 800-600-3782.
Dirs: H. M. Chapman, T. H. Cruikshank, W. E. Green, W. R. Howell, C. M. Lillis, G. A. Lorch, W. G. Lowrie, F. T. Macinnis, S. J. Malcolm, J. D. Stoney, J. H. Williams.

Founded: in 1908.
Domicile: Delaware.
Employees: 6,619.
S&P Analyst: Craig K. Shere, CFA /GG

Winn-Dixie Stores

Recommendation: **HOLD** ★★★☆☆
SELL SELL HOLD BUY BUY

12-Month Target Price: **$3.50**
(as of October 20, 2004)

WIN has an approximate 0.01% weighting in the **S&P 500**

Sector: Consumer Staples
Sub-Industry: Food Retail
Peer Group: Food Chain Cos. - Large

Summary: Jacksonville, FL-based Winn-Dixie Stores is one of the largest supermarket operators in the highly competitive Sunbelt.

Quantitative Evaluations

S&P Earnings & Dividend Rank: B

| D | C | B- | **B** | B+ | A- | A | A+ |

S&P Fair Value Rank: NR

| 1 | 2 | 3 | 4 | 5 |
Lowest   Highest

Fair Value Calc.: NA

S&P Investability Quotient Percentile
92%

WIN scored higher than 92% of all companies for which an S&P Report is available.

Volatility: High

| Low | Average | **High** |

Technical Evaluation: Neutral
Since 11/04, the technical indicators for WIN have been Neutral.

Relative Strength Rank: Weak
23
1 Lowest   Highest 99

| Price as of 11/12/04: | $4.07 | 2005E S&P Core EPS: | $-2.46 |

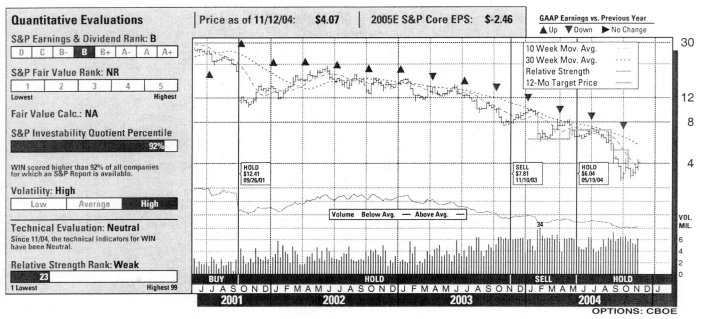

GAAP Earnings vs. Previous Year ▲ Up ▼ Down ▶ No Change

- 10 Week Mov. Avg.
- 30 Week Mov. Avg.
- Relative Strength
- 12-Mo Target Price

HOLD $12.41 09/26/01   SELL $7.81 11/10/03   HOLD $6.04 05/19/04

Volume   Below Avg. — Above Avg.

BUY   HOLD   SELL   HOLD
J J A S O N D J F M A M J J A S O N D J F M A M J J A S O N D J F M A M J J A S O N D J
2001   2002   2003   2004

OPTIONS: CBOE

Analyst commentary prepared by Joseph Agnese/PMW/JWP

Highlights October 22, 2004

- We expect total sales to decline in the low single digits in FY 05 (Jun.), on negative comparable-store sales growth and lost sales due to store disruptions as the company implements a store remodelling strategy. Remodeling efforts are focusing on increasing average customer transaction size by improving the company's perishables business. Overall, we believe benefits from remodeling will not be felt until FY 06. Meanwhile, we expect increased competitor store openings and more intense industry pricing competition to restrict revenue growth in FY 05.

- We think gross margins will narrow. We believe lower pricing will outweigh improved shrink-reduction efforts and greater efficiencies achieved through enhanced centralized procurement processes. However, we see operating margins benefiting from a reduction of about 10,000 in WIN's workforce, as part of an asset rationalization plan. Also as part of the plan, the company expects to generate significant savings via improved buying practices and renegotiated service contracts.

- With interest expense expected to decline, due to lower debt levels, we see an FY 05 operating loss of $0.24 a share, versus an operating loss of $0.26 a share in FY 04.

Investment Rationale/Risk October 22, 2004

- We would hold existing positions. The company recently began to make significant investments in pricing and promotions in an effort to achieve comparable-store sales growth. Reacting to lower than expected sales and EPS growth, WIN also began to rationalize non-core assets, focusing on maintaining share and revitalizing stores in its core markets. We do not believe the company's major remodeling strategy will guarantee revenue gains, as we believe that WIN operates in a highly competitive environment in which more than 70% of its stores compete head to head with Wal-Mart (WMT: accumulate, $52), but we believe these strategic initiatives will lead to a stronger competitive position and improve growth prospects for the longer term.

- Risks to our opinion and target price include potential liquidity problems, as the company continues to operate with negative free cash flow in an increasingly competitive environment.

- Our 12-month target price of $3.50 is based on our enterprise value to EBITDA analysis. Applying a multiple of 4.5X to 5.0X to our FY 06 EBITDA estimate of $150 million and subtracting our estimated debt value of $300 million, we arrive at an average equity value of $3.50 a share.

Key Stock Statistics

S&P Oper. EPS 2005E	-0.24	52-week Range	$10.10-2.97
P/E on S&P Oper. EPS 2005E	NM	12 Month P/E	NM
S&P Oper. EPS 2006E	-0.10	Beta	0.49
Yield (%)	Nil	Shareholders	36,868
Dividend Rate/Share	Nil	Market Cap (B)	$0.579
Shares Outstanding (M)	142.2		

Value of $10,000 invested five years ago: **$ 1,497**

Dividend Data Dividends have been paid since 1934

Amount ($)	Date Decl.	Ex-Div. Date	Stock of Record	Payment Date
0.050	Oct. 20	Oct. 30	Nov. 03	Nov. 17 '03
0.050	Jan. 20	Jan. 29	Feb. 02	Feb. 17 '04

Revenues/Earnings Data Fiscal year ending June 30

Revenues (Million $)

	2005	2004	2003	2002	2001	2000
1Q	2,337	2,419	2,833	2,808	2,941	3,162
2Q	—	3,228	3,786	3,768	3,956	3,060
3Q	—	2,428	2,822	2,902	3,016	3,199
4Q	—	2,558	2,727	2,857	2,990	3,060
Yr.	—	10,633	12,168	12,334	12,903	13,698

Earnings Per Share ($)

	2005	2004	2003	2002	2001	2000
1Q	-0.88	0.04	0.25	0.22	0.07	0.15
2Q	E-0.07	-0.47	0.65	0.30	0.09	-1.70
3Q	E-0.07	0.08	0.36	0.38	0.08	0.07
4Q	E-0.02	-0.01	0.44	0.37	0.09	-1.70
Yr.	E-0.24	-0.36	1.70	1.35	0.32	-1.57

Next earnings report expected: late-January Source: S&P, Company Reports
EPS Estimates based on S&P Operating Earnings; historical GAAP earnings are as reported.

Winn-Dixie Stores, Inc.

Recommendation: **HOLD** ★ ★ ★ ☆ ☆   12-Month Target Price: **$3.50** (as of October 20, 2004)

Business Summary October 22, 2004

Winn-Dixie is one of the largest U.S. food retailers in terms of supermarket sales. The company's operating strategy focuses on maintaining low-price leadership by offering high-quality food and variety at the lowest possible prices. At the end of FY 04 (Jun.), WIN operated 1,049 stores in 12 U.S. states and the Bahamas.

The company is currently in the process of exiting, either by sale or closure, stores located in market areas that it has designated as non-core. The total number of core stores operated at the end of FY 04 was 947, distributed as follows: Florida (440), Alabama (112), Georgia (96), North Carolina (92), Louisiana (78), Mississippi (60), South Carolina (50), Tennessee (7), the Bahamas (12), and Indiana (1). Stores operated under the names Winn-Dixie and Winn-Dixie Market-place banners.

WIN's stores averaged 44,600 sq. ft.. Total retail space at the end of FY 04 totaled 46.8, down from 47.6 million sq. ft in FY 03. In FY 04, the company opened 11 new stores, enlarged or remodeled 48 and implemented an image makeover in 331. Over 57% of total stores have been opened, enlarged, remodeled, or made over in the past five years.

Store sales in FY 04 totaled $10.6 billion, down 3.6% from those of FY 03, reflecting increased competition from other retail formats, a de-emphasis of certain limited aspect of its promotional program on advertised special offers and price reductions without a corresponding increase in volumes. In FY 04, average store sales declined 5.7%; identical-store sales (for stores open for the full fiscal year, including enlargements) decreased 6.0%; and comparable-store sales (including

replacement stores) were down 5.9%. Gross profits narrowed to 26.4% of sales, from 28.4%, primarily due to the implementation of price reductions. Operating and administrative expenses increased to 26.7% of sales, from 25.7%, reflecting increased advertising, utility and occupancy costs.

The company is developing and pursuing five strategic initiatives announced in FY 04. These initiatives include asset rationalization, expense reductions, and three brand-related initiatives. WIN aims to refocus on the core markets that it thinks offer the best opportunities for success, and to locate and exit non-core markets in which it has low market share and limited opportunities to gain share. Core markets are generally those in which the company holds the first, second or third market share position. As part of its plan, WIN will exit a total of 156 stores. During the FY 04 fourth quarter, the company began to exit these stores through sale or closure. In addition, WIN plans to exit three of its 14 distribution centers, and all of its manufacturing operations.

As part of WIN's three strategic brand-related initiatives, the company plans to improve in-store customer service, implement an image makeover program for its stores, and improve its brand positioning. WIN is implementing these initiatives in a lead market of 92 stores in the Miami-Ft. Lauderdale market area. The lead market program is designed to test and refine the company's new approach, and to measure its impact on a smaller scale before moving ahead with the program throughout core markets. WIN anticipates that all stores in its lead market will include these new programs and offerings by March 2005.

Company Financials Fiscal Year ending June 30

Per Share Data ($)

(Year Ended June 30)	2004	2003	2002	2001	2000	1999	1998	1997	1996	1995
Tangible Bk. Val.	5.85	6.68	5.15	4.83	6.03	9.50	9.19	8.97	8.84	8.17
Cash Flow	0.84	5.16	2.60	1.63	0.19	3.18	3.55	3.30	3.30	2.89
Earnings	-0.36	1.70	1.35	0.32	-1.57	1.23	1.33	1.36	1.69	1.56
S&P Core Earnings	-0.34	1.46	1.29	0.32	NA	NA	NA	NA	NA	NA
Dividends	0.15	0.20	0.36	1.02	1.02	1.02	1.02	0.96	0.89	0.78
Payout Ratio	NM	12%	26%	NM	NM	83%	77%	71%	53%	50%
Prices - High	10.10	16.65	20.40	33.12	24.75	46.68	62.81	44.00	39.00	37.62
- Low	2.97	7.50	11.71	10.22	13.43	22.31	28.62	29.87	31.00	25.56
P/E Ratio - High	NM	10	15	NM	NM	38	47	32	23	24
- Low	NM	4	9	32	NM	18	22	22	18	16

Income Statement Analysis (Million $)

	2004	2003	2002	2001	2000	1999	1998	1997	1996	1995
Revs.	10,633	12,168	12,334	12,903	13,698	14,137	13,617	13,219	12,955	11,788
Oper. Inc.	139	475	542	457	287	499	579	513	538	463
Depr.	169	166	176	184	257	292	330	291	247	201
Int. Exp.	14.4	40.4	57.8	52.8	47.1	30.0	28.0	22.0	21.0	14.3
Pretax Inc.	-87.5	641	308	73.6	-302	296	318	319	387	354
Eff. Tax Rate	NM	12.7%	38.5%	38.5%	NM	38.5%	37.4%	36.1%	34.1%	34.4%
Net Inc.	-50.8	560	190	45.3	-229	182	199	204	256	232
S&P Core Earnings	-48.3	205	182	45.3	NA	NA	NA	NA	NA	NA

Balance Sheet & Other Fin. Data (Million $)

	2004	2003	2002	2001	2000	1999	1998	1997	1996	1995
Cash	76.1	147	246	121	29.6	25.0	24.0	14.1	32.0	30.4
Curr. Assets	1,351	1,473	1,638	1,599	1,472	1,798	1,736	1,588	1,501	1,456
Total Assets	2,619	2,790	2,938	3,042	2,747	3,149	3,069	2,921	2,649	2,483
Curr. Liab.	939	1,019	1,110	1,150	1,422	1,547	1,507	1,393	1,112	1,030
LT Debt	314	332	565	726	32.2	38.0	49.0	54.0	54.0	78.0
Common Equity	1,198	1,270	812	1,064	1,164	1,412	1,369	1,337	1,343	1,241
Total Cap.	1,512	1,602	1,378	1,790	1,196	1,450	1,418	1,391	1,404	1,319
Cap. Exp.	204	177	83.5	313	214	346	370	423	362	372
Cash Flow	118	726	365	229	27.8	474	529	495	503	433
Curr. Ratio	1.4	1.4	1.5	1.4	1.0	1.2	1.2	1.1	1.4	1.4
% LT Debt of Cap.	20.8	20.7	41.0	40.6	2.7	2.6	3.5	3.9	4.3	5.9
% Net Inc.of Revs.	NM	4.6	1.5	0.4	NM	1.3	1.5	1.5	2.0	2.0
% Ret. on Assets	NM	19.6	6.3	1.6	NM	5.9	6.6	7.3	10.0	10.0
% Ret. on Equity	NM	48.2	23.9	4.1	NM	13.1	14.7	15.2	19.9	20.2

Data as orig reptd.; bef. results of disc opers/spec. items. Per share data adj. for stk. divs.; EPS diluted. E-Estimated. NA-Not Available. NM-Not Meaningful. NR-Not Ranked. UR-Under Review.

Office: 5050 Edgewood Court, Jacksonville, FL 32254-3601.
Telephone: 904-783-5000.
Website: http://www.winn-dixie.com
Pres & CEO: F. Lazaran.
SVP, CFO & Investor Contact: R. McCook 904-783-5000.

SVP & General Counsel: L.B. Appel.
VP & Chief Acctg Officer: D.M. Byrum.
VP & Treas: K.D. Hardee.
Dirs: J. Anderson, J. Dasburg, T. W. Davis, T. K. Fowler, E. Mehrer, Jr., J. B. North, C. T. Rider, H. J. Skelton, C. P. Stephens, R. Townsend.

Founded: in 1928.
Domicile: Florida.
Employees: 89,000.
S&P Analyst: Joseph Agnese/PMW/JWP

Worthington Industries

Recommendation: HOLD ★★★☆☆   12-Month Target Price: **$23.00**
SELL SELL HOLD BUY BUY   (as of September 22, 2004)

WOR has an approximate 0.02% weighting in the **S&P 500**

Sector: Materials
Sub-Industry: Steel
Peer Group: Steel Distribution and Processing

Summary: WOR is the largest U.S. processor of close-tolerance steel.

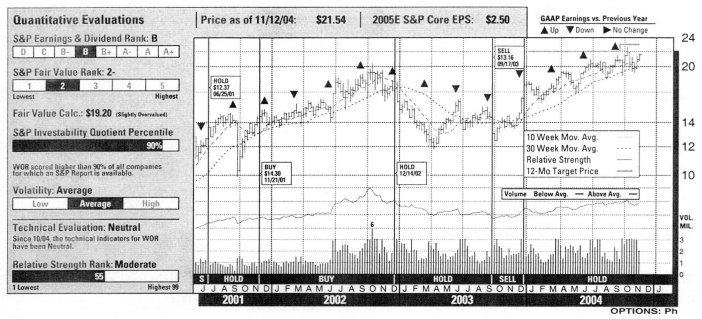

Quantitative Evaluations

S&P Earnings & Dividend Rank: B

| D | C | B- | B | B+ | A- | A | A+ |

S&P Fair Value Rank: 2-

| 1 | 2 | 3 | 4 | 5 |
Lowest ... Highest

Fair Value Calc.: $19.20 (Slightly Overvalued)

S&P Investability Quotient Percentile
90%

WOR scored higher than 90% of all companies for which an S&P Report is available.

Volatility: Average
| Low | Average | High |

Technical Evaluation: Neutral
Since 10/04, the technical indicators for WOR have been Neutral.

Relative Strength Rank: Moderate
55
1 Lowest ... Highest 99

Price as of 11/12/04: $21.54   2005E S&P Core EPS: $2.50

GAAP Earnings vs. Previous Year
▲ Up ▼ Down ▶ No Change

Chart legend:
- 10 Week Mov. Avg.
- 30 Week Mov. Avg.
- Relative Strength
- 12-Mo Target Price

Volume Below Avg. — Above Avg.

Annotations: HOLD $12.37 06/25/01 · BUY $14.30 11/21/01 · HOLD 12/14/02 · SELL $13.16 09/17/03

OPTIONS: Ph

Analyst commentary prepared by Leo J. Larkin/CB/JWP

Highlights September 23, 2004

- Following an increase of 7.2% in FY 04 (May), we see FY 05 sales, excluding the acquisition of the cylinder assets of Western Industries, up approximately 40%. Our forecast assumes 4.3% GDP growth in calendar 2004 and 3.4% growth in calendar 2005 and higher prices in steel processing and metal framing. We also anticipate flat North American automotive output in calendar 2004, after a 3.1% drop in calendar 2003. We see the automotive output cut as the main reason for WOR's meager 2.2% FY 04 sales rise in the processed steel products segment. We also expect a pickup in demand from the construction industry, boosting metal framing. We see pressure cylinder sales flat to up slightly, excluding acquisitions. Aided by higher capacity utilization, merger savings in metal framing and the divestment of the money-losing Decatur plant, we expect FY 05 operating profit to rise. Further aided by a large gain in equity income, FY 05 EPS should post a sizable gain.

- For the longer term, we see EPS benefiting from market share gains in steel processing and metal framing.

- According to statistics compiled by Ward's Automotive, North American vehicle production increased 1.2% in the first eight months of 2004. For all of 2003, North American vehicle production fell 3.1%.

Investment Rationale/Risk September 23, 2004

- We view WOR shares as worth holding as a play on the expansion in the economy, for consolidation in the steel processing and metal framing industries and for current income. As we anticipate a large EPS gain in FY 05, we believe the current dividend is sustainable. Following a much stronger than expected first quarter, we increased our FY 05 estimate to $2.50 from $1.80. Nevertheless, given that we expect FY 05 to represent peak or near peak EPS, we would not add to holdings.

- The main risk to our recommendation and target price is lower than expected EPS due to unanticipated weakness in WOR's end markets or to a failure to achieve merger savings in metal framing. Another risk is that the recent acquisition of Western Industries' cylinder assets could prove dilutive. Lower EPS combined with rising capital spending could strain the dividend given that free cash flow has just barely covered the dividend in recent years.

- Our 12-month target price is $23, which assumes that the stock will trade at a P/E multiple of 9X, at the low end of its historical range for the past 10 years. We believe the P/E will be low given the possibility that FY 05 could represent peak EPS.

Key Stock Statistics

S&P Oper. EPS 2005E	2.25	52-week Range	$22.73-13.45
P/E on S&P Oper. EPS 2005E	9.6	12 Month P/E	13.6
Yield (%)	3.0%	Beta	0.69
Dividend Rate/Share	0.64	Shareholders	8,718
Shares Outstanding (M)	87.6	Market Cap (B)	$ 1.9

Value of $10,000 invested five years ago: **$ 16,105**

Dividend Data Dividends have been paid since 1968

Amount ($)	Date Decl.	Ex-Div. Date	Stock of Record	Payment Date
0.160	Nov. 20	Dec. 11	Dec. 15	Dec. 29 '03
0.160	Feb. 19	Mar. 11	Mar. 15	Mar. 29 '04
0.160	May. 24	Jun. 14	Jun. 15	Jun. 29 '04
0.160	Aug. 19	Sep. 13	Sep. 15	Sep. 29 '04

Revenues/Earnings Data Fiscal year ending May 31

Revenues (Million $)

	2005	2004	2003	2002	2001	2000
1Q	769.3	498.0	525.5	409.6	484.2	462.9
2Q	—	540.1	567.9	410.4	457.4	473.3
3Q	—	558.1	536.6	405.7	418.7	486.5
4Q	—	782.9	590.0	519.3	465.8	539.8
Yr.	—	2,379	2,220	1,745	1,826	1,963

Earnings Per Share ($)

	2005	2004	2003	2002	2001	2000
1Q	0.66	0.07	0.32	0.17	0.15	0.27
2Q	E0.50	0.20	0.24	0.13	0.08	0.28
3Q	E0.40	0.28	0.13	-0.53	0.02	0.26
4Q	E0.69	0.45	0.18	0.31	0.17	0.25
Yr.	E2.25	1.00	0.87	0.08	0.42	1.06

Next earnings report expected: mid-December Source: S&P, Company Reports
EPS Estimates based on S&P Operating Earnings; historical GAAP earnings are as reported.

STANDARD &POOR'S

Worthington Industries, Inc.

Stock Report
November 13, 2004
NYSE Symbol: **WOR**

Recommendation: HOLD ★ ★ ★ ☆ ☆ 12-Month Target Price: **$23.00** (as of September 22, 2004)

Business Summary September 23, 2004

Worthington Industries is the largest U.S. processor of close-tolerance steel, and a manufacturer of metal products.

The Steel Processing Products segment, which provided 58% of sales and $18 million of operating profit in FY 04 (May), is comprised of two businesses: Worthington Steel Co. and Gerstenslager Co., both of which are intermediate processors of flat-rolled steel.

WOR buys coils of wide, open-tolerance sheet steel from major steel mills, and processes them to the orders of more than 1,000 industrial customers in the automotive, appliance, electrical, machinery, communication, leisure time and other industries. Its processing capabilities include picking, slitting, rolling, annealing, edging, tension leveling, cut-to-length, configured blanking, painting, nickel plating and hot dipped galvanizing. The company's competitors in steel processing are Shiloh Industries, Gibraltar Steel, Steel Technologies, Olympic Steel, Ryerson Tull, Friedman Industries, and Huntco Inc. Shipments totaled 3,806,000 tons in FY 04, versus 3,890,000 tons in FY 03.

Gerstenslager Co. manufactures automotive after-market body panels for the U.S. market. Major customers include domestic and transplant automotive and heavy duty truck manufacturers.

Metal Framing (28% of sales, $63.8 million of operating profit) consists of Dietrich Industries, Inc., which makes metal framing products for the commercial and residential building industries. Major customers include building products distribu-

tors, commercial and residential contractors, and gypsum producers. Shipments totaled 781,000 tons in FY 04, versus 694,000 tons in FY 03.

Pressure Cylinders (14% of sales, $29.4 million of operating profit) consists of Worthington Cylinders Corp. This business produces disposable and reusable steel and aluminum cylinders, sold primarily to producers and distributors of refrigerant gases, and refillable steel and aluminum cylinders, used to hold liquefied petroleum gas. Unit shipments were 14,670,000 units in FY 04, versus 15,235,000 units in FY 03.

As part of a strategy to selectively develop new products, markets and technological capabilities, while expanding its international presence, WOR participates in four consolidated joint ventures (Spartan Steel Coating, L.L.C., Worthington S.A., Worthington Tank, Ltda., and Worthington Gastec, a.s.) and four unconsolidated joint ventures (Worthington Armstrong, Worthington Specialty Processing, TWB Co., and Acerex S.A. de C.V.). Equity income in FY 04 totaled $41.1 million, versus $30.0 million in FY 03.

On September 20, 2004, WOR announced that it had completed the purchase, for $64.5 million, of the propane and specialty gas cylinder assets of Western Industries, Inc. The propane and specialty gas cylinder group manufactures cylinders for hand torches, camping stoves, portable heaters and table top grills. WOR expects the acquistion to be modestly accretive in the first year.

Company Financials Fiscal Year ending May 31

Per Share Data ($)

(Year Ended May 31)	2004	2003	2002	2001	2000	1999	1998	1997	1996	1995
Tangible Bk. Val.	6.48	6.04	6.21	6.67	6.92	7.18	7.08	6.38	6.32	6.49
Cash Flow	1.77	1.67	0.88	1.24	1.86	1.74	1.48	1.50	1.44	1.66
Earnings	1.00	0.87	0.08	0.42	1.06	0.90	0.85	0.97	1.01	1.29
S&P Core Earnings	0.95	0.79	0.01	0.39	NA	NA	NA	NA	NA	NA
Dividends	0.64	0.64	0.64	0.60	0.59	0.56	0.52	0.36	0.56	0.40
Payout Ratio	64%	74%	NM	143%	56%	62%	61%	37%	55%	31%

Cal. Yrs.	2003	2002	2001	2000	1999	1998	1997	1996	1995	1994
Prices - High	18.23	20.40	15.24	17.00	17.68	19.56	22.00	22.50	23.25	23.50
- Low	11.80	13.50	7.62	6.37	11.06	10.37	15.12	17.50	16.62	17.50
P/E Ratio - High	18	23	NM	40	17	22	26	23	23	18
- Low	12	16	NM	15	10	12	18	18	16	14

Income Statement Analysis (Million $)

	2004	2003	2002	2001	2000	1999	1998	1997	1996	1995
Revs.	2,379	2,220	1,745	1,826	1,963	1,763	1,624	1,912	1,478	1,484
Oper. Inc.	247	190	168	142	240	225	197	206	166	188
Depr.	67.3	69.4	68.9	70.6	71.0	78.5	61.5	51.4	39.2	34.1
Int. Exp.	22.2	24.8	22.7	33.4	39.8	43.1	25.6	18.4	8.35	6.04
Pretax Inc.	127	118	10.2	56.0	151	133	131	151	148	187
Eff. Tax Rate	31.9%	36.5%	36.5%	36.5%	37.5%	37.0%	37.0%	38.0%	38.1%	37.5%
Net Inc.	86.8	75.2	6.50	35.6	94.2	83.6	82.3	93.3	91.3	117
S&P Core Earnings	83.6	67.3	0.83	33.5	NA	NA	NA	NA	NA	NA

Balance Sheet & Other Fin. Data (Million $)

	2004	2003	2002	2001	2000	1999	1998	1997	1996	1995
Cash	1.98	1.14	0.50	0.19	0.54	7.64	3.79	7.20	19.0	2.00
Curr. Assets	833	506	490	450	624	624	643	594	476	452
Total Assets	1,643	1,478	1,457	1,476	1,674	1,687	1,842	1,561	1,220	917
Curr. Liab.	475	318	339	307	433	428	410	247	151	179
LT Debt	288	290	289	309	362	366	440	450	299	53.5
Common Equity	680	636	606	650	673	690	780	716	640	590
Total Cap.	1,115	1,110	1,085	1,150	1,215	1,228	1,407	1,296	1,052	720
Cap. Exp.	29.6	25.0	39.1	62.9	71.5	108	309	173	109	61.5
Cash Flow	154	145	75.4	106	165	162	144	145	131	151
Curr. Ratio	1.8	1.6	1.4	1.5	1.4	1.5	1.6	2.4	3.1	2.5
% LT Debt of Cap.	25.9	26.1	26.6	26.9	29.8	29.8	31.3	34.8	28.4	7.4
% Net Inc.of Revs.	3.6	3.4	0.4	1.9	4.8	4.7	5.1	4.9	6.2	7.9
% Ret. on Assets	5.6	5.1	0.4	2.3	5.6	4.7	4.8	6.6	8.5	13.6
% Ret. on Equity	13.2	12.1	1.0	5.4	13.8	11.4	11.0	13.5	14.8	21.3

Data as orig reptd.; bef. results of disc opers/spec. items. Per share data adj. for stk. divs.; EPS diluted. E-Estimated. NA-Not Available. NM-Not Meaningful. NR-Not Ranked. UR-Under Review.

Office: 200 Old Wilson Bridge Rd, Columbus, OH 43085-4769.
Telephone: 614-438-3210.
Website: http://www.worthingtonindustries.com
Chrmn & CEO: J.P. McConnell.
Pres & CFO: J.S. Christie.
VP, Secy & General Counsel: D.T. Brinkman.

Treas: R.I. Rombeiro.
Investor Contact: A.M. Sanders 614-840-3133.
Dirs: J. B. Blystone, J. S. Christie, W. S. Dietrich, II, M. J. Endres, P. Karmanos, Jr., J. R. Kasich, J. H. McConnell, S. A. Ribeau, M. F. Schiavo.

Founded: in 1955.
Domicile: Ohio.
Employees: 6,700.
S&P Analyst: Leo J. Larkin/CB/JWP

Wrigley (Wm.) Jr.

Recommendation: **BUY** ★★★★★
SELL | SELL | HOLD | BUY | BUY

12-Month Target Price: **$78.00**
(as of November 15, 2004)

WWY has an approximate 0.14% weighting in the **S&P 500**

Sector: Consumer Staples
Sub-Industry: Packaged Foods & Meats
Peer Group: Larger Food Manufacturers

Summary: This company is the world's largest producer of chewing gum, with approximately 60% of the U.S. market. The Wrigley family controls 51% of the supervoting Class B stock.

Quantitative Evaluations

S&P Earnings & Dividend Rank: A+

D	C	B-	B	B+	A-	A	A+

S&P Fair Value Rank: 2

1	2	3	4	5
Lowest				Highest

Fair Value Calc.: $61.40 (Slightly Overvalued)

S&P Investability Quotient Percentile

100%

WWY scored higher than 100% of all companies for which an S&P Report is available.

Volatility: Low

Low	Average	High

Technical Evaluation: Bullish
Since 10/04, the technical indicators for WWY have been Bullish.

Relative Strength Rank: Moderate

	60	
1 Lowest		Highest 99

Price as of 11/15/04:	$68.08	2004E S&P Core EPS:	$2.16

GAAP Earnings vs. Previous Year
▲ Up ▼ Down ► No Change

BUY
$60.25
07/28/04

10 Week Mov. Avg.
30 Week Mov. Avg.
Relative Strength
12-Mo Target Price

Volume Below Avg. — Above Avg.

HOLD | BUY

J J A S O N D J F M A M J J A S O N D J F M A M J J A S O N D J F M A M J J A S O N D J
2001 **2002** **2003** **2004**

OPTIONS: ASE

Analyst commentary prepared by Richard Joy/MF/BK

Highlights July 30, 2004

- We expect net sales to increase more than 15% in 2004, reflecting worldwide volume gains, product mix improvements, favorable foreign exchange and contributions from certain confectionery businesses acquired in April 2004 from Joyco Group, a subsidiary of privately held Spanish food conglomerate Agrilomen. We believe new products should help North American sales advance at a high single digit rate in 2004, while we expect international sales growth of more than 20% on contributions from Joyco and strong volume gains in Eastern Europe, Russia and Asia. We see gross margins benefiting from modestly higher prices and an improved product mix, though likely restricted somewhat by the inclusion of Joyco sales and costs from new product introductions. An increase in advertising and promotional spending to support new gum products will likely be in line with sales growth.

- Following modest share repurchases, we expect EPS to grow 12% in 2004, to $2.22, from $1.98 in 2003. For 2005, we expect EPS to grow 12% to $2.48. For the longer term, we project annual EPS growth of 10% to 12%.

- Our 2004 and 2005 Standard & Poor's Core Earnings per share projections, reflecting estimated stock option expense of $0.06 per share and a modest pension adjustment, are $2.16 and $2.42, respectively.

Investment Rationale/Risk July 30, 2004

- We believe the shares are attractive, in light of our view of WWY's relatively high and improving operating profitability, clean balance sheet, dominant and growing U.S. market share (about 60%), and impressive global distribution infrastructure. Volume and earnings growth has been strong in recent quarters, reflecting successful new product introductions and strong international growth. Free cash flow continues to grow, and will likely continue to fund niche acquisitions and share repurchases. Recently trading at a P/E multiple of approximately 24X our 2005 EPS estimate, a premium to the S&P 500 and to those of other packaged food companies, but at the low end of WWY's historical range, we believe the shares are undervalued.

- Risks to our recommendation and target price include competitive pressures in WWY's markets, consumer acceptance of new product introductions and foreign currency movements.

- Our analysis of discounted cash flows, using a weighted average cost of capital of 8.5%, suggests an intrinsic value for the shares in the high $60s to low $70s. We have a 12-month target price of $69, which is derived from our analysis of peers and our discounted free cash flow model.

Key Stock Statistics

S&P Core EPS 2005E	2.42	52-week Range	$67.92-54.44
S&P Oper. EPS 2004E	2.22	12 Month P/E	31.5
P/E on S&P Oper. EPS 2004E	30.3	Beta	0.06
S&P Oper. EPS 2005E	2.50	Shareholders	40,379
Yield (%)	1.4%	Market Cap (B)	$ 13.0
Dividend Rate/Share	0.94	Shares Outstanding (M)	224.4

Value of $10,000 invested five years ago: **$ 18,168**

Dividend Data Dividends have been paid since 1913

Amount ($)	Date Decl.	Ex-Div. Date	Stock of Record	Payment Date
0.235	Jan. 28	Apr. 13	Apr. 15	May. 03 '04
0.235	May. 25	Jul. 13	Jul. 15	Aug. 02 '04
0.235	Aug. 18	Oct. 13	Oct. 15	Nov. 01 '04
0.235	Oct. 26	Jan. 12	Jan. 14	Feb. 01 '05

Revenues/Earnings Data Fiscal year ending December 31

Revenues (Million $)

	2004	2003	2002	2001	2000	1999
1Q	812.1	672.4	599.0	561.6	507.0	484.9
2Q	957.9	792.6	708.5	623.9	574.4	537.4
3Q	916.7	782.9	699.5	597.5	539.4	512.7
4Q	—	821.2	739.3	646.6	524.9	544.1
Yr.	—	3,069	2,746	2,430	2,146	2,079

Earnings Per Share ($)

	2004	2003	2002	2001	2000	1999
1Q	0.49	0.43	0.38	0.36	0.33	0.30
2Q	0.62	0.56	0.49	0.44	0.41	0.38
3Q	0.56	0.50	0.44	0.41	0.37	0.34
4Q	E0.55	0.49	0.48	0.40	0.35	0.32
Yr.	E2.22	1.98	1.78	1.61	1.45	1.33

Next earnings report expected: late-January Source: S&P, Company Reports
EPS Estimates based on S&P Operating Earnings; historical GAAP earnings are as reported.

Wm. Wrigley Jr. Company

Recommendation: **BUY** ★★★★★   12-Month Target Price: **$78.00** (as of November 15, 2004)

Business Summary July 30, 2004

Since 1891, Wrigley has concentrated its operations essentially on one line of business: the manufacture and marketing of chewing gum. The company is the world's largest gum manufacturer, accounting for more than 40% of total chewing gum sales volume worldwide. Principal products include Wrigley's Spearmint, Doublemint, Juicy Fruit, Big Red, Winterfresh and Extra. Other products include Airwaves, Freedent, Ice White, Orbit, P.K. and Hubba Bubba (bubble gum). Chewing gum and other confectionery products account for over 90% of total worldwide sales and earnings.

Finished gum is manufactured in four factories in the U.S. and 11 factories in other countries. Three wholly owned associated domestic companies also manufacture products other than finished chewing gum: L. A. Dreyfus Co. produces chewing gum base for Wrigley and other customers; Northwestern Flavors, Inc., processes flavorings and rectifies mint oil for Wrigley and ingredients for other food-related industries; and The Wrico Packaging division produces a large portion of the company's domestic printed and other wrapping supplies.

The Amurol Confections subsidiary, which manufactures and markets children's bubble gum items (Big League Chew, Bubble Tape) and other uniquely packaged confections, also includes various non-gum items, such as a line of suckers, dextrose candy, liquid gel candy, and hard roll candies as an important part of its total business. Amurol is also developing export markets, with the largest currently being Canada, Brazil and Japan.

By geographic area, sales contributions in 2003 were: Americas, consisting of the U.S., Canada and Latin America, 39%; the EMEAI region, consisting of Europe, the Middle East, Africa and India, 47%; Asia, 11%; and the Pacific, 3%. In alphabetical order, WWY's 10 largest markets outside of the U.S. in 2003 were Australia, Canada, China, France, Germany, Poland, Russia, Spain, Taiwan, and the U.K. WWY brands are sold in more than 150 countries and territories. Asia is the company's fastest growing region.

New products accounted for 17% of sales in 2003, down from 23% in 2002 and 20% in 2001. In addition to new flavors and product line extensions, several new products deliver benefits including breath freshening, tooth whitening, oral care, vitamin delivery, as well as sore throat and cough relief. These increasingly sophisticated products are consistent with the company's strategy of boosting the core chewing gum business, while also improving profitability.

The chewing gum business is an intensely competitive one in the U.S. and most international markets. The company estimates that there are approximately 14 U.S. chewing gum manufacturers, with Wrigley brands accounting for about 60% of total domestic chewing gum product unit sales. Principal U.S. competitors are the Adams Confections division of Cadbury Schweppes, and Hershey Foods Corporation.

Company Financials Fiscal Year ending December 31

Per Share Data ($)

(Year Ended December 31)	2003	2002	2001	2000	1999	1998	1997	1996	1995	1994
Tangible Bk. Val.	8.10	6.77	5.67	2.51	4.98	4.98	4.25	3.87	3.44	2.96
Cash Flow	2.52	2.16	1.91	1.70	1.59	1.55	1.39	1.20	1.16	1.17
Earnings	1.98	1.78	1.61	1.45	1.33	1.32	1.17	0.99	0.97	0.99
S&P Core Earnings	1.95	1.66	1.50	NA	NA	NA	NA	NA	NA	NA
Dividends	0.86	0.81	0.74	0.70	0.67	0.65	0.59	0.51	0.48	0.45
Payout Ratio	44%	45%	46%	48%	50%	49%	50%	51%	50%	45%
Prices - High	58.90	58.90	53.30	48.31	50.31	52.15	41.03	31.43	27.00	26.93
- Low	51.05	44.21	42.93	29.93	33.25	35.46	27.28	24.18	21.43	19.06
P/E Ratio - High	30	33	33	33	38	40	35	32	28	27
- Low	26	25	27	21	25	27	23	24	22	19

Income Statement Analysis (Million $)

	2003	2002	2001	2000	1999	1998	1997	1996	1995	1994
Revs.	3,069	2,746	2,430	2,146	2,062	2,005	1,937	1,836	1,754	1,597
Oper. Inc.	769	671	582	521	489	468	432	412	381	331
Depr.	120	85.6	68.3	57.9	61.3	55.8	50.4	47.3	43.8	41.1
Int. Exp.	Nil	Nil	Nil	Nil	0.71	0.61	0.96	1.10	1.96	1.49
Pretax Inc.	652	583	527	479	444	441	394	359	350	353
Eff. Tax Rate	31.6%	31.2%	31.2%	31.4%	30.7%	30.9%	31.1%	35.9%	36.1%	34.7%
Net Inc.	446	402	363	329	308	305	272	230	224	231
S&P Core Earnings	438	374	336	NA	NA	NA	NA	NA	NA	NA

Balance Sheet & Other Fin. Data (Million $)

	2003	2002	2001	2000	1999	1998	1997	1996	1995	1994
Cash	505	279	308	301	288	215	207	301	232	230
Curr. Assets	1,291	1,006	914	829	804	843	798	729	672	623
Total Assets	2,520	2,108	1,766	1,575	1,548	1,521	1,343	1,234	1,099	979
Curr. Liab.	465	386	332	288	252	219	226	218	213	210
LT Debt	Nil	Nil	Nil	Nil	Nil	Nil	Nil	Nil	Nil	Nil
Common Equity	1,821	1,523	1,276	1,133	1,139	1,157	985	897	797	688
Total Cap.	1,904	1,593	1,319	1,173	1,184	1,197	1,016	922	816	704
Cap. Exp.	220	217	182	125	128	148	127	102	103	87.0
Cash Flow	566	487	431	387	369	360	322	278	268	272
Curr. Ratio	2.8	2.6	2.7	2.9	3.2	3.9	3.5	3.3	3.2	3.0
% LT Debt of Cap.	Nil	Nil	Nil	Nil	Nil	Nil	Nil	Nil	Nil	Nil
% Net Inc.of Revs.	14.5	14.6	14.9	15.3	14.9	15.2	14.0	12.5	12.8	14.4
% Ret. on Assets	19.3	20.7	21.7	21.1	20.1	21.3	21.1	19.7	21.5	25.7
% Ret. on Equity	26.7	28.7	30.1	29.0	26.8	28.4	28.9	27.2	30.1	36.5

Data as orig reptd.; bef. results of disc opers/spec. items. Per share data adj. for stk. divs.; EPS diluted. E-Estimated. NA-Not Available. NM-Not Meaningful. NR-Not Ranked. UR-Under Review.

Office: 410 North Michigan Avenue, Chicago, IL 60611.
Telephone: 312-644-2121.
Website: http://www.wrigley.com
Chrmn, Pres & CEO: W. Wrigley, Jr.
COO: R. Waters.
CFO: R. Gamoran.

Treas: A.J. Schneider.
Secy & General Counsel: H. Malovany.
Investor Contact: K. McGrail 312-645-4754.
Dirs: J. F. Bard, H. B. Bernick, T. A. Knowlton, P. S. Pritzker, M. R. Rich, S. B. Sample, A. Shumate, R. K. Smucker, W. Wrigley, Jr.

Founded: in 1910.
Domicile: Delaware.
Employees: 12,000.
S&P Analyst: Richard Joy/MF/BK

Wyeth

Recommendation: HOLD ★★★☆☆
SELL | SELL | HOLD | BUY | BUY

12-Month Target Price: **$43.00**
(as of November 11, 2004)

WYE has an approximate 0.49% weighting in the **S&P 500**

Sector: Health Care
Sub-Industry: Pharmaceuticals
Peer Group: Ethical Pharmaceuticals - Major

Summary: Wyeth (formerly American Home Products Corp.) is a leading maker of prescription drugs and OTC medications.

Quantitative Evaluations

S&P Earnings & Dividend Rank: B

| D | C | B- | B | B+ | A- | A | A+ |

S&P Fair Value Rank: 5

| 1 | 2 | 3 | 4 | **5** |
| Lowest | | | | Highest |

Fair Value Calc.: $47.10 (Slightly Undervalued)

S&P Investability Quotient Percentile
93%

WYE scored higher than 93% of all companies for which an S&P Report is available.

Volatility: Average

| Low | Average | High |

Technical Evaluation: Bullish
Since 10/04, the technical indicators for WYE have been Bullish.

Relative Strength Rank: Moderate
56
1 Lowest — Highest 99

Price as of 11/12/04: $40.28 | **2004E S&P Core EPS:** $2.43

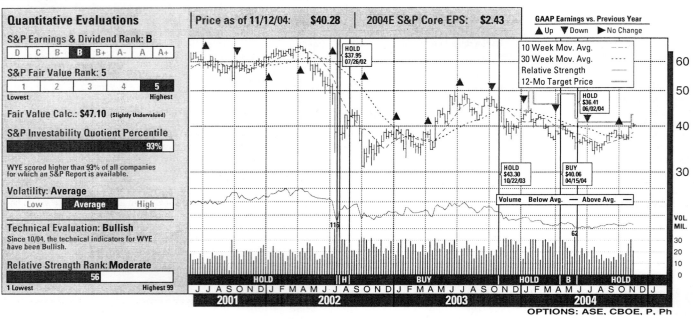

GAAP Earnings vs. Previous Year ▲ Up ▼ Down ▶ No Change

10 Week Mov. Avg.
30 Week Mov. Avg.
Relative Strength
12-Mo Target Price

OPTIONS: ASE, CBOE, P, Ph

Analyst commentary prepared by H. B. Saftlas/PMW/JWP

Highlights 15-NOV-04

- We project 2005 revenue growth in the high single digits, paced by strong momentum in sales of established products and contributions from new drugs. Sales of Prevnar broad-based pediatric vaccine are expected to climb 70%, to about $1.7 billion, boosted by recent manufacturing capacity additions, higher dosing schedules, and further expansion in international markets. We also see further robust growth for Effexor antidepressant and Enbrel anti-inflammatory agent, helped by expanded indications and line extensions. However, we forecast relatively modest sales gains in Protonix proton pump inhibitor (PPI) gastrointestinal drug, as inexpensive generic and OTC rivals have resulted in substantial discounting in the PPI market. Sales of Premarin hormone replacement products are likely to remain relatively flat.

- We expect gross margins to remain at 73% to 74%. We see increases in SG&A costs pacing our projected gain in revenues, but we forecast a 14% rise in R&D spending to fund WYE's growing R&D pipeline. Interest expense is also expected to increase, while other income will probably decline.

- We estimate 2005 operating EPS at $2.85, up from a projected $2.65 (before nonrecurring items) in 2004. After estimated stock option and pension expenses, we project S&P Core EPS of $2.65 for 2005, after $2.43 for 2004.

Investment Rationale/Risk 15-NOV-04

- We have a hold recommendation on the shares. WYE posted better than expected earnings over the past two quarters, buoyed, in our view, by strong demand for key products and good control over operating costs. We think the company's R&D pipeline looks better, with seven Phase III compounds, each with what we see as $1 billion sales potential, and another five with peak sales potential of $500 million each. However, the company continues to be burdened by mounting phen-fen related liabilities. WYE made no change in its $3 billion diet drug reserve in the third quarter, but we believe significant future liabilities are likely, based on the large number of claims outstanding in the class settlement and opt-out (persons suing the company as individuals) groups.

- Risks to our recommendation and target price include the possibility of significantly greater diet drug liabilities, and a failure to successfully develop and commercialize pipeline compounds.

- Our 12-month target price of $43 is derived by applying a P/E multiple of 15.1X to our 2005 EPS estimate of $2.85. Our target price approximates our calculation of intrinsic value based on our DCF model, which assumes decelerating free cash flow growth over 10 years and a 7.3% weighted average cost of capital.

Key Stock Statistics

S&P Core EPS 2005E	2.65	52-week Range	$44.70-33.50
S&P Oper. EPS 2004E	2.65	12 Month P/E	16.2
P/E on S&P Oper. EPS 2004E	15.2	Beta	0.75
S&P Oper. EPS 2005E	2.85	Shareholders	57,354
Yield (%)	2.3%	Market Cap (B)	$ 53.7
Dividend Rate/Share	0.92	Shares Outstanding (M)	1334.2

Value of $10,000 invested five years ago: **$ 7,942**

Dividend Data Dividends have been paid since 1919

Amount ($)	Date Decl.	Ex-Div. Date	Stock of Record	Payment Date
0.230	Jan. 27	Feb. 11	Feb. 13	Mar. 01 '04
0.230	Apr. 22	May. 11	May. 13	Jun. 01 '04
0.230	Jun. 16	Aug. 11	Aug. 13	Sep. 01 '04
0.230	Sep. 30	Nov. 09	Nov. 12	Dec. 01 '04

Revenues/Earnings Data Fiscal year ending December 31

Revenues (Million $)

	2004	2003	2002	2001	2000	1999
1Q	4,015	3,689	3,644	3,449	3,206	3,442
2Q	4,223	3,747	3,503	3,216	3,041	3,319
3Q	4,472	4,082	3,624	3,736	3,509	3,321
4Q	—	4,333	3,814	3,727	3,506	3,467
Yr.	—	15,851	14,584	14,129	13,263	13,550

Earnings Per Share ($)

	2004	2003	2002	2001	2000	1999
1Q	0.56	0.96	0.65	0.55	1.32	0.49
2Q	0.62	0.65	0.45	0.36	0.31	0.30
3Q	1.06	-0.32	1.05	0.19	0.58	-2.20
4Q	E0.70	0.25	1.18	0.62	-2.91	0.45
Yr.	E2.65	1.54	3.33	1.72	-0.69	-0.94

Next earnings report expected: late-January Source: S&P, Company Reports
EPS Estimates based on S&P Operating Earnings; historical GAAP earnings are as reported.

Recommendation: **HOLD** ★ ★ ★ ☆ ☆   12-Month Target Price: **$43.00** (as of November 11, 2004)

Business Summary 15-NOV-04

This maker of popular consumer medications such as Anacin and Advil pain relievers also produces a wide range of prescription drugs, with special emphasis on women's health care. Corporate strategy in recent years has focused on higher-margin products, while divesting less profitable businesses. In recent years, the company sold its medical device, food products and agricultural businesses. The company changed its name to Wyeth, from American Home Products Corp., in March 2002.

Human prescription pharmaceuticals accounted for 80% of total sales in 2003, consumer health care products for 15%, and animal health products for 5%. Foreign operations are significant, accounting for 40% of sales in 2003.

WYE is the world's leading maker of women's drugs, with its popular line of Premarin estrogen and PremPro/Premphase estrogen/progestin hormone replacement therapy (HRT) products (sales of $1.3 billion in 2003), and oral contraceptives such as Triphasal, Lo/Ovral and Alesse. The HRT business has been negatively affected by clinical studies released in mid-2002 that highlighted cardiovascular and cancer risks with HRT products. Addressing that issue, WYE now offers a line of low dose Premarin and PremPro products that provide efficacy similar to older HRT products, but are believed to entail reduced safety risks.

Other principal drugs are Effexor (sales of $2.7 billion in 2003), an antidepressant that works on both serotonin and norepinephrine; Protonix ($1.5 billion), a treatment for heartburn caused by gastroesophageal erosive reflux disease; and Prevnar ($946 million), a broad-based pediatric vaccine. The company also offers

Cordarone, Veralan and Ziac cardiovasculars; Lodine, Oruvail and Naprelan anti-arthritics; Suprax, Zosyn and Minocin anti-infectives; and Refacto, a factor VIII treatment for hemophilia A. WYE also markets Enbrel, a treatment for rheumatoid arthritis, in conjunction with Amgen, Inc.; and Altace, a cardiovascular, through a co-marketing pact with King Pharmaceuticals, Inc.

The Whitehall and A.H. Robins divisions offer a broad range of OTC medications such as Advil and Anacin analgesics, Dimetapp and Robitussin for coughs and colds, Primatene for asthma, Preparation H for hemorrhoids, and Centrum and Solgar vitamins.

R&D spending in 2003 totaled $2.1 billion, equal to 13.2% of sales. The R&D pipeline includes more than 60 compounds in development, covering a wide range of therapeutic categories. Key pipeline products include treatments for cancer, infection, diabetes, asthma, Alzheimer's disease, pain, arthritis, schizophrenia, hepatitis C, and other conditions.

WYE has set aside over $16.6 billion for settlements and litigation charges associated with lawsuits filed in connection with its discontinued Redux and Pondimin diet drugs. At the end September 2004, an additional $3 billion had been reserved for potential liabilities. About 117,370 matrix claims (alleging significant heart valve disease) had been filed as of October 13, 2004. In addition, a number of opt-out forms had been filed, representing alleged injured persons who decided not to participate in WYE's class action settlement, and were expected to pursue separate legal actions.

Company Financials Fiscal Year ending December 31

Per Share Data ($)

(Year Ended December 31)	2003	2002	2001	2000	1999	1998	1997	1996	1995	1994
Tangible Bk. Val.	4.01	3.22	0.17	NM	NM	1.23	NM	NM	NM	-4.03
Cash Flow	1.94	3.72	2.17	-0.28	-0.42	2.35	4.18	2.00	1.90	1.49
Earnings	1.54	3.33	1.72	-0.69	-0.94	1.85	1.56	1.48	1.35	1.24
S&P Core Earnings	1.78	1.73	1.92	NA	NA	NA	NA	NA	NA	NA
Dividends	0.92	0.92	0.92	0.92	0.91	0.87	0.83	0.78	0.76	0.73
Payout Ratio	60%	28%	53%	NM	NM	47%	53%	53%	56%	58%
Prices - High	49.95	66.51	63.80	65.25	70.25	58.75	42.43	33.25	24.96	16.81
- Low	32.75	28.25	52.00	39.37	36.50	37.75	28.50	23.53	15.43	13.84
P/E Ratio - High	32	20	37	NM	NM	32	27	22	18	14
- Low	21	8	30	NM	NM	20	18	16	11	11

Income Statement Analysis (Million $)

	2003	2002	2001	2000	1999	1998	1997	1996	1995	1994
Revs.	15,851	14,584	14,129	13,263	13,550	13,463	14,196	14,088	13,376	8,996
Oper. Inc.	4,450	4,060	4,299	3,808	3,759	3,931	3,946	3,634	3,191	2,484
Depr.	538	485	608	534	682	665	701	658	679	306
Int. Exp.	103	202	146	239	343	323	462	563	605	115
Pretax Inc.	2,362	6,097	2,869	-1,101	-1,926	3,585	2,815	2,755	2,439	2,030
Eff. Tax Rate	13.1%	27.1%	20.3%	NM	NM	31.0%	27.4%	31.6%	31.1%	24.7%
Net Inc.	2,051	4,447	2,285	-901	-1,227	2,474	2,043	1,883	1,680	1,528
S&P Core Earnings	2,379	2,313	2,551	NA	NA	NA	NA	NA	NA	NA

Balance Sheet & Other Fin. Data (Million $)

	2003	2002	2001	2000	1999	1998	1997	1996	1995	1994
Cash	7,180	3,947	3,027	2,985	2,413	1,301	1,051	1,544	2,020	1,944
Curr. Assets	14,962	11,596	9,767	10,181	9,738	7,956	7,361	7,470	7,986	7,821
Total Assets	31,032	25,995	22,968	21,092	23,906	21,079	20,825	20,785	21,363	21,675
Curr. Liab.	8,430	5,476	7,257	9,742	7,110	4,211	4,327	4,338	4,556	4,618
LT Debt	8,076	7,546	7,357	2,395	3,669	3,859	5,032	6,021	7,802	9,973
Common Equity	9,294	8,156	4,073	2,818	6,216	9,615	8,176	6,962	5,543	4,254
Total Cap.	17,371	15,702	11,430	5,213	9,885	13,695	13,415	13,179	13,659	14,551
Cap. Exp.	1,909	1,932	1,924	1,682	1,000	810	830	652	638	473
Cash Flow	2,589	4,932	2,893	-367	-545	3,139	2,744	2,541	2,359	1,834
Curr. Ratio	1.8	2.1	1.3	1.0	1.4	1.9	1.7	1.7	1.8	1.7
% LT Debt of Cap.	46.5	48.1	64.4	45.9	37.1	28.2	37.5	45.7	57.1	68.5
% Net Inc.of Revs.	12.9	30.5	16.2	NM	NM	18.4	14.4	13.4	12.6	17.0
% Ret. on Assets	7.2	18.2	10.4	NM	NM	11.8	9.8	8.9	7.8	10.4
% Ret. on Equity	23.5	72.7	66.3	NM	NM	27.8	27.0	30.1	34.3	37.8

Data as orig reptd.; bef. results of disc opers/spec. items. Per share data adj. for stk. divs.; EPS diluted. E-Estimated. NA-Not Available. NM-Not Meaningful. NR-Not Ranked. UR-Under Review.

Office: Five Giralda Farms, Madison, NJ 07940-0874.
Telephone: 973-660-5000.
Website: http://www.wyeth.com
Chrmn, Pres & CEO: R. Essner.
EVP & CFO: K. J. Martin.
EVP: B. J. Poussot.

SVP & General Counsel: L. V. Stein.
Investor Contact: Justin R. Victoria (973-660-5000).
Dirs: C. L. Alexander, Jr., F. A. Bennack, Jr., R. L. Carrion, R. Essner, J. D. Feerick, R. S. Langer, J. P. Mascotte, M. L. Polan, I. G. Seidenberg, W. V. Shipley, J. R. Torell III.

Founded: in 1926.
Domicile: Delaware.
Employees: 52,385.
S&P Analyst: H. B. Saftlas/PMW/JWP

The McGraw·Hill Companies

Xcel Energy

Recommendation: **HOLD** ★ ★ ★ ☆
SELL SELL HOLD BUY BUY

12-Month Target Price: $18.00
(as of September 20, 2004)

XEL has an approximate 0.07% weighting in the **S&P 500**

Sector: Utilities
Sub-Industry: Electric Utilities
Peer Group: Electric & Gas- Larger

Summary: This energy holding company was created through the August 2000 merger of Minneapolis-based Northern States Power and Denver-based New Century Energies.

Quantitative Evaluations

S&P Earnings & Dividend Rank: B

| D | C | B- | **B** | B+ | A- | A | A+ |

S&P Fair Value Rank: 3

| 1 | 2 | **3** | 4 | 5 |
| Lowest | | | | Highest |

Fair Value Calc.: $17.80 (Fairly Valued)

S&P Investability Quotient Percentile

62%

XEL scored higher than 62% of all companies for which an S&P Report is available.

Volatility: Low

| **Low** | Average | High |

Technical Evaluation: Bullish
Since 11/04, the technical indicators for XEL have been Bullish.

Relative Strength Rank: Moderate

46

| 1 Lowest | | Highest 99 |

Price as of 11/17/04: $18.02 | **2004E S&P Core EPS:** $0.94

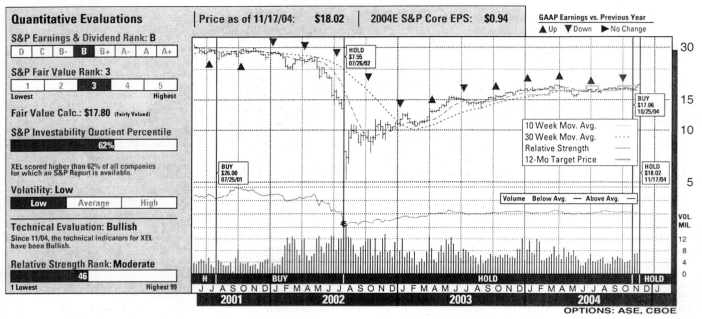

GAAP Earnings vs. Previous Year
▲ Up ▼ Down ► No Change

HOLD $7.55 07/26/02

BUY $17.06 10/25/04

BUY $26.00 07/25/01

HOLD $18.02 11/17/04

- 10 Week Mov. Avg.
- 30 Week Mov. Avg.
- Relative Strength
- 12-Mo Target Price

Volume Below Avg. — Above Avg.

VOL. MIL.

H	BUY	HOLD	HOLD
J J A S O N D	J F M A M J J A S O N D	J F M A M J J A S O N D	J F M A M J J A S O N D	J
2001	**2002**	**2003**	**2004**

OPTIONS: ASE, CBOE

Analyst commentary prepared by Justin McCann/CB/BK

Highlights 17-NOV-04

- The STARS recommendation for Xcel Energy, Inc. (XEL) has recently been changed to 3 from 4. The Highlights section of this Stock Report will be updated accordingly.

Investment Rationale/Risk 17-NOV-04

- The Investment Rationale/Risk section of this Stock Report will be updated shortly. For the latest news story on Xcel Energy, Inc. (XEL) from MarketScope, see below.

11/17/04 04:05 pm EST... S&P DOWNGRADES SHARES OF XCEL ENERGY TO HOLD FROM BUY (XEL 17.99***): Following the recent rise in XEL's shares, we believe the stock is now fairly valued at an approximate peer P/E multiple. We do not expect the recent approval of a renewable energy measure by Colorado voters to have a significant impact on the company. The measure called for the state's utilities to increase the use of renewable energy to 10% of their total by 2015. Since the measure includes wind power, XEL expects to exceed the requirement by the end of 2005. We are maintaining our 12-month target price of $18, as well as our EPS estimates of $1.25 for '04 and $1.30 for '05. /J.McCann

Key Stock Statistics

S&P Core EPS 2005E	1.04	52-week Range	$18.34-15.48
S&P Oper. EPS 2004E	1.25	12 Month P/E	9.8
P/E on S&P Oper. EPS 2004E	14.7	Beta	0.63
S&P Oper. EPS 2005E	1.30	Shareholders	121,900
Yield (%)	4.6%	Market Cap (B)	$ 7.2
Dividend Rate/Share	0.83	Shares Outstanding (M)	400.3

Value of $10,000 invested five years ago: **NA**

Dividend Data Dividends have been paid since 1910

Amount ($)	Date Decl.	Ex-Div. Date	Stock of Record	Payment Date
0.188	Dec. 10	Dec. 30	Jan. 02	Jan. 20 '04
0.188	Mar. 17	Mar. 31	Apr. 02	Apr. 20 '04
0.208	May. 20	Jun. 30	Jul. 02	Jul. 20 '04
0.208	Aug. 25	Sep. 29	Oct. 01	Oct. 20 '04

Revenues/Earnings Data Fiscal year ending December 31

Revenues (Million $)

	2004	2003	2002	2001	2000	1999
1Q	2,291	2,086	2,371	4,231	793.0	743.2
2Q	1,807	1,722	2,227	3,699	679.0	659.4
3Q	2,009	2,020	2,473	3,763	2,562	813.5
4Q	—	2,110	2,454	3,336	4,980	685.2
Yr.	—	7,938	9,524	15,028	11,592	2,869

Earnings Per Share ($)

	2004	2003	2002	2001	2000	1999
1Q	0.35	0.31	0.26	0.61	0.30	0.34
2Q	0.20	0.14	0.22	0.49	0.39	0.06
3Q	0.40	0.43	-4.10	0.79	0.29	0.72
4Q	E0.30	0.36	-0.54	0.38	0.40	0.32
Yr.	E1.25	1.23	-4.36	2.27	1.54	1.43

Next earnings report expected: late-January Source: S&P, Company Reports
EPS Estimates based on S&P Operating Earnings; historical GAAP earnings are as reported.

Xcel Energy, Inc.

Recommendation: **HOLD** ★ ★ ★ ☆ ☆   12-Month Target Price: **$18.00** (as of September 20, 2004)

Business Summary October 28, 2004

In August 2000, New Century Energies merged into Northern States Power Co. (NSP), which was renamed Xcel Energy.

Xcel Energy owns five utilities, serving electric and gas customers in 11 states. The Northern States Power utilities include NSP Minnesota, which serves about 1.3 million electric customers and 430,000 gas customers in Minnesota, North Dakota, and South Dakota; NSP Wisconsin, which serves about 235,000 electric customers and 95,000 gas customers in northwestern Wisconsin and the western portion of the Upper Peninsula of Michigan. Minnesota-based Black Mountain Gas Co. was sold in October 2003.

The utilities acquired from New Century Energies were: Public Service Co. of Colorado, which serves 1.3 million electric customers and 1.2 million gas customers in Colorado (including the Denver metropolitan area); Southwestern Public Service Co., which serves 390,000 electric customers in portions of Texas, New Mexico, Oklahoma and Kansas; and Cheyenne Light Fuel and Power Co. (CLF&P), which serves 38,000 electric customers and 31,000 gas customers in and around Cheyenne, WY. In January 2004, XEL reached an agreement to sell CLF&P, subject to regulatory approvals.

In 2003, residential customers accounted for 30.5% of electric revenues (30.9% in 2002); commercial and industrial 52.2% (51.4%); wholesale 13.5% (13.2%); other 2.0% (2.7%); and public authorities and other retail 1.8% (1.9%).

Residential customers accounted for 60.7% of gas revenues in 2003 (60.3% in 2002); commercial and industrial 35.4% (32.6%); and transportation and other 3.9% (7.1%).

NSP operates two nuclear plants: the single unit 583 mw Monticello plant, and the Prairie Island plant, which has two units totaling 1,082 mw.

On December 5, 2003, the company divested its ownership interest in NRG Energy, which was involved in independent power projects in the U.S. and internationally. In 2000 and 2001, XEL sold 26% of NRG's shares to the public. In June 2002, it reacquired the publicly held NRG shares. In May 2003, NRG filed for bankruptcy protection. On December 5, 2003, it completed a reorganization and emerged from bankruptcy.

Other non-regulated businesses include Eloigne, which invests in projects qualifying for low income housing tax credits; e prime, a provider of energy related products and services; Xcel Energy Utility Engineering, a provider of construction management services, with subsidiaries that include Quixx, which invests in non-utility power generation projects; and Planergy International, which provides energy services to industrial, commercial and utility customer. On September 27, 2004, XEL announced its intention to sell Seren Innovations, which offers high speed information access through automated communications systems. It expects to complete the sale during the first quarter of 2005.

In December 2003, directors approved plans to exit the remaining businesses of Xcel Energy International. In January 2003, XEL sold Viking Gas Transmission Co., for net proceeds of $124 million.

Company Financials Fiscal Year ending December 31

Per Share Data ($)

(Year Ended December 31)	2003	2002	2001	2000	1999	1998	1997	1996	1995	1994
Tangible Bk. Val.	12.95	11.44	17.91	15.79	15.67	15.58	15.23	15.42	14.82	14.13
Earnings	1.23	-4.36	2.27	1.54	1.43	1.84	1.70	1.91	1.96	1.73
S&P Core Earnings	1.03	-4.57	1.68	NA	NA	NA	NA	NA	NA	NA
Dividends	0.75	1.13	1.50	1.47	1.44	1.42	1.40	1.37	1.34	1.31
Payout Ratio	61%	NM	66%	96%	101%	77%	82%	72%	69%	76%
Prices - High	17.40	28.49	31.85	30.00	27.93	30.81	29.43	26.68	24.75	23.50
- Low	10.40	5.12	24.18	16.12	19.31	25.68	22.25	22.25	21.25	19.37
P/E Ratio - High	14	NM	14	19	20	17	17	14	13	14
- Low	8	NM	11	10	14	14	13	12	11	11

Income Statement Analysis (Million $)

	2003	2002	2001	2000	1999	1998	1997	1996	1995	1994
Revs.	7,938	9,524	15,028	11,592	2,869	2,819	2,734	2,654	2,569	2,487
Depr.	756	1,037	949	792	356	338	326	306	290	274
Maint.	NA	NA	NA	NA	179	181	165	156	158	170
Fxd. Chgs. Cov.	2.50	1.54	2.37	2.54	1.86	2.64	7.80	3.33	3.36	3.55
Constr. Credits	NA	NA	NA	NA	7.00	15.8	16.6	18.9	17.2	12.3
Eff. Tax Rate	23.7%	NM	28.2%	34.2%	22.8%	27.1%	29.0%	37.0%	35.6%	34.7%
Net Inc.	510	-1,661	785	546	224	282	237	275	276	244
S&P Core Earnings	417	-1,745	579	NA	NA	NA	NA	NA	NA	NA

Balance Sheet & Other Fin. Data (Million $)

	2003	2002	2001	2000	1999	1998	1997	1996	1995	1994
Gross Prop.	22,371	29,119	31,770	25,000	13,478	11,049	10,460	8,741	8,407	8,109
Cap. Exp.	951	1,503	5,366	2,196	462	411	433	412	401	409
Net Prop.	13,667	18,816	21,165	15,273	8,146	6,020	5,759	4,338	4,310	4,274
Capitalization:										
LT Debt	6,519	7,044	12,612	8,060	3,653	2,051	1,879	1,593	1,542	1,463
% LT Debt	55.0	59.6	66.7	58.7	57.8	44.2	42.2	40.1	40.5	40.6
Pfd.	105	105	105	105	104	105	200	240	240	240
% Pfd.	0.89	0.89	0.56	0.76	1.65	2.26	4.50	6.10	6.30	6.70
Common	5,222	4,665	6,194	5,562	2,558	2,482	2,372	2,136	2,027	1,897
% Common	44.1	39.5	32.8	40.5	40.5	53.5	53.3	53.8	53.2	52.7
Total Cap.	14,017	13,303	22,040	15,996	7,246	5,581	5,382	4,923	4,813	4,624
% Oper. Ratio	88.1	78.0	87.1	87.0	85.9	85.6	85.0	86.2	86.5	87.6
% Earn. on Net Prop.	8.0	13.0	10.7	11.2	4.8	6.2	NA	8.5	8.1	7.3
% Return on Revs.	6.4	NM	5.2	4.7	7.8	10.0	8.7	10.3	10.7	9.8
% Return On Invest. Capital	7.3	12.4	10.9	10.3	7.5	11.5	9.2	10.5	8.5	7.8
% Return On Com. Equity	10.1	NM	13.5	10.0	8.7	11.4	NA	12.6	13.4	12.4

Data as orig reptd. (for Northern States Power pr. to Aug. 21, 2000); bef. results of disc opers/spec. items. Per share data adj. for stk. divs.; EPS diluted. E-Estimated. NA-Not Available. NM-Not Meaningful. NR-Not Ranked.

Office: 800 Nicollet Mall, Minneapolis, MN 55402-5667.
Telephone: 612-330-5500.
Website: http://www.nspco.com
Chrmn & CEO: W.H. Brunetti.
Pres & COO: R.C. Kelly.
VP & Treas: G. Tyson.
VP & Secy: C.J. Hart.

VP & General Counsel: G.R. Johnson.
Investor Contact: R.J. Kolkmann 612-330-6622.
Dirs: R. H. Anderson, W. H. Brunetti, C. C. Burgess, D. A. Christensen, R. R. Hemminghaus, A. B. Hirschfeld, R. C. Kelly, D. W. Leatherdale, A. F. Moreno, R. R. Peterson, M. R. Preska, A. P. Sampson, W. T. Stephens.

Founded: in 1909.
Domicile: Minnesota.
Employees: 11,048.
S&P Analyst: Justin McCann/CB/BK

Xerox Corp.

Recommendation: **HOLD** ★★★☆☆
SELL SELL HOLD BUY BUY

12-Month Target Price: **$15.00**
(as of April 30, 2004)

XRX has an approximate 0.12% weighting in the **S&P 500**

Sector: Information Technology
Sub-Industry: Office Electronics
Peer Group: Office Electronics

Summary: XRX serves the document processing market worldwide, offering a complete line of copiers, electronic printers, and other office and computer equipment.

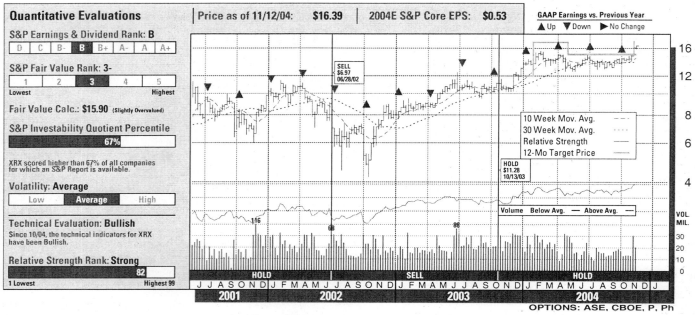

| Quantitative Evaluations | Price as of 11/12/04: | $16.39 | 2004E S&P Core EPS: | $0.53 |

S&P Earnings & Dividend Rank: B
D C B- **B** B+ A- A A+

S&P Fair Value Rank: 3-
1 2 **3** 4 5
Lowest Highest

Fair Value Calc.: $15.90 (Slightly Overvalued)

S&P Investability Quotient Percentile
67%
XRX scored higher than 67% of all companies for which an S&P Report is available.

Volatility: Average
Low **Average** High

Technical Evaluation: Bullish
Since 10/04, the technical indicators for XRX have been Bullish.

Relative Strength Rank: Strong
82
1 Lowest Highest 99

GAAP Earnings vs. Previous Year
▲ Up ▼ Down ▶ No Change

10 Week Mov. Avg. ---
30 Week Mov. Avg. ·····
Relative Strength ——
12-Mo Target Price ——

OPTIONS: ASE, CBOE, P, Ph

Analyst commentary prepared by Richard N. Stice, CFA /MF/JWP

Highlights October 27, 2004

- We expect 2005 revenues to increase about 3%, following our projection of a modest decline in 2004. We see a turnaround as likely to result from an expected pickup in corporate IT spending, improving business conditions in developing markets and various new product offerings.

- We believe gross margins will widen, as a more favorable business mix and manufacturing efficiencies outweigh ongoing pricing pressures. We expect R&D expenses to remain near 5% of revenues as the company continues to focus on technological development. We see interest income declining, as cash balances are likely to be used to pay down nearly $4.5 billion in debt scheduled to mature over the next five quarters.

- We forecast 2005 operating EPS of $0.91, up 17% from 2004's expected $0.78. Our 2005 and 2004 Standard & Poor's Core Earnings per share estimates are $0.72 and $0.53, respectively, reflecting projected pension and stock option expenses.

Investment Rationale/Risk October 27, 2004

- We believe the company's turnaround efforts have yielded positive results. We think that XRX has strengthened its balance sheet, reduced expenses, bolstered its product offerings and expanded EBITDA margins. However, we believe there remain hurdles for the company to overcome. We think demand for office products remains lackluster, and see competition intensifying. In addition, we still view debt levels as high. As a result, we would not add to positions.

- Risks to our recommendation and target price include increasing competitive threats, an inability to expand upon existing color technologies, prolonged adverse pricing conditions, the failure to meet debt obligations and instability in overseas markets.

- The shares are trading at a premium to the level of the S&P 500 on the basis of P/E multiple to growth ratio, but at a discount to our intrinsic value calculation, based on our discounted cash flow analysis. Combining the two metrics leads to our 12-month target price of $15.

Key Stock Statistics

S&P Core EPS 2005E	0.72	52-week Range	$17.24-10.17
S&P Oper. EPS 2004E	0.78	12 Month P/E	18.6
P/E on S&P Oper. EPS 2004E	21.0	Beta	1.98
S&P Oper. EPS 2005E	0.91	Shareholders	56,326
Yield (%)	Nil	Market Cap (B)	$ 13.8
Dividend Rate/Share	Nil	Shares Outstanding (M)	840.2

Value of $10,000 invested five years ago: **$ 6,531**

Dividend Data

Cash dividends were suspended in 2001.

Revenues/Earnings Data Fiscal year ending December 31

Revenues (Million $)

	2004	2003	2002	2001	2000	1999
1Q	3,827	3,757	3,858	4,291	4,540	4,300
2Q	3,853	3,920	3,952	4,283	4,778	4,862
3Q	3,716	3,732	3,793	4,052	4,552	4,628
4Q	—	4,292	4,246	4,382	4,831	5,438
Yr.	—	15,701	15,849	17,008	18,701	19,228

Earnings Per Share ($)

	2004	2003	2002	2001	2000	1999
1Q	0.17	-0.10	-0.07	0.27	-0.38	0.48
2Q	0.21	0.09	0.12	0.14	0.28	0.62
3Q	0.17	0.11	0.04	-0.05	-0.22	0.47
4Q	E0.23	0.22	0.01	-0.23	-0.15	0.41
Yr.	E0.78	0.36	0.10	-0.17	-0.44	1.96

Next earnings report expected: late-January Source: S&P, Company Reports
EPS Estimates based on S&P Operating Earnings; historical GAAP earnings are as reported.

Xerox Corporation

Recommendation: **HOLD** ★ ★ ★ ☆ ☆   12-Month Target Price: **$15.00** (as of April 30, 2004)

Business Summary October 27, 2004

Xerox believes the document industry is undergoing a fundamental transformation that includes a continuing transition from older light lens devices to digital technology, a transition from black and white to color, management of publishing and printing jobs over the Internet, use of variable data to create customized documents, and an increase in mobile workers using hand-held devices. Documents are increasingly created and stored in digital electronic form and the Internet is increasing the amount of information that can be accessed in the form of electronic documents. As a result, the company sees important areas for growth including color systems in both Office and Production environments, the replacement of multiple single-function office devices with multifunction systems, and the transition of low-end offset printing to digital technology.

XRX competes in the monochrome (black and white) and the color segments, providing what it believes to be the industry's broadest range of document products, solutions and services. Products include printing and publishing systems, digital multi-function devices (which can print, copy, scan and fax), digital copiers, laser and solid ink printers, fax machines, document management software, and supplies such as toner, paper and ink. XRX also provides software and solutions intended to help businesses easily print books or create personalized documents for customers. Services include operating in-house production centers, developing online document repositories and analyzing how customers can most efficiently create and share documents in the office.

In 2003, revenues from major segments were as follows: production 29% (28% in 2002), office 49% (48%), developing markets 10% (11%) and other 12% (13%).

In the production segment, XRX offers monochrome and color systems for three main customer environments: production publishing, transaction printing and enterprise-wide printing. It says it is the only manufacturer in the market that provides a complete family of production publishing systems from 65 to 180 impressions per minute. New products introduced in 2003 include the DocuPrint 850, the 2101 Digital Copier/Printer and the DocuColor 5252 Digital Production Press.

The office market includes global, national and small to medium sized commercial customers as well as government, education and other public sector customers. Office systems and services encompass monochrome devices at speeds up to 90 pages per minute and color devices up to 40 pages per minute. XRX plans to drive the market to color printing and copying by making color as easy, fast and affordable as traditional black and white.

The developing markets business includes marketing, direct sales, distribution programs and service operations for XRX's products, supplies and services in Latin America, the Middle East, India, Eurasia, Russia and Africa. More than 120 countries are included in the segment, with Brazil accounting for about 40% of segment revenues in 2003.

International operations provided 46% of total revenues in 2003, up from 43% in 2002. The company's largest interest outside the U.S. is Xerox Ltd., which operates predominantly in Europe.

Company Financials Fiscal Year ending December 31

Per Share Data ($)

(Year Ended December 31)	2003	2002	2001	2000	1999	1998	1997	1996	1995	1994
Tangible Bk. Val.	1.57	NM	0.52	2.86	4.79	4.76	5.54	5.79	5.02	6.12
Cash Flow	1.25	1.38	1.72	0.96	3.13	2.00	2.96	2.95	2.83	2.16
Earnings	0.36	0.10	-0.17	-0.44	1.96	0.80	2.02	1.75	1.70	1.12
S&P Core Earnings	0.53	-0.17	-1.33	NA	NA	NA	NA	NA	NA	NA
Dividends	Nil	Nil	0.05	0.65	0.78	0.70	0.64	0.58	0.50	0.50
Payout Ratio	Nil	Nil	NM	NM	40%	87%	32%	33%	29%	45%
Prices - High	13.89	11.45	11.35	29.31	63.93	60.81	44.00	29.12	24.10	18.79
- Low	7.90	4.20	4.68	3.75	19.00	33.09	25.75	19.89	16.08	14.62
P/E Ratio - High	39	NM	NM	NM	33	76	22	17	14	17
- Low	22	NM	NM	NM	10	41	13	11	9	13

Income Statement Analysis (Million $)

	2003	2002	2001	2000	1999	1998	1997	1996	1995	1994
Revs.	15,701	15,849	17,008	18,701	19,228	19,449	18,166	17,378	16,611	16,831
Oper. Inc.	2,585	2,803	3,011	1,946	3,815	3,685	3,400	3,161	3,016	1,961
Depr.	748	1,035	1,332	948	935	821	739	715	660	681
Int. Exp.	362	401	457	605	547	570	520	513	509	714
Pretax Inc.	494	306	418	-323	2,104	837	2,268	1,821	1,847	1,558
Eff. Tax Rate	27.1%	19.6%	NM	NM	30.0%	24.7%	32.1%	38.4%	33.3%	35.4%
Net Inc.	360	154	-109	-257	1,424	585	1,452	1,206	1,174	794
S&P Core Earnings	434	-128	-931	NA	NA	NA	NA	NA	NA	NA

Balance Sheet & Other Fin. Data (Million $)

	2003	2002	2001	2000	1999	1998	1997	1996	1995	1994
Cash	2,477	2,887	3,990	1,741	126	79.0	75.0	104	130	1,058
Curr. Assets	10,335	11,019	12,600	13,022	11,985	12,475	10,766	10,152	9,833	NA
Total Assets	24,591	25,458	27,689	29,475	28,814	30,024	27,732	26,818	25,969	38,585
Curr. Liab.	7,569	7,787	10,260	6,268	7,950	8,507	7,692	7,204	6,999	NA
LT Debt	8,739	11,485	11,815	16,042	11,632	11,505	9,416	8,424	7,867	7,780
Common Equity	3,291	1,893	1,820	3,493	4,911	4,857	4,985	4,985	3,878	4,177
Total Cap.	13,418	14,001	14,313	20,323	17,339	17,173	15,233	14,355	12,490	13,214
Cap. Exp.	197	146	219	452	594	566	520	510	438	389
Cash Flow	1,037	1,116	1,209	638	2,305	1,350	2,134	1,921	1,834	1,402
Curr. Ratio	1.4	1.4	1.2	2.1	1.5	1.5	1.4	1.4	1.4	NA
% LT Debt of Cap.	65.1	82.0	82.5	78.9	67.1	67.0	61.8	58.7	63.0	58.9
% Net Inc.of Revs.	2.3	1.0	NM	NM	7.4	3.0	8.0	6.9	7.1	4.7
% Ret. on Assets	1.4	0.6	NM	NM	4.8	2.0	5.3	4.6	4.4	2.0
% Ret. on Equity	11.1	4.4	NM	NM	28.1	10.7	29.8	27.8	29.2	17.5

Data as orig reptd.; bef. results of disc opers/spec. items. Per share data adj. for stk. divs. Bold denotes primary EPS - prior periods restated. E-Estimated. NA-Not Available. NM-Not Meaningful. NR-Not Ranked. UR-Under Review.

Office: 800 Long Ridge Road, Stamford, CT 06904-1600.
Telephone: 203-968-3000.
Website: http://www.xerox.com
Chrmn & CEO: A.M. Mulcahy.
SVP & CFO: L.A. Zimmerman.
SVP & CTO: H.J. Gallaire.

VP & Chief Acctg Officer: G.R. Kabureck.
VP & Treas: R.L. Seegal.
VP & Investor Contact: J.H. Lesco .
Dirs: G. A. Britt, R. Harrington, W. Hunter, A. A. Johnson, V. E. Jordan, Jr., Y. Kobayashi, H. Kopper, R. S. Larsen, A. M. Mulcahy, N. J. Nicholas, Jr., J. E. Pepper, A. Reese, S. Robert.

Founded: in 1906.
Domicile: New York.
Employees: 61,100.
S&P Analyst: Richard N. Stice, CFA /MF/JWP

Xilinx, Inc.

Recommendation: **HOLD** ★★★☆☆
SELL SELL HOLD BUY BUY

12-Month Target Price: $33.00
(as of October 22, 2004)

XLNX has an approximate 0.10% weighting in the **S&P 500**

Sector: Information Technology
Sub-Industry: Semiconductors
Peer Group: Semiconductors - Logic - Larger Cos.

Summary: XLNX is the world's largest supplier of programmable logic chips and related development system software.

Quantitative Evaluations

S&P Earnings & Dividend Rank: B

| D | C | B- | **B** | B+ | A- | A | A+ |

S&P Fair Value Rank: 2-

| 1 | **2** | 3 | 4 | 5 |
| Lowest | | | | Highest |

Fair Value Calc.: $26.90 (Slightly Overvalued)

S&P Investability Quotient Percentile

92%

XLNX scored higher than 92% of all companies for which an S&P Report is available.

Volatility: Average

| Low | **Average** | High |

Technical Evaluation: Bullish

Since 10/04, the technical indicators for XLNX have been Bullish.

Relative Strength Rank: Moderate

53

| 1 Lowest | | Highest 99 |

Price as of 11/12/04: **$30.63**   2005E S&P Core EPS: **$0.75**

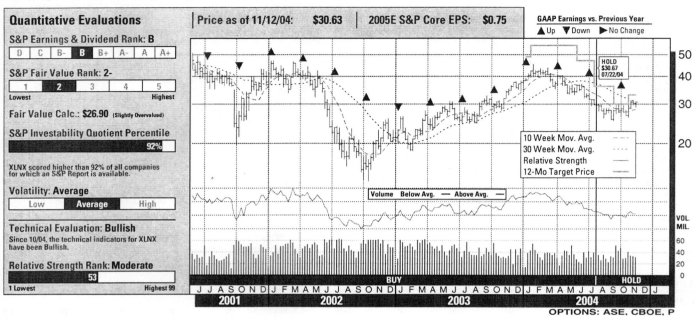

GAAP Earnings vs. Previous Year
▲ Up ▼ Down ► No Change

HOLD
$30.67
07/22/04

- 10 Week Mov. Avg.
- 30 Week Mov. Avg.
- Relative Strength
- 12-Mo Target Price

Volume   Below Avg. — Above Avg.

BUY   HOLD

J J A S O N D | J F M A M J J A S O N D | J F M A M J J A S O N D | J F M A M J J A S O N D | J
2001 | 2002 | 2003 | 2004

OPTIONS: ASE, CBOE, P

Analyst commentary prepared by Amrit Tewary/MF/JWP

Highlights October 27, 2004

- We project that sales will climb 15% in FY 05 (Mar.), as the current semiconductor industry upcycle continues. For FY 06, we see revenue growth moderating to about 8%. We expect new products to drive growth over the next few years.

- We see the gross margin widening to 64.5% in FY 05 and 65.9% in FY 06, from 62.1% in FY 04. We believe the adoption of advanced production techniques is leading to reduced costs. We expect the operating margin to widen to 26.2% in FY 05 and 30.3% in FY 06, from 25.3% in FY 04, as revenues rise faster than R&D and SG&A costs.

- We estimate operating EPS of $0.95 for FY 05 and $1.20 for FY 06. We project FY 05 Standard & Poor's Core Earnings of $0.75 and $1.00 for FY 06, after $0.20 of stock option expense that we estimate for each year. On April 22, XLNX initiated a quarterly cash dividend of $0.05, payable June 2, and extended its share buyback program.

Investment Rationale/Risk October 27, 2004

- We would hold the shares. Despite the year-to-date decline in the stock price, we think current valuation multiples are warranted, in light of what we see as elevated near-term macro uncertainty. Also, we believe multiple expansion is unlikely over the next 12 months for most chip stocks, as we enter what we believe will be the latter stage of the current industry upcycle. In addition, based on our view that inventory levels in the distribution channel are at or above optimal levels, we expect distributors and OEMs to be cautious in their ordering. Lastly, recent increases in XLNX's own inventory also gives us some concern.

- Risks to our opinion and target price include industry cyclicality, competition, dependence on chip foundry partners for production, rising inventory, and reliance on stock-based compensation that we view as moderately high versus peers.

- Our 12-month target price of $33 is derived by applying a P/E of 33X, below the stock's average historical multiple, to our forward 12-month EPS estimate of $0.99. Our target price also applies a price-to-sales ratio of 8.5X, below historical norms, to our FY 05 sales per share estimate. We expect the stock to trade at a discount to historical average multiples, in light of what we see as heightened macro and inventory risks.

Key Stock Statistics

S&P Core EPS 2006E	1.00	52-week Range	$45.40-25.21
S&P Oper. EPS 2005E	0.95	12 Month P/E	28.6
P/E on S&P Oper. EPS 2005E	32.2	Beta	2.43
S&P Oper. EPS 2006E	1.20	Shareholders	180,000
Yield (%)	0.7%	Market Cap (B)	$ 10.7
Dividend Rate/Share	0.20	Shares Outstanding (M)	348.3

Value of $10,000 invested five years ago: **$ 6,866**

Dividend Data Dividends have been paid since 2004

Amount ($)	Date Decl.	Ex-Div. Date	Stock of Record	Payment Date
0.050	Apr. 22	May. 10	May. 12	Jun. 02 '04
0.050	Jul. 22	Aug. 16	Aug. 18	Sep. 01 '04
0.050	Oct. 26	Nov. 15	Nov. 17	Dec. 01 '04

Revenues/Earnings Data Fiscal year ending March 31

Revenues (Million $)

	2005	2004	2003	2002	2001	2000
1Q	423.6	313.3	289.9	289.3	364.9	211.4
2Q	403.3	315.6	277.9	224.7	437.4	238.8
3Q	—	365.6	282.7	228.1	450.1	264.3
4Q	—	403.4	305.5	273.5	407.0	306.6
Yr.	—	1,398	1,156	1,016	1,659	1,021

Earnings Per Share ($)

	2005	2004	2003	2002	2001	2000
1Q	0.26	0.13	0.12	0.05	0.27	0.15
2Q	0.24	0.16	0.11	-0.53	0.32	0.17
3Q	E0.21	0.19	-0.01	0.03	-0.03	0.20
4Q	E0.23	0.36	0.14	0.10	-0.49	1.36
Yr.	E0.95	0.85	0.36	-0.34	0.10	1.90

Next earnings report expected: late-January Source: S&P, Company Reports
EPS Estimates based on S&P Operating Earnings; historical GAAP earnings are as reported.

The **McGraw·Hill** Companies

Xilinx, Inc.

Recommendation: **HOLD** ★ ★ ★ ☆ ☆   12-Month Target Price: **$33.00** (as of October 22, 2004)

Business Summary October 27, 2004

Founded in 1984, Xilinx is the world's leading supplier of programmable logic devices based on market share. These devices, commonly known as PLD chips, include field programmable gate arrays (FPGAs) and complex programmable logic devices (CPLDs). They are standard integrated circuits that are programmed by customers to perform desired logic operations. The company believes it provides high levels of integration and creates significant time and cost savings for electronic equipment manufacturers in the telecommunications, networking, computing and industrial markets.

FPGAs account for the vast majority of sales, but the company also derives revenue from development and system software tools, and field engineering support. In FY 04 (Mar.), revenues were derived 42% from the U.S. (49% in FY 03), 19% (22%) from Europe, 15% (15%) from Japan, and 24% (14%) from Asia Pacific and other regions.

XLNX's FPGAs are proprietary integrated circuits designed by the company; they provide a combination of the high logic density usually associated with custom gate arrays, the time-to-market advantages of programmable logic and the availability of a standard product. XLNX has several product families, including the XC4000, Coolrunner, Spartan and Virtex lines. The Virtex-II Pro product line, introduced in March 2002, is a platform for programmable systems, enabling very high-bandwidth system-on-a-chip designs with the flexibility and low development cost of programmable logic.

Company products are classified as new, mainstream, base and support. New products accounted for 32% of FY 04 sales (20% in FY 03). Mainstream products accounted for 49% of FY 04 revenues (60%). Base products represented 12% of sales in FY 04 (14%). Support products contributed 7% of FY 04 sales (6%).

As a fabless semiconductor maker, XLNX does not directly manufacture wafers for its products. Instead, it contracts for wafer production from chip foundries, including United Microelectronics Corp. (UMC) in Taiwan, Seiko Epson Corp. in Japan, and IBM in the U.S. The company maintained an equity position in UMC of about 367 million shares as of March 2004.

Revenue by end-market in FY 04 was divided as follows: 50% (55% in FY 03) communications, 19% (21%), storage and servers, and 31% (24%) consumer, industrial and other. Over time, PLD chips have evolved to become sufficiently small and low in cost to address markets traditionally served by application specific integrated circuits (ASICs). New generations of PLDs are making headway in digital consumer electronics areas. Introduced in April 2003, the Spartan-3 family of chips aims at high-volume markets, including LCD TVs, video on demand services, and blade servers.

Company Financials Fiscal Year ending March 31

Per Share Data ($)

(Year Ended March 31)	2004	2003	2002	2001	2000	1999	1998	1997	1996	1995
Tangible Bk. Val.	6.79	5.44	5.26	5.82	5.68	2.81	1.89	1.67	1.28	0.87
Cash Flow	1.05	0.57	-0.02	0.36	2.03	0.52	0.50	0.43	0.39	0.24
Earnings	0.85	0.36	-0.34	0.10	1.90	0.42	0.40	0.35	0.32	0.20
S&P Core Earnings	0.57	0.05	-0.31	0.35	NA	NA	NA	NA	NA	NA
Dividends	Nil	Nil	Nil	Nil	Nil	Nil	Nil	Nil	Nil	Nil
Payout Ratio	Nil	Nil	Nil	Nil	Nil	Nil	Nil	Nil	Nil	Nil
Cal. Yrs.	2003	2002	2001	2000	1999	1998	1997	1996	1995	1994
Prices - High	39.20	47.15	59.25	98.31	48.56	16.75	14.62	11.62	13.87	5.16
- Low	18.50	13.50	19.52	35.25	15.31	7.43	7.12	6.12	4.52	2.41
P/E Ratio - High	46	NM	NM	NM	26	40	37	33	43	26
- Low	22	NM	NM	NM	8	18	18	18	14	12

Income Statement Analysis (Million $)

	2004	2003	2002	2001	2000	1999	1998	1997	1996	1995
Revs.	1,398	1,156	1,016	1,659	1,021	662	614	568	561	355
Oper. Inc.	412	283	87.3	586	371	214	207	192	208	107
Depr.	67.9	72.5	106	93.5	44.2	32.1	32.7	28.0	22.5	12.2
Int. Exp.	Nil	Nil	0.06	0.17	Nil	11.9	13.9	14.6	5.60	10.3
Pretax Inc.	351	170	-193	61.1	1,030	184	183	166	171	94.8
Eff. Tax Rate	13.6%	26.0%	NM	42.3%	36.7%	29.8%	30.9%	33.4%	40.6%	37.5%
Net Inc.	303	126	-114	35.3	652	129	127	110	102	59.3
S&P Core Earnings	204	18.1	-103	132	NA	NA	NA	NA	NA	NA

Balance Sheet & Other Fin. Data (Million $)

	2004	2003	2002	2001	2000	1999	1998	1997	1996	1995
Cash	337	214	230	209	85.5	53.6	167	216	378	123
Curr. Assets	1,302	1,175	999	1,102	1,041	658	600	602	539	256
Total Assets	2,937	2,422	2,335	2,502	2,349	1,070	941	848	721	321
Curr. Liab.	381	314	196	350	245	167	126	97.3	103	76.1
LT Debt	Nil	Nil	Nil	Nil	Nil	Nil	250	250	250	0.87
Common Equity	2,483	1,951	1,904	1,918	1,777	879	550	491	368	244
Total Cap.	2,556	2,108	2,140	2,152	2,104	903	816	751	618	245
Cap. Exp.	41.0	46.0	94.9	223	144	40.9	29.7	26.8	60.5	26.2
Cash Flow	371	198	-7.51	129	697	161	159	138	124	71.5
Curr. Ratio	3.4	3.7	5.1	3.1	4.3	3.9	4.8	6.2	5.2	3.4
% LT Debt of Cap.	Nil	Nil	Nil	Nil	Nil	Nil	30.6	33.3	40.4	0.4
% Net Inc.of Revs.	21.7	10.9	NM	2.1	63.9	19.5	20.6	19.4	18.1	16.7
% Ret. on Assets	11.3	5.3	NM	1.5	38.2	12.8	14.2	14.1	19.5	21.5
% Ret. on Equity	13.7	6.5	NM	1.9	49.1	18.1	24.3	25.7	33.1	28.2

Data as orig reptd.; bef. results of disc opers/spec. items. Per share data adj. for stk. divs.; EPS diluted. E-Estimated. NA-Not Available. NM-Not Meaningful. NR-Not Ranked. UR-Under Review.

Office: 2100 Logic Drive, San Jose, CA 95124-3400.
Telephone: 408-559-7778.
Email: ir@xilinx.com
Website: http://www.xilinx.com
Chrmn, Pres & CEO: W.P. Roelandts.

SVP & CFO: K. Chellam.
VP, Secy & General Counsel: T.R. Lavelle.
Investor Contact: M. Quillard 408-879-4988.
Dirs: J. L. Doyle, J. G. Fishman, P. T. Gianos, W. G. Howard, Jr., H. E. Hughes, Jr., W. P. Roelandts, R. W. Sevcik, B. Vanderslice.

Founded: in 1984.
Domicile: Delaware.
Employees: 2,770.
S&P Analyst: Amrit Tewary/MF/JWP

XL Capital Ltd

Recommendation: **HOLD** ★★★☆☆ 12-Month Target Price: **$80.00**
(as of October 15, 2004)

XL has an approximate 0.09% weighting in the **S&P 500**

Sector: Financials
Sub-Industry: Property & Casualty Insurance
Peer Group: Commercial/Specialty Insurers

Summary: XL, which originally provided excess liability insurance coverage to commercial enterprises worldwide, has expanded into reinsurance and other risk management services.

Quantitative Evaluations

S&P Earnings & Dividend Rank: B-

| D | C | B- | B | B+ | A- | A | A+ |

S&P Fair Value Rank: 2-

| 1 | 2 | 3 | 4 | 5 |
| Lowest | | | | Highest |

Fair Value Calc.: $62.00 (Overvalued)

S&P Investability Quotient Percentile   **94%**

XL scored higher than 94% of all companies for which an S&P Report is available.

Volatility: Low

| Low | Average | High |

Technical Evaluation: Bearish

Since 10/04, the technical indicators for XL have been Bearish.

Relative Strength Rank: Moderate   **44**

| 1 Lowest | Highest 99 |

Price as of 11/12/04: **$74.25**   **2004E S&P Core EPS:** **$8.81**

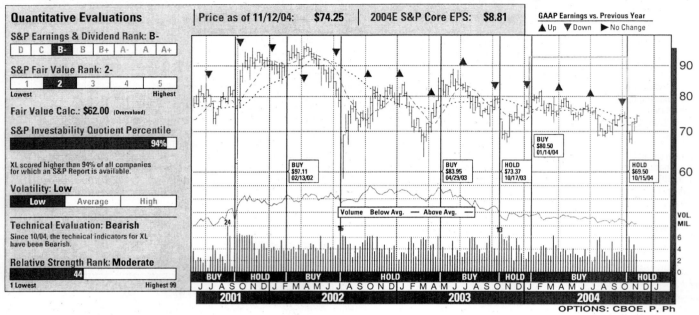

GAAP Earnings vs. Previous Year
▲ Up   ▼ Down   ▶ No Change

OPTIONS: CBOE, P, Ph

Analyst commentary prepared by Catherine Seifert/CB/BK

Highlights November 04, 2004

- We believe earned premium growth in 2005 will not be as robust as the 12% to 14% rate of growth we anticipate for 2004. This is largely due to a reduction in the writing of certain types of life insurance and annuity reinsurance, and to heightened price competition in a number of XL's core property-casualty insurance and reinsurance lines of coverage.

- Net investment income growth will likely not be as strong, reflecting the possibility that the company may incur some modest writedowns in its bond portfolio.

- The rebound in operating earnings that we see for 2005, to $10.35 a share, is skewed by third quarter 2004 after-tax catastrophe losses totaling $420.1 million from numerous hurricanes. Largely as a result of those claims, we anticipate that operating earnings per share will total $6.65 a share in 2004. Our 2004 estimate assumes there will not be any large one-time reserve boosts taken. Operating earnings per share of $2.12 reported in 2003 included a fourth quarter after-tax charge of $647 million (about $4.73 per share). The charge relates to a reserve increase that was necessitated by adverse loss trends in a number of XL's reinsurance policies that were underwritten during 1997-2001.

Investment Rationale/Risk November 04, 2004

- We recently downgraded our opinion on the shares to hold, from accumulate, for two primary reasons. First, we viewed XL's catastrophe loss exposure as outsized relative to its market share. Second, we believe the headline risk associated with the New York Attorney General's probe of certain sales and marketing practices within the insurance industry may pressure the shares in the near term. Longer term, we think the reforms that will likely emerge from this probe could increase competition among underwriters.

- Risks to our opinion and target price include the possibility of a deterioration in claim trends, another terrorist attack in the U.S., and a sharp increase in premium price competition. There is also a risk that the investigation into certain insurance marketing practices by numerous state Attorneys General could widen.

- Our 12-month target price of $80 reflects our more cautious stance toward XL. Our revised target price assumes that the shares continue to trade at the low end of XL's historical range; and that the shares trade at a discount of approximately 20% to the peer group average. In light of the uncertainty surrounding the Attorney General investigations, valuations for the entire sector have come under pressure. We believe XL's discount to its peers is still warranted, in light of the relatively higher than industry average risk profile of XL's business mix that we see.

Key Stock Statistics

S&P Oper. EPS 2004E	6.65	52-week Range	$82.00-66.70
P/E on S&P Oper. EPS 2004E	11.2	12 Month P/E	19.7
S&P Oper. EPS 2005E	10.35	Beta	0.57
Yield (%)	2.6%	Shareholders	1,002
Dividend Rate/Share	1.96	Market Cap (B)	$ 10.3
Shares Outstanding (M)	138.7		

Value of $10,000 invested five years ago: **$ 15,148**

Dividend Data Dividends have been paid since 1992

Amount ($)	Date Decl.	Ex-Div. Date	Stock of Record	Payment Date
0.490	Feb. 03	Mar. 04	Mar. 08	Mar. 31 '04
0.490	May. 03	Jun. 03	Jun. 07	Jun. 30 '04
0.490	Jul. 28	Sep. 01	Sep. 06	Sep. 30 '04
0.490	Oct. 29	Dec. 02	Dec. 06	Dec. 31 '04

Revenues/Earnings Data Fiscal year ending December 31

Revenues (Million $)

	2004	2003	2002	2001	2000	1999
1Q	2,157	1,792	1,165	767.1	714.2	593.1
2Q	3,179	1,892	1,168	791.7	674.0	585.1
3Q	2,370	1,969	2,340	845.0	694.6	646.8
4Q	—	2,363	1,942	1,654	634.7	686.0
Yr.	—	8,017	6,578	4,057	2,717	2,500

Earnings Per Share ($)

	2004	2003	2002	2001	2000	1999
1Q	3.25	1.74	0.65	1.73	1.77	1.58
2Q	2.62	2.51	-0.68	1.01	1.13	0.48
3Q	0.16	0.71	1.34	-6.70	1.10	1.07
4Q	—	-2.29	1.56	-0.64	0.01	0.56
Yr.	—	2.69	2.88	-4.55	3	3.62

Next earnings report expected: mid-February Source: S&P, Company Reports
EPS Estimates based on S&P Operating Earnings; historical GAAP earnings are as reported.

XL Capital Ltd

Recommendation: **HOLD** ★ ★ ★ ☆ ☆   12-Month Target Price: **$80.00** (as of October 15, 2004)

Business Summary November 05, 2004

XL Capital, a Bermuda-based specialty insurer, was formed in 1986 by a consortium of Fortune 500 companies to provide excess liability coverage. Since then, the company has expanded its operations (mostly through acquisitions) to include insurance, reinsurance, and other financial services. XL is a registered Bermuda insurance company, subject to regulation and supervision in Bermuda. Net written premiums total $7.6 billion in 2003 (up 8.6% from $7.0 billion in 2002) and were divided: casualty insurance 28%, casualty reinsurance 16%, other property coverage 16%, marine, energy, aviation and satellite 13%, life and annuity operations 10%, accident, health and other insurance 5%, property catastrophe 4%, other reinsurance 4%, and financial operations 4%. The combined loss and expense ratio worsened during 2003, to 102.6% from 97.0% in 2002. The loss ratio increased to 75.3% in 2003 from 68.0% in 2002, while the expense ratio improved to 27.3% in 2003 from 29.0% in 2002.

Insurance business written includes general liability, as well as other specialized types of liability coverage, like directors' and officers' liability and professional and employment practices liability. An array of property coverage, as well as marine and aviation insurance, and surety coverage, is also underwritten. Rein-

surance business written includes treaty and facultative reinsurance to primary insurers of casualty risk. Some of the reinsurance lines include general liability, professional liability, automobile, workers' compensation, commercial and personal property risks, accident and health, and fidelity and surety. The financial services unit provides insurance and reinsurance solutions for complex financial risks. Products offered include financial insurance and reinsurance, credit enhancement swaps, and other collateralized transactions.

To help broaden its product offerings, the company has made a number of acquisitions. Among the more significant acquisitions was the August 1998 purchase of the 73% of Mid Ocean Ltd. (a Cayman Islands reinsurer) that it did not already own, for stock valued at about $2.2 billion. In June 1999, XL acquired property-casualty reinsurer NAC Re for $1.01 billion in stock. XL has also made many smaller investments, including stakes in Highfields Capital Management L.P. (March 1999) and MKP Capital Management (August 1999). In July 2001, the company acquired Winterthur International, the large commercial account property casualty insurer, for about $405 million in cash. In January 2002, XL increased its ownership of Le Mans Re to 67%.

Company Financials Fiscal Year ending December 31

Per Share Data ($)

(Year Ended December 31)	2003	2002	2001	2000	1999	1998	1997	1996	1995	1994
Tangible Bk. Val.	37.07	36.13	28.35	31.86	30.91	29.67	26.20	24.27	25.54	15.73
Oper. Earnings	NA	5.10	-3.67	4.52	3.63	4.36	3.95	3.14	2.74	2.20
Earnings	2.69	2.88	-4.55	4.03	3.62	6.20	7.84	5.39	3.22	1.32
S&P Core Earnings	1.80	3.50	-4.38	NA	NA	NA	NA	NA	NA	NA
Dividends	1.92	1.88	1.84	1.80	1.76	1.64	1.36	0.95	0.70	0.61
Payout Ratio	71%	65%	NM	45%	49%	26%	17%	18%	22%	46%
Prices - High	88.87	98.48	96.50	89.25	75.75	84.00	65.18	40.25	32.75	22.68
- Low	63.49	58.45	61.50	39.00	41.93	59.12	36.87	29.81	19.31	18.00
P/E Ratio - High	33	34	NM	22	21	14	8	7	10	17
- Low	24	20	NM	10	12	10	5	6	6	14

Income Statement Analysis (Million $)

	2003	2002	2001	2000	1999	1998	1997	1996	1995	1994
Premium Inc.	6,969	5,990	3,476	2,035	1,750	685	541	518	558	521
Net Invest. Inc.	780	735	563	543	525	279	217	199	200	182
Oth. Revs.	268	-147	18.0	140	236	253	402	265	101	-70.2
Total Revs.	8,017	6,578	4,057	2,717	2,511	1,218	1,159	982	859	633
Pretax Inc.	451	442	-764	451	431	594	682	497	335	145
Net Oper. Inc.	NA	701	-465	NA	NA	NA	NA	288	283	239
Net Inc.	412	406	-576	506	471	588	677	494	333	144
S&P Core Earnings	250	481	-555	NA	NA	NA	NA	NA	NA	NA

Balance Sheet & Other Fin. Data (Million $)

	2003	2002	2001	2000	1999	1998	1997	1996	1995	1994
Cash & Equiv.	2,698	3,785	2,044	1,074	669	503	395	308	727	516
Premiums Due	4,847	4,833	2,182	1,120	1,126	690	363	345	234	118
Invest. Assets: Bonds	19,494	14,483	10,832	8,605	7,581	5,213	3,417	2,961	2,517	2,286
Invest. Assets: Stocks	583	575	548	557	1,136	1,129	838	812	838	492
Invest. Assets: Loans	Nil	Nil	Nil	Nil	Nil	Nil	Nil	Nil	Nil	Nil
Invest. Assets: Total	22,821	17,956	13,741	10,472	9,768	6,616	4,255	3,733	3,355	2,944
Deferred Policy Costs	778	688	394	309	276	98.0	22.0	30.0	41.0	35.7
Total Assets	40,764	35,647	27,963	16,942	15,091	10,109	6,088	5,032	4,725	3,853
Debt	1,905	1,878	1,605	450	411	Nil	Nil	Nil	Nil	Nil
Common Equity	10,171	6,569	5,437	5,574	5,577	4,818	2,479	2,116	2,006	1,684
Prop. & Cas. Loss Ratio	75.3	68.0	105.0	70.4	69.1	57.0	67.6	78.3	79.0	78.1
Prop. & Cas. Expense Ratio	27.3	29.0	34.9	36.4	34.3	26.3	18.2	15.3	15.0	15.6
Prop. & Cas. Combined Ratio	102.6	97.0	139.9	106.8	103.4	83.3	85.8	93.6	94.0	93.7
% Return On Revs.	5.2	6.0	NM	18.6	19.9	48.3	77.2	50.3	38.7	22.7
% Ret. on Equity	3.9	6.6	NM	9.1	8.4	16.1	29.5	24.0	18.0	8.2

Data as orig reptd.; bef. results of disc opers/spec. items. Prior to 1999, yrs. ended Nov. 30. Per share data adj. for stk. divs.; EPS diluted (primary prior to 1998). E-Estimated. NA-Not Available. NM-Not Meaningful. NR-Not Ranked. EPS est. excl. real. inv. gains/losses; historical EPS data incl. them.

Office: XL House, One Bermudiana Road, Hamilton HM 11, Bermuda.
Telephone: 441-292-8515.
Website: http://www.xl-capital.com
Chrmn: M.J. Esposito, Jr.
Pres & CEO: B.M. O'Hara.
EVP, CFO & Treas: J.M. de St. Paer.

EVP, Secy & General Counsel: P.S. Giordano.
SVP & Investor Contact: S.C. Hoy 441-294-7201.
Dirs: R. L. Bornheutter, D. R. Comey, M. P. Esposito, Jr., R. R. Glauber, P. Jeanbart, J. Loudon, E. M. McQuade, B. M. O'Hara, R. S. Parker, C. Rance, A. Senter, J. T. Thornton, E. E. Thrower, J. Weiser.

Founded: in 1986.
Domicile: Cayman Islands.
Employees: 3,350.
S&P Analyst: Catherine Seifert/CB/BK

Recommendation: **BUY** ★★★★☆
SELL SELL HOLD BUY BUY

12-Month Target Price: $41.00
(as of October 13, 2004)

YHOO has an approximate 0.47% weighting in the **S&P 500**

Sector: Information Technology
Sub-Industry: Internet Software & Services
Peer Group: Internet Content - General

Summary: YHOO offers online content and services. In October 2003, it acquired Overture Services for an estimated $1.9 billion in cash and stock.

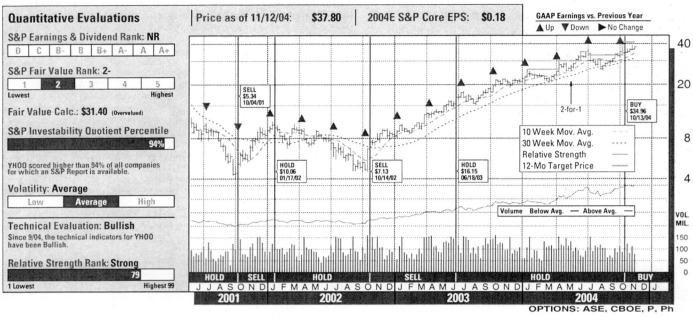

Quantitative Evaluations

S&P Earnings & Dividend Rank: NR

| D | C | B- | B | B+ | A- | A | A+ |

S&P Fair Value Rank: 2-

| 1 Lowest | 2 | 3 | 4 | 5 Highest |

Fair Value Calc.: $31.40 (Overvalued)

S&P Investability Quotient Percentile
94%

YHOO scored higher than 94% of all companies for which an S&P Report is available.

Volatility: Average

| Low | Average | High |

Technical Evaluation: Bullish
Since 9/04, the technical indicators for YHOO have been Bullish.

Relative Strength Rank: Strong
79
1 Lowest   Highest 99

Price as of 11/12/04: $37.80 | **2004E S&P Core EPS:** $0.18

GAAP Earnings vs. Previous Year
▲ Up ▼ Down ► No Change

10 Week Mov. Avg.
30 Week Mov. Avg.
Relative Strength
12-Mo Target Price

Volume   Below Avg. — Above Avg.

OPTIONS: ASE, CBOE, P, Ph

Analyst commentary prepared by Scott H. Kessler/CB/JWP

Highlights October 13, 2004

- We project that 2005 revenues will climb 33%, excluding traffic acquisition costs. In October 2003, YHOO purchased sponsored search company Overture Services (which generated $668 million in 2002 revenues).

- We expect marketing services revenues (84% of 2004 third quarter revenues) to continue to benefit from secular growth in branded advertising and sponsored search. We think fee revenue (11%) will be bolstered by YHOO's co-branded Internet access services with SBC Communications, British Telecommunications and Rogers Cable. We expect listings revenues (4%) to be aided by market share gains and international expansion at HotJobs and growth at the Yahoo! Personals dating service.

- We expect operating, EBITDA and net margins to widen sequentially in 2005, reflecting increasing leverage, and cost reductions and efficiencies related to the integration of recent acquisitions. The notable disparity between our per-share operating and Standard & Poor's Core Earnings estimates reflects material projected stock option expenses.

Investment Rationale/Risk October 13, 2004

- Although YHOO has diversified beyond online marketing, its financial results are still largely driven by this segment, which we believe started a material rebound in the 2003 third quarter. We expect this business to provide for annual revenue growth exceeding 28% over the next three years, as marketers commit an increasing percentage of their advertising budgets to the Internet. We believe YHOO's market leadership (in terms of traffic, users and revenues), international presence, growth characteristics and profitable business model have appeal.

- Risks to our recommendation and target price include increasing competition in online advertising and services (particularly from the likes of Google and Microsoft). We believe Microsoft's interest in the Internet search segment could result in the termination of its sponsored search partnership with YHOO.

- Based on our discounted cash flow model, with assumptions that include weighted average cost of capital of 14.3%, annual growth in free cash flow averaging 73% through 2008, and a perpetuity growth rate of 3%, our 12-month target price is $41. YHOO trades at a premium to the S&P 500 and its peers based on P/E and P/E to growth, which we think is warranted given the company's notable competitive advantages.

Key Stock Statistics

S&P Core EPS 2005E	0.36	52-week Range	$39.25-18.98
S&P Oper. EPS 2004E	0.34	12 Month P/E	NM
P/E on S&P Oper. EPS 2004E	NM	Beta	NA
S&P Oper. EPS 2005E	0.52	Shareholders	10,180
Yield (%)	Nil	Market Cap (B)	$ 52.0
Dividend Rate/Share	Nil	Shares Outstanding (M)	1374.8

Value of $10,000 invested five years ago: **$ 7,926**

Dividend Data

Amount ($)	Date Decl.	Ex-Div. Date	Stock of Record	Payment Date
2-for-1	Apr. 08	May. 12	Apr. 26	May. 11 '04

Revenues/Earnings Data Fiscal year ending December 31

Revenues (Million $)

	2004	2003	2002	2001	2000	1999
1Q	757.8	282.9	192.7	180.2	230.8	86.04
2Q	832.3	321.4	225.8	182.2	272.9	115.2
3Q	906.7	356.8	248.8	166.1	295.6	155.1
4Q	—	663.9	285.8	188.9	310.9	201.1
Yr.	—	1,625	953.1	717.4	1,110	588.6

Earnings Per Share ($)

	2004	2003	2002	2001	2000	1999
1Q	0.07	0.04	0.01	-0.01	0.06	0.02
2Q	0.08	0.04	0.02	-0.05	0.05	-0.02
3Q	0.17	0.05	0.03	-0.02	0.04	0.01
4Q	E0.10	0.06	0.04	-0.01	-0.09	0.04
Yr.	E0.34	0.18	0.09	-0.08	0.06	0.05

Next earnings report expected: mid-January Source: S&P, Company Reports
EPS Estimates based on S&P Operating Earnings; historical GAAP earnings are as reported.

Yahoo! Inc.

Recommendation: **BUY** ★★★★☆   12-Month Target Price: **$41.00** (as of October 13, 2004)

Business Summary October 14, 2004

Originally designed to function primarily as an online navigational guide, Yahoo! has transformed its flagship website into a destination that millions of Internet users use to find information, communicate with others, and purchase goods and services. Primary categories for YHOO's properties and services are Search and Marketplace (including search, yellow pages, maps, city guides, classified advertisements and information in the autos and real estate areas, shopping, auctions, travel, HotJobs, and small business); Information and Content (general, financial, sports, weather, entertainment, and health news and information; music, through the LAUNCH service; games; Network Services, including the Yahoo! front page and My Yahoo!); Communications and Consumer Services (premium Internet packages, e-mail, instant messaging, community offerings, photo-sharing, dating services and Yahoo! Mobile); and Affiliate Services, including pay-for-performance advertising, paid inclusion, and algorithmic search services. YHOO's total number of registered users worldwide (excluding Yahoo! Japan) grew to 300 million as of June 2004, from 236 million a year earlier. Active registered users rose to 146 million, from 116 million.

Historically, YHOO has derived a majority of its revenues from the sale of advertisements on its websites (marketing services accounted for 74% and 68% of 2003 and 2002 revenues, respectively). Revenues are derived from rich-media advertisements, sponsorship and text-link advertisements (including pay-for-performance search advertisements), paid inclusion, algorithmic searches, and transaction revenue.

Fee revenue (18%, 22%) is generated from consumer and business services, including SBC Yahoo! DSL and Dial, Yahoo! Personals, Small Business Services, Yahoo! Mail, and Yahoo! Enterprise Solutions. Listings revenue (8%, 10%) is contributed by access to the HotJobs database, classifieds from Yahoo! Autos and Yahoo! Real Estate, and other search services. Fee paying customers rose to 5.8 million as of March 2004, from 2.9 million a year earlier, largely reflecting growth in the SBC Yahoo! and BT Yahoo! Broadband access services.

YHOO provides products and services in 13 languages in more than 20 countries, including localized versions of Yahoo! in Argentina, Australia, Brazil, Canada, China, France, Germany, Hong Kong, India, Ireland, Italy, Japan, Mexico, New Zealand, Singapore, South Korea, Spain, and the U.K. As of December 2002, the company owned interests of about 70% in Yahoo! Europe, 34% in Yahoo! Japan, and 67% in Yahoo! Korea.

As of December 2003, SOFTBANK and its consolidated affiliates owned about a 4% equity interest in the company, down from 20% in 2001.

In April 2003, YHOO sold zero coupon senior convertible notes due in 2008, for net proceeds of $732 million.

Company Financials Fiscal Year ending December 31

Per Share Data ($)

(Year Ended December 31)	2003	2002	2001	2000	1999	1998	1997	1996	1995	1994
Tangible Bk. Val.	1.64	1.47	1.52	1.69	1.11	0.62	0.16	0.16	0.16	NA
Cash Flow	0.31	0.18	0.03	0.11	0.09	0.04	-0.03	0.00	0.00	NA
Earnings	0.18	0.09	-0.08	0.06	0.05	0.03	-0.03	0.00	0.00	NA
S&P Core Earnings	0.03	-0.32	-0.85	NA	NA	NA	NA	NA	NA	NA
Dividends	Nil	Nil	Nil	Nil	Nil	Nil	Nil	Nil	Nil	NA
Payout Ratio	Nil	Nil	Nil	Nil	Nil	Nil	Nil	Nil	Nil	NA
Prices - High	22.74	10.67	21.68	125.03	112.00	35.75	4.43	1.79	NA	NA
- Low	8.25	4.47	4.01	12.53	27.50	3.60	0.69	0.54	NA	NA
P/E Ratio - High	NM	NM	NM	NM	NM	NM	NM	NM	NM	NA
- Low	NM	NM	NM	NM	NM	NM	NM	NM	NM	NA

Income Statement Analysis (Million $)

	2003	2002	2001	2000	1999	1998	1997	1996	1995	1994
Revs.	1,625	953	717	1,110	589	203	67.4	19.1	1.36	NA
Oper. Inc.	477	198	34.5	390	197	58.4	-0.95	-6.40	-0.55	NA
Depr.	160	109	131	69.1	42.3	10.2	2.55	0.39	0.13	NA
Int. Exp.	Nil	Nil	Nil	Nil	Nil	Nil	Nil	Nil	NA	NA
Pretax Inc.	391	180	-81.1	264	104	43.3	-23.6	-2.30	-0.63	NA
Eff. Tax Rate	37.6%	39.7%	NM	71.2%	39.0%	41.1%	NM	NM	Nil	NA
Net Inc.	238	107	-92.8	70.8	61.1	25.6	-22.9	-2.30	-0.63	NA
S&P Core Earnings	35.5	-377	-966	NA	NA	NA	NA	NA	NA	NA

Balance Sheet & Other Fin. Data (Million $)

	2003	2002	2001	2000	1999	1998	1997	1996	1995	1994
Cash	714	311	926	1,150	234	125	62.5	92.5	100	NA
Curr. Assets	1,722	970	1,052	1,291	946	467	107	97.6	NA	NA
Total Assets	5,932	2,790	2,379	2,270	1,470	622	142	110	101	NA
Curr. Liab.	708	412	359	311	192	80.0	23.5	7.70	NA	NA
LT Debt	750	Nil	Nil	Nil	Nil	Nil	Nil	Nil	0.10	NA
Common Equity	4,363	2,262	1,967	1,897	1,261	536	118	102	100	NA
Total Cap.	5,151	2,294	1,997	1,926	1,265	540	118	102	100	NA
Cap. Exp.	117	51.6	86.2	94.4	49.5	11.9	6.60	2.40	0.11	NA
Cash Flow	398	216	37.8	140	103	35.8	-20.3	-1.91	-0.50	NA
Curr. Ratio	2.4	2.4	2.9	4.1	4.9	5.8	4.6	12.6	NA	NA
% LT Debt of Cap.	14.6	Nil	Nil	Nil	Nil	Nil	Nil	Nil	0.1	NA
% Net Inc.of Revs.	14.6	11.2	NM	6.4	10.4	12.6	NM	NM	NM	NA
% Ret. on Assets	5.5	4.1	NM	3.7	5.4	6.7	NM	NM	NA	NA
% Ret. on Equity	7.2	5.1	NM	4.5	6.3	7.8	NM	NM	NA	NA

Data as orig reptd.; bef. results of disc opers/spec. items. Per share data adj. for stk. divs.; EPS diluted. E-Estimated. NA-Not Available. NM-Not Meaningful. NR-Not Ranked. UR-Under Review.

Office: 701 First Avenue, Sunnyvale, CA 94089.
Telephone: 408-349-3300.
Email: investor_relations@yahoo-inc.com
Website: http://www.yahoo.com
Chrmn & CEO: T.S. Semel.
COO: D. Rosensweig.

EVP & CFO: S.L. Decker.
SVP, Secy & General Counsel: M. Callahan.
Investor Contact: N. Leverich 408-349-3300.
Dirs: R. Bostock, R. W. Burkle, E. Hippeau, A. Kern, R. Kotick, E. R. Kozel, T. Semel, G. L. Wilson, J. Yang.

Founded: in 1995.
Domicile: Delaware.
Employees: 5,500.
S&P Analyst: Scott H. Kessler/CB/JWP

Yum! Brands

Recommendation: HOLD ★★★☆☆
SELL | SELL | HOLD | BUY | BUY

12-Month Target Price: **$44.00**
(as of October 07, 2004)

YUM has an approximate 0.12% weighting in the **S&P 500**

Sector: Consumer Discretionary
Sub-Industry: Restaurants
Peer Group: Fast-food - Larger

Summary: YUM is the world's largest fast-food business, with more than 33,000 KFC, Pizza Hut and Taco Bell units.

Quantitative Evaluations

S&P Earnings & Dividend Rank: NR

| D | C | B- | B | B+ | A- | A | A+ |

S&P Fair Value Rank: 1+

| 1 | 2 | 3 | 4 | 5 |

Lowest / Highest

Fair Value Calc.: $37.10 (Overvalued)

S&P Investability Quotient Percentile

95%

YUM scored higher than 95% of all companies for which an S&P Report is available.

Volatility: Low

| Low | Average | High |

Technical Evaluation: Bullish
Since 8/04, the technical indicators for YUM have been Bullish.

Relative Strength Rank: Moderate

64

1 Lowest / Highest 99

Price as of 11/12/04: $44.95 **2004E S&P Core EPS:** $2.22

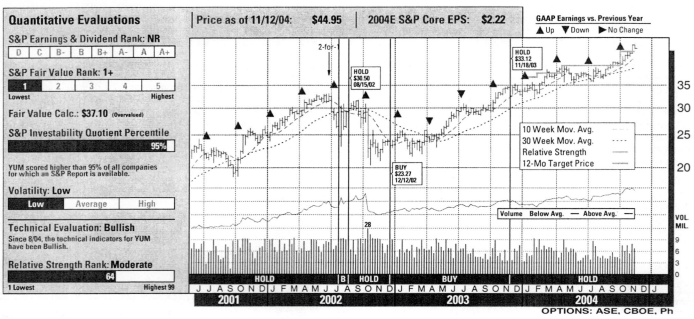

GAAP Earnings vs. Previous Year ▲ Up ▼ Down ► No Change

OPTIONS: ASE, CBOE, Ph

Analyst commentary prepared by Dennis Milton/MF/BK

Highlights October 08, 2004

- The company believes it can grow earnings by 10% annually over the next several years through global expansion, the multi-branding of U.S. restaurants, and improvement in the profitability of its base global business. YUM plans to open at least 1,000 restaurants annually, focusing on international expansion, especially in China and Europe. The company also intends to multi-brand at least 500 restaurants annually for the next several years. It expects multi-branding to boost revenues 20% to 30% per unit.

- We expect 2004 revenues to grow 8% to 9%, paced by international expansion, higher average unit volumes at multi-branded units, and a blended same-store sales increase of about 2%. We see wider profit margins, reflecting the leveraging of fixed costs over a larger sales base and a lower effective tax rate, partially offset by higher food costs.

- We project 2004 EPS of $2.35, up from $2.06 in 2003, excluding one-time items. We arrive at our 2004 Standard & Poor's Core Earnings per share estimate of $2.22 by subtracting $0.13 for projected stock option expense. Our 2005 EPS estimate of $2.60 is based on continued international expansion and same store sales growth of about 2%.

Investment Rationale/Risk October 08, 2004

- At 18X our 2004 EPS estimate of $2.35, YUM shares trade at a slight premium to fast food peers. We believe this valuation fairly reflects YUM's growth potential. While we are impressed with the company's expansion prospects, especially in China, stiff competition in the fast-food industry and operating difficulties at KFC may limit sales and profitability in the company's core U.S. business.

- Risks to our recommendation and target price include faster than expected food cost hikes, currency exchange rate risk, and costs associated with international expansion.

- Our 12-month target price of $44 assumes a P/E multiple of 17X applied to our 2005 EPS estimate of $2.60. Based on our cash flow model, which assumes revenue growth of 5% to 7% annually for the next several years, followed by gradually declining growth rates, the shares are trading near their intrinsic value.

Key Stock Statistics

S&P Core EPS 2005E	2.45	52-week Range	$46.17-32.00
S&P Oper. EPS 2004E	2.35	12 Month P/E	19.1
P/E on S&P Oper. EPS 2004E	19.1	Beta	0.38
S&P Oper. EPS 2005E	2.60	Shareholders	101,000
Yield (%)	0.9%	Market Cap (B)	$13.2
Dividend Rate/Share	0.40	Shares Outstanding (M)	292.9

Value of $10,000 invested five years ago: **$22,865**

Dividend Data Dividends have been paid since 2004

Amount ($)	Date Decl.	Ex-Div. Date	Stock of Record	Payment Date
0.100	May. 20	Jul. 14	Jul. 16	Aug. 06 '04
0.100	Sep. 24	Oct. 13	Oct. 15	Nov. 05 '04

Revenues/Earnings Data Fiscal year ending December 31

Revenues (Million $)

	2004	2003	2002	2001	2000	1999
1Q	1,970	1,802	1,614	1,506	1,597	1,813
2Q	2,077	1,936	1,767	1,605	1,656	1,886
3Q	2,179	1,989	1,915	1,640	1,658	1,812
4Q	—	2,653	2,461	2,202	2,182	2,311
Yr.	—	8,380	7,757	6,953	7,093	7,822

Earnings Per Share ($)

	2004	2003	2002	2001	2000	1999
1Q	0.47	0.39	0.40	0.30	0.40	0.33
2Q	0.58	0.40	0.45	0.38	0.36	0.55
3Q	0.61	0.53	0.47	0.41	0.20	0.61
4Q	E0.72	0.70	0.56	0.54	0.43	0.47
Yr.	E2.35	2.02	1.88	1.62	1.39	1.96

Next earnings report expected: mid-February Source: S&P, Company Reports
EPS Estimates based on S&P Operating Earnings; historical GAAP earnings are as reported.

Yum! Brands, Inc.

Recommendation: **HOLD** ★ ★ ★ ☆ ☆   12-Month Target Price: **$44.00** (as of October 07, 2004)

Business Summary October 08, 2004

Yum! Brands has the world's largest quick service restaurant (QSR) system, with more than 33,000 KFC, Pizza Hut and Taco Bell restaurants in more than 100 countries and territories. In 2003, the company's brands generated nearly $8.4 billion in worldwide revenues, up 8.0% from 2002. In May 2002, YUM acquired Long John Silver's and A&W All American Food restaurants, adding about $1.1 billion in annual revenues.

YUM has four operating companies, organized around major concepts: KFC, Pizza Hut, Taco Bell, and TRI (international operations). In each concept, units are operated by the company as well as by independent franchisees, licensees, or unconsolidated affiliates. Over the past several years, YUM rebalanced its system toward increased franchisee ownership, to focus resources on growth opportunities. At the end of 2003, 24% of worldwide units were operated by YUM , 65% by franchisees, 7% by licensees, and 5% by unconsolidated affiliates. Company-owned units accounted for 89% of total revenues in 2003.

KFC (originally Kentucky Fried Chicken) is the leader in the U.S. chicken QSR segment, with about a 45% market share. At the end of 2003, it operated 5,456 units in the U.S. and 7,293 units internationally.

Pizza Hut is the world's largest restaurant chain specializing in ready-to-eat pizza products. As of December 2003, it operated 6,400 units in the U.S. and 4,462 units internationally, and led the U.S. pizza QSR segment with about a 15% market share.

Taco Bell is the leader in the U.S. Mexican food QSR segment, with about a 65%

market share. At the end of 2003, It operated 5,027 units in the U.S. and 204 units internationally.

In 2003, TRI accounted for 33% of total revenues, up from 31% in 2002. At the end of 2003, it had 12,171 total units in operation. International markets include Australia, Canada, China, Korea, and the U.K.

The company is pursuing a three-pronged growth strategy. First, with more than 12,000 international restaurants, it believes it has the operational scale to execute an international growth strategy. YUM is committed to doubling its international business in the next eight to 10 years by adding at least 1,000 units annually. Second, the company believes it can accelerate U.S. growth through multi-branding, i.e., placing two or more of its brands within the same restaurant. YUM believes giving customers more food choices could add $100,000 to $400,000 in annual sales per restaurant. At the end of 2003, the company had 2,148 multi-branded units worldwide, and it planned to expand to nearly 4,000 multi-branded units by the end of 2006. Finally, through its goal of operational excellence, the company believes it can secure 2% blended same-store sales growth, as well as wider margins at existing restaurants.

The company purchased $278 million of its shares in 2003 and $956 million of its shares since 1998.

YUM does not expense stock option grants. Expensing options would have cut EPS by $0.11, $0.12 and $0.12 in 2003, 2002 and 2001, respectively.

Company Financials Fiscal Year ending December 31

Per Share Data ($)

(Year Ended December 31)	2003	2002	2001	2000	1999	1998	1997	1996	1995	1994
Tangible Bk. Val.	0.83	NM	NM	NM	NM	NM	NA	NM	NA	NA
Cash Flow	3.33	3.07	2.78	2.57	3.17	2.76	1.40	NM	NA	NA
Earnings	2.02	1.88	1.62	1.39	1.96	1.42	-0.36	0.43	NA	NA
S&P Core Earnings	2.07	1.60	1.36	NA	NA	NA	NA	NA	NA	NA
Dividends	Nil	Nil	Nil	Nil	Nil	Nil	Nil	NA	NA	NA
Payout Ratio	Nil	Nil	Nil	Nil	Nil	Nil	Nil	NA	NA	NA
Prices - High	35.41	33.17	26.65	19.28	36.93	25.43	18.12	NA	NA	NA
- Low	21.54	20.35	15.78	11.78	17.50	12.53	13.93	NA	NA	NA
P/E Ratio - High	18	18	16	14	19	18	NM	NA	NA	NA
- Low	11	11	10	9	9	9	NM	NA	NA	NA

Income Statement Analysis (Million $)

	2003	2002	2001	2000	1999	1998	1997	1996	1995	1994
Revs.	8,380	7,757	6,953	7,093	7,822	8,468	9,681	9,838	NA	NA
Oper. Inc.	1,471	1,375	1,220	1,217	1,280	1,185	1,198	NA	NA	NA
Depr.	401	370	354	354	386	417	536	NA	NA	NA
Int. Exp.	173	172	158	176	202	272	276	NA	NA	NA
Pretax Inc.	886	858	733	684	1,038	756	-35.0	308	NA	NA
Eff. Tax Rate	30.2%	32.1%	32.9%	39.6%	39.6%	41.1%	NM	57.5%	NA	NA
Net Inc.	618	583	492	413	627	445	-111	131	NA	NA
S&P Core Earnings	632	494	416	NA	NA	NA	NA	NA	NA	NA

Balance Sheet & Other Fin. Data (Million $)

	2003	2002	2001	2000	1999	1998	1997	1996	1995	1994
Cash	192	130	110	133	89.0	121	268	157	NA	NA
Curr. Assets	806	730	547	688	486	625	683	819	NA	NA
Total Assets	5,620	5,400	4,388	4,149	3,961	4,531	5,098	5,976	NA	NA
Curr. Liab.	1,461	1,520	1,805	1,216	1,298	1,473	1,579	1,382	NA	NA
LT Debt	2,056	2,299	1,552	2,397	2,391	3,436	4,551	4,674	NA	NA
Common Equity	1,120	594	104	-322	-560	-1,163	-1,620	-835	NA	NA
Total Cap.	3,176	2,893	1,656	2,085	1,838	2,338	2,964	4,139	NA	NA
Cap. Exp.	663	760	636	572	470	460	541	NA	NA	NA
Cash Flow	1,019	953	846	767	1,013	862	425	NA	NA	NA
Curr. Ratio	0.6	0.5	0.3	0.6	0.4	0.4	0.4	0.6	NA	NA
% LT Debt of Cap.	64.7	79.5	93.7	115.0	130.1	147.0	153.5	113.0	NA	NA
% Net Inc.of Revs.	7.4	7.5	7.1	5.8	8.0	5.3	NM	1.3	NA	NA
% Ret. on Assets	11.2	11.9	11.5	10.2	14.8	9.2	NM	NM	NA	NA
% Ret. on Equity	72.1	167.0	NM	NM	NM	NM	NM	NM	NA	NA

Data as orig. reptd. (pro forma in 1996; balance sheet as of June 14, 1997); bef. results of disc. opers. and/or spec. items. Per share data adj. for stk. divs.; EPS diluted (primary prior to 1998). E-Estimated. NA-Not Available. NM-Not Meaningful. NR-Not Ranked.

Office: 1441 Gardiner Lane, Louisville, KY 40213.
Telephone: 502-874-8300.
Email: yum.investors@yum.com
Website: http://www.yum.com
Chrmn & CEO: D.C. Novak.
COO & CFO: D. Deno.

SVP & Treas: C. Kreidler.
SVP, Secy & General Counsel: C.L. Campbell.
VP & Investor Contact: T. Jerzyk 888-298-6986.
Investor Contact: Q. Nghe 888-298-6986.
Dirs: M. Ferragamo, J. D. Grissom, B. G. Hill, R. Holland, Jr., K. G. Langone, D. C. Novak, A. E. Pearson, T. M. Ryan, J. Trujillo, R. J. Ulrich.

Founded: in 1997.
Domicile: North Carolina.
Employees: 265,000.
S&P Analyst: Dennis Milton/MF/BK

Zimmer Holdings

Recommendation: **HOLD** ★★★☆☆
SELL SELL HOLD BUY BUY

12-Month Target Price: $77.00
(as of October 26, 2004)

ZMH has an approximate 0.18% weighting in the **S&P 500**

Sector: Health Care
Sub-Industry: Health Care Equipment
Peer Group: Orthopedic Products

Summary: Zimmer Holdings, spun off by Bristol-Myers Squibb in August 2001, manufactures orthopedic reconstructive implants and fracture management products.

Quantitative Evaluations	**Price as of 11/12/04:** $79.75 **2004E S&P Core EPS:** $2.09

GAAP Earnings vs. Previous Year
▲ Up ▼ Down ▶ No Change

Quantitative Evaluations

S&P Earnings & Dividend Rank: NR

D	C	B-	B	B+	A-	A	A+

S&P Fair Value Rank: 4-

1	2	3	**4**	5
Lowest				Highest

Fair Value Calc.: $83.70 (Slightly Undervalued)

S&P Investability Quotient Percentile

92%

ZMH scored higher than 92% of all companies for which an S&P Report is available.

Volatility: Average

Low	**Average**	High

Technical Evaluation: Bullish
Since 11/04, the technical indicators for ZMH have been Bullish.

Relative Strength Rank: Moderate

51

1 Lowest	Highest 99

10 Week Mov. Avg.
30 Week Mov. Avg.
Relative Strength
12-Mo Target Price

Volume Below Avg. — Above Avg. —

HOLD $28.10 08/16/01
BUY $33.60 04/25/02
HOLD $77.17 09/27/04

HOLD   BUY   HOLD
J J A S O N D | J F M A M J J A S O N D | J F M A M J J A S O N D | J F M A M J J A S O N D | J F M A M J J A S O N D | J
2001 **2002** **2003** **2004**

Analyst commentary prepared by Robert M. Gold/PMW/GG

Highlights October 28, 2004

- In our view, the 2003 acquisition of Swiss orthopedics device manufacturer Centerpulse made ZMH the leading global manufacturer of hip and knee implants, and gave it a foothold in the dynamic spinal surgery market. We think operating synergies from Centerpulse will drive three-year sales growth of 16% to 18%, with EPS growth moving toward 20% to 25%, both exceeding projections for the S&P 500 and ZMH's orthopedic peers.

- We project 2004 revenues of $2.95 billion, including an approximate 3% boost from currency, and think unit pricing increases in the reconstructive orthopedic joint markets will generate an additional 2% to 3% of revenue growth in 2004. Aided by a more favorable product mix and higher unit selling prices, we see 2004 gross margins of 75.5%. SG&A expenses should consume 38.5% of sales, and R&D costs 6%. Looking to 2005, we see revenues advancing nearly 14%, to $3.35 billion, aided by new product launches, improvement in the U.S. spinal category, and improved performance in Europe.

- We expect interest costs to rise, due to borrowings associated with the Centerpulse deal, although efforts to quickly retire this debt could enable interest expense to fall below our estimate. After taxes projected at 31.5%, and before special charges, we project 2004 EPS of $2.34, and see 2005 EPS of $2.80. Our 2004 S&P Core EPS estimate is $2.09; we believe the divergence between our operating and S&P Core EPS projections is modest relative to that of device peers.

Key Stock Statistics

S&P Oper. EPS 2004E	2.34	52-week Range	$89.44-62.94
P/E on S&P Oper. EPS 2004E	34.1	12 Month P/E	53.9
S&P Oper. EPS 2005E	2.80	Beta	NA
Yield (%)	Nil	Shareholders	531,000
Dividend Rate/Share	Nil	Market Cap (B)	$ 19.6
Shares Outstanding (M)	245.3		

Value of $10,000 invested five years ago: **NA**

Dividend Data

No cash dividends have been paid.

Investment Rationale/Risk October 28, 2004

- With the stock near our 12-month target price of $77, we would hold existing positions. We expect minimal near-term valuation expansion. We view ZMH as well positioned across the orthopedic joint replacement markets, and believe that investor concerns regarding a slowdown in unit demand and unit pricing in this area are unfounded, as shown by the second quarter performance of the company and its peers. However, with over 40% of sales generated overseas, we think ZMH faces some challenging comparisons in 2005, with less favorable foreign currency fluctuations. Nevertheless, we regard the shares as a core holding in a diversified health care portfolio.

- Risks to our recommendation and target price include failure to integrate Centerpulse in a timely manner, unfavorable Medicare reimbursements, adverse patent litigation outcomes, increased competition in core markets, and additional valuation erosion in the medical device subsector.

- Our 12-month target price is $77. At that level, the shares would have a 2005 P/E to growth (PEG) ratio of 1.2X, based on our estimates, in line with that of orthopedic peers. On a P/E multiple basis, our target price assumes a 2005 multiple of 28X and a 2005 price to sales multiple of nearly 4.5X, premiums to the orthopedics sector that we think are justified by ZMH's leading share in several product categories.

Revenues/Earnings Data Fiscal year ending December 31

Revenues (Million $)

	2004	2003	2002	2001	2000	1999
1Q	742.2	390.1	319.1	286.0	—	—
2Q	737.4	411.1	345.6	294.3	—	—
3Q	700.2	398.2	337.5	286.7	—	—
4Q	—	701.6	370.2	311.6	—	—
Yr.	—	1,901	1,372	1,179	1,041	—

Earnings Per Share ($)

	2004	2003	2002	2001	2000	1999
1Q	0.40	0.41	0.28	0.16	—	—
2Q	0.47	0.45	0.34	0.22	—	—
3Q	0.52	0.43	0.33	0.14	—	—
4Q	E0.64	0.15	0.37	0.22	—	—
Yr.	E2.34	1.38	1.31	0.77	0.81	—

Next earnings report expected: early-February Source: S&P, Company Reports
EPS Estimates based on S&P Operating Earnings; historical GAAP earnings are as reported.

Zimmer Holdings, Inc.

Recommendation: **HOLD** ★ ★ ★ ☆ ☆   12-Month Target Price: **$77.00** (as of October 26, 2004)

Business Summary October 28, 2004

Zimmer Holdings primarily designs, develops, manufactures and markets orthopedic reconstructive implants and fracture management products. The former division of Bristol-Myers Squibb was spun off to BMY shareholders in August 2001.

Zimmer's reconstructive implants (80% of 2003 sales) are used to restore function lost due to disease or trauma in joints such as knees, hips, shoulders and elbows. The company offers a wide range of products for specialized knee procedures, including The NexGen Complete Knee Solution, The NexGen Legacy, The NexGen Revision Knee, the M/G Unicompartmental Knee System, and the Prolong Highly Crosslinked Polyethylene Articular Surface material. Hip replacement products include the VerSys Hip System, the ZMR Hip System, the Trilogy Acetabular System and a line of specialty hip products. ZMH also sells the Coonrad/Moorey product line of elbow replacement implant products.

In the spine/trauma area (10%), the company sells devices used to reattach or stabilize damaged bone and tissue to support the body's natural healing process. The most common stabilization of bone fractures involves the internal fixation of bone fragments, which can involve the use of an assortment of plates, screws, rods, wires and pins. ZMH offers a line of products designed for use in fracture fixation.

ZMH makes and markets other orthopedic surgical products (10%), used by surgeons both for orthopedic and for non-orthopedic procedures. Products include tourniquets, blood management systems, wound debridgement products, powered surgical instruments, pain management devices, and orthopedic

softgoods that provide support and/or heat retention and compression for trauma of the knee, ankle, back and upper extremities, including the shoulder, elbow, neck and wrist.

The company has operations in more than 24 countries, and markets its products in about 80 countries. The largest region is the Americas, accounting for 64% of 2003 sales, with the U.S. accounting for the bulk of sales in the region. The Asia/Pacific region accounted for 17% of 2003 sales, with Japan accounting for most of these sales. Europe accounted for 19% of 2003 sales, with the principal contributors being France, Germany, Italy, Spain, and the U.K.

In October 2003, ZMH acquired Swiss orthopedics device maker Centerpulse AG, for cash and common stock valued at $3.4 billion. The company recorded $79.6 million (pretax) of related charges in 2003, and anticipates that another $128 million of pretax charges will be incurred in 2004. In April 2004, ZMH acquired privately-held Implex Corp. for $98.6 million in cash and an undisclosed amount of potential future payments contingent on the growth of Implex product sales through 2006. Zimmer believes Implex gives it flexibility in the development of Travecular Metal Technology for reconstructive joint and spinal devices.

R&D spending totaled $105.8 million in 2003, equal to 5.6% of sales. On a proforma basis to include Centerpulse, R&D spending in 2003 was $149 million. At the end of 2003, the company had about 42 major projects in its research pipeline, including about 12 projects added via the Centerpulse acquisition.

Company Financials Fiscal Year ending December 31

Per Share Data ($)

(Year Ended December 31)	2003	2002	2001	2000	1999	1998	1997	1996	1995	1994
Tangible Bk. Val.	0.38	1.88	0.41	NM	NA	NA	NA	NA	NA	NA
Cash Flow	1.87	1.43	0.89	0.92	NA	NA	NA	NA	NA	NA
Earnings	1.38	1.31	0.77	0.81	NA	NA	NA	NA	NA	NA
S&P Core Earnings	1.31	1.24	0.70	NA	NA	NA	NA	NA	NA	NA
Dividends	Nil	Nil	Nil	NA	NA	NA	NA	NA	NA	NA
Payout Ratio	Nil	Nil	Nil	NA	NA	NA	NA	NA	NA	NA
Prices - High	71.85	43.00	33.30	NA	NA	NA	NA	NA	NA	NA
- Low	38.02	28.00	24.70	NA	NA	NA	NA	NA	NA	NA
P/E Ratio - High	52	33	43	NA	NA	NA	NA	NA	NA	NA
- Low	28	21	32	NA	NA	NA	NA	NA	NA	NA

Income Statement Analysis (Million $)

	2003	2002	2001	2000	1999	1998	1997	1996	1995	1994
Revs.	1,901	1,372	1,179	1,041	NA	NA	NA	NA	NA	NA
Oper. Inc.	645	426	272	291	NA	NA	NA	NA	NA	NA
Depr.	103	25.0	23.4	23.0	NA	NA	NA	NA	NA	NA
Int. Exp.	13.0	12.0	7.40	29.0	NA	NA	NA	NA	NA	NA
Pretax Inc.	439	389	241	239	NA	NA	NA	NA	NA	NA
Eff. Tax Rate	33.4%	33.7%	37.8%	34.3%	NA	NA	NA	NA	NA	NA
Net Inc.	291	258	150	157	NA	NA	NA	NA	NA	NA
S&P Core Earnings	277	244	137	NA	NA	NA	NA	NA	NA	NA

Balance Sheet & Other Fin. Data (Million $)

	2003	2002	2001	2000	1999	1998	1997	1996	1995	1994
Cash	78.0	16.0	18.4	50.0	NA	NA	NA	NA	NA	NA
Curr. Assets	1,339	612	509	487	NA	NA	NA	NA	NA	NA
Total Assets	5,156	859	745	669	NA	NA	NA	NA	NA	NA
Curr. Liab.	645	401	373	217	NA	NA	NA	NA	NA	NA
LT Debt	1,008	Nil	214	500	NA	NA	NA	NA	NA	NA
Common Equity	3,143	366	78.7	-48.0	NA	NA	NA	NA	NA	NA
Total Cap.	4,158	366	293	452	NA	NA	NA	NA	NA	NA
Cap. Exp.	45.0	34.0	54.7	NA	NA	NA	NA	NA	NA	NA
Cash Flow	394	283	173	180	NA	NA	NA	NA	NA	NA
Curr. Ratio	2.1	1.5	1.4	2.2	NA	NA	NA	NA	NA	NA
% LT Debt of Cap.	24.2	Nil	73.0	110.6	NA	NA	NA	NA	NA	NA
% Net Inc.of Revs.	15.3	18.9	12.7	15.1	NA	NA	NA	NA	NA	NA
% Ret. on Assets	9.7	32.1	22.4	NA	NA	NA	NA	NA	NA	NA
% Ret. on Equity	10.6	115.0	NM	NA	NA	NA	NA	NA	NA	NA

Data as orig reptd.; bef. results of disc opers/spec. items. Per share data adj. for stk. divs.; EPS diluted. Pro forma data in 2000; balance sheet & book value as of Mar. 31, 2001. E-Estimated. NA-Not Available. NM-Not Meaningful. NR-Not Ranked.

Office: 345 East Main Street, Warsaw, IN 46580.
Telephone: 574-267-6131.
Email: zimmer.infoperson@zimmer.com
Website: http://www.zimmer.com
Chrmn, Pres & CEO: J.R. Elliott.

EVP, CFO & Investor Contact: S.R. Leno 574-372-4790.
EVP, Secy & General Counsel: D.C. Dvorak.
Dirs: J. R. Elliott, L. C. Glasscock, R. E. Herzlinger, J. L. McGoldrick, A. A. White III.

Founded: in 1927.
Domicile: Delaware.
Employees: 6,500.
S&P Analyst: Robert M. Gold/PMW/GG

Zions Bancorporation

Recommendation: **BUY** ★★★★☆   12-Month Target Price: **$70.00**
(as of October 20, 2004)

ZION has an approximate 0.06% weighting in the **S&P 500**

Sector: Financials
Sub-Industry: Regional Banks
Peer Group: Rocky Mountain/Plains Regional Banks

Summary: ZION has 400 full-service banking offices in eight western states. At September 30, 2004, it had assets of $30.7 billion and deposits of $23.2 billion.

Quantitative Evaluations

S&P Earnings & Dividend Rank: A

| D | C | B- | B | B+ | A- | A | A+ |

S&P Fair Value Rank: 4

| 1 | 2 | 3 | 4 | 5 |
| Lowest | | | | Highest |

Fair Value Calc.: $66.30 (Slightly Overvalued)

S&P Investability Quotient Percentile

95%

ZION scored higher than 95% of all companies for which an S&P Report is available.

Volatility: Low

| Low | Average | High |

Technical Evaluation: Bullish
Since 10/04, the technical indicators for ZION have been Bullish.

Relative Strength Rank: Moderate

68

| 1 Lowest | | Highest 99 |

Price as of 11/12/04: **$68.24** | **2004E S&P Core EPS:** **$4.33**

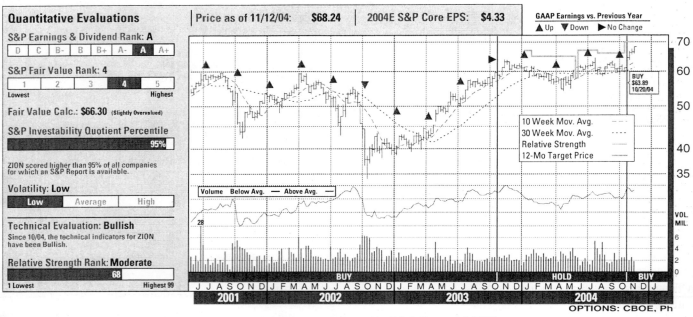

Analyst commentary prepared by Erik J. Eisenstein/MF/BK

OPTIONS: CBOE, Ph

Highlights October 21, 2004

- We see loan growth of 10% in 2005, reflecting improved demand for commercial credit in what we view as economically attractive geographical markets. We anticipate that ZION's asset yields will benefit from higher short term rates in the coming year. As a result, we project a wider net interest margin on a year-over-year basis and a 12% increase in net interest income. We were encouraged by the sequential improvement in asset quality during the third quarter of 2004. Despite 10% forecasted loan growth, we see only a 1% increase in loan loss provisions.

- Our 2004 forecast assumes a 2% increase in noninterest income, despite a less vibrant mortgage origination market, due to service charges on a larger expected deposit base. We see expenses up about 9%, a bit less than loan growth, reflecting projected benefits of efforts to streamline the Colorado branch network.

- Overall, we project 10% growth in 2005 EPS from continuing operations, to $4.90, from $4.47 seen in 2004. Our Standard & Poor's Core Earnings estimates for 2004 and 2005 are $4.33 and $4.78 a share, respectively, reflecting our view of stock-based compensation expense.

Investment Rationale/Risk October 21, 2004

- We believe ZION's potential for profit growth significantly exceeds that of its peers. The bank operates in western states, which we find attractive based on demographic and economic growth prospects that we see. We believe this represents an opportunity for Zion to gain market share. In addition, we expect credit quality, interest margins, and fee income sources to benefit particularly from a continued economic recovery. Based on our view of above-average intermediate and longer-term fundamentals, we project 11% average EPS growth in the five years beyond 2005, above that of most regional banks.

- Risks to our recommendation and target price include the possibility that the economic recovery will not be as strong as anticipated, restricting gains in credit quality and net interest margins.

- Our 12-month target price of $70 is derived by applying a P/E to growth (PEG) multiple of 1.30X, in line with that of other regional banks, to our 2005 EPS and five-year EPS growth projections. Based on our view of ZION's potential appreciation, and on the stock's 2.1% dividend yield, we recommend accumulating the shares on a total return basis.

Key Stock Statistics

S&P Core EPS 2005E	4.78	52-week Range	$68.24-54.08
S&P Oper. EPS 2004E	4.47	12 Month P/E	15.7
P/E on S&P Oper. EPS 2004E	15.3	Beta	0.29
S&P Oper. EPS 2005E	4.90	Shareholders	6,506
Yield (%)	1.9%	Market Cap (B)	$ 6.1
Dividend Rate/Share	1.28	Shares Outstanding (M)	89.7

Value of $10,000 invested five years ago: **$ 11,552**

Dividend Data Dividends have been paid since 1966

Amount ($)	Date Decl.	Ex-Div. Date	Stock of Record	Payment Date
0.300	Jan. 20	Feb. 09	Feb. 11	Feb. 25 '04
0.320	Apr. 30	May. 10	May. 12	May. 26 '04
0.320	Jul. 19	Aug. 09	Aug. 11	Aug. 25 '04
0.320	Oct. 18	Nov. 08	Nov. 10	Nov. 24 '04

Revenues/Earnings Data Fiscal year ending December 31

Revenues (Million $)

	2004	2003	2002	2001	2000	1999
1Q	457.4	445.7	460.8	518.7	343.3	364.0
2Q	469.8	454.3	472.7	501.3	467.2	375.9
3Q	492.6	539.6	441.4	509.6	499.8	385.7
4Q	—	449.8	462.2	481.1	508.1	500.3
Yr.	—	1,889	1,833	2,011	1,818	1,626

Earnings Per Share ($)

	2004	2003	2002	2001	2000	1999
1Q	1.10	0.96	0.89	0.80	-0.33	0.61
2Q	1.09	1.02	0.92	0.79	0.69	0.66
3Q	1.13	0.71	0.71	0.78	0.74	0.69
4Q	E1.16	1.05	0.92	0.78	0.75	0.49
Yr.	E4.47	3.74	3.44	3.15	1.86	2.26

Next earnings report expected: late-January Source: S&P, Company Reports
EPS Estimates based on S&P Operating Earnings; historical GAAP earnings are as reported.

Zions Bancorporation

Recommendation: **BUY** ★★★★☆   12-Month Target Price: **$70.00** (as of October 20, 2004)

Business Summary October 21, 2004

Zions Bancorporation is a financial service holding company for community banks in the western U.S. With assets of $30.9 billion and deposits of $23.2 billion at September 30, 2004, the company operated 400 full-service banking offices, in Arizona, California, Colorado, Idaho, Nevada, New Mexico, Utah and Washington.

ZION believes it benefits from its local-oriented operating model, which employs decentralized decision making. At the same time, the company seeks to leverage its resources and operate more efficiently by using a common set of systems and back office utilities.

For several years, the company has been expanding from its Salt Lake City base, acquiring banks in neighboring states, including Colorado, Nevada and California. In November 2002, ZION acquired Arizona-based Frontier State Bank, with six branches.

Subsidiaries provide various financial services and products to individual, commercial and government customers, like all commercial banks, but the vast majority of revenues is from net interest income, the difference between interest received on loans and other investments and interest paid on funds borrowed. At December 31, 2003, total loans of $20.0 billion were divided as follows: commercial 39%; commercial real estate 31%; consumer 28%; loans held for sale 1% and other 1%.

Poor asset quality can have a significant impact on bank profitability. Banks reserve for existing and potential nonperforming assets on a regular basis. At December 31, 2003, the allowance for loan losses covered 1.35% of loans and leases outstanding, versus 1.47% a year earlier. Asset quality improved in 2003; nonperforming assets decreased to 0.12% of net loans and leases, from 0.20% in 2002.

ZION also offers lease origination, discount brokerage, venture capital, and insurance services. In October 2002, the company acquired Utah-based insurance agency Grant-Hatch & Associates, Inc. Inc. In May 2002, ZION announced the sale of its Digital Signature Trust subsidiary to Indentrus, a provider of digital trust services to business customers, in exchange for a 33% interest in the combined company. In September 2003, ZION sold its Lexign, Inc., unit, an electronic document management and workflow provider, incurring a pretax loss on the sale of $2.4 million. In April 2004, the company acquired Van der Moolen UK Ltd., a U.K. odd-lot electronic bond trader, which will conduct business as Zions Bank International Ltd. The transaction was seen increasing ZION's electronic bond trading volume by 20%.

In June 2004, directors authorized the repurchase of up to $50 million in common stock.

Company Financials Fiscal Year ending December 31

Per Share Data ($)

(Year Ended December 31)	2003	2002	2001	2000	1999	1998	1997	1996	1995	1994
Tangible Bk. Val.	20.96	17.21	15.19	13.06	11.61	9.44	7.76	7.98	6.99	5.96
Earnings	3.74	3.44	3.15	1.86	2.26	1.91	1.89	1.71	1.38	1.09
S&P Core Earnings	4.42	3.17	2.42	NA	NA	NA	NA	NA	NA	NA
Dividends	1.02	0.80	0.80	0.89	0.86	0.52	0.58	0.32	0.35	0.29
Payout Ratio	27%	23%	25%	48%	38%	27%	30%	18%	25%	27%
Prices - High	63.86	59.65	64.00	62.87	75.87	62.50	46.00	26.00	20.37	10.50
- Low	39.31	34.14	42.30	32.00	48.25	37.87	25.43	16.25	8.87	8.37
P/E Ratio - High	17	17	20	34	34	33	24	15	15	10
- Low	11	10	13	17	21	20	13	10	6	8

Income Statement Analysis (Million $)

	2003	2002	2001	2000	1999	1998	1997	1996	1995	1994
Net Int. Inc.	1,095	1,035	950	803	741	544	352	260	227	199
Tax Equiv. Adj.	NA	NA	NA	NA	16.2	8.84	6.90	7.10	5.30	4.70
Non Int. Inc.	426	402	388	274	270	199	143	111	86.9	73.5
Loan Loss Prov.	69.9	71.9	73.2	31.8	18.0	12.2	6.17	3.54	2.80	1.99
Exp./Op. Revs.	63.7%	59.8%	63.9%	75.9%	66.4%	68.3%	60.9%	56.6%	59.1%	63.2%
Pretax Inc.	546	481	440	243	309	218	188	153	122	94.7
Eff. Tax Rate	39.1%	34.9%	35.8%	32.8%	35.5%	32.5%	34.8%	34.0%	33.5%	32.6%
Net Inc.	340	317	290	162	194	147	122	101	81.3	63.8
% Net Int. Marg.	4.45	4.56	4.64	4.27	4.31	4.60	4.27	4.56	4.50	4.07
S&P Core Earnings	402	292	223	NA	NA	NA	NA	NA	NA	NA

Balance Sheet & Other Fin. Data (Million $)

	2003	2002	2001	2000	1999	1998	1997	1996	1995	1994
Money Mkt. Assets	569	543	280	528	525	804	898	648	751	403
Inv. Securities	5,402	4,238	3,463	4,188	4,437	3,488	2,629	1,776	1,477	1,663
Com'l Loans	10,404	13,648	4,110	3,615	3,311	2,905	1,393	944	821	496
Other Loans	9,613	5,195	13,304	10,843	9,133	7,777	3,521	2,509	2,017	1,920
Total Assets	28,558	26,566	24,304	21,939	20,281	16,649	9,522	6,485	5,621	4,934
Demand Deposits	5,883	5,117	4,481	3,586	3,277	3,170	1,783	1,160	999	886
Time Deposits	15,014	15,015	13,361	11,484	10,786	8,622	5,071	3,392	3,098	2,820
LT Debt	1,843	1,310	781	420	453	511	470	252	142	160
Common Equity	2,540	2,374	2,281	1,779	1,660	1,014	655	507	429	366
% Ret. on Assets	1.2	1.2	1.3	0.8	1.0	1.1	1.5	1.7	1.5	1.3
% Ret. on Equity	13.8	13.6	14.3	9.4	12.5	17.6	21.0	21.6	20.5	18.8
% Loan Loss Resv.	0.9	1.4	1.5	1.3	1.6	1.9	1.7	2.0	2.4	2.8
% Loans/Deposits	142.6	96.0	97.0	96.6	91.0	79.8	71.1	75.8	68.5	68.3
% Equity to Assets	8.9	9.2	8.8	8.1	8.1	6.4	7.3	7.7	7.5	7.0

Data as orig reptd.; bef. results of disc opers/spec. items. Per share data adj. for stk. divs. Bold denotes primary EPS - prior periods restated. E-Estimated. NA-Not Available. NM-Not Meaningful. NR-Not Ranked. UR-Under Review.

Office: 1 South Main Street, Salt Lake City, UT 84111-1904.
Telephone: 801-524-4787.
Website: http://www.zionsbancorporation.com
Chrmn & CEO: H.H. Simmons.

EVP & CFO: D. Arnold.
Investor Contact: C.B. Hinckley 801-524-4985.
Dirs: J. C. Atkin, R. D. Cash, P. Frobes, R. H. Madsen, R. B. Porter, S. D. Quinn, L. E. Simmons, H. H. Simmons, S. T. Williams.

Founded: in 1961.
Domicile: Utah.
Employees: 7,896.
S&P Analyst: Erik J. Eisenstein/MF/BK